# A Pocket Botanical Dictionary, By J. Paxton Assisted By Prof. Lindley

Joseph Paxton, John Lindley

A POCKET

# BOTANICAL DICTIONARY.

# A POCKET

# BOTANICAL DICTIONARY,

COMPRISING THE

NAMES, HISTORY, AND CULTURE OF ALL PLANTS KNOWN
IN BRITAIN;

WITH A FULL EXPLANATION OF TECHNICAL TERMS.

BY

## JOSEPH PAXTON, F.L.S., H.S., &c.

ASSISTED BY

PROFESSOR LINDLEY, Ph.D., F.R.S., &c. &c.

## LONDON:

J. ANDREWS, 167, NEW BOND STREET;

AND W. S. ORR AND CO., PATERNOSTER ROW.

MDCCCXL.

LONDON:
BRADBURY AND EVANS, PRINTERS, WHITEFRIARS.

# PREFACE.

WHEN an author offers to the public a work, the greater part of the information contained in which is already available in detached fragments or other forms, his first duty is to exhibit the propriety of its publication; and prove, beyond question, that he has been instigated to his task by no unworthy desire of fame, but by a distinct and certified persuasion of its demand and utility.

Happily, in the present case, we are enabled to court scrutiny into our motives, being fully prepared to explain and justify them. During the numerous interviews enjoyed by us with the leading patrons of floriculture, the want of a pocket companion, such as that now furnished, has ever been especially and forcibly urged. There are, it is true, Catalogues, Encyclopædias, Lexicons, and Cultural Directories, all highly valuable in their respective spheres, and essential adjuncts to a gardener's or amateur's library : but they are too elaborate, verbose, technical, or uninteresting, to be readily and thoroughly appropriated ; the expense, also, of several is necessarily enormous, and beyond the means of the great majority of those who thirst after botanical and floricultural literature; and no single one, much less a set, embracing all the subjects of this Dictionary, is conveniently portable, or can ever be carried, without discomfort, beyond the porch of the proprietor's domicile.

Comprehensive compendiums, in which scientific and popular details are abridged, combined, and thus brought within the pecuniary reach as well as easy examination of those whose income and time are subjected to many other more pressing exactions, are highly commendable if attentively and clearly arranged; but their usefulness is in proportion to the precision and accuracy of the manner in which they are compiled.

THE POCKET BOTANICAL DICTIONARY, then, has been prepared solely as an instant resource and standard of consultation ; and for this purpose will be found invaluable to the professors and lovers of horticulture, in all its branches and of every grade. Within its columns is compressed all the most important information relative to admired plants which its small size and avowed design would admit. With this in his pocket, the possessor or cultivator of plants may perambulate his own garden, visit those of his friends or public establishments, and attend floricultural exhibitions, in the full assurance that if any particular object engage his attention, he may at once derive every fact of interest respecting both it and its congeners which is yet known in this country, and form an idea of the facility or difficulty, and consequent expense, attending its conservation. Such is, cursorily, the prime purport of this publication, and the aim of its author. To supersede the necessity for attaching the meaning of every specific appellation, and at the same time to afford the most ample means for acquiring a knowledge of all the phrases peculiar to the science, a voluminous glossary has been incorporated; wherein, in addition to the more abstruse Latin terms, a number of ordinary words that are used botanically in a peculiar sense are fully explained.

One inestimable quality of a popular synopsis of any sort, is the discreet abridgment of uninteresting matter, and detailed record of merely the most attractive particulars. On the judicious selection and proper apportionment of desirable intelligence, the value of a summary entirely rests. In this respect we have much to claim for the volume to which the present address is prefixed. On account of the extreme scarcity, or non-existence in Britain, of many plants, considerable perplexity has been experienced in assigning to each species its due share of honour. For this reason, if a few plants are unjustly elevated, and others improperly debased, some little allowance may fairly be expected. Those indigenous species which are ranked with the ornamental sorts, are not to be regarded as worthless because of their commonness, but may be cultivated with advantage in the more secluded and sylvan flower borders.

To take a general glance at the arrangement and composition of this DICTIONARY, it will be better to show more lucidly the intent and application of each separate point, and afterwards advert to the abbreviations. Compactness and facile portability being the primary and principal elements of the design, condensation of the letter-press was an inevitable result. On this score, however, we have just grounds for eulogising our printers, as nothing can be more beautiful or perfect than the mechanical execution of the work; while the objection that might attach to the minuteness of the type, is completely removed by its exceeding clearness.

Under the head of each genus, besides the authority for its name, its origin, and position, both in the Linnæan and Natural System, a concise outline is given of its most striking members, with adequate instructions for their cultivation, and observations on their particular medicinal or useful properties. In conformity to the principle of giving prominence to only the most interesting subjects, the worthless genera are passed over with a slight statement of their insignificance; and to prevent repetition, reference is occasionally made to other genera for directions on treatment, when the habits of both closely correspond. For all the suggestions on culture, we hold ourselves, for the most part, responsible; the notes in those instances where we have no personal cognizance being extracted from the best authors, with the usual acknowledgments. Immediately succeeding the above-named sketches, a list of specific synonymes is furnished, with figures of allusion affixed to each, and similar ones to the species they represent, by which the observer may instantly perceive what names are applied to the same plant, that in the last or descriptive text being always the most authentic.

In the enumeration of genera and species, we are indebted chiefly to Mr. Geo. Don's *General System of Gardening and Botany*, Dr. Lindley's *Introduction to the Natural System*, and Mr. Loudon's *Arboretum et Fruticetum Britannicum*, comparing these with all other catalogues extant,—of which Loudon's *Hortus Britannicus* is the principal and best,—and adopting such readings as are most obviously correct. We rely greatly on our own rigid research into these matters, having been engaged in it for several years, but still more so on a careful revision of both MSS. and printed proofs, undertaken by Dr. Lindley in the most disinterested and kind manner. Nevertheless, such is the typographical diminutiveness, that we cannot imagine but some errors have eluded us. Should it reach another edition, we shall have great pleasure in effecting any emendations which our correspondents or friends may discover and communicate. It will be manifest that two distinct courses have been followed with regard to the ornamental and trivial species. Possessing nothing to recommend them to notice, or to render the enrolment of their habits, native country, &c., at all desirable, we have arranged the latter in aggregated groups; after their more interesting allies where these exist, and directly following the general remarks on those genera which comprise no ornamental species. On the description of each meritorious plant included in the columns opposite its appellation, we shall descant more largely, when considering the abbreviations.

Respecting the number of scientific terms herein explained, we may be allowed to say that no other popular glossary contains such a copious collection. Their explication is in exact accordance with the views of the most learned botanists, merely being reduced to dimensions which best comport with simplicity and conciseness.

Considering the immense field which this volume occupies, the accentuation of generic, specific, and all purely botanical names that are not Anglicised, must be regarded as a highly valuable characteristic. By the extreme perspicuity of the marks employed, their full and universal adaptation, and the fact that they were all supplied by the first botanist in England, (Dr. Lindley,) the botanic student or other assiduous examiner will here meet with a fund of accurate instruction in this particular, to which only the most laboured and extremely expensive publication can at all pretend.

It might be assumed that the signs used are sufficiently common to require no comment; but, for the benefit of the less informed, we shall just show the manner in which they apply. In the first place, the vowel in each word over which the primary accent occurs, sustains all the *emphasis* of the syllabic pronunciation, independently of the real nature of the sign. Further, the employment of the long quantity ( ¯ ) or the short quantity ( ˘ ) simply denotes that the vowel above which they are placed is to be sounded long and broadly, or short and abruptly. To vary our expression, the short vowel is perpetually pronounced in conjunction with the next consonant, and the long one has its own distinct and final sound, as if the letter were doubled, but the voice rested on each. In all cases when the last syllable but one is marked long ( ¯ ), the accent falls on that syllable; and when the last syllable but one is marked short ( ˘ ), the accent falls on the last syllable but two. Thus Romānŭs would be accented Románus, and trĭcŏlŏr would be accented trícolor, although the i on which the accent is placed is short. It is extremely important to bear this in mind.

To reduce the work to the smallest practicable size, it has been found requisite to abridge the language conveying many of the details, and that this may be rightly comprehended, we shall now enter on its elucidation. First, the numerical figures which follow the recognised specific names in the general list, and such as precede the synonymes, have, as before hinted, a direct connexion with each other, establishing the identity. Thus, in page 1, under the genus ACACIA, the synonyme " 1. A. acicularis " is but another appellation for " A. Brownei 1," in the ensuing text; " 2. Mimosa tortuosa," is synonymous with " A. Burmanniana 2 ;" and so on, in like manner, throughout the whole. Next, the authorities for the generic names are very often shortened, and a list of all those, with the country in which they rose to celebrity, will be subjoined. Again, the descriptive peculiarities of species are classed in seven columns, in which the colours of the flowers, —the month during which they commonly blossom,—their habitude, whether as concerns the temperature they receive, their duration, or general nature,—their native climate, and the year in which they were first introduced to Britain,—are all duly registered. Where either or several of these circumstances are omitted, it is to be inferred that they have not been accurately ascertained. In the case of Epiphytes, Palms, and Grasses, they are simply noted as such, since their habits are universally the same. All other trifling particulars are regularly and efficiently interpreted in the catalogue of abbreviations.

Having thus specified the objects, classification, and utility of the work, we have only to commend it to the kind indulgence of the public, convinced that, whatever may be its failings—and in such an extensive compilation some defects must naturally be anticipated—they are neither glaring, momentous, nor, notwithstanding the smallness of the type, equal to those of any similar production. To the gardener, and all who cultivate or delight in acquainting themselves with plants, either for enrichment or amusement; but emphatically to such persons as wish to study the nature and history of vegetation in the garden, where alone they can hope these features to be permanently impressed on the memory, the BOTANICAL POCKET DICTIONARY has claims which nothing at present existing or likely to be issued can supplant or diminish.

JOSEPH PAXTON.

CHATSWORTH,
   *July*, 1840.

*h*

# AUTHORITIES FOR GENERIC TITLES.

*Ach.* for *Acharius.* A Swedish botanist and examiner of Lichens.
*Adams, F.* A Russian botanist and traveller in Siberia.
*Adanson.* A French traveller and botanist.
*Afzelius.* A professor in Sweden, and traveller in Sierra Leone.
*Agardh.* A Swedish professor, bishop, and writer on Algaceous plants.
*Aiton.* The manager of the Royal Kew Gardens.
*Albertini.* Author of some dissertations on Fungi.
*Allioni.* A botanist of Italy.
*Anderson.* A London writer on Pæonies.
*Andr.* for *Andrews.* An eminent English botanical artist.
*Andrzejowski.* A Russian botanist.
*Aublet.* A Frenchman who travelled in Guiana.

*Bancroft.* A physician resident in Jamaica.
*Banks.* A celebrated English traveller and promoter of science.
*Bartl.* for *Bartling.* A botanist of Gottingen.
*Barton.* Once a professor at Philadelphia.
*Bauhin, Caspar.* A German botanist of the sixteenth century.
*Baumgarten.* A botanist of Transylvania.
*Beauvois* for *Palisot de Beauvois.* A French botanist and traveller in Africa.
*Benth.* for *Bentham.* An English botanist, and secretary to the London Horticultural Society.
*Bergius.* A Swede, and writer on Cape plants.
*Berkley.* An English clergyman and writer on Fungi.
*Bernhardi.* A botanist of Italy.
*Bertolini.* A writer on Italian plants.
*Besser.* A professor in Russia.
*Birberstein.* A Russian botanist, and writer upon the plants of Caucasus.
*Blume.* A Dutch botanist and traveller in Java.
*Boerhaave.* An ancient botanist and physician.
*Bohmer.* A German and writer on botany.
*Bojer.* A botanist of the Mauritius.
*Borkhausen.* An examiner of the plants of Hesse Darmstadt.
*Bory* for *Bory de St. Vincent.* A French botanist and traveller.
*Bot. Reg.* for *Botanical Register.* A botanical monthly periodical, commenced by Ker and now conducted by Lindley.
*Bot. Rep.* for *Botanical Repository.* A botanical periodical, formerly conducted by Andrews and others.
*Bridel.* A German author on Mosses.
*Brignoli.* A botanist of Verona.
*Brongniart.* A botanist of France.
*Browne, Patrick.* An Irish botanist and writer on the plants of Jamaica.
*Brown, R.* An English botanist and traveller in New Holland.
*Bulliard.* A Frenchman and investigator of Fungi.
*Burmann.* A Dutch writer on botany and patron of Linnæus.

*Carmichael.* A Scotch botanist.
*Cassini, H.* A French writer on Composite plants.
*Casanilles.* A botanist at Madrid.
*Chamisso.* A German traveller and botanist.
*Choisy.* A botanist of Switzerland.
*Colebrook.* An English writer on the Flora of India.
*Colladon, J. F.* A botanist of Geneva.
*Commelin.* A botanist of Holland.
*Commerson.* A French traveller and botanist.
*Corda.* A German botanist.
*Correa* for *Correa de Serra.* A Portuguese botanist, diplomatist, and writer on botanical subjects.
*Coulter.* An Irish physician and traveller in Mexico.
*Cronis.* An Austrian Botanist.
*Cunn. A.* for *A. Cunningham.* A British collector for the Kew Gardens.
*Cusson.* A Swiss observer of Umbelliferæ.
*Cyrilli.* An Italian botanist.

*Dec.* for *Decandolle.* A French botanist now resident as professor at Geneva.
*Desfon.* for *Desfontaines.* A French traveller and botanist in Algiers.
*Desmazieres.* A botanist of France.
*Desvaux.* A French botanist.
*Dickson.* An English examiner of Cryptogamia.

*Dillenius.* A German writer on botany, especially Mosses, settled in England when he was gardener to Gerard, at Eltham.
*Dillwyn.* An English investigator of Confervæ.
*Ditmar.* A botanist of Holland.
*Don, D.* Librarian to the Linnæan Society and botanist.
*Don, G.* An English botanist and traveller.
*Douglas.* A collector of plants in North America for the Horticultural Society of London.
*Dryander.* A Swedish botanist and long a librarian to Sir Joseph Banks.
*Dumont,* for *Dumont Courset.* A French gardening author.

*E. Botany* for *English Botany.* A periodical containing coloured figures of British plants by Sowerby and Sir J. E. Smith.
*Ehrhart.* A botanist of Germany.
*Elliot.* An American botanist who wrote on the plants of Carolina.
*Ellis.* An English writer on marine plants.
*Endlicher.* A German botanist.

*Fensl.* An Austrian botanist.
*Feuille.* A French Jesuit who wrote on the plants of Chile.
*Fischer.* A Russian botanist, and director of the Botanical Garden, St. Petersburg.
*Flora Peru.* for *Flora Peruviana.* A work on the plants of Chile and Peru by Ruiz and Pavon, two Spanish botanists.
*Flugge.* A German writer on Grasses.
*Forskahl.* A Danish naturalist who travelled in Arabia.
*Forster.* A traveller in the South Pacific Ocean.
*Fougerous* for *Fougerous de Bondaroux.* A French botanist of the last century.
*Fries.* A writer on Fungi in Sweden.

*Gærtner.* A German writer on the structure of fruit and seeds.
*Gaudich.* for *Gaudichaud.* A French botanist and voyager.
*Gingins.* A French botanist.
*Gmelin.* A Russian botanist and traveller in Siberia.
*Greville.* An English author on Cryptogamic botany.
*Gronovius.* A Dutch botanist.

*Haller.* A botanist and physician of Switzerland.
*Hamilton.* A Scotch botanist and Indian traveller, sometimes called Buchanan.
*Harvey.* A writer on Cryptogamic and Cape plants.
*Haworth.* An English author on succulent plants.
*Hedwig.* A German writer on Cryptogamic plants.
*Herbert.* An English writer on Amaryllidaceous plants.
*Hilaire.* A French botanist and traveller in Brazil.
*Hill.* An English botanical writer.
*Hoffmann.* A German botanical author.
*Hooker.* A professor of botany at Glasgow.
*Hort. Kew.* for *Hortus Kewensis.* A catalogue of the plants in the Royal Kew Gardens.
*Host.* An Austrian botanical writer.
*Hudson.* An investigator of British plants.
*Humboldt and Bonpland.* Botanists and travellers in America, &c.

*Jack.* An English writer on the plants of the Indian Archipelago.
*Jackson.* An English botanist.
*Jacq.* for *Jacquin.* An Austrian botanist.
*Jussieu.* A French systematical botanist.

*Kæmpfer.* A traveller in Japan.
*Kalm.* A Swedish pupil of Linnæus who travelled in N. America.
*Kaulfuss.* A German writer upon Ferns.
*Ker.* A describer of plants in Bot. Reg.
*Knowles and Westcott.* Editors of the Floral Cabinet.
*Koch.* A professor of botany at Erlangen.
*Kœnig.* A German naturalist who travelled in the East Indies.
*Kunth.* A Prussian botanist who assisted in the arrangement and publication of the plants found in America by Humboldt and Bonpland.

*Kunze.*     A German writer upon minute Cryptogamic plants.

*Labillar.* for *Labil'ardicra.*   A French botanist, and traveller in Syria, New Holland, &c.
*Lagasca.*     A botanist of Spain.
*La Llave.*     A Mexican botanist.
*Lamarck.*     A French naturalist who wrote largely upon botany about the end of the eighteenth century.
*Lambert, A. B.*     An English patron of botany.
*Lamouroux.*     A French writer upon marine plants.
*Lehmann.*     A German botanist and director of the Botanical Garden of Hamburgh.
*L'Herit.* for *L'Heritier.*   A French botanist.
*Lindley.*     Professor of botany in University College, London.
*Link.*     A botanist of Prussia.
*Linn.* for *Linnæus.*   The great Swedish naturalist.
*Llav.* for *Llavarza.*   A Mexican botanist.
*Læfling.*     A Swedish traveller and botanist.
*Loureiro.*     A Portuguese monk who wrote on the plants of Cochinchina.
*Lyngbye.*     A Danish writer on submarine Cryptogamic plants.

*Marcgraav.*     One of the early naturalists who explored Brazil.
*Martius.*     A Bavarian naturalist and traveller in Brazil.
*Medicus.*     A German botanist.
*Merat.*     A French writer on the flowers of Paris.
*Meyer.*     A botanist of Germany.
*Mich.* for *Michaux.*   A French botanist who wrote on the plants of North America.
*Micheli.*     A Florentine microscopical botanist.
*Mikan.*     A German author on the Brazilian Flora.
*Miller.*     One of the ablest scientific English garden botanists.
*Mirbel.*     A French physiological botanist.
*Mœnch.*     A German systematical botanist.
*Mohring.*     A writer on Cryptogamia in Germany.
*Molina.*     An Italian naturalist who wrote upon the flowers of Chile.
*Mutis.*     A Spanish botanist and correspondent of Linnæus.

*Necker.*     A German botanical writer.
*Nees.*     A German botanist and professor.
*Noronha.*     A Spanish botanist who visited the Philippines.
*Nuttall.*     An American traveller and botanist.

*Ortega.*     A botanist of Spain.

*Pavon.*     One of the authors of the Spanish Flora Peruviana.
*Pers.* for *Persoon.*   A French botanist.
*Pliny.*     An ancient naturalist.
*Plumier.*     A French botanist and traveller in the West Indies.
*Pohl.*     A botanist of Germany who travelled in Brazil.
*Poiteau.*     A French artist and botanist.
*Poppig* and *Endlicher.*   German botanists, the former a traveller in South America.
*Presl.*     A German systematical botanist.
*Pursh.*     A Prussian gardener who wrote a Flora of North America.

*Rafin.* for *Rafinesque-Schmalz.*   A North American botanical writer.
*Ramond.*     A French botanist who wrote concerning the flowers of the Pyrenees.
*Reich.* for *Reichard.*   A German botanist.
*Reichenbach.*     A botanist of Germany.
*Retz.*     A German botanist who wrote on the flowers of Scandinavia.
*Rheede.*     A Dutch gentleman under whose orders the Hortus Malabaricus was published.
*Rich.* for *Richard.*   A French botanist and traveller in Demerara.
*Rivinus.*     A German botanist.
*Robil.* for *Robillard.*   A French botanist.
*Rochel.*     Superintendant of the garden at Pesth.

*Rolander.*     A botanist of Sweden.
*Romer* and *Schultes.*   German botanists, and editors of the Systema Vegetabilium of Linnæus.
*Roscoe.*     An English botanical author.
*Roth.*     A German writer on botany.
*Rotboll.*     A Danish botanist.
*Rox.* for *Roxburgh.*   A botanist of India, formerly in charge of the botanic garden Calcutta.
*Rudge.*     An English botanical amateur.
*Ruiz* and *Pavon.*   See Flora Peruviana.
*Rumphius.*     A botanical author of the Herbarium Amboinense.

*Salis.* for *Salisbury.*   An English botanist.
*Salm Dyck* for the *Prince of Salm Dyck.*   An illustrious German amateur.
*Savi.*     A botanist of Italy.
*Schlech.* for *Schlechtendahl.*   A German botanist.
*Schmidt.*     A Bohemian botanist.
*Schousb.* for *Schousboe.*   A Danish consul at Tangiers, author of a work on Morocco plants.
*Schrader.*     A German botanist.
*Schreber.*     A botanist of Germany.
*Schumacher.*     A Danish botanist, who described many Sierra Leone plants.
*Scopoli.*     A botanist of Italy who wrote on the flowers of Carniola.
*Seringe.*     A French botanist.
*Sibthorp.*     An English traveller in Greece, and botanist.
*Sims.*     An English garden botanist.
*Smith, Sir J. E.*   An English botanist, founder of the Linnæan Society.
*Solander.*     A botanist of Sweden who sailed round the world with Banks and Cook.
*Sonnerat.*     A French traveller in the East Indies.
*Spach.*     A writer in the Annales des Sciences Naturelles.
*Sparmann.*     A Swedish traveller at the Cape of Good Hope.
*Sprengel.*     A German botanist and antiquary.
*Stackhouse.*     An English writer on marine plants.
*Sternberg.*     A noble botanist of Germany.
*Swartz.*     A Swedish botanist who visited the West Indies, and published an account of the native plants.
*Sweet.*     An English garden botanist.

*Thouars* for *Du Petit Thouars.*   A French physiologist and traveller in Madagascar.
*Thun.* for *Thunberg.*   A Swedish botanist and traveller.
*Tode.*     A German author on Fungi.
*Tournefort.*     An ancient French traveller and botanist.
*Trentepohl.*     A botanist of Germany.
*Trinius.*     A Russian writer on Gramineæ.
*Turpin.*     A French botanist and draftsman.
*Turra.*     A botanist of Italy.

*Vahl.*     A Danish botanical author.
*Vaillant.*     A French traveller and botanist.
*Vandelli.*     A botanist of Portugal who wrote on the plants of Brazil.
*Vauch.* for *Vaucher.*   A Swiss writer on Confervæ.
*Vela.*
*Velloza.*     A Brazilian botanist.
*Ventenat.*     A French garden botanist.
*Villars.*     A botanist of France who wrote on the plants of Dauphiny.

*Wallich.*     Superintendent of the Calcutta botanic garden.
*Walter.*     A writer on the plants of Carolina.
*Weber.*     A German Cryptogamic botanist.
*Wendland.*     A German garden botanist.
*Willd.* for *Willdenow.*   A Prussian botanical writer.

*Zea.*     A botanist of Spain.

# ABBREVIATIONS.

## FIRST COLUMN.
### COLOURS OF THE FLOWERS.

| | |
|---|---|
| Apetal | destitute of conspicuous petals. |
| bh. | bluish. |
| bld. | blood-coloured. |
| blk. | black or blackish. |
| blu. | blue or bluish. |
| brk. eld. | brick red. |
| br. brn. | brown. |
| brnsh. | brownish. |
| br. brt. | bright. |
| carm. | carmine-coloured. |
| crim. | crimson. |
| dk. drk. | dark. |
| gn. gr. grn. | green. |
| grnsh. gsh. | greenish. |
| lgt. lt. | light. |
| li. lil. | lilac-coloured. |
| or. oran. | orange-coloured. |
| pa. | pale. |
| pnk. | pink. |
| pksh. | pinkish. |
| pur. | purple. |
| pursh. purpsh. | purplish. |
| rich p. | rich purple. |
| rdsh. | reddish. |
| ro. | rose-coloured. |
| saff. | saffron-coloured. |
| salm. | salmon-coloured. |
| scar. scr. | scarlet. |
| spot. | spotted. |
| strip. | striped. |
| varieg. | variegated. |
| vermil. | vermilion-coloured. |
| vio. | violet-coloured. |
| wht. w. whtsh. | white or whitish. |
| yel. | yellow. |
| yelsh. ysh. | yellowish. |

## SECOND COLUMN.
### PERIOD OF FLOWERING.

| | |
|---|---|
| 1. | January. |
| 2. | February. |
| 3. | March. |
| 4. | April. |
| 5. | May. |
| 6. | June. |
| 7. | July. |
| 8. | August. |
| 9. | September. |
| 10. | October. |
| 11. | November. |
| 12. | December. |

## THIRD COLUMN.
### TEMPERATURE REQUIRED.

| | |
|---|---|
| F. | Frame plant. |
| G. | Greenhouse plant. |
| H. | Hardy plant. |
| S. | Stove plant. |

## FOURTH COLUMN.
### HABITUDE.

| | |
|---|---|
| Aq. | Aquatic. |
| Bl. | Bulbous. |
| Cl. | Climbing. |
| Cr. | Creeping. |
| De. | Deciduous. |
| Epi. Epiphy. | Epiphyte. |
| Ev. | Evergreen. |
| Fu. | Fusiform-rooted. |
| Her. | Herbaceous. |
| Ter. | Terrestrial. |
| Tr. | Trailing. |
| Tu. | Tuberous-rooted. |
| Tw. | Twining. |

## FIFTH COLUMN.
### HABIT AND DURATION.

| | |
|---|---|
| A. | Annual. |
| B. | Biennial. |
| Bl. | Bulbous plant. |
| Cl. | Climber. |
| Cr. | Creeper. |
| P. | Perennial. |
| S. | Shrub. |
| T. | Tree. |
| Tr. | Trailing plant. |
| Tu. | Tuberous-rooted plant. |

## SIXTH COLUMN.
### NATIVE COUNTRY.

| | |
|---|---|
| Adriat Is. | Adriatic Islands. |
| Alp. Eur. | European Alps. |
| Amer. hyb. | American hybrid. |
| A. Minor | Asia Minor. |
| Apenn. | Apennines. |
| Archipel. | Grecian Archipelago. |
| Asiatic G. | Asiatic Gulf. |
| Baff. B. | Baffin's Bay. |
| Barba. | Barbary. |
| B. Ayres. | Buenos Ayres. |
| Californ. | California. |
| Cappadoc. | Cappadocia. |
| Carthag. | Carthagena. |
| Casp. Sea. | Caspian Sea. |
| Casp. Sho. | Caspian Shores. |
| Carpa. Mo. | Carpathian Mountains. |
| C. G. H. | Cape of Good Hope. |
| Cherson. | Chersonesus. |
| Coromand. | Coromandel. |
| Cordill. | Cordilleras. |
| E. Ind. | East Indies. |
| Eng. hyb. | English hybrid. |
| Falk. Is. | Falkland Islands. |
| Ft. Vancou. | Fort Vancouver. |
| Guayaq. | Guayaquil. |
| Huds. B. | Hudson's Bay. |
| I. France | Isle of France. |
| I. Skye | Isle of Skye. |
| Kamtsch. | Kamtschatka. |
| K. Geo.'s Sd. | King George's Sound. |
| Louisia. | Louisiana. |
| Madagas. | Madagascar. |
| Magell. | Magellan. |
| Maran. | Maranha. |
| Martiniq. | Martinique. |
| Mediterr. | Mediterranean Islands. |
| Montpel. | Montpelier. |
| Moreton B. | Moreton Bay. |
| Mosambi. | Mosambique. |
| M. Video | Monte Video. |
| N. Africa | North Africa. |
| N. Amer. | North America. |
| N. Caledon. | New Caledonia. |
| N. Eur. | North Europe. |
| Newfoundl. | Newfoundland. |
| N. Grenada | New Grenada. |
| N. Holl. | New Holland. |
| N. Patag. | North Patagonia. |
| N. Spain | New Spain. |
| N. S. W. | New South Wales. |
| N. Zeal. | New Zealand. |
| Organ Mts. | Organ Mountains. |
| Pennsyl. | Pennsylvania. |
| Philadel. | Philadelphia. |
| Rio Jan. | Rio Janeiro. |
| S. Amer. | South America. |
| San. Cruz. | Santa Cruz. |
| Scandin. | Scandinavia. |
| S. Austral. | South Australia. |
| S. Carol. | South Carolina. |
| S. Eur. | South Europe. |
| S. France | South France. |
| S. Leone | Sierra Leone. |
| St. Domin. | St. Domingo. |
| St. Vinc. | St. Vincent. |
| S. Sea Is. | South Sea Islands. |
| Switz. | Switzerland. |
| Sw. River, Swan R. | Swan River. |
| Tranqueb. | Tranquebar. |
| Valpar. | Valparaiso. |
| V. D. L. or V. Die. L. | Van Diemen's Land. |
| W. Ind. | West Indies. |
| W. Ind. Is. | West India Islands. |

# A POCKET

# BOTANICAL DICTIONARY.

———◆———

**ABIES**, see *Pinus.*

**ABILDGAARDIA**, *Vahl.* After Professor Abildgaard, of Copenhagen. *Linn.* 3, Or. 1, Nat. Or. *Cyperaceæ.* Worthless dwarf species of grass-like plants; increased by division, and grown in any common soil.

| | | | | |
|---|---|---|---|---|
| monostachya | . . | Apetal | . . 6, Grass. N. Holl. . . | 1819 |
| tristachya | . . . | Apetal | . . 6, Grass. N. Holl. . . | 1824 |

**ABORTION**, imperfect or untimely development.

**ABROMA**, *Linn.* From *a*, privative, and *broma*, food; unfit to be eaten. *Linn.* 18, Or. 1, Nat. Or. *Sterculiaceæ.* Handsome free-flowering species of easy culture, delighting in a compost of loam and peat. Propagated with ease from seeds, or cuttings. The bark of *A. augusta* furnishes a very tough fibrous tissue, suited for manufacturing into cordage.

| | | | | |
|---|---|---|---|---|
| augusta | . . . | Purple | . . 8, S. Ev. T. E. Indies . | 1770 |
| fastuosa | . . . | Purple | . . 8, S. Ev. T. N. S. W. . | 1800 |

**ABRONIA**, *Jussieu.* From *abros*, delicate; referring to the involucrum. *Linn.* 5, Or. 1, Nat. Or. *Nyctaginaceæ.* Handsome trailing plants, multiplied by division, and grown in sandy peat. *Synonyme:* 1. *Tricratus admirabilis.*

| | | | | |
|---|---|---|---|---|
| mellifera | . . | White | . 7, H. De. Tr. California . | 1826 |
| umbellata, 1 | . | Red | . . 4, H. Ev. Tr. California . | 1823 |

**ABRUPT**, blunt, broken off.

**ABRUPTLY-PINNATE.** Pinnate leaves, terminating without an odd leaflet.

**ABRUS**, *Linn.* From *abros*, soft; in allusion to the delicacy of the leaves. *Linn.* 17, Or. 4, Nat. Or. *Leguminosæ.* This pretty climbing species (Wild Liquorice) must have a strong heat to enable it to flower well. It delights in loam and peat, and is propagated readily from cuttings, in sand, under a glass. The roots have the property of the liquorice of the shops, while the seeds, if eaten in any quantity, produce violent headache.

| | | | | |
|---|---|---|---|---|
| precatorius | . . | Pa. pur. | . 4, S. Da. cl. W. Indies . | 1680 |

**ABUTA**, *Aublet.* From *Abouta* or *Abuta*, its name in Guiana. *Linn.* 22, Or. 10, Nat. Or. *Menispermaceæ.* An ornamental evergreen climber. Loam and peat, divisions. From the branches of this plant a drink is made by the natives of Cayenne, and used by them against obstructions of the liver.

| | | | | |
|---|---|---|---|---|
| rufescens | . | Grn. Yell. | . S. Ev. cl. Guiana . | 1820 |

**ACACIA**, *Necker.* From *ac*, a point, or *akazo*, to sharpen; many of the species having thorns or prickles. *Linn.* 23, Or. 1, Nat. Or. *Leguminosæ, Mimoseæ.* Very ornamental plants of neat growth, and elegant foliage. All grow well in sandy loam and peat, and cuttings taken off at a joint root freely in sand, under a glass; portions of the strong roots planted in soil, in heat, leaving the points out, produce young plants; but the best plants are obtained from seed. The hardy species require to be slightly protected in severe weather. The bark of some species furnishes the tanning principle in a great degree, particularly *A. arabica*; the bark of which is largely used in tanning leather, and is in India regarded as a powerful tonic. Gums are yielded in considerable quantities by some species; and in India an intoxicating principle is obtained from other species. *Synonymes:* 1. *A. acicularis.* 2. *Mimosa tortuosa.* 3. *A. strigosa.* 4. *M. giraffæ.* 5. *A. prostrata.* 6. *A. viscosa.* 7. *A. stolonifera.* 8. *M. marginata.* 9. *A. floribunda.* 10. *A. linearis.* 11. *A. mollissima.* 12. *A. impressa.* 13. *M. nigricans.* 14. *A. ambigua.* 15. *M. verticillata.* 16. *M. verticillata.*

| Species | Colour | Habit | Country | Date |
|---|---|---|---|---|
| abietina | . . Yellow | . 5, G. Ev. S. | N. Holl. | 1823 |
| acanthocarpa | . Pa. red. | . 8. Ev. S. | N. Spain | 1822 |
| acantholoba | . White | . 8. Ev. S. | S. Amer. | 1823 |
| acapulcensis | . White | . 8. Ev. S. | Acapulco | 1825 |
| affinis | . . Yellow | . 5, G. Ev. S. | N. Holl. | 1822 |
| alata | . . Yellow | . 5, G. Ev. S. | N. Holl. | 1803 |
| amara | . . White | . 8. Ev. T. | E. Ind. | 1816 |
| amœna | . . Yellow | . 8. Ev. S. | N. Holl. | 1820 |
| anceps | . . Yellow | . 5, G. Ev. S. | N. Holl. | 1820 |
| angulata | . . Yellow | . 6, G. Ev. S. | N. Holl. | 1820 |
| angustifolia | . Yellow | . 4, G. Ev. S. | N. S. W. | 1816 |
| arabica | . . White | . 8. Ev. T. | E. Ind. | 1820 |
| arborea | . . Pink | . 8. Ev. T. | Jamaica | 1768 |
| arenosa | . . | . 8. Ev. S. | Caracas | 1816 |
| armata | . . Yellow | . 5, G. Ev. S. | N. Holl. | 1803 |
| Arrophala | . . | . G. Ev. T. | Nepal. | 1818 |
| asparagoides | . Yellow | . 5, G. Ev. S. | N. Holl. | 1818 |
| aspera | . . Yellow | . 5, G. Ev. S. | N. Holl. | 1824 |
| Bancroftiana | . | . 8. Ev. T. | Jamaica | |
| biflora | . . Yellow | . 5, G. Ev. S. | N. Holl. | 1803 |
| binervata | . . Yellow | . 5, G. Ev. S. | N. Holl. | 1824 |
| bivenosa | . . Yellow | . 5, G. Ev. S. | N. Holl. | 1824 |
| brachyacantha | . | . 8. Ev. T. | S. Amer. | 1824 |
| brasiliensis | . | . 8. Ev. T. | Brasil | 1825 |
| brevifolia | . . Yellow | . 5, G. Ev. S. | N. Holl. | 1820 |
| brevipes | . . Yellow | . G. Ev. S. | N. S. W. | |
| Brownei, 1 | . Yellow | . 6, G. Ev. S. | N. S. W. | 1796 |
| Brunoni | . . Yellow | . 5, G. Ev. S. | N. Holl. | 1824 |
| braxifolia | . . Yellow | . 4, G. Ev. S. | N. Holl. | 1824 |
| Burmanniana, 2 | . | . 8. Ev. S. | Ceylon | 1818 |
| caesia | . . Yellow, | . 8. Ev. T. | E. Ind. | 1773 |
| cafra | . . Yel. wht. | . G. Ev. T. | C. G. H. | 1800 |
| calamifolia | . Yellow | . 5, G. Ev. S. | N. Holl. | 1823 |
| canaliculata | . Yellow | . 5, G. Ev. S. | N. Holl. | 1824 |
| caracasana | . Purple, | . 8. Ev. S. | Caracas | 1817 |
| cassioides | . White | . 8. Ev. T. | | 1820 |
| Catechu | . . Pa. yel. | . 8. Ev. T. | E. Ind. | 1790 |
| centrophylla | . White | . 8. Ev. T. | Jamaica | 1818 |
| Ceratonia | . . White | . 8. Ev. T. | S. Amer. | 1800 |
| chrysostachys | . | . 8. Ev. T. | Maurit. | 1824 |
| ciliata, 3 | . Yellow | . 5, G. Ev. S. | N. Holl. | 1803 |
| cinerascens | . Yellow | . 5, G. Ev. S. | N. Holl. | 1824 |
| cochlearis | . . Yellow | . 5, G. Ev. S. | N. Holl. | 1818 |
| concinna | . . White | . 8. Ev. S. | E. Ind. | 1823 |
| Concordiana | . | . 8. Ev. T. | E. Ind. | 1818 |
| conferta | . . Yellow | . 4, G. Ev. S. | N. Holl. | 1824 |
| contorta | . . White | . 8. Ev. T. | Brasil | 1825 |
| copallina | . | . 8. Ev. T. | | 1825 |
| coriacea | . . Yellow | . 5, G. Ev. S. | N. Holl. | 1825 |
| cornigera | . . Pa. yell. | . 8. Ev. T. | S. Amer. | 1692 |
| coronillæfolia, 4 | . | . 8. Ev. S. | N. Africa | 1817 |
| Courrantiana | . | . G. Ev. T. | Canaries | 1818 |
| crassicarpa | . Yellow | . 4, G. Ev. S. | N. Holl. | 1824 |
| crassiuscula | . Yellow | . 5, G. Ev. S. | N. Holl. | 1824 |
| Cyclops | . . Yellow | . 5, G. Ev. S. | N. Holl. | 1824 |
| daviesifolia | . Yellow | . 5, G. Ev. S. | N. Holl. | 1817 |
| dealbata | . . Yellow | . 5, G. Ev. S. | N. Holl. | 1823 |
| decipiens | . . Yellow | . 5, G. Ev. S. | N. Holl. | 1802 |
| præmorsa | . . Yellow | . 5, G. Ev. S. | N. Holl. | 1830 |
| decurrens | . . Yellow | . 6, G. Ev. S. | N. S. W. | 1790 |

[ 1 ]

B

| Name | Colour | No. | Grp | Type | S/T | Habitat | Year |
|---|---|---|---|---|---|---|---|
| detinens | Yellow | 5, | G. | Ev. | S. | N. Holl. | 1828 |
| diffusa, 5 | Yellow | 5, | G. | Ev. | S. | N. S. W. | 1814 |
| Dillwyniaefolia | Yellow | 5, | G. | Ev. | S. | N. Holl. | 1828 |
| diptera | White | | 8. | Ev. | T. | S. Amer. | 1818 |
| discolor | Yellow | 5, | G. | Ev. | S. | N. S. W. | 1784 |
| divaricata | White | 4, | G. | Ev. | S. | N. Holl. | 1827 |
| dodonaeifolia, 6 | Yellow | 5, | G. | Ev. | S. | N. Holl. | 1818 |
| dolabriformis | Yellow | 6, | G. | Ev. | S. | N. Holl. | 1814 |
| doratoxylon | Yellow | | 8. | Ev. | S. | N. Holl. | 1822 |
| dumosa | | | 8. | Ev. | T. | E. Ind. | 1818 |
| eburnea | Yellow | | 8. | Ev. | S. | E. Ind. | 1792 |
| echioides | Yellow | 5, | G. | Ev. | S. | N. Holl. | 1824 |
| edulis | | | 8. | Ev. | T. | E. Ind. | 1820 |
| eglandulosa | Yellow | 5, | G. | Ev. | S. | N. Holl. | 1824 |
| elata | | | 8. | Ev. | T. | E. Ind. | 1820 |
| elephantorhiza | | | G. | Ev. | T. | C. G. H. | 1818 |
| elongata | Yellow | 5, | G. | Ev. | S. | N. Holl. | 1824 |
| emarginata | Yellow | 4, | G. | Ev. | S. | N. Holl. | 1824 |
| esculenta | White | | 8. | Ev. | T. | N. Spain | 1825 |
| Esterhasia | Yellow | 5, | G. | Ev. | S. | N. Holl. | 1824 |
| falcata | Yellow | 5, | G. | Ev. | S. | N. S. W. | 1790 |
| falciformis | Yellow | 5, | G. | Ev. | S. | N. Holl. | 1818 |
| Farnesiana | Yellow | 7, | S. | Ev. | T. | St. Domin. | 1656 |
| ferruginea | | | 8. | Ev. | S. | E. Ind. | 1818 |
| filicina | | | 8. | Ev. | T. | Mexico | 1825 |
| flexuosa | | | 8. | Ev. | S. | Cumana | 1824 |
| floribunda | Yellow | 5, | G. | Ev. | S. | N. S. W. | 1796 |
| formosa | White | | 8. | Ev. | S. | Mexico | 1825 |
| frondosa | White | | 8. | Ev. | T. | E. Ind. | 1816 |
| fruticosa | | | 8. | Ev. | S. | E. Ind. | 1820 |
| fuscata | | | 8. | Ev. | S. | T. | 1824 |
| genistifolia | Yellow | 5, | G. | Ev. | S. | N. S. W | 1825 |
| Giraffae | | | 8. | Ev. | T. | C. G. H. | 1816 |
| glauca | White | 7, | G. | Ev. | S. | America | 1690 |
| glaucescens | Yellow | 6, | G. | Ev. | S. | N. S. W. | 1790 |
| grata | | | 8. | Ev. | S. | Brazil | 1820 |
| graveolens | Yellow | 5, | G. | Ev. | S. | N. Holl. | 1820 |
| guianensis | White | | 8. | Ev. | T. | Cayenne | 1803 |
| guayaquilensis | | | 8. | Ev. | S. | Guiaquil | 1818 |
| Guilandina | Yellow | | 8. | Ev. | cl. | Cayenne | 1820 |
| gummifera | | | G. | Ev. | T. | Guinea | 1823 |
| hastulata | Yellow | 5, | G. | Ev. | S. | N. Holl. | 1824 |
| hebecephala | Yellow | 4, | G. | Ev. | S. | N. Holl. | 1817 |
| hebeclada, 7 | | | 8. | Ev. | T. | C. G. H. | 1816 |
| haematoxylon | Yel.-wht. | | 8. | Ev. | T. | C. G. H. | 1816 |
| heteracantha | | | G. | Ev. | T. | C. G. H. | 1816 |
| heteromalla | Yellow | 6, | G. | Ev. | S. | N. Holl. | 1818 |
| heterophylla | Yellow | 5, | G. | Ev. | S. | N. Holl. | 1824 |
| hispidissima | White | | G. | Ev. | S. | Jamaica | 1800 |
| hispidula | Yellow | 4, | G. | Ev. | S. | N. S. W. | 1794 |
| homomalla | Yellow | 6, | G. | Ev. | S. | N. Holl. | 1822 |
| hybrida | Yellow | 5, | G. | Ev. | S. | Hybrid | 1822 |
| indica | | | 8. | Ev. | S. | E. Ind. | 1800 |
| intermedia | Yellow | | G. | Ev. | S. | N. Holl. | |
| intertexta | Yellow | 5, | G. | Ev. | S. | N. Holl. | 1824 |
| Intsia | Yel.-wht. | | 8. | Ev. | T. | E. Ind. | 1778 |
| Jacaranda | | | 8. | Ev. | T. | S. Amer. | 1825 |
| Julibrissin | White | 8, | H. | De. | T. | Levant | 1745 |
| juniperina | Yellow | | 8. | Ev. | S. | N. S. W. | 1790 |
| Kalkora | | | 8. | Ev. | T. | E. Ind. | 1818 |
| Lambertiana | Purple | 5, | G. | Ev. | S. | Mexico | 1818 |
| lanigera | Yellow | 4, | G. | Ev. | S. | N. Holl. | 1824 |
| latisiliqua | Pink | 5, | S. | Ev. | S. | W. Ind. | 1777 |
| latronum | White | | 8. | Ev. | T. | E. Ind. | 1824 |
| laurifolia | Yellow | | 8. | Ev. | T. | Tanna | 1775 |
| Lebbek | Pink | 5, | S. | Ev. | T. | Egypt | 1823 |
| lenticifolia | | | 8. | Ev. | T. | Mexico | 1824 |
| leproea | Yellow | 5, | G. | Ev. | S. | N. Holl. | 1817 |
| leptophylla | | | 8. | Ev. | T. | S. Amer. | 1824 |
| leucocephala | White | 7, | S. | Ev. | T. | E. Ind. | 1823 |
| leucophloea | Pa.-yel. | | 8. | Ev. | T. | E. Ind. | 1812 |
| leucophylla | Yellow | 5, | G. | Ev. | S. | N. Holl. | 1822 |
| linearis | Yellow | 5, | G. | Ev. | S. | N. S. W. | 1820 |
| lineata | Yellow | 4, | G. | Ev. | S. | N. Holl. | 1824 |
| linifolia | Yellow | 5, | G. | Ev. | S. | N. S. W. | 1790 |
| litakunensis | | | G. | Ev. | S. | Litakun | 1816 |
| lomatocarpa, 8 | Pa. yel. | | 8. | Ev. | T. | E. Ind. | 1824 |
| longifolia, 9 | Yellow | 4, | G. | Ev. | S. | N. S. W. | 1792 |
| longissima, 10 | Yellow | 5, | G. | Ev. | S. | N. S. W. | 1819 |
| lophantha | Yellow | 6, | G. | Ev. | S. | N. Holl. | 1803 |
| lophanthoides | Yellow | | 8. | Ev. | S. | Jamaica | 1820 |
| lucida | | | 8. | Ev. | T. | E. Ind. | 1820 |
| lunata | Yellow | | 8. | Ev. | T. | V. Die. I. | 1810 |
| macranthoides | | | 8. | Ev. | T. | Jamaica | 1820 |
| Manglium | Yellow | | 8. | Ev. | S. | E. Ind. | 1820 |
| marginata | Yellow | 5, | G. | Ev. | S. | N. S. W. | 1803 |
| maroccana | | | G. | Ev. | S. | Morocco | 1823 |
| melanoxylon | Yellow | 5, | G. | Ev. | S. | V. Die. L | 1818 |
| microphylla | | | 8. | Ev. | S. | Caraccas | 1826 |
| mollis, 11 | Yellow | 7, | S. | Ev. | S. | N. Holl. | 1810 |
| monacantha | White | | 8. | Ev. | T. | Brazil | 1818 |
| mucronata | Yellow | 5, | G. | Ev. | S. | N. Holl. | 1818 |
| mucronulata | Yellow | 5, | G. | Ev. | S. | N. Holl. | 1824 |
| multinervia | Yellow | 4, | G. | Ev. | S. | N. Holl. | 1824 |
| myrtifolia | Pa.-yel. | 5, | G. | Ev. | S. | N. S. W. | 1789 |
| nervosa | Yellow | 5, | G. | Ev. | S. | N. Holl. | 1824 |
| nigricans | Yellow | 6, | G. | Ev. | S. | N. Holl. | 1808 |
| obtusata | Yellow | 5, | G. | Ev. | S. | N. Holl. | 1824 |
| obtusifolia | Yellow | 5, | G. | Ev. | S. | N. Holl. | 1822 |
| odoratissima | White | | 8. | Ev. | T. | E. Ind. | 1790 |
| oleifolia | Yellow | 5, | G. | Ev. | S. | N. Holl. | 1824 |
| oligophylla | Yellow | | 8. | Ev. | S. | | 1817 |
| ornithophora | Yellow | 5, | G. | Ev. | S. | N. Holl. | 1824 |
| oxycedrus | Yellow | 5, | G. | Ev. | S. | N. Holl. | 1824 |
| papuliformis | Yellow | 4, | G. | Ev. | S. | N. Holl. | 1824 |
| patula | | | 8. | Ev. | T. | S. Amer. | 1818 |
| pedunculata | | | 8. | Ev. | T. | E. Ind. | 1822 |
| pendula | Yellow | 5, | G. | Ev. | S. | N. Holl. | 1824 |
| pennata | Yellow | | 8. | Ev. | T. | E. Ind. | 1773 |
| penninervia, 12 | Yellow | | 8. | Ev. | S. | N. Holl. | 1824 |
| pentadenia | Yellow | 4, | G. | Ev. | S. | N. Holl. | |
| peregrina | White | 7, | S. | Ev. | S. | S. Amer. | 1780 |
| peruviana | Yellow | | 8. | Ev. | T. | Peru | 1820 |
| pilosa | White | | 8. | Ev. | T. | Jamaica | 1800 |
| platyphylla | Yellow | 6, | S. | Ev. | S. | N. Holl. | 1820 |
| plectocarpa | Yellow | 4, | G. | Ev. | S. | N. Holl. | 1824 |
| plumosa | Yellow | | 8. | Da. | cl. | | |
| podalyriaefolia | Yellow | | 8. | Ev. | S. | N. Holl. | 1824 |
| polygalaefolia | Yellow | 4, | G. | Ev. | S. | N. Holl. | 1824 |
| polyphylla | White | | 8. | Ev. | S. | N. Holl. | 1824 |
| portoricensis | White | 7, | S. | Ev. | S. | W. Ind. | 1824 |
| praenans | Yellow | | G. | Ev. | cl. | | |
| prismatica | Yellow | | 8. | Ev. | S. | | 1818 |
| procera | Pa.-yel. | | 8. | Ev. | T. | E. Ind. | 1816 |
| prominens | Yellow | | 8. | Ev. | S. | N. Holl. | 1824 |
| pubescens | Yellow | 5, | G. | Ev. | S. | N. S. W. | 1790 |
| pugioniformis | Yellow | 5, | G. | Ev. | S. | N. Holl. | 1818 |
| pulchella | Yellow | 6, | G. | Ev. | S. | N. Holl. | 1803 |
| pulcherrima | | | 8. | Ev. | S. | Brazil | 1823 |
| pyrifolia | Yellow | 5, | G. | Ev. | S. | N. Holl. | 1824 |
| quadrangularis | White | 8, | S. | Ev. | S. | | 1825 |
| quadrilateralis | Yellow | | 8. | Ev. | S. | N. Holl. | 1824 |
| reticulata | White | | G. | Ev. | S. | C. G.H. | 1816 |
| rhodacantha | Yellow | | 8. | Ev. | T. | | |
| Richardsoni | Yellow | 6, | S. | Ev. | S. | N. Holl. | 1822 |
| rigens | Yellow | 5, | G. | Ev. | S. | N. Holl. | 1824 |
| robusta | | | G. | Ev. | S. | C. G. H. | 1816 |
| Rohriana, 13 | White | | 8. | Ev. | T. | | 1823 |
| Roesli | | | 8. | Ev. | T. | | 1822 |
| rubida | Yellow | 5, | G. | Ev. | S. | N. Holl. | 1823 |
| ruscifolia | Yellow | 4, | G. | Ev. | S. | N. Holl. | 1824 |
| rutaefolia | Yellow | | 8. | Ev. | S. | | 1810 |
| saligna | Yellow | 5, | G. | Ev. | S. | N. Holl. | 1818 |
| sapindoides | Yellow | | G. | Ev. | T. | Moreton B. | 1820 |
| sarmentosa | | | 8. | Ev. | cl. | | 1820 |
| scandens | Purple | | 8. | Ev. | cl. | India | 1780 |
| seleroxylon | | | 8. | Ev. | S. | W. Ind. | 1822 |
| semicordata | | | 8. | Ev. | T. | E. Ind. | 1820 |
| Senegal | White | | 8. | Ev. | T. | Africa | 1823 |
| Seriosa | | | 8. | Ev. | T. | E. Ind. | 1822 |
| Smithiana | | | 8. | Ev. | T. | | |
| Sophorae | Yellow | 5, | G. | Ev. | S. | V. Die. I. | 1805 |
| speciosa | Purple | 8, | S. | Ev. | S. | E. Ind. | 1742 |
| Spini | Red-yel. | | 8. | Ev. | T. | | |
| stipulata | White | | 8. | Ev. | T. | Bengal | 1800 |
| stricta | Yellow | 3, | G. | Ev. | S. | N. S. W. | 1790 |
| strombulifera | | | G. | Ev. | S. | Peru | 1825 |
| suaveolens, 14 | Yellow | 4, | G. | Ev. | S. | N. S. W. | 1790 |
| subulata | Yellow | 5, | G. | Ev. | S. | N. Holl. | 1824 |
| sulcata | Yellow | 7, | G. | Ev. | S. | N. Holl. | 1803 |
| Sundra | Yellow | | 8. | Ev. | T. | E. Ind. | 1789 |
| tamarindifolia | White | | 8. | Ev. | S. | W. Ind. | 1774 |
| taxifolia | Yellow | 5, | G. | Ev. | S. | N. Holl. | 1823 |
| tetragona | White | 6, | H. | Ev. | S. | Caraccas | 1820 |
| tomentosa | | | 8. | Ev. | S. | E. Ind. | 1816 |
| tortuosa | | | 8. | Ev. | S. | Jamaica | 1824 |
| trapesoides | Yellow | 4, | G. | Ev. | S. | N. Holl. | 1810 |
| trichodes | Pa.-yel. | | 8. | Ev. | S. | Peru | 1818 |
| trigonocarpa | Yellow | 5, | G. | Ev. | S. | N. Holl. | 1824 |
| tsinervata | Yellow | 4, | G. | Ev. | S. | N. Holl. | 1820 |
| tristis | Yellow | 3, | G. | Ev. | S. | N. Holl. | 1822 |
| umbrosa | Yellow | | 8. | Ev. | S. | N. Holl. | 1824 |
| uncinata | Yellow | 4, | G. | Ev. | S. | N. S. W. | 1819 |
| undulaefolia | Yellow | 5, | G. | Ev. | S. | N. Holl. | 1824 |
| vaga | White | | 8. | Ev. | T. | Brazil | 1818 |
| venusta | Pink | | 8. | Ev. | T. | S. Amer. | 1816 |
| vera | White | 7, | S. | Ev. | T. | Egypt | 1596 |
| verniciflua | Yellow | 5, | G. | Ev. | S. | N. Holl. | 1818 |
| verticillata | Yellow | 4, | G. | Ev. | S. | V. Die. I. | 1780 |
| angusta, 15 | Yellow | 4, | G. | Ev. | S. | | 1780 |
| latifolia, 16 | Yellow | 4, | G. | Ev. | S. | | 1780 |
| vestita | Yellow | 6, | G. | Ev. | S. | N. Holl. | 1820 |
| villosa | White | | 8. | Ev. | S. | Jamaica | 1800 |
| virescens | | | 8. | Ev. | T. | S. Amer. | 1820 |
| virgata | Yellow | | 8. | Ev. | S. | N. Holl. | 1824 |
| viridiflora | Wht.-green | | 8. | Ev. | T. | S. Amer. | 1824 |
| viridiramis | Yellow | | G. | Ev. | S. | C. G. H. | 1816 |
| Wallichiana | | | 8. | Ev. | T. | E. Ind. | 1820 |

ACAENA, *Linn.* From *akaina*, a thorn; in allusion to the thorns or bristles on the calyx or fruit. *Linn.* 2, Or. 1, Nat. Or. *Sanguisorbeæ.* Humble, shrubby, very curious plants, growing well in sandy loam and peat. Cuttings will root planted in soil, and protected by a frame or hand-glass.

| Name | Colour | No. | Grp | Type | S/T | Habitat | Year |
|---|---|---|---|---|---|---|---|
| adscendens | Green | 5, | H. | Her. | P. | Magellan | 1822 |
| argentea | Green | 5, | H. | Her. | P. | Chile | 1822 |
| latebrosa | Green | 5, | H. | Her. | P. | C. G. H. | 1822 |

| | | | | | | | |
|---|---|---|---|---|---|---|---|
| lævigātā | . . | . Green | . 7, | G. Her. | P. | Magell. | . 1790 |
| lūcidā | . . | . Green | . 5, | H. Her. | P. | Falk. Is. | . 1777 |
| magellānicā | . | . Yellow | . 5, | G. Her. | P. | Magell. | . 1823 |
| myriophyllā | . | . Green | . 5, | H. Her. | P. | Mendoza | . 1828 |
| ovalifôliā | . . | . Green | . 5, | H. Her. | P. | Peru | . 1802 |
| ovina | . . | . Green | . 6, | H. Her. | P. | N. Holl. | . 1818 |
| pinnatifīdā | . | . Green | . 5, | G. Her. | P. | Chile. | . 1822 |
| Sanguisôrbæ | . | . Green | . 6, | H. Her. | P. | N. Zeal. | . 1796 |

**ACĀLŸPHĀ, Linn.** From a, privative, kalos, pleasant, and aphe, touch. Linn. 21, Or. 1, Nat. Or. *Euphorbiaceæ.* Worthless species of the easiest culture, for which see genus *Abildgaardia—alopecuroīdēā, brachystāchyā, caroliniānā, ciliātā, cuspidātā, diversifôliā, hispidā, indicā, integrifôliā, lævigātā, macrostāchyā, môllis, pauciflôrā, polystāchyā, prunifôliā, rēptāns, rūbrā, scabrôsā, virgātā, virginicā.*

**ACANTHOPHIPPIŪM, Blum.** The meaning of the name is not explained. Linn. 20, Or. 1, Nat. Or. *Orchidaceæ.* A. bicolor is a very curious and rather rare plant; in habit it much resembles *A. geodorum,* only it has pseudo-bulbs instead of tubers, while its rich flowers are produced from near the base of the shoots. *A. striatum* is described as being very much inferior. They will thrive well with the same treatment as *Bletia,* provided they have a great deal of heat and moisture during the growing season.

| | | | | | |
|---|---|---|---|---|---|
| bicôlôr | . . . | . Yel-red | . 6, | S. Epi. | Ceylon | . 1833 |
| striātum | . . . | . White | . 6, | S. Epi. | Nepal | . . |
| sylhetense | . . | . White | . 6, | S. Epi. | Sylhet | . 1837 |

**ACĀNTHŪS, Linn.** From akantha, a spine, some of the species being spiny. Bear's Breech, Linn. 14, Or. 2, Nat. Or. *Acanthaceæ.* Coarse, yet stately, herbaceous plants, flourishing in almost any soil or situation, and are increased by divisions or by seed with great facility. *A. mollis* is said to be emollient; and it is conjectured that the leaf of this plant furnished the ancients with the elegant Acanthus leaf of their architecture.

| | | | | | | | |
|---|---|---|---|---|---|---|---|
| carduifôlius | . | . Blue | . 8, | G. Her. | P. | C. G. H. | . 1816 |
| hispanicus | . | . White | . 8, | H. Her. | P. | Spain | . 1700 |
| ilicifôlius | . . | . | . | S. Ev. | S. | E. Ind. | . 1759 |
| mollis | . . . | . Pur. wht. | 8, | H. Her. | P. | Italy | . 1548 |
| niger | . . . | . White | . 8, | H. Her. | P. | Portugal | . 1759 |
| spinosissimus | . | . Pur. wht. | 8, | H. Her. | P. | S. Eur. | . 1629 |
| spinôsus | . . | . Pur. wht. | 8, | H. Her. | P. | Italy | . 1629 |

**ACĀRNĀ, Willdenow.** Theophrastus describes a thistle under that name. Linn. 19, Or. 1, Nat. Or. *Compositæ.* Insignificant plants, void of any known merit. For culture and propagation, see genus *Abuta.* Synonyme: 1. *Atractylis cancellata—cancellātā* 1, *gummifera.*

**ACAULIS,** without a stem.

**ACCESSARY,** something added to the usual number of organs.

**ACCRETE,** grown together.

**ACCUMBENT,** lying on something else.

**ACER, Linn.** The word, in Latin, signifies vigorous, or sharp, and comes from *ac,* meaning a point, in Celtic. The name is used to designate this genus on account of the wood having formerly been much sought after for manufacturing into heads of pikes and lances. Linn. 23, Or. 1, Nat. Or. *Aceraceæ.* For the most part beautiful trees, of considerable size, generally employed in forming avenues or the back of shrubberies. The soil they delight most to grow in is open sandy loam, in which also, cuttings will strike freely in the open air; or by layers put down in the autumn they may be increased; but all the best plants are obtained from seed, which should be sown soon after gathering. From the sap of *A. saccharinum* the North Americans make a very good sort of sugar, in considerable quantities; other species possess, more or less, in the sap this saccharine property. Synonymes: 1. *A. eriocarpon.* 2. *A. sempervirens.* 3. *A. spicatum.* 4. *A. striatum, hybridum.*

| | | | | | | | |
|---|---|---|---|---|---|---|---|
| austriacum | . | . Green | . 5, | H. De. | T. | Austria | . |
| barbātum | . | . Orn. yel. | . 5, | H. De. | T. | N. Amer. | . 1812 |
| campēstrē | . | . Orn. yel. | . 5, | H. De. | T. | Britain | . |
| collīnum | . | . Orn. yel. | . 5, | H. De. | T. | France | . |
| variegātum | . | . Orn. yel. | . 5, | H. De. | T. | Britain | . |
| circinātum | . | . Orn. yel. | . 4, | H. De. | T. | Columbia | . 1827 |
| creticum | . | . | . 5, | H. De. | S. | Levant | . 1752 |
| dasycārpum, 1 | . | . Orn. yel. | . 4, | H. De. | T. | N. Amer. | . 1725 |
| heterophyllum, 2 | . | Orn. yel. | . 5, | H. Ev. | S. | Levant | . 1759 |
| hybridum | . | . Green | . 4, | H. De. | T. | Amer. hyb. | . 1790 |
| ibericum | . | . Green | . | H. De. | T. | Asiatic G. | . 1826 |
| lobātum | . | . Green | . | H. De. | T. | Siberia | . 1820 |

| | | | | | | | |
|---|---|---|---|---|---|---|---|
| macrophyllum | . Green | . | . 5, | H. De. | T. | N. Amer. | . 1826 |
| montānum, 3 | . Orn. yel. | . | . 4, | H. De. | T. | N. Amer. | . 1750 |
| monspessulānum | . Orn. yel. | . | . 4, | H. De. | S. | France | . 1789 |
| nigrum | . . . | . Orn. yel. | . 4, | H. De. | T. | N. Amer. | . 1812 |
| oblôngum | . . | . Orn. wht. | . | F. Ev. | T. | Nepal | . 1824 |
| obtusātum | . . | . Orn. yel. | . 5, | H. De. | S. | Hungary | . 1825 |
| obtusifôlium | . | . Orn. yel. | . 5, | H. De. | S. | Crete | . |
| opalifôlium | . | . Orn. yel. | . 5, | H. De. | S. | France | . 1826 |
| ôpälis | . . . | . Orn. yel. | . 5, | H. De. | T. | Italy | . 1752 |
| palmātum | . | . Green | . | H. De. | T. | Japan | . 1820 |
| pennsylvänicūm, 4 | Orn. yel. | . | . 5, | H. De. | T. | N. Amer. | . 1755 |
| platanoīdēs | . | . Orn. yel. | . 6, | H. De. | T. | Europe | . 1683 |
| laciniātum | . | . Orn. yel. | . 6, | H. De. | T. | Europe | . 1683 |
| Lobelii | . . | . Orn. yel. | . 6, | H. De. | T. | Naples | . |
| variegātum | . | . Orn. yel. | . 6, | H. De. | T. | Europe | . 1683 |
| Pseūdo-Plātānūs | Orn. yel. | . | . 4, | H. De. | T. | Britain | . |
| purpūreūm | . | . Purple | . 5, | H. De. | T. | | . 1828 |
| subobtūsūm | . | . Orn. yel. | . 5, | H. De. | T. | | . |
| variegātum | . | . Orn. yel. | . 5, | H. De. | T. | Britain | . |
| rūbrum | . . | . Red | . 4, | H. De. | T. | N. Amer. | . 1656 |
| saccharīnum | . | . Yellow | . 4, | H. De. | T. | N. Amer. | . 1735 |
| tatāricum | . . | . Orn. yel. | . 5, | H. De. | T. | Tartary | . 1759 |

**ACĒRĀS, Robert Brown.** From a, privative, and keras, horn, on account of the spur being absent. Linn. 20, Or. 1, Nat. Or. *Orchidaceæ.* A very curious species, rather troublesome to cultivate. A light loamy soil, mixed with chalk, delights it most, and it can only be increased by seeds.

| | | | | | | | |
|---|---|---|---|---|---|---|---|
| anthropôphôrā | . Green | . | . 6, | H. Tu. | P. | England | . |
| secundiflôrā | . | . Violet | . 7, | F. Tu. | P. | S. Eur. | . 1829 |

**ACĒRĀTŪM, Decandolle.** Derived from a, privative, and keras, a horn; implying that the anthers are destitute of horns. Linn. 11, Or. 1, Nat. Or. *Elæocarpaceæ.* An interesting species, grown in peat and loam; multiplied from cuttings.

| | | | | | | |
|---|---|---|---|---|---|---|
| oppositifôlium | . White | . | . 8. | S. Ev. | S. | Amboyna | . 1818 |

**ACEROSE,** fine and slender, with a sharp point.

**ACETARIOUS,** any thing belonging to the salad tribe of plants.

**ACETOSE,** sour, tart, acid.

**ACHILLĒA, Linn.** Named after Achilles, a pupil of Chiron, and the first who used the plant so called in medicine. Linn. 19, Or. 2, Nat. Or. *Asteraceæ,* or *Compositæ.* Showy, free-flowering species, succeeding well in any common soil, and readily increased by dividing the roots. *A. tomentosa* is, by its bright yellow flowers, well suited for ornamenting rock-work. The dried leaves of *A. Ptarmica,* powdered, and taken up the nostrils, excite sneezing. *A. moschata* is sudorific and acrid, and makes a wholesome food for cattle. Synonymes: 1. *A. serrata.* 2. *A. ambigua.* 3. *A. filicifolia.* 4. *A. ochroleuca.* 5. *A. helvetica.*

| | | | | | | | |
|---|---|---|---|---|---|---|---|
| abrotanifôliā | . Yellow | . | . 7, | H. Her. | P. | Levant | . 1789 |
| acuminātā | . White | . | . 8, | H. Her. | P. | | . 1830 |
| ægyptīācā | . Pa. yel. | . | . 8, | G. Ev. | S. | Levant | . 1640 |
| Agerātūm | . Yellow | . | . 9, | H. Her. | P. | S. Eur. | . 1570 |
| albidā | . . | . Pa. yel. | . 7, | H. Her. | P. | | . 1819 |
| alpinā | . . | . White | . 9, | H. Her. | P. | Siberia | . 1781 |
| anglicā, 1 | . | . White | . 8, | H. Her. | P. | Britain | . |
| anthemoīdēs | . | . Pa. yel. | . 7, | H. Her. | P. | | . |
| asplenifôliā | . | . Pink | . 7, | H. Her. | P. | N. Amer. | . 1803 |
| atrātā | . . | . White | . 8, | H. Her. | P. | Austria | . 1596 |
| aūrēā | . . | . Yellow | . 7, | H. Her. | P. | Levant | . 1739 |
| auriculātā | . | . Yellow | . 7, | H. Her. | P. | A. Minor | . 1827 |
| biserrātā | . | . White | . 6, | H. Her. | P. | Albania | . 1820 |
| chamæmēlifôliā | . White | . | . 7, | H. Her. | P. | France | . 1825 |
| Clavennæ | . | . White | . 6, | H. Her. | P. | Austria | . 1656 |
| coarctātā | . | . Yellow | . 8, | H. Her. | P. | S. Eur. | . 1816 |
| compāctā | . | . Pa. yel. | . 7, | H. Her. | P. | | . 1803 |
| coronopifôliā | . | . Pa. yel. | . 7, | H. Her. | P. | Levant | . 1823 |
| cretica | . . | . White | . 7, | H. Her. | P. | Candia | . 1739 |
| cristātā | . . | . White | . 7, | H. Her. | P. | Italy | . 1784 |
| crithmifôliā | . | . White | . 7, | H. Her. | P. | Hungary | . 1804 |
| decolôrāns | . | . Wht. yel. | . 7, | H. Her. | P. | | . 1798 |
| decūmbens | . | . Yellow | . 7, | H. Ev. | Tr. | Kamtsch. | . 1816 |
| Eupatôrium, 3 | . White | . | . 7, | H. Her. | P. | Casp. sho. | . 1803 |
| falcātā | . . | . Pa. yel. | . 7, | H. Her. | P. | Levant | . 1739 |
| Gerberi | . | . Pa. yel. | . 7, | H. Her. | P. | Siberia | . 1821 |
| glomerātā | . | . Yellow | . 7, | H. Her. | P. | Caucasus | . 1818 |
| grandiflôrā | . | . White | . 7, | H. Her. | P. | Caucasus | . 1818 |
| Herba-rôtā | . | . White | . 7, | H. Her. | P. | France | . 1640 |
| holoserīceā | . | . White | . 8, | H. Her. | P. | Parnassus | . 1817 |
| imbricātā | . | . Yellow | . 7, | H. Her. | P. | Persia | . 1818 |
| impātiēns | . | . White | . 8, | H. Her. | P. | Siberia | . 1759 |
| lanātā | . . | . White | . 7, | H. Her. | P. | | . 1804 |
| leptophyllā | . | . Pa. yel. | . 7, | H. Her. | P. | Tauria | . 1816 |
| ligustica | . | . White | . 7, | H. Her. | P. | Italy | . 1791 |
| lingulātā | . | . White | . 7, | H. Her. | P. | Hungary | . 1815 |
| macrophyllā | . | . White | . 7, | H. Her. | P. | Italy | . 1710 |
| micrantha | . | . Yellow | . 8, | H. Her. | P. | Levant | . 1805 |
| microphyllā | . | . White | . 8, | H. Her. | P. | Spain | . 1800 |
| Millefôlium | . | . White | . 8, | H. Her. | P. | Britain | . |
| mongôlicā | . | . White | . 7, | H. Her. | P. | Siberia | . 1819 |

| | | | | | | |
|---|---|---|---|---|---|---|
| moschātā | . | White | . 6, | H. Her. P. | Italy | . 1775 |
| myriophyllā | . | White | . 8, | H. Her. P. | | . 1798 |
| nāna | . | White | . 7, | H. Her. P. | Italy | . 1769 |
| nobīlis | . | White | . 7, | H. Her. P. | Germany | . 1640 |
| ochroleūcā | . | Pa. yel. | . 8, | H. Her. P. | | . 1804 |
| odorātā | . | White | . 7, | H. Her. P. | Spain | . 1789 |
| paucīflorā | . | Yellow | . 7, | H. Her. P. | Spain | . 1810 |
| pectinātā, 4 | . | Pa. yel. | . 8, | H. Her. P. | Hungary | . 1801 |
| Ptarmicā | . | White | . 7, | H. Her. P. | Britain | . |
| flōre-plēnō | . | White | . 8, | H. Her. P. | | . |
| pubēscens | . | Lgt. yel. | . 8, | H. Her. P. | Levant | . 1789 |
| punctātā | . | Straw | . 7, | H. Her. P. | Naples | . 1820 |
| recurvifōliā | . | White | . 7, | H. Her. P. | Pyrenees | . 1820 |
| Santolīnā | . | Pa. yel. | . 7, | H. Her. P. | Levant | . 1759 |
| santolinōīdēs | . | White | . 7, | H. Her. P. | Spain | . |
| serrātā | . | White | . 8, | H. Her. P. | Switzerland | 1686 |
| setāceā | . | White | . 7, | H. Her. P. | Hungary | . 1805 |
| speciōsā | . | White | . 8, | H. Her. P. | | . 1804 |
| squarrōsā | . | White | . 7, | H. Her. P. | | . 1775 |
| tanacetifōliā | . | Pink | . 7, | H. Her. P. | Switzerland | 1820 |
| tenuifōliā | . | Yellow | . 7, | H. Her. P. | Switzerland | 1658 |
| taūricā | . | Pa. yel. | . 7, | H. Her. P. | Tauria | . 1818 |
| tomentōsā | . | Yellow | . 7, | H. Her. P. | Britain | . |
| valleslācā, 5 | . | White | . 7, | H. Her. P. | Switzerland | 1819 |

*Bannātīcā, dentīfera, distans 2, dubia, heterophȳllā, intermedia, magna, Millefōliōm rubrum, montana, polyphȳllā, rosea, stricta.*

ACHLȲS, *Decandolle.* From *achlys,* meaning obscure, in allusion to the obscurity of the genus. *Linn.* 13, Or. 1, Nat. Or. *Berberaceæ.* A tuberous-rooted plant, of little beauty, multiplied by cuttings, and grown in sandy loam.

| | | | | | | |
|---|---|---|---|---|---|---|
| triphȳllā | . | White | . 5, | H. Ev. T. | N. Amer. | 1827 |

ACNĀNTHĒS, *Agardh.* Derived from *achne,* froth of the ocean, and *anthos,* flower. *Linn.* 24, Or. 7, Nat. Or. *Algæ.* Curious aquatic productions, said to separate by degrees into fragments: between every articulation or joint is one or more crystalline points—*brēvīpēs, lōngīpēs, unipunctātā.*

ACHNODŌNTŌN, *Palisot de Beauvois.* From *achne,* a chaff, or husk, and *odon,* a tooth. *Linn.* 3, Or. 2, Nat. Or. *Graminaceæ.* Very insignificant plants, of the easiest culture, for which see *Abildgaardia.* Synonyme: 1. *Phalaris bellardi. Bellārdī* 1. *līnēæ.*

ACHRĀS, *Linn.* The Greek name for the pear, or from *ac,* meaning a point, in Celtic, in allusion to the stiff spines with which the tree is covered. *Linn.* 5, Or. 1, Nat. Or. *Sapotaceæ.* These plants, in this country, possess little merit, but in the West Indies the fruit produced by some of the species is much esteemed. *A. sapota* yields a fruit as large as a quince, the flesh of which is as *yellow* as a carrot; it has an agreeable smell, and very rich taste; the seeds, two in number, are aperient and diuretic; rich loamy soil; cuttings.

| | | | | | |
|---|---|---|---|---|---|
| australis | . | | G. Ev. T. | N. Holl. | . 1827 |
| Sapōta | . | White | S. Ev. T. | S. Amer. | . 1731 |
| Zapotīllā | . | White | S. Ev. T. | S. Amer. | . 1731 |

ACHYRĀNTHĒS, *Linn.* Achuron, chaff, and *anthos,* a flower, in allusion to the chaffy nature of the floral leaves. *Linn.* 5, Or. 1, Nat. Or. *Amarantaceæ.* Uninteresting species, of easy culture. *A. pōrrigēns* is the most handsome species.

| | | | | | | |
|---|---|---|---|---|---|---|
| argentēā | . | White | . 8. | S. Ev. S. | Sicily | . 1713 |
| aspērā | . | Pink | . 4. | S. Ev. S. | India | . 1751 |
| australis | . | White | . 6, | G. Ev. S. | N. Holl. | . 1823 |
| brachiātā | . | White | . 7, | G. | A. E. Ind. | . 1824 |
| crispā | . | Wht. grn. | 7, | G. Ev. S. | S. Amer. | . 1810 |
| dichōtōmā | . | Green | . 8, | H. | A. N. Amer. | . |
| fruticōsā | . | Purple | . 6, | G. Ev. S. | E. Ind. | . 1820 |
| nivēā | . | White | . 6, | G. Ev. S. | Canaries | . 1780 |
| obtusifōliā | . | Pink | . 8, | S. Ev. S. | | . |
| pōrrigēns | . | Purple | . 7, | S. Ev. S. | | . 1802 |
| pubēscens | . | Pink | . 6, | G. Ev. S. | | . 1821 |
| verticillātā | . | White | . 7, | G. Ev. S. | C. G. H. | . 1820 |
| virgātā | . | Wht. grn. | 7, | G. Ev. S. | W. Ind. | . 1817 |

ACHYRŌNYĀ, *Willd.* From *achuron,* chaff, in allusion to the chaffy hairs on the branches and leaves. *Linn.* 17, Or. 4, Nat. Or. *Leguminosæ Papilionaceæ.* The species is of easy culture.

| | | | | | | |
|---|---|---|---|---|---|---|
| villōsā | . | Yellow | . 7, | G. Ev. S. | N. Holl. | . 1819 |

ACHYROPHŌRŪS, *D. Don.* Achuron, chaff, and *phoreo,* to bear; the receptacle being chaffy. *Linn.* 19, Or. 1, Nat. Or. *Compositæ.* Mere weeds, of the easiest culture and propagation. Synonymes: 1. *Hypochæris helvetica.* 2. *H. maculata.* 3. *H. radicata—helvēticā* 1, *maculātā* 2, *radicātā* 3.

ACIĀNTHŪS, *Robert Brown.* From *akis,* a point, and *anthos,* a flower; in reference to the bristly tips of the flower. *Linn.* 20, Or. 1, Nat. Or. *Orchidaceæ.* Brown, small-flowered, tuberous-rooted plants; multiplied by divisions, and grown in loam and peat.

| | | | | | | |
|---|---|---|---|---|---|---|
| caudātūs | . | Brown | . 5, | G. Ev. Tu. | N. Holl. | . 1824 |
| exsērtūs | . | Brown | . 5, | G. Ev. Tu. | N. Holl. | . 1822 |
| fornicātūs | . | Brown | . 5, | G. Ev. Tu. | N. Holl. | . 1822 |

ACICĀRPŪ, *Jussieu.* From *akis,* a point, and *karphe, palea;* on account of the palea being spiny. *Linn.* 19, Or. 4, Nat. Or. *Calyceraceæ.* A curious dwarf species, succeeding in peat and loam; propagated from divisions.

| | | | | | |
|---|---|---|---|---|---|
| spatulātā | . | . | . | S. Her. P. | Brazil | . 1824 |

ACICŪLĀE, needle-shaped.

ACIDŌTŌN, *Swartz.* From *akidotos,* pointed; in allusion to the stinging hairs on the leaves. *Linn.* 21, Or. 9, Nat. Or. *Euphorbiaceæ.* A worthless species, easily grown and propagated:—*Grēns.*

ACINĀCIFŌRM, scimitar-like shaped.

ACIŌTIS, *D. Don.* From *akis,* a point, and *ous,* an ear; in allusion to the petals. *Linn.* 10, Or. 1, Nat. Or. *Melastomaceæ.* Pretty species, particularly *aquatica;* may be propagated and grown the same as the genus *Melastoma.* Synonymes: 1. *Rhexia aquatica. Melastoma aquatica.* 2. *Melastoma discolor.*

| | | | | | | |
|---|---|---|---|---|---|---|
| aquaticā, 1 | . | . | Wht. red | 6, S. Ev. S. | S. Amer. | . 1793 |
| discolōr, 2 | . | . | Wht. red | 6, S. Ev. S. | Trinidad | . 1816 |

ACĪS, *Salisbury.* Taken from *Acis,* a shepherd, the son of Faunus. *Linn.* 6, Or. 1, Nat. Or. *Amaryllidaceæ.* This is a genus of pretty, dwarf, bulbous-rooted plants, delighting in sandy soil, and multiplied by offsets. Synonymes: 1. *Leucojum autumnale.* 2. *L. roseum.* 3. *L. tricophyllum.*

| | | | | | | |
|---|---|---|---|---|---|---|
| autumnālīs, 1 | . | Pink | . 9, | H. De. Bu. | Portugal | . 1629 |
| grandiflōrūs | . | White | . 8, | H. De. Bu. | Numidia | . 1820 |
| rōsēūs, 2 | . | Red | . 8, | H. De. Bu. | Corsica | . 1820 |
| trichophȳllūs, 3 | . | White | . 4, | H. De. Bu. | Spain | . 1820 |

ACISANTHĒRĀ, *Jussieu.* Taken from *akis,* a point, and *anthos,* an anther, on account of the anthers being pointed. *Linn.* 10, Or. 1, Nat. Or. *Melastomaceæ.* A curious evergreen shrub, for propagation and culture may be referred to *Melastoma.* Synonyme: 1. *Rhexia acisanthera.*

| | | | | | |
|---|---|---|---|---|---|
| quadrātā, 1 | . | . | . | S. Ev. S. | Jamaica | 1804 |

ACMADĒNĪĀ, *Bartl.* Taken from *akme,* a point, and *aden,* a gland; in allusion to glands on the anthers. *Linn.* 5, Or. 1, Nat. Or. *Rutaceæ.* A handsome little species, for culture and propagation, see *Dioema.* Synonyme: 1. *Adenandra tetragona.*

| | | | | | | |
|---|---|---|---|---|---|---|
| tetragōnā, 1 | . | White | . 6, | G. Ev. S. | C. G. H. | . 1798 |

ACMĒLLĀ, *Rich.* Taken from *akme,* a point; in allusion to the pricking taste of the foliage. *Linn.* 19, Or. 2, Nat. Or. *Compositæ.* Uninteresting dwarf, trailing species; for culture, &c., see genus *Galinsogea.* Synonymes: 1. *Spilanthes Acmella.* 2. *S. repens.*

| | | | | | | |
|---|---|---|---|---|---|---|
| occidentālīs | . | Yellow | . 7, | H. Tr. A. | S. Amer. | . 1825 |
| rēpēns, 2 | . | Yellow | . 7, | H. Tr. A. | Carolina | . 1818 |

*Maurilānd, 1.*

ACMĒNĀ, *Decandolle.* Derived from *Acmena,* a nymph of Venus. *Linn.* 12, Or. 1, Nat. Or. *Myrtaceæ.* An ornamental species; for culture, &c., see *Tristanea.* Synonyme: 1. *Metrosideros floribunda.*

| | | | | | | |
|---|---|---|---|---|---|---|
| florībundā, 1 | . | White | . 7, | G. Ev. S. | N. Holl. | . 1788 |

ACNĪDĀ, *Linn.* Taken from *a,* privative, and *knide,* nettle; the plant being like a nettle, but without stings. *Linn.* 22, Or. 6, Nat. Or. *Chenopodiaceæ.* An uninteresting species; for culture, &c., see *Cannabis:—cannabīnā.*

ACONĪTŪM, *Tournefort.* The name is given on account of some species being found plentiful about Acone, a town in Bithynia. *Linn.* 13, Or. 3, Nat. Or. *Ranunculaceæ.* Ornamental, tall, free-flowering, very hardy plants, succeeding well under the shade of trees; increased by division or by seeds. All the species are to be dreaded, being highly poisonous. *A. napellus,* and *cammarum,* are diuretic, and acrid in a high degree. The aconite has, however, become of great service in many very troublesome disorders. In Sweden favourable operations have been effected by an extract of the juice of the leaves of *A. napellus* in cases of rheumatism and intermittent fevers, applied in doses of from a grain to a scruple twice a day or oftener. A much larger dose has also been safely administered. Synonymes: 1. *A. inclinatum.* 2.

[ 4 ]

*A. altissimum.* 3. *A. pyrenaicum.* 4. *A. strictum.*
5. *A. pallidum.* 6. *A. Cammarum.* 7. *A. Napellus
pubescens.* 8. *A. laxum.*

| Species | Colour | No. | H. | Dur. | Type | Country | Year |
|---|---|---|---|---|---|---|---|
| acuminatum | Blue | 7, | H. | De. | Tu. | Switz. | 1819 |
| acutum | Blue | 6, | H. | De. | Tu. | S. Eur. | 1821 |
| albidum | White | 6, | H. | De. | Tu. | Europe | 1824 |
| album | White | 7, | H. | Her. | P. | Levant | 1752 |
| amænum | Blue | 6, | H. | De. | Tu. | S. Eur. | |
| ampliflorum | Blue | 6, | H. | De. | Tu. | Austria | 1823 |
| angustifolium | Blue | 6, | H. | De. | Tu. | Europe | 1824 |
| Anthora | Pa. yel. | 7, | H. | Her. | P. | Pyrenees | 1596 |
| Anthoroideum, 1 | Pa. yel. | 7, | H. | Her. | P. | Jura | 1821 |
| australe | Purple | 7, | H. | De. | Tu. | Denmark | 1821 |
| barbatum | Pa. yel. | 6, | H. | Her. | P. | Siberia | 1807 |
| Bernhardianum | Blue | 6, | H. | De. | Tu. | Europe | 1824 |
| biflorum | Pa. blue | 6, | H. | De. | Tu. | Siberia | 1817 |
| Bräunii | Blue | 7, | H. | De. | Tu. | Switzerl. | 1821 |
| callybotryon | Blue | 6, | H. | De. | Tu. | S. Eur. | |
| Cammarum | Purple | 8, | H. | De. | Tu. | Austria | 1752 |
| carpaticum | Purple | 7, | H. | Her. | P. | Carp. mo. | 1810 |
| cernuum | Blue | 7, | H. | De. | Tu. | Switzerl. | 1800 |
|   flexicaule | Blue | 7, | H. | De. | Tu. | Switzerl. | 1819 |
|   pauciflorum | Blue | 7, | H. | De. | Tu. | Switzerl. | 1821 |
|   ramosum | Blue | 7, | H. | De. | Tu. | | |
| chinense | Blue | 9, | H. | Her. | P. | China | 1833 |
| Clusii | Blue | 7, | H. | De. | Tu. | Switzerl. | 1819 |
| commutatum | Blue | 6, | H. | De. | Tu. | S. Eur. | 1823 |
| Cynoctonum, 2 | Pa. yel. | 7, | H. | Her. | P. | France | 1820 |
| Decandollii | Pa. yel. | 7, | H. | Her. | P. | Siberia | 1823 |
| decorum | Blue | 6, | H. | De. | Tu. | Pyrenees | 1824 |
| delphinifolium | Blue | 6, | H. | De. | Tu. | N. Amer. | 1804 |
| elatum | Blue | 6, | H. | De. | Tu. | Europe | 1822 |
| eminens | Blue | 6, | H. | De. | Tu. | Europe | 1800 |
| eriostemon | Blue | 6, | H. | De. | Tu. | Europe | 1821 |
| eulophum | Pa. yel. | 6, | H. | Her. | P. | Caucasus | 1821 |
| eustachyon | Blue | 6, | H. | De. | Tu. | Europe | 1824 |
| exaltatum | Blue | 7, | H. | De. | Tu. | Siberia | 1819 |
| flaccidum | Blue | 7, | H. | De. | Tu. | Siberia | 1822 |
| Florkeanum | Blue | 7, | H. | De. | Tu. | Siberia | 1822 |
|   bicolor | Blu. wht. | 6, | H. | De. | Tu. | Switzerl. | 1801 |
| formosum | Blue | 7, | H. | De. | Tu. | S. Eur. | 1824 |
| Fünkii | Blue | 6, | H. | De. | Tu. | Switzerl. | 1825 |
| Galactonum | Blue | 6, | H. | De. | Tu. | Hungary | 1822 |
| gibbosum | Blue | 7, | H. | De. | Tu. | Caucasus | 1818 |
| Gmelini | Blue | 7, | H. | De. | Tu. | Siberia | 1821 |
| gracile | Blue | 7, | H. | De. | Tu. | Switzerl. | 1821 |
| grandiflorum | Pa. yel. | 7, | H. | Her. | P. | Jura | 1821 |
| Halleri | Blue | 6, | H. | De. | Tu. | S. Eur. | 1821 |
|   bicolor | Blue | 6, | H. | De. | Tu. | Switzerl. | 1820 |
| hamatum | Pa. blue | 7, | H. | De. | Tu. | Italy | 1810 |
| hebegynum | Purple | 7, | H. | De. | Tu. | Switzerl. | 1819 |
|   multifidum | Purple | 7, | H. | De. | Tu. | Switzerl. | 1819 |
| hians | Blue | 6, | H. | De. | Tu. | S. Eur. | 1823 |
| hispidum | Pa. yel. | 6, | H. | De. | Tu. | Siberia | 1823 |
| Höppii | Blue | 6, | H. | De. | Tu. | Carinthia | 1823 |
| illimitum | Blue | 7, | H. | De. | Tu. | | 1821 |
| intermedium | Blue | 7, | H. | De. | Tu. | | 1820 |
| inunctum | Blue | 6, | H. | De. | Tu. | Europe | 1822 |
| Jacquini | Pa. yel. | 7, | H. | Her. | P. | Austria | 1800 |
| japonicum | Flesh | 8, | H. | De. | Tu. | Japan | 1790 |
|   cæruleum | Blue | 7, | H. | De. | Tu. | Japan | 1700 |
| Kalleanum | Blue | 6, | H. | De. | Tu. | S. Eur. | 1820 |
|   pygmæum | Blue | 6, | H. | De. | Tu. | S. Eur. | 1822 |
| Kohleri | Blue | 6, | H. | De. | Tu. | Europe | 1824 |
| lacinioeum | Blue | 7, | H. | De. | Tu. | Switzerl. | 1820 |
| latum | Blue | 6, | H. | De. | Tu. | S. Eur. | 1820 |
| Lamarckii, 3 | Pa. yel. | 7, | H. | Her. | P. | Pyrenees | 1817 |
| laxiflorum | Pa. yel. | 7, | H. | Her. | P. | Switzerl. | 1823 |
| larum | Blue | 6, | H. | De. | Tu. | S. Eur. | 1820 |
| leucanthum | White | 6, | H. | De. | Tu. | | 1823 |
| lupicidum | Pa. yel. | 7, | H. | De. | Tu. | Europe | 1821 |
| lycoctonum | Purple | 7, | H. | Her. | P. | Alp. Eur. | 1596 |
| macrophyllum | Pa. yel. | 7, | H. | Her. | P. | | |
| maximum | Blue | 7, | H. | De. | Tu. | Kamtsch. | 1823 |
| melectonum | Blue | 6, | H. | De. | Tu. | | 1821 |
| Meyeri | Blue | 6, | H. | De. | Tu. | Switzerl. | 1825 |
| moldavicum | Purplish | 8, | H. | Her. | P. | Moldav. | 1830 |
| mollis | Blue | 7, | H. | De. | Tu. | | 1820 |
| Napellus | Blue | 6, | H. | De. | Tu. | Europe | 1596 |
|   albus | White | 6, | H. | De. | Tu. | Switzerl. | 1819 |
|   rubellus | Blue | 6, | H. | De. | Tu. | Switzerl. | 1819 |
| nasutum | Purple | 7, | H. | De. | Tu. | Siberia | 1818 |
| nemorosum | Pa. yel. | 7, | H. | Her. | P. | Caucasus | 1823 |
| neomontanum | Blue | 7, | H. | De. | Tu. | Europe | 1799 |
| neubergense, 4 | Blue | 6, | H. | De. | Tu. | S. Eur. | 1822 |
| nitidum | Blue | 7, | H. | De. | Tu. | Switzerl. | 1825 |
| Nuttallii, 5 | Pa. blue | 8, | H. | Her. | P. | N. Amer. | 1822 |
| ochroleucum | Lgt. yel. | 7, | H. | Her. | P. | Caucasus | 1794 |
| oligocarpum | Blue | 7, | H. | De. | Tu. | Europe | 1823 |
| Ottonianum | Blue | 6, | H. | De. | Tu. | Europe | 1824 |
| Pallasii | Pa. yel. | 7, | H. | Her. | P. | Siberia | 1821 |
| paniculatum | Pa. blue | 7, | H. | Her. | P. | France | 1815 |
| plicatum | Blue | 6, | H. | De. | Tu. | Switzerl. | 1825 |
| productum | Blue | 7, | H. | De. | Tu. | Siberia | 1821 |
| pubescens | Blue | 6, | H. | De. | Tu. | Europe | 1824 |
| pyrenaicum | Yellow | 6, | H. | Her. | P. | Pyrenees | 1739 |
| recognitum | Blue | 6, | H. | De. | Tu. | | 1820 |
| rectum | Pa. yel. | 7, | H. | Her. | P. | Europe | 1824 |
| rigidum | Blue | 6, | H. | De. | Tu. | Switzerl. | 1825 |
| grandiflorum | Blue | 6, | H. | De. | Tu. | Siberia | 1822 |
| rostratum | Blue | 7, | H. | De. | Tu. | Switzerl. | 1810 |
|   piloniscetidum, 6 | Purple | 7, | H. | De. | Tu. | Carp. mo. | 1800 |
| rubicundum | Purple | 7, | H. | Her. | P. | Siberia | 1819 |
| rhynchanthum | Pur. blu. | 7, | H. | De. | Tu. | Switzerl. | 1821 |
|   bicolor | Wht. blu. | 7, | H. | De. | Tu. | Switzerl. | 1821 |
| Schleicheri, 7 | Blue | 6, | H. | De. | Tu. | Switzerl. | 1821 |
| semigaleatum | Blue | 6, | H. | De. | Tu. | Siberia | 1818 |
| septentrionale | Blue | 7, | H. | Her. | P. | N. Eur. | 1800 |
| speciosum | Blue | 7, | H. | De. | Tu. | | 1823 |
| Sprengelii | Blue | 6, | H. | De. | Tu. | Europe | 1824 |
| squarrosum | Blue | 7, | H. | De. | Tu. | Siberia | 1822 |
| Stoerckianum | Blue | 8, | H. | Her. | P. | Austria | 1824 |
| strictum | Blue | 6, | H. | De. | Tu. | Siberia | 1824 |
| tauricum, 8 | Blue | 6, | H. | De. | Tu. | Tauria | 1752 |
| theriophonum | Pa. yel. | 6, | H. | Her. | P. | Europe | 1824 |
| tortuosum | Pur. blue | 7, | H. | De. | Tu. | | 1812 |
| toxicum | Blue | 6, | H. | De. | Tu. | Switzerl. | 1825 |
| tragoctonum | Pa. yel. | 7, | H. | Her. | P. | Switzerl. | 1822 |
| umbrosum | Blue | 7, | H. | De. | Tu. | Switzerl. | 1825 |
| uncinatum | Blue | 7, | H. | De. | Tu. | N. Amer. | 1768 |
|   Michauxianum | Blue | 7, | H. | De. | Tu. | N. Amer. | 1800 |
| variegatum | Pur. wht. | 7, | H. | De. | Tu. | S. Eur. | 1597 |
|   albiflorum | White | 7, | H. | De. | Tu. | Switzerl. | 1819 |
|   bicolor | Wht. blu. | 7, | H. | De. | Tu. | Switzerl. | 1821 |
|   cœruleum | Blue | 7, | H. | De. | Tu. | Switzerl. | 1819 |
| venustum | Blue | 7, | H. | De. | Tu. | Switzerl. | 1823 |
| veralcolor | Blu. yel. | 8, | H. | Her. | P. | Siberia | 1820 |
| virgatum | Blue | 6, | H. | De. | Tu. | S. Eur. | 1822 |
| volubile | Blue | 7, | H. | De. | Tu. | Siberia | 1799 |
| Vulparia | Pa. yel. | 7, | H. | Her. | P. | Alp. Eur. | 1821 |
| Willdenovii | Blue | 7, | H. | De. | Tu. | Europe | 1823 |
| zooctonum | Blue | 6, | H. | De. | Tu. | Switzerl. | 1825 |

ACORUS, *Linn.* Derived from *a*, privative, and *kore*, pupil of the eye, in reference to its medical properties. *Linn.* 6, Or. 1, Nat. Or. *Acoraceæ.* Marshy plants, of the easiest culture. *A. Calamus* is extremely useful, and Linnæus says, the roots powdered, might supply the place of foreign spices; it is very aromatic and stimulant.

| | | | | | | | |
|---|---|---|---|---|---|---|---|
| Calamus | Apetal. | 6, | H. | Aq. | P. | Britain | |
| gramineus | Apetal. | 2, | H. | Her. | P. | China | 1796 |
| terrestris | Apetal. | 6, | H. | Her. | P. | China | 1822 |

ACREMONIUM, *Link.* Derived from *akremon*, a branch, in reference to the clustered thecæ. *Linn.* 24, Or. 9, Nat. Or. *Fungi.* Very curious plants, found growing generally upon dead sticks—*fuscum, verticillatum.*
ACRE, sharp, pungent.
ACROCEPHALUS, *Bentham.* The name is derived from *akron*, summit, *kephale*, head; on account of the flowers being on the top of the branches. *Linn.* 14, Or. 1, Nat. Or. *Labiatæ.* A plant of little beauty; increased from slips, and grown in sandy loam. *Synonyme: Lumnitzera capitata.*

| | | | | | | | |
|---|---|---|---|---|---|---|---|
| capitatus, 1 | White | 7, | H. | A. | | China | 1806 |

ACROCOMIA, *Martius.* The leaves are in tufts, hence the derivation of the name, *akros*, top, and *kome*, tuft. *Linn.* 21, Or. 6, Nat. Or. *Palmaceæ.* This genus comprehends a portion of those majestic species of palms which, by their towering stems and gigantic foliage, soar to the height of thirty or forty feet, and give a feature of exquisite grandeur to the character of the countries they inhabit. They prefer a light sandy loam; and to grow them well, an atmosphere very moist and warm is indispensable. They are increased from suckers. *A. aculeata* is reported to have a trunk the size of a man's body, and the leaves prickly and longer than those of the *Cocos.* It produces a fruit the shape and size of a crab, with a thin, sweetish, astringent pulp, within which is a nut inclosing a white sweet eatable kernel. *Synonymes:* 1. *Cocos aculeata.* 2. *C. fusiformis.* 3. *Bactris globosa-minor.*

| | | | | |
|---|---|---|---|---|
| aculeata, 1 | | Palm. | W. Ind. | 1796 |
| fusiformis, 2 | | Palm. | Trinidad | 1731 |
| globosa | | Palm. | St. Vinc. | 1824 |
| guianensis | | Palm. | Demerara | 1824 |
| horrida | | Palm. | Trinidad | 1825 |
| minor, 3 | | Palm. | Trinidad | 1820 |
| sclerocarpa | | Palm. | W. Ind. | 1731 |
| tenuifolia | | Palm. | Brasil | 1824 |

ACROGLOCHIN, *Schrader.* Taken from *akros*, summit, and *glochin*, spear point. *Linn.* 21, Or. 1, Nat. Or. *Chenopodiaceæ.* An insignificant species, grown in any common soil, and increased from suckers. *Synonyme:* 1. *Amaranthus Acroglochin—chenopodioïdes* 1.
ACROPERA, *Lindley.* From *acros*, the extremity, and *pera*, a small sack, because of the saccate appen-

dage at the apex of the labellum. *Linn.* 20, Or. 1, Nat. Or. *Orchidaceæ.* A very singular and rather pretty plant, producing its pale yellow and spotted purple flowers in pendent racemes. For culture and propagation, see *Stanhopea.* Synonymes: 1. *Maxillaria galeata.*

Loddigesii . . . Yel. & spot. 8, S. Epi. Mexico . . 1828

ACROSPERMŪM, *Tode.* Derived from *akros,* summit, and *sperma,* seed, in reference to the tumids on the apex of the plant emitting sporules. *Linn.* 24, Or. 9, Nat. Or. *Fungi.* Interesting and minute productions, existing as parasites upon decayed vegetables—*compressŭm, cornŭtŭm.*

ACROSPORĪŪM, *Nees.* This word is taken from *akros,* top, and *spora,* sporule, implying that the latter occupies the summit of the filaments. *Linn.* 24, Or. 9, Nat. Or. *Fungi.* Minute species found upon the leaves of grasses and rotten oranges—*fasciculatŭm, monilioides.*

ACROSTICHŪM, *Linn.* Supposed to refer to the beginning of a verse, on account of the back surfaces of the leaves being so lined as to resemble in some degree the commencement of lines in poetry. *Linn.* 24, Or. 1, Nat. Or. *Polypodiaceæ.* Very interesting species of tropical ferns, delighting mostly in a mixture of loam and peat. They may be increased either by dividing at the roots, or by seed. *A. aureum* sometimes grows to the height of four, five, and even six feet. *A. alcicorne* is a curious species common in our plant houses.

| | | | | | |
|---|---|---|---|---|---|
| alcicornĕ . . | . Brown | . 9, Parasite. | N. S. W. | . 1808 |
| appendiculatŭm . | . Brown | . 7, S. Her. | P. W. Ind. | . 1824 |
| aŭrĕŭm . . | . Brown | . 8, S. Her. | P. W. Ind. | . 1815 |
| crinitŭm . . | . Brown | . 7, S. Her. | P. W. Ind. | . 1793 |
| flagellifĕrŭm . | . Brown | . 8. Her. | P. E. Ind. | . 1828 |
| fimbriatŭm . . | . Brown | . 8. Her. | P. Brazil | . 1824 |
| glandulŏsŭm . | . Brown | . 8. Her. | P. Jamaica | . 1825 |
| grandĕ . . | . Brown | . G. Her. | P. Moreton, B. | 1828 |
| longifolĭŭm . | . Brown | . 8, 8. Her. | P. Jamaica | . 1817 |
| simplĕx . . | . Brown | . 8. Her. | P. Jamaica | . 1793 |
| Stemmariă . . | . Brown | . 7, Parasite. | Guinea | . 1823 |

ACROTRĬCHĔ, *Robert Brown.* Derived from *akros,* a point, and *thrix,* hair; in reference to the hairy corolla. *Linn.* 6, Or. 1, Nat. Or. *Epacridaceæ.* Very ornamental but dwarf species; for culture and propagation, see *Achyronia.*

| | | | | | |
|---|---|---|---|---|---|
| cordată . . | . White | . 6. S. Ev. S. | N. Holl. | . 1823 |
| divaricată . | . White | . 5. S. Ev. S. | N. Holl. | . 1824 |
| ovalifolĭă . | . White | . 3, G. Ev. S. | N. Holl. | . 1823 |

ACTÆĂ, *Linn.* *Aktæa,* an elm, in allusion to the resemblance the leaves bear to those of the elm. *Linn.* 13, Or. 1, Nat. Or. *Ranunculaceæ.* Dwarf species of little beauty, for culture &c., see *Aconitum.* Synonymes: 1. *A. brachypetala, Americana.* 2. *A. brachypetala, rubra.*

| | | | | |
|---|---|---|---|---|
| albă, 1 . . | . White | . 5, H. Her. | P. N. Amer. | . |
| rubră, 2 . . | . White | . 5, H. Her. | P. N. Amer. | . |
| spicată . . | . White | . 5, H. Her. | P. Britain | . |

ACTINOCĀRPŪS, *Robert Brown.* The derivation of the name is from *aktin,* ray, and *karpos,* fruit, in allusion to its radiated appearance. *Linn.* 6, Or. 4, Nat. Or. *Alismaceæ.* Interesting floating aquatics, thriving only in water, or in moist situations. *A. minor* is a native of New South Wales, and grows well in a pot of sandy peat immersed in water; seeds. Synonymes: 1 *Alisma Damasonium, Damasonium stellatum.*

| | | | | |
|---|---|---|---|---|
| Damasonĭŭm, 1 | . White | . 7, H. Aq. | P. England | . |
| minŏr . . | . White | . 6, G. Aq. | P. N. S. W. | . |

ACTINOCHLŎĂ, *Willd.* The name is derived from *aktin,* a ray, and *chloa,* grass, resemblance to grass. *Linn.* 3, Or. 2, Nat. Or. *Gramineæ.* Weeds of the simplest culture. Synonymes: 1. *Chondrosium procumbens.* 2. *C. tenue.—Hirsŭtă, procumbens* 1; *prostrata, tenŭis* 2.

ACTINOMĔRĬS, *Nuttall.* The name is taken from *aktin,* ray, and *meris,* part; alluding to the radiated appearance peculiar to these plants. *Linn.* 19, Or. 3, Nat. Or. *Compositæ.* Ornamental species; for culture, &c., see *Calliopsis.* Synonymes: 1. *Coreopsis alata.* 2. *C. procera.* 3. *C. alternifolia, Verbesina Coreopsis.*

| | | | | | |
|---|---|---|---|---|---|
| alată, 1 . | . Yellow | . 7, H. Her. | P. S. Amer. | . 1803 |
| helianthoĭdĕs | . Yellow | . 7, H. Her. | P. S. Amer. | . 1825 |
| procĕră, 2 . | . Yellow | . 9, H. Her. | P. N. Amer. | . 1766 |
| squarrŏsă, 3 . | . Yellow | . 7, H. Her. | P. N. Amer. | . 1640 |

ACTINOTHYRĬŪM, *Kunze.* Compounded from *aktin,* a ray, and *thyrion,* a door, alluding to the radiated integument of the sporidem. *Linn.* 24, Or. 9, Nat. Or. *Fungi.* The species appears in the early part of the year upon the culms of grasses, and is orbicular, and almost black.—*Graminis.*

ACTINŌTŬS, *Labillar.* Derived from *actinotos,* radiated, in reference to the rayed appearance of the involucrum. *Linn.* 5, Or. 2, Nat. Or. *Umbelliferæ.* An interesting plant with curious leaves, increased by divisions, and grown in loamy soil. Synonyme: 1. *Eriocalia major.*

Helianthi . . White . 6, G. Her. P. N. Holl. . 1821

ACUTANGULAR, having sharp, or acute angles.

ACUMINATE, cuspidate, having a long tapering point.

ACUTE, terminating abruptly in a sharp point.

ACĬNŎS, *Persoon.* The name is supposed to be the Greek name of a balsamic plant. *Linn.* 14, Or. 1, Nat. Or. *Labiatæ.* Most of the species are handsome, particularly *A. vulgaris.* For culture &c., see *Thymus.* Synonymes: 1. *Thymus grandiflorus.* 2. *T. herba-baroni.* 3. *T. acynoides, heterophyllus.* 4. *T. suaveolens.* 5. *T. acynos.*

| | | | | |
|---|---|---|---|---|
| alpinŭs . . | . Purple | . 8, G. | B. Austria | . 1731 |
| grandiflorŭs, 1 | . Purple | . 7, H. Tr. | B. | . 1810 |
| graveŏlĕns . | . Purple | . 7, H. Ev. S. | Crimea | . 1820 |
| herbă-barŏnĭ, 2 | . Purple | . 7, H. Ev. S. | Corsica | . 1820 |
| heterophyllŭs, 3 | . Purple | . 6, H. | A. Italy | . 1822 |
| patavinŭs . | . Flesh | . 7, H. | B. S. Eur. | . 1776 |
| purpurascĕns . | . Purple | . 6, H. | B. Spain | . 1820 |
| rotundifolĭŭs . | . Purple | . 6, H. Ev. | S. Spain | . 1820 |
| suaveŏlĕns, 4 . | . Red | . 7, H. | A. Greece | . 1817 |
| vulgâris, 5 . | . Violet | . 7, H. | A. Britain | . |
| villŏsŭs . . | . Red | . 7, H. | A. Germany | . 1817 |

ADĂMĬĂ, *Wallich.* Named in honour of John Adam, M.D., of Calcutta. *Linn.* 14, Or. 2, Nat. Or. *Saxifragaceæ.* An ornamental species cultivated in peat and loam, and propagated from cuttings in sand, under a glass.

cyaneă . . . S. Ev. S. E. Ind. . . 1829

ADAM's needle. See *Yucca.*

ADANSONĬĂ, *Linn.* Dedicated to Michael Adanson, a celebrated French botanist. *Linn.* 16, Or. 8, Nat. Or. *Sterculiaceæ.* The largest tree in the world is the Adansonia or Baobab-tree, the trunk of which has been found with a diameter of thirty feet; but its height is not in proportion. "It is emollient and mucilaginous in all its parts. The leaves dried and reduced to powder constitute Lalo, a favourite article with the Africans, which they mix daily with their food, for the purpose of diminishing the excessive perspiration to which they are subject in those climates, and even Europeans find it serviceable in cases of diarrhœa, fevers, and other maladies. The fruit is, perhaps, the most useful part of the tree. Its pulp is slightly acid and agreeable, and frequently eaten ; while the juice is expressed from it, mixed with sugar, and constitutes a drink, which is valued as a specific in putrid and pestilential fevers."—*Hooker, Bot. Mag.* 2792. It delights in rich loamy soil, and cuttings of the large ripened wood, strike best in a pot of sand, in a moist heat under a glass.

digitată . . . White . S. Ev. T. Guinea . . 1724

ADDER's-TONGUE. See *Ophioglossum.*

ADELĬĂ, *Linn.* The common generic name is taken from the minute parts of fructification, and is derived from *a,* privative, and *delos,* visible. *Linn.* 22, Or. 13, Nat. Or. *Euphorbiaceæ.* Ornamental shrubs, cultivated in peat and loam, and increased from cuttings.

| | | | | | |
|---|---|---|---|---|---|
| Acidŏtŏn . . | . Grn. wht. | . 6, S. Ev. S. | Jamaica | . 1768 |
| Bernardĭă . | . Green | . 7, S. Ev. S. | Jamaica | . 1768 |
| Ricinella . | . Grn. wht. | . 7, S. Ev. S. | Jamaica | . 1768 |

ADENANDRĂ, *Willd.* The derivation is from *aden,* a gland, and *aner,* a male, or stamen, in allusion to the appearance of the stamens. *Linn.* 5, Or. 1, Nat. Or. *Rutaceæ.* Beautiful little shrubs with a pleasing appearance, succeeding well in sandy peat, mixed with a little turfy loam, and propagated easily by cuttings from the young branches planted in a pot of sand, under a glass, but not plunged. Synonymes: 1. *Diosma linearis.* 2. *D. marginata.* 3. *D. villosa.*

[ 6 ]

| | | | | | |
|---|---|---|---|---|---|
| acuminata . . . | White . | 6, G. Ev. S. | C. G. H. | 1812 |
| andina . . . | Red . | 6, G. Ev. S. | C. G. H. | 1796 |
| coriacea . . | Pink . | 6, G. Ev. S. | C. G. H. | 1790 |
| fragrans . . | Pink . | 6, G. Ev. S. | C. G. H. | 1812 |
| linearis, 1 . . | White . | 6, G. Ev. S. | C. G. H. | 1800 |
| marginata, 2 . | Pink . | 6, G. Ev. S. | C. G. H. | 1806 |
| speciosa . . | Pink . | 6, G. Ev. S. | C. G. H. | 1789 |
| multiflora . . | Pink . | 6, G. Ev. S. | C. G. H. | 1790 |
| pauciflora . . | Pink . | 6, G. Ev. S. | C. G. H. | 1790 |
| umbellata . . | Pink . | 6, G. Ev. S. | C. G. H. | 1790 |
| uniflora . . | Pink . | 6, G. Ev. S. | C. G. H. | 1775 |
| villosa, 3 . . | Pink . | 6, G. Ev. S. | C. G. H. | 1796 |

ADENANTHERA, *Linn.* The name is derived from *aden*, a gland, and *anthera*, an anther, in allusion to a gland on each anther. Linn. 10, Or. 1, Nat. Or. *Leguminosæ, Mimosæ.* Handsome trees, thriving well in a mixture of loam and peat, and cuttings, with the leaves not shortened, root readily in a pot of sand, plunged in heat under a glass. *A. Pavonia* is one of the largest trees in the E. Indies, and its timber is esteemed on account of its solidity; by the natives the leaves are powdered and used in their ceremonies, and the common people eat the seeds.

| | | | | | |
|---|---|---|---|---|---|
| falcata . . . | Yellow . | 8. Ev. S. | E. Ind. . | 1812 |
| Pavonina . . . | Yel. wht. . | 7, S. Ev. S. | E. Ind. . . | 1759 |

ADENANTHOS, *Labill.* The name is from *aden*, a gland, and *anthos*, a flower; in reference to the gland on the flower. Linn. 4, Or. 1, Nat. Or. *Proteaceæ.* Handsome species, requiring, like all *Proteaceæ*, great attention in cultivation. They grow in sandy peat, and increase from cuttings in sand under a glass.

| | | | | | |
|---|---|---|---|---|---|
| cuneata . . . | Red . . | G. Ev. S. | N. Holl. . | 1824 |
| obovata . . . | Red . . | 7, G. Ev. S. | N. Holl. . | 1826 |
| sericea . . . | Red . . | G. Ev. S. | N. Holl. . | 1824 |

ADENOCARPUS, *Decandolle.* From *aden*, a gland, and *karpos*, fruit; in allusion to the fruit being beset with glands. Linn. 16, Or. 6, Nat. Or. *Leguminosæ.* When in flower these are splendid plants, and may be managed like the hardy species of *Cytisus. A. foliolosus* and *frankenioides* must be sheltered in frosty weather. *Synonymes:* 1. *Cytisus foliolosus.* 2. *Genista viscosa.* 3. *Cytisus hispanicus.* 4. *C. complicatus.* 5. *Spartium complicatum, C. complicatus.* 6. *S. complicatum, C. telonensis.*

| | | | | | |
|---|---|---|---|---|---|
| foliolosus, 1 . | Yellow . | 5, G. Ev. S. | Canaries . | 1629 |
| frankenioides, 2 | Yellow . | 6, G. Ev. S. | Canaries . | 1815 |
| hispanicus, 3 . | Yellow . | 6, H. De. S. | Spain . | 1816 |
| intermedius, 4 | Yellow . | 6, H. De. S. | Sicily . |  |
| parvifolius, 5 . | Yellow . | 6, H. De. S. | S. France . | 1800 |
| telonensis, 6 | Yellow . | 6, H. De. S. | S. France . | 1800 |

ADENOPHORA, *Fischer.* The derivation is from *aden*, a gland, and *phoreo*, to bear. Linn. 5, Or. 1, Nat. Or. *Campanulaceæ.* These are pretty border flowers, will grow in common soil, and increase from seeds, but will not allow of being divided at the roots. *Synonymes:* 1. *Campanula communis.* 2. *C. coronopifolia.* 3. *C. tricuspidata.* 4. *C. Fischeri.* 5. *C. intermedia.* 6. *C. Lamarkiana.* 7. *C. coronata.* 8. *C. pereskiæfolia.* 9. *C. periplocifolia.* 10. *C. Rabelaisiana.* 11. *C. stylosa.* 12. *C. verticillata.*

| | | | | | |
|---|---|---|---|---|---|
| communis, 1 . | Pa. blue . | 7, H. Her. P. | Siberia . | 1810 |
| hybrida . . | Pa. blue . | 6, H. Her. P. | Siberia . | 1816 |
| suaveolens . . | Pa. blue . | 6, H. Her. P. | Siberia . | 1816 |
| coronopifolia, 2 . | Blue . . | 6, H. Her. P. | Dahuria . | 1822 |
| denticulata, 3 . | Pa. blue . | 7, H. Her. P. | Siberia . | 1817 |
| Fischeri . . | Pa. blue . | 8, H. Her. P. | Siberia . | 1819 |
| Ornelini . . | Pa. blue . | 6, H. Her. P. | Siberia . | 1820 |
| intermedia, 5 . | Pa. blue . | 8, H. Her. P. | Siberia . | 1819 |
| Lamarkiana, 6 . | Pa. blue . | 7, H. Her. P. | Siberia . | 1824 |
| marsupiiflora, 7 | Pa. blue . | 7, H. Her. P. |  | 1818 |
| pereskiæfolia, 8 | Pa. blue . | 6, H. Her. P. | Siberia . | 1821 |
| periplocifolia, 9 | Pa. blue . | 8, H. Her. P. | Siberia . | 1824 |
| Rabelaisiana, 10 | Blue . . | 8, H. Her. P. | Siberia . | 1823 |
| reticulata . . | Pa. blue . | 7, H. Her. P. | Siberia . | 1820 |
| stylosa, 11 . | Pa. blue . | 6, H. Her. P. | Siberia . | 1820 |
| verticillata, 12 | Lgt. blue . | 6, H. Her. P. | Siberia . | 1783 |

ADENOTRICHIA, *Lindley.* Taken from *aden*, a gland, and *thris*, hair; the plant being remarkable for an intermixture of hairs and glands. Linn. 19, Or. 2, Nat. Or. *Compositæ.* A species of little beauty and of easy cultivation.

| | | | | | |
|---|---|---|---|---|---|
| amplexicaulis . | Yellow . | 5, G. Her. P. | Chile . . | 1826 |

ADESMIA, *Decandolle.* Derived from *a*, without, and *desmos*, a bond; in reference to the stamens being free. Linn. 16, Or. 6, Nat. Or. *Leguminosæ papi-*
[ 7 ]

*lionaceæ.* Interesting trailing plants. The annual species, sown in pots on a hotbed in spring, and hardened by degrees, will succeed well. The perennial species grow in loam and sandy peat; and cuttings strike in sand under a glass : the stove species increase best from seeds. *Synonymes:* 1. *Hedysarum muricatum.* 2. *Æschynomene papposa.*

| | | | | | |
|---|---|---|---|---|---|
| glutinosa . . | Yellow . | G. Ev. S. | Chile . | 1831 |
| Loudonia . . | Yellow . | 5, G. Ev. S. | Valparaiso . | 1832 |
| microphylla . | Yellow . | F. Ev. S. | Valparaiso . | 1830 |
| muricata, 1 . | Yellow . | 6, G. De. Tr. | Patagonia . | 1798 |
| papposa, 2 . | Yellow . | 6, G. De. Tr. | Chile . | 1823 |
| pendula . . | Yellow . | 6, F. De. Tr. | B. Ayres . | 1825 |
| uspallatensis . | Yellow . | 7, G. Ev. S. | Chile . | 1832 |
| viscosa . . | Yellow . | 8, H. | S. Chile . | 1831 |

ADGLUTINATED, glued to any thing; generally applied to filaments and anthers.

ADIANTUM, *Linn.* Derived from *adiantos*, dry. Pliny says, it is in vain to plunge the *adiantum* in water, for it always remains dry. Linn. 24, Or. 1, Nat. Or. *Polypodiaceæ.* Elegant species of ferns with beautiful leaves. They succeed well in a mixture of loam and peat, but they appear to thrive best if planted in loose rock-work where there is a good drainage; and may be increased by divisions or by seeds. *A. pedatum*, and *Capillus-Veneris*, are pectoral and lenitive. *Synonymes:* 1. *A. trigonum.*

| | | | | | |
|---|---|---|---|---|---|
| assimile, 1 . | Brown . | 7, G. Her. P. | N. Holl. | 1823 |
| Capillus-Veneris . | Brown . | 7, G. Her. P. | Britain . |  |
| cuneatum . . | Brown . | 8, G. Her. P. | Brazil . | 1820 |
| deltoideum . | Brown . | 8, S. Her. P. | S. Amer. | 1820 |
| formosum . . | Brown . | 7, G. Her. P. | N. Holl. | 1820 |
| hispidulum . | Brown . | 8, G. Her. P. | N. Holl. | 1822 |
| lunatum . . | Brown . | 7, S. Her. P. | Mexico . | 1823 |
| macrophyllum . | Brown . | 7, S. Her. P. | Jamaica . | 1793 |
| pilum . . | Brown . | 7, S. Her. P. | Brazil . | 1824 |
| pedatum . . | Brown . | 7, S. Her. P. | N. Amer. | 1640 |
| pubescens . . | Brown . | 4, H. Her. P. | N. Holl. | 1830 |
| pulverulentum . | Brown . | 7, G. Her. P. | W. Ind. | 1793 |
| radiatum . . | Brown . | 7, S. Her. P. | W. Ind. | 1776 |
| reniforme . . | Brown . | 7, G. Her. P. | Madeira | 1699 |
| rhomboideum . | Brown . | 7, G. Her. P. | S. Amer. | 1820 |
| serrulatum . | Brown . | 8, S. Her. P. | Jamaica | 1822 |
| tenerum . . | Brown . | 7, S. Her. P. | Jamaica | 1793 |
| ternatum . . | Brown . | 7, S. Her. P. | S. Amer. | 1819 |
| trapeziforme . | Brown . | 8, S. Her. P. | W. Ind. | 1793 |
| virium . . | Brown . | 7, S. Her. P. | S. Amer. | 1820 |
| villosum . . | Brown . | 7, S. Her. P. | Jamaica | 1775 |

ADINA, *Salisbury.* The name is taken from *adinos*, clustered; on account of the flowers being in heads. Linn. 4, Or. 1, Nat. Or. *Cinchonaceæ.* The species is a pretty little plant; for culture &c., see *Nauclea. Synonyme:* 1. *Nauclea Adina.*

| | | | | | |
|---|---|---|---|---|---|
| globiflora . . . | White . | 7, S. Ev. S. | China . | 1804 |

ADLUMIA, *Rafin.* Given in reference to the purplish fringy character of the flowers. Linn. 17, Or. 2, Nat. Or. *Fumariaceæ.* This interesting climbing species requires to be supported by stakes; it succeeds well in common soil, and increases readily from seeds sown in a damp situation. *Synonyme:* 1. *Corydalis fungosa.*

| | | | | | |
|---|---|---|---|---|---|
| cirrhosa, 1 . . . | White . | 8, H. cl. B. | N. Amer. . | 1778 |

ADNATE, adhering; applied to leaves, which being very erect, compress the stem: and to anthers when they are attached to the filaments by their whole length.

ADONIS, *Linn.* It is said that this plant sprung from the blood of Adonis when wounded by a boar, alluding to the blood-red colour of the flowers of many of the species. Adonis is stated to have been a great favourite with Venus. Linn. 13, Or. 6, Nat. Or. *Ranunculaceæ.* Pretty free flowering species; especially *A. vernalis* and *A. autumnalis*, both of which are favourites in the flower garden. They all succeed well in any common soil; the annual species are easily increased from seeds, and the perennial either from seed or by dividing the root. *Synonymes:* 1. *A. miniata.* 2. *A. vernalis, Mentzelii.*

| | | | | | |
|---|---|---|---|---|---|
| æstivalis, 1 . | Scarlet . | 6, H. | A. S. Eur. | 1629 |
| apennina, 2 . | Yellow . | 4, H. Her. P. | Alp. Eur. |  |
| autumnalis . | Crimson . | 4, H. | A. Britain . |  |
| citrina . . | Orange . | 6, H. | A. S. Eur. | 1819 |
| davurica . . | Yellow . | 4, H. Her. P. | Siberia . | 1827 |
| distorta . . | Yellow . | 4, H. Her. P. | Naples . | 1827 |
| flammea . . | Yellow . | 6, H. | A. Austria | 1800 |
| flava . . | Yellow . | 6, H. | A. S. Eur. | 1800 |
| microcarpa . . | Flesh . | 6, H. | A. Spain . | 1824 |

| | | | | | |
|---|---|---|---|---|---|
| pyrenāicā . . . | . Yellow | . 7, H. Her. | P. Pyrenees | 1817 |
| sibīricā . . . | . Yellow | . 4, H. Her. | P. Siberia | 1827 |
| vernālis . . . | . Yellow | . 3, H. Her. | P. Europe | 1829 |
| volgēnsis . . | . 6, H. Her. | P. Volga | | 1818 |

**ADŎXĂ,** *Linn.* Derived from *a*, privative, and *doxa*, glory; alluding to the want of show in the flowers, these being of the same colour as the leaves. *Linn.* 8, Or. 4, Nat. Or. *Oraliaceæ.* The plant is very dwarf and interesting, flourishing best under the shade of trees; it is increased by offsets.

| | | | | |
|---|---|---|---|---|
| Moschatellīnā . | . Grn. yel. | . 4, H. Tu. Her. | Britain . . |

**ADULT,** full grown.

**ADUNCOUS,** crooked, twisted, or hooked.

**ÆCIDĬŬM,** *Pers.* Taken from *aikion*, a wheel, and *eidos*, like; like pustules. *Linn.* 24, Or. 9, Nat. Or. *Fungi.* These plants are found upon the leaves of other vegetables, and one of them is known to agriculturists under the name of red gum. This species usually grows inside the glumes of the calyx, under the epidermis, which, when the plant is ripe, bursts and emits a powder of bright orange colour. It does not appear to be materially injurious to the grains; and it has been found upon branded leaves. Before the cuticle which covers the fungus bursts, it has much the appearance of a pustule upon the human body.—*Loudon's Ency. of Plants.*—*Albēscēns, Allĭi, Berbērĭdis, Bŭnĭi, Cālĭhæ, confērtŭm, cornūtŭm, Epĭlŏbĭi, Grossulārĭæ, Jacobæa,lacerātŭm, Legŭmĭnosārŭm, leucospērmŭm, Mēnthæ, Pĕrĭclўmĕnĭ, Pĭnĭ, Prenānthĭs, Prīmŭlæ, Ranunculacedrŭm, Rhāmnĭ, rubēllŭm, Tarāxăcĭ, Thalĭctrĭ, Tussĭlāgĭnĭs, Urtĭcæ, Vĭolārŭm.*

**ÆŎLŎPS,** *Linn.* Supposed to possess a remedy for a disease of one corner of the eye; hence the name. *Linn.* 23, Or. 1, Nat. Or. *Gramineæ.* Uninteresting hardy species of grass of the simplest culture. *Synonyme.*—*Æ. triuncĭālis.*—*Æ. caudātā, cylĭndrĭca, hŷstrĭx, ovāta, squarrōsă, triarĭstātā, triuncĭalis.*

**ÆŎŪRĬTĬ,** *Persoon.* Derived from *aigeiros*, a poplar; the species being first discovered on it. *Linn.* 24, Or. 9, Nat. Or. *Fungi.* Exceedingly minute productions found generally on dead wood—*cāndĭdā, sĕtosa.*

**ÆŎLPHĬLĬ,** *Linn.* A favourite of goats, hence the name, *aix*, a goat, and *philos*, dear. *Linn.* 4, Or. 1, Nat. Or. *Verbenaceæ.* Handsome species delighting in open loamy soil, and propagated from cuttings in sand in heat, under a glass.

| | | | | | |
|---|---|---|---|---|---|
| arborēscēns . . | . White . | . 8. Ev. S. | Trinidad | . 1823 |
| diffūsā . . . | . Yellow . | . 7, 8. Ev. S. | W. Ind. | . 1824 |
| elātā . . . | . Pa. yel. . | . 8, 8. Ev. S. | W. Ind. | . 1823 |
| fœtĭdā . . . | . Lilac . | . 7, 8. Ev. S. | W. Ind. | . 1820 |
| martinicēnsis . | . White . | . 9, 8. Ev. S. | W. Ind. | . 1780 |
| obovātā . . . | . Yellow . | . 8. Ev. S. | W. Ind. | . 1804 |
| trĭfĭdā . . . | . White . | . 6, 8. Ev. S. | Jamaica | . 1826 |

**ÆGLE,** *Correa.* The word is from *ægle*, one of the Hesperides. *Linn.* 13, Or. 1, Nat. Or. *Aurantiaceæ.* The fragrant flowers of this ornamental shrub (the Bengal Quince) are succeeded by a fruit resembling an orange, which is thus spoken of by Mr. Don,—"The fruit is much larger than that of *Feronia elephantium*, and is very delicious to the taste, and exquisitely fragrant. It is not only nutritious, but possesses an aperient quality which is particularly serviceable in habitual costiveness; it contains a large quantity of exceedingly tenacious transparent gluten, which may be drawn out when fresh into fine threads, two or three yards in length." From the rind, the Dutch in Ceylon prepare a perfume.

| | | | | |
|---|---|---|---|---|
| Mārmălōs . . . | . Wht. red. | . 8. Ev. S. E. Ind. | . . 1759 |

**ÆGOPŎDĬŬM,** *Linn.* The resemblance of the leaves to a foot, hence the derivation, from *aix*, a goat, and *podion*, a little foot. *Linn.* 5, Or. 2, Nat. Or. *Umbelliferæ.* Common goat-weed. A troublesome weed: the leaves smell like Angelica, and may be eaten in salads.

| | | | | |
|---|---|---|---|---|
| Podagrārĭă . . | . White . | . 6, H. Her. P. Britain . . |
| variegātā . . . | . White . | . 6, H. Her. P. England . . |

**ÆGOPŎGŎN,** *Humboldt.* Compounded from *aix*, a goat, and *pogon*, a beard. *Linn.* 3, Or. 2, Nat. Or. *Gramineæ.* Curious species of grass of easy culture.

| | | | | | |
|---|---|---|---|---|---|
| pusillūs . . . | . Apetal. | . 7, Grass. S. Amer. | . 1822 |
| trisetūs . . . | . Apetal. | . 7, Grass. S. Amer. | . 1822 |

**ÆŎLLĀNTHŬS,** *Martius.* The flowers are subject to vary, hence the name from *aiollo*, to vary, and *anthos*, flower. *Linn.* 14, Or. 2, Nat. Or. *Labiatæ.* This interesting species delights in sandy loam, and is increased freely from seeds.

| | | | | |
|---|---|---|---|---|
| suavēŏlens . . | . White . | . 7, S. | A. Brazil | . 1825 |

**ÆQUILATERAL,** equal sided.

**ÆRĂNTHŬS,** *Lindley.* From *aer*, air, and *anthos*, a flower; in allusion to the manner in which the plant grows. *Linn.* 20, Or. 1, Nat. Or. *Orchidaceæ.* This is a very singular plant, with large, solitary, and scentless flowers. It requires the same treatment as *Vanda.*

| | | | | |
|---|---|---|---|---|
| grandiflora . . | . Yell. Grn. | . 6. S. Epi. | Madagasc. | . 1823 |

**ÆRĬDES,** *Loureiro.* Named from *aer*, the air, because it possesses the power of living almost entirely upon the matter which it absorbs from the atmosphere. *Linn.* 20, Or. 1, Nat. Or. *Orchidaceæ.* The flowers produced by some of the plants are delightfully fragrant, as *A. odorata*, the flowers of which are a rather delicate, light flesh colour, and disposed in a loose, drooping spike, from six inches to a foot long, which grows from the axils of the leaves. For culture and propagation, see *Vanda.* *Synonymes:* 1. *Epidendrum subulatum.* 2. *Aerides cornuta.*

| | | | | | |
|---|---|---|---|---|---|
| affinē . . . | . | . 8. Epi. | Sylhet | . 1837 |
| cylindricum, 1 | . | . 8. Epi. | E. Ind. | . |
| odontŏchilum . | . | . 8. Epi. | Sylhet | . 1837 |
| odorātă, 2 . . | . Wht. ll. | . 8, 8. Epi. | E. Ind. | . 1800 |
| Wightianum . . | . | . 8. Epi. | E. Ind. | . 1800 |

**ÆRŬĂ,** *Forskahl.* Taken from *eroua*, its Arabic name. *Linn.* 5, Or. 1, Nat. Or. *Amarantaceæ.* Interesting little plants of easy culture. *Synonyme:* 1. *Celosia lanata.*

| | | | | | |
|---|---|---|---|---|---|
| javānĭcă . . . | . White | . 6, S. Her. P. E. Ind. | . . 1768 |
| lanātă, 1 . . . | . White | . 6, S. Her. P. E. Ind. | . . 1691 |

**ÆRŬGINOUS,** having a colour like verdigris.

**ÆSCHYNŎMĔNĔ,** *Linn.* Derived from *aischuno*,—supposed to be a little sensitive. *Linn.* 17, Or. 4, Nat. Or. *Leguminosæ, Papilionaceæ.* Ornamental plants requiring, Sweet says, "a strong heat to preserve the species through the winter; good loam suits them best, and cuttings root in heat under a glass." *Synonymes:* 1. *Æ. viscidula.* 2. *Æ. prostrata.*

| | | | | | |
|---|---|---|---|---|---|
| americānā . . | . Yellow | . 7, S. | A. Jamaica | . 1732 |
| aspĕră . . . | . Yellow | . 6, S. | A. E. Ind. | . 1759 |
| crēpĭtans . . | . Yellow | . 7, S. Ev. S. | Caraccas | . 1820 |
| hispĭdă . . . | . Yellow | . H. | A. N. Amer. | . 1803 |
| indĭcă . . . | . Yellow | . 6, S. | A. E. Ind. | . 1799 |
| pātŭlā . . . | . Yellow | . 7, S. Ev. S. | Maurit. | . 1826 |
| pendŭlă . . . | . Yellow | . 7, S. Ev. S. | Maurit. | . 1826 |
| pūmĭlă . . . | . Yellow | . 7, S. | A. E. Ind. | . 1818 |
| sensitĭvă . . | . White | . S. Ev. S. | W. Ind. | . 1733 |
| subviscōsā, 1 . | . Yellow | . 7, S. | A. E. Ind. | . 1816 |
| viscĭdŭlă, 2 . | . Yellow | . 7, G. | A. Florida | . 1816 |

**ÆSCHYNANTHŬS,** *Jack.* From *aischuno*, to be ashamed, and *anthos*, a flower. *Linn.* 14, Or. 2, Nat. Or. *Cyrtandraceæ.* These are truly beautiful plants, and deserving a place in every collection. *Æ. grandiflora* produces its beautiful deep scarlet flowers, at the extremity of the young shoots, in clusters of from twenty to thirty flowers in each cluster, and contrasting well with the thick, fleshy, dark-green leaves. It is an epiphyte, and is found to thrive best in chopped moss, and broken pots; it will also grow freely upon the old stumps of trees prepared for the purpose. *Æ. Roxburghii* requires a mixture of equal portions of very turfy loam and fresh leaf mould, with a little sand, and to be kept in a moist shady stove. They are easily increased by cuttings.

| | | | | | |
|---|---|---|---|---|---|
| grandiflora . . | . Scarlet | . 8, S. Epi. E. Ind. | . . 1837 |
| Roxburghii . . | . Scarlet | . 7, S. Ev. E. Ind. | . . 1837 |

**ÆSCŬLŬS,** *Linn.* The name is given to a kind of oak which bears an edible fruit, and is derived from *esca*, food or nourishment. *Linn.* 7, Or. 1, Nat. Or. *Æsculaceæ.* Showy trees of considerable magnitude, well adapted for planting singly in parks or lawns, having at all times a pleasing appearance, but more especially when in flower. A deep loamy soil suits them, and they may be increased either by layering, grafting, or budding, and some produce good seed, by which they can be

[ 8 ]

with advantage increased. The bark has been used successfully in intermittent fevers, and with good success in dyeing yellow colours. *Synonyme:* 1. *Æ. carnea,*

| | | | | | | | |
|---|---|---|---|---|---|---|---|
| glabra | . . . | Orn. yel. | . 5, | H. De. | T. | N. Amer. | . 1812 |
| Hippocastanûm | . | White . | . 5, | H. De. | T. | Asia | . 1629 |
| variegatûm | . . | White . | . 5, | H. De. | T. | Asia | . 1629 |
| ohiotênsis | . . | White . | . 5, | H. De. | T. | N. Amer. | . |
| pállida | . . . | Orn. yel. | . 6, | H. De. | T. | N. Amer. | . 1812 |
| rubicunda, 1 | . . | Red . | . 6, | H. De. | T. | N. Amer. | . 1830 |

ÆSTIVATION, applied to the calyx and corolla of a flower when in the bud, before expansion.

ÆSTUOUS, scorching, glowing, like summer.

ÆTHALIÔM, *Link.* The name is taken from *aithales,* splendid; alluding to its showy appearance *Linn.* 24, Or. 9, Nat. Or. *Fungi.* This species appears in autumn, on the bark in stoves—*flavûm.*

ÆTHIONÈMA, *R. Brown.* Derived from *aitho,* to scorch, and *nema,* a filament; in allusion perhaps to some sunburnt appearance in the stamens. *Linn.* 15, Or. *Siliculosa,* Nat. Or. *Cruciferæ, Lepidinæ.* Pretty alpine plants, adapted for ornamenting rock-work; they grow well in common soil, and may be increased either by seeds or cuttings. *Synonymes:* 1. *Thlaspi arabicum.* 2. *T. saxatile.*

| | | | | | | |
|---|---|---|---|---|---|---|
| Buxbaûmii, 1 | . | Pa. red | . 6, | H. | A. Levant | . 1823 |
| gracile | . . . | Pa. red | . 6, | H. | A. Carnio | . 1823 |
| membranaceûm | . | Lilac | . 7, | H. Her. | P. Persia | . 1829 |
| monospermûm | . | Pa. pur. | . 7, | H. Her. | P. Spain | . 1778 |
| parviflorûm | . . | Lilac | . 7, | H. Her. | P. Persia | . 1830 |
| saxatile, 2 | . . | Flesh | . 6, | H. | A. S. Eur. | . 1759 |

ÆTHIÔNIA, *D. Don.* Derived from *Æthion,* one of Phœbus's horses. *Linn.* 19, Or. 1, Nat. Or. *Compositæ.* An ornamental species, for culture, &c., see *Hieracium.* *Synonymes:* 1. *Crepis filiformis.* 2. *Hieracium fruticosum.*

| | | | | | | |
|---|---|---|---|---|---|---|
| fruticosa, 2 | . | Yellow | . 6, | G. Ev. S. | Madeira | . 1785 |
| filiformis, 1 | | | | | | |

ÆTHÚSA, *Linn.* The name alludes to the dangerous acridity of the plants, and is derived from *aithusso,* to heat or make hot. *Linn.* 5, Or. 2, Nat. Or. *Umbelliferæ.* Quite hardy species, of little beauty and of the simplest culture. The stem and leaves of *Æ. Cynapium* are poisonous, and contain a peculiar alkali called cynopia.

| | | | | | | |
|---|---|---|---|---|---|---|
| Cynapiûm | . . . | White | . 7, | H. | A. Britain | . |
| elata | . . . | White | . 8, | H. | A. | . 1781 |

AFRICAN ALMOND, see *Brabejum.*

AFRICAN FLEABANE, see *Tarchonanthus.*

AFRICAN LILY, see *Agapanthus.*

AFRICAN MARIGOLD, see *Tagetes erecta.*

AGAPANTHUS, *L'Héritière.* Named in allusion to the lovely and showy flowers, from *agape,* love, and *anthos,* flower. *Linn.* 6, Or. 4, Nat. Or. *Liliaceæ.* Showy plants producing large umbels of bright blue flowers. They are nearly hardy, and will grow well in any common soil, provided they have plenty of pot room. Suckers.

| | | | | | |
|---|---|---|---|---|---|
| minor | . . . | Blue | . 8, | G. Tu. | P. C. G. H. | . |
| praecox | . . . | Pur. blue | . 6, | G. Tu. | P. C. G. H. | . |
| umbellatûs | . . | Blue | . 8, | G. Tu. | P. C. G. H. | . 1692 |
| albidûs | . . . | Whitish | . 9, | G. Her. | P. C. G. H. | . |
| variegatûs | . . | Blue | . 4, | G. Tu. | P. | . |

AGARICUS, *Linn.* Derived from *Agaria,* the name of a town in Sarmatia. *Linn.* 24, Or. 9, Nat. Or. *Fungi.* A more extensive genus than this is not known in the whole vegetable kingdom. Some species, as the common mushroom, *A. campestris, A. vaginatus,* &c., are well known for the wholesomeness of the food which is prepared from them. Others, as *A. muscarius, A. necator,* &c., are very dangerous poisons; indeed, the latter quality exists more or less in so many species, and these resemble those that are wholesome so nearly as to render it advisable to be exceedingly cautious in the use of any, for the most dreadful effects are well known to have resulted from want of caution in this respect. We shall here briefly notice the cultivation of the common mushroom in houses erected for the purpose, referring the reader for details to *Loudon's Encyclopædia of Gardening,* where a copious account of the different modes of culture, preparing spawn, formation of houses, &c., is laid down. Collect a sufficient quantity of

[ 9 ]

fresh horse droppings as free from straw as possible, lay it in an open shed in a heap or ridge; here it will heat violently, and in consequence should be now and then turned for sweetening; after this has subsided to moderation, it will be in a fit state for forming into a bed. In the process of making the bed, the dung should be put on in small quantities and beat firmly and equally together until it is the required size: in this state let it remain until the highest degree of heat to which it is capable of coming is ascertained, which may be readily done by inserting a heat-stick and pressing it with the hand: if not found violent, the spawn may be broken up into pieces of two or three inches square, and put into holes about three inches in depth, by six inches asunder, over its surface: after this throw a very small quantity of well-broken droppings over the whole. In this state let it remain for two or three weeks, when a loamy soil may be put on about an inch or an inch and a half thick and gently patted with the spade. If the temperature of the house be kept about sixty or sixty-five degrees, mushrooms may be expected in six weeks. It is not well to water the beds much, particularly when bearing; it is much better to throw a little water over the path and flues, which will both improve the colour and flavour of the mushrooms without being attended with those bad effects frequently resulting from watering, viz. that of destroying the young stock; and turning brown those already fit for table. *Synonymes:* 1. *A. auratus.* 2. *A. spongiosus.* 3. *A. puniceus.* 4. *A. clavatus.* 5. *A. agrestis.* 6. *A. rhæoides.* 7. *Viridarius.* 8. *A. varius, proliferus.* 9. *A. pileolarius.* 10. *A. croceus.* 11. *Resupinatus.* 12. *A. cornutus.* 13. *A. adustus.* 14. *A. flexuosus.* 15. *A. scariosus.* 16. *A. caseus.* 17. *A. reticulatus.* 18. *A. fulvus.* 19. *A. rosellus.* 20. *A. serosus.* 21. *A. rubescens.* 22. *A. coronatus.* 23. *A adnatus.* 24. *A. ficoides.* 25. *A. alumnus.* 26. *Merulius androsaceus.*—*Acris, adônis, adhesivus, adûstûs, a. elephantînûs, ædematôpûs coralloidês, æruginôsûs, æstûâns, albo-brûnnéûs, âlbûs, alcalînûs, alliâcéûs, elutâcéûs, a. xânthôpûs* 1, *androsâcéûs, applicâtûs, âquilûs, armeniâcûs, aromâtichs, âspêr, asprêlûs, atro-âlbûs, atro-rûfûs, aurantî-ferruginéûs, aurantîâcûs, aurântîûs, aûréûs, aurinêllûs, biênnâtûs, Boltôni, bombycînûs, brûnnéûs* 2, *bulbôsûs, cæspitôsûs, callochrôûs, callôsûs vârîûs, camârophgllûs, campestris, cândicâns, caperâtûs, cârneô-âlbûs, cârnéûs* 3, *carnôsûs, castânéûs, caulicinâlîs, cepæstîpês, cerâcéûs, chalgbéûs, chrysôdôn, cilicioidês, cinnamôméûs, clâvûs, clypeolârîûs felînûs, c.Meleâgris, coccinéûs, cochleâtûs, collinîtûs, collinûs, columbêttâ, côlûs, compréssûs, conchâtûs, cônflûens, cônicûs, conîgénûs, conspersûs, constrictûs, controvêrsûs, cortioâlîs, eretâcéûs, cristâtûs, cruêntûs, cûcûmis, cuspidâtûs, cyathîfôrmis* 4, *dealbâtûs* 5, *decâstês, deliciôsûs, depâllens, depressûs, diatrêtûs, disseminâtûs, drqînûs, dryôphilûs, dûlcis, Dunâlii, ebûrnéûs nitêns, êlégâns, emêticûs Gêorgii, epichqsiam, epiphgllûs, epiptergglûs, equêstris, ericéûs, ericetôrûs, esculêntûs, evernîûs, excoriâtûs, fasciculâris, fastibilis, fêrtilis, fibûld, filipês, fimbriâtûs, fimipûtris, flabelliformis, flâccidû, flâmmâns* 6, *flâvidûs, flexuôsûs, fœtens, fœtidûs, frâgrâns, fucâtûs, fûlvûs, furcâtûs, furfurâcéûs* 7, *furfurôsûs, fusco-purpûréûs, fûstîpês, galiôpûs, galericulâtûs* 8, *gambôsûs, geophgllûs, Gêorgii, gibbûs, gigantéûs, gilvûs* 9, *glûucôpûs, glycyôsmûs, grâcilis, grammopôdîûs, granulôsûs* 10, *griseocgânûs, hæmâtôpûs, haustellâtûs* 11, *helvolûs, helvûs, hippopînûs, hortênsis, Hudsôni, hgbridûs, hypnôrûm, hypothêjûs, hgsgînûs, illinîtûs, Inûyûs* 12, *inornâtûs, involûtûs* 13, *juncicôld, laccâtûs amethgstinûs, lachrymabûndûs, lâctéûs, lanuginôsûs, laterâlis, laterîtiûs, leoninûs, lepidûs monstrôsûs, lignâtilis, littôréûs, longicâûlis* 14, *lûridûs, luteoâlbûs, lûtéûs, majâlis, maritîmûs, mastrucâtûs, malaltucûs, mêlitéûs elâsticûs, laricinûs, millûs, millisimûs, môllis, mâcidûs, murâlis, muricâtûs* 15, *inequâlis, murinâcéûs, murinûs, muscârîûs, mutabilis, Mgômgcês, Mgosôtis, nebulâris* 16, *necâtôr, nidûlâns, niti-ûs, nivâlis, nûcéûs, nûdûs, obêsûs, obliquûs, odorâtûs, olivâcéô-âlbûs, opâcûs, oreâdês, ostreâtûs, ovâlis, ovînûs, pâllidûs, phalloidês verrucôsûs virêscêns, palmâtûs, pantherînûs, papilionâcéûs, papyrâcéûs, parasîticûs, pâscûûs, peliûnthinus, pel-*

c

lūcĭdŭs, pĕrfŏrāns, perŏnātŭs, persŏnātŭs, petaloīdĕs, pezizoīdĕs, phlĕbŏphŏrŭs 17, phŏlĭdĕŭs, pĭlĭpĕs, pĭpĕrātŭs, pistillārĭs, platyphȳllŭs, plŭmbĕŭs, plŭmŏsŭs, plŭtĕŭs, pŏlītŭs, pŏlygrāmmŭs, pŏlnĕŭs, pŏrphȳrĭŭs, pŏrrĭgĕns, prăcŏx appendicŭlātŭs, p. delĭcātŭs, prasĭnŭs, praĭēnsĭs 18, p. clavafŏrmĭs, p. ĕrĭcēŭs, prŏcērŭs, prŭnŭlŭs, psittăcīnŭs, pterĭgēnŭs 19, pŭnĭcēŭs, pūrŭs, pyrŏgālŭs, pyxĭdātŭs, quĭĕtŭs 20, racemŏsŭs, radĭcātŭs, rameālĭs, rhodŏphŏlĭŭs, rĭmŏsŭs, rŏsēŭs, rŏtŭlă, rŭbĕr, rŭbēscēns, rŭfŭs 21, Rŭssŭlă, rŭtĭlănŭs, sangŭĭnēŭs, scăbĕr, scŭārhŭs, scorŏdŏnĭŭs, scrŏbĭcŭlātŭs, sējunctŭs, semĭglŏbātŭs, semĭovātŭs 22, sēptĭcŭs, serŏtĭnŭs, sĭnŭātŭs, spĭlomĕŭs, spĭnĭpĕs, splēndēns, spŭmŏsŭs, squămŏsŭs, squarrŏsŭs, stellātŭs, stercŏrārĭŭs 23, stipātŭs, ellĭptĭcŭs 24, strŏbĭlīnŭs, stylŏbātŭs, subdŭlcĭs, sublanātŭs, sulphūrēŭs, tanacētĭŭs, tĕnĕr, tentăcŭlŭm, testācēŭs, thejŏgālŭs, tĭgrīnŭs, Tĭthymalīnŭs, tĭtŭbāns tormĭnŏsŭs, tŏrtĭlĭs, torulŏsŭs, tŏrvŭs, tremŭlŭs, tŭbĕrŏsŭs 25, turbĭnātŭs, turfŏsŭs, tūrgĭdŭs, ulmārĭŭs, ustălĭs, ŭvĭdŭs, vaccĭnŭs, vagĭnātŭs fulvŭs, v. hyalīnŭs, v. plŭmbĕŭs, v. vulvĭnātŭs, Vaillāntĭī 26, varĭābĭlĭs, vellēŭs, velŭtĭpĕs, vērnŭs, versĭcŏlŏr, vĭĕtŭs, vĭolācēŭs, vĭrgātŭs, vĭrgĭnēŭs, vĭrĭdĭs, vulgārĭs, vulpīnŭs.

**AGĂSTĂCHȲS**, *R. Brown.* So named in reference to its fine flowers. From *agatos*, admirable, and *stachys*, a spike. Linn. 4, Or. 1, Nat. Or. *Proteaceæ.* A pretty species, for culture, &c. see *Persoonia.*

odorātă . . . . . Pa. yel. . 6, G. Ev. S. N. Holl. . 1826

**AGASȲLLĬS**, *Sprengel.* The Greek name for the Ammoniac plant. Linn. 5, Or. 2, Nat. Or. *Umbelliferæ.* An uninteresting species of easy culture. Synonymes: 1. *Cachrys latifolia, Siler caucasicum.* —Caucásĭcă 1.

**AGĂTHĂ͞EA,** *H. Cassini.* Named from *agathos,* excellent; on account of its beautiful flowers. Linn. 19, Or. 2, Nat. Or. *Compositæ.* For culture, &c. see *Cineraria.* Synonymes: 1. *Cineraria amelloīdes.* 2. *C. linifolia.*

cœlēstĭs, 1 . . Blue . . 6, G. Ev. S. C. G. H. . 1759
linifŏlĭă, 2 . . Blue . . 6, G. Ev. S. C. G. H. . 1800

**AGĂTHŎPHȲLLŬM**, *Jussieu.* The name refers to the pleasant clove-like smell of the leaf, and is derived from *agathos,* good, and *phyllon,* a leaf. Linn. 11, Or. 1, Nat. Or. *Lauraceæ,* Madagascar Nutmeg. This ornamental tree grows well in good peat, or open rich loam; it is propagated from cuttings with ease, in sand, in heat. The bark and dried fruit are aromatic, especially the latter.

aromătĭcŭm . . White . . S. Ev. T. Madag. . 1823

**AGĂTHŎSMĂ,** *Willden.* Derived from *agathos,* good, and *osma,* smell. Linn. 5, Or. 1, Nat. Or. *Rutaceæ.* The plants are ornamental, and smell like *Diosmas.* For culture, &c. see that genus. The Hottentots use the dried and powdered leaves of *A. pulchella,* with the grease of which they anoint their bodies; this according to Thunberg, gives them almost an unbearable smell. Synonymes: 1. *Diosma ambigua.* 2. *D. orbiculāris.* 3. *Bucco prolifera.*

acumĭnātă . . . Violet . 5, G. Ev. S. C. G. H. . 1812
ambĭgŭă, 1 . . White . . 5, G. Ev. S. C. G. H. . 1810
brevĭfŏlĭă . . . Purple . 5, G. Ev. S. C. G. H. . 1818
Brunĭādĕs . . . Purple . 5, G. Ev. S. C. G. H. . 1820
cerefŏlĭă . . . White . . 5, G. Ev. S. C. G. H. . 1774
cĭlĭātă . . . . White . . 5, G. Ev. S. C. G. H. . 1774
erēctă . . . . Blue wht. 5, G. Ev. S. C. G. H. . 1816
hĭrtă . . . . Purple . 5, G. Ev. S. C. G. H. . 1794
  exsĭccātă . . Purple . 5, G. Ev. S. C. G. H. . 1794
  purpūrĕă . . Purple . 5, G. Ev. S. C. G. H. . 1794
  Ventenātĭănă . Purple . 5, G. Ev. S. C. G. H. . 1794
hĭspĭdă . . . Violet . 5, G. Ev. S. C. G. H. . 1786
imbrĭcătă . . . Pink . . 5, G. Ev. S. C. G. H. . 1774
linifŏlĭă . . . White . 5, G. Ev. S. C. G. H. . 1823
orbĭcŭlārĭs, 2 . White . 5, G. Ev. S. C. G. H. . 1800
prolĭferă, 3 . . White . 5, G. Ev. S. C. G. H. . 1790
pŭbēscēns . . . White . 5, G. Ev. S. C. G. H. . 1798
reflēxă . . . Purple . 5, G. Ev. S. C. G. H. . 1820
rŭgŏsă . . . White . 5, G. Ev. S. C. G. H. . 1790
vestĭtă . . . White . 5, G. Ev. S C. G. H. . 1824
villŏsă . . . Violet . 5, G. Ev. S. C. G. H. . 1786

**AGĂTHȲRSŬS**, *D. Don.* The flowers are very pretty, hence the name is derived from *agathos,* pretty, and *thyrsus,* a thyrse. Linn. 19, Or. 1, Nat. Or. *Compositæ.* For culture, &c. see *Sonchus.* Synonymes: 1. *Sonchus agrestis.* 2. *S. alpinus.* 3. *S.*

cacalĭæfŏlĭŭs. 4. *S. cyaneus.* 5. *S. floridanus.* 6. *S. lapponicus.* 7. *S. Plumieri.* 8. *S. sibiricus.* 9. *S. tataricus.*

alpīnŭs, 2 . . Blue . . 7, H. . A. Scotland
cyanĕŭs, 4 . . Blue . . 7, H. Her. P. Nepal . 1820
florĭdānŭs, 5 . Blue . . 7, H. . B. Iberia . 1820
lapponĭcŭs, 6 . Blue . . 7, H. Her. P. N. Amer. 1713
Plumĭĕrī, 7 . Blue . . 8, H. Her. P. Lapland . 1804
sĭbīrĭcŭs, 8 . Blue . . 8, H. Her. P. Pyrenees . 1794
tatărĭcŭs, 9 . Blue . . 8, H. Her. P. Siberia . 1784

**AGĂTĬ,** *Rheede.* Agati is its name in the Sanscrit language. Linn. 17, Or. 4, Nat. Or. *Leguminosæ.* Tall ornamental species. For culture, &c., see *Sesbania.* Synonymes: 1. *Sesbanea coccinea.* 2. *S. grandiflora.*

coccīnĕă, 1 . . Red . . 8, S. Ev. T. E. Ind. . 1768
grandiflŏră, 2 . Red . . 8, S. Ev. T. E. Ind. . 1820

**AGĂVĔ,** *Linn.* The name has been altered from *agauos,* admirable. Linn. 6, Or. 1, Nat. Or. *Amaryllidaceæ.* To this highly interesting genus belongs the *A. Americana,* or American aloe. This plant has been said to flower only once in a hundred years, but it is now known to flower sooner or later, according to the treatment it receives. The readiest way to throw it into flower is to apply bottom heat, and treat it as the pineapple. All the species thrive well in rich loamy soil, mixed with a very little rotten dung, decayed vegetable mould, and brick rubbish; they require but little water, and are propagated by suckers from the root. Synonyme: 1. *A. spicata.*

americānă . . Yellow . 8, G. Ev. S. S. Amer. . 1640
  varĭēgātă . . Yellow . 8, G. Ev. S. S. Amer. . 1640
angustĭfŏlĭă . . Green . . 8, S. Ev. S. . 1790
brachystăchȳs, 1 Green . . 8, S. Ev. S. Mexico . 1826
flăccĭdă . . . Green . . 8, S. Ev. S. S. Amer. . 1790
Karatto . . . Green . . 8, S. Ev. S. S. Amer. . 1768
lūrĭdă . . . Green . . 6, S. Ev. S. Vera Cruz 1731
mexĭcānă . . Green . . 8, S. Ev. S. Mexico . 1817
Millĕrĭ . . . Green . . 8, S. Ev. S. . 1768
polyacanthă . . Green . . 8, S. Ev. S. . 1800
saponārĭă . . Brown . 7, G. Ev. S. Peru . 1838
virgĭnĭcă . . Purple . F. Ev. S. N. Amer. . 1765
vivĭpără . . . Green . . 9, S. Ev. S. S. Amer. . 1731
univĭttātă . . Green . . 8, S. Ev. S. Mexico . 1830
yuccæfŏlĭă . . Yellow . 8, S. Ev. S. . 1819

**AGĔRĂTŬM,** *Linn.* The colours are constant, or as might be rendered, always clear; hence the name is compounded of *a,* privative, and *geras,* old. Linn. 19, Or. 1, Nat. Or. *Compositæ.* The species are ornamental, and grow freely in light rich soil; cuttings root freely in soil under a glass. Synonyme: 1. *A. obtusifolium.*

angustĭfŏlĭŭm . White . . 7, G. . A. M. Video . 1827
cærūlĕŭm, 1 . Blue . . 7, G. . A. W. Ind. . 1800
conyzoīdĕs . . Lgt. blue . 7, H. . A. America . 1714
latĭfŏlĭŭm . . . White . . 7, H. . A. Peru . 1800
mexĭcānŭm . . Blue . . 6, H. . A. Mexico . 1822
strĭctŭm . . . White . . 6, H. . A. Nepal . 1821

**AGGLOMERATE,** } collected into a heap or head.
**AGGLOMERATED,** }

**AGGREGATE,** } gathered together, applied to the in-
**AGGREGATED,** } florescence.

**AGNŎSTŬS,** *A. Cunn.* Agnostos, unknown. Linn. 4, Or. not known, Nat. Or. *Proteaceæ.* This is a most beautiful plant, on account of its erect clear growth, and large interesting pinnatifid foliage. It thrives well in sandy peat, but must not be over-watered, and probably may be increased by cuttings.

sĭnŭātă . . . . . G. Ev. T. Moren. Bay 1830

**AGRIMONIA,** *Tournefort.* Given by the Greeks to a plant supposed useful in the cataract of the eye; from *argos,* white. Linn. 11, Or. 2, Nat. Or. *Rosaceæ.* Ornamental species of easy culture. A decoction of *A. Eupatoria* makes a wholesome gargle.

dahūrĭcă . . . Yellow . 8, H. Her. P. Dahuria . 1811
Eupatŏrĭă . . . Yellow . 6, H. Her. P. Britain
nepalēnsĭs . . . Yellow . 7, H. Her. P. Nepal . 1820
odorātă . . . Yellow . 7, H. Her. P. Italy . 1640
parviflŏră . . . Yellow . 7, H. Her. P. N. Amer. 1768
pilŏsă . . . . Yellow . 7, H. Her. P. Siberia . 1819
rēpēns . . . . Yellow . 8, H. Her. P. Levant . 1737
strĭātă . . . White . 7, H. Her. P. N. Amer. 1812
suavēŏlēns . . . Yellow . 7, H. Her. P. Virginia . 1810

**AGRIMONY,** see Agrimonia.

**AGRŎPȲRŬM,** *Palisot de Beauvois.* Derived from *agros,* a field, and *pyros,* wheat. Linn. 3, Or. 2, Nat. Or

*Gramineæ.* Mere weeds, of the simplest culture. *Synonymes:* 1. *Triticum giganteum, T. elongatum.* 2. *T. panicum.* 3. *T. pectinatum.* 4. *T. repens.*—*Acûtûm, angustifolium, caninûm, cristâtûm, dasyanthûm, densiflôrûm, desertôrûm, distichûm, elongâtûm,* 1, *glaûcûm, imbricâtûm, intermêdiûm, jûncêûm* 2, *littôrâlê, muricâtûm, obtusiflôrûm, pectinâtûm* 3, *pectiniförmê, prostrâtûm, pûngêns, rêpêns* 4, *arvênsê, capillârê, dumetôrûm, Leersiânûm, subulâtûm, Vaillantiânûm, rigidûm, rupêstrê, sibivicum, subulâtûm, variegâtûm.*

AGROSTEMMÂ, *Linn.* Derived from *agros*, a field, and *stemma*, a crown; in reference to the beauty of the flowers. *Linn.* 10, Or. 4, Nat. Or. *Silenaceæ*, Rose Campion. The species are well adapted for flower borders, where, when in flower, they are very ornamental. They grow well in any common soil, and increase by divisions or seed. *Synonymes:* 1. *A. perennans.* 2. *Lychnis pyrenaica.*

| | | | | | |
|---|---|---|---|---|---|
| Bungeânâ | . . | Scarlet | . 7, H. Her. P. | Russia | . 1834 |
| decûmbêns, 1 | . | Crimson | . 7, H. Her. P. | | |
| pyrenáirâ, 2 | . | Pa. rose | . 6, H. Her. P. | Pyrenees | . 1819 |
| suecica | . . | Pink | . 8, H. Her. P. | Sweden | . 1824 |

AGROSTIS, *Linn.* This is the Greek name for all grasses, from *agros*, a field. *Linn.* 3, Or. 2, Nat. Or. *Gramineæ.* Bent Grass. Plants of simple culture.

| | | | | | |
|---|---|---|---|---|---|
| alba | . | Apetal | . 7, Grass. | Britain | . |
| purpurâscêns | . | Apetal | . 7, Grass. | Britain | . |
| vivipârâ | . | Apetal | . 7, Grass. | Britain | . |
| pauciflôrâ | . | Apetal | . 7, Grass. | Switzerl. | . 1824 |
| spica-vênti | . | Apetal | . 7, Grass. | England | . |
| stolonifêrâ | . | Apetal | . 7, Grass. | Britain | . |
| angustifôliâ | . | Apetal | . 7, Grass. | Britain | . |
| aristâtâ | . | Apetal | . 7, Grass. | Britain | . |
| latifôlia | . | Apetal | . 7, Grass. | Britain | . |
| nemorâlis | . | Apetal | . 7, Grass. | Britain | . |
| palustris | . | Apetal | . 7, Grass. | Britain | . |

*Æmûlâ, ambigûa, âspêrâ, Billardiêrî, captênsis, capillâris, dêbilis, decûmbêns, diffûsâ, dûbiâ, dûlcis, Forstêrî, frondôsâ, gigantêâ, hispidâ, interrûptâ, Jûrtesî, latifôliâ, maritimâ, neglêctâ, pâllidâ, pâtulâ, plebêiâ, purpûrêâ, retrofrâctâ, spiridâ, sylvâticâ, tenêllâ, Tenôrii, tenuifôliâ, valentinâ, vâriâ, versicôlor, verticillâtâ, virginicâ, vulgâris, variegâti.*

AGRÛMI, a name given to any kind of lemon by the Italians.

AGYNEIA, *Linn.* Possessed of neither style nor stigma, hence the name from *a*, privative, and *gyne*, a female. *Linn.* 21, Or. 1, Nat. Or. *Euphorbiaceæ.* Uninteresting plants, succeeding in loam, and increased readily from seeds or suckers—*impûbês, puber.*

AGYRIÛM, *Fries.* Derived from *agyris*, a cluster, the species being generally found in crowds or clusters. *Linn.* 24, Or. 9, Nat. Or. *Fungi.* Curious dot-like productions, appearing like crusty spots upon dead wood—*cæstûm, rûfûm.*

AILANTUS, *Willdenow.* Derived from *ailanto*, (tree of heaven); the name of one species in the Moluccas, "*A. glandulosa* is a tree which may be compared to a gigantic stag's-horn sumach; it has very large leaves, unequally pinnate, with footstalks from one to two feet in length; and numerous flowers in a terminating pedicel, which exhale a disagreeable odour. The tree grows very fast, and on very poor soil, especially if it be calcareous. If the bark be wounded a resinous juice flows out, which hardens in a few days. The wood is hard, heavy, glossy, like satin, and susceptible of a very fine polish. It is propagated by cuttings of the roots. In general the trees bear only male flowers, but in France it has produced both male and female flowers, and fruit twice in ten years."—*Loudon's Ency. of Plants.*

| | | | | | |
|---|---|---|---|---|---|
| excêlsâ | . . . | Green | . . | H. De. T. E. Ind. | . 1800 |
| glandulôsâ | . . | Green | . . | H. De. T. China | . 1751 |

AIRA, *Willdenow.* Applied by the Greeks to *Lolium temulentum*, in reference to the deleterious qualities of that plant. *Linn.* 3, Or. 2, Nat. Or. *Gramineæ* Grasses of the simplest culture. *Synonyme:* 1. *Phalaris semineutra.*

| | | | | | |
|---|---|---|---|---|---|
| arundinâceâ | . . | Apetal | . . 6, Grass. | Cumana | . 1817 |
| semineutrâ, 1 | . | Apetal | . 7, Grass. | Hungary | . 1812 |

*Atropurpûreâ, caryophyllâtâ, flexuôsâ, glabrâtâ, hâmilis, lendigêrâ, pâllêns, pulchêllâ, refrâctâ, versicôlor.*

[ 11 ]

AIROPSIS, *Desvaux.* Named from its resemblance to the genus *aira*; from *aira*, hair-grass, and *opsis*, like. *Linn.* 3, Or. 2, Nat. Or. *Gramineæ.* For culture, &c., see Aira. *Synonymes:* 1. *Aira brevifôlia.* 2. *Poa agrostidea, Aira agrostidea.*

| | | | | | |
|---|---|---|---|---|---|
| brevifôlia, 1 | . | Apetal | . 7, Grass. | Missouri | . 1818 |
| Candollei 2 | . | Apetal | . 7, Grass. | S. Eur. | . 1820 |

*Globôsâ, obtusâta.*

AIR-PLANT, see *Aerides.*

AITONIA, *Linn., Junior.* In honour of Mr. William Aiton, the king's head gardener at Kew. *Linn.* 16, Or. 5, Nat. Or. *Meliaceæ.* A pretty and interesting species, thriving well in loam and peat. Cuttings if taken off when young will root in sand, under a glass in heat, if not suffered to remain damp.

| | | | | | |
|---|---|---|---|---|---|
| capênsis | . . . | Pink | . 7, G. Ev. S. C. G. H. | | . 1777 |

AIZOON, *Linn.* These plants live under almost any treatment; hence the name is derived from *aei*, always, and *zoon*, alive. *Linn.* 12, Or. 2, Nat. Or. *Tetragoniaceæ.* Not worth growing, except in botanical collections. For culture, &c., see *Mesembryanthemum.*

| | | | | | |
|---|---|---|---|---|---|
| canariênse | . | Yellow | . 8, G. | A. Canaries | . 1781 |
| glinoidês | . | Yellow | . 7, G. Ev. S. C. G. H. | | . 1774 |
| hispânicûm | . | Apetal | . 7, G. | A. Spain | . 1728 |
| lanceolâtûm | . | Pink | . 8, G. | B. C. G. H. | . 1752 |
| perfoliâtûm | . | Pink | . 7, G. Ev. S. C. G. H. | | . 1818 |

AJUGA, *Linn.* The derivation of the name is from *a*, privative, and *zugon*, a yoke. *Linn.* 14. Or. 1, Nat. Or. *Labiatæ*, Bugle. These dwarf species have a pretty appearance when in flower, planted near the front of borders, &c. They are easily cultivated, and increased by divisions or seeds.

| | | | | | |
|---|---|---|---|---|---|
| alpinâ | . . | Blue | . 8, H. Her. P. | England | . |
| australis | . | Blue | . 7, H. Her. P. N. Holl. | | . 1822 |
| Chamæpitys | . | Yellow | . 7. H. | A. England | . |
| foliôsâ | . | Blue | . 8, H. Her. P. Switzerl. | | . 1826 |
| genevênsis | . | Flesh | . 7, H. Her. P. Switzerl. | | . 1656 |
| integrifôlia | . | Blue | . 6, H. Her. P. Nepal | | . 1821 |
| Iva | . | Yellow | . 7, H. | A. S. Eur. | . 1759 |
| orientâlis | . | Blue | . 6, H. Her. P. Levant | | . 1752 |
| pyramidâlis | . | Purple | . 5, H. Her. P. Britain | | . |
| rêptans | . | Blue | . 5, H. Her. P. Britain | | . |
| albâ | . | White | . 5, H. Her. P. Britain | | . |
| rûbrâ | . | Red | . 5, H. Her. P. Britain | | . |
| rupêstris | . | Blue | . 5, H. Her. P. Switzerl. | | . 1826 |

AKEE-TREE, see *Blighia sapida.*

AKENIÛM, an indehiscent pericarp, containing a single seed, which does not adhere to it.

ALANGIÛM, *Jussieu.* Its name in Malabar. *Linn.* 12, Or. 1, Nat. Or. *Alangiaceæ.* Tall ornamental trees, thriving in light sandy loam, or loam, mixed with peat. Cuttings strike in sand, in heat, under a glass.

| | | | | | |
|---|---|---|---|---|---|
| decapêtalûm | . | Pa. pur. | . 8. Ev. T. E. Ind. | | . 1779 |
| hexapêtalûm | . | Purple | . 8. Ev. T. E. Ind. | | . 1826 |

ALBUCA, *Linn.* The name is given, somewhat injudiciously, to the colour of the flowers, from *albus*, white; only a few of the species having white flowers. *Linn.* 6, Or. 1, Nat. Or. *Liliaceæ.* The species are handsome, and thrive well in sandy loam mixed with a little peat. The suckers from the old bulb, or leaves taken off with a scale from the old bulb, will produce young plants. *Synonymes:* 1. *Anthericum exuviatum.* 2. *A. fragrans.*

| | | | | | |
|---|---|---|---|---|---|
| abyssinicâ | . . | White | . 8, G. | Bl. Abyssinia | 1818 |
| altissimâ | . | White | . 5, G. | Bl. C. G. H. | . 1789 |
| aûreâ | . | Grn. yel. | . 6, G. | Bl. C. G. H. | . 1818 |
| caudâtâ | . | Yellow | . 6, G. | Bl. C. G. H. | . 1791 |
| coarctâtâ | . | White | . 6, G. | Bl. C. G. H. | . 1774 |
| exuviâtâ, 1 | . | White | . 6, G. | Bl. C. G. H. | . 1795 |
| fastigiâtâ | . | White | . 6, G. | Bl. C. G. H. | . 1774 |
| filifôlia | . | Yellow | . 6, G. | Bl. C. G. H. | . 1820 |
| flaccidâ | . | Yel. grn. | . 6, G. | Bl. C. G. H. | . 1791 |
| fragrâns | . | Yel. grn. | . 7, G. | Bl. C. G. H. | . 1791 |
| fûgâx, 2 | . | Grn. yel. | . 7, G. | Bl. C. G. H. | . 1791 |
| major | . | Grn. yel. | . 5, G. | Bl. C. G. H. | . 1759 |
| minor | . | Yellow | . 5, G. | Bl. C. G. H. | . 1768 |
| physôdês | . | White | . 6, G. | Bl. C. G. H. | . 1804 |
| setôsâ | . | Green | . 6, G. | Bl. C. G. H. | . 1795 |
| spirâlis | . | White | . 6, G. | Bl. C. G. H. | . 1795 |
| viridiflôrâ | . | Green | . 6, G. | Bl. C. G. H. | . 1794 |
| viscôsâ | . | Wht. grn. | . 6, G. | Bl. C. G. H. | . 1779 |
| vittâtâ | . | Yel. grn. | . 6, G. | Bl. C. G. H. | . 1802 |

ALBUMEN, the substance under the inner coat of the testa of seeds, surrounding the embryo.

**ALBÚRNÚM**, the young wood before it comes to a proper consistence.

**ALCHEMILLA**, *Linn.* The word is from *Alkemelyeh*, its Arabic name. *Linn.* 4, Or. 1, Nat. Or. *Rosaceæ*. Many of the species are ornamental, and well adapted for planting near the front of borders, or for adorning rock-work. They succeed well in any common soil, if not over-wet, and may be increased from seeds or divisions. *A. vulgaris* is astringent, and slightly tonic. *Synonymes*: 1. *A. arvensis*, *Aphanes arvensis*. 2. *Alchemilla montana*.

| | | | | | |
|---|---|---|---|---|---|
| alpína | . . | Green | . 6, H. Her. P. Britain | . |
| capénsis | . . | Green | . 6, G. Her. P. C. G. H. | . 1818 |
| físsa | . . | Green | . 7, H. Her. P. Switzerl. | 1826 |
| hybrída, 9 | . | Green | . 7, H. Her. P. Britain | . |
| pentaphylla | . | White | . 7, H. Her. P. Switzerl. | 1784 |
| pubéscens | . | Green | . 7, H. Her. P. Caucasus | 1813 |
| serícéa | . . | Green | . 7, H. Her. P. Caucasus | 1818 |
| Sibbaldiæfólia | . | White | . 6, G. Her. P. Mexico | . 1823 |
| vulgáris | . . | Green | . 7, H. Her. P. Britain | . |
| glábra | . | Green | . 7, H. Her. P. Pyrenees | . 1817 |
| variegáta | . | Green | . 7, H. Her. P. Britain | . |

*Aphánes* 1, *cornucopioides*.

**ALCÍNA**, *Cavanilles*. Named in honour of Fr. Ign. Alcina, a Spanish naturalist. *Linn.* 19, Or. 4, Nat. Or. *Compositæ*. A species of little interest and easy cultivation—*Perfoliáta*.

**ALCYONÍDIÚM**, *Agardh.* So called, from *Halkioneion*, the foam of the sea, among which the plants referred to this genus are naturally produced. *Linn.* 24, Or. 7, Nat. Or. *Algæ*. This also is supposed to be the nidus of animalcula. Lamouroux, who originally fixed it here, afterwards referred it to Zoophites; in which last opinion, Gaillon agrees with him, declaring that he has actually seen the animalcula nestling in it. D'Orbigny and Ellis consider it the ova of a testaceous animal. *Defráctúm, diáphánúm, flavéscens.*

**ALDER**, see *Alnus*.

**ALDROVÁNDA**, *Linn.* In honour of Ulysses Aldrovandus, an old Italian botanist. *Linn.* 5, Or. 5, Nat. Or. *Droseraceæ*. We refer for culture, &c. of this curious little aquatic, to *Actinocarpus*.

| | | | | | |
|---|---|---|---|---|---|
| vesiculósa | . . | White | . 7, H. Aq. P. Italy | . . 1823 |

**ALECTÓRIA**, *Acharius.* The name is derived from *Alektor*, unmarried, because of the uncertainty respecting the male flowers. *Linn.* 24, Or. 8, Nat. Or. *Lichenes.* *A. jubata* occasionally supplies the rein-deer with food; for which purpose the Laplanders cut down the trees, that the lichen may be devoured from the topmost branches.— *Jubátâ.j. chalybliformis, sarmentósa.*

**ALEMBIC**, a vessel acting like a still.

**ALETRIS**, *Linn.* The whole plant appears covered with a powdery dust; hence the propriety of the name, from *Aleton*, meal. *Linn.* 6, Or. 1, Nat. Or. *Liliaceæ.* Interesting species, delighting in a shady situation, and peat or leaf soil. They are increased from offsets. *A. farinosa* has bitter roots, which act as a tonic and stomachic given in small doses, but a mixture of twenty grains produces much nausea, with a tendency to vomit. *Synonyme*: 1. *A. alba.*

| | | | | | |
|---|---|---|---|---|---|
| aúrea | . . . | Yellow | . H. Hr | P. N. Amer. | . 1811 |
| farinósa, 1 | . . | White | . H. Hr | P. N. Amer. | . 1768 |

**ALEURÍTES**, *Forster.* Derived from *aleurites*, mealy; in allusion to the farinaceous substance with which the whole plant is covered. *Linn.* 21, Or. 10, Nat. Or. *Euphorbiaceæ.* Handsome plants, succeeding well in loamy soil, and increased from ripe cuttings with the leaves left on, in a pot of sand, in heat, under a glass.

| | | | | | |
|---|---|---|---|---|---|
| trilóba | . . | Apetal. | . S. Ev. T. Society Is. . 1793 |

**ALEXANDRIAN LAUREL**, see *Ruscus racemosus.*

**ALHÁGI**, *Tournefort.* The Arabic name of the plant. *Linn.* 17, Or. 4, Nat. Or. *Leguminosæ. Manna.* These interesting plants must have the protection of the greenhouse in winter. They grow best in sandy loam and peat; and young cuttings in sand under a glass in heat, will root; but seeds when obtainable, sown in a hotbed, make the best plants. *Manna* is a natural exudation from the leaves and branches of *A. maurorum*, and is yielded only in hot weather. *Synonymes*: 1. *Hedysarum Pseudo-Alhagi. Maunæ caspica.* 2. *H. alhagi Manna hebraica.*

| | | | | | |
|---|---|---|---|---|---|
| camelórúm | . | Red | . . 7, F. Her. P. Siberia | . . 1816 |
| maurórúm | . . | Red | . . 7, G. Ev. S. Egypt | . . 1714 |

**ALIBERTIA**, *A. Richard.* In honour of M. Alibert, a famous French chemist. *Linn.* 5, Or. 1, Nat. Or. *Cinchonaceæ.* An interesting tree, which may be referred to *Hamelia*, for culture and propagation. *Synonyme: Melanopsidium nigrum.*

| | | | | | |
|---|---|---|---|---|---|
| edúlis | . . . | Cream-cld. | S. Ev. T. Guiana | . . 1823 |

**ALÍSMA**, *Linn.* The name is of Celtic origin, from *alis*, water. Water Plantain. *Linn.* 6, Or. 1, Nat. Or. *Alismaceæ.* Pretty little aquatics; for culture, &c., see *Actinocarpus. A. Plantago* is recommended in hydrophobia.

| | | | | | |
|---|---|---|---|---|---|
| cordifólia | . . | White | . 7, S. Aq. P. W. Ind. | . . 1810 |
| lanceolátá | . | Pur. wht. | 7, H. Aq. P. Britain | . . |
| nátans | . . | White | . 7, H. Aq. P. Wales | . . |
| parnassiæfólia | . | White | . 7, F. Aq. P. Italy | . . 1820 |
| parvifióra | . . | White | . 7, H. Aq. P. N. Amer. | . 1816 |
| Plantágo | . . | Pur. wht. | 7, H. Aq. P. Britain | . . |
| ranunculoídes | . | Purple | . 8, H. Aq. P. Britain | . . |
| répens | . . . | Wht. pur. | 8, H. Aq. P. Wales, Engl. | . |
| triviális | . . | White | . 7, H. Aq. P. N. Amer. | . 1816 |

**ALKALI**, any substance which mingled with acid produces fermentation.

**ALLAMÁNDA**, *Willdenow.* Named in memory of Dr. Frederic Allamand, professor at Leyden. *Linn.* 5, Or. 1, Nat. Or. *Apocynaceæ.* This handsome and free-flowering plant delights in rich loamy soil, and may be multiplied freely from cuttings in sand in moist heat. An infusion of the leaves makes a valuable cathartic.

| | | | | | |
|---|---|---|---|---|---|
| cathártica | . . | Yellow | . 7, S. Ev. S. Guiana | . 1785 |

**ALLANTÓDIA**, *Bot. Reg.* The cylindrical indusia resembles a kind of pudding called a sausage, hence the derivation of the name, from *allantos*, a sausage. *Linn.* 24, Or. 1, Nat. Or. *Polypodiaceæ.* Ornamental species of Ferns; for culture, &c., see *Polypodium. Synonymes*: 1 *Polypodium axillare.* 2. *P. umbrosum.*

| | | | | | |
|---|---|---|---|---|---|
| austrális | . . | Brown | . 7, G. Her. P. V. Die. L. | . 1820 |
| axilláris, 1 | . | Brown | . 7, G. Her. P. Madeira | . 1779 |
| ténera | . . | Brown | . 7, G. Her. P. N. Holl. | . 1820 |
| umbrósa, 2 | . | Brown | . 7, G. Her. P. Madeira | . 1779 |

**ALLIÁRIA**, *Adanson.* The name refers to the strong garlic smell; and is derived from *allium*, garlic. *Linn.* 15, Nat. Or. *Cruciferæ.* Mere weeds, of the simplest culture. *Synonyme*: 1. *Erysimum alliaria —brachycárpa, officinalis,* 1.

**ALLIÓNIA**, *Linn.* In memory of Charles Allioni, a botanist at Turin. *Linn.* 4, Or. 1, Nat. Or. *Nyctagynaceæ.* These interesting annuals delight in sandy peat or loam.

| | | | | | |
|---|---|---|---|---|---|
| incarnátá | . . | Flesh | . 8, H. | A. Cumana | . 1820 |
| ováta | . . . | Purple | . 7, H. | A. N. Amer. | . 1827 |
| violácéá | . . | Violet | . 7, H. | A. Cumana | . 1820 |

**ALLIÚM**, *Linn.* Derived from the Celtic *all*, signifying hot, or burning. *Linn.* 6, Or. 1, Nat. Or. *Liliaceæ.* Most of the species are pretty. They succeed in common soil, and increase abundantly from offsets. The Onion, Leek, Garlic, Shallot, Chives, &c., all agree in their stimulant, diuretic, and expectorant effects, differing in degree of activity. *Synonymes*: 1. *A. carneum.* 2. *Amaryllis caspia.* 3. *Allium campestre.* 4. *A. flavescens.* 5. *A. fœtidum.* 6. *A. baicalense, spirale, senescens.* 7. *A. roseum, ambiguum.* 8. *A. paniculatum.* 9. *A. monspessulanum.* 10. *A. tataricum.* 11. *A. virescens.* 12. *A. scorodoprasum.* 13. *Scilla paradoxa.* 14. *A. paniculatum.* 15. *A. vineale.* 16. *A. stellatum album, angulosum.* 17. *A. bisulcum.* 18. *A. tenuifolium.* 19. *A. glaucum, palustre.* 20. *Ornithogalum gramineum.* 21. *A. deflexum.* 22. *A. ambiguum, graminifolium, tricolorum.* 23. *A. ciliatum.* 24. *A. Ampeloprasum.*

| | | | | | |
|---|---|---|---|---|---|
| acutangúlúm | . | Red | . . 6, H. Bl. P. | . 1816 |
| acutiflórúm | . | Red | . . 6, H. Bl. P. France | . 1819 |
| acútúm | . . | Red | . . 7, H. Bl. P. | . 1819 |
| alládúm | . . | White | . 6, H. Bl. P. Crimea | . 1820 |
| amœnúm 1 | . | Red | . . 5, H. Bl. P. France | . 1821 |
| ampelopræsúm | . | Purple | . 7, H. Bl. P. England | . |
| Andersónii | . | Purple | . 6, H. Bl. P. Siberia | . 1818 |
| angulósúm | . . | Lgt. pur. | 6, H. Bl. P. Germany | . 1739 |
| arenárіúm | . | Purple | . 6, H. Bl. P. Britain | . |
| ascalónicúm | . | Purple | . 6, H. Bl. P. Palestine | . 1546 |
| májús | . | Purple | . 7, H. Bl. P. S. Eur. | . |
| aspérúm | . . | Purple | . 8, H. Bl. P. S. Eur. | . 1800 |
| atropurpúréúm | . | Drk. pur. | 7, H. Bl. P. Hungary | . 1821 |
| azúréúm | . . | Blue | . 10, H. Bl. P. | . 1830 |
| brachystémón | . | White | . 6, H. Bl. P. Europe | . 1819 |
| canadénsé | . . | Purple | . 6, H. Bl. P. N. Amer | 1739 |
| carinátúm | . . | Grn. yel. | 6, H. Bl. P. England | . |

cárneûm . . Ps. pur. 6, H. Bl. P. . . 1815
caroliniânûm . Red . 6, H. Bl. P. N. Amer. 1818
cáspicûm, 2 . White . 4, H. Bl. P. Crimea . 1822
caucásicûm . White . 6, H. Bl. P. Caucasus .
Cèpa . . . White . 6, H. Bl. B.
  aggregâtûm . White . 6, H. Bl. P.
  pauciflôrûm . White . 6, H. Bl. P.
cepæfôrmê . White . 8, H. Bl. P. . . 1824
cêrnûûm . . Red . 6, H. Rl. P. N. Amer. 1806
Chamæmôlý . White . 1, H. Bl. P. S. Eur. . 1774
cinêrêûm . . Straw . 7, H. Bl. P. Siberia . 1829
Clusiânûm . White . 7, H. Bl. P. S. Eur. . 1803
confertûm, 3 . Purple . 8, H. Bl. P. Europe .
congêstûm . Purple . 5, H. Bl. P. Siberia . 1818
controvêrsûm . Purple . 6, H. Bl. P. . . 1816
Cowáni . . White . 6, H. Bl. P. Chile . 1822
danubiálê . . Red . . 6, H. Bl. P. Germany 1818
denudâtûm, 4 . Wht. red 8, H. Bl. P. Siberia . 1819
descéndâns . Drk. pur. 7, H. Bl. P. Switzerl. . 1796
erêctûm . . White . 6, H. Bl. P. C. G. H. . 1823
euô̂mûn . . White . 6, H. Bl. P. . . 1829
exsêrtûm . . White . 7, H. Bl. P. Russia . 1818
Fischêri . . Lilac . 7, H. Bl. P. Siberia . 1829
fistulôsûm . . Grn. yel. 4, H. Bl. P. Siberia . 1629
flávûm . . . Yellow . 6, H. Bl. P. Austria . 1759
flêxûm, 5 . . Drk. pur. 7, H. Bl. P.
foliolôsûm . . Purple . 7, H. Bl. P. . . 1817
frágrâns . . White . 9, H. Bl. P. W. Ind. . 1822
fûscûm . . . Brown . 7, H. Bl. P. Hungary . 1820
glandulôsûm . White . 6, H. Bl. P. . . 1829
gláucûm, 6 . . Pink . 6, H. Bl. P. Siberia . 1800
globôsûm . . Purple . 8, H. Bl. P. Caucasus . 1821
guttâtûm . . White . 7, H. Bl. P. Odessa . 1819
Halléri . . . Pa. red . 7, H. Bl. P. S. Eur. . 1818
illýricûm . . Purple . 7, H. Bl. P. Austria . 1820
incarnâtûm, 7 . Red . . 5, H. Bl. P. Greece . 1812
intermédiûm, 8 . White . 8, H. Bl. P. S. Eur. . 1827
juncifôliûm . White . 5, H. Bl. P. Chile . 1826
láxûm . . . Red . . 6, H. Bl. P. Siberia . 1817
lineârê . . . Wht. red 6, H. Bl. P. Siberia . 1752
littorêûm, 9 . Purple . 7, H. Bl. P. Italy . . 1818
longifôliûm . . Drk. pur. 7, H. Bl. P. Mexico . 1826
longispáthûm . Brown . 7, H. Bl. P. France . 1810
mágicûm . . Grn. wht. 6, H. Bl. P. Austria . 1596
majâle . . . White . 6, H. Bl. P. Italy . . 1824
médiûm . . . White . 6, H. Bl. P. Hungary . 1820
Môly . . . Yellow . 6, H. Bl. P. S. Eur. . 1604
montânûm . . Red . . 7, H. Bl. P. Greece . 1818
moschâtûm . Wht. pur. 8, H. Bl. P. S. Eur. . 1823
mutábile . . Red . . 6, H. Bl. P. N. Amer. 1824
multiflôrûm . Red . . 6, H. Bl. P. N. Africa 1800
narcissiflôrûm . Purple . 6, H. Bl. P. France .
neapolitânûm . White . 6, H. Bl. P. Naples . 1823
nigrûm . . . White . 7, H. Bl. P. Barbary . 1818
nudicâulê . . . . . H. Bl. P. . . 1829
nûtâns . . . Red . . 7, H. Bl. P. Siberia . 1785
obliquûm . . White . 6, H. Bl. P. Siberia . 1759
ochrolêûcûm . Cream . 7, H. Bl. P. Hungary . 1816
odôrûm, 10 . White . 6, H. Bl. P. S. Eur. . 1820
olerâcêûm, 11 . Pa. yel. 6, H. Bl. P. England .
Ophioscôrôdon, 12 Ph. red . 8, H. Bl. P. Greece .
oxypétâlûm . White . 8, H. Bl. P. . . 1818
Pallâsii . . . Red . . 6, H. Bl. P. Russia . 1819
pállêns . . . Pale . . 6, H. Bl. P. S. Eur. . 1779
paniculâtûm . Pale . . 6, H. Bl. P. S. Eur. . 1780
paradôxûm, 13 . White . 4, H. Bl. P. Caucasus . 1823
parviflôrûm . Purple . 6, H. Bl. P. S. Eur. . 1781
pedemontânûm . Red . . 7, H. Bl. P. Piedmont 1817
pendulînûm . White . 4, H. Bl. P. Italy . . 1825
Pôrrûm . . . White . 4, H. Bl. B. Switzerl. . 1562
proliférûm . . White . 7, H. Bl. P. . . 1820
prostrâtûm . . Red . . 7, H. Bl. P. Siberia . 1823
pruniâtûm . . Red . . 7, H. Bl. P. Spain . 1819
pulchêllûm, 14 . Scarlet . 7, H. Bl. P. Tauria . 1810
Pûrshii, 15 . . Pink . . 8, H. Bl. P. N. Amer. 1818
pusíllûm . . White . 7, H. Bl. P. Italy . . 1826
ramôsûm . . Pa. yel. 6, H. Bl. P. Siberia . 1819
reticulâtûm, 16 . White . 6, H. Bl. P. N. Amer. 1800
rôsêûm . . . Pa. pur. 6, H. Bl. P. France . 1752
rotúndûm . . Purple . 7, H. Bl. P. S. Eur. . 1820
rubéllûm . . Red . . 7, H. Bl. P. Caucasus . 1825
rûbêns, 17 . . Purple . 6, H. Bl. P. Germany . 1805
rubicúndûm . Red . . 7, H. Bl. P. C. G. H. . 1804
rupêstrê . . . Red . . 6, H. Bl. P. Crimea . 1824
sativûm . . . White . 6, H. Bl. P. Sicily . 1548
saxatîlê . . . White . 6, H. Bl. P. Crimea . 1823
Schœnoprâsûm, 18 Flesh . 5, H. Bl. P. Britain .
Scorodoprásûm . Lt. pur. 7, H. Bl. P. Denmark 1596
scorzonerœfôliûm Yellow . 6, H. Bl. P. S. Eur. . 1820
senéscêns . . White . 6, H. Bl. P. Germany . 1596
serôtinûm . . Red . . 8, H. Bl. P. Switzerl. . 1820
sibíricûm, 19 . Pa. red . 7, H. Bl. P. Siberia . 1777
sículûm . . . Grn. pur. 7, H. Bl. E. Sicily . 1832
sphærocéphâlûm . Red . . 7, H. Bl. P. Europe . 1759
spôrtûm . . . Purple . 6, H. Bl. P. Siberia . 1820
stellâtûm . . Lilac . . 6, H. Bl. P. N. Amer. 1811
striâtûm . . . White . 6, H. Bl. P. Carolina . 1800
striâtêllûm, 20 . Wht. yel. 4, H. Bl. P. Chile . 1823
strictûm, 21 . . Pink . . 7, H. Bl. P. . . 1821

[ 13 ]

suavêôlêns, 22 . White . 6, H. Bl. P. Austria . 1801
subhirsûtûm, 23 . White . 5, H. Bl. P. S. Eur. . 1596
Synnôtii . . . Pa. red . 7, H. Bl. P. C. G. H. . 1825
tenuiflôrûm . . Pink . . 7, H. Bl. P. Italy . . 1824
tricôcêûm . . White . 6, H. Bl. P. N. Amer. 1770
triquêtrûm . . White . 5, H. Bl. P. Spain . 1789
ursînûm . . . White . 4, H. Bl. P. Britain .
verrucôsûm . . Pa. pur. 5, H. Bl. P. C. G. H. . 1825
Victoriâlis . . Grn. yel. 5, F. Bl. P. Austria . 1789
  angustifôliûm . Grn. yel. 4, H. Bl. P. Scotland .
vineálê . . . Purple . 6, H. Bl. P. Britain .
violâcêûm . . Violet . 6, H. Bl. P. S. Eur. . 1823
Waldsteinii, 24 . Purple . 6, H. Bl. P. Hungary . 1826

**ALLOSÔRÛS**, *Bernhardi*. Named from *allos*, various, and *soros*, heap; in allusion to the changing of the sori. *Linn.* 24, *Or.* 1, Nat. Or. *Polypodiaceæ.* An interesting native species of fern, of easy culture. *Synonymes*: 1. *Pteris crispa, Osmunda crispa.*

crispûs, 1 . . Brown . . 7, H. Her. P. Britain .

**ALLSEED**, see *Polycarpon.*
**ALLSPICE**, see *Calycanthus.*
**ALLSPICE-TREE**, see *Pimenta.*
**ALMOND**, see *Amygdalus.*

**ALNUS**, *Tournefort.* Compounded from *al*, near, and *lan*, the edge of a river; in allusion to the situation where the species grow. *Linn.* 21, *Or.* 4, Nat. Or. *Betulaceæ.* Timber trees, thriving best in very moist situations. The wood is employed for under-water purposes, turnery, &c.; the sap is yellow. They are propagated by layers or seeds, and the bark possesses the tanning principle in a considerable degree.

canadénsis . . Apetal . 6, H. De. T. Canada .
cordifôliâ . . Apetal . 6, H. De. T. Naples . 1818
glaûca . . . Apetal . 6, H. De. T. N. Amer. 1820
glutinôsa . . Apetal . 4, H. De. T. Britain .
  emarginâtâ . Apetal . 4, H. De. T. Britain .
  foliis-variegâtis Apetal . 4, H. De. T. Britain .
  inciâa . . . Apetal . 4, H. De. T. Britain .
  laciniâta . . Apetal . 4, H. De. T. Britain .
  quercifôliâ . Apetal . 4, H. De. T. Britain .
incâna . . . Apetal . 6, H. De. T. Europe . 1780
  angulâta . . Apetal . 6, H. De. T.
  pinnâta . . Apetal . 6, H. De. T. Europe .
macrocárpâ . . Apetal . 6, H. De. T.
macrophýllâ . Apetal . 6, H. De. T. Naples .
oblongâtâ . . Apetal . 6, H. De. T. S. Eur. . 1730
  elliptica . . Apetal . 6, H. De. T.
oxyacanthifôliâ . Apetal . 6, H. De. T.
pûmila . . . Apetal . 6, H. De. T.
rûbra . . . Apetal . 6, H. De. T.
serrulâta . . Apetal . 6, H. De. T. N. Amer. 1769
subrotúnda . . Apetal . 4, H. De. T.
undulâta . . Apetal . 6, H. De. T. N. Amer. 1782

**ALOE**, *Linn.* Derived from *alloeh*, the Arabic name for this genus. *Linn.* 6, *Or.* 1, Nat. Or. *Liliaceæ.* Very interesting and curious succulent plants, thriving well in open sandy loam and peat, mixed with a little reduced manure; the pots must be well drained and the plants cautiously watered, especially in winter. They increase by suckers, or leaves laid on, or very slightly planted in a pot of mould. Socotrine aloes are obtained from *A. spicata*, and an inferior sort is attributable to *A. perfoliata.* *Synonymes*: 1. *A. humilis.* 2. *A. mitræformis.* 3. *humilis, incurva.* 4. *A. picta.* 5. *A. striata.* 6. *A. barbadensis.*

acuminâta, 1 . Orange . 4, G. Ev. S. C. G. H. . 1795
albispina . . Scarlet . 4, G. Ev. S. C. G. H. . 1796
albocincta . . Orange . 6, G. Ev. S. . . 1812
arborêscêns . Red . . 4, G. Ev. S. C. G. H. . 1781
aristâta . . . Orange . 5, G. Her. P. C. G. H. . 1801
brevifôliâ . . Orange . 4, G. Ev. S. C. G. H. . 1810
cæsiâ . . . Orange . 7, G. Ev. S. C. G. H. . 1818
  elátiôr . . Red . . 6, G. Ev. S. C. G. H. . 1821
chinénsis . . Yellow . 6, G. Ev. S. C. G. H. . 1821
ciliâris . . . Red . . 6, G. Ev. S. C. G. H. . 1821
Commelini, 2 . . . . G. Ev. S. C. G. H. . 1819
depréssa . . Orange . 8, G. Ev. S. C. G. H. . 1731
dichôtômâ . . Red . . 7, G. Ev. S. C. G. H. . 1780
dístâns . . . Red . . 7, G. Ev. S. C. G. H. . 1732
  depréssa . . Red . . 7, G. Ev. S. C. G. H. . 1820
  refléxâ . . Red . . 7, G. Ev. S. C. G. H. . 1820
echinâta . . . . . . G. Ev. S. C. G. H. . 1820
flavispina . . Red . . 8, G. Ev. S. C. G. H. . 1793
frutéscêns . . Red . . 4, G. Ev. S. C. G. H. . 1818
glaûca . . . Red . . 4, G. Ev. S. C. G. H. . 1731
  rhodacánthâ . Red . . 4, G. Ev. S. C. G. H. . 1731
grácilis . . . Orange . 6, G. Ev. S. C. G. H. . 1822
húmilis . . . Orange . 6, G. Ev. S. C. G. H. . 1781
incúrvâ, 3 . . Orange . 5, G. Ev. S. C. G. H. . 1795
latifôliâ . . . Scarlet . 7, G. Ev. S. C. G. H. . 1795

| | | | | |
|---|---|---|---|---|
| lineātā . . . | Scarlet | . | G. Ev. S. C. G. H. | . 1789 |
| glaucescēns . | Scarlet | . | G. Ev. S. C. G. H. | . 1786 |
| micracanthā . | Pink | . 7, | G. Ev. S. C. G. H. | . 1819 |
| mitræformis . | Red | . 6, | G. Ev. S. C. G. H. | . 1732 |
| nobilis . . | Blue | . 8, | G. Ev. S. C. G. H. | . 1800 |
| obscūrā. 4 . | Red | . 7, | G. Ev. S. C. G. H. | . 1819 |
| glaucior . . | Red | . 7, | G. Ev. S. C. G. H. | . 1819 |
| māgnidēns . | Red | . 7, | G. Ev. S. C. G. H. | . 1890 |
| pallēscēns . . | Red | . 7, | G. Ev. S. C. G. H. | . 1820 |
| paniculātā, 5 . | Scarlet | . 7, | G. Ev. S. C. G. H. | . 1795 |
| plūridēns . . | Red | . 7, | G. Ev. S. C. G. H. | . 1823 |
| prolīferā . . | Orange | . 4, | G. Ev. S. C. G. H. | . 1819 |
| majōr . . | Orange | . 4, | G. Ev. S. C. G. H. | . 1819 |
| purpurascēns . | Purple | . 8, | G. Ev. S. C. G. H. | . 1789 |
| saponāriā . . | Red | . 7, | G. Ev. S. C. G. H. | . 1727 |
| luteo-striātā . | Red | . 7, | G. Ev. S. C. G. H. | . 1821 |
| sērrā . . | Orange | . 7, | G. Ev. S. C. G. H. | . 1818 |
| serrulātā . . | Red | . 7, | G. Ev. S. C. G. H. | . 1789 |
| socotrīna . . | Red | . 3, | G. Ev. S. C. G. H. | . 1731 |
| spicātā . . | Red | . | G. Ev. S. C. G. H. | . 1795 |
| spinosior . . | Red | . 4, | G. Ev. S. C. G. H. | . 1820 |
| striātūlā . . | Red | . 6, | G. Ev. S. C. G. H. | . 1821 |
| suberēctā . . | Scarlet | . 4, | G. Ev. S. C. G. H. | . 1789 |
| æmiguttātā . | Orange | . 5, | G. Ev. S. C. G. H. | . 1819 |
| subtuberculātā . | Orange | . 6, | G. Ev. S. C. G. H. | . 1690 |
| tenuifōliā . . | Orange | . 6, | G. Her. P. C. G. H. | . 1821 |
| tentior . . | Yellow | . 6, | G. Ev. S. C. G. H. | . 1821 |
| tuberculātā . | Orange | . 4, | G. Ev. S. C. G. H. | . 1796 |
| variegātā . . | Pink | . 6, | G. Ev. S. C. G. H. | . 1790 |
| virēns . . | Yellow | . 6, | G. Ev. S. C. G. H. | . 1790 |
| vulgāris, 6 . | Yellow | . 6, | G. Ev. S. C. G. H. | . 1596 |
| xanthacanthā . | Orange | . 6, | G. Ev. S. C. G. H. | . 1817 |

**ALOMIA**, *Kunth.* The name is gathered from *a*, privative, and *loma*, a fringe. *Linn.* 19, Or. 1, Nat. Or. *Compositæ.* An ornamental dwarf evergreen; grown in sandy loam, and increased from cuttings.

| | | | | |
|---|---|---|---|---|
| ageratoidēs . . | White | . 7, | F. Ev. P. N. Spain | . 1824 |

**ALONSOA**, *Ruiz and Pavon.* So named, after Zanoni Alonso, by the authors of the Flora Peruviana. *Linn.* 14, Or. 2, Nat. Or. *Scrophulariaceæ.* These pretty free-flowering species, which make such an interesting show in the flower-garden, may be successfully grown in rich mould; and multiplied plentifully from cuttings or seeds. *Synonymes*: 1. *Hemimeris urticifolia, Celsia urticifolia*. 2. *Celsia linearis, Hemimeris coccinea*.

| | | | | |
|---|---|---|---|---|
| acutifoliā . . | Scarlet | . 6, | G. Ev. S. Peru | . 1790 |
| caulialātā . . | Scarlet | . 6, | F. Her. P. Chile | . 1823 |
| incisifōliā, 1 . | Scarlet | . 6, | G. Ev. S. Chile | . 1795 |
| intermēdiā . . | Scarlet | . 6, | G. Ev. S. Hybrid | . |
| lineāris, 2 . . | Scarlet | . 6, | G. Ev. S. Peru | . 1790 |

**ALOPECURUS**, *Willdenow.* Called the fox-tail grass; hence the name from *alopex*, a fox, and *oura*, a tail. *Linn.* 3, Or. 2, Nat. Or. *Gramineæ.* Useful species of grass. *A. pratensis* possesses the requisites of quantity, quality, and earliness, in a superior degree. Any garden soil, divisions, or seeds.

| | | | | |
|---|---|---|---|---|
| alpinūs . . | Apetal | . 6, | Grass. Scotland | . |
| arundinācēūs . | Apetal | . 7, | Grass. Europe | . 1826 |
| brachystachys . | Apetal | . 7, | Grass. Siberia | . 1820 |
| colobachnoidēs . | Apetal | . 7, | Grass. Siberia | . 1826 |
| macrostachys . | Apetal | . 7, | Grass. Barbary | . 1826 |
| nigricāns . . | Apetal | . 4, | Grass. Europe | . 1815 |
| pratēnsis . . | Apetal | . 7, | Grass. Britain | . |

*Agrēstis, bulbōsūs, echinātūs, fulvūs, geniculātūs, ramōsūs, utriculātūs, ventricōsūs.*

**ALOYSIA**, *Ortega.* Named in compliment to Maria Louisa, Queen of Spain, by Don Antonio Palan, botanist at Madrid. *Linn.* 15, Or. 2, Nat. Or. *Verbenaceæ.* Justly esteemed for its citron-scented leaves, with which most people are acquainted. Rich mould suits it, and cuttings strike freely in sandy soil. *Synonyme*: 1. *Verbena triphylla.*

| | | | | |
|---|---|---|---|---|
| citriodōrā . . | Pa. pur. | . 8, | G. De. S. Chile | . 1784 |

**ALPINIA**, *Linn.* In memory of Prosper Alpini, an Italian botanist. *Linn.* 1, Or. 1, Nat. Or. *Zingiberaceæ.* These handsome species, to succeed well, require rich sandy soil, and to be grown at large in a hot humid atmosphere. They are increased by divisions at the roots. The root or rhizoma of *A. racemosa* and *Galanga*, are aromatic. *Synonymes*: 1. *Cardamomum medium*. 2. *A. bracteata.*

| | | | | |
|---|---|---|---|---|
| Allūghās . . | Red | . 2, S. Her. P. E. Ind. | . 1796 |
| antillārūm . . | Flesh | . 5, S. Her. P. W. Ind. | . 1826 |
| auriculātā . . | Red. yel. | . 8. Her. P. E. Ind. | . 1814 |
| bracteātā . . | White | . 5, S. Her. P. E. Ind. | . 1824 |
| calcarātā . . | White | . 9, S. Her. P. E. Ind. | . 1800 |
| Cardamōmūm . | White | . 8. S. Her. P. E. Ind. | . 1815 |

| | | | | |
|---|---|---|---|---|
| cērnūā . . . | Pink | . 4, S. Her. P. E. Ind. | . 1804 |
| comōsā . . | White | . 5, S. Her. P. Caraccas | . 1752 |
| difflēsā . . | Pur. blu. yel. | 4, S. Her. P. E. Ind. | . 1818 |
| exaltātā . . | Red yel. | . 8. Her. P. Surinam | . 1820 |
| Galāngā . . | Wht. yel. | . 10, S. Her. P. E. Ind. | . |
| linguæfōrmis . | Red | . 7, S. Her. P. E. Ind. | . 1820 |
| magnifica . . | Red | . 7, S. Her. P. Maurit. | . 1820 |
| malaccēnsis . . | White | . 4, S. Her. P. E. Ind. | . 1799 |
| mēdiā, 1 . . | Red | . 7, S. Her. P. E. Ind. | . 1815 |
| mūticā . . | White | . 8, S. Her. P. E. Ind. | . 1811 |
| nūtāns . . | Pink | . 5, S. Her. P. E. Ind. | . 1792 |
| occidentālis . . | White | . 7, S. Her. P. Jamaica | . 1793 |
| penicillātā . . | Pink | . 5, G. Her. P. China | . |
| punīceā . . | Scarlet | . 6, S. Her. P. E. Ind. | . 1820 |
| racemōsā . . | White | . 8, S. Her. P. W. Ind. | . 1752 |
| Roscoeānā, 2 . | Red | . 5, S. Her. P. E. Ind. | . 1823 |
| spicātā . . | | . 8. Her. P. Sumatra | . 1822 |
| striātā . . | | . 8 Her. P. E. Ind. | . 1818 |
| tubulātā . . | Red | . 7, S. Her. P. Demerara | . 1820 |

**ALSINE**, *Linn.* The name is derived from *alsos*, signifying a shaded place; in allusion to the situation the plant thrives best in. *Linn.* 5, Or. 3, Nat. Or. *Alsinaceæ.* Curious plants of simple culture.

| | | | | |
|---|---|---|---|---|
| molluginēa . . | White | . 7, H. | A. Spain | . 1816 |
| mucronātā . . | White | . 7, H. | A. S. Eur. | . 1777 |
| pubēscens . . | White | . 7, H. | A. | . 1810 |
| segetālis . . | White | . 7, H. | A. France | . 1805 |

*Mēdiā.*

**ALSODEIA**, *Du Petit Thouars.* Derived from *alsodes*, leafy; in reference to the plants being thickly beset with leaves. *Linn.* 5, Or. 3, Nat. Or. *Violaceæ.* These ornamental species succeed in a mixture of loam and peat, and propagate freely from cuttings in sand.

| | | | | |
|---|---|---|---|---|
| latifōlia . . | White | . 8. Ev. S. Madaga. | . 1824 |
| pauciflōrā . . | White | . 8. Ev. S. Madagas. | . 1824 |

**ALSOPHILA**, *Bot. Reg.* The name refers to the habitation of the plant, and is gathered from *alsos*, grove, and *phileo*, to love. *Linn.* 24, Or. 1, Nat. Or. *Polypodiaceæ.* This interesting species may be grown in peat and loam, and increased by divisions.

| | | | | |
|---|---|---|---|---|
| austrālis . . | Brown | . | G. Her. P. N. Holl. | . 1823 |

**ALSTONIA**, *R. Brown.* In memory of Dr. Alston, a professor of medicine at Edinburgh. *Linn.* 5, Or. 1, Nat. Or. *Apocynaceæ.* Pretty species, for culture, &c., see *Nerium.* *Synonymes*: 1. *A. oleandrifolia, Nerium tinctorium.*

| | | | | |
|---|---|---|---|---|
| scholāris, 1 . . | White | . 5, S. Ev. S. E. Ind. | . 1824 |
| venenātā . . | White | . 6, S. Ev. S. E. Ind. | . 1825 |

**ALSTRŒMERIA**, *Linn.* Named in honour of Baron Claudius Alstrœmer, a Swedish botanist. *Linn.* 6, Or. 1, Nat. Or. *Amaryllidaceæ.* The species of this beautiful genus, Sweet observes, "thrive best in a mixture of full one third sand, rather more than a third of turfy loam, and the rest turfy peat; several species succeed well out in the open air, planted about six inches deep, by the side of a south wall, in sandy soil." The stove species also succeed well in the same compost; they are increased by dividing the roots, or by seeds, which must be sown as soon as ripe. *A. Ligtu* is delightfully fragrant. *A. salsilla* is diaphoretic and diuretic. From *A. pallida* a kind of arrow-root is prepared in Chile. *Synonymes*: 1. *A. Hookeri.* 2. *A. Simsii.*

| | | | | |
|---|---|---|---|---|
| acutifoliā . . | Red. yel. | . 9, F. De. Tw. Mexico | . 1820 |
| aurantiācā . . | Orange | . 6, G. Bl. P. Valpar. | . 1831 |
| edūlis . . | Red | . 7, S. De. Tw. Trinidad | . 1820 |
| Flos-Martial . | Wht. pur. | . 6, S. Tu. P. Chile | . 1822 |
| hæmanthā . . | Oran. red. | . 7, S. Tu. P. Chile | . 1830 |
| hirtūlā . . | Red yel. | . 7, H. De. Tw. Mexico | . 1824 |
| Ligtu . . | Scarlet | . 8, S. Tu. P. Peru | . 1776 |
| Neillii . . | Pa. Rose | . 6, G. Tu. P. Mendoza | . 1827 |
| oculātā . . | Ro. pur. | . 6, G. De. Cl. Valpar. | . 1831 |
| ovātā . . | Red. yel. | . 6, H. De. Tw. Chile | . 1824 |
| pallīdā . . | Pink red | . 6, G. Tu. P. Chile | . 1827 |
| pauciflōrā . . | Oran. grn. | . 9, S. De. Tw. Caraccas | . 1823 |
| Pelegrīnā . . | Striped | . 7, G. Tu. P. Peru | . 1753 |
| psittacīnā . . | Crimson | . 9, F. Tu. P. Mexico | . 1829 |
| pulchēlla, 1 . | Scarlet | . 8, S. Tu. P. Chile | . 1822 |
| pilōsā . . | Scarlet | . 10, S. Tu. P. Chile | . |
| rōsēā. 2 . . | Pink | . 7, S. Tu. P. Peru | . 1824 |
| Salsilla . . | Grn. crim. | . 6, S. De. Tw. S. Amer. | . 1806 |

**ALTERNANTHERA**, *R. Brown.* The name refers to the stamens being alternately fertile and barren. *Linn.* 5, Or. 1, Nat. Or. *Amarantaceæ.* The biennial species of this interesting genus should be sown on a gentle heating hotbed, in peaty soil. The stove and greenhouse species succeed well in any light

[ 14 ]

rich soil, and propagate freely from cuttings. *Synonyme:* 1. *A. axillaris.*

| Achyrantha | . | White | . 7, 8. | Her. | P. | B. Ayres | . 1782 |
|---|---|---|---|---|---|---|---|
| canescens | . | White | . 7, 8. | Her. | P. | Cumana | . 1825 |
| caracasana | . | White | . 7, 8. | Her. | P. | Trinidad | . 1819 |
| ficoides | . | Green | . 7, 8. | Her. | P. | S. Amer. | . 1821 |
| frutescens | . | White | . 7, G. | Ev. | S. | Peru | . 1820 |
| polygonoides | . | White | . 7, G. | Her. | P. | America | . 1731 |
| procumbens | . | White | . 7, 8. | Her. | P. | Brazil | . 1818 |
| sericea | . | White | . 7, 8. | Her. | P. | Quito | . 1820 |
| senallis | . | Brown | . 8, 8. | B. | E. Ind. | . 1778 |
| spinosa, 1 | . | Yellow | . 6, 8. | A. | . 1823 |

ALTERNATING, alternate with anything mentioned.

ALTHÆA, *Linn.* Derived from *altheo,* to cure; from the medicinal qualities of some of the species. *Linn.* 16, Or. 8, Nat. Or. *Malvaceæ.* Tall free-flowering plants: the biennial and annual kinds should be sown in the open border in spring, and transplanted when sufficiently strong. The herbaceous kinds may be increased by dividing the roots, or by seeds. *A. rosea,* the parent of the many beautiful varieties of Hollyhock, yields a blue colouring matter equal to indigo. *Synonymes:* 1. *A. leucantha.* 2. *A. grandiflora.*

| acaulis | . | . | Purple | . 7, H. | A. | Aleppo | . 1680 |
|---|---|---|---|---|---|---|---|
| cannabina | . | . | Purple | . 7, H. | Her. | P. | S. Eur. | . 1597 |
| cariba | . | . | Pink | . 4, 8. | B. | W. Ind. | . 1816 |
| ficifolia | . | . | Orange | . 7, H. | B. | Levant | . 1597 |
| flexuosa | . | . | Pink | . 7, H. | Her. | P. | E. Ind. | . 1803 |
| Froloviana | . | . | . | H. | B. | Siberia | . 1827 |
| hirsuta | . | . | White | . 7, H. | A. | Britain | . |
| Ludwigii | . | . | Pink | . 7, H. | A. | Sicily | . 1791 |
| narbonensis | . | . | Pink | . 8, H. | Her. | P. | S. Eur. | . 1780 |
| nudiflora, 1 | . | . | White | . 7, H. | Her. | P. | Siberia | . 1827 |
| officinalis | . | . | Flesh | . 7, H. | Her. | P. | Britain | . |
| pallida | . | . | Pa. red. | . 7, H. | B. | Hungary | . 1805 |
| rosea | . | . | Red | . 8, H. | B. | China | . 1573 |
|   biloba, 2 | . | . | Red | . 7, H. | B. | S. Eur. | . |
| Sieberi | . | . | Purple | . 7, H. | B. | Sicily | . 1829 |
| sinensis | . | . | Red | . 7, H. | A. | China | . 1818 |
| striata | . | . | White | . 7, H. | B. | . |
| taurinensis | . | . | Red | . 8, H. | Her. | P. | Turin | . 1817 |

ALTINGIA, *Noronha.* Named in memory of Alting, a worthy German botanist. *Linn.* 22, Or. 12, Nat. Or. *Coniferæ.* These handsome-growing trees attain a great magnitude and height, especially *A. excelsa,* which averages one hundred feet in height; they prefer deep loamy soil; and young plants may with care be struck from portions of the fully-ripened wood taken off at the joints, and planted in a pot of sand, under a glass, but not plunged or exposed to the sun. Seeds, when such can be obtained, produce the best plants. *Synonyme:* 1. *Araucaria excelsa.*

| Cunninghami | . Apetal | . G. Ev. | T. | N. Holl. | . 1824 |
|---|---|---|---|---|---|
| excelsa, 1 | . | . Apetal | . G. Ev. | T. | Norfolk Is. | . 1795 |

ALTISSIMA, tallest, highest.

ALVEOLATE, having the appearance of honey.

ALVINE, belonging to the intestines.

ALYSICARPUS, *Necker.* Derived from *alysis,* a chain, and *karpus,* a fruit; in allusion to the chain-like appearance of the legume. *Linn.* 17, Or. 4, Nat. Or. *Leguminosæ.* Plants of the simplest culture. *Synonymes:* 1. *Hedysarum bupleurifolium, gramineum.* 2. *H. nummularifolium.* 3. *H. styracifolium.* 4. *H. vaginale.*

| buplerifolius, 1 | . | Purple | . 7, 8. | Her. | P. | E. Ind. | . 1793 |
|---|---|---|---|---|---|---|---|
| montifer | . | Purple | . 7, 8. | Her. | P. | E. Ind. | . 1816 |

*Nummularifolius* 2. *Styracifolius* 3. *vaginalis* 4.

ALYSSUM, *Linn.* Derived from *a,* privative, and *lyssa,* rage; from a notion among the ancients of the plant possessing the power of allaying anger. *Linn.* 15, Or. 1, Nat. Or. *Cruciferæ.* These neat and interesting species are well adapted for ornamenting rock-work, or for the front of flower-beds. They increase readily either from seeds, cuttings, or divisions, and grow well in any common soil. *Synonyme:* 1. *A. alpestre.*

| alpestre | . | Yellow | . 6, H. | Her. | P. | S. Eur. | . 1825 |
|---|---|---|---|---|---|---|---|
| argenteum | . | Yellow | . 4, H. | Her. | P. | Switzerl. | . |
| atlanticum | . | Yellow | . 4, H. | Ev. | S. | Crete | . 1817 |
| Bertoloni | . | Yellow | . 7, H. | Her. | P. | Switzerl. | . 1823 |
| cuneifolium | . | Yellow | . 7, H. | Her. | P. | Italy | . 1820 |
| diffusum | . | Yellow | . 7, H. | Her. | P. | Italy | . 1820 |
| gemonense | . | Yellow | . 4, H. | Ev. | S. | Europe | . |
| hirsutum | . | Yellow | . 6, H. | A. | Tauria | . 1817 |
| Marschallianum | . | Yellow | . 4, H. | Her. | P. | Caucasus | . 1820 |
| montanum | . | Yellow | . 6, H. | Her. | P. | Germany | . 1713 |

[ 15 ]

| murale | . | . | Yellow | . 7, H. | Her. | P. | Hungary | . 1820 |
|---|---|---|---|---|---|---|---|
| obtusifolium | . | Yellow | . 4, H. | Ev. | S. | Tauria | . 1828 |
| olympicum | . | Yellow | . 6, H. | Her. | P. | . 1790 |
| orientale | . | Yellow | . 4, H. | Ev. | S. | Crete | . |
| saxatile | . | Yellow | . 6, H. | Ev. | S. | Candia | . 1710 |
| serpyllifolium | . | Yellow | . 8, H. | Ev. | S. | S. Eur. | . 1822 |
| spatulatum | . | Yellow | . 4, H. | Ev. | S. | Siberia | . 1818 |
| tortuosum | . | Yellow | . 4, H. | Her. | P. | Hungary | . 1804 |
| umbellatum | . | Yellow | . 7, H. | A. | Tauria | . 1821 |
| vernale | . | Yellow | . 6, H. | Ev. | S. | . 1819 |
| Wulfenianum | . | Yellow | . 8, H. | Her. | P. | Carinthia | . 1819 |

*Calycinum, campestre, micropetalum, minimum, rostratum.*

ALYXIA, *R. Brown.* Taken from *alyxis,* anxiety; in allusion to the heavy aspect of the plant. *Linn.* 5, Or. 1, Nat. Or. *Apocynaceæ.* Curious species of easy culture, growing well in sandy loam mixed with a little peat, cuttings of the ripened wood planted in a pot of sand under a glass, plunged in heat, will root freely. *Synonymes:* 1. *Gynopogon Alyxia, Alyxia Forsteri.* 2. *A. Richardsonia.*

| daphnoides | . | White | . 4, G. | Ev. | S. | Norfolk Is. | . 1831 |
|---|---|---|---|---|---|---|---|
| Forsteri | . | White | . G. | Ev. | S. | Norfolk Is. | . 1831 |
| Gynopogon, 1 | . | White | . G. | Ev. | S. | Norfolk Is. | . 1831 |
| pugioniformis | . | White | . G. | Ev. | S. | Moreton B. | . 1820 |
| ruscifolia, 2 | . | White | . G. | Ev. | S. | N. Holl. | . 1820 |

ALZATEA, *Ruiz and Pavon.* Named in honour of Joseph A. de Alzaty, a Spanish naturalist. *Linn.* 5, Or. 1, Nat. Or. *Celastraceæ.* An ornamental tree, for culture, &c. see *Celastrus.*

| verticillata | . | . | . | G. Ev. | T. | Peru | . 1824 |
|---|---|---|---|---|---|---|

AMABILE, pleasing, amiable.

AMARANTHUS, *Linn.* Derived from *a,* privative, and *mairaino,* to wither; in reference to the length of time some of the flowers retain their bright colours. *Linn.* 21, Or. 5, Nat. Or. *Amarantaceæ.* Some species of this genus are pretty; the hardy kinds merely require sowing in the open border; the less hardy should be sown in a gentle-heating hotbed, and when old enough, potted off singly, observing to give plenty of pot-room, good rich soil, and water. *A. obtusifolia* is diuretic. *Synonymes:* 1. *Chenopodium caudatum.*

| atropurpureus | . | Purple | . 9, H. | A. | E. Ind. | . 1820 |
|---|---|---|---|---|---|---|
| bicolor | . | Red grn. | . 8, H. | A. | E. Ind. | . 1802 |
| caracasanus | . | Red | . 7, H. | A. | Caraccas | . 1818 |
| caudatus | . | Red | . 8, H. | A. | E. Ind. | . 1596 |
|   maximus | . | Red | . 8, H. | A. | . 1820 |
| celosioides | . | Red | . 7, H. | A. | S. Amer. | . 1818 |
| cruentus | . | Drk. red. | . 7, H. | A. | China | . 1798 |
| fasciatus | . | Red | . 7, H. | A. | E. Ind. | . 1816 |
| flavus | . | Lgt. yel. | . 8, H. | A. | India | . 1759 |
| frumentaceus | . | Red | . 8, H. | A. | E. Ind. | . 1823 |
| becticus | . | Pink | . 8, H. | A. | . 1796 |
| hypochondriacus | . | Dark red | . 7, H. | A. | Virginia | . 1684 |
| lanceæfolius | . | Red | . 7, H. | A. | E. Ind. | . 1816 |
| melancholicus | . | Purple | . 7, H. | A. | E. Ind. | . 1731 |
| oleraceus | . | Pa. red | . 7, H. | A. | E. Ind. | . 1764 |
| paniculatus | . | Green | . 8, H. | A. | N. Amer. | . 1798 |
| sanguineus | . | Red | . 8, H. | A. | Bahama | . 1775 |
| speciosus | . | Red | . 7, H. | A. | Nepal | . 1819 |
| tricolor | . | Red yel. | . 8, H. | A. | E. Ind. | . 1548 |

*Albus, angustifolius, Berchtoldii, Blitum, bullatus, campestris, cauliflorus, chlorostachys, curvifolius, deflexus, gangeticus, giganteus, gracilis, 1: græcizans, hybridus, inamænus, incomtus, interruptus, lætus, lineatus, lividus, mangostanus, pallidus, parisiensis, persicarioides, polygamus, polygonoides, polystachys, prostratus, pumilus, retroflexus, rigidus, scandens, speciosus, spicatus, spinosus, strictus, sylvestris, tenuifolius, tristis, viridis, xanthus.*

AMARYLLIS, *Linn.* The name of a nymph celebrated by the poet Virgil. *Linn.* 6, Or. 1, Nat. Or. *Amaryllidaceæ.* This interesting and beautiful genus of bulbous plants, may be successfully grown in the following manner. The bulbs of the stove species should be turned out of the pots in autumn, and laid on a shelf or other dry place till spring, when they should be potted and introduced into the hothouse, giving them, as they progress, plenty of water. *A. reticulata* and *striatifolia* will not bear turning out, as they flower better by remaining in the pot all the year. The greenhouse species must also be turned out of the pots and dried, and in the spring potted, and encouraged to flower. The soil should comprise equal portions of turfy loam and peat, with a fair quantity of sand; the pots should be drained well. They are increased by offsets

from the bulbs. *Synonymes*: 1. *A. spectabilis*. 2.
*A. vittata, Harrisoni.* 3. *A. maranensis.*

| | | | | | | | |
|---|---|---|---|---|---|---|---|
| amābilis | . . | Varieg. | 6, | G. De. | Bl. | Hybrid | 1822 |
| amœna | . . | Red | 6, | 8. De. | Bl. | Hybrid | 1821 |
| atrōrūbens | . . | Dk. red | 8, | 8. De. | Bl. | Hybrid | 1821 |
| angūstā | . . | Scarlet | 12, | 8. De. | Bl. | Hybrid | 1822 |
| aūlicā | . . | Orn. scar. | 7, | H. De. | Bl | Brazil | 1810 |
| platypetālā | . . | Orange | 8, | 8. De. | Bl. | Brazil | 1824 |
| Belladōnna | . . | Red | 7, | H. De. | Bl. | Hybrid | 1821 |
| pāllidā | . . | Flesh | 8, | H. De. | Bl. | W. Ind. | 1712 |
| campanulātā | . . | Pur. scar. | 8, | 8. De. | Bl. | Hybrid | 1822 |
| canaliculātā | . . | Scarlet | 8, | 8. De. | Bl. | Hybrid | 1822 |
| coccīneā | . . | Scarlet | 8, | 8. De. | Bl. | Hybrid | 1821 |
| compāctā | . . | Red | 8, | 8. De. | Bl. | Hybrid | 1821 |
| consanguīneā | . . | Orange | 8, | 8. De. | Bl. | Hybrid | 1821 |
| costātā | . . | Striped | 8, | 8. De. | Bl. | Hybrid | 1821 |
| crispiflōrā | . . | Scarlet | 6, | G. De. | Bl. | Brazil | 1822 |
| crocātā | . . | Vermil. | 4, | 8. De. | Bl. | Brazil | 1815 |
| regīnæ | . . | Scarlet | 8, | 8. De. | Bl. | Hybrid | 1810 |
| delēctā | . . | Dark red | 8, | G. De. | Bl. | Hybrid | 1822 |
| decōrā | . . | Striped | 7, | 8. De. | Bl. | Hybrid | 1821 |
| discōlor | . . | Striped | 8, | 8. De. | Bl. | Hybrid | 1821 |
| equēstris | . . | Scarlet | 8, | 8. De. | Bl. | W. Ind. | 1710 |
| major | . . | Scarlet | 8, | 8. De. | Bl. | W. Ind. | 1710 |
| plēnā | . . | Scarlet | 8, | 8. De. | Bl. | W. Ind. | 1809 |
| expānsā | . . | Dark red | 8, | 8. De. | Bl. | Hybrid | 1821 |
| Forbēsii | . . | Pur. wht. | 7, | G. De. | Bl. | C. G. H. | 1823 |
| purpūreā | . . | Purple | 7, | G. De. | Bl. | C. G. H. | 1823 |
| formosīssimā | . . | Dark red | 7, | G. De. | Bl. | N. Amer. | 1658 |
| fūlgidā | . . | Vermil. | 4, | 8. De. | Bl. | Brazil | 1810 |
| vittātā | . . | Violet | 8, | 8. De. | Bl. | Hybrid | 1820 |
| glaucēscens | . . | Red | 7, | G. De. | Bl. | Hybrid | 1822 |
| grandiflōrā | . . | Striped | 8, | 8. De. | Bl. | Hybrid | 1821 |
| Hoodii | . . | Scarlet | 8, | 8. De. | Bl. | Hybrid | 1822 |
| ignēscens | . . | Flame | 6, | G. De. | Bl. | Hybrid | 1822 |
| imperiālis | . . | Scarlet | 8, | G. De. | Bl. | Hybrid | 1822 |
| intermēdiā | . . | Striped | 8, | 8. De. | Bl. | Brazil | 1821 |
| Johnsōni, 1 | . . | Striped | 8, | G. De. | Bl. | Hybrid | 1810 |
| kermesīnā | . . | Carmine | 6, | 8. De. | Bl. | Brazil | 1833 |
| macrānthā | . . | Red | 8, | 8. De. | Bl. | Hybrid | 1822 |
| multistriātā | . . | Striped | 8, | 8. De. | Bl. | Hybrid | 1822 |
| nervifōliā | . . | Pur. red | 8, | 8. De. | Bl. | Hybrid | 1821 |
| pallēscens | . . | Pur. red | 7, | S. De. | Bl. | C. G. H. | |
| patentīssimā | . . | Crimson | 8, | 8. De. | Bl. | Hybrid | 1821 |
| pātens | . . | Purple | 8, | 8. De. | Bl. | Hybrid | 1821 |
| phœnīceā | . . | Purple | 6, | 8. De. | Bl. | Hybrid | 1822 |
| prīnceps | . . | Scarlet | 8, | 8. De. | Bl. | Hybrid | 1822 |
| princīpis | . . | Scarlet | 8, | 8. De. | Bl. | Hybrid | 1830 |
| psittacīnā | . . | Orn. scar. | 7, | 8. De. | Bl. | Brazil | 1816 |
| pudīcā | . . | Pink | 6, | G. De. | Bl. | C. G. H. | 1795 |
| pūlchrā | . . | Pur. wht. | 8, | G. De. | Bl. | Hybrid | 1823 |
| punctātā | . . | Pa. red | 8, | 8. De. | Bl. | Hybrid | 1822 |
| purpurāscens | . . | Purple | 6, | 8. De. | Bl. | Hybrid | 1822 |
| quadricōlor | . . | Striped | 8, | 8. De. | Bl. | Hybrid | 1822 |
| recurvātā | . . | Striped | 5, | 8. De. | Bl. | Hybrid | 1822 |
| recurviflōrā | . . | Red | 8, | 8. De. | Bl. | Hybrid | 1822 |
| regīnæ | . . | Scarlet | 6, | 8. De. | Bl. | America | 1725 |
| pulverulēntā | . . | Scarlet | 6, | 8. De. | Bl. | Hybrid | 1820 |
| vittātā | . . | Scarlet | 8, | 8. De. | Bl. | Hybrid | 1820 |
| reticulātā | . . | Scarlet | 4, | 8. De. | Bl. | Brazil | 1777 |
| retiflōrā | . . | Scarlet | 6, | 8. De. | Bl. | Hybrid | 1822 |
| retinērviā | . . | Scarlet | 6, | 8. De. | Bl. | W. Ind. | 1822 |
| ringens | . . | Red wht. | 8, | 8. De. | Bl. | Hybrid | 1821 |
| rōseā-ālbā | . . | Red wht. | 8, | 8. De. | Bl. | Hybrid | 1821 |
| rubēscens | . . | Red | 4, | 8. De. | Bl. | Hybrid | |
| rubicūndā | . . | Red | 6, | 8. De. | Bl. | Hybrid | 1823 |
| rūbro-crōceā | . . | Red saff. | 8, | 8. De. | Bl. | Hybrid | 1822 |
| rugōsā | . . | Striped | 5, | 8. De. | Bl. | Hybrid | 1821 |
| rūtilā | . . | Scarlet | 4, | 8. De. | Bl. | Brazil | 1815 |
| sexmaculātā | . . | Copper | 8, | 8. De. | Bl. | Hybrid | 1822 |
| spathāceā | . . | Red | 8, | 8. De. | Bl. | Hybrid | 1821 |
| splēndens | . . | Scarlet | 8, | 8. De. | Bl. | Hybrid | 1821 |
| stenānthā | . . | Red | 4, | 8. De. | Bl. | Hybrid | 1821 |
| striatiflōrā | . . | Striped | 7, | 8. De. | Bl. | Hybrid | 1821 |
| striatifōliā | . . | Purple | 8, | 8. De. | Bl. | Brazil | 1815 |
| stylōsā, 3 | . . | Red | 4, | 8. De. | Bl. | Maranhao | 1823 |
| subbarbātā | . . | Scarlet | 8, | 8. De. | Bl. | Brazil | 1823 |
| sulcātā | . . | Striped | 5, | 8. De. | Bl. | Hybrid | 1821 |
| supērbā | . . | Striped | 8, | 8. De. | Bl. | Hybrid | 1821 |
| tortuliflōrā | . . | Scarlet | 6, | 8. De. | Bl. | Hybrid | 1822 |
| tortuōsā | . . | Orn. scar. | 8, | 8. De. | Bl. | Hybrid | 1822 |
| undulāmflōrā | . . | Pur. wht. | 6, | 8. De. | Bl. | Hybrid | 1822 |
| variābilis | . . | Red wht. | 6, | 8. De. | Bl. | C. G. H. | 1821 |
| variegātā | . . | Striped | 6, | 8. De. | Bl. | Hybrid | 1821 |
| versicōlor | . . | Varieg. | 9, | 8. De. | Bl. | Hybrid | 1821 |
| vittātā | . . | Striped | 4, | G. De. | Bl. | C. G. H. | 1769 |
| major | . . | Striped | 6, | G. De. | Bl. | Hybrid | 1774 |
| vittīferā | . . | Striped | 4, | 8. De. | Bl. | Hybrid | 1823 |

*Accēdens, advēnā, A. cerīnā, Andersōnii, Annesleyānā,
attenuātā, blāndā, bracteātā, breviflōrā, brevifōliā,
calyptrātā, carnēscens, Colvilli, consobrīnā, cūpreā,
dioīcā, flāmmeā, fulvā, imbūtā, lateritiā, lineātā 2,
miniātā, mutābilis, nervōsā, obscūrā, pāllidā, palli-
flōrā, pulverulātā, P. longipedunculātā, pumīlis,
solandræflōrā, S. purpurāscens, rūbro-strīātā,
tutāricā, trĭcōlor, Vallēti, ventōsā, Wellsiānā.*
AMASŌNIĀ, *Linn.* In memory of Thomas Amason,

an American traveller. *Linn.* 14, Or. 2, Nat. Or.
*Verbenaceæ*. These are interesting plants, and may
be successfully grown in sandy loam, and increased
from suckers. *Synonyme*: 1. *Talygala campestris*.

| | | | | | | | |
|---|---|---|---|---|---|---|---|
| erēctā, 1 | . . | Yellow | 9, | 8. Her. | P. | Maranh. | 1823 |
| punīceā | . . | Yellow | 9, | 8. Her. | P. | Trinidad | 1825 |

AMBIGUOUS, doubtful or uncertain.

AMBRŌSIĀ, *Linnæus.* A poetical name, expressive
of the food of the heathen gods. *Linn.* 21, Or. 5,
Nat. Or. *Compositæ*. Uninteresting species, of the
simplest culture. *Synonyme*: 1. *A. absinthifolia—
artemisiæfōliā, cumanēnsis, elātior, heterophŷllā* 1,
*integrifōliā, maritimā, paniculātā, trifīdā.*

AMELĀNCHIĒR, *Medicus.* According to Clusius, this
is the only Savoy name for the Medlar. *Linn.* 12,
Or. 2, Nat. Or. *Pomaceæ*. These ornamental free-
flowering bushes, make a gay display when standing in the distant part of pleasure-ground. For
culture, &c., see *Cotoneaster*. *Synonymes* : 1.
*Mespilus canadensis, Pyrus sanguinea.* 2. *Mespilus
Amelanchier.*

| | | | | | | | |
|---|---|---|---|---|---|---|---|
| Botryāpiūm | . . | White | 5, | H. De. | S. | N. Amer. | 1746 |
| ovālis | . . | White | 5, | H. De. | S. | N. Amer. | 1800 |
| sanguīneā, 1 | . . | White | 5, | H. De. | S. | N. Amer. | 1800 |
| vulgāris, 2 | . . | White | 5, | H. De. | S. | S. Eur. | 1596 |

AMELLŪS, *Willdenow.* Employed by Virgil, for a fine
flower found on the banks of the river Mella.
*Linn.* 19, Or. 2, Nat. Or. *Compositæ*. Interesting
species, succeeding well in a loamy soil, and cuttings
planted under a glass root freely. *Synonymes*: 1.
*Sideranthus spinulosus.* 2. *S. villosus.*

| | | | | | | | |
|---|---|---|---|---|---|---|---|
| Lychnītis | . . | Violet | 7, | G. Ev. | T. | C. G. H. | 1768 |
| spinulōsus, 1 | . . | Yellow | 8, | H. Her. | P. | Missouri | 1811 |
| villōsus, 2 | . . | Yellow | 8, | H. Her. | P. | Missouri | 1811 |

AMENT, } A catkin, mode of inflorescence; as the
AMENTUM, } Hazel and Willow.

AMERICAN ALOE, see *Agave Americana.*

AMERICAN COWSLIP, see *Dodecatheon.*

AMERIMNON, *Patrick Browne.* A Greek name for the
house-leek ; derived from *a*, privative, and *merimna*,
care ; in allusion to the little attention the plant
requires. *Linn.* 16, Or. 6, Nat. Or. *Leguminosæ*.
Ornamental shrubs ; for culture, &c., see *Pterocarpus.*

| | | | | | | | |
|---|---|---|---|---|---|---|---|
| Brownēi | . . | White | 8, | S. Ev. | T. | W. Ind. | 1793 |
| strigulōsum | . . | White | 8, | S. Ev. | S. | Trinidad | 1817 |

AMETHŸSTEĀ, *Willdenow.* The name is given in
allusion to the colour of the flowers, from *amethy-
stos*, the amethyst. *Linn.* 2, Or. 1, Nat. Or. *Labiatæ*.
A pretty blue-flowered annual ; it grows in peaty
soil, and matures an abundance of seed.

| | | | | | | | |
|---|---|---|---|---|---|---|---|
| cærūleā | . . | Blue | 7, | H. | A. | Siberia | 1759 |

AMETHŸSTINOUS, violet-coloured.

AMHERSTIĀ, *Wallich.* In honour of the Rt. Hon.
Countess Amherst and her daughter Lady Sarah
Amherst ; the zealous friends and promoters of
every branch of Natural History, but especially
Botany. *Linn.* 17, Or. 4, Nat. Or. *Leguminosæ*.
This truly noble object first became known to Dr.
Wallich, through the medium of a Mr. Crawford,
in August 1826, who originally discovered it in
Martaban, the E. Indies ; the former gentleman
afterwards found it, as he himself states, "growing
near a decayed Kioum, (a sort of monastery,) together with numerous individuals of *Jonesia Asoca*
and *Mesua ferrea* ; it was profusely ornamented
with pendulous racemes of large vermilion-coloured
blossoms, unequalled in the flora of the E. Indies,
and perhaps not surpassed in magnificence and
elegance in any part of the world."—*Wallich's
Plantæ Asiaticæ Rariores.* The ground, he states,
was strewed even at a distance with its flowers,
which are daily offered to the images in the ad-
joining caves. He transported it to the Botanic Garden, Calcutta, where it was seen by Mr. J. Gibson,
who very fortunately succeeded in bringing a plant
alive to the collection at Chatsworth. It appears
to delight in a rich strong loam, and may be propagated by cuttings of the half-ripened wood,
planted in sand, under a glass, in heat ; or by
ringing the stems of the old plant.

| | | | | | | | |
|---|---|---|---|---|---|---|---|
| nobīlis | . . | Rich ver. | 8. Ev. | T. | E. Ind. | 1837 |

AMICIĀ, *Humboldt and Bonpland.* In memory of J.
B. Amici, a noted physician. *Linn.* 16, Or. 6, Nat.

Or. *Leguminosæ*. This interesting evergreen climber delights in open loamy soil, and increases readily from cuttings.

| | | | | | |
|---|---|---|---|---|---|
| sigómèrìs | . . . | Yellow | . 6, S. Ev. Cl. Mexico | . 1826 |

**AMIROLÀ**, *Persoon*. Derivation unknown. *Linn*. 21, Or. 9. Nat. Or. *Sapindaceæ*. An ornamental tree, thriving in peat and loam, and increased from cuttings in sand. Synonyme: 1. *Lagunea nitida*.

| | | | | | |
|---|---|---|---|---|---|
| nítidà, 1 | | | S. Ev. T. Peru | . 1824 |

**AMMANNÌA**, *Linn*. In honour of John Ammann, a physician and botanist at Petersburgh. *Linn*. 4, Or. 1, Nat. Or. *Lythraceæ*. Species of no beauty; for culture, &c., see *Balsamina*.

| | | | | | |
|---|---|---|---|---|---|
| verticillatà | . . | White | . 8, H. | A. Guinea . | . 1819 |

*Ægyptíacà, auriculàtà, baccíferà, cúspicà, débilìs, diffúsà, húmilìs, latifòlìà, multiflòrà, octàndrà, pentàndrà, racemòsà, ramòsìòr, rotundifòlià, rùbrà, sanguinolèntà, víridìs, Wormskiòldìì.*

**AMMI**, *Linn*. The plant delights to grow in sandy places, hence the name from *ammos*, sand. *Linn*. 5, Or. 2, Nat. Or. *Umbelliferæ*. Weeds of the simplest culture. Synonyme: 1. *Bunium acaule*.

*Acaùlè 1, anethifòlìùm, Boehèri, daucifòlìùm, ferulæfòlìùm, glaucifòlìùm, màjùs, Visnàgà.*

**AMMÒNÌÙM**, *R. Brown*. Derived from *ammos*, sand, and *bio*, to live; in reference to the situation where it grows. *Linn*. 19. Or 1, Nat. Or. *Compositæ*. Pretty species of the easiest culture.

| | | | | | |
|---|---|---|---|---|---|
| alàtùm | . . . | White | . 6, F. Her. | P. N. Holl. | 1822 |
| plantagíneùm | . | White | . 8, G. Her. | P. N. Holl. | . 1827 |

**AMMYRSÌNÈ**, *Pursh*. Derived from *ammos*, sand, and *myrsine*, a myrtle. *Linn*. 10, Or. 1, Nat. Or. *Ericaceæ*. These interesting species should be grown in peat, and sheltered in winter in a frame or pit. They increase from layers. Synonyme: 1. *Ledum buxifolium, Leiophyllum thymifolium*.

| | | | | | |
|---|---|---|---|---|---|
| buxifòlìà, 1 | . | White | . 5, H. Ev. S. N. Amer. | . 1736 |
| prostràtà | . | . White | . 6, H. Ev. S. N. Amer. | |

**AMÒMÙM**, *Linn*. Derived from *a*, privative, and *momos*, impurity; in allusion to the counter-poison qualities some species are supposed to possess. *Linn*. 1, Or. 1, Nat. Or. *Scitamineæ*. Ornamental stove-plants, requiring similar treatment to *Alpinia*. In Bengal, the fruit of *A. aromaticum* is used, and the greater sort of *Cardamoms* is yielded by *A. Grana-Paradisi*.

| | | | | | |
|---|---|---|---|---|---|
| aculeàtùm | . . | Orange | . 5, S. Her. | P. E. Ind. | . 1819 |
| Afzàlii | . . | Pink | . 5, S. Her. | P. S. Leone | . 1795 |
| angustifòlìùm | . | Red | . 5, S. Her. | P. Madagas. | |
| aromàtìcùm | . | Pur. yel. | . 6, S. Her. | P. E. Ind. | . 1823 |
| Cardamòmùm | . | Pa. bru. | . 6, S. Her. | P. E. Ind. | . 1820 |
| dealbàtùm | . | White | . 4, S. Her. | P. Bengal | . 1819 |
| Grana-Paradìsi | . | Red | . 3, S. Her. | P. Madagas. | |
| grandiflòrùm | . | White | . 7, S. Her. | P. S. Leone | . 1795 |
| latifòlìùm | . | Pur. yel. | . 6, S. Her. | P. S. Leone | . 1824 |
| máxìmùm | . | White | . 6, S. Her. | P. E. Ind. | |
| seríceùm | . | White | . 7, S. Her. | P. E. Ind. | . 1819 |
| subulàtùm | . | Yellow | . 4, S. Her. | P. Bengal | . 1822 |
| sylvéstrè | . | White | . 4, S. Her. | P. W. Ind. | . 1819 |

**AMÒRPHÀ**, *Linn*. The name is derived from *a*, privative, and *morpha*, form; alluding to the deformity of the corolla. *Linn*. 16, Or. 6, Nat. Or. *Leguminosæ*. Elegant free-flowering shrubs, thriving well in common soil, and increased by layers, or cuttings taken off at a joint, and planted early in autumn, in a sheltered situation. The more tender species require the protection of a mat in severe weather. Synonymes: 1. *A. nana*. 2. *A. pubescens*.

| | | | | | |
|---|---|---|---|---|---|
| canéscèns | . | Blue | . 7, F. De. | S. Missouri | . 1812 |
| eròceò-lanàtà | . | Purple | . 7, H. De. | S. N. Amer. | . 1820 |
| frágrans, 1 | . | Purple | . 7, H. De. | S. N. Amer. | . 1800 |
| fruticòsà | . | Purple | . 7, H. De. | S. Carolina | . 1724 |
| emarginàtà | . | Purple | . 7, H. De. | S. Carolina | . 1724 |
| microphyllà | . | Purple | . 6, H. De. | S. Carolina | |
| glàbrà | . | Purple | . 7, F. Her. | P. N. Amer. | . 1818 |
| herbàceà, 2 | . | Blue | . 7, F. Her. | P. Carolina | . 1803 |
| Lewìsii | . | Purple | . 7, F. De. | S. N. Amer. | . 1820 |
| microphyllà | . | Purple | . 8, F. De. | S. Missouri | . 1811 |
| nànà | . | Blue | . 8, F. De. | S. Missouri | . 1811 |

**AMPELÒPSÌS**, *Michaux*. These plants resemble the vine; hence the name from *ampelos*, a vine, and *opsis*, resemblance. *Linn*. 5, Or. 1, Nat. Or. *Vitaceæ*. This genus of interesting plants comprehends the Virginian creeper, so well known for its adaptation to cover walls, bowers, and trellis-work. They

grow in common soil, and increase from layers or cuttings. Synonymes: 1. *Cissus ampelopsis*. 2. *C. quinquefolius*.

| | | | | | |
|---|---|---|---|---|---|
| bipinnàtà | . . | Pur. grn. | . 8, H. De. S. N. Amer. | . 1700 |
| cordàtà, 1 | . | Pur. grn. | . 5, H. De. Cl. N. Amer. | . 1803 |
| hederàceà, 2 | . | Pur. grn. | . 7, H. De. Cl. N. Amer. | . 1729 |
| hirsùtà | . | Pur. grn. | . 5, H. De. Cl. N. Amer. | . 1806 |

**AMPELYGÒNÙM**, *Lindley*. The name is in allusion to the grape-like fruit. *Linn*. 8, Or. 8, Nat. Or. *Polygalaceæ*. This species is very interesting, and will thrive in sandy loam and a little peat, and will readily increase from seeds. This is one of the species from which indigo of fine quality is obtained.

| | | | | | |
|---|---|---|---|---|---|
| chinénsè | . . | Yelsh. wht. | 7, G. Her. P. E. Ind. | . 1837 |

**AMPHERÈPHÌS**, *Kunth*. Derived from *ampherephis*, well covered; in allusion to the double involucrum. *Linn*. 19, Or 1, Nat. Or. *Compositæ*. Pretty annuals, of easy culture.

| | | | | | |
|---|---|---|---|---|---|
| aristàtà | . | Purple | . 7, H. | A. Caracas | . 1824 |
| intermèdìà | . | Purple | . 8, H. | A. Brazil | . 1821 |
| mútìcà | . | Purple | . 7, H. | A. S. Amer. | . 1808 |

**AMPHIBIOUS**, growing either in or out of the water.

**AMPHICÀRPÀ**, *Elliot*. The name is derived from *amphi*, on both sides, and *karpus*, fruit; in allusion to the fact of the plants bearing pods both on the roots and on the stems. *Linn*. 17, Or. 4, Nat. Or. *Leguminosæ*. Ornamental deciduous twiners; for culture, &c., see *Clitoria*. Synonymes: 1. *G. comosa*. 2. *G. monoica*. 3. *G. filosa, sarmentosa*.

| | | | | | |
|---|---|---|---|---|---|
| monòìcà, 2 | . | Apetal | . 9, H. De. Tw. N. Amer. | . 1781 |
| sarmentòsà, 3 | . | Apetal | . 9, H. De. Tw. N. Amer. | . 1820 |

*Comòsà, 1*

**AMPHICHORDÀ**, *Fries*. Compounded from *amphis*, signifying on either or each side, and *chorda*, a chord. *Linn*. 24, Or. 9, Nat. Or. *Fungi*. A dusty or porous substance, found on rotten trunks under ground in the autumn—*farinàcèà*.

**AMPHICÒMÈ**, *Royle*. From *amphi*, around, and *kome*, hair; in allusion to the structure of the seeds. *Linn*. 14, Or. 2, Nat. Or. *Bignoniaceæ*. Dr. Lindley describes this as a very elegant and rather slender perennial, probably hardy enough to stand out if planted in any dry situation or on rock-work, and protected during winter from the wet and most severe frosts. It thrives best in loamy soil mixed with a little sandy peat. and may be increased by seeds or cuttings of the young shoots.

| | | | | | |
|---|---|---|---|---|---|
| argùtà | . . | Lilac | . 8, H. Ev. P. Himalaya Mts. | |

**AMPHILÒBÌÙM**, *Kunth*. Derived from *amphi*, round, and *lobos*, a pod; in allusion to the round fruit. *Linn*. 14, Or. 2, Nat. Or. *Bignoniaceæ*. A pretty evergreen climber; for culture, &c., see *Bignonia*. Synonyme: 1. *Bignonia paniculata*.

| | | | | | |
|---|---|---|---|---|---|
| paniculàtùm, 1 | . | Purple | . 8, Ev. Cl. W. Ind. | . 1733 |

**AMPHICARPUS**, round-fruited.

**AMPHIPÒGÒN**, *R. Brown*. Compounded from *amphi*, round, and *pogon*, a beard. *Linn*. 3, Or. 2, Nat. Or. *Gramineæ*. A curious species of grass of the easiest culture.

| | | | | | |
|---|---|---|---|---|---|
| strìctùm | . . | Apetal | . 6, Grass. N. Holl. | . 1823 |

**AMPHISPÒRÌÙM**, *Link*. Compounded from *amphi*, on either or each side, and *sporia*, a sporule. *Linn*. 24, Or. 9, Nat. Or. *Fungi*. Yellow particles observable on hyacinths grown in glasses.—*Versicòlòr*.

**AMPLEXICAULIS**, stem-clasping.

**AMSÒNÌÀ**, *Walter*. In memory of Charles Amson, a traveller in America. *Linn*. 5, Or. 1, Nat. Or. *Apocynaceæ*. Pretty species, succeeding well in common soil, and increased freely from cuttings under a glass, or by dividing at the roots. Synonyme: 1. *Tabernæmontana Amsonia*.

| | | | | | |
|---|---|---|---|---|---|
| angustifòlìà | . | Blue | . 6, H. Her. P. N. Amer. | . 1774 |
| latifòlìà, 1 | . | Blue | . 6, H. Her. P. N. Amer. | . 1759 |
| salicifòlìà | . | Blue | . 6, H. Her. P. N. Amer. | . 1812 |

**AMYGDÀLÙS**, *Linn*. Derived from *amysso*, to lacerate; in allusion to the fissured shell. *Linn*. 12, Or. 1, Nat. Or. *Rosaceæ*. The tall and coarse portion of these ornamental early-flowering plants may be advantageously disposed of in large plantations, and the dwarf kinds in small shrubberies at the front of the large ones. The common way of increasing them is by budding on the plum stock, or on the bitter almond. Rich mould is a proper medium for them. They are most valued for producing their showy pink blossoms early in the season, sooner than almost any other shrubs. *Synonyme:* 1. *Prunus sinensis.*

| | | | | | | | |
|---|---|---|---|---|---|---|---|
| communis . . | Red | . . | 4. H. De. T. | Barbary | 1548 |
| amara | Red | . . | 4. H. De. T. | Barbary | 1548 |
| fragi is . | Red | . . | 4. H. De. T. | Barbary | |
| macrocarpa | Red | . . | 4. H. De. T. | Barbary | |
| persicoides | Red | . . | 4. H. De. T. | Barbary | |
| incana | Red | . . | 4. H. De. S. | Caucasus | |
| nana | Red | . . | 4. H. De. S. | Russia | 1683 |
| campestris | Red | . . | 4. H. De. S. | Podolia | 1818 |
| georgica | Red | . . | 4. H. De. S. | Georgia | 1818 |
| orientalis | Red | . . | 4. H. De. S. | Levant | 1756 |
| pumila, 1 | Red | . . | 4. H. De. S. | China | 1683 |
| sibirica | Red | . . | 4. H. De. S. | Siberia | 1890 |

**AMYLACEOUS,** possessing the properties of starch.
**AMYRIS,** *Linn.* From *a*, intensive, and *myron*, balm, or *myrrha*, myrrh; in allusion to the strong perfume of the species *Linn.* 8, Or. 1, Nat. Or. *Amyridaceæ.* Ornamental trees, succeeding well in an equal mixture of loam and peat, and are propagated from cuttings in sand under a glass. *A. toxifera* is poisonous. *Synonymes:* 1. *A. elemifera.* 2. *A. balsamifera.*

| | | | | | | |
|---|---|---|---|---|---|---|
| acuminata | White | . . | 8. S. Ev. T. | E. Ind. | 1823 |
| brasiliensis | White | . 8. S. Ev. T. | Brazil | 1823 |
| heptaphylla | White | . . | 8. S. Ev. T. | E. Ind. | 1823 |
| Lunani | White | . 7. S. Ev. T. | Jamaica | 1820 |
| maritima | White | . 8. S. Ev. T. | S. Amer. | 1810 |
| nana | White | . . | 8. S. Ev. T. | E. Ind. | 1822 |
| Plumieri, 1 | White | . . | 8. S. Ev. T. | W. Ind. | 1820 |
| sylvatica | White | . 7. S. Ev. T. | Carthage | 1793 |
| Tecomaca | White | . . | 8. S. Ev. T. | Mexico | 1827 |
| toxifera, 2 | White | . . | 8. S. Ev. T. | W. Ind. | 1818 |

**ANABASIS,** *Linn.* Equisitum, was so named by the Greeks. *Linn.* 5, Or. 2, Nat. Or. *Chenopodiaceæ.* Curious species of the simplest culture. *Synonyme:* 1. *Salsola articulata.*

| | | | | | | |
|---|---|---|---|---|---|---|
| aphylla, 1 | Green | . 7. S. Ev. S. | A. Minor | 1817 |
| florida | Green | . 7. H. | A. Iberia | 1817 |
| oppositiflora | Grn. yel. | . 7. H. | A. Russia | 1825 |
| tamariscifolia | Green | . 7. G. Ev. S. | Spain | 1752 |

**ANACAMPSEROS,** *Ehrhart.* Compounded from *anacampto*, to induce to return, and *eros*, love; the name of a plant to which the ancients attributed the quality of restoring the passion *love.* *Linn.* 11, Or. 1, Nat. Or. *Portulacaceæ.* A genus of curious succulent plants; for culture, &c. see *Aloe.* *Synonymes:* 1. *Rulingia polyphylla.* 2. *Talinum anacampseros, Rulingia Anacampseros.* 3. *R. varians.*

| | | | | | | |
|---|---|---|---|---|---|---|
| angustifolia | Pink | . 7. S. Ev. S. | C. G. H. | 1820 |
| arachnoides | Pink | . 8. G. Ev. S. | C. G. H. | 1790 |
| filamentosa | Pink | . 9. G. Ev. S. | C. G. H. | 1795 |
| intermedia | Pink | . 7. G. Ev. S. | C. G. H. | 1824 |
| lanceolata | Pink | . 9. G. Ev. S. | C. G. H. | 1796 |
| polyphylla, 1 | Pink | . 8. G. Ev. S. | C. G. H. | 1818 |
| rotundifolia, 2 | Pink | . 8. G. Ev. S. | C. G. H. | 1732 |
| rubens | Red | . 8. S. Ev. S. | C. G. H. | 1796 |
| rufescens | Pink | . 7. G. Ev. S. | C. G. H. | 1818 |
| varians, 3 | Pink | . 8. G. Ev. S. | C. G. H. | 1818 |

**ANACAMPTIS,** *Richard.* Named from *anacampto*, to turn back; in allusion to the reflexed state of the pollen masses. *Linn.* 20, Or. 1, Nat. Or. *Orchidaceæ* An interesting native species, very similar to our orchis; cultivation simple. *Synonyme:* 1. *Orchis pyramidalis.*

| | | | | | | |
|---|---|---|---|---|---|---|
| pyramidalis | . Red | . . | 7. H. Ter. | Britain | . . |

**ANACANTHOUS,** spineless.
**ANACARDIUM,** *Roxburgh.* The name refers to the form of the nut; hence the derivation from *ana*, like, and *kardia*, heart. *Linn.* 23, Or. 2, Nat. Or. *Anacardiaceæ.* These ornamental trees thrive in light loamy soil, and cuttings with their leaves on, taken from the ripe wood, will strike in sand, in heat, under a glass. *A. occidentale* is thus spoken of by Mr. Sander:—" This elegant tree, bearing panicled corymbs of sweet smelling flowers, succeeded by an edible fruit of the pomme kind of a yellow or red colour. This fruit or apple has a sub-acid flavour, with some degree of astringency."

| | | | | | | |
|---|---|---|---|---|---|---|
| occidentale | . Grn. red. | . . | 8. Ev. T. | W. Ind. | . 1699 |
| indicum | . Grn. red. | . . | 8. Ev. T. | E. Ind. | . . 1699 |

**ANACYCLUS,** *Linn.* Derived from *a*, privative, and *anthos*, a flower, and *kyklos*, a circle; in allusion to the rows of ovaries placed round the disk. *Linn.* 19, Or. 2, Nat. Or. *Compositæ.* Hardy annuals,

requiring only to be sown in the open ground. *Synonymes:* 1. *Santolina anthemoides.* 2. *Anthemis valentina.*

| | | | | | | |
|---|---|---|---|---|---|---|
| aureus | . . | . Yellow | . 8, H. | A. Levant | . 1570 |
| clavatus | . . | . White | . 8, H. | A. Barbary | . 1810 |
| radiatus, 2 | . | . Yellow | . 8, H. | A. S. Eur. | . 1506 |

*Anthemoides* 1, *creticus, divaricatus, orientalis, valentinus.*

**ANADENIA,** *R. Brown.* Named from *a*, privative, and *aden*, a gland; the nectariferous gland is wanting. *Linn.* 4, Or. 1, Nat. Or. *Proteaceæ.* A handsome species, cultivated in peat and loam, and multiplied by cuttings in sand under a glass.

| | | | | | | |
|---|---|---|---|---|---|---|
| pulchella | . . | . Yellow | . G. Ev. S. | N. Holl. | . 1824 |

**ANAGALLIS,** *Tournefort.* The power of removing despondency is attributed to this genus, hence the name from *anagelao*, to laugh. *Linn.* 5, Or. 1, Nat. Or. *Primulaceæ.* Very pretty interesting species, of easy culture. Sow the hardy annuals in the open ground, and the biennials in pots in the greenhouse or a frame, and plant them out when strong enough. They increase from cuttings planted in any common soil under a glass. Orfila destroyed a dog by making him swallow three drachms of the extract of *A. arvensis.* *Synonymes:* 1. *A. phænicea.* 2. *A. collina.*

| | | | | | | |
|---|---|---|---|---|---|---|
| carnea | . . | . Flesh | . 8, H. | A. Switzerl. | 1819 |
| fruticosa, 2 | . | . Vermilion | . 8, G. | B. Morocco | 1803 |
| indica | . . | . Blue | . 7, H. | A. Nepal. | 1824 |
| latifolia | . . | . Purple | . 8, G. | B. Spain | 1759 |
| linifolia | . . | . Blue | . 8, G. | B. Portugal | 1796 |
| Marryatta | . | . Copper | . 7, F. Ev. | Tr. Hybrid | 1838 |
| Monelli | . . | . Blue | . 7, G. Her. | P. Italy | 1648 |
| lilacina | . . | . Lilac | . 8, G. Her. | P. | 1835 |
| W illmoreana | . | . Pur. blue | . 9, G. Her. | P. Madeira | 1834 |
| tenell. | . . | . Pink | . 7, H. De. | Cr. Britain | |
| Webbiana | . | . Blue | . 7, F. Ev. | Tr. Portugal | 1828 |
| Wellsiana | . | . Copper | . 8, F. Ev. | Tr. Eng. hyb. | 1830 |

*Arvensis,* 1; *cærulea.*

**ANAGYRIS,** *Tournefort.* Named in allusion to the curved pod; from *ana*, backward, and *gyros*, a circle. *Linn.* 10, Or. 1, Nat. Or. *Leguminosæ.* Ornamental trees, growing in peat and loam, or any light rich soil, and multiplied from cuttings or seeds. The seeds of *A. fœtida*, if eaten in any quantity, produce headach.

| | | | | | | |
|---|---|---|---|---|---|---|
| fœtida | . . | . Yellow | . 4, F. Ev. S. | Spain | . 1570 |
| glauca | . . | . Yellow | . 4, F. Ev. S. | S. Eur. | . 1800 |
| latifolia | . . | . Yellow | . 4, G. Ev. S. | Teneriffe | . 1815 |

**ANANASSA,** *Thunberg.* From *naeas*, the Guiana name. *Linn.* 6, Or. 1, Nat. Or. *Bromeliaceæ.* The plants that yield this very superior fruit, so much esteemed for its sweet aromatic flavour, were first cultivated in this country at Sir Matthew Dickers, at Richmond, where fruit was first produced in 1715. There are now as many as thirty distinct kinds described in our gardens, but of these only a few merit cultivation; these are the common broad-leaved Queen, Ripley Queen, and Lemon Queen, Black Jamaica, New and Old Providence, Antigua, Montserrat, and two or three others of very good quality. There are many ways of cultivating these plants; our experience dictates the following Young plants should be potted in a compost of open sandy loam, mixed with a small proportion of either deer, sheep, or horse-droppings; the pots should be well drained and plunged into a tan-bed at about 75 degrees of heat; as the plants increase give them additional pot-room, using the same soil as before. In fine weather admit air the first thing in the morning—7 o'clock, and close the house early in the afternoon—3 o'clock; when the paths should be watered and the plants syringed over the tops, which will cause the atmosphere to be very moist; in this state the plants will thrive surprisingly. Fruiting plants must not be grown in an over-moist atmosphere, but should have when such can be given a freer circulation of air, or the fruit will be of an inferior flavour. The temperature in winter should be 70 or 75 degrees, in summer 80 or 85 degrees, and when closed in the afternoon 100 or 110 degrees. The best plants are obtained from suckers, but new or very rare sorts are often obtained from the crown of the fruit. After the fruit is cut, the stools should be plunged in a strong bottom-heat, and strong suckers equal to year-old plants may be soon taken off. *Synonymes:* 1. *Bromelia lucida.* 2. *B. ananas*

| | | | | | |
|---|---|---|---|---|---|
| bracteatā | . . | Crimson | . 4, S. Her. P. Brazil | . . | 1820 |
| debilis, 1 | . . | Crimson | . 4, S. Her. P. | | |
| lucida, 1 | . . | Pink | . 8. Her. P. S. Amer. | . | |
| nitiva, 2 | . . | Purple | . 8. Her. P. S. Amer. | . | 1690 |

**ANANTHERIX**, *Nuttall*. Derived from *a*, without, and *antherix*, an awn, the appendage being wanting. *Linn*. 9, Or. 2, Nat. Or. *Asclepiadaceæ*. An interesting species; for culture, &c., see *Asclepias*. Synonyme: 1. *Asclepias viridis*.

| | | | | | |
|---|---|---|---|---|---|
| viridis, 1 | . . | Grn. yel. | . 8. H. Her. P. N. Amer. | . | 1818 |

**ANARRHINUM**, *Desfont*. The name is gathered from *a*, privative, and *rhin*, nose; the plants being allied to *Antirrhinum*, but the flowers quite different. *Linn*. 14, Or. 2, Nat. Or. *Scrophulariaceæ*. These pretty biennials succeed well if sown in the open borders.

| | | | | | |
|---|---|---|---|---|---|
| bellidifolium | . | Blue | . 7, H. | B. France | . 1629 |
| fruticosum | . | White | . 8. H. | B. S. Eur. | . . 1826 |
| pubescens | . | White | . 8, H. | B. S. Eur. | . . 1818 |

**ANASTATICA**, *Linn*. This plant, however dry, will recover its original form, if immersed in water; hence the name from *anastasis*, resurrection. *Linn*. 15, Or. 1, Nat. Or. *Cruciferæ*. Rose of Jericho. A curious dwarf species, of easy culture.

| | | | | | |
|---|---|---|---|---|---|
| hierochuntina | . | White | . 7, F. | A. Levant | . . 1597 |

**ANATHERUM**, *Palisot de Beauvois*. Named in allusion to the awnless valves of the calyx, from *a*, privative, and *ather*, awn. *Linn*. 23, Or. 1, Nat. Or. *Gramineæ*. Uninteresting species, of easy culture. Synonymes: 1. *Andropogon muricatus, squarrosus*. 2. *A. muticum*—*Muricatum* 1, *muticum* 2, *virginicum*.

**ANASTOMOSING**, uniting of vessels, veins, or nerves.

**ANATOMICUM**, dissected, laciniated.

**ANCEPS**, two-edged.

**ANCHIETEA**, *Hill*. In memory of P. Anchietea, a Brazilian writer on plants. *Linn*. 5, Or. 1, Nat. Or. *Violaceæ*. An ornamental species; for culture, &c. see *Calyptrion*. Synonyme: 1. *Calyptrion pyrifolium*.

| | | | | | |
|---|---|---|---|---|---|
| pyrifolia, 1 | . . | White | . 7, S. Ev. Cl. Brazil | . . | 1822 |

**ANCHOVY-PEAR**, see *Grias cauliflora*.

**ANCHUSA**, *Linn*. A. *tinctoria* was anciently used for staining the skin; hence the name, from *agchoresa*, paint for the skin. *Linn*. 5, Or. 1, Nat. Or. *Boragineæ*. The hardy annual and biennial species of this ornamental genus succeed well sown in the open borders. A. *capensis* should be raised in a frame, and treated as a greenhouse plant. The roots of *A. tinctoria* and *virginica* furnish a reddish brown substance used by dyers. Synonymes: 1. *Myosotis obtusa*. 2. *A. angustifolia*. 3. *Myosotis macrophylla*. 4. *A. zeylanica*.

| | | | | | |
|---|---|---|---|---|---|
| Azardhii | . . | Blue | . 2, H. Her. P. Siberia | . | 1820 |
| amœna | . . | Blue | . 6, H. | A. S. Eur. | . 1817 |
| angustifolia | . . | Purple | . 5, H. Her. P. S. Eur. | . | 1640 |
| ægyptiaca | . . | Blue | . 5, H. | B. Egypt | . 1817 |
| Barrelieri, 1 | . . | Blue | . 7, H. Her. P. S. Eur. | . | 1820 |
| capensis | . . | Blue | . 6, G. | B. C. G. H. | . 1800 |
| Gmelini | . . | Blue | . 8, H. | B. Podolia | . 1817 |
| lanata | . . | Blue | . 7, H. Her. P. Egypt | . | 1817 |
| hybrida | . . | Wht. blue | . 7, H. | A. Italy | . 1820 |
| incarnata | . . | Flesh | . 7, H. Her. P. S. Eur. | . | 1816 |
| latifolia | . . | Blue | . 5, H. | B. | . 1826 |
| leptophylla, 2 | . . | Purple | . 8, H. Her. P. Europe | . | 1640 |
| longifolia | . . | Blue | . 7, H. Her. P. Italy | . | 1819 |
| maculata | . . | Blue | . 5, H. Her. P. Russia | . | 1824 |
| Milleri | . . | Blue | . 6, H. | A. | . 1824 |
| myosotidiflora, 3 | . | Pink | . 8, H. Her. P. Levant | . | 1713 |
| officinalis | . . | Blue | . 8, H. Her. P. Tauria | . | 1825 |
| ochroleuca | . . | Purple | . 7, H. Her. P. Britain | . | |
| italica | . . | Pa. yel. | . 8, H. Her. P. Caucasus | . | 1810 |
| paniculata | . . | Red | . 5, H. Her. P. S. Eur. | . | 1597 |
| procera | . . | Blue | . 5, H. Her. P. Madeira | . | 1777 |
| rupestris | . . | Blue | . 7, H. Her. P. Galicia | . | 1824 |
| sericea | . . | Pur. yel. | . 7, H. Her. P. Siberia | . | 1802 |
| styloid | . . | Blue | . 5, H. | A. Siberia | . 1802 |
| tomentosa, 4 | . . | Blue | . 5, H. | A. Ceylon | . 1820 |
| tinctoria | . . | White | . 8, H. Her. P. Montpel. | . | 1596 |
| undulata | . . | Purple | . 7, H. Her. P. Spain | . | 1752 |
| verrucosa | . . | Blue | . 7, H. | A. S. Eur. | . 1821 |

*Lycopsoides*.

**ANDERSONIA**, *R. Brown*. In memory of Messrs. W. A. W. and G. Anderson, great promoters of Botany. *Linn*. 5, Or. 1, Nat. Or. *Epacridaceæ*. A very pretty species, multiplied from portions of the young shoots, in sand, under a glass, and grown in sandy peat soil carefully watered.

| | | | | | |
|---|---|---|---|---|---|
| sprengelioides | . . | Pink | . 6, G. Ev. S. N. Holl. | . | 1803 |

**ANDIRA**, *Lamarck*. Its Brazilian name. *Linn*. 17, Or. 4, Nat. Or. *Leguminosæ*. Large ornamental

[ 19 ]

---

trees; for culture, &c., see *Geoffroya*. Synonymes: 1. *Geoffroya inermis*. 2. *G. racemosa*.

| | | | | | |
|---|---|---|---|---|---|
| inermis, 1 | . . | Purple | . 8. Ev. T. W. Ind | . | 1778 |
| racemosa, 2 | . . | Purple | . 8. Ev. T. Trinidad | . | 1818 |

**ANDRACHNE**, *Linn*. The name of the Purslain in Greece. *Linn*. 21, Or. 10, Nat. Or. *Euphorbiaceæ*. Bastard Orpine. A weed, of simple culture—*telephioides*.

**ANDRÆA**, *Hedwig*. Named in honour of J. G. R. Andrew, a German professor. *Linn*. 24, Or. 5, Nat. Or. *Musci*. This remarkable genus differs from all other mosses, in having a thread, which splits into four valves, cohering at their ends by means of the persistent lid; it agrees with *Sphagnum*, in having no footstalk, but in its room an elongated receptacle, and appears to be a transition from *Musci* to *Hepaticæ*. This is, however, only apparent. All the species are natives of rocks or mountains, and are remarkable for their nearly black, or dark-brown colour.—*London's Encyclopædia of Plants*—*alpina, nivalis, Rothii, rupestris*.

**ANDROGYNOUS**, producing male and female flowers on the same plant, or on the same spike, or head.

**ANDROSÆNIA**, *Decandolle*. In memory of Ant. Andrzejowski, a Russian botanist. *Linn*. 15, Or. 1, Nat. Or. *Cruciferæ*. Mere weeds, of the simplest culture. Synonymes: 1. *Sisymbrium Sieversianum*. 2. *S. integrifolium*. 3. *S. pectinatum, Hesperis pinnata*. 4. *Cheiranthus pinnatifidus,—eglandulosa*, 1; *integrifolia*, 2, *pectinata*, 3; *pinnatifida*, 4.

**ANDROCYMBIUM**, *Linn*. The name is derived from *aner*, anther, and *kimbion*, a saucer, in allusion to the peculiar form of the stamens and their appendages. *Linn*. 6, Or. 3, Nat. Or. *Melanthaceæ*. Interesting bulbous-rooted plants; for culture, &c. see *Melanthium*. Synonyme: 1. *Melanthium eucomoides*.

| | | | | | |
|---|---|---|---|---|---|
| eucomoides, 1 | . | Green | . 4, G. Bl. P. C. G. H. | . | 1794 |
| melanthioides | . | White | . 7, G. Bl. P. C. G. H. | . | 1823 |
| volutare | . | White | . 4, G. Bl. P. C. G. H. | . | 1816 |

**ANDROMACHIA**, *Kunth*. Named after Andromachus a physician to Nero. *Linn*. 19, Or. 2, Nat. Or. *Compositæ*. An uninteresting species of easy culture —*Igniaria*.

**ANDROMEDA**, *Linn*. Named after the virgin Andromeda. *Linn*. 10, Or. 1, Nat. Or. *Ericaceæ*. Very ornamental and interesting species, delighting in peat soil, and increased plentifully from layers and seeds. The seed should be sown in pots, and very thinly covered, for if deep in the soil they will rot; the young plants should be planted out in the spring. Synonymes: 1. *A. lucida, populifolia, reticulata, laurina*. 2. *A. Walteri*. 3. *A. spinulosa*. 4. *A. nitida, lucida*. 5. *A. polifolia, latifolia*. 6. *A. paniculata*. 7. *A. pubescens*.

| | | | | | |
|---|---|---|---|---|---|
| acuminata, 1 | . | White | . 8, H. Ev. S. N. Amer. | . | 1765 |
| angustifolia | . | White | . 3, H. Ev. S. N. Amer. | . | 1748 |
| arborea | . | White | . 8, H. Ev. T. N. Amer. | . | 1752 |
| axillaris | . | White | . 6, H. Ev. S. N. Amer. | . | 1765 |
| longifolia, 2 | . | White | . 7, H. Ev. S. N. Amer. | . | |
| buxifolia | . | Pink | . 8. Ev. S. Mauritius | . | 1822 |
| calyculata | . | White | . 4, H. Ev. S. N. Amer. | . | 1748 |
| latifolia | . | White | . 3, H. Ev. S. Newfoundl. | . | 1748 |
| nana | . | White | . 3, H. Ev. S. | | |
| ventricosa | . | White | . 3, H. Ev. S. Russia | . | 1748 |
| candicans | . | White | . 6, H. Ev. S. N. Amer. | . | |
| Catesbæi, 3 | . | White | . 6, H. Ev. S. N. Amer. | . | 1793 |
| coriacea, 4 | . | Pink | . 7, H. Ev. S. N. Amer. | . | 1765 |
| rubra | . | Red | . 7, H. Ev. S. N. Amer. | . | 1765 |
| eriopå | . | White | . 8, H. Ev. S. N. Amer. | . | 1824 |
| dealbata | . | Pink | . 4, H. Ev. S. | | |
| fasciculata | . | White | . 8. Ev. T. Jamaica | . | 1824 |
| floribunda | . | White | . 6, H. Ev. S. N. Amer. | . | 1812 |
| glaucophylla, 5 | . | Pink | . 7, H. Ev. S. N. Amer. | . | |
| hypnoides | . | Wht. red | . 6, F. De. Cr. Lapland | . | 1798 |
| jamaicensis | . | White | . 8. Ev. S. Jamaica | . | 1793 |
| japonica | . | White | . G. Ev. T. Japan | . | 1806 |
| mariana | . | White | . 6, H. Ev. S. N. Amer. | . | 1736 |
| oblonga | . | White | . 6, H. Ev. S. N. Amer. | . | 1736 |
| ovalis | . | White | . 6, H. Ev. S. N. Amer. | . | 1736 |
| ovalifolia | . | White | . G. Ev. T. Nepal | . | 1825 |
| pilulifera | . | White | . 6, H. Ev. S. | | |
| polifolia | . | Pink | . 7, H. Ev. S. | | |
| grandiflora | . | Pink | . 4. H. Ev. S. Ingria | . | 1790 |
| latifolia | . | Pink | . 7, H. Ev. S. N. Amer. | . | |
| media | . | White | . 7, H. Ev. S. Britain | . | |
| minima | . | Pink | . 4. H. Ev. S. | | |
| oleifolia | . | Pink | . 4. H. Ev. S. | | |
| revoluta | . | Pink | . 4. H. Ev. S. N. Eur. | . | 1783 |
| subulata | . | Pink | . 7, H. Ev. S. | | |

| | | | | | |
|---|---|---|---|---|---|
| racemósa, 6 | White | 6, H. Ev. S. | N. Amer. | 1736 |
| latifólia | White | 7, H. Ev. S. | N. Amer. | |
| stricta | White | 7, H. Ev. S. | N. Amer. | |
| rosmarinifólia | Pink | 7, H. Ev. S. | N. Amer. | |
| rubiginósa, 7 | White | 8. Ev. S. | W. Ind. | |
| salicifólia | Pa. grn. | 8, H. Ev. S. | Maurit. | 1825 |
| sinénsis | Blush | 6, G. Ev. S. | China | 1826 |
| speciósa | White | 8, H. Ev. S. | Carolina | 1800 |
| glauca | Pink | 8, H. Ev. S. | | |
| nitida | White | 8, H. Ev. S. | Carolina | 1800 |
| pulverulénta | White | 7, H. Ev. S. | Carolina | 1800 |
| spicáta | White | 6, H. Ev. S. | N. Amer. | |
| tetragóna | White | 4, F. Ev. S. | Lapland | 1810 |

ANDROPŌGŎN, *Willdenow.* The little tufts of hairs on the flowers resemble a man's beard; hence the name from *aner*, a man, and *pogon*, a beard. *Linn.* 23, Or. 1, Nat. Or. *Gramineæ.* Uninteresting species of grass, of the simplest culture. *Synonyme:* 1 *Andropogon larus—angustifólia, annulátus, argénteus, comósus, furcátus, hirtus, Ischæmum, lagurõīdes, saccharõīdes, serrátus,* 1.

ANDRŌSĀCĒ, *Linn.* Named in reference to the resemblance of the round hollow leaf to an ancient buckler; from *aner*, a man, and *sakos*, a buckler. *Linn.* 5, Or. 1, Nat. Or. *Primulaceæ.* Pretty species, succeeding well in small pots, in a mixture of turfy loam and peat, cautiously watered. They increase from seeds, or by divisions.

| | | | | | |
|---|---|---|---|---|---|
| acaúlis | White | 7, H. | B. Siberia | 1825 |
| alismóīdes | White | 9, H. H. | B. Siberia | 1830 |
| brevifólia | White | 5, F. | B. S. France | 1825 |
| cárnea | Flesh | 4, H. Her. P. | Switzerl. | 1768 |
| carináta | Yellow | 4, H. Her. P. | N. Amer. | 1826 |
| Chamæjásme | Pink | 7, F. Her. P. | Austria | 1768 |
| elongáta | White | 4, H. | A. Austria | 1776 |
| filiformis | White | 5, H. | A. Siberia | 1820 |
| láctea | White | 7, F. Her. P. | Austria | 1752 |
| lactiflóra | White | 8, K. | B. Siberia | 1806 |
| lineáris | White | 4, H. Her. P. | N. Amer. | 1806 |
| macrocárpa | White | 7, H. | A. Siberia | 1827 |
| máxima | White | 4, H. | A. Austria | 1797 |
| nána | White | 4, H. | A. Denmark | 1803 |
| obtusifólia | Pink | 4, H. | A. Italy | 1817 |
| septentrionális | White | 5, H. | A. Russia | 1755 |
| villósa | Pink | 5, H. Her. P. | Pyrenees | 1790 |

ANDROSÆMŪM, *Allioni.* The name is given in allusion to the colour of the juice; from *aner*, a man, and *haima*, blood. *Linn.* 18, Or. 8, Nat. Or. *Hypericaceæ.* Tutsan. An interesting native species, simply cultivated. *Synonyme:* 1. *Hypericum Androsæmum.*

| | | | | | |
|---|---|---|---|---|---|
| officinále, 1 | Yellow | 8, H. Her. P | Britain | |

ANDRÝALA, *Linn.* Not explained. *Linn.* 19, Or. 1, Nat. Or. *Compositæ.* The species are rather pretty, and will grow well in common soil; they increase by seeds or divisions. *Synonymes:* 1, *A. lyrata.* 2. *Crepis incana.*

| | | | | | |
|---|---|---|---|---|---|
| argéntea, 1 | Yellow | 8, H. | B. Pyrenees | 1817 |
| cheiranthifólia | Yellow | 7, G. Her. P. | Madeira | 1777 |
| erithmifólia | Yellow | 8, G. | B. Madeira | 1778 |
| incána, 2 | Yellow | 6, H. | B. Pyrenees | 1818 |
| integrifólia | Yellow | 8, H. | B. S. Eur. | 1711 |
| nigricans | Yellow | 8, H. | A. Barbary | 1804 |
| pinnatifída | Yellow | 7, G. | B. Madeira | 1778 |
| ragusína | Yellow | 8, G. Her. P. | Archipel. | 1753 |
| runcináta | Yellow | 7, H. | B. S. Eur. | 1731 |

ANEILĒMĀ, *R. Brown.* The involucrum is wanting; hence the name from *a*, without, and *eilema*, involucrum. *Linn.* 3, Or. 1, Nat. Or. *Commelinaceæ.* Interesting species; for culture, &c. see *Commelina.*

| | | | | | |
|---|---|---|---|---|---|
| acuminátā | Blue | 8, S. Ev. | Cr. N. Holl. | 1822 |
| æquinoctiális | Blue | 7, S. Ev. | Tr. Guinea | 1820 |
| affínis | Blue | 8, G. Ev. | Cr. N. Holl. | 1820 |
| ambígua | Blue | 7, S. Her. P | S. Leone | 1822 |
| biflóra | Blue | 8, S. Ev. | Tr. N. Holl. | 1822 |
| longifólia | Blue | 7, S. Her. P. | Mozambi. | 1825 |
| nudicaúlis | Blue | 7, S. Ev. | Tr. E. Ind. | 1818 |
| nudiflóra | Blue | 7, G. B. | Tr. E. Ind. | 1824 |
| serruláta | Blue | 8, S. Ev. | Tr. Trinidad | 1824 |
| sinica | Pur. blue | 5, G. Her. P. | China | 1820 |
| spiráta | Blue | 7, G. Ev. | Cr. E. Ind. | 1783 |

ANEMIA, *Swartz.* Named in allusion to the naked inflorescence, from *aneimon*, naked. *Linn.* 24, Or. 1, Nat. Or. *Osmundaceæ.* Ornamental species of ferns, succeeding well in open loamy soil, and increased by dividing the roots, or by seeds. *Synonymes:* 1. *Osmunda humilis.* 2. *O. Phillitidis.*

| | | | | | |
|---|---|---|---|---|---|
| adiantifólia | Brown | 8, S. Her. P. | W. Ind. | 1793 |
| coccínea | Brown | 8, S. Her. P. | | 1830 |

| | | | | | |
|---|---|---|---|---|---|
| collína | Brown | 8, S. Her. P. | Brazil | 1829 |
| flexuósa | Brown | 8. Her. P. | S. Amer. | 1831 |
| fraxinifólia | Brown | 6, S. Her. P. | Brazil | 1828 |
| hirsúta | Brown | 8, S. Her. P. | Jamaica | 1794 |
| húmilis, 1 | Brown | 7, S. Her. P. | N. Amer. | 1823 |
| laciniáta | Brown | 8, S. Her. P. | W. Ind. | 1794 |
| lanceoláta | Brown | 8, S. Her. P. | W. Ind. | 1820 |
| répens | Brown | 8, S. Her. P. | Brazil | 1831 |
| Phillítidis, 2 | Brown | 6, S. Her. P. | Trinidad | 1830 |

ANEMŌNE, *Linn.* Many of the species inhabit elevated windy places; hence the name, from *anemos*, the wind. *Linn.* 13, Or. 6, Nat. Or. *Ranunculaceæ.* Very showy, free-flowering species, succeeding best in light loamy soil. They increase variously, from divisions, offsets, or seeds, and the greenhouse species may be propagated from cuttings in light loam under a glass. *Synonymes:* 1. *A. ochotensis.* 2. *A. fragifera.* 3. *Clematis capensis.* 4. *A. tenella.* 5. *A. stellata, versicolor.* 6. *A. alpina.* 7. *A. cuneifolia.* 8. *A. hortensia, pavonia.* 9. *A. apiifolia.*

| | | | | | |
|---|---|---|---|---|---|
| alba, 1 | White | 6, H. Her. P. | Siberia | 1820 |
| albána | White | 5, H. Her. P. | Caucasus | 1821 |
| alpína | White | H. Her. P. | Austria | 1658 |
| apennína | Blue | 4, H. Tu. P. | England | |
| acutipétala | Blue | 5, H. Her P. | Switzerl. | 1819 |
| baldénsis, 2 | White | 5, H. Tu. P. | Switzerl. | 1792 |
| cærúlea | Blue | 5, H. Tu. P. | Siberia | 1826 |
| capénsis, 3 | Purple | 4, G. Her. P. | C. G. H. | 1795 |
| caroliniána, 4 | White | 4, H. Tu. P. | Carolina | 1824 |
| cérnua | Red wht. | 5, H. Her. P. | Japan | 1806 |
| coronária | Striped | 6, H. Tu. P. | Levant | 1596 |
| pléna | Striped | 4, H. Tu. P. | | |
| dahúrica | Flesh | 5, H. Her. P. | Dahuria | 1819 |
| deltoídea | White | 5, H. Her. P. | Columbia | 1827 |
| dichótoma | Red wht. | 5, H. Her. P. | N. Amer. | 1768 |
| Fischeriána | White | 4, H. Her. P. | Siberia | 1827 |
| Halléri | Purple | 4, H. Her. P. | Switzerl. | 1816 |
| horténsis, 5 | Striped | 4, H. Tu. P. | Italy | 1597 |
| Hudsoniána | White | 5, H. Her. P. | N. Amer. | 1827 |
| lancifólia | White | 4, H. Her. P. | N. Amer. | 1822 |
| micrántha, 6 | Wht. pur. | 7, H. Her. P. | Austria | 1800 |
| multifida | White | 6, H. Her. P. | Magellan | 1824 |
| narcisiflóra | White | 5, H. Her. P. | Siberia | 1773 |
| nemorósa | Wht. red | 4, H. Tu. P. | Britain | |
| flore-pléno | Wht. red | 4, H. Tu. P. | Britain | |
| Nuttalliána | White | 7, H. Her. P. | N. Amer. | 1827 |
| obsoléta | Purple | 5, H. Her. P. | Germany | |
| palmáta | White | 5, H. Tu. P. | Portugal | 1597 |
| flore-albído | Whitish | 5, H. Tu. P. | | |
| flore-flavo | Yellow | 5, H. Tu. P. | Portugal | 1597 |
| flore-pléno | Yellow | 5, H. Tu. P. | | |
| parviflóra, 7 | White | 5, H. Her. P. | N. Amer. | 1824 |
| pátens | Lgt. yel. | 4, H. Her. P. | Siberia | 1752 |
| ochroleúca | Cream | 4, H. Her. P. | Siberia | 1752 |
| pavonína | Red | 4, H. Tu. P. | France | |
| flore-pléno | Red | 5, H. Tu. P. | Europe | |
| fúlgens, 8 | Red | 5, H. Tu. P. | S. Eur. | 1818 |
| pennsylvánica | White | 5, H. Her. P. | N. Amer. | 1766 |
| praténsis | Drk. pur. | 5, H. Her. P. | Germany | 1731 |
| Pulsatilla | Violet | 5, H. Her. P. | England | |
| quinquefólia | White | 4, H. Tu. P. | N. Amer. | 1817 |
| ranunculóides | Yellow | 4, H. Tu. P. | England | |
| refléxa | Yellow | 4, H. Tu. P. | Siberia | 1818 |
| Richardsónia | Yellow | 6, H. Her. P. | N. Amer. | 1827 |
| sibírica | White | 5, H. Her. P. | Siberia | 1804 |
| stelláta | White | 6, H. Her. P. | Italy | 1597 |
| purpúrea | Purple | 5, H. Tu. P. | Italy | 1597 |
| sulphúrea, 9 | Sulphur | 5, H. Her. P. | Europe | 1816 |
| sylvéstris | White | 5, H. Her. P. | Germany | 1596 |
| trifólia | White | 4, H. Her. P. | France | 1597 |
| umbelláta | Blue | 5, H. Tu. P. | Levant | 1824 |
| uralénsis | Blue | 5, H. Her. P. | Siberia | 1824 |
| vernális | White | 4, H. Her. P. | Switzerl. | 1752 |
| flore-lúteo | Yellow | 4, H. Her. P. | S. Eur. | |
| virginiána | White | 5, H. Her. P. | N. Amer. | 1772 |
| vitifólia | White | 7, H. Her. P. | Nepal | 1829 |

ANĒTHŪM, *Linn.* Named in allusion to the quick growth; from *ano*, upwards, and *theo*, to run. *Linn.* 5, Or. 2, Nat. Or. *Umbelliferæ.* Useful species, succeeding in any common soil, and increased plentifully from seeds. The seed is used in the manufacture of gin, and in medicine as a carminative. *Synonyme:* 1. *Meum Fæniculum.*

| | | | | | |
|---|---|---|---|---|---|
| Fæniculum, 1 | Yellow | 8, H. Her. P. | England | |
| dúlce | Yellow | 8, H. Her. P. | Italy | |
| gravéolens | Yellow | 7, H. | B. Spain | 1570 |
| piperátum | Yellow | 7, H. | B. Italy | 1824 |
| Sówa | Yellow | 7, H. | A. E. Ind. | 1810 |

*Segétum.*

ANFRACTUOUS, full of turning and winding passages.
ANGĒLICA, *Linn.* Named after its supposed angelic virtues. *Linn.* 14, Or. 2, Nat. Or. *Scrophulariaceæ.* Uninteresting species, of the simplest culture. *Synonyme:* 1. *Imperatoria verticillaris—flavéscens,*

lucida, Raxoulii; *sylvestris, triquinata, verticillaris,* 1.

ANGELICA-TREE, see *Aralia spinosa.*

ANGOBONIA, *Kunth.* From *angelon,* its name in the Caraccas. Linn. 14, Or. 2, Nat. Or. *Scrophularinaceæ.* An elegant flowering species, thriving in light rich soil or turfy loam and peat, carefully watered. Cuttings planted in the same kind of soil, under a glass, root freely if a little air is occasionally admitted to them.

| salicarifolia | . | Lgt. blue | 8, S. Her. P. S. Amer. | 1818 |

ANGIANTHUS, *Wendland.* Compounded from *aggos,* vessel, and *anthos,* a flower. Linn. 19, Or. 5, Nat. Or. *Compositæ.* An ornamental species; for culture, &c., see *Cassinia.* Synonyme: 1. *Cassinia aurea.*

| aureus, 1 | . | Yellow | 7, G. Her. P. N. Holl. | 1803 |

ANGIONIDIUM, *Greville.* Derived from *aggeion,* a vessel, and *eidos,* like. Linn. 24, Or. 9, Nat. Or. *Fungi.* A minute production, found upon dead sticks and other decomposing vegetables in autumn. Synonyme: 1. *Reticularia sinuosa—sinuosum,* 1.

ANGOPHORA, *Cavanilles.* In allusion to the make of the fruit; from *aggos,* a vessel, and *phero,* to bear. Linn. 19, Or. 4, Nat. Or. *Myrtaceæ.* Ornamental species; for culture, &c., see *Metrosideros.* Synonymes: 1. *Metrosideros hispidus.* 2. *M. costatus.*

| cordifolia, 1 | . | Yellow | 8, G. Ev. S. N. Holl. | 1789 |
| lanceolata, 2 | . | Yellow | 8, G. Ev. S. N. Holl. | 1816 |

ANORÆCUM, *Thouars.* Altered from *angurek,* the Malayan name of such plants. Linn. 20, Or. 1, Nat. Or. *Orchidaceæ.* Some fine plants are described as belonging to this genus, among which *A. eburnum* is the most beautiful; it is a very rare plant, and not, as we are aware, possessed by more than three or four individuals in this country. It is a remarkably slow-growing plant, and has only flowered once in the country. For culture and propagation see *Vanda.*

| caudatum | . | Wht. grn. | 8, S. Epi. S. Leone | 1834 |
| clandestinum | . | White | 9, S. Epi. S. Leone | 1834 |
| distichum | . | White | 9, S. Epi. S. Leone | 1834 |
| eburnum | . | White | 1, S. Epi. Madagas. | 1826 |
| luridum | . | Brown | 9, S. Epi. S. Leone | 1822 |
| micranthum | . | White | 10, S. Epi. S. Leone | |
| odoratissimum | . | | S. Epi. | |
| teretifolium | . | White | S. Epi. S. Leone | |

ANGULATE, cornered, having sharp angles.

ANGUILLARIA, *R. Brown.* Named in allusion to the twisted seed; from *anguilla,* an eel. Linn. 6, Or. 3, Nat. Or. *Melanthaceæ.* Interesting dwarf species, growing well in sandy peat, and are multiplied from offsets.

| biglandulosa | . | Purple | 5, F. Her. P. N. Holl. | 1826 |
| dioica | . | Purple | 5, F. Her. P. N. S. W. | 1826 |
| indica | . | Drk. pur. | 6, F. Her. P. Tranqueb. | 1818 |

ANGUINEA, signifying a snake.

ANGULATE, forming angles.

ANGULARLY-TOOTHED, toothed so as to form angles.

ANGURIA, *Linn.* A Grecian name for the cucumber. Linn. 21, Or. 2, Nat. Or. *Cucurbitaceæ.* Interesting species of the easiest culture.

| pedati | . | Yellow | 7, S. Ev. Cl. S. Amer. | 1820 |
| trilobata | . | Pink | 7, S. Ev. Cl. Carthage | 1793 |
| trifoliata | . | Yellow | 7, S. Ev. Cl. St. Domin. | |
| umbrosa | . | Yellow | 7, S. Ev. Cl. S. Amer. | 1827 |

ANICTANGIUM, *Hedwig.* Compounded from *anoiktos,* open, and *aggeion,* a vase; referring to the open nature of the theca. Small mosses, found in small depressed tufts in summer on rocks, &c. Synonymes: 1. *Gymnostomum ciliatum.* 2. *G. imberbe.*—*Ciliatum,* 1. *imberbe,* 2.

ANIGOZANTHOS, *R. Brown.* Named in allusion to the long conspicuous scapes upon which the flowers are raised. Linn. 6, Or. 1, Nat. Or. *Hæmodoraceæ.* Interesting species, succeeding in sandy peat, well watered, and increased by dividing the roots. Synonyme: 1. *Schwagrichenia flavida.*

| flavida, 1 | . | Yellow | 6, G. Her. P. N. Holl. | 1808 |
| Manglesii | . | Green | 5, G. Her. P. S. River | 1833 |
| an ustifolia | . | Grn. red | 7, G. Her. P. N. Holl. | 1836 |
| rufa | . | Rufous | 7, G. Her. P. N. Holl. | 1824 |

ANIMAL OAT, see *Avena sterilis.*

ANISACANTHA, *R. Brown.* Derived from *anisos,* unequal, and *akantha,* a spine. Linn. 4, Or. 1, Nat.

[ 21 ]

Or. *Chenopodiaceæ.* A very curious species, of easy culture.

| divaricata | . | | G. Ev. S. N. Holl. | 1824 |

ANTHANTHUS, *Willdenow.* Named from *anisos,* unequal, and *anthos,* a flower. Linn. 18, Or. 1, Nat. Or. *Iridaceæ.* Ornamental bulbous-rooted plants; for culture, &c., see *Antholyza.* Synonymes: 1. *Antholyza Cunonia. Gladiolus Cunonia.* 2. *Gladiolus quadrangularis. G. abbreviatus.*

| Cunonia, 1 | . | Scarlet | 6, G. Bl. P. C. G. H. | 1756 |
| quadrangularis, 2 | Yellow | 4, G. Bl. P. C. G. H. | 1700 |
| splendens | . | Scarlet | 6, G. Bl. P. C. G. H. | 1828 |

ANISE, see *Tragium Anisum.*

ANISEED-TREE, see *Illicium.*

ANISOCHILUS, *Wallich.* Derived from *anisos,* unequal, and *cheilos,* a lip. Linn. 14, Or. 1, Nat. Or. *Labiatæ.* An ornamental species; for culture, &c., see *Lavandula.* The juice mixed with powdered sugar candy, is prescribed in India in cynanche. Synonyme: 1. *Lavandula carnosa.*

| carnosa | . | Lilac | 8, S. Her. P. E. Ind. | 1778 |

ANISODUS, *Link.* Named in allusion to the unequal divisions of the calyx; from *anisos,* unequal, and *odous,* a tooth. Linn. 5, Or. 1, Nat. Or. *Solanaceæ.* Synonymes: 1. *Nicandra anomala.* 2. *Whitleya stramonifolia.*

| luridus, 1 | . | Lurid | 9, H. Her. P. Nepal | 1824 |
| stramonifolius, 2 | Yel. grn. | 9, H. Her. P. Nepal | 1824 |

ANISOMELES, *R. Brown.* Named from *anisos,* unequal, and *melos,* a member. Linn. 14, Or. 1, Nat. Or. *Labiatæ.* Ornamental species; for culture, &c., see *Nepeta.* Synonymes: 1. *Ajuga furcata.* 2. *Nepeta malabarica.*

| furcata, 1 | . | Blue | 8, G. Ev. S. Nepal | 1824 |
| malabarica, 2 | . | Violet | 8, S. Ev. S. E. Ind. | 1823 |
| moschata | . | Purple | 8, S. Ev. S. N. Holl. | 1824 |
| ovata | . | Pink | 8, S. | A. E. Ind. | 1823 |

ANNULATIONS, rings or circles.

ANNULAR, circular, producing a ring or circle.

ANODA, *Cavanilles.* Named in reference to the impervious capsule cells; from *anodos,* signifying impervious. Linn. 16, Or. 8, Nat. Or. *Malvaceæ.* Uninteresting species; for culture, &c. see *Sida.* Synonymes: 1. *Sida hastata.* 2. *S. cristata.* 3. *S. crenatiflora.* 4. *S. deltoides.* 5. *S. cristata.*—*Acerifolia* 1, *Dilleniana* 2, *hastata, incarnata, parviflora* 3, *triangularis* 4, *triloba* 5.

ANODONTIA, *Decandolle.* From *a,* destitute, and *odontos,* a tooth, alluding to the stamens. Linn. 15, Or. 1, Nat. Or. *Cruciferæ.* Ornamental species; for culture, &c. see *Alyssum.* Synonymes: 1. *Alyssum dasycarpum.* 2. *Al. edentulum.* 3. *Al. halimifolium.* 4. *Al. macrocarpum.* 5. *Al. rupestre.* 6. *Al. spinosum.*

| dasycarpa, 1 | . | Yellow | 7, H. | A. Siberia | 1819 |
| macrocarpa, 4 | . | White | 6, F. Ev. S. France | 1823 |
| obovata | . | Yellow | H. Her. P. | 1830 |
| spinosa, 6 | . | White | 6, F. Ev. S. S. Eur. | 1683 |

edentula 2, halimifolia 3, rupestris 5.

ANŒCTOCHILUS, *Blume.* Supposed to be from *anoiktos,* open, and *cheilos,* a lip; in allusion to the spreading apex of that organ. Linn. 20, Or. 1, Nat. Or. *Orchidaceæ.* This is a very interesting little plant, with rather inconspicuous flowers and very handsome leaves, which are admirably and singularly painted with transverse yellowish lines upon a rich brown ground. The plant is described as a native of Java and Ceylon, but his Grace the Duke of Devonshire's collector found it on the Khoseea Hills, from whence he brought living plants in 1837, and which are thriving in great beauty in the orchideæ house at Chatsworth. It requires the same treatment as the other East Indian terrestrial orchidaceæ.

| setaceus | . | Wht. grn. | 6, S. Ter. E. Ind. | 1836 |

ANOMATHECA, *Ker.* Named from *anomos,* singular, and *theca,* a capsule. Linn. 3, Or. 1, Nat. Or. *Iridaceæ.* Very interesting free-flowering species, succeeding in common soil, and multiplied plentifully from seeds. *A. cruenta* makes a pretty show when planted in a bed by itself in the flower-garden, where its neat blossoms are produced in abundance.

| cruenta | . | Blood | 7, F. Bl. P. C. G. H. | 1830 |
| juncea | . | Lilac | 5, G. Bl. P. C. G. H. | 1791 |

**ANŎMŎDŎN**, *Hooker.* Compounded from *anomos*, irregular, and *odous*, a tooth; in allusion to the singular nature of the peristoma. *Linn.* 24, Or. 5, Nat. Or. *Musci.* The plants have dark, blackish green, long cylindrical, straggling stems, and are found on the wilds of Dartmoor. *Synonymes:* 1. *Neckera curtipendula.* 2. *Hypnum viticulosum, curtipendulum* 1, *viticulosum* 2.

**ANŎNA**, *Adanson.* From Menona, its Banda name. *Linn.* 13, Or. 6, Nat. Or. *Anonaceæ.* An interesting genus, comprising for the most part fruit-bearing plants, preferring a moist heat and rich loamy soil, well watered. Ripened cuttings, in sand, under a glass, root readily; and fresh seed obtained from the tropics, sown in pots, and plunged in a strong hotbed, will speedily furnish good plants. The fruit is a pretty berry of a sub-acid taste, often as large as an orange, but in general more like a plum. *A. cherimolia* produces a succulent fruit of a dark purple colour, containing a soft sweet mucilage, and is much esteemed by the Peruvians. *A. reticulata* yields a yellowish, sometimes reddish fruit, of the consistence of custard, and is much esteemed by some people. *A. palustris* bears a smooth, heart-shaped, sweet-scented fruit, of an agreeable taste, but is a strong narcotic; the wood of this plant is so remarkable for its soft, spongy nature, as to be employed in Brazil as a substitute for corks. *Synonyme:* 1. *A. tripetala.*

| | | | | | | |
|---|---|---|---|---|---|---|
| amplexicaulis | Yel. grn. | 8. | Ev. | S. | Maurit. | 1824 |
| asiatica | Yel. grn. | 8. | Ev. | S. | Asia | 1816 |
| Cherimolia, 1 | Brown | 8. | S. Ev. | T. S. | Amer. | 1739 |
| cinerea | Yel. grn. | 8. | S. Ev. | T. | W. Ind. | 1818 |
| glabra | Brown | 8. | S. Ev. | T. | Carolina | 1774 |
| laurifolia | Brown | 8. | S. Ev. | T. | W. Ind. | 1773 |
| longifolia | Yel. grn. | 8. | S. Ev. | T. | Guiana | 1820 |
| mexicana | Yel. grn. | 8. | S. Ev. | S. | Mexico | 1823 |
| muricata | Yel. grn. | 8. | S. Ev. | E. Ind. | | 1820 |
| muricata | Grn. yel. | 8. | S. Ev. | T. | W. Ind. | 1656 |
| obtusifolia | Yel. grn. | 8. | S. Ev. | T. | W. Ind. | 1810 |
| paludosa | Green | 8. | S. Ev. | S. | Guiana | 1803 |
| pa lustris | Yellow | 8. | S. Ev. | W. | Ind. | 1731 |
| punctata | Yel. grn. | 8. | S. Ev. | S. | Trinidad | 1818 |
| reticulata | Wht. grn. | 8. | S. Ev. | T. S. | Amer. | 1690 |
| senegalensis | Yel. grn. | 8. | S. Ev. | S. | Guinea | 1824 |
| squamosa | Wht. grn. | 8. | S. Ev. | S. | Amer. | 1731 |

**ANSERRINOUS**, relating to geese.

**ANTENNARIA**, *R. Brown.* In reference to the down of the pappus, which is like the antennæ of some insects. *Linn.* 19, Or. 2, Nat. Or. *Compositæ.* Mostly interesting species; for culture, &c., see *Gnaphalium. Synonyme:* 1. *Gnaphalium alpinum.*

| | | | | | | |
|---|---|---|---|---|---|---|
| alpina | Pink | 6. | H. Her. | P. | Alp. Eur. | 1775 |
| carpatica, 1 | Pink | 6. | H. Her. | P. | Carp. mo. | 1775 |
| contorta | White | 7. | F. Her. | P. | Nepal | 1821 |
| dioica | Pink | 6. | H. Her. | P. | Britain | |
| hyperborea | Whitish | 6. | H. Ev. | Cr. | Skye | |
| margaritacea | White | 7. | H. Her. | P. | England | |
| plantaginea | White | 7. | H. Her. | P. | Virginia | 1759 |
| triplinervis | White | 8. | F. Her. | P. | Nepal | 1823 |

**ANTERIOR**, growing in front of any thing.

**ANTHELMINTIC**, capable of killing worms.

**ANTHEMIS**, *Linn.* In allusion to the great production of flowers; from *anthemon*, a flower. *Linn.* 19, Or. 2, Nat. Or. *Compositæ.* These species are more useful than ornamental, and may be grown in common soil, and increased from seed. *A. nobilis* is a very useful herb, and is employed medicinally as a tonic carminative anodyne, and when taken in large doses it proves a powerful emetic. *Synonymes:* 1. *A. maritima.* 2. *A. saxatilis.* 3. *A. peregrina.* 4. *A. incrassata.* 5. *Pyrethrum orientale.*

| | | | | | | |
|---|---|---|---|---|---|---|
| alpina | White | 7. | H. Her. | P. | Austria | 1824 |
| altissima | White | 7. | H. | A. | S. Eur. | 1731 |
| apifolia | White | 7. | G. Her. | P. | China | 1819 |
| austriaca | White | 8. | H. | A. | Austria | 1759 |
| Barrelieri | White | 8. | H. De. | Tr. | Italy | 1825 |
| carpatica | White | 6. | H. Her. | P. | Carpat. | 1820 |
| Chamomilla | White | 7. | H. Her. | P. | S. Eur. | 1807 |
| Chia | White | 5. | H. | A. | Chio | 1731 |
| coronopifolia | White | 6. | H. Her. | P. | Spain | 1818 |
| Cota | White | 4. | H. | A. | Italy | 1714 |
| discoidea | Yellow | 7. | H. | A. | Italy | 1800 |
| fallax | White | 7. | H. | A. | | 1825 |
| fruticulosa | White | 8. | H. Her. | P. | Caucas. | 1820 |
| fuscata | White | 7. | H. | A. | Portugal | 1805 |
| globosa | White | 7. | G. Her. | P. | S. Eur. | 1570 |
| grandiflora | White | 7. | H. Her. | P. | S. Eur. | 1825 |
| iberica | White | 8. | H. Her. | P. | Iberia | 1820 |
| incrassata | White | 7. | H. Her. | P. | France | 1818 |
| Hitalbiti, 2 | White | 6. | H. Her. | P. | Hungary | 1823 |
| maritima | White | 7. | H. | A. | Mediter. | 1800 |

| | | | | | | |
|---|---|---|---|---|---|---|
| Marchalliana | Yellow | 7. | H. Her. | P. | Caucas. | 1816 |
| melampodia | White | 8. | H. Her. | P. | Egypt | 1819 |
| mixta | White | 8. | H. | A. | France | 1731 |
| montana | Purple | 7. | H. Her. | P. | Italy | 1759 |
| nobilis | White | 8. | H. Ev. | Cr. | Britain | |
| flore-pleno | White | 8. | H. Ev. | Cr. | Britain | |
| petræa | White | 7. | H. De. | Tr. | Italy | 1825 |
| pubescens | White | 7. | H. Her. | P. | S. Eur. | 1803 |
| punctata | White | 8. | G. Ev. | S. | Barbary | 1818 |
| Pyrethrum | White | 5. | H. Her. | P. | S. Eur. | 1570 |
| rigescens | White | 8. | H. Her. | P. | Caucas. | 1805 |
| Rudolphiana, 5 | Yellow | 7. | H. Her. | P. | Caucas. | 1824 |
| ruthenica | White | 6. | H. | A. | Tauria | 1822 |
| saxatilis | White | 7. | H. Her. | P. | Hungary | 1807 |
| tinctoria | Yellow | 6. | H. Her. | P. | Britain | |
| tomentosa | White | 7. | H. Her. | P. | Levant | 1795 |
| Triumfetti | Pa. yel. | 8. | H. | B. | Switzerl. | 1819 |

*Anglica* 1, *arvensis, Cotula, nicæensis* 3, *pedunculata* 4, *peregrina, racemosa, retusa, secundiramea.*

**ANTHEPHŎRA**, *Schreber.* Compounded from *anthos*, a flower, and *phoreo*, to bear. *Linn.* 3, Or. 2, Nat. Or. *Gramineæ.* An interesting species of grass, of easy culture. *Synonymes:* 1. *Tripsacum hermaphroditum, Cenchrus lævigatus.*

| | | | | | | |
|---|---|---|---|---|---|---|
| elegans, 1 | Apetal | 8. | Grass. | Jamaica | | 1776 |

**ANTHERICŬM**, *Linn.* Applied by the Greeks to the stem of the asphodel. *Linn.* 6, Or. 1, Nat. Or. *Liliaceæ.* This interesting genus comprises both bulbous and shrubby species, and all may be grown in a mixture of loam and peat, with the addition of a little sand. The shrubby species propagate readily from cuttings; and from the bulbous kinds offsets may be obtained. Most of them perfect seed. None of the species will thrive if over-watered, and the bulbous kinds should not have any water in winter. *Synonyme:* 1. *Scilla pomeridiana.*

| | | | | | | |
|---|---|---|---|---|---|---|
| albucoides | White | 7. | G. Her. | P. | C. G. H. | 1788 |
| bipedunculatum | White | 5. | G. Her. | P. | C. G. H. | 1825 |
| canaliculatum | Wht. grn. | 5. | G. Her. | P. | C. G. H. | 1774 |
| rufum | Copper | 6. | G. Her. | P. | C. G. H. | |
| erectum | White | 6. | F. Her. | P. | C. G. H. | 1800 |
| falcatum | White | 7. | G. Her. | P. | C. G. H. | 1825 |
| filifolium | White | 5. | G. Her. | P. | C. G. H. | 1820 |
| filiforme | White | 4. | G. Her. | P. | C. G. H. | 1775 |
| flexifolium | White | 6. | G. Her. | P. | C. G. H. | 1795 |
| floribundum | White | 4. | G. Her. | P. | C. G. H. | 1774 |
| fragrans | White | 5. | G. Her. | P. | C. G. H. | 1795 |
| graminifolium | White | 6. | G. Her. | P. | C. G. H. | 1794 |
| hirsutum | White | 7. | G. Her. | P. | C. G. H. | 1820 |
| longifolium | White | 6. | G. Her. | P. | C. G. H. | 1824 |
| pilosum | White | 7. | G. Her. | P. | C. G. H. | 1825 |
| plumosum | White | 8. | F. Her. | P. | Chile | 1822 |
| pomeridianum, 1 | White | 6. | G. Her. | P. | C. G. H. | 1819 |
| revolutum | White | 10. | G. Her. | P. | C. G. H. | 1731 |
| serotinum | White | 7. | H. Her. | P. | Britain | |
| spirale | White | 6. | G. Her. | P. | C. G. H. | 1824 |
| squameum | White | 7. | G. Her. | P. | C. G. H. | 1820 |
| sulphureum | Pur. yel. | 7. | H. Her. | P. | Hungary | 1823 |
| triflorum | White | 9. | G. Her. | P. | C. G. H. | 1787 |
| undulatum | White | 7. | G. Her. | P. | C. G. H. | 1825 |
| vespertinum | White | 6. | G. Her. | P. | C. G. H. | 1802 |
| villosum | White | 7. | G. Her. | P. | C. G. H. | 1826 |

**ANTHERIFEROUS**, bearing anthers.

**ANTHERS**, the male parts of a flower, containing the fecundating matter.

**ANTHINA**, *Fries.* Derived from *anthinus*, florid; referring to the colour. *Linn.* 24, Or. 9, Nat. Or. *Fungi.* Minute productions, found on the decayed and decaying leaves—*minuta.*

**ANTHISTIRIA**, *Willdenow.* Named in allusion to the very stiff stubble, from *anthisteri. Linn.* 23, Or. 1, Nat. Or. *Gramineæ.* Uninteresting species, of simple culture. *Synonymes:* 1. *Andropogon quadrivalvis —australis, ciliata.*

**ANTHOCERCIS**, *Labillardière.* Named in reference to the radiated corolla, from *anthos*, a flower, and *kirkis*, a ray. *Linn.* 14, Or. 2, Nat. Or. *Scrophulariaceæ.* These pretty species succeed well in a mixture of loam and peat, with the pots well drained, and the plants carefully watered; cuttings root in sand under a glass.

| | | | | | | |
|---|---|---|---|---|---|---|
| albicans | White | 6. | G. Ev. | S. | N. Holl. | 1824 |
| littorea | White | 7. | G. Ev. | S. | N. Holl. | 1803 |
| viscosa | White | 5. | G. Ev. | S. | N. Holl. | 1822 |

**ANTHOCEROS**, *E. Botany.* From *anthos*, a flower, and *keroeis*, a horn; alluding to the horn-like form of the theca. *Linn.* 24, Or. 7, Nat. Or. *Hepaticæ.* Small frondose plants, with long, slender, two-valved theca, in habit resembling *Jungermannia, major, multifidus, punctatus.*

**ANTHOCLEISTA**, *Afzelius.* From *anthos*, a flower, and

*elatior*, shut up. *Linn.* 5, Or. 1, Nat. Or. *Apocynaceæ.* An ornamental tree, thriving well in peat and loam, and increased from cuttings.

| macrophyllā | . . White | . 8. Ev. T. S. Leone | . 1820 |
|---|---|---|---|

**ANTHŌDŌN,** *Ruiz and Pavon.* Derived from *anthos*, a flower, and *odous*, a tooth. *Linn.* 3, Or. 1, Nat. Or. *Hippocrataceæ.* Interesting evergreen species, growing in rich loam and peat, and propagated from cuttings in sand under a glass.

| ellipticūm | . . . Yel. grn. | . 8. Ev. S. Rio Jan. | . 1818 |
|---|---|---|---|
| paniculatūm | . . . Yel. grn. | . 8. Ev. S. Rio Jan. | . 1818 |

**ANTHOLŌMĀ,** *La Billardière.* Named from *anthos*, a flower, and *loma*, a fringe. *Linn.* 13, Or. 1, Nat. Or. *Marcgraaviaceæ.* A beautiful tree, preferring rich loam, mixed with a little peat; ripened cuttings root in sand under a glass.

| montanā | . . . | . 8. Ev. S. N. Holl. | . 1810 |
|---|---|---|---|

**ANTHŌPHŌRŪM,** the receptacle on which the petals, stamens, and ovary are seated.

**ANTHOLȲZĀ,** *Linn.* A figurative name, from *anthos*, a flower, and *lyssa*, rage; the flowers look like the mouth of an animal ready to bite. *Linn.* 3, Or. 1, Nat. Or. *Iridaceæ.* An interesting genus of bulbous plants, thriving well in sandy soil under a south wall; the roots should be planted deep enough so as to be out of the reach of severe frost; they increase easily from offsets. Synonyme: 1. *A. æthiopica vitigera.*

| æthiopicā | . . . Scr. grn. | . 6, H. Bl. P. C. G. H. | . 1759 |
|---|---|---|---|
| montanā | . . . Brown | . 6, H. Bl. P. C. G. H. | . |
| præaltā, 1 | . . . Orange | . 2, H. Bl. P. C. G. H. | . |

**ANTHOSPĒRMŪM,** *Linn.* From *anthos*, a flower, and *sperma*, seed. *Linn.* 22, Or. 4, Nat. Or *Rubiaceæ.* Amber Tree. An interesting species, delighting in loam and peat, and cuttings strike freely in soil.

| æthiōpicūm | . . Grn. wht. | 6, G. Ev. S. C. G. H. | . 1692 |
|---|---|---|---|

**ANTHOXĀNTHŪM,** *Linn.* From *anthos*, a flower, and *xanthus*, yellow. *Linn.* 2, Or. 2, Nat. Or. *Gramineæ.* Spring Grass. Interesting species of grass, of the simplest culture. It is the dried herbage of *A. odoratum* that gives the sweet peculiar fragrance in meadow hay, said to depend on the presence of benzoic acid.

| arārūm | . . . Apetal | . 6, Grass. Morocco | . 1810 |
|---|---|---|---|
| galcllē | . . . Apetal | . 3, Grass. Sicily | . 1820 |
| odoratūm | . . . Apetal | . 5, Grass. Britain | . . |
| laxūm | . . . Apetal | . 5, Grass. Britain | . . |
| pubescūm | . . . Apetal | . 5, Grass. Britain | . . |
| ramosūm | . . . Apetal | . 5, Grass. Britain | . . |
| ovatūm | . . . Apetal | . 7, Grass. Spain | . . 1821 |

**ANTHRĪSCŪS,** *Persoon.* The name of a plant described by Pliny resembling *Scandix.* *Linn.* 5, Or. 2, Nat. Or. *Umbelliferæ.* Uninteresting species, of the simplest culture. Synonyme: 1. *Scandix Anthriscus*—*fumarioīdēs*, *hispidā*, *nemorōsā*, *nodōsā*, *tauricā*, *trichospērmā*, *tuberculātā*, *vulgāris* 1.

**ANTHȲLLIS,** *Linn.* From *anthos*, a flower, and *ioulos*, down; in reference to the flowers being usually downy. *Linn.* 16, Or. 5, Nat. Or. *Leguminosæ.* Beautiful free-flowering species, proper for ornamenting rock-work. The hardy perennial and annual kinds thrive well in a warm situation and light soil. The greenhouse and frame kinds succeed best in sandy loam and peat, and increase plentifully from seeds, and sometimes from cuttings. Synonymes 1. *Vulneraria rubriflora.* 2. *A. cornicina.* 3. *Vulneraria polyphylla.* 4. *A. rustica.*

| alpinā | . . . Yellow | . 8, H. Her. P. Britain | . . |
|---|---|---|---|
| aspalāthī | . . . Yellow | . 7, G. Ev. S. C. G. H. | . 1824 |
| Barbā Jōvis | . . . Pa. yel. | . 4, O. Ev. S. S. Eur. | . 1640 |
| cornicīnā | . . . White | . 7, H. | A. Spain | . 1759 |
| cytisoīdēs | . . . White | . 6, G. Ev. S. Spain | . 1731 |
| Dillenī, 1 | . . . Red | . 7, H. Her. P. S. Eur. | . 1816 |
| echinātā | . . . Purple | . 6, G. Ev. S. S. Eur. | . . |
| erinacea | . . . Purple | . 5, F. Ev. S. Spain | . 1759 |
| Gerārdī | . . . White | . 8, H. Her. P. Provence | . 1806 |
| hamōsā, 2 | . . . Pa. yel. | . 7, H. | A. Barbary | . 1821 |
| Hermānnīā | . . . Yellow | . 7, F. Ev. S. Levant | . 1739 |
| heterophyllā | . . . Pink | . 7, G. Ev. S. S. Eur. | . 1768 |
| lotoīdēs | . . . Yellow | . 7, H. | A. Spain | . 1739 |
| montānā | . . . Purple | . 7, H. Her. P. S. Eur. | . 1759 |
| alba | . . . White | . 7, H. Her. P. S. Eur. | . 1818 |
| onobrychoīdēs | . . . Yellow | . 7, H. Her. P. Spain | . 1817 |
| polyodphalā | . . . Yellow | . 7, H. Her. P. Barbary | . 1829 |
| polyphyllā, 3 | . . . Yellow | . 7, H. Her. P. S. Eur. | . 1816 |
| tenuifoliā | . . . Yellow | . 7, G. Ev. S. C. G. H. | . 1818 |

[ 23 ]

| tetraphyllā | . . . Yellow | . 7, H. | A. S. Eur. | . 1640 |
|---|---|---|---|---|
| Vulnerārīā | . . . Yellow | . 7, H. Her. P. Britain | . . |
| albiflorā, 4 | . . . White | . 7, H. Her. P. Britain | . . |
| rubrā | . . . Red | . 7, H. Her. P. Britain | . . |
| Webbiānā | . . . Pa. rose | . 6, H. Her. P. Teneriffe | . 1829 |

**ANTI-APHRODISIACAL,** any thing which checks the desire of sexual intercourse.

**ANTIDĒSMĀ,** *Linn.* So called from the use of the bark in making ropes; from *anti*, like, and *desmos*, bond. *Linn.* 22, Or. 5, Nat. Or. *Stilagineæ.* Plants requiring a rich loamy soil; ripened cuttings with their leaves on, root in sand, in a moist heat.

| guineēnsis | . . . Apetal | . 8. Ev. S. Guinea | . 1825 |
|---|---|---|---|
| pubescēns | . . . Apetal | . 8. Ev. S. E Ind. | . 1818 |
| zeylānicā | . . . Apetal | . 8. Ev. S. Ceylon | . 1821 |

*Alexitērīā, paniculata.*

**ANTI-PESTILENTIAL,** efficacious against pestilence.

**ANTI-PHRASIS,** the use of words in a sense opposite to that of some neighbouring parallel sentence.

**ANTIRRHĪNŪM,** *Linn.* Derived from *anti*, similar, and *rhin*, nose; the flowers of most of the species bear a perfect resemblance to the snout of some animal. *Linn.* 14, Or. 2, Nat. Or. *Scrophulariaceæ.* Very pretty flowering species, succeeding well in common soil, and increased plentifully from cuttings or seeds.

| angustifōlīūm | . . . Pink | . 8, H. Her. P. Europe | . 1817 |
|---|---|---|---|
| Asarīnā | . . . White | . 7, F. Ev. Tr. Italy | . 1699 |
| calycinūm | . . . Red | . 7, H. | A. Spain | . 1810 |
| glandulōsūm | . . . Ro. yel. | . 9, H. | A. Californ. | . 1834 |
| majūs | . . . Pink | . 7, H. Her. P. England | . |
| bicolōr | . . . Scr. wht. | . 7, H. Her. P. England | . |
| caryophylloīdēs | . Scar. stpd. | . 7, H. Her. P. Gard. hyb. | . |
| coccineā | . . . Scarlet | . 7, H. Her. P. England | . |
| florē-plēnō | . . . Flesh | . 7, H. Her. P. England | . |
| variegātūm | . . . Red | . 7, H. Her. P. England | . |
| mēdīūm | . . . Pink | . 8, H. Her. P. Europe | . 1821 |
| meoanthūm | . . . Pink | . 8, H. Her. P. S. Eur. | . 1817 |
| mōlle | . . . White | . 8, F. Ev. F. Spain | . 1752 |
| montevidēnsē | . . . Red | . 7, H. | A. Mt. Video. | . 1829 |
| Orōntīūm | . . . Flesh | . 8, H. | A. Britain | . |
| sempervirēns | . . . Pink | . 8, H. Her. P. Pyrenees | . 1821 |
| alcalūm | . . . White | . 7, H. Her. P. Sicily | . 1804 |

**ANTRŌPHȲŪM,** *Kaulfuss.* Named in reference to its native places of habitation, from *antron*, a cavern, and *phio*, to grow. *Linn.* 24, Or. 1, Nat. Or. *Polypodiaceæ.* An interesting species of fern, of easy culture. Synonyme: 1. *Hemionitis lanceolata.*

| lanceolatūm, 1 | . Brown | . 8, S. Her. P. W. Ind. | . 1793 |
|---|---|---|---|

**ANTI-SCROPHULOUS,** efficacious against scurvy, anti-scorbutic.

**ANTISEPTIC,** efficacious against putrefaction.

**ANTWERP HOLLYHOCK,** see *Althæa ficifolia.*

**ANȲCHĪA,** *Michx.* Named from its affinity to *Paronychia.* *Linn.* 5, Or. 1, Nat. Or. *Illecebraceæ.* An ornamental species; for culture, &c. see *Paronychia.* Synonyme: 1. *Queria canadensis.*

| dichōtōmā | . . . Green | . 7, H. | B. N. Amer. | . 1806 |
|---|---|---|---|---|

**AŌTŪS,** *Smith.* The ear-like appendages are wanting; hence the name from *a*, privative, and *ous*, ear. *Linn.* 10, Or. 1, Nat. Or. *Leguminosæ.* Pretty greenhouse species; for culture, &c., see *Pultenæa.*

| incanā | . . . Yellow | . 6, G. Ev. S. N. Holl. | . 1824 |
|---|---|---|---|
| villōsā | . . . Yellow | . 6, G. Ev. S. N. Holl. | . 1790 |
| ericoīdēs | . . . Yellow | . 6, G. Ev. S. N. Holl. | . 1810 |
| ferrugīnēā | . . . Yellow | . 6, G. Ev. S. N. Holl. | . 1820 |
| virgātā | . . . Yellow | . 6, G. Ev. S. N. Holl. | . |

**APARGĪA,** *Scopoli.* A name applied by the Greeks to a plant now unknown. *Linn.* 19, Or. 1, Nat. Or. *Compositæ.* Herbaceous plants, of simple culture. Synonyme: 1. *A. cichoracea.*

| aurantīacā | . . . Orange | . 6, H. Her. P. Hungary | . 1816 |
|---|---|---|---|

*alpina, aspera, caucasica, coronopifolia, crispa, crocea, dubia, fasciculata* 1, *Gouani, hastilis, hispida, hyoseroides, incana, macrorhiza, strigosa, Taraxaci, Villarsi.*

**APEĪBĀ,** *Margraav.* A name given by the natives of Brazil, to *Apeiba Tibourbou.* *Linn.* 13, Or. 1, Nat. Or. *Tiliaceæ.* Beautiful trees, with large leaves and fine yellow flowers, thriving well in loam and peat, and propagated by cuttings of the ripened wood, in sand, in heat, under a glass, carefully watered. The best way to make them flower in this country, is by ringing the large branches, and by this means checking the flow of the sap. Synonymes: 1. *A. hispida.* 2. *A. hirsuta.*

| | | | | |
|---|---|---|---|---|
| áspérá . . . | Yellow | . S. Ev. T. | Cayenne | . 1792 |
| lùria . . . | Green | . S. Ev. T. | Cayenne | . 1817 |
| Petoúmó, 1 . . | Yellow | . S. Ev. T. | S. Amer. | . 1817 |
| Tiboúrboú, 2 . | Yellow | . S. Ev. T. | S. Amer. | . 1756 |

APERIENT, possessing a slight purgative quality.

APERTUS, open, expanded.

APETALOUS, without petals.

APEX, the summit of anything.

APHANANTHÉ, *Link.* Derived from *aphanos*, obscure, and *anthos*, flower; in allusion to the flowers being destitute of beauty. *Linn.* 8, Or. 2, Nat. Or. *Amarantaceæ.* A curious species, grown in peat and loam; cuttings.

| | | | | |
|---|---|---|---|---|
| celosioídés . . . | Wht. grn. | 7, G. Ev. S. | Brazil | . 1813 |

APHANOCHILÚS, *Benth.* From *aphanos*, obscure, and *cheílos*, a lip, in reference to the obscurity of the lip of the flower. *Linn.* 14, Or. 1. Nat. Or. *Labiatæ.* An ornamental species; for culture, &c., see *Mentha.* Synonyme: 1. *Mentha blanda.*

| | | | | |
|---|---|---|---|---|
| incísùs . . . | White | . 9, H. Her. | P. Nepal | . 1824 |

APHELANDRÀ, *R. Brown.* From *apheles*, simple, and *aner*, a male; the anthers being one-celled. *Linn.* 15, Or. 2, Nat. Or. *Acanthaceæ.* This splendid stove species, to succeed well, should have a good turfy loam and peat, and be grown in proportioned sized pots, judiciously drained; when the plant is in a growing state, it should have a good supply of water at the roots, and frequently a powerful syringing on the leaves, &c. Synonymes: 1. *Ruellia cristata, Justicia pulcherrima.*

| | | | | |
|---|---|---|---|---|
| cristátá, 1 . . | Scarlet | . 8, S. Ev. S. | W. Ind. | . 1733 |

APHELEXIS, *D. Don.* From *apheles*, simple, and *exis*, habit; in reference to the habit of the species. *Linn.* 19, Or. 2, Nat. Or. *Compositæ.* Ornamental species; for culture, &c., see *Elichrysum.* Synonymes: 1. *Elichrysum ericoides.* 2. *E. fasciculatum.* 3. *E. spectabile, pinifolium.* 4. *E. sesamoides. Xeranthemum sesamoides.*

| | | | | |
|---|---|---|---|---|
| ericoídés, 1 . | White | . 6, G. Ev. S. | C. G. H. | . 1796 |
| fasciculátá, 2 . | Pur. yel. | . 7, G. Ev. S. | C. G. H. | . 1799 |
| alba . | White | . 7, G. Ev. S. | C. G. H. | . 1799 |
| rúbrá . | Red | . 7, G. Ev. S. | C. G. H. | . 1799 |
| versícólór . | Varieg. | . 7, G. Ev. S. | C. G. H. | . 1799 |
| húmílis, 3 . | Pink | . 5, G. Ev. S. | C. G. H. | . 1810 |
| sesamoídés, 4 . | Pur. wht. | . 5, G. Ev. S. | C. G. H. | . 1739 |

APHTHOUS, resembling something covered with little ulcers.

APHYLLANTHES, *Linn.* Its stems are like a rush, and bear on their summit a little tuft of flowers; hence the name from *aphyllos*, leafless, and *anthos*, flower. *Linn.* 6, Or. 1, Nat. Or. *Liliaceæ.* This pretty species delights in peat that is somewhat sandy, and increases by dividing the roots or by seeds.

| | | | | |
|---|---|---|---|---|
| monspeliénsis . | Red | . 6, F. Her. | P. France | . 1791 |

APICRA, *Willdenow.* Derived from *apikros*, not bitter; probably in allusion to the taste not being like bitter aloes. *Linn.* 6, Or. 1, Nat. Or. *Liliaceæ.* Very interesting species of succulents; for culture, &c. see *Aloe.* Synonymes: 1. *Aloe spiralis.* 2. *Apicra pseudo rigida.*

| | | | | |
|---|---|---|---|---|
| áspérá . . . | Grey | . 6, G. Ev. S. | C. G. H. | . 1795 |
| aspérúlá . . | Grey | . 6, G. Ev. S. | C. G. H. | . 1824 |
| bicarínátá . . | Grey | . 6, G. Ev. S. | C. G. H. | . 1820 |
| bullulátá . . | Grey | . 5, G. Ev. S. | C. G. H. | . |
| foliólosá . . | Grey | . 7, G. Ev. S. | C. G. H. | . 1795 |
| imbricátá, 1 . | Grey | . 6, G. Ev. S. | C. G. H. | . 1731 |
| nígrá . . | Grey | . 7, G. Ev. S. | C. G. H. | . 1823 |
| pentagóná . . | Grey | . 6, G. Ev. S. | C. G. H. | . 1731 |
| tortá . . | Grey | . 6, G. Ev. S. | C. G. H. | . 1800 |
| rígídá, 2 . . | Grey | . 6, G. Ev. S. | C. G. H. | . 1820 |
| spírális . . | Grey | . 6, G. Ev. S. | C. G. H. | . 1790 |
| spírálís . . | Grey | . 8, G. Ev. S. | C. G. H. | . 1808 |

APICULATUM, the flowers resembling a bee.

APICULATE,
APICULATED, } terminating in a little point.

APIFERA, like a bee.

APIÓS, *Boerhaave.* From *apion*, a pear; in reference to the form of the roots. *Linn.* 17, Or. 4, *Leguminosæ.* An ornamental species; for culture, &c., see *Clitoria.* The roots may be eaten with safety. Synonyme: 1. *Glycine apios.*

| | | | | |
|---|---|---|---|---|
| tuberósá . . . | Brown pak. | 8, H. Tu. | P. N. Amer. | . 1640 |

APIUM, *Linn.* Derived from the Celtic word *apon*, water; in allusion to the place where the plants grow. *Linn.* 5, Or. 2, Nat. Or. *Umbelliferæ.* The mode of cultivating these plants is so well known, that we need not mention it here.

| | | | | |
|---|---|---|---|---|
| gravéólens . . . | White | . 7, H. | B. Britain | . . |

*fractophyllum, prostratum, romanum, ternatum.*

APLECTRUM, *Nuttall.* From *a*, without, and *plektron*, a spur; the flower is spurless. *Linn.* 20, Or. 1, Nat. Or. *Orchidaceæ.* A curious little plant growing freely in sandy peat, and increased by offsets.

| | | | | |
|---|---|---|---|---|
| hiemále . . . | Brown | . H. Ter. | N. Amer. | . 1827 |

APLOPHYLLUM, *Jussieu.* From *aploos*, simple, *phyllon*, a leaf. The leaves are simple. *Linn.* 10, Or. 1, Nat. Or. *Rutaceæ.* Uninteresting species, of easy culture. Synonymes: 1. *Ruta dahurica.* 2. *R. linifolia.* 3. *R. patavina.* 4. *R. pubescens.* 5. *R. suaveolens.* 6. *R. villosa—Buxbaumii, dahurica 1, linifolium2, patavinum 3, pubescens 4, suaveolens 5, tuberculatum, villosum 6.*

APLÚDÁ, *Linn.* Derived from *apluda*, chaff; the resemblance of the involucres to chaff. *Linn.* 23, Or. 1, Nat. Or. *Gramineæ.* An uninteresting species, of the easiest cultivation. Synonyme: 1. *Andropogon involucratus—aristátá, 1.*

APOCYNUM, *Linn.* Derived from *apo*, away, and *kyon*, a dog; supposed to be mortal if eaten by dogs. *Linn.* 5, Or. 1, Nat. Or. *Apocynaceæ.* Plants of little beauty, but easy culture; *A. androsæmifolium* is acrid, and blisters the skin. The stalks of *A. cannabinum* afford the North American Indians a substitute for hemp, of which they make twine, bags, fishing-nets, and lines, also linen for their own wear.

| | | | | |
|---|---|---|---|---|
| androsæmifóliúm | Striped | . 8, H. Her. | P. N. Amer. | . 1688 |
| cannábinúm | . Yellow | . 8, H. Her. | P. N. Amer. | . 1699 |
| hypericifóliúm | . White | . 6, H. Her. | P. N. Amer. | . 1758 |
| venétúm | . White | . 6, H. Her. | P. Adriat Is. | . 1690 |

APONOGETON, *Thun.* The name is derived because of the species growing in water; from the Celtic *apon*, water, and the Greek word *geiton*, near. *Linn.* 6, Or. 3, Nat. Or. *Saururaceæ.* Interesting aquatics, succeeding well if planted in loam and peat, and placed in a tub of water. Offsets or seeds.

| | | | | |
|---|---|---|---|---|
| angustifóliúm | . White | . 7, G. Aq. P. | C. G. H. | . 1788 |
| crispúm | . White | . 8, S. Aq. P. | Ceylon | . 1820 |
| distáchyón | . White | . 5, S. Aq. P. | C. G. H. | . 1788 |
| monostáchyón | . Pink | . 9, S. Aq. P. | E. Ind. | . 1803 |

APOPHYSIS, a swelling beneath the theca of mosses.

APORUM, *Blume.* From *aporux*, a running-shoot; from the appearance of the plant. *Linn.* 20, Or. 1, Nat. Or. *Orchidaceæ.* This genus possesses little to recommend it to the lovers of this beautiful tribe. Its insignificant flowers are produced from the axils of its bright green leaves. It thrives well with the same treatment as *Vanda.* Synonyme: 1. *Dendrobium anceps.*

| | | | | |
|---|---|---|---|---|
| anceps, 1 . . | Yelsh. all | . S. Epi. | E. Ind. | . . 1826 |

APPENDAGE, that which is attached.

APPENDANT,
APPENDENT, } hanging, approaching, pendulous.

APPENDICULATE,
APPENDICULATED, } furnished with appendages.

APPENDIX, anything attached.

APPRESSED, pressed close to any thing.

APPROXIMATE,
APPROXIMATING, } near together.

APTEROUS, without the membranous margins, by botanists called wings.

AQUARTIA, *Jacq.* In honour of B. Aquart, Jacquin's companion in America. *Linn.* 4, Or. 1, Nat. Or. *Solanaceæ.* A species of little beauty, and easy culture.

| | | | | |
|---|---|---|---|---|
| tomentósá . . . | White | . . S. Ev. S. | S. Amer. | . 1819 |

AQUATIC, growing in water.

AQUILARIA, *Linn.* The wood is called *bois d'aigle*, or eagle wood, in Malacca; hence the name from *aquila*, an eagle. *Linn.* 10, Or. 2, Nat. Or. *Aquilariaceæ.* An ornamental evergreen shrub, succeeding in loam and peat, and propagated from cuttings, under a glass, in heat. Synonyme: 1. *A. ovata.*

| | | | | |
|---|---|---|---|---|
| malaccénsis . . | Wht. grn. | . 8. S. Ev. S. | Malacca | . 1823 |

AQUILEGIA, *Linn.* From *aquila*, an eagle; alluding to the form of the petal. *Linn.* 13, Or. 5, Nat. Or. *Ranunculaceæ.* The species of this ornamental genus may be grown in common soil, and increased plentifully from seeds. Synonymes: 1. *A. glan-*

*dulosa. 2. A. atropurpurea. 3. A. alpina grandi-flora. 4. A. bicolor. 5. A. vulgaris, dahurica.*

| | | | | |
|---|---|---|---|---|
| alpina | Blue | 6, H. Her. P. | Switzerl. | 1781 |
| anemonoides, 1 | Purple | 7, H. Her. P. | Altaia | 1827 |
| atropurpurea | Purple | 6, H. Her. P. | Siberia | |
|   Fischeriana, 2 | Purple | 6, H. Her. P. | Siberia | 1827 |
| canadensis | Red oran. | 6, H. Her. P. | N. Amer. | 1640 |
| davurica | Purple | 6, H. Her. P. | Davuria | 1827 |
| formosa | Red oran. | 6, H. Her. P. | Kamtsch. | 1832 |
| Garnieriana | Pur. strip. | 6, H. Her. P. | Eng. hyb. | 1829 |
| glandulosa | Wht. blue | 6, H. Her. P. | Siberia | 1822 |
|   concolor | Violet | 7, H. Her. P. | Altaia | 1822 |
| grandiflora, 3 | Blue | 6, H. Her. P. | Siberia | 1818 |
| hybrida, 4 | Purple | 6, H. Her. P. | Siberia | |
| parviflora | Purple | 6, H. Her. P. | Siberia | 1819 |
| pyrenaica | Blue | 7, H. Her. P. | Pyrenees | 1818 |
| sibirica, 5 | Blue wht. | 6, H. Her. P. | Siberia | 1806 |
| viridiflora | Grn. yel. | 6, H. Her. P. | Siberia | 1780 |
| viscosa | Purple | 6, H. Her. P. | Montpel. | 1752 |
| vulgaris | Blue | 6, H. Her. P. | Britain | |
|   corniculata | Blue wht. | 6, H. Her. P. | Europe | |
|   degener | Blue wht. | 6, H. Her. P. | Europe | |
|   inversa | Blue wht. | 6, H. Her. P. | Europe | |
|   stellata | Blue wht. | 6, H. Her. P. | Europe | |

AQUILINUS, like an eagle.

ARABIS, *Linn.* Originally from Arabia, but this name is not very precise, as the species are found in many parts of the world. *Linn.* 15, Nat. Or. *Cruciferæ.* Mostly interesting species, adapted for ornamenting rock-work; they are propagated from seeds or cuttings. Synonymes: 1. *A. cau-casica.* 2. *Turritis stricta.* 3. *A. aspera.* 4. *Tur-ritis patula.* 5. *Turritis alpina.* 6. *A bellidifolia, ciliaris.* 7. *Hesperis verna.*

| | | | | |
|---|---|---|---|---|
| albida, 1 | White | 7, H. Ev. Tr. | Caucasus | 1798 |
| alpestris | White | 7, H. Ev. B. | Switzerl. | 1819 |
| alpina | Wht. yel. | 5, H. Ev. Tr. | Switzerl. | 1596 |
|   Clusiana | White | 5, H. Ev. Tr. | Pyrenees | 1596 |
|   nana | White | 5, H. Ev. Tr. | Switzerl. | 1819 |
| ambigua | White | 7, H. B. | Siberia | 1824 |
| arenosa | Pink | 7, H. A. | Germany | 1798 |
| bellidifolia | Wht. yel. | 6, H. Her. P. | Switzerl. | 1778 |
| caerulea | Pa. blue | 6, H. Her. P. | Switzerl. | 1793 |
| ciliata, 5 | White | 6, H. B. | Ireland | |
| crispata | White | 5, H. Ev. Tr. | Carniola | 1818 |
| curtisiliqua | White | 6, H. B. | N. Eur. | 1825 |
| dasycarpa | White | 6, H. Her. P. | Podolia | 1827 |
| lasioloba | White | 6, H. B. | Mexico | 1820 |
| longifolia | White | 6, H. Ev. Tr. | Persia | 1820 |
| lucida | White | 6, H. Her. P. | Hungary | 1790 |
|   variegata | White | 6, H. Her. P. | Gardens | |
| mollis | White | 6, H. Her. Tr. | Caucasus | 1817 |
| nutans | White | 6, H. Her. P. | Switzerl. | 1658 |
| ovirensis | Pa. red | 6, H. Ev. Tr. | Carinthia | 1824 |
| petraea | White | 6, H. Ev. Tr. | Austria | 1800 |
|   hastulata | Purple | 6, H. Ev. Tr. | Britain | |
|   hispida | White | 6, H. Ev. Tr. | Scotland | |
|   praecox | | | | |
|   variegata | White | 6, H. Ev. Cr. | Gardens | |
| procurrens | White | 6, H. Ev. Tr. | Hungary | 1819 |
| pumila, 6 | White | 6, H. Ev. Tr. | Austria | 1816 |
| retrofracta | Bluish | 6, H. Her. P. | N. Amer. | 1827 |
| rosea | Rose | 2, H. Her. P. | Calabria | 1832 |
| Schivereckiana | White | 6, H. Ev. Tr. | Austria | 1826 |
| stellulata | White | 6, H. Ev. Tr. | Italy | 1817 |
| stenopetala | White | 6, H. B. | | 1818 |
| stolonifera | White | 6, H. Ev. Tr. | Carniola | 1818 |
| stricta | Cream | 5, H. Her. P. | England | |
| toxophylla | White | 7, H. B. | Volga | 1823 |
| undulata | White | 6, H. Ev. Tr. S. Eur. | | 1810 |
| verna, 7 | Purple | 5, H. A. | France | 1710 |

*Allionii 2, auriculata 3, A. dasycarpa, A. patula 4, A. recta, canadensis, cebennensis, collina, Halleri, hirsuta, incana, lævigata, lyrata, muralis, Patrini-ana, pendula, præcox, pubescens, sagittata, S. lon-gisiliqua, S. oblongata, S. ovata, subglabrata, saxa-tilis, serpyllifolia, spatulata, Thaliana, T. parviflora, Turrita, T. pendula, T. umbrosa.*

ARACHIS, *Linn.* From a, privative, and rachis, a branch; the plant bears no branches. *Linn.* 17, Or. 4, Nat. Or. *Leguminosæ Cæsalpinieæ.* This very singular plant has the property of forcing the fruit or pods as they increase in size into the earth, where they ripen their seeds, hence the trivial name earth-nut. It grows in sandy loam singly in pots, and is multiplied from offsets. In South Carolina the seed is roasted, and used as chocolate; it further affords a thin limpid oil, proper for lamps, a purpose to which it is applied in Cochin-China.

| | | | | |
|---|---|---|---|---|
| hypogaea | Yellow | 6, S. A. | S. Amer. | 1812 |

ARACHNOIDEUS, covered with capillary filaments.

ARALIA, *Linn.* A name of unknown meaning, under

which one species was sent to Fagon from Quebec in 1764, by a French physician. *Linn.* 5, Or. 5, Nat. Or. *Araliaceæ.* These fine species succeed well in common soil, and cuttings, cut off at a joint where the wood is ripe, and planted in a sheltered situation, soon strike root. *A. nudicaulis* is used in North America as a substitute for sarsa-parilla. Synonymes: 1. *Hedera aculeata.* 2. *H. arborea.* 3. *H. capitata.* 4. *Panax fragrans.* 5. *Aralia hispida.*

| | | | | |
|---|---|---|---|---|
| aculeata, 1 | White | 8. Ev. T. | Nepal | 1820 |
| arborea, 2 | Green | 8. Ev. T. | Jamaica | 1820 |
| capitata, 3 | Green | 8. Ev. S. | W. Ind. | |
| cochleata | White | 8. Ev. S. | K. Ind. | 1820 |
| digitata | White | 8. Ev. T. | E. Ind. | 1817 |
| ferruginea | White | 8. Ev. T. | Trinidad | 1826 |
| fragrans, 4 | White | 8. Ev. S. | Nepal | 1818 |
| hispida | White | 7, H. De. S. | N. Amer. | 1799 |
| micans | White | 8. Ev. T. | Trinidad | 1826 |
| macrophylla | White | G. Ev. S. | Norfolk Is. | 1831 |
| Muhlenbergiana, 5 | White | 7, H. Her. P. | N. Amer. | |
| nudicaulis | White | 7, H. Her. P. | N. Amer. | 1731 |
| pentaphylla | White | G. Ev. T. | Japan | 1810 |
| pubescens | White | G. Ev. S. | W. Ind. | 1818 |
| racemosa | White | 7, H. Her. P. | N. Amer. | 1658 |
| sambucifolia | White | 8, G. Ev. S. | N. Holl. | 1823 |
| spinosa | White | H. De. S. | Virginia | 1688 |
| umbraculifera | White | 8. Ev. P. | E. Ind. | 1819 |

ARANIFEROUS, resembling a spider.

ARAUCARIA, *Ruiz and Pavon.* Derived from arau-canos, its name in Chile. *Linn.* 22, Or. 13, Nat. Or. *Coniferæ.* This, says Sweet, may be termed the handsomest genus of plants with which we are acquainted. *A. imbricata* in particular is certainly one of the grandest plants known. It will thrive well in the open air, with the protection of a mat or two in very severe weather, and when got pretty large will no doubt be perfectly hardy. Rich open loam suits them well; and propagation may be effected in the same manner as recommended for *Altingia.*

| | | | | |
|---|---|---|---|---|
| brasiliana | Apetal | G. Ev. T. | Brazil | 1819 |
| imbricata | Apetal | G. Ev. T. | Chile | 1796 |

ARBOREUS, being a tree, as distinguished from fru-tescent.

ARBORESCENT, having a tendency to become a tree.

ARBOR-VITÆ, see *Thuja.*

ARBUTUS, *Linn.* From the Celtic arboise, austere-bush, rough fruit. *Linn.* 10, Or. 1, Nat. Or. *Eri-caceæ.* Elegant shrubs, especially *A. unedo,* which is covered with blossoms, and sometimes with fruit throughout the months of October and November. They succeed well in open loamy soil, mixed with a little sandy peat, and increased by seeds, or by budding and inarching on each other: the dwarfer kinds root readily by layers. From the flowers of *A. unedo* an agreeable wine is prepared in the island of Corsica. The fruit when taken in any quantity is narcotic. Synonyme: 1. *A. hybrida.*

| | | | | |
|---|---|---|---|---|
| Andrachne | White | 4, H. Ev. S. | Levant | 1724 |
| andrachnoides, 1 | Wht. grn. | 4, H. Ev. S. | | |
| canariensis | Wht. grn. | 6, G. Ev. S. | Canaries | 1796 |
| densiflora | White | G. Ev. T. | Mexico | 1826 |
| laurifolia | White | G. Ev. T. | Mexico | 1825 |
| Menziesii | White | H. Ev. S. | N. Amer. | 1827 |
| Milleri | | H. Ev. S. | Hybrid | 1825 |
| mucronata | White | G. Ev. Tr. | Magellan | 1828 |
| pilosa | White | 5, H. Ev. S. | Mexico | 1829 |
| phillyreaefolia | White | G. Ev. S. | Peru | 1812 |
| procera | White | H. Ev. S. | N. Amer. | 1825 |
| pumila | White | G. Ev. S. | Magellan | 1825 |
| serratifolia | Wht. grn. | | | |
| Unedo | White | 10, H. Ev. S. | Ireland | |
|   crispa | White | 10, H. Ev. S. | | |
|   integrifolia | Pink | 10, H. Ev. S. | | |
|   plena | Wht. grn. | 10, H. Ev. S. | | |
|   salicifolia | White | 10, H. Ev. S. | | |
|   schizopetala | White | 10, H. Ev. S. | | |
|   rubra | Pink | 10, H. Ev. S. | | |

ARCHANGEL, see *Lamium.*

ARCHANGELI, see *Archangelica.*

ARCHANGELICA, *Hoffman.* From arche, chief, and angelica. So named, from its supposed archangelic virtues. *Linn.* 5, Or. 2, Nat. Or. *Umbelliferæ.* Ornamental species; for culture, &c. see *Angelica.* Synonymes: 1. *Angelica atropurpurea.* 2. *A. arch-angelica.*

| | | | | |
|---|---|---|---|---|
| officinalis, 2 | Green | 7, H. B. | England | |

*Atropurpurea 1.*

E

**Arctium, Linn.** From *arktos*, a bear; in allusion to the rough bristly fruit. *Linn.* 19, Or. 1, Nat. Or. *Compositæ.* Mere weeds, of the simplest culture. The seeds of *A. Bardana* are diuretic, diaphoretic, and gently purgative. Synonymes: 1. *A. tomentosa.* 2. *A. major—Bardana* 1, *Lappa* 2, *minds.*

**Arctopus, Linn.** From *arktos*, a bear, and *pous*, a foot; alluding to the spines which beset the plant, and which have been compared to the claws of a bear. *Linn.* 23, Or. 2, Nat. Or. *Umbelliferæ.* An interesting species, which should be grown in a mixture of peat, sand, and loam, and it may be increased by dividing the plant or by seeds.

echinatus . . . Green . . 5, G. Her. P. C. G. H. . 1774

**Arctostaphylos, Adanson.** Derived from *arktos*, a bear, and *staphyle*, a grape; in allusion to the roughness of the fruit. *Linn.* 10, Or. 1, Nat. Or. *Ericaceæ.* Interesting species; for culture, &c. see *Arbutus.* Synonymes: 1. *Arbutus alpina.* 2. *A. Uva-ursi.*

alpina, 1 . . . Flesh . . 4, H. De. Tr. Scotland .
Uva-ursi, 2 . . White . . 4, H. Ev. Tr. Britain .
tomentosa . . White . . H. Ev. S. N. Amer. . 1826

**Arctotheca, Wendland.** From *arktos*, a bear, and *theke*, capsule; so named from the roughness of the fruit. *Linn.* 19, Or. 3, Nat. Or. *Compositæ.* Ornamental species, grown in turfy loam, or loam and peat, and increased by divisions. Synonyme: 1. *Arctotis scapigera.*

hirta . . . Yellow . 7, G. Her. P. C. G. H. . 1820
repens, 1 . . Yellow . 7, G. Her. P. C. G. H. . 1793

**Arctotis, Linn.** Derived from *arktos*, a bear, and *ous*, an ear; shaggy fruit. *Linn.* 19, Or. 4, Nat. Or. *Compositæ.* Showy interesting species; for culture, &c. see *Arctotheca.*

acaulis . . . Yel. red . 5, G. Her. P. C. G. H. . 1759
angustifolia . . Purple . 8, G. Her. S. C. G. H. . 1789
arborescens . . Wht. pak. 7, G. Ev. S. C. G. H. . 1818
argentea . . . Orange . 8, G. B. C. G. H. . 1774
aspera . . . Yellow . 7, G. Ev. S. C. G. H. . 1710
aureola . . . Orange . 8, G. Ev. S. C. G. H. . 1710
auriculata . . Yellow . 7, G. Ev. S. C. G. H. . 1795
bicolor . . . Wht. red . 7, G. Ev. S. C. G. H. . 1812
Cinerariа . . Yel. oran. 7, G. Her. P. C. G. H. . 1824
cuprea . . . Yel. pur. . 7, G. C. G. H. . 1823
decumbens . . Yellow . 8, G. Her. P. C. G. H. . 1790
decurrens . . Wht. red . 7, G. Ev. S. C. G. H. . 1794
elatior . . . Yel. pur. . 7, G. Ev. S. C. G. H. . 1820
fastuosa . . . Oran. red . 6, G. B. C. G. H. . 1795
flaccida . . . Wht. red . 6, G. A. C. G. H. . 1794
glabrata . . . Yel. pur. . 6, G. Ev. S. C. G. H. . 1820
glaucophylla . . Yel. pur. . 7, G. Her. P. C. G. H. . 1794
grandiflora . . Pa. yel. . 5, G. B. C. G. H. . 1774
maculata . . . Wht. oran. 6, G. Ev. S. C. G. H. . 1812
melanocicla . . Wht. pur. 6, G. Ev. S. C. G. H. . 1812
paniculata . . Wht. red . 7, G. Ev. S. C. G. H. . 1816
plantaginea . . Orange . 6, G. Her. P. C. G. H. . 1768
reptans . . . Wht. red . 7, G. Her. P. C. G. H. . 1795
revoluta . . . Yellow . 6, G. Her. P. C. G. H. . 1820
rosea . . . . Pink . . 9, G. Ev. S. C. G. H. . 1793
speciosa . . . Yellow . 6, G. Ev. S. C. G. H. . 1812
spinulosa . . . Orange . 6, G. A. C. G. H. . 1795
squarrosa . . Oran. pur. 6, G. Ev. S. C. G. H. . 1825
tricolor . . . Wht. red . 6, G. Her. P. C. G. H. . 1794
undulata . . . Orange . 6, G. Her. P. C. G. H. . 1795
virgata . . . Yellow . 7, H. A. C. G. H. . 1816

**Arcuate,** } bent like a bow, forming an arch.
**Arcuated,** }

**Arcyria, Persoon.** So called from *arkys*, a net; alluding to the net-like appearance of the fibres. *Linn.* 24, Or. 9, Nat. Or. *Fungi.* Extremely small productions, found upon rotten wood. Synonymes: 1. *Trichia denudata, flava, incarnata, leucocephala, punicea* 1.

**Ardens,** bright, glowing, burnished.

**Ardisia, Swartz.** A name derived from *ardis*, a spear-point; alluding to the acute segments of the corolla. *Linn.* 5, Or. 1, Nat. Or. *Myrsineæ.* Mostly handsome free-flowering species, of easy culture, succeeding well in a mixture of loam and peat; cuttings root freely in sand, plunged in heat, under a glass; or they may be increased from portions of the root, planted in a pot of mould leaving the points out, and plunged in a brisk bottom-heat. Synonymes 1. *Icacorea guianensis.* 2. *Ardisia crenata.* 3. *Myrsine Heberdenia.* 4. *Ardisia crenulata.* 5. *A. umbellata.* 6. *A. pyramidalis.*

acuminata, 1 . . . . 7, S. Ev. S. Guiana . . 1803
canaliculata . . . . 7, S. Ev. S. . . . 1821

canariensis . . . Red . 7, G. Ev. S. Canaries . 1820
colorata . . . Red . 7, S. Ev. S. E. Ind. . 1816
complanata . . Pink . 8, Ev. S. Penang . 1824
coriacea . . . Scarlet . 8. Ev. S. Antilles . 1824
crenulata . . . Red . 7, S. Ev. S. W. Ind. . 1809
elegans, 2 . . . Red . 8, S. Ev. S. E. Ind. . 1809
excelsa, 3 . . . Red . 7, G. Ev. T. Madeira . 1784
hymenandra . . Pink . 7, G. Ev. S. Silhet . 1828
humilis . . . Red . 7, S. Ev. S. Ceylon . 1820
lanceolata . . . Red . 7, S. Ev. S. E. Ind. . 1820
lateriflora . . . White . 8. Ev. S. W. Ind. . 1793
lentiginosa, 4 . . White all 8. Ev. S. China . 1814
littoralis, 5 . . . Red . 7, S. Ev. S. E. Ind. . 1809
macrocarpa . . Flesh . G. Ev. S. Nepal . 1824
odontophylla . . Salm. red . 7, S. Ev. S. Bengal . 1834
paniculata, 6 . . Red . 7, S. Ev. T. E. Ind. . 1818
pubescens . . . . 7, S. Ev. S. . . 1820
punctata . . . White . 7, S. Ev. S. China . 1823
pyramidalis . . Red . 7, S. Ev. T. Santa Cruz. 1818
serrulata . . . Red . 7, S. Ev. S. W. Ind. . 1821
solanacea . . . Red . 8, S. Ev. S. E. Ind. . 1798
thyrsiflora . . Pink . G. Ev. S. Nepal . 1824
tenuifolia . . . Red . 7, S. Ev. T. W. Ind. . 1820

**Arduina, Linn.** In honour of Pietro Arduini, curator of the economical garden of Padua. *Linn.* 5, Or. 1, Nat. Or. *Apocynaceæ.* This pretty species may be treated as recommended for *Carissa.*

bispinosa . . . White . 6, G. Ev. S. C. G. H. . 1760

**Areca, Linn.** When an old tree, it is called in Malabar *areec*, when quite young, *Perynga.* *Linn.* 21, Or. 10, Nat. Or. *Palmaceæ.* This most beautiful genus of palms succeeds best in light sandy loam, and can be increased only from seeds. The well-known Betel Nut is the fruit of *A. Catechu*, and remarkable for its narcotic or intoxicating power; from the fruit is prepared a kind of spurious *Catechu.* Ainslie, 1—65. It seems to me, however, doubtful whether the intoxicating effect of the Betel Nut, which is cut in slices, folded in the aromatic leaves of the Betel pepper Nut (Piper Betel), and chewed in the mouth like tobacco, is not owing to the Piper leaf, in which it is wrapped when eaten, rather than to any special property of its own.—*Lindley's Introd. to the Nat. Syst.,* 2nd Edit.

Catechu . . . White . . Palm. E. Ind. . 1690
crinita . . . . White . . Palm. S. France . 1824
exilis . . . . . Palm. W. Ind. . 1823
humilis . . . White . Palm. E. Ind. . 1814
lutescens . . . White . Palm I. France . 1824
Manicot . . . . Palm. S. Amer. . 1822
montana . . . . Palm. S. Amer. . 1820
oleracea . . . White . Palm. W. Ind. . 1656
rubra . . . . Palm. Maurit. . 1823
triandra . . . . Palm. E. Ind. . 1825

**Aremonia, Decandolle.** Said to be altered from *Agrimonia.* *Linn.* 8, Or. 2, Nat. Or. *Rosaceæ.* Merely ornamental; for culture, &c. see *Agrimonia.* Synonyme: 1. *Agrimonia agrimonoides.*

agrimonoides . Yellow . 7, H. Her. P. Italy . . 1739

**Arenaria,** growing among sand.

**Arenaria, Linn.** From *arena*, sand; referring to the sandy situation in which most of the species are found. *Linn.* 10, Or. 3, Nat. Or. *Alsinaceæ.* Diminutive plants, of the easiest culture. Synonymes: 1. *A. Villarsii.* 2. *A. macrocarpa.* 3. *A. sibirica.* 4. *A. fastigiata.* 5. *A. liniflora.* 6. *A. filifolia.* 7. *A. glaberrima.* 8. *A. marginata.* 9. *A. marina.* 10. *A. androsacea.* 11. *A. cherlerifolia.* 12. *A. heteromalla.* 13. *A. pungens.* 14. *A. viscosa.*

austriaca, 1 . . White . . 7, H. Her. P. Austria . 1793
balearica . . . White . . 7, H. Ev. Tr. Majorca . 1787
breviscaule . . White . . 7, H. Her. P. Alp. Eur. . 1823
cæspitosa . . . White . . 7, H. Her. P. Switzerl. . 1826
calycina . . . White . . 7, H. . A. Barbary . 1816
calyculata . . White . . 7, H. Her. P. Hungary . 1817
canadensis . . Red . . 7, H. . A. N. Amer. . 1812
cæsdcana, 2 . . White . . 7, H. Her. P. . . 1817
capillacea . . White . . 7, H. . A. Piedmont . 1819
capillaris, 3 . . White . . 7, H. Her. P. Siberia . 1820
cherlerioides . . White . . 7, H. Her. P. France .
ciliata . . . . White . . 6, H. Her. P. Ireland .
coimbricensis . . White . . 7, H. . A. Portugal . 1817
dahurica . . . White . . 7, H. Her. P. Dahuria . 1824
densa . . . . White . . 7, H. Her. P. Hungary . 1824
fasciculata, 4 . . White . . 7, H. . A. Scotland .
filifolia . . . White . . 7, H. Her. P. Arabia .
formosa . . . White . . 6, H. Her. P. Dahuria . 1824
Gerardi, 5 . . White . . 6, H. Her. P. France . 1822
glandulosa . . Purple . 6, H. . A. Europe . 1820
glomerata . . White . . 7, H. . A. Tauria . 1818

| | | | | | |
|---|---|---|---|---|---|
| graminifolia, 6 | White | 7, H. Her. P. | Siberia | . 1817 | |
| glaberrima, 7 | White | 7, H. Her. P. | Caucasus | . 1816 | |
| grandiflora | White | 7, H. Her. P. | Switzerl. | 1783 | |
| Halmii | White | 7, H. Her. P. | Siberia | . 1826 | |
| hirsuta | White | 7, H. Her. P. | Caucasus | . 1820 | |
| imbricata | White | 7, H. Her. P. | Caucasus | . 1820 | |
| juniperina | White | 7, H. Her. P. | Siberia | . 1800 | |
| lanceolata | White | 6, H. Her. P. | Switzerl. | . 1823 | |
| laricifolia | White | 8, H. Her. P. | Britain | | |
| longifolia | White | 7, H. Her. P. | Siberia | . 1823 | |
| macrocarpa | White | 7, H. Her. P. | N. Amer. | . 1810 | |
| marina, 8 | Purple | 7, H. Her. P. | Germany | . 1793 | |
| marginata | White | 7, H. De. Tr. | Caucasus | . 1818 | |
| mediterranea | White | 6, H. A. | Mediterr. | . 1843 | |
| montana | White | 6, H. Her. P. | France | . 1800 | |
| multicaulis | White | 7, H. Her. P. | Europe | . 1814 | |
| nardifolia | White | 7, H. Her. P. | Siberia | . 1827 | |
| otitoidea, 10 | White | 7, H. Her. P. | Siberia | . 1820 | |
| pendula | White | 7, H. Her. P. | Hungary | . 1816 | |
| peploides | White | 6, H. Ev. Cr. | Britain | | |
| pinifolia | White | 7, H. Her. P. | Caucasus | . 1823 | |
| polygonoides | Red | 7, H. Her. P. | Switzerl. | 1822 | |
| procera | White | 7, H. Her. P. | Siberia | . 1820 | |
| procumbens | Purple | 7, F. De. Tr. | Egypt | . 1801 | |
| pubescens | White | 7, H. Her. P. | Archipel. | . 1820 | |
| purpurea | White | 7, H. | A. Spain | . 1823 | |
| ramosissima | White | 7, H. | B. Hungary | . 1816 | |
| recurva | White | 7, H. Her. P. | Alps | . 1822 | |
| rigida | White | 7, H. Her. P. | Siberia | . 1823 | |
| rostrata | White | 8, H. Her. P. | Hungary | . 1816 | |
| rubra | Purple | 7, H. | A. Britain | | |
| rubella, 11 | Red | 7, H. Her. P. | Scotland | | |
| anlina | Purple | 7, H. | A. Bohemia | . 1820 | |
| saxatilis | White | 7, H. Her. P. | Germany | . 1732 | |
| scabra | White | 7, H. Her. P. | Alp. Eur. | . 1822 | |
| setacea, 12 | White | 7, H. Her. P. | France | | |
| striata | White | 7, H. Her. P. | Switzerl. | 1683 | |
| stricta | White | 7, H. Her. P. | N. Amer. | . 1812 | |
| subulata, 13 | White | 6, H. Her. P. | Caucasus | . 1822 | |
| tenuifolia | White | 7, H. | A. England | | |
| Barrelieri | White | 7, H. | A. S. France | 1820 | |
| hybrida | White | 7, H. | A. S. France | 1827 | |
| viscidula, 14 | White | 7, H. | A. France | . 1818 | |
| tetraquetra | White | 8, H. Her. P. | Pyrenees | . 1731 | |
| triflora | White | 7, H. Her. P. | S. Eur. | . 1816 | |
| triandra | White | 7, H. | A. | . 1817 | |
| trinervis | White | 6, H. | A. Britain | | |
| verna | White | 7, H. Her. P. | Britain | | |
| verticillata | White | 7, H. Her. P. | Armenia | . 1823 | |
| uliginosa | White | 7, H. Her. P. | Switzerl. | 1819 | |

*Media*, 9, *serpyllifolia*.

AREOLÆ, little spaces or areas on the surface of anything; the spaces between the cracks in the lichens are the areolæ.

ARETHUSA, *Swartz*. A nymph of Diana's, who was changed into a fountain; applied to this genus on account of the habit of the plants. *Linn.* 20, Or. 1, Nat. Or. *Orchidaceæ*. The species of this genus are handsome, especially *A. bulbosa*, which has a large fine lilac flower terminating each stem; it requires to be kept in the greenhouse, and to be grown in a peaty soil, very moist, with the pots well drained. *A. plicata* does not require to be kept quite so moist.

| | | | | | |
|---|---|---|---|---|---|
| bulbosa | Wht. ro. | 6, G. Ter. | Carolina | | |
| plicata | | 7, S. Ter. | E. Ind. | . 1806 | |

ARETIA, *Willdenow*. Called after Benoit Aretius, a Swiss, professor in the university of Berne. *Linn.* 5, Or. 1, Nat. Or. *Primulaceæ*. Minute interesting species, growing best on rock-work or in pots. Sandy loam and peat suit them, and they are multiplied by dividing the roots. *Synonyme:* 1. *Androsace aretia*.

| | | | | | |
|---|---|---|---|---|---|
| alpina | Pink | 6, H. Her. P. | Switzerl. | 1775 | |
| argentea | White | 6, F. Her. P. | Switzerl. | 1826 | |
| helvetica, 1 | White | 6, H. Her. P. | Switzerl. | 1775 | |
| pubescens | White | 6, H. Her. P. | Switzerl. | 1824 | |
| Vitaliana | Yellow | 6, H. Her. P. | Pyrenees | . 1787 | |

ARGANIA, *Schousb*. From *argam*, its aboriginal name. *Linn.* 5, Or. 1, Nat. Or. *Sapotaceæ*. A very fine tree, succeeding in common soil, and increased freely by layers or cuttings. The wood is so close and hard, as to sink in water. *Synonymes:* 1. *Sideroxylon spinosum*, *Elæodendron argania*.

| | | | | | |
|---|---|---|---|---|---|
| sideroxylon, 1 | Grn. yel. | 7, S. Ev. T. | Morocco | . 1711 | |

ARGEMONE, *Tournefort*. Named from its supposed medicinal qualities; from *argema*, cataract of the eye. *Linn.* 13, Or. 1, Nat. Or. *Papaveraceæ*. Very interesting dwarf species, succeeding well in common soil, and increased by suckers. *Synonyme:* 1. *intermedia*.

[ 27 ]

| | | | | | |
|---|---|---|---|---|---|
| albiflora | White | 7, H. | A. Mexico | . 1821 | |
| Barclaiana, 1 | Cream | 6, F. Her. P. | Mexico | . 1827 | |
| grandiflora | White | 7, H. Her. P. | Mexico | . 1827 | |
| mexicana | Yellow | 7, H. | A. Mexico | . 1592 | |
| ochroleuca | Sulphur | 7, H. | A. Mexico | . 1827 | |

ARGOLASIA, *Jussieu*. Named from *argos*, white, and *lasios*, woolly; in reference to the calyx being white and velvety on the outside. *Linn.* 6, Or. 1, Nat. Or. *Hæmodoraceæ*. An ornamental species; for culture, &c., see *Lophiola*. *Synonyme:* 1. *Lanaria plumosa*.

| | | | | | |
|---|---|---|---|---|---|
| plumosa | White | G. Her. P. C. G. H. | | . 1787 | |

ARGYREIA, *Loureiro*. Named in reference to the white silvery texture of the leaves; from *argyreios*, silvery. *Linn.* 5, Or. 1, Nat. Or. *Convolvulaceæ*. A very fine genus of extensive growing climbers, requiring a good deal of time and pot-room before they flower. *A. cuneifolia* is dwarf, and produces an abundance of elegant flowers: light rich soil, or sandy loam and peat mixed, suit them well; cuttings in the same kind of soil, under a glass, root freely. *Synonymes:* 1. *Lettsomia bona-nox*. 2. *L. cuneata*. 3. *L. cymosa*. 4. *L. ornata*. 5. *L. pomacea*. 6. *Ipomæa speciosa*, *Lettsomia nervosa*. 7. *L. splendens*. 8. *L. uniflora*.

| | | | | | |
|---|---|---|---|---|---|
| bona-nox, 1 | White | 8. Ev. Tu. | E. Ind. | . 1799 | |
| cuneata, 2 | Purple | 8. 8. Ev. Tu. | E. Ind. | . 1822 | |
| cymosa, 3 | Pink | 8. Ev. Tu. | E. Ind. | . 1823 | |
| ornata, 4 | White | 8. Ev. Tu. | E. Ind. | . 1824 | |
| pomacea, 5 | Pink | 8. Ev. Tu. | E. Ind. | . 1818 | |
| speciosa, 6 | Red | 7, 8. Ev. Tu. | E. Ind. | . 1818 | |
| splendens, 7 | Pink | 8. Ev. Tu. | E. Ind. | . 1820 | |
| uniflora, 8 | White | 8. Ev. Tu. | E. Ind. | . 1817 | |

ARIDITY, dryness.

ARIETINUM, resembling a ram's head.

ARIL, } a process of the placenta adhering to the
ARILLUS, } hilum of seeds; a peculiar substance covering the seeds.

ARILLATE, having that peculiar appendage called arillus. A term only applied to seeds.

ARISTATE, } having a beard or awn, as the glume of
ARISTATED, } barley.

ARISARUM, *Tournefort*. A Greek word. *Linn.* 21, Or. 9, Nat. Or. *Araceæ*. A curious plant, of little interest, and easily grown in sandy loam, with a little peat. *Synonyme:* 1. *Arum arisarum*.

| | | | | | |
|---|---|---|---|---|---|
| vulgare, 1 | Lgt. yel. | 5, F. Her. P. | S. Eur. | . 1596 | |

ARISTEA, *Ker*. Named in reference to the bearded leaves, from *arista*, a point, or beard. *Linn.* 3, Or. 1, Nat. Or. *Iridaceæ*. A pretty genus, thriving well in loam and peat, and increased by seeds or divisions. *A. capitata* should be planted in peat.

| | | | | | |
|---|---|---|---|---|---|
| capitata | Blue | 7, G. Her. P. C. G. H. | | . 1790 | |
| cyanea | Blue | 6, G. Her. P. C. G. H. | | . 1759 | |
| melaleuca | Pa. blue | 6, G. Her. P. C. G. H. | | . 1796 | |
| pusilla | Blue | 7, G. Her. P. C. G. H. | | . 1806 | |
| spiralis | Pa. blue | 5, G. Her. P. C. G. H. | | . 1795 | |

ARISTIDA, *Linn*. Derived from *arista*, an ear of corn. *Linn.* 3, Or. 2, Nat. Or. *Gramineæ*. These plants are not worth cultivating.

| | | | | | |
|---|---|---|---|---|---|
| stipoides | Apetal | 6, Grass. | N. Holl. | . 1826 | |
| vagans | Apetal | 6, Grass. | N. Holl. | . 1816 | |

ARISTOLOCHIA, *Linn*. So named from *aristos*, best, and *locheia*, parturition; its supposed medical qualities. *Linn.* 20, Or. 3, Nat. Or. *Aristolochiaceæ*. This is a remarkable genus, the flowers having more or less the appearance of a horn. The most suitable compost is a mixture of sandy loam and peat, with a very little well-decomposed dung. Cuttings root readily in sand, under a glass in heat. *Synonymes:* 1. *A. ringens*. 2. *A. trilobata*.

| | | | | | |
|---|---|---|---|---|---|
| acuminata | Purple | 8. Ev. Cl. | Maurit. | . 1822 | |
| arborescens | Yel. pur. | 7, G. Ev. S. | America | . 1737 | |
| Arkana | Purple | 7, H. De. Cl. | Arkansas | . 1824 | |
| barbata | Purple | 8. Ev. Cl. | Caraccas | . 1796 | |
| bilobata | Purple | 8. Ev. Cl. | | . 1824 | |
| bætica | Purple | 6, H. De. Cl. | Spain | . 1596 | |
| bracteata | Purple | 7, 8. Ev. Tr. | E. Ind. | . 1793 | |
| brasiliensis, 1 | Yellow | 8. Ev. Cl. | Brasil | . 1830 | |
| caudata | Lurid | 6, 8. De. Tu. | Brasil | . 1828 | |
| chilensis | Pur. grn. | 9, F. De. Cl. | W. Ind. | . 1832 | |
| fœtens | Pur. yel. | 6, 8. Ev. Cl. | W. Ind. | . 1832 | |
| Clematitis | Yellow | 7, H. Her. P. | Britain | | |
| cymbifera | Purple | 8. Ev. Cl. | St. Paul. | . 1829 | |
| fœtida | | 7, 8. Ev. Cl. | Mexico | . 1822 | |
| glauca | Purple | 7, G. Ev. Cl. | Barbary | . 1785 | |
| grandiflora | | 8. Ev. Cl. | Jamaica | . 1824 | |

| hastātā | . . . | . | . | 7, S. Ev. Cl. Cuba | . | 1822 |
| hirtā | . . . | . Purple | . | 6, G. Her. P. Chio | . | 1759 |
| indīcā | . . . | . Purple | . | 7, S. Ev. Cl. E. Ind. | . | 1780 |
| labiōsā | . . . | . Pur. grn. yl. | 7, | H. De. Tr. S. Eur. | . | 1548 |
| lōngā | . . . | . Purple | . | 7, S. Ev. Cl. N. Spain | . | 1759 |
| māximā | . . . | . Purple | . | 7, S. Ev. Cl. Jamaica | . | 1737 |
| odoratissimā | . . | . Purple | . | H. Her. P. Italy | . | 1640 |
| pallīdā | . . | . Wht. pur. | . | 8, S. Ev. Cl. Caraccas | . | 1823 |
| panduriformis | . | . | . | 8, S. Ev. Cl. Caraccas | . | 1823 |
| Pistolōchiā | . | . Purple | . | H. De. Tr. S. Eur. | . | 1597 |
| ringēns | . | . Pur. grn. yl. | 7, S. Ev. Cl. Brazil | . | 1820 |
| rotūndā | . | . Drk. pur. | 7, G. Her. P. S. Eur. | . | 1596 |
| saccātā | . | . Purpah. red | 9, S. Ev. Tu. Silhet | . | 1829 |
| sagittātā | . | . Purple | . | 7, H. Her. P. N. Amer. | . | 1819 |
| sempērvirēns | . | . Purple | . | 6, G. Ev. Tr. Candia | . | 1727 |
| Serpentāriā | . | . Drk. pur. | 7, H. De. Tr. N. Amer. | . | 1632 |
| Siphō | . . . | . Yel. brn. | 7, H. De. Cl. N. Amer. | . | 1763 |
| surinamēnsis, 2 | . | . Yellow | . | 8, S. Ev. Cl. Surinam | . | 1823 |
| tomentōsā | . | . Purple | . | 7, H. De. Cl. N. Amer. | . | 1799 |
| trifīdā | . | . Green | . | 8, S. De. Tu. Caraccas | . |  |
| trilobātā | . | . Purple | . | 6, S. Ev. Cl. S. Amer. | . | 1775 |

**ARISTOTĒLIA,** *Willdenow.* In memory of the celebrated Aristotle. *Linn.* 11, Or. 1, Nat. Or. *Philadelphaceæ.* This as a shrub is showy, but its flowers have little beauty. In a warm situation it grows freely, in common soil, and ripened cuttings soon take, as do also layers. It produces a berry.

| Mācqui | . . . | . Wht. grn. | 5, H. Ev. S. Chile | . | 1785 |
| variegātā | . . | . Wht. grn. | 5, F. Ev. S. Gardens | . |  |

**ARMENĪACA,** *Tournefort.* Named from the apricot being originally from *Armenia. Linn.* 12, Or. 1, Nat. Or. *Amygdaleæ.* A genus of valuable fruit trees, as is at once apparent from its containing the well-known apricot. The species all thrive well in a rich loamy soil, and are best increased by budding on kind free-growing plum stocks. *A. vulgaris,* or common apricot, produces a round, yellow, firmish-fleshed fruit, little less esteemed than the peach or nectarine; it is used fresh from the tree at the dessert, and is also made into jellies, preserves, &c.; from the clarified juice the Chinese make lozenges, which, dissolved by water, yield a grateful beverage; the nut yields a kind of oil, and the young shoots a fine golden colour to wool. *Synonymes:* 1. *Prunus brigantiaca.* 2. *P. dasycarpa.* 3. *P. sibirica.* 4. *P. armeniaca.*

| brigantiāca, 1 | . | . Pink | . | 4, H. De. S. S. Eur. | . | 1819 |
| dasycārpa, 2 | . | . White | . | 4, H. De. T. | . | 1800 |
| persicifōlia | . | . Pink | . | 4, H. De. T. | . | 1800 |
| sibīrica, 3 | . | . Pink | . | 4, H. De. S. Siberia | . | 1788 |
| vulgāris, 4 | . | . White | . | 4, H. De. T. Levant | . | 1548 |
| cordifōlia | . | . White | . | 8, H. De. T. Levant | . | 1548 |
| ovalifōlia | . | . White | . | 8, H. De. T. Levant | . | 1548 |

**ARMĒRIA,** *Willdenow. Armeria* is the Latin name of Sweetwilliam. *Linn.* 5, Or. 5, Nat. Or. *Plumbaginaceæ.* These plants though dwarf are handsome, and well adapted for ornamenting rock-work; they may also be grown in pots, in sandy, open, rich soil. *A. vulgaris,* or common thrift, is considered next to box the most valuable for edging walks, borders, &c. *Synonyme:* 1. *Statice armeria.*

| alliāceā | . . | . White | . | 6, H. Her. P. Spain | . | 1798 |
| alpīnā | . . | . Purple | . | 7, H. Her. P. Carinthia | . |  |
| arenāriā | . | . Pink | . | 6, H. Her. P. France | . |  |
| cephalōtis | . | . Pink | . | 6, H. Her. P. Europe | . | 1800 |
| denticulātā | . | . Flesh | . | 6, H. Her. P. Naples | . | 1816 |
| dianthoīdēs | . | . Pink | . | 6, H. Her. P. Europe | . | 1810 |
| fasciculātā | . | . Purple | . | 7, G. Ev. S. Portugal | . |  |
| hīrta | . . | . Pink | . | 6, H. Her. P. N. Africa | . | 1820 |
| hūmilis | . | . Pink | . | 6, H. Her. P. S. Eur. | . | 1817 |
| juniperifōlia | . | . Pink | . | 6, H. Her. P. Spain | . | 1818 |
| latifōlia | . | . Lgt. red | 7, H. Her. P. Algarbia | . | 1740 |
| littorālis | . | . Pink | . | 7, H. Her. P. S. Eur. | . |  |
| maritīma, 1 | . | . Red | . | 7, H. Her. P. Britain | . |  |
| montāna | . | . Pink | . | 6, H. Her. P. Scotland | . |  |
| pinifōlia | . | . Pink | . | 6, H. Her. P. Portugal | . |  |
| plantaginea | . | . Red | . | 6, H. Her. P. S. Eur. | . | 1818 |
| pūngens | . | . Pink | . | 6, H. Her. P. Spain | . | 1818 |
| scorzonerafōlia | . | . Scarlet | 6, H. Her. P. S. Eur. | . | 1816 |
| vulgāris | . | . Red | . | 7, H. Her. P. Europe | . |  |

**ARMILLĀRIS,** like a bracelet.

**ĀRNICĀ,** *Linnæus.* Derived from *arnakis,* a lamb's skin, because of the likeness of the leaves. *Linn.* 19, Or. 2, Nat. Or. *Compositæ.* The species are dwarf and interesting. *A. montana* is a powerful sternutatory, and has besides many and important medicinal properties. *Synonyme:* 1. *A. montana.*

| Clūsii | . . | . Yellow | . | 7, H. Her. P. Switzerl. | . | 1819 |
| cordāta | . | . Yellow | . | 7, H. Her. P. Switzerl. | . | 1819 |
| cōrsica | . | . Yellow | . | 7, H. Her. P. Corsica | . | 1824 |
| Doronicum | . | . Yellow | . | 7, H. Her. P. Austria | . | 1816 |

| glaciālis | . . | . Yellow | . | 7, H. Her. P. Switzerl. | . | 1823 |
| helvetica, 1 | . | . Yellow | . | 7, H. Her. P. Switzerl. | . | 1819 |
| laxigāra | . | . Yellow | . | 7, H. Her. P. Italy | . | 1827 |
| montāna | . | . Yellow | . | 7, H. Her. P. Europe | . | 1731 |
| scorpioīdēs | . | . Yellow | . | 7, H. Her. P. Austria | . | 1710 |

**ARNOPŌGŌN,** *Willdenow.* Taken from *arnos,* lamb, and *pogon,* beard; in allusion to the bearded seeds. *Linn.* 19, Or. 1, Nat. Or. *Compositæ.* These are pretty flowering plants, and easily cultivated; the seed merely requires sowing in the border, and treating as other annuals. *Synonymes:* 1. *Urospermum capense.* 2. *U. Dalechampii.*

| āspēr | . . . | . Yellow | . | 7, H. | . | A. Montpel. | . 1774 |
| capēnsis, 1 | . | . Yellow | . | 7, H. | . | B. C. G. H. | . 1816 |
| Dalechāmpii, 2 | . | . Lgt. yel. | 7, H. Her. P. S. Eur. | . | 1739 |
| picroīdēs | . | . Yellow | . | 7, H. | . | A. S. Eur. | . 1683 |

**ARRACĀCHA,** *Bancroft.* The name given to the plant by the Spaniards in South America. *Linn.* 5, Or. 2, Nat. Or. *Umbelliferæ.* Perennial South American herbs of a salubrious quality, extensively cultivated for culinary purposes, and propagated by planting pieces of the root, in each of which is an eye or shoot. *Synonyme:* 1. *Conium arracacha.*

| esculēnta, 1 | . | . Brash | . | 7, S. Tu. P. Santa Fe. | . | 1823 |

**ARŌMĀ,** the spicy quality of a thing.

**ARRHENATHĒRUM,** *Palisot de Beauvois.* Derived from *arrhen,* male, and *ather,* a point; the male spikes being furnished with awns. *Linn.* 23, Or. 1, Nat. Or. *Gramineæ.* Species of grass, of great use, though but little beauty; cultivation easy. *Synonymes:* 1. *Holcus avenaceus, Avena elatior.* 2. *Holcus bulbosus, Avena bulbosa.*

| avenācēum, 1 | . | . Apetal | . | 6, Grass. Britain | . |  |
| mūticum | . | . Apetal | . | 7, Grass. Scotland | . |  |
| bulbōsum, 2 | . | . Apetal | . | 7, Grass. Germany | . |  |

**ARRŌSUS,** gnawed, bitten.

**ARROW-GRASS,** see *Triglochin.*

**ARROW-HEAD,** see *Sagittaria.*

**ARROW-ROOT,** see *Maranta.*

**ARTĀBŌTRYS,** *R. Brown.* This name was suggested by the curious tendril belonging to the peduncle, by which the growing fruit is suspended on the nearest support; from *aratao,* to suspend, *botrys,* grapes. *Linn.* 13, Or. 6, Nat. Or. *Anonaceæ.* This species is very ornamental, growing about six feet high, and is easily cultivated in sandy loam, mixed with a little peat, and propagated from ripened cuttings in sand, under a glass. *Synonyme:* 1. *A. hexapetala.*

| odoratissimā | . | . Brown | . | 7, S. Ev. S. China | . | 1758 |

**ARTANĒMĀ,** *D. Don.* A tooth is borne on one side of each of the longer filaments; whence the name, from *aratao,* to support, *nema,* a filament. *Linn.* 14, Or. 1, Nat. Or. *Scrophulariaceæ.* This is an interesting plant, with the aspect of a mimulus, producing large showy blossoms. It has been treated in the greenhouse, but will succeed in the open border in summer, in loam and peat; seeds. *Synonymes:* 1. *Torenia scabra.*

| fimbriātum | . | . Pa. blue | 8, G. Ev. S. Moreton B. | 1830 |

**ARTĒDIA,** *Linnæus.* In honour of Peter Artedi, a Swedish naturalist, one of the first who attempted to divide umbelliferous plants into genera. *Linn.* 5, Or. 2, Nat. Or. *Umbelliferæ.* An uninteresting species, of the simplest culture—*squamata.*

**ARTEMISIA,** *Linnæus.* Artemis, one of the names of Diana; the plant is said to have been named after Diana, on account of its being used in bringing on precocious puberty. *Linn.* 19, Or. 1, Nat. Or. *Compositæ.* Some species of this genus are pretty, others merely ornamental, while some are wholly uninteresting; their silvery leaves have a showy effect in rock-work, for which places they are well suited; they grow in almost any soil, and are increased readily from divisions, cuttings, and seeds. *A. chinensis,* and some other species, yield the moxa of China, a substance used as a cautery, by burning it upon parts affected with gout and rheumatism. In India *A. indica* is considered a powerful deobstruent and antispasmodic; and the leaves of *A. maderaspatana* are esteemed a valuable stomachic medicine. *Synonymes:* 1. *A. caucasica.* 2. *A. leucanthemifolia.* 3. *A. nutans, cernua.* 4. *A. rupestris.* 5. *A. Redowskii.* 6. *A. inodora.* 7. *A. glacialis, rupestris.* 8. *A. rupestris.* 9. *A. splendens.*

| | | | | |
|---|---|---|---|---|
| Abrŏtănŭm | Yel. grn. | 8, H. De. | S. Europe | 1548 |
| áfrá | White | 8, G. Ev. | S. | |
| alpïnă, 1 | Yel. grn. | 7, H. Her. | P. Caucasus | 1804 |
| arborěscěns | | 7, H. Ev. | S. Levant | 1640 |
| argěntěă | Yel. grn. | 6, G. Ev. | S. Madeira | 1777 |
| aŭstrïăcă | Brown | 9, H. Her. | P. Austria | 1597 |
| cærŭlěscěns | Yellow | 9, H. Ev. | S. England | |
| chïněnsis | Yellow | 7, G. Her. | P. China | 1818 |
| Drăcŭncŭlŭs | Wht. grn. | 7, H. Her. | P. S. Eur. | 1548 |
| frïgïdă | Yel. grn. | 8, H. Her. | P. Siberia | 1826 |
| furcătă | Yel. grn. | 7, H. Her. | P. Siberia | 1820 |
| găllïcă | Brown | 8, H. Her. | P. Britain | |
| glăcïălis | Yel. grn. | 7, H. Her. | P. Switzerl. | 1739 |
| glaŭcă | Green | 7, H. Her. | P. Siberia | 1806 |
| grœnländïcă | Yel. grn. | 7, H. Her. | P. Greenland | 1810 |
| helvětïcă | Yel. grn. | 7, H. Her. | P. Switzerl. | 1819 |
| indïcă | Yel. grn. | 9, H. Her. | P. E. Ind. | 1796 |
| Jŭdăïcă | Yellow | 8, F. Ev. | S. | 1774 |
| lactïflŏră | Pa. wht. | 11, G. Her. | S. Nepal | 1823 |
| lednïcěnsis | Yellow | 7, H. De. | S. Carpat. | 1826 |
| marïtïmă | Brown | 7, H. Her. | P. Britain | |
| Marschallïănă, 6 | Yellow | 7, H. Her. | P. Caucas. | 1816 |
| Mŏxă | Yellow | 10, G. Ev. | S. China | |
| Mŭtěllïnă, 7 | Yellow | 7, H. Her. | P. Alp. Eur. | 1815 |
| nïvěă | Green | 6, H. Her. | P. Siberia | 1815 |
| norvěgïcă, 8 | Yellow | 7, H. Her. | P. Norway | 1818 |
| orïěntălis | Yel. grn. | 7, H. Her. | P. Armenia | 1810 |
| Pallăsĭĭ | Yel. grn. | 7, H. Her. | P. Siberia | 1820 |
| palmătă | Green | 6, F. Ev. | S. Siberia | |
| pěctïnătă | Brown | 6, H. | A. Dauria | 1806 |
| pědŭncŭlăria, 9 | Yellow | 7, H. Her. | P. Caucasus | 1818 |
| pŏntïcă | Yellow | 9, H. Her. | P. Austria | 1570 |
| pŏtěntillæfŏliă | | 7, H. Her. | P. Siberia | 1818 |
| rămŏsă | | G. Ev. | S. Canaries | 1816 |
| rěpěns | Brown | 6, H. Her. | Tr. Tartary | 1805 |
| rŭpěstris | Brown | 8, H. Her. | P. Siberia | 1748 |
| sălïnă | Wht. grn. | 8, H. Her. | P. Hungary | 1823 |
| Santŏnïcă | Wht. grn. | 9, H. Ev. | S. Siberia | 1596 |
| saxătïlis | Brown | 7, H. Her. | P. Hungary | |
| scŏpărïă | Wht. grn. | 8, H. | A. Hungary | 1796 |
| sěrïcěă | White | 6, H. Her. | P. Siberia | 1796 |
| spïcătă | Brown | 6, H. Her. | P. Switzerl. | 1790 |
| taŭrïcă | Wht. grn. | 7, H. Her. | P. Tauria | 1818 |
| těnŭifŏliă | Yel. grn. | 10, G. Ev. | S. China | 1732 |
| valěntïnă | Yel. grn. | 7, F. Ev. | S. Spain | 1739 |
| vallěsïăcă | Lgt. yel. | 7, G. Ev. | S. Italy | 1739 |
| Wŭlfěnĭĭ | Yel. grn. | 7, H. Her. | P. Switzerl. | 1819 |

*Absinthïŭm, albïda, ambïgua, anethïfŏliă, annua, armeniaca, arragŏněnsis, Balsamïta, biennis, camphorătă, campestris, c. alpina, cănă, canaděnsis, caněscěns, caucăsïcă, caudătă, chamæmelïfŏliă, coarctătă, crïthmïfŏliă, desertŏrŭm 2, dracunculŏïděs 3, fascïculătă, frăgrăns, gnaphalïoïděs, herbăcěă, hirsŭtă, hispănïcă, hŭmïlis 4, inclsa, incŭltă, inodŏră 5, insïpïdă, integrïfŏliă, Japŏnïcă, lacinïătă, longïfŏliă, mexïcănă, mollïssïmă, monogўnă, monteviděnsis, neglěctă, nŭtans, odŏratïssïmă, palŭstris, parvïflŏră, paucïflŏră, prŏcěră, prŏcŭmběns, serrătă, Sieversïănă, subcaněscěns, tanacetïfŏliă, viridïfŏliă, vulgăris.*

**Arthōnïă.** The meaning unexplained. Linn. 24, Or. 8, Nat. Or. Lichenes. Curious species, growing from a quarter of a foot to three feet high, and found chiefly on the bark of old trees.—*Astrŏïděă, impŏlītă, ignēă, obscŭră, Swartzïănă.*

**Arthraïtïcŭs,** gouty, swollen.

**Arthrŏpŏdïŭm,** R. Brown. Derived from arthron, a joint, and pous, a foot; the foot-stalks of the flowers being jointed. Linn. 6, Or. 1, Nat. Or. Liliaceæ. Some species of this genus are very pretty, viz. *A. minus* and *fimbriatum*; others are ornamental; and the whole succeed in sandy loam and peat, and increase freely by divisions or seeds. Synonymes: 1. *A. minus.* 2. *Anthericum pendulum.*

| | | | | |
|---|---|---|---|---|
| cirrătum | White | 6, G. Her. | P. N. Zeal. | 1821 |
| fimbriătum | White | 7, G. Her. | P. N. Holl. | 1822 |
| mïnŭs | White | 7, G. Her. | P. N. Holl. | 1823 |
| panïculătŭm, 1 | White | 8, G. Bi. | P. N. S. W. | 1800 |
| pendŭlŭm, 2 | White | 7, G. Her. | P. Teneriffe | 1816 |

**Arthrŏstěmmă,** Pavon. From arthron, a joint, and stemon, a stamen; their stamens or connectives being jointed. Linn. 8, Or. 1, Nat. Or. Melastomaceæ. A beautiful plant, about two feet high, with palish lilac-coloured flowers; it grows in loam, mixed with a little peat, and increases from cuttings. Synonyme: 1. *Rhexia versicolor.*

| | | | | |
|---|---|---|---|---|
| versïcŏlŏr, 1 | Pink | 8, S. Ev. | S. Brazil | 1825 |
| altïdŭm | Pa. lil. | 7, G. Ev. | S. B. Ayres | 1830 |

**Artĭchoke,** see *Cynara.*

**Artĭculate,** } jointed, having joints.
**Artĭculated,** }

**Artĭculation,** the places where one thing is jointed with another.

**Artŏcărpŭs,** Linn. From artos, bread, and carpus, fruit; in allusion to the well-known name and uses of the bread-fruit. Linn. 21, Or. 1, Nat. Or. Urticaceæ. To this genus belongs the bread-fruit tree of the South Sea Islands They are difficult to cultivate in this country; a light rich loamy soil is best adapted to them. Sweet says, "they have been generally treated too tenderly, and not allowed sufficient air. They appear to be of the same nature as the fig, to which they are nearly allied. Large cuttings root freely in a pot of sand, plunged under a hand-glass, in a moist heat, with all their leaves entire; if the leaves are shortened, it is a great chance if they succeed." For further particulars respecting this very valuable genus, see *Loudon's Encyclopædia of Plants.*

| | | | | |
|---|---|---|---|---|
| incïsă | Wht. grn. | 8. Ev. T. | S. Sea Is. | 1793 |
| nuclfěră | Wht. grn. | 8. Ev. T. | E. Ind. | 1793 |
| integrïfŏliă | Wht. grn. | 6, 8. Ev. T. | E. Ind. | 1778 |
| heterŏphўllă | Wht. grn. | 8. Ev. T. | E. Ind. | 1778 |

**Ărŭm,** Linnæus. Formerly aron, supposed to be an ancient Egyptian word. Linn. 21, Or. 9, Nat. Or. Araceæ. This genus contains some very handsome species, while others are only useful on account of their medicinal qualities; the flowers are generally very disagreeable, hence they are not favourites; they all succeed in any common soil, and increase with little trouble from offsets. Synonymes: 1. *Tacca phalifera.* 2. *A. gramineum.*

| | | | | |
|---|---|---|---|---|
| atrŏ-rŭběns | Brown | 7, H. Her. | P. N. Amer. | 1758 |
| bulbïfěrŭm | Purple | 4, H. Her. | P. Bengal | 1813 |
| campanulătŭm, 1 | Purple | 5, S. Her. | P. E. Ind. | 1817 |
| Cŏlŏcăsïă | Green | 8. Tu. | P. Levant | 1551 |
| erïnïtŭm | Brown | 4, F. Her. | P. Minorca | 1777 |
| divarïcătŭm | Green | 7, S. Tu. | P. E. Ind. | 1759 |
| Dracŏntïŭm | Green | 6, H. Her. | P. N. Amer. | 1759 |
| Dracŭncŭlŭs | Brown | 7, H. Her. | P. S. Eur. | 1548 |
| flagellïfŏrmě | Brown | 5, S. Her. | P. Bengal | 1819 |
| gramïněŭm | | 6, H. Her. | P. | 1823 |
| hederăcěŭm | Purple | 6, Epiphy. | W. Ind. | 1793 |
| indïcŭm | Brown | 8. Ev. | S. China | 1824 |
| itălïcŭm | Lgt. yel. | 6, H. Her. | P. Italy | 1683 |
| integrïfŏliŭm | Green | 6, S. Ev. | S. | 1825 |
| lingulătŭm | | Epiphy. | W. Ind. | 1793 |
| margïnătŭm | | 8. Her. | P. E. Ind. | 1820 |
| macrŏrhïzŏn | Green | 8. Tu. | P. E. Ind. | 1803 |
| mïnŭtŭm | Purple | 7, S. Tu. | P. E. Ind. | 1802 |
| obtusïlŏbŭm | | 8. Her. | P. | 1824 |
| orïěntălě | | 6, H. Her. | P. Tauria | 1820 |
| orïzænsě | Purple | 6, S. Tu. | P. S. Amer. | 1820 |
| palmătŭm | | H. Her. | P. | 1825 |
| pědătŭm | | 8. Her. | P. S. Amer. | 1820 |
| pentaphўllŭm | | 8. Her. | P. E. Ind. | 1818 |
| pïctŭm | | H. Her. | P. Corsica | 1800 |
| polyphўllŏm | | 8. Her. | P. S. Amer. | 1818 |
| prŏbŏscïděŭm | | 7, H Her. | P. Apenn. | 1818 |
| rămŏsŭm | | 6, S. Ev. | S. | 1810 |
| rïngěns | | 6, G. Her. | P. Japan | 1800 |
| sagittïfŏliŭm | | 8. Her. | P. | 1824 |
| spïrălě | Brown | 5, S. Her. | P. China | 1816 |
| syrïăcŭm, 2 | | 6, H. Her. | P. Egypt | 1820 |
| těnŭifŏliŭm | White | 6, H. Her. | P. S. Eur. | 1570 |
| ternătŭm | Purple | 7, F. Her. | P. Japan | 1774 |
| trïlŏbătŭm | Purple | 6, S. Tu. | P. Ceylon | 1714 |
| auricŭlătŭm | Purple | 6, S. Tu. | P. Ceylon | 1714 |
| trïphўllŭm | Purple | 6, H. Her. | P. N. Amer. | 1664 |
| zebrïnŭm | Brown | 6, H. Her. | P. N. Amer. | 1664 |
| věnŏsŭm | Purple | 8, S. Her. | P. | 1794 |

*maculătŭm.*

**Arundïnăcěæ,** reed-like.

**Arundïnărïă,** Michaux. An alteration of the word arundo, a reed. Linn. 3, Or. 2, Nat. Or. Arundinaceæ. These plants are only fit for general collections; their culture is simple, and young plants are obtained from seeds. Synonymes: 1. *Ludolphia glaucěscěns.* *Pănïcŭm glaucěscěns.*

| | | | | |
|---|---|---|---|---|
| glaucěscěns, 1 | Apetal | Grass. E. Ind. | | 1818 |
| macrŏspěrmă | Apetal | 6, Grass. N. Amer. | | 1809 |

**Arŭndŏ,** Beauvois. An ancient name of doubtful origin, supposed by some to be from the Latin arundo, a reed; and by a recent author to be from the Celtic aru, water. Linn. 3, Or. 2, Nat. Or. Gramineæ. These are mere weeds. *A. Donax,* var. versicolor, is regarded by some on account of its striped leaves. *A. Donax* is grown in France and Italy for fishing-rods, fence-wood, training vines to, &c.

| | | | | |
|---|---|---|---|---|
| Dŏnax | Apetal | 7, Grass. | S. Eur. | 1648 |
| versïcŏlŏr | Apetal | 7, Grass. | S. Eur. | 1648 |

*festucăcěă, tenax.*

**Ăsărŭm,** Linnæus. From a, privative, and saron,

feminine; the application of the term unexplained. *Linn.* 11, Or. 1, Nat. Or. *Aristolochieæ.* This is a remarkable genus of dwarf plants, on account of their curious flowers, which are frequently overlooked among the leaves; it is best to plant them near the front of borders, on account of their dwarf character, any common soil suits them, and portions of the root make young plants. The leaves and roots of *A. europæum* are emetic, cathartic, and diuretic.

| | | | | | | |
|---|---|---|---|---|---|---|
| arifolium . . | . Brown | . 6, | H. Her. | P. | N. Amer. | . 1823 |
| canadense . . | . Brown | . 6, | H. Her. | P. | Canada | . 1713 |
| europæum . . | . Purple | . 5, | H. Her. | P. | England | |
| grandifolium . | . Brown | . 5, | H. Her. | P. | N. Amer. | . 1890 |
| virginicum . . | . Brown | . 5, | H. Her. | P. | Virginia | . 1759 |

ASCARICIDA, *Cassini.* Derived from *ascaris*, an intestinal worm, and *cædo*, to kill, because of its medical properties. *Linn.* 19, Or. 1, Nat. Or. *Compositæ.* Interesting, dwarfish annuals, easily cultivated, with the treatment in common practice for stove annuals. *Synonymes:* 1. *Vernonia anthelmintica.* 2. *V. triplinervia.*

| | | | | | | |
|---|---|---|---|---|---|---|
| anthelmintica, 1 | . Purple | . 8, | S. | A. | E. Ind. | . 1770 |
| triplinervia, 2 | . Purple | . 11, | S. | A. | Brazil | . 1825 |

ASCENDENT, } at first trailing on the ground, then
ASCENDING, } rising erect, forming a curve.

ASCI, small tubes, which contain the sporules of cryptogamous plants.

ASCIGEROUS, having asci.

ASCLEPIAS, *Linnæus.* The Greek name of the Æsculapius of the Latins. *Linn.* 5, Or. 2, Nat. Or. *Asclepiadaceæ.* This is a genus of tall-growing herbaceous plants, which thrive best in peat, or any very light soil. They require a good deal of room to show their characters. and are readily propagated by seeds, or dividing the roots. *A. syriaca* is very odoriferous, and in Canada, when in flower, charms the traveller, especially when passing through woods in the evening. The French there eat the tender shoots in spring, as we do asparagus. The natives make a sugar of the flowers, gathering them in the morning, when they are covered with dew, and collect the cotton from the pods to fill their beds. On account of the silkiness of this cotton, Parkinson calls it Virginian silk. The roots of *A. decumbens* are diaphoretic and sudorific, and have the singular property of exciting general perspiration, without increasing the heat of the body; it is used in Virginia against pleurisy. *A. tuberosa* is used in the United States as a mild cathartic, as a remedy for a variety of disorders. *Synonymes:* 1. *A. laurifolia.* 2. *Cynanchum Ipecacuanha.* 3. *A. connivens.* 4. *A. purpurascens.* 5. *A. hybrida.*

| | | | | | | |
|---|---|---|---|---|---|---|
| acuminata, 1 | . Red | . 7, | H. Her. | P. | N. Amer. | . 1826 |
| alexiaca . . | . Green | . | H. Ev. | Tw. | Ceylon | . 1816 |
| amœna . . | . Purple | . 8, | H. Her. | P. | N. Amer. | . 1732 |
| amplexicaulis . | . Red | . 7, | H. Her. | P. | N. Amer. | . 1816 |
| angustifolia . | . White | . 7, | H. Her. | P. | Mexico | . 1817 |
| asthmatica, 2 | . White | . 7, | S. Ev. | Tw. | Ceylon | . 1810 |
| cinerea . . | . Brown | . 7, | H. Her. | P. | N. Amer. | . 1825 |
| citrifolia . . | . White | . 7, | S. Her. | P. | N. Amer. | . 1818 |
| curassavica . | . Scarlet | . 7, | S. Her. | P. | S. Amer. | . 1692 |
| alba . . | . White | . 7, | S. Her. | P. | S. Amer. | |
| debilis . . | . White | . 7, | H. Her. | P. | N. Amer. | . 1818 |
| decumbens . | . Orange | . 7, | H. Tu. | P. | N. Amer. | . 1781 |
| exaltata, 3 | . Purple | . 7, | H. Her. | P. | N. Amer. | . 1800 |
| Greeniana | . White | . | 8. | Ev. | S. | . 1828 |
| incarnata . | . Purple | . 7, | H. Her. | P. | N. Amer. | . 1710 |
| Linaria . . | . White | . 7, | G. Her. | P. | Mexico | . 1802 |
| linifolia . . | . White | . 7, | H. Her. | P. | Mexico | . 1818 |
| longifolia . . | . Pa. pur. | . 7, | H. Her. | P. | N. Amer. | . 1816 |
| mexicana . . | . White | . 7, | G. Ev. | - | Mexico | . 1821 |
| nivea . . | . White | . 8, | H. Her. | P. | N. Amer. | . 1740 |
| obtusifolia, 4 | . Purple | . 7, | H. Her. | P. | N. Amer. | . 1820 |
| parviflora . | . White | . 9, | G. Her. | P. | N. Amer. | . 1774 |
| paupercula . | . Red | . 7, | H. Her. | P. | N. Amer. | . 1817 |
| phytolaccoides | . Purple | . 7, | H. Her. | P. | N. Amer. | . 1812 |
| polystachya . | . White | . 7, | H. Her. | P. | N. Amer. | . 1825 |
| pulchra . | . Purple | . 7, | H. Her. | P. | N. Amer. | |
| purpurascens, 5 | . Purple | . 7, | H. Her. | P. | N. Amer. | . 1732 |
| quadrifolia . | . Wht. red | . 7, | H. Her. | P. | N. Amer. | . 1820 |
| rosea . . | . Red | . 7, | G. Her. | P. | Mexico | . 1824 |
| rubra . . | . Red | . 7, | H. Her. | P. | Virginia | . 1825 |
| salicifolia . | . White | . 7, | G. Her. | P. | Mexico | . 1817 |
| syriaca . | . Purple | . 7, | H. Her. | P. | N. Amer. | . 1629 |
| tuberosa . . | . Orange | . 6, | H. Tu. | P. | N. Amer. | . 1690 |
| variegata . . | . White | . 7, | H. Her. | P. | N. Amer. | . 1597 |
| verticillata . | . Wht. grn. | . 7, | H. Her. | P. | N. Amer. | . 1759 |
| viridis . . | . White | . 7, | H. Her. | P. | N. Amer. | . 1820 |

ASCOBOLUS, *Persoon.* From *askos*, a bladder, and *ballo*, to eject; in allusion to the principal peculiarity of the genus. *Linn.* 24, Or. 9, Nat. Or. *Fungi.* A curious production found chiefly on old cow soil—*furfuraceus.*

ASCOPHORA, *Tode.* From *askos*, a term used to denote a peculiar kind of receptacle of sporules, and *phoreo*, to bear. *Linn.* 24, Or. 9, Nat. Or. *Fungi.* This is mere mould, as seen upon old paste, &c.—*mucedo.*

ASCYRUM, *Linnæus.* From *a*, privative, and *skyros*, hard; plants soft to the touch. *Linn.* 16, Or. 8, Nat. Or. *Hypericaceæ.* The species are dwarf and curious, and succeed well with the treatment given to *Hypericums.*

| | | | | | | |
|---|---|---|---|---|---|---|
| amplexicaule . | . Yellow | . 8, | G. Ev. | S. | N. Amer. | . 1823 |
| crux-Andreæ | . Yellow | . 7, | G. Ev. | S. | N. Amer. | . 1759 |
| hypericoides | . Yellow | . 8, | G. Ev. | S. | N. Amer. | . 1759 |
| pumilum . . | . Yellow | . 7, | F. Her. | P. | Georgia | . 1806 |
| stans . . | . Yellow | . 8, | G. Ev. | S. | N. Amer. | . 1816 |

ASH-TREE, see *Fraxinus.*

ASIATIC POISON-BULB, see *Crinum asiaticum.*

ASIMINA, *Adanson.* A name of Canadian origin, meaning unknown. *Linn.* 13, Or. 6, Nat. Or. *Anonaceæ.* Ornamental shrubs, from one to three feet high; they succeed best in peat and loam, and are of easy propagation by layering the branches. *Synonyme:* 1. *Anona triloba.*

| | | | | | | |
|---|---|---|---|---|---|---|
| grandiflora . . | . White | . 6, | H. De. | S. | Georgia | . 1820 |
| parviflora . | . Brown | . 5, | H. De. | S. | N. Amer. | . 1806 |
| pygmæa . | . White | . | H. De. | S. | N. Amer. | . 1812 |
| triloba, 1 | . Pa. pur. | . 8, | H. De. | S. | China | . 1822 |

ASPALATHUS, *Linnæus.* Said to be derived from *a*, privative, and *spao*, to extract; in reference to the thorns. *Linn.* 16, Or. 6, Nat. Or. *Leguminosæ.* "All the species are rather ornamental when in flower. A mixture of loam, peat, and sand, is the soil best adapted for them; and young cuttings of all will strike in sand, under bell-glasses, but the glasses must be wiped occasionally, or the cuttings are very liable to damp off."—*Don's System of Gard. and Botany.*

| | | | | | | |
|---|---|---|---|---|---|---|
| affinis . . | . Yellow | . 7, | G. Ev. | S. | C. G. H. | . 1822 |
| albens . . | . White | . 7, | G. Ev. | S. | C. G. H. | . 1774 |
| araneosa . | . Yellow | . 7, | G. Ev. | S. | C. G. H. | . 1795 |
| argentea . | . Yellow | . 7, | G. Ev. | S. | C. G. H. | . 1759 |
| asparagoides | . Yellow | . 7, | G. Ev. | S. | C. G. H. | . 1812 |
| astroites . | . Yellow | . 7, | G. Ev. | S. | C. G. H. | . 1818 |
| callosa . . | . Yellow | . 7, | G. Ev. | S. | C. G. H. | . 1812 |
| candicans . | . Yellow | . 7, | G. Ev. | S. | C. G. H. | . 1774 |
| carnosa . | . Yellow | . 7, | G. Ev. | S. | C. G. H. | . 1795 |
| capitata . | . Yellow | . 7, | G. Ev. | S. | C. G. H. | . 1823 |
| Chenopoda . | . Yellow | . 7, | G. Ev. | S. | C. G. H. | . 1759 |
| ciliaris . | . Yellow | . 7, | G. Ev. | S. | C. G. H. | . 1799 |
| crassifolia . | . Yellow | . 7, | G. Ev. | S. | C. G. H. | . 1800 |
| ericifolia . | . Yellow | . 7, | G. Ev. | S. | C. G. H. | . 1789 |
| galioides . | . Yellow | . 7, | G. Ev. | Tr. | C. G. H. | . 1817 |
| genistoides . | . Yellow | . 7, | G. Ev. | S. | C. G. H. | . 1816 |
| globosa . . | . Orange | . 7, | G. Ev. | S. | C. G. H. | . 1802 |
| hispida . . | . Yellow | . 7, | G. Ev. | S. | C. G. H. | . 1818 |
| hystrix . . | . Yellow | . 7, | G. Ev. | S. | C. G. H. | . 1824 |
| indica . . | . Red | . 7, | G. Ev. | S. | E. Ind. | . 1759 |
| laricina . . | . Yellow | . 7, | G. Ev. | S. | C. G. H. | . 1823 |
| mucronata . | . Yellow | . 7, | G. Ev. | S. | C. G. H. | . 1796 |
| multiflora . | . Yellow | . 7, | G. Ev. | S. | C. G. H. | . 1818 |
| pedunculata | . Yellow | . 7, | G. Ev. | S. | C. G. H. | . 1775 |
| quinquefolia . | . Yellow | . 7, | G. Ev. | S. | C. G. H. | . 1816 |
| sericea . | . Yellow | . 7, | G. Ev. | S. | C. G. H. | . 1816 |
| spinosa . | . Yellow | . 7, | G. Ev. | S. | C. G. H. | . 1824 |
| squarrosa . | . Yellow | . 7, | G. Ev. | S. | C. G. H. | . 1823 |
| subulata . | . Yellow | . 7, | G. Ev. | S. | C. G. H. | . 1789 |
| thymifolia . | . Yellow | . 7, | G. Ev. | S. | C. G. H. | . 1825 |
| uniflora . | . Yellow | . 7, | G. Ev. | S. | C. G. H. | . 1812 |

ASPHALTUS, *Linnæus.* Derived from *a*, intensive, and *sparasso*, to tear, some of the species being armed with strong prickles. *Linn.* 6, Or. 1, Nat. Or. *Liliaceæ.* The character and mode of treating this favourite genus is known by all; suffice it to say, that they are most successful in good rich light soil, and may be multiplied by seeds or divisions.

| | | | | | | |
|---|---|---|---|---|---|---|
| acutifolius . | . Wht. grn. | . | F. Ev. | S. | Spain | . 1640 |
| æthiopicus . | . White | . | G. Ev. | S. | C. G. H. | . 1816 |
| albus . . | . White | . | F. Ev. | S. | Spain | . 1540 |
| amarus . . | . Green | . 7, | H. Her. | P. | France | . 1824 |
| aphyllus . | . White | . | F. Ev. | S. | S. Eur. | . 1640 |
| asiaticus . | . White | . | G. Ev. | S. | Asia | . 1759 |
| Broussonetii | . | . | H. Her. | P. | Canaries | . 1822 |
| capensis . | . Green | . 4, | G. Ev. | S. | C. G. H. | . 1691 |
| dahuricus . | . Green | . 4, | H. Her. | P. | Dauria | . 1823 |
| declinatus . | . Wht. grn. | . | F. Her. | P. | C. G. H. | . 1759 |
| decumbens . | . Wht. grn. | . 4, | G. Her. | P. | C. G. H. | . 1792 |
| dependens . | . White | . | G. Ev. | Tw. | C. G. H. | . 1819 |
| falcatus . | . Wht. grn. | . | 8. | Ev. | S. | E. Ind. | . 1792 |

| | | | | | |
|---|---|---|---|---|---|
| flexuòsūs | Wht. grn. | 7, S. Ev. S. | C. O. H. | 1800 |
| hòrridūs | White . | 6, F. Ev. Tw. | S. Eur. | 1800 |
| longifolius | White . | 7, H. Her. P. | Siberia | 1827 |
| marìtìmūs | Green . | 6, H. Her. P. | Caspian | 1823 |
| officinàlis | Green . | 7, H. Her. P. | England | |
| plocamoldës | | | Teneriffe | 1829 |
| racemòsūs | Wht. grn. | G. Ev. S. | E. Ind. | 1808 |
| retrofractūs | White . | 7, G. Ev. Tw. | Africa | 1759 |
| sarmentòsūs | Wht. grn. | 8, S. Ev. Tw. | Ceylon | 1810 |
| scándèns | Green . | G. Ev. Tw. | C. O. H. | 1796 |
| Smithiànūs | | | Teneriffe | 1829 |
| stipulàcèūs | White . | G. Ev. Tw. | C. O. H. | 1821 |
| subulàtūs | | F. Ev. S. | C. O. H. | 1811 |
| sylvàtìcūs | Green . | 7, H. Her. P. | Hungary | 1819 |
| verticillàris | White . | 7, H. Her. P. | Caucasus | 1752 |

ASPÀSIA, *Lindley*. From *aspazomai*, I embrace, in allusion to the manner in which the column is embraced by the labellum. *Linn.* 20, Or. 1, Nat. Or. *Orchidaceæ.* Elegant plants, with the aspect of epidendrum. The flowers of *A. variegatum* are deliciously sweet in the morning. For culture and propagation, see *Stanhopea*.

| | | | | | |
|---|---|---|---|---|---|
| epidendroldēs | Wht. yel. | 8. Epi. | Panama . | 1833 |
| variegàtā | 2, 8. Epi. | Panama . | 1836 |

ASPEN, see *Populus tremula*.

ÀSPERÀ, harsh, rugged.

ASPRÈLLA, see *Elymus hystrix*.

ASPERGÍLLUS, *Micheli*. From *aspergillum*, because of its resemblance to the brush with which the holy water is scattered in catholic ceremonies. *Linn.* 24, Or. 9, Nat. Or *Fungi*. Mere mouldiness, found in patches upon rotten substances, and damp species in herbariums—*glaucus, làneus, penicillàtus, vìrens.*

ASPERÙGO, *Linnæus*. Derived, on account of its asperity, from *asper*, rough. *Linn.* 5, Or. 1, Nat. Or. *Boraginaceæ*. Altogether uninteresting, except in a botanical point of view.

| | | | | | |
|---|---|---|---|---|---|
| procùmbèns | Blue . | 4, H. Tr. A | Britain . . |

ASPERÙLA, *Linnæus*. A diminutive of *asper*, rough; leaves. *Linn.* 4, Or. 1, Nat. Or. *Stellatæ*. *A. arvensis* is a mere weed; all the rest of the species are pretty, and excepting *cynanchica*, remarkable for thriving under the shade of trees, in moist soil. The scent of *A. odorata* is quite pleasant, and has been used for flavouring wine, perfuming clothes, &c. An infusion of *A. cynanchica* is astringent, and is used as a gargle. *A. odorata* is diuretic. *Synonymes* : l. *A. rivalis.* 2. *Galium glaucum.* 3. *A. repens.* 4. *Galium humifusum.* 5 *A. incana.*

| | | | | | |
|---|---|---|---|---|---|
| alpìnā | White . | 7, H. Her. P. | Caucasus | 1820 |
| Aparìnē, 1 | White . | 7, H. Her. P. | S. Eur. | 1818 |
| arcadiènsis | Red . | 4, H. Her. P. | Arcadia | 1819 |
| aristàtā | Yellow . | 7, H. Her. P. | S. Eur. | 1823 |
| brevifòlia | Purple . | 7, F. Ev. | Tr. Europe | 1825 |
| crassifòlìā | White . | 7, H. Her. P. | Levant | 1775 |
| cynánchicā | Flesh . | 7, H. Her. P. | England | |
| galioldēs, 2 | White . | 7, H. Her. P. | S. Eur. | 1710 |
| hirsùtā, 3 | White . | 6, H. Her. P. | Portugal | 1819 |
| hirtā | Purple . | 7, H. Her. P. | Pyrenees | 1817 |
| humifùsa, 4 | White . | 7, H. Her. Tr. | Caucasus | 1818 |
| lævigàtā | White . | 6, H. Her. P. | S. Eur. | 1775 |
| longiflòrā | Yel. pur. | 7, H. Her. P. | Hungary | 1821 |
| longifòlìā | Red . | 7, H. Her. P. | S. Eur. | 1820 |
| montànā | Pink . | 7, H. Her. P. | Hungary | 1801 |
| nìtìdā | Pink . | 8, H. Her. P. | Greece | 1829 |
| odoràtā | White . | 7, H. Her. P. | Britain | |
| pyrenàìcā | Flesh . | 7, H. Her. P. | Spain | 1821 |
| rìgìdā | Red . | 7, H. Her. P. | Greece | 1819 |
| scàbrā | White . | 7, H. Her. P. | Italy | |
| supìnā | Pink . | 6, H. Her. P. | Caucasus | 1821 |
| taurìnā | White . | 6, H. Her. P. | Italy | 1789 |
| tinctòrìā | Pink . | 7, H. Her. P. | Europe | 1764 |
| tomentòsā, 5 | Red . | 7, H. Her. P. | S. Eur. | 1817 |

*arvensis.*

ASPHÓDELUS, *Linnæus*. From *a*, privative, and *sphallo*, to supplant; a flower not to be surpassed. *Linn.* 6, Or. 1, Nat. Or. *Liliaceæ.* These plants are of a bold aspect, and when in flower very ornamental; common soil suits them well, and young plants are obtained without difficulty from the roots.

| | | | | | |
|---|---|---|---|---|---|
| æstìvūs | White . | 7, H. Her. P. | Spain | 1820 |
| albūs | White . | 4, H. Her. P. | S. Eur. | |
| clavàtūs | White . | 7, S. | A. E. Ind. | 1806 |
| erètìcūs | Yellow . | 6, H. Her. P. | Candia | 1821 |
| fistulòsūs | White . | 8, H. Her. P. | S. Eur. | 1596 |
| intermèdìūs | White . | 7, G. | Canaries | 1822 |
| lùtèūs | Yellow . | 6, H. Her. P. | Sicily | 1596 |
| prolìferūs | White . | 8, H. | A. Armenia | 1824 |
| ramòsūs | White . | 4, H. Her. P. | S. Eur. | 1551 |
| sìbìrìcūs | Pa. yel. | 5, H. Her. P. | Siberia | 1829 |
| tauricūs | White . | 6, H. Her. P. | Tauria | 1812 |
| tenuìor | White . | 7, H. Her. P. | Siberia | 1824 |

ASPICÀRPA, *Richard*. The form of the fruit resembles a shield ; hence the name from *aspis*, a shield, and *karpos*, fruit. *Linn.* 1, Or. 2, Nat. Or. *Malpighiaceæ.* A twining plant of little interest, and easy cultivation.

| | | | | | |
|---|---|---|---|---|---|
| ùrèns | Apetal . | 7, S. De. Tw. | S. Amer. | 1821 |

ASPIDÍSTRA, *Ker*. From *aspidiscon*, a little round shield ; the form of the flower. *Linn.* 8, Or. 1, Nat. Or. *Acoraceæ.* A curious plant, remarkable for producing its flowers under the surface of the soil ; any common soil ; suckers.

| | | | | | |
|---|---|---|---|---|---|
| lùrìdā | Purple . | 7, S. Her. P. | China | 1822 |
| punctàtā | Purple . | 3, S. Her. P. | China | 1824 |

ASPÍDIUM, *Swartz*. From *aspidion*, a little buckler; because of the form of the indusium. *Linn.* 24, Or. 1, Nat. Or. *Polypodiaceæ.* One of the pretty and very interesting genera of Ferns. A mixture of loam and peat, and a sheltered situation, are very suitable for them ; they are multiplied by seeds, or divisions. *Synonymes* : 1. *Nephrodium acrostichoides.* 2. *N. decompositum.* 3. *Cyathea dentata.* 4 *Aspidium trapezoides.* 5. *Polypodium fragrans.* 6. *Nephrod. unitum.*

| | | | | | |
|---|---|---|---|---|---|
| acrosticholdēs, 1 | Brown | 7, H. Her. P. | N. Amer. | |
| aculeàtūm | Brown | 7, H. Her. P. | Britain . | |
| æmùlūm | Brown | 7, G. Her. P. | Madeira | 1779 |
| alpìnūm | Brown | 7, H. Her. P. | S. Eur. | 1825 |
| angulàrē | Brown | 7, H. Her. P. | Hungary | 1819 |
| atomàrìūm | Brown | 7, H. Her. P. | N. Amer. | 1820 |
| auriculàtūm | Brown | 7, S. Her. P. | E. Ind. | 1793 |
| bulbìferūm | Brown | 7, H. Her. P. | N. Amer. | 1638 |
| cicutàrìūm | Brown | 7, S. Her. P. | Jamaica | 1820 |
| cordifòlìūm | Brown | 6, S. Her. P. | Jamaica | 1824 |
| coriàcèūm | Brown | 7, G. Her. P. | V. D. L. | 1821 |
| cristàtūm | Brown | 7, H. Her. P. | England | |
| decompòsìtūm, 2 | Brown | 7, G. Her. P. | N. Holl. | 1820 |
| dentàtūm, 3 | Brown | 6, H. Her. P. | Wales | |
| dilatàtūm | Brown | 6, H. Her. P. | Britain | |
| dumetòrūm | Brown | 7, H. Her. P. | Britain | |
| elongàtūm | Brown | 6, G. Her. P. | Madeira | 1779 |
| exaltàtūm | Brown | 7, S. Her. P. | Jamaica | 1793 |
| Fìlìx-mās | Brown | 7, H. Her. P. | Britain | |
| fragìlē | Brown | 7, H. Her. P. | Britain | |
| frágrans | Brown | 7, H. Her. P. | Siberia | 1820 |
| intermèdìūm | Brown | 7, H. Her. P. | N. Amer. | 1823 |
| indivìsūm | Brown | 7, S. Her. P. | Jamaica | 1824 |
| irrìgùūm | Brown | 7, H. Her. P. | Britain | |
| lobàtūm | Brown | 7, H. Her. P. | England | |
| Lonchìtis | Brown | 7, H. Her. P. | Britain | |
| macrophyllūm | Brown | 8, S. Her. P. | W. Ind. | 1816 |
| marginàlē | Brown | 7, H. Her. P. | N. Amer. | 1772 |
| mòllē | Brown | 7, S. Her. P. | Caraccas | 1824 |
| montànūm | Brown | 6, H. Her. P. | Switzerl. | 1819 |
| mucronàtūm | Brown | 6, S. Her. P. | Jamaica | 1820 |
| noveboracènsē | Brown | 7, H. Her. P. | N. Amer. | 1812 |
| Orèoptèris | Brown | 8, H. Her. P. | Britain | |
| parasìtìcūm | Brown | 6, S. Her. P. | E. Ind. | 1824 |
| pàtèns | Brown | 7, S. Ev. S. | Jamaica | 1784 |
| pectinàtūm, 4 | Brown | 7, S. Her. P. | W. Ind. | 1820 |
| propìnquūm | Brown | 7, S. Her. P. | E. Ind. | 1793 |
| pubèscèns | Brown | 7, S. Her. P. | Jamaica | 1817 |
| règìūm | Brown | 7, S. Her. P. | Britain | |
| rhètìcūm | Brown | 6, H. Her. P. | Britain | |
| rhizophyllūm | Brown | 7, H. Her. P. | Jamaica | 1820 |
| rìgìdūm, 5 | Brown | 7, H. Her. P. | S. Eur. | 1816 |
| Sèrrā | Brown | 7, S. Her. P. | Jamaica | 1819 |
| spinulòsūm | Brown | 7, H. Her. P. | Britain | |
| Thelyptèris | Brown | 7, H. Her. P. | Britain | |
| trapezoldēs | Brown | 7, S. Her. P. | Jamaica | 1824 |
| trifoliàtūm | Brown | 7, S. Her. P. | W. Ind. | 1769 |
| unìtūm, 6 | Brown | 8, S. Her. P. | N. Holl. | 1793 |
| villòsūm | Brown | 7, S. Her. P. | W. Ind. | 1793 |

ASPLÉNIUM, *Linnæus*. From *a*, privative, and *splen*, spleen; its supposed medicinal qualities. *Linn.* 24, Or. 1, Nat. Or. *Polypodiaceæ.* For culture, &c., see *Aspidium*. Synonymes : 1. *A. germanicum.* 2. *Nephrodium asplenioides, Aspidium asplenioides.* 3. *Polypodium Filix-fæmina.* 4. *Aspidium fontanum, Polypodium fontanum.* 5. *Aspidium Halleri, Athyrium Halleri.* 6. *Nephrodium Filix-fæmina, Aspidium angustum.* 7. *A. obliquum.* 8. *A. glandulosum, Vallis-clausæ.* 9. *A. rhizophorum.* 10. *A. acrostichoides.*

| | | | | | |
|---|---|---|---|---|---|
| acùtūm | Brown | 4, G. Her. P. | Teneriffe | 1818 |
| Adiantum-nìgrūm | Brown | 8, H. Her. P. | Britain . | |
| alternifòlìūm, 1 | Brown | 7, H. Her. P. | Scotland | |
| angustifòlìūm | Brown | 7, H. Her. P. | N. Amer. | 1812 |
| Athyrìum, 2 | Brown | 8, H. Her. P. | N. Amer. | 1823 |
| attenuàtūm | Brown | 7, G. Her. P. | N. Holl. | 1824 |
| bipartìtūm | Brown | 8, S. Her. P. | Jamaica | 1820 |
| bisectūm | Brown | 7, S. Her. P. | Jamaica | 1821 |
| brasiliènsē | Brown | 7, S. Her. P. | Brazil | 1822 |

| Species | Colour | Conditions | Country | Year |
|---|---|---|---|---|
| bulbíferum | Brown | 7, G. Her. P. | N. Zeal. | 1820 |
| cicutarium | Brown | 8, S. Her. P. | W. Ind. | 1820 |
| cultrifolium | Brown | 8. Her. P. | W. Ind. | 1820 |
| dentatum | Brown | 7, S. Her. P. | W. Ind. | 1820 |
| difforme | Brown | 8, G. Her. P. | N. Holl. | 1823 |
| diversifolium | Brown | 6, G. Her. P. | Norf. Is. | 1821 |
| ebeneum | Brown | 7, H. Her. P. | N. Amer. | 1779 |
| falcatum | Brown | 7, G. Her. P. | N. Holl. | 1825 |
| Filix-fæmina, 3 | Brown | 4. H. Her. P. | Britain | |
| flabellifolium | Brown | 7, S. Her. P. | N. Holl. | 1820 |
| fontanum, 4 | Brown | 7, H. Her. P. | England | |
| formosum | Brown | 6, S. Her. P. | W. Ind. | 1822 |
| fragrans | Brown | 8, S. Her. P. | Jamaica | 1793 |
| Hallëri. 5 | Brown | 7, H. Her. P. | Switzerl. | 1819 |
| lanceolatum | Brown | 8, H. Her. P. | England | |
| maderense | Brown | 6, H. Her. P. | Madeira | 1828 |
| marinum | Brown | 7, H. Her. P. | Britain | |
| melanocaulon | Brown | 7, H. Her. P. | N. Amer. | 1812 |
| Michauxi, 6 | Brown | 8, H. Her. P. | N. Amer. | 1823 |
| monanthemum | Brown | 7, G. Her. P. | C. G. H. | 1790 |
| montanum | Brown | 7, H. Her. P. | N. Amer. | 1812 |
| Nidus | Brown | 8, S. Her. P. | E. Ind. | 1820 |
| obtusatum, 7 | Brown | 7, G. Her. P. | N. Holl. | 1824 |
| palmatum | Brown | 7, G. Her. P. | S. Eur. | 1816 |
| Petrarchæ, 8 | Brown | 8, H. Her. P. | France | 1819 |
| præmorsum | Brown | 8, S. Her. P. | Jamaica | 1793 |
| pumilum | Brown | 7, H. Her. P. | W. Ind. | 1823 |
| radicans, 9 | Brown | 6, S. Her. P. | W. Ind. | 1820 |
| rhizophorum | Brown | 8, S. Her. P. | Jamaica | 1793 |
| rhizophyllum | Brown | 7, H. Her. P. | N. Amer. | 1680 |
| Ruta-muraria | Brown | 7, H. Her. P. | Britain | |
| septentrionale | Brown | 7, H. Her. P. | Britain | |
| serratum | Brown | 8, S. Her. P. | W. Ind. | 1793 |
| Shepherdi | Brown | 8, S. Her. P. | N. Holl. | 1820 |
| striatum | Brown | 8, S. Her. P. | W. Ind. | 1793 |
| thelypteroides, 10 | Brown | 7, H. Her. P. | N. Amer. | 1823 |
| Trichomanes | Brown | 7, H. Her. P. | Britain | |
| viride | Brown | 6, H. Her. P. | Britain | |
| viviparum | Brown | 8, S. Her. P. | Maurit. | 1820 |
| zamiæfolium | Brown | 7, S. Her. P. | Caraccas | 1820 |

ASĒŌNIX, *Cavanilles.* In honour of Ignatius Deasso, a distinguished Spanish botanist. Linn. 16, Or. 7, Nat. Or. *Sterculiaceæ.* These plants are ornamental and of easy cultivation in sandy soil; cuttings are propagated without difficulty in sand or sandy loam, in heat.

| Species | Colour | Conditions | Country | Year |
|---|---|---|---|---|
| populnea | White | 8. Ev. T. | Bourbon | 1820 |
| viburnoïdes | White | 8. Ev. T. | Bourbon | 1822 |

ASSURGENT, rising upwards.

ASTARTEA, *Decandolle.* A mythological name; Astarte, in Syria Venus. Linn. 18, Or. 2, Nat. Or. *Myrtaceæ* An ornamental species, three feet high; for culture, &c., see *Melaleuca.* Synonyme: 1. *Melaleuca fascicularis.*

| Species | Colour | Conditions | Country | Year |
|---|---|---|---|---|
| fascicularis, 1 | | G. Ev. S. | N. Holl. | |

ASTELMA, *R. Brown.* From *a,* privative, and *stelma,* crown, in allusion to the construction of the fruit. Linn. 19, Or. 2, Nat. Or. *Compositæ.* Beautiful flowering plants, especially *A. eximium;* they grow about three feet high and thrive well in sandy peat soil; the pots must be well drained, and the soil carefully watered, or they do not progress freely, but on the contrary, the whole plant appears to languish; they delight in a situation near the glass, with a free admission of air; they increase by seeds, sown in light open soil, or cuttings in sand, or sandy soil, without difficulty. Synonymes: 1. *Elichryseum canescens.* 2. *E. fragrans.* 3. *E. imbricatum.* 4. *Gnaphalium milleflorum.* 5. *Elichrysum retortum.* 6. *E. speciosissimum.* 7. *E. spirale.* 8. *E. Stæhelina.* 9. *E. variegatum.*

| Species | Colour | Conditions | Country | Year |
|---|---|---|---|---|
| canescens, 1 | Purple | 6, G. Ev. S. | C. G. H. | 1794 |
| eximium | Crimson | 7, G. Ev. S. | C. G. H. | 1793 |
| fragrans, 2 | Pink | 7, G. Ev. S. | C. G. H. | 1803 |
| imbricatum, 3 | White | 8, G. Ev. S. | C. G. H. | 1820 |
| milleflorum, 4 | Pa. pur. | 7, G. Ev. S. | C. G. H. | 1802 |
| retortum | White | 7, G. Ev. S. | C. G. H. | 1732 |
| speciosissimum, 6 | White | 8, G. Ev. S. | C. G. H. | 1691 |
| spirale, 7 | White | 9, G. Ev. S. | C. G. H. | 1801 |
| Stæhelina, 8 | White | G. Ev. S. | C. G. H. | 1801 |
| variegatum, 9 | Brn. wht. | 6, G. Ev. S. | C. G. H. | 1801 |

ASTEPHANUS, *R. Brown.* From *a,* privative, and *stephanos,* crown; in reference to the stamens. Linn. 5, Or. 2, Nat. Or. *Asclepiadaceæ.* These are twining plants of considerable beauty, growing about four feet high, in peat and loam, and are increased by divisions.

| Species | Colour | Conditions | Country | Year |
|---|---|---|---|---|
| linearis | White | 7, G. Ev. Tw. | C. G. H. | 1816 |
| triflorus | White | 7, G. Ev. Tw. | C. G. H. | 1816 |

ASTER, *Linnæus.* From aster, a star; the flowers resemble little stars from the rays of their circumference. Linn. 19, Or. 2, Nat. Or. *Compositæ.* Many species of this extensive genus are stately and handsome plants, such as *A. puniceus, pulchellus,* &c.: the expanded flowers, which appear in autumn when others are over, have been compared to a star, from the numerous rays of the circumference; they succeed in any soil or situation, and the herbaceous kinds increase abundantly from suckers. *A. argophyllus* is a very rapid-growing species, and forms an ornamental tree when planted in the border of a conservatory: its leaves have also a fine fragrance resembling musk. Synonymes: 1. *A. pumilus.* 2. *A. pennsylvanicus.* 3. *A. umbellatus.* 4. *A. dracunculoides.* 5. *Solidago bicolor.* 6. *A. biennis.* 7. *A. Marylandica.* 8. *A. scoparius.* 9. *A. pubescens.* 10. *A. carneus.* 11. *Grindelia siberica.* 12. *A. glaucus.* 13. *A. lucidus.* 14. *A. leucanthemus* 15. *A. expansus.* 16. *A. parviflorus.* 17. *A. ledifolius.* 18. *A. villosus.* 19. *A. fruticulosus.* 20. *A. pinifolius.* 21. *A. amœnus.* 22. *A. alpinus ramosus.* 23. *A. glaucus cyaneus.* 24. *A. virgatus.* 25. *A. hungaricus.* 26. *A. virginicus.* 27. *A. dentatus, ferruginea.* 28. *A. patulus, strictus.*

| Species | Colour | Conditions | Country | Year |
|---|---|---|---|---|
| abbreviatus | Blue | 8, H. Her. P. | N. Amer. | |
| acris | Blue | 8, H. Her. P. | S. Eur. | 1731 |
| aculeatus | White | 6, G. Ev. S. | N. Holl. | 1818 |
| acuminatus | Pa. red | 9, H. Her. P. | N. Amer. | 1806 |
| adulterinus | Violet | 9, H. Her. P. | N. Amer. | |
| æstivus | Blue | 7, H. Her. P. | N. Amer. | 1776 |
| albus | White | 8, H. Her. P. | N. Amer. | |
| Alpinus | Purple | 6. H. Her. P. | Europe | 1658 |
|   flore-albo | White | 7, H. Her. P. | Europe | 1827 |
|   ramosus | Blue | 6, H. Her. P. | Europe | |
| altaicus, 1 | Blue | 6. H. Her. P. | Siberia | 1804 |
| alwartensis | Red | 5, H. Her. P. | Caucasus | 1807 |
| Amellus | Purple | 8, H. Her. P. | Italy | 1596 |
|   angustifolius | Pa. blue | 8, G. Ev. S. | S. Eur. | 1596 |
| amelloïdes | Violet | 7, H. Her. P. | Podolia | 1824 |
| amplexicaulis, 2 | Blue | 10, H. Her. P. | N. Amer. | |
| amygdalinus, 3 | White | 8, H. Her. P. | N. Amer. | 1759 |
| angustifolius | Pa. blue | 7, G. Ev. S. | C. G. H. | 1804 |
| argenteus | Purple | 8, H. Her. P. | N. Amer. | 1801 |
| argophyllus | White | 7, G. Ev. S. | V. D. L. | 1804 |
| artemisiflorus, 4 | White | 9, H. Her. P. | N. Amer. | |
| bellidiflorus | Pa. red | 9, H. Her. P. | N. Amer. | |
| biflorus | Violet | 8, H. Her. P. | Caucasus | 1820 |
| blandus | Pa. blue | 10, H. Her. P. | N. Amer. | 1800 |
| bicolor, 5 | Wht. yel. | 9, H. Her. P. | N. Amer. | 1759 |
| canescens, 6 | Violet | 9. H. B. | N. Amer. | 1812 |
| canus | Purple | 8, H. Her. P. | Hungary | 1816 |
| carolinianus | Purple | 9, G. Ev. S. | Carolina | |
| caucaseus | Purple | 7, H. Her. P. | Caucasus | 1804 |
| ciliatus | White | 9, H. Her. P. | N. Amer. | |
| concinnus | Purple | 10, H. Her. P. | N. Amer. | 1800 |
| concolor | Purple | 10, H. Her. P. | N. Amer. | 1759 |
| conyzoides, 7 | White | 9, H. Her. P. | N. Amer.? | 1778 |
| cordifolius | Blue | 7, H. Her. P. | N. Amer. | 1759 |
| coridifolius | Pa. blue | 10, H. Her. P. | N. Amer. | |
| cornifolius | White | 10, H. Her. P. | N. Amer. | 1811 |
| corymbosus | White | 10, H. Her. P. | N. Amer. | 1765 |
| Cymbalaria | White | 9, G. Ev. S. | C. G. H. | 1796 |
| cyaneus | Blue | 9, H. Her. P. | N. Amer. | 1789 |
| desertorum | Blue | 7, H. Her. P. | Siberia | 1820 |
| diffusus, 8 | White | 10, H. Her. P. | N. Amer. | 1777 |
| divaricatus | White | 9, H. Her. P. | N. Amer. | 1800 |
| dracunculoïdes | White | 11, H. Her. P. | Tauria | 1811 |
| dumosus | White | 10, H. Her. P. | N. Amer. | 1784 |
| elegans | Blue | 9, H. Her. P. | | 1790 |
| eminens, 9 | Light | 10, H. flor. P. | N. Amer. | |
| ericoïdes | White | 9, H. Her. P. | N. Amer. | 1758 |
| erubescens | Red | 6, G. Ev. S. | N. Holl. | |
| exasperatus | White | 9, G. Ev. S. | C. G. H. | 1823 |
| alifolius | White | 5, G. Ev. S. | C. G. H. | 1812 |
| firmus | Red | 8, H. Her. P. | N. Amer. | 1816 |
| floribundus | Purple | 9, H. Her. P. | N. Amer. | |
| foliolatus | Pa. blue | 10, H. Her. P. | N. Amer. | 1788 |
| foliosus | White | 9, H. Her. P. | N. Amer. | 1799 |
| fragilis, 10 | Flesh | 9, H. Her. P. | N. Amer. | 1800 |
| fruticulosus | Blue | 5, G. Ev. S. | C. G. H. | 1759 |
| gracilis | Green | 9, H. Her. P. | N. Amer. | |
| graminifolius | Pa. pur. | 10, H. Her. P. | | |
| grandiflorus | Blue | 11, H. Her. P. | N. Amer. | 1720 |
| graveolens | | H. Her. P. | Arkansas | 1826 |
| heterophyllus | White | 8, H. Her. P. | N. Amer. | 1811 |
| hispidus | White | 9, H. Her. P. | China | 1804 |
| humilis | White | 9, H. Her. P. | N. Amer. | 1699 |
| hyssopifolius | Pa. pur. | 9, H. Her. P. | N. Amer. | 1683 |
| ibericus | Purple | 8, H. Her. P. | Iberia | |
| incisus, 11 | Blue | 8, H. Her. P. | Siberia | 1818 |
| inuloïdes | Red | 8, H. Her. P. | Nepal | |
| junceus | Flesh | 9, H. Her. P. | N. Amer. | 1758 |
| lævigatus, 12 | Flesh | 9, H. Her. P. | N. Amer. | 1794 |
| lævis, 13 | Blue | 9, H. Her. P. | N. Amer. | 1758 |
| lanceolatus | White | 9, H. Her. P. | N. Amer. | 1811 |
| laxus, 14 | White | 10, H. Her. P. | N. Amer. | |

| Name | Colour | Height, Culture | Native | Date |
|---|---|---|---|---|
| laxiflorus | | 9, H. Her. P. | N. Amer. | |
| linariifolius | Pa. blue | 9, H. Her. P. | N. Amer. | 1699 |
| linifolius | White | 7, H. Her. P. | N. Amer. | 1739 |
| liratus | White | 6, G. Ev. S. | N. S. W. | 1812 |
| longifolius | White | 10, H. Her. P. | N. Amer. | 1798 |
| lusitanicus | Blue | 6, H. Her. P. | Spain | 1826 |
| luxurians, 15 | Blue | 9, H. Her. P. | N. Amer. | 1816 |
| macrophyllus | White | 8, H. Her. P. | N. Amer. | 1739 |
| marginatus | Violet | 7, H. Her. P. | N. Gran. | 1827 |
| montanus | | 8, H. Her. P. | Carolina | |
| multiflorus | White | 9, H. Her. P. | N. Amer. | 1732 |
| mutabilis | Purple | 9, H. Her. P. | N. Amer. | 1710 |
| myrsinoides | Pa. pur. | 5, G. Ev. S. | N. Holl. | 1825 |
| myrtifolius | White | 8, H. Her. P. | | 1812 |
| nemoralis, 17 | Lilac | 8, H. Her. P. | N. Amer. | 1778 |
| Novæ-Angliæ | Purple | 9, H. Her. P. | N. Amer. | 1710 |
| ruber | Red | 7, H. Her. P. | N. Amer. | 1812 |
| Novi-Belgii | Pur. blue | 9, H. Her. P. | N. Amer. | 1710 |
| nudiflorus | Purple | 8, H. Her. P. | N. Amer. | |
| oblongifolius | Lilac | 7, H. Her. P. | N. Amer. | 1797 |
| obtusatus | White | 6, G. Ev. S. | C. G. H. | 1793 |
| pallens | Violet | 9, H. Her. P. | N. Amer. | |
| paludosus | Blue | 8, H. Her. P. | N. Amer. | 1784 |
| paniculatus | Blue | 9, H. Her. P. | N. Amer. | 1640 |
| pannonicus | Violet | 7, H. Her. P. | Hungary | 1815 |
| patens | Purple | 10, H. Her. P. | N. Amer. | 1773 |
| pauciflorus | White | 9, H. Her. P. | Missouri | |
| pendulus | White | 9, H. Her. P. | N. Amer. | 1758 |
| peregrinus | Blue | 7, H. Her. P. | N. Amer. | |
| phlogifolius | Violet | 9, H. Her. P. | N. Amer. | 1797 |
| pilosus, 18 | Pa. blue | 9, H. Her. P. | N. Amer. | 1812 |
| plantaginæfolius | White | 8, H. Her. P. | N. Amer. | |
| pluriflorus, 19 | White | 6, G. Ev. S. | C. G. H. | 1759 |
| polyphyllus, 20 | White | 9, H. Her. P. | N. Amer. | |
| præaltus | Vermil. | 9, H. Her. P. | N. Amer. | 1800 |
| præcox | Violet | 7, H. Her. P. | N. Amer. | 1800 |
| prenanthoides | Blue | 9, H. Her. P. | N. Amer. | 1821 |
| pulchellus | Purple | 6, H. Her. P. | Armenia | |
| pulcherrimus | Blue | 9, H. Her. P. | N. Amer. | 1810 |
| punctatus | Violet | 8, H. Her. P. | Hungary | 1815 |
| puniceus, 21 | Blue | 8, H. Her. P. | N. Amer. | 1710 |
| demissus | Blue | 9, H. Her. P. | Gardens | 1820 |
| pyrenæus | Violet | 7, H. Her. P. | Pyrenees | |
| radula | White | 10, H. Her. P. | N. Amer. | 1785 |
| ramosus, 22 | Pur. red | 6, H. Her. P. | N. Amer. | 1816 |
| recurvatus | Pa. blue | 8, H. Her. P. | N. Amer. | 1800 |
| reflexus | Crimson | 7, G. Ev. S. | C. G. H. | 1759 |
| reticulatus | White | 9, H. Her. P. | N. Amer. | 1812 |
| rigidulus | Blue | 9, H. Her. P. | N. Amer. | 1816 |
| rigidus | Purple | 9, H. Her. P. | N. Amer. | 1759 |
| rivularis | White | 8, H. Her. P. | N. Amer. | 1820 |
| rubricaulis, 23 | Purple | 9, H. Her. P. | N. Amer. | 1815 |
| sagittæfolius | Blue | 6, H. Her. P. | N. Amer. | 1700 |
| salicifolius, 24 | Flesh | 9, H. Her. P. | N. Amer. | 1760 |
| saliguus, 25 | White | 9, H. Her. P. | Germany | 1815 |
| sanguineus | Blue | 9, H. Her. P. | N. Amer. | |
| Schreberi | White | 8, H. Her. P. | N. Amer. | |
| sericeus | Blue | 8, G. Ev. S. | C. G. H. | 1786 |
| serotinus | Blue | 8, H. Her. P. | N. Amer. | |
| sessiliflorus | Red | 10, H. Her. P. | N. Amer. | 1700 |
| sibiricus | Blue | 8, H. Her. P. | Siberia | 1768 |
| simplex, 26 | Wht. pur. | 9, H. Her. P. | N. Amer. | |
| solidaginoides | White | 8, H. Her. P. | N. Amer. | 1699 |
| sparsiflorus | Pa. pur. | 10, H. Her. P. | N. Amer. | 1798 |
| spectabilis | Blue | 8, H. Her. P. | N. Amer. | 1777 |
| spurius | Blue | 9, H. Her. P. | N. Amer. | 1789 |
| squarrosus | Blue | 6, H. Her. P. | N. Amer. | 1801 |
| stellulatus | Violet | 0, G. Ev. T. | V. D. L. | 1823 |
| strictus | Violet | 10, H. Her. P. | N. Amer. | 1806 |
| subulatus | Pa. blue | 9, H. Her. P. | N. Amer. | |
| surculosus | Purple | 9, H. Her. P. | N. Amer. | |
| tardiflorus | Blue | 9, H. Her. P. | N. Amer. | 1775 |
| tataricus | White | 8, H. Her. P. | Tartary | 1818 |
| tenellus | Blue | 8, G. | B. C. G. H. | 1769 |
| tenuifolius | White | 8, H. Her. P. | N. Amer. | 1723 |
| tomentosus, 27 | Pink | 7, G. Ev. S. | N. S. W. | 1725 |
| tortifolius | Purple | 9, H. Her. P. | N. Amer. | |
| Tradescanti | White | 8, H. Her. P. | N. Amer. | 1633 |
| trinervis | White | 8, H. Her. P. | Nepal | 1818 |
| Tripolium | Blue | 8, H. Her. P. | Britain | |
| undulatus | Purple | 9, H. Her. P. | N. Amer. | 1699 |
| versicolor | Wht. pur. | 8, H. Her. P. | N. Amer. | 1790 |
| villosus | White | 5, G. Ev. S. | C. G. H. | 1812 |
| vimineus, 28 | Blue | 9, H. Her. P. | N. Amer. | 1800 |

*divergens, miser* 16.

ASTERIAS, stellate, starry.

ASTEROCEPHALUS, *Vaillant*. From *aster*, a star, *kephale*, head; in allusion to the seed. *Linn.* 4, Or. 1, Nat. Or. *Dipsaceæ*. Very showy plants, growing about two feet high in common soil, and may be readily increased from seeds or cuttings, under a hand-glass, in the same kind of soil. Synonymes: 1. *Scabiosa africana*. 2. *S. agrestis*. 3. *S. altissima, africana, indurata*. 4. *S. amœna, nitida*. 5. *S. argentea*. 6. *S. atropurpurea*. 7. *S. bannatica, Columnæ*. 8. *S. Bieberstcinii*. 9. *S. canescens*. 10. *S. capillata, mollis*. 11. *S. caucasea*. 12. *S. ceratophylla pilosa*. 13. *S. Colum-*

baria. 14. *S. commutata*. 15. *S. crenata, coronopifolia*. 16. *S. cretica*. 17. *S. elegans*. 18. *S. graminifolia*. 19. *S. gramuntia*. 20. *S. grandiflora*. 21. *S. holosericea*. 22. *S. incana*. 23. *S. intermedia*. 24. *S. isetensis*. 25. *S. legionensis*. 26. *S. lucida*. 27. *S. lutea*. 28. *S. lyrata*. 29. *S. maritima*. 30. *S. micrantha*. 31. *S. mollissima*. 32. *S. neglecta*. 33. *S. nitens, lucida*. 34. *S. ochroleuca*. 35. *S. palæstina*. 36. *S. paucisetus*. 37. *S. pectinata*. 38. *S. prolifera*. 39. *S. pyrenaica*. 40. *S. rotata*. 41. *S. rupestris*. 42. *S. rutæfolia*. 43. *S. saxatilis*. 44. *S. Scopolii*. 45. *S. setifera*. 46. *S. sicula*. 47. *S. silenifolia*. 48. *S. simplex*. 49. *S. stellata, laxiflora*. 50. *S. tomentosa*. 51. *S. ucranica*. 52. *S. urceolata*. 53. *Webbiana*.

| Name | Colour | Height, Culture | Native | Date |
|---|---|---|---|---|
| africanus, 1 | White | 8, G. Ev. S. | Africa | 1690 |
| agrestis, 2 | Purple | 8, H. Her. P. | Hungary | 1818 |
| altissimus, 3 | Blue | 8, G. Ev. S. | Africa | 1819 |
| amœnus, 4 | Purple | 6, H. Her. P. | | 1820 |
| argenteus, 5 | White | 8, H. Her. P. | Levant | 1713 |
| atropurpureus, 6 | Brown | 7, H. A. | E. Ind. | 1629 |
| albus | White | 7, H. A. | E. Ind. | 1629 |
| carneus | Flesh | 7, H. A. | E. Ind. | 1629 |
| proliferus | Purple | 7, H. A. | E. Ind. | 1629 |
| roseus | Red | 7, H. A. | E. Ind. | 1629 |
| variegatus | Varieg. | 7, H. A. | E. Ind. | 1629 |
| bannaticus, 7 | Pink | 7, H. Her. P. | Hungary | 1802 |
| Biebersteinii, 8 | Pink | 7, H. A. | Iberia | 1823 |
| canescens, 9 | Lilac | 7, H. Her. P. | Hungary | 1802 |
| capillatus, 10 | Violet | 7, H. Her. P. | | 1820 |
| caucaseus, 11 | Blue | 8, H. Her. P. | Caucasus | 1803 |
| ceratophyllus, 12 | Red | 7, H. Her. P. | Italy | 1826 |
| columbarius, 13 | Purple | 7, H. Her. P. | Britain | |
| commutatus, 14 | Blue | 7, H. Her. P. | Siberia | 1826 |
| crenatus, 15 | Flesh | 7, H. Her. P. | Italy | 1825 |
| creticus, 16 | Purple | 6, G. Ev. S. | Crete | 1596 |
| elegans, 17 | Lgt. blue | 6, H. Her. P. | S. Eur. | 1813 |
| graminifolius, 18 | Blue | 7, H. Her. P. | Switzerl. | 1683 |
| gramuntius, 19 | Lgt. blue | 7, H. Her. P. | S. Eur. | 1597 |
| grandiflorus, 20 | White | 7, H. A. | Barbary | 1804 |
| holosericeus, 21 | Blue | 7, H. Her. P. | Pyrenees | 1818 |
| incanus, 22 | Red | 7, H. Her. P. | Europe | 1826 |
| intermedius, 23 | Blue | 7, H. Her. P. | S. Eur. | 1824 |
| isetensis, 24 | White | 7, H. Her. P. | Siberia | 1801 |
| legionensis, 25 | Pink | 7, H. A. | Spain | 1820 |
| lucidus, 26 | Blue | 7, H. Her. P. | Dauphiny | 1800 |
| luteus, 27 | Yellow | 6, H. Her. P. | Russia | 1820 |
| lyratus, 28 | Purple | 7, G. Her. P. | Turkey | 1799 |
| maritimus, 29 | Purple | 7, H. A. | Italy | 1683 |
| micranthus, 30 | Pink | 7, H. Her. P. | Armenia | 1825 |
| mollissimus, 31 | White | 6, H. Her. P. | Italy | 1820 |
| neglectus, 32 | Red | 7, H. A. | Germany | 1825 |
| nitens, 33 | | 6, H. Her. P. | Azores | 1779 |
| ochroleucus, 34 | Yellow | 7, H. Her. P. | Germany | 1517 |
| palæstinus, 35 | Citron | 7, H. A. | Palestine | 1771 |
| paucisetus, 36 | Straw | 7, H. Her. P. | S. Eur. | 1827 |
| pectinatus, 37 | Violet | 7, H. A. | Arabia | 1824 |
| proliferus, 38 | Yellow | 7, H. A. | Egypt | 1683 |
| pyrenaicus, 39 | Purple | 7, H. Her. P. | S. France | 1819 |
| rotatus, 40 | Pink | 7, H. A. | Iberia | 1823 |
| rupestris, 41 | Pink | 7, H. Her. P. | Caucasus | 1824 |
| rutæfolius, 42 | Scarlet | 7, H. Her. P. | Sicily | 1804 |
| saxatilis, 43 | Pink | 7, H. A. | Spain | 1827 |
| Scopolii, 44 | Straw | 7, H. Her. P. | S. Eur. | 1818 |
| setiferus, 45 | White | 7, H. Her. P. | S. France | 1823 |
| siculus, 46 | Pink | 7, H. A. | Sicily | 1783 |
| silenifolius, 47 | Red | 7, H. Her. P. | Hungary | 1826 |
| simplex, 48 | White | 7, H. A. | S. Eur. | 1820 |
| stellatus, 49 | Blue | 7, H. A. | Spain | 1596 |
| tomentosus, 50 | Blue | 7, H. Her. P. | Spain | 1827 |
| ucranicus, 51 | Lgt. yel. | 7, H. Her. P. | Ukraine | 1795 |
| urceolatus, 52 | Yellow | 7, H. Her. P. | Barbary | 1804 |
| Webbianus, 53 | White | 7, H. Her. P. | Mt. Ida | 1818 |

ASTEROMA, *Decandolle*. Supposed to be named from *aster*, on account of their resemblance to a star. *Linn.* 24, Or. 9, Nat. Or. *Fungi*. The substances referred to this genus are merely cobweb lines, discernible upon the leaves of elm, ash, and sometimes apple-trees.—*Alchemillæ, Fraxini, Padi, Prunellæ, Pyri, Ulmi*.

ASTEROPHORA, *Dittmar*. Named from *aster*, a star, and *phoreo* to bear. *Linn.* 24, Or. 9, Nat. Or. *Fungi*. This curious production is said to be peculiar to rotten mushrooms—*lycoperdoides*.

ASTILBE, *Hamilton*. From *a*, privative, and *stilbe*, brightness; plants opaque. *Linn.* 10, Or. 2, Nat. Or. *Saxifragaceæ*. This plant is ornamental, attaining two feet in height; it grows best in open peat, and is multiplied by divisions. Synonyme: 1. *Tiarella biternata*.

| Name | Colour | Height, Culture | Native | Date |
|---|---|---|---|---|
| decandra, 1 | White | 6, H. Her. P. | Carolina | 1812 |

ASTRAGALUS, *Linnaeus*. From *astragalos*, vertebra, or talus, the seeds being squeezed into a squarish

F

form in some of the species. It is also a name given by the Greeks to one of their leguminous plants. Linn. 17, Or. 4, Nat. Or. *Leguminosæ*. This genus is extensive, and the species are many of them very handsome, and well suited for the flower-garden; the herbaceous kinds merely require planting in the open air; the annual kinds sowing where they are to flower. *A. lotoides* is the handsomest, and should be sown in a moderately-heating hotbed, and planted out in the borders when sufficiently strong. *Synonymes*: 1. *A. carnosus*. 2. *A. macrorhizus*. 3. *A. virescens*. 4. *A. malacaphyllus*. 5. *Phaca vesicaria*. 6. *A. tragacanthoides*. 7. *A. tenuifolius*. 8. *A. sinicus*. 9. *A. micranthus*. 10. *Phaca triangularis*. 11. *A. albidus*. 12. *A. alopecuroides*.

| | | | | | |
|---|---|---|---|---|---|
| acutifolius | . . | . | 7, H. Her. P. | Switzerl. | 1826 |
| adsúrgens | . . | Purple | 7, H. Her. P. | Siberia | 1820 |
| prostrátus | . . | Purple | 7, H. De. Tr. | Siberia | 1818 |
| adúncus | . . | Purple | 7, H. Her. P. | Caucasus | 1819 |
| ægicerás | . . | Pa. yel. | 7, H. Tr. A. | | 1818 |
| alopécias | . . | Yellow | 6, H. Her. P. | Siberia | 1810 |
| alopecuroídes | . | Lgt. yel. | 7, H. Her. P. | Spain | 1737 |
| Ammodýtes | . . | White | 7, H. Ev. S. | Siberia | 1820 |
| annuláris | . . | Purple | 7, H. Tr. A. | Egypt | 1810 |
| arenárius | . . | Blue | 7, H. De. Tr. | Germany | 1768 |
| aristátus | . . | Purple | 7, H. Ev. S. | Pyrenees | 1791 |
| ásper | . . | Pa. yel. | 7, H. Her. P. | Astracan | 1796 |
| austríacus | . . | Pa. blue | 7, H. Tr. A. | S. Eur. | 1640 |
| bǽticus | . . | Pa. yel. | 7, H. Tr. A. | S. Eur. | 1759 |
| baicalensis | . . | Yellow | 8, H. Her. P. | Siberia | 1830 |
| bayonénsis | . . | Purple | 7, H. Her. P. | France | 1816 |
| brachycárpus | . | Purple | 7, H. De. Tr. | Caucasus | 1820 |
| brachýceras | . | Yellow | 7, H. | Tauria | 1828 |
| brevifórus | . . | Purple | 7, F. Ev. S. | Armenia | 1826 |
| búceras | . . | Pa. yel. | 7, H. Tr. A. | | 1818 |
| buchtornénsis | . | Yellow | 6, H. Her. P. | Siberia | 1818 |
| canadénsis | . . | Pa. yel. | 7, H. Her. P. | N. Amer. | 1732 |
| canaliculátus | . | White | 7, H. | A. | 1816 |
| caprínus | . . | Pa. yel. | 7, H. Her. P. | Barbary | 1683 |
| capitátus | . . | Pa. yel. | 7, H. Her. P. | Levant | 1759 |
| caroliniánus | . | Grn. yel. | 7, H. Her. P. | N. Amer. | 1732 |
| caryocárpus, 1 | . | Purple | 7, H. Her. B. | Spain | 1800 |
| caucásicus | . . | White | 7, H. Ev. S. | Caucasus | 1824 |
| chinénsis | . . | Pa. yel. | 7, G. Her. P. | China | 1795 |
| chlorostáchys | . | Grn. yel. | 9, H. Her. P. | Nepal | 1824 |
| christiánus | . . | Pa. yel. | 7, H. Her. P. | Armenia | 1737 |
| Cícer | . . | Yellow | 7, H. Tr. A. | Europe | 1570 |
| contortuplicátus | . | Pa. yel. | 7, H. Tr. A. | Siberia | 1764 |
| cruciátus | . . | Violet | 7, H. Tr. A. | | 1820 |
| cymbaecárpus | . | White | 7, H. Tr. A. | Spain | 1800 |
| dahúricus | . . | Purple | 6, H. Her. P. | Dahuria | 1822 |
| dasyglóttis | . . | Purple | 7, H. De. Tr. | Siberia | 1818 |
| depréssus | . . | Pa. yel. | 7, H. De. Tr. | Europe | 1772 |
| diffúsus | . . | Pa. yel. | 7, H. Her. P. | Caspia | 1820 |
| Doniánus, 2 | . | Purple | 7, H. De. Tr. | Nepal | 1818 |
| emarginátus | . | Pa. yel. | 8, H. Her. P. | S. Eur. | 1825 |
| epiglóttis | . . | Pa. yel. | 7, H. De. Tr. S. Eur. | | 1737 |
| exscápus | . . | Yellow | 7, H. Her. P. | Hungary | 1827 |
| falcátus, 3 | . | Grn. yel. | 7, H. Her. P. | Siberia | |
| falcifórmis | . | Pa. yel. | 7, H. Her. P. | Algiers | 1816 |
| fruticósus | . . | Violet | 7, H. De. S. | Siberia | 1804 |
| galegifórmis, 4 | . | Yel. grn. | 6, H. Her. P. | Siberia | 1729 |
| Gláux | . . | Purple | 7, H. Tr. A. | Spain | 1596 |
| glycyphylloídes | . | Pa. yel. | 7, H. De. Tr. | Iberia | 1818 |
| glycyphýllus | . | Yel. grn. | 7, H. De. Tr. | Britain | |
| grácilis | . . | Purple | 6, H. Her. P. | N. Amer. | 1821 |
| Halicácabus | . | Pa. yel. | 6, H. Her. P. | Armenia | 1806 |
| hamósus | . . | Pa. yel. | 6, H. De. Tr. | Spain | 1683 |
| macrocárpus | . | Pa. yel. | 6, H. De. Tr. S. Eur. | | 1820 |
| hypoglóttis | . | Purple | 7, H. De. | Britain | |
| incánus | . . | Purple | 7, H. Her. P. | Montpel. | 1759 |
| inflátus | . . | Purple | 7, H Her. P. | Mendoza | 1827 |
| lanígerus, 6 | . | Yellow | 6, H. Her. P. | Egypt | 1791 |
| Laxmánni | . . | Purple | 8, H. De. Tr. | Siberia | 1814 |
| leontínus | . . | Blue | 7, H. Her. P. | Austria | 1816 |
| leptophýllus | . | White | 7, H. Her. P. | Barbary | 1811 |
| leucophǽus | . | Wht. yel. | 7, H. De. Tr. | | 1776 |
| linaerifólius, 7 | . | Purple | 7, H. Her. P. | Siberia | 1780 |
| longiflórus | . . | Yellow | 7, H. Her. P. | Tartary | 1806 |
| lotoídes, 8 | . | Red | 8, H. Tr. A. | China | 1763 |
| mareóticus | . . | Lilac | 7, H. Tr. A. | Egypt | 1817 |
| máximus | . . | Yellow | 6, H. Her. P. | America | |
| melilotoídes | . | Purple | 6, H. Her. P. | Siberia | 1785 |
| micránthus | . | Pa. yel. | 7, H. Her. P. | | 1800 |
| microphýllus | . | Yellow | 6, H. Her. P. | Siberia | 1773 |
| monspessulánus | . | Purple | 7, H. Ev. Tr. | France | 1710 |
| albus | . . | White | 7, H. Her. P. S. Eur. | | |
| narbonénsis | . | Pa. yel. | 7, H. Her. P. | S. Eur. | 1789 |
| negléctus | . . | Purple | 7, H. Her. P. | Siberia | 1826 |
| Nuttalliánus, 9 | . | Blue | 7, H. Tr. A. | America | 1820 |
| odorátus | . . | Pa. yel. | 7, H. Her. P. | S. Eur. | 1820 |
| onobrychioídes | . | Purple | 7, H. Her. P. | Iberia | 1819 |
| Onobrýchis | . | Purple | 7, H. De. Tr. | Austria | 1640 |
| otóptérus | . . | Pa. blue | 7, H. Her. P. | Altai | 1817 |
| oxyglóttis | . . | Blue | 7, H. Tr. A. | Tauria | 1817 |
| Pállasii | . . | Purple | 7, H. Her. P. | Caspia | 1818 |
| pallescens | . . | Pa. yel. | 6, H. Her. P. | Siberia | |

| | | | | | |
|---|---|---|---|---|---|
| pentaglóttis | . | Purple | 7, H. Tr. A | Spain | 1789 |
| physódes | . . | Purple | 7, H. Her. P. | Siberia | 1759 |
| platyphýllus | . | Pa. yel. | 7, H. De. Tr. | Siberia | 1824 |
| pónticus | . . | Pa. yel. | 7, H. Her. P. | Tauria | 1820 |
| Potérium | . . | White | 7, H. Ev. S. | Levant | 1640 |
| procúmbens | . | Yel. blue | 5, F. Her. P. | Chile | 1832 |
| purpúreus | . . | Purple | 7, H. De. Tr. S. France | | 1820 |
| réptans | . . | White | 7, G. Ev. Cr. | Mexico | 1818 |
| reticuláris | . . | Blue | 7, H. | A. Iberia | 1828 |
| semiloculáris | . | Pa. yel. | 7, H. Her. P. | Siberia | 1804 |
| sesámeus | . . | Pa. blue | 7, H. Tr. A. | S. Eur. | 1616 |
| scorpioídes | . | Pa. blue | 7, H. | A. Spain | 1816 |
| stélla | . . | Blue | 7, H. De. Tr. S. Eur. | | 1658 |
| stipulátus | . . | Yellow | 6, H. Her. P. | Nepal | 1822 |
| subulátus | . . | Purple | 7, H. Her. P. | Siberia | 1820 |
| succuléntus | . | Purple | 7, H. Her. P. | N. Amer. | 1827 |
| sulcátus | . . | Lgt. blue | 7, H. Her. P. | Siberia | 1785 |
| taúricus | . . | Purple | 7, H. Her. P. | Tauria | 1826 |
| testiculátus | . | Flesh wht. | 7, H. Her. P. | Tauria | 1818 |
| tomentósus | . | Pa. yel. | 7, F. Her. P. | Egypt | 1800 |
| Tragacánthā | . | Pa. yel. | 7, H. Ev. S. | S. Eur. | 1640 |
| trianguláris, 10 | . | Pa. yel. | 7, H. | A. | 1818 |
| tribuloídes | . | Purple | 7, H. Tr. A. | Egypt | 1617 |
| triméstris | . . | Pa. yel. | 7, H. Tr. A. | Egypt | 1730 |
| trimórphus | . | Purple | 7, H. Tr. A. | S. Eur. | 1816 |
| túmidus | . . | Pa. yel. | 7, H. Ev. S. | Egypt | 1816 |
| uliginósus | . . | Pa. yel. | 7, H. Her. P. | Siberia | 1752 |
| utríger | . . | Yellow | 7, H. Her. P. | Russia | 1818 |
| vesicárius, 11 | . | Wht. yel. | 7, H. De. Tr. | Europe | 1737 |
| vimíneus | . . | Purple | 7, H. Her. P. | Siberia | 1816 |
| virgátus | . . | Violet | 7, H. De. S. | Siberia | 1806 |
| vulpínus, 12 | . | Lgt. yel. | 7, H. Her. P. | Caucas. | 1815 |

**ASTRÁNTHUS**, *Loureiro*. Named from *astron*, a star, and *anthos*, a flower; segments radiating in a star-like manner. Linn. 8, Or. 1, Nat. Or. *Homalineæ*. This species is curious, it grows about four feet high, and will succeed in any rich soil; cuttings in sand strike freely.

| | | | | |
|---|---|---|---|---|
| cochin-chinénsis | . White | . 7, G. Ev. S. | China | . . 1822 |

**ASTRÁNTIA**, *Linnæus*. From *astron*, a star, and *anti*, comparison; in reference to the appearance of the umbels of flowers. Linn. 5, Or. 2, Nat. Or. *Umbelliferæ*. This is a pretty genus; the plants grow from half a foot to two feet high, and succeed well in the flower-border. *A. minor* requires to be grown in pots, and protected in a pit or frame in winter; increased by seeds. *Synonymes*: 1. *A. intermedia*. 2. *A. helliborifolia heterophylla*.

| | | | | |
|---|---|---|---|---|
| carniólica | . . | Striped | 6, H Her. P. Carniola | 1812 |
| caucásica, 1 | . | Pink | 7, H. Her. P. Caucasus | 1818 |
| májor | . . | Striped | 6, H. Her. P. Alp. Eur. | 1596 |
| máxima, 2 | . | Pink | 7, H. Her. P. Caucasus | 1804 |
| minor | . . | Pink | 6, H. Her. P. Switzerl. | 1686 |
| paucifóra | . | White | 7, H. Her. P. Sicily | 1820 |

**ASTRAPÆX**, *Lindley*. Named from *astrape*, lightning, bright colour of the flowers. Linn. 16, Or. 7, Nat. Or. *Sterculiaceæ*. These are splendid plants, especially *A. Wallichii*, which may be considered one of the finest plants that ever was introduced; when loaded with its magnificent flowers, we think nothing can exceed its grandeur; there are other species in the collections about London, but we have not yet seen their flowers; they grow freely in any rich soil, or a mixture of loam and peat suits them very well; young cuttings planted in mould, and placed under a hand glass in heat, will soon strike root.

| | | | | |
|---|---|---|---|---|
| tiliæfólia | . . . | | 8. Ev. T. Bourbon. | 1824 |
| viscósa | . . | Pink | 8. Ev. T. Madagas. | 1823 |
| Wállichii | . | Pink | 7, S. Ev. T. Madagas. | 1820 |

**ASTROCÁRYUM**, *Meyer*. From *astron*, a star, and *karyon*, nut; in allusion to the fruit. Linn. 21, Or. 6, Nat. Or. *Palmaceæ*. A genus of very ornamental trees, attaining the height of from ten to forty feet, thriving in rich loamy soil best, and increased plentifully from seeds.

| | | | | |
|---|---|---|---|---|
| acaúle | . . . | | Pa. m. Brazil | . . 1820 |
| aculeátum | . . | | Palm. Guiana | . . 1824 |
| campéstre | . . | | Palm. Brazil | . . 1826 |
| Murumúrū | . | | Palm Brazil | . . 1825 |
| vulgáre | . . | | Palm. Brazil | . . 1825 |

**ASTROLÓBIUM**, *Decandolle*. From *astron*, a star, and *lobos*, a pod; in reference to the disposition of the pods. Linn. 17, Or. 4, Nat. Or. *Leguminosæ*. Very pretty dwarf annuals, with an abundance of yellow flowers; they grow freely in any soil, and ripen abundance of seed, by which they may be multiplied. *Synonymes*: 1. *Ornithopus durus*. 2. *O. ebracteatus*. 3. *O. repandus*. 4. *O. scorpioides*.

| | | | | | | |
|---|---|---|---|---|---|---|
| durum, 1 | . | . Yellow | . 7, H. | A. Spain | . | 1816 |
| ebracteatum, 2 | . | . Yellow | . 7, H. | A. S. Eur. | . | 1700 |
| repandum, 8 | . | . Yellow | . 7, H. | A. Barbary | . | 1805 |
| scorpioides, 4 | . | . Yellow | . 7, H. | A. S. Eur. | . | 1506 |

ASTROLŎMĂ, *Robert Brown.* From *astron,* a star, and *loma,* a fringe; the limb of the corolla being bearded. *Linn.* 5, Or. 1, Nat. Or. *Epacrideæ.* This most beautiful genus should be in every collection; they make little bushes about a foot high, and thrive best in sandy loam and peat mixed, with the pots well drained, and the plants cautiously watered; cuttings root in sand under a glass.

| | | | | | | |
|---|---|---|---|---|---|---|
| denticulatum | . | Pa. red. | . 7, G. Ev. S. N. Holl. | . | 1824 |
| humifūsŭm | . | . Scarlet | . 7, G. Ev. S. N. S. W. | . | 1807 |

ASTROSPŎRĬŬM, *Kunze.* From *aster,* a star, and *spora,* a sporule, alluding to the form of the sporules. *Linn.* 24, Or. 9, Nat. Or. *Fungi.* A minute curious black substance, discovered on dead beech branches —*Hoffmanni.*

ATALANTHŬS, *D. Don.* From *atalos,* soft, and *anthos,* a flower; in reference to the softness of the flowers. *Linn.* 19, Or. 1, Nat. Or. *Compositæ.* These are species of little beauty, and easy cultivation—*arbŏreus, pinnatus, spinosus.*

ATALANTĬA, *Correa.* The fruit of this shrub is of a golden yellow colour, whence the name from Atalanta the daughter of Schœnus; so swift that she promised to marry him who outran her, and by casting three golden apples in her way, she was overtaken by Hippomenes. *Linn.* 10, Or. 1, Nat. Or. *Aurantiaceæ.* This species is represented as being ornamental, and attaining four feet in height; it succeeds in any rich soil, and increases freely from cuttings in sand under a glass in heat. *Synonyme:* 1. *Limonium monophyllum.*

| | | | | | | |
|---|---|---|---|---|---|---|
| monophylla, 1 | . White | . . 7, S. Ev. S. E. Ind. | . | 1777 |

ATAMASCŎ-LILY, see *Zephyranthes Atamasco.*

ATHAMANTĂ, *Koch.* Some of the species are found upon Mount Athamas in Sicily; whence the name. *Linn.* 5, Or. 2, Nat. Or. *Umbelliferæ.* These are chiefly weeds, of very easy culture. *Synonymes:* 1. *Ligusticum Cervaria.* 2. *Cachrys panacifolia.*

| | | | | | | |
|---|---|---|---|---|---|---|
| condensata | . | . White | . 8, H. Her. P. Siberia | . | 1773 |
| macedonica | . | . White | . 7, H. Her. P. Greece | . | 1596 |
| Matthiolii | . | . White | . 7, H. Her. P. Carniola | . | 1802 |
| tortuosa | . | . White | . 7, F. Her. P. S. Eur. | . | 1826 |

*Annŭă, carvifŏlĭă, Cervărĭă* 1, *cretensis, incănă, lasiănthă, panacifŏlĭă* 2, *sibirĭcă, sicŭlă.*

ATHANASĬA, *Cassini.* From *a,* privative, and *thanatos,* death; in allusion to the length of time the flowers last. *Linn.* 19, Or. 1, Nat. Or. *Compositæ.* This is a genus of Cape plants, growing from half a foot to two feet high; some of them are very pretty, and all succeed well in loamy soil, and increase from cuttings in sand under a glass. *Synonyme:* 1. *A. lanuginosa.*

| | | | | | | |
|---|---|---|---|---|---|---|
| canescens, 1 | . | . Yellow | . 7, G. Ev. S. C. G. H. | . | 1820 |
| capitata | . | . Yellow | . 8, G. Ev. S. C. G. H. | . | 1774 |
| crenata | . | . Yellow | . 7, G. Ev. S. C. G. H. | . | 1816 |
| crithmifolia | . | . Yellow | . 7, G. Ev. S. C. G. H. | . | 1783 |
| cuneifolia | . | . Yellow | . 7, G. Ev. S. C. G. H. | . | 1816 |
| dentata | . | . Yellow | . 7, G. Ev. S. C. G. H. | . | 1759 |
| filiformis | . | . Yellow | . 8, G. Ev. S. C. G. H. | . | 1787 |
| longifolia | . | . Yellow | . 7, G. Ev. S. C. G. H. | . | 1800 |
| parviflora | . | . Yellow | . 4, G. Ev. S. C. G. H. | . | 1731 |
| pectinata | . | . Yellow | . 7, G. Ev. S. C. G. H. | . | 1774 |
| pinnata | . | . Yellow | . 7, G. Ev. S. C. G. H. | . | 1818 |
| pubescens | . | . Yellow | . 7, G. Ev. S. C. G. H. | . | 1768 |
| punctata | . | . Yellow | . 6, G. Ev. S. C. G. H. | . | 1822 |
| tomentosa | . | . Yellow | . 5, G. Ev. S. C. G. H. | . | 1774 |
| tricuspis | . | . Yellow | . 7, G. Ev. S. C. G. H. | . | 1816 |
| trifurcata | . | . Yellow | . 7, G. Ev. S. C. G. H. | . | 1710 |
| virgata | . | . Yellow | . 7, G. Ev. S. C. G. H. | . | 1815 |

ATHEROPŎGŎN, *Willdenow.* From *ather,* awn, and *pogon,* a beard; on account of the awns being bearded. *Linn.* 23, Or. 1, Nat. Or. *Gramineæ.* This is a species of grass said to be very pretty; the cultivation and propagation simple. *Synonyme:* 1. *Chloris curtipendula, Dinebra curtipendula.*

| | | | | | | |
|---|---|---|---|---|---|---|
| apludoides, 1 | . . Apetal | . 8, Grass. S. Eur. | . | 1768 |

ATHEROSPERMĂ, *Labillardiere.* From *ather,* awn, *sperma,* seed; the seeds being furnished with awns. *Linn.* 21, Or. 8, Nat. Or. *Atherospermaceæ.* An ornamental tree, attaining the height of twenty-two feet; it grows in loam and peat, and may be increased from cuttings.

| | | | | | | |
|---|---|---|---|---|---|---|
| moschata | . | . . White . | . 6, G. Ev. T. N. Holl. | . | 1824 |

[ 35 ]

ATHRIXĬA, *Ker.* From *a,* privative, and *thrix,* a hair; the receptacle being without hairs. *Linn.* 19, Or. 2, Nat. Or. *Compositæ.* This is a rather low, ornamental Cape shrub, succeeding in a loamy soil, and increased from cuttings.

| | | | | | | |
|---|---|---|---|---|---|---|
| capensis | . | . . Red | . 4, G. Ev. S. C. G. H. | . | 1821 |

ATRACTŎBŎLŬS, *Tode.* The bladder which contains the sporules is fusiform, and is ejected from the base of the capsule as soon as the operculum is thrown off; whence the name, from *atracktos,* a spindle, and *boleo,* to eject. *Linn.* 24. Or. 9, Nat. Or. *Fungi.* Merely a white powdery substance found on wood, stones, &c.—*ubiquitārius.*

ATRACTYLIS, *Linnæus.* The stems are light, and fit to make spindles; whence the name is derived from *atraktos,* a spindle. *Linn.* 19, Or. 1, Nat. Or. *Compositæ.* This species is fit only for general collections; culture and propagation easy—*humilis.*

ATRAGENE, *Linnæus.* A name given to a species of Clematis by Theophrastus. *Linn.* 13, Or. 6, Nat. Or. *Ranunculaceæ.* This is a valuable and handsome genus of climbing plants, well adapted for training like Clematis, over bowers, trellis-work, and places where climbing plants are desirable; they grow in any common soil, and young plants may be obtained from cuttings under a glass, or layers. Seeds are sometimes produced, which should be sown in pans, and potted off, and attended. *Synonymes:* 1. *Clematis verticillaris.* 2. *Atragene alpina, Clematis alpina.* 3. *Clematis occidentalis.* 4. *C. ochotensis.* 5. *C. sibirica.*

| | | | | | | |
|---|---|---|---|---|---|---|
| americana, 1 | . | . Purple | . 6, H. De. Cl. N. Amer. | . | 1797 |
| obliqua | . | . Purple | . 6, H. De. Cl. N. Amer. | . | 1797 |
| austriaca, 2 | . | . Brn. yel. | . 7, H. De. Cl. Austria | . | 1792 |
| occidentalis, 3. | . | . | . 7, H. De. Cl. | . | 1818 |
| ochotensis, 4 | . | . White . | . 6, H. De. Cl. Siberia | . | 1818 |
| sibirica, 5 | . | . Wht. yel. | . 7, H. De. Cl. Siberia | . | 1753 |

ATRAPHAXIS, *Linnæus.* Derived from *a,* privative, and *trepho,* to nourish, a plant yielding no nourishment; a name given by the Greeks to the Atriplex of the Latins. *Linn.* 6, Or. 2, Nat. Or. *Polygonaceæ.* The species of this genus are curious; they grow about two feet high, and thrive in a loamy soil, and increase from layers.

| | | | | | | |
|---|---|---|---|---|---|---|
| spinosa | . | . . Apetal | . 8, F. Ev. S. Levant | . | 1732 |
| undulata | . | . . Apetal | . 6, F. Ev. S. C. G. H. | . | 1732 |

ATRIPLEX, *Linnæus.* From *ater,* black; the same name as *Atraphaxia.* *Linn.* 23, Or. 1, Nat. Or. *Chenopodiaceæ.* These are straggling plants of little beauty, and the simplest culture and propagation. *Synonymes:* 1. *A. nitens.* 2. *A. rosea.* 3. *A. tatarica.* 4. *Calligonum canescens.* 5. *A. prostrata.* 6. *A. patula.* 7. *A. hastata.* 8. *A. incisa.* 9. *Obione sibirica.*

| | | | | | | |
|---|---|---|---|---|---|---|
| Halimus | . | . . Green | . 7, H. Ev. S. Spain | . | 1640 |
| hortensis | . | . . Green | . 7, H. A. Tartary | . | 1548 |
| rubra | . | . . Green | . 7, H. A. Tartary | . | 1548 |
| portulacoides | . | . Green | . 6, H. Ev. S. Britain. | . | |

*Acuminātă* 1, *ălbă* 2, *ălbĭcăns, angustifŏlĭă, campestris* 3, *canescens* 4, *decumbens* 5, *diffusa, erecta, glauca, hastata* 6, *incana laciniata, linifolia, littoralis, microsperma, montevidensis, oblongifolia, obtusata, parvifolia, patula* 7, *pedunculata, prostrata, reniformis, rosea* 8, *sibirica* 9, *sulcata, tatarica, triangularis, venata, verticillata, virgata.*

ATROPĂ, *Linnæus.* In allusion to the very poisonous fruit; from Atropos, one of the Fates, whose duty it was to cut the thread of human life. *Linn.* 5, Or. 1, Nat. Or. *Solanaceæ.* Both poisonous species, only fit for botanical collections. The leaves of *A. Belladonna* are narcotic and exciting.

| | | | | | | |
|---|---|---|---|---|---|---|
| arborescens | . | . White | . 7, G. Ev. S. Jamaica | . | 1733 |
| Belladonna | . | . Violet . | . 6, H. Her. P. Britain | . | |

ATTALĔA, *Humboldt.* Derived from *attalus,* magnificent; in allusion to the beauty of the trees. *Linn.* 21, Or. 9, Nat. Or. *Palmaceæ.* A fine genus of ornamental Palm trees, attaining the height of from ten to seventy feet; they thrive in any rich soil, and increase from seeds.

| | | | | | |
|---|---|---|---|---|---|
| compta | . | . . . | . Palm. Brasil | . | 1820 |
| excelsa | . | . . . | . Palm. Brasil | . | 1826 |
| funifera | . | . . . | . Palm. Brasil | . | 1824 |
| humilis | . | . . . | . Palm. Brasile. | . | 1820 |
| Rósaei | . | . . . | . Palm. Brasil | . | 1825 |
| speciosa | . | . . . | . Palm. Brasil | . | 1826 |
| spectabilis | . | . . . | . Palm. Brasil | . | 1824 |

ATTENUATE,
ATTENUATED, } tapering gradually to a point.

AUBRIÈTIA, *Adanson.* In honour of M. Aubriet, a famous French botanical draughtsman. *Linn.* 15, Nat. Or. *Cruciferæ.* These are very ornamental either in the flower-garden or on rock-work, as they produce their purple flowers for such a length of time; they delight in an open dry situation, and are multiplied by dividing the roots, or cuttings, under a glass. *Synonymes :* 1. *Farsetia deltoidea, Alyssum deltoideum.* 2. *Draba hesperidiflora.* 3. *Arabis purpurea.*

deltoideä, 1 . . Purple . 4, H. Ev. Tr. Levant . . 1710
hesperidiflorä, 2 . Purple . 3, H. Ev. Tr. S Eur. . . 1823
purpureä, 3 . . Purple . 4, H. Ev. Tr. Greece . . 1820

AUCUBA, *Kæmpfer.* The name of the shrub in Japan. *Linn.* 21, Or. 4, Nat. Or. *Cornaceæ.* This is a fine hardy shrub, and its beautiful blotched leaves make it generally admired, particularly as it is clothed with leaves all the year; it is proper for standing singly on a small grass-plot, or in clumps amongst other shrubs in a conspicuous place. Cuttings root readily under hand-glasses, in the common garden soil.

japónicä . . . Apetal . 6, H. Ev. S. Japan . . 1783

AUCUPARIUS, having a tendency to attract birds.

AUDIBÈRTIA, *Bentham.* In honour of M. Audibert, of Tarascon, a celebrated nurseryman. *Linn.* 2, Or. 1, Nat. Or. *Labiatæ.* An interesting little plant about a foot and half high, and bearing palish-blue flowers; it grows in any common soil, and increases from seeds. *Synonyme:* 1. *Salvia carnosa.*

incänä . . . . Pa. blue . 3, H. Ev. S. Columbia . 1827

AUDOUÏNIA, *Brongniart.* In honour of V. Audouin, a profound entomologist and friend of Brongniart. *Linn.* 5, Or. 1, Nat. Or. *Bruniaceæ.* An ornamental genus; for culture, &c., see the genus *Diosma.* *Synonyme:* 1. *Diosma capitata.*

capitätä . . . . Purple . 6, G. Ev. S. C. G. H. . 1790

AUGUSTUS, grand, stately, magnificent.

AULAX, *Bergius.* Named from *aulax,* a furrow; the under side of the leaves of the original species being furrowed. *Linn.* 22, Or. 4, Nat. Or. *Proteaceæ.* This is a pretty genus; the species attain from one to two feet high and bear yellow flowers; they succeed best in a very sandy loam, with a good drainage; ripened cuttings taken off at a joint, and planted in a pot of sand, will strike root readily under a hand-glass.

pinifoliä . . . Yellow . 8, G. Ev. S. C. G. H. . 1780
umbellätä . . . Yellow . 7, G. Ev. S. C. G. H. . 1774

AURICOMUS, a head or tuft like hair, of a gold colour.

AURICULATE,
AURICULATED, } having ear-like appendages.
AURICLED,

AURICULATELY-SAGITTATE, eared at the base, so as to give the leaf the appearance of the head of an arrow.

AURICULATELY STEM-CLASPING, having auricles at the base of the leaves, clasping the stem.

AVÈNA, *Linnæus.* A name of obscure origin, supposed to be from the Celtic aten, from *etan,* to eat; whence our word oat has been obtained. *Linn.* 3, Or. 2, Nat. Or. *Gramineæ.* The species of this genus are easy of cultivation, and uninteresting in point of beauty.

nüdä . . . . Apetal . 6, Grass.
orientälis . . . Apetal . 6, Grass.
praténsis . . . Apetal . 6, Grass. Britain . . 1798
sativä . . . . Apetal . 6, Grass.
leucospērmä . Apetal . 6, Grass.
melanospērmä . Apetal . 6, Grass.
stèrilis . . . . Apetal . 6, Grass. Barbary . . 1640

Albä, brèvis, bromöides, fállax, fátuä, hirsütä, planicúlmis, précôx, púmilä, sempèrvirèns, setácëä, versicölor.

AVÈNS, see Geum.

AVÈRRHÒA, *Linnæus.* In honour of Averrhoes, of Cordova, in Spain, a celebrated physician. *Linn.* 10, Or. 4, Nat. Or. *Oxalidaceæ.* The species are evergreen trees, singular for the fruit growing frequently on the trunk itself below the leaves: the flowers grow in racemes; the fruit is a five-celled pomme. *A. Bilimbi* is a beautiful tree, with a green, fleshy, oblong fruit, the thickness of the finger, filled with a grateful acid juice; the sub-

stance and seeds not unlike those of the cucumber. Both species form handsome plants in our stoves, growing freely; and ripened cuttings root readily in sand, under a hand-glass.

Bilimbi . . . . Red yel. . 3, S. Ev. S. E. Ind. . . 1791
Carambölä . . . Grn. red . 8, S. Ev. S. Ceylon . . 1733

AVICÈNNIA, *Linnæus.* In honour of Avicenna, a celebrated Persian philosopher and physician. *Linn.* 14, Or. 2, Nat. Or. *Myoporaceæ.* The bark of *A. tomentosa* is in great use at Rio Janeiro for tanning, but it is not worth culture in this country—*tomentosä.*

AVICULAR, fit for bird's meat.

AWL-SHAPED, narrow-pointed, like an awl.

AWNED, terminating in an awn, or sharp point.

AWNEDLY-ACUMINATED, tapering to a point, and terminating in an awn.

AWNS, the beard of any thing.

AXIL,
AXILLA, } literally the arm-pit; in plants applied to the angle formed by the union of the leaf and stem.

AXIL-FLOWERING, flowering in the axils of the leaves.

AXILLARY, placed in the axils or axillæ.

AXIS, the line real or imaginary that passes through any thing; the axis of a spike of flowers is the stem to which the flowers are attached.

AXONOPUS, *Beauvois.* Derived from *axon,* axis, and *pous,* a foot; in reference to the structure of the plant. *Linn.* 3, Or. 2, Nat. Or. *Gramineæ.* Species of grass, possessing little that is interesting.

cimicinüs . . . Apetal . . 7, Grass. India . . 1788

aürëus, digitätüs.

AXYRIS, *Linnæus.* From *axyros,* rough; on account of the leaves. *Linn.* 21, Or. 3, Nat. Or. *Chenopodiaceæ.* The species of this genus are mere weeds, of the easiest culture, &c.—*amaranthöidës, hġbridä, prosträtä.*

AYÈNIA, *Linnæus.* In honour of the Duke d'Ayen, of the house of Noailles. *Linn.* 5, Or. 1, Nat. Or. *Sterculiaceæ.* The species are curious and grow from one to two feet high, producing purple and scarlet flowers in rich soil, and are multiplied by cuttings in sand.

lævigätä . . . Scarlet . S. Ev. S. Jamaica .
pusillä . . . Purple . 3, S. B. Jamaica . 1756

AZALEA, *Linnæus.* From *azaleos,* dry, arid; habitation of the plant. *Linn.* 5, Or. 1, Nat. Or. *Ericaceæ.* This is a beautiful genus, universally admired for its white, orange, purple, scarlet, and variegated flowers, which are invariably produced in great profusion. They all thrive best in sandy peat or very sandy loam; and cuttings taken off close to the plant will root in sand, under a glass placed in heat, or they may be multiplied from seeds, &c. *A. indica* is a greenhouse plant of great beauty, it should stand out in the open air in summer in a partially shaded situation, and in the winter in a cool part of the greenhouse; the beautiful varieties require the same treatment.

arborëscèns . . Red . . 6, H. De. S. N. Amer. . 1818
bicölor . . . . Scarlet . 6, H. De. S. N. Amer. . 1734
canèscèns . . . Red . . 6, H. De. S. N. Amer. . 1812
calendulâcëä . . Orange . 6, H. De. S. N. Amer. . 1806
chrysolêctä . . Yellow . 6, H. De. S. N. Amer. .
crócëä . . . . Saffron . 6, H. De. S. N. Amer. .
cūprëä . . . . Copper . 6, H. De. S. N. Amer. .
flammëä . . . Red . . 6, H. De. S. N. Amer. . 1812
grandiflorä . . . Orange . 6, H. De. S. N. Amer. .
ignëscèns . . . Red . . 6, H. De. S. N. Amer. .
lèpidä . . . . Varieg. . 6, H. De. S. N. Amer. .
splèndèns . . . Orange . 6, H. De. S. Hybrid .
Stapletoniänä . Rosy . . 6, H. De. S. Hybrid .
subcūprëä . . . Copper . 6, H. De. S. Hybrid .
triūmphäns . . Orange . 6, H. De. S. N. Amer. .
Daniel siänä . . Carmine . 6, H. De. S. China . . 1830
glaücä . . . . White . 6, H. De. S. N. Amer. . 1734
hispidä . . . . White . 6, H. De. S. N. Amer. . 1734
indicä . . . . Scarlet . 6, G. Ev. S. China . 1808
aurantiäcä . . Orange . 4, G. Ev. S. China . 1822
ignëscèns . . . Brown . 4, H. Ev. S. China .
phœnicëä . . . Purple . 4, G. Ev. S. China . 1824
purpurëö-plénä . Purple . 5, G. Ev. S. China . 1819
variegätä . . . Striped . 6, G. Ev. S. China . 1824
ledifoliüm, . . White . 4, G. Ev. S. China . 1824
Mortêrii . . . . Flesh . 5, H. De. S. Hybrid .
prüitäns . . . . Copper . 6, H. De. S. Hybrid .
nitidä . . . . . White . 4, H. De. S. N. Amer. . 1812
nudiflorä . . . Scr. Pink . 6, H. De. S. N. Amer. . 1734
albä . . . . White . 6, H. De. S. N. Amer. .

| | | | |
|---|---|---|---|
| alba-plēnā . . | White . . | 6, H. De. S. N. Amer. . | |
| blandā . . | Blush . . | 6, H. De. S. N. Amer. . | |
| cārnēā . . | Pa. red . | 6, H. De. S. N. Amer. . | 1734 |
| caroliniānā . | Scarlet . | 6, H. De. S. N. Amer. . | |
| CobūrghII . . | Scarlet . | 6, H. De. S. N. Amer. . | |
| coccīneā . . | Scarlet . | 6, H. De. S. N. Amer. . | |
| corymbōsā . | Scarlet . | 6, H. De. S. N. Amer. . | |
| crispā . . | Pink . . | 6, H. De. S. N. Amer. . | |
| cumulātā . . | Scr. pink . | 6, H. De. S. N. Amer. . | |
| discōlor . . | Wht. scr. . | 6, H. De. S. N. Amer. . | |
| fastigiātā . . | Pink . . | 6, H. De. S. N. Amer. . | |
| florīdā . . | Pink . . | 6, H. De. S. N. Amer. . | |
| globōsā . . | Pink . . | 6, H. De. S. N. Amer. . | |
| glomerātā . . | Pink . . | 6, H. De. S. N. Amer. . | |
| incānā . . | Pink . . | 6, H. De. S. N. Amer. . | |
| incarnātā . . | Flesh . . | 6, H. De. S. N. Amer. . | |
| mirābilis . . | Scarlet . | 6, H. De. S. N. Amer. . | |
| magnifīcā . . | Scarlet . | 6, H. De. S. N. Amer. . | |
| montānā . . | Scarlet . | 6, H. De. S. N. Amer. . | |
| pallīdā . . | Pa. red . | 6, H. De. S. N. Amer. . | |
| paludōsā . . | Pa. red . | 6, H. De. S. N. Amer. . | |
| papilionācēā . | Striped . | 6, H. De. S. N. Amer. . | |
| partītā . . | Wht. red . | 6, H. De. S. N. Amer. . | |
| parvifflōrā . . | | 6, H. De. S. N. Amer. . | |
| prolīfērā . . | | 6, H. De. S. N. Amer. . | |
| pūmīlā . . | White . . | 6, H. De. S. N. Amer. . | |
| purpurāscēns . | Purple . | 6, H. De. S. N. Amer. . | |
| purpūrēā . . | Purple . | 6, H. De. S. N. Amer. . | |
| purpūrēō-plēnā . | Purple . | 6, H. De. S. N. Amer. . | |
| rōsēā . . | Red . . | 6, H. De. S. N. Amer. . | |
| rubērrīmā . | Drk. red . | 6, H. De. S. N. Amer. . | |
| rubēscēns . . | Red . . | 6, H. De. S. N. Amer. . | |
| rubicūndā . . | Red . . | 6, H. De. S. N. Amer. . | |
| rūbrā . . | Red . . | 6, H. De. S. N. Amer. . | |
| rūtīlāns . . | Drk. red . | 6, H. De. S. N. Amer. . | |
| scintillāns . . | Orange . | 6, H. De. S. Hybrid . . | 1827 |
| semidūplēx . . | White . . | 6, H. De. S. N. Amer. . | |
| stamīnēā . . | Red . . | 6, H. De. S. N. Amer. . | |
| stellātā . . | Red . . | 6, H. De. S. N. Amer. . | |
| thyrsifflōrā . . | Drk. scr. . | 6, H. De. S. Seedling. . | 1827 |
| tricōlor . . | Scr. wht. . | 6, H. De. S. N. Amer. . | |
| variābilīs . . | Red . . | 6, H. De. S. N. Amer. . | |
| variegātā . . | Red wht. . | 6, H. De. S. N. Amer. . | |
| versicōlor . . | Red wht. . | 6, H. De. S. N. Amer. . | |

| | | | |
|---|---|---|---|
| violācēā . . | Violet . . | 6, H. De. S. N. Amer. . | |
| pontīca . . | Yellow . | 6, H. De. S. Turkey . . | 1793 |
| albiflōrā . . | White . . | 5, H. De. S. Turkey . . | |
| cuprēā . . | Copper . | 6, H. De. S. Turkey . | |
| glaūcā . . | Yellow . | 6, H. De. S. Turkey . | |
| pallīdā . . | Pa. yel. . | 4, H. De. S. Turkey . | |
| tricōlor . . | Pa. red . | 4, H. De. S. Turkey . | |
| versīcōlor . | Yel. rose . | 5, H. Ev. S. Hybrid . . | 1827 |
| sinēnsis . . | Yellow . | 5, G. Ev. S. China . . | 1823 |
| speciōsā . . | Scarlet . | 6, H. De. S. N. Amer. . | |
| acutifōlīā . . | | 6, H. De. S. N. Amer. . | |
| aurāntīā . . | Orange . | 6, H. De. S. N. Amer. . | |
| ciliātā . . | | 6, H. De. S. N. Amer. . | |
| crispā . . | Scarlet . | 6, H. De. S. N. Amer. . | |
| cucullātā . . | | 6, H. De. S. N. Amer. . | |
| mājōr . . | Scarlet . | 6, H. De. S. N. Amer. . | |
| oblīquā . . | | 6, H. De. S. N. Amer. . | |
| prunifōlīā . . | | 6, H. De. S. N. Amer. . | |
| revolūtā . . | | 6, H. De. S. N. Amer. . | |
| tortulifōlīā . . | | 6, H. De. S. N. Amer. . | |
| undulātā . . | | 6, H. De. S. N. Amer. . | |
| viscōsā . . | White . . | 7, H. De. S. N. Amer. . | 1734 |
| crispā . . | White . . | 7, H. De. S. N. Amer. . | |
| dealbātā . . | White . . | 7, H. De. S. N. Amer. . | |
| fissā . . | White . . | 7, H. De. S. N. Amer. . | |
| odorātā . . | White . . | 7, H. De. S. N. Amer. . | |
| penicillātā . | White . . | 7, H. De. S. N. Amer. . | |
| pubēscēns . . | White . . | 7, H. De. S. N. Amer. . | |
| rubēscēns . . | White . . | 7, H. De. S. N. Amer. . | |
| variegātā . . | White . . | 7, H. De. S. N. Amer. . | |
| vittātā . . | White . . | 7, H. De. S. N. Amer. . | |

AZĀRĀ, *Ruiz et Pavon.* In honour of Joseph Nicolas Azara, a Spanish promoter of botany. *Linn.* 13, Or. 1, Nat. Or. *Bixaceæ.* An ornamental tree eighteen feet high, which Mr. Don recommends to be grown in loam and sand; and ripened cuttings, he says, will root if planted in sand, placed under a glass, in a moderate heat.

| | | | |
|---|---|---|---|
| dentātā . . . . | Yellow . . | G. Ev. S. Chile . . | 1830 |
| integrifōlīā . . | | G. Ev. S. Conception | 1832 |

AZŪRĒĪ, sky-blue coloured.

# B.

BABIĀNĀ, *Ker.* Derived by Mr. J. B. Ker, from *babianer*, because the roots are the favourite food of baboons. *Linn.* 3, Or. 1, Nat. Or. *Iridaceæ.* Handsome species, succeeding well in a mixture of sand, loam, and peat, freely watered when the plants are growing; but after flowering keep them dry till October, when they require repotting. During the suspension of water, keep them quite cool till new roots are made in the pots, after which a little more heat will cause them to flower strong. Protected from frost they succeed well in a south border, or the bulbs may be planted in spring and taken up again in autumn. Offsets or seeds. Synonymes: 1. *Ixia stricta.* 2. *I. villosa.* 3. *Gladiolus nanus.*

| | | | |
|---|---|---|---|
| angustifōlīā, 1 . | Varieg. . | 6, G. Bl. P. C. G. H. | 1757 |
| distīchā . . | Blue . . | 6, G. Bl. P. C. G. H. | 1774 |
| mucronātā . . | Purple . | 6, G. Bl. P. C. G. H. | 1825 |
| nānā, 3 . . | Blue . . | 4, G. Bl. P. C. G. H. | 1807 |
| obtusifōlīā, 2 . | Blue . . | 6, G. Bl. P. C. G. H. | 1825 |
| plicātā . . | Purple . | 6, G. Bl. P. C. G. H. | 1774 |
| purpūrēā . . | Purple . | 6, G. Bl. P. C. G. H. | 1806 |
| ringēns . . | Purple . | 6, G. Bl. P. C. G. H. | 1752 |
| rubrocyānēā . | Blue red . | 4, G. Bl. P. C. G. H. | 1794 |
| sambucīnā . . | Blue . . | 6, G. Bl. P. C. G. H. | 1799 |
| spathācēā . . | Lgt. blue . | 6, G. Bl. P. C. G. H. | 1801 |
| strictā . . | Blue wht. . | 6, G. Bl. P. C. G. H. | 1757 |
| sulphūrēā . . | Yellow . | 6, G. Bl. P. C. G. H. | 1795 |
| tenuiflōrā . . | Purple . | 6, G. Bl. P. C. G. H. | 1825 |
| ThunbergII . | Wht. red . | 4, G. Bl. P. C. G. H. | 1774 |
| tubātā . . | Yel. red . | 6, G. Bl. P. C. G. H. | 1774 |
| tubiflōrā . . | Drk. red . | 6, G. Bl. P. C. G. H. | 1774 |
| villōsā . . | Purple . | 8, G. Bl. P. C. G. H. | 1778 |

BACĀZĪĀ, *Flora Peru.* In honour of George Bacaz, a botanist at Carthagena. *Linn.* 19, Or. 1, Nat. Or. *Compositæ.* An interesting plant, growing well in peat and loam; cuttings.

| | | | |
|---|---|---|---|
| spinōsā . . . . | | 6, G. Ev. S. Peru . . | 1825 |

BACCĀTE, berried, fleshy.

BACCĀTŪS, berry-bearing.

BACCHĀRIS, *Linn.* By the Greeks, to a plant dedicated to Bacchus. *Linn.* 19, Or. 2, Nat. Or. *Compositæ.* This genus, called the Ploughman's Spikenard, consists of ornamental species, of easy culture and propagation. Loam and peat; cuttings in sand, under a glass. Synonymes: 1. *Molina parviflora.* 2. *Calea scoparia.*

| | | | |
|---|---|---|---|
| adnātā . . | Purple . | 8, S. Ev. S. S. Amer. . | 1823 |
| alātā . . | Pa. yel. . | 12, G. Ev. S. . | 1829 |
| angustifōlīā . | White . | 7, G. Ev. S. N. Amer. . | 1812 |
| confērtā . . | | S. Ev. S. Mexico . . | 1826 |
| Dioscōrīdīs . | White . | 0, F. Ev. S. Levant . | |
| glomeruliflōrā . | White . | 8, H. De. S. N. Amer. . | 1817 |
| glutinōsā . . | | S. Ev. S. Peru . . | 1824 |
| halimifōlīā . | White . | 10, H. De. S. N. Amer. . | 1683 |
| indīcā . . | | S. Ev. S. E. Ind. . | 1819 |
| ivæfōlīā . . | White . | 7, G. Ev. S. America . | 1696 |
| parviflōrā, 1 . | | S. Ev. S. Peru . . | 1820 |
| scopārīā, 2 . | Cream cl. . | 7, S. Ev. S. Jamaica . | 1820 |

BĀCTRIS, *Jacquin.* From *baktron*, a cane; on account of the small stems being used for walking-sticks. *Linn.* 21, Or. 6, Nat. Or. *Palmaceæ.* Fine species of *Palms*, thriving well in sandy loam, and only increased by seeds. *B. minor* produces a fruit the size of a common cherry, which contains an acid juice, not very pleasant to the taste. *B. major* produces a nut with a solid kernel, eaten in Carthagena.

| | | | |
|---|---|---|---|
| caryotæfōlīā . . | | Palm. Brazil . . | 1825 |
| cuspidātā . . | | Palm. Brazil . . | 1826 |
| guianēnsis . . | | Palm. Guiana . . | 1820 |
| macracānthā . . | | Palm. Brazil . . | 1823 |
| mājōr . . . . | | Palm. Carthag. . | 1800 |
| mīnōr . . . . | | Palm. S. Amer. . | 1691 |
| pectinātā . . . | | Palm. Brazil . . | 1825 |

BADGER'S-BANE, see *Aconitum meloctonum.*

BÆCKĪĀ, *Linn.* Taken from A. Bæck, a physician to the king of Sweden. *Linn.* 1, Or. 1, Nat. Or. *Myrtaceæ.* Very interesting plants, delighting in sandy loam and peat. Cuttings root readily in sand, under a glass.

| | | | |
|---|---|---|---|
| camphorātā . | White . | 7, G. Ev. S. N. Holl. . | 1818 |
| densifōlīā . . | White . | 9, G. Ev. S. N. S. W. . | |
| diosmæfōlīā . | White . | 8, G. Ev. S. N. Holl. . | 1824 |
| frutēscēns . | White . | 11, G. Ev. S. China . | 1806 |
| grācīlis . . | White . | G. Ev. S. N. Holl. . | 1826 |
| linifōlīā . . | White . | 8, G. Ev. S. N. Holl. . | 1818 |

| | | | | |
|---|---|---|---|---|
| ramosíssimā | . . White | . | O. Ev. 8. N. Holl. | 1824 |
| saxícolā | . . White | 7, G. Ev. 8. N. Holl. | | 1824 |
| virgātā | . . White | 9, G. Ev. 8. N. Caledo. | | 1806 |

**BÆOMÝCES**, *Acharius.* Derived from *baios*, small, and *mykes*, fungus; the resemblance of the fructication to a fungus. *Linn.* 24, Or. 9, Nat. Or. *Fungi.* The species appear like some small kinds of *Agaricus* or *Helvella*, and are generally found upon heath, oaks, or sandstone—*cæspititius, microphýllus, róseus, rūfus.*

**BAGGED**, swelled like a sack, or bag.

**BALANTIUM**, *Kaulf.* From *balantion*, a purse; on account of the form of the indusium. *Linn.* 24, Or. 1, Nat. Or. *Polypodiaceæ.* An interesting species of fern, growing in peat and loam, and increased by divisions. *Synonyme:* 1 *Dicksonia culcita.*

| | | | | |
|---|---|---|---|---|
| cūl-ītā, 1 | . . Brown | . 8, S. Fern. Madeira. | | . |

**BALBISIA**, *Cav.* In honour of John Baptist Balbis, a writer on botany. *Linn.* 10, Or. 5, Nat. Or. *Oxalidaceæ.* A handsome plant, succeeding best in the greenhouse, in loam and peat. It must be watered with great caution; cuttings. *Synonymes:* 1. *Ledocarpum pedunculare. Cruickshanksia cistiflora.*

| | | | | |
|---|---|---|---|---|
| pedunculārīs, 1 | . Yellow | . 8, G. Ev. 8. Chile | | . 1825 |

**BALL**, applied to the round central part of the flower of Stapelia.

**BALLŌTA**, *Linn.* Named from *ballo*, to reject, on account of its offensive odour; hence the trivial name. Stinking Horehound. *Linn.* 14, Or. 1, Nat. Or. *Labiatæ.* Mere weeds, of the easiest culture. *Synonyme:* 1. *B. fœtidā—ālbā, distichā, nīgrā, 1, vulgāris.*

**BALM**, see *Melissā.*

**BALM OF GILEAD**, see *Dracocephālūm canariénsē.*

**BALSAM**, see *Impātiēns.*

**BALSAM APPLE**, see *Momördicā balsamīnēā.*

**BALSAMĪNĀ**, *Rivinus.* Called *balassan* by the Arabs, from which most probably the name balsamina has sprung. *Linn.* 5, Or. 1, Nat. Or. *Balsaminaceæ.* That beautiful and popular annual the garden balsam, with its white, red, pink, purple, lilac, and finely-variegated carnation-like flowers, belongs to this genus. All the species are ornamental, and may be grown with success by the following mode of treatment, recommended in Don's Miller's Gard. Dic.:—"The seeds of these plants should be sown on a moderate hotbed, in spring, and when the plants are about two or three inches high, they should be planted in separate small pots, taking care to shade them until they have taken fresh root, replacing them in the hotbed, after which they should have a moderate share of free air admitted to them when the weather is favourable, to prevent their being drawn up tall and weak; they should then be shifted from size to size of pots, until the plants have grown the size required, and when in flower they may be placed in the greenhouse, where they will make a very showy appearance, and seed freely." A light, very rich soil, composed of rotten dung, loam, and leaf mould, with a little sand, suits them best, plentifully watered. They do not root readily by cuttings; but may be increased abundantly from seeds, which in general ripen. The juice of the balsam used with alum is employed by the Japanese to dye their nails red. *Synonyme:* 1. *Impatiens balsamina.*

| | | | | |
|---|---|---|---|---|
| bīfīdā | . . . Red | . 8, G. | A. Japan | . 1820 |
| capēnsīs | . . . Red | . 8, G. | A. C. G. H. | 1818 |
| chinēnsīs | . . Purple | 8, G. | A. China | . 1824 |
| coccīneā | . . . Scarlet | 8, S. | A. E. Ind. | 1808 |
| cornūtā | . . . Red | . 8, G. | A. Ceylon | . 1826 |
| hortēnsīs, 1 | . . Red | . 9, S. | A. E. Ind. | . 1596 |
| latīfōlīā | . . . Pa. red | 8, G. | A. E. Ind. | . 1818 |
| madagascariēnsīs | . Red | . 8, G. | A. Madagas. | 1824 |
| mīnōr | . . . Red | . 8, G. | A. E. Ind. | 1817 |
| mysorēnsīs | . . Red | . 8, G. | A. Mysore | . 1820 |

**BALSAMĪTĀ**, *Desfon.* From *balsamon*, balm; in reference to its strong balsamic smell. *Linn.* 19, Or. 1, Nat. Or. *Compositæ.* Plants of little interest, and easy culture. *Synonyme:* 1. *Tanacētūm ānnūūm.*

| | | | | |
|---|---|---|---|---|
| grandīflōrā | . . Yellow | . 7, F. | B. Algiers. | . 1821 |
| vulgārīs | . . Yel. grn. | 8, H. Her. P. Italy | | . 1568 |

*ageratifōlīā, annua* 1, *virgata.*

**BALSAMODENDRON**, *Kunth.* From *balsamon*, balsam, and *dendron*, tree. *Linn.* 8, Or. 1, Nat. Or. *Burseraceæ.* An ornamental tree, growing well in

sandy loam and peat, and ripened cuttings root freely in sand, under a glass, in heat. This tree yields the gum elemi of the East, which is distinct from the American elemi. *Synonyme:* 1. *Amyris zelanica.*

| | | | | |
|---|---|---|---|---|
| zeylānīcūm, 1 | . . | 8. Ev. T. Ceylon | | . . |

**BALTIMORA**, *Linn.* In honour of Lord Baltimore, proprietor of Maryland. *Linn.* 19, Or. 4, Nat. Or. *Compositæ.* Uninteresting species, of easy culture —*ālbā, recta.*

**BALSAM OF CAPIVI**, see *Copaifērā.*

**BALSAM TREE**, see *Clūsiā.*

**BAMBOO CANE**, see *Bambūsā.*

**BAMBŪSĀ**, *Schrader.* From *bambos*, its name in India. *Linn.* 6, Or. 1, Nat. Or. *Gramineæ.* This genus contains the bamboo-cane; the species are interesting, and in rich loamy soil they grow rapidly to a great height in our stoves if well watered; they increase by offsets. *B. arundinaceæ* is very useful for a very great variety of domestic purposes; in the E. Indies, cottages are almost entirely made of it, bridges, boxes, cups, baskets, mats, paper, and masts for boats, are also made of it. It is likewise employed for fences for gardens, &c., and it is commonly used instead of pipes for conveying water. The substance called tabasher, is a secreted siliceous matter, found at the joints of the bamboo.

| | | | | |
|---|---|---|---|---|
| aristātā | . . . Apetal. | . Grass. E. Ind. | | . 1824 |
| arundinaceā | . . Apetal. | . Grass. E. Ind. | | . 1730 |
| glaúcā | . . . Apetal. | . Grass. E. Ind. | | . 1826 |
| nīgrā | . . . Apetal. | . Grass. E. Ind. | | . 1825 |
| pubēscēns | . . Apetal. | . Grass. E. Ind. | | . 1826 |
| spīnōsā | . . . Apetal. | . Grass. E. Ind. | | . 1820 |
| strictā | . . . Apetal. | . Grass. E. Ind. | | . 1824 |
| verticillātā | . . Apetal. | . Grass. India | | . 1803 |

**BANANA TREE**, *see Mūsā sapiēntūm.*

**BANE-BERRY**, see *Actēā.*

**BANDS**, applied to the spaces between the lines, or ribs of the fruit of umbelliferous plants.

**BANGIA**, *Agardh.* Named in honour of Christian Frederick Bang. *Linn.* 24, Or. 7, Nat. Or. *Algeæ.* Curious productions, appearing on marine rocks about the sea coast—*atropurpūrēd, fusco-purpūrēd, calophýllā, Laminārīæ.*

**BANISTĒRĪĀ**, *Linn.* In memory of the Rev. John Banister, a diligent botanist. *Linn.* 10, Or. 3, Nat. Or. *Malpighiaceæ.* Interesting species, with beautiful foliage, as *B. splendens.* They succeed in loam and sand, or a mixture of loam and sandy peat; ripened cuttings root in sand, under a glass, in heat. *Synonyme:* 1. *B. heterophylla, B. fulgens.*

| | | | | |
|---|---|---|---|---|
| ciliātā | . . . Yellow | . 8. Ev. Tw. Brasil | | . 1796 |
| ferrugīneā | . . Yellow | . 8. Ev. | Brasil | . 1820 |
| fulgēns | . . . Yellow | . 8. Ev. | W. Ind. | . 1759 |
| Humboldtiānā | . Yellow | . 8. Ev. | S. Amer. | . 1824 |
| laurifōlīā | . . Yellow | . 8. Ev. | Jamaica | . 1733 |
| ovātā | . . . Yellow | . 7, 8. Ev. | St. Domin. | . 1810 |
| periplocæfōlīā | . Yellow | . 7, 8. Ev. S. | Porto Rico | . 1818 |
| sericeā | . . . Yellow | . 7, 8. Ev. Tw. Brasil | | . 1810 |
| splēndēns, 1 | . . Yellow | . 8. Ev. 8. | S. Amer. | . 1812 |
| tenūīs | . . . Yellow | . G. Ev. Tw. B. Ayres | | . |
| tomentōsā | . . Yellow | . 7, 8. Ev. Tw. S. Amer. | | . 1820 |
| zanzibārīcā | . . Yellow | . 8. Ev. Tw. Zanzibar | | . 1824 |

**BANKSIA**, *Robert Brown.* In honour of Sir Joseph Banks, Bart. Pres. R.S.; a distinguished patron of science in general, particularly Natural History. *Linn.* 4, Or. 1, Nat. Or. *Proteaceæ.* This is a handsome and interesting genus. The species, to succeed well, must be treated in the following manner recommended by Sweet. "The pots must be well drained, which should be done in the following manner:—place a piece of potsherd about half way over the hole at the bottom of the pot, then lay another piece against it that it may be hollow, afterwards put some smaller pieces all around them, and some more broken very small on the top of these. All plants belonging to the *Proteaceæ* should be drained in the same manner, as the roots are very fond of running amongst the broken potsherds, and there is not so much danger of their being overwatered; care must be taken not to let them flag for want of water, as they seldom recover if allowed to get very dry; they should also be placed in an airy part of the greenhouse when in doors, as nothing is more beneficial to them than a free circulation of air. Cuttings are generally supposed to be difficult to root, but they will root readily if properly managed; let them be well ripened before they are taken off; then cut them at a joint, and plant them in pots of sand, without shortening any of the leaves, except on the part that is planted in the sand, where they should be taken off quite close, the less depth they are planted in the pots the better, if they only stand firm, when the sand is well closed round them; then place them under hand-glasses in the propagating house, but not plunge them in heat, the glasses must be frequently taken off to give them air, and dry them, or they are apt to damp off; when they are rooted, the sooner they are potted off in small pots the better, as the sand is liable to canker their roots, if left too long in it; when potted off they should be placed in a close frame, but not on heat, as a bottom-heat will destroy their roots, when they must be hardened to the air by degrees. Plants raised in this way have better roots, grow faster, and flower sooner, than plants raised from seeds: in raising them from seeds, they should be sown in the same kind of soil as the plants are grown in, and placed in the greenhouse, or if it is in summer they will come up sooner, if placed out in the open air; they will soon make their appearance, when they should be potted off in small pots, for if left in the seed pots too long they are apt to die, and are more difficult to move with safety." *Synonymes*: 1. *B. ledifolia, B. littoralis.*

| | | | | |
|---|---|---|---|---|
| æmùlä | . | Green | . 8, G. Ev. S. N. S. W. | 1788 |
| attenuätä | . | Yellow | . G. Ev. S. N. S. W. | 1794 |
| austrälis | . | Green | . G. Ev. S. N. S. W. | 1812 |
| Baüèri | . | | . G. Ev. S. N. Holl. | 1830 |
| Bäxtèri | . | | . G. Ev. S. N. Holl. | 1830 |
| Brównii | . | | . G. Ev. S. N. Holl. | 1830 |
| Cälèyi | . | | . G. Ev. S. N. Holl. | 1830 |
| coccinèä | . | Scarlet | . G. Ev. S. N. Holl. | 1803 |
| collìna | . | Yellow | . G. Ev. S. N. S. W. | 1800 |
| cömpar | . | Yellow | . G. Ev. S. N. Holl. | 1824 |
| Cunninghämii, 1 | Pa. yel. | . G. Ev. S. N. Holl. | 1822 |
| dentätä | . | Yellow | . G. Ev. S. N. S. W. | 1822 |
| deprèssä | . | Yellow | . G. Ev. S. N. Holl. | 1824 |
| dryandroìdès | . | Yellow | . G. Ev. S. N. Holl. | 1824 |
| elätiör | . | Yellow | . G. Ev. S. N. Holl. | 1824 |
| ericifòlià | . | Yellow | . G. Ev. S. N. S. W. | 1788 |
| Goódii | . | | . G. Ev. S. N. Holl. | 1830 |
| grändis | . | Yellow | . G. Ev. S. N. W. | 1794 |
| insulàris | . | Yellow | . G. Ev. S. N. S. W. | 1822 |
| integrifòliä | . | Yellow | . G. Ev. S. N. S. W. | 1788 |
| latifòlià | . | Green | . 7, G. Ev. S. N. W. | 1802 |
| littoràlis | . | Orange | . G. Ev. S. N. Holl. | 1803 |
| marcèscens | . | Yellow | . G. Ev. S. N. Holl. | 1794 |
| marginätä | . | Yellow | . 7, G. Ev. S. N. S. W. | 1804 |
| mèdià | . | Yellow | . G. Ev. S. N. Holl. | 1824 |
| nòtäns | . | Yellow | . 6, G. Ev. S. N. Holl. | 1803 |
| oblongifòliä | . | Yellow | . 7, G. Ev. S. N. S. W. | 1805 |
| occidentàlis | . | Yellow | . G. Ev. S. N. Holl. | 1808 |
| paludòsä | . | Yellow | . 3, G. Ev. S. N. S. W. | 1805 |
| prosträtä | . | Yellow | . G. Ev. S. N. Holl. | 1824 |
| pulchèllä | . | Yellow | . G. Ev. S. N. Holl. | 1805 |
| quercifòliä | . | Yellow | . G. Ev. S. N. Holl. | 1805 |
| rèpäns | . | Yellow | . G. Ev. S. N. Holl. | 1803 |
| serràtä | . | Yellow | . 8, G. Ev. S. N. S. W. | 1788 |
| Solàndrä | . | | . G. Ev. S. N. Holl. | 1830 |
| speciòsä | . | Yellow | . 7, G. Ev. S. N. Holl. | 1805 |
| spinulòsä | . | Yellow | . 8, G. Ev. S. N. S. W. | 1788 |
| sphaerocärpä | . | Yellow | . G. Ev. S. N. Holl. | 1803 |
| verticillàtä | . | Yellow | . 8, G. Ev. T. N. Holl. | 1794 |

BAOBAB TREE, see *Adansònià.*

BÁPHIÄ, *Afzelius.* Taken from *baphe*, from its use in dyeing. *Linn.* 10, Or. 1, Nat. Or. *Leguminosæ.* The genus yields what cabinet-makers call ringwood.

| | | | | |
|---|---|---|---|---|
| nitìdä | . | White | . 8, S. Ev. T. S. Leone | 1793 |

BAPTÍSIÄ, *Robert Brown.* From *bapto*, to dye; in allusion to the dyeing properties possessed by some species. *Linn.* 10, Or. 1, Nat. Or. *Leguminosæ.* Ornamental border plants, succeeding in common loamy soil, and multiplied by divisions. The roots and leaves of *B. tinctoria* are antiseptic and astringent. *Synonyme*: 1. *Podalyria uniflora.*

| | | | | |
|---|---|---|---|---|
| alba | . | White | . 6, H. Her. P. N. Amer. | 1724 |
| austràlis | . | Blue | . 6, H. Her. P. N. Amer. | 1758 |
| exaltätä | . | White | . 6, H. Her. P. N. Amer. | 1724 |
| lanceolätä, 1 | Yellow | . 7, H. Her. P. N. Amer. | 1818 |
| minör | . | Blue | . 6, H. Her. P. N. Amer. | 1829 |
| mollis | . | Blue | . 6, H. Her. P. N. Amer. | 1824 |
| perfoliätä | . | Yellow | . 8, F. Her. P. Carolina | 1732 |
| tinctòriä | . | Yellow | . 7, H. Her. P. N. Amer. | 1750 |
| villòsä | . | Yellow | . 8, H. Her. P. N. Amer. | 1811 |

BARBACÈNIÄ, *Vandelli.* From *Barbacena*, the governor of Minas Geraes. *Linn.* 6, Or. 1, Nat. Or. Bro-

*meliaceæ.* An interesting species, growing in sandy loam, and multiplied by divisions.

| | | | | |
|---|---|---|---|---|
| purpúrää | . | Purple | . 7, S. Har. P. Brazil | 1825 |

BARBADOES CEDAR, see *Junìpèrùs barbadènsis.*
BARBADOES CHERRY, see *Malpìghiä.*
BARBADOES GOOSEBERRY, see *Perèskiä.*
BARBADOES LILY, see *Amaryllis equestris.*

BARBARÈÄ, *Robert Brown.* On account of its being formerly called the herb of St. Barbara. *Linn.* 15, Nat. Or. *Cruciferæ.* Plants of easy culture. The genus is called the Winter Cress. *Synonymes*: 1. *Cheiranthus ibericus.* 2. *Sisymbrium Barbarea.* 3. *Erysimum præcox.* 4. *E. Barbarea.*

| | | | | |
|---|---|---|---|---|
| præcox, 3 | . | Yellow | . 10, H. Her. P. England | |
| vulgàris, 4 | . | Yellow | . 7, H. Her. P. Britain | . . |

*ibericä* 1, *plantaginèä* 2, *taúricä.*

BARBIÈRIÄ, *Decan.* In compliment to J. B. G. Barbier, M.D. *Linn.* 17, Or. 4, Nat. Or. *Leguminosæ.* An ornamental species, grown in sandy peat, and multiplied by cuttings. *Synonymes*: 1. *Clitoria polyphylla. Galactia pinnata.*

| | | | | |
|---|---|---|---|---|
| polyphyllä, 1 | . | Purple | . 8. Ev. S. S. Amer. | 1818 |

BARLÈRIÄ, *Linn.* In honour of the Rev. James Barrelier, a Dominican, and M.D. of Paris. *Linn.* 14, Or. 2, Nat. Or. *Acanthaceæ.* These interesting dwarfish plants flower freely if grown in loam and peat, mixed with a little rotten dung; and strike readily from cuttings made of the young wood, planted in soil, and placed under a glass. *Synonymes*: 1. *B. mitis, Justicia flava, Eranthemum flavum.* 2. *Dicliptera spinosa.*

| | | | | |
|---|---|---|---|---|
| alba | . | White | . 7, S. Ev. S. N. Holl. | 1815 |
| buxifòliä | . | White | . 7, S. Ev. S. E. Ind. | 1768 |
| cærùlèä | . | Blue | . 7, S. Ev. S. E. Ind. | 1823 |
| cristätä | . | Blue | . 7, S. Ev. S. E. Ind. | 1796 |
| dichótomä | . | Purple | . 7, S. Ev. S. E. Ind. | 1823 |
| flavä, 1 | . | Yellow | . 7, S. Ev. S. E. Ind. | 1816 |
| longifòliä | . | White | . 8, S. B. E. Ind. | 1781 |
| longiflòrä | . | | . 7, S. Ev. S. E. Ind. | 1816 |
| lupulìnä, 2 | . | Yellow | . 8, S. Ev. S. Mauritius | 1824 |
| Priónitis | . | Orange | . 7, S. Ev. S. E. Ind. | 1759 |
| purpúrèä | . | Purple | . 9, S. Ev. S. E. Ind. | 1814 |
| solanifòliä | . | Blue | . 8, S. Ev. S. W. Ind. | |
| strigòsä | . | Blue | . 7, S. Ev. S. E. Ind. | 1820 |

BARLEY, see *Hördèûm.*

BARNÀRDIÄ, *Lindley.* In honour of E. Barnard, F.L.S. *Linn.* 6, Or. 1, Nat. Or. *Liliaceæ.* This pretty species succeeds well in peat and loam mixed, and increases by offsets.

| | | | | |
|---|---|---|---|---|
| scilloìdès | . | Pa. blue | . 5, F. BL Siberia | 1819 |

BARRED, marked in spaces with a paler colour, resembling bars.

BARREN-WORT, see *Epimèdiûm.*

BARRINGTÒNIÄ, *Forster.* Dedicated to the Hon. Daines Barrington, F.R.S .&c. *Linn.* 16, Or. 8, Nat. Or. *Myrtaceæ.* This very handsome, lofty-growing species, is rather scarce in our stoves, and somewhat difficult to preserve in a healthy state. It must be grown in a moist, warm atmosphere, not by any means under 60 degrees, and planted in loam and peat mixed. Cuttings in a moist heat, root in sand, under a glass. *B. speciosa* yields a reddish-brown drupe, the seed of which, mixed with the bait, inebriates fish.

| | | | | |
|---|---|---|---|---|
| speciòsä | . | Scarlet | . 8. Ev. T. E. Ind. | 1786 |

BARTHOLÌNÄ, *R. Brown.* In memory of the great Danish anatomist and physiologist Thomas Bartholin. *Linn.* 20, Or. 1, Nat. Or. *Orchidaceæ.* A singular species, very difficult to preserve in our collections. It requires a very sandy loam, and a light part of the greenhouse; it is very probable, that if they had more light in their growing season, they would be much easier preserved. *Synonyme*: 1. *Arèthùsä pèctìnätä.*

| | | | | |
|---|---|---|---|---|
| pèctìnätä | . | Lilac | . 11, G. Ter. C. G. H. | 1787 |

BARTÒNIÄ, *Pursh.* In honour of Dr. B. S. Barton, a botanist in Philadelphia. *Linn.* 12, Or. 1, Nat. Or. *Loasaceæ.* Beautiful plants with large yellow and white flowers, which open in the night, and effuse around them a delightful odour. Sweet says, they should be raised in a gentle hotbed, and when up, potted, and protected in the greenhouse in winter. *Synonyme*: 1. *B. decapetala.*

| | | | | | |
|---|---|---|---|---|---|
| albēscēns | . . . White . | . H. | . A. Chile | . | . 1831 |
| aūreā | . . . Gold. yel. | 6, H. | . A. California | | 1834 |
| nūdā | . . . White . | 8, F. | . B. Missouri | | 1811 |
| ornātā, 1 | . . White . | 8, F. | . B. Missouri | | 1811 |

**BARTRĂMĬĂ**, *Hedwig*. So called in honour of J. Bartram, an Anglo-American, to whose researches in N. America the gardens of Europe owe many of their finest trees. *Linn.* 24, Or. 5, Nat. Or. *Muscl.* This is an elegant genus of mosses, remarkable for their green leaves, and spherical capsules. The genus approaches nearly to *Bryum*, but differs in almost every species having spherical capsules, and the sixteen broad segments of the inner peristome instead of being entire, or only perforated, are cleft like the teeth of a *Dicranum.—Loudon's Ency. of Plants.* Synonymes: 1. *Bryum fontanum—arcuātā, fontānā, f. mājōr* 1, *f. mărchĭcā, grăcĭlis, Hallerĭānā, ĭthyphŷllā, pomĭfōrmĭs, p. mājŏr, p. mĭnŏr.*

**BĂRTSĬĂ**, *Linn.* Dedicated to his friend John Barsch, M.D. *Linn.* 14, Or. 2, Nat. Or. *Scrophularĭaceæ.* Curious plants, of difficult cultivation. They succeed best in a shady bog border, or in pots kept moist; they also do pretty well in a moderately exposed situation sown in sandy soil.

| | | | | | |
|---|---|---|---|---|---|
| alpīnā | . . . Purple . | 8, H. | . A. Britain | . | |
| latĭfōlĭā | . . . Purple . | 8, H. | . A. S. Europe | . | |
| odontĭtēs | . . . Pink . | 8, H. | . A. Britain | . | |
| viscōsā | . . . Yellow . | 7, H. | . A. Britain | . | |

**BARYŎSMĂ**, *Willd.* From the powerful scent of the leaves. *Linn.* 5, Or. 1, Nat. Or. *Rutaceæ.* Pretty species; for culture, &c., see *Diosma.* Synonymes: 1. *Diosma latifolia, D. serratifolia, D. odorata, Bucco crenata.* 2. *Diosma tinifolia.* 3. *Agathosma latifolia.* 4. *Agathosma pulchella.*

| | | | | | |
|---|---|---|---|---|---|
| betulīnā | . . . White . | 6, G. Ev. S. | C. G. H. | . | 1790 |
| crenulātā, 1 | . . Bluish . | 4, G. Ev. S. | C. G. H. | . | |
| diōĭcā, 2 | . . . White . | 6, G. Ev. S. | C. G. H. | . | 1816 |
| latĭfōlĭā, 3 | . . White . | 7, G. Ev. S. | C. G. H. | . | 1769 |
| ovātā | . . . White . | 6, G. Ev. S. | C. G. H. | . | 1790 |
| pulchēllā, 4 | . . Purple . | 6, G. Ev. S. | C. G. H. | . | 1787 |

**BASĒLLĂ**, *Linn.* Its Malabar name. *Linn.* 5, Or. 3, Nat. Or. *Chenopodiaceæ.* Some species are pretty; *B. lucida* when in fruit is very interesting. The seed should be sown on a gentle hotbed, or in pots in the hothouse, and afterwards planted out singly in small pots, and placed among the tender annuals. The species furnish a summer spinach in Paris and China.

| | | | | | |
|---|---|---|---|---|---|
| ālbā | . . . White . | 8, S. | B. E. Ind. | . | 1688 |
| cordĭfōlĭā | . . Pa. pur. | 8, S. Cl. | B. E. Ind. | . | 1802 |
| lūcĭdā | . . . White . | 8, S. Cl. | B. E. Ind. | . | 1802 |
| margĭnātā | . . . | 7, S. Tw. | B. Mexico | . | 1824 |
| nĭgrā | . . . White . | 8, S. Cl. | B. China | . | 1822 |
| ramōsā | . . . | 8, S. Ev. Cl. | | | |
| rūbrā | . . . Pink . | 8, S. Cl. | B. E. Ind. | . | 1731 |
| tuberōsā | . . Purple . | 9, S. Tu. | B. S. Amer. | . | 1824 |

**BASIL**, see *Ocȳmum.*

**BASILAR**, at the base of anything, usually the embryo when situated at the bottom of the seed.

**BĂSSĬĂ**, *Linn.* In honour of Ferdinando Bassi, Curator of the Botanic Garden at Bologna. *Linn.* 11, Or. 1, Nat. Or. *Sapotaceæ.* Handsome lofty-growing trees, thriving well in light loam and peat, mixed; ripened cuttings in sand, under a glass, strike root freely. *B. butyracea* yields a thick oil-like butter, and *B. longifolia* is prescribed in rheumatic affections.

| | | | | | |
|---|---|---|---|---|---|
| butyrācēā | . . . | S. Ev. T. Nepal | | . | 1823 |
| latĭfōlĭā | . . . Yellow | S. Ev. T. E. Ind. | | . | 1799 |
| longĭfōlĭā | . . . | S. Ev. T. E. Ind. | | . | 1811 |

**BASTARD ACĂCĬĂ**, see *Robĭnĭă Pseudo-acācĭā.*
**BASTARD ACMĚLLĂ**, see *Spilănthēs Pseudo-acmēllā.*
**BASTARD ATŌCĬŎN**, see *Silene Pseudo-atōcĭŏn.*
**BASTARD BALM**, see *Melĭttĭs.*
**BASTARD BOX**, see *Polȳgălă Chamæbūxŭs.*
**BASTARD CABBAGE-TREE**, see *Geŏffrŏyā.*
**BASTARD CEDAR**, see *Guazūmă.*
**BASTARD CHERRY**, see *Cĕrăsŭs Pseudo-cĕrăsŭs.*
**BASTARD CINNAMON**, see *Cinnamŏmŭm Cassĭa.*
**BASTARD CORK-TREE**, see *Quĕrcŭs Pseudo-sūbĕr.*
**BASTARD CRĂCCĂ**, see *Vĭcĭā Pseudo-crăccā.*
**BASTARD CYPRŬS**, see *Cărĕx Pseudo-cyprŭs.*
**BASTARD DICTĂMNŬS**, see *Berĭngĕrĭā Pseudo-dictamnus.*
**BASTARD GROUND-PINE**, see *Teūcrĭŭm Pseudo-chamæpĭtȳs.*

**BASTARD HARE'S-EAR**, see *Phȳllĭs.*
**BASTARD HYSSOP**, see *Teūcrĭŭm Pseudo-hyssōpŭs.*
**BASTARD INDIGO**, see *Amŏrphă.*
**BASTARD JASMINE**, see *Andrŏsăcĕ chamæjăsmĕ.*
**BASTARD LUPINE**, see *Trĭfŏlĭŭm Lupināstĕr.*
**BASTARD MANCHINEEL**, see *Camerărĭă.*
**BASTARD MOUSE-EAR**, see *Hierācĭŭm Pseudo-pilosēllă.*
**BASTARD ŎLBĬĂ**, see *Lavatĕră Pseudo-ōlbĭā.*
**BASTARD ORPINE**, see *Andrăchnĕ.*
**BASTARD PIMPERNEL**, see *Centūncŭlŭs bicŏrnĭs.*
**BASTARD QUINCE**, see *Pȳrŭs-chamæmespĭlŭs.*
**BASTARD ROCKET**, see *Brăssĭcă Pseudo-erucāstrŭm.*
**BASTARD TOAD-FLAX**, see *Thĕsĭŭm.*
**BASTARD VERVAIN**, see *Stachytărphĕtă.*
**BASTARD VETCH**, see *Phăcă.*
**BASTARD WINDFLOWER**, see *Gentiānă Pseudo-pneumonănthĕ.*
**BASTARD WOODSAGE**, see *Teūcrĭŭm Pseudo-scorodōnĭā.*

**BATEMĂNNĬĂ**, *Lindley.* In compliment to James Bateman, Esq. of Knypersley Hall, Cheshire, an ardent collector and successful cultivator of Orchidaceæ, and author of that splendid work, the "Orchidaceæ of Mexico and Guatemala." *Linn.* 20, Or. 1, Nat. Or. *Orchidaceæ.* A very pretty species, well deserving a place in every collection; it somewhat resembles a Maxillaria, with a pendulous raceme of flowers from the base of the pseudo-bulbs; the sepals and petals are brownish-purple within, green without, and a white labellum. It requires the same treatment as *Stanhopea*, and other similar genera.

| | | | | | |
|---|---|---|---|---|---|
| Collĕyī | . . . Pur. grn. | . 8, S. Epi. Demerara | | . | 1834 |

**BATRACHOSPĒRMŬM**, *Agardh.* From *batrachos*, frog, and *sperma*, seed. Name refers to the situation where the species grow. *Linn.* 24, Or. 7, Nat. Or. *Algæ.* The species are interesting, having more or less the appearance of a necklace, especially *B. monilĭfōrmĕ*; they grow mostly in marshes—*monilĭfōrmĕ, M. delĕrtŭm, M. purpurāscēns, M. simplĭcĭŭs, M. stagnălĕ; văgŭm, V. tenuĭssĭmŭm.*

**BĂTSCHĬĂ**, *Michaux.* In honour of John George Batsch, a professor of botany in Germany. *Linn.* 5, Or. 1, Nat. Or. *Boraginaceæ.* Pretty dwarf species, succeeding in common soil, and increased by seeds or divisions. Synonymes: 1. *Lithospermum canescens.* 2. *L. hirtum, Batschia caroliniensis.*

| | | | | | |
|---|---|---|---|---|---|
| canēscēns, 1 | . . Yellow | . 7, H. Her. | P. N. Amer. | . | 1826 |
| Gmelĭnī, 2 | . . Yellow | . 6, H. Her. | P. Carolina | . | 1812 |
| longĭflōrā | . . Yellow | . 6, H. Her. | P. Missouri | . | 1812 |
| serĭcēā | . . . Yellow | . 7, H. Her. | P. N. Amer. | . | 1825 |

**BATTĂRRĔĂ**, *Persoon.* Named in honour of Antonia Battarra. *Linn.* 24, Or. 9, Nat. Or. *Fungi.* A very curious plant, found only in Britain, where it is very rare. The volva or wrapper, is about the size of a hen's egg, originally in three slightly coriaceous layers, hollow internally, which rises suddenly to its full height of about twelve inches; the stalk carries up on its summit full half the innermost layer of the volva, which is white and smooth within, and covered externally with copious brown sporules, intermixed with fibre.—*Loudon's Ency. of Plants—phallōĭdēs.*

**BAUĔRĂ**, *Andr.* In memory of Francis and Ferdinand Bauer, botanical draughtsmen of the highest celebrity. *Linn.* 13, Or. 2, Nat. Or. *Baueraceæ.* Pretty, free-flowering species, of easy culture; a mixture of sand and peat suits them, and young cuttings root readily in sand or soil, under a glass.

| | | | | | |
|---|---|---|---|---|---|
| hūmĭlĭs | . . . . Red | . 9, G. Ev. S. | N. S. W. | . | 1804 |
| rubĭæfōlĭā | . . Pink | . 9, G. Ev. S. | N. S. W. | . | 1793 |

**BAUHĬNĬĂ**, *Plumier.* In memory of John and Caspar Bauhin, botanists of the sixteenth century. *Linn.* 10, Or. 1, Nat. Or. *Leguminosæ.* Showy interesting species, some of them particularly so when in bloom; they succeed well in a mixture of sand, loam, and peat; and cuttings taken when the wood is neither ripe nor very young (observing to dress off the leaves), and planted in sand, under a glass in a moist heat, will strike root. The dried leaves and young buds of *B. tomentosa* are prescribed in dysenteric affections; the bark of *B. variegata* is used in tanning and drying leather, and that of *B. racemosa* is employed in making rope. Synonymes: 1. *B. anguina.* 2. *B. retusa, divaricata.* 3. *B. aculeata.*

| | | | | | |
|---|---|---|---|---|---|
| aculeàtà | . White . | . 8. Ev. 8. | W. Ind. | . 1737 |
| acuminàtà | . White . | . 7, 8. Ev. 8. | E. Ind. | . 1808 |
| americàna | . White . | . 8. Ev. 8. | S. Amer. | . 1800 |
| anatòmicà | . White . | . 8. Ev. 8. | S. Amer. | . 1806 |
| armàtà | . White . | . 8. Ev. Cl. | Brazil | . 1824 |
| aurìtà | . White . | . 8. Ev. 8. | Jamaica | . 1756 |
| càndidà | . White . | . 6, 8. Ev. 8. | E. Ind. | . 1777 |
| chinénsis | . Red . | . 8. Ev. 8. | China | . 1800 |
| corymbósà, 1 | . White . | . 8. Ev. Cl. | E. Ind. | . 1818 |
| cumanénsis | . White . | . 7, 8. Ev. Cl. | Cumana | . 1826 |
| divaricàtà | . White . | . 7, 8. Ev. 8. | W. Ind. | . 1748 |
| emarginàtà | . White . | . 8. Ev. 8. | Carthag. | . 1700 |
| ferrugìneà | . White . | . 8. Ev. Cl. | E. Ind. | . 1820 |
| forficàtà | . White . | . 8. Ev. 8. | Brazil | . 1823 |
| glàbrà | . White . | . 8. Ev. Cl. | Carthag. | . 1810 |
| glaucéscens | . White . | . 8. Ev. 8. | Cumana | . 1817 |
| grandiflòrà | . White . | . 8. Ev. 8. | Peru | . 1820 |
| guianénsis | . White . | . 8. Ev. Cl. | Guiana | . 1820 |
| heterophyllà | . White . | . 8. Ev. 8. | Caraccas | . 1824 |
| indicà | . White . | . 8. Ev. 8. | E. Ind. | . 1820 |
| inérmis | . Yel. red . | . 8. Ev. 8. | Acapulco | . 1810 |
| Lamarkiànà, 2 | . White . | . 8. Ev. 8. | S. Amer. | . 1818 |
| latifòlià | . White . | . 8. Ev. 8. | W. Ind. | . 1818 |
| leptopetàlà | . Yel. grn. . | . 8. Ev. 8. | N. Spain | . 1818 |
| lunàrià | . White . | . 8. Ev. 8. | Acapulco | . 1820 |
| madagascariénsis | . White . | . 8. Ev. 8. | Madagas. | . 1826 |
| malabàricà | . White . | . 8. Ev. Cl. | E. Ind. | . 1810 |
| microphyllà | . White . | . 8. Ev. 8. | S. Amer. | . 1817 |
| multinérvià | . White . | . 8. Ev. 8. | Caraccas | . 1808 |
| parviflòrà | . White . | . 8. Ev. 8. | E. Ind. | . 1820 |
| Paulàtià | . White . | . 8. Ev. 8. | Panama | . 1737 |
| porrécta | . White . | . 8. Ev. 8. | W. Ind. | . 1823 |
| pubéscens | . White . | . 8. Ev. 8. | Jamaica | . 1778 |
| purpùreà | . Purple . | . 8. Ev. 8. | E. Ind. | . 1778 |
| racemòsà | . Pa. pink . | . 8. Ev. Cl. | E. Ind. | . 1790 |
| retùsà | . White . | . 8. Ev. 8. | E. Ind. | . 1820 |
| ruféscens | . Pa. red . | . 8. Ev. 8. | Africa | . 1810 |
| scándens | . Wht. yel. . | . 8. Ev. Cl. | E. Ind. | . 1790 |
| semibìfidà | . White . | . 8. Ev. Cl. | E. Ind. | . 1817 |
| spathàceà | . White . | . 8. Ev. 8. | Mexico | . 1823 |
| speciòsà | . White . | . 8. Ev. Cl. | | . 1820 |
| subrotundifòlià | . White . | . 8. Ev. 8. | Acapulco | . 1820 |
| tomentòsà | . Yel. wht. . | . 8. Ev. Cl. | E. Ind. | . 1808 |
| triàndrà | . White . | . 8. Ev. Cl. | E. Ind. | . 1823 |
| ungùlà. 3 | . White . | . 8. Ev. 8. | Caraccas | . 1817 |
| variegàtà | . Striped . | . 6, 8. Ev. 8. | E. Ind. | . 1690 |

BAWD-MONEY, see *Mèum.*

BAY TREE, see *Laûrùs nòbilis.*

BEAD TREE, see *Mèlià.*

BEAK, anything like the beak of a bird, hard sharp points.

BEAN, see *Fàbà.*

BEAN CAPER, see *Zygophyllûm.*

BEAN TREFOIL, see *Anàgyris.*

BEARBIND, see *Calystègià.*

BEARDLETTED, possessed of small awns.

BEAR's-BREECH, see *Acànthûs.*

BEAR's-EAR SANICLE, see *Cortùsà.*

BEAR's-FOOT, see *Hellèbôrûs fœtidûs.*

BEAR's-GRAPE, see *Arctostaphylôs ûvâ ûrsî.*

BEAST's-BANE, see *Acônîtûm theriôphônûm.*

BEAUFORTIÀ, *Robert Brown.* In compliment to Mary, Duchess of Beaufort, a botanical patroness. *Linn.* 18, Or. 2, Nat. Or. *Myrtaceæ.* Very splendid and desirable species; for culture, &c., see *Tristania.*

| | | | | | |
|---|---|---|---|---|---|
| carinàtà | . Scarlet . | . | G. Ev. 8. | N. Holl. | . 1823 |
| Dampÿerì | . Pink . | . 5, | G. Ev. 8. | Hartog's Is. | |
| decussàtà | . Scarlet . | . 5, | G. Ev. 8. | N. Holl. | . 1803 |
| »pùrsà | . Red . | . | G. Ev. 8. | N. Holl. | . 1803 |
| spléndens | . . | . | G. Ev. 8. | N. Holl. | . 1830 |

BEAUMONTIÀ, *Wallich.* In memory of Diana, the lady of Colonel T. Beaumont, of Bretton Hall. *Linn.* 5, Or. 1, Nat. Or. *Apocynaceæ.* Beautiful species, especially *B. grandiflora.* They succeed well in loam, or loam and peat mixed, and are propagated from cuttings, or seed, in sandy soil under a glass.

| | | | | | |
|---|---|---|---|---|---|
| grandiflòrà | . White . | . 6, 8. Ev. Tw. | E. Ind. | . 1820 |
| longifòlià | . White . | . 8. Ev. Tw. | E. Ind. | . 1818 |

BECKMANNIÀ, *Host.* Dedicated to Mr. Beckman, the author of "The History of Inventions." *Linn.* 3, Or. 2, Nat. Or. *Graminæ.* An uninteresting species, of the simplest culture. *Synonyme:* 1. *Cynosurus erucæformis, erucíformis* 1.

BED-STRAW, see *Gàlliûm.*

BEECH, see *Fàgùs.*

BEET, see *Bètà.*

BEGONIÀ, *Linn.* In honour of Michael Begon, a Frenchman, and promoter of botany. *Linn.* 21, Or. 9, Nat. Or. *Begoniaceæ.* An interesting, somewhat succulent genus, peculiar for the leaves being oblique at their base. They succeed well in very

[ 41 ]

rich soil, and cuttings root readily. Some species are useful in cases of scurvy. *Synonymes:* 1. *B. maculata.* 2. *Evansiana.* 3. *Glabra.*

| | | | | | |
|---|---|---|---|---|---|
| acuminàtà | . White . | . 7, 8. Ev. 8. | Jamaica | . 1790 |
| acutifòlià | . White . | . 8, 8. Ev. 8. | W. Ind. | . 1816 |
| argyrostigmà, 1 | . White . | . 8, 8. Ev. 8. | Brasil | . 1819 |
| bulbìferà | . Wht. pnk. | . 7, G. Her. P. | Peru | . 1827 |
| dichotòmà | . White . | . 7, 8. Ev. 8. | Caraccas | . 1800 |
| dipetàlà | . Pink . | . 7, 8. Ev. 8. | Bombay | . 1827 |
| dìpterà | . White . | . 6, 8. Ev. 8. | C. G. H. | . 1822 |
| discôlôr, 2 | . White . | . 5, 8. Ev. 8. | China | . 1804 |
| distìchà | . White . | . 9, 8. Her. P. | Brasil | . 1819 |
| diversifòlià | . Pink . | . 7, 8. Her. P. | Mexico | . 1829 |
| dùbià | . White . | . 7, 8. Her. P. | Brasil | . 1818 |
| Fischerì | . . | . 6, 8. Ev. 8. | S. Amer. | . 1835 |
| geraniifòlià | . Wht. red . | . 9, 8. Tu. P. | Lima | . 1833 |
| heracleifòlià | . . | . 8. Tu. P. | | . 1831 |
| hirsùtà | . White . | . 6, 8. | B. W. Ind. | . 1789 |
| hirtéllà | . White . | . 9, 8. Her. P. | | . 1824 |
| hùmilis | . White . | . 9, 8. | B. W. Ind. | . 1788 |
| incarnàtà | . Pink . | . 8. | | . 1829 |
| insìgnis | . Pink . | . 12, 8. Ev. 8. | S. Amer. | . 1826 |
| longìpes | . White . | . 7, 8. Ev. 8. | Mexico | . 1828 |
| lùcidà | . White . | . 8, 8. Ev 8. | W. Ind. | . 1816 |
| macrophyllà | . White . | . 7, 8. Ev. 8. | Jamaica | . 1793 |
| Martiàna | . Pink . | . 8, 8. Tu. P. | Brasil | . 1829 |
| monòptera | . White . | . 8, 8. Tu. P. | Brasil | . 1829 |
| multibulbillòsà | . White . | . 8. Tu. P. | Brasil | . 1830 |
| nìtidà | . White . | . 8, 8. Ev. 8. | Jamaica | . 1777 |
| octopetala | . Gsh. wht. | . 10, 8. Tu. P. | Peru | . 1835 |
| odoràtà | . White . | . 9, 8. Her. P. | | . 1824 |
| palmàtà | . White . | . 8, 8. Ev. 8. | Nepal | . 1819 |
| papillòsà | . Pink . | . 7, 8. Ev. 8. | Brasil | . 1826 |
| pàtùla | . White . | . 8, 8. Ev. 8. | W. Ind. | . 1818 |
| pauciflòrà | . White . | . 9, 8. Her. P. | | . 1816 |
| petalòidés | . Ro. wht. . | . 5, 8. Ev. 8. | Brasil | . 1822 |
| pìctà | . Pink . | . 8, 8. Tu. P. | Nepal | . 1818 |
| platanifòlià | . Pink . | . 8, 8. Ev. 8. | Brasil | . 1829 |
| pulchélla | . White . | . 7, 8. | A. Brasil | . 1823 |
| renifòrmis | . White . | . 7, 8. Ev. 8. | Brasil | . 1818 |
| sanguìneà | . . | . 8, 8. Ev. 8. | Brasil | . 1829 |
| scándens, 3 | . White . | . 8, 8. Ev. Cl. | Guiana | . 1822 |
| semperflòrens | . Pink . | . 8, 8. Ev. 8. | Brasil | . 1829 |
| spatulàtà | . White . | . 9, 8. Her. P. | W. Ind. | . 1819 |
| suaveòlens | . White . | . 8, 8. Ev. 8. | W. Ind. | . 1816 |
| tuberòsà | . White . | . 8, 8. Tu. P. | Amboyna | . 1810 |
| ulmifòlià | . White . | . 7, 8. Ev. 8. | S. Amer. | . 1822 |
| undulàtà | . White . | . 7, 8. Ev. 8. | Brasil | . 1825 |
| villòsà | . Pink . | . 7, 8. | A. S. Amer. | |

BEJARIÀ, *Mutis.* In memory of M. Bejar, a Spanish botanist. *Linn.* 11, Or. 1, Nat. Or. *Ericaceæ.* Beautiful species, of easy culture, succeeding well in loam and peat; and cuttings root readily under a glass in heat.

| | | | | | |
|---|---|---|---|---|---|
| glaúcà | . Purple . | . 6, 8. Ev. 8. | N. Grena. | . 1826 |
| racemòsà | . Purple . | . 6, G. Ev. 8. | Florida | . 1810 |

BELLADONNA LILY, see *Amaryllis Belladonnà.*

BELLEISLE CRESS, see *Barbàréà præcòx.*

BELLEVALIÀ, *La Peyrouse.* In memory of P. R. Belleval, a French botanist. *Linn* 6, Or. 1, Nat. Or. *Liliaceæ.* An interesting species, succeeding in common soil, and increased by suckers. *Synonymes:* 1. *Scilla romana, Hyacinthus romanus.*

| | | | | | |
|---|---|---|---|---|---|
| operculàta, 1 | . White . | . 5, H. Bl. P. | Italy | . 1596 |

BELL FLOWER, see *Campànûlà.*

BELLIDIASTRÙM, *Micheli.* From *bellis* and *astrum,* resembling a daisy. *Linn.* 19, Or. 2, Nat. Or. *Compositæ.* An ornamental species, succeeding in peat and loam, and increased by divisions. *Synonyme:* 1. *Arnica Bellidiastrum.*

| | | | | | |
|---|---|---|---|---|---|
| Michelì | . White . | . 6, H. Her. P. | Austria | . 1570 |

BELLIS, *Linn.* In allusion to the pretty flowers. *Linn.* 19, Or. 2, Nat. Or. *Compositæ.* This comprehends the common daisy, the merits and the culture of which must be familiar to every one.

| | | | | | |
|---|---|---|---|---|---|
| ánnùà | . White . | . 5, H. | A. S. Eur. | . 1759 |
| hybrìdà | . White . | . 4, H. Her. P. | Italy | . 1824 |
| perénnis | . White . | . 6, H. Her. P. | Britain | |
| fistulòsà | . Red . | . 6, H. Her. P. | | |
| horténsis | . Red . | . 6, H. Her. P. | | |
| prolìferà | . Striped . | . 6, H. Her. P. | | |
| sylvéstris | . White . | . 6, H. Her. P. | Portugal | . 1797 |

BELLIUM, *Linn.* From *bellis,* daisy; the flowers being similar to those of the daisy. *Linn.* 19 Or. 2, Nat. Or. *Compositæ.* Pretty species, succeeding best in sandy peat, or peat and common soil mixed; seeds or divisions.

| | | | | | |
|---|---|---|---|---|---|
| bellidioìdés | . White . | . 7, H. | A. Italy | . 1796 |
| crassifòlium | . Wht. yel. | 6, F. Ev. P. | Sardinia | . 1831 |
| minùtùm | . White . | . 8, H. Her. P. | Levant | . 1772 |

BELOPERÒNÈ, *Nees.* Named in reference to the arrow-

G

shaped connectivum; from *belos*, an arrow, and *perone*, a band, or strap. *Linn.* 2, Or. 1, Nat. Or. *Acanthaceæ.* A pretty species, easily cultivated, and multiplied by cuttings.

| | | | | | |
|---|---|---|---|---|---|
| oblongătă | . . . Ro. pur. | . 9, S. Ev. S. | Brazil | . | 1832 |

BENGAL QUINCE, see *Aglĕ mărmĕlŏs.*

BENINCĂSĂ, *Savi.* From Count Benincasa, an Italian nobleman. *Linn.* 23, Or. 1, Nat. Or. *Cucurbitaceæ.* A worthless species, of the easiest culture. Synonyme: 1. *Cucurbita cerifera—cerifĕră* 1.

BENJAMIN TREE, see *Ficŭs Benjamĭnă.*

BENJAMIN TREE, see *Laŭrŭs Bĕnzŏin.*

BENT-GRASS, see *Agrŏstis.*

BENTHĂMĬĂ, *Lindl.* In honour of George Bentham, secretary of the London Horticultural Society. *Linn.* 4, Or. 1, Nat. Or. *Cornaceæ.* A very handsome plant, sufficiently hardy to bear our severest winters, if guarded from the cold cutting winds, and unusually sharp frosts, by a mat. The flowers, which appear in profusion during summer, are succeeded by an abundance of large, globular, reddish-yellow, eatable fruit, of an insipid though not unpleasant taste. It succeeds best in common garden loamy soil, and is easily increased by seeds or layers. The best situation for it is against a south wall, where it grows freely, and looks well.

| | | | | | |
|---|---|---|---|---|---|
| fragiferă | . . . Ysh. red | . 8, H. Ev. S. | E. Ind. | . | 1825 |

BERĂRDĬĂ, *Villars.* Named after Mr. Berard, a botanist of Grenoble. *Linn.* 19, Or. 1, Nat. Or. *Compositæ.* A pretty species, of very easy culture. Synonymes: 1. *Brunia palæacea.* 2. *B. phylicoides.*

| | | | | | |
|---|---|---|---|---|---|
| palĕăcĕă, 1 | . . White | . 7, G. Ev. S. | C. G. H. | . | 1791 |
| phylicoidĕs, 2 | . . White | . 7, G. Ev. S. | C. G. H. | . | 1805 |

BERBĔRĬS, *Linn.* From berberys, its name in Arabia. *Linn.* 6, Or. 2, Nat. Or. *Berberaceæ.* This genus comprises the common berberry, and the species are very ornamental whilst growing plants. They thrive in any common soil, but prefer one rather light; cuttings or layers take freely in the open ground. The fruit makes an agreeable jelly, and, as a medicine, is considered an agreeable and grateful astringent acid. The bark of the root boiled is used in Poland to dye yellow; the colour is best when boiled in ley. Synonymes: 1. *Chitria.* 2. *Vulgaris iberica.*

| | | | | | |
|---|---|---|---|---|---|
| aristătă, 1 | . . Yellow | . 4, H. Ev. S. | Nepal | . | 1820 |
| asiatică | . . Yellow | . H. Ev. S. | Nepal | . | 1823 |
| buxifolĭă | . . Yellow | . F. Ev. S. | Stra. of Mag. | . | 1827 |
| canadĕnsis | . . Yellow | . 5, H. De. S. | Canada | . | 1759 |
| cratægĭnă | . . Yellow | . H. De. S. | Asia Minor | . | 1829 |
| crĕtică | . . Yellow | . 6, H. De. S. | Candia | . | 1759 |
| serratifolĭă | . . Yellow | . 5, H. De. S. | Candia | . | 1759 |
| daŭrică | . . Yellow | . 5, H. De. S. | Dauria | . | 1818 |
| dĕalbătă | . . Yellow | . 5, H. Ev. S. | Mexico | . | 1833 |
| dŭlcis | . . Yellow | . 8. H. Ev. S. | Magellan | . | 1830 |
| emarginătă | . . Yellow | . 5, H. Ev. S. | Siberia | . | 1790 |
| empetrifolĭă | . . Yellow | . 5, F. Ev. S. | Stra. of Mag. | . | 1827 |
| heterophyllă | . . Yellow | . 5, H. Ev. S. | Magellan | . | 1805 |
| iberică, 2 | . . Yellow | . 5, H. De. S. | Iberia | . | 1818 |
| ilicifolĭă | . . Yellow | . 7, H. Ev. S. | T. del Fue. | . | 1791 |
| inĕrmis | . . Yellow | . F. Ev. S. | Stra. of Mag. | . | 1827 |
| provinciălis | . . Yellow | . 6, H. De. S. | France | . | 1821 |
| ruscifolĭă | . . Yellow | . 5, G. Ev. S. | B. Ayres | . | 1823 |
| sibirică | . . Yellow | . 7, H. De. S. | Siberia | . | 1790 |
| sinĕnsis | . . Yellow | . 4, H. De. S. | China | . | 1815 |
| tenuifolĭă | . . | . H. Ev. S. | Vera Cruz. | . | 1836 |
| vulgăris | . . Yellow | . 4, H. De. S. | England | . | |
| alba | . . Yellow | . 4, H. De. S. | | | |
| aspĕrmă | . . Yellow | . 4, H. De. S. | Europe | . | |
| lŭtĕa | . . Yellow | . 5, H. De. S. | Europe | . | |
| nigră | . . Yellow | . 4, H. De. S. | Europe | . | |
| purpŭrĕă | . . Yellow | . 4, H. De. S. | Europe | . | |
| violacĕă | . . Yellow | . 4, H. De. S. | | | |
| Wallichiănă | . . Yellow | . 5, F. Ev. S. | Nepal | . | 1820 |

BERBERRY, see *Bĕrbĕris.*

BERCHĔMĬĂ, *Necker.* In honour of M. Berchem, a French botanist. *Linn.* 5, Or. 1, Nat. Or. *Rhamnaceæ.* The species succeed in sandy loam and peat, and are interesting. They increase either by cuttings or seeds. To the roots of *B. volubilis*, antisyphilitic virtues are ascribed. Synonymes: 1. *Rhamnus lineatus, Œnoplia lineata.* 2. *Rhamnus volubilis, Œnoplia volubilis.*

| | | | | | |
|---|---|---|---|---|---|
| lineătŭs, 1 | . . Green | . 6, G. Ev. Cl. | China | . | 1804 |
| volŭbĭlis, 2 | . . Green | . 6, H. De. Tw. | Carolina | . | 1714 |

BERCKHĔYĬĂ, *Greville.* Dedicated to John Lefranc de Berckhey, a Dutch botanist. *Linn.* 19, Or. 3, Nat.

---

Or. *Compositæ.* The species are ornamental, and succeed well in a mixture of loam and peat; cuttings planted in common soil, root readily under a glass.

| | | | | | |
|---|---|---|---|---|---|
| cĕrnŭă | . . Yellow | . 6, S. | B. C. G. H. | . | 1774 |
| cuneătă | . . Yellow | . 6, G. Ev. S. | C. G. H. | . | 1812 |
| cynaroidĕs | . . Yellow | . 6, H. Her. | P. C. G. H. | . | 1789 |
| grandiflŏră | . . Yellow | . 7, G. Ev. S. | C. G. H. | . | 1812 |
| incănă | . . Yellow | . 7, G. Ev. S. | C. G. H. | . | 1789 |
| obovătă | . . Yellow | . 7, G. Ev. S. | C. G. H. | . | 1794 |
| palmătă | . . Yellow | . 7, G. Ev. S. | C. G. H. | . | 1800 |
| pectinătă | . . Yellow | . 8, G. Ev. S. | C. G. H. | . | 1818 |
| spinosissĭmă | . . Yellow | . 7, G. Her. | P. C. G. H. | . | 1821 |
| uniflŏră | . . Yellow | . 7, G. Ev. S. | C. G. H. | . | 1815 |

BERGAMOT, see *Menthă odorătă.*

BERGĔRĂ, *König.* In compliment to C. J. Berger, a botanist at Kiel. *Linn.* 10, Or. 1, Nat. Or. *Aurantiaceæ.* Curious and interesting species, succeeding in sandy loam, and multiplied by layers or cuttings. The leaves of *B. Königii* are stomachic and tonic, and an infusion of them toasted allays vomiting.

| | | | | | |
|---|---|---|---|---|---|
| integĕrrĭmă | . . White | . 6, S. Ev. S. | W. Ind. | . | 1823 |
| Königĭĭ | . . White | . 6, S. Ev. S. | E. Ind. | . | 1820 |

BERGĬĂ, *Linn.* In honour of P. J. Bergius, M.D. *Linn.* 10, Or 4, Nat. Or. *Elatinaceæ.* This curious little species may be grown in sandy soil, and increased plentifully by seeds.

| | | | | | |
|---|---|---|---|---|---|
| verticillătă | . . Wht. red | . 6, H. | A. Egypt | . | 1820 |

BERINGĔRĬĂ, *Necker.* supposed to be a man's name. *Linn.* 14, Or. 1, Nat. Or. *Labiatæ.* Ornamental species; for culture, &c., see *Marrubium.* Synonymes: 1. *Marrubium acetabulosum.* 2. *M. africanum.* 3. *M. cinereum.* 4. *M. crispum.* 5. *M. hirsutum.* 6. *M. hispanicum.* 7. *M. orientale.* 8. *M. Pseudo-dictamnus.*

| | | | | | |
|---|---|---|---|---|---|
| acetabulosă, 1 | . . Purple | . 7, F. Ev. S. | Candia | . | 1676 |
| africănă, 2 | . . Purple | . 8, H. Her. | P. C. G. H. | . | 1710 |
| cinĕrĕă, 3 | . . Pa. pur. | . 7, H. Her. | P. Spain | . | 1823 |
| crispă, 4 | . . Pa. pur. | . 7, H. Her. | P. S. Eur. | . | 1714 |
| hirsŭtă, 5 | . . Pa. pur. | . 6, H. Her. | P. | | |
| hispănĭcă, 6 | . . Purple | . 7, H. Her. | P. Spain | . | 1714 |
| orientălis, 7 | . . Purple | . 7, H. Her. | P. S. Eur. | . | 1821 |
| Pseudo-dictamnus, 8 | Purple | . 7, F. Ev. | P. Candia | . | 1596 |

BERKELĔYĬĂ, *Greville.* In honour of the Rev. Mr. Berkely, an English cryptogamist. *Linn.* 24, Or. 7, Nat. Or. *Algeæ.* A very small, interesting marine production—*fragilis.*

BERMUDA CEDAR, see *Junipĕrŭs bermudiănă.*

BERRĂYĂ, *Rox.* In memory of Dr. Berry, who first introduced it into Calcutta. *Linn.* 13, Or. 1, Nat. Or. *Tiliaceæ.* An ornamental tree, succeeding well in rich loam and peat mixed; cuttings planted in sandy soil root well under a glass. *B. amomilla* furnishes the fine light timber employed in making the Massoola boats of Madras, and called Trincomalee.

| | | | | | |
|---|---|---|---|---|---|
| amomilla | . . . | . 7, S. Ev. T. | E. Ind. | . . | 1800 |

BERTĔRĬĂ, *Dec.* Named in compliment to C. J. Bertero, an esteemed friend of Decandolle's. *Linn.* 15, Nat. Or. *Cruciferæ.* The species are ornamental, and of easy cultivation: sandy soil suits them, and young plants are obtained either from seeds or cuttings. Synonymes: 1. *Farsetia incana.* 2. *Farsetia mutabilis.*

| | | | | | |
|---|---|---|---|---|---|
| incănă, 1 | . . White | . 7, H. | B. Europe | . | 1640 |
| mutăbĭlis, 2 | . . Wht. pnk. | . 7, H. Her. | P. Levant | . | 1802 |
| obliquă | . . White | . 7, F. Ev. S. | Sicily | . | 1823 |

BERTHOLLĔTĬĂ, *Humb.* and *Bonp.* In memory of L. C. Berthollet, a meritorious chemist. *Linn.* 13, Or. 1, Nat. Or. *Lecythidaceæ.* This tall ornamental tree yields the nuts known in shops under the name of Brazilian nuts. It succeeds in sand, peat, and loam, and may be increased by cuttings in sand, or in a sandy soil.

| | | | | | |
|---|---|---|---|---|---|
| excelsă | . . . | . S. Ev. T. | Para | . . . |

BERZĔLĬĂ, *Brongniart.* Dedicated to the celebrated chemist Berzelius. *Linn.* 5, Or. 1, Nat. Or. *Bruniaceæ.* These pretty species delight in a mixture of rather sandy peat and loam. Cuttings take readily in sand, under a glass. Synonymes: 1. *Brunia abrotanoides.* 2. *B. lanuginosa.*

| | | | | | |
|---|---|---|---|---|---|
| abrotanoidĕs, 1 | . White | . 6, G. Ev. S. | C. G. H. | . | 1787 |
| lanuginŏsă, 2 | . White | . 7, G. Ev. S. | C. G. H. | . | 1774 |

BESLĔRĬĂ, *Linn.* Named in memory of Basil Besler,

an apothecary at Nuremberg. *Linn.* 14, Or. 2, Nat. Or. *Gesneriaceæ.* A pretty and interesting genus, delighting in very light rich soil. Sweet says, cuttings strike freely by merely sticking them, without protection, in the tan-bed. *Synonyme:* 1. *B. bicolor.*

| | | | | | |
|---|---|---|---|---|---|
| coccinea | Yellow | S. Ev. S. | Guiana | 1819 |
| cristata | Yellow | 6, S. Ev. Cl. | W. Ind. | 1739 |
| dichrus, 1 | Red yel. | 7, S. Ev. S. | Brazil | 1826 |
| grandifolia | Yellow | 8, S. Ev. S. | Brazil | 1823 |
| hirtella | Yellow | 7, S. Ev. S. | Brazil | 1824 |
| incarnata | Yellow | S. Her. P. | Guiana | 1820 |
| lutea | Yellow | 7, S. Ev. S. | Guiana | 1739 |
| melittifolia | Orange | 6, S. Ev. S. | Guiana | 1739 |
| mollis | Yellow | 8, S. Ev. S. | Amer. | 1828 |
| pulchella | Yellow | 8, S. Ev. S. | Trinidad | 1806 |
| serrulata | Pur. yel. | S. Ev. Cl. | W. Ind. | 1806 |
| violacea | Yellow | S. Ev. Cl. | Guiana | 1824 |

BETA, *Linn.* From the Celtic *bett,* signifying red; alluding to the red colour of the roots. *Linn.* 5, Or. 2, Nat. Or. *Chenopodiaceæ.* The beet-root is the type of this genus; the uses of which are well known; the species succeed well in common garden soil, treated as other culinary roots. *B. patula* does best kept in the greenhouse. *B. cicla* is used as spinach; and in Germany and Switzerland the midrib of the leaf is boiled, and eaten with gravy or melted butter.

| | | | | |
|---|---|---|---|---|
| cicla | Green | 8, H. B. | Portugal | 1670 |
| crispa | Green | 8, H. B. | S. Eur. | 1800 |
| macrorhiza | Green | 8, H. B. | Caucasus | 1820 |
| maritima | Green | 8, H. B. | Britain | |
| trigyna | White | 7, H. Her. P. | Hungary | 1796 |
| vulgaris | Green | 8, H. B. | Europe | 1548 |
| lutea | Green | 8, H. B. | S. Eur. | |
| rubra | Green | 8, H. B. | S. Eur. | |
| viridis | Green | 8, H. B. | S. Eur. | |

BETLE NUT, see *Pipĕr Betle.*

BETONICA, *Linn.* From *beutonic,* its Celtic name. *Linn.* 14, Or. 1, Nat. Or. *Labiatæ.* These handsome dwarf species are well adapted for ornamenting the margins of flower-borders, or rock-work. They grow in any common soil, and increase plentifully from suckers. *B. officinalis* when fresh intoxicates, and the dried leaves excite sneezing.

| | | | | |
|---|---|---|---|---|
| alopecurus | Red | 7, H. Her. P. | S. Eur. | 1759 |
| grandiflora | Purple | 5, H. Her. P. | Siberia | 1800 |
| hirsuta | Purple | 6, H. Her. P. | Italy | 1710 |
| incana | Flesh | 6, H. Her. P. | Italy | 1759 |
| macroura | Pa. red. | 7, H. Her. P. | Europe | 1820 |
| nivea | Red | 7, H. Her. P. | Caucasus | 1820 |
| officinalis | Purple | 8, H. Her. P. | Britain | |
| alba | White | 8, H. Her. P. | Britain | |
| orientalis | Lt. pur. | 6, H. Her. P. | Levant | 1787 |
| stricta | Purple | 6, H. Her. P. | Denmark | 1592 |

BETONY, see *Betŏnĭcă.*

BETONY, see *Teŭcrĭŭm betŏnĭcŭm.*

BETULA, *Linn.* From *betu,* its Celtic name. *Linn.* 21, Or. 4, Nat. Or. *Betulaceæ.* This is a popular genus, and best known by its common name, the beech. The species are for the most part lofty-growing trees, and very ornamental. *B. pendula* has a graceful and pleasing growth; the species *pumila* and *nana* are dwarfer-growing kinds, but very pretty and interesting. They thrive in any soil, and are commonly increased by grafting or budding on the larger and more plentiful kinds, the latter being raised from seed; the dwarfest species are best when produced from layers. *Synonyme:* 1. *Alnus viridis.*

| | | | | |
|---|---|---|---|---|
| alba | Apetal | 4, H. De. T. | Britain | |
| dalecarlica | Apetal | 5, H. De. T. | Europe | |
| macrocarpa | Apetal | 6, H. De. T. | Europe | |
| verrucosa | Apetal | 4, H. De. T. | Britain | |
| carpinifolia | Apetal | 7, H. Ev. S. | N. Amer. | 1759 |
| daurica | Apetal | 7, H. De. T. | Siberia | 1785 |
| parvifolia | Apetal | 7, H. De. T. | Siberia | |
| excelsa | Apetal | 7, H. De. T. | N. Amer. | 1767 |
| fruticosa | Apetal | 6, H. De. S. | Siberia | 1818 |
| lanulosa | Apetal | 7, H. De. T. | N. Amer. | 1817 |
| lenta | Apetal | 7, H. De. T. | N. Amer. | 1759 |
| lutea | Apetal | 5, H. De. S. | N. Amer. | |
| nana | Apetal | 5, H. De. S. | N. Amer. | |
| macrophylla | Apetal | 5, H. De. S. | Switzerl. | 1819 |
| stricta | Apetal | 5, H. De. S. | Siberia | |
| nigra | Apetal | 7, H. De. T. | N. Amer. | 1736 |
| ovata, 1 | Apetal | 5, H. De. S. | Hungary | 1890 |
| papyracea | Apetal | 6, H. De. T. | N. Amer. | 1750 |
| pendula | Apetal | 6, H. De. T. | Britain | |
| pontica | Apetal | 5, H. Ev. S. | Turkey | |
| populifolia | Apetal | 7, H. Ev. T. | N. Amer. | 1750 |

| | | | | |
|---|---|---|---|---|
| pubescens | Apetal | 6, H. De. T. | Germany | 1812 |
| pumila | Apetal | 5, H. De. S. | N. Amer. | 1762 |
| rubra | Apetal | 7, H. De. T. | Canada | |
| tristis | Apetal | 5, H. De. T. | Kamtsch. | |

BIALATA, two-winged.

BICEPS, having two heads.

BICORNIS, two-horned.

BIDENTATE, having twin, or a double row of, teeth.

BIENNIAL, of the continuance of two years. A plant is said to be biennial which takes two years to mature its fruit, and then dies.

BIFARIOUS, disposed in two rows.

BIFID, opening with a cleft nearly divided in two.

BIDENS, so called from *bis,* twice, and *dens,* a tooth; alluding to the seed. *Linn.* 19, Or. 1, Nat. Or. *Compositæ.* These species are mostly uninteresting; a few, however are worth cultivating. They grow readily in common soil, and increase from seeds, suckers, or divisions, according to their habits and duration. *Synonymes:* 1. *Coreopsis coronata.* 2. *B. odorata.* 3. *B. tripartita.*

| | | | | |
|---|---|---|---|---|
| Bertoriana, 1 | Yellow | 5, S. Her. P. | Porto Rico | 1787 |
| bipinnata | Yellow | 7, H. A. | N. Amer. | 1687 |
| crithmifolia | Yellow | 6, G. Her. P. | Mexico | 1824 |
| cynapifolia | Yellow | G. A. | Cuba | 1827 |
| grandiflora, 2 | Yellow | 6, H. A. | S. Amer. | 1800 |
| heterophylla | Yellow | 8, G. Her. P. | Mexico | 1803 |
| leucantha | White | 7, H. A. | S. Amer. | |
| macrosperma | Yellow | 6, H. A. | Siberia | 1819 |
| odorata | White | 6, H. A. | Mexico | 1825 |
| procera | Yellow | 11, H. Her. P. | Mexico | 1822 |
| repens, 3 | Yellow | 7, H. De. Cr. | Nepal | 1819 |
| sambucifolia | Yellow | 7, H. Her. P. | S. Amer. | 1801 |

*Angustifolia, bullata, cernua, chinensis, connata, chrysantha, chrysanthemoides, foliosa, frondosa, helianthoides, hirtella, luxurians, nudiflora, parviflora, pilosa, procumbens, reflexa, striata, tripartita.*

BIFORIS, *Sprengel.* The name is compounded from *bis,* double, or two, and *foris,* a flap; in reference to the shape of the fruit. *Linn.* 5, Or. 2, Nat. Or. *Umbelliferæ.* Uninteresting species, of the simplest culture. *Synonymes:* 1. *Coriandrum testiculatum.* 2. *C. testiculatum—radicans* 1, *testiculatum* 2.

BIFRENARIA, *Lindley.* So named from *bis,* twice, and *frænum;* in allusion to the double strap or *frænum* that connects the pollen masses with their gland. *Linn.* 20, Or. 1, Nat. Or. *Orchidaceæ.* A genus of very pretty plants when in flower, especially *B. aurantiaca,* the flowers of which are deep orange yellow, mottled with deep brown spots. For culture and propagation see *Maxillaria,* to which the genus is near akin. *Synonyme:* 1. *Maxillaria atropurpurea.*

| | | | | |
|---|---|---|---|---|
| atropurpurea, 1 | Drk. pur. | S. Epi. | Rio Jan. | 1828 |
| aurantiaca | Or. spot. | 9, S. Epi. | Demerara | |

BIFRONS, two-faced.

BIGELOVIA, see *Borrĕrĭă.*

BIGEMINATE, twin, each division bearing a pair of leaflets.

BIGLANDULAR, having two or double glands.

BIGLUMIS, having two husks, or chaffy scales.

BIGNONIA, *Linn.* In memory of Abbé Bignon, librarian to Louis XIV. *Linn.* 14, Or. 2, Nat. Or. *Bignoniaceæ.* The species are trees or shrubs, inhabitants of hot climates. The leaves are opposite, pinnate, ternate, or conjugate; the flowers in panicles, large and handsome, of various colours, red, blue, yellow, or white, and eminently beautiful. The stove sorts grow freely in loam and peat, and young cuttings root in sand under a handglass. The species grow in any soil, but will not flower well unless the situation be warm; they are increased by cuttings of the roots, by layers, or by young cuttings in a gentle heat, under a handglass or frame. *B. radicans* is a well-known much-admired species, capable of living in the open air in this country against a wall.—*Loud. Ency. of Plants.* The young shoots of *B. Chirere* are sometimes manufactured into wicker-work. *Synonymes:* 1. *Jacaranda alba.* 2. *B. heterophylla.* 3. *Jacaranda echinata.* 4 *Tomentosa.* 5. *Millingtonia hortensis.* 6. *Incarvillea—tomentosa.*

| | | | | |
|---|---|---|---|---|
| alba, 1 | White | S. Ev. Cl. | Guiana | 1823 |
| alliacea | Yellow | S. Ev. Cl. | W. Ind. | 1790 |
| amoena | Yellow | S. Ev. T. | E. Ind. | 1828 |
| apurensis | Yellow | S. Ev. Cl. | Orinoco | 1824 |
| aequinoctialis | Yellow | 6, S. Ev. Cl. | Guiana | 1768 |

| | | | | |
|---|---|---|---|---|
| maculiflóra | Yellow | 8. Ev. T. | Mexico | |
| bijúga | | 8. Ev. S. | Madagas. | 1822 |
| clandícans | | 8. Ev. Cl. | Cayenne | 1820 |
| capreolátå | Scarlet | 6, H. Da. Cl. | N. Amer. | 1710 |
| Chamberlaynll | Yellow | 8, 8. Ev. Cl. | Brazil | 1820 |
| Chicå | | 8. Ev. Cl. | Orinoco | 1819 |
| chirárå, 2 | Red. or. | 8. Ev. Cl. | Guiana | 1824 |
| chryanthå | Yellow | 8. Ev. T. | Guiana | 1823 |
| chrysoleucå | Yel. wht. | 7, 8. Ev. Cl. | S. Amer. | 1824 |
| Clematís | | 8. Ev. Cl. | Caracas | 1820 |
| crenata | | 8. Ev. Cl. | E. Ind. | 1823 |
| crucigerå | Yel. scar. | 8. Ev. Cl. | S. Amer. | 1759 |
| decipiens | | 8. Ev. Cl. | E. Ind. | 1823 |
| diversifolíå | | 8. Ev. Cl. | Mexico | 1825 |
| echinátå, 3 | Purple | 8. Ev. Cl. | S. Amer. | 1804 |
| elongátå | Purple | 8. Ev. Cl. | S. Amer. | 1820 |
| floribundå | White | 8. Ev. Cl. | Caracas | 1816 |
| fluviatíle | Yellow | 8. Ev. S. | Guiana | 1824 |
| grácilis | Yellow | 4, 8. Ev. Cl. | S. Amer. | 1810 |
| grandifolíå | Pur. red | 6, 8. Ev. Cl. | Caracas | 1816 |
| incarnátå | Wht. or. | 8. Ev. Cl. | Guiana | 1820 |
| indicå | Purple | 8. Ev. T. | India | 1775 |
| jasminifolíå | White | 8. Ev. Cl. | Orinoco | 1826 |
| jasminoídes | Purple | O. Ev. Cl. | Moreton B. | 1830 |
| lactiflorå | White | 5, 8. Ev. Cl. | Santa Cruz | 1823 |
| latifolíå | Yellow | 8. Ev. Cl. | Cayenne | 1823 |
| laurifolíå | | 8. Ev. Cl. | Guiana | 1804 |
| Leucóxylon | Pink | 8. Ev. T. | W. Ind. | 1759 |
| littorális | Pink red | 8. Ev. Cl. | Mexico | 1824 |
| lúcidå | | 8. Ev. Cl. | E. Ind. | 1823 |
| mccanthå, 4 | Pink | 6, 8. Ev. Cl. | N. Holl. | |
| móllis, 4 | | 8. Ev. Cl. | Guiana | 1818 |
| mollíssimå | | 8. Ev. Cl. | Caracas | 1820 |
| multifidå | | 8. Ev. Cl. | E. Ind. | 1823 |
| pállidå | White | 7, 8. Ev. Cl. | W. Ind. | 1823 |
| pictå | Varieg. | 8. Ev. Cl. | S. Amer. | 1822 |
| pubéscens | Yellow | 6, 8. Ev. Cl. | Campeachy | 1759 |
| purpúreå | Purple | 8. Ev. S. | S. Amer. | 1822 |
| quadranguláris | | 8. Ev. Cl. | E. Ind. | 1823 |
| rigéscens | Pink | 6, 8. Ev. Cl. | Caracas | 1823 |
| salicifolíå | Yellow | 8. Ev. Cl. | Trinidad | 1824 |
| serratifolíå | Yellow | 8. Ev. T. | W. Ind. | 1822 |
| spectábilis | Purple | 8. Ev. Cl. | W. Ind. | 1820 |
| spicátå | | 8. Ev. Cl. | Trinidad | 1822 |
| staminåd | Yellow | 8. Ev. Cl. | Hispani. | 1825 |
| suberóså, 5 | White | 8. Ev. T. | E. Ind. | 1820 |
| tomentóså, 6 | | 8. Ev. T. | Japan | 1820 |
| triphylla | White | 8. Ev. S. | S. Amer. | 1733 |
| úngula | Yellow | 8. Ev. Cl. | Caracas | 1759 |
| variábilis | Yel. wht. | 8. Ev. Cl. | W. Ind. | 1819 |
| venósta | Orange | 9, 8. Ev. Cl. | S. Amer. | 1816 |
| viridiflorå | Green | 8. Ev. Cl. | S. Amer. | 1823 |

BILbous, yoked together, coupled.
BILABIATE, having two lips.
BILBERRY, see *Vaccinium myrtillus*.
BILOBED, divided so as to form two lobes.
BILIMBI TREE, see *Averrhóa Bilimbi*.
BILLARDIERÅ, *Smith*. In honour of Julien Labillardiere, a French botanist and traveller. *Linn.* 5, Or. 1, Nat. Or. *Pittosporaceæ.* Handsome climbers, especially *B. longiflora*, which is an abundant flowerer, and produces a handsome blue berry. Good rich open loam mixed with peat suits them well, and cuttings root in sand, under a glass; they may also be raised from seed.

| | | | | |
|---|---|---|---|---|
| angustifolíå | Cream | 7, G. Ev. Cl. | N. Holl. | 1820 |
| longiflorå | Crimson | 7, G. Ev. Cl. | V. D. L. | 1810 |
| mutábilis | Crimson | 8, G. Ev. Cl. | N. S. W. | 1795 |
| ovális | Gra. yel. | 6, G. Ev. Cl. | V. D. L. | 1833 |
| parviflorå | Blue | 7, G. Ev. Cl. | N. Holl. | 1825 |
| scándens | Purple | 7, G. Ev. Cl. | N. S. W. | 1790 |

BILLBERGIÅ, *Thunberg*. Named after J. G. Billberg, a Swedish botanist. *Linn.* 6, Or. 1, Nat. Or. *Bromeliaceæ.* The species are handsome, especially when well cultivated, the flowers are very showy, and in some species they are produced in abundance; for culture, &c., see *Bromelia.* Synonymes: 1. *Tillandsia amena, Bromelia pallida.* 2. *B. melanantha.* 3. *B. iridiflora.* 4. *B. nudicaulis.* 5. *B. pyramidalis.* 6. *B. zebrina.*

| | | | | |
|---|---|---|---|---|
| aménå, 1 | Yellow | 6, Epiphy. | S. Amer. | 1817 |
| bicolor | Ro. blue | 5, Epiphy. | Rio Jan. | 1829 |
| clavátå, 2 | Blue | 3, Epiphy. | Trinidad | 1824 |
| cruéntå | Blue red | 8, Epiphy. | Rio Jan. | 1824 |
| fasciátå | Blue red | 8, Epiphy. | Rio Jan. | 1825 |
| iridifolíå, 3 | Scar. yel. | 8, Epiphy. | Rio Jan. | 1825 |
| nudicaulis, 4 | Crimson | 5, Epiphy. | Trinidad | 1822 |
| purpúreå | Ro. purple | 10, Epiphy. | Brasil | |
| pyramidális, 5 | Crimson | 3, Epiphy. | Rio Jan. | 1817 |
| zebrinå, 6 | | 6, Epiphy. | S. Amer. | 1826 |

BILLÓTIÅ, *J. F. Colladon.* After M. Teophila Billoti, of Turin. *Linn.* 18, Or. 2, Nat. Or. *Cinchonaceæ.* An interesting and ornamental evergreen of easy culture.

| | | | | |
|---|---|---|---|---|
| aceróså | Red | 8, G. Ev. S. | N. Holl. | 1816 |

BINATA, two growing together.
BINDWEED, see *Convólvulus.*
BINDWEED, see *Smilåx aspérå.*
BIOPHÝTUM, *Decan.* So called from *bios*, life, and *phýton*, a plant; in allusion to the irritability of the leaves and pods, which latter open when touched. *Linn.* 10, Or. 4, Nat. Or. *Oxalidaceæ.* A very pretty, and when grown as in China nine inches high, a remarkable annual; the leaves are prettily pinnated, which with the rich yellow flowers, have an interesting appearance. Cultivated in common soil, and raised plentifully from seeds. Synonyme: 1. *Oxalis sensitiva.*

| | | | | |
|---|---|---|---|---|
| sensitívum, 1 | Yellow | 7, H. | A. China | 1823 |

BIOVULATE, containing two ova, or young seeds; seeds before they are mature are called ova.
BIRCH, see *Bétulå.*
BIRCH, see *Cárpinus Bétulås.*
BIRD-CHERRY, see *Cérasus pádus.*
BIRD-PEPPER, see *Cápsicum báccátum.*
BIRD'S-BILL, see *Trigonélla ornithopodioídes.*
BIRD'S-EYE, see *Primúlå farinóså.*
BIRD'S-FOOT, see *Ornithópus.*
BIRD'S-FOOT, see *Euphórbiå ornithópus.*
BIRD'S-FOOT TREFOIL, see *Lótus.*
BIRD'S-NEST, see *Asplénium Nídus.*
BIRD'S-TONGUE, see *Ornithoglóssum.*
BIRTHWORT, see *Aristolóchiå.*
BISCUTÉLLÅ, *Linn.* Named from *bis*, double, or two, and *scutella*, a saucer; the form of the seed-vessel when bursting. *Linn.* 15, Nat. Or. *Cruciferæ.* Interesting plants, adapted for rock-work; they may also be grown in pots with other alpine plants, in loam and peat, which suits them well; increased from seeds.

| | | | | |
|---|---|---|---|---|
| ambígua | Yellow | 6, H. Her. P. | S. Italy | 1820 |
| ápula | Yellow | 7, H. | A. Italy | 1710 |
| auriculátå | Yellow | 6, H. Her. A. | Pyrenee | 1683 |
| cichoriifolíå | Yellow | 6, H. Her. A. | S. France | 1820 |
| ciliátå | Yellow | 6, H. | A. France | 1820 |
| Colúmnæ | Yellow | 6, H. | A. S. Italy | 1823 |
| coronopifolíå | Yellow | 6, H. Her. P. | Italy | 1790 |
| depréssa | Yellow | 6, H. | A. Egypt | 1811 |
| erigerifolíå | Yellow | 6, H. | A. S. Eur. | |
| eriocárpå | Y llow | 6, H. | A. S. Eur. | 1820 |
| híspidå | Yellow | 6, H. | A. S. Eur. | 1824 |
| lævigátå | Yellow | 6, H. Her. P. | Italy | 1777 |
| alpéstris | Yellow | 6, H. Her. P. | Hungary | 1816 |
| leiocárpå | Yellow | 6, H. | A. Levant | 1816 |
| lyrátå | Yellow | 7, H. | A. Spain | 1799 |
| marítimå | Yellow | 6, H. | A. Naples | 1824 |
| microcárpå | Yellow | 6, H. | A. S. Eur. | 1818 |
| montánå | Yellow | H. Her. P. | Spain | 1823 |
| obovátå | Yellow | 6, H. | A. Europe | 1817 |
| raphanifolíå | Yellow | 7, H. Her. A. | Sicily | 1822 |
| saxátilis | Yellow | 6, H. Her. P. | S. Eur. | 1821 |
| sempérvirens | Yellow | 6, H. Her. P. | Spain | 1784 |
| stenophýllå | Yellow | 6, H. Her. P. | Spain | 1826 |

BISACCATE, having two little bags, or pouches.
BISCUTATE, resembling two bucklers.
BISERRATE, twice cut, like the teeth of a saw.
BISERRÚLÅ, *Linn.* Derived from *bis*, twice, and *serrula*, a small saw; the pods being furnished with teeth something like a saw. *Linn.* 17, Or. 4, Nat. Or. *Leguminosæ.* This genus is known by the name of Hatchet Vetch, and comprehends an interesting species, which may be cultivated in sandy loam or peat, and increased from seeds.

| | | | | |
|---|---|---|---|---|
| Peláciñus | Purple | 7, H. | A. S. Eur. | 1640 |

BISHOP'S-WEED, see *Sisón Ammi.*
BISULCATA, doubly furrowed,
BITERNATE, divided into two, thrice over.
BITTER OAK, see *Quércus Cérris.*
BITTER SWEET, see *Solánum Dulcamárå.*
BITTER VETCH, see *Orobus.*
BITUMINOUS, clammy, adhesive.
BIVAGINATE, having double sheaths, or covers.
BIVONÆÅ, *Decan.* Dedicated to Antoine Bivona Bernardi, a professor of botany in Sicily. *Linn.* 15, Nat. Or. *Cruciferæ.* A pretty species, the seeds sown in sandy dry soil, where they are intended to remain, will succeed well. Synonyme: 1. *Thlaspi luteum—lútéå* 1.
BIXÅ, *Linn.* Its name in South America. *Linn.* 13, Or. 1, Nat. Or. *Bixaceæ.* These trees grow to a large size before they can be got to flower from seed. But if cuttings be taken from a flowering plant and struck, they may be brought to flower

when small plants. Loam and peat suit them well, and cuttings root freely in sand, under a glass, in heat.—*G. Don.*

| | | | | | | |
|---|---|---|---|---|---|---|
| Orellānā | . | . Pink | . 6, S. Ev. T. W. Ind. | . 1690 |
| purpūréā | . | . Purple | . 7, S. Ev. T. E. Ind. | . 1817 |
| Urucurānā | . | . Pink | . 7, S. Ev. T. Brazil | . 1820 |

BLACK ADIANTUM, see *Asplēnīūm adīāntūm nigrūm*.
BLACK BRYONY, see *Tāmūs*.
BLACK SALTWORT, see *Glaūx marītīmā*.
BLACK VARNISH TREE, see *Melanorrhæā*.
BLACKWĒLLĪĀ, *Commelin*. In compliment to Elizabeth Blackwell, a botanical artist. *Linn.* 11, Or. 5, Nat. Or. *Homaliaceæ*. The foliage of these plants is pretty, but the flowers have nothing to recommend them. They delight in sandy peat, and are propagated with facility from cuttings.

| | | | | | |
|---|---|---|---|---|---|
| axillārīs | . | . White | . 8. Ev. S. Madag. | . 1824 |
| grandiflōrā | . | . White | . 8, G. Ev. S. China | . 1824 |
| integrifōlīā | . | . White | . 8. Ev. S. Madag. | . 1823 |
| padiflōrā | . | . White | . 8, G. Ev. S. Chile | . 1827 |
| panicūlātā | . | . White | . S. Ev. S. Bourbon | . 1820 |
| spirālīs | . | . White | . 8. Ev. S. E. Ind. | . 1820 |

BLĀĒRĪĀ, *Linn.* In compliment to Patrick Blair, a physician at Boston, in Lincolnshire. *Linn.* 4, Nat. Or. *Ericeæ*. The species are interesting, and may be cultivated the same as the genus *Erica*.

| | | | | |
|---|---|---|---|---|
| articūlātā | . | . Pink | . 5, G. Ev. S. C. G. H. | . 1795 |
| ciliārīs | . | . White | . 6, G. Ev. S. C. G. H. | . 1795 |
| deprēssā | . | | . 6, G. Ev. S. C. G. H. | . 1816 |
| dumōsā | . | | . 6, G. Ev. S. C. G. H. | . 1806 |
| ericoīdēs | . | . Purple | . 9, G. Ev. S. C. G. H. | . 1774 |
| fascicūlātā | . | | . 6, G. Ev. S. C. G. H. | . 1812 |
| glabellā | . | | . 6, G. Ev. S. C. G. H. | . 1816 |
| muscōsā | . | . Pink | . 7, G. Ev. S. C. G. H. | . 1774 |
| paucifōlīā | . | | . 6, G. Ev. S. C. G. H. | . 1812 |
| purpūréā | . | . Purple | . 5, G. Ev. S. C. G. H. | . 1791 |
| scabrā | . | . Purple | . 5, G. Ev. S. C. G. H. | . 1824 |

BLĀKĒĀ, *Linn.* In memory of Martin Blake, an active promoter of useful knowledge. *Linn.* 11, Or. 1, Nat. Or. *Melastomaceæ*. These species are said to be among the most beautiful plants of the W. Indies. They grow well in peat, or peat and loam mixed; cuttings taken from quite ripened wood, planted in sand, and plunged in a moist heat, root readily.

| | | | | |
|---|---|---|---|---|
| quinquenērvīā | . | White | . 6, S. Ev. S. Trinidad | . 1820 |
| trinērvīā | . | White | . 6, S. Ev. S. Jamaica | . 1789 |

BLANCHING, making white, by being grown in a dark place, or by being covered with any thing.
BLAND, fair, beautiful.
BLANDFŌRDĪĀ, *Smith*. Dedicated to George, Marquis of Blandford. *Linn.* 6, Or. 1, Nat. Or. *Liliaceæ*. These beautiful species grow freely in an equal mixture of sandy loam and peat, and thrive planted out in a conservatory, much better than when grown in pots. They increase from suckers or seeds.

| | | | | |
|---|---|---|---|---|
| grandiflōrā | . | . Crimson | . 7, G. Her. P. N. S. W. | . 1812 |
| nōbīlīs | . | . Orange | . 7, G. Her. P. N. S. W. | . 1803 |

BLATTĀRĪŪS, relating to moths, like moths.
BLĒCHNŪM, *Linn.* Derived from *blechnon*, a Greek name for a Fern. *Linn.* 24, Or. 1, Nat. Or. *Polypodiaceæ*. Very interesting species of Ferns, they delight to grow in the openings of rockwork, in sandy loam and peat mixed; they divide readily at the roots, and may very readily be increased by seeds. *Synonymes*: 1. *canadense*. 2. *stramineum*.

| | | | | |
|---|---|---|---|---|
| australē | . | . Brown | . 6, G. Her. P. C. G. H. | . 1691 |
| brasilīēnsē, 1 | . | . Brown | . 6, S. Her. P. Brazil | . 1820 |
| cartilāgīnēūm | . | . Brown | . 7, G. Her. P. N. Holl. | . 1820 |
| glandulōsūm | . | . Brown | . 4, S. Her. P. Brazil | . 1823 |
| grācīlē | . | . Brown | . 11, S. Her. P. Brazil | . 1830 |
| lanceōlā | . | . Brown | . 9, S. | P. Brazil | . 1829 |
| laevigātūm | . | . Brown | . 7, G. Her. P. N. Holl. | . 1821 |
| longifōlīūm | . | . Brown | . 7. S. Her. P. Caraccas | . 1820 |
| occidentālē | . | . Brown | . 8, S. Her. P. Brazil | . 1823 |
| pectīnātūm | . | . Brown | . 8, S. Her. P. S. Amer. | . 1827 |
| polypodioīdēs | . | . Brown | . 9, S. Her. P. Brazil | . 1829 |
| serrulātūm | . | . Brown | . 7, H. Her. P. Florida | . 1819 |
| strīātūm, 2 | . | . Brown | . 7, G. Her. P. N. Holl. | . 1824 |

BLĒCHŪM, *Jussieu*. Taken from the Greek name of a plant resembling marjoram. *Linn.* 14, Or. 2, Nat. Or. *Acanthaceæ*. Species of considerable beauty; for culture, &c., see *Justicia*.

| | | | | |
|---|---|---|---|---|
| angustifōlīūm | . | . Blue | . 6, S. Her. P. Jamaica | . 1824 |
| Brasilīānē | . | . Blue | . 6, S. Her. P. Brazil | . 1824 |
| Brōwnē | . | | . 6, S. Her. P. W. Ind. | . 1780 |
| laxiflōrūm | . | . White | . 6, S. Her. P. Jamaica | . 1818 |

BLĒPHĀRĪS, *Jussieu*. Derived from *blepharis*, the

eyelash; in allusion to the bracteas of the calyx. *Linn.* 14, Or. 2, Nat. Or. *Acanthaceæ*. The species are ornamental, and may be referred to *Acanthus* for culture, &c. *Synonyme*: 1. *Acanthus capensis*.

| | | | | |
|---|---|---|---|---|
| boerhaavīæfōlīā | . | Blue | . 7, S. | A. E. Ind. | . 1821 |
| capēnsīs | . | . Blue | . 7, G. | B. C. G. H. | . 1816 |
| furcātā | . | | . 7, G. Ev. S. | C. G. H. | . 1816 |
| linearifōlīā | . | . Blue | . 7, S. | A. Guinea. | . 1823 |
| procūmbēns | . | | . 7, G. Ev. T. C. G. H. | . 1825 |

BLĒPHĪLĪĀ, *Rafin.* The derivation is from *blepharis*, eyelash; the sepals being fringed. *Linn.* 2, Or. 1, Nat. Or. *Labiatæ*. These species are ornamental, and for culture, &c., may be referred to *Monarda*.

| | | | | |
|---|---|---|---|---|
| ciliātā | . | . Red | . 7, H. Her. P. N. Amer. | |
| hirsūtā | . | . Purple | . 8, H. Her. P. N. Amer. | . 1798 |

BLĒTĪĀ, *Ruiz and Pavon*. In honour of Don Louis Blet, a Spanish physician and botanist. *Linn.* 20, Or. 1, Nat. Or. *Orchidaceæ*. This is, when in flower, a handsome genus of tuberous-rooted plants. They succeed well when grown in a mixture of sandy peat and light loam, with the pots well drained, and treated as follows:—As soon as the leaves die down, remove the plants to a cooler house, where they should be kept dry for three or four months; then they must be repotted, and placed in a brisk moist heat; and when growing freely, liberally supplied with water. They are easily increased by dividing the roots, which should be done at the time of potting. *Synonymes*: 1. *B. pallida, Cymbidium floridum*. 2. *C. hyacinthinum*. 3. *C. altum, Limodorum altum*. 4. *B. Shepherdii*.

| | | | | |
|---|---|---|---|---|
| acutipetālā | . | . Purple | . 9, G. Ter. America | . |
| capitātā | . | | . 6, S. Ter. W. Ind. | . 1795 |
| flōrīdā, 1 | . | . Rose | . 2, S. Ter. Trinidad | . 1786 |
| grācīlīs | . | . Yelsh. pur. 6, S. Ter. Mexico | . 1830 |
| guinéēnsīs | . | . Purple | . 8. Ter. S. Leone | . 1822 |
| hāvānēnsīs | . | . Purple | . 4, S. Ter. Havannah | . 1835 |
| hyacinthīnā, 2 | . | . Ro. pink | . 8. Ter. China | . 1802 |
| patūlā | . | . Purple | . 8. Ter. Hayti | . |
| rēflexā | . | . Pur. grn. | . 8, S. Ter. Mexico | . |
| verecūndā, 3 | . | . Purple | . 8, S. Ter. W. Ind. | . 1733 |
| Shepherdīī, 4 | . | Ro. purple 9, S. Ter. W. Ind. | . 1788 |

BLĪGHĪĀ, *Hortus Kew*. Dedicated to Capt. Bligh, who first carried the bread-fruit to the W. Indies. *Linn.* 8, Or. 1, Nat. Or. *Sapindaceæ*. This is called Akee Tree, and is a plant much esteemed in Africa and the W. Indies on account of its fruit, which is as large as a goose's egg, and of a reddish, or yellow colour; the aril is eatable, of a sub-acid flavour, and considered very grateful, particularly in the W. Indies. It grows in loam and peat; and cuttings, with the leaves not taken off, root in sand, under a glass.

| | | | | |
|---|---|---|---|---|
| sāpīdā | . | . White | . 8. Ev. T. Africa | . 1793 |

BLIGHT, a vague term, signifying a pestilence amongst plants, caused by the attack of insects, or parasitical fungi; or by some epidemic affection of the atmosphere.
BLISTERED, the surface being raised, as the skin is when blistered.
BLĪTŪM, *Linn.* The derivation is doubtful, but it is most probably taken from *bliton*, insipid. *Linn.* 1, Or. 2, Nat. Or. *Chenopodiaceæ*. These plants are only worth cultivation for the strawberry-like fruit which succeeds the flowers; hence the trivial name Strawberry Blite; they succeed well sown in the open ground.

| | | | | |
|---|---|---|---|---|
| capitātūm | . | . Apetal | . 7, H. | A. Austria | . 1633 |
| marītīmūm | . | . Apetal | . 7, H. | A. N. Amer. | . 1825 |
| virgātūm | . | . Apetal | . 7, H. | A. S. Eur. | . 1680 |

*chenopodioīdēs, petiolārē.*
BLUMENBĀCHĪĀ, *Schrader*. In compliment to J. F. Blumenbach. *Linn.* 19, Or. 1, Nat. Or. *Loasaceæ*. The species are ornamental; for culture, &c., see *Loasa*. *Synonyme*: 1. *Loasa palmata*.

| | | | | |
|---|---|---|---|---|
| insignīs, 1 | . | . White | . 7, H. Tr. A. Monte VI. | . 1826 |
| multifīdā | . | . Grn. red | . 7, H. | A. B. Ayres | . 1826 |

BOBĀRTĪĀ. Dedicated to Jacob Bobart, a worthy professor of botany at Oxford. *Linn.* 3, Or. 1, Nat. Or. *Iridaceæ*. The species are rather showy, and may be referred to *Marica* for culture, &c. *Synonymes*: 1. *Marica gladiata, Moræa gladiata*. 2. *Moræa spathacea*.

| | | | | |
|---|---|---|---|---|
| aurantīācā | . | . Orange | . 3, H. Her. P. Belgia | . 1827 |
| gladiātā, 1 | . | . Yellow | . 6, G. Her. P. C. G. H. | . 1816 |
| spathāceā, 2 | . | . Yellow | . 6, G. Her. P. C. G. H. | . 1798 |

BOCCŌNĬA, *Linn.* The name is derived from a Sicilian monk, named Paolo Boccone, M.D. *Linn.* 11, Or. 1, Nat. Or. *Papaveraceæ.* The species are ornamental, and *B. frutescens* has pretty foliage. They are easily cultivated in loamy soil, and increased from cuttings in sand, in a gentle heat, placed under a glass.

| frutescens | . . | Wht. yel. | 2, S. Ev. S. W. Ind. | . 1739 |
| integrifolia | . . | White . | 2, S. Ev. S. Mexico | . 1820 |

BŒBĔRĂ, *Willdenow.* Taken from Bœber, a Russian professor of botany. *Linn.* 19, Or. 2, Nat. Or. *Compositæ.* The species are pretty, and of easy cultivation. *Synonymes:* 1. *Dyssodia glutinosa.* 2. *D. porophylla.*

| chrysanthemoídæ, 1 | Yellow . | 10, H. | A. Carolina | . 1821 |
| incāna | . . . | Golden . | 9, G. Ev. S. Mexico | . 1828 |

*porophȳlla,* 2.

BŒHMĔRĬA, *Jacquin.* In memory of George Rudolph Bœhmer, a German botanist. *Linn.* 21, Or. 4, Nat. Or. *Nyctaginaceæ.* The species are uninteresting, and of the easiest culture. *Synonyme:* 1. *Urtica arborea.*

| rubescēns, 1 | . . Green . | 4, G. Ev. S. Canaries | . 1779 |

*castaneæfōlĭa, caudāta, cylindrĭca, elongāta, frondōsa, frutescēns, hirta, interruptā, lateriflōra, macrophȳlla, platyphȳlla, ramiflōra, rotundifōlĭa, salicifōlĭa.*

BŒRHAAVĬA, *Linn.* So called in honour of the famous Dutch physician, who is said to have been the first of the many friends and patrons of Linnæus. *Linn.* 1, Or. 1, Nat. Or. *Nyctaginaceæ.* The species are of very simple cultivation, and possess but little beauty.

| diffūsa | . . . White . | 9, S. Ev. Tr. India | . 1690 |
| discolōr | . . . Red . | 8, S. Her. P. Guayaq. | . 1825 |
| erēctā | . . . White . | 7, S. Her. P. India | . 1733 |
| excelsā | . . . Red . | 8, S. Ev. S. S Amer. | . 1820 |
| hirsūtā | . . . Scarlet . | 6, S. Ev. Tr. Jamaica | . 1733 |
| plumbagineā | . Red . | 8, S. Her. P. Spain | . 1820 |
| procumbēns | . . Red . | 8, S. Ev. Tr. E. Ind. | . 1800 |
| scandēns | . . Green . | 8, S. Ev. Cl. Jamaica | . 1691 |
| viscōsā | . . . Scarlet . | 6, S. Ev. Tr. Peru | . 1821 |

BOLBOPHYLLŪM, *Thouars.* From *bolbos,* a bulb, and *phyllon,* a leaf; the leaves universally rise from a pseudo-bulb. *Linn.* 20, Or. 1, Nat. Or. *Orchidaceæ.* This is a most singular and interesting genus of plants, which to thrive well must be grown in a strong damp heat, potted, and otherwise treated as the genera *Epidendrum, Stanhopea,* &c. *Synonymes:* 1. *Anisopetalum Careyanum.* 2. *Tribrachia pendula.*

| barbigĕrūm | . . Crimson . | 6, S. Epi. S. Leone | . 1835 |
| bracteolātūm | . . Yel. pur. | 7 S. Epi. Demerara | . 1836 |
| Carĕyānūm, 1 | . Brn. pur. | 10, S. Epi. Nepal | . 1823 |
| cocoīnūm | . . Flesh . | 10, S. Epi. S. Leone | . 1835 |
| cuprĕūm | . . Copper . | 8, S. Epi. Manilla | . 1837 |
| leopardinūm | . Ysh. grn. | 8, S. Epi. E. Ind. | . 1837 |
| recūrvūm | . . Grn. wht. | 9, S. Epi. S. Leone | . 1822 |
| saltatōrĭūm | . | 12, S. Epi. S. Leone | . 1835 |
| setigĕrūm | . . Purple . | S. Epi. Demerara | |
| tetragonūm | . . | S. Epi. S. Leone | |
| umbellātūm | . . Yellow . | S. Epi. E. Ind. | . 1837 |

BŌLDŎA, *Lagasca.* In memory of D. Boldo, a Spanish botanist. *Linn.* 3, Or. 1, Nat. Or. *Nyctaginaceæ.* Ornamental species, succeeding in sandy peat, and propagated by cuttings. *Synonyme:* 1. *Salpianthus arenarius.*

| lanceolātā, 1 | . Purple | 6, S. Ev. S. W. Ind. | . 1824 |
| purpurascēns | . Varieg. | 6, S. Her. P. Cuba | . 1820 |

BOLE, trunk of a tree.

BŌLĔTŬS, *Dillenius.* Named from *bolos,* a mass, in reference to its massy or globular form. *Linn.* 24, Or. 9, Nat. Or. *Fungi.* Curious productions, found in woods and groves, pastures, or on old trees. The species are succulent, and have their parts in the greatest perfection of any *Fungi. B. granulatus* is eatable, as is *B. sub-tomentosus,* and *B. edulis* is excellent when cooked. The *Boleti* when wounded, heal much in the same manner as the flesh of animals. *Synonymes:* 1. *B. rubeolus—cyanascens, edulis, lactiflōrus, lūridus* 1, *lutēns, piperātus, scabĕr, S. aurantiācus. S. bovinus, subtomentōsus, S. sanguinĕus, variegātus.*

BŌLĔŬM, *Desvaux.* The name is taken from the round pods; and is derived from *bolos,* a ball. *Linn.* 15, Nat. Or. *Cruciferæ.* An ornamental species, succeeding best in rather sandy peat; it ripens

seed, from which it may be plentifully increased. *Synonyme:* 1. *Vella aspera.*

| aspĕrūm | . . . Cream . | 6, F. Ev. S. Spain | . . 1818 |

BOLIVĂRĬA, *Schlech.* The name is given in honour of the great Bolivar. *Linn.* 2, Or. 1, Nat. Or. *Jasminaceæ.* An interesting species, delighting in a mixture of loam and peat, and propagates readily from cuttings.

| trifĭda | . . . Yellow . | 6, G. Ev. S. Chile | . . 1823 |

BOLTŌNĬA, *L. Herit.* Dedicated to J. B. Bolton, an English professor of botany. *Linn.* 19, Or. 2, Nat. Or. *Compositæ.* Very interesting species, so much like some of those of the genus *Aster,* that they may be referred for culture, &c. to that genus.

| asteroídæ | . . . Flesh . | 9, H. Her. P. N. Amer. | . 1758 |
| glastifōlĭa | . . . Pink . | 9, H. Her. P. N. Amer. | . 1758 |

BŌMBĂX, *Linn.* The name is derived from *bombax,* cotton; in allusion to the wool in the pods. *Linn.* 16, Or. 8, Nat. Or. *Sterculiaceæ.* The genus is trivially named the Silk Cotton Tree, and the species thrive well in a sandy loamy soil; half-ripened cuttings taken off at a joint, and planted in sand, under a glass, in a moist heat, root readily. The seeds of many of the species are enveloped in long hairs, like those of the true Cotton; it is found, however, that they cannot be manufactured, in consequence of no adhesion between the hairs. The woolly coat of the seeds of some of the species is employed in different countries for stuffing cushions, &c. The trunk of *B. Ceiba* is spiny, and said to be one of the highest trees in both Indies; the wood is light and of little value, but is sometimes used for canoes. The wood cut into boards, and steeped some time in lime-water, will endure the action of the air many years. The cotton in which the seed is enveloped, is used by the poor inhabitants for stuffing chairs, pillows, &c., but is seldom or never used for beds, it being thought unwholesome to sleep upon. *Synonymes:* 1. *quinatum.* 2. *heptaphyllum.* 3. *heptaphyllum.*

| Ceibā, 1 | . . . White . | S. Ev. T. S. Amer. | . 1692 |
| globōsūm | . . . | S. Ev. T. Guiana | . 1824 |
| malabāricūm, 2 | Scarlet . | S. Ev. T. Malabar | |
| septenātūm, 3 | . White . | S. Ev. T. Carthag. | . 1699 |

BONAPARTĔA, *Ruiz and Pavon.* In memory of Napoleon Bonaparte. *Linn.* 6, Or. 1, Nat. Or. *Bromeliaceæ.* This species has a singularly graceful appearance, by the naturally drooping tendency of its rush-like leaves. It grows well in sandy rich loam, and increases without difficulty from seed.

| gracĭlis | . . . . | Epiphy. Mexico | . 1828 |
| juncĕa | . . . Blue . | Epiphy. Peru | . 1800 |

BONĀTĔA, *Willdenow.* In honour of M. Bonat, a celebrated botanist and professor at Padua. *Linn.* 20, Or. 1, Nat. Or. *Orchidaceæ.* A curious species, with remarkably formed green and white, slightly fragrant flowers. For culture and propagation, see *Blettia. Synonymes:* 1. *Orchis speciosa.*

| speciōsā | . . . Grn. wht. | 6, S. Ter. C. G. H. | . 1820 |

BONNĂYĂ, *Link.* In memory of Bonnay, a German botanist. *Linn.* 2, Or. 1, Nat. Or. *Scrophulariaceæ.* The species are dwarf-growing plants of considerable interest; for culture, &c., see *Gratiola. Synonyme:* 1. *Gratiola veronicæfolia.*

| brachiātā | . . . White . | S. S. A. Brasil | . . 1823 |
| reptāns | . . . Blue . | 7, S. Ev. Cr. E. Ind. | . 1820 |
| veronicæfōlĭa, 1 | . Pale . | 8, S. Cr. R. E. Ind. | . 1796 |

BONNEMAISŌNĬA, *Agardh.* Named in honour of M. Bonnemaison, a French cryptogamist. *Linn.* 24, Or. 7, Nat. Or. *Algæ.* A very delicate, finely-branched species, much like asparagus, rather plentiful about the sea-shore—*asparagoides.*

BONNĔTĬA, *Schreber.* In honour of C. Bonnet, a celebrated naturalist. *Linn.* 13, Or. 1, Nat. Or. *Ternstromiaceæ.* An elegant species, doing well in a mixture of loam and peat; ripened cuttings in a moderate heat, root freely in sand, under a glass.

| palustris | . . . Red . | S. Ev. T. Trinidad | . 1819 |

BŌNTĬA, *Linn.* Dedicated to James Bont, a Dutch physician. *Linn.* 14, Or. 2, Nat. Or. *Myoporaceæ.* An interesting plant, with the appearance of a *Daphne;* it succeeds in loam and peat, and cuttings root readily in sand, under a glass, in heat.

| daphnoídēs | . . . Yel. pur. | 6, S. Ev. T. W. Ind. | . 1690 |

**BóraĠŏ**, *Linn.* So called from the nourishing qualities of the herb. *Linn.* 5, Or. 1, Nat. Or. *Boraginaceæ.* Pretty dwarf species, succeeding in any common soil, and are increased by divisions or seeds. The leaves of *B. officinalis* may be used as a salad, and has been much reputed as a cordial.

| | | | | | |
|---|---|---|---|---|---|
| crassifòliă | . . | Pink | . 6, H. Her. | P. Persia . | 1822 |
| crética | . . | Blue | . 5, H. Her. | P. Crete . | 1823 |
| laxiflòră | . . | Blue | . 6, H. Tr. | B. Corsica | 1813 |
| longifòliă | . . | Blue | . 7, H. | A. S. Eur. | 1825 |
| officinalis | . . | Blue | . 8, H. | A. England | |
| albiflòră | . . | White | . 8, H. | A. England | |
| orientalis | . . | Blue | . 6, H. Her. | P. Turkey | . 1752 |

**BorÁssŭs**, *Linn.* The immortal Linnæus applied this name to the spatha of the date. *Linn.* 22, Or. 6, Nat. Or. *Palmaceæ.* This fine species grows upwards of thirty feet high, and yields a fruit the size and shape of a child's head; it thrives well in a mixture of loam and peat, and propagates from seeds. From the sap of the trunk a sugar and wine is made of considerable value.

| | | | | |
|---|---|---|---|---|
| flabelliformis | . . Wht. grn. | . Palm. E. Ind. | . . 1771 |

**BoabŏnYĬ**, *Willdenow.* Dedicated to Gaston de Bourbon, Duke of Orleans, son of Henry IV. of France. *Linn.* 16, Or. 6, Nat. Or. *Leguminosæ.* The species are very showy when in flower, and thrive well in peat and loam; and cuttings of the young wood in sand, placed under a glass, root freely.

| | | | | | |
|---|---|---|---|---|---|
| barbàtă | . . . | Yellow | . 7, G. Ev. S. | C. G. H. | . 1822 |
| ciliàtă | . . . | Yellow | . 7, G. Ev. S. | C. G. H. | . 1816 |
| cordàtă | . . . | Yellow | . 8, G. Ev. S. | C. G. H. | . 1759 |
| crenàtă | . . . | Yellow | . 7, G. Ev. S. | C. G. H. | . 1774 |
| ericifòliă | . . . | Pink | . 1, G. Ev. S. | C. G. H. | . 1821 |
| lanceolàtă | . . . | Yellow | . 7, G. Ev. S. | C. G. H. | . 1752 |
| ruscifòliă | . . . | Yellow | . 7, G. Ev. S. | C. G. H. | . 1790 |
| trinérviă | . . . | Yellow | . 7, G. Ev. S. | C. G. H. | . 1759 |
| undulàtă | . . . | Yellow | . 7, G. Ev. S. | C. G. H. | . 1812 |

**BorkhaŭsĬă**, *Bohmer.* Dedicated to Moritz Borkhausen, a German professor of botany. *Linn.* 19, Or. 1, Nat. Or. *Compositæ.* Species of no beauty except *B. alpina*, which is rather pretty and interesting; they are all easily cultivated. *Synonymes:* 1. *Crepis alpina.* 2. *Hieracium stipitatum.* 3. *Lagoseris bursifolia.* 4. *Crepis fœtida.* 5. *Lagoseris intybacea.* 6. *L. leontodontoides.* 7. *Crepis nicæensis.* 8. *Lagoseris raphanifolia.* 9. *Crepis rubra.* 10. *C. senecioides.* 11. *L. versicolor.*

| | | | | |
|---|---|---|---|---|
| alpìnă, 1 | . . . Yellow | . 7, H. | A. Italy | . . 1739 |

*apargioìdĕs* 2, *ăspĕră, bellidifòliă, bursifòliă* 3, *Candòliĕi, caroliniănă, fœtidă* 4, *gravĕŏlēns, hispìdă, intybàcĕă* 5, *leontodontoìdĕs* 6, *macrophyllă, nicæensis* 7, *raphanifòliă* 8, *rùbră* 9, *senecioìdĕs.* *Suffreniànă, taraxacifòliă, versicòlor.*

**BorŏnYă**, *Sims.* In memory of Francis Boroni, an Italian attendant of Dr. Sibthorp. *Linn.* 8, Or. 1, Nat. Or. *Proteaceæ.* A very pretty and interesting genus of New Holland plants. The species flower remarkably free, and some may be seen in bloom at almost any time of the year. They grow best in sandy peat mixed with a few broken shreds, and the pots, which should not be large, must be judiciously drained, as the plants are very liable to suffer from over watering. Cuttings taken at a joint, planted in sand, and placed under a glass in a frame, observing to dry up the damp now and then, will, if carefully tended, make roots.

| | | | | | |
|---|---|---|---|---|---|
| alàtă | . . . | Red | . 5, G. Ev. S. | N. Holl. | . 1825 |
| anemonæfòliă | . | Red | . 5, G. Ev. S. | N. Holl. | . 1824 |
| crenulàtă | . . | Red | . 7, G. Ev. S. | Kg. Geo's. Sd. | |
| denticulàtă | . . | Red | . G. Ev. S. | N. Holl. | . 1823 |
| ledifòliă | . . | Red | . 5, G. Ev. S. | N. S. W. | . 1814 |
| parodòxă | . . | Red | . 3, G. Ev. S. | N. Holl. | . 1825 |
| pilosmă | . . | Red | . G. Ev. S. | N. Holl. | . 1826 |
| pinnàtă | . . | Purple | . 3, G. Ev. S. | N. S. W. | . 1794 |
| polygalæfòliă | . | Red | . 5, G. Ev. S. | N. Holl. | . 1824 |
| serrulàtă | . . | Scarlet | . 6, G. Ev. S. | N. S. W. | . 1816 |
| tetrandră | . . | Red | . 5, G. Ev. S. | N. Holl. | . 1824 |

**BorrÉră**, *Ach.* In honour of J. W. Borrer, F.L.S., a British cryptogamist. *Linn.* 24, Or. 8, Nat. Or. *Lichenaceæ.* An exceedingly interesting genus to the cryptogamist, on account of the natural habit of the species—*atlántică, chrysophthálmă, ciliáris, flavĭcăns, furfuràcĕă, leucòmĕlă, tenéllă.*

**BorrÉriă**, *Meyer.* Derivation same as *Borrera. Linn.* 4, Or. 1, Nat. Or. *Cinchonaceæ.* Pretty little plants, of easy culture, in any common soil; and cuttings of the perennial and shrubby kinds root readily in

sand under a glass. *B. stricta* must be treated as a tender biennial. *Synonymes:* 1. *Spermacoce verticillata, Bigelovia commula.* 2. *S. stricta, B. stricta.* 3. *S. verticillata, B. verticillata.*

| | | | | | |
|---|---|---|---|---|---|
| commútàtă, 1 | . . | White | . 6, S. Her. | P. W. Ind. | . 1818 |
| strícta, 2 | . . | White | . 7, G. | R. E. Ind. | . 1820 |
| verticillàtă, 3 | . | White | . 7, S. Ev. | S. Africa | . 1782 |

**BorYĬ**, *Willdenow.* Dedicated to Colonel Bory de St. Vincent, a French traveller and promoter of natural history. *Linn.* 22, Or. 2, Nat. Or. *Liliaceæ.* The species are uninteresting, and easily cultivated—*acuminàtă, ligustrìnă, nìtidă, porulòsă, prionoìdĕs, retŭsă.*

**BŏscĬă**, *Lamarck.* Dedicated to Louis Bosc, a French professor of agriculture. *Linn.* 11, Or. 1, Nat. Or. *Capparidaceæ.* The species is ornamental, and may be referred to *Cratæva* for culture, &c. *Synonyme:* 1. *Podoria Senegalensis.*

| | | | | |
|---|---|---|---|---|
| senegalénsis | . . | S. Ev. S. | Senegal | . 1824 |

**BósĬă**, *Linn.* In compliment to Ernest Gottlieb Bose, a professor of botany in Germany. *Linn.* 5, Or. 2, Nat. Or. *Phytolaccaceæ.* An ornamental species, succeeding in loam and peat mixed; and cuttings in sand, under a glass, placed in heat, strike readily.

| | | | | |
|---|---|---|---|---|
| Yervamòră | . . Rufous | . G. Ev. S. | Canaries | . 1728 |

**BoswéllYĬ**, *Roxburgh.* Dedicated to Dr. John Boswell, of Edinburgh. *Linn.* 10, Or. 1, Nat. Or. *Burseraceæ.* Ornamental trees of easy culture, thriving best in loam and peat, and are propagated with facility from cuttings in sand, under a glass. The genus is called the Olibanum Tree. *B. serrata* yields a resin called olibanum, which yields a grateful incense, and possesses stimulant, astringent, and diaphoretic qualities. *B. glabra* furnishes a coarse resin, used for pitching the bottom of ships. The resin of both species is used in India as a frankincense and as pitch.

| | | | | | |
|---|---|---|---|---|---|
| glabră | . . | Pa. yel. | . 8. Ev. T. | Coromand. | . 1823 |
| serràtă | . . | Pa. yel. | . 8. Ev. T. | E. Ind. | . . 1820 |

**BOTANY BAY TREE**, see *Smilax glycyphyllă.*

**BotrÝchĬs**, *Willdenow.* So called from *botrys*, a raceme, and *keras*, a horn; the horn-like raceme. *Linn.* 4, Or. 1, Nat. Or. *Aquifoliaceæ.* An interesting species; for culture, &c., see *Banksia.*

| | | | | |
|---|---|---|---|---|
| laurìnŭm | . . | G. Ev. S. | N. Holl. | . 1823 |

**BotrÝchĬŭm**, *Swartz.* The derivation is from *botrys*, a bunch; in reference to the form of the fructification, which is much like a bunch of grapes. *Linn.* 24, Or. 1, Nat. Or. *Ophioglossiaceæ.* The genus is well known by the name of *Moonwort.* The species are curious and interesting plants; see *Adiantum* for culture, &c. *B. virginicum* is the largest of the American ferns, and is named the rattlesnake, on account of its generally being found growing where those reptiles abound. *Synonymes:* 1. *Gracilis.* 2. *Osmunda Lunària.*

| | | | | | |
|---|---|---|---|---|---|
| australe | . . | Brown | . 6, F. Her. | P. N. Holl. | . 1823 |
| dissèctum, 1 | . | Brown | . 7, H. Her. | P. N. Amer. | . 1806 |
| fumarioìdĕs | . | Brown | . 7, H. Her. | P. Carolina | . 1806 |
| Lunària, 2 | . . | Brown | . 5, H. Her. | P. Britain | . |
| obliquŭm | . . | Brown | . 8, H. Her. | P. N. Amer. | . 1821 |
| virginìcŭm | . . | Brown | . 8, H. Her. | P. N. Amer. | . 1790 |

**BotrÝtis**, *Michaux.* Name alludes to the little round seeds, or seed-vessels, resembling a bunch of grapes, and derived from *botrys*, a cluster of grapes. *Linn.* 24, Or. 9, Nat. Or. *Fungi.* Minute productions. *B. parasitica* is found on that plant called the Shepherd's Purse, viz. *Capsélla Bùrsă păstòris—agaricìnă, dénsă, diffùsă, effùsă, leucospòră, macrospòră, murìnă, nìgră, parasitìcă, polyspòră.*

**BourrÉrĬă**, *Gærtner.* Named in memory of Bourrer, an apothecary of Nuremberg. *Linn.* 5, Or. 1, Nat. Or. *Cordiaceæ.* Ornamental trees of easy cultivation; for the mode of which, see the genus *Ehretia. Synonyme:* 1. *Ehretia Bourrèrìă.*

| | | | | | |
|---|---|---|---|---|---|
| exsùccă | . . | White | . 8. Ev. T. W. Ind. | | . 1804 |
| succuléntă, 1 | . | White | . 8. Ev. T. W. Ind. | | . 1758 |

**BoŭssingaŭltYĬ**, *H. B.* and Kunth named this genus in honour of J. B. Boussingault, a celebrated naturalist and traveller. *Linn.* 5, Or. 1, Nat. Or. *Chenopodiaceæ.* This is described as a most desirable stove plant, of rapid growth, and bearing copious and graceful racemes of deliciously fragrant flowers. It grows in any common garden soil, and may be increased by seed. At Glasnevin, near Dublin, the plant has stood the winter in the open air, planted at the bottom of a wall.

basellioides . . . White . . 7, F. Bl. P. S. Amer. . 1836

**BOUVARDIA**, *Salis*. In memory of Dr. Bouvard, superintendant of the royal Paris botanic garden. *Linn.* 4, Or. 1, Nat. Or. *Rubiaceæ*. This is a beautiful genus, worthy of extensive cultivation. B. *triphylla* is a free flowerer, and thrives in a cool part of the greenhouse ; B. *versicolor* is rather more tender, and thrives best in a warmer situation in summer, but requires to be cool in winter. They grow in a mixture of loam and peat, and young plants may be obtained from cuttings, which strike in the same kind of soil, in heat ; they may also be propagated by pieces of the root, planted in good soil, in heat. *Synonyme:* 1. B. *Jacquinii*, *Houstonia coccinea*.

| | | | | |
|---|---|---|---|---|
| longiflora | . . . | White | . 8. Ev. S. Mexico | . 1827 |
| triphylla, 1 | . . . | Scarlet | . 7, G. Ev. S. Mexico | . 1794 |
| pubescens | . . . | Scarlet | . 7, G. Ev. S. Mexico | . 1794 |
| glabra | . . . | Scarlet | . 7, G. Ev. S. Mexico | . 1794 |
| versicolor | . . . | Red | . 8, G. Ev. S. S. Amer. | . 1814 |

**BOVISTA**, *Persoon*. Latinised from its German name *bofist*. *Linn.* 24, Or. 9, Nat. Or. *Fungi*. Striking productions. Bulliard mentions having seen many of eighteen, twenty, and twenty-three inches in diameter ; and on the authority of others, affirms them to attain the enormous bulk of nearly nine feet in circumference. B. *gigantea* is the largest of the genus or order, measuring two feet in diameter. The flesh is at first white, afterwards of a greenish-yellow, lastly of a brown grey, the outer peridium cracks, and peels off in large flakes on being handled.—*Loudon's Ency. of Plants—gigantea, nigrescens.*

**BOWIEA**, *Haworth*. In memory of J. Bowie, a collector of plants for the Kew gardens. *Linn.* 6, Or. 1, Nat. Or. *Liliaceæ*. Curious plants, succeeding in fibrous sandy peat, and multiplied by offsets or suckers.

| | | | | |
|---|---|---|---|---|
| Africana | . . . | Red grn. | . 10, G. Ev. S. C. G. H. | . 1823 |
| myriacantha | . . . | Red grn. | . 5, G. Ev. S. C. G. H. | . 1823 |

**BOWLESIA**, *Romer and Schultes*. Named in honour of Mr. Bowles, an Irish botanist. *Linn.* 5, Or. 2, Nat. Or. *Umbelliferæ*. A minute curious plant, will grow in any common soil, and is increased by divisions.

| | | | | |
|---|---|---|---|---|
| tenera | . . . | Grn. yel. | . 7, F. Ev. Cr. M. Video | . 1827 |

**BRABEJUM**, *Linn.* Named from *brabeion*, a sceptre ; applying to the racemes of flowers. *Linn.* 23, Or. 1, Nat. Or. *Proteaceæ*. An ornamental tree, succeeding best in open sandy loam and peat ; cuttings of the ripened wood root without difficulty, in sand, under a glass.

| | | | | |
|---|---|---|---|---|
| stellatum | . . . | White | . 3, G. Ev. S. C. G. H. | . 1731 |

**BRACHIATE**, having arms or branches usually placed opposite to each other at right angles with the main stem, and crossing each other alternately.

**BRACHYLÆNA**, *R. Brown*. From *brachys*, short, and *læna*, cloak ; in allusion to the form of the calyx. *Linn.* 19, Or. 2, Nat. Or. *Compositæ*. An ornamental plant, for the culture of which, see *Baccharis*. *Synonymes:* 1. *Baccharis nereifolia*, *Tarchonanthus dentata*.

| | | | | |
|---|---|---|---|---|
| nereifolia, 1 | . . | White | . 9, G. Ev. S. C. G. R. | . 1752 |

**BRACHYPODIUM**, *Beauvois*. Taken from *brachys*, short, and *pous*, a foot ; in reference to the short stalks of the spikelets *Linn.* 3, Or 2, Nat. Or. *Gramineæ*. Mere weeds, of the simplest culture. *Synonymes:* 1. *Triticum asperum*, *Festuca rigida*. 2. *Triticum loliaceum*. 3. *Bromus pinnatus*. 4. B. *rupestris*. 5. B. *sylvaticus*. 6. *Brachypodium nardus—asperum* 1, *brunciale*, *brevisetum*, *cæspitosum*, *distachyon*, *Halleri*, *loliaceum* 2, *longifolium*, *obtusifolium*, *phænicoïdes*, *pinnatum* 3, *ramosum*, *retusum*, *rupestre* 4, *strigosum*, *sylvaticum* 5, *tenellum* 6, *Tenorianum*, *tenuiculum*, *tenuiflorum*, *uniolodes*, *unilaterale*.

**BRACHYSEMA**, *R. Brown*. Derived from *brachys*, short, and *sema*, standard ; the flowers having a very short standard. *Linn.* 10, Or. 1, Nat. Or. *Leguminosæ*. Very handsome climbing species, especially B. *latifolia*, thriving well in an equal mixture of sandy loam and peat ; they are increased by layers, or cuttings planted in sand, under a glass,

in heat, root freely. They may also be increased by seeds, which are sometimes produced. These plants are well suited for training up the columns of the conservatory or greenhouse.

| | | | | |
|---|---|---|---|---|
| latifolium | . . . | Crimson | . 5, G. Ev. Cl. N. Holl. | . 1803 |
| undulatum | . . . | Green | . 3, G. Ev. Cl. N. S. W. | . 1820 |

**BRACHYSTELMA**, *R. Brown*. Named from the word *brachys*, short, and *stelma*, a crown ; in allusion to the short coronal processes of the flowers. *Linn.* 5, Or. 2, Nat. Or. *Asclepiadaceæ*. A curious plant, grows well in sandy loam, and is increased by cuttings.

| | | | | |
|---|---|---|---|---|
| crispum | . . . | Br. yel. | . 9, S. Tu. P. C. G. H. | . 1829 |
| tuberosum | . . . | Purple | . 6, S. Tu. P. C. G. H. | . 1821 |

**BRACTEAS**, small leaves placed near the calyx on the peduncle or pedicel.

**BRADLEIA**, *Gaertner*. In honour of Richard Bradly, a professor of botany at Cambridge. *Linn.* 21, Or. 10, Nat. Or. *Euphorbiaceæ*. Curious plants, of little interest. They succeed in loamy soil, and multiply from cuttings.

| | | | | |
|---|---|---|---|---|
| nitida | . . . | | S. Ev. S. E. Ind. | . 1820 |
| sinica | . . . | | . 7, S. Ev. S. China | . 1816 |

**BRACTEÆ**, small leaves placed near the calyx, on the peduncle or pedicel.

**BRACTEATE**, furnished with bractea.

**BRACTEOLÆ**, little bracteæ.

**BRASSAVOLA**, *R. Brown*. Named after Antonio Musa Brassavola, a noble Venetian, and one of the most enlightened botanists of his day. *Linn.* 20, Or. 1, Nat. Or. *Orchidaceæ*. The plants of this genus are deserving a place in every collection of orchidaceæ, having, when in flower, a delightfully fragrant odour. They require to be propagated, and otherwise treated, as *Stanhopea*. *Synonymes:* 1. *Epidendrum cucullatum*, *Cymbidium cucullatum*. 2. C. *nodosum*, *Epidendrum nodosum*.

| | | | | |
|---|---|---|---|---|
| angustata | . . . | Ysh. grn. | . 6, S. Epi. Demerara | . |
| cordata | . . . | Wht. grn. | . 5, S. Epi. Brazil | . |
| cucullata, 1 | . . . | White | . 6, S. Epi. W. Ind. | . 1790 |
| elegans | . . . | Lilac | . 8, S. Epi. Antigua | . |
| nodosa, 2 | . . . | Wht. grn. | . 1, S. Epi. Jamaica | . 1830 |
| Perrinii | . . . | Wht. grn. | . 9, S. Epi. Rio Jan. | . |
| tuberculata | . . . | Wht. yel. | . 7, S. Epi. Brasil | . 1827 |

**BRASSIA**, *R. Brown*. In commemoration of the late Mr. Brass, a skilful botanical traveller and draughtsman. *Linn.* 20, Or. 1, Nat. Or. *Orchidaceæ*. This is a fine genus of plants, all of which are delightfully fragrant when in flower. The flowers are mostly yellowish green, spotted with purple. For culture and propagation, see *Stanhopea*. *Synonymes:* 1. *Epidendrum caudatum*, *Malaxis caudata*.

| | | | | |
|---|---|---|---|---|
| caudata, 1 | . . . | Ysh. grn. | . 2, S. Epi. W. Ind. | . 1823 |
| Lanceana | . . . | Ysh. spot. | . 1, S. Epi. Surinam. | . 1833 |
| macrostachya | . . . | Grn. brn. | . S. Epi. Demerara | . |
| maculata | . . . | Wht. spot. | . 4, S. Epi. Jamaica | . 1806 |

**BRASSICA**, *Linn.* From *bresic*, the Celtic name of the cabbage. *Linn.* 15, Or. 2, Nat. Or. *Cruciferæ*. In this genus we have the well known cabbage, with its many varieties, and many other familiar potherbs and roots. It is wonderful to look upon the common cabbage (B. *oleracea*) with its varieties, and observe the exceeding great difference in appearance and qualities, particularly when we compare the original types as found on our shores, with wavy sea green leaves tending to no head, and flowering like wild mustard or charlock, with the cauliflower and red cabbage, &c. As their culture is generally well known, we shall dwell upon it here as briefly as possible ; the cabbage and its varieties require a very strong rich soil, or they will not come to a good size. The turnip also does well only in good rich soil, and indeed the whole tribe thrive best in open loamy soil, enriched with manure. They all produce an abundance of seeds, which must be sown at those periods which experience has shown to be the best, for bringing their produce to perfection at certain seasons. *Synonymes:* 1. B. *sempervirens*. 2. *Raphanus cheiranthifolia*. 3. *Sisymbrium valentinum—balearica* 1, *campestris*, C. *napa Brassica*, C. *communis*, C. *rutabaga*, C. *oleifera*, C. *pabularia*, *cheiranthifolia* 2, *cheiranthos*, *chinensis*, *elongata*, E. *rucastrum*, *fruticulosa*, *Gravina*, *Heléniana*, *humilis*, *incana*, *lævigata*, *monensis*, *montana*, *Napus*, N. *esculenta*, N.

álbūs, N. flāvūs, N. nigrĭcāns, olĕĭfĕrūs 2, olerācĕā, O. asparagoídes, O. cauliflōrā, O. commūnis, O. cōnĭcā, O. costātā, O. crīspā, O. deprēssā, O. ellīptĭcā, O. gemmĭfĕrā, O. mājŏr, O. obovātā, O. oblōngā, O. palmĭfōlĭā, O. quercĭfōlĭā, O. ramōsā, O. rūbrā, O. sabéllĭcā, O. sphærĭcā, O. vulgārĭs, pinnātĭfĭdā, poly-mōrphā, præcŏx, Pseudo-erucāstrūm, Rāpā, R. deprēssā, R. oblōngā, R. olĕĭfĕrā, repāndā, Richĕrĭī, subulārĭā, Tournefŏrtĭī, valentīnā 3, violācĕā.

BRAYĂ, Sternberg. In memory of Count Bray, a German botanist. Linn. 15, Or. 2, Nat. Or. Crucifèræ. Curious minute species, with purple flowers. They thrive best in loamy soil mixed with a little fibrous peat, and are multiplied by seeds.

| | | | |
|---|---|---|---|
| alpīnā . . . . | Purple | . 6, H. Hĕr. P. Carinthia . | 1823 |
| pilōsā . . . . | Purple | . 5, H. Ev. S. N. Amer. . | 1827 |

BREMONTIĔRĂ, Dec. In memory of M. Bremontier, an agriculturist. Linn. 17, Or. 4, Nat. Or. Leguminòsæ. An ornamental interesting plant, thriving in sandy loam, and is multiplied by cuttings in sand, under a glass, in heat.

| | | | |
|---|---|---|---|
| Ammŏxÿlŏn . . | Purple | . 8. Ev. S. Mauritius . | 1826 |

BRÉXĬĂ, Noronha. Named from brexis, rain; on account of the protection afforded against rain by some of the large leaves. Linn. 5, Or. 1, Nat. Or. Brexiaceæ. Excellent stove plants, with very beautiful foliage. They all grow freely and look well planted in large pots, in turfy loam and peat mixed. Cuttings take readily in any state, except that the leaves must not be moved, planted in sand, under a glass, in heat. A bud at the base of an entire leaf will strike, and make a young plant, if put in a little sand, under a glass, and put in the propagating house.

| | | | |
|---|---|---|---|
| chrysophylla . . | | 8. Ev. T. Mauritius . | 1820 |
| madagascariénsis . | Green | . 6, 8. Ev. T. Madagas. . | 1812 |
| spinōsā . . . . | Green | . 6, 8. Ev. T. Madagas. . | 1812 |

BRIDÉLĬĂ, Willdenow. Named after the great muscologist, Professor Bridel. Linn. 23, Or. 1, Nat. Or. Euphorbiàceæ. Small shrubs or trees, with little beauty, and easily cultivated. Synonyme: 1. Clusia scandens.

| | | | |
|---|---|---|---|
| montānā . . . | Apetal | . 8. Ev. T. E. Ind. . . | 1825 |
| scāndēns, 1 . . | Apetal | . 8, S. Ev. Cl. E. Ind. . . | 1804 |
| spinōsā . . . . | Apetal | . 6, S. Ev. S. E. Ind. . | 1803 |

BRIGNÒLĬĂ, Bertoloni. Named in compliment to J. L. Brignoli, a professor at Vienna. Linn. 5, Or. 2, Nat. Or. Umbelliferæ. A species of trifling beauty and easy culture. Synonyme: 1. Sium siculum.

| | | | |
|---|---|---|---|
| panacĭfōlĭā, 1 . . | White . | . 7, H. Hĕr. P. Sicily . | 1686 |

BRISTLES, rigid hairs.
BRISTLY-TOOTHED, bristles like teeth, or with the teeth ending each in a bristle.

BRĬZĂ, Linn. Named from brizo, to nod, on account of the quaking character of the spikelets. Linn. 3, Or. 2, Nat. Or. Gramíneæ. Although mere weeds, some species are pretty and interesting, as B. minor, rubra, Clusii, &c. The whole are of easy cultivation.

| | | | |
|---|---|---|---|
| Clūsĭī . . . . | Apetal | . 6, Grass. S. Eur. . | 1820 |
| elātĭŏr . . . . | Apetal | . 7, Grass. Greece . | 1817 |
| genĭculātā . . . | Apetal | . 6, Grass. C. G. H. . | 1816 |
| hūmĭlĭs . . . . | Apetal | . 6, Grass. Caucasus . | 1825 |
| māxĭmā . . . . | Apetal | . 6, Grass. S. Eur. . | 1633 |
| mĕdĭā . . . . | Apetal | . 5, Grass. Britain . | |
| mĭnŏr . . . . | Apetal | . 7, Grass. England . | |
| rūbrā . . . . | Apetal | . 6, Grass. S. Eur. . | 1820 |
| vĭrēns . . . . | Apetal | . 6, Grass. Spain . | 1800 |

BRODIÆ̆Ă, Sir J. E. Smith. In honour of James J. Brodie, a Scotch Cryptogamist. Linn. 3, Or. 1, Nat. Or. Liliàceæ. Very curious bulbs, with lilac, blue, and white flowers. They may be successfully grown in sandy peat, and increased chiefly by offsets of the root. Synonyme: 1. Hookeria coronaria.

| | | | |
|---|---|---|---|
| congéstā . . . | Blue . | . 7, G. Bl. P. Georgia . | 1806 |
| grandiflōrā, 1 . . | Blue . | . 6, F. Bl. P. N. Amer. . | 1806 |

BRÒMÉLĬĂ, Linn. So called after Olaus Bromel, a Swedish botanist. Linn. 6, Or. 1, Nat. Or. Bromelláceæ. This is a genus of very handsome plants, among which the Pine Apple was lately included. They are of easy culture providing they have a sufficiency of heat, and are potted in good rich open loamy soil; they must be watered carefully, that is, giving a good supply when growing, but in the

[ 49 ]

winter a very little is sufficient. The pots should be well drained, and as the plants are, like the Pine Apple, subject to injurious attacks of the scale, &c. they should be carefully looked over and washed; indeed, these plants may be said to do best with the treatment successfully applied to the Pine Apple. Rope is manufactured from a species of the genus in Brazil, called Grawartha.

| | | | | |
|---|---|---|---|---|
| acángī . . . . | | 8. Hĕr. P. Brazil | . | 1822 |
| bractēātā . . . | Pink . | 9, S. Hĕr. P. Jamaica | . | 1785 |
| chrysánthā . . . | Blue . | 8. Hĕr. P. Caraccas | . | 1819 |
| cruéntā . . . . | Blk. wht. | 8, 8. Hĕr. P. Rio. Jan. | . | 1824 |
| discŏlŏr . . . . | Pink . | 4, 8. Ev. S. S. Amer. | | |
| exūdāns . . . . | Yellow . | 10, Epiphy. W. Ind. | . | 1820 |
| fastuōsā . . . . | Purple . | 8, 8. Hĕr. P. S. Amer. | . | 1815 |
| hūmĭlĭs . . . . | Pink . | 8, 8. Hĕr. P. | . | 1789 |
| Karātās . . . . | Pink . | 8. Hĕr. P. W. Ind. | . | 1739 |
| lingŭlātā . . . . | Yellow . | 5, 8. Hĕr. P. S. Amer. | . | 1759 |
| panĭculĭgĕrā . . . | | 5, 8 Hĕr. P. W. Ind. | . | 1822 |
| Pinguin . . . . | Red . | 3, 8. Hĕr. P. W. Ind. | . | 1690 |
| nemĭsserrātā . . | Green . | 8. Hĕr. P. S. Amer. | . | |
| nemĭliflōrā . . . | | 7, 8. Hĕr. P. S. Amer. | . | 1826 |
| sylvéstrĭs . . . | Crimson . | 7, 8. Hĕr. P. S. Amer. | . | 1820 |

BRÒMŬS, Linn. So called from bromos, the Greek name for a wild oat. Linn. 3, Or. 1, Nat. Or. Gramíneæ. The whole are uninteresting, and in point of culture simply managed. Synonymes: 1. Festuca gigantea. 2. F. triflora—Alopecūrūs, altīssĭmūs, arvēnsĭs, āspĕr, austrālĭs, Bieberstĕĭnĭī, cilĭātūs, commutātūs, confĕrtūs, elongātūs, erēctūs, festucoídes, Gaudĭnĭ, gigantēūs 1, G. longĭfōlĭūs, G. triflōrūs 2, glaūcūs, hirsutīssĭmūs, hūmĭlĭs, jubātūs, lanceolātūs, lanuginōsūs, lāxūs, ligūstrĭcūs, longiflōrūs, madrĭtēnsĭs, māxĭmūs, mōllĭs, multiflōrūs, parvĭflōrūs, pendulīnūs, pilōsūs, pratēnsĭs, pubēscēns, pūrgāns, racemōsūs, rigĭdūs, scabērrĭmūs, scopārĭūs, secalīnūs, squarrōsūs, stenophgĭllūs, stērĭlĭs, tectōrŭm, tōrtĭlĭs, variegātūs, velutīnūs, vestītūs, volgénsĭs.

BRONGNIÁRTĬĂ, Humb. Bonpl. and Kunth. In honour of M. Adolphe Brongniart, a French botanist. Linn. 17, Or. 4, Nat. Or. Leguminòsæ. A valuable species, having flesh-coloured flowers. It is cultivated best in loam and peat, with a little sand; and increased by cuttings in sand, in heat, under a glass.

| | | | |
|---|---|---|---|
| podalyrioídēs . . | Flesh . | . 9, G. Ev. S. N. Spain . | 1827 |

BRÒSĬMŬM, Swartz. Named from brosĭmos, good to eat; in allusion to the eatable fruit. Linn. 23, Or. 2, Nat. Or. Urticàceæ. Alicastrum is common in the woods of Jamaica; the timber is not despicable, but the leaves and young branches are more useful, and a hearty fattening fodder for all sorts of cattle. The fruit, boiled with salt fish, pork, or beef, or pickle, has frequently been the support of the negroes and poorer sorts of white people in times of scarcity, and proved a wholesome and not unpleasant food; when roasted, it eats something like our common chestnut, and is called bread nut. The leaves and young shoots are full of gum, which renders them disagreeable to most cattle at first; but they soon grow very fond of them. B. spurium is also common in woods in the W. Indies; but its timber is of little value. In our stoves both species thrive well, and like loamy soil, and old cuttings with their leaves on, root in sand, in moist heat. —Lou. Ency. of Plants.

| | | | |
|---|---|---|---|
| Alicāstrūm . . | Apetal . | S. Ev. S. Jamaica . | 1776 |
| spūrĭūm . . . | Apetal . | 8. Ev. S. Jamaica . | 1789 |

BRÒSSÆ̆Ă, Linn. Named after Gui de la Brosse, physician to Louis XIII. Linn. 5, Or. 1. Not sufficiently known to be referred to any natural order. As far as we know of this plant, it is a shrub, like a cistus, with scarlet flowers half an inch long. It will no doubt grow in sandy peaty soil, and raise from cuttings in sand.

| | | | |
|---|---|---|---|
| coccĭnĕā . . . | Scarlet . | 8. Ev. S. S. Amer. . | |

BRÒTÉRĂ, Willd. So called, in memory of Felix A. Brotero, a Portuguese botanist, and professor at Coimbra. Linn. 19, Or. 5, Nat. Or. Compòsitæ. An interesting plant, with blue flowers, grows in loam, mixed with peat, and propagates by dividing the roots. Synonyme: 1. Onobroma corymbosa.

| | | | |
|---|---|---|---|
| corymbōsā . . . | Blue . | . 6, H. Hĕr. P. S. Eur. . . | 1640 |

BROUGHTÒNĬĂ, Brown. In honour of Mr. Arthur Broughton, an English botanist. Linn. 20, Or. 1, Nat. Or. Orchidàceæ. B. sanguinea, the only species

H

we have seen flower, is a very desirable plant, producing its fine crimson flowers in terminal racemes. They require a free supply of water when in a free-growing state. For culture and propagation see *Stanhopea*.

| | | | |
|---|---|---|---|
| nitida | . . . Red | . 6, S. Epi. E. Ind. | . 1824 |
| sanguinea | . . Crimson | . 8, S. Epi. Jamaica | . 1793 |

**BROUSSONETIA**, *Ventenat*. In compliment to P. N. V. Broussonet, a French naturalist and traveller. *Linn.* 22, Or. 4, Nat. Or. *Urticaceæ*. Ornamental and fast-growing fruit trees, with large, various-shaped leaves, which differ in the male and female plants, so much as not to be easily distinguished one from the other. The fruit is no larger than peas; and in China and Japan B. papyrifera is cultivated for the sake of its young shoots, which are used in the same manner as osiers here; the outer bark, when separated from the wood and inner bark, will make tolerably good paper. The juice is also used in China as glue in gilding leather and paper. From the bark of this tree is made the finest and whitest cloth, worn by the highest ranks in Otaheite and the Sandwich Islands. The cloth of the breadfruit tree is inferior in whiteness and softness to it, consequently worn by the commoner people. They grow in any open soil, and increase readily by cuttings. *Synonyme*: 1. *Morus papyrifera*.

| | | | |
|---|---|---|---|
| papyrifera, 1 | . . Apetal | . 6, H. De. T. Japan | . 1751 |
| spatulata | . . Apetal | . 6, H. De. T. Japan | . 1824 |

**BROWALLIA**, *Linn*. Named in honour of J. Browallius, bishop of Abo. *Linn.* 14, Or. 2, Nat. Or. *Scrophulariaceæ*. Very handsome plants, on account of their blue and white flowers. They are easily cultivated in common soil, if sandy, much the better, and increased by seeds. *Synonyme*: 1. *B. lactea*.

| | | | |
|---|---|---|---|
| demissa | . . . Blue | . S. G. A. S. Amer. | . 1735 |
| elata | . . . Blue | . S. G. A. Peru | . 1768 |
| elongata, 1 | . . Blue wht. | 7, G. A. | |
| grandiflora | . . Lilac | . 7, G. A. Peru | . 1829 |

**BROWNEA**, *Wild*. In memory of Dr. Patrick Browne. *Linn.* 16, Or. 3, Nat. Or. *Leguminosæ*. This, though rare in our collections, is a splendid genus. The species succeed in sandy loam and peat, if the pots be well drained, and the soil carefully watered, particularly in winter. Cuttings of the ripe wood in sand, put in a moist heat under a glass, may be brought to root. *Synonyme*: 1. *B. speciosa*.

| | | | |
|---|---|---|---|
| coccinea | . . . Scarlet | . 7, S. Ev. S. W. Ind. | . 1793 |
| grandiceps | . . Red | . 8. S. Ev. S. Caraccas | . 1829 |
| latifolia | . . . Scarlet | . 8. S. Ev. S. Trinidad | . 1824 |
| racemosa | . . . Rose | . 8. S. Ev. S. Caraccas | . 1826 |
| rosea, 1 | . . . Scarlet | . 7, S. Ev. S. Trinidad | . 1820 |

**BROWNLOWIA**, *Roxburgh*. In compliment to the late Lady Brownlow, daughter of Sir A. Hume. *Linn.* 13, Or. 1, Nat. Or. *Tiliaceæ*. A large, tall-growing tree, of considerable beauty, thriving in a sandy, loamy soil, and increased by cuttings without difficulty.

| | | | |
|---|---|---|---|
| elata | . . . Yellow | . 8. Ev. T. E. Ind. | . 1820 |

**BRUCEA**, *L. Héritier*. In memory of J. Bruce, the traveller in Abyssinia. *Linn.* 12, Or. 4, Nat. Or. *Zanthoxylaceæ*. Evergreen ornamental shrubs, thriving in an open loamy soil mixed with a little peat; and propagated from half or wholly ripened cuttings, in sand or soil, under glass.

| | | | |
|---|---|---|---|
| ferruginea | . . . Green | . 4, S. Ev. S. Abyssinia | . 1775 |
| gracilis | . . . Yel. grn. | . S. Ev. S. Ind. | . 1820 |
| sumatrana | . . . Green | . 5, S. Ev. S. E. Ind. | . 1820 |

**BRUGMANSIA**, *Persoon*. Named in honour of Professor S. J. Brugmans. *Linn.* 5, Or. 1, Nat. Or. *Solanaceæ*. The species of this genus are among the greatest ornaments of our conservatories; B. arborea in particular; this species never thrives well but when planted out in a border, and must be plentifully watered, allowing plenty of room for the branches; thus treated, the number, size, and fine white colour of the flowers will be surprising. All the species are great feeders, and require good soil, and a deal of room to grow them fine. They are easily propagated from cuttings; or the eyes taken off, like vines, and put in good soil in heat, will strike readily. *Synonymes*: 1. Sanguinea. 2. Datura arborea. 3. D. arborea.

| | | | |
|---|---|---|---|
| bicolor, 1 | . . . Dk. red | . 8, G. Ev. S. Peru | . 1833 |
| candida, 2 | . . . White | . 8, G. Ev. S. Peru | . 1818 |

| | | | |
|---|---|---|---|
| suaveolens 3 | . . White | . 8, G. Ev. S. Peru | . 1733 |
| Waymanii | . . . Wht. pur. | 5, S. Ev. T. S. Amer. | . 1827 |

**BRUNIA**, *Linn*. In memory of Cornelius Brun, a traveller in the Levant and Russia. *Linn.* 5, Or. 1, Nat. Or. *Escalloniaceæ*. This, observes Mr. Sweet, is a pretty Cape genus; its species are pretty bushy shrubs, with heath-like leaves, and are handsomest while young. The flowers are not so showy as in many other genera, but some of them are very elegant. A sandy peat soil suits them best, with a moderate supply of water; young cuttings, planted in sand under a bell-glass, strike root freely.—*Bot. Cult.* 153.

| | | | |
|---|---|---|---|
| alopecuroides | . . White | . . G. Ev. S. C. G. H. | . 1816 |
| arachnoidea | . . White | . 6, G. Ev. S. C. G. H. | . 1820 |
| comosa | . . . White | . 7, G. Ev. S. C. G. H. | . 1820 |
| deusta | . . . White | . 7, G. Ev. S. C. G. H. | . 1820 |
| elegans | . . . White | . 7, G. Ev. S. C. G. H. | . 1817 |
| ericoides | . . . White | . 7, G. Ev. S. C. G. H. | . 1804 |
| formosa | . . . White | . . G. Ev. S. C. G. H. | . 1817 |
| fragarioides | . . White | . 6, G. Ev. S. C. G. H. | . 1794 |
| globosa | . . . White | . 7, G. Ev. S. C. G. H. | . 1816 |
| hirsuta | . . . White | . 7, G. Ev. S. C. G. H. | . 1820 |
| lævis | . . . White | . 7, G. Ev. S. C. G. H. | . 1822 |
| laxa | . . . White | . 7, G. Ev. S. C. G. H. | . 1805 |
| macrophylla | . . White | . 7, G. Ev. S. C. G. H. | . 1815 |
| nodiflora | . . . White | . 7, G. Ev. S. C. G. H. | . 1786 |
| plumosa | . . . White | . 7, G. Ev. S. C. G. H. | . 1824 |
| squarrosa | . . . White | . 7, G. Ev. S. C. G. H. | . 1820 |
| superba | . . . White | . 6, G. Ev. S. C. G. H. | . 1791 |
| verticillata | . . White | . 7, G. Ev. S. C. G. H. | . 1794 |

**BRUNNICHIA**, *Banks*. Named in memory of one P. Brunnich, a Danish naturalist. *Linn.* 10, Or. 3, Nat. Or. *Polygonaceæ*. An evergreen climber, of some merit; it grows readily in a loamy soil, and roots freely from cuttings.

| | | | |
|---|---|---|---|
| cirrhosa | . . . Pink | . . 7, G. Ev. Cl. Carolina | . 1787 |

**BRUNONIA**, *Smith*. Named in compliment to Robert Brown, Esq., D.C.L., &c. &c. *Linn.* 5, Or. 1, Nat. Or. *Brunoniaceæ*. A most interesting fragrant perennial; for the growth of which, a frame or cool greenhouse is recommended.

| | | | |
|---|---|---|---|
| australis | . . . Blue | . H. Her. P. N. Holl. | . 1834 |

**BRUNSFELSIA**, *Linn*. In memory of Otho Brunsfels, of Mentz, a carthusian monk and physician. *Linn.* 14, Or. 2, Nat. Or. *Scrophulariaceæ*. Handsome-growing, fine-flowering shrubs, with neat foliage, and showy white or purple flowers. They succeed well in a good rich soil; and cuttings root readily in sand or soil under a glass in heat.

| | | | |
|---|---|---|---|
| americana | . . . Pa. yel. | . 6, S. Ev. S. W. Ind. | . 1735 |
| angustifolia | . . Pa. yel. | . 7, S. Ev. S. W. Ind. | |
| latifolia | . . . Pa. yel. | . 6, S. Ev. S. W. Ind. | |
| montana | . . . White | . 7, S. Ev. S. Amer. | . 1820 |
| undulata | . . . White | . 7, S. Ev. S. Jamaica | . 1780 |
| violacea | . . . Livid | . 7, S. Ev. S. W. Ind. | . 1815 |

**BRUNSVIGIA**, *Ker*. So called in honour of the family of Brunswick. *Linn.* 6, Or. 1, Nat. Or. *Amaryllidaceæ*. This, observes Mr. Sweet, is a beautiful bulbous genus, "some of the bulbs grow to a great size, and require large pots to have them flower in perfection; or if planted out in the open borders in spring, there will be a better chance of their flowering; taking the bulbs up again in autumn, and keeping them through the winter; or the best way to succeed well with them is to have a pit built on purpose, so as to be occasionally covered with the lights to keep off too much wet, and to be covered close in severe weather, as they cannot bear the frost; the mould must be made for them of full one-third sand, more than one-third of turfy loam, and the rest peat; all well mixed together, but not chopped too small, as the roots run better through it for being rough and hollow; when in full growth and flower they require a frequent supply of water, but none while dormant; all the greenhouse species of *Amaryllideæ* will succeed best in this way."—*Bot. Cult.*, 190. *Synonymes*: 1. *Hæmanthus ciliaris*. 2. *Ammocharis coranica*. 3. *Amaryllis coranica, pallida*. 4. *Disticha, Buphane disticha*. 5. *Ammocharis falcata*. 6. *Amaryllis laticoma, Nerine laticoma*. 7. *Amaryllis orientalis*. 8. *Hæmanthus toxicarius*.

| | | | |
|---|---|---|---|
| ciliaris, 1 | . . . Black | . 8, G. Bl. P. C. G. H. | . 1752 |
| coranica, 2 | . . . Pink | . 9, G. Bl. P. C. G. H. | . 1815 |
| pallida, 3 | . . . Pale | . 9, G. Bl. P. C. G. H. | . 1826 |
| disticha, 4 | . . . Red | . 9, G. Bl. P. C. G. H. | . 1823 |
| falcata, 5 | . . . Red | . 5, G. Bl. P. C. G. H. | . 1774 |

| | | | |
|---|---|---|---|
| grandiflòrá . . | Pink . | 8, G. BL. P. C. G. H. | 1827 |
| Josephinä . . | Scarlet | 7, G. BL. P. C. G. H. | 1814 |
| minòr . . | Scarlet | 7, G. BL. P. C. G. H. | 1814 |
| striàtà . . | Scarlet | 7, G. BL. P. C. G. H. | 1823 |
| lúcidä, 6 . . | Pink . | 8, G. BL. P. C. G. H. | 1818 |
| marginàtä . . | Scarlet | 9, G. BL. P. C. G. H. | 1795 |
| minòr . . | Pink . | 7, G. BL. P. C. G. H. | 1822 |
| multiflòrä, 7 . | Red . | 7, G. BL. P. C. G. H. | 1752 |
| rädülä . . | Red . | 6, G. BL. P. C. G. H. | 1790 |
| striàtä . . | Pink . | 7, G. BL. P. C. G. H. | 1823 |
| toxicàriä . . | Pink . | 10, G. BL. P. C. G. H. | 1774 |

BRYÁ, *Brown*. From the word *bryo*, to sprout; so named on account of the germination of the seed commencing while on the plant. *Linn.* 16, Or. 6, Nat. Or. *Leguminosæ*. Tallish evergreen ornamental shrubs, succeeding well in very rich soil, and increased readily by cuttings or seed in heat. *Synonyme:* 1. *Amerrimum Ebenus*.

| | | | |
|---|---|---|---|
| Ebènûs, 1 . . | Yel. grn. | 7, S. Ev. S. Jamaica | 1718 |
| Leonënsis . . | Yel. grn. | 8. Ev. S. S. Leone | 1824 |

BRYOBÍÚM, *Lindley*. Name not explained. *Linn.* 20, Or. 1, Nat. Or. *Orchidaceæ*. A plant of no beauty, and very easy culture.

| | | | |
|---|---|---|---|
| pubëscëns . . | Green . | 8. Epi. E. Ind. . . | |

BRYÒNÍÁ, *Linn.* Named in allusion to the quick growth of the stems, from *bryo*, to sprout. *Linn.* 21, Or. 10, Nat. Or. *Cucurbitaceæ*. Straggling plants of little interest, and easy culture. "The root of *Bryonia* is powerfully purgative, but if properly cooked, becomes wholesome; those of *B. rostrata* are used in India internally, in electuary, in cases of piles, it is also used in the form of powder as a demulcent; *B. cordifolia* is cooling, and useful in expectorants. The root of *B. Epigæa* was once considered to be the esteemed Calomba Root, on account of its nearness in quality. The young shoots and leaves of *B. scabra*, after roasting, are aperient.—*Lind. Intro. Nat. System—africàná, albá, cordàtä, crëticä, dioïcä, disëctä, divïsä, epigæä, ficifòliä, filifòrmïs, Gàrcini, grändïs, laciniòsä, latebròsä, nítïdä, palmàtä, pinnatífïdä, quinquelòbä, scàbrä, scabrëllä, tenëllä, trilobàtä, verrucòsä.*

BRYOPHÝLLÚM, *Salisbury*. So named from *bryo*, to grow, and *phyllon*, a leaf; in reference to the circumstance of the leaf when laid upon damp earth emitting roots, whence arise young plants. *Linn.* 8, Or. 4, Nat. Or. *Crassulaceæ*. Of this curious plant, Mr. Loudon observes, it requires very little water, and the pots to be well drained; it flowers best plunged in tan heat; rich loamy soil suits it best. *Synonyme:* 1. *Cotyledon calycinum*.

| | | | |
|---|---|---|---|
| calycìnúm, 1 . | Grn pur. | 6, S. Ev. S. E. Ind. . . | 1800 |

BRYÒPSIS, *Aghardh*. The little branches resemble moss; hence the name *bryon*, moss, and *opsis*, resemblance. *Linn.* 24, Or. 7, Nat. Or. *Algæ*. Interesting marine productions, growing in fine feathery tufts—*compòsïtä, plumòsä*.

BRYÚM, *Hedwig*. Named from *bryo*, to abound; abounding in great plenty. *Linn.* 24, Or. 5, Nat. Or. *Musci*. Dwarf species, generally found growing in wet places. *B. triquetrum* has been only met with upon the border of some lakes in the north of Ireland. *Synonymes:* 1. *Mnium androgynum*. 2. *Bryum stellare*. 3. *Compactum*. 4. *Aureum*. 5. *Nigricans*. 6. *Linum, cubitale—alpìnúm, andrògynûm* 1, *argëntëüm cæspitítïûm, C. mäjüs, C. minòr, capillàrë* 2, *cärnûm, crüdûm, cuspidàtûm, dealbàtüm, demïssûm, elongàtûm, hörnûm, inúdcëüm, ligulàtüm, marginàtûm, nütäns* 3, *palüstrë, punctàtûm, pyrifòrmë* 4, *ròsëûm, rostràtûm, Tozeri, trichòdës, triquëtrûm, turbinàtûm* 5, *ventricòsûm* 6, *Zïërïï*.

BUBÒN, *Linn.* Named from *boubon*, signifying the groin; in allusion to its medicinal qualities. *Linn.* 5, Or. 2, Nat. Or. *Umbelliferæ*. Curious plants, of little beauty and easy cultivation. *Synonymes:* 1. *Selinum gallanum*. 2. *Farula lævigata*.

| | | | |
|---|---|---|---|
| gálbänûm, 1 . | Yel. grn. | 7, G. Ev. S. C. G. H. | 1596 |
| gummiferûm . | Pa. yel. | 7, G. Ev. S. C. G. H. | 1731 |
| lævigàtüm, 2 . | Yellow . | 8, G. Ev. S. C. G. H. | 1774 |

BUCHANÀNÍÁ, *Roxburgh*. Named in honour of F. Buchanan, now Hamilton, M.D. *Linn.* 10, Or. 4, Nat. Or. *Anacardiaceæ*. Fruit-bearing trees of no particular value; they grow well in light loamy soil; and cuttings root in sand, under a glass, in heat. *Synonymes:* 1. *Mangifera axillaris, Spondias axillaris*.

[ 51 ]

| | | | |
|---|---|---|---|
| angustifòliä, 1 | White . | 8. Ev. T. E. Ind. . | 1820 |
| latifòliä . . . | White . | 8. Ev. T. E. Ind. . | 1820 |

BUCHNÈRÍÁ, *Linn.* After J. G. Buchner, a German naturalist. *Linn.* 14, Or. 2, Nat. Or. *Scrophulariaceæ*. Species of little interest; they grow in loamy soil, and are increased by seeds. *Synonyme:* 1. *Biflora*.

| | | | |
|---|---|---|---|
| americàná . . | Blue . | 7, H. Her. P. N. Amer. . | 1733 |

*hispidä, urticæfòliä* 1.

BOCÌDÁ, *Linn.* Named from *bous*, an ox; the fruit being like an ox's horn. *Linn.* 10, Or. 2, Nat. Or. *Combretaceæ*. A fine tree, of considerable value on account of its useful qualities; it grows best in loam and peat; and ripened cuttings planted in sand, and plunged in heat, under a glass, root readily. The bark is greatly esteemed by the tanners.

| | | | |
|---|---|---|---|
| Bücërüs . . . | Yel. wht. | 8, S. Ev. T. Jamaica | 1793 |

BUD, the flower, or leaves before expansion, are said to be in the bud.

BUDDLÈÁ, *Linn.* In memory of Adam Buddle, an English botanist. *Linn.* 4, Or. 1, Nat. Or. *Scrophulariaceæ*. A genus of very handsome shrubs, especially *B. globosa*, which flowers freely in the open air of Britain, providing it has a warm situation; one against a south wall is best. *B. Neemda* is one of the most beautiful plants of India, bearing a profusion of handsome white flowers. They delight in a loamy soil, mixed with a little peat, and young plants are obtained by laying the branches, or from cuttings, which root in sandy mould without difficulty.

| | | | |
|---|---|---|---|
| americàná . . | Yellow . | 8, S. Ev. S. Mexico . | 1826 |
| brasiliënsis . . | Orange . | 8. Ev. S. Brasil . | 1822 |
| connàtä . . . | Orange . | 5, S. Ev. S. Peru . | 1826 |
| diversifòliä . . | | 8. Ev. S. Java . | 1823 |
| globòsä . . . | Orange . | 5, H. Ev. S. Chile . | 1774 |
| heterophýllä . | Yellow . | 5, S. Ev. S. S. Amer. . | |
| madagascariënsis | Orange . | 8. Ev. S. Madeira . | 1824 |
| Neëmdä . . . | White . | 6, S. Ev. S. Nepal . | 1824 |
| paniculàtä . . | White . | 5, S. Ev. S. Nepal . | 1823 |
| salicifòliä . . | | 8. Ev. S. S. Amer. . | 1823 |
| salignä . . . | White . | 8, G. Ev. S. C. G. H. | 1816 |
| salvifòliä . . | Crimson . | 8, G. Ev. S. C. G. H. | 1760 |

BUFFALO CLOVER, see *Trifòlïûm pensylvànïcûm*.

BUFFÒNÍÁ, *Wild.* Named after Count de Buffon, the noted naturalist. *Linn.* 4, Or. 2, Nat. Or. *Alsinaceæ*. Dwarf curious species, of easy culture. *Synonyme:* 1. *B. annus*.

| | | | |
|---|---|---|---|
| perënnïs . . | White . | 6, H. Her. P. France . | 1817 |
| tenuifòliä, 1 . | White . | 6, H. | A. England |

BUGAINVILLÈÁ, *Commerson*. Named after De Bougainville, a French navigator. *Linn.* 8, Or. 8, Nat. Or. *Nyctaginaceæ*. A showy evergreen climber, succeeding in loam, and increased by cuttings.

| | | | |
|---|---|---|---|
| spectàbïlïs . . | Pink . | 8. Ev. Cl. S. Amer. . | 1829 |

BUGLE, see *Ajúgä*.

BUGLOSS, see *Anchùsä*.

BUGWORT, see *Cimicifùgä*.

BULBÍNE, *Wild.* From *bolbos*, a bulb. *Linn.* 6, Or. 1, Nat. Or. *Liliaceæ*. The species are showy, fragrant, and of easy culture; and increase rapidly by cuttings.—*Lou. Ency. of Plants—Synonymes:* 1. *Anthericum annuum*. 2. *Bulbosum*. 3. *Asphodeloides*. 4. *Hispidum*. 5. *Latifolium*. 6. *Nutans*. 7. *Præmorsa*. 8. *Scabrum*. 9. *Semibarbatum*. 10. *Triquetrum*.

| | | | |
|---|---|---|---|
| aloïdes . . . | Yellow . | 6, G. Her. P. C. G. H. | 1732 |
| ännüä, 1 . . | Yellow . | 5, H. Her. A. C. G. H. | 1731 |
| asphodeloïdës, 2 | White . | 7, F. Her. P. C. G. H. | 1759 |
| austràlïs, 3 . | Yellow . | 6, G. Bu. P. N. Holl. | 1820 |
| bisulcàtä . . | Yellow . | 11, H. BL. P. C. G. H. | 1823 |
| ciliàtä . . . | Yellow . | 5, G. Her. P. C. G. H. | 1823 |
| frutëscëns . . | Yellow . | 6, G. Ev. S. C. G. H. | 1702 |
| glaücä . . . | White . | G. BL. P. Chile . | 1828 |
| gramïnëä . . | Yellow . | 5, G. Her. P. C. G. H. | 1824 |
| hispïdä, 4 . . | White . | 5, G. Her. P. C. G. H. | 1774 |
| latifòliä, 5 . . | White . | 7, G. Her. P. C. G. H. | 1812 |
| longiscàpä . . | Yellow . | 6, G. Her. P. C. G. H. | 1759 |
| mesembryanthoïdës | Yellow . | 5, G. Her. P. C. G. H. | 1822 |
| nütäns, 6 . . | Yellow . | 7, G. Her. P. C. G. H. | 1820 |
| præmòrsä, 7 . | Yellow . | 6, G. Her. P. C. G. H. | 1818 |
| pugioniförmïs . | Yellow . | 5, G. Her. P. C. G. H. | 1795 |
| rostràtä . . . | Yellow . | 6, G. Ev. S. C. G. H. | 1812 |
| scàbrä, 8 . . | Yellow . | 6, G. Her. P. C. G. H. | 1825 |
| semibarbàtä, 9 . | Yellow . | 7, G. Her. P. C. G. H. | 1820 |
| suàvïs . . . | Yellow . | 5, G. Ev. S. N. Holl. | 1826 |
| triquëträ, 10 . | Yellow . | 6, G. Her. P. C. G. H. | 1825 |

BULBIFEROUS, bulb-bearing.

BULBOCHÆTÆ, *Agardh*. Named in reference to the stiff bristly end of the primary filaments, from *bolbos*, bulb, and *chaite*, bristles. Linn. 24, Or. 7, Nat. Or. *Algæ*. Found in autumn in delicate tufts about lakes and rivers—*setigerd*.

BULBS, under-ground buds, resembling roots, and consisting of numerous fleshy scales, placed one over the other.

BULBOCŎDIŬM, *Willd*. Named from *bolbos*, bulb, and *kodion*, wool; the bulb being wrapped in a woolly covering. Linn. 6, Or. 1, Nat. Or. *Melanthaceæ*. Very beautiful dwarf species, worthy of careful cultivation: they grow best in sandy loam and peat; and young plants are obtained from the roots. Synonyme: 1. *Colchicum versicolor*.

| | | | | | | |
|---|---|---|---|---|---|---|
| vẽrnŭm . . . | . Purple | . 2, H | Bl. | P. | Spain | . 1629 |
| versicŏlŏr, I | . Purple | . 8, H. | Bl. | P. | Crimea | . 1820 |

BULOXÆIX, *Fries*. The species assume something the form of a bag; hence the name from *bulga*, a leather bag. Linn. 24, Or. 9, Nat. Or. *Fungi*. Minute species, frequent upon dead oaks and other decaying trees—*inquindns, sarcoides*.

BULLACE TREE, see *Prūnūs insititĭd*.

BULLATE, garnished with studs, like bubbles.

BULL GRAPE, see *Vitis rotundifōlĭd*.

BULLIARDÆ, *Dec.* In memory of M. Bulliard, a French botanist. Linn. 4, Or. 3, Nat. Or. *Crassulaceæ*. A curious little annual aquatic. The soil for it is loam and peat; seeds.

| | | | | | |
|---|---|---|---|---|---|
| Vaillantĭ . . . | . White | . 7, H. | | A. S. Europe | . 1825 |

BUMÆLDÆ, *Thunberg*. In memory of J. A. de Bumalda, a botanist of Bologna. Linn. 5, Or. 2, Nat. Or. *Staphyleaceæ*. A curious evergreen, with little to recommend it; any common soil suits it; seeds. Synonyme: 1. *Staphylea Bumalda*.

| | | | | | |
|---|---|---|---|---|---|
| trifōlĭā . . . | . | . 8, G. | Ev. | S. Japan | . 1812 |

BUMELĬÆ, *Swartz*. The Greeks gave this name to the common ash. Linn. 5, Or. 1, Nat. Or. *Sapotaceæ*. These are plants of grand foliage, but no great beauty of blossom. Some of the species are robust enough to bear our winters in the open air, but they are rather tender, and require to be placed in a sheltered situation, or against a warm wall, and covered with mats during winter; cuttings root in sand, under a glass. The stove species are low W. Indian trees, and known under the name of bully-tree. They thrive well in loamy soil, or loam and peat; and cuttings will root, but, according to Sweet, not freely, in sand under a hand-glass, being well ripened before they are taken off.—*Lou. Ency. of Plants*—Synonymes: 1. *Sideroxylon lycioides*. 2. *Chrysophyllum macrophyllum*. 3. *Achras salicifolia*. 4. *Sideroxylon strigosum*. 5. *S. tenax*.

| | | | | | | |
|---|---|---|---|---|---|---|
| barbõnĭcā . . | . White | . | 8. | Ev. | T. Bourbon | . 1825 |
| cuneātā . . . | . White | . 7, | 8. | Ev. | T. W. Ind. | . 1823 |
| fœtidĭssĭmā . . | . White | . | 8, | H. | De. | S. Carolina | . 1806 |
| lanugĭnōsā . . | . White | . 8, | H. | De. | S. Carolina | . 1806 |
| lycioĭdēs, 1 . . | . White | . | H. | De. | S. N. Amer. | . 1758 |
| nervõsā, 2 . . | . White | . | 8. | Ev. | T. Guiana | . 1820 |
| nĭgrā . . . | . White | . | 8. | Ev. | F. W. Ind. | . 1806 |
| oblongĭfōlĭā . . | . White | . 7, | H. | De. | S. N. Amer. | . 1818 |
| reclĭnātā . . | . White | . 6, | H. | De. | S. Carolina | . 1806 |
| rotundĭfŏlĭā . | . White | . | 8. | Ev. | T. W. Ind. | |
| salicĭfŏlĭā, 3 . | . White | . | 8. | Ev. | T. S. Amer. | . 1758 |
| serrātā . . . | . White | . | H. | De. | S. Missouri | . 1812 |
| strĭgōsā, 4 . . | . White | . | 7, | F. | Ev. | T. N. Amer. | . 1818 |
| tēnāx, 5 . . . | . White | . 7, | H. | De. | T. Carniola | . 1765 |

BUNCHŎSĬÆ, *Jussieu*. From *bunchos*, coffee; the seeds resembling that article. Linn. 10, Or. 1, Nat. Or. *Malpighĭaceæ*. A genus of ornamental tallish shrubs; they thrive best in a mixture of loam, peat, and sand; cuttings of the ripe wood root very well in sand, in heat, under a glass. Synonymes: 1 *Malpighia canescens*. 2. *M. glandulĭfera*. 3. *M. glandulosa*. 4. *M. media*. 5. *M. nitida*. 6. *M. polystachya*. 7. *M. tuberculata*.

| | | | | | | |
|---|---|---|---|---|---|---|
| argĕntĕā . . | . Yellow | . 7, | 8. | Ev. | S. Caraccas | . 1810 |
| canĕscĕns, 1 . | . Yellow | . 7, | 8. | Ev. | T. W. Ind. | . 1742 |
| cumanĕnsĭs . | . Yellow | . 9, | 8. | Ev. | S. Cumana | . 1820 |
| glandulĭferā, 2 | . Yellow | . 4, | 8. | Ev. | S. W. Ind. | . 1806 |
| glandulōsā, 3 . | . Yellow | . 4, | 8. | Ev. | S. W. Ind. | . 1804 |
| mẽdĭā, 4 . . | . Yellow | . 7, | 8. | Ev. | S. W. Ind. | . 1790 |
| nĭtĭdā, 5 . . | . Red | . 7, | 8. | Ev. | S. St. Domin. | . 1800 |
| odŏrātā . . | . Yellow | . 7, | 8. | Ev. | S. Carthag. | . 1806 |

| | | | | | | |
|---|---|---|---|---|---|---|
| panĭculāta . . | . Purple | . 6, | 8. | Ev. | S. Jamaica | . 1820 |
| polystãchyā, 6 | . Yellow | . 4, | 8. | Ev. | S. W. Ind. | . 1806 |
| tuberculātā, 7 . | . Yellow | . 6, | 8. | Ev. | S. Caraccas | . 1806 |

BUNĬÆS, *Linn.* Bunios, a hill; alluding to the habitation. Linn. 15, Or. 1, Nat. Or. *Cruciferæ*. Hardy annuals, of no interest—*aspérd, Erucâgd, orientâlis.*

BŬNĬUM, *Linn.* Same as Bunias. Linn. 5, Or. 2, Nat. Or. *Umbelliferæ*. Mere weeds of the simplest culture. Synonymes: 1. *Flexuosum*. 2. *Bulbocastanum—ammoides* 1, Bulbocastanum, flexuosum 2, pyrenæum.

BUPLEŬRŬM, *Linn.* Not satisfactorily explained. Linn. 5, Or. 2, Nat. Or. *Umbelliferæ*. A very natural and remarkable genus, on account of the leaves being for the most part quite entire. They succeed in any common soil. The annual species merely require sowing in the open border early in spring; the perennial kinds may be increased by offsets, or seeds. Synonymes: 1. Tenoria canescens. 2. T. difforme. 3. T. frutescens. 4. T. fruticosum. 5. T. coriaceum. 6. T. plantagineum. 7. B. junceum. 8. T. spinosum.

| | | | | | | |
|---|---|---|---|---|---|---|
| argulõsŭm . . | . Grn. yel. | . 6, | H. | Her. | P. Switzerl. | . 1759 |
| aŭrĕŭm . . | . Grn. yel. | . 5, | H. | Her. | P. Siberia | . 1820 |
| baldẽnsĕ . . | . Grn. yel. | . 7, | H. | Her. | P. Mt. Baldo | . 1817 |
| Burserĭānŭm . | . Grn. yel. | . 7, | H. | Her. | P. | . 1817 |
| canĕscĕns, 1 . | . Yellow | . 8, | G. | Ev. | S. Barbary | . 1809 |
| caricĭfŏlĭŭm . | . Grn. yel. | . 7, | H. | Her. | P. France | . 1817 |
| diffŏrmĕ, 2 . | . Yellow | . 8, | G. | Ev. | S. C. G. H. | . 1752 |
| exaltātŭm . . | . Grn. yel. | . 7, | H. | Her. | P. Tauria | . 1807 |
| falcātŭm . . | . Grn. yel. | . 8, | H. | Her. | P. Germany | . 1739 |
| frutĕscĕns, 3 . | . Yellow | . 8, | H. | Ev. | S. Spain | . 1752 |
| frutĭcōsŭm, 4 . | . Yellow | . 7, | F. | Ev. | S. Eur. | . 1596 |
| Gerārdĭ . . | . Grn. yel. | . 7, | H. | | A. S. Eur. | . 1804 |
| Gibraltărĭcā, 5 | . Yellow | . 7, | F. | Ev. | S. Gibraltar | . 1784 |
| grãcĭlĕ . . | . Grn. yel. | . 7, | H. | | A. S. Eur. | . 1819 |
| gramĭnĭfŏlĭŭm | . Grn. yel. | . 6, | H. | Her. | P. Switzerl. | . 1768 |
| heterophŷllŭm | . Yellow | . 6, | H. | | A. Egypt. | . 1818 |
| jŭncĕŭm . . | . Grn. yel. | . 7, | H. | | A. S. Eur. | . 1772 |
| lancĭfŏlĭŭm . | . Grn. yel. | . 7, | H. | | B. Tauria | . 1820 |
| longĭfŏlĭŭm . | . Grn. yel. | . 6, | H. | Her. | P. Switzerl. | . 1713 |
| nodĭflōrŭm . | . Grn. yel. | . 7, | H. | | A. Greece | . 1823 |
| nŭdŭm . . | . Grn. yel. | . 10, | G. | Her. | P. C. G. H. | . 1778 |
| Odontĭtēs . . | . Grn. yel. | . 7, | H. | | A. Italy | . 1749 |
| oppŏsĭtĭfŏlĭŭm | . Grn. yel. | . 7, | H. | | A. Pyrenees | . 1819 |
| panĭculātŭm . | . Yellow | . 7, | H. De. | | P. Spain | . 1824 |
| petræŭm . . | . Grn. yel. | . 7, | H. | Her. | P. Switzerl. | . 1768 |
| plantagĭnĕŭm, 6 | . Yellow | . 7, | F. | Ev. | S. Mt. Atlas | . 1810 |
| Pollĭchĭĭ, 7 . | . Grn. yel. | . 7, | H. | | A. Palestine | . 1818 |
| polyphŷllŭm . | . Grn. yel. | . 5, | H. | Her. | P. Caucasus | . 1823 |
| pyrenāicŭm . | . Grn. yel. | . 7, | H. | | A. Pyrenees | |
| ranunculoĭdēs . | . Grn. yel. | . 7, | H. | Her. | P. France | . 1790 |
| rĭgĭdŭm . . | . Grn. yel. | . 6, | H. Her. | | P. England | . 1820 |
| rotundĭfŏlĭŭm . | . Grn. yel. | . 7, | H. | | A. Spain | |
| seral-compŏsĭtŭm | . Grn. yel. | . 7, | H. | | A. Spain | . 1778 |
| sibirĭcŭm . . | . Grn. yel. | . 7, | H. Her. | | P. Siberia | . 1826 |
| spĭnōsŭm, 8 . | . Yellow | . 7, | H. | Ev. | S. Spain | . 1752 |
| stellātŭm . . | . Grn. yel. | . 6, | H. | | P. Switzerl. | . 1775 |
| subovātŭm . | . Yellow | . 6, | H. | | A. Spain | . 1819 |
| tenuĭssĭmŭm . | . Grn. yel. | . 7, | H. | | A. England | |
| trĭfĭdŭm . . | . Yellow | . 7, | H. | | B. Italy | . 1824 |

BUPHTHĂLMŬM, *Linn.* Named in allusion to the resemblance the disk of the flowers bears to an ox's eye, from *bous*, ox, and *ophthalmos*, eye. Linn. 19, Or. 2, Nat. Or. *Compositæ*. The plants of this genus are very showy and ornamental. The greenhouse species do well in a loamy soil; and increase from cuttings, under a glass: the herbaceous species thrive in common garden mould; and increase by suckers: the annual species only require sowing in the open ground. Synonyme: 1. *Coriaceum*.

| | | | | | | |
|---|---|---|---|---|---|---|
| aquãtĭcŭm . . | . Yellow | . 7, | H. | | A. S. Eur. | . 1731 |
| grandĭflōrŭm . | . Yellow | . 8, | H. | Her. | P. Austria | . 1722 |
| lævĭgātŭm, 1 . | . Yellow | . 8, | G. | Ev. | S. Teneriffe | . 1800 |
| marĭtĭmŭm . . | . Yellow | . 8, | F. | Her. | P. Sicily | . 1640 |
| salicĭfŏlĭŭm . | . Yellow | . 9, | H. | Her. | P. Austria | . 1759 |
| serĭcĕŭm . . | . Yellow | . 6, | G. | Ev. | S. Canaries | . 1779 |
| specĭosĭssĭmŭm . | . Yellow | . 7, | H. | Her. | P. S. Eur. | . 1826 |
| spĭnōsŭm . . | . Yellow | . 7, | H. | | A. Spain | . 1570 |
| stenophŷllŭm . | . Yellow | . 6, | G. | Ev. | S. Canaries | . 1818 |

BUR, see *Centathẽcă Cappăcĭā*.

BURCHÄRDĬÆ, *R. Brown*. In honour of Henry Burchard, M.D., a botanical author. Linn. 6, Or. 1, Nat. Or. *Melanthaceæ*. A species of considerable beauty, thriving best in sandy peat, or peat mixed with a little loam; offsets or divisions.

| | | | | | |
|---|---|---|---|---|---|
| umbellāta . . | . Wht. grn | . 8, G. | Her. | P. N. Holl. | . 1820 |

BURCHĔLLĬÆ, *R. Brown*. In compliment to W. Burchell, a traveller in Africa. Linn. 5, Or. 1, Nat.

Or. *Cinchonaceæ*. Handsome species, especially *B. capensis*; they require open rich soil, and to be carefully watered, and they will flower well. *Synonyme*: 1. *Parviflora*.

| | | | | | | |
|---|---|---|---|---|---|---|
| bubalinā, 1 | . | . | Scarlet | . 5, S. Ev. S. C. G. H. | . 1818 |
| capénsis | . . | . | Scarlet | . 3, S. Ev. S. C. G. H. | . |

BURDOCK, see *Arctium*.

BURLINGTŌNIĀ. *Lindley* dedicated this lovely genus to the amiable and accomplished Countess of Burlington. *Linn.* 20, Or. 1, Nat. Or. *Orchidaceæ*. The species belonging to this genus are of great beauty, each of which rivals the other in loveliness of colour and delightful fragrance of their flowers. The species belonging to this and some other genera grow best upon wood with a little moss on their roots, and fastened to the wood with tempered copper or metallic wire. Oak branches with several arms or forks protruding in different directions are the most suitable wood for them. *B. rigida* is a very curious-growing species, producing the small pseudo-bulbs at the end of the wiry-like rhizoma. When the plants make their growth a little moss should be fastened to the oak branch for the young shoots to root and fasten themselves to. Copious watering overhead and likewise a strong heat are necessary when the plants are growing, but when they are torpid they should be kept cool and dry. They are increased by dividing the bulbs.

| | | | | | | |
|---|---|---|---|---|---|---|
| cándidā | . . . | . | White | . 4, S. Epi. Demerara | . 1834 |
| rígidā | . . | . | | 8. Epi. Brazil | . . |

BURNET, see *Poterium*.
BURNET SAXIFRAGE, see *Pimpinella*.
BUR PARSLEY, see *Caucalis*.
BUR REED, see *Sparganium*.
BURRY, covered with hooked stiff hairs, like the heads of bur or burdock.

BURSĀRIĀ, *Cavanilles*. Named from *bursa*, signifying a pouch. *Linn.* 5, Or. 1, Nat. Or. *Pittosporaceæ*. A pretty species desirable for a greenhouse or conservatory, being an abundant flowerer, and very showy when covered with its elegant little white blossoms. An equal mixture of sandy loam and peat is the best soil for it; and young cuttings are not difficult to root in sand under a little glass.—*Bot. Cul.*

| | | | | | | |
|---|---|---|---|---|---|---|
| spinōsā | . . . | . | White | . 10, G. Ev. S. N. S. W. | . 1793 |

BURSĒRĀ, *Jacquin*. In memory of Joachim Burser, a botanist in Naples. *Linn.* 23, Or. 2, Nat. Or. *Burseraceæ*. Large trees of considerable value: they grow in loam and peat; and increase by cuttings or seeds. *B. gummifera* abounds in a watery balsamic fluid, which however soon becomes inspissated by exposure to the air. Hedges are made of it by the Spanish residents in S. America, who call it *Almacigo*. It is also said to possess identical properties with *Quassia*.

| | | | | | | |
|---|---|---|---|---|---|---|
| gummiférā | . . | . | Wht. grn. | . | 8. Ev. T. W. Ind. | . 1690 |
| serrātā | . . | . . | | 8. Ev. T. E. Ind. | . 1818 |

BURTŌNIĀ, *R. Brown*. Named in honour of D. Burton, who collected for the Kew Garden. *Linn.* 10, Or. 1, Nat. Or. *Leguminosæ*. This pretty New Holland genus, says Mr. Sweet, requires more than ordinary treatment to keep it in good health; an equal mixture of very sandy loam and peat is the best soil for it, and the pots to be well drained, with small potsherds, that the water may pass off freely, as nothing is more injurious to it than too much water. Young cuttings are not difficult to root, planted in sand under a bell-glass; it may also be raised from seeds, which are sometimes produced.—*Bot. Cul.* 181. *Synonyme*: 1. *Gompholobium minus*.

| | | | | | | |
|---|---|---|---|---|---|---|
| confértā | . . | . | Violet | . 7, G. Ev. S. N. Holl. | . 1830 |
| minōr, 1 | . | . | Yellow | . 5, G. Ev. S. N. Holl. | . 1812 |
| scābrā | . . | . | Yellow | . 6, G. Ev. S. N. Holl. | . 1803 |
| sessiliflōrā | . . | . | Yellow | . 6, G. Ev. S. N. Holl. | . 1824 |

BUTCHER'S BROOM, see *Ruscus*.

BŪTĒĀ, *Roxburgh*. In compliment to John, Earl of Bute, a lover and patron of botany. *Linn.* 17, Or. 1, Nat. Or. *Leguminosæ*. This most splendid genus is rare in our collections, though easily grown, and not difficult to propagate. They grow best in loam and peat; and cuttings taken off at a joint, and planted singly in pots with their leaves on, will soon root, if not suffered to get damp, which should be continually guarded against. It is desirable to plunge them in a moist heat. The

flowers of *B. frondosa* and *superba* yield a beautiful dye, and the roots are capable of being made into strong rope.

| | | | | | | |
|---|---|---|---|---|---|---|
| frondōsā | . . | . | Scarlet | . | 8. Ev. S. E. Ind. | . . 1796 |
| parviflōrā | . . | . | Scarlet | . | 8. Ev. S. Coroman. | . 1818 |
| supérbā | . . | . | Scarlet | . | 8. Ev. S. E. Ind. | . . 1798 |

BŪTŌMŪS, *Linn.* The leaves of this plant are said to cause the mouths of cattle to bleed that crop it; hence the name from *bous*, ox, and *temno*, to cut. *Linn.* 9, Or. 3, Nat. Or. *Butomaceæ*. This genus contains that beautiful plant the flowering rush, a native of the margins of our rivers, ditches, &c.; both species are aquatic, and may be increased with little difficulty.

| | | | | | | |
|---|---|---|---|---|---|---|
| latifōlius | . . | . | White | . 6, H. Aq. P. Nepal | . . 1823 |
| umbellātus | . . | . | Pink | . 6, H. Aq. P. Britain | . . |

BUTTER AND EGGS, see *Narcissus*.
BUTTER BUR, see *Tussilāgō petasītes*.
BUTTERFLY PLANT, see *Oncidium Papilio*.
BUTTER-NUT, see *Jūglāns cinēreā*.
BUTTERWORT, see *Pinguicula*.
BUTTON FLOWER, see *Gōmphiā*.
BUTTON TREE, see *Conocārpus*.
BUTTON-WEED, see *Spermacōce*.
BUTTON-WOOD, see *Cephalānthus*.

BUXBAŌMIĀ, *Linn.* In memory of J. C. Buxbaum, a German botanist. *Linn.* 24, Or. 5, Nat. Or. *Musci*. A most singular minute plant, without apparent leaves, more like a species of fungus than a moss, found generally in summer in fir-woods, &c.—*aphglla*.

BŌXŪS, *Linn.* Supposed to have been taken from *pyknos*, dense; in reference to the wood. *Linn.* 21, Or. 4, Nat. Or. *Euphorbiaceæ*. This is an excellent genus of hardy evergreen shrubs; *B. balearicus* does much better however when it is slightly protected in severe weather. They thrive in most situations; and are propagated by suckers, or layers, without difficulty. The timber is very hard and smooth, and not apt to warp: it is used by the turner, engraver, mathematical instrument maker, comb, pipe, and flute maker; and the roots by the inlayer and cabinet maker. Wheels, skewers, pins, pegs for musical instruments, nutcrackers, button-moulds, weavers' shuttles, hollersticks, bump-sticks, rollers, rolling-pins, tops, screws, spoons, knife-handles, combs, &c., are made of it, as well as many other useful articles.

| | | | | | | |
|---|---|---|---|---|---|---|
| austrālis | . . | . | | G. Ev. S. N. Holl. | . 1820 |
| baleāricā | . | . | Yel. grn. | . 7, H. Ev. S. Minorca | . 1780 |
| chinénsis | . . | . | Yel. grn. | . 10, G. Ev. S. China | . 1802 |
| sempervīrens | . | . | Yel. grn. | . 4, H. Ev. S. England | . |
| angustifōliā | . | . | Yel. grn. | . 4, H. Ev. S. | |
| suffruticōsā | . | . | Yel. grn. | . | H. Ev. S. | |

BYBLIS, *Salisbury*. Byblis was the daughter of Miletus. *Linn.* 5, Or. 5, Nat. Or. *Droseraceæ*. A minute, very pretty aquatic; it should be planted in loamy soil, and immersed in water; seeds.

| | | | | | | |
|---|---|---|---|---|---|---|
| liniflōrā | . . | . | Blue | . 5, G. Aq. P. N. Holl. | . 1800 |

BYRSŌNIMĀ, *Richard*. Derived from *byrsa*, hide; useful for tanning. *Linn.* 10, Or. 3, Nat. Or. *Malpighiaceæ*. These are handsome stove plants, thriving exceedingly in a rich soil, or loam and peat mixed suits them. Cuttings of the ripe wood planted in sand, under a glass, in heat root freely. *Synonymes*: 1. *Malpighia altissima*. 2. *M. coriacea*. 3. *M. crassifolia*. 4. *M. lucida*. 5. *M. Moureila*. 6. *M. macrophylla*. 7. *M. pallida*. 8. *M. verbascifolia*. 9. *M. volubilis*.

| | | | | | | |
|---|---|---|---|---|---|---|
| altissimā, 1 | . | . | White | . 7, S. Ev. S. | Guiana | . 1820 |
| chrysophyllā | . | . | Yellow | . 8, S. Ev. S. | Orinoco | . 1823 |
| coriāceā, 2 | . | . | White | . 6, S. Ev. T. | Jamaica | . 1814 |
| crassifōliā, 3 | . | . | Yellow | . 7, S. Ev. T. | Guiana | . 1793 |
| laurifōliā | . | . | Yellow | . 7, S. Ev. T. | Cumana | . 1824 |
| lúcidā, 4 | . | . | Pink | . 7, S. Ev. S. | W. Ind. | . 1759 |
| Moureilā, 5 | . | . | Yellow | . 8, S. Ev. T. | S. Amer. | . 1823 |
| nervōsā, 6 | . | . | Yellow | . 7, S. Ev. S. | Brazil | . 1820 |
| pallidā, 7 | . | . | Pale | . | 8. S. Ev. S. | Cayenne | . 1820 |
| reticulātā | . | . | Pur. yel. | . 7, S. Ev. S. | Cayenne | . 1823 |
| spicātā | . | . | Yellow | . 8, S. Ev. S. | Antilles | . 1810 |
| verbascifōliā, 8 | . | . | Pa. red | . 7, S. Ev. S. | Guiana | . 1810 |
| volūbilis, 9 | . | . | Yellow | . 8, S. Ev. Tw. W. Ind. | . 1793 |

BYSSOCLĀDIŪM, *Agardh*. Compounded from *byssos*, fine flax, and *klados*, a branch; alluding to the fine branches. *Linn.* 24, Or. 7, Nat. Or. *Algeæ*. A singular production, said to grow in places overflowed with water, and on windows—*fenestrale*.

**BYTTNORŎŎN**, *Wild.* The word alludes to the throat of the corolla being closed by hairs, and derived from *byo*, to close, and *pogon*, beard. *Linn.* 14, Or. 1, Nat. Or. *Labiatæ.* The species are ornamental, and thrive best in a mixture of loam and peat; and cuttings put in sand or soil root readily.

| | | | | | |
|---|---|---|---|---|---|
| canariénsis | . . | Pa. pur. | 7, G. Ev. S. | Canaries | . 1714 |
| origanifólius | . . | Pa. pur. | 7, G. Ev. S. | Canaries | . 1815 |
| plumósus | . . | Pa. pur. | 6, G. Ev. S. | Canaries | . 1779 |
| punctātus | . . | Pa. pur. | 8, G. Ev. S. | Madeira | . 1775 |

**BYTTNĒRIĀ**, *Loeffling.* In memory of S. A. Buttner, a professor at Gottingen. *Linn.* 5, Or. 1, Nat. Or. *Sterculiaceæ.* The species are not very interesting; for culture, &c., see *Commersonia.* *Synonyme :* 1. *Commersonia dasyphylla.*

| | | | | | |
|---|---|---|---|---|---|
| dasyphylla. 1 | . | White. | . 6, G. Ev. S. V. D. L. | . 1780 |
| hermannifólĭa | . | | G. Ev. S. N. Holl. | . 1822 |
| microphylla | . | Wht. pur. | 8. Ev. S. S. Amer. | . 1816 |
| scābrā | . | Purple | . 7. S. Ev. S. W. Ind. | . 1793 |

*catalpæfóliā, cordātā, grandifóliā, herbācĕā.*

# C.

**CACALĪĀ**, *Linn.* Named from *kakos*, pernicious, and *lian*, exceedingly. *Linn.* 19, Or. 1, Nat. Or. *Compositæ.* A genus remarkable for the fleshy awkward-looking stems, and discoloured leaves of many of the species. They grow in a mixture of sandy loam, brick-rubbish, and decomposed dung well reduced; they require little water, especially when growing, and the pots must be well drained. Cuttings taken off, and dried for a few days to heal the wound, strike readily; when sufficiently struck, they should be potted off, using the same kind of soil recommended for old plants, and carefully watered. *Synonymes :* 1. *Kleinia tomentosa.* 2. *C. tomentosa.* 3. *C. pugioniformis.* 4. *C. macrophyllum.*

| | | | | | |
|---|---|---|---|---|---|
| albifrons | . | White | . 7, H. Her. P. | Austria | . 1739 |
| alpīnā | . . | Purple | . 7, H. Her. P. | Austria | . 1739 |
| Anteuphórbĭum | . | Yellow | . 2, G. Ev. S. | C. G. H. | . 1696 |
| appendiculāta | . | Yellow | . G. Ev. S. | Teneriffe | . 1815 |
| articulāta | . | Yellow | . 9, G. Ev. S. | C. G. H. | . 1775 |
| atriplicifóliā | . | 8, H. Her. P. | N. Amer. | . 1669 |
| bicŏlŏr | . . | Purple | . 7, S. De. S. | E. Ind. | . 1804 |
| carnósā | . | Yellow | . 6, G. Ev. S. | C. G. H. | . 1757 |
| coccīneā | . | Orange | . 6, H. A. | | . 1799 |
| cordifóliā | . | White | . 8, H. Tu. P. | Mexico | . 1823 |
| cylindrĭcā | . | Yellow | . 6, G. Ev. S. | C. G. H. | . 1818 |
| ficóĭdĕs | . | Yellow | . 8, G. Ev. S. | C. G. H. | . 1710 |
| hastāta | . | White | . 9, H. Her. P. | Siberia | . 1780 |
| Haworthīī, 1 | . | Yellow | . G. Ev. S. | C. G. H. | . 1795 |
| Kleinīā | . | Yellow | . 9, G. Ev. S. | Canaries | . 1732 |
| leucophýllā, 2 . | Pa. yel. | . 9, H. Her. P. | S. Eur. | . 1819 |
| longifóliā, 3 | . | Yellow | . G. Ev. S. | | . 1820 |
| ovālis | . | Yellow | . 7, S. Ev. S. | E. Ind. | . 1834 |
| papillāris | . | Yellow | . 8, G. Ev. S. | C. G. H. | . 1727 |
| radicāns | . | Yellow | . 7, G. Ev. Cr. | C. G. H. | . 1823 |
| reniformis | . | White | . 7, H. Her. P. | N. Amer. | . 1801 |
| rēpēns | . | Yellow | . 8, G. Ev. S. | C. G. H. | . 1759 |
| reticulāta | . | Yellow | . G. Ev. S. | Bourbon | . 1823 |
| rhombifóliā, 4. | Yellow | . 8, H. Her. P. | Siberia | . 1816 |
| sagittāta | . | Or. pur. | 8. A. | Java | . 1823 |
| scándens | . | Or. pur. | 4, G. Ev. Tw. C. G. H. | . 1814 |
| sonchifóliā | . | Pink | . 7, S. A. | E. Ind. | . 1768 |
| suavéŏlēns | . | White | . 8, H. Her. P. | N. Amer. | . 1752 |
| tomentósā | . | Yellow | . G. Ev. S. | C. G. H. | . 1795 |
| tuberósā | . | | . 8, H. Tu. P. | N. Amer. | . 1812 |

*peltātā, radulæfóliā, runcinātā.*

**CĀCHRỸS**, *Linn.* Not satisfactorily explained. *Linn.* 5, Or. 5, Nat. Or. *Umbelliferæ.* The species are uninteresting, and the culture of them is easy. *Synonyme :* 1. *Laserpitium ferulaceum—alāta* 1, *alpīnā, athamantoĭdēs, crētĭcā, Libanōtĭs, microcārpā, Morisōnĭ, odontālgĭcā, seselŏĭdēs, taūrĭcā.*

**CĀCTŬS**, *Linn.* A name used by Theophrastus to describe a spiny plant. *Linn.* 12, Or. 1, Nat. Or. *Cactaceæ.* This genus is commonly called the melon thistle. The species are very interesting in appearance, and variable in structure. They succeed best in sandy loam, mixed with brick and lime rubbish, and a little peat, or rotten dung, at all times carefully watered. Cuttings root readily if a little dried before planting. *Synonyme :* 1. *C. nobilis.*

| | | | | | |
|---|---|---|---|---|---|
| corrugātŭs | . . . | | S. Ev. S. | Chile | . 1824 |
| foliósŭs | . . . | | S. Ev. S. | Chile | . 1824 |
| redūctŭs, 1 | . . . | | S. Ev. S. | Mexico | . 1796 |
| senīlis | . . . | | S. Ev. S. | Mexico | . 1823 |

**CĀDĪĀ**, *Forskahl.* From the Arabic name *gadhy.* *Linn.* 10, Or. 1, Nat. Or. *Leguminosæ.* This rather curious species succeeds in light loamy soil, and cuttings root in sand, under a glass, in heat. *Synonyme :* 1. *C. varia.*

| | | | | | |
|---|---|---|---|---|---|
| purpūrĕā, 1 | . | Wht. pur. | 6, S. Ev. S. | Arabia | . 1775 |

**CADŪCŬS**, falling off soon.

**CÆLESTĪNĬĀ**, *Cassini.* Named from *cælestes*, celestial; alluding to the sky-blue colour of the flowers. *Linn.* 19, Or. 1, Nat. Or. *Compositæ.* Showy species of easy culture, common open soil suits them; seeds. *Synonymes :* 1. *Eupatorium cæruleum.* 2. *E. micranthum, Ageratum cælestinum.*

| | | | | | |
|---|---|---|---|---|---|
| ageratoĭdēs | . | Blue | . 8, G. Her. P. N. Spain | |
| cærūlĕā, 1 | . | Blue | . 7, F. Her. P. N. Amer. | . 1732 |
| micránthā, 2 | . | Blue | . 7, F. Ev. S. S. Amer. | . 1800 |

**CÆNÓPTĔRĬĀ**, *Bergius.* Derived from *kainos*, new, and *pteris*, a fern. *Linn.* 24, Or. 1, Nat. Or. *Polypodiaceæ.* Small interesting ferns; peat mixed with a little loam suits them, and they are chiefly increased by divisions. *Synonymes :* 1. *Asplenium laxum, Darea, Appendiculata.* 2. *Asplenium Odontites Darea, Odontites.*

| | | | | | |
|---|---|---|---|---|---|
| appendiculāta, 1 | . | Brown | . 7, G. Ev. S. N. Holl. | . 1822 |
| odontītes, 2 | . | Brown | . 7, G. Ev. S. N. Holl. | . 1822 |

**CÆSALPĪNĬĀ**, *Plumier.* In memory of Andreas Cæsalpinus, chief physician to Pope Clement VIII. *Linn.* 10, Or. 1, Nat. Or. *Leguminosæ.* This genus as a whole is of considerable importance, but the species in point of beauty have little to recommend them; they all grow well in sand, peat, and open loam mixed. *C. Sappan* yields the sappan wood of India. From the seeds of *C. oleosperma* an oil is expressed; and the Brazil-wood of commerce is obtained from the *C. Brasiliensis.*

| | | | | | |
|---|---|---|---|---|---|
| bahamēnsis | . | White | . 8. Ev. S. | Bahama | . 1820 |
| bĭjūgā | . | Yellow | . 8. Ev. T. | Jamaica | . 1770 |
| brasiliénsis | . | Orange | . 8. Ev. T. | Jamaica | . 1739 |
| Cacalacŏ | . | Yellow | . 8. Ev. S. | Mexico | . 1824 |
| cassioĭdēs | . | Yellow | . 8. Ev. S. | S. Amer. | . 1821 |
| chinénsis | . | Yellow | . 8. Ev. S. | E. Ind. | . 1820 |
| Crĭstā | . | Wht. yel. | . 8. Ev. T. | Jamaica | |
| enneaphýllā | . | Yellow | . 8. Ev. S. | E. Ind. | . 1816 |
| Gillieslī | . | | . 8. De. S. | Mendoza | . 1829 |
| mimosoĭdēs | . | Yellow | . 8. Ev. S. | E. Ind. | . 1906 |
| mucronātā | . | Yellow | . 8. Ev. S. | Brazil | . 1823 |
| Nūgā | . | Yellow | . 8. Ev. S. | E. Ind. | . 1801 |
| oleospérmā | . | Yellow | . 8. Ev. S. | E. Ind. | . 1820 |
| paniculāta | . | Yellow | . 8. Ev. S. | Malabar | . 1817 |
| procērā | . | Yellow | . 8. Ev. T. | Cuba | . 1824 |
| punctāta | . | Yellow | . 8. Ev. S. | Brazil | . 1820 |
| Sappan | . | Yellow | . 8. Ev. T. | E. Ind. | . 1773 |
| scándens | . | Yellow | . 8. Ev. Cl. | E. Ind. | . 1800 |
| suberósa | . | Yellow | . 8. Ev. S. | E. Ind. | . 1823 |
| tortuósā | . | Yellow | . 8. Ev. S. | Malabar | . 1820 |
| vesicāriā | . | Yellow | . 8. Ev. S. | E. Ind. | . 1820 |

**CÆSĪĀ**, *R. Brown.* In honour of Frederick Cæsius. *Linn.* 6, Or. 1, Nat. Or. *Tiliaceæ.* A showy species, sandy loam and peat suit it, and young plants are obtained from seeds.

| | | | | | |
|---|---|---|---|---|---|
| vittātā | . . . | Pa. blue. | . 7, G. Tu. P. N. S. W. | . 1816 |

**CÆSIOUS**, grey.

**CÆSPITOSE**, growing in little tufts.

**CÆSŪLĬĀ**, *Roxburgh.* From *cæsos*, beaten; appearing as if trampled upon. *Linn.* 19, Or. 1, Nat. Or. *Compositæ.* Not interesting, culture simple. *Synonyme :* 1. *Meyera orientalis—axillāris* 1.

**CAJĀNŬS**, *Dec.* From *catjang*, its name in Malabar. *Linn.* 17, Or. 1, Nat. Or. *Leguminosæ.* The species are highly useful for food in some places. They grow well in sandy loam; and increase from seed. The seed of *C. flavus* is much eaten by poor people, and negroes, and is esteemed a wholesome pulse. The plant is cultivated in Jamaica for feeding pigeons, whence its name; and in the island of Martinico, even the better sort of people hold it in estimation. *Synonymes :* 1. *Cytisus Pseudocajan.* 2. *C. Cajan.*

| bicolör, 1 | Yellow | 7, 8. Ev. S. E. Ind. | 1800 |
|---|---|---|---|
| flavus, 2 | Yellow | 7, 8. Ev. S. E. Ind. | 1687 |

**CAKILE**, *Tournefort.* An Arabic term for these plants. *Linn.* 15, Or. 1, Nat. Or *Cruciferæ.* Annual species of little beauty; cultivation simple. *Synonyme*: 1. *Maritima sinuatifolia.*

| ægyptiaca, 1 | Purple | 7, H. | A. Egypt | |
|---|---|---|---|---|
| americana | Purple | 7, H. | A. America | 1823 |
| maritima | Purple | 7, H. | A. Britain | |

**CALABASH**, see *Crescentia.*
**CALABA TREE**, see *Calophyllum Calaba.*
**CALADENIA**, *R. Brown.* From *kalos*, beautiful, and *aden*, a gland; in reference to the disc of the labellum being finely beset with glands. *Linn.* 20. Or. 1, Nat. Or. *Orchidaceæ.* A genus of pretty orchideous plants, growing well in a mixture composed of peat, loam, and sand in equal parts. They should be kept in a cool frame, and carefully watered, when not in a growing state; increased by dividing the roots.

| alata | | 6, F. Ter. N. Holl. | 1823 |
|---|---|---|---|
| alba | White | 7, F. Ter. N. Holl. | 1810 |
| cærulea | Blue | 7, F. Ter. N. Holl. | 1804 |
| carnea | Flesh | 7, F. Ter. N. Holl. | 1826 |
| testacea | | 7, F. Ter. N. Holl. | 1824 |

**CALADIUM**, *Ventenat.* Meaning not explained. *Linn.* 21, Or. 9, Nat. Or. *Araceæ.* The species of this genus are interesting on account of having singularly spotted stems, and pretty neat, often green foliage. Several grow best in water, and the whole grow well if planted in rich soil, and may be propagated from tubers. C. *seguinum* is a native of the W. Indies and S. America, and called the dumb-cane, and grows five or six feet high. This plant has the power, when chewed, of swelling the tongue, and destroying the power of speech. Dr. Hooker gives an account of a gardener who incautiously bit a piece of the dumb-cane, when his tongue swelled to such a degree, that he could not move it, he became utterly incapable of speaking, and was confined to the house for several days; he also adds, that it is said to impart an indelible stain to linen.—*Ex. Bot.* P. Brown states, that its stalk is employed to bring sugar to a good grain when it is too viscid, and cannot be made to granulate properly by the application of lime alone. *Synonymes*: 1. *Arum cucullatum* 2. *A. grandifolium.* 3. *C. seguinum maculatum.* 4. *C. grandifolium.* 5. *Arum virginicum.* 6. *A. xanthorhizum.*

| arborescens | White | 6, S. Ev. S. W. Ind. | 1759 |
|---|---|---|---|
| arboreum | White | 8. Ev. S. Cumana | 1820 |
| auritum | White | 8. Ev. S. America | 1739 |
| bicolör | White | 6, S. Her. P. Madeira | 1773 |
| cucullatum, 1 | Green | 3, S. Ev. S. China | 1826 |
| edule | White | 8. Her. P. Guiana | 1800 |
| esculentum | White | 8. Her. P. America | 1739 |
| fragrantissimum | Red | Parasite. Demerara | 1832 |
| grandifolium, 2 | White | 6, S. Ev. S. Caraccas | 1803 |
| helleborifolium | White | 6, S. Ev. S. Caraccas | 1796 |
| lacerum | White | 8. Ev. S. Caraccas | 1822 |
| lividum | Dingy | 9, S. Her. P. W. Ind. | 1828 |
| maculatum, 3 | Green | 3, S. Ev. S. S. Amer. | 1820 |
| nymphæifolium | White | 8. Her. P. E. Ind. | 1800 |
| odoratum | White | 8. Her. P. Pegu | 1818 |
| ovatum | White | 8. Her. P. E. Ind. | 1818 |
| pedatum | White | 8. Her. P. Brazil | 1824 |
| pinnatifidum | White | 8. Her. P. Caraccas | 1817 |
| pumilum | White | 8. Her. P. Nepal | 1820 |
| sagittifolium | White | 8. Her. P. W. Ind. | 1710 |
| scandens | White | 8. Her. P. Guinea | 1822 |
| seguinum | White | 8, S. Ev. S. America | 1759 |
| small. 4 | White | 4, S. Ev. Cl. | |
| tripartitum | White | 8. Ev. S. Caraccas | 1816 |
| virginicum, 5 | | 6, H. Her. P. Virginia | 1759 |
| viviparum | Green | 5, S. Her. P. E. Ind. | 1817 |
| xanthorhizum, 6 | White | 8. Ev. S. | 1822 |
| zaminifolium | Yellow | 8. Her. P. Brasil | |

**CALAMAGROSTIS**, *Adanson.* Taken from *calamos*, a reed, and *agrostis*, grass. *Linn.* 3, Or. 2, Nat. Or. *Gramineæ.* Mere weeds of simple culture. *Synonymes*: 1. *Arundo epigejos.* 2. *A. Pseudophragmites.* 3. *C. sylvatica.* 4. *Arundo Calamagrostis* 5. *Agrostis Calamagrostis.* 6. *Arundo stricta.* 7. *C. arundinacea.* 8. *Arundo humilis—acutiflora, confinis, effusa* 1, *glauca, Halleriana* 2, *Hostii* 3, *lanceolata* 4, *Langsdorffii, laxa, littorea, montana, speciosa* 5, *stricta* 6, *strigosa, sylvatica* 7, *tenella* 8, *varia.*

**CALAMARIÆ**, plants resembling reeds.

**CALAMIFORME**, reed or quill-shaped.
**CALAMINT**, see *Calamintha.*
**CALAMINTHA**, *Pursh.* From *kalos*, beautiful, and *mintha*, mint. *Linn.* 14, Or. 1, Nat. Or. *Labiatæ.* The species of this genus have little to recommend them; all that can be said is, that they are ornamental; they grow without difficulty in common loamy soil, and are increased by suckers. *Synonymes*: 1. *Thymus caroliniana.* 2. *Melissa grandiflora.* 3. *Nepeta marifolia.* 4. *Melissa Nepeta.* 5. *M. calamintha, Thymus Calamintha.*

| alba | White | 7, H. Her. P. Hungary | 1818 |
|---|---|---|---|
| caroliniana, 1 | Flame | 6, H. Her. P. Carolina | 1804 |
| cretica | Purple | 6, F. Ev. S. S. Eur. | 1596 |
| fruticosa | Purple | 8, F. Ev. S. Spain | 1752 |
| grandiflora, 2 | Red | 7, H. Her. P. Italy | 1596 |
| variegata | Red | 7, H. Her. P. | |
| marifolia, 3 | Purple | 6, H. Her. P. Spain | 1788 |
| Nepeta, 4 | Blue | 8, H. Her. P. England | |
| vulgaris, 5 | Red | 7, H. Her. P. England | |

**CALAMPELIS**, *D. Don.* Compounded from *kalos*, pretty, and *ampelis*, a vine, its habit of growth being to ramble like that plant. *Linn.* 14, Or. 2, Nat. Or. *Bignoniaceæ.* This is a species of great merit, capable of enduring the open air; when in full flower it has an elegant appearance; the situation for it is against a south wall, trained up a pillar, over a vase, &c. Any light loamy soil suits it; and young plants from cuttings are readily obtained. *Synonyme*: 1. *Eccremocarpus scaber.*

| scabra, 1 | Orange | 7, F. Ev. Cl. Chile | 1824 |
|---|---|---|---|

**CALAMUS**, *Linn.* Taken from *kalam*, signifying a reed, in Arabic. *Linn.* 6, Or. 1, Nat. Or. *Palmaceæ.* This is a fine genus, holding a middle station between the grasses and palms, with the habit of the former and inflorescence of the latter. They succeed best in a moist atmosphere in rich sandy loam, and are increased by seed. The resin called dragon's-blood is obtained by wounding C. *Draco.* C. *salacca* is cultivated for its fruit, which is about the size of a walnut, and covered with scales like those of a lizard; within these scales are two or three sweet yellow kernels.

| albus | | Palm. E. Ind. | 1812 |
|---|---|---|---|
| Draco | | Palm. E. Ind. | 1819 |
| niger | Green | Palm. E. Ind. | 1824 |
| rudentum | Green | Palm. E. Ind. | 1819 |
| verus | Green | Palm. Cochin China | 1824 |
| Zalacca | Green | Palm. E. Ind. | 1812 |

**CALANDRINIA**, *Humboldt and Bonpland.* In honour of J. L. Calandrini, a German botanist. *Linn.* 11, Or. 1, Nat. Or. *Portulacaceæ.* The species of this genus are very pretty, and grow well in loam and peat carefully incorporated; multiplied from seeds or cuttings. *Synonymes*: 1. *Talinum ciliatum.* 2. *T. paniculatum.*

| arenaria | Or. red | 7, H. Her. P. Valpar. | 1831 |
|---|---|---|---|
| ascendens | Purple | 8, H. Her. P. Brasil | |
| ciliata, 1 | Purple | 8, S. A. Chile | 1823 |
| discolor | Rose | 7, G. Her. P. Chile | 1834 |
| grandiflora | Purple | 7, S. Her. P. Chile | 1826 |
| paniculata, 2 | Purple | 7, S. Her. P. S. Amer. | 1816 |
| speciosa | Purple | 6, H. Her. P. California | 1831 |

**CALANTHE**, *R. Brown.* From *kalos*, beautiful, and *anthos*, a flower; literally a "pretty blossom." *Linn.* 20, Or. 1, Nat. Or. *Orchidaceæ.* This is a genus of very pretty plants when in flower. They require a light airy part of the house, otherwise the flowers will not open freely, neither will their colour be so good. The plants must never be saturated with water; in every other respect they require the same treatment as is recommended for the *Bletias.*

| bicolör | Yellow | G. Ter. Japan | 1837 |
|---|---|---|---|
| densiflora | Yelsh. | 9, S. Ter. E. Ind. | 1837 |
| discolor | White | G. Ter. Japan | 1837 |
| furcata | White | G. Ter. Luzon Is. | 1836 |
| Sieboldii | | S. Ter. E. Ind. | 1837 |
| veratrifolia | White | 4, S. Ter. Java | 1819 |

**CALATHEA**, *Meyer.* The name applies to the form of the stigma, and is derived from *kalathos*, a basket or cup. *Linn.* 1, Or. 1, Nat. Or. *Marantaceæ.* The plants of this genus are interesting and ornamental. C. *zebrina* is much admired on account of the stripes on the leaves, which resemble the marks on a zebra's back; whence the specific name. They grow well in the stove, in sandy peat; and are increased by divisions. *Synonyms:* 1. *Maranta zebrina.*

| | | | | | | |
|---|---|---|---|---|---|---|
| Allouyá | . . | White | . 9. | S. Her. | P. | Trinidad . 1824 |
| flavéscens | . . | Yellow | . 8. | S. Her. | P. | Brasil . 1832 |
| grandifólia | . . | Yellow | . 7. | S. Her. | P. | Rio Jan. . 1826 |
| longibracteátá | . . | Purple | . 4. | S. Her. | P. | Brasil . 1826 |
| maciláutá | . . | White | . 12. | S. Her. | P. | Rio Jan. . 1826 |
| orbiculátá | . . | Yellow | . 8. | S. Her. | P. | W. Ind. . 1830 |
| Róssii | . . | . . | . 4. | S. Her. | P. | Brasil . 1825 |
| villósá | . . | . . | . 4. | S. Her. | P. | Brasil . 1825 |
| violáceá | . . | Purple | . 7. | S. Her. | P. | Brasil . 1815 |
| zebrina, 1 | . . | Red yel. | . 8. | S. Her. | P. | Brasil . 1815 |

CALATHIAN VIOLET, see *Gentiána pneumonánthé.*
CALCARATE, spurred, having a spur.
CALCAREOUS, chalky.
CALCEIFORM, like a little shoe.
CALCEOLÁRIA, *Linn.* Named from *calceolus,* alluding to the form of the corolla. *Linn.* 2, Or. 1, Nat. Or. *Scrophulariaceæ.* This is a favourite genus, and contains some very showy species, from which an almost countless number of handsome hybrids have been raised and are raising. The herbaceous and shrubby kinds are chiefly cultivated. They thrive in a turfy loam, peat and sand mixed, or any kind of rich, open, sandy garden mould seems to suit them. The place most favourable to their successful growth is a pit or frame, where they must be potted and watered with judgment. Some cultivators turn them out in the flower-garden, where they make a brilliant display; others flower them in pots, with perfect success in the greenhouse; the latter way is generally preferred for the rare and superior kinds. Young cuttings planted in soil, under a glass, root freely; they are also increased from seed, which it is recommended to sow as soon as ripe. The annual species require to be sown in heat, and when up, potted off, and afterwards brought on for flowering in the greenhouse. *Synonymes:* 1. *Tinctoria.* 2. *Diffusa.* 3. *Floribunda.* 4. *Anomala, pendula.*

| | | | | | | |
|---|---|---|---|---|---|---|
| angustiflóra | . . | Yellow | . 6. | G. Ev. S. | | Peru . 1830 |
| arachnoídeá, 1 | . . | Purple | . 6. | G. Her. P. | | Chile . 1827 |
| ascéndens | . . | Yellow | . 7. | G. Ev. S. | | Cordill. 1826 |
| Atkinsoniá | . . | Yel. red | . 7. | G. Her. P. | | Hybrid. 1830 |
| bicolór, 2 | . . | Yellow | . 8. | G. Ev. S. | | Peru . 1829 |
| chiloénsis | . . | Yellow | . 8. | G. Ev. S. | | Chiloe . 1830 |
| connátá, 3 | . . | Yellow | . G. | R. | | Chile . 1824 |
| corymbósá | . . | Yellow | . 6. | G. Her. P. | | Chile . 1822 |
| crenatiflóra, 4 | . . | Yel. spot. | . 6. | F. Her. P. | | Chile . 1831 |
| Fothergillí | . . | Orange | . 4. | F. Her. P. | | Falk. Is. 1777 |
| Gellaniáná | . . | Ochre | . G. | Her. P. | | Hybrid 1830 |
| Herbertiáná | . . | Yellow | . 6. | G. Her. P. | | Chile . 1828 |
| parviflóra | . . | Yellow | . 4. | G. Ev. S. | | Valparaiso 1836 |
| biáns | . . | Yellow | . 6. | G. Her. Hybrid | | 1830 |
| Hopeáná | . . | Yellow | . 8. | F. Ev. S. | | Chile . 1822 |
| integrifóliá | . . | Yellow | . 8. | F. Ev. S. | | Chile . 1822 |
| angustifóliá | . . | Yellow | . 8. | G. Her. P. | | Chile . 1822 |
| viscosíssimá | . . | Yellow | . 8. | G. Ev. S. | | Chile . 1832 |
| Knyperaliénsis | . . | Yel. or. | . G. | Her. P. | | Hybrid 1834 |
| Martiáná | . . | Yel. spot. | . 7. | G. Her. P. | | Hybrid 1830 |
| mirábilis | . . | Purple | . G. | Her. P. | | Hybrid 1834 |
| Morrisoní | . . | Ochre | . 6. | G. Ev. S. | | Hybrid 1830 |
| péndulá | . . | Yel. spot. | . 7. | G. Her. P. | | Chile . 1831 |
| pinnátá | . . | Yellow | . 7. | G. | A. | Peru . 1773 |
| plantaginéá | . . | Yellow | . 8. | G. Her. P. | | Chile . 1827 |
| polifóliá | . . | Yellow | . 7. | G. Her. P. | | Chile . 1826 |
| polyánthá | . . | Yellow | . 5. | G. Her. P. | | Hybrid 1830 |
| purpúreá | . . | Purple | . 7. | G. Her. P. | | Chile . 1827 |
| élegáns | . . | Pa. pur. | . 6. | G. Her. P. | | Chile . 1832 |
| pictá | . . | Wht. pur. | . 6. | G. Her. P. | | Chile . 1832 |
| rugósá | . . | Yellow | . 8. | F. Ev. S. | | Chile . 1822 |
| scabiosæfóliá | . . | Yellow | . 5. | G. Her. P. | | Chile . 1822 |
| séssilis | . . | Yellow | . 9. | F. Ev. S. | | Valparaiso 1832 |
| thyrsiflóra | . . | Yellow | . 6. | G. Ev. S. | | Chile . 1827 |
| Wheelérí | . . | Purple | . 5. | F. Her. P. | | Hybrid 1831 |
| Youngíi | . . | Ochre | . 5. | G. Her. P. | | Hybrid 1830 |
| átrá | . . | Dark | . 5. | G. Her. P. | | Hybrid 1830 |
| dilectá | . . | Brown | . 5. | G. Her. P. | | Hybrid 1830 |
| pallidiór | . . | Pale | . 5. | G. Her. P. | | Hybrid 1830 |

CALDÁSIA, *Willd.* In memory of J. Caldas, a Bogotan naturalist. *Linn.* 5, Or. 1, Nat. Or. *Umbelliferæ.* This very handsome species thrives well in sandy peat mixed with a little loam; seeds. *Synonyme:* 1. *Bonplandia geminiflora.*

| | | | | | |
|---|---|---|---|---|---|
| heterophyllá | . . | Blue | . 7. S. | A. N. Spain | 1813 |

CÁLEA, *R. Brown.* Derived from *kalos,* beautiful; in allusion to the showy flowers. *Linn.* 19, Or. 1, Nat. Or. *Compositæ.* The species are very showy, and easily cultivated; a loamy soil mixed with peat is best; cuttings take without difficulty in soil or sand.

cordifóliá . . . . 8. Ev. S. Jamaica . 1822
jamaicénsis . . Purple . 6. S. Ev. S. W. Ind. . 1789
solidáginéá . . . . 8. Ev. S. Caraccas . 1817

CALEÁCTE, *R. Brown.* From *kalos,* beauty, and *akte,* sea-shore; the species being ornamental there. *Linn.* 19, Or. 1, Nat. Or. *Compositæ.* A showy species of easy culture and propagation. *Synonyme:* 1. *Solidago urticæfolia.*

urticæfóliá, 1 . Yellow . 7. S. Ev. S. Vera Cruz 1740

CÁLEÁNÁ, *R. Brown.* In honour of George Caley, some time superintendant of the Botanic Garden St. Vincent. *Linn.* 20, Or. 1, Nat. Or. *Orchidaceæ.* A genus of pretty plants, requiring the same treatment as the *Caladenias.*

majór . . . Gra. brn. . 6. G. Ter. N. S. W. . 1810
minór . . . Gra. brn. . 6. G. Ter. N. Holl. . 1822

CALÉNDULÁ, *Linn.* Named from *calendæ,* the first day of the month; there being flowers almost any month in the year. *Linn.* 19, Or. 4, Nat. Or. *Compositæ.* A genus of showy plants, among which is the old and well-known *C. officinalis,* or common marigold. This species was formerly used in soups and broths, but is now little regarded. The greenhouse species thrive well in loam and peat mixed; and cuttings root freely in sand, under a glass. The half-hardy annuals it is recommended to sow in a gentle heating hotbed, from whence they must be transplanted into the open ground; the hardy kinds merely require to be sown in the open borders. *Synonyme:* 1. *C. ægyptiaca.*

| | | | | | | |
|---|---|---|---|---|---|---|
| arboréscens | . | Yellow | . 12. | G. Ev. S. | C. G. H. | . 1774 |
| arvénsis | . | Yellow | . 6. | H. | A. | Europe . 1597 |
| chrysanthemifóliá | Yellow | . 4. | G. Ev. S. | | C. G. H. | . 1790 |
| dentátá | . | Yellow | . 5. | G. Ev. S. | C. G. H. | . 1790 |
| denticulátá | . | Yellow | . 12. | G. Ev. S. | Barbary | . 1821 |
| fruticósá | . | Yellow | . 6. | G. Ev. S. | C. G. H. | . 1752 |
| graminifóliá | . | Yellow | . 6. | G. Her. | P. | C. G. H. . 1731 |
| hybridá | . | White | . 6. | H. | A. | C. G. H. . 1752 |
| incáná | . | Yellow | . 7. | H. | A. | Barbary . 1796 |
| mexicáná | . | Yellow | . 8. | H. | A. | Mexico . 1829 |
| muricátá | . | Yellow | . 12. | G. Ev. S. | C. G. H. | |
| nudicaúlis | . | Wht. pur. | . 7. | H. | A. | C. G. H. . 1731 |
| officinális | . | Orange | . 6. | H. | A. | S. Eur. . 1573 |
| pléná | . | Orange | . 6. | H. | A. | |
| oppositifóliá | . | Yellow | . 8. | G. Ev. S. | C. G. H. | . 1774 |
| pluviális | . | White | . 6. | H. | A. | C. G. H. . 1699 |
| sánctá | . | Yellow | . 6. | H. | A. | Levant . 1731 |
| sícülá | . | Yellow | . 6. | H. | A. | Sicily . 1816 |
| stellátá | . | Yellow | . 7. | H. | A. | Barbary . 1795 |
| suffruticósá | . | Yellow | . 12. | G. Ev. S. | C. G. H. | . 1823 |
| Trágus | . | Wht. pur. | . 6. | G. Ev. S. | C. G. H. | . 1774 |
| fláccidá | . | Orange | . 6. | G. Ev. S. | C. G. H. | . 1774 |
| viscósá | . | Orange | . 8. | G. Ev. S. | C. G. H. | . 1790 |

CALÉPÍNÁ, *Adanson.* Not explained. *Linn.* 15, Or. 1, Nat. Or. *Cruciferæ.* A curious annual, of easy culture. *Synonyme:* 1. *Myagrum iberioides.*

corvini . . . . White . . 5. H. A. S. Eur. . . 1816

CALYCÍUM, *Acharius.* The name is expressive of the organs of reproduction; and derived from *kalypion,* a little cup. *Linn.* 24, Or. 8, Nat. Or. *Lichenes.* Curious white or grey productions appearing in patches on wood or boards exposed to the air—*aciculáré, æruginósá, cantharéllum, capitellátum, chrysocéphálum, claviculáré, cúrtum, débilé, ferrugínéum, hyperéllum, ínquínans, microcéphálá, róscidum, sphærocéphálum, stigonéllum, terebinéllum, tigilláré.*

CÁLLA, *Linn.* From *kalos,* beauty. *Linn.* 7, Or. 1, Nat. Or. *Araceæ.* These species are showy and worth cultivation, they grow freely in any rich soil; and increase by seeds, or divisions. *Synonyme:* 1. *Dracontium pertusum.*

aromáticá . . . White . . 7. G. Her. P. China . 1818
occúltá . . . White . . 5. G. Her. P. China . 1817
palústris . . . White . . 7. G. Aq. P. N. Amer. . 1768
pertúsá, 1 . . . White . . 5. G. Ev. Cr. W. Ind. . 1752

CALLICÁRPÁ, *Linn.* Named in reference to the pretty berries; from *kalos,* beautiful, and *karpos,* fruit. *Linn.* 4, Or. 1, Nat. Or. *Verbenaceæ.* The species of this genus are handsome, and succeed well in loam and peat mixed. Cuttings strike without difficulty in sand or soil. The bark of *C. Lantana* has a peculiar subaromatic and slightly bitter taste, and is chewed by the Cingalese, when they cannot obtain *betle* leaves; the Malays reckon the plant diuretic.—*Lind. Nat. System of Botany.* *Synonyme:* 1. *C. tomentosa.*

| | | | | | | |
|---|---|---|---|---|---|---|
| americāna | . . | Red | . 6, | G. De. S. | N. Amer. | . 1724 |
| arbórea | . . | Purple | . 8, | S. Ev. T. | E. Ind. | . 1820 |
| cāna, 1 | . . | Purple | . 8, | S. Ev. S. | E. Ind. | . 1799 |
| ferruginēā | . . | Blue | . 6, | S. Ev. S. | Jamaica | . 1794 |
| inclnā | . . | Red | . 7, | S. Ev. S. | E. Ind. | . 1800 |
| lanāta | . . | Purple | . 6, | S. Ev. S. | E. Ind. | . 1788 |
| lanceolārā | . . | Purple | . 7, | S. Ev. S. | E. Ind. | . 1822 |
| longifólīā | . . | White | . 4, | S. Ev. S. | China | . 1825 |
| macrophyllā | | Pink | | S. Ev. S. | India | . 1808 |
| purpúrea | . . | Purple | . 7, | S. Ev. S. | E. Ind. | . 1822 |
| reticulātā | . . | Red | . 7, | S. Ev. S. | Jamaica | . 1820 |
| rubellā | . . | Red | . 8, | S. Ev. S. | China | . 1822 |

CALLICHROÍ, *Fischer and Meyer.* From *kalos*, beautiful, and *chros*, colour; in reference to the colour of its flowers. Linn. 19, Or. 2, Nat. Or. *Compositæ.* This little plant is well entitled to a place in every flower-border, as well on account of its dwarf and slender habit as of its rich golden-coloured flowers. It grows well in common garden soil, and is increased from seed, which should be reared on a hotbed.

| | | | | | | |
|---|---|---|---|---|---|---|
| platyglóssā | . . | Yellow | . 10, | H. | A. California | 1835 |

CALLICŌMĀ, *Bot. Rep.* The name is expressive of the pretty bunches of yellow flowers; and is derived from *kalos*, beautiful, and *kome*, hair. Linn. 11, Or. 2, Nat. Or. *Cunoniaceæ.* A very showy plant, cultivated with ease in fibrous peat and sand; and cuttings root readily in sand, under a glass.

| | | | | | | |
|---|---|---|---|---|---|---|
| serratifólīā | . . | Yellow | . 6, | G. Ev. S. | N. S. W. | . 1793 |

CALLIGŌNŪM, *Linn.* Derived from *kalos*, beautiful, and *gonum*, a joint; there being joints instead of leaves. Linn. 11, Or. 4, Nat. Or. *Polygonaceæ.* This species is showy, and requires sandy open loam to grow it well; cuttings.

| | | | | | | |
|---|---|---|---|---|---|---|
| Pallásū | . . . | Grn. wht. | 8, H. | Ev. S. | Casp. Sea . | 1780 |

CALLIŌPEĀ, *D. Don.* So called from *Calliope*, one of the Muses. Linn. 19, Or. 1, Nat. Or. *Compositæ.* This is a pretty dwarf genus, succeeding in any loamy soil, and increased by divisions. Synonyme 1. *Leontodon aureum.*

| | | | | | | |
|---|---|---|---|---|---|---|
| aúrea | . . . | Yellow | . 6, H. Her. | P. Italy | . | 1769 |

CALLIŌPSĪ, *Reich.* Derived from *kallistos*, beautiful, and *opsis*, eye; in allusion to the beautiful bright eye of the flower. Linn. 19, Or. 2, Nat. Or. *Compositæ.* The flowers of these plants are extremely pretty, and well suited for the flower-garden. The perennial kinds grow in any loamy soil, and the annuals merely require sowing; the tender species should be sown in a slight hotbed, and afterwards transplanted. *Synonymes:* 1. *Coreopsis tinctoria.* 2. *Coreopsis palmata.* 3. *Coreopsis rosea.*

| | | | | | | |
|---|---|---|---|---|---|---|
| Atkinsoniānā | . | Yel. brn. | . | H. | A. Columbia | . 1826 |
| bicólor, 1 | . . | Yellow | . 6, | H. | A. Arkansas | . 1822 |
| palmātā, 2 | . . | Yellow | . 6, | H. Her. | P. Louisiana | . 1823 |
| rósēā, 3 | . . | Red | . 7, | H. Her. | P. N. Carna | 1778 |

CALLIPRŌRĀ, *Lindley.* Derived from *kalos*, pretty, and *prora*, a front; in allusion to its pretty appearance. Linn. 6, Or. 1, Nat. Or. *Liliaceæ.* This is a very handsome hardy bulbous species, succeeding well in a shaded peat border, and increased freely from offsets.

| | | | | | | |
|---|---|---|---|---|---|---|
| lútēā | . . . | Yellow | . 8, | H. Bu. | P. California | . 1831 |

CALLISACĪ, *Fischer.* The name alludes to the seeds; and is taken from *kalos*, beautiful, and *sakos*, a buckler. Linn. 5, Or. 2, Nat. Or. *Umbelliferæ.* A species of little beauty, and easily cultivated—*dahúricā.*

CALLISĪĀ, *Linn.* This is a pretty species, hence the propriety of the name from *kalos*, pretty. Linn. 3, Or. 11, Nat. Or. *Liliaceæ.* This plant succeeds in sandy fibrous peat, and is increased by divisions.

| | | | | | | |
|---|---|---|---|---|---|---|
| répens | . . . | Blue | . 6, | S. Tu. | P. W. Ind. | . 1776 |

CALLISTĀCHYS, *Ventenat.* The name is expressive of the fine spikes of flowers; and is derived from *kalos*, beautiful, and *stachys*, a spike. Linn. 10, Or. 1, Nat. Or. *Leguminosæ.* Beautiful shrubs, of easy and free growth; sandy peat and loam is the best soil for them; and young plants are readily obtained from cuttings, in sand.

| | | | | | | |
|---|---|---|---|---|---|---|
| cuneātā | . . . | Yellow | . 7, | G. Ev. S. | N. Holl. | . 1824 |
| lanceolātā | . . | Yellow | . 6, | G. Ev. S. | N. Holl. | . 1815 |
| linariæfólīā | . | Yellow | . 6, | G. Ev. S. | N. Holl. | . 1824 |
| ovātā | . . . | Yellow | . 6, | G. Ev. S. | N. Holl. | . 1815 |
| retānā | . . . | Yellow | . 7, | S. Ev. S. | N. Holl. | . 1830 |

CALLISTEMMĀ, *R. Brown.* The name refers to the beautiful flowers; and is derived from *kallistos*, prettiest, and *stemma*, a crown. Linn. 19, Or. 2, Nat. Or. *Compositæ.* The species of this genus are well known in the garden for the beauty of their flowers, and the little trouble required to bring them to perfection. The seeds should be sown in a gentle hotbed in spring, and the plants removed to the flower borders, or they may be sown as soon as the weather permits in the open air, where they are wished to flower. *Synonymes:* 1. *Aster chinensis.* 2. *A. indicus.*

| | | | | | | |
|---|---|---|---|---|---|---|
| horténsā, 1 | . . | Blue | . 7, | H. | A. China | . 1731 |
| álbūm | . . | White | . 7, | H. | A. China | . 1731 |
| rubrūm | . . | Red | . 7, | H. | A. China | . 1731 |
| variegātūm | . . | Varieg. | . 7, | H. | A. China | . 1731 |
| múltiplex | . | Varieg. | . 7, | H. | A. China | . 1731 |
| brachyánthūm | . | Blue | . 7, | H. | A. China | . 1731 |
| indicūm, 2 | . . | Blue | . 7, | H. | A. E. Ind. | . 1820 |

CALLISTĒMŌN, *R. Brown.* The name refers to the beautiful scarlet colour of the stamens of some species; and is derived from *kallistos*, beautiful, and *stemon*, a stamen. Linn. 12, Or. 1, Nat. Or. *Leguminosæ.* These are species of great beauty, and should be cultivated in all conservatory or greenhouse collections; particularly those with scarlet or crimson flowers. Loam, peat, and sand, is the best soil for them; and ripened cuttings strike readily in sand, or sandy loam, under a glass: they are also sometimes increased from seeds. *Synonymes:* 1. *Metrosideros citrinus.* 2. *M. lophanthus.* 3. *M. rugulosus.* 4. *M. salignus.* 5. *M. speciosus.* 6. *M. viminalis.*

| | | | | | | |
|---|---|---|---|---|---|---|
| formósūs | . . | | | G. Ev. S. | N. Holl. | . 1824 |
| lanceolātūs, 1 | . | Crimson | . 6, | G. Ev. S. | N. S. W. | . 1788 |
| leptostáchyūs | . | Green | . 6, | G. Ev. S. | N. Holl. | . 1820 |
| linearifólīūs | . | Red | . 5, | G. Ev. S. | N. S. W. | . 1820 |
| lineáris | . . | Scarlet | . 6, | G. Ev. S. | N. S. W. | . 1788 |
| lophanthūs, 2 | . | Purple | . 6, | G. Ev. S. | N. S. W. | . 1800 |
| marginātūs | . . | | | G. Ev. S. | N. S. W. | . 1816 |
| microphyllūs | . | | | G. Ev. S. | N. Holl. | . 1824 |
| microstáchyūm | . | Red | . 3, | G. Ev. S. | N. Holl. | . 1836 |
| pinifólīūs | . . | Green | . 6, | G. Ev. S. | N. S. W. | . |
| púngens | . . | | | 5, | G. Ev. S. | N. S. W. | . 1827 |
| rígidūs | . . | Crimson | . 4, | G. Ev. S. | N. Holl. | . 1800 |
| rugulósūs, 3 | . | Pink | . 4, | G. Ev. S. | N. S. W. | . 1821 |
| salígnūs, 4 | . . | | | 6, | G. Ev. S. | N. Holl. | . 1788 |
| scábēr | . . | | | 7, | G. Ev. S. | N. Holl. | . 1820 |
| sempérflórens | . | Crimson | . 4, | G. Ev. S. | N. S. W. | . 1818 |
| speciōsūs, 5 | . | Crimson | . 4, | G. Ev. S. | N. S. W. | . 1822 |
| viminālis, 6 | . | Red | . 4, | G. Ev. S. | N. S. W. | . 1800 |
| viridiflórūs | . . | Green | . 7, | G. Ev. S. | N. Holl. | . 1818 |

CALLITRĪCHĒ, *Wild.* Named from *kalos*, beautiful, and *thrix*, hair; applied by Pliny to a plant, which had the colour of beautiful hair. Linn. 1, Or. 2, Nat. Or. *Callitrichaceæ.* Plants not worth cultivating; the seeds do well thrown into a pond. *Synonymes:* 1. *C. aquatica—autumnalis, pedunculata, verna* 1, *V. aquatica.*

CALLITRIS, *Ventenat.* From *kalos*, beautiful; in allusion to its beautiful appearance. Linn. 21, Or. 9, Nat. Or. *Coniferæ.* This is a beautiful species, growing twenty or thirty feet high; like the rest of the family, it delights in sandy loam; and increases from seed. *Synonymes:* 1. *Thuja articulala.* 2. *Cupressus triquetra.*

| | | | | | | |
|---|---|---|---|---|---|---|
| cupressifórmis | . | | | G. Ev. T. | N. Holl. | . 1826 |
| quadriválvis, 1 | . | Apetal | . 2, | G. Ev. T. | Barbary | . 1815 |
| triquétrā, 2 | . | Apetal | . 4, | G. Ev. T. | C. G. H. | . 1820 |

CALLOSE, callous, hardened.

CALLOUSLY-GLANDULAR, having hardened glands.

CALLOUSLY-SERRATED, having hardened serratures.

CALOCERĀ, *Fries.* *Kalos*, beautiful, and *keros*, a horn; in allusion to the divisions of the plants. Linn. 24, Or. 9, Nat. Or. *Fungi.* These are remarkable productions found under the bark of various trees —*córnēā, tuberósā.*

CALOCHILUS, *Brown.* From *kalos*, beautiful, and *cheilos*, a lip. Linn. 20, Or. 1, Nat. Or. *Orchidaceæ.* A genus of bulbous-rooted plants, very showy when in flower. The sepals are yellowish-green, and the lip purple, covered with rich brown hairs. They will grow in the greenhouse; but they do best in the stove, treated as the *Bletias.*

| | | | | | | |
|---|---|---|---|---|---|---|
| campéstris | . . | Grn. brn. | . | G. Ter. | N. Holl. | . 1824 |
| paludósūs | . . | Brown | . | G. Ter. | N. Holl. | . 1823 |

CALOCHŌRTŪS, *Pursh.* From *kalos*, handsome, and *chortus*, grass. Linn. 6, Or. 3, Nat. Or. *Liliaceæ.*

This is a splendid genus of plants. The soil most suitable for them is sandy peat, and a little loam; if the plants are grown in pots, they must be carefully drained, and the soil only watered as the growth happens to require it. In the winter they must be treated like other frame bulbs. When the roots recommence growing, shift them into new soil. They increase from offsets.

| | | | | |
|---|---|---|---|---|
| alăgăns . . . | White . | 6, F. Bu. P. | Columbia | . 1826 |
| lŭtĕūs . . . | Yel. spot. | 9, F. Bu. P. | California | . 1831 |
| macrocărpūs . | Purple . | 8, F. Bu. P. | Columbia | . 1826 |
| nĭtĭdūs . . . | Purple . | 8, F. Bu. P. | Columbia | . 1826 |
| splĕndĕns . . | Wht. spot. | 8, F. Bu. P. | California | . 1832 |
| venŭstŭs . . . | Lilac . | 8, F. Bu. P. | California | . 1836 |

CALODĔNDRON, *Thunberg.* Derived from *kalos,* beautiful, and *dendron,* a tree; in reference to the beauty of this plant. *Linn.* 5, Or. 1, Nat. Or. *Rutaceæ.* A tall-growing ornamental tree, succeeding in loamy soil; and increases from cuttings.

| | | | |
|---|---|---|---|
| capĕnsĕ . . . | Pink . . | G. Ev. T. C. G. H. | . 1789 |

CALŎPHĂCĂ, *Fischer.* Taken from *kalos,* beautiful, and *phake,* lentil. *Linn.* 17, Or. 4, Nat. Or. *Leguminosæ.* An ornamental species; it grows best in sandy loam; and is multiplied by seeds. *Synonyme:* 1. *Cytisus niger, pinnatus, Wolgaricus.*

| | | | |
|---|---|---|---|
| Wolgărĭcă, 1 . | Yellow . | 5, H. De. S. Siberia . | 1786 |

CALŎPHĂNĔS, *D. Don.* Taken from *kalos,* beautiful, and *phaino,* to appear; alluding to the flowers. *Linn.* 14, Or. 2, Nat. Or. *Acanthaceæ.* This is an interesting addition to our hardy border flowers; it succeeds best in loam and peat; and is readily increased by parting the roots. *Synonyme:* 1. *Ruellia oblongifolia.*

| | | | |
|---|---|---|---|
| oblongĭfŏlĭă . . | Blue . . | 8, H. Her. P. Carolina . | 1832 |

CALOPHYLLŬM, *Linn.* Expressive of the beautiful leaf; and taken from *kalos,* beautiful, and *phyllon,* a leaf. *Linn.* 13, Or. 1, Nat. Or. *Guttiferæ.* Large-growing timber trees of considerable value. Sandy loam suits them best; and young plants are easily procured from cuttings. *Synonyme:* 1. *Calaba.*

| | | | |
|---|---|---|---|
| Calăba . . . | White . | 8. Ev. T. India . . | 1780 |
| Inophyllum . | White . | 8. Ev. T. E. Ind. . | 1793 |
| spŭrĭūm, 1 . . | White . | 8. Ev. T. Malabar . | 1800 |
| Tacamahăcă . | White . | 8. Ev. T. Bourbon . | 1822 |

CALOPŎGŎN, *R. Brown.* From *kalos,* beautiful, and *pogon,* a beard; the lip is beautifully fringed. *Linn.* 20, Or. 1, Nat. Or. *Orchideæ.* This is a beautiful greenhouse plant, producing a few purple flowers on a stem, from twelve to eighteen inches high. It will grow well in peat and loam, and may be increased by dividing the tuberous roots. *Synonyme:* 1. *Limodorum tuberosum.*

| | | | |
|---|---|---|---|
| pulchĕllŭs . . | Purple . | 7, G. Ter. N. Amer. . | 1771 |

CALOSTĔMMĂ, *R. Brown.* From *kalos,* beautiful, and *stemma,* a crown; alluding to the flowers. *Linn.* 6, Or. 1, Nat. Or. *Amaryllideæ.* These are handsome bulbous species, of tolerably easy culture; they thrive best in sandy loam and a little peat mixed; and are increased from offsets.

| | | | |
|---|---|---|---|
| albŭm . . . | White . | 6, G. Bu. P. N. Holl. . | 1824 |
| lutĕūm . . . | Yellow . | 11, G. Bu. P. N. Holl. . | 1819 |
| purpŭrĕūm . . | Purple . | 11, G. Bu. P. N. Holl. . | 1819 |

CALOTHĂMNŬS, *Labillardière.* So called from *kalos,* beautiful, and *thamnos,* a shrub. *Linn.* 18, Or. 2, Nat. Or. *Myrtaceæ.* Beautiful shrubs; they succeed well in sandy peat; and cuttings root freely in sand, or sandy mould, under a glass.

| | | | |
|---|---|---|---|
| clavătă . . . | Scarlet . | 7, G. Ev. S. N. Holl. . | 1824 |
| grăcĭlĭs . . . | Scarlet . | 7, G. Ev. S. N. Holl. . | 1803 |
| quadrĭfĭdă . . | Scarlet . | 7, G. Ev. S. N. Holl. . | 1803 |
| villŏsă . . . | Scarlet . | 7, G. Ev. S. N. Holl. . | 1803 |

CALŎTHRĬX, *Agardh.* The name applies to the beauty of the filaments; and is taken fram *kalos,* beautiful, and *thrix,* a hair. *Linn.* 24, Or. 7, Nat. Or. *Algæ.* Minute, curious marine productions, found in little patches sometimes floating—*confervicolor, distorta, fasciculata, landta, L. fuscescens, luteola, mirabilis, nivea, scopulorum.*

CALŎTĬS, *R. Brown.* A derivation from *kalos,* beautiful, and *ous,* an ear; alluding to the paleæ of the pappus. *Linn.* 19, Or. 2, Nat. Or. *Compositæ.* This species has wedge-shaped leaves, and is very

pretty; it is multiplied by divisions, and grown successfully in any common soil.

| | | | | |
|---|---|---|---|---|
| cunĕĭfŏlĭă . . . | Blue . | 6, G. Her. P. N. Holl. | | . 1819 |

CALŎTRŎPĬS, *R. Brown.* Taken from *kalos,* beautiful, and *tropis,* a keel; alluding to the keel of the flower. *Linn.* 5, Or. 2, Nat. Or. *Asclepiadaceæ.* Any rich soil suits these beautiful species, young plants of which are readily obtained from cuttings, or seeds. *Synonyme:* 1. *Asclepias gigantea.*

| | | | |
|---|---|---|---|
| gigantĕă, 1 . . | White . | 8, G. Ev. S. E. Ind. . . | 1690 |
| procĕră . . . | White . | 8, G. Ev. S. Persia . . | 1714 |

CĂLTHĂ, *Linn.* A syncope of *kalathos,* a goblet; in allusion to the likeness of the form of the corolla to a golden cup. *Linn.* 13, Or. 1, Nat. Or. *Ranunculaceæ.* The species are showy, and do best in a moist situation, but will grow and flower in a common border. Seeds, or divisions. *Synonyme:* 1. *Ficarioides.*

| | | | |
|---|---|---|---|
| asarĭfŏlĭă . . . | Yellow . | 4, H. Her. P. Unilas . | 1824 |
| bĭflŏră . . . | White . | 6, H. Her. P. N. Amer. | 1827 |
| flabellĭfŏlĭă . . | Yellow . | 4, H. Her. P. N. Amer. | 1818 |
| leptosĕpălă . . | Yellow . | 5, H. Her. P. N. Amer. | 1827 |
| mĭnŏr . . . | Yellow . | 4, H. Her. P. Britain . | |
| nătăns . . . | Yellow . | 5, H. Her. P. Siberia . | 1816 |
| palŭstrĭs . . . | Yellow . | 4, H. Her. P. Britain . | |
| flore-plĕnŏ . . | Yellow . | 4, H. Her. P. | |
| parnassĭfŏlĭă . . | Yellow . | 6, H. Her. P. N. Amer. . | 1815 |
| radĭcăns . . . | Yellow . | 4, H. Her. P. Scotland . | |

CALTROPS, see *Tribulus.*

CALYCĂNTHŬS, *Linn.* From *kalyx,* a calyx, and *anthos,* a flower; in allusion to the colour of the calyx. *Linn.* 12, Or. 3, Nat. Or. *Calycanthaceæ.* This is a valuable genus, with delightful fragrant flowers. They succeed in open loamy soil, and multiply by layers.

| | | | |
|---|---|---|---|
| fĕrtĭlĭs . . . | Brown . | 6, H. De. S. Carolina . | 1726 |
| flŏrĭdŭs . . . | Brown . | 6, H. De. S. Carolina . | 1726 |
| laevĭgătŭs . . | Brown . | 6, H. De. S. N. Amer. . | 1806 |
| oblongĭfŏlĭŭs . | Brown . | 5, H. De. S. N. Amer. . | 1890 |
| pennsylvănĭcŭs . | Brown . | 5, H. De. S. Pennsyl. . | 1820 |

CALYCIFORM, formed like a calyx.

CALYCINE, of or belonging to the calyx.

CALYCULATE, } having bracteas resembling an ex-
CALYCULATED, } ternal, or additional calyx.

CALYPSO, *Salisbury.* Said to be from *kalypto,* to conceal; in allusion to the habitat of the plant. *Linn.* 20, Or. 1, Nat. Or. *Orchideæ.* This is a small, but extremely pretty species, well deserving a place in every garden. It grows best in sandy loam and peat, in a frame or warm border, by a south wall, and is increased by offsets from the bulbs. *Synonyme:* 1. *C. americana.*

| | | | |
|---|---|---|---|
| borĕālĭs . . . | Ro. brn. | 1, F. Ter. N. Amer. . | 1820 |

CALYPTRĂ, applied to the body which covers the theca in mosses; anything in the shape of an extinguisher.

CALYPTRĂNTHĔS, *Swartz.* From *kalyptra,* a veil, and *anthos,* a flower; in allusion to the peculiar manner in which the united segments of the calyx fall off. *Linn.* 12, Or. 1, Nat. Or. *Myrtaceæ.* Strong-growing ornamental timber trees, of easy management. Sandy peat suits them; and young plants are obtained by layering the branches.

| | | | |
|---|---|---|---|
| Chytracŏlĭă . . | White . | 4, S. Ev. T. Jamaica . | 1778 |
| Zuzygĭŭm . . | White . | 6, S. Ev. T. W. Ind. . | 1778 |

CALYPTRĬŎN, *Gingins.* Derived from *kalyptra,* a veil, and *ion,* a violet. *Linn.* 5, Or. 1, Nat. Or. *Violaceæ.* Pretty species: peat and loam suits it; and young plants are procured from seeds. *Synonyme:* 1. *Viola Hybanthus, Ionidium Hybanthus.*

| | | | |
|---|---|---|---|
| Aublĕtĭĭ, 1 . . | Cream . | 8. Ev. Cl. Guiana . . | 1823 |

CALYSTĔGĬĂ, *Loureiro.* Named from *kalyx,* calyx, and *stega,* a covering. *Linn.* 5, Or. 1, Nat. Or. *Convolvulaceæ.* Only a few of these species are interesting. They all succeed in common loamy soil, and are increased by divisions. *Synonymes:* 1. *Convolvulus sepium.* 2. *Convolvulus spithamæus.* 3. *Convolvulus stans.*

| | | | |
|---|---|---|---|
| dahŭrĭcă . . . | Pink . | 7, H. De. Tr. Dahuria . | 1823 |
| marginătă . . | Pink . | 5, H. De. Tr. N. Holl. . | 1834 |
| sĕpĭŭm, 1 . . | Wht. grn. | 9, H. De. Tw. Australia . | 1837 |
| incarnătă . . | Red . | 7, H. De. Tw. N. Amer. | |
| Soldanĕllă . . | Flame . | 7, H. De. Tr. Britain . | |

| | | | | | | |
|---|---|---|---|---|---|---|
| spithamæa | . . | White | . 7, H. De. | Tw. | N. Amer. | 1796 |
| sylvéstris, 2 | . | White | . 7, H. De. | Tw. | Hungary | 1815 |
| tomentosa, 3 | . | . 6, H. De. | Tr. | N. Amer. | 1818 |

*Catesbeàná, paradóxá, reniförmis.*

CALYTHRIX, *Labillardière.* So called from *kalyx*, a calyx, and *thrix*, hair. *Linn.* 12, Or. 1, Nat. Or. *Myrtaceæ.* These are handsome evergreens, of easy culture; sandy peat and loam mixed suits them; and cuttings take readily in sand, under a glass.

| | | | | | |
|---|---|---|---|---|---|
| ericoídés | . . | White | . G. Ev. 8. | N. Holl. | 1824 |
| floribúndá | . . | White | . G. Ev. 8. | N. Holl. | 1820 |
| glàbrá | . . | White | . 5, G. Ev. 8. | N. Holl. | 1818 |
| pubéscéns | . . | White | . G. Ev. 8. | N. Holl. | 1824 |
| scàbrá | . . | White | . 6, G. Ev. 8. | S. Austra. | 1824 |

CAMELINA, *Crantz.* From *chamai*, on the ground, and *linon*, flax; in allusion to its dwarf habit. *Linn.* 15, Or. 1, Nat. Or. *Cruciferæ.* The species have but little beauty, and require to be sown in the open border. *C. sativa* is cultivated in some parts of Europe for the sake of the oil which is obtained from the seeds. *Synonymes*: 1. *Myagrum sativum.* 2. *Cheiranthus sylvestris.*

| | | | | | |
|---|---|---|---|---|---|
| sativa, 1 | . . | Yellow | . 5, H. | A. Britain | . . |
| pilósá, 2 | . . | Yellow | . 5, H. | A. Britain | . . |
| glabràtá | . . | Yellow | . 5, H. | A. | |

*austriàcá, barbarexfòliá, dentátá, microcárpá.*

CÁLYX, the outer envelope of a flower.

CAMÁSSIA, *Lindley.* From *quamass*, or *camass*, its native name in N. America. *Linn.* 6, Or. 1, Nat. Or. *Asphodeleæ.* The flowers of this beautiful plant are nearly two inches in diameter. Dr. Lindley scarcely remembers to have ever seen a more strikingly handsome bulbous plant. It requires a peat border, under a north wall; increased by seeds.

| | | | | | |
|---|---|---|---|---|---|
| esculéntá | . . | Purple | . 7, H. Bu. P. | Columbia | . 1827 |

CAMELLIA, *Ker.* Named in honour of George Joseph Kamel, or Camellus, a Moravian Jesuit, and traveller in Asia. *Linn.* 16, Or. 8, Nat. Or. *Ternstræmiaceæ.* "All the species of Camellia are universally admired by every collector of plants, on account of their beautiful rose-like flowers, and elegant dark-green shining laurel-like leaves. They are very hardy greenhouse plants and are easy of culture, requiring only to be sheltered from severe frost. The best soil for them is an equal quantity of good sandy loam and peat. Messrs. Loddiges find that light loam alone answers as well, or better; and in the Comte de Vande's gardens at Bayswater, rotten dung is mixed with loam and peat. The pots should be well drained with pieces of potsherds, that they may not get soddened with too much wet, as nothing injures them more than over-watering, particularly when they are not·in a growing state. When growing freely, they can scarcely have too much, and they should be watered over the leaves with a fine rose-pot; they are readily increased by cuttings, or inarching on the common kinds. The cuttings should be taken off at a joint as soon as they are ripened, and planted in sand, under a glass, where they will soon strike root; when this is the case they should be planted singly in small pots, and set in a close frame, and they must be afterwards hardened to the air by degrees."—*Sweet.* The season most proper to give the Camellias a general potting is February and March. After this, put them into a peach-house or vinery, or a warm greenhouse, and give the plants plenty of water while they are making their young shoots; when the season's growth is completed, and the flower-buds formed, the back of the greenhouse or even a well-sheltered north border will suit them, for they will be seriously injured if exposed to the rays of the sun. A regular succession of flowers may be obtained from autumn till July, if attention is paid to shifting the plants· to the warm atmosphere of a vinery, or pinery, &c., and to one a few degrees colder, and so on till they come to expand their flowers in the greenhouse, which in rough, bleak, cold weather, should be kept closed. The seeds of *C. oleifera* yield an excellent table oil.

| | | | | | |
|---|---|---|---|---|---|
| euryoídés | . . . | White | . 5, G. Ev. 8. | China | . 1824 |
| hybrida | . . . | . G. Ev. 8. | Leige | |
| japónicá | . . . | Red | . 5, G. Ev. 8. | China | . 1739 |

*Acutipétálá, Aitònià, álbá, A. plèná, A. semidúplés, A. símplèx, A. variegátá, altheiflòrá, Amhérstiá, amplíssimá, anemoneflòrá, A. álbá, A. cárneá, A. Knightii, A. ròseá, A. striátá, Antwerpénsis, apúngá, árdéns, argéntéá, atropurpúreá, atròrúbéns, atro-violáceá, aucubæfòliá, augústá, Bedfordii, blándá, brooksiáná, Bruxellénsis, Bucklándi, burlesiáná, candidíssimá, Candolleáná, cardinális, cárneá, cerasiná, Chamléril, Chandléril, Clintònii, Cliveáná, coccíneá, cólá, Colvíllii, compáctá, C. rúbrá, Comptoniáná,·conchiflòrá, concíná, concólór, conspicuá, corallíná, coronátá, crassinèrvis, curvatiflòrá, Dahliæflòrá, decórá, delicatíssimá, Derbyáná, dilécá, dianthiflòrá, Donkelaárii, Dorséttii, Egertònii, Eclíptís, eléctá, élégáns, elegantíssimá, Elphinstònii, excélsá, exímiá, fasciculáris, fimbriátá, floriáná, fláccidá, flammèòlá, flavéscéns, floribándá, flòridá, Flòyli, fòlíis-variegátís, Fòrdii, Francfortensis, fulgéns, gaussònii, Gillsii, gloriósá, grandiflòrá, Grisfínii, hallsii, haylóckii, hélvòlá, heptanguláris, Herbértii, heterophýllá, hexanguláris, Hibbértii, hóvéi, húmilis, ignéscéns, imbricátá, I. álbá, imperiális, incarnátá, insígnis, I. álbá, involútá, Johnsònii, Kermesiná, láctéá, Lambértii, Lancmániá, latifòliá, Leéthii, Leeáná, Lefevreáná, Lehmánnii, líndbriá, Lindleyáná, Lippòldii, longifòliá, lúcidá, látá-álbá, macrophýllá, marmorátá, Mastérii, máximá, minátá, mutábilis, myrtifòliá, náná, nankinénsis, níveá, nobilíssimá, ochroléucá, ornátá, oxoniénsis, pæoniflòrá, papaverácéá, paradóxá, Párksii, parthoniáná, parviflòrá, penicillátá, perféctá, picturátá, platypétálá, plumáriá, pompóná, prégnáns, Préssii, princéps, pulchéllá, pulchérrimá, punctátá, ranunculiflòrá, Reevésii, regíná, respléndéns, Rivinii, rosácéá, rosaflòrá, róséá-mándi, róséá-sinénsis, róseá, roseáná, Róssii, rotundifòliá, roulíni, rubicándá, rúbrá, rúbrá-punctátá, rubricaúlis, rugosíssimá, Sabiniáná, sanguíneá, semi-plèná, serícéá, Símsii, Soulangeáná, spatulátá, specìósá, spectábilis, Spoffòrthiáná, Spoffòrthiá-cárneá, spolíférá, staminádi, supíná, Swéétii, tricólór, triúmpháns, vandésii-cárneá, vandésii-supérbá, variábilis, variegátá plèná, V. símplèx, venósá, versicólór, Weimáriá, Welbankiáná, Wiltònii, Wòòsii.*

| | | | | | |
|---|---|---|---|---|---|
| Kíssi | . . . | White | . 5, G. Ev. 8. | China | . 1823 |
| oleiférá | . . . | White | . 5, G. Ev. 8. | China | . 1819 |
| reticulátá | . . . | Red | . 4, G. Ev. 8. | China | . 1824 |
| Sasánquá | . . . | White | . 2, G. Ev. 8. | China | . 1811 |
| plèná-álbá | . . | White | . 2, G. Ev. 8. | China | . 1824 |
| plèná-rúbrá | . . | Red | . 2, G. Ev. 8. | China | . 1818 |
| semi-plèná | . . | Red | . 2, G. Ev. 8. | China | . 1811 |

CAMERARIA, *Linn.* In memory of Joachim Camerarius, a physician and botanist of Nuremberg. *Linn.* 5, Or. 1, Nat. Or. *Apocynaceæ.* The species of this genus are handsome flowering plants, of easy culture; they succeed best in loam and peat mixed; and cuttings root in sand, under a glass, in heat. *Synonyme:* 1. *Wrightia dubia.*

| | | | | | |
|---|---|---|---|---|---|
| angustifòliá | . . | White | . 9, S. Ev. 8. | S. Amer. | . 1752 |
| dùbiá, 1 | . . . | Orange | . 6, S. Ev. 8. | E. Ind. | . 1812 |
| latifòliá | . . . | White | . 8, S. Ev. T. | Havannah | . 1733 |

CAMPÁNULA, *Linn.* The name is a diminutive of *campana*, a bell; on account of the resemblance thereto of the corolla. *Linn.* 5, Or. 1, Nat. Or. *Campanulaceæ.* This is a showy and well-known genus; some of the species are tall-growing handsome plants, while others scarcely rise more than a few inches from the ground. They are all of easy culture in the border of the flower-garden or shrubbery, where the hardy kinds merely require sowing; the less hardy kinds should be sown on a hotbed, or in the greenhouse, and when up potted off. The roots of *C. Rapunculus* are occasionally eaten. *Synonymes:* 1. *Rupestris.* 2. *Roella decumbens.* 3. *C. capitata.* 4. *Neglecta.* 5. *Spatulata.* 6. *Speciosa.* 7. *Diffusa.* 8. *Betonicæfolia.* 9. *Adenophora liliifolia.* 10. *C. baldensis.* 11. *Multiflora.* 12. *Glomerata petræa.* 13. *Lobelioides.* 14. *Gummifera.* 15. *Glomerata dahurica.* 16. *Planiflora.* 17. *Flexuosa.*

| | | | | | |
|---|---|---|---|---|---|
| acuminátá | . . | Blue | . 8, H. Her. P. | N. Amer. | . 1826 |
| Adàmi | . . | Blue | . 7, H. | B. Caucasus | . 1821 |
| affínis | . . | Blue | . 7, H. | B. S. Eur. | . 1824 |
| aggregátá | . . | Blue | . 8, H. Her. P. | Bavaria | . 1817 |
| alliariæfòliá | . . | Blue | . 7, H. Her. P. | Caucasus | . 1803 |
| Allionii | . . | Blue | . 7, H. Her. P. | S. France | . 1820 |
| alpíná | . . | Blue | . 7, H. Her. P. | Switzerl. | . 1779 |
| Alpìni | . . | Blue | . 6, H. Her. P. | Italy | . 1800 |

| | | | | |
|---|---|---|---|---|
| americàna | Blue | 7, H. | B. Pennsyl. | 1763 |
| angustifòlìa | Blue | 7, H. Her. P. | France | 1818 |
| Arménà | Blue | 7, H. | B. Russia | 1826 |
| aùrèa | Yellow | 8, G. Ev. S. | Madeira | 1777 |
|   angustifòlìa | Yellow | 8, G. Ev. S. | Madeira | 1777 |
|   latifòlìa | Yellow | 8, G. Ev. S. | Madeira | 1777 |
| azùrèa | Ll. blue | 6, H. Her. P. | Switzerl. | 1778 |
| barbàtà | Blue | 6, H. Her. P. | Italy | 1752 |
|   cyànèa | Blue | 7, H. Her. P. | | 1836 |
| Barrelieri | Blue | 9, H. Her. P. | | |
| Bellardi | Blue | 6, H. Her. P. | Italy | 1813 |
| bellidifòlìa | Blue | 7, H. | B. Pyrenees | 1823 |
| betonicæfòlìa | Blue | 7, H. | B. Greece | 1890 |
| Biebersteniànà, 1 | Blue | 7, H. Her. P. | Caucasus | 1890 |
| bononiénsis | Blue | 8, H. Her. P. | Italy | 1773 |
| Broussonetiànà | Blue | 7, H. | A. Mogadore | 1825 |
| cæspitòsà | Blue | 7, H. Her. P. | Austria | 1819 |
| calycìnà | Blue | 7, H. Her. P. | Tauria | 1820 |
| capénsis, 2 | Blue | 7, G. | A. C. G. H. | 1803 |
| carpàtìca | Blue | 7, H. Her. P. | Carp. Alps | 1774 |
| caucàsìcà | Purple | 7, H. Her. P. | Caucasus | 1804 |
| ceniàlà | Blue | 6, H. Her. P. | Switzerl. | 1775 |
| cephalànthà | Blue | 8, H. Her. P. | Russia | 1817 |
| cephalòtes | Blue | 6, H. Her. P. | | 1818 |
| cærùlà | Blue | 7, G. | B. C. G. H. | 1804 |
| Cervicàrìa | Ll. blue | 7, H. | B. Germany | 1808 |
| cervicaroìdes | Blue | 7, H. Her. P. | Italy | 1822 |
| cichoràceà, 3 | Blue | 7, H. Her. P. | Greece | 1768 |
| collìnà | Blue | 7, H. Her. P. | Caucasus | 1803 |
| congéstà | Blue | 7, H. Her. P. | France | 1823 |
| corymbòsà | Blue | 6, H. | B. Crete | 1890 |
| crenàtà, 4 | Blue | 7, H. Her. P. | Russia | 1890 |
| dehìscens | Blue | 7, G. | A. E. Ind. | 1818 |
| dichòtòmà | Blue | 7, H. | A. Sicily | 1890 |
| divérgens, 5 | Blue | 6, H. | A. Hungary | 1814 |
| drabæfòlìa | Pa. blue | 6, H. | A. Athens | 1823 |
| Elatìnè | Pa. blue | 7, H. Her. Tr. | S. Eur. | 1823 |
| élégans, 6 | Pa. blue | 7, H. Her. P. | Siberia | 1811 |
| elliptìcà | Blue | 7, H. Her. P. | Hungary | 1826 |
| eriocàrpà | Purple | 6, H. Her. P. | Caucasus | 1823 |
| Erìnùs | Pa. blue | 7, H. | A. S. Eur. | 1768 |
| erinoìdes | Pa. blue | 7, H. | A. Africa | 1823 |
| excìsà | Blue | 5, H. Her. P. | Switzerl. | 1890 |
| foliòsà | Blue | 7, H. Her. P. | Italy | 1826 |
| glomeràtà | Violet | 5, H. Her. P. | Britain | |
|   flòrè-albò | White | 5, H. Her. P. | Britain | |
|   plènà-àlbà | White | 5, H. Her. P. | Britain | |
| fràgìlis, 7 | Blue | 8, F. Her. P. | Alps | 1826 |
|   hirsùtà | Blue | 8, F. Her. P. | Italy | 1833 |
| gargànìcà | Pa. blue | 7, H. Tr. | B. Mt. St. Ang. | 1830 |
| gràcìlìs | Blue | 6, G. | B. N. S. W. | 1794 |
| graminifòlìa | Blue | 7, H. Her. P. | Hungary | 1817 |
| gummìferà, 8 | Blue | 7, H. Her. P. | Caucasus | 1817 |
| hederàceà | Blue | 5, H. Her. P. | C. G. H. | 1817 |
| Herminìi | Blue | 7, H. | A. Portugal | 1823 |
| heterodòxà | Blue | 7, H. Her. P. | Hungary | 1824 |
| hispìdùlà | Blue | 7, H. | A. C. G. H. | 1817 |
| infundìbùlùm | Purple | 7, H. Her. P. | Siberia | 1825 |
| infundibulifòrmis | Blue | 7, H. Her. P. | Siberia | 1822 |
| laciniàtà | Blue | 6, H. Her. P. | Greece | 1788 |
| lactiflòrà | Blue | 8, H. Her. P. | Iberia | 1816 |
| lamiifòlìà | Pa. yel. | 6, H. Her. P. | Iberia | 1823 |
| lanceolàtà | Blue | 7, H. Her. P. | France | 1819 |
| lanuginòsà | Blue | 6, H. | B. | 1814 |
| latifòlìa | White | 7, H. Her. P. | Britain | |
|   flòrè-albò | White | 7, H. Her. P. | | |
| liliifòlìa, 9 | Blue | 5, H. Her. P. | Siberia | 1784 |
| lingulàtà | Violet | 7, H. Her. P. | Hungary | 1804 |
| linifòlìa | Blue | 7, H. Her. P. | Switzerl. | 1819 |
| littoràlìs | Blue | 8, G. | B. N. Holl. | 1890 |
| Lœflìngìi | Blue | 7, H. | A. S. Eur. | 1818 |
| longifòlìa | Blue | 7, H. Her. P. | Pyrenees | 1890 |
| Lòrèi, 10 | Purple | 6, H. | A. Italy | 1824 |
| lyràtà | Violet | 7, H. | A. S. Eur. | 1823 |
| macrànthà | Purple | 8, H. Her. P. | Russia | 1822 |
|   polyànthà | Blue | 5, H. Her. P. | Russia | 1830 |
| macrostàchyà, 11 | Blue | 6, H. | B. Hungary | 1814 |
| Mèdìùm | Blue | 7, H. | B. Germany | 1597 |
|   àlbùm | White | 7, H. | B. | |
| microphylla | Blue | 6, H. Her. P. | Hungary | 1820 |
| mòllìs | Purple | 6, G. Her. P. | Sicily | 1788 |
| mùràlìs | Blue | 8, F. Her. P. | S. Eur. | 1835 |
| neglécta | Blue | 7, H. | B. | 1818 |
| nìceénsìs, 12 | Purple | 6, H. Her. P. | Piedmont | 1890 |
| nìtìdà | White | 7, H. Her. P. | N. Amer. | 1731 |
|   cærùleà | Blue | 7, H. Her. P. | N. Amer. | 1731 |
| Nuttallìi | Blue | 7, H. Her. P. | N. Amer. | 1829 |
| oblìquà | Blue | 6, H. | B. | 1813 |
| obliquifòlìà | Blue | 7, H. Her. P. | Italy | 1823 |
| Ottoniànà | Blue | 8, G. Ev. S. | C. G. H. | 1825 |
| parviflòrà | Blue | 7, H. Her. P. | Iberia | 1819 |
| pàtùlà | Violet | 7, H. | B. Britain | |
| peregrìnà | Blue | 7, H. | B. C. G. H. | 1794 |
| persicifòlìà | Blue | 8, H. Her. P. | Europe | 1596 |
|   àlbà | White | 8, H. Her. P. | Europe | 1596 |
|   àlbà-plènà | White | 8, H. Her. P. | Europe | 1596 |
|   plènà | Blue | 8, H. Her. P. | Europe | 1596 |
|   gràndìs | Blue | 8, H. Her. P. | Europe | 1596 |
|   màxìmà | Blue | 8, H. Her. P. | Europe | 1596 |

| | | | | |
|---|---|---|---|---|
| planiflòrà | Blue | 8, H. Her. P. | Siberia | 1817 |
| pubéscens | Blue | 7, H. Her. P. | Bohemia | |
| pùlla | Blue | 6, H. Her. P. | Austria | 1779 |
| pùmìlà | Blue | 7, H. Her. P. | Switzerl. | |
| punctàtà | White | 7, H. | A. Siberia | 1813 |
| pusìlla | Blue | 6, H. Her. P. | Switzerl. | 1821 |
| pyramidàlìs | Blue | 7, H. Her. P. | Carniola | 1594 |
|   flòrè-albò | White | 7, H. Her. P. | Europe | |
| quadrìfìdà | Blue | 6, H. Her. P. | N. Holl. | 1820 |
| ramosìssìmà, 13 | Blue | 7, H. | A. Greece | 1820 |
| Rainèrà | Blue | 7, H. Her. P. | Italy | 1826 |
| Rapùncùlùs | Blue | 7, H. Her. P. | Britain | |
| Rapunculoìdes | Blue | 6, H. Her. P. | England | |
| rhomboìdeà | Blue | 7, H. Her. P. | Switzerl. | 1775 |
| rigéscens | Blue | 7, H. Her. P. | Siberia | 1820 |
| rotundifòlìa | Blue | 7, H. Her. P. | Britain | |
|   flòrè-albò | White | 7, H. Her. P. | Britain | |
| ruthénìcà | Blue | 7, H. Her. P. | Caucasus | 1815 |
| sarmàtìcà, 14 | Blue | 7, H. Her. P. | Siberia | 1803 |
| saxàtìlis | Blue | 6, H. Her. P. | Candia | 1768 |
| Scheuchzeri | Blue | 7, H. Her. P. | Europe | 1813 |
| sibìrìcà | Blue | 8, H. | B. Siberia | 1783 |
| sìmplex | Blue | 7, H. Her. P. | S. France | 1819 |
| spatulàtà | Blue | 7, H. | B. Greece | 1817 |
| speciòsà, 15 | Purple | 5, H. Her. P. | Siberia | 1825 |
| spicàtà | Blue | 7, H. | B. Switzerl. | 1786 |
| sprètà | Blue | 7, H. Her. P. | Siberia | 1820 |
| strìctà | Blue | 6, H. | B. Syria | 1819 |
| tenuifòlìa | Violet | 7, H. Her. P. | Hungary | 1817 |
| thyrsoìdeà | Blue | 7, H. Her. P. | Switzerl. | 1785 |
| tomentòsà | White | 6, H. Her. P. | Levant | 1810 |
| Trachèlìùm | Blue | 7, H. Her. P. | Britain | |
|   àlbà | White | 7, H. Her. P. | Britain | |
|   àlbà-plènà | White | 7, H. Her. P. | Britain | |
|   plènà | Blue | 7, H. Her. P. | Britain | |
| trachelioìdes | Blue | 7, H. Her. P. | Caucasus | 1817 |
| trichocalycìnà | Blue | 7, H. Her. P. | Italy | 1823 |
| urticifòlìa | Blue | 7, H. Her. P. | Germany | 1800 |
| Vandàsi | Cream | 6, H. Her. P. | | |
| velutìnà | Blue | 7, H. | B. S. Eur. | 1826 |
| virgàtà | Blue | 7, H. Her. P. | N. Amer. | 1823 |
| versìcolòr, 16 | Striped | 8, H. Her. P. | Siberia | 1788 |
| violæfòlìa | Blue | 7, H. | B. Siberia | 1817 |
| Waldsteiniànà,17 | Blue | 6, H. Her. P. | Hungary | 1824 |
| Zòysìi | Dk. blue | 7, H. Her. P. | Carniola | 1813 |

CAMPANULATE, bell-shaped.

CAMPÈLIA, *Richard*. So named from *kampe*, a bending, and *helios*, the sun. *Linn.* 6, *Or.* 1, *Nat. Or.* *Commelinæ*. An interesting plant, growing in any rich soil, and increased by seeds. Synonymes: 1. *Tradescantia zanonia*.

| | | | | |
|---|---|---|---|---|
| Zanònìa, 1 | Blue | 8, S. Her. P. | W. Ind. | 1759 |

CAMPHORÒSMÀ, *Linn.* Named from *camphora*, camphor, and *osme*, a smell; the former a Latin and the latter a Greek word. *Linn.* 4, *Or.* 1, *Nat. Or.* *Chenopodiaceæ*. The species have but little beauty. *C. monspeliaca* abounds with a volatile oily salt, and is warm and stimulating.

| | | | | |
|---|---|---|---|---|
| monspellàcà | Apetal. | 8, G. Ev. S. | S. Eur. | 1640 |

*acùtà, ovàtà.*

CAMPHOR TREE, see *Cinnamòmùm camphòrà.*

CAMPION, see *Cucùbàlùs.*

CAMPYLÀNTHÙS, *Roth*. Named from *kampylos*, a curve, and *anthos*, a flower. *Linn.* 2, *Or.* 1, *Nat. Or.* *Primulaceæ*. An ornamental plant, succeeding in sandy loam and peat; and increased from cuttings in sand, under a glass.

| | | | | |
|---|---|---|---|---|
| salsoloìdes | Purple | 8, G. Ev. S. | Teneriffe | 1825 |

CANADA RICE, see *Zizànìà aqùàtìcà.*

CANADIAN MUGWORT, see *Artemìsìà canadénsis.*

CANALICULATE, channelled, furrowed.

CANARÌNÀ, *Linn.* So called from the species being natives of the Canaries. *Linn.* 6, *Or.* 1, *Nat. Or.* *Campanulaceæ*. These are desirable plants, producing pretty flowers in the autumn and winter. Unless the roots are placed in the stove after they begin to grow in the spring, they do not flower so well in the greenhouse. A mixture of light loam and peat is the best soil for them; plants are procured from cuttings, which strike in soil, or by dividing of the roots.

| | | | | |
|---|---|---|---|---|
| Campànùlà | Orange | 2, G. Her. P. | Canaries | 1696 |
| lævigàtà | Orange | 2, G. Her. P. | Canaries | 1825 |

CANARY GRASS, see *Phàlàrìs.*

CANAVÀLÌÀ, *Dec.* Canavali is its name in Malabar. *Linn.* 16, *Or.* 6, *Nat. Or.* *Leguminosæ*. These species have but little to recommend them; for culture, &c., see *Dolichos.* Synonymes: 1. *Dolichos ensiformis.* 2. *D. obtusifolius.* 3. *D. roseus.*

[ 60 ]

| | | | | | |
|---|---|---|---|---|---|
| bonariénsis . . | Purple | 7, 8. | De. Cl. | B. Ayres . | |
| ensifórmis, 1 . | Purple | 7, 8. | A. | E. Ind. . | 1778 |
| gladiáta . . | Wht. red | 6, 8. | Ev. Tw. | E. Ind. . | 1790 |
| obtusifólia, 2 . | Purple | 7, 8. | Ev. Tw. | E. Ind. . | 1820 |
| emarginátá . | Purple | 7, 8. | Ev. Tw. | E. Ind. . | 1800 |
| róséa, 3 . . | Purple | 7, 8. | Ev. Cr. | Jamaica . | 1812 |

CANCELLATE, like lattice-work.

CANDLEBERRY MYRTLE, see *Myrīcā*.

CANDOLLĒA, *Labillardière*. In honour of Augustus Pyramus Decandolle, F.M.R.S. and L.S., Professor of Botany at Geneva, author of many approved botanical works. He is one of the first botanists of the present age. *Linn.* 18, Or. 2, Nat. Or. *Dilleniaceæ*. A beautiful shrub, thriving best in a mixture of loam, peat, and sand; cuttings, in the same kind of soil, root readily, under a glass.

| | | | | | |
|---|---|---|---|---|---|
| cuneifórmis . . | Yellow | 7, G. | Ev. S. | N. Holl. . | 1824 |

CANDY CARROT, see *Athamāntā Matthīōlā*.

CANDYTUFT, see *Ibērīs*.

CANE-BRAKE, see *Arundinācēā*.

CANĒLLĀ, *P. Browne.* From *canna*, a reed; in allusion to the bark being rolled like cinnamon. *Linn.* 16, Or. 5, Nat. Or. *Guttiferæ*. These are valuable and ornamental trees, about fifteen feet high, best cultivated in loam, peat, and sand; cuttings of the well-ripened wood taken off at a joint will root in sand in a moist heat; they must not be deprived of any of their leaves. Sweet recommends large old cuttings as the best. The bark is aromatic and pungent.

| | | | | | |
|---|---|---|---|---|---|
| alba . . . . | White . | 8. | Ev. T. | W. Ind. . | 1735 |
| laurifólia . . | White . | 8. | Ev. T. | S. Amer. . | 1820 |

CANESCENT, hoary, approaching to white.

CANINĒ, pertaining to dogs.

CĀNNĀ, *Linn.* The Celtic name for a cane or mat. *Linn.* 2, Or. 1, Nat. Or. *Marantaceæ*. This, says Mr. Sweet, is a genus worthy of cultivation in all collections, as its lively flowers are produced in great abundance, and at all seasons; many species are now in our collections; the most splendid is *iridiflora*, which is amongst the handsomest plants of the stove; rich light soil suits the species best: they are propagated by divisions at the root, or by seeds, which they produce in abundance.—*Bot. Cult.* 43. Synonyme: 1. *C. chinensis.*

| | | | | | |
|---|---|---|---|---|---|
| achīrās . . . | Drk. red | 8, S. | Her. | P. Mendoza | 1829 |
| angustifólia . | Scarlet | 4, S. | Her. | P. S. Amer. | 1824 |
| aurantiácā . . | Orange | 12, S. | Her. | P. Brazil | 1824 |
| cárneā . . . | Flesh | 12, S. | Her. | P. Brazil | 1822 |
| coccínēā . . | Scarlet | 12, S. | Her. | P. S. Amer. | 1731 |
| compáctā . . | Red . | 4, S. | Her. | P. E. Ind. | 1820 |
| crócēā . . . | Red . | 5, S. | Her. | P. | 1823 |
| denudátā . . | Scarlet | 6, S. | Her. | P. Brazil | 1818 |
| latifóliā . . | Red . | 7, S. | Her. | P. Brazil | 1818 |
| discólor . . | Scarlet | 11, S. | Her. | P. Trinidad | 1827 |
| edúlis . . . | Red . | 9, S. | Her. | P. Peru | 1820 |
| esculéntā . . | Red . | 12, S. | Her. | P. S. Amer. | 1822 |
| excélsa . . . | Scarlet | 2, S. | Her. | P. Brazil | 1820 |
| flaccídā . . | Red . | 7, S. | Her. | P. S. Carol. | 1788 |
| gigántēā . . | Red yel. | 12, S. | Her. | P. S. Amer. | 1809 |
| glaúcā . . . | Yellow | 7, S. | Her. | P. S. Amer. | 1730 |
| rúfā . . . | Brown | 7, S. | Her. | P. S. Amer. | |
| índícā . . . | Scarlet | 12, S. | Her. | P. India | 1570 |
| maculátā . . | Red yel. | 12, S. | Her. | P. India | |
| iridiflórā . . | Red . | 12, S. | Her. | P. Peru | 1816 |
| júncēā . . . | Red . | 5, S. | Her. | P. Indies | 1820 |
| lagunénsis . . | Yellow | 9, S. | Her. | P. Laguna | 1828 |
| Lambérti . . | Scarlet | 6, S. | Her. | P. Trinidad | 1819 |
| lanceolátā . . | Red . | 12, S. | Her. | P. Brazil | 1825 |
| lanuginósā . . | Scarlet | 4, S. | Her. | P. Marant. | 1823 |
| latifóliā . . | Pink . | 12, S. | Her. | P. Brazil | 1820 |
| limbátā . . . | Red . | 12, S. | Her. | P. Brazil | 1818 |
| lútēā . . . | Yellow | 10, S. | Her. | P. E. Ind. | 1629 |
| occidentális . | Red yel. | 6, S. | Her. | P. W. Ind. | 1822 |
| orientális, 1 . | Red . | 6, S. | Her. | P. E. Ind. | 1820 |
| flávā . . . | Yellow | 6, S. | Her. | P. E. Ind. | 1820 |
| pallídā . . . | Pa. yel. | 6, S. | Her. | P. W. Ind. | 1820 |
| latifóliā . . | Yellow | 6, S. | Her. | P. W. Ind. | 1820 |
| pátens . . . | Red yel. | 5, S. | Her. | P. Rio Jan. | 1778 |
| pedunculátā . | Orange | 10, S. | Her. | P. | 1820 |
| polymórphā . | Red . | 12, S. | Her. | P. S. Amer. | 1825 |
| Roscōēā . . | Yellow | 5, S. | Her. | P. China | 1835 |
| rúbrā . . . | Red . | 12, S. | Her. | P. W. Ind. | 1820 |
| rubricaúlis . | Red . | 5, S. | Her. | P. | 1821 |
| sanguínēā . . | Red . | 12, S. | Her. | P. S. Amer. | 1820 |
| speciósā . . | Red . | 8, S. | Her. | P. S. Amer. | 1820 |
| sylvéstris . . | Scarlet | 12, S. | Her. | P. S. Amer. | 1820 |
| variábilis . . | Red . | 12, S. | Her. | P. India | 1822 |

CĀNNĀBIS, *Linn.* So called from *ganeh*, its Arabic name, and from the Celtic appellation *can*, reed, and *ab*, small. *Linn.* 22, Or. 5, Nat. Or. *Urticaceæ*.

One species of this genus produces the hemp. The hemp to which we owe so many of our comforts is *C. sativa.* Neither is handsome, and they require only to be sown in the open ground and kept clean. A most powerfully narcotic gum resin.

| | | | | | |
|---|---|---|---|---|---|
| indíca . . . . | Green . | 8, H. | | A. E. Ind. . | 1800 |
| sativa . . . | Orn. wht. | 6, H. | | A. India . | |

CANTERBURY BELLS, see *Campānūlā mēdium.*

CANTHARĒLLŪS, *F. Adams.* An alteration of the French name *chanterelle*. *Linn.* 24, Or. 9, Nat. Or. *Fungi*. Interesting productions. *C. cibarius* is one of the best of our eatable mushrooms. The best way of preserving them for use, is to string them in rows, and after they have become flaccid, to hang them in a dry place where they can have plenty of air. They then form a delicious ingredient in rich gravies, &c. Synonyme: 1. *Merulius purpuratus, aurantiacus, cibarius, cinereus, cornucoploides 1, lobatus, lutescens, umbonatus, undulatus.*

CĀNTHĬŬM, *Lambert.* Cantix is the Malabar name. *Linn.* 5, Or. 1, Nat. Or. *Cinchonaceæ*. This is an ornamental shrub, and will grow in any rich soil; cuttings.

| | | | | | |
|---|---|---|---|---|---|
| dúbíum . . . | White . | 7, G. | Ev. S. | E. Ind. . | 1824 |

CAPE JASMINE, see *Gardēnĭā flōrĭdā.*

CAPE PHILLYREA, see *Cassīnē capēnsis.*

CAPER SPURGE, see *Euphōrbĭā Lāthyris.*

CAPER TREE, see *Cāppāris.*

CAPILLARY, }
CAPILLACEOUS, } very slender, like a hair.

CAPILLARY-MULTIFID, divided in slender hair-like segments.

CAPILLATE, hairy, stringy.

CAPITATE, growing in a head; a stigma is capitate, when it is large, round, and blunt.

CAPITELLATE, }
CAPITULAR, } growing in small heads.
CAPITULATE, }

CAPNOPHYLLUM, *Gærtner.* So called from *kapnos*, smoke, and *phyllon*, a leaf. *Linn.* 5, Or. 2, Nat. Or. *Umbelliferæ*. A mere weed. Synonymes: 1. *Conium africanum, Rumia capensis—africānd 1.*

CĀPPĀRĬS, *Linn.* So called from the Arabic *kapar*, capers. *Linn.* 13, Or. 1, Nat. Or. *Capparidaceæ*. This is a genus of ornamental low shrubs; they grow well in a mixture of loam and peat: and cuttings root in sand, in heat, under a glass. *C. spinosa* is a good free-flowering species, when allowed plenty of room. The flower-buds of the caper form a well-known pickle; they are stimulant, antiscorbutic, and aperient; and the bark is said to be diuretic. Synonymes: 1. *acutifolia, acuminata.* 2. *Octandra.* 3. *Fontanesii.* 4. *Arborescens.* 5. *Uncinata.*

| | | | | | |
|---|---|---|---|---|---|
| acuminátā . . | White . | 8. | Ev. | S. E. Ind. . | 1822 |
| ægyptiácā . . | White . | 8. | Ev. | S. Egypt . | 1822 |
| amygdalínā . . | White . | 8. | Ev. | S. W. Ind. . | 1818 |
| aphylla . . . | White . | 8. | Ev. | S. E. Ind. . | 1822 |
| auriculátā . . | White . | 8. | Ev. | S. | |
| Brēasil . . . | White . | 8. | Ev. | S. Gold Coast | 1793 |
| Breynia . . . | White . | 8. | Ev. | S. W. Ind. . | 1752 |
| chinénsis, 1 . | White . | 7, | 8. | S. S. Amer. . | 1827 |
| cynophallóphōrā | Grn. wht. | 8. | Ev. | S. W. Ind. . | 1752 |
| Eustachíānā . | Striped | 8. | Ev. | S. St. Eust. . | 1822 |
| ferrugínēā, 2 . | White . | 8. | Ev. | S. Jamaica . | |
| frondósā . . | Green . | 8. | Ev. | S. Carthag. . | 1800 |
| herbácēā . . | White . | F. | Her. | P. Tauria . | 1818 |
| jamaicénsis . | White . | 8. | Ev. | S. Jamaica . | 1793 |
| linéāris . . . | White . | 8. | Ev. | S. W. Ind. . | 1793 |
| mariánā . . . | White . | 8. | Ev. | S. Timor . | 1820 |
| odoratissímā . | White . | 8. | Ev. | S. Caraccas . | 1814 |
| ovátā, 3 . . | White . | 6, | F. De. | S. S. Eur. . | |
| peltátā . . . | White . | G. | Ev. | S. Trinidad . | 1827 |
| pulchérrímā, 4 | White . | 8. | Ev. | S. Carthag. . | 1700 |
| malígnā . . . | White . | 8. | Ev. | S. Santa Cruz | 1807 |
| sepiáríā . . | White . | 8. | Ev. | S. E. Ind. . | 1823 |
| spinósā . . . | White . | 6, | F. De. | S. S. Eur. . | 1596 |
| tenuisíliquā . | White . | 8. | Ev. | S. Caraccas . | 1823 |
| torulósā, 5 . | White . | 8. | Ev. | S. W. Ind. . | 1822 |
| triflórā . . . | White . | 8. | Ev. | S. S. Amer. . | |
| undulátā . . | White . | 8. | Ev. | S. | |
| verrucósā . . | White . | 8. | Ev. | S. Carthagena | 1820 |
| zeylánicā . . | White . | | 8 Ev. | S. Ceylon . | 1819 |

CAPRĀRĬA, *Linn.* The leaves of this genus are liked by goats; hence the name, from *caper*, a goat. *Linn.* 14, Or. 2, Nat. Or. *Scrophulariaceæ*. Uninteresting species, of easy culture—*biflórā, cuneātā, hūmilis, lanceolátā, undulátā.*

CAPREOLATE, having tendrils.

**CAPRIFOLIUM**, *Romer* and *Schultes*. Called poetically goat-leaf; and is derived from *caper*, a goat, and *folium*, a leaf; in reference to the climbing and twining habit of the plant. Linn. 5, Or. 1, Nat. Or. *Caprifoliaceæ*. This is a genus of favourite climbing plants, well adapted for planting against walls, bowers, or trellis-work. Common soil suits them; and cuttings taken off early in autumn readily root in a shady border. Synonymes: 1. *Lonicera glabratum*. 2. *Cap. pubescens*. 3. *L. caprifolium*. 4. *Caprifolium japonicum*.

| | | | | | |
|---|---|---|---|---|---|
| chinénse, 1 | Orange | 8, F. Ev. Tw. | China | 1806 |
| elliséum | Yellow | 5, F. De. Tw. | Missouri | 1825 |
| dioïcum | Purple | 6, H. De. Tw. | N. Amer. | 1776 |
| Douglassii | Orange | K, H. De. Cl. | N. Amer. | 1824 |
| etruscum | Orange | 5, H. De. Tw. | Italy | |
| flávum | Yellow | 5, H. De. Tw. | Carolina | 1810 |
| hirsútum, 2 | Yellow | 5, H. De. Tw. | Canada | 1822 |
| hispidúlum | Rose | 7, H. Ev. Tw. | S. Amer. | 1833 |
| grátum | Red | 7, H. Ev. Tw. | N. Amer. | 1730 |
| impléxum | Red yel. | 7, H. Ev. Tw. | Minorca | 1772 |
| itálicum, 2 | Pur. yel. | 6, H. De. Tw. | England | |
| rúbrum | Red | 6, H. De. Tw. | S. Eur. | |
| japónicum | Red | 6, F. Ev. Tw. | China | 1806 |
| longiflórum | Yel. wht. | 7, H. De. Cl. | China | 1826 |
| nepalénse, 3 | Orange | 7, F. Ev. Tw. | Nepal | 1807 |
| occidentále | Orange | 7, H. De. Tw. | Ft. Vancou. | 1824 |
| Periclyménum | Yellow | 6, H. De. Tw. | Britain | |
|   Belgica | Yellow | 6, H. De. Tw. | | |
|   quercifólium | Yel. red | 6, H. De. Tw. | | |
|   serótinum | Yel. red | 6, H. De. Tw. | | |
|   variegátum | Yel. red | 6, H. De. Tw. | Britain | |
| sempérvirens | Scarlet | 6, H. Ev. Tw. | N. Amer. | 1656 |
|   minus | Scarlet | 6, F. Ev. Tw. | Carolina | 1656 |

**CAPSELLA**, *Moench*. So called from a diminution of capsule. Linn. 15, Or. 1, Nat. Or. *Cruciferæ*. Weedy plants. Synonyme: 1. *Thlaspi bursa-pastoris*—*bursd-pastóris* 1, *apétála*, B. *coronopifólia*, B. *integrifólia*, B. *minór*.

**CAPSICUM**, *Linn.* So named from *kapto*, to bite; on account of the hot, pungent qualities of the pericarp. Linn. 5, Or. 1, Nat. Or. *Solanaceæ*. This genus is ornamental, but chiefly cultivated for its fruit, which is much used in pickles; they are easily cultivated in any rich open soil; and readily increased from seeds. Synonyme: 1. *Cerasiforme*.

| | | | | |
|---|---|---|---|---|
| angulósum | White | 6, H. | A. India | |
| ánnuum | White | 6, H. | A. India | 1548 |
| baccátum | White | 6, S. Ev. S. | | 1731 |
| bicólor | Purple | 6, S. Ev. S. | W. Ind. | 1804 |
| cerasiflórum | White | 6, S. Ev. S. | | 1823 |
| cerasifórmě | Pa. yel. | 6, S. | A. W. Ind. | 1739 |
| eduícum | White | 6, S. | A. Guiana | 1820 |
| conoídes | White | 4, S. Ev. S. | India | 1750 |
| cordifórmě | White | 6, H. | A. India | |
| frutéscens | Pa. yel. | 7, S. Ev. S. | India | 1656 |
|   tortulósum | White | 6, S. Ev. S. | E. Ind. | 1820 |
| globifórum | White | 6, S. Ev. S. | Guiana | 1824 |
| grósum | White | 7, S. | B. India | 1759 |
|   globósum | White | 7, S. Ev. S. | E. Ind. | |
| lúteum | White | 7, S. Ev. S. | E. Ind. | |
| lóngum | White | 6, H. | A. India | 1548 |
| lúteum | White | 7, S. Ev. S. | E. Ind. | 1820 |
| micránthum | White | 5, S. Ev. S. | Brazil | 1820 |
| microcárpon | White | 5, S. Ev. S. | | |
| Millěrii, 1 | White | 6, O. | A. W. Ind. | 1824 |
| ovátum | White | 7, S. Ev. S. | | 1824 |
| péndulum | White | 7, S. | | 1750 |
| pyramidále | White | 5, S. Ev. S. | Egypt | 1750 |
| sinénse | White | 7, S. Ev. S. | India | 1807 |
| sphǽricum | White | 5, S. Ev. S. | | 1807 |
| tetragónum | White | 6, H. | A. India | |
| ústulátum | White | 6, S. | A. Chile | |

**CARAGANA**, *A. B. Lambert*. So called from *carachana*, its name in Tartary. Linn. 17, Or. 4, Nat. Or. *Leguminosæ*. This is a handsome genus; most of the species are well adapted for shrubberies; they a sandy open loam is the best soil for them; they are multiplied either by grafts, layers, or seeds. Synonymes: 1. *Robinia Altagana*. 2. *R. Caragana*. 3. *R. frutescens*. 4. *R. mollis-tomentosa*.

| | | | | |
|---|---|---|---|---|
| Altagána, 1 | Yellow | 5, H. De. S. | Siberia | 1789 |
| arboréscens, 2 | Yellow | 5, H. De. T. | Siberia | 1752 |
| inérmis | Yellow | 5, H. De. S. | Siberia | 1820 |
| arenária | Yellow | 6, H. De. S. | Siberia | 1802 |
| Chamlágú | Yellow | 5, H. De. S. | China | 1773 |
| férox | Yellow | 6, H. De. S. | Siberia | |
| frutéscens | Yellow | 4, H. De. S. | Siberia | 1752 |
| grandiflóra | Yellow | 6, H. De. S. | Iberia | 1823 |
| cubáta | Yellow | H. De. S. | Siberia | 1796 |
| macracántha | Yellow | H. De. S. | Siberia | |
| microphylla | Yellow | 6, H. De. S. | Russia | 1819 |
| móllis | Yellow | 5, H. De. S. | Tauria | 1818 |
| pygmǽa | Yellow | 5, H. De. S. | Siberia | 1751 |

| | | | | |
|---|---|---|---|---|
| Redowski | Yellow | 6, H. De. S. | Siberia | 1827 |
| spinósa | Yellow | 5, H. De. S. | Siberia | 1775 |
| tragacanthoídes | Yellow | 5, H. De. S. | Siberia | 1816 |

**CARAGUATA**, *Plumier*. Its name in S. America. Linn. 6, Or. 1, Nat. Or. *Bromeliaceæ*. An interesting plant, but with no great beauty; for culture, &c., see Bromelia. Synonyme: 1. *Tillandsia lingulata*.

| | | | | |
|---|---|---|---|---|
| linguláta | Yellow | 6, Epiphy. | Jamaica | 1795 |

**CARALLIA**, *Roxburgh*. From *Carillie*, the name of C. *lucida* in the Telinga language in Hindoostan. Linn. 11, Or. 1, Nat. Or. *Rhizophoraceæ*. An ornamental stove tree, about twenty feet high, succeeding best in a mixture of sandy peat and loam, and may be increased from cuttings in sand, under a glass.

| | | | | |
|---|---|---|---|---|
| lúcida | Yellow | 8. Ev. T. | E. Ind. | 1820 |

**CARALLUMA**, *R. Brown*. Its Indian name. Linn. 5, Or. 2, Nat. Or. *Asclepiadaceæ*. This succulent genus of curious plants is allied to *Stapelia*; they vary in height from one to two feet. The best soil for them seems to be a mixture of loam and brick rubbish. The pots require to be well drained, and the plants cautiously watered, except about the time of flowering, when they ought to have a liberal supply. Cuttings root freely, if they are allowed to dry before planted, till they begin to shrivel.

| | | | | |
|---|---|---|---|---|
| adscéndens, 1 | Pink | 7, S. Ev. S. | E. Ind. | 1804 |
| crenuláta | Pa. yel. | 8. Ev. S. | E. Ind. | 1829 |
| fimbriáta | Pa. yel. | 8. Ev. S. | E. Ind. | 1829 |
| umbelláta | Pink | 8. Ev. S. | E. Ind. | 1804 |

**CARAPA**, *Aublet*. From *Caraipe*, the name of C. *guianensis* in Guiana. Linn. 10, Or. 1, Nat. Or. *Meliaceæ*. A fine genus of stove plants, not common in collections; they succeed best in loam and sandy peat mixed, and are increased readily by cuttings in sand, plunged in heat, under a glass.

| | | | | |
|---|---|---|---|---|
| guianénsis | Yellow | 8. Ev. T. | Guiana | 1824 |
| guineénsis, 1 | Yellow | 8. Ev. T. | S. Leone | 1793 |
| moluccénsis | Yellow | 8. Ev. T. | E. Ind. | 1820 |
| procéra | Yellow | 8. Ev. T. | W. Ind. | |

**CARAWAY**, see *Cárum Cárui*.

**CARBONIXED**, burned to coal.

**CARDAMINE**, *Linn.* From *kardia*, the heart, *damas*, to subdue; stomachic quality of the plants, or perhaps a diminutive of *kardamon*, watercress, the taste being similar. Linn. 15, Nat. Or. *Cruciferæ*. An interesting genus, of the simplest culture and propagation.

| | | | | |
|---|---|---|---|---|
| amára | White | 4, H. Her. P. | Britain | |
| asarifólia | White | 6, H. Her. P. | Italy | 1710 |
| bellidifólia | White | 4, H. Her. P. | Scotland | |
| alpína, 1 | White | 4, H. Her. P. | Austria | 1658 |
| Chelidónia | White | 6, H. Her. P. | Italy | 1739 |
| glaúca | White | 6, H. Her. P. | Calabria | 1827 |
| latifólia | Purple | 6, H. Her. P. | Spain | 1710 |
| macrophýlla | Purple | 4, H. Her. P. | Siberia | 1824 |
| praténsis | Purple | 4, H. Her. P. | Britain | |
|   plěna | Purple | 4, H. Her. P. | | |
| thalictroídes | White | 6, H. | A. Piedmont | 1818 |
| trifólia | White | 5, H. Her. P. | Switzerl. | 1629 |
| uliginósa | White | 4, H. Her. P. | Tauria | 1819 |

*africána*, *alpína*, *chilénsis*, *dentáta*, *granulósa*, *hirsúta*, *impátiens*, *parviflóra*, *pensylvánica*, *prorépens*, *resedifólia*, *rhomboídea*, *rotundifólia*, *sylvática*, *umbrósa*.

**CARDINAL FLOWER**, see *Lobélia cardinális*.

**CARDINALIS**, principal, chief; scarlet.

**CARDIOSPERMUM**, *Linn.* From *kardia*, a heart, and *sperma*, seed; in allusion to the shape of the seeds. Linn. 8, Or. 3, Nat. Or. *Sapindaceæ*. The species of this singular genus require to be sown in a hot-bed frame, or in the stove in any light soil.

| | | | | |
|---|---|---|---|---|
| canéscens | | 8. | E. Ind. | 1822 |
| coluteoídes | White | 7, S. Ev. Cl. | Caraccas | 1818 |
| Carindum | Wht. grn. | 7, S. | A. Brazil | 1750 |
| grandiflórum | White | 7, S. Ev. Cl. | Jamaica | 1817 |
| Halicácabum | White | 7, S. Cl. | E. Ind. | 1594 |
| hirsútum | White | 7, S. Ev. Cl. | Guinea | 1822 |
| pubéscens | Scarlet | 6, S. Ev. Cl. | N. Spain | 1822 |

**CARDOON**, see *Cýnara cardúnculus*.

**CARDOPATUM**, *Jussieu*. *Carduus*, a thistle, and *patos*, beaten path; in allusion to the appearance of the plant, and the place it inhabits. Linn. 19, Or. 1, Nat. Or. *Compositæ*. An uninteresting herbaceous plant, of simple cultivation, and is increased by dividing the root—*corymbósum*.

CARDÚNCĚLŬS, *Adanson.* From the diminutive, *cardunculus*, of cardoon. *Linn.* 19, Or. 1, Nat. Or. *Compositæ.* A genus of pretty herbaceous plants, succeeding well in common soil, and increased by dividing the roots. *Synonymes:* 1. *Carthamus mitissimus.* 2. *C. carduncellus.*

| | | | | | | |
|---|---|---|---|---|---|---|
| mitissimŭs, 1 | . | Blue | . | 6, H. Her. P. France | . | 1776 |
| vulgāris, 2 | . | Blue | . | 5, H. Her. P. France | . | 1784 |

CĀRDÚŬS, *Linn.* From *ard*, in Celtic, meaning a point, the plants being mostly spiny. *Linn.* 19, Or. 1, Nat. Or. *Compositæ.* A coarse, though somewhat ornamental and numerous genus of plants, growing from one to four feet high; they succeed in any common soil, and are multiplied by seeds or divisions. *Synonymes:* 1. *Onopordum deltoideum.* 2. *Carlina pyrenaica.*

| | | | | | | |
|---|---|---|---|---|---|---|
| alātŭs | . | Purple | . | 7, H. | B. | 1812 |
| albidŭs | . | Purple | . | 7, H. | A. Tauria | 1816 |
| alpestrŭs | . | Purple | . | 7, H. Her. P. Croatia | . | 1805 |
| atriplicifōliŭs, 1 | . | Purple | . | 8, H. Her. P. Siberia | . | 1784 |
| arabicŭs | . | Purple | . | 7, H. | A. Arabia | 1789 |
| arctioĭdēs | . | Purple | . | 7, H. Her. P. Carniola | . | 1804 |
| argentātŭs | . | Purple | . | 7, H. | A. Egypt | 1789 |
| Argemōnŭ | . | Purple | . | 7, H. Her. P. Pyrenees | . | 1810 |
| cándicāns | . | Purple | . | 7, H. | B. Hungary | 1805 |
| carlinæfōliŭs | . | Purple | . | 7, H. | B. Pyrenees | 1804 |
| carlinoĭdēs, 2 | . | Purple | . | 7, H. | B. Pyrenees | 1784 |
| cinĕrĕŭs | . | Purple | . | 7, H. | A. Caucasus | 1818 |
| clavulātŭs | . | Purple | . | 7, H. | A. Canaries | 1827 |
| collīnŭs | . | Purple | . | 7, H. | B. Hungary | 1818 |
| corymbōsŭs | . | Purple | . | 7, H. | B. Naples | 1824 |
| crassifōliŭs | . | Purple | . | 7, H. | P. | 1805 |
| crispŭs | . | Purple | . | 7, H. | B. Europe | 1804 |
| deflorātŭs | . | Red | . | 8, H. Her. P. Austria | . | 1670 |
| dūbiŭs | . | Purple | . | 7, H. Her. P. | | 1816 |
| hamulōsŭs | . | Purple | . | 6, H. | B. Hungary | 1802 |
| lanuginōsŭs | . | Purple | . | 7, H. | B. Armenia | 1820 |
| leucánthŭs | . | Purple | . | 7, H. | A. Spain | 1816 |
| leucŏgrăphŭs | . | Purple | . | 6, H. | A. Italy | 1752 |
| macrocěphálŭs | . | Purple | . | 7, H. Her. P. Numidia | . | 1827 |
| mĕdiŭs | . | Purple | . | 6, H. Her. P. Piedmont | . | 1819 |
| montōsŭs | . | Purple | . | 7, H. | B. S. Eur. | 1820 |
| nigrěscēns | . | Purple | . | 7, H. | B. S. France | 1819 |
| nūtāns | . | Purple | . | 7, H. | A. Britain | |
| onopordioĭdēs | . | Purple | . | 7, H. Her. P. Iberia | . | 1818 |
| oriēntālis | . | Purple | . | 7, H. Her. P. Iberia | . | 1804 |
| parvifōrŭs | . | Purple | . | 7, H. Her. P. S. Eur. | . | 1781 |
| peregrinŭs | . | Purple | . | 7, H. | A. | 1816 |
| Personātā | . | Purple | . | 7, H. | B. Austria | 1776 |
| podacánthŭs | . | Purple | . | 7, H. Her. P. France | . | 1819 |
| pycnocéphálŭs | . | Purple | . | 7, H. Her. P. S. Eur. | . | 1739 |
| seminūdŭs | . | Purple | . | 7, H. | B. Caucasus | 1819 |
| uncinātŭs | . | Purple | . | 7, H. | B. Tauria | 1817 |
| volgēnsis | . | Purple | . | 7, H. | A. Volga | 1820 |

*acanthoĭdēs, tenuiflōrŭs.*

CĀRĚX, *Linn.* From *careo*, to want; the upper spikes being without seeds. *Linn.* 21, Or. 3, Nat. Or. *Cyperaceæ.* This genus is extensive, and the species are uninteresting; part of them are natives of marshy situations, and a few do best on dry sandy eminences; they seed freely, by which they are increased. *Synonymes:* 1. *C. scotica.* 2. *C. straminea* —*acuminātā, acūtā, alba, alpestris, ambleocarpā, ampullācěā, ānceps, angustifōliā, appréssā, aquătilis, arenāriā, ātrātā, axillāris, bicŏlŏr, binērvis, brachystăchyā brixoĭdēs, bullātā, Burbaŭmiā, cæspitōsā, capillāris, chordorhīzā, ciliātā, clandestīnā, collīnā, conglobātā, crinītā, cūrtā, curvŭlā, cyperoĭdēs, Davalliānā, depauperātā, digitātā, dioīcā, distāns, divisā, divŭlsā, elongātā, extēnsā, ferruginēā, flāvā, filifōrmis, fimbriātā, flexuōsa, ferriā, fætidā, Fraseriānā, fulvā, glareōsa, granulāris, hirtā, hordeifōrmis, incūrvā, intermēdiā, invērsā, jūncēā, juncifōliā, lævigātā, lagopodioĭdēs, leporīnā, leuco-glōchin, limōsā, lobātā, loliācěā, lōngipēs, leucōrum, Michelii, Mielichhfěrā 1, microstăchyā, mucronātā, multiflōrā, muricātā, nemorōsā, nĭtidā, norvégicā, nŭtāns, Œdērii, ovālis, palléscēns, paludōsā, panicěā, paniculātā, paradōxā, pauciflōrā, pēndŭlā, phæostăchyā 2, pilōsā, pilulifěrā, plantaginěā, podocărpā, præcŏx, pseūdō-cypěrŭs, pulicăris, pŭllā, pyrenāicā, rarifōrā, recŭrvā, remōtā, rēpēns, rigidā, ripāriā, rŏstā, rostrātā, rupēstris, salīnā, saxātilis, schænoĭdēs, Schrebērī scopāriā, secalīnā, speirostăchyā, sphærostăchyā, stellŭlātā, stenophŏllā, stictocărpā, stipātā, străminēā, strictā, strigōsā, sylvăticā, tenēllā, teretiascŭlā, thuringiăicā, tomentōsā, umbrōsā, ustulātā, Văhlii, vesicāriā, vulpīnā.*

CARĚYA, *Roxburgh.* In honour of the Rev. William Carey, of Serampore, a distinguished botanist. *Linn.* 16, Or. 8, Nat. Or. *Myrtaceæ.* C. *herbacea*

is a most splendid herbaceous stove-plant, of rather difficult culture; it must be grown in a mixture of light loam and sandy peat, carefully watered at all times, particularly in winter, and the pot properly drained; and the mode of raising it is by dividing the roots.

| | | | | | |
|---|---|---|---|---|---|
| arbōrěā | . . . | Red yal. | 8. Ev. T. E. Ind. | . . | 1823 |
| herbácěā | . . . | Red | 7, 8. Her. P. E. Ind. | . . | 1808 |
| sphérĭcā | . . . | Red | 8. Ev. 8. E. Ind. | . . | 1808 |

CARGILLYA, *R. Brown.* In honour of James Cargill, M.D., of Aberdeen. *Linn.* 23, Or. 2, Nat. Or. *Ebenaceæ.* An interesting genus of greenhouse plants, that succeed best grown in a mixture of peat and open loam, and are increased by cuttings in sand, or sandy soil, under a glass.

| | | | | |
|---|---|---|---|---|
| australis | . . . | G. Ev. T. N. Holl. | . | 1816 |
| laxa | . . . | G. Ev. T. N. Holl. | . | 1827 |

CĀRĬCĀ, *Linn.* Erroneously supposed to be a native of Caria. *Linn.* 22, Or. 9, Nat. Or. *Papayaceæ.* The plants of this genus are ornamental, and grow best in loamy soil; full-grown cuttings root at once, if the leaves are not taken off, planted in sand, under a glass, in heat.

| | | | | | |
|---|---|---|---|---|---|
| cauliflōrā | . . . | Green | . . | 8. Ev. T. Caraccas | 1806 |
| citrifōrmis | . . . | Wht. grn. | 8. Ev. T. Lima | . . | 1820 |
| microcărpā | . . . | Wht. grn. | 8. Ev. T. Caraccas | . . | 1806 |
| monōĭcā | . . . | Wht. grn. | 8. Ev. T. | . . | 1818 |
| Papāyă | . . . | Green | . 7, 8. Ev. 8. India | . . | 1690 |
| pyrifōrmis | . . . | | 8. Ev. T. Guiana | . . | 1823 |
| spinōsā, 1 | . . . | Wht. grn. | 8. Ev. T. Guiana | . . | 1821 |

CARINA, a keel like that of a boat, also the lower petal of a papilionaceous flower.

CARINĀTE, keel-shaped.

CARINATELY-WINGED, having a wing like a keel.

CARINATELY-CONCAVE, hollowed so as to resemble a keel externally.

CARIŎPsĬs, a one-celled, small, indehiscent pericarp, adhering to the seed which it contains, as the grain of grasses.

CARIssĀ, *Linn.* Derivation not known. *Linn.* 5, Or. 1, Nat. Or. *Apocynaceæ.* This is an ornamental genus, the species attain from six to twenty feet high, and to succeed well require a mixture of peat and loam; and to grow in pots, should be carefully drained, as the plants are impatient of much water. Cuttings root freely in sand, under a glass, in heat.

| | | | | | |
|---|---|---|---|---|---|
| carándas | . . | White | . 7, 8. Ev. T. E. Ind. | . . | 1790 |
| lanceōlātā | . . | White | . 7, 8. Ev. T. N. Holl. | . . | 1822 |
| ovātā | . . | White | . 8, 8. Ev. T. N. Holl. | . . | 1819 |
| spinārŭm | . . | White | . 7, 8. Ev. T. E. Ind. | . . | 1819 |
| Xylopicrŏn | . . | White | . 7, 8. Ev. T. Mauritius | . . | 1820 |

CARLĪNA, *Linn.* Named after the famous Charlemagne, whose army was cured of the plague by it. *Linn.* 19, Or. 1, Nat. Or. *Compositæ.* Interesting plants, attaining from one to three feet high, and succeeding well in garden soil; they are easily increased from seeds. *Synonymes:* 1. *C. sulphurea.* 2. *C. bracteata.*

| | | | | | |
|---|---|---|---|---|---|
| acanthifōliā | . . | White | . 6, H. Her. P. Carniola | . | 1818 |
| acaūlis | . . | White | . 6, H. Her. P. Italy | . | 1640 |
| caulěscēns | . . | White | . 6, H. Her. P. Switzerl. | . | 1819 |
| aggregātā | . . | White | . 7, H. Her. P. Hungary | . | 1804 |
| Bieberstein iānā | . . | | . 8, H. Her. P. Caucasus | . | 1816 |
| corymbōsā | . . | Yellow | . 7, H. Her. P. S. Eur. | . | 1640 |
| lanātā | . . | Purple | . 6, H. | A. S. Eur. | 1683 |
| lyrātā | . . | | . 6, O. | B. C. G. H. | 1816 |
| racemōsā, 1 | . . | Yellow | . 7, H. | A. Spain | 1658 |
| sicŭlā, 2 | . . | | . 7, H. | B. Sicily | 1827 |
| simplex | . . | White | . 6, H. Her. P. Hungary | . | 1816 |

*vulgāris.*

CARLINE THISTLE, see *Carlīnā.*

CARLOWIZIA, *Mænch.* After Carlowiz, some unknown botanist. *Linn.* 19, Or. 1, Nat. Or. *Compositæ.* This is a pretty greenhouse shrub, attaining the height of three feet; it thrives best when grown in sandy loam; cuttings root freely in sand, under a glass. *Synonyme:* 1. *Onobroma salicifolium.*

| | | | | |
|---|---|---|---|---|
| salicifōliŭs, 1 | . . | Yellow | . 8, G. Ev. 8. Madeira | . 1784 |

CARLUDŎVĬCĀ, *Ruiz* and *Pavon.* Named in honour of Charles IV. of Spain, and Louisa his Queen, noble patrons of botany. *Linn.* 21, Or. 9, Nat. Or. *Cyclanthaceæ.* These are ornamental low palm-like plants; they grow best in a mixture of sandy peat and loam, and are multiplied by suckers.

*Synonymes:* 1. *Salmia angustifolia.* 2. *Ludovia funifera.*

| | | | |
|---|---|---|---|
| angustifoliā, 1 | Grn. yel. | 8. Her. P. Peru | 1818 |
| funifera, 2 | White | 8. Ev. Cl. Trinidad | 1824 |
| jamaicensis | White | 8. Ev. Cl. Jamaica | 1825 |
| latifolia | Green | 7, 8. Her. P. Peru | 1818 |
| palmata | White | 7, 8. Her. P. Peru | 1818 |

CARMICHAELIA, *R. Brown.* In honour of the late Captain Dugald Carmichael, F.H.S., author of the "Flora of Tristan da Acunha." *Linn.* 17, Or. 4, Nat. Or. *Leguminosæ.* A pretty greenhouse shrub, succeeding well in sandy peat, and increased by cuttings in sand under a glass. *Synonyme:* 1. *Lotus australis.*

| | | | |
|---|---|---|---|
| australis, 1 | Blue | 6, G. Ev. S. N. Holl. | 1800 |

CARMINATIVES, medicines which remove flatulence.
CARNATION, see *Diánthus caryophýllus.*
CARNOSE, fleshy, thick substance.
CAROB TREE, see *Ceratōnia.*
CAROLINEA, *Linn.* In honour of Sophia Caroline, Margravine of Baden. *Linn.* 16, Or. 8, Nat. Or. *Sterculiaceæ.* Splendid species, growing from fifteen to twenty feet high; they delight in a rich loamy soil; and cuttings, not deprived of their leaves, root in sand under a glass in heat.

| | | | |
|---|---|---|---|
| alba | White | 7, 8. Ev. T. Brasil | 1817 |
| insignis | Red | 8. Ev. T. W. Ind. | 1796 |
| minor | Red yel. gr. | 7, 8. Ev. T. Guiana | 1798 |
| princeps | Red yel. gr. | 8. Ev. T. W. Ind. | 1787 |

CARPELLA,  the small parts of which compound fruits
CARPELS,  } are formed.
CARPESIUM, *Linn.* From *karpesion,* a bit of straw, the appearance of the leaves of the involucrum. *Linn.* 19, Or. 1, Nat. Or. *Compositæ.* Plants of little beauty, and easy management in light rich soil; seeds—*abrotanoides, cernuum.*
CARPINUS, *Linn.* From the Celtic, *car,* wood, *pinda,* head; the wood being fit for the yokes of cattle. *Linn.* 5, Or. 1, Nat. Or. *Apocynaceæ.* Ornamental trees, from twelve to thirty feet high; some of the species make good hedges for shelter, as they grow quick, and are easily managed; they are raised from seeds or layers without difficulty.

| | | | |
|---|---|---|---|
| americana | Apetal | H. De. T. N. Amer. | 1812 |
| Bētulus | Apetal | 8, H. De. T. Britain | |
| incisa | Apetal | 4, H. De. T. | |
| quercifolia | Apetal | 5, H. De. T. Europe | |
| variegata | Apetal | 8, H. De. T. Britain | |
| orientalis | Apetal | H. De. T. Levant | 1739 |

CARPODINUS, *R. Brown.* From *karpos,* fruit, and *dinos,* a circle; the fruit being round. *Linn.* 5, Or. 1, Nat. Or. *Apocynaceæ.* A fruiting shrub, attaining about eight feet high, and growing well in a mixture of open loam and sandy peat, and increased, without difficulty, from cuttings.

| | | | |
|---|---|---|---|
| dulcis | Green | 6, S. S. Leone | 1822 |

CARPODONTOS, *Labillardière.* From *karpos,* a fruit, and *odontos,* toothed; the cells or carpels toothed at the apex. *Linn.* 13, Or. 6, Nat. Or. *Hypericaceæ.* An ornamental greenhouse plant, growing to the height of twenty feet; it thrives best in peat and loam mixed, and cuttings root freely in sand, under a glass.

| | | | |
|---|---|---|---|
| lucida | | G. Ev. T. N. Holl. | 1820 |

CARPOLOGY, the science which treats of the structure of fruits and seeds.
CARRICHTERA, *Decandolle.* Probably without meaning. *Linn.* 15, Nat. Or. *Cruciferæ.* This is a pretty annual, growing well when sown in the open ground in a dry situation. *Synonyme:* 1. *Vella annua.*

| | | | |
|---|---|---|---|
| Vella, 1 | Yellow | 6, H. A. England | |

CARROT, see *Daucus.*
CARTHAMUS, *Tournefort.* From its Arabic name *quortom,* to paint; the flowers yield a fine colour. *Linn.* 19, Or. 1, Nat. Or. *Compositæ.* Interesting annuals, requiring to be sown on a gentle hotbed, and afterwards transplanted where they are intended to flower.

| | | | |
|---|---|---|---|
| oxyacantha | Yellow | 7, H. A. Caucasus | 1818 |
| tinctorius | Orange | 6, H. A. Egypt | 1551 |

CARTILAGINOUS, gristly.
CARTONEMA, *R. Brown.* From *kartos,* shorn, and *nema,* a filament; in allusion to the stamens. *Linn.*

6, Or. 1, Nat. Or. *Commelinaceæ.* A pretty annual, requiring merely to be sown in sandy peat, and treated in the stove.

| | | | |
|---|---|---|---|
| spicatum | Blue | 7, 8. Her. P. N. Holl. | 1822 |

CARUM, *Koch.* From Caria, in Asia Minor, being originally found there. *Linn.* 5, Or. 2, Nat. Or. *Umbelliferæ.* One species of this genus, *C. Carui,* produces the seeds so generally known by the name of caraway seeds; they are hardy biennials, and require merely to be sown in the open ground.

| | | | |
|---|---|---|---|
| carui | White | 5, H. Her. P. Britain | |

*Amplex.*
CARUNCLE, a small protuberance.
CARUNCULARIA, *Haworth.* Derived from *caruncula,* a fleshy protuberance; in reference to the flowers. *Linn.* 5, Or. 2, Nat. Or. *Asclepiadaceæ.* A curious succulent plant; for culture, &c., see *Stapelia.* *Synonyme:* 1. *Stapelia pedunculata.*

| | | | |
|---|---|---|---|
| pedunculata, 1 | Br. pur. | 7, 8. Ev. S. C. G. H. | 1790 |

CARYA, *Nuttall.* From *caryon,* signifying a nut; in allusion to the fruit. *Linn.* 21, Or. 9, Nat. Or. *Juglandaceæ.* A genus of timber-trees, growing about thirty feet high; they succeed in common soil, and increase by seeds or layers. *Synonymes:* 1. *Juglans squamosa, alba.* 2. *J. amara.* 3. *J. compressa.* 4. *J. obcordata.* 5. *J. angustifolia, olivæformis.* 6. *J. porcina.* 7. *J. sulcata.*

| | | | |
|---|---|---|---|
| alba, 1 | Apetal | 4, H. De. T. N. Amer. | 1629 |
| amara, 2 | Apetal | 4, H. De. T. N. Amer. | 1800 |
| compressa, 3 | Apetal | 4, H. De. T. N. Amer. | 1730 |
| laciniosa | Apetal | 4, H. De. T. N. Amer. | |
| microcarpa | Apetal | 4, H. De. T. N. Amer. | |
| obcordata, 4 | Apetal | 5, H. De. T. N. Amer. | 1812 |
| olivæformis, 5 | Apetal | 4, H. De. T. N. Amer. | |
| porcina, 6 | Apetal | 5, H. De. T. N. Amer. | 1799 |
| glabra | Apetal | 5, H. De. T. N. Amer. | |
| sulcata, 7 | Apetal | 4, H. De. T. N. Amer. | 1804 |
| tomentosa | Apetal | 4, H. De. T. N. Amer. | |
| maxima | Apetal | 5, H. De. T. Philadel. | |

CARYOCAR, *Linn.* From *karyon,* a nut; the species bear large fruit, containing an eatable nut. *Linn.* 13, Or. 4, Nat. Or. *Rhizobolaceæ.* A genus of fruit-bearing trees, attaining the height of a hundred feet; in our stoves they thrive best in sandy open loam or a mixture of loam and peat, and may be increased by cuttings in sand, under a glass. *Synonyme:* 1. *Pekea tuberculata.*

| | | | |
|---|---|---|---|
| glabrum | Green | 8. Ev. T. Guiana | 1820 |
| nuciferum | Red. yel. | 8. Ev. T. Guiana | |
| tomentosum, 1 | White | 8. Ev. T. Guiana | 1820 |

CARYOPHYLLUS, *Linn.* From *karyon,* a nut, and *phyllon,* a leaf; referring to the appearance of the flower-buds. *Linn.* 12, Or. 1, Nat. Or. *Myrtaceæ.* The species *aromaticus* grows to about twenty feet high, and produces the article known as cloves. It grows best in a mixture of sandy peat and loam in a strong steady heat. The species is rather scarce, owing to the difficulty of keeping them in winter; cuttings in sand root readily under a glass, in a moist heat.

| | | | |
|---|---|---|---|
| aromaticus | Yel. wht. | 8. Ev. T. Moluccas | 1797 |

CARYOTA, *Linn.* The Greeks applied this name to a cultivated date. *Linn.* 21, Or. 9, Nat. Or. *Palmaceæ.* A noble and beautiful genus of palms, growing to the height of twenty feet; the best way of treating them is in sandy loam, and a warm moist atmosphere; increased by seeds.

| | | | |
|---|---|---|---|
| horrida | | Palm. S. Amer. | 1823 |
| mitis | White | Palm. China | 1820 |
| urens | White | Palm. E. Ind. | 1788 |

CASEARIA, *Jacquin.* In honour of J. Casearius, the co-operator of Rheede in the Hortus Malabaricus. *Linn.* 10, Or. 1, Nat. Or. *Samydaceæ.* Interesting stove shrubs, growing from four to eight feet high; they all thrive well in sandy loam, and are increased by cuttings in sand under a glass in heat. *Synonymes:* 1. *C. decandra.* 2. *Iroucana guianensis.*

| | | | |
|---|---|---|---|
| hirsuta | Yel. grn. | 8. Ev. S. Jamaica | 1825 |
| parviflora, 1 | Yel. grn. | 8. Ev. S. S. Amer. | 1818 |
| parvifolia | Yel. grn. | 8. Ev. S. Martinlq. | 1827 |
| ramiflora, 2 | Yel. grn. | 8. Ev. S. Guiana | 1824 |
| serrulata | Wht. grn. | 8. Ev. S. Jamaica | 1818 |
| sylvestris | Wht. grn. | 8. Ev. S. Jamaica | 1823 |

CASHEW-NUT, see *Anacardium.*

CameXvI, see Jániphá Mánihót.

CIssIX, *Linn.* According to Olaus Celsus, this name is to be traced to the Hebrew Ketzioth, and latinised by Cassia. *Linn.* 10, Or. 1, Nat. Or. *Leguminosæ.* This is a numerous genus of ornamental plants, growing from one to fifteen feet high; they delight in a light, loamy soil, or loam and peat mixed; some produce seed in abundance, but cuttings strike freely in sand under a glass in a little heat. *Synonymes:* 1. *C. acuminata.* 2. *C. flexuosa.* 3. *C. crispa.* 4. *C. grandiflora.* 5. *C. orientalis, acutiloba.* 6. *C. Senna.* 7. *C. procumbens.* 8. *C. cernua.* 9. *C. arborescens.* 10. *C. multiglandulosa.* 11. *C. chinensis.* 12. *C. dimidiata.*

| | | | | | | | |
|---|---|---|---|---|---|---|---|
| acapulcěnsis | . | Yellow | . | 6, 8. Ev. S. | Acapulco | . | 1893 |
| æschynőměně | . | Yellow | . | 6, 8. | A. W. Ind. | . | 1810 |
| ægyptiácǎ | . | Yellow | . | 5, G. Ev. S. | Egypt | . | 1822 |
| alátǎ | . | Yellow | . | 8. Ev. S. | W. Ind. | . | 1731 |
| angustissimǎ | . | Yellow | . | 7, 8. | A. E. Ind. | . | 1820 |
| apoucouttǎ, 1 | . | Yellow | . | 8. Ev. S. | Surinam | . | 1820 |
| arenáriǎ | . | Yellow | . | 7, 8. Ev. S. | Maypures | . | 1819 |
| artemisioïdes | . | Yellow | . | 6, G. Ev. S. | N. Holl. | . | 1820 |
| áspěrǎ | . | Yellow | . | 7, 8. | A. Georgia | . | 1818 |
| atomáriǎ | . | Yellow | . | 8. Ev. S. | N. Amer. | . | 1810 |
| auriculátǎ | . | Yellow | . | 8. Ev. S. | E. Ind. | . | 1777 |
| austrális | . | Yellow | . | 7, G. Ev. S. | N. Holl. | . | 1824 |
| aversiflórǎ | . | Yellow | . | 7, 8. Ev. S. | Brazil | . | 1820 |
| bacilláris | . | Yellow | . | 8. Ev. S. | E. Ind. | . | 1789 |
| Barclayǎnǎ | . | Yellow | . | 7, G. Ev. S. | N. Holl. | . | 1827 |
| Bertéri | . | Yellow | . | 6, G. Ev. S. | W. Ind. | . | 1827 |
| bicapsuláris | . | Yellow | . | 5, G. Ev. S. | W. Ind. | . | 1789 |
| biflórǎ | . | Yellow | . | 8, G. Ev. S. | W. Ind. | . | 1766 |
| bifoliátǎ | . | Yellow | . | 6, G. Ev. S. | Brazil | . | 1820 |
| bracteátǎ | . | Yellow | . | 8, G. Ev. S. | W. Ind. | . | 1822 |
| brevifóliǎ | . | Yellow | . | 6, G. Ev. S. | Madagas. | . | 1824 |
| Burmánnǎ, 2 | . | Yellow | . | 9, F. | A. C. G. H. | . | 1810 |
| capénsis | . | Yellow | . | 6, G. Ev. S. | C. G. H. | . | 1816 |
| chamæcristǎ | . | Yellow | . | 7, | America | . | 1699 |
| chinénsis | . | Yellow | . | 8, G. Ev. S. | China | . | 1807 |
| ciliáris | . | Yellow | . | 6, 8. Her. P. | E. Ind. | . | 1817 |
| ciliátǎ | . | Yellow | . | 8. Ev. S. | Cuba | . | 1820 |
| coromandeliánǎ | . | Yellow | . | 6, 8. Ev. S. | Coroman. | . | 1823 |
| corymbósǎ | . | Yellow | . | 7, 8. Ev. S. | B. Ayres | . | 1796 |
| cuspidátǎ | . | Yellow | . | 7, 8. Ev. S. | S. Amer. | . | 1820 |
| diphyllǎ | . | Yellow | . | 6, 8. Ev. S. | W. Ind. | . | 1781 |
| dispǎr | . | Yellow | . | 8. Ev. S. | S. Amer. | . | 1824 |
| elliptieǎ | . | Yellow | . | 6, 8. Ev. S. | Trinidad | . | 1818 |
| emarginátǎ | . | Yellow | . | 5, 8. Ev. S. | Jamaica | . | 1759 |
| fastigiátǎ | . | Yellow | . | 6, 8. Ev. S. | E. Ind. | . | 1818 |
| flexuósǎ | . | Yellow | . | 7, 8. | A. Brasil | . | 1810 |
| floribúndǎ | . | Yellow | . | 8. | A. New Spain | . | 1818 |
| flóridǎ | . | Yellow | . | 6, 8. | A. E. Ind. | . | 1820 |
| frondósǎ, 8 | . | Yellow | . | 4, G. Ev. S. | W. Ind. | . | 1796 |
| geminiflórǎ | . | Yellow | . | 6, 8. Ev. S. | Mexico | . | 1824 |
| glandulósǎ | . | Yellow | . | 2, 8. | A. W. Ind. | . | 1822 |
| glaucǎ | . | Yellow | . | 6, 8. Ev. S. | E. Ind. | . | 1818 |
| glutinósǎ | . | Yellow | . | 6, G. Ev. S. | N. Holl. | . | 1818 |
| gracíllis | . | Yellow | . | 6, 8. Ev. S. | Orinoco | . | 1817 |
| Herbertiánǎ | . | Yellow | . | 11, 8. Ev. S. | Barba. | . | 1828 |
| hírtǎ | . | Yellow | . | 8, 8. Ev. S. | N. Amer. | . | 1820 |
| hirsútǎ | . | Yellow | . | 7, 8. Ev. S. | America | . | 1778 |
| húmilis | . | Yellow | . | 6, 8. | B. S. Amer. | . | 1800 |
| itálicǎ | . | Yellow | . | 6, 8. | A. S. Eur. | . | |
| lævigátǎ, 4 | . | Yellow | . | 7, 8. Ev. S. | | | |
| lanceolátǎ, 5 | . | Yellow | . | 7, 8. Ev. S. | Levant | . | |
| ligustrínǎ | . | Yellow | . | 8, 8. Ev. S. | Bahama | . | 1726 |
| lineáris | . | Yellow | . | 6, G. Ev. S. | Carolina | . | 1800 |
| lineátǎ | . | Yellow | . | 6, 8. Ev. S. | Jamaica | . | 1818 |
| longisiliquǎ | . | Yellow | . | 6, 8. Ev. S. | W. Ind. | . | 1800 |
| latoídes | . | Yellow | . | 6, 8. Ev. S. | Trinidad | . | 1820 |
| macranthérǎ | . | Yellow | . | 6, 8. Ev. S. | Brasil | . | 1824 |
| marginátǎ | . | Yellow | . | 6, 8. Ev. S. | Surinam | . | 1823 |
| marilándicǎ | . | Yellow | . | 9, H. Her. P. | N. Amer. | . | 1823 |
| mexicánǎ | . | Yellow | . | 6, 8. Ev. S. | Mexico | . | 1824 |
| microphyllǎ | . | Yellow | . | 7, 8. | A. San. Cruz | . | 1800 |
| mimosoídes | . | Yellow | . | 7, 8. | A. Ceylon | . | 1806 |
| mollissimǎ | . | Yellow | . | 8. Ev. S. | S. Amer. | . | 1820 |
| nictitǎns | . | Yellow | . | 7, H. | A. N. Amer. | . | 1800 |
| nigrícǎns | . | Yellow | . | 6, G. Ev. S. | Egypt | . | 1817 |
| obovátǎ, 6 | . | Yellow | . | 7, 8. | A. Egypt | . | 1640 |
| occidentális | . | Yellow | . | 6, 8. Ev. S. | W. Ind. | . | 1759 |
| pállidǎ | . | Pa. yel. | . | 6, 8. Ev. S. | S. Amer. | . | 1818 |
| Parkeriánǎ | . | Yellow | . | 8, 8. Ev. S. | Demerara | . | 1817 |
| patǔlǎ | . | Yellow | . | 8, 8. Ev. S. | W. Ind. | . | 1778 |
| pendǔlǎ | . | Yellow | . | 7, 8. Ev. S. | S. Amer. | . | 1820 |
| pentagónǎ | . | Yellow | . | 6, 8. Her. P. | Peru | . | 1700 |
| pilósǎ | . | Yellow | . | 6, 8. Her. P. | Jamaica | . | 1818 |
| plantasiliquǎ | . | Yellow | . | 6, 8. Ev. S. | W. Ind. | . | 1822 |
| polyphyllǎ | . | Yellow | . | 6, 8. Ev. S. | W. Ind. | . | 1816 |
| prostrátǎ | . | Yellow | . | 6, 8. Ev. S. | Tr. S. Amer. | . | 1819 |
| pubéscens | . | Yellow | . | 6, 8. Ev. S. | S. Amer. | . | 1819 |
| pulchéllǎ | . | Yellow | . | 7, G. Ev. S. | Mauritius | . | 1825 |
| pumílǎ, 7 | . | Yellow | . | 6, 8. Tr. | A. E. Ind. | . | 1814 |
| purpúrěǎ | . | Yellow | . | 7, 8. Ev. S. | E. Ind. | . | 1821 |
| quinquanguláris | . | Yellow | . | 6, 8. Ev. S. | Cayenne | . | 1818 |
| reticulátǎ | . | Yellow | . | 8, 8. Ev. S. | S. Amer. | . | 1821 |
| Richardiánǎ | . | Yellow | . | 7, 8. Ev. S. | Cumana | . | 1823 |

[ 65 ]

| | | | | | | | |
|---|---|---|---|---|---|---|---|
| robinioídes | . | Yellow | . | 7, 8. Ev. S. | S. Amer. | . | 1823 |
| ruscifóliǎ | . | Yellow | . | 6, G. Ev. S. | Madeira | . | 1816 |
| sennoídes | . | Yellow | . | 7, 8. Ev. S. | E. Ind. | . | 1808 |
| sophórǎ | . | Yellow | . | 7, 8. Ev. S. | E. Ind. | . | 1658 |
| speciósǎ | . | Yellow | . | 6, 8. Ev. S. | Brazil | . | 1816 |
| spectábilis | . | Yellow | . | 6, 8. Ev. S. | Caraccas | . | 1820 |
| stipuláceǎ | . | Yellow | . | 8. Ev. S. | Chili | . | 1781 |
| sulcáta, 8 | . | Yellow | . | 6, 8. Ev. S. | S. Amer. | . | 1820 |
| tarántǎn | . | Yellow | . | 7, 8. Ev. S. | Cumana | . | 1817 |
| tenéllǎ | . | Yellow | . | 7, 8. Ev. S. | Oronoco | . | 1820 |
| Thonníngii | . | Yellow | . | 6, 8. | A. Guinea | . | 1824 |
| tomentósǎ, 9 | . | Yellow | . | 7, 8. Ev. T. | S. Amer. | . | 1822 |
| torósǎ, 10 | . | Yellow | . | 6, 8. Ev. S. | China | . | 1816 |
| triflórǎ | . | Yellow | . | 6, 8. | A. W. Ind. | . | 1816 |
| viminǎǎ | . | Yellow | . | 8. Ev. S. | W. Ind. | . | 1786 |
| virgátǎ | . | Yellow | . | 6, 8. Ev. S. | W. Ind. | . | 1810 |
| Wallichiánǎ, 11 | Yellow | . | 6, 8. | A. Nepal | . | . | 1817 |

*Abǎts, ligustrinoídes, obtusifóliǎ, procúmběns, sericěǎ, sulphǔrěǎ 12, Tagěrǎ, Tórǎ.*

CassíNě, *Linn.* The name applied to it by the Indians of Florida. *Linn.* 5, Or. 8, Nat. Or. *Aquifoliaceæ.* An ornamental genus, from one to six feet high; and one species, *C. excelsa*, grows eighteen feet high. They thrive in a composition of loam and peat, and cuttings of the matured wood root freely in sand under a glass.

| | | | | | | | |
|---|---|---|---|---|---|---|---|
| æthiópicǎ | . | . | White. | 7, G. Ev. S. | C. G. H. | . | |
| barbárǎ | . | . | White. | 7, G. Ev. S. | C. G. H. | . | 1818 |
| capénsis | . | . | White. | 7, G. Ev. S. | C. G. H. | . | 1629 |
| Cólpóon | . | . | White. | G. Ev. S. | C. G. H. | . | 1791 |
| excélsǎ | . | . | | G. Ev. S. | Nepal | . | 1820 |
| Maurocéniǎ | . | White. | G. Ev. S. | C. G. H. | . | . | 1690 |
| oppositifóliǎ | . | White. | G. Ev. S. | | | | |

CassínIX, *R. Brown.* In honour of M. Henri Cassini, a celebrated French botanist. *Linn.* 19, Or. 5, Nat. Or. *Compositæ.* The species of this genus are pretty, and may be successfully cultivated in a mixture of loam and peat; they are multiplied by dividing at the root, by cuttings, and by seed, without difficulty.

| | | | | | | | |
|---|---|---|---|---|---|---|---|
| affínis | . | . | . | 5, G. Ev. S. | N. Holl. | . | 1820 |
| aúrěǎ | . | . | Yellow | 7, G. Her. P. | N. Holl. | . | 1803 |
| leptophyllǎ | . | White. | 8, G. Ev. S. | N. Zeal. | . | . | 1821 |
| longifóliǎ | . | . | . | 5, G. Ev. S. | N. Holl. | . | 1822 |
| spectábilis | . | . | Yellow | 7, H. Ev. A. | N. Holl. | . | 1818 |

CassIOBERRY BUSH, see *Viburnum lævigátum.*

CassÝTHǍ, *Linn.* The Greek name of the *Cuscuta,* which it much resembles. *Linn.* 9, Or. 1, Nat. Or. *Cassythaceæ.* This is a curious parasite, resembling very much the habit and character of the genus *Cuscuta,* and will succeed with the same treatment; which see.

| | | | | | | | |
|---|---|---|---|---|---|---|---|
| filifórmis | . | . | White . | 5, Parasite. | E. Ind. | . | 1796 |
| glabéllǎ | . | . | White . | 5, Parasite. | N. Holl. | . | 1823 |

CastǍnEǍ, *Gærtner.* From its being originally found in the territory of Castanea, in Thessaly. *Linn.* 21, Or. 9, Nat. Or. *Corylaceæ.* Ornamental timber trees, of variable heights, from ten to fifty feet; some are raised from seed; the varieties are frequently multiplied by grafting on the common kinds. *Synonyme:* 1. *Fagus Castanea.*

| | | | | | | | |
|---|---|---|---|---|---|---|---|
| americánǎ | . | . | Green . | 5, H. De. T. | America | . | |
| chinénsis | . | . | Green . | 5, H. De. T. | China | . | |
| indicǎ | . | . | . | 8. Ev. T. | E. Ind. | . | 1827 |
| pumílǎ | . | Grn. yel. | 7, H. De. T. | N. Amer. | . | . | 1699 |
| véscǎ, 1 | . | . | Green . | 6, H. De. T. | England | . | |
| asplenifóliǎ | . | Green . | 6, H. De. T. | Europe | . | . | |
| fóliis-aúrěis | . | Green . | 6, H. De. T. | | | | |
| médiǎ | . | . | Green . | 6, H. De. T. | Europe | . | |

CastanospÉrmǔm, *Hooker.* The seeds taste like chesnuts; whence the name, from *castanea*, a chesnut, and *sperma*, a seed. *Linn.* 10, Or. 1, Nat. Or. *Leguminosæ.* An ornamental fruit-tree, growing upwards of forty feet high, and delights in any loamy soil, and may be increased by layers.

| | | | | | | | |
|---|---|---|---|---|---|---|---|
| austrálě | . | . | Saffron | . | G. Ev. T. | N. Holl. | . 1828 |

CastÉLIǍ, *Turpin.* After M. Castel, author of a poem upon plants. *Linn.* 8, Or. 1, Nat. Or. *Ochnaceæ.* An interesting stove shrub, four feet high; it requires a mixture of peat and loam to grow in, and is increased by cuttings in sand, in heat under a glass.

| | | | | | | |
|---|---|---|---|---|---|---|
| erěctǎ | . . . . | 8. Ev. T. | W. Ind. | . 1821 |

CastillEjǍ, *Mutis.* After Don Castilleja, a Spanish botanist, and friend of Mutis. *Linn.* 14, Or. 2, Nat. Or. *Scrophulariaceæ.* A genus of ornamental plants, of easy management; the stove species succeed well in a mixture of loam and peat, and are increased by cuttings; the herbaceous and annual kinds may be grown in sandy peat, and increased by dividing the roots or seeds. *Synonyme:* 1. *Bartsia pallida.*

| | | | | | |
|---|---|---|---|---|---|
| integrifolia | . . | | 8. Ev. | 8. S. Amer. | 1825 |
| morananais | . . | | 8. Ev. | 8. Mexico | 1825 |
| pallida, 1 | . Lgt. pur. | 7, H. Her. | P. Siberia | . 1782 |
| septentrionalis | . Wht. grn. | 8, H. | A. Labrador | . 1824 |

CASTOR-OIL PLANT, see *Ricinus communis.*

CASUARINA, *Linn.* Supposed to be named from the resemblance the leaves bear to the feathers of the *Cassowary,* of the same country. *Linn.* 21, Or. 1, Nat. Or. *Casuaraceæ.* These are very interesting plants, on account of their rush-like, frequently drooping, appearance; they grow from ten to fifteen feet high, and are very desirable, from the circumstance of their flowering so late in the season; they grow very well in a mixture of sandy loam and peat, and cuttings root in sand under a glass.

| | | | | | |
|---|---|---|---|---|---|
| distyla | . Apetal | | G. Ev. T. N. Holl. | . 1812 |
| equisetifolia | . Apetal | 9, | G. Ev. T. S. Sea Isl. | 1776 |
| glauca | . Apetal | | G. Ev. T. N. Holl. | . 1824 |
| muricata | . Apetal | | G. Ev. T. E. Ind. | . 1822 |
| nodiflora | . Apetal | | G. Ev. T. N. Caled. | . 1823 |
| quadrivalvis | . Apetal | | G. Ev. T. N. S. W. | . 1812 |
| stricta | . Apetal | 5, | G. Ev. T. N. S. W. | . 1775 |
| tenuissima | . Apetal | | G. Ev. T. N. Holl. | . 1825 |
| torulosa | . Apetal | | G. Ev. T. N. S. W. | . 1772 |

CATABROSA, *Beauvois.* Derived from *katabrosis,* signifying food. *Linn.* 3, Or. 2, Nat. Or. *Gramineæ.* A curious aquatic genus of grasses, that require to be grown in a cistern, or pan of water; divisions. *Synonyme:* 1. *Aira aquatica.*

| | | | | | |
|---|---|---|---|---|---|
| aquatica, 1 | . Apetal | . 6, H. Aq. | P. England | . |
| viridula | . Apetal | . 6, H. Aq. | P. | . 1816 |

CATALPA, *Jussieu.* Its name in India. *Linn.* 2, Or. 1, Nat. Or. *Bignoniaceæ.* *C. syringæfolia* is excellently adapted for planting singly on lawns, or about the skirts of pleasure-grounds; it grows freely in a mixture of loam and peat, and is propagated readily by means of seed, layers, or cuttings. *Synonyme:* 1. *Bignonia microphylla.*

| | | | | | |
|---|---|---|---|---|---|
| longissima, | . . | 8. Ev. | T. W. Ind. | . 1777 |
| microphylla, 1 | . . | 8. Ev. | T. Hispaniola | . 1820 |
| syringæfolia | . White | . 7, H. De. | T. N. Amer. | . 1726 |

CATANANCHE, *Linn.* *Katanagke,* strong incentive; used by the women of Thessaly in philtres and love potions. *Linn.* 19, Or. 1, Nat. Or. *Compositæ.* A pretty genus, that succeeds well in common soil, and may be increased by seeds, or dividing at the roots.

| | | | | | |
|---|---|---|---|---|---|
| cærulea | . Blue | . 8, H. Her. | P. S. Eur. | . 1596 |
| bicolor | . Wht. blue | 8, H. Her. | P. Gardens | . 1827 |
| lutea | . Yellow | . 6, H. | A. Candia | . 1640 |

CATAPHRACTA, clothed in mail.

CATARRHAL, of or belonging to a cold.

CATASETUM, *Richard.* Not explained. *Linn.* 20, Or. 1, Nat. Or. *Orchidaceæ.* All the species of this genus are strong, rapid-growing plants, and from the singular formation of the flowers, they well deserve a place in every collection. They should be kept cool and dry when torpid, forced gently into growth, and when growing freely, kept in a strong heat, and copiously supplied with water: this treatment should be applied to all plants of a similar habit. They require to be potted in the same kind of soil, and in a similar manner to the *Stanhopeas* and *Gongoras. Synonymes:* 1. *C. Claveringi.* 2. *C. floribundum.*

| | | | | | |
|---|---|---|---|---|---|
| atratum | . Dark | . 7, 8. Epi. | Brasil | . |
| cristatum | . Green | . 8, 8. Epi. | Brasil | . 1823 |
| Hookeri | . Grn. brn. | 10, 8. Epi. | Brasil | . 1818 |
| luridum | . Grn. brn. | 10, 8. Epi. | Brasil | . |
| maculatum | . Grn. pur. | 8. Epi. | N. Grenada | . 1836 |
| Milleri | . Pur. spot. | 9, 8. Epi. | Brasil | . 1837 |
| poriferum | . Grn. pur. | 8. Epi. | Demerara | . 1837 |
| purum | . Green | . 10, 8. Epi. | Brasil | . |
| semiapertum | . Green | . 1, 8. Epi. | Brasil | . 1824 |
| tridentatum | . Yel. brn. | 4, 8. Epi. | Brasil | . 1822 |
| Claveringi, 1 | . Yel. brn. | 8, 8. Epi. | Brasil | . 1822 |
| floribundum, 2 | . Yel. brn. | 11, 8. Epi. | Trinidad | . 1824 |
| trifidum | . Green | . 6, 8. Epi. | Trinidad | . |

CATCHFLY, see *Silene.*

CATERPILLAR, see *Scorpiurus.*

CATESBÆA, *Gronovius.* After Mark Catesby, author of the Natural History of Carolina. *Linn.* 4, Or. 1,

Nat. Or. *Cinchonaceæ.* An ornamental genus, the species of which attain from two to twelve feet high; they thrive best in light turfy loam, and peat soil. Being very subject to the attacks of insects, great watchfulness is required to keep them clear, or the plants never succeed or flower. Cuttings root in sand under a glass, in heat.

| | | | | | |
|---|---|---|---|---|---|
| latifolia | . . Yellow | . 6, 8. Ev. | T. W. Ind. | . 1823 |
| parviflora | . . . White | . 6, 8. Ev. | S. Jamaica | . 1810 |
| spinosa | . . . Yellow | . 6, 8. Ev. | S. I. Provi. | . 1726 |

CATHARANTHUS, *Don.* From *katharos,* pure, and *anthos,* a flower; on account of the neat and beautiful flowers. *Linn.* 5, Or. 1, Nat. Or. *Apocynaceæ.* The species of this genus are well worth cultivating in every collection of plants. *C. roseus* and its varieties succeed well in common garden soil, and are readily increased by cuttings or seeds. The seeds of *C. pusillus* should be sown in a pot full of light rich soil, and placed in a hotbed, and afterwards treated as other tender annuals. *Synonymes:* 1. *Vinca pusilla.* 2. *V. rosea.*

| | | | | | |
|---|---|---|---|---|---|
| pusillus | . . . Blue | . 8, S. | A. Tranquebar | 1778 |
| roseus | . . . Rose eld. | . 5, 8. Ev. | S. E. Ind. | . 1726 |
| albus | . . . White | . 6, 8. Ev. | S. E. Ind. | . |
| ocellatus | . . . Wht. pur. | 6, 8. Ev. | S. E. Ind. | . |

CATHARTIC, purgative.

CATHOLIC, generally useful, excellent in a medicinal sense.

CATKIN, inflorescence of the natural order *Amentaceæ,* as the willow.

CATMINT, see *Nepeta.*

CAT'S EAR, see *Hypochæris.*

CAT'S TAIL, see *Typha.*

CAT'S-TAIL GRASS, see *Phleum.*

CAT THYME, see *Teucrium marum.*

CATTLEYA, *Lindley.* In honour of William Cattley, Esq., of Barnet, Hertfordshire, a famous patron of botany, and one of the most ardent collectors of rare plants of his day. *Linn.* 20, Or. 1, Nat. Or. *Orchidaceæ.* Some of the species of this splendid genus of plants are most magnificent when in flower, as *C. crispa, labiata,* and *Mossiæ;* and these three vie with each other in the beauty of their flowers: when they are well grown, each of these has generally from four to six flowers on a spike; in *C. crispa* the sepals and petals are pure white, the latter much curled, while the lip or labellum is purple in the inside, and white outside. The flowers of *C. labiata* are very large and showy, the sepals and petals being a delicate rose-colour, and somewhat curled; the outside of the labellum is also rose-colour, and the inside blotched, and striped with deep carmine. The flowers of *C. Mossiæ* very much resemble those of *labiata,* only they are larger, the circumference of the flower being about twenty-four inches. All the other species are highly deserving of cultivation, if only for the splendour of their flowers. For culture and propagation they may be referred to the *Stanhopeas.*

| | | | | | |
|---|---|---|---|---|---|
| bicolor | . . . Olive grn. | 9, 8. Epi. | Brasil | . 1837 |
| crispa | . . . Wht. pur. | 9, 8. Epi. | Brasil | . 1826 |
| elatior | . . . Grn. spot. | 8. Epi. | Brasil | . 1827 |
| Forbesii | . . . Wht. yel. | 6, 8. Epi. | Brasil | . 1823 |
| guttata | . . . Grn. spot. | 4, 8. Epi. | Brasil | . 1827 |
| Russelliana | . . . Grn. spot. | 8. Epi. | Brasil | . 1838 |
| Harrisoniæ | . . . Vio. yel. | 4, 8. Epi. | Brasil | . 1824 |
| intermedia | . . . Vio. yel. | 4, 8. Epi. | Brasil | . 1833 |
| pallida | . . . Lgt. red | 6, 8. Epi. | Brasil | . 1818 |
| labiata | . . . Crim. lilac. | 5, 8. Epi. | Brasil | . 1818 |
| Loddigesii | . . . Vio. lilac. | 8, 8. Epi. | Brasil | . 1815 |
| Mossiæ | . . . Crim. lilac. | 7, 8. Epi. | La Guayra | . 1836 |
| Perrinii | . . . Purple | . 8. Epi. | Brasil | . |
| pumila | . . . Purple | . 4, 8. Epi. | S. Amer. | . 1837 |

CAUCALIS, *Hoffmannsegg.* A name used by Hippocrates and Theophrastus. *Linn.* 5, Or. 2, Nat. Or. *Umbelliferæ.* The plants have little beauty, and are easily managed by merely sowing the seed in the open ground—*daucoides, glabra, hispida, latifolia, leptophylla, mauritanica, pumila.*

CAUDATE, tailed, being like a tail.

CAUDEX, the trunk or stem of a tree.

CAUDICULA, a small membranous process, on which the pollen of orchidaceous plants is fixed.

CAULESCENT, acquiring a stem.

CAULIALATA, wing-stemmed.

CAULICULE, the little stem of the embryo which unites the cotyledons with the radicle.

CAULIFLOWER, see *Brassica oleracea cauliflora.*

**CAULINE**, belonging to the stem.

**CAULOPHYLLUM**, *Michaux*. From *kaulos*, a stem, and *phyllon*, a leaf; being so terminated by the stalks, its leaves appear a continuation of the stem. *Linn.* 6, Or. 1, Nat. Or. *Berberaceæ*. A singular plant that requires to be grown in sandy peat, and is increased by dividing the roots. *Synonyme:* 1. *Leontice thalictroides.*

| | | | | | |
|---|---|---|---|---|---|
| thalictroīdēs, 1 | . | Yel. grn. | . 5, H. Tu. P. N. Amer. | . 1755 |

**CAUSTIC**, having a burning quality.

**CAVUS**, hollow, full of holes.

**CEANOTHUS**, *Linn*. From *kenteo*, to prick; a name used by Theophrastus to denote a spiny plant. *Linn.* 5, Or. 1, Nat. Or. *Rhamnaceæ*. A genus of showy plants, growing from one to twenty feet high; they thrive well in peat and loam; cuttings strike in sand, under a glass. *Synonymes:* 1 *C. cæruleus.* 2. *Rhamnus capensis.* 3. *R. lævigatus.* 4. *R. mystacinus.* 5. *R. sphærospermus.* 6. *Celastrus zeylanicus.*

| | | | | | |
|---|---|---|---|---|---|
| americānūs | . | White | . 7, H. De. 8. N. Amer. | . 1713 |
| azurēūs, 1 | . | Pa. blue | . 4, G. Ev. 8. Mexico | . 1818 |
| capēnsīs, 2 | . | White | . 6, G. Ev. 8. C. G. H. | . 1823 |
| collīnūs | . | Light | . 7, H. Ev. 8. N. Amer. | . 1827 |
| infēctūs | . | . | 8. Ev. 8. Mexico | . 1824 |
| intermēdīūs | . | White | . 6, H. De. 8. N. Amer. | . 1812 |
| lævigātūs, 3 | . | Grn. yel. | . 8. Ev. 8. W. Ind. | . 1818 |
| macrocārpūs | . | Yellow | . 7, 8. Ev. 8. N. Spain | . 1824 |
| microphyllūs | . | White | . 6, H. De. 8. N. Amer. | . 1806 |
| Mocīniānūs | . | . | 8. Ev. 8. Mexico | . 1824 |
| mystacīnūs, 4 | . | Wht. grn. | 11, 8. Ev. 8. Africa | . 1775 |
| nepalēnsīs | . | Yellow | . H. De. 8. Nepal | . 1820 |
| ovātūs | . | White | . 7, H. De. 8. N. Amer. | . 1818 |
| perēnnīs | . | White | . 8. H. Her. P. Carolina | . 1822 |
| sanguinēūs | . | White | . 6, H. De. 8. Missouri | . 1812 |
| sphærocārpūs, 5 | . | Grn. yel. | . 8. Ev. 8. Jamaica | . 1824 |
| tardiflōrūs | . | White | . 9, H. De. 8. N. Amer. | . 1820 |
| zeylānīcūs, 6 | . | White | . 8. Ev. T. Ceylon | . 1818 |

**CECROPIA**, *Linn*. After Cecrops, king of Athens, whose legs were fabled to be snakes. *Linn.* 22, Or. 2, Nat. Or. *Urticaceæ*. Beautiful plants, attaining upwards of fifteen feet high, they have five peltate leaves, which give the plant a fine appearance; a mixture of loam and peat suits them, and strong cuttings planted in sand, under a glass, with a little heat, root freely.

| | | | | | |
|---|---|---|---|---|---|
| concōlōr | . | Apetal | . 8. Ev. T. Brazil | . 1822 |
| palmātā | . | Apetal | . 8. Ev. T. Brazil | . 1820 |
| peltātā | . | Apetal | . 8. Ev. T. Jamaica | . 1778 |

**CEDAR OF GOA**, see *Cupréssūs lusitānīcā.*

**CEDAR OF LEBANON**, see *Cédrūs Libānī.*

**CEDRELA**, *Linn.* From *cedrus*, the cedar-tree; the wood has an aromatic resinous scent like it. *Linn.* 5, Or. 1, Nat. Or. *Cedrelaceæ*. A genus of tallish timber trees, they do well in open loam, and young plants are procured from cuttings in sand, under a glass.

| | | | | | |
|---|---|---|---|---|---|
| odorātā | . | Pink | . 8. Ev. T. W Ind. | . 1739 |
| Toōnā | . | Yellow | . 8. Ev. T. E. Ind. | . 1823 |
| velutīnā | . | . | 8. Ev. T. | |

**CEDRUS**, *Miller*. Found plentifully on the banks of a brook in Judæa, named Cedron; whence the name. *Linn.* 21, Or. 10, Nat. Or. *Coniferæ.* The two species of this genus are not only ornamental but highly valuable for the fine timber they yield, and grow ninety feet high; they delight in sandy loamy soil, and are increased by seeds generally, but *C. Deodara* takes readily grafted upon the common larch. *Synonyme:* 1. *Pinus Cedrus.*

| | | | | | |
|---|---|---|---|---|---|
| Deodārā | . | Apetal | . 5, H. Ev. T. Nepal | . 1822 |
| Libānī | . | Apetal | . 5, H. Ev. T. Levant | . 1683 |

**CELASTRUS**, *Linn.* From *celas*, the latter season; the fruit remains on the tree all winter. *Linn.* 5, Or. 1, Nat. Or. *Celastraceæ*. This is a genus composed of ornamental plants, varying in height from two to twenty feet; the species thrive best in a mixture of sandy loam and peat; the ripened cuttings root freely in sand, under a glass. The leaves of *C. edulis* and *nutans* are said to be stimulant, and are used in medicine. *Synonymes:* 1. *C. emarginatus.* 2. *Cassine lævigata.*

| | | | | | |
|---|---|---|---|---|---|
| bullātūs | . | White | . 7, H. De. Cl. Virginia | . 1759 |
| buxifolīūs | . | White | . 5, G. Ev. 8. C. G. H. | . 1752 |
| cassinoīdēs | . | White | . 8, G. Ev. 8. Canaries | . 1779 |
| ebrulūs | . | White | . 5, G. Ev. 8. C. G. H. | . 1817 |
| cymōsūs | . | White | . 7, G. Ev. 8. C. G. H. | . 1815 |
| emarginātūs | . | . | G. Ev. 8. C. G. H. | . 1820 |

| | | | | | |
|---|---|---|---|---|---|
| flexuōsūs | . | White | . 5, G. Ev. 8. C. G. H. | . 1820 |
| ilicīnūs | . | White | . G. Ev. 8. C. G. H. | . 1817 |
| laurīnūs | . | White | . 6, G. Ev. 8. C. G. H. | . 1818 |
| lineārīs | . | White | . 8, G. Ev. 8. C. G. H. | . 1818 |
| lucīdūs | . | White | . 5, G. Ev. 8. C. G. H. | . 1752 |
| mexicānūs | . | . | 8. Ev. 8. Mexico | . 1824 |
| multiflōrūs | . | White | . 5, 8. Ev. T. 8. Eur. | . 1816 |
| myrtifolīūs | . | White | . 8. Ev. T. Jamaica | . 1810 |
| nūtāns | . | White | . 8. Ev. Cl. E. Ind. | . 1810 |
| oleoīdēs | . | White | . 5, G. Ev. 8. C. G. H. | . 1824 |
| pterocārpūs | . | White | . 7, G. Ev. 8. C. G. H. | . 1824 |
| punctātūs | . | . | G. Ev. Cl. Japan | . 1817 |
| pyracānthūs | . | White | . 5, G. Ev. 8. C. G. H. | . 1742 |
| quadrangulārīs | . | White | . 8. Ev. 8. Brazil | . 1820 |
| retūsūs, 1 | . | Yellow | . G. Ev. 8. Peru | . 1824 |
| rigīdūs | . | Yellow | . 5, G. Ev. 8. C. G. H. | . 1818 |
| scāndēns | . | Yellow | . 5, H. De. Cl. N. Amer. | . 1736 |
| tetragōnūs | . | White | . G. Ev. 8. C. G. H. | . 1816 |
| tricuspidātūs, 2 | . | White | . 5, G. Ev. 8. C. G. H. | . 1818 |
| trigynūs | . | . | 5, 8. Ev. 8. L France | . 1824 |
| undātūs | . | White | . 5, G. Ev. 8. C. G. H. | . 1826 |

**CELANDINE**, see *Chelidōnīūm.*

**CELANDINE**, see *Boccōnīā frutēscēns.*

**CELERY**, see *Apīūm gravēolēns.*

**CELL**, the hollow part of a capsule, in which the seeds are lodged, and the part of the anthers which contains the pollen.

**CELLULAR**, composed of cells.

**CELOSIA**, *Linn*. From *kelos*, burnt; the flowers of some of the species appear as it were singed or burnt. *Linn.* 5, Or. 1, Nat. Or. *Amarantaceæ.* These are all ornamental or curious plants, growing from one to five feet high; the species should be sown in a hotbed frame, or in a hothouse, and when of a sufficient strength, they should be transplanted into single pots, and placed amongst other hothouse or greenhouse annuals.

| | | | | | |
|---|---|---|---|---|---|
| argentēā | . | Lgt. flesh. | 7, 8. | A. China | . 1740 |
| lineārīs | . | Flesh | 6, G. | A. E. Ind. | . 1714 |
| castrēnsīs | . | Purple | 7, 8. | A. E. Ind. | . 1739 |
| cērnūā | . | Purple | 7, 8. | A. E. Ind. | . 1809 |
| coccīnēā | . | Pink | 7, 8. | A. China | . 1597 |
| comōsā | . | Pink | 7, 8. | A. E. Ind. | . 1802 |
| cristātā | . | Drk. red | 7, 8. | A. Asia | . 1570 |
| compāctā | . | Drk. red | 7, G. | A. Asia | . 1570 |
| elātā | . | Drk. red | 7, G. | A. Asia | . 1570 |
| flavēscēns | . | Yellow | 7, G. | A. Asia | . 1570 |
| dichōtōmā | . | Yellow | 7, 8. | A. E. Ind. | . 1824 |
| echinātā | . | Purple | 7, 8. Ev. 8. Orinoco | . 1821 |
| glaūcā | . | White | 7, G. Ev. 8. C. G. H. | . 1818 |
| margaritācēā, 1 | . | Yellow | 8, 8. | A. W. Ind. | . 1817 |
| Monsōnīā | . | White | 8, 8. | A. E. Ind. | . 1778 |
| nītīdā | . | Purple | 8, 8. | A. Malabar | . 1766 |
| nodiflōrā | . | Green | 8, 8. | A. E. Ind. | . 1780 |
| pyramidālīs | . | White | 7, 8. | A. E. Ind. | . 1820 |

**CELSIA**, *Linn*. In honour of Olaus Celsius, D.D. professor of oriental languages in the university of Upsal, and friend of Linnæus. *Linn.* 14, Or. 2, Nat. Or. *Scrophulariaceæ.* This is a genus of ornamental plants, from two to six feet high; its species must be raised on a mild hotbed, and then transplanted in pots, as it is necessary they have the protection of a stove or greenhouse during winter.

| | | | | | |
|---|---|---|---|---|---|
| Arctūrūs | . | Yellow | . 8, F. | B. Candia | . 1780 |
| betonicæfolīā | . | Yellow | . 7, F. | B. N. Africa | |
| coromandeliānā | . | Yellow | . 7, 8. | A. E. Ind. | . 1783 |
| crētīcā | . | Yellow | . 7, F. | B. Crete | . 1752 |
| heterophyllā | . | Yellow | . 7, F. | B | . 1829 |
| lanātā | . | Yellow | . 7, F. Ev. 8. | | . 1818 |
| lanceolātā | . | Yellow | . 7, F. | B. Levant | . 1816 |
| orientālīs | . | Brn. yel. | . 7, H. | A. Levant | . 1713 |
| viscōsā | . | Yellow | . 7, 8. | A. | . 1816 |

**CELSUS**, upright, stately, tall.

**CELTIS**, *Linn*. One of the ancient names given to the *Lotus. Linn.* 23, Or. 1, Nat. Or. *Ulmaceæ.* This is an ornamental genus of trees and shrubs, varying in height from six to fifty feet; the most of them do very well in any common garden soil, and are very suitable for the back of shrubberies and plantations; increased by seeds or layers. *Synonyme:* 1. *C. cordifolia.*

| | | | | | |
|---|---|---|---|---|---|
| aculeātā | . | Green | . 8. Ev. T. Jamaica | . 1791 |
| australīs | . | Green | . 5, H. De. T. 8. Eur. | . 1796 |
| crassifolīā, 1 | . | Green | . 4, H. De. T. N. Amer. | . 1812 |
| lævigātā | . | Green | . 4, H. De. T. Louisiana | |
| līmā | . | Grn. yel. | . 8. Ev. T. W. Ind. | . 1823 |
| micranthā | . | Green | . 8, 8. Ev. T. Jamaica | . 1739 |
| occidentālīs | . | Green | . 4, H. De. F. N. Amer. | . 1656 |
| cordātā | . | Green | . 4, H. De. F. N. Amer. | |
| scabriūscūlā, 2 | . | Green | . 4, H. De. F. N. Amer. | |
| orientālīs | . | Grn. yel. | . 8. Ev. T. E. Ind. | . 1820 |

| | | | | |
|---|---|---|---|---|
| pūmīlă | Green | 6, H. De. | S. N. Amer. | 1812 |
| sinensis | Green | H. De. | T. Asia | 1820 |
| Tournefōrtī | Green | H. De. | S. Levant | 1739 |

**CEMBRA**, signifying a pine.

**CENĀNGĪŪM**, *Fries*. From *kenos*, empty, and *aggeion*, a vessel; in reference to the empty or hollow receptacle. *Linn.* 24, *Or.* 9, *Nat. Or. Fungi*. Minute species of *Fungi*, appearing generally upon plum and cherry barks, and as well upon the Mountain Ash and dead Firs—*Aucupārīā, Cērāsī, ferruginōsūm, Prunāstrī, quercīnūm*.

**CENCHRŪS**, *Linn*. From *kegchros*, the oriental name of the millet. *Linn.* 3, *Or.* 1, *Nat. Or. Gramineæ*. These, as well as the greater part of the *Gramineæ*, are very curious; the species of this genus grow from one to two feet high, and the principal part of them only require to be sown in the open ground.

| | | | | |
|---|---|---|---|---|
| australis | Apetal | 7, Gram. | N. Holl. | 1822 |
| echinatus | Apetal | 9, Gram. | W. Ind. | 1691 |
| spinifex | Apetal | 5, Gram. | S. Amer. | 1820 |
| tribuloidēs | Apetal | 6, Gram. | N. Amer. | 1818 |

**CENIA**, *Commelin*. Derived from *kenos*, empty; in allusion to its inflated calyx. *Linn.* 19, *Or.* 2, *Nat. Or. Compositæ*. *Synonyme*: 1. *Lidbeckia turbinata*—*turbinātā*, 1.

**CENISIA**, growing on Mount Cenis.

**CENŌMYCE**, *Acharius*. From *kenos*, empty, and *mykes*, a fungus; alluding to the hollowness of the little receptacles. *Linn.* 24, *Or.* 8, *Nat. Or. Lichenes*. An extensive genus of interesting *Lichens*, discoverable upon moor and mountain land, and also upon old wood, &c.—*alcicōrnis, bacillāris, bellidiflōrā, cervicōrnis, cocciferā, C. cornucopioīdēs, defōrmis, delicātā, digitātā, ecmocymā, E. grācilis, endivierfōlīa, fimbriātā, F. cornutā, F. radiātā, furcātā, F. subulātā, gonoregā, G. anomēā, papillārīā, pyxidātā, racemōsā, rangiferinā, R. pūngens, spardesā, uncīālīs, vermiculāris.*

**CENTAŪRĪA**, *Linn*. With one of these plants, the Centaur Chiron cured the wound made in his foot by the arrow of Hercules. *Linn.* 19, *Or.* 3, *Nat. Or. Compositæ*. The species of this genus are, for the greater part, ornamental plants, growing from half a foot to five feet high. The hardy annual and biennial kinds need only to be sown in the open ground; the half-hardy ones should be sown on a mild hotbed, where they must remain till strong enough to be planted out in the borders. *Synonymes*: 1. *C. ceratophylla*. 2. *C. caucasica*. 3. *C. exaltata*. 4. *C. argyrophylla*. 5. *C. linarifolia*. 6. *C. sibirica*. 7. *C. sulphurea*. 8. *C. leucantha*. 9. *C. virgata*. 10. *C. rigescens*. 11. *C. zannonii*. 12. *C. variegata*.

| | | | | | | |
|---|---|---|---|---|---|---|
| acanthōdēs | Purple | 7, H. Her. | P. | | | 1827 |
| Adāmī | Yellow | 7, | A. | Siberia | | 1804 |
| ægyptīācā | White | 7, F. Her. | P. | Egypt | | 1790 |
| alātā | Yellow | 8, H. Her. | P. | Tartary | | 1781 |
| alba | White | 7, H. Her. | P. | Spain | | 1597 |
| alpīnā | Yellow | 7, H. Her. | P. | Italy | | 1640 |
| amārā | Purple | 7, H. Her. | P. | Italy | | |
| grandiflōrā | Purple | 7, H. Her. | P. | Switzerl. | | 1819 |
| pinnatīfidā | Purple | 7, H. Her. | P. | Switzerl. | | 1819 |
| americānā, 1 | Red | 7, | A. | N. Amer. | | 1824 |
| āpūlā | Yellow | 7, | A. | N. Africa | | 1817 |
| arachnoīdēs, 1 | Yellow | 7, | B. | Italy | | 1820 |
| arenārīā | Purple | 8, H. Her. | P. | S. Eur. | | 1778 |
| argentēā | Pa. yel. | 7, F. Ev. | S. | Candia | | 1739 |
| argūtă | | 8, F. Ev. | S. | Canaries | | 1829 |
| āsperā | Purple | 8, H. Her. | P. | S. Eur. | | 1772 |
| astracānīcā | Purple | 7, H. Her. | P. | Astracan | | 1818 |
| atropurpūrēā | Purple | 7, H. Her. | P. | Hungary | | 1802 |
| aūrēā | Yellow | 8, H. Her. | P. | S. Eur. | | 1758 |
| austrīācā | Purple | 8, H. Her. | P. | Austria | | 1815 |
| axillāris | Purple | 7, H. Her. | P. | Austria | | 1823 |
| babylōnīcā | Yellow | 7, H. Her. | P. | Levant | | 1710 |
| Balsamītā | Yellow | 7, H. Her. | P. | Syria | | 1820 |
| Barrelièrī | Purple | 7, H. Her. | P. | Hungary | | 1820 |
| benedīctā | Yellow | 8, | A. | Spain | | 1548 |
| bractēātā | Purple | 7, H. Her. | P. | S. Eur. | | 1817 |
| Calcitrapă | Pink | 7, H. Her. | P. | England | | |
| calcitrapoīdēs | Purple | 6, H. Her. | P. | Levant | | 1683 |
| calocēphalā | Yellow | 7, H. Her. | P. | Levant | | 1816 |
| calophylla | Yellow | 7, H. Her. | P. | S. Eur. | | 1816 |
| cancellātă | Yellow | 7, | A. | N. Amer. | | 1824 |
| capillātă | Purple | 7, H. Her. | P. | Siberia | | 1810 |
| centauroīdēs | Yellow | 6, H. Her. | P. | S. Eur. | | 1739 |
| centaurīum | Yellow | 7, H. Her. | P. | Italy | | 1596 |
| cheiranthifōlīa, 2 | Pa. yel. | 7, H. Her. | P. | Caucasus | | 1820 |
| cichorācēā | Purple | 7, H. Her. | P. | Caucasus | | 1816 |
| cicutæfōlīa | Purple | 7, H. Her. | P. | Podolia | | 1820 |
| Cinerārīā | Purple | 7, F. Her. | P. | Italy | | 1710 |
| cinerēā | Purple | 6, H. Her. | P. | Italy | | 1710 |

| | | | | | | |
|---|---|---|---|---|---|---|
| coarctātā | Yellow | 7, H. | | A. | N. Africa | 1827 |
| collīnă | Yellow | 6, H. Her. | | P. | S. Eur. | 1596 |
| concinnā | Yellow | 8, H. Her. | | P. | Caucasus | 1818 |
| coriācēā | Purple | 6, H. Her. | | P. | Hungary | 1804 |
| coronopifōlīā, 3 | Yellow | 6, H. Her. | | A. | Levant | 1739 |
| Crocodīlīūm | Purple | 7, H. Her. | | A. | Levant | 1777 |
| cruentā | Purple | 7, H. Her. | | A. | | 1816 |
| Crūpīnă | Flesh | 8, H. | | P. | Italy | 1596 |
| crupioīdēs | Copper | 7, H. | | A. | N. Africa | 1818 |
| Cyānŭs | Blue | 7, H. | | A. | Britain | |
| dealbātā | Purple | 8, H. Her. | | P. | Caucasus | 1804 |
| deciplēns | Purple | 7, H. Her. | | P. | France | 1816 |
| declinātā | Purple | 8, H. Her. | | P. | Caucasus | 1821 |
| decumbēns | Purple | 7, H. Her. | | P. | France | 1815 |
| depressā | Blue | 7, H. | | A. | Caucasus | 1818 |
| dedstă | Drk. red | 8, H. Her. | | P. | Naples | 1818 |
| dilūtă | Pa. pur. | 7, H. Her. | | P. | S. Eur. | 1781 |
| dissectă | Purple | 7, H. Her. | | P. | Naples | 1823 |
| elātā | Yellow | 8, H. Her. | | P. | Maurit. | 1820 |
| elongātă | Purple | 8, H. Her. | | P. | Barbary | 1823 |
| eriōphŏră | Yellow | 8, H. Her. | | P. | Portugal | 1714 |
| eriophyllă | Yellow | 7, H. Her. | | P. | | 1827 |
| ferōx | Yellow | 8, H. Her. | | P. | Barbary | 1790 |
| Fischērī | Blue | 7, H. Her. | | P. | Russia | 1820 |
| flosculōsā | Purple | 7, H. Her. | | P. | Italy | 1818 |
| glastifōlīa | Yellow | 7, H. Her. | | P. | Siberia | 1731 |
| glaucā | Pa. yel. | 6, H. | | A. | Caucasus | 1806 |
| hybrīdā | Purple | 7, H. Her. | | P. | Switzerl. | 1819 |
| hyssopifōlīā | Purple | 7, F. Ev. | | S. | Spain | 1812 |
| ibērīcă | Purple | 7, H. | | B. | Iberia | 1818 |
| incānă | Purple | 8, H. Her. | | P. | Naples | 1822 |
| intybācēā | Purple | 8, H. Her. | | P. | S. Eur. | 1778 |
| Isnārdī | Purple | 7, H. | | A. | Britain | |
| jacobææfōlīā, 4 | Yellow | 7, H. | | P. | | 1818 |
| leucantha | White | 8, H. Her. | | P. | S. France | 1816 |
| leucophyllă | Purple | 7, H. Her. | | P. | Caucasus | 1823 |
| limbātă | Purple | 7, H. Her. | | P. | Portugal | 1818 |
| lingulātă | Blue | 7, H. Her. | | P. | Spain | 1824 |
| linifōlīā, 5 | Purple | 7, H. Her. | | P. | Spain | 1827 |
| Lippīī | Pa. pur. | 6, H. | | A. | Egypt | 1793 |
| macrocēphală | Yellow | 7, H. Her. | | P. | Caucasus | 1805 |
| maculātă | Purple | 7, H. Her. | | P. | Siberia | 1816 |
| maculōsă | Purple | 7, H. Her. | | P. | Siberia | 1816 |
| Marschalliānă, 6 | Purple | 7, H. Her. | | P. | Caucasus | 1820 |
| melitēnsis | Yellow | 7, H. | | A. | Malta | 1710 |
| mollis | Blue | 7, H. Her. | | P. | Hungary | 1818 |
| montānă | Blue | 7, H. Her. | | P. | Austria | 1596 |
| moschātă | Purple | 7, H. | | A. | Persia | 1629 |
| muricātă | Purple | 8, H. Her. | | P. | Spain | 1621 |
| myacanthă | Purple | 8, H. Her. | | P. | France | 1820 |
| napifōlīă | Purple | 7, H. | | A. | Candia | 1691 |
| neglēctă, 7 | Yellow | 7, H. Her. | | P. | Podolia | 1820 |
| nervōsă | Purple | 7, H. Her. | | P. | S. Eur. | 1815 |
| nicæēnsis | Yellow | 7, H. | | A. | Nice | 1819 |
| nītens | Purple | 7, H. Her. | | P. | Caucasus | 1823 |
| ochroleūcă, 8 | Pa. yel. | 7, H. Her. | | P. | Caucasus | 1801 |
| orientālis | Yellow | 7, H. Her. | | P. | Siberia | 1759 |
| ornātā | Yellow | 7, H. Her. | | P. | Spain | 1818 |
| ovīnă | Purple | 8, H. Her. | | P. | Caucasus | 1802 |
| pallēscens | Yellow | 7, H. | | A. | Egypt | 1816 |
| paniculātā | Purple | 7, H. Her. | | P. | Europe | 1640 |
| parviflōrā | Violet | 6, H. Her. | | P. | Barbary | 1823 |
| pectinātă | Purple | 8, H. Her. | | P. | France | 1727 |
| peregrīnā | Yellow | 7, H. Her. | | P. | S. Eur. | 1749 |
| phrygīă | Purple | 8, H. Her. | | P. | Switzerl. | 1633 |
| ambigūă | Purple | 8, H. Her. | | P. | Switzerl. | 1819 |
| polyacanthă | Purple | 7, H. Her. | | P. | Portugal | 1804 |
| polymōrphă, 9 | Purple | 7, H. Her. | | P. | Spain | 1819 |
| Poussīnī | Purple | 7, H. Her. | | P. | S. France | 1824 |
| pratēnsis | Purple | 7, H. Her. | | P. | France | 1817 |
| procumbēns | Purple | 6, H. Her. | | T. | S. Eur. | 1821 |
| pubēscens | Yellow | 7, H. Her. | | P. | | 1804 |
| pulchērrimă | Yellow | 7, H. Her. | | P. | Armenia | 1816 |
| pullātă | Purple | 7, H. Her. | | P. | S. Eur. | 1759 |
| radiātā | White | 7, H. Her. | | P. | Siberia | 1804 |
| ragusīnă | Yellow | 7, G. Ev. | | S. | Candia | 1710 |
| reflexă | Yellow | 7, H. Her. | | P. | Iberia | 1801 |
| rēpens | Yellow | 7, H. Her. | | P. | Levant | 1739 |
| rigidă, 10 | Purple | 7, H. Her. | | P. | | 1823 |
| rivulāris | Brown | 7, H. Her. | | P. | Portugal | 1812 |
| romāna, 11 | Red | 7, H. Her. | | P. | Rome | 1739 |
| rupestris | Purple | 7, H. Her. | | P. | Italy | 1805 |
| ruthēnīcă | Pa. yel. | 8, H. Her. | | P. | Russia | 1806 |
| sabulōsă | White | 7, H. Her. | | P. | Siberia | 1820 |
| salicifōlīă | Purple | 7, H. Her. | | P. | Caucasus | 1823 |
| salmantīcă | Purple | 8, H. | | S. | S. Eur. | 1596 |
| sanguinēă | Purple | 7, H. Her. | | P. | | 1827 |
| sempervīrens | Red yel. | 7, G. Ev. | | S. | Spain | 1683 |
| Seridis | Purple | 7, H. Her. | | P. | Spain | 1686 |
| sebana, 12 | Blue | 7, H. Her. | | P. | S. Eur. | 1816 |
| sibīrīcă | Purple | 7, H. Her. | | P. | Siberia | 1780 |
| sichlă | Yellow | 7, H. | | A. | Sicily | 1710 |
| solstitīālis | Yellow | 7, H. | | A. | England | |
| sonchifōlīa | Purple | 8, H. Her. | | P. | Mediter. | 1780 |
| sordidā | Purple | 7, H. Her. | | P. | | 1818 |
| spatulātā | Blue | 7, H. Her. | | P. | Naples | 1825 |
| sphærocēphală | Purple | 7, H. Her. | | P. | S. Eur. | 1683 |
| splēndens | Purple | 7, H. Her. | | P. | Spain | 1597 |
| spinōsă | Purple | 7, F. Her. | | P. | Candia | 1640 |

| | | | | | | |
|---|---|---|---|---|---|---|
| spinulosa | . . | Purple | . 7, H. Her. P. | Hungary | . | 1896 |
| stereophylla | . . | Purple | . 7, H. Her. P. | Podolia | . | 1820 |
| Stevenii | . . | Yellow | . 7, H. B. | Caucasus | . | 1820 |
| Stœbe | . . | Red yel. | . 6, H. Her. P. | Austria | . | 1759 |
| straminea | . . | Yellow | . 7, H. A. | Egypt. | . | 1801 |
| stricta | . . | Blue | . 7, H. Her. P. | Hungary | . | 1816 |
| suaveolens | . . | Yellow | . 7, H. A. | Levant | . | 1683 |
| sulphurea | . . | Yellow | . 7, H. A. | | . | 1815 |
| tatarica | . . | Yellow | . 7, H. Her. P. | Tartary | . | 1801 |
| tenuiflora | . . | Purple | . 7, H. Her. P. | Siberia | . | 1820 |
| transalpina | . . | Purple | . 7, H. Her. P. | Switzerl. | . | 1819 |
| trichocephala | . . | Purple | . 7, H. Her. P. | Siberia | . | 1805 |
| trinervia | . . | Purple | . 7, H. Her. P. | Podolia | . | 1816 |
| uliginosa | . . | Yellow | . 7, H. Her. P. | Portugal | . | 1816 |
| uniflora | . . | Purple | . 7, H. Her. P. | S. Eur. | . | 1819 |
| verutum | . . | Yellow | . 7, H. A. | Levant | . | 1780 |
| vochinensis | . . | Purple | . 7, H. Her. P. | Austria | . | 1817 |
| xanthina | . . | Yellow | . 7, H. Her. P. | | | |

*Jáceă, nígră 13, nigréscens, Scabiósă, tagánă, Triumfétti.*

CENTOTHECA, *Desfontaines.* From *kenteo*, to prick, and *theca*, a sheath; in reference to the prickly sheath. *Linn.* 3, Or. 2, Nat. Or. *Gramineæ.* A curious grass, of the simplest culture. *Synonyme:* 1. *Cenchrus lappaceus.*

| | | | | | | |
|---|---|---|---|---|---|---|
| lappacea, 1 | . . | Apetal | . 7, Gram. | E. Ind. | . . | 1778 |

CENTRAL-PLACENTA, a column in the centre of fruits to which the seeds are attached.

CENTRANTHUS, *Decandolle.* From *kentron*, a spur, and *anthos*, a flower; the corolla being furnished with a spur at the base. *Linn.* 10, Or. 1, Nat. Or. *Valerianaceæ.* The plants are ornamental, growing from one foot to one and a half high; they succeed in any common garden soil, in the open borders; seeds.

| | | | | | | |
|---|---|---|---|---|---|---|
| angustifolius | . . | Crimson | . 6, H. Her. P. | S. Eur. | . | 1759 |
| calcitrapa | . . | Purple | . 6, H. | A. Portugal | . | 1683 |
| ruber | . . | Crimson | . 6, H. Her. P. | Britain | . | |
| flore-albo | . . | White | . 6, H. Her. P. | Britain | . | |

CENTROCARPHA, *D. Don.* From *kentron*, a sharp point, and *karphe*, chaff; the paleæ being bristly. *Linn.* 19, Or. 3, Nat. Or. *Compositæ.* An interesting genus of herbaceous plants, that thrive well in common soil, and are increased by dividing the roots, and by seeds. *Synonymes:* 1. *C. acutifolia, Rudbeckia Newmani.*

| | | | | | | |
|---|---|---|---|---|---|---|
| chrysomela, 1 | . . | Yellow | . 8, H. Her. P. | S. Amer. | . | 1821 |
| chrysantha | . . | Yellow | . 8, H. Her. P. | Gardens | . | |
| fulgida | . . | Yellow | . 7, H. Her. P. | N. Amer. | . | 1760 |
| gracilis | . . | Yellow | . 9, H. Her. P. | N. Amer. | . | 1825 |
| grandiflora | . . | Yellow | . 9, H. Her. P. | N. Amer. | . | 1830 |
| hirta | . . | Yellow | . 7, H. Her. P. | N. Amer. | . | 1714 |
| radula | . . | Yellow | . 9, F. Her. | B. | | |
| spathulata | . . | Yellow | . 9, F. Her. P. | N. Amer. | . | 1825 |
| subtomentosa | . . | Yellow | . 8, H. Her. P. | N. Amer. | . | 1812 |
| triloba | . . | Yellow | . 8, H. | B. N. Amer. | . | 1699 |

CENTROCLINIUM, *D. Don.* Derived from *kentron*, a sharp point, and *kline*, a bed. *Linn.* 19, Or. 2, Nat. Or. *Compositæ.* A genus of ornamental stove plants, succeeding best when grown in a light vegetable soil; seeds.

| | | | | | | |
|---|---|---|---|---|---|---|
| appressum | . . | Rosy | . 1, S. Ev. S. | Peru | . | 1830 |
| reflexum | . . | Rosy | . 8, S. | A. Peru | . | 1830 |

CENTROSPERMUM, *Sprengel.* From *kentron*, a spur, and *sperma*, a seed; alluding to the spiny points of the pappus. *Linn.* 19, Or. 2, Nat. Or. *Compositæ.* A pretty annual, that requires sowing in the open border, in common garden soil.

| | | | | | | |
|---|---|---|---|---|---|---|
| chrysanthum | . | Yellow | . 7, H. | A. Spain | . | 1823 |

CENTAURY, see *Centauréa.*

CENTUNCULUS, *Linn.* The name applied by the Romans to a small plant, found in cultivated land. *Linn.* 4, Or. 1, Nat. Or. *Primulaceæ.* A curious annual, of easy culture in sandy loam.

| | | | | | | |
|---|---|---|---|---|---|---|
| minimus | . . | Flesh | . 6, H. | A. Britain | . . | |

CEPHAELIS, *Swartz.* From *kephale*, a head; the flowers disposed in heads. *Linn.* 5, Or. 1, Nat. Or. *Cinchonaceæ.* An ornamental genus of plants, from one to fifteen feet high; they thrive well in a mixture of peat and sandy loam, and cuttings strike root freely under a glass. *Synonymes:* 1. *C. calycina.* 2. *Tapagomia purpurea.* 3. *T. violacea.*

| | | | | | | |
|---|---|---|---|---|---|---|
| axillaris, 1 | . . | White | . 4, S. Ev. S. | Brazil | . | 1816 |
| elata | . . | Purple | . S. Ev. S. | Jamaica | . | 1793 |
| involucrata | . . | White | . 7, S. Ev. S. | Guiana | . | 1826 |
| pedunculata | . . | White | . 2, S. Ev. S. | Leone | . | |
| punicea | . . | White | . 7, S. Ev. S. | Jamaica | . | 1820 |
| purpurea, 2 | . . | Wht. pur. | . 5, S. Ev. Tr. | Trinidad | . | 1821 |
| tomentosa | . . | Brown | . 8, S. Ev. S. | Trinidad | . | 1825 |
| violacea, 3 | . . | White | . 6, S. Ev. Tr. | W. Ind. | . | 1818 |

[ 69 ]

CEPHALANTHERA, *Richard.* From *kephale*, a head, and *anthera*, an anther. *Linn.* 20, Or. 1, Nat. Or. *Orchidaceæ.* A genus of very pretty plants, succeeding well in peat and loam, and increased by dividing the roots. *Synonymes:* 1. *Epipactis ensifolia.* 2. *E. pallens.* 3. *E. rubra.*

| | | | | | | |
|---|---|---|---|---|---|---|
| ensifolia, 1 | . . | White | . 6, H. Ter. Britain | . . | | |
| pallens, 2 | . . | White | . 6, H. Ter. Britain | . . | | |
| rubra, 3 | . . | Purple | . 6, H. Ter. Britain | . . | | |

CEPHALANTHUS, *Linn.* From *kephale*, a head, and *anthos*, a flower; referring to the flowers being disposed in globular heads. *Linn.* 4, Or. 1, Nat. Or. *Cinchonaceæ.* An ornamental shrub, growing seven feet high; the soil best for it is a mixture of sandy peat and loam; propagation is easy, the ripened cuttings root readily under a glass, or by layers.

| | | | | | | |
|---|---|---|---|---|---|---|
| occidentalis | . . | White | . 8, H. De. S. | N. Amer. | . | 1735 |
| brachypodus | . | White | . 8, H. De. S. | N. Amer. | . . | |

CEPHALIC, medicinal to the head.

CEPHALOPHORA, *Cavanilles.* From *kephale*, a head, and *phoreo*, to bear; the flowers are united in little heads. *Linn.* 19, Or. 1, Nat. Or. *Compositæ.* An annual of little beauty, and easy culture. *Synonymes:* 1. *Hymenopappus glaucus, Grœmia aromatica—glauca, 1.*

CEPHALOTRICHUM, *Link.* From *kephale*, a head, and *thrix*, a hair; the heads being covered with hairs. *Linn.* 24, Or. 9, Nat. Or. *Fungi.* A minute fungus discernible in general on decayed or decaying branches—*nanum.*

CEPHALOTUS, *R. Brown.* From *kephalotes*, headed; its filaments of stamens are capitate. *Linn.* 11, Or. 6, Nat. Or. *Cephalotaceæ.* A most curious little plant of rather difficult management, it should be potted in chopped moss, and boggy soil, mixed, the pots well drained, and the plants carefully watered. A glass should be placed over it at all times, and if allowed plenty of light and a temperature of 65 or 70 degrees, offsets treated in the same manner will speedily make roots.

| | | | | | | |
|---|---|---|---|---|---|---|
| follicularis | . . | White | . G. Her. P. N. Holl. | . | 1822 |  |

CERACEOUS, wax-like.

CERAMIUM, *Rochel.* Derived from *keromion*, a pitcher; from the resemblance of the capsules. *Linn.* 24, Or. 7, Nat. Or. *Algæ.* An extensive genus of seaweeds—*arbuscula, Borreri, corymbosum, Daviesii, diaphanum, D. pilosum, floridulum, Hookeri, interruptum, lanuginosum, patens, pedicellatum, pinnulatum, pluma, plumula, repens, roseum, Rothii, rubrum, tetragonum, tetricum, thujoides, Turneri, versicolor.*

CERANTHERA, *Beauvois.* From *keras*, a horn, and *anthera*, an anther; the lobes of the anthers being terminated by a bristle. *Linn.* 5, Or. 1, Nat. Or. *Violaceæ.* An ornamental genus of stove plants, growing about six feet high; it must be grown in sandy loam, and will increase by cuttings in sand, under a glass and in heat.

| | | | | | | |
|---|---|---|---|---|---|---|
| subintegrifolia | . | White | . 6, S. Ev. S. | Guinea | . | 1824 |

CERASCINOUS, deep red, cherry-coloured.

CERASTIUM, *Linn.* From *keras*, a horn; because many of the species have capsules like an ox's horn. *Linn.* 10, Or. 4, Nat. Or. *Alsinaceæ.* A genus of little interest; they vary in height from half a foot to two feet high. The herbaceous kinds have a pretty appearance on rock-work. Any light loamy soil suits them; seeds or suckers.

| | | | | | | |
|---|---|---|---|---|---|---|
| alpinum | . . | White | . 6, H. Ev. Tr. | Britain | . | |
| glaciale | . . | White | . 6, H. Ev. Tr. | Switzerl. | . | 1814 |
| grandiflorum | . . | White | . 6, H. Her. Tr. | Siberia | . | 1818 |
| lanatum | . . | White | . 6, H. Her. Tr. | Alps | . | 1819 |
| latifolium | . . | White | . 6, H. Her. Tr. | Britain | . | |
| pusillum | . . | White | . 6, H. | A. Siberia | . | 1824 |
| sylvaticum | . . | White | . 6, H. Her. Cr. | Hungary | . | 1820 |

*Anomalum, arvense, barbulosum, Biebersteinii, brachypetalum, campanulatum, caucasicum, dahuricum, dichotomum, diffusum, dioicum, glandulosum, gracile, hirsutum, holosteoides, inflatum, maritimum, matrense, maximum, nemorale, ovale, ovatum, pennsylvanicum, pentandrum, perfoliatum, pilosum, pubescens, ruderatum, rupestre, semidecandrum, serpyllifolium, Sprengelii, stellarioides, strictum, S. suffruticosum, tauricum, Tenorianum, tetrandrum, tomentosum, viscosum, vulgatum.*

CERASUS, *Jussieu.* Reported to have been first

brought from Cerasus, a town of Pontus, in Asia. *Linn.* 12, Or. 1, Nat. Or. *Rosaceæ*. A valuable genus of fruit trees, that grow well in any common soil, and are increased by seeds, budding, or grafting, with perfect ease. Synonymes: 1. *C. macrophylla*. 2. *Prunus rubra*. 3. *P. pubescens*. 4. *C. salicina*. 6. *Prunus serrulata*.

| | | | | | |
|---|---|---|---|---|---|
| avium | White | 4, H. | De. | T. | England |
| macrocarpa | White | 4, H. | De. | T. | Switzerl. |
| multiplex | White | 4, H. | De. | T. | |
| pallida | White | 4, H. | De. | T. | |
| sylvestris | White | 4, H. | De. | T. | Britain |
| borealis | White | 5, H. | De. | T. | N. Amer. | 1822 |
| canadensis | White | 5, H. | De. | T. | Canada | 1820 |
| caproniana | White | 4, H. | De. | T. | S. Eur. | |
| cordigera | White | 4, H. | De. | T. | |
| gobbetta | White | 4, H. | De. | T. | |
| griotta | White | 4, H. | De. | T. | |
| Montmorencyana | White | 4, H. | De. | T. | |
| multiplex | White | 4, H. | De. | T. | |
| pallescens | White | 4, H. | De. | T. | |
| persicifolia | White | 4, H. | De. | T. | |
| polygyna | White | 4, H. | De. | T. | |
| variegata | White | 4, H. | De. | T. | |
| caroliniana | White | 5, H. | Ev. | T. | Carolina | 1759 |
| Chamæcerasus | White | 5, H. | De. | S. | Austria | 1597 |
| chicasa | White | 5, H. | De. | S. | N. Amer. | 1806 |
| depressa | White | 4, H. | De. | S. | S. Eur. | 1805 |
| duracina | White | 4, H. | De. | T. | S. Eur. | |
| cordigera | White | 4, H. | De. | T. | |
| mammillaria, 1 | White | 4, H. | De. | T. | |
| obtusata | White | 4, H. | De. | T. | |
| hyemalis | White | 5, H. | De. | S. | N. Amer. | 1805 |
| japonica | Pink | 4, H. | De. | S. | Japan | 1810 |
| multiplex | Pink | 4, H. | De. | S. | Japan | 1810 |
| Juliana | White | 4, H. | De. | T. | S. Eur. | |
| Heaumeana | White | 4, H. | De. | T. | |
| pendula | White | 4, H. | De. | T. | S. Eur. | 1821 |
| Laurocerasus | White | 4, H. | Ev. | S. | Levant | 1629 |
| lusitanica | White | 5, H. | Ev. | S. | Portugal | 1648 |
| Mahaleb | White | 4, H. | Ev. | T. | Austria | 1714 |
| fructo-flavo | White | 5, H. | De. | T. | S. Eur. | |
| latifolia | White | 5, H. | De. | T. | S. Eur. | |
| nepalensis | White | 5, F. | De. | T. | Nepal | 1820 |
| occidentalis | White | 8. | Ev. | T. | Jamaica | 1629 |
| Padus | White | 4, H. | De. | T. | Britain | |
| bracteosa | White | 4, H. | De. | T. | Europe | |
| parviflora | White | 5, H. | De. | T. | N. Eur. | |
| rubra, 2 | White | 4, H. | De. | T. | Britain | |
| vulgaris | White | 4, H. | De. | T. | Britain | |
| pensylvanica | White | 5, H. | De. | T. | N. Amer. | 1773 |
| persicifolia | White | 5, H. | De. | S. | Crete | |
| prostrata | Pink | 4, H. | De. | S. | Crete | 1802 |
| Pseudo-cerasus | White | 4, H. | De. | S. | China | 1821 |
| pubescens, 3 | White | 4, H. | De. | S. | N. Amer. | 1806 |
| pumila | White | 5, H. | De. | S. | N. Amer. | 1756 |
| pygmæa, 4 | White | 5, H. | De. | S. | N. Amer. | 1823 |
| semperflorens | White | 4, F. | De. | T. | China | 1822 |
| se-siliflora | White | 4, H. | De. | T. | |
| serotina | White | 6, H. | De. | T. | N. Amer. | 1629 |
| serrulata, 5 | White | 4, F. | De. | S. | China | 1822 |
| sphærocarpa | White | 8, S. | Ev. | S. | Jamaica | 1820 |
| virginiana | White | 5, H. | De. | T. | Virginia | 1724 |

**Ceratiola**, *Michaux*. From *keration*, a little horn; in allusion to the stigma having the appearance of a horn. *Linn.* 21, Or. 2, Nat. Or. *Empetraceæ*. This is a very pretty greenhouse under-shrub, that should be grown in a sandy peat, and may be increased by cuttings potted in sand, under a glass.

| | | | | | |
|---|---|---|---|---|---|
| ericoides | Brown | 6, F. | Ev. | S. | N. Amer. | 1826 |

**Ceratium**, *Albertini*. From *keration*, a little horn; because the plants resemble small horns. *Linn.* 24, Or. 9, Nat. Or. *Fungi*. These are minute plants, generally found growing on dead wood in the form of little horns—*hydnoides*.

**Ceratocarpus**, *Linn.* From *keras*, a horn, and *karpos*, fruit; in reference to the calyx being two-horned. *Linn.* 21, Or. 1, Nat. Or. *Chenopodiaceæ*. An uninteresting annual, only requiring to be sown in the open border—*arenarius*.

**Ceratocephalus**, *Mœnch.* From *keras*, a horn, and *kephale*, a head; on account of the end of the seeds in the heads of the capsules being horned. *Linn.* 5, Or. 6, Nat. Or. *Ranunculaceæ*. A somewhat curious genus of plants, only requiring to be sown in the open border, and treated as other hardy annuals. Synonyme: 1. *Ranunculus falcatus*.

| | | | | | |
|---|---|---|---|---|---|
| falcatus | Yellow | 5, H. | | A. | S. Eur. | 1739 |
| orthoceras, 1 | Yellow | 5, H. | | A. | Caucasus | 1816 |

**Ceratochloa**, *Decandolle*. From *keras*, horn, and *chloa*, grass; in reference to the seeds having three little horns. *Linn.* 3, Or. 2, Nat. Or. *Gramineæ*.

An uninteresting grass, requiring only to be sown in common soil. Synonyme: 1. *Festuca unioloides—unioloides* 1.

**Ceratonia**, *Linn.* From *keration*, a horn or pod; in allusion to the shape of the pods. *Linn.* 23, Or. 2, Nat. Or. *Leguminosæ*. Scarcely worth cultivating, except for botanical collections; it grows to the height of fifteen feet, in a mixture of loam and peat; cuttings in sand will strike under a glass.

| | | | | | |
|---|---|---|---|---|---|
| siliqua | Red yel. | 9, G. | Ev. | T. | Levant | 1570 |

**Ceratopetalum**, *Smith.* Derived from *keras*, a horn, and *petalon*, a petal; in reference to the form of the petals. *Linn.* 10, Or. 1, Nat. Or. *Cunoniaceæ.* A fine greenhouse plant, growing best in a sandy loam, and increased by cuttings in sand under a glass.

| | | | | | |
|---|---|---|---|---|---|
| gummiferum | Yellow | G. | Ev. | T. | N. Holl. | 1820 |

**Ceratophyllum**, *Linn.* From *keras*, a horn, and *phyllon*, a leaf; the petals are cut so as to appear like a stag's horn. *Linn.* 21, Or. 9, Nat. Or. *Urticaceæ*. Uninteresting water plants, thriving in any pond, and easily raised by seeds—*demersum, submersum*.

**Ceratophyllus**, leaves like the upper part of a stag's horn.

**Ceratoanthes**, *Jussieu*. From *keras*, a horn, and *anthos*, a flower; referring to the inner segments. *Linn.* 21, Or. 10, Nat. Or. *Cucurbitaceæ.* A climbing plant, of no beauty, and grows in any common soil; increased by dividing the roots. Synonyme: 1. *Trichosanthes tuberosa, corniculata—tuberosa* 1.

**Cerbera**, *Linn.* Named from its poisonous qualities, in allusion to the dog Cerberus, whose bite was poisonous. *Linn.* 5, Or. 1, Nat. Or. *Apocynaceæ.* An ornamental genus of stove plants, succeeding well in a rich mould, and cuttings in sand root freely under a glass in heat. The fruit of *C. Ahouai* is a deadly poison. The Indians put small stones into the empty nuts, with which they ornament their legs; and the bark of *C. Odallam* is purgative.

| | | | | | |
|---|---|---|---|---|---|
| Ahouai | Yellow | 6, S. | Ev. | T. | Brazil | 1739 |
| fruticosa | Red | 6, S. | Ev. | S. | Pegu | 1819 |
| maculata | White | 6, S. | Ev. | T. | Bourbon | 1782 |
| ovata | Yellow | 8. | Ev. | S. | N. Spain | |
| Thevetia | Yellow | 6, S. | Ev. | T. | S. Amer. | 1735 |
| thevetioides | Yellow | 6, S. | Ev. | S. | N. Spain | 1800 |

**Cerbera**, see *Tanghinia*.

**Cercis**, *Linn.* From *kerkis*, a shuttlecock; a name given to this tree by Theophrastus. *Linn.* 10, Or. 1, Nat. Or. *Leguminosæ*. This is a beautiful genus of ornamental trees, flowering early in spring, and looking very pretty planted singly on a lawn, or trained to a wall or trellis; they grow to the height of twenty feet, and prefer an open loamy soil: plentifully increased from seeds.

| | | | | | |
|---|---|---|---|---|---|
| canadensis | Pa. red | 5, H. | De. | T. | N. Amer. | 1730 |
| siliquastrum | Red | 5, H. | De. | T. | S. Eur. | 1596 |
| flore-albo | White | 5, H. | De. | T. | S. Eur. | |
| parviflorum | Purple | 5, H. | De. | T. | Bucharia | 1827 |

**Cereris**, *Persoon.* From the goddess Ceres, the inventor of tillage. *Linn.* 3, Or. 2, Nat. Or. *Gramineæ*. This is a very pretty grass, that requires to be grown in a greenhouse, and succeeds in any common soil; increased by seeds. Synonyme: 1. *Paspalum membranaceum*.

| | | | | | |
|---|---|---|---|---|---|
| elegans | Apetal | 7, G. | Her. | P. | Peru | 1816 |

**Cereus**, *Decandolle*. From *cereus*, signifying pliant, like wax; referring to the shoots of some of the species being easily bent. *Linn.* 12, Or. 1, Nat. Or. *Cactaceæ*. A most beautiful genus, belonging to *Cactaceæ*; some of the species produce the most splendid flowers that are grown in our stoves; they succeed well in a sandy loam, the pots being well drained; in winter they require little or no water, but as soon as the flower-buds appear, they should have a good supply; increased by cuttings, which should be laid to dry a few days before being planted.

| | | | | | |
|---|---|---|---|---|---|
| Æthiops | | S. | Ev. | S. | Brazil | 1829 |
| affinis | White | S. | Ev. | S. | |
| albisetosus | | S. | Ev. | S. | St. Domin. | 1816 |
| albispinus | | S. | Ev. | S. | St. Domin. | 1816 |
| amblygonus | | S. | Ev. | S. | B. Ayres | 1836 |
| arcuatus | White | S. | Ev. | S. | | 1835 |
| bifrons | | S. | Ev. | S. | | 1818 |

| Species | Colour | | Origin | Date |
|---|---|---|---|---|
| Bonariénse | | 8. Ev. S. | B. Ayres | 1836 |
| céclûs | Grey | 8. Ev. S. | | 1836 |
| cándicâns | | 8. Ev. S. | | |
| Chilôénsis | | 8. Ev. S. | Chile | 1825 |
| Chiloénsoïdés | | 8. Ev. S. | Chile | |
| coccínêûs | Scarlet | 9, 8. Ev. S. | Brazil | |
| cœrúlêscêns | Blue | 8. Ev. S. | Brazil | |
| Colvíllî | Rose | 8. Ev. S. | Hybrid | |
| costátûs | | 8. Ev. S. | Peru | 1690 |
| crenulátûs | | 8. Ev. S. | W. Ind. | 1822 |
| cylíndricûs | | 8. Ev. S. | Peru | 1799 |
| Déppei | | 8. Ev. S. | Peru | 1799 |
| divaricátûs | | 8. Ev. S. | Mexico | 1826 |
| ebúrnéûs | | 8. Ev. S. | S. Amer. | 1818 |
| erióphôrûs | Red | 8. Ev. S. | | 1835 |
| euphorbioïdés | | 8. Ev. S. | S. Amer. | |
| exténûs | | 8. Ev. S. | | |
| Eyrésîî | Wht. grn. | 8. Ev. S. | | 1829 |
| feróx | | 8. Ev. S. | Brazil | 1827 |
| fimbriátûs | White | 8. Ev. S. | St. Domin. | 1836 |
| flagellifórmis | Pink | 8. Ev. S. | Peru | 1690 |
| flagrifórmis | | 8. Ev. S. | | 1834 |
| flavispínûs | | 8. Ev. S. | W. Ind. | |
| formôsûs | White | 8. Ev. S. | S. Amer. | 1834 |
| fulvispinôsûs | | 8 Ev. S. | S. Amer. | 1796 |
| gemmátûs | | 8. Ev. S. | | 1835 |
| glaucéscêns | | 8. Ev. S. | B. Ayres | 1836 |
| glaúcûs | | 8. Ev. S. | Brazil | 1835 |
| graciliôr | | 8. Ev. S. | | 1835 |
| grácilis | | 8. Ev. S. | S. Amer. | |
| grandiflôrûs | Wht. yel. | 8. Ev. S. | Jamaica | 1700 |
| grándis | | 8. Ev. S. | Brazil | |
| grísêûs | Grey | 8. Ev. S. | | 1809 |
| Hawórthîî | | 8. Ev. S. | Caribbees | 1711 |
| heptagônûs | White | 7, 8. Ev. S. | W. Ind. | 1728 |
| heteracánthûs | | 8. Ev. S. | B. Ayres | 1836 |
| hexagônûs | White | 8, 8. Ev. S. | Surinam | 1690 |
| húmilis | | 8. Ev. S. | S. Amer. | 1827 |
| Hýstrix | | 8. Ev. S. | | 1808 |
| incrustátûs | | 8. Ev. S. | | 1826 |
| Jamacárû | White | 8. Ev. S. | Brazil | 1835 |
| lætévírêns | | 8. Ev. S. | | 1836 |
| Lanceânûs | Scarlet | 8. Ev. S. | | 1834 |
| lanuginôsûs | White | 8, 8. Ev. S. | W. Ind. | 1690 |
| leptacánthûs | | 8. Ev. S. | | 1826 |
| leptóphis | | 8. Ev. S. | | 1835 |
| leucánthûs | Wht. pur. | 8. Ev. S. | | 1830 |
| macracánthûs | | 8. Ev. S. | | 1830 |
| mágnûs | | 8. Ev. S. | St. Domin. | 1829 |
| Martiánûs | Purple | 8. Ev. S. | | 1835 |
| monstrôsûs | Red wht. | 8. Ev. S. | S. Amer. | 1816 |
| multangulâris | | 8. Ev. S. | S. Amer. | 1815 |
| múltiplêx | Scarlet | 8. Ev. S. | St. Domin. | 1829 |
| myosúrûs | | 8. Ev. S. | | 1828 |
| myriacánthûs | | 8. Ev. S. | Chile | 1815 |
| myriocaúlôn | | 8. Ev. S. | | 1835 |
| myriophýllûs | Brown | 8. Ev. S. | | 1815 |
| Napoleónis | Grn. wht. | 8. Ev. S. | | 1834 |
| nígêr | | 8. Ev. S. | S. Amer. | 1820 |
| nigrícâns | | 8. Ev. S. | | 1835 |
| nigrospínûs | | 8. Ev. S. | B. Ayres | 1836 |
| nóbilis | Pink | 8. Ev. S. | W. Ind. | 1811 |
| nycticállis | | 8. Ev. S. | | 1834 |
| obtúsûs | | 8. Ev. S. | | 1820 |
| ochroleúcûs | Ochre | 8. Ev. S. | | 1835 |
| Oiférsîî | | 8. Ev. S. | Brazil | 1836 |
| ovátûs | | 8. Ev. S. | Chile | 1827 |
| oxygônûs | Pink | 8. Ev. S. | Brazil | 1829 |
| pallidûs | | 8. Ev. S. | St. Domin. | 1826 |
| pentagônûs | White | 7, 8. Ev. S. | S. Amer. | 1769 |
| pentálophus | | | | |
|   subarticulátûs | Lilac | 8. Ev. S. | Mexico | |
| peruviánûs | Red | 8, 8. Ev. S. | Peru | 1728 |
| Pitahaýâ | | 8. Ev. S. | Carthagena | 1836 |
| polygônûs | White | 8. Ev. S. | Chi's | 1827 |
| polymórphûs | | 8. Ev. S. | Chile | 1827 |
| prismáticûs | | 8. Ev. S. | | 1820 |
| propínquûs | | 8. Ev. S. | | 1826 |
| quadrangulâris | | 8. Ev. S. | S. Amer. | 1829 |
| radícâns | | 8. Ev. S. | B. Ayres | 1836 |
| ramôsûs | | 8. Ev. S. | | |
| regális | White | 8. Ev. S. | | |
| repándûs | White | 8, 8. Ev. S. | W. Ind. | 1728 |
| réptâns | | 8. Ev. S. | | 1813 |
| rosêûs | Rose | 8. Ev. S. | | 1826 |
| Royéni | White | 8. Ev. S. | S. Amer. | 1728 |
| Russélliânûs | | 8. Ev. S. | Demerara | 1836 |
| Scbrákîî | | 8. Ev. S. | | 1835 |
| senílis | Red | 8. Ev. S. | Mexico | 1823 |
| serpentínûs | Wht. pur. | 8. Ev. S. | Peru | |
| setôsûs | | 8. Ev. S. | Brazil | |
| stéllâtûs | | 8. Ev. S. | Brazil | 1828 |
| Smíthîî | | 8. Ev. S. | | 1835 |
| speciosíssimûs | Crimson | 7, 8. Ev. S. | S. Amer. | 1836 |
| spinôsûs | | 8. Ev. S. | | 1815 |
| spinibárbis | | 8. Ev. S. | Brazil | 1828 |
| squamulôsûs | | 8. Ev. S. | Brazil | |
| strictûs | | 8. Ev. S. | S. Amer. | 1822 |

| Species | Colour | | Origin | Date |
|---|---|---|---|---|
| strigôsûs | | 8. Ev. S. | | 1815 |
| subrepándûs | | 8. Ev. S. | | 1817 |
| tenuátûs | | 8. Ev. S. | | 1836 |
| tenúis | Red | 8. Ev. S. | Brazil | |
| tenuispínûs | | 8. Ev. S. | | |
| tenuissímûs | | 8. Ev. S. | | 1835 |
| tetragônûs | White | 7, 8. Ev. S. | S. Amer. | 1810 |
| tortuôsûs | | 8. Ev. S. | B. Ayres | 1816 |
| triangulâris | White | 8, 8. Ev. S. | W. Ind. | 1690 |
| trigônûs | White | 8. Ev. S. | S. Amer. | 1809 |
| triquétêr | | 8. Ev. S. | S. Amer. | 1794 |
| triptéris | | 8. Ev. S. | | |
| tubiflôrûs | White | 8. Ev. S. | | 1830 |
| turbinátûs | | 8. Ev. S. | | 1835 |
| undátûs | | 8. Ev. S. | China | 1829 |
| undulátûs | | 8. Ev. S. | | |
| válidûs | | 8. Ev. S. | S. Amer. | 1826 |
| variábilis | | 8. Ev. S. | | 1836 |

CERÍNTHE, *Linn.* From *keros*, wax, and *anthos*, a flower; in reference to the attraction for bees in the flowers. *Linn.* 5, Or. 1, Nat. Or. *Boraginaceæ.* The species of this genus are all ornamental annual, or biennial plants, requiring only to be sown in common soil.

| Species | Colour | | Origin | Date |
|---|---|---|---|---|
| áspêrâ | Yel. pur. | 7, H. | A. S. France | 1633 |
| maculátâ | Yel. red | 7, H. | B. S. France | 1804 |
| májôr | Yellow | 7, H. | A. S. France | 1596 |
| mínôr | Yel. pur. | 7, H. | A. Austria | 1570 |
| retórtâ | Wht. grn. | 7, H. Tw. | A. Levant | 1825 |

CERNUOUS, nodding, drooping, pendulous.

CEROPEGIA, *Linn.* From *keros*, wax, and *pege*, a fountain; literally a fountain of wax. *Linn.* 5, Or. 2, Nat. Or. *Asclepiadaceæ.* A curious genus of stove plants, that require to be grown in a sandy loam, and increased by cuttings potted in sand, and placed in a little heat.

| Species | Colour | | Origin | Date |
|---|---|---|---|---|
| acuminátâ | Purple | 6, S. Tu. P. | Coroman. | 1820 |
| africánâ | Yellow | 8. Ev. Tw. | E. Ind. | 1823 |
| aphýllâ | White | 6, G. Ev. Tw. | | 1817 |
| austrális | | G. Ev. Tw. | N. Holl. | 1820 |
| bulbôsâ | Red grn. | 5, 8. Tu. P. | E. Ind. | 1821 |
| dichótômâ | White | 7, G. Ev. S. | E. Ind. | 1804 |
| élegâns | Purple | 8, 8. De. Tw. | E. Ind. | 1828 |
| júncêâ | Yellow | 8. Ev. S. | E. Ind. | 1822 |
| Laishîî | | 9, 8. De. Cl. | Bombay | 1833 |
| sinuátâ | Pa. red | 7, G. Ev. Tw. | C. G. H. | 1818 |
| stapeliæfórmis | Purple | 7, 8. Ev. Tr. | C. G. H. | 1826 |
| tuberôsâ | Red grn. | 5, 8. Tu. P. | E. Ind. | 1821 |
| Wrightîî | Grn. pur. | 8, 8. De. Cl. | E. Ind. | 1832 |

CERRIS, ancient name for the bitter oak.

CERVINOUS, tawny, deer-coloured.

CESTRINUS, *Cassini.* After Cestrinus the son of Helenus and Andromache. *Linn.* 19, Or. 1, Nat. Or. *Compositæ.* An ornamental herbaceous plant, that grows well in common soil, and is increased freely by dividing at the root. *Synonymes : 1. Serratula acaulis, Cynara acaulis.*

| Species | Colour | | Origin | Date |
|---|---|---|---|---|
| carthamoïdês, 1 | Purple | 7, H. Her. P. | Barbary | 1797 |

CESTRUM, *Linn.* The Greek name for betony, but it has no relation to the plant which now bears that name. *Linn.* 5, Or. 1, Nat. Or. *Cestraceæ.* This is a genus of little beauty, and of easy culture; all the species grow well in a mixture of peat and loam, and are increased by cuttings; the fruit of all the species is poisonous.

| Species | Colour | | Origin | Date |
|---|---|---|---|---|
| acuminátûm | Gsh. yel. | 9, G. Ev. S. | Mexico | 1824 |
| alaternoïdês | Pa. yel. | 8, 8. Ev. S | Trinidad | 1824 |
| angustifôlium | White | 6, 8. Ev. S. | W. Ind. | 1820 |
| auriculátûm | Green | 6, 8. Ev. S. | Peru | 1774 |
| bracteátûm | Green | 4, 8. Ev. S. | Brazil | 1818 |
| cauliflôrûm | White | 5, G. Ev. S. | | 1821 |
| citrifôlium | Yellow | 6, G. Ev. S. | | 1821 |
| confértûm | Yellow | 6, 8. Ev. S. | Peru | 1820 |
| diúrnûm | White | 11, 8. Ev. S. | W. Ind. | 1732 |
| fœtidíssimûm | White | 6, 8. Ev. S. | E. Ind. | |
| fastigiátûm | White | 11, 8. Ev. S. | W. Ind. | |
| hírtûm | White | 6, 8. Ev. S. | Trinidad | 1800 |
| latifôlium | White | 6, 8. Ev. S. | W. Ind. | 1818 |
| laurifôlium | White | 6, 8. Ev. S. | W. Ind. | 1691 |
| lycioïdês | White | 7, G. Ev. S. | C. G. H. | 1826 |
| macrophýllûm | White | 6, 8. Ev. S. | W. Ind. | 1812 |
| noctúrnûm | White | 11, 8. Ev. S. | E. Ind. | 1732 |
| odontospérmûm | White | 7, 8. Ev. S. | W. Ind. | 1793 |
| Párquî | Pa. yel. | 6, G. Ev. S. | Chile | 1787 |
| pendulínûm | Grn. wht. | 6, 8. Ev. S. | Caracas | 1824 |
| salicifôlium | Grn. wht. | 6, 8. Ev. S. | Caracas | |
| suberôsûm | Sulphur | 6, 8. Ev. S. | | 1815 |
| tinctórîûm | White | 5, 8. Ev. S. | Caracas | 1823 |
| tomentôsûm | Yellow | 6, 8. Ev. S. | S. Amer. | 1790 |
| undulátûm | Yellow | G. Ev. T. | Peru | 1825 |
| venenátûm | White | 6, 8. Ev. S. | C. G. H. | 1787 |
| vespertínûm | Green | 6, 8. Ev. S. | W. Ind. | 1759 |

CETRARIA, *Acharius*. From *cetra*, a buckler; in reference to the receptacle being buckler-shaped. Linn. 24, Or. 8, Nat. Or. *Lichenes*. Is a genus of lichens; some of the species are used for food in Iceland and Lapland. *C. islandica* and *nivalis* are used as tonic, demulcent, and nutrient—*glaûcâ, G. fallâx, islândicâ, juniperinâ, J. Pindstrî, nivâlis, sepincôld*.

CEUTHOSPORA, *Fries*. From *keutho*, to hide, and *spora*, a sporule; in allusion to the sporules being hidden. Linn. 24, Or. 9, Nat. Or. *Fungi*. A genus of very minute fungi, found on decaying holly, laurel, and other leaves—*Laûrí, phacidioîdês, phæôcòmês*.

CHÆNANTHE, *Lindley*. Not explained. Linn. 20, Or. 1, Nat. Or. *Orchidaceæ*. This is described as a most singular plant, but no figure of it has yet appeared. It will most probably be found to succeed best when treated as is recommended for the genus *Vanda*.

Barkëri  . . .  S. Epi. Para  . . . 1837

CHÆTACHLÆNA, *D. Don*. From *chaite*, a bristle, and *chlaina*, a covering; the points of the involucre being covered. Linn. 19, Or. 2, Nat. Or. *Compositæ*. This is an ornamental, greenhouse, herbaceous plant, succeeding best in sandy loam; seed.

odorâtâ  . .  Red  .  8, G. Her. P. Chile  .  1830

CHÆROPHYLLUM, *Hoffmansegg*. From *chairo*, to rejoice, and *phyllon*, a leaf; alluding to the smell of the leaves. Linn. 5, Or. 2, Nat. Or. *Umbelliferæ*. An uninteresting genus of plants, varying in height from one to three feet; the annual and biennial species are best sown in the open ground in common soil. Synonyme: 1. *Myrrhis bulbosa*.

aromâticûm  .  White  .  7, H. Her. P. Germany  . 1726
tenuifoliûm  .  White  .  5, H. Her. P. S. Eur.  .  1818

*Angelicæfoliûm, aûreûm, Biebersteinii, bulbôsûm 1, capênsê, cicutâriûm, colorâtûm, divaricâtûm, hirsûtûm, hûmilê, hŷbridûm, maculâtûm, monogônûm, nítidûm, prôcumbêns, rôseûm, têmûlûm, torquâtûm.*

CHÆTANTHERA, *Ruiz et Pavon*. From *chaite*, a bristle, and *anthera*, an anther; because the anther is furnished with a hairy tuft. Linn. 19, Or. 2, Nat. Or. *Compositæ*. This is a pretty genus of herbaceous plants, which thrive best when sown in a mixture of peat and loam, increased by dividing at the roots. Synonyme: 1. *Perdicium Chilense*.

chilénsis, 1  . . .  7, G. Her. P. Chile  .  1827
ciliâtâ  . . .  7, G. Her. P. Chile  .  1822

CHÆTARIA, *Beauvois*. Derived from *chaite*, an awn or bristle. Linn. 3, Or. 2, Nat. Or. *Gramineæ*. This is an interesting genus of grasses, that grow well if sown in any common soil. Synonyme: 1. *Aristida adscensionis—adscensionis* 1, *cærulescens, divaricata, hystrix*.

CHÆTOCALYX, *Decandolle*. From *chaite*, a bristle, and *kalyx*, calyx; the calyx is covered with bristles. Linn. 17, Or. 4, Nat. Or. *Leguminosæ*. Is an ornamental stove climber, that thrives well in a mixture of peat and loam; increased by cuttings. Synonyme: 1. *Glycine vincentina*.

vincentinâ, 1  .  Yellow  .  6, S. Ev. Tu. St. Vincent 1823

CHÆTOGASTRA, *Decandolle*. From *chaite*, a bristle, and *gaster*, a belly; alluding to the tube of the calyx being covered with hairy scales. Linn. 10, Or. 1, Nat. Or. *Melastomaceæ*. Interesting plants, succeeding well in a mixture of peat and loam, and increased by seeds.

grâcilis  . .  Red li.  . .  S. Her. P. Brasil  . 1834
lanceolâtâ, 1  .  White  .  1, 8.    A. Trinidad  . 1820

CHÆTOMIUM, *Kunze*. Named from *chaite*, a bristle; in allusion to the hairy appearance of the plants. Linn. 24, Or. 9, Nat. Or. *Fungi*. This is a minute species of *Fungus*, found growing on damp straw, &c.—*elâtûm*.

CHÆTOPHORA, *Agardh*. From *chaite*, a bristle, and *phoreo*, to bear; the filaments being terminated by a bristle-like point. Linn. 24, Or. 7, Nat. Or. *Algæ*. This is a curious genus of *Algæ*, found growing on marine rocks, in lakes, ditches, &c.—*endiviæfoliâ, E. crâssâ, pelitîâ, pisifôrmis* 1, *tuberculôsâ*.

CHÆTOSPORA, *Agardh*. From *chaite*, a bristle, and *spora*, a seed; the sporules are placed on fine divisions of the filaments. Linn. 24, Or. 7, Nat. Or.

*Algæ*. A fine genus of *Algæ*, found growing on the sea-shore—*Wiggii*.

CHÆTOSPORA, *R. Brown*. From *chaite*, a bristle or awn; and *spora*, a seed. Linn. 3, Or. 1, Nat. Or. *Cyperaceæ*. An uninteresting genus of grasses, that grow well in a boggy situation; increased by dividing at the roots. Synonyme: 1. *Schœnus ferrugineus*.

turbinâtâ  . .  Apetal  .  7, Grass. N. Holl.  .  1820

ferruginëâ, 1.

CHÆTURUS, *Link*. From *chaite*, a bristle, and *oura*, a tail; in reference to the silky appearance of the panicles. Linn. 3, Or. 2, Nat. Or. *Gramineæ*. An uninteresting grass, that grows in any common soil—*fasciculâtâ*.

CHAFF-FLOWER, see *Alternantherâ Achyranthâ*.

CHAFFY, bearing processes like chaff.

CHAILLETIA, *Decandolle*. In honour of M. Chaillet, a Swiss botanist. Linn. 5, Or. 1, Nat. Or. *Chailletiaceæ*. A poisonous greenhouse shrub, that grows about five feet high, succeeding well in a mixture of peat and loam, and increased by cuttings potted in sand, under a glass.

toxicâriâ  . .  White  .  6, G. Ev. S. S. Leone  . 1824

CHALAZA, a spot on the seed, indicating where the vessels of the raphe terminate.

CHAMÆDOREA, *Willdenow*. From *chamai*, dwarf, and *dorea*, a gift; supposed to refer to the flowers being near the ground. Linn. 22, Or. 6, Nat. Or. *Palmaceæ*. An ornamental genus of Palms, growing from eight to ten feet high; they thrive best in a sandy loam in a moist heat. Synonyme: 1. *Nunezia fragrans*.

fragrâns, 1  .  White  .  Palm. Trinidad  . 1820
grâcilis  . .  Wht. grn.  .  Palm. Caraccas  . 1803

CHAMÆLEDON, *Link*. From *chamai*, dwarf, and *ledon*, a kind of cistus; from its having the appearance of a cistus. Linn. 5, Or. 1, Nat. Or. *Ericaceæ*. This is one of the most interesting of our native plants; it delights in a sandy peat, and may be increased by layers. Synonymes: 1. *Azalea procumbens, Loiseleuria procumbens*.

procûmbêns, 1  .  Pink  .  4, H. Ev. S. Britain  . .

CHAMÆLIRIUM, *Willdenow*. Derived from *chamai*, ground, and *leirion*, a lily; on account of the appearance of the plant. Linn. 22, Or. 6, Nat. Or. *Melanthaceæ*. An ornamental herbaceous plant, that grows best in a mixture of peat and loam, and is increased by dividing at the roots. Synonymes: 1. *Veratrum luteum, Helonias lutea, dioica, Melanthium densum*.

carolinianûm, 1  .  Yellow  .  7, H. Her. P. N. Amer.  . 1759

CHAMÆROPS, *Linn*. *Chamai*, on the ground, *rhops*, a twig; alluding to the low growth of the plants. Linn. 23, Or. 2, Nat. Or. *Palmaceæ*. A handsome genus of the Palm tribe, attaining thirty feet in height, and delighting best in a rich loamy soil; and with the exception of *C. guianensis* and *gracilis*, they do very well in a common greenhouse. Synonyme: 1. *Corypha palmata*.

excêlsâ  . . .  Grn. wht.  .  Palm. Nepal  .  1822
grâcilis  . . .  Grn. wht.  .  Palm. S. Amer.  . 1822
guianênsis  . .  Grn. wht.  .  Palm. Guiana  .  1824
hûmilis  . . .  Grn. wht.   2, Palm. S. Eur.  .  1731
hystrix  . . .  Grn. wht.  .  Palm. Georgia  . 1801
Palmêttô, 1  . .  Grn. wht.  .  Palm. Carolina  . 1809
serrulâtâ  . .  Grn. wht.  .  Palm. N. Amer.  . 1809

CHAMISSOA, *Humbt. et Bonpl*. In honour of M. Chamisso, the companion of Kotzebue. Linn. 5, Or. 1, Nat. Or. *Amarantaceæ*. This is a beautiful stove plant, attaining the height of five feet; it thrives well in common soil, and may be increased from cuttings. Synonyme: 1. *Achyranthes altissima*.

altissimâ, 1  .  Yellow  .  7, S. Ev. S. Jamaica  .  1816

CHAMOMILE, see *Anthemis*.

CHANNEL-LEAVED, folded together, so as to resemble a channel for conducting water.

CHAPTALIA, *Ventenat*. In honour of M. Chaptal, a celebrated French chemist. Linn. 19, Or. 4, Nat. Or. *Compositæ*. This is a pretty hardy herbaceous plant, that succeeds well in common soil, and increases by dividing the roots. Synonyme: 1. *Tussilago integrifolia*.

tomentôsâ, 1  .  White  .  5, H. Her. P. N. Amer.  . 1806

CHĀRĀ, *Linn.* From *chairo*, to delight; in allusion to its habitation. *Linn.* 24, Or. 7, Nat. Or. *Algæ.* A curious and interesting genus, requiring to be grown in ponds or cisterns, in a peat soil—*áspĕrā, hĭspĭdā, vulgārĭs.*

CHARLES'S SCEPTRE, see *Pedicularis Sceptrum carolīnum.*

CHARLOCK, see *Sinapis arvensis.*

CHARLWOODIĀ, *Sweet.* In honour of G. Charlwood, F.L.S., an enthusiastic English botanist. *Linn.* 6, Or. 1, Nat. Or. *Liliaceæ.* This is a beautiful stove genus, that attains the height of ten feet; the species thrive well in a mixture of peat and loam, and are increased by cuttings in sand, under a glass, in heat. *Synonymes:* 1. *Dracæna australis.* 2. *D. indivisa.* 3. *D. stricta.*

| | | | |
|---|---|---|---|
| australis, 1 | . . Blue wht. | 8. Ev. T. N. Zeal. | . 1823 |
| congesta | . . Pa. blue | . 3, 8. Ev. T. N. Holl. | . 1822 |
| indivisa, 2. | . . Blue | . 8, 8. Ev. T. N. Zeal. | . |
| stricta, 3 | . . Blue | . 8, 8. Ev. T. N. Zeal. | . 1820 |

CHARRED, blackened by fire.

CHASMŌNIĀ, *Presb.* From *chasmao*, to gape wide; in reference to the calyx being spread open. *Linn.* 14, Or. 1, Nat. Or. *Labiatæ.* An ornamental annual, that only requires sowing in common soil. *Synonyme:* 1. *Moluccella spinosa.*

| | | | |
|---|---|---|---|
| incisa, 1 | . . . Pink | . 7, H. | A. Levant . . 1596 |

CHEESE RENNET, see *Galium verum.*

CHEILĀNTHĒS, *Swartz.* From *cheilos*, a lip, and *anthos*, a flower; in allusion to the form of the indusium. *Linn.* 24, Or. 1, Nat. Or. *Polypodiaceæ.* This is a beautiful genus of ferns, that succeed best when grown in a mixture of peat and loam, and increase by dividing the roots. *Synonymes:* 1. *Polypodium fragrans.* 2. *Pteris gracilis.* 3. *Notholæna cheilanthoides.* 4. *Adiantum pteroides.* 5. *Nephrodium lanosum.*

| | | | | |
|---|---|---|---|---|
| caudata | . . . | Brown | . 6, G. Her. P. N. Holl. | . 1824 |
| crenulata | . . . | Brown | . 8. Her. P. | . 1831 |
| cuneata | . . . | Brown | . 8. Her. P. | . 1831 |
| ferruginea | . . . | Brown | . 6, 8. Her. P. | . 1816 |
| fragrans, 1. | . . | Brown | . 8, G. Her. P. Madeira | . 1778 |
| gracilis, 2 | . . | Brown | . 7, H. Her. P. N. Amer. | . 1823 |
| hirta | . . . | Brown | . 6, G. Her. P. C. G. H. | . 1806 |
| lendigera | . . | Brown | . 6, 8. Her. P. N. Spain | . |
| microphylla, 3 | | Brown | . 6, G. Her. P. W. Ind. | . 1823 |
| odora | . . . | Brown | . 6, F. Her. P. Switzerl. | . 1819 |
| pteroides, 4 | . . | Brown | . 7, G. Her. P. C. G. H. | . 1775 |
| repens | . . . | Brown | . 7, 8. Her. P. W. Ind. | . 1824 |
| spectabilis | . . | Brown | . 9, 8. Her. P. Brazil | . 1829 |
| vestita, 5 | . . | Brown | . 8, H. Her. P. N. Amer. | . 1812 |

CHEIRĀNTHŪS, *Linn.* Derived from its Arabic name *kheyrey*, and *anthos*, a flower. *Linn.* 15, Nat. Or. *Cruciferæ.* These are all ornamental dwarfish plants, and the common kinds thrive well in light soil, the rest require it somewhat richer, and the protection of a frame or greenhouse in winter. *Synonyme:* 1. *C. dubius.*

| | | | | |
|---|---|---|---|---|
| alpinus | . . . | . Yellow | . 5, G. Ev. 8. S. Eur. . . | 1810 |
| arboreus | . . . | . Yellow | . 5, G. Ev. 8. Egypt . . | 1827 |
| Cheiri | . . . | . Orange | . 5, F. Ev. 8. S. Eur. . | 1573 |
| ferrugineus | . | . Brown | . 5, F. Ev. 8. S. Eur. . | 1573 |
| flavescens | . | . Yellow | . 5, F. Ev. 8. S. Eur. . | 1573 |
| flore-pleno | . | . Yellow | . 5, F. Ev. 8. | |
| grandiflorus | . | . Yellow | . 5, F. Ev. 8. S. Eur. . | 1573 |
| hæmanthus | . | . Blood | . 5, F. Ev. 8. S. Eur. . | 1573 |
| maximus | . . | . Yellow | . 5, F. Ev. 8. S. Eur. . | 1573 |
| patulus | . . | . Yellow | . 5, F. Ev. 8. S. Eur. . | 1573 |
| sanguineus | . | . Drk. brn. | . 5, F. Ev. 8. | |
| serratus | . . | . Yellow | . 5, F. Ev. 8. S. Eur. . | 1573 |
| thyrsoidea | . | . Blood | . 5, F. Ev. 8. S. Eur. . | 1573 |
| varius | . . | . Varieg. | . 5, F. Ev. 8. S. Eur. . | 1573 |
| firmus | . . | . Yellow | . 6, F. Ev. 8. Europe . | 1816 |
| fruticulosus | . | . Yellow | . 5, H. Her. P. Britain . | |
| linifolius | . . | . Purple | . 4, G. Ev. 8. Spain . . | 1815 |
| mutabilis | . | . Yel. pur. | . 4, G. Ev. 8. Madeira | 1777 |
| longifolius | . | . Wht. pur. | . 4, G. Ev. 8. Madeira | 1815 |
| ochroleucus, 1 | | . Pa. yel. | . 4, H. Her. P. Switzerl. | 1822 |
| scoparius | . . | . Wht pur. | . 6, G. Ev. 8. Teneriffe | 1812 |
| æruginosus | . | . Rusty | . 6, G. Ev. 8. Teneriffe | 1812 |
| chamæleo | . | . Yel. pur. | . 6, G. Ev. 8. Teneriffe | 1812 |
| semperflorens | . | . White | . G. Ev. 8. Barbary | 1815 |
| frutescens | . | . White | . 5, G. Ev. 8. Teneriffe | 1815 |
| tenuifolius | . | . Yellow | . 6, G. Ev. 8. Madeira | 1777 |

CHEIROSTĒMŌN, *Humboldt* and *Bonpland.* From *cheir*, the hand, and *stemon*, a stamen; on account of their having five stamens, and the filaments united at the base. *Linn.* 16, Or. 6, Nat. Or. *Sterculiaceæ.* This is a very handsome plant, on account of its five-lobed leaves; it grows about thirty feet high,

[ 78 ]

in a sandy loam, and cuttings with their leaves entire, potted in peaty soil, plunged in heat, root freely.

| | | | |
|---|---|---|---|
| platanoïdes | . . . | 8. Ev. T. N. Spain | . 1820 |

CHELIDŌNIŪM, *Linn.* The plant is said to flower at the arrival and dry up at the departure of the swallows; whence the name, from *cheledon*, a swallow. *Linn.* 13, Or. 1, Nat. Or. *Papaveraceæ.* The species of this genus are interesting, and succeed well in common garden soil. *Synonyme:* 1. *C. dahuricum.*

| | | | |
|---|---|---|---|
| grandiflorum, 1 | . Yellow | . 5, H. Her. P. Dahuria | . 1820 |
| laciniatum | . . | . Yellow | . 5, H. Her. P. S. Eur. . . |
| majus | | | |

CHELŌNE, *Linn.* From *chelone*, a tortoise; to the back of which, the helmet of the flowers is fancifully compared. *Linn.* 14, Or. 2, Nat. Or. *Scrophularieæ.* This is a beautiful hardy herbaceous genus, that ought to have a place in every collection; the species succeed well in a mixture of peat and loam, and are increased by dividing the roots. *Synonyme:* 1. *C. major.*

| | | | | |
|---|---|---|---|---|
| barbata | . . . | . Scarlet | . 7, H. Her. P. Mexico | . 1794 |
| centranthifolia | | . Scarlet | . 9, H. Her. P. California | . 1834 |
| gentianoïdes | . | . Oran. scar. | . 7, F. Her. P. Mexico | . 1825 |
| glabra | . . . | . White | . 8, H. Her. P. N. Amer. | . 1730 |
| Lyōni, 1 | . . . | . Purple | . 8, H. Her. P. N. Amer. | . 1812 |
| nemorosa | . . | . Purple | . 8, H. Her. P. N. Amer. | . 1827 |
| obliqua | . . | . Purple | . 8, H. Her. P. N. Amer. | . 1752 |

CHENŌLEĀ, *Linn.* Supposed to be derived from *chen*, a goose, and *leia*, prey. *Linn.* 5, Or. 1, Nat. Or. *Chenopodiceæ.* The beauty of this plant consists in its silvery leaves; its height is seldom more than one foot, and any rich light soil will suit it; cuttings root freely placed under a glass.

| | | | |
|---|---|---|---|
| diffusa | . . . | . Green | . 8, G. Ev. 8. C. G. H. . . 1758 |

CHENOPŌDIŪM, *Linn.* From *chen*, a goose, and *pous*, a foot; in reference to many of the species having leaves similar to the webbed feet of the goose. *Linn.* 5, Or. 2, Nat. Or. *Chenopodiaceæ.* A genus of so little beauty, that its species are for the greatest part only grown in botanical collections; when grown they require to be sown on a sandy soil in the open border. *Synonymes:* 1. *Salsola fruticosa.* 2. *S. divergens.* 3. *C. erosum.* 4. *Salsola salsa.* 5. *C. fœtidum.* 6. *Salsola salsa.*

| | | | | |
|---|---|---|---|---|
| ambrosioïdes | . | . Green | . 8, H. | A. Mexico . . 1640 |
| fruticosum, 1 | . | . Green | . 8, H. Ev. 8. England . | |
| Quinōa | . . . | . Green | . 7, H. | A. Peru . . 1822 |
| rubrum | . . . | . Green | . 7, H. | A. Peru . . 1822 |

*acuminātŭm, acutifōliŭm, ālbŭm, Ā crassifōliŭm, A. integrifōliŭm, A. subrotŭndŭm, A. viridĕ, altissimŭm, anthelminticŭm, aristātŭm, atriplicis, Biebersteiniānŭm, blitoïdĕs, Bōnŭs-Henrīcŭs, botryoïdĕs, Bōtrys, Carthaginēnsĕ, caudātŭm, chrysomelanospermŭm, crassifōliŭm, ficifōliŭm, fœtidŭm, gigantĕŭm, glaucŭm, gravēolens, guineēnsĕ, hirsūtŭm, hortēnsĕ 2, humifūsĕ, hybridŭm, incīsŭm, lanceolātŭm, laterālĕ, marginātŭm, maritimŭm, multifidŭm, murālĕ, olidŭm, opulifōliŭm 3, Pallasiānŭm, parvifōliŭm, pūtulŭm, petiolārĕ, polyspermŭm, punctulātŭm, radiātŭm, rhombifōliŭm, rŭbrŭm, salsŭm 4, Schraderiānŭm 5, sepiŭm, serotinŭm, setigerŭm, spicātŭm 6, suffruticōsŭm, ŭrbicŭm.*

CHERLERIĀ, *Haller.* In honour of John Henry Cherler, who assisted John Bauhin in his history of plants. *Linn.* 10, Or. 3, Nat. Or. *Alsinaceæ.* This is an ornamental plant, and has a good effect upon rockwork; it grows best in a sandy loam and peat, and may be increased by dividing the roots, or by cuttings.

| | | | |
|---|---|---|---|
| sedoïdes | . . . | . Yel. wht. | 7, H. Her. P. Scotland . |

CHERRY, see *Cerasus.*

CHERVIL, see *Daucus Gingidium.*

CHERVIL, see *Chærophyllum.*

CHESNUT, see *Castānĕa.*

CHICASAW PLUM, see *Cerasus chicasa.*

CHICKLING VETCH, see *Lathyrus sativus.*

CHICK PEA, see *Cicer.*

CHICKWEED, see *Alsine.*

CHILOCHLŌA, *Beauvois.* Derived from *chilos*, fodder, and *chloa*, grass. *Linn.* 3, Or. 2, Nat. Or. *Gramineæ.* A genus of grasses of no particular beauty, that only require to be sown in the open ground. *Synonymes:* 1. *Phleum annuum.* 2. *P. arenaria.* 3. *P.*

L

*paniculatum.* 4. *P. Bœhmeri—annua* 1, *arenaria* 2, *aspera* 8, *Bœhmeri* 4, *cuspidata.*

CHILODIX, *R. Brown.* From *cheilos*, a lip, and *odous*, a tooth; alluding to the lip being toothed. *Linn.* 14, Or. 1, Nat. Or. *Labiatæ.* The species of this genus are ornamental greenhouse shrubs, that succeed well in a mixture of peat and loam, and increase by cuttings potted in sand, under a glass.

| | | | | | |
|---|---|---|---|---|---|
| australis | Violet | 7, | G. Ev. S. | N. Holl. | |
| scutellarioidea | Violet | 9, | G. Ev. S. | N. Holl. | 1829 |

CHILOGLOTTIS, *R. Brown.* From *cheilos*, a lip, and *glotta*, a tongue; alluding to the tongue-like appendage to the lip. *Linn.* 20, Or. 1, Nat. Or. *Orchidaceæ.* An ornamental bulbous-rooted plant, growing well in a mixture of light turfy loam, turfy peat, and sand; and kept either in the greenhouse or in a frame.

| | | | | | |
|---|---|---|---|---|---|
| diphylla | Red | | F. Ter. N. Holl. | | |

CHIMAPHILA, *Pursh.* From *cheima*, winter, and *phileo*, to love; the plants are green in winter. *Linn.* 10, Or. 1, Nat. Or. *Pyrolaceæ.* This is a genus of ornamental and medicinal plants, but difficult of cultivation; they succeed best planted out in peat soil, and there left to remain, as they cannot bear to be disturbed; cuttings. *Synonymes:* 1. *Pyrola umbellata.* 2. *P. maculata.*

| | | | | | |
|---|---|---|---|---|---|
| corymbosa, 1 | White | 6, | H. Her. P. N. Amer. | | 1752 |
| maculata, 2 | Pink | 6, | H. Her. P. N. Amer. | | 1752 |

CHIMONANTHUS, *Lindley.* From *cheimon*, winter, and *anthos*, a flower; alluding to the time of its flowering. *Linn.* 12, Or. 3, Nat. Or. *Calycanthaceæ.* This genus is deserving of a place in all collections, on account of its delightful fragrance; it will endure our winters in the open air, but when grown in the conservatory it is seen to the most advantage, as the flowers are liable to be injured when unprotected. It will grow in any soil, but prefers a mixture of loam and peat; increased by layers or young cuttings potted in sand, under a glass, plunged in a little heat. *Synonyme:* 1. *Calycanthus præcox.*

| | | | | | |
|---|---|---|---|---|---|
| fragrans, 1 | Yel. red | 12, | H. De. S. | Japan | 1766 |
| grandiflorus | Yellow | 12, | H. De. S. | | |
| parviflorus | Pa. yel. | 12, | H. De. S. | Japan | 1818 |

CHINA ASTER, see *Callistemà.*

CHINA ROSE, see *Hibiscus ròsā-sinênsis.*

CHINESE TREE, see *Pæònià Mòutàn.*

CHIOCOCCA, *P. Brown.* From *chion*, snow, and *kokkos*, a berry; referring to the berries, which are white, hence the name snowberry. *Linn.* 5, Or. 1, Nat. Or. *Cinchonaceæ.* Ornamental plants growing from three to six feet high; they thrive well in a mixture of loam and peat, and are increased by cuttings in sand, placed under a glass. *C. anguifuga* is a violent emetic and purgative.

| | | | | | |
|---|---|---|---|---|---|
| anguifuga | White | 7, | S. Ev. S. | Brasil | 1824 |
| racemosa | White | 9, | S. Ev. S. | Jamaica | 1729 |

CHIONANTHUS, *Linn.* From *chion*, white or snow, and *anthos*, a flower; the flowers are pure white. *Linn.* 2, Or. 1, Nat. Or. *Oleaceæ.* An ornamental genus of plants, varying in height from seven to thirty feet; the best plants are raised from seeds, but they may be increased by budding or grafting on the common ash.

| | | | | | |
|---|---|---|---|---|---|
| axillaris | White | 6, | S. De. S. | E. Ind. | 1810 |
| maritima | White | 6, | H. De. S. | N. Amer. | 1736 |
| virginica | White | 6, | H. De. T. | N. Amer. | 1736 |

CHIRONIA, *Linn.* After Chiron, one of the fathers of medicine and botany; he is represented to have been the son of Saturn. *Linn.* 5, Or. 1, Nat. Or. *Gentianaceæ.* The species of this genus are pretty, growing to the height of two feet: peat soil, or peat with a little loam mixed, suits them best; they ought to be frequently raised from cuttings, as the species are not long-lived plants; cuttings strike freely in peat, placed under a glass.

| | | | | | |
|---|---|---|---|---|---|
| angustifolià | Red | 7, | G. Ev. S. | C. G. H. | 1800 |
| baccifera | Yellow | 6, | G. Ev. S. | C. G. H. | 1759 |
| decussata | Red | 7, | G. Ev. S. | C. G. H. | 1789 |
| frutescens | Red | 7, | G. Ev. S. | C. G. H. | 1756 |
| albiflora | White | 7, | G. Ev. S. | C. G. H. | 1756 |
| jasminoides | Purple | 5, | G. Ev. S. | C. G. H. | 1812 |
| linoides | Red | 8, | G. Ev. S. | C. G. H. | 1787 |
| lychnoides | Purple | 5, | G. Ev. S. | C. G. H. | 1816 |
| nudicaulis | Purple | 7, | G. Ev. S. | C. G. H. | 1816 |

| | | | | | |
|---|---|---|---|---|---|
| peduncularis | Purple | 7, | G. Ev. S. | C. G. H. | 1830 |
| serpyllifolia | Yellow | 8, | G. Ev. S. | C. G. H. | 1829 |
| tetragona | Yellow | 7, | G. Ev. S. | C. G. H. | 1824 |

CHITONIA, *D. Don.* From *chiton*, a coat of mail; in allusion to the seeds being covered with scales. *Linn.* 10, Or. 1, Nat. Or. *Melastomaceæ.* This is a genus of ornamental stove plants, growing from three to twenty feet high; they succeed well in a mixture of peat and loam, and are increased readily by cuttings planted in sand under a glass. *Synonymes:* 1. *Melastoma albicans.* 2. *M. Fothergilla, Fothergilla mirabilis.* 3. *M. pyramidalis.* 4. *M. Tamoniana, M. Swartziana.*

| | | | | | |
|---|---|---|---|---|---|
| albicans, 1 | White | 8. Ev. S. | Mexico | | 1815 |
| Fothergilla, 2 | Purple | 8. Ev. T. S. Amer. | | | 1815 |
| macrophylla | White | 8. Ev. S. | Trinidad | | 1820 |
| pyramidalis, 3 | White | 7, S. Ev. S. | Trinidad | | 1817 |
| Tamonia, 4 | Purple | 8. Ev. T. W. Ind. | | | 1815 |

CHIVES, see *Allium Schœnopràsum.*

CHLIDANTHUS, *Herbert.* From *chlideios*, delicate, and *anthos*, a flower; alluding to the delicate texture of the flowers. *Linn.* 6, Or. 1, Nat. Or. *Amaryllidaceæ.* This is a pretty plant, requiring to be grown in a composition of two-thirds sandy loam, and one-third sand and peat; bulbs that are planted out in the spring will flower in summer, but they should be taken up in the autumn. *Synonyme:* 1. *Pancratium luteum.*

| | | | | | |
|---|---|---|---|---|---|
| fragrans, 1 | Yellow | 5, G. Bu. P. B. Ayres | | | 1820 |

CHLOANTHES, *R. Brown.* Named from *chloa*, grass, and *anthos*, a flower; on account of the green flowers. *Linn.* 14, Or. 2, Nat. Or. *Verbenaceæ.* An ornamental genus; the species grow to the height of two feet, and require a mixture of loam and peat; cuttings, when young, root freely in the same soil, under a glass.

| | | | | | |
|---|---|---|---|---|---|
| glandulosa | Grn. yel. | 7, | G. Ev. S. | N. Holl. | 1824 |
| rosmarinifolia | Grn. yel. | 7, | G. Ev. S. | N. Holl. | 1823 |
| Stœchadis | Grn. yel. | 7, | G. Ev. S. | N. Holl. | 1822 |

CHLORA, *Linn.* From *chloros*, green. The flowers of *C. perfoliata* are a perfect green when dried, but yellow when fresh; hence the name Yellow-wort. *Linn.* 8, Or. 1, Nat. Or. *Gentianaceæ.* This is a pretty genus, and the species well worth cultivating as hardy annuals; they only require to be sown in the open borders as soon as the seeds are ripe. *Synonyme:* 1. *C. dubia.*

| | | | | | |
|---|---|---|---|---|---|
| imperfoliata, 1 | Yellow | 6, | H. | A. Italy | 1823 |
| perfoliata | Yellow | 6, | H. | A. Britain | |

CHLORANTHUS, *Swartz.* The flowers are green; whence the name, from *chloros*, green, and *anthos*, a flower. *Linn.* 1, Or. 1, Nat. Or. *Chloranthaceæ.* This is a very curious genus of plants, not growing more than a foot, or a foot and a half high. They grow well in a mixture of loam and peat, and cuttings root freely in peat under a glass.

| | | | | | |
|---|---|---|---|---|---|
| inconspicuus | Apetal | 5, S. Ev. S. | China | | 1781 |
| monander | Apetal | 6, S. Ev. S. | China | | 1817 |
| monostachys | Apetal | 4. S. Her. P. | China | | 1819 |

CHLORIDIUM, *Link.* From *chloros*, pallid, and *eidos*, appearance; alluding to the appearance of the plants. *Linn.* 24, Or. 9, Nat. Or. *Fungi.* Insignificant plants, growing on decayed wood—griseum.

CHLORIS, *Swartz.* From *chloros*, green; alluding to the colour of the herbage. *Linn.* 23, Or. 1, Nat. Or. *Gramineæ.* The tender species should be raised on a hotbed, and require altogether to be grown with other tender annuals. *Synonyme:* 1. *C. Durandiana.*

| | | | | | |
|---|---|---|---|---|---|
| barbata | Apetal | 6, Grass. | E. Ind. | | 1777 |
| ciliata | Apetal | 8, Grass. | Jamaica | | 1779 |
| compressa | Apetal | 7, Grass. | S. France | | 1820 |
| dolichostachya | Apetal | 7, Grass. | Phil. Is. | | 1822 |
| elegans | Apetal | 7, Grass. | S. Amer. | | 1818 |
| fasciculata | Apetal | 7, Grass. | Brasil | | 1827 |
| gracilis, 1 | Apetal | 7, Grass. | | | 1824 |
| inflata | Apetal | 7, Grass. | California | | 1826 |
| pallida | Apetal | 8, Grass. | S. France | | 1816 |
| polydactyla | Apetal | 7, Grass. | Jamaica | | 1810 |
| radiata | Apetal | 8, Grass. | W. Ind. | | 1739 |
| rettusa | Apetal | 7, Grass. | B. Ayres | | 1824 |
| Roxburghiana | Apetal | 7, Grass. | E. Ind. | | 1820 |
| truncata | Apetal | 7, Grass. | N. Holl. | | 1818 |
| ventricosa | Apetal | 7, Grass. | N. Holl. | | 1820 |

CHLOROCOCCUM, *Greville.* Derived from *chloros*, green, and *kokkos*, a berry; on account of their appearance. *Linn.* 24, Or. 7, Nat. Or. *Algæ.* This is a very curious genus, belonging to *Algæ,* found growing on trunks of trees and old walls. *Synonyme:* 1. *Lepraria botryoides—murorum, vulgare* l.

CHLORÓPHŸTÜM, *Ker.* From *chloros,* green, and *phyton,* a plant; referring to the appearance of the plants. *Linn.* 24, Or. 7, Nat. Or. *Algæ.* A curious genus, growing from one to two feet high; they do best in a compost of turfy loam, peat and sand. *Synonyme:* 1. *Anthericum alatum.*

| | | | | | | | |
|---|---|---|---|---|---|---|---|
| elatüm, 1 | . . | White. | . | 8, S. Her. P. C. G. H. | . 1751 |
| inornatüm | . . | White. | . | 7, S. Her. P. S. Leone | |
| orchidiastrüm | . . | White. | . | 8. Her. P. S. Leone | . 1822 |

CHLOROSIS, the green sickness; a disease so called.

CHLORÓXŸLÖN, *Decandolle.* From *chloros,* green, and *xylon,* wood; on account of the green or deep yellow colour of the wood. *Linn.* 10, Or. 1, Nat. Or. *Cedrelaceæ.* This is a fine timber tree, growing to the height of one hundred feet; it grows well in our stoves, in a mixture of loam and peat; cuttings. *Synonyme:* 1. *Swietenia chloroxylon.*

| | | | | | | |
|---|---|---|---|---|---|---|
| Swietenia, 1 | . . | White . | . | 8. Ev. T. E. Ind. | . 1820 |

CHOCOLATE-NUT, see *Theobrōmā.*

CHOISŸÀ, *Kunth.* In honour of M. Choisy, a Genevese botanist. *Linn.* 10, Or. 1, Nat. Or. *Rutaceæ.* This is an ornamental shrub, growing about six feet high; it thrives well in a mixture of peat and loam, and may be increased by cuttings in sand under a glass.

| | | | | | | |
|---|---|---|---|---|---|---|
| ternata | . . . | White. | . 7, S. Ev. S. Mexico . | . 1825 |

CHOKE, see *Cérāstium hyemālis.*

CHOKÓ, see *Sechiüm.*

CHOMÉLIA, *Jacquin.* After J. B. Chomel, M.D., physician to Louis XV. *Linn.* 4, Or. 1, Nat. Or. *Cinchonaceæ.* The species are ornamental plants, growing from five to twelve feet in height; they thrive well in a mixture of loam and peat, and cuttings root freely under a glass in heat. *Synonymes:* 1. *Ixora fasciculata.* 2. *I. spinosa.*

| | | | | | | |
|---|---|---|---|---|---|---|
| fasciculata, 1 | . . | White. | . | 8. Ev. S. W. Ind. | . 1825 |
| spinosa, 2 | . . | White. | . | 8. Ev. S. W. Ind. | . 1793 |

CHÓNDRIA, *Agardh.* From *chondros,* a cartilage; on account of the fronds being cartilaginous. *Linn.* 24, Or. 7, Nat. Or. *Algæ.* A curious genus, belonging to *Algæ;* all the species are found growing in the ocean—*articulāta, clavellōsā, dasyphŷllā, kaliformis, obtūsā, ovālis, pinnatifīdā, tenuissīmā.*

CHONDRILLA, *Linn.* From *chondros,* a lump; the plants bear lumps of gummy matter on the stems. *Linn.* 19, Or. 1, Nat. Or. *Compositæ.* Uninteresting plants; the species grow best planted in a sandy soil, and are increased by dividing the roots—*gramīnēā, jūncēā, latifōliā.*

CHORDARIA, *Link.* Named on account of the resemblance of the plants to a cord, from *chordea,* a cord. *Linn.* 24, Or. 7, Nat. Or. *Algæ.* A very remarkable genus of *Algæ,* found growing in the ocean—*flagelliformis.*

CHORDORHIZA, cord-rooted.

CHORISPÓRA, *Decandolle.* From *choris,* separately, and *spora,* a seed; the seeds are separated from each other in the pods. *Linn.* 15, Nat. Or. *Cruciferæ.* The species of this genus are pretty, and only require sowing in the open ground, and treating like other hardy annuals. *Synonymes:* 1. *Raphanus tenellus.* 2. *R. arcuatus.*

| | | | | | | |
|---|---|---|---|---|---|---|
| tenella, 1 | . . | Purple | . 6, H. | A. Siberia . | . 1780 |
| arcuata, 2 | . . | Purple | . 6, H. | A. Siberia . | |

*ibērica, sibīrica.*

CHORŌZĒMÀ. From *choros,* a dance, and *zema,* a drink; this name was suggested to Labillardiére, who originally discovered the plant upon the southwest coast of New Holland, at the foot of the mountains, near a spot, where, after finding many salt springs, his party met with an ample supply of fresh water. *Linn.* 10, Or. 1, Nat. Or. *Leguminosæ.* This is a very pretty genus, C. *Henchmanni* is beautiful; they grow from one to two feet high, and succeed best in an equal mixture of peat, loam, and sand, and increase from cuttings, but the best plants are obtained from seed, which ripen in abundance.

| | | | | | | |
|---|---|---|---|---|---|---|
| cordata | . . . | Red | . 4, G. Ev. S. N. S. W. | |
| Henchmanni | . . | Scarlet | . 8, G. Ev. S. N. Holl. | . 1824 |
| ilicifolia | . . | Yel. red | . 8, G. Ev. S. N. Holl. | . 1803 |

[ 75 ]

| | | | | | | |
|---|---|---|---|---|---|---|
| nana | . . . | Yel. red | . 4, G. Ev. S. N. Holl. | . 1803 |
| ovata | . . . | Scarlet | . 8, G. Ev. S. N. Holl. | . 1830 |
| rhombea | . . . | Yellow | . 5, G. Ev. S. N. Holl. | . 1803 |
| spartioides | . . | Yel. red | . 6, G. Ev. S. N. Holl. | . 1832 |
| triangulare | . . | Scarlet | . 4, G. Ev. S. N. Holl. | . 1830 |

CHRISTMAS ROSE, see *Hellēborus niger.*

CHRIST'S EYE, see *Inula Ocūlus Christi.*

CHRIST'S THORN, see *Paliūrus.*

CHRÖÖLÉPIS, *Agardh.* From *chroos,* skin, and *lepo,* to decorticate; in allusion to the change undergone by the inner membrane, which becomes powdery. *Linn.* 24, Or. 7, Nat. Or. *Algæ.* This is a curious genus of *Algæ,* found growing on rocks, trees, and old walls—*ebēnēis, jolithūs, lichenicōlā, odorātus, rubicūndus.*

CHRYSALIS-LIKE, like the chrysalis of an insect.

CHRYSANTHĔLLÛM, *Richard.* A diminutive of Chrysanthemum. *Linn.* 19, Or. 2, Nat. Or. *Compositæ.* An uninteresting stove annual, that will grow well sown in any common soil. *Synonyme:* 1. *Verbesina mutica, Collæa procumbens—procūmbēns,* 1.

CHRYSANTHĔMÛM, *Linn.* From *chrysos,* gold, and *anthemon,* a flower; alluding to the colour of some of the flowers being yellow. *Linn.* 19, Or. 2, Nat. Or. *Compositæ.* The species and varieties of this genus are very numerous and of great beauty, when a large quantity of them are grown together; the greenhouse species thrive well in any light soil, and young cuttings root freely taken off young, and potted in sand under a glass. *Synonyme:* 1. *C. indicum.*

| | | | | | | |
|---|---|---|---|---|---|---|
| absinthiifolium | . White . | . | H. Her. P. | Siberia . | . 1824 |
| Achilleæ . . | . White . | . 7, H. Her. P. | Italy . | . 1775 |
| anomalum . | . White . | . 6, F. Ev. S. | Spain . | . 1811 |
| arcticum . . | . White . | . 7, H. Her. P. | Kamtsch. | . 1801 |
| argenteum . | . White . | . 7, H. Her. P. | Levant . | . 1781 |
| atratum . . | . White . | . 7, H. Her. P. | Austria . | . 1781 |
| lobatum . . | . White . | . 7, H. Her. P. | Switzerl. | . 1819 |
| carinatum . | . Wht. pur. | 8, H. | A. | Barbary | . 1796 |
| coronarium . | . Yellow . | 8, H. | A. | Sicily . | . 1629 |
| daucifolium . | . White . | . 7, H. Her. P. | | . 1820 |
| graminifolium | . White . | . 6, H. Her. P. | Montpel. | . 1739 |
| heterophyllum | . White . | . 7, H. Her. P. | Switzerl. | . 1806 |
| indicum . . | . Yellow . | . 9, H. Her. P. | China . | |
| italicum . . | . Pa. yel. | . 6, H. De. | Tr. Italy . | . 1796 |
| lanceolatum . | . White . | . 6, H. Her. P. | Hungary | . 1817 |
| leucanthemum | . White . | . 6, H. Her. P. | Britain . | |
| mexicanum . | . White . | . 8, H. Her. P. | Mexico . | . 1825 |
| monspeliense | . White . | . 7, H. Her. P. | Montpel. | . 1739 |
| montanum . | . White . | . 6, H. Her. P. | France . | . 1759 |
| Myconis . | . Yellow . | . 7, H. | A. | Italy . | . 1775 |
| paludosum . | . White . | . 6, H. Her. P. | Barbary | . 1810 |
| parpusillum . | . White . | . 6, H. Her. P. | France . | . 1825 |
| pinnatifidum | . White . | . 7, G. Ev. S. | Madeira | . 1777 |
| pumilum . . | . White . | . 8, H. | A. | | . 1806 |
| radicans . . | . White . | . 7, G. Ev. S. | Spain . | . 1810 |
| rotundifolium | . White . | . 6, H. Her. P. | Hungary | . 1817 |
| segetum . . | . Yellow . | . 7, H. | A. | Britain . | |
| sinense . . | . Varieg. | . 10, H. Her. P. | China . | . 1764 |
| sylvestre . . | . White . | . 6, H. Her. P. | | . 1804 |
| tanacetifolium | . White . | . 7, H. Her. P. | A. Minor | . 1818 |
| tripartitum, 1 | . Yellow . | . 10, H. Her. P. | E. Ind. . | . 1800 |

CHRYSEIS, *Lindley.* After Chryseis, a celebrated Homeric beauty; alluding to the colour of the flowers. *Linn.* 13, Or. 4, Nat. Or. *Papaveraceæ.* The species of this genus are very handsome when in flower, and on that account well deserving of a place in every flower-garden. They succeed well in any rich soil, and must be annually raised from seed sown on a gentle hotbed early in spring, and afterwards planted out in the open border, where they will produce their flowers and seeds in autumn. If there is any convenience for protecting the young plants during winter, the seed should be sown in autumn, as by that means the plants will flower much earlier and produce seeds with greater certainty. *Synonymes:* 1. *Eschscholtzia Californica.* 2. *E. crocea.*

| | | | | | | |
|---|---|---|---|---|---|---|
| californica, 1 | . Yellow | . 9, H. Tu. P. California | . 1826 |
| compacta | . . Yellow | . 8, H. Tu. P. California | . 1833 |
| crocea, 2, | . . Saffron | . 8, H. Tu. P. California | . 1833 |

CHRYSIPHIALA, *Ker.* From *chrysos,* gold, and *phiale,* a goblet; in allusion to the golden cup-like flowers. *Linn.* 6, Or. 1, Nat. Or. *Amaryllidaceæ.* This is a pretty genus of bulbs, that require to be grown in a light loam, and are increased by offsets. *Synonyme:* 1. *Stenomison flava.*

| | | | | | | |
|---|---|---|---|---|---|---|
| crocea | . . . | Copper | . 5, G. Bu. P. S. Amer. | . 1820 |
| curvidentata | . . | Yellow | . 10, G. Bu. P. Peru . | . 1825 |
| flava, 1 . . | . Orange | . 5, G. Bu. P. Peru . | . 1820 |
| panciflora | . . | Orange | . 5, G. Bu. P. Peru . | . 1822 |

**CHRYSOBĂLĂNŬS**, *Linn.* From *chrysos*, gold, and *balanos*, an acorn; some of the species bear yellow fruit. *Linn.* 12, Or. 1, Nat. Or. *Chrysobalanaceæ*. A genus of fruiting shrubs, succeeding best when grown in a mixture of loam and peat; increased by layers or cuttings in sand, under a glass. In the W. Indies the fruit of *C. Icaco* is eaten, under the name of cocoa-plum.

| | | | | | |
|---|---|---|---|---|---|
| Icaco | . . . | White . | . 8. Ev. S. W. Ind. | . 1752 |
| oblongifōliŭs | . . | White . | . 5, G. Ev. S. Georgia | . 1812 |

**CHRYSŎCŎMĂ**, *Decandolle.* From *chrysos*, gold, and *kome*, hair; the stems are terminated by tufts of yellow flowers. *Linn.* 19, Or. 1, Nat. Or. *Compositæ*. This is an ornamental genus of plants, the species growing from half a foot to six feet high; they succeed best in a mixture of loam and peat, and cuttings taken off when ripe, root freely under a glass.

| | | | | | |
|---|---|---|---|---|---|
| biflŏrā | . . . | Blue . | . 8, H. Her. P. Siberia | . 1741 |
| cernŭă | . . . | White . | . 7, G. Ev. S. C. G. H. | . 1712 |
| ciliārĭs | . . . | White . | . 8, G. Ev. S. C. G. H. | . 1759 |
| ComaŭreĂ | . . | Yellow | . 7, G. Ev. S. C. G. H. | . 1731 |
| denticulātă | . . | Yellow | . 7, G. Ev. S. |
| dracunculoīdēs | . | Yellow | . 8, H. Her. P. Siberia . |
| Lynosÿrīs | . . | Yellow | . 9, H. Her. P. Europe . | . 1596 |
| nivĕă | . . . | Yellow | . 7, G. Ev. S. C. G. H. | . 1816 |
| nudātă | . . . | Yellow | . 9, H. Her. P. Carolina | . 1818 |
| patŭlă | . . . | Yellow | . 7, G. Ev. S. C. G. H. | . 1810 |
| scābră | . . . | White . | . 8, G. Ev. S. C. G. H. | . 1732 |
| squamātă | . . | Yellow | . 5, G. Her. P. N. S. W. | . 1837 |
| villōsă | . . . | Yellow | . 8. H. Her. P. Hungary | . 1799 |
| virgātă | . . . | Yellow | . 9, H. Her. P. N. Amer. | . 1821 |

**CHRYSŎGŎNŬM**, *Linn.* From *chrysos*, gold, and *gonu*, a knee or joint; the flowers are generally produced at the joints of the stem. *Linn.* 19, Or. 4, Nat. Or. *Compositæ*. This is a very pretty herbaceous plant, that thrives best in peat and loam, and is increased by dividing the roots.

| | | | | | |
|---|---|---|---|---|---|
| virginiānŭm | . | Yellow | . 5, H. Her. P. N. Amer. | |

**CHRYSŎPHŸLLŬM**, *Linn.* From *chrysos*, gold, and *phyllon*, a leaf; in allusion to the under surface of the leaves being covered with dense shining hairs of a bright yellow colour. *Linn.* 5, Or. 1, Nat. Or. *Sapotaceæ*. This is a fruit-bearing genus; the species grow from fifteen to fifty feet high, and one species, *C. macrophyllum*, attains the height of one hundred feet, with most splendid foliage; they do well in a mixture of loam and peat; and cuttings of the ripened wood root freely in sand under a glass, with a good moist heat.

| | | | | | |
|---|---|---|---|---|---|
| angustifōliŭm . | . White . | . 8. Ev. T. W. Ind. | . 1819 |
| argēntĕŭm . | . White . | . 8. Ev. T. Martinique | . 1758 |
| Cainĭtŏ . . | . White . | . 5, S. Ev. T. W. Ind. | . 1737 |
| cærŭleŭm . | . White . | . 5, S. Ev. T. S. Amer. | . 1737 |
| jamaicĕnsĕ . | . White . | . 5, S. Ev. T. Jamaica | . 1737 |
| microphyllŭm . | . White . | . 5, G. Ev. T. S. Amer. | . 1800 |
| glābrŭm . . | . White . | . 8. Ev. T. Martinique | . 1823 |
| macrophyllŭm . | . White . | . 8. Ev. T. S. Leone | . 1824 |
| monopÿrēnŭm . | . Brown . | . 8. Ev. T. W. Ind. | . 1819 |

**CHRYSŎPŎGŎN**, *Trinius.* From *chrysos*, gold, and *pogon*, a beard; in allusion to the yellow awns. *Linn.* 23, Or. 1, Nat. Or. *Gramineæ*. An uninteresting grass, that only needs to be sown in any common soil. Synonymes: 1. *Andropogon gryllus, Holcus gryllus, Pollinia gryllus—gryllus* 1.

**CHRYSOSPLĒNĬŬM**, *Linn.* From *chrysos*, gold, and *splen*, the spleen; in reference to the colour of the flowers, and the supposed medicinal virtues of the plant. *Linn.* 10, Or. 2, Nat. Or. *Saxifragaceæ*. This is a curious and rather pretty genus; they require a moist situation. Our native species are found in the greatest perfection upon the banks of small rivulets; increased by dividing the roots.

| | | | | | |
|---|---|---|---|---|---|
| alternifōliŭm . | . Yellow | . 4, H. Her. P. Britain . | |
| nepalensĕ . . | . Yellow | . 4, H. Her. P. Nepal . | . 1820 |
| oppositifōliŭm . | . Yellow | . 4, H. Her. P. Britain . | |

**CHRYSŎSTĔMMĂ**, *Lessing.* From *chrysos*, gold, and *stemma*, a crown; alluding to the colour of the flowers. *Linn.* 19, Or. 3, Nat. Or. *Compositæ*. This very pretty species deserves to be cultivated in every flower-border. For culture and propagation see *Coreopsis*. Synonymes: 1. *Coreopsis tripteris*.

| | | | | | |
|---|---|---|---|---|---|
| triptĕrĭs . . | . Yellow | . 8, H. Her. P. N. Amer. | . 1837 |

**CHRYSŎŬRŬS**, *Persoon.* From *chrysos*, gold, and *oura*, a tail; alluding to the compact heads of flowers. *Linn.* 3, Or. 2, Nat. Or. *Gramineæ*. This is a genus

of grasses, some of which are very ornamental; they only require to be sown in any common soil. Synonymes: 1. *C. cynosuroides, Cynosurus aureus.* 2. *Cynosurus elegans.*

| | | | | | |
|---|---|---|---|---|---|
| aŭrĕŭs . . | . Apetal | . 7, Gras. S. Eur. | . 1824 |
| elegans 2 . . | . Apetal | . 7, Gras. S. Eur. | . 1816 |

*Aureus* 1, *echinatus.*

**CHŶSĬS**, *Lindley.* From *chusis*, a melting; because the pollen-masses are as it were fused together. *Linn.* 20, Or. 1, Nat. Or. *Orchidaceæ*. This is a splendid but very rare species. In its native country it is found growing suspended by long fibrous roots from the branches of trees, so that the pseudo-bulbs, which grow to a great length (and are also very brittle when growing), hang downwards, and wave in the wind. The flower is very showy, the colour being very bright, its texture firm, and its surface even and waxy. The labellum is beautifully marked with crimson veins. It succeeds well with the treatment recommended for the genus *Vanda*.

| | | | | | |
|---|---|---|---|---|---|
| aŭrĕă . . . | . Yellow | . 5, S. Epi. Venezuela | . 1834 |

**CĪBĀRĬOUS**, good for food, esculent.

**CĪBŎTĬŬM**, *Kaulfuss.* From *kibotion*, a little chest; in reference to the form of the indusium. *Linn.* 24, Or. 1, Nat. Or. *Polypodiaceæ*. This is a beautiful tree fern from N. Holland, where it grows to the height of thirty feet; it requires to be grown in a mixture of loam and peat, and is increased by dividing the roots. Synonyme. 1. *Dicksonia antarctica.*

| | | | | | |
|---|---|---|---|---|---|
| Billardiĕrĭ, 1 . | . Brown . | . G. Ev. T. N. Holl. | . 1824 |

**CĬCCĂ**, *Linn.* Supposed to be a man's name. *Linn.* 21, Or. 4, Nat. Or. *Euphorbiaceæ*. Is a fruit tree, growing to the height of twenty feet; it thrives best in sandy loam, and strong cuttings root freely if planted with their leaves on in sand, under a glass.

| | | | | | |
|---|---|---|---|---|---|
| distĭchă . . | . Green . | . S. Ev. T. E. Ind . | . 1796 |

**CĬCĔR**, *Tournefort.* From *kykis*, force, or strength; in reference to its qualities. *Linn.* 17, Or. 4, Nat. Or. *Leguminosæ*. This genus is cultivated in the south of Europe for the same purpose as the lentil in this country; it only requires to be sown in common soil, but it is too delicate for field culture in this country.

| | | | | | |
|---|---|---|---|---|---|
| arietīnŭm . . | . Purple | . 7, H.    A. S. Eur. | . 1548 |

**CĬCHŌRĬUM**, *Linn.* The Greeks adopted this name from the Egyptians. *Linn.* 19, Or. 1, Nat. Or. *Compositæ*. This is a genus of uninteresting plants, with the exception of *C. Endivia*, which is very valuable as a salad; the tender species should be sown on a hotbed, and afterwards transplanted.

| | | | | | |
|---|---|---|---|---|---|
| Endivĭă . . | . Blue . | . 7, H.    A. E. Ind. | . 1548 |
| Intybŭs . . | . Blue . | . 7, H. Her. P. Britain . | |

*divaricātum, pumilum, spinosum.*

**CĬCŪTĂ**, *Linn.* A name of doubtful meaning, used by Pliny. *Linn.* 5, Or. 2, Nat. Or. *Umbelliferæ*. The species of this genus are of little interest, growing from one to three feet high; they delight in a humid situation, and are easily raised from seeds. The roots of *C. virosa* are poisonous.

| | | | | | |
|---|---|---|---|---|---|
| maculātă . . | . White . | . 7, H. Her. P. N. Amer. | . 1759 |
| virosă . . | . White . | . 7, H. Her. P. Britain . | |

*bulbifera, datrica.*

**CĬLIÆ**, hairs like those of the eyelash.

**CĬLIĀTED,** } eyelash-haired.
**CĬLIĀRY,** }

**CĬLIATELY-TOOTHED**, having teeth like the hairs of the eyelash.

**CĬLIARY-SCABROUS**, having rough ciliated margins.

**CĬLIATELY-PLUMOSE**, having long hairs on the edges, like the feathers of a quill.

**CĬMICĬFŬGĂ**, *Linn.* From *cimex*, a bug, and *fugo*, to drive away; referring to the virtues which the plants are supposed to possess. *Linn.* 13, Or. 5, Nat. Or. *Ranunculaceæ*. A curious genus; the species grow from two to four feet high. They thrive well in any common soil, and are increased by seeds, or dividing the roots. Synonymes: 1. *Achæa podocarpa.* 2. *A. Cimicifuga.*

| | | | | | |
|---|---|---|---|---|---|
| americānă, 1 . | . Wht. yel. | . 7, H. Her. P. Carolina | . 1824 |
| cordifōliă . . | . Wht. yel. | . 6, H. Her. P. N. Amer. | . 1812 |
| fœtĭdă, 2 . . | . Lgt. yel. | . 6, H. Her. P. Siberia | . 1777 |
| palmātă . . | . Wht. yel. | . 7, H. Her. P. N. Amer. | . 1812 |

CINCHŌNĀ, *Linn.* In honour of the Countess de Cinchon, vice-queen of Peru, who was cured of a fever in 1638 by this remedy. *Linn.* 5, Or. 1, Nat. Or. *Cinchonaceæ.* It is from this genus that the celebrated Peruvian bark is obtained ; it is not common in collections, owing to its being rather difficult to keep. The best soil for it is loam and peat ; and cuttings, if taken off when ripe, and planted in a pot of sand under a glass in heat, will strike.

| | | | | | |
|---|---|---|---|---|---|
| officinalis | . . . | . Red | . . 7, 8. Ev. | T. Peru | . . 1810 |
| scabrā | . . . | . Red | . . 8. Ev. S. | | . 1820 |

CINCLIDŌTŪS, *Beauvois.* From *kigklis*, lattice, and *odous*, a tooth ; the ciliæ of the peristome are united in parcels, in a peculiar netted manner. *Linn.* 24, Or. 5, Nat. Or. *Musci.* A pretty genus, belonging to *Musci*, found growing in streams of fresh water. *Synonyme:* 1. *Fontinalis minor—fontinaloïdes* 1.

CINERĀRĪĀ, *Linn.* From *cineres*, ashes ; referring to the soft white down which covers the surfaces of the leaves. *Linn.* 19, Or. 2, Nat. Or. *Compositæ.* This is a pretty genus of plants, the species of which grow generally from one to three feet high ; they thrive best in a mixture of loam and peat, and young cuttings root freely under a glass.

| | | | | | |
|---|---|---|---|---|---|
| Altoniānā | . . | . Yellow | . 7, 8. Ev. S. | | |
| alba | . . . | . White . | 2, G. Ev. S. | C. G. H. | . 1825 |
| alpestris | . . | . Yellow | . 5, H. Her. P. | Switzerl. | 1819 |
| alpinā | . . | . Yellow | . 7, H. Her. P. | Switzerl. | 1819 |
| americānā | . . | . Yellow | . 8. Ev. S. | Grenada | . 1825 |
| angustifoliā | . | . Yellow | . 7, G. Ev. S. | Mexico | . 1825 |
| aurantiācā | . | . Orange | . 6, H. Her. P. | Switzerl. | 1819 |
| aūrēā | . . | . Yellow | . 7, H. Her. P. | Siberia | . 1827 |
| auritā | . . | . Purple | . 6, G. Ev. S. | Madeira | . 1777 |
| bicōlōr, 1 | . | . Yellow | . 7, G. Ev. S. | Austria | |
| cacalioīdēs | . | . Yellow | . 7, G. Ev. S. | C. G. H. | . 1816 |
| canadēnsis | . | . Yellow | . 7, H. Her. P. | Canada | . 1739 |
| canēscēns, 2 | . | . Yellow | . 6, G. Ev. S. | C. G. H. | . 1790 |
| campēstris | . | . Yellow | . 5, H. Her. P. | Europe | . |
| caucasicā | . | . Yellow | . 7, G. Her. P. | C. G. H. | . 1759 |
| crassifoliā | . | . Yellow | . 7, H. Her. P. | Carinthia | . 1827 |
| crispā | . . | . Yellow | . 7, H. Her. P. | Switzerl. | . 1818 |
| discōlōr | . . | . White . | 7, 8. Ev. S. | Jamaica | . 1804 |
| elātīor | . . | . White . | 7, G. Her. P. | | |
| geïfoliā | . . | . Yellow | . 8, G. Ev. S. | C. G. H. | . 1710 |
| gigantēā | . . | . White . | 7, H. Her. P. | Cape Horn | . 1801 |
| glābrātā | . . | . Yellow | . 7, 8. Ev. S. | Jamaica | . 1822 |
| hamifoliā | . . | . Yellow | . 7, G. Ev. S. | C. G. H. | . 1754 |
| hybridā | . . | . Yellow | . 2, G. Ev. S. | | |
| incānā | . . | . Yellow | . 7, G. Ev. S. | Jamaica | . 1823 |
| integrifoliā | . | . Yellow | . 5, H. Her. P. | England | |
| lactēā | . . | . White . | 6, G. Ev. S. | | . 1816 |
| lanātā | . . | . Purple | . 6, G. Ev. S. | Canaries | . 1780 |
| lævigātā | . . | . Yellow | . 7, H. Her. P. | Siberia | . 1819 |
| lobātā | . . | . Yellow | . 7, G. Ev. S. | C. G. H. | . 1774 |
| longifoliā | . . | . Yellow | . 7, H. Her. P. | Austria | . 1792 |
| lūcidā | . . | . Yellow | . 7, 8. Ev. S. | W. Ind. | |
| macrophyllā | . | . Yellow | . 7, H. Her. P. | Altai Mts. | 1831 |
| malvæfoliā | . | . Yellow | . 8, G. Her. P. | Azores | . 1777 |
| maritima | . . | . Yellow | . 8, H. Ev. S. | S. Eur. | . 1633 |
| palūstris | . . | . Yellow | . 6, H. Her. P. | England | |
| purpūrēā | . . | . Yellow | . 7, H. Her. P. | Gallicia | . 1821 |
| parviflōrā | . . | . Yellow | . 7, H. Her. P. | Caucasus | . 1820 |
| Petasītēs | . . | . Yellow | . 2, G. Ev. S. | Mexico | . 1812 |
| populifoliā | . . | . Red . | 7, G. Ev. S. | Canaries | . 1780 |
| præcōx | . . | . Yellow | . 2, G. Ev. S. | Mexico | . 1824 |
| pulchēllā | . . | . Purple | . 2, G. Ev. S. | Canaries | . 1818 |
| racemōsā | . . | . Yellow | . 7, H. Her. P. | Caucasus | . 1820 |
| renifoliā | . . | . Yellow | . 5, H. Her. P. | Russia | . 1833 |
| rivulāris | . . | . Yellow | . 7, H. Her. P. | Hungary | . 1816 |
| salicifoliā | . . | . Yellow | . 7, G. Ev. S. | Mexico | . 1827 |
| sexpiflōrā | . . | . Yellow | . 7, G. Ev. S. | C. G. H. | . 1829 |
| sibiricā | . . | . Yellow | . 7, H. Her. P. | Siberia | . 1784 |
| spatulæfoliā, 4 | . | . Yellow | . 5, H. Her. P. | Germany | . 1820 |
| speciōsā | . . | . Yellow | . 7, H. Her. P. | Siberia | . 1815 |
| suēticā | . . | . Yellow | . 7, H. Her. P. | Switzerl. | . 1819 |
| tussilaginoīdēs | | | | | |
| Waterhousēānā | Red | . 4, G. Her. P. | Hybrid | . 1835 |
| vestītā | . . | . Yellow | . 8, G. Ev. S. | C. G. H. | . 1824 |
| viscōsā | . . | . Yellow | . 7, G. | B. C. G. H. | . 1774 |

CINEREOUS, coloured like ashes, grey.

CINEREOUSLY-CANESCENT, between white and ash-coloured.

CINEREOUSLY-GLAUCOUS, between sea-green and ash-coloured.

CINEREOUSLY-PUBESCENT, covered with grey pubescence.

CINGALESE, inhabitants of, or belonging to Ceylon.

CINNĀ, *Linn.* The ancient name of a grass growing in Cilicia. *Linn.* 1, Or. 2, Nat. Or. *Gramineæ.* This is a curious grass, that succeeds well sown in any common soil.

| | | | | |
|---|---|---|---|---|
| arundinācēā | . . | . 7, | Canada | . . 1799 |

CINNĀMŌMŪM, *R. Brown.* Derived from the Arabic, *kinamon*, cinnamon. *Linn.* 9, Or. 1, Nat. Or. *Lauraceæ.* This is a genus of stove plants of considerable beauty, and some of them are highly valuable. It is from the inner bark of *C. verum* that the cinnamon of commerce is obtained ; and *C. camphora* is the plant from which camphor is prepared. All the species succeed well in a mixture of loam and peat ; and cuttings of the ripened wood root freely in sand under a glass. *Synonymes:* 1. *Laurus Beiolgota.* 2. *L. camphora.* 3. *L. cassia, L. cinnamomum.* 4. *L. Cullaban.* 5. *L. dulce, L. Burmanni.* 6. *L. glauca.* 7. *L. gracilis.* 8. *L. Malabatrum.* 9. *L. montana.* 10. *L. nitida.* 11. *L. cinnamomum, cassia.*

| | | | | | |
|---|---|---|---|---|---|
| Beiolgōtā, 1 | . | . Yel. grn. | . 8. Ev. T. E. Ind. | . . | 1818 |
| Camphōrā, 2 | . | . Grn. wht. | 5, 8. Ev. T. Japan | . . | 1727 |
| Cassia, 3 | . | . Yel. grn. | . 6, 8. Ev. T. Ceylon | . . | 1768 |
| Cullabān, 4 | . | . Yel. grn. | . 8. Ev. T. E. Ind. | . . | 1823 |
| dūlcē, 5 | . | . Wht. yel. | . 8. Ev. T. E. Ind. | . . | 1820 |
| glaūcūm, 6 | . | . Pa. yel. | . 8. Ev. T. Japan | . . | 1800 |
| grācĭlĕ, 7 | . | . Yel. grn. | . 8. Ev. T. E. Ind. | . . | 1820 |
| Malabātrūm, 8 | . | . Yel. grn. | . 8. Ev. T. E. Ind. | . . | 1805 |
| montānūm, 9 | . | . Wht. grn. | . 8. Ev. T. W. Ind. | . . | 1810 |
| nitidūm, 10 | . | . White . | . 8. Ev. T. E. Ind. | . . | 1823 |
| vērūm, 11 | . | . Green . | . 7, 8. Ev. T. E. Ind. | . . | 1768 |

CINNAMON, see *Cinnamōmūm.*

CINQUEFOIL, see *Potentīllā.*

CIRCÆĀ, *Linn.* After Circe, the famous enchantress ; the fruit, from being covered with hooked prickles, lays hold of the clothes of passengers, as Circe is said to have done by her enchantment. *Linn.* 2, Or. 1, Nat. Or. *Onagraceæ.* Ornamental species, growing in any common soil, and increased by offsets.

| | | | | | |
|---|---|---|---|---|---|
| alpinā | . . . | . Red | . . 7, H. Her. P. | Britain | . . |
| intermēdiā | . . | . Red | . . 7, H. Her. P. | Europe | . 1821 |
| lutetiānā | . . | . Red | . . 7, H. Her. P. | Britain | . . |

CIRCINATE, curled round like a sheep crook.

CIRCINAL, resembling a circle.

CIRCINATELY-REVOLUTE, curled round like a circle.

CIRRHÆĀ, *Lindley.* The part of the flower called the rostellum is prolonged in the form of a small tendril or *cirrhus* ; hence the name. *Linn.* 20, Or. 1, Nat. Or. *Orchidaceæ.* This is an interesting genus of orchideous plants. The flowers of all the species are of a green or yellowish colour ; and in some, the sepals and petals are beautifully spotted with rich orange. For culture and propagation see *Stanhopea.* *Synonymes:* 1. *Cymbidium dependens.* 2. *Gongora viridi purpurea.*

| | | | | | |
|---|---|---|---|---|---|
| fuscolūtēā | . . . | . Yel. grn. | . 7, 8. Epi. | Brazil | . . |
| Loddigēsii, 1 | . | . Yellowish | . 5, 8. Epi. | Brazil | . 1827 |
| obtusātā | . . . | . Yel. red | . 9, 8. Epi. | Rio Jan. | . 1835 |
| tristis | . . . | . Pur. grn. | . 6, 8. Epi. | Mexico | . 1834 |
| viridipurpūrēā, 2 | . | . Pur. grn. | . 6, 8. Epi. | Brazil | . . |
| Warrēānā | . . | . Yelsh. grn. | . 6, 8. Epi. | Brazil | . . |

CIRRHIFEROUS, bearing tendrils, or claspers.

CIRRHOPĒTĀLŪM, *Lindley.* From *cirrhus*, a tendril, and *petalon*, a petal ; in allusion to the form of the flowers. *Linn.* 20, Or. 1, Nat. Or. *Orchidaceæ.* *C. Thouarsii* is a most singular species, with long, strap-shaped sepals, growing from one side of the flowers, while the petals are very small, yellow, spotted finely with red. The rhizoma of this species elongates very much, and is in a growing state always at the extremity ; on this account it is requisite, in potting, to keep the active part nearest the side of the pot from which it grows away. The other species have much smaller flowers, without anything striking about them. For culture, &c., they may be referred to *Stanhopea.*

| | | | | | |
|---|---|---|---|---|---|
| cæspitōsūm | . . . | . Pa. yel. | . 8, 8. Epi. | Khooseea | . 1837 |
| cornūtūm | . . . | . Purple | . 8, 8. Epi. | Khooseea | . 1837 |
| Thouārsii | . . . | . Yel. red. | . 7, 8. Epi. | So. Isles | . 1836 |

CIRRHOSE, }
CIRRHOUS, } tendrilled, having claspers, like the pea.

CIRSIŪM, *Vaillant.* From *kirsos*, a swelled vein ; from its supposed healing properties. *Linn.* 19, Or. 1, Nat. Or. *Compositæ.* This is an ornamental genus of hardy herbaceous plants, that succeed well in any common soil, and are increased by dividing the roots, or by seeds. *Synonymes:* 1. *Cnicus acarna, Carlina acarna.* 2. *Carduus pratensis.* 3. *C. arvensis, Serratula arvensis.* 4. *Cnicus horridus.* 5. *Cirsium horridus.* 6. *Cnicus nivalis.* 7. *Carduus cichoraceus.* 8. *Cnicus cynaroides.* 9. *Carduus fimbriatus.* 10. *Carduus giganteus, Cnicus firma.* 11. *Cnicus elatior.* 12. *Cnicus heteromallus.* 13. *Cnicus*

*hybridus.* 14. *Carduus igniarius.* 15. *Cnicus inerme.*
16. *Carduus italicus.* 17. *Cnicus lanceolatus.* 18.
*Cnicus leucocephalus.* 19. *Carthamus mareoticus.*
20. *Cnicus medius.* 21. *Cnicus glaber.* 22. *Cnicus
orientalis.* 23. *Cnicus paludosus.* 24. *Carduus palustris.* 25. *Carduus paniculatus.* 26. *Carduus pauciflorus.* 27. *Cnicus pazcuarensis.* 28. *Cnicus pinnatifidus.* 29. *Carduus polyanthemus.* 30. *Cnicus
pungens.* 31. *Carduus pyrenaicus.* 32. *Cnicus salisburgensis.* 33. *Carlina echinus.* 34. *Cnicus strictus.*
35. *C. Verutum.* 36. *Carduus virginianus.*

| | | | | | |
|---|---|---|---|---|---|
| acärnä, 1 | . | Purple . | 8, H. | A. Spain | . 1683 |
| acaulé | . | Purple . | 7, H. Her. | P. Britain | . |
| afrüm | . | Purple . | 6, H. | B. Barbary | . 1800 |
| altissimüm | . | Purple . | 7, H. Her. | P. N. Amer. | . 1726 |
| ambigüum | . | Purple . | 7, H. Her. | P. Mt. Cenis | . 1820 |
| angulätüm | . | Purple . | 7, H. Her. | P. Switzerl. | . 1819 |
| arachnoidēūm | . | Purple . | 7, H. Her. | P. Tauria | . 1818 |
| Bertolini, 4 | . | Yellow . | 7, H. Her. | P. Italy | . 1820 |
| bæticüm, 5 | . | Yellow . | 7, H. Her. | P. Spain | . 1824 |
| cänüm | . | Purple . | 7, H. Bl. | P. Austria | . 1633 |
| carniölicüm | . | Pa. yel. . | 7, H. Her. | P. Carniola | . 1792 |
| cassäbönæ | . | Purple . | 7, F. | B. S. Eur. | . 1714 |
| cērnüüm | . | Purple . | 7, H. | B. Mexico | . 1827 |
| Cervini | . | | 7, H. Her. | P. Switzerl. | . 1825 |
| cichorácēüm, 6 | Purple . | 8, F. | B. Naples | . 1816 |
| ciliätüm | . | Purple . | 8, H. Her. | P. Siberia | . 1787 |
| cynaroidēs, 7 | . | Purple . | 7, H. | B. Crete | . 1827 |
| dealbätüm | . | Purple . | 7, H. | B. Caucasus | . 1820 |
| desertörüm | . | Purple . | 7, H. Her. | P. Siberia | . 1824 |
| diacänthüm | . | Purple . | 7, F. | B. Syria | . 1800 |
| discolör | . | Purple . | 6, H. | B. N. Amer. | . 1803 |
| echinätüm | . | Purple . | 8, H. Her. | P. Barbary | . 1817 |
| echinocéphalüm | Purple . | 7, H. Her. | P. Caucasus | . 1826 |
| elätüs, 8 | . | Purple . | 8, H. Her. | P. | . 1823 |
| erióphörüm | . | Purple . | 7, H. | B. Britain | . |
| Eriathalēs | . | Pa. yel. . | 7, H. Her. | P. France | . 1752 |
| ferōx | . | White . | 7, H. | B. S. Eur. | . 1683 |
| fimbriätüm, 9 | . | Purple . | 7, H. Her. | P. Caucasus | . 1816 |
| gigantēūm, 10 | . | Crimson . | 7, H | B. Sicily | . 1820 |
| glutinösüm | . | Pa. yel. . | 7, H. | B. S. Eur. | . 1816 |
| Hallëri | . | Purple . | 7, H. Her. | P. S. Eur. | . 1816 |
| heleniöidēs | . | Purple . | 7, H. Her. | P. Siberia | . 1804 |
| heteromallüm, 11 | Purple . | 7, H. | B. Nepal | . 1820 |
| heterophyllüm | . | Purple . | 7, H. Her. | P. Britain | . |
| hörridüm, 12 | . | Purple . | 8, H. | B. Iberia | . 1823 |
| hybridüm, 13 | . | Pa. yel. . | 7, H. Her. | P. Switzerl. | . 1819 |
| igniärüm, 14 | . | Purple . | 7, H. | B. Russia | . 1826 |
| incänüm | . | Purple . | 7, H. | B. Caucasus | . 1820 |
| inermē, 15 | . | Purple . | 7, H. Her. | P. | . 1824 |
| italicüm, 16 | . | Purple . | 7, H. Her. | P. Italy | . 1815 |
| lactēūm | . | Pa. yel. . | 7, H. Her. | P. Switzerl. | . 1819 |
| lanceolätüm, 17 | . | Purple . | 7, H. | B. Britain | . |
| laniflörüm | . | Purple' . | 7, H. Her. | P. Tauria | . 1819 |
| lappácēüm | . | Purple . | 7, H. | B. Caucasus | . 1821 |
| leucocéphalüm, 18 | Yel. wht. | 7, H. Her. | P. Crete | . 1816 |
| mareöticüm, 19 | . | White . | 7, F. Her. | P. Egypt | . 1827 |
| mädiüm, 20 | . | Purple . | 7, H. Her. | P. Piedmont | . 1819 |
| mitē . | . | Purple . | 7, H. | B. Siberia | . 1820 |
| monspessulänüm | . | Purple . | 6, H. Her. | P. Montp. | . 1596 |
| munitüm | . | Purple . | 7, H. | B. Caucasus | . 1816 |
| müticüm, 21 | . | Purple . | 7, H. Her. | P. N. Amer. | . 1820 |
| neglectüm | . | Purple . | 7, H. Her. | P. Siberia | . 1827 |
| nudiflörüm | . | Purple . | 8, H. Her. | P. Switzerl. | . 1817 |
| obvallätüm | . | Purple . | 7, H. Her. | P. Caucasus | . 1816 |
| ochrolēūcüm | . | Pa. yel. . | 7, H. Her. | P. Switzerl. | . 1801 |
| oleräcēüm | . | Pa. yel. . | 7, H. Her. | P. Europe | . 1570 |
| orgyálē | . | Purple . | 7, H. Her. | P. | . 1823 |
| orientälē, 22 | . | Purple . | 7, H. | B. Asia Minor | . 1827 |
| paludösüm, 23 | . | Purple . | 7, H. Her. | P. Switzerl. | . 1819 |
| paniculätüm, 25 | . | Purple . | 6, H. | B. S. Eur. | . 1781 |
| pauciflörüm, 26 | . | Purple . | 7, H. | B. Hungary | . 1816 |
| pascuarēnsē, 27 | . | Purple . | 7, H. | B. Mexico | . 1827 |
| pinnatifidüm, 28 . | Purple . | 7, H. | A. Spain | . 1820 |
| polyanthemüm, 29 | Pink . | 6, H. | B. Rome | . 1739 |
| püngēns, 30 | . | Purple . | 7, H. | B. S. Eur. | . 1820 |
| pyrenäicüm, 31 | . | Purple . | 7, H. Her. | P. Pyrenees | . 1816 |
| rigēns | . | Yellow . | 7, H. Her. | P. Switzerl. | . 1775 |
| rivulärē | . | White . | 7, H. Her. | P. Hungary | . 1804 |
| rufescēns | . | White . | 7, H. Her. | P. Pyrenees | . 1816 |
| Salisburgēnsē, 32 | Purple . | 7, H. Her. | P. Europe | . 1816 |
| sclerändüm, 33 | . | Pa. wht. . | 7, H. | B. Caucasus | . 1820 |
| semipectinätüm | . | Pa. wht. . | 7, H. Her. | P. Siberia | . 1819 |
| serratuloidēs | . | Purple . | 8, H. Her. | P. Siberia | . 1752 |
| serrulätüm | . | Purple . | 7, H. Her. | P. Tauria | . 1819 |
| setösüm | . | Purple . | 6, H. | A. Silesia | . 1822 |
| spinosissimüm | . | Pa. yel. . | 7, H. Her. | P. Switzerl. | . 1759 |
| squarrösüm | . | Purple . | 7, H. | B. Siberia | . 1818 |
| stellätüm | . | Purple . | 6, H. | A. Italy | . 1665 |
| strictüm, 34 | . | Purple . | 8, H. Her. | P. Naples | . 1819 |
| strigösüm | . | Purple . | 7, H. | B. Caucasus | . 1825 |
| syriäcüm | . | Purple . | 7, H. Her. | P. Levant | . 1771 |
| tatäricüm | . | White . | 7, H. Her. | P. Siberia | . 1775 |
| tuberösüm | . | Purple . | 7, H. Her. | P. England | . |
| uliginösüm | . | Purple . | 6, H. Her. | P. Caucasus | . 1820 |
| verütum, 35 | . | Purple . | 7, H. | B. Nepal | . 1820 |
| virginiänüm, 36 | . | Purple . | 7, H. Her. | P. Virginia | . 1824 |

*anglicüm* 2, *arvénsē* 3, *Forstēri, palüstrē* 24.

**CISSÄMPELÖS,** *Linn.* From *kissos,* ivy, and *ampelos,* a
vine, having the character of the ivy in its rambling branches, and that of the vine, from the fruit
being in racemes. *Linn.* 22, Or. 13, Nat. Or. *Menispermaceæ.* This is a genus of beautiful stove
climbers; the species thrive well in a sandy peat,
and are increased by cuttings planted in sand,
under a glass.

| | | | | | |
|---|---|---|---|---|---|
| caapëbä | . | Green . | . 7, S. Ev. Tw. S. Amer. | . 1788 |
| capénsis | . | Green . | . 8, Ev. Tw. C. G. H. | . 1775 |
| hirsütä | . | Yel. grn. | . G. Ev. Tw. Nepal | . 1819 |
| mauritiänä | . | Yel. grn. | . 8. Ev. Tw. Mauritius | . 1824 |
| microcärpä | . | Yel. grn. | . 8. Ev. Tw. W. Ind. | . 1823 |
| Pareirä | . | Green . | . 7, S. Ev. Tw. S. Amer. | . 1733 |

**CISSÜS,** *Linn.* From the Greek, *kissos,* ivy; said also
to come from the Arabic word, *qissos,* signifying
the same plant. *Linn.* 4, Or. 1, Nat. Or. *Vitaceæ.*
This is a genus of climbers, some of the species of
which are very ornamental; they are free growers,
and delight in a light rich soil. Cuttings are easily
rooted under a glass in a moist heat.

| | | | | |
|---|---|---|---|---|
| äcidä | . | Green . | . S. Ev. Cl. Jamaica | . 1692 |
| antärcticä | . | Green . | . 7, G. Ev. Cl. N. S. W. | . 1790 |
| capénsis | . | Green . | . G. Ev. Cl. C. G. H. | . 1792 |
| cäsiä | . | Green . | . S. Ev. Cl. S. Leone | . 1822 |
| diversifoliä, 1 | . | Green . | . S. Ev. Cl. | . 1822 |
| elongätä | . | Green . | . G. Ev. Cl. E. Ind. | . 1818 |
| glandulösä | . | Green . | . S. Ev. Cl. E. Ind. | . 1819 |
| glaucä | . | Green . | . S. Ev. Cl. E. Ind. | . 1818 |
| ovätä | . | Green . | . S. Ev. Cl. Guadaloupe | 1822 |
| pentaphyllä | . | Green . | . 7, G. Ev. Cl. Japan | . 1790 |
| puncticulösä | . | Green . | . S. Ev. Cl. Cayenne | . 1818 |
| quadrangulärïs | . | Green . | . S. Ev. Cl. E. Ind. | . 1790 |
| quinätä | . | Green . | . 7, G. Ev. Cl. C. G. H. | . 1790 |
| Sicyoïdēs | . | Green . | . S. Ev. Cl. Jamaica | . 1768 |
| trifoliätä | . | Green . | . S. Ev. Cl. E. Ind. | . 1818 |
| trilobätä | . | Green . | . 7, S. Ev. Cl. E. Ind. | . 1822 |
| vitigineä | . | Green . | . S. Ev. Cl. India | . 1772 |

*adnätä, alätä, angustifoliä, auriculätä, carnösä, lati-
foliä, microcärpä, orientälis, quinquefoliä, rēpēns,
smilacïnä.*

**CISTÜS,** *Tournefort.* From the Greek, *kistos,* which
is derived from *kiste,* meaning a box or capsule; on
account of the remarkable shape of the capsule.
*Linn.* 13, Or. 1, Nat. Or. *Cistaceæ.* This is a beautiful genus of plants, varying in height from one to
four feet; they are considered hardy, but there are
some of them that require protection in winter,
either in a greenhouse or cold frame, but most of
the species will pass the winter in the open air, if
the weather be not very severe; but it is the best
plan to keep some of all the sorts in pots, that they
may be more easily protected from severe weather,
when they may be turned out in the borders in
spring, where they will flower freely. They do
well in common soil, and are increased by layers, or
ripened cuttings placed under a glass, or seeds.
*Synonymes:* 1. *C. salvifolius.* 2. *C. ladaniferus, ste-
nophyllus.* 3. *C. undulatus.* 4. *C. villosus, virescens.*
5. *C. ladaniferus, undulatus.*

| | | | | | |
|---|---|---|---|---|---|
| acutifoliüs, 1 | . | White . | . 8, H. Ev. S. S. Eur. | . |
| albidüs | . | Pa. pur. . | 6, H. Ev. S. Spain | . 1640 |
| asperifoliüs | . | White . | 6, H. Ev. S. Spain | . |
| candidissimüs | . | Pa. red . | 6, H. Ev. S. Canaries | . 1817 |
| canéscēns | . | Red . | 6, H. Ev. S. | . |
| Clüsii | . | White . | 6, H. Ev. S. Spain | . 1810 |
| complicätüs | . | Red . | 6, H. Ev. S. Spain | . 1818 |
| Corboriänsis | . | White . | 6, H. Ev. S. Spain | . 1656 |
| cordifoliüs | . | White . | 6, H. Ev. S. | . 1800 |
| crēticüs | . | Purple . | 7, H. Ev. S. Levant | . 1731 |
| taüricüs | . | Purple . | 6, H. Ev. S. Tauria | . 1817 |
| crispüs | . | Purple . | 6, H. Ev. S. Portugal | . 1656 |
| cupaniänüs | . | White . | 6, F. Ev. S. Sicily | . |
| cymösüs | . | Purple . | 6, H. Ev. S. | . |
| cyprïüs, 2 | . | White . | 6, H. Ev. S. Greece | . 1800 |
| Dunaliänüs, 3 | . | Purple . | 5, H. Ev. S. | . |
| florentïnüs | . | White . | 6, H. Ev. S. Italy | . 1825 |
| heterophyllüs | . | Purple . | 6, H. Ev. S. Algiers | . |
| hirsütüs | . | White . | 6, H. Ev. S. Portugal | . 1656 |
| incänüs | . | Purple . | 7, H. Ev. S. Eur. | . 1596 |
| ladaniferüs | . | White . | 6, H. Ev. S. Spain | . 1629 |
| albiflörüs | . | White . | 6, H. Ev. S. Spain | . |
| maculätüs | . | White . | 6, H. Ev. S. Spain | . 1700 |
| latifoliüs | . | White . | 6, F. Ev. S. Barbary | . |
| laurifoliüs | . | White . | 6, H. Ev. S. Spain | . 1731 |
| laxüs | . | White . | 6, H. Ev. S. Spain | . 1656 |
| Lëdon | . | White . | 6, H. Ev. S. France | . 1730 |
| longifoliüs | . | White . | 6, H. Ev. S. S. Eur. | . 1800 |
| monspeliénsis | . | White . | 6, H. Ev. S. S. Eur. | . 1656 |
| oblongifoliüs | . | White . | 6, H. Ev. S. S. Eur. | . |
| obtusifoliüs | . | White . | 6, H. Ev. S. | . |
| parviflörüs | . | Pa. red . | 6, H. Ev. S. Crete | . 1800 |

| | | | |
|---|---|---|---|
| platyspalus | Red | 6, H. Ev. S. | |
| populifolius | White | 5, H. Ev. S. Spain | 1656 |
| pedicspalus | White | 6, H. Ev. S. | |
| purpureus | Purple | 6, H. Ev. S. | |
| rotandifolius, 4 | Purple | 6, H. Ev. S. S. Eur. | |
| salvifolius | White | 6, H. Ev. S. S. Eur. | 1548 |
| sericotis | Red | 6, H. Ev. S. Spain | 1826 |
| undulatus, 5 | White | 6, H. Ev. S. S. Eur. | 1800 |
| vaginatus | Pa. pur. | 4, H. Ev. S. Teneriffe | 1779 |
| villosus | Purple | 6, H. Ev. S. S. Eur. | 1640 |

CITHAREXYLUM, *Linn.* From *kithara*, a lyre, and *xylon*, wood, erroneously supposed to be applicable to making musical instruments; hence the name fiddle-wood. *Linn.* 14, Or. 2, Nat. Or. *Verbenaceæ.* An ornamental genus; the species vary in height from six to ten feet. They thrive best in a mixture of peat and loam, and cuttings root freely in sand under a glass.

| | | | |
|---|---|---|---|
| caudatum | White | 8. Ev. T. Jamaica | 1763 |
| cinereum | White | 8. Ev. T. W. Ind. | 1739 |
| dentatum | | 8. Ev. T. E. Ind. | 1824 |
| molle | White | 8. Ev. T. W. Ind. | 1816 |
| pentandrum | White | 8. Ev. S. Porto Rico | 1815 |
| quadrangulare | White | 8. Ev. T. Jamaica | 1759 |
| sericeum | | 8. Ev. T. E. Ind. | 1824 |
| subserratum | White | 8. Ev. T. W. Ind. | 1820 |
| villosum | | 8. Ev. T. St. Domin. | 1784 |

CITRIOBATUS, *Cunningham.* Derived from *citros*, a citron, and *batos*, a thorn; in reference to the small orange-coloured fruit, which resembles an orange; hence it is called by the colonists orange thorn. *Linn.* 5, Or. 1, Nat. Or. *Pittosporaceæ.* The species of this little known genus will probably be found to succeed best in sandy peat, and a little loam, well mixed. The pots should be carefully drained.

| | | | |
|---|---|---|---|
| multiflorus | | G. Ev. S. N. Holl. | 1818 |
| pauciflorus | | G. Ev. S. N. Holl. | 1822 |

CITRON, see *Citrus.*

CITRUS, *Linn.* This genus is said to have its name from the town Citron, in Judea. *Linn.* 18, Or. 2, Nat. Or. *Aurantiaceæ.* This is an ornamental genus of fruit trees, growing from three to fifteen feet high; they thrive best in a good loamy soil, mixed with a quantity of rotten dung. They do not like much pot-room, nor too much water, when in a growing state. The different kinds are procured by budding or grafting on common stocks, which, as soon as operated upon, should be placed in some close frame, in a moderate dung heat. Stocks for working upon are raised from any oranges, lemons, &c. They are sometimes raised from cuttings, in which case they produce fruit when very small plants.

| | | | |
|---|---|---|---|
| angulata | White | G. Ev. T. E. Ind. | |
| aurantium | White | G. Ev. T. Asia | 1595 |
| buxifolia | White | 6, G. Ev. S. China | |
| decumana | White | 6, G. Ev. T. India | 1724 |
| hystrix | White | 6, G. Ev. T. E. Ind. | |
| japonica | White | 6, G. Ev. T. Japan | |
| Limetta | White | 6, G. Ev. T. Asia | 1648 |
| Limonum | White | 6, G. Ev. T. Asia | 1648 |
| madurensis | White | 6, G. Ev. T. China | |
| margarita | White | 6, G. Ev. T. China | |
| Medica | White | 6, G. Ev. S. Asia | |
| nobilis | White | 6, G. Ev. S. China | 1805 |
| minor | White | 6, G. Ev. S. China | 1805 |
| spinosissima | White | 6, G. Ev. T. Cayenne | |
| vulgaris | White | 6, G. Ev. T. Asia | |
| myrtifolia | White | 6, G. Ev. S. Asia | |

CLADANTHUS, *Cassini.* From *klados*, a branch, and *anthos*, a flower; referring to the situation of the flowers. *Linn.* 19, Or. 2, Nat. Or. *Compositæ.* Interesting dwarf plants, of simple culture. This is a pretty annual, growing about a foot and a half high; it only requires to be sown in common soil. *Synonyme:* 1. *Anthemis arabica.*

| | | | |
|---|---|---|---|
| arabicus, 1 | Yellow | 7, H. A. Barbary | 1759 |
| canescens | Yellow | 6, F. Ev. S. Canaries | 1829 |

CLADIUM, *P. Browne.* From *klados*, a branch or twig; referring to the appearance of the plant. *Linn.* 2, Or. 1, Nat. Or. *Cyperaceæ.* The species are curious, and best cultivated in wet boggy soil. *Synonyme:* 1. *Schœnus acutus.*

| | | | |
|---|---|---|---|
| glomeratum | Apetal | 6, Grass. N. Holl. | 1816 |
| junceum | Apetal | 7, Grass. N. Holl. | 1820 |
| occidentale | Apetal | 6, Grass. Jamaica | 1820 |
| schoenoides, 1 | Apetal | 7, Grass. N. Holl. | 1823 |

germanicum.

CLADOSPORIUM, *Link.* From *klados*, a branch, and

*spora*, a sporule; on account of the sporules being attached to the branches of the fungi. *Linn.* 24, Or. 9, Nat. Or. *Fungi.* Minute species of *Fungi*, found most frequently upon old decaying wood— *herbarum, velutinum.*

CLADOSTACHYS, *D. Don.* From *klados*, a branch, and *stachys*, a spike, in reference to the manner of its flowering. *Linn.* 5, Or. 1, Nat. Or. *Amarantaceæ.* The species possess little beauty. For culture, &c., see *Achyranthes.* *Synonymes:* 1. *Achyranthes alternifolia, Desmochaeta alternifolia.* 3. *A. muricata, Chamissoa muricata.*

| | | | |
|---|---|---|---|
| alternifolia, 1 | Purple | 9, G. R. E. Ind. | 1789 |
| frutescens, 2 | Green | 9, S. Ev. S. E. Ind. | 1777 |

CLADOSTEPHUS, *Agardh.* From *klados*, a branch, and *stephos*, a crown; in reference to the whorled branches. *Linn.* 24, Or. 7, Nat. Or. *Algæ.* Marine productions, of an interesting character—*myriophyllum, spongiosus.*

CLAMMY, viscid, sticky.

CLANDESTINE, hidden, secret, private.

CLARKIA, *Pursh.* In honour of Captain Clarke, who accompanied Captain Lewis in his journey to the Rocky Mountains. *Linn.* 8, Or. 1, Nat. Or. *Onagraceæ.* A genus of annuals, which make a beautiful display in the flower-borders during summer. They succeed well merely sown in the open ground, where they are to flower; seeds ripen in great plenty.

| | | | |
|---|---|---|---|
| elegans | Ro. pur. | 7, H. A. California | 1832 |
| gauroides | Pink | 8, H. A. California | 1835 |
| pulchella | Purple | 6, H. A. N. Amer. | 1826 |
| flore-albo | White | 6, H. A. N. Amer. | 1826 |

CLARY, see *Salvia Sclarea.*

CLATHRATE, latticed, divided like lattice-work.

CLAUSENA, *Burmann.* The meaning unexplained. *Linn.* 10, Or. 1, Nat. Or. *Aurantiaceæ.* An ornamental tree, growing upwards of twenty feet high, and cultivated best in rich loam. Cuttings may be rooted in sand, under a glass. *Synonyme:* 1. *Limonia pentaphylla.*

| | | | |
|---|---|---|---|
| pentaphylla, 1 | White | 7, S. Ev. T. Coroman. | 1800 |

CLAVA HERCULIS, see *Zanthoxylon.*

CLAVARIA, *Vaillant.* From *clava*, a club; in reference to the form of the species. *Linn.* 24, Or. 9, Nat. Or. *Fungi.* Striking species of *Fungi*, growing from the eighth of an inch to a foot high, but the majority average from one to three inches. They are found upon trees of various kinds, sometimes in meadows, and at others, in dense shady places, where the soil is damp—*abietina, acuta, Ardenla, botrytis, ceranoides, cinerea, coralloides, cornea, corniculata, cristata, fimbriata, flava, fragilis, fusiformis, helvola, inæqualis, pistillaris, pratensis, rugosa, setipes, stricta, uncialis, vermicularis.*

CLAVATE, } shaped like a club, the thick end upper-
CLAVATED, } most.

CLAVELLOSE, having club-like processes.

CLAVUS, a name for the ergot, a disease in corn.

CLAVIJA, *Ruiz and Pavon.* In honour of J. Clavijo Faxardo, a Spanish naturalist. *Linn.* 5, Or. 1, Nat. Or. *Myrsineæ.* A very ornamental genus, growing in peat and loam, and cuttings might strike in the same kind of soil, under a glass, in heat. The trees grow about twenty feet high. *Synonymes:* 1. *C. macrophylla.* 2. *Theophrasta longifolia.*

| | | | |
|---|---|---|---|
| macrocarpa, 1 | White | 8. Ev. S. Peru | 1816 |
| ornata | Orange | 8. Ev. S. Caracas | 1828 |

CLAWS, the narrow end of petals.

CLAYTONIA, *Linn.* In honour of John Clayton, a collector of plants in Virginia, which were published by Gronovius in his Flora Virginica. *Linn.* 5, Or. 1, Nat. Or. *Portulacaceæ.* The species of this genus are very pretty; the perennial species grow best in a border of peat soil. The annual kinds only require sowing in the open border, in peaty soil. *Synonymes:* 1. *C. virginica.* 3. *C. bifida.*

| | | | |
|---|---|---|---|
| acutifolia | White | H. Tu. P. Siberia | 1827 |
| acutiflora, 1 | White | 5, H. Tu. P. N. Amer. | |
| alsinoides | White | 5, H. A. England | |
| caroliniana | Pink | 4, H. Tu. P. N. Amer. | 1789 |
| grandiflora | Pink | 4, H. Tu. P. N. Amer. | |
| gypsophiloides | Pink | 10, H. A. California | 1835 |
| joanneana | White | 6, H. A. Siberia | 1818 |
| lanceolata | White | 4, H. Tu. P. N. Amer. | 1812 |
| longifolia | White | 4, H. Tu. P. N. Amer. | 1827 |

| | | | | |
|---|---|---|---|---|
| perfoliātā | White | 6, H. | A. N. Amer. | 1794 |
| polyphylla | Pink | 4, H. Tu. | P. N. Amer. | 1827 |
| sibīrica | Red | 6, H. | A. Siberia | 1768 |
| unalaschkénsis, 2 | White | 6, H. | A. Russia | 1820 |
| Vestiānā | Rose | H. Her. | P. Altai | 1827 |
| virginiānā | White | H. Her. | P. N. Amer | 1740 |

CLEARING-NUT, see *Strychnos potatorum.*

CLEAVERS, see *Galium Aparine.*

CLEFT, divided, but not to the base, split.

CLEISÓSTOMA, *Blume.* Not explained. *Linn.* 20, Or. 1, Nat. Or. *Orchidaceæ.* The species of this genus are described as rather insignificant, the flowers being small, and of a dingy colour. They succeed best on wood, treated as the *Burlingtonias.*

| | | | | |
|---|---|---|---|---|
| rōsēā | Straw cld. | 9, S. Epi. | Manilla | 1837 |
| tridentātā | Redsh. wht. | 8. Epi. | N. Holl. | 1838 |

CLEMATIS, *Linn.* From *klema,* a vine branch; because most of the species climb like the vine. *Linn.* 13, Or. 6, Nat. Or. *Ranunculaceæ.* A numerous and highly ornamental genus of, for the most part, climbing plants. The greenhouse species are very desirable where climbers are wanted; they grow well in any light soil, or loam and peat; cuttings root freely under a glass. The same treatment is required for the stove kinds. The hardy kinds grow in any common garden soil, and are well adapted for trellis-work, or for training against a wall. They are readily increased by laying the young shoots in July or October. The herbaceous kinds are increased by dividing the plants at the root early in spring. *Synonymes*: 1. *C. calycina.* 2. *C. australis.* 3. *C. fragrans.* 4. *C. cirrhosa.* 5. *C. cordata.* 6. *C. bracteata.*

| | | | | |
|---|---|---|---|---|
| americānā | White | S. Ev. Cl. | S. Amer. | |
| angustifōliā | White | 6, H. Her. | P. Austria | 1787 |
| aristātā | Grn. yel. | 6, G. De. Cl. | N. Holl. | 1812 |
| baleārica, 1 | Yel. wht. | 2, F. Ev. Cl. | Minorca | 1783 |
| brachiātā | Yel. grn. | 10, G. H. Cl. | C. G. H. | |
| brasiliānā | White | 8, H. De. Cl. | Brasil | 1823 |
| caerūleā | Violet | 4, H. De. Cl. | Japan | 1836 |
| campaniflorā | Purple | 7, H. De. Cl. | Spain | 1810 |
| caripénsis | White | 8. Ev. Cl. | Trinidad | 1820 |
| chinénsis | Yel. wht. | F. Cl. Cl. | China | 1820 |
| cirrhōsā | Wht. grn. | 4, H. Ev. Cl. | Spain | 1596 |
| coriāceā, 2 | White | G. Ev. Cl. | N. Holl. | 1821 |
| crispā | Pa. pur. | 8, H. De. Cl. | N. Amer. | 1796 |
| cylindrica | Blue | 8, H. Her. | P. N. Amer. | 1802 |
| dahūrica | Yel. grn. | 9, H. De. Cl. | Dahuria | 1820 |
| dioīca | Grn. yel. | 8, H. Ev. Cl. | W. Ind. | 1733 |
| diversifōliā | White | 4, H. Her. | P. | |
| erectā | White | 7, H. Her. | P. Austria | 1597 |
| hispānica | White | 7, H. Her. | P. Spain | 1800 |
| Flammūlā | White | 8, H. De. Cl. | France | 1596 |
| maritīmā | White | 7, H. De. Cl. | S. Eur. | |
| rotundifōliā, 3 | White | 8, H. De. Cl. | France | 1596 |
| vulgāris | White | 8, H. De. Cl. | France | |
| flōridā | White | 6, H. De. Cl. | Japan | 1776 |
| flōre-plēnō | White | 6, H. De. Cl. | | |
| glaūcā | Pa. yel. | 4, H. De. Cl. | Siberia | |
| glycinoīdēs | | G. Ev. Cl. | N. Holl. | 1826 |
| grandiflorā | Yel. grn. | 8. Ev. Cl. | S. Leone | 1823 |
| hedysarifōliā | White | 8. Ev. Cl. | E. Ind. | 1819 |
| integrifōliā | Blue | 7, H. Her. | P. Hungary | 1596 |
| angustifōliā | Blue | 7, H. Her. | P. Hungary | |
| elongāta | Blue | 8, H. Her. | P. Europe | |
| lineariloba | White | 7, G. Her. | P. Carolina | 1823 |
| Massoniānā | | H. E. Cl. | C. G. H. | |
| montānā | White | 6, H. De. Cl. | Nepal | 1831 |
| ochroleūca | Li. yel. | 6, H. De. | P. N. Amer. | 1767 |
| odorātā | | 6, G. Ev. Cl. | E. Ind. | 1831 |
| orientālis | Yel. wht. | 8, H. De. Cl. | Levant | 1731 |
| paniculātā | White | 7, H. De. Cl. | Japan | 1800 |
| pedicellātā, 4 | Wht. grn. | 7, H. Ev. Cl. | Majorca | |
| reticulātā | Purple | 7, H. De. Cl. | N. Amer. | 1812 |
| semitrilobā | Wht. grn. | 6, H. Ev. Cl. | Spain | |
| Simsii, 5 | Purple | 7, H. De. Cl. | N. Amer. | 1812 |
| smilacifōliā | Purple | 8. Ev. Cl. | E. Ind. | 1824 |
| triternātā | White | H. De. Cl. | | 1800 |
| Viornā | Purple | 8, H. De. Cl. | N. Amer. | 1730 |
| viornoīdēs | Lilac | 8, H. De. Cl. | N. Amer. | 1828 |
| virginiānā | Green | 7, H. De. Cl. | N. Amer. | 1767 |
| bracteātā, 6 | G-h. wht. | 6, H. De. Cl. | N. Amer. | 1767 |
| Vitalbā | White | 8, H. De. Cl. | England | |
| integrātā | White | 8, H. De. Cl. | England | |
| Viticélla | Purple | 8, H. De. Cl. | Spain | 1569 |
| caerūleā | Blue | 7, H. De. Cl. | Spain | 1659 |
| plēnā | Purple | 8, H. De. Cl. | | |
| purpūreā | Purple | 7, H. De. Cl. | Spain | |
| sansibarénsis | | G. Ev. Cl. | Zanzibar | 1820 |

CLEOME, *Linn.* From *kleio,* to shut; alluding to the parts of the flower. *Linn.* 15, Nat. Or. *Capparidaceæ.* The species of this genus are very pretty, and free-flowering; the stove kinds require a rich light soil, and cuttings root freely under a glass. Some of the annual species require sowing in a hotbed frame, or in a hothouse, and when potted off, to be placed among the tender annuals. The hardier kinds may be sown on a hotbed, and when of sufficient size, planted out in sheltered situations in the flower-borders. *Synonymes*: 1. *C. ornithopodioides.* 2. *C. spinosa.*

| | | | | |
|---|---|---|---|---|
| aculeātā | White | 6, S. | A. S. Amer. | 1817 |
| arābica | Yellow | 6, H. | A. Arabia | 1794 |
| arbōrēā | White | 6, S. Ev. | S. Caracoas | 1817 |
| cardinālis | Red | 7, S. | A. Mexico | 1823 |
| Dilleniana, 1 | White | 6, H. | A. Levant | 1732 |
| diffūsa | Green | 6, S. | A. Brazil | 1823 |
| gigantēā | White | 6, S. Ev. | S. S. Amer. | 1774 |
| heptaphylla | White | 7, S. | A. Jamaica | 1817 |
| Houstoni | White | 8. | A. W. Ind. | 1730 |
| ibērica | White | 8. | A. Iberia | 1820 |
| monophylla | Yellow | 6, S. | A. E. Ind. | 1759 |
| zeylānica | Yellow | 6, S. | A. E. Ind. | 1759 |
| polygāmā | White | 6, S. | A. W. Ind. | 1824 |
| procūmbēns | Yellow | 6, S. He | P. W. Ind. | 1798 |
| pubéscens | Red | 7, H. | A. | 1815 |
| pūngēns, 2 | White | 7, S. | B. W. Ind. | 1812 |
| rōsēā | Red | 6, S. | A. Brazil | 1825 |
| speciosissimā | Purple | 7, H. | A. Mexico | 1827 |
| spinōsā | White | 6, S. | B. W. Ind. | 1731 |
| violāceā | Purple | 6, H. | A. Portugal | 1776 |
| virgātā | White | 6, H. | A. Persia | 1820 |

CLEONIA, *Linn.* A Greek name, employed by Theophrastus. *Linn.* 14, Or. 1, Nat. Or. *Labiatæ.* This pretty species merely requires sowing in the open border, and treating as other hardy annuals.

| | | | | |
|---|---|---|---|---|
| lusitānica | Li. blue | 6, H. | A. Portugal | 1710 |

CLERODENDRUM, *Linn.* *Kleros,* lot, and *dendron,* a tree; in allusion to the uncertain medicinal properties of the species. *Linn.* 14, Or. 2, Nat. Or. *Verbenaceæ.* A beautiful genus, varying in height from three to eight feet; they succeed best in a rich soil, composed of loam, rotten dung, and sandy peat. Young cuttings root freely in sand or soil, under a glass. *C. speciosissimum* is the most splendid. *Synonymes*: 1. *Volkameria buxifolia.* 2. *C. ovatum, V. madagascariense.* 3. *V. angustifolia.* 4. *Leucosceptrum canum.* 5. *Siphonanthus indica.*

| | | | | |
|---|---|---|---|---|
| angustifōliūm | | 8. Ev. | S. Maurit. | 1824 |
| attenuātūm | | 8. Ev. | S. N. Holl. | 1824 |
| buxifōliūm, 1 | White | 8. Ev. | S. | 1820 |
| calamitōsūm | | 8, 8. Ev. | S. E. Ind. | 1823 |
| cērnūūm | | 8. Ev. | S. E. Ind. | 1823 |
| coromandelianūm 2 | | 8. Ev. | S. Maurit. | 1823 |
| costātūm | | 8. Ev. | S. N. Holl. | 1823 |
| emirnénsē | White | 2, 8. Ev. | S. Madagas. | 1822 |
| floribūndūm | Lilac | 7, 8. Ev. | S. Madagas. | 1825 |
| foétidūm | | 8. Ev. | S. Nepal | 1820 |
| fortunātūm | | 7, 8. Ev. | S. E. Ind. | 1784 |
| fragrāns | Wht red | 10, 8. Ev. | S. China | 1790 |
| flōre-plēnō | Wht red | 10, 8. Ev. | S. China | 1790 |
| glaūcūm | | 8. Ev. | S. E. Ind. | 1825 |
| hastātūm | White | 6. S. Ev. | S. E. Ind. | 1825 |
| helianthifōliūm | | 8. Ev. | S. E. Ind. | 1824 |
| heterophyllūm, 3 | White | 8, S. Ev. | S. Maurit. | 1805 |
| inérmē | White | 7, S. Ev. | S. E. Ind. | 1692 |
| infortunātūm | | 8. Ev. | S. E. Ind. | |
| Leucosceptrūm, 4 | White | 8. Ev. | S. Nepal | 1826 |
| ligustrīnūm | White | 9, S. Ev. | S. Maurit. | 1789 |
| lividūm | White | 11, S. Ev. | S. China | 1824 |
| macrophyllūm | Wht. blue | 7, S. Ev. | S. E. Ind. | 1815 |
| nūtāns | White | 11, S. Ev. | S. E. Ind. | 1825 |
| odorātūm | Red | 8. Ev. | S. Nepal | 1823 |
| paniculātūm | Scarlet | 8, S. Ev. | S. Java | 1809 |
| phlomoīdēs | White | 8, S. Ev. | S. E. Ind. | 1820 |
| salicifōliūm | | 8. Ev. | S. Nepal | 1824 |
| serrātūm | | 8. Ev. | S. E. Ind. | 1822 |
| Siphonánthus, 5 | White | 8. Ev. | S. E. Ind. | 1796 |
| speciosissimūm | Scarlet | 8, S. Ev. | S. | 1835 |
| squamātūm | Scarlet | 8, S. Ev. | S. China | 1790 |
| ternifōliūm | | 8. Ev. | S. Nepal | 1823 |
| tomentōsūm | White | 4, G. Ev. | S. N. S. W. | 1794 |
| trichotōmūm | | G. Ev. | S. Japan | 1800 |
| urticaefōliūm | | 8. Ev. | S. E. Ind. | 1824 |
| verticillātūm | White | 8, S. Ev. | S. Nepal | 1818 |
| violāceūm | Violet | 8. Ev. | S. | 1822 |
| viscōsūm | White | 7, S. Ev. | S. E. Ind. | 1796 |
| volūbile | White | 8. Ev. | Cl. Guinea | 1823 |

CLETHRA, *Linn.* From *klethra,* the Greek name of the alder; on account of the resemblance it bears to that plant. *Linn.* 10, Or. 1, Nat. Or. *Ericaceæ.* All the species of this genus are ornamental, growing from two to ten feet high. The greenhouse kinds are well suited for conservatories, succeeding best in peat earth, or light sandy loam; cuttings taken off, not too ripe, will root freely in sand, under a glass. The hardy kinds, where the soil will suit them, are well adapted for the front of shrubberies, and require the same kind of soil as the greenhouse species. It is usual to increase them by layers; but cuttings root readily in sand, under a glass. All the kinds may be raised from seeds.

| | | | | |
|---|---|---|---|---|
| acuminata | White | 9, H. De. S. | Carolina | 1806 |
| alnifolia | White | 9, H. De. S. | N. Amer. | 1731 |
| arborea | White | 9, G. Ev. S. | Madeira | 1784 |
| minor | White | 9, G. Ev. S. | Madeira | |
| variegata | White | 8, G. Ev. S. | Madeira | |
| ferruginea | | G. Ev. S. | Peru | 1800 |
| nana | White | 8, H. De. S. | | 1820 |
| paniculata | White | 9, H. De. S. | N. Amer. | 1770 |
| scabra | White | 9, H. De. S. | Georgia | 1806 |
| tinifolia | White | S. Ev. T. | Jamaica | 1825 |
| tomentosa | White | 9, H. De. S. | N. Amer. | 1731 |

CLEYERA, *Thunberg*. In honour of Andrew Cleyer, M.D., a Dutch botanist, once resident at Batavia. *Linn.* 13, Or. 1, Nat. Or. *Ternstromiaceæ.* An ornamental greenhouse plant, about five feet high; it grows well in sandy peat, and is increased by cuttings under a glass.

| | | | | |
|---|---|---|---|---|
| japonica | | G. Ev. S. | Japan | 1820 |

CLIANTHUS, *Solander*. From *kleios*, glory, and *anthos*, a flower; in reference to the noble appearance of the species of this genus. *Linn.* 17, Or. 4, Nat. Or. *Leguminosæ.* A very elegant plant, resembling the *Sutherlandia frutescens* when in flower; it attains the height of eight or ten feet; it grows well in an equal mixture of loam, peat, and sand; it does best when planted in the border of the conservatory, and will also flourish against a south wall when protected from frost and cold; cuttings root in the kind of soil recommended for growing it, when placed under a glass.

| | | | | |
|---|---|---|---|---|
| puniceus, 1 | Crimson | 5, F. Ev. S. | N. Zeal. | 1832 |

CLIDEMIA. In honour of Clidemi, an ancient Greek botanist. *Linn.* 10, Or. 1, Nat. Or. *Melastomaceæ.* The species of this genus are not very showy. For culture and propagation, see *Melastoma. Synonymes:* 1. *Melastoma alata.* 2. *M. cernua.* 3. *M. elegans.* 4. *M. hirta.* 5. *M. rubra.* 6. *M. velutina.*

| | | | | |
|---|---|---|---|---|
| aggregata | White | 7, S. Ev. S. | Peru | 1820 |
| agrestis | White | 7, S. Ev. S. | Guiana | 1822 |
| alata, 1 | White | 7, S. Ev. S. | Maran. | 1819 |
| cernua, 2 | White | 7, S. Ev. S. | Peru | 1820 |
| elegans, 3 | White | 7, S. Ev. S. | Maran. | 1822 |
| hirta, 4 | Purple | 8, S. Ev. S. | Jamaica | 1740 |
| holosericea | White | 7, S. Ev. S. | Brazil | 1820 |
| microphylla | White | 7, S. Ev. S. | S. Amer. | 1817 |
| nivea | White | 7, S. Ev. S. | S. Amer. | 1823 |
| rubra, 5 | Purple | 4, S. Ev. S. | Guiana | 1783 |
| spicata | White | 7, S. Ev. S. | Guiana | 1793 |
| velutina, 6 | White | 7, S. Ev. S. | W. Ind. | 1816 |

CLIFFORTIA, *Linn.* In honour of George Cliffort, a merchant of Amsterdam, and one of the patrons of Linnæus. *Linn.* 22, Or. 12, Nat. Or. *Rosaceæ.* These species are only worthy of cultivation on account of their singular habit; they succeed well in an equal mixture of peat and loam, and cuttings of the young wood root freely in sand, under a glass.

| | | | | |
|---|---|---|---|---|
| cinerea | Grn. wht. | 6, G. Ev. S. | C. G. H. | 1800 |
| cordifolia | Grn. wht. | 6, G. Ev. S. | C. G. H. | 1820 |
| crenata | Grn. wht. | G. Ev. S. | E. Ind. | 1791 |
| cuneata | Grn. wht. | 4, G. Ev. S. | C. G. H. | 1787 |
| ericæfolia | Grn. wht. | 7, G. Ev. S. | C. G. H. | 1799 |
| falcata | Grn. wht. | 6, G. Ev. S. | C. G. H. | 1818 |
| ilicifolia | Grn. wht. | 7, G. Ev. S. | C. G. H. | 1714 |
| obcordata | Grn. wht. | 7, G. Ev. S. | C. G. H. | 1790 |
| obliqua | Grn. wht. | 6, G. Ev. S. | C. G. H. | 1816 |
| pulchella | Grn. wht. | 4, G. Ev. S. | C. G. H. | 1795 |
| ruscifolia | Grn. wht. | 6, G. Ev. S. | C. G. H. | 1752 |
| sarmentosa | White | 7, G. Ev. S. | C. G. H. | 1793 |
| strobilifera | Grn. wht. | 6, G. Ev. S. | | 1818 |
| ternata | Grn. wht. | 6, G. Ev. S. | C. G. H. | 1818 |
| tridentata | Grn. wht. | 6, G. Ev. S. | C. G. H. | |
| trifoliata | Grn. wht. | 6, G. Ev. S. | C. G. H. | 1752 |

CLINANDRIUM, that part of the column of orchideous plants in which the anther lies.

CLINOPODIUM, *Linn.* From *kline*, a bed, and *pous*, a foot; the flowers have been compared to the castor of a bedpost. *Linn.* 14, Or. 1, Nat. Or. *Labiatæ.* Rather ornamental plants, growing about a foot high; they do well in any common soil, and increase freely by division of the roots, or by seeds.

| | | | | |
|---|---|---|---|---|
| ægyptiacum | Purple | 7, H. Her. P. | Egypt | 1759 |
| origanifolium | Pink | 7, H. Her. P. | S. Eur. | 1825 |
| vulgare | Pink | 7, H. Her. P. | Britain | |

CLINTONIA, *Douglas.* In honour of De Witt Clinton, late governor of the state of New York. *Linn.* 16, Or. 2, Nat. Or. *Lobeliaceæ.* Very pretty border plants, producing an abundance of flowers; the seeds merely require sowing in the flower-borders in spring; they produce an abundance of seeds.

| | | | | |
|---|---|---|---|---|
| elegans | Blue | 7, H. | A. Columbia | 1827 |
| pulchella | Blue wht. | 8, G. | A. Columbia | 1831 |

CLITORIA, *Linn.* From *clitoris*, an anatomical term; a resemblance to the configuration of which has been fancied to exist in the flower. *Linn.* 17, Or. 4, Nat. Or. *Leguminosæ.* The species of this genus are mostly climbers, with large elegant pea-flowers: they succeed best in a mixture of loam, peat, and sand; cuttings will root under a glass, in heat, but the best method of increasing them is by seed, which sometimes ripens in this country. The annual species requires the same treatment as other tender annuals.

| | | | | |
|---|---|---|---|---|
| arborescens | Pink | 8, S. Ev. S. | Trinidad | 1804 |
| braziliana | Pink | 7, S. Tr. A. | Brazil | 1759 |
| coccinea | Scarlet | 7, S. Ev. Tw. | Brazil | 1820 |
| formosa | Pink | 7, S. Ev. Tw. | Orinoco | 1823 |
| gracilis | Blue | 7, S. Ev. Tw. | S. Amer. | 1824 |
| heterophylla | Blue | 7, S. Ev. Tw. | E. Ind. | 1812 |
| lasciva | | 7, G. Ev. Tw. | Madagas. | 1826 |
| mariana | Blue | 8, F. De. Tw. | N. Amer. | 1759 |
| mexicana | Purple | 10, G. Ev. Tw. | N. Amer. | 1759 |
| Plumieri | Wht. red | 10, S. Ev. Tw. | W. Ind. | |
| Ternata | Blue | 7, S. Ev. Tw. | E. Ind. | 1739 |
| virginiana | Blue | 7, S. Ev. Tw. | America | 1732 |

CLIVIA, *Lindley.* Named in honour of the Duchess of Northumberland. *Linn.* 6, Or. 1, Nat. Or. *Amaryllidaceæ.* A beautiful plant, requiring a warm part of the greenhouse, or a cool part of the stove; the soil it grows best in is a rich loam, with about a third part sand; when growing freely, it requires a plentiful supply of water; it may be increased by divisions, or seeds. *Synonyme:* 1. *Imatophyllum Aitoni.*

| | | | | |
|---|---|---|---|---|
| nobilis, 1 | Red yel. | 7, G. Ev. Bl. | C. G. H. | 1823 |

CLOSED, that which is closed up, leaving no aperture; pressed together, not spreading.

CLOSE-PRESSED, when any thing lies quite close upon a surface.

CLOUDBERRY, see *Rubus chamæmorus.*

CLOVE, see *Dianthus caryophyllus.*

CLOVEN, forked.

CLOVER, see *Trifolium.*

CLOVER-TREE, see *Caryophyllus.*

CLOWN'S ALLHEAL, see *Stachys palustris.*

CLUB GRASS, see *Corynephorus.*

CLUB MOSS, see *Lycopodium.*

CLUB RUSH, see *Scirpus.*

CLUSIA, *Linn.* In honour of Charles de l'Ecluse, of Artois, a celebrated botanist, who died in 1609. *Linn.* 23, Or. 1, Nat. Or. *Guttiferæ.* A very ornamental genus of trees growing, under cultivation, thirty feet high; they require a light sandy loam, and the pots must be well drained. Cuttings root freely in sand, under a glass. In tropical climates they are found growing on other trees.

| | | | | |
|---|---|---|---|---|
| alba | White | S. Ev. T. | S. Amer. | 1752 |
| flava | Yellow | S. Ev. T. | Jamaica | 1759 |
| rosea | Red | 7, S. Ev. T. | Carolina | 1692 |
| venosa | White | S. Ev. T. | S. Amer. | 1733 |

CLUSTERED, disposed in clusters.

CLUTIA, *Aiton.* Named after Outgers Cluyt, a Dutchman, who was professor of botany at Leyden. *Linn.* 22, Or. 3, Nat. Or. *Euphorbiaceæ.* Ornamental species, thriving in a mixture of loam and peat; cuttings of the young wood root freely in sand, under a glass.

| | | | | |
|---|---|---|---|---|
| alaternoides | White | 7, G. Ev. S. | C. G. H. | 1692 |
| collina | White | 8, G. Ev. S. | E. Ind. | 1807 |
| daphnoides | White | 5, G. Ev. S. | C. G. H. | 1731 |
| ericoides | White | 4, G. Ev. S. | C. G. H. | 1790 |
| heterophylla | White | 5, G. Ev. S. | C. G. H. | 1818 |
| patula | White | 8, G. Ev. S. | E. Ind. | 1812 |
| polifolia | White | 5, G. Ev. S. | C. G. H. | 1790 |
| polygonoides | White | 4, G. Ev. S. | C. G. H. | 1790 |
| pubescens | White | 4, G. Ev. S. | C. G. H. | 1800 |
| pulchella | White | 4, G. Ev. S. | C. G. H. | 1739 |
| tenuifolia | White | 6, G. Ev. S. | C. G. H. | 1817 |
| tomentosa | White | 4, G. Ev. S. | C. G. H. | 1812 |

CLYPEATE, buckler-shaped.

CLYPEOLA, *Gærtner.* From *clypeus*, a buckler; in

M

allusion to its buckler-like silicle. *Linn.* 15, Nat. Or. *Cruciferæ.* Pretty annuals, which only require sowing in the open ground, and to be treated as other hardy annuals. .

| | | | | |
|---|---|---|---|---|
| Ion Thlåspi | . . | Yellow | . 6, H. | A. S. Eur. . . 1710 |
| eriōphōrā | . . . | White | . 6, H. | A. Spain . . 1820 |

CNEMIDOSTĀCHỸS, *Martius.* Derived from *knemis*, the spoke of a wheel, and *stachys*, a spike. *Linn.* 21, Or. 2, Nat. Or. *Euphorbiaceæ.* A worthless stove annual, growing in sandy peat—*Chamelæd.*

CNEŌRŪM, *Linn.* Theophrastus gave the name *cneoron* to some shrub resembling an olive. *Linn.* 3, Or. 1, Nat. Or. *Surianaceæ.* Beautiful species, delighting in a mixture of peat and loam, and cuttings root freely in sand, under a glass.

| | | | | |
|---|---|---|---|---|
| pulverulentūm | . | Yellow | . 6, G. Ev. S. Madeira | . 1822 |
| tricōccūm | . | Yellow | . 6, G. Ev. S. S. Eur. | . 1793 |

CNESTĪS, *Jussieu.* From *knao*, to scratch; in reference to the prickly capsules. *Linn.* 10, Or. 4, Nat. Or. *Connaraceæ.* Ornamental shrubs; see *Connarus*, for culture and propagation.

| | | | | |
|---|---|---|---|---|
| corniculātā | . | Purple | . 8. Ev. S. Guinea | . 1793 |
| glābrā | . | Wht. grn. | 8. Ev. S. Maurit. | . 1823 |
| polyphyllā | . . | Purple | . S. Ev. S. Maurit. | . 1823 |

CNĪDIŪM, *Cusson.* The ancient name of Orach. *Linn.* 5, Or. 2, Nat. Or. *Umbelliferæ.* Worthless herbaceous plants; for culture and propagation, see *Sěsělī.* *Synonymes:* 1. *Smyrnum atropurpureum.* 2. *Selinum canadense.* 3. *Angelica Fischeri—atropurpureum* 1, *canadense* 2, *Fischeri* 3, *Monnieri*, *pyrenæum.*

COADUNATE, united, soldered together.

COĀGŪLĀNS, congealing together.

COARCTATE, pressed together.

COBÆA, *Cavanilles.* In honour of B. Cobo, a Spanish botanist. *Linn.* 5, Or. 1, Nat. Or. *Polemoniaceæ.* A very fast growing climber, well adapted to a conservatory; it thrives well in the open air in summer, and looks well growing up by the side of a house; if the wall be rough on which it runs, the tendrils will catch fast hold of the crevices and support the branches without any assistance; it may be increased by cuttings, which will root under a glass, in a little moist heat, but it is best to raise it from seeds, which ripen in abundance.

| | | | | |
|---|---|---|---|---|
| scāndēns | . | Purple | . 8, F. Ev. Cl. Mexico | . 1792 |

COBŪRGHĪA, *Herbert.* In honour of Prince Leopold of Saxe-Coburgh, now King of Belgium. *Linn.* 6, Or. 1, Nat. Or. *Amaryllidaceæ.* Handsome species, requiring the same treatment as *Pancratium.* *Synonyme:* 1. *Pancratium incarnatum.*

| | | | | |
|---|---|---|---|---|
| fulvā | . . | Tawny | . G. Bu. P. S. Amer. | . 1829 |
| incarnātā, 1 | . | Scarlet | . 8, F. Bu. P. Quito | . 1826 |

COBWEBBED, covered with loose hairs, as if with a cobweb.

COCCOCYPSĒLŪM, *Swartz.* From *kokkos*, fruit, and *kypsele*, a vase; alluding to the shape of the berries. *Linn.* 4, Or. 1, Nat. Or. *Cinchonaceæ.* An uninteresting stove herbaceous plant, growing in sandy loam, and multiplied by cuttings in sand, under a glass—*rěpēns.*

COCCŌLŌBĀ, *Linn.* From *kokkos*, a berry, and *lobos*, a lobe; in allusion to the character of the fruit. *Linn.* 8, Or. 3, Nat. Or. *Polygonaceæ.* The Sea-side Grape is an ornamental genus, varying in height from fifteen to eighty feet, the species are remarkable for their large leaves. They grow well in a mixture of loam and peat, and cuttings of the ripened wood, taken off at a joint, will root freely under a glass, in sand; the leaves of the cuttings must not be shortened. *Synonyme:* 1. *Coccoloba parviflora.*

| | | | | |
|---|---|---|---|---|
| acuminātā | . . | Wht. grn. | 8. Ev. T. N. Grana. | . 1820 |
| barbadēnsis | . . | Wht. grn. | 8. Ev. T. Barbadoes | . !790 |
| brasiliēnsis | . . | Wht. grn. | 8. Ev. T. Brazil | . 1825 |
| diversifōliā | . . | Wht. grn. | 8, 8. Ev. T. St. Domin. | . 1818 |
| excoriātā | . . | Wht. grn. | 8. Ev. T. W. Ind. | . 1733 |
| flavēscēns | . . | Wht. grn. | 8. Ev. T. St. Domin. | . 1820 |
| latifōliā | . . | Wht. grn. | 8. Ev. T. S. Amer. | . 1812 |
| laurifōliā | . . | Wht. grn. | 8, 8. Ev. T. Caraccas | . 1822 |
| longifōliā | . . | Wht. grn. | 8. Ev. T. W. Ind. | . 1810 |
| microstāchyā | . . | Wht. grn. | 8. Ev. T. W. Ind. | . 1824 |
| nīveā | . . | Wht. grn. | 8. Ev. T. Jamaica | . 1818 |
| obovātā | . . | Wht. grn. | 8. Ev. T. S. Amer. | . 1824 |
| obtusifōliā | . . | Wht. grn. | 8. Ev. T. Carthag. | . 1822 |
| orbiculāris | . . | Wht. grn. | 8. Ev. T. S. Amer. | . 1825 |
| pubēscēns | . . | Wht. grn. | 8. Ev. T. W. Ind | . 1690 |

| | | | | |
|---|---|---|---|---|
| punctātā | . . | Wht. grn. | 8. Ev. T. W. Ind. | . 1733 |
| tenuifōliā | . . | Wht. grn. | 8. Ev. T. Jamaica | . 1820 |
| uvifērā, 1 | . . | Wht. grn. | 8. Ev. T. W. Ind. | . 1690 |
| vīrēns | . . | Wht. grn. | 8. Ev. T. W. Ind. | . 1825 |

CŌCCŪLŪS, a kind of cell, which opens with elasticity.

CŌCCŪLŪS, *Decandolle.* Derived from *coccos*, the systematic name of the cochineal; given to this genus because most of the species bear scarlet berries. *Linn.* 22, Or. 6, Nat. Or. *Menispermaceæ.* An interesting genus of plants, remarkable for their medicinal virtues. The species do well in a mixture of loam and peat, and cuttings root freely under a glass. *C. crispus* is used in intermittent fevers and liver complaints; a poisonous principle called picrotoxia has been detected in the seed of *C. suberosus.* *Synonyme:* 1. *Menispermum coculus.*

| | | | | |
|---|---|---|---|---|
| cordifōliūs | . . | Wht. grn. | 8. Ev. Cl. E. Ind. | . 1820 |
| crispūs | . . | Wht. grn. | 8. Ev. Cl. E. Ind. | . 1822 |
| incānūs | . . | Wht. grn. | 8. Ev. Cl. E. Ind. | . 1820 |
| laurifōliūs | . . | Wht. grn. | 8. Ev. Cl. E. Ind. | . 1816 |
| orbiculātūs | . . | Grn. yel. | 8. Ev. Cl. E. Ind. | . 1790 |
| palmātūs | . . | Wht. grn. | 8. Ev. Cl. E. Ind. | . 1800 |
| Plukenētiī, 1 | . | Grn. yel. | 8. Ev. Cl. E. Ind. | . 1790 |
| rotundifōliūs | . . | Wht. grn. | 8. Ev. Cl. | . 1820 |
| suberōsūs | . . | Wht. grn. | 8. Ev. Cl. E. Ind. | . 1800 |
| tomentōsūs | . . | Wht. grn. | 8. Ev. Cl. E. Ind. | . 1819 |
| villōsūs | . . | Grn. yel. | 8. Ev. Cl. E. Ind. | . 1800 |
| hirsūtūs | . . | Grn. yel. | 8. Ev. Cl. E. Ind. | . 1800 |

COCHLEĀRIX, *Tournefort.* From *cochlear*, a spoon; the leaves are hollowed like the bowl of a spoon. *Linn.* 15, Nat. Or. *Cruciferæ.* Plants of little interest with the exception of *C. Armoracea*, the common Horse-radish, which should be planted in February or October in a deep rich soil; the best way of increasing it is by slips from the root. The smaller perennial kinds do best in pots or rock-work. The annuals and biennials merely require sowing in the open border, which should be done directly after the seeds have ripened. *Synonymes:* 1. *C. pusilla.* 2. *Myagrum saxatile.*

| | | | | |
|---|---|---|---|---|
| anglicā | . . | White | . 5, H. | A. Britain . |
| Armorācēā | . . | White | . 5, H. Fu. P. England | . |
| dānicā | . . | White | . 5, H. | A. Britain . |
| fenestrātā | . . | White | . 5, H. | B. Greenland | . 1820 |
| gronlandicā | . . | Flesh | . 5, H. | B. Scotland | . |
| integrifōliā | . . | White | . 5, H. | B. Siberia | . 1822 |
| officinālis | . . | White | . 4, F. | B. Britain | . |
| minor | . . | White | . 4, H. | B. Britain | . |
| rotundifōliā | . . | White | . 4, H. | B. Britain | . |
| pyrenāicā | . . | White | . 4, H. | B. Pyrenees | . 1820 |

*acaulis* 1, *auriculātā*, *glastifōliā*, *macrocārpā*, *saxatilis* 2.

COCHLEATE, twisted to resemble the shell of a snail.

COCHLOSPĒRMŪM, *Kunth.* From *kochlo*, to twist, and *sperma*, a seed; alluding to the somewhat twisted seeds. *Linn.* 16, Or. 3, Nat. Or. *Ternstromiaceæ.* Magnificent trees, attaining the height of sixty feet, the best soil for them is loam and peat; cuttings not too ripe, taken off at a joint, will root in sand, under a glass, in a moist heat. *Synonymes:* 1. *Bombax Gossypium*, *B. grandiflorum.* 2. *B. vitifolium.*

| | | | | |
|---|---|---|---|---|
| Gossypiūm, 1 | . | Yellow | . 5. Ev. T. E. Ind. | . 1824 |
| serratifōliūm, 2 | . | Yellow | . 8. Ev. T. Mexico | . 1820 |

COCK'S-COMB, see *Celōsiā.*

COCK'S-COMB, see *Rhinānthūs Cristā-gālli.*

COCK'S-COMB, see *Erythrinā Cristā-gālli.*

COCK'S-FOOT, see *Echinochlōā Crūs-gālli.*

COCK'S-FOOT GRASS, see *Dāctỹlis.*

COCK'S-SPUR, see *Cratægūs Crūs-gālli.*

COCOA-NUT TREE, see *Cōcōs.*

COCOA PLUM, see *Chrysobālnūs.*

CŌCŌS, *Linn.* From the Portuguese word *coco*; the end of the nut resembles a monkey's head. *Linn.* 21, Or. 6, Nat. Or. *Palmaceæ.* The cocoa-nut tree belongs to this elegant genus. The species grow upwards of fifty feet high, and are cultivated best in a mixture of loam and peat or light sandy loam, in a warm moist atmosphere. They do not succeed well in our collections, probably from being too much exposed to the sun, as they thrive best in the shade in their native country. *Synonyme:* 1. *C. comosa.*

| | | | | |
|---|---|---|---|---|
| flexuōsā | . . . | . . | Palm. Brazil | . 1825 |
| nucifērā | . . . | Pa. grn. | Palm. E. Ind. | . 1690 |
| plumōsā, 1 | . . | Pa. grn. | Palm. Brazil | . 1825 |

CODĀRIŪM, *Solander.* Derived from *kodarion*, a leathern pouch; in reference to the pods. *Linn.* 2,

Or. 1, Nat. Or. *Leguminosœ*. Ornamental trees, from twelve to twenty feet high. For culture and propagation, see *Copaifêrâ*.

| | | | | | |
|---|---|---|---|---|---|
| acutifolium | . | Pa. red | . 2, S. Ev. T. S. Leone | . 1800 |
| obtusifolium | . | Pa. red | . 2, S. Ev. S. S. Leone | . 1824 |

CŌDĬŬM, *Stackhouse*. From *kodion*, a skin; on account of the appearance of the species. *Linn.* 24, Or. 7, Nat. Or. *Algæ*. Marine productions of little interest—*bŭrsâ, tomentôsâm.*

CODLINS AND CREAM, see *Epilôbĭūm hĭrsūtūm.*

CŎDŌN, *Linn.* From *kodon*, a little bell, referring to the shape of the corolla. *Linn.* 10, Or. 1, Nat. Or. *Hydrolaceæ.* A curious plant, thriving in a mixture of loam and peat; it requires to be kept with the greenhouse plants.

| | | | | | |
|---|---|---|---|---|---|
| Royênî | . . . | White | . 9, G. | B. C. G. H. | . 1801 |

CODŌNŌPHŌRĀ, *Linn.* From *kodon*, a little bell, and *phoreo*, to bear; alluding to the flowers. *Linn.* 14, Or. 2, Nat. Or. *Gesneraceœ.* Ornamental plants. For culture, &c., see *Gesnĕrĭâ.* Synonymes: 1. *Gesnera pasinata. G. tomentosa.*

| | | | | | |
|---|---|---|---|---|---|
| grandiflôrâ, 1 | . | Scarlet | . 6, S. Ev. S Brazil | . 1818 |
| lanceolâtâ, 2 | . | Scarlet | . 6, S. Ev. S. S. Amer. | . 1752 |

CŒLĪX, *Lindley.* Not explained. *Linn.* 20, Or. 1, Nat. Or. *Orchidaceæ.* This is described as being a very curiously formed plant, and requiring the same treatment as *Stanhopea.* Synonymes:1.*Cymbidium tripterum, Epidendrum tripterum.*

| | | | | | |
|---|---|---|---|---|---|
| Hauârânâ | . . . | White | . 6, S. Epi. Jamaica | . 1790 |

CŒLŌGŸNĒ, *Lindley.* From *koilos*, hollow, and *gyne*, a female; in allusion to the form of the stigma. *Linn.* 20, Or. 1, Nat. Or. *Orchidaceæ.* The species of this genus are all very handsome when in flower, and therefore deserve to be in every collection of Orchideous plants. From most of the species having been introduced but a short time, they are rather rare in most collections. They should be grown in a hot damp heat, and otherwise treated as the *Stanhopeas.* Synonymes: 1. *Cœlogyne punctulata.*

| | | | | | |
|---|---|---|---|---|---|
| barbâtâ | . . . | Wht. yel. | 12, S. Epi. Khossea | . 1837 |
| cristâtâ | . . . | | 8. Epi. Nepal | . 1837 |
| elâtâ | . . . | | 8. Epi. Khossea | . 1837 |
| fimbriâtâ | . . . | Wht. brn. | 9, S. Epi. Nepal | . |
| flaccida | . . . | | 1, S. Epi. Nepal | . |
| Gardneriânâ | . . . | White | . 11, S. Epi. Khossea | . 1837 |
| interrūptâ | . . . | White | . 8. Epi. Khossea | . 1837 |
| longicaulis | . . . | Wht. yel. | 8. Epi. Khossea | . 1837 |
| maculâtâ | . . . | | 8. Epi. Khossea | . 1837 |
| mêdîâ | . . . | Wht. yel. | 8. Epi. Khossea | . 1837 |
| nîtîdâ | . . . | Yellow | . 8. Epi. E. Ind. | . 1822 |
| ocellâtâ | . . . | Yellow | . 8. Epi. E. Ind. | . 1822 |
| ovâlis | . . . | Wht. brn. | 10, S. Epi. E. Ind. | . |
| prolifêrâ | . . . | Yellowish | . 8. Epi. Khossea | . 1837 |
| rĭgĭdâ | . . . | Yellow | . 8. Epi. Khossea | . 1837 |
| undulâtâ | . . . | White | . 8. Epi. Khossea | . 1837 |
| Wallichiânâ | . . . | Rose | . 8. Epi. Khossea | . 1837 |

CŎFFÆ, *Linn.* Named from Coffee, a province of Narea in Africa, where it grows in abundance. *Linn.* 5, Or. 1, Nat. Or. *Cinchonaceæ.* The Coffee-tree is a very ornamental plant, succeeding well in peat and loam, and if kept clean and free from insects it will flower and fruit abundantly; to grow well, it must have a good supply of water and plenty of pot-room; cuttings of the ripened wood root readily in sand, under a glass, in a moist heat. Coffee is the roasted seeds of this plant, and owes its character to a peculiar chemical principle called Caffein. Synonymes: 1. *Tetramerium paniculatum.*

| | | | | | |
|---|---|---|---|---|---|
| arâbĭcâ | . . | White | . 9, S. Ev. S. Yemen. | . 1696 |
| paniculâtâ, 1 | . | White | . 8. Ev. S. Guiana | . 1822 |

COFFEE-TREE, see *Coffêâ.*

COOWOOD TREE, see *Laûrûs Chlorôxŷlŏn.*

COHERING, connected.

CŎĬX, *Linn.* A name applied by Theophrastus, to a reed-leaved plant. *Linn.* 21, Or. 3, Nat. Or. *Gramineæ.* A genus of curious tropical grasses, growing freely in light rich soil; they produce both flowers and seeds in great plenty.

| | | | | | |
|---|---|---|---|---|---|
| agrêsĭs | . . | Apetal | . Gram. E. Ind. | . 1812 |
| arundinâcêâ | . . | Apetal | . 7, Gram. Mexico | . 1818 |
| exaltâtâ | . . | Apetal | . 6, Gram. China | . 1816 |
| Kœnigĭĭ | . . | Apetal | . 7, Gram. E. Ind. | . 1818 |
| lachrŷmâ | . . | Apetal | . 6, Gram. E. Ind. | . 1596 |

CŎLĀ, see *Stercûlĭâ acumĭnâtâ.*

COLBERTĬĀ, *Salisbury.* In honour of John Baptist

Colbert, Marquis of Seignelai, a famous French statesman and patron of botany: died 1683. *Linn.* 12, Or. 5, Nat. Or. *Dilleniaceæ.* A beautiful genus of trees, resembling *Dillenia*, to which genus they may be referred for culture and propagation.

| | | | | | |
|---|---|---|---|---|---|
| coromandelĭânâ, 1 | Yellow | . 4, S. Ev. T. Coroman. | . 1808 |
| scabrêllâ | . . . | Yellow | . 8. Ev. T. Nepal | . 1820 |

CŎLCHĬCŬM, *Linn.* Named after Colchis, its native country. *Linn.* 6, Or. 3, Nat. Or. *Melanthaceæ.* An ornamental genus of bulbs, growing best in a light loamy soil, and increased by offsets from the bulbs, or from seeds. Synonymes: 1. *Merendera montana.*

| | | | | | |
|---|---|---|---|---|---|
| alpĭnûm | . . . | Purple | . 7, H. Bu. P. Apennin. | . 1820 |
| arenârĭûm | . . . | Purple | . 9, H. Bu. P. Hungary | . 1816 |
| autumnâlê | . . . | Purple | . 9, H. Bu. P. Britain | . |
| album | . . . | White | . 9, H. Bu. P. Britain | . |
| foliis-variegâtis | Purple | . 9, H. Bu. P. Britain | . |
| flore-plêno | . . . | Purple | . 9, H. Bu. P. Britain | . |
| byzântĭûm | . . . | Purple | . 9, H. Bu. P. Levant | . 1629 |
| chionênsê | . . . | Purple | . 11, H. Bu. P. Chio | . |
| crociflôrûm | . . . | Purple | . 8, H. Bu. P. S. Eur. | . |
| montânûm, 1 | . . | Purple | . 8, H. Bu. P. S. Eur. | . 1819 |
| tessellâtûm | . . . | Purple | . 9, H. Bu. P. S. Eur. | . 1600 |
| umbrôsûm | . . . | Pink | . 9, H. Bu. P. Crimea | . 1819 |
| variegâtûm | . . . | Purple | . 9, H. Bu. P. Greece | . 1629 |

CŎLDĒNĬĀ, *Linn.* In honour of C. Colden, a zealous North American botanist. *Linn.* 4, Or. 3, Nat. Or. *Boraginaceæ.* A pretty stove annual, requiring the same treatment as other tender annuals.

| | | | | | |
|---|---|---|---|---|---|
| procumbêns | . . | White | . 7, S. Tr. A. E. Ind. | . 1699 |

CŎLEBRŌŌKĬĀ, *Smith.* In honour of H. T. Colebrooke, an accomplished botanist. *Linn.* 14, Or. 2, Nat. Or. *Labiatæ.* A beautiful genus of shrub, growing about three feet high, succeeding best in a mixture of peat and loam; increased by cuttings in sand, under a glass.

| | | | | | |
|---|---|---|---|---|---|
| oppositifolĭâ | . . | White | . G. Ev. S. Nepal | . 1820 |
| ternifolĭâ | . . | White | . G. Ev. S. E. Ind. | . 1823 |

CŎLFONĒMĬĀ, *Bartling.* From *keleosa*, a sheath, and *nema*, a filament; in allusion to the manner in which the filaments are fixed. *Linn.* 5, Or. 1, Nat. Or. *Rutaceæ.* A very beautiful little shrub. For culture and propagation, see *Adenândrâ.* Synonyme: 1. *Diosma alba.*

| | | | | | |
|---|---|---|---|---|---|
| albâ, 1 | . . . | White | . 6, G. Ev. S. C. G. H | . 1798 |

CŎLEORHĪZĀ, a little sheath, which tips the radicle in cruciferous plants.

CŎLĒŬS, *Loureiro.* Derived from *koleos*, a sheath; referring to the manner in which the stamens are united. *Linn.* 14, Or. 1, Nat. Or. *Labiatæ.* Shrubs of some merit, requiring to be grown in a mixture of loam and peat, and increased by cuttings in sand, under a glass, in heat. Synonymes: 1. *C. amboinicus, Gesnera odorata.* 2. *Plectanthus barbatus, P. Forskohldi.* 3. *P. fruticosus.*

| | | | | | |
|---|---|---|---|---|---|
| aromâtĭcûs, 1 | . . | | 5, S. Ev. S. India | . 1826 |
| barbâtûs, 2 | . . | Blue | . 10, S. Ev. S. Abyssinia | . 1806 |
| fruticôsûs, 3 | . . | Blue | . 7, G. Ev. S. C. G. H. | . 1774 |

COLLAPSING, the act of closing or falling together.

CŎLLĒMĀ, *Hoffmann.* From the Greek *kolla*, glue; all the species are gelatinous. *Linn.* 24, Or. 9, Nat. Or. *Lichenes.* A rather extensive genus of *Lichenes*, varying from half an inch to three inches high, found in a variety of situations, some being on the trunks and roots of trees, some on rocks, and others on old walls and dry banks, &c.—*Burgesii, chelêûm, corrugâtûm, cretâcêûm, crispûm, fasciculârê, flaccîdûm, fluvĭâlê, frâgrâns, fŭrvûm, granulâtûm, lâcerûm, melênûm, M. marginâlê, multipartîtûm, muscicôlâ, nigrêscêns, nigrûm, palmâtûm, plicâtĭlê, saturnĭnûm, Schradêrĭ, scotĭnûm, S. sinuâtûm, spongĭôsûm, subtĭlê, tĭnâx, tenuĭssĭmûm, tremellôĭdês.*

CŎLLETĬĀ. A name given by Commerson, in honour of his friend and countryman M. Collet, a writer upon the plants of Brest. *Linn.* 5, Or. 1, Nat. Or. *Rhamnaceæ.* Ornamental shrubs, varying from two to five feet high. For culture and propagation, see *Retanĭllâ.* Synonymes: 1. *C. ferox.* 2. *C. horrida.*

| | | | | | |
|---|---|---|---|---|---|
| hŏrrĭdâ, 1 | . . | Grh. wht. | 5, F. Ev. S. Chile | . 1823 |
| serratifolĭâ | . . | Yellow | . 6, S. Ev. S. Peru | . 1822 |
| spinôsâ, 2 | . . | Apetal | . 6, S. Ev. S. Peru | . 1823 |

CŎLLIGUĀŸĀ, *Molina.* The name given to it by the natives. *Linn.* 21, Or. 10, Nat. Or. *Euphorbiaceæ.*

A shrub of considerable merit, though little known in cultivation.

| | | | | | |
|---|---|---|---|---|---|
| odorífera | Yel. wht. | G. Ev. S. Chile | 1831 |

**COLLÍNSYX**, *Nuttall.* In honour of Zac. Collins, vice-president of the Academy of Natural Sciences, Philadelphia. *Linn.* 14, *Or.* 2, *Nat. Or. Scrophulariacee.* A most elegant genus of hardy annuals: the seeds of the different kinds need only to be sown in the borders of the flower-garden early in spring, they will then flower beautifully during summer, and ripen plenty of seeds; to obtain flowering plants early in spring, the seed must be sown in autumn.

| | | | | | |
|---|---|---|---|---|---|
| bicólor | Pur. wht | 6. H. | A. California | 1833 |
| grandiflóra | Pk. blue | 6. H. | A. Columbia | 1826 |
| heterophýllá | Lilac | 7. H. | A. Columbia | 1838 |
| parviflóra | Pur. blue | 6, H. Tr. | A. Columbia | 1826 |
| vérná | Pur. blue | 6, H. | A. N. Amer. | 1826 |

**COLLINSÓNYX.** Named by Linnæus in honour of his friend Peter Collinson, F.R.S., a distinguished promoter of botany. *Linn.* 2, *Or.* 1, *Nat. Or. Labiate.* A genus of pretty plants, growing upwards of three feet high; they succeed well in common garden soil, particularly if they are planted in a moist situation; they are increased by dividing them at the roots.

| | | | | | |
|---|---|---|---|---|---|
| anisátá | Yellow | 10, H. Her. | P. Carolina | 1806 |
| canadénsis | Li. yel. | 9, H. Her. | P. N. Amer. | 1735 |
| cordátá | Li. yel. | 9, H. Her. | P. N. Amer. | 1734 |
| ovátá | Li. yel. | 9, H. Her. | P. N. Amer. | 1734 |
| ovális | Yellow | 8, H. Her. | P. Carolina | 1812 |
| scabriúsculá | Red yel. | 8, G. Her. | P. E. Flor. | 1776 |
| tuberósá | Yellow | 8, H. Tu. | P. Carolina | 1806 |

**COLLÓMYX**, *Nuttall.* Derived from *kolla*, glue; referring to the seeds. *Linn.* 5, *Or.* 1, *Nat. Or. Polemoniacee.* A genus of annuals, possessing little beauty in their flowers; they require the same treatment as *Collinsia*. Synonyme: 1. *C. laterita.*

| | | | | | |
|---|---|---|---|---|---|
| coccíneá, 1. | Brick | 7, H. | A. Chile | 1832 |
| grandiflóra | Pink | 7, H. | A. Columbia | 1826 |
| heterophýllá | Pink | 7, H. | A. Columbia | 1826 |
| linearis | Red | 6, H. | A. N. Amer. | 1826 |

**COLOGÁNYX**, *Kunth.* In honour of the family of Cologan, of Port Orotavo in Teneriffe, from whom the men of science visiting that island experience the greatest hospitality. *Linn.* 17, *Or.* 4, *Nat. Or. Leguminose.* A beautiful genus of climbers. For culture and propagation, see *Clitoria.* Synonyme: 1. *Clitoria Broussonetii.*

| | | | | | |
|---|---|---|---|---|---|
| angustifólia | Violet | 8. Ev. Tw. | Mexico | 1827 |
| Broussonètii, 1 | Violet | 8. Ev. Tw. | | 1827 |

**COLOPHÓNYX**, *Commerson.* Its name in the Isle of France is Bois de Colophone. *Linn.* 6, *Or.* 1, *Nat. Or. Burseracee.* An ornamental tree, scarcely known in collections. For culture and propagation, see *Boswellia.*

| | | | | | |
|---|---|---|---|---|---|
| mauritiáná | Purple | 8. Ev. T. | Mauritius | 1826 |

**COLÓRINS**, changeable, coloured.
**COLORÁTE**, coloured, painted.
**CÓLPÓÓN**, see *Fusánus.*
**CÓLPÓÓN-TREE**, see *Cassiné Cólpóón.*
**COLT's-FOOT**, see *Tussilágo.*
**COLUBRÍNÁ**, *Richard.* From *koluber*, a snake; alluding to the appearance of the twisted stamens. *Linn.* 5, *Or.* 1, *Nat. Or. Rhamnacee.* Plants of little beauty, and scarcely worth cultivating except in general collections; loam and peat suits them, and cuttings of the young wood root readily in sand, under a glass. Synonymes: 1. *Ceanothus asiaticus.* 2. *C. cubensis.* 3. *C. colubrina.* 4. *C. reclinatus.*

| | | | | | |
|---|---|---|---|---|---|
| asiática, 1 | Pa. yel. | 7, G. Ev. S. | Ceylon | 1691 |
| cubénsis, 2 | Crimson | 8. Ev. S. | Cuba | 1820 |
| ferruginósá, 3 | Green | 7, 8. Ev. T. | Bahama | 1762 |
| reclinátá, 4 | Green | 8, 8. Ev. S. | Jamaica | 1758 |

**COLUBRÍNÁ**, relating to snakes.
**COLUMBINE**, see *Aquilégia.*
**COLUMBÍNÚS**, resembling a dove in shape or colour.
**COLUMBLLÍX.** Named by Jacquin after the celebrated Geoponic writer, L. J. M. Columella, a Spaniard, who flourished about forty-two years A.C. *Linn.* 19, *Or.* 2, *Nat. Or. Columelliacee.* A worthless greenhouse biennial, growing in any common soil. Synonyme: 1. *Nestlera biennis—biénnis* 1.
**COLÚMNEÁ**, *Plumier.* In honour of Fabius Columna, of the noble family of Colonna, in Italy. *Linn.* 14,

Or. 2, Nat. Or. *Gesneracee.* Pretty flowering plants, growing well in a mixture of loam and peat, and striking readily from cuttings: the plants must be carefully watered or they will soon rot; they require a dry part of the house.

| | | | | | |
|---|---|---|---|---|---|
| hirsútá | Pa. pur. | 9, 8. Ev. S. | Jamaica | 1780 |
| rútilans | Purple | 9. S. Ev. S. | Jamaica | 1823 |
| scándens | Scarlet | 8, S. Ev. Cl. | W. Ind. | 1759 |
| trifoliátá | Blue | 9, S. Ev. S. | | 1823 |

**COLÚRYX**, *R. Brown.* From *kolouros*, deprived of a tail; in reference to the seed wanting that appendage. *Linn.* 12, *Or.* 3, *Nat. Or. Rosacee.* A pretty species, thriving best in a mixture of peat and loam, and increased by divisions. Synonyme: 1. *Geum potentilloides.*

| | | | | | |
|---|---|---|---|---|---|
| potentilloídés, 1 | Orange | 6, H. Her. | P. Siberia | 1780 |

**COLÚTEÁ**, *Linn.* Supposed to be from *koluo*, to amputate; they are said to die if the branches are cut off. *Linn.* 17, *Or.* 4, *Nat. Or. Leguminose.* All the species of Bladder-Senna, on account of the great profusion of flowers, and their continuing in flower the most of the season, are well adapted for the shrubbery; they thrive in any common soil, and are increased by seeds, or cuttings planted in the autumn. *C. arborescens* is purgative. Synonyme: 1. *C. Pocockii.*

| | | | | | |
|---|---|---|---|---|---|
| arboréscens | Yellow | 7, H. De. S. | France | 1548 |
| cruénta | Scarlet | 6, H. De. S. | Levant | 1710 |
| haléppicá, 1 | Yellow | 8, H. De. S. | Levant | 1752 |
| médiá | Orange | 7, H. De. S. | | |
| nepalénsis | Yellow | 8, H. De. S. | Nepal | 1822 |

**COLVÍLLEÁ**, *Bojer.* In honour of Sir Charles Colville, Governor of the Mauritius. *Linn.* 10, *Or.* 1, *Nat. Or. Leguminose.* A splendid tree, from forty to fifty feet high; nothing is at present known of its cultivation.

| | | | | | |
|---|---|---|---|---|---|
| racemósá | Scarlet | 8. Ev. T. | Madagas. | |

**COMÁNDRÁ**, *Nuttall.* Derived from *kome*, hair, and *aner*, anther; in allusion to the tuft of hair attached to the anthers. *Linn.* 5, *Or.* 1, *Nat. Or. Santalacee.* A hardy plant of some merit, thriving in a mixture of loam and peat, and increased by divisions. Synonymes: 1. *Thesium umbellatum, Hamiltonia umbellatum.*

| | | | | | |
|---|---|---|---|---|---|
| umbellátá, 1 | Green | H. Her. | P. N. Amer. | 1782 |

**COMARÓPSIS**, *Richard.* From *komaron*, the comarum, and *opsis*, appearance; because of its resemblance to Marsh Cinquefoil. *Linn.* 12, *Or.* 3, *Nat. Or. Rosacee.* Pretty herbaceous plants. For culture and propagation, see *Geum.* Synonymes: 1. *Dalibarda fragarioides, Waldsteinia Doniana.* 2. *D. fragarioides.*

| | | | | | |
|---|---|---|---|---|---|
| Doniáná, 1 | Yellow | 5, H. Her. | P. N. Amer. | 1800 |
| fragarioídés, 2 | White | 5, H. Her. | P. N. Amer. | 1803 |

**COMÁRÚM**, *Linn.* Derived from *komaron*, the arbutus; on account of the similarity of its fruit. *Linn.* 12, *Or.* 3, *Nat. Or. Rosacee.* An interesting plant, growing in any moist soil, and increased by divisions. Synonyme: 1. *Potentilla comarum.*

| | | | | | |
|---|---|---|---|---|---|
| palústré, 1 | Purple | 6, H. Her. | P. Britain | |

**COMÁTÚS**, tufted.
**COMBRÉTÚM**, *Læffling.* A name given to a climbing plant by Pliny. *Linn.* 8, *Or.* 1, *Nat. Or. Combretacee.* Plants surpassed by few in the elegance and brilliancy of their blossoms; they all thrive well in loam and peat, and cuttings of the young wood root readily in a pot of sand, in a moist heat, with a glass over them. The climbing species are well adapted to training up the rafters, or covering the trellis-work in a stove. Synonyme: 1. *C. laxum.*

| | | | | | |
|---|---|---|---|---|---|
| élegans | Scarlet | 5, S. Ev. Cl. | Brazil | 1820 |
| farinósúm | Oran. red | 5, S. Ev. Cl. | Mexico | 1825 |
| grandiflórúm | Scarlet | 5, S. Ev. S. | Sierra Leone | 1824 |
| nánúm | White | 8. Ev. S. | Nepal | 1825 |
| paniculátúm | Scarlet | 9, S. Ev. Cl. | Guinea | 1824 |
| racemósúm | White | 5, S. Ev. Cl. | Benin | 1826 |
| secúndúm, 1 | Viv. str. | 5, S. Ev. Cl. | Trinidad | 1818 |

**COMÓSPERMÁ**, *Labillardière.* From *kome*, the hair of the head; and *sperma*, a seed; alluding to the tuft of hairs at the end of the seed. *Linn.* 14, *Or.* 5, *Nat. Or. Polygalacee.* These species are well worthy of cultivation, succeeding best in sandy loam and peat, and young cuttings will root freely in sand, under a glass.

| | | | | | | |
|---|---|---|---|---|---|---|
| cordifòlia | Purple | 8, G. Ev. S. | N. Holl. | 1822 |
| ericina | Purple | 6, G. Ev. S. | N. Holl. | 1822 |
| grácilis | Blue | 4, G. De. Tw. | Australia | 1834 |

**COMFREY**, see *Sỹmphỹtum.*

**COMMELÌNA**, *Linn.* In honour of J. and G. Commelin, famous Dutch botanists. *Linn.* 3, Or. 1, Nat. Or. *Commelinaceæ.* Some of the plants of this genus are very handsome; the stove kinds grow freely in a mixture of sandy loam and peat, and are increased by divisions or seeds. The hardy kinds thrive in common garden soil, and are increased by offsets from the roots, or by seeds; the annual species require the same treatment as other hardy and tender annuals.

| | | | | | |
|---|---|---|---|---|---|
| africàna | Blue | 7, G. Ev. Tr. | C. G. H. | 1759 |
| angustifòlia | Blue | 6, F. Ev. Tr. | Carolina | 1827 |
| bengalènsis | Blue | 6, S. Ev. Tr. | Bengal | 1794 |
| Cajennènsis | Blue | 6, S. Ev. Tr. | Guiana | 1823 |
| caripènsis | Blue | 6, S. Her. P. | Trinidad | 1826 |
| caroliniàna | Pur. blue | H. Ev. Tr. | America | 1732 |
| ecclèsia | Blue | 6, S. Her. P. | | 1813 |
| commùnis | Pur. blue | 6, H. A. | America | 1732 |
| cucullàta | Blue | 7, G. A. | Brazil | 1825 |
| cyànea | Blue | 7, G. Ev. Tr. | N. Holl. | 1820 |
| deficiens | Blue | 8, S. Ev. Tr. | Brazil | 1823 |
| dianthifòlia | Blue | 7, S. Tw. P. | | 1816 |
| dùbia | Blue | 6, S. Ev. Tr. | | 1818 |
| erècta | Blue | 8, H. Her. P. | Virginia | 1782 |
| fasciculàta | Blue | 6, H. Her. P. | Lima | 1817 |
| grácilis | Blue | 7, G. Her. P. | Lima | 1830 |
| hirtèlla | Blue | 6, H. Her. P. | N. Amer. | 1820 |
| longicaùlis | Blue | 8, S. Ev. Tr. | Caracas | 1806 |
| mollis | Blue | 8, S. Ev. Tr. | Caracas | 1804 |
| oblìqua | Blue | 6, S. Ev. Tr. | | 1820 |
| pallìda | Blue | 6, S. Ev. Tr. | Trinidad | 1820 |
| parviflòra | Blue | 6, S. Ev. Tr. | | 1824 |
| polygàma | Blue | 6, S. Ev. Tr. | China | 1818 |
| tuberòsa | Blue | 8, S. Her. P. | Mexico | 1732 |
| virginica | Blue | 6, H. Ev. Tr. | Virginia | 1779 |

**COMMERSÒNIA**, *Forster.* In honour of Philibert Commerson, M.D., a French botanist and traveller, who died in 1774. *Linn.* 5, Or. 5, Nat. Or. *Sterculiaceæ.* These ornamental shrubs thrive well in a mixture of peat and loam, and cuttings of the ripened wood will root readily in sand, under a glass, in heat.

| | | | | | |
|---|---|---|---|---|---|
| echinàta | White | 8. Ev. S. | Moluccas | 1820 |
| platyphỹlla | White | 6, 8. Ev. S. | Moluccas | 1806 |

**COMMINUTED**, pulverised, pounded.

**COMOCLÀDIA**, *P. Browne.* From *kome*, a tuft, and *klados*, a branch; the leaves being crowded at the tops of the branches. *Linn.* 8, Or. 1, Nat. Or. *Anacardiaceæ.* Ornamental trees, from fifteen to twenty feet high, succeeding well in a mixture of peat and loam, or any light rich soil; ripened cuttings will root in sand, under a glass, in heat.

| | | | | | |
|---|---|---|---|---|---|
| dentàta | Red | 7, S. Ev. S. | W. Ind. | 1790 |
| ilicifòlia | Red | 8. Ev. S. | Caribbee Is. | 1789 |
| integrifòlia | Red | 8. Ev. S. | Jamaica | 1778 |

**COMPACT**, close, crowded.

**COMPARÈTTIA**, *Pœppig and Endlicher.* Named after Andreas Comparetti, professor at Padua, and an eminent writer upon vegetable physiology. *Linn.* 20, Or. 1, Nat. Or. *Orchidaceæ.* This is a splendid but a very rare genus of plants, well worth cultivating for the brilliant colour of the flowers, and their very curious structure. They will be found to succeed well potted in good fibrous peat, and the pots efficiently drained with broken potsherds, which should be carried up the centre of the peat. The plants should be raised above the pot according to their size, in the same way as the *Stanhopeas.*

| | | | | | |
|---|---|---|---|---|---|
| coccínea | Scarlet | 8, S. Epi. | Brazil | 1838 |

**COMPLANATE**, flattened.

**COMPLICATE**, folded together.

**COMPOUND**, used in botany to express the union of several things into one.

**COMPRESSED**, pressed together, flattened.

**COMPTÒNIA**, *Banks.* In honour of Henry Compton, Lord Bishop of London, an ardent cultivator of exotics. *Linn.* 21, Or. 8, Nat. Or. *Myricaceæ.* A pretty shrub, growing about four feet high in light sandy loam or peat soil; increased by layers.

| | | | | | |
|---|---|---|---|---|---|
| asplenifòlia | Brown | 4, H. De. S. | N. Amer. | 1714 |

**CONANTHÈRA**, *Ruiz et Pavon.* From *konos*, a cone, and *anthera*, an anther; the anthers being united into a cone. *Linn.* 6, Or. 1, Nat. Or. *Liliaceæ.* A pretty genus of bulbs, growing best in light sandy

loam; increased by offsets. *Synonyme:* 1. *C. bifolia.*

| | | | | | |
|---|---|---|---|---|---|
| bifòlia | Blue | 4, G. Bu. P. | Chile | 1823 |
| Simsii, 1 | Blue | 4, G. Bu. P. | Chile | 1823 |

**CONCAVE**, hollow.

**CONCENTRIC**, points, or lines, at equal distances from a common centre.

**CONCRETE**, formed into one mass, joined together.

**CONDÀLIA**, *Cavanilles.* In honour of A. Condal, a Spanish botanist. *Linn.* 5, Or. 1, Nat. Or. *Rhamnaceæ.* A curious plant, growing about two feet high; cultivated in any common soil, and increased by cuttings. *Synonyme:* 1. *Zizyphus myrtoides.*

| | | | | | |
|---|---|---|---|---|---|
| microphỹlla, 1 | Green | F. Ev. S. | Chile | 1824 |

**CONDENSATE**, bundled, growing close.

**CONDYLOCÀRPUS**, *Hoffman.* From *kondyle*, a knob, and *karpos*, fruit; in allusion to the fruit. *Linn.* 5, Or. 2, Nat. Or. *Umbelliferæ.* The species are of the simplest culture. *Synonymes:* 1. *Tordylium apulum.* 2. *T. humile.* 3. *T. officinale—apulum* 1, *humile* 2, *officinale* 3.

**CONE**, a particular kind of compound fruit.

**CONFERRUMINATE**, united together so as to be undistinguishable.

**CONFÈRVA**, *Agardh.* Derived from the Latin *conferrumino*, to consolidate; because of the close coherence. *Linn.* 24, Or. 7, Nat. Or. *Algæ.* A very extensive and interesting genus of *Algæ*, found chiefly in the ocean, lakes, pools, ditches, &c.— *ægagròpila, ærea, æruginòsa, alpìna, árctà, áspera, bombycìna, Brownii, capillàris, càrnea, catenàta, collàbens, congregàta, cràssa, crispàta, cùrta, dissìliens, distàns, ericetòrum, fasciàta, ferrugìnea, flácca, fláccida, flavèscens, floccòsa, fráctà, fucòrum, glomeràta, heteròchloa, hormoìdes, Hutchìnsiæ, implèxa, intricàta, isogòna, lanòsa, linum, melagònium, mucòsum, pàtens, P. prolìfera, pellùcida, refrácta, ripària, rivulàris, R. ánglica, rupéstris, serìcea, stellàris, tortuòsa, tumidàta, vaucheriæfòrmis, vesicàta, V. fuscèscens, Youngàna, zonàta.*

**CONFLUENT**, running into one another at the base or apex.

**CONGLUTINATE**, glued together into one mass.

**CONICAL**, shaped like a cone.

**CONICALLY-SUBULATE**, between cone and awl-shaped, thickest at the base.

**CONICO-CYLINDRICAL**, form of a cylinder, but tapering to a point.

**CONICO-SUBULATE**, awl-shaped and conical, tapering to a point.

**CONIC-OVATE**, between egg-shaped and conical.

**CONJUGATE**, joined in pairs; chiefly applied to leaves.

**CONÌUM.** Derived, according to Linnæus, from *konis*, dust or powder; the application of the term is not evident. *Linn.* 5, Or. 2, Nat. Or. *Umbelliferæ.* The annual species of this genus merely require sowing in the open ground in autumn; the stove species delights in a rich mould, and is increased by dividing the roots. In the south of Europe *C. maculatum* is a dangerous poison, while in Russia and the Crimea it is innocuous and eatable.

| | | | | | |
|---|---|---|---|---|---|
| croàticum | White | 7, H. Her. P. | Hungary | 1818 |
| maculàtum | White | 6, H. B. | Britain | |
| moschàtum | White | 6, S. Fu. P. | S. Amer. | 1824 |

**CONNÀRUS**, *Linn.* From *connaros*, the name of a tree described by Athenæus. *Linn.* 16, Or. 6, Nat. Or. *Connaraceæ.* The species of this genus are ornamental plants, growing from six to eight feet high; they succeed best in a mixture of peat and loam, and increase by cuttings of the ripened wood in sand, under a glass, in heat.

| | | | | | |
|---|---|---|---|---|---|
| nitìdus | White | S. Ev. S. | Silhet | 1824 |
| paniculàtus | White | S. Ev. S. | Chittagong | 1824 |
| pubèscens | White | S. Ev. S. | Guiana | 1822 |

**CONNÀTUS**, joined together at the base.

**CONNIVING**, converging, lying close together.

**CONOCÀRPUS**, *Linn.* From *konos*, a cone, and *karpos*, a fruit; the fruit is so closely imbricated in a head as to resemble a fir cone. *Linn.* 5, Or. 1, Nat. Or. *Combretaceæ.* Ornamental shrubs. For culture and propagation, see *Bucida.* The bark of *C. racemosus* is much used in Rio Janeiro for tanning.

| | | | | | |
|---|---|---|---|---|---|
| acutifòlius | Pa. yel. | S. Ev. S. | Amer. | 1824 |
| erèctus | White | S. Ev. S. | Jamaica | 1752 |
| procùmbens | Pa. yel. | S. Ev. S. | Cuba | 1700 |
| racemòsus | White | S. Ev. S. | Amer. | 1820 |

CONOCĔPHĂLŬS, *Blume*. From *konos*, a cone, and *kephale*, a head; referring to the form of the flowers. *Linn.* 21, Or. 4, Nat. Or. *Urticaceæ*. A curious plant, growing about ten feet high; cultivated in peat and loam, and increased by cuttings in sand, under a glass, in heat.

| | | | | | |
|---|---|---|---|---|---|
| naucleiflŏrŭs, 1 | Yellow | | 8. Ev. 8. | Chittagong | 1820 |

CONOID, cone-shaped.

CONOPŌDĬUM, *Koch*. From *konos*, a cone, and *podion*, a little foot; form of flowers. *Linn.* 5, Or. 2, Nat. Or. *Umbelliferæ*. Plants of little beauty; may be grown in any common soil, and increased by dividing the roots. *Synonymes*: 1. *Sison canadense*. 2. *Myrrhis Claytoni*. 3. *Bunium denudatum*.

| | | | | | |
|---|---|---|---|---|---|
| Claytoni, 2 | White | | 7, H. Her. P. | N. Amer. | 1806 |

*canadĕnsĕ* 1, *denudātŭm* 3.

CONŎPSĔUM, resembling a gnat.

CONOSPĔRMŬM, *Smith*. From *konos*, a cone, and *sperma*, a seed. *Linn.* 4, Or. 1, Nat. Or. *Proteaceæ*. An ornamental genus of plants, thriving well in sandy peat, and readily increased by cuttings in sand, under a glass.

| | | | | |
|---|---|---|---|---|
| acinacifolĭŭm | White | 7, G. Ev. 8. N. Holl. | 1824 |
| cærūlĕŭm | Blue | 6, G. Ev. 8. N. Holl. | 1830 |
| capitātŭm | Blue | 7, G. Ev. 8. N. Holl. | 1824 |
| ellipticŭm | White | 6, G. Ev. 8. N. Holl. | 1822 |
| ericĭfolĭŭm | White | 7, G. Ev. 8. N. Holl. | 1820 |
| longifolĭŭm | White | 7, G. Ev. 8. N. Holl. | 1824 |
| taxifolĭŭm | White | 7, G. Ev. 8. N. Holl. | 1824 |
| tenuifolĭŭm | White | 7, G. Ev. 8. N. Holl. | 1824 |
| triplinervĭŭm | | G. Ev. 8. N. Holl. | 1830 |

CONŎSTŎMŬM, *Swartz*. From *konos*, a cone, and *stoma*, a mouth; the teeth of the theca are united. *Linn.* 24, Or. 5, Nat. Or. *Musci*. A curious species of moss, found during summer on some of the Scotch mountains. *Synonyme*: 1. *Grimmia conostoma-boreālē* 1.

CONOSTYLĬS, *R. Brown*. From *konos*, a cone, and *stylos*, a style; the styles are united. *Linn.* 6, Or. 1, Nat. Or. *Hæmodoraceæ*. Rather an ornamental genus, growing about a foot high; sandy peat suits them, and they are increased by dividing the roots.

| | | | | |
|---|---|---|---|---|
| aculeātă | | G. Her. P. N. Holl. | 1820 |
| serrulātă | | G. Her. P. N. Holl. | 1824 |
| setigĕră | | G. Her. P. N. Holl. | 1825 |

CONSPĔRSŬS, scattered, or sprinkled.

CONSTRICTED, tightened, or contracted in some particular place.

CONTORTUPLICATE, twisted in plaits.

CONTRACTED, narrowed in some particular place.

CONTRAJĔRVĂ-ROOT, see *Dorstĕnĭă Contrajĕrvă*.

CONVALLĂRĬĂ, *Linn*. From the Latin *convallis*, a valley; in allusion to the situation where it grows. *Linn.* 6, Or. 1, Nat. Or. *Liliaceæ*. The Lily of the Valley is a sweet little plant, thriving in any common soil; it will do well in any shady situation where few other plants will succeed; it is multiplied by dividing the roots.

| | | | | | |
|---|---|---|---|---|---|
| majālis | White | 5, H. Her. P. | Britain | |
| flŏrĕ-plēnŏ | White | 5, H. Her. P. | Britain | |
| rūbră | Flesh | 5, H. Her. P. | Britain | |

CONVEX, rising in a circular form.

CONVOLUTE, rolled together, or over each other.

CONVOLVŬLŬS, *Linn*. Derived from the Latin *convolvere*, to entwine or wind about; in reference to the habit of the plants. *Linn.* 5, Or. 1, Nat. Or. *Convolvulaceæ*. Being mostly showy plants, the tender species are best adapted to stoves and conservatories: they are best cultivated in loam and peat, and cuttings strike very freely in sand, under a glass; the half-hardy annual kinds should be sown on a gentle hotbed, and when of sufficient size planted out into the open border, the hardy kinds only require sowing in the open ground; the stove and greenhouse annuals and biennials require to be sown in the stove, and treated as other stove and greenhouse annuals and biennials. The roots of *C. arvensis* and *macrocarpus* abound in a milky juice which is highly purgative, and the roots of *C. floridus* and *scoparius* are used as sternutatories. *Synonymes*: 1. *C. Pseudo-siculus*. 2. *C. decumbens*.

| | | | | | |
|---|---|---|---|---|---|
| albivēnĭŭs | Pa. pink | 6, S. Ev. Cl. | Algoa | 1823 |
| althæoīdēs | Pink | 6, H. De. Tw. | Levant | 1597 |
| arborescĕns | | 8. Ev. 8. | Mexico | 1818 |
| bicolŏr | Wht. pur. | 7, 8. Tw. A. | Isle Fra. | 1818 |
| bicuspidātŭs | Purple | 6, H. De. Tw. | Davuria | 1818 |
| bonariĕnsis | White | 7, H. De. Tw. | Chile | 1817 |
| bryonifolĭŭs | Pink | 7, G. De. Tw. | China | 1802 |
| canariĕnsis | Pink | 6, G. Ev. Tw. | Canaries | 1690 |
| cantabricŭs | Pink | 6, H. De. Tr. | 8. Eur. | 1640 |
| chinĕnsis | Purple | 7, H. De. Tw. | China | 1817 |
| ciliātŭs | Pink | 7, 8. Ev. Tw. | Cayenne | 1816 |
| Cneorŭm | Pink | 6, G. Ev. 8. | Levant | 1640 |
| cŏrsĭcŭs | Pink | 6, H. De. Tw. | Corsica | 1824 |
| Dorycnĭŭm | Flesh | 7, H. De. Tr. | Levant | 1806 |
| ebracteātŭs | White | 7, H. De. Tr. | | 1819 |
| elongātŭs, 1 | White | 7, H. Tw. A. | Canaries | 1815 |
| emarginātŭs | Purple | 7, H. De. Tw. | | 1817 |
| erubescĕns | Pink | 7, G. Tw. B. | N. S. W. | 1803 |
| evolvuloīdēs, 2 | Red | 7, G. A. | 8. Eur. | 1820 |
| farinōsŭs | Pink | 5, G. Ev. Tw. | Madeira | 1777 |
| florĭdŭs | Pink | 8, G. Ev. Tr. | Canaries | 1799 |
| Gerardī | Pink | 6, H. De. Tr. | 8. Eur. | |
| glabĕr | White | 5, 8. Ev. Tw. | Cayenne | 1806 |
| guianĕnsis | White | 8, 8. Ev. Tw. | Guiana | 1823 |
| Hermānnĭā | White | 8, G. Ev. Tw. | Peru | 1799 |
| hirtŭs | Blue | 7, 8. Tr. A. | E. Ind. | 1804 |
| imperātī | Yellow | 7, H. De. Cr. | Naples | 1824 |
| lanuginōsŭs | White | 7, H. Tw. | Levant | 1818 |
| lineārĭs | Pink | 6, G. Ev. 8. | 8. Eur. | 1770 |
| lineātŭs | Purple | 6, H. De. Tr. | 8. Eur. | 1770 |
| macrocārpŭs | Purple | 7, 8. Tw. A. | 8. Amer. | 1752 |
| māxĭmŭs | Pink | 7, 8. Ev. Tw. | Ceylon | 1799 |
| ochrācĕŭs | Yellow | 7, 8. Ev. Tw. | Guinea | 1825 |
| pannifolĭŭs | Blue | 8, G. Ev. Tw. | Canaries | 1805 |
| pentapetaloīdēs | Li. blue | 7, H. Tr. A. | Majorca | 1789 |
| pentanthŭs | Li. blue | 8, 8. Ev. Tw. | E. Ind. | 1808 |
| quinquefolĭŭs | White | 7, 8. Tw. A. | W. Ind. | 1808 |
| reptāns | Purple | 7, 8. Ev. Cr. | E. Ind. | 1806 |
| salvĭfolĭŭs | Pink | 7, H. De. Tw. | Palestine | 1825 |
| saxātĭlĭs | White | 7, G. Ev. Tr. | 8. Eur. | 1796 |
| Scammōnĭă | Wht. par. | 7, H. De. Tw. | Levant | 1596 |
| scopārĭŭs | White | 8, G. Ev. Tr. | Canaries | 1733 |
| scrobiculātŭs | Pa. red. | 8. Ev. Tr. | 8. Amer. | 1825 |
| Sibthŏrpĭī | White | 7, H. De. Tr. | France | 1823 |
| sicŭlŭs | Li. blue | 7, H. Tr. A. | 8. Eur. | 1640 |
| suffruticōsŭs | Pink | 7, G. Ev. Tw. | Madeira | 1788 |
| tiliācĕŭs | Purple | 7, G. Ev. Tw. | Brazil | 1820 |
| tricolŏr | Striped | 7, H. A. | 8. Eur. | 1629 |
| albiflŏrŭs | White | 7, H. A. | 8. Eur. | 1629 |
| verticillātŭs | Blue | 8, 8. Ev. Tw. | W. Ind. | 1819 |

*arvĕnsĭs, bogotĕnsĭs, dentātŭs, filicaulĭs, hirsūtŭs, intermēdĭŭs, itālĭcŭs, micrānthŭs, multifĭdŭs, serōtĭnŭs.*

CONYZĂ, *Linn*. From *konis*, dust; because it was supposed to have the power, when it was powdered and sprinkled, of driving away flies, whence the name Flea (Fly)-bane. *Linn.* 19, Or. 2, Nat. Or. *Compositæ*. Plants of no beauty. The stove and greenhouse shrubby kinds grow well in loam and peat; young cuttings root under a glass. The hardy herbaceous kinds grow in any garden soil, and increase by divisions or seeds. The hardy and tender kinds require the same treatment as other hardy and tender annuals. *Synonyme*: 1. *Conyza candida*.

| | | | | |
|---|---|---|---|---|
| gnistelloīdēs | Yellow | 8. Ev. 8. 8. Amer. | 1824 |
| odorātă | Purple | 7, 8. Ev. 8. India | 1759 |

*ægyptĭācă, amœnă, amplexicaulĭs, arborescĕns, aurĭtă, axillārĭs, balsamifĕră, bifrōns, camphorātă, cāndĭdă, carolinĕnsĭs, chinĕnsĭs, cinĕrĕă, fastigĭātă, fœtĭdă, geminiflŏră, glomerātă, Gouānī, hirsūtă, incīsă, inuloīdēs, limonifolĭă 1, marylāndĭcă, paniculātă, pātŭlă, pinnatĭfĭdă, prolifĕră, purpurascĕns, rigĭdă, rugōsă, rupĕstrĭs, saxātĭlĭs, sericĕă, sicŭlă, sŏrdĭdă, spatulātă, squarrōsă, Tenŏrĭī, thapsoīdēs, verbascifolĭŭm, virgātă.*

COŎKĬĂ, *Sonnerat*. In memory of the celebrated circumnavigator Capt. James Cook, R.N., who was killed in the Sandwich Islands in 1779. *Linn.* 10, Or. 1, Nat. Or. *Aurantiaceæ*. An ornamental stove tree, requiring to be cultivated in a mixture of loam and peat, and cuttings of the ripened wood with their leaves on will root in sand, under a glass, in a moist heat. A fruit called wampee, which is highly esteemed in China and the Indian archipelago, is the produce of this tree.

| | | | | |
|---|---|---|---|---|
| punctātă | White | 8. Ev. T. China | 1795 |

COOPĔRĬĂ, *Herbert*. In compliment to Mr. Joseph Cooper, one of the most zealous and successful cultivators of rare plants in this kingdom, and who has had, for upwards of twenty years, the management of the botanic garden at Wentworth House, the property and residence of Earl Fitzwilliam. *Linn.* 6, Or. 1, Nat. Or. *Amaryllidaceæ*. Very interesting flowering bulbs; a sandy compost appears to suit them well, with a copious supply of water they increase freely from seed. The flower is fragrant, smelling like a primrose, and is produced at night.

| | | | | | |
|---|---|---|---|---|---|
| chlorānthēs | . Wht. grn. | . G. Bu. P. | Mexico | . 1835 |
| Drummōndīī | . Wht. red | . G. Bu. P. | Mexico | . 1835 |

COPAYFĒRĀ, *Linn.* Derived from the Brazilian name, *copaiba*, and *fero*, to bear. The balsam of Capevi is the produce of this genus. *Linn.* 10, Or. 1, Nat. Or. *Amyridaceæ.* Valuable species, because of their medical properties. They are best cultivated in sandy loam; ripened cuttings will root in sand, under a glass, in heat.

| | | | | | |
|---|---|---|---|---|---|
| guianēnsīs | . White. | . S. Ev. T. | Guiana | . 1826 |
| officinālīs | . White. | . S. Ev. T. | S. Amer. | . 1774 |

COPRĪNŪS, *Persoon.* Named from *kopria*, dung; species found on dunghills. *Linn.* 24, Or. 9, Nat. Or. *Fungi.* The species of this genus are found on dunghills, trunks of trees, shady damp places, &c. —*atramentārīūs, cinērēūs, comātūs, domēstīcūs, ephēmērūs, Lagōpūs, micaceus, vīrēns, pīlācēūs, plicātīlīs, rudīātūs.*

COPTIS, *Salisbury.* From *kopto*, to cut; in allusion to the divisions of the leaves. *Linn.* 13, Or. 6, Nat. Or. *Ranunculaceæ.* A pretty species, well worthy of a place in every garden, succeeding well in a bed of peat soil, or grown in pots, and protected in severe weather, increased by divisions or seeds. In the United States, the root of this plant is a popular remedy for apthous affections of the mouth in children. *Synonyme*: 1. *Helleborus trifolius.*

| | | | | | |
|---|---|---|---|---|---|
| trifoliātā, 1 | . Brown | . 5, H. Her. P. | N. Amer. | . 1782 |

CORALLOID, like coral.

CORAL TREE, see *Erythrīnā corallodēndrōn.*

CORALLŌRHĪZĀ, *Swartz.* Said to be from *korallion*, a coral, and *rhiza*, a root. *Linn.* 20, Or. 1, Nat. Or. *Orchidaceæ.* A genus of curious, bulbous-rooted, perfectly hardy plants. They grow well in peat and loam, and are readily increased by divisions.

| | | | | | |
|---|---|---|---|---|---|
| innātā | . Green | . 6, H. Ter. | Scotland |
| multiflōrā | . Green | . 6, H. Ter. | N. Amer. | . 1824 |
| odontorhīzā | . Green | . 6, H. Ter. | N. Amer. | . 1824 |

CORANIC POISON-BULB, see *Brunsvīgīā cordācā.*

CORBULĀRĪĀ, *Haworth.* From *corbula*, a little basket; in reference to the shape of the nectary. *Linn.* 6, Or. 1, Nat. Or. *Amaryllidaceæ.* An ornamental species, thriving best in a light loamy soil in a sheltered situation; it also succeeds well in pots treated as a bulbous frame plant. *Synonyme*: 1. *Narcissus bulbocodium.*

| | | | | | |
|---|---|---|---|---|---|
| serotīnā, 1 | . Yellow | . 3, H. Bu. P. | Portugal | . 1629 |

CORCHŌRŪS, *Linn.* From *kore*, a pupil, and *koreo*, to purge; in allusion to the laxative qualities of *C. olitorius. Linn.* 13, Or. 1, Nat. Or. *Tiliaceæ.* A genus of stove shrubs and annuals, of easy cultivation. In India, fishing lines and nets, rice bags, and a coarse kind of linen are made from *C. capsularis.*

| | | | | | |
|---|---|---|---|---|---|
| hirtūs | . Yellow | . 7, S. Ev. S. | S. Amer. | . 1820 |
| pilolobūs | . Yellow | . 7, S. Ev. S. | S. Amer. | . 1818 |
| tridēns | . Yellow | . 7, S. Ev. S. | Senegal | . 1824 |

*acutiāngūlūs, æstūāns, capsulārīs, hirsūtūs, olitōrīūs, siliqūōsūs, triloculārīs.*

CORDATE, formed like a heart.

CORDATE, when joined by a hyphen to another word, signifies a figure between the two, as cordate-reniform, a figure between heart-shaped and kidney-shaped: cordate-auriculate, having auricles at the base, so as to give the leaf the figure of a heart.

CORDIĀ, *Linn.* In honour of E. Cordus, a German botanist of the sixteenth century. *Linn.* 5, Or. 1, Nat. Or. *Cordiaceæ.* An ornamental genus, many of the species being fine timber-trees, upwards of sixty feet high; best cultivated in loam and peat, and cuttings root freely in sand, under a glass, in heat. The flesh of the fruit of *C. Myxa* and *Sebestena* is succulent, mucilaginous, and emollient. *Synonymes*: 1. *Varronia alba.* 2. *V. alnifolia.* 3. *V. angustifolia.* 4. *V. monosperma.* 5. *V. bullata, V. globosa.* 6. *V. lineata.* 7. *V. martinicensis.* 8. *V. mirabiloides.*

| | | | | | |
|---|---|---|---|---|---|
| albā, 1 | . White. | . S. Ev. S. | Trinidad | . 1820 |
| alnifōlīā, 2 | . White. | . S. Ev. S. | | . 1818 |
| angustifōlīā, 3 | . White. | . S. Ev. S. | Santa Cruz | 1808 |
| collocōcā | . Green | . S. Ev. T. | Jamaica | . 1759 |
| corymbōsā, 4 | . White. | . S. Ev. T. | Caraccas | . 1800 |

| | | | | | |
|---|---|---|---|---|---|
| dentātā | . White | . 8. Ev. T. | Curacoa | . 1819 |
| dichōtōmā | . Pink | . 8. Ev. T. | N. Holl. | . 1824 |
| Dillēnīī | . Orange | . 4, 8. Ev. T. | Bahama | . 1700 |
| domēstīcā | . Orange | . 8. Ev. T. | E. Ind. | . 1820 |
| ellipticā | . White | . 8. Ev. T. | W. Ind. | . 1804 |
| flavēscēns | . White | . 8. Ev. S. | Guiana | . 1823 |
| Geraschānthūs | . Pink | . 5, 8. Ev. T. | W. Ind. | . 1789 |
| globosā, 5 | . White | . 8, 8. Ev. S. | Jamaica | . 1818 |
| grandiflōrā | . White | . 9, G. Ev. S. | S. Amer. | . 1827 |
| lævis | . Red | . 7, 8. Ev. F. | Trinidad | . 1826 |
| lineātā, 6 | . White | . 8. Ev. S. | W. Ind. | . 1793 |
| macrophyllā | . White | . 8. Ev. T. | W. Ind. | . 1752 |
| martinicēnsīs, 7 | . White | . 8, 8. Ev. S. | Martiniq. | . 1795 |
| micrānthā | . White | . 8. Ev. T. | Guiana | . 1822 |
| mirabilōīdēs, 8 | . White | . 9, 8. Ev. T. | Hispaniola | . 1793 |
| monoīcā | . White | . 4, 8. Ev. T. | E. Ind. | . 1799 |
| Myxā | . White | . 8. Ev. T. | E. Ind. | . 1644 |
| nervōsā | . White | . 8. Ev. T. | E. Ind. | . 1820 |
| nodōsā | . White | . 6, 8. Ev. S. | Guiana | . 1808 |
| obliquā | . White | . 8. Ev. T. | E. Ind. | . 1818 |
| parviflōrā | . White | . 8. Ev. T. | Jamaica | . 1819 |
| reticulātā | . Yellow | . 8. Ev. T. | E. Ind. | . 1820 |
| rugōsā | . Orange | . 8. Ev. T. | S. Amer. | . 1825 |
| Sebestēnā | . White | . 7, 8. Ev. T. | W. Ind. | . 1728 |
| spinēscēns | . White | . 8. Ev. T. | E. Ind. | . 1824 |

CORDIGĒRĀ, heart-lipped.

CORDYLĪNĒ, *Commerson.* From *kordyle*, signifying a club. *Linn.* 6, Or. 1, Nat. Or. *Liliaceæ.* Ornamental shrubs, cultivated in a mixture of peat and loam, or any light vegetable soil; readily increased by suckers.

| | | | | | |
|---|---|---|---|---|---|
| cannæfōlīā | . | . S. Ev. S. | N. Holl. | . 1820 |
| hemichrysā | . | . S. Ev. S. | Bourbon | . 1823 |

CORĒMĀ, *D. Don.* From *corema*, a broom; in allusion to the habit of the plant. *Linn.* 22, Or. 3, Nat. Or. *Empetraceæ.* An ornamental dwarf shrub, succeeding well in sandy peat, and increased by layers.

| | | | | | |
|---|---|---|---|---|---|
| albā, 1 | . Apetal | . 4, H. Ev. S. | Portugal | . 1774 |

CORĒMĪŪM, *Nees.* From *korema*, filth; found there. *Linn.* 24, Or. 9, Nat. Or. *Fungi.* A very minute fungus, found on old paste, &c.—*glaūcūm.*

CORĪŌPSIS, *Linn.* From *koris*, a bug, and *opsis*, appearance; because of the resemblance of the seeds. *Linn.* 19, Or. 3, Nat. Or. *Compositæ.* A very pretty genus of plants, the stove perennial kinds grow freely in any rich light soil, and cuttings root under a glass; some of the hardy kinds are tall growing plants well adapted to the back of flower borders, or vacant places in the shrubbery, some of the smaller species are very handsome, and may be planted near the front; they are increased by divisions of the roots. The hardy and tender annuals and biennials require the same treatment as other hardy and tender annuals and biennials.

| | | | | | |
|---|---|---|---|---|---|
| albā | . White | . 6, S. Ev. | Tw. Jamaica | . 1699 |
| angustifōlīā | . Yellow | . 7, H. Her. P. | N. Amer. | . 1778 |
| argūtā | . Yellow | . 8, H. Her. P. | Carolina | . |
| aūrēā | . Yellow | . 8, H. Her. P. | N. Amer. | . 1785 |
| auriculātā | . Yellow | . 7, H. Her. P. | N. Amer. | . 1699 |
| chrysānthā | . Yellow | . 8, S. B. | W. Ind. | . 1752 |
| coronātā | . Yel. brn. | . 7, H. Her. P. | Mexico | . 1835 |
| crassifōlīā | . Yellow | . 9, H. Her. P. | Carolina | . 1786 |
| dichōtōmā | . Yellow | . 8, H. Her. P. | Carolina | . 1827 |
| diversifōlīā | . Blood | . 7, H. A. | N. Amer. | . 1833 |
| ferulæfōlīā | . Yellow | . 10, F. Her. P. | Mexico | . 1799 |
| silifōlīā | . Yellow | . 8, H. A. | Texas | . 1835 |
| grandiflōrā | . Yellow | . 8, H. Her. P. | N. Amer. | . 1826 |
| incisā | . Yellow | . 10, S. Ev. | Tw. W. Ind. | . |
| integrifōlīā | . Yellow | . 7, H. Her. P. | Carolina | . |
| lanceolātā | . Yellow | . 8, H. B. | Carolina | . 1724 |
| latifōlīā | . Yellow | . 8, H. Her. P. | N. Amer. | . 1786 |
| lōngīpēs | . Yellow | . 4, H. A. | Texas | . 1835 |
| rēptāns | . Yellow | . 7, S. Tw. A. | W. Ind. | . 1792 |
| senifōlīā | . Yellow | . 8, H. Her. P. | N. Amer. | . 1812 |
| tenuifōlīā | . Yellow | . 7, H. Her. P. | N. Amer. | . 1780 |
| trichospērmā | . Yellow | . 8, H. B. | N. Jersey | . 1818 |
| verticillātā | . Yellow | . 8, H. Her. P. | N. Amer. | . 1750 |

*amplexicaūlīs.*

CORKOPSIS, see *Chrȳsostēmmā.*

CORIACEOUS, thick, tough, like leather.

CORIANDER, see *Coriāndrūm.*

CORIĀNDRŪM, *Hoffmann.* From *koris*, a bug; alluding to the smell of the leaves. *Linn.* 5, Or. 2, Nat. Or. *Umbelliferæ.* A species of little beauty, which only requires to be sown in the open ground. The fruit is a well-known warm, and agreeable aromatic.

| | | | | | |
|---|---|---|---|---|---|
| satīvūm | . White | . 6, H. A. | England |

CORIĀRĪĀ, *Linn.* From *corium*, a hide. *Linn.* 22, Or. 9, Nat. Or. *Coriariaceæ.* Ornamental shrubs, the hardy species succeeds well in the open border, and is readily increased by cuttings of the roots, or by suckers. The other species thrives well in a mixture of sand, loam, and peat, and cuttings under a glass, in the same kind of soil, will root freely. *C. myrtifolia* is not only used in tanning leather, but also for staining black. Its fruit is poisonous.

| | | | | | |
|---|---|---|---|---|---|
| myrtifolia | . . | Green | . 6, H. Ev. S. S. Eur. | . 1629 |
| sarmentosa | . | Green | . 6, G. Ev. S. N. Zeal. | . 1822 |

**CŎRĬS**, *Linn.* A Greek name, used by Dioscorides. *Linn.* 5, Or. 1, Nat. Or. *Primulaceæ.* An ornamental little plant, rather of a succulent nature, growing in peat and loam, with the pots well drained and a limited supply of water; it produces seeds in great plenty.

| | | | | |
|---|---|---|---|---|
| monspeliensis | . | Lilac | . 6, G. | B. S. Eur. | . 1640 |

**CORISPĔRMŬM**, *Linn.* From *koris*, a bug, or tick, and *sperma*, a seed. *Linn.* 1, Or. 2, Nat. Or. *Chenopodiaceæ.* Worthless hardy annuals, which merely require sowing in the open ground—*canēscēns, glomerātūm, hyssopifōlĭūm, intermēdĭūm, Marschāllĭĭ, nĭtĭdūm, pātēns, pūngēns, Redōwskĭĭ, sabulōsūm, squarrōsūm, tĕnŭĕ.*

**CORK-TREE,** see *Quercus sǔbĕr.*

**CORKWOOD,** see *Anōnā palūstrĭs.*

**CORN-COCKLE,** see *Lўchnis Gĭthāgŏ.*

**CORNELIAN CHERRY,** see *Cornus māscŭlā.*

**CORN-FLAG,** see *Gladiōlūs bullātūs.*

**CORNICULATED,** furnished with little horns.

**CORNICULĀRĬA**, *Acharius.* From *corniculus*, a little horn; referring to the divisions of the thallus. *Linn.* 24, Or. 9, Nat. Or. *Lichenes.* A genus of *Lichenes* found on mountains and alpine rocks—*aculeātā, A. spadīcĕā, bĭcŏlŏr, heteromāllā, lanātā, ochrolēūcā, pulēscēns, trīstis.*

**CORNISH MONEYWORT,** see *Sĭbthōrpĭā europœā.*

**CORNUCŎPĬÆ**, *Linn.* From *cornu*, a horn, and *copia*, plenty; the spike inclosed in the involucrum resembles the horn of plenty. *Linn.* 3, Or. 1, Nat. Or. *Gramineæ.* This is an annual grass, that only requires to be sown in the open ground.

| | | | | |
|---|---|---|---|---|
| cucullātŭm | . . . | Apetal | . 8, Grass. | Levant | . 1788 |

**CŎRNŬS**, *Tournefort.* Derived from *cornu*, a horn; the wood being thought as hard and durable as horn. *Linn.* 14, Or. 1, Nat. Or. *Cornaceæ.* This is an ornamental genus, consisting principally of trees and shrubs, that succeed well in any common soil; they are increased by seeds or by layers, the herbaceous species are generally grown in pots, but they grow well in a bed of peat, and are increased by dividing the roots. The bark of *C. florida* and *sericea* is said to rank among the best tonics of N. America.

| | | | | |
|---|---|---|---|---|
| alba | . . . | White | . 7, H. De. | T. Siberia | . 1741 |
| rŭgŏsā | . . | White | . 7, H. De. | T. Siberia | . 1820 |
| alternifōlĭā | . | White | . 7, H. De. | T. N. Amer. | . 1760 |
| canadēnsis | . | White | . 7, H. Her. | P. Canada | . 1774 |
| circinātā | . | White | . 7, H. De. | S. N. Amer. | . 1784 |
| flŏrĭdā | . | White | . 7, H. De. | T. N. Amer. | . 1731 |
| māscŭlā | . | Yellow | . 2, H. De. | T. Austria | . 596 |
| variegātā | . | Yellow | . 6, H. De. | T. Austria | . 1596 |
| oblōngā | . | Purple | . H. De. | T. Nepal | . 1818 |
| panĭculātā | . | White | . 6, H. De. | S. Britain | . 1758 |
| sanguĭneā | . | White | . 6, H. De. | S. Britain | . |
| variegātā | . | White | . 6, H. De. | S. Britain | . |
| serĭceā | . | White | . 8, H. De. | S. N. Amer. | . 1683 |
| sibīrĭcā | . | White | . 7, H. De. | S. Siberia | . 1824 |
| strĭctā | . | White | . 6, H. De. | T. N. Amer. | . 1758 |
| variegātā | . | White | . 6, H. De. | T. N. Amer. | . 1758 |
| suēcĭcā | . | White | . 4, H. Her. | P. Britain | . |

**CORNŪTĀ,** horned, furnished with horns.

**CORNŪTĬA**, *Linn.* Named after Jacques Cornutus, a French physician and traveller. *Linn.* 2, Or. 1, Nat. Or. *Verbenaceæ.* An ornamental shrub growing about six feet high, succeeding well in a mixture of loam and peat; cuttings strike freely in sand, under a glass.

| | | | | |
|---|---|---|---|---|
| pyramidātā | . | Blue | . 7, S. Ev. S. | Mexico | . 1733 |

**CORNWRED,** see *Biscrrŭlā Pelecīnŭs.*

**COROLLA,** the coloured part of a flower, composed of a petal or petals. The term is only applied when the calyx is persistent, otherwise it is called a perianth.

**CORŎNĀ,** a crown; in botany applied to the crownlike cup, which is found at the orifice of the tube of the corolla in *Narcissus, Pancratium,* and some others.

**CORONILLA**, *Necker.* Derived from *corona*, a crown; in reference to the arrangement of the flowers. *Linn.* 17, Or. 4, Nat. Or. *Leguminosæ.* An interesting genus: several of the greenhouse species are very pretty flowering shrubs, and grow well in a mixture of peat and loam, and may be increased by cuttings or seeds, which ripen in abundance; the herbaceous species are some of them best grown in pots, such as *C. coronata* and *minima*, as they require the protection of a frame in severe weather; increased by seeds or dividing at the roots: the hardy annual kinds only require to be sown in the open ground.

| | | | | |
|---|---|---|---|---|
| argēntĕā | . . . | Yellow | . 5, F. Ev. S. | Crete | . 1664 |
| cappadŏcĭcā, 1 | . | White | . 7, H. Her. P. | Cappadoc. | . 1800 |
| coronātā | . | Yellow | . 6, F. Her. P. | S. Eur. | . 1776 |
| crētĭcā | . | Striped | . 6, H. | A. Candia | . 1731 |
| Emĕrŭs | . | Red yel. | . 4, H. De. S. | France | . 1596 |
| glaŭcā | . | Yellow | . 7, F. Ev. S. | France | . 1722 |
| variegātā | . | Yellow | . 8, F. Ev. S. | Gardens | . |
| globōsā | . | White | . 9, H. De. Cr. | Crete | . 1800 |
| ibērĭcā | . | Yellow | . 7, H. De. Tr. | Iberia | . 1822 |
| jūncĕā | . | Yellow | . 6, H. Ev. S. | France | . 1656 |
| minĭmā | . | Yellow | . 7, H. Her. P. | S. Eur. | . 1658 |
| montānā, 2 | . | Yellow | . 6, F. Her. P. | Switzerl. | . 1776 |
| pentaphyllā | . | Yellow | . 6, F. Ev. S. | Algiers | . 1700 |
| squamātā | . | White | . 6, H. Her. P. | Crete | . 1820 |
| vārĭā | . | Pink | . 9, H. De. Cr. | Europe | . 1597 |
| valentīnā, 3 | . | Yellow | . 8, F. Ev. S. | S. Eur. | . 1596 |
| viminālĭs | . | Yellow | . 8, F. Ev. S. | Mogad. | . 1798 |

**CORPUSCLE,** a small body, a particle of anything.

**CORRǢA**, *Smith.* In honour of Joseph Correa da Serra, a distinguished Portuguese botanist. *Linn.* 8, Or. 1, Nat. Or. *Rutaceæ.* The species of this genus are pretty greenhouse shrubs, growing from three to six feet high; they succeed best in a mixture of equal parts of sand and loam; the species are increased by cuttings, which should not be planted too thick, as they are liable to damp off. *C. speciosa*, which is allowed to be the most difficult, may be increased by inarching upon the common sorts.

| | | | | |
|---|---|---|---|---|
| albā | . . . | White | . 6, G. Ev. S. | N. S. W. | . 1793 |
| pulchēllā | . | Scarlet | . 6, G. Ev. S. | N. Holl. | . 1824 |
| rŭfā | . | White | . 6, G. Ev. S. | N. Holl. | . 1821 |
| specĭōsā | . | Scarlet | . 6, G. Ev. S. | N. S. W. | . 1806 |
| vĭrēns | . | Green | . 7, G. Ev. S. | N. S. W. | . 1800 |

**CORRIGIŎLĂ**, *Linn.* A diminutive of *corrigia*, a leathern thong; from the habit of the plants. *Linn.* 5, Or. 3, Nat. Or. *Illicebraceæ.* These are pretty annuals, only requiring to be sown in the open ground, and to be treated as other hardy annuals.

| | | | | |
|---|---|---|---|---|
| capēnsĭs | . . . | White | . 7, H. Tr. A. | C. G. H. | . 1819 |
| littorālĭs | . | White | . 7, H. Tr. A. | England | . |
| telephiifōlĭā | . | White | . 7, H. De. Tr. | S. Eur. | . 1822 |

**CORROBORANT,** strengthening.

**CORROSIVE,** having the power to eat away.

**CORRUGATED,** wrinkled, or shrivelled.

**CORTICAL,** belonging to the bark.

**CORTICATE,** like bark.

**CORTŪSĂ**, *Linn.* In honour of J. A. Cortusus, professor of botany at Padua. *Linn.* 5, Or. 1, Nat. Or. *Primulaceæ.* This is an ornamental plant, that succeeds well grown in a pot in a mixture of peat and loam, but requires to be protected in severe weather; it is increased by dividing the roots, or by seeds.

| | | | | |
|---|---|---|---|---|
| Matthĭŏlĭ | . . . | Red | . 4, H. Her. P. | Austria | . 1596 |

**CORVISĀRTĬA.** Named by Merat, in honour of M. Corvisart. *Linn.* 19, Or. 2, Nat. Or. *Compositæ.* Plants not remarkable for much beauty, that grow well in common soil, and are increased by dividing the roots. *Synonymes:* 1. *Inula caucasica.* 2. *I. Helenium.*

| | | | | |
|---|---|---|---|---|
| caucāsĭcā 1 | . | Yellow | . 7, H. Her. P. | Caucasus | . 1818 |
| Helenĭŭm, 2 | . | Yellow | . 7, H. Her. P. | Britain | . |

**CORYĀNTHĔS**, *Hooker.* From *korys*, a helmet, and *anthos*, a flower; in allusion to the large helmet-like appendage to the lip of the flower. *Linn.* 20, Or. 1, Nat. Or. *Orchidaceæ.* The species of this genus ought to be extensively cultivated, because of their splendid and very curiously-formed flowers. The most extraordinary species of this genus is *C. macrantha,* of which the following is an abridged description, extracted from the *Botanical Register.* "The plant has the habit of a *Stanhopea,* and pushes forth from the base of its pseudo-bulbs a pendulous scape, on which two or three flowers are developed; each flower is placed at the end of a long, stiff, cylindrical-furrowed ovary, and when expanded, measures something more than six inches from the tip of one sepal to that of the opposite one. The sepals and petals are nearly of the same colour, being of an ochrey yellow, spotted irregularly with dull purple. The lip is as fleshy and solid in its texture as the sepals and petals are delicate; it is seated on a deep purple stalk, nearly an inch long, this stalk terminates in a hemispherical greenish-purple cup or cap; and the latter contracting at its front edge, extends forward into a sort of second stalk of a very vivid blood-colour, the sides of which are thinner than the centre, turned back, and marked with four or five very deep, solid, sharp-edged plaits. These edges again expand and form a second cup, less lobed than the first, thinning away very much to the edges, of a broadly conical figure, with a diameter of at least two inches at the orifice; this second cup is of an ochrey yellow, streaked and spotted with pale crimson, and seems intended to catch a watery secretion, which drips into it from two succulent horns, taking their origin in the base of the column, and hanging over the centre of the cup."—*Bot. Reg.* vol. xxii. t. 1841. The genus requires the same treatment as is recommended for *Stanhopea*. Synonymes: 1. *Gongora macrantha*. 2. *G. speciosa.*

| | | | | | |
|---|---|---|---|---|---|
| macrántha, 1 | . | Brn. yel. | . 6, S. Epi. Caraccas . | |
| maculáta | 2 | . Yel. spot. | . 6, S. Epi. Demerara | . 1829 |
| speciósa, 2 | . | Yel. grn. | . 5, S. Epi. Brazil | . 1826 |

CORYCÁRPÚS, *Zea.* From *korys*, a helmet, and *karpos*, a fruit; in allusion to the shape of the fruit. *Linn.* 2, Or. 2, Nat. Or. *Gramineæ.* A curious grass, only requiring to be sown in any common soil. Synonyme: 1. *Festuca diandra.*

| | | | | |
|---|---|---|---|---|
| arundinácea, 1 | . Apetal . | . 4, Grass. N. Amer. | . 1810 |

CORÝCIÚM, *Swartz.* From *korys*, a helmet; appearance of the flower. *Linn.* 20, Or. 1, Nat. Or. *Orchidaceæ.* The species of this genus will succeed well in an equal mixture of sandy loam and peat, planted out in a pit or frame. They will also grow, when planted about six inches deep, in a warm border, and protected by some slight covering, in frosty weather, but to be exposed when the weather is fine and mild; increased by divisions.

| | | | | |
|---|---|---|---|---|
| crispúm | . . . | Yellow | . 7, F. Ter. C. G. H. . | . 1825 |
| orobanchóídes | . | Yellow | . 7, F. Ter. C. G. H. . | . 1825 |

CORÝDÁLIS, *Decandolle.* One of the Greek names of Fumitory; from *korydalos*, a lark; because the spur of the flower resembles the spur of that bird. *Linn.* 17, Or. 2, Nat. Or. *Papaveraceæ.* This is a beautiful genus, the species of which grow from one to six feet high; the delicate kinds thrive best in a mixture of peat and loam, and are very ornamental in flower-borders; the annual kinds only require sowing in the open border; seeds. Synonymes: 1. *Fumaria solida.* 2. *F. fabacea.* 3. *F. sempervirens.* 4. *F. pauciflora.* 5. *F. cava albiflora.*

| | | | | | | |
|---|---|---|---|---|---|---|
| acaúlis | . . | Pa. yel. | . 7, H. | A. Hungary | . 1825 |
| angustifóliá | . | Purple | . 2, H. Tu. | P. Iberia | . 1819 |
| aúrea | . . | Yellow | . 6, H. | B. N. Amer. | . 1812 |
| bracteáta | . | Pa. yel. | . 2, H. Tu. | P. Siberia | . 1820 |
| bicalcaráta | . | Pink | . 6, H. Tu. | P. | |
| brevifóra | . | Pa. yel. | . 6, H. | A. Kamtsch. | . 1824 |
| bulbósa, 1 | . | Pink | . 2, H. Tu. | P. Britain | . |
| capnoídes | . | White | . 7, H. | B. S. Eur. | . 1596 |
| caucásicá, 2 | . | Purple | . 2, H. Tu. | P. Caucasus | . 1823 |
| claviculáta | . | Wht. yel. | . 6, H. Cl. | A. Britain | . |
| fabácea | . | Purple | . 2, H. Tu. | P. Germany | . 1815 |
| Gebleri | . | | . 5, H. Tu. | P. Altai | . 1827 |
| glaúcá, 3 | . | Yel. pur. | . 7, H. | A. N. Amer. | . 1683 |
| impátiens | . | Yellow | . 5, H. | A. Siberia | . 1823 |
| látea | . | Yellow | . 7, H. Her. | P. England | . |
| longifóra | . | Pa. rose | . 4, H. Tu. | P. Altai | . 1832 |
| Marshalliáná | . | Purple | . 2, H. Tu. | P. Tauria | . 1824 |
| nóbilis | . | Li. yel. | . 5, H. Tu. | P. Siberia | . 1783 |
| pæoniæfóliá | . | Purple | . 2, H. Her. | P. Siberia | . 1830 |
| pauciflóra, 4 | . | Purple | . 2, H. Tu. | P. Siberia | . 1819 |
| sibírica | . | Yellow | . 7, H. Her. | P. Siberia | . 1810 |
| strícta | . | Yellow | . 6, H. | B. Siberia | . 1827 |
| tuberósa | . | Purple | . 2, H. Tu. | P. Europe | . 1596 |
| albiflóra, 5 | . | White | . 2, H. Tu. | P. Europe | . 1596 |
| uralensis | . | Pa. yel. | . 8, H. | B. Kamtsch. | . 1824 |

CORÝLÚS, *Linn.* From *korys*, a helmet; referring to the calyx enwrapping the fruit. *Linn.* 21, Or. 9, Nat. Or. *Cupuliferæ.* The species of this genus are

[ 89 ]

generally cultivated for the sake of their fruit; they will thrive well in any common garden soil, and may be raised from seed; but to have any variety true to its kind, they must be raised from suckers or layers.

| | | | | | | |
|---|---|---|---|---|---|---|
| americáná | . . | Apetal | . 4, H. De. S. | N. Amer. | . |
| Avelláná | . . | Apetal | . 2, H. De. S. | Britain | . |
| alba | . . | Apetal | . 2, H. De. S. | Spain | . |
| barcelonénsis | . | Apetal | . 2, H. De. S. | Spain | . |
| crispá | . | Apetal | . 2, H. De. S. | | |
| glomeráta | . | Apetal | . 2, H. De. S. | | |
| grándis | . | Apetal | . 2, H. De. S. | | |
| ováta | . | Apetal | . 2, H. De. S. | | |
| púmilá | . | Apetal | . 2, H. De. S. | | |
| rúbra | . | Apetal | . 2, H. De. S. | | |
| variegátá | . | Apetal | . 2, H. De. S. | | |
| heterophýllús | . | Yel. red | . H. De. S. | Danube | . 1829 |
| húmilis | . | Apetal | . 2, H. De. S. | N. Amer. | . 1798 |
| Colúrná | . | Apetal | . 2, H. De. S. | Constant. | . 1665 |
| rostráta | . | Apetal | . 2, H. De. S. | N. Amer. | . 1745 |
| tubulósa | . | Apetal | . 2, H. De. S. | Eur. | . 1759 |

CORYMB, a raceme or panicle, in which the stalks of the lower flowers are longer than those of the upper, so that the flowers are all on the same level.

CORYMBOSELY-CYMOSE, between a corymb and a cyme.

CORYMBULOSE, formed of many small corymbs.

CORYNEPHÓRÁ, *Agardh.* From *koryne*, a club, and *phoreo*, to bear; the last articulation of the jointed beard is club-shaped. *Linn.* 24, Or. 7, Nat. Or. *Algæ.* Curious plants, found growing on the sea-shore. Synonyme: *Rivularia tuberiformis—marina* 1.

CORYNEPHÓRÚS, *Beauvois.* From *koryne*, a club, and *phoreo*, to bear; the last articulation of the jointed beard is club-shaped. *Linn.* 3, Or. 2, Nat. Or. *Gramineæ.* Uninteresting species of grass, requiring only to be sown in common soil. Synonyme: 1. *Aira canescens.*

| | | | | |
|---|---|---|---|---|
| articulátús | . . . | Apetal | . 7, Grass. S. Eur. | . 1816 |

canéscens 1.

CORÝNÉÚM, *Nees.* So called from *koryne*, a club; in allusion to the form of the plants. *Linn.* 24, Or. 8, Nat. Or. *Fungi.* Very minute species of *Fungi*, discernible upon old decaying branches—*pulvinátúm.*

CORÝNOCÁRPÚS, *Forster.* This name is derived from *koryne*, a club, and *karpos*, a fruit; in reference to the form of the seed-vessel. *Linn.* 5, Or. 1, Nat. Or. *Myrsineæ.* An ornamental plant, of easy culture and propagation.

| | | | |
|---|---|---|---|
| lævigátús | . . . | G. Ev. T. N. Zeal. | . 1823 |

CORÝPHÁ, *Linn.* From *koryphe*, the summit; the leaves are only on the top of the trees. *Linn.* 6, Or. 1, Nat. Or. *Palmaceæ.* This is a beautiful genus of the Palm tribe, growing in their native country from 15 to 150 feet high; they should have a strong moist heat, and a sandy loam to grow them well.

| | | | | |
|---|---|---|---|---|
| austrális | . | Apetal | . Palm. N. Holl. | . 1824 |
| eláta | . | Apetal | . Palm. E. Ind. | . 1825 |
| glaucéscens | . | Apetal | . Palm. E. Ind. | . 1820 |
| heterophýllús | . | Apetal | . Palm. Danube | . 1829 |
| Púmós | . | Apetal | . Palm. Cuba | . 1824 |
| tectórúm | . | Apetal | . Palm. W. Ind. | . 1825 |
| umbraculíferá | . | Apetal | . Palm. E. Ind. | . 1742 |
| Utan | . | Apetal | . Palm. Moluccas | . 1825 |

CORYSÁNTHÉS, *R. Brown.* From *korys*, a helmet, and *anthos*, a flower; in allusion to the large helmet-like appendage to the flower. *Linn.* 20, Or. 1, Nat. Or. *Orchidaceæ.* The species of this genus are well worth cultivating; for which, see *Corycium.*

| | | | | |
|---|---|---|---|---|
| bicalcaráta | . . | Drk. brn. | . 7, F. Ter. N. Holl. | . 1823 |
| fimbriáta | . . | Drk. brn. | . 7, F. Ter. N. Holl. | . 1824 |
| unguiculáta | . . | Drk. brn. | . 7, F. Ter. N. Holl. | . 1822 |

COSCÍNIÚM, *Colebrooke.* From *koskinion*, a little sieve; in reference to the cotyledons being perforated. *Linn.* 22, Or. 6, Nat. Or. *Menispermaceæ.* This is a climbing plant of pleasing habit, that grows well in a mixture of loam and peat, and is increased by dividing the roots. Synonyme: 1. *Menispermum fenestratum.*

| | | | |
|---|---|---|---|
| fenestrátúm, 1 | . Yel. grn. | . 8. Ev. Cl. Ceylon | . 1800 |

CÓSMEÁ, *Willdenow.* From *kosmos*, an ornament; in allusion to the ornamental flowers. *Linn.* 19, Or. 2, Nat. Or. *Compositæ.* The species of this genus are mostly pretty annuals, that require to be sown on a gentle hotbed, and when large enough transplanted into the greenhouse or open borders.

N

| | | | | | | |
|---|---|---|---|---|---|---|
| bipinnáta | . . | Purple | . 7, G. | A. Mexico | . 1799 |
| chrysanthemifólia | Yellow | . 10, G. | A. S. Amer. | 1826 |
| crithmifólia | . | Yellow | . 9, G. | A. Mexico | . 1825 |
| lútea | . . | Yellow | . 10, G. | A. Mexico | 1811 |
| parviflóra | . | White | . 7, H. | A. Mexico | . 1800 |
| sulphúrea | . | Yellow | . 7, H. | A. Mexico | . 1799 |
| tenélla | . | Yellow | . 10, G. | A. Mexico | . 1824 |

COSMÈLIA, *R. Brown.* From *kosmeo*, to adorn; in reference to the beauty of the flowers. *Linn.* 5, Or. 1, Nat. Or. *Epacrideæ.* This is a pretty plant, growing about a foot and a half high; it succeeds best in a sandy peat soil, and may be increased freely from cuttings in the same compost.

| rúbra | . . | Red | . | | G. Ev. S. N. Holl. | . 1826 |

COSMÉTIC, beautifying.

COSMŪS, *Cavanilles.* From *kosmos*, beautiful; in allusion to the appearance of the species. *Linn.* 19, Or. 2, Nat. Or. *Compositæ.* This is a genus of very beautiful plants, well deserving of extensive cultivation. The flowers are not very much unlike those of a single dahlia, to which the genus bears a close resemblance; and the perennial species requires exactly the same treatment. *C. tenuifolius* being an annual, the seeds must therefore be sown on a hotbed early in spring, and planted out in the flower-garden about the end of May; but a few plants should be kept in the greenhouse, from which the seeds should be gathered.

| diversifólius | . | Lilac | . 9, H. Tu. P. N. Amer. | . 1835 |
| scabiosöides | . | Scarlet | . 9, G. Tu. P. Mexico | . |
| tenuifólius | . | Purple | . 9, H. | A. Mexico | . 1836 |

COSSIGNYA, *Commerson.* In honour of M. Cossigny, a French naturalist, who presented Commerson with an herbarium of the plants of Coromandel. *Linn.* 6, Or. 2, Nat. Or. *Sapindaceæ.* This is a pretty stove plant, growing well in a mixture of peat and loam; and cuttings, in sand, root freely under a glass.

| borbónica | . | | | | S. Ev. S. Maurit. | . 1824 |

COSTÁTE, ribbed, having longitudinal elevations.

COSTMARY, see *Balsamíta.*

COSTŪS, *Linn.* Derived from its Arabic name, *Gosth.* *Linn.* 1, Or. 1, Nat. Or. *Scitamineæ.* This is an ornamental genus of plants, growing well in a mixture of peat and loam, and are increased by dividing the roots, or by seed. Synonymes: 1. *C. afer hirsutus.* 2. *C. speciosus angustifolius.* 3. *Alpinia spiralis.*

| áfer | . . | White | . 6, S. Her. P. S. Leone | 1822 |
| arábicus | . | White | . 8, S. Her. P. Indies | . 1752 |
| discólor | . | White | . 6, S. Her. P. Maran. | . 1823 |
| lanátus | . | | . 5, S. Her. P. S. Amer. | . 1820 |
| maculátus, 1 | . | White | . 7, S. Her. P. S. Leone | 1822 |
| nepalénsis, 2 | . | White | . 7, S. Her. P. E. Ind. | . 1799 |
| píctus | . | Yel. pur. | . 7, S. Her. P. Mexico | . 1832 |
| Pisónis | . | Crimson | . 6, S. Her. P. Maran. | . 1823 |
| speciósus | . | White | . 8, S. Her. P. E. Ind. | . 1799 |
| spicátus | . | Yellow | . 6, S. Her. P. W. Ind. | . 1793 |
| spirális, 3 | . | Scarlet | . 11, S. Her. P. St. Vincent | |
| villosíssimus | . | Yellow | . 11, S. Her. P. St. Vincent | 1822 |

COTONEÁSTER, *Medicus.* From *cotoneum*, a quince-tree; in reference to the downy leaves of this genus being similar to the quince. *Linn.* 12, Or. 2, Nat. Or. *Rosaceæ.* These are hardy ornamental shrubs, growing about four feet high; they thrive well in any common soil, and are increased by layers. Synonymes: 1. *Pyrus Missia.* 2. *P. microphylla, uva-ursi.* 3. *Mespilus Cotoneaster.*

| acumináta | . | Pink | . 4, H. De. S. Nepal | . 1820 |
| affínis | . | Pink | . 4, H. De. S. Nepal | . 1820 |
| frígida, 1 | . | Wht. grn. | . 4, H. De. S. Nepal | . 1824 |
| laxiflóra | . | Pink | . 4, H. De. S. | . 1826 |
| melanocárpa | . | | . 4, H. De. S. | |
| microphýlla | . | White | . 4, H. De. S. Nepal | . 1825 |
| nummulária | . | Wht. grn. | . 4, H. De. S. Nepal | . 1824 |
| rotundifólia, 2 | . | White | . 4, H. Ev. S. Nepal | . 1820 |
| tomentósa | . | Pink | . 4, H. De. S. | . 1759 |
| vulgáris, 3 | . | Pink | . 4, H. De. S. Europe | . 1656 |
| depréssa | . | White | . 4, H. De. S. Europe | . |
| erythrocárpa | . | White | . 4, H. De. S. Europe | . |
| melanocárpa | . | White | . 4, H. De. S. Europe | . |

COTTON, see *Gossýpium.*

COTTON GRASS, see *Eriophórum.*

COTTON ROSE, see *Filágo pygmæa.*

COTTON THISTLE, see *Onopórdum.*

CÓTŪLA, *Linn.* A diminutive of *cota*, an old name of a species of *Anthemis.* *Linn.* 19, Or. 2, Nat. Or. *Compositæ.* This is a genus of very little interest; the tender species require to be sown on a gentle

hotbed, or in the stove, but the hardy kinds need only to be sown in the open air.

| aúrea | . . | Yellow | . 7, H. | A. Spain | . 1818 |
| nudicaúlis | . | Yellow | . 7, H. | A. C. G. H. | . 1816 |

*anthemoídes, coronopifólia, sphæránthá, tanacetifólia, viscósa.*

COTYLÈDON, seed leaf, the first leaf from seed.

COTYLÈDON, *Linn.* From *kotyle*, a cavity; in allusion to the cup-like leaves. *Linn.* 10, Or. 4, Nat. Or. *Crassulaceæ.* A numerous and rather ornamental genus of succulents; they succeed best in a sandy loam, and the pots must be well drained, as they do not thrive with too much water at their roots. Cuttings taken off and dried in the sun for a few days root freely. Synonymes: 1. *C. purpurea.* 2. *C. papillaris.* 3. *Onostachys malacophyllum.* 4. *C. ramosissima.* 5. *C. mucronata.*

| altérnans | . | | . 7, G. Ev. S. C. G. H. | . 1816 |
| cacaliöídes | . | Yellow | . 5, G. Ev. S. C. G. H. | . 1818 |
| canaliculáta | . | | . 5, G. Ev. S. C. G. H. | . 1818 |
| clavifólia | . | Purple | . 9, G. Her. P. C. G. H. | . 1824 |
| corúscans | . | Orange | . 6, G. Ev. S. C. G. H. | . 1818 |
| crassifólia | . | | . | G. | P. C. G. H. | . 1824 |
| cristáta | . | Varieg. | . 9, G. Her. P. C. G. H. | . 1818 |
| cuneáta | . | | . 8, G. Ev. S. C. G. H. | . 1818 |
| cuneifórmis | . | | . | G. Ev. S. C. G. H. | . 1823 |
| curviflóra, 1 | . | Orange | . 18, G. Ev. S. C. G. H. | . 1818 |
| decussáta, 2 | . | Scarlet | . 8, G. Ev. S. C. G. H. | . 1819 |
| dichótoma | . | | . 6, G. Ev. S. C. G. H. | . 1818 |
| eláta | . | | . 6, G. Ev. S. C. G. H. | . 1818 |
| fasciculáris | . | Red | . 7, G. Ev. S. C. G. H. | . 1759 |
| grácilis | . | | . 6, G. Ev. S. C. G. H. | . 1800 |
| hemisphæríca | . | Wht. pur. | . 6, G. Ev. S. C. G. H. | . 1731 |
| interjécta | . | | . 7, G. Ev. S. C. G. H. | . 1824 |
| jasminiflóra | . | | . | G. Ev. S. C. G. H. | . 1818 |
| maculáta | . | Wht. pur. | . 6, G. Ev. S. C. G. H. | . 1818 |
| Malacophýllum, 3 | Pa. yel. | . 6, H. | S. Dauria | . 1815 |
| mammilláris | . | Wht. pur. | . 6, G. Ev. S. C. G. H. | . 1818 |
| oblónga | . | Red | . 8, G. Ev. S. C. G. H. | . 1690 |
| orbiculáta | . | Red | . 7, G. Ev. S. C. G. H. | . 1793 |
| ováta | . | Red | . 8, G. Ev. S. C. G. H. | . 1789 |
| papilláris | . | Red | . 7, G. Ev. S. C. G. H. | . 1822 |
| ramósa, 4 | . | | . 8, G. Ev. S. C. G. H. | . 1748 |
| ramo-íssima | . | | . 5, G. Ev. S. C. G. H. | . 1816 |
| rhombifólia | . | | . 6, G. Ev. S. C. G. H. | . 1823 |
| rotundifólia | . | | . 6, G. Ev. S. C. G. H. | . 1826 |
| spúria | . | | . 7, G. Ev. S. C. G. H. | . 1731 |
| tricuspidáta | . | | . 7, G. Ev. S. C. G. H. | . 1823 |
| triflóra | . | Pk. wht. | . 6, G. Ev. S. C. G. H. | . 1821 |
| tuberculósa | . | Orange | . 7, G. Ev. S. C. G. H. | . 1820 |
| unduláta, 5 | . | | . 6, G. Ev. S. C. G. H. | . 1818 |
| unguláta | . | | . 5, G. Ev. S. C. G. H. | . 1818 |
| víridis | . | | . | G. Ev. S. C. G. H. | . 1824 |

COUCH GRASS, see *Agropýrum répens.*

COULTÈRIA, *Humboldt and Bonpl.* In honour of Thomas Coulter, M.D., a botanical author. *Linn.* 10, Or. 1, Nat. Or. *Leguminosæ.* An ornamental genus of stove shrubs, from twelve to fifteen feet high; they grow well in a mixture of peat and loam, and are increased by seeds. Synonymes: 1. *Poinciana tarra, Cæsalpina tinctoria.*

| hórrida | . | Orange | . | S. Ev. S. Carthage | . 1824 |
| tinctória, 1 | . | Orange | . 8, H. Ev. S. Carthage | . 1822 |

COUROÚRDE, see *Lagenária vulgáris*; var.

COUTÁREA, *Aublet.* Derived from *coutari*, the name applied to it in Guiana. *Linn.* 5, Or. 1, Nat. Or. *Cinchonaceæ.* This is a beautiful plant, growing to the height of twelve feet, and thriving best in sandy peat; increased by cuttings. Synonymes: 1. *Portlandia hexandra.*

| speciósa, 1 | . | Purple | . | S. Ev. S. Guiana | . 1803 |

COUTOURÉA, *Aublet.* The name given to it in Guiana. *Linn.* 4, Or. 1, Nat. Or. *Gentianaceæ.* The species of this genus require a mixture of peat and loam; increased by seed, which must be sown in a hotbed frame, or in the stove. Synonymes: 1. *Exacum ramosum.* 2. *E. spicatum.* 3. *E. verticillata, Gentiana verticillata.*

| ramósa, 1 | . | White | . 7, S. | A. Brasil | . 1824 |
| spicáta, 2 | . | White | . 7, S. | B. Maran. | . 1823 |
| verticilláta, 3 | . | White | . 7, S. | B. Trinidad | . 1818 |

COWÁNIA, *D. Don.* In commemoration of the services rendered to botany by the late Mr. James Cowan, a merchant who visited and introduced a number of plants from Mexico and Peru. *Linn.* 12, Or. 3, Nat. Or. *Rosaceæ.* A very beautiful and interesting shrub, about two feet high, with large showy blossoms resembling the rose; if it should prove sufficiently hardy to endure our winters, it will be a very great acquisition to the ornamental shrubbery. It requires to be grown in sandy peat, and may be increased by divisions, though it has, as yet, been found extremely difficult to propagate.

plicātā . . . . Red . . 6, H. Ev. S. Mexico .

COWBANE, see Cicūtā.
COWBERRY, see Vaccīnīum Vītis Idēā.
COWDIE PINE, see Dammāra austrālis.
COW-GRASS, see Trifōlīum mēdīum.
COW-HERB, see Sapōnārīā vaccārīā.
COW-ITCH, see Mucūnā.
COW-PARSLEY, see Herāclēum pānīcēs.
COW-PARSNEP, see Herāclēum.
COWSLIP, see Prīmūlā vēris.
COW-WHEAT, see Meldmpȳrum.

CRĀMBE, Tournefort. The Greek name for Sea-kale, or Sea-cabbage. Linn. 15, Nat. Or. Cruciferæ. Some of the species are much valued, and cultivated as vegetables. They require a good rich soil, and may be increased by dividing the roots, or by seed.

| | | | | |
|---|---|---|---|---|
| cordifōliā . . . . | White . | . 5, H. Tu. | P. Caucasus | . 1822 |
| maritimā . . . . | White . | . 5, H. Tu. | P. Britain . | |
| tatārīcā . . . . | White . | . 6, H. Tu. | P. Siberia . | . 1754 |

āspērā, fīliformīs, fruticōsā, hispānīcā, orientālis, pinnātīfīdā, renīformīs, strigōsā.

CRANBERRY, see Oxycōccus palūstris.
CRANE'S-BILL, see Gerānīum.
CRANIOLĀRĪĀ, Linn. Derived from kranion, a skull; on account of the fancied resemblance in the capsules. Linn. 14, Or. 2, Nat. Or. Pedaliaceæ. A greenhouse species, growing about two feet high, and succeeding in any light sandy soil, in which it merely requires sowing. Synonyme: 1. Martynia craniolaria.

ānnūā, 1 . . . White . . 7, G.     A. S. Amer. . 1733

CRASPĒDĪĀ, Forster. Derived from craspedon, a fringe; in allusion to the flowers. Linn. 19, Or. 1, Nat. Or. Compositæ. Curious plants, preferring a light loamy soil, and propagated readily by cuttings in sand, under a glass. Synonyme: 1. Richea glauca.

| | | | | |
|---|---|---|---|---|
| glaūcā, 1 . . . | Yellow . | . 4, H. Her. | P. N. Holl. | . 1826 |
| macrocēphālā . . | Yeh. wht. . | F. Ev. | P. V. D. L. | . 1834 |
| plebēīā . . . | | G. Ev. | S. N. Holl. | . 1828 |

CRĀSSŪLĀ, Linn. A diminutive of crassus, thick; in reference to the fleshy leaves and stems. Linn. 5, Or. 5, Nat. Or. Crassulaceæ. Succulent species, thriving best in a mixture of sandy loam and brick rubbish, care being taken to have the pots well drained; cuttings taken off and laid for two or three days in the sun to dry, take root freely. Synonymes: 1. Turgosia aloides. 2. T. capitellata. 3. T. pertusa. 4. T. linguæfolia. 5. T. obovata. 6. T. tomentosa. 7. T. turrita.

| | | | | | | |
|---|---|---|---|---|---|---|
| acutifōlīā . . | White . | . 7, | G. Ev. | S. | Greece | . 1795 |
| albiflōrā . . | White . | . 6, | G. | S. | C. G. H. | . 1800 |
| aloīdes, 1 . . | White . | . 7, | G. | B. | C. G. H. | . 1774 |
| arborēscens . . | Pink . | . 5, | G. Ev. | S. | C. G. A. | . 1789 |
| bibractēātā . . | White . | . 8, | G. Ev. | S. | C. G. H. | . 1823 |
| mājor . . | White . | . 8, | G. Ev. | S. | C. G. H. | . 1823 |
| biconvēxā . . | White . | . 8, | G. Ev. | S. | C. G. H. | . 1800 |
| biplanātā . . | White . | . 9, | G. Ev. | S. | C. G. H. | . 1823 |
| bullulātā . . | Yellow . | . 8, | G. Ev. | S. | C. G. H. | . 1800 |
| capitellātā, 2 . | White . | . 7, | G. | B. | C. G. H. | . 1774 |
| centauroīdes . | Pink . | . 5, | G. | B. | C. G. H. | . 1774 |
| ciliātā . . | Yellow . | . 7, | G. Ev. | S. | C. G. H. | . 1782 |
| mēdīā . . | Yellow . | . 7, | G. Ev. | S. | C. G. H. | . 1818 |
| minor . . | Yellow . | . 7, | G. Ev. | S. | C. G. H. | . 1818 |
| coccinēllā . . | Scarlet . | . 7, | G. Ev. | S. | C. G. H. | . 1823 |
| columnāris . | White . | . | G. Ev. | S. | C. G. H. | . 1789 |
| tomentōsā . . | | | G. Ev. | S. | C. G. H. | . 1818 |
| cordātā . . | Pink . | . 6, | G. Ev. | S. | C. G. H. | . 1774 |
| corymbulōsā, 3. | White . | . 11, | G. | B. | C. G. H. | . 1818 |
| cotylēdōnis . | White . | . | G. Ev. | P. | C. G. H. | . 1800 |
| dejēctā . . | White . | . 7, | G. Ev. | S. | C. G. H. | . 1820 |
| diffūsā . . | Pink . | . 6, | G. | A. | C. G. H. | . 1774 |
| ericoīdes . | White . | . 9, | G. Ev. | S. | C. G. H. | . 1820 |
| expānsā . . | White . | . 6, | G. | A. | C. G. H. | . 1774 |
| filicaūlis . . | White . | . 8, | G. Ev. | S. | C. G. H. | . 1820 |
| fruticulōsā . | White . | . | G. Ev. | S. | C. G. H. | |
| glabrā, 1 . . | White . | . 8, | G. | A. | C. G. H. | . 1774 |
| glomerātā . . | White . | . 9, | G. | A. | C. G. H. | . 1774 |
| imbricātā . . | White . | . 6, | G. Ev. | S. | C. G. H. | . 1760 |
| lactēā . . | White . | . 9, | G. Ev. | S. | C. G. H. | . 1774 |
| lineolātā . . | Yellow . | . 7, | G. | B. | C. G. H. | . 1774 |
| linguæfōlīā, 4 | White . | . 8, | G. | B. | C. G. H. | . 1803 |
| Magnōlii . . | White . | . 6, | G. | A. | S. Eur. | . 1800 |
| marginālis . | Pa. yel. . | . 7, | G. Ev. | S. | C. G. H. | . 1774 |
| moschātā . . | White . | . 9, | G. | A. | N. S. W. | . 1794 |

[ 91 ]

| | | | | | | |
|---|---|---|---|---|---|---|
| oblīquā . . | Red . | . 4, | G. Ev. | S. | C. G. H. | . 1759 |
| obovātā, 5 . | White . | . 6, | G. | B. | C. G. H. | . 1818 |
| obtūsā . . | | | G. Ev. | S. | C. C. H. | . 1812 |
| orbiculāris . | Pink . | . 8, | G. Her. | P. | C. G. H. | . 1731 |
| perfilātā . . | Pink . | . 9, | G. Ev. | S. | C. G. H. | . 1785 |
| pellūcīdā . . | Pink . | . 8, | G. Ev. | S. | C. G. H. | . 1732 |
| pertusīlā . . | White . | . 10, | G. | B. | C. G. H. | . 1814 |
| pulchēllā . . | Red . | . 5, | G. | A. | C. G. H. | . 1810 |
| punctātā . . | White . | . 6, | G. Ev. | S. | C. G. H. | . 1759 |
| ramōsā . . | Pink . | . 7, | G. Ev. | S. | C. G. H. | . 1774 |
| ramulīflōrā . | White . | . 6, | G. Ev. | S. | C. G. H. | . 1822 |
| retrofleχā . | Yellow . | . 6, | G. | A. | C. G. H. | . 1788 |
| revolvēns . | White . | . 8, | G. Ev. | S. | C. G. H. | . 1820 |
| rosulāris . | White . | . 7, | G. Her. | P. | C. G. H. | . 1819 |
| rotundifōlīā . | White . | . 8, | G. Ev. | S. | C. G. H. | . 1820 |
| rūbēns . . | Pink . | . 5, | G. | A. | Italy | . 1759 |
| scābrā . . | Pa. yel. . | . 6, | G. Ev. | S. | C. G. H. | . 1730 |
| scabrēllā . . | | | G. Ev. | S. | C. G. H. | . 1810 |
| spārsā . . | White . | . 6, | G. | B. | C. G. H. | . 1774 |
| spathulātā . | White . | . 8, | G. Ev. | S. | C. G. H. | . 1774 |
| squamulōsā . | White . | . 7, | G. Ev. | S. | C. G. H. | . 1817 |
| subulātā . . | | . 6, | G. | A. | C. G. H. | . 1800 |
| telephioīdes . | White . | . 7, | G. Ev. | S. | C. G. H. | . 1818 |
| tetragōnā . | White . | . 8, | G. Ev. | S. | C. G. H. | . 1711 |
| tomentōsā, 6 | White . | . 4, | G. | B. | C. G. H. | . 1818 |
| tūrrītā, 7 . | White . | . 8, | G. | B. | C. G. H. | . 1818 |
| verticillāris . | Pink . | . 6, | G. | A. | S. Eur. | . 1788 |

CRASSIFŌLĪĀ, thick-leaved.

CRATÆGŪS, Linn. From kratos, strength; in allusion to the strength and hardness of the wood. Linn. 12, Or. 2, Nat. Or. Rosaceæ. A very ornamental genus, chiefly composed of low, hardy trees, or shrubs. Young plants may be obtained from seeds, and they may also be multiplied by buds, or grafts. Synonymes: 1. C. glandulosa. 2. C. indentata. 3. Coccinea spinosa. 4. Mespilus linearis. 5. M. nana. 6. Cratægus lobata. 7. Pyrus cratægifolia. 8. Cratægus Oliveriana. 9. C. laciniata. 10. C. edulis. 11. C. incisa. 12. C. Celsiana.

| | | | | | | |
|---|---|---|---|---|---|---|
| alpīnā . . | White . | . 5, H. | De. | T. | Italy | |
| apiifōlīā . . | White . | . 5, H. | De. | T. | N. Amer. | . 1812 |
| Arōniā . . | White . | . 5, H. | De. | T. | S. Eur. | . 1810 |
| Azarōlūs . | White . | . 5, H. | De. | T. | S. Eur. | . 1640 |
| carpātīcā . | White . | . 5, H. | De. | T. | Carpat. Mo. | |
| coccinēā . . | White . | . 5, H. | De. | T. | N. Amer. | . 1683 |
| glandulōsā, 1 | White . | . 5, H. | De. | T. | N. Amer. | . 1759 |
| indentātā, 2 | White . | . 5, H. | De. | T. | N. Amer. | |
| maximā, 3 | White . | . 5, H. | De. | T. | N. Amer. | |
| corallīnā . | White . | . 5, H. | De. | T. | France | |
| cordātā . . | White . | . 5, H. | De. | T. | N. Amer. | . 1738 |
| crenulātā . | White . | . 5, H. | Ev. | S. | Nepal | . 1820 |
| Crūs-gāllī . | White . | . 5, H. | De. | T. | N. Amer. | . 1691 |
| lineāris, 4 | White . | . 5, H. | De. | T. | N. Amer. | |
| nānā, 5 | White . | . 5, H. | De. | T. | N. Amer. | |
| pyracanthifōlīā | White . | . 5, H. | De. | T. | N. Amer. | |
| salicifōlīā | White . | . 5, H. | De. | T. | N. Amer. | |
| splendēns | White . | . 5, H. | De. | T. | N. Amer. | |
| Douglasii | White . | . 5, H. | De. | T. | N. Amer. | . 1830 |
| ellipticā | White . | . 5, H. | De. | T. | N. Amer. | . 1765 |
| ericocārpā | White . | . 5, H. | De. | T. | Britain | |
| flexā . . | White . | . 5, H. | De. | T. | | . 1810 |
| flabellātā | White . | . 5, H. | De. | T. | S. Eur. | |
| flāvā . . | White . | . 5, H. | De. | T. | N. Amer. | . 1724 |
| lobātā, 6 | White . | . 5, H. | De. | S. | | |
| florentīnā, 7 | White . | . 5, H. | De. | T. | | . 1800 |
| florīdā . . | White . | . 5, H. | De. | T. | N. Amer. | |
| glabrā . . | White . | . 5, H. | De. | T. | N. Amer. | . 1818 |
| heterophyllā | White . | . 5, H. | De. | T. | N. Amer. | . 1816 |
| laciniātā | White . | . 5, H. | De. | T. | Sicily | . 1816 |
| latifōlīā . | White . | . 5, H. | De. | T. | N. Amer. | . 1820 |
| lucīdā . . | White . | . 5, H. | De. | T. | N. Amer. | |
| maroccānā | White . | . 5, H. | De. | T. | Barbary | . 1822 |
| melanocārpā | White . | . 5, H. | De. | T. | Tauria | . 1820 |
| mexicānā | White . | . 5, F. | Ev. | T. | Mexico | . 1823 |
| monogynā | White . | . 5, H. | De. | T. | Siberia | |
| nigrā . . | White . | . 5, H. | De. | T. | Hungary | . 1819 |
| odoratissimā | White . | . 5, H. | De. | T. | Crimea | |
| orientālis . | White . | . 5, H. | De. | T. | S. Eur. | . 1810 |
| ovalifōlīā | White . | . 5, H. | De. | T. | N. Amer. | . 1810 |
| oxyacanthā | White . | . 5, H. | De. | T. | Britain | |
| aūrēā | White . | . 5, H. | De. | T. | | |
| mājor | White . | . 5, H. | De. | T. | | |
| Oliveriānā, 8 | White . | . 5, H. | De. | T. | Asia Minor. | 1820 |
| plēnā | White . | . 5, H. | De. | T. | | |
| præcōx | White . | . 5, H. | De. | T. | | |
| punīcēā | Scarlet . | . 5, H. | De. | T. | | |
| rōsēā, 9 | Red . | . 5, H. | De. | T. | | |
| oxyacanthoīdes | White . | . 5, H. | De. | T. | France | . 1822 |
| parvifōlīā | White . | . 5, H. | De. | T. | N. Amer. | . 1704 |
| grossularisæfōlīā | White . | . 5, H. | De. | T. | N. Amer. | |
| pentagynā | White . | . 5, H. | De. | T. | Hungary | . 1820 |
| Poiretiānā | White . | . 5, H. | De. | T. | Hungary | . 1810 |
| Priestiānā | White . | . 5, H. | De. | T. | | . 1810 |
| prunellifōlīā | White . | . 5, H. | De. | T. | | |
| prunifōlīā | White . | . 5, H. | De. | T. | N. Amer. | . 1818 |
| punctātā | White . | . | H. | De. | T. | N. Amer. | . 1746 |
| purpūrēā | White . | . 5, H. | De. | T. | | . 1822 |

| | | | | |
|---|---|---|---|---|
| Pyracantha | White | 5, H. Ev. T. | S. Eur. | 1629 |
| pyrifolia, 10 | White | 6, H. De. T. | N. Amer. | 1765 |
| sanguinea | White | 5, H. De. T. | Siberia | 1810 |
| spathulata | White | 5, H. De. T. | N. Amer. | 1805 |
| spinosissima | White | 5, H. De. T. | Europe | |
| tanacetifolia | White | 5, H. De. T. | Greece | 1789 |
| glabra | White | 5, H. De. T. | Germany | 1816 |
| Leeana, 11 | White | 6. H. De. T. | Hybrid | |
| taurica, 12 | White | 7, H. De. T. | Tauria | 1800 |
| viridis | White | 5, H. De. T. | Carolina | 1810 |

CRATÆVA, *Linn.* After Cratævus, a Greek botanist, who lived in the time of Hippocrates. *Linn.* 11, Or. 1, Nat. Or. *Capparidaceæ.* Ornamental stove trees, growing from twelve to twenty feet high; they prefer a rich strong soil, and may be propagated by cuttings in sand, under a glass, in heat. *Synonymes:* 1. *Capparis trifoliata.* 2. *C. trifoliata.*

| | | | | |
|---|---|---|---|---|
| gynandra | White | 8. Ev. T. | Jamaica | 1789 |
| Roxburghii, 1 | White | 8. Ev. T. | E. Ind. | 1822 |
| tapia | White | 8. Ev. T. | India | 1752 |
| tapioides, 2 | White | 8. Ev. T. | S. Amer. | 1820 |

CRATERIUM, *Trentepohl.* Derived from *krater*, a cup; in reference to the form of the peridium. *Linn.* 24, Or. 9, Nat. Or. *Fungi.* Curious minute species, found growing on mosses in damp places. *Synonyme:* 1. *Cyathus minutus—leucocephalum, vulgare* 1.

CREEPING, spread upon the ground, and rooting at the joints.

CREEPING FIORIN, see *Agrostis stolonifera.*

CREPIS, *Linn.* A name given to a plant by Pliny, of which he gave no description. *Linn.* 19, Or. 1, Nat. Or. *Compositæ.* Uninteresting species, succeeding in any common border soil, in which they merely require sowing. *Synonymes:* 1. *C. Gmelini.* 2. *Prenanthes hieraciæfolia.* 3. *Lagoseris taurinensis.* 4. *C. graminifolia—agrestis, bannatica, biennis, cernua, chondrilloides, cinerea, corymbosa, croatica, diffusa, Dioscoridis, heterosperma, hieraciotdes, lacera, latifolia, lodomiriensis, macrorhiza, neglecta, parviflora, pinnatifida, pulchra* 2, *rhagadioloides, rigens, rigida, scabra, segetum, Sprengeriana, taurinensis* 3, *tectorum, tenuifolia* 4, *virens.*

CRENATE, having round notches.
CRENULATE, having small round notches.

CRESCENTIA, *Linn.* In memory of Pietro Crescenti, of Bologna, an agricultural author of the sixteenth century. *Linn.* 14, Or. 2, Nat. Or. *Bignoniaceæ.* A genus of handsome stove trees; they will thrive in a mixture of loam and peat, and cuttings of the ripened wood root freely in sand, in heat.

| | | | | |
|---|---|---|---|---|
| acuminata | Orn. wht. | 8. Ev. T. | Cuba | 1822 |
| cucurbitina | White | 8. Ev. T. | W. Ind. | 1733 |
| Cujete | White | 8. Ev. T. | Jamaica | 1690 |

CRESS, see *Lepidium sativum.*

CRESSA, *Linn.* From *cressa*, a native of Crete; the plant is plentiful there. *Linn.* 5, Or. 2, Nat. Or. *Convolvulaceæ.* This is a curious annual, growing about six inches high, and should be sown in sandy peat.

| | | | | |
|---|---|---|---|---|
| cretica | Purple | 7, H. Tr. A. | Levant | 1822 |

CRESS ROCKET, see *Vella.*

CREST, applied to some elevated appendage, terminating a particular organ; a stamen is crested when the filament projects beyond the anther, and becomes dilated.

CRETACEOUSLY-PRUINOSE, covered with white glittering spots, or pustules.

CRETAN CARROT, see *Athamanta cretica.*

CRIBRARIA, *Schrader.* From *cribrum*, a sieve; in reference to the upper part of the peridium being perforated. *Linn.* 24, Or. 9, Nat. Or. *Fungi.* A small species, found on pine bark, &c—*micropus.*

CRIBRIFORM, riddled with holes, like a sieve.
CRINITUS, hairy, having long hairs.

CRINUM, *Linn.* From *krinon*, the Greek name of the lily. *Linn.* 6, Or. 1, Nat. Or. *Amaryllidaceæ.* This is a fine genus of bulbous plants; many of the species are very beautiful. The flowers of most of them are delightfully fragrant, and are produced freely in large umbels. They prefer a mixture of rich loam, peat, and sand, and are increased by offsets, which are produced in abundance. *Synonymes:* 1. *C. superbum.* 2. *campanulatum.* 3. *toxicarium.* 4. *brevifolium.* 5. *Amaryllis longifolia.* 6. *C. capense, viridiflorum.* 7. *A. ornata.* 8. *C. rubrolimbo.* 9. *A. australasica.* 10. *A. giganteum.* 11. *A. revoluta, C. revoluta.* 12. *A. insignis.* 13. *A. moluccanum.* 14. *A. zeylanica*

| | | | | |
|---|---|---|---|---|
| algoense | Red wht. | 8, S. Bu. P. | C. G. H. | 1826 |
| amabile, 1 | Purple | 7, S. Bu. P. | E. Ind. | 1810 |
| americanum | White | 7, S. Bu. P. | S. Amer. | 1752 |
| amœnum | White | 8. Bu. P. | E. Ind. | 1810 |
| lævé | White | 8. Bu. P. | E. Ind. | 1819 |
| angustifolium | White | 8. Bu. P. | E. Ind. | 1819 |
| angustifolium | White | 6, G. Bu. P. | N. Holl. | 1824 |
| angustum | Pink | 7, S. Bu. P. | Maurit. | 1818 |
| anomalum | White | 7, S. Bu. P. | China | 1822 |
| aquaticum, 2 | Pink | 8, S. Bu. P. | C. G. H. | 1820 |
| arenarium | White | 5, S. Bu. P. | N. Holl. | 1822 |
| blandum | Blue | 5, S. Bu. P. | N. Holl. | 1821 |
| asiaticum, 3 | White | 7, S. Bu. P. | China | 1732 |
| augustum | Wht. red | 7, S. Bu. P. | E. Ind. | 1819 |
| Baconi | Red wht. | 7, S. Bu. P. | Eng. hyb. | 1826 |
| brachyandrum | White | 7, S. Bu. P. | N. Holl. | 1819 |
| bracteatum, 4 | White | 7, S. Bu. P. | Maurit. | 1810 |
| angustifolium | White | 7, S. Bu. P. | Maurit. | 1810 |
| brevilimbum | | 7, S. Bu. P. | Pacific Isl. | 1820 |
| Broussonetti | Red wht. | 7, S. Bu. P. | Guinea | 1740 |
| caffrum | Red wht. | 9, S. Bu. P. | C. G. H. | 1825 |
| canaliculatum | White | 7, S. Bu. P. | E. Ind. | 1810 |
| canalifolium | | 7, S. Bu. P. | E. Ind. | 1820 |
| capense, 5 | Pink | 7, H. Bu. P. | C. G. H. | 1752 |
| Gowenii | Pink | 6, H. Bu. P. | Hybrid | |
| careyanum | White | 7, S. Bu. P. | Maurit. | 1821 |
| Commelini | White | 6, S. Bu. P. | S. Amer. | 1796 |
| confertum | White | 6, S. Bu. P. | N. Holl. | 1822 |
| crassifolium, 6 | Pink | 9, G. Bu. P. | C. G. H. | 1774 |
| cruentum | Red | 7, S. Bu. P. | E. Ind. | 1810 |
| declinatum | White | 5, S. Bu. P. | Silhet | 1818 |
| defixum | White | 8, S. Bu. P. | E. Ind. | 1810 |
| distichum, 7 | Wht. pur. | 6, S. Bu. P. | Guinea | 1774 |
| elegans | White | 9, S. Bu. P. | E. Ind. | 1823 |
| ensifolium | White | 7, S. Bu. P. | Pegu | 1819 |
| erubescens, 8 | Pa. wht. | 7, S. Bu. P. | W. Ind. | 1789 |
| herbiceum | White | 7, S. Bu. P. | Berbice | 1819 |
| majus | Red wht. | 7, S. Bu. P. | S. Amer. | 1789 |
| minus | Red wht. | 7, S. Bu. P. | S. Amer. | 1789 |
| viridifolium | White | 7, S. Bu. P. | Demerara | 1819 |
| erythrophyllum | Red wht. | 7, S. Bu. P. | E. Ind. | 1825 |
| exaltatum | | 8, S. Bu. P. | E. Ind. | 1820 |
| flaccidum, 9 | Pink | 7, G. Bu. P. | N. Holl. | 1816 |
| formosum | | 7, S. Bu. P. | Brazil | 1820 |
| giganteum, 10 | White | 7, S. Bu. P. | Guinea | 1792 |
| Herberti, 11 | Pink | 9, H. Bu. P. | C. G. H. | 1774 |
| humile | White | 10, S. Bu. P. | | 1822 |
| hybridum | Pink | 7, S. Bu. P. | Hybrid | 1820 |
| insigne, 12 | Pink | 11, S. Bu. P. | E. Ind. | 1819 |
| Lancei | Red wht. | 7, S. Bu. P. | Surinam | 1825 |
| latifolium | Pink | 7, S. Bu. P. | E. Ind. | 1805 |
| longiflorum | Purple | 7, G. Bu. P. | C. G. H. | 1816 |
| longifolium | White | 7, G. Bu. P. | Bengal | 1810 |
| lorifolium | White | 7, G. Bu. P. | Pegu | 1819 |
| macrocarpum | | 7, G. Bu. P. | Pegu | 1820 |
| mauritianum | Pink | 8, G. Bu. P. | Maurit. | 1812 |
| moluccanum, 13 | Pink | 7, G. Bu. P. | Moluccas | 1819 |
| multiflorum | White | 7, G. Bu. P. | | 1822 |
| pedunculatum | White | 7, S. Bu. P. | N. S. W. | 1790 |
| plicatum | White | 7, G. Bu. P. | China | 1818 |
| procerum | White | 7, S. Bu. P. | Pegu | 1820 |
| purpurascens | Purple | 6, S. Bu. P. | Fernan. Po | 1826 |
| revolutum | White | 6, S. Bu. P. | Maranh. | 1823 |
| riparium | Pink | 7, G. Bu. P. | C. G. H. | 1816 |
| scabrum | Pink | 5, S. Bu. P. | Azores | 1810 |
| sinicum | White | 8. Bu. P. | China | 1819 |
| speciosum | Pink | 7, S. Bu. P. | E. Ind. | 1819 |
| strictum | White | 9, S. Bu. P. | | 1824 |
| submersum | Pink | 7, S. Bu. P. | Rio Jan. | 1820 |
| sumatranum | White | 7, S. Bu. P. | Sumatra | 1810 |
| undulatum | White | 11, S. Bu. P. | Maranh. | 1824 |
| venustum | Wht. red | 7, S. Bu. P. | E. Ind. | 1821 |
| verecundum | Pa. red | 7, S. Bu. P. | E. Ind. | 1820 |
| Yuccæoides | Red wht. | 6, S. Bu. P. | Guinea | 1740 |
| zeylanicum, 14 | Purple | 7, S. Bu. P. | Ceylon | 1771 |

CRISP, curled, much undulated.

CRISTARIA, *Cavanilles.* From *crista*, a crest; in reference to the form of the capsules. *Linn.* 16, Or. 8, Nat. Or. *Malvaceæ.* A pretty little hardy herbaceous plant, requiring to be planted in peat soil; to thrive, it may be increased by division or seeds. *Synonyme:* 1. *Malva coccinea.*

| | | | | |
|---|---|---|---|---|
| coccinea, 1 | Scarlet | 8, H. Her. P. | Missouri | 1811 |

CRISTATE, crested, tufted.

CRITHMUM, *Tournefort.* Derived from *krithe*, barley; in allusion to the singularity of the seeds. *Linn.* 5, Or. 2, Nat. Or. *Umbelliferæ.* Curious species, not succeeding well under any cultivation. Sandy or gravelly soil is best for them, with a plentiful supply of water, to which a little soda should be added now and then; increased by division. *Synonyme:* 1. *Tenoria canadensis.*

| | | | | |
|---|---|---|---|---|
| latifolium, 1 | Yellow | 7, G. Her. P. | Canaries | 1780 |
| maritimum | White | 8, H. Her. P. | Britain | |

CROCUS, *Linn.* A Chaldean name, applied by Theophrastus. *Linn.* 3, Or. 1, Nat. Or. *Iridaceæ*. This is a well-known and much-admired genus. The species and varieties are very pretty and ornamental in flower-beds, borders, &c. They will grow well in any light sandy soil, and may be increased by offsets or seeds.

| | | | | | | |
|---|---|---|---|---|---|---|
| albiflōrŭs | . | White | . | 2, H. Bu. P. | Austria | . |
| argentĕŭs | . | Wht. brn. | 2, H. Bu. P. | | |
| aûrĕŭs | . | Yellow | . | 2, H. Bu. P. | Greece | . |
| biflōrŭs | . | White | . | 2, H. Bu. P. | Crimea | . | 1629 |
| impertī | . | Lilac | . | 2, H. Bu. P. | Naples | . | 1830 |
| lāctĕŭs | . | Pa. yel. | . | 3, H. Bu. P. | | |
| lagenæflōrŭs | . | Red yel. | . | 2, H. Bu. P. | Greece | . |
| flāvŭs | . | Pa. yel. | . | 2, H. Bu. P. | Greece | . |
| lūtĕŭs | . | Yellow | . | 2, H. Bu. P. | Turkey | . | 1629 |
| maulācŭs | . | Yellow | . | 2, H. Bu. P. | Greece | . | 1629 |
| minimŭs | . | Purple | . | 2, H. Bu. P. | | 1629 |
| nudiflōrŭs | . | Violet | . | 9, H. Bu. P. | England | . |
| odōrŭs | . | | . | 9, H. Bu. P. | Naples | . | 1830 |
| Pallasī | . | Lilac | . | 9, H. Bu. P. | Crimea | . | 1821 |
| pusillŭs | . | Wht. blue | 2, H. Bu. P. | Naples | . | 1824 |
| reticulātŭs | . | Blue | . | 2, H. Bu. P. | Crimea | . |
| sativŭs | . | Violet | . | 9, H. Bu. P. | England | . |
| serōtīnŭs | . | Violet | . | 10, H. Bu. P. | S. Eur. | . | 1629 |
| stellāris | . | Yellow | . | 2, H. Bu. | | |
| striātŭs | . | White | . | 2, H. Bu. P. | | 1830 |
| suavĕōlĕns | . | | . | 9, H. Bu. P. | Naples | . | 1830 |
| sulphūrĕŭs | . | Yellow | . | 2, H. Bu. P. | S. Eur. | . | 1629 |
| flāvŭs | . | Pa. yel. | . | 2, H. Bu. P. | S. Eur. | . | 1629 |
| Susiānŭs | . | Yellow | . | 2, H. Bu. P. | Turkey | . | 1605 |
| Thomasī | . | Blue | . | 9, H. Bu. P. | Naples | . | 1830 |
| variegātŭs | . | Varieg. | . | 2, H. Bu. P. | Levant | . | 1629 |
| vērnŭs | . | Purple | . | 2, H. Bu. P. | England | . |
| leucorhynchŭs | Wht. blue | 2, H. Bu. P. | | |
| neapolitānŭs | Pur. blue | 2, H. Bu. P. | Naples | . |
| obovātŭs | . | Purple | . | 2, H. Bu. P. | S. Eur. | . |
| pictŭs | . | Pa. wht. | 2, H. Bu. P. | | |
| versicōlŏr | . | Purple | . | 2, H. Bu. P. | S. Eur. | . | 1629 |

CRŎCŬS BLIGHT, see *Rhizoctōnĭā Crocōrŭm.*

CROSSĀNDRĀ, *Salisbury.* From *krossos*, a fringe, and *aner*, a male, or anther; in reference to the anthers being fringed. *Linn.* 14, Or. 2, Nat. Or. *Acanthaceæ.* A beautiful, free-flowering stove shrub, succeeding well in any light rich soil, and easily propagated by cuttings in sand. *Synonyms:* 1. *Harrachia speciosa, Ruellia infundibuliformis.*

| | | | | | |
|---|---|---|---|---|---|
| undulæfōlĭā, 1 | . | Or. Scar. | . 3, S. Ev. S. E. Ind. | . . | 1800 |

CROSSWORT, see *Crucianēllā.*

CROSSWORT, see *Valantĭā cruciātā.*

CROTALĀRĬĀ, *Linn.* Derived from *krotalon*, a castanet; the seeds are in inflated pods, and rattle when shaken. *Linn.* 16, Or. 7, Nat. Or. *Leguminosæ.* This is a numerous genus, some species of which are very ornamental. *C. juncea* is said to be a valuable fodder; they require a mixture of loam and peat. The perennial kinds may be increased by cuttings in sand, under a glass. The annual and biennial kinds merely require sowing. *Synonyms:* 1. *sericea.* 2. *hirta.* 3. *Trifoliastrum.* 4. *chinensis.* 5. *lævigata.* 6. *stricta, anthylloides.* 7. *cærulea.* 8. *incanescens.*

| | | | | | |
|---|---|---|---|---|---|
| acuminātā | . | Yellow | . 7, F. | A. C. G. H. | 1820 |
| alātā | . | Pa. yel. | . 7, S. | B. Nepal | 1818 |
| anagyrōīdēs | . | Yellow | . 7, S. Ev. | S. Trinidad | 1823 |
| angulātā | . | Yellow | . 6, S. | A. S. Amer. | 1700 |
| anthyllōīdēs | . | Yellow | . 8, S. Ev. | S. E. Ind. | 1789 |
| argentĕā | . | Yellow | . 6, O. Ev. | S. C. G. H. | 1823 |
| Berteriānā | . | Yellow | . 6, S. Ev. | S. W. Ind. | 1818 |
| bialātā | . | Yellow | . 6, S. | A. | 1820 |
| bifariā | . | Yellow | . 7, S. | A. E. Ind. | 1817 |
| bractĕātā | . | Yellow | . 7, S. | A. E. Ind. | 1820 |
| Brownĕī | . | Yellow | . 7, S. Ev. | S. Jamaica | 1816 |
| Burmannī, 1 | . | Yellow | . 7, S. | A. E. Ind. | 1800 |
| cajanifōlĭā | . | Yellow | . 8, S. Ev. | S. S. Amer. | 1824 |
| calycinā | . | Blue | . 6, S. | A. E. Ind. | 1816 |
| chinēnsis | . | Yellow | . 6, S. Ev. | S. China | 1818 |
| cubēnsis, 2 | . | Yellow | . 5, S. | A. Cuba | 1820 |
| cytisōīdēs | . | Yellow | . 7, S. Ev. | S. E. Ind. | 1826 |
| dichōtōmā | . | Yellow | . 7, G. Ev. | S. Mexico | 1824 |
| foliōsā | . | Yellow | . 6, S. Ev. | S. E. Ind. | 1818 |
| fruticōsā | . | Yellow | . 6, S. Ev. | S. Jamaica | 1716 |
| fulvā | . | Yellow | . 6, S. | A. E. Ind. | 1817 |
| glaucā | . | Yellow | . 7, S. | A. Guinea | 1824 |
| hirsūtā | . | Yellow | . 7, S. | A. E. Ind. | 1818 |
| Langsdorfī | . | Yellow | . 6, S. | A. | 1820 |
| linifōlĭā | . | Yellow | . 7, S. Ev. | S. Nepal | 1820 |
| medicaginĕā, 3 | Yel. grn. | . 6, S. Ev. | S. E. Ind. | 1816 |
| microphyllā | . | Yellow | . 7, S. Tr. | A. Arabia | 1820 |
| Novæ Hollandĭæ | Purple | . 6, S. Ev. | P. N. Holl. | 1823 |
| obscūrā | . | Yellow | . 6, G. Ev. | S. C. G. H. | 1820 |
| ovālīs | . | Yellow | . 7, F. | A. Carolina | 1810 |
| paniculātā, 4 | . | Yellow | . 6, S. Ev. | S. Java | 1820 |
| pellītā | . | Yellow | . 7, S. Ev. | S. Jamaica | 1820 |
| pendūlā | . | Yellow | . 8, S. Ev. | S. Jamaica | 1820 |

| | | | | | |
|---|---|---|---|---|---|
| procumbēns | . | Yellow | . 6, S. Her. | P. Mexico | . 1823 |
| pūmilā | . | Yellow | . 6, S. Tr. | A. Cuba | . 1823 |
| purpurāscēns | . | Purple | . 7, S. | A. Madagas. | . 1825 |
| Purshiī, 5 | . | Yellow | . 6, F. | A. N. Amer. | . 1800 |
| Roxburghiānā, 6 | Yellow | . 6, S. Ev. | S. E. Ind. | . 1820 |
| senegalēnsis | . | Yellow | . 6, S. | A. Senegal | . 1819 |
| spectābilīs | . | Purple | . 7, S. | A. E. Ind. | . 1820 |
| stipulārīs | . | Yellow | . 7, S. | A. Cayenne | . 1823 |
| striātā | . | Yel. red. | . 8, Ev. | S. Maurit. | . 1831 |
| tenuifōlĭā | . | Yellow | . 6, S. Ev. | S. E. Ind. | . 1816 |
| thebaīcā | . | Yellow | . 6, G. Ev. | S. Egypt | . 1818 |
| trianthā | . | Yellow | . 6, S. | A. Mexico | . 1824 |
| tuberōsā | . | Purple | . 6, G. | A Nepal | . 1821 |
| tūrgīdā | . | Yellow | . 7, S. Ev. | S. | . 1820 |
| verrucōsā, 7 | . | Blue | . 7, S. | A. W. Ind. | . 1731 |
| acuminātā | . | Blue | . 7, S. | A. E. Ind. | . 1731 |
| villōsā | . | Yellow | . 7, S. | A. C. G. H. | . 1824 |
| virgātā | . | Yellow | . 6, S. Ev. | S. E. Ind. | . 1816 |

*angustifōlĭā, arborēscēns 8, axillārīs, benghalēnsis, biflōrā, curtātā, diffūsā, fenestrātā, hirtā, incānā, juncĕā, laburnifōlĭā, latifōlĭā, micāns, micrānthā, nepalēnsis, orixēnsis, pallidā, parviflōrā, Paulinā, platycārpā, prostrātā, pulchēllā, pulchērrimā, pulchrā, purpūrĕā, quinquefōlĭā, retūsā, rubiginōsā, sagittālis, Saltiānā, semperflōrēns, strictā, tetragōnā, vitellīnā.*

CRŎTŌN, *Linn.* From *kroton*, a tick: in reference to the resemblance of the seeds. *Linn.* 21, Or. 10, Nat. Or. *Euphorbiaceæ.* A genus (with the exception of one or two species) of little interest. The bark of *C. cascarilla* is aromatic; and the seeds of *C. Tiglium* are purgative. They will all succeed in a mixture of three parts loam, and one peat; and cuttings, with the leaves left on, root freely in sand, under a glass, in heat. *Synonymes:* 1. *digitata.* 2. *Aleurites ambinux.*

| | | | | | |
|---|---|---|---|---|---|
| Eleutērĭā | . | Wht. grn. | 7, S. Ev. | S. Jamaica | . 1748 |
| glabellā | . | Wht. grn. | 8, S. Ev. | S. Jamaica | . 1778 |
| linĕārĭs | . | Wht. grn. | 7, S. Ev. | S. W. Ind. | . 1778 |
| pictā | . | Wht. grn. | 7, S. Ev. | S. E. Ind. | . 1810 |
| rosmarinifōlĭā | . | | 6, G. Ev. | S. N. Holl. | . 1824 |
| Tiglĭum | . | Wht. grn. | 8, S. Ev. | S. E. Ind. | . 1796 |
| variegātā | . | Wht. grn. | 8, S. Ev. | S. E. Ind. | . 1804 |
| crispā | . | Wht. grn. | 8, S. Ev. | S. E. Ind. | . 1804 |
| mediā | . | Wht. grn. | 7, S. Ev. | S. E. Ind. | . 1804 |

*argentĕā, aromāticā, astroītēs, cascarillā, castaneæfōlĭā, digitātā, flabellifōlĭā, flāvus, glandulōsā, gossypifōlĭā 1, hibiscifōlĭā, hūmilis, lācerā, lobātā, lūcidā, macrophyllā, maritīmā, micāns, moluccānā 2, nitēns, nivĕā, palūstris, penicillātā, pūngēns, rosmarinifōlĭā, tomentōsā, xalapēnsis.*

CRŎWĔĀ, *Smith.* In honour of James Crow, of Norwich, an excellent British botanist, and a great collector of willows. *Linn.* 10, Or. 1, Nat. Or. *Rutaceæ.* Delightful greenhouse shrubs, producing their beautiful purple flowers throughout the greatest part of the year; they succeed in loam and peat, and cuttings root freely in sand, under a glass.

| | | | | | |
|---|---|---|---|---|---|
| latifōlĭā | . | Purple | . 7, G. Ev. | S. N. S. W. | . 1825 |
| salignā | . | Purple | . 9, G. Ev. | S. N. S. W. | . 1796 |

CROWFOOT, see *Ranōncŭlŭs.*

CROW's-FOOT, see *Echinōchlŏā cŭs cŏrvī.*

CROWNED, terminated by anything.

CROZŎPHŎRĀ, *Necker.* The meaning is not explained. *Linn.* 21, Or. 10, Nat. Or. *Euphorbiaceæ.* An annual species, of simple culture, succeeding in any light soil. The preparation called turnsol is chiefly obtained from this plant. *Synonyme:* 1. *Croton tinctoria.*

| | | | | | |
|---|---|---|---|---|---|
| tinctōrĭā, 1 | . | Wht. grn. | 7, H. | A. S. Eur. | . 1570 |

CRUCIANĒLLĀ, *Linn.* A diminutive of *crux*, a cross; alluding to the leaves being placed crosswise. *Linn.* 4, Or. 1, Nat. Or. *Stellatæ.* The greenhouse species of this genus grow freely in a mixture of loam and peat, and may be increased by cuttings; the annual kinds merely require sowing in the open border.

| | | | | | |
|---|---|---|---|---|---|
| ægyptĭācā | . | Yellow | . 6, H. | A. Egypt | . 1800 |
| americānā | . | Yellow | . 7, G. Ev | S. Amer. | . 1780 |
| angustifōlĭā | . | Yellow | . 6, H. | A. France | . 1658 |
| anōmalā | . | Yellow | . 7, H. Her. | P. Caucasus | . 1820 |
| ciliātā | . | Yellow | . 7, H. | A. Levant | . 1805 |
| glomerātā | . | Yellow | . 7, H. Her. | P. Iberia | . 1824 |
| latifōlĭā | . | Green | . 6, H. | A. France | . 1633 |
| maritīmā | . | Yellow | . 7, G. Ev. | S. France | . 1640 |
| mollugīnōīdēs | . | Green | . 7, H. Her. | P. Caucasus | . 1801 |
| monspelliācā | . | Yellow | . 7, H. | A. France | . 1791 |
| pātŭlā | . | Yellow | . 6, H. | A. Spain | . 1793 |
| pubēscēns | . | Purple | . 7, H. Her. | P. Candia | . 1799 |
| stylōsā | . | Pink | . 7, H Her. | P. Persia | . |
| tuberculōsā | . | Yellow | . 7, H. | A. Spain | . 1826 |

CRUCIATE, a flower is cruciate when four petals are placed opposite each other, at right angles.

CRUCIFEROUS, the name of a particular family of plants bearing cruciate flowers.

CRYBE, *Lindley.* From *krubeis*, concealed; in allusion to the manner in which the column is hidden by the floral envelopes. *Linn.* 20, Or. 1, Nat. Or. *Orchidaceæ.* This plant is only remarkable for never expanding its singular, club-shaped, rose-coloured flowers. It requires the same treatment as *Bletia.*

| | | | | | |
|---|---|---|---|---|---|
| róseã | . . . | Rose | . 6, S. Ter. Mexico | . . 183- |

CRYPSIS, *Aiton.* From *krypto*, to conceal; referring to the flowers being concealed among the leaves. *Linn.* 3, Or. 3, Nat. Or. *Gramineæ.* Uninteresting species of grass, merely requiring to be sown in any common soil. Synonyme: 1. *Heleochloa alopecuroides, Phalaris crypsoides—aculeãtã, alopecuroĩdẽs* 1, *schænoĩdẽs.*

CRYPTĂNDRĂ, *Smith.* From *kryptos*, hidden, and *aner*, a man; alluding to the stamens being concealed. *Linn.* 5, Or. 1, Nat. Or. *Rhamnaceæ.* A singular genus; the species grow well in sandy peat, and young plants may be obtained from cuttings.

| | | | | | |
|---|---|---|---|---|---|
| amárã | . . . | White | . 5, G. Ev. S. N. Holl. | . 1821 |
| ericifõllã | . . . | White | . 5, G. Ev. S. N. Holl. | . 1821 |
| obovãtã | . . . | White | . 5, G. Ev. S. N. Holl. | . 1825 |
| spinẽscẽns | . . . | White | . 5, G. Ev. S. N. Holl. | . 1824 |

CRYPTARRHĔNĂ, *R. Brown.* From *kryptos*, hidden, and *arren*, a male. *Linn.* 20, Or. 1, Nat. Or. *Orchidaceæ.* The small, yellowish-green flowers of this species are produced on a loose spike. For culture and propagation, see *Bletia.*

| | | | | |
|---|---|---|---|---|
| lunãtã | . . . | Yelsh. grn. | S. Ter. Jamaica | . . 1815 |

CRYPTOCĂRYĂ, *R. Brown.* From *kryptos*, hidden, and *karya*, a nut; alluding to the fruit being covered. Greenhouse shrubs, growing about sixteen feet high; they will succeed in sandy peat, and plants may be obtained from cuttings.

| | | | | |
|---|---|---|---|---|
| glaucẽscẽns | . . | Wht. yel. | 4, G. Ev. S. N. Holl. | . 1818 |
| obovãtã | . . | Wht. yel. | 4, G. Ev. S. N. Holl. | . 1820 |

CRYPTOCHĪLŬS, *Wallich.* From *kryptos*, hidden, and *cheilos*, a lip; the labellum is not easily seen, on account of the contraction of the mouth of the calyx. *Linn.* 20, Or. 1, Nat. Or. *Orchidaceæ.* A very interesting species, well worth a place in every collection of orchideous plants. It produces its brilliant scarlet flowers on a one-sided spike. For culture and propagation, see *Stanhopea.*

| | | | | |
|---|---|---|---|---|
| sanguĩnẽã | . . . | Scarlet | . 6, S. Epi. Nepal | . . |

CRYPTOLĔPĬS, *R. Brown.* From *kryptos*, hidden, and *lepis*, a scale; in reference to the seeds. *Linn.* 5, Or. 1, Nat. Or. *Apocynaceæ.* An interesting climbing species, growing well in a mixture of peat and loam, and multiplied by cuttings under a glass, in sand.

| | | | | |
|---|---|---|---|---|
| élẽgãns | . . . . | | S. Ev. Tw. Brasil | . . 1824 |

CRYPTŎMŸCĔS, *Greville.* Derived from *kryptos*, hidden, and *mikes*, a small fungus; alluding to the smallness of the plants. *Linn.* 24, Or. 9, Nat. Or. *Fungi.* A curious species found on willow branches—*Watchll.*

CRYPTOSPĔRMŬM, *Persoon.* From *kryptos*, hidden, and *sperma*, a seed; in allusion to the seeds being concealed in the involucrum. *Linn.* 4, Or. 1, Nat. Or. *Cinchonaceæ.* A plant of little merit, growing freely, and increased by cuttings. Synonyme: 1. *Opercularia paleata—Yoũngĩĩ* 1.

CRYPTOSTĕGIĂ, *R. Brown.* From *kryptos*, concealed, and *stege*, a covering; referring to the corona being concealed within the tube of the corolla. *Linn.* 5, Or. 2, Nat. Or. *Asclepiadaceæ.* Beautiful, climbing plants, succeeding in a mixture of loam and peat; and cuttings will root freely in sand, under a glass, in heat.

| | | | | |
|---|---|---|---|---|
| grandiflõrã | . . | Pink | . 6, S. Ev. Tw. India | . 1818 |
| madagascariẽnsis | . | Pink | . 7, S. Ev. Tw. Madag. | . 1826 |

CRYPTOSTĔMMĂ, *R. Brown.* From *kryptos*, hidden, and *stemma*, a crown; the crown of the grains being concealed in wood. *Linn.* 19, Or. 3, Nat. Or. *Compositæ.* Annual species, requiring to be sown in a gentle hotbed, and, when of a sufficient strength,

planted out in the open borders, where they will flower, and look very well.

| | | | | | |
|---|---|---|---|---|---|
| calendulãceŭm | . | Yellow | . 7, H. | A. C. G. H. | . 1752 |
| hypochondrĩacŭm | Yellow | . 7, H. | A. C. G. H. | . 1781 |
| runcinãtŭm | . . | Yellow | . 7, H. | A. C. G. H. | . 1794 |

CRYPTŏsTŸLĬs, *R. Brown.* From *kryptos*, hidden, and *stylos*, a style. *Linn.* 20, Or. 1, Nat. Or. *Orchidaceæ.* The species of this genus are curious, and succeed best in an equal mixture of turfy loam, peat, and sand; divisions.

| | | | | | |
|---|---|---|---|---|---|
| ẽrẽctã | . . . | Drk. bra. | . 6, G. Ter. N. Holl. | | 1824 |
| longifõlĩã | . . . | Drk. bra. | . 6, G. Ter. N. Holl. | | 1822 |

CRYSTALLINE, resembling crystals.

CŬBĬCŬs, cubical, die-shaped.

CUCKOO-FLOWER, see *Lychnis flosc̆ŭcŭli.*

CUCKOO-FLOWER, see *Cardamine pratensis.*

CUCŬBĂLŬs, *Gærtner.* Altered from *Căcŏbŏlŭs*, which is derived from *kakos*, bad, and *bolos*, a shoot; meaning a plant which is destructive to the soil. *Linn.* 10, Or. 3, Nat. Or. *Silenaceæ.* A common plant, of little interest, thriving in any common soil, and increasing either by seeds, or division—*baccĩfer.*

CUCULLATE; a leaf is cucullate when its edge is curved inwards, so as to resemble the cowl of a monk.

CUCUMBER, see *Cŭcŭmis.*

CŬCŬMĬs, *Linn.* Derived from *curvus*, crooked; referring to the shape of the fruit. *Linn.* 21, Or. 10, Nat. Or. *Cucurbitaceæ.* This is a well-known and extensively cultivated genus, chiefly for culinary purposes. The *C. colocynthis* produces the colocynth of the shops. The whole of the species require to be sown in a hotbed, and, when of sufficient size and strength, to be planted out in frames, or under a hand-glass, in a good rich soil. Synonyme: 1. *Cucurbita citrullus.*

| | | | | | |
|---|---|---|---|---|---|
| africãnŭs | . . | Yellow | . 7, F. Tr. A. C. G. H. | | |
| Angũrĩã | . . . | Yellow | . 7, F. Tr. A. Jamaica | | 1692 |
| Ciãtã | . . . | Yellow | . 6, F. Tr. A. Levant | | 1759 |
| Citrŭllŭs, 1 | . | Yellow | . 6, F. Tr. A. S. Eur. | | 1597 |
| Jace | . . | Yellow | . 7, F. Tr. A. | | 1597 |
| Pastẽcã | . . | Yellow | . 7, F. Tr. A. | | 1597 |
| Colocynthis | . . | Yellow | . 6, F. Tr. A. C. G. H. | | 1551 |
| delĩcĩõsŭs | . . | Yellow | . 7, F. Tr. A. E. Ind. | | 1818 |
| Dudãĩm | . . | Yellow | . 6, F. Tr. A. Levant | | 1705 |
| flexuõsŭs | . . | Yellow | . 6, F. Tr. A. E. Ind. | | 1597 |
| integrifõlĩŭs | . . | Yellow | . 7, F. Tr. A. E. Ind. | | 1820 |
| jamaicẽnsis | . . | Yellow | . 7, F. Tr. A. Jamaica | | 1824 |
| linẽãtŭs | . . | Yellow | . 7, F. Tr. A. Guiana | | 1825 |
| maculãtŭs | . . | Yellow | . 7, F. Tr. A. Guinea | | 1820 |
| maderaspãtãnŭs | . | Yellow | . 7, F. Tr. A. E. Ind. | | 1805 |
| Mẽlõ | . . . | Yellow | . 7, F. Tr. A. | | 1570 |
| Cantalŭpĭ | . | Yellow | . 7, F. Tr. A. | | 1570 |
| melitẽnsis | . | Yellow | . 7, F. Tr. A. | | 1570 |
| reticulãtŭs | . | Yellow | . 7, F. Tr. A. | | 1570 |
| Momõrdĭcã | . | Yellow | . 7, F. Tr. A. E. Ind. | | 1820 |
| muricãtŭs | . . | Yellow | . 7, F. Tr. A. E. Ind. | | 1817 |
| prophetãrŭm | . | Yellow | . 7, F. Tr. A. Levant | | 1777 |
| pubẽscẽns | . . | Yellow | . 7, F. Tr. A. | | 1815 |
| satĩvŭs | . . | Yellow | . 8, H. Tr. A. E. Ind. | | 1597 |
| albŭs | . | Yellow | . 7, H. Tr. A. | | |
| fastigiãtŭs | . | Yellow | . 7, H. Tr. A. | | |
| flãvŭs | . | Yellow | . 7, H. Tr. A. | | |
| variegãtŭs | . | Yellow | . 7, H. Tr. A. | | |
| virĭdĭs | . | Yellow | . 7, F. Tr. A. E. Ind. | | 1597 |
| utilĩssĭmŭs | . | Yellow | . 7, F. Tr. A. E. Ind. | | 1820 |

CŬCŬRBĬTĂ, *Linn.* From *curvitas*, crookedness; in allusion to the shape. *Linn.* 21, Or. 10, Nat. Or. *Cucurbitaceæ.* For culture, &c., see *Cucumis,* to which genus this is nearly allied.

| | | | | | |
|---|---|---|---|---|---|
| aurantĩãcã | . | Yellow | . 7, F. Tr. A. | | 1802 |
| orãngĩnã | . | Yellow | . 7, F. Tr. A. | | 1802 |
| colocynthoĩdẽs | . | Yellow | . 7, F. Tr. A. | | 1802 |
| mãxĭmã | . . | Yellow | . 7, H. Tr. A. | | |
| Melopẽpõ | . . | Yellow | . 6, H. Tr. A. | | 1597 |
| moschãtã | . . | Yellow | . 7, H. Tr. A. | | |
| ovĩferã | . . | Yellow | . 8, H. Tr. A. Astracan. | | |
| grisẽã | . | Yellow | . 7, H. Tr. A. | | |
| pyrĩfõrmĭs | . | Yellow | . 7, H. Tr. A. | | |
| subglobõsã | . | Yellow | . 7, H. Tr. A. | | |
| Pẽpõ | . . . | Yellow | . 7, H. Tr. A. Levant | | 1570 |
| oblõngã | . | Yellow | . 7, H. Tr. A. | | 1570 |
| subrotŭndã | . | Yellow | . 7, H. Tr. A. Levant | | 1570 |
| Potĩrã | . . | Yellow | . 7, H. Tr. A. | | |
| gourgẽrã | . | Yellow | . 7, H. Tr. A. | | |
| virĭdĭs | . | Yellow | . 7, H. Tr. A. | | |
| ulcerãrĭã | . . | Yellow | . 7, H. Tr. A. Chile | | 1824 |
| subverrucõsã | . | Yellow | . 6, H. Tr. A. | | |
| verrucõsã | . . | Yellow | . 7, H. Tr. A. | | 1658 |

CŬICĬTĬŬM, *Humboldt and Bonpland.* From *culcita*, a stuffed bed; referring to the heads of palæœ. *Linn.*

19, Or. 1, Nat. Or. *Compositæ*. An ornamental, greenhouse plant, growing well in any common soil, and propagated by cuttings. *Synonyme:* 1. *Cacalia salicina*.

salicinūm, 1 . . Yellow . 6, G. Ev. S. N. Holl. . 1820

CULLŪMĬA, *R. Brown*. In honour of Sir Thomas Cullum, Bart., F.L.S., a great promoter of botany. *Linn.* 19, Or. 3, Nat. Or. *Compositæ*. Curious species, growing well in a mixture of peat and loam, and cuttings will strike root in soil, under a glass, in heat.

| | | | |
|---|---|---|---|
| ciliāris . . . . | Yellow | . 5, G. Ev. S. C. G. H. | . 1774 |
| setōsā . . . . | Yellow | . 7, G. Ev. S. C. G. H. | . 1780 |
| squarrōsā . . . | Yellow | . 7, G. Ev. S. C. G. H. | . 1786 |

CULM, the stem of grasses, scitamineous plants, and the like.

CULMIFEROUS, producing culms.

CULTRATE, } shaped like a pruning-knife.
CULTRIFORM, }

CUMIN, see *Cuminūm*.

CUMIN, see *Lagœcia*.

CUMINŪM, *Bauhin*. Altered from *quamoun*, its Arabic name. *Linn.* 5, Or. 2, Nat. Or. *Umbelliferæ*. A plant of little beauty, and merely requires to be sown in any open border, to succeed.

Cyminum . . . White . . 6, H. A. Egypt . . 1594

CUMMINGĬĀ, *D. Don*. In honour of Lady Gordon Cumming, of Altyre, near Forres, Scotland. *Linn.* 6, Or. 1, Nat. Or. *Liliaceæ*. Pretty frame bulbs, with blue flowers; a mixture of loam and peat suits them, and they are multiplied by offsets. *Synonyme:* 1. *Conanthera campanulata*.

| | | | |
|---|---|---|---|
| campanulātā, 1 | Blue . . | 8, F. Bu. P. Chile | . 1823 |
| tenélla . . . | Blue . . | 11, F. Bu. P. Chile | . 1829 |
| trimaculātā . . | Blue . . | 12, F. Bu. P. Chile | . 1829 |

CUMULATE, heaped, overflowed.

CUNEATE, wedge-shaped.

CUNEIFORM-OVATE, between wedge-shaped and egg-shaped.

CUNĪLA, *Linn*. The derivation of this word is doubtful; by some botanists it is supposed to be from *konos*, a cone, and by others, to be from *Cunila*, the name of a town. *Linn.* 2, Or. 1, Nat. Or. *Labiatæ*. Pretty species. *C. coccinea* requires the heat of a greenhouse, and will succeed in a mixture of loam and peat. *C. mariana* will thrive in the open border, in any common soil; they may both be increased by division. *C. mariana* is used beneficially in slight fevers and colds, with a view to excite perspiration.

| | | | |
|---|---|---|---|
| coccinēa . . . | Scarlet . . | 9, G. Her. P. N. Amer. | . 1823 |
| mariānā . . . | Red . . | 9, H. Her. P. N. Amer. | . 1759 |

CUNNINGHAMĬĀ, *Richard*. In honour of J. and A. Cunningham, botanists and travellers in New South Wales. *Linn.* 21, Or. 10, Nat. Or. *Coniferæ*. This is a very handsome species; it succeeds best in a mixture of peat and loam, and may be propagated by cuttings, or seeds. It will grow freely planted out in a warm situation, if protected during the winter from severe frost. *Synonyme:* 1. *Pinus lanceolata, Belis jaculiflora, C. lanceolata.*

sinénsis, 1 . . Apetal . G. Ev. T. China . . 1804

CUNŌNĬĀ, *Linn*. In honour of John Christian Cuno, of Amsterdam, who described his own garden in verse, in 1750. *Linn.* 10, Or. 2, Nat. Or. *Cunoniaceæ*. An ornamental, greenhouse tree, attaining a height of twenty feet; it prefers a mixture of sandy loam and peat, and cuttings root in sand, under a glass, in heat.

capēnsis . . . White . . 8, G. Ev. T. C. G. H. . 1816

CUP, anything in the shape of a cup.

CUPĀNĬĀ, *Plumier*. In memory of Father Francis Cupani, an Italian monk, and botanical author, who died in 1710. *Linn.* 8, Or. 1, Nat. Or. *Sapindaceæ*. An ornamental stove genus. The species vary in height from six to twenty feet; they flourish in a mixture of equal parts peat and loam, and young plants may be obtained from cuttings, under a glass, in sand. *Synonyme:* 1. *Molinia canescens*.

| | | | |
|---|---|---|---|
| canéscens, 1 . . | White . . | 8. Ev. T. E. Ind. | . 1818 |
| dentātā . . . . | White . . | 8. Ev. T. Mexico . | . 1824 |
| excélsa . . . . | White . . | 8. Ev. T. Mexico . | . 1824 |
| glābrā . . . . | White . . | 5, 8. Ev. T. Jamaica | . 1822 |

[ 95 ]

---

| | | | |
|---|---|---|---|
| saponarioïdēs . . | White . | 4, 8. Ev. 8. W. Ind. | . 1810 |
| setĭgerā . . . | White . | 11, 8. Ev. T. C. Moret. B. | . 1820 |
| tomentōsā . . . | White . | 8. Ev. T. W. Ind. | . 1818 |

CŪPHĒĀ, *Jacquin*. Derived from *kuphos*, curved; in reference to the form of the capsule. *Linn.* 11, Or. 1, Nat. Or. *Lythraceæ*. This is rather a pretty genus; the stove species require to be grown in sandy loam, and are propagated by cuttings. The annual kinds should be raised in a gentle hotbed, and when strong enough, may be potted off, and kept in the greenhouse. *Synonyme:* 1. *Melvillea speciosa*.

| | | | |
|---|---|---|---|
| circæoïdēs . . | Purple . | 9, G. | A. S. Amer. | . 1821 |
| decándrā . . | Purple . | 7, 8. Ev. 8. | Jamaica | . 1789 |
| grācĭlis . . | Purple . | 7, 8. Ev. 8. | Orinoco . | . 1824 |
| lanceolātā . . | Purple . | 8. | B. Mexico . | . 1796 |
| Llavēā . . | Purple . | 6, F. Ev. 8. | Mexico . | . 1830 |
| Melvilliā, 1 . . | Scarlet . | 8, 8. Her. P. | Guiana . | . 1823 |
| micropétalā . . | Purple . | 7, 8. Ev. 8. | Mexico . | . 1824 |
| multiflōrā . . | Purple . | 9, 8. Ev. 8. | Mexico . | . 1824 |
| parviflōrā . . | Pink . . | 11, 8. Ev. 8. | Demerara | . 1824 |
| procúmbēns . . | Pa. pur. | 8, 8. | A. Mexico . | . 1816 |
| racemōsā . . | Purple . | 6, 8. Ev. 8. | W. Ind. | . 1820 |
| serpyllifōliā . . | Red . | 8, 8. Ev. 8. | Trinidad | . 1822 |
| viscosissĭmā . . | Purple . | 7, G. | A. America | . 1776 |
| virgātā . . | Purple . | 8, G. | A. Mexico . | . 1824 |

CŪPĬĀ, *Decandolle*. Cupi is the Malabar name of one of the species. *Linn.* 5, Or. 1, Nat. Or. *Cinchonaceæ*. The species of this genus deserve to be in every collection of plants, being very showy when in blossom, and the flowers very fragrant. For culture and propagation, see *Rondeletia*. *Synonymes:* 1. *Webera coriacea*. 2. *W. corymbosa*. 3. *W. cymosa.*

| | | | |
|---|---|---|---|
| coriācea, 1 . . | White . . | 8. Ev. 8. E. Ind. . | . 1828 |
| corymbōsā, 2 . | White . . | 8. Ev. 8. E. Ind. . | . 1759 |
| cymōsā, 3 . . | White . . | 8. Ev. 8. E. Ind. . | . 1811 |

CUPRĒSSŪS, *Linn*. From *kuo*, to produce, and *parisos*, equal; in reference to the branches being regular. *Linn.* 21, Or. 10, Nat. Or. *Coniferæ*. The species comprising this genus are handsome, evergreen trees, varying in height from ten to forty feet. The hardy kinds are beautiful ornaments for lawns, grass plots, &c. They prefer a good, rich, loamy soil, and are generally multiplied by seeds; but cuttings may be made to root, under a glass, in the shade. *Synonymes:* 1. *glauca*. 2. *Thuja sphæroidea.*

| | | | |
|---|---|---|---|
| austrālis . . | Apetal . | 4, G. Ev. T. N. Holl. | |
| bacciformis . . | Apetal . | 5, H. Ev. T. | . 1818 |
| lusitānĭca, 1 . . | Apetal . | 4, F. Ev. T. Goa . . | . 1683 |
| péndŭla . . | Apetal . | 5, G. Ev. T. Japan . | . 1808 |
| sempervĭrens . . | Apetal . | 5, H. Ev. T. Candia . | . 1548 |
|   horizontālis . | Apetal . | 5, H. Ev. T. Mediter. | |
| strícta . . | Apetal . | 5, H. Ev. T. Mediter. | |
| thyoïdēs, 2 . . | Apetal . | 5, H. Ev. T. N. Amer. | . 1736 |
| torulōsā . . | Apetal . | 5, H. Ev. T. Nepal . | . 1824 |

CŪPRĒŪS, copper-coloured.

CUPŪLĀ, the cup of an acorn, and such-like fruits.

CUPULATE, shaped like a cup, or a reversed bell.

CURATĚLLĂ, *Linn*. From *kureno*, to shave; in reference to the leaves being used in Guiana for polishing bows, sabres, &c. *Linn.* 13, Or. 2, Nat. Or. *Dilleniaceæ*. Stove shrubs of some beauty, succeeding in sandy loam, and cuttings, made of the ripened wood, root freely in sand, under a glass.

| | | | |
|---|---|---|---|
| alātā . . . . | White . . | 8. Ev. 8. Guiana . . | |
| americānā . . | White . . | 8. Ev. 8. 8. Amer. . | |

CURCŪLĬGŌ, *Gærtner*. Derived from *curculio*, a weevil; the seeds have a process resembling the beak of that animal. *Linn.* 6, Or. 1, Nat. Or. *Amaryllidaceæ*. Pretty, herbaceous species, succeeding in a mixture of loam and peat, and increased by offsets.

| | | | |
|---|---|---|---|
| brevifōlĭā . . | Yellow . | 6, 8. Her. P. E. Ind. . | . 1804 |
| latifōlĭā . . | Yellow . | 6, 8. Her. P. Penla Pin. | . 1804 |
| orchioïdēs . . | Yellow . | 6, 8. Her. P. E. Ind. . | . 1800 |
| plicātā . . | Yellow . | 6, G. Her. P. C. G. H. | . 1788 |
|   glābrā . . | Yellow . | 6, G. Her. P. C. G. H. | . 1788 |
| recurvātā . . | Yellow . | 8. Her. P. Bengal . | . 1805 |
| sumatrānā . . | Yellow . | 7, 8. Her. P. Sumatra | . 1818 |

CURCŪMĂ, *Linn*. Derived from *kurkum*, its Arabic name. *Linn.* 1, Or. 1, Nat. Or. *Scitamineæ*. Interesting species, thriving well in a rich, light soil, and increased by offsets, from the root. Turmeric is obtained from *C. longa*; it is cordial and stomachic, and considered by the native doctors of India an excellent application in powder for cleansing foul ulcers. A kind of arrow-root is prepared from *C. angustifolia*.

| Name | Colour | Time | Habit | Native | Year |
|---|---|---|---|---|---|
| æruginösä | Red yel. | 5, 8. | Her. P. | E. Ind. | 1807 |
| amädä | Red yel. | 4, 8. | Her. P. | Bengal | 1819 |
| angustifòliä | Yellow | 7, 8. | Her. P. | E. Ind. | 1822 |
| aromáticä | Yellow | 6, 8. | Her. P. | E. Ind. | 1804 |
| cæsiä | Yellow | 5, 8. | Her. P. | Bengal | 1819 |
| comösä | Red yel. | 5, 8. | Her. P. | E. Ind. | 1819 |
| elätä | Crimson | 5, 8. | Her. P. | E. Ind. | 1819 |
| ferruginsä | Yellow | 5, 8. | Her. P. | E. Ind. | 1819 |
| latifòlia | Yellow | 5, 8. | Her. P. | E. Ind. | 1820 |
| leucorhizä | Red yel. | 5, 8. | Her. P. | E. Ind. | 1819 |
| lòngä | | 8, 8. | Her. P. | E. Ind. | 1759 |
| montänä | Red wht. | 5, 8. | Her. P. | E. Ind. | 1824 |
| parviflòrä | Wht. vio. | 1, 8. | Her. P. | Rome | 1828 |
| petiolätä | Blue | 8, 8. | Her. P. | Pegu | 1822 |
| reclinätä | Pink | 4, 8. | Her. P. | E. Ind. | 1824 |
| rubéscens | Red | 7, 8. | Her. P. | E. Ind. | 1805 |
| rubricaulis | Yellow | 5, 8. | Her. P. | E. Ind. | 1822 |
| viridiflòrä | Yel. grn. | 8. | Her. P. | Sumatra | 1822 |
| xanthorhizä | Red | 5, 8. | Her. P. | Amboyna | 1819 |
| sedoäriä | Red | 7, 8. | Her. P. | E. Ind. | 1797 |
| serúmbét | Yellow | 7, 8. | Her. P. | E. Ind. | 1807 |

CURRANT, see Ribes.

CURTA, broken off, curtailed.

CURTISIA, Aiton. In honour of the late William Curtis, the founder of the Botanical Magazine. Linn. 3, Or. 1, Nat. Or. Aquifoliaceæ. This, in its native country, is a timber tree, attaining the height of eighty feet, and from which the Hottentots and Caffres make the shafts of their javelins. It succeeds in loam and peat, and cuttings strike readily in sand.

| Name | Colour | Habit | Native | Year |
|---|---|---|---|---|
| faginsä | Pale | G. Ev. T. | C. G. H. | 1775 |

CURTOGYNE, Haworth. From kurtos, curved, and gyne, a style; referring to the gibbous ovaria. Linn. 5, Or. 5, Nat. Or. Crassulaceæ. Greenhouse species, flourishing in sandy loam, and propagated by cuttings, which should be laid a few days in the sun to dry. Synonyme: 1. Crassula undata.

| Name | Colour | Time | Habit | Native | Year |
|---|---|---|---|---|---|
| undäiä, 1 | White | 8, | G. Ev. S. | C. G. H. | 1818 |
| undulätä | White | 8, | G. Ev. S. | C. G. H. | 1797 |
| undösä | White | 8, | G. Ev. S. | C. G. H. | 1824 |

CUSCÜTA, Linn. Derived from its Arabic name, kechout. Linn. 5, Or. 2, Nat. Or. Cuscutaceæ. A genus of curious parasitical plants. They will grow on almost any plant they can lay hold of, producing, in the autumn, abundance of sweet-scented flowers. Synonyme: 1. Reflexa verrucosa.

| Name | Colour | Time | Habit | Native | Year |
|---|---|---|---|---|---|
| americänä | Wht. yel. | 8, | Parasite. | S. Amer. | 1816 |
| austràlis | White | 8, | Parasite. | N. Holl. | 1818 |
| chilänsis | White | 8, | Parasite. | Chile | 1821 |
| chinénsis | White | 8, | Parasite. | China | 1808 |
| Epithymüm | White | 7, | Parasite. | Britain | |
| europæä | White | 9, | Parasite. | Britain | |
| Hookéri, 1 | White | 8, | Parasite. | E. Ind. | 1823 |
| verrucösä | White | 8, | Parasite. | Nepal | 1821 |

CUSSÖNIA, Thunberg. In honour of Pette Cusson, a celebrated French botanist, and professor at Montpellier. Linn. 5, Or. 2, Nat. Or. Araliaceæ. Greenhouse shrubs, succeeding well in a mixture of peat and loam, and cuttings root freely in sand, under a glass.

| Name | Colour | Habit | Native | Year |
|---|---|---|---|---|
| spicätä | Green | G. Ev. S. | C. G. H. | 1789 |
| thyrsiflòrä | Green | G. Ev. S. | C. G. H. | 1795 |
| triptèris | Green | G. Ev. S. | C. G. H. | 1816 |

CUSTARD APPLE, see Anòna.

CUTANEOUS, relating to the skin.

CUTICLE, the scarf skin, or epidermis.

CUT-TOOTHED, cut and toothed at the same time.

CYAMÖRSIS, Decandolle. From kyamos, a bean, and opsis, resemblance; on account of the plant resembling a bean. Linn. 16, Or. 6, Nat. Or. Leguminosæ. An annual species, of some beauty, growing freely in any common soil. Synonymes: 1. Dolichos psoraleoides, D. fabæformis, Psoralea tetragonolobus, Lupinus trifoliatus.

| Name | Colour | Time | Habit | Native | Year |
|---|---|---|---|---|---|
| psoraloìdes, 1 | Purple | 7, H. | A. | Arabia | 1818 |

CYANÉLLÄ, Linn. A diminutive of kyanos, blue; alluding to the flowers. Linn. 6, Or. 1, Nat. Or. Liliaceæ. These are pretty bulbous plants, thriving in a mixture of sandy loam and peat, and increased by offsets.

| Name | Colour | Time | Habit | Native | Year |
|---|---|---|---|---|---|
| alba | White | 7, | G. Bu. P. | C. G. H. | 1819 |
| capénsis | Blue | 7, | G. Bu. P. | C. G. H. | 1768 |
| lineätä | Striped | 7, | G. Bu. P. | C. G. H. | 1816 |
| lùteä | Yellow | 7, | G. Bu. P. | C. G. H. | 1788 |
| orchidiflòrä | Blue | 8, | G. Bu. P. | C. G. H. | 1826 |

CYANÖTIS, D. Don. Derived from kyanos, blue, and ous, an ear; referring to the flowers. Linn. 6, Or. 1, Nat. Or. Commelinaceæ. Pretty species, requiring a good rich soil. C. barbata may be increased by division.

| Name | Colour | Time | Habit | Native | Year |
|---|---|---|---|---|---|
| axilläris | Blue | 8, | G. | B. E. Ind. | 1822 |
| barbätä | Blue | 8, | H. Her. P. | Nepal | 1824 |
| cristätä | Blue | 8, | G. | B. Ceylon | 1770 |

CYATHEA, Smith. From kyatheion, a little cup; in allusion to the indusium being cup-shaped. Linn. 24, Or. 1, Nat. Or. Polypodiaceæ. This is a genus of fine tropical ferns, mostly arborescent, growing from fifteen to twenty feet high. They succeed best in a mixture of peat and loam, and are increased by division, or seeds. Synonyme: 1. arborea.

| Name | Colour | Habit | Native | Year |
|---|---|---|---|---|
| arbörea | Brown | 8. Ev. T. | W. Ind. | 1793 |
| excélsa, 1 | Brown | 8. Ev. T. | Maurit. | 1825 |

CYATHIFORM, cup-shaped, concave.

CYATHÖDES, Labillardière. From kyathos, a cup, and eidos, like; because the nectary resembles that vessel. Linn. 5, Or. 1, Nat. Or. Epacridaceæ. Greenhouse shrubs, worth cultivating; they thrive in a mixture of peat and loam, and young plants may be obtained from cuttings.

| Name | Colour | Time | Habit | Native | Year |
|---|---|---|---|---|---|
| acerösa | White | 7, | G. Ev. S. | N. Holl. | 1823 |
| glaucä | White | 4, | G. Ev. T. | V. D. L. | 1818 |
| Oxycèdrus | White | 4, | G. Ev. S. | V. D. L. | 1822 |

CYCAS, Linn. The Greek name of a palm, said to grow in Ethiopia. Linn. 22, Or. 12, Nat. Or. Cycadaceæ. This is a fine ornamental genus of stove plants, requiring to be grown in good rich loam, with a liberal supply of water. Young plants may be obtained from suckers, which are sometimes produced. From the soft stem of C. circinalis a kind of sago is produced.

| Name | Colour | Time | Habit | Native | Year |
|---|---|---|---|---|---|
| angulätä | Apetal | | 8. Her. P. | N. Holl. | 1824 |
| circinàlis | Apetal | | 8. Her. P. | E. Ind. | 1700 |
| glaucä | Apetal | | 8. Her. P. | E. Ind. | 1818 |
| revolütä | Apetal | 7, | 8. Her. P. | China | 1737 |
| squarrösä | Apetal | | 8. Her. P. | E. Ind. | 1824 |

CYCLAMEN, Linn. Derived from kyclicos, circular; referring to the round leaves. Linn. 5, Or. 1, Nat. Or. Primulaceæ. Pretty bulbous species, thriving well in a mixture of sandy loam and vegetable mould; they may be increased by seeds, which should be sown as soon as they are ripe. All the species are famous for their acridity, yet it is the principal food of the wild boars of Sicily, hence the common name of sowbread. Synonymes: 1. Clusii. 2. europæum.

| Name | Colour | Time | Habit | Native | Year |
|---|---|---|---|---|---|
| coüm | Li. red | 2, | H. Tu. P. | S. Eur. | 1596 |
| europæüm, 1 | Li. red | 8, | H. Tu. P. | Switzerl. | 1596 |
| hederifòliüm, 2 | Purple | 4, | H. Tu. P. | Britain | |
| albidüm | White | 7, | H. Tu. P. | Britain | |
| purpurascéns | Purple | 7, | H. Tu. P. | Britain | |
| ibèricüm | | | H. Tu. P. | Asiatic G. | 1831 |
| latifòliüm | Red | 4, | H. Tu. P. | S. Eur. | 1800 |
| linearifòliüm | Purple | 4, | H. Tu. P. | S. Eur. | 1824 |
| neapolitànüm | Red | 4, | H. Tu. P. | Italy | 1824 |
| persicüm | Red wht. | 2, | G. Tu. P. | Cyprus | 1731 |
| albiflòrüm | White | 2, | G. Tu. P. | Cyprus | 1731 |
| inodòrüm | Red wht. | 2, | G. Tu. P. | Cyprus | 1731 |
| odorätüm | Red wht. | 2, | G. Tu. P. | Cyprus | 1731 |
| laciniätüm | Red wht. | 4, | G. Tu. P. | | |
| repändüm | | 4, | G. Tu. P. | Greece | 1816 |
| vernüm | Purple | 4, | H. Tu. P. | S. Eur. | |

CYCLANTHUS, Poiteau. From kyclos, a circle, and anthos, a flower; in allusion to the disposition of the flowers. Linn. 21, Or. 9, Nat. Or. Cyclanthaceæ. A curious stove perennial, flourishing in a mixture of loam and peat, and multiplied by suckers.

| Name | Colour | Habit | Native | Year |
|---|---|---|---|---|
| Plumièri | Green | 8. Her. P. | Trinidad | 1820 |

CYCLONÖTHRA, Sweet. From kyklos, a circle, and bothros, a pit; alluding to the sepals being circular. Linn. 6, Or. 1, Nat. Or. Liliaceæ. Beautiful species of bulbous plants, thriving well in an equal mixture of loam, peat, and sand. They may be readily increased by the little viviparous bulbs that are produced on the upper part of the stem. Synonymes: 1. Fritillaria barbata. 2. Cyclobothra barbata. 3. Fritillaria purpurea.

| Name | Colour | Time | Habit | Native | Year |
|---|---|---|---|---|---|
| alba, 1 | White | 8, | H. Bu. P. | California | 1832 |
| barbätä | Yellow | 8, | F. Bu. P. | Mexico | 1827 |
| lùteä, 2 | Yellow | 9, | G. Bu. P. | Mexico | 1827 |
| pulchélla | Yellow | 8, | H. Bu. P. | California | 1832 |
| purpùrea, 3 | Pur. grn. | 8, | F. Bu. P. | Mexico | 1827 |

CYCLÖPIA, Ventenat. From kyclos, and pous, a foot; in allusion to the shape of the base of the pods. Linn. 10, Or. 1, Nat. Or. Leguminosæ. Greenhouse shrubs, with little to recommend them; they grow freely in a mixture of peat and loam, and propagate freely by cuttings. *Synonymes:* 1. *Sophora galioides, Aspalathus callosa.* 2. *Genista buxifolia.*

| | | | | | |
|---|---|---|---|---|---|
| galioides, 1 | . | Yellow | . 7, G. Ev. S. C. G. H. | . 1820 |
| genistoides | . . | Yellow | . 7, G. Ev. S. C. G. H. | . 1787 |
| latifolia, 2 | . . | Yellow | . 7, G. Ev. S. C. G. H. | . 1820 |
| tenuifolia | . . | Yellow | . 7, G. De. S. C. G. H. | . 1809 |

CYCNŌCHES, *Lindley.* From *kyknos*, a swan, and *auchen*, the neck; in allusion to the column, which is long, and gracefully curved, like the neck of a swan. *Linn.* 20, Or. 1, Nat. Or. *Orchidaceæ.* The species of this genus are well worth cultivating, especially C. *Loddigesii*, which has large and delightfully fragrant flowers. The sepals and petals of this species are of a brownish-green colour, with darker spots, and bearing a strong resemblance to the expanded wings of a swan. They require a strong heat, and a plentiful supply of water when growing, and to be otherwise treated as the *Stanhopeas.*

| | | | | | |
|---|---|---|---|---|---|
| Loddigesii | . . . | Wht. grn. | 5, S. Epi. Surinam | . 1830 |
| ventricosa | . . | Grn. wht. | . 8. Epi. Guatemala | . 1835 |

CYDŌNIA, *Tournefort.* Supposed to be named from its being a native of Kydon, in the Island of Crete. *Linn.* 12, Or. 2, Nat. Or. *Rosaceæ.* A genus of fruit trees. C. *japonica* is one of the handsomest hardy shrubs, producing its beautiful scarlet, or white flowers, in great abundance. C. *vulgaris*, the quince, is well known, and cultivated for its fruit. They will thrive in any soil, and may be multiplied by suckers.

| | | | | | |
|---|---|---|---|---|---|
| japonica | . . . | Scarlet all | H. De. S. Japan | . 1815 |
| alba | . . . | White all | . H. De. S. | |
| sinensis | . . . | Pink | . 5, H. De. S. China | . 1818 |
| vulgaris | . . | White | . 5, H. De. T. Austria | . 1573 |
| lusitanica | . | White | . 5, H. De. T. Spain | |
| maliformis | . . | White | . 5, H. De. T. | . 1573 |
| oblonga | . . | White | . 5, H. De. T. Europe | |

CYLINDRICAL, cylinder-shaped, round.
CYLINDRICALLY-GLOBOSE, a form between a cylinder and a sphere.
CYLINDROSPORIUM, *Linn.* From *kylindros*, a cylinder, and *spora*, a sporule; alluding to the cylindrical-shaped sporule. *Linn.* 24, Or. 9, Nat. Or. *Fungi.* A minute species, growing on cabbage leaves—*concentricum.*
CYLISTA, *Aiton.* Derived from *kylix*, a calyx; in allusion to the very large calyx. *Linn.* 17, Or. 4, Nat. Or. *Leguminosæ.* An ornamental climbing genus; the species grow well in a mixture of loam and peat, and cuttings of the young wood root well in sand, under a glass.

| | | | | | |
|---|---|---|---|---|---|
| albiflora | . . | White | . 4, S. Ev. Tw. Maurit. | |
| scariosa | . . | Yellow | . S. Ev. Tw. E. Ind. | . 1806 |
| tomentosa | . . | Yellow | . S. Ev. Tw. E. Ind. | . 1816 |
| villosa | . . . | Yellow | . 4, S. Ev. Tw. C. G. H. | . 1776 |

CYMBARIA, *Linn.* Derived from *kymbe*, a boat; referring to the shape of the fruit. *Linn.* 14, Or. 2, Nat. Or. *Scrophulariaceæ.* This is a curious plant, growing about a foot high, and producing yellow flowers; it will flourish in any common soil, and may be increased by dividing the roots.

| | | | | | |
|---|---|---|---|---|---|
| daurica | . . . | Yellow | . 6, H. Her. P. Tauria | . 1796 |

CYMBIDIUM, *Swarts.* From *kymbos*, a hollow recess; in allusion to the labellum. *Linn.* 20, Or. 1, Nat. Or. *Orchidaceæ.* Several of the species of this genus are remarkably handsome when in flower, and therefore deserve to be extensively cultivated. The *epiphytal* kinds may be referred to *Stanhopea*, and the *terrestrial*, to *Bletia*, for culture and propagation.

| | | | | | |
|---|---|---|---|---|---|
| aloifolium | . . | Pur. yel. | 9, S. Ter. E. Ind. | . 1789 |
| ensifolium | . . | Yel. strip. | 9, S. Ter. E. Ind. | . 1780 |
| cetriatum | . . | Grn. red | 6, S. Epi. China | |
| Finlaysonianum | . | | S. Epi. Cochin China | |
| Gibsonii | . . | Wht. red | 1, S. Ter. Sylhet | . 1837 |
| giganteum | . . | Brn. pur. | . S. Epi. Nepal | . 1837 |
| lancifolium | . . | Wht. red | 9, S. Ter. Nepal | . 1822 |
| marginatum | . . | Yel. pur. | . S. Epi. Brazil | |
| ochroleucum | . . | Yellow | . S. Epi. Trinidad | |
| sinense | . . . | Pur. grn. | . S. Ter. China | . 1793 |
| tristo | . . . | Purple | . S. Ter. Nepal | |
| virescens | . . | Greenish | 5, S. Epi. Japan | |
| xiphifolium | . . | Green | . 10, S. Ter. China | . 1814 |

CYMBIFORM, boat-shaped.

CYMBOPŌGON, *Sprengel.* From *kymbe*, a boat, and *pogon*, a beard; the valves of the calyx are boat-shaped. *Linn.* 23, Or. 1, Nat. Or. *Gramineæ.* A species of grass, remarkable for its fragrance; loam and peat suits it, in which it merely requires to be sown. *Synonyme:* 1. *Andropogon Schænanthus.*

| | | | | | |
|---|---|---|---|---|---|
| Schænanthus, 1 | . Apetal | . Grass. E. Ind. | . 1786 |

CYME, a mode of inflorescence resembling a flattened panicle, as that of the *Elder.*
CYMINOSMA, *Gærtner.* *Kyminon*, cumin seed, and *osme*, smell; the fruit smells like cumin seed. *Linn.* 8, Or. 1, Nat. Or. *Rutaceæ.* Curious evergreen shrubs. They flourish in a mixture of loam and peat, and cuttings root freely in sand, under a glass. *Synonymes:* 1. *Gela oblongifolia.* 2. *Jambolifera odorata.* 3. *J. pedunculata.*

| | | | | | |
|---|---|---|---|---|---|
| oblongifolia, 1 | . | White | . 7, G. Ev. S. N. S. W. | . 1824 |
| odorata, 2 | . | Green | . 6, S. Ev. S. China | . 1824 |
| pedunculata, 3 | . | Green | . 6, S. Ev. S. E. Ind. | . 1800 |

CYMOSE, flowering in cymes.
CYNANCHUM, *Linn.* From *kuon*, a dog, and *agche*, to strangle; alluding to its poisonous qualities. *Linn.* 5, Or. 2, Nat. Or. *Asclepiadaceæ.* Most of the species of this genus are perennial twiners, requiring the heat of the stove, or greenhouse; they may be grown in a good loamy soil, and will readily increase by cuttings. The hardy kinds thrive in any border soil. In Egypt, the leaves of C. *Arghel* are used for adulterating senna. *Synonymes:* 1. *Oleifolia.* 2. *Asclepias davurica.* 3. *A. villosa.* 4. *A. vincetoxicum.*

| | | | | | |
|---|---|---|---|---|---|
| acutum | . . | White | . 7, H. Her. P. Spain | . 1596 |
| Arghel, 1 | . . | Grh. wht. | 6, G. Ev. S. Egypt | . 1831 |
| capense | . | White | . 7, G. Ev. Tw. C. G. H. | . 1820 |
| cirrhosum | . . | | H. De. Tw. | . 1825 |
| crassifolium | . | Green | . G. Ev. Tw. C. G. H. | . 1816 |
| excelsum | . | White | . 7, H. De. Tw. Barbary | . 1816 |
| fimbriatum | . | Purple | . 7, S. Ev. Tw. Cumana | . 1826 |
| foetidum | . | White | . 7, S. Ev. Tw. Mexico | . 1820 |
| fuscatum | . | Brown | . 7, H. Her. P. | . 1817 |
| Heynianum | . | White | . 8. Ev. Tw. E. Ind. | . 1825 |
| hirsutum | . | | . 8. Ev. Tw. Trinidad | . 1825 |
| luteum | . | Yellow | . 6, H. Her. P. Europe | . 1596 |
| medium | . | White | . 6, H. Her. P. | |
| melanthos | . | Purple | . 7, H. De. Tw. | . 1818 |
| monspeliacum | . | White | . 8, H. Her. P. S. Eur. | . 1596 |
| mucronatum | . | Green | . 7, S. Ev. Tw. Trinidad | . 1804 |
| nigrum | . | White | . 7, H. Her. P. S. Eur. | . 1596 |
| pauciflorum | . | Green | . 8. Ev. Tw. Tranqueb. | . 1820 |
| pilosum | . | White | . 7, G. Ev. Tw. C. G. H. | . 1796 |
| roseum, 2 | . | Purple | . 7, H. De. Tw. Davuria | . 1818 |
| sibiricum | . | Green | . 7, H. Her. P. Siberia | . 1775 |
| undatum | . | Green | . 7, S. Ev. Tw. W. Ind. | . 1803 |
| villosum, 3 | . | White | . 7, H. De. Tw. | . 1821 |
| Vincetoxicum, 4 | . | White | . 7, H. Her. P. Europe | . 1596 |
| viridiflorum | . | Green | . 11, S. Ev. Tw. E. Ind. | . 1814 |

CYNARA, *Vaillant.* From *kuon*, a dog; in reference to the spines of the involucrum. *Linn.* 19, Or. 1, Nat. Or. *Compositæ.* This genus produces the artichoke, so much grown for culinary purposes. They all delight in a good rich soil, and may be increased by seeds. The Arabians consider the root of C. *scolymus* an aperient; the gum of it is called *kunkirgeed*, and placed by them among their emetics. *Synonyme:* 1. *Stobæa glomerata.*

| | | | | | |
|---|---|---|---|---|---|
| cardunculus | . | Blue | . 8, H. Her. P. Candia | . 1658 |
| ferox | . | Blue | . 7, H. Her. P. Italy | . 1820 |
| glomerata, 1 | . | Blue | . 8, F. Her. P. C. G. H. | . 1824 |
| horrida | . | Purple | . 8, G. Her. P. Madeira | . 1768 |
| integrifolia | . | Blue | . 7, H. Her. P. Spain | |
| pygmæa | . | Purple | . 7, H. Her. P. Spain | . 1820 |
| Scolymus | . | Purple | . 8, H. Her. P. S. Eur. | . 1548 |
| spinosissima | . | Blue | . 7, H. Her. P. Sicily | . 1826 |

humilis.

CYNODON, *Richard.* Derived from *kuon*, a dog, and *odous*, a tooth. *Linn.* 3, Or. 2, Nat. Or. *Gramineæ.* Grasses, succeeding in any common soil, in which they merely require sowing. In India, a cooling drink is prepared from the roots of C. *Dactylon.* *Synonyme:* 1. *Panicum Dactylon—Dactylon* 1.

| | | | | | |
|---|---|---|---|---|---|
| Indica | . . | Apetal | . 7. H. Cr. A. E. Ind. | |

*Dactylon* 1, *linearis, præcox, stellatus, virgatus.*

CYNOGLOSSUM, *Linn.* From *kuon*, a dog, and *glossa*, a tongue; the leaves resemble a dog's tongue, whence the common name of the genus, Hound's Tongue. *Linn.* 5, Or. 1, Nat. Or. *Boraginaceæ.* The species are pretty border plants, succeeding in any common soil, and readily multiplied by

o

division. *Synonymes*: 1. *C. virginicum.* 2. *hirsutum.* 3. *Anchusa lanata.*

| | | | | | | |
|---|---|---|---|---|---|---|
| amplexicaulĕ, 1 | Blue | . | 6, H. Her. | P. | N. Amer. | 1812 |
| apenninŭm . | Red | . | 5, H. | B. | Italy | 1731 |
| australĕ . | Pa. red | . | 6, G. Her. | P. | N. Holl. | 1820 |
| bicŏlŏr . | Wht. pur. | . | 7, H. | B. | Germany | 1820 |
| canĕscĕns, 2 | Blue | . | 7, H. | A. | E. Ind. | 1819 |
| cheirifŏlĭŭm, 3 | Blue | . | 6, H. | B. | Levant | 1596 |
| clandestīnŭm | Brown | . | 7, H. | B. | Spain | 1821 |
| columnæ . | Blue | . | 7, H. | B. | Apennines | 1825 |
| Dioscŏrĭdĭs | Purple | . | 7, H. | B. | France | 1820 |
| elongātŭm . | Flesh | . | 7, H. | B. | | 1819 |
| glomerātŭm | | . | 6, H. | B. | N. Amer. | 1812 |
| grandiflŏrŭm | Blue wht. | | H. Her. | P. | India | 183.. |
| Hænkii . | Blue pur. | 7, H. | B. | Bohemia | 1819 | |
| hirsūtŭm . | Blue | . | 7, H. | A. | C. G. H. | 1806 |
| holosericĕŭm | Violet | . | 7, H. | B. | Siberia | 1821 |
| magellĕnsĕ . | Purple | . | 6, H. Her. | P. | Naples | 1823 |
| officinālĕ . | Pur. red | . | 6, H. | B. | Britain | |
| pictŭm . | Li. blue | . | 8, H. | B. | Madeira | 1658 |
| sylvătĭcŭm . | Blue | . | 6, H. | B. | Britain | |
| umbellātŭm | Purple | . | 6, H. | B. | Hungary | 1817 |

CYNOMĔTRX, *Linn.* From *kyon*, a dog, and *metra*, the matrix; referring to the form of the pods. *Linn.* 10, Or. 1, Nat. Or. *Leguminosæ.* Stove trees, growing from twenty to thirty feet high, thriving well in a mixture of loam and sandy peat, and ripened cuttings will root in sand, under a glass.

| | | | | | | |
|---|---|---|---|---|---|---|
| cauliflŏrā . | Red | . | 8. Ev. T. E. Ind. | . | 1804 |
| polyāndrā . | Red | . | 8. Ev. T. E. Ind. | . | 1822 |

CYNŎRCHĬS, *Thouars.* From *kuon*, a dog, and *orchis*, Dog-orchis. *Linn.* 20, Or. 1, Nat. Or. *Orchidaceæ.* This species is one of the representatives in tropical countries of the terrestrial Orchises of Europe. It has a smell resembling that of *Orchis mascula.* It succeeds best in sandy loam, in a moist part of the house, and is increased by dividing the roots.

| | | | | | | |
|---|---|---|---|---|---|---|
| fastigiātā | . | Red. grn. . 3, S. Ter. Is. of France . 1835 |

CYNOSŬRŬS, *Beauvois.* From *kuon*, a dog, and *oura*, a tail; from its resemblance to a dog's tail, whence the name dog's-tail grass. *Linn.* 3, Or. 2, Nat. Or. *Gramineæ.* This species is esteemed one of the best fodder grasses in Europe; it will succeed in any soil.

| | | | |
|---|---|---|---|
| cristātŭs . . . . | Apetal | . 8, Grass. Britain . . |

CYPĔLLX, *Herbert.* From *kypellon*, a goblet; in reference to the shape of the flowers. *Linn.* 16, Or. 1, Nat. Or. *Iridaceæ.* The species of this genus are rendered ornamental by their beautiful flowers; they delight in sandy peat, and may be multiplied by offsets. *Synonyme*: 1. *Moræa Herberti, Tigridia Herberti.*

| | | | | | | |
|---|---|---|---|---|---|---|
| Drummŏndii . | Pur. yel. | . 6, G. Bu. P. San. Fe. | . 1834 |
| Herbĕrti, 1 . . | Vermil. | . 7, G. Bu. P. B. Ayres | . 1823 |

CYPĔRŬS, *Linn.* Supposed to be derived from *Cypris*, a name of Venus, from the roots of some of the species being aphrodisiacal. *Linn.* 3, Or. 1, Nat. Or. *Cyperaceæ.* A genus of grass-looking plants, many of them growing best in water, or a wet situation; any soil suits them, and they may be increased by division.

| | | | | | |
|---|---|---|---|---|---|
| Aitŏni . . . | Apetal | . 6, Grass. | C. G. H. | |
| alopecuroīdĕs . | Apetal | . 5, Grass. | C. G. H. | . 1804 |
| alternifŏlĭŭs . | Apetal | . 2, Grass. | Madag. | . 1781 |
| bādĭŭs . . . | Apetal | . 7, Grass. | Algiers | . 1800 |
| conglomerātŭs . | Apetal | . 7, Grass. | Arabia | . 1820 |
| distāns . . . | Apetal | . 7, Grass. | W. Ind. | . 1820 |
| dūbĭŭs . . . | Apetal | . 7, Grass. | E. Ind. | . 1802 |
| erubĕscĕns . . | Apetal | . 5, Grass. | | . 1820 |
| esculēntŭs . . | Apetal | . 7, H. Tw. P. | S. Eur. | . 1597 |
| fastigiātŭs . . | Apetal | . 6, Grass. | E. Ind. | . 1800 |
| flavĕscĕns . . | Apetal | . 7, Grass. | Germany | . 1776 |
| fūscŭs . . . | Apetal | . 8, Grass. | England | |
| glomerātŭs . . | Apetal | . 7, Grass. | Italy | . 1804 |
| irĭā . . . . | Apetal | . 7, Grass. | E. Ind. | . 1802 |
| kyllingoīdĕs . | Apetal | . 7, Grass. | N. Amer. | . 1828 |
| lōngŭs . . . | Apetal | . 7, Grass. | England | |
| lūzūlā . . . | Apetal | . 7, Grass. | W. Ind. | |
| nilŏtĭcŭs . . | Apetal | . 8, Grass. | Egypt | . 1810 |
| paniculātŭs . . | Apetal | . 6, Grass. | E. Ind... | . 1804 |
| pannŏnĭcŭs . . | Apetal | . 7, Grass. | Hungary | . 1781 |
| strigŏsŭs . . | Apetal | . 8, Grass. | W. Ind. | . 1786 |
| tenēllŭs . . . | Apetal | . 5, Grass. | C. G. H. | . 1819 |
| vĕgĕtŭs . . . | Apetal | . 7, Grass. | America | . 1790 |
| viscŏsŭs . . . | Apetal | . 6, Grass. | Jamaica | . 1781 |

*articulātŭs, australĭs, brizĕŭs, carĭcīnŭs, compāctŭs, comprēssŭs, cruēntŭs, diffōrmĭs, dīvĕs, fascĭculārĭs, hȳdrā, leucocĕphălŭs, ligulārĭs, Mōnii, mucronātŭs, pallĕscĕns, Pangōrĕi, paramattĕnsĭs, pătĕns, pătŭlŭs,*

*polycĕphălŭs, polystāchȳs, prostrātŭs, rĭgĭdŭs, tenuĭflōrŭs, trīsŭlcŭs.*

CYPHĬĀ, *Bergius.* From *kyphos*, curved; in reference to the stigma being gibbous. *Linn.* 5, Or. 1, Nat. Or. *Goodeniaceæ.* A pretty genus; the species require a mixture of peat, loam, and sand, and may be increased by taking off the young shoots as they begin to grow, and planting them in sand. The annual species merely require sowing. *Synonymes*: 1. *Lobelia cardamines.* 2. *L. volubilis.*

| | | | | | | |
|---|---|---|---|---|---|---|
| bulbōsā . . . | Pa. blue | . 3, G. | A. C. G. H. | . 1791 |
| cardamĭnĕs, 1 . | . 7, S. Her. | P. C. G. H. | . 1823 | | |
| incīsā . . . | Pa. red | . 7, G. | A. C. G. H. | . 1819 |
| Phytĕūmā . . | Pink | . 2, G. Tu. | P. C. G. H. | . 1822 |
| volūbĭlĭs, 2 . | Pa. blue | . 7, G. | A. C. G. H. | . 1795 |

CYPRĔSS, see *Cuprēssŭs.*

CYPRIPĔDĬŬM, *Linn.* From *Cypris*, one of Venus's names, and *podion*, a slipper; hence the name, Venus's, or Ladies' Slipper. *Linn.* 20, Or. 2, Nat. Or. *Orchidaceæ.* The Cypripediums are remarkably handsome when in flower, and on that account, they deserve a place in every collection. They are all of the easiest culture. The hardy species succeed well in peat soil, either kept in a frame, or planted out in a shady border. The species, natives of America, require to be protected from severe frost and rain. The stove kinds require the same treatment as other stove terrestrial orchidaceæ. *Synonyme*: 1. *C. humile.*

| | | | | | | |
|---|---|---|---|---|---|---|
| acaulĕ, 1 . . | Ra. pur. | . 5, H. Ter. | N. Amer. | . 1786 |
| albŭm . . . | White | . 5, H. Ter. | N. Amer. | . 1800 |
| arietīnŭm . . | Grn. ro. | . 4, H. Ter. | Canada | . 1808 |
| Calcĕŏlŭs . . | Yellow | . 6, H. Ter. | England | . |
| helvĕtĭcŭm . | Yellow | . 6, H. Ter. | Switzerl. | . 1825 |
| cāndĭdŭm . . | White | . 6, H. Ter. | N. Amer. | . 1826 |
| insignĕ . . . | Pur. grn. | . 6, S. Ter. | Nepal | . 1819 |
| macrānthŏs . . | Purple | . 5, H. Ter. | Siberia | . 1822 |
| parviflōrŭm . . | Yellowish | . 6, H. Ter. | N. Amer. | . 1759 |
| pubĕscĕns . . | Yel. pur. | . 6, H. Ter. | N. Amer. | . 1790 |
| purpurātŭm . . | Purple | . 9, H. Ter. | Archipel. | . 1836 |
| spectābĭlĕ . . | Wht. pur. | . 6, H. Ter. | N. Amer. | . 1731 |
| venūstŭm . . | Grn. pur. | . 10, S. Ter. | Nepal | . 1816 |

CYRILLX, *Linn.* In honour of Dominico Cyrillo, M.D., a professor of botany at Naples, and Fellow of the Royal Society of London. *Linn.* 5, Or. 1, Nat. Or. *Celastraceæ.* A genus of pretty shrubs, that grow well in a mixture of sandy loam and peat. Young cuttings root in sand, under a glass.

| | | | | | | |
|---|---|---|---|---|---|---|
| Antillārŭm . . | White | . 7, G. Ev. S. | Antilles | . 1824 |
| carolinĭānā . . | White | . 7, G. Ev. S. | Carolina | . 1765 |

CYRTĂNTHŬS, *Aiton.* From *kyrtos*, curved, and *anthos*, a flower; the tube of the flower is long and round. *Linn.* 6, Or. 1, Nat. Or. *Amaryllidaceæ.* Handsome Cape bulbs, succeeding in a mixture of turfy loam, sand, and peat, and a liberal supply of water, when in a growing state. They may be increased readily from offsets.

| | | | | | | |
|---|---|---|---|---|---|---|
| angustifŏlĭŭs . | Orange | . 5, G. Bu. | P. C. G. H. | . 1774 |
| cārnĕŭs . . . | Flesh | . 8, G. Bu. | P. C. G. H. | . |
| collīnŭs . . . | Crimson | . 6, G. Bu. | P. C. G. H. | . 1816 |
| obliquŭs . . . | Grn. or. | . 6, G. Bu. | P. C. G. H. | . 1774 |
| odōrŭs . . . | Crimson | . 6, G. Bu. | P. C. G. H. | . 1818 |
| pallĭdŭs . . . | Pink | . 6, G. Bu. | P. C. G. H. | . 1822 |
| spirālĭs . . . | Scarlet | . 6, G. Bu. | P. C. G. H. | . 1790 |
| striātŭs . . . | Orange | . 7, G. Bu. | P. C. G. H. | . |
| ventricōsŭs . . | Red | . 6, G. Bu. | P. C. G. H. | . 1770 |

CYRTŎCHĬLŬM, *Kunth.* From *cyrtos*, concave, and *cheilos*, a lip. *Linn.* 20, Or. 1, Nat. Or. *Orchidaceæ.* The species of this genus are small, but remarkably pretty when in blossom, and will probably be found to succeed best with the treatment recommended for the genus *Burlingtonia.*

| | | | | | | |
|---|---|---|---|---|---|---|
| bictoniēnsĕ . . | Red | . 10, S. Epi. | Guatemala | . 1836 |
| flavĕscĕns . . | Yellowish | 6, S. Epi. | Mexico | . 183.. |
| maculātŭm . . | Grn. pur. | . 8, S. Epi. | Vera Cruz | . 1837 |
| mystacīnŭm . . | Yellowish | 10, S. Epi. | Peru | . 1836 |

CYRTŎPĔRX, *Lindley.* Not explained. *Linn.* 20, Or. 1, Nat. Or. *Orchidaceæ.* This is a splendid species when in flower. It is easily cultivated with the treatment given to *Stanhopeas*, and the like: and it is readily increased by separating the thick stem, with a portion of the rooting rhizoma attached. *Synonyme*: 1. *Cyrtopodium Woodfordii.*

| | | | | | | |
|---|---|---|---|---|---|---|
| Woodfŏrdii, 1 . | Pink | . 9, S. Epi. S. Amer. | . 1814 |

CYRTOPŎDĬŬM, *R. Brown.* From *cyrtos*, hollow, and *pous*, a foot; alluding to the curved stalk of the labellum of *C. Andersonii.* *Linn.* 20, Or. 1. Nat.

Or. *Orchideæ*. This is a genus of plants well worth cultivating for the sake of their fine, yellow, sweet-scented flowers. They succeed well, treated as the genus *Stanhopea*.

Andersonii . . . Yellow . 4. S. Epi. St. Vincent . 1804
flavum . . . . Yellow . 8. Epi. . . . . 1831
punctatum . . . Yel. red . 4. S. Epi. Brazil . .

CYRTOSTŸLIS, *R. Brown*. From *cyrtos*, convex, and *stylos*, a style. *Linn.* 20, Or. 1, Nat. Or. *Orchideæ*. A very curious species, succeeding well with the same treatment as is recommended for the genus *Corycium*.

reniformis . . . . 6. F. Ter. N. Holl. . 1823

CYSTICAPNOS, *Boerhaave*. From *kystis*, a bladder, and *kapnos*, a Greek name for fumitory; in allusion to the bladdery capsules. *Linn.* 17, Or. 2, Nat. Or. *Papaveraceæ*. Annual species, requiring to be sown in a gentle hotbed, and afterwards transplanted into the open ground, where they will flower well. Synonyme: 1. *Fumaria vesicaria*.

africana, 1 . . . Wht. red . 6, H. Cl. A. C. G. H. . 1696
alexandriná . . . Wht. red . 6, H. Cl. A. Alexan. . 1837

CYSTOSEIRA, *Agardh*. From *kystis*, a bladder, and *seira*, a chain; in reference to the upper parts of the fronds appearing like little bladders chained together. *Linn.* 24, Or. 7, Nat. Or. *Algæ*. Species of sea-weed, found at all seasons of the year in the open ocean—*abrotanifolia, barbata, discors, ericoides, fibrosa, granulata, siliquosa, S. denudata, S. minor*.

CYSTOSPORA, *Fries*. From *kystis*, a bladder, and *spora*, a sporule; the sporules appear like little bladders. *Linn.* 24, Or. 9, Nat. Or. *Fungi*. Minute species, growing on dead branches, leaves, &c.—*chrysosperma, guttifera, leucosperma, Rosarum*.

CYTISUS, *Linn.* Derived from *Cythrus*, one of the Cyclades, one of the species being first found there. *Linn.* 16, Or. 6, Nat. Or. *Leguminosæ*. This is a very ornamental genus. The species are fine, hardy, free-flowering trees and shrubs, succeeding in almost any soil, and readily increased by seeds, layers, grafts, or buds. Synonymes: 1. *Spartium multiflorum*. 2. *C. pauciflorus*. 3. *Spartium spinosum, villosum*. 4. *C. elongatus*. 5. *Spartium nubigenum*. 6. *S. patens*. 7. *S. spinosum*.

| | | | | | | | |
|---|---|---|---|---|---|---|---|
| mollis . . . | . | Yellow . | 5, | H. De. S. | Stromboli | . 1826 |
| albidus . . . | . | White . | 6, | H. De. S. | S. Eur. | |
| albus, 1 . . | . | White . | 5, | H. De. S. | Portugal | . 1752 |
|   incarnatus . | . | Flesh | 5, | H. De. S. | Portugal | . 1752 |
| alpinus . . . | . | Yellow . | 6, | H. De. T. | Europe | . 1596 |
| argenteus . . | . | Yellow . | 5, | H. De. S. | France | . 1739 |
| austriacus . . | . | Yellow . | 7, | H. De. S. | Austria | . 1741 |
| biflorus . . . | . | Yellow . | 5, | H. De. S. | Hungary | . 1760 |
| calycinus, 2 . | . | Yellow . | 8, | H. De. S. | Tauria | . 1820 |
| capitatus . . | . | Yellow . | 7, | H. De. S. | Austria | . 1774 |
| ciliatus . . . | . | Yellow . | 7, | H. De. S. | Carpathia | . 1817 |
| elegans . . . | . | Yellow . | 6, | G. Ev. S. | C. G. H. | . 1821 |
| elongatus . . | . | Yellow . | 5, | H. De. S. | Hungary | . 1804 |
| falcatus . . . | . | Yellow . | 7, | H. De. S. | Hungary | . 1816 |
| glomeratus . . | . | | | 8. Ev. S. | Zanzibar | . 1826 |
| grandiflorus . | . | Yellow . | 6, | H. De. S. | Portugal | . 1816 |
| hirsutus . . | . | Yellow . | 7, | H. De. S. | S. Eur. | . 1789 |
| Laburnum . . | . | Yellow . | 5, | H. De. T. | Switserl. | . 1596 |
|   purpurascens | . | Purple . | 7, | H. Ev. T. | Hybrid | . 1828 |
| laniger, 3 . . | . | Yellow . | 6, | F. Ev. S. | Spain . | . 1821 |
| leucanthus . . | . | Pa. yel. | 6, | H. De. S. | Hungary | . 1806 |
| mollis . . . | . | Yellow . | 6, | H. De. S. | | . 1818 |
| multiflorus, 4 . | . | Yellow . | 6, | H. De. S. | Europe | . 1800 |
| nanus . . . | . | Yellow . | 6, | H. De. S. | Levant | . 1816 |
| nigricans . . | . | Yellow . | 6, | H. De. S. | Austria | . 1730 |
| nubigenus, 5 . | . | Yellow . | 5, | G. Ev. S. | Teneriffe | . 1779 |
| orientalis . . | . | Yellow . | 6, | H. De. S. | S. Eur. | . 1818 |
| patens, 6 . . | . | Yellow . | 6, | H. De. S. | Portugal | . 1752 |
| polytrichus . | . | Yellow . | 6, | H. De. S. | Tauria | . 1818 |
| proliferus . . | . | Yellow . | 4, | G. Ev. S. | Canaries | . 1779 |
| purpureus . . | . | Purple . | 6, | H. De. S. | Austria | . 1792 |
|   albiflorus . | . | White . | 6, | H. De. S. | Austria | |
| pygmæus . . | . | Yellow . | 6, | H. De. S. | Galecca | |
| racemosus . . | . | Yellow . | 7, | H. Ev. S. | | . 1835 |
| ruthenicus . . | . | Yellow . | 6, | H. De. S. | Russia | . 1817 |
| scoparius . . | . | Yellow . | 6, | H. De. S. | England | |
|   albus . . | . | White . | 6, | H. De. S. | England | |
| sessiliflorus . | . | Yellow . | 7, | H. De. S. | Italy . | . 1629 |
| spinosus, 7 . | . | Yellow . | 6 | H. Ev. S. | S. Eur. | . 1596 |
| supinus . . . | . | Yellow . | 6, | H. De. S. | S. Eur. | . 1755 |
| triflorus . . | . | Yellow . | 6, | H. De. S. | Spain . | . 1640 |

CZACKIA, *Andrezjouski*. In honour of Andrezousky Czack, a Russian botanist. *Linn.* 6, Or. 1, Nat. Or. *Liliaceæ*. A pretty species, producing abundance of elegant flowers; it prefers a good rich loam, and an open situation. It is readily increased by seeds, or dividing the roots. Synonyme: 1. *Anthericum liliastrum*.

liliastrum, 1 . . White . . 5, H. Her. P. S. Eur. . . 1629

# D.

DACRYDIUM, *Banks*. Derived from *dakru*, a tear; in reference to the gummy exudation. *Linn.* 21, Or. 10, Nat. Or. *Taxaceæ*. These are ornamental plants, resembling the spruce in appearance, except that the branches are somewhat pendulous; hence the English name of *D. cupressinum*, New Zealand Spruce. A mixture of sandy loam and peat suits them, and ripened cuttings root in sand, under a glass. Synonyme: 1. *Juniperus elata*.

cupressinum . . . G. Ev. T. N. Zeal. . 1825
elatum, 1 . . . G. Ev. T. Pulo Pea. . 1830

DACRYMYCES, *Nees*. From *dakru*, a tear, and *myke*, a fungus; in allusion to the deliquescent nature of the plants. *Linn.* 24, Or. 9, Nat. Or. *Fungi*. Curious and minute species of *Fungi*, found usually upon dead and partially rotten wood, in the early part of the season—*moriformis, stillatus*.

DACTYLICAPNOS, *Wallich*. From *dactylos*, a finger, and *kapnos*, fumitory; alluding to the berries being finger-shaped. *Linn.* 17, Or. 2, Nat. Or. *Papaveraceæ*. An interesting annual, of a climbing character, succeeding in any sandy soil. Synonyme: 1. *Dielytra scandens*.

thalictrifolia, 1 . Yel. brn. . F. Ev. Cl. Nepal . . 1831

DACTYLIS, *Linn.* From *dactylos*, a finger; the head is divided so as fancifully to resemble fingers. *Linn.* 3, Or. 2, Nat. Or. *Gramineæ*. An uninteresting genus of grasses, of easy culture and propagation.

glomerata . . . Apetal . . Grass. Britain . .
variegata . . . Apetal . . Grass. Gardens . .

*ascendens, cynosuroides, glauca, glaucescens, hispanica, littoralis, maritima, patens, repens*.

DACTYLOCTENIUM, *Willd.* From *dactylos*, a finger,

[ 99 ]

and *kteis*, a comb; alluding to the digitate spikes. *Linn.* 3, Or. 2, Nat. Or. *Gramineæ*. A plant of little merit, and of easy culture. Synonyme: 1. *Cynosurus ægyptiacus*.

ægyptiacum, 1 . Apetal . . 8, Grass. Egypt . . 1770

DÆDALEA, *Persoon*. From *dædaleus*, artificial; artificial-like arrangement of sinuosities. *Linn.* 24, Or. 9, Nat. Or. *Fungi*. Very minute species of *Fungi*, found at all seasons on rotten wood, trunks of trees, &c.—*angusta, betulina, biennis, confragosa, gibbosa, quercina, unicolor*.

DÆMIA, *R. Brown*. The name given to it in Arabia, where the first plant was found. *Linn.* 5, Or. 2, Nat. Or. *Asclepiadaceæ*. An ornamental genus of twining plants, thriving best in a mixture of sandy loam and peat. Cuttings root freely in sand, or sandy soil, under a glass. Synonymes: 1. *Cynanchum bicolor*. 2. *C. extensum*. 3. *Asclepias scandens*.

bicolor, 1 . . . White . 7, S. Ev. Tw. E. Ind. . . 1806
cordata . . . White . 7, S. Ev. Tw. Arabia . . 1824
extensa, 2 . . White . 7, S. Ev. Tw. E. Ind. . . 1777
scandens, 3 . . White . 7, S. Ev. Tw. Gambia . . 1824

DAFFODIL, see *Narcissus*.

DAHLIA, *Cavanilles*. In honour of Andrew Dahl, a celebrated Swedish botanist, and pupil of Linnæus. *Linn.* 19, Or. 2, Nat. Or. *Compositæ*. This exceedingly beautiful genus comprises almost an indefinite number of varieties, all more or less showy in the flower-garden in the autumn, when most other flowers have faded. They are all of easy cultivation, growing freely in almost any soil, particularly if of a sandy open nature. They may be raised plentifully from seeds, which should be sown early in the spring. After the flowering season is over, and the frost has damaged the leaves and branches, the roots should be taken up, and placed in a secure dry place, excluded from frost, till spring, when they should be divided and propagated, and brought on, by dung heat, in frames, for planting out in the flower-garden in May or June. Cuttings will root with great facility, by merely breaking or cutting off the young shoots, and planting them in small pots, in a warm frame heat; but this practice, as seeds grow so readily, except for very rare kinds, is more troublesome than profitable. *Synonymes:* 1. *Dahlia frustranea-fulgens.* 2. *Georgina pinnata.*

| | | | | |
|---|---|---|---|---|
| Cervantesii | . Scarlet | . 8, H. Her. P. | Mexico | . . |
| crocata, 1 | . Scarlet | . 7, H. Tu. P. | Mexico | . . 1802 |
| frustrata | . Scarlet | . 10, H. Tu. P. | Mexico | . . 1802 |
| aurantia | . Orange | . 10, H. Tu. P. | Mexico | . . 1802 |
| erecta | . Yellow | . 10, H. Tu. P. | Mexico | . . 1802 |
| lutea | . Sulphur | . 10, H. Tu. P. | Mexico | . . 1802 |
| superflua, 2 | . Purple | . 10, H. Tu. P. | Mexico | . . 1789 |

DAIS, *Linn.* The derivation of the name is unknown. *Linn.* 10, Or. 1, Nat. Or. *Thymelaceæ.* This is an interesting species, much like the *Rhus cotinus,* in its leaves; it grows in a mixture of peat and loam, and is increased from cuttings of the roots, kept in a warm situation, and sometimes from seeds.

| | | | | |
|---|---|---|---|---|
| cotinifolia | . . . Wht. grn. | 6, G. Ev. S. | C.G.H. | . 1776 |

DAISY, see *Bellis.*

DALBERGIA, *Linn.* In honour of Nicholas Dalberg, a Swedish botanist. *Linn.* 19, Or. 4, Nat. Or. *Leguminosæ.* Ornamental stove species, delighting most in sandy loam and peat; cuttings strike, if planted in sand, under a glass.

| | | | | |
|---|---|---|---|---|
| alata | . . . White | . S. Ev. T. | E. Ind. | . . 1823 |
| Barclayi | . . . Blue | . S. Ev. Cl. | Maurit. | . 1823 |
| Crowei | . . . White | . S. Ev. T. | E. Ind. | . . 1823 |
| emarginata | . . . White | . S. Ev. T. | E. Ind. | . . 1823 |
| frondosa | . . . White | . S. Ev. T. | E. Ind. | . . 1818 |
| latifolia | . . . White | . S. Ev. T. | E. Ind. | . . 1811 |
| marginata | . . . White | . S. Ev. Cl. | E. Ind. | . . 1823 |
| ougeinensis | . . . White | . S. Ev. T. | E. Ind. | . . 1820 |
| paniculata | . . . White | . S. Ev. T. | E. Ind. | . . 1811 |
| rimosa | . . . White | . S. Ev. Cl. | E. Ind. | . . 1823 |
| robusta | . . . White | . S. Ev. T. | E. Ind. | . . 1816 |
| rubiginosa | . . . White | . S. Ev. T. | E. Ind. | . . 1811 |
| scandens | . . . White | . S. Ev. Cl. | E. Ind. | . . 1812 |
| Sissoo | . . . White | . S. Ev. T. | E. Ind. | . . 1820 |
| stipulacea | . . . White | . S. Ev. T. | E. Ind. | . . 1820 |
| tamarindifolia | . . White | . S. Ev. Cl. | E. Ind. | . . 1820 |
| Talfairii | . . . White | . S. Ev. Cl. | Maurit. | . 1823 |
| timoriensis | . . . White | . S. Ev. T. | E. Ind. | . . 1826 |
| volubilis | . . . White | . S. Ev. Tw. | E. Ind. | . . 1818 |

DALEA, *Linn.* In honour of Thomas Dale, an English botanist of the last century. *Linn.* 16, Or. 4, Nat. Or. *Leguminosæ.* All the species of this genus are almost destitute of interest; they grow best in loam and peat. The shrubby and perennial kinds are increased by cuttings planted in sand, under a glass. The tender annual species must be sown on a gentle hotbed, and, when of sufficient size, transplanted into the open borders. *Synonymes:* 1. *Psoralea laxiflora.* 2. *P. leporina.* 3. *P. Dalea.*

| | | | | |
|---|---|---|---|---|
| alopecuroides, 1 | . Pa. blue | . 7, H. A. | Mississippi | 1812 |
| aurea | . . . Yellow | . 7, H. Her. P. | Louisiana | . 1811 |
| bicolor | . . . Yel. blue | . 7, S. Her. P. | S. Amer. | . 1817 |
| citriodora | . . . Pink | . 10, S. A. | N. Spain | . 1780 |
| Cliffortiana | . Blue | . 7, H. A. | Vera Cruz | . 1787 |
| enneaphylla | . Pink | . 7, S. Ev. S. | W. Ind. | . 1772 |
| Lagopus, 2 | . White | . 7, F. A. | Mexico | . 1780 |
| laxiflora, 3 | . Violet | . 10, H. Her. P. | Louisiana | . 1811 |
| mutabilis | . . Purple | . 10, G. Her. P. | Mexico | . 1818 |
| nutans | . . . Violet | . 7, S. Her. P. | Mexico | . 1824 |
| phymatodes | . White | . 7, G. Ev. S. | Caraccas | . 1819 |
| reclinata | . . . Violet | . 7, S. Ev. Tr. | Mexico | . 1820 |
| sericea | . . . Violet | . 7, S. Her. P. | Mexico | . 1824 |
| Thouini | . . . Blue | . 7, G. A. | | . 1816 |
| tuberculata | . . Purple | . 7, S. Ev. S. | Mexico | . 1824 |

DALECHAMPIA, *Linn.* In honour of James Dalechamp, a celebrated French botanist, who died in 1588. *Linn.* 2, Or. 1, Nat. Or. *Euphorbiaceæ.* Pretty climbing plants, thriving well in a mixture of loam and peat. Cuttings root freely in sand.

| | | | | |
|---|---|---|---|---|
| brasiliensis | . . . Grn. yel. | 7, S. Ev. Cl. | Brazil | . 1824 |
| ficifolia | . . . Grn. yel. | 7, S. Ev. Cl. | Brazil | . 1820 |
| scandens | . . . Grn. yel. | 6, S. Ev. Cl. | W. Ind. | . 1739 |

DALIBARDA, *Linn.* Named after Denis Dalibard, a French botanist. *Linn.* 12, Or. 2, Nat. Or. *Rosaceæ.* A curious plant, well suited for decorating rockwork, or the front of flower-borders; it requires protecting in severe weather, and is increased by division. *Synonyme:* 1. *D. repens.*

| | | | | |
|---|---|---|---|---|
| violoides | . . . White | . 5, H. Her. P. | N. Amer. | . 1768 |

DALRYMPLEA, see *Turpinia.*

DALTONIA. Named by Hooker in honour of the Rev. James Dalton, an excellent English muscologist. *Linn.* 24, Or. 5, Nat. Or. *Musci.* Pretty dwarf species of moss. *D. splachnoides* is only found growing, and that sparingly, by the side of a small stream on the Secawn Mountain, in the neighbourhood of Dublin. *Synonymes:* 1. *Neckera heteromalla.* 2. *Neckera splachnoides—heteromalla* 1, *splachnoides* 2.

DAMASONIUM, *Schreber.* From *damazo,* to subdue; in reference to its once supposed medicinal qualities. *Linn.* 6, Or. 4, Nat. Or. *Hydrocharaceæ.* Handsome aquatics. *D. indicum* is reputed to possess the power of removing the venom of the sea-dog.

| | | | | |
|---|---|---|---|---|
| indicum | . . . White | . 8, S. Aq. P. | E. Ind. | . . 1800 |
| ovalifolium | . . White | . 8, G. Aq. P. | N. Holl. | . 1824 |

DAMMARA, *Mirbel.* The name of the species in Amboyna. *Linn.* 21, Or. 10, Nat. Or. *Coniferæ.* A very handsome genus of *Coniferæ,* thriving well in a mixture of sandy loam, but of difficult propagation. The only successful mode, is to take off the cuttings as soon as ripened, and plant them in a pot of sand, under a glass, in a gentle bottom heat. Liquid storax is thought to be yielded by the species of this genus. *Synonyme:* 1. *Pinus Dammara, Agathis loranthifolia.*

| | | | | |
|---|---|---|---|---|
| australis, 1 | . . Apetal | . S. Ev. T. | N. Zeal. | . 1821 |
| orientalis, 1 | . . Apetal | . S. Ev. T. | Amboyna | . 1804 |

DAMMAR PINE, see *Dammara.*

DAMPIERA. Named by Brown, in memory of Captain William Dampier, the celebrated circumnavigator. *Linn.* 5, Or. 1, Nat. Or. *Scævolaceæ.* Ornamental species, succeeding well in a mixture of peat and loam; cuttings of the young wood root freely, in sand, under a glass.

| | | | | |
|---|---|---|---|---|
| ovalifolia | . . . Blue | . 7, G. Her. P. | N. Holl. | . 1824 |
| stricta | . . . Blue | . 7, G. Her. P. | N. S. W. | . 1814 |

DANAA, *Smith.* In honour of Pierre Martin Dana, a writer on the plants of Piedmont. *Linn.* 24, Or. 1, Nat. Or. *Danæaceæ.* An ornamental species of fern, growing well in a mixture of peat and loam, and increased by divisions of the root.

| | | | | |
|---|---|---|---|---|
| alata | . . . . Brown | . S. Her. P. | W. Ind. | . . 1823 |

DANCING-GIRLS, see *Mantisia Saltatoria.*

DANDELION, see *Leontodon.*

DANTHONIA, *Decandolle.* In honour of M. Danthoine, a French botanist. *Linn.* 3, Or. 2, Nat. Or. *Gramineæ.* A worthless genus of grasses, of simple cultivation. *Synonymes:* 1. *Avena provincialis.* 2. *A. semiannularis.* 3. *A. glumacea.* 4. *A. strigosa—calycina, curvifolia, longifolia, macrantha, pilosa, provincialis* 1, *semiannularis* 2, *sericea, spicata* 3, *strigosa* 4.

DAPHNE, *Linn.* From *daio,* to burn, and *phone,* a noise; it crackles when burning. *Linn.* 8, Or. 1, Nat. Or. *Thymelaceæ.* All handsome dwarf shrubs, mostly evergreens, excellently suited for planting near the front of shrubberies. The branches of *D. Cneorum* are procumbent, stretching to a great distance; whence it makes a beautiful rock plant. All the species prefer a peaty soil, and are readily increased by grafting on the common Spurge Laurel (*D. Laureola*), which may be plentifully raised from seed. In the South of Europe, *D. Gnidium* is used to dye wool yellow. The berries of *D. Laureola* are poisonous to all animals except birds. *Synonymes:* 1. *D. Dauphinii.* 2. *D. collina, neapolitana.* 3. *D. cannabina.* 4. *D. oleæfolia.* 5. *Passerina Tarton-vaira.* 6. *P. villosa.* 7. *P. Thymelæa.*

| | | | | |
|---|---|---|---|---|
| alpina | . . . White | . 6, H. Ev. S. | Italy | . . 1759 |
| altaica | . . . White | . 4, H. Ev. S. | Siberia | . 1796 |
| australis | . . . Pink | . 4, H. Ev. S. | Naples | . . |
| chinensis | . . . Yellow | . 5, G. Ev. S. | China | . 1825 |
| Cneorum | . . . Pink | . 7, H. Ev. S. | Austria | . 1752 |
| collina | . . . Purple | . 8, H. Ev. S. | Italy | . 1752 |
| Gnidium | . . . White | . 7, H. Ev. S. | Spain | . 1597 |
| hybrida, 1 | . . Red | . 6, G. Ev. S. | Hybrid | . 1827 |
| indica | . . . White | . 6, G. Ev. S. | China | . 1800 |
| Laureola | . . . Green | . 2, H. Ev. S. | Britain | . |
| Mezereum | . . Pink | . 3, H. De. S. | England | . |
| album | . . . . | . 3, H. De. S. | | |
| autumnale | . . Red | . 8, H. De. S. | Europe | . . |
| rubrum | . . . Pink | . 3, H. De. S. | England | . . |
| neapolitana, 2 | . Purple | . 8, H. Ev. S. | Naples | . 1822 |
| odora | . . . Pak. wht. | 3, G. Ev. S. | China | . 1771 |
| rubra | . . . Pink | . 4, G. Ev. S. | China | . 1831 |
| variegata | . . . White | . 10, G. Ev. S. | Japan | . 1800 |
| oleoides | . . . White | . H. Ev. S. | Crete | . 1815 |

| papyracea, 3 | . . . | White | . 5, G. Ev. S. | Nepal | . 1824 |
| pontica | . . . | Grn. yel. | 4, H. Ev. S | Pontus | . 1759 |
| rubra | . . . | Red | . 4, G. Ev. S. | Hybrid | . 1827 |
| pubescens | . . . | Yellow | . 4, H. Ev. S. | Austria | . 1810 |
| sericea, 4 | . . . | White | . 4, H. Ev. S. | Crete | . 1820 |
| striata | . . . | Purple | . 5, H. Ev. S | Switzerl. | 1819 |
| Tarton-raira, 5 | | White | . 6, H. Ev. S. | France | . 1640 |
| tinifolia | . . . | | . S. Ev. S. | Jamaica | . 1773 |
| tomentosa, 6 | . | White | . 6, F. Ev. S. | Asia | . 1800 |
| Thymelæa, 7 | . | Yellow | . 6, H. Ev. S. | Spain | . 1815 |

DARLINGTÒNIA, *Decandolle.* In honour of Dr. Darlington, an American botanist. *Linn.* 5, Or. 1, Nat. Or. *Leguminosæ.* The soil best adapted to these pretty plants, is peat and sand, mixed with vegetable mould. They do best grown in pots, among the Alpine plants. They may be increased by dividing at the roots, or by young cuttings in sand, under a glass. *Synonymes:* 1. *Acacia brachyloba.* 2. *Mimosa glandulosa, Acacia glandulosa.*

| brachylòba, 1 | . . | White | . 9, F. Her. P. N. Amer. | . 1803 |
| glandulòsa, 2 | . | White | . 9, F. Her. P. N. Amer. | . 1806 |

DARNEL, see *Lòlium temulèntum.*

DARWINÌA, *Rudge.* In honour of Dr Darwin, the celebrated author of the poem entitled the Botanic Garden. *Linn.* 10, Or. 1, Nat. Or. *Myrtaceæ.* These very singular plants grow well in a mixture of loam, peat, and sand, and cuttings of the young wood strike freely in sand, under a glass.

| fasciculàta | . . . | | . 6, G. Ev. S. N. Holl. | . 1820 |
| taxifòlia | . . . | | . 6, G. Ev. S. N. Holl. | . 1824 |

DASYCÀRPÒS, hairy-fruited.

DATE-PALM, see *Phœnix.*

DATE-PLUM, see *Diòspýros.*

DATÍSCA, *Willdenow.* Meaning unknown. *Linn.* 22, Or. 10, Nat. Or. *Datiscaceæ.* Hardy herbaceous plants, growing in any common garden soil, to the height of four feet. They are increased by divisions at the roots.

| cannabìna | . . . | Yellow | . 8, H. Her. P. Candia | . 1640 |
| hirta | . . . | Grn. yel. | . 6, H. Her. P. Pennsylv. | . 1826 |

DATÙRA, *Linn.* An alteration of the Arabic name, *tdtòrah. Linn.* 5, Or. 1, Nat. Or. *Solanaceæ.* An ornamental genus, but chiefly composed of plants possessing very deleterious qualities. The seeds of *D. ceratocaulon* will sometimes remain in the ground for several years before they vegetate. The seeds of all the species require to be sown early in spring, on a hotbed, and when of sufficient size, they should be transplanted into a warm border, where they will flower better than if kept in pots. In the United States, the juice of *D. stramonium* is used in doses of from twenty to thirty grains, in cases of epilepsy, or of mania without fever.

| ceratocaulòn | . . | White | . 8, H. | A. S. Amer. | . 1805 |
| fastuòsa | . . . | Purple | . 8, H. | A. Egypt | . 1629 |
| feròx | . . . | White | . 8, H. | A. China | . 1781 |
| guayaquilensis | . | White | . 8, H. | A. Guayaquil | . 1826 |
| lævis | . . . | White | . 7, H. | A. Africa | . 1700 |
| Mètel | . . . | White | . 7, H. | A. Asia | . 1596 |
| muricàta | . . | White | . 5, H. | A. | . 1820 |
| Stramònium | . . | White | . 8, H. | A. England | |
| Tatùla | . . . | Blue | . 8, H. | A. N. Amer. | . 1629 |

DAUBENTÒNIA, *Decandolle.* In honour of M. Daubenton, a celebrated naturalist. *Linn.* 17, Or. 4, Nat. Or. *Leguminosæ.* Very handsome plants; for culture and propagation, see *Piscidia. Synonymes:* 1. *Æschynomene longifòlia, Piscidia longifùlia.* 2. *Æschynomene punìcea.*

| longifòlia, 1 | . . | Yellow | . 7, S. Ev. S. N. Spain | 1820 |
| punìcea, 2 | . . | Vermiln. | . 7, S. Ev. S. N. Spain | 1820 |

DAUBÈNYA. Dr. Lindley named this genus after Dr. Charles Daubeny, the present professor of botany at Oxford, and well known for his physiological researches. *Linn.* 6, Or. 1, Nat. Or. *Liliaceæ.* This is a very pretty, as well as a singular little plant, producing its beautiful yellow flowers in an umbel, larger than a crown piece. It will grow well in sandy loam and peat, and may be increased from offsets.

| aùrea | . . . . | Yellow | . 6, G. Bu. P. C. G. H. | . 1832 |

DAÙCUS, *Tournefort.* From *daio,* to make hot; in allusion to its supposed effect in medicine. *Linn.* 5, Or. 2, Nat. Or. *Umbelliferæ.* Some of the species of this genus are very useful, as D. Carota, and its varieties, yield the esculent root, so well known

under the name of Carrot. They grow well in any common soil; the seeds require to be sown towards the end of March, or beginning of April.

| Caròta | . . . | White | . 6, H. | B. Britain | . . |
| aurantìa | . . | White | . 6, H. | B. Europe | . . |
| hortènsis | . . | White | . 5, H. | B. Europe | . . |
| præcòx | . . | White | . 6, H. | B. Europe | . . |

*aùreus, crinìtus, Gingìdium, gùmmifer, hispìdus, littoràlis, lùcidus, marìtimus, mauritànicus, meifòlius, montevidénsis, parvifòrus, polýgamus.*

DAVÀLLIA, *Smith.* In honour of Edmund Davall, a Swiss botanist. *Linn.* 24, Or. 1, Nat. Or. *Polypodiaceæ.* This is a genus of very beautiful ferns. The rootstock of *D. canariensis* curves over the side of the pot in which it grows, and being covered with close brown hair, it very much resembles a hare's-foot; hence it is commonly called the hare's-foot fern. The species thrive well in a mixture of peat and loam, and may be increased by seeds at the roots, or by seeds. *Synonyms:* 1. *Trichomanes gibberosa.*

| canariénsis | . . | Brown | . 6, G Her. P. Canaries | . 1699 |
| concavadénsis | . | Brown | . 8. Her. P. Brasil | . 1823 |
| dùbia | . . . | Brown | . 6, G. Her. P. N. Holl. | . 1826 |
| élegàns | . . . | Brown | . 6, G. Her. P. N. Holl. | . 1824 |
| flaccida | . . | Brown | . 6, G. Her. P. N. Holl. | . 1820 |
| gibberòsa, 1 | . . | Brown | . 6, G. Her. P. N. Holl. | . 1825 |
| pyxidàta | . . | Brown | . 6, G. Her. P. N. S. W. | . 1808 |

DAVIÈSIA, *Smith.* In honour of the Rev. Hugh Davies, F.L.S., a Welch botanist. *Linn.* 10, Or. 1, Nat. Or. *Leguminosæ.* The species are all very handsome plants when in flower; they do best in an equal mixture of loam, peat, and sand; cuttings nearly ripened, of all the species, will root readily in sand, under a glass. *Synonyms:* 1. *Daviesia glauca.*

| aciculàris | . . . | Yellow | . 6, G. Ev. S. N. S. W. | . 1804 |
| alàta | . . . | Yellow | . 6, G. Ev. S. N. S. W. | . 1818 |
| cordàta | . . . | Yellow | . 6, G. Ev. S. N. Holl. | . 1824 |
| corymbòsa | . . | Wht. red | . 7, G. Ev. S. N. Holl. | . 1804 |
| incrassàta | . . | Yellow | . 6, G. Ev. S. N. Holl. | . 1820 |
| juniperìna | . . | Yellow | . 5, G. Ev. S. N. Holl. | . 1825 |
| júncea | . . . | Yellow | . 7, G. Ev. S. N. Holl. | . 1823 |
| latifòlia | . . . | Yellow | . 6, G. Ev. S. N. Holl. | . 1805 |
| leptophýlla | . . | Yellow | . 7, G. Ev. S. N. S. W. | . 1824 |
| lineàris | . . . | Yellow | . 7, G. Ev. S. N. S. W. | . 1817 |
| mimosoìdes, 1 | . | Yellow | . 5, G. Ev. S. N. S. W. | . 1809 |
| physòdes | . . | Yellow | . 5, G. Ev. S. N. Holl. | . 1824 |
| racemulòsa | . . | Yellow | . 7, G. Ev. S. N. Holl. | . 1823 |
| squarròsa | . . | Yellow | . 6, G. Ev. S. N. Holl. | . 1824 |
| ulicìna | . . . | Yellow | . 6, G. Ev. S. N. S. W. | . 1792 |
| umbellulàta | . . | Yellow | . 6, G. Ev. S. N. Holl. | . 1816 |
| virgàta | . . . | Tawny | . 7, G. Ev. S. Blue Mts. | . 1827 |

DAY LILY, see *Hemerocàllis.*

DEADLY CARROT, see *Thàpsia.*

DEADLY NIGHTSHADE, see *Atròpa Belladònna.*

DEAD NETTLE, see *Galeòbdòlon.*

DÈBILE, weak, feeble, slender.

DECANDROUS, having ten stamens.

DECAPHÝLLOUS, ten-leaved.

DECIDUOUS, falling off. Leaves which are shed annually are said to be deciduous; as are trees that annually lose their leaves.

DECIDUOUS CYPRESS, see *Taxodium distichum.*

DECIPIÈNS, deceiving, by resembling something else.

DECLINATE, curved downwards.

DECOCTION, a preparation or digest, by boiling water.

DECÒDÒN, *Gmelin.* From *deka,* ten, and *odous* (*odontos*), a tooth; referring to the calyx having ten teeth. *Linn.* 10, Or. 1, Nat. Or. *Lythraceæ.* This is a handsome border plant when in flower, growing in any common soil, and increased by dividing the plant at the roots. *Synonyme:* 1. *Nesæa verticillata.*

| verticillàta, 1 | . | Purple | . 8, H. Her. P. N. Amer. | . 1759 |

DECOMPOUND: a leaf is said to be decompound when it is often pinnated; a panicle, when its branches are also panicled.

DECORTICATED, disbarked.

DECUMÀRIA, *Linn.* From *decuma,* a tenth; in reference to the tenfold structure of some of the flowers and fruit. *Linn.* 11, Or. 1, Nat. Or. *Philadelphaceæ.* The species of this genus are ornamental, and well adapted to training against a wall or trellis; they grow well in any common soil, and may be increased by layers, or cuttings placed in sand, under a glass.

| barbàra | . . . | White | . 7, H. De. Tw. Carolina | . 1785 |
| prostràta | . . | White | . 7, H. De. Tr. N. Amer. | . 1820 |
| sarmentòsa | . . | White | . 7, H. De. Tw. Carolina | . 1758 |

DECUMBENT, lying down.

DECURRENT, running down.

DECURSIVE, having a tendency to run down.

DECUSSATE, when two right lines cross each other at right angles, they are said to be decussate.

DEERINGIA, *R. Brown.* In memory of Dr. Charles Deering, an English botanical author. *Linn.* 5, Or. 1, Nat. Or. *Amarantaceæ.* Curious but weak-growing plants. The seed requires to be sown in a hothouse, or hotbed, and when of sufficient size, the plants may be potted off, and placed among the stove plants.

| celosioides | . . . | White | . 9, S. | B. E. Ind. | . 1804 |
| indica | . . . . | White | . 10, S. | B. E. Ind. | . 1804 |

DEFLEXED, turned downwards.

DEFOLIATUS, deprived of leaves.

DEGRAPHIS, *Trinius.* Derived from *dis,* twice, and *grapho,* to mark. *Linn.* 3, Or. 2, Nat. Or. *Gramineæ.* Worthless species of grass, growing in any common soil, and increased by divisions at the roots. *Synonymes:* 1. *Phalaris arundinacea.* 2. *Arundo colorata—americana* 1, *arundinacea* 2, *variegata.*

DEHISCENT, gaping; an expression applied to the mode in which the anthers or the fruit burst open, and discharge their contents.

DELESSERIA, *Lamour.* In honour of M. Benjamin Delessert, a famous French botanical patron. *Linn.* 24, Or. 7, Nat. Or. *Algæ.* Beautiful species, of mostly deep green *Algæ,* found in the ocean, and on the sea-shore—*alata, A. angustissima, A. dilatata, Bonnemaisoni, glandulosa, hypoglossum, lacerata, ocellata, Plocamium, punctata, ruscifolia, sanguinea, sinuosa.*

DELIMA, *Linn.* From *delimo,* to file, or shave off; the leaves are used for polishing. *Linn.* 13, Or. 1, Nat. Or. *Dilleniaceæ.* Very fine climbing plants, growing best in loam, peat, and sand mixed; ripened cuttings root in sand, under a glass, in heat.

| nitida | . . . . | | S. Ev. Cl. | Trinidad | . 1830 |
| sarmentosa, 1 | . . | Yellow | S. Ev. Cl. | Ceylon | . 1820 |

DELIQUESCENT, melting away upon exposure to air.

DELPHINIUM, *Linn.* From *delphin,* a dolphin; in reference to the supposed resemblance in the nectary of the plant to the imaginary figures of the dolphin. *Linn.* 13, Or. 3, Nat. Or. *Ranunculaceæ.* All the species of Larkspur are showy, and valuable as border flowers, especially *D. Ajacis* and *Consolida,* both of which are universally grown among the border annuals. The herbaceous and perennial kinds are increased by divisions, or seeds, and the annual and biennial kinds merely require sowing in the open border, where they will flower and seed freely. *D. Consolida* is regarded as a simple astringent. *Synonymes:* 1. *D. tridactylon.* 2. *D. hirsutum.* 3. *D. intermedium.* 4. *D. junceum.* 5. *D. ambiguum.*

| aconiti | . . . | Purple | . 6, H. | A. | Levant | . 1801 |
| Ajacis | . . . | Pink | . 6, H. | A. | Switzerl. | . 1573 |
| flore-pleno | . . | Varieg. | . 6, H. | A. | Europe | . 1573 |
| albiflorum | . . | White | . 7, H. Her. P. | | Armenia | . 1823 |
| alpinum | . . . | Blue | . 7, H. Her. P. | | Hungary | . 1816 |
| altaicum | . . . | Blue | . 7, H. Her. P. | | Altaia | . 1829 |
| ambiguum | . . . | Blue | . 6, H. | A. | Barbary | . 1759 |
| amœnum | . . . | Pa. blue | . 7, H. Her. P. | | Siberia | . 1818 |
| astreum | . . . | Lgt. blue | . 7, H. Her. P. | | Carolina | . 1805 |
| Barlowii | . . . | Dk. blue | . 8, H. Her. P. | | Eng. hyb. | |
| cardiopetalum | . | Blue | . 6, H. | A. | Pyrenees | . 1818 |
| cheilanthum | . . | Dk. blue | . 5, H. Her. P. | | Siberia | . 1819 |
| multiplex | . . | Az. blue | . 7, H. Her. P. | | | |
| chinense | . . . | Blue | . 7, H. | A. | China | . 1818 |
| Consolida | . . . | Blue | . 4, H. | A. | England | |
| flore-pleno | . . | Varieg. | . 6, H. | A. | England | |
| cuneatum | . . . | Blue | . 7, H. Her. P. | | Siberia | . 1818 |
| dasycarpum | . . | Blue | . 7, H. Her. P. | | Caucasus | . 1819 |
| dictyocarpum | . | Blue | . 7, H. Her. P. | | Siberia | . 1817 |
| elatum | . . . . | Blue | . 7, H. Her. P. | | Siberia | . 1597 |
| elegans | . . . | Blue | . 7, H. Her. P. | | N. Amer. | |
| flore-pleno | . . | Blue | . 7, H. Her. P. | | N. Amer. | . 1741 |
| exaltatum, 1 | . . | Blue | . 7, H. Her. P. | | N. Amer. | . 1758 |
| fissum | . . . . | Blue | . 6, H. Her. P. | | Hungary | . 1816 |
| flexuosum | . . | Blue | . 5, H. Her. P. | | Caucasus | . 1820 |
| grandiflorum | . | Dk. blue | . 7, H. Her. P. | | Siberia | . 1816 |
| album | . . . | White | . 7, H. Her. P. | | Gardens | . 1816 |
| flore-pleno | . . | Dk. blue | . 6, H. Her. P. | | | |
| pallidum | . . . | Blue | . 6, H. Her. P. | | Gardens | . 1820 |
| hybridum, 2 | . . | Blue | . 7, H. Her. P. | | Siberia | . 1794 |
| intermedium | . . | Blue | . 8, H. Her. P. | | Silesia | . 1710 |
| cœrulescens | . . | Lt. blue | . 7, H. Her. P. | | | . 1836 |
| laxum | . . . . | Blue | . 5, H. Her. P. | | | |
| leptostachyum 3 | | Blue | . 5, H. Her. P. | | Pyrenees | |
| pallidum | . . | Blue | . 7, H. Her. P. | | | . 1836 |
| pilosissimum | . | Blue | . 7, H. Her. P. | | Siberia | |
| ranunculifolium | | Blue | . 7, H. Her. P. | | Pyrenees | |
| sapphirinum | . | Blue | . 7, H. Her. P. | | | |
| laxiflorum | . . | Blue | . 7, H. Her. P. | | Siberia | |
| Menziesii | . . | Blue | . 7, H. Tu. P. | | N. Amer. | . 1826 |
| mesoleucum | . | Blue | . 7, H. Her. P. | | | . 1822 |
| montanum | . . | Blue | . 7, H. Her. P. | | Switzerl. | . 1819 |
| bracteosum | . | Blue | . 6, H. Her. P. | | S. Eur. | . 1816 |
| ochroleucum | . | White | . 6, H. Her. P. | | Iberia | . 1823 |
| Oliverianum | . | Blue | . 6, H. | A. | S. Eur. | . 1826 |
| palmatifidum | . | Blue | . 7, H. Her. P. | | Siberia | . 1824 |
| glabellum | . . | Blue | . 7, H. Her. P. | | Siberia | . 1817 |
| pentagynum | . | Blue | . 7, H. Her. P. | | S. Eur. | . 1819 |
| peregrinum, 4 . | | Blue | . 7, H. | A. | Italy | . 1629 |
| pictum | . . . | Lgt. blue | 6, H. | B. | S. Eur. | . 1816 |
| pseudo-peregrinum | Red | . 6, H. Her. P. | | | Siberia | . 1823 |
| pubescens, 5 | . | Blue | . 8, H. | A. | Mediterr. | . 1816 |
| puniceum | . . | Purple | . 7, H. Her. P. | | Siberia | . 1785 |
| Requienii | . . | Blue | . 7, H. | B. | Majorca | . 1834 |
| revolutum | . . | Pa. blue | . 4, H. Her. P. | | | |
| speciosum | . . | Blue | . 7, H. Her. P. | | Caucasus | . 1816 |
| spurium | . . | Blue | . 8, H. Her. P. | | Siberia | . 1810 |
| Staphisagria | . | Lgt. blue | 7, H. | B. | S. Eur. | . 1596 |
| tenuissimum | . | Purple | . 8, H. | A. | Greece | . 1835 |
| tricorne | . . | Blue | . 7, H. Her. P. | | N. Amer. | . 1806 |
| triste | . . . | Blue | . 7, H. Her. P. | | Dahuria | . 1819 |
| urceolatum | . | Blue | . 6, H. Her. P. | | | . 1801 |
| velutinum | . . | Blue | . 7, H. Her. P. | | Italy | . 1819 |
| villosum | . . | Blue | . 7, H. Her. P. | | Caucasus | . 1818 |
| vimineum | . . | Blue | . 8, H. Her. P. | | N. Amer. | . 1835 |
| virgatum | . . | Blue | . 6, H. | A. | Syria | . 1823 |

DELTA-LEAVED, shaped like the Greek Δ.

DELTOIDES, triangular.

DEMATIUM, *Persoon.* From a diminutive of *dema,* a bundle; in reference to the mode of growth. *Linn.* 24, Or. 9, Nat. Or. *Fungi.* An extremely minute species of *Fungi,* of a bluish colour, found on the stems of herbs in autumn—*articulatum.*

DEMULCENT, having the property of softening anything.

DENDROBIUM, *Swartz.* From *dendron,* a tree, and *bios,* life; in the places of their natural growth, the species are generally found upon trees. *Linn.* 20, Or. 1, Nat. Or. *Orchidaceæ.* No orchidaceous plants contribute more to the gaiety of the stove, than the species of this splendid genus. *D. nobile, chrysanthum, Gibsonii, fimbriatum, densiflorum,* and many others, are equalled by few, and certainly not surpassed, in the beauty of their flowers, by any other orchidaceous plants; and if the following directions be attended to, they will be found very easy of culture:—All orchidaceous plants require (to cultivate them successfully), a season of growth, a season of rest, and a season for flowering; all of which should coincide, as much as possible, with the corresponding seasons of those parts of the globe which they so profusely inhabit; and the species of this genus should especially be subjected to a change of treatment assimilating as much as possible to that before mentioned, without which, they will never flower in perfection. In India, three seasons only are known; the hot, or dry season, which is succeeded by the rainy season, and the cold, or winter season. In the hot season, all, or the greater part, of the plants belonging to this genus produce their flowers; in the rainy season, they make their shoots; and during the cold season, they have a period of repose. The different seasons being so well known, it is very easy to imitate them in our hothouses, and by attending to these simple rules, we should be enabled to flower the species of this more abundantly than those of any other orchidaceous genus, besides which, they might be easily induced to flower in this country at any season of the year. *D. chrysanthum, Pierardii,* and some others, grow well when fastened singly on pieces of wood, and treated as is recommended under *Burlingtonia;* but they all succeed well when potted in very turfy peat, raised above the pot, in the same way as is recommended in potting *Stanhopeas.* A strong moist heat is indispensable in the growing season, when they may be frequently slightly syringed over-head. They will be found to succeed best in a warmer part of the house than the *Stanhopeas* require. They are propagated by detaching one or more of the stems while in a dormant state, taking care not to injure the roots, and potting it carefully in turfy peat soil, and not much raised above the pot, which must be carefully drained; the pot should then be plunged in a gentle bottom heat, where the plant will speedily produce new shoots. *Synonymes:* 1. *D. cucullatum.* 2. *D. pusillum.*

| | | | | | | |
|---|---|---|---|---|---|---|
| amulūm | . . | Wht. bra. | 12, 8. | Epi. | N. Holl. | 1823 |
| aggregatūm | . . | Yellow | 4, 8. | Epi. | India | . . |
| amplūm | . . | Straw cld. | 8. | Epi. | Khooseea | 1837 |
| aūreūm | . . | Yellow | 8. | Epi. | Ceylon | . . |
| cærulēscens | . . | Sky blue | 4, 8. | Epi. | Khooseea | 1837 |
| calamiformē | . . | | 8. | Epi. | | |
| calceolārī | . . | Or. pink | 6, 8. | Epi. | E. Ind. | 1820 |
| canaliculātūm | . . | | 8. | Epi. | N. Holl. | 1824 |
| candidūm | . . | White | 8. | Epi. | Khooseea | 1837 |
| chrysanthūm | . . | Yellow | 2, 8. | Epi. | Nepal | 1838 |
| crumenātūm | . . | White | 4, 8. | Epi. | Sumatra | 1822 |
| cūpreūm | . . | Red buff | 6, 8. | Epi. | E. Ind. | 1825 |
| Dalhousiānūm | . . | Pur. rose | 8. | Epi. | Brazil | 1837 |
| densiflōrūm | . . | Orange | 6, 8. | Epi. | Nepal | 1829 |
| denūdāns | . . | Wht. grn. | 8. | Epi. | Khooseea | 1837 |
| fimbriātūm | . . | Yellow | 5, 8. | Epi. | Nepal | 1823 |
| formōsūm | . . | White | 5, 8. | Epi. | Khooseea | 1837 |
| Gibsōnii | . . | Orange | 6, 8. | Epi. | Khooseea | 1837 |
| heterocārpūm | . . | Pa. yel. | 8. | Epi. | Khooseea | 1837 |
| insigne | . . | Yelsh. grn. | 8. | Epi. | Khooseea | 1837 |
| Jenkinsii | . . | | 8. | Epi. | Assam | 1837 |
| linguæfōrmē | . . | Purple | 8. | Epi. | N. S. W. | 1810 |
| longicōrnū | . . | White | 5, 8. | Epi. | Nepal | 1823 |
| macrōstāchyūm | . . | Yellow | 6, 8. | Epi. | Ceylon | 1829 |
| moniliformē | . . | Blue | 4, 8. | Epi. | Japan | 1824 |
| moschātūm | . . | Ro. buff | 5, 8. | Epi. | E. Ind. | 1823 |
| multicaulē | . . | White | 8. | Epi. | E. Ind. | 1837 |
| nōbilē | . . | Gn. yel. pk. | 8. | Epi. | China | . . |
| Pierārdii, 1 | . . | Whitish | 4, 8. | Epi. | E. Ind. | 1815 |
| pulchellūm | . . | Yellow | 4, 8. | Epi. | E. Ind. | . . |
| pygmæūm, 2 | . . | | 8. | Epi. | E. Ind. | . . |
| ramōsūm | . . | | 8. | Epi. | E. Ind. | . . |
| rigidūm | . . | | 8. | Epi. | N. Holl. | 1824 |
| secundūm | . . | Ro. pur. | 7, 8. | Epi. | Malacca | 1828 |
| speciosūm | . . | Yel. wht. | 1, 8. | Epi. | N. Holl. | 1824 |
| stupōsūm | . . | White | 5, 8. | Epi. | Khooseea | 1837 |
| sulcatūm | . . | Orange | 4, 8. | Epi. | Khooseea | 1837 |
| teretifolīūm | . . | Purple | 8. | Epi. | N. Holl. | 1823 |
| transpārens | . . | Rose | 8. | Epi. | Nepal | . . |

**DENDROMĒCŌN,** *Bentham.* From *dendron,* a tree, and *mekon,* a poppy; alluding to the shrubby habit and affinity of the plant. *Linn.* 13, Or. 1, Nat. Or. *Papaveraceæ.* This is rather a remarkable plant, thriving in any common garden soil, and increased by seeds.

| | | | | | | |
|---|---|---|---|---|---|---|
| rigidūm | . . | Yellow | . 5, F. | Ev. 8. | California | 1833 |

**DENSŪM,** thick, tufted, bundled.

**DENTĀRĪA,** *Tournefort.* From *dens,* a tooth; alluding to the tooth-like structure of the roots; whence the English name, Toothwort. *Linn.* 15, Nat. Or. *Cruciferæ.* This is a genus of very ornamental plants, well worthy of cultivation in every garden. They succeed best in a light, rich, sandy soil, in a moist shady situation; they may be multiplied by divisions, or seeds.

| | | | | | | |
|---|---|---|---|---|---|---|
| bulbifera | . . | Purple | . 4, H. | Tu. P. | England | . . |
| digitāta | . . | Pa. pur. | 5, H. | Tu. P. | Switzerl. | 1656 |
| diphylla | . . | Wht. pur. | 5, H. | Tu. P. | N. Amer. | . . |
| enneaphylla | . . | Pa. yel. | 5, H. | Tu. P. | Austria | 1656 |
| glandulōsa | . . | Lgt. pur. | 5, H. | Tu. P. | Hungary | 1815 |
| laciniāta | . . | White | 5, H. | Tu. P. | N. Amer. | 1822 |
| māxima | . . | Pa. pur. | 5, H. | Tu. P. | N. Amer. | 1823 |
| pinnāta | . . | Pa. pur. | 5, H. | Tu. P. | Switzerl. | 1633 |
| polyphylla | . . | Purple | 5, H. | Tu. P. | Hungary | 1818 |
| quinquefolia | . . | Purple | 5, H. | Tu. P. | Tauria | 1820 |
| tenuifolia | . . | Lgt. pur. | 5, H. | Tu. P. | Siberia | 1825 |
| trifolia | . . | White | 5, H. | Tu. P. | Hungary | 1824 |

**DENTATE,** having the margin divided into incisions, resembling teeth.

**DENTATELY-CILIATED,** having the margin toothed, and tipped with hairs.

**DENTATELY-SINUATED,** scolloped and toothed.

**DENTELLA,** *Forster.* From a diminutive of *dens,* a tooth; each side of the segments of the corolla is furnished with a small tooth. *Linn.* 5, Or. 1, Nat. Or. *Cinchonaceæ.* A small, creeping plant, the seeds of which require to be sown on a hotbed in spring, and when of sufficient size, they may be planted out into the open border. *Synonyme:* 1. *Oldenlandia repens.*

| | | | | | | |
|---|---|---|---|---|---|---|
| repens, 1 | . . | White | . . F. | | A. E. Ind. | 1802 |

**DENTICULATE,** the margins finely and slightly toothed.

**DENTICULATELY-CILIATED,** having the margin so finely toothed as to appear edged with hairs.

**DENTICULATIONS,** very small teeth.

**DENTIFORM,** tooth-shaped.

[ 103 ]

**DENTIFRICE,** powder made to scour the teeth.

**DEOBSTRUENT,** having the power of removing obstructions; a term in medicine.

**DEPAUPERATE,** impoverished, poor.

**DEPENDENT,** hanging down.

**DEPRESSED,** pressed downwards, low.

**DEPURATED,** purified, cleansed.

**DESCENDENS,** growing downwards.

**DESCHĀMPSĪA,** *Beauvois.* In honour of M. Deschamps, M.D., a celebrated French botanist. *Linn.* 3, Or. 2, Nat. Or. *Gramineæ.* A genus of grasses, which will grow in any common soil, and is increased by divisions, or seeds. *Synonymes:* 1. *Aira bottnica.* 2. *A. cæspitosa.* 3. *A. lævigata.* 4. *A. montana.* 5. *A. paludosa.*

| | | | | | | |
|---|---|---|---|---|---|---|
| bottnica, 1 | . . | Apetal | . . 6, Gram. | Bottnia | . . 1816 |
| cæspitōsa | . . | | | | |
| vivipāra | . . | Apetal | . . 6, Gram. | Britain | . . |
| glomerāta | . . | Apetal | . . 6, Gram. | Scotland | . . |
| lævigāta, 3 | . . | Apetal | . . 6, Gram. | Scotland | . . |

*alpīna, ambigūa, cæspitōsa 2, discōlor, jūncēa, montāna 4, mēdīa, paludōsa 5.*

**DESMĀNTHŪS,** *Willdenow.* From *desme,* a bundle, and *anthos,* a flower; the flowers are collected into bundles, or spikes. *Linn.* 23, Or. 1, Nat. Or. *Leguminosæ.* Some of the species of this genus are rather ornamental, while others are not worth cultivating. They like a mixture of peat and loam, and young cuttings root freely in sand, under a glass. The aquatic kinds require to be grown in large tubs, with five or six inches of soil in the bottom, and filled up with water. The tubs should be placed in a warm situation in the stove, where the plants will grow, and produce seeds, from which they may be increased.

| | | | | | | |
|---|---|---|---|---|---|---|
| callistāchys | . . | Red yel. | 7, 8. | Ev. 8. | Teneriffe | 1824 |
| lacūstris | . . | White | 7, 8. | Aq. P. S. | Amer. | 1818 |
| leptostāchys | . . | White | 7, 8. | Ev. 8. | Guinea | 1825 |
| strictūs | . . | White | 7, 8. | Ev. 8. | W. Ind. | 1800 |
| triquētrus | . . | White | 7, 8. | Aq. P. E. | Ind. | 1820 |

*cinērēus, diffūsus, divērgēns, nātāns, plēnūs, punctātus, virgātus.*

**DESMIDIŪM,** *Agardh.* From *desmos,* a bond; on account of the parts cohering when in a state of dissolution. *Linn.* 24, Or. 7, Nat. Or. *Algæ.* Two minute species of green *Algæ,* found in summer in still waters. *Synonyme:* 1. *Conferva dissiliens—cylindrica* 1, *Swartzii.*

**DESMOCHÆTA,** *Decandolle.* From *desmos,* a bond, and *chaite,* a hair; in allusion to the coherence of the flowers. *Linn.* 5, Or. 1, Nat. Or. *Amarantaceæ.* This is a genus of ornamental plants, requiring a soil composed of a mixture of sandy loam and peat. They are variously increased by cuttings, seeds, or dividing the roots; the former root readily in sand, in heat, under a glass. *Synonymes:* 1. *Achyranthes lappacea.* 2. *A. patula.*

| | | | | | | |
|---|---|---|---|---|---|---|
| atropurpūrea, 1 | . . | Purple | 9, 8. | Ev. 8. | E. Ind. | 1759 |
| flavēscens | . . | Yellow | 8, G. | A. E. Ind. | | 1822 |
| globōsa | . . | Pa. red | 8, G. | A. E. Ind. | | 1817 |
| micranthā | . . | Yellow | 7, G. | A. E. Ind. | | 1820 |
| patūla, 2 | . . | White | 9, 8. | Her. P. M. Ind. | | 1822 |
| prostrāta | . . | Grn. pur. | 7, G. | Ev. 8. | E. Ind. | 1793 |
| tomentōsa | . . | White | 8, G. | Ev. 8. | E. Ind. | 1818 |
| uncināta | . . | | 8, G. | A. E. Ind. | | 1820 |

**DESMŌDIŪM,** *Decandolle.* From *desmos,* a bond; alluding to the stamens being joined. *Linn.* 17, Or. 4, Nat. Or. *Leguminosæ.* A few species of this genus are very handsome, while the rest have little or no beauty. A mixture of sandy loam and peat suits them, and young plants may be obtained from cuttings planted in sand, under a glass, in heat, or by seeds. *D. diffusum* is a valuable fodder plant. *Synonymes:* 1. *Hedysarum glutinosum.* 2. *H. aparines.* 3. *H. adscendens.* 4. *H. canadense.* 5. *H. canescens.* 6. *H. capitatum.* 7. *H. cuspidatum.* 8. *H. gangeticum.* 9. *H. gyrans.* 10. *H. latifolium.* 11. *H. maculatum.* 12. *H. malacophyllum.* 13. *H. marilandicum.* 14. *H. multiflorum.* 15. *H. obtusum.* 16. *H. paniculatum.* 17. *H. canescens.* 18. *H. sagittatum.* 19. *H. serotinum.* 20. *H. tomentosum.* 21. *H. tortuosum.* 22. *H. trigonum.* 23. *H. triflorum.* 24. *H. triquetrum.* 25. *H. umbellatum.* 26. *H. viridiflorum.*

| | | | | | | |
|---|---|---|---|---|---|---|
| acuminātūm, 1 | . . | Purple | 7, 8. | Her. B. | N. Amer. | 1805 |
| alātūm | . . | Purple | 7, 8. | | E. Ind. | 1817 |
| angustifolīūm | . . | Purple | 7, 8. | Ev. 8. | Mexico | 1824 |

| | | | | | | |
|---|---|---|---|---|---|---|
| auriculātūm | Purple | 7, 8. | B. | Timor | 1819 |
| bracteātūm | Purple | 7, H. Her. | P. | N. Amer. | 1818 |
| brasiliēnsē | Purple | 7, 8. Ev. | 8. | Brazil | 1819 |
| cajanifolīūm | Blue | 7, 8. Ev. | 8. | Caraccas | 1820 |
| cephalōtēs | Purple | 7, H. | 8. | E. Ind. | 1823 |
| ciliārē | Violet | 7, H. Her. | P. | N. Amer. | 1822 |
| cinērēūm | Purple | 7, 8. Ev. | 8. | Mexico | 1820 |
| collīnūm | Purple | 7, 8. Ev. | 8. | E. Ind. | 1816 |
| dūbīūm | Pa. red | 7, 8. Ev. | 8. | Nepal | 1824 |
| glabellūm | Purple | 7, H. Her. | P. | N. Amer. | |
| gȳrāna, 9 | Purple | 7, 8. | B. | E. Ind. | 1775 |
| gyroīdēs | | 7, 8. | B. | E. Ind. | 1817 |
| hamōsūm | Purple | 7, 8. Ev. | 8. | E. Ind. | 1818 |
| incānūm | Purple | 7, 8. Ev. | 8. | Jamaica | 1818 |
| lāctēūm | Purple | 7, 8. Ev. | 8. | Maurit. | 1826 |
| lasiocarpūm | Purple | 7, 8. Ev. | 8. | Guinea | 1823 |
| latifolīūm, 10 | Purple | 7, 8. Ev. | 8. | China | 1818 |
| nudiflōrūm | Purple | 7, 8. Her. | P. | N. Amer. | 1723 |
| nūtāns | Purple | 7, 8. Ev. | 8. | E. Ind. | 1823 |
| paniculātūm, 16 | Purple | 7, H. Her. | P. | N. Amer. | 1781 |
| pauciflōrum | White | 7, H. De. | Tr. N. Amer. | | 1818 |
| pseudo-triquētrum | | 7, 8. | B. | Nepal | 1820 |
| reniformē | | 7, 8. | B. | E. Ind. | 1820 |
| rotundifolīūm, 17 | White | 7, H. De. | Tr. N. Amer. | | 1738 |
| spectābilē | Purple | 7, 8. Ev. | 8. | Maurit. | 1826 |
| stipulācēūm | Purple | 7, 8. Her. | P. | Mexico | 1824 |
| supīnūm | Purple | 7, 8. Ev. | Tr. W. Ind. | | 1816 |
| triquētrūm, 24 | Purple | 7, 8. | B. | E. Ind. | 1802 |
| trinērvīūm | Purple | 7, 8. Ev. | 8. | | 1820 |

*Aparīnēs 2, adscēndēns, cærūlēūm, aspērūm, canadēnsē 4, canēscēns 5, capitātūm, cuspidātūm 7, diffūsūm, diversifolīūm, gangēticūm 8, guianēnsē, heterophylīūm, Lechinaūlīī, maculātā 11, malacophyllūm 12, marilāndicum 13, multiflōrūm 14, obtūsūm 15, retūsūm, sagittātūm 18, serōtīnūm 19, spirālē, tenēllūm, tomentōsūm 20, tortuōsūm 21, trigōnūm 22, triflōrūm 23, umbellātūm 25, viridiflōrūm 26.*

DESMŎNCŬS, *Martius.* From *desmos*, a bond, and *ogkos*, a hook; the tendrils at the apex of the leaves are connected. *Linn.* 21, Or. 6, Nat. Or. *Palmaceæ.* A very ornamental genus of palms, delighting in sandy loam, and requiring precisely the same treatment as the other genera belonging to the same tribe.

| | | | | |
|---|---|---|---|---|
| americānūs | | Palm. | St. Vincent | 1824 |
| dūbīūs | | Palm. | Trinidad | 1824 |
| orthacānthūs | | Palm. | Brazil | 1822 |
| polyacānthūs | | Palm. | Brazil | 1822 |

DESPUMATE, to throw off, in froth or scum.

DETERGENT, DETERSIVE, having the power of cleansing.

DEVIL'S BIT, see *Succīsā.*

DEVIL'S MILK, see *Euphōrbiā Pēplūs.*

DEWBERRY, see *Rūbūs cæsīūs.*

DEUTZIA. *Thunberg* named this genus in compliment to John Deutz, sheriff of Amsterdam, and one of his patrons. *Linn.* 10, Or. 3, Nat. Or. *Philadelphaceæ.* A very ornamental plant, producing white flowers, not so large as the snowdrop, but many together, in numerous clusters, at the tips of the branches; the foliage is dark green. It thrives in any garden soil, and may be propagated with facility by cuttings, or layers.

| | | | | | |
|---|---|---|---|---|---|
| scābrā | . 5, H. De. 8. | Japan | . 1833 |

DIADELPHOUS, when stamens are connected into two bodies.

DIANDROUS, having two stamens.

DIANĒLLĀ, *Lambert.* Derived from Diana, the sylvan goddess; on account of the plants growing in woods. *Linn.* 6, Or. 1, Nat. Or. *Liliaceæ.* A genus of very ornamental plants, requiring, to grow them well, a mixture of loam and peat; they are easily increased by divisions, or seeds. *Synonyme:* 1. *Dracæna ensifolia.*

| | | | | | |
|---|---|---|---|---|---|
| cærūlēā | Blue | 6, G. Tu. P. | N. Holl. | 1783 |
| congēstā | Blue | 6, G. Tu. P. | N. Holl. | 1820 |
| divaricātā | Blue | 7, G. Tu. P. | N. S. W. | 1805 |
| ensifolīā, 1 | White | 8, 8. Tu. P. | E. Ind. | 1731 |
| lævis | Blue | 8, G. Tu. P. | N. Holl. | 1822 |
| longifolīā | Blue | 8, G. Tu. P. | N. Holl. | 1822 |
| nemorōsā | Blue | 8, 8. Tu. P. | E. Ind. | 1731 |
| revolūtā | Blue | 8, G. Tu. P. | N. Holl. | 1823 |
| strumōsā | Blue | 3, G. Tu. P. | N. Holl. | 1822 |

DIĀNTHŬS, *Linn.* From *dios*, divine, and *anthos*, a flower; in reference to the fragrance of the blossoms, and the unrivalled neatness of the flowers. *Linn.* 13, Or. 2, Nat. Or. *Silenaceæ.* A truly beautiful and ornamental genus, containing some of the most prized flowers we possess, on account of the beauty and fragrance of their flowers, and their foliage, which is as green and vivid in winter as it is in

summer. The rarer kinds should be grown in pots, so that they can be protected in winter. They all delight in light loamy soil, mixed with a little rotten dung, or decayed leaves and sand. They may be increased by seeds, or cuttings; the last method is preferable. The cuttings should be planted out under a glass, about the middle of June, and if they be planted on a gentle hotbed, they will be ready for planting out in about three weeks. The annual and biennial kinds merely require sowing in the open border, where they will grow and flower freely. *Synonymes:* 1. *D. scaber.* 2. *D. glaucophyllus.* 3. *D. pumilus.* 4. *D. atrorubens.* 5. *D. orientalis.* 6. *D. neglectus.* 7. *D. furcatus.* 8. *D. Willdenovii.* 9. *D. petræus.* 10. *D. procumbens.* 11. *D. pallens.* 12. *D. petræus.* 13. *D. moschatus, dubius.* 14. *D. ochroleucus.* 15. *D. Birisigniani.* 16. *D. virgineus.* 17. *D. pungens, rupestris.*

| | | | | | |
|---|---|---|---|---|---|
| aggregātūs | Pink | 6, H. | B. | | 1817 |
| albēns | White | 8, G. Her. | P. | C. G. H. | 1787 |
| alpēstris | Red | 6, H. | A. | Europe | 1817 |
| alpīnūs | Red | 6, H. Her. | P. | Austria | 1759 |
| arbōrēūs | Pink | 7, F. Ev. | 8. | Greece | 1820 |
| arbūscūlā | Red | 7, F. Ev. | 8. | China | 1824 |
| arenārīūs | Purple | 8, H. Her. | P. | Europe | |
| Armērīā | Red | 6, H. | A. | England | |
| armerioīdēs | Red | 6, H. | A. | New Jersey | 1826 |
| aspēr, 1 | Pink | 7, H. Her. | P. | Switzerl. | 1822 |
| atrōrubēns | Crimson | 8, H. Her. | P. | Italy | 1802 |
| attenuātūs | Red | 7, H. Her. | P. | Spain | 1822 |
| Balbīsīī, 2 | Red | 8, H. Her. | P. | Genoa | 1817 |
| barbātūs | Pink | 7, H. Her. | P. | Germany | 1573 |
| latifolīūs, 3 | Scarlet | 7, H. Her. | P. | | 1826 |
| bicolōr | Pink | 7, H. Her. | P. | Tauria | 1816 |
| buchtormānsis | Red | 7, H. Her. | P. | Russia | 1826 |
| cæsīūs | Flesh | 7, H. Her. | P. | Britain | |
| campēstris | Wht. red | 8, H. Her. | P. | Tauria | 1815 |
| capitātūs, 4 | Purple | 8, H. Her. | P. | Caucasus | 1822 |
| caroliniānūs | Purple | 6, H. Her. | P. | N. Amer. | 1811 |
| Carthusianōrūm | Red | 7, H. Her. | P. | Germany | 1573 |
| caryophylloīdēs | Red | 6, H. Her. | P. | | 1817 |
| Caryophyllūs | Flesh | 6, H. Her. | P. | England | |
| flōre-plēnō | Crimson | 8, H. Her. | P. | England | |
| fruticōsūs | Crimson | 8, H. Her. | P. | England | |
| imbricātūs | Flesh | 8, H. Her. | P. | England | |
| caucāsicūs | Purple | 7, H. Her. | P. | Caucasus | 1803 |
| cephalōtēs | Pink | 7, H. Her. | P. | | 1823 |
| chinēnsis | Red | 7, H. | B. | China | 1713 |
| ciliātūs | Pink | 7, H. Her. | P. | Naples | 1829 |
| clavātūs | Flesh | 7, H. Her. | P. | | |
| collīnūs | White | 8, H Her. | P. | Hungary | 1800 |
| crenātūs | Flesh | 8, G. Her. | P. | C. G. H. | 1817 |
| deltoīdēs | Flesh | 6, H. Her. | P. | Britain | |
| dentātūs | Red | 7, H. Her. | P. | Siberia | 1826 |
| diffūsūs | Red | 7, H. Her. | P. | Cyprus | 1820 |
| diminūtūs | Pink | 7, H. Her. | P. | 8. Eur. | 1771 |
| discolōr | Pink | 7, H. Her. | P. | Caucasus | 1803 |
| divaricātūs | Purple | 7, H. Her. | P. | Greece | 1822 |
| erubēscēns | Blush | 7, H. Her. | P. | Pyrenees | 1825 |
| ferruginēūs | Brown | 7, H. Her. | P. | Italy | 1756 |
| sulphūrēūs | Sulphur | 8, H. | B. | Italy | 1826 |
| fimbriātūs, 5 | Brown | 7, H. Her. | P. | Iberia | 1815 |
| Fischērī | Red | 6, H. Her. | P. | Russia | 1820 |
| albūs | White | 8, H. Her. | P. | Gardens | 1820 |
| frāgrāns | White | 7, H. Her. | P. | Austria | 1804 |
| fruticōsūs | Pink | 7, F. Ev. | 8. | Greece | 1815 |
| furcātūs | Pa. red | 7, H. Her. | P. | Piedmont | 1819 |
| gallicūs | Purple | 7, H. Her. | P. | 8. France | |
| gigantēūs | Purple | 8, H. Her. | P. | Greece | 1824 |
| glaciālis, 6 | Red | 7, H. Her. | P. | 8. Eur. | 1820 |
| glaucophyllūs | Red | 7, H. Her. | P. | | 1827 |
| glaucūs | White | 6, H. Her. | P. | Britain | |
| guttātūs | Red | 7, H. Her. | P. | Caucasus | 1816 |
| hirtūs | Red | 7, H. Her. | P. | France | 1821 |
| Hornemānnī, 7 | Red | 8, H. Her. | P. | Italy | |
| hortēnsis | Red | 7, H. Her. | P. | Hungary | 1805 |
| hyssopifolīūs | Pink | 8, H. Her. | P. | Europe | 1810 |
| ibēricūs, 8 | Purple | 7, H. Her. | P. | Iberia | 1817 |
| japonicūs | Pink | 6, F. Her. | P. | China | 1804 |
| latifolīūs | Pink | 6, H. Her. | P. | | |
| leptopētalūs | White | 6, H. Her. | P. | Caucasus | 1814 |
| Libanōtis | White | 7, H. Her. | P. | Lebanon | 1830 |
| Liboschitziānūs, 9 | White | 7, H. Her. | P. | Tauria | 1817 |
| longicaūlis | White | 7, H. | B. | | 1820 |
| marginātūs | White | 7, H. | B. | 8. Eur. | 1820 |
| monadēlphūs, 10 | Wht. pink | 8, H. Her. | P. | Levant | |
| monspessulānūs | Red | 7, H. Her. | P. | Montpel. | 1764 |
| montānūs | Red | 7, H. Her. | P. | Caucasus | 1803 |
| Mussīnī | White | 6, H. Her. | P. | Caucasus | 1823 |
| nānūs | Crimson | 6, H. Her. | P. | Switzerl. | 1820 |
| nitīdūs | Red | 7, H. Her. | P. | Carpath. | 1822 |
| pallidiflōrūs, 11 | Purple | 7, H. Her. | P. | Siberia | 1817 |
| petræūs | White | 7, H. Her. | P. | Hungary | 1804 |
| flōribūs majoribūs, 12 | Pink | 6, H. Her. | P. | | 1804 |
| Poiretiānūs | Purple | 8, H. Her. | P. | | 1816 |

| | | | | | |
|---|---|---|---|---|---|
| flōrē-plēnō | . Purple | 4, H. Her. P. | Greece | . | 1820 |
| polymórphūs | . Red | 8, H. Her. P. | Crimea | . | 1822 |
| diūtinūs | . Red | 7, H. Her. P. | Hungary | . | 1816 |
| pomeridiānūs | . Yellow | 7, H. Her. P. | Levant | . | 1804 |
| plumārīūs, 13 | . Wht. pur. | 7, H. Her. P. | S. Eur. | . | 1629 |
| plumōsūs | . Wht. li. | 6, H. Her. P. | M. Bald. | | |
| pratēnsīs, 14 | . Wht. yel. | 8, H. Her. P. | Crimea | . | 1820 |
| prólifer | . Pink | 7, H. | A. England | | |
| prostrātūs | . Red | 9, H. Ev. S. | C. G. H. | . | 1824 |
| Pseud-Armēriā | . Purple | 8, H. Her. P. | Crimea | . | 1820 |
| pubēscēns | . Red | 7, H. | A. Greece | . | 1820 |
| pulchéllūs | . Wht. red | 6, H. Her. P. | Siberia | . | 1827 |
| punctātūs | . Pa. li. | 8, H. Her. P. | | | |
| pūngēns | . Pink | 8, H. Her. P. | Spain | . | 1781 |
| rīgīdūs | . Red | 7, H. Her. P. | Casp. Sea | . | 1802 |
| rupicōlā, 15 | . Red | 6, H. Her. P. | Italy | . | 1820 |
| ruthēnīcūs | . Purple | 6, H. Her. P. | Russia | . | 1816 |
| saxātīlīs | . White | 6, H. Her. P. | S. Eur. | . | 1816 |
| serōtinūs | . Purple | 8, H. Her. P. | Hungary | . | 1804 |
| serrātūs | . Pink | 6, H. Her. P. | Pyrenees | . | 1827 |
| sīcūlūs | . Red | 8, H. Her. P. | Sicily | . | 1829 |
| squarrōsūs | . White | 6, H. Her. P. | Tauria | . | 1817 |
| Sternbergīī | . Red | 6, H. Her. P. | | | |
| suavēolēns | . White | 8, H. Her. P. | | . | 1820 |
| suāvīs | . Pink | 7, H. Her. P. | | | |
| suffruticōsūs | . Pink | 8, F. Ev. S. | Siberia | . | 1804 |
| supērbūs | . White | 8, H. Her. P. | Europe | . | 1596 |
| sylvātīcūs | . Red | 6, H. Her. P. | Ratisbon | . | 1815 |
| sylvéstrīs, 16 | . Red | 7, H. Her. P. | S. Eur. | . | 1732 |
| tēnēr | . Red | 8, H. Her. P. | Europe | . | 1817 |
| versīcolōr | . Red | 8, H. Her. P. | Russia | . | 1823 |
| vîrgineūs, 17 | . Red | 6, H. Her. P. | Montpel. | . | 1816 |

DIAPĒNSIA. Named by Linnæus from *diapente*, composed of five; alluding to the flowers being five-cleft. *Linn.* 5, Or. 1, Nat. Or. *Diapensiaceæ*. A very pretty little alpine plant, but rather difficult to cultivate, as too much moisture is very apt to kill it. In its native country, it is continually covered with snow in winter, which protects it from the severe dry frosts. It succeeds best grown in small pots, in peat soil, with the protection of a frame in winter. It is increased by seeds, or divisions.

| | | | | |
|---|---|---|---|---|
| lappōnicā | . . White | . 7, H. Her. P. | Lapland | . 1801 |

DIAPHANOUS, transparent.

DIAPHORETIC, promoting perspiration.

DIASCIA, *Link.* From *dis*, twice, and *askion*, a little bladder; because of the two protuberances at the base of the corolla. *Linn.* 14, Or. 2, Nat. Or. *Scrophulariaceæ*. A Cape annual, of no value—*Berginā*.

DIATŌMA, *Decandolle*. From *diatome*, separation; the filaments are divided into joints. *Linn.* 24, Or. 7, Nat. Or. *Algæ*. Very minute species of yellow and green *Algæ*, found at all seasons of the year in the ocean, ditches, and on the sea-coast—*Biddulphiānūm, elongātūm, flocculōsūm, marīnūm, obliquātūm, striātūlūm, tēnūē*.

DICĒRA, *Forster*. From *dis*, double, and *keras*, a horn; the anthers are terminated by two horns, or bristles. *Linn.* 11, Or. 1, Nat. Or. *Elæocarpaceæ*. A rambling shrub, growing to the height of about two feet. It succeeds well in a mixture of loam and peat; and cuttings of the ripened wood root in sand, under a glass. *Synonymes:* 1. *Elæocarpus dentatus, Eriostemon dentatus.*

| | | | | |
|---|---|---|---|---|
| dentātā, 1 | . . White | . 7, G. Ev. S. | New Zeal. | 1810 |

DICĒRMA, *Decandolle*. From *dis*, twice, and *erma*, a prop; the calyx is propped at the base by two bracts. *Linn.* 17, Or. 4, Nat. Or. *Leguminosæ*. A genus of very elegant shrubs, about three feet high, growing in a mixture of loam and peat; they may be increased by young cuttings, planted in sand, under a glass, or by seeds. *Synonymes:* 1. *Hedysarum biarticulatum.* 2. *Zornia elegans, Hedysarum elegans.* 3. *Zornia pulchella.*

| | | | | |
|---|---|---|---|---|
| biarticulātūm, 1 | . Yellow | . 7, S. Ev. S. | E. Ind. | . 1808 |
| ēlēgans, 2 | . Yellow | . 7, S. Ev. S. | China | . 1819 |
| pulchēllūm, 3 | . Yellow | . 7, S. Ev. S. | E. Ind. | . 1798 |

DICHÆA, *Lindley*. From *dichi*, in two rows; in allusion to the arrangement of the leaves. *Linn.* 20, Or. 1, Nat. Or. *Orchidaceæ*. This is a small, uninteresting little plant, succeeding best when treated as the genus *Burlingtonia. Synonymes:* 1. *Cymbidium graminoides, Epidendrum graminoides.*

| | | | | |
|---|---|---|---|---|
| graminōīdēs | . . Grn. yel. | . 6, S. Epi. | Demerara | . 1823 |

DICHILUS, *Decandolle*. From *dis*, twice, and *cheilos*, a lip; in allusion to the calyx being deeply two-

lipped. *Linn.* 16, Or. 6, Nat. Or. *Leguminosæ*. A pretty little shrub; for culture and propagation, see *Loddigesia*.

| | | | | |
|---|---|---|---|---|
| Lebeckioīdēs | . Wht. yel. | 4, G. Ev. S. | C. G. H. | . 1826 |

DICHONDRA, *Forster*. From *dis*, twice, and *chondros*, a grain; in allusion to the form of the capsules. *Linn.* 5, Or. 2, Nat. Or. *Nolanaceæ*. Little creeping inconspicuous plants, seldom to be met with in collections; they grow well in peat and loam, and may be increased by cuttings.

| | | | | |
|---|---|---|---|---|
| argéntēā | . . White | . 7, G. Ev. Cr. | W. Ind. | . 1800 |
| carolinēnsīs | . . White | . 7, F. Ev. Cr. | Carolina | . 1810 |
| repēns | . . White | . 7, G. Ev. Cr. | N. S. W. | . 1803 |
| rotundifōliā | . . White | . 7, G. Ev. Cr. | | . 1819 |
| serīcēā | . . White | . 7, S. Ev. Cr. | Jamaica | . 1793 |

DICHORIZĀNDRA, *Mikan*. From *dis*, twice, *chorizo*, to part, and *aner*, an anther; in reference to the anthers being two-cleft. *Linn.* 6, Or. 1, Nat. Or. *Commelinaceæ*. Beautiful herbaceous plants, resembling *Commelina* in their foliage, and may be referred to that genus for culture and propagation.

| | | | | |
|---|---|---|---|---|
| grācilīs | . . Blue | . 8, S. Her. P. | Brasil | . . |
| oxypétālā | . . Red | . 8, S. Her. P. | Brasil | . . 1810 |
| pictā | . . Blue | . 9, S. Her. P. | S. Amer. | . 1830 |
| pubērūlā | . . Blue | . 8, S. Her. P. | Brasil | . . 1823 |
| thyraīflōrā | . . Blue | . 8, S. Her. P. | Brasil | . . 1822 |

DICHOSMA. Derived from *dicha*, without, and *osme*, a smell. *Linn.* 5, Or. 1, Nat. Or. *Rutaceæ*. An ornamental species; for culture, &c., see *Diosma. Synonyme:* 1. *Diosma bifida.*

| | | | |
|---|---|---|---|
| bīfīdā | . . . White | . 5, G. Ev. S. | C. G. H. |

DICHOSPŌRIŪM, *Nees*. From *dicha*, double, and *spora*, a sporule; in allusion to the double coat of the peridium. *Linn.* 24, Or. 9, Nat. Or. *Fungi*. An extremely minute species, found on the bark of oak trees in autumn. *Synonyme:* 1. *Spumaria physaroides—aggregatum* 1.

DICHOTOMOUS, a stem that ramifies in pairs.

DICOCCOUS, having two cocci.

DICKSONIA, *L'Heritier*. In honour of James Dickson, a famous British cryptogamic botanist. *Linn.* 24, Or. 1, Nat. Or. *Polypodiaceæ*. A very ornamental genus of ferns, containing the tree-fern of St. Helena, which has often been brought in a living state to this country, but it rarely survives many months. The species do well in a mixture of loam and peat, and are readily increased by divisions, or seeds.

| | | | | |
|---|---|---|---|---|
| adiantoīdēs | . . Brown | . 11, S. Ev. S. | W. Ind. | . 1828 |
| arborēscēns | . . Brown | . 9, S. Ev. T. | St. Helena | . 1786 |
| dīssēctā | . . Brown | . 8, S. Her. P. | Jamaica | . 1793 |
| pilosiūscūlā | . . Brown | . 8, S. Her. P. | N. Amer. | . 1811 |

DICLIPTERA, *Jussieu*. From *dis*, double, and *kleio*, to shut; in allusion to the two-valved fruit. *Linn.* 2, Or. 1, Nat. Or. *Acanthaceæ*. An ornamental genus, nearly allied to *Justicia*, to which genus it may be referred for culture and propagation.

| | | | | |
|---|---|---|---|---|
| assūrgēns | . . . Red | . 7, S. Ev. S. | W. Ind. | . 1818 |
| bivalvis | . . . Purple | . 6, S. Ev. S. | E. Ind. | . 1818 |
| chinēnsīs | . . Pa. blue | . 9, G. Her. P. | E. Ind. | . 1816 |
| hexangulārīs | . . Red | . 7, S. | A. S. Amer. | . 1788 |
| martinicēnsīs | . Purple | . 7, S. Ev. S. | W. Ind. | . 1818 |
| pectinātā | . . . Blue | . 6, S. Ev. S. | E. Ind. | . 1798 |
| peruviānā | . . . Purple | . 6, S. Ev. S. | Peru | . . 1818 |
| resupinātā | . . Wht. pur. | 8, S. | A. S. Amer. | . 1805 |
| retūsā | . . . Purple | . 7, S. Her. P. | W. Ind. | . 1821 |
| scorpioīdēs | . . . | . 7, S. Ev. S. | Vera Cruz | . 1802 |
| verticillārīs | . . Purple | . 5, G. Ev. S. | C. G. H. | . 1826 |

DICRANUM, *Hedwig*. From *dikranos*, two-headed; in reference to the divisions of the teeth of the capsule. *Linn.* 24, Or. 5, Nat. Or. *Musci*. A fine genus of mosses; many of the species form broad masses of turfy vegetation, giving a beautiful character to the face of the earth where they grow. They are found at all seasons, and almost in every situation. *Synonymes:* 1. *Hypnum adiantoides.* 2. *Dicranum viridulum, osmundoides.* 3. *D. pusillum, uncinatum.* 4. *Trichostomum piliferum.* 5. *D. flagellare.* 6. *Hypnum taxifolium.* 7. *D. callistomum.* —*adiantoides* 1, *bryoides* 2, *cerviculatum* 3, *crispum, falcatum, flavescens, flexuosum, fulvellum, glaucum, heteromallum, latifolium* 4, *longifolium, pellucidum, polycarpon, Schreberianum, scoparium, fuscescens-majus, Scottianum* 5, *spurium, squarrosum; Starkii, strumiferum, subulatum, taxifolium, undulatum, varium, luridum, rufescens, viride* 7, *virens.*

P

DICRĪPTĂ, *Lindley*. From *dis*, two, and *cryptos*, hidden; alluding to the structure of the four pollen masses. *Linn.* 20, Or. 1, Nat. Or. *Orchidaceæ*. A curious species, with solitary flowers, requiring the same treatment as the *Stanhopeas*. Synonyme: 1. *Heterotaxis crassifolia.*

Bauĕrĭ . . . Yellow . 6, S. Epi. Jamaica . 1823

DICTĂMNŬS, *Linn.* An ancient name supposed to have been given because the leaves resemble those of the Ash; hence the English name, Fraxinella. *Linn.* 10, Or. 1, Nat. Or. *Rutaceæ.* A genus of very ornamental plants, deserving a place in every flower-border. D. *Fraxinella*, when rubbed, emits a fine odour, something like that of lemon-peel; this fine scent is strongest in the pedicels of the flowers. The species succeed well in any common garden soil, and may be increased by seeds, which ripen freely. The roots were formerly esteemed as a sudorific and vermifuge. Synonyme: 1. *D. albus.*

albŭs . . . . White . 6, H. Her. P. Germany . 1596
angustifolĭŭs . . Lilac . 6, H. Her. P. Altai . 1821
Fraxinĕllă, 1 . . Purple . 6, H. Her. P. Germany . 1596

DICTȲDĬŬM, *Schrader*. From *diktyon*, a net, and *eidos*, similar; alluding to the resemblance of the peridium. *Linn.* 24, Or. 9, Nat. Or. *Fungi.* A very minute, black, pinheaded species, to be found at all seasons on rotten wood—*cernuum.*

DIDĔLTĂ, *L'Heritier.* From *dis*, double, and *delta*, the Greek letter equivalent to the English D; in reference to the double receptacle. *Linn.* 19, Or. 3, Nat. Or. *Compositæ.* Shrubs, with little to recommend them, growing well in peat and loam, mixed; and may be increased by cuttings—*carnosum, spinosum.*

DIDĔSMŬS, *Desfontaines.* From *dis*, twice, and *desmos*, a bond; the pod is jointed like two links of a chain. *Linn.* 15, Nat. Or. *Cruciferæ.* Uninteresting annuals, of the simplest culture. Synonymes: 1. *Myagrum ægyptiacum.* 2. *Sinapis bipinnata—ægyptiaca* 1, *bipinnata* 2.

DIDYMĬŬM, *Schrader.* From *didymos*, double; in allusion to the inner and outer peridium. *Linn.* 24, Or. 9, Nat. Or. *Fungi.* A very small species of *Fungi*, occasionally seen on dead leaves—*globosum.*

DIDYMŎDŌN, *Hedwig.* From *didymos*, double, and *odous*, a tooth; the teeth of the fringe are in pairs. *Linn.* 24, Or. 5, Nat. Or. *Musci.* A genus of chiefly greenish mosses, found in spring and summer on mountain rocks and moist banks. D. *inclinatum* is only to be met with in this country, upon the mountains of Cunnemara, in Ireland. Synonymes: 1. *Trichostomum capillaceum.* 2. *T. flexifolium.* 3. *Grimmia heteromalla.* 4. *G. inclinata.* 5. *G. atrovirens.* 6. *D. Bruntoni.* 7. *Bryum bipartitum, Dicranum Celsii, D. strictum, Trichostomum papillosum.* 8. *T. rigidulum.* 9. *T. trifarium, linoides—capillaceum* 1, *flexifolium* 2, *glaucescens, heteromallum* 3, *inclinatum* 4, *nervosum* 5, *obscurum* 6, *purpureum* 7, *rigidulum* 8, *trifarium* 9.

DIDYMOUS, two united; applied to the fruit when they appear twin.

DIDYNAMOUS, having two long stamens and two short ones in the same flower, each pair being collateral.

DIELȲTRĂ, *Borkhausen.* From *dis*, double, and *elytron*, a sheath; the base of the flower is furnished with two sheath-like spurs. *Linn.* 17, Or. 2, Nat. Or. *Papaveraceæ.* A genus of very desirable herbaceous plants. Any light rich soil suits them, and they are easily increased by divisions, or seeds. Synonymes: 1. *Corydalis canadensis.* 2. *Fumaria cucullaria.* 3. *F. eximia.* 4. *Corydalis tenuifolia.*

bracteŏsă . . . White . 6, H. Her. P. N. Amer. . 1823
canadĕnsĭs, 1 . . White . 6, H. Her. P. N. Amer. . 1819
cucullărĭă, 2 . . White . 6, H. Her. P. N. Amer. . 1731
exīmĭă, 3 . . Flesh . 6, H. Her. P. N. Amer. . 1812
formŏsă . . . Flesh . 6, H. Her. P. N. Amer. . 1796
lachenalĭæflōră . Purple . 6, H. Her. P. Siberia . 1826
specĭŏsă . . . Flesh . 6, H. Her. P. . 1810
spectăbĭlĭs . . Purple . 6, H. Her. P. Siberia . 1810
tenuĭfolĭă, 4 . . Purple . 6, H. Her. P. Kamtch. . 1820

DIENĬX, *Lindley.* From *dis*, two, and *enia*, a strap; in allusion to the attachment of the pollen-masses. *Linn.* 20, Or. 1, Nat. Or. *Orchidaceæ.* This is described as a plant of no beauty. Turfy peat soil, and an efficient drainage, will be found to suit it.

cordătă . . . Green . 8. Epi. Mexico . 1837

DIERVĬLLĂ, *Tournefort.* In compliment to M. Dier-

ville, a French surgeon. *Linn.* 5, Or. 1, Nat. Or. *Caprifoliaceæ.* A very desirable plant for the front of shrubberies, growing from three to four feet high, in any common soil; it may readily be increased by cuttings, put into the ground in autumn and spring, or by suckers, which it throws up in great quantities from the roots. Synonyme: 1. D. *canadensis*, Lonicera *Diervilla.*

lutĕă, 1 . . . Yellow . 6, H. De. S. N. Amer. . 1739

DIETETICS, relating to food, or diet.

DIFFORM, different forms; used to express irregularity.

DIFFUSE, scattered, widely spread.

DIĔTĔS, *Salisbury.* From *dis*, twice, and *etes*, an associate; the genus is nearly related to *Iris* and *Moræa.* *Linn.* 3, Or. 1, Nat. Or. *Iridaceæ.* The plants of this genus are very ornamental, and for culture, &c., may be referred to *Iris.* Synonymes: 1. *Iris bicolor.* 2. *Moræa catenulata.* 3. *Iris moræoides, Moræa iridioides.*

bicolŏr, 1 . . Yel. drk. . 6, F. Her. P.
catenulătă, 2 . Wht. brn. 6, F. Her. P. Madagas. 1826
iridioĭdĕs, 3 . . Wht. brn. 7, F. Her. P. C. G. H. . 1758

DIGITĀLIS, *Linn.* Derived from *digitale*, the finger of a glove; in allusion to the resemblance the flower bears to the finger of a glove. *Linn.* 14, Or. 2, Nat. Or. *Scrophulariaceæ.* The species are mostly very showy border flowers, growing in any common garden soil. The tender kinds are best planted in pots, so that they may have the protection of the frame in winter. According to Decandolle, the powdered leaves, or an extract of them, produce vomiting, dejection, and vertigo, increase the secretion of saliva and urine, lower the pulse, and even cause death. Synonymes: 1. D. *grandiflora.* 2. *parviflora.* 3. *intermedia.* 4. *ambigua.* 5. *erubescens.*

ambīgŭă, 1 . . Lgt. yel. . 7, H. Her. P. Switzerl. . 1596
aūrĕă . . . Brown . 7, H. Her. P. Greece . 1816
eriostăchȳă . . Brn. yel. . 7, H. . B. Russia . 1827
ferrugĭnĕă . . Brown . 7, H. . B. Italy . 1597
fuscĕscĕns . . Red . 7, H. Her. P. Hungary . 1823
fulvă . . . Brown . 6, H. Her. P.
lacinĭătă . . Yellow . 6, H. Her. P. Spain . 1827
lævigātă . . Yellow . 7, H. Her. P. Hungary . 1816
lanātă . . . Yellow . 6, H. Her. P. Hungary . 1789
leucophæă . . Wht. brn. 6, H. Her. P. Greece . 1788
lutĕă, 2 . . . Lgt. yel. . 7, H. Her. P. France . 1629
lutĕscĕns . . Yellow . 7, H. Her. P.
medĭă, 3 . . . Yellow . 6, H. Her. P. Germany . 1817
micrănthă . . Yel. brn. . 7, H. Her. P. Switzerl. . 1817
minŏr . . . Purple . 7, H. Her. P. Spain . 1789
obscūră . . . Orange . 6, F. Ev. S. Spain . 1778
ochroleūcă, 4 . White . 6, H. Her. P. Europe .
orientālis . . White . 6, H. Her. P. Levant . 1820
parvĭflōră . . Brown . 7, H. Her. P. . 1798
purpurăscĕns, 5 Pink . 6, H. Her. P. Germany . 1776
purpūrĕă . . Purple . 7, H. . B. Britain .
albă . . . . White . 7, H. . B. Britain .
rĭgĭdă . . . Yel. red . 6, H. Her. P.
Thăpsĭ . . . Purple . 6, H. Her. P. Spain . 1752
tomentŏsă . . Red . . 7, H. Her. P. Portugal . 1818
tubiflōră . . Yellow . 6, H. Her. P.

DIGITATED, fingered, shaped like the hand spread open.

DIGITĀRĬĂ, *Schrader.* Derived from *digitus*, a finger; alluding to the singular manner in which the heads are divided. *Linn.* 3, Or. 2, Nat. Or. *Gramineæ.* A genus of grasses, all the species of which are uninteresting. They grow in any common soil, and may be multiplied by seeds. Synonymes: 1. D. *humifusa.* 2. *Milium filiforme—ægyptiaca, affinis, barbata, biformis, ciliaris, eriogona, filiformis, glabra* 1, *linearis, marginata, paspaloides, Roxburghii* 2, *sanguinalis, villosa.*

DIGITIFORM, formed like fingers.

DIGYNOUS, two styles, or female organs.

DILATED, widened.

DILĂTRĬS, *Linn.* Meaning unexplained. *Linn.* 3, Or. 1, Nat. Or. *Hæmodoraceæ.* Ornamental plants, growing about a foot high in sandy peat; they are readily propagated by seeds, or divisions.

corymbŏsă . . Purple . 5, G. Her. P. C. G. H. . 1790
paniculātă . . Blue . 6, G. Her. P. C. G. H. . 1825
viscŏsă . . . Blue . . G. Her. P. C. G. H. . 1795

DILL, see *Anethum.*

DILLĔNĬĂ, *Linn.* After the celebrated professor of botany at Oxford, John James Dillenius, author of *Hortus Elthamensis*, &c. *Linn.* 13, Or. 6, Nat. Or. *Dilleniaceæ.* A splendid tree, which thrives well

[ 106 ]

in the collections of this country. It grows best in a light loamy soil, or loam and peat; ripened cuttings, not deprived of any of their leaves, will root in sand, under a glass, in heat. The young calyxes are used in curries by the inhabitants of Bengal.

| | | | | |
|---|---|---|---|---|
| specióså | . . . Wht. yel . | 8. Ev. T. E. Ind. | . . . | 1800 |

**DILLWŸNIA,** *Smith.* In honour of Lewis Weston Dillwyn, F.R.S., L.S., &c., a well-known British botanist. *Linn.* 10, Or. 1, Nat. Or. *Leguminosæ.* Very elegant shrubs when in flower, and well worthy of cultivation in every collection. They grow from one to four feet high, in an equal mixture of loam, peat, and sand, with the pots well drained. Cuttings of the young wood root freely in sand, under a glass.

| | | | | |
|---|---|---|---|---|
| acicularis | . . . Yellow | . 5, G. Ev. 8. N. Holl. | . 1826 |
| cinerascens | . . . Yellow | . 5, G. Ev. 8. N. S. W. | . 1819 |
| ericifolia | . . . Yellow | . 5, G. Ev. 8. N. S. W. | . 1794 |
| floribunda | . . . Yellow | . 5, G. Ev. 8. N. S. W. | . 1794 |
| glabarrima | . . . Yellow | . 5, G. Ev. 8. N. S. W. | . 1800 |
| juniperina | . . . Yellow | . 5, G. Ev. 8. V. D. L. | . 1818 |
| parvifolia | . . . Yellow | . 5, G. Ev. 8. N. S. W. | . 1800 |
| phylicoides | . . . Yellow | . 5, G. Ev. 8. N. Holl. | . 1824 |
| rudis | . . . Yellow | . 4, G. Ev. 8. N. Holl. | . 1824 |
| brevifolia | . . . Yellow | . 4, G. Ev. 8. N. Holl. | . 1824 |
| hispidula | . . . Yellow | . 5, G. Ev. 8. N. Holl. | . 1824 |
| teretifolia | . . . Yellow | . 5, G. Ev. 8. N. Holl. | . 1824 |
| sericea | . . . Yellow | . 4, G. Ev. 8. N. Holl. | . 1824 |
| tenuifolia | . . . Yellow | . 5, G. Ev. 8. N. Holl. | . 1824 |

**DIMIDIATE,** divided into two parts.

**DINEBRA,** *Beauvois.* Its Arabic name. *Linn.* 3, Or. 2, Nat. Or. *Gramineæ.* An annual species, growing in any garden soil, and increased by seeds.

| | | | | |
|---|---|---|---|---|
| arabica | . . . Apetal. | . 6, Grass. E. Ind. | . . . 1804 |

**DINEMA,** *Lindley.* Not explained. *Linn.* 20, Or. 1, Nat. Or. *Orchidaceæ.* A very pretty plant; for culture and propagation, see *Stanhopea.* Synonyme: 1. *Epidendrum polybulbon.*

| | | | | |
|---|---|---|---|---|
| polybulbon | . . White . | 12, S. Epi. Jamaica | . 1822 |

**DINETUS,** *Sweet.* From *dinetos*, that may be twined; in allusion to the habit of the plants. *Linn.* 5, Or. 1, Nat. Or. *Convolvulaceæ.* A very ornamental genus; the perennial species thrives well in any rich light soil. Young cuttings, in the same sort of soil, under a glass, in heat, will soon root. D. *racemosa* grows very fast in a sheltered situation, and is well adapted to make a good covering for a temporary arbour. It is increased from seed, which is ripened in abundance. Synonymes: 1. *Porana paniculata.* 2. *P. racemosa.*

| | | | | |
|---|---|---|---|---|
| paniculata, 1 | . . White | . 8, S. Ev. Tw. E. Ind. | . 1823 |
| racemosa, 2 | . . White | . 8, H. Tw. A. Nepal | . 1823 |

**DIOCLEA,** *H. Bet. Kunth.* In memory of Diocles Carystinus, an ancient Greek botanist. *Linn.* 17, Or. 4, Nat. Or. *Leguminosæ.* A twining shrub, growing in any common soil, increased by cuttings in sand, under a glass, in heat. Synonyme: 1. *Dolichos multis—mollis.*

**DIODIA,** *Linn.* From *diodos*, a passage; many of the species grow by the way-sides. *Linn.* 4, Or. 1, Nat. Or. *Cinchonaceæ.* A genus of rather pretty trailing shrubs, of simple cultivation. A light soil suits them best; and cuttings, in the same kind of soil, root freely if placed in heat.

| | | | | |
|---|---|---|---|---|
| prostrata | . . White | . 6, S. Ev. Tr. W. Ind. | . 1818 |
| sarmentosa | . . White | . 7, S. Ev. Tr. W. Ind. | . 1821 |
| verticillata | . . White | . 6, S. Ev. Tr. W. Ind. | . 1821 |
| virginica | . . White | . 6, H. De. Tr. Virginia | . 1890 |

**DIŒCIOUS,** when a plant bears female flowers on one individual, and males on another.

**DIOMEDEA,** *Cassini.* Named after Diomeda, the daughter of Phorbas. *Linn.* 19, Or. 2, Nat. Or. *Compositæ.* A genus of ornamental shrubs, with silvery leaves; they succeed well in any rich light soil; and cuttings root freely, in the same kind of soil, under a glass. Synonymes: 1. *Bupthalmum frutescens.* 2. *B. arborescens.*

| | | | | |
|---|---|---|---|---|
| argentea | . . . Yellow | . 6, G. Ev. 8. S. Amer. | . 1824 |
| bidentata, 1 | . . Yellow | . 7, G. Ev. 8. W. Ind. | . 1696 |
| glabrata, 2 | . . Yellow | . 6, G. Ev. 8. S. Amer. | . 1699 |

**DIONÆA,** *Linn.* Dione, one of the names of Venus. *Linn.* 10, Or. 1, Nat. Or. *Cephalotaceæ.* This is a very singular little plant in respect to its leaves, which are of an anomalous form, and have a curious motion, by which they catch insects; whence the

[ 107 ]

specific name, *Muscipula,* a fly-trap. The petiole of the leaf is winged. The extreme part is that which acts as a trap. As soon as the insect enters, the lobes of the leaf fold together, and remain so as long as the insect continues to struggle; but as soon as it is quiet, the leaf opens, and permits it to escape. The plant thrives best in small pots, in peat earth, and some dwarf species of moss placed underneath in the pot; the pots should then be placed in a pan of water, and set in a cool place in the stove, with a glass over them, but not close, else they will be liable to damp. Seeds are sometimes produced, by which they may be increased, but the readier way is to divide the plants at the root. It has also been found, that if a leaf be taken off, and placed on damp moss, it will emit a young plant from its edge.

| | | | | |
|---|---|---|---|---|
| Muscipula | . . . White . | . 7, S. Her. P. Carolina | . 1788 |

**DIOSCOREA,** *Linn.* Named after Pedacius Dioscorides, a famous Greek physician. *Linn.* 24, Or. 6, Nat. Or. *Dioscoreaceæ.* The Yam is cultivated in tropical climates for the sake of the roots, which are used in a similar way to potatoes, and are much esteemed by the natives. They are chiefly climbing plants; some of them have very handsome foliage. They succeed well in any light rich soil, and are readily increased by dividing their roots.

| | | | | |
|---|---|---|---|---|
| aculeata | . . . Green . | . 8. Tw. P. E. Ind. | . 1803 |
| alata | . . . Green . | . 8. Tw. P. India | . 1739 |
| brasiliensis | . . . Green . | . 8. Tw. P. Brazil | . 1823 |
| bulbifera | . . . Green . | . 7, 8. Tw. P. E. Ind. | . 1692 |
| cinnamomifolia | . Grn. yel. | . 8. Tw. P. Rio Jan. | . 1827 |
| pentaphylla | . . . Green . | . 8. Tw. P. E. Ind. | . 1768 |
| sativa | . . . Green . | . 8. Tw. P. W. Ind. | . 1733 |

*altissima, anguina, angustifolia, atropurpurea, coriacea, crispata, fasciculata, glabra, globosa, heterophylla, leonensis, nepalensis, Nummularia, oppositifolia, piperifolia, pulchella, purpurea, quaternata, quinqueloba, rubella, scabra, trifida, trifoliata, triphylla, villosa.*

**DIOSMA,** *Linn.* From *dios*, divine, and *osme*, smell; the bruised leaves have an exquisite smell. *Linn.* 5, Or. 1, Nat. Or. *Rutaceæ.* This is a genus of truly beautiful, heath-like shrubs, growing from one to four feet high. To grow them well, they must have a mixture of peat and sand, and a little turfy loam in the bottom of the pot, over the shreds. Young cuttings, planted in sand, with a glass over them, will root freely, without any heat.

| | | | | |
|---|---|---|---|---|
| cordata | . . . White . | . 5, G. Ev. 8. C. G. H. | . 1823 |
| corymbosa | . . . White . | . 5, G. Ev. 8. C. G. H. | . 1818 |
| cupressina | . . . Pink . | . 5, G. Ev. 8. C. G. H. | . 1790 |
| ericoidea | . . . White . | . 6, G. Ev. 8. C. G. H. | . 1756 |
| fœtidissima | . . . White . | . 6, G. Ev. 8. C. G. H. | . 1824 |
| hirsuta | . . . Pink . | . 5, G. Ev. 8. C. G. H. | . 1731 |
| hybrida | . . . White . | . 5, G. Ev. 8. C. G. H. | . 1823 |
| longifolia | . . . White . | . 5, G. Ev. 8. C. G. H. | |
| oppositifolia | . . . White . | . 6, G. Ev. 8. C. G. H. | . 1752 |
| pectinata | . . . Blue . | . 5, G. Ev. 8. C. G. H. | . 1812 |
| punctata | . . . White . | . 6, G. Ev. 8. C. G. H. | . 1823 |
| rubra | . . . Red . | . 8, G. Ev. 8. C. G. H. | . 1752 |
| scoparia | . . . White . | . 6, G. Ev. 8. C. G. H. | . 1812 |
| sphærocephala | . White . | . 5, G. Ev. 8. C. G. H. | |
| squamosa | . . . | . 6, G. Ev. 8. C. G. H. | . 1818 |
| subulata | . . . White . | . 6, G. Ev. 8. C. G. H. | . 1818 |
| succulenta | . . . White . | . 6, G. Ev. 8. C. G. H. | |
| tenella | . . . White . | . 5, G. Ev. 8. C. G. H. | . 1823 |
| tenuissima | . . . White . | . 7, G. Ev. 8. C. G. H. | . 1820 |
| tenuifolia | . . . White . | . 6, G. Ev. 8. C. G. H. | |
| tetragona | . . . White . | . 6, G. Ev. 8. C. G. H. | . 1789 |
| ulicina | . . . White . | . 6, G. Ev. 8. C. G. H. | . 1823 |
| virgata | . . . White . | . 6, G. Ev. 8. C. G. H. | . 1820 |

**DIOSPYROS,** *Linn.* From *dios*, divine, and *pyros*, a pear; resemblance of the fruit. *Linn.* 23, Or. 2, Nat. Or. *Ebenaceæ.* Ornamental and highly valuable timber trees, from fifteen to thirty feet high. The species grow in any light loamy soil, and may be increased by ripened cuttings, planted in sand, under a glass. The European species, D. *Lotus*, produced that famous fruit, which, according to the ancient romancers, caused oblivion. Some of the species are very remarkable for the hardness of the wood, such as D. *Ebenus, Ebenaster, Mabola,* and *Melanoxylon,* and for the eatable quality of the fruit; the former is well known under the name of Ebony and Ironwood. The bark of D. *virginiana* is said to be febrifugal. The fruit of D. *Embryopteris* is so glutinous as to be used in Bengal for paying boats.

| | | | | | | |
|---|---|---|---|---|---|---|
| chloroxylòn | . | White . . | S. Ev. | T. E. Ind. | . . | 1822 |
| cordifòlià | . . | Wht. gra. | S. Ev. | T. E. Ind. | . . | 1794 |
| discòlòr . | . . | | G. Ev. | T. Philippine | . | 1823 |
| Ebenàstèr | . | | S.' Ev. | T. Bengal | . . | 1792 |
| Ebènùm | . . | White . . | S. Ev. | T. E. Ind. | . . | 1792 |
| edùlïs . . | . | | S. Ev. | T. E. Ind. | . . | 1824 |
| Embryòptèris | . Wht. gra. . | 7. | S. Ev. | T. E. Ind. | . . | 1818 |
| hirsùtà . | . | | S. Ev. | T. Ceylon | . . | 1820 |
| Kàkï . . | . | Wht. gra. | G. Ev. | T. Japan | . . | 1789 |
| lobàtà . . | . | | G. Ev. | T. China | . . | 1822 |
| Lòtùs . . | . | Yel. gra. . | 6, | H. Ev. | T. Italy | . . | 1596 |
| lùcïdà . . | . | Yellow . | 6, | H. Ev. | T. N. Amer. | . | 1820 |
| lycioïdès . | . | | S. Ev. S. | | . | 1806 |
| Mabòlà . | . | Yel. gra. | S. Ev. | S. Philip. Is. | . | 1822 |
| melanòxylòn | . White . . | | S. Ev. | T. E. Ind. | . . | 1817 |
| montànà . | . | Wht. gra. | G. Ev. | S. E. Ind. | . . | 1822 |
| obovàtà . | . | Wht. gra. | S. Ev. | T. W. Ind. | . . | 1796 |
| pubescèns | . Yel. gra. . | 4, | H. Ev. | T. N. Amer. | . | 1812 |
| reticulàtà | . | | G. Ev. | T. Maurit. | . | 1824 |
| rugulòsà | . | | G. Ev. | T. N. Holl. | . | 1823 |
| sylvàtïcà | . | White . . | S. Ev. | T. E. Ind. | . . | 1812 |
| vaccinioïdès | . White . . | 5, | G. Ev. | S. China | . . | 1823 |
| virginiànà | . Yel. gra. . | 6, | H. Ev. | T. N. Amer. | . | 1629 |
| dùlcïs . . | . | Yellow . | 7, | H. Ev. | T. America | . | 1629 |

**DIÒRÏS,** *Schreber.* From *dis,* double, and *ous,* an ear; the flowers possess two ear-like appendages at the base of the florets. *Linn.* 21, Or. 4, Nat. Or. *Chenopodiaceæ.* Shrubs of little beauty, thriving in any light soil, and increased by layers, or cuttings, under a glass. *Synonyme:* 1. *Atriplex pedunculata.*

| | | | | | |
|---|---|---|---|---|---|
| ceratoïdès | . . | Apetal | . 3, | H. De. S. Siberia | . . 1780 |

*atriplicinà* 1, *candidissimà.*

**DIPHÀCÀ,** *Loureiro.* From *dis,* twice, and *phake,* a lentil, or pea; the pods are composed of two one-seeded joints. *Linn.* 17, Or. 4, Nat. Or. *Leguminosæ.* An ornamental shrub, about eight feet high, nearly allied to *Dalbergia.* It requires the same treatment as other greenhouse plants. *Synonyme:* 1. *Dalbergia Diphaca.*

| | | | | |
|---|---|---|---|---|
| cochinchinènsïs | . White . . | G. Ev. S. China | . . |

**DIPHYLLEÏX,** *Michaux.* From *dis,* double, and *phyllon,* a leaf; in allusion to the stems bearing only two alternate leaves each. *Linn.* 6, Or. 1, Nat. Or. *Berberaceæ.* A very pretty plant, growing freely in any rich light soil, and multiplied by divisions.

| | | | | |
|---|---|---|---|---|
| cymòsà | . . | White . | 5, H. Her. P. N. Amer. | . 1812 |

**DIPHYSÀ,** *Jacquin.* From *dis,* twice, and *physa,* a bladder; the pods are furnished with a membranous bladder on each side. *Linn.* 17, Or. 4, Nat. Or. *Leguminosæ.* An ornamental shrub, from six to ten feet high; the soil best adapted to it is a mixture of loam, peat, and sand. Young cuttings will root in sand, under a glass, in heat.

| | | | | |
|---|---|---|---|---|
| carthaginènsïs | . Yellow . . | S. Ev. S. Carthago | . 1827 |

**DIPHYSCÏÙM,** *Weber.* From *dis,* twice, and *physkion,* a vesicle; in reference to the shell of the theca being double. *Linn.* 24, Or. 5, Nat. Or. *Musci.* A very little plant, found in woods, and on rocks in Alpine situations. The stems are exceedingly short, and grow in densely matted patches. *Synonyme:* 1. *Buxbaumia foliosa—foliòsum.*

**DIPLÀCHNÈ,** *Beauvois.* From *diploos,* double, and *achne,* chaff. *Linn.* 3, Or. 2, Nat. Or. *Gramineæ.* An uninteresting species of grass, of simple culture. *Synonyme:* 1. *Festuca polystachya—fasciculàris* 1.

**DIPLÀCÙS,** *Nuttall.* From *dis,* two, and *plakos,* a placenta; alluding to the splitting of the capsule, to each valve of which is attached a large placenta, and under its edges are found the slender subulate seeds. *Linn.* 14, Or. 2, Nat. Or. *Scrophulariaceæ.* A genus of very elegant plants, especially *D. puniceus,* which will prove a very great ornament to our gardens. The species will succeed well in rich sandy loam, and may be increased by cuttings. *D. puniceus* is at present very scarce in this country. *Synonyme:* 1. *Mimulus glutinosus.*

| | | | | |
|---|---|---|---|---|
| glutinòsùs, 1 | . Orange all . | G. Ev. S. California | . 1794 |
| punïcèùs . | . Scarlet all . | F. Ev. S. California | . 1837 |

**DIPLÀSÏÀ,** *Richard.* From *diplaso,* to double; in reference to the glumes. *Linn.* 3, Or. 1, Nat. Or. *Cyperaceæ.* A plant with little to recommend it, growing in any common soil, and increased by divisions.

| | | | | |
|---|---|---|---|---|
| karatifòlïà | . . | Apetal | . 3, Gram. Guiana | . . 1825 |

**DIPLÀZÏÙM,** *Swartz.* From *diplazo,* to double; in allusion to the indusia being double. *Linn.* 24, Or.

1, Nat. Or. *Polypodiaceæ.* A very handsome and ornamental genus of ferns. *D. auriculatum* forms a tree about ten feet high. The plants succeed well in loam and peat, and may be either increased by seeds, or divisions; the latter is the more preferable method. *Synonymes:* 1. *Asplenium arboreum.* 2. *Hemionitis esculenta.* 3. *H. grandifolia.* 4. *Asplenium ambiguum.* 5. *A. plantagineum.*

| | | | | | |
|---|---|---|---|---|---|
| arborescèns | . Brown | . 8, S. Ev. | T. Maurit. | . 1826 |
| auriculàtùm, 1 | . Brown | . 8, S. Ev. | T. Caracoes | . 1820 |
| castaneæfòlïùm | . Brown | . 7, S. Her. | P. Guiana | . 1824 |
| esculèntùm, 2 | . Brown | . 8, S. Her. | P. E. Ind. | . 1822 |
| grandifòlïùm, 3 | . Brown | . 8, S. Her. | P. Jamaica | . 1793 |
| juglandifòlïùm | . Brown | . 8, S. Her. | P. Jamaica | . 1820 |
| malabàricùm, 4 | . Brown | . 8, S. Her. | P. E. Ind. | . 1818 |
| plantaginèùm, 5 | . Brown | . 8, S. Her. | P. W. Ind. | . 1819 |
| serampurèùs | . Brown | . 8, S. Her. | P. Serampore | . 1820 |

**DIPLÒCÒMÀ,** *D. Don.* From *diploos,* double, and *koma,* hair; the pappus is of two forms. *Linn.* 19, Or. 2, Nat. Or. *Compositæ.* A pretty plant, succeeding well in common garden soil. The plants require protection in winter, therefore it is best to grow a few plants in pots, to stand in the frame in winter, as those in the ground are apt to suffer if not well attended to; it may be increased by seeds, or divisions. *Synonyme:* 1. *Doronicum villosum.*

| | | | | |
|---|---|---|---|---|
| villòsà, 1 | . . . Yellow . | 6, H. Her. P. Mexico | . . 1826 |

**DIPLÒLÈPÏS,** *R. Brown.* From *diploos,* double, and *lepis,* a scale. *Linn.* 5, Or. 2, Nat. Or. *Asclepiadaceæ.* An uninteresting genus of climbing plants, growing freely in any rich light soil; young cuttings root in sand, under a glass, in heat. The root of *D. vomitoria* is prized by the Indian doctors for its expectorant and diaphoretic qualities—*apiculàtà, ovàtà, vomitòrïà.*

**DIPLOPÀPPÙS,** *Cassini.* From *diploos,* double, and *pappos,* pappus; the fruit is furnished with a double row of bristles. *Linn.* 19, Or. 2, Nat. Or. *Compositæ.* A very handsome, shrubby species, growing to the height of about two feet, producing its flowers in heads, with the rays rich lilac, and the disc a bright yellow. It succeeds well in sandy loam, and is increased by cuttings. It will grow and flower well in a hot exposed situation in the open ground, in summer, but requires the protection of a frame in winter.

| | | | | |
|---|---|---|---|---|
| incànûs | . . . Lgt. yel. | 8, F. Ev. S. California | . 1822 |

**DIPLOPHYLLÙM,** *Lehmann.* Derived from *diploos,* double, and *phyllon,* a leaf; in allusion to the two-leaved calyx. *Linn.* 2, Or. 1, Nat. Or. *Scrophulariaceæ.* A border annual, the seeds of which need only be sown in the open border early in spring. *Synonyme:* 1. *Veronica Crista-galli.*

| | | | | |
|---|---|---|---|---|
| veronicæfòrmè, 1 | . Blue . | 4, H. Tr. A. Caucasus | . 1813 |

**DIPLOTÀXÏS,** *Decandolle.* From *diploos,* double, and *taxis,* a series; the seeds are disposed in two rows in each cell. *Linn.* 15, Nat. Or. *Cruciferæ.* Uninteresting annuals, which merely require sowing in the open border, where they will grow, flower, and produce their seed in abundance. *Synonymes:* 1. *Sisymbrium catholicum.* 2. *Sinapis crassifolia.* 3. *Sinapis erucoides.* 4. *Sisymbrium murale.* 5. *Sisymbrium pendulum.* 6. *Sisymbrium tenuifolium.* 7. *Sinapis virgata—Barrelieri, catholica* 1, *crassifolia* 2, *erucoides* 3, *hispida, muralis* 4, *pendula* 5, *saxatilis, tenuifolia* 6, *viminea, virgata* 7.

**DIPLOTHÈMÏÙM,** *Martius.* Derived from *diploos,* double, and *thema,* a spathe. *Linn.* 21, Or. 9, Nat. Or. *Palmaceæ.* Ornamental plants, growing to the height of about ten feet, and requiring the same treatment as *Caryota,* and other genera of the order.

| | | | | |
|---|---|---|---|---|
| campestrè | . . . | Palm. Brazil | . . 1823 |
| maritïmùm | . . . | Palm. Brazil | . . 1823 |

**DIPÒDÏÙM,** *R. Brown.* From *dis,* two, and *pous podos,* a foot; referring to the threads of the pollen masses. *Linn.* 20, Or. 1, Nat. Or. *Orchidaceæ.* A very curious, leafless plant, with rather pretty purplish flowers. For culture and propagation, see *Bletia.* *Synonyme:* 1. *Dendrobium punctatum.*

| | | | | |
|---|---|---|---|---|
| punctàtùm | . . . Purplish . | 12, S. Ter. N. Holl. | . 1822 |

**DIPSÀCÙS,** *Tournefort.* Supposed to be from *dipsao,* to thirst; in consequence of the leaves holding water; *dipsakos* is also the Greek name for the disease called diabetes, which is always accompanied by great thirst. *Linn.* 4, Or. 1, Nat. Or. *Dipsaceæ.*

Curious species, some of which are pretty flowering plants, especially *D. pilosus.* They grow well in any common soil, and are readily increased by seeds. *D. fullonum* is extensively cultivated in the west of England, the dried heads of which furnish the teasel used by fullers in dressing cloth.

| | | | | | |
|---|---|---|---|---|---|
| feròx | . . . | . Purple . | 7, H. | B. S. Eur. . . | 1818 |
| fullònûm | . . . | . Purple . | 7, H. | B. Britain . | . |
| Gmelìnî | . . . | . Blue . | 7, H. | B. Caucasus | .1820 |
| inèrmis | . . . | . White . | H. | B. Nepal . | .1823 |
| laciniàtûs | . . | . Purple . | 7, H. | B. Germany | .1683 |
| pilòsûs | . . . | . White . | 8, H. | B. Britain . | . |

sylvèstris.

DIPTÈRIX, *Schreber.* From *dis*, double, and *pterix*, a wing; the two upper lobes of the calyx appear like two wings. Linn. 17, Or. 4, Nat. Or. *Leguminosæ.* An ornamental tree, attaining the height of sixty feet. It requires to be grown in a loamy soil, and ripened cuttings root in sand, under a glass, in a moist heat. The seeds of this tree are the Tongo, or Tonquin-beans, so well known as giving a pleasant scent to snuff. *Synonyme:* 1. *Baryosma Tongo.*

| | | | | | |
|---|---|---|---|---|---|
| odoràta, 1 | . . . | . Purple . | 8. Ev. T. | Guiana . | . 1793 |

DIPTÈROUS, applied to anything which has two wings.

DIRCA, *Linn.* Derived from *dirka*, signifying a fountain; in reference to the habitation of the plant. Linn. 8, Or. 1, Nat. Or. *Thymelaceæ.* An ornamental little shrub, found growing in the marshes of North America. It succeeds well in sandy loam, and is propagated by layers, or seeds. It is so tough that the twigs are used for baskets, &c.; whence the English name, Leather Wood.

| | | | | | |
|---|---|---|---|---|---|
| palûstris | . . . | . Yellow . | 3, H. | De. S. Virginia | . 1750 |

DISA, *Linn.* Meaning unknown. Linn. 20, Or. 1, Nat. Or. *Orchidaceæ.* A genus of interesting, tuberous-rooted plants, thriving well in an equal mixture of peat, loam, and sand, and increased by separating the roots. They require to be very carefully watered when not in a growing state.

| | | | | |
|---|---|---|---|---|
| bracteàtâ . . . | . Green . | 6, G. Ter. | C. G. H. . | . 1818 |
| chrysostàchyâ . | . Yellow . | 6, G. Ter. | C. G. H. . | . |
| cornûtâ . . . | . Pa. blue | 6, G. Ter. | C. G. H. . | . 1805 |
| dracònis . . . | . Wht. pur. | 6, G. Ter. | C. G. H. . | . 1823 |
| ferruginèâ . . | . Brown | 6, G. Ter. | C. G. H. . | . 1820 |
| flexuòsâ . . | | G. Ter. | C. G. H. . | . 1823 |
| graminifòliâ . | . Blue | 6, G. Ter. | C. G. H. . | . 1825 |
| grandiflòrâ . | . Scarlet | 7, G. Ter. | C. G. H. . | . 1825 |
| lácerâ . . | . White . | 6, G. Ter. | C. G. H. . | . 1826 |
| maculàtâ . | . Blue . | 6, G. Ter. | C. G. H. . | . 1816 |
| prasinàtâ . | . Grn. red | 6, G. Ter. | C. G. H. . | . 1815 |
| spatulàtâ . | . Pa. blue | 6, G. Ter. | C. G. H. . | . 1805 |

DISANDRA, *Linn.* Named from *dys*, difficult, and *aner*, an anther; the number of the anthers varies. Linn. 7, Or. 1, Nat. Or. *Scrophulariaceæ.* A pretty trailing plant, which, when raised, its pendant branches, and little yellow flowers, have a very pretty appearance. It will grow well in any rich light soil, and is propagated by divisions, or cuttings, with or without a glass, in a shady situation.

| | | | | |
|---|---|---|---|---|
| prostràtâ | . . . | . Yellow . | 6, G. Ev. Tr. Madeira | . 1771 |

DISCHIDIA, *R. Brown.* From *dis*, twice, and *schizo*, to split; application unexplained. Linn. 5, Or. 2, Nat. Or. *Asclepiadaceæ.* Ornamental plants, growing in any light sandy soil; and cuttings will root very freely in the same kind of soil, without any glass.

| | | | | |
|---|---|---|---|---|
| bengalènsis | . . | . White . | 9, S. Ev. Tr. India | . 1819 |
| nummulàrîs | . . | . White . | 8, S. Ev. Tr. Amboyna | . |

DISCOID, any thing dilated into something which may be compared to a disk.

DISCUS, or DISK, the fleshy annular process that surrounds the ovarium of many flowers; also the surface of a leaf; also the centre of a head of flowers of *Compositæ.*

DISCUTIENT, having the power to scatter the matter of tumours.

DISEMMA, *Labillardière.* From *dis*, double, and *stemma*, a crown; the crown of the flower is double Linn. 16, Or. 2, Nat. Or. *Passifloraceæ.* A genus, comprising two splendid and curious shrubs, requiring the same treatment, in culture and propagation, as *Passiflora. Synonymes:* 1. *Passiflora adiantifolia, Murucuia adiantifolia.* 2. *Passiflora Herbertiana, Murucuia Herbertiana.*

| | | | | |
|---|---|---|---|---|
| adiantifòliâ, 1 | . . | . Orange . | 7, S. Ev. Cl. Norfolk Is. | . 1792 |
| Herbertiànâ, 2 | . | . Grn. wht. | 7, S. Ev. Cl. N. Holl. | . 1821 |

DISERMIS, smooth, without thorns.

[ 109 ]

DISOMORPHOUS, two-shaped.

DISPÈRIS, *Swartz.* From *dis*, two, and *pera*, a pouch; in allusion to the appearance of the two outer lateral segments of the perianth. Linn. 20, Or. 1, Nat. Or. *Orchidaceæ.* A tuberous-rooted genus, requiring the same treatment as *Disa.*

| | | | | |
|---|---|---|---|---|
| capènsis . . . | . Scarlet . | 7, G. Ter. | C. G. H. . | . 1816 |
| cucullàtâ . . | . Purple . | 6, G. Ter. | C. G. H. . | . 1822 |
| secûndâ . . . | . Purple . | 6, G. Ter. | C. G. H. . | . 1787 |

DISPÈRMUS, two-seeded.

DISPÒRUM, *Salisbury.* From *dis*, twice, and *poros*, a pore. Linn. 6, Or. 1, Nat. Or. *Melanthaceæ.* Pretty species, which may be successfully grown in two-thirds peat, and one-third loam; they will succeed in a warm border, if carefully protected from severe frosts: they may be increased by dividing the roots, or by seeds. *Synonyme:* 1. *Uvularia chinensis.*

| | | | | |
|---|---|---|---|---|
| fúlvûm, 1 | . . . | . Brown . | 10, G. Her. P. China | . 1801 |
| parviflòrûm | . . | . Yellow . | 7, G. Her. P. Nepal | . 1820 |

DISSÈCTX, lacinated, deeply cut into very fine segments.

DISSÈPIMENTS, the partitions by which a seed-vessel is divided internally.

DISSÒDÒN, *Greville.* From *dis*, twice, and *odous*, a tooth. Linn. 24, Or. 5, Nat. Or. *Musci.* A genus of little, dark, and pale green plants, inhabiting, during summer, mountains and alpine bogs. *Synonymes:* 1. *Splachnum Frælichianum, S. reticulatum.* 2. *Weissia splachnoides—Frælichiânûm* 1, *splachnoîdes* 2.

DISSOLÈNX, *Loureiro.* From *dis*, double, and *solen*, a tube; in allusion to the double tube of the corolla. Linn. 5, Or. 1, Nat. Or. *Apocynaceæ.* A pretty species, growing in a rich light soil; and cuttings, planted in sand, under a glass, in heat, will soon root. *Synonyme:* 1. *Cerbera chinensis.*

| | | | | |
|---|---|---|---|---|
| verticillàtâ | . . . | | G. Ev. S. China | . . 1812 |

DISTACHYÒN, two-spiked.

DISTÈNTUS, distended, inflated.

DISTICHOUS, two-rowed; producing leaves or flowers in two opposite rows.

DITTÒLX, *Fries.* From *dittos*, double, and *ioulous*, down; in reference to the downy nature of the pubescence. Linn. 24, Or. 9, Nat. Or. *Fungi.* A species of *Fungi*, which grows upon dry wood, from the autumn till spring. It is one of the species of dry rot, and very injurious to the timber on which the plants vegetate—*radicàtâ.*

DITRICHOTOMOUS, divided into twos or threes; a stem continually divided into double or treble ramifications.

DITTANY OF CRETE, see *Origanum Dictamnus.*

DIURETIC, having the power of promoting the flow of urine.

DIURIS, *R. Brown.* From *dis*, double, and *oura*, a tail; alluding to the lateral lobes of the labellum. Linn. 20, Or. 1, Nat. Or. *Orchidaceæ.* The species of this genus succeed well with the same treatment as *Disa.*

| | | | | |
|---|---|---|---|---|
| álbâ . . . . | . White . | 6, G. Ter. | N. Holl. . | . |
| aûreâ . . . | . Yellow . | 6, G. Ter. | N. S. W. . | . 1810 |
| elongàtâ . . | . Pink . | 5, G. Ter. | N. Holl. . | . 1822 |
| longifòliâ . . | . Pink . | 7, G. Ter. | N. Holl. . | . 1824 |
| maculàtâ . . | . Yel. spot. | 4, G. Ter. | N. S. W. . | . 1823 |
| pedunculàtâ . | . Yellow . | 5, G. Ter. | N. Holl. . | . 1826 |
| sulphùreâ . . | . Pa. yel. | 6, G. Ter. | N. Holl. . | . 1823 |

DIÙRNÛM, daily.

DIVARICATE, growing in a straggling manner.

DIVERGENT, } growing far asunder; applied to
DIVERGING, } branches and leaves.

DOCK, see *Rûmêx.*

DODARTIX, *Linn.* In honour of F. Dodart, M.D., a French botanist. Linn. 14, Or. 2, Nat. Or. *Scrophularineæ.* A species of little beauty, thriving in any light rich soil, and increased from seeds, or divisions.

| | | | | |
|---|---|---|---|---|
| orientàlis | . . . | . Purple . | 7, H. Her. P. Levant | . . 1752 |

DODDER, see *Cûscûtâ.*

DODECANDROUS, having twelve stamens.

DODECATHÈON, *Linn.* From *dodeka*, twelve, and *theos*, a divinity; twelve gods, or divinities of the Romans; a name absurdly applied to a plant, native of a world the Romans did not know, and resembling in no particular any plant of their writers. Linn. 5, Or. 1, Nat. Or. *Primulaceæ.* Very ornamental plants when in flower, and well worthy a place in every collection. The species grow best in a light loamy soil, and are easily increased by dividing the roots.

| | | | | | | |
|---|---|---|---|---|---|---|
| integrifōliūm | . Lgt. pur. | 4, | H. Her. | P. N. Amer. | . 1829 |
| Meadīa | . Lgt. pur. | 5, | H. Her. | P. Virginia | . 1744 |
| albiflōrūm | . White . | 5, | H. Her. | P. Gardens | . 1824 |
| elēgāns | . Rosy . | 5, | H. Her. | P. Gardens | . 1827 |
| gigāntēūm | . Lilac . | 5, | H. Her. | P. Gardens | . 1819 |
| lilacīnūm | . Lilac . | 5, | H. Her. | P. Gardens | . 1824 |

DODONÆI, *Linn.* In honour of Rembert Dodoens, known by the name of Dodonæus, a famous botanist and physician. *Linn.* 8, Or. 1, Nat. Or. *Sapindaceæ.* Plants scarcely worth cultivating, except in general collections. They thrive well in loam and peat, or any light soil; cuttings will root in sand, under a glass; those of the stove species must be placed in heat. *Synonymes:* 1. *D. heterophylla.* 2. *D. viscosa, angustifolia.* 8. *D. angustifolia.*

| | | | | | | |
|---|---|---|---|---|---|---|
| angustissimā | . Green . | 6, | G. Ev. S. | | . 1828 |
| asplenifōliā | . Green . | 6, | G. Ev. S. N. Holl. | | . 1820 |
| attenuātā | . Green . | 6, | G. Ev. S. N. Holl. | | . 1820 |
| Burmanniānā | . Green . | 6, | S. Ev. S. E. Ind. | | . 1800 |
| cuneātā | . Green . | 6, | G. Ev. S. N. Holl. | | . 1820 |
| dioīcā, 1 | . Green . | 6, | S. Ev. S. E. Ind. | | . 1819 |
| elæagnoīdes | . Green . | 6, | S. Ev. S. S. Domin. | | . 1800 |
| filifōrmis | . Green . | 6, | S. Ev. S. | | . 1820 |
| jamaicēnsis, 2 | . Green . | 6, | G. Ev. S. Jamaica | | . 1810 |
| laurifōliā | . Green . | 6, | S. Ev. S. N. Holl. | | . 1823 |
| microcārpā | . Green . | 6, | S. Ev. S. Bourbon | | . 1824 |
| pinnātā | . Green . | 6, | G. Ev. S. N. Holl. | | . 1824 |
| salicifōliā, 3 | . Green . | 6, | G. Ev. S. N. Holl. | | . 1820 |
| scābrā | . Green . | 6, | G. Ev. S. N. Holl. | | . 1820 |
| truncātā | . Green . | 6, | G. Ev. S. N. Holl. | | . 1820 |

*bialātā, oblongifōliā, pauliniæfōliā, triquētrā, viscōsā.*

DOG BRAMBLE, see *Ribes Cynosbāti.*

DOG POISON, see *Æthūsā Cynāpiūm.*

DOG'S-BANE, see *Apōcȳnūm.*

DOG'S-CABBAGE, see *Thelygōnūm Cynocrāmbē.*

DOG'S-TAIL GRASS, see *Cynosūrūs.*

DOG'S-TOOTH VIOLET, see *Erythrōniūm.*

DOGWOOD, see *Cōrnūs.*

DOLABRIFORM, axe-shaped.

DŌLICHŌS, *Linn.* From *dolichos,* long; in reference to the long twining stems. *Linn.* 17, Or. 4, Nat. Or. *Leguminosæ.* D. *Jacquinii* and D. *lignosus* are about all that are worth cultivating for ornament. Any rich light soil will suit them, and they may be increased by seeds, or cuttings; if by cuttings, they must be planted in sand, under a glass; the stove kinds in heat. *Synonyme:* 1. *Phaseolus vexillatus.*

| | | | | | | |
|---|---|---|---|---|---|---|
| angulōsus | . Yellow . | 7, | H. Tr. A. | N. Amer. | . 1820 |
| capēnsis | . Yellow . | 7, | G. Ev. Tw. | C. G. H. | . 1823 |
| Cātiāng | . Purple . | 7, | S. A. | E. Ind. | . 1793 |
| frutēscēns | . Pa. yel. . | 7, | S. Ev. S. | Nepal . | . 1820 |
| gangēticūs | . | 7, | S. Ev. Tw. | Jamaica | . 1816 |
| hirsūtūs | . Purple . | 7, | H. Tw. | China . | . 1802 |
| heterophȳllūs | . | 7, | H. Tw. A. | Canaries | . 1810 |
| Jacquinii | . White . | 7, | S. Ev. Tw. | S. Amer. | . 1800 |
| lignōsūs | . Purple . | 7, | G. Ev. Tw. | E. Ind. | . 1776 |
| lobātūs | . Yellow . | 6, | H. Tw. A. | C. G. H. | . 1800 |
| Lāblā | . Wht. blue . | 7, | H. A. | Egypt . | . 1818 |
| melanophthālmūs | . | 8, | H. A. | Italy . | . 1800 |
| monachālis | . Pa. red . | 7, | H. A. | Spain . | . 1816 |
| sinēnsis | . Pa. red . | 7, | H. Tw. A. | India . | . 1776 |
| sphærospērmūs | . | 6, | S. A. | Jamaica | . 1816 |
| vexillātūs, 1 | . Yellow . | 7, | G. Tw. A. | W. Ind. | . 1780 |

*biflōrūs, latīūs, pilōsūs, reticulātūs, sesquipedālīs, octafōliūs, tetraspērmūs, tranquebāricūs, unguiculātūs.*

DOLIOCĀRPŪS, *Rolander.* From *dolios,* deceitful, and *karpos,* a fruit; the fruit, though beautiful, is poisonous. *Linn.* 13, Or. 1, Nat. Or. *Dilleniaceæ.* An ornamental plant; for propagation and culture, see *Tetracera. Synonyme:* 1. *Tetracera Calinea, Calinea scandens.*

| | | | | | | |
|---|---|---|---|---|---|---|
| Calinēā, 1 | . Yellow . | 7, | S. Ev. Cl. | Guiana . | . 1822 |

DOMBEYĀ, *Cavanilles.* In honour of Joseph Dombey, a French botanist and traveller in Peru and Chili. *Linn.* 16, Or. 7, Nat. Or. *Sterculiaceæ.* Ornamental plants, growing freely in sandy loam and peat; cuttings of the young wood will root freely, if put in sand, under a glass, in a moist heat.

| | | | | | | |
|---|---|---|---|---|---|---|
| cannabīnā | . White . | 8, | S. Ev. T. | Mauritius | . |
| cordifōliā | . Red . | | S. Ev. S. E. Ind. | | . 1820 |
| ferruginēā | . White . | | S. Ev. T. | Mauritius | . 1815 |
| ovātā | . White . | | S. Ev. T. | Bourbon | . 1822 |
| punctātā | . White . | | S. Ev. T. | Bourbon | . 1820 |
| tiliæfōliā | . White . | | S. Ev. T. | Bourbon | . 1820 |

DŌNDĪA, *Sprengel.* In honour of Dondie Duprée, a

French botanist. *Linn.* 5, Or. 2, Nat. Or. *Umbelliferæ.* A very pretty little plant, requiring an equal mixture of loam and peat; it may be increased by seeds, or divisions. *Synonyme:* 1. *Astruntia Epipactis.*

| | | | | | | |
|---|---|---|---|---|---|---|
| Epipāctis, 1 | . Yellow . | 4, | H. Her. | P. Alps . | . 1823 |

DOŌDIA, *R. Brown.* In honour of Samuel Doody, a London apothecary, one of the earliest British cryptogamic botanists. *Linn.* 24, Or. 1, Nat. Or. *Polypodiaceæ.* Very handsome ferns, growing well in loam and peat, and easily increased, either by seeds or divisions. *Synonyme:* 1. *Woodwardia caudata.*

| | | | | | | |
|---|---|---|---|---|---|---|
| asperā | . Brown . | 6, | G. Her. | P. N. S. W. | . 1808 |
| caudātā, 1 | . Brown . | 6, | G. Her. | P. N. Holl. | . 1820 |
| mediā | . Brown . | 6, | G. Her. | P. N. Holl. | . 1823 |

DORONĪCŪM, *Linn.* Altered from *Doronigi,* its Arabic name. *Linn.* 19, Or. 2, Nat. Or. *Compositæ.* An ornamental genus, and from the plants flowering early in spring, they are well deserving of cultivation; they grow in any garden soil, and may be increased with facility by dividing at the root. *Synonyme:* 1. *D. orientale.*

| | | | | | | |
|---|---|---|---|---|---|---|
| altāicūm | . White . | 7, | H. Her. | P. Siberia | . 1783 |
| austrīācūm | . Yellow . | 7, | H. Her. | P. Austria | . 1816 |
| caucāsicūm, 1 | . Yellow . | 7, | H. Her. | P. Caucasus | . 1815 |
| colūmnā | . Yellow . | 5, | H. Her. | P. Italy . | . 1824 |
| Pardalīanchēs | . Yellow . | 5, | H. Her. | P. Britain | . |
| plantaginēūm | . Yellow . | 5, | H. Her. | P. S. Eur. | . 1570 |
| scorpioīdēs | . Yellow . | 5, | H. Her. | P. Germany | . |

DORSAL, growing on the back.

DORSTĒNIA, *Linn.* In memory of Theodore Dorsten, a German botanist. *Linn.* 4, Or. 1, Nat. Or. *Urticaceæ.* Very curious plants, growing freely in any light rich soil, and may be multiplied with facility by parting the roots, or by seeds.

| | | | | | | |
|---|---|---|---|---|---|---|
| arifōliā | . Green . | 6, | S. Her. | P. Brasil | . 1822 |
| brasiliēnsis | . Green . | 6, | S. Her. | P. Brasil | . 1792 |
| ceratosānthēs | . Green . | 6, | S. Her. | P. S. Amer. | . 1826 |
| cordifōliā | . Green . | 6, | S. Her. | P. W. Ind. | . 1822 |
| contrajērvā | . Green . | 6, | S. Her. | P. S. Amer. | . 1748 |
| Drakēnā | . Green . | 6, | S. Her. | P. Vera Cruz | . 1818 |
| Houstōni | . Green . | 6, | S. Her. | P. S. Amer. | . 1747 |
| tubicīnā | . Green . | 6, | S. Her. | P. Trinidad | . 1817 |

DORTMĀNNĀ, *Don.* After one Dortmann, said to be a Dutch apothecary. *Linn.* 5, Or. 1, Nat. Or. *Lobeliaceæ.* The species of this genus are singular and beautiful plants, but require a good deal of care in cultivation. D. *lacustris* succeeds best planted in a pot of gravel, and placed in a pond or cistern, so that the plants may be about six inches under the water. The *other* species may be grown in a pot half filled with peat earth, and the rest with sphagnum, in which the plants must be set, and the pot placed in shallow water, so as not to immerse the plants. They may be increased by division. *Synonymes:* 1. *Lobelia Dortmanna.* 2. *L. paludosa.*

| | | | | | | |
|---|---|---|---|---|---|---|
| lacūstris, 1 | . Pa. blue . | 7, | H. Her. | P. Britain | . |
| paludōsā, 2 | . Pa. blue . | 7, | H. Her. | P. N. Amer. | . |

DORYĀNTHĒS. Named by Correa de Serra, from *dory,* a spear, and *anthe,* flower; because of the long, straight flower-stem. *Linn.* 6, Or. 1, Nat. Or. *Amaryllidaceæ.* Rather an ornamental plant, requiring a warm part of the greenhouse, or a cool part of the stove; the latter is preferable. It may be increased from suckers, which are seldom to be obtained, except by cutting a large plant down, or taking out the heart of the plant; in either case, it will throw out suckers.

| | | | | | | |
|---|---|---|---|---|---|---|
| excēlsā | . Cream . | 7, | G. Her. | P. N. S. W. | . 1800 |

DORYCNIŪM, *Tournefort.* From *dory,* a spear; the ancient plant was used to poison spears. *Linn.* 17, Or. 4, Nat. Or. *Leguminosæ.* Very handsome plants, of simple culture, succeeding best in a dry soil. They may be increased by seeds, which they ripen in abundance. *Synonymes:* 1. *Lotus hirsulus.* 2. *D. ibericum.* 3. *L. parviflorus.* 4. *L. rectus.* 5. *L. subbiflorus.* 6. *D. monspeliense, Lotus Dorycnium.* 7. *D. hirsutum, incanum, Lotus tomentosus, sericeus, affinis.*

| | | | | | | |
|---|---|---|---|---|---|---|
| herbāceūm | . White . | 7, | H. Her. | P. S. Eur. | . 1802 |
| hirsūtūm, 1 | . Red wht. . | 7, | H. Ev. S. | S. Eur. | . 1683 |
| latifōliūm, 2 | . White . | 7, | H. Her. | P. Iberia | . 1818 |
| parviflōrūm, 3 | . Yel. grn. . | 7, | H. Tr. A. | S. Eur. | . 1810 |
| rēctūm, 4 | . Red . | 7, | H. Ev. S. | S. Eur. | . 1640 |
| subbiflōrūm, 5 | . | 7, | H. A. | Spain . | . 1820 |
| suffruticōsūm, 6 | . White . | 7, | G. Ev. S. | S. Eur. | . 1640 |
| tomentōsūm, 7 | . Red wht. . | 7, | H. Ev. S. | S. Eur. | . 1817 |

DOTHIDĔX, *Fries.* Derived from *dothien*, a tubercle, and *eidos*, similar. *Linn.* 24, Or. 9, Nat. Or. *Fungi.* Mostly dark species, growing upon stems of grass, and leaves of trees—*ălnĕā, betulīnā, Gerănĭī, Himăntĭā, Plĕrĭdĭs, ribĕsĭā, Robertiănā, Ulmi.*

DOTS—may be pellucid, resinous, or hairy.

DOUGLASĬA. Named by Dr. Lindley, some years ago, in compliment to Mr. Douglas, whose zeal in collecting seeds and plants, and whose untimely end, have richly earned for him a niche in the long gallery of departed science. *Linn.* 5, Or. 1, Nat. Or. *Primulaceæ.* This is a very beautiful, but scarce, little plant, growing pretty freely in peat and sand, and ripening its seed in small quantity. Mr. Douglas transmitted the seed, from which this interesting plant was raised, from the Rocky Mountains, where he first found it among the snow, and afterwards from California.

| nivalis | . . . . | Purple | . 6, H. Her. P. Rky. Mts. . 1827 |

DOWN'S-FOOT, see *Gerănĭŭm mŏllĕ.*

DOWN, soft, short hairs.

DOWNY-VILLOUS, covered with long soft hairs.

DOWNY-PUBESCENT, soft, short down, closely pressed to the surface.

DRĂBĂ, *Decandolle.* From *drabe*, acrid, biting; taste of the leaves. *Linn.* 15, Nat. Or. *Cruciferæ.* Some of the species of this genus are very pretty, being well adapted for ornamenting rock-work, or growing in pots, among other alpine plants. A mixture of loam and peat suits them best, and they increase with facility, either by dividing at the root, or by seeds. *Synonymes:* 1. *D. aizoides.* 2. *D. incana.* 3. *D. androsacea.* 4. *D. lutea, longipes.* 5. *D. contorta.* 6. *D. androsacea.* 7. *D. hirta.* 8. *D. hirta.* 9. *D. hirta.*

| aizoīdēs | . . . | Yellow | . 3, H. Her. P. Wales . . |
| Aisoŏn . . . | . | Yellow | . 5, H. Her. P. Carinthia . 1823 |
| alpīnā . . . | . | Yellow | . 4, H. Her. P. Lapland . 1820 |
| millefŏlĭa-pilōsis | Yellow | . 8, H. Her. P. Greenland . 1820 |
| aūreā . . . | . | Yellow | . 6, H. . B. Denmark . 1820 |
| austriăcā . . | . | White | . 6, H. Her. P. Austria . 1824 |
| brachystēmŏn, 1 | . | Yellow | . 6, H. Her. P. Switzerl. . 1819 |
| brunisfŏlĭā . . | . | Yellow | . 6, H. Her. P. Caucasus . 1820 |
| bryoīdēs . . | . | Yellow | . 5, H. Her. P. Tauria . 1820 |
| ciliārĭs . . | . | Yellow | . 3, H. Her. P. Switzerl. . 1731 |
| cinĕreā . . | . | White | . 7, H. . B. Siberia . 1818 |
| confūsā, 2 . . | . | White | . 7, H. . B. N. Eur. . |
| corymbōsā . . | . | White | . 5, H. Her. P. Baff. B. . 1823 |
| crassifŏlĭā . . | . | Yellow | . 6, H. Her. P. N. Amer. . 1826 |
| cuspidātā . . | . | Yellow | . 8, H. Her. P. Iberia . 1820 |
| daūrĭcā . . | . | White | . 7, H. . B. Dauria . 1824 |
| ericæfŏlĭā . . | . | Yellow | . 6, H. Her. P. Caucasus . 1821 |
| fladniēnsĭs, 3 . | . | White | . 6, H. Her. P. Switzerl. . 1819 |
| glaciālĭs . . | . | Yellow | . 6, H. Her. P. Siberia . 1826 |
| Ōmalĭā . . | . | Yellow | . 6, H. Her. P. Siberia . 1823 |
| grācĭlĭs, 4 . . | . | Yellow | . 6, H. . A. N. Amer. . 1827 |
| helvĕtĭcā . . | . | Yellow | . 6, H. Her. P. Switzerl. . 1819 |
| hirta . . . | . | White | . 6, H. Her. P. N. Eur. . 1823 |
| incānā, 5 . . | . | White | . 5, H. . B. Britain . |
| incompta . . | . | Yellow | . 4, H. Her. P. Caucasus . 1821 |
| lapponĭcā, 6 . | . | White | . 4, H. Her. P. Lapland . 1810 |
| lasiocārpā . . | . | White | . 5, H. Her. P. . . 1820 |
| latēā . . . | . | Yellow | . 6, H. . A. S. Eur. . 1824 |
| murālĭs . . | . | White | . 6, H. . A. England . |
| muricĕllā, 7 . | . | White | . 6, H. Her. P. Lapland . 1810 |
| nemorālĭs . . | . | Yellow | . 6, H. . A. Europe . 1759 |
| nivālĭs . . | . | White | . 5, H. Her. P. Switzerl. . 1824 |
| oblongātā . . | . | White | . 5, H. Her. P. Baff. B. . 1823 |
| pilōsā . . | . | White | . 6, H. Her. P. Siberia . 1825 |
| rĕpēns . . | . | Yellow | . 6, H. Her. P. Siberia . 1818 |
| rupestrĭs, 8 . | . | Yellow | . 6, H. Her. P. Scotland . |
| siliquōsā . . | . | White | . 6, Hf Her. P. Caucasus . 1822 |
| stellātā, 9 . | . | White | . 6, H. Her. P. Pyrenees . 1820 |
| tomentōsā . . | . | White | . 6, H. Her. P. Switzerl. . 1819 |

*nummulārĭā.*

DRACÆNĂ, *Linn.* From *drakaina*, a female dragon; the inspissated juice becomes a powder, like the dragon's-blood. *Linn.* 6, Or. 1, Nat. Or. *Liliaceæ.* Very ornamental trees, well worthy of being cultivated in every collection of stove plants. They thrive well in a light, loamy soil; large cuttings root freely by being stuck in the tan, provided there be a strong heat. In Java, the root of *D. terminalis* is considered a valuable medicine in dysenteric affections. The substance called Gum Dragon, so well known in medicine, is the juice of *D. Draco.* *Synonyme:* 1. *D. marginata.*

| arbōreā . . | . | White | . 5, S. Ev. T. S. Leone . 1800 |
| brasiliēnsĭs . | . | White | . S. Ev. S. Brasil . 1825 |
| rērnĭā . . | . | White | . 5, S. Ev. T. Mauritius . |
| Drăcō . . | . | White | . S. Ev. T. E. Ind. . . 1640 |

[ 111 ]

ensifolĭā

| | | | S. Ev. S. | . 1800 |
| ferrēā . . | . | White | . 4, S. Ev. T. China | . 1771 |
| frăgrāns . . | . | White | . 4, S. Ev. T. Africa | . 1768 |
| interruptā . . | . | White | . 6, S. Ev. S. S. Leone | . 1793 |
| leonēnsĭs . . | . | White | . 6, S. Ev. S. S. Leone | . 1824 |
| mauritiănā . . | . | White | . 5, S. Ev. S. Mauritius | . 1825 |
| nodōsā . . | . | White | . S. Ev. S. | . 1820 |
| nūtāns . . | . | Brown | . 7, G. Ev. S. N. Holl. | . 1820 |
| ovātā . . | . | White | . 8, S. Ev. S. S. Leone | . |
| purpūreā . . | . | White | . 6, S. Ev. T. E. Ind. | . 1820 |
| reflexā . . | . | White | . 6, S. Ev. S. Madagas. | . 1819 |
| striătā . . | . | White | . 4, S. Ev. S. C. G. H. | . 1820 |
| surculōsā . . | . | White | . 7, S. Ev. S. S. Leone | . 1821 |
| terminālĭs . . | . | White | . 6, S. Ev. T. E. Ind. | . 1820 |
| tessellātā, 1 . | . | | . S. Ev. T. Madagas. | . 1816 |
| umbraculĭferā . | . | White | . S. Ev. T. Mauritius | . 1783 |
| undulātā . . | . | White | . G. Ev. S. C. G. H. | . 1816 |

DRACOCĔPHĂLŬM, *Linn.* From *drakon*, a dragon, and *kephale*, head; the appearance of the heads of the flowers. *Linn.* 15, Or. 1, Nat. Or. *Labiatæ.* Most of the species are ornamental, and as such, they deserve a place in every garden. They succeed well in common garden soil. Some of the tender perennial kinds require the protection of a frame in winter, and, on that account, they ought to be grown in pots; they increase readily by dividing at the roots. The annual kinds merely require sowing in a rich, light soil, in the open ground, where they will flower beautifully. *Synonyme:* 1. *D. grandiflorum.*

| altaīensĕ, 1 . | . | Purple | . 7, H. De. S. Georgia . 1759 |
| argunēnsĕ . | . | Blue | . 7, H. Her. P. Siberia . 1822 |
| austriăcŭm . | . | Blue | . 6, H. Her. P. Austria . 1597 |
| botryoīdēs . | . | Purple | . 7, H. Her. P. Siberia . 1822 |
| canariēnsĕ . | . | Pa. pur. | . 8, G. Ev. S. Canaries . 1697 |
| canēscēns . | . | Blue | . 7, H. . A. Levant . 1711 |
| chamædryoīdēs | . | Blue | . 7, F. Ev. Tr. . 1823 |
| ibĕrĭcŭm . | . | Blue | . 7, H. Her. P. Iberia . 1820 |
| moldăvĭcŭm . | . | Blue | . 7, H. . A. Moldavia . 1596 |
| albiflōrŭm . | . | White | . 7, H. . A. Moldavia . 1596 |
| nūtāns . . | . | Blue | . 7, H. Her. P. Siberia . 1731 |
| origanoīdēs . | . | | . 7, F. Ev. Tr. Siberia . 1829 |
| palmātŭm . | . | Purple | . 7, H. Her. P. Siberia . 1815 |
| parviflōrŭm . | . | Blue | . 7, H. Her. P. N. Amer. . 1825 |
| peltātŭm . | . | Purple | . 7, H. Her. P. Levant . 1711 |
| peregrīnŭm . | . | Purple | . 7, H. . A. Siberia . 1759 |
| Ruyschiānŭm . | . | Blue | . 7, H. Her. P. N. Eur. . 1699 |
| sibĭrĭcŭm . | . | Blue | . 8, H. Her. P. Siberia . 1760 |
| thymiflōrŭm . | . | Purple | . 7, H. . A. Siberia . 1752 |

DRACŎNĬA, spotted like a serpent.

DRACONTĬŬM, *Linn.* From *drakon*, a dragon; the stems are spotted like the skin of a snake. *Linn.* 7, Or. 1, Nat. Or. *Araceæ.* Curious species, delighting in a rich, light loam, and increased by dividing the roots. In India, the prepared root of *D. polyphyllum* is supposed to possess antispasmodic virtues, and is a valuable remedy in asthma.

| polyphyllŭm . | . | Apetal | . 5, S. Ev. Cr. India . 1759 |
| spinōsŭm . | . | Apetal | . 4, S. Ev. Cr. Ceylon . 1759 |

DRACOPHŸLLŬM, *Labillardière.* From *drakon*, a dragon, and *phyllon*, a leaf; the leaves resemble those of *Dracæna Draco.* *Linn.* 3, Or. 1, Nat. Or. *Epacridaceæ.* Ornamental shrubs; for culture and propagation, see *Andersonia.*

| capitātŭm . | . | | . G. Ev. S. N. Holl. . 1820 |
| longifolĭŭm . | . | White | . 6, G. Ev. S. N. Holl. . 1824 |
| secŭndŭm . | . | White | . 6, G. Ev. S. N. Holl. . 1823 |

DRAGON, see *Dracontĭŭm.*

DRAGON'S-HEAD, see *Dracocĕphălŭm.*

DRAGON-TREE, see *Dracæna Dracŏ.*

DRAPARNALDĬA, *Bory de St. Vincent.* In honour of J. P. R. Draparnald, a French botanist. *Linn.* 24, Or. 7, Nat. Or. *Algæ.* Small, bright green plants, found at all seasons in pools and rivulets—*glomerata, plumosa, tenuis.*

DRASTIC, applied to purgative medicines which act violently.

DREPANOCĂRPŬS, *Meyer.* From *drepanon*, a sickle, and *carpos*, a fruit; alluding to the shape of the pods. *Linn.* 17, Or. 6, Nat. Or. *Leguminosæ.* Rather an ornamental shrub, from six to ten feet high. For culture and propagation, see *Pterocarpus.* *Synonyme:* 1. *Pterocarpus lunatus.*

| lunātĭs . . | . | White | . S. Ev. S. S. Amer. . 1792 |

DREPANOPHŸLLŬM, *Kunth.* From *drepanon*, a sickle, and *phyllon*, a leaf; alluding to the falcate leaves. *Linn.* 5, Or. 2, Nat. Or. *Umbelliferæ.* A worthless, herbaceous perennial, growing in any soil; increased by divisions. *Synonyme:* 1. *Sium Falcaria* —*agrestĕ* 1.

DRIMIA, *Jacquin.* From *drimys*, acrid; the juice of the roots is so acrid as to cause inflammation when applied to the skin. *Linn.* 6, Or. 1, Nat. Or. *Liliaceæ.* An ornamental genus, when the plants are in flower; they require a mixture of sandy loam and leaf mould, or peat soil. When not in a growing state, they require but little water, and when potted just before they begin to grow, they will flower freely. *Synonyme:* 1. *D. lanceæfolia, Hyacinthus revolutus, Lachenalia reflexa.*

| | | | | |
|---|---|---|---|---|
| acuminata . . . | Brown . | 8, G. Bl. P. C. G. H. | . 1829 |
| altissima . . . | Wht. grn. | 8, G. Bl. P. C. G. H. | . 1791 |
| ciliaris . . . | Pur. wht . | 8, G. Bl. P. C. C. H. | . 1800 |
| elata . . . | Red grn. | 10, G. Bl. P. C. G. H. | . 1799 |
| lanceæfolia . . . | Purple . | 9, G. Bl. P. C. G. H. | . 1800 |
| lanceolata . . . | Yel. grn. | 9, G. Bl. P. C. G. H. | . 1774 |
| longipedunculata . | Grn. pur. | 9, G. Bl. P. C. G. H. | . 1800 |
| media . . . | White . | 8, G. Bl. P. C. G. H. | . 1820 |
| purpurascens . . | Purple . | 8, G. Bl. P. C. G. H. | . 1818 |
| pusilla . . . | Green . | 5, G. Bl. P. C. G. H. | . 1793 |
| revoluta, 1 . . | Green . | 5, G. Bl. P. C. G. H. | . 1774 |
| undulata . . . | Grn. str. | 5, G. Bl. P. C. G. H. | . 1819 |
| villosa . . . | Green . | 8, G. Bl. P. C. G. H. | . 1826 |

DRIMYS, *Forster.* From *drimys*, acrid; the juice of the root causes inflammation when applied to the skin. *Linn.* 13, Or. 4, Nat. Or. *Winteraceæ.* Valuable trees, from twelve to forty feet high, requiring a mixture of loam, peat, and sand; ripened cuttings would probably root, if planted in sand, under a glass. The winter bark, which resembles that of cinnamon, is the produce of *D. Winteri. Synonyme:* 1. *Wintera aromatica.*

| | | | | |
|---|---|---|---|---|
| chilensis . . . | White . | G. Ev. T. Chile | . 1829 |
| Winteri, 1 . . | White . | G. Ev. T. Magellan | . 1827 |

DRINKER'S-NUT, see *Strychnos potatorum.*

DROPWORT, see *Spiræa filipendula.*

DROSERA. From *droseros*, dewy; the plants are beset with glandular hairs, which makes them appear as if covered with dew. *Linn.* 5, Or. 5, Nat. Or. *Droseraceæ.* This is a most singular and beautiful genus of plants, whose leaves are ornamented with red, glandular hairs, discharging from their ends a drop of viscid acrid juice. These hairs are so irritable as to contract when touched, imprisoning insects, after the manner of *Dionæa Muscipula.* In their native state, they are found growing on mossy turfy bogs. The best way to grow them, is to plant them in small pots, about three parts full of peat earth, and some sphagnum planted on it; the plants should then be planted in the moss, and the pots placed in pans of water, and even then, the hardy species grow best in the greenhouse. They are all increased by seeds, which should be allowed to sow themselves. *Synonyme:* 1. *D. intermedia.*

| | | | | |
|---|---|---|---|---|
| acaulis . . . | White . | 7, G. Aq. P. C. G. H. | . 1823 |
| americana . . . | White . | 7, H. Aq. P. N. Amer. | . 1840 |
| anglica . . . | Wht. red. | 7, H. Aq. P. England | . . |
| binata . . . | White . | 7, G. Aq. P. N. Holl. | . 1821 |
| filiformis . . . | Purple . | 7, H. Aq. P. N. Jersey | . 1811 |
| linearis . . . | Purple . | 7, H. Aq. P. N. Amer. | . 1818 |
| longifolia, 1 . . | Wht. red | 7, H. Aq. P. Britain | . . |
| pauciflora . . . | White . | 7, G. Aq. P. C. G. H. | . 1823 |
| rotundifolia . . | White . | 7, H. Aq. P. Britain | . . |

DRUMMONDIA, *Decandolle.* Named after Mr. Thomas Drummond, a well-known naturalist, and zealous collector of plants, chiefly in the United States; he died at Havannah, in March, 1835. *Linn.* 5, Or. 2, Nat. Or. *Saxifrageæ.* This is a very pretty little plant, well adapted for the front of flower-borders, or to grow on rockwork. It grows most luxuriantly in peat, though it succeeds in any light soil; divisions. *Synonyme:* 1. *Mitella pentandra.*

| | | | |
|---|---|---|---|
| mitelloides . . . | Yellowish | 6, H. Her. P. Rky. Mts. | . 1827 |

DRUNKEN DARNEL, see *Lolium temulentum.*

DRUPE, a kind of fruit, consisting of a fleshy, succulent rind, and containing a hard stone in the middle.

DRUSA, *Decandolle.* In honour of M. Le Dru, a French botanist and traveller. *Linn.* 5, Or. 2, Nat. Or. *Umbelliferæ.* A hardy annual, the seeds of which merely require sowing in a warm situation—*oppositifolia.*

DRYANDRA, *R. Brown.* In honour of Jonas Dryander, a distinguished Swedish botanist. *Linn.* 4, Or. 1, Nat. Or. *Proteaceæ.* A splendid genus of plants, nearly related to *Banksia.* All the species thrive well in an equal mixture of turfy loam, peat, and sand. The pots require to be well drained, and

the potsherds broken very small, because the roots are fond of running among them. Cuttings taken off at a joint, in August or September, and planted in sand, without shortening the leaves, will readily root, if placed on a gentle hotbed, (but not plunged,) under a glass; but they must be covered, so as the frost cannot injure them. As soon as rooted, they must be potted off, as the sand would injure the roots if they were too long in it; after being potted off, they should be placed in a close frame, and hardened to the air by degrees. The cuttings will do equally well if put in early in spring, just as they are beginning to push out young wood.

| | | | | |
|---|---|---|---|---|
| arctotoides . . . | Yellow . | G. Ev. S. N. Holl. | . 1830 |
| armata . . . | Yellow . | G. Ev. S. N. Holl. | . 1803 |
| Baxteri . . . | Yellow . | G. Ev. S. N. Holl. | . 1824 |
| blechnifolia . . | Yellow . | G. Ev. S. N. Holl. | . 1824 |
| calophylla . . | | G. Ev. S. N. Holl. | . 1830 |
| cuneata . . . | Yellow . | 6, G. Ev. S. N. Holl. | . 1803 |
| brevifolia . . | Yellow . | 6, G. Ev. S. N. Holl. | . 1803 |
| longifolia . . | Yellow . | 6, G. Ev. S. N. Holl. | . 1803 |
| floribunda . . . | Yellow . | G. Ev. S. N. Holl. | . 1803 |
| foliolata . . . | | G. Ev. S. N. Holl. | . 1830 |
| formosa . . . | Yellow . | G. Ev. S. N. Holl. | . 1803 |
| longifolia . . . | Yellow . | G. Ev. S. N. Holl. | . 1803 |
| mucronulata . . | Yellow . | G. Ev. S. N. Holl. | . 1824 |
| nervosa . . . | Yellow . | G. Ev. S. N. Holl. | . 1824 |
| nivea . . . | Yellow . | G. Ev. S. N. Holl. | . 1805 |
| obtusa . . . | Yellow . | G. Ev. S. N. Holl. | . 1803 |
| plumosa . . . | Yellow . | G. Ev. S. N. Holl. | . 1803 |
| pteridifolia . . | Yellow . | G. Ev. S. N. Holl. | . 1824 |
| tenuifolia . . . | Yellow . | 4, G. Ev. S. N. Holl. | . 1803 |

DRYAS, *Linn.* From *dryades*, or nymphs of the oaks; because the leaves bear some resemblance to those of the oak. *Linn.* 12, Or. 3, Nat. Or. *Rosaceæ.* A delicate genus of plants, which succeed best in a border of peat soil; but they require to be protected in winter. They may be increased either from cuttings, seeds, or divisions. *Synonymes:* 1. *D. octopetala.* 2. *D. integrifolia.*

| | | | | |
|---|---|---|---|---|
| Drummondi, 1 . | White . | 7, F. Ev. T. N. Amer. | . 1828 |
| integrifolia . . | White . | 7, F. Ev. T. Greenland | . 1824 |
| octopetala . . | White . | 7, H. Ev. T. Britain . | . |
| americana . . | White . | 7, H. Ev. T. N. Amer. | . 1830 |
| tenella, 2 . . | White . | 7, F. Ev. T. Canada . | . 1820 |

DRYMARIA, *Willdenow.* From *drymys*, a forest; habitation of the species. *Linn.* 5, Or. 3, Nat. Or. *Illecebraceæ.* Plants of no value; they need only to be sown on a hotbed early in spring. In the month of May, they may be planted out into a warm border. *Synonyme*; 1. *Holosteum cordatum.*

| | | | | |
|---|---|---|---|---|
| cordata, 1 . . | White . | 7, S. Ev. Cr. Jamaica | . 1800 |
| gracilis . . . | White . | 7, S. Ev. Cr. Brazil | . 1829 |

DRYMONIA, *Martius.* From *drumonia*, woodland; the plant inhabits forests. *Linn.* 14, Or. 2, Nat. Or. *Gesneraceæ.* An ornamental plant. For culture and propagation, see *Besleria. Synonyme:* 1. *Besleria serrulata.*

| | | | |
|---|---|---|---|
| bicolor . . . | Purp. yel. | S. Ev. Cl. W. Ind. | . 1806 |

DRYPETES. Named by Vahl, from *drypto*, to lacerate; plant spiny. *Linn.* 22, Or. 4, Nat. Or. *Euphorbiaceæ.* An ornamental shrub, about six feet high, growing in a mixture of loam and peat; cuttings will root in sand, under a glass, in heat. *Synonyme:* 1. *Schæfferia lateriflora.*

| | | | |
|---|---|---|---|
| crocea, 1 . . . | | 6, S. Ev. S. W. Ind. | . 1820 |

DRYPIS, *Linn.* From *dripto*, to tear; the leaves are armed with stiff spines. *Linn.* 5, Or. 3, Nat. Or. *Silenaceæ.* This beautiful little plant is well adapted for ornamenting rock-work, in which situation it flowers in the greatest profusion. It may be increased by cuttings, planted in sand, under a glass, or by seeds, sown in an equal mixture of loam, peat, and sand, and when the plants get of sufficient size, they ought to be planted on the top of rock-work, where they must not be suffered to get dry till they are well established.

| | | | |
|---|---|---|---|
| spinosa . . . | Pa. blue . | 6, H. Ev. S. Italy . | . 1775 |

DUCK'S-FOOT, see *Podophyllum.*

DUCKWEED, see *Lemna.*

DULCIS, sweet, nectariferous.

DULICHIUM, *Persoon.* The name of the island where the plant was first found. *Linn.* 3, Or. 1, Nat. Or. *Cyperaceæ.* A curious perennial species, growing in peaty soil, and increased by divisions.

| | | | |
|---|---|---|---|
| spathaceum . . | Apetal. . | 7, Gras. N. Amer. | . 1818 |

DUMĂSĬĂ, *Decandolle*. In honour of M. Dumas, one of the editors of Annales des Sciences Naturelles. *Linn.* 17, Or. 4, Nat. Or. *Leguminosæ*. Ornamental plants; for culture and propagation, see *Clitoria*.

| | | | |
|---|---|---|---|
| pubéscĕns . . . | Yellow | . 10, G. Ev. Tw. Nepal . | 1824 |
| villósā . . . . | Pa. yel. | . 10, G. Ev. Tw. Nepal . | 1824 |

DUMB CANE, see *Calădĭŭm seguīnŭm*.

DUMĔRĬLĬĂ, *Leysser*. In honour of M. A. M. Constant Dumeril, a French naturalist. *Linn.* 19, Or. 1, Nat. Or. *Compositæ*. Rather a pretty shrub, growing about three feet high, in any common garden soil, and increased by cuttings.

| | | | |
|---|---|---|---|
| paniculátā . . | Purple | . 8, S. Ev. S. Columbia . | 1825 |

DŬMOSE, bushy, shrubby.

DŬRANTĂ, *Linn.* After Castor Durantes, a physician and botanist, who died in 1590. *Linn.* 14, Or. 2, Nat. Or. *Verbenaceæ*. A very pretty and free-flowering genus, successfully grown in a mixture of loam and peat. Cuttings root freely, planted in sand, under a glass, in heat. *Synonymes:* 1. *D. microphylla.* 2. *D. dentata.*

| | | | |
|---|---|---|---|
| argĕntĕā . . . | Blue | . 8. Ev. S. E. Ind. . | 1824 |
| Elliatā, 1 . . . | Blue | . 8, S. Ev. S. W. Ind. . | 1739 |
| inérmis . . . | Blue | . 8, S. Ev. S. S. Amer. . | 1739 |
| macrocărpā, 2 . | Blue | . 8. Ev. S. W. Ind. . | 1818 |
| Mutisĭĭ . . . | Blue | . 8. Ev. S. W. Ind. . | 1820 |
| Plumĭĕrĭ . . . | Blue | . 10, S. Ev. S. S. Amer. . | 1733 |
| xalapĕnsĭs . . | Blue | . 8. Ev. S. Mexico . | 1822 |

DŬRĬŎ, *Linn.* Duryon, in the Malay language, is the name of the fruit. *Linn.* 18, Or. 1, Nat. Or. *Sterculiaceæ*. This tree thrives well in a rich loamy soil; and cuttings, not too ripe, taken off at a joint, with their leaves entire, will root in sand, under a glass, in a moist heat. The fruit of this tree is about the size of a man's head, and is said to be the most delicious of all the fruits of India. The axil-like substance, which contains the kernel, is the eatable part of it, and most resembles cream; yet it is accompanied by such an intolerable stench, that, according to Rumphius and Valentyn, it is, by law, forbidden to throw them out, near any public path, in Amboyna. The smell is said to be similar to that of some putrid animal substances; yet, all agree, that if the first repugnance is once overcome, no fruit is more agreeable than the *durion*. The fruit is also used as a bait to entrap the civet-cat; hence the specific name.

| | | | |
|---|---|---|---|
| zibethinŭs . . . | White | . 8. Ev. T. E. Ind. . | 1825 |

DŬRĬŎscŭLĂ, rather hard, or rigid.

DURMAST, see *Quĕrcŭs pubĕscĕns*.

DŎRŎs, hard, stubborn, rough.

DUTCH RUSH, see *Equisĕtŭm hyemālĕ*.

DŬVĂLĬĂ, *Haworth*. In honour of M. Duval, a celebrated French botanist. *Linn.* 5, Or. 2, Nat. Or. *Asclepiadaceæ*. A curious genus of succulent plants, nearly related to *Stapelia*, to which they may be referred for culture, &c. *Synonymes:* 1. *Stapelia hirtella.* 2. *D. radiata.* 3. *Stapelia reclinata.* 4. *S. replicata.*

| | | | |
|---|---|---|---|
| cæspitósā . . . | Purple | . 5, S. Ev. S. C. G. H. . | 1790 |
| compáctā . . | Brown | . 8, S. Ev. S. C. G. H. . | 1800 |
| élĕgăns . . . | Purple | . 8, S. Ev. S. C. G. H. . | 1795 |
| glomerátā . . | Brown | . 8, S. Ev. S. C. G. H. . | 1804 |
| hirtélla, 1 . . | Purple | . 6, S. Ev. S. C. G. H. . | |
| Jacquiniánā, 2 | Purple | . 8, S. Ev. S. C. G. H. . | 1802 |
| lævigátā . . | Brown | . 8, S. Ev. S. C. G. H. . | 1800 |
| maclŏdĕs . . | Brown | . 8, S. Ev. S. C. G. H. . | |
| radiátā . . . | Purple | . 8, S. Ev. S. C. G. H. . | 1795 |
| reclinátā, 3 . | Purple | . 8, S. Ev. S. C. G. H. . | 1795 |
| replicátā, 4 . | Purple | . 8, S. Ev. S. C. G. H. . | 1812 |
| tuberculátā . | Brown | . 8, S. Ev. S. C. G. H. . | 1808 |

DŬVĂŎĂ, *Kunth.* In honour of M. Duvau, a French botanist. *Linn.* 21, Or. 7, Nat. Or. *Anacardiaceæ*. Rather an ornamental genus; for culture and propagation, see greenhouse species of *Rhus*.

| | | | |
|---|---|---|---|
| dentátā . . . | White | . 6, G. Ev. S. Owhyhee . | 1795 |
| depéndĕns . . | White | . G. Ev. S. Chile . | 1790 |
| ovátā . . . | Grnsh. | . G. Ev. S. Chile . | 1824 |
| latifóliā . . . | Yellsh. | . G. Ev. S. Chile . | 1830 |

DWARF FAN-PALM, see *Chamærops hŭmĭlĭs*.

DWARF MOLY, see *Allĭŭm Chamæmŏly*.

DŶCKĬĂ, *Schultes, Jun.* In honour of the Prince Salm-Dyck, one of the most liberal and intelligent patrons of science of the present day. *Linn.* 6, Or. 3, Nat. Or. *Bromeliaceæ*. A very handsome plant, agreeing in many particulars with the Aloe, to which genus it may be referred for culture and propagation.

| | | | |
|---|---|---|---|
| rariflórā . . . | Orange | . 6, G. Her. P. Brazil . | 1832 |

DYER'S GREEN WEED, see *Genĭstă tinctōrĭā*.

DYER'S LITTLE YELLOW WEED, see *Rĕsĕdă lutĕŏlă*.

DYSŎPHŸLLĂ, *Blume.* From *dysodes*, fetid, and *phyllon*, a leaf; in reference to the smell of the leaves. *Linn.* 14, Or. 1, Nat. Or. *Labiatæ*. Plants nearly related to *Mentha*, for which, see culture and propagation. *Synonymes:* 1. *Mentha pumila, verticillata.* 2. *M. quadrifolia.*

| | | | |
|---|---|---|---|
| pūmĭlă, 1 . . | Purple | . 8, H. Her. P. Nepal . | 1826 |
| quadrifóliă, 2 . | Purple | . 7, G. Ev. S. Nepal . | 1820 |

DYSPĔPSĬĂ, difficulty of digestion.

# E.

EARED, having ears, or appendages.

EARTH NUT, see *Bŭnĭŭm*.

EARTH TONGUE, see *Geoglŏssŭm*.

EAST INDIA MUGWORT, see *Artemĭsĭă hirsūtă*.

EBĔNĔŎs, black, ebony-coloured.

EBĔNŬs, *Linn.* From *abnous*, the Arabic name for ebony, or *ebenus* of the Romans. *Linn.* 16, Or. 6, Nat. Or. *Ebenaceæ*. These are pretty little dwarf plants, with pink flowers; they require a peaty soil, added to a little loam, to grow in, and are increased by seeds. *Synonymes:* 1. *Anthyllis cretica.* 2. *A. pinnata.*

| | | | |
|---|---|---|---|
| crĕtĭcă, 1 . . | Pink | . 6, G. Ev. S. Candia . | 1787 |
| pinnátā, 2 . . | Pink | . 6, G. | B. Barbary . | 1796 |

EBONY, see *Diŏspўrŏs ĕbĕnŭs*.

ECASTAPHŶLLŬM, *P. Browne.* From *hecastos*, each, and *phyllon*, a leaf; the leaves of some of the species are composed of only one leaflet. *Linn.* 17, Or. 4, Nat. Or. *Leguminosæ*. Ornamental shrubs, growing about ten feet high; they succeed in rich soil, and are increased by cuttings of the ripened wood, planted in sand, under a glass, in heat. *Synonyme:* 1. *Pterocarpus Ecastaphyllum.*

| | | | |
|---|---|---|---|
| Brownĕĭ, 1 . . | Wht. red | . 8. Ev. S. W. Ind. . | 1733 |
| Plumĭĕrĭ . . . | White | . 8. Ev. S. S. Amer. . | 1820 |
| Siebĕrĭ . . . | Wht. red | . 8. Ev. S. S. Guinea . | 1824 |

ECAUDATE, spikeless, without a stem.

ECCREMOCĂRPŬs, *Ruiz et Pavon.* From *ekkremes*, pendent, and *karpos*, fruit; the fruit is pendent. *Linn.* 14, Or. 2, Nat. Or. *Bignoniaceæ*. An exceedingly ornamental plant, well adapted for training over bowers, columns, trellis-work, &c., like Clematis, Honeysuckles, &c.; it should be planted in a mixture of sand, loam, and peat; cuttings root at once, in sand, or soil, with or without a glass.

| | | | |
|---|---|---|---|
| longiflórŭs . . | Orange | . 7, G. Ev. Cl. Peru . | 1825 |

ECHĔVĔRĬĂ, *Decandolle.* In honour of M. Echeveri, author of the splendid drawings of the Flora Mexicana. *Linn.* 10, Or. 4, Nat. Or. *Crassulaceæ*. Among succulents, this genus is one of great beauty. *E. gibbiflora* is disposed to grow rather straggling; nevertheless, it is worthy of a place in every collection, on account of its strong, shining leaves, and orangy-scarlet flowers. To grow them well, they require a soil composed of sandy loam, and a little peat, mixed with reduced rubbish of bricks, &c. At all seasons they should be cautiously watered, particularly in winter. They increase from cuttings, dried a few days before being put in the soil. *Synonymes:* 1. *Cotyledon cæspitosa.* 2. *C. coccinea.*

| | | | |
|---|---|---|---|
| cæspitósā, 1 . | Yellow | . 7, G. Her. P. California . | 1796 |
| coccínĕā, 2 . | Scarlet | . 10, G. Ev. S. Mexico . | 1816 |
| gibbiflórā . . | Yel. pink | . 9, G. Ev. S. Mexico . | 1826 |
| grandifóliā . . | Orange | . 10, G. Ev. S. Mexico . | 1828 |
| lŭrĭdā . . . | Scarlet | . 7, S. Her. P. Mexico . | 1830 |
| racemósā . . | Crimson | . 10, S. Her. P. Mexico . | 1836 |
| secŭndā . . . | Scarlet | . 6, S. Ev. S. Mexico . | 1837 |

ECHINĂCĔĂ, *Mœnch.* Derived from *echinus*, a hedge-

Q

hog; the prickly scales of the receptacle give that appearance. *Linn*. 19, Or. 3, Nat. Or. *Compositæ.* These plants are ornamental, growing from one to two feet high, and of bold habits. For culture, &c., see *Coreopsis*. *Synonymes:* 1. *Coreopsis heterophylla*. 2. *Rudbeckia napifolia*. 3. *R. purpurea*. 4. *R. serotina*.

| | | | | | |
|---|---|---|---|---|---|
| Dicksoni | . | Lilac . | 8, H. Her. P. | Mexico . | |
| heterophylla, 1 | . | Purple . | 10, H. Her. P. | Mexico . | 1829 |
| intermedia | . | Red . | 9, H. Her. P. | Eng. hyb. | 1826 |
| napifolia, 2 | . | Red . | 7, F. Her. P. | N. Spain | 1824 |
| purpurea, 3 | . | Red . | 9, H. Her. P. | N. Amer. | 1699 |
| serotina, 4 | . | Red . | 9, H. Her. P. | N. Amer. | 1816 |

ECHINATED, covered with prickles, like an echinus, or hedgehog.

ECHINARIA, *Desfontaines*. From *echinus*, a hedgehog; the prickly heads may be fancied to resemble little hedgehogs. *Linn*. 3, Or. 2, Nat. Or. *Gramineæ.* A curious little annual, growing in any common soil, and increased by cuttings. *Synonyme:* 1. *Cenchrus capitatus, Sesleria echinata.*

| | | | | |
|---|---|---|---|---|
| capitata, 1 | . | Apetal . | 7, Grass. 8. Eur. | . 1771 |

ECHINELLA, *Agardh*. From *echinus*, a hedgehog; bristly appearance of the plants. *Linn*. 24, Or. 7, Nat. Or. *Algæ.* A very minute species of green *Alga*, found in lakes, and, by some naturalists, believed to be animalcula—*articulata*.

ECHINOCACTUS, *Salm-Dyck*. From *echinos*, a hedgehog, and *cactus*; a name given by Theophrastus to a spiny plant. *Linn*. 12, Or. 1, Nat. Or. *Cactaceæ.* These are plants of great beauty and interest, on account of their singular and grotesque structure, the arrangement of their spines, and the beauty of their flowers. The soil best suited for them, is sandy peat, a little loam, and a little lime, or brick rubbish, all of which must be well mixed together. They must be watered very sparingly at all times, but more so in winter. They are increased from offsets, which must be dried a few days before being put in to strike. These plants, and *Mammillarias*, are sometimes much infested with red spider, which is very troublesome. The effectual way of exterminating them, is to shed a little dry sulphur over the plant infested, and they will soon disappear, and as soon return, if not carefully watched. *Synonymes:* 1. *Cereus abnormis*. 2. *E. platacantha, Cactus latispina*. 3. *Cereus cylindricus*. 4. *Cactus depressa*. 5. *Cereus gibbosus*. 6. *Cereus hystrix*. 7. *Cereus imbricatus*. 8. *Cactus intorta*. 9. *Cactus erinaceus*. 10. *Cactus parvispinus*. 11. *Cactus recurvus, nobilis*.

| | | | | | |
|---|---|---|---|---|---|
| abnormis, 1 | . | White . | 7, 8. Ev. 8. | S. Amer. | 1818 |
| acutus | . | Yellow . | 9, 8. Ev. 8. | M. Video | 1836 |
| acutangularis | . | Yellow . | 9, 8. Ev. 8. | | 1835 |
| Anconianus | . | | 8. Ev. 8. | Ancona | 1834 |
| arcuatus | . | | 8. Ev. 8. | M. Video | |
| centeterius | . | Lil. red . | 9, 8. Ev. 8. | | 1836 |
| coccineus | . | | 9, 8. Ev. 8. | | 1835 |
| cornigerus, 2 | . | Purple . | 8. Ev. 8. | Mexico . | 1823 |
| corynodes | . | Yellow . | 9, 8. Ev. 8. | | 1835 |
| crispatus | . | Purple . | 8. Ev. 8. | Mexico . | 1826 |
| cylindricus, 3 | . | | 8. Ev. 8. | Peru . | 1799 |
| denatus | . | | 8. Ev. 8. | Mexico . | 1829 |
| Deppei | . | | 8. Ev. 8. | Mexico . | 1829 |
| depressus, 4 | . | | 8. Ev. 8. | S. Amer. | 1796 |
| echinatus | . | | 9, 8. Ev. 8. | Mexico . | 1830 |
| exsculptus | . | | 9, 8. Ev. 8. | | 1836 |
| Eyriesii | . | Wht. yel. | 8. Ev. 8. | Mexico . | 1829 |
| glaucus | . | Wht. grn. | 7, 8. Ev. 8. | | |
| formosus | . | | 8. Ev. 8. | Mexico . | 1830 |
| gibbosus, 5 | . | White . | 7, 8. Ev. 8. | Jamaica | 1808 |
| Gillesii | . | | 9, 8. Ev. 8. | Mexico . | 1830 |
| gladiatus | . | | 7, 8. Ev. 8. | Mexico . | |
| hamatus | . | | 8. Ev. 8. | B. Ayres | 1833 |
| hystrix, 6 | . | | 8. Ev. 8. | | 1808 |
| imbricatus, 7 | . | | 8. Ev. 8. | | 1820 |
| inflatus | . | | 8. Ev. 8. | Chile . | 1828 |
| intortus, 8 | . | Purple . | 6, 8. Ev. 8. | Antigua | 1768 |
| intricatus | . | | 8. Ev. 8. | M. Video | |
| erinaceus, 9 | . | | 7, 8. Ev. 8. | | 1818 |
| Linkii | . | Yellow . | 9, 8. Ev. 8. | Mexico . | 1835 |
| Mackieanus | . | Yel. wht. | 10, 8. Ev. 8. | Chile . | 1836 |
| mammillarioides | . | Yel. red . | 10, 8. Ev. 8. | Chile . | 1836 |
| melocactiformis | . | White . | 8. Ev. 8. | Mexico . | |
| monacanthus | . | | 8. Ev. 8. | Jamaica | |
| montevideanus | . | | 8. Ev. 8. | M. Video | |
| obvallatus | . | Purple . | 8. Ev. 8. | Mexico . | |
| orthacanthus | . | | 8. Ev. 8. | M. Video | |
| Ottonis | . | Yellow . | 9, 8. Ev. 8. | Mexico . | 1829 |
| oxyacanthus | . | | 8. Ev. 8. | | 1830 |
| oxygonus | . | Pa. rose . | 8. Ev. 8. | Brasil | 1831 |

| | | | | | |
|---|---|---|---|---|---|
| pachycentrus | . | | 8. Ev. 8. | | |
| parvispinus, 10 | . | | 8. Ev. 8. | S. Amer. | |
| platyacanthus | . | | 8. Ev. 8. | Mexico . | 1837 |
| polyacanthus | . | | 8. Ev. 8. | Brazil | 1837 |
| recurvus, 11 | . | | 8. Ev. 8. | Mexico . | 1796 |
| rhodanthus | . | Rosy . | 9, 8. Ev. 8. | | 1835 |
| robustus | . | | 9, 8. Ev. 8. | | 1835 |
| Salmianus | . | Grey . | 8. Ev. 8. | Curacoa | |
| scopa | . | Yellow . | 8. Ev. 8. | Brasil | 1836 |
| spinis-albis | . | Yellow . | 6, 8. Ev. 8. | Brasil | 1836 |
| Sellowi | . | | 8. Ev. 8. | M. Video | 1836 |
| sessiliflorus | . | | 8. Ev. 8. | | 1834 |
| spinosissimus | . | | 8. Ev. 8. | | 1834 |
| spiralis | . | | 8. Ev. 8. | | 1835 |
| subgibbosus | . | | 8. Ev. 8. | Valparaiso | 1830 |
| subuliferus | . | | 8. Ev. 8. | Mexico . | |
| sulcatus | . | | 8. Ev. 8. | Mexico . | 1829 |
| tenuispinus | . | Yellow . | 9, 8. Ev. 8. | Brasil | 1835 |
| tephracanthos | . | | 8. Ev. 8. | Brasil | 1825 |
| thelephorus | . | | 8. Ev. 8. | | 1834 |
| tuberculatus | . | | 8. Ev. 8. | Mexico . | 1826 |
| tubiflorus | . | White . | 8. Ev. 8. | Mexico . | 1836 |
| xanthacanthus | . | | 8. Ev. 8. | | 1835 |

ECHINOCHLOA, *Beauvois*. From *echinos*, a hedgehog, and *chloa*, grass; alluding to the prickly heads of flowers. *Linn*. 3, Or. 2, Nat. Or. *Gramineæ.* Hardy annuals, fit only to be grown in botanic gardens. *Synonymes:* 1. *Panicum stagninum*. 2. *P. crus-galli*.

| | | | | |
|---|---|---|---|---|
| crus-galli, 2 | . | Apetal . | 7, Grass. Britain | |
| setigera | . | Apetal . | 7, Grass. E. Ind. | . 1830 |

*commutata* 1, *crus-curvi, echinata, erythrosperma, intermedia, stagnina.*

ECHINOPHORA, *Tournefort*. From *echinos*, a hedgehog, and *phoreo*, to bear; the involucrum is covered with stiff spines. *Linn*. 5, Or. 2, Nat. Or. *Umbelliferæ.* Rather interesting plants, succeeding in any common soil, and increased by dividing the roots.

| | | | | |
|---|---|---|---|---|
| spinosa | . | White . | 7, H. Her. P. | England . |
| tenuifolia | . | White . | 7, H. Her. P. | Apulia . 1731 |
| trichophylla | . | White . | 7, H. Her. P. | Levant . 1820 |

ECHINOPOGON, *Beauvois*. From *echinos*, prickly, and *pogon*, a beard. *Linn*. 3, Or. 2, Nat. Or. *Gramineæ.* A mere weed, of the simplest culture. *Synonyme:* 1. *Agrostis ovatus—ovatus.*

ECHINOPS, *Linn*. From *echinos*, a hedgehog, and *opsis*, aspect; in allusion to the hedgehog-like heads of flowers. *Linn*. 19, Or. 5, Nat. Or. *Compositæ.* Coarse plants, of considerable beauty, attaining from one to five feet high. They are well adapted for borders, on account of their stiff growth; any common soil suits them, and young plants are obtained by dividing the roots. In Spain, they use the flower of *E. strigosus* for tinder. *Synonymes:* 1. *E. persicus.*

| | | | | | |
|---|---|---|---|---|---|
| exaltatus | . | White . | 7, H. Her. P. | Austria | 1817 |
| horridus, 1 | . | Blue . | 7, H. | B. Persia | 1818 |
| humilis | . | Blue . | 7, H. | B. Caucasus | 1816 |
| lanuginosus | . | Blue . | 7, H. | B. Levant | 1786 |
| paniculatus | . | Blue . | 7, H. Her. P. | Spain | 1815 |
| polycephalus | . | Blue . | 7, H. Her. P. | S. Eur. | 1816 |
| Ritro | . | Blue . | 7, H. Her. P. | Europe | 1570 |
| ruthenicus | . | Blue . | 7, H. Her. P. | Russia | 1816 |
| sphærocephalus | . | Lgt. blue . | 7, H. Her. P. | Austria | 1596 |
| spinosus | . | White . | 7, H. Her. P. | Egypt | 1597 |
| strictus | . | Pa. blue . | 7, H. Her. P. | Europe | 1822 |
| strigosus | . | White . | 7, H. | A. Spain | 1789 |
| tauricus | . | Blue . | 8, H. | B. Tauria | 1816 |
| tenuifolius | . | Blue . | 7, H. Her. P. | Russia | 1820 |
| virgatus | . | Blue . | 6, H. Her. P. | S. Eur. | 1820 |
| viscosus | . | Blue . | 8, H. | B. Caucasus | 1818 |

ECHINOSPERMUM, *Swartz*. From *echinos*, a hedgehog, and *sperma*, seed, the seeds are very prickly. *Linn*. 5, Or. 1, Nat. Or. *Boraginaceæ.* These plants are not worth cultivating, except in general collections. *Synonymes:* 1. *Myosotis Lappula*. 2. *M. marginata*. 3. *M. virginica*.

| | | | | |
|---|---|---|---|---|
| virginicum, 3 | . | Blue . | 6, H. | B. Virginia . 1699 |

*barbatum, deflexum, Lappula* 1, *marginatum* 2, *patalum, Redowskii.*

ECHITES, *Linn*. From *echis*, a viper; referring to the smooth, twining shoots. *Linn*. 5, Or. 1, Nat. Or. *Apocynaceæ.* This is a most beautiful genus of evergreen twiners; they grow freely in a mixture of loam and peat, and are increased readily from cuttings in sand, under a glass. The bark of *E. antidysenterica* is astringent and febrifugal.

| | | | | | |
|---|---|---|---|---|---|
| antidysenterica | . | Pink . | 8, E. Ev. Tw. E. Ind. | | 1821 |
| biflora | . | White . | 7, S. Ev. Tw. W. Ind. | | 1793 |
| bispinosa | . | Pink . | 9, G. Ev. S. | C. G. H. | 1795 |
| caryophyllata | . | Pa. yel. | 10, S. Ev. Tw. E. Ind. | | 1812 |
| cymosa | . | | 7, S. Ev. Tw. E. Ind. | | 1828 |

| | | | | | |
|---|---|---|---|---|---|
| difförmis | Pa. yel. | 7, G. Ev. Tw. | Carolina | 1806 |
| domingénsis | Yellow | 6, S. Ev. Tw. | W. Ind. | 1820 |
| frutéscens | | 8. Ev. Tw. | E. Ind. | 1816 |
| grandiflörä | Pink | 8. Ev. Tw. | E. Ind. | 1893 |
| Hoyáll | Yellow | 6, S. Ev. Tw. | E. Ind. | 1818 |
| longiflörä | White | 6, S. Ev. Tw. | Brasil | 1816 |
| malabáricä | Red | 6, S. Ev. Tw. | Malabar | 1822 |
| paniculátä | Yellow | 7, S. Ev. Tw. | S. Amer. | 1823 |
| peltátä | | 8. Ev. Tw. | Trinidad | 1896 |
| reticulátä | Yellow | 7, S. Ev. Tw. | E. Ind. | 1818 |
| Richárdii | Yellow | 7, S. Ev. Tw. | Guiana | 1824 |
| rubricaúlis | Yellow | 7, S. Ev. Tw. | Guiana | 1824 |
| stelláris | Ro. yel. | 7, S. Ev. Tw. | Rio Jan. | |
| suberéctä | Yellow | 7, S. Ev. Tw. | Jamaica | 1759 |
| tortéä | Yellow | 7, S. Ev. Tw. | Jamaica | 1778 |
| umbellátä | Yellow | 7, S. Ev. Tw. | Jamaica | 1783 |

ECHÏÖM, *Linn.* From *echis*, a viper; the seeds resemble the head of the viper. *Linn.* 5, Or. 1, Nat. Or. *Boraginaceæ.* This is a very pretty genus of shrubs, growing from two to six feet high, in a mixture of loam and peat. Cuttings will root in the same kind of soil, under a glass; but they are more readily increased by layers, which soon take root if laid down in the young wood, with a little nick cut in the shoot. Seeds are frequently produced, from which they may also be increased. *Synonymes:* 1. *E. formosum.* 2. *E. grandiflorum.* 3. *E. hispidum, elegans.*

| | | | | | |
|---|---|---|---|---|---|
| aculeátüm | White | 6, G. Ev. S. | Canaries | 1815 |
| ambigüüm | Wht. red | 7, G. Ev. S. | Canaries | 1890 |
| argentéüm | Blue | 6, G. Ev. S. | C. G. H. | 1789 |
| austrálé | Purple | 8, H. | A. S. Eur. | 1824 |
| bifröns | Wht. red | 6, G. Ev. S. | Canaries | 1820 |
| brachyánthüm | White | 6, G. Ev. S. | C. G. H. | 1819 |
| cándicáns | Blue | 6, G. Ev. S. | Madeira | 1777 |
| capitátüm | Red | 6, G. Ev. S. | C. G. H. | 1819 |
| caudátüm | Red | 7, G. Her. P. | C. G. H. | 1818 |
| créticüm | Red | 4, H. | A. Levant | 1683 |
| cynoglossoïdés | Blue | 7, G. Ev. S. | Canaries | 1816 |
| denssifíörüm | Blue | 6, G. Ev. S. | Canaries | 1820 |
| diffüsüm | Pink | 6, H. | A. Crete | 1817 |
| fastuösüm | Purple | 4, G. Ev. S. | Canaries | 1779 |
| feroclssímüm | Blue | 6, G. Ev. S. | Madeira | 1794 |
| folióüm | White | 7, G. Ev. S. | Canaries | 1815 |
| fruticösüm | Pink | 5, G. Ev. S. | C. G. H. | 1769 |
| gigantéüm | White | 6, G. Ev. S. | Canaries | 1779 |
| glábrüm | White | 5, G. Ev. S. | C. G. H. | 1791 |
| glaucophyllüm | Violet | 5, G. Ev. S. | C. G. H. | 1792 |
| grandiflörüm, 1 | Pink | 6, G. Ev. S. | Madeira | 1787 |
| hispídüm | White | 6, G. Ev. S. | C. G. H. | 1818 |
| italícüm | White | 7, H. | B. Jersey | |
| lævigátüm | Blue | 7, G. Ev. S. | C. G. H. | 1774 |
| lasiophyllüm | White | 5, G. Ev. S. | C. G. H. | 1819 |
| lineátüm | White | 7, G. Ev. S. | Canaries | 1815 |
| longiflörüm | Blue | 7, G. Ev. S. | C. G. H. | 1806 |
| lusitánicüm | Violet | 6, H. | A. S. Eur. | 1731 |
| macránthüm, 2 | Violet | 7, H. | A. Barbary | 1818 |
| macrophyllüm | Blue | 7, G. Ev. S. | Canaries | 1823 |
| maritímüm | Blue | 7, H. | A. Italy | 1815 |
| Mertênsii | Blue | 6, H. Her. P. | Spain | 1824 |
| micránthüm | Violet | 6, H. | A. Barbary | 1824 |
| mölle | White | 6, G. Ev. S. | Teneriffe | 1820 |
| nervösüm | Purple | 7, G. Ev. S. | Madeira | 1777 |
| orientálé | Pa. blue | 6, H. | A. Levant | 1780 |
| paniculátüm | White | 7, G. Ev. S. | C. G. H. | 1815 |
| parviflörüm | Blue | 7, H. | A. Barbary | 1798 |
| plantaginoïdés | White | 6, H. | A. S. Eur. | 1826 |
| plantaginéüm | Purple | 7, H. | A. Italy | 1776 |
| prostrátüm | Red | 7, H. Her. P. | Egypt | 1825 |
| pyramidátüm | Blue | 7, G. Ev. S. | C. G. H. | 1890 |
| pyrenæüm | White | 7, H. | B. Pyrenees | 1815 |
| rubrüm | Red | 6, H. | B. Hungary | 1791 |
| salmánticüm | Pink | 7, H. | A. Spain | 1819 |
| scábrüm | Pur. blue | 7, G. Ev. S. | C. G. H. | 1820 |
| Sibthörpii, 3 | Red | 6, H. | B. Europe | 1824 |
| simpléx | White | 6, G. Ev. S. | Teneriffe | 1820 |
| spicátüm | White | 7, G. Her. P. | C. G. H. | 1790 |
| strictüm | Blue | 6, G. Ev. S. | Canaries | 1779 |
| strigösüm | Violet | 8, G. Ev. S. | C. G. H. | 1821 |
| tenüé | Blue | 7, H. | B. Sicily | 1824 |
| thyrsoïdéüm | Blue | 8, H. | R. S. Eur. | 1820 |
| tuberculátüm | Violet | 8, H. | B. Spain | 1820 |
| verrucösüm | White | 7, G. Ev. S. | C. G. H. | 1822 |
| violáceüm | Blue | 6, H. | B. Austria | 1658 |
| viréscens | White | 7, G. Ev. S. | Canaries | 1820 |
| vulgáré | Red | 7, H. | B. Britain | |
| flöré-albö | White | 7, H. | B. Britain | |

ECLÏPTÄ. From *ekleipo*, to be deficient; the seed-crown and wing are wanting. *Linn.* 19, Or. 2, Nat. Or. *Compositæ.* Uninteresting annuals and biennials of easy culture—*erèctä, latifölïä, procúmbëns, prostrátä, punctátä, undulátä.*

ECOSTÁTÆ, having no nerves on the leaf.

ECTROCÁRPÜS, *Lyngbye.* From *ektos*, outside, and *karpos*, a fruit; the theca is not inclosed. *Linn.*

24, Or. 7, Nat. Or. *Algæ.* Mostly dark green marine productions, found in spring and summer—*brachiátüs, granulösüs, tomentösüs, siliculösüs atrö-virëns-ferrugineüs.*

ECTOSTRÖMÄ, *Fries.* From *ektos*, without, and *stroma*, a hair. *Linn.* 24, Or. 9, Nat. Or. *Fungi.* Very minute species, to be met with during summer and autumn on the *Iris*, and decayed laurel leaves; whence their specific names—*Iridis, Laúri.*

EDENTÚLÖS, not toothed.

EDÍBLE, eatable.

EDWÁRDSÏÄ, *Salisbury.* In honour of Sydenham Edwards, a celebrated English botanical draughtsman. *Linn.* 10, Or. 1, Nat. Or. *Leguminosæ.* A very ornamental genus of plants, which will survive our winters if planted against a warm wall, and protected from very severe frosts. They vary in height from four to twelve feet; they thrive best in sandy peat, and increase readily from cuttings. *Synonyme:* 1. *Sophora sericea.*

| | | | | | |
|---|---|---|---|---|---|
| chilénsis | Yellow | 6, G. Ev. T. | Chile | 1822 |
| chrysophyllä | Yellow | 5, F. De. S. | N. Zeal. | |
| grandiflörä | Yellow | 5, F. De. S. | N. Zeal. | 1772 |
| microphyllä | Yellow | 5, F. De. S. | N. Zeal. | 1772 |
| minímä | Yellow | 5, F. De. S. | N. Zeal. | 1818 |
| nítidä | Yellow | 8. Ev. S. | Bourbon | 1820 |

EFFÚSE, applied to inflorescence, and means a kind of panicle with a very loose arrangement.

EGG-BEARER, see *Solánüm orígénüm.*

EGLÁNTINE, see *Rösä lútéä.*

EGLÁNTINE, see *Rübüs Eglantérïä.*

EGYPTIAN LOTUS, see *Nymphéä Lötüs.*

EGYPTIAN THORN, see *Acácïä vérä.*

EHRÉTÏÄ, *Linn.* In honour of D. G. Ehret, a celebrated German botanical draughtsman. *Linn.* 5, Or. 1, Nat. Or. *Ehretiaceæ.* Stove plants, of much beauty, from eight to twenty-five feet high. They delight in loam and peat, and cuttings root in the same kind of soil, or in sand, under a glass, in heat.

| | | | | | |
|---|---|---|---|---|---|
| acuminátä | White | 7, G. Ev. T. | N. Holl. | 1820 |
| asperä | White | 8. Ev. T. | E. Ind. | 1795 |
| buxifölïä | White | 8. Ev. S. | E. Ind. | 1823 |
| divaricátä | White | 8. Ev. T. | Havannah | 1820 |
| dúbïä | White | 8. Ev. T. | Jamaica | 1825 |
| internödïä | White | 8. Ev. S. | Antilles | 1819 |
| lævis | White | 8. Ev. T. | E. Ind. | 1823 |
| laxä | White | 8. Ev. S. | Bourbon | 1826 |
| microphyllä | White | 7, 8. Ev. S. | E. Ind. | 1818 |
| serrátä | White | 8. Ev. S. | E. Ind. | 1823 |
| tinifölïä | White | 6, 8. Ev. T. | Jámaica | 1734 |

EHRHÁRTÏÄ, *Smith.* In honour of F. Ehrhart, a Swiss naturalist. *Linn.* 6, Or. 1, Nat. Or. *Gramineæ.* Plants which are only interesting in botanical collections. *Synonyme:* 1. *Aira capensis.*

| | | | | | |
|---|---|---|---|---|---|
| panicéä | Apetal | 7, Grass. | C. G. H. | 1790 |

*calycína 1, distichiphylla, gigantea.*

EKEBÉRGÏÄ. Sparmann named this genus in compliment to C. Gustavus Ekeberg, captain of a Swedish East Indiaman, who took him out to China. *Linn.* 10, Or. 1, Nat. Or. *Meliaceæ.* A very ornamental tree, growing about twenty feet high; a mixture of loam and peat suits it, and young plants may be raised from cuttings, planted in sand, under a glass, in heat.

| | | | | | |
|---|---|---|---|---|---|
| capénsis | White | 7, G. Ev. T. | C. G. H. | 1789 |

ELÆÁGNÜS, *Linn.* From *elaia*, an olive, and *agnos*, a chaste tree; resemblance the tree bears. *Linn.* 4, Or. 1, Nat. Or. *Elæagnaceæ.* These are ornamental, largish-growing trees, or shrubs, of easy culture, thriving in any open soil, and are increased by layers or cuttings of the ripened wood, planted in a warm situation early in autumn. The fruit of *E. arborea*, and *conferta*, is eaten in Nepal; and in Persia the fruit of *E. orientalis* is used as a dessert, under the name of Zinzeyd.

| | | | | | |
|---|---|---|---|---|---|
| acuminátä | Apetal | G. Ev. S. | | |
| angustifölïä | Yellow | 7, H. De. T. | S. Eur. | 1633 |
| arbörëä | Apetal | 7, G. Ev. T. | Nepal | 1819 |
| argentéä | Apetal | H. De. T. | N. Amer. | 1813 |
| confertä | White | H. De. S. | Nepal | 1825 |
| latifölïä | Apetal | 7, 8. Ev. S. | E. Ind. | 1712 |
| orientális | Apetal | 7, G. Ev. T. | Levant | 1748 |

ELÆIS, *Jacquin.* From *elaia*, olive; the natives of Guinea express an oil from the fruit of this plant, as the Greeks do from their olives; whence the name. *Linn.* 22, Or. 6, Nat. Or. *Palmaceæ.* Beautiful species of palms, requiring a strong heat, and rich sandy loam, to grow in, and may be increased by suckers. Palm oil is chiefly obtained from *E. guineensis*, and the best kind of palm wine is also said to be obtained from the same tree.

| | | | | |
|---|---|---|---|---|
| guineensis | . . | Grn. wht. | . Palm. Guinea . | 1730 |
| melanocócca | . . | Grn. wht. | . Palm. N. Granada . | 1821 |
| occidentalis | . . | Grn. wht. | . Palm. Jamaica . | 1820 |
| pernambucánă | . . | Grn. wht. | . Palm. Brazil . | 1825 |

ELÆOCÁRPÚS, *Linn.* From *elaia*, an olive, and *karpos*, a fruit; the fruit has been compared to an olive. *Linn.* 11, Or. 1, Nat. Or. *Elæocarpaceæ.* Very beautiful plants, from ten to twenty feet high. *E. cyaneus* is excellently adapted for a conservatory. They grow best in a mixture of loam and peat, and ripened cuttings strike in sand, or soil, under a glass, in a moderate heat; they are sometimes raised from seeds. *Synonyme:* 1. *E. reticulata.*

| | | | | |
|---|---|---|---|---|
| cyáneŭs, 1 | . . | White | . 7, G. Ev. S. N. Holl. | 1803 |
| grandiflŏrŭs | . . | White | . 8. Ev. T. E. Ind. | 1829 |
| serrátŭs | . . | | . 8. Ev. T. E. Ind. | 1774 |

ELÆODÉNDRÓN, *Jacquin.* From *elaia*, an olive, and *dendron*, a tree; the fruit is like that of an olive, and the seeds are oily. *Linn.* 5, Or. 1, Nat. Or. *Celastraceæ.* This is an ornamental genus of plants, growing from three to twelve feet high; they delight in loam and peat, and cuttings root in sand, under a glass, in heat. *Synonymes:* 1. *Portenschlagia australis, Lamarckia dentata.* 2. *Schrebera albens, Senacia glauca, Mangifera glauca.* 3. *Rubentia olivina.* 4. *Cassine xylocarpa.*

| | | | | |
|---|---|---|---|---|
| austrálĭs, 1 | . . | Grn. wht. | . 7, G. Ev. S. N. S. W. | 1796 |
| glaúcŭm, 2 | . . | Green | . 8. Ev. S. Ceylon | 1824 |
| integrifolĭŭm | . . | Grn. wht. | . 7, G. Ev. S. N. Holl. | |
| orientálĕ, 3 | . . | Grn. yel. | . 8. Ev. T. Maurit. | 1771 |
| xylocárpŭm, 4 | . . | Grn. yel. | . 8. Ev. S. Antilles | 1816 |

ELÁPHRIŬM, *Jacquin.* From *elaphros*, contemptible; the wood being of no value. *Linn.* 8, Or. 1, Nat. Or. *Burseriaceæ.* A tallish-growing, ornamental tree, with white flowers; it succeeds well in peat and loam, and young plants are readily obtained from cuttings in sand, or sandy mould, under a glass, in heat. *Synonyme:* 1. *Fagara Elaphrium.*

| | | | | |
|---|---|---|---|---|
| glábrŭm, 1 | . . | White | . 8. Ev. T. Carthag. | 1818 |

ÉLÁTÉ, *Aiton.* A name adopted from the Greeks. *Linn.* 21, Or. 6, Nat. Or. *Palmaceæ.* This is a fine palm, bearing fruit much like a wild plum. In the East Indies, the people chew it like the Areca nut, with the leaf of the betel, pepper, and quick-lime. Elephants eat the fruit-stalks with avidity, on account of their sweetness. In our stoves, to grow the plant well, it must have a strong heat, and good rich loam; increased by suckers.

| | | | | |
|---|---|---|---|---|
| sylvéstrĭs | . . | Green | . 5, Palm. E. Ind. | 1763 |

ELATÉRIŬM, *Linn.* From *elater*, an impeller; in reference to the elastic seed-vessel. *Linn.* 21, Or. 10, Nat. Or. *Cucurbitaceæ.* A singular genus of plants, on account of the elastic seed-vessel; they have little beauty, and require the same treatment as *Cucurbita.*

| | | | | |
|---|---|---|---|---|
| carthaginénsĕ | . . | Yellow | . 6, H. Tw. A. Carthage | 1823 |
| tamoídĕs | . . | Yellow | . 6, H. Tw. A. Mexico | 1820 |

ELÁTÍNĔ, *Linn.* From *elate*, signifying a fir in Greek; its leaves have been compared to those of the fir-tree. *Linn.* 8, Or. 4, Nat. Or. *Elatinaceæ.* Curious little aquatic plants, of no beauty; they merely require sowing by the side of a pond, or rivulet, in the open air. *Synonyme:* 1. *E. triandra, hexandra, Hydropiper.*

| | | | | |
|---|---|---|---|---|
| Hydropípĕr | . . | White | . 8, H. Aq. A. S. Eur. | . . |
| tripétală, 1 | . . | Flesh | . 8, H. Aq. A. Britain | . . |

ELDER, see *Sambucus.*

ELECAMPANE, see *Corvisártiă Helénĭŭm.*

ELECTUARY, a medicine of conserves and powders, of the consistence of honey.

ELEGÍA, *Thunberg.* From *elegos*, lamentation; in reference to the sad colour of the plants. *Linn.* 22, Or. 3, Nat. Or. *Gramineæ.* The species of this genus are only worth cultivating in botanical collections; they grow in a loamy soil, and are multiplied by divisions—*juncĕă, racemósă.*

ELEIÓTIS, *Decandolle.* From *eleios*, a dormouse, and *ous otos*, an ear; the leaves are shaped like the ears of a dormouse. *Linn.* 17, Or. 4, Nat. Or. *Leguminosæ.* A stove biennial, of no interest whatever.

*Synonymes:* Hedysarum sororium, Hallia sororia, Onobrychis sororia—sororia.

ELEÓCHÁRIS, *R. Brown.* From *helos*, a marsh, and *chairo*, to delight; in allusion to the place where the plants delight to grow. *Linn.* 3, Or. 1, Nat. Or. *Gramineæ.* Mostly insignificant bog plants, which can only be recommended where there are botanical collections. *Synonymes:* 1. *Scirpus acicularis.* 2. *S. multicaulis.*

| | | | | |
|---|---|---|---|---|
| acútă | . . . | Apetal | . 7, Gram. N. Holl. | 1819 |
| geniculátă | . . . | Apetal | . 7, Gram. W. Ind. | 1822 |
| glaucéscĕns | . . . | Apetal | . 7, Gram. N. Amer. | 1820 |
| multicaúlĭs, 2 | . . . | Apetal | . 7, Gram. Britain | . . |
| obtúsă | . . . | Apetal | . 6, Gram. N. Amer. | 1818 |
| ténuĭs | . . . | Apetal | . 7, Gram. N. Amer. | 1824 |

*aciculárĭs* 1, *ovata, palustris.*

ELEPHANTIASIS, a species of leprosy, in which the limbs become prodigiously swollen.

ELEPHÁNTÓPÚS, *Cassini.* From *elephas*, an elephant, and *pous*, a foot; the radical leaves resemble an elephant's foot. *Linn.* 19, Or. 5, Nat. Or. *Compositæ.* The plants of this genus possess but very little beauty; they grow in any common soil, and are multiplied from seeds and offsets. On the coast of Malabar, a decoction of the leaves and roots of *E. scaber* is given in cases of dysuria—*angustifolĭŭs, carolinĭánŭs, mŏllĭs, nudicaúlĭs, nudiflŏrŭs, scábĕr, spicátŭs, tomentósŭs.*

ELEPHANT'S-FOOT, see *Elephántópŭs.*

ELEPHANT'S-FOOT, see *Testudinárĭă Elephántĭpĕs.*

ELEUSÍNĔ, *Gærtner.* Derived from *Eleusis*, one of the appellations of Ceres. *Linn.* 3, Or. 2, Nat. Or. *Gramineæ.* Species of grass, of little beauty, and easy culture. *Synonyme:* 1. *Cynosurus indicus.*

| | | | | |
|---|---|---|---|---|
| calycínă | . . . | Apetal | . 3, Gram. E. Ind. | 1820 |
| corácaná | . . . | Apetal | . 3, Gram. E. Ind. | 1714 |
| índicá, 1 | . . . | Apetal | . 3, Gram. E. Ind. | 1714 |
| verticillátă | . . . | Apetal | . 3, Gram. E. Ind. | 1820 |

ELEVATED, anything that rises above the surface.

ELICHRÝSŬM. From *helios*, sun, and *chrysos*, gold; in allusion to the brilliant flowers. *Linn.* 19, Or. 2, Nat. Or. *Compositæ.* This genus is greatly admired on account of the beautiful flowers of some of the species. The soil in which they grow best, is a mixture of three parts peat, and one part sandy loam. Cuttings will strike in the same kind of soil, if they are taken off at a joint; some of the species seed freely, from which they may be increased. *Synonymes:* 1. *Gnaphalium acuminatum.* 2. *G. angustifolium.* 3. *G. apiculatum.* 4. *G. arboreum.* 5. *G. arenarium.* 6. *G. candidissimum.* 7. *G. cephalotus.* 8. *G. congestum.* 9. *G. conicum.* 10. *G. crassifolium.* 11. *G. crispum.* 12. *G. cymosum.* 13. *G. dasyanthum.* 14. *G. diosmæfolium.* 15. *G. discolor.* 16. *G. divaricatum.* 17. *G. ericoides.* 18. *G. fœtidum.* 19. *G. flaccidum.* 20. *Astelma fruticans, G. fruticans, grandiflorum.* 21. *G. grandiflorum.* 22. *G. graveolens.* 23. *G. helianthemifolium.* 24. *Elich-splendens.* 25. *G. ignescens.* 26. *G. italicum.* 27. *G. lasiocaulon.* 28. *G. maritimum.* 29. *G. odoratissimum.* 30. *G. orientale.* 31. *G. patulum.* 32. *G. rutilans.* 33. *G. Stæchas.* 34. *G. tephrodes.* 35. *G. teretifolium.*

| | | | | |
|---|---|---|---|---|
| acuminátŭm, 1 | . . . | White | . 7, G. Ev. S. C.G.H. | 1823 |
| angustifolĭŭm, 2 | . | Yellow | . 8, F. Ev. S. Naples | . . |
| apiculátŭm, 3 | . | Yellow | . G. Her. P. V.D.L. | 1804 |
| arbórĕŭm, 4 | . . | White | . 5, G. Ev. S. C.G.H. | 1770 |
| arenárĭŭm, 5 | . | Yellow | . 8, H. Her. P. Europe | 1789 |
| argéntĕŭm | . | White | . 6, G. Her. P. C.G.H. | 1800 |
| bicŏlŏr | . | Yellow | . 7, H. | A. V.D.L. | 1825 |
| bracteátŭm | . | Pa. yel. | . 7, H. | A. N. Holl. | 1799 |
| involucro-álbĭdŏ | . | Yellow | . 7, H. | A. | 1823 |
| candidíssĭmŭm, 6 | . | Pa. yel. | . 6, H. Her. P. Caspian | 1822 |
| cephalótŭs, 7 | . | Pink | . 6, G. Ev. S. C.G.H. | 1789 |
| congestátŭm, 8 | . | Purple | . 6, G. Ev. S. C.G.H. | 1791 |
| cónĭcŭm, 9 | . | Yellow | . 7, H. Ev. S. S. Eur. | 1824 |
| crassifolĭŭm, 10 | . | Yellow | . 8, G. Ev. S. C.G.H. | 1774 |
| crispŭm, 11 | . | Pink | . G. Her. P. C.G.H. | 1809 |
| cylindrícŭm | . | Yellow | . 6, G. Her. P. C.G.H. | 1780 |
| cymósŭm, 12 | . | Yellow | . 6, G. Ev. S. Africa | 1781 |
| dasyánthŭm, 13 | . | Yellow | . 7, G. Ev. S. C.G.H. | 1812 |
| dealbátŭm | . | White | . G. Her. P. V.D.L. | 1812 |
| diosmæfolĭŭm, 14 | . | White | . 6, G. Ev. S. C.G.H. | 1812 |
| discolórŭm, 15 | . | Brown | . 7, G. Ev. S. C.G.H. | 1815 |
| divaricátŭm, 16 | . | White | . 7, G. Ev. S. C.G.H. | 1820 |
| ericoídĕs, 17 | . | Pink | . 6, G. Ev. S. C.G.H. | 1774 |
| fœtidŭm, 18 | . | Lgt. yel. | . 8, G. | S. C.G.H. | 1822 |
| flaccidŭm, 19 | . | Yellow | . 7, G. Her. P. Brazil | 1826 |
| fruticósŭm, 20 | . | Yellow | . 6, G. Ev. S. C.G.H. | 1779 |
| fulgidŭm | . . . | Yellow | . 7, G. Ev. S. C.G.H. | 1774 |

| | | | | | | | |
|---|---|---|---|---|---|---|---|
| grandiflôrūm, 21 | . | White | . 7, | G. Ev. | S. | C. G. H. | . 1731 |
| gravēolēns, 22 | . | Yellow | . 6, | H. Her. | P. | Tauria | . 1819 |
| helianthemifôliūm 23 | | White | . 7, | G. Ev. | S. | C. G. H. | . 1774 |
| herbāceūm, 24 | . | Yellow | . 7, | G. Her. | P. | C. G. H. | . 1802 |
| ignēscēns, 25 | . | Red | . 8, | G. Ev. | S. | C. G. H. | . 1731 |
| incānūm | . | Pa. yel. | . 5 | G. Her. | P. | V. D. L. | . 1826 |
| itālicūm, 26 | . | Yellow | . 8, | G. Her. | P. | Italy | . 1826 |
| laniocaūlōn, 27 | . | White | . 8, | G. Ev. | S. | C. G. H. | . 1823 |
| maritimūm, 28 | . | White | . 8, | G. Ev. | S. | C. G. H. | . 1772 |
| microphyllūm | . | Wht. yel. | 7, | G. Ev. | S. | C. G. H. | . 1823 |
| odoratissimūm, 29 | . | Yellow | . 6, | G. Her. | P. | C. G. H. | . 1691 |
| orientālē, 30 | . | Yellow | . 6, | G. Ev. | S. | Africa | . 1629 |
| paniculātūm | . | White | . 7, | G. Ev. | S. | C. G. H. | . 1800 |
| pātūlūm, 31 | . | White | . 5, | G. Ev. | S. | C. G. H. | . 1771 |
| rigidūm | . | White | . 7, | G. Ev. | S. | C. G. H. | . 1801 |
| rūtilāns, 32 | . | Red yel. | 6, | G. Her. | S. | C. G. H. | . 1731 |
| Stœchās, 33 | . | Yellow | . 8, | H. Ev. | S. | Europe | . 1629 |
| tephrodēs, 34 | . | Yel. wht. | 7, | G. Ev. | S. | C. G. H. | . 1823 |
| teretifolium, 35 | . | Brown | . 7, | G. Ev. | S. | C. G. H. | . 1812 |

ELLIŌTTĬX, *Nuttall.* In honour of Stephen Elliot, a North American botanist. *Linn.* 8, Or. 1, Nat. Or. *Ericaceæ.* An ornamental species, succeeding best in a little sandy loam, mixed with peat; it is increased by layers.

racemōsā . . . White . 6, F. Ev. S. Georgia . .

ELLĬSĬX, *Linn.* In honour of J. Ellis, F.R.S., a distinguished English naturalist. *Linn.* 5, Or. 1, Nat. Or. *Hydrophyllaceæ.* A curious little species, of very easy culture.

Nyctēlēā . . . White . 7, H. A. Virginia . 1755

ELLEBOCĂRPŬS, *Kaulfuss.* Derived from *en*, in, *lobos*, a pod, and *karpos*, fruit; in reference to the divisions of the fronds. *Linn.* 24, Or. 1. Nat. Or. *Gleicheniaceæ.* An ornamental species of fern, of considerable beauty; it grows in a loamy soil, and is increased by dividing the roots.

oleracēūs . . . Brown . 8, S. Her. P. Tranqueb. . 1818

ELLIPSOID, like an ellipsis.
ELLIPTIC-LANCEOLATE, a form between elliptic and lanceolate.
ELISĒNĬ, *Herbert.* An ancient name of romance. *Linn.* 6, Or. 1, Nat. Or. *Amaryllidaceæ.* This splendid species will form a welcome addition to the cultivators of bulbous plants. It will no doubt be found to succeed well with the treatment commonly given to *Pancratiums*, and the like.

longipētālā . . White . 6, S. Bl. P. Lima . . 1837

ELM TREE, see *Ulmus.*
ELŌDĒX, *Richard.* From *elodes*, a marsh; the habitation of the plants. *Linn.* 3, Or. 3, Nat. Or. *Hydrocharaceæ.* Interesting aquatics; for culture, &c., see *Plumieria.*

guianēnsīs . . . White . 7. S. Aq. A. Guiana . 1820
pulchēllā . . . . S. Aq. A. E. Ind. . 1831

ELONGATED, lengthened.
ELSHŌLTZĬX, *Willdenow.* In honour of J. S. Elsholtz, a Prussian botanist. *Linn.* 14, Or. 1, Nat. Or. *Labiatæ.* The species are not ornamental, and may be referred to *Hyssopus*, for culture, &c. Synonyme: 1. *Hyssopus cristatus.*

cristātā . . . Pink . 6, H. A. Siberia . 1789
paniculātā, 1 . Pink . 7, H. B. E. Ind. . 1820
ocymoīdēs.

ELȲMŬS. According to *Linnæus*, it is named from *elyo*, to cover. *Linn.* 3, Or. 1, Nat. Or. *Gramineæ.* The plants of this genus are of little beauty or interest, except in botanical collections; they grow in any soil, and are increased by seeds, or divisions. Synonyme: 1. *Asperella hystrix.*

crinītūs . . . Apetal . 6, Grass. Smyrna . 1806
geniculātūs . . . Apetal . 7, Grass. England . .
gigantēūs . . . Apetal . 7, Grass. N. Amer. . 1790
hystrix, 1 . . . Apetal . 6, Grass. Crimea . 1770
mexicānūs . . . Apetal . 7, Grass. Mexico . 1823

*arenārīūs, canadēnsīs, Caput-Medūsæ, europæūs, glaucifôlīūs, hordeifôrmīs, intermēdīūs, jūncēūs, philadēlphīcūs, pseudo-hystrīx, racemôsūs, sabulôsūs, sibirīcūs, striātūs, tēnēr, villôsūs, virginīcūs.*

ELȲNĬ, *Schrader.* Supposed to be from *elyo*, to cover. *Linn.* 3, Or. 1, Nat. Or. *Gramineæ.* A dwarf species of grass, of little interest, and very easy culture. Synonymes: 1. *Carex Bellardi, myosuroides.*

spicātā, 1 . . Apetal . 6, Grass. Europe . 1819

ELYTRĀRĬX, *Vahl.* From *elytron*, an envelope; in allusion to the scaly stem. *Linn.* 2, Or. 1, Nat.

Or. *Acanthaceæ.* A genus of uninteresting stove biennials, growing in sandy peat. Synonyme: 1. *Justicia acaulis—caulescens, crenata* 1, *imbricata, lyrata, marginata, ramosa, virgata.*

EMARGINATE, having a small notch at the end.
EMBĒLĬX, *Linn.* In Ceylon, the plant is called *Æmbelia.* *Linn.* 5, Or. 1, Nat. Or. *Myrsinaceæ.* A fine East Indian tree, growing twenty feet high; loam and peat mixed suit it, and young plants are readily obtained from cuttings in sand, under a glass, in heat. The plant is said to be cathartic.

robūstā . . . . Wht. grn. 8. Ev. T. E. Ind. . 1823

EMBLĬCX, *Gærtner.* The name of the plant in the Moluccas. *Linn.* 21, Or. 10, Nat. Or. *Euphorbiaceæ.* Interesting, evergreen shrubs, growing from three to twelve feet high; a mixture of peat and sand suits them. Cuttings root readily in sand, under a glass, in heat. Synonymes: 1. *Phyllanthus Emblica.* 2. *P. racemosus.*

officinālis, 1 . . Pa. yel. . 7, S. Ev. S. E. Ind. . 1768
racemōsā, 2 . . Grn. yel. . 7, S. Ev. S. E. Ind. . 1793

EMBOSSED, projecting from the surface, like the boss or umbo of a round shield, or target.
EMBOTHRĬŪM, *Forster.* From *en*, in, and *bothrion*, a little pit; in allusion to the anthers. *Linn.* 4, Or. 1, Nat. Or. *Proteaceæ.* This is described as a very handsome plant, growing about three feet high; like most of the *Proteaceæ*, it delights in sandy peat soil, and cuttings, in sand or soil, readily produce roots.

strobilinūm . . . Grn. yel. . 4, G. Ev. S. N. Holl. . 1824

EMBRACING; a leaf is said to embrace a stem when it clasps it round with its base.
EMETIC, that which produces vomiting.
EMĒX, *Necker.* An anagram of Rumex. *Linn.* 6, Or. 3, Nat. Or. *Polygonaceæ.* This species is only worth cultivating in general collections. Synonyme: 1. *Rumex spinosus.*

spinôsūs . . . Green . 7, H. Tr. A. Candia . . 1556

EMMENAGOGUE, any medicine that promotes menstruation.
EMOLLIENT, softening.
EMPĒTRŌM, *Linn.* From *en*, upon, and *petros*, a rock; alluding to the place of growth. *Linn.* 22, Or. 3, Nat. Or. *Empetraceæ.* These are interesting dwarf plants, of easy culture, delighting in elevated, particularly exposed situations, on dry, barren, moorish, or even boggy soil. The little berries they produce are eaten by children, but are not wholesome if eaten in large quantities.

nigrūm . . . . Apetal . 4, H. Ev. S. Britain . .
rubrūm . . . . Brn. pur. . H. Ev. S. S. Amer. . 1833

EMPLEŪRŪM, *Solander.* From *en*, in, and *pleuron*, the membrane which envelops the lungs; the seeds are attached to a coriaceous membrane. *Linn.* 21, Or. 4, Nat. Or. *Rutaceæ.* A good greenhouse plant, with pretty pinkish flowers. It grows about three feet high; for culture, &c., see *Diosma.*

serrulātūm . . . Pink . . 6, G. Ev. S. C. G. H. . 1774

EMULSIONS, medicines made of bruised oily seeds and fluid.
ENARTHROCĂRPŬS, *Labillardière.* From *ennea*, nine, *arthron*, a joint, and *karpos*, fruit; the pod has nine or ten seeds in the lower joint. *Linn.* 15, Nat. Or. *Cruciferæ.* These are insignificant hardy annuals, only fit for botanical collections. Synonyme: 1. *Raphanus pterocarpus—arcuātūs, pterocărpūs* 1.

ENCALȲPTX, *Hedwig.* From *en*, within, and *kalypter*, a covering; the calyptra is unusually large, entirely enclosing the thecæ. *Linn.* 24, Or. 5, Nat. Or. *Musci.* Small, mostly greenish plants, found at all seasons on mountains, moist rocks, &c. Synonyme: 1. *Bryum extinctorium—ciliata, alpina, concolor, rhaptocarpa, streptocarpa, vulgaris* 1.

ENCELĬX, *Adanson.* Derived from *egchelion*, a little eel; in allusion to the appearance of the seeds. *Linn.* 19, Or. 3, Nat. Or. *Compositæ.* Very pretty dwarfish shrubs, growing best in loamy soil, or loam and peat mixed. Cuttings strike with ease in sand, under a glass, if not over-watered. Synonymes: 1. *Pallasia halimifolia.* 2. *P. grandiflora.*

canescēns, 1 . . Orange . 7, G. Ev. S. Peru . . 1786
halimifôliā, 2 . . Yellow . 7, G. Ev. S. Mexico . 1826

**ENCHANTER'S NIGHTSHADE**, see *Circæa*.

**ENCŒLIUM**, *Agardh*. From *en*, within, and *koilos*, hollow; the fronds are tubular and hollow. *Linn.* 24, Or. 7, Nat. Or. *Algæ*. Plants found during the summer and autumn on the sea-coast. Synonyme: 1. *Ulva fistulosa—bullosum*, Lyngbyanum 1.

**ENDIVE**, see *Cichōrium endivia*.

**ENDOCARP**, the inner lining of fruits, which forms the cells.

**ENDOCARPŎN**, *Hedwig*. From *endon*, within, and *karpos*, a fruit; the receptacles are deeply imbedded in the leaf. *Linn.* 24, Or. 8, Nat. Or. *Lichenes*. Green and greyish species, found most plentiful in summer, on rocks. Synonyme: 1. *Lichen fuscellus—complicatum*, Hedwigii *lachnatum*, *leptophyllum*, *miniatum*, *pallidum*, *parasiticum*, *samaragdalum*, *sinopicum*, *tephroïdes* 1, *Weberi*.

**ENERVIS**, having no veins.

**ENGLISH MERCURY**, see *Chenopōdium Bōnus Henrĭcus*.

**ENKIANTHUS**, *Loureiro*. From *enkous*, pregnant, and *anthos*, a flower; the flowers are swollen. *Linn.* 10, Or. 1, Nat. Or. *Ericaceæ*. Most beautiful greenhouse plants, which *Sweet* says, "have been considered difficult to propagate. The difficulty is now removed, as ripened cuttings root readily, planted in pots of sand, and placed under a handglass, without bottom heat. The best soil for them is an equal mixture of sandy loam and peat, and care must be taken not to over-water them, when not in a growing state. When they become pretty large, they are the greatest ornament for the greenhouse, or conservatory."

quinqueflōria . . Pink . 5, G. Ev. S. China . . 1812
reticulātus . . . Pink . 1, G. Ev. S. China . . 1822

**ENODIS**, without knots, smooth.

**ENDOPLEURA**, the inner coat of seeds, under the spermodermis.

**ENSATE**, or **ENSIFORM**, shaped like a sword, with a straight blade.

**ENTADA**, *Adanson*. The name given to one of the species in Malabar. *Linn.* 23, Or. 1, Nat. Or. *Leguminosæ*. Ornamental stove climbers, of easy culture; loam and peat are the best soil for the plants, and sand for cuttings, in which they soon take root, if under a glass, in heat. The natives use the seeds of *E. Purætha* for washing the hair. Synonymes: 1. *Adenanthera scandens*. 2. *Mimosa scandens*. 3. *M. Entada*. 4. *M. polystachya*. 5. *M. scandens*.

Adenanthēra, 1 . White . . S. Ev. Cl. S. Sea Isl. . 1817
Gigalobĭum, 2 . . White . . S. Ev. Cl. W. Ind. . 1819
monostāchya, 3 . White . . S. Ev. Cl. Malabar . 1800
polystāchya, 4 . White . . S. Ev. Cl. W. Ind. . 1816
Purætha, 5 . . White . . S. Ev. Cl. E. Ind. . . 1780

**ENTELEA**, *R. Brown*. From *enteles*; alluding to the stamens being all perfect. *Linn.* 13, Or. 1, Nat. Or. *Tiliaceæ*. These plants are well worth cultivating; they thrive best in garden loam, mixed with a little sandy peat, and are propagated by cuttings in sand.

arborescens . . White . . 5, G. Ev. T. N. Zeal. . 1820
palmāta . . . White . . G. Ev. S.

**EPACRIS**, *Forster*. From *epi*, upon, and *akros*, the top; in reference to the species growing on the tops of hills. *Linn.* 5, Or. 1, Nat. Or. *Epacridaceæ*. Very elegant greenhouse plants, growing in general from two to four feet high; they grow best in a very sandy peat soil, and the rougher and more turfy the soil is, the better the plants will thrive. If the plants are to be turned out of doors from the greenhouse in summer, they ought, just before, to be shifted into fresh pots and soil, otherwise, the roots being so fine, the hot sun against the pots is apt to destroy the points of them, and frequently kills the plant altogether. Cuttings taken from the tips of the young shoots, and planted in sand, under a glass, in autumn, winter, or spring, will root readily; but they will not strike so freely in summer. When rooted, they should be potted singly in small pots, and set in a close frame, and hardened to the air by degrees.

apiculāta . . . . . 5, G. Ev. S. N. Holl. . 1825
campanulāta . . Dp. blush. 4, G. Ev. S. N. Holl. . 1830
  alba . . . . White . . 4, G. Ev. S. N. S. W. . 1830
cerœflōra . . . White . . 4, G. Ev. S. V. D. L. . 1831
exsērta . . . . White . . 4, G. Ev. S. V. D. L. . 1812
grandiflōra . . . Scarlet . 3, G. Ev. S. N. S. W. . 1803

heterōnēma . . . White . 6, G. Ev. S. N. Holl. . 1823
impressa . . . . Crimson . 6, G. Ev. S. N. Holl. . 1824
microphylla . . . . . . 6, G. Ev. S. N. Holl. . 1822
mucronulāta . . Red . . . 5, G. Ev. S. N. Holl. . 1824
nivālis . . . . . White . 2, G. Ev. S. N. Holl. . 1829
obtusifōlia . . . White . 5, G. Ev. S. N. S. W. . 1804
onomæflōra . . . Red . . . 6, G. Ev. S. N. Holl. . 1823
paludōsa . . . . Pa. red . 6, G. Ev. S. N. Holl. . 1825
pulchēlla . . . . Pink . . 5, G. Ev. S. N. S. W. . 1804
purpurascens . . Purple . 2, G. Ev. S. N. S. W. . 1803
  rūbra . . . . Red . . . 2, G. Ev. S. N. S. W. . 1803
ruscifōlia . . . . . . . 5, G. Ev. S. N. Holl. . 1824
spārsa . . . . . White . 5, G. Ev. S. N. Holl. . 1826
variābĭlis . . . . Pink . . 5, G. Ev. S. N. S. W. . 1829

**EPHEDRA**, *Linn.* The Greek name for the herb horsetail; because of the resemblance. *Linn.* 22, Or. 12, Nat. Or. *Gnetaceæ*. This is a curious genus of plants, succeeding in any common garden soil, and young plants are obtained by layering the shoots or branches. "The berries," says Mr. Loudon, "ripen in July and August; they are sweetish, mucous, and leave a little heat in the throat. They are eaten by the Russian peasants, and by the wandering hordes of all Great Tartary."

altissĭma . . . Apetal. . . F. Ev. Tw. Barbary . 1825
distāchya . . . Apetal. 6, H. Ev. S. France . . 1570
monostāchya . . Apetal. 10, H. Ev. S. Siberia . . 1772

**EPHEMERIS**, thing of a day's continuance.

**EPICARP**, the outside covering of a fruit.

**EPIDENDRUM**, *Linn.* From *epi*, upon, and *dendron*, a tree; the plants are usually found growing on the branches of trees. *Linn.* 20, Or. 1, Nat. Or. *Orchidaceæ*. This is a very extensive genus of *epiphytes*, many of which are highly deserving of culture, either for the beauty or delicious fragrance of their flowers. They thrive best when grown in a good strong heat, and a plentiful supply of water; they may be potted, and otherwise treated as the *Stanhopeas*. Synonymes: 1. *Epidendrum ellipticum*. 2. *E. ciliare*. 3. *E. lineatum*. 4. *E. anceps*. 5. *Epithecia glauca*. 6. *Encyclia patens*. 7. *Hormidium uniflorum*. 8. *Encyclia viridiflora*.

semilūm . . . . Lilac . . 2, S. Epi. Para . . 1835
altissĭmum . . . Yel. brn. . S. Epi. Bahamas . 1837
armeniācum . . . Yellow . . S. Epi. Brazil
aromatĭcum . . . Yellow . 5, S. Epi. Guatemala . 1835
aspērum . . . . Yelsh. . . S. Epi. Mexico
aurantiācum . . Orange . . S. Epi. Guatemala . 1835
bicornūtum . . . White . . 4, S. Epi. Jamaica
bifĭdum . . . . . Yel. grn. 7, S. Epi. W. Ind.
Boothiānum . . . Green . . 9, S. Epi. Cuba . . 1835
calamārium . . . Yelsh. grn. 10, S. Epi. Brazil . . 1837
cauliflōrum . . . Yellow . . S. Epi. Rio Jan. . 183—
chloranthum . . Green . . 4, S. Epi. Demerara . 183—
chloroleucum . . Grn. wht. 9, S. Epi. Demerara . 1836
ciliāre . . . . . White . . 7, S. Epi. Martinique . 1790
clavātum . . . . Grn. wht. 7, S. Epi. Cumana . 1834
cochleātum . . . Purple . . 8, S. Epi. W. Ind. . 1799
conopsēum . . . Green . . . S. Epi. Florida
crassifōlium, 1 . Pink . . . 4, S. Epi. St. Vincent
cucullātum . . . White . . . S. Epi. Para
cuspidātum, 2 . White . . 6, S. Epi. Mexico . 1808
dichotōmum . . Green . . . S. Epi. Demerara . 1836
diffūsum . . . . Green . . 4, S. Epi. Jamaica . 1816
ellipticum . . . Rose . . . 4, S. Epi. Brazil . . 1834
elongātum . . . Red . . . 5, S. Epi. W. Ind. . 1798
equitans . . . . Brown . . . S. Epi. Vera Cruz . 1836
floribundum . . Grn. blue 10, S. Epi. Mexico
frāgrans, 3 . . . White . . 9, S. Epi. Jamaica . 1778
fucātum . . . . Grn. blue 7, S. Epi. Havannah . 1835
fuscātum, 4 . . . Green . . 4, S. Epi. Jamaica . 1790
glaucum, 5 . . . Grn. purp. 6, S. Epi. Mexico . 1837
gracĭle . . . . . Red grn. . S. Epi. Bahamas
Harrisōniæ . . . Grnh. wht. . S. Epi. Brazil
ionosmum . . . Green . . . S. Epi. Essequibo
lacērum . . . . Pa. pink 11, S. Epi. Havannah . 1835
lividum . . . . Purple . . S. Epi. Columbia
longicōllis . . . Yellow . . S. Epi. Demerara . 1836
macrochīlum . . Brn. wht. 7, S. Epi. Mexico . 1836
noctūrnum . . . White . . 9, S. Epi. Martinique . 1836
  latifōlium . . . Yel. wht. 10, S. Epi. W. Ind. . 1836
nūtans . . . . . Green . . 7, S. Epi. Jamaica . 1793
ochracēum . . . Yellow . 7, S. Epi. Guatemala . 1835
odoratissĭmum, 6 Dingy grn. 8, S. Epi. Rio Jan. . 1827
oncidioïdes . . . Yel. brn. 6, S. Epi. S. Amer.
pachyanthum . . Green . . . S. Epi. Guiana . 1827
papiliōrum . . . Grn. wht. 6, S. Epi. Mexico . 1837
pastōris . . . . Olive . . . S. Epi. Mexico . 1837
pātens . . . . . White . 10, S. Epi. St. Vincent
pictum . . . . . Yel. crims. . S. Epi. Demerara
primulīnum . . Yel. brn. . 6, S. Epi. Bahamas . 1837
pygmæum . . . Wht. rose 11, S. Epi. Brazil . 1830
rhizophōrum . . . . . . S. Epi. Guatemala . 1836
rigĭdum . . . . . Yelsh. wht. 6, S. Epi. Jamaica . 1836

| | | | | | | |
|---|---|---|---|---|---|---|
| Schomburgkii | . | Scarlet | . . | 8. Epl. | Guiana | . | 1837 |
| aceundum | . | Red | . . | 9, 8. Epi. | W. Ind. | . | 1798 |
| selligerum | . . | | | 8. Epi. | Mexico | . | 1836 |
| Skinnerl | . | Grn. wht. | 7, 8. Epi. | Comana | . | 1834 |
| smaragdinum | . | Green | . | 3, 8. Epi. | Demerara | . | 183-. |
| stenopetalum | . | Rose | . | 3, 8. Epi. | Jamaica | . |
| tessellatum | . | Yel. brn. | 6, 8. Epi. | Guatemala. | 1836 |
| tibicinis | . . | Rose | . . | 8. Epi. | Honduras | . | 1836 |
| tridactylum | . | Brn. yel. | . | 5, 8. Epi. | Brazil | . | 183-. |
| umbellatum | . | Green | . | 1, 8. Epi. | Jamaica | . | 1793 |
| uniflorum, 7 | . | Yelsh. grn. | . | 8. Epi. | Mexico | . | 1837 |
| variegatum | . | Grn. wht. | . | 1, 8. Epi. | Rio Jan. | . | 1829 |
| coriaceum | . | Grn. purp. | . | 8. Epi. | Demerara |
| varicosum | . | Green | .' | 8. Epi. | Guatemala. | 1836 |
| verrucosum | . | Grn. brn. | . | 8. Epi. | Jamaica | . | 1825 |
| vesicatum | . | White | . . | 8. Epi. | Brazil | . |
| virescens | . | Green | . . | 7, 8. Epi. | Dominica | . |
| viridiflorum. 8 | . | Green | . | 2, 8. Epi. | Brazil | . |

**EPIDERMIS,** the outer skin of a plant.

**EPIGÆA,** *Linn.* From *epi*, upon, and *gaia*, the earth; alluding to the trailing habit of the plant. *Linn.* 10, Or. 1, Nat. Or. *Ericaceæ.* These are very pretty trailing plants, and to grow well, they require a sandy peat soil, mixed with a very little loam, and are most readily increased from layers.

| | | | | | | |
|---|---|---|---|---|---|---|
| repens | . . . | White | . | 7, H. Ev. Tr. | N. Amer. | . | 1736 |
| rubicunda | . . | Red | . | 3, H. Ev. Tr. | | . | 1836 |

**EPILOBIUM,** *Linn.* From *epi*, upon, and *lobos*, a lobe; the flowers have the appearance of being seated on the top of the pod. *Linn.* 8, Or. 1, Nat. Or. *Onagraceæ.* Many of the species of this genus are very ornamental, as *E. angustifolium*, while a few others, such as *E. montanum*, are mere weeds. They all grow well in common soil, and are either increased by seeds, or by dividing the roots. *Synonymes:* 1. *E. Halleri.* 2. *E. molle.* 3. *E. squamatum.*

| | | | | | | |
|---|---|---|---|---|---|---|
| alpestre | . . . | Purple | . | 6, H. Her. | P. Switzerl. | . | 1820 |
| angustifolium | . | Purple | . | 7, H. Her. | P. Britain | . |
| album | . . | White | . | 7, H. Her. | P. Britain | . |
| angustissimum | . | Purple | . | 7, H. Her. | P. Alps Eur. | . | 1775 |
| coloratum | . | Purple | . | 6, H. Her. | P. N. Amer. | . | 1805 |
| crassifolium | . | Red | . | 6, H. Her. | P. | . | 1829 |
| dahuricum | . . | White | . | 6, H. | A. Dahuria | . | 1822 |
| Dodonæi, 1 | . | Purple | . | 7, H. Her. | P. France | . | 1700 |
| hirsutum | . | Purple | . | 7, H. Aq. | P. Britain | . |
| variegatum | . | Rosy | . | 6, H. Her. | P. England | . |
| lanceolatum | . | Purple | . | 7, H. Her. | P. Italy | . | 1810 |
| latifolium | . | Red | . | 6, H. Her. | P. N. Eur. | . | 1779 |
| obscurum | . | Purple | . | 7, H. Her. | P. Europe | . | 1815 |
| parviflorum, 2 | . | Purple | . | 7, H. Her. | P. Britain | . |
| rosmarinifolium, 3 | Purple | . | 6, H. Her. | P. N. Amer. | . | 1800 |
| epictum | . | Purple | . | 6, H. Her. | P. N. Amer. | . |
| strictum | . | Purple | . | 7, H. Her. | P. Pennsyl. | . | 1817 |
| tomentosum | . | Purple | . | 6, H. Her. | P. Asia | . | 1818 |
| villosum | . | Purple | . | 7, G. Her. | P. C. G. H. | . | 1799 |

*alpinum, alsinifolium, montanum, palustre, roseum, tetragonum.*

**EPIMEDIUM,** *Linn.* From *epi*, upon, and Media; the plants were said to grow in Media. *Linn.* 4, Or. 1, Nat. Or. *Berberaceæ.* Elegant little plants, succeeding best in sandy peat soil, and may be increased by dividing the roots. *E. grandiflorum* requires to be grown in a cold frame, with the same kind of soil as recommended for the others.

| | | | | | | |
|---|---|---|---|---|---|---|
| alpinum | . . | Blood | . | 5, H. De. Cr. | England | . |
| diphyllum | . | Red | . | 6, H. Her. | P. Japan | . | 1830 |
| grandiflorum | . | White | . | 4, F. Her. | P. Japan | . | 1836 |
| hexandrum | . | Lilac | . | 6, H. Her. | P. N. Amer. | . | 1827 |
| violaceum | . | Wht. vio. | . | 4, H. Her. | P. Japan | . | 1837 |

**EPIPACTIS,** *Haller.* From *epipegnus*, to coagulate; alluding to its supposed effect on milk. *Linn.* 20, Or. 1, Nat. Or. *Orchidaceæ.* Pretty plants, thriving well in the flower-border, or in pots, in a mixture of peat and loam, very sparingly watered when in a torpid state. They are increased by divisions of the roots.

| | | | | | |
|---|---|---|---|---|---|
| latifolia | . . | Purple | . | 7, H. Ter. | Britain | . |
| palustris | . . | Purple | . | 7, H. Ter. | Britain | . |
| purpurata | . | Purple | . | 6, H. Ter. | England | . |

**EPIPHYLLOUS,** growing upon the leaves.

**EPIPHYLLUM,** *Haworth.* From *epi*, upon, and *phyllon*, a leaf; alluding to the flowers growing from the flat branches, which appear like leaves. *Linn.* 12, Or. 1, Nat. Or. *Cactaceæ.* These splendid-flowering plants are the pride of every well-furnished garden. Their culture and propagation are the same as that recommended for *Cereus*, and the other genera of this order. *Synonymes:* 1. *Cactus phyllanthus.* 2.

[ 119 ]

*C. phyllanthoides.* 3. *C. speciosa, elegans.* 4. *C. truncata.*

| | | | | | | |
|---|---|---|---|---|---|---|
| Ackermanni | . | Scarlet | . | 6, S. Ev. S. | Mexico | . | 1829 |
| alatum | . . | White | . | 6, S. Ev. S. | N. Amer. | . | 1810 |
| coccineum | . | Scarlet | . | 6, S. Ev. S. | Brazil | . | 1828 |
| crispatum | . . | | | 8, S. Ev. S. | Brazil | . | 1829 |
| Hookeri, 1 | . | White | . | 6, S. Ev. S. | S. Amer. | . |
| phyllanthoides, 2 | . | Pa. red | . | 8, S. Ev. S. | Jamaica | . | 1817 |
| Phyllanthus | . | White | . | 6, S. Ev. S. | S. Amer. | . | 1810 |
| ramulosum | . . | | | 8, S. Ev. S. | | . | 1835 |
| rhombeum | . . | | | 8, S. Ev. S. | | . | 1835 |
| speciosum, 3 | . | Red | . | 6, S. Ev. S. | Brazil | . | 1810 |
| truncatum, 4 | . | Pink | . | 8, S. Ev. S. | Brazil | . | 1818 |
| coccineum | . | Scarlet | . | 6, S. Ev. S. | | . | 1818 |

**EPIPHYTES,** plants which grow upon other plants without deriving any nutriment from them.

**EPISTOMEOUS,** spigot-shaped.

**EQUAL,** applied to petals and sepals when they are equal in size and shape with each other.

**EQUISETIS,** fancied resemblance to a horse's head.

**EQUIDISTANT,** equally distant.

**EQUILATERAL,** having equal sides.

**EQUISETUM,** *Linn.* From *equus*, a horse, and *seta*, hair; in allusion to the fine hair-like branches. *Linn.* 24, Or. 2, Nat. Or. *Equisetaceæ.* Although looked upon as mere weeds, they have a very interesting aspect when seen growing in their natural situations; they are found in boggy places, and multiplied by divisions—*arvense, Drummondii, fluviatile, hyemale, limosum, palustre, pratense, scirpoides, sylvaticum, umbrosum, variegatum.*

**EQUITANT,** a mode of arrangement of leaves with respect to each other, in which the sides or edges alternately overlap each other.

**ERAGROSTIS,** *Beauvois.* From *eros*, love, and *agrostis*, grass; in allusion to the beautiful dancing spikelets; whence the English name, Love Grass. *Linn.* 3, Or. 2, Nat. Or. *Gramineæ.* Pretty species of grass, growing about a foot high, in any common soil. *Synonymes:* 1. *Poa cynosuroides.* 2. *P. mexicana.* 3. *P. Eragrostis.*

| | | | | | |
|---|---|---|---|---|---|
| ægyptiaca | . . | Apetal | . | 7, Grass. | Egypt | . | 1812 |
| capillaris | . . | Apetal | . | 7, Grass. | N. Amer. | . | 1819 |
| cynosuroides, 1 | . | Apetal | . | 7, Grass. | Egypt | . | 1824 |
| decipiens | . . | Apetal | . | 7, Grass. | | . | 1819 |
| mexicana, 2 | . | Apetal | . | 7, Grass. | | . | 1785 |
| pilosa | . . | Apetal | . | 7, Grass. | Italy | . | 1804 |
| pomformis, 3 | . | Apetal | . | 7, Grass. | Greece | . | 1699 |
| punctata | . . | Apetal | . | 7, Grass. | Malabar. | . | 1820 |
| purpurascens | . | Apetal | . | 7, Grass. | | . | 1817 |
| tenella | . . | Apetal | . | 7, Grass. | E. Ind. | . | 1781 |
| tephrosanthes | . | Apetal | . | 7, Grass. | Martinique | . | 1818 |
| verticillata | . | Apetal | . | 7, Grass. | S. Eur. | . | 1820 |

**ERANTHEMUM,** *R. Brown.* From *ear*, spring, and *anthos*, a flower; applied by the ancients to their *Anthemis.* *Linn.* 2, Or. 1, Nat. Or. *Acanthaceæ.* The species of this genus are very pretty, and succeed well in sandy peat soil, and cuttings take readily in sand, under a glass, in heat.

| | | | | | |
|---|---|---|---|---|---|
| ambiguum | . . | Red | . | 7, S. Ev. S. | | . | 1821 |
| bicolor | . . | Wht. red | 7, S. Ev. S. | Lucena | . | 1802 |
| capense | . . | Purple | . | 6, G. Ev. S. | E. Ind. | . | 1818 |
| crenulatum | . | Lilac | . | 10, S. Ev. S. | Nepal | . | 1824 |
| elegans | . . | Scarlet | . | 6, S. Ev. S. | Guinea | . | 1824 |
| facundum | . | Lilac | . | 6, S. Ev. S. | Brazil | . | 1829 |
| pulchellum | . | Blue | . | 4, S. Ev. S. | E. Ind. | . | 1796 |
| roseum | . . | Red | . | 5, S. Ev. S. | E. Ind. | . | 1820 |
| epinosum | . . | | | 7, S. Ev. S. | W. Ind. | . | 1733 |
| strictum | . . | Purple | . | 4, S. Ev. S. | Nepal | . | 1818 |
| variable | . | Purple | . | 6, G. Ev. S. | N. Holl. | . | 1820 |

**ERANTHIS,** *Salisbury.* From *erao*, to love, and *anthos*, a flower; the bright yellow flowers are produced in winter. *Linn.* 13, Or. 6, Nat. Or. *Ranunculaceæ.* The species are dwarf, ornamental plants, of easy culture. *Synonyme:* 1. *Helleborus hyemalis.*

| | | | | | |
|---|---|---|---|---|---|
| hyemalis, 1 | . | Yellow | . | 2, H. Tu. | P. Italy | . | 1596 |
| sibirica | . | Yellow | . | 3, H. Tu. | P. Siberia | . | 1826 |

**ERECTLY-SPREADING,** between erect and spreading.

**EREMURUS,** *Bieberstein.* From *eremos*, solitary, and *oura*, tail; spikes solitary. *Linn.* 6, Or. 1, Nat. Or. *Liliaceæ.* An ornamental species; for culture, &c., see *Asphodelus.* *Synonyme:* 1. *Asphodelus altaicus.*

| | | | | | |
|---|---|---|---|---|---|
| spectabilis | . . | Yellow | . | 5, H. Her. | P. Siberia | . | 1800 |

**ERIA,** *Lindley.* From *erion*, wool; in allusion to the woolliness of the flower. *Linn.* 20, Or. 1, Nat. Or. *Orchidaceæ.* The species of this genus are very pretty when in flower. They require the same treatment as the *Stanhopeas*, &c. *Synonymes*: 1. *E. pubescens*.

| | | | | |
|---|---|---|---|---|
| callòsa | . . . | | S. Epi. Chira | 1837 |
| clavàtà | . . . | White | S. Epi. Chira | 1837 |
| clavicaùlis | . . . | Wht. yel. | S. Epi. Chira | 1837 |
| densiflòra | . . . | Wht. yel. | S. Epi. Chira | 1837 |
| excavàtà | . . . | | S. Epi. Nepal | |
| flàvà, l | . . . | Yellow | 2, S. Epi. Nepal | 1830 |
| longicaùlis | . . . | White | S. Epi. Chira | 1837 |
| maculàtà | . . . | Grsh. yel. | S. Epi. E. Ind. | |
| pùmilà | . . . | Pink | S. Epi. E. Ind. | |
| pùsilla | . . . | | S. Epi. Chara | 1837 |
| ròsea | . . . | Ro. wht. | S. Epi. China | 1824 |
| mollìsà | . . . | Yelsh. | 2, S. Epi. Java | |

**ERIÀNTHUS**, *R. Brown*. From *erion*, wool, and *achne*, a glume; the glumes are woolly. *Linn.* 3, *Or.* 2, *Nat. Or. Gramineæ*. A curious species of grass, succeeding in any common soil. *Synonyme*: 1. *Aira truncata*.

| | | | | |
|---|---|---|---|---|
| obtusà, l | . . . | Apetal | 5, Gram. N. Amer. | 1819 |

**ERIÀNTHUS**, *Richard*. From *erica*, wool, and *anthos*, a flower. *Linn.* 3, *Or.* 3, *Nat. Or. Gramineæ*. These pretty plants succeed best in loam, mixed with a little peat; they are increased by divisions. *Synonymes*: 1. *Saccharum brevibarbe*. 2. *S. giganteum*.

| | | | | |
|---|---|---|---|---|
| brevibarbis, l | . . . | Apetal | 7, Gram. N. Amer. | 1822 |
| saccharoìdes, 2 | . . . | Apetal | 7, Gram. N. Amer. | 1822 |

**ERÌCA**, *Linn.* The *Erica* of Pliny, which is derived from *erice* or *ereice*, to break; some of the species are supposed to have the quality of breaking stone in the bladder. *Linn.* 8, *Or.* 1, *Nat. Or. Ericaceæ*. This is a genus comprising a great number of very beautiful and interesting plants, but not so much cultivated as they ought to be, on account of the supposed difficulty in managing and propagating them; but the greatest difficulty lies in getting proper soil for them, without which they will not thrive. Sweet says, the free-growing kinds thrive best in good black peat, and like largish pots to grow in. The dwarf and hard-wooded kinds must have a very sandy peat, and smaller pots, well drained with potsherds, over which a few bits of rough turfy peat should be placed; they also require less water than the free-growing kinds, as they grow chiefly at the Cape on the tops and sides of mountains, and in the crevices of rocks, and such like situations, chiefly in very sandy soil, and but little of it; they all require a good deal of air, and must not be crowded too thick together. Too much fire heat in winter will hurt them as much as anything, as they only require to be kept from frost; most of the kinds might be preserved through the winter in frames: the only difficulty is to keep the damp from them. Cuttings of most species strike readily, by taking off the very tender tops of the shoots, and planting them in sand, under glasses. The strong growing kinds require the cuttings to be rather larger than the others, and some of the stunted growing kinds should be kept in the stove a little while when they begin to grow, to draw them to a sufficient length of young wood, or cuttings cannot be procured; as soon as rooted, they should be potted off singly into small pots, and placed in a close frame, and hardened by degrees. The hardy sorts require to be grown in the same kind of soil; cuttings planted in sand, under a glass, will root freely; they may also be increased by layers. *Synonymes*: 1. *Erica cylindrica*. 2. *E. amœna*. 3. *E. florida*. 4. *E. aristata minor*. 5. *E. Linnæana superba*. 6. *E. pulchella*. 7. *E. quadriflora*. 8. *E. cuniculata minor*. 9. *E. calycina*. 10. *E. eriocephala*. 11. *E. inaperta*. 12. *E. sessiliflora*. 13. *E. calycina*. 14. *E. mirabilia*. 15. *E. rupestris*. 16. *E. transparens*. 17. *E. articulata*. 18. *E. peltata*. 19. *E. octophylla, coronata*. 20. *E. Walkeriana*. 21. *E. glandulosa*. 22. *E. divaricata*. 23. *E. Petiveriana*. 24. *E. incarnata*. 25. *E. pubescens*. 26. *E. gracilis*. 27. *E. sordida*. 28. *E. Linnæana perspicua*. 29. *E. pinea*. 30. *E. pubescens*. 31. *E. glomerata*. 32. *E. Patersoniana coccinea*. 33. *E. ciliata*. 34. *E. pellucida rubra*. 35. *E. calyculata*. 36. *E. pinifolia*. 37. *E. cupressina*. 38. *E. nutans*. 39. *E. pulchella*. 40. *E. peduncularis*. 41. *E. tricolor*. 42. *E. axillaris*. 43. *E. pubescens*. 44. *E. pugionifolia*. 45. *E. ferox*. 46. *E. pubescens minima*. 47. *E. pedunculata*. 48. *E. Cassonii*. 49. *E. cernua*. 50. *Calluna vulgaris*.

| | | | | | |
|---|---|---|---|---|---|
| absinthoìdes | . . | Purple | 5, G. Ev. S | C. G. H. | 1792 |
| actùà | . . | Purple | 5, G. Ev. S | C. G. H. | 1822 |
| acuminàtà | . . | Red | 6, G. Ev. S | C. G. H. | 1800 |
| pallìdà | . . | Pa. red | 6, G. Ev. S | C. G. H. | 1830 |
| acùtà | . . | Red | 6, G. Ev. S | C. G. H. | 1799 |
| acutàngùlà | . . | White | 4, G. Ev. S | C. G. H. | 1810 |
| adenophorà | . . | White | 6, G. Ev. S | C. G. H. | 1810 |
| aggregàtà | . . | Purple | 7, G. Ev. S | C. G. H. | 1830 |
| àlbà | . . | White | 7, G. Ev. S | C. G. H. | 1822 |
| Aitonìànà | . . | Wht. pur. | 8, G. Ev. S | C. G. H. | 1790 |
| albàns | . . | White | 7, G. Ev. S | C. G. H. | 1789 |
| àlbìdà | . . | White | 7, G. Ev. S | C. G. H. | 1825 |
| aldepurpùròìdes | . . | Pa. pur. | 5, G. Ev. S | C. G. H. | 1810 |
| ambìguà, l | . . | Purple | 5, G. Ev. S | C. G. H. | 1798 |
| ambìguà, 2 | . . | Purple | 6, G. Ev. S | C. G. H. | 1795 |
| ampullàceà | . . | Wht. red | 6, G. Ev. S | C. G. H. | 1790 |
| ampullaceòìdes | . . | Red yel. | 6, G. Ev. S | C. G. H. | 1800 |
| andromedæflorà | . . | Pink | 5, G. Ev. S | C. G. H. | 1802 |
| anthèrà, 3 | . . | Red | 6, G. Ev. S | C. G. H. | 1800 |
| anthìnà | . . | Red | 6, G. Ev. S | C. G. H. | 1811 |
| apèrtà | . . | | 4, G. Ev. S | C. G. H. | 1830 |
| Aphànà | . . | | 5, G. Ev. S | C. G. H. | 1830 |
| approximàtà | . . | Red | 6, G. Ev. S | C. G. H. | 1823 |
| arbòreà | . . | White | 4, F. Ev. S | Eur. | 1658 |
| squarròsà | . . | White | 4, F. Ev. S | Europe | 1800 |
| stylòsà | . . | White | 4, F. Ev. S | Eur. | 1658 |
| arbùscùlà | . . | Red | 5, G. Ev. S | C. G. H. | 1810 |
| Archeriànà | . . | Dk. scar. | 9, G. Ev. S | C. G. H. | 1796 |
| aretùsà | . . | | 7, G. Ev. S | C. G. H. | 1800 |
| àrdens | . . | Scarlet | 5, G. Ev. S | C. G. H. | 1800 |
| argentiflòrà | . . | White | 6, G. Ev. S | C. G. H. | 1800 |
| aristàtà | . . | Dk. pur. wht. | 6, G. Ev. S | C. G. H. | 1801 |
| aristèlà | . . | Red | 6, G. Ev. S | C. G. H. | 1806 |
| armàtà | . . | | 6, G. Ev. S | C. G. H. | 1816 |
| àsperà | . . | Yellow | 5, G. Ev. S | C. G. H. | 1802 |
| assùrgens | . . | White | 5, G. Ev. S | C. G. H. | 1821 |
| auriculàris | . . | Purple | 6, G. Ev. S | C. G. H. | 1800 |
| aùreà | . . | Orange | 8, G. Ev. S | C. G. H. | 1799 |
| australis | . . | Purple | 5, H. Ev. S | Spain | 1769 |
| axillàris | . . | Pink | 6, G. Ev. S | C. G. H. | 1798 |
| bàccans | . . | Purple | 5, G. Ev. S | C. G. H. | 1774 |
| Bandoniànà | . . | Purple | 7, G. Ev. S | C. G. H. | 1810 |
| Banksiànà | . . | Wht. pur. | 4, G. Ev. S | C. G. H. | 1787 |
| àlbà | . . | White | 6, G. Ev. S | C. G. H. | 1812 |
| purpùreà | . . | Purple | 6, G. Ev. S | C. G. H. | 1800 |
| répens | . . | Red | 6, G. Ev. S | C. G. H. | 1800 |
| barbàtà | . . | White | 7, G. Ev. S | C. G. H. | 1799 |
| màjor | . . | Red | 6, G. Ev. S | C. G. H. | 1800 |
| minor | . . | Red | 6, G. Ev. S | C. G. H. | 1800 |
| Beaumontiànà | . . | Purple | 6, G. Ev. S | C. G. H. | 1830 |
| Bedfordiànà, 5 | . . | Red pur. | 4, G. Ev. S | C. G. H. | 1800 |
| bèlla, 6 | . . | Red | 5, G. Ev. S | C. G. H. | 1800 |
| Bergiànà, 7 | . . | Purple | 6, G. Ev. S | C. G. H. | 1787 |
| bicòlor | . . | Ora. red | 7, G. Ev. S | C. G. H. | 1790 |
| bìflòrà | . . | White | 5, G. Ev. S | C. G. H. | 1819 |
| blànda | . . | Pur. oran. | 5, G. Ev. S | C. G. H. | 1798 |
| Blandfordiànà | . . | Yellow | 5, G. Ev. S | C. G. H. | 1803 |
| fùscà | . . | Dk. yel. | 5, G. Ev. S | C. G. H. | 1803 |
| Bonplandiànà | . . | Pa. yel. | 7, G. Ev. S | C. G. H. | 1818 |
| borbonìæfòlià | . . | | 5, G. Ev. S | C. G. H. | 1816 |
| Bowieànà | . . | White | 10, G. Ev. S | C. G. H. | 1822 |
| brachiàlis | . . | | 7, G. Ev. S | C. G. H. | 1792 |
| bracteàtà | . . | Red | 6, G. Ev. S | C. G. H. | 1800 |
| bracteolàris | . . | Red | 5, G. Ev. S | C. G. H. | 1800 |
| brevifòlià | . . | | 4, G. Ev. S | C. G. H. | 1800 |
| Breadleyànà | . . | Red | | G. Ev. S | C. G. H. | 1800 |
| brumàlis | . . | White | 5, G. Ev. S | C. G. H. | 1774 |
| bryanthà | . . | White | 6, G. Ev. S | C. G. H. | 1812 |
| buccinæfòrmis | . . | Pink | 6, G. Ev. S | C. G. H. | 1818 |
| cæsià | . . | Red | 6, G. Ev. S | C. G. H. | 1800 |
| càffrà | . . | White | 5, G. Ev. S | C. G. H. | 1802 |
| spicàtà | . . | White | 9, G. Ev. S | C. G. H. | 1800 |
| callòsa, 8 | . . | Red | 6, G. Ev. S | C. G. H. | 1822 |
| calcòttìànà | . . | Flesh | 5, G. Ev. S | Eng. hyb. | 1810 |
| calycìnà | . . | Purple | 6, G. Ev. S | C. G. H. | 1799 |
| calycinoìdes, 9 | . . | Red pur. | 8, G. Ev. S | C. G. H. | 1789 |
| calyculàtà | . . | Purple | 6, G. Ev. S | C. G. H. | 1800 |
| campanulàtà | . . | Yellow | 5, G. Ev. S | C. G. H. | 1791 |
| canalicùlàtà | . . | Red | 5, G. Ev. S | C. G. H. | 1799 |
| canèscens, 10 | . . | Pink | 5, G. Ev. S | C. G. H. | 1790 |
| cantharifòrmis | . . | White | 6, G. Ev. S | C. G. H. | 1829 |
| càpax | . . | | 6, G. Ev. S | C. G. H. | 1806 |
| capitàtà | . . | Yellow | 6, G. Ev. S | C. G. H. | 1774 |
| cardùifòlià | . . | Purple | 7, G. Ev. S | C. G. H. | 1806 |
| carinàtà | . . | Purple | 5, G. Ev. S | C. G. H. | 1830 |
| carìnùlà | . . | Purple | 8, G. Ev. S | C. G. H. | 1818 |
| càrneà | . . | Pa. pur. | 2, H. Ev. S | Germany | 1763 |
| herbàceà | . . | Pink | 2, H. Ev. S | Germany | |
| carneòlà | . . | Pink | 7, G. Ev. S | C. G. H. | 1810 |
| carneolàtà | . . | Red pur. | 8, G. Ev. S | C. G. H. | 1810 |
| catervæfòlià | . . | Red | 5, G. Ev. S | C. G. H. | 1790 |
| Celsiànà | . . | Or. rose | 5, G. Ev. S | C. G. H. | 1810 |
| cephalòtes | . . | Purple | 5, G. Ev. S | C. G. H. | 1812 |
| cerinthoìdes | . . | Dk. scar. | 9, G. Ev. S | C. G. H. | 1774 |
| màjor | . . | Scarlet | 5, G. Ev. S | C. G. H. | 1800 |
| nàná | . . | Scarlet | 5, G. Ev. S | C. G. H. | 1800 |
| cèrnùà | . . | Purple | 10, G. Ev. S | C. G. H. | 1791 |
| cerviciflòrà, 11 | . . | | 5, G. Ev. S | C. G. H. | 1810 |
| chlamydiflòrà | . . | Purple | 8, G. Ev. S | C. G. H. | 1801 |

| Name | Colour | | Date |
|---|---|---|---|
| chlorōlōmä . | Crim. grn. | 11, G. Ev. S. C. G. H. | |
| ciliāris . | Purple . | 8, H. Ev. S. Cornwall | |
| ciliciflōrā . | | 6, G. Ev. S. C. G. H. | 1800 |
| cinerāscēns | Purple . | 5, G. Ev. S. C. G. H. | 1810 |
| cinerēa . | Purple | 8, H. Ev. S. Britain | |
| alba . | White . | 8, H. Ev. S. Britain | |
| atropurpūrēā | Dk. pur. | 8, H. Ev. S. Britain | |
| cārnēā | Flesh | 8, H. Ev. S. Britain | |
| prolifērā . | Purple | 7, H. Ev. S. Britain | |
| rūbrā | Red | 8, H. Ev. S. Britain | |
| strictā | Purple | 7, H. Ev. S. Britain | |
| cistifoliā . | White . | 5, G. Ev. S. C. G. H. | 1823 |
| clavātā . | Green . | 7, G. Ev. S. C. G. H. | 1800 |
| clavaeflōrā, 12 . | Green . | G. Ev. S. C. G. H. | 1799 |
| Cliffordiānā | White . | 4, G. Ev. S. C. G. H. | 1812 |
| Clintōniā . | | 7, G. Ev. S. C. G. H. | 1816 |
| coarctātā | Purple . | 7, G. Ev. S. C. G. H. | 1801 |
| coccinēā | Scarlet | G. Ev. S. C. G. H. | 1788 |
| codonōdēs . | Pa. rose | H. Ev. S. | |
| colōrāns | Wht. red | 5, G. Ev. S. C. G. H. | 1817 |
| comōsā . | Red . | 6, G. Ev. S. C. G. H. | 1787 |
| alba . | White . | 6, G. Ev. S. C. G. H. | 1787 |
| rūbra . | Red | 6, G. Ev. S. C. G. H. | 1787 |
| complanātā | Yellow | 6, G. Ev. S. C. G. H. | 1820 |
| Comptoniānā | Purple . | 6, G. Ev. S. C. G. H. | 1802 |
| cōncāvā . | Pa. pur. | 4, G. Ev. S. C. G. H. | 1773 |
| concinnā . | Flesh . | 9, G. Ev. S. C. G. H. | 1820 |
| cōncōlōr . | | 6, G. Ev. S. C. G. H. | 1800 |
| confērtā | White . | 6, G. Ev. S. C. G. H. | 1818 |
| confertiflōrā | White . | 5, G. Ev. S. C. G. H. | |
| confertifoliā . | | 5, G. Ev. S. C. G. H. | |
| congēstā | White . | 6, G. Ev. S. C. G. H. | 1820 |
| cōnicā | Purple . | 6, G. Ev. S. C. G. H. | 1820 |
| cōnspicūā | Dk. yel. | 7, G. Ev. S. C. G. H. | 1774 |
| constāntiā | Purple . | 6, G. Ev. S. C. G. H. | 1810 |
| cordātā | White . | 5, G. Ev. S. C. G. H. | 1799 |
| corifoliā, 13 . | Pa. pur. | 10, G. Ev. S. C. G. H. | 1774 |
| corydalis . | | 7, G. Ev. S. C. G. H. | |
| costātā . | Pink . | 4, G. Ev. S. C. G. H. | 1795 |
| supērbā . | Scarlet | 5, G. Ev. S. C. G. H. | |
| Coventryānā | Pink . | 5, G. Ev. S. C. G. H. | 1801 |
| cristaeflōrā | Pa. pur. | G. Ev. S. C. G. H. | 1803 |
| cristāta | Red | 6, G. Ev. S. C. G. H. | 1826 |
| croceātā . | Purple . | 6, G. Ev. S. C. G. H. | |
| cruciformis . | Purple | 8, G. Ev. S. C. G. H. | 1800 |
| cruēntā . | Dk. pur. | 7, G. Ev. S. C. G. H. | 1774 |
| cūbicā . | Purple | 6, G. Ev. S. C. G. H. | 1790 |
| majōr | Purple | 6, G. Ev. S. C. G. H. | 1800 |
| cumulaeflōrā | Purple . | 6, G. Ev. S. C. G. H. | 1801 |
| curviflōrā | Yellow | 8, G. Ev. S. C. G. H. | 1774 |
| rubra . | Red | 8, G. Ev. S. C. G. H. | 1800 |
| Cushiniānā | | 9, G. Ev. S. C. G. H. | 1816 |
| cuspidigērā | | 3, G. Ev. S. C. G. H. | 1796 |
| cylindricā | White . | 6, G. Ev. S. C. G. H. | 1823 |
| cyrillaeflōrā | | 7, G. Ev. S. C. G. H. | 1800 |
| daphnaeflōrā | Pa. pur. | 4, G. Ev. S. C. G. H. | 1791 |
| daphnoidēs, 14 | White . | 5, G. Ev. S. C. G. H. | 1800 |
| declinātā | Purple | 9, G. Ev. S. C. G. H. | 1820 |
| decōrāns | Purple | 6, G. Ev. S. C. G. H. | 1790 |
| decōrā | White . | 7, G. Ev. S. C. G. H. | 1810 |
| deflēxā | Grn. yel. | 3, G. Ev. S. C. G. H. | 1818 |
| dēnsā | Red | 6, G. Ev. S. C. G. H. | 1810 |
| densiflōrā | Purple | 6, G. Ev. S. C. G. H. | 1811 |
| denticulātā | Purple | 4, G. Ev. S. C. G. H. | 1821 |
| deprēssā, 15 | Yellow | 7, G. Ev. S. C. G. H. | 1789 |
| dianthiflōrā | Purple | 6, G. Ev. S. C. G. H. | 1796 |
| diaphānā, 16 | Purple | 6, G. Ev. S. C. G. H. | 1796 |
| dichotōmā | Rose | 6, G. Ev. S. C. G. H. | 1827 |
| discolōr | Red grn. | 7, G. Ev. S. C. G. H. | 1788 |
| Dicksoniā | White . | 6, G. Ev. S. C. G. H. | 1809 |
| alba | White . | 6, G. Ev. S. C. G. H. | 1809 |
| rūbra | Red | 5, G. Ev. S. C. G. H. | 1809 |
| diosmaeflōrā | | 5, G. Ev. S. C. G. H. | 1792 |
| dioicflōrā | | 7, G. Ev. S. C. G. H. | 1794 |
| doliiformis . | | 7, G. Ev. S. C. G. H. | 1796 |
| Doniānā | | 6, G. Ev. S. C. G. H. | 1812 |
| dumōsā | Purple | 6, G. Ev. S. C. G. H. | 1812 |
| echiiflōrā | Scarlet | 4, G. Ev. S. C. G. H. | 1796 |
| coccinēā | Scarlet | 4, G. Ev. S. C. G. H. | 1812 |
| purpūrā | Purple | 4, G. Ev. S. C. G. H. | 1809 |
| supērbā | Scarlet | 4, G. Ev. S. C. G. H. | 1800 |
| elātā | Orange | 8, G. Ev. S. C. G. H. | 1790 |
| elegāns | Green | 8, G. Ev. S. C. G. H. | 1799 |
| elongātā | White . | 5, G. Ev. S. C. G. H. | 1810 |
| emarginātā | Purple | 6, G. Ev. S. C. G. H. | 1802 |
| empetrifoliā | | 8, G. Ev. S. C. G. H. | 1798 |
| empetrifoliā | Yellow | 6, G. Ev. S. C. G. H. | 1774 |
| empetroidēs | Lgt. flesh | 6, G. Ev. S. C. G. H. | 1798 |
| ephēmeriā | Yel. grn. | 5, G. Ev. S. C. G. H. | 1810 |
| equisetifoliā, 17 | Purple | 7, G. Ev. S. C. G. H. | 1809 |
| eriōcā | Pa. pink | 4, G. Ev. S. C. G. H. | 1817 |
| erubescēns | Flesh | 6, G. Ev. S. C. G. H. | 1800 |
| exigua | Pink | 6, G. Ev. S. C. G. H. | 1790 |
| eximiā | Scarlet | 6, G. Ev. S. C. G. H. | 1800 |
| expānsā | Scarlet | 7, G. Ev. S. C. G. H. | 1812 |
| exsumptā | Purple | 7, G. Ev. S. C. G. H. | 1811 |
| exsūrta, 18 . | Purple | 6, G. Ev. S. C. G. H. | 1820 |
| exsūrgēns | Dk. oran. | G. Ev. S. C. G. H. | 1792 |
| cārneā . | Orange | G. Ev. S. C. G. H. | 1800 |
| grandiflōrā . | Orange | all G. Ev. S. C. G. H. | 1800 |
| majōr . | Orange | all G. Ev. S. C. G. H. | 1800 |
| pallidā . | Pa. red | all G. Ev. S. C. G. H. | 1810 |
| exūdāns . | Red | 10, G. Ev. S. C. G. H. | 1810 |
| Eweriānā | Pink | 8, G. Ev. S. C. G. H. | 1798 |
| glabrā | Pink | 7, G. Ev. S. C. G. H. | 1800 |
| longiflōrā | Red | 6, G. Ev. S. C. G. H. | 1798 |
| pilōsā | Red | 8, G. Ev. S. C. G. H. | 1798 |
| speciōsā | Red | 8, G. Ev. S. C. G. H. | 1798 |
| fabrilis . | Purple | 6, G. Ev. S. C. G. H. | 1791 |
| fallax . | Purple | 5, G. Ev. S. C. G. H. | 1800 |
| fascicularis, 19 | Purple | 4, G. Ev. S. C. G. H. | 1787 |
| fastigiātā, 20 | White | 7, G. Ev. S. C. G. H. | 1797 |
| fatuātā . | Pa. pur. | 5, G. Ev. S. C. G. H. | 1795 |
| ferrugineā | Red | 5, G. Ev. S. C. G. H. | 1798 |
| fēctā . | | 6, G. Ev. S. C. G. H. | 1812 |
| fībūlā . | Purple | 7, G. Ev. S. C. G. H. | 1823 |
| filamentōsā | Purple | 5, G. Ev. S. C. G. H. | 1800 |
| filiformis . | | 6, G. Ev. S. C. G. H. | |
| fimbriātā | Pa. pur. | 4, G. Ev. S. C. G. H. | 1800 |
| finitimā . | | 5, G. Ev. S. C. G. H. | 1820 |
| fistulaeflōrā | White | 9, G. Ev. S. C. G. H. | 1800 |
| flaccidā . | White . | 5, G. Ev. S. C. G. H. | 1822 |
| flagellāris | Pa. yel. | 5, G. Ev. S. C. G. H. | 1820 |
| flagelliformis | Purple | 5, G. Ev. S. C. G. H. | 1800 |
| flammeā | Lgt. yel. | 6, G. Ev. S. C. G. H. | 1798 |
| flāvā . | Yellow | 6, G. Ev. S. C. G. H. | 1795 |
| imbricātā | Yellow | 7, G. Ev. S. C. G. H. | 1795 |
| flexicaulis, 21 | White | 6, G. Ev. S. C. G. H. | 1800 |
| flexuōsā, 22 | White . | 5, G. Ev. S. C. G. H. | 1792 |
| floribūnda | Pa. pink | 5, G. Ev. S. C. G. H. | 1800 |
| florida . | Red | 6, G. Ev. S. C. G. H. | 1802 |
| campanulātā | Red | 5, G. Ev. S. Hybrid | 1837 |
| moschātā | Red | 5, G. Ev. S. C. G. H. | |
| foliōsā | Yellow | G. Ev. S. C. G. H. | 1800 |
| folliculāris, 23 | Yellow | 4, G. Ev. S. C. G. H. | 1794 |
| formōsā | Red | 8, G. Ev. S. C. G. H. | 1795 |
| alba | White . | 8, G. Ev. S. C. G. H. | 1795 |
| rūbra | Red | 8, G. Ev. S. C. G. H. | 1795 |
| fragrāns | Purple | 4, G. Ev. S. C. G. H. | 1808 |
| fucātā | Purple | 4, G. Ev. S. C. G. H. | 1819 |
| fūgax | Purple | 5, G. Ev. S. C. G. H. | 1800 |
| furfurōsā | Red | 10, G. Ev. S. C. G. H. | 1789 |
| gelidā | Grn. wht. | 5, G. Ev. S. C. G. H. | 1799 |
| albēns | White . | 6, G. Ev. S. C. G. H. | 1820 |
| geniatmfoliā | Purple | 8, G. Ev. S. C. G. H. | |
| gilvā | Yellow | 6, G. Ev. S. C. G. H. | 1820 |
| glabrā | White . | 6, G. Ev. S. C. G. H. | 1820 |
| glandulōsā | Red oran. | 2, G. Ev. S. C. G. H. | 1820 |
| glaucā | Dk. pur. | 6, G. Ev. S. C. G. H. | 1792 |
| globōsā | Pink | 8, G. Ev. S. C. G. H. | 1789 |
| glomerātā | Purple | 3, G. Ev. S. C. G. H. | 1780 |
| glutinōsā | Purple | 8, G. Ev. S. C. G. H. | 1797 |
| droseroidēs | Purple | 8, G. Ev. S. C. G. H. | 1787 |
| gnaphaloidēs | White . | 5, G. Ev. S. C. G. H. | 1812 |
| gracilis . | Pur. red | 8, G. Ev. S. C. G. H. | 1794 |
| grandiflōrā | Yellow | 7, G. Ev. S. C. G. H. | 1785 |
| humilis . | Yellow | 5, G. Ev. S. C. G. H. | 1806 |
| grandinōsā | White . | 8, G. Ev. S. C. G. H. | 1810 |
| guttaeflōrā, 24 | Red | 6, G. Ev. S. C. G. H. | 1701 |
| Halicacābā | Yellow | 6, G. Ev. S. C. G. H. | 1780 |
| Hartnelli | Purple | 7, G. Ev. S. C. G. H. | 1820 |
| helianthemifoliā | White . | 6, G. Ev. S. C. G. H. | 1796 |
| Hibbertiānā | Oran. yel. | 7, G. Ev. S. C. G. H. | 1800 |
| hirsūtā . | Wht. pur. | 4, G. Ev. S. C. G. H. | 1800 |
| hirtā . | | 5, G. Ev. S. C. G. H. | 1795 |
| hirtiflōrā, 25 | Purple | 5, G. Ev. S. C. G. H. | 1790 |
| hispidā . | Pink | 7, G. Ev. S. C. G. H. | 1791 |
| holoserceā . | | 4, G. Ev. S. C. G. H. | 1800 |
| horizontalis . | Pink | 7, G. Ev. S. C. G. H. | 1800 |
| Humeānā | Pink | 8, G. Ev. S. C. G. H. | 1808 |
| humifūsā | Purple | 4, G. Ev. S. Tr. C. G. H. | |
| hyacinthoidēs | Pink | 7, G. Ev. S. C. G. H. | 1798 |
| hyssopifoliā | | 7, G. Ev. S. C. G. H. | 1800 |
| ignēscēns | Red | 5, G. Ev. S. C. G. H. | 1792 |
| imbecilla, 26 | Purple | 6, G. Ev. S. C. G. H. | 1793 |
| imbricātā | Pink | 6, G. Ev. S. C. G. H. | 1786 |
| imperialis | Scarlet | 6, G. Ev. S. C. G. H. | 1802 |
| incānā | White . | 7, G. Ev. S. C. G. H. | 1810 |
| rūbra | Red | 7, G. Ev. S. C. G. H. | 1810 |
| incarnātā | Pa. red | 6, G. Ev. S. C. G. H. | 1792 |
| incurvā | White . | 6, G. Ev. S. C. G. H. | 1802 |
| inflātā | Wht. red | 7, G. Ev. S. C. G. H. | 1809 |
| infundibulāris | Purple | 4, G. Ev. S. C. G. H. | 1821 |
| infundibuliformis | Pa. red | 6, G. Ev. S. C. G. H. | 1802 |
| insolātā | Yel. grn. | 6, G. Ev. S. C. G. H. | 1810 |
| intertixtā | Yellow | 6, G. Ev. S. C. G. H. | 1818 |
| intervallāris | Purple | 6, G. Ev. S. C. G. H. | 1800 |
| Irbyānā | Wht. grn. | 6, G. Ev. S. C. G. H. | 1800 |
| jasminiflōrā | Wht. pink | 8, G. Ev. S. C. G. H. | 1794 |
| alba | White . | 8, G. Ev. S. C. G. H. | |
| jubātā | | 8, G. Ev. S. C. G. H. | 1800 |
| juliānā | Red | 7, G. Ev. S. C. G. H. | 1800 |
| lablātā | | 7, G. Ev. S. C. G. H. | 1800 |
| lachnaefoliā | White . | 6, G. Ev. S. C. G. H. | 1798 |
| lasticolōr | White . | 8, G. Ev. S. C. G. H. | 1818 |
| lactiflōrā | White . | 8, G. Ev. S. C. G. H. | 1820 |
| laevis | White | 5, G. Ev. S. C. G. H. | 1821 |

| | | | | |
|---|---|---|---|---|
| ălbă . . . . | White . | . 5, G. Ev. S. | C. G. H. | . 1801 |
| Lambertiānă . | . White . | . 6, G. Ev. S. | C. G. H. | . 1800 |
| lanātă . . . | . Orange | . 3, G. Ev. S. | C. G. H. | . 1775 |
| lanceolātă . . | . White . | . 9, G. Ev. S. | C. G. H. | . 1791 |
| laniflōră, 27 . | . Lgt. scar. . | G. Ev. S. | C. G. H. | . 1790 |
| lanuginōsă . . | . Pūr. yel. | . 4, G. Ev. S. | C. G. H. | . 1803 |
| lascīvă . . . . | | . 7, G. Ev. S. | C. G. H. | . 1800 |
| lasiophyllă . . | . Purple | . 6, G. Ev. S. | C. G. H. | . 1816 |
| laterālis . . | . Red . | . 5, G. Ev. S. | C. G. H. | . 1791 |
| latifōliă . . . | . Red . | . 6, G. Ev. S. | C. G. H. | . 1800 |
| lavandulæfōliă . | | . 6, G. Ev. S. | C. G. H. | . 1795 |
| Lawsōni . . . | . Flesh . | . 5, G. Ev. S. | C. G. H. | . 1802 |
| lāxă . . . . | . Purple | . 4, G. Ev. S. | C. G. H. | . 1800 |
| Leeānă . . . | . Oran. yel. | . 4, G. Ev. S. | C. G. H. | . 1788 |
| leucānthēră . | . White . | . 3, G. Ev. S. | C. G. H. | . 1803 |
| linifōliă . . | . Purple | . 6, G. Ev. S. | C. G. H. | . 1796 |
| Linnæānă, 28 . | . Pur. wht. | . 3, G. Ev. S. | C. G. H. | . 1790 |
| Linnæoīdēs . | . Pur. red | . 4, G. Ev. S. | C. G. H. | . 1812 |
| linoīdēs . . . | . Red . | . 8, G. Ev. S. | C. G. H. | . |
| lituiflōră . . | | . 7, G. Ev. S. | C. G. H. | . 1796 |
| Loddigēsiī . . | . Flame cld. | 7, G. Ev. S. | C. G. H. | . 1830 |
| longiflōră . . | . Red oran. | 5, G. Ev. S. | C. G. H. | . 1812 |
| longifōliă, 29 . | . Red . | . 4, G. Ev. S. | C. G. H. | . 1787 |
| longipedunculātă | . Pink . | . 7, G. Ev. S. | C. G. H. | . 1805 |
| lūcĭdă . . . . | . Purple | . 5, G. Ev. S. | C. G. H. | . 1800 |
| lūteă . . . . | . Pa. yel. | . 3, G. Ev. S. | C. G. H. | . 1774 |
| ălbă . . . . | . Pa. yel. | . 6, G. Ev. S. | C. G. H. | . 1810 |
| lyrigēră . . . | | . 3, G. Ev. S. | C. G. H. | . 1790 |
| magnifĭcă . . | . Purple | . 9, G. Ev. S. | C. G. H. | . 1800 |
| malleāris . . | . Red . | . 6, G. Ev. S. | C. G. H. | . 1803 |
| mammōsă . . | . Purple | . 8, G. Ev. S. | C. G. H. | . 1762 |
| mĭnŏr . . | . Purple | . 8, G. Ev. S. | C. G. H. | . 1800 |
| pāllĭdă . . | . Pa. red | . 8, G. Ev. S. | C. G. H. | . 1810 |
| margaritācĕă . | . White . | . 7, G. Ev. S. | C. G. H. | . 1775 |
| marifōliă . . | . White . | . 6, G. Ev. S. | C. G. H. | . 1773 |
| Massōni . . | . Red grn. | . 8, G. Ev. S. | C. G. H. | . 1787 |
| mĭnŏr . . | . Red grn. | . 8, G. Ev. S. | C. G. H. | . |
| mediterrānĕă . | . Purple | . 4, H. Ev. S. | Portugal | . 1648 |
| melanthēră . | . Pa. pur. | . 6, G. Ev. S. | C. G. H. | . 1803 |
| melăstōmă . . | . Red brn. | . 6, G. Ev. S. | C. G. H. | . 1795 |
| mellĭfēră . . | . Purple | . 4, G. Ev. S. | C. G. H. | . 1820 |
| metulæflōră . | . Orange | . 4, G. Ev. S. | C. G. H. | . 1798 |
| microphyllă . | . Purple | . 9, G. Ev. S. | C. G. H. | . 1820 |
| micrŏstōmă . | . Purple | . 9, G. Ev. S. | C. G. H. | . 1810 |
| mĭnĭmă . . . | . Red . | . 6, G. Ev. S. | C. G. H. | . 1810 |
| mirābĭlis . . | . Purple | . 5, G. Ev. S. | C. G. H. | . 1800 |
| mitræfōrmis, 30 | . Red . | . 6, G. Ev. S. | C. G. H. | . 1800 |
| modēstă . . | . Purple | . 4, G. Ev. S. | C. G. H. | . 1800 |
| mōllĭs . . . | . Purple | . 5, G. Ev. S. | C. G. H. | . 1790 |
| mollissĭmă . . | . White . | . 5, G. Ev. S. | C. G. H. | . |
| monadĕlphă . | . Pink . | . 6, G. Ev. S. | C. G. H. | . 1789 |
| Monsoniānă . | . White . | . 7, G. Ev. S. | C. G. H. | . 1787 |
| montānă . . | . Purple | . 10, G. Ev. S. | C. G. H. | . 1818 |
| moschātă . . | . Green . | . 6, G. Ev. S | C. G. H. | . 1805 |
| mucōsă . . . | . Red . | . 6, G. Ev. S. | C. G. H. | . 1787 |
| mucronātă . . | . Purple | . 6, G. Ev. S. | C. G. H. | . 1800 |
| multiflōră . . | . Flesh . | . 8, H. Ev. S. | France . | . 1731 |
| ălbă . . . | . White . | . 8, H. Ev. S. | Europe . | . |
| mūndă . . . | . Purple | . 5, G. Ev. S. | C. G. H. | . |
| mūndūlă . . | . Purple | . 6, G. Ev. S. | C. G. H. | . 1810 |
| mājŏr . . | . Purple | . 6, G. Ev. S. | C. G. H. | . 1810 |
| Muscāri . . | . White . | . 5, G. Ev. S. | C. G. H. | . 1790 |
| muscaroīdēs . | . Yel. grn. | . 6, G. Ev. S. | C. G. H. | . 1800 |
| mutābĭlis . . | . Crimson | . 5, G. Ev. S. | C. G. H. | . 1798 |
| nānă . . . | . Yellow | . 7, G. Ev. S. | C. G. H. | . 1792 |
| nidiflōră . . | | . 8, G. Ev. S. | C. G. H. | . 1800 |
| niduläriă . . | . Pink . | . 4, G. Ev. S. | C. G. H. | . 1809 |
| nigrĭcāns . . | | . 7, G. Ev. S. | C. G. H. | . 1816 |
| nigrītă . . . | . White . | . 4, G. Ev. S. | C. G. H. | . 1790 |
| nĭtēns . . . | . Purple | . 7, G. Ev. S. | C. G. H. | . 1810 |
| nĭtĭdă . . . | . White . | . 8, G. Ev. S. | C. G. H. | . 1800 |
| nĭvĕă . . . | . White . | . 4, G. Ev. S. | C. G. H. | . 1816 |
| Niveniānă . . | . Purple | . 4, G. Ev. S. | C. G. H. | . 1799 |
| mĭnŏr . . | . Purple | . 4, G. Ev. S. | C. G. H. | . 1812 |
| nōbĭlis . . . | . Purple | . 6, G. Ev. S. | C. G. H. | . 1818 |
| nodiflōră . . | . Red . | . 5, G. Ev. S. | C. G. H. | . 1799 |
| nolæflōră, 31 . | . White . | . 2, G. Ev. S. | C. G. H. | . 1818 |
| notābĭlis . . | . Purple | . 6, G. Ev. S. | C. G. H. | . 1816 |
| nudiflōră . . | . Dk. yel. | . 7, G. Ev. S. | C. G. H. | . 1788 |
| obcordātă . . | . Red . | . 5, G. Ev. S. | C. G. H. | . 1791 |
| oblīquă . . . | . Purple | . 8, G. Ev. S. | C. G. H. | . 1800 |
| obtūsă . . . | . Purple | . 9, G. Ev. S. | C. G. H. | . 1789 |
| octagōnă . . | . Purple | . G. Ev. S. | C. G. H. | . 1810 |
| octofāriă . . | | . 6, G. Ev. S. | C. G. H. | . 1816 |
| odorātă . . . | . Pink . | . 6, G. Ev. S. | C. G. H. | . 1829 |
| ōllūlă . . . | . Pink . | . 6, G. Ev. S. | C. G. H. | . 1804 |
| oncosmæflōră . | . Pur. red | . 8, G. Ev. S. | C. G. H. | . 1802 |
| oppositifōliă . | . Yellow | . 6, G. Ev. S. | C. G. H. | . 1789 |
| rūbră . . . | . White . | . 4, G. Ev. S. | C. G. H. | . 1802 |
| orbātă . . . | . Red . | . 5, G. Ev. S. | C. G. H. | . 1810 |
| orbiculāris . . | | G. Ev. S. | C. G. H. | . 1810 |
| ostrīnă . . . | . Purple | . 8, G. Ev. S. | C. G. H. | . 1820 |
| ovaliflōră . . | . Purple | . 6, G. Ev. S. | C. G. H. | . 1817 |
| ovātă . . . | . Purple | . 6, G. Ev. S. | C. G. H. | . 1811 |
| oxycoccifōliă . | . Red . | . 8, G. Ev. Tr. | C. G. H. | . 1791 |
| pachyphyllă . | | G. Ev. S. | C. G. H. | . 1800 |
| pāllēns . . . | . Pa. red | . 7, G. Ev. S. | C. G. H. | . 1800 |
| pāllĭdă . . . | . Pur. red | . 5, G. Ev. S. | C. G. H. | . 1818 |
| rūbră . . . | . Red . | . 5, G. Ev. S. | C. G. H. | . 1812 |

| | | | | |
|---|---|---|---|---|
| palliiflōră . . | . Purple . | 5, G. Ev. S. | C. G. H. | . 1796 |
| palūstris . . | . Flesh . . | 7, G. Ev. S. | C. G. H. | . 1799 |
| paniculātă . . | . Red . . | 8, G. Ev. S. | C. G. H. | . 1774 |
| ălbă . . . . | . White . . | 8, G. Ev. S. | C. G. H. | . 1774 |
| pannōsă . . | . Purple . | 4, G. Ev. S. | C. G. H. | . |
| parīlis . . . . | . | 6, G. Ev. S. | C. G. H. | . 1789 |
| Parmentieriānă | . Pa. pur. . | 7, G. Ev. S. | C. G. H. | . 1810 |
| rōsĕă . . . . | . Red . . | 7, G. Ev. S. | C. G. H. | . 1810 |
| parviflōră . . | . Pink . . | 6, G. Ev. S. | C. G. H. | . 1790 |
| Passerīnă . . | . White . . | 5, G. Ev. S. | C. G. H. | . 1800 |
| pătēns . . . . | . Purple . | 4, G. Ev. S. | C. G. H. | . 1800 |
| Patersoniānă, 32 | . Yellow . | 5, G. Ev. S. | C. G. H. | . 1791 |
| coccĭnĕă . . | . Scarlet . | 5, G. Ev. S. | C. G. H. | . 1810 |
| mājŏr . . . | . Yellow . | 5, G. Ev. S. | C. G. H. | . |
| monstrōsă . | . Yellow . | 5, G. Ev. S. | C. G. H. | . |
| Patersonioīdēs | . Oran. red . | 6, G. Ev. S. | C. G. H. | . 1800 |
| pavettæflōră . . | . | 6, G. Ev. S. | C. G. H. | . 1800 |
| pectinifōliă . | . Red . . | 8, G. Ev. S. | C. G. H. | . 1800 |
| pedunculātă, 33 | . Purple . | 10, G. Ev. S. | C. G. H. | . 1818 |
| pellūcĭdă . . . | White . . | 9, G. Ev. S. | C. G. H. | . 1800 |
| pellucidioīdēs, 34 | Red pur. . | 9, G. Ev. S. | C. G. H. | . 1808 |
| pēndūlă . . . . | . Purple . | 7, G. Ev. S. | C. G. H. | . 1791 |
| penicillātă . . | . Rose . . | 5, G. Ev. S. | C. G. H. | . 1792 |
| penicilliflōră, 35 | . Wht. brn. | 5, G. Ev. S. | C. G. H. | . 1774 |
| periplocæflōră . | . Purple . | 10, G. Ev. S. | C. G. H. | . 1792 |
| perlātă . . . . | . Purple . | 6, G. Ev. S. | C. G. H. | . 1810 |
| persolūtă . . | . Purple . | 4, G. Ev. S. | C. G. H. | . 1774 |
| ălbă . . . . | . White . . | 3, G. Ev. S. | C. G. H. | . 1800 |
| rūbră . . . . | . Red . . | 3, G. Ev. S. | C. G. H. | . 1800 |
| perspĭcŭă . . . | . Wht. pur. | 5, G. Ev. S. | C. G. H. | . 1790 |
| nānă . . . . | . Pink . . | 4, G. Ev. S. | C. G. H. | . 1800 |
| perspicuoīdēs . | . Red pur. . | 5, G. Ev. S. | C. G. H. | . 1800 |
| patiolātă . . | . Pa. pur. . | 5, G. Ev. S. | C. G. H. | . 1774 |
| Petivērii . . | . Yellow . | 5, G. Ev. S. | C. G. H. | . 1774 |
| coccĭnĕă . . | . Scarlet . | 5, G. Ev. S. | C. G. H. | . |
| fūscă . . . . | . Brown . | 5, G. Ev. S. | C. G. H. | . 1801 |
| Pezīză . . . . | . White . . | 6, G. Ev. S. | C. G. H. | . 1812 |
| phylicoīdēs . | . White . . | 5, G. Ev. S. | C. G. H. | . 1800 |
| physōdēs . . | . White . . | 5, G. Ev. S. | C. G. H. | . 1788 |
| pĭctă . . . . | . Oran. yel. | 7, G. Ev. S. | C. G. H. | . 1820 |
| pilōsă . . . . | . Green . . | 6, G. Ev. S. | C. G. H. | . 1800 |
| pilulĭfēră . . . | . Red . . | 5, G. Ev. S. | C. G. H. | . 1789 |
| pinastrifōliă . | . Scarlet . | 8, G. Ev. S. | C. G. H. | . 1800 |
| rūbră . . . . | . Red . . | 8, G. Ev. S. | C. G. H. | . 1810 |
| pīnĕă . . . . | . Red . . | 10, G. Ev. S. | C. G. H. | . 1790 |
| dĭscŏlŏr . . . | . Red . . | 10, G. Ev. S. | C. G. H. | . |
| echioīdēs . . | . Red . . | 10, G. Ev. S. | C. G. H. | . |
| favoīdēs . . . | . Red . . | 10, G. Ev. S. | C. G. H. | . |
| pulchellă . . | . Red . . | 10, G. Ev. S. | C. G. H. | . |
| purpūrĕă . . | . Purple . | 8, G. Ev. S. | C. G. H. | . 1806 |
| spirālis . . . | . Red . . | 10, G. Ev. S. | C. G. H. | . |
| pityophyllă, 36 | . White . . | 4, G. Ev. S. | C. G. H. | . 1810 |
| dĭscŏlŏr . . . | . Pur. red . | 7, G. Ev. S. | C. G. H. | . 1810 |
| spirālis . . . | . Wht. pur. | 7, G. Ev. S. | C. G. H. | . 1800 |
| planifōliă . . | . Purple . | 8, G. Ev. S. | C. G. H. | . 1795 |
| Plukenētii . . | . Red . . | 5, G. Ev. S. | C. G. H. | . 1774 |
| pāllĭdă . . . | . Pa. red . | 6, G. Ev. S. | C. G. H. | . 1794 |
| Pohlmānni . . . | . | G. Ev. S. | C. G. H. | . 1812 |
| prăcŏx . . . . | . Purple . | G. Ev. S. | C. G. H. | . 1820 |
| prægnāns . . . | . Red . . | 8, G. Ev. S. | C. G. H. | . 1796 |
| præstāns . . . | . White . . | 8, G. Ev. S. | C. G. H. | . 1810 |
| primuloīdēs . | . Pur. red . | 5, G. Ev. S. | C. G. H. | . 1802 |
| prīncēps . . . | . Scarlet . | 6, G. Ev. S. | C. G. H. | . 1800 |
| cārnĕă . . . | . Flesh . . | 6, G. Ev. S. | C. G. H. | . 1804 |
| procēră . . . . | . White . . | 5, G. Ev. S. | C. G. H. | . 1791 |
| procūmbēns, 37 | . Purple . | 6, G. Ev. S. | C. G. H. | . 1800 |
| propēndēns . . | . Purple . | 7, G. Ev. S. | C. G. H. | . 1800 |
| protrūdēns . . | . White . . | 4, G. Ev. S. | C. G. H. | . 1805 |
| pseūdo-vēstītă . | . Pink . . | 5, G. Ev. S. | Hybrid . | . |
| pubēscēns . . | . Purple . | 6, G. Ev. S. | C. G. H. | . 1790 |
| mĭnŏr . . . | . Red . . | 6, G. Ev. S. | C. G. H. | . 1802 |
| pubescēntiŏr . | . Red . . | 6, G. Ev. S. | C. G. H. | . 1802 |
| pubigēră . . . | . | 8, G. Ev. S. | C. G. H. | . 1792 |
| pudibūndă, 38 . | . Purple . | 8, G. Ev. S. | C. G. H. | . 1810 |
| pulchēllă . . . | . Red . . | 7, G. Ev. S. | C. G. H. | . 1792 |
| pulverulēntă . | . Purple . | 7, G. Ev. S. | C. G. H. | . 1820 |
| pulvinifōrmis . | . | 8, G. Ev. S. | C. G. H. | . 1800 |
| pūmĭlă . . . . | . Purple . | 6, G. Ev. S. | C. G. H. | . 1812 |
| pūră . . . . . | . White . . | 8, G. Ev. S. | C. G. H. | . 1807 |
| puriālis . . . . | . Purple . | 9, G. Ev. S. | C. G. H. | . 1810 |
| purpūrĕă . . . | . Lgt. pur. . | G. Ev. S. | C. G. H. | . 1789 |
| pusīllă . . . . | . Purple . | 6, G. Ev. S. | C. G. H. | . |
| pygmæă . . . | . Purple . | 8, G. Ev. S. | C. G. H. | . 1806 |
| pyramidālis . . | . Pink . . | 3, G. Ev. S. | C. G. H. | . 1787 |
| pyramidifōrmis | . Purple . | 10, G. Ev. S. | C. G. H. | . 1818 |
| pyrolæflōră . . | . White . . | 6, G. Ev. S. | C. G. H. | . 1790 |
| quadrangulāris | . Purple . | 6, G. Ev. S. | C. G. H. | . 1800 |
| quadrātă . . . | . White . . | 5, G. Ev. S. | C. G. H. | . 1829 |
| quadriflōră . . | . | 5, G. Ev. S. | C. G. H. | . 1800 |
| racemōsă . . . | . Pink . . | 4, G. Ev. S. | C. G. H. | . 1795 |
| racemĭfēră . . . | . Red . . | 5, G. Ev. S. | C. G. H. | . 1803 |
| radiātă . . . . | . Crimson . | 9, G. Ev. S. | C. G. H. | . 1798 |
| ramentācĕă . . | . Dk. red . | 9, G. Ev. S. | C. G. H. | . 1786 |
| ramulōsă . . . | . Purple . | 6, H. Ev. S. | S. Eur. . | . 1800 |
| rūbră . . . | . Red . . | 6, H. Ev. S. | S. Eur. . | . 1800 |
| recurvātă . . | . Purple . | 5, G. Ev. S. | C. G. H. | . 1810 |
| reflēxă . . . . | . White . . | 5, G. Ev. S. | C. G. H. | . 1820 |
| refūlgēns . . | . Scarlet . | 5, G. Ev. S. | C. G. H. | . 1800 |
| regērmĭnāns . | . Red . . | 6, G. Ev. S. | C. G. H. | . 1791 |

| | | | | | |
|---|---|---|---|---|---|
| álbá | White | 6, G. Ev. | 8. C. G. H. | 1810 |
| resinósá | Orange | 6, G. Ev. | 8. C. G. H. | 1803 |
| retórtá | Pk. wht. | 6, G. Ev. | 8. C. G. H. | 1787 |
| retroflèxá, 39 | White | 8, G. Ev. | 8. C. G. H. | 1787 |
| rigidá | Pink | 7, G. Ev. | 8. C. G. H. | 1820 |
| rigidifóliá | Purple | 6, G. Ev. | 8. C. G. H. | 1818 |
| Rollinsónii | Purple | 6, G. Ev. | 8. C. G. H. | 1820 |
| rósá | Lgt. red | 8, G. Ev. | 8 C. G. H. | 1798 |
| rostéllá | White | 5, G. Ev. | 8. C. G. H. | 1810 |
| rubéllá | Pink | 6, G. Ev. | 8. C. G. H. | 1814 |
| rúbéns, 40 | Dk. red | 7, G. Ev. | 8. C. G. H. | 1810 |
| rúbidá | Wht. red | G. Ev. | 8. C. G. H. | 1826 |
| rugósá | Purple | 5, G. Ev. | 8. C. G. H. | 1800 |
| Russelliáná | Pink | 5, G. Ev. | 8. C. G. H. | 1820 |
| sacciflórá | | 4, G. Ev. | 8. C. G. H. | 1800 |
| Sainsburyáná | Purple | 7, G. Ev. | 8. C. G. H. | 1800 |
| sálax | White | 4, G. Ev. | 8. C. G. H. | 1796 |
| sanguineá | Crimson | 4, G. Ev. | 8. C. G. H. | 1815 |
| sanguinoléntá | Cream cld. | 6, G. Ev. | 8. C. G. H. | 1818 |
| Savileáná | Red | 6, G. Ev. | 8. C. G. H. | 1800 |
| scabriúsculá | White | 5, G. Ev. | 8. C. G. H. | 1805 |
| scariósá | Purple | 6, G. Ev. | 8. C. G. H. | 1800 |
| sceptriformis | | 8, G. Ev. | 8. C. G. H. | 1790 |
| Scholliáná | Purple | 5, G. Ev. | 8. C. G. H. | 1810 |
| scopáriá | Green | 4, G. Ev. | 8. C. G. H. | 1770 |
| minimá | Green | 4, G. Ev. | 8. C. G. H. | 1800 |
| Sebáná | Orange | 4, G. Ev. | 8. C. G. H. | 1774 |
| fúscá | Brown | 5, G. Ev. | 8. C. G. H. | 1812 |
| lútéá | Yellow | 5, G. Ev. | 8. C. G. H. | 1800 |
| minór | Orange | 5, G. Ev. | 8. C. G. H. | 1810 |
| selaginifóliá | | 4, G. Ev. | 8. C. G. H. | 1801 |
| serpyllifóliá | White | 6, G. Ev. | 8. C. G. H. | 1810 |
| serratifóliá | Orange | 10, G. Ev. | 8. C. G. H. | 1790 |
| serrulátá | | G. Ev. | 8. C. G. H. | 1810 |
| setáceá | White | 3, G. Ev. | 8. C. G. H. | 1796 |
| sexfáriá | | 6, G. Ev. | 8. C. G. H. | 1774 |
| Shannoniáná | Wht. pur. | 6, G. Ev. | 8. C. G. H. | 1816 |
| sicæfóliá | | 4, G. Ev. | 8. C. G. H. | |
| siculá | Red | 5, F. Ev. | 8. Sicily | 1819 |
| simpliciflórá | Orange | 4, G. Ev. | 8. C. G. H. | 1774 |
| Smithiáná | Purple | 4, G. Ev. | 8. C. G. H. | 1791 |
| socciflórá | Green | 4, G. Ev. | 8. C. G. H. | 1799 |
| Solandriáná | Pink | 6, G. Ev. | 8. C. G. H. | 1800 |
| sórdidá | Red | 7, G. Ev. | 8. C. G. H. | 1810 |
| Sparmánni | Dk. oran. | 6, G. Ev. | 8. C. G. H. | 1794 |
| spársá | Purple | 4, G. Ev. | 8. C. G. H. | 1810 |
| speciósá | Red grn. | 7, G. Ev. | 8. C. G. H. | 1800 |
| spicátá | Lgt. yel. | G. Ev. | 8. C. G. H. | 1789 |
| spirális | | G. Ev. | 8. C. G. H. | 1820 |
| spléndens | Scarlet | 7, G. Ev. | 8. C. G. H. | 1792 |
| spléndidá | Scarlet | 6, G. Ev. | 8. C. G. H. | 1820 |
| Sprengélii, 41 | Yel. pur. | 6, G. Ev. | 8. C. G. H. | 1806 |
| spumósá | White | 6, G. Ev. | 8. C. G. H. | 1786 |
| spúriá | Purple | 6, G. Ev. | 8. C. G. H. | 1796 |
| squamæflórá | | 4, G. Ev. | 8. C. G. H. | 1796 |
| squamósá | Flesh | 5, G. Ev. | 8. C. G. H. | 1794 |
| squarrósá | | 5, G. Ev. | 8. C. G. H. | 1800 |
| stagnális | | 4, G. Ev. | 8. C. G. H. | 1790 |
| stamineá | Red | 6, G. Ev. | 8. C. G. H. | 1799 |
| stellifera | Purple | 5, G. Ev. | 8. Hybrid | 1800 |
| stelláris | Purple | 6, G. Ev. | 8. C. G. H. | 1810 |
| stellátá | Purple | 5, G. Ev. | 8. C. G. H. | 1806 |
| strícta | Purple | 9, H. Ev. | 8. Eur. | 1795 |
| strigósá, 42 | Pa. red | 4, G. Ev. | 8. C. G. H. | 1798 |
| struthiolæflórá | | G. Ev. | 8. C. G. H. | |
| styláris | | 6, G. Ev. | 8. C. G. H. | 1812 |
| stylósá | | 6, G. Ev. | 8. C. G. H. | 1789 |
| suavéolens | Pink | 8, G. Ev. | 8. C. G. H. | 1800 |
| subulátá | Purple | 8, G. Ev. | 8. C. G. H. | 1817 |
| sulphúreá | Yellow | 6, G. Ev. | 8. C. G. H. | 1805 |
| Swainsónii | Red pur. | 8, G. Ev. | 8. C. G. H. | 1794 |
| tardiflórá, 43 | Purple | 6, G. Ev. | 8. C. G. H. | 1790 |
| taxiflórá | Purple | 9, G. Ev. | 8. C. G. H. | 1798 |
| tegulæfóliá | | 4, G. Ev. | 8. C. G. H. | 1800 |
| Templeáná | Red pur. | 7, G. Ev. | 8. C. G. H. | 1820 |
| tenélla | Purple | 6, G. Ev. | 8. C. G. H. | 1791 |
| tenuiflórá | Lgt. yel. | 5, G. Ev. | 8. C. G. H. | 1800 |
| álbá | White | 5, G. Ev. | 8. C. G. H. | 1818 |
| tenuifóliá | Pink | 7, G. Ev. | 8. C. G. H. | 1794 |
| ténüis | Red | 7, G. Ev. | 8. C. G. H. | 1800 |
| tenuíssimá | Red | 4, G. Ev. | 8. C. G. H. | 1803 |
| tetragóná, 44 | Lgt. yel. | 8, G. Ev. | 8. C. G. H. | 1789 |
| Tetrálix | Flesh | 7, H. Ev. | 8. Britain | |
| álbá | White | 7, H. Ev. | 8. Britain | |
| cárneá | Flesh | 7, H. Ev. | 8. Britain | |
| Mackaiáná | Flesh | 7, H. Ev. | 8. Ireland | |
| teucrifóliá | | 7, G. Ev. | 8. C G. H. | 1812 |
| thalictræflórá | Yellow | 7, G. Ev. | 8. C. G. H. | 1820 |
| Thunbergiáná | Orange | 6, G. Ev. | 8. C. G. H. | 1794 |
| thymifóliá | Purple | 7, G. Ev. | 8. C. G. H. | 1789 |
| tiaræflórá | Red | 6, G. Ev. | 8. C. G. H. | 1800 |
| togátá | Red | 6, G. Ev. | 8. C. G. H. | |
| tomentósá | Purple | 6, G. Ev. | 8. C. G. H. | 1788 |
| tortuósá | | 5, G. Ev. | 8. C. G. H. | 1816 |
| tótta, 45 | Purple | 6, G. Ev. | 8. C. G. H. | 1810 |
| tragulæflórá | | 6, G. Ev. | 8. C. G. H. | 1800 |
| translúcens | Red | 6, G. Ev. | 8. C. G. H. | 1797 |
| transpárens | White | 5, G. Ev. | 8. C. G. H. | 1800 |
| tricéps | White | 6, G. Ev. | 8. C. G. H. | 1820 |

[ 123 ]

| | | | | | |
|---|---|---|---|---|---|
| tricólor | Red grn. | 6, G. Ev. | 8. C. G. H. | 1810 |
| májor | Red grn. | 6, G. Ev. | 8. C. G. H. | 1810 |
| minór | Red grn. | 6, G. Ev. | 8. C. G. H. | 1810 |
| supérbá | Pink | 7, G. Ev. | 8. Hybrid | |
| triflórá | White | 4, G. Ev. | 8. C. G. H. | 1774 |
| triphýllá | Red yel. | 9, G. Ev. | 8. C. G. H. | 1822 |
| trіumphâns | White | 4, G. Ev. | 8. C. G. H. | 1802 |
| troesúlá | Wht. pink | 4, G. Ev. | 8. C. G. H. | 1800 |
| rúbrá | Red | 4, G. Ev. | 8. C. G. H. | 1810 |
| tuberculáris | Purple | 4, G. Ev. | 8. C. G. H. | 1790 |
| tubiflórá | Pink | 5, G. Ev. | 8. C. G. H. | 1775 |
| tubiúsculá, 46 | Red | 4, G. Ev. | 8. C. G. H. | 1800 |
| túmidá | Scarlet | 7, G. Ev. | 8. C. G. H. | 1812 |
| turbiniflórá | | 6, G. Ev. | 8. C. G. H. | 1793 |
| túrgidá | Purple | 5, G. Ev. | 8. C. G. H. | 1821 |
| turrígerá | Red | 7, G. Ev. | 8. C. G. H. | 1796 |
| umbellátá | Purple | 6, F. Ev. | 8. Portugal | 1782 |
| undulátá | Rose | 8, G. Ev. | 8. C. G. H. | 1827 |
| úncia, 47 | Purple | 6, G. Ev. | 8. C. G. H. | 1800 |
| urceoláris | White | 6, G. Ev. | 8. C. G. H. | 1778 |
| ursíná | | 6, G. Ev. | 8. C. G. H. | 1812 |
| vágans | Red | 7, H. Ev. | 8. Cornwall | |
| álbá | White | 7, H. Ev. | 8. Cornwall | |
| purpurácens | Purple | 7, H. Ev. | 8. Cornwall | |
| rubéscens | Pa. red | 7, H. Ev. | 8. Cornwall | |
| tenéllá | Red yel. | 7, H. Ev. | 8. Europe | |
| váriá, 48 | Pur. yel. | 7, G. Ev. | 8. C. G. H. | 1810 |
| velitáris | | 3, G. Ev. | 8. C. G. H. | 1790 |
| velleriflórá | White | 4, G. Ev. | 8. C. G. H. | 1774 |
| ventricósá | Flesh | 6, G. Ev. | 8. C. G. H. | 1787 |
| álbá | White | 6, G. Ev. | 8. C. G. H. | |
| cárneá | Flesh | 6, G. Ev. | 8. C. G. H. | |
| coccíneá | Scarlet | 6, G. Ev. | 8. C. G. H. | |
| erécta | Flesh | 6, G. Ev. | 8. C. G. H. | |
| hirsúta | Flesh | 6, G. Ev. | 8. C. G. H. | |
| náná | Flesh | 6, G. Ev. | 8. C. G. H. | |
| stellifera | Flesh | 6, G. Ev. | 8. C. G. H. | |
| supérbá | Scarlet | 6, G. Ev. | 8. C. G. H. | |
| verecúnda, 49 | Yel. pink | 7, G. Ev. | 8. C. G. H. | 1800 |
| vernális | Pink | 3, G. Ev. | 8. C. G. H. | 1827 |
| verniciflúá | Purple | 6, G. Ev. | 8. C. G. H. | 1804 |
| veralcólor | Oran. red | 8, G. Ev. | 8. C. G. H. | 1790 |
| májor | Red wht. | 7, G. Ev. | 8. C. G. H. | 1800 |
| verticillátá | Scarlet | 8, G. Ev. | 8. C. G. H. | 1774 |
| májor | Scarlet | 9, G. Ev. | 8. C. G. H. | 1800 |
| vesiculáris | | 5, G. Ev. | 8. C. G. H. | 1796 |
| vestítúa | | 6, G. Ev. | 8. C. G. H. | 1795 |
| vestítá | White | 6, G. Ev. | 8. C. G. H. | 1789 |
| álbá | White | G. Ev. | 8. C. G. H. | 1789 |
| blándá | Pink | 5, G. Ev. | 8. C. G. H. | 1827 |
| coccíneá | Scarlet | G. Ev. | 8. C. G. H. | 1789 |
| élégans | Purple | G. Ev. | 8. C. G. H. | 1810 |
| fúlgidá | Orange | G. Ev. | 8. C. G. H. | 1789 |
| incarnátá | Pink | G. Ev. | 8. C. G. H. | 1789 |
| lútéa | Yellow | G. Ev. | 8. C. G. H. | 1789 |
| mutábilis | Scar. wht. | G. Ev. | 8. C. G. H. | 1800 |
| purpúreá | Purple | 6, G. Ev. | 8. C. G. H. | 1789 |
| rósea | Lgt. red | 6, G. Ev. | 8. C. G. H. | 1789 |
| villósá | White | 4, G. Ev. | 8. C. G. H. | 1800 |
| villosiúsculá | Rose | 7, G. Ev. | 8. C. G. H. | 1820 |
| viréscens | Yel. grn. | 5, G. Ev. | 8. C. G. H. | 1820 |
| virgáta | Purple | 9, G. Ev. | 8. C. G. H. | 1818 |
| viridiflórá | Orange | 7, G. Ev. | 8. C. G. H. | 1810 |
| viridipurpúréá | Grn. pur. | 6, F. Ev. | 8. Portugal | |
| víridis | Dk. grn. | 7, G. Ev. | 8. C. G. H. | 1800 |
| viscáriá | Red | 5, G. Ev. | 8. C. G. H. | 1774 |
| vulgáris, 50 | Purple | 4, H. Ev. | 8. Britain | |
| álbá | White | 4, H. Ev. | 8. Britain | |
| coccíneá | Scarlet | 4, H. Ev. | 8. Britain | |
| decúmbens | Red | 4, H. Ev. | 8. Britain | |
| flóre-plèno | Purple | 4, H. Ev. | 8. Britain | |
| spicáta | Red | 4, H. Ev. | 8. Britain | |
| tomentósá | Red | 4, H. Ev. | 8. Britain | |
| variegáta | Red | 4, H. Ev. | 8. Britain | |
| Willmórei | Pink | 7, G. Ev. | 8. Hybrid | 1837 |
| xeranthemifóliá | | 7, G. Ev. | 8. C. G. H. | 1812 |

ERIGÉRON, *Linn.* From *er*, spring, and *geron*, an old man; the plants become old in the beginning of the season. *Linn.* 19, Or. 2, Nat. Or. *Compositæ.* This genus comprehends many exceedingly handsome species, varying from a few inches to two feet or more high, and producing a great and copious display of blossom; they will grow in almost any soil, and are increased with facility from either seeds or divisions. In the United States, *E. heterophyllus*, and *E. philadelphicus*, are used as diuretics. Synonymes: 1. *E. Serpentarius*. 2. *Conyza chilensis*. 3. *Aster bonariensis*. 4. *A. annuus*. 5. *Conyza ambigua*.

| | | | | | |
|---|---|---|---|---|---|
| ácris | Blue | 7, H. | B. Britain | |
| alpínus | Purple | 7, H. Her. | P. Scotland | |
| armeriæfóliús | Purple | 8, H. Her. | P. N. Amer. | 1829 |
| áspér | Purple | 8, H. Her. | P. N. Amer. | 1828 |
| asteroídes | White | 7, H. Her. | P. Huds. Bay | 1776 |
| átticus | Purple | 7, H. Her. | P. Attica | 1816 |
| austrális | | H. | A. 8. Eur. | 1827 |

| | | | | | | |
|---|---|---|---|---|---|---|
| bellidifōlius, 1 | . Purple | . 7, | H. Her. | P. | N. Amer. | . 1790 |
| bomariánsis | . Purple | . 7, | H. | A. | S. Amer. | . 1732 |
| canadénsis | . White | . 8, | H. | A. | England | . |
| caroliniánus | . Purple | . 7, | H. Her. | P. | N. Amer. | 1727 |
| caucásicus | . Purple | . 7, | H. Her. | P. | Caucasus | . 1821 |
| chilánsis, 2 | . Yellow | . 9, | H. | B. | Chile | . 1816 |
| chinénsis | . White | . 8, | H. | A. | China | . 1818 |
| compósitus | . Wht. red | . 7, | H. Her. | P. | N. Amer. | . 1811 |
| contórtus | . Pa. pur. | . 7, | H. | B. | | . 1826 |
| delphinifōlius | . Purple | . 8, | G. | B. | S. Amer. | . 1816 |
| divaricátus | . White | . 8, | H. | B. | Mississippi | 1818 |
| glabéllus | . Blue | . 8, | H. Her. | P. | N. Amer. | . 1825 |
| glaúcus, 3 | . Purple all | . G. Ev. | S. | S. Amer. | . 1812 |
| gramíneus | . Purple | . 7, | H. Her. | P. | Siberia | . 1824 |
| grandiflórus | . Purple | . 7, | H. Her. | P. | Switzerl. | . 1819 |
| gravēólens | . Yellow | . 7, | H. | A. | S. Eur. | . 1633 |
| heterophýllus, 4 | . White | . 7, | H. | B. | N. Amer. | . 1640 |
| húmilis | . Flesh | . 8, | H. Her. | P. | N. Amer. | . 1828 |
| involucrátus | . | . 8, | Her. | P. | Brazil | . 1828 |
| jamaicénsis | . Purple | . 8, | A. | Jamaica | . 1818 |
| lævigátus | . White | . 7, | H. | B. | Cayenne | . 1822 |
| Lehmánni | . Lilac | . 8, | H. Her. | P. | | . 1828 |
| linifōlius, 5 | . Purple | . 7, | H. | A. | S. Amer. | . |
| longifōlius | . Purple | . 7, | H. Her. | P. | N. Amer. | . 1830 |
| nudicaúlis | . White | . 7, | H. Her. | P. | N. Amer. | . 1812 |
| philadélphicus | . Purple | . 7, | H. Her. | P. | N. Amer. | . 1778 |
| podólicus | . Purple | . 7, | H. | B. | Podolia | . 1821 |
| purpúreus | . Purple | . 8, | H. Her. | P. | Huds. Bay | . 1776 |
| pusíllus | . White | . 8, | H. | A. | N. Amer. | . 1823 |
| rupéstris | . Purple | . 7, | H. Her. | P. | Switzerl. | . 1819 |
| strigósus | . White | . 7, | H. | B. | N. Amer. | . 1816 |
| unifórus | . Purple | . 8, | H. Her. | P. | Scotland | . |
| Villársii | . Purple | . 7, | H. Her. | P. | Piedmont | . 1804 |

ERINĚUM, *Fries*. From *erinos*, a hedgehog; because of its erinaceous appearance. *Linn.* 24, Or. 9, Nat. Or. *Fungi*. Very minute species, mostly brown or whitish; they are found growing in little tufts, on various kinds of leaves—*acerīnum, ālnēum, aûrēum, betulīnum, clandestīnum, fagīnēum, grisēum, Juglándis, lantēum, Pâdi, populīnum, Pseudo-plátāni, purpurāscens, pyrīnum, rōsēum, Sōrbi, tiliācēum, tortuōsum, Vĭtis.*

ERINŬS, prickly, rough.

ERINŬS, *Linn.* Meaning unknown. Erinos is the wild fig-tree. *Linn.* 14, Or. 2, Nat. Or. *Scrophulariaceæ*. These are pretty dwarf species, and should be in every collection of Alpines. If the soil is sandy, they will succeed well, and young plants are easily obtained from seeds, or divisions.

| | | | | | | |
|---|---|---|---|---|---|---|
| alpínus | . . . | . Blue | . . | 3, H. Her. | P. Pyrenees | . 1739 |
| fragrans | . . . | . Wht. yel. | 5, G. Ev. | S. C. G. H. | . 1776 |
| hispánicus | . . | . Red | . 3, H. Her. | P. Spain | . 1739 |
| Lychnídeá | . . | . Yel. wht. | 5, G. Ev. | S. C. G. H. | . |
| tristis | . . . | . Purple | 5, G. Ev. | S. C. G. H. | . 1825 |

ERIOBÓTRYX, *Lindley*. From *erion*, wool, and *botrys*, a bunch of grapes; the raceme is very woolly. *Linn.* 12, Or. 2, Nat. Or. *Rosaceæ*. E. japonica is the loquat tree of Japan, and is deserving of the most extensive culture, both as a plant of ornament and utility. The flowers are produced in terminal bunches in January, and the fruit ripens, and is fit for table, in April. Plants may be obtained from cuttings, seeds, or grafting. By cuttings, take off the young ripe wood in June, each cutting about two inches long, always cut off at a joint; plant them in a pot of sand, under a glass, plunged up to the rim of the pot in a brisk heat, and they will soon root. By seeds, as soon as they are gathered, they must be sown in a pot of fine-sifted leaf-mould, and the pot plunged in a brisk heat; the soil should be covered with moss, to prevent the surface drying, and in about a fortnight young plants will make their appearance. When about an inch high, they should be planted singly into thimble pots, in a mixture of leaf and heath-mould broken very fine; plunge the pots again in a hotbed till they require another potting, after which, treat them as old plants. The best stock for grafting on is the Whitethorn, and for plants grown in the stove, the end of October is the best time for grafting, and if growing out of doors, grafting may readily be performed at the usual grafting season. *Synonymes*: 1. *Mespilus cuila*. 2. *M. japonica*.

| | | | | | |
|---|---|---|---|---|---|
| ellíptica, 1 | . | . White | . | F. Ev. T. Nepal | . 1828 |
| japónica, 2 | . | . White | . 10, F. Ev. T. Japan | . 1787 |

ERIOCAŮLON, *Linn.* From *erion*, wool, and *caulon*, a stem; in allusion to the woolly stems. *Linn.* 3, Or. 2, Nat. Or. *Restiaceæ*. Very interesting plants, particularly *E. septangulare*, which flourishes ex-

ceedingly well in Scotland, where, in some parts, it is found in abundance.

| | | | | | |
|---|---|---|---|---|---|
| austrále | . . . | . White | . 6, G. | P. N. Holl. | . 1820 |
| decangulāre | . . | . White | . 7, H. Aq. | P. N. Amer. | . 1826 |
| fasciculátum | . . | . White | . 7, S. | A. Guiana | . 1825 |
| septangulāre | . | . White | . 9, H. Aq. | P. Scotland | . |

ERIOCÉPHALUS, *Linn.* From *erion*, wool, and *kephale*, a head; the woolly seeds are collected into heads. *Linn.* 19, Or. 4, Nat. Or. *Compositæ*. Cape evergreen shrubs, of considerable beauty, sometimes growing to the height of six feet. They are cultivated with success in peat and sandy loam mixed, and cuttings root freely in sand, or sandy soil.

| | | | | |
|---|---|---|---|---|
| africánus | . . . | . Yellow | . 2, G. Ev. S. C. G. H. | . 1732 |
| decussátus | . . | . Yellow | . 4, G. Ev. S. C. G. H. | . 1816 |
| purpúreus | . . | . Purple | . 4, G. Ev. S. C. G. H. | . 1816 |
| racemósus | . . | . Yellow | . 3, G. Ev. S. C. G. H. | . 1739 |
| spinéscens | . . | . Yellow | . 5, G. Ev. S. C. G. H. | . 1816 |

ERIOCHÍLUS, *R. Brown*. From *erion*, wool, and *cheilos*, a lip; alluding to the disk of the labellum being pubescent. *Linn.* 20, Or. 1, Nat. Or. *Orchidaceæ*. This plant thrives best in an equal mixture of light turfy loam, peat, and sand, with the pots well drained, to let the water pass off readily; increased by divisions of the roots. *Synonyme*: 1. *Epipactis cucullata*.

| | | | | |
|---|---|---|---|---|
| autumnalis | . . . | . Red | . 10, G. Ter. N. Holl. | . 1823 |

ERIOCÓMA, *Kunth*. Derived from *erion*, wool, and *kome*, hair; alluding to the woolly palea. *Linn.* 19, Or. 2, Nat. Or. *Compositæ*. Very pretty Mexican shrubs, growing about three feet high, and cultivated in almost any common soil, and cuttings root freely in sand, or sandy soil.

| | | | | |
|---|---|---|---|---|
| floribúnda | . . . | . White | . 10, F. Ev. S. Mexico | . 1828 |
| fragrans | . . . | . White | . 9, F. Ev. S. Mexico | . 1828 |

ERIODÉNDRON, *Decandolle*. From *erion*, wool, and *dendron*, a tree; the capsule is filled with a fine, silky, woolly substance. *Linn.* 16, Or. 8, Nat. Or. *Sterculiaceæ*. These are noble plants, growing from fifty to a hundred feet high, in a strong, humid heat, and good rich loam and sandy peat mixed; they may be increased from seeds. The woolly coat of the seeds of some of the species is used in different countries for stuffing cushions, and similar purposes. *Synonymes*: 1. *Bombax pentandrum*. 2. *B. caribæum*. 3. *Bombax erianthos*.

| | | | | |
|---|---|---|---|---|
| anfractuósum, 1 | . | . Scarlet | . S. Ev. T. E. Ind. | . 1789 |
| caribǽum, 2 | . | . Cream | . S. Ev. T. W. Ind. | . 1739 |
| guineénsé | . | . Scarlet | . S. Ev. T. Guinea | . 1826 |
| leianthērum, 3 | . | . Scarlet | . S. Ev. S. Brazil | . 1818 |

ERIOGÓNUM, *Michaux*. From *erion*, wool, and *gonu*, a joint; alluding to the stems being woolly at the joints. *Linn.* 9, Or. 1, Nat. Or. *Polygonaceæ*. The species of this genus are very pretty, and easily cultivated in loam and peat, and young plants are obtained with ease from seeds. *Synonyme*: 1. *E. flavum*.

| | | | | |
|---|---|---|---|---|
| compósitum | . | . Yel. wht. | . 6, H. Her. P. N. Albion | . |
| longifōlium | . | . Yellow | . 6, H. Her. P. N. Amer. | . 1822 |
| pauciflórum | . | . Yellow | . 6, H. Her. P. Louisiana | . 1820 |
| sericéum, 1 | . | . Yellow | . 7, H. Her. P. Missouri | . 1811 |
| tomentósum | . | . Yellow | . 5, H. Her. P. Carolina | . 1811 |

ERIOLǼNA, *Decandolle*. From *erion*, wool, and *chlaina*, a cloak; the calyx is woolly. *Linn.* 16, Or. 8, Nat. Or. *Sterculiaceæ*. These plants are described as being pretty, growing in sandy peat, and multiplied from cuttings.

| | | | | |
|---|---|---|---|---|
| Candóllei | . | . Yellow | . 12, G. Ev. T. Prome | . 1828 |
| Wallíchii | . | . Red | . G. Ev. S. E. Ind. | . 1822 |

ERIOPHÓRUM, *Linn.* From *erion*, wool, and *phoreo*, to bear; the seeds are covered with a woolly substance. *Linn.* 3, Or. 1, Nat. Or. *Gramineæ*. Very interesting plants, found in boggy situations, and may be increased by divisions. It is remarkable for having the seeds covered with a wool-like cottony substance; whence the English name, Cotton Grass.

| | | | | |
|---|---|---|---|---|
| angustifōlium | . . | . Apetal | . 4, Gram. Britain | . . |
| capitátum | . . | . Apetal | . 3, Gram. Scotland | . . |
| gracile | . . | . Apetal | . 7, Gram. Scotland | . . |
| polystáchyon | . . | . Apetal | . 6, Gram. Britain | . . |
| pubéscens | . . | . Apetal | . 3, Gram. England | . . |
| vaginátum | . . | . Apetal | . 6, Gram. Britain | . . |
| virgínicum | . . | . Apetal | . 6, Gram. N. Amer. | . 1830 |

ERIOPHÓRUS, woolly-headed.

**ERIOPHYLLUM,** *Lagasca.* From *erion,* wool, and *phyllon,* a leaf; in allusion to the silky, wool-like substance covering the leaves. *Linn.* 19, Or. 2, Nat. Or. *Compositæ.* The species are pretty, and will thrive in any common soil, and young plants grow well from divisions of the roots. *Synonymes:* 1. *Trichophyllum lanatum, Actinella lanata.* 2. *Trichophyllum oppositifolium.*

| | | | | |
|---|---|---|---|---|
| cæspitosum, 1 | Yellow | 5, H. Ev. Tr. | N. Amer. | 1826 |
| oppositifolium, 2 | Yellow | H. Her. P. | Missouri | |

**ERIOSPERMUM,** *Jacquin.* From *erion,* wool, and *sperma,* a seed; in allusion to the woolly envelope of the seeds. *Linn.* 6, Or. 1, Nat. Or. *Liliaceæ.* Ornamental Cape bulbs when in flower; they grow freely in sandy peat, and may be increased from suckers. *Synonymes:* 1. *E. latifolium.* 2. *Ornithogalum paradoxum.*

| | | | | |
|---|---|---|---|---|
| Bellendeni, 1 | Lgt. blue | 7, G. Bl. P. | C. G. H. | 1806 |
| folioliferum | Yel. grn. | 7, G. Bl. P. | C. G. H. | 1806 |
| lancemfolium | Lgt. blue | 7, G. Bl. P. | C. G. H. | 1795 |
| lanuginosum | Wht. grn. | 7, G. Bl. P. | C. G. H. | 1820 |
| latifolium | Lgt. blue | 7, G. Bl. P. | C. G. H. | 1800 |
| paradoxum, 2 | | 7, G. Bl. P. | C. G. H. | 1825 |
| parvifolium | Drk. blue | 7, G. Bl. P. | C. G. H. | 1795 |
| pubescens | Wht. grn. | 7, G. Bl. P. | C. G. H. | 1820 |

**ERIOSTEMON,** *Smith.* From *erion,* wool, and *stemon,* a stamen; because of the woolly stamens. *Linn.* 10, Or. 1, Nat. Or. *Rutaceæ.* Beautiful New Holland shrubs, varying from one to three feet high. They grow best in very sandy peat and a little loam mixed, and increase readily from cuttings in sand, or sandy soil.

| | | | | |
|---|---|---|---|---|
| buxifolius | Pink | 5, G. Ev. S. | N. Holl. | 1824 |
| cuspidatus | Red | 6, G. Ev. S. | N. Holl. | 1824 |
| ericifolius | Red | 6, G. Ev. S. | N. Holl. | 1824 |
| gracilis | Lilac | 7, G. Ev. S. | N. Holl. | 1831 |
| lanceolatus | Red | 6, G. Ev. S. | N. Holl. | 1823 |
| linearifolius | Red | 6, G. Ev. S. | N. Holl. | 1823 |
| myoporoides | White | 9, G. Ev. S. | N. Holl. | 1824 |
| obovatus | Red | 5, G. Ev. S. | N. Holl. | 1824 |
| salicifolius | Red | 6, G. Ev S. | N. Holl. | 1824 |
| squametus | Red | 6, G. Ev. S. | N. Holl. | 1822 |

**ERISMA,** *Rudge.* From *erisma,* strife; so named from the anomalous form of the genus, which is at so much variance with others. *Linn.* 1, Or. 1, Nat. Or. *Vochyaceæ.* An ornamental plant, thriving well in a mixture of peat and loam, and cuttings of the ripened wood will root in sand, under a glass, in heat.

| | | | | |
|---|---|---|---|---|
| floribunda | Blue | 10, S. Ev. T. | Guiana | 1825 |

**ERITHALIS,** *P. Browne.* From *erithallo,* to grow green; alluding to the deep green, shining leaves. *Linn.* 5, Or. 1, Nat. Or. *Cinchonaceæ.* A pretty genus of trees, succeeding well in the stove in a strong heat, and rich loam, mixed with a little peat; cuttings root readily in sand, under a glass, in heat.

| | | | | |
|---|---|---|---|---|
| fruticosa | White | 7, S. Ev. T. | Jamaica | 1793 |
| Timon | | S. Ev. T. | E. Ind. | 1823 |

**ERNODEA,** *Swartz.* From *ernodes,* branched; the plant is much branched. *Linn.* 4, Or. 1, Nat. Or. *Cinchonaceæ.* This is, though a dwarf, a very pretty plant, and succeeds best in gravelly soil; young plants are obtained by dividing the roots. *Synonyme:* 1. *Asperula calabrica, Pavetta fœtidissima.*

| | | | | |
|---|---|---|---|---|
| montana, 1 | Red | 6, F. Ev. Tr. | Sicily | 1820 |

**ERODIUM,** *L'Heritier.* From *erodios,* a heron; the carpels resemble the head and beak of that bird. *Linn.* 16, Or. 2, Nat. Or. *Geraniaceæ.* An extensive genus of plants, of considerable beauty; they thrive well in any common soil, with the usual treatment. *Synonymes:* 1. *E. alpinum.* 2. *E. graveolens.* 3. *E. chamædryoides, Geranium Reichardi.* 4. *E. multicaule, ruthenicum.* 5. *E. multifidum.*

| | | | | |
|---|---|---|---|---|
| alpinum | Red | 6, H. Her. P. | Italy | 1814 |
| anthemidifolium | Purple | 6, H. Her. P. | Iberia | 1820 |
| Botrys | Blue | 6, H. | A. Italy | 1818 |
| caucalifolium, 1 | Purple | 6, H. Her. P. | France | 1816 |
| cicutifolium | Purple | 6, H. | A. France | 1816 |
| crassifolium | Scarlet | 6, F. Her. P. | Cyprus | 1788 |
| glandulosum, 2 | Purple | 7, F. Her. P. | Spain | 1798 |
| Gussoni | Pa. pur. | 6, H. Her. P. | Naples | 1821 |
| hirtum | Purple | 7, H. Her. P. | Egypt | 1818 |
| hymenodes | Pink | 7, F. Her. P. | Barbary | 1789 |
| incarnatum | Flesh | 6, G. Ev. S. | C. G. H. | 1787 |
| laciniatum | Red | 6, F. Her. P. | Crete | 1794 |

| | | | | |
|---|---|---|---|---|
| maineboides | Blue | 7, H. | A. S. Eur. | 1596 |
| malapoides | Purple | 6, H. Her. P. | N. Africa | 1800 |
| corsicum | Purple | 6, H. Her. P. | Corsica | 1817 |
| melastigmatum | Purple | 6, F. Her. P. | | 1828 |
| moschatum | Purple | 6, H. | A. England | |
| muricatum | Red | 7, H. | A. | 1827 |
| murinum | Blue | 7, H. | A. N. Africa | 1818 |
| petræum | Purple | 7, H. Her. P. | S. Eur. | 1640 |
| pilosum | Dk. pur. | 7, H. | A. France | 1800 |
| pimpinellifolium | Purple | 7, H. | A. S. Eur. | 1800 |
| Reichardi, 3 | White | 7, F. Her. P. | Minorca | 1783 |
| ribifolium | Purple | 6, H. | A. C. G. H. | |
| romanum | Purple | 5, H. | B. Rome | 1724 |
| serotinum, 4 | Blue | 8, H. Her. P. | Siberia | 1821 |
| Stephanianum, 5 | Blue | 6, H. Her. P. | Dahuria | 1820 |
| stylatum | Purple | 6, H. Her. P. | | 1826 |

*bipinnatum, chium, cicônium, cicutârium, glaucophyllum, gruinum, littoreum, maritimum.*

**EROPHILA,** *Decandolle.* From *er,* the spring, and *phileo,* to love; alluding to the time of flowering. *Linn.* 15, Nat. Or. *Cruciferæ.* Minute plants, one of which, *E. vulgaris,* is a native of Britain, and better known by the name of *Draba verna;* it is very pretty in spring when seen growing upon old walls, and other like places, where it is generally abundant. Any soil seems to suit these plants; but if it consists chiefly of loam, so much the better they will grow; seed is produced in abundance. *Synonymes:* 1. *Draba præcox.* 2. *D. verna.*

| | | | | |
|---|---|---|---|---|
| americana | White | 3, H. | A. N. Amer. | 1816 |
| præcox, 1 | White | 3, H. | A. Caucasus | 1820 |
| vulgaris, 2 | White | 3, H. | A. Britain | |

**EROSE,** gnawed, bitten; a term used to denote a particular kind of irregular denticulation.

**EROSELY-TOOTHED,** the teeth are gnawed, or erose.

**ERRHINE,** promoting a discharge of mucus from the nostrils.

**ERPETION,** *Decandolle.* From *erpetos,* creeping, and *ion,* the Greek name for violet; in reference to the creeping rooting stems. *Linn.* 5, Or. 1, Nat. Or. *Violaceæ.* Small, but pretty evergreen creepers, of much interest; they grow in sandy peat, and are multiplied by parting the roots. *Synonymes:* 1. *Viola hederacea.* 2. *V. hederacea Blatines.*

| | | | | |
|---|---|---|---|---|
| hederacea, 1 | Pa. blue | 7, F. Ev. Cr. | N. Holl. | 1823 |
| reniformis, 2 | Pa. blue | 7, F. Ev. Cr. | N. Holl. | 1823 |

**ERUBESCENT,** reddish, blush-coloured.

**ERUCA,** *Tournefort.* From *uro,* to burn; the seeds have a burning taste, and when applied to the skin, cause blisters. *Linn.* 15, Nat. Or. *Cruciferæ.* These plants possess but little to recommend them; they will grow in any common soil, and may be increased from seed. *Synonyma:* 1. *Brassica Eruca.*

| | | | | |
|---|---|---|---|---|
| hispida | White | 7, H. | A. Naples | 1800 |
| sativa, 1 | Pa. yel. | 7, H. | A. S. Eur. | 1573 |
| alba-glabra | White | 7, H. | A. S. Eur. | 1577 |
| alba-pilosa | White | 7, H. | A. S. Eur. | 1577 |
| eruoides | Pa. yel. | 7, H. | A. S. Eur. | 1577 |
| exotica | Yellow | 7, H. | A. S. Eur. | 1577 |
| flava-glabra | Yellow | 7, H. | A. S. Eur. | 1577 |
| flava-pilosa | Yellow | 7, H. | A. S. Eur. | 1577 |
| turgida | Yellow | 7, H. | A. S. Eur. | 1577 |
| vesicaria | Pa. yel. | 7, H. | A. Spain | 1820 |

**ERUCARIA,** *Gærtner.* Said to be from *eruca,* a rocket, because of its analogy. *Linn.* 15, Nat. Or. *Cruciferæ.* These are uninteresting dwarf annuals, of the simplest culture. *Synonymes:* 1. *Cordylocarpus lævigatus.* 2. *Brassica crassifolia.* 3. *Sinapis hispanica—aleppica 1, crassifolia 2, tenuifolia 3.*

**ERVUM,** *Linn.* From *erw,* tilled land, in Celtic; some of the species are a pest in cultivated ground. *Linn.* 17, Or. 4, Nat. Or. *Leguminosæ.* Plants with little to recommend them; they are of the simplest culture. *Synonymes:* 1. *Vicia Ervilia, Ervilia sativa.* 2. *Vicia gracilis.* 3. *E soloniense, uniflorum, Cicer ervoides.* 4. *Vicia articulata, Lathyrus monanthos.* 5. *E. lentoides.*

| | | | | |
|---|---|---|---|---|
| Ervilia, 1 | Purple | 6, H. Cl. | A. S. Eur. | 1596 |
| Lens | Pa. blue | 6, H. Cl. | A. France | 1548 |
| monânthos, 4 | Purple | 6, H. Cl. | A. S. Eur. | 1798 |

*dispermum, Ervilia 1, gracile 2, hirsutum, Lenticula 3, nigricans 5, pubescens, tetraspermum.*

**ERYNGO,** see **Eryngium.**

**ERYNGIUM,** *Tournefort.* From *ereugo,* to belch; according to Dioscorides, this plant is a specific against all complaints arising from flatulence. *Linn.* 5, Or. 2, Nat. Or. *Umbelliferæ.* Most of the species of this extensive genus are extremely ornamental and beautiful, more especially the hardier kinds, which are, on that account, particularly well adapted for the flower-border. They thrive best in a light sandy soil, though they will all grow in any common garden soil. The greenhouse and frame kinds should be grown in pots, so that they may be sheltered in winter. They are readily increased by seeds, or dividing at the roots. The roots of *E. campestre* are slightly aromatic.

| | | | | | | | |
|---|---|---|---|---|---|---|---|
| alpīnŭm | . | Blue | . | 7, H. Her. P. | Switzerl. | . | 1597 |
| amethystīnŭm | . | Lgt. blue | 7, H. Her. P. | Styria | . | 1648 |
| AndersŏnII | . | Blue | . | 7, H. Her. P. | | . | 1800 |
| aquātĭcŭm | . | White | . | 8, H. Her. P. | N. Amer. | . | 1699 |
| Aquĭfŏlĭŭm | . | Blue | . | 8, H. Her. P. | S. Spain | . | 1816 |
| asperĭfŏlĭŭm | . | White | . | 7, H. Her. P. | | . | 1820 |
| azūrĕŭm | . | Blue | . | 7, H. Her. P. | S. Eur. | . | 1790 |
| Bourgati | . | Pa. blue | . | 7, H. Her. P. | S. France | . | 1731 |
| bromeliæfŏlĭŭm | White | . | 7, H. Her. P. | N. Spain | . | 1824 |
| cærūlĕŭm | . | Blue | . | 7, H. Her. P. | Caspian . | . | 1816 |
| campĕstrĕ | . | Blue | . | 7, H. Her. P. | Britain | | |
| CervantesII | . | Green | . | 8, G. Her. P. | Mexico | . | 1820 |
| comŏsŭm | . | Blue | . | 7, G. Her. P. | N. Spain | . | 1818 |
| cornĭcŭlātŭm | . | Green | . | 7, H. Her. P. | Portugal | . | 1808 |
| dichŏtŏmŭm | . | Blue | . | 7, H. Her. P. | S. Eur. | . | 1820 |
| dilatātŭm | . | Blue | . | 7, H. Her. P. | Portugal | . | 1821 |
| ebracteātŭm | . | White | . | 7, G. Her. P. | B. Ayres | . | 1817 |
| fœtĭdŭm | . | Green | . | 9, S. Her. P. | W. Ind. | . | 1714 |
| galĭoĭdēs | . | Green | . | 7, H. Her. P. | Portugal | . | 1810 |
| gigantēŭm | . | Blue | . | 7, H. Her. P. | Caucasus | . | 1820 |
| glomerātŭm | . | Blue | . | 7, H. Her. P. | S. Eur. | . | 1826 |
| grăcĭlĕ | . | Blue | . | 7, S. Her. P. | N. Spain | . | 1824 |
| longĭfŏlĭŭm | . | White | . | 7, S. Her. P. | Mexico | . | 1820 |
| marĭtĭmŭm | . | Blue | . | 7, H. Her. P. | Britain | | |
| ovīnŭm | . | White | . | 7, G. Her. P. | N. Holl. | . | 1824 |
| plānŭm | . | Lgt. blue | 7, H. Her. P. | Europe | . | 1596 |
| pusĭllŭm | . | Green | . | 7, H. Her. P. | Spain | . | 1640 |
| rĭgĭdŭm | . | Blue | . | 7, H. Her. P. | France | . | 1816 |
| serrātŭm | . | Blue | . | 7, G. Her. P. | N. Spain | . | 1800 |
| tĕnŭĕ | . | Blue | . | 7, H. | | B. Spain | . | 1824 |
| trĭcuspĭdātŭm | . | Green | . | 9, H. | | B. Spain | . | 1699 |
| trĭquĕtrŭm | . | Blue | . | 7, H. Her. P. | S. Eur. | . | 1824 |
| virgātŭm | . | Lgt. blue | 6, H. Her. P. | N. Amer. | . | 1810 |
| virgĭniānŭm | . | Blue | . | 8, H. Her. P. | N. Amer. | | |

ERYSĬMŬM, *Gærtner.* From *erion*, to draw, to cure; it is reckoned a powerful cure for a sore throat; it is also said to draw and produce blisters. *Linn.* 15, Nat. Or. *Cruciferæ.* An extensive genus, of little merit. The herbaceous kinds thrive well in common soil, or in a mixture of loam and peat; they may be increased by cuttings, under a glass. The annual and biennial species merely require sowing in the open border *Synonymes*: 1. *Brassica alpina.* 2. *E. diffusum.* 3. *Cheiranthus virgatus.* 4. *Brassica austriaca.* 5. *Cheiranthus bicolor.* 6. *C. alpinus.* 7. *C. collinus.* 8. *C. decumbens.* 9. *C. dubius.* 10. *C. firmus.* 11. *C. helveticus.* 12. *C. armeniacus.* 13. *C. erysimoides.* 14. *C. leptophyllus.* 15. *E. grandiflorum.* 16. *E. grandiflorum.* 17. *Brassica orientalis.* 18. *Cheiranthus rhaticus.* 19. *C. quadrangularis.* 20. *C. siliculosus.* 21. *C. strigosus.* 22. *C. hieracifolius.* 23. *C. versicolor.*

| | | | | | | | |
|---|---|---|---|---|---|---|---|
| altissĭmŭm | . | Yellow | 6, H. | | B. | Germany | . 1818 |
| AndrzejoskiānŭmII 2 | Yellow | . | 6, H. | | B. | Tauria | . 1818 |
| aūrĕŭm | . . | Yellow | . | 6, H. | | B. | Caucasus | . 1820 |
| bĭcŏlŏr, 5 | . . | Yellow | . | 5, H. | | B. | Switzerl. | . 1819 |
| canĕscĕns, 6 | . | Yellow | . | 5, H. | | B. | S. Eur. | . 1816 |
| collīnŭm, 7 . | . | Yellow | . | 5, H. | | B. | Caucasus | . 1823 |
| decŭmbĕns, 8 | . | Yellow | . | 6, H. | | B. | Switzerl. | . 1819 |
| firmŭm, 10 . | . | Yellow | . | 7, H. | | B. | Switzerl. | . 1819 |
| hieracĭfŏlĭŭm | . | Yellow | . | 7, H. | | B. | N. Eur. | . 1819 |
| ibērĭcŭm, 12 | . | Yellow | . | 5, H. | | B. | Armenia | . 1808 |
| intermĕdĭŭm | . | Yellow | . | 6, H. | | B. | Switzerl. | . 1819 |
| leptophyllŭm, 14 | . | Yellow | . | 6, H. | | B. | Iberia | . 1821 |
| longĭfŏlĭŭm, 16 | . | Yellow | . | 6, H. | | B. | S. Eur. | . 1823 |
| longĭsĭlĭquŏsŭm | . | Yellow | . | 6, H. | | B. | Switzerl. | . 1819 |
| pătŭlŭm | . . | Yellow | . | 6, H. | | B. | S. Eur. | . 1820 |
| perfŏliātŭm, 17 | . | White | . | 5, H. | | A. | Austria | . 1818 |
| pŭmĭlŭm | . . | Yellow | . | 5, H. | | B. | Switzerl. | . 1819 |
| quadrĭcŏrnĕ | . | Yellow | . | 6, H. | | A. | Siberia | . 1821 |
| RedōwskiII | . | White | . | 6, H. | | B. | Siberia | . 1821 |
| rhætĭcŭm, 18 | . | Yellow | . | 5, H. | | B. | Switzerl. | . 1819 |
| strĭgŏsŭm, 21 | . | Yellow | . | 6, H. | | B. | Siberia | . 1806 |
| strĭctŭm, 22 | . | Yellow | . | 6, H. | | B. | Austria | . 1819 |
| suffrutĭcŏsŭm, 23 | . | Yellow | . | 6, H. Ev. | B. | Europe | . 1820 |
| versĭcŏlŏr, 23 | . | Varieg. | . | 5, H. Her. P. | Caucasus | . 1825 |

*alpīnŭm* 1, *angustĭfŏlĭŭm* 3, *aspĕrŭm*, *austrīăcŭm* 4, *cheiranthoīdēs*, *cuspĭdātŭm*, *diffūsŭm*, *dŭbĭŭm* 9, *exaltātŭm*, *helvĕtĭcŭm*, *lanceolātŭm* 13, *leptŏstĭglŭm* 15, *Marschalliānŭm*, *odorātŭm*, *repāndŭm*, *sessĭlĭflōrŭm* 19, *sĭcŭlŭm*, *sĭlĭcŭlōsŭm* 20, *virgātŭm.*

ERYSĬPHÆ, *Decandolle.* The name given to mildew by the Greeks. *Linn.* 24, Or. 9, Nat. Or. *Fungi.* Very minute, mostly whitish species, found most

commonly in autumn, on a great variety of plants, shrubs, and trees—*adŭncă, Pŏpŭlī, Prunāstrī, bĭcŏrnĭs, commūnĭs, Cichoracĕārŭm, Legŭmĭnŏsārŭm, Pŏlygŏnĕārŭm, Ranunculacĕārŭm, Umbellĭfĕrārŭm, dĭvărĭcātă, deprĕssă, Artemĭsĭæ, Bardānă, fŭlgĭnĕă, guttātă, coryli, Ulmōrŭm, lamprocărpă, penĭcĭllātă, Berbĕrĭdĭs, Grossulărĭă.*

ERYTHRÆA, *Richard.* From *erythros*, red; alluding to the colour of the flowers. *Linn.* 5, Or. 1, Nat. Or. *Gentianaceæ.* The species of this genus are pretty, but not easy of cultivation. The herbaceous species require an open, loamy soil, and may be increased by divisions. The annuals and biennials require sowing in the open border, in autumn, or they will not come up. *Synonymes*: 1. *Chironia Centaurium.* 2. *C. littoralis.* 3. *C. pulchella.*

| | | | | | | | |
|---|---|---|---|---|---|---|---|
| aggregātă | . | Red | . | 7, H. | | B. | S. Eur. | . 1824 |
| Cachanlăhŭĕn | . | Pink | . | 7, F. | | A. | Chile | . 1825 |
| Centaūrĭŭm, 1 | . | Pink | . | 7, H. | | A. | Britain | |
| confĕrtă | . . | Pink | . | 6, G. Her. P. | Spain | . 1824 |
| latĭfŏlĭă | . . | Pink | . | 6, H. | | A. | Britain | |
| littŏrālĭs, 2 | . | Pink | . | 5, H. | | A. | England | |
| lūtĕă | . . | Yellow | . | 7, H. | | A. | S. Eur. | . 1824 |
| marĭtĭmă | . . | Yellow | . | 7, G. Her. P. | S. Eur. | . 1777 |
| Massŏnī | . | Yellow | . | 7, F. Her. P. | Azores | . 1777 |
| pulchĕllă, 3 | . | Pink | . | 6, H. | | A. | England | |
| spĭcātă | . | Pink | . | 7, H. | | A. | S. France | . 1820 |

ERYTHRĬNĂ, *Linn.* From *erythros*, red; in reference to the colour of the flowers. *Linn.* 17, Or. 4, Nat. Or. *Leguminosæ.* These are all splendid plants, with fine large leaves, and beautiful, brilliant, scarlet, or red flowers; the compost best suited for them is one part fresh maiden loam, one part sandy peat, and one part of horse-dung, well rotted and pulverised. The whole should be well incorporated and chopped, and also well exposed during frost in winter. As soon as the plants have done growing, cut them down, and set them in a cool greenhouse, where they may be kept quite dry till the end of November, when they may be potted into fresh soil, and pots of a proper size. When potted, water, and set them in a house where the heat is about sixty degrees, and about March they will flower in perfection. When the plants are again out of flower, cut them down, as before, to five or six eyes, according to the strength of the stems; re-pot them, and place them in the stove until they have taken root, and made shoots from nine to twelve inches, when they must be removed to a house of the temperature of from fifty-five to sixty degrees, allowing them plenty of light; they must be frequently syringed, to prevent the attacks of the red spider. Continue this treatment till they show flower, then allow them plenty of air and moisture, and they will flower freely again in July, after which, it is advisable to give them their winter. Cuttings taken off at a joint, without depriving them of their leaves, root readily in sand, under a hand-glass, in a moist heat. *E. Crista-galli*, and *E. laurifolia*, will thrive and flower freely in warm sheltered situations out of doors; in such a situation, they are killed to the stump in winter without they are cut down to about four inches of the stem, and sheltered by an inverted flower-pot. *Synonymes*: 1. *E. velutina.* 2. *E. arborea.*

| | | | | | | | |
|---|---|---|---|---|---|---|---|
| abyssĭnĭcă | . | Scarlet | . | 8, S. Ev. S. | Abyssinia | . 1820 |
| acŭleātīssĭmă | . | Scarlet | . | 8, S. Ev. T. | E. Ind. | . 1800 |
| arborĕscĕns | . | Scarlet | . | 8, S. Ev. T. | E. Ind. | . 1818 |
| austrālĭs | . . | | | 8, S. Ev. T. | Moreton B. | . 1830 |
| caffră | . . | Scarlet | . | 8, S. Ev. S. | C. G. H. | . 1816 |
| cārnĕă | . . | Pink | . | 5, S. Ev. T. | Vera Cruz. | . 1738 |
| Corallodendrŭm | . | Scarlet | . | 5, S. Ev. T. | W. Ind. | . 1690 |
| Crista-gallī | . | Scarlet | . | 8, S. Ev. T. | Brasil | . 1771 |
| enneāndră, 1 | . | Scarlet | . | 8, S. Ev. | | |
| fulgĕns | . . | Scarlet | . | 8, S. Ev. S. | E. Ind. | . 1801 |
| fŭscă | . . | Scarlet | . | 8, S. Ev. T. | E. Ind. | . 1800 |
| glaūcă | . . | Scarlet | . | 8, S. Ev. T. | Caraccas | . 1823 |
| herbācĕă | . . | Scarlet | . | 7, G. Her. P. | Carolina | . 1824 |
| hŏrrĭdă | . . | Scarlet | . | 8, S. Ev. S. | Mexico | . 1824 |
| incānă | . . | Scarlet | . | 8, S. Ev. T. | E. Ind. | . 1820 |
| indĭcă | . . | Scarlet | . | 8, S. Ev. T. | E. Ind. | . 1814 |
| laurĭfŏlĭă | . . | Scarlet | . | 8, S. Her. P. | S. Amer. | . 1800 |
| macrophyllă | . . | Scarlet | . | 8, S. Ev. T. | Teneriffe | . 1822 |
| mĭtĭs | . . | Scarlet | . | 8, S. Ev. T. | Caraccas | . 1790 |
| nānă | . . | Scarlet | . | G. De. S. | | . 1823 |
| ovalĭfŏlĭă | . . | Scarlet | . | 8, S. Ev. S. | E. Ind. | . 1816 |
| ovālĭs | . . | Scarlet | . | 8, S. Ev. S. | Nepal | . 1820 |
| pĭctă | . . | Scarlet | . | 8, S. Ev. S. | E. Ind. | . 1696 |
| piscĭdĭoīdēs | . | Scarlet | . | 8, S. Ev. T. | E. Ind. | . 1800 |
| polĭanthĕs | . . | Scarlet | . | 8, S. Ev. S. | S. Amer. | . 1820 |

[ 196 ]

| | | | | |
|---|---|---|---|---|
| portoricensis . | . Scarlet . | 8. Ev. 8. | Porto Rico . | 1800 |
| resupinata . | . Scarlet . | 8. Her. P. | E. Ind. . | 1823 |
| rubrinervia . | . Scarlet . | 8. Ev. T. | Bogota . | 1823 |
| secundiflora . | . Scarlet . | 8. Ev. T. | Brazil . | 1820 |
| spathacea . | . Scarlet . | 8. Ev. T. | W. Ind. . | 1824 |
| speciosa . | . Scarlet . | 9, 8. Ev. T. | W. Ind. . | 1805 |
| stricta . | . Scarlet . | 8. Ev. 8. | E. Ind. . | 1816 |
| suberosa . | . Scarlet . | 8. Ev. T. | E. Ind. . | 1816 |
| umbrosa, 2 . | . Scarlet . | 8. Ev. T. | Caraccas . | 1817 |
| velutina . | . Scarlet . | 8. Ev. T. | Caraccas . | 1810 |

ERYTHROLÆNA, *Sweet.* From *erythros*, red, and *chlæna*, a cloak; alluding to the scales of the calyx. *Linn.* 19, Or. 1, Nat. Or. *Compositæ.* A very pretty Mexican species, producing its scarlet and orange flowers in abundance; it delights in a rich soil, and young plants are readily obtained from seed.

| | | | | |
|---|---|---|---|---|
| conspicua . | . Scar. oran. | 9, H. | B. Mexico . | 1825 |

ERYTHRONIUM, *Linn.* From *erythros*, red; in allusion to the colour of the leaves and flowers. *Linn.* 6, Or. 1, Nat. Or. *Liliaceæ.* These are handsome, though dwarf-growing plants. They all thrive in common garden soil, except *E. lanceolatum*, which requires a peat soil, or it will not succeed; they are increased from offsets. Synonyme: 1. *E. americanum.*

| | | | | |
|---|---|---|---|---|
| albidum . | . White . | 4, H. Bl. P. | Louisiana . | 1824 |
| Dens canis . | . Red lilac . | 3, H. Bl. P. | Europe . | 1596 |
| albidum . | . White . | 3, H. Bl. P. | Italy . | 1596 |
| rubrum . | . Red lilac . | 3, H. Bl. P. | Europe . | 1596 |
| grandiflorum . | . Yellow . | 5, H. Bl. P. | N. Amer. . | 1826 |
| lanceolatum, 1 . | . Yellow . | 4, H. Bl. P. | N. Amer. . | 1665 |

ERYTHROPHLÆUM, *R. Brown.* From *erythros*, red; in reference to the red juice which flows from the tree when cut. *Linn.* 10, Or. 1, Nat. Or. *Leguminosæ.* This is a lofty and an ornamental tree, growing about a hundred feet high. The natives of many parts of Western Africa use the red juice of the tree as an ordeal, to detect the guilt of those accused of any crime. The juice is taken in large draughts, and those who are not sufficiently strong to stand this ordeal, are pronounced guilty, and those who are, are considered innocent; whence the tree is called Gregre-tree, or Ordeal-tree. Synonyme: 1. *Afzelia grandis.*

| | | | | |
|---|---|---|---|---|
| guineense . | . Pa. yel. . | 8. Ev. T. | S. Leone . | 1793 |

ERYTHROXYLON, *Linn.* From *erythros*, red, and *xylon*, wood; the wood of the trees is red. *Linn.* 10, Or. 3, Nat. Or. *Malpighiaceæ.* These trees are not possessed of much beauty. They require to be grown in a mixture of peat and loam, and cuttings, not too ripe, will root in sand, under a glass, in a moist heat.

| | | | | |
|---|---|---|---|---|
| havanense . | . Yel. grn. . | 8. Ev. T. | Havannah . | 1822 |
| hypericifolium . | . Yel. grn. . | 8. Ev. T. | Maurit. . | 1818 |
| laurifolium . | . Yel. grn. . | 8. Ev. T. | Maurit. . | 1823 |

ESCALLONIA, *Mutis.* In honour of Escallon, a Spanish traveller in South America, who first found the species in New Granada. *Linn.* 5, Or. 1, Nat. Or. *Escalloniaceæ.* All the species of this genus are very fine, evergreen, greenhouse shrubs, several of which are sufficiently hardy to stand our winters when planted against a south wall, with the protection of a mat in severe weather. They grow best in a mixture of peat, sand, and loam; cuttings taken off as soon as the wood is ripened, will root readily if planted in sand, under a glass. Synonyme: 1. *E. bifida.*

| | | | | |
|---|---|---|---|---|
| discolor . | . White . | 8. Ev. S. | S. Amer. . | 1830 |
| glandulosa . | . Red . | 9, G. Ev. S. | Chile . | 1827 |
| illinita . | . White . | 8, G. Ev. S. | Chile . | 1830 |
| montevidensis, 1 . | . White . | 8, G. Ev. S. | Monte Vid. | 1827 |
| pulverulenta . | . | G. Ev. S. | Chile . | 1831 |
| rubra . | . Red . | 9, G. Ev. S. | Chile . | 1827 |
| viscosa . | . White . | G. Ev. S. | Mendoza . | 1829 |

ESCHAROTIC, having the power to scar or burn the skin.

ESCHSCHOLTZIA, see *Chryseïs.*

ESCULENT, good for food.

ETHULIA, *Cassini.* Meaning unknown. *Linn.* 19, Or. 1, Nat. Or. *Compositæ.* Stove annuals, not worth cultivating, except in botanical collections. Synonyms: 1. *E. sinapifolia, brasiliensis, conyzoides, divaricata, integrifolia* 1.

EUCALYPTUS, *L'Heritier.* From *eu*, well, and *kalypto*, to cover; the limb of the calyx covers the flower before expansion, and afterwards falls off in the

shape of a lid, or cover. *Linn.* 12, Or. 1, Nat. Or. *Myrtaceæ.* All the species of this genus are very tall and handsome, and as they grow fast, are well adapted for conservatories. *E. perfoliata* will endure the open air against a south wall, in which situation it looks very handsome, on account of its hoary, bluish foliage, and neat growth of the branches. They delight to grow in a mixture of peat, loam, and sand; and cuttings, not too ripe, root readily in sand, under a glass. A kind of gum, called *kino*, is got from *E. resinifera*, and sold in the medicine bazaars of India; and various other species yield a large quantity of tannin, which is extracted from the trees in New Holland, and sent to the English market, and is said to be twice as powerful in its operations as oak-bark. Synonyme: 1. *E. cordata.*

| | | | | |
|---|---|---|---|---|
| alata . | . White . | G. Ev. T. | N. Holl. | 1816 |
| albicaulis . | . White . | G. Ev. T. | N. Holl. | 1810 |
| amygdalina . | . White . | G. Ev. S. | V. D. L. | 1820 |
| angustifolia . | . White . | G. Ev. T. | N. Holl. | 1810 |
| botryoides . | . White . | 6, G. Ev. T. | N. Holl. | 1803 |
| capitellata . | . White . | G. Ev. T. | N. Holl. | 1804 |
| cornuta . | . White . | G. Ev. T. | N. Holl. | 1803 |
| corymbosa . | . White . | G. Ev. T. | N. S. W. | 1788 |
| cotinifolia . | . White . | G. Ev. T. | N. Holl. | 1818 |
| curvula . | . White . | G. Ev. T. | N. Holl. | |
| elongata . | . White . | G. Ev. T. | N. Holl. | 1823 |
| eugenioides . | . White . | G. Ev. T. | N. Holl. | |
| globulus . | . White . | G. Ev. T. | N. Holl. | 1810 |
| hæmastoma . | . White . | G. Ev. T. | N. Holl. | 1803 |
| heterophylla . | . White . | G. Ev. T. | N. Holl. | 1820 |
| hirsuta . | . White . | G. Ev. T. | N. Holl. | |
| hypericifolia . | . White . | G. Ev. T. | N. Holl. | 1823 |
| incrassata . | . White . | G. Ev. T. | N. Holl. | 1816 |
| longifolia . | . White . | 6, G. Ev. T. | N. Holl. | |
| marginata . | . White . | G. Ev. T. | N. Holl. | 1794 |
| media . | . White . | G. Ev. T. | N. Holl. | 1823 |
| microphylla . | . White . | G. Ev. T. | N. Holl. | 1823 |
| mucronata . | . White . | G. Ev. T. | N. Holl. | 1823 |
| multiflora . | . White . | G. Ev. T. | N. Holl. | 1820 |
| myrtifolia . | . White . | G. Ev. S. | N. Holl. | 1823 |
| obliqua . | . White . | 7, G. Ev. T. | V. D. L. | 1774 |
| orbicularis . | . White . | G. Ev. T. | N. Holl. | 1816 |
| ovata . | . White . | G. Ev. T. | N. Holl. | 1820 |
| paniculata . | . White . | G. Ev. T. | N. S. W. | 1804 |
| pauciflora . | . White . | G. Ev. T. | N. Holl. | |
| perfoliata . | . White . | G. Ev. T. | N. Holl. | 1820 |
| pernicifolia . | . White . | 7, G. Ev. T. | C. G. H. | 1817 |
| phillyreoides . | . White . | G. Ev. T. | N. Holl. | 1820 |
| pilularis . | . White . | G. Ev. T. | N. S. W. | 1804 |
| piperita . | . White . | G. Ev. T. | N. S. W. | 1788 |
| pulchella . | . White . | G. Ev. T. | N. Holl. | 1820 |
| pulverulenta, 1 . | . White . | 6, G. Ev. T. | N. Holl. | 1816 |
| pulvigera . | . White . | G. Ev. T. | N. Holl. | 1824 |
| purpurascens . | . White . | G. Ev. T. | N. Holl. | 1823 |
| resinifera . | . White . | 5, G. Ev. T. | N. S. W. | 1788 |
| reticulata . | . White . | G. Ev. S. | N. Holl. | 1823 |
| robusta . | . White . | 8, G. Ev. T. | N. S. W. | 1794 |
| rostrata . | . White . | G. Ev. T. | N. S. W. | 1804 |
| saligna . | . White . | G. Ev. T. | N. S. W. | 1804 |
| scabra . | . White . | G. Ev. T. | N. Holl. | 1810 |
| stenophylla . | . White . | G. Ev. T. | N. Holl. | 1823 |
| stricta . | . White . | G. Ev. T. | N. Holl. | |
| tereticornis . | . White . | G. Ev. T. | N. Holl. | 1804 |
| triantha . | . White . | G. Ev. T. | N. Holl. | 1823 |
| undulata . | . White . | G. Ev. T. | N. Holl. | 1820 |
| verrucosa . | . White . | G. Ev. T. | N. Holl. | 1820 |
| viminalis . | . White . | G. Ev. T. | N. Holl. | 1810 |
| virgata . | . White . | G. Ev. T. | N. Holl. | |

EUCHARIDIUM, *Fischer and Meyer.* From *eucharis*, agreeable; in allusion to the appearance of the plant. *Linn.* 8, Or. 1, Nat. Or. *Onagraceæ.* A pretty little plant, nearly allied to *Clarkia*; it flowers about six weeks from the time of germination, and is perfectly hardy.

| | | | | |
|---|---|---|---|---|
| concinnum . | . Purple . | 6, H. | A. N. Amer. . | 1836 |

EUCHILUS, *R. Brown.* From *eu*, well, or good, and *cheilos*, a lip; the upper lip of the calyx is very large. *Linn.* 10, Or. 1, Nat. Or. *Leguminosæ.* A very pretty plant when in flower. For culture and propagation, see *Pultenæa.*

| | | | | |
|---|---|---|---|---|
| obcordatus . | . Yellow . | 4, G. Ev. S. | N. Holl. . | 1803 |

EUCHROMA, *Nuttall.* From *eu*, well, or good, and *chroma*, a colour; alluding to the colour of the bracteas. *Linn.* 14, Or. 2, Nat. Or. *Scrophulariaceæ.* Dwarf ornamental plants, of easy culture. Synonymes: 1. *Bartsia coccinea, Castilleja coccinea.* 2. *Castilleja sessiliflora, grandiflora.*

| | | | | |
|---|---|---|---|---|
| coccinea, 1 . | . Yellow . | 7, H. | A. N. Amer. . | 1787 |
| grandiflora, 2 . | . Pur. yel. . | 7, H. Her. P. | Louisiana . | 1811 |

EUCLEA, *Linn.* Derived from *eukleia*, glory; alluding to the beautiful evergreen foliage. *Linn.* 22, Or. 10, Nat. Or. *Euphorbiaceæ.* These are very ornamental shrubs, succeeding in peat and loam mixed, and multiplied from cuttings.

| | | | | | |
|---|---|---|---|---|---|
| racemosa | . . | White | . 11, G. Ev. S. C. G. H. | . 1772 |
| undulata | . . | White | . G. Ev. S. C. G. H. | . 1794 |

EUCLIDIUM, *R. Brown.* From *eu*, well, and *kleidoo*, to shut up; on account of the well-closed seedpods. *Linn.* 15, Nat. Or. *Cruciferæ.* Plants which are only worth growing in general collections. *Synonymes:* 1. *Bunias syriaca.* 2. *Vella tenuissima.*

| | | | | | |
|---|---|---|---|---|---|
| syriacum, 1 | . | White | . 7, H. | A. Levant | . 1778 |
| tataricum, 2 | . | White | . 7, H. | A. Tartary | . 1821 |

EUCOMIS, *Linn.* From *eukomes*, beautiful-haired; alluding to the tufted crown of the flower-spike. *Linn.* 6, Or. 1, Nat. Or. *Liliaceæ.* Ornamental plants, succeeding in any rich soil, and increased from offsets.

| | | | | | |
|---|---|---|---|---|---|
| bifolia | . . . | Lgt. grn. | . 4, G. Her. P. C. G. H. | . 1792 |
| nana | . . . | Brown | . 5, G. Her. P. C. G. H. | . 1774 |
| punctata | . . | Grn. brn. | . 4, G. Her. P. C. G. H. | . 1783 |
| purpureocaulis | . | Grn. brn. | . 4, G. Her. P. C. G. H. | . 1794 |
| regia | . . | Green | . 8, G. Her. P. C. G. H. | . 1702 |
| striata | . . | Green | . G. Her. P. C. G. H. | . 1790 |
| undulata | . . | Green | . 4, G. Her. P. C. G. H. | . 1760 |

EUCROSIA, *Ker.* From *eu*, well, and *krossos*, a fringe; in allusion to the beautiful fringe of the flower, formed by the cup of the stamens. *Linn.* 6, Or. 1, Nat. Or. *Amaryllidaceæ.* This is a very pretty bulb, with orange-coloured flowers; it thrives in light loam, and is increased from offsets.

| | | | | | |
|---|---|---|---|---|---|
| bicolor | . . . . | Orange | . 4, G. Bl. P. C. Horn | . 1816 |

EUDESMIA, *R. Brown.* From *eu*, well, and *desma*, a bundle; the stamens are connected into bundles. *Linn.* 18, Or. 2, Nat. Or. *Myrtaceæ.* An ornamental evergreen tree, about sixteen feet high, and producing an abundance of flowers; it thrives in sandy peat, and is increased by cuttings planted in sand, under a glass.

| | | | | | |
|---|---|---|---|---|---|
| tetragona | . . | Red | . 7, G. Ev. T. N. Holl. | . 1824 |

EUGENIA, *Linn.* In honour of Prince Eugene of Savoy, a great patron of botany. *Linn.* 12, Or. 1, Nat. Or. *Myrtaceæ.* A very ornamental and highly useful genus of plants, requiring the same treatment in culture and propagation as *Jambosa.*

| | | | | | |
|---|---|---|---|---|---|
| acuminata | . . | White | . 6, S. Ev. S. E. Ind. | . 1820 |
| auriculata | . . | White | . S. Ev. S. | . 1825 |
| axillaris | . . | White | . 9, S. Ev. S. Jamaica | . 1793 |
| balsamica | . . | White | . S. Ev. S. | . 1816 |
| baruonsis | . . | White | . S. Ev. S. S. Amer. | |
| bracteata | . . | White | . S. Ev. S. E. Ind. | . 1890 |
| buxifolia | . . | White | . 5, G. Ev. S. W. Ind. | . 1818 |
| coracoides | . . | White | . S. Ev. S. E. Ind. | . 1822 |
| elliptica | . . | White | . 7, G. Ev. S. N. S. W. | . 1790 |
| floribunda | . . | White | . S. Ev. S. W. Ind. | . 1890 |
| fragrans | . . | White | . 4, S. Ev. S. Jamaica | . 1790 |
| glandulifera | . . | White | . S. Ev. S. E. Ind. | . 1825 |
| glauca | . . | White | . S. Ev. S. | . 1822 |
| gracilis | . . | White | . S. Ev. S. E. Ind. | . 1825 |
| javanica | . . | White | . S. Ev. S. Java | . 1822 |
| latifolia | . . | White | . S. Ev. S. Guiana | . 1793 |
| ligustrina | . . | White | . 8, S. Ev. S. Hispani. | . 1793 |
| macrocarpa | . . | White | . S. Ev. S. E. Ind. | . 1822 |
| Mini | . . | White | . S. Ev. S. Guiana | . 1842 |
| obovata | . . | White | . S. Ev. S. l. France | . 1828 |
| obtusifolia | . . | White | . S. Ev. S. E. Ind. | . 1821 |
| petalomoides | . . | White | . S. Ev. S. E. Ind. | . 1825 |
| pulchella | . . | White | . S. Ev. S. E. Ind. | . 1824 |
| rugosa | . . | White | . S. Ev. S. E. Ind. | . 1824 |
| sinemariensis | . . | White | . 6, S. Ev. S. Guiana | . 1823 |
| sumatrana | . . | White | . S. Ev. S. Sumatra | . 1822 |
| ternifolia | . . | White | . S. Ev. S. E. Ind. | . 1822 |
| uniflora | . . | White | . 2, S. Ev. S. Brazil | . 1759 |

EULOPHIA, *R. Brown.* From *eulophos*, a handsome crest; in allusion to the labellum bearing elevated lines, or ridges. *Linn.* 20, Or. 1, Nat. Or. *Orchidaceæ.* This is a very pretty genus of tuberous-rooted plants. They must be kept perfectly dry when in a torpid state, and may be in every other respect treated as *Bletias.*

| | | | | | |
|---|---|---|---|---|---|
| barbata | . . . | | . 7, G. Ter. C. G. H. | . 1825 |
| carata | . . . | Yelsh. | . G. Ter. C. G. H. | . 1822 |
| guineensis | . . | Pur. brn. | . 9, S. Ter. S. Leone | . 1822 |
| longicornis | . . | | . 7, G. Ter. C. G. H. | . 1825 |
| lurida | . . | Yel. brn. | . 1, S. Epi. S. Leone | |
| macrostachya | . | Yel. grn. | . 10, S. Ter. Ceylon | |
| trintis | . . | Dark | . 6, G. Ter. C. G. H. | . 1825 |
| virens | . . | Orn. yel. | . 7, S. Ter. E. Ind. | . 1825 |

EUNOMIA, *Decandolle.* From *eu*, well, and *nomos*, order; because the leaves are opposite, and the seeds twin. *Linn.* 15, Nat. Or. *Cruciferæ.* This is a pretty little plant, growing freely in sand, loam, and peat, and increased by cuttings in the same kind of soil, under a glass, or by seed. *Synonyme:* 1. *Lepidium oppositifolium.*

| | | | | | |
|---|---|---|---|---|---|
| oppositifolia, 1 | . | White | . 6, F. Her. P. Syria | . 1827 |

EUONYMUS, *Linn.* From *eu*, good, and *onoma*, a name, well named. *Linn.* 5, Or. 1, Nat. Or. *Celastraceæ.* This is a genus of largish and ornamental shrubs, well suited for large shrubberies. *E. atropurpureus*, and *E. latifolius*, are the most showy; any situation or soil will suit them. They increase by seed, or cuttings of the ripened wood, put in in autumn, will take root. *Synonyme:* 1. *E. scandens.*

| | | | | | |
|---|---|---|---|---|---|
| americanus | . | Pink | . 6, H. De. S. N. Amer. | . 1683 |
| angustifolius | . | Yel. red | . 6, H. Ev. S. N. Amer. | . 1806 |
| atropurpureus | . | Purple | . 6, H. De. S. N. Amer. | . 1756 |
| bullatus | . | Pink | . 6, G. Ev. S. Nepal | . 1828 |
| chinensis | . | Pink | . 5, F. De. S. China | . 1820 |
| echinatus | . | White | . 5, F. De. S. Nepal | . 1824 |
| europæus | . | White | . 6, H. De. S. Britain | |
| foliis-variegatis | White | . 5, H. Ev. T. Britain | |
| leucocarpus | . | White | . 6, H. De. S. Britain | |
| pumilus | . | White | . 6, H. De. S. | |
| grandiflorus | . | White | . 6, F. Ev. S. Nepal | . 1824 |
| grossus | . | White | . 5, H. Ev. S. Nepal | . 1824 |
| Hamiltonianus | . | White | . 3, F. Ev. T. Nepal | . 1825 |
| japonicus | . | Pink | . 7, F. Ev. S. Japan | . 1804 |
| latifolius | . | Green | . 6, H. De. S. Austria | . 1730 |
| lucidus | . | White | . 5, H. Ev. S. Nepal | . 1820 |
| micranthus | . | White | . H. De. S. Nepal | . 1820 |
| nanus | . | | . H. De. S. Caucasus | . 1825 |
| obovatus | . | Pink | . 6, H. De. S. N. Amer. | . 1820 |
| sarmentosus, 1 | . | Yellow | . 5, H. De. S. N. Amer. | . 1824 |
| verrucosus | . | Green | . 6, H. De. S. Austria | . 1763 |

EUPATORIUM. Linnæus derived the name from Mithridates Eupator, who used it as a counterpoison. *Linn.* 19, Or. 1, Nat. Or. *Compositæ.* Some species of this genus are very ornamental, as *E. floribundum*, while others, as *E. coriaceum*, are quite uninteresting. They require a mixture of peat and loam to grow in, and young plants are obtained from seeds without difficulty. *E. Ayapana* has been famed for curing the bite of serpents, and an infusion of its leaves forms excellent diet-drink, and when fresh bruised, is said to be very useful for cleaning the face of a foul ulcer. *E. perfoliatum* is tonic, stomachic, and febrifugal. *Synonymes:* 1. *E. nepalense.* 2. *E. atriplicifolium.* 3. *E. molle, Ageratum guianense.* 4. *E. cordatum.* 5. *Eriopappus paniculatus.* 6. *E. Dalea.* 7. *E. atriplicifolium.*

| | | | | | |
|---|---|---|---|---|---|
| acuminatum, 1 | . | | . 8, G. Ev. S. | Nepal | . 1819 |
| ageratoides | . | White | . 9, H. Her. P. | N. Amer. | . 1640 |
| album | . | White | . 8, H. Her. P. | N. Amer. | . 1820 |
| altissimum | . | Pink | . 9, H. Her. P. | S. Amer. | . 1699 |
| aromaticum | . | White | . 7, H. Her. P. | N. Amer. | . 1739 |
| Ayapana | . | | . 8, S. Ev. P. | Brazil | . 1821 |
| candens | . | Pur. yel. | . 8, S. Ev. S. | Jamaica | . 1821 |
| cannabinum | . | Pink | . 6, H. Her. P. | Britain | |
| ceanothifolium | . | White | . 8, H. Her. P. | | . 1824 |
| chamædrifolium | Blue | . 8, S. Ev. S. | S. Amer. | . 1822 |
| coronopifolium | . | White | . 8, H. Her. P. | Carolina | . 1824 |
| Dalea | . | Pink | . 8, S. Ev. S. | Jamaica | . 1778 |
| deltoideum | . | Purple | . 8, S. Her. P. | S. Amer. | . 1822 |
| fœniculaceum | . | Pa. yel. | . 8, H. Her. P. | N. Amer. | . 1807 |
| floribundum | . | Blue | . 7, S. Ev. S. | S. Amer. | . 1823 |
| Fraseri | . | White | . 8, H. Her. P. | Carolina | . 1820 |
| glandulosum | . | White | . 8, S. Her. P. | Mexico | . 1826 |
| hyssopifolium | . | White | . 8, H. Her. P. | N. Amer. | . 1699 |
| ivaefolium | . | White | . 8, S. Ev. Tw. | N. Grenada | . 1820 |
| ivæfolium | . | Pink | . 9, S. Her. P. | Jamaica | . 1794 |
| lævifolium | . | Pink | . 9, S. Her. P. | | . 1822 |
| lanceolatum | . | White | . 7, H. Her. P. | N. Amer. | . 1819 |
| linearifolium | . | White | . 8, H. Her. P. | N. Amer. | . 1820 |
| macrophyllum, 3 | White | . 9, S. Her. P. | Jamaica | . 1823 |
| maculatum | . | Purple | . 9, H. Her. P. | N. Amer. | . 1656 |
| melissoides, 4 | . | White | . 8, H. Her. P. | N. Amer. | . 1811 |
| montanum | . | | . 7, H. Ev. S. | Jamaica | . 1820 |
| nutans | . | | . 8, G. Her. S. | Mexico | . 1827 |
| odoratum | . | Pink | . 8, S. Her. P. | Jamaica | . 1752 |
| paniculatum, 5 | . | Pink | . 8, S. Her. P. | S. Amer. | . 1818 |
| parviflorum, 6 | . | | . 8, S. Ev. S. | Jamaica | . 1826 |
| perfoliatum | . | White | . 7, H. Her. P. | N. Amer. | . 1699 |
| pubescens | . | White | . 7, H. Her. P. | N. Amer. | . 1819 |
| punctatum | . | Purple | . 9, H. Her. P. | N. Amer. | . 1815 |
| purpureum | . | Pink | . 8, H. Her. P. | N. Amer. | . 1640 |
| rotundifolium | . | White | . 7, H. Her. P. | N. Amer. | . 1699 |
| salviæfolium | . | Pink | . 7, H. Her. P. | N. Amer. | . 1814 |
| scandens | . | Yellow | . 8, S. Ev. Tw. | S. Amer. | . 1821 |

| | | | | | | | |
|---|---|---|---|---|---|---|---|
| serōtĭnŭm | Violet | 10, | H. | Her. | P. | N. Amer. | 1824 |
| sessilifōlĭŭm | White | 9, | H. | Her. | P. | N. Amer. | 1777 |
| squarrōsŭm | Purple | 8, | G. | Her. | P. | Mexico | 1827 |
| syrĭăcŭm | Purple | 8, | H. | Her. | P. | Syria | 1807 |
| teucriifōlĭŭm | White | 9, | H. | Her. | P. | N. Amer. | 1816 |
| trifoliātŭm | Purple | 8, | H. | Her. | P. | N. Amer. | 1768 |
| truncātŭm | White | 9, | H. | Her. | P. | N. Amer. | 1800 |
| urticæfōlĭŭm | Pink | 9, | F. | Her. | P. | S. Amer. | 1803 |
| veronicæfōlĭŭm | Blue | 8, | S. | Ev. | S. | Mexico | 1825 |
| verticillātŭm | Purple | 8, | H. | Her. | P. | N. Amer. | 1811 |
| villōsŭm | | | S. | Ev. | S. | Jamaica | |
| xalapĕnsĕ | White | 7, | S. | Ev. | S. | Mexico | 1826 |

*baccharoīdēs, coriācĕŭm, macrānthŭm 2, parviflōrŭm 6, populifōlĭŭm, pulchĕllŭm, repāndŭm 7, triflōrŭm.*

EUPHŌRBIĂ. Linnæus named this genus after Euphorbus, a physician to Juba, King of Mauritania. *Linn.* 11, Or. 3, Nat. Or. *Euphorbiaceæ.* This is an exceedingly variable, and very extensive genus of plants, comprising a number of very handsome species, as well as a number that are entirely unworthy of cultivation. Many of the stove and greenhouse species are of a succulent nature, therefore require to be grown in a dry soil, consisting of loam, and old brick and lime rubbish; they require but little water; those that are not of a succulent nature require a light rich soil, and plenty of moisture. They all abound in a milky juice. Sweet says, "The way we have succeeded best in striking the cuttings, is to stick them in the tan among the pots, in a good heat, and not cover them with any glass; but the best way of getting good plants is from seed, which will ripen plentifully if care be taken to fertilize the stigmas with the pollen when in bloom." The hardy perennial species thrive in any common garden soil, and increase by divisions of the roots, or by seeds. The hardy annuals and biennials merely require sowing in the open ground. The tender kinds must be sown in the hothouse, or in a hotbed frame, and when potted off, must be set with other tender annuals and biennials. The root of *E. Ipecacuanha* is said to be equal to the true *Ipecacuanha*. *E. antiquorum, canariensis*, and some other fleshy species, produce the drug *Euphorbium*, which is the inspissated milky juice of such plants. The native practitioners of India prescribe internally the juice of the leaves of *nereifolia* as a purge and deobstruent. The Tamool doctors of India give the leaves and seeds of *E. thymifolia* in worm cases. In India, the fresh acrid juice of *E. Tirucalli* is used as a vesicatory. The juice of *E. heptagona*, according to Virey, furnishes the Ethiopians with a deadly poison for their arrows. *Synonymes:* 1. *E. bupleuroides.* 2. *Medusa major.* 3. *Treisia tuberculata.* 4. *Dactylanthes globosa.* 5. *Treisia clava.* 6. *T. hystrix.* 7. *E. virgata.* 8. *Dactylanthes patula.* 9. *Tithymalus pendulus.* 10. *E. minima.* 11. *E. rigida.* 12. *E. Jacquiniflora.* 13. *Tithymalus geniculatus.* 14. *Tithymalus repandus.* 15. *Croton clutioides.*

| | | | | | | | |
|---|---|---|---|---|---|---|---|
| affinis | Apetal | 6, | H. | Her. | P. | Europe | 1820 |
| aleppică | Apetal | 7, | F. | Her. | P. | Crete | 1789 |
| ambiguă | Apetal | 5, | H. | Her. | P. | Hungary | 1817 |
| amygdaloīdēs | Apetal | 4, | H. | Ev. | S. | England | |
| anacampseroīdēs | Apetal | | S. | Ev. | S. | S. Amer. | |
| anacānthă | Apetal | 9, | S. | Ev. | S. | C. G. H. | 1727 |
| angulātă | Apetal | 8, | H. | Her. | P. | Austria | 1821 |
| angustifōlĭă | Yellow | 7, | H. | Her. | P. | Trinidad | 1827 |
| antiquōrŭm | Apetal | 4, | S. | Ev. | S. | E. Ind. | 1768 |
| aphyllă | Apetal | | G. | Ev. | S. | Teneriffe | 1815 |
| Apĭos | Apetal | 7, | G. | Ev. | S. | Candia | 1596 |
| atlāntică, 1 | Apetal | 6, | H. | Her. | P. | S. Eur. | 1818 |
| atropurpŭrĕă | Apetal | 7, | G. | Ev. | S. | Teneriffe | 1815 |
| balsamifĕră | Apetal | 6, | G. | Ev. | S. | Canaries | 1779 |
| biglandulōsă | Apetal | | S. | Ev. | S. | Bourbon | 1808 |
| biumbellātă | Apetal | | H. | Her. | P. | Barbary | 1780 |
| Bojeri | Scarlet | 11, | S. | Ev. | S. | Madagascar | |
| brasiliĕnsis | Apetal | 8, | H. | | A. | Brazil | 1826 |
| bracteātă | Apetal | 8, | S. | Ev. | S. | | 1809 |
| bupleurifōlĭă | Apetal | 8, | S. | Ev. | S. | C. G. H. | 1791 |
| canariĕnsis | Apetal | 7, | S. | Ev. | S. | Canaries | 1697 |
| canēscēns | Apetal | | H | | A. | Spain | 1818 |
| cœrulēscēns | Apetal | 6, | S. | Ev. | S. | C. G. H. | 1824 |
| cæspitōsă | Apetal | 7, | H. | Her. | P. | Italy | 1820 |
| Caput-Medūsæ, 2 | Apetal | 8, | S. | Ev. | S. | Africa | 1731 |
| pūmĭlă | Apetal | 8, | S. | Ev. | S. | C. G. H. | 1768 |
| carniōlĭcă | Apetal | 8, | H. | Her. | P. | Carniola | 1796 |
| Charăcĭăs | Apetal | 7, | H. | Ev. | S. | England | |
| cereifōrmis | Apetal | 4, | S. | Ev. | S. | C. G. H. | 1731 |
| clāvă, 3 | Apetal | 7, | S. | Ev. | S. | C. G. H. | 1774 |
| congēstă | Apetal | 6, | H. | Her. | P. | Spain | 1817 |
| Cordeăriānă | Apetal | 5, | H. | Her. | P. | S. Eur. | 1824 |

| | | | | | | | |
|---|---|---|---|---|---|---|---|
| coriifōlĭă | Apetal | 5, | G. | Ev. | S. | C. G. H. | 1800 |
| cotinifōlĭă | Apetal | 7, | S. | Ev. | S. | S. Amer. | 1690 |
| crispă | Apetal | 7, | S. | Ev. | S. | C. G. H. | 1819 |
| cruentātă | Apetal | 7, | G. | Her. | P. | St. Louis | 1831 |
| cucumerĭnă | Apetal | 6, | S. | Ev. | S. | C. G. H. | |
| cyathŏphŏră | Apetal | 7, | S. | Her. | P. | S. Amer. | 1800 |
| Cyparissĭăs | Apetal | 7, | H. | Her. | P. | England | |
| dendroīdēs | Apetal | 7, | H. | Ev. | S. | Italy | 1768 |
| denticulātă | Apetal | 6, | H. | Her. | P. | S. Eur. | 1810 |
| diversifōlĭă | Apetal | 5, | H. | | A. | S. Eur. | 1823 |
| dūlcis | Apetal | 7, | H. | Her. | P. | S. Eur. | 1759 |
| enneagōnă | Apetal | 6, | S. | Ev. | S. | C. G. H. | 1790 |
| epithymoīdēs | Apetal | 5, | H. | Her. | P. | Austria | 1805 |
| erōsă | Apetal | 12, | S. | Ev. | S. | C. G. H. | 1805 |
| Erythrīnă | Apetal | 7, | G. | Her. | P. | C. G. H. | 1823 |
| Esūlă | Apetal | 6, | H. | Her. | P. | Britain | |
| flavicōmă | Apetal | 7, | H. | Her. | P. | S. France | 1820 |
| fructuspīnă | Apetal | 8, | S. | Ev. | S. | C. G. H. | 1731 |
| gemĭnātă | Apetal | 8, | S. | Ev. | S. | C. G. H. | 1731 |
| fruticōsă | Apetal | 6, | F. | Ev. | S. | Sicily | 1824 |
| fūlgēns | Scarlet | 8, | S. | Ev. | S. | Mexico | 1836 |
| geminispīnă | Apetal | | S. | Ev. | S. | Mexico | 1823 |
| genistoīdēs | Apetal | 7, | G. | Ev. | S. | C. G. H. | 1808 |
| globōsă, 4 | Apetal | 7, | H. | | A. | | 1818 |
| grāndidēns | Apetal | 7, | S. | Ev. | S. | C. G. H. | 1823 |
| grandifōlĭă | Apetal | | S. | Ev. | S. | S. Leone | 1798 |
| hamātă | Apetal | | G. | Ev. | S. | C. G. H. | 1795 |
| Hawōrthĭi, 5 | Apetal | 5, | S. | Ev. | S. | C. G. H. | 1800 |
| heterophyllă | Apetal | | S. | Ev. | S. | S. Amer. | 1800 |
| heptagōnă | Apetal | 9, | S. | Ev. | S. | C. G. H. | 1731 |
| rūbră | Apetal | 9, | S. | Ev. | S. | C. G. H. | 1731 |
| hibērnĭcă | Apetal | 6, | H. | Her. | P. | Britain | |
| hirtă | Apetal | 7, | S. | | A. | E. Ind. | 1818 |
| humifūsă | Apetal | 6, | H. | | A. | Europe | 1817 |
| hystrix, 6 | Apetal | 7, | S. | Ev. | S. | C. G. H. | 1695 |
| imbricātă | Apetal | 8, | F. | Ev. | S. | Portugal | 1804 |
| Isātis | Apetal | 8, | H. | Her. | P. | Spain | 1820 |
| jūncĕă | Apetal | 7, | G. | Her. | P. | Madeira | 1779 |
| lactĕă | Apetal | 7, | S. | Ev. | S. | E. Ind. | 1804 |
| lætă | Apetal | 6, | G. | Ev. | S. | | 1758 |
| Lamārkĭi, 7 | Apetal | 7, | S. | Ev. | S. | C. G. H. | 1808 |
| lanifĕră | Apetal | | S. | Ev. | S. | Mexico | 1828 |
| laurifōlĭă | Apetal | | S. | Ev. | S. | Peru | 1820 |
| leptophyllă | Apetal | 7, | H. | | A. | S. Eur. | 1817 |
| linarifōlĭă | Apetal | | S. | Ev. | S. | | 1794 |
| linifōlĭă | Apetal | | S. | Ev. | S. | W. Ind. | 1774 |
| lineāris | Apetal | 7, | S. | Ev. | S. | Vera Cruz | 1824 |
| longifōlĭă | Apetal | 6, | H. | Her. | P. | Nepal | 1828 |
| lophogōnă | Apetal | | S. | Ev. | S. | Madagascar | 1824 |
| lūcĭdă | Apetal | 6, | H. | Her. | P. | Hungary | 1818 |
| magnimāmmă | Apetal | | S. | Ev. | S. | Mexico | 1823 |
| mammillāris | Apetal | 7, | S. | Ev. | S. | C. G. H. | 1759 |
| marginātă | Apetal | 6, | G. | Her. | P. | S. Amer. | 1824 |
| mauritānĭcă | Apetal | 7, | G. | Ev. | S. | Maurit. | 1782 |
| mellifĕră | Apetal | 7, | G. | Ev. | S. | Madeira | 1784 |
| meloformis | Apetal | 7, | S. | Ev. | S. | C. G. H. | 1774 |
| Mercuriālis | Apetal | 7, | H. | Her. | P. | N. Amer. | 1820 |
| multicorymbōsă | Apetal | 7, | H. | Her. | P. | | 1805 |
| myrtifōlĭă | Apetal | 7, | S. | Ev. | S. | C. G. H. | 1699 |
| neapolitānă | Apetal | 7, | H. | | A. | Naples | 1816 |
| neriifōlĭă | Apetal | 6, | S. | Ev. | S. | India | 1690 |
| nudiflōră | Apetal | 8, | S. | Ev. | S. | | 1800 |
| nummulariæfōlĭă | Apetal | 7, | G. | Ev. | S. | | 1800 |
| obscūră | Apetal | 6, | H. | | A. | S. France | 1817 |
| odontophyllă | Apetal | | S. | Ev. | S. | C. G. H. | 1824 |
| officinārŭm | Apetal | 6, | S. | Ev. | S. | Africa | 1597 |
| ophthalmĭcă | Apetal | 7, | S. | | A. | Rio Jan. | 1824 |
| ornithŏpŭs | Apetal | 7, | G. | Ev. | S. | C. G. H. | 1816 |
| parviflōră | Apetal | 7, | S. | | A. | Ceylon | 1820 |
| Parălĭăs | Apetal | 8, | F. | Her. | P. | England | |
| suffruticōsă | Apetal | 8, | F. | Ev. | S. | Europe | |
| pătŭlă, 8 | Apetal | 8, | S. | Ev. | S. | C. G. H. | 1768 |
| pēndŭlă, 9 | Apetal | | S. | Ev. | S. | | 1808 |
| pentagōnă | Apetal | | S. | Ev. | S. | C. G. H. | 1824 |
| petaloīdēs, 11 | Apetal | 7, | H. | Ev. | S. | | 1795 |
| petiolāris | Apetal | 5, | S. | Ev. | S. | W. Ind. | 1800 |
| piscatōrĭă | Apetal | | G. | Ev. | S. | Canaries | 1777 |
| Pithyūsă | Apetal | 6, | F. | Ev. | S. | S. Eur. | 1741 |
| plumōsă | Apetal | 7, | H. | | A. | | 1816 |
| polygōnă | Apetal | 8, | S. | Ev. | S. | C. G. H. | 1790 |
| portlāndĭcă | Apetal | 6, | H. | Her. | P. | Britain | |
| portulacoīdēs | Apetal | 4, | H. | Her. | P. | N. Amer. | 1816 |
| procūmbēns | Apetal | 8, | S. | Ev. | S. | C. G. H. | 1768 |
| prolifĕră | Apetal | 5, | H. | Her. | P. | Nepal | 1820 |
| prunifōlĭă, 12 | Apetal | 8, | G. | | B. | | 1799 |
| pubēscēns | Apetal | 7, | H. | | A. | S. Eur. | 1817 |
| punĭcĕă | Apetal | 4, | G. | Ev. | S. | Jamaica | 1778 |
| purpurātă | Apetal | 6, | H. | Her. | P. | France | 1820 |
| pyrifōlĭă | Apetal | | S. | Ev. | S. | Maurit. | |
| reflēxă | Apetal | 6, | H. | Her. | P. | | 1826 |
| repāndă, 13 | Apetal | 8, | S. | Ev. | S. | E. Ind. | 1808 |
| rĭgĭdă | Apetal | 6, | H. | Her. | P. | Caucasus | 1818 |
| rūbră | Apetal | 6, | H. | | A. | France | 1818 |
| saxātĭlis | Apetal | 6, | H. | Her. | P. | Austria | 1817 |
| scordifōlĭă | Apetal | 7, | S. | | A. | Africa | 1823 |
| serpyllifōlĭă | Apetal | 7, | H. | | A. | S. Amer. | 1817 |
| serrātă | Apetal | 7, | F. | Her. | P. | S. Eur. | 1710 |
| seticōrnis | Apetal | 7, | H. | | A. | Italy | 1820 |
| silenifōlĭă | Apetal | 6, | S. | Ev. | S. | C. G. H. | 1821 |

| | | | | | | |
|---|---|---|---|---|---|---|
| glauca | . . | Apetal | . 7, S. Ev. S. | C. G. H. | . 1821 |
| spathulifolia | . | Apetal | . 8, G. Ev. S. | | . 1800 |
| spinosa | . . | Apetal | . 6, F. Ev. S. | Levant | . 1710 |
| splendens | . . | Scarlet | . 6, S. Ev. S. | L. France | . 1826 |
| squarrosa | . . | Apetal | . 8. Ev. S. | | |
| stellaespina | . | Apetal | . 8. Ev. S. | C. G. H. | . 1824 |
| tannensis, 14 | . | Apetal | . 7. H. | A. N. Heb. | . 1827 |
| taurica | . . . | Apetal | . 6, H. | A. Tauria | . 1820 |
| taurianais | . | Apetal | . 7, H. Her. P. | Italy | . 1818 |
| terracina | . . | Apetal | . 7, H. | A. Europe | . 1810 |
| tessellata | . . | Apetal | . 8, S. Ev. S. | | . 1768 |
| tetragona | . . | Apetal | . 8. Ev. S. | | |
| Tirucalli | . . . | Apetal | . 8. Ev. S. | India | . 1690 |
| toxicaria | . . | Apetal | . 7, S. Ev. S. | Guinea | . 1793 |
| trigona | . . . | Apetal | . 7, S. Ev. S. | E. Ind. | . 1768 |
| trigynocarpa | . | Apetal | . 6, H. Her. P. | | . 1823 |
| truncata | . . . | Apetal | . 7, H. Her. S. | S. Eur. | . 1820 |
| tuberculata | . . | Apetal | . 12, S. Ev. S. | C. G. H. | . 1815 |
| tuberosa | . . . | Apetal | . 7, S. Ev. S. | C. G. H. | . 1808 |
| uncinata | . . . | Apetal | . 7, S. Ev. S. | C. G. H. | . 1794 |
| undulata | . . . | Apetal | . 6, H. Her. P. | Caucasus | . 1818 |
| uniflora | . . . | Apetal | . 8, S. Tu. P. | S. Amer. | . 1827 |
| Valeriana | . . . | Apetal | . 7, H. Her. P. | Siberia | . 1818 |
| varians | . . . | Apetal | . 8, S. Ev. S. | E. Ind. | . 1800 |
| variegata | . . | Apetal | . 4, H. | A. Louisiana | . 1811 |
| veneta | . . . | Apetal | . 7, F. Ev. S. | Europe | . 1820 |
| villosa | . . . | Apetal | . 6, H. Her. P. | Hungary | . 1820 |

acuminata, agraria, androsaemifolia, Aplos, bialata, Chamaesyce, ceratocarpa, condylocarpa, condensa, coralloides, corollata, cretica, crispata, dentata, diffusa, emarginata, exigua, falcata, fragifera, Gerardiana, glaucescens, glaucophylla, glareosa, helioscopia, hypericifolia, hyssopifolia, Humboldtii, Ipecacuanha, juncoides, Kanzel, Lathyris, literata, maculata, micrantha, microphylla, Myrsinites, nicaensis, ocymoidea, orientalis, pallida, palustris, Peplis, Peplus, peploides, picta, pilosa, pilulifera, platyphyllos, polygonifolia, procera, prostrata, provincialis, pterococca, retusa, rosea, salicifolia, segetalis, serrulata, stricta, sylvatica, thymifolia, uralensis, valentina, verrucosa, virgata.

EUPHORIA, *Jussieu.* From *euphorus*, fertile; alluding to the fruit. Linn. 8, Or. 1, Nat. Or. *Sapindaceae.* A genus of fruit-bearing trees, attaining from fifteen to twenty feet high, and thriving in any rich mould; they may be increased either by layers or seed. Synonymes: 1. *Dimocarpus Litchi.* 2. *D. Longan.* 3. *Nephelium lappaceum, Scytalia Rambootan.*

| | | | | | |
|---|---|---|---|---|---|
| Litchi, 1 | . . | White | . 5, S. Ev. T. | China | . 1786 |
| Longana, 2 | . | White | . 5, S. Ev. T. | China | . 1786 |
| Nephelium, 3 | . | White | . 5, S. Ev. T. | E. Ind. | . 1809 |
| verticillata | . . | Wht. red | . 5, S. Ev. T. | E. Ind. | . 1820 |

EUPHRASIA, *Linn.* From *euphraino*, to delight; the plant has been supposed to cure blindness. Linn. 14, Or. 2, Nat. Or. *Scrophulariaceae.* These are interesting plants, particularly *E. officinalis*; they thrive with the most common treatment. *E. officinalis* is slightly bitter and aromatic. Synonyme: 1. *E. salisburgensis.*

| | | | | | |
|---|---|---|---|---|---|
| alpina, 1 | . | Purple | . 7, H. | A. Europe | . 1827 |
| linifolia | . . | Purple | . 8, H. | A. France | . 1826 |
| lutea | . . . | Purple | . 8, H. | A. S. Eur. | . 1816 |
| officinalis | . . | Purple | . 8, H. | A. Britain | . |

EUPOMATIA, *R. Brown.* From *eu*, well, and *poma*, a lid; the flower is covered before expansion, in the manner of an extinguisher. Linn. 12, Or. 3, Nat. Or. *Anonaceae.* An interesting, laurel-like shrub, succeeding in sandy peat and loam mixed; it is increased by cuttings, or seeds.

| | | | |
|---|---|---|---|
| laurina | . . . | G. Ev. S. N. Holl. | . 1824 |

EUROTIUM, *Link.* From *euros*, the Greek name of a kind of mouldiness. Linn. 24, Or. 9, Nat. Or. *Fungi.* Yellow and white *Fungi*, found at all seasons on dried plants, and rose-bushes—*herbariorum, Rosarum.*

EURYA, *Thunberg.* From *eurys*, large; alluding to the large flowers. Linn. 23, Or. 1, Nat. Or. *Ternstraemiaceae.* Evergreen shrubs, described as being very pretty; they succeed best in peat and loam, and are multiplied by cuttings in sand, or very sandy mould, under a glass, in heat.

| | | | | | |
|---|---|---|---|---|---|
| chinensis | . . | White | . 6, S. Ev. S. | China | . 1823 |
| multiflora | . . | White | . F. Ev. S. | Nepal | . 1823 |

EURYALE, *Salisbury.* From *Euryale*, one of the Gorgons; alluding to the thorny menacing habit of the plant. Linn. 13, Or. 1, Nat. Or. *Nymphaeaceae.* This is a very handsome plant, on account of its fine large leaves, which float on the surface of the water, in which it requires to be constantly grown. The only way of propagating it is by seed, which is readily obtained by shaking the pollen on the stigma when the flowers are well expanded. Synonyme: 1. *Anneslea spinosa.*

| | | | | | |
|---|---|---|---|---|---|
| ferox | . . . . | Red | . . 8, S. Aq. P. | India | . . 1809 |

EURYBIA, *Cassini.* From *eurubies*, wide-spreading; alluding to its creeping offsets. Linn. 19, Or. 2, Nat. Or. *Compositae.* Rather a pretty plant, each corymb usually consisting of numerous heads of flowers. For culture and propagation, see *Aster.* Synonymes; 1. *Aster corymbosus, A. cordifolius.*

| | | | | | |
|---|---|---|---|---|---|
| corymbosa, 1 | . | White | . 7, H. Her. P. | N. Amer. | . 1765 |

EURYCLES, *Salisbury.* From *eurys*, broad, and *kleio*, to close up; the perianth is shut up by the tube of the stamens. Linn. 6, Or. 1, Nat. Or. *Amaryllidaceae.* Ornamental plants, growing about two feet high. For culture and propagation, see *Pancratium.* Synonymes: 1. *Pancratium amboinense, Proiphys amboinensis.* 2. *P. australasicum.* 3. *Crinum nervosum.*

| | | | | | |
|---|---|---|---|---|---|
| amboinensis, 1 | . | White | . 5, S. Bl. P. | Amboyna | . 1759 |
| australasica, 2 | . | White | . 5, S. Bl. P. | N. Holl. | . 1821 |
| Cunninghamii | . | White | . 8, S. Bl. P. | N. Holl. | . 1826 |
| nervosa, 3 | . . | White | . 8, S. Bl. P. | E. Ind. | . 1822 |

EUSTACHYS, *Desfontaines.* From *eu*, well, and *stachys*, a spike; alluding to the large flower spike. Linn. 23, Or. 1, Nat. Or. *Gramineae.* A pretty species of grass, of the easiest culture. Synonyme: 1. *Chloris petraea, Agrostis complanata.*

| | | | | | |
|---|---|---|---|---|---|
| petraea, 1 | . . . | Apetal | . 7, Grass. | Jamaica | . . 1779 |

EUSTEGIA, *R. Brown.* Derived from *eu*, good, and *stege*, a covering. Linn. 5, Or. 2, Nat. Or. *Asclepiadaceae.* This plant is described as being very ornamental; it will grow well in peat and loam, and is increased from cuttings in sand. Synonyme: 1. *Apocynum hastatum.*

| | | | | | |
|---|---|---|---|---|---|
| hastata, 1 | . . . | White | . . 7, G. Ev. Tr. | C. G. H. | . 1816 |

EUSTOMA, *Salisbury.* From *eustoma*, beautiful mouth; referring to the flower. Linn. 5, Or. 1, Nat. Or. *Gentianaceae.* A very pretty annual, requiring to be sown on a gentle hotbed and transplanted into the open border, where it will produce flowers and seed in abundance.

| | | | | | |
|---|---|---|---|---|---|
| silenifolia | . . . | White | . 7, H. | A. L. Provid. | . 1804 |

EUSTREPHUS, *R. Brown.* From *eu*, well, and *strepho*, to twine; twining habit of the plants. Linn. 6, Or. 1, Nat. Or. *Liliaceae.* These are very pretty evergreen twiners, and if carefully managed, they will succeed in sandy peat. Young plants are obtained from cuttings without any difficulty.

| | | | | | |
|---|---|---|---|---|---|
| angustifolius | . . | Pa. pur. | . 7, G. Ev. Tw. | N. S. W. | . 1820 |
| latifolius | . . . | Pa. pur. | . 6, G. Ev. Tw. | N. S. W. | . 1800 |

EUTAXIA, *R. Brown.* From *eutaxia*, modesty; in allusion to the delicate appearance of the plants when in flower. Linn. 10, Or. 1, Nat. Or. *Leguminosae.* The plants of this genus are very pretty, and thrive best in a mixture of loam and peat. To have handsome bushy plants, the tops should be frequently plucked off, and in potting, plenty of drainage should be given. Cuttings root readily planted in sand, under a glass. Synonyme: 1. *Dillwynia pungens.*

| | | | | | |
|---|---|---|---|---|---|
| Baxteri | . . . | Yellow | . G. Ev. S. | N. Holl. | . 1830 |
| myrtifolia | . . | Orange | . 8, G. Ev. S. | N. Holl. | . 1803 |
| pungens, 1 | . . | Orange | . 5, G. Ev. S. | N. Holl. | . 1825 |

EUTERPE, *Gaertner.* From *euterpe*, pleasing; alluding to the habit of the species. Linn. 21, Or. 6, Nat. Or. *Palmaceae.* This is a fine genus of palms; some of the species grow upwards of forty feet high. To grow them well, they require a sandy loamy soil, and plenty of heat; they are increased from seed. Mr. Loudon has the following notice of *E. oleracea*:—"It is the highest of the American palms. The sheaths of the leaves are very close, and form the green top of the trunk, a foot and a half in length. The inhabitants cut off this top, take out the white heart, of two or three inches in diameter, consisting of the leaves closely folded together, and eat it either raw, with pepper and salt, or fried with butter, like the artichoke." —*Ency of Plants.* Synonymes: 1. *Areca oleracea.* 2. *A. spicata.*

| | | | | |
|---|---|---|---|---|
| caribæa . . . . | | Palm. | W. Ind. . | 1656 |
| globosa . . . . | | Palm. | Maurit. . | 1819 |
| oleracea, 1 . . . | | Palm. | Brasil . | 1800 |
| pisiformis, 2 . . . | | Palm. | Madagas. . | 1819 |

**EUTHÁLES,** *R. Brown.* From *eu*, well, and *thaleo*, to push, or sprout. *Linn.* 5, Or. 1, Nat. Or. *Goodeniaceæ.* This species is pretty, and will succeed well in loam and peat mixed; it is increased without any difficulty, by cuttings.

| | | | | |
|---|---|---|---|---|
| trinervis . . . | Pur. yel. . 7, G. Her. | P. N. Holl. . | 1803 |

**EUTHÁMIA,** *Nuttall.* From *eu*, well, and *thames*, crowded; in allusion to the flowers. *Linn.* 19, Or. 1, Nat. Or. *Compositæ.* Ornamental plants. For culture and propagation, see *Chrysocoma.* Synonymes: 1. *Chrysocoma graminifolia, Solidago lanceolata.* 2. *S. tenuifolia.*

| | | | | |
|---|---|---|---|---|
| graminifolia, 1 . | Yellow . 9, H. Her. | P. N. Amer. . | 1758 |
| tenuifolia, 2 . | Yellow . 10, H. Her. | P. N. Amer. . | 1758 |

**EUTÓCA,** *R. Brown.* From *eutokos*, fruitful; alluding to the great number of seeds. *Linn.* 5, Or. 1, Nat. Or. *Hydrophyllaceæ.* The plants of this genus are very pretty. The seeds require to be sown in the flower-border early in spring, in light soil, where they will flower abundantly if not allowed to grow too thick.

| | | | | |
|---|---|---|---|---|
| divaricata . . | Lgt. vio. . 5, H. | A. California . | 1833 |
| Franklini . . | Pink . . 5, H. | B. N. Amer. . | 1827 |
| multiflora . . | Pink . . 6, H. | B. N. Amer. . | 1836 |
| sericea . . . | Blue . . 6, H. | B. N. Amer. . | 1827 |
| Wrangeliana . | Blue . . 6, H. | A. California . | 1835 |

**EUXÉNIA,** *Chamisso.* From *eu*, beautiful, and *xenos*, a stranger. *Linn.* 19, Or. 5, Nat. Or. *Compositæ.* This is described as a very pretty plant, growing well in peat and loam, and increased from cuttings in sand, under a glass.

| | | | | |
|---|---|---|---|---|
| grata . . . | Yellow . . G. Ev. S. | Chile . . | 1825 |

**EVEN;** applied to a surface when it is not wrinkled or curled.

**EVANESCENT,** quickly vanishing.

**EVENING FLOWER,** see *Hesperántha.*

**EVERGREEN THORN,** see *Cratægus Pyracántha.*

**EVERLASTING,** see *Gnaphálium.*

**EVERLASTING PEA,** see *Láthyrus latifólius.*

**EVÉRNIA,** *Acharius.* From *eurnes*, well-branched. *Linn.* 24, Or. 8, Nat. Or. *Lichenes.* A small bushy plant, of a greenish white colour; it is found at all seasons on heaths, and is used in dyeing. Synonyme: 1. *Lichen stictoceros—Prunastri* 1.

**EVÓDIA,** *Forster.* From *evodia*, a sweet smell; plant scented. *Linn.* 4, Or. 1, Nat. Or. *Rutaceæ.* An ornamental, evergreen, East Indian shrub, succeeding in sandy loam, and is increased from cuttings planted in sand, under a glass, in heat. Synonyme: 1. *Fagara triphylla.*

| | | | | |
|---|---|---|---|---|
| triphylla, 1 . | White . . S. Ev. S. | E. Ind. . . | 1821 |

**EVOLVED,** unfolded.

**EVÓLVULUS,** *Linn.* From *evolvo*, to roll out, not twining, opposite to *Convolvulus. Linn.* 5, Or. 2, Nat. Or. *Convolvulaceæ.* All the species of this genus bear very handsome flowers. They are chiefly plants of very easy culture. The annuals require to be raised on a moderate hotbed, and when potted off, to be treated like other tender annuals. Synonyme: 1. *E. sericeus.*

| | | | | |
|---|---|---|---|---|
| alsinoides . . | Blue . . 7, G. Tr. A. | E. Ind. . | 1817 |
| emarginatus . | Blue . . 9, S. Tr. A. | E. Ind. . | 1816 |
| gangeticus . . | Blue . . 7, S. Tr. A. | E. Ind. . | 1820 |
| hirsutus . . | Blue . . 7, S. Tr. A. | Trinidad . | 1818 |
| incanus, 1 . | Blue . . 7, S. Tr. A. | S. Amer. . | 1810 |
| latifolius . . | White . . 6, S. Ev. Tw. | Brasil . | 1819 |
| linifolius . . | Blue . . 8, H. Tr. A. | Jamaica . | 1732 |
| nummularius . | Blue . . 9, S. Tr. A. | Jamaica . | 1816 |
| Nuttallianus . | Blue . . 7, H. Tr. A. | N. Amer. . | 1824 |
| sericeus . . . | White . . 7, S. Tr. A. | W. Ind. . | 1816 |
| villosus . . . | Blue . . 7, S. Ev. Tr. | S. Amer. . | 1810 |

**EXÁCUM,** *Linn.* From *ex*, out of, and *ago*, to drive; it is said to have the property of expelling poison. *Linn.* 4, Or. 1, Nat. Or. *Gentianaceæ.* These are pretty annuals, requiring to be sown in the open air, in peat soil, and a moist situation.

| | | | | |
|---|---|---|---|---|
| pulchellum . | Pink . . 6, H. | A. N. Jersey . | 1826 |
| tetragonum . | Blue . . 8, H. | A. Nepal . | 1820 |

**EXARILLATE,** without aril.

**EXCÆCÁRIA,** *Linn.* From *excæco*, to blind; it is said the juice has the power to cause the loss of sight. *Linn.* 22, Or. 13, Nat. Or. *Euphorbiaceæ.* Handsome, stove, evergreen species, thriving well in open loamy soil; they are increased by cuttings in sand, under a glass, in heat. The juice of *E. agallocha* affects the eyes with intense pain. Rumphius says, "When sailors have been sent ashore to cut fuel, and accidentally rubbed their eyes with the juice of it, they became blinded, and ran about like distracted beings, and some of them finally lost their sight."—*Nat. Syst. Bot.*, p. 115.

| | | | | |
|---|---|---|---|---|
| Agallocha . . | White . . 5, S. Ev. S. | E. Ind. . . | 1820 |
| glandulosa . . | White . . 5, S. Ev. S. | Jamaica . | 1821 |
| serrata . . . | White . . 5, S. Ev. S. | Chile . . | 1796 |

**EXSCÁPUS,** without a stalk.

**EXCENTRICAL,** out of the centre.

**EXCIPÚLA,** *Fries.* From *excipio*, to catch, alluding to the roughness of the plant to the touch. *Linn.* 24, Or. 9, Nat. Or. *Fungi.* A minute species of black *Fungi*, found in autumn upon dead raspberry stems—*Rubi.*

**EXCISA,** bluntly cut off.

**EXCORIATE,** stripped of the skin.

**EXCURRENT,** projecting beyond the edge or point of any thing.

**EXIDIA,** *Fries.* From *exidio*, to exude; alluding to the sporules exuding from the receptacle. *Linn.* 24, Or. 9, Nat. Or. *Fungi.* Brownish species, found in autumn and winter on various species of trees—*auriculata, rubescenti-fusca, flaccida, glandulosa, recisa.*

**EXILÁRIA,** *Greville.* From *exilis*, slender; habit of the plants. *Linn.* 24, Or. 7, Nat. Or. *Algæ.* Greenish, very minute species, found in summer in the sea, and various watery places—*circularis, fasciculata, flabellata, fulgens.*

**EXIGUUS,** mean, small.

**EXOCÁRPUS,** *Labillardière.* From *exo*, outside, and *karpos*, fruit; the seed is situated on a large fleshy receptacle. *Linn.* 21, Or. 5, Nat. Or. *Thymelaceæ.* These are large-growing plants, especially *E. cupressiformis*, which is described as a timber tree. They require a mixture of peat and loam to grow in, and cuttings take freely in sand, under a glass.

| | | | | |
|---|---|---|---|---|
| cupressiformis . | Apetal . . G. Ev. T. | V. D. L. . | 1824 |
| humifusus . . | Apetal . . G. Ev. Tr. | V. D. L. . | 1824 |
| strictus . . | Apetal . . G. Ev. S. | N. Holl. . | 1822 |

**EXOSPORIUM,** *Link.* From *exo*, outside, and *spora*, a sporule. *Linn.* 24, Or. 9, Nat. Or. *Fungi.* A very minute plant, found growing at any season on the lime-tree branches—*Tiliæ.*

**EXOSTEMMA,** *Decandolle.* From *exo*, without, and *stemma*, a crown; alluding to the exserted stamens. *Linn.* 5, Or. 1, Nat. Or. *Cinchonaceæ.* Trees, attaining from twenty to thirty feet high. *E. floribundum* is described as a timber tree. They all require to be grown in loam and peat, and are increased from cuttings in sand, under a glass, in heat.

| | | | | |
|---|---|---|---|---|
| brachycarpum . | White . . 8, S. Ev. T. | Jamaica . | 1828 |
| caribæum . . | White . . 8, S. Ev. T. | W. Ind. . | 1780 |
| floribundum . | White . . 8, S. Ev. T. | W. Ind. . | 1794 |
| longiflorum . | White . . 6, S. Ev. T. | Caraccas . | 1820 |

**EXPECTORANT,** anything that promotes the discharge of mucus from the chest.

**EXSERTED,** projecting much beyond something else.

**EXSICCATED,** dried up.

**EXTRA-AXILLARY,** growing from above or below the axils of the leaves, or branches.

**EXTRA-FOLIACEOUS,** away from the leaves, or inserted in a different place from them.

**EXSUCCOUS,** dry, sapless.

**EXSURGENT,** growing upwards.

**EXUVIA,** whatever is cast off from plants.

**EYEBRIGHT,** see *Euphrásia.*

# F.

FĀBĂ, *Decandolle*. From *phago*, to eat; the esculent seeds of the common bean are well known. *Linn.* 14, Or. 4, Nat. Or. *Leguminosæ.* This species, and its garden varieties, are well known, on account of their seeds being so much used in cookery. They only require to be sown in the open ground. *Synonyme:* 1. *Vicia Faba.*

| | | | | | | |
|---|---|---|---|---|---|---|
| vulgāris, 1 | . | White | . 7, H. | A. | Egypt | . |
| equīnā | . . | Purple | . 7, H. | A. | | |

FABĀGŎ, *Tournefort*. From *faba*, a bean; resemblance of the leaves. *Linn.* 10, Or. 1, Nat. Or. *Zygophyllaceæ.* This species thrives well in a light soil, and a dry situation; it is increased from seed. *Synonyme:* 1. *Zygophyllum fabago.*

| | | | | | | |
|---|---|---|---|---|---|---|
| mājŏr, 1 | . . . | Wht. saf. | 7, H. Her. P. | Syria | . . 1596 |

FABRĬCĬĂ, *Gærtner*. In honour of J. C. Fabricius, the celebrated Danish entomologist. *Linn.* 12, Or. 1, Nat. Or. *Myrtaceæ.* Ornamental plants, well adapted for conservatories, as they require to grow to a good size before they will flower. For culture and propagation, see *Leptospermum.*

| | | | | | | |
|---|---|---|---|---|---|---|
| lævigātā | . . | Yellow | . 6, G. Ev. S. | N. S. W. | . 1788 |
| myrtifōliā | . . | Yellow | . G. Ev. S. | N. Holl. | . |
| sericeā | . . | Yellow | . 6, G. Ev. S. | N. Holl. | 1820 |
| strictā | . . . | | 6, G. Ev. S. | N. Holl. | 1827 |

FÆCŬLĂ, the nutritious powder of wheat, or other things; the albumen of some seeds.

FAGĀRĂ, see *Xanthöxÿlum.*

FAGELĬĂ, *Necker*. Supposed to be the name of some botanist known to Necker. *Linn.* 17, Or. 4, Nat. Or. *Leguminosæ.* A very desirable greenhouse or conservatory plant, requiring the same treatment as *Kennedya.* *Synonyme:* 1. *Glycine bituminosa.*

| | | | | | | |
|---|---|---|---|---|---|---|
| bituminōsā, 1 | . Yel. pur. | . 6, G. Ev. Tw. | C.G.H. | . . 1774 |

FAGŌNĬĂ, *Linn.* In honour of M. Fagon, a Frenchman, and great patron of botany. *Linn.* 10, Or. 1, Nat. Or. *Zygophyllaceæ.* These plants do not possess much to recommend them. They grow well in loam, peat, and sand, mixed, and cuttings root freely when planted in sand, under a glass.

| | | | | | | |
|---|---|---|---|---|---|---|
| arābĭcă | . . . | Purple | . 7, G. Ev. S. | Arabia | . 1759 |
| crētĭcă | . . . | Purple | . 7, G. Ev. S. | Candia | . 1739 |
| glutinōsă | . . | Red | . 6, G. Ev. Tr. | Egypt | . 1820 |

FAGRÆĂ. Named by Thunberg, after his friend J. T. Fagræus, M.D. *Linn.* 5, Or. 1, Nat. Or. *Loganiaceæ.* These are ornamental stove plants, thriving well in sandy loam and peat; cuttings of the young wood root readily in sand, under a glass, in heat. *Synonyme:* 1. *Willughbeia zeylanica.*

| | | | | | | |
|---|---|---|---|---|---|---|
| obovātā | . . . | White | . 8. Ev. T. | Silhet | . 1816 |
| zeylānĭcă, 1 | . | White | . 8. Ev. T. | Ceylon | . 1816 |

FĀGŬS. From *phago*, to eat; in early ages the nuts of the Beech-tree were used as food. *Linn.* 21, Or. 9, Nat. Or. *Corylaceæ.* Handsome and very ornamental timber trees, particularly *F. sylvatica*, which is one of the handsomest and best adapted of trees for planting singly in parks, or lawns. The Beech-tree thrives best in a chalky clay, or loamy soil, preferring a sheltered situation. They may all be increased by seed, budding, or grafting. The timber is brittle, but much used by turners, joiners, and millwrights.

| | | | | | | |
|---|---|---|---|---|---|---|
| antārctĭcă | . . | Apetal | . H. De. T. | Magellan | . 1830 |
| betuloīdēs | . . | Apetal | . H. Ev. T. | Magellan | . 1830 |
| ferruginēā | . . | Apetal | . 6, H. De. T. | N. Amer. | . 1766 |
| sylvātĭcă | . . | Apetal | . 6, H. De. T. | Britain | . . |
| atrōrūbēns | . | Apetal | . 6, H. De. T. | | |
| incīsā | . . | Apetal | . 6, H. De. T. | | |

FALCATE, } bent like a sickle.
FALCIFORM, }

FĀLKĬĂ. Named by Linnæus in honour of J. P. Falk, a Swedish botanist, who died in 1774. *Linn.* 5, Or. 2, Nat. Or. *Nolanaceæ.* A desirable little creeper, which grows readily in a mixture of peat

and loam, and young plants are easily procured from cuttings in the same kind of soil, under a glass.

| | | | | | | |
|---|---|---|---|---|---|---|
| rēpēns | . | Pink | . 7, G. Ev. Cr. | C.G.H. | . 1774 |

FALSE ARMERIA, see *Diānthŭs Pseudo-arměrĭā.*

FALSELY TWO-VALVED; imperfectly two-valved, or having two valves with an origin different from that of ordinary valves.

FAN-NERVED, the nerves disposed like a fan.

FAN PALM, see *Corÿphă.*

FARĀMĔĂ, *Aublet*. Meaning of the name not given. *Linn.* 5, Or. 1, Nat. Or. *Cinchonaceæ.* This shrub is well deserving of culture on account of its sweet-scented flowers, which are about the size of those of the jasmine. It succeeds well in a mixture of turfy loam, peat, and sand, and may be increased by ripened cuttings planted in sand, under a glass, in a moist heat. The plants require plenty of pot-room, and a liberal supply of water. *Synonyme:* 1. *Tetramerium odoratissimum.*

| | | | | | | |
|---|---|---|---|---|---|---|
| odoratissĭmā | . . | White | . 8. Ev. S. | W. Ind. | . 1793 |

FARINACEOUS, full of flour.

FARĪNĂ, meal.

FARINACEOUSLY TOMENTOSE, } covered with a mealy
FARINOSELY-TOMENTOSE, } kind of down.

FARSETĬĂ, *Turra*. In honour of Philip Farseti, a noble Venetian botanist. *Linn.* 15, Nat. Or. *Cruciferæ.* The frame species of this interesting genus thrive well in any light soil, and cuttings strike readily in the same kind of soil, under a glass. The perennial kinds are well suited for rock-work, or for the front of flower-borders; they may be increased from cuttings planted under a glass, or from seed. The annual species merely require sowing where intended to flower. *Synonymes:* 1. *Alyssum cheiranthifolium.* 2. *F. ægyptiaca, Cheiranthus Farsetia.* 3. *Alyssum clypeatum.* 4. *Lunaria græca.*

| | | | | | | |
|---|---|---|---|---|---|---|
| cheiranthifōliă, 1 | Yellow | . 7, H. | A. | Levant | . 1818 |
| cheiranthoīdēs, 2 | . Wht. pur. | 7, F. Ev. S. | Levant | . 1788 |
| clypeātă, 3 | . . | Yellow | . 7, H. Her. P. | S. Eur. | . 1596 |
| eriocārpă | . . | Yellow | . 7, F. Ev. S. | Greece | . 1820 |
| lunarioīdēs, 4 | . | Yellow | . 7, F. Ev. S. | Archip. | . 1731 |
| suffruticōsă | . . | Violet | . 4, F. Ev. S. | Persia | . 1823 |

FASCIATED, having pale bands or transverse spots.

FASCICLED, in bundles, or parcels.

FASCICLES, parcels, or bundles.

FASCICULATE, } arranged in bundles, or parcels.
FASCICULAR, }

FASCICLED-WHORLED, arranged in parcels, but forming a whorl, or circle.

FASCICLED-RACEMES, racemes collected into parcels.

FASCICULATELY-TUBEROUS, } roots composed of parcels
FASCICLED-TUBEROUS, } of tubers.

FASTIGIATE, tapering to a narrow point, like a pyramid.

FASTIGIATELY-BRANCHED, the branches becoming gradually shorter from the base to the apex.

FAUCES, the gaping part of monopetalous flowers.

FAVOSE, pitted, like the cells of a honeycomb.

FAVOSELY-SCROBICULATE, excavated in little pits or hollows.

FEATHER-GRASS, see *Stipa pennata.*

FEATHER-NERVED, the nerves disposed like the feathers of a pen.

FEBRIFUGE, } efficacious in moderating fevers.
FEBRIFUGAL, }

FECULENT, muddy, thick with sediment.

FECUNDATION, the act of making fruitful.

FĔDĬĂ, *Mœnch*. Derived from *fedus*, an ancient word, signifying a kid. *Linn.* 2, Or. 1, Nat. Or. *Valerianaceæ.* An extremely ornamental annual, the seeds of which merely require to be sown in the open border in spring.

| | | | | | | |
|---|---|---|---|---|---|---|
| cornucōpiă | . . | Red | . 7, H. | A. S. Eur. | . 1796 |

FELWORT, see *Sivērsĭă.*

FEMALE FERN, see *Asplēnĭŭm Filĭx fœmĭnă.*

**FENESTRALIS**, having holes, or gaps.

**FENNEL**, see *Anethum fœniculum*.

**FENNEL-FLOWER**, see *Nigella*.

**FENUGREEK**, see *Trigonella*.

**FERNANDEZIA**, *Ruiz and Pavon*. Named after George Garcias Fernandez, a Spanish botanist, who is unknown except through the medium of this genus. *Linn.* 20, Or. 1, Nat. Or. *Orchidaceæ*. Small plants not possessed of much beauty. They may be cultivated in good turfy peat, broken into small pieces, mixed with a few potsherds. The pots must be well drained, and the plants kept in a hot damp stove.

| | | | | | | |
|---|---|---|---|---|---|---|
| acuta | . . . | . Yel. red | . 6, S. | Epi. | Trinidad | . 1834 |
| elegans | . . . | . Yellow | . 6, S. | Epi. | Trinidad | . 1817 |

**FERNELIA**, *Commerson*. After J. Fernel, physician to Henry II. of France, who died in 1558. *Linn.* 4, Or. 1, Nat. Or. *Cinchonaceæ*. Elegant little plants, with fine glossy leaves, well worthy a place in every collection. They succeed well in a mixture of turfy loam and peat, and cuttings planted in sand, under a glass, will root freely in the stove. *Synonyms*: 1. *Coccocypselum buxifolium*.

| | | | | | | |
|---|---|---|---|---|---|---|
| buxifolia, 1 | . . | . | S. Ev. S. 1. | France | . 1816 |
| obovata | . . . | . | S. Ev. S. 1. | France | . 1816 |

**FERRARIA**, *Linn.* In honour of J. B. Ferrari, an Italian botanist. *Linn.* 16, Or. 1, Nat. Or. *Iridaceæ*. Rather ornamental plants when in flower, succeeding best in a mixture of sandy loam and peat; when in a dormant state, they should be kept quite dry. As soon as they begin to grow they should receive a fresh potting, and a regular supply of water. If grown in a warm border, in sandy soil, the bulbs should be planted about six inches deep, and protected from severe weather; they are increased by offsets, or seeds. *Synonyms*: 1. *Ferrariola viridiflora*.

| | | | | | |
|---|---|---|---|---|---|
| angustifolia | . . | . Brown | . 6, G. Bl. P. C. G. H. | . | . 1825 |
| antherosa, 1 | . . | . Grn. brn. | . 6, G. Bl. P. C. G. H. | . | . 1800 |
| atrata | . . . | . Drk. pur. | . 6, H. Bl. P. C. G. H. | . | . |
| divaricata | . . | . Brown | . 6, G. Bl. P. C. G. H. | . | . 1825 |
| elongata | . . | . Drk. pur. | . 7, F. Bl. P. M. Video | . | . 1828 |
| obtusifolia | . . | . Brown | . 6, G. Bl. P. C. G. H. | . | . 1825 |
| uncinata | . . | . Brown | . 6, G. Bl. P. C. G. H. | . | . 1825 |
| undulata | . . | . Grn. brn. | . 4, G. Bl. P. C. G. H. | . | . 1775 |

**FERRUGINOUS**, iron-coloured, rusty.

**FERULA**, *Tournefort*. From *ferio*, to strike; stems used as rods. *Linn.* 5, Or. 2, Nat. Or. *Umbelliferæ*. All the species of Ferula, or *Giant-fennel*, are strong-growing plants. They do well in any garden soil, and are easily increased by seeds. *Synonyms*: 1. *F. nodiflora*. 2. *Peucedanum obtusifolium*. 3. *F. asafœtida*. 4. *Peucedanum sibiricum*. 5. *Cicuta venenata*.

| | | | | | |
|---|---|---|---|---|---|
| asafœtida | . . | . Yellow | . 7, H. Her. P. | Persia | . |
| campestris | . . | . Yellow | . 6, H. Her. P. | Tauria | . 1829 |
| capillaris | . . | . Yellow | . 6, H. Her. P. | Spain | . 1820 |
| caspica | . . | . Yellow | . 7, H. Her. P. | Caucasus | . 1819 |
| communis | . . | . Yellow | . 7, H. Her. P. | S. Eur. | . 1597 |
| Ferulago, 1 | . | . Yellow | . 7, H. Her. P. | S. Eur. | . |
| glauca | . . | . Pa. yel. | . 7, H. Her. P. | Italy | . 1596 |
| longifolia | . . | . Yellow | . 7, H. Her. P. | Siberia | . 1820 |
| macedis | . . | . Yellow | . 7, H. Her. P. | Levant | . 1810 |
| nuda | . . . | . Yellow | . 7, H. Her. P. | Siberia | . 1821 |
| obtusifolia, 2 | . | . Green | . 7, H. Her. P. | Greece | . 1819 |
| orientalis | . . | . Yellow | . 7, H. Her. P. | Levant | . 1759 |
| persica, 3 | . . | . Yellow | . 8, H. Her. P. | Persia | . 1782 |
| pubescens | . . | . Yellow | . 7, H. Her. P. | Siberia | . 1820 |
| sibirica, 4 | . . | . Yellow | . 7, H. Her. P. | Siberia | . 1816 |
| stricta | . . | . Yellow | . 7, H. Her. P. C. G. H. | . | . 1818 |
| sylvatica | . . | . Yellow | . 6, H. Her. P. | Podolia | . 1822 |
| tingitana | . . | . Yellow | . 7, H. Her. P. | Barbary | . 1680 |
| villosa, 5 | . . | . White | . 7, H. Her. P. | N. Amer. | . 1824 |

**FERULAGO**, *Koch*. From *ferio*, same as Ferula. *Linn.* 5, Or. 2, Nat. Or. *Umbelliferæ*. Plants very nearly related to *Ferula*, and requiring precisely the same treatment. *Synonyms*: 1. *Ferula nodiflora*. 2. *F. thyrsiflora*.

| | | | | | |
|---|---|---|---|---|---|
| nodiflora, 1 | . | . Yellow | . 7, H. Her. P. | S. Eur. | . 1596 |
| thyrsiflora, 2 | . | . White | . 6, H. Her. P. | Crete | . 1825 |

**FESTUCA**. Linnæus derived this name from the Celtic word *fest*, signifying pasture, or food. *Linn.* 3, Or. 2, Nat. Or. *Gramineæ*. This genus affords some valuable fodder grasses, grows best in a loamy soil, and is increased from seeds.

| | | | | | |
|---|---|---|---|---|---|
| cambrica | . . | . Apetal | . 7, Gram. | Wales | . |
| cynosuroides | . | . Apetal | . 7, Gram. | S. Eur. | . 1820 |

| | | | | | |
|---|---|---|---|---|---|
| duriuscula | . . | . Apetal | . 6, Gram. | Britain | . |
| glabra | . . | . Apetal | . 7, Gram. | Britain | . |
| glauca | . . | . Apetal | . 7, Gram. | S. Eur. | . |
| hirsuta | . . | . Apetal | . 7, Gram. | Germany | . 1818 |
| hordeiformis | . | . Apetal | . 7, Gram. | Britain | . |
| lævis | . . | . Apetal | . 6, Gram. | Russia | . 1806 |
| ovina | . . | . Apetal | . 6, Gram. | Britain | . |
| tenuifolia | . . | . Apetal | . 7, Gram. | Britain | . |
| varia | . . | . Apetal | . 7, Gram. | S. Eur. | . 1823 |
| vivipara | . . | . Apetal | . 7, Gram. | Britain | . |

alpestris, alpina, amethystina, aspera, baledrica, bulbosa, cæsia, capillata, ciliata, curvula, dumetorum, Fenas, fallax, flavescens, glomerata, grandiflora, Halleri, heterophylla, laxa, mexicana, natans, pallens, pannonica, pubescens, rubens, rubra, scabra, serotina, stricta, tenella, triflora, vaginata, vallesiaca, xanthina.

**FEVERFEW**, see *Pyrethrum*.

**FEVERWORT**, see *Triosteum*.

**FIBRILLOSE**, covered with little strings, or fibres.

**FIBROUS**, composed of fibres.

**FICULIFORMIS**, button-shaped.

**FICARIA**, *Dillenius*. Derived from *ficus*, a fig; the roots bear tubercles resembling little figs. *Linn.* 13, Or. 6, Nat. Or. *Ranunculaceæ*. These desirable plants succeed best if planted in any common soil, under the shade of trees. They are increased by separating the tubers in autumn. *Synonyms*: 1. *F. ranunculoides*.

| | | | | | |
|---|---|---|---|---|---|
| verna, 1 | . . | . Yellow | . 5, H. Tu. P. | Britain | . |
| pallida | . . | . Pa. yel. | . 5, H. Tu. P. | Gardens | . |
| plena | . . | . Yellow | . 5, H. Tu. P. | Britain | . |

**FICUS**, *Linn.* The derivation of the name is unknown. *Linn.* 23, Or. 2, Nat. Or. *Urticaceæ*. This is an extensive but easily cultivated genus of plants, some of which are very desirable, especially *F. elastica*, which is one of the most noted. They all thrive well in any light rich soil, or in loam and peat. Cuttings, with their leaves uninjured, root in sand; the stove species in heat. *F. elastica* is famed for producing a species of Indian rubber. The glutinous juice of *F. indica* is applied to the teeth and gums to ease the toothach; the Hindoos consider the bark a powerful tonic, and use it in diabetes. *F. racemosa* is slightly astringent, and the juice of the root is also a powerful tonic. *F. religiosa* is the celebrated Banyan Tree of India, the seeds of which are supposed to be cooling and alterative. *Synonyms*: 1. *cerasiformis*. 2. *scabra*, *glandulosa*. 3. *nitida*. 4. *venosa*, *leucosticta*. 5. *virens*. 6. *scabra*. 7. *speciosa*, *indica*.

| | | | | | |
|---|---|---|---|---|---|
| acuminata, 1 | . | . Apetal | . S. Ev. S. | Silhet | . 1820 |
| Afzelii | . . | . Apetal | . S. Ev. T. | S. Leone | . 1823 |
| americana | . . | . Apetal | . S. Ev. S. | Guiana | . 1820 |
| aquatica | . . | . Apetal | . S. Ev. T. | E. Ind. | . 1758 |
| arbutifolia | . . | . Apetal | . S. Ev. S. | . | . 1825 |
| aspera | . . | . Apetal | . 5, G. Ev. S. | N. Holl. | . 1807 |
| aurantiaca | . . | . Apetal | . S. Ev. T. | . | . 1824 |
| australis | . . | . Apetal | . 5, G. Ev. S. | N. S. W. | . 1789 |
| benghalensis | . | . Apetal | . 5, S. Ev. T. | E. Ind. | . 1690 |
| Benjamina | . . | . Apetal | . S. Ev. T. | E. Ind. | . 1757 |
| brasiliensis | . . | . Apetal | . S. Ev. S. | Brazil | . 1822 |
| Brassii | . . | . Apetal | . S. Ev. T. | S. Leone | . 1822 |
| calyculata | . . | . Apetal | . S. Ev. T. | N. Spain | . 1600 |
| capensis | . . | . Apetal | . G. Ev. S. | C. G. H. | . 1816 |
| Carica | . . | . Apetal | . 6, G. De. T. | S. Eur. | . 1548 |
| ciliolosa | . . | . Apetal | . G. Ev. S. | . | . 1823 |
| comosa | . . | . Apetal | . S. Ev. T. | E. Ind. | . 1818 |
| cordata | . . | . Apetal | . G. Ev. S. | C. G. H. | . 1802 |
| coriacea | . . | . Apetal | . S. Ev. T. | E. Ind. | . 1772 |
| coronata | . . | . Apetal | . 6, S. Ev. T. | . | . 1800 |
| costata | . . | . Apetal | . S. Ev. T. | E. Ind. | . 1768 |
| cotinifolia | . . | . Apetal | . S. Ev. T. | Mexico | . 1826 |
| crassinervia | . | . Apetal | . S. Ev. T. | S. Amer. | . 1823 |
| dumosa | . . | . Apetal | . S. Ev. S. | . | . 1825 |
| elastica | . . | . Apetal | . S. Ev. T. | E. Ind. | . 1815 |
| elliptica | . . | . Apetal | . S. Ev. T. | S. Amer. | . 1824 |
| exasperata, 2 | . | . Apetal | . S. Ev. S. | Guinea | . 1800 |
| glabrata | . . | . Apetal | . S. Ev. T. | Caraccas | . 1816 |
| glomerata | . . | . Apetal | . S. Ev. T. | E. Ind. | . 1818 |
| heterophylla | . | . Apetal | . S. Ev. T. | Malabar | . 1816 |
| Hookeri, 3 | . . | . Apetal | . S. Ev. S. | W. Ind. | . 1816 |
| indica | . . | . Apetal | . S. Ev. T. | E. Ind. | . 1759 |
| infectoria | . . | . Apetal | . S. Ev. T. | W. Ind. | . 1762 |
| lævigata | . . | . Apetal | . S. Ev. T. | W. Ind. | . 1823 |
| lanceolata | . . | . Apetal | . S. Ev. T. | E. Ind. | . 1873 |
| lasiophylla | . . | . Apetal | . S. Ev. T. | . | . 1820 |
| lentiginosa | . . | . Apetal | . S. Ev. T. | W. Ind. | . 1820 |
| leucostoma, 4 | . | . Apetal | . S. Ev. T. | E. Ind. | . 1768 |
| Lichtensteinii | . | . Apetal | . S. Ev. S. | C. G. H. | . 1824 |
| Loganii | . . | . Apetal | . S. Ev. T. | Caraccas | . 1824 |
| longifolia | . . | . Apetal | . S. Ev. S. | E. Ind. | . 1825 |
| lucida | . . | . Apetal | . S. Ev. T. | . | . 1772 |

| | | | |
|---|---|---|---|
| lutescens . . | . Apetal | 6, 8. Ev. 8. | . 1824 |
| macrophylla . . | . Apetal | G. Ev. T. N. Holl. | |
| martinicensis, δ | . Apetal | G. Ev. T. W. Ind. | . 1759 |
| microcarpa . . | . Apetal | G. Ev. T. Guinea . | . 1819 |
| Mantia . . | . Apetal | G. Ev. S. N. Holl. | . 1822 |
| myrtifolia . . | . Apetal | 8. Ev. T. | . 1824 |
| nitida . . | . Apetal | 6, 8. Ev. S. E. Ind. | . 1796 |
| nymphæifolia . . | . Apetal | 8. Ev. T. E. Ind. | . 1759 |
| oblongata . . | . Apetal | 8. Ev. T. C. G. H. | . 1825 |
| obtusata . . | . Apetal | 8. Ev. S. | . 1821 |
| obtusifolia . . | . Apetal | 8. Ev. T. Mexico . | . 1823 |
| oppositifolia, δ . | . Apetal | 8. Ev. S. E. Ind. | . 1802 |
| pedunculata . . | . Apetal | 8. Ev. S. S. Amer. | . 1776 |
| pendula . . | . Apetal | 8. Ev. T. | . 1824 |
| pertusa . . | . Apetal | 8. Ev. S. S. Amer. | . 1780 |
| populnea . . | . Apetal | 8. Ev. T. S. Amer. | . 1812 |
| pumila . . | . Apetal | G. Ev. Tr. China . | . 1769 |
| racemosa . . | . Apetal | 8. Ev. S. E. Ind. | . 1759 |
| religiosa . . | . Apetal | 8. Ev. T. E. Ind. | . 1731 |
| repens . . | . Apetal | 8. Ev. Cr. E. Ind. | . 1805 |
| retusa . . | . Apetal | 8. Ev. T. E. Ind. | . 1793 |
| rubiginosa . . | . Apetal | 8. Ev. T. Brasil | . 1824 |
| rugosa . . | . Apetal | 8. Ev. S. S. Leone | . 1826 |
| sagittata . . | . Apetal | 8. Ev. Cr. E. Ind. | . 1810 |
| salicifolia, 7 . | . Apetal | G. Ev. T. Arabia | |
| stipulata . . | . Apetal | G. Ev. Cr. China . | . 1771 |
| superstitiosa . . | . Apetal | 8. Ev. S. | . 1768 |
| terebrata . . | . Apetal | 8. Ev. T. Maurit. | . 1822 |
| tinctoria . . | . Apetal | 6, 8. Ev T. Society Is. | . 1793 |
| tomentosa . . | . Apetal | 8. Ev. T. E. Ind. | . 1816 |
| ulmifolia . . | . Apetal | 8. Ev. S. Philipp. | . 1813 |
| urophylla . . | . Apetal | 6, 8. Ev. S. India . | . 1829 |
| venosa . . | . Apetal | 8. Ev. T. E. Ind. | . 1763 |
| virgata . . | . Apetal | 8. Ev. T. E. Ind. | . 1816 |
| viscifolia . . | . Apetal | 8. Ev. T. | . 1820 |

FIDDLE-WOOD, see *Citharexylum.*

FIELDIA, *A. Cunningham.* In honour of Baron Field, once chief judge of New South Wales. *Linn.* 14, Or. 1, Nat. Or. *Bignoniaceæ.* An ornamental species, which may be successfully grown in a mixture of loam and peat; cuttings will root readily in sand, under a glass, if their leaves are left entire.

| | | | |
|---|---|---|---|
| australis . . | . White. | . 7, G. Ev. Cr. N. Holl. | . 1826 |

FIELD MADDER, see *Rubia.*

FIG MARIGOLD, see *Mesembryanthemum.*

FIG TREE, see *Ficus.*

FIGWORT, see *Scrophularia.*

FILAGO, *Linn.* From *filum,* a thread; the plant appears as if covered with cotton, or down; whence the name Cotton Rose. *Linn.* 19, Or. 2, Nat. Or. *Composita.* A worthless annual, which merely requires sowing in the open border. *Synonyme:* 1. *Evax pygmæa*—pygmæa 1.

FILAMENTOSE, thready, or cotton-like.

FILBERT, see *Corylus Avellana.*

FILIFORM, like a thread in form.

FILMY LEAF, see *Hymenophyllum.*

FIMBRIATE, fringed round the margin.

FIMBRISTYLIS, *Vahl.* From *fimbria,* a fringe, and *stylus,* a style; the style is fringed. *Linn.* 3, Or. 1, Nat. Or. *Cyperaceæ.* Herbaceous species of grass, requiring to be grown in ponds or ditches; Increased by seeds—*annua, dichotoma, diphylla, puberula.*

FINGER-PARTED; five lobes resembling the human hand.

FINGER GRASS, see *Digitaria.*

FIORIN, see *Agrostis stolonifera.*

FIR, see *Pinus.*

FIRM, hardish, tending to solidity.

FISTULAR, } hollow, like a pipe.
FISTULOUS, }

FISTULINA, *Bulliard.* From *fistula,* a pipe. *Linn.* 24, Or. 9, Nat. Or. *Fungi.* A crimson-like plant, growing in patches about six inches high, most conspicuous in autumn—*hepatica.*

FLABELLATE, fan-shaped.

FLACCID, feeble, weak.

FLACOURTIA, L'Heritier named this genus in honour of Etienne Flacourt, a botanist, and a director of the French East India Company in 1648. *Linn.* 22, Or. 12, Nat. Or. *Flacourtiaceæ.* These are ornamental fruit trees, or shrubs, from four to twenty feet high, and very successfully grown in loam and peat; cuttings root freely in sand, under a glass, in heat. *F. Ramontchi* bears leaves and fruit similar to those of the plum. The natives eat the fruit, which is sweet, but leaves a slight bitterish taste in the mouth.

| | | | |
|---|---|---|---|
| cataphracta . . | . White . | 8. Ev. S. E. Ind. | . 1804 |
| flavescens . . | . White . | 8. Ev. S. Guinea . | . 1780 |

| | | | |
|---|---|---|---|
| inermis . . | . White . | 8. Ev. T. E. Ind. | . 1819 |
| Ramontchi . | . White . | 7, 8. Ev. S. Madagas. | . 1775 |
| rhamnoides . | . White . | 8. Ev. S. C. G. H. | . 1816 |
| rotundifolia . | . White . | 8. Ev. S. E. Ind. | . 1820 |
| sapida . . | . White . | 8. Ev. S. E. Ind. | . 1800 |
| sepiaria . . | . White . | 8. Ev. S. E Ind. | . 1816 |

FLAGELLARIA, *Linn.* From *flagellum,* alluding to the long flexible branches. *Linn.* 6, Or. 3, Nat. Or. *Juncaceæ.* A curious plant, growing about seven feet high in a mixture of peat and loam; it may be readily increased by suckers. The leaves of this plant are said to be astringent and vulnerary.

| | | | |
|---|---|---|---|
| indica . . . | . White. | . 6, 8. Ev. Cl. India | . 1782 |

FLAGELLÆ, runners without leaves.

FLAGELLIFORM, in form of runners, creeping along the ground.

FLAVESCENS, pale yellow.

FLAT, plane, level.

FLAVERIA, *Jussieu.* From *flavus,* yellow; because in Chili the plants are used for dyeing that colour. *Linn.* 19, Or. 5, Nat. Or. *Compositæ.* Annuals and biennials of no value. They require to be sown in heat, and when potted off, treated as other tender plants. *Synonymes:* 1. *Milleria contrayerba.* 2. *M. angustifolia.* 3. *Flaveria linearis.*

| | | | |
|---|---|---|---|
| Contrayerba, 1 . | . Yellow . | 8, 8. B. Peru . | . 1794 |

*angustifolia* 2, *maritima* 3.

FLAX, see *Linum.*

FLAX LILY, see *Phormium.*

FLAX STAR, see *Lysimachia Linum-stellatum.*

FLEABANE, see *Conyza.*

FLEAWORT, see *Inula Pulicaria.*

FLEAWORT, see *Plantago Psyllium.*

FLEMINGIA, *Roxburgh.* In honour of John Fleming, M.D., F.R.S., F.L.S., &c., an acute botanist, and formerly president of the East India Company's medical establishment in Bengal. *Linn.* 17, Or. 4, Nat. Or. *Leguminosæ.* Plants only worth cultivating in collections. They succeed in any light soil, and cuttings will root in sand, under a glass, in heat.

| | | | |
|---|---|---|---|
| procumbens . . | . Purple | 8, 8. Ev. Tr. E. Ind. . | . 1816 |
| prostrata . . | . Purple | 8, 8. Ev. Tr. E. Ind. . | . 1816 |

*congesta, lineata, nana, semialata, stricta.*

FLEXILE, easily bent in different directions, pliable.

FLEXUOUS, having a bent or undulating direction, zigzag.

FLINDERSIA, *R. Brown.* In compliment to Captain M. Flinders, R.N., who, accompanied by the famous botanist and naturalist Robert Brown, explored the coast of New Holland in the beginning of the present century. *Linn.* 10, Or. 1, Nat. Or. *Cedrelaceæ.* This is a fine tall-growing tree, the wood of which is employed by the natives for various domestic uses; indeed, it is said to be very little inferior to mahogany. It succeeds well in loam and peat, and cuttings of the ripened wood, with their leaves not cut, will root in sand, under a glass.

| | | | |
|---|---|---|---|
| australis . . . | . White. | . G. Ev. T. N. Holl. | . 1823 |

FLIX-WEED, see *Sisymbrium Sophia.*

FLOCCOSE, } covered with little tufts, like wool.
FLOCKY, }

FLOCCOSELY-TOMENTOSE, down, disposed in little tufts.

FLORAL, of or belonging to a flower.

FLORAL-ENVELOPES, the calyx, and corolla, which envelop the inner parts of the flower, are so called.

FLORETS, little flowers; chiefly applied to compositæ, and grasses.

FLOSCULOSUS, composite flowers, consisting of many tubular monopetalous florets.

FLOWER FENCE, see *Poinciana.*

FLOWERING ASH, see *Ornus.*

FLOWERING RUSH, see *Butomus.*

FLOWER OF JOVE, see *Lychnis flos Jovis.*

FLUGGEA, *Willdenow.* In honour of John Flugge, a German cryptogamic botanist. *Linn.* 22, Or. 6, Nat. Or. *Euphorbiaceæ.* An evergreen shrub of no beauty, and of the simplest culture—*leucopyrus.*

FLUITANS, floating.

FLY, see *Lonicera Xylosteum.*

FŒTENS, stinking.

FŒTIDIA, *A. Cunningham.* From *fœtidus,* fetid; alluding to the smell of the wood. *Linn.* 12, Or. 3, Nat.

Or. *Myrtaceæ.* An ornamental tree, about twenty-five feet high; it requires a turfy loam, mixed with a little peat, and ripened cuttings will soon root if planted in sand, under a glass, in heat.

mauritiàna . . . White . . S. Ev. T. Maurit. . . 1825

FOLIACEOUS, having the texture of leaves.

FOLIATE; when a leaf is divided into leaflets, it is called 1, 2, 3, 5, or 10-foliate, according to the number of leaflets.

FOLLICLE, a particular kind of two-valved seed-vessel, such as that of *Pæony.*

FOLLICULAR, like a follicle.

FONTANESIA, *Labillardière.* In honour of the celebrated Desfontaines, professor of botany at Paris. *Linn.* 2, Or. 1, Nat. Or. *Oleaceæ.* If this very ornamental species is planted out in the open ground, it will require a little protection in severe weather. It thrives well in any common soil, and may be easily increased by layers, or cuttings, under a glass.

phillyræoìdes . . Yellow . 8. F. De. S. Syria . . 1787

FONTINALIS, *Linn.* From *fons,* a fountain; alluding to the place of growth. *Linn.* 24, Or. 5, Nat. Or. *Musci.* Greenish-looking plants, most conspicuous in the summer season. *F. antipyretica* is very common, floating in large masses in rivers and pools of water—*antipyrética, capillácéā, squamósā.*

FOOLS' PARSLEY, see *Æthúsa.*

FOOTSTALKS, the stalks of leaves, &c.

FORFICATUS, pince, or nipper-shaped.

FORMOSA, handsome, ornamental.

FORNICATE, arched.

FORSKAHLIA, *Linn.* In honour of Peter Forskahl, a traveller in Egypt. *Linn.* 21, Or. 6, Nat. Or. *Urticaceæ.* Curious little plants, somewhat resembling the nettle. *F. candida* thrives well in any light rich soil, and cuttings root readily in the same kind of soil, under a glass. The annual kinds require to be sown in a gentle hotbed, and when of sufficient size, transplanted into the open ground.

angustifòliā . . . Wht grn. 7, H. . . A. Teneriffe . 1779
càndida . . . . Wht grn. 7, G. Her. P. C.G.H. . 1774
tenacissimā . . . Wht grn. 7, H. . . A. Egypt . . 1767

FOTHERGILLIA, *Linn.* In memory of John Fothergill, M.D., an eminent physician of London, and patron of botany. *Linn.* 13, Or. 2, Nat. Or. *Hamamelaceæ.* Beautiful shrubs when in leaf and flower, growing from three to six feet high, and bearing pretty, white, sweet-scented flowers. In the shrubbery, they thrive well in a peat soil, and may be increased by layers in spring or autumn, or by seed, which is annually imported from America. *Synonymes:* 1. *F. Gardeni.* 2. *F. major.*

alnifòliā . . . White . . 5, H. De. S. N. Amer. . 1765
acútā, 1 . . . White . . 6, H. De. S. N. Amer. . 1765
obtúsā, 2 . . . White . . 6, H. De. S. N. Amer. . 1765
serótina . . . White . . 8, H. De. S. N. Amer. . 1765

FOVEATE, }
FOVEOLATE, } pitted, full of little pits.

FOVEOLÆ, little pits, or hollows.

FOXBANE, see *Aconítùm Vulpàrià.*

FOXGLOVE, see *Digitàlis.*

FOX-TAIL GRASS, see *Alopecúrùs.*

FRAGARIA, *Linn.* From *fragrans,* fragrant; the perfumed fruit of the strawberry is well known. *Linn.* 12, Or. 1, Nat. Or. *Rosaceæ.* The cultivation and propagation of this plant is so familiar to every one, as are also the wholesomeness and deliciousness of the fruit, that neither need be particularised here any further than that seeds, sown early in spring, will generally fruit the same year very late in autumn. *Synonyme:* 1. *grandiflóra.*

bonariénsis . . . Apetal . 6, H. Her. P. B. Ayres . .
Breslingii . . . White . . 5, H. Her. P. France . .
calycìnā, 1 . . . White . . 4, H. Her. P. France . .
canadénsis . . . White . . 5, H. Her. P. N. Amer. .
chiliénsis . . . White . . 5, H. Her. P. S. Amer. . 1727
collìnā . . . . White . . 6, H. Her. P. Germany . 1768
elàtior . . . . White . . 5, H. Her. P. Britain . .
grandiflórā . . . White . . 5, H. Her. P. Surinam . 1759
índicā . . . . Yellow . 7, H. Her. Cr. India . . 1805
majaúféā . . . White . . 5, H. Her. P. France . .
monophýllā . . . White . . 5, H. Her. P. . . . . 1778
platanoídēs . . . Red . . 5, H. Her. P. N. Amer. .
véscā . . . . White . . 5, H. Her. P. Britain . .
virginiánā . . . White . . 4, H. Her. P. N. Amer. . 1629

FRAGILLARIA, *Lyngbye.* From *fragilis,* brittle; alluding to the nature of the plants. *Linn.* 24, Or. 7, Nat. Or. *Algæ.* Green and brown tufts of *Algæ,* found in rivulets and watery places—*Ayemális, pectinális.*

FRANCISCIA, *Pohl.* In honour of Francis, emperor of Austria, a patron of botany. *Linn.* 14, Or. 2, Nat. Or. *Scrophulariaceæ.* An ornamental dwarfish shrub, requiring a mixture of peat and loam. Cuttings root in sand, under a glass, in heat. *Synonyme:* 1. *F. Hopeana.*

uniflórā, 1 . . . Wht. pur. 7, S. Ev. S. Brazil . . 1826

FRANCOA. *Cavanilles* named this genus after F. Franco, a Valencian promoter of botany in the sixteenth century. *Linn.* 8, Or. 4, Nat. Or. *Francoaceæ.* Beautiful plants when in flower, and well worthy a place in every collection. They may be planted out in the open ground, in a warm sheltered situation, with a slight protection in severe weather. They can only be increased by seeds.

appendiculátā . . Purple . 7, H. Her. P. Chile . . 1830
ramósā . . . . White . 7, H. Her. P. Chile . . 1831
sonchifòliā . . . Purple . 7, H. Her. P. Chile . . 1830

FRANKENIA. Named by Linnæus in honour of John Frankenius, professor of botany at Upsal, who died in 1661. *Linn.* 6, Or. 1, Nat. Or. *Frankeniaceæ.* Truly beautiful, little evergreen shrubs, or herbs. The hardy kinds are particularly well adapted for ornamenting rock-work, or they may be grown in small pots, and placed among the alpine plants. The greenhouse species should be placed on the front shelf in winter. All the species grow well in loam, peat, and sand, with the pots well drained; they are easily increased by cuttings planted in sand, under a glass, by seeds, or divisions of the roots. *Synonymes:* 1. *hispida.* *hirsuta.*

corymbósā . . . Red . . 7, H. Ev. Tr. Barbary . 1819
ericifòliā . . . Red . . 7, G. Ev. Tr. Canaries . 1816
hirsùta, 1 . . . Ll. blue . 7, H. Ev. Tr. Siberia . . 1789
intermédiā, 2 . . White . . 7, H. Ev. Tr. S. Eur. . 1817
lævis . . . . Flesh . 7, H. Ev. Cr. England . .
móllis . . . . Red . . 7, H. Ev. Tr. Caucasus . 1824
nodiflórā . . . Flesh . 6, G. Ev. Tr. C. G. H. . 1818
Nóthriā . . . . Flesh . 7, H. Ev. Cr. C. G. H. . 1816
pauciflórā . . . Pink . 7, G. Ev. S. N. Holl. . 1824
pulverulántā . . . Red . . 7, H. Tr. A. England . .

FRANKINCENSE, see *Pìnùs Tédā.*

FRANSERIA, *Cavanilles.* In honour of Antony Franzer, a botanist. *Linn.* 21, Or. 5, Nat. Or. *Compositæ.* Greenhouse shrubs of no interest. They grow in peat and loam, and may be increased by cuttings—*ambrosioídes, artemisioídes.*

FRASERA. Michaux dedicated this genus in honour of John Fraser, an indefatigable collector of North American plants. *Linn.* 4, Or. 1, Nat. Or. *Gentianaceæ.* A very curious little plant, found in the morasses of North America, and successfully cultivated in peat soil, and increased by seeds, or divisions. The root of this plant is a pure and excellent bitter. *Synonyme:* 1. *Walteri.*

carolinénsis, 1 . . Grn. yel. . 7, H. . . P. Carolina . 1795

FRAXINUS, *Linn.* From *phraxis,* a separation; the wood is used in making hedges. *Linn.* 23, Or. 2, Nat. Or. *Oleaceæ.* Most of the species are large-growing trees, well suited for plantations. *F. excelsior* is one of the most useful of our native timber trees; its wood is much used by coachmakers, wheelwrights, and for many implements used in husbandry. Any of the kinds may be increased by budding or grafting on the common ash, but they are most frequently raised from seeds, which do not vegetate till the second year. The bark of several of the species yields a concrete discharge called *manna,* which is a sweet and gentle purgative. *Synonymes:* 1. *discolor.* 2. *crispa.* 3. *simplicifolia.* 4. *nigra.*

acuminátā . . . Green . 5, H. De. T. N. Amer. . 1723
álbā . . . . Green . 5, H. De. T. N. Amer. . 1823
amarissimā . . . Green . 5, H. De. T. . .
americánā . . . Green . 5, H. De. T. N. Amer. . 1723
appéndicā . . . Green . 5, H. De. T. . .
appendiculátā . . Green . 5, H. De. T. . .
argéntéā . . . Green . 6, H. De. T. Corsica . 1825
atróvìrens . . . Green . 5, H. De. S. Britain . .
caroliniánā . . . Green . 6, H. De. T. N. Amer. . 1783
cinéréā . . . . Green . 5, H. De. T. N. Amer. . 1824

| | | | | | |
|---|---|---|---|---|---|
| elliptica | Green | 5, H. De. T. | N. Amer. | 1825 |
| epiptera, 1 | Green | 5, H. De. T. | N. Amer. | 1823 |
| excelsior, 2 | Green | 5, H. De. T. | Britain | |
| argentea | Green | 5, H. De. T. | Britain | |
| aurea | Green | 5, H. De. T. | Britain | |
| erosa | Green | 5, H. De. T. | Britain | |
| fungosa | Green | 5, H. De. T. | Britain | |
| horisontalis | Green | 5, H. De. T. | | |
| jaspidea | Green | 5, H. De. T. | | |
| nana | Green | 5, H. De. T. | Britain | |
| pendula | Green | 5, H. De. T. | Britain | |
| striata | Green | 5, H. De. T. | Britain | |
| verticillaris | Green | 5, H. De. T. | Britain | |
| expansa | Green | 5, H. De. T. | N. Amer. | 1824 |
| fusca | Green | 5, H. De. T. | N. Amer. | 1823 |
| heterophylla, 3 | Green | 5, H. De. T. | England | |
| juglandifolia | Green | 5, H. De. T. | N. Amer. | 1783 |
| lancea | Green | 5, H. De. T. | N. Amer. | 1820 |
| lentiscifolia | Green | 5, H. De. T. | Aleppo | 1710 |
| pendula | Green | 6, H. De. T. | Germany | 1833 |
| longifolia | Green | 5, H. De. T. | N. Amer. | 1824 |
| lucida | Green | 5, H. De. T. | | |
| macrophylla | Green | 5, H. De. T. | | 1823 |
| mixta | Green | 5, H. De. T. | N. Amer. | 1824 |
| nana | Green | 6, H. De. T. | | |
| nigra | Green | 5, H. De. T. | N. Amer. | 1825 |
| ovata | Green | 5, H. De. T. | N. Amer. | |
| oxycarpa | Green | 5, H. De. T. | Caucasus | 1815 |
| oxyphylla | Green | H. De. T. | S. Eur. | 1821 |
| pallida | Green | 5, H. De. T. | | |
| pannosa | Green | 5, H. De. T. | Carolina | 1820 |
| parvifolia | Green | 5, H. De. T | Levant | 1822 |
| platycarpa | Green | 5, H. De. T. | N. Amer. | 1820 |
| pubescens, 4 | Green | 4, H. De. T. | N. Amer. | 1811 |
| pulverulenta | Green | 5, H. De. T. | N. Amer. | 1824 |
| quadrangulata | Green | 5, H. De. T. | N. Amer. | 1822 |
| Richardi | Green | 5, H. De. T. | N. Amer. | |
| rubicunda | Green | 5, H. De. T. | N. Amer. | 1824 |
| rufa | Green | 5, H. De. T. | N. Amer. | 1822 |
| sambucifolia | Green | 5, H. De. T. | N. Amer. | 1800 |
| verrucosa | Green | 5, H. De. T. | England | |
| virens | Green | 5, H. De. T. | | |
| variegata | Green | 4, H. De. T. | | |
| viridis | Green | 5, H. De. T. | N. Amer. | 1824 |

FREE, apart from each other, not connected together.

FRENCH MARIGOLD, see *Tagetes patula*.

FREZIERA, *Swartz.* Named in compliment to A. F. Frezier, a French traveller in Chili and the South Sea. *Linn.* 13, Or. 1, Nat. Or. *Ternstromiaceæ.* An ornamental, tall-growing tree, with the habit of *Laurus.* It requires to be grown in a mixture of sand, loam, and peat; and cuttings take, when planted in sand, under a glass, in heat.

| | | | | |
|---|---|---|---|---|
| theoides | White | S. Ev. T. | Jamaica | 1818 |

FRIAR'S-COWL, see *Arisarum*.

FRIESIA, *Decandolle.* In honour of the celebrated cryptogamic botanist Elias Fries, M.D., professor of botany in the university of Lund. *Linn.* 11, Or. 1, Nat. Or. *Malvaceæ.* An ornamental shrub, from three to six feet high; it grows freely in a mixture of turfy loam and peat, and ripened cuttings will root without difficulty, in a pot of sand. *Synonyme*: 1. *Elæocarpus peduncularis.*

| | | | | |
|---|---|---|---|---|
| peduncularis, 1 | White | G. Ev. S. V. D. L. | 1818 |

FRINGED, having a border like a fringe.

FRINGE TOOTHED, the border toothed so as to appear fringed.

FRINGE-TREE, see *Chimonanthus*.

FRITILLARIA, *Linn.* From *fritillus*, a chessboard; alluding to the chequered sepals of the flowers. *Linn.* 6, Or. 1, Nat. Or. *Liliaceæ.* These plants have very singular and showy flowers. They will all succeed well in a sandy soil, in the open ground, and may be increased by offsets. *Synonymes*: 1. *Lilium Kamschatkense.* 2. *F. latifolia*, *minor.* 3. *pyrenaica.* 4. *meleagris, alba.* 5. *Lilium pudicum.* 6. *F. racemosa.* 7. *F. racemosa, minor.*

| | | | | | |
|---|---|---|---|---|---|
| alba | White | 5, H. Bl. P. | N. Amer. | |
| cuprea | Copper | 7, H. Bl. P. | Mexico | 1830 |
| imperialis | Dk. yel. | 4, H. Bl. P. | Persia | 1596 |
| flava | Yellow | 4, H. Bl. P. | Persia | 1596 |
| rubra | Red | 4, H. Bl. P. | Persia | 1596 |
| lanceolata, 1 | Dk. pur. | 5, H. Bl. P. | Kamtschat. | 1759 |
| latifolia | Red | 4, H. Bl. P. | Caucasus | 1604 |
| leucantha | White | 5, H. Bl. P. | Siberia | 1822 |
| lusitanica | Br. pur. | 5, H. Bl. P. | Spain | 1825 |
| lutea | Yellow | 5, H. Bl. P. | Caucasus | 1812 |
| meleagris | Purple | 5, H. Bl. P. | Britain | |
| multiplex | Purple | 4, H. Bl. P. | Gardens | |
| meleagroides | Purple | 4, H. Bl. P. | Siberia | 1824 |
| messanensis | Br. pur. | 6, H. Bl. P. | Italy | 1825 |
| minor | Pur. spo. | 4, H. Bl. P. | Altai Mts. | 1830 |

| | | | | | |
|---|---|---|---|---|---|
| nervosa, 2 | Dk. pur. | 5, H. Bl. P. | Caucasus | 1826 |
| nigra, 3 | Yel. pur. | 5, H. Bl. P. | Pyrenees | 1596 |
| obliqua | Br. pur. | 4, H. Bl. P. | Caucasus | |
| persica | Brown | 5, H. Bl. P. | Persia | 1596 |
| minima | Brown | 5, H. Bl. P. | Persia | 1596 |
| præcox, 4 | White | 5, H. Bl. P. | Europe | |
| pudica, 5 | Pur. yel. | 5, H. Bl. P. | N. Amer. | 1824 |
| pyrenaica, 6 | Dk. pur. | 5, H. Bl. P. | | 1605 |
| ruthenica | Purple | 5, H. Bl. P. | Caucasus | 1826 |
| tenella, 7 | Purple | 5, H. Bl. P. | Caucasus | 1826 |
| tulipifolia | Br. pur. | 5, H. Bl. P. | Crimea | 1822 |
| verticillata | Purple | 4, H. Bl. P. | Crimea | 1823 |

FRITILLARY, see *Fritillaria*.

FROG-BIT, see *Hydrocharis*.

FROG-ORCHIS, see *Gymnadenia viridis*.

FRONDS, the leaves of palms and ferns.

FROSTED, covered with glittering particles

FRUCTIFEROUS, that which bears fruit.

FRUCTIFICATION, all those parts composing the fruit of plants.

FRUTESCENT, }
FRUTICOSE, } shrubby

FRUTESCENT CELANDINE, see *Bocconia frutescens*.

FRUTICULOSE, applied to a little shrub.

FUCATUS, coloured, stained.

FUCHSIA, *Plumier.* In honour of the celebrated German botanist, Leonard Fuchs, author of Historia Stirpium, in 1549. *Linn.* 8, Or. 1, Nat. Or. *Onagraceæ.* A most beautiful and well-known genus of plants, well worthy a place in every garden, especially *F. fulgens*, a recently introduced species, and said to be "probably the most beautiful plant of the temperate flora of Mexico." A mixture of loam and peat suits them well, but they will grow equally well in any light rich soil; and young cuttings will root freely in sand, under a glass, which must occasionally be taken off to give them air, or they are very liable to damp. *Synonymes:* 1. *Skinnera excorticata.* 2. *F. decussata.*

| | | | | | |
|---|---|---|---|---|---|
| apetala | Purple | 9, G. Ev. S. | Chile | 1824 |
| arborescens | Pink | 10, G. Ev. S. | Mexico | 1824 |
| bacillaris | Rosy | 9, G. De. S. | Mexico | 1829 |
| coccinea | Scar. pur. | 8, G. Ev. S. | Chile | 1788 |
| conica | Scar. pur. | 8, G. Ev. S. | Chile | 1825 |
| discolor | Pur. red | 8, G. Ev. S. | Pt. Fam. | 1830 |
| excorticata, 1 | Grn. pur. | 7, G. Ev. S. | N. Zeal. | 1824 |
| fulgens | Vermil. | 7, G. Ev. S. | Mexico | 183-- |
| globosa | Crim. pur. | 7, G. Ev. S. | Hybrid | 1830 |
| elegans | Scarlet | 6 G. Ev. S. | Eng. hyb. | 1836 |
| gracilis, 2 | Scar. pur. | 8, G. Ev. S. | Chile | 1823 |
| multiflora | Scar. pur. | 8, G. Ev. S. | Chile | 1824 |
| hybrida | Scarlet | 8, G. Ev. S. | Hybrid | 1825 |
| lycioides | Red | 7, G. Ev. S. | Chile | 1796 |
| macrostemon | Scar. pur. | 7, G. Ev. S. | Chile | 1823 |
| recurvata | Violet | G. Ev. S. | Hybrid | 1835 |
| microphylla | Scar. pur. | 8, G. Ev. S. | Mexico | 1828 |
| parviflora | Red | 8, G. Ev. S. | Mexico | 1824 |
| tenella | Scar. pur. | 8, G. Ev. S. | Chile | 1824 |
| thymifolia | Red | 8, G. Ev. S. | Mexico | 1828 |
| venusta | Purple | 10, G. Ev. S. | Mexico | 1825 |
| virgata | Scar. pur. | 8, G. Ev. S. | Mexico | 1825 |

FUCUS, *Linn.* Derived from *phukos*, a Greek name for sea-weed. *Linn.* 24, Or. 7, Nat. Or. *Algæ.* All the species of this genus are common on the sea-coasts, especially *F. vesiculosus*, which is much employed in the manufacture of kelp, and in some of the Scottish islands it is the chief support of horses, cattle, and sheep, in the winter months; while *F. serratus* is the chief food of the cattle in Norway—*canaliculatus, ceranoides, distichus, loreus, nodosus, Mackaii, serratus, tuberculatus, vesiculosus, laterifractus, linearis, longifractus, subcostatus.*

FUGACIOUS, lasting but for a short time.

FUIRENA, *Rottboll.* In honour of G. Fuiren, a Danish botanist. *Linn.* 3, Or. 1, Nat. Or. *Cyperaceæ.* A curious species of grass, growing best in a boggy soil, and increased by divisions.

| | | | | |
|---|---|---|---|---|
| umbellata | Apetal | 6, Grass. | W. Ind. | 1825 |

FULCRA, scales and stipules.

FULGENT, bright, glittering, shining.

FULVOUS, tawny-yellow, or fox-coloured.

FUMARIA, *Linn.* From *fumus*, smoke; alluding to the disagreeable smell of the plant. Our English word Fumitory, is derived from the French name of the genus *Fumeterre.* *Linn.* 17, Or. 2, Nat. Or. *Fumariaceæ.* *F. capreolata* and *media* are the only two species worthy of extensive culture; they do best sown under a hedge, to which they will attach themselves and make a beautiful appearance. They only require sowing in the open ground. *Synonyme*: 1. *F. capreolata*.

| | | | | | | |
|---|---|---|---|---|---|---|
| capreolátă | . | . Flesh | . | 7, H. Cl. A. | Europe . | . |
| Burchéllíi | . | . | 4, H. | A. C. G. H. | . | 1816 |
| densiflórá | . | . Pink | . | 7, H. | A. Montpel. | . 1824 |
| média, 1 | . | . Flesh | . | 7, H. | A. Britain . | . |
| micránthá | . | . Pink | . | 7, H. | A. Spain | . 1823 |
| spícátá | . | . Flesh | . | 7, H. | A. S. Eur. . | . 1714 |
| Vaillántíi | . | . Pink | . | 7, H. | A. England | . |

*officinális*, *parviflórá*.

FUMITORY, see *Fumáriă*.

FUMÓSÚS, strong-scented.

FUNÁRIĂ, *Linn*. From *funis*, a rope; alluding to the twisted formation of the fruit-stalks. *Linn*. 24, Or. 5, Nat. Or. *Musci*. Minute species of moss, found growing in tufts on rocks and cottage roofs, during the winter and spring months—*hibérnică*, *hygrométricá*, *Muhlenbérgíi*.

FUNGOUS, having the consistence of a mushroom.

FUNICLE, a little stalk, by which the seed is attached to the placenta.

FÚNKIĂ. Named by Sprengel in honour of Henry Funk, a German cryptogamist. *Linn*. 6, Or. 1, Nat. Or. *Liliaceæ*. Ornamental species, requiring a warm situation in the flower-garden, otherwise they will not flower well; they are easily multiplied by dividing the roots. *Synonymes*: 1. *Hemerocallis lanceæfolia*. 2. *H. cærulea*. 3. *H. japonica*.

| | | | | | |
|---|---|---|---|---|---|
| albo-marginátá | . Lilac | . | 7, G. Her. | P. Japan | . 1837 |
| lancæfólíá, 1 | . Lilac | . | 8, H. Her. | P. Japan | . 1829 |
| ovátá, 2 | . . Blue | . | 6, H. Her. | P. Japan | . 1790 |
| Sieboldiáná | . Lilac | . | 6, H. Her. | P. Japan | . 1830 |
| subcordátá, 3 | . White | . | 8, H. Her. | P. Japan | . 1790 |

FÚRCATE, forked.

FURCATELY-DIVIDED, divided in a furcate manner.

FURCELLÁRIĂ, *Lamour*. From *furcella*, a little fork;

alluding to the arrangement of the fronds. *Linn*. 24, Or. 7, Nat. Or. *Algæ*. A small plant, most conspicuous in spring and autumn—*fastigiátá*.

FURCRÆĂ. Named by Ventenat, in honour of M. Fourcroy, a celebrated French chemist. *Linn*. 6, Or. 1, Nat. Or. *Bromeliaceæ*. A noble genus of plants, resembling in a great measure the genus *Agave*, and requiring the same treatment. *Synonyme*: 1. *Agave fœtida*.

| | | | | | |
|---|---|---|---|---|---|
| austrális | . . . | | 8, Her. P. N. Holl. | . 1811 |
| Cántúlá . | . . . | | 8, Her. P. China | . 1818 |
| cubénsís | . . Green | . | 8, Her. P. S. Amer. | . 1739 |
| gigántéá, 1 | . . Green | . 8, Her. P. S. Amer. | . 1690 |
| madagascariénsís | . . | | 8, Her. P. Madagas. | . 1825 |
| rígídá | . . . | | 8, Her. P. S. Amer. | . 1768 |
| tuberósá | . . Green | . 8, Her. P. S. Amer. | 1739 |

FURFURACEOUS, scaly, mealy, scurfy.

FURROWED, having longitudinal furrows, or channels.

FUSÁNÚS, *Linn*. Derived from the French, *fusain*, a spindle tree; on account of the resemblance of the leaves and fruit. *Linn*. 23, Or. 1, Nat. Or. *Santalaceæ*. A worthless, evergreen, Cape shrub, requiring the same treatment as other Cape greenhouse shrubs—*comprēssús*.

FUSÁRIÚM, *Link*. From *fusus*, a spindle; alluding to the shape of the sporules. *Linn*. 24, Or. 9, Nat. Or. *Fungi*. An extremely minute species, of a pinkish colour, found chiefly in spring on dead nettle stems—*tremelloídēs*.

FUSCOUS, blackish-brown.

FUSÍDIÚM, *Fries*. From *fusus*, a spindle; the sporidia are spindle-shaped. *Linn*. 24, Or. 9, Nat. Or. *Fungi*. Whitish-coloured species, chiefly to be met with in autumn on dead beech leaves—*cándídúm*, *flavovírēns*, *grisēúm*.

FUSIFORM, spindle-shaped, like the root of a carrot.

FUSTIC-WOOD, see *Maclúră tinctóriă*.

# G.

GÆRTNERĂ, *Lamarck*. In honour of J. Gærtner, M.D., F.R.S., a celebrated botanist. *Linn*. 10, Or. 1, Nat. Or. *Loganiaceæ*. These plants are ornamental, and thrive well in a mixture of loam and peat, and cuttings root readily in sandy soil, under a glass, in heat. *Synonymes*: 1. *Hiptage obtusifolia*. 2. *H mandablota*.

| | | | | | |
|---|---|---|---|---|---|
| obtusifólíá, 1 | . White | . . | 8, Ev. Tw. China | . 1810 |
| racemósá, 2 | . Wht. yel. . 4, 8, Ev. Tw. E. Ind. . | . 1793 |

GÁGEĂ, *Salisbury*. In honour of Sir Thomas Gage, a botanical amateur. *Linn*. 6, Or. 1, Nat. Or. *Liliaceæ*. The species of this genus are very handsome, and thrive well in any light soil, in the open ground, and may be readily increased from offsets. *Synonymes*: 1. *Ornithogalum bohemicum*. 2. *O. luteum*. 3. *O. luteum*, *Gagea lutea*. 4. *O. pygmæum*. 5. *Anthericum serotinum*. 6. *O. minimum*, *arvense*. 7. *O. striatum*. 8. *O. uniflorum*.

| | | | | | |
|---|---|---|---|---|---|
| bohémicá, 1 | . Yellow | . 4, H. Bl. | P. Bohemia | . 1825 |
| bracteolária, 2 | . Yellow | . 4, H. Bl. | P. Europe | . 1817 |
| bulbíferá | . . . | . 5, H. Bl. | P. Tauria | . 1829 |
| chloránthá | . Yellow | . 4, H. Bl. | P. Siberia | . 1819 |
| circinátá | . Yellow | . 5, H. Bl. | P. Siberia | . 1789 |
| fasciculária, 3 | . Yellow | . 4, H. Bl. | P. Britain | . |
| glaúcá | . . Yellow | . 4, H. Bl. | P. Switzerl. | . 1825 |
| Liotárdí | . . . | . 5, H. Bl. | P. S. Eur. | . 1825 |
| podólicá | . . . | . 5, H. Bl. | P. Podolia | . 1827 |
| pusílá | . . Yellow | . 4, H. Bl. | P. Bohemia | . 1825 |
| pygmæá, 4 | . Yellow | . 4, H. Bl. | P. Spain | . 1825 |
| serótíná, 5 | . . Yellow | . 6, H. Bl. | P. Wales | . |
| spatháceá | . . Yellow | . 5, H. Bl. | P. Germany | . 1759 |
| stellária, 6 | . Yellow | . 5, H. Bl. | P. Sweden | . 1759 |
| Sternbérgíi | . Yellow | . 4, H. Bl. | P. Switzerl. | . 1826 |
| striátá, 7 | . . Yellow | . 7, H. Bl. | P. Europe | . 1826 |
| sylvática | . . Yellow | . 4, H. Bl. | P. Europe | . |
| uniflórá, 8 | . Yellow | . 5, H. Bl. | P. Siberia | . 1781 |
| villósá | . . Yellow | . 4, H. Bl. | P. Caucasus | . 1825 |

GAGNEBINĂ, *Necker*. The meaning unknown. *Linn*. 10, Or. 1, Nat. Or. *Leguminosæ*. Very ornamental evergreen shrubs, growing about six feet high. For culture and propagation, see *Mimosa*. *Synonymes*: 1. *Mimosa pterocarpa*. 2. *Acacia tamariscina*.

| | | | | | |
|---|---|---|---|---|---|
| axillária, 1 | . . Yellow | . 8, Ev. S. Maurit. . | . 1824 |
| tamariscína, 2 | . Yellow | . 8, Ev. S. Maurit. . | . 1824 |

GAILLÁRDĬĂ. Named by Fougeroux, in honour of

M. Gaillard de Marentonneau, an amateur botanist. *Linn*. 19, Or. 3, Nat. Or. *Compositæ*. Ornamental species, particularly G. bicolor; they grow well in any common soil, and increase readily by dividing the roots. *Synonymes*: 1. *Virgilia helodes*. 2. *G. bicolor Drummondii*.

| | | | | | |
|---|---|---|---|---|---|
| aristátá | . . . Orange | . 8, H. Her. | P. N. Amer. | . 1812 |
| bícólor, 1 | . . Yellow | . 8, H. Her. | P. N. Amer. | . 1787 |
| pícta, 2 | . . Yellow | . 8, H. Her. | P. Louisiana | . 1833 |
| Richardsóní | . . Orange | . 7, H. Her. | P. N. Amer. | . 1829 |

GALACTĬĂ, *P. Browne*. From *gala*, milk. G. pendula yields a milky juice when cut or broken. *Linn*. 17, Or. 4, Nat. Or. *Leguminosæ*. These are very handsome plants, especially G. pendula, which is a very desirable twiner. They require precisely the same treatment in culture and propagation as *Clitoria*, except that the North American species do not require to be grown in heat. *Synonymes*: 1. *Ervum volubile*. 2. *Hedysarum volubile*.

| | | | | | |
|---|---|---|---|---|---|
| glabéllá, 1 | . . Purple | . 7, H. De. Tw. N. Amer. | . |
| móllis, 2 | . . Purple | . 7, H. De. Tw. N. Amer. | . 1827 |
| péndúlá | . . Red | . 7, S. Ev. Tw. Jamaica | . 1794 |
| seríceá | . . . | . 7, S. Ev. Tw. Bourbon | . 1824 |

GALACTÍTES, *Mœnch*. From *gala*, milk; alluding to the white veins of the leaves. *Linn*. 19, Or. 3, Nat. Or. *Compositæ*. Very pretty annuals, which only require to be sown in the open border in spring. *Synonyme*: 1. *Centaurea Galactites*.

| | | | | | |
|---|---|---|---|---|---|
| austrális | . . . Purple | . 7, H. | A. N. Holl. | . 1824 |
| tomentósá, 1 | . Purple | . 7, H. | A. S. Eur. . | . 1738 |

GALACTODÉNDRÓN, *Kunth*. Derived from *gala*, milk, and *dendron*, a tree. *Linn*. 23, Or. 2, Nat. Or. *Urticaceæ*. This is a lofty-growing tree, attaining the height of fifty feet; it may be grown in a mixture of peat and loam, and may probably be increased by cuttings.

| | | | | |
|---|---|---|---|---|
| utílé | . . . | | 8, Ev. T. Caraccas | . 1829 |

GALANGALE, see *Kæmpferiă*.

GALÁNTHÚS, *Linn*. From *gala*, milk, and *anthos*, a flower; alluding to the milk-white flowers. *Linn*. 6, Or. 1, Nat. Or. *Amaryllidaceæ*. These are dwarf, but very pretty species, of the simplest culture.

| | | | | | |
|---|---|---|---|---|---|
| nivàlis | . . . | White | . 2, H. Bl. P. | Britain | . . |
| plicàtus | . . . | White | . 2, H. Bl. P. | Crimea | . 1818 |

GÁLÁX, *Linn.* From *gala*, milk; alluding to the whiteness of the flower. *Linn.* 5, Or. 1, Nat. Or. *Pyrolaceæ.* The species is pretty, and succeeds best in peaty soil, in a moist situation; it is readily increased by divisions. *Synonyme:* 1. *Blandfordia cordata.*

| | | | | | |
|---|---|---|---|---|---|
| aphyllà | . . . | White | . 7, H. Her. P. | N. Amer. | . 1786 |

GALÁXIÁ, *Thunberg.* From *galaktiao*, to abound in milk. *Linn.* 16, Or. 1, Nat. Or. *Iridaceæ.* These are very pretty Cape bulbs, and grow best in a sandy peat soil; they are easily increased from offsets.

| | | | | | |
|---|---|---|---|---|---|
| graminéà | . . | Lgt. yel. | . 7, G. Bl. P. | C. G. H. | . 1795 |
| grandiflorà | . | Drk. yel. | . 7, G. Bl. P. | C. G. H. | . 1799 |
| mucronulàris | . | Purple | . 7, G. Bl. P. | C. G. H. | . 1799 |
| ovàtà | . . . | Drk. yel. | . 7, G. Bl. P. | C. G. H. | . 1799 |
| versìcolòr | . | Purple | . 7, G. Bl. P. | C. G. H. | . 1799 |

GALEÁNDRÁ, *Lindley.* The meaning of the name is unexplained. *Linn.* 20, Or. 1, Nat. Or. *Orchidaceæ.* A pretty little plant, thriving well with the treatment given to the genus *Bletia.* *Synonyme:* 1. *Eulophia gracilis.*

| | | | | | |
|---|---|---|---|---|---|
| graèilis | . . . | Grn. yel. | . 5, S. Ter. | | . 1822 |

GALEATE, helmeted; the upper lip of a ringent corolla is the galea of that corolla.

GALEÓX, *Tournefort.* From *gala*, milk; the plants are said to increase the milk of such animals as eat of them. *Linn.* 16, Or. 6, Nat. Or. *Leguminosæ.* Ornamental, tallish plants, well suited for flowerborders, provided they have plenty of room. They are readily increased by dividing the roots, or by seeds.

| | | | | | |
|---|---|---|---|---|---|
| bilobà | . . . | Blue | . 7, H. Her. P. | | . 1823 |
| officinàlis | . . | Blue | . 7, H. Her. P. | Spain | . 1568 |
| alba | . . . | White | . 7, H. Her. P. | Spain | |
| orientàlis | . . | Blue | . 7, H. Her. P. | Levant | . 1801 |
| persìcà | . . . | White | . 7, H. Her. P. | Persia | . 1826 |
| lilacìnà | . . . | Lilac | . 6, H. Her. P. | Persia | . 1830 |
| tricòlòr | . . . | Blue | . 7, H. Her. P. | | . 1823 |

GALÉNÍÁ, *Linnæus.* After C. Galenus, a celebrated physician of Pergamus. *Linn.* 8, Or. 2, Nat. Or. *Chenopodiaceæ.* A species of little beauty, succeeding in peat and loam; and young plants are readily obtained from cuttings.

| | | | | | |
|---|---|---|---|---|---|
| africànà | . . . | White | . 7, G. Ev. S. | C. G. H. | . 1759 |

GALEÓRDÓLÓN, *Hudson.* From *gale*, weasel, and *bdolos*, fœtid smell; alluding to the smell of the species. *Linn.* 14, Or. 1, Nat. Or. *Labiatæ.* A pretty plant, found abundantly in most parts of England in marshy places; increased by divisions.

| | | | | | |
|---|---|---|---|---|---|
| lùtèùm | . . . | Yellow | . 6, H. Her. P. | Britain | . . |

GALEÓPSIS, *Linn.* From *gale*, weasel, and *opsis*, resemblance; the mouth of the corolla is gaping like that of the animal. *Linn.* 14, Or. 1, Nat. Or. *Labiatæ.* Annual weeds, common in corn-fields, and therefore unworthy of cultivation. *Synonymes:* 1. *cannabina.* 2. *ochroleuca—angustifolia, canescens, Ladanum, parviflora, pubescens, Tetrahit, versicolor* 1, *villosa* 2.

GALERICULATE, having a tuft or plume.

GALINSÓGÍÁ, *Ruiz and Pavon.* In honour of M. M. Galinsoga, superintendant of the Madrid botanic garden. *Linn.* 19, Or. 2, Nat. Or. *Compositæ.* A genus of little beauty; the seeds may be sown in the open border in spring.

| | | | | | |
|---|---|---|---|---|---|
| balbisioìdès | . | Yellow | 8, H. | A. | Mexico | . 1825 |

*parviflorà, trilobàtà.*

GALIPÍÁ, *Aublet.* The name given to the plant in Guiana. *Linn.* 2, Or. 1, Nat. Or. *Rutaceæ.* These plants are described as being handsome, and attaining the height of four feet. They succeed well in peaty soil, and are increased by cuttings in sand, under a glass, in heat.

| | | | | | |
|---|---|---|---|---|---|
| odoratìssìmá | . | White | . 5, S. Ev. S. | Rio Jan. | . . |
| trifoliàtà | . . | Green | . 8, S. Ev. S. | Guiana | . 1816 |

GÁLÍÓM, *Linn.* From *gala*, milk; the flowers of G. *verum* are used for curdling milk. *Linn.* 4, Or. 1, Nat. Or. *Stellatæ.* This is an extensive genus of plants, of very little merit. They all grow well in common garden soil. The herbaceous kinds are increased by dividing the roots, and the annuals

need only be sown in the open ground. *Synonymes:* 1. *glaucum.* 2. *reflexum, Valantia taurica.* 3. *G. anisophyllum.* 4 *Valantia cucullaria.* 5. *G. vernum.* 6. *saxatile.* 7. *murale.* 8. *hispidum.* 9. *saccharatum, Valantia aparine.*

| | | | | | |
|---|---|---|---|---|---|
| campanulàtùm, 1 | White | . 7, H. Her. P. | S. Eur. | . 1821 |
| græcùm | . . . | Purple | . 7, H. Her. P. | Candia | . 1798 |
| hirsùtùm | . . . | White | . 8, F. Her. P. | Teneriffe | . 1830 |
| purpùreùm | . . | Purple | . 7, H. Her. P. | Switzerl. | . 1831 |
| rùbrùm | . . . | Purple | . 7, H. Her. P. | Italy | . 1597 |
| suaveòlèns | . . | White | . 7, | A. N. Eur. | . 1821 |
| taùrìcùm, 2 | . | Yellow | . 7, H. Her. P. | Tauria | . 1818 |

*alpèstrè* 3, *ânglìcùm, aparìnè, aristàtùm, austrìâcùm, baldènsè, Boccônî, boreàlè, brevìfolìûm, campèstrè, capillàrè, caucàsicùm, cìnèrèûm, cucullàrià* 4, *dèbìlî, diffùsûm, divarìcâtûm, ellìptìcùm, erèctûm, fràgìlê, fruticôsûm, glâbrûm, Hallèrì* 5, *helòdès, helvètìcûm* 6, *infèstûm, lævè, linifolìûm, lithospermifolìûm, lûcìdûm, marìtìmûm, megalospèrmûm, microcârpûm, microspèrmûm, minìmûm* 7, *mollûgô, montânûm, oblìqûm, palûstrè, parìsìènsè, pilôsûm, pubèscèns, pùmìlûm, pusìllûm, rigìdûm, rotundìfolìûm, rubìoìdês, satureifolìûm, saxàtìlè, scabèrrìmûm* 8, *scàbrûm, spûrìûm, sylvâtîcûm, supìnûm, tenuìfolìûm, tenuìssìmûm, trìcôrnè, trìfîdûm, tyrolènsè, ulìgìnôsûm, valantìoìdès, verrucôsûm* 9, *vêrûm, verticillàtûm, Villàrsìî, villôsûm, Witherìngìî.*

GALPHÍMÍÁ, *Cavanilles.* An anagram of Malpighia. *Linn.* 10, Or. 8, Nat. Or. *Malpighiaceæ.* Handsome shrubs, thriving well in a mixture of loam and peat, and cuttings of the ripened wood will root in sand, under a glass, in heat.

| | | | | | |
|---|---|---|---|---|---|
| glaucà | . . . | Yellow | . 8. Ev. Tw. | Mexico | . 1829 |
| hìrsùtà | . . . | Yellow | . 9, S. Ev. S. | Mexico | . 1824 |

GAMBOGE, see *Garcinia Gambogia.*

GAMÓSEPALOUS, when the sepals are joined at the edge.

GARCÍNÍÁ, *Linn.* In honour of Laurent Garcin, M.D., F.R.S., an oriental traveller. *Linn.* 11, Or. 1, Nat. Or. *Guttiferæ.* This is a valuable and much admired genus of fruit-bearing trees. The plants thrive best in a light loamy soil with a little peat mixed: they require a strong moist heat to flourish well, and ripened cuttings will root in sand, under a glass, in a moist heat. In Loudon's Encyclopædia of Plants, the following description is given of G. *Mangostana*—"This tree bears a fruit which, in the East Indies, ranks with that of the pineapple. It rises with a taper stem, sending out many branches, not unlike a fir-tree, with oval leaves, seven or eight inches long. The flower is like that of a single rose; the fruit round, the size of a middling orange; the shell is like that of the pomegranate, the inside of a rose colour, divided by thin partitions, as in oranges, in which the seeds are lodged, surrounded by a soft juicy pulp, of a delicious flavour, partaking of the strawberry and the grape, and is esteemed one of the richest fruits in the world. According to Dr. Garcin, it is esteemed the most delicious of the East Indian fruits, and a great deal of it may be eaten without any inconvenience; it is the only fruit which sick people are allowed to eat without scruple. It is given with safety in almost every disorder; and we are told that Dr. Solander, in the last stage of a putrid fever in Batavia, found himself insensibly recovering by sucking this delicious and refreshing fruit. The pulp has a most happy mixture of the tart and sweet, and is no less salutary than pleasant."

| | | | | | |
|---|---|---|---|---|---|
| còrneà | . . . | Yellow | . 8. Ev. T. | E. Ind. | . 1823 |
| Còwà | . . . | Yellow | . 8 Ev. T. | E. Ind. | . 1822 |
| Gambògìà | . . | Yellow | . 8. Ev. T. | E. Ind. | . 1820 |
| Mangostànà | . | Purple | . 8. Ev. T. | Java | . 1789 |

GARDEN BALSAM, see *Justicia pectoralis.*

GARDÉNÍÁ, *Ellis.* Named in compliment to Alexander Garden, M.D., of Charleston, Carolina, a correspondent of Ellis and Linnæus. *Linn.* 5, Or. 1, Nat. Or. *Cinchonaceæ.* This is a splendid genus of plants, producing their sweet-scented flowers very freely. They require a mixture of loam and peat; and the stove kinds, a strong moist heat and plenty of water at the roots. Cuttings of all root readily if not too ripe when taken off, planted in sand, under a glass, in a moist heat, with the pots plunged. *Synonymes:* 1. *Mussænda spinosa.* 2. *Canthium coronatum, Posoqueria dumetorum.* 3.

[ 138 ]

*Posoqueria fragrans.* 4. *P. longispina.* 5. *nutans.*
6. *Canthium chinense.* 7. *Mussænda tetracantha.*

| | | | |
|---|---|---|---|
| amœna | Pink | 7, G. Ev. S. China | |
| angustifolia | White | G. Ev. S. | 1823 |
| armata, 1 | White | 7, S. Ev. S. W. Ind. | 1813 |
| campanulata | | 8. Ev. S. E. Ind. | 1815 |
| dumetorum | White | 7, S. Ev. S. E. Ind. | 1777 |
| florida | Pa. yel. | 8, G. Ev. S. China | 1754 |
| picta | Pa. yel. | 8, G. Ev. S. China | 1754 |
| simplici | White | 1, S. Ev. S. E. Ind. | 1831 |
| fragrans, 3 | White | 8. Ev. S. E. Ind. | 1820 |
| latifolia | Pa. yel. | 8. Ev. S. E. Ind. | 1787 |
| longispina, 4 | White | 7, S. Ev. S. E. Ind. | 1812 |
| lucida | White | 8. Ev. S. E. Ind. | 1819 |
| mexicana | White | 7, S. Ev. S. Mexico | 1817 |
| micrantha | White | 8. Ev. S. China | 1806 |
| montana | White | 8. Ev. S. E. Ind. | 1819 |
| Mussænda | White | 8. Ev. S. Carthage | 1820 |
| nutans, 5 | White | 7, S. Ev. S. E. Ind. | 1820 |
| pannea | Yellow | 6, S. Ev. S. S. Amer. | 1830 |
| parviflora | White | 6, S. Ev. S. E. Ind. | 1818 |
| Pavetta | White | 7, S. Ev. S. E. Ind. | 1817 |
| propinqua | White | 7, S. Ev. S. E. Ind. | 1823 |
| pubescens | | 8. Ev. S. E. Ind. | 1824 |
| radicans | White | 6, G. Ev. S. China | 1804 |
| Rothmannia | Pa. yel. | 7, G. Ev. S. C. G. H. | 1774 |
| spinosa, 6 | White | 7, S. Ev. S. China | 1800 |
| tetracantha, 7 | White | 7, S. Ev. S. S. Amer. | 1820 |
| theobromæfolia | White | 8. Ev. S. S. Amer. | |
| Thunbergii | White | 2, G. Ev. S. C. G. H. | 1773 |
| uliginosa | White | 7, S. Ev. S. E. Ind. | 1802 |

GARDEN ROCAMBOLE, see *Allium ophioscordon.*

GARDOQUIA, *Ruiz and Pavon.* In honour of Don Diego Gardoqui, a Spaniard, who greatly promoted the publication of the Flora Peruviana. *Linn.* 14, Or. 2, Nat. Or. *Labiatæ.* These plants are well worthy of cultivation, on account of their large showy flowers, especially *G. Hookeri.* A mixture of equal parts of sand, loam, and peat, suits the species well; and cuttings root readily in the same kind of soil, under a glass.

| | | | |
|---|---|---|---|
| betonicoides | Purple | 10, G. Her. P. Mexico | 1837 |
| discolor | Purple | 6, S. Ev. S. Chile | 1827 |
| Gillieaii | Lilac | G. Ev. S. Chile | 1828 |
| Hookeri | Scarlet | 6, G. Ev. S. Carolina | 1832 |

GARIDELLA, *Linn.* In honour of Pierre Garidel, M.D., a botanical author of Provence in the beginning of last century. *Linn.* 10, Or. 3, Nat. Or. *Ranunculaceæ.* An inconspicuous plant, merely requiring to be sown in the open border in spring.

| | | | |
|---|---|---|---|
| Nigellastrum | Br. grn. | 7, H. A. France | 1736 |

GARLAND FLOWER, see *Pleurandra Cneorum.*
GARLIC, see *Allium.*
GARLIC PEAR, see *Cratæva.*
GARRYA. Named by Douglas, in compliment to Nicholas Garry, Esq., of the Hudson's Bay Company, to whose assistance he was much indebted during his travels. *Linn.* 21, Or. 4, Nat. Or. *Garryaceæ.* This is described as being an ornamental shrub, very similar in appearance to *Viburnum,* and said to be the greatest botanical curiosity in all Mr. Douglas's collections. It prefers a loamy soil, and may be readily increased by layers.

| | | | |
|---|---|---|---|
| elliptica | Green | 9, H. Ev. S. N. Califor. | 1828 |

GARUGA, *Roxburgh.* The Telingas call it Garuga, or Garoogoo. *Linn.* 10, Or. 1, Nat. Or. *Burseraceæ.* An ornamental plant, attaining the height of twenty feet; for culture and propagation, see *Boswellia.*

| | | | |
|---|---|---|---|
| pinnata | Yellow | 8. Ev. T. E. Ind. | 1808 |

GASTERIA, *Haworth.* Derived from *gaster,* the belly; alluding to the enlarged base of the flowers. *Linn.* 6, Or. 1, Nat. Or. *Liliaceæ.* These plants are all extremely interesting, and remarkable for producing their leaves, more or less regular, in two rows. Sandy loam, a little leaf-mould, and peat, well mixed together, with a small quantity of brick rubbish, is the best compost for them; and being of a very succulent nature, they require to be only very moderately watered at any time, particularly when not growing. They all increase from suckers, or leaves, which will produce young plants from their base, as *Furcræa* and *Aloe.* Synonymes: 1. *longifolia.* 2. *nigricans.* 3. *nigricans fasciata.*

| | | | |
|---|---|---|---|
| acinacifolia | Orange | 7, G. Ev. S. C. G. H. | 1819 |
| minor | Scar. red | 7, G. Ev. S. C. G. H. | 1820 |
| angulata, 1 | Red | 7, G. Ev. S. C. G. H. | 1791 |
| minor | Red | 8, G. Ev. S. C. G. H. | 1820 |
| angustifolia | Red | 6, G. Ev. S. C. G. H. | 1731 |
| longifolia | Red | 7, G. Ev. S. C. G. H. | 1796 |

| | | | |
|---|---|---|---|
| bicolor | | G. Ev. S. C. G. H. | 1824 |
| brevifolia | Red | 7, G. Ev. S. C. G. H. | 1809 |
| perviridis | Scar. red | 7, G. Ev. S. C. G. H. | 1820 |
| candicans | Red | 7, G. Ev. S. C. G. H. | 1822 |
| carinata | Red | 7, G. Ev. S. C. G. H. | 1731 |
| conspurcata | Red | 6, G. Ev. S. C. G. H. | 1796 |
| crassifolia | Red | 7, G. Ev. S. C. G. H. | 1820 |
| decipiens, 2 | Scar. red | 7, G. Ev. S. C. G. H. | 1820 |
| disticha | Scar. red | 7, G. Ev. S. C. G. H. | 1820 |
| major | Scar. red | 7, G. Ev. S. C. G. H. | 1820 |
| ensifolia | Red | 7, G. Ev. S. C. G. H. | 1823 |
| excavata | Red | G. Ev. S. C. G. H. | 1824 |
| obliqua | Red | 7, G. Ev. S. C. G. H. | 1759 |
| fasciata, 3 | Red | 7, G. Ev. S. C. G. H. | 1820 |
| laxa | Scar. red | 7, G. Ev. S. C. G. H. | 1820 |
| formosa | Scar. red | 7, G. Ev. S. C. G. H. | 1820 |
| glabra | Red | 7, G. Ev. S. C. G. H. | 1796 |
| minor | Scar. red | 7, G. Ev. S. C. G. H. | 1820 |
| intermedia | Red | 7, G. Ev. S. C. G. H. | 1790 |
| asperrima | Red | 7, G. Ev. S. C. G. H. | 1820 |
| lævior | Scar. red | 7, G. Ev. S. C. G. H. | 1820 |
| longior | Scar. red | 7, G. Ev. S. C. G. H. | 1820 |
| lætepunctata | Scar. red | 7, G. Ev. S. C. G. H. | 1820 |
| denticulata | Scar. red | 7, G. Ev. S. C. G. H. | 1822 |
| lævia | Red | 7, G. Ev. S. C. G. H. | 1820 |
| linita | Scar. red | 7, G. Ev. S. C. G. H. | 1820 |
| maculata | Scar. red | 7, G. Ev. S. C. G. H. | 1759 |
| fallax | Scar. red | 7, G. Ev. S. C. G. H. | 1820 |
| mollis | Red | 7, G. Ev. S. C. G. H. | 1823 |
| nigricans | Red | 7, G. Ev. S. C. G. H. | 1790 |
| marmorata | Red | 7, G. Ev. S. C. G. H. | 1820 |
| nitens | Red | 7, G. Ev. S. C. G. H. | 1820 |
| brevior | Scar. red | 7, G. Ev. S. C. G. H. | 1820 |
| nitida | Red | 7, G. Ev. S. C. G. H. | 1820 |
| grandipunctata | Red | 7, G. Ev. S. C. G. H. | 1822 |
| obtusa | Red | 7, G. Ev. S. C. G. H. | 1820 |
| obtusifolia | Red | 7, G. Ev. S. C. G. H. | 1796 |
| parva | Scar. red | 7, G. Ev. S. C. G. H. | 1820 |
| picta | Scar. red | 7, G. Ev. S. C. G. H. | 1820 |
| pluripunctata | Scar. red | 7, G. Ev. S. C. G. H. | 1820 |
| magnipunctata | Scar. red | 7, G. Ev. S. C. G. H. | 1823 |
| pulchra | Scar. red | 7, G. Ev. S. C. G. H. | 1759 |
| repens | Red | 7, G. Ev. S. C. G. H. | 1821 |
| rotata | Scar. red | 7, G. Ev. S. C. G. H. | 1820 |
| strigata | Scar. red | 7, G. Ev. S. C. G. H. | 1820 |
| subcarinata | Orange | 7, G. Ev. S. C. G. H. | 1818 |
| viridior | Red | 7, G. Ev. S. C. G. H. | 1820 |
| subnigricans | Scar. red | 7, G. Ev. S. C. G. H. | 1820 |
| glabrior | Scar. red | 7, G. Ev. S. C. G. H. | 1826 |
| subverrucosa | Red | 7, G. Ev. S. C. G. H. | 1820 |
| parvipunctata | Scar. red | 7, G. Ev. S. C. G. H. | 1820 |
| sulcata | Scar. red | 7, G. Ev. S. C. G. H. | 1820 |
| trigona | Scar. red | 7, G. Ev. S. C. G. H. | 1820 |
| undata | Scar. red | 7, G. Ev. S. C. G. H. | 1820 |
| venusta | Scar. red | 7, G. Ev. S. C. G. H. | 1820 |
| verrucosa | Red | 7, G. Ev. S. C. G. H. | 1731 |

GASTONIA. Dedicated by Commerson, to Gaston de Bourbon, son of Henry IV. of France, a promoter of botany. *Linn.* 11, Or. 5, Nat. Or. *Araliaceæ.* Rather an ornamental shrub, requiring a soil composed of a mixture of sand, loam, and peat; and cuttings root readily when planted in sand, under a glass, in heat.

| | | | |
|---|---|---|---|
| palmata | Wht. grn. | 3, S. Ev. S. | 1818 |

GASTRIDIUM, *Beauvois.* Derived from *gastridion,* a little swelling. *Linn.* 3, Or. 2, Nat. Or. *Gramineæ.* Plants of little interest, and of the easiest culture. Synonyme: 1. *Milium lendigerum.*

| | | | |
|---|---|---|---|
| australe, 1 | Apetal | 7, Grass. Britain | |
| muticum | Apetal | 7, Grass. Sicily | 1819 |

GASTROCARPHA, *Don.* From *gaster,* the belly, and *karphe,* chaff; alluding to the form of the receptacle. *Linn.* 19, Or. 4, Nat. Or. *Compositæ.* This is an ornamental plant, succeeding in any common soil, and increased readily from seeds.

| | | | |
|---|---|---|---|
| runcinata | White | 7, F. Her. P. Chile | 1827 |

GASTROCHILUS, *Wallich.* From *gaster,* the belly, and *cheilos,* a lip; alluding to the bellied lip. *Linn.* 1, Or. 1, Nat. Or. *Scitamineæ.* This species is described as being ornamental, succeeding well in sandy loam, and may be increased by divisions.

| | | | |
|---|---|---|---|
| pulcherrimus | Yel. pink | 8, S. Her. P. Rangoon | 1828 |

GASTRODIA, *R. Brown.* From *gaster,* the belly, and *odous,* a tooth; referring to the top of the column. *Linn.* 20, Or. 1, Nat. Or. *Orchidaceæ.* A curious herbaceous species, succeeding in peat and loam mixed, and increased by divisions of the roots.

| | | | |
|---|---|---|---|
| sesamoides | White | G. Ter. N. Holl. | 1826 |

GASTROLOBIUM, *R. Brown.* From *gaster,* the belly, and *lobos,* a pod; the pods are inflated. *Linn.* 10, Or. 1, Nat. Or. *Leguminosæ.* These are very elegant little shrubs. For culture and propagation, see *Pultenæa.*

| | | | | |
|---|---|---|---|---|
| bīlōbŭm | . . . | Yellow | . 5, G. Ev. S. N. Holl. | . 1803 |
| retūsŭm | . . . | Or. scar. | . 5, G. Ev. S. N. Holl. | . 1830 |

GASTRONĒMÁ, *Herbert.* From *gaster*, the belly, and *nema*, a filament; the filaments are inflated. Linn. 6, Or. 1, Nat. Or. *Amaryllidaceæ.* This is a very pretty plant; for culture and propagation, see *Cyrtanthus.* Synonyme: 1. *Cyrtanthus uniflorus.*

| | | | | |
|---|---|---|---|---|
| clavātŭm | . . . | White | . 5, G. Bl. P. C. G. H. | . 1816 |

GAUDICHAUDÍÁ, *H. B. and Kunth.* In honour of Charles Gaudichaud, the naturalist, who accompanied Freycinet in his voyage round the world. Linn. 5, Or. 1, Nat. Or. *Malpighiaceæ.* An ornamental plant, succeeding best in light turfy loam and peat mixed; cuttings, if ripened, root well in sand, under a glass, in heat.

| | | | | |
|---|---|---|---|---|
| cynanchoīdēs | . Yellow | . 8. Ev. Tw. Mexico. | . 1824 |

GAUDINÍÁ, *Beauvois.* In honour of M. Gaudin, a Swiss botanist. Linn. 3, Or. 2, Nat. Or. *Gramineæ.* Uninteresting, and easily cultivated. Synonyme: 1. *Avena fragilis—frāgĭlĭs* 1.

GAULTHĒRÍÁ, *Kalm.* After Gaulthier, a physician and botanist of Canada. Linn. 10, Or. 1, Nat. Or. *Ericaceæ.* These are highly ornamental shrubs, thriving best in a peat soil. The greenhouse kinds should be treated the same as other hardy greenhouse plants. They are all readily increased by layers. The succulent fruits of *G. procumbens* and *G. shallon* are sometimes used as food.

| | | | | |
|---|---|---|---|---|
| antīpōdā | . . | White | . G. Ev. S. N. Zeal. | . 1820 |
| frāgrāns | . . | Pur. red | . G. Ev. S. Nepal | . 1824 |
| procūmbēns | . . | White | . 7, H. Ev. Cr. N. Amer. | . 1762 |
| shāllon | . . | White | . 5, H. Ev. S. N. Amer. | . 1826 |

GAŪRÁ, *Linn.* From *gauros*, superb; in reference to the beautiful flowers of some of the species. Linn. 8, Or. 1, Nat. Or. *Onagraceæ.* All the species of this genus are well worthy of extensive cultivation. *G. fruticosa*, and the perennial kinds, thrive well in any light rich soil; the former may be increased from cuttings, and the latter by seed. The annuals and biennials require the same treatment as other hardy and tender annuals and biennials.

| | | | | |
|---|---|---|---|---|
| angustĭfōlĭā | . . | Pink | . 8, H. Her. P. | |
| biēnnīs | . . | Red wht. | . 9, H. Her. P. N. Amer. | . 1762 |
| coccīnēā | . . | Scarlet | . 4, H. Her. P. Louisiana | . 1811 |
| frutīcōsā | . . | Red wht. | . 8. Ev. S. Amer. | . 1815 |
| œnotherœflōrā | . | Purple | . 7, H. | B. S. Amer. | . 1816 |
| mutābĭlĭs | . . | Yellow | . 7, F. | B. N. Amer. | . 1795 |
| parvĭflōrā | . . | Yellow | . 8, H. | B. N. Amer. | . 1835 |
| trĭpĕtāla | . . | Pink | . 8, H. | A. Mexico | . 1804 |

GAZĂNÍÁ, *Gærtner.* From *gaza*, riches; alluding to the splendour of the flowers. Linn. 19, Or. 3, Nat. Or. *Compositæ.* Very showy and interesting plants, of easy management. Peat and loam suits them best, and young plants are obtained from cuttings in sand, under a glass. *G. subulata* may also be increased by dividing the roots. Synonyme: 1. *Gorteria rigens.*

| | | | | |
|---|---|---|---|---|
| heterophyllā | . . | Orange | . 7, G. Her. P. C. G. H. | . 1812 |
| pavōnĭā | . . | Yellow | . 7, G. Her. P. C. G. H. | . 1804 |
| rīgēns, 1 | . . | Orange | . 6, G. Ev. S. C. G. H. | . 1755 |
| subulātā | . . | Yellow | . 7, G. Her. P. C. G. H. | . 1792 |
| unĭflōrā | . . | Yellow | . 7, G. Ev. S. C. G. H. | . 1816 |

GEASTRŬM, *Michaux.* From *ge*, the earth, and *aster*, a star; star-like appearance of the plants. Linn. 24, Or. 9, Nat. Or. *Fungi.* Small, mostly brownish species, found most plentiful in pine-woods and pastures during the autumn months. Synonyme: 1. *Lycoperdon recolligens—coliforme, multĭfĭdum* 1, *quadrĭfĭdum, Woodwardi.*

GEISSOMĒRÍÁ, *Lindley.* From *geisson*, a tile, and *meris*, a part; in allusion to the imbricated calyx. Linn. 14, Or. 2, Nat. Or. *Acanthaceæ.* This is a very handsome species; rich soil, comprising loam and rotten dung, suits it best; and cuttings root without difficulty, either in sand or soil, under a glass, in heat.

| | | | | |
|---|---|---|---|---|
| longĭflōrā | . . | Scarlet | . 7, S. Ev. S. Brasil | . . 1826 |

GEISSORHIZÁ, *Ker.* From *geisson*, a tile, and *rhiza*, a root; shape of the root. Linn. 3, Or. 1, Nat. Or. *Iridaceæ.* Handsome Cape bulbs; for culture, &c., see *Galaxiā.*

| | | | | |
|---|---|---|---|---|
| cĭlĭārīs | . . . | | . 5, G. Bl. P. C. G. H. | |
| exclsā | . . . | White | . 5, G. Bl. P. C. G. H. | . 1789 |
| hĭrtā | . . . | White | . 5, G. Bl. P. C. G. H. | . 1825 |
| ĭmbrĭcātā | . . . | Varieg. | . 5, G. Bl. P. C. G. H. | . 1825 |
| jūncēā | . . . | White | . 7, G. Bl. P. C. G. H. | . 1822 |
| Larōchēī | . . . | Violet | . 5, G. Bl. P. C. G. H. | . 1790 |
| obtūsātā | . . . | Yellow | . 5, G. Bl. P. C. G. H. | . 1801 |
| secūndā | . . . | White | . 5, G. Bl. P. C. G. H. | . 1795 |
| albēscēns | . . | White | . 5, G. Bl. P. C. G. H. | . 1795 |
| cœrūlēā | . . | Blue | . 5, G. Bl. P. C. G. H. | . 1795 |
| sētācēā | . . . | Sulphur | . 7, G. Bl. P. C. G. H. | . 1809 |
| subulātā | . . . | Yellow | . 5, G. Bl. P. C. G. H. | . 1825 |
| vāgīnātā | . . . | Yel. blue | . 5, G. Bl. P. C. G. H. | . 1824 |

GEITONOPLĒSIŬM, *Cunningham.* From *geiton*, neighbour, and *plesion*, near; alluding to the scrambling habit of the plants. Linn. 6, Or. 1, Nat. Or. *Liliaceæ.* These are described as being curious and ornamental plants, requiring to be grown in a mixture of peat and loam, or sandy peat; and increasing by cuttings in sand, under a glass. Synonymes: 1. *Luzuriaga cymosa.* 2. *L. montana.*

| | | | | |
|---|---|---|---|---|
| aspērŭm | . . . | | G. Her. P. N. Holl. | . 1831 |
| cymōsŭm, 1 | . | Green | . G. Ev. Tw. N. S. W. | . 1825 |
| montānŭm, 2 | . | Green | . G. Her. P. N. Holl. | . 1820 |

GĒÍÁ, *Loureiro.* From *geleo*, to shine; supposed to refer to the leaves. Linn. 8, Or. 1, Nat. Or. *Rutaceæ.* Ornamental plants, succeeding in sandy peat, and increased by cuttings planted in sand, under a glass. Synonyme: 1. *Selas lanceolata.*

| | | | | |
|---|---|---|---|---|
| lanceolātā, 1 | . . | Yellow | . G. Ev. S. Cochin-Ch. | 1820 |
| oblongĭfōlĭā | . | Wht. grn. | 6, G. Ev. T. N. Holl. | . 1823 |

GELATINE, jelly, a term in chemistry.

GELATINOUS, consisting of jelly.

GELĬDŬS, cold, frigid.

GELŌNÍŬM, *Roxburgh.* The meaning unknown. Linn. 22, Or. 2, Nat. Or. *Euphorbiaceæ.* Uninteresting stove shrubs, of the easiest culture—*bĭfārĭŭm, fascĭculātŭm, lanceolātŭm.*

GELSĒMÍŬM, *Jussieu.* An Italian name of the Jasmine. In America the species is known under the name of *Carolina Jessamine.* Linn. 5, Or. 1, Nat. Or. *Bignoniaceæ.* This species is not possessed of much beauty; it thrives best in sandy peat, and cuttings root readily under a glass. Synonyme: 1. *Bignonia sempervirens.*

| | | | | |
|---|---|---|---|---|
| sempērvīrēns | . . | Yellow | . 6, F. Ev. Cl. N. Amer. | . 1640 |

GEMINATA, twin, producing flowers or leaves, in pairs.

GEMMÆ, leaf buds, as distinguished from alabastra, or flower-buds.

GEMMIFEROUS, bearing buds.

GENICULATE, swollen jointed.

GENIPÁ, *Plumier.* From *genepapa*, the name of one of the species in Guiana. Linn. 5, Or. 1, Nat. Or. *Cinchonaceæ.* A genus of fruit-bearing trees. The fruit produced by *G. americana* is said to be excellent, and is in much request in Dutch Guiana, where it is called Marmalade Box; for culture, see *Gardenia.* Synonyme: 1. *Gardenia esculenta.*

| | | | | |
|---|---|---|---|---|
| americānā | . . . | Pa. yel. | . 8. Ev. T. S. Amer. | . 1779 |
| edūlīs | . . . | White | . 8. Ev. T. Guiana | . 1824 |
| esculēntā, 1 | . . . | | . 8. Ev. T. China | . 1823 |
| Meriānā | . . . | White | . 8. Ev. T. Cayenne | . 1800 |
| oblongĭfōlĭā | . . | Yellow | . 8. Ev. T. Peru | . 1821 |

GENIP-TREE, see *Genipá.*

GENISTÁ, *Lamarck.* Derived from the Celtic word *gen*, a small bush. Linn. 10, Or. 6, Nat. Or. *Leguminosæ.* These are all exceedingly ornamental, and free-flowering plants. The greenhouse and frame kinds thrive best in a mixture of loam, peat, and sand; and young cuttings planted in sand, under a glass, root very readily. The hardy species are particularly adapted for the front of shrubberies, on account of their generally low growth; they may be increased from layers, or seeds. Some of the species are purgatives, and others are diuretics. Synonymes: 1. *Spartium æthnense.* 2. *angulatum.* 3. *aphyllum.* 4. *cinereum.* 5. *sericeum.* 6. *congestum.* 7. *ferox.* 8. *linifolium.* 9. *monospermum.* 10. *parviflorum.* 11. *patens.* 12. *Genista prostrata.* 13. *Spartium purgans.* 14. *radiatum.* 15. *Genista januensis.* 16. *Spartium Scorpius.* 17. *sphærocarpon.* 18. *umbellatum.* 19. *virgatum.*

| | | | | |
|---|---|---|---|---|
| æthnēnsĭs, 1 | . . | Yellow | . 7, H. Ev. S. Sicily | . . 1816 |
| ānglĭcā | . . . | Yellow | . 7, H. Ev. S. Britain | . |
| angulātā, 2 | . . | Yellow | . 6, H. Ev. S. Maryland | . 1739 |
| anxantĭcā | . . | Yellow | . 7, H. Ev. S. Italy | . 1818 |
| aphyllā, 3 | . . | Violet | . 7, H. De. S. Siberia | . 1800 |

| | | | | |
|---|---|---|---|---|
| bracteolata | . | Yellow | 5, F. Ev. S. | . 1823 |
| canariensis | . | Yellow | 6, G. Ev. S. Canaries | . 1659 |
| candicans | . | Yellow | 6, H. Ev. S. Spain | . 1735 |
| cinerea, 4 | . | Yellow | 7, H. Ev. S. Eur. | . |
| clavata, 5 | . | Yellow | 6, G. Ev. S. Mogadore | . 1812 |
| congesta, 6 | . | Yellow | 6, G. De. S. Teneriffe | . |
| decumbens | . | Yellow | 6, H. Ev. Tr. Burgundy | . 1775 |
| diffusa | . | Yellow | 6, H. Ev. S. Hungary | . 1816 |
| ephedroides | . | Yellow | 6, H. De. S. Barbary | . 1832 |
| ferox, 7 | . | Yellow | 7, F. Ev. S. Barbary | . 1800 |
| florida | . | Yellow | 7, H. Ev. S. Spain | . 1752 |
| germanica | . | Yellow | 7, H. Ev. S. Germany | . 1778 |
| hispanica | . | Yellow | 7, H. Ev. S. Spain | . 1759 |
| horrida | . | Yellow | 7, H. Ev. S. Pyrenees | . 1821 |
| humifusa | . | Yellow | 7, H. De. Tr. S. France | . 1819 |
| italica | . | Yellow | 7, H. Ev. S. Italy | . |
| linifolia, 8 | . | Yellow | 6, F. Ev. S. Spain | . 1739 |
| lusitanica | . | Yellow | 5, H. Ev. S. Portugal | . 1771 |
| mantica | . | Yellow | 7, H. Ev. S. S. Eur. | . 1816 |
| monosperma, 9 | . | Yellow | 7, F. De. S. S. Eur. | . 1690 |
| ovata | . | Yellow | 7, H. Ev. S. Hungary | . 1816 |
| parviflora, 10 | . | Yellow | 7, H. Ev. S. S. Eur. | . 1817 |
| patens, 11 | . | Yellow | 6, H. Ev. S. Spain | . |
| patula | . | Yellow | 7, H. Ev. S. Caucasus | . 1818 |
| pilocarpa | . | Yellow | 7, H. Ev. S. | . 1823 |
| pilosa | . | Yellow | 6, H. Ev. S. England | . |
| polygalæfolia | . | Yellow | 7, H. Ev. S. Spain | . 1820 |
| procumbens, 12 | . | Yellow | 7, H. Ev. Tr. Hungary | . 1816 |
| purgans, 13 | . | Pa. yel. | 7, H. De. S. S. France | . 1768 |
| radiata, 14 | . | Yellow | 7, H. Ev. S. Italy | . 1758 |
| sagittalis | . | Yellow | 6, H. Ev. S. Germany | . 1570 |
| scariosa, 15 | . | Yellow | 7, H. Ev. S. Italy | . 1821 |
| Scorpius, 16 | . | Yellow | 4, H. De. S. S. Eur. | . 1570 |
| sericea | . | Yellow | 6, H. Ev. S. Austria | . 1812 |
| sibirica | . | Yellow | 7, H. Ev. S. Siberia | . 1785 |
| sphærocarpa, 17 | . | Yellow | 7, G. De. S. S. Eur. | . 1731 |
| sylvestris | . | Yellow | 7, H. Ev. S. Hungary | . 1818 |
| tetragona | . | Yellow | 7, H. De. Tr. Podolia | . 1822 |
| tinctoria | . | Yellow | 7, H. Ev. S. Britain | . |
| triacanthos | . | Yellow | 7, H. Ev. S. Spain | . |
| triangularis | . | Yellow | 6, H. Ev. S. Hungary | . 1815 |
| triquetra | . | Yellow | 6, H. Ev. S. Corsica | . 1770 |
| umbellata, 18 | . | Yellow | 6, F. Ev. S. Barbary | . 1799 |
| virgata, 19 | . | Yellow | 6, H. De. S. Madeira | . 1777 |

GENITALS, styles and stamens.

GENTIAN, see *Gentiana*.

GENTIANA, Linn. After Gentius, King of Illyria, who first experienced the virtues of the plants. Linn. 5, Or. 2, Nat. Or. *Gentianaceæ*. This is an extremely beautiful genus of plants; most of the herbaceous kinds grow well in a rich light soil, but some require to be grown in peat; indeed, all will grow much stronger in it. Some of the species should be grown in pots, and placed among alpine plants, and protected in winter; some of them may be increased by divisions. The annual and biennial kinds may be sown in a dry sandy situation, in the open border; but they must be sown as soon as ripe, because if left till spring before they are sown, they will not, very probably, come up till the second year. The stems and roots of most of the species, especially *G. Amarella, campestris, cruciata, lutea,* and *purpurea*, are tonic, stomachic, and febrifugal. *Synonymes:* 1. quinqueflora. 2. ciliata. 3. fimbriata. 4. ciliata. 5. amarelloides.

| | | | | |
|---|---|---|---|---|
| æstiva | . | Blue | 7, H. Her. Cr. Austria | . 1818 |
| acaulis | . | Blue | 5, H. Her. Cr. Wales | . |
| angustifolia | . | Blue | 5, H. Her. Cr. Alps | . 1819 |
| adscendens | . | Blue | 7, H. Her. P. Siberia | . 1799 |
| decumbens | . | Blue | 6, H. Her. P. Siberia | . 1799 |
| algida | . | White | 7, H. Her. P. Siberia | . 1808 |
| alpina | . | Blue | 7, H. Her. Cr. Alps | . 1817 |
| altaica | . | Purple | 5, H. Her. P. Siberia | . 1824 |
| Amarella | . | Purple | 8, H.   A. Britain | . |
| angulosa | . | Purple | . H. Her. P. Altai | . 1824 |
| angustifolia | . | Purple | 7, H.   A. N. Amer. | . 1812 |
| asclepiadea | . | Blue | 7, H. Her. P. Austria | . 1629 |
| aurea, 1 | . | Yellow | 8, H. Her. P. Norway | . 1823 |
| barbata, 2 | . | Blue | 8, H.   B. Siberia | . 1764 |
| bavarica | . | Blue | 7, H. Her. Cr. Germany | . 1775 |
| biloba | . | Yellow | 7, H. Her. P. Alps | . 1820 |
| brachyphylla | . | Blue | 5, H. Her. Cr. Switzerl. | . 1819 |
| Burseri | . | Yellow | 7, H. Her. P. Pyrenees | . 1820 |
| campanulata | . | Sulphur | 7, H. Her. P. Switzerl. | . 1819 |
| campestris | . | Purple | 8, H.   A. Britain | . |
| cariathiaca | . | Blue | 8, H.   A. Switzerl. | . 1817 |
| Catesbæi | . | Blue | 7, H. Her. P. N. Amer. | . 1803 |
| caucasica | . | Violet | 7, H.   B. Caucasus | . 1804 |
| ciliata | . | Blue | 7, H. Her. P. Germany | . 1759 |
| clavata | . | Blue | 7, H. Her. P. | . 1820 |
| cristata, 3 | . | Blue | 7, H.   B. N. Amer. | . 1804 |
| cruciata | . | Dk. blue | 7, H. Her. P. Austria | . 1596 |
| fimbriata, 4 | . | Blue | 8, H. Her. P. Caucasus | . 1818 |
| frigida | . | White | 7, H. Her. P. Syria | . 1817 |
| gelida | . | Blue | 7, H. Her. P. Siberia | . 1807 |
| germanica | . | Blue | 8, H.   A. Germany | . 1818 |

| | | | | |
|---|---|---|---|---|
| glacialis | . | Blue | 7, H.   A. Alps | . 1819 |
| humilis | . | Purple | 4, H.   A. Caucasus | . 1824 |
| hybrida | . | Yel. pur. | 7, H. Her. P. Switzerl. | . 1817 |
| imbricata | . | Blue | 7, H. Her. P. Switzerl. | . 1819 |
| incarnata | . | Pink | 9, H. Her. P. N. Amer. | . 1812 |
| intermedia | . | Purple | 9, H. Her. P. N. Amer. | . 1820 |
| linearis | . | Blue | 8, H. Her. P. Carolina | . 1816 |
| lutea | . | Yellow | 7, H. Her. P. Alps | . 1596 |
| macrophylla | . | Blue | 7, H. Her. P. Siberia | . 1796 |
| nivalis | . | Blue | 8, H.   A. Scotland | . |
| obtusifolia | . | Yellow | 7, H.   A. Switzerl. | . 1826 |
| ochroleuca | . | Purple | 8, H. Her. P. N. Amer. | . 1803 |
| pannonica | . | Purple | 7, H. Her. P. Alps | . |
| Pneumonanthe | . | Blue | 8, H. Her. P. England | . |
| guttata | . | Blue | 8, H. Her. P. | . |
| pratensis | . | Blue | 7, H.   A. Siberia | . 1817 |
| Pseudo-pneumonanthe | . | Blue | 8, H. Her. P. N. Amer. | . 1800 |
| pumila | . | Blue | 5, H. Her. Cr. Switzerl. | . 1817 |
| punctata | . | Yellow | 7, H. Her. P. Alps | . 1775 |
| purpurea | . | Blue | 7, H. Her. P. Alps | . 1768 |
| flore-albo | . | White | 7, H. Her. P. Alps Eur. | . 1823 |
| pyrenaica, 5 | . | Blue | 7, H. Her. P. Pyrenees | . 1825 |
| quinqueflora | . | Blue | 8, H. Her. P. N. Amer. | . 1824 |
| saponaria | . | Blue | 8, H. Her. P. N. Amer. | . 1776 |
| flore-albo | . | White | 9, H. Her. P. N. Amer. | . 1826 |
| septemfida | . | Blue | 7, H. Her. P. Persia | . 1804 |
| guttata | . | Blue | 6, H. Her. P. Levant | . 1804 |
| triflora | . | Blue | 7, H. Her. P. Siberia | . 1807 |
| umbellata | . | Purple | 6, H. Her. P. Caucasus | . 1823 |
| utriculosa | . | Purple | 4, H. Her. P. S. Eur. | . 1822 |
| verna | . | Blue | 5, H. Her. Cr. England | . |

GEODORUM, Jackson. From *ge*, the earth, and *doron*, a gift. Linn. 20, Or. 1, Nat. Or. *Orchidaceæ*. These are rather interesting plants, succeeding well in a hot, damp stove, with the same treatment as is recommended for *Bletia*.

| | | | | |
|---|---|---|---|---|
| citrinum | . | Yellow | 9, S. Ter. E. Ind. | . 1800 |
| dilatatum | . | Pink | 7, S. Ter. E. Ind. | . 1800 |
| fucatum | . | Rose | 7, S. Ter. Ceylon | . 1822 |
| pallidum | . |   | 8, S. Ter. Sylhet | . 1837 |
| purpureum | . | Purple | 7, S. Ter. E. Ind. | . 1800 |

GEOFFROYA, Jacquin. In honour of M. E. F. Geoffroy, author of Materia Medica, who died in 1781. Linn. 17, Or. 4, Nat. Or. *Leguminosæ*. Stove trees, from twenty to thirty feet high; loam and peat mixed suit them well, and cuttings root freely in sand, under a glass, in heat.

| | | | | |
|---|---|---|---|---|
| spinosa | . | Yellow | 8. Ev. T. S. Amer. | . 1818 |
| violacea | . | Violet | 8. Ev. T. Guiana | . 1823 |

GEOGLOSSUM, Persoon. From *ge*, the earth, and *glossa*, tongue; alluding to the form of the plants. Linn. 24, Or. 2, Nat. Or. *Fungi*. Small species of a brownish colour, found in autumn among grass, and in moist meadows; whence the English name Earth Tongue—*glabrum, hirsutum, viride, viscosum*.

GEONOMA, Willdenow. From *geonomos*, skilled in agriculture; the species are difficult to propagate. Linn. 22, Or. 6, Nat. Or. *Palmaceæ*. A fine genus of Palms, the species of which grow from four to twenty feet high. They require to be grown in a rich sandy loam, and a strong heat. They can only be increased from seed which, in this country, is seldom produced.

| | | | | |
|---|---|---|---|---|
| acaulis | . | Apetal | . Palm. Brasil | . 1823 |
| macrostachys | . | Apetal | . Palm. Brasil | . 1823 |
| pinnatifrons | . | Apetal | . Palm. Caraccas | . 1821 |
| Schottiana | . | Apetal | . Palm. Brasil | . 1820 |
| simplicifrons | . | Apetal | . Palm. Trinidad | . 1818 |
| Spixiana | . | Apetal | . Palm. Brasil | . 1824 |

GEOPHILA, Don. From *ge*, the earth, and *phileo*, to love; alluding to the trailing habit of the plant. Linn. 5, Or. 1, Nat. Or. *Cinchonaceæ*. A minute species, of not much beauty, and easy cultivation. *Synonyme:* 1. Psychotria herbacea.

| | | | | |
|---|---|---|---|---|
| reniformis, 1 | . | Pa. red | 6, S. Her. Tr. W. Ind. | . 1793 |

GERANIUM. Named by Linnæus from *geranos*, a crane; in allusion to the crane-like beak terminating the carpels. Linn. 16, Or. 6, Nat. Or. *Geraniaceæ*. Some species of this extensive genus produce very handsome flowers, while others are mere weeds. The greenhouse and frame kinds thrive in loam and peat, mixed with vegetable soil, and are easily increased from cuttings or seeds. The hardy kinds do well in the open border; *G. argenteum*, however, requires to be protected in winter: they ripen seeds freely, from which they may be increased. The annual kinds merely require to be sown in the open border. In North America, they consider the root of *G. maculatum* a valuable astringent, and in North Wales, *G. Robertianum* is used in nephritic complaints. *Synonymes:* 1. *varium.* 2. *albanum.* 3. *prostratum.* 4. *Londesii.* 5. *pyrenaicum, nemorum.*

| | | | | | | |
|---|---|---|---|---|---|---|
| aconitifolium | . White | . 6, | H. Her. | P. | Switzerl. | . 1775 |
| albiflorum | . Whtsh. | 7, | H. Her. | P. | N. Amer. | . 1827 |
| altaicum | . Pa. red | 7, | H. Her. | P. | Altai | . 1818 |
| anemonefolium | . Red | . 8, | G. Ev. | S. | Madeira | . 1788 |
| angulatum | . Purple | . 6, | H. Her. | P. | | . 1789 |
| argenteum | . Striped | 7, | F. Her. | P. | S. Eur. | . 1699 |
| batrachioides | . Blue | . 7, | H. Her. | P. | Europe | . 1817 |
| Briceanum | . White | . 6, | H. | A. | Bristol | . |
| caeruleum | . Blue | . 7, | H. Her. | P. | Dahuria | . 1824 |
| canescens | . Pink | . 6, | F. Her. | P. | C.G.H. | . 1787 |
| cinereum, 1 | . Red | . 8, | H. Her. | P. | Pyrenees | . |
| collinum | . Purple | . 7, | H. Her. | P. | Siberia | . 1815 |
| cristatum, 2 | . Red | . 7, | H. Her. | P. | Iberia | . 1820 |
| dahuricum | . Purple | . 6, | H. Her. | P. | Dahuria | . 1820 |
| eriostemon | . Blue | . 7, | H. Her. | P. | Siberia | . 1822 |
| pallidum | . Pa. blue | 8, | H. Her. | P. | Nepal | . 1822 |
| fuscum | . Brown | . 7, | H. Her. | P. | S. Eur. | . 1759 |
| gymnocaulon | . Blue | . 7, | H. Her. | P. | Iberia | . 1814 |
| ibericum | . Blue | . 7, | H. Her. | P. | Levant | . 1802 |
| incanum | . Pink | . 6, | F. Her. | P. | C.G.H. | . 1701 |
| inodorum | . Pa. red | 6, | H. | A. | N. Amer. | . 1800 |
| Lamberti | . Red | . 7, | H. Her. | P. | Nepal | . 1824 |
| lancastriense, 3 | . Striped | 6, | H. De. | Tr. | Britain | . |
| longipes, 4 | . Lilac | . 7, | H. Her. | P. | | . 1823 |
| lucidum | . Pink | . 6, | H. Her. | P. | Britain | . |
| macrorhizum | . Purple | . 6, | H. Her. | P. | Italy | . 1576 |
| maculatum | . Purple | . 7, | H. Her. | P. | N. Amer. | . 1732 |
| multifidum | . Red | . 8, | H. Her. | P. | C.G.H. | . 1817 |
| nemorosum, 5 | . Purple | . 7, | H. Her. | P. | Italy | . 1821 |
| nepalense | . Red | . 6, | H. Her. | P. | Nepal | . 1818 |
| nodosum | . Purple | . 7, | H. Her. | P. | England | . |
| palustre | . Purple | . 7, | H. Her. | P. | Germany | . 1732 |
| parviflorum | . Purple | . 6, | H. Her. | P. | V.D.L. | . 1816 |
| phaeum | . Black | . 5, | H. Her. | P. | England | . |
| pilosum | . Purple | . 7, | H. Her. | P. | N. Zeal. | . 1821 |
| pratense | . Blue | . 6, | H. Her. | P. | Britain | . |
| dauricum | . Blue | . 6, | H. Her. | P. | Dauria | . 1818 |
| flore-albo | . White | . 6, | H. Her. | P. | Britain | . |
| flore-pleno | . Blue | . 6, | H. Her. | P. | Scotland | . |
| flore-variegato | Varieg. | 7, | H. Her. | P. | Britain | . |
| purpureum | . Purple | . 7, | H. | A. | Switzerl. | . 1819 |
| pyrenaicum | . Purple | . 6, | H. Her. | P. | Britain | . |
| reflexum | . Red | . 7, | H. Her. | P. | Italy | . 1758 |
| sanguineum | . Blood | . 7, | H. Her. | P. | Britain | . |
| villosissimum | . Blood | . 7, | H. De. | Tr. | Europe | . |
| sibiricum | . White | . 7, | H. Her. | P. | Siberia | . 1758 |
| striatum | . Striped | 8, | H. Her. | P. | Italy | . 1629 |
| sylvaticum | . Blue | . 6, | H. Her. | P. | Britain | . |
| tuberosum | . Pink | . 7, | H. Her. | P. | Italy | . 1596 |
| ramosum | . Purple | . 7, | H. Her. | P. | S. Eur. | . |
| umbrosum | . Purple | . 7, | H. Her. | P. | Hungary | . 1804 |
| villosum | . Blue | . 7, | H. | A. | Italy | . 1820 |
| Vlassovianum | . Red | . 7, | H. Her. | P. | Crimea | . 1821 |
| Wallichianum | . Striped | 7, | H. Her. | P. | Nepal | . 1819 |

*bohemicum, Carolinianum, columbinum, dissectum, divaricatum, lucidum, molle, pallens, pusillum, Robertianum, rotundifolium, villosum.*

**GERARDIA**, *Linn.* In honour of John Gerard, a famous old English botanist, and author of Gerard's Herbal, published in 1597. *Linn.* 14, Or. 2, Nat. Or. *Scrophulariaceæ.* These are handsome plants, growing well in a peaty soil. The perennial kinds may be increased by cuttings planted under a glass; but the best way of obtaining young plants is by seed.

| | | | | | | |
|---|---|---|---|---|---|---|
| aphylla | . Rose | . 7, | H. | A. | Carolina | . 1834 |
| delphinifolia | . Pink | . 7, | S. Her. | P. | E. Ind. | . 1800 |
| flava | . Yellow | . 7, | H. Her. | P. | N. Amer. | . 1796 |
| maritima | . Yellow | . 7, | H. | B. | N. Amer. | . 1823 |
| purpurea | . Purple | . 7, | H. | B. | N. Amer. | . 1772 |
| quercifolia | . Yellow | . 7, | H. Her. | P. | N. Amer. | . 1812 |
| tenuifolia | . Purple | . 7, | H. | B. | N. Amer. | . 1812 |

**GERBERA**, Gronovius named this genus in compliment to J. Gerber, a naturalist and traveller in Russia. *Linn.* 19, Or. 2, Nat. Or. *Compositæ.* A very pretty plant, of easy management; it thrives in a mixture of sandy loam and peat, and is increased the same way as other tender biennials.

| | | | | | |
|---|---|---|---|---|---|
| crenata | . Purple | . 7, | G. | B. C.G.H. | . 1822 |

**GERM**, or **GERMEN**, the old name of the ovary.
**GERMINATION**, the first act of vegetation in the seed.
**GERMAN MADWORT**, see *Asperugo.*
**GEROPOGON**, *Linn.* From *geron*, old man, and *pogon*, a beard; alluding to the appearance of the seed. *Linn.* 19, Or. 1, Nat. Or. *Compositæ.* Very pretty plants, of easy culture; they grow in any common soil.

| | | | | | | |
|---|---|---|---|---|---|---|
| calyculatus | . Pink | . 7, | H. Her. | P. | Italy | . 1774 |
| glaber | . Pink | . 7, | H. | A. | Italy | . 1704 |
| hirsutus | . Red | . 7, | H. | A. | Italy | . 1759 |

**GESNERA**, *Linn.* Named by Linnæus, after the famous botanist, Conrad Gesner, of Zurich. *Linn.* 14, Or. 2, Nat. Or. *Gesneraceæ.* These are very handsome species, thriving well in any light rich soil; and cuttings root readily in sand or soil, under a glass, in heat. *Synonyme:* 1. *pendulina.*

| | | | | | | |
|---|---|---|---|---|---|---|
| acaulis | . Scarlet | . 8, | S. Her. | P. | Jamaica | . 1793 |
| allagophylla | . Orange | . 7, | S. Her. | P. | Brasil | . 1834 |
| aggregata, 1 | . Scarlet | . 6, | S. Her. | P. | Brasil | . 1816 |
| bulbosa | . Scarlet | . 6, | S. Her. | P. | Brasil | . 1816 |
| calycina | . | . | 8, | S. Ev. | S. | Jamaica | . |
| Cooperi | . Scarlet | . | S. Her. | P. | Brasil | . 1829 |
| corymbosa | . Scarlet | . 7, | S. Ev. | S. | Jamaica | . 1822 |
| Douglasi | . Red yel. | 9, | S. Her. | P. | Rio Jan. | . 1826 |
| verticillata | . Crimson | 5, | S. Her. | P. | Rio Jan. | . 1835 |
| elongata | . Scarlet | . 9, | S. Ev. | S. | S. Amer. | . 1835 |
| faucialis | . Scarlet | . 7, | S. Her. | P. | Brasil | . 1833 |
| hirsuta | . Scarlet | . 7, | S. Ev. | S. | Cumana | . 1826 |
| humilis | . Scarlet | . | 8, | S. Ev. | S. | Cuba | . |
| lateritia | . Scarlet | . 7, | S. Her. | P. | Brasil | . 1834 |
| Lindleyi | . Scur. yel. | 7, | S. Her. | P. | Brasil | . 1825 |
| macrostachya | . Scarlet | . 7, | S. Her. | P. | Rio Jan. | . 1825 |
| Marchii | . Scarlet | . 9, | S. Her. | P. | Organ Mts. | . 1837 |
| rupestris | . Scarlet | . 8, | S. Her. | P. | | . 1835 |
| scabra | . Scarlet | . 8, | S. Ev. | S. | Jamaica | . 1830 |
| Sellowii | . Scarlet | . 8, | S. Her. | P. | Brasil | . 1835 |
| spicata | . Scarlet | . 8, | S. Her. | P. | N. Granada | . 1831 |
| Suttoni | . Scarlet | . 7, | S. Her. | P. | Rio Jan. | . 1833 |
| tubiflora | . Scarlet | . 8, | S. Her. | S. | S. Amer. | . 1815 |
| rutila | . Scarlet | . 8, | S. Ev. | S. | Brasil | . 1825 |

**GETHYLLIS**, *Linn.* From *getheo*, to rejoice; alluding to the perfume of the flowers. *Linn.* 6, Or. 1, Nat. Or. *Amaryllideæ.* These small, ornamental, Cape plants, Sweet says, "thrive best in a mixture of sandy loam and peat, and require but little water when not in a growing state; they are increased by offsets from the bulbs, or by seeds."

| | | | | | | |
|---|---|---|---|---|---|---|
| afra | . White | . 7, | G. Bl. | P. | C.G.H. | . 1820 |
| ciliaris | . White | . 7, | G. Bl. | P. | C.G.H. | . 1788 |
| lanceolata | . White | . 7, | G. Bl. | P. | C.G.H. | . 1790 |
| spiralis | . White | . 7, | G. Bl. | P. | C.G.H. | . 1780 |
| villosa | . White | . 7, | G. Bl. | P. | C.G.H. | . 1787 |

**GETONIX.** Named by Roxburgh, who does not give the derivation. *Linn.* 10, Or. 1, Nat. Or. *Combretaceæ.* Ornamental evergreen climbers, succeeding in loam and peat, and multiplied from cuttings in sand, in heat, under a glass.

| | | | | | | |
|---|---|---|---|---|---|---|
| floribunda | . Yel. grn. | 8, | S. Ev. Cl. | E. Ind. | . 1815 |
| nutans | . Apetal | . 8, | S. Ev. Cl. | E. Ind. | . 1816 |

**GEUM**, *Linn.* From *geyo*, to give a relish; because of the roots of *G. urbanum.* *Linn.* 12, Or. 3, Nat. Or. *Rosaceæ.* This is an ornamental genus, indeed some of the species, as *G. coccineum*, are extremely handsome. They all grow well in any rich light loamy soil, and are increased by dividing the roots, or by seeds. *G. urbanum* and *rivale* have been, for efficacy, compared to *Cinchona.* *Synonymes:* 1 *canadense.* 2. *coccineum.* 3. *sylvaticum.* 4. *incli natum.* 5. *Adamsia rotundifolia.*

| | | | | | | |
|---|---|---|---|---|---|---|
| agrimonioides | . White | . 7, | H. Her. | P. | N. Amer. | . 1811 |
| album, 1 | . White | . 7, | H. Her. | P. | N. Amer. | . 1730 |
| atlanticum, 2 | . Yellow | . 7, | H. Her. | P. | S. Eur. | . 1810 |
| brachypetalum | . Yellow | . 7, | H. Her. | P. | | . 1818 |
| canadense | . Yellow | . 7, | H. Her. | P. | Canada | . 1810 |
| chiloense, 3 | . Copper | . 7, | H. Her. | P. | Chile | . 1826 |
| grandiflorum | . Scarlet | . 7, | H. Her. | P. | | . |
| ciliatum | . Yellow | . 7, | H. Her. | P. | N. Amer. | . 1818 |
| heterophyllum | . White | . 7, | H. Her. | P. | | . 1816 |
| hybridum | . Red brn. | 7, | H. Her. | P. | Europe | . |
| intermedium | . Yellow | . 7, | H. Her. | P. | Volhinia | . 1794 |
| macrophyllum | . Yellow | . 7, | H. Her. | P. | Kamtsch. | . 1804 |
| nutans | . Yellow | . 7, | H. Her. | P. | N. Amer. | . 1825 |
| Portenschlagianum | Yellow | . 7, | H. Her. | P. | | . 1820 |
| pyrenaicum, 4 | . Yellow | . 7, | H. Her. | P. | Pyrenees | . 1804 |
| radiatum | . Yellow | . 7, | H. Her. | P. | N. Amer. | . 1815 |
| ranunculoides, 5 | . Yellow | . 7, | H. Her. | P. | | . 1823 |
| rivale | . Yellow | . 6, | H. Her. | P. | Britain | . |
| intermedium | . Yellow | . 6, | H. Her. | P. | Germany | . 1794 |
| rotundifolium, 6 | . Yellow | . 7, | H. Her. | P. | Russia | . 1820 |
| strictum | . Striped | 6, | H. Her. | P. | N. Amer. | . 1778 |
| urbanum | . Yellow | . 7, | H. Her. | P. | Britain | . |
| virginianum | . White | . 7, | H. Her. | P. | N. Amer. | . |

**GHINIA**, *Swartz.* After Ghini, an Italian botanist. *Linn.* 2, Or. 1, Nat. Or. *Verbenaceæ.* A curious little plant, of easy culture in sandy open loam. The seeds require to be sown in pots, which must be placed in a hothouse, and when the seedlings are of sufficient size, potted off, and treated as other tender annuals.

spinósá . . . . Purple . 8, S.   A. W. Ind. . . 1733

GIANT FENNEL, see *Fěrŭlă.*

GIBBOUS, protuberant, swelled.

GILIA, *Ruiz and Pavon.* In honour of P. S. Gil, a Spanish botanist. *Linn.* 5, Or. 1, Nat. Or. *Polemoniaceæ.* This is an extremely pretty genus; all the species deserve a place in every flower-garden. The seeds merely require to be sown in the open borders in spring, where they will produce their pretty flowers in abundance. *Synonymes:* 1. *pulchella, Cantua aggregata, Ipomopsis elegans.* 2. *Ipomopsis inconspicua, Cantua parviflora.*

| | | | | |
|---|---|---|---|---|
| achilleæfóliă . . . | . Pink . | 8, H. | A. California | . 1838 |
| aggregáta, 1 . . | . Scarlet . | 7, G. | B. America | . 1822 |
| capitátá . . . | . Blue . | 7, H. | A. Columbia | . 1826 |
| grácilis . . . | . Pink . | 7, H. | A. N. Amer. | . 1826 |
| laciniátá . . . | . Blue . | 7, H. | A. Chile | . 1831 |
| parviflórá, 2 . | . Blue . | 10, H. | A. America | . 1793 |
| púngéns . . . | . Pink . | 7, H. | A. N. Amer. | . 1827 |
| tricŏlŏr . . . | . Pur. or. | 8, H. | A. California | . 1833 |
| flóribûs-albicántĭbûs | White . | 7, H. | A. California | . 1833 |

GILLĚNIA. Named by Mœnch, probably after Gillen, some obscure botanist. *Linn.* 12, Or. 2, Nat. Or. *Rosaceæ.* Ornamental plants; for culture and propagation, see *Spiræa.* The roots are emetic, and probably tonic. *Synonymes:* 1. *Spiræa trifoliata.* 2. *S. stipulacea.*

| | | | | |
|---|---|---|---|---|
| stipulácéá, 2 . | . Red wht. | 7, H. Her. | P. N. Amer. | . 1805 |
| trifoliátá, 1 . | . Red wht. | 7, H. Her. | P. N. Amer. | . 1713 |

GILLIĚSIA, *Lindley.* Named after Dr. Gillies, of Mendoza, in Chili. *Linn.* 16, Or. 3, Nat. Or. *Gilliesiaceæ.* This species succeeds well in a warm border, consisting of loam and peat, with a little protection in winter; it is, however, scarcely worth cultivating. It is increased by offsets.

| | | | | |
|---|---|---|---|---|
| gramíněă . . . | . Green . | 8, F. Bl. | P. Chile | . 1825 |

GILVA, flesh, or ash-coloured.

GINGER, see *Zingibĕr.*

GINGERBREAD TREE, see *Parinărĭŭm macrophyllŭm.*

GINSENG, see *Pǎnǎx quinquefŏlĭŭm.*

GIRDED, surrounded by any thing.

GISĚKIA, *Linn.* In honour of P. D. Giseke, a Danish botanist. *Linn.* 5, Or. 5, Nat. Or. *Phytolaccaceæ.* A curious little plant, requiring the same treatment as other tender annuals.

| | | | | |
|---|---|---|---|---|
| pharnaceoídés . | . Pa. grn. | 6, S. | A. E. Ind. . | . 1782 |

GLABROUS, smooth, destitute of hairs.

GLACIALIS, having a frozen appearance.

GLADIATE, shaped like a short straight sword.

GLADIŎLŭs, *Linn.* From *gladius,* a sword; alluding to the sword-shaped leaves. *Linn.* 3, Or. 1, Nat. Or. *Iridaceæ.* This is an extensive genus, consisting chiefly of beautiful flowering Cape bulbs. Sweet says, " the species thrive best in a mixture of very sandy loam, and decayed leaves, or peat soil, and require no water after they have done flowering till they begin to grow afresh. In the month of October, they should be taken out of their pots, and replanted in fresh soil, when they should be set in a cool frame, or some such place, as they require to be only protected from frost till such time as their pots are full of young roots.; then they may be set in a warmer situation, and watered regularly, and they will flower freely. The hardy species thrive well in a light sandy soil, and are rapidly increased, as well as the tender kinds, by offsets from the bulbs; they require to be planted in a warm south border. If intended to remain in the ground all the winter, the smaller bulbs must be planted six inches deep, and the larger ones eight inches, so as to be out of the reach of frost; they should also be covered with a little dry litter in severe frost, or they may be taken up in autumn, and laid to dry all the winter where the frost cannot hurt them; they must then be planted early in spring, and they will generally flower well."

| | | | | |
|---|---|---|---|---|
| alátús . . . | . Scar. yel. | 6, G. Bl. | P. C. G. H. | . 1795 |
| algoénsis . . | . Orange | 7, G. Bl. | P. C. G. H. | . 1824 |
| albidús . . | . White . | 6, G. Bl. | P. C. G. H. | . 1774 |
| pictús . . | . Red wht. | 7, G Bl. | P. C. G. H. | . 1794 |
| angústús . . | . Yellow | 6, | Bl. | P. C. G. H. | . 1756 |
| blandús . . | . Flesh . | 6, . Bl. | P. C. G. H. | . 1774 |
| brevifóliús . . | . Pink . | 6, G. Bl. | P. C. G. H. | . 1802 |
| byzantínús . . | . Red . | 7, H. Bl. | P. Turkey | . 1629 |

| | | | | |
|---|---|---|---|---|
| campanulátús . | . Lgt. pur. | 5, G. Bl. | P. C. G. H. | . 1794 |
| cardinális . . | . Red . | 7, G. Bl. | P. C. G. H. | . 1789 |
| carnéús . . | . Flesh . | 6, G. Bl. | P. C. G. H. | . 1796 |
| cochleátús . . | . Wht. red . | 8, G. Bl. | P. C. G. H. | . 1829 |
| Colvíllí . . | . Scar. yel. | 7, G. Bl. | P. Hybrid . | . 1824 |
| commúnis . . | . Red . | 7, H. Bl. | P. S. Eur. | . 1596 |
| carnéús . . | . Flesh . | 7, H. Bl. | P. S. Eur. | . 1696 |
| cóncŏlŏr . . | . Yellow | 6, G. Bl. | P. C. G. H. | . 1790 |
| cuspidátús . . | . Wht. brn. | 5, G. Bl. | P. C. G. H. | . 1795 |
| debílís . . | . White . | 5, G. Bl. | P. C. G. H. | . |
| edúlís . . | . White . | 6, G. Bl. | P. C. G. H. | . 1816 |
| flexuósús . . | . Orange | 6, G. Bl. | P. C. G. H. | . 1825 |
| floribúndús . . | . Citron . | 7, G. Bl. | P. C. G. H. | . 1748 |
| grácilís . . | . Blue wht. | 4, G. Bl. | P. C. G. H. | . 1800 |
| hastátús . . | . Flesh . | 5, G. Bl. | P. C. G. H. | . 1816 |
| hirsútús . . | . Pink . | 6, G. Bl. | P. C. G. H. | . 1795 |
| hyálinús . . | . Yel. red . | 6, G. Bl. | P. C. G. H. | . 1825 |
| imbricátús . . | . Red . | 6, H. Bl. | P. Russia . | . 1820 |
| involútús . . | . Pink . | 6, G. Bl. | P. C. G. H. | . 1757 |
| Milléri . . | . Violet . | 5, G. Bl. | P. C. G. H. | . 1751 |
| Mortónĭús . . | . White . | G. Bl. | P. S. Africa | . 1837 |
| namaquénsis . . | . Orange | 6, G. Bl. | P. C. G. H. | . 1800 |
| natalénsis . . | . Scar. yel. | 8, G. Bl. | P. Natal River | . 1830 |
| permeábílís . . | . Orange | 6, G. Bl. | P. C. G. H. | . 1825 |
| recúrvús . . | . Striped | 5, G. Bl. | P. C. G. H. | . 1758 |
| ségétúm . . | . Purple | 7, G. Bl. | P. S. Eur. | . 1596 |
| tenéllús . . | . Yellow | 6, G. Bl. | P. C. G. H. | . 1825 |
| ténúís . . | . Red . | 6, H. Bl. | P. Tauria . | . 1823 |
| trichonemifóliús | . Yellow | 6, G. Bl. | P. C. G. H. | . 1800 |
| trimaculátús . | . Red wht. | 6, G. Bl. | P. C. G. H. | . 1794 |
| tristís . . | . Brn. red | 7, G. Bl. | P. C. G. H. | . 1745 |
| undulátús . . | . Pink . | 5, G. Bl. | P. C. G. H. | . 1760 |
| carnéús . . | . Flesh . | 5, G. Bl. | P. C. G. H. | . 1760 |
| pállidús . . | . Pink . | 5, G. Bl. | P. C. G. H. | . 1760 |
| versicŏlŏr . . | . Brown . | 6, G. Bl. | P. C. G. H. | . 1794 |
| binérvis . . | . Pink . | 6, G. Bl. | P. C. G. H. | . 1806 |
| tenúĭŏr . . | . Varieg. | 6, G. Bl | P. C. G. H. | . 1779 |
| viperátús . . | . Grn. wht. | 5, G. Bl. | P. C. G. H. | . 1787 |
| Watsónĭús . . | . Red . | 3, G. Bl. | P. C. G. H. | . 1791 |
| variegátús . . | . Red wht. | 4, G. Bl. | P. C. G. H. | . 1801 |

GLADWIN, see *Iris fœtidĭssĭmă.*

GLANDULAR, furnished with glands.

GLANDULARLY-CRENATED,
GLANDULARLY-SERRATED, } having crenatures or serratures tipped with glands.

GLANDULARLY-MURICATED, covered with tubercles tipped with glands.

GLANDULARLY-TOOTHED, margins toothed, with the teeth bearing glands.

GLANDULIFEROUS, bearing glands.

GLAREÓSÚS, flourishing in gravelly soils.

GLASSWORT, see *Salicŏrnĭă.*

GLASTONBURY THORN, see *Cratǣgús Oxyacănthă,* var.

GLAUCESCENT, having something of a bluish hoary appearance.

GLAUCĬÚM, *Tournefort.* From *glaukos,* glaucous; alluding to the colour of the plants. *Linn.* 13, Or. 1, Nat. Or. *Papaveraceæ.* Very pretty plants, some of which are particularly handsome in the flower-borders, where they flower and ripen seed in abundance, which has only to be sown in the open border. *Synonymes:* 1. *G. luteum.* 2. *corniculatum.*

| | | | | |
|---|---|---|---|---|
| flávúm, 1 . . | . Yellow | 8, H. | B. Britain . | . |
| fulvúm . . . | . Orange | 8, H. | B. S. Eur. . | . 1802 |
| pérsicúm . . | . Red . | 8, H. | A. Volhynia | . 1829 |
| phœnicéúm, 2 | . Purple | 7, H. | A. England | . |
| flaviflórúm . | . Yellow | 7, H. | A. Tauria . | . 1823 |
| rúbrúm . . | . Red . | 7, H. | A. Greece | . 1818 |
| tricŏlŏr . . | . Red . | 7, H. | A. Persia . | . 1828 |

GLAUCOUS, having a hoary grey surface.

GLAUX, *Linn.* From *glaukos,* grey; in allusion to the colour of the leaves. *Linn.* 5, Or. 1, Nat. Or. *Primulaceæ.* This is a pretty little plant, of easy management in open sandy loam; and is increased from seeds.

| | | | | |
|---|---|---|---|---|
| marítímá . . | . Flesh . | 4, H. Her. | Tr. Britain . | . |

GLECHŌMA, *Linn.* Derived from the Greek *glechon,* signifying a sort of thyme. *Linn.* 14, Or. 2, Nat. Or. *Labiatæ.* Plants requiring no particular management. G. *hederacea* is useful in the preparation of slightly tonic beverages.

| | | | | |
|---|---|---|---|---|
| hederáceá . | . Blue . | 5, H. Ev. | Tr. Britain . | . |
| rŏséá . . | . Rose . | 5, H. Ev. Cr. | England | . |
| variegáta . | . Blue . | 5, H. Ev. Cr. | England | . |
| hirsúta . . | . Pink . | 5, H. Ev. Cr. | Hungary | . |

GLEDĬTSCHIA, *Linn.* In honour of Gottlieb Gleditsch, once a professor at Berlin, and a defender of Linnæus against Siegesbeck, and author of many botanical works. *Linn.* 23, Or. 2, Nat. Or. *Leguminosæ.* A most ornamental genus of trees, very remarkable for their acacia-like leaves, and the branching thorns which are produced on the stems of some of the species. They grow in any kind of soil, and are increased by seeds, which are usually procured from the native countries of the trees. A bed must be prepared, in which the seeds may be sown an inch deep, and if the spring is dry, they will not vegetate till the following year. *Synonyme*: 1. *orientalis*. 2. *lævis*.

| | | | | | | |
|---|---|---|---|---|---|---|
| brachycárpá | . Green | . 7, H. De. T. | N. Amer. | |
| cáspicá | . Green | . 7, H. De. T. | Caspia | . 1822 |
| feróx, 1 . | . Green | . 7, H. De. T. | | |
| hórridá | . Green | . 7, H. De. T. | China | . 1774 |
| purpúreá | . Green | . 7, H. De. T. | China | . 1774 |
| latisiliquá | . Green | . 7, H. De. T. | | |
| macránthá . | . Green | . 7, H. De. T. | | |
| micracánthōs | . Green | . 7, H. De. T. | | |
| monospérmá | . Green | . 7, H. De. T. | N. Amer. | . 1728 |
| sinénsis . | . Green | . F. De. T. | China | . 1812 |
| inérmis | . Green | . H. De. T. | | |
| triacánthōs | . Green | . H. De. T. | N. Amer. | . 1700 |
| inérmis, 2 | . Green | . 7, H. De. T. | | |

GLEICHĒNĬX, *Smith*. In honour of the Baron P. F. Von Gleichen, a German botanist. *Linn.* 24, Or. 1, Nat. Or. *Gleicheniaceæ*. These are pretty plants, and will, in general, succeed in peat and loam, and increase from divisions of the roots.

| | | | | | |
|---|---|---|---|---|---|
| flabellátá | . Brown | . 7, S. Her. P. | N. Holl. | . 1823 |
| microphýllá | . Brown | . 7, S. Her. P. | N. Holl. | . 1823 |
| pectinátá | . Brown | . 8, S. Her. P. | Trinidad | . 1824 |
| pubéscens | . Brown | . 8, S. Her. P. | S. Amer. | . 1822 |
| spelúncæ | . Brown | . 7, S. Her. P. | N. Holl. | . 1824 |

GLĪNŪS, *Linn.* A name given by Theophrastus to the Maple. *Linn.* 11, Or. 5, Nat. Or. *Ficoideæ*. A greenhouse annual, of simple culture—*lotoídes*.

GLŌBBĀ, *Roscoe*. The name given to it in the Moluccas. *Linn.* 10, Or. 1, Nat. Or. *Scitamineæ*. These are very pretty plants, especially *G. Careyana*. They attain from one to two feet high, and are cultivated in sandy open loam; they increase by parting the roots. *Synonyme*: 1. *G. Hura*.

| | | | | | |
|---|---|---|---|---|---|
| bulbíferá | . Yellow | . 7, S. Her. P. | E. Ind. | . 1820 |
| Careyáná | . Yellow | . 8, S. Her. P. | Pegu | . 1822 |
| erécta | . White | . 7, S. Her. P. | E. Ind. | . 1820 |
| marantiná | . Yellow | . 7, S. Her. P. | E. Ind. | . 1800 |
| orixénsis | . Pink | . 7, S. Her. P. | E. Ind. | . 1819 |
| péndulá | . Yellow | . 7, S. Her. P. | E. Ind. | . 1822 |
| racemósá, 1 | . Yellow | . 7, S. Her. P. | Ceylon | . 1812 |
| sessiliflórá | . Yellow | . 8, S. Her. P. | Pegu | . 1807 |

GLOBE AMARANTH, see *Gomphréna*.
GLOBE FLOWER, see *Tróllius*.
GLOBE THISTLE, see *Echīnōps*.
GLOBOSE,
GLOBULAR, } round or spherical.
GLOBOSELY-ELLIPTICAL, between spherical and oval.
GLOBULOSE, a diminutive of globose.
GLOBULĀRĬX, *Linn.* So named because the flowers are produced in globose heads. *Linn.* 4, Or. 1, Nat. Or. *Globulariaceæ*. This is a very handsome genus; the greenhouse species thrive well in a mixture of loam and peat, and the hardy kinds do well in sandy light soil. *G. vulgaris* is said to do best in peat. They increase freely by cuttings in sand or soil, or by seeds. *Synonymes*: 1. *vulgaris*. 2. *salicina*.

| | | | | | |
|---|---|---|---|---|---|
| Alypúm | . Pale | . 8, G. Her. P. | S. Eur. | . 1640 |
| integrifolíúm | . Pale | . 8, G. Her. P. | S. Eur. | |
| bellidifolíá | . Red | . 7, H. Her. P. | Italy | . 1825 |
| cordifolíá | . Blue | . 7, H. Her. P. | Germany | . 1633 |
| linifolíá, 1 | . Blue | . 6, H. Her. P. | Spain | . 1818 |
| longifolíá, 2 | . White | . 7, G. Her. P. | Madeira | . 1775 |
| nāná | . Blue | . 7, H. Her. P. | France | . 1824 |
| nudicaulis | . Blue | . 7, H. Her. P. | Germany | . 1629 |
| spinósá | . Blue | . 7, H. Her. P. | Spain | . 1640 |
| vulgáris | . Blue | . 6, H. Her. P. | Europe | . 1640 |

GLOBŪLĒX, *Haworth*. From *globulos*, a globule, or small globe; the petals are tipped with waxy globules. *Linn.* 5, Or. 5, Nat. Or. *Crassulaceæ*. These are interesting succulent plants, which may be successfully cultivated in sandy loam, and a little peat mixed with a small portion of brick rubbish. They require to be very carefully watered, especially when not in a free growing state. Cuttings, after drying a day or two, will root readily in the same kind of soil, or in sand. *Synonyme*: 1. *Crassula cultrata*.

| | | | | |
|---|---|---|---|---|
| atropurpúreá | . Purple | . 8, G. Her. P. C. G. H. | . 1823 |
| canéscens | . White | . 7, G. Her. P. C. G. H. | . 1800 |
| capitátá | . White | . 7, G. Her. P. C. G. H. | . 1819 |
| cultrátá, 1 | . White | . 7, G. Her. P. C. G. H. | . 1732 |
| hispídá | . White | . 11, G. Her. P. C. G. H. | . 1823 |

| | | | | |
|---|---|---|---|---|
| impréssá | . White | . 8, G. Her. P. C. G. H. | . 1820 |
| minōr | . White | . 8, G. Her. P. C. G. H. | . 1820 |
| linguá | . White | . 7, G. Her. P. C. G. H. | . 1823 |
| lingúlá | . White | . 7, G. Her. P. C. G. H. | . 1823 |
| mesembryanthoídes | . White | . 8, G. Her. P. C. G. H. | . 1820 |
| altiōr | . White | . 8, G. Her. P. C. G. H. | . 1820 |
| móllis | . White | . 8, G. Her. P. C. G. H. | . 1774 |
| nudicaulis | . White | . 8, G. Her. P. C. G. H. | . 1732 |
| obvallátá | . White | . 7, G. Her. P. C. G. H. | . 1795 |
| paniculátá | . White | . 8, G. Her. P. C. G. H. | . 1823 |
| radícáns | . White | . 8, G. Her. P. C. G. H. | . 1823 |
| subincáná | . White | . 8, G. Her. P. C. G. H. | . 1823 |
| erécta | . White | . 8, G. Her. P. C. G. H. | . 1823 |
| sulcátá | . White | . 8, G. Her. P. C. G. H. | . 1818 |

GLOCHIDATE, having hairs, the ends of which are split and hooked back.
GLOMERATE,
GLOMERATED, } gathered into round heaps, or heads.
GLORIŌSĀ, *Linn.* Derived from *gloriosus*, glorious; because of the magnificent flowers. *Linn.* 6, Or. 1, Nat. Or. *Liliaceæ*. This is a truly handsome and curious genus of plants, well worthy of cultivation in every collection of stove plants. The following method of treatment is given by the late Mr. Sweet:—"We have found them succeed best, and flower luxuriantly, by being planted in rather more than one-third turfy loam, full one-third white sand, and the remainder peat; as soon as planted, to be set in a hotbed frame till they have begun to grow; then move them to a warm part of the hothouse, and as they grow, train them up a stick, or wire, where they will flower, and if a little pains be taken to fertilize the stigmas with the pollen when in bloom, they will produce plenty of seeds, which should be sown as soon as gathered. After flowering, the stems must be let die down, and they require no more water; the pots may then be laid on their sides, in a dry situation, and there left till the March following, when they should be planted." Young plants are generally obtained by dividing the roots; they are also raised from seeds. *Synonyme*: 1. *simplex*.

| | | | | |
|---|---|---|---|---|
| nepalénsis, 1 | . Yellow | . 6, F. Bl. P. | Nepal | . 1825 |
| simpléx | . Blue | . 7, S. Bl. P. | Senegal | . 1756 |
| superbá | . Orange | . 7, S. Bl. P. | E. Ind. | . 1690 |
| viréscens | . Orange | . 8, S. Bl. P. | Mozamb. | . 1823 |

GLORIŌSŪS, superb, grand.
GLOSSŌDIX, *R. Brown*. From *glossa*, a tongue, and *eidos*, like; alluding to the tongue-like appendage within the flower. *Linn.* 20, Or. 1, Nat. Or. *Orchidaceæ*. Pretty plants, thriving well in sandy loam and peat, and increased by offsets from the roots. They require very little water when not in a growing state.

| | | | | |
|---|---|---|---|---|
| majōr | . Blue | . 6, G. Ter. | N. Holl. | . 1810 |
| minōr | . Blue | . 6, G. Ter. | N. Holl. | . 1810 |

GLOSSŪLĀ, *Lindley*. From *glossa*, a tongue; in allusion to the tongue-like segments of the labellum. *Linn.* 20, Or. 1, Nat. Or. *Orchidaceæ*. A curious species, with very minute green flowers. It requires the heat of the stove, and to be otherwise treated like *Glossodia*.

| | | | | |
|---|---|---|---|---|
| tentaculátá | . Green | . 12, S. Ter. | China | . 1824 |

GLOTTĬDĬUM, *Desfontaines*. From *glotta*, a tongue; the valves of the legume separate into two membranes each, which have been compared to the superior opening of the larynx. *Linn.* 17, Or. 4, Nat. Or. *Leguminosæ*. A tall growing plant, the seeds of which require to be sown in peat and sand, and placed in heat, and when of sufficient size, planted singly in the same kind of soil, and shifted into larger pots as they grow. *Synonyme*: 1. *Phaca floridana, Sesbania disperma, Æschynomene platycarpa*.

| | | | | |
|---|---|---|---|---|
| floridánúm, 1 | . Yellow | . 7, G. | A. Florida | . 1816 |

GLOXĪNĬX, *L'Heritier*. Named in honour of P. B. Gloxin, a botanist of Colmar. *Linn.* 14, Or. 2, Nat. Or. *Gesneraceæ*. A splendid genus of plants, well deserving of extensive cultivation; they thrive best in a rich soil, consisting of loam, peat, and sand, in equal quantities, with a little vegetable soil, well mixed together. In the summer, they should have a plentiful supply of water; in winter, they require very little water. *G. maculata* is easily increased by divisions. The leaves of most of the others, if taken off close to the stem, and planted, will soon make young plants.

| | | | | |
|---|---|---|---|---|
| caulescens | Purple | 7, 8. Her. P. Pernam. | 1896 |
| hirsuta | Blue | 7, 8. Her. P. 8. Amer. | 1824 |
| maculata | Purple | 9, 8. Her. P. 8. Amer. | 1789 |
| maxima | Pa. wht. | 7, 8. Her. P. Hybrid | 1827 |
| speciosa | Purple | 9, 8. Her. P. 8 Amer. | 1815 |
| alba | White | 9, 8. Her. P. 8 Amer. | |

**GLUMACEOUS;** plants are said to be glumaceous when their flowers are like those of grasses.

**GLUME,** a part of the floral envelopes of a grass.

**GLUTEN,** glue.

**GLUTINOUS, GLUTINOSE,** } adhesive, gluey.

**GLYCERIA,** *R. Brown.* From *glykeros,* sweet; alluding to the herbage. *Linn.* 3, Or. 2, Nat. Or. *Gramineæ.* An aquatic of no interest or beauty; it is of the simplest culture. *Synonyme:* 1. *Festuca fluitans—fluitans.*

**GLYCINE,** *Linn.* From *glykys,* sweet; the leaves and roots of some of the species are sweet. *Linn.* 17, Or. 4, Nat. Or. *Leguminosæ.* A beautiful genus of plants, producing their pretty flowers in fascicles, or racemes, from the axils of the leaves; for culture and propagation, see *Clitoria.*

| | | | | |
|---|---|---|---|---|
| biloba | Violet | 11, G. Ev. | Mexico | 1827 |
| clandestina | Pa. yel. | 7, 8. Ev. Tw. N. Holl. | 1824 |
| hedysaroides | Purple | 7, 8. Ev. 8. Guinea | 1823 |
| heterophylla | Yellow | 7, G. Ev. Tw. C. G. H. | 1825 |
| minima | Purple | 7, G. Ev. Tw. N. Holl. | 1818 |
| mollis | Yellow | 7, 8. Ev. Tw. W. Ind. | 1824 |
| secunda | Yellow | 7, G. Ev. Tr. | |
| striata | Yellow | 7, 8. Ev. Tw. 8. Amer. | 1818 |

*dubilis, parviflora.*

**GLYCOSMIS,** *Correa.* From *glykys,* sweet, and *osme,* smell; alluding to the sweet-scented flowers. *Linn.* 10, Or. 1, Nat. Or. *Amarantaceæ.* These trees are said to attain the height of twenty feet, and thrive well in a rich mould. They may be increased by cuttings in sand, under a glass, in heat. *Synonyme:* 1. *Limonia pentaphylla.*

| | | | | |
|---|---|---|---|---|
| arborea | White | 7, 8. Ev. T. E. Ind. | 1796 |
| pentaphylla, 1 | White | 7, 8. Ev. T. E. Ind. | 1790 |

**GLYCYRRHIZA,** *Tournefort.* From *glykys,* sweet, and *rhiza,* a root; the sweetness of the root of the Liquorice is well known. *Linn.* 17, Or. 4, Nat. Or. *Leguminosæ.* A deep light sandy loam suits all the species of this genus, and they are readily increased by slips from the roots with eyes, and planting them in spring. The sweet, subacrid, mucilaginous juice is much esteemed as a pectoral. *Synonymes:* 1. *aspera, hispida.* 2. *Liquiritia officinalis.*

| | | | | |
|---|---|---|---|---|
| asperrima | Blue | 7, H. Her. P. Siberia | 1795 |
| echinata | Pale | 7, H. Her. P. Italy | 1596 |
| fœtida | Pa. yel. | 7, H. Her. P. Africa | 1817 |
| glabra, 2 | Pa. blue | 7, H. Her. P. Italy | 1562 |
| glandulifera | Pale | 7, H. Her. P. Hungary | 1805 |
| hirsuta | Pale | 7, H. Her. P. Levant | 1739 |
| lepidota | Pale | 7, H. Her. P. Missouri | 1811 |
| uralensis | Pa. blue | 7, H. Her. P. Siberia | 1818 |

**GLYPHOMITRION,** *Bridel.* From *glypho,* to emboss, and *mitrion,* a little diadem. *Linn.* 24, Or. 5, Nat. Or. *Musci.* Small tufts of mo s, found on rocks in the spring. *Synonyme:* 1. *Grimmia Daviesii, Encalypta Daviesii—Daviesii.*

**GMELINA,** *Linn.* In honour of George Gmelin, a celebrated German naturalist and traveller. *Linn.* 14, Or. 2, Nat. Or. *Verbenaceæ.* This is a genus of fine plants, though they seldom flower in this country. They grow best in rich loam, mixed with a little peat, requiring a very strong heat to grow them well. They may be increased without difficulty by cuttings, planted in sand, in heat, under a glass.

| | | | | |
|---|---|---|---|---|
| arborea | Yellow | 8. Ev. T. E. Ind. | 1894 |
| asiatica | Yellow | 8. Ev. T. E. Ind. | 1792 |
| parviflora | Orange | 8. Ev. T. E. Ind. | 1817 |
| speciosissima | White | G. Ev. T. Nepal | 1823 |
| villosa | | 8. Ev. T. E. Ind. | 1818 |

**GNAPHALIUM,** *Linn.* From *gnaphalon,* soft down; alluding to the woolly covering of the plants. *Linn.* 19, Or. 2, Nat. Or. *Compositæ.* Some of these are interesting plants, on account of the quality the flowers possess of retaining their colours after they are gathered from the plants. They grow in any rich light soil, and the shrubby and herbaceous kinds may be increased by cuttings and divisions. The annual and biennial kinds require the same treatment as other tender and hardy annuals and biennials. *Synonymes:* 1. *Filago arvensis.* 2. *F. cephaloidea.* 3. *Gnaphalium spicatum.* 4. *F. gallica.*

5. *germanica.* 6. *alpestris.* 7. *Lagopus.* 8. *montana.* 9. *G. spatulata.* 10. *F. pusilla.* 11. *pyramidala.* 12. *recta.* 13. *sphærica.* 14. *G. alpinum.* 15. *F. sylvatica.* 16. *Gnaphalium multicaule.*

| | | | | |
|---|---|---|---|---|
| albescens | White | 8. Ev. 8. Jamaica | 1793 |
| involucratum | Br. yel. | 7, H. Her P. N. Zeal. | 1699 |
| obtusifolium | Yellow | 7, H. | A. N. Amer. | 1732 |
| purpureum | Purple | 7, G. | B. N. Amer. | 1732 |
| sanguineum | Crimson | 7, H. Her. B. Egypt | 1768 |
| undulatum | Yel. wht. | 7, H. | A. Africa | 1732 |

*americanum, arvense* 1, *cephaloideum* 2, *coarctatum* 3, *decurrens, gallicum* 4, *germanicum* 5, *Lagopus* 6, *luteo-album, minimum* 7, *montanum* 8, *pensylvanicum* 9, *pusillum* 10, *pyramidatum* 11, *rectum* 12, *sphæricum* 13, *supinum* 14, *sylvaticum* 15, *uliginosum* 16.

**GNETUM,** *Linn.* Derived from *gnemon;* the name given to it in the island of Ternate. *Linn.* 21, Or. 1, Nat. Or. *Gnetaceæ.* This plant will grow in sandy peat and loam mixed; it is multiplied by cuttings in sand, under a glass, in heat. In Amboyna, they eat the seeds roasted, boiled, or fried, and the tasteless green leaves form a favourite vegetable, in lieu of spinach.

| | | | | |
|---|---|---|---|---|
| Gnemon | | 8. Ev. T. E. Ind. | 1815 |

**GNIDIA,** *Linn.* The ancient name of the Laurel. *Linn.* 8, Or. 1, Nat. Or. *Thymelaceæ.* The species of *Gnidia* are very pretty, and thrive well in a peat soil, if carefully watered, in which respect they require particular attention, as they have very tender roots. They are rather difficult to propagate, particularly *G. radiata;* the shoots should be taken off when young, planted in sand, under a glass, and placed where there is not much damp. *Synonymes:* 1. *denudata.* 2. *acerosa.*

| | | | | |
|---|---|---|---|---|
| argentea | Pa. yel. | 6, G. Ev. 8. C. G. H. | 1826 |
| biflora | Pa. yel. | 6, G. Ev. 8. C. G. H. | 1800 |
| capitata | Pa. yel. | 7, G. Ev. 8. C. G. H. | 1788 |
| flava | Yellow | 6, G. Ev. 8. C. G. H. | 1825 |
| imberbis | Pa. yel. | 6, G. Ev. 8. C. G. H. | 1792 |
| imbricata, 1 | Pa. yel. | 6, G. Ev. 8. C. G. H. | 1820 |
| juniperifolia, 2 | Pa. yel. | 6, G. Ev. 8. C. G. H. | 1810 |
| lævigata | Pa. yel. | 6, G. Ev. 8. C. G. H. | 1822 |
| linoides | Pa. yel. | 6, G. Ev. 8. C. G. H. | 1824 |
| pinifolia | Pa. yel. | 6, G. Ev. 8. C. G. H. | 1768 |
| ochroleuca | Pa. yel. | 6, G. Ev. 8. C. G. H. | 1820 |
| oppositifolia | Pa. yel. | 6, G. Ev. 8. C. G. H. | 1783 |
| radiata | Pa. yel. | 6, G. Ev. 8. C. G. H. | 1818 |
| sericea | Pa. yel. | 7, G. Ev. 8. C. G. H. | 1786 |
| simplex | Pa. yel. | 6, G. Ev. 8. C. G. H. | 1786 |
| stricta | Pa. yel. | 6, G. Ev. 8. C. G. H. | 1818 |
| tomentosa | Pa. yel. | 6, G. Ev. 8. C. G H. | 1820 |

**GOAT-ROOT,** see *Ononis Natrix.*

**GOAT's-BANE,** see *Aconitum tragoctonum.*

**GOAT's-BEARD,** see *Spiræa aruncus.*

**GOAT's-FOOT,** see *Oxalis caprina.*

**GOAT's-ORIGANUM,** see *Thymus Tragoriganum.*

**GOAT's-RUE,** see *Galega.*

**GOAT's-THORN,** see *Astragalus Tragacantha.*

**GOAT's-WHEAT,** see *Tragopogrum.*

**GOATWEED,** see *Capraria biflora.*

**GODETIA.** Named by Spach, a German botanist, resident in Paris; it is probably a Latinised proper name. *Linn.* 8, Or. 1, Nat. Or. *Onagraceæ.* Very pretty annuals, well worthy of a place in every garden; they are nearly related to *Œnothera,* to which genus they may be referred for culture, &c.

| | | | | |
|---|---|---|---|---|
| lepida | Pink | 8, H. | A. Californ. | 1835 |
| rubicunda | Pa. flame | 8, H. | A. Californ. | 1835 |
| vinosa | Blush | 7, H. | A. Californ. | 1835 |

**GODOYA.** Ruiz and Pavon dedicated this genus to Emmanuel Godoy, Duke of Arcadia, and Prince of the Peace, a noble Spaniard, and a protector of botany. *Linn.* 13, Or. 1, Nat. Or. *Hypericaceæ.* This is described as an elegant tree, thriving well in a mixture of peat and loam; and cuttings, if ripened, root freely in sand, in heat, under a glass.

| | | | | |
|---|---|---|---|---|
| geminiflora | Yellow | 8. Ev. 8. Brazil | 1820 |

**GOLDBACHIA,** *Decandolle.* In honour of G. L. Goldbach, a Russian botanist, who communicated many observations on *Cruciferæ* to Decandolle. *Linn.* 15, Nat. Or. *Cruciferæ.* We know little of this plant, but it is described as ornamental, and doing well when sown in the open border, in common soil. *Synonyme:* 1. *Raphanus lævigatus.*

| | | | | |
|---|---|---|---|---|
| lævigata | Pa. yel. | 7, H. | A. Astracan | 1827 |

**GOLDEN-HAIR,** see *Chrysocoma comaurea.*

**GOLDEN-ROD,** see *Bæta.*

U

GOLDEN-ROD, see *Leóntice Chrysogònum.*
GOLDEN-ROD, see *Solidàgo.*
GOLDEN-SAXIFRAGE, see *Chrysosplènium.*
GOLDEN-THISTLE, see *Scólymus.*
GOLDEN-THISTLE, see *Protèa Scólymus.*
GOLDFÙSSIA, *Nees.* In compliment to Dr. Goldfuss, professor of natural history at Bonn upon the Rhine. *Linn.* 14, Or. 2, Nat. Or. *Acanthàceæ.* This ornamental shrub is well known in gardens under another name, *Ruellia anisophylla.* For culture and propagation, see *Ruellia. Synonyme:* 1. *Ruellia anisophylla.*

anisophýlla    .   Blue    .   7, 8. Ev. S. Silhet   .   1833

GOLD OF PLEASURE, see *Camelìna.*
GOLDYLOCKS, see *Chrysocòma.*
GOMOPETALOUS, more properly GAMOPETALOUS, mono-petalous.
GÒMPHIA, *Schreber.* From *gomphos,* a club; alluding to the shape of the fruit. *Linn.* 10, Or. 1, Nat. Or. *Ochnàceæ.* A very pretty genus of plants, from three to five feet high; they thrive in sandy loam, and young plants are obtained from cuttings in sand, in heat, under a glass. *Synonyme:* 1. *Ochna zeylanica.*

| | | | |
|---|---|---|---|
| jabotapíta   .   . | Yellow | .   8. Ev. S. Jamaica | .   1820 |
| lævigàta   .   . | Yellow | .   8. Ev. S. | .   1820 |
| laurifòlia   .   . | Yellow | .   8. Ev. S. Jamaica | .   1823 |
| nítida   .   . | Yellow | .   8. Ev. S. Jamaica | .   1803 |
| obtusifòlia   . | Yellow | .   8. Ev. S. Jamaica | .   1803 |
| zeylánica, 1 | Yellow | .   8. Ev. S. Ceylon | .   1823 |

GOMPHOCÁRPUS, *R. Brown.* From *gomphos,* a club, and *karpos,* a fruit; alluding to the club-shaped fruit. *Linn.* 5, Or. 2, Nat. Or. *Asclepiadàceæ.* This is a pretty Cape genus, succeeding in a mixture of loam and peat; and cuttings planted in sand, under a glass, in heat, will root freely. They are also sometimes raised from seeds. *Synonyme:* 1. *Asclepias arborescens.*

| | | | |
|---|---|---|---|
| arboréscens, ]   . | White | . 12, G. Ev. S. C. G. H. | . 1714 |
| críspus   .   . | Yellow | .   7, G. Ev. S. C. G. H. | . 1714 |
| fruticòsus   .   . | White | .   7, G. Ev. S. C. G. H. | . 1714 |

GOMPHOLÒBIUM, *Smith.* From *gomphos,* a club, and *lobos,* a pod; the pod is club or wedge-shaped. *Linn.* 10, Or. 1, Nat. Or. *Leguminòsæ.* A splendid genus of New Holland plants, succeeding in sandy loam and peat; but they must be very carefully watered, or they will sicken, and die, as they are very delicate, and impatient of moisture. Cuttings take without difficulty in sand, under a glass. *Synonymes:* 1. *fimbriatum.* 2. *fimbriatum.*

| | | | |
|---|---|---|---|
| barbigérum, 1   . | Yellow | .   6, G. Ev. S. N. Holl. | . 1824 |
| capitàtum   .   . | Yellow | .   7, G. Ev. S. N. Holl. | . 1830 |
| glabràtum   .   . | Yellow | .   6, G. Ev. S. N. Holl. | . 1820 |
| glaucéscens   . | Yellow | .   6, G. Ev. S. N. Holl. | . 1824 |
| grandiflòrum   . | Yellow | .   6, G. Ev. S. N. S. W. | . 1803 |
|    setifòlium   . | Yellow | .   6, G. Ev. S. N. S. W. | . 1826 |
| Knightiànum   . | Yellow | .   8, G. Ev. S. N. Holl. | . 1830 |
| lanàtum   .   . | Yellow | .   5, G. Ev. S. N. Holl. | . 1824 |
| latifòlium, 2   . | Yellow | .   5, G. Ev. S. N. S. W. | . 1803 |
| marginàtum   . | Yellow | .   5, G. Ev. S. N. Holl. | . 1820 |
| mirbelioìdes   . | Yellow | .   5, G. Ev. S. N. Holl. | . 1822 |
| pedunculàre   . | Yellow | .   5, G. B. N. Holl. | . 1824 |
| pinnàtum   .   . | Yellow | .   5, G. B. N. Holl. | . 1820 |
| polymórphum   . | Yellow | .   6, G. Ev. S. N. Holl. | . 1803 |
| reticulàtum   . | Yellow | .   5, G. Ev. S. N. Holl. | . 1824 |
| tenéllum   .   . | Yellow | .   5, G. Ev. S. N. Holl. | . 1824 |
| tetrathecoìdes   . | Yellow | .   5, G. Ev. S. N. Holl. | . 1824 |
| tomentòsum   . | Yellow | .   5, G. Ev. S. N. Holl. | . 1803 |
| venulòsum   . | Purple | .   6, G. Ev. S. N. Holl. | . 1830 |
| venústum   .   . | Yellow | .   5, G. Ev. S. N. Holl. | . 1803 |
| virgàtum   .   . | Yellow | .   5, G. Ev. S. N. Holl. | . 1820 |

GOMPHONÈMA, *Agardh.* From *gomphos,* a club, and *nema,* a filament; filaments wedge-shaped. *Linn.* 24, Or. 7, Nat. Or. *Algæ.* Minute plants, of a yellowish colour, found in lakes and alpine rivulets—*geminàtum, minutíssimum, paradóxum.*
GOMPHRÈNA, *Linn.* From *gomphos,* a club; alluding to the shape of the flowers. *Linn.* 5, Or. 1, Nat. Or. *Amarantàceæ.* The Globe Amaranth, which is the type of this genus, is well known for its round heads of purple and white flowers. They will succeed in rich mould; but to grow them very fine, they require a great deal of attention to shifting, watering, &c.; they all increase from seeds, and the shrubby kinds from cuttings also.

| | | | |
|---|---|---|---|
| amaranthoìdes   . | White | .   8, S. B. E. Ind. | . 1820 |
| arboréscens   . | White | .   9, G. Ev. S. S. Amer. | . 1802 |
| decúmbens   . | Purple | .   7, S. B. Mexico | . 1826 |
| globòsa   .   . | Red | .   7, S. A. India | . 1714 |

| | | | | |
|---|---|---|---|---|
| albà   .   .   . | White | .   7, 8. | A. India | . 1714 |
| láctea   .   . | White | .   7, 8. Ev. S. S. Amer. | | . 1823 |
| lanàta   .   . | White | .   7, G. | B. N. Holl. | . 1824 |
| perénnis   . | Pa. yel. | .   8, S. Her. P. S. Amer. | | . 1732 |

GÒMPHUS, *Fries.* From *gomphos,* a club; in reference to the shape of the plants. *Linn.* 24, Or. 9, Nat. Or. *Fungi.* Small species, found in pine woods during the summer and autumn months—*glutinòsus, rútilus.*
GOMÙTUS, *Rumphius.* Its name in Malabar. *Linn.* 21, Or. 9, Nat. Or. *Palmàceæ.* This is a fine palm, described as growing upwards of forty feet high; it requires a strong heat, and rich mould, and can only be increased by seeds.

saccharífer   .   .   .      Palm. Moluccas   .   1820

GONGÒRA, *Ruiz and Pavon.* In honour of D. Antonio Cabellero y Gongora, once Viceroy of New Granada, and a zealous patron of the celebrated Mutis. *Linn.* 20, Or. 1, Nat. Or. *Orchidàceæ.* The plants belonging to this genus are highly deserving of cultivation, as well on account of the extraordinary forms assumed by their flowers, as for their delicious perfume. For culture and propagation, see *Stanhopea.*

| | | | |
|---|---|---|---|
| atropurpùrea   . | Dk. pur. | .   6, S. Epi. Trinidad | . 1824 |
| maculàta   .   . | Yel. spot. | .   5, S. Epi. Demerara | . 1832 |

GONIOCÁRPUS, *Thunberg.* From *gonia,* an angle, and *karpos,* a fruit; in allusion to the angular fruit. *Linn.* 4, Or. 3, Nat. Or. *Onagràceæ.* This is a somewhat curious species, merely requiring to be sown in the open ground.

micránthus   .   White .   7, H.   A. China   . 1806

GONOLÒBUS, *Richard.* From *gonia,* an angle, and *lobos,* a pod; the pods are angular. *Linn.* 5, Or. 2, Nat. Or. *Asclepiadàceæ.* Pretty twining plants; the stove and greenhouse species thrive well in loam and peat, and cuttings root readily in sand, under a glass. The hardy kinds grow best in a warm dryish situation, in any light soil, or in peat; they are increased by divisions, or seeds. *Synonymes:* 1. *G. hirsutus.* 2. *Cynanchum discolor.* 3. *C. maritimum.* 4. *Gonolobus viridiflorus.*

| | | | |
|---|---|---|---|
| carolinénsis, 1   . | Purple | .   7, G. De. Tw. Carolina | . 1824 |
| crispiflòrus   . | Wht. grn. | .   8, S. De. Tw. S. Amer. | . 1741 |
| diademàtus   . | Green | .   9, S. Ev. Tw. Mexico | . 1819 |
| discôlor, 2   .   . | Green | .   7, H. De. Tw. N. Amer. | . 1809 |
| echinàtus   .   . | | .   8, S. Ev. Tw. | |
| grandiflòrus   . | Green | .   7, S. De. Tw. Trinidad | . 1826 |
| hirsùtus   .   . | Purple | .   6, H. De. Tw. N. Amer. | . 1806 |
| lævis   .   . | Purple | .   7, H. De. Tw. N. Amer. | . 1806 |
| macrophýllus   . | Yellow | .   7, H. De. Tw. N. Amer. | . 1822 |
| marítimus, 3   . | Green | .   6, S. Ev. Tw. Carthage | . 1823 |
| niger   .   .   . | Dk. pur. | . 10, S. Ev. Tw. Mexico | . 1825 |
| Nuttaliànus, 4   . | Green | .   7, H. De. Tw. Mississippi | . 1822 |
| oblìquus   .   . | | .   7, H. De. Tw. Carolina | . 1818 |
| planiflòrus   . | Green | .   7, S. Ev. Tw. Trinidad | . 1818 |
| prostràtus   . | Green | .   7, S. De. Tr. Mexico | . 1823 |
| racemòsus   . | White | .   7, S. Ev. Tw. Caracas | . 1823 |
| rostràtus   .   . | | .   8, S. Ev. Tw. Trinidad | . 1824 |
| suberòsus   .   . | Green | .   8, S. Ev. Tw. N. America | . 1732 |
| uniflòrus   .   . | White | .   8, S. De. Tw. Mexico | . 1825 |
| viridiflòrus   . | Green | .   9, S. Ev. Tw. S. Amer. | . 1826 |

GONIOSTÈMON, *Haworth.* From *gonia,* an angle, and *stemon,* a stamen; alluding to the shape of the stamens. *Linn.* 5, Or. 2, Nat. Or. *Asclepiadàceæ.* This is a genus of curious succulent plants, nearly related to *Stapelia*; which genus see for culture and propagation. *Synonyme:* 1. *Stapelia divaricata.*

| | | | |
|---|---|---|---|
| divaricàtus, 1   . | Flesh | .   8, S. Ev. S. C. G. H. | . 1793 |
| pallidus   .   . | Pa. blue | .   8, S. Ev. S. C. G. H. | . 1818 |
| strictus   .   . | Pa. blue | .   8, S. Ev. S. C. G. H. | . 1814 |

GOODÈNIA. Named by Smith in honour of Dr. Goodenough, Bishop of Carlisle, and a botanical author. *Linn.* 5, Or. 2, Nat. Or. *Goodeniàceæ.* A very elegant genus of plants, requiring to be grown in a mixture of peat and loam; and young plants are freely obtained from cuttings in sand, under a glass; they are also raised from seeds.

| | | | |
|---|---|---|---|
| bellidifòlia   . | Yellow | .   7, G. Her. P. N. Holl. | . 1823 |
| grácilis   .   . | Yellow | .   7, G. Her. P. N. Holl. | . 1822 |
| grandiflòra   . | Yellow | .   7, G. Ev. P. N. S. W. | . 1803 |
| hederàcea   . | Yellow | .   7, G. Ev. S. N. Holl. | . 1813 |
| heterophýlla   . | Pa. red | .   7, G. Ev. S. N. Holl. | . 1826 |
| ovàta   .   . | Yellow | .   7, G. Ev. S. N. S. W. | . 1793 |
| paniculàta   . | Yellow | .   7, G. Her. P. N. Holl. | . 1823 |

GOOD HENRY, see *Chenopòdium Bònus-Henrìcus.*
GOODÌA, *Salisbury.* In honour of Peter Good, a collector of seeds in New Holland for the botanic

garden at Kew. *Linn.* 16, Or. 6, Nat. Or. *Leguminosæ.* This is a very elegant genus of little shrubs, succeeding in a mixture of loam and peat; and young cuttings root freely in sand, under a glass. They may be raised from seeds, which generally ripen in abundance.

| | | | | |
|---|---|---|---|---|
| latifolia . . . . | Yellow | . 6, G. Ev. 8. V. D. L. | . 1793 |
| p-lyspermă . | Yellow | . 6, G. Ev. 8. V. D. L. | . 1790 |
| pubéscena . . | Yellow | . 6, G. Ev. 8. V. D. L. | . 1805 |

GOOD-NIGHT, see *Argyreiă bōnd-nōx.*

GOODYĒRĂ, *R. Brown.* In honour of John Goodyer, a British botanist. *Linn.* 20, Or. 1, Nat. Or. *Orchidaceæ.* These are rather pretty free-flowering plants. The stove kinds do best in sandy peat, mixed with a little leaf-mould. The hardy kinds do best in sandy peat, and are readily increased by divisions of the roots. *Synonyme:* 1. *Neottia repens.*

| | | | |
|---|---|---|---|
| di-cŏlŏr . . . . | White | . 11, 8. Ter. 8. Amer. | . 1815 |
| procērā . . | White | . 6, 8. Ter. Nepal | . 1821 |
| pubéscens . . | White | . 7. H. Ter. N. Amer. | . 1802 |
| rēpěns, 1 . | White | . 7. H. Ter. Scotland | . |
| tessellătă . . | White | . 7. H. Ter. N. Amer. | . 1821 |

GOOSEBERRY, see *Rībĕs Grossulārĭă.*
GOOSE-CORN, see *Jūncŭs squamōsŭs.*
GOOSE-FOOT, see *Chenŏpŏdĭŭm.*
GOOSE-FOOT, see *Aspalāthŭs Chenŏpŏdă.*
GOOSE-TANSY, see *Potentīllă Anserīnă.*

GORDŌNĬĂ, *Ellis.* In honour of Alexander Gordon, a celebrated nurseryman at Mile End, London, who lived in the time of Miller. *Linn.* 16, Or. 8, Nat. Or. *Ternstromiaceæ.* This is a genus of elegant plants, well deserving of extensive cultivation on account of their large and beautiful flowers. The plants are hardy enough to stand our British winters in the open air, yet the young shoots often get injured, owing to the shortness of our summer not suffering them to ripen the wood, or even to flower in perfection; they should therefore be treated as greenhouse plants. The best soil for them is peat, mixed with a little loam; they are readily increased by layers, or cuttings in sand, under a glass. *G. Hæmatoxylon* requires to be grown in the stove; and cuttings of the ripened wood will root in sand, under a glass, in heat. *Synonyme:* 1. *Lacathea florida.*

| | | | |
|---|---|---|---|
| Franklinĭ . . | White | . 9, H. De. 8. N. Amer. | . 1774 |
| Hæmatŏxylŏn . | White | . 8. Ev. T. Jamaica | . 1820 |
| Lasiānthŭs . | Yellow | . 9, H. De. 8. N. Amer. | . 1739 |
| pubéscens, 1 . | White | . 7. H. De. 8. Carolina | . 1774 |

GORTĒRĬĂ, *Linn.* In honour of David Gorter, a Dutch professor of botany at Hardewych. *Linn.* 19, Or. 3, Nat. Or. *Compositæ.* This is a dwarf Cape plant, of little beauty and easy culture.

| | | | |
|---|---|---|---|
| personātă . . | Yellow | . 8, G. A. C. G. H. | . 1774 |

GOSSÝPĬŬM, *Linn.* From *gos,* or *gothn,* an Arabic word, signifying a soft substance; whence the Latin and English name of the genus. The name of the Cotton-tree in Egypt is *Gotnenssigtar.* *Linn.* 16, Or. 8, Nat. Or. *Malvaceæ.* This is a highly valuable genus of plants, especially the species *barbadense* and *herbaceum,* the former being extensively cultivated in the West Indies, and the latter in the South of Europe. A light rich soil and a moist heat suit all the species best. Cuttings of the shrubby kinds, if not too ripe, will root freely in a light soil, under a glass; they may also be increased by seeds. The annual and biennial species should be sown in pots in spring, and placed in heat, and when the plants are of sufficient size, they should be planted singly into small pots, and shifted as they grow.

| | | | | |
|---|---|---|---|---|
| acuminātŭm . . | Yellow | . 7, 8. Ev. 8. E. Ind. | . 1822 |
| arbŏrĕŭm . . | Yellow | . 7, 8. Ev. T. E. Ind. | . 1694 |
| barbadénsĕ . . | Yellow | . 9, 8. B. Barbadoes | . 1759 |
| herbăcĕŭm . . | Yellow | . 7, 8. A. E. Ind. | . 1594 |
| hirsŭtŭm . . | Yellow | . 7, G. B. S. Amer. | . 1731 |
| Indĭcŭm . . | Yellow | . 8, 8. B. E. Ind. | . 1800 |
| latifŏlĭŭm . . | Yellow | . 7, 8. Ev. 8. | . 1800 |
| micrānthŭm . . | Yellow | . 7, 8. B. Persia | . 1820 |
| obtusifŏlĭŭm . . | Yellow | . 7, 8. Ev. 8. E. Ind. | . |
| religiŏsŭm . . | Yellow | . 7, 6. Her. P. India | . 1777 |
| vitifŏlĭŭm . . | Yellow | . 7, 8. A. E. Ind. | . 1805 |

GOUĂNĬĂ, *Linn.* In honour of Anthony Gouan, once professor of botany at Montpelier, and author of the Hortus Monspeliensis. *Linn.* 23, Or. 2, Nat. Or. *Ranunculaceæ.* Interesting evergreen climbers,

growing about ten feet high, and succeeding well in a mixture of peat and loam; cuttings root freely in sand, under a glass, in heat

| | | | | |
|---|---|---|---|---|
| cordifŏlĭa . . | Yellow | . 8. Ev. Cl. Rio Jan. | . 1820 |
| domingēnsĭa . . | Yellow | . 8. Ev. Cl. W. Ind. | . 1739 |
| integrifŏlĭă . . | Grn. yel. | . 8. Ev. Cl. | . 1800 |
| mauritĭāna . . | Grn. yel. | . 8. Ev. Cl. Mauritius | . 1823 |
| tilimfŏlĭa . . | Yellow | . 7, 8. Ev. Cl. E. Ind. | . 1810 |
| tomentŏsă . . | Grn. yel. | . 8. Ev. Cl. W. Ind. | . 1823 |

GOURD, see *Cucūrbĭtă.*
GOUTWEED, see *Ægopŏdĭŭm.*

GOWĒNĬĂ, *Lindley.* In compliment to J. R. Gowen, Esq., the originator of some splendid hybrid *Rhododendrons,* &c., at Highclere. *Linn.* 20, Or. 1, Nat. Or. *Orchidaceæ.* These are two remarkably handsome plants when in flower. For culture and propagation, see *Bletia.*

| | | | |
|---|---|---|---|
| liliācĕă . . . | White | . 7, 8. Ter. Mexico | . . |
| supērbă . . | Yellow | . 3, 8. Ter. Xalapa | . 1828 |

GRABŌWSKĬĂ. Schlechtendahl named this genus in compliment to Mr. H. Grabowsky, an apothecary, and a botanical author of Ohlaf, in Silesia. *Linn.* 5, Or. 1, Nat. Or. *Solanaceæ.* A curious spiny, scrambling shrub, in appearance much like *Atriplex Halimus.* It is said to be sufficiently hardy to stand our winters when planted against a south wall. The soil best suited for it is a mixture of peat and loam, and it may be increased from cuttings without any difficulty. *Synonymes:* 1. *Lycium boerhaaviæfolium, Ehretia halamifolia.*

| | | | |
|---|---|---|---|
| boerhaaviæfŏlĭă . | Pa. pur. | . 4, H. Ev. 8. Peru | . . 1780 |

GRAIN-OF-PARADISE, see *Amōmŭm Grānd-Parādĭsĭ.*

GRAMMĂNTHĒS, *Decandolle.* From *gramma,* a writing, and *anthos,* a flower; on account of the segments of the corolla having the appearance of the letter V on them. *Linn.* 5, Or. 5, Nat. Or. *Crassulaceæ.* The seeds of this pretty little succulent plant should be thinly sown in carefully drained pots, filled with loam and a little lime rubbish mixed. *Synonymes: Vauanthes chloraflora, Crassula dichotoma.*

| | | | |
|---|---|---|---|
| chloræflŏră . . | Yellow | . 7, 8. A. C. G. H. | . 1774 |

GRAMMATOPHÝLLŬM, *Blume.* Name unexplained. *Linn.* 20, Or. 1, Nat. Or. *Orchidaceæ.* This is a fine species, but very rare in collections. It appears to grow well in a hot part of the house, treated the same as the genus *Stanhopea.*

| | | | |
|---|---|---|---|
| multiflŏrŭm . . . | | 8. Epl. Manilla | . 1837 |

GRĂNGĒĬĂ, *Adanson.* Probably after Grange, some person known to Adanson. *Linn.* 19, Or. 1, Nat. Or. *Compositæ.* Annuals of little beauty; they may be sown in the open border, or raised on a gentle hotbed, and transplanted. *Synonymes:* 1. *Cotula latifolia.* 2. *C. cuneifolia.*

| | | | |
|---|---|---|---|
| cinĕrĕă . . . | Yellow | . 7, H. A. Egypt | . 1818 |
| decŭmbĕns . . | Yellow | . 7, H. A. N. Holl. | . 1816 |
| ranchifŏlĭă . . | Yellow | . 7, H. A. Caucasus | . 1821 |

bicŏlŏr 1, chinēnsĭs 2, maderaspatānă, minĭmă.

GRANGĒRĬĂ. Commerson dedicated this genus to N. Granger, a traveller in Egypt and Persia. *Linn.* 11, Or. 1, Nat. Or. *Chrysobalanaceæ.* A stove plant, described as ornamental, and succeeding in peat and loam; it is increased from cuttings.

| | | | |
|---|---|---|---|
| borbŏnĭeă . . . | White | . 8. Ev. T. Bourbon | . 1823 |

GRANIFORM, formed like grains of corn.
GRANULAR, } covered, as if with grains.
GRANULATED, }
GRANULIFEROUS, bearing grains.
GRAPE, see *Vitis vinifera.*
GRAPE-HYACINTH, see *Muscārĭ.*
GRAPE-PEAR, see *Amelānchĭĕr Botrýăpĭŭm.*

GRĂPHĬS, *Acharius.* From *grapho,* to write; in reference to the apothecia being like writing. *Linn.* 24, Or. 8, Nat. Or. *Lichenes.* Species found at all seasons of the year, chiefly on the bark of trees—dendrĭtĭcă, ĕlĕgăns, hyĕllĭ, scrīptă, S. cĕrăsĭ, S. pulverulēntă, serpentīnă.

GRASS-OF-PARNASSUS, see *Parnāssĭă.*

GRĂTĬŎLĂ, *Linn.* From *gratia,* grace of God; on account of its supposed medicinal virtues. *Linn.* 2, Or. 1, Nat. Or. *Scrophulariaceæ.* Some species of this genus are very pretty free-flowering plants, thriving well in any rich moist soil, and are readily multiplied by divisions of the roots. The leaves and roots of *G. officinalis* act as purgatives and emetics.

| | | | | | | | |
|---|---|---|---|---|---|---|---|
| aūrĕa | . . . | . Yellow | . 6, H. Her. | P. N. Amer. | . 1820 |
| latifolia | . . . | . White | . 7, G. Her. | P. N. Holl. | . 1822 |
| officinalis | . . . | . Lgt. blue | . 7, H. Her. | P. Europe | . 1568 |
| quadridentata | . . . | . White | . 6, H. Her. | P. N. Amer. | . 1821 |
| tetragóna | . . . | . Blue | . 8, F. Her. | P. B. Ayres | . 1830 |
| virginĕa | . . . | . Yellow | . 8, H. Her. | P. Virginia | . 1759 |

GRĀTŭs, grateful, agreeable.
GRAVĕŏLĕNs, strongly-scented.
GREAT BURNET, see *Sanguisŏrbă*.
GREAT CENTAURRA, see *Centaūrĕā Centaūrĭum*.
GREAT MACAW TREE, see *Acrocŏmĭă fusĭfŏrmĭs*.
GREEK VALERIAN, see *Polemōnĭum*.
GREEN DRAGON, see *Arūm Dracōntĭum*.
GREENISH-GLAUCOUS, between a grey and green colour.
GREEN LAVER, see *Ulvă Lactūcă*.
GREGARIOUS, herding together.
GREVĬLLĔă, *R. Brown*. In honour of C. F. Greville, a patron of botany. *Linn.* 4, Or. 1, Nat. Or. *Proteaceæ*. This is a handsome genus of New Holland plants, which require to be grown in an equal mixture of sand, loam, and peat; and ripened cuttings root without difficulty in sand, under a glass. Seed is frequently produced by some of the species, by which young plants may also be obtained. *Synonymes:* 1. *blechnifolia.* 2. *concinna.*

| | | | | | | |
|---|---|---|---|---|---|---|
| acanthifōlĭā | . . | . Purple | . 6, G. Ev. S. | N. S. W. | . 1824 |
| acuminātā | . . | . Red | . 6, G. Ev. S. | N. S. W. | . 1805 |
| arenārĭă | . . | . Pink | . 6, G. Ev. S. | N. S. W. | . 1803 |
| aspĕrā | . . | . Pink | . 6, G. Ev. S. | N. S. W. | . 1824 |
| asplenifōlĭā | . . | . Pink | . 7, G. Ev. S. | N. S. W. | . 1806 |
| Bauĕrĭ | . . | . Red | . 6, G. Ev. S. | N. Holl. | . 1824 |
| berberifōlĭā | . . | . Red | . 6, G. Ev. S. | N. S. W. | . 1821 |
| buxifōlĭā | . . | . Pink | . 6, G. Ev. S. | N. S. W. | . 1790 |
| Caleyĭ, 1 | . . | . Red | . 6, G. Ev. S. | Moreton B. | . 1830 |
| canĕscĕns | . . | . Gn. taw. | . G. Ev. S. | Pt. Jack. | . 1824 |
| cinĕrĕă | . . | . Red | . 6, G. Ev. S. | N. Holl. | . 1822 |
| collīnă | . . | . Pink | . 6, G. Ev. S. | N. S. W. | . 1812 |
| concīnnā | . . | . Purple | . 6, G. Ev. S. | N. S. W. | . 1824 |
| dūbĭă | . . | . Violet | . 6, G. Ev. S. | N. S. W. | . 1820 |
| Flindĕrsĭĭ | . . | . Purple | . 6, G. Ev. S. | N. S. W. | . 1824 |
| heterophyllă | . . | . White | . 6, G. Ev. S. | N. Holl. | . 1821 |
| juniperīnă | . . | . Pink | . 6, G. Ev. S. | N. S. W. | . 1822 |
| linearis | . . | . White | . 6, G. Ev. S. | N. S. W. | . 1790 |
| albă | . . | . White | . 6, G. Ev. S. | N. Holl. | . 1790 |
| incarnātă | . . | . Flesh | . 6, G. Ev. S. | N. S. W. | . 1790 |
| montānă | . . | . Violet | . 6, G. Ev. S. | N. S. W. | . 1822 |
| mucronifōlĭā | . . | . Violet | . 6, G. Ev. S. | N. S. W. | . 1824 |
| mucronulātă | . . | . Pink | . 6, G. Ev. S. | N. S. W. | . 1809 |
| phyllicoīdĕs | . . | . Red | . 6, G. Ev. S. | N. Holl. | . 1823 |
| planifōlĭā, 2 | . . | . Orange | . 6, G. Ev. S. | N. Holl. | . 1822 |
| podalyriæfōlĭā | . . | . Red | . 6, G. Ev. S. | N. Holl. | . 1821 |
| podocarpifōlĭā | . . | . Red | . 6, G. Ev. S. | N. Holl. | . 1824 |
| pubĕscĕns | . . | . Red | . 6, G. Ev. S. | N. Holl. | . 1822 |
| punīcĕă | . . | . Purple | . 6, G. Ev. S. | N. Holl. | . 1822 |
| ripārĭă | . . | . Pink | . 6, G. Ev. S. | N. S. W. | . 1791 |
| robūstă | . . | . Orange | . 6, G. Ev. T. | Pt. Jack. | . 1829 |
| rosmarinifōlĭā | . . | . Red | . 6, G. Ev. S. | N. S. W. | . 1824 |
| sericĕă | . . | . Pink | . 6, G. Ev. S. | N. S. W. | . 1790 |
| strictă | . . | . Pink | . 6, G. Ev. S. | N. S. W. | . 1820 |
| stylōsă | . . | . Red | . 6, G. Ev. S. | N. S. W. | . 1809 |
| sulphūrĕă | . . | . Pa. yel. | . 6, G. Ev. S. | N. S. W. | . 1824 |
| trifurcātă | . . | . Red | . 6, G. Ev. S. | N. Holl. | . 1821 |

GRĔWĬă, *Jussieu*. In honour of Nehemiah Grew, M.D., F.R.S., a famous English vegetable physiologist, who died in 1711. *Linn.* 13, Or. 1, Nat. Or. *Tiliaceæ*. These are shrubs, with elm-looking leaves, but not possessed of any great beauty; they succeed in sandy loam and peat, and cuttings root in sand, under a glass, in heat. The fruit of *G. asiatica* is acrid and pleasant; it is much used in the manufacture of sherbet. *Synonymes:* 1. *Mallococca crenata.* 2. *G. hirsuta.*

| | | | | | | |
|---|---|---|---|---|---|---|
| affīnĭs | . . . | . Green | . | 8, Ev. S. | China | . 1824 |
| asiātĭcă | . . . | . Purple | . 7, | 8, Ev. S. | E. Ind. | . 1792 |
| aspĕrā | . . . | . White | . | 8, Ev. S. | E. Ind. | . 1818 |
| bicolŏr | . . . | . White | . | 8, Ev. S. | Guinea | . 1818 |
| bracteātă | . . . | . Purple | . 6, | 8, Ev. S. | E. Ind. | . 1820 |
| carpinifōlĭā | . . . | . White | . | 8, Ev. S. | Guinea | . 1823 |
| flāvă | . . . | . Yellow | . | 8, Ev. S. | C. G. H. | . 1819 |
| hirsūtă | . . . | . Purple | . | 8, Ev. S. | E. Ind. | . 1816 |
| Mallocōccă, 1 | . . . | . Pa. pur. | . | 8, Ev. S. | E. Ind. | . 1792 |
| Mĭcrŏcŏs | . . . | . Green | . | 8, Ev. S. | E. Ind. | . 1799 |
| obtusifōlĭā | . . . | . Red | . | 8, Ev. S. | C. G. H. | . 1818 |
| occidentalis | . . . | . Purple | . 8, | G. Ev. S. | C. G. H. | . 1690 |
| oppositifōlĭā | . . . | . Purple | . | 8, Ev. S. | Nepal | . 1818 |
| orientalis | . . . | . Purple | . 7, | S. Ev. S. | E. Ind. | . 1767 |
| ovalifōlĭā | . . . | . White | . 8, | S. Ev. S. | E. Ind. | . 1818 |
| paniculātă | . . . | . White | . | S. Ev. S. | E. Ind. | . 1816 |
| pilōsă | . . . | . White | . | 8, Ev. S. | E. Ind. | . 1804 |
| Rŏthĭĭ | . . . | . White | . | 8, Ev. S. | E. Ind. | . 1819 |
| salvifōlĭā | . . . | . White | . 8, | S. Ev. S. | E. Ind. | . 1818 |

| | | | | | | |
|---|---|---|---|---|---|---|
| serrulātă | . . | . White | . 8, | S. Ev. S. | E. Ind. | . 1818 |
| subinæqualĭs | . . | . White | . 8, | S. Ev. S. | E. Ind. | . 1816 |
| terebinthĭnacĕă | . . | . White | . | G. Ev. S. | | . 1820 |
| tiliæfōlĭā | . . | . White | . | S. Ev. S. | E. Ind. | . 1812 |
| tomentōsă, 2 | . . | . Purple | . | S. Ev. S. | Java | . 1820 |
| ulmifōlĭā | . . | . White | . | S. Ev. S. | E. Ind. | . 1816 |
| umbellātă | . . | . Purple | . | S. Ev. S. | E. Ind. | . 1816 |
| villōsă | . . | . White | . 8, | S. Ev. S. | E. Ind. | . 1816 |

GRĪĀs, *Linn.* From *grao*, to eat; the fruit is edible. *Linn.* 13, Or. 1, Nat. Or. *Myrtaceæ*. This is an elegant fruit-bearing tree, from thirty to fifty feet high, with leaves about three feet long, and large flowers growing out of the stem and old branches; it thrives best in a loamy soil, and large cuttings will root under a handglass, in heat. In the West Indies, the fruit is eaten under the name of *Anchovy Pear*. It is of a brown russet colour, and the size and shape of an alligator's egg. It is pickled, and eaten in the same way as the East Indian mango, and is very similar to that fruit in taste. Don says, " to grow it for fruit, it should be planted in a border, and trained near the light."

| | | | | | | |
|---|---|---|---|---|---|---|
| cauliflōră | . . . | . White | . | 8. Ev. T. | Jamaica | . 1768 |

GRIĒLŭM, *Linn.* From *grielum*, old, grey; hoary aspect of the plants. *Linn.* 10, Or. 4, Nat. Or. *Rosaceæ*. Pretty Cape plants, said to thrive best in sandy gravel, with the pots well drained, as they are very impatient of water. Cuttings root with the greatest ease in the same kind of soil, with or without glasses.

| | | | | | | |
|---|---|---|---|---|---|---|
| humifūsŭm | . . | . Yellow | . 5, | G. Her. | P. C. G. H. | . 1825 |
| lacinĭātŭm | . . | . Yellow | . 8, | G. Her. | P. C. G. H. | . 1825 |
| tenuifōlĭŭm | . . | . Yellow | . 5, | G. Her. | P. C. G. H. | . 1780 |

GRIFFINĬă, *Ker*. In honour of William Griffin, Esq., of South Lambeth. *Linn.* 6, Or. 1, Nat. Or. *Amaryllidaceæ*. These are very pretty bulbous plants, which, Mr. Sweet says, " succeed best in a mixture of rather more than one-third turfy loam, a third of white sand, and the rest peat, keeping them quite dry when in a dormant state; but as soon as they begin to grow, or show bloom, they must be well supplied with water. An airy situation suits them best; they may be increased by offsets from the bulbs, or by seeds."

| | | | | | | |
|---|---|---|---|---|---|---|
| hyacinthīnă | . . | . Blue | . 7, | S. Bl. | P. S. Amer. | . 1815 |
| intermedĭă | . . | . Blue | . 4, | S. Bl. | P. Brazil | . 1823 |
| parviflōră | . . | . Pa. pur. | . 8, | S. Bl. | P. S. Amer. | . 1815 |

GRIFFITHSĬă, *Agardh*. In honour of Mrs. Griffiths, of Devonshire, who has made many discoveries in marine vegetation. *Linn.* 24, Or. 7, Nat. Or. *Algæ*. Small, red-coloured species, found on the sea shore most plentiful in summer—*barbātā, corallīnă, equisetifōlĭā, multifĭdă, setācĕă.*

GRIMMĬă, *Hedwig*. In honour of J. F. Grimm, a German botanist. *Linn.* 24, Or. 5, Nat. Or. *Musci*. Small plants, growing in roundish tufts. *G. pulvinata* is very common on the tops of old walls and houses; it forms little cushion-like, brownish-green tufts, or lumps. *Synonyme:* 1. *Dicranum ovale—apocărpă, nigra-virĭdĭs, strictă, Donĭānă, leucophæă, maritīmă, ovātă* 1, *pulvinātă, saxicŏlă, spirālĭs, torquātă, trichophỹllă, unicolŏr.*

GRINDĔLĬă, *Willdenow*. Named after Grindel, a German botanist. *Linn.* 19, Or. 2, Nat. Or. *Compositæ*. Elegant plants, with very neat foliage and yellow flowers; they succeed without difficulty in loam and peat, and readily increase from cuttings in sand, under a glass. *Synonymes:* 1. *Donia ciliata.* 2. *G. angustifolia.* 3. *Donia glutinosa.* 4. *D. squarrosa.*

| | | | | | | |
|---|---|---|---|---|---|---|
| angustifōlĭă | . . | . Yellow | . 8, | G. Her. | P. Mexico | . 1822 |
| ciliātă, 1 | . . | . Yellow | . 8, | H. | B. N. Amer. | . 1821 |
| coronopifōlĭă | . . | . Yellow | . 8, | G. Ev. | S. Mexico | . 1826 |
| Duvalĭĭ, 2 | . . | . Yellow | . 8, | G. Ev. | S. Mexico | . 1829 |
| glutinōsă, 3 | . . | . Yellow | . | G. Ev. | S. Mexico | . 1803 |
| inuloīdĕs | . . | . Yellow | . 8, | G. Ev. | S. Mexico | . 1815 |
| Lambĕrtĭĭ | . . | . Yellow | . 8, | G. Ev. | S. Mexico | . 1816 |
| spatulātă | . . | . Yellow | . 8, | G. Ev. | S. Mexico | . 1819 |
| squarrōsă, 4 | . . | . Yellow | . 8, | H. | P. Missouri | . 1811 |

GRISLĔă, *Linn.* In honour of G. Grisley, a Portuguese surgeon, and botanical author. *Linn.* 8, Or. 1, Nat. Or. *Lythraceæ*. Interesting stove shrubs, thriving best in a mixture of sandy peat and loam, and increased by cuttings in sand, under a glass, in heat.

| | | | | | | |
|---|---|---|---|---|---|---|
| secūndă | . . . | . | . | S. Ev. S. | Cumana | . 1820 |
| tomentōsă | . . . | . Red | . 6, | S. Ev. S. | E. Ind. | . 1804 |

GRŏNȲĬ, *Lindley*. Named in honour of Lord Grey, of Groby, a munificent patron of horticulture, and a most zealous cultivator of orchidaceous epiphytes. He died in 1836. *Linn.* 20, Or. 1, Nat. Or. *Orchidaceæ*. This is a very curious and pretty species, nearly allied to *Cymbidium*. The flowers are pale ochre colour, beautifully spotted with purple, and are produced on a pendulous raceme. For culture and propagation, see *Stanhopea*.

Ambŏretĭ  .  .  .  Ochre spot. 9, S. Epi. Brasil  .  1829

GROMWELL, see *Lithospĕrmŭm*.

GRONŏVĬĬ, *Linn.* In honour of J. F. Gronovius, a botanist of Leyden. *Linn.* 5, Or. 1, Nat. Or. *Loasaceæ*. Plants of little beauty, and easy cultivation; they are increased by seeds.

Humboldtĭānă  .  Yellow  .  7, S. Cl. B. S. Amer.  .  1820
scándĕns  .  .  .  Grn. yel.  .  6, S. Cl. B. Jamaica  .  1731

GROOVED, furrowed, channelled, marked with grooves.

GRŏSsŭM, thick, fat.

GROUND-CHERRY, see *Cĕrăsŭs Chamæcĕrăsŭs*.

GROUND-CISTUS, see *Rhododĕndrŏn Chamæcistŭs*.

GROUND-CRISTA, see *Căssĭă Chamæcrĭstă*.

GROUND-CYPRESS, see *Santŏlĭnă Chamæcyparĭssŭs*.

GROUND-IVY, see *Glechŏmă*.

GROUND-PINE, see *Ajŭgă Chamæpĭtȳs*.

GROUNDSEL, see *Senĕcĭŏ*.

GROUNDNEL, see *Hyoscȳămŭs Senecĭŏnĭs*.

GROVE-DOCK, see *Rŭmĕx Nemolapăthŭm*.

GRUMOSE, clubbed, knotted.

GRȲLLŭS, a cricket.

GUAĬ̆CUM, *Linn.* Guaiac is the South American name of the tree. *Linn.* 10, Or. 1, Nat. Or. *Zygophyllaceæ*. Lofty, ornamental-growing trees, cultivated in rich loam; ripened cuttings, taken off at a joint, will root in sand, under a glass, in heat; but great care must be taken not to break the fibres when the cuttings are rooted, as they are very brittle. The species are well known for their exciting properties. The bark and wood of *G. officinale* is bitter and acrid, and is chiefly used in sudorifics, diaphoretics, or alteratives. *Synonyme:* 1. *Zygophyllum arboreum*.

arbŏreŭm, 1  .  Blue  .    S. Ev. T. Trinidad  .  1816
officinale  .  .  Blue  .  8, S. Ev. T. W. Ind.  .  1694
verticale  .  .  Blue  .    S. Ev. T. W. Ind.  .  1820

GUĬ̆RĔĬ, *Linn.* From *Guara*, the name given to one of the species by the natives of Cuba. *Linn.* 8, Or. 1, Nat. Or. *Meliaceæ*. These are tall-growing trees; the soil best adapted to them is loam, mixed with a little sand; and cuttings of the ripened wood, with the leaves not shortened, will root in sand, in heat, under a glass. *Synonymes:* 1. *trichilioides*. 2. *trichilioides*.

grandiflŏră, 1  .  White  .  6, S. Ev. T. S. Amer.  .  1752
ramiflŏră  .  .  White  .    S. Ev. T. Porto Rico.  1824
Swartzĭĭ, 2  .  .  White  .  6, S. Ev. T. Jamaica  .  1818

GUATTĔRĬĬ, *Ruiz and Pavon.* In honour of John Baptiste Guatteri, an Italian botanist, and once professor at Parma. *Linn.* 13, Or. 6, Nat. Or. *Anonaceæ*. This is a splendid genus of plants, succeeding in a mixture of loam, peat, and sand. Young plants are readily obtained by cuttings planted in sand, under a glass, in heat. *Synonyme:* 1. *Uvaria lanceolata*.

cerasoĭdĕs  .  .  Green  .    S. Ev. S. E. Ind.  .  1820
laurifŏlĭă  .  .  White  .    S. Ev. S. Jamaica  .  1818
rūfă  .  .  .  .  Brown  .  7, S. Ev. S. China  .  1822
suberŏsă  .  .  .  White  .    S. Ev. S. E. Ind.  .  1820
virgătă, 1  .  .  White  .    S. Ev. T. Jamaica  .  1793

GUAVA, see *Psĭdĭŭm*.

GUAZŭMĬ, *Plumier.* The name of the plant in Mexico. *Linn.* 18, Or. 1, Nat. Or. *Sterculiaceæ*. These are ornamental trees, described as growing from twenty to forty feet high; they thrive in a mixture of peat and loam, and increase from cuttings in sand, or soil, under a glass, in heat. *Synonymes:* 1. *Bubroma guazuma, Theobroma guazuma*. 2. *Bubroma polybotryum*.

polybŏtrȳă, 2  .  .         S. Ev. T. Brasil  .  1816
tomentŏsă  .  .         S. Ev. T. Cumana  .  1820
ulmifŏlĭă, 1  .  Yellow  .    S. Ev. T. Jamaica  .  1739

GUELDER-ROSE, see *Vibŭrnŭm ŏpŭlŭs*.

GUERNSEY-LILY, see *Nerĭnĕ sarniĕnsĭs*.

GUETTĂRDĬ, *Ventenat.* In honour of Etienne Guettard,

a French botanist. *Linn.* 21, Or. 6, Nat. Or. *Cinchonaceæ*. Splendid trees, attaining from upwards of twenty feet high; they succeed best in peat and loam mixed; and cuttings strike in sand without any difficulty. *Synonymes:* 1. *Laugeria hirsuta.* 2. *L. lucida.* 3. *L. odorata.* 4. *Mathiola scabra.*

hirsūtă, 1  .  .  .        S. Ev. T. Peru  .  1820
lūcĭdă, 2  .  .         S. Ev. T. Jamaica  .  1818
odorātă, 3  .  .         S. Ev. T. Jamaica  .  1818
rugŏsă  .  .  .        S. Ev. T. W. Ind.  .  1793
tomentŏsă  .  .         S. Ev. T. Jamaica  .  1820
scābră, 4  .  .         S. Ev. T. W. Ind.  .  1818
speciŏsă, 4  .  .  Scarlet  .  S. Ev. T. E. Ind.  .  1771

GUILANDĬNĬ, *Jussieu.* In honour of Melchior Guilandina, of Prussia, a great traveller, and a professor of botany at Padua, who died in 1589. *Linn.* 10, Or. 1, Nat. Or. *Leguminosæ*. These are pretty stove shrubs, of easy culture in sandy peat, mixed with a little loam; and young plants are obtained either by cuttings, or by seeds, without difficulty. The native practitioners of India suppose the kernels of *G. Bonducella* to possess powerful tonic virtues.

Bŏndūc  .  .  .  Yellow  .  S. Ev. S. India  .  1640
Bonducĕllă  .  .  Yellow  .  S. Ev. S. E. Ind.  .  1700

GUINEA-PEACH, see *Sarcocĕphălŭs*.

GUINEA-PLUM, see *Parinărĭŭm excĕlsŭm*.

GULDENSTĂDTĬ, *Fischer.* In honour of J. A. Guldenstædt, a Russian naturalist. *Linn.* 17, Or. 4, Nat. Or. *Leguminosæ*. A dwarf plant, of little beauty, and very simple culture. *Synonyme:* 1. *Astragalus pauciflorus*.

pauciflŏră, 1  .  Red  .  7, H. Her. P. Siberia  .  1827

GUM-ARABIC TREE, see *Acăcĭă arăbĭcă*.

GUM-CISTUS, see *Cĭstŭs Ladanĭfĕrŭs*.

GUMMIFEROUS, producing gum.

GUM-SUCCORY, see *Chondrĭllă*.

GUM-TREE, see *Eucalȳptŭs robŭstă*.

GUNDĔLĬĬ, *Tournefort.* From Andrew Gundelscheimer, a German botanist, and first discoverer of the plant. *Linn.* 19, Or. 5, Nat. Or. *Compositæ*. A curious plant, though possessed of no great beauty; it does best in sandy peat, and is readily increased by divisions.

Tournefŏrtĭĭ  .  Lgt. grn.  .  7, H. Her. P. Levant  .  1739

GUNNĔRĬ, *Linn.* In honour of E. Gunner, Bishop of Drontheim, a good botanist. *Linn.* 2, Or. 1, Nat. Or. *Urticaceæ*. A curious Cape plant, growing best in rich mould kept moist; it is increased by divisions.

perpĕnsă  .  .  .  Purple  .  7, G. Her. P. C. G. H.  .  1688

GŬNNĬĬ, *Lindley.* In compliment to Ronald Gunn, Esq., a zealous investigator of the botany of Van Diemen's Land. *Linn.* 20, Or. 1, Nat. Or. *Orchidaceæ*. This is a curious little plant, with dingy purple flowers, succeeding well with the treatment recommended for *Burlingtonia*.

pictă  .  .  .  .  Purple  .  6, S. Epi. Sidney    1837

GUSTĂVĬĬ, Linnæus dedicated this genus to his patron Gustavus III. of Sweden, who presented a large collection of Indian plants to him. *Linn.* 16, Or. 8, Nat. Or. *Myrtaceæ*. This is a truly splendid plant, growing upwards of ten feet high; it thrives well in any rich soil, and increases from cuttings in sand, in heat, under a glass.

augŭstă  .  .  .  White  .  S. Ev. T. Guiana  .  1794

GUZMĂNNĬĬ, *Ruiz and Pavon.* In honour of A. Guzman, a naturalist. *Linn.* 6, Or. 1, Nat. Or. *Bromeliaceæ*. This is a pretty species, and will do well in any rich mould; it is increased by suckers.

tricŏlŏr  .  .  Grn. scar.  4, S. Her. P. S. Amer.  .  1820

GYMNADĔNĬĬ, *R. Brown.* From *gymnos*, naked, and *aden*, a gland; in allusion to the gland of the pollen masses. *Linn.* 20, Or. 1, Nat. Or. *Orchidaceæ*. The plants of this genus do best in sandy loam and peat, and if grown in pots, they must be well drained, and very little water given to them when not in a growing state; they are increased by divisions of the roots. *Synonymes:* 1. *Orchis conopsea.* 2. *Habenaria tridentata.*

conōpsĕă, 1  .  Purple  .  6, H. Ter. Britain  .  .
cucullātă  .  .  White  .  6, H. Ter. Podolia  .  .
odoratissĭmă  .  White  .  6, H. Ter. Switserl.  .  1824
tridentātă, 2  .  White  .  6, H. Ter. Canada  .  1820

GYMNÈMA, *R. Brown.* From *gymnos,* naked, and *nema,* a thread; in reference to the stamens. *Linn.* 5, Or. 2. Nat. Or. *Asclepiadaceæ.* Interesting stove twiners, easily cultivated in loam and peat; cuttings take in sand, in heat, under a glass. The milky juice yielded by *G. lactiferum* is used by the Cingalese for food, who also use the leaves when boiled. Indigo of excellent quality is obtained from *G. tingens.* Synonymes: 1. *Asclepias tenacissima.* 2. *A. tingens.*

| | | | | |
|---|---|---|---|---|
| lactiferum . . . | | 8. Ev. Tw. Ceylon | . 1824 |
| sylvestre . . | . Green | 8. Ev. Tw. Ceylon | . 1816 |
| tenacissimum, 1 | . Yellow | 8. Ev. Tw. E. Ind. | . 1806 |
| tingens, 2 . . | . Yellow | 7, 8. Ev. Tw. E. Ind. | . 1823 |

GYMNOCLÀDUS, *Lamarck.* From *gymnos,* naked, and *klados,* a branch; appearance of the branches. *Linn.* 22, Or. 9, Nat. Or. *Leguminosæ.* A very handsome hardy tree, growing well in open loamy soil, and is propagated by cuttings of the roots.

| | | | | |
|---|---|---|---|---|
| canadénsis . . | . White | H. De. T. Canada. | . 1748 |

GYMNOGRÀMMA, *Desfontaines.* From *gymnos,* naked, and *gramma,* writing; alluding to the naked sori. *Linn.* 24, Or. 1, Nat. Or. *Polypodiaceæ.* The species of this genus are among the most interesting of the Fern tribe, and not difficult of cultivation, growing well in a mixture of loam and peat; and young plants are obtained by divisions of the roots. Synonymes: 1. *Acrostichum calomelanos.* 2. *A. chrysophylla.* 3. *A. leptophylla.* 4. *Hemionitis pedata.* 5. *H. rufa.* 6. *H. tartarea.* 7. *Acrostichum trifoliata.*

| | | | |
|---|---|---|---|
| calomélanos, 1 | . Brown | 7, 8. Her. P. W. Ind. | . 1790 |
| chrysophylla, 2 | . Brown | 7, 8. Her. P. W. Ind. | . 1824 |
| leptophylla, 3. | . Brown | 7. H. Her. P. S. Eur. | . 1819 |
| myriophylla | . Brown | 8. Her. P. Brasil | . 1824 |
| pedata, 4 . | . Brown | 6, 8. Her. P. N. Spain | . 1822 |
| peruviana . | . Brown | 8. Her. P. Peru . | . 1822 |
| rufa, 5 . . | . Brown | 6, 8. Her. P. Jamaica | . 1793 |
| sulphúrea . | . Brown | 7, 8. Her. P. Jamaica | . 1808 |
| tartarea, 6 . | . Brown | 8, 8. Her. P. W. Ind. | . 1817 |
| tomentosa . | . Brown | 7, 8. Her. P. Brasil . | . 1831 |
| trifoliata, 7 | . Brown | 7, 8. Her. P. Jamaica | . 1810 |

GYMNOLÒMIA, *Humbt., Bonp., and Kunth.* From *gymnos,* naked, and *loma,* a border; in reference to the margin of the grains. *Linn.* 19, Or. 3, Nat. Or. *Compositæ.* An interesting genus of stove shrubs, particularly the species *maculata,* which is very pretty; they require a mixture of loam and peat, and young plants are obtained from cuttings in soil, under a glass, in heat, without difficulty. *G. maculata* is very readily increased by divisions of the roots.

| | | | | |
|---|---|---|---|---|
| connáta . . | . Yellow | 10, 8. Ev. S. Brasil | . 1821 |
| maculáta . . | . Yellow | 6, 8. Ev. S. W. Ind. | . 1821 |
| triplinérvia . | . Yellow | 10, 8. Ev. S. N. Spain | . 1825 |

GYMNOSTÀCHYS, *R. Brown.* From *gymnos,* naked, and *stachys,* a spike. *Linn.* 4, Or. 1, Nat. Or. *Acoraceæ.* This is a pretty plant, of easy culture in peat and loam, and is increased by suckers.

| | | | | |
|---|---|---|---|---|
| ánceps . . . . | | 6, G. Her. P. N. Holl. | . 1820 |

GYMNOSTÒMUM, *Hedwig.* From *gymnos,* naked, and *stoma,* a mouth; alluding to the open orifice of the theca. *Linn.* 24, Or. 4, Nat. Or. *Musci.* A numerous genus of plants, growing in tufts and patches of various colours, found at every season, and in almost every situation. Synonymes: 1. *luteolum.* 2. *stelligerum.* 3. *obtusum.* 4. *æruginosum.* 5. *paucifolium.* 6. *intermedium.* 7. *Grimmia Forsteri-æstivum* 1, *conicum, curviróstrum* 2, *Donidàum, fasciculàre, Griffithsiànum, Heîmii* 3, *lappónicum, microstòmum, ovàtum, gràcile, vulgàre, pyrifórme, rupéstre* 4, *tènue* 5, *truncàtulum* 6, *viridissimum* 7, *Wilsòni.*

GYNANDRÒPSIS, *Decandolle.* From *gyne,* a female, *aner, andros,* a male, and *opsis,* resemblance; the stamens appear as if inserted on the top of the ovary. *Linn.* 15, Nat. Or. *Capparidaceæ.* These are very pretty plants; for culture, &c., see *Cleome.* Synonymes: 1. *Cleome candelabrum.* 2. *C. pentaphylla.* 3. *triphylla.* 4. *speciosa.* 5. *triphylla.*

| | | | | |
|---|---|---|---|---|
| candelábrum, 1 | . Red | . 7, H. | A. S. Amer. | . 1824 |
| pentaphýlla, 2 | . White | . 7, S. | A. E. Ind. | . 1640 |
| pulchélla | . White | . 6, H. | A. Marash. | . 1825 |
| semillifióra, 3 | . White | . 7, H. | A. W. Ind. | . 1820 |
| speciósa, 4 . | . White | . 7, S. | B. Carthag. | . 1818 |
| triphýlla, 5 | . White | . 7, H. | A. W. Ind. | . 1816 |

GYNANDROUS, having the stamens and style combined in one body.

GYNOBASE, a fleshy receptacle, bearing separate fruits.

GYNOBASIC, having a gynobase.

GYNOPHORE, a lengthened receptacle, bearing the petals, stamens, and pistils, but not the calyx.

GYNOUS; flowers are said to be 3, 4, 5, &c., gynous, when they contain so many styles.

GYPSOPHILA, *Linn.* From *gypsos,* chalk, and *phileo,* to love; in reference to the favourite habitat of the plants. *Linn.* 10, Or. 2, Nat. Or. *Silenaceæ.* The plants of this genus do not possess much beauty; they are all easily cultivated in any open soil, and the herbaceous kinds are increased by cuttings. The annuals need only be sown in the open border. Synonyme: 1. *scorzoneræfolia.*

| | | | | |
|---|---|---|---|---|
| acutifòlia | . White | . 7, H. Her. P. | Siberia | 1820 |
| adscéndens | . White | . 7, H. Her. P. | S. Eur. | 1800 |
| altíssima | . Striped | 7, H. Her. P. | Siberia | 1759 |
| arenária | . White | . 7, H. Her. P. | Hungary | 1801 |
| collína | . White | . 7, H. Her. P. | Podolia | 1821 |
| erética | . White | . 7, H. Her. P. | Crete | 1810 |
| dúbia | . White | . 7, H. Her. P. | | 1815 |
| élegans | . White | . 7, H. Her. P. | Crimea | 1828 |
| fastigiáta | . White | . 6, H. Her. P. | Germany | 1759 |
| glaúca | . White | . 8, H. Her. P. | Caucasus | 1822 |
| glomeráta | . Pa. red | 7, H. Her. P. | Tauria | 1818 |
| graminea | . Red | . 8, H. Her. Tr. | Greece | 1810 |
| grandifióra | . White | . 7, H. Her. P. | | 1800 |
| murális | . Red | . 8, H. | A. | Germany | 1739 |
| paniculáta | . White | . 8, H. Her. P. | Siberia | 1759 |
| perfoliáta | . Flame | 7, H. Her. P. | Spain | 1732 |
| prostráta | . Red | . 8, H. Her. Tr. | Siberia | 1759 |
| pubéscens | . White | . 6, H. Her. P. | Siberia | 1829 |
| répens | . Striped | 7, H. Her. Tr. | Siberia | 1774 |
| rígida | . Pink | . 7, H. Her. Tr. | France | 1769 |
| sabulósa, 1 | . White | . 7, H. Her. P. | Tauria | 1817 |
| Saxifrága | . Pink | . 7, H. Her. Tr. | Germany | 1774 |
| serótina | . White | . 8, H. | A. | Europe | 1818 |
| Steveni | . White | . 7, H. Her. P. | Iberia | 1822 |
| Strúthium | . White | . 7, H. Her. P. | Spain | 1729 |
| tenélla | . White | . 7, H. | A. | Europe | 1816 |
| tenuifòlia | . Red | . 7, H. Her. P. | Caucasus | 1824 |
| viscósa | . White | . 6, H. | A. | Levant | 1773 |

GYROCÁRPUS, *Jacquin.* From *gyro,* to turn round, and *karpos,* a fruit; in allusion to the fruit moving in the air. *Linn.* 23, Or. 1, Nat. Or. *Illigeraceæ.* These plants are described as being very ornamental, and of easy cultivation in loam and peat. Cuttings strike readily in sand, in heat, under a glass. Synonymes: 1. *G. Jacquinii.* 2. *Jacquinii.*

| | | | | |
|---|---|---|---|---|
| americánus, 1 | . Yellow | S. Ev. T. W. Ind. | . 1816 |
| asiáticus, 2 | . Yellow | S. Ev. T. E. Ind. | . 1818 |

GYRÒPHORA, *Acharius.* From *gyros,* a circle, and *phoreo,* to bear; alluding to the disk of the shield. *Linn.* 24, Or. 8, Nat. Or. *Lichenes.* Very interesting plants of the Lichen tribe, found growing chiefly upon exposed rocks, or granite stones; some of the species are peculiar to the Highlands of Scotland—*cylíndrica, deústa, erósa, glàbra, polyphýlla, murína, pelltíta, proboscídea, árctica, pustuláta.*

GYROSE, turned round like a crook.

GYROSTÈMON, *Desfontaines.* From *gyros,* a circle, and *stemon,* a stamen; in reference to the concentric arrangement of the stamens. *Linn.* 22, Or. 12, Nat. Or. *Euphorbiaceæ.* This is described as being rather an ornamental tree, and thriving in loam and peat; it may be increased by cuttings in sand. Synonyme: 1. *Codonocarpus australis.*

| | | | | |
|---|---|---|---|---|
| attenuátus . . . | | G. Ev. T. Moreton | . 1830 |

# H.

HABENĀRĬA, *Willldenow.* From *habena*, a rein, or thong; in allusion to the long strap-shaped spur. *Linn.* 20, Or. 1, Nat. Or. *Orchidaceæ.* This is a genus of interesting plants, well deserving of a place in every collection. The hardy kinds will grow well in the open border, with a slight protection for the American species in severe, frosty, or rainy weather. The stove species grow best in a mixture of leaf-mould and peat, placed in a hot, damp part of the house when in a growing state; but like the genus *Bletia*, after the plants have lost their leaves, and the roots become dormant, they require to be kept cool and dry until the roots begin to push, when the plants should be repotted, and again placed in a hot and moist heat. They are all increased by divisions of the roots. *Synonyme:* 1. *Orchis foliosa.*

| | | | | | |
|---|---|---|---|---|---|
| alāta, 1 | . | Yellow | 6, S. Ter. W. Ind. | | 1823 |
| bifolĭā | . | White | 6, H. Ter. Britain. | | |
| grācĭlĭs | . | Yel. red | 7, S. Ter. E. Ind. | | 1823 |
| leptŏcēris | . | Orn. wht. | 10, S. Ter. | | 1824 |
| longicaudā | . | Grnh. wht. | 8. Ter. Demerara | 183.. | |
| macrŏcēris | . | White | 6, S. Ter. W. Ind. | | 1825 |
| marginātā | . | Yellow | 7, S. Ter. E. Ind. | | 1822 |
| membrānĕcĕā | . | | 7, S. Ter. S. Leona. | | 1826 |
| ochrŏleūcā | . | Pa. yel. | 6, S. Ter. N. Holl. | | 1824 |
| procērā | . | Green | 8, H. Ter. N. Amer. | | 1822 |

HABIT, features, or general appearance of a plant.
HĀBĬTĀT, habitation, locality, native country.
HABLITZĬĀ, *Bieberstein.* In honour of C. Von Hablitz, a traveller, and author of Travels in the Crimea. *Linn.* 5, Or. 1, Nat. Or. *Chenopodiaceæ.* We know nothing of this plant; indeed, it is very possible it is not in the country. It may be increased by cuttings, or seeds.

| | | | | |
|---|---|---|---|---|
| tamnoīdēs | . | White | 9, H. De. Cl. Caucasus | 1828 |

HABRĀNTHŬS, *Herbert.* From *habros*, delicate, and *anthos*, a flower. *Linn.* 6, Or. 1, Nat. Or. *Amaryllidaceæ.* All the species of this genus are pretty when in flower. A mixture of three parts sandy loam, and one part peat, suits the various species of this genus. They may be increased by offsets from the roots, or by seeds, which are frequently produced in abundance.

| | | | | | | |
|---|---|---|---|---|---|---|
| angustūs | . | Red | 8, G. Bl. P. | Brazil | | 1822 |
| Andersonī | . | Yel. red | 5, G. Bl. P. | M. Video | | 1829 |
| texānūs | . | Yellow | G. Bl. P. | Texas | | 1834 |
| Bagnoldī | . | Yellow | 10, F. Bl. P. | Chile | | 1829 |
| bifĭdūs | . | Pink | 6, G. Bl. P. | B. Ayres | | 1823 |
| gracĭlĭfolĭūs | . | White | 1, H. Bl. P. | S. Amer. | | 1821 |
| Boothiānūs | . | Pink | 10, H. Bl. P. | B. Ayres | | 1836 |
| lorĭfolĭūs | . | Pink | 6, G. Bl. P. | S. Amer. | | 1821 |
| miniātūs | . | Red | 7, F. Bl. P. | Chile | | 1832 |
| pallĭdūs | . | Pink | 6, G. Bl. P. | Valparaiso | | 1830 |
| pūmĭlūs | . | Red | 9, G. Bk iP. | Chile | | 1831 |
| phycelloīdēs | . | Scarlet | 6, G. Bl. P. | Chile | | 1905 |
| robūstūs | . | Red | 6, G. Bl. P. | B. Ayres | | 1827 |
| rosĕūs | . | Rose | 6, F. Bl. P. | Chiloe | | 1828 |
| spathācĕūs | . | | 8, G. Bl. P. | B. Ayres | | 1825 |
| versĭcŏlŏr | . | Pink | 9, H. Bl. P. | S. Amer. | | 1821 |

HÆMADĬCTYŎN, *Lindley.* From *haima*, blood, and *dyktyon*, a net; alluding to the colour of the veins of the leaves. *Linn.* 5, Or. 1, Nat. Or. *Apocynaceæ.* A very ornamental plant, with beautifully-veined leaves; the soil best adapted to it is a mixture of loam and peat, and cuttings of the young wood root readily in sand, under a glass, in heat. *Synonymes:* 1. *Echites sanguinolenta, nutans.*

| | | | | |
|---|---|---|---|---|
| venōsūm, l | . | Yellow | 7, S. Ev. Tw. W. Ind. | 1821 |

HÆMĀNTHŬS, *Linn.* From *haima*, blood, and *anthos*, a flower; colour of some of the flowers. *Linn.* 6, Or. 1, Nat. Or. *Amaryllidaceæ.* A genus of fine bulbous plants; all the species succeed well in sandy loam, mixed with a little peat. They do not require to be watered when in a dormant state, in consequence of which, the bulbs ripen, and afterwards flower freely; increased by offsets.

| | | | | |
|---|---|---|---|---|
| albĭfŏs | . | White | 6, G. Bl. P. C. G. H. | 1791 |
| amaryllŏīdēs | . | Pink | 8, G. Bl. P. C. G. H. | 1825 |

[ 151 ]

| | | | | |
|---|---|---|---|---|
| cārnēūs | . | Pink | 6, G. Bl. P. C. G. H. | 1819 |
| carinātūs | . | Pink | 8, G. Bl. P. C. G. H. | 1759 |
| coarctātūs | . | Pink | 9, G. Bl. P. C. G. H. | 1795 |
| coccinēūs | . | Red | 9, G. Bl. P. C. G. H. | 1629 |
| crănăpēs | . | Red | 5, G. Bl. P. C. G. H. | 1820 |
| hūmĭlĭs | . | Scarlet | 9, G. Bl. P. C. G. H. | 1825 |
| hyalocārpūs | . | Red | 7, G. Bl. P. C. G. H. | 1822 |
| lancæfolĭūs | . | Red | 10, G. Bl. P. C. G. H. | 1794 |
| maculātūs | . | | 6, G Bl. P. C. G. H. | 1790 |
| moschātūs | . | Red | 9, G. Bl. P. C. G. H. | 1816 |
| multiflōrūs | . | Scarlet | 6, S. Bl. P. S. Leone | 1788 |
| orbiculārĭs | . | White | 7, G. Bl. P. C. G. H. | 1820 |
| pumĭlĭo | . | Pink | 8, G. Bl. P. C. G. H. | 1789 |
| pubēscēns | . | White | 7, G. Bl. P. C. G. H. | 1774 |
| puniceūs | . | Scarlet | 6, G. Bl. P. C. G. H. | 1722 |
| quadrivalvĭs | . | Flame | 9, G. Bl. P. C. G. H. | 1790 |
| rotundĭfolĭūs | . | Scarlet | 7, G. Bl. P. C. G. H. | 1790 |
| sanguinēūs | . | Crimson | 8, G. Bl. P. C. G. H. | 1820 |
| tigrinūs | . | Flame | 4, G. Bl. P. C. G. H. | 1790 |

HÆMATŎDĒS, blood-coloured.
HÆMATŎXYLŎN, *Linn.* From *haima*, blood, and *xylon*, wood; logwood is well known for its red colour. *Linn.* 10, Or. 1, Nat. Or. *Leguminosæ.* The logwood tree attains the height of twenty feet; it grows well in a mixture of loam, peat, and a little sand, and it may be increased by cuttings in sand, in heat, under a glass, or by seeds, which are very frequently received in this country from the West Indies. The bark and the wood are slightly astringent. The wood is chiefly used in dyeing.

| | | | | |
|---|---|---|---|---|
| campechiānūm | . | Yellow | 8. Ev. T. S. Amer. | 1724 |

HÆMODŎRŬM, *Smith.* From *haima*, blood, and *doron*, a gift; colour of the flowers. *Linn.* 3, Or. 2, Nat. Or. *Hæmodoraceæ.* Ornamental plants, growing freely in loam and peat; they are readily increased by divisions of the roots.

| | | | | |
|---|---|---|---|---|
| planĭfolĭūm | . | Orange | 8, G. Her. P. N. S. W. | 1810 |
| teretĭfolĭūm | . | Orange | 8, G. Her. P. N. Holl. | 1822 |

HAIR GRASS, see *Aīra.*
HĀKĒĀ, *Schrader.* In honour of Baron Hake, a German promoter of botany. *Linn.* 4, Or. 1, Nat. Or. *Proteaceæ.* A genus of very desirable New Holland plants; they require to be grown in a soil composed of equal parts of loam, peat, and sand. It is necessary to drain the pots well, so that the plants are not injured by too much water. Cuttings of the ripened wood root without difficulty in sand, under a glass.

| | | | | | |
|---|---|---|---|---|---|
| aciculārĭs | . | White | 6, G. Ev. S. N. S. W. | | 1790 |
| angustĭfolĭā | . | White | 6, G. Ev. S. N. Holl. | | 1824 |
| acanthophyllā | . | White | G. Ev. S. N. S. W. | | 1821 |
| amplexicaulĭs | . | White | G. Ev. S. N. Holl. | | 1803 |
| Baxterī | . | White | G. Ev. S. N. Holl. | | 1830 |
| canēscēns | . | White | 7, G. Ev. S. N. Holl. | | 1800 |
| carduĭfolĭā | . | White | 5, G. Ev. S. N. Holl. | | 1825 |
| ceratophyllā | . | Brown | 6, G. Ev. S. N. Holl. | | 1824 |
| clavātā | . | White | 7, G Ev. S. N. Holl. | | 1824 |
| cinerĕā | . | White | 6, G. Ev. S. N. Holl. | | 1803 |
| cucullātā | . | White | 6, G. Ev. S. N. Holl. | | 1824 |
| dactyloīdēs | . | White | 7, G. Ev. S. N. Holl. | | 1790 |
| echinātā | . | White | 6, G. Ev. S. N. Holl. | | 1824 |
| elliptĭcā | . | White | 7, G. Ev. S. N. Holl. | | 1794 |
| epiglottĭs | . | White | 5, G. Ev. S. N. Holl. | | 1819 |
| ferruginĕā | . | White | 6, G. Ev. S. N. Holl. | | 1825 |
| flexĭlĭs | . | White | G. Ev. S. N. Holl. | | 1824 |
| florĭdā | . | White | G. Ev. S. N. Holl. | | 1803 |
| gibbosā | . | White | 6, G. Ev. S. N. S. W. | | 1790 |
| ilicĭfolĭā | . | White | 8, G. Ev. S. N. Holl. | | 1803 |
| Lambertī | . | White | G. Ev. S. N. S. W. | | 1825 |
| lanĭgerā | . | White | 6, G. Ev. S. N. Holl. | | 1820 |
| latĭfolĭā | . | White | G. Ev. S. N. Holl. | | 1825 |
| laurĭnā | . | | G. Ev. S. N. Holl. | | 1830 |
| lineārĭs | . | White | 5, G. Ev. S. N. Holl. | | 1824 |
| longĭfolĭā | . | White | 5, G. Ev. S. N. Holl. | | 1825 |
| marginātā | . | White | 7, G. Ev. S. N. Holl. | | 1824 |
| microcārpā | . | White | 5, G. Ev. S. V. D. L. | | 1819 |
| nitĭdā | . | White | 6, G. Ev. S. N. Holl. | | 1803 |
| oblĭquā | . | White | 5, G. Ev. S. N. Holl. | | 1803 |
| oleĭfolĭā | . | White | 6, G. Ev. S. N. Holl. | | 1794 |
| parĭlĭs | . | White | 5, G. Ev. S. V. D. L. | | 1795 |
| pectinātā | . | White | 5, G. Ev. S. N. Holl. | | 1810 |
| petrophiloīdēs | . | White | G. Ev. S. N. Holl. | | 1825 |
| propinquā | . | White | 5, G Ev. S. N. S. W. | | 1824 |
| prostrātā | . | White | 6, G. Ev. S. N. Holl. | | 1833 |

| | | | | |
|---|---|---|---|---|
| pugioniförmis . | White . | G. Ev. S. | N. S. W. | 1796 |
| repánda . | White . | 6, G. Ev. S. | N. Holl. | 1824 |
| ruscifölia . | White . | 7, G. Ev. S. | N. Holl. | 1824 |
| salignä . | White . | 4, G. Ev. S. | N. Holl. | 1791 |
| suaveölens . | White . | G. Ev. S. | N. Holl. | 1803 |
| subulátä . | White . | 5, G. Ev. S. | N. S. W | 1824 |
| sulcátä . | White . | 5, G. Ev. S. | N. Holl. | 1890 |
| trifurcátä . | White . | 6, G. Ev. S. | N. Holl. | 1824 |
| tuberculátä . | | G. Ev. S. | N. Holl. | 1830 |
| ulicinä . | White . | G. Ev. S. | N. S. W. | 1824 |
| undulátä . | White . | 5, G. Ev. S. | N. Holl. | 1803 |
| váriä . | White . | 7, G. Ev. S. | N. Holl. | 1825 |

HALBERD-WEED, see *Neuroland*.

HALÈSIA, *Linn.* In honour of S. Hales, D.D., F.R.S., a vegetable physiologist. *Linn.* 11, Or. 1, Nat. Or. *Ebenaceæ.* All the species of the Snowdrop tree are most beautiful and valuable shrubs, on account of their flowering so early in the season; they grow freely in any common garden soil, and multiply by cuttings of the roots, or by layers.

| | | | | |
|---|---|---|---|---|
| tetráptêrä . | White . | 5, H. De. S. | Carolina | 1756 |
| parvíflörä . | White . | 5, H. De. S. | N. Amer. | 1802 |
| díptêrä . | White . | 4, H. De. S. | N. Amer. | 1758 |

HALIMODÈNDRŎN, *Flscher.* From *halimos*, maritime, and *dendron*, a tree; in allusion to the shrub growing in dry, naked, salt fields, by the river Irtis, in Siberia. *Linn.* 17, Or. 4, Nat. Or. *Leguminosæ.* These are very beautiful shrubs, well worthy of a place in every garden; for culture and propagation, see *Caragana.* Synonymes: 1. *Robinia Halodendron*, *Caragana argentea.* 2. *Robinia triflora.*

| | | | | |
|---|---|---|---|---|
| argentêûm, 1 . | Pink . | 5, H. De. S. | Siberia | 1779 |
| brachysêmä . | Pink . | 6, H. De. S. | Siberia | |
| subvirêscêns, 2 . | Pink . | 5, H. De. S. | Siberia | |

HALISERIS, *Agardh.* From *hals*, the sea, and *seris*, lettuce; in reference to the membranous fronds. *Linn.* 24, Or. 7, Nat. Or. *Algæ.* A species, with some likeness of a Polypodium; it is olive-green, and found in the ocean at all seasons of the year— *polypodioïdês.*

HALLÈRIA, *Linn.* In honour of Albert Haller, M.D., a distinguished botanical author. *Linn.* 14, Or. 2, Nat. Or. *Scrophulariaceæ.* A genus of ornamental shrubs, requiring to be grown in a light rich soil; cuttings root readily in sand, or soil, under a glass. They require an airy part of the greenhouse, and plenty of water in summer.

| | | | | |
|---|---|---|---|---|
| ellípticä . | Scarlet . | 7, G. Ev. S. | C. G. H. | 1816 |
| lúcidä . | Scarlet . | 7, G. Ev. S. | C. G. H. | 1752 |

HXLIA, *Thunberg.* In compliment to Berger Martin Hall, a pupil of Linnæus. *Linn.* 16, Or. 6, Nat. Or. *Leguminosæ.* Herbaceous plants, with little to recommend them to the cultivator; they thrive best in sandy loam and peat, and cuttings of the young wood root freely in sand, under a glass. They sometimes ripen seed, from which plants may also be obtained.

| | | | | |
|---|---|---|---|---|
| imbricátä . | Pink . | 8, G. Ev. S. | C. G. H. | 1812 |

*alátä, asarínä, cordátä, fláccidä.*

HALORXGIS, *Forster.* From *hals*, the sea, and *rhax*, berry of grapes. *Linn.* 8, Or. 4, Nat. Or. *Onagraceæ.* These are rather curious plants, thriving well in a mixture of loam and peat, and increased readily by cuttings in sand, under a glass.

| | | | | |
|---|---|---|---|---|
| Cercödiä . | Grn. red . | 6, G. Ev. S. | N. Zeal. | 1772 |
| prostrátä . | Grn. red . | 7, G. Ev. S. | N. Zeal. | 1820 |

HALYMÈNIA, *Agardh.* From *hals*, the sea, and *hymen*, a membrane; alluding to the membranous fronds. *Linn.* 24, Or. 7, Nat. Or. *Algæ.* Interesting marine plants, with flat, membranous fronds. *H. edulis* is the true, and *H. palmata* the common Dulse, both of which are eaten in Scotland—*adälis-médiä, furcellátä, ligulátä, Opûntiä, palmátä-marginíferä-sarniênsis, purpurāscêns-crispátä.*

HAMAMÈLIS, *Linn.* From *hama*, with, and *melon*, an apple; the fruit accompanies the flower. *Linn.* 4, Or. 2, Nat. Or. *Hamamelaceæ.* The species of Witch-hazel are ornamental trees, producing a fruit something like a nut. They succeed in any common soil, and are commonly increased by layers.

| | | | | |
|---|---|---|---|---|
| macrophýllä . | Yellow . | 5, H. De. T. | N. Amer. | 1812 |
| virginiäna . | Yellow . | 4, H. De. T. | N. Amer. | |

HAMÈLIA. Named by Jacquin, in honour of the distinguished botanist H. L. Du Hamel Du Monceau, who died in 1782. *Linn.* 5, Or. 1, Nat. Or. *Cinchonaceæ.* This genus consists of handsome, free-flowering shrubs, easily cultivated in peat and loam; and cuttings, planted in the same kind of soil, root readily in a moist heat, under a glass. Synonyme: 1. *H. odorata.*

| | | | | |
|---|---|---|---|---|
| axillaris . | Yellow . | 8, S. Ev. S. | W. Ind. | 1822 |
| chrysánthä . | Yellow . | 11, S. Ev. S. | Jamaica | 1822 |
| pátêns . | Yellow . | 7, S. Ev. S. | Hispaniola | 1752 |
| sphærocärpä . | Orange . | 7, S. Ev. S. | Mexico | 1811 |
| ventricösä . | Yellow . | 9, S. Ev. S. | W. Ind. | 1778 |

HAMILTŎNIA, *Roxburgh.* In honour of Mr. Hamilton, of Woodlands, near Philadelphia, an eminent botanist, and the first to erect a conservatory in North America, for the preservation of plants of hot climates. *Linn.* 22, Or. 3, Nat. Or. *Cinchonaceæ.* These plants are very desirable on account of their producing flowers very freely, which are delightfully fragrant; loam and peat suit them best, and cuttings root readily in sand, under a glass, in a moist heat. Synonymes: 1. *Spermadictyon azureum.* 2. *S. suaveolens.*

| | | | | |
|---|---|---|---|---|
| scábrä, 1 . | Pa. blue . | 1, S. Ev. S. | Nepal | 1823 |
| suaveölens, 2 . | White . | 10, S. Ev. S. | E. Ind. | 1818 |

HAMÔSUS, hooked, bent.

HAPALOSTÈPHIÙM, *Don.* From *hapalis*, soft, and *stephos*, a crown; alluding to the hairy receptacle. *Linn.* 19, Or. 1, Nat. Or. *Compositæ.* The plants included in this genus are well adapted for rock-work, or the front of flower-borders; they grow freely in any light rich soil, and increase by dividing the roots, or by seeds. Synonymes: 1. *Crepis austriaca.* 2. *Hieracium grandiflorum.* 3. *lyratum.* 4. *paludosum.* 5. *blattarioïdes, Lepicaune multicaulis.* 6. *Hieracium pyrenaicum.* 7. *sibiricum, Crepis sibirica.* 8. *Lepicaune spinulosa.*

| | | | | |
|---|---|---|---|---|
| austriäcûm, 1 . | Yellow . | 7, H. Her. P. | Pyrenees | 1728 |
| grandiflörûm, 2 . | Yellow . | | H. Her. P. | Switzerl. | 1791 |
| lyrätûm, 3 . | Yellow . | | H. Her. P. | Siberia | 1777 |
| paludösûm, 4 . | Yellow . | 8, H. Her. P. | Britain | |
| pilösûm, 5 . | Yellow . | | H. Her. P. | Pyrenees | 1728 |
| pyrenaïcûm, 6 . | Yellow . | | H. Her. P. | Pyrenees | 1723 |
| sibïrïcûm, 7 . | Yellow . | | H. Her. P. | Siberia | 1755 |
| spinulösûm, 8 . | Yellow . | | H. Her. P. | Pyrenees | 1820 |

HARD-GRASS, see *Ophiurus*.
HARD-GRASS, see *Sclerochloä*.

HARDWICKIA. Roxburgh named this genus in compliment to Major-General Thomas Hardwicke, F.R.S., L.S., &c., of the East India Company's Artillery. *Linn.* 10, Or. 1, Nat. Or. *Leguminosæ.* Trees from forty to fifty feet high; a light loamy soil suits them well, and good sized cuttings root readily in sand, under a glass, in heat.

| | | | | |
|---|---|---|---|---|
| binátä . | Yellow . | 3, S. Ev. T. | E. Ind. | 1820 |
| pinnátä . | Yellow . | 4, S. Ev. T. | E. Ind. | 1818 |

HAREBELLS, see *Campánulä rotundifölia*.
HARE'S EAR, see *Erýsimûm austriäcûm*.
HARE'S-EAR, see *Buplêûrûm*.
HARE'S-FOOT, see *Ochrömä Lagôpûs*.
HARE'S-FOOT FERN, see *Davalliä canariénsis*.
HARE'S-TAIL GRASS, see *Lagûrûs*.
HARICOT D'ORLEANS, see *Phasëölûs sphæricûs.*

HARÔNOX, *P. Thouars.* The native name of the species is Ronga. *Linn.* 18, Or. 2, Nat. Or. *Hypericaceæ.* A tall, ornamental-growing shrub, thriving well in a mixture of loam and peat; plants may be obtained from cuttings of the ripened wood, planted in sand, under a glass, in heat. Synonyme: 1. *paniculata.*

| | | | | |
|---|---|---|---|---|
| madagascariénsis, 1 | Yellow . | 7, S. Ev. S. | Madagas. | 1825 |

HARPXLYCE, *Don.* After Harpalyce, daughter of Lycurgus. *Linn.* 19, Or. 1, Nat. Or. *Compositæ.* The species of this genus are not possessed of much interest; they grow well in any garden soil, and the perennial kinds may be increased by seeds, or divisions; the annual species by seed, sown in the open border. Synonymes: 1. *Prenanthes alba.* 2. *altissima.* 3. *cordata.* 4. *serpentaria.* 5. *virgata.*

| | | | | |
|---|---|---|---|---|
| albä, 1 . | White . | 7, H. Her. P. | N. Amer. | 1762 |
| altíssimä, 2 . | Yellow . | 7, H. Her. P. | N. Amer. | 1696 |
| cordätä, 3 . | Pa. yel. . | 7, H. Her. P. | N. Amer. | 1816 |
| vimínêä . | Yellow . | 7, H. | B. Austria | 1816 |

*serpentáriä 4, virgätä 5.*

HARRISÔNIA. Hooker named this genus in honour of Mrs. Harrison, of Aighburg, near Liverpool, who first introduced the plant. *Linn.* 5, Or. 2, Nat. Or.

*Asclepiadaceæ.* An ornamental shrub, well worthy of extensive cultivation; for culture and propagation, see *Gomphocarpus.*

| lonicaroides | . | Scarlet | . 7, S. Ev. S. | Brazil | . 1825 |
|---|---|---|---|---|---|

HARTOGIA, *Thunberg.* In honour of J. Hartog, a Dutch naturalist and traveller at the Cape. *Linn.* 5, Or. 1, Nat. Or. *Aquifoliaceæ.* An ornamental tallish-growing shrub, nearly related to *Myginda*; for culture and propagation, see *Cassine.*

| capensis | . | . | . 6, G. Ev. S. | C. G. H. | . 1800 |
|---|---|---|---|---|---|

HART'S-TONGUE, see *Scolopendrium.*
HART'S-TONGUE, see *Polypodium Phyllitidis.*
HARTWEGIA, *Lindley.* In compliment to Mr. Theodore Hartweg, a successful collector of Mexican plants for the Horticultural Society of London, and who discovered this his genus. *Linn.* 20, Or. 1, Nat. Or. *Orchidaceæ.* A curious little plant, with delicate purple flowers; it requires to be treated similar to other Mexican orchidaceæ.

| purpurea | . | . | Purple | . 8, S. Epi. | Vera Cruz | . 1837 |
|---|---|---|---|---|---|---|

HARTWORT, see *Tordylium.*
HASSAGAY-TREE, see *Curtisia.*
HASSELQUISTIA. Named by Linnæus, in honour of his pupil Frederick Hasselquist, M.D., who travelled in the Holy Land, &c., and died at Smyrna, in 1752. *Linn.* 5, Or. 2, Nat. Or. *Umbelliferæ.* Mere annual weeds, natives of Egypt; they grow in any common soil—*ægyptiaca, cordata.*

HASTATE, formed like the head of a halbert.
HASTATELY-LANCEOLATE, between halbert-shaped and lance-shaped.
HASTATELY-SAGITTATE, between halbert-shaped and arrow-shaped.
HATCHET-VETCH, see *Biserrula.*
HAULM, dead stems of herbs.
HAUTBOY, see *Fragaria.*
HAWKWEED, see *Hieracium.*
HAWORTHIA. Prince Salm-Dyck named this genus in compliment to A. H. Haworth, F.L.S., a distinguished English botanist. *Linn.* 6, Or. 1, Nat. Or. *Liliaceæ.* Haworthia is a singular and highly interesting genus of succulent plants, nearly related to the genera *Aloe* and *Gasteria*, and they require the same treatment as those genera. *Synonymes:* 1. *Aloe atrovirens.* 2. *A. margaritifera minima.* 3. *Haworthia concava.* 4. *rigida.* 5. *Aloe margaritifera.* 6. *Haworthia fasciata.* 7. *Aloe rigida.* 8. *A. venosa.* 9. *A. viscosa.*

| albicans | . | . | Grey | . 7, G. Ev. S. | C. G. H. | . 1795 |
|---|---|---|---|---|---|---|
| altilinea | . | . | Grey | . 8, G. Ev. S. | C. G. H. | . 1824 |
| angustifolia | . | . | Grey | . 6, G. Ev. S. | C. G. H. | . 1824 |
| arachnoides | . | . | Grey | . 8, G. Ev. S. | C. G. H. | . 1727 |
|   minor | . | . | Grey | . 8, G. Ev. S. | C. G. H. | . 1819 |
| aristata | . | . | Grey | . 6, G. Ev. S. | C. G. H. | . 1820 |
| asperiuscula | . | . | Grey | . 6, G. Ev. S. | C. G. H. | . 1818 |
| atrovirens, 1 | . | . | Grey | . 5, G. Ev. S. | C. G. H. | . 1823 |
| attenuata | . | . | Grey | . 7, G. Ev. S. | C. G. H. | . 1790 |
| brevis, 2 | . | . | Grey | . 6, G. Ev. S. | C. G. H. | . 1810 |
| chloracantha | . | . | Grey | . 8, G. Ev. S. | C. G. H. | . 1820 |
| claripata | . | . | Grey | . 6, G. Ev. S. | C. G. H. | . 1824 |
| coarctata | . | . | Grey | . 8, G. Ev. S. | C. G. H. | . 1821 |
| coadunata | . | . | Grey | . 8, G. Ev. S. | C. G. H. | . 1823 |
| cordifolia | . | . | Grey | . 8, G. Ev. S. | C. G. H. | . 1817 |
| curta | . | . | Grey | . 7, G. Ev. S. | C. G. H. | . 1816 |
| cuspidata | . | . | Grey | . 8, G. Ev. S. | C. G. H. | . 1819 |
| cymbiformis, 3 | . | . | Grey | . 6, G. Ev. S. | C. G. H. | . 1795 |
| denticulata | . | . | Grey | . 8, G. Ev. S. | C. G. H. | . 1819 |
| erecta | . | . | Grey | . 8, G. Ev. S. | C. G. H. | . 1818 |
| expansa, 4 | . | . | Grey | . 8, G. Ev. S. | C. G. H. | . 1795 |
| fasciata | . | . | Grey | . 8, G. Ev. S. | C. G. H. | . 1818 |
|   major | . | . | Grey | . 7, G. Ev. S. | C. G. H. | . 1820 |
| granata, 5 | . | . | Grey | . 7, G. Ev. S. | C. G. H. | . 1735 |
| hybrida | . | . | Grey | . 7, G. Ev. S. | C. G. H. | . 1821 |
| indurata | . | . | Grey | . 6, G. Ev. S. | C. G. H. | . 1820 |
| laeta-virens | . | . | Grey | . 8, G. Ev. S. | C. G. H. | . 1819 |
| lavis | . | . | Grey | . 8, G. Ev. S. | C. G. H. | . 1820 |
| limpida | . | . | Grey | . 8, G. Ev. S. | C. G. H. | . 1819 |
| margaritifera | . | . | Grey | . 7, G. Ev. S. | C. G. H. | . 1739 |
| minor | . | . | Grey | . 6, G. Ev. S. | C. G. H. | . |
| mirabilis | . | . | Grey | . 7, G. Ev. S. | C. G. H. | . 1795 |
| multifaria | . | . | Grey | . 7, G. Ev. S. | C. G. H. | . 1824 |
| mucronata | . | . | Grey | . 7, G. Ev. S. | C. G. H. | . 1820 |
| mutica | . | . | Grey | . 7, G. Ev. S. | C. G. H. | . 1820 |
| nigricans | . | . | Grey | . 8, G. Ev. S. | C. G. H. | . 1822 |
| nitida | . | . | Grey | . 7, G. Ev. S. | C. G. H. | . 1825 |
| obtusa | . | . | Grey | . 6, G. Ev. S. | C. G. H. | . 1824 |
| pallida | . | . | Grey | . 6, G. Ev. S. | C. G. H. | . 1820 |
| planifolia | . | . | Grey | . 4, G. Ev. S. | C. G. H. | . 1824 |
| papillosa | . | . | Grey | . 6, G. Ev. S. | C. G. H. | . 1820 |
| semipapillosa | . | . | Grey | . 6, G. Ev. S. | C. G. H. | . 1820 |

| parva | . | . | Grey | . 5, G. Ev. S. | C. G. H. | . 1821 |
|---|---|---|---|---|---|---|
| pseudo-tortuosa | . | Grey | . 7, G. Ev. S. | C. G. H. | . 1818 |
| pumila | . | . | Grey | . 5, G. Ev. S. | C. G. H. | . 1752 |
| radula | . | . | Grey | . 5, G. Ev. S. | C. G. H. | . 1805 |
|   asperior | . | . | Grey | . 8, G. Ev. S. | C. G. H. | . 1820 |
|   lavior | . | . | Grey | . 8, G. Ev. S. | C. G. H. | . 1825 |
|   pluriperlata | . | Grey | . 8, G. Ev. S. | C. G. H. | . 1820 |
| ramifera | . | . | Grey | . 8, G. Ev. S. | C. G. H. | . 1821 |
| recurva | . | . | Grey | . 8, G. Ev. S. | C. G. H. | . 1795 |
| Reinwardti, 6 | . | Grey | . 6, G. Ev. S. | C. G. H. | . 1820 |
| reticulata | . | . | Grey | . 6, G. Ev. S. | C. G. H. | . 1794 |
| retusa | . | . | Grey | . 6, G. Ev. S. | C. G. H. | . 1720 |
| scabra | . | . | Grey | . 6, G. Ev. S. | C. G. H. | . 1818 |
| semimargaritifera | | Grey | . 4, G. Ev. S. | C. G. H. | . 1819 |
|   major | . | . | Grey | . 4, G. Ev. S. | C. G. H. | . 1819 |
|   minor | . | . | Grey | . 4, G. Ev. S. | C. G. H. | . 1819 |
|   multiperlata | . | Grey | . 4, G. Ev. S. | C. G. H. | . 1819 |
| semiglabrata | . | Grey | . 6, G. Ev. S. | C. G. H. | . 1811 |
| setata | . | . | Grey | . 6, G. Ev. S. | C. G. H. | . 1820 |
|   major | . | . | Grey | . 7, G. Ev. S. | C. G. H. | . 1820 |
|   media | . | . | Grey | . 7, G. Ev. S. | C. G. H. | . 1820 |
|   nigricans | . | Grey | . 7, G. Ev. S. | C. G. H. | . 1820 |
| sordida | . | . | Grey | . 7, G. Ev. S. | C. G. H. | . 1820 |
| tessellata | . | . | Grey | . 6, G. Ev. S. | C. G. H. | . 1823 |
| torquata | . | . | Grey | . 8, G. Ev. S. | C. G. H. | . 1823 |
| tortella | . | . | Grey | . 7, G. Ev. S. | C. G. H. | . 1817 |
| tortuosa, 7 | . | . | Grey | . 7, G. Ev. S. | C. G. H. | . 1794 |
| translucens | . | . | Grey | . 6, G. Ev. S. | C. G. H. | . 1795 |
| turgida | . | . | Grey | . 8, G. Ev. S. | C. G. H. | . 1819 |
| venosa, 8 | . | . | Grey | . 6, G. Ev. S. | C. G. H. | . 1820 |
| virescens | . | . | Grey | . 8, G. Ev. S. | C. G. H. | . 1819 |
|   minor | . | . | Grey | . 8, G. Ev. S. | C. G. H. | . 1819 |
| viscosa, 9 | . | . | Grey | . 8, G. Ev. S. | C. G. H. | . 1727 |

HAWTHORN, see *Cratægus.*
HAWTHORN, see *Rhus Oxyacantha.*
HAYLOCKIA. Herbert named this genus in honour of his very intelligent gardener Matthew Haylock. *Linn.* 6, Or. 1, Nat. Or. *Amaryllideæ.* This is rather a pretty bulb when in flower, and it may be successfully grown in sandy loam; it is easily increased from offsets from the bulbs.

| pusilla | . | . | . | Straw | . 9, F. Bl. | P. B. Ayres | . 1829 |
|---|---|---|---|---|---|---|---|

HAZEL, see *Corylus.*
HEART'S-EASE, see *Viola tricolor.*
HEART-SEED, see *Cardiospermum.*
HEATH, see *Erica.*
HEBENSTREITIA, *Linn.* In honour of J. E. Hebenstreit, M.D., professor of botany at Leipsic. *Linn.* 14, Or. 2, Nat. Or. *Selaginaceæ.* This is a genus of pretty under-shrubs, with very neat foliage and modest flowers; they thrive best in a mixture of sandy loam and peat, and young plants are readily obtained from cuttings in the same kind of soil, under a glass. *Synonyme:* 1. *H. aurea.*

| albiflora | . | . | White | . 7, G. Ev. S. | C. G. H. | . 1822 |
|---|---|---|---|---|---|---|
| capitata | . | . | White | . 6, G. Ev. S. | C. G. H. | . 1823 |
| chamaedrifolia | . | White | . G. Ev. S. | C. G. H. | . 1822 |
| ciliata | . | . | White | . 6, G. Ev. S. | C. G. H. | . 1815 |
| cordata | . | . | White | . 7, G. Ev. S. | C. G. H. | . 1774 |
| dentata | . | . | White | . 7, G. A. | C. G. H. | . 1789 |
| erinoides | . | . | White | . 5, G. Ev. S. | C. G. H. | . 1816 |
| fruticosa | . | . | White | . 8, G. Ev. S. | C. G. H. | . 1816 |
| integrifolia, 1 | . | White | . 5, G. Ev. S. | C. G. H. | . 1792 |
| scabra | . | . | White | . 6, G. Ev. S. | C. G. H. | . 1820 |

HEDEOMA, *Persoon.* Hedeoma is a Greek name for Mint. *Linn.* 2, Or. 1, Nat. Or. *Labiatæ.* The seeds of these plants merely require to be sown in the open border in spring

| pulegioides | . | Blue | . 7, H. | A. N. Amer. | . 1777 |
|---|---|---|---|---|---|
| thymoides | . | Red | . 7, H. | A. France | . 1699 |

HEDERA, *Swartz.* The name appears to be derived from *hedra*, a Celtic word, signifying a cord, and the English name, Ivy, is derived from *iw*, a word in the same language, signifying green, from its being always green. *Linn.* 5, Or. 1, Nat. Or. *Araliaceæ.* The common Ivy is very often employed for covering naked buildings, or trees, which latter it invariably kills; it is increased by slips, taken off, and planted where they are to grow. The tender kinds will grow in any soil, though they appear to grow better in a very light one.

| Helix | . | . | Green | . 9, H. Ev. Cl. | Britain | . . |
|---|---|---|---|---|---|---|
| arborescens | . | Green | . H. Ev. Cl. | | |
| canariensis | . | Green | . H. Ev. Cl. | Canaries | . |
| chrysocarpa | . | Green | . H. Ev. Cl. | India | . |
| vulgaris | . | . | Green | . H. Ev. Cl. | Britain | . . |

HEDGE-GARLIC, see *Alliaria.*
HEDGE-HYSSOP, see *Gratiola.*
HEDGE-MUSTARD, see *Erysimum.*

x

HEDGE-NETTLE, see *Stachys.*

HEDWIGIA, *Swartz.* In honour of John Hedwig, the celebrated muscologist, who died in 1799. *Linn.* 8, Or. 1, Nat. Or. *Burseraceæ.* A tall-growing ornamental tree, thriving in peat and loam, with a little sand mixed; cuttings root readily in sand, under a glass, in heat.

| | | | | | |
|---|---|---|---|---|---|
| balsamifera | . White | . 8, S. Ev. T. W. Ind. | . 1820 |

HEDYCHIUM, *König.* From *hedys*, sweet, and *chion*, snow; alluding to the sweet-scented snow-white flowers of some of the species. *Linn.* 1, Or. 1, Nat. Or. *Scitamineæ.* The species of *Hedychium*, or Garland Flower, are all highly-prized flowering plants, more particularly *H. angustifolium* and *H. coronarium*; they are all well worthy of extensive cultivation. They all grow freely in rich light soil, and to flower them well, they require a large pot, with a plentiful supply of water when in a growing state; they are readily increased by dividing the roots. *Synonymes:* 1. *angustifolium.* 2. *angustifolium.*

| | | | | |
|---|---|---|---|---|
| acuminātūm | . White | . 7, S. Her. P. E. Ind. | . 1820 |
| angustifōliūm | . Scarlet | . 8, S. Her. P. E. Ind. | . 1815 |
| aurantiācūm, 1 | . Orange | . 7, S. Her. P. E. Ind. | . 1812 |
| cārnēūm | . Pink | . 8, S. Her. P. E. Ind. | . 1823 |
| coccīnēūm, 2 | . Scarlet | . 7, S. Her. P. E. Ind. | . 1815 |
| coronārīūm | . Yellow | . 8. S. Her. P. E. Ind. | . 1791 |
| elātūm | . Pa. red | . 8. S. Her. P. E. Ind. | . 1818 |
| ellipticūm | . White | . 8, S. Her. P. E. Ind. | . 1804 |
| flavēscēns | . Yellow | . 6. S. Her. P. India | . 1822 |
| flāvūm | . Yellow | . 7, S. Her. P. Nepal | . 1822 |
| Gardneriānūm | . Yellow | . 7, S. Her. P. E. Ind. | . 1819 |
| glaūcūm | . White | . 7, S. Her. P. India | . 1822 |
| grācīlē | . White | . 6. S. Her. P. Bengal | . 1823 |
| heteromallūm | . Yellow | . 7, S. Her. P. India | . 1822 |
| longifōliūm | . Red | . 6. S. Her. P. E. Ind. | . 1819 |
| māximūm | . White | . 8, S. Her. P. E. Ind. | . 1820 |
| specīōsūm | . Pa. yel. | . 8, S. Her. P. E. Ind. | . 1823 |
| spicātūm | . Yellow | . 6. S. Her. P. India | . 1810 |
| stenopetalūm | . White | . 4, S. Her. P. India | . 1830 |
| thyrsiformē | . White | . 7, S. Her. P. Nepal | . 1818 |
| urophyllūm | . Yellow | . 8, S. Her. P. India | . 1823 |
| villōsūm | . Cream | . 7, S. Her. P. E. Ind. | . 1823 |

HEDYOTIS, *Linn.* From *hedys*, sweet, and *ous*, an ear; alluding to the sweet-scented ear-like leaves. *Linn.* 4, Or. 1, Nat. Or. *Cinchonaceæ.* Stove annuals, of neither interest nor value; they are readily grown both in peat and loam. *Synonymes:* 1. *Spermacoce biflora.* 2. *Oldenlandia diffusa.* 3. *O. ramosissima*—*biflora* 1, *cymōsa, diffusa* 2, *herbācēa, lāctēa, ramosissima* 3, *umbellāta.*

HEDYPNOIS, *Tournefort.* From *hedys*, sweet, and *pneo*, to breathe; in reference to its having the power of scenting the breath. *Linn.* 19, Or. 1, Nat. Or. *Compositæ.* Hardy annuals, of no interest; the species need only be sown in the open ground— *coronopifōliā, crēticā, mauritānicā, monspeliēnsis, pēndālā, rhagadioloīdēs, tubæformis.*

HEDYSARUM, *Linn.* From *hedysaron*, the name of a papillonaceous plant described by Theophrastus. *Linn.* 17, Or. 4, Nat. Or. *Leguminosæ.* Almost all the species of this genus are very handsome flowering plants, producing racemes of very beautiful pea flowers, particularly adapted for flowerborders, or rock-work. They grow freely in a light rich soil, or loam and peat, and the herbaceous kinds are increased by dividing the roots in spring, or by seeds. The seeds of the annual and biennial kinds only require sowing in the open border in spring. *Synonyme:* 1. *H. sibiricum.* 2. *H. alpinum.* 3. *H. obscurum altaicum.* 4. *H. humile.*

| | | | | |
|---|---|---|---|---|
| alpīnūm, 1 | . Purple | . 6, H. Her. P. Siberia | . 1798 |
| pedicelare, 2 | . Purple | . 6, H. Her. P. Siberia | |
| altaicūm | . Purple | . 7, H. Her. P. Siberia | . 1818 |
| brachysēmium, 3 | . Purple | . 7, H. Her. P. Siberia | . 1817 |
| cāndidūm | . Purple | . 5, H. Her. P. Tauria | . 1824 |
| hūmilē, 4 | . Purple | . 6, H. Her. P. Tauria | . 1817 |
| carnōsūm | . Purple | . 7, H. Her. P. Barbary | . 1820 |
| caucāsēūm | . Purple | . 7, H. Her. P. Caucasus | . 1820 |
| consanguīnēūm | . Purple | . 7, H. Her. P. Siberia | . 1820 |
| coronārīūm | . Scarlet | . 6, H. | B. Italy | . 1596 |
| cretācēūm | . Purple | . 6, H. Her. P. Siberia | . 1819 |
| fruticōsūm | . Purple | . 6, H. De. S. Siberia | . 1782 |
| grandiflōrūm | . Purple | . 6, H. Her. P. Tauria | . 1821 |
| ībērīcūm | . Purple | . 7, H. Her. P. Iberia | . 1818 |
| lasiocarpūm | . Purple | . H. Her. P. Siberia | . 1816 |
| obscūrūm | . Purple | . 7, H. Her. P. Alps | . 1640 |
| pāllidūm | . Pa. red | . 6, H. Her. P. N. Africa | . 1820 |
| rōsēūm | . Pink | . 8, H. Her. P. Caucasus | . 1803 |

| | | | | |
|---|---|---|---|---|
| rutidocārpūm | . Purple | . 8, H. Her. P. Siberia | . 1826 |
| splēndēns | . Cream | . 7, H. Her. P. Siberia | . 1819 |
| taūricūm | . Pa. pur. | . 7, H. Her. P. Tauria | . 1804 |
| vārīūm | . White | . 7, H. Her. P. S. Eur. | . 1820 |

*argēntūm, flexuōsūm, hāmilī, spinosissimum.*

HEIMIA, *Link.* In honour of Dr. Heim, a celebrated Berlin physician. *Linn.* 11, Or. 1, Nat. Or. *Lythraceæ.* These plants are very pretty when in blossom; they grow well in an equal mixture of loam and peat, with a little sand. They only require to be protected from frost in winter, which may easily be done if the plants are against a south wall; if in pots, they should be removed into the greenhouse. Cuttings strike freely either in sand or soil, under a glass. *Synonyme:* 1. *Nesæa salicifolia.*

| | | | | |
|---|---|---|---|---|
| lineārifōliā | . Yellow | . F. Ev. S. S. Amer. | . 1829 |
| myrtifōliā | . Yellow | . 8. F. Ev. S. Amer. | . 1826 |
| salicifōliā, 1 | . Yellow | . 8. F. Ev. S. Mexico | . 1821 |

HEISTERIA. Named by Linnæus, in honour of Laurence Heister, once professor of botany at Helmstadt, who died in 1758. *Linn.* 10, Or. 1, Nat. Or. *Olacaceæ.* This is a tree which attains the height of about fifteen feet, and is cultivated in a mixture of loam, peat, and sand; and cuttings will root in sand, under a glass, in heat. The wood of this tree is the partridge-wood of the cabinet-makers.

| | | | | |
|---|---|---|---|---|
| coccīnēā | . Scarlet | . 8. Ev. T. W. Ind. | . 1822 |

HELENIUM, *Linn.* Named after the celebrated Helen. *Linn.* 19, Or. 2, Nat. Or. *Compositæ.* Very pretty tallish-growing plants, well adapted for flowerborders; they will grow freely in any common garden soil. The herbaceous species may be increased by dividing the roots. The annuals and biennials require the same treatment as is generally given to such species.

| | | | | |
|---|---|---|---|---|
| autumnālē | . Yellow | . 9, H. Her. P. N. Amer. | . 1729 |
| canaliculātūm | . Yellow | . 8, H. Her. P. N. Amer. | . 1800 |
| mexicānūm | . Yellow | . 8, H. Her. P. Mexico | . 1825 |
| pubēscēns | . Yellow | . 8, H. Her. P. N. Amer. | . 1776 |
| pūmilūm | . Yellow | . 8, H. Her. P. | . 1818 |
| quadridentātūm | . Yellow | . 8, H. | A. Louisiana | . 1790 |
| quadripartītūm | . Yellow | . 9, O. | B. | . 1823 |
| undulātūm | . Yellow | . 9, H. Her. P. California | . 1830 |

HELIANTHEMUM, *Tournefort.* From *helios*, sun, and *anthemon*, flower; in allusion to the yellow flowers. *Linn.* 13, Or. 1, Nat. Or. *Cistaceæ.* This is a very showy, free-flowering genus of plants, comprising some of the prettiest little shrubs in cultivation, for ornamenting rock-work. In winter, some of the species require the protection of a frame, or greenhouse, and on that account, require to be grown in pots; they all thrive well in a mixture of sandy loam and peat. The shrubby kinds may be increased by cuttings, under a hand-glass, in a sheltered situation, or by seeds, by which the annual species are also to be raised. *Synonymes:* 1. *viscidulum.* 2. *roseum.* 3. *salicifolium.* 4. *campevicifolium.*

| | | | | |
|---|---|---|---|---|
| acuminātūm | . Yellow | . 6, H. Ev. Tr. Nice | . 1820 |
| ægyptiacūm | . White | . 6, H. | A. Egypt | . 1764 |
| algarvēnsē | . Yellow | . 7, F. Ev. S. Portugal | . 1800 |
| alpēstrē | . Yellow | . 6, H. Ev. Tr. Germany | . 1818 |
| Andersōnī | . Yellow | . 5, H. Ev. Tr. Hybrid | . 1828 |
| angustifōliūm | . Yellow | . 6, H. Ev. Tr. | . 1800 |
| apennīnūm | . White | . 6, H. Ev. S. Italy | . 1731 |
| arābicūm, 1 | . Yellow | . 7, H. Ev. S. S. Eur. | . 1826 |
| atriplicifōliūm | . Yellow | . 6, H. Ev. S. Spain | . 1656 |
| barbātūm | . Yellow | . 6, H. Ev. S. Spain | . 1820 |
| Barrēliērī | . Yellow | . 6, H. Ev. S. Italy | . 1825 |
| brasiliēnsē | . Yellow | . 6, H. Ev. S. Brasil | . 1823 |
| canadēnsē | . Yellow | . 6. H. Her. P. N. Amer. | . 1799 |
| canariēnsē | . Yellow | . 6, F. Ev. S. Canaries | . 1790 |
| cāndidūm | . Yellow | . 6, H. Ev. S. Spain | |
| canēscēns, 2 | . Red | . 6, H. Ev. S. | |
| cānūm | . Yellow | . 6, H. Ev. Tr. S. Eur. | . 1772 |
| carolinīānūm | . Yellow | . 7, H. Her. P. Carolina | . 1823 |
| cheiranthoīdēs | . Yellow | . 6, H. Ev. S. Portugal | . 1818 |
| ciliātūm | . Red | . 6, H. Ev. S. S. Eur. | |
| cinērēūm | . Yellow | . 7, F. Ev. S. Spain | |
| confērtūm | . Yellow | . 8, F. Ev. S. Teneriffe | |
| confūsūm | . White | . 6, H. Ev. Tr. S. Eur. | |
| crassifōliūm | . Yellow | . 6, F. Ev. S. Barbary | . 1818 |
| crōcēūm | . Yellow | . 7, H. Ev. Tr. Spain | . 1800 |
| cūprēūm | . Red | . 6, H. Ev. Tr. Hybrid | |
| denticulātūm, 3 | Yellow | . 6, H. | A. France | . 1818 |
| dichōtōmūm | . Yellow | . 7, H. Ev. Tr. Spain | . 1826 |
| diversifōliūm | . Flame | . 6, H. Ev. S. Europe | |
| ellipticūm | . Yellow | . 7, F. Ev. S. Egypt | |
| ericoīdēs | . Yellow | . 6, F. Ev. S. S. Eur. | |

| | | | | | |
|---|---|---|---|---|---|
| eriocaulòn | Yellow | H. | A. | Spain | 1817 |
| erio-epalòn | Yellow | H. Ev. | Tr. | Hybrid | |
| farinòsũm | White | 6, H. Ev. | S. | Spain | |
| fœtidũm | White | 6, H. Ev. | Tr. | | 1800 |
| formòsũm | Yellow | F. Ev. | S. | Portugal | 1780 |
| Fumáná | Yellow | 6, H. Ev. | S. | France | 1752 |
| glaũcum | Yellow | 7, H. Ev. | S. | Spain | 1815 |
| globulariæfolìũm | Yellow | 6, H. Her. | P. | Portugal | 1826 |
| glomeràtũm | Yellow | 6, F. Ev. | S. | Mexico | 1823 |
| glutinòsũm | Yellow | 7, H. Ev. | S. | S. Eur. | 1790 |
| grandiflòrũm | Yellow | 6, H. Ev. | Tr. | Italy | 1800 |
| guttàtũm | Yellow | 6, H. | A. | England | |
| halimifolìũm | Yellow | 7, H. Ev. | S. | Spain | 1656 |
| hirtũm | Yellow | 6, H. Ev. | S. | Spain | 1759 |
| hispidũm | White | H. Ev. | Tr. | S. Eur. | 1816 |
| hyssopifolìũm | Yellow | 5, H. Ev. | Tr. | Italy | |
| eũprèũm | Copper | 5, H. Ev. | Tr. | Naples | |
| mũltiplex | Copper | 5, H. Ev. | Tr. | Italy | |
| erocèũm | Copper | 6, H. Ev. | Tr. | Europe | |
| inconspicũũm | Yellow | 6, H. | A. | Spain | 1819 |
| involucràtũm | Yellow | F. Ev. | S. | Spain | 1826 |
| itàlicũm | Yellow | 8, V. Ev. | Tr. | Italy | 1799 |
| juniperìnũm | Yellow | 7, V. Ev. | S. | S. Eur. | 1800 |
| kahìricũm | Yellow | 6, F. Ev. | S. | Egypt | 1820 |
| Lagàscæ | Yellow | 7, F. Ev. | Tr. | Spain | 1826 |
| lanceolàtum | White | 6, H. Ev. | Tr. | Hybrid | |
| lasiánthũm | Yellow | 6, F. Ev. | S. | Spain | 1826 |
| lavandulæfolìũm | Yellow | 6, H. Ev. | S. | S. France | 1817 |
| làvæ | Yellow | 6 F. Ev. | S. | Spain | 1826 |
| lævìpes | Yellow | 7, H. Ev. | S. | France | 1690 |
| ledifolìũm | Yellow | 6, H. | A. | England | |
| leptophýllũm | Yellow | H. Ev. | Tr. | Spain | 1818 |
| libanòtis | Yellow | H. Ev. | S. | S. Eur. | 1752 |
| lignòsũm | Yellow | 6, H. Ev. | S. | S. Eur. | 1806 |
| lineàré | White | 6, F. Ev. | S. | S. Eur. | 1818 |
| Lippiì | Yellow | F. Ev. | S. | Egypt | 1820 |
| lucidũm | Yellow | 6, H. Ev. | Tr. | | 1826 |
| lunulàtũm | Yellow | 7, H. Ev. | S. | Spain | 1826 |
| macrànthũm | Wht. yel. | 7, H. Ev. | Tr. | | |
| mũltiplex | Wht. yel. | 6, H. Ev. | Tr. | Europe | |
| majoranifolìũm | Yel. wht. | 6, H. Ev. | S. | | |
| marifolìũm | Yellow | 5, H. Ev. | Tr. | S. Eur. | |
| microphýllũm | Yellow | 6, H. Ev. | S. | Europe | 1800 |
| Millèrì | Yellow | 6, H. Ev. | Tr. | S. Eur. | |
| mòllè | Yellow | 7, F. Ev. | S. | Spain | 1817 |
| mutàbilè | Red yel. | 7, H. Ev. | Tr. | Spain | 1829 |
| ròsèũm | Red | 7, H. Ev. | S. | S. Eur. | |
| nilòticũm | Yellow | 6, H. | A. | S. Eur. | 1817 |
| majũs | Yellow | H. | A. | Europe | 1817 |
| procũmbèns | Yellow | H. | A. | France | 1816 |
| nudicaulè | Yellow | 6, H. Ev. | S. | Spain | 1826 |
| nummulàrìũm | Yellow | 7, H. Ev. | Tr. | Spain | 1752 |
| obovàtũm | Yellow | F. Ev. | S. | Spain | 1826 |
| obscũrũm | Yellow | 6, H. Ev. | Tr. | Europe | 1816 |
| ocymoìdès, 4 | Yellow | 6, F. Ev. | S. | Spain | 1800 |
| cœlùdicũm | Yellow | 7, H. Ev. | Tr. | Germany | 1816 |
| origanifolìũm | Yellow | F. Ev. | Tr. | Spain | 1795 |
| ovàtũm | Yellow | H. Ev. | Tr. | Geneva | 1818 |
| paniculàtũm | Yellow | 7, F. Ev. | S. | Spain | 1826 |
| penicillàtũm | Yellow | 6, H. Ev. | Tr. | Spain | 1817 |
| pilòsũm | White | 7, H. Ev. | Tr. | S. France | 1731 |
| plantagìnèũm | Yellow | H. | A. | S. Eur. | 1823 |
| polifolìũm | White | 6, H. Ev. | Tr. | England | |
| procũmbèns | Yellow | H. Ev. | T. | S. Eur. | |
| pulchèllũm | Yellow | 5, H. Ev. | Tr. | S. Eur. | 1820 |
| pulverulèntũm | White | 6, H. Ev. | Tr. | France | |
| punctàtũm | Yellow | 7, H. | A. | S. France | 1816 |
| racemòsũm | White | 7, H. Ev. | S. | S. Eur. | 1820 |
| ramuliflòrũm | Yellow | 6, H. Her. | P. | Carolina | 1823 |
| rhodànthũm | Red | 6, H. Ev. | Tr. | Spain | 1800 |
| ròsèũm | Pink | 6, H. Ev. | Tr. | S. Eur. | 1815 |
| mũltiplex | Pink | 6, H. Ev. | Tr. | | 1815 |
| rosmarinifolìũm | Pa. yel. | 6, H. Her. | P. | Canada | 1823 |
| rugòsũm | Yellow | 6, F. Ev. | S. | Portugal | 1800 |
| salicifolìũm | Yellow | 7, H. | A. | S. Eur. | 1759 |
| sanguinèũm | Yellow | 6, H. | | Spain | 1826 |
| scabròsũm | Yellow | H. Ev. | S. | Portugal | 1775 |
| serpyllifolìũm | Yellow | 7, H. Ev. | S. | England | 1731 |
| squamàtũm | Yellow | 6, F. Ev. | S. | Spain | 1815 |
| stœchadifolìũm | Yellow | H. Ev. | S. | Spain | 1816 |
| stramìnèũm | Straw | H. Ev. | Tr. | Europe | |
| mũltiplex | Striped | H. Ev. | Tr. | Europe | |
| strictũm | White | 6, F. Ev. | S. | Spain | 1820 |
| sulphũrèũm | Pa. yel. | H. Ev. | Tr. | Spain | 1795 |
| surrejànũm | Yellow | 8, H. Ev. | Tr. | England | |
| taũricũm | Yellow | 6, H. Ev. | Tr. | Tauria | |
| thymifolìũm | Yellow | 7, H. Ev. | S. | Spain | 1658 |
| tomentòsũm | Yellow | 7 F. Ev. | Tr. | Scotland | |
| Tuberàrìa | Yellow | 6, H. Her. | P. | S. Eur. | 1752 |
| umbellàtũm | White | 7, F. Ev. | S. | S. Eur. | 1731 |
| variegàtũm | Red wht. | 6, H. Ev. | Tr. | Hybrid | |
| vеnùstũm | Red | 6, H. Ev. | Tr. | S. Eur. | 1800 |
| flòre-plèno | Red | 6, H. Ev. | Tr. | S. Eur. | 1800 |
| versicòlor | Red wht. | 7, H. Ev. | S. | S. Eur. | 1800 |
| villòsũm | Yellow | 7, H. | A. | Spain | 1823 |
| vineàlè | Yellow | H. Ev. | Tr. | Germany | 1817 |
| violàcèũm | White | H. Ev. | Tr. | Spain | 1826 |
| virgàtũm | White | 6, H. Ev. | S. | Barbary | 1818 |
| virìde | Yellow | F. Ev. | S. | Italy | 1825 |

[ 155 ]

| | | | | | |
|---|---|---|---|---|---|
| vulgàré | Yellow | 6, H. Ev. | Tr. | Britain | |
| plènũm | Yellow | 6, H. Ev. | Tr. | | |

HELIÀNTHŨS, *Linn.* From *helios*, sun, and *anthos*, a flower; on account of the brilliant colour of the flowers, and from the erroneous idea that the flowers always turned towards the sun. *Linn.* 19, Or. 2, Nat. Or. *Compositæ.* The sun-flower is a highly ornamental and extensive genus of plants, and from their tall growth they are particularly adapted to the back of flower borders or the front of shrubberies, in which situation they make a splendid appearance in autumn; they grow well in any common garden soil, the tender kinds being protected in winter. They are all easily increased by seed, which is ripened in abundance; the annual kinds should be raised on a hotbed in spring, and when of sufficient size, transplanted into the open border, where they will grow and flower beautifully. *Synonymes:* 1. *H. pubescens.* 2. *asper.*

| | | | | | |
|---|---|---|---|---|---|
| angustifolìũs | Yellow | 9, H. Her. | P. | N. Amer. | 1789 |
| altìssimũs | Yellow | 8, H. Her. | P. | N. Amer. | 1731 |
| ànnũûs | Yellow | 7, H. | A. | S. Amer. | 1596 |
| atrorùbèns | Yellow | 8, H. Her. | P. | N. Amer. | 1732 |
| cornifolìũs | Yellow | 8, H. Her. | P. | Mexico | 1825 |
| decapétalũs | Yellow | 9, H. Her. | P. | N. Amer. | 1759 |
| diffùsũs | Yellow | H. Her. | P. | N. Amer. | 1821 |
| divaricàtũs | Yellow | H. Her. | P. | N. Amer. | 1759 |
| excèlsũs | Yellow | H. Her. | P. | Mexico | 1820 |
| gigantèûs | Yellow | H. Her. | P. | N. Amer. | 1714 |
| Hookèrì, 1 | Yellow | 9, H. Her. | P. | | |
| indicũs | Yellow | 7, H. | A. | Egypt | 1785 |
| lætiflòrũs | Yellow | 8, H. Her. | P. | N. Amer. | 1810 |
| lenticulàrìs | Yellow | H. Her. | P. | | 1827 |
| lineàris | Yellow | 9, H. Her. | P. | Mexico | 1823 |
| longifolìũs | Yellow | H. Her. | P. | Georgia | 1812 |
| macrophýllũs | Yellow | H. Her. | P. | N. Amer. | 1800 |
| missùricũs | Yellow | H. Her. | P. | Missouri | 1821 |
| mòllis | Yellow | 8, H. Her. | P. | N. Amer. | 1805 |
| multiflòrũs | Yellow | H. Her. | P. | N. Amer. | 1597 |
| plènũs | Yellow | H. Her. | P. | N. Amer. | 1797 |
| ovàtũs | Yellow | H. | A. | Mexico | 1829 |
| parviflòrũs | Yellow | 7, H. Her. | P. | Mexico | 1826 |
| pátens | Yellow | 8, H. Her. | P. | N. Amer. | 1829 |
| pauciflòrũs | Yellow | 8, H. Her. | P. | Louisiana | 1824 |
| petiolàrìs, 2 | Yellow | 9, H. | A. | Arkansas | 1826 |
| prostràtũs | Yellow | 8, H. De. | Tr. | N. Amer. | 1800 |
| pubèscèns | Yellow | H. Her. | P. | N. Amer. | 1759 |
| specìòsũs | Yellow | 8, H. | A. | Jorulla | 1828 |
| strumòsũs | Yellow | H. Her. | P. | N. Amer. | 1710 |
| trachelifolìũs | Yellow | 9, H. Her. | P. | N. Amer. | 1825 |
| trilobàtũs | Yellow | 9, H. Her. | P. | Mexico | 1824 |
| tubæformis | Yellow | 7, H. | A. | Mexico | 1799 |
| tuberòsũs | Yellow | 8, H. Tw. | P. | Brazil | 1617 |
| villòsũs | Yellow | 8, H. Her. | P. | N. Amer. | 1820 |

HELICHRÝSŨM, see *Elichrysũm.*

HELICÒNÌA, *Linn.* Derived from *Helicon*, the mountain of the Muses; from its affinity to the genus *Musa.* *Linn.* 5, Or. 2, Nat. Or. *Musaceæ.* A rich loamy soil mixed with sand is best adapted for these curious plants, and to flower them in perfection they require plenty of pot-room and a strong heat; young plants are easily obtained by division of the roots. *Synonymes:* 1. *buccinata.* 2. *psittacorum.*

| | | | | | |
|---|---|---|---|---|---|
| Balìsa | Orange | 8, S. Her. | P. | Maranh. | 1823 |
| bicolòr | Wht. crim. | 8. Her. | P. | Brazil | 1828 |
| Bìhaì | Orange | 7, S. Her. | P. | W. Ind. | 1786 |
| Brasiliènsis | Scarlet | 8, S. Her. | P. | Brazil | 1820 |
| caribèæ | Orange | 7, S. Her. | P. | W. Ind. | 1798 |
| dealbàtã | | 8. Her. | P. | | |
| hirsùtã | Orange | 7, S. Her. | P. | S. Amer. | 1800 |
| hùmìlis | Scarlet | 8. Her. | P. | Caraccas | 1798 |
| indica, 1 | | 8. Her. | P. | Madaga. | 1818 |
| psittacòrũm | Orange | 8, S. Her. | P. | W. Ind. | 1797 |
| pulverulèntã | Osh. scar. | 7, S. Her. | P. | S. Amer. | 1830 |
| Swartziàná, 2 | Yellow | 7, S. Her. | P. | Jamaica | 1800 |

HELICOSPÒRÌŨM, *Nees.* From *helikos*, twisted, and *spora*, a sporule; in reference to the twisted sporules. *Linn.* 24, Or. 9, Nat. Or. *Fungi.* An extremely minute greenish species, found in autumn about the foot of trees—*sègetũm.*

HELICTÈRĘS, *Linn.* From *helix*, a screw; in reference to the carpels being twisted. *Linn.* 16, Or. 7, Nat. Or. *Sterculiaceæ.* A genus of free-flowering shrubs, not possessed of much beauty; they grow freely in a mixture of loam and peat, and cuttings taken off at a joint, root readily in sand, under a glass, in heat.

| | | | | | |
|---|---|---|---|---|---|
| barùënsis | White | 9, S. Ev. | S. | W. Ind. | 1789 |
| elongàtã | Yellow | S. Ev. | S. | E. Ind. | 1831 |
| ferrugìnàtã | Yellow | 6, S. Ev. | S. | Brazil | 1823 |
| guasumæfolìã | Purple | S. Ev. | S. | Orinoco | 1820 |

| Isŏrā | Yellow | 6, S. Ev. S. | Malabar | 1733 |
| jamaicensis | White | S. Ev. S. | E. Ind. | 1823 |
| verbascifolia | Brown | S. Ev. S. | Brazil | 1818 |
| virgata | Red | S. Ev. S. | E. Ind. | 1830 |

**HELIOCARPUS**, *Linn.* From *helios*, the sun, and *karpos*, a fruit; the valves of the capsule are beautifully fringed, which gives them the appearance of a little sun. *Linn.* 11, Or. 1, Nat. Or. *Tiliaceæ.* An ornamental shrub, from fourteen to twenty feet high: it thrives in a mixture of sand, loam, and peat; and cuttings of the young wood will root in sand, under a glass, in a moderate heat.

| americanus | Purple | S. Ev. S. | Vera Cruz | 1733 |

**HELIOPHILA**, *Linn.* From *helios*, the sun, and *phileo*, to love; on account of the plants growing in places exposed to the sun. *Linn.* 15, Nat. Or. *Cruciferæ.* A genus of pretty little plants, mostly annuals; they are well worthy of extensive cultivation, thriving well in sandy loam and peat; cuttings of the shrubby kinds strike readily in sand, under a glass, or they may be increased by seeds. The annuals should be sown early in spring, in pots, and placed in the greenhouse or a gentle hotbed; and in May they may be planted out in the open border. *Synonymes:* 1. *Pilosa incisa.* 2. *Cleome capensis, Cheiranthus strictus.* 3. *Peltaria capensis.* 4. *Heliophila pinnata.* 5. *H. integrifolia.* 6. *H. pinnata.*

| amplexicaulis | Wht. pur. | 7, H. | A. C. G. H. | 1774 |
| araboides, 1 | Brown | 6, H. | A. C. G. H. | 1768 |
| cleomoides, 2 | Yellow | 7, G. Ev. S. | A. C. G. H. | 1802 |
| coronopifolia | Violet | 7, H. | A. C. G. H. | 1778 |
| crithmifolia | Violet | 7, H. | A. C. G. H. | 1816 |
| diffusa | White | 6, H. | A. C. G. H. | 1818 |
| digitata | Brown | 6, H. | A. C. G. H. | 1819 |
| dissecta | Blue | 6, H. | A. C. G. H. | 1792 |
| pinnata | White | 6, H. | A. C. G. H. | 1792 |
| foeniculacea | Purple | 6, H. | A. C. G. H. | 1774 |
| filiformis | Pa. pur. | 6, H. | A. C. G. H. | 1786 |
| incana | Purple | 6, G. Ev. S. | C. G. H. | 1774 |
| lepidioides | White | 6, H. | A. C. G. H. | 1818 |
| linearifolia | Blue | 6, G. Ev. S. | C. G. H. | 1819 |
| pectinata | White | 6, H. | A. C. G. H. | 1819 |
| peltaria, 3 | White | 6, H. | A. C. G. H. | 1820 |
| pendula, 4 | Yel. wht. | 7, H. | A. C. G. H. | 1792 |
| pilosa, 5 | Blue | 7, H. | A. C. G. H. | 1768 |
| platysiliqua | Purple | 7, G. Ev. S. | C. G. H. | 1774 |
| pusilla | White | 6, H. | A. C. G. H. | 1824 |
| rivalis | White | 6, H. | A. C. G. H. | 1819 |
| scoparia | Red | 6, G. Ev. S. | C. G. H. | 1802 |
| stricta | Blue | 6, H. | A. C. G. H. | 1823 |
| trifida, 6 | Purple | 6, H. | A. C. G. H. | 1819 |

**HELIOPSIS**, *Persoon.* From *helios*, the sun, and *opsis*, appearance; alluding to the brilliant colour of the flowers. *Linn.* 19, Or. 2, Nat. Or. *Compositæ.* These are tall growing plants, well suited for the back of flower borders, where they flower beautifully in autumn. The annual kinds require the same treatment as those of the genus *Helianthus*; while the herbaceous kinds may be freely increased by dividing the roots. *Synonymes:* 1. *Acmella bupthalmoides, Bupthalmum scabrum.* 2. *B. helianthoides.*

| canescens | Yellow | 8, H. Her. P. | Mexico | 1818 |
| lævis, 2 | Yellow | 8, H. Her. P. | N. Amer. | 1714 |
| scabra | Yellow | 8, H. Her. P. | N. Amer. | 1824 |

*bupthalmoides* 1, *dubia.*

**HELIOTROPIUM**, *Linn.* From *helios*, the sun, and *trope*, twining; the flowers are said to turn towards the sun. *Linn.* 5, Or. 1, Nat. Or. *Ehratiaceæ.* Some of the plants of this genus are highly valued for the fragrance of their flowers, and are therefore to be met with in most gardens; they succeed freely in any rich light soil, and cuttings of the shrubby kinds taken off when young, readily strike in the same kind of soil. The annuals and biennials require the same treatment as other hardy and tender annuals and biennials. *Synonymes:* 1. *H. grandiflorum.* 2. *H. chenopodioides.* 3. *Myosotis linifolia.*

| brevifolium | White | 8. Tr. B. | Nepal | 1824 |
| capense | White | H. | A. C. G. H. | 1824 |
| commutatum | White | 8, H. | A. S. Eur. | 1800 |
| coromandelinum | White | | A. E. Ind. | 1812 |
| corymbosum, 1 | Lilac | 7, G. Ev. S. | Peru | 1800 |
| curassavicum | White | 6, F. | A. W. Ind. | 1731 |
| chenopodioides 2 | White | 6, H. | A. S. Amer. | 1823 |
| europæum | White | 8 H. | A. S. Eur. | 1562 |
| humile | White | 6, S. Ev. S. | W. Ind. | 1752 |
| linifolium, 3 | White | 7, G. Ev. S. | C. G. H. | 1815 |
| maroccanum | White | 6, G. Ev. S. | Morocco | 1823 |
| oblongifolium | White | 7, H. | A. S. Eur. | 1824 |
| obovatum | Brown | 6, H. | A. Nepal | 1825 |
| parviflorum | White | 8, S. | B. W. Ind. | 1732 |
| peruvianum | Lilac | 7, G. De. S. | Peru | 1757 |
| hybridum | Lilac | 7, G. De. S. | Hybrid | 1815 |
| prostratum | White | 6, H. | A. N. Holl. | 1826 |
| undulatum | LL brn. | 7, G. Ev. S. | N. Africa | 1820 |
| zeylanicum | White | 8. Her. P. | Ceylon | 1818 |

**HELLEBORUS**, *Linn.* From *helein*, to cause death, and *bora*, food; the poisonous qualities of the plants. *Linn.* 13, Or. 6, Nat. Or. *Ranunculaceæ.* These plants thrive well in any common soil, growing best under the shade of trees; and are readily increased by divisions or seeds. The poisonous qualities of this genus are well known. *Synonyme:* 1. *trifolius.*

| atrorubens | Purple | 3, H. Her. P. | Hungary | 1820 |
| dumetorum | Green | 3, H. Her. P. | Hungary | 1817 |
| foetidus | Green | 3, H. Her. P. | England | |
| lividus | Purple | 3, H. Her. P. | Corsica | 1710 |
| integrilobus, 1 | Purple | 2, F. Her. P. | Corsica | 1710 |
| niger | Pink | 3, H. Her. P. | Austria | 1596 |
| angustifolius | Pink | 3, H. Her. P. | Austria | 1596 |
| odorus | Green | 3, H. Her. P. | Hungary | 1817 |
| purpurascens | Pur. grn. | 3, H. Her. P. | Hungary | 1817 |
| vernalis | White | 2, H. Her. P. | Austria | 1596 |
| viridis | Green | 3, H. Her. P. | Britain | |

**HELLENIA**, *Willdenow.* In honour of C. N. Hellenius, professor at Abo. *Linn.* 1, Or. 1, Nat. Or. *Scitamineæ.* Ornamental plants; for culture and propagation, see *Hedychium.*

| abnormis | White | 6, S. Her. P. | China | 1824 |
| cærulea | White | 8. Her. P. | N. Holl. | 1820 |
| chinensis | White | 8. Her. P. | China | 1825 |

**HELMET-SHAPED**, see *Galeate.*

**HELMINTHIA**, *Jussieu.* From *helminthion*, a little worm; because of the resemblance of the rugose seeds. *Linn.* 19, Or. 1, Nat. Or. *Compositæ.* The seeds of this species only require to be sown in the open border. *Synonyme: Picris echioides.*

| echioides | Yellow | 6, H. | A. Britain | |

**HELMISPORIUM**, *Link.* From *helmins*, a worm, and *spora*, a sporule; shape of the sporules. *Linn.* 24, Or. 9, Nat. Or. *Fungi.* Patches of very minute black *Fungi*, found on dead wood, and branches of trees—*macrocarpon, velutinum.*

**HELONIAS**, *Linn.* From *helos*, a marsh; in reference to the habitat of the plants. *Linn.* 6, Or. 3, Nat. Or. *Melanthaceæ.* These are ornamental plants, delighting in peat soil and a moist situation, where they will grow and flower profusely; they increase readily by dividing the roots, or by seeds. *Synonymes:* 1. *H. latifolia.* 2. *H. læta.*

| angustifolia | White | 5, H. Her. P. | N. Amer. | 1823 |
| bullata, 1 | Purple | 4, H. Her. P. | N. Amer. | 1758 |
| erythrosperma, 2 | White | 6, H. Her. P. | N. Amer. | 1770 |

**HELOSCIADIUM**, *Koch.* From *helos*, a marsh, and *skiadon*, an umbel; an umbelliferous plant, inhabiting marshes. *Linn.* 5, Or. 2, Nat. Or. *Umbelliferæ.* Mere weeds, growing in ponds or rivulets, like other hardy aquatics. *Synonymes:* 1. *Sison Ammi.* 2. *S. bulbosum.* 3. *S. inudatum.* 4. *Sium nodiflorum.* 5. *Sison repens*—*Ammi* 1, *bulbosum* 2, *inundatum* 3, *nodiflorum* 4, *repens* 5.

**HELVELLA**, *Linn.* A name employed by Cicero, as the name of a fungus. *Linn.* 24, Or. 9, Nat. Or. *Fungi.* These species are found in spring and autumn in woods, fields, &c.—*elastica, esculenta, infula, leucophæa, mitra.*

**HEMEROCALLIS**, *Linn.* From *hemera*, a day, and *kallos*, beauty; alluding to the beauty and duration of the flowers. *Linn.* 6, Or. 1, Nat. Or. *Liliaceæ.* This is an ornamental genus of flowering plants, of the simplest culture, thriving well in any light loamy soil, and readily increased by divisions.

| disticha | Orange | 5, H. Her. P. | China | 1798 |
| flava | Yellow | 6, H. Her. P. | Siberia | 1596 |
| fulva | Fulvous | 7, H. Her. P. | Levant | 1596 |
| graminea | Li. yel. | 6, H. Her. P. | Siberia | 1759 |
| Sieboldi | Pink | 9, H. Her. P. | Japan | 1833 |

**HEMICLIDIA**, *R. Brown.* Supposed to be from *hemisus*, half, and *kleio*, to shut up. *Linn.* 4, Or. 1, Nat. Or. *Proteaceæ.* A fine greenhouse plant; for culture and propagation, see *Dryandra. Synonyme:* 1. *Dryandra falcata.*

| Baxteri, 1 | Yellow | 6, G. Ev. S. | Lucky Bay | 1824 |

HEMIDÈSMÛS, *R. Brown.* From *hemisus*, half, and *desmos*, a tie; alluding to the filaments. *Linn.* 5, Or. 2, Nat. Or. *Asclepiadaceæ.* A pretty climbing species, thriving well in a mixture of loam and peat; young plants are very freely obtained by cuttings planted in sand, under a glass, in a little heat. A decoction of the roots is recommended by European practitioners in cutaneous diseases, scrofula, and venereal affections.

indicûs . . . . Green . . S. Ev. Tw. Ceylon . . 1796

HEMIMÈRIs, *Linn.* From *hemisus*, half, and *meris*, a part; the flowers appear as if parted. *Linn.* 2, Or. 1, Nat. Or *Scrophulariaceæ.* An ornamental plant, growing well in a mixture of loam and peat; and young cuttings, planted in the same kind of soil, root freely.

montànâ . . . . . 7, S. Her. P. C. G. H. . 1816

HEMIONÌTÏs, *Linn.* From *hemionos*, a mule; the species is supposed to be barren. *Linn.* 24, Or. 1, Nat. Or. *Polypodiaceæ.* A very elegant little fern, thriving well in a mixture of sandy loam and peat, and readily increased by dividing the roots.

palmatâ . . . . . . 7, S. Her. P. W. Ind. . 1793

HEMLOCK, see *Conïûm.*
HEMLOCK-SPRUCE, see *Pÿnûs canadènsis.*
HEMP, see *Cànnâbis.*
HEMP-AGRIMONY, see *Eupatörïûm cannabïnûm*
HEMP-NETTLE, see *Galeöpsis.*
HEN-AND-CHICKENS, see *Bèllis perènnis prolïferâ*
HENBANE, see *Hyoscÿâmûs.*
HENBIT, see *Lâmïûm amplexicaûlê.*
HENNA-PLANT, see *Lawsönïâ inermis.*

HEPÀTICĂ, *Linn.* From *hepaticos*, relating to the liver; the lobes of the leaves have been compared to the lobes of the liver. *Linn.* 13, Or. 6, Nat. Or. *Ranunculaceæ.* These are very pretty plants, and on account of their being abundant flowerers, and the flowers of much variety in shade and colour, they are all universal favourites in the flower-garden. They grow best in a light loam or peat soil, and increase readily by dividing the roots in spring. *Synonyme;* 1. *Anemone hepatica.*

acutilöbâ . . . . Blue . . 3, H. Her. P. N. Amer. . 1818
americàna . . . . Blue . . 3, H. Her. P. N. Amer. . 1800
angulöâ . . . . Blue . . 3, H. Her. P. N. Amer.
trilöbâ, 1 . . . . Pink . . 4, H. Her. P. England

HEPATICOUS, liver-coloured, lobed like the liver.

HERACÀNTHĂ, *Link.* From *heros*, noble, and *akantha*, a thorn; alluding to the beauty of the plants. *Linn.* 19, Or. 1, Nat. Or. *Compositæ.* Very pretty annuals; the seed should be sown on a gentle hotbed, and when of sufficient size, transplanted into the flower borders. *Synonymes:* 1. *Carthamus armenius.* 2. *C. lanatus.* 3. *C. creticus.* 4. *C. tauricus, Onobroma dentata.*

armènïâ, 1 . . . Yellow . 6, H.    A. Armenia . 1816
crètïcâ, 2 . . . . White . . 6, H.    A. Candia . 1731
lanàtâ, 3 . . . . Yellow . 7, H.    A. S. Eur. . 1596
taûrïcâ, 4 . . . Yellow . 6, H.    A. Caucasus . 1818

HERÀCLÈÛM, *Linn.* From *Heracles*, a plant sacred to Hercules. *Linn.* 5, Or. 2, Nat. Or. *Umbelliferæ.* Strong coarse growing plants, only worth cultivating in botanical collections; any common soil suits them; and they are all easily increased by seed. *Synonymes:* 1. *H. angustifolium.* 2. *H. sibiricum.* 3. *H. gummiferum.* 4. *H. amplifolium.* 5. *H. elegans.* 6. *H. laciniatum.*

alpìnûm . . . . White . . 6, H. Her. P. Switzerl. . 1739
aspèrûm . . . . White . 7, H.    B. Caucasus . 1818
caucàsïcûm . . . White . . 6, H.    B. Caucasus . 1818
lanàtûm . . . . White . . 6, H. Her. P. N. Amer. . 1810
ligusticifölïûm . . White . . 6, H.    B. Tauria . 1816
màsîmûm . . . . White . . 6, H. Her. P. S. France . 1810
pubèscène, 3 . . . White . 7, H.    B. Caucasus . 1823
pyrenàïcûm . . . White . . 6, H.    B. Pyrenees . 1798
specîôsûm . . . . White . . 6, H.    B. Siberia . 1817
Sphondylïûm
  élègàns, 5 . . . White . . 5, H.    B. Britain .
  lacinätûm, 6 . White . . 5, H.    B. Austria . 1800
villôsûm . . . . White . . 5, H.    B. Austria . 1900
villôsûm . . . . White . . 6, H.    B. Siberia . 1826

*austrïâcûm, flavèscèns, F. angustifölïûm* 1, *F. latifölïûm* 2, *longifölïûm, Panàcês, taûrïcûm, verrucôsûm.*

HERBACEOUS-PLANT, a plant, the stem of which perishes annually.

HERBÈRTÏĂ, *Sweet.* In honour of the Hon. and Rev. William Herbert, of Spofforth, a distinguished botanist, and author of a Monograph on Amarylli-

daceæ, 1837. *Linn.* 16, Or. 1, Nat. Or. *Iridaceæ.* A very pretty species, growing well in an equal mixture of loam, peat, and sand; with protection in winter, the species will grow as well in the open border, as in the frame; it is increased by seeds.

pulchèllâ . . . Blue pur.. 7, F. Bu. P. Chile . . 1827

HERB-PARIS, see *Paris quadrifölïâ.*
HERB-ROBERT, see *Gerânïûm Robertïânûm.*
HERCULES's-CLUB, see *Zanthöxÿlûm clàvâ Hercûlis.*

HERITIÈRĂ, *Aiton.* In honour of Charles Louis L'Heritier de Bautelle, a celebrated French botanist and author; he died in 1800. *Linn.* 21, Or. 10, Nat. Or. *Sterculiaceæ.* This genus, the Looking-glass Plant, consists of large handsome growing trees, and is easily cultivated in sandy loam and peat; large ripened cuttings root in sand, under a glass, in a moist heat.

littoràlis . . . . Red . . S. Ev. T. E. Ind. . . 1780
minôr . . . . . . S. Ev. T. Mauritius . 1824

HERMÀNNÏĂ, *Linn.* In honour of Paul Hermann, a botanist and traveller in Ceylon; he died in 1695. *Linn.* 16, Or. 2, Nat. Or. *Sterculiaceæ.* Pretty flowering plants, well worth a place in every garden; they all grow well in any light rich soil, and young cuttings will root readily in the same kind of soil, under a glass. *Synonymes:* 1. *H. rotundifolia.* 2. *Mahernia grandiflora.* 3. *H. latifolia.*

alnifölïâ . . . Yellow . 3, G. Ev. S. C. G. H. . 1728
althæifölïâ . . . Yellow . 4, G. Ev. S. C. G. H. . 1728
angulàris . . . Yellow . 4, G. Ev. S. C. G. H. . 1791
argèntâ . . . . Or. yel. . 5, G. Ev. S. C. G. H. . 1820
bryonifölïâ . . . Yellow . 6, G. Ev. S. C. G. H. . 1818
càndïcàns . . . Yellow . 5, G. Ev. S. C. G. H. . 1774
coronopifölïâ . . Yellow . 6, G. Ev. S. C. G. H. . 1823
cuneifölïâ . . . Yellow . 3, G. Ev. S. C. G. H. . 1791
decûmbèns . . . Yellow . 5, G. Ev. S. C. G. H. . 1821
denudàtâ . . . . Yellow . 6, G. Ev. S. C. G. H. . 1774
dioæmæfölïâ . . . Yellow . 4, G. Ev. S. C. G. H. . 1795
disermæfölïâ . . Or. red . 4, G. Ev. S. C. G. H. . 1795
distïchâ, 1 . . . Yellow . 6, G. Ev. S. C. G. H. . 1789
filifölïâ . . . . Yellow .   G. Ev. S. C. G. H. . 1816
flàmmèâ . . . . Orange . 12, G. Ev. S. C. G. H. . 1794
frâgràns . . . . Yellow .   G. Ev. S. C. G. H. . 1822
glandulôsâ . . . Yellow . 6, G. Ev. S. C. G. H. . 1822
grandifölïâ, 2 . . Red . . all G. Ev. S. C. G. H. . 1791
hirsûtâ . . . . Yellow . 5, G. Ev. S. C. G. H. . 1790
holoserïcêâ . . . Yellow . 6, G. Ev. S. C. G. H. . 1792
hyssopifölïâ . . . Straw . 5, G. Ev. S. C. G. H. . 1725
incìsâ . . . . . Yellow . 6, G. Ev. S. C. G. H. . 1816
involucràtâ . . . Yellow . 5, G. Ev. S. C. G. H. . 1794
lavandulæfölïâ . . Yellow . 6, G. Ev. S. C. G. H. . 1728
melochinïdes . . . Yellow .   G. Ev. S. C. G. H. . 1818
mìcàns, 3 . . . . Yellow . 5, G. Ev. S. C. G. H. . 1790
mòllis . . . . . Yellow . 5, G. Ev. S. C. G. H. . 1814
multiflôrâ . . . Yellow . 4, G. Ev. S. C. G. H. . 1791
odoràtâ . . . . Yellow . 5, G. Ev. S. C. G. H. . 1780
plicàtâ . . . . Yellow . 11, G. Ev. S. C. G. H. . 1774
procûmbèns . . . Yellow . 5, G. Ev. S. C. G. H. . 1792
pulverulèntâ . . Yellow . 6, G. Ev. S. C. G. H. . 1820
salvifölïâ . . . Yellow . 5, G. Ev. S. C. G. H. . 1795
scàbrâ . . . . . Yellow . 4, G. Ev. S. C. G. H. . 1789
scordifölïâ . . . Yellow . 6, G. Ev. S. 0. G. H. . 1794
tenuifölïâ . . . Yellow . 6, G. Ev. S. C. G. H. .
trifölïàtâ . . . Yellow .   G. Ev. S. C. G. H. . 1752
trifurcàtâ . . . Purple . 5, G. Ev. S. C. G. H. . 1789
triphÿllâ . . . . Yellow . 6, G. Ev. S. C. G. H. . 1819
velutìnâ . . . . Yellow .   G. Ev. S. C. G. H. . 1818

HERMAPHRODITE, consisting of two sexes.

HERMÀs, *Linn.* The meaning of the name is unknown. *Linn.* 23, Or. 1, Nat. Or. *Umbelliferæ.* This is a genus of inconspicuous, stunted-looking plants, thriving well in peat, sand, and loam mixed. They may either be increased by seeds, or cuttings. *Synonyme:* 1. *H. depauperata.*

cilìàta . . . . Grn. yel. . 5, G. Her. P. C. G. H. . 1816
gigantèâ . . . . Green . . 5, G. Her. P. C. G. H. . 1794
villôsâ, 1 . . . Green . . 5, G. Her. P. C. G. H. . 1795

HERMÌNÏÛM, *R. Brown.* The meaning of the name is not explained. *Linn.* 20, Or. 1, Nat. Or. *Orchidaceæ.* The species of this genus are pretty, and grow freely in chalky soil, or in a mixture of loam, peat, and sand; they increase by divisions of the roots. *Synonymes:* 1. *Ophrys alpina, Chamorchis alpina.* 2. *Ophrys monorchis.*

alpìnûm, 1 . . . White . 5, F. Ter. Switzerl. . 1824
congèstûm . . . . Green . 11, G. Ter. Madeira .
monorchis, 2 . . . Green . 6, H. Ter. England .

HERNÀNDÏĂ, *Linn.* In honour of Francisco Hernandez, M.D., a Spanish botanist. *Linn.* 21, Or.

3, Nat. Or. *Hernandiaceæ*. The species of this genus are elegant and lofty-growing trees, succeeding well in sandy loam and peat; and ripened cuttings, not divested of their leaves, will root readily in sand, under a glass. The juice of the leaves of *H. sonora* is a powerful depilatory; it destroys hair, without pain, wherever it is applied.

| | | | | |
|---|---|---|---|---|
| guianensis | . . . | 8. Ev. T. Guiana | . | 1820 |
| ovigera | . . . | 8. Ev. T. E. Ind. | | |
| sonora | . . . | 8. Ev. T. E. Ind. | . | 1693 |

**HERNIARIA,** *Linn.* From *hernia*, a rupture; because of its supposed effect in curing it. *Linn.* 5, Or. 2, Nat. Or. *Illecebraceæ*. The species of this genus are not of very much interest, but of the simplest culture. Synonyme: 1. *hirsuta*.

| | | | | |
|---|---|---|---|---|
| alpīnā | . . | Green | . 6, H. De. Tr. S. Eur. | 1822 |
| annūā | . . | Green | . 7, H. Tr. A. Spain | 1824 |
| cinerēā | . . | Green | . 6, H. Tr. A. Montpel. | 1823 |
| fruticōsā | . . | Green | . 6, H. Ev. S. Spain | 1814 |
| glabrā | . . | Green | . 7, H. De. Tr. England | |
| hirsūtā | . . 1 | Green | . 7, H. De. Tr. England | |
| incānā, 1 | . . | Green | . 7, H. De. Tr. S. Eur. | 1822 |
| polygonoīdēs | . | Green | . 6, G. Ev. S. S. Eur. | 1752 |

**HERON'S-BILL,** see *Erodium*.

**HERPESTIS,** *Gærtner.* From *herpestes*, anything that creeps; alluding to the habit of the plants. *Linn.* 14, Or. 2, Nat. Or. *Scrophulariaceæ*. Some of the species of this genus are very pretty; others are mere weeds. They all thrive well in a rich soil, and are readily increased by seeds, or divisions.

| | | | | |
|---|---|---|---|---|
| cuneifōliā | . . | Blue | . 8. H. Aq. P. N. Amer. | 1812 |
| Monnierī | . . | Li. blue | . 8, 8. Aq. P. S. Amer. | 1772 |
| strictā | . . | Blue | . 8, 8. Aq. P. | 1824 |

*amplexicaulis, Brownii, micrantha, portulacacea, rotundifolia.*

**HERRERIA,** *Ruiz and Pavon.* In honour of C. A. de Herrera, a Spanish agriculturist. *Linn.* 6, Or. 1, Nat. Or. *Liliaceæ*. These are handsome plants, growing freely in a mixture of loam and peat, and are increased by divisions.

| | | | | |
|---|---|---|---|---|
| parviflōrā | . . | Grn. yel. | . 6, 8. Ev. Tw. Brasil | 1824 |
| stellātā | . . | Grn. yel. | . 6, 8. Ev. Tw. Chile | 1825 |

**HESPERANTHA,** *Ker.* From *hespera*, an evening, and *anthos*, a flower; the flowers are produced in the evening. *Linn.* 3, Or. 1, Nat. Or. *Iridaceæ*. A genus of rather pretty flowering bulbs; for culture and propagation, see *Gladiolus*. Synonyme: 1. *Ixia anguita*.

| | | | | |
|---|---|---|---|---|
| angūstā, 1 | . . | White | . 5, G. Bl. P. C. G. H. | 1825 |
| cinnamōmeā | . . | Violet | . 4, G. Bl. P. C. G. H. | 1787 |
| falcātā | . . | Violet | . 4, G. Bl. P. C. G. H. | 1787 |
| graminifōliā | . . | Violet | . 3, G. Bl. P. C. G. H. | 1808 |
| pilōsā | . . | Violet | . 4, G. Bl. P. C. G. H. | 1811 |
| radiātā | . . | Violet | . 3, G. Bl. P. C. G. H. | 1794 |

**HESPERIS,** *Linn.* From *hesperos*, the evening; the flowers of most of the species of Rocket are more fragrant towards evening. *Linn.* 15, Nat. Or. *Cruciferæ*. The Rocket is a well-known flower in every garden. The herbaceous kinds do best in a light rich soil, and attention must be paid to frequent transplanting and dividing, or they will not grow, particularly *H. matronalis* and its varieties; the best time for doing it is when they begin to spring afresh from the root after flowering. The seed of the annual and biennial kinds merely require sowing in the open border. Synonymes: 1. *H. sibirica*. 2. *H. inodora*. 3. *H. bituminosa*.

| | | | | |
|---|---|---|---|---|
| apricā | . . . | Purple | . 6, H. Her. P. Siberia | . 1822 |
| elātā | . . . | Pink | . 6, H. B. Europe | . 1824 |
| excelsā | . . . | White | . 6, H. Her. P. | 1828 |
| frāgrāns | . . . | Purple | . 6, H. B. Siberia | . 1821 |
| grandiflōrā | . . | Wht. pur. 7, H. | B. | 1820 |
| heterophyllā | . . | Red | . 6, H. B. Italy | . 1823 |
| laciniātā | . . | Purple | . 5, H. Her. P. S. France | . 1816 |
| matronālis | . . | Purple | . 6, H. Her. P. Europe | . 1597 |
| hortensis | . . | Purple | . 6, H. Her. P. Europe | . 1759 |
| albiflōrā | . . | White | . 6, H. Her. P. Europe | . 1759 |
| albo-plēnā | . . | White | . 6, H. Her. P. Europe | . 1597 |
| foliiflōrā | . . | Green | . 6, H. Her. P. Europe | . 1597 |
| purpureo-plēnā | Red | . 6, H. Her. P. Europe | . 1597 | |
| variegātā | . . | Wht. red | . 6, H. Her. P. Europe | . 1597 |
| sibirica, 1 | . . | Purple | . 6, H. Her. P. Siberia | . 1800 |
| sylvestris, 2 | . . | Pink | . 6, H. Her. P. Britain | |
| pulchellā | . . | Red | . 7, H. A. Levant | . 1827 |
| pygmēā | . . | Purple | . 6, H. A. Syria | . 1828 |
| ramosissimā | . . | Red | . 7, H. A. Algiers | . 1819 |
| repāndā | . . | Purple | . 6, H. Her. B. Spain | . 1821 |
| runcinātā | . . | Wht. pur. 6, H. B. Hungary | . 1804 | |

| | | | | |
|---|---|---|---|---|
| bituminōsā, 3 | Wht. pur. 6, H. B. | | | |
| speciōsā | . . . | Ro. pur. | . 4, H. Her. P. Siberia | . 1829 |
| tristis | . . . | Purple | . 6, H. B. Austria | . 1629 |

**HESPEROSCORDUM,** *Lindley.* From *hesperos*, the west, and *skordon*, garlic; an alliaceous plant, growing in the western hemisphere. *Linn.* 6, Or. 1, Nat. Or. *Liliaceæ*. These are rather pretty species, growing well in light sandy soil, and increased by offsets, or seeds. *H. hyacinthinum* requires protection in winter. Synonyme: 1. *Brodiæa grandiflora*.

| | | | | |
|---|---|---|---|---|
| hyacinthinūm, 1 | . Blue | . 7, F. Bl. P. | 1826 |
| lūteūm | . . | White | . 7, H. Bl. P. California | . 1833 |

**HETERANTHERA,** *Beauvois.* From *heteros*, variable, and *aner*, an anther; the anthers are variable. *Linn.* 3, Or. 1, Nat. Or. *Pontederaceæ*. This is a genus of ornamental aquatics. The hardy species may be grown by the side of a pond or rivulet; the other kinds require the same treatment as other tender aquatics. Synonyme: 1. *Leptanthes reniformis*.

| | | | | |
|---|---|---|---|---|
| acūtā, 1 | . . | White | . 6, G. Aq. P. Virginia | . 1812 |
| limōsā | . . | Blue | . 7, H. Aq. P. N. Amer. | . 1822 |
| reniformis | . . | White | . 7, 8. Aq. P. S. Amer. | . 1824 |

**HETEROMORPHA,** *Chamisso.* From *heteros*, diverse, and *morpha*, form; in allusion to the leaves. *Linn.* 5, Or. 2, Nat. Or. *Umbelliferæ*. This shrub thrives well in any common garden soil, and is freely increased by cuttings. Synonyme: 1. *Tenoria arborescens*.

| | | | |
|---|---|---|---|
| arborēscens | . | Yellow | . 8, G. Ev. S. C. G. H. | . 1816 |

**HETEROPOGON,** *Persoon.* From *heteros*, variable, and *pogon*, a beard. *Linn.* 21, Or. 3, Nat. Or. *Gramineæ*. Species of grass, not worth cultivating in any collection. Synonymes: 1. *glaber*. 2. *Andropogon contortus—Allionii* 1, *contortus* 2.

**HETEROPTERIS,** *H. B. and Kunth.* From *heteros*, variable, and *pteron*, a wing; the wings of the carpels are various in size and shape. *Linn.* 10, Or. 3, Nat. Or. *Malpighiaceæ*. The plants of this genus are for the most part handsome climbers, thriving well in sand, peat, and loam; and cuttings of the ripened wood will root in sand, under a glass, in heat. Synonymes: 1. *Banisteria brachiata*. 2. *chrysophylla*. 3. *nitida*. 4. *purpurea*.

| | | | | |
|---|---|---|---|---|
| appendiculātā | . | Yellow | . 8. Ev. Cl. St. Vincent | 1820 |
| brachiātā, 1 | . | Yellow | . 8. Ev. Cl. W. Ind. | 1759 |
| cærūleā | . . | Blue | . 8. Ev. Cl. W. Ind. | 1823 |
| chrysophyllā, 2 | . | Yellow | . 8. Ev. Cl. Brasil | 1793 |
| floribūndā | . . | Blue | . 8. Ev. Cl. Mexico | 1824 |
| nitidā, 3 | . . | Yellow | . 8. Ev. S. Brasil | 1809 |
| rūfā | . . | Yellow | . 8. Ev. S. Brasil | 1809 |
| parvifoliā | . | Purple | . 8. Ev. Cl. W. Ind. | 1820 |
| purpūreā, 4 | . | Purple | . 8. Ev. Cl. W. Ind. | 1759 |

**HETEROSPERMUM,** *Willdenow.* From *heteros*, various, and *sperma*, a seed; alluding to the variable size and shape of the seed. *Linn.* 19, Or. 2, Nat. Or. *Compositæ*. An annual of little value; it requires to be raised on a gentle hotbed, and afterwards transplanted into the flower-border.

| | | | |
|---|---|---|---|
| pinnatūm | . . . | Yellow | . 8, H. A. New Spain 1799 |

**HETEROSPHÆRIA,** *Greville.* From *heteros*, variable, and *sphaira*, a sphere. *Linn.* 24, Or. 9, Nat. Or. *Fungi*. A black shining fungus, found growing on the stems of dead herbs—*patella*.

**HEUCHERA,** *Linn.* In honour of John Henry de Heucher, professor of medicine at Wittenberg, and a botanical author. *Linn.* 5, Or. 2, Nat. Or. *Saxifragaceæ*. A genus of very neat, though not showy, American plants, growing well in any light garden soil, and very easily increased by dividing the plants at the root. *H. americana* is a powerful astringent.

| | | | | |
|---|---|---|---|---|
| americānā | . . | Purple | . 5, H. Her. P. N. Amer. | . 1656 |
| caulēscens | . . | White | . 6, H. Her. P. Carolina | . 1812 |
| cylindrāceā | . . | Green | . 5, H. Her. P. N. Amer. | . 182.. |
| glabrā | . . | Pink | . 5, H. Her. P. N. Amer. | . 1827 |
| hispidā | . . | Purple | . 6, H. Her. P. Virginia | . 1826 |
| micranthā | . . | Yel. grn. | . 7, H. Her. P. Columbia | . 1827 |
| pubēscens | . . | Pk. vio. | . 6, H. Her. P. N. Amer. | . 1812 |
| Richardsonii | . . | Green | . H. Her. P. N. Amer. | . 1827 |
| villōsā | . . | Violet | . 5, H. Her. P. Canada | . 1812 |

**HEXAGONAL,** six-sided.

**HEXANDROUS,** having six stamens.

**HEXANGULAR,** six-angled.

**HEXAPETALOUS,** having six petals.

**HEYLANDIA,** *Decandolle.* In honour of M. Heyland,

an artist employed by Decandolle. *Linn.* 16, Or. 6, Nat. Or. *Leguminosæ.* Stove shrubs, otherwise requiring the same treatment as *Hallia.* Synonyms: 1. *Hallia monophylla—hebecarpa* 1, *leiocarpa.*

HẼVNEÃ, *Roxburgh.* In honour of B. Heyne, M.D., a German botanist and traveller in India. *Linn.* 10, Or. 1, Nat. Or. *Meliaceæ.* Ornamental-growing trees, about twenty feet high; they require to be grown in loam and peat, and ripened cuttings, with their leaves whole, will root in sand, under a glass, in heat.

| | | | | | | | |
|---|---|---|---|---|---|---|---|
| quinquejūgā | . . | White | . . | 8. | Ev. | T. Java | . 1816 |
| trijūgā | . . . | White | . . | 9, 8. | Ev. | T. Nepal | . 1819 |

HĪANS, gaping, opening wide.

HIBBĔRTĬĀ, *Anderson.* In honour of George Hibbert, F.R.S., L.S., once eminently distinguished for his love of plants; for a length of time he maintained Mr. Niven, a famous collector of plants, at the Cape. *Linn* 13, Or. 3, Nat. Or. *Dilleniaceæ.* All the species of *Hibbertia* are well worthy of a place in every collection of plants; they grow from one to three feet high, and succeed best in equal quantities of sandy loam and peat. Cuttings, put in in the same kind of soil, either in spring or summer, will root freely under a glass. Synonyms: 1. *H. corifolia.*

| | | | | | | | |
|---|---|---|---|---|---|---|---|
| cistifolĭā | . . | Yellow | . 6, | G. Ev. | 8. | N. Holl. | . 1826 |
| Cunninghamĭ | . . | Yellow | . 6, | G. Ev. | 8. | K. G. Sound | 1832 |
| dentātā | . . | Yellow | . | G. Ev. | Tw. | N. Holl. | . 1814 |
| grossularimfolĭā | . | Yellow | . 5, | G. Ev. | Tr. | N. Holl. | . 1816 |
| linearĭs | . . . | Yellow | . 6, | G. Ev. | 8. | N. Holl. | . 1821 |
| obtusifolĭā | . . | Yellow | . | G. Ev. | 8. | V. D. L. | . 1824 |
| pedunculātā, 1 | . | Yellow | . 6, | G. Ev. | 8. | N. Holl. | . 1821 |
| salĭgnā | . . | Yellow | . 7, | G. Ev. | 8 | N. Holl. | . 1823 |
| virgātā | . . | Yellow | . 7, | G. Ev. | 8. | N. Holl. | . 1822 |
| volūbĭlĭs | . . | Yellow | . 6, | G. Ev. | Tw. | C. G. H. | . 1790 |

HĪBĪSCŬS, *Linn.* Said to be derived from *ibis,* a stork, which is said to chew some of the species. *Linn.* 16, Or. 8, Nat. Or. *Malvaceæ.* All the species of this extensive genus are very showy flowering plants, and therefore deserve to be extensively cultivated. The shrubby, stove, and greenhouse kinds all require the same treatment, growing best in a mixture of loam and peat; and cuttings root readily in sand, under a glass, the stove kinds in heat. *H. syriacus* thrives well in any common garden soil, and is easily increased by layers, or seeds, while its varieties may be grafted one on the other, or they may be raised from cuttings planted under a hand-glass. The hardy herbaceous kinds are particularly showy; they are marshy plants, and require to be grown in a rather moist soil, with protection in winter. The hardy annuals merely require to be sown in the open ground. The tender biennials and annuals require to be sown in pots, and treated as other tender annuals and biennials. The petals of *H. rosa sinensis* are astringent, and a few species, such as *H. sabdariffa* and *suratiensis,* are slightly acid. Synonymes: 1. *H. palustris.* 2. *H. racemosus.* 3. *H. digitatus.* 4. *H. ficulneus.* 5. *H. grandiflorus.* 6. *H. aculeatus.*

| | | | | | | | |
|---|---|---|---|---|---|---|---|
| Abelmöschŭs | . | Yellow | . 8, | 8. Ev. | 8. | India | . 1640 |
| acerifolĭŭs | . . | Pink | . 4, | G. Ev. | 8. | E. Ind. | . 1798 |
| æthiöpĭcŭs | . . | Purple | . 8, | 8. Ev. | T. | C. G. H. | . 1774 |
| squādcŭs, 1 | . | White | . 7, | H. Her. | P. | 8. Eur. | . 1819 |
| Bāmĭā | . . | Yellow | . 7, | 8. | A. | Africa | . 1818 |
| bifurcātŭs | . . | Purple | . 6, | 8. Ev. | 8. | Brazil | . 1825 |
| borbönĭcŭs | . . | Yellow | . 7, | 8. Ev. | 8. | Bourbon | . 1820 |
| Camerönĭ | . . | Rosy | . 6, | 8. Ev. | 8. | Madagas. | . 1837 |
| cannabĭnŭs | . . | Wht. pur. | 6, | G. | B. | E. Ind. | . 1759 |
| cancellātŭs, 2 | . | Yellow | . 7, | 8. Ev. | 8. | E. Ind. | . 1817 |
| clandestĭnŭs | . . | Cream | . 7, | 8. Ev. | 8. | Guinea | . 1822 |
| clypeātŭs | . . | Yellow | . 8, | 8. Ev. | 8. | Jamaica | . 1759 |
| digitātŭs | . . | Wht. red | 8, | 8. | A. | Brazil | . 1816 |
| Kerianŭs, 3 | . | Wht. red | 8, | 8. | B. | Brazil | . 1816 |
| divaricātŭs | . . | Sulphur . | 7, | G. Ev. | 8. | Moreton B. | . 1829 |
| diversifolĭŭs, 4 | . | Yellow | . 6, | 8. Ev. | 8. | E. Ind. | . 1798 |
| eriocarpŭs | . . | Yellow | . 8, | 8. Ev. | 8. | Bengal | . 1823 |
| esculentŭs | . . | Yellow | . 6, | 8. | A. | W. Ind. | . 1692 |
| ferrugĭneŭs | . . | Scarlet | . | 8. Ev. | 8. | Madagas. | . 1824 |
| ficulnĕtŭs | . . | Yel. pur. | 6, | 8. Ev. | 8. | Ceylon | . 1732 |
| ficuloidĕs | . . | Yellow | . 6, | 8. Ev. | 8. | | . 1822 |
| furcātŭs | . . | Yellow | . 8, | 8. Her. | P. | E. Ind. | . 1816 |
| Genĕvĭl | . . | Rose | . 7, | 8. Ev. | 8. | Maurit. | . |
| gossýpinŭs | . . | Yellow | . 7, | G. Ev. | 8. | C. G. H. | . 1818 |
| grandiflorŭs | . . | Flame | . 7, | F. Her. | P. | Georgia | . 1816 |
| heterophyllŭs, 5 | . | Wht. red | 8, | G. Ev. | 8. | N. S. W. | . 1803 |
| hispĭdŭs | . . | Yel. brn. | 7, | G. Ev. | 8. | C. G. H. | . |
| incānŭs | . . | Yellow | . 9, | H. Her. | P. | Carolina | . 1806 |
| Manpĭĕ | . . | Pink | . | 8. Ev. | 8. | E. Ind. | . 1806 |

| | | | | | | | |
|---|---|---|---|---|---|---|---|
| lilacĭnŭs | . . | Lilac | . | 8. | Ev. | 8. N. Holl. | . 1836 |
| liliiflorŭs | . . | Scarlet | . 6, | G. Ev. | 8. | Bourbon | . 1822 |
| hybrĭdŭs | . . | Scarlet | . 7, | 8. Ev. | 8. | Maurit. | . 1828 |
| Lindlei | . . . | Purple | . 12, | 8. Ev. | 8. | India | . 1823 |
| longiflorŭs | . . | Pa. yel. | . 8, | 8. | A. | E. Ind. | . 1817 |
| Mänĭhöt | . . | Yellow | . 7, | 8. | Her. | P. E. Ind. | . 1712 |
| membranāceŭs | . | Pink | . | 8. | Ev. | T. | . 1816 |
| micranthŭs | . . | Purple | . | 8. | Ev. | 8. E. Ind. | . 1794 |
| militarĭs | . . | Purple | . 8, | G. Her. | P. | N. Amer. | . 1804 |
| Moschĕutŏs | . . | Wht. pak. | 8, | H. Her. | P. | N. Amer. | . |
| mutābĭlĭs | . . | White | . 11, | 8. | Ev. | 8. E. Ind. | . 1690 |
| obtusifolĭŭs | . . | Yellow | . 7, | 8. | | A. E. Ind. | . 1820 |
| palŭstrĭs | . . | Pink | . 8, | H. | Her. | P. N. Amer. | . 1759 |
| parviflorŭs | . . | Yellow | . 7, | 8. | Ev. | 8. 8. Amer. | . 1828 |
| pedunculātŭs | . . | Red | . 8, | 8. | Ev. | 8. C. G. H. | . 1812 |
| pentacarpŏs | . . | Li. red | . 8, | H. | Her. | P. Venice | . 1752 |
| phœnĭceŭs | . . | Purple | . 7, | 8. | Ev. | T. E. Ind. | . 1796 |
| pulchellŭs | . . | Yellow | . 7, | 8. | Ev. | 8. K. Ind. | . 1820 |
| radiātŭs | . . | Yellow | . 7, | 8. | | A. E. Ind. | . 1790 |
| rhombifolĭŭs | . . | Purple | . 7, | 8. | Ev. | 8. E. Ind. | . 1823 |
| Richardsŏnĭ | . . | Yellow | . 8, | G. | Ev. | 8. N. S. W. | . |
| Rŏsā-malabārĭcā | . | Scarlet | . 8, | 8. | Ev. | 8. E. Ind. | . |
| Rosa-sĭnensĭs | . . | Red | . 7, | 8. | Ev. | T. E. Ind. | . 1731 |
| carnĕā-plĕnā | . | Flesh | . 7, | 8. | Ev. | T. E. Ind. | . 1731 |
| flāvā-plĕnā | . | Yellow | . 7, | 8. | Ev. | T. E. Ind. | . |
| lŭtĕā | . | Yellow | . 7, | 8. | Ev. | T. E. Ind. | . 1823 |
| rŭbrā-plĕnā | . | Red | . 7, | 8. | Ev. | T. E. Ind. | . |
| variegātā-plĕnā | | Striped | . 7, | 8. | Ev. | T. E. Ind. | . |
| rŏseŭs | . . | Pink | . 8, | H. | Her. | P. France | . 1827 |
| Sabdarĭffā | . . | Yellow | . 7, | G. | | B. E. Ind. | . 1596 |
| scābĕr, 6 | . . | Yellow | . 8, | F. | Her. | P. Carolina | . 1810 |
| senegalénsĭs | . . | Yellow | . 6, | 8. | Ev. | 8. Guinea | . 1824 |
| setösŭs | . . | Yellow | . 7, | 8. | Ev. | 8. E. Ind. | . 1800 |
| speciōsŭs | . . | Scarlet | . 7, | F. | Her. | P. N. Amer. | . 1804 |
| spirālĭs | . . | Yel. red | . 6, | 8. | Ev. | 8. Mexico | . 1823 |
| splendĕns | . . | Rose | . 6, | 8. | Ev. | 8. N. Holl. | . 1823 |
| suratténsĭs | . . | Yellow | . 8, | 8. | | A. E. Ind. | . 1731 |
| syrĭācŭs | . . | Purple | . 8, | H. | De. | 8. Syria | . 1596 |
| albŭs | . . | White | . 8, | H. | De. | 8. | |
| albŭs-plĕnŭs | . | White | . 8, | H. | De. | 8. | |
| marginātŭs | . | Pur. wht. | 8, | H. | De. | 8. Syria | . |
| purpūreŭs | . | Purple | . 8, | H. | De. | 8. | |
| purpūreŏ-plĕnŭs | | Purple | . 8, | H. | De. | 8. | |
| rŭber | . . | Red | . 8, | H. | De. | 8. | |
| variegātŭs | . | Striped | . 8, | H. | De. | 8. | |
| tetraphyllŭs | . . | Yellow | . 7, | 8. | | A. Bengal | . 1818 |
| trĭlŏbŭs | . . | Yellow | . 7, | 8. | Ev. | 8. W. Ind. | . 1818 |
| Triönum | . . | Yel. brn. | 7, | H. | | A. Italy | . 1596 |
| tubulōsŭs | . . | Yellow | . 8, | 8 | Ev. | 8. E. Ind. | . 1796 |
| unĭdĕns | . . | Yellow | . 7, | 8. | | A. Brazil | . 1822 |
| velutĭnŭs | . . | White | . 7, | 8. | Ev. | 8. Timor | . 1818 |
| vesicārĭŭs | . . | Yel. brn. | 7, | H. | | A. Africa | . 1713 |
| virgĭnĭcŭs | . . | Red | . 8, | H. | Her. | P. Virginia | . 1798 |
| vitifolĭŭs | . . | Yellow | . 8, | 8. | | A. E. Ind. | . 1690 |

HICKORY-TREE, see *Cārӯā ālbā.*

HIĔMĀLĬS, pertaining to winter.

HIĔRĂCĬŬM, *Linn.* From *hieras,* a hawk; being supposed to sharpen the sight of birds of prey. *Linn.* 19, Or. 1, Nat. Or. *Compositæ.* An extensive genus of pretty flowering plants; the dwarf herbaceous kinds are remarkably adapted for rock-work, or the front of flower-borders, the taller kinds at the back; they may either be increased by seeds, or divisions. *H. fruticosum* is readily increased by cuttings in mould, under a glass. The annual species need only be sown in the open border. Synonymes: 1. *H. verbascifolium.* 2. *H. auricula collinum.* 3. *H. sabaudum.* 4. *H. prenanthoides.* 5. *H. collinum.* 6. *H. collinum cymosum.* 7. *H. montanum.* 8. *Lepicaune prunellæfolia.* 9. *H. integrifolium.* 10. *Andryala lanata.*

| | | | | | | | |
|---|---|---|---|---|---|---|---|
| alpestrĕ | . . | Yellow | . 7, | H. Her. | P. | Switzerl. | . 1822 |
| alpĭnŭm | . . | Yellow | . 7, | H. Her. | P. | Britain | . |
| amplexicaŭlĕ | . . | Yellow | . 7, | H. Her. | P. | Pyrenees | . 1739 |
| pulmonarĭoĭdĕs | | Yellow | . 7, | H. Her. | P. | Switzerl. | . 1819 |
| anchusæfolĭŭm, 1 | | Yellow | . 7, | H. Her. | P. | Italy | . 1816 |
| andryaloĭdĕs | . . | Yellow | . 7, | H. Her. | P. | Switzerl. | . 1819 |
| Liottardĭ | . . | Yellow | . 7, | H. Her. | P. | Switzerl. | . 1819 |
| angustifolĭŭm | . . | Yellow | . 7, | H. Her. | P. | Switzerl. | . 1823 |
| aurantĭācŭm | . . | Orange | . 6, | H. Her. | Cr. | Scotland | . |
| flāvŭm | . . | Yellow | . 6, | H. Her. | Cr. | Switzerl. | . 1819 |
| auriculā | . . | Yellow | . 6, | H. Her. | Cr. | England | . |
| auriculātŭm | . . | Yellow | . 7, | H. Her. | P. | | . 1816 |
| Bauhĭnĭ | . . | Yellow | . 6, | H. Her. | Cr. | Germany | . 1816 |
| Bessĕriānŭm, 2 | . | Yellow | . 6, | H. Her. | Cr. | Germany | . 1816 |
| bifĭdŭm | . . | Yellow | . 6, | H. Her. | P. | Hungary | . |
| bifurcātŭm | . . | Yellow | . 6, | H. Her. | P. | Tauria | . 1820 |
| boreālĕ, 3 | . . | Yellow | . 7, | H. Her. | P. | N. Eur. | . |
| bracteolātŭm | . . | Yellow | . 8, | H. Her. | P. | Europe | . 1823 |
| calcārĕŭm | . . | Yellow | . 7, | H. Her. | P. | Europe | . 1816 |
| canadénsĕ | . . | Yellow | . 8, | H. Her. | P. | Canada | . 1800 |
| canéscĕns | . . | Yellow | . 8, | H. Her. | P. | Switzerl. | . 1820 |
| cerinthoĭdĕs | . . | Yellow | . 8, | H. Her. | P. | Scotland | . |
| chondrilloĭdĕs | . . | Yellow | . 6, | H. Her. | P. | Austria | . 1640 |
| ciliātŭm | . . | Yellow | . 7, | H. Her. | P. | Crete | . 1824 |
| collīnŭm | . . | Yellow | . 5, | H. Her. | Cr. | Switzerl. | . 1819 |

| | | | | |
|---|---|---|---|---|
| compositum | . Yellow | . 7, H. Her. P. | Pyrenees | . 1819 |
| corymbosum | . Yellow | . 6, H. Her. P. | | 1817 |
| crassifolium | . Yellow | . 6, H. Her. P. | Hungary | . 1820 |
| croaticum | . Yellow | . 7, H. Her. P. | Hungary | . 1820 |
| croceum | . Yellow | . 6, H. Her. P. | Siberia | . 1818 |
| cydoniæfolium | . Yellow | . 7, H. Her. P. | France | . 1816 |
| cymosum | . Yellow | . 5, H. Her. Cr. | Europe | . 1789 |
| dentatum | . Yellow | . 7, H. Her. P. | Switzerl. | . 1819 |
| denticulatum, 4 | . Yellow | . 7, H. Her. Cr. | Scotland | |
| dubium | . Yellow | . 7, H. Her. Cr. | Britain | |
| echioides | . Yellow | . 7, H. Her. P. | Hungary | . 1802 |
| elongatum | . Yellow | . 7, H. Her. P. | Switzerl. | . 1819 |
| eriophorum | . Yellow | . 8, H. Her. P. | S. Eur. | . 1817 |
| eriophyllum | . Yellow | . 6, H. Her. P. | | |
| fallax | . Yellow | . 7, H. Her. Cr. | | . 1816 |
| fasciculatum | . Yellow | . 7, H. Her. P. | Canada | |
| flagellare, 5 | . Yellow | . 5, H. Her. Cr. | | . 1816 |
| flexuosum | . Yellow | . 7, H. Her. P. | Hungary | . 1804 |
| florentinum | . Yellow | . 7, H. Her. Cr. | Germany | . 1791 |
| foliosum | . Yellow | . 7, H. Her. P. | Hungary | . 1805 |
| fruticosum | . Yellow | . 7, H. G. Ev. S. | Madeira | . 1785 |
| glabratum | . Yellow | . 7, H. Her. P. | Switzerl. | . 1819 |
| tubulosum | . Yellow | . 7, H. Her. P. | Switzerl. | . 1819 |
| glaucum | . Yellow | . 6, H. Her. P. | S. Eur. | . 1807 |
| glutinosum | . Yellow | . 7, H. | A. S. Eur. | . 1796 |
| Gmelini | . Yellow | . 6, H. Her. P. | Siberia | . 1798 |
| Gochnati, 6 | . Yellow | . 6, H. Her. Cr. | Switzerl. | . 1819 |
| Gronovii | . Yellow | . 6, H. Her. P. | N. Amer. | . 1798 |
| Halleri | . Yellow | . 7, H. Her. P. | Britain | |
| Hoppeanum | . Yellow | . 7, H. Her. P. | Switzerl. | . 1819 |
| humile | . Yellow | . 7, H. Her. P. | Germany | . 1804 |
| brachiatum | . Yellow | . 6, H. Her. P. | Switzerl. | . 1819 |
| hybridum | . Yellow | . 7, H. Her. P. | Switzerl. | . 1816 |
| incanum | . Yellow | . 7, H. Her. P. | Caucasus | . 1817 |
| incarnatum, 7. | . Pink | . 6, H. Her. P. | Carniola | . 1815 |
| incisum | . Yellow | . 7, H. Her. P. | Switzerl. | . 1819 |
| intybaceum | . Yellow | . 7, H. Her. P. | Europe | . 1794 |
| Kalmii | . Yellow | . 7, H. Her. P. | Pennsyl. | . 1794 |
| lævigatum | . Yellow | . 8, H. Her. P. | | . 1804 |
| lanatum | . Yellow | . 7, H. Her. P. | Hungary | . 1820 |
| lapeanoides | . Yellow | . 7, H. Her. P. | Pyrenees | . 1819 |
| latifolium | . Yellow | . 7, H. Her. P. | Croatia | . 1820 |
| Lawsoni | . Yellow | . 6, H. Her. P. | Britain | |
| longifolium | . Yellow | . 7, H. Her. P. | | . 1821 |
| macrophyllum | . Yellow | . 7, H. Her. P. | Canada | . 1825 |
| maculatum | . Yellow | . 8, H. Her. P. | Britain | |
| Milleri | . Yellow | . 7, H. Her. P. | | . 1820 |
| molle | . Yellow | . 8, H. Her. P. | Scotland | |
| montanum | . Yellow | . 7, H. Her. P. | S. Eur. | . 1775 |
| nigrescens | . Yellow | . 7, H. Her. P. | | . 1801 |
| ovatum | . Yellow | . 7, H. Her. P. | Switzerl. | . 1819 |
| pallescens | . Yellow | . 7, H. Her. P. | Hungary | . 1818 |
| paniculatum | . Yellow | . 7, H. Her. P. | Canada | . 1800 |
| parviflorum | . Yellow | . 6, H. Her. P. | Switzerl. | . 1819 |
| picridifolium | . Yellow | . 7, H. Her. P. | Switzerl. | . 1819 |
| pictum | . Yellow | . 7, H. Her. P. | Switzerl. | . 1819 |
| pilocephalum | . Yellow | . 7, H. Her. P. | | . 1823 |
| Pilosella | . Yellow | . 6, H. Her. Cr. | Britain | |
| Peleteriana | . Yellow | . 6, H. Her. Cr. | Switzerl. | . 1819 |
| Pseudo-Pilosella | . Yellow | . 6, H. Her. Cr. | Switzerl. | . 1819 |
| piloselliforme | . Yellow | . 6, H. Her. Cr. | Switzerl. | . 1819 |
| piloselloides | . Yellow | . 6, H. Her. Cr. | Switzerl. | . 1819 |
| porrifolium | . Yellow | . 7, H. Her. P. | Austria | . 1640 |
| præaltum | . Yellow | . 6, H. Her. Cr. | Switzerl. | . 1819 |
| præmorsum | . Yellow | . 6, H. Her. P. | Switzerl. | . 1818 |
| prenanthoides | . Yellow | . 7, H. Her. P. | Scotland | |
| prostratum | . Yellow | . 7, H. Her. Cr. S. Eur. | | . 1822 |
| prunellæfolium, 8 | . Yellow | . 7, H. Her. P. | Switzerl. | . 1820 |
| pulmonarioides | . Yellow | . 7, H. Her. P. | France | . 1819 |
| pulmonarium | . Yellow | . 7, H. Her. P. | Scotland | |
| pumilum | . Yellow | . 7, H. Her. P. | Switzerl. | . 1819 |
| tubulosum | . Yellow | . 7, H. Her. P. | Switzerl. | . 1819 |
| pusillum | . Yellow | . 7, H. Her. P. | Labrador | . 1800 |
| racemosum | . Yellow | . 7, H. Her. P. | Hungary | . 1816 |
| ramosum | . Yellow | . 8, H. Her. P. | Hungary | . 1805 |
| repens | . Yellow | . 7, H. Her. Cr. | Switzerl. | . 1819 |
| rotundatum | . Yellow | . 7, H. Her. P. | Hungary | . 1817 |
| rupestre | . Yellow | . 6, H. Her. P. | Switzerl. | . 1820 |
| subaudum | . Yellow | . 7, H. Her. P. | Italy | . 1700 |
| saxatile | . Yellow | . 7, H. Her. P. | Austria | . 1801 |
| Schraderi | . Yellow | . 7, H. Her. P. | Switzerl. | . 1819 |
| sonchifolium | . Yellow | . 6, H. Her. P. | Caucasus | . 1821 |
| speciosissimum | . Yellow | . 8, H. Her. P. | S. Eur. | . 1821 |
| speciosum | . Yellow | . 7, H. Her. P. | | . 1818 |
| staticifolium | . Yellow | . 6, H. Her. P. | Europe | . 1804 |
| Sternbergii | . Yellow | . 7, H. Her. P. | Switzerl. | . 1819 |
| stipitatum | . Yellow | . 7, H. Her. P. | Switzerl. | . 1819 |
| stoloniferum | . Yellow | . 6, H. Her. Cr. | Switzerl. | . 1820 |
| subnudum | . Yellow | . 6, H. Her. P. | Switzerl. | . 1819 |
| succisæfolium, 9 | . Yellow | . 6, H. Her. P. | Switzerl. | . 1819 |
| sudeticum | . Yellow | . 6, H. Her. P. | Switzerl. | . 1819 |
| sylvaticum | . Yellow | . 7, H. Her. P. | Britain | |
| tricocephalum | . Yellow | . 7, H. Her. P. | | . 1823 |
| umbellatum | . Yellow | . 8, H. Her. P. | Britain | |
| undulatum | . Yellow | . 7, H. Her. P. | Spain | . 1778 |
| veldepilosum | . Yellow | . 7, H. Her. P. | Switzerl. | . 1819 |
| venosum | . Yellow | . 6, H. Her. P. | N. Amer. | . 1790 |
| verbascifolium, 10 | . Yellow | . 6, H. Her. P. | S. Eur. | . 1732 |
| verruculatum | . Yellow | . 7, H. Her. P. | | . 1821 |

| | | | | |
|---|---|---|---|---|
| villosum | . Yellow | . 7. H. Her. P. | Scotland | |
| virescens | . Yellow | . 7. H. Her. P. | Switzerl. | . 1819 |
| virgatum | . Yellow | . 7. H. Her. P. | N. Amer. | . 1816 |

*murorum, Lachenalii, maculatum, obtusifolium, sylvaticum.*

**HIEROCHLOE**, *Gmelin*. From *hieros*, holy, and *chloe*, grass. Linn. 3, Or. 2, Nat. Or. *Gramineæ*. A genus of perennial grasses, growing freely in any common garden soil, and increased by seeds, which are produced in abundance. *Synonymes:* 1. *Holcus borealis.* 2. *H. odoratus.*

| | | | | |
|---|---|---|---|---|
| australis | . . . . Apetal | . 6, Grass. | S. Eur. | . . 1777 |
| borealis, 1 | . . . . Apetal | . 6, Grass. | Scotland | |
| fragrans, 2 | . . . . Apetal | . 6, Grass. | N. Amer. | . 1777 |

**HILLIA**, *Jacquin*. In honour of Sir John Hill, the author of many botanical works. Linn. 6, Or. 1, Nat. Or. *Cinchonaceæ*. These are ornamental species, of easy culture in a mixture of turfy loam, peat, and sand; and cuttings root readily in the same kind of soil, or sand, under a glass, in heat.

| | | | | |
|---|---|---|---|---|
| longiflora | . . . White | . 8, S. Ev. S. W. Ind. | . 1789 |
| tetrandra | . . . White | . 6, S. Ev. S. Jamaica | . 1793 |

**HILUM**, the scar, or mark in a seed, which indicates the place by which it adhered to the placentæ.

**HIPPEASTRUM**, *Herbert*. From *hippeus*, a knight, and *astron*, a star; Knights' Star. Linn. 6, Or. 1, Nat. Or. *Amaryllidaceæ*. A genus of pretty flowering species, separated from *Amaryllis* by the Hon. and Rev. W. Herbert, who has added several species already known under the genus *Amaryllis*. These plants require the same treatment as those belonging to the genus before alluded to.

| | | | | |
|---|---|---|---|---|
| brevifolium | . Wht. red. 4, S. Bl. P. B. Ayres | . 1836 |
| organense | . . . . | S. Bl. P. Org. Mts. | . 1837 |

**HIPPIA**, *Linn.* From *hippos*, a horse; because horses were fond of the original plant, Chickweed. Linn. 19, Or. 4, Nat. Or. *Compositæ*. Uninteresting plants, of the simplest culture—*frutescens, integrifolia*.

**HIPPION**, *Schmidt*. From *hippos*, a horse, and *ion*, a violet. Linn. 5, Or. 1, Nat. Or. *Gentianaceæ*. Pretty little plants, requiring to be treated the same as other tender biennials. *Synonymes:* 1. *Exacum hyssopifolium*. 2. *E. verticillatum*. 3. *E. viscosum.*

| | | | | |
|---|---|---|---|---|
| hyssopifolium, 1 | . Fulvous . 7, S. | B. E. Ind. | . 1825 |
| verticillatum, 2 | . White . 7, S. | B. Trinidad | . 1817 |
| viscosum, 3 | . Yellow . 6, G. | B. Canaries | . 1781 |

**HIPPOCRATEA**, *Linn.* In honour of Hippocrates, who is regarded as one of the fathers of botany. Linn. 3, Or. 1, Nat. Or. *Hippocrataceæ*. A genus of mostly climbing shrubs, with very minute flowers; the plants are only worth cultivating in collections. Loam and peat suits them well, and cuttings root readily in sand, under a glass, in heat. *Synonymes:* 1. *scandens*. 2. *volubilis.*

| | | | | |
|---|---|---|---|---|
| arborea | . . . Grn. wht. | 8. Ev. Cl. E. Ind. | . 1818 |
| obcordata, 1 | . . Grn. wht. | 8. Ev. Cl. W. Ind. | . 1819 |
| obtusifolia | . . Grn. wht. | 8. Ev. Cl. E. Ind. | . 1818 |
| ovata, 2 | . . . Grn. wht. | 8. Ev. Cl. S. Amer. | . 1793 |

**HIPPOCREPIS**, *Linn.* From *hippos*, a horse, and *crepis*, a shoe; alluding to the appearance of the curved recesses of the pods. Linn. 17, Or. 4, Nat. Or. *Leguminosæ*. The plants of this genus are all remarkably neat and beautiful, and highly deserving a place in every garden. *H. balearica* thrives well in loam and peat, and cuttings root readily in sand, under a glass. The herbaceous kinds grow well in any light sandy soil, and look well when planted on a bank, or rock-work. The seeds of the annual kinds should be sown early in spring, in the open border. *Synonyme:* 1. *comosa.*

| | | | | |
|---|---|---|---|---|
| balearica | . . Yellow . 5, G. Ev. S. | Minorca | . 1776 |
| biflora | . . . Yellow . 6, H. | A. | . 1816 |
| ciliata | . . . Yellow . 6, H. | A. S. Eur. | . 1818 |
| comosa | . . Yellow . 4, H. Her. Tr. | England | |
| glauca | . . Yellow . 5, H. Her. Tr. | | . 1819 |
| helvetica, 1 | . Yellow . 5, H. Her. Tr. | Switzer. | . 1819 |
| monocarpa | . . Yellow . 5, H. | A. | Caucasus | . 1824 |
| multisiliquosa | . Yellow . 7, H. | A. S. Eur. | . 1683 |
| unisiliquosa | . Yellow . 6, H. | A. S. Eur. | . 1570 |

**HIPPOMANE**, *Linn.* From *hippos*, a horse, and *mane*, madness; alluding to the effects of the original plant. Linn. 21, Or. 10, Nat. Or. *Euphorbiaceæ*. The Manchineel-tree grows to an immense size in its native country, and abounds in a white milky juice, which is highly poisonous, therefore, it is very necessary in cutting the plant, not to let any of the juice touch the skin, as a single drop would be sufficient to make the hands swell and itch very much. A mixture of sandy loam and peat suits it, and cuttings root readily in sand, under a glass, in heat.

Mancinella . . . Green . . . S. Ev. T. W. Ind. . 1690

HIPPOMARATHRUM, *Linn.* From *hippos*, a horse, and *marathron*, fennel. *Linn.* 5, Or. 2, Nat. Or. *Umbelliferæ*. A curious species, of very easy culture and propagation.

siculum . . . . Yellow . 7, H. Her. P. Sicily . . 1640

HIPPOPHAE, *Linn.* From *hippos*, a horse, and *phao*, to destroy; in reference to the supposed poisonous qualities of the seeds. *Linn.* 22, Or. 4, Nat. Or. *Eleagnaceæ*. Ornamental trees, growing in any common soil, and may be readily increased by layers, or cuttings of the roots

rhamnoides . . Apetal . 5, H. De. T. England .
angustifolia . . Apetal . 5, H. De. T. S. Eur. .
sibirica . . . . Apetal . 4, H. De. T. Siberia .
salicifolia . . . Apetal . H. De. S. Nepal . . 1822

HIPPURIS, *Linn.* From *hippos*, a mare, and *oura*, a tail; the stem resembles a mare's tail, from the crowded whorls of very narrow hair-like leaves. *Linn.* 1, Or. 1, Nat. Or. *Onagraceæ*. A curious aquatic, growing best in a ditch, pond, or marshy situation.

vulgaris . . . Apetal . 5, H. Aq. P. Britain . .

HIRÆA, *Jacquin.* In honour of J. N. de la Hire, a French botanist, who died in 1727. *Linn.* 10, Or. 3, Nat. Or. *Malpighiaceæ*. These are pretty climbers, growing best in a mixture of sandy loam and peat; and cuttings of the ripened wood root readily in sand, under a glass, in heat.

indica . . . . White . 7, S. Ev. Cl. E. Ind. . 1820
nutans . . . . White . 7, S. Ev. Cl. E. Ind. . 1820
odorata . . . . Yellow . S. Ev. Cl. Guinea . 1823
reclinata . . . Yellow . 7, S. Ev. Cl. W. Ind. .

HIRSUTE, rough, with soft hairs.
HIRTELLA, *Linn.* From *hirtus*, hairy; the young branches. *Linn.* 5, Or. 1, Nat. Or. *Chrysobalanaceæ*. The flowers of these curious tropical timber trees are rarely seen in this country; they delight in a mixture of peat and loam, and cuttings will root freely in sand, under a glass, in heat. *Synonymes:* 1. *americana.* 2. *paniculata.*

racemosa, 1 . . Violet . . S. Ev. T. Guiana . 1782
triandra, 2 . . White . . S. Ev. T. Jamaica . 1810

HISPID, rough, with stiff hairs.
HOARY, covered with white down.
HOFFMANSEGGIA, *Cavanilles.* In honour of J. C. Hoffmansegg, a distinguished naturalist, and with Link, author of the Flore Portugaise, Berlin, 1806. *Linn.* 10, Or. 1, Nat. Or. *Leguminosæ*. An interesting dwarf shrub, growing well in peat and loam; and cuttings, if not too ripe, will root in sand, under a glass, in heat.

falcaria . . . Yellow . 7, S. Her. P. Chile . . 1806

HOG-NUT, see *Carya obcordata.*
HOG-PLUM, see *Spondias.*
HOGWEED, see *Boerhaavia.*
HOITZIA, *Jussieu.* Derived from *Hoitzil*, the name given to it in Peru. *Linn.* 5, Or. 1, Nat. Or. *Polemoniaceæ*. Handsome species, succeeding well in equal portions of sandy loam and peat; and cuttings root freely when placed under a glass, in the same kind of soil.

coerulea . . . Blue . . O. Ev. S. Mexico . 1824
coccinea . . . Scarlet . O. Ev. S. Mexico . 1824
glandulosa . . . Pa. red . O. Ev. T. Mexico . 1825

HOLCUS, *Linn.* From *helko*, to extract; the original plant was supposed to possess the power of extracting thorns. *Linn.* 23, Or. 1, Nat. Or. *Gramineæ*. A genus of grasses, which delights to grow in light loamy soil; increased by seeds, or divisions.

lanatus . . . . Apetal . 6, Grass. Britain . .
mollis . . . . Apetal . 7, Grass. Britain . .

HOLIGARNA, *Roxburgh.* The name of the tree in the language of Karnata. *Linn.* 23, Or. 1, Nat. Or.

[ 161 ]

*Anacardiaceæ*. This species is a very tall-growing tree; for culture and propagation, see *Anacardium.*

longifolia . . . White . . S. Ev. T. E. Ind. . . 1828

HOLLY, see *Ilex.*
HOLLYHOCK, see *Althæa rosea.*
HOLMSKIOLDIA, *Reta.* In honour of Theodore Holmskiold, a Danish botanical author. *Linn.* 14, Or. 2, Nat. Or. *Labiatæ.* Rather curious and interesting plants, succeeding well in an equal mixture of loam, peat, and sand; and cuttings of the young wood root freely in the same kind of soil, under a glass, in heat. *Synonymes:* 1. *Hastingia coccinea.* 2. *Hastingia scandens.*

sanguinea, 1 . . Scarlet . . S. Ev. S. E. Ind. . . 1796
scandens, 2 . . Scarlet . 5, S. Ev. Cl. E. Ind. . . 1824

HOLOSERICEA, silky, pubescent.
HOLOSTEUM, *Linn.* From *holos*, all, and *osteon*, a bone; applied by antiphrasis to this plant, which is soft and delicate. *Linn.* 3, Or. 3, Nat. Or. *Alsinaceæ.* These species merely require to be sown in the open ground.

spergulioides . . White . 7, H. A. Egypt . . 1829
umbellatum . . . Pink . 7, H. A. England .

diandrum.

HOMALIUM, *Jacquin.* From *homalos*, regular; the stamens are regularly divided into 3-stamened fascicles. *Linn.* 18, Or. 4, Nat. Or. *Homaliaceæ.* The flower of this species is rather insignificant. The plant grows in a mixture of loam and peat; and cuttings, nearly ripened, root readily in sand, under a glass, in heat.

racemosum . . . White . 6, S. Ev. T. W. Ind. . 1816

HOMOGENEOUS, having a uniform nature, principle, or composition.
HOMERIA, *Ventenat.* Named after the distinguished father of epic poetry, Homer. *Linn.* 16, Or. 1, Nat. Or. *Iridaceæ.* This is a beautiful genus of bulbous plants; they delight to grow in an equal mixture of loam, peat, and sand. When they are in a dormant state, they should be kept free from moisture; but when growing, they should be plentifully supplied with water. They are increased by offsets from the bulbs, or by seeds. *Synonymes:* 1. *Moræa collina.* 2. *elegans.* 3. *collina exaltata.* 4. *collina miniata minor.* 5. *flexuosa.* 6. *spicata.* 7. *virgata.*

collina, 1 . . . Purple . 5, G. Bl. P. C. G. H. . 1768
elegans, 2 . . . Vermil. . 5, G. Bl. P. C. G. H. . 1825
exaltata, 3 . . . Vermil. . 5, G. Bl. P. C. G. H. . 1768
flaccida, 4 . . . Vermil. . 5, G. Bl. P. C. G. H. . 1810
flexuosa, 5 . . . Yellow . 5, G. Bl. P. C. G. H. . 1802
lineata . . . . Vermil. . 5, G. Bl. P. C. G. H. . 1825
miniata . . . . Vermil. . 5, G. Bl. P. C. G. H. . 1799
porrifolia . . . Vermil. . 5, G. Bl. P. C. G. H. . 1825
spicata, 6 . . . Yellow . 5, G. Bl. P. C. G. H. . 1785
virgata, 7 . . . Purple . 5, G. Bl. P. C. G. H. . 1825

HOMER'S MOLY, see *Allium magicum.*
HONESTY, see *Lunaria.*
HONEY-BERRY, see *Melicocca.*
HONEY-FLOWER, see *Melianthus.*
HONEY-GARLIC, see *Nectaroscordum.*
HONEY-LOCUST TREE, see *Gleditschia triacanthos.*
HONEY-PORE, the pore in flowers which secretes honey.
HONEY-SCALES, the scales in flowers which secrete honey.
HONEY-SPOTS, the spots in flowers which secrete honey.
HONEYSUCKLE, see *Lonicera.*
HONEYWORT, see *Cerinthe.*
HONEYWORT, see *Steon.*
HOODED, being curved or hollowed at the end, into the form of a hood.
HOODED MILFOIL, see *Utricularia.*
HOOKERIA, *Smith.* In honour of Sir William Jackson Hooker, LL.D., F.R.S., &c., the present professor of botany in the university of Glasgow, one of the most distinguished of modern botanists. *Linn.* 24, Or. 5, Nat. Or. *Musci.* This is described as a very beautiful genus of plants, resembling *Hypnum.* One of the species, *H. læte-virens*, has only been discovered as yet in a bog near Cork—*læte-virens, lucens.*

HOOP-ASH, see *Celtis crassifolia.*
HOOP-PETTICOAT, see *Narcissus bulbocodium.*
HOP, see *Humulus.*
HOP-HORNBEAM, see *Ostrya.*
HOP-LIKE TREFOIL, see *Medicago lupulina.*

Y

HŎRDĔŬM, *Linn.* According to Bodæus, the name is derived from *hordus*, heavy; because bread made with barley is very heavy. *Linn.* 3, Or. 2, Nat. Or. *Gramineæ.* The species of this genus are among the most useful plants we possess; corn, like barley, are among their products. The seeds of the various species have only to be sown in the open ground.

| | | | | | |
|---|---|---|---|---|---|
| cœlĕstĕ | . | . Apetal . | 7, Grass. Levant | . . |
| complanātum | . . | . Apetal . | 7, Grass. S. Eur. | . | 1819 |
| distichŏn | . . | . Apetal . | 7, Grass. Tartary | . . |
| imbĕrbĕ | . . | . Apetal . | 7, Grass. Tartary | . . |
| hexastichŏn | . . | . Apetal . | 7, Grass. | . . |
| hystrix | . . | . Apetal . | 6, Grass. Spain | . | 1821 |
| jubātum | . . | . Apetal . | 7, Grass. N. Amer. | . | 1782 |
| nepalĕnsĕ | . . | . Apetal . | 7, Grass. Nepal | . | 1817 |
| nigrum | . . | . Apetal . | 7, Grass. S. Eur. | . | 1818 |
| nŭdŭm | . . | . Apetal . | 7, Grass. Tartary | . . |
| secalīnum | . . | . Apetal . | 7, Grass. Europe | . . |
| vulgārĕ | . . | . Apetal . | 7, Grass. Sicily | . . |
| gigantĕum | . . | . Apetal . | 7, Grass. Levant | . . |
| Zeocritŏn | . . | . Apetal . | 8, Grass. | . . |

*bulbōsŭm, capĕnsĕ, maritīmŭm, murīnŭm, pratĕnsĕ, strictŭm.*

HOREHOUND, see *Marrŭbĭŭm.*

HORKĔLĬA, *Schlechtendahl.* In honour of John Horkel, professor of botany at Berlin. *Linn.* 10, Or. 1, Nat. Or. *Rosaceæ.* These are rather pretty herbaceous plants, growing freely in any common garden soil, and increased by seeds, or divisions.

| | | | | |
|---|---|---|---|---|
| congĕstă | . . | . White . | 8, H. Her. P. California | . 1826 |
| fŭscă | . . | . Wht. brn. | 7, H. Her. P. N. Amer. | . . |

HORMINUM CLARY, see *Sălvĭă Hormīnŭm.*

HŎRMĬNŬM, *Linn.* From *hormao*, to excite; medicinal qualities of the plant. *Linn.* 14, Or. 1, Nat. Or. *Labiatæ.* This is a very beautiful plant when in blossom; it grows well in the open border in summer, but if allowed to remain in that situation during winter, it is apt to be killed by damp; it is readily increased by divisions, or seeds.

| | | | | |
|---|---|---|---|---|
| pyrenāĭcŭm | . . | . Blue . | 6, H. Her. P. Pyrenees | . 1820 |

HORN; any stiff awl-shaped process is called a horn.

HORNBEAM, see *Carpīnŭs.*

HORNEMANNĬA, *Willdenow.* In honour of Professor Hornemann, of Copenhagen. *Linn.* 14, Or. 2, Nat. Or. *Scrophulariaceæ.* A little inconspicuous species, of greater rarity than beauty, and of simple culture. Synonyme: 1. *Gratiola goodeniæfolia.*

| | | | | |
|---|---|---|---|---|
| bĭcŏlŏr, 1 | . . | . Blue . | . 8, S. A. E. Ind. | . 1816 |

HORNGRASS, see *Ceratŏchlŏă.*

HORN OF PLENTY, see *Fĕdĭă cornucōpĭă.*

HORN-POPPY, see *Glauciŭm.*

HORNWORT, see *Ceratophyllŭm.*

HORSE-CHESTNUT, see *Æscŭlŭs.*

HORSE-POPPY, see *Seslĭ Hippomărăthrŭm.*

HORSE-RADISH, see *Cochlearĭă armorācĭă.*

HORSE-RADISH TREE, see *Moringă.*

HORSESHOE VETCH, see *Hippŏcrĕpĭs.*

HORSETAIL, see *Equisĕtŭm.*

HORSETAIL TREE, see *Casuarīnă.*

HORSE-THISTLE, see *Cīrsĭŭm.*

HŏsĂCKĬA. Named by Douglas in honour of David Hosack, M.D., F.R.S., professor of botany in the university of New York. *Linn.* 17, Or. 4, Nat. Or. *Leguminosæ.* The plants of this genus are showy, and well adapted for borders and rock-work. They grow in common garden soil, and are increased by divisions, or seeds. Synonymes: 1. *Lotus pinnatus.* 2. *L. sericeus.*

| | | | | |
|---|---|---|---|---|
| bĭcŏlŏr, 1 | . . | . Yel. wht. | 8, H. Her. P. N. Amer. | . 1826 |
| decumbĕns | . . | . Yellow . | 8, H. Her. P. N. Amer. | . 1827 |
| parviflŏră | . . | . Yellow . | 8, H. Her. P. N. Amer. | . 1827 |
| Purshĭană, 2 | . . | . Yellow . | 7, H. Her. P. N. Amer. | . 1824 |

HŏstĂ, *Jacquin.* In honour of N. T. Host, a German botanist. *Linn.* 2, Or. 1, Nat. Or. *Verbenaceæ.* Handsome shrubs, growing freely in peat and loam, and increased by cuttings in sand, under a glass, in heat. Synonyme: 1. *Cornutia punctata.*

| | | | | |
|---|---|---|---|---|
| cœrūlĕă, 1 | . . | . Blue . | 7, S. Ev. S. Mexico | . 1733 |
| latifōlĭă | . . | . Blue . | 7, S. Ev. S. Mexico | . 1824 |
| longifōlĭă | . . | . Blue . | 7, S. Ev. S. Mexico | . 1826 |

HOTTENTOT-BREAD, see *Dioscōrĕă.*

HOTTENTOT-CHERRY, see *Cassīnĕ maurocĕnĭă.*

HOTTENTOT-FIG, see *Mesembryanthĕmŭm edŭlĕ.*

HŬTTŎNĬA, *Linn.* In honour of P. Hotton, a professor in the university of Leyden; he died in 1709. *Linn.*

5, Or. 1, Nat. Or. *Primulaceæ.* This is a singular and pretty aquatic species, producing its flowers in large bundles; it should be grown in a pond or ditch, and increased by divisions.

| | | | | |
|---|---|---|---|---|
| palŭstrĭs | . . | . Flesh . | . 8, H. Aq. P. England | . . |

HOUND'S-TONGUE, see *Cynoglŏssŭm.*

HOUSELEEK, see *Sempervīvŭm.*

HOUSTŎNĬA, *Linn.* In honour of William Houston, M.D., a famous British botanist; he died in 1788. *Linn.* 4, Or. 1, Nat. Or. *Gentianaceæ.* The species of this elegant genus are well adapted for ornamenting flower borders or rock-work; they grow best in a peaty soil, and increase freely by divisions.

| | | | | |
|---|---|---|---|---|
| albiflŏră | . . | . White . | 6, H. Her. P. N. Amer. | . 1828 |
| cœrūlĕă | . . | . Blue . | 6, H. Her. P. N. Amer. | . 1785 |
| longifōlĭă | . . | . Scarlet . | H. Her. P. N. Amer. | . |
| purpūrĕă | . . | . Purple . | 7, H. Her. P. N. Amer. | . 1800 |
| serpyllifōlĭă | . . | . White . | 7, H. Her. P. N. Amer. | . 1826 |

HOUTTUYNĬA, *Thunberg.* After Houttuyn, the celebrated virtuoso of Amsterdam. *Linn.* 3, Or. 3, Nat. Or. *Saururaceæ.* The species are worth cultivating. They thrive well in any light rich soil, in a very moist situation, and increase by divisions or seeds.

| | | | | |
|---|---|---|---|---|
| cordātă | . . | . Yel. grn. | 6, G. Her. P. Japan | . 1820 |
| fœtĭdă | . . | . Yel. grn. | 7, G. Her. P. Japan | . 1800 |

HŎVĔĂ, *R. Brown.* In honour of Anthony Pantaleon Hove, a Polish botanist, and traveller in the Crimea and Persia. *Linn.* 14, Or. 6, Nat. Or. *Leguminosæ.* The plants of this genus are truly elegant when in flower, and particularly well adapted for ornamenting the conservatory and greenhouse. They delight in a mixture of sand, loam, and peat, and may be increased by young cuttings in sand, under a glass. Synonyme: 1. *Poiretia elliptica.* 2. *P. linearis.* 3. *H. lanigera.*

| | | | | |
|---|---|---|---|---|
| apiculātă | . . | . Purplish . | 5, G. Ev. S. N. Holl. | . 1824 |
| acutifōlĭă | . . | . Purple . | 4, G. Ev. S. N. Holl. | . 1823 |
| Cĕlsĭĭ | . . | . Blue . | 6, G. Ev. S. N. Holl. | . 1818 |
| crispă | . . | . Purple . | 2, G. Ev. S. Sw. River | . 1837 |
| elliptĭcă, 1 | . . | . Purple . | 4, G. Ev. S. N. Holl. | . 1817 |
| Manglĕsĭĭ | . . | . Purple . | 1, G. Ev. S. Sw. River | . 1837 |
| lanceolātă | . . | . Purple . | 5, G. Ev. S. N. Holl. | . 1805 |
| latifōlĭă | . . | . Purple . | 6, G. Ev. S. N. Holl. | . 1820 |
| linēārĭs, 2 | . . | . Purple . | 7, G. Ev. S. N. S. W. | . 1796 |
| longifōlĭă | . . | . Purple . | 7, G. Ev. S. N. S. W. | . 1805 |
| mucronātă | . . | . Purple . | 6, G. Ev. S. N. Holl. | . 1824 |
| pannŏsă, 3 | . . | . Purple . | 6, G. Ev. S. N. Holl. | . 1824 |
| pūngens | . . | . Blue . | G. Ev. S. Sw. River | . 1837 |
| purpūrĕă | . . | . Purple . | 6, G. Ev. S. N. Holl. | . 1820 |
| rosmarinifōlĭă | . . | . Blue . | 6, G. Ev. S. N. Holl. | . 1824 |
| villōsă | . . | . Lilac . | 4, G. Ev. S. N. Holl. | . 1829 |

HOVĔNĬA, *Thunberg.* In honour of David Hoven, a senator of Amsterdam, who contributed to the success of the travels of Thunberg. *Linn.* 5, Or. 1, Nat. Or. *Rhamnaceæ.* These are small fruit-bearing trees, growing to the height of eight or ten feet, and producing a fruit which is said to taste like the Bergamot pear. They grow freely in a mixture of loam and peat; and cuttings of the ripened wood root freely in sand, under a glass. Synonymes: 1. *H. acerba,* 2. *H. dulcis.*

| | | | | |
|---|---|---|---|---|
| dulcis, 1 | . . | . White . | 7, G. Ev. T. Japan | . 1812 |
| insequālĭs, 2 | . . | . White . | G. Ev. T. Nepal | . 1820 |

HŎĬĂ, *R. Brown.* In honour of Thomas Hoy, F.L.S. late gardener to the Duke of Northumberland, at Sion House; he died in 1821. *Linn.* 5, Or. 2, Nat. Or. *Asclepiadaceæ.* The plants of this genus bear very handsome waxy flowers, well known to all cultivators. They will grow in almost any soil, but loam, peat, and sand, suits them best; cuttings planted in a moist heat, will root freely; even a leaf, taken off close to the plant, and planted in mould, in a little heat, will root and produce a plant. Synonymes: 1. *H. lanceolata, H. pallida.*

| | | | | |
|---|---|---|---|---|
| australis | . . | . White . | 8. Ev. Tw. N. Holl. | . 1820 |
| carnŏsă | . . | . Pink . | 7, S. Ev. Tw. Asia | . 1802 |
| coriācĕă | . . | . Wht. yel. | 8, S. Ev. Tw. Manilla | . 1838 |
| crassifōlĭă | . . | . | 8. Ev. Tw. China | . 1817 |
| fŭscă | . . | . Brownish . | 8. Ev. Tw. Sylhet | . 1837 |
| parasitĭcă, 1 | . . | . Yellow . | 8, S. Ev. Tw. E. Ind. | . . |
| Potsĭĭ | . . | . Yellow . | 8. Ev. Tw. E. Ind. | . 1824 |
| trinĕrvis | . . | . Yellow . | 7, S. Ev. Tw. China | . 1824 |

HUDSŎNĬA, *Linn.* In honour of William Hudson, F.R.S., a London apothecary, and author of the Flora Anglica, 1778. *Linn.* 11, Or. 1, Nat. Or.

*Cistaceæ.* These are pretty little heath-like shrubs, rather difficult to cultivate; they grow best in a peat soil, in a shady situation. They require the protection of glass in winter, and should therefore be grown in pots. They may either be increased by layers, or ripened cuttings, in sand, under a glass.

| | | | | | | | |
|---|---|---|---|---|---|---|---|
| ericoídes | . . | . Yellow | . 6, | F. Ev. S. | N. Amer. | . 1805 |
| Nuttalli | . . | . Yellow | . 7, | F. Ev. S. | N. Amer. | . |
| tomentósá | . . | . Yellow | . 5, | F. Ev. S. | N. Amer. | . 1826 |

HUÈRNÌA, *R. Brown.* In honour of Justus Huernius, an early collector of Cape plants, and from whose drawing the first account of *Stapelia* was taken. *Linn.* 5, Or. 2, Nat. Or. *Asclepiadaceæ.* These plants are related to the genus *Stapelia;* which see, for culture and propagation. *Synonymes:* 1. *Stapelia ocellata.* 2. *S. reticulata.*

| | | | | | | | |
|---|---|---|---|---|---|---|---|
| barbátá | . . | . Wht. stri. | 8, | S. Ev. S. | C. G. H. | . 1795 |
| campanulátá | . | . Wht. stri. | 8, | S. Ev. S. | C. G. H. | . 1795 |
| clavígèrá | . | . Yel. stri. | 9, | S. Ev. S. | C. G. H. | . 1795 |
| crispá | . . | . | | S. Ev. S. | C. G. H. | . |
| guttátá | . . | . Yel. stri. | 9, | S. Ev. S. | C. G. H. | . 1795 |
| húmilis | . . | . Yel. stri. | 9, | S. Ev. S. | C. G. H. | . 1795 |
| lentíginósá | . | . Yel. stri. | 9, | S. Ev. S. | C. G. H. | . 1795 |
| ocellátá, 1 | . | . Yel. stri. | 9, | S. Ev. S. | C. G. H. | . |
| reticulátá, 2 | . | . Pnk. stri. | 8, | S. Ev. S. | C. G. H. | . 1793 |
| tubátá | . . | . Yel. stri. | 9, | S. Ev. S. | C. G. H. | . 1805 |
| venústá | . . | . Yel. stri. | 6, | S. Ev. S. | C. G. H. | . 1795 |

HUGÒNÌA, *Linn.* In honour of John Hugon, an English botanical author in 1771. *Linn.* 16, Or. 6, Nat. Or. *Hugoniaceæ.* The plants of this genus thrive well in a mixture of loam, peat, and sand; and cuttings of the ripened wood will root freely in sand, under a glass, in heat.

| | | | | | | | |
|---|---|---|---|---|---|---|---|
| mystáx | . . | . Yellow | . 6, | S. Ev. S. | Ceylon | . 1818 |
| serrátá | . . | . Yellow | . 8, | S. Ev. S. | Maurit. | . 1820 |

HUMBLE-PLANT, see *Mimósá pudícá.*

HÙMEA, *Smith.* In honour of the Lady of the late Sir Abraham Hume, Bart. of Wormleybury, Herts. *Linn.* 19, Or. 1, Nat. Or. *Compositæ.* An elegant species, flowering well in a warm situation in the open border; it requires to be raised on a gentle hotbed, and when of sufficient size, potted off, and treated as a greenhouse plant till the second year, when it may be turned out into the open border, where it will grow and flower much better, than if confined in pots.

| | | | | | | |
|---|---|---|---|---|---|---|
| élègans | . . . | . Red | . . 7, | G. | B. N. S. W. | . 1800 |

HÙMIFÙSÙS, prostrate, diffuse.

HÙMÌLÌS, humble, small, low.

HÙMÙLÙS, *Linn.* From *humus,* the ground; the plant, if not supported, creeps along the ground. *Linn.* 22, Or. 5, Nat. Or. *Urticaceæ.* This is the well-known Hop, which is so extensively cultivated in some parts of England. It looks well grown as a temporary arbour in summer, as its leaves are very large, and make a fine shade; deep loamy soil suits it best, and it may be increased by divisions or seeds.

| | | | | | | |
|---|---|---|---|---|---|---|
| Lúpùlùs | . . . | Yellow | . 7, | H. Her. Cl. | Britain. | . . |

HUNGARIAN LÒTÙS, see *Nymphǽá thermàlis.*

HUNNEMÀNNÌA, *Sweet.* In honour of John Hunnemann, a zealous botanist, and to whom the British gardens are indebted for a great number of plants. *Linn.* 13, Or. 1, Nat. Or. *Papaveraceæ.* This is a very handsome plant when in flower, requiring much the same treatment as *Humea.*

| | | | | | | |
|---|---|---|---|---|---|---|
| fumariæfòlìá | . | . Yellow | . F. Her. P. | Mexico. | . 1827 |

HÙRA, *Linn.* The name of the plant in South America. *Linn.* 21, Or. 11, Nat. Or. *Euphorbiaceæ.* The species of Sandbox tree grow well in a light loamy soil, or loam and peat mixed; large cuttings of the ripened wood will root in sand, under a glass, in heat.

| | | | | | | |
|---|---|---|---|---|---|---|
| crépítans | . . | . Wht. yel. | . 8, Ev. T. | S. Amer. | . 1733 |
| strépens | . . | . Wht. yel. | . 8. Ev. T. | S. Amer. | . . |

HUSKS, the dry envelopes of either flowers or fruits.

HUTCHINSÌA, *R. Brown.* In compliment to Miss Hutchins, an accomplished Irish cryptogamist. *Linn.* 15, Nat. Or. *Cruciferæ.* This is a genus of pretty alpine plants; the herbaceous kinds do best in sandy loam and peat, and are easily increased by cuttings under a hand-glass. The annual species delight in a dry situation on a rockery. *Synonymes:* 1. *Lepidium alpinum.* 2. *calycinum.* 3.

*petræum.* 4. *procumbens.* 5. *Iberis rotundifolia.* 6. *I. stylosa.*

| | | | | | |
|---|---|---|---|---|---|
| alpína, 1 | . . | . White | . 5. H. Her. P. | S. Eur. | . 1775 |
| brevístylá | . . | . White | . 5, H. Her. P. | Syria | . 1825 |
| calycína, 2 | . . | . White | . 4. H. Her. P. | Siberia | . 1823 |
| cepæfòlìá | . . | . Pink | . 6, H. Her. P. | Carinthia | . 1824 |
| petrǽá, 3 | . . | . White | . 4, H. | A. England | . |
| procumbens, 4 | . | . White | . 5, H. | A. S. Eur. | . 1823 |
| púmìlá | . . | . White | . 6, H. Her. P. | Caucasus | . 1821 |
| rotundifòlìá, 5 | . | Wht. pur. | 6, H. Her. P. | S. Eur. | . 1759 |
| stylòsá, 6 | . . | . Wht. pink | 6, H. Her. P. | Caucasus | . 1824 |

HYACÌNTHÙS, *Linn.* A boy killed by Zephyrus. *Linn.* 6, Or. 1, Nat. Or. *Liliaceæ.* These beautiful and well-known plants are easily cultivated in light sandy loam, and readily increase by offsets from the bulbs. The hyacinth forces well, and few bulbs do better in water. *Synonyme:* 1. *Zuccagnia viridis.*

| | | | | | |
|---|---|---|---|---|---|
| amethýstínùs | . . | . Blue | . 4, H. Bu. P. | S. Eur. | . 1759 |
| brumàlís | . . | . Various | . 2, H. Bu. P. | | |
| orientàlís | . . | . Blue | . 3, H. Bu. P. | Levant | . 1596 |
| álbùs | . . | . White | . 3, H. Bu. P. | | . 1596 |
| flàvùs | . . | . Yellow | . 3, H. Bu. P. | | . 1596 |
| múltíplèx | . . | . Varieg. | . 4, H. Bu. P. | | . 1596 |
| rùber | . . | . Red | . 3, H. Bu. P. | | . 1596 |
| semíplénùs | . . | . Varieg. | . 3, H. Bu. P. | | . 1596 |
| spicátùs | . . | . Blush | . 2, H. Bu. P. | Zante | . 1826 |
| víridís, 1 | . . | . Green | . 3, G. Bl. P. | C. G. H. | . 1774 |

HYACINTH, see *Hyacínthùs.*

HYÆNÀNCHÈ, *Lambert.* From *hyæna,* the hyæna, and *agcho,* to strangle; poisonous quality of the fruit. *Linn.* 22, Or. 10, Nat. Or. *Euphorbiaceæ.* A shrub from six to eight feet high, of very easy culture. In the colony of the Cape of Good Hope, the powdered fruit is used to poison hyænas. *Synonyme:* 1. *Toxicodendron capense.*

| | | | | | |
|---|---|---|---|---|---|
| globòsá, 1 | . . | . Wht. grn. | 6, G. Ev. S. | C. G. H. | . 1783 |

HYÆNA POISON, see *Hyænánchè.*

HYALÌNE, crystalline, transparent.

HYBRID, partaking of the nature of two species.

HÝDNÙM, *Linn.* From *hydnon,* a Greek word, signifying a truffle. *Linn.* 24, Or. 9, Nat. Or. *Fungi.* Some of the species of this genus are eatable, as *H. coralloides;* they are chiefly found under the trunks of trees, in moist situations—*auriscálpium, bárbá-Jòvis, coralloìdes, crispúm, erináctúm, ferruginósúm, gelatinósúm, imbricátúm, membranácèúm, mínimúm, ochrácèúm, rádúlá, repándúm-squamósúm, rufèscèns, spatulátúm.*

HYDRÀNGEA, *Linn.* From *hydor,* water, and *aggeion,* a vessel; the capsule of some of the species has been compared to a cup. *Linn.* 10, Or. 2, Nat. Or. *Saxifrageæ.* Dwarf shrubs, which are very pretty when in flower; they are well suited for the front of shrubberies, growing in any common soil; and ripened cuttings root freely planted in any sheltered situation. *Synonymes:* 1. *Hortensia opuloides.* 2. *Hydrangea radiata.*

| | | | | | |
|---|---|---|---|---|---|
| arboréscens | . . | . White | . 7, H. De. S. | Virginia | . 1736 |
| cordátá | . . | . White | . 7, H. De. S. | Carolina | . 1806 |
| heteromállá | . . | . White | . 4, H. De. S. | Nepal | . 1821 |
| horténsìs, 1 | . . | . Pink | . 5, H. De. S. | China | . 1740 |
| nívéá, 2 | . . | . White | . 7, H. De. S. | Carolina | . 1786 |
| quercifòlìá | . . | . White | . 7, H. De. S. | Florida | . 1803 |

HYDRÀGOGUE, any thing which removes dropsy.

HYDRÀSTÌS, *Linn.* From *hydor,* water; plants growing in humid places. *Linn.* 14, Or. 1, Nat. Or. *Ranunculaceæ.* An ornamental species, succeeding well in a moist situation, in loam and peat, and increased by tubers of the roots.

| | | | | | |
|---|---|---|---|---|---|
| canadénsís | . . | . Green | . 5, H. Her. P. | N. Amer. | . 1759 |

HYDRÒCHÀRÌS, *Linn.* From *hydor,* water, and *charis,* grace; a pretty aquatic. *Linn.* 22, Or. 3, Nat. Or. *Hydrocharaceæ.* This little plant is one of the prettiest ornaments of our still waters; it looks very pretty grown in a tub or cistern of water, and is readily increased by seeds, or runners, which root at the joints.

| | | | | | |
|---|---|---|---|---|---|
| mórsùs-ránǽ | . | . White | . 6, H. Aq. P. | Britain | . . |

HYDRÒCHLÒA, *Link.* From *hydor,* water, and *chloa,* grass; aquatic grass. *Linn.* 3, Or. 2, Nat. Or. *Gramineæ.* Mere weeds, of the simplest culture. *Synonymes:* 1. *Poa aquatica, Glyceria aquatica.* 2. *P. arundinacea.* 3. *P. distans.* 4. *P. maritima, Glyceria maritima—aquáticá* 1, *arundinácèá* 2, *distáns* 3, *marítímá* 4.

HYDROCÒTÝLE, *Tournefort.* From *hydor,* water, and

cotyle, a cavity; in reference to the plants growing in moist situations, and the leaves being hollowed like cups. *Linn.* 5, Or. 2, Nat. Or. *Umbelliferæ.* Uninteresting plants, growing in peat soil in wet situations; increased by divisions. *Synonyme:* 1. *H. hirsuta—americānd, asiāticā, bonariēnsis, nepalēnsis, nūtāns, peduncularis, plebēiā, ranunculoīdēs, repāndā, sibthorpioīdēs, trilobā, umbellātā, villōsā, vulgāris.*

spicātā, 1 . . . Green . 7, 8. Her. P. India . . 1810

HYDRODICTYON, *Kunth.* From *hydor,* water, and *dictyon,* a net; reticulate structure of the plants. *Linn.* 24, Or. 7, Nat. Or. *Algæ.* A curious aquatic production, resembling a net—*utriculātum.*

HYDROLEX, *Linn.* From *hydor,* water, and *elaia,* oil; alluding to the situation and oily nature of the plant. *Linn.* 5, Or. 2, Nat. Or. *Hydroleaceæ.* Rather handsome plants when in flower, succeeding well in loam and peat; and cuttings will root in sand, under a glass, in heat. *Synonyme:* 1. *caroliniana.*

quadrivalvis, 1 . Pa. blue . 7, S. Her. P. Carolina . 1824
spinosa . . . . Blue . 6, S. Ev. S. S. Amer. . 1791

HYDROPELTIS, *Michaux.* From *hydor,* water, and *pelte,* a buckler; the plant grows in water, and the leaves are like a buckler. *Linn.* 13, Or. 6, Nat. Or. *Nymphæaceæ.* This very pretty plant is seldom to be met with in our gardens, it being very difficult to grow; it requires to be kept in a cistern or pond of water, and may be increased by offsets. *Synonyme:* 1. *Brasenia peltata.*

purpūrea, 1 . . Red . . 7, F. Aq. P. N. Amer. . 1798

HYDROPHYLLUM, *Linn.* From *hydor,* water, and *phyllon,* a leaf. *Linn.* 5, Or. 1, Nat. Or. *Hydrophyllacea.* Dwarf, neat-foliaged plants, inhabiting the marshes of North America; any rich soil suits them in a moist situation; and they may be increased by suckers.

canadēnsē . . . White . 5, H. Her. P. Canada · 1759
virginicum . . . Blue . 6, H. Her. P. N. Amer. . 1789

HYDROTÆNIA, *Lindley.* The petals have a triangular glandular bar at their base, which points upwards and secretes honey; whence the name. *Linn.* , Or. , Nat. Or. *Iridaceæ.* A curious genus, found in mountain pastures, near the Real del Monte mines in Mexico. The plant looks like a *Tigridia,* and bears flowers resembling *Fritillaria pyrenaica,* only smaller. For culture, &c., see *Tigridia.*

Meleāgris . . . Yellow . 7, H. Bl. P. Mexico . . 1837

HYGROCROCIS, *Agardh.* From *hygros,* moist, and *krokis,* a little tuft. *Linn.* 24, Or. 7, Nat. Or. *Algæ.* These plants are only found in chemical solutions of vegetable matter, such as ink, rose water, &c.—*atramēnti, barytica, pallida, Rōsā, sanguinēā, typhlodērmā, vīni.*

HYGROMETRICAL, indicating the approach of water.

HYGROPHILA, *R. Brown.* From *hygros,* moist, and *phileo,* to love, alluding to the habitat of the plant. *Linn.* 14, Or. 2, Nat. Or. *Acanthaceæ.* A pretty plant, growing freely in a rich light soil; and young cuttings root freely in the same kind of soil, under a glass, in heat. *Synonyme:* 1. *Ruellia ringens.*

ringēns . . . . 8. Ev. Tr. E. Ind. . . 1820

HYMENÆA, *Linn.* From *Hymen,* god of marriage; in reference to the two leaflets. *Linn.* 10, Or. 1, Nat. Or. *Leguminosæ.* The species of Locust-tree are highly ornamental; they delight to grow in loam and peat, and cuttings will root in sand, under a glass, in heat. *Synonyme:* 1. *Trachylobium Martianum.*

Candolliāna . . White . . 8. Ev. T. Acapulco . 1824
Coūrbaril . . . Yel. pur. . 8. Ev. T. W. Ind. . 1688
verrucōsā, 1 . . . 8. Ev. T. Madagas. . 1808

HYMENANTHERA, *R. Brown.* From *hymen,* a membrane, and *anthera,* an anther, the termination of the anthers. *Linn.* 5, Or. 1, Nat. Or. *Polygalaceæ.* An ornamental shrub, about six feet high; it grows freely in peat and loam, and cuttings root in sand, under a glass, in heat.

dentātā . . . . Yellow . 5, G. Ev. S. N. Holl. . 1824

HYMENELLA, *Fries.* From *hymen,* a membrane; the

plants are scaly. *Linn.* 24, Or. 9, Nat. Or. *Fungi.* Small productions, found on nettle stems—*vulgāris.*

HYMENOCARPUS, *Savi.* From *hymen,* a membrane, and *karpos,* a fruit; alluding to the membranous legumes. *Linn.* 17, Or. 4, Nat. Or. *Leguminosæ.* Little inconspicuous plants, of the simplest culture. *Synonymes:* 1. *Medicago circinata.* 2. *M. nummularia.* 3. *M. radiata.*

circinātus, 1 . Yellow . 7, H. Tr. A. Italy . . 1640
nummulārius, 2 . Yellow . 8, H. Tr. A. S. France . 1640
radiātus, 3 . . . Yellow . 6, H. A. Italy . . 1629

HYMENODICTYON, *Wallich.* From *hymen,* a membrane, and *diktyon,* a net; the seeds are girded by a reticulated membrane. *Linn.* 5, Or. 1, Nat. Or. *Cinchonaceæ.* Ornamental trees, from twenty to thirty feet high; for culture and propagation, see *Cinchona. Synonymes:* 1. *Cinchona excelsa.* 2. *C. thyrsiflora.*

excelsum, 1 . . Grn. yel. . 7, S. Ev. T. E. Ind. . . 1820
thyrsiflōrum, 2 . Grn. yel. . 6, S. Ev. T. E. Ind. . . 1819

HYMENOGYNE, *Haworth.* From *hymen,* a membrane, and *gyne,* a woman. *Linn.* 12, Or. 2, Nat. Or. *Ficoideæ.* A plant of no great beauty, and requiring the same treatment as other tender annuals. *Synonyme:* 1. *Mesembryanthemum glabrum.*

glabrā, 1 . . . Pa. yel. . 8, G. A. C. G. H. . 1787

HYMENOPAPPUS, *L'Heritier.* From *hymen,* a membrane, and *pappos,* a pappus; in reference to the membranous crown of the seeds. *Linn.* 19, Or. 1, Nat. Or. *Compositæ.* Half-hardy annuals, of little beauty, and easy culture. *Synonyme:* 1. *Stevia pedata.*

pedātus, 1 . . . White . 8, H. A. S. Amer. . 1803
scabiosētus . . . White . 8, H. A. Carolina . 1816
*tenuifōlius.*

HYMENOPHYLLUM, *Smith.* From *hymen,* a membrane, and *phyllon,* a leaf; alluding to the leaves. *Linn.* 24, Or. 1, Nat. Or. *Gleicheniaceæ.* The species of this genus rank among the most elegant of the Ferns, and do best when grown in small pots, in a mixture of loam and peat, and increase freely by seed, or dividing the roots.

tunbridgēnsē . . Brown . 6, H. Her. P. Britain . .
Wilsōni . . . Brown . 6, H. Her. P. Britain . .

HYOSCYAMUS, see *Physochlaina.*

HYOSCYAMUS, *Linn.* From *hyos,* a hog, and *kyamos,* a bean; the fruit is eaten by the swine. *Linn.* 5, Or. 1, Nat. Or. *Solanaceæ.* The species of *Henbane* are all of the easiest culture. The shrubby and herbaceous kinds are well adapted for planting on rock-work during summer, but in winter they require the protection of glass; and are increased by cuttings or seeds. The annual and biennial kinds merely require sowing in the open ground. Henbane has been long used as a medicine. *Synonyme:* 1. *H. niger annuus.*

auriculātus . . Yellow . 6, H. A. Naples . . 1823
canariēnsis . . . Yellow . 12, G. Ev. S. Canaries . 1816
Datūra . . . Yellow . 5, F. Ev. S. Egypt . . 1829
niger . . . . Yel. pur. . 6, H. B. Britain . .

*agrēstis* 1, *albūs, aurēus, micrānthus, mūticus, pallidus, pusillus, seneciōnis.*

HYOSERIS, *Linn.* From *hyos,* a hog, and *seris,* succory; swine's-succory. *Linn.* 19, Or. 1, Nat. Or. *Compositæ.* Uninteresting herbaceous plants, of the simplest culture—*arenāriā, lūcidā, radiātā, scābrā.*

HYPECOUM, *Linn.* From *hypecheo,* to rattle; in reference to the noise made by the seeds in the pods. *Linn.* 4, Or. 2, Nat. Or. *Papaveraceæ.* These are very pretty plants; the seed has only to be sown in the open ground.

erectum . . . Yellow . 5, H. A. Siberia . 1759
pendulum . . . Yellow . 6, H. Tr. A. S. France . 1640
procumbēns . . Yellow . 7, H. Tr. A. S. Eur. . 1596

HYPERBOREUS, northern.

HYPERCATHARSIS, a medicine that produces too powerful effects as a purgative.

HYPERICUM, *Linn.* The name is said to be derived from *uper* and *eicon,* an image; the superior part of the flower represents a figure. *Linn.* 18, Or. 2, Nat. Or. *Hypericaceæ.* The most part of the species of this extensive genus are showy plants. The greenhouse and frame shrubby kinds do well in loam and peat, and young cuttings root freely in sand, under a glass. The hardy shrubs are well fitted for the front of shrubberies, being dwarf and showy, and growing in any soil, and increased by divisions or seeds, as well as the herbaceous kinds, which thrive well in any common soil. The seeds of the annual species have only to be sown in the open ground in spring. *Synonymes*: 1. *H. mono-gynum*. 2. *delphinense*. 3. *Kohlianum*. 4. *nervo-sum*. 5. *aspalathoides*. 6. *Elodea campanulata*.

| | | | | |
|---|---|---|---|---|
| ægyptīācům . . | Yellow | 6, G. Ev. S. | Egypt . . | 1787 |
| æthiōpicům . . | Yellow | 7, G. Ev. S. | C. G. H. | 1817 |
| amœnům . . | Yellow | 7, H. Her. P. | Carolina | 1802 |
| angulōsům . . | Yellow | 6, H. Her. P. | N. Amer. | 1812 |
| Ascýron . . | Yellow | 6, H. Her. P. | Siberia | 1774 |
| ascyroīdés . . | Yellow | 6, H. Her. P. | N. Amer. | 1812 |
| attenuātům . . | Yellow | 7, H. Her. P. | Dahuria | 1822 |
| balearicům . . | Yellow | 5, F. Ev. S. | Majorca | 1714 |
| barbātům . . | Yellow | 7, H. Her. P. | Scotland | |
| calabricům . . | Yellow | 8, H. Her. P. | Calabria | 1816 |
| calycinům . . | Yellow | 7, H. De. S. | Ireland . | |
| canadensé . . | Yellow | 8, H. Her. P. | N. Amer. | 1770 |
| canariénsé . . | Yellow | 8, G. Ev. S. | Canaries | 1699 |
| chinênsé, 1 . | Yellow | 6, G. Ev. S. | China . | 1753 |
| ciliātům . . | Yellow | 7, F. Her. P. | Levant . | 1739 |
| cochin-chinênsé | Red | 7, G. Ev. S. | China . | 1821 |
| cordifōlium . . | Yellow | F. Ev. S. | Nepal . | 1825 |
| Cōris . . . | Yellow | 6, F. Ev. S. | Levant . | 1640 |
| crispům . . | Yellow | 7, F. Her. P. | Greece . | 1688 |
| dentātům . . | Yellow | 8, H. Her. P. | Medit. . | 1820 |
| dolabriformé . | Yellow | 6, H. Her. P. | N. Amer. | 1821 |
| dūbīům, 2 . | Yellow | 7, H. Her. P. | Britain . | |
| elātům . . | Yellow | 7, H. De. S. | N. Amer. | 1762 |
| ēlégáns, 3 . | Yellow | 6, H. Her. P. | Siberia . | 1822 |
| elōdés . . | Yellow | 7, H. Her. P. | Britain . | |
| elodioīdés, 4 . | Sulphur | 7, H. Her. P. | Nepal . | 1820 |
| empetrifōlium . | Yellow | 7, F. Ev. S. | S. Eur. . | 1820 |
| erioīdés . . | Yellow | 6, F. Ev. S. | Spain . | 1821 |
| fasciculātům, 5 . | Yellow | 7, F. De. S. | Carolina | 1811 |
| fimbriātům . . | Yellow | 7, H. Her. P. | Pyrenees | 1821 |
| floribundům . . | Yellow | 6, G. De. S. | Madeira | 1779 |
| foliōsům . . | Yellow | 8, G. Ev. S. | Azores . | 1778 |
| frondōsům . . | Yellow | 7, H. De. S. | N. Amer. | 1806 |
| Geblēri . . | Yellow | 7, H. De. S. | Altai . | 1829 |
| glandulōsům . | Yellow | 6, G. Ev. S. | Madeira | 1777 |
| glaūcům . . | Yellow | 8, F. De. S. | N. Amer. | 1812 |
| grandiflōrům . | Yellow | 7, G. Ev. S. | Teneriffe | 1718 |
| heterophýllům . | Yellow | 7, G. Ev. S. | Persia . | 1812 |
| hircinům . . | Yellow | 8, H. De. S. | S. Eur. . | 1640 |
| minůs . . | Yellow | 8, H. De. S. | S. Eur. . | |
| hirsūtům . . | Yellow | 6, H. Her. P. | Britain . | |
| humifūsům . . | Yellow | 7, H. De. Tr. | Britain . | |
| hyssopifōlium . | Yellow | 7, H. Her. P. | S. Eur. . | 1823 |
| involūtům . . | Yellow | 7, H. Her. P. | N. S. W. | 1822 |
| japōnicům . . | Yellow | 7, H. Her. P. | Nepal . | 1823 |
| Kalmiānům . . | Yellow | 6, H. De. S. | N. Amer. | 1759 |
| lævigātům . . | Yellow | 8, H. Her. P. | N. Amer. | 1772 |
| Liottárdi . . | Yellow | 7, H. Tr. B. | Switzerl. | 1819 |
| montānům . . | Yellow | 7, H. Her. P. | Britain . | |
| myrtifōlium . . | Yellow | 7, H. Her. P. | N. Amer. | 1818 |
| nudiflōrům . . | Yellow | 7, H. Her. P. | N. Amer. | 1811 |
| nummulārīům . | Yellow | 6, H. De. Cr. | S. Eur. . | 1823 |
| oblongifōlium . | Yellow | 6, G. Ev. S. | Nepal . | 1823 |
| olýmpicům . . | Yellow | 8, H. Ev. S. | Levant . | 1706 |
| palūdōsům . . | Yellow | 7, H. Her. P. | N. Amer. | 1821 |
| pātůlům . . | Yellow | 6, H. Ev. S. | Nepal . | 1823 |
| perforātům . . | Yellow | 7, H. Her. P. | Britain . | |
| perfolīātům . . | Yellow | 7, H. Her. P. | Italy . . | 1785 |
| procůmbéns . . | Yellow | 8, H. Her. P. | N. Amer. | 1822 |
| prolificům . . | Yellow | 7, H. De. S. | N. Amer. | 1758 |
| pūlchrům . . | Yellow | 7, H. Her. P. | Britain . | |
| punctātům . . | Yellow | 6, H. De. S. | N. Amer. | 1823 |
| pusīllům . . | Yellow | 7, F. De. Tr. | N. S. W. | 1818 |
| pyramidātům . | Yellow | 7, H. Her. P. | Canada . | 1759 |
| quadrangůlům . | Yellow | 7, H. Her. P. | Britain . | |
| quinquenervium | Yellow | 7, H. Her. P. | N. Amer. | 1759 |
| rosmarinifōlium . | Yellow | 7, F. De. S. | Carolina | 1812 |
| serpyllifōlium . | Yellow | 7, H. Ev. S. | Levant . | 1688 |
| simplex . . | Yellow | 7, H. | A. N. Amer. | 1826 |
| tomentōsům . . | Yellow | 8, H. Her. P. | S. Eur. . | 1648 |
| triplinervé . . | Yellow | 7, H. Her. P. | N. Amer. | 1821 |
| uralům . . | Yellow | 7, H. De. S. | Nepal . | 1823 |
| verticillātům . | Yellow | 8, G. Ev. S. | C. G. H. | 1784 |
| virgātům . . | Yellow | 7, H. Her. P. | N. Amer. | 1820 |
| virginicům, 6 . | Yellow | 8, H. Her. P. | N. Amer. | 1800 |

**HYPHÆNÉ**, *Gærtner*. From *hyphaino*, to entwine; alluding to the fibres of the fruit. Linn. 22, Or. 6, Nat. Or. *Palmaceæ*. An ornamental palm-tree, growing best in strong sandy loam. *Synonyme*: 1. *Cucifera thebaica*.

| | | | | |
|---|---|---|---|---|
| coriāceã, 1 . . | | Palm. Egypt . . | | 1824 |

**HYPNÚM**, *Linn*. *Hypnos* was a name used for a moss by the Greeks. Linn. 24, Or. 5, Nat. Or. *Musci*. This is the most extensive genus among mosses, and known without difficulty by the prostrate, pin-

[ 165 ]

nated, bright green branches. *H. crista-castrensis* is said to be the most rare and beautiful of all the British species. *Synonymes*: 1. *serrulatum*. 2. *ni-groviride*. 3. *dubium, fallax*. 4. *confertum*. 5. *flu-viatile, adnatum*. 6. *alpinum*. 7. *implexum*. 8. *Stokesii, Swartzii*. 9. *recognitum*. 10. *illecebrum*. 11. *crenulatum*. 12. *subtile*. 13. *intricatum—abie-tinum, adůncům-rugōsům, ālbīcāns, alopecūrům, alpēstré, Blandōvii, blāndům, brevirōstré, catenu-lātům, commutātům, confěrtům* 1, *cordifōlium, cristā-castrénsé, cupressifōrmé* 2-*polyánthēs, curvātům, cuspidātům, denticulātům angustifōlium-obtusifō-lium, dimōrphům, filicīnům* 3, *flagellāré, flūitāus, Hallēri, lōrěům, lutēscēns, mōllé, mollūscům, murālé* 4, *nītēns, palūstré* 5, *piliférům, plumōsům* 6, *poly-mōrphům, populěům* 7, *prælōngům* 8, *prolíférům* 9, *pārům* 10, *reflēxům, ripārium, rugulōsům, rusci-fōlium, rutābūlům* 11, *salebrōsům, Schrebēri, scor-pioīdés, sěrpēns* 12, *silesiānům, splēndēns, squarrō-sům, stellātům-squarrulōsům, stramīněům, striātům, tenēllům, trifāriům, triquetrům, undulātům, unci-nātům, velutīnům* 13.

**HYPOCALÝPTůs**, *Thunberg*. From *hypo*, under, and *kalypto*, to veil. Linn. 16, Or. 4, Nat. Or. *Legu-minosæ*. A plant well worthy of cultivation. It thrives well in an equal mixture of sandy loam and peat; and young cuttings root readily in pots of sand, under a glass. *Synonyme*: 1. *Crotalaria cordifolia*.

| | | | | |
|---|---|---|---|---|
| obcordātům, 1 . | Purple | 6, G. Ev. S. | C. G. H. | 1823 |

**HYPOCHÆRĬs**, *Linn*. From *hypo*, for, and *choiras*, a pig; the plants are eaten by them. Linn. 19, Or. 1, Nat. Or. *Compositæ*. Weeds of the easiest cul-ture—*arachnītés, Balbīsii, canēscēns, dimōrphā, glābrā, hīspidā, macrorhīzā, minīmā*.

**HYPOCRATERIFORM**, salver-shaped.

**HYPÆLÝTRůM**, *Richard*. From *elytron*, a covering, and *hypo*, under; the bracteas are under the glumes. Linn. 3, Or. 1, Nat. Or. *Cyperaceæ*. A curious species, succeeding best in loam and peat, and increased by divisions.

| | | | | |
|---|---|---|---|---|
| argentěům . . . | Wht. pur. | 7, Grass. | E. Ind. . | 1824 |

**HYPOGÆA**, subterranean.

**HYPOGYNOUS**, situate below the ovarium.

**HYPOĒSTĒs**, *Solander*. From *hypoestes*, an under garment; in reference to the covering of the in-volucrum. Linn. 2, Or. 1, Nat. Or. *Acanthaceæ*. Ornamental plants; for culture and propagation, see *Justicia*. *Synonyme*: 1. *Micranthus cochin-chinensis*.

| | | | | |
|---|---|---|---|---|
| cochin-chinēnsís, 1 | White . | 7, S. De. Cl. | China . | |
| fastuōsã . . | Red . | 6, S. Ev. S. | E. Ind. . | 1818 |
| involucrātã . | White . | 7, S. Ev. S. | E. Ind. . | 1811 |
| purpūrēã . . | Purple . | 5, S. Her. P. | China . | 1822 |
| sěrpēns . . . | | 7, S. Ev. S. | Australia | 1820 |

**HYPOLÆNA**, *R. Brown*. From *hypo*, under, and *chlaina*, a cloak; alluding to the base of the fruit. Linn. 22, Or. 2, Nat. Or. *Restiaceæ*. Curious plants, of very easy culture in sandy peat; and increased by divisions of the root.

| | | | | |
|---|---|---|---|---|
| exsulcã . . . | Apetal . | 6, Grass. | N. Holl. . | 1821 |
| fastigiātã . . | Apetal . | 6, Grass. | N. Holl. . | 1820 |

**HYPOLÝTRům**, *Vahl*. From *hypo*, underneath, and *elytron*, involucrum. Linn. 3, Or. 1, Nat. Or. *Cype-raceæ*. Rather an interesting species, of simple culture, and increased by seeds.

| | | | | |
|---|---|---|---|---|
| senegalēnsé . . | Apetal . | 7, Grass. | Senegal . | 1824 |

**HYPOPHYLLOUS**, situated under the leaf.

**HYPŌXĬs**, *Linn*. From *hypo*, beneath, and *oxys*, sharp; referring to the base of the capsule. Linn. 6, Or. 1, Nat. Or. *Amaryllidaceæ*. A genus of no great beauty, thriving well in sandy loam and peat, or decayed leaves. While dormant, they do not require any water, and when they begin to grow, they should be fresh potted, and regularly watered; they are easily increased by offsets from the roots.

| | | | | |
|---|---|---|---|---|
| albã . . . . | White . | 6, G. Her. P. | C. G. H. | 1806 |
| aquaticã . . | Yellow . | 6, G. Aq. P. | C. G. H. | 1787 |
| breviscāpã . . | Yellow . | 5, G. Her. P. | Brazil . | 1823 |
| carolīnēnsé . . | Yellow . | 6, G. Her. P. | Carolina | 1822 |
| decůmbéns . . | Yellow . | 7, S. Her. P. | Jamaica | 1755 |
| ēlégáns . . . | Wht. blue | 5, G. Her. P. | C. G. H. | 1752 |
| erěctã . . . | Yellow . | 6, H. Her. P. | N. Amer. | 1752 |
| hygrometricã . . | Yellow . | 7, G. Her. P. | N. Holl. | 1820 |
| júncēã . . . | Yellow . | 6, F. Her. P. | Carolina | 1787 |

| | | | | | | | |
|---|---|---|---|---|---|---|---|
| linearis | . . . | Yellow | . | 5, G. Her. | P. | C. G. H. | . 1792 |
| obtusa | . . . | Yellow | . | 6, G. Her. | P. | C. G. H. | . 1816 |
| obliqua | . . . | Yellow | . | 7, G. Her. | P. | C. G. H. | . 1795 |
| ovata | . . . | Yellow | . | 2, G. Her. | P. | C. G. H. | . 1806 |
| pratensis | . . . | Yellow | . | 4, G. Her. | P. | N. Holl. | . 1824 |
| ramosa | . . . | Yellow | . | 6, G. Bu. | P. | C. G. H. | . 1829 |
| scabra | . . . | Yellow | . | 8, F. Bu. | P. | C. G. H. | . 1823 |
| serrata | . . . | Yellow | . | 6, H. Her. | P. | C. G. H. | . 1788 |
| sobolifera | . . . | Yellow | . | 6, H. Her. | P. | C. G. H. | . 1774 |
| stellata | . . . | Wht. blue | . | 5, G. Her. | P. | C. G. H. | . 1752 |
| stellipilis | . . . | Yellow | . | 7, G. Her. | P. | C. G. H. | . 1821 |
| veratrifolia | . . . | Yellow | . | 6, H. Her. | P. | C. G. H. | . 1778 |
| villosa | . . . | Yellow | . | 6, H. Her. | P. | C. G. H. | . 1774 |

HÝPTIS, *Jacquin.* From *hyptios*, resupinate; because the limb of the corolla is turned on its back. *Linn.* 14, Or. 1, Nat. Or. *Labiatæ.* Plants of little merit. The shrubby and herbaceous kinds should be treated as other stove and greenhouse plants, and are readily increased by cuttings. The annuals and biennials require the same treatment as other hardy and tender annuals and biennials. *Synonymes:* 1. *H. persica, Nepeta pectinata.* 2. *H. ebracteata, H. Plumieri.*

| | | | | | | |
|---|---|---|---|---|---|---|
| albida | . . . | White | . | 6. S. Ev. S. | Mexico | . 1825 |
| brevipes | . . | Lilac | . | 7, S. Her. P. | S. Amer. | . 1822 |
| capitata | . . | Pa. pur. | . | 8. | B. W. Ind. | . 1714 |
| pectinata, 1 | . | Purple | . | 12, S. Her. P. | W. Ind. | . 1776 |

ICED, covered with shiny particles, like icicles.

ICE-DROPS, resembling icicles.

ICELAND-MOSS, see *Cetrária islándica.*

ICE-PLANT, see *Mesembryánthémum crystallínum.*

ICHNOCÁRPÚS, *R. Brown.* From *ichnos*, a vestige, and *karpos*, fruit. *Linn.* 5, Or. 1, Nat. Or. *Apocynaceæ.* An ornamental stove shrub, of easy management in peat and loam; and cuttings take in sand without difficulty. *Synonyme:* 1. *Apocynum frutescens.*

| | | | | | |
|---|---|---|---|---|---|
| frutescens | . . | Purple | . 7, S. Ev. Tw. | E. Ind. | . 1759 |

ICÍCA, *Aublet.* The name of the plant in Guiana. *Linn.* 10, Or. 1, Nat. Or. *Burseraceæ.* These are ornamental trees, attaining upwards of thirty feet high; for culture, &c., see *Amyris.* Synonymes: 1. *Amyris guianensis.* 2. *A. heterophylla.*

| | | | | | |
|---|---|---|---|---|---|
| caneándra | . | White | . | S. Ev. T. | Guiana | . 1822 |
| guianensis, 1 | . | White | . | S. Ev. T. | Guiana | . 1823 |
| heterophylla, 2 | . | White | . | S. Ev. T. | Guiana | . 1826 |
| Tacamahaca | . | White | . | S. Ev. T. | Trinidad | . 1819 |

ICOSÁNDROUS, having twenty or more stamens.

ÍLEX, *Linn.* Name originally from the Celtic, *oe*, or *ac*, signifying a point; on account of the prickly leaves. *Linn.* 4, Or. 8, Nat. Or. *Aquifoliaceæ.* A genus of trees and shrubs well known for their

# I.

IBĒRIS, *Linn.* From the country called Iberia, now Spain; on account of the original species being found there. *Linn.* 15, Nat. Or. *Cruciferæ.* The species of this genus are all very pretty plants of easy culture, and well known in our gardens under the name of Candytuft. *I. umbellata* is a great favourite, and generally found in every flower-garden collection. *Synonymes:* 1. *E. cepæfolia.*

| | | | | | | |
|---|---|---|---|---|---|---|
| amara | . . . | White | . 6, H. | | A. England | |
| ciliata | . . . | White | . 6, H. | | B. Provence | . 1802 |
| confertà | . . . | White | . 6, H. Ev. S. | | Spain | . 1827 |
| contracta , | . . | White | . 5, H. Ev. | | Spain | . 1824 |
| corifolia | . . . | White | . 6, H. Ev. S. | | S. Eur. | . 1739 |
| coronaria | . . . | White | . 7, H. | | A. | . 1886 |
| Garrexiana | . . | White | . 6, H. Ev. S. | | Piedmont | . 1820 |
| gibraltarica | . . | Wht. pink | . 5, G. Ev. S. | | Gibraltar | . 1732 |
| intermedia | . . | White | . 6, H. | | B. France | . 1823 |
| Lagascana | . . | White | . 7, H. | | A. Spain | . 1822 |
| linifolia | . . . | White | . 6, H. | | B. S. Eur. | . 1759 |
| nana | . . . | Wht. pur. | . 6, H. | | B. Dauphiny | . 1822 |
| odorata | . . . | White | . 6, H. | | A. Crete | . 1806 |
| pinnata | . . . | White | . 7, H. | | A. S. Eur. | . 1596 |
| pubescens | . . | Pa. vio. | . 6, H. Ev. S. | | | |
| saxatilis | . . . | White | . 5, H. Ev. S. | | S. Eur. | . 1739 |
| sempervirens | . . | White | . 6, H. Ev. S. | | Sicily | . 1679 |
| sempervirens | . . | White | . 5, H. Ev. S. | | Candia | . 1731 |
| spatulata | . . | Purple | . 6, H. | | A. Pyrenees | . 1802 |
| tenrica | . . . | White | . 5, H. | | B. Caucasus | . 1802 |
| Tenoreana, 1 | . | Pa. pur. | . 6, H. Her. | | P. Naples | . 1802 |
| umbellata | . . | Purple | . 6, H. | | A. S. Eur. | . 1596 |
| violacea | . . . | Purple | . 6, H. | | A. | . 1782 |

| | | | | | | |
|---|---|---|---|---|---|---|
| radiata | . | Purple | . | 8, S. Her. | P. | Carolina | . 1690 |
| recurvata | . | Purple | . | 7, S. Her. | P. | Cayenne | . 1820 |
| stachyoides | . | | . | 7, G. Her. | P. | W. Ind. | . 1824 |

*chamædrys, Polyánthos, polystáchya, scopária, spicáta, suavēolēns, 2.*

HYSSOP, see *Hyssópus.*

HYSSÓPÚS, *Linn.* The derivation of this word is rather uncertain. By some it is said to be from the Hebrew, *ezob*; others assert it to be from the Arabic, *azzof. Linn.* 14, Or. 1, Nat. Or. *Labiatæ.* The cultivation of this genus is well known to everybody. *Synonymes:* 1. *H. orientalis.* 2. *H. Schleicheri.*

| | | | | | | |
|---|---|---|---|---|---|---|
| officinalis | . . | . | Blue | . 6, H. Ev. S. | S. Eur. . | . 1548 |
| angustifolius, 1 | Blue | . 7, H. Ev. S. | Caucasus | | | |
| canescens, 2 | . | Blue | . 6, H. Ev. S. | Switzerl. | . 1819 | |

HYSTĒRIÚM, *Fries.* From *hysteresis*, penury; alluding to its appearance on infested trees. *Linn.* 24, Or. 9, Nat. Or. *Fungi.* Minute plants, found growing upon the bark of trees, &c.—*angustátum, arundináceum, conigēnum, degēnērans, foliicólum, Fráxini, graminēum, Junipēri, lineáre, maculáre, melaleúcum, Pinástri, pulicáre, quercínum, Rúbi, várium.*

HÝSTRIX, bristly, like a porcupine.

elegant character, evergreen prickly foliage, and their adaptation to lawns. Many varieties have resulted from culture, which are distinguished by the variegation and size of the leaves, and the colour of the fruit. They grow well in any soil, but best in a dryish situation, where there is a good depth of loam. They are increased by budding or grafting on the common kinds; but cuttings of the ripened wood will root under a glass, in a sheltered situation. *I. paraguensis* is used as tea, and yields the famous beverage called Maté in Brazil. *Synonyme:* 1. *Ilex nata.*

| | | | | | |
|---|---|---|---|---|---|
| angustifolia | . . | . White | . 5, F. Ev. S. | Carolina | . 1806 |
| Aquifolium | . | . White | . 5, H. Ev. T. | Britain | |
| albo-marginátum | White | . 5, H. Ev. S. | Britain | | |
| aureo-marginátum | White | . 5, H. Ev. S. | Britain | | |
| crassifólium | . | . White | . 5, H. Ev. T. | Britain | |
| ferox | . | . White | . 5, H. Ev. S. | Britain | |
| flavum | . | . White | . 5, H. Ev. S. | Britain | |
| heterophýllum | . | . White | . 5, H. Ev. T. | Britain | |
| médio-pictum | . | . White | . 5, H. Ev. S. | Britain | |
| recúrvum | . | . White | . 5, H. Ev. S. | Britain | |
| balearica | . . | . White | . 5, H. Ev. T. | Minorca | . 1815 |
| canariénsis | . | . White | . 5, H. Ev. T. | Canaries | . 1820 |
| Cassíne | . | . White | . 5, H. Ev. T. | Carolina | . 1700 |
| chinénsis | . | . White | . 7, G. Ev. S. | China | . 1814 |
| Dahóon | . | . White | . 5, H. Ev. S. | Carolina | . 1726 |
| laxiflóra | . | . White | . 5, H. Ev. T. | Carolina | . 1811 |
| myrtifólia | . | . White | . 7, S. Ev. S. | W. Ind. | . 1806 |
| opaca | . | . White | . 5, H. Ev. T. | Carolina | . 1744 |
| paraguensis | . | . White | . 8. Ev. S. | Paraguay | . 1822 |
| Peradó | . | . Pink | . 5, G. Ev. T. | Madeira | . 1760 |
| recúrva, 1 | . | . White | . 5, H. Ev. T. | | |
| salicifolia | . | . White | . 5, S. Ev. S. | Maurit. | . 1818 |
| vomitória | . | . White | . 7, H. Ev. T. | Florida | . 1700 |

ILLECĒBRÚM, *Linn.* From *Illecebra* of Pliny, which is derived from *illicio*, to allure; pretty enticing plants. *Linn.* 5, Or. 1, Nat. Or. *Illecebraceæ.* Interesting dwarf plants. *I. verticillatum* is found in England in boggy places, and is very pretty. They grow in any soil, and increase from seed without difficulty. *Synonyme:* 1. *Paronychia cymosa.*

| | | | | | |
|---|---|---|---|---|---|
| cymósum, 1 | . | . White | . 7, H. Tr. | A. S. Eur. | . 1820 |
| diffusum | . | . White | . 6, G. Her. | P. Trinidad | . 1817 |
| glomeratum | . | . White | . 6, S. Her. | P. Brazil | . 1820 |
| gomphrenoides | . | . White | . 6, S. | A. Peru | . 1810 |
| leucrum | . | . White | . 6, H. Tr. | A. C. G. H. | . 1818 |
| verticillatum | . | . White | . 7, H. Tr. | A. England | |

ILLICÍÚM, *Linn.* From *illicio*, to allure; because of the agreeable perfume of the species. *Linn.* 13, Or. 6, Nat. Or. *Winteraceæ.* The species of this useful genus thrive well in a light loamy soil, and are readily increased by layers. Cuttings of the ripened wood root readily in sand, under a glass, in heat. *I. anisatum* and *I. floridanum* are considered powerful stomachics and carminatives.

| | | | | | | |
|---|---|---|---|---|---|---|
| anisātūm | . . . Red | . 5, F. Ev. 8. | Japan | . 1790 |
| floridānūm | . . Red | . 5, F. Ev. 8. | Florida | . 1766 |
| parvifiōrūm | . . Yellow | . 5, F. Ev. 8. | Florida | . 1790 |

ILLOSPŌRIŪM, *Martius*. From *illo*, to envelop, and *sporos*, a sporule. *Linn*. 24, Or. 9, Nat. Or. *Fungi*. A very small rose-coloured fungus, appearing in autumn on *Borrera ciliaris*, and some others—*rōsēūm*.

IMBĒRBIS, smooth, without a beard.

IMBRICATE, laid one over another, like tiles.

IMMARGINATE, without a margin.

IMMERSED, buried, applied to the leaves of aquatics when they grow under the water, and to the ovary when buried in the disk.

IMPĀTIĒNS, *Rivinus*. From *impatiens*, impatient; applied to this genus because the elastic valves of the capsules burst when touched, and throw the seed out with great force. *Linn*. 5, Or. 1, Nat. Or. *Balsaminaceæ*. This is a genus of very beautiful and singular plants, all deserving a place in every collection. *I. natans* should be grown in a large pot of water, in rich loamy soil, in a warm part of the stove, and increased by seeds sown in spring. *I. scapiflora* thrives well in a light rich soil, with careful watering in winter. The frame species should be sown on a gentle hotbed in spring, and when about two inches high, they may be planted out into the open border. The seeds of the hardy kinds should be sown in the open border in a shady situation. *Synonyme* · 1. *biflora*.

| | | | | | |
|---|---|---|---|---|---|
| cristātā | . . . Yellow | . 8, H. | A. China | . 1837 |
| discolor | . . . Yellow | . 8, H. | A. Nepal | . 1820 |
| fulvā, 1 | . . Dk. yel. | 6, H. Aq. | A. N. Amer. | |
| Noli-me-tāngērē | . Yellow | . 8, H. | A. England | |
| pallīdā | . . . Yellow | . 8, H. | A. N. Amer. | . 1812 |
| parvifiōrā | . . Yellow | . 8, H. Aq. | A. Russia | . 1820 |
| scapifiōrā | . . Lilac | . 8, S. Bl. | P. E. Ind. | . 1835 |
| trifiōrā | . . . Pa. red | . 8, F. | A. Ceylon | . 1818 |
| tripētālā | . . Red | . 8, F. | A. Nepal | . 1825 |

IMPERĀTĪ, *Cyrilli*. After Ferrante Imperati, a Neapolitan botanist of the sixteenth century. *Linn*. 8, Or. 2, Nat. Or. *Gramineæ*. Pretty species of grass, of the commonest culture. *Synonyme*: 1. *Saccharum spontaneum*.

| | | | | | |
|---|---|---|---|---|---|
| arundinācēā | . . Apetal | . 7, Gram. 8. Eur. | | . 1817 |
| spontānēā, 1 | . Apetal | . 7, Gram. | Africa | . 1824 |

IMPERATŌRĪĀ. Named by Linnæus from its supposed forceful medicinal virtues. *Linn*. 5, Or. 2, Nat. Or. *Umbelliferæ*. Plants of no great beauty, and of the simplest culture; increased by divisions, except *I. mexicana*, which is raised from seeds.

| | | | | | |
|---|---|---|---|---|---|
| angustifōlīā | . . Purple | . 7, H. Her. P. S. Eur. | | . 1819 |
| mexicānā | . . Ora. yel. | . 7, H. Her. P. Mexico | . 1818 |
| Ostruthīūm | . . Pink | . 6, H. Her. P. Scotland | |

IMPLEXUS, folded or plaited.

INAMŒNUS, unpleasant, disagreeable.

INCANUS, hoary, mouldy-coloured.

INCISED, cut, separated by incisions.

INCLAUDENT, not closing.

INCOMPLETE, not full.

INCOMPTUS, slovenly, rough, unpolished.

INCONSPICUOUS, obscure, ill defined.

INCRASSATED, becoming thicker by degrees.

INCUMBENT, lying upon any thing.

INCURVED, bending inwards.

INDEHISCENT, not dehiscing.

INDIAN BAY, see *Laūrūs Indicā*.

INDIAN BLUE, see *Nymphǣā cyānēā*.

INDIAN CORN, see *Zēā*.

INDIAN CRESS, see *Tropēōlūm*.

INDIAN CUCUMBER, see *Medēōlā virginicā*.

INDIAN DOOB-GRASS, see *Cynōdōn Indicā*.

INDIAN FIG, see *Opūntiā*.

INDIAN HAWTHORN, see *Raphiōlēpis*.

INDIAN HEART, see *Cardiospērmūm corindūm*.

INDIAN LOTUS, see *Nymphǣā Lōtūs*.

INDIAN MADDER, see *Hedyōtis*.

INDIAN MILLET, see *Sōrghūm vulgārē*.

INDIAN SHOT, see *Cannā Indicā*.

INDIAN TOBACCO, see *Cannābis Indicā*.

INDIGENOUS, native of a country.

INDIGO, see *Indigōferā*.

INDIGŌFĒRĀ, *Linn*. From *indigo*, a blue dyestuff, a corruption of *Indicum*, Indian, and *fero*, to bear; most of the species produce the well known dye called Indigo. *Linn*. 17, Or. 4, Nat. Or. *Leguminosæ*. An extensive genus of rather elegant plants,

[ 167 ]

the shrubby kinds of which are well worthy of cultivation. The stove and greenhouse shrubby kinds thrive best in a mixture of sandy loam and peat, and may be increased without difficulty by cuttings of the young wood planted in sand, under a glass, in heat. The annual and biennial kinds must be raised from seeds sown in a hotbed in spring, and when the plants have grown a sufficient height, they may be planted singly into pots, and treated as other tender annuals and biennials. The powdered leaf of *I. Anil* is used in hepatitis. *Indigo* is produced from various species of this genus, especially from *I. tinctoria*. *Synonymes* · 1. *I. tinctoria, brachycarpa*. 2. *I. filifolia*. 3. *I. hirsuta*. 4. *Lebeckia nuda*. 5. *I. angulata*. 6. *I. cærulea*.

| | | | | | |
|---|---|---|---|---|---|
| amœnā | . . . Purple | . 3, G. Ev. 8. | C. G. H. | . 1774 |
| angustifōlīā | . Purple | . 8, G. Ev. 8. | C. G. H. | . 1774 |
| Anil | . . . Purple | . 7, G. Ev. 8. | W. Ind. | . 1731 |
| argentēā | . . Purple | . 7, G. Ev. 8. | E. Ind. | . 1776 |
| aspalathoīdēs | . Purple | . 6, G. Ev. 8. | Ceylon | . 1817 |
| atropurpūrēā | . Purple | . 7, G. Ev. 8. | Nepal | . 1816 |
| australis | . . . Pink | . 4, G. Ev. 8. | N. S. W. | . 1790 |
| candicāns | . . Red | . 7, G. Ev. 8. | C. G. H. | . 1774 |
| coriācēā | . . Purple | . 7, G. Ev. 8. | C. G. H. | . 1774 |
| cytisoīdēs | . . Red | . 7, G. Ev. 8. | C. G. H. | . 1774 |
| denudātā | . . Purple | . 6, G. Ev. 8. | C. G. H. | . 1790 |
| diphylla | . . . Purple | . 7, 8. | A. Africa | . 1816 |
| divaricātā | . . Red | . 7, G. Ev. 8. | | |
| endreaphylla | . Scarlet | . 7, 8. De. | Tr. Guinea | . 1823 |
| enneaphylla | . Purple | . 7, 8. Tr. | A. E. Ind. | . 1776 |
| filifōlīā | . . . Purple | . 8, G. Ev. 8. | C. G. H. | . 1812 |
| filifōrmis | . . Purple | . 7, 8. Ev. 8. | C. G. H. | . 1822 |
| frāgrāns | . . Purple | . 7, G. Ev. 8. | E. Ind. | . 1816 |
| frutescēns | . . Purple | . 7, G. Ev. 8. | C. G. H. | . 1822 |
| fūsca | . . . Flesh | . 7, 8. | A. Guinea | . 1823 |
| glabrā | . . . Red | . 7, 8. Tr. | A. E. Ind. | . 1820 |
| glandulōsā | . . Purple | . 7, 8. | A. E. Ind. | . 1820 |
| Guatimālā, 1 | . Purple | . 7, G. Ev. 8. | W. Ind. | . 1800 |
| hedysaroīdēs | . Purple | . 7, G. Ev. 8. | E. Ind. | . 1822 |
| hirsūtā | . . Drk. pur. | . 7, 8. Ev. 8. | Guinea | . 1823 |
| incana | . . . Pink | . 8, G. Ev. 8. | C. G. H. | . 1812 |
| laterītīā, 3 | . . Purple | . 8, 8. Tr. | A. Guinea | . 1806 |
| Leschenaultī | . Purple | . 7, G. | A. E. Ind. | . 1820 |
| leptostāchyā | . Purple | . 6, 8. Ev. 8. | E. Ind. | . 1818 |
| linifōlīā | . . . Red | . 7, 8. Tr. | A. E. Ind. | . 1792 |
| lotoīdēs | . . Red | . 7, G. Ev. 8. | C. G. H. | . 1800 |
| nūdā, 4 | . . . Purple | . 6, S. Ev. 8. | C. G. H. | . 1820 |
| procūmbēns | . . Blood | . 6, G. Her. P. | C. G. H. | . 1818 |
| psoraloīdēs | . . Red | . 8, G. Ev. 8. | C. G. H. | . 1758 |
| rigidā | . . . Red | . 7, 8. Ev. 8. | E. Ind. | . 1816 |
| sarmentōsā | . . Purple | . 7, G. Her. P. | C. G. H. | . 1786 |
| spinōsā | . . . Purple | . 6, G. Ev. 8. | Arabia | . 1820 |
| sylvatīcā, 5 | . Rosy lil. | . 6, G. Ev. 8. | N. Holl. | . 1825 |
| tinctōrīā, 6 | . . Pink | . 7, 8. Ev. 8. | E. Ind. | . 1731 |
| trifōlīātā | . . Purple | . 7, 8. | A. E. Ind. | . 1816 |
| trītā | . . . Red | . 7, 8. | A. E. Ind. | . 1802 |
| violācēā | . . Pa. rose | . 6, G. Ev. 8. | E. Ind. | . 1819 |
| virgātā | . . . Purple | . 8, S. Ev. 8. | E. Ind. | . 1820 |
| viscōsā | . . . Red | . 5, 8. | A. E. Ind. | . 1806 |

*juncēā 2, stipulāris*.

INDURATED, hardened.

INDUSIŪM, the membrane that incloses the thecæ of ferns.

INERMIS, smooth, unarmed.

INFECTORIUS, dyeing, staining.

INFERIOR, any thing placed below the ovary; the lowest of any thing.

INFLATED, blown up, full of air.

INFLEXED, bent inwards.

INFLORESCENCE, disposition of flowers.

INFUNDIBULIFORM, funnel-shaped.

INGĀ, *Plumier*. The South American name of *I. vera*, adopted by Marcgraff. *Linn*. 23, Or. 1, Nat. Or. *Leguminosæ*. The whole of these plants are described as ornamental, and as attaining even thirty feet high. They are of easy culture in peat and loam, and are readily multiplied by cuttings in soil or sand, under a glass, in heat. *I. dulcis* is well known for the sweet juice which flows from its leaves when they are put into the mouth and bruised. *Synonymes*: 1. *Acacia grandiflora*. 2. *I. marginata, Mimosa fagifolia*. 3. *M. Houstoni, Acacia Houstoni*. 4. *I. afxelioides*. 5. *Mimosa fagifolia*. 6. *M. xylocarpa*.

| | | | | | |
|---|---|---|---|---|---|
| affinis | . . . Pink | . 8. Ev. T. | Brasil | . 1800 |
| alba | . . . White | . 8. Ev. T. | Cayenne | . 1804 |
| anōmālā, 1 | . Red | . 6, S. Ev. T. | Mexico | . 1729 |
| Burgōni, 2 | . . Pink | . 8. Ev. T. | Guiana | . 1752 |
| circinalis | . . Pink | . 8. Ev. T. | W. Ind. | . 1796 |
| contōsā | . . Pink | . 8. Ev. T. | Jamaica | . 1818 |
| dulcis | . . . Pink | . 8. Ev. T. | E. Ind. | . 1800 |
| emarginātā | . . Purple | . 8. Ev. T. | Mexico | . 1825 |

| | | | | | | | |
|---|---|---|---|---|---|---|---|
| foetida | . . | Pink | . . | 8. Ev. | T. | W. Ind. | 1816 |
| fastuosa | . . | Red | . . | 8. Ev. | T. | Caraccas | 1820 |
| Feuillei | . . | White | . . | 8. Ev. | 8. | Lima | 1824 |
| Houstoni, 3 | . . | Purple | . 7, 8. Ev. | 8. | Mexico | . | 1729 |
| hymenoides, 4 | . . | Pink | . . | 8. Ev. | T. | Cayenne | 1823 |
| latifolia | . . | Purple | . 5, 8. Ev. | T. | W. Ind. | 1768 |
| laurina, 5 | . . | White | . . | 8. Ev. | T. | S. Amer. | 1818 |
| marginata | . . | Pink | . . | 8. Ev. | T. | S. Amer. | 1820 |
| microphylla | . . | Pink | . . | 8. Ev. | 8. | Cumana | 1817 |
| pulcherrima | . . | . . | . . | 8. Ev. | T. | Mexico | 1822 |
| punctata | . . | Pink | . . | 8. Ev. | 8. | Caraccas | 1818 |
| purpurea | . . | Purple | . 4, 8. Ev. | 8. | W. Ind. | 1733 |
| quassiaefolia | . . | . . | . . | 8. Ev. | T. | Brazil | 1820 |
| setifera | . . | Pink | . . | 8. Ev. | T. | Guiana | 1824 |
| spuria | . . | White | . . | 8. Ev. | 8. | Cumana | 1820 |
| tergemina | . . | Pink | . . | 8. Ev. | 8. | W. Ind. | 1820 |
| unguis-cati | . . | Pink | . . | 8. Ev. | T. | W. Ind. | 1670 |
| velutina | . . | . . | . . | 8. Ev. | T. | Para | 1820 |
| vera | . . | White | . 7, 8. Ev. | T. | W. Ind. | 1739 |
| xylocarpa, 6 | . . | Pink | . . | 8. Ev. | T. | E. Ind. | 1816 |

INNOCUOUS, harmless.

INOCARPUS, *Forster*. From *is*, a fibre, and *karpos*, a fruit; alluding to the fibrous envelopes. *Linn.* 10, Or. 1, Nat. Or. *Hernandiaceæ*. This species, known as the Otaheite Chestnut, thrives well in a mixture of loam and peat; and cuttings of the ripened wood will root in sand, under a glass. "It is a lofty tree, with alternate leaves, and flowers in racemes, succeeded by nuts called *Rutta*, in Otaheite. The kernel of these is kidney-shaped, about an inch in diameter, and is eaten roasted by the inhabitants of the Society and Friendly Isles, the New Hebrides, New Guinea, the Molucca Isles, &c. It is sweetish, but less pleasant than the chestnut, harder, and less farinaceous. The bark is astringent, and is used in the dysentery."—*Loudon's Ency. of Plants.*

| | | | | | | |
|---|---|---|---|---|---|---|
| edulis | . . | White | . 7, 8. Ev. | T. | S. Sea Is. | 1793 |

INODORUS, without smell.

INOPS, poor, deficient, wanting.

INORNATUS, unadorned, of mean appearance.

INQUINANS, stained, dyed.

INSPISSATED, thickened; spoken of sap, or other liquor.

INSTITIALE, *Fries*. From *instita*, a fringe; alluding to the appearance of the plants. *Linn.* 24, Or. 9, Nat. Or. *Fungi*. Minute brown species, most conspicuous in autumn on plastered walls, old rotten wood, &c. *Synonymes:* 1. *Lycoperdon radiatum*. 2. *L. agariciforme*—*Agariciformis* 1, *radiata* 2.

INTEGUMENT, the outer covering of seeds.

INTENERATING, having the power of softening.

INTERMEDIATE, between two, the middle one of anything.

INTERNODES, the space between the joints of plants.

INTRAPETIOLAR, between the petioles on each side.

INTERSTICES, spaces between one thing and another.

INTRAMARGINAL, within the margin.

INTRUDED, thrust in, intruding.

INUNDATUM, submersed, growing under water.

INULA, *Linn.* A corruption of *Helenium*. *Linn.* 19, Or. 1, Nat. Or. *Compositæ*. These are species of no particular merit; they succeed in any common garden soil, and may be propagated either from seeds, or divisions of the roots. *Synonymes:* 1. *Pulicaria arabica*. 2. *I. montana*. 3. *I. oculus Christi, helenoides*. 4. *Pulicaria dysenterica*. 5. *P. vulgaris*. 6. *Erigeron glutinosus*. 7. *E. tuberosus*. 8. *I. thapsoides*. 9. *Pulicaria villosa*. 10. *Erigeron viscosus*.

| | | | | | | | |
|---|---|---|---|---|---|---|---|
| bifrons | . . | Yellow | . 7, | H. Her. | P. | S. Eur. | 1713 |
| britannica | . . | Yellow | . 8, | H. Her. | P. | Germany | 1759 |
| Bubonium | . . | Yellow | . 8, | H. Her. | P. | Austria | 1801 |
| calycina, 2 | . . | Yellow | . 7, | H. Her. | P. | Sicily | 1768 |
| campestris, 3 | . . | Yellow | . 8, | H. Her. | P. | Podolia | 1823 |
| conyzoides | . . | Yellow | . 7, | H. Her. | P. | Crete | 1810 |
| crithmifolia | . . | Yellow | . 8, | H. Her. | P. | England | |
| crithmoides | . . | Yellow | . 8, | F. Ev. | 8. | Greece | 1800 |
| ensifolia | . . | Yellow | . 7, | H. Her. | P. | Austria | 1793 |
| foetida | . . | Yellow | . 8, | H. | A. | Malta | 1688 |
| germanica | . . | Yellow | . 7, | H. Her. | P. | Germany | 1759 |
| glandulosa | . . | Yellow | . 7, | H. Her. | P. | Georgia | 1804 |
| gossypina | . . | Yellow | . 8, | H. Her. | P. | N. Amer. | 1823 |
| graminifolia | . . | Yellow | . 7, | H. Her. | P. | N. Amer. | |
| grandiflora | . . | Yellow | . 7, | H. Her. | P. | Caucasus | 1810 |
| hirta | . . | Yellow | . 7, | H. Her. | P. | Austria | 1759 |
| hybrida | . . | Yellow | . 7, | H. Her. | P. | Podolia | 1818 |
| mariana | . . | Yellow | . 7, | H. Her. | P. | N. Amer. | 1742 |
| mollis | . . | Yellow | . 7, | H. Her. | P. | | |
| montana | . . | Yellow | . 8, | H. Her. | P. | S. Eur. | 1759 |
| Oculus Christi | . . | Yellow | . 7, | H. Her. | P. | Austria | 1759 |

| | | | | | | | |
|---|---|---|---|---|---|---|---|
| odora | . . | Yellow | . 7, | H. Her. | P. | S. Eur. | 1821 |
| provincialis | . . | Yellow | . 8, | H. Her. | P. | France | 1776 |
| quadridentata | . . | Yellow | . 8, | H. Her. | P. | Spain | 1820 |
| salicina | . . | Yellow | . 7, | H. Her. | P. | N. Eur. | 1648 |
| saturejoides | . . | Yellow | . 7, | H. Her. | P. | Vera Cruz | 1733 |
| saxatilis, 6 | . . | Yellow | . 7, | H. Her. | P. | S. Eur. | 1816 |
| squarrosa | . . | Yellow | . 7, | H. Her. | P. | Italy | 1768 |
| suaveolens | . . | Yellow | . 7, | H. Her. | P. | S. Eur. | 1758 |
| tuberosa, 7 | . . | Yellow | . 8, | H. Tw. | P. | S. Eur. | 1640 |
| Vaillanti | . . | Yellow | . 9, | H. Her. | P. | France | 1739 |
| verbascifolia, 8 | . . | Yellow | . 7, | H. Her. | P. | Caucasus | 1819 |
| villosa, 9 | . . | Yellow | . 8, | H. | A. | N. Amer. | 1811 |
| viscosa, 10 | . . | Yellow | . 7, | F. Her. | P. | S. Eur. | 1596 |

*arabica* 1, *dysenterica* 4, *indica*, *paludosa*, *Pulicaria* 5, *undulata*.

INVERSE, inverted, upside down.

INVOLUCEL, the partial involucra of umbelliferous plants.

INVOLUCRATE, having an involucre.

INVOLUCRATED, covered with an involucre.

INVOLUCRE, or INVOLUCRUM, the bracteas which surround the flowers or umbels.

INVOLUTE, rolled inwards.

IONIDIUM, *Ventenat*. From *ion*, a violet, and *eidos*, similar; resemblance. *Linn.* 5, Or. 1, Nat. Or. *Violaceæ*. Ornamental species; for culture, &c., see Solea. *Synonymes:* 1. *Viola capensis*. 2. *Solea verticillata*. 3. *S. stricta*.

| | | | | | | | |
|---|---|---|---|---|---|---|---|
| capense, 1 | . . | White | . 6, | G. Ev. | 8. | C. G. H. | 1824 |
| polygalaefolium, 2 | Grn. yel. | . 6, | G. Ev. | 8. | S. Amer. | 1797 |
| Sprengelianum, 3 | White | . 6, | F. Her. | P. | Pennsylv. | 1818 |
| strictum | . . | White | . 8, | H. Her. | P. | W. Ind. | 1824 |
| verbenaceum | . . | Pa. blue | . 9, | 8. Her. | P. | Mexico | 1823 |

IONOPSIS, *Humboldt and Kunth*. Literally Violet-faced; from *ion*, a violet, and *opsis*, look. *Linn.* 20, Or. 1, Nat. Or. *Orchidaceæ*. The plants of this genus are small, and difficult to preserve in our collections. We find that they grow best on wood, in the same manner as *Burlingtonia*.

| | | | | | | | |
|---|---|---|---|---|---|---|---|
| tenera | . . | White | . 5, | 8. Epi. | | Havannah | 1836 |
| tersa | . . | Li. strip. | . 5, | 8. Epi. | | Demerara | |
| utricularioides | . . | Wht. pur. | . 10, | 8. Epi. | | Trinidad | 1822 |

IPOMŒA, *Linn.* From *ips*, bindweed, and *homoios*, similar; alluding to the twining habit of the plants. *Linn.* 5, Or. 1, Nat. Or. *Convolvulaceæ*. A most beautiful genus of plants, well adapted for the rafters, columns, and pillars of the stove, also for trellis-work. *I. Horsfalliæ* is excellently suited for training to a trellis, where its beautiful bright scarlet flowers have a lovely appearance. They thrive in loam and peat, mixed with a little dung; and the perennial kinds are multiplied from cuttings in sand without difficulty. The annual and biennial kinds should be raised on a hotbed in spring, and afterwards treated as other half-hardy and tender annuals and biennials. The roots of *I. Quamoclit* are sternutatory. *Synonymes:* 1. *I. salicifolia*. 2. *I. palmata, Convolvulus cairicus*. 3. *I. tuberculata*. 4. *C. fastigiatus*. 5. *I. angustifolia, I. denticulata*. 6. *I. rubro-cærulea*. 7. *C. Jalapa*. 8. *I. Michauxii*. 9. *C. panduratus*. 10. *I. maritima*. 11. *C. pilosus*. 12. *C. umbellatus*. 13. *C. stipulaceus*. 14. *I. stipulacea*. 15. *C. vitifolius*.

| | | | | | | | |
|---|---|---|---|---|---|---|---|
| acuminata | . . | Purple | . 7, | 8. Ev. | Tw. | W. Ind. | 1818 |
| Aitoni | . . | Pa. pur | . 6, | 8. Ev. | | CL | |
| albivenia | . . | Yellow | . 9, | 8. Ev. | Tw. | Algoa Bay | 1824 |
| Buchanani, 1 | . . | White | . 5, | 8. De. | Tw. | Bengal | 1816 |
| cairica, 2 | . . | Red | . 7, | 8. Ev. | Tw. | Egypt | 1680 |
| campanulata | . . | Pur. wht. | . 8, | H. Ev. | Tw. | E. Ind. | 1800 |
| candicans | . . | White | . 7, | 8. Ev. | Tw. | N. Amer. | 1776 |
| carolina | . . | Purple | . 7, | 8. De. | Tw. | Carolina | 1789 |
| chryseides | . . | Yellow | . 7, | 8. De. | Tw. | China | 1817 |
| corymbosa | . . | White | . 7, | 8. Ev. | Tw. | E. Ind. | 1823 |
| cymosa | . . | White | . 7, | 8. De. | Tw. | E. Ind. | 1820 |
| dasysperma, 3 | . . | Sulphur | . 8, | 8. De. | Tw. | E. Ind. | 1815 |
| dissecta | . . | White | . 7, | G. Ev. | Tw. | Tropics | 1812 |
| fastigiata, 4 | . . | Purple | . 6, | 8. Ev. | Tw. | W. Ind. | 1816 |
| filicaulis, 5 | . . | Yellow | . 7, | 8. | A. | E. Ind. | 1778 |
| filiforme | . . | Purple | . 8, | 8. Ev. | Tw. | Martinico | 1823 |
| grandiflora | . . | White | . 9, | 8. Ev. | Tw. | E. Ind. | 1802 |
| hepaticifolia | . . | Purple | . 8, | 8. Ev. | Tw. | Ceylon | 1759 |
| Hookeri, 6 | . . | Wht. red | . 8, | 8. Ev. | Tw. | Mexico | 1830 |
| Horsfalliæ | . . | Rose-col. | . 10, | 8. Ev. | Tw. | E. Ind. | 1833 |
| involucrata | . . | Red | . 7, | 8. De. | Tw. | Guinea | 1823 |
| Jalapa, 7 | . . | Red | . 8, | 8. Tu. | P. | America | 1733 |
| lacunosa | . . | White | . 6, | H. De. | Tw. | N. Amer. | 1640 |
| latifolia | . . | White | . 8, | 8. De. | Tw. | W. Ind. | |
| leucantha | . . | White | . 8, | 8. De. | Tw. | S. Amer. | 1823 |
| macrorhiza | . . | White | . 8, | G. Tu. | P. | Georgia | 1815 |
| rubra, 8 | . . | Red pur. | . 8, | 8. Ev. | Tw. | Mexico | 1815 |
| multiflora | . . | Pink | . 6, | 8. De. | Tw. | Jamaica | |

| | | | | | | |
|---|---|---|---|---|---|---|
| muricātă | Bl. pur. | 8, S. | | A. | E. Ind. | 1777 |
| mutābilis | Blue | 7, S. | Ev. | Tw. | S. Amer. | 1812 |
| noctilūcă | White | 8, S. | Ev. | Tw. | E. Ind. | 1820 |
| obscūră | White | 7, S. | De. | Tw. | E. Ind. | 1732 |
| ochrăcĕă | Yellow | 8, S. | De. | Tw. | Guinea | 1826 |
| pandurātă, 9 | Wht. pur. | 6, H. | De. | Tw. | N. Amer. | 1732 |
| parviflōră | Purplish | 7, S. | De. | Tw. | W. Ind. | 1822 |
| pĕndŭlă | Pink | 7, G. | Ev. | Tw. | N. S. W. | 1805 |
| pes-căpræ, 10 | Purple | 6, S. | Ev. | Cr. | India | 1776 |
| pes-tigrĭdis | Red | 8, S. | De. | Tw. | E. Ind. | 1732 |
| pilōsă, 11 | Pink | 8, S. | De. | Tw. | E. Ind. | 1815 |
| platĕnsis | Violet | 7, S. | Ev. | Tw. | Plata | 1817 |
| polyănthes, 12 | Yellow | 8, S. | Ev. | Tw. | W. Ind. | 1739 |
| pudibŭndă | Rose-col. | 8, S. | Ev. | Tw. | St. Vincent | 1822 |
| repăndă | Scarlet | 7, S. | Ev. | Tw. | S. Amer. | 1798 |
| rĕptans | Purple | 7, S. | Ev. | Cr. | E. Ind. | 1806 |
| Roxbūrghiĭ | White | 8, S. | | B. | E. Ind. | 1799 |
| sagittifōlĭă | Rose | 7, H. | De. | Tw. | Carolina | 1819 |
| Sellōwiĭ | | G. | De. | Cl. | | 1831 |
| sepiărĭă | Red | 7, S. | Ev. | Tw. | E. Ind. | 1817 |
| sessiliflōră | White | 8, S. | Ev. | Tw. | Nepal | 1816 |
| setōsă | Purple | 8, S. | De. | Tw. | Brazil | |
| sibĭrĭcă | Flesh | 7, H. | De. | Tw. | Siberia | 1779 |
| sinuată | White | 7, H. | Ev. | Tw. | Florida | 1813 |
| solanifōlĭă | Pink | 7, S. | De. | Tw. | America | 1759 |
| stipulăcĕă, 13 | Purple | 9, S. | Ev. | Cr. | E. Ind. | 1805 |
| tamnifōlĭă | Blue | 7, S. | De. | Tw. | Carolina | 1732 |
| trichocărpă | Pa. pur. | 7, H. | De. | Tw. | Carolina | 1732 |
| tridentātă | Yellow | 7, S. | | A. | E. Ind. | 1778 |
| triquĕtră | Purple | 7, S. | Ev. | Tw. | W. Ind. | |
| tuberculātă, 14 | | 7, S. | Ev. | Tw. | Bourbon | 1818 |
| tuberōsă | Pa. yel. | 8, S. | Tu. | P. | W. Ind. | 1731 |
|   uniflōră | | 8, S. | Tu. | P. | S. Amer. | 1731 |
| Turpēthŭm | White | 8, S. | Ev. | Tw. | E. Ind. | 1752 |
| tyrianthĭnă | Purple | 10, S. | Ev. | Tw. | Mexico | |
| umbellātă | Scarlet | 6, S. | Ev. | Tw. | S. Amer. | 1739 |
| violăcĕă | Purple | 8, S. | De. | Tw. | S. Amer. | 1792 |
| vitifōlĭă, 15 | Yellow | 7, S. | Ev. | Tw. | E. Ind. | 1820 |

Ipomœă, see *Batatas*.
Ipomœă, see *Leptocallis*.
Ipomœă, see *Pharbitis*.
Ipomœă, see *Quamoclit*.
Ipomœă, see *Rivea*.
Ipomœă, see *Shutereia*.

Ipomŏpsis, *Micheli*. From *ipo*, to strike forcibly, and *opsis*, sight; alluding to the dazzling colour of the flowers. *Linn.* 5, Or. 1, Nat. Or. *Polemoniaceæ*. A very beautiful genus of plants, but rather difficult to cultivate. The following is our mode of treatment:—About the end of July the seed should be sown very thinly in small pots, large sixties, well crocked, and filled with peat and loam, both sandy, and in equal parts, and placed in a cold frame, where the seed will soon vegetate, during which time the least possible water is given. When the plants begin to show signs of leaves, they are thinned out to three or four in each pot; in about a week after this, they should be removed into a rather light and airy part of the greenhouse, where they remain all winter. During winter, over-watering, and drips from the roof of the house, must be carefully avoided. In spring, they are shifted into forty-eight-sized pots, well drained, and the same kind of soil as before; in doing this, great care must be taken not to injure the roots. In this sized pot they will generally be found to flower. Out of the four plants left after thinning, it is rare that more than two remain in each pot, one of which may be destroyed if the other appears healthy and well established; if not, let both remain. In the course of their growth, water cannot be too cautiously given, especially just before the plants break into flower. Thus nourished, in an airy situation near the glass, they flower splendidly in July and August, and continue beautiful for a long time. *Synonyme*: 1. *Gilia pulchella*.

| | | | | | | |
|---|---|---|---|---|---|---|
| ĕlĕgāns | Scarlet | 7, H. | | B. | N. Amer. | 1820 |

Irĕsĭnĕ, *Willdenow*. From *eiros*, wool; referring to the woolly appearance of the branches. *Linn.* 22, Or. 5, Nat. Or. *Amarantaceæ*. The plants of this genus are very pretty, and may be cultivated in sandy loam and peat, mixed with a little decayed dung. They increase from seeds by merely sowing them on a gentle hotbed.

| | | | | | | |
|---|---|---|---|---|---|---|
| celosioīdēs | White | 7, F. | Her. | P. | S. Amer. | 1733 |
| diffūsă | White | 7, F. | Her. | P. | S. Amer. | 1818 |
| elātiŏr | White | 7, G. | | A. | Antilles | 1820 |
| elongātă | White | 7, F. | Her. | P. | S. Amer. | 1822 |
| flavēscēns | White | 7, F. | Her. | P. | S. Amer. | 1824 |

Īrĭs, *Linn.* From *iris*, the eye; alluding to the variety and beauty of the colours of the flower. *Linn.* 3, Or. 1, Nat. Or. *Iridaceæ*. The genus *Iris* has long been, as it still continues to be, a great favourite in the flower-garden. "The sword-leaved sorts," says Sweet, "do best in a light loamy soil, and increase freely by suckers from the roots, or by seeds. The tuberous-rooted ones are more difficult to cultivate, and thrive best in a mixture of loam, peat, and sand, as does also the tribe to which *I. persica* belongs, as *I. alata*, *caucasica*, *reticulata*, &c. The common bulbous species do well in common garden soil, the more sandy the better." *I. tuberosa* is purgative, and *I. versicolor* and *verna* are used in the United States as cathartics. *Synonymes*: 1. *I. gracilis*. 2. *Vieusseuxia iridioides*. 3. *I. spatulata*. 4. *I. tripetala*. 5. *I. nepalensis*. 6. *I. paradoxa*. 7. *I. stenogyna*. 8. *I. aphylla*. 9. *I. tripetula*. 10. *I. pumila*, *I. violacea*.

| | | | | | | |
|---|---|---|---|---|---|---|
| acūtă | Blue | 5, H. | Her. | P. | | |
| alātă | Blue | 6, H. | Bl. | P. | Algiers | 1801 |
| amœnă | Blue | 5, H. | Her. | P. | | 1821 |
| arenārĭă | Yellow | 6, H. | Her. | P. | Hungary | 1802 |
| aūrĕă | Yellow | 6, H. | Her. | P. | Germany | 1826 |
| biflōră | Purple | 6, H. | Her. | P. | S. Eur. | 1596 |
| biglūmis | Blue | 4, H. | Her. | P. | Siberia | 1811 |
| bohĕmĭcă | Blue | 5, H. | Her. | P. | Bohemia | 1825 |
| Boltoniānă, 1 | Blue | 5, H. | Her. | P. | N. Amer. | 1825 |
| brachycūspis | Purple | 5, H. | Her. | P. | Siberia | 1819 |
| caucăsĭcă | Yellow | 7, H. | Her. | P. | Caucasus | 1821 |
| chinĕnsis | Pa. blue | H. | Her. | P. | China | 1792 |
| clandestīnă | | 5, G. | Her. | P. | Brazil | 1829 |
| cœlestīnă | Blue | 6, F. | Her. | P. | N. Amer. | 1824 |
| crassifōlĭă | Pa. blue | 6, G. | Her. | P. | C. G. H. | 1830 |
| cristātă | Pa. blue | 6, H. | Her. | P. | N. Amer. | 1756 |
| cūprĕă | Orange | 6, H. | Her. | P. | N. Amer. | 1812 |
| curtopĕtălă, 2 | Yel. blue | 5, H. | Her. | P. | | 1823 |
| deflĕxă | Lilac | 6, G. | Her. | P. | Nepal | 1888 |
| desertōrŭm, 3 | Blue | 7, H. | Her. | P. | Russia | 1811 |
| dichŏtŏmă | Lgt. blue | 8, H. | Her. | P. | Dauria | 1784 |
| ēlĕgāns | Yellow | 7, H. | Her. | P. | | 1823 |
| flavēscēns | Yellow | 5, H. | Her. | P. | | 1818 |
| flavissĭmă | Yellow | 5, H. | Her. | P. | Siberia | 1814 |
| flexuōsă | White | 5, H. | Her. | P. | Germany | 1810 |
| florentīnă | White | 5, H. | Her. | P. | S. Eur. | 1596 |
| fœtidissĭmă | Livid | 6, H. | Her. | P. | Britain | |
|   variegātă | Livid | 6, H. | Her. | P. | Britain | |
| furcātă | Blue | 8, H. | Her. | P. | Tauria | 1822 |
| germănĭcă | Blue | 5, H. | Her. | P. | Germany | 1573 |
| gramĭnĕă | Striped | 6, H. | Her. | P. | Austria | 1597 |
| Guldenstädtiĭ | Yellow | 4, H. | Her. | P. | Siberia | 1757 |
| halŏphĭlă | Blue | 8, H. | Her. | P. | Siberia | 1780 |
| Hookĕri, 4 | Purple | 5, H. | Her. | P. | N. Amer. | 1826 |
| Hūmei, 5 | Blue | 4, H. | Her. | P. | Nepal | 1822 |
| hŭmĭlis | Blue | 4, H. | Her. | P. | Caucasus | 1812 |
| hungărĭcă | Violet | 5, H. | Her. | P. | Hungary | 1815 |
| ibĕrĭcă, 6 | Red | 5, H. | Her. | P. | Iberia | 1820 |
| lĭvĭdă | Livid | 4, H. | Her. | P. | Levant | |
| longiflōră | | 5, H. | Her. | P. | | 1824 |
| longifōlĭă | Greenish | 4, H. | Her. | P. | Naples | 1829 |
| longispăthă | Purple | 7, H. | Her. | P. | Siberia | 1823 |
| lūrĭdă | Brown | 4, H. | Her. | P. | S. Eur. | 1758 |
| lusitānĭcă | Blue | 4, H. | Bl. | P. | Portugal | 1796 |
| lutĕscēns | Yellow | 4, H. | Her. | P. | Germany | 1748 |
| Monnieri | Yellow | 5, H. | Her. | P. | Greece | 1820 |
| neglĕctă | Pa. blue | 5, H. | Her. | P. | | |
| nepalĕnsis | Blue | 4, H. | Her. | P. | Nepal | 1823 |
| nertchinskĭă | Blue | 5, H. | Her. | P. | Siberia | 1831 |
| nŏthă | Blue | 5, H. | Her. | P. | Italy | 1820 |
| nudicaūlis | Blue | 5, H. | Her. | P. | | 1820 |
| ochroleūcă, 7 | Lgt. yel. | 7, H. | Her. | P. | Levant | 1757 |
| odorātă | Blue | 6, H. | Her. | P. | | 1821 |
| orientālis | Lgt. blue | 5, H. | Her. | P. | China | 1790 |
| Pallāsii | Blue | 5, H. | Her. | P. | Tartary | 1820 |
|   chinĕnsis | Blue | 5, H. | Her. | P. | China | 1820 |
| pallĭdă | Pa. blue | 5, H. | Her. | P. | Turkey | 1596 |
| pērsĭcă | Blue yel. | 5, H. | Bl. | P. | Persia | 1629 |
| plicātă | Wht. blue | 6, H. | Her. | P. | | 1821 |
| prismătĭcă | Purple | 5, H. | Her. | P. | N. Amer. | 1812 |
| Pseūd-ăcŏrŭs | Yellow | 6, H. | Her. | P. | Britain | |
|   pallĭdă-flāvă | Pa. yel. | 6, H. | Her. | P. | N. Amer. | 1812 |
| pūmĭlă | Purple | 5, H. | Her. | P. | Austria | 1596 |
| reticulātă | Blue | 8, H. | Her. | P. | Iberia | 1821 |
| ruthēnĭcă | Blue | 5, H. | Her. | P. | Siberia | 1804 |
| sambucīnă | Lgt. blue | 6, H. | Her. | P. | S. Eur. | 1658 |
| scariōsă | Blue | 5, H. | Her. | P. | Russia | 1826 |
| sibĭrĭcă | Lgt. blue | 5, H. | Her. | P. | Siberia | 1596 |
|   flōrĕ-ălbō | White | 5, H. | Her. | P. | Siberia | 1596 |
| sōrdĭdă | White | 5, H. | Her. | P. | | 1819 |
| spathulātă | Pa. blue | 6, H. | Her. | P. | Germany | 1759 |
| spūrĭă | Pa. blue | 5, H. | Her. | P. | Siberia | 1759 |
| squalēns | Striped | 5, H. | Her. | P. | S. Eur. | 1768 |
| stenŏgynă | Yellow | 6, H. | Her. | P. | | 1819 |
| sub-biflōră | Violet | 7, H. | Her. | P. | Portugal | 1596 |
| susiānă | Striped | 4, H. | Her. | P. | Levant | 1596 |
| Swērtii, 8 | White | 5, H. | Her. | P. | | 1819 |
| tangĕrĭcă | Blue | 7, H. | Her. | P. | Tangiers | 1820 |
| taūrĭcă | Yellow | 6, H. | Her. | P. | Tauria | 1827 |
| tĕnăx | Purple | 7, H. | Her. | P. | California | 1826 |

| | | | | | |
|---|---|---|---|---|---|
| tenuifòliã | Lgt. blue | 5, H. Bl. | P. Dauria | 1796 |
| tridentàtã, 9 | Blue | 5, H. Her. | P. N. Amer. | 1820 |
| trifiòrã | Blue | 6, H. Her. | P. Italy | 1821 |
| tuberòsã | Grn. blue | 8, H. Bl. | P. Levant | 1597 |
| variegàtã | Striped | 5, H. Her. | P. Hungary | 1597 |
| venticòsã | Pa. blue | 6, H. Her. | P. Dauria | 1800 |
| vèrnã | Purple | 4, H. Her. | P. Virginia | 1748 |
| versicölör | Varieg. | 5, H. Her. | P. N. Amer. | 1732 |
| violàcëã, 10 | Violet | 5, H. Her. | P. S. Eur. | 1800 |
| viràscëns | Yellow | 5, H. Her. | P. | 1820 |
| virginìcã | Blue | 6, H. Her. | P. N. Amer. | 1758 |
| Xìphìũm | Blu. yel. | 6, H. Bl. | P. Spain | 1596 |
| xiphioìdës | Blu. yel. | 6, H. Bl. | P. Spain | 1571 |

IRISH-HEATH, see *Menzìësìã polifòlìã.*
IRON-TREE, see *Siderödëndrön.*
IRON-WOOD, see *Sideröxỹlön.*
IRON-WOOD, see *Argànìã Sideröxỹlön.*
IRONWORT, see *Sidéritìs.*

ISÀCHNE, *P. Browne.* From *isos*, equal, and *achne*, a glume. *Linn.* 3, Or. 2, Nat. Or. *Gramineæ.* A species of grass, of little interest, and common culture—*australis.*

ISÀNTHŨS, *Micheli.* From *isos*, equal, and *anthos*, a flower; in reference to the regularity of the corolla. *Linn.* 14, Or. 1, Nat. Or. *Labiatæ.* A somewhat interesting annual, cultivated in sandy peat, and propagated from seeds. *Synonyme:* 1. *Trichostema brachiatum.*

| | | | | | |
|---|---|---|---|---|---|
| cœrulèũs | Blue | 7, H. | A. N. Amer. | 1818 |

ISÀRIÃ, *Persoon.* From *isos*, equal; on account of the regularity of the filaments. *Linn.* 24, Or. 9, Nat. Or. *Fungi.* A white species, found during the spring months on some species of *Trichia—microscòpìcã.*

ISÀTIS, *Caspar Bauhin.* From *isazo*, to make equal; the plant was believed, by its simple application, to destroy all roughness of the skin. *Linn.* 15, Nat. Or. *Cruciferæ.* The species of this genus have not much beauty, and cannot be recommended except for general collections. They thrive with the commonest management, and increase from seeds. *I. alpina* may be increased by dividing the roots. *Synonymes:* 1. *I. megacarpa.* 2. *I. dasycarpa.*

| | | | | | |
|---|---|---|---|---|---|
| alëppìcã | Yellow | 6, H. | A. Levant | 1739 |
| alpìnã | Yellow | 6, H. Her. | P. Italy | 1800 |
| armènã | Yellow | 7, H. | A. Levant | 1825 |
| campèstris | Yellow | 7, H. | B. Persia | 1820 |
| cànëscëns | Yellow | 5, H. | B. S. Eur. | 1822 |
| ibèrìcã | Yellow | 6, H. | B. Iberia | 1823 |
| latisilìquã | Yellow | 5, H. | B. Persia | 1821 |
| littoràlis | Yellow | 5, H. | B. Tauria | 1822 |
| lusitànìcã | Yellow | 6, H. | A. Portugal | 1739 |
| mæòtìcã, 1 | Yellow | 5, H. | B. Azof | 1828 |
| oblongàtã, 2 | Yellow | 5, H. | B. Bdeal | 1829 |
| præcòx | Yellow | 7, H. | B. Hungary | 1820 |
| taùrìcã | Yellow | 7, H. | B. Tauria | 1820 |
| tinctòrìã | Yellow | 7, H. | B. England | |

*bannàtìcã, hebecàrpã, orientàlis.*

ISCHÆMŨM, *Beauvois.* From *ischo*, to stop, and *haima*, blood; because of its supposed medicinal qualities. *Linn.* 23, Or. 1, Nat. Or. *Gramineæ.* Uninteresting species, of the easiest culture—*aristàtũm, austràlë, rugòsũm.*

ISÈRTIÃ, *Schreber.* Named after P. E. Isert, a German surgeon, in the Danish service at Accra. *Linn.* 6, Or. 1, Nat. Or. *Cinchonaceæ.* This is described as a very showy species, succeeding in sandy loam and peat, and increased by cuttings in sand, under a glass, in heat. *Synonyme:* 1. *Guettarda coccinea.*

| | | | | | |
|---|---|---|---|---|---|
| coccìnëã | Scarlet | 7, S. Ev. | S. Guinea | 1820 |

ISIDÌŨM, *Acharius.* From *isos*, equal; because of the small difference that exists between the podetia. *Linn.* 24, Or. 8, Nat. Or. *Lichenes.* Small species, found most plentiful in autumn and winter on rocks and trunks of old trees. *I. Westringii* is used in dyeing—*coccòdës, corallìnũm, microstìctìcũm, phymatòdës, phragmēũm, Westrìngìĩ.*

ISMÈLIÃ, *Cassini.* Origin of name unknown. *Linn.* 19, Or. 2, Nat. Or. *Compositæ.* This is described as an elegant little shrub, from one to two feet high, succeeding best in a light sandy soil, and increased both by cuttings and seeds.

| | | | | | |
|---|---|---|---|---|---|
| madëtènsis | Straw. | 5, F. Ev. | S. Madeira | 1834 |

ISMÈNÈ, *Herbert.* Ismene the daughter of Œdipus and Jocasta. *Linn.* 6, Or. 1, Nat. Or. *Amaryllidaceæ.* These species are all beautiful, and worthy of extensive cultivation; for which, see *Amaryllis.*

*Synonymes:* 1. *Pancratium Amancaes.* 2. *P. calathinum.*

| | | | | | |
|---|---|---|---|---|---|
| Amancàës, 1 | Yellow | 6, S. Bl. | P. Peru | 1804 |
| sulphùrëã | Sulphur | 6, S. Bl. | P. Hybrid | 1829 |
| calàthìnũm | White | 6, S. Bl. | P. Brazil | 1800 |
| Knìghtìĩ | White | 8, S. Bl. | P. Florida | 1836 |
| Macleànã | White | 6, S. Bl. | P. Lima | 1837 |
| nùtãns, 2 | White | 6, S. Bl. | P. Brazil | 1800 |

ISNÀRDIÃ, *Linn.* In memory of Antoine Dante Isnard, member of the Academy of Sciences. *Linn.* 4, Or. 1, Nat. Or. *Onagraceæ.* Mere weeds, found in marshy situations—*alternìfòlìã, palùstris.*

ISOCÀRPHÃ, *R. Brown.* From *isos*, equal, and *karphe*, chaff; regularity of the chaff of the receptacle. *Linn.* 19, Or. 1, Nat. Or. *Compositæ.* An uninteresting plant, of common cultivation—*oppositìfòlìã.*

ISOCHÌLŨS, *R. Brown.* From *isos*, equal, and *cheilos*, a lip. *Linn.* 20, Or. 1, Nat. Or. *Orchidaceæ.* The flowers produced by these plants are very insignificant. For culture and propagation, see *Stanhopea.*

| | | | | | |
|---|---|---|---|---|---|
| graminifòlìũm | Grn. yel. | 5, S. Epi. | Jamaica | 1823 |
| lineàrë | Pink | 4, S. Epi. | Martinique | 1791 |
| livìdũm | Livid | 8, S. Epi. | Mexico | |
| prolìfërũm | White | 8, S. Epi. | Jamaica | 1793 |

ISOÈTÈS, *Linn.* From *isos*, equal, and *etos*, the year; plant the same throughout the year. *Linn.* 24, Or. 4, Nat. Or. *Lycopodiaceæ.* A curious little aquatic, found in some lakes in this country.

| | | | | | |
|---|---|---|---|---|---|
| lacùstris | Brown | 7, H. Aq. | P. Britain | |

ISÒLÈPIS, *R. Brown.* From *isos*, equal, and *lepis*, a scale; alluding to the regularity of the scales. *Linn.* 3, Or. 1, Nat. Or. *Cyperaceæ.* Curious species, growing freely in any common soil, and increased by seeds, suckers, and divisions. *Synonymes:* 1. *Scirpus fluitans.* 2. *S. gracilis.* 3. *S. densus.*

| | | | | | |
|---|---|---|---|---|---|
| australis | Apetal | 7, Gras. | S. Eur. | |
| complanàtã | Apetal | 7, Gras. | E. Ind. | 1823 |
| fliùtãns, 1 | Apetal | 7, Gras. | Britain | |
| Holoschœnös | Apetal | 7, Gras. | England | |
| nodòsã, 2 | Apetal | 7, Gras. | N. Holl. | 1820 |
| romànã | Apetal | 7, Gras. | Austria | |
| setàcëã | Apetal | 7, Gras. | Britain | |
| tenuìssìmã, 3 | Apetal | 7, Gras. | Nepal | 1821 |

ISOPLÈXIS, *Lindley.* Derived from *isos*, equal, and *pleco*, to plait; on account of the upper segment of the corolla being equal in length to the lip. *Linn.* 14, Or. 2, Nat. Or. *Scrophulariaceæ.* This is a genus of remarkably showy plants when in blossom. They grow well in a light rich soil, and may be increased either by cuttings under a glass, or by seed. *Synonymes:* 1. *Digitalis canariensis.* 2. *D. sceptrum.*

| | | | | | |
|---|---|---|---|---|---|
| canariènsis, 1 | Yellow | 6, G. Ev. | S. Canaries | 1698 |
| sceptrũm, 2 | Yel. brn. | 7, G. Ev. | S. Madeira | 1777 |

ISOPÒGÒN, *R. Brown.* Derived from *isos*, equal, and *pogon*, a beard. *Linn.* 4, Or. 1, Nat. Or. *Proteaceæ.* A fine genus of evergreen shrubs, invariably from New Holland; for culture, &c., see *Protea.* *Synonyme:* 1. *Protea divaricata.*

| | | | | | |
|---|---|---|---|---|---|
| anemonifòlìũs | Yellow | 7, G. Ev. | S. N. Holl. | 1791 |
| anethifòlìũs | Pale | 4, G. Ev. | S. N. Holl. | 1796 |
| attenuàtũs | Pale | 4, G. Ev. | S. N. Holl. | 1822 |
| axillàris | Pale | 4, G. Ev. | S. N. Holl. | 1824 |
| Baxtèrì | Rose | 4, G. Ev. | S. N. Holl. | 1831 |
| ceratophỹllũs | Pale | 4, G. Ev. | S. N. Holl. | 1824 |
| divaricàtũs, 1 | Pale | 5, G. Ev. | S. N. Holl. | 1824 |
| formòsũs | Rose | 4, G. Ev. | R. N. Holl. | 1805 |
| longifòlìũs | Yellow | 4, G. Ev. | S. N. Holl. | 1823 |
| Loudòni | Purple | 6, G. Ev. | S. K. G.'s Snd. | 1830 |
| pulycëphàlũs | Pale | 5, G. Ev. | S. N. Holl. | 1824 |
| propinquũs | Pale | 5, G. Ev. | S. N. Holl. | 1824 |
| spatulàris | Purple | G. Ev. | S. | |
| lineàris | Purple | 9, G. Ev. | S. K. G.'s Sed. | 1830 |
| teretifòlìũs | Pale | 4, G. Ev. | S. N. Holl. | 1823 |
| trilòbũs | Pale | 5, G. Ev. | S. N. Holl. | 1803 |

ISOPỸRŨM, *Linn.* From *isos*, equal, and *pyros*, wheat; the Greeks gave this name to a plant resembling *Nigella*, the seeds of which have the same taste. *Linn.* 13, Or. 6, Nat. Or. *Ranunculaceæ.* Pretty plants, succeeding with the simplest cultivation in loamy soil, and increased by seeds. *I. thalictroides* may be also increased by divisions.

| | | | | | |
|---|---|---|---|---|---|
| fumarioìdës | Wht. grn. | 6, H. | A. Siberia | 1741 |
| thalictroìdës | Wht. grn. | 4, H. Her. | P. Italy | 1759 |

ITALIAN BEECH, see *Quèrcus Escûlûs.*

ITÈA, *Linn. Itea* is the Greek name of the willow, and applied to this genus on account of the quick growth of the species. *Linn.* 5, Or. 1, Nat. Or. *Escalloniaceæ.* An interesting North American shrub, cultivated in open fibrous sandy peat, and multiplied without great difficulty from layers.

| | | | | | | |
|---|---|---|---|---|---|---|
| virgínica | . . . | White . | . 7, H. De. S. N. Amer. | . 1774 |

IVA. Supposed to be from *Yua,* a name used by the older botanists; applied to this genus by Linnæus, because the smell of the plants resembles that of the ancient *Iva. Linn.* 19, Or. 5, Nat. Or. *Compositæ.* These species are not very interesting; they grow in any common soil, and increase from seeds. *I. frutescens* may also be increased by cuttings.

| | | | | | | |
|---|---|---|---|---|---|---|
| frutéscens | . . . | White . | . 8, H. Ev. S. N. Amer. | . 1711 |

ánnuâ, cíliâtâ.

IVY, see *Hèdèrâ.*

IXIA, *Linn. Ixia,* bird-lime; because of the viscid nature of some of the species. *Linn.* 3, Or. 1, Nat. Or. *Iridaceæ.* A genus of very handsome plants when in flower. Sweet recommends them to be grown in a mixture of sandy loam and decayed leaves, or peat soil. When they have done flowering, they require no water till they begin to grow afresh. In October, they should be fresh potted, and set in a cool frame, as they only require to be protected from frost till their pots are well filled with roots; then they may be set on the shelves of the greenhouse, and watered regularly, and they will flower well. The species of this genus, and some other bulbous-rooted genera, succeed best in a pit, covered with lights in very cold or wet weather. Most of the species will grow well in a south border, in the open air, planted from five to six inches deep, in a light sandy soil, near a wall, and to be covered with dry litter in severe weather; they will then flower much stronger than if grown in pots, and they may be increased by offsets from the bulbs, or by seeds.

| | | | | | |
|---|---|---|---|---|---|
| amœnâ | . . . | Red | . 4, G. Bl. P. C. G. H. | . 1822 |
| aristâtâ | . . . | Pink | . 4, G. Bl. P. C. G. H. | . 1800 |
| atâlica | . . . | Pink | . 4, G. Bl. P. C. G. H. | . 1774 |
| capillâris | . . . | Violet | . 4, G. Bl. P. C. G. H. | . 1774 |
| capitâtâ | . . . | Wht. blue | 5, G. Bl. P. C. G. H. | . 1780 |
| columellâris | . . . | Varieg. | . 3, G. Bl. P. C. G. H. | . 1790 |
| cônica | . . . | Orange | . 4. G. Bl. P. C. G. H. | . 1757 |
| crateroídæ | . . . | Drk. yel. | . 5, G. Bl. P. C. G. H. | . 1778 |
| crispâ | . . . | Blue | . 4, G. Bl. P. C. G. H. | . 1787 |

| | | | | | |
|---|---|---|---|---|---|
| dùbia | . . . | Red | . 4, G. Bl. P. C. G. H. | . |
| erécta | . . . | White | . 6, G. Bl. P. C. G. H. | . 1757 |
| incarnâtâ | . | Flesh | . 5, G. Bl. P. C. G. H. | . 1757 |
| lùtea | . | Yellow | . 5, G. Bl. P. C. G. H. | . 1757 |
| flexuósâ | . . . | Pink | . 4, G. Bl. P. C. G. H. | . 1757 |
| furcâtâ | . . . | Pink | . 4, G. Bl. P. C. G. H. | . 1800 |
| hybrída | . . . | White . | . 6, G. Bl. P. C. G. H. | . 1757 |
| incarnâtâ | . . . | Flesh | . 5, G. Bl. P. C. G. H. | . |
| leucánthâ | . . . | White . | . 4, G. Bl. P. C. G. H. | . 1779 |
| lineâris | . . . | White . | . 5, G. Bl. P. C. G. H. | . 1796 |
| maculâtâ | . . . | Wht. brn. | . 4, G. Bl. P. C. G. H. | . 1780 |
| ochroleúcâ | . . . | Pur. yel. | . 5, G. Bl. P. C. G. H. | . 1780 |
| monadélphâ | . | Blue | . 5, G. Bl. P. C. G. H. | . 1792 |
| cûrtâ | . . . | Orange | . 4, G. Bl. P. C. G. H. | . 1792 |
| ovâtâ | . . . | Red | . 4, G. Bl. P. C. G. H. | . 1780 |
| pátens | . . . | Purple | . 4, G. Bl. P. C. G. H. | . 1779 |
| retùsâ | . . . | Lgt. yel. | . 4, G. Bl. P. C. G. H. | . 1793 |
| scillâris | . . . | Varieg. | . 1, G. Bl. P. C. G. H. | . 1787 |
| viridiflórâ | . . . | Green | . 5, G. Bl. P. C. G. H. | . 1780 |

IXODÎA, *R. Brown.* From *ixodes,* viscid; in allusion to the nature of the plants. *Linn.* 19, Or. 1, Nat. Or. *Compositæ.* This is a pretty shrub, and may be successfully grown in a mixture of peat and sand, and propagated from cuttings of the young wood in sand, under a glass.

| | | | | | |
|---|---|---|---|---|---|
| achilleoídes | . . . | White . | . 6, G. Ev. S. N. Holl. | . 1803 |

IXÔRÂ, *Linn.* After Iswara, a Malabar deity, to which the flowers of some are offered. *Linn.* 4, Or. 1, Nat. Or. *Cinchonaceæ.* A beautiful genus of East Indian shrubs, easily cultivated in our stoves. They require a sandy open soil, composed of loam and peat, in which they grow well provided they are kept clear of insects, which is easily effected by well washing the whole plant with a good syringe while growing. They propagate from cuttings in sand, or sandy soil, under a glass, in heat. *Synonymes*: 1. *I. Pavetta.* 2. *I. alba.* 3. *I. parviflora.* 4. *I. longifolia.* 5. *I. coccínea.* *I. flammea.*

| | | | | | |
|---|---|---|---|---|---|
| arbórea, 1 | . . . | Scarlet | . 8, S. Ev. S. E. Ind. | . 1800 |
| Bandhùcâ | . . . | Scarlet | . 7, S. Ev. S. E. Ind. | . 1815 |
| barbâtâ | . . . | White . | . 8, S. Ev. S. E. Ind. | . 1823 |
| blánda, 2 | . . . | White . | . 8, S. Ev. S. E. Ind. | . 1768 |
| brachiâtâ | . . . | White . | . 8, S. Ev. S. E. Ind. | . 1823 |
| crocâtâ | . . . | Orange | . 8, S. Ev. S. China | . 1822 |
| cuneifólîa | . . . | White . | . 6, S. Ev. S. E. Ind. | . 1822 |
| deciplens, 3 | . . . | White . | . 8, S. Ev. S. E. Ind. | . 1806 |
| flâvâ | . . . | Scarlet | . 7, S. Ev. S. E. Ind. | . 1825 |
| fúlgens, 4 | . . . | Orange | . 8, S. Ev. S. E. Ind. | . 1823 |
| grandiflórâ | . . . | Red | . 8, S. Ev. S. E. Ind. | . 1814 |
| incarnâtâ | . . . | Purple | . 6, S. Ev. S. Moluccas | . 1822 |
| róseâ | . . . | Rose | . 7, S. Ev. S. Bengal | . 1819 |
| strícta, 5 | . . . | Scarlet | . 7, S. Ev. S. Moluccas | . 1690 |

# J.

JABORÓSÂ, *Jussieu.* Derived from the Arabic, *Jaborose*; a name applied to the Mandrake, from its affinity to it. *Linn.* 5, Or. 1, Nat. Or. *Solanaceæ.* Pretty little plants, thriving well in any light rich soil, and may be easily increased by cuttings or divisions.

| | | | | | |
|---|---|---|---|---|---|
| integrifólîa | . . . | White . | . 3, H. Her. P. B. Ayres | . |
| runcinâtâ | . | Orn. yel. | . G. Her. P. Plata | . 1831 |

JACARÂNDÂ, *Jussieu.* The name of *J. brasiliana* in Brazil. *Linn.* 14, Or. 2, Nat. Or. *Bignoniaceæ.* These are fine lofty trees, with the elegant habit of the fine-leaved *Acacias.* The soil best suited for them is loam, peat, and sand; and cuttings, with the leaves whole, of the half-ripened wood, will root in sand, under a glass. The best way to get them to flower, is to keep the plants dry in winter. *Synonymes*: 1. *Bignonia cærulea.* 2. *B. procera.* 3. *J. Rhombifolia.* 4. *J. ovalifolia.*

| | | | | | |
|---|---|---|---|---|---|
| bahamênsis, 1 | . | Blue | . 7, S. Ev. T. Bahamas | . 1824 |
| brasiliâna | . . . | Yellow | . S. Ev. T. Brasil | . 1820 |
| Copâîa, 2 | . . . | Blue | . S. Ev. T. Guiana | . 1793 |
| filicifólîa, 3 | . . . | Blue | . S. Ev. T. W. Ind. | . 1800 |
| mimosifólîa, 4 | . . . | Blue | . 4, S. Ev. T. Brasil | . 1818 |
| pubéscens | . . . | Blue | . S. Ev. T. | . 1825 |
| tomentósâ | . . . | Purple | . S. Ev. T. Brasil | . 1824 |

JACA TREE, see *Artocárpûs integrifólîâ.*

JACK-IN-A-BOX, see *Hernándiâ.*

JACKSÔNIA, *R. Brown.* In honour of George Jackson, an acute Scotch botanist, once librarian to the distinguished A. B. Lambert, Esq., F.R.S., V.P. L.S., &c. *Linn.* 10, Or. 1, Nat. Or. *Leguminosæ.* A genus of pretty plants, growing readily in light loam and peat, and easily increased by cuttings in sand, under a glass. *Synonyme*: 1. *Daviesia reticulata.*

| | | | | | |
|---|---|---|---|---|---|
| furcellâtâ | . . . | Yellow | . 6, G. Ev. S. N. Holl. | . 1824 |
| reticulâtâ, 1 | . | Yellow | . 6, G. Ev. S. N. Holl. | . 1820 |
| scopâria | . . . | Yellow | . 7, G. Ev. S. N. S. W. | . 1803 |
| spinósâ | . . . | Yellow | . 7, G. Ev. S. N. Holl. | . 1803 |

JACOBÆÂ LILY, see *Amarýllis formosíssimâ.*

JACQUÍNIA, *Linn.* In honour of the celebrated botanist, N. J. Von Jacquin, professor at Vienna. *Linn.* 5, Or. 1, Nat. Or. *Myrsinaceæ.* A genus of very desirable plants, on account of the beauty of their flowers. They are of easy culture in a mixture of sand and peat. It is thought that watering these plants occasionally with salted water, has a tendency to make them grow and flower more freely. Cuttings will root in sand, under a glass, in heat; but they are by no means easy of propagation.

| | | | | | |
|---|---|---|---|---|---|
| arbórea | . . . | White . | . 7, S. Ev. T. W. Ind. | . 1829 |
| armillâris | . . . | White . | . 6, S. Ev. T. W. Ind. | . 1768 |
| aurantíaca | . . . | Orange | . 6, S. Ev. S. Sandw. Is. | . 1796 |
| lineâris | . . . | Red | . 6, S. Ev. S. W. Ind. | . 1823 |
| macrocárpâ | . . . | Orange | . 6, S. Ev. S. Mexico . | . 1825 |
| ruscifólîa | . . . | White . | . S. Ev. S. S. Amer. | . 1759 |

JAGGED, cut in a coarse manner.

JALAP, see *Mirábilis Jalápâ.*

JALAP, see *Ipomæa Jalāpā*.
JAMAICA DOGWOOD, see *Psidīā Erythrīnā*.
JAMAICA EBONY, see *Brȳā Ebēnūs*.
JAMAICA MILKWOOD, see *Brōsīmūm spūrīūm*.
JAMAICA REDWOOD, see *Gordōnīā Hæmatōxȳlōn*.
JAMAICA ROSE, see *Merīānā*.
JAMBOLANA TREE, see *Calyptrānthēs Jambolānā*.
JAMBŌSĀ, *Rumphius*. Altered from *Schambu*, the Malay name of one of the species. *Linn.* 12, Or. 1, Nat. Or. *Myrtaceæ*. The plants of this genus are possessed of some beauty, growing readily in loam and peat; but they do not produce their flowers till the plants attain a good size. Cuttings of the ripened wood root freely in sand, under a glass, in heat. Synonymes: 1. *Eugenia amplexicaulis*. 2. *E. aquea*. 3. *E. myrtifolia*, *E. australis*. 4. *E. macrophylla*. 5. *E. malaccensis*. 6. *E. Jambos*.

| | | | | | |
|---|---|---|---|---|---|
| amplexicaulis, 1 | . White | . 6, S. Ev. T. E. Ind. | . 1823 |
| aquea, 2 | . White | . 8. Ev. T. E. Ind. | . 1820 |
| australis, 3 | . White | . 6, G. Ev. T. N. Holl. | . 1800 |
| macrophylla, 4 | . White | . 8. Ev. T. E. Ind. | . 1820 |
| malaccensis | . Scarlet | . 7, S. Ev. T. E. Ind. | . 1768 |
| purpūrēā, 5 | . Purple | . 8, S. Ev. T. E. Ind. | . 1768 |
| vulgāris, 6 | . Grn. yel. | . 4, S. Ev. T. E. Ind. | . 1768 |

JANĪPHĀ, *Kunth*. Derived from *Janipaba*, the Brazilian name of the plant. *Linn.* 21, Or. 1, Nat. Or. *Euphorbiaceæ*. A genus of interesting plants; for culture and propagation, see *Jatropha*. Synonymes: 1. *Jatropha Lœflingii*. 2. *J. Manihot*.

| | | | | |
|---|---|---|---|---|
| maculifolia | . Brown | . 8. Ev. S. N. Spain | . 1826 |
| angustifolia | . Brown | . 8. Ev. S. Brazil | . 1829 |
| fœtida | . Brown | . 8. Ev. S. Mexico | . 1824 |
| Lœflingii, 1 | . Brown | . 7, S. Ev. S. Carthag. | . 1820 |
| Manihot, 2 | . Brown | . 7, S. Ev. S. S. Amer. | . 1739 |

JASIŌNĒ, *Linn.* A name applied by Theophrastus to a wild pot-herb now unknown. *Linn.* 5, Or. 1, Nat. Or. *Lobeliaceæ*. The species of this genus are very elegant when in blossom, and well adapted for ornamenting rock-work. They all prefer to grow in a peat soil, and require the protection of a frame in severe weather, and may be increased by divisions of the roots, cuttings, or seeds.

| | | | | |
|---|---|---|---|---|
| hūmīlis | . Blue | . 7, H. Her. P. S. France | . 1824 |
| montāna | . Blue | . 6, H. | A. Britain | . |
| perēnnis | . Blue | . 7, H. Her. P. France | . 1787 |

JASMINE, see *Jasmīnum*.
JASMĪNUM. Linnæus derives the name from *ia*, a violet, and *osme*, smell; some assert that it is from *yasmyn*, the Arabic name of the plant. *Linn.* 2, Or. 1, Nat. Or. *Jasminaceæ*. The species of this very elegant genus are familiar to every one. The stove and greenhouse kinds thrive well in a mixture of sand, loam, and peat; and cuttings of the ripened wood root freely in soil or sand, under a glass, in heat. The hardy kinds thrive well in any common soil, and are easily increased by cuttings planted under a glass. They are remarkably well adapted for training over an arbour, or against a wall, or trellis-work. The genuine oil of Jasmine of the shops is the produce of *J. grandiflorum* and *officinale*; but a similar perfume is obtained from *J. Sambac*. Synonymes: 1. *J. Wallichianum*. 2. *J. flexile*.

| | | | | |
|---|---|---|---|---|
| acuminātum | . White | . 6, S. Ev. Cl. N. Holl. | . 1820 |
| angustifolīum | . White | . 8. Ev. Tw. E. Ind. | . 1816 |
| arborēscēns | . White | . 8. Ev. S. E. Ind. | . 1824 |
| auriculātum | . White | . 7, S. Ev. Tw. E. Ind. | . 1790 |
| azōrīcūm | . White | . 7, G. Ev. Tw. Madeira | . 1724 |
| bracteātūm | . White | . 4, S. Ev. Cl. E. Ind. | . 1818 |
| campanulātūm | . White | . 8. Ev. S. | . 1812 |
| capēnsē | . White | . 5, G. Ev. S. C. G. H. | . 1816 |
| dispermūm | . White | . G. Ev. Cl. Nepal | . 1825 |
| elongātūm | . White | . 8. Ev. Cl. E. Ind. | . 1820 |
| flexile | . White | . 4, S. Ev. Cl. E. Ind. | . 1825 |
| frūtīcāns | . Yellow | . 7, H. De. S. S. Eur. | . 1570 |
| glaūcūm | . White | . 8, G. Ev. Cl. C. G. H. | . 1774 |
| grācīle | . White | . G. Ev. Cl. Norfolk Is. | 1791 |
| grandiflōrūm | . White | . 7, G. Ev. Cl. India | . 1629 |
| heterophyllūm | . White | . 6, H. Ev. S. Nepal | . 1820 |
| hirsūtūm | . White | . 8. Ev. S. E. Ind. | . 1759 |
| hūmīlē | . Yellow | . 7, H. De. S. S. Eur. | . 1656 |
| lanceolārīūm | . White | . G. Ev. Cl. Silhet | . 1826 |
| latifolīūm | . White | . 6, S. Ev. Tw. E. Ind. | . 1819 |
| laurifolīūm | . White | . 6, S. Ev. Cl. E. Ind. | . 1812 |
| odoratissīmūm | . White | . 6, G. Ev. Cl. Madeira | . 1656 |
| officinale | . White | . 7, H. Ev. Cl. E. Ind. | . 1548 |
| fol. argentēis | . White | . 7, H. De. Cl. E. Ind. | . |
| fol. aūrēis | . White | . 7, H. De. Cl. E. Ind. | . |

| | | | | |
|---|---|---|---|---|
| flōrībūs plēnīs | . White | . 7, H. De. Cl. E. Ind. | . |
| paniculātūm | . White | . 1, S. Ev. Cl. China | . 1818 |
| pubīgērūm, 1 | . Yellow | . 6, H. Ev. Cl. Nepal | . 1827 |
| revolūtūm | . Yellow | . 6, S. Ev. Cl. E. Ind. | . 1812 |
| Sāmbāc | . White | all S. Ev. Tw. E. Ind. | . 1665 |
| flore-plēnō | . White | all S. Ev. Tw. E. Ind. | . 1790 |
| trifolīātūm | . White | all S. Ev. Tw. E. Ind. | . 1730 |
| scāndēns | . White | . 8, S. Ev. Tw. E. Ind. | . 1820 |
| simplicifolīūm | . White | . 6, S. Ev. Cl. S. Seas | . 1800 |
| tortuōsūm, 2 | . White | . 6, G. Ev. Cl. C. G. H. | . 1818 |
| trinērvē | . White | . 1, S. Ev. Cl. E. Ind. | . 1804 |
| undulātūm | . White | . 1, S. Ev. Cl. China | . 1819 |

JATRŌPHĀ, *Linn.* From *iatros*, physician, and *trophe*, food; in allusion to the medicinal properties of the plants. *Linn.* 21, Or. 10, Nat. Or. *Euphorbiaceæ*. The species of this genus are only valuable in a medicinal point of view. They thrive well in sandy loam and peat, in small pots, with little water. Most of the species ripen seed freely if care be taken to fertilise the stigmas with the pollen. Cuttings root very readily stuck in the tan, in a strong heat. The seeds of *J. Curcas* are purgative and emetic; an oil is obtained from them, which is a valuable external application in itch.

| | | | | |
|---|---|---|---|---|
| australis | . | . 8. Ev. S. N. Holl. | . |
| coccīnēā | . Scarlet | . 8. Ev. S. Cuba | . 1824 |
| Cūrcās | . Green | . 8. Ev. S. S. Amer. | . 1731 |
| frāgrāns | . | . S. Ev. S. Cuba | . 1822 |
| glandulōsā | . | . 8. Ev. S. Arabia | . 1824 |
| gossypifolīā | . Green | . 6, S. Ev. S. W. Ind. | . 1690 |
| herbācēā | . Green | . 7, S. | A. Vera Cruz | . 1759 |
| integērrīmā | . Scarlet | . 6, S. Ev. S. Cuba | . 1809 |
| multīfīdā | . Green | . 7, S. Ev. S. S. Amer. | . 1696 |
| pandurœfolīā | . Scarlet | . 7, S. Ev. S. Cuba | . 1800 |
| peltātā | . | . 8. Ev. S. S. Amer. | . 1825 |
| ūrēns | . Green | . 6, S. Ev. S. Brazil | . 1690 |

napæifolīā.
JEFFERSŌNĪĀ. Dedicated by Barton, to Mr. Jefferson, the celebrated president of the United States. *Linn.* 8, Or. 1, Nat. Or. *Ranunculaceæ*. This is a pretty hardy plant, very curious, from the peculiar mode of dehiscence of its capsule. It grows well in any common garden soil, and may be increased by dividing the roots, or by seeds. Synonyme: 1. *Podophyllum diphyllum*.

| | | | | |
|---|---|---|---|---|
| diphylla, 1 | . White | . 5, H. Her. P. N. Amer. | . 1792 |

JERSEY THISTLE, see *Centaūrēā Isnārdī*.
JERUSALEM ARTICHOKE, see *Heliānthūs tuberōsūs*.
JERUSALEM SAGE, see *Phlōmīs fruticōsā*.
JEW'S-EAR, see *Exidīā auriculā*.
JOB'S TEARS, see *Cōīx*.
JŌHNĪĀ. Named by Roxburgh, in honour of the Rev. Dr. John, a missionary, once resident in Tranquebar. *Linn.* 3, Or. 1, Nat. Or. *Celastraceæ*. Very handsome shrubs, producing edible fruit. They do well in loam and peat; and cuttings of the ripened wood will root in sand, under a glass, in a moist heat.

| | | | | |
|---|---|---|---|---|
| coromandelīnā | . Yel. grn. | . 8. Ev. Cl. E. Ind. | . 1820 |
| salacioīdēs | . Orange | . 8. Ev. S. E. Ind. | . 1822 |

JOINTS, the places at which the pieces of the stem are articulated with each other.
JOLLIFFĪĀ. Named by Bojer, in compliment to his friend M. Jolliffe. *Linn.* 22, Or. 18, Nat. Or. *Cucurbitaceæ*. This is a splendid plant, producing its curious and beautiful flowers in great profusion; but it requires a large space to grow in, and to be frequently pruned in, before it flowers. It grows well in sandy loam and a little peat. It is much better to raise it from cuttings of the flowering shoots, as they will flower much earlier; they will root without difficulty in soil or sand, under a glass, in heat. Synonyme: 1. *Telfairia pedata*, *Feuillea pedata*.

| | | | | |
|---|---|---|---|---|
| africāna, 1 | . Purple | . 7, S. Ev. Tw. Zanzibar | . 1825 |

JONESĪĀ, *Roxburgh*. In honour of the distinguished scholar and botanist, Sir William Jones. *Linn.* 7, Or. 1, Nat. Or. *Leguminosæ*. The species of this genus are highly fragrant, and well worthy of a place in every collection. They thrive well in a mixture of sandy loam and peat; and large cuttings root freely under a glass, in heat. Synonyme: 1. *J. pinnata*.

| | | | | |
|---|---|---|---|---|
| Asōcā, 1 | . Orange | . 8. Ev. T. E. Ind. | . 1796 |
| scāndēns | . Orange | . 8. Ev. Cl. E. Ind. | . 1820 |

JOSSINĪĀ, *Commerson*. The derivation not known

but most probably a man's name. *Linn.* 12, Or. 1, Nat. Or. *Myrtaceæ.* This plant is well worth cultivating for the sake of its beautiful foliage, independently of its handsome large flowers; for culture and propagation, see *Psidium.*

| | | | | |
|---|---|---|---|---|
| orbiculata | . . . White . . | 8. Ev. 8. Mauritius . 1823 |

JOUTAY, see *Oséëá.*
JOVE'S BEARD, see *Hydnum barbâ Jovis.*
JOVE'S FRUIT, see *Laûrus Diospyrōs.*
JUBĀTŪS, crested, maned.
JUDAS TREE, see *Cèrcis.*
JUGĀTŪS, coupled together.
JŪGLĀNS, *Linn.* From *Jovis glans*; literally the nut of Jove. *Linn.* 21, Or. 9, Nat. Or. *Juglandaceæ.* The well-known *Walnut-tree* is among the species of this ornamental genus. They are all tall, stately growing trees, well adapted for parks and lawns. They grow freely in any rich loamy soil, and are raised from seeds. *J. cinerea* is esteemed anthelmintic and cathartic. Synonyme: 1. *J. heterophylla, J. filicifolia.*

| | | | | |
|---|---|---|---|---|
| cinerea | . . . Apetal . | 4, H. De. T. N. Amer. . 1656 |
| fraxinifolia | . . Apetal . | 4, H. De. T. N. Amer. |
| nigra | . . . Apetal . | 4, H. De. T. N. Amer. . 1629 |
| pterocarpa | . . Apetal . | 4, H. De. T. N. Amer. |
| rëgia | . . . Apetal . | 4, H. De. T. Persia . . 1562 |
| laciniata, 1 | . Apetal . | 4, H. De. T. Persia . |
| maxima | . . . Apetal . | 4, H. De. T. Persia . |
| serōtina | . . . Apetal . | 4, H. De. T. Persia . |
| tenēra | . . . Apetal . | 4, H. De. T. Persia . |

JULY FLOWER, see *Prosōpis juliflōrā.*
JŪNCŪS. Linnæus derived the name, from *jungo*, to join; in allusion to the first ropes being made from rushes. *Linn.* 6, Or. 1, Nat. Or. *Juncaceæ.* All the species of Rush do best cultivated in a moist situation, some of them entirely in water, and others in a peat soil; they may be increased by seeds, or dividing the roots. In Japan, they cultivate *J. effusus* for making floor-mats. Synonymes: 1. *J. helodes, arcticus.* 2. *J. compressus.* 3. *J. gracilis, tenuis.* 4. *J. biglumis.*

| | | | | |
|---|---|---|---|---|
| acūtūs | . . . Apetal . | 7, Grass. Britain . . |
| conglomerātūs | . . Apetal . | 6, Grass. Britain . . |
| effūsūs | . . . Apetal . | 5, Grass. Britain . . |
| Gesnerī, 3 | . . . Apetal . | 7, Grass. Scotland . . |
| glaūcūs | . . . Apetal . | 7, Grass. England . . |
| maritimūs | . . . Apetal . | 8, Grass. Britain . . |

*acutiflōrūs, ārctīcūs, aristātūs, bāltīcūs* 1, *biglūmis, bottnīcūs, bufōnīūs, bulbōsūs* 2, *capitātūs, castānēūs, cænōsūs, filifōrmis, Jacquīnī* 4, *lampocārpūs, monānthōs, obtusiflōrūs, pauciflōrūs, planifōlīūs, plebēīūs, polycēphālūs, pygmæūs, squarrōsūs, subverticillātūs, supīnūs, Tenagēiā, tēnūis, trifīdūs, triglūmis, uliginōsūs, vaginātūs, valvātūs.*

JUNGERMĀNNĪA, *Nees.* In honour of the German botanist, Louis Jungermann, who died in 1653. *Linn.* 24, Or. 6, Nat. Or. *Jungermanniaceæ.* This is a very extensive genus of obscure plants, found at all seasons of the year, and generally in little patches, formed by their creeping stems, upon trees, or rocks, or on the earth in damp places—*albēscēns, albīcāns, anōmālā, asplenīoīdēs, barbātā, bicuspidātā, bidentātā, Blāsīā, byssācēā, calyptrifōlīā, capitātā, cilīāris, cochleariformīs, complanātā, comprēssā, concinnātā, connīvēns, cordifōlīā, crenulātā, cuneifōlīā, curvifōlīā, decipīēns, Dicksōnī, dilatātā, Donīānā, emarginātā, epiphyllā, exclsā, exsēctā, Franciscī, furcātā, hamatifōlīā, heterophyllā, hibērnīcā, Hookērī, Hutchīnsīæ, hyalīnā, inclsā, inflātā, iulācēā, juniperīnā, lævigātā, lanceolātā, laxifōlīā, Mackāīī, minūtā, minutīssimā, multifīdā, nemorōsā, obtusifōlīā, orcadēnsis, pīnguīs, planifōlīā, platyphyllā, polyānthōs, pubēscēns, pumīlā, pusīllā, rēptāns, resupīnātā, scalāris, serpyllifōlīā, setācēā, setifōrmis, sphærocārpā, Spāgnī, spinulōsā, stipulācēā, Tamariscī, Taylōrī, tomentēllā, Trichomānis, trichophyllā, trilobātā, Turnērī, umbrōsā, undulātā, ventricōsā, viticulōsā, Wōdsīī.*

JUNIPER, see *Junipērūs.*
JUNĪPĒRŪS, *Linn.* Derived from the Celtic, *juniperus*, rough, or rude; in allusion to the stiff habit of the shrubs. *Linn.* 22, Or. 13, Nat. Or. *Coniferæ.* This genus is too well known to need to be particularised here. All the species will grow in sandy loam, and some in any common garden soil, as *J. Sabina.* They are mostly raised from seeds, though cuttings will strike when planted in a

( 178 )

sheltered situation, under a hand-glass. The stimulating and diuretic powers of the Savin (*J. Sabina*) are well known. The berries of *J. communis* are well known for the flavour they give to gin. Synonymes: 1. *J. canadensis.* 2. *J. nana.* 3. *J. suecica.* 4. *J. alpina.* 5. *J. prostrata, J. repens.* 6. *J. tamariscifolia.* 7. *J. caroliniana.*

| | | | | |
|---|---|---|---|---|
| barbadēnsis | . . Apetal . | F. Ev. T. W. Ind. | 1759 |
| bermūdiānā | . . Apetal . | 5, F. Ev. T. Bermudas . | 1683 |
| chinēnsis | . . Apetal . | 5, H. Ev. 8. China . . | 1804 |
| Smithīī | . . . Apetal . | F. Ev. 8. Nepal . . |
| commūnīs | . . Apetal . | 5, H. Ev. 8. Britain . . |
| canadēnsis, 1 | . Apetal . | 5, H. Ev. 8. Canada . . | 1820 |
| nānā, 2 | . . Apetal . | 5, H. Ev. 8. Siberia . . |
| oblōngā | . . Apetal . | 6, H. Ev. 8. |
| suēcīcā, 3 | . . Apetal . | 5, H. Ev. 8. N. Eur. . . |
| cracōvīā | . . Apetal . | 5, H. Ev. 8. Poland . . | 1820 |
| daūrīcā | . . Apetal . | 7, H. Ev. 8. Dauria . . | 1791 |
| drupācēā | . . Apetal . | 5, H. Ev. 8. Syria . . | 1820 |
| excelsā | . . Apetal . | H. Ev. T. Siberia . . | 1806 |
| lycia | . . Apetal . | 5, H. Ev. 8. 8. Eur. . | 1750 |
| macrocārpā | . . Apetal . | H. Ev. 8. Greece . |
| Oxycēdrūs | . . Apetal . | 5, H. Ev. 8. Spain . . | 1739 |
| phœnīcēā | . . Apetal . | 5, H. Ev. 8. 8. Eur. . | 1683 |
| recūrvā | . . Apetal . | 5, H. Ev. 8. Nepal . . | 1817 |
| Sabīnā | . . Apetal . | 5, H. Ev. 8. 8. Eur. . . | 1548 |
| alpīnā, 4 | . . Apetal . | 5, H. Ev. 8. |
| prostrātā, 5 | . Apetal . | 5, H. Ev. 8. N. Amer. . |
| tamariscifōlīā, 6 | Apetal . | H. Ev. 8. 8. Eur. . . | 1548 |
| variegātā | . . Apetal . | 5, H. Ev. 8. Europe . . |
| squamātā | . . Apetal . | 5, H. Ev. 8. Nepal . . | 1824 |
| aquamōsā | . . Apetal . | H. Ev. 8 E Ind. . |
| thurīferā | . . Apetal . | 5, H. Ev. 8. Spain . . | 1752 |
| uvīferā | . . Apetal . | H. Ev. 8. C. Horn . . |
| virginiānā, 7 | . Apetal . | 5, H. Ev. 8. N. Amer. . | 1664 |
| hūmīlis | . . . Apetal . | 5, H. Ev. 8. India . . | 1800 |

JUPITER'S BEARD, see *Anthyllis Bārbā Jovis.*
JUSSIĒÆ. Named by Linnæus, in memory of Antoine de Jussieu, demonstrator of plants in the Royal Gardens at Paris, and uncle of the celebrated Antoine Laurent de Jussieu. *Linn.* 10, Or. 1, Nat. Or. *Onagraceæ.* Rather obscure aquatics, growing freely in a pot or tub of water, and readily increased by cuttings. The biennials are raised from seeds. Synonymes: 1. *J. acuminata.* 2. *J. villosa.*

| | | | | |
|---|---|---|---|---|
| arēctā | . . . Yellow . | 8, S. Aq. B. S. Amer. . | 1739 |
| frutēscēns | . . Yellow . | 6, S. Ev. 8. | 1824 |
| grandiflōrā | . . Yellow . | 8, G. Aq. P. Carolina . | 1812 |
| hīrtā | . . . Yellow . | 7, S. Aq. B. S. Amer. . | 1816 |
| leptocārpā | . . Yellow . | 7, S. Aq. B. S. Amer. . | 1817 |
| linifolīā | . . . Yellow . | 7, S. Aq. B. N. Amer. . | 1824 |
| ovalifōlīā | . . Yellow . | 8, S. Aq. B. E. Ind. . | 1810 |
| rēpēns | . . . Yellow . | 8, S. Aq. P. W. Ind. . | 1817 |
| scābrā | . . . Yellow . | 7, S. Aq. P. S. Amer. . | 1816 |
| suffruticōsā, 1 | . Yellow . | 8, S. Aq. P. India . . | 1808 |
| variabīlis, 2 | . Yellow . | 8, S. Aq. B. W. Ind. . | 1826 |

JUSTICIA, *Linn.* In honour of J. Justice, an eminent Scotch horticulturist and botanist. *Linn.* 2, Or. 1, Nat. Or. *Acanthaceæ.* An extensive, highly interesting and ornamental genus of plants, which mostly flower very freely. The stove and greenhouse shrubby and herbaceous kinds, grow well in any light soil, or loam and peat mixed, and may be multiplied by cuttings in sand, under a glass, the stove kinds in heat. The seeds of the annual and biennial kinds must be raised in pots, in a hothouse, or hotbed frame, and when transplanted, treated as other tender annuals and biennials. The flowers, leaves, and roots of *J. Adhatoda* are said to possess antispasmodic qualities. *J. Ecbolium* is supposed to be diuretic. *J. paniculata* is the base of the French bitter tincture called *Drogue Amère,* which is highly valued for its stomachic and tonic properties. Synonymes: 1. *J. quadrangularis.* 2. *J. flavicoma.* 3. *eustachiana.* 4. *oblongata.* 5. *tinctoria.*

| | | | | |
|---|---|---|---|---|
| Adhatoda | . . . Purple . | 8. Ev. T. Ceylon . . | 1699 |
| albā | . . . White . | 6, 8. Ev. 8. E. Ind. . | 1816 |
| amabīlis | . . . | 8. Ev. 8. |
| aspērūlā, 1 | . . Pink . | 8. Ev. 8. Indies . . | 1829 |
| Betōnīcā | . . . White . | 5, 8. Ev. 8. E. Ind. . | 1737 |
| bicalyculātā | . . Lilac . | 8, 8. A. E. Ind. . | 1775 |
| bracteolātā | . . Purple . | 7, 8. Ev. 8. Caraccas . | 1823 |
| calytrīchā, 2 | . Yellow . | 2, 8. Ev. 8. Brazil . | 1824 |
| caracasānā | . . Violet . | 5, 8. Ev. Tr. Caraccas . | 1822 |
| cārnēā | . . . Flesh . | 8, 8. Ev. 8. Rio Jan. . | 1827 |
| carthaginēnsis | . Purple . | 7, 8. Ev. 8. Carthag. . | 1792 |
| cilīāris | . . . White . | 7, 8. A. W. Ind. . | 1780 |
| coccīnēā | . . . Scarlet . | 5, 8. Ev. 8. Amer. . | 1770 |
| comātā | . . . Purple . | 7, 8. Her. P. Jamaica . | 1795 |
| cuspidātā | . . . | 7, 8. Ev. 8. Arabia . | 1820 |

| | | | |
|---|---|---|---|
| diffusa | White | 6, S. Ev. S. | E. Ind. | 1816 |
| Ecbolium | Blue | 6, S. Ev. S. | E. Ind. | 1759 |
| echioides | Red | 4, S. Her. P. | E. Ind. | 1820 |
| elongata | Red | 6, S. Her. P. | E. Ind. | 1812 |
| eustachiana | Orange | 3, S. Ev. S. | St. Eustace | 1799 |
| formosa | Purple | 5, S. Ev. S. | | 1818 |
| furcata | Violet | 4, S. Ev. Tr. | Peru | 1795 |
| Gendarussa | Lilac | 6, S. Ev. S. | E. Ind. | 1800 |
| geniculata | Purple | 6, S. Ev. S. | W. Ind. | 1820 |
| guttata | Yellow | 4, S. Her. P. | E. Ind. | 1823 |
| hispida | Yel. wht. | 5, S. Her. P. | S. Leone | 1824 |
| humifusa | Pink | 6, S. Ev. Tr. | Jamaica | 1820 |
| humilis | White | 6, F. Her. P. | N. Amer. | 1818 |
| hyssopifolia | Yellow | 5, G. Ev. S. | Canaries | 1690 |
| Koriana. 3 | White | 6, S. Ev. S. | E. Ind. | 1790 |
| lanceolata | Red | 4, S. Ev. S. | E. Ind. | 1818 |
| lithospermifolia | Purple | 4, S. Ev. Tr. | Peru | 1796 |
| lucida | Scarlet | 7, S. Ev. S. | W. Ind. | 1795 |
| maculata | Pink | 3, S. Ev. S. | E. Ind. | 1824 |
| nasuta | White | 6, S. Ev. S. | E. Ind. | 1790 |
| nemorosa | Purple | 5, S. Her. P. | W. Ind. | 1795 |
| nigricans | White | 6, G. Ev. S. | China | 1819 |
| nitida | White | 6, S. Ev. S. | W. Ind. | 1790 |
| nodosa, 4 | Red | 8, S. Ev. S. | Brazil | 1820 |
| orchioides | | 8, G. Ev. S. | C. G. H. | 1774 |

| | | | |
|---|---|---|---|
| paniculata | Pink | 7, S. Ev. S. | E. Ind. | 1811 |
| pectoralis | Purple | 5, S. Her. P. | W. Ind. | 1787 |
| pedunculosa | Lilac | 7, F. Her. P. | N. Amer. | 1759 |
| periplocifolia | Pink | 6, S. Ev. S. | A. Amer. | 1799 |
| picta | Crimson | 7, S. Ev. S. | E. Ind. | 1780 |
|   lurido-sanguinea | Crimson | 7, S. Ev. S. | E. Ind. | 1780 |
| plumbaginifolia | Violet | 7, S. Ev. S. | W. Ind. | 1819 |
| polysperma | Pa. blue | 7, G. Tr. B. | E. Ind. | 1818 |
| polystachya | Pink | 6, S. Ev. S. | Guiana | 1821 |
| procumbens | Purple | 7, S. Ev. Tr. | E. Ind. | 1796 |
| pumila | | 6, S. Ev. S. | S. Amer. | 1820 |
| quadrifida | Scarlet | 6, S. Ev. S. | Mexico | 1795 |
| quinquangularis | Purple | 7, S. Ev. Tr. | E. Ind. | 1820 |
| ramosissima | Purple | 6, S. Ev. S. | E. Ind. | 1825 |
| reflexiflora | Purple | 6, S. Her. P. | W. Ind. | 1824 |
| Roxburghiana, 5 | Pink | 8, S. Ev. S. | E. Ind. | 1815 |
| salicina | Red | 8, S. Ev. S. | Peru | 1816 |
| salviaeflora | Scarlet | 7, S. Ev. S. | Mexico | 1824 |
| secunda | Red | 6, S. Ev. S. | W. Ind. | 1798 |
| speciosa | Purple | 8, S. Ev. S. | E. Ind. | 1826 |
| thyrsiflora | Scarlet | 8, S. Ev. S. | E. Ind. | 1812 |
| variegata | Red | 5, S. Ev. S. | Guiana | 1825 |
| ventricosa | Wht. red | 6, S. Ev. S. | China | 1826 |
| venusta | Purple | 8, S. Ev. S. | Bengal | |
| vitellina | Yellow | 6, S. Ev. S. | E. Ind. | 1818 |

# K.

KÆMPFERIA, Linn. In honour of E. Kæmpfer, a German naturalist, who died in 1716. Linn. 1, Or. 1, Nat. Or. Scitamineæ. A curious genus of stemless plants, easily cultivated provided they are carefully watered, requiring but little when not in a growing state. They grow best in sandy loam and peat mixed, and are easily increased by divisions of the roots.

| | | | |
|---|---|---|---|
| angustifolia | Wht. blue | 3, S. Her. P. | E. Ind. | 1797 |
| elegans | Purple | 8, S. Her. P. | Pegu | 1828 |
| Galanga | Wht. pur. | 7, S. Her. P. | E. Ind. | 1728 |
| latifolia | White | 5, S. Her. P. | E. Ind. | 1803 |
| marginata | Blue | 7, S. Her. P. | E. Ind. | 1822 |
| ovalifolia | Blue | 6, S. Her. P. | Malacca | 1822 |
| pandurata | Purple | 10, S. Her. P. | E. Ind. | 1797 |
| Roscoeana | White | 10, S. Her. P. | E. Ind. | 1827 |
| rotunda | Red wht. | 7, S. Her. P. | E. Ind. | 1764 |

KAGENECKIA, Ruiz and Pavon. In honour of Count Frederick Kageneck, a patron of botany. Linn. 12, Or. 2, Nat. Or. Rosaceæ. This is described as a very tall ornamental-growing tree, succeeding in loam, peat, and sand; ripened cuttings will probably root in sand, under a glass, in a little heat.

| | | | |
|---|---|---|---|
| crataegoides | White | F. Ev. T. | Chile | 1831 |

KALANCHOE, Adanson. The Chinese name of one of the species. Linn. 8, Or. 4, Nat. Or. Crassulaceæ. This is a pretty genus of succulent plants, requiring but little water when not in a free-growing state. They appear to do best in a mixture of loam and sand. They are very easily increased by cuttings, which should be taken off, and laid to dry a few days before planting; they will then root in a few days. Synonymes: 1. Verea acutiflora. 2. V. crenata. 3. Crassula rotundifolia.

| | | | |
|---|---|---|---|
| acutiflora, 1 | White | 8, S. Ev. S. | E. Ind. | 1806 |
| aegyptiaca | Yellow | 7, S. Ev. S. | Egypt | 1820 |
| ceratophylla | Yellow | 7, S. Ev. S. | China | 1820 |
| crenata, 2 | Yellow | 8, S. Ev. S. | S. Leone | 1793 |
| laciniata | Yellow | 7, S. Ev. S. | E. Ind. | 1781 |
| rotundifolia, 3 | White | 4, S. Ev. S. | C. G. H. | 1820 |
| spatulata | Yellow | 7, S. Ev. S. | China | 1820 |

KALIFORM, formed like Salsola Kali, a sea-coast plant.

KALMIA, Linn. In honour of Peter Kalm, professor at Abo, in Sweden, and author of Travels in America, 1753. Linn. 10, Or. 1, Nat. Or. Ericaceæ. The plants of this genus rank among the most handsome of our hardy shrubs. They do best when grown in a peat soil, though they will grow in a very sandy loam; they may be increased by layers or seeds, and when raised from the latter, they require the same treatment as that recommended for Rhododendron.

| | | | |
|---|---|---|---|
| angustifolia | Red | 6, H. Ev. S. | N. Amer. | 1786 |
| foliis-variegatis | Red | 6, H. Ev. S. | N. Amer. | |
| minima | Red | 6, H. Ev. S. | N. Amer. | |
| nana | Red | 6, H. Ev. S. | N. Amer. | |
| ovata | Red | 6, H. Ev. S. | N. Amer. | |
| pumila | Red | 6, H. Ev. S. | N. Amer. | |

| | | | |
|---|---|---|---|
| rosea | Red | 6, H. Ev. S. | N. Amer. | |
| rubra | Red | 6, H. Ev. S. | N. Amer. | |
| cuneata | Wht. red | 6, H. Ev. S. | Carolina | 1820 |
| glauca | Purple | 4, H. Ev. S. | N. Amer. | 1767 |
|   rosmarinifolia | Red | 4, H. Ev. S. | N. Amer. | 1812 |
| hirsuta | Red | 8, H. Ev. S. | N. Amer. | 1786 |
| latifolia | Red | 6, H. Ev. S. | N. Amer. | 1734 |

KALOSANTHES, Haworth. From kalos, beautiful, and anthos, a flower. Linn. 5, Or. 5, Nat. Or. Crassulaceæ. A truly handsome genus of succulent plants, well worthy of extensive cultivation for the beauty of their flowers; for culture and propagation, see Globulea. Synonyme: 1. Crassula coccinea.

| | | | |
|---|---|---|---|
| bicolor | Yel. scar. | 6, G. Ev. S. | C. G. H. | 1810 |
| biconvexa | White | 7, G. Ev. S. | C. G. H. | 1823 |
| coccinea, 1 | Scarlet | 7, G. Ev. S. | C. G. H. | 1710 |
|   flore-albo | White | 7, G. Ev. S. | C. G. H. | 1811 |
| cymosa | Red | 6, G. Ev. S. | C. G. H. | 1800 |
| jasminea | White | 4, G. Ev. S. | C. G. H. | 1815 |
| media | Red | 6, G. Ev. S. | C. G. H. | 1810 |
| odoratissima | Pink | 6, G. Ev. S. | C. G. H. | 1793 |
| versicolor | White | 5, G. Ev. S. | C. G. H. | 1817 |

KANGURU VINE, see Cissus antarcticus.

KAULFUSSIA, Blume. In honour of Frederick Kaulfuss, M.D., professor of botany at Halle. Linn. 19, Or. 2, Nat. Or. Compositæ. This is a pretty little annual, with bright blue flowers, succeeding well in any light loamy soil.

| | | | |
|---|---|---|---|
| amelloides | Blue | 7, H. | A. C. G. H. | 1819 |

KEEL; when the midrib of a leaf or petal is sharp, and elevated externally, it is called a keel.

KENNEDYA, Ventenat. In honour of Mr. Kennedy, formerly of the firm of Lee and Kennedy, the once celebrated nurserymen of Hammersmith. Linn. 17, Or. 4, Nat. Or. Leguminosæ. A very beautiful genus of conservatory or greenhouse climbers, succeeding well in sandy loam and peat, and easily propagated from cuttings of the young wood in sand, in a little bottom heat, with a glass over them. Synonyme: 1. K. dilatata. 2. latifolia.

| | | | |
|---|---|---|---|
| apetala | Apetal | G. Ev. Tw. | | 1824 |
| coccinea | Scarlet | 6, G. Ev. Tw. | N. Holl. | 1803 |
| Comptoniana | Blue | 4, G. Ev. Tw. | N. Holl. | 1803 |
| heterophylla | | G. Ev. Tw. | N. Holl. | 1824 |
| inophylla, 1 | Scarlet | G. Ev. Tw. | N. Holl. | 1824 |
| macrophylla | Purple | G. Ev. Tw. | S. River | 1835 |
| Marryattae | Scarlet | 4, G. Ev. Tw. | Australia | 1834 |
| monophylla | Purple | 5, G. Ev. Tw. | N. Holl. | 1790 |
|   longeracemosa | Pink | G. Ev. Tw. | N. S. W. | 1828 |
| nigricans | Pur. grn. | 3, G. Ev. Tw. | N. Holl. | 1832 |
| ovata, 2 | Purple | 6, G. Ev. Tw. | N. Holl. | 1818 |
| parviflora | | G. Ev. Tw. | N. Holl. | 1824 |
| prostrata | Scarlet | 4, G. Ev. Tr. | N. S. W. | 1790 |
|   minor | Red | 6, G. Ev. Tw. Cr. | N. Holl. | 1836 |
| rubicunda | Dk. red | 6, G. Ev. Tw. | N. S. W. | 1788 |
| sericea | Scarlet | G. Ev. Tw. | N. Holl. | 1824 |
| Sterlingii | Scarlet | G. Ev. Tw. | S. River | 1834 |

KERRIA, Decandolle. In honour of Mr. Kerr, sometime superintendant of the botanic garden in Ceylon. Linn. 12, Or. 2, Nat. Or. Rosaceæ. This truly beautiful plant is an old and well-known inhabitant of our gardens; it will grow in any common soil, and cuttings of the young wood taken off at a joint, will root readily if planted under a hand-glass. *Synonyme:* 1. *Corchorus japonicus.*

japónicã, 1 . . Yellow all H. De. S. Japan . . 1700

KIDNEY-BEAN, see *Phaséŏlūs.*

KIDNEY-VETCH, see *Anthŏllis.*

KIGGELÀRÏÅ, *Linn.* In honour of Francis Kiggelar, a Dutch botanical author. *Linn.* 22, Or. 9, Nat. Or. *Flacourtiaceæ.* Plants only worth cultivating in general collections: they are of common culture, and increased by cuttings.

africanã . . . Wht. grn. 6, S. Ev. T. C. G. H. . 1683
integrifolÏa . . . Wht. grn. 6, S. Ev. T. C. G. H. . 1819

KIRGANĒLÏÅ, *Jussieu.* From *Kirganeli,* the name of the plant in Malabar. *Linn.* 21, Or. 10, Nat. Or. *Euphorbiaceæ.* This plant will grow well in a mixture of loam and peat; and ripened cuttings will root in sand, under a glass, in a moist bottom heat. *Synonyme:* 1. *Phyllanthus kirganelia.*

elágãns . . . . . 7, S. Ev. S. Maurit. . 1820

KITAIBĒLÏÅ, *Willdenow.* In honour of Paul Kitaibel, M.D., professor of botany at Pest, in Hungary. *Linn.* 16, Or. 8, Nat. Or. *Malvaceæ.* A tall, mallow-like, herbaceous plant, succeeding in any common soil, and easily increased by seeds, which it ripens in abundance.

vitifolÏã . . . White . 8, H. Her. P. Hungary . 1801

KLEINHŎVÏÅ, *Linn.* In honour of M. Kleinhoff, formerly director of the botanic garden in Java. *Linn.* 16, Or. 7, Nat. Or. *Sterculiaceæ.* A handsome species, flowering throughout the year, and seldom being without fruit, which is, however, of little value. It succeeds well in peat and loam; and cuttings root in sand, under a glass, in heat.

hóspÏtã . . . Pink all S. Ev. T. Moluccas . 1800

KLEINÏÅ. Named by Linnæus, in honour of James Henry Klein, a German botanist. *Linn.* 19, Or. 1, Nat. Or. *Compositæ.* The species of this genus are of very little interest, and of the simplest culture and propagation.

viridiflorã . . . Green . . 7, S. Ev. S. Mexico . . 1823

*colorātã, Porophŷllūm, rudērālis, suffrutícōsã, tagetoídēs.*

KNAPPÏÅ, *Smith.* In compliment to Mr. M. Knapp, a writer on British grasses. *Linn.* 3, Or. 2, Nat. Or. *Gramineæ.* This is one of the least of the British grasses, and merely requires sowing in any common soil.

agrostídēã . . . . Apetal . 7, Gram. Wales . .

KNAPWEED, see *Centaūrēã scabiōsã.*

KNAPWEED, see *Centaūrēã Jácēã.*

KNAUTÏÅ, *Coulter.* In honour of C. Knaut, a physician, and botanical author at Halle, in Saxony, who died in 1694. *Linn.* 4, Or. 1, Nat. Or. *Dipsaceæ.* Plants of little beauty, growing in any soil or situation. *Synonymes:* 1. *Scabiosa arvensis.* 2. *S. collina.* 3. *S. ciliata.* 4. *S. diversifolia.* 5. *S. hybrida.* 6. *S. montana.* 7. *S. orientalis.* 8. *S. propontica.* 9. *S. sylvatica.* 10. *S. integrifolia.* 11. *S. longifolia.*

arvēnsis, 1 . . Bl. pur. . 8, H. Her. P. Britain . .
collínã, 2 . . Bluish . 8, H. Her. P. Europe . .
vulgārīs . . Bluish . 8, H. Her. P. Britain . .
cilíātã, 3 . . White . 7, H. Her. P. Moravia . 1802
diversifolÏã, 4 . Violet . 6, H. Her. P. Transylv. . 1826
hybrídã, 5 . . Pa. pur. . 6, H. A. S. Eur. . 1819
montánã, 6 . . White . 7, H. Her. P. Caucasus . 1820
orientális, 7 . . Red . 8, H. A. Levant . 1713
propontica, 8 . Purple . 8, H. A. Levant . 1768
sylvátícã, 9 . . Red . . 7, H. Her. P. Europe . 1633
integrifolÏã, 10 Cream . . 7, H. Her. P. Europe . 1748
longifolÏã, 11 Lilac . . 7, H. Her. P. Hungary . 1802

KNAWEL, see *Sclerānthūs.*

KNEED, or KNEE-JOINTED, bent like the knee-joint.

KNIGHTÏÅ, *R. Brown.* In honour of the late distinguished president of the Horticultural Society, Thomas Andrew Knight, Esq., F.R.S., &c., who died in 1838. *Linn.* 4, Or. 1, Nat. Or. *Proteaceæ.* This is described as a fine ornamental tree, requiring much the same treatment as *Hakea,* and some other New Holland genera.

excélsã . . . . Flesh . . G. Ev. T. N. Zeal. . 1824

KNOT-GRASS, see *Illecēbrūm.*

KNOWLTŎNÏÅ, *Salisbury.* After Thomas Knowlton, once curator of the botanic garden at Eltham. *Linn.* 13, Or. 6, Nat. Or. *Ranunculaceæ.* Curious species, but of no great beauty. They succeed well in loam and peat, and are increased by dividing the roots, or by seeds. *Synonymes:* 1. *Adonis hirsuta.* 2. *A. capensis.*

daucifolÏã . . . G. Her. P. C. G. H. . 1822
gracÏlis . . . Yel. grn. . 4, G. Her. P. C. G. H. . 1820
hirsútã, 1 . . Yel. grn. . 4, G. Her. P. C. G. H. . 1823
rigïdã, 2 . . Yel. grn. . 4, G. Her. P. C. G. H. . 1780
vesicatŏrÏã . . Yel. grn. . 3, G. Her. P. C. G. H. . 1801

KNŎXÏÅ, *Linn.* In honour of Robert Knox, who lived many years in Ceylon, and published a relation of it in 1781. *Linn.* 4, Or. 1, Nat. Or. *Cinchonaceæ.* The species of this genus are rather ornamental, and succeed well in sandy loam and peat; and young cuttings planted in mould or sand, under a glass, will root readily. *Synonymes:* 1. *Spermacoce Roxburghii.* 2. *K. corymbosa, S. sumatrensis.* 3. *K. umbellata, S. teres.*

lævis, 1 . . . Pink . . 7, S. A. Bengal . 1818
sumatrēnsis, 2 . White . 7, S. Ev. S. E. Ind. . 1818
tēres, 3 . . . White . 7, S. Ev. S. E. Ind. . 1820
zeylánícã . . . White . 7, S. Ev. S. Ceylon . 1826

KOBRĒSÏÅ, *Willdenow.* After Dr. Kobres, a German, and a great promoter of botany. *Linn.* 21, Or. 3, Nat. Or. *Cyperaceæ.* A mere weed, of the simplest culture. *Synonyme:* 1. *Schænus monoica—caricínã.*

KŎCHÏÅ, *Roth.* In honour of M. Koch, a German botanist. *Linn.* 5, Or. 2, Nat. Or. *Chenopodiaceæ.* The species of this genus are not possessed of much beauty. The seed has only to be sown in the open ground. *Synonyme.* 1. *Chenopodium arenarium.*

arenárÏã, 1 . . . Wht. grn. 5, H. A. Hungary . 1822
dasyánthã . . . Green . 7, H. A. Caucasus . 1823
eriŏphŏrã . . . Green . 6, H. A. Spain . .
hys"sopifolÏã . . Green . 7, H. A. Siberia . . 1801
muricātã . . . Green . 7, H. A. Egypt . 1773
prostrátã . . . Green . 7, H. De. Cr. S. Eur. . 1780
scopárÏã . . . Green . 6, H. A. Greece . 1629
sedoídēs . . . . Green . 5, H. A. Crimea . 1821
trigýnã . . . . Green . 6, H. A. Spain . 1804

KŒLĒRÏÅ, *Link.* Named in honour of M. Kœhler, professor of natural history at Mayence. *Linn.* 3, Or. 2, Nat. Or. *Gramineæ.* Mere weeds, of the commonest cultivation. *Synonyme:* 1. *Aira cristata.*

glabrã, 1 . . . . Apetal . 7, Grass. Britain . .

*ægyptíacã, brachystāchŷã, cristātã, glaucã, grandiflòrã, hirsūtã, hīspïdã, lobātã, macrānthã, pennsylvánícã, phleoídēs, pubēscēns, tuberōsã, vallesíacã, villōsã.*

KŒNIGÏÅ. Linnæus named this genus after Samuel Kœnig, a Swiss mathematician. *Linn.* 3, Or. 3, Nat. Or. *Polygaleæ.* This is a curious inconspicuous species, of greater rarity than beauty; it will grow sown in any common soil in the open border.

islandícã . . . Apetal . . 4, H. A. Iceland . . 1773

KOLREUTĒRÏÅ, *Linn.* In honour of the celebrated German botanist, J. G. Kolreuter. *Linn.* 8, Or. 1, Nat. Or. *Sapindaceæ.* This is a very handsome plant, growing well in any common soil; it should be planted in a sheltered situation, as it will not flower if too much exposed; it is readily increased by layers or cuttings of the roots.

paniculátã . . . Yellow . 7, H. De. T. China . . 1763

KONIGÏÅ, *R. Brown.* In honour of Charles Konig, F.R.S., L.S., superintendent of the natural history department in the British Museum. *Linn.* 15, Nat. Or. *Cruciferæ.* K. *maritima variegata* is a pretty little undershrub; it grows in any common soil, and may be increased by cuttings planted under a glass. K. *maritima* is increased from seed sown in the open border. *Synonyme:* 1. *Alyssum maritimum, Adysetum maritimum, Glyce maritima.*

marítïmã, 1 . . White . . 7, H. A England .
variegátã . . . White . 7, G. Ev. S.

KRAMĒRÏÅ, *Læfling.* In honour of J. G. H. and W. H. Kramer, two German botanists. *Linn.* 14, Or. 2, Nat. Or. *Polygaleæ.* This is described as an ornamental shrub, succeeding in sandy loam and peat; cuttings will root in sand, under a glass, in heat. The species is tonic, and excessively astringent.

| pauciflora . . . | | 8. Ev. S. Mexico . | . 1824 |

KRIGIA, *Schreber.* In honour of Dr. David Kreig, a German botanist. Linn. 19, Or. 1, Nat. Or. Composite. *K. virginica* is rather a pretty little grassy-leaved annual; it, as well as *K. caroliniana*, has only to be sown in spring, in any open loamy soil. The other species will grow well in the same kind of soil, and may be increased by divisions. Synonymes: 1. *Troximum virginicum.* 2. *Hyoseris caroliniana.* 3. *Troximum Dandelion.* 4. *Hyoseris virginica.*

| virginica, 4 . . | Yellow . 6, H. | A. N. Amer. | . 1811 |

*amplexicaulis* 1, *caroliniana* 2, *Dandelion* 3.

KRUBERA, *Hoffmann.* After John Julius Kruber, M.D., a promoter of botany. Linn. 5, Or. 2, Nat. Or. *Umbelliferæ.* The seed of this species only requires sowing in a light soil in the open border, in spring. Synonyme: 1. *Ulospermum dichotomum.*

| leptophylla . . | White . . 6, H. | A. S. Eur. . | . 1596 |

KUHNIA, *Linn.* In honour of Adam Kuhn, of Pennsylvania, a pupil of Linnæus. Linn. 19, Or. 1, Nat. Or. Composite. Ornamental little plants, succeeding well in a mixture of peat and sandy loam, and increased by divisions. Synonymes: 1.

*Critonia Kuhnia.* 2. *C. eupatorioides.* 3. *Kleinia linearifolia, Jaumea linearis.*

| Critonia, 1 . . . | White . . | 7, H. Her. P. N. Amer. | . 1816 |
| eupatorioides, 2 . | White . . | 7, H. Her. P. N. Amer. | . 1812 |
| linearifolia, 3 . . | | G. Her. P. Brazil | . 1829 |
| rosmarinifolia . . | White . . | 7, G. Her. P. Cuba | . 1823 |

KUNTHIA. Humboldt named this genus in honour of his friend Charles Sigismund Kunth, a famous Prussian botanist. Linn. 21, Or. 6, Nat. Or. *Palmaceæ.* This is described as an ornamental palm, growing in any rich mould, and increased only by seeds.

| montana . . . | | Palm. N. Grenada . | . 1829 |

KYDIA, *Roxburgh.* In honour of Colonel Robert Kyd, the first director of the Calcutta botanic garden. Linn. 16, Or. 7, Nat. Or. *Sterculiaceæ.* An ornamental genus, succeeding well in light turfy loam and peat, well mixed; and increased by cuttings, not too ripe, planted in sand, under a glass, on a bottom heat.

| calycina . . . | White . . | 8. Ev. S. E. Ind. . | . 1818 |
| fraterna . . . | White . . | 8. Ev. S. E. Ind. . | . 1823 |

KYLLINGIA, *Linn.* In honour of P. Kylling, a Danish botanist, who died in 1696. Linn. 3, Or. 1, Nat. Or. *Cyperaceæ.* Mere weeds, of the simplest culture—*brevifolia, intermedia, monocephala, polycephala, triceps, uncinata.*

# L.

LABELLUM, the front segment of an orchidaceous or other flower, the lower petal, the lip.

LABIATE, having a lip, or lips.

LABIOSA, large, or broad-lipped.

LABLAVIA, *Adanson.* Lablab is the Arabic name of *Convolvulus,* with which this has no affinity except in the twining habit. Linn. 17, Or. 4, Nat. Or. *Leguminosæ.* The seeds of the annual kinds may be sown in pots, and kept in the hothouse until May, when, if the weather is fine, they may be planted in a sheltered situation in the open ground, and supported in the same way as scarlet-runners. The greenhouse species are readily increased by cuttings. Synonymes: 1. *Dolichos cultratus.* 2. *D. albus.* 3. *D. bengalensis, Lablab bengalensis.* 4. *L. purpureus, D. purpureus.* 5. *D. Lablab.*

| cultrata, 1 . . | White . | 7, G. Tw. A. Japan . | . 1816 |
| leucocarpa . . | White . | 7, S. Tw. A. E. Ind. . | . 1816 |
| microcarpa . . | Purple . | 7, S. Tw. A. E. Ind. . | . 1818 |
| nankinica . . | White . | 7, G. Tw. A. China . | . 1714 |
| perennans, 2 . . | White . | 7, G. De. Tw. China . | . 1820 |
| vulgaris, 5 . . | Violet . | 7, S. De. Tw. E. Ind. . | . 1794 |
| albiflora, 3 . . | White . | 8, S. De. Tw. E. Ind. . | . 1800 |
| purpurea, 4 . . | Purple . | 7, S. De. Tw. E. Ind. . | . 1790 |

LACEBRAKE, see *Lagetta linteäria.*

LACERATE, } torn, appearing torn.
LACERATED, }

LACERATELY-TOOTHED, toothed in a coarse irregular manner.

LACHENALIA, *Jacquin.* In honour of W. de la Chenal, a botanical author. Linn. 6, Or. 2, Nat. Or. *Liliaceæ.* This is a genus of pretty, though rather diminutive plants, seldom attaining a foot in height. They bear forcing remarkably well, and may be made to flower at almost any season. The soil best adapted to the growth of these plants is a mixture of peat and sand. Care must be taken to give them little or no water when not in a growing state. They may be increased by offsets, or by seeds.

| anguinea . . | White . | 4, G. Bl. P. C. G. H. | . 1825 |
| angustifolia . . | White . | 4, G. Bl. P. C. G. H. | . 1793 |
| bifolia . . | Pink . | 4, G. Bl. P. C. G. H. | . 1813 |
| contaminata . . | White . | 3, G. Bl. P. C. G. H. | . 1774 |
| flava . . | Yellow . | 5, G. Bl. P. C. G. H. | . 1790 |
| fragrans . . | Wht. red . | 4, G. Bl. P. C. G. H. | . 1798 |
| glaucina . . | Grn. wht. | 5, G. Bl. P. C. G. H. | . 1795 |
| glauca . . | Pur. red . | 5, H. Bl. P. Persia . | . 1825 |
| hyacinthoides . | Wht. red . | 5, G. Bl. P. C. G. H. | . 1812 |
| isopetala . . | Wht. pur. | 5, G. Bl. P. C. G. H. | . 1804 |
| lanceaefolia . . | Wht. grn. | 5, G. Bl. P. C. G. H. | . 1818 |
| liliiflora . . | White . | 4, G. Bl. P. C. G. H. | . 1825 |
| lucida . . | Pink . | 4, G. Bl. P. C. G. H. | . 1798 |
| luteola . . | Yel. red . | 3, G. Bl. P. C. G. H. | . 1774 |

| maculata . . | Yel. red . | 3, G. Bl P. C. G. H. | . 1774 |
| mutabilis . . | Blue . | 11, G. Bl. P. C. G. H. | . 1825 |
| nervosa . . | Pink . | 4, G. Bl. P. C. G. H. | . 1810 |
| orchioides . . | Grn. wht. | 3, G. Bl. P. C. G. H. | . 1752 |
| pallida . . | Pa. blue . | 5, G. Bl. P. C. G. H. | . 1782 |
| minor . . | Pa. blue . | G. Bl. P. C. G. H. | . 1782 |
| patula . . | Wht. pink | 4, G. Bl. P. C. G. H. | . 1795 |
| pendula . . | Red yel. | 4, G. Bl. P. C. G. H. | . 1789 |
| maculata . . | Red yel. | 4, F. Bl. P. C. G. H. | . 1789 |
| punctata . . | Purple . | 4, F. Bl. P. C. G. H. | . 1824 |
| purpurea . . | Purple . | 4, G. Bl. P. C. G. H. | . 1826 |
| purpureo-caerulea | Purple . | 4, G. Bl. P. C. G. H. | . 1796 |
| pusilla . . | White . | 6, G. Bl. P. C. G. H. | . 1825 |
| pustulata . . | Pur. grn. | 2, G. Bl. P. C. G. H. | . 1790 |
| quadricolor . . | Scar. yel. | 3, G. Bl. P. C. G. H. | . 1774 |
| colorata . . | Scar. yel. | 4, G. Bl. P. C. G. H. | . 1774 |
| racemosa . . | Wht. grn. | 5, G. Bl. P. C. G. H. | . 1811 |
| rosea . . | Pink . | 5, G. Bl. P. C. G. H. | . 1800 |
| rubida . . | Red . | 9, G. Bl. P. C. G. H. | . 1803 |
| serotina . . | Pink . | 8, F. Bl. P. C. G. H. | . 1820 |
| sessiliflora . . | Red . | 5, G. Bl. P. C. G. H. | . 1804 |
| tricolor . . | Red yel. | 4, G. Bl. P. C. G. H. | . 1774 |
| unicolor . . | Pink . | 5, G. Bl. P. C. G. H. | . 1806 |
| uniflora . . | Wht. blue | 3, G. Bl. P. C. G. H. | . 1795 |
| violacea . . | Violet . | 3, G. Bl. P. C. G. H. | . 1795 |

LACHNÆA, *Linn.* Derived from *lachne*, down; alluding to the downy clothing of the corolla. Linn. 8, Or. 1, Nat. Or. *Thymelaceæ.* Interesting Cape plants, with pretty woolly heads of white or purple flowers. They succeed well in sandy peat, with the pots carefully drained; and young plants may be obtained from cuttings in sand, under a glass. Synonymes: 1. *Gnidia filamentosa.* 2. *Passerina conglomerata.*

| buxifolia, 1 . . | White . | 5, S. Ev. S. C. G. H. | . 1800 |
| conglomerata, 2 . | White . | 6, G. Ev. S. C. G. H. | . 1773 |
| eriocephala . . | White . | 5, G. Ev. S. C. G. H. | . 1798 |
| glauca . . | White . | 6, G. Ev. S. C. G. H. | . 1800 |
| purpurea . . | Purple . | 4, G. Ev. S. C. G. H. | . 1800 |

LACHNANTHES, *Ellis.* From *lachne*, wool, and *anthos*, a flower; in allusion to the flowers, which are woolly. Linn. 3, Or. 1, Nat. Or. *Hæmodoraceæ.* A pretty plant; for culture and propagation, see *Dilatris.* Synonyme: 1. *Dilatris tinctoria, D. Heritiera.*

| tinctoria, 1 . . | Pink . | 7, G. Her. P. N. Amer. | . 1812 |

LACHRYMA, weeping, drooping.

LACINIATE, jagged, cut.

LACTUCA, *Linn.* Derived from *lac*, milk; on account of the milky juice which exudes from the plants when broken. Linn. 19, Or. 1, Nat. Or. *Compositæ.* Among others, this genus contains the well-known "Lettuce," with the culture of which every one is familiar. *L. virosa* yields an extract resembling opium in its qualities, but less likely to produce the consequences attending the use of that drug. *Synonyme*: 1. *sonchoides*.

| | | | | | |
|---|---|---|---|---|---|
| crispā | Yellow | 6, H. | A. | | 1570 |
| intybācēā | Yellow | 7, H. | A. 8. Amer. | | 1781 |
| palmātā | Yellow | 6, H. | A. | | 1683 |
| quercīnā | Yellow | 5, H. | A. Sweden | | 1686 |
| sativā | Yellow | 6, H. | A. | | 1562 |
| seguiānā | Purple | 7, H. | A. Piedmont | | 1822 |
| virōsā | Yellow | 7, H. | A. Britain | | |

*altissimā, augustānā, canadēnsis, Chaīēll, cichoriifōlā 1, crētica, elongātā, gramīnēā, indīca, integrifōlā, maculātā, perēnnis, sagittātā, salīgnā, scariōlā, sonchifōlā, strīctā, tenērrimā, tuberōsā, villōsā, viminēā.*

LACTĒSCENT, yielding milky juice.

LACŪNÆ, little pits, or depressions; applied to vessels when they are full of air.

LACŪNOSE, covered with pits, or depressions.

LACŪSTRIS, growing in lakes, or pools.

LADIES'-SLIPPER, see *Cypripēdium*.

LADY'S-SMOCK, see *Cardaminē*.

LADIES' TRACES, see *Neōttia spīrālis*.

LADIES' TRACES, see *Spirānthēs*.

LADY FERN, see *Aspīdium Thelŷptērum*.

LÆLIX. Named by Lindley, who does not give the derivation. *Linn.* 20, Or. 1, Nat. Or. *Orchidaceæ*. These are splendid plants, approaching in beauty to some of the finer *Cattleyas*. The sepals and petals of *L. anceps*, and its variety, are pale lilac; the central lobe of the labellum is a beautiful deep purple, and the mouth of the tubular part yellow and white. *L. grandiflora* has never flowered in this country, and is found rather difficult to grow. The others are of very easy cultivation, requiring precisely the same treatment as their rivals, the *Cattleyas*.

| | | | | | |
|---|---|---|---|---|---|
| albīdā | White | 8. Epi. | Oaxaca | | 1838 |
| anceps | Ro. pur. | 12, 8. Epi. | Mexico | | |
| Barkeriānā | Purple | 12, 8. Epi. | Mexico | | 1833 |
| autumnālis | Red | 9, 8. Epi. | Mexico | | 1836 |
| furfurācēā | Rose | 11, 8. Epi. | Mexico | | 1838 |
| grandiflōrā | | 8. Epi. | Xalapa | | |
| majālis | Violet | 8. Epi. | Mexico | | 1838 |

LÆTIX, *Linn.* In honour of Jean de Laet, of Antwerp, who published a Latin history of America, dedicated to King Charles I. of England. *Linn.* 13, Or. 1, Nat. Or. *Bixaceæ*. Rather a pretty shrub; for culture and propagation, see *Ludia*.

| | | | | | |
|---|---|---|---|---|---|
| Thāmnīā | White | 7, 8. Ev. 8. W. Ind. | | | 1824 |

LÆTUS, cheerful, bright.

LÆVIGĀTUS, smooth, soft.

LAGASCĪA, *Cavanilles*. In honour of Don Mariana Lagasca, professor of botany at Madrid. *Linn.* 19, Or. 1, Nat. Or. *Compositæ*. A pretty little plant, requiring precisely the same treatment as other stove annuals.

| | | | | | |
|---|---|---|---|---|---|
| mollis | White | 7, 8. | A. 8. Amer. | | 1815 |

LAGENĀRIX, *Seringe*. From *lagena*, a bottle; because of the bottle-shaped fruit of some of the species. *Linn.* 21, Or. 10, Nat. Or. *Cucurbitaceæ*. The well-known vegetable, the "Gourd," is the produce of this species and its varieties; for culture, &c., see *Cucurbita*. *Synonyme*: 1. *Cucurbita Lagenaria*.

| | | | | | |
|---|---|---|---|---|---|
| vulgāris, 1 | Yellow | 8, H. Tr. | A. India | | 1597 |
| clavātā | Yellow | 8, H. Tr. | A. India | | 1597 |
| deprēssā | Yellow | 8, H. Tr. | A. India | | 1597 |
| courgourdā | Yellow | 8, H. | A. India | | 1597 |
| turbinātā | Yellow | 8, H. Tr. | A. India | | 1597 |

LAGERSTRŒMIX, *Linn.* In honour of Magnus Lagerstrœm, of Gottenburgh. *Linn.* 23, Or. 1, Nat. Or. *Lythraceæ*. A most splendid genus of plants, especially *L. regina*, the flowers of which are produced in panicles; they are at first pale rose-coloured, and gradually deepen to a beautiful purple. The soil best adapted to these plants is a mixture of peat and loam. All the species, except *L. indica* and its variety, are rather difficult to cultivate; they require a strong heat, and very little water in winter. In summer, they grow freely, and require plenty of room to grow, with a good supply of water; cuttings root readily in sand, under a glass, in heat.

| | | | | | |
|---|---|---|---|---|---|
| grandiflōrā | Red | 7, 8. Ev. 8. | E. Ind. | | 1818 |
| indīca | Flesh | 7, 8. Ev. 8. | E. Ind. | | 1759 |
| rōsēā | Rose | 8, G. Ev. 8. | China | | 1825 |
| parviflōrā | White | 8. Ev. 8. | E. Ind. | | 1818 |
| regīnæ | Red | 8. Ev. 8. | E. Ind. | | 1792 |

LAGETTX, *Jussieu*. Lagetto is the name of the species in Jamaica. *Linn.* 8, Or. 1, Nat. Or. *Thymelaceæ*. This species grows well in loam and peat; and cuttings of the ripened wood root readily in sand, under a glass, in heat. *Synonyme*: 1. *Daphne Lagetta*.

| | | | | | |
|---|---|---|---|---|---|
| lintēārīā | White | 8. Ev. 8. Jamaica | | | 1793 |

LAGŌECIX, *Linn.* From *lagos*, a hare, and *oikos*, a house; the seeds enveloped in the hairy involucrum have been compared to young leverets. *Linn.* 5, Or. 2, Nat. Or. *Umbelliferæ*. The seeds of this plant should be sown soon after they are ripe, in autumn, because if deferred till spring, they commonly remain a year, and sometimes longer, before they grow

| | | | | | |
|---|---|---|---|---|---|
| cuminoīdēs | Grn. wnt. | 6, H. | A. Levant | | 1640 |

LAGONYCHIUM, *Bieberstein*. From *lagos*, a hare, and *onychion*, a little nail; in allusion to the spines on the plant. *Linn.* 10, Or. 1, Nat. Or. *Leguminosæ*. This plant will succeed in a warm situation in the open border, if protected by a mat in severe weather in winter. It may be increased either by seeds, layers, or cuttings, taken off at a joint when very young, and planted in sand, under a glass. *Synonymes*:1. *Acacia Stephaniana*, *Mimosa micrantha*.

| | | | | | |
|---|---|---|---|---|---|
| Stephaniānūm | Yellow | 7, F. Ev. 8. Persia | | | 1816 |

LAGŌPUS, resembling the foot of a hare.

LAGOSĒRIS, *Bieberstein*. From *lagos*, a hare, and *seris*, succory. *Linn.* 19, Or. 1, Nat. Or. *Compositæ*. Obscure plants, of the simplest culture. *Synonyme*: 1. *Crepis nemausensis—nemausensis* 1, *taūricā*.

LAGUNÆX, *Cavanilles*. In honour of Andreas Laguna, a Spanish physician and botanist of the sixteenth century. *Linn.* 16, Or. 8, Nat. Or. *Malvaceæ*. Annuals of no interest; they will grow in any light loamy soil. *Synonyme*: 1. *L. angulata—lobātā, sinuātā* 1.

LAGŪRUS, *Linn.* From *lagos*, a hare, and *oura*, a tail; on account of the resemblance of its heads. *Linn.* 3, Or. 2, Nat. Or. *Gramineæ*. A mere weed, growing in any soil or situation.

| | | | | | |
|---|---|---|---|---|---|
| ovātūs | Apetal | 6, Grass. N. Hou. | | | 1820 |

LAHAYX, *Ræmer and Schultes*. In honour of M. Lahaye, a diligent botanical gardener. *Linn.* 5, Or. 1, Nat. Or. *Illecebraceæ*. This is a genus of rather pretty plants. The shrubby and herbaceous kinds grow well in sandy peat, and may be increased by cuttings planted in sand. The annuals require similar treatment to other hardy and tender annuals. *Synonymes*: 1. *Hayea alsinifolia*. 2. *Mollia aristata*. 3. *M. diffusa*. *Illecebrum divaricatum*. 4. *I. latifolium*. 5. *Hayea polycarpoides*.

| | | | | | |
|---|---|---|---|---|---|
| alsinifōliā, 1 | White | 7, H. Tr. | A. 8. Eur. | | 1817 |
| aristātā, 2 | White | 6, G. Ev. 8. | Canaries | | 1780 |
| corymbōsā | White | 6, 8. Ev. 8. | Ceylon | | 1823 |
| diffūsā, 3 | White | 7, G. | A. Canaries | | 1779 |
| gnaphalioīdēs | White | 6, G. Ev. 8. | N. Africa | | 1818 |
| latifōlīā, 4 | White | 7, G. Ev. 8. | Teneriffe | | 1810 |
| minuartoīdēs | White | 7, H. Tr. | A. Spain | | 1826 |
| polycarpoīdēs, 5 | White | 7, G. Her. P. | Sicily | | 1817 |
| stellātā | White | 7, 8. Ev. 8. | Guinea | | 1820 |
| tenuifōlīā | White | 7, 8. Ev. 8. 8. | Leone | | 1817 |

LALAGX, *Lindley*. Lalage, the name of a lively witty dame, immortalized by Horace, and applied to this plant on account of its gay and lively-looking colours. *Linn.* 15, Or. 6, Nat. Or. *Leguminosæ*. This is one of the prettiest of the New Holland leguminous plants. It requires an airy part of the greenhouse, and to be similarly treated to the genus *Hovea*.

| | | | | | |
|---|---|---|---|---|---|
| ornātā | Yel. pur. | 4, 8. Ev. 8. N. Holl. | | | 1830 |

LAMBERTIX. Named by Smith, in honour of Aylmer Bourke Lambert, Esq., F.R.S., V.P. L.S., one of the most liberal botanists in Europe, and the possessor of a splendid herbarium, open to every man of science. *Linn.* 4, Or. 1, Nat. Or. *Proteaceæ*. Very handsome plants, succeeding well in loam and peat, with the pots carefully drained. Water must, at all seasons, be very cautiously supplied; for if once the soil in the pots gets saturated, the plants will soon become sickly, and perish. Cuttings taken off at a joint, before they begin to push, will root in sand, under a glass, if secured from damp.

| | | | | | |
|---|---|---|---|---|---|
| echinātā | . . . | | 7, G. Ev. S. N. Holl. | . 1824 |
| ericifoliā | . . . | | G. Ev. S. N. Holl. | . 1830 |
| formōsā | . . . | Red | . 7, G. Ev. S. N. S. W. | . 1788 |
| inērmis | . . . | | G. Ev. S. N. Holl. | . 1824 |
| longifoliā | . . . | Red | . 7, G. Ev. S. N. Holl. | . 1826 |
| propinquā | . . . | | 7, G. Ev. S. N. Holl. | . 1830 |
| uniflōrā | . . . | | 7, G. Ev. S. N. Holl. | . 1824 |

LAMB'S LETTUCE, see *Valerianēlla.*

LAMELLATE, } divided internally by little plates.
LAMELLATED, }

LAMELLOSE, having little plates.

LĀMINĀ, applied to a leaf of a plant considered without a petiole.

LAMINĀRIĀ, *Lamour.* Named because of the sori upon the laminæ of the fronds. Linn. 24, Or. 7, Nat. Or. *Algæ.* Interesting species of sea-weed. In Iceland, an extract is obtained from L. *saccharina,* which is used by the poorer inhabitants as a substitute for sugar—*agārūm, bulbōsā, dēbilis, digitātā, esculentā, latifoliā, Phyllītis, saccharinā-bullātā.*

LĀMIŪM, *Linn.* Derived from *lamios.* the throat; on account of the form of the flowers. Linn. 14, Or. 1, Nat. Or. *Labiatæ.* Plants of very little merit, if we except L. *Orvala.* They will grow in any common soil, and are increased by divisions and seeds. Synonyme: 1. L. *maculatum.*

| | | | | | |
|---|---|---|---|---|---|
| bifidūm | . . | White | . 6, H. | A Britain | |
| flexuōsūm | . . | | 4, H. Her. P | Naples | . 1824 |
| hirsūtūm | . . | Purple | . 6, H. Her. P. | S. Eur. | |
| longiflōrūm, 1 | | Pink | . 3, H. Her. P. | S. Eur. | |
| multifidūm | . . | Purple | . 4, H. | A. Levant | . 1782 |
| Orvālā | . . | Purple | . 6, H. Her. P. | Italy | . 1596 |
| tomentōsūm | . . | White | . 6, H. | A. Armenia | |

*albūm, amplexicaūlē, gargānicūm, incisūm, lævigātūm, maculātūm, mōllē, moschātūm, purpūrēūm, ālbidūm, rugōsūm.*

LAMPWICK, see *Phlōmis Lychnītis.*

LANCASHIRE ASPHODEL, see *Narthēcīūm ossifrāgūm.*

LANCEOLATE, lance or spear shaped.

LANCEWOOD, see *Guattēriā virgātā.*

LANDRA, see *Rāphānūs Lāndrā.*

LANTĀNĀ. An ancient name of *Viburnum,* and applied to this genus by Linnæus because of its affinity. Linn. 14, Or. 2, Nat. Or. *Verbenaceæ.* These plants are rapid growers, forming small bushy shrubs, and producing their pink, yellow, orange, or changeable-coloured heads of flowers in great abundance, which have a somewhat agreeable aromatic flavour. Any loamy soil suits them; and they are increased readily by cuttings in sand, in heat. Synonyme: 1. *parvifoliu.*

| | | | | | |
|---|---|---|---|---|---|
| aculeātā | . . | Red | . 6, S. Ev. S. | W. Ind. | . 1692 |
| albā | . . . | White | . 7, S. | S. Amer. | |
| ānnūā | . . . | Flesh | . 7, S. | S. Amer. | . 1733 |
| brasiliēnsis | . . | White | . 6, S. Ev. S. | Brazil | . 1823 |
| cammārā | . . | Red or. | . 6, S. Ev. S. | W. Ind. | . 1691 |
| coccinēā | . . | Scarlet | . 6, S. Ev. S. | S. Amer. | . 1824 |
| crocēā | . . | Copper | . 8, S. Ev. S. | Jamaica | . 1818 |
| fucātā | . . | Pink | . 6, S. Ev. S. | S. Amer. | . 1822 |
| geminātā | . . | Purple | . 6, S. Ev. S. | Trinidad | . 1819 |
| hirtā | . . . | | 8, S. Ev. S. | Mexico | . 1825 |
| hispidā | . . | Purple | . 7, S. Ev. S. | Mexico | . 1824 |
| hōrridā | . . | Red | . 6, S. Ev. S. | Mexico | . 1824 |
| involucrātā | . . | Pink | . 6, S. Ev. S. | W. Ind. | . 1690 |
| lavandulācēā | . . | Red | . 7, S. Ev. S. | S. Amer. | . 1820 |
| Lockhārtii | . . | White | . 8, S. Ev. S. | Trinidad | . 1820 |
| melissifoliā | . . | Yellow | . 8, S. Ev. S. | W. Ind. | . 1732 |
| mixtā | . . . | | 9, S. Ev. S. | W. Ind. | . 1732 |
| mollis | . . | Red wht. | . 7, S. Ev. S. | Mexico | . 1828 |
| nivēā | . . | White | . 8, S. Ev. S. | E. Ind. | |
| mutabilis | | Yel. rose | . 8, S. | | |
| odorātā | . . | White | . 8, S. Ev. S. | W. Ind. | . 1758 |
| pilōsā | . . | Purple | . 7, S. Ev. S. | Cuba | . 1823 |
| purpūrēā | . . | Purple | . 7, S. Ev. S. | S. Amer. | . 1820 |
| rādūlā | . . | Purple | . 8, S. Ev. S. | W. Ind. | . 1803 |
| rēctā, 1 | . . | Purple | . 7, S. Ev. S. | Jamaica | . 1758 |
| salviæfoliā | . . | Red | . 8, S. Ev. S. | C. G. H. | . 1823 |
| scābrida | . . | | 9, S. Ev. S. | W. Ind. | . 1774 |
| strictā | . . | Pa. pur. | . 7, S. Ev. S. | Jamaica | . 1733 |
| trifoliā | . . | Purple | . 7, S. Ev. S. | W. Ind. | . 1733 |
| violacēā | . . | Violet | . 7, S. Ev. S. | S. Amer. | . 1818 |

LANUGINŌSŪS, woolly

LAPPĀGŌ, *Schreber.* From *lappa,* burdock; because of its rough prickly flowers. Linn. 3, Or. 2, Nat. Or. *Gramineæ.* A plant of little beauty. The flowers are furnished with small prickles, similar to those of *Arctium Lappa,* or Burdock; whence the name. It will grow in any soil

| | | | | | |
|---|---|---|---|---|---|
| racemōsā | . . . . | Apetal | . 7, Grass. S. Eur. | . 1771 |

LAPSĀNĀ, *Linn.* From *lapazo,* to purge; in allusion to its once supposed medicinal virtues. Linn. 19, Or. 1, Nat. Or. *Compositæ.* Plants of little interest, and of the commonest culture. Synonymes: 1. *Hyoseris fœtida, Arnoseris fœtida.* 2. *H. minima, A. minima.*

| | | | | | |
|---|---|---|---|---|---|
| grandiflōrā | . . | Yellow | . 7, H. Her. P. | Caucasus | . 1816 |
| pubēscēns | . . | Yellow | . 7, H. | A Europe | . 1816 |

*commūnis, crispā, fœtidā 1, intermēdiā, lyrātā, pusillā 2.*

LARBRĒX, *Hilaire.* Named after the Abbé Larbré, a botanical author. Linn. 10, Or. 3, Nat. Or. *Alsinaceæ.* A small uninteresting weed, succeeding in any common wet soil. Synonymes: 1. *Stellaria aquatica, uliginosa—aquāticā* 1.

LARCH, see *Lārix.*

LĀRIX, *Decandolle.* From tne Celtic, *lar,* fat; on account of the tree producing an abundance of resin. Linn. 21, Or. 10, Nat. Or. *Coniferæ.* All the species of this genus are highly ornamental, and some of them are extensively cultivated for their timber, which is adapted to a variety of useful purposes. The larch grows rapidly in almost any soil, and in any situation, yet its timber can only be brought to perfection when the trees are grown in a clear dry atmosphere, on a cold-bottomed soil, rather moist on the surface. Young plants are obtained from seed, which should be sown in April, on finely-prepared soil. After the seeds are sown, a light roller should be drawn over the bed, to press the seeds firmly into the earth, and they should then have a thin covering of soil. The plants are generally allowed to remain two years in the seed-bed, and afterwards planted into nursery lines, or where they are finally to remain. As the Larch vegetates earlier than most other trees, and suffers more if removed after it has begun to grow, it ought to be transplanted in autumn, or early in spring. We have adopted the names of the species and varieties as given by Mr. Loudon in his very valuable work, the *Arboretum et Fruticetum Britannicum.* Synonymes: 1. Pinus laricina, P. microcarpa, Abies microcarpa. 2. L. pendula, Pinus pendula, P. intermedia, Abies pendula. 3. L. prolifera. 4. L. microcarpa, P. microcarpa. 5. L. dahurica. 6. L. intermedia, P. intermedia. 7. L. sibirica, L. rossica, Pinus L. sibirica.

| | | | | | |
|---|---|---|---|---|---|
| americānā, 1 | . | Apetal | . 3, H. De. T. | N. Amer. | . 1739 |
| pēndūlā, 2 | . | Apetal | . 3, H. De. T. | N. Amer. | . 1739 |
| prolifērā, 3 | . | Apetal | . 3, H. De. T. | | |
| rūbrā, 4 | . | Apetal | . 3, H. De. T. | N. Amer. | . 1760 |
| europēā | . | Apetal | . 3, H. De. T. | Germany | . 1629 |
| commūnis | . | Apetal | . 3, H. De. T. | Germany | . 1629 |
| compactā | . | Apetal | . 3, H. De. T. | | |
| dahūricā, 5 | . | Apetal | . 3, H. De. T. | Dahuria | . 1827 |
| flore-albō | . | Apetal | . 3, H. De. T. | Tyrol | |
| flore-rūbrō | . | Apetal | . 3, H. De. T. | Germany | . 1629 |
| intermēdiā, 6 | . | Apetal | . 3, H. De. T. | Altai | . 1816 |
| lāxā | . | Apetal | . 3, H. De. T. | | |
| pēndūlā | . | Apetal | . 3, H. De. T. | Tyrol | |
| rēpēns | . | Apetal | . 3, H. De. T. | | |
| sibiricā, 7 | . | Apetal | . 3, H. De. S. | Siberia | . 1824 |

LARKSPUR, see *Delphīnīūm.*

LĀRRĒX, *Cavanilles.* In honour of John Anthony de Larrea, a Spanish promoter of the sciences. Linn. 10, Or. 1, Nat. Or. *Zygophyllaceæ.* A mixture of loam, peat, and sand, is best adapted to the growth of these pretty shrubs; and young cuttings will root freely in sand, under a glass.

| | | | | | |
|---|---|---|---|---|---|
| divaricātā | . . | Yellow | . 7, G. Ev. S. B. Ayres | . 1829 |
| nitidā | . . | Yellow | . 6, G. Ev. S. S. Amer. | . 1823 |

LASERPITIUM, *Tournefort.* From *laser,* its gum, and *pix,* pitch; the name of the ancient Silphium. Linn. 5, Or. 2, Nat. Or. *Umbelliferæ.* Mere weeds, growing in any common soil. Synonymes: 1. L. trilobum. 2. L. Libanotis. 3. Cnidium carvifolium. 4. L. Halleri. 5. L. pilosum—*aquilegifoliūm* 1, *archangēlicūm, āspērūm* 2, *athamāniæ, aūrēūm, caucāsicūm* 3, *gāllicūm, G. angustifoliūm, hirsūtūm* 4, *hispidūm* 5, *latifoliūm, marginātūm, meoīdēs, peucedanoīdēs, pilōsūm, pruthēnicūm, scābrum, Silēr, triquētrūm.*

LASERWORT, see *Laserpītīūm.*

LASERWORT, see *Thāpsīā Laserpītīī.*

LASIĀNDRĀ, *Decandolle.* From *lasios,* hairy, and *andros,* a male; alluding to the hairy stamens. Linn. 10, Or. 1, Nat. Or. *Melastomaceæ.* This elegant genus of shrubs well deserves a place in every stove; their large purple blossoms are rather freely produced in panicles. They require to be grown in a mixture of loam, peat, and sand; and cuttings of the young wood will root without difficulty, if planted in the same kind of soil, under a glass, in heat. *Synonymes:* 1. *Pleroma holosericeum, Rhexia holosericea.* 2. *Pleroma Fontanesii, Melastoma granulosa.*

| | | | | | | |
|---|---|---|---|---|---|---|
| argentéum, 1 | . | Purple | . 7, S. Ev. S. Rio Jan. | . 1816 |
| Fontanesiàna, 2 | . | Purple | . S. Ev. S. Rio Jan. | . |

**LASIOBŌTRYS**, *Kunze.* From *lasios*, woolly, and *botrys*, a bunch of grapes. *Linn.* 24, Or. 9, Nat. Or. *Fungi.* This species is found beneath the epidermis of honeysuckle leaves; when mature, it is of a black colour, and generally situated on a paler or colourless portion of the leaf.—*Lonicèræ.*

**LASIOPĒTĂLUM**, *Cassini.* From *lasios*, woolly, and *petalon*, a petal. *Linn.* 16, Or. 7, Nat. Or. *Sterculiaceæ.* These are small bushy shrubs, producing an agreeable contrast in the greenhouse by their ferrugineous leaves and woolly-petalled flowers. They grow in loam and peat, and are increased by ripened cuttings, under a glass.

| | | | | |
|---|---|---|---|---|
| ferrugineúm | . | White | . 6, G. Ev. S. N. Holl. | 1791 |
| parvifórum | . | White | . 6, G. Ev. S. N. Holl. | 1810 |

**LASIŌPŬS**, *Cassini.* From *lasios*, hairy, and *pous*, a foot; alluding to the woolly footstalks of its heads of flowers. *Linn.* 19, Or. 2, Nat. Or. *Compositæ.* This plant has little beauty to recommend it; any common soil suits it, and it may be increased by divisions.

| | | | | |
|---|---|---|---|---|
| oncholdæ | . | Yellow | . 8, H. Her. P. Armenia | . 1834 |

**LASIOSPĒRMUM**, *Lagasca.* From *lasios*, woolly, and *sperma*, a seed; woolly texture of the seeds. *Linn.* 19, Or. 1, Nat. Or. *Compositæ.* Rather pretty plants, of the simplest culture and propagation. *Synonymes:* 1. *Santolina anthemoides.* 2. *crithmifolia.* 3. *eriosperma.* 4. *alpina, erecta.* 5. *rigida.*

| | | | | |
|---|---|---|---|---|
| anthemoldes, 1 | . | Yellow | . 8, H. Ev. Tr. Italy | . 1727 |
| crithmifolìum, 2 | . | Yellow | . 8, F. Ev. Tr. Macedon. | . 1817 |
| eriospérmum, 3 | . | Yellow | . 8, F. Ev. Tr. Italy | . 1816 |
| pedunculare, 4 | . | Yellow | . 7, H. Ev. Tr. Italy | . 1798 |
| rigidùm, 5 | . | Yellow | . 8, F. Ev. Tr. Greece | . 1816 |

**LASTHĒNYX**, *Decandolle.* The meaning of the name not explained. *Linn.* 19, Or. 2, Nat. Or. *Compositæ.* These are rather pretty plants, well adapted for the beds of the flower-border. The seeds should be sown early in spring, or in the previous autumn.

| | | | | |
|---|---|---|---|---|
| califórnica | . | Yellow | . 5, H. A. California | . 1834 |
| glabrátá | . | Yellow | . 5, H. A. California | . 1834 |

**LATĀNIX**, *Commerson.* Latanier is the name of the plant in the Isle of Bourbon. *Linn.* 22, Or. 13, Nat. Or. *Palmaceæ.* A genus of fine middle-sized palms, with plaited fan-like fronds. They delight in a rich strong loam, with a tolerable supply of water. *Synonyme:* 1. *chinensis.*

| | | | | |
|---|---|---|---|---|
| borbónica, 1 | . | Orn. wht. | . Palm. Bourbon | . 1816 |
| glaucophylla | . | Orn. wht. | . Palm. E. Ind. | . 1823 |
| rúbra | . | Orn. wht. | . Palm. Maurit. | . 1788 |

**LATĒRAL**, on one side, or on the sides.

**LATHRĀEX**, *Linn.* From *lathraios*, concealed; in allusion to the plant being found in concealed places. *Linn.* 14, Or. 2, Nat. Or. *Orobanchaceæ.* A very curious little plant, furnished with white fleshy scales in the place of leaves. It is very shy of cultivation, and may be increased by carefully dividing the roots.

| | | | | |
|---|---|---|---|---|
| Squamaria | . | Green | . 4, H. Her. P. Britain | . . |

**LĀTHYRUS**, *Linn.* From *la*, augmentative, and *thouros*, anything exciting; in allusion to the medicinal qualities of the seeds. *Linn.* 17, Or. 4, Nat. Or. *Leguminosæ.* This genus is formed for the most part of very handsome plants when in flower, the larger kinds being well adapted for arbours or shrubberies, where they must be supplied with branches to support them. Any common soil suits them; they are increased by seeds, and some of the perennial kinds by dividing the roots. The seeds of *L. Aphaca* produce intense headach if eaten in any quantity, while the roots of *L. tuberosus* are said to be wholesome food

| | | | | |
|---|---|---|---|---|
| alátùs | . | Purple | . 7, H. Cl. A. Italy | . 1823 |
| altaïcus | . | | H. Her. P. Altai | . 1832 |
| amphicárpus | . | Pink | . 6, H. A. Levant | . 1680 |
| angulátùs | . | Red | . 6, H. A. S. Eur. | . 1683 |

| | | | | | | |
|---|---|---|---|---|---|---|
| ánnûûs | . . | Yellow | . 7, H. Cl. A. S. Eur. | . 162? |
| Aphàca | . . | Yellow | . 6, H. Cl. A. England | . |
| Armitageánûs | . | Pur. blue | 5, H. De. S. Brasil | . 1824 |
| articulátùs | . | Fsh. wht. | 7, H. Cl. A. S. Eur. | . 1640 |
| auriculátùs | . | Purple | . 7, H. Cl. A. S. Eur. | . 1800 |
| califórnicûs | . | Purple | . 6, H. De. Cl. Californ. | . 1826 |
| Cícêrá | . | Red | . 6, H. Cl. A. S. Eur. | . 1633 |
| ciliátûs | . . | | 8, H. A. Naples | . 1832 |
| Clymènûm | . | Blue | . 6, H. Cl. A. Levant | . 1713 |
| cornútûs | . | Purple | . 7, H. Cl. A. | . 1818 |
| decaphýllûs | . | Red lil. | 6, H. De. Cl. N. Amer. | . 1827 |
| grandiflórûs | . | Rose | . 7, H. De. Cl. S. Eur. | . 1814 |
| heládês | . . | Purple | . 7, H. Cl. A. | . 1827 |
| heterophýllûs | . | Flesh | . 8, H. De. Cl. Europe | . 1731 |
| hirsútûs | . | Purple | . 7, H. Cl. A. England | . |
| hírtûs | . . | Purple | . 7, H. A. Europe | . 1800 |
| inconspicûûs | . | Purple | . 7, H. A. Levant | . 1739 |
| incúrvûs | . | Blue | . 7, H. De. Cl. Russia | . 1808 |
| intermédiûs | . | Red | . 8, H. De. Cl. N. Eur. | . 1820 |
| itálicûs | . . | Pink | . 8, H. Cl. A. Italy | . |
| latifolíús | . . | | 8, H. De. Cl. England | . |
| albiflórûs | . | White | . 8, H. De. Cl. Gardens | . |
| leptophýllûs | . | Purple | . 6, H. A. Caucasus | . 1818 |
| longipedunculátûs | Red | . 7, H. A. | . 1817 |
| lusitánicûs | . . | | 7, H. Cl. A. Spain | . 1827 |
| magellánicûs | . | Pur. blue | 6, H. De. Cl. C. Horn. | . 1744 |
| micránthûs | . | Purple | . 4, H. A. S. France | . 1816 |
| mutábilis | . | Pur. red | 7, H. De. Cl. Siberia | . 1825 |
| myrtifolíús | . | Red | . 5, H. De. Cl. Philadel. | . 1822 |
| Nissòlìá | . | Crimson | . 6, H. A. England | . |
| odorátûs | . | Varieg. | . 7, H. Cl. A. Sicily | . 1700 |
| palústris | . | Pa. pur. | 6, H. De. Cl. Britain | . |
| pisifórmis | . | Purple | . 7, H. De. Cl. Siberia | . 1795 |
| polymórphûs | . | Pa. pur. | 7, H. De. Cl. Missouri | . 1824 |
| praténsis | . | Yellow | . 7, H. De. Cl. Britain | . |
| purpûrèó-cærulèscens | . } | Pur. blue | 8, H. De. Tw. Brasil | . 1836 |
| purpûrèûs | . | Purple | . 7, H. Cl. A. Crete | . |
| ròsêûs | . | Red | . 7, H. De. Cl. Iberia | . 1822 |
| rotundifolìûs | . | Rose | . 7, H. De. Cl. Tauria | . 1822 |
| satívûs | . | White | . H. Cl. A. S Eur. | . 1640 |
| setifolìûs | . | Red | . 6, H. A. S. Eur. | . 1739 |
| sphäricûs | . | Crimson | . 6, H. A. S. Eur. | . 1801 |
| spûrìûs | . | Purple | . 7, H. Cl. A. | . 1815 |
| stipulácêûs | . | Purple | . 7, H. Cl. De. Cl. N. York | . 1816 |
| sylvéstris | . | Purple | . 7, H. De. Cl. Britain | . |
| tenuifolìûs | . | Blue | . 7, H. Cl. A. N. Africa | . 1820 |
| tingitánûs | . | Dk. pur. | 7, H. Cl. A. Barbary | . 1680 |
| tuberósûs | . | Red | . 7, H. De. Cl. Holland | . 1596 |
| túmidûs | . | Red | . 7, H. Cl. A. Piedmont | . 1817 |
| venósûs | . | Wht. red | 6, H. De. Cl. Pennsyl. | . |

**LAUREL**, see *Laūrûs.*
**LAUREL CHERRY**, see *Cĕrăsûs Laurocĕrăsûs.*
**LAURESTINE**, see *Vibûrnûm Tínûs.*

**LAUROPHYLLÛS**, *Thunberg.* From *laurus*, a laurel, and *phyllon*, a leaf; in allusion to the similarity of the foliage. *Linn.* 23, Or. 2, Nat. Or. *Urticaceæ.* A shrub of no great beauty, from six to seven feet high, producing its minute green flowers in panicles; it thrives in loam and peat, and may be increased by layers.

| | | | | |
|---|---|---|---|---|
| capénsis | . . | Green | . . G. Ev. S. C. G. H. | . 1801 |

**LAŪRÛS**, *Pliny.* From the Celtic word *blaur*, (laur, the b is dropped) signifying green, in allusion to the foliage of the plants. *Linn.* 9, Or. 1, Nat. Or. *Lauraceæ.* This is a very handsome and interesting genus of plants. The stove and greenhouse kinds do well in a mixture of sandy loam and peat, and ripened cuttings generally root freely in sand, under a glass; the stove species in a moist heat. Among the most interesting and valuable of the hardy kinds is *L. nobilis*, or bay-tree, which is injured by severe frost: it is, therefore, best to protect the plants with mats when young; they will grow freely in the common garden soil, and in the warmer counties where the weather does not hurt them, they attain the size of trees. *L. Benzoin, L. Sassafras*, and several others, are deciduous, and in some situations attain a great size. They may be increased by layers, or cuttings of the roots. The bark of *L. Benzoin* is stimulant and tonic, and in North America it is used in intermittent fevers. In *L. fœtens* an acrid red, or violet juice, is particularly abundant. All the species are more or less aromatic and stomachic. *Synonymes:* 1. *Evosmus albidus.* 2. *Laurus Borbonia.*

| | | | | |
|---|---|---|---|---|
| æstivális | . | Yellow | . 4, H. De. S. N. Amer. | . 1775 |
| aggregátá | . | Orn. yel. | G. Ev. S. China | . 1821 |
| albida, 1 | . | Yellow | . H. De. S. Carolina | . 1824 |
| Bénzôin | . | Yel. grn. | 4, H. De. S. N. Amer. | . 1688 |
| bullátá | . | Green | . 6, G. Ev. S. C. G. H. | . 1823 |
| canariénsis | . | Yel. grn. | G. Ev. T. Canaries | . 1815 |
| caroliénsis, 2 | . | Yel. grn. | 5, H. Ev. T. N. Amer. | . 1806 |

| glabra | . . | Yel. grn. | 5, | H. | Ev. | T. | N. Amer. | 1806 |
|---|---|---|---|---|---|---|---|---|
| obtusa | . . | Yel. grn. | 4, | H. | Ev. | T. | Carolina | 1806 |
| pubescens | . . | Yel. grn. | 4, | H. | Ev. | T. | N. Amer. | 1806 |
| Catesbiana | . . | White | | H. | De. | S. | Carolina | 1820 |
| Chloroxylon | | Grn. wht. | | S. | Ev. | T. | W. Ind. | 1778 |
| coriacea | . . | White | | S. | Ev. | T. | W. Ind. | 1810 |
| crassifolia | . . | White | | S. | Ev. | T. | Cayenne | 1800 |
| Diospyrus | . . | Grn. yel. | 4, | H. | De. | S. | N. Amer. | 1810 |
| exaltata | . . | Wht. yel. | | S. | Ev. | T. | Jamaica | 1800 |
| floribunda | . . | Yel. grn. | | S. | Ev. | T. | W. Ind. | 1800 |
| foetens | . . | Grn. yel. | | G. | Ev. | T. | Madeira | 1760 |
| geniculata | . . | Yellow | 4, | H. | De. | S. | N. Amer. | 1759 |
| indica | . . | Grn. yel. | 7, | G. | Ev. | T. | Madeira | 1665 |
| nivea | . . | | | R. | Ev. | T. | | 1820 |
| nobilis | . . | Yel. wht. | | H. | Ev. | T. | S. Eur. | 1561 |
| crispa | . . | Yel. wht. | 5, | H. | Ev. | T. | | |
| flore-pleno | . | Yel. wht. | 5, | H. | Ev. | T. | | |
| latifolia | . . | Yel. wht. | 5, | F. | Ev. | T. | Asia | . |
| salicifolia | . | Yel. wht. | 4, | H. | Ev. | S. | | |
| undulata | . . | Yel. wht. | 4, | H. | Ev. | T. | | |
| variegata | . | Yel. wht. | 5, | H. | Ev. | T. | | |
| palma | . . | Wht. yel. | | S. | Ev. | S. | W. Ind. | 1824 |
| pendula | . . | | | S. | Ev. | T. | Jamaica | 1800 |
| salicifolia | . | Yel. grn. | 4, | S. | Ev. | T. | W. Ind. | 1826 |
| Sassafras | . . | Grn. yel. | 6, | H. | De. | S. | N. Amer. | 1633 |
| splendens | . . | Yel. grn. | | S. | Ev. | T. | E. Ind. | 1800 |
| thymiflora | . | Yel. grn. | | H. | Ev. | T. | Madagas | 1810 |

**LAVANDULA**, *Linn.* From *lavo*, to wash; in allusion to the use made of its distilled water. *Linn.* 14, Or. 1, Nat. Or. *Labiatæ*. The hardy kinds are the only plants of this genus worth cultivating; they are much esteemed for the fragrance of their flowers, and are most valued when grown in a dry gravelly soil; they are freely increased by cuttings planted in a shady situation. The frame kinds do well in any light rich soil, and are readily increased from young cuttings in the same kind of soil. *Synonyme* : 1. *L. formosa.*

| abrotanoides | . | Lilac | . | 7, | G. | Ev. | S. | Canaries | 1699 |
|---|---|---|---|---|---|---|---|---|---|
| dentata | . . | Lilac | . | 8, | F. | Ev. | S. | S. Eur. | 1597 |
| heterophylla | . | Lilac | . | 6, | H. | Ev. | S. | Hybrid | 1816 |
| latifolia | . . | Lilac | . | 8, | H. | Ev. | S. | S. Eur. | 1568 |
| multifida | . . | Lilac | . | 8, | G. | | S. | S. Eur. | 1597 |
| pinnata | . . | Lilac | . | 6, | G. | Ev. | S. | Madeira | 1777 |
| pubescens, 1 | | Lilac | . | 6, | G. | Ev. | S. | | 1816 |
| spica | . . | Lilac | . | 8, | H. | Ev. | S. | S. Eur. | 1568 |
| Stœchas | . . | Lilac | . | 6, | H. | Ev. | S. | S. Eur. | 1568 |
| vera | . . | Blue | . | 7, | H. | Ev. | S. | S. Eur. | 1568 |
| viridis | . . | Purple | . | 6, | F. | Ev. | S. | Madeira | 1777 |

**LAVATERA**, *Tournefort.* In honour of his friends, the two Lavaters, famous physicians and naturalists of Zurich. *Linn.* 16, Or. 8, Nat. Or. *Malvaceæ.* The greenhouse and frame kinds grow well in any light soil, and are readily increased by cuttings of the ripened wood, planted in the same kind of soil, under a glass. The hardy herbaceous species grow freely in any common soil, and increase by divisions or seeds. The annuals and biennials need only be sown in the open border in spring. *Synonymes*: 1. *Empedoclis.* 2. *undulata.*

| acerifolia | . . | Pink | . | 7, | F. | Ev. | S. | Teneriffe | 1820 |
|---|---|---|---|---|---|---|---|---|---|
| africana | . . | Pink | . | 6, | F. | Ev. | S. | Spain | 1820 |
| ambigua | . . | Purple | . | 8, | H. | | A. | Naples | 1824 |
| arborea | . . | Purple | . | 8, | H. | | B. | Britain | |
| australis | . . | Purple | . | 8, | H. | | A. | S. Eur. | 1820 |
| biennis | . . | Red | . | 8, | H. | | A. | Caucasus | 1819 |
| cretica | . . | Ll. blue | . | 7, | H. | | A. | Candia | 1723 |
| flava, 1 | . . | Yellow | . | 7, | H. | | A. | Sicily | 1818 |
| hispida | . . | Pink | . | 6, | F. | Ev. | S. | Algiers | 1804 |
| lanceolata | . | Purple | . | 8, | H. | | A. | Europe | 1817 |
| lusitanica | . | Purple | . | 8, | F. | Ev. | S. | Portugal | 1748 |
| maritima | . . | White | . | 6, | F. | Ev. | S. | S. Eur. | 1597 |
| micans | . . | Purple | . | 6, | F. | Ev. | S. | Spain | 1796 |
| neapolitana | . | Purple | . | 8, | H. | Her. | P. | Naples | 1818 |
| Olbia | . . | Red pur. | . | 8, | F. | Ev. | S. | Provence | 1570 |
| phœnicea | . . | Pink | . | 6, | G. | Ev. | S. | Canaries | 1816 |
| plebeia | . . | Pale | . | 9, | G. | Her. | P. | N. Holl. | 1820 |
| Pseudo-Olbia, 2 | | Red | . | 8, | F. | Ev. | S. | | 1817 |
| punctata | . . | Pale | . | 8, | H. | | A. | Italy | 1800 |
| salvifoliensis | . | Pink | . | 7, | H. | | B. | | 1821 |
| sylvestris | . | Purple | . | 8, | H. | | A. | Portugal | 1817 |
| thuringiaca | . | Ll. blue | . | 8, | H. | Her. | P. | Germany | 1731 |
| triloba | . . | Ll. pur. | . | 8, | H. | | A. | Spain | 1759 |
| trimestris | . | Flesh | . | 6, | H. | | A. | Spain | 1633 |
| unguiculata | . | Lilac | . | 8, | F. | Ev. | S. | Samos | 1807 |

**LAVENDER**, see *Lavandula.*
**LAVENDER COTTON**, see *Santolina.*
**LAVENIA**, *Swartz.* Supposed to be of Cingalese origin. *Linn.* 19, Or. 1, Nat. Or. *Compositæ.* Mere annual weeds, growing in any common soil—*decumbens, erecta.*
**LAVRADIA**, *Velloza.* In honour of the Marquis of Lavradio, a distinguished patron of botany. *Linn.*

*b,* Or. 1, Nat. Or. *Violaceæ.* This is a very elegant shrub, requiring a mixture of loam, peat, and sand; and cuttings root freely under a glass, in sand, in heat.

| montana | . . . | Purple | . | S. | Ev. | S. | Brazil | . 1826 |
|---|---|---|---|---|---|---|---|---|

**LAWSONIA**, *Linn.* In honour of Isaac Lawson, M.D., author of a Voyage to Carolina. *Linn.* 8, Or. 1, Nat. Or. *Lythraceæ.* Ornamental trees, producing their flowers in panicles or racemes; for culture and propagation, see *Lavradia.* The Egyptian women obtain a paste from the powdered leaves, with which they stain their fingers and feet an orange colour; this they esteem an ornament. It will last for several weeks before there is occasion to renew it. *Synonyme*: 1. *L. inermis, L. spinosa.*

| alba, 1 | . . . | White | . | S. | Ev. | T. | E. Ind. | . 1752 |
|---|---|---|---|---|---|---|---|---|
| purpurea | . . | Purple | . | S. | Ev. | T. | E. Ind. | . 1820 |

**LAX**, loose, supple.
**LAXMANNIA**, *R. Brown.* In honour of E. Laxman, a Siberian traveller. *Linn.* 6, Or. 1, Nat. Or. *Liliaceæ.* An interesting plant, growing freely in loam and peat, and readily increased by divisions.

| gracilis | . . . | Pur. wht. | 6, | G. | Her. | P. | N. Holl. | . 1824 |
|---|---|---|---|---|---|---|---|---|

**LEADWORT**, see *Plumbago.*
**LEAFLETS**, small parts of compound leaves.
**LEAFY**, covered with leaves, or of the consistence of a leaf.
**LEANGIUM**, *Link.* From *leios*, smooth, and *aggeion*, a vessel; alluding to the peridium. *Linn.* 24, Or. 9, Nat. Or. *Fungi.* A genus of minute wart-like *Fungi*, found upon the leaves of mosses, and decaying trunks of trees—*floriforme, Trevelyani.*
**LEATHERWOOD**, see *Dirca.*
**LEATHERY**, thick, of the consistence of leather.
**LEBECKIA**, *Thunberg.* After Lebeck, some unknown botanist. *Linn.* 16, Or. 6, Nat. Or. *Leguminosa.* Plants of some beauty, succeeding in sandy loam and peat, and multiplied by seeds, or cuttings in sand, under a glass.

| contaminata | . | Yellow | . | 4, | G. | Ev. | S. | C. G. H. | . 1787 |
|---|---|---|---|---|---|---|---|---|---|
| cytisoides | . | Yellow | . | 4, | G. | Ev. | S. | C. G. H. | . 1774 |
| sepiaria | . . | Yellow | . | 4, | G. | Ev. | S. | C. G. H. | . 1820 |
| sericea | . . | Yellow | . | 4, | G. | Ev. | S. | C. G. H. | . 1774 |
| subnuda | . . | Yellow | . | 4, | G. | Ev. | S. | C. G. H. | . 1824 |
| subternata | . | Yellow | . | 4, | G. | Ev. | S. | C. G. H. | . 1824 |

**LEBRETONIA**, see *Pavonia.*
**LECANORA**, *Acharius.* From *lekane*, a basin; alluding to the form of the shields. *Linn.* 24, Or. 8, Nat. Or. *Lichenes.* This genus comprises some valuable plants. *L. atra, hæmatomma, parella,* and *tartarea,* are used in dyeing, especially the latter, which is in much request for dyeing woollen yarn—*albella, apochræa, argopholis, atra, brannea, candelaris, polyearpa, carneo-lutea, cerina, cervina, chlorolouca, circinata, coarctata, crassa, effusa, elegans, epigæa, erythrella, frustulosa, fulgens, galactina, gelida, glaucoma, hæmatomma, porphyria, Hagenii, crenulata, Hookeri, hypnorum, lentigera, murorum, oculata, parella, periclea, exigua, rabra, rubricosa, salicina, saxicola, sophodes, Stoneii, subfusca, tartarea-frigida, tuberculosa, Turneri, upsaliensis, varia, ventosa, virella, vitellina.*
**LECHEA**, *Linn.* After G. Leche, a Swedish botanist, who died in 1764. *Linn.* 3, Or. 3, Nat. Or. *Cistaceæ.* Small plants, of no beauty, and the commonest culture. *Synonyme*: 1. *L. major.*

| minor | . . . | White | . | 7, | H. | Her. | P. | Canada. | . 1802 |
|---|---|---|---|---|---|---|---|---|---|
| racemulosa | . | White | . | 7, | H. | Her. | P. | N. Amer. | . 1816 |
| tenuifolia | . . | White | . | 6, | H. | Her. | P. | Virginia | . 1823 |
| thymifolia | . . | White | . | 7, | H. | Her. | P. | Canada | . 1790 |
| villosa, 1 | . . | White | . | 7, | H. | Her. | P. | N. Amer. | . 1812 |

**LECHENAULTIA**, *R. Brown.* Named in compliment to M. Lechenault, a French botanist and traveller. *Linn.* 5, Or. 1, Nat. Or. *Goodeniaceæ.* Very elegant plants when in blossom. They grow best in a mixture of turfy loam, peat, and sand; and cuttings of the young wood root readily in the same kind of soil, under a glass. *Synonyme*; 1. *L. Baxteri.*

| oblata, 1 | . . | Orange | . | 6, | G. | Ev. | S. | N. Holl. | . 1824 |
|---|---|---|---|---|---|---|---|---|---|
| formosa | . . | Scarlet | . | 6, | G. | Ev. | S. | N. Holl. | . 1824 |

**LECIDEA**, *Acharius.* From *lekis*, a saucer, and *eidos*, like; in allusion to the saucer-like shields. *Linn.* 24, Or. 8, Nat. Or. *Lichenes.* A very extensive genus of *Fungi*, found in almost every situation, and at all seasons of the year. *Synonymes*: 1. *Lichen*

escharoides. 2. Lichen atrocarpus. 3. Lichen calvus
—abietina, alabastrina, albă, albō-cærulăscĕns, tŭrgĭdă, anōmălă, anthracĭna, aromătĭcă, ătrŏ-cinĕrĕă, ătrŏ-ălbă, ătrŏ-virĕns, geogrăphĭcă, ătrŏ flăvă, ătrŏrăfă, cæsĭŏ-rŭfă, cândĭdă, canăscĕns, carnĕŏlă, cinĕrĕŏ-fŭscă, citrinĕllă, cŏnflŭĕns, conspurcătă, coracĭnă, cortĭcŏlă, dædălĕă, declpĭĕns, decŏlōrăns, granulōsă 1, dolōsă, Ehrhartiănă, epipŏllă, escharoĭdĕs, fumōsă 2, fŭscŏ-ătră, fŭscŏ-lŭtĕă, ichmadŏphĭlă, immĕrsă, incănă, lapĭctădă, Lightfŏŏtĭă, lăcĭdă, lŭrĭdă, lutĕŏlă, lutĕŏ-ălbă, marmŏrĕă, melĭzĕă, mĭcrophŷllă, miscĕllă, Œdĕrĭ, orŏsthĕă, parasĕmă, pĕtrĕă, pholidĭŏtă, pŏlŷtrŏpă, quĕrnĕă, rĭvulōsă, rubĭfōrmĭs, rupĕstrĭs 3, sabulĕtōrŭm, gĕŏchrŏă, sanguinărĭă, scabrōsă, scalārĭs, silĭcĕă, spĕĭrĕă, sulphŭrĕă, uligĭnōsă, verruculōsă, vesiculārĭs, virĭdĕscĕns.

LECŶTHĬS, Læffling. From lecythos, an oil-jar; in allusion to the form of the seed-vessels. Linn. 13, Or. 1, Nat. Or. Lecythidaceæ. The soil best adapted to these plants is a mixture of loam and sand, and they require to be kept in a strong heat. Cuttings of the ripened wood will root in sand, under a glass, in heat. The fleshy seeds of Lecythis are eatable, but leave a bitter taste in the mouth.

| | | | | | |
|---|---|---|---|---|---|
| adatĭmōn | . . | . Yel. wht. | 8. Ev. 8. | Maranh. | . 1825 |
| amără | . . | . Yel. wht. | 8. Ev. 8. | Guiana . | . 1825 |
| bractĕătă | . . | . Yel. wht. | 8. Ev. 8. | Maranh. | . 1825 |
| grandiflōră | . . | . Yel. wht. | 8. Ev. 8. | Trinidad | . 1824 |
| mĭnŏr | . . | . Yel. wht. | 8. Ev. 8. | Carthage | . 1825 |
| parviflōră | . . | . Yel. wht. | 8. Ev. 8. | Trinidad | . 1825 |

LEDEBŪRĬĂ, Link. After M. Ledebour, a botanical author. Linn. 5, Or. 2, Nat. Or. Umbelliferæ. L. hyacinthina is possessed of some beauty, and is of very simple cultivation. Synonyme: 1. Tragium tauricum.

| | | | | | |
|---|---|---|---|---|---|
| hyacĭnthĭnă | . . | . Grnsh. wht. | 0. Bu. P. E. Ind. . | . 1832 |

pimpinellŏĭdĕs 1.
LEDON GUM, see Cistŭs Lĕdŏn.
LEDŬM, Linn. From ledon, the Greek name for a plant now known as the Cistus Ledum. In foliage the present genus agrees with the plant of the ancients. Linn. 10, Or. 1, Nat. Or. Ericaceæ. This is an ornamental genus of plants, well suited for the shrubbery, where they form a fine contrast to Rhododendrons. They thrive best in bog earth, and young plants are obtained from layers, treated in the same way as the Rhododendron. Synonyme: 1. L. grœnlandicum.

| | | | | | | |
|---|---|---|---|---|---|---|
| canadĕnsĕ, 1 | . | . White | . 4, | H. Ev. S. | Canada . | . |
| latĭfŏlĭŭm | . | . White | . 4, | H. Ev. S. | N. Amer. | . 1763 |
| palŭstrĕ | . | . White | . 4, | H. Ev. S. | Europe . | . 1762 |
| decŭmbĕns | . | . White | . 4, | H. Ev. S. | Hud. Bay | . 1762 |

LEĔA, Linn. In honour of James Lee, founder of the Hammersmith nursery, and whose grandson is the present proprietor. Linn. 5, Or. 1, Nat. Or. Vitaceæ. Plants only worthy of cultivation in general collections. A mixture of loam and peat suits them well, and good sized cuttings root freely in sand, under a glass, in heat.

| | | | | | | |
|---|---|---|---|---|---|---|
| æquătă | . . | . Green | . 8. Ev. | 8. E. Ind. . | . 1777 |
| crĭspă | . . | . White | . 8. Her. | P. C. G. H. . | . 1767 |
| hĭrtă | . . | . Green | . 10, 8. Ev. | 8. E. Ind. . | . 1823 |
| macrophŷllă | . | . White | . 8. Ev. | 8. E. Ind. . | . 1806 |
| robŭstă | . . | . Green | . 11, 8. Ev. | 8. E. Ind. . | . 1823 |
| sambucĭnă | . | . Yellow | . 10, 8. Ev. | 8. E. Ind. . | . 1790 |

LEE CHEE, see Euphŏrĭă Lĭtchĭ.
LEEK, see Allĭŭm Pŏrrŭm.
LEĔRSĬĂ, Swartz. After J. D. Leers, a German botanist. Linn. 3, Or. 2, Nat. Or. Gramineæ. These plants possess little to recommend them. They grow readily in any common soil, and are increased by seeds.

| | | | | | |
|---|---|---|---|---|---|
| austrālĭs | . . . | . Apetal | . 7, | Grass. | N. Holl. . | . 1819 |
| oryzoĭdĕs | . . | . Apetal | . 7, | Grass. | Levant . | . 1793 |
| virginĭcă | . . | . Apetal | . 7, | Grass. | N. Amer. | . 1770 |

LEGUME, } a pod, the fruit of leguminous plants.
LEGUMEN, }

LEGUMINOUS, plants which bear legumes, or pods, such as the pea, the bean, &c.
LEIMANTHĬŬM, Michaux. From leimon, a meadow, and anthos, a flower. Linn. 23, Or. 1, Nat. Or. Melanthaceæ. These plants are worth cultivating. They thrive well in a peat soil, in a damp situation, and are increased by seeds. Synonymes: 1.

Melanthium hybridum, latifolium, racemosum. 2. monoicum, polygamum. 3. virginicum, Helonias virginica, Veratrum virginicum.

| | | | | | |
|---|---|---|---|---|---|
| hybrĭdŭm, 1 | . | . White | . 6, | H. Her. P. N. Amer. | . 1822 |
| monoĭcŭm, 2 | . | . Brown | . 6, H. Her. P. N. Amer. | . 1817 |
| virginĭcŭm, 8 | . | . Brown | . 6, H. Her. P. N. Amer. | . 1768 |

LEMANĔĂ, Bory. In honour of M. Leman, a French botanist. Linn. 24, Or. 7, Nat. Or. Algæ. This is rather a curious genus; the species are always found floating in fresh water rivers—fluviătĭlĭsmĕdĭă, torulōsă.

LEMNĂ, Linn. From lepis, a scale; in reference to the form of the plants. Linn. 21, Or. 1, Nat. Or. Pistiaceæ. Annual weeds, found floating in stagnant water, and known to most under the name of Duckweed—gĭbbă, mĭnŏr, polyrhĭză, trĭsŭlcă.

LEMON-GRASS, see Cymbopŏgŏn Schœnănthŭs.
LENS, see Ervŭm Lĕns.
LENTICULAR, lens, or pea-shaped.
LENTIGĬNŌSŬS, freckled, pimpled.
LENTIL, see Ervŭm Lĕns.
LEOCARPŬS, Link. From leios, smooth, and karpos, a fruit; in allusion to the smooth peridium. Linn. 24, Or. 9, Nat. Or. Fungi. This is found in clusters on rotten wood, and has the appearance of being varnished with vermilion. Synonyme: 1. Lycoperdon fragile—vernicōsŭs 1.

LEONŌTĬS, Persoon. From leon, a lion, and ous, an ear; in reference to the fancied resemblance in the corolla. Linn. 14, Or. 1, Nat. Or. Labiatæ. Fine ornamental plants. They require to be grown in loam and peat, and should have plenty of air to allow of their flowering in perfection. Cuttings root in sand, under a glass, in heat. L. nepetifolia requires the treatment commonly given to tender annuals. Synonymes: 1. Phlomis Leonurus. 2. P. Leonitis.

| | | | | | |
|---|---|---|---|---|---|
| intermĕdĭă | . | . Orange | . 9, S. Ev. 8. | C. G. H. | . 1822 |
| Leonūrŭs, 1 | . | . Scarlet | . 11, G. Ev. 8. | C. G. H. | . 1712 |
| nepetæfŏlĭă | . | . Orange | . 9, 8. | A. E. Ind. . | . 1778 |
| ovătă, 2 | . | . Orange | . 6, 8. | A. C. G. H. | . 1713 |

LEONTĬCĔ, Linn. Abridged from Leontopetalon, which is derived from leon, a lion, and petalon, a leaf; because of the resemblance of the leaf of L. leontopetalon to the impression of a lion's foot. Linn. 6, Or. 1, Nat. Or. Berberaceæ. Plants of little beauty, succeeding in any common soil, and increased by offsets, or seeds.

| | | | | | |
|---|---|---|---|---|---|
| altăĭcă | . . . | . Yellow | . 4, | F. Tu. P. Siberia . | . 1822 |
| Chrysŏgŏnŭm | . | . Yellow | . 8, F. Tu. P. Levant . | . 1740 |
| leontopĕtălŏn | . | . Yellow | . 4, F. Tu. P. Levant . | . 1597 |
| odessănă | . . | . Yellow | . 4, F. Tu. P. Odessa . | . 1828 |
| vesicărĭă | . . | . Yellow | . 5, F. Tu. P. Siberia . | . 1821 |

LEONTŎDŎN, Linn. From leon, a lion, and odous, a tooth; in allusion to the tooth-like divisions of the leaves. Linn. 19, Or. 1, Nat. Or. Compositæ. Herbaceous plants, of no value. They grow in any common soil, and increase freely by seeds, or divisions of the roots. Synonymes: 1. Prenanthes bulbosus. 2. Taraxacum ceratophorum. 3. T. glaucanthum. 4. T. bicolor. 5. Leontodon lividus. 6. L. alpinus—alpīnŭs, bessarābĭcŭs, bulbōsŭs 1, cichorācĕŭs, ceratŏphŏrŭs 2, corniculātŭs, eriŏpŏdĕs, erythrospĕrmŭs, glaucănthŏs 3, glaucĕscĕns, lævĭgătŭs, leucānthŏs 4, nĭgrĭcăns, obovātŭs, palăstrĭs, serŏtĭnŭs, Stevĕnĭĭ, tarăxăcŭm.

LEONTOPŎDĬŬM, R. Brown. From leon, a lion, and pous, a foot; the heads of the flowers have been fancifully likened to a lion's foot. Linn. 19, Or. 2, Nat. Or. Compositæ. This plant does best cultivated in peat soil; it is well suited for ornamenting rock-work, and is increased by seeds, or divisions of the roots. Synonymes: 1. vulgare, Gnaphalium Leontopodium.

| | | | | | |
|---|---|---|---|---|---|
| helvĕtĭcŭm, 1 | . | . Yellow | . 6, | H. Her. P. Austria . | . 1776 |

LEONŪRŬS, Linn. From leon, a lion, and oura, a tail; in allusion to the appearance of the spike of flowers. Linn. 14, Or. 1, Nat. Or. Labiatæ. The herbaceous species grow freely in common garden soil, and increase readily by seeds. The other kinds require to be treated similar to other hardy and half-hardy annuals and biennials. Synonymes: 1. L. crispus. 2. L. villosus, L. condensatus. 3. L. heterophyllus. 4. L. altaicus, L. multifidus.

| | | | | | |
|---|---|---|---|---|---|
| cardĭăcă | . . | . Red | . 6, H. Her. P. | Britain . | . |
| crĭspŭs, 1 | . | . Red | . 7, H. Her. P. | Siberia . | . 1658 |

| villōsūs, 2 | . | Purple | . 7, H. Her. P. Tauria . . | 1820 |
| alcārūs | . . | Pink | . 6, H. Her. P. Nepal . . | 1824 |
| lanātūs | . | Yellow | . 7, H. Her. P. Siberia . . | 1752 |
| Marrubiastrūm | . | Purple | . 6, H.    A. Europe . . | 1710 |
| multifidūs | . . | Purple | . 6, H.    A.        . . | 1817 |
| neglēctūs | . | Purple | . 7, H.    B. S. Eur. . | 1818 |
| sibirīcūs, 3 | . | Red | . 7, H.    B. Siberia . . | 1759 |
| tatārīcūs, 4 | . | Flesh | . 9, H.    B. Russia . . | 1756 |

LEOPARD'S-BANE, see Dorōnīcŭm.

LEOPARD'S BANE, see Arnīcā Dorōnīcā.

LEOPOLDINĬA. Named by Martius, in memory of the late Empress of Brazil. *Linn.* 21, Or. 6, Nat. Or. *Palmaceæ.* A fine palm, requiring similar treatment to other Brazilian palms.

| pŭlchrā | . | Palm. Brazil . . . | 1825 |

LEOTĬA, *Hill.* The meaning is not explained. *Linn.* 24, Or. 9, Nat. Or. *Fungi.* A genus of very little interest, found on the ground in moist woods, or on trees—*infundibuliformis, imbricā, nānā.*

LEPANTHĔS, *Swartz.* From *lepos,* bark, or *lepis,* small, and *anthos,* a flower; the plants of this genus have very small flowers, and grow upon the bark of trees. *Linn.* 20, Or. 1, Nat. Or. *Orchidaceæ.* This is one of the most pigmy of orchideæ, with the habit of a *Pleurothallis.* It can only be grown under a bell-glass, among damp moss, in a cool part of the house.

| tridentātā | . . . Yel. pur. | . 1, S. Epi. Jamaica |

LEPECHINĬA, *Willdenow.* In honour of John Lepechin, a Russian botanist. *Linn.* 14, Or. 1, Nat. Or. *Labiatæ.* Rather pretty plants, growing well in a mixture of peat and loam, and increased by cuttings, planted under a glass. *L. spicata* requires to be protected in frosty weather. *Synonyme:* 1. *Horminum caulescens.*

| chenopodifolĭā | . | Red | . 7, H. Her. P. Siberia . . | 1818 |
| spicātā, 1 | . . | Pa. yel. | . 7, F. Her. P. Mexico . . | 1800 |

LEPIDAGATHIS, *Willdenow.* From *lepis,* a scale, and *agathis,* a ball. *Linn.* 14, Or. 2, Nat. Or. *Acanthaceæ.* This genus is nearly related to *Justicia;* it thrives well in any light rich soil; and cuttings of the young wood, planted in the same kind of soil, and placed under a glass, will root in a very short time.

| cristātā | . . . | S. Her. P. E. Ind. . . | 1820 |

LEPIDĬUM, *R. Brown.* From *lepis,* a scale; in allusion to the shape of the pods, which appear like little scales. *Linn.* 15, Nat. Or. *Cruciferæ.* Most of these plants are uninteresting, and none of them pretty. *L. sativum* is the well-known garden cress. They are all easily increased by seeds sown in the open ground. *Synonymes:* 1. *Thlaspi campestre.* 2. *Cochlearia Draba.* 3. *Thlaspi hirtum.* 4. *Lepidium graminifolium.* 5. *L. graminifolium.*

| satīvūm | . . | White | . 6, H.    A. Persia . . | 1548 |
| crispūm | . . | White | . 6, H.    A. Persia . . | 1548 |
| latifolĭūm | . . | White | . 6, H.    A. Persia . . | 1548 |

*affīnē, bonariensē, campestrē* 1, *capensē, cardaminēs, chalepensē, cordātūm, coronopifolĭūm, crassifolĭūm, Cummingiānūm, cuneifolĭūm, densiflōrūm, divaricātūm, Drabā* 2, *Eklonīī, Gussōnī, hirtūm* 3, *hyssopifolĭūm, Ibērĭs* 4, *incīsūm, latifolĭūm, lineārē, lyrātūm, Menziēsĭī, micranthūm, Novæ-Hollāndĭæ, olerācēūm, perfolĭātūm, Piscidĭūm, ruderālē, spinōsūm, subulātūm, suffrutīcōsūm* 5, *vesicārĭūm, virginĭcūm.*

LEPIDOSPERMĀ, *Labillardière.* From *lepis,* a scale, and *sperma,* a seed; in allusion to the scaly appearance of the seeds. *Linn.* 3, Or. 1, Nat. Or. *Cyperaceæ.* This plant is not possessed of much interest; it will grow in any kind of soil, and is increased by divisions.

| gladiātā | . . . . Apetal . | . 7, Grass. N. Holl. . | 1819 |

LEPIDOTED, covered with scurfy dots.

LEPRARĬA, *Linn.* From *lepra,* leprosy; the plants on which the species grow appear as if diseased with leprosy. *Linn.* 24, Or. 8, Nat. Or. *Lichenes.* Found most common on old pales, or rocks. They are generally of a yellowish cast. *L. ochracea* is one of the Lichens used in dyeing—*chlorīnā, flāvā, ochrācēā, vīrēscēns.*

LEPROUS, covered with spots, or scales.

LEPROUSLY-SILVERY, } covered with white or silvery
LEPROUSLY-WHITE,  } scales, or scurf, resembling the leprosy.

LEPROUSLY-TOMENTOSE, covered with shaggy down, having the appearance of leprosy.

LEPTALĔUM, *Decandolle.* From *leptaleos,* slender; in allusion to the slender filiform leaves. *Linn.* 15, Nat. Or. *Cruciferæ.* The seed of this annual species has only to be sown in the open ground. *Synonyme:* 1. *Sisymbrium filifolium.*

| filifolĭūm, 1 | . . Yellow | . 6, H.    A. Siberia . . | 1820 |

LEPTANDRĀ, *Nuttall.* From *leptos,* slender, and *aner,* an anther. *Linn.* 2, Or. 1, Nat. Or. *Scrophulariaceæ.* The plants of this genus are well adapted for ornamenting flower-borders, and are readily increased by divisions of the roots. *Synonymes:* 1. *Veronica sibirica.* 2. *V. virginica.*

| sibirĭcā, 1 | . . | Blue | . 7, H. Her. P. Dauria . . | 1779 |
| virginĭcā, 2 | . . | White | . 7, H. Her. P. Virginia . . | 1714 |
| incarnātā | . . | Flesh | . 7, H. Her. P. Virginia . . | 1714 |

LEPTANTHŬS, *Michaux.* From *leptos,* slender, and *anthos,* a flower; the tube of the flower is long and slender. *Linn.* 3, Or. 1, Nat. Or. *Pontederaceæ.* This species may be preserved in a peat soil, in a very moist situation; it is increased by offsets.

| graminĕūs | . . . Yellow . 7, H. Aq. P. N. Amer. . | 1823 |

LEPTOCARPÆĀ, *Decandolle.* From *leptos,* slender, and *karpos,* a fruit; in allusion to the slender fruitpods. *Linn.* 15, Nat. Or. *Cruciferæ.* The seed of this annual should be sown in the open ground early in spring. *Synonymes:* 1. *Turritis Loeselii, Sisymbrium Loeselii—Loeselīī* 1.

LEPTOCARPŬS, *R. Brown.* From *leptos,* slender, and *karpos,* a fruit. *Linn.* 22, Or. 3, Nat. Or. *Restiaceæ.* A mere weed, requiring to be grown in the greenhouse, and increased by divisions. *Synonyme:* 1. *Schœnodum tenax—tēnāx* 1.

LEPTOCHLŌĀ, *Beauvois.* From *leptos,* slender, and *chloa,* grass; in allusion to the slender habit of the plants. *Linn.* 3, Or. 2, Nat. Or. *Gramineæ.* This genus consists for the most part of annuals. They grow in any soil, and are increased by seeds. *Synonyme:* 1. *Poa chinensis.*

| cynosuroidēs | . . | Apetal | . 5, Grass. E. Ind. . . | 1824 |
| domingensīs | . . | Apetal | . 6, Grass. W. Ind. . . | 1820 |
| filiformīs, 1 | . . | Apetal | . 7, Grass. China . . | 1820 |
| procērā | . . | Apetal | . 7, Grass. Brasil . . | 1823 |
| tenerrīmā | . . | Apetal | . 6, Grass. China . . | 1820 |
| virgātā | . . | Apetal | . 7, Grass. W. Ind. . . | 1727 |

LEPTOMERĬĀ, *R. Brown.* From *leptos,* slender, and *meris,* a part. *Linn.* 5, Or. 1, Nat. Or. *Santalaceæ.* Ornamental plants, succeeding well in a soil composed of loam and peat in equal parts; and cuttings of the ripened wood will root readily in sand, under a glass. *Synonyme:* 1. *Thesium drupaceum.*

| acīdā | . . . | White | . . G. Ev. S. N. Holl. . | 1823 |
| Billardĭerī, 1 | . . | White | . . G. Ev. S. N. Holl. . | 1823 |

LEPTOMĬTŬS, *Agardh.* From *leptos,* slender, and *mitos,* a thread. *Linn.* 24, Or. 7, Nat. Or. *Algæ.* These plants are found floating in the water. They consist of very slender intertangled filaments, from the extreme fineness of which the generic name is contrived—*clavātūs, lactēūs, minutissīmūs, nānūs.*

LEPTOPHYLLŬS, slender-leaved.

LEPTOSIPHŌN, *Bentham.* From *leptos,* slender, and *siphon,* a tube; in allusion to the slenderness of the tube of the corolla. *Linn.* 5, Or. 1, Nat. Or. *Polemoniaceæ.* These are very elegant annuals, well worthy of a place in every flower-border. The seed should be sown in a peat soil. Seeds sown in autumn will flower in April and May, and seed sown in spring will produce flowers in autumn.

| androsācēūs | . . Blue wht. | 8, H.    A. California . | 1833 |
| densiflōrūs | . . Purple | . 6, H.    A. California . | 1833 |
| corollā-albā | . . White | . 6, H.    A. California . | 1833 |

LEPTOSPERMŬM, *Forster.* From *leptos,* slender, and *sperma,* a seed; in allusion to the small narrow seeds. *Linn.* 12, Or. 1, Nat. Or. *Myrtaceæ.* All the plants of this genus are well worthy of extensive cultivation, as well for the neatness of their foliage as for the beauty of their blossoms. They thrive best in a mixture of loam, peat, and sand, and cuttings root in sand, under a glass; they may also be raised from seeds, but plants from cuttings are preferable, as they flower when young, and those raised from seeds do not flower till they become large. *Synonymes:* 1. *Billotia flexuosa.* 2. *L. grandifolium.* 3. *B. marginata.* 4. *L. stellatum.*

| arachnoidēūm | . . White | . 6, G. Ev. S. N. S. W. . | 1795 |
| attenuātūm | . . White | . 6, G. Ev. S. N. S. W. . | 1795 |

| | | | | |
|---|---|---|---|---|
| baccātūm . . | . White . | 6, G. Ev. S. N. Holl. | 1790 |
| emarginātūm . | . White . | 6, G. Ev. S. N. Holl. | 1818 |
| flavéscēns . . | . White . | 6, G. Ev. S. N. Holl. | 1787 |
| flexuosūm, 1 . | . White . | 6, G. Ev. S. N. Holl. | 1823 |
| grandiflorūm, 2 | . White . | 6, G. Ev. S. N. Holl. | 1810 |
| imbricātūm . . | . White . | 6, G. Ev. S. N. Holl. | 1823 |
| juniperīnūm . . | . White . | 6, G. Ev. S. N. Holl. | 1790 |
| lanīgerūm . . | . White . | 6, G. Ev. S. N. Holl. | 1774 |
| marginātūm, 3 . | . White . | 6, G. Ev. S. N. Holl. | 1820 |
| multicaulē . . | . White . | 6, G. Ev. S. N. Holl. | 1824 |
| obliqūūm . . | . White . | 6, G. Ev. S. N. Holl. | 1800 |
| obtūsūm . . | . White . | 6, G. Ev. S. | 1820 |
| parvifolīūm . . | . White . | 6, G. Ev. S. N. Holl. | 1789 |
| pendūlūm . . | . White . | 7, G. Ev. S. N. Holl. | |
| porophyllūm . | . White . | 6, G. Ev. S. N. S. W. | 1800 |
| scopārīūm . . | . White . | 6, G. Ev. S. N. Zeal. | 1772 |
| grandiflorūm . | . White . | 7, G. Ev. S. Pt. Jack. | 1817 |
| rubricaulē . . | . White . | 6, G. Ev. S. N. S. W. | 1817 |
| serīcēūm . . | . White . | 6, G. Ev. S. N. S. W. | 1818 |
| squarrōsūm . . | . White . | 7, G. Ev. S. N. Holl. | |
| thymifolīūm . . | . White . | 6, G. Ev. S. N. Holl. | 1824 |
| triloculārē . . | . White . | 6, G. Ev. S. N. Holl. | 1800 |
| tuberculātūm, 4 | . White . | 6, G. Ev. S. N. Holl. | 1816 |

**LEPTOSTĒLMĀ**, *D. Don.* From *leptos*, slender, and *stelma*, a crown. *Linn.* 19, Or. 2, Nat. Or. *Compositæ.* This is a strong-growing plant, attaining the height of seven or eight feet; the flowers are produced in large panicles. It will grow well in a rich light soil, protected from severe frosts, and may be increased by seeds, or by separating the roots.

| | | | | |
|---|---|---|---|---|
| maximūm . . . . | . Whitsh. | 9, F. Her. P. Mexico . . | 1827 |

**LEPTOSTRŌMĀ**, *Fries.* From *leptos*, thin, and *stroma*, a layer; in allusion to the thin consistence of the species. *Linn.* 24, Or. 9, Nat. Or. *Fungi.* These species are found on the stalks of ferns, and on the leaves of some plants—*caricīnūm, filicīnūm, scirpīnūm, Spiræā.*

**LEPTOTĒS**, *Lindley.* From *leptos*, slender; in allusion to the leaves. *Linn.* 20, Or. 1, Nat. Or. *Orchidaceæ.* This is a pretty little species, growing rather freely among broken potsherds, decayed vegetable matter, and moss, and may be increased by divisions.

| | | | | |
|---|---|---|---|---|
| bicolōr . . . . | . Wht. red | 4, S. Epi. Brasil . . | 1831 |

**LEPYRŌDIĀ**. *R. Brown.* From *lepyrodes*, scaly; because the bracteas are within the scales of the spike. *Linn.* 22, Or. 3, Nat. Or. *Restiaceæ.* This plant requires the protection of the greenhouse. A mixture of light sand, loam, and peat, in equal portions, suits it well, and it may be increased by dividing the roots.

| | | | | |
|---|---|---|---|---|
| gracīlīs . . . . | . Apetal. . | 5, Grass. N. Holl. . . | 1824 |

**LĒRIĀ.** Named by Decandolle, in compliment to his friend M. Leri. *Linn.* 19, Or. 2, Nat. Or. *Compositæ.* Mere biennial weeds. They are natives of the West Indies. *Synonymes:* 1. *Tussilago nutans—albicāns, nūtāns* 1, *pumilā.*

**LĒSKĒĀ**, *Hedwig.* In honour of N. G. Leske, professor of natural history at Marburg. *Linn.* 24, Or. 5, Nat. Or. *Fungi.* A genus of mosses, sometimes united to *Hypnum*, which it very much resembles in habit. They are found during spring and summer on the trunks of trees, &c. *Synonymes:* 1. *Hypnum atrovirens, attenuatum.* 2. *Pterogonium rotundifolium.* 3. *Hypnum medium, inundatum—complanātā, dendroīdēs, incurvātā* 1, *iulācēā* 2, *polyānthā, polycārpā* 3, *pulchēllā, ruffescēns, serīcēā, trichomanoīdēs.*

**LESPĒDEZĀ**, *Michaux.* In honour of M. Lespedez, once governor of Florida, and a great patron of botany. *Linn.* 17, Or. 4, Nat. Or. *Leguminosæ.* Very showy plants when in flower. The herbaceous kinds grow well in peat borders, and are increased by dividing the roots in spring. The shrubby kinds must be grown in a mixture of sand and peat; and cuttings of the young wood root readily in sand, under a glass. The seeds of the annual kinds should be sown in a peat border, in a sheltered situation. *Synonymes:* 1. *Anthyllis cuneata.* 2. *Hedysarum junceum.* 3. *L. hirta.* 4. *L. divergens.* 5. *L. reticulata.* 6. *L. sessilliflora.*

| | | | | |
|---|---|---|---|---|
| angustifolīā . . | . Pa. pur. | 6, H. Her. P. N. Amer. | 1800 |
| capitātā . . . | . Striped . | 6, H. Her. P. N. Amer. | 1789 |
| ericāērpā, 1 . . | . Violet . | 7, O. Ev. S. Nepal . . | 1819 |
| fruticōsā . . . | . Purple . | 7, H. De. S. Virginia . | 1739 |
| glomerātā . . . | . Purple . | 7, S. Tw. A. E. Ind. . . | 1819 |
| juncēā, 2 . . . | . White . | 7, H. Ev. S. Siberia . . | 1776 |
| polystāchyā . . | . White . | 7, H. Her. P. N. Amer. . | 1789 |

| | | | | |
|---|---|---|---|---|
| procūmbēns . | . Purple | . 7, H. De. Tr. N. Amer. . | 1816 |
| prostrātā . . | . Purple | . 7, H. De. Tr. N. Amer. . | 1810 |
| Stūvei . . . | . Purple | . 7, H. A. N. Amer. . | 1824 |
| villōsā, 3 . . | . White . | 7, H. Her. P. N. Amer. . | 1819 |
| violācēā . . | . Violet . | 7, H. Her. P. N. Amer. . | 1789 |
| divergēns, 4 . | . Violet . | 7, H. Her. P. N. Amer. . | 1800 |
| reticulātā, 5 . | . Purple | . H. Her. P. N. Amer. . | 1816 |
| sessiliflorā, 6 | . Purple | . 7, H. Her. P. N. Amer. . | |

**LESSĒRTIĀ**, *Decandolle.* In honour of the Baron Benjamin Delessert, of Paris, a most distinguished promoter of botany, and author of the *Icones*, published at Paris, in 1823. *Linn.* 10, Or. 10, Nat. Or. *Leguminosæ.* The shrubby and herbaceous kinds are elegant little plants, requiring the same treatment as *Swainsonia.* The annual species should be sown in pots early in spring, and placed in the greenhouse, and when about two inches high, to be planted singly into small pots, and shifted into larger ones as they grow.

| | | | | |
|---|---|---|---|---|
| annūā . . . . | . Red . | 6, G. A. C. G. H. . | 1731 |
| annulārīs . . | . Purple | . 7, G. A. C. G. H. . | 1816 |
| brachystāchyā | . Purple | . 7, G. Ev. S. C. G. H. . | 1826 |
| diffūsā . . . | . Red . | 7, G. Tr. A. C. G. H. . | 1792 |
| falcifōrmīs . . | . Purple | . 7, G. Ev. S. C. G. H. . | 1826 |
| fruticōsā . . | . Purple | . 7, G. Ev. S. C. G. H. . | 1826 |
| perēnnāns . . | . Red . | 8, G. Her. P. C. G. H. . | 1776 |
| procūmbēns . | . Purple | . 6, G. Her. P. C. G. H. . | 1753 |
| pūlchrā . . . | . Red . | 5, G. Ev. S. C. G. H. . | 1817 |

**LESTIBUDĒSIĀ**, *Thouars.* In honour of F. J. Lestiboudois, a Flemish botanist. *Linn.* 5, Or. 1, Nat. Or. *Amarantaceæ.* These plants are not possessed of much beauty. A light rich soil suits all the species well. *Synonyme:* 1. *Celosia paniculata.*

| | | | | |
|---|---|---|---|---|
| paniculātā, 1 . | . Pa. yel. | . 7, S. B. Jamaica . | 1733 |
| trigynā . . . | . White . | 8, S. B. Senegal. . | 1777 |
| virgātā . . . | . Green . | 9, S. Ev. S. . | 1815 |

**LETTSŌMIĀ**, *Ruiz and Pavon.* In honour of J. C. Lettsom, M.D., F.R.S., a famous English naturalist, and author of a work on the Means of Preserving Objects of Natural History in 1772. *Linn.* 13, Or. 1, Nat. Or. *Ternstromiaceæ.* A very beautiful shrub. It must be grown in the stove, in the same kind of soil as recommended for *Leptomeria.*

| | | | | |
|---|---|---|---|---|
| tomentōsā . . . | . White . | . 8. Ev. S. Peru . . | 1823 |

**LETTUCE**, see *Lactūcā.*

**LEUCADĒNDRŌN**, *Linn.* From *leukos*, white, and *dendron*, a tree; in allusion to the white leaves. *Linn.* 14, Or. 2, Nat. Or. *Proteaceæ.* A genus of splendid evergreen shrubs, with handsome foliage, and heads of yellow flowers. *L. argenteum*, or the Silvertree, grows to the height of fifteen or twenty feet, with beautiful silky leaves; it is on that account admirably adapted for ornamenting conservatories. They grow best in loam and peat, with a small portion of sand, provided the pots are carefully drained, and not overwatered. Cuttings of the ripened wood will root readily planted in sand, under a glass. *Synonyme:* 1. *Protea stellaris.*

| | | | | |
|---|---|---|---|---|
| abietīnūm . . | . Yellow | . 7, G. Ev. S. C. G. H. . | 1789 |
| adscendēns . . | . Yellow | . 7, G. Ev. S. C. G. H. . | 1774 |
| æmūlūm . . | . Yellow | . 7, G. Ev. S. C. G. H. . | 1789 |
| angustātūm . . | . Yellow | . 6, G. Ev. S. C. G. H. . | 1820 |
| argentēūm . . | . Yellow | . 8, G. Ev. S. C. G. H. . | 1693 |
| buxifolīūm . . | . Yellow | . G. Ev. S. C. G. H. . | 1812 |
| caudātūm . . | . Yellow | . 5, G. Ev. S. C. G. H. . | 1800 |
| cinerēūm . . | . Yellow | . 7, G. Ev. S. C. G. H. . | 1774 |
| concāvūm . . | . Yellow | . 6, G. Ev. S. C. G. H. . | 1818 |
| concinnūm . . | . Yellow | . G. Ev. S. C. G. H. . | 1800 |
| concolōr . . | . Yellow | . 5, G. Ev. S. C. G. H. . | 1774 |
| corymbōsūm . | . Yellow | . 4, G. Ev. S. C. G. H. . | 1790 |
| decōrūm . . | . Yellow | . G. Ev. S. C. G. H. . | 1790 |
| decūrrēns . . | . Yellow | . G. Ev. S. C. G. H. . | 1812 |
| florīdūm . . | . Yellow | . 4, G. Ev. S. C. G. H. . | 1795 |
| fuscifōrūm, 1 . | . Yellow | . 5, G. Ev. S. C. G. H. . | |
| glabrūm . . | . Yellow | . G. Ev. S. C. G. H. . | 1810 |
| Globulārīs . . | . Yellow | . 4, G. Ev. S. C. G. H. . | 1810 |
| grandiflorūm . | . Yellow | . 4, G. Ev. S. C. G. H. . | 1789 |
| imbricātūm . | . Yellow | . G. Ev. S. C. G. H. . | 1790 |
| inflēxūm . . | . Yellow | . 4, G. Ev. S. C. G. H. . | 1800 |
| Levisānūs . . | . Yellow | . 5, G. Ev. S. C. G. H. . | 1774 |
| linifolīūm . . | . Yellow | . 5, G. Ev. S. C. G. H. . | |
| marginātūm . | . Yellow | . 5, G. Ev. S. C. G. H. . | 1800 |
| ovālē . . . | . Yellow | . 5, G. Ev. S. C. G. H. . | 1818 |
| platyspērmūm . | . Yellow | . 5, G. Ev. S. C. G. H. . | 1818 |
| plumōsūm . . | . Yellow | . 7, G. Ev. S. C. G. H. . | 1774 |
| pubēscēns . . | . Yellow | . 4, G. Ev. S. C. G. H. . | 1819 |
| retūsūm . . | . Yellow | . 5, G. Ev. S. C. G. H. . | 1810 |
| salignūm . . | . Yellow | . 5, G. Ev. S. C. G. H. . | 1774 |
| scābrūm . . | . Yellow | . G. Ev. S. C. G. H. . | 1812 |
| serīcēūm . . | . Yellow | . 5, G. Ev. S. C. G. H. . | 1817 |

| | | | | | |
|---|---|---|---|---|---|
| spatulātūm | . . Yellow | . 5, G. Ev. S. C. G. H. | . 1818 |
| squarrōsūm | . . Yellow | . G. Ev. S. C. G. H. | . 1894 |
| strictūm | . . Yellow | . 6, G. Ev. S. C. G. H. | . 1795 |
| törtūm | . . Yellow | . 6, G. Ev. S. C. G. H. | . 1790 |
| uliginōsūm | . . Yellow | . 5, G. Ev. S. C. G. H. | . 1795 |
| venōsūm | . . Yellow | . 5, G. Ev. S. C. G. H. | . 1816 |
| virgātūm | . . Yellow | . 6, G. Ev. S. C. G. H. | |

**Lēūcās**, *Burmann.* From *leukos*, white; because o the downy whiteness of the flowers. *Linn.* 14, Or. 1, Nat. Or. *Labiatæ.* These plants are not possessed of much beauty. They will grow freely in any common soil. *Synonymes:* 1. *L. Plunkenetii.* 2. *Phlomis chinensis.* 3. *P. zeylanica.* 4. *P. martinicensis.*

| | | | | | |
|---|---|---|---|---|---|
| biflōrā | . . . | White | . 2, G. | A. Ceylon | . 1819 |
| cephalōtēs | . . | White | . 3, S. | A. E. Ind. | . 1818 |
| chinēnsis, 2 | . | White | . 7, S. | A. China | . 1820 |
| flāccĭdā | . . | White | . 3, G. | A. N. Holl. | . 1823 |
| linifōliā, 3 | . . | White | . 3, S. | A. E. Ind. | . 1816 |

*aspera* 1, *indica, martinicensis* 4, *urticæfolia, zeylanica.*

**Lēūcocārpūs**, *G. Don.* From *leukos*, white, and *karpos*, a berry; in allusion to the white fruit. *Linn.* 14, Or. 2, Nat. Or. *Scrophulariaceæ.* A curious little plant, growing best in peat and loam. *Synonyme:* 1. *Mimulus perfoliatus.*

| | | | | | |
|---|---|---|---|---|---|
| alātūs, 1 | . . | White | . F. | A. Vera Cruz. | . 1830 |

**Leucocōrȳnē**, *Lindley.* From *leukos*, white, and *koryne*, a club; because of the white sterile anthers. *Linn.* 3, Or. 1, Nat. Or. *Liliaceæ.* These plants will succeed well in a light sandy soil, and increase by offsets from the bulbs, or by seeds. *Synonymes:* 1. *Brodiæa alliacea.* 2. *B. ixioides.*

| | | | | | |
|---|---|---|---|---|---|
| alliacēā, 1 | . . | White | . | F. Bl. P. Chile | . 1825 |
| ixioīdēs, 2 | . . | Lilac | . 10, | F. Bl. P. Chile | . 1821 |
| odorātā | . . . | White | . 3, | F. Bl. P. Valparaiso | . 1826 |

**Lēūcŏdŏn**, *Schweigger.* From *leukos*, white, and *odous*, a tooth; on account of the colour and shape of the peristome. *Linn.* 24, Or. 5, Nat. Or. *Musci.* A species of moss, with long stems, creeping over stones, the bark of trees, &c. *Synonyme:* 1. *Dicranum sciuroides—sciuroides* 1.

**Lēūcōĭŭm**, *Linn.* From *leukos*, white, and *ion*, a violet; in reference to the colour of the flower; whence the English name, Snow-flake. *Linn.* 6, Or. 1, Nat. Or. *Amaryllidaceæ.* Hardy bulbs, growing to the height of twelve or eighteen inches, and producing spikes of pretty white flowers, like the Snow-drop. Sandy loam suits them best, and they are increased by offsets from the bulbs.

| | | | | | |
|---|---|---|---|---|---|
| æstivūm | . . . | White | . 5, H. Bl. P. England | . |
| pulchēllūm | . . | White | . 4, H. Bl. P. | |
| vērnūm | . . . | White | . 2, H. Bl. P. Germany | . 1596 |
| carpāthicūm | . . | White | . 2, H. Bl. P. C . . M. | . 1816 |
| mūltĭplēx | . . | White | . 3, H. Bl. P. Gardens | |

**Lēūcopŏgŏn**, *R. Brown.* From *leukos*, white, and *pogon*, a beard; because of the white hairs with which the limb of the corolla is bearded. *Linn.* 5, Or. 1, Nat. Or. *Epacridaceæ.* These plants are well worth a place in every greenhouse. They will grow well in an equal mixture of sandy loam and peat, with the pots well drained, and care must be taken never to overwater them. The tops of the very young shoots, taken off, and planted in sand, under a glass, will root freely. *Synonymes:* 1. *Styphelia obovatus.* 2. *S. Richei.* *L. parviflorus.*

| | | | | | |
|---|---|---|---|---|---|
| amplexicaūlis | . | White | . . G. Ev. S. N. S. W. | . 1815 |
| apprēssūs | . . | White | . 6, G. Ev. S. N. Holl. | . 1820 |
| collīnūs | . . . | White | . 5, G. Ev. S. V. D. L. | . 1824 |
| ericoīdēs | . . . | White | . . G. Ev. S. N. S. W. | . 1815 |
| interrūptūs | . . | White | . 6, G. Ev. S. N. Holl. | . 1826 |
| juniperoīdēs | . . | White | . 5, G. Ev. S. N. S. W. | . 1804 |
| lanceolātūs | . . | White | . 5, G. Ev. S. N. S. W. | . 1790 |
| microphyllūs | . . | White | . 6, G. Ev. S. N. Holl. | . 1818 |
| obovātūs, 1 | . . | White | . 6, G. Ev. S. N. Holl. | . 1824 |
| polystāchys | . . | White | . 6, G. Ev. S. N. Holl. | . 1826 |
| Richēī, 2 | . . . | White | . 6, G. Ev. S. N. Holl. | . 1822 |
| setĭgerā | . . . | White | . . G. Ev. S. N. Holl. | . 1824 |
| striātūs | . . . | White | . 6, G. Ev. S. N. Holl. | . 1823 |
| verticillātūs | . . | | . . G. Ev. S. K. G. S. | . 1837 |
| virgātūs | . . . | White | . 6, G. Ev. S. N. Holl. | . 1824 |

**Lēūcospērmūm**, *R. Brown.* From *leukos*, white, and *sperma*, a seed; in allusion to the downy seeds. *Linn.* 4, Or. 1, Nat. Or. *Proteaceæ.* An interesting genus of plants, with entire downy, or hairy leaves, and terminal heads of yellow flowers; for culture and propagation, see *Protea*, to which this genus is nearly allied. *Synonymes:* 1. *Protea candicans.* 2. *Leucodendron grandiflorum.*

| | | | | | |
|---|---|---|---|---|---|
| attenuātūm | . . | Yellow | . 6, G. Ev. S. C. G. H. | . 1820 |
| candĭcāns, 1 | . . | Yellow | . 6, G. Ev. S. C. G. H. | . 1790 |
| conocārpūm | . . | Yellow | . 6, G. Ev. S. C. G. H. | . 1774 |
| ellĭptĭcūm | . . | Yellow | . 6, G. Ev. S. C. G. H. | . 1803 |
| formōsūm | . . | Yellow | . 7, G. Ev. S. C. G. H. | . 1784 |
| grandiflōrūm, 2 | . | Yellow | . 6, G. Ev. S. C. G. H. | . 1800 |
| hypophyllūm | . . | Yellow | . 6, G. Ev. S. C. G. H. | . 1787 |
| lineārē | . . . | Yellow | . 7, G. Ev. S. C. G. H. | . 1774 |
| mēdĭūm | . . . | Orange | . 7, G. Ev. S. C. G. H. | . 1794 |
| pārĭlē | . . . | Yellow | . 8, G. Ev. S. C. G. H. | . 1789 |
| pātŭlūm | . . . | Yellow | . 8, G. Ev. S. C. G. H. | . 1823 |
| puberūm | . . . | Yellow | . 6, G. Ev. S. C. G. H. | . 1774 |
| spatulātūm | . . | Yellow | . 6, G. Ev. S. C. G. H. | . 1825 |
| tomentōsūm | . . | Yellow | . 6, G. Ev. S. C. G. H. | . 1789 |
| töttūm | . . . | Yellow | . 7, G. Ev. S. C. G. H. | . 1774 |

**Lēūcorhīzā**, white-rooted.

**Lēūcostēmmā**, *Bentham.* Derived from *leukos*, white, and *stemma*, a crown; on account of the white downy seeds. *Linn.* 4, Or. 1, Nat. Or. *Compositæ.* This is a very fine species, well deserving of extensive cultivation. It may be referred to *Elichrysum* for culture and propagation. *Synonyme:* 1. *Elichrysum vestitum.*

| | | | | | |
|---|---|---|---|---|---|
| vestītūm, 1 | . . | White | . 8, G. Ev. S. C. G. H. | . 1774 |

**Lēūcōxȳlŏn**, white-wooded.

**Lēūzēā**. Named by Decandolle, in honour of his friend De Leuze. *Linn.* 19, Or. 3, Nat. Or. *Compositæ.* These are dwarf ornamental plants, seldom exceeding nine inches in height, and producing large purple flowers. Any common garden soil suits them, and they may be increased by divisions of the roots, or by seeds. *Synonymes:* 1. *Cnicus carthamoides.* 2. *Centaurea conifera.* 3. *Cirsium salinum, Centaurea altaica.*

| | | | | | |
|---|---|---|---|---|---|
| altāīcā | . . . | Purple | . 8, H. Her. P. Siberia | . 1822 |
| austrālis | . . . | Purple | . 8, H. Her. P. N. Holl. | . 1821 |
| carthamoīdēs, 1 | . | Purple | . 8, H. Her. P. Siberia | . 1816 |
| conĭferā, 2 | . . | Purple | . 7, H. Her. P. S. Eur. | . 1683 |
| salīna, 3 | . . . | Purple | . 6, H. Her. P. Siberia | . 1817 |

**Lēvĭstĭcūm**, *Koch.* From *levo*, to assuage; the plant is said to relieve flatulency. *Linn.* 5, Or. 2, Nat. Or. *Umbelliferæ.* This plant succeeds well in common garden soil, and is easily increased by seeds. *Synonyme:* 1. *Ligusticum levisticum.*

| | | | | | |
|---|---|---|---|---|---|
| officĭnālē, 1 | . . | Pa. yel. | . 6, H. Her. P. Italy | . 1596 |

**Lēwĭsĭā**, *Pursh.* In honour of Captain M. Lewis, who accompanied Captain Clarke to the Rocky Mountains. *Linn.* 13, Or. 1, Nat. Or. *Cactaceæ.* Light loam and brick rubbish is a good soil for this plant, and it may be increased by dividing the roots, or by seeds.

| | | | | | |
|---|---|---|---|---|---|
| redivīvā | . . . | Rose | . . H. Her. P. N. Amer. | . 1826 |

**Lēȳssērā**, *Linn.* In honour of Frederick William Leysser, a famous German botanist. *Linn.* 19, Or. 2, Nat. Or. *Compositæ.* Ornamental plants, requiring to be grown in a peat soil, mixed with a little loam; and cuttings, planted in the same kind of soil, under a glass, will root without difficulty. *Synonyme:* 1. *Stæhelina gnaphaloides.*

| | | | | | |
|---|---|---|---|---|---|
| ciliātā | . . . | Orange | . 8, G. Ev. S. C. G. H. | . 1816 |
| gnaphaloīdēs | . . | Orange | . 8, G. Ev. S. C. G. H. | . 1774 |
| polifōliā | . . . | Orange | . 8, G. Ev. S. C. G. H. | . 1820 |
| squarrōsā, 1 | . . | Orange | . 8, G. Ev. S. C. G. H. | . 1815 |

**Lēȳcestērĭā**. Wallich named this genus in honour of his friend William Leycester, once chief judge at Bengal, a munificent and zealous patron of horticulture. *Linn.* 5, Or. 1, Nat. Or. *Caprifoliaceæ.* This is an elegant and most beautiful shrub when in flower, from the contrast of the deep green hue of its stem and leaves, with the purple colour of the large bracteas and the berries. A light soil suits it best, and it is readily increased by cuttings taken off in autumn or spring, or by seeds. It is well adapted to the front of shrubberies. It will require the protection of a mat in winter.

| | | | | | |
|---|---|---|---|---|---|
| formōsā | . . . | Wht pur. | 8, H. Ev. S. Nepal | . 1824 |

**Lĭātrĭs**, *Schreber.* The meaning of the name is not known. *Linn.* 19, Or. 1, Nat. Or. *Compositæ.* These are very charming little plants, with spikes of purple or pink flowers. It is best to take them out of the border in winter, and preserve in pots of sandy loam and peat, and in spring they may be planted out in the open border in the same kind of soil. Young plants are easily obtained by divisions.

| bellidifólia | . | . | Pink | . | 8, F. Her. P. N. Amer. | . |
| boreális | . | . | Pink | . | 8, H. Her. P. N. Amer. | . |
| corymbósa | . | . | Purple | . | 9, F. Her. P. Carolina | 1825 |
| cylindrica | . | . | Pink | . | 9, H. Her. P. N. Amer. | 1811 |
| elegans | . | . | Purple | . | 9, H. Her. P. N. Amer. | 1787 |
| grácilis | . | . | Purple | . | 9, F. Her. P. Carolina | 1818 |
| graminifólia | . | . | Pink | . | 9, H. Her. P. N. Amer. | . |
| heterophýlla | . | . | Purple | . | 7, H. Her. P. N. Amer. | 1790 |
| intermédia | . | . | Purple | . | 9, H. Her. P. N. Amer. | 1823 |
| odoratíssima | . | . | Purple | . | 9, F. Her. P. Carolina | 1786 |
| paniculáta | . | . | Purple | . | 8, F. Her. P. Carolina | 1826 |
| pilósa | . | . | Purple | . | 9, H. Her. P. N. Amer. | 1783 |
| pumila | . | . | Purple | . | 9, H. Her. P. N. Amer. | . |
| pycnostáchya | . | . | Purple | . | 9, H. Her. P. N. Amer. | 1732 |
| scariósa | . | . | Purple | . | 7, H. Her. P. N. Amer. | 1739 |
| sphæroídea | . | . | Purple | . | 9, H. Her. P. N. Amer. | 1817 |
| squarrósa | . | . | Purple | . | 7, H. Her. P. N. Amer. | 1732 |
| spicáta | . | . | Purple | . | 9, H. Her. P. N. Amer. | 1732 |
| tenuifólia | . | . | Purple | . | 9, H. Her. P. Carolina | 1820 |
| turbináta | . | . | Purple | . | 9, H. Her. P. N. Amer. | 1823 |

LIBER, the inner bark.

LIBERTIA, *Sprengel*. In compliment to Mademoiselle M. A. Libert de Malmédy, a Belgian lady, to whom the French Flora is indebted for a great number of new species. *Linn.* 16, Or. 1, Nat. Or. *Iridaceæ*. This ornamental species thrives well in an equal mixture of loam and peat, and may be increased by dividing the roots. Synonyme: 1. *Sisyrinchium formosum.*

| formósa | . | . | . | White | . | 5, F. Her. P. Chiloe | . . | 1831 |

LICEA, *Schrader*. The meaning is not explained. *Linn.* 24, Or. 9, Nat. Or. *Fungi*. A species about the size of a pin's head, found chiefly on rotten wood—*fragifórmis*.

LICHINA, *Agardh*. Derived from *Lichen*; on account of the resemblance. *Linn.* 24, Or. 7, Nat. Or. *Algæ*. By some botanists, this genus has been referred to the *Lichens*, and by others they are said to be *Algæ* in one stage of their existence, and *Lichens* in another—*confínis, pygmæd.*

LICHTENSTEINIA, *Chamisso*. In honour of M. Von Lichtenstein, a celebrated German botanist, and professor of medicine at Berlin. *Linn.* 5, Or. 2, Nat. Or. *Umbelliferæ*. Pretty plants, with blue flowers. They grow well in sandy loam, and young plants are readily obtained from seeds. Synonyme: 1. *Cymation lævigatum.*

| lævigáta, 1 | . | . | Blue | . | . | G. Her. P. C. G. H. | . | 1824 |
| undulata | . | . | Blue | . | 7, G. Her. P. C. G. H. | . | 1814 |

LICUALA, *Rumphius*. The name of the species in the Macassar language. *Linn.* 6, Or. 1, Nat. Or. *Palmaceæ*. These are very beautiful palms, requiring a sandy loam and strong moist heat to grow in. In Macassar, they make tobacco-pipes of the narrow leaves, while the middle broad one is used for wrapping up fruit, &c.

| peltáta | . | . | . | Wht. yel. | . | Palm. E. Ind. | . . | 1825 |
| spinósa | . | . | . | Wht. grn. | . | Palm. E. Ind. | . . | 1802 |

LID, the calyx which falls off from the flower in a single piece.

LIDBECKIA, *Berger*. In honour of E. G. Lidbeck, an acute Swedish botanist. *Linn.* 19, Or. 2, Nat. Or. *Compositæ*. Ornamental plants; for culture and propagation, see *Leyssera*. Synonyme: 1. *Cotula quinqueloba.*

| lobáta, 1 | . | . | Yellow | . | 5, G. Ev. S. C. G. H. | . | 1800 |
| pectináta | . | . | Yellow | . | 5, G. Ev. S. C. G. H. | . | 1744 |

LIGHTFOOTIA, *L'Heritier*. In honour of the Rev. J. Lightfoot, author of the first Flora Scotica. *Linn.* 5, Or. 1, Nat. Or. *Campanulaceæ*. Ornamental under shrubs, growing freely in a mixture of loam and peat; and young cuttings root readily in the same kind of soil, under a glass. Synonymes: 1. *tenella.* 2. *Campanula fruticosa, interrupta.*

| Loddigesii, 1 | . | . | Pa. blue | . | 7, G. Ev. S. C. G. H. | . | 1822 |
| oxycoccoídes | . | . | Blue | . | 7, G. Ev. S. C. G. H. | . | 1787 |
| subuláta, 2 | . | . | Blue | . | 8, G. Ev. S. C. G. H. | . | 1787 |

LIGNEOUS, woody.

LIGNUM VITÆ TREE, see *Guaiacum.*

LIGULA, the membrane at the top of the petiole of grasses.

LIGULATE, strap-shaped.

LIGUSTICUM, *Koch*. So named because of some of the species growing in Liguria. *Linn.* 5, Or. 2, Nat. Or. *Umbelliferæ*. Hardy herbaceous and biennial plants not worth cultivating. They will grow in any soil, and are increased by seeds. Synonymes:

1. *Sison peregrinum.* 2. *Cnidium pyrenaicum.* 3. *Selinum Seguieri—alátum* 1, *baléaricum, cándicans, ferulaceum* 2, *obtusifólium, peregrínum, pyrenaicum, scóticum, Seguieri* 3, *Sprengélii.*

LIGUSTRUM, *Linn.* From *ligare*, to tie; in allusion to the very flexible branches. *Linn.* 2, Or. 1, Nat. Or. *Oleaceæ*. These plants are well suited for making hedges, especially the evergreen varieties of *L. vulgare. L. lucidum,* and its *variety,* if grown in the open air, will require protecting in winter; they are easily increased by cuttings. Synonyme: 1. *L. nepalense.*

| lúcidum | . | . | White | . | 6, F. Ev. S. China | . | 1794 |
| floribúndum | . | . | White | . | 7, F. Ev. S. China | . | 1794 |
| spicátum, 1 | . | . | White | . | 6, H. De. S. Nepal | . | 1823 |
| vulgáre | . | . | White | . | 6, H. De. S. Britain | . |
| angustifólium | . | White | . | 6, H. De. S. Britain | . |
| chlorocárpum | . | White | . | 6, H. Ev. S. Britain | . |
| leucocárpum | . | White | . | 6, H. De. S. Britain | . |
| sempervírens | . | White | . | 6, H. Ev. S. Italy | . |
| variegátum | . | White | . | 6, H. De. S. Britain | . |
| xanthocárpum | . | White | . | 6, H. De. S. Italy | . |

LILAC, see *Syringa.*

LILIUM, *Tournefort*. Derived from the Celtic word *li*, signifying whiteness; on account of the beautiful white flowers of the original species. *Linn.* 6, Or. 1, Nat. Or. *Liliaceæ*. This is a fine ornamental and well-known genus; most of the species succeed in a light rich soil, but the American species should be grown in peat. All the kinds are readily increased by offsets from the bulbs. In Kamtschatka, the root of *L. Pomponium* is cultivated the same as the potato is in this country. Synonymes: 1. *L. fulgens.* 2. *L. autumnale.* 3. *L. speciosissimum.* 4. *L. lancifolium.* 5. *L. lancifolium-roseum.* 6. *L. pennsylvanicum.*

| Andínum | . | . | Scarlet | . | 7, H. Bl. P. N. Amer. | . | 1819 |
| atrosanguíneum, 1 | Drk. red | . | 7, G. Bl. P. Japan | . | 1835 |
| aurantiáceum | . | Orange | . | 7, F. Bl. P. Japan | . | 1835 |
| aurantíum | . | Drk. or. | . | 7, H. Bl. P. Italy | . | 1835 |
| flóre-plénó | . | Drk. or. | . | 6, H. Bl. P. |
| minus | . | . | Orange | . | 6, H. Bl. P. |
| variegátum | . | Drk. or. | . | 6, H. Bl. P. |
| bulbíferum | . | Orange | . | 6, H. Bl. P. Italy | . | 1596 |
| minus | . | . | Orange | . | 6, H. Bl. P. |
| umbellátum | . | Orange | . | 6, H. Bl. P. Italy | . | 1596 |
| variegátum | . | Orange | . | 6, H. Bl. P. |
| Buschiánum | . | Orange | . | 6, H. Bl. P. Siberia | . | 1829 |
| canadénse | . | Lgt. or. | . | 7, H. Bl. P. N. Amer. | . | 1629 |
| rúbrum | . | Orange | . | 7, H. Bl. P. N. Amer. | . | 1629 |
| candídum | . | White | . | 6, H. Bl. P. Levant | . | 1596 |
| spicátum | . | White | . | 6, H. Bl. P. |
| striátum | . | White | . | 6, H. Bl. P. |
| variegátum | . | White | . | 6, H. Bl. P. |
| Caroliniánum, 2 | Orange | . | 7, H. Bl. P. N. Amer. | . | 1819 |
| Catesbéi | . | Scarlet | . | 7, H. Bl. P. China | . | 1806 |
| Chalcedónicum | . | Scarlet | . | 7, H. Bl. P. Levant | . | 1796 |
| concólor | . | Red | . | 7, H. Bl. P. China | . | 1806 |
| corúscans | . | Scarlet | . | 8, G. Bl. P. |
| cróceum | . | Yellow | . | 7, H. Bl. P. | . | 1596 |
| exímium, 3 | . | White | . | 7, G. Bl. P. Japan | . | 1834 |
| glábrum | . | Orange | . | 6, H. Bl. P. | . | 1596 |
| japónicum | . | White | . | 7, H. Bl. P. China | . | 1804 |
| latifólium | . | Orange | . | 7, H. Bl. P. Europe | . | 1820 |
| longifólium | . | White | . | 8, H. Bl. P. China | . | 1820 |
| Martágon | . | Purple | . | 7, H. Bl. P. Germany | . | 1596 |
| albó-plénó | . | White | . | 7, H. Bl. P. Germany | . |
| pubéscens | . | Orange | . | 6, H. Bl. P. Germany | . | 1596 |
| sepális-albis | . | White | . | 7, H. Bl. P. Germany | . |
| sepális-plurimis | Purple | . | 7, H. Bl. P. Gardens |
| monadélphum | . | Yellow | . | 6, H. Bl. P. Caucasus | . | 1820 |
| Nepalénse | . | White | . | 7, H. Bl. P. Nepal | . | 1825 |
| penduliflórum | . | Copper col. | 6, H. Bl. P. N. Amer. | . | 1820 |
| peregrínum | . | White | . | 6, H. Bl. P. C. G. H. | . | 1824 |
| philadélphicum | . | Scarlet | . | 7, H. Bl. P. N. Amer. | . | 1757 |
| Pomponium | . | Red | . | 7, H. Bl. P. Siberia | . | 1659 |
| flóre-plénó | . | Red | . | 6, H. Bl. P. |
| pumílum | . | Scarlet | . | 7, H. Bl. P. Dauria | . | 1816 |
| pyrenáicum | . | Drk. or. | . | 7, H. Bl. P. Pyrenees | . | 1596 |
| flóre-plénó | . | Yellow | . | 7, H. Bl. P. |
| sibíricum | . | Yellow | . | 7, H. Bl. P. Siberia | . |
| speciósum, 4 | . | Orange | . | 8, H. Bl. P. Japan | . | 1833 |
| punctátum, 5 | . | Wht. spot. | 7, G. Bl. P. Japan | . | 1835 |
| spectábile, 6 | . | Lgt. or. | . | 6, H. Bl. P. Dauria | . | 1754 |
| tenuifólium | . | Scarlet | . | 6, H. Bl. P. Siberia | . | 1820 |
| Thunbergiánum | . | Or. scar. | . | 7, G. Bl. P. Japan | . | 1835 |
| tigrínum | . | Orange | . | 7, H. Bl. P. China | . | 1804 |

LILY, see *Lilium.*

LILY HYACINTH, see *Scilla Lilio-hyacinthus.*

LILY-OF-THE-VALLEY, see *Convallaria.*

LILY PINK, see *Aphyllanthes.*

LILY THORN, see *Catesbæa.*

LIMBATE, having an expanded end; or being bordered by something.

**Limb**, the border of a flower.

**Lime**, see *Citrus Limonium*.

**Lime-tree**, see *Tilia*.

**Limeum**, *Linn.* From *loimos*, a pest; on account of the supposed poisonous qualities of the plant. *Linn.* 7, Or. 3, Nat. Or. *Illecebraceæ*. A mixture of sandy loam and peat suits this species best; and cuttings root readily under a glass.

| | | | | | | |
|---|---|---|---|---|---|---|
| africanum . . | . White . | . 6, | G. Her. | P. | C. G. H. | . 1774 |

**Limnanthes**, *R. Brown*. From *limne*, a marsh, and *anthos*, a flower; in allusion to the habitat of the plant. *Linn.* 10, Or. 1, Nat. Or. *Limnanthaceæ*. This plant is well deserving of a place in every collection, on account of the elegance and beauty of its flowers, which are slightly fragrant. It requires to be grown in a moist and shady situation, and it is increased by seeds, which ripen pretty freely.

| | | | | | | |
|---|---|---|---|---|---|---|
| Douglasii . . | . Wht. yel. | . H. Tr. | A. | Californ. | 1833 |

**Limnocharis**, *Bonpland*. From *limne*, a pool, and *chairo*, to delight; in allusion to the habitat of the species. *Linn.* 13, Or. 1, Nat. Or. *Commelinaceæ*. Handsome aquatic plants, of easy culture in a tub or cistern of water, and increased either by runners or seeds.

| | | | | | | |
|---|---|---|---|---|---|---|
| Humboldtii . | . Yellow . | . 6, | S. Aq. | P. | B. Ayres | . 1831 |
| Plumieri . . | . Pa. yel. | . 7, | S. Aq. | P. | Brasil . | . 1822 |

**Limonia**, *Linn.* From *limoun*, the Arabic name of the Citron. *Linn.* 10, Or. 1, Nat. Or. *Aurantiaceæ*. This genus is nearly allied to *Citrus*. The plants should be grown in a mixture of loam and peat, with a little rotten dung added; and cuttings will root in sand, under a glass, plunged in a moist heat.

| | | | | | |
|---|---|---|---|---|---|
| australis . . | . White . | . G. Ev. T. | N. Holl. | . 1830 |
| citrifolia . . | . White . | . G. Ev. S. | China . | . 1800 |
| crenulata . . | . White . | . G. Ev. S. | E. Ind. | . 1808 |
| parviflora . . | . White . | . G. Ev. S. | China . | |
| scandens . . | . White . | . G. Ev. Cl. | China . | . 1800 |

**Limosella**, *Linn.* From *limus*, mud; in allusion to the habitation of the species; whence the English name Mudwort. *Linn.* 14, Or. 2, Nat. Or. *Scrophulariaceæ*. The seeds of this sub-aquatic should be sown near a pond or rivulet.

| | | | | | |
|---|---|---|---|---|---|
| aquatica . . | . Flesh . | . 8, H. Aq. | A. | Britain . | . |

**Limosus**, muddy, growing in mud.

**Limpidus**, clear, transparent.

**Linanthus**, *Bentham*. From *linon*, flax, and *anthos*, a flower. *Linn.* 5, Or. 1, Nat. Or. *Polemoniaceæ*. An ornamental annual, succeeding well when sown in the open border in spring.

| | | | | | |
|---|---|---|---|---|---|
| dichotomus . | . Pink . | . H. | A. | Californ. | . 1833 |

**Linaria**, *Tournefort*. From *linum*, flax; on account of the similarity of the leaves. *Linn.* 14, Or. 2, Nat. Or. *Scrophulariaceæ*. This genus for the most part consists of annuals, well adapted for ornamenting rock-work. *L. triornithophora* is remarkable for the form of its flowers, which bears some little resemblance to three little birds seated in the spur. They thrive best in a light sandy loam, and are readily multiplied by seeds. Synonymes: 1. *speciosa*. 2. *Antirrhinum lanigerum*. 3. *A. fruticans*. 4. *A. linarioides* 5. *spurium*. 6. *A. Linaria*. 7. *A. odorum*. 8. *strictum*. 9. *L. striata*. 10. *Antir. lusitanicum*, *pedunculatum*.

| | | | | | |
|---|---|---|---|---|---|
| acutiloba . . | . Purple . | . 8, H. Ev. | Tr. Siberia | . 1825 |
| ægyptiaca . . | . Yel. pur. | . 7, | A. Egypt . | . 1771 |
| æquitriloba . | . Purple . | . 6, H. Ev. | Tr. Sardinia | . 1829 |
| alpina . . . | . Blue . | . 7, H. Ev. | Tr. Austria | . 1570 |
| alsinifolia . | . Blue . | . 6, H. | A. Corsica | . 1824 |
| amethystina . | . Blue yel. | . 7, H. | A. Spain . | . 1788 |
| arenaria . . | . Yellow . | . 7, H. Tr. | A. S. Eur. | . 1822 |
| arvensis . . | . Pur. blue | . 7, H. | A. S. Eur. | . |
| bipartita, 1 . | . Purple . | . 8, H. Her. | P. Barbary | . 1815 |
| bipunctata . | . Yellow . | . 7, H. | A. Spain . | . 1749 |
| canadensis . | . Violet . | . 7, H. | A. N. Amer. | . 1812 |
| caucasica . . | . Yellow . | . 7, H. Tr. | A. Caucasus | . 1818 |
| chalepensis . | . White . | . 6, H. | A. Levant . | . 1680 |
| circinata . . | . Yellow . | . 6, | N. Africa | . 1833 |
| cirrhosa . . | . Pa. blue | . 7, H. Tr. | A. Egypt . | . 1771 |
| cretacea . . | . | . 7, H. | A. Siberia | . 1827 |
| Cymbalaria . | . Violet . | . 5, H. Ev. | Tr. England | . |
| alba . . | . White . | . 6, H. Ev. | Tr. Gardens | . |
| variegata . | . Violet . | . 6, H. Ev. | Tr. Gardens | . |
| dalmatica . . | . Yellow . | . 6, F. Ev. | S. Levant . | . 1731 |
| dealbata, 2 . | . Yellow . | . 8, H. Tr. | A. Portugal | . 1820 |
| delphinioides | . Blue . | . 8, H. | A. Russia . | . 1838 |
| diffusa . . . | . | . 7, H. | A. Spain . | . 1826 |

---

| | | | | | | |
|---|---|---|---|---|---|---|
| Elatine . . | . Yellow . | . 8, | H. Tr. | A. | England . | |
| elatinoides . | . Yellow . | . 8, | H. Tr. | A. S. Eur. | . 1821 |
| flava . . | . Yellow . | . 7, | H. | A. N. Africa | . 1820 |
| fruticans, 3 . | . Yellow . | . 6, | G. Ev. | S. C. G. H. | . 1822 |
| galioides . . | . Blue . | . 7, | H. Her. | P. S. Eur. | |
| genistæfolia . | . Yellow . | . 7, | H. Her. | P. Austria | . 1704 |
| glauca . . | . Pur. vio. | . 7, | H. | A. S. Eur. | . 1800 |
| Hælava . . | . Purple . | . 7, | H. | A. Egypt . | . 1803 |
| heterophylla . | . Yel. brn. | . 7, | H. Her. | P. N. Africa | . 1825 |
| hirta . . | . Purple . | . 8, | H. | A. Spain . | . 1759 |
| incarnata . . | . Flesh . | . 6, | H. | A. Spain . | . 1819 |
| juncea . . | . Yel. brn. | . 7, | H. | A. Spain . | . 1780 |
| lanigera, 5 . | . Yellow . | . 7, | H. Tr. | A. Portugal | . 1818 |
| latifolia . . | . Yellow . | . 8, | H. | A. Portugal | . 1818 |
| linifolia, 6 . | . Yellow . | . 7, | H. Her. | P. Caucasus | . 1820 |
| littoralis . . | . Yellow . | . 6, | H. Tr. | A. Austria | . 1820 |
| Loeselii, 7 . | . Blue . | . 7, | H. | A. Tauria . | . 1823 |
| lusitanica . | . Blue . | . 8, | H. | A. Spain . | . 1819 |
| macroura, 8 . | . Yellow . | . 8, | H. Her. | P. Crimea | . 1822 |
| marginata . | . Yelsh. . | . 8, | H. Her. | P. Barbary | . 1820 |
| micrantha . . | . Yellow . | . 6, | H. Tr. | A. Spain . | . 1820 |
| minor . . | . Violet . | . 8, | H. | A. England | |
| monspessulana, 9 | Blue . | . 7, | H. Her. | P. S. France | |
| alba . . | . White . | . 7, | H. Her. | P. | |
| multicaulis . | . White . | . 6, | H. | A. Levant . | . 1728 |
| origanifolia . | . Blue . | . 8, | F. Ev. | S. S. Eur. | . 1785 |
| Pelisseriana . | . Violet . | . 8, | H. | A. S. Eur. | . 1640 |
| pilosa . . | . Purple . | . 8, | H. Ev. | Tr. Pyrenees | . 1800 |
| procera . . | . Pa. blue | . 7, | H. Her. | P. | |
| pubescens . . | . Pale . | . 8, | H. Ev. | Tr. Naples | . 1820 |
| purpurascens . | . Purple . | . 6, | H. | B. S. Eur. | . 1829 |
| purpurea . . | . Purple . | . 8, | H. Her. | P. S. Eur. | . 1648 |
| pyrenaica . . | . Yellow . | . 6, | H. | A. Pyrenees | . 1821 |
| reflexa . . | . Yel. pur. | . 7, | H. | A. S. Eur. | . 1810 |
| repens . . | . Green . | . 8, | H. Cr. | A. England | |
| reticulata . . | . Purple . | . 6, | F. Her. | A. Algiers | . 1788 |
| rubrifolia . . | . Blue . | . 6, | H. | A. S. France | . 1826 |
| saxatilis . . | . Yellow . | . 8, | H. Ev. | Tr. Spain | . 1819 |
| scoparia . . | . Yellow . | . 6, | G. Ev. | S. Teneriffe | . 1816 |
| sibirifolia . . | . Yellow . | . 7, | H. Her. | P. Armenia | . 1819 |
| simplex . . | . Purple . | . 7, | H. | A. S. Eur. | . 1816 |
| spartea . . | . Yellow . | . 8, | H. | A. Spain . | . 1772 |
| spuria . . | . Yellow . | . 8, | H. Tr. | A. England | |
| supina . . | . Yellow . | . 7, | H. Tr. | A. Spain . | . 1728 |
| thymifolia . | . Blue . | . 6, | H. | A. S. Eur. | . 1818 |
| transtagana, 10 | Blue . | . 6, | H. | A. Portugal | . 1810 |
| triornithophora | Purple . | . 8, | F. Her. | P. Portugal | . 1710 |
| triphylla . . | . Yel. pur. | . 8, | H. | A. Sicily . | . 1596 |
| tristis . . | . Brown . | . 7, | F. Her. | P. Spain . | . 1727 |
| lutea . . | . Yellow . | . 8, | F. Her. | P. Gardens | |
| versicolor . . | . Pur. yel. | . 8, | H. | A. France . | . 1777 |
| villosa . . | . Blue . | . 7, | F. Her. | P. Spain . | . 1786 |
| virgata . . | . Blue . | . 8, | H. | A. N. Africa | . 1817 |
| viscosa . . | . Brown . | . 7, | H. | A. Spain . | . 1786 |
| vulgaris . . | . Yellow . | . 8, | H. Her. | P. Britain . | |
| Peloria . . | . Yellow . | . 8, | H. Her. | P. Britain . | |

**Lincoxia**, *Linn.* Probably from *Lincon*, the name of some botanist. *Linn.* 5, Or. 2, Nat. Or. *Bruniaceæ*. Ornamental plants; for culture and propagation, see *Diosma*. Synonymes: 1. *Diosma cuspidata*. 2. *deusta*.

| | | | | | |
|---|---|---|---|---|---|
| alopecuroides . | . White . | . 5, G. Ev. | S. C. G. H. | . 1816 |
| cuspidata, 1 . | . White . | . 5, G. Ev. | S. C. G. H. | . 1825 |
| thymifolia, 2 . | . White . | . 5, G. Ev. | S. C. G. H. | . 1825 |

**Lindernia**, *Linn.* In honour of F. B. Von Lindern, M.D., of Strasburg, a botanical author. *Linn.* 14, Or. 2, Nat. Or. *Scrophulariaceæ*. The seed of this plant has only to be sown in the flower-borders.

| | | | | | |
|---|---|---|---|---|---|
| Pyxidaria . . | . Blue . | . 7, H. | A. S. Eur. | . 1789 |

**Lindsæa**, *Dryander*. In honour of Mr. Lindsey, an English writer on the germination of mosses. *Linn.* 24, Or. 1, Nat. Or. *Polypodiaceæ*. A very handsome genus of Ferns, which will grow well in an equal mixture of sandy loam and peat, and it may be increased by divisions of the roots, or by seeds, which must be sown on a pot of earth, watered, and covered over with moss, till they make their appearance.

| | | | | | |
|---|---|---|---|---|---|
| falcata . . | . Brown . | . 5, S. Her. | P. Trinidad | . 1819 |
| linearis . . | . Brown . | . 5, G. Her. | P. N. Holl. | . 1820 |
| media . . | . Brown . | . 5, G. Her. | P. N. Holl. | . 1823 |
| microphylla . | . Brown . | . 5, G. Her. | P. N. Holl. | . 1820 |
| trapeziformis . | . Brown . | . 5, S. Her. | P. S. Amer. | . 1819 |

**Linear**, narrow, when the two sides are nearly parallel.

**Lined**, having lines, or streaks.

**Linguiform,** } tongue-shaped.
**Linguiate,** }

**Linnæa**. Dr. J. F. Gronovius, with the concurrence of Linnæus, selected this little depressed, abject, early-flowering, long-overlooked northern plant, to transmit the illustrious name of Linnæus to posterity. *Linn.* 14, Or. 2, Nat. Or. *Caprifoliaceæ*.

This elegant little plant is not only a native of the land which gave birth to Linnæus, but also of Lapland, Norway, Russia, Germany, Switzerland, Savoy, Siberia, &c. In Scotland, the plant was first found in an old fir-wood at Inglismaldie, on the borders of Mearns-shire, in 1795, and since then in several similar situations in the highlands of Scotland. In North America, it has been found in a number of districts, but most plentiful in Canada. It should be grown in a peat border, in a shady situation, where it will grow and flower freely. It will also grow luxuriantly in large pots, filled with peat earth; it is easily increased by separating the creeping stems when rooted. The American plants are commonly stronger than the European ones.

| borealis . . . . | Flesh . . | 6, H. Ev. Tr. Scotland . | |

LINOCIERA, *Swartz*. In honour of G. Linocier, a French physician. Linn. 2, Or. 1, Nat. Or. *Oleaceæ.* These plants are not possessed of much beauty. They grow well in sandy loam and peat, and are increased by cuttings in sand, under a glass, in heat.

| compacta | . . | White. . | 8. Ev. T. W. Ind. | . 1793 |
| cotinifolia | . . | White. . | 8. Ev. T. Ceylon | . 1818 |
| ligustrina | . . | White. . | 8. Ev. T. E. Ind. | . 1820 |

LINUM, *Linn.* From the Celtic word *llin*, a thread; whence the Greek, *linon*, and the Latin, *linum*. Linn. 5, Or. 5, Nat. Or. *Linaceæ.* These plants are mostly ornamental, and well worth cultivating in every collection. The greenhouse and frame kinds grow best in a mixture of loam and peat, and cuttings root freely under a glass. The hardy shrubby kinds do well in any light soil, and are increased by cuttings under a glass. The hardy herbaceous species are well suited for ornamenting flower-borders; but the dwarf kinds do best on rock-work, or even grown in pots, that they may be protected by a frame in frosty or very wet weather; they may be increased by divisions of the roots, by cuttings, or by seeds. The annual and biennial species should be sown in the open ground in April. *Synonymes:* 1. *perenne.* 2. *tenuifolium, bicolor.* 3. *angustifolium, decumbens.* 4. *angustifolium.* 5. *austriacum, perenne.* 6. *austriacum.*

| æthiopicum | . | Yellow | . | 6, G. Ev. | 8. | C. G. H. | . 1771 |
| africanum | . | Yellow | . | 6, G. Ev. | 8. | C. G. H. | . 1771 |
| agreste | . | Lilac | . | H. Her. | P. | Portugal | . 1826 |
| alpinum | . | Blue | . | 7, H. Her. | P. | Austria . | . 1739 |
| album | . | White. | . | 7, H. Her. | P. | Gardens | |
| altaicum | . | Blue | . | 7, H. Her. | P. | Altai . | 1829 |
| anglicum, 1 | . | Blue | . | 6, H. Her. | P. | England | |
| album | . | White. | . | 6, H. Her. | P. | Gardens | |
| angustifolium | . | Purple | . | 7, H. Her. | P. | England | |
| arboreum | . | Yellow | . | 5, G. Ev. | 8. | Candia . | . 1788 |
| ascyrifolium | . | White. | . | 7, H. Her. | P. | Portugal | . 1800 |
| aureum | . | Yellow | . | 6, H. | A. | Hungary | . 1820 |
| austriacum | . | Blue | . | 6, H. Her. | P. | Austria . | . 1775 |
| Berlandieri | . | Yel. or. | . | 9, F. | A. | Bijar . | . 1835 |
| bicolor, 2 | . | Yel. blue | . | 6, H. | A. | Morocco | . 1820 |
| campanulatum | . | Yellow | . | 7, H. Her. | P. | Europe . | . 1795 |
| capitatum | . | Yellow | . | 6, H. Her. | P. | Austria . | . 1816 |
| catharticum | . | White. | . | 7, H. | A. | Britain . | |
| Cummingi | . | White. | . | 7, G. Ev. | 8. | Chile . | . 1830 |
| dahuricum | . | Yellow | . | 6, H. Her. | P. | Dahuria | . 1816 |
| decumbens, 3 | . | Red | . | 6, H. Her. | P. | N. Africa | . 1817 |
| diffusum | . | Blue | . | 6, H. Her. | P. | | 1823 |
| flavum | . | Yellow | . | 7, H. Her. | P. | Austria . | . 1793 |
| gallicum | . | Yellow | . | 7, H. | A. | France . | . 1777 |
| grandiflorum | . | Blue | . | 6, H. Her. | P. | S. Eur. . | . 1820 |
| hirsutum | . | Blue | . | 7, H. Her. | P. | Austria . | . 1759 |
| hypericifolium | . | Purple | . | 6, H. Her. | P. | Caucasus | . 1807 |
| Lewisii | . | Blue | . | 6, H. Her. | P. | N. Amer. | . 1820 |
| luteolum | . | Yellow | . | 6, H. | A. | Tauria . | . 1820 |
| marginatum, 4 | . | Blue | . | 6, H. Her. | | | . 1810 |
| maritimum | . | Yellow | . | 7, H. Her. | P. | S. Eur. . | . 1596 |
| mexicanum | . | | . | 6, F. Her. | P. | Mexico . | . 1838 |
| monogynum | . | White. | . | 7, H. Her. | P. | N. Zeal. | . 1822 |
| montanum | . | Blue | . | 6, H. Her. | P. | Switzerl. | . 1817 |
| narbonense | . | Blue | . | 6, F. Her. | P. | S. France | . 1759 |
| nervosum | . | Blue | . | 6, H. Her. | P. | Hungary | . 1822 |
| nodiflorum | . | White. | . | 7, H. Her. | P. | Italy . | . 1759 |
| pallescens | . | Lilac | . | 1, H. Her. | P. | Siberia . | . 1831 |
| quadrifolium | . | Yellow | . | 5, G. Ev. | 8. | C. G. H. | . 1787 |
| reflexum | . | Blue | . | 7, H. Her. | P. | S. Eur. . | . 1777 |
| rigidum | . | Pa. yel. | . | 7, H. | A. | Missouri | . 1807 |
| salsoloides | . | Pink | . | 6, H. Ev. | 8. | S. Eur. . | . 1810 |
| sibiricum | . | Blue | . | 6, H. Her. | P. | Siberia . | . 1775 |
| squamulosum, 6 | . | Blue | . | 7, H. Her. | P. | Tauria . | . 1819 |
| striatum | . | Blue | . | 6, H. | A. | Carolina | . 1817 |
| strictum | . | Yellow | . | 6, H. | B. | S. Eur. . | . 1759 |
| suffruticosum | . | Pink | . | 8, G. Ev. | 8. | Spain . | . 1759 |
| tauricum | . | Yellow | . | 6, H. Ev. | 8. | Tauria . | . 1818 |
| tenuifolium | . | Pink | . | 6, H. Her. | P. | Europe . | . 1759 |

| trigynum | . . | . | Yellow | . | 6, G. Ev. | 8. | E. Ind. . | . 1799 |
| usitatissimum | . . | . | Blue | . | 6, H. | A. | Britain . | |
| viscosum | . . | . | Purple | . | 7, H. Her. | P. | S. Eur. . | . 1818 |
| virginianum | . . | . | Yellow | . | 7, H. Her. | P. | N. Amer. | . 1807 |

**catharticum, nodiflorum.**

LION'S-EAR, see *Leonotis.*

LION'S-FOOT, see *Leontopodium.*

LION'S-LEAF, see *Leóntice Leontopétalon*

LION'S-TAIL, see *Leonotis Leonúra.*

LIP, the lower petal of any irregular flower.

LIPARIA, *Linn.* From *liparos*, brilliant;, in allusion to the shining surface of the leaves. Linn. 14, Or. 10, Nat. Or. *Leguminosæ.* Rather an ornamental plant, and requires to be treated the same as *Priestleya.*

| sphærica | . . . | Orange | . 7, G. Ev. | 8. C. G. H. | . 1794 |

LIPARIS, *Richard.* Dr. Lindley thinks it is probable that the name is derived from *liparos*, unctuous; in allusion to the soft surface of the leaves of some of the species. Linn. 20, Or. 1, Nat. Or. *Orchidaceæ.* This is rather an extensive genus of plants, some of which are very pretty when in flower. The *terrestrial* kinds require the treatment of *Bletia*, and the *epiphytes* may be referred to *Stanhopea.*

| atrata | . . . | Yelsh. grn. | | 8. Epi. | China . | . 1837 |
| cæspitosa | . . . | | | 8. Epi. | Bourbon | |
| cylindrostachya | . | | | 8. Ter. | E. Ind. . | . 1837 |
| elata | . . . | Brn. grn. | . | 9, 8. Epi. | Rio Jan. | . 1826 |
| elegans | . . . | | | 8. Ter. | E. Ind. . | |
| flavescens | . . . | Yellow | . | 8. Ter. | Bourbon | |
| foliosa | . . . | Green | . | 9, 8. Ter. | Maurit. . | . 1823 |
| guineensis | . . . | Green | . | 8. Ter. | S. Leone | . 1832 |
| liliifolia | . . . | Green | . | 7, 8. Ter. | N. Amer. | . 1758 |
| longipes | . . . | Wht. yel. | . | 11, 8. Epi. | Ceylon . | |
| nepalensis | . . . | Green | . | 6, 8. Ter. | Nepal . | |
| pendula | . . . | Green | . | 8. Epi. | India . | |
| priochilus | . . . | Orange | . | 7, 8. Ter. | China . | . 1830 |
| purpurascens | . . | Purple | . | 8. Ter. | I. Bourbon | |
| Walkeriæ | . . . | Purple | . | 8. Ter. | Ceylon . | |

LIPOSTOMA, *G. Don.* From *leipo*, to fall from, and *stoma*, a mouth; lid from capsule. Linn. 4, Or. 1, Nat. Or. *Cinchonaceæ.* This plant is well worth a place in every collection. The flower is a very fine blue, with a yellow throat; for culture and propagation, see *Richardsonia.* *Synonymes:* 1. *Hedyotis campanulæflora, Æginetia capitata.*

| campanuliflora, 1 Blue . . . 7, S. Ev. T. Brasil . . 1825 |

LIPPED, having lips.

LIPPIA, *Linn.* In honour of Augustus Lippi, a French physician and traveller in Abyssinia. Linn. 14, Or. 2, Nat. Or. *Verbenaceæ.* Any rich light soil will suit these plants, and cuttings of the young wood will root readily in sand, under a glass.

| dulcis | . . . . | White | . 8. Her. | P. Trinidad | . 1837 |
| purpurea | . . . | Red | . 6, 8. Ev. | 8. Mexico | . 1823 |

LIQUIDAMBAR, *Linn.* From *liquidus*, liquid; *amber*, amber; in allusion to the gum which exudes from the trees. Linn. 21, Or. 9, Nat. Or. *Balsamaceæ.* Ornamental hardy trees. L. *styraciflua*, or Sweet Gum-tree, attains a great height, and in form and habit bears a strong resemblance to the Maple. They grow freely in any common soil, and plants are obtained from cuttings, or seeds. *Synonyms:* 1. *orientale.*

| imberbe, 1 | . . . | Apetal | . 8, H. De. T. Levant . | . 1759 |
| styraciflua | . . . | Apetal | . 8, H. De. T. N. Amer. | . 1683 |

LIQUORICE, see *Glycyrrhiza.*

LIRIODENDRON, *Jussieu.* From *leirion*, a lily, and *dendron*, a tree; the flower produced by this tree bears some resemblance to a lily, but is more like a tulip. Linn. 13, Or. 6, Nat. Or. *Magnoliaceæ.* The Tulip-tree grows to a considerable height before it will produce its flowers, which are large. It is well suited for planting singly on lawns, or for forming avenues. It is generally increased from imported seeds, which should be sown in March, in a light rich soil, well exposed to the sun, and covering them about half an inch deep. They commonly remain two years in the ground before they come up. From the tonic quality of L. *tulipifera*, it has been said to be equal to Peruvian bark. The wood of this tree is smooth and fine-grained, very easily wrought, and not liable to split. It is used in carving and ornamental work, but is generally used in this country to make the panels of coach and chaise bodies.

| | | | | | | |
|---|---|---|---|---|---|---|
| tulipiferä | . . | Yel. red | 6, H. De. T. | N. Amer. | . 1663 |
| obtusifolia | . . | Yel. red | 6, H. De. T. | Pennsyl. | . 1663 |

**LISIANTHUS**, *Linn.* From *lysis*, dissolution, and *anthos*, a flower; in allusion to its being a powerful cathartic. *Linn.* 5, Or. 1, Nat. Or. *Gentianaceæ.* A mixture of loam, sand, and peat is the soil best suited for these ornamental plants. Cuttings of the shrubby and herbaceous kinds strike freely in sand, under a glass. *L. Russellianus* is the most splendid of the genus; it was discovered by the lamented Drummond in Texas, who described it as "not excelled in beauty by any plant." The flower is large, handsome, borne in a terminal panicle; the corolla is as large as a tulip, of a fine rich purple, with a very deep eye in the centre. The flower continues perfect for two or three weeks. By forcing it early in the spring, and planting out in the open border, it will probably be found to flower as freely as *Phlox Drummondii.* It is figured as an annual, but is very likely to prove biennial. *Synonymes*; 1. *Eustoma silenifolia.* 2. *L. angustifolius.*

| | | | | | | |
|---|---|---|---|---|---|---|
| acutangulus | . . | Yellow | 7, 8. | Her. P. | Peru | . 1820 |
| alatus | . . | White | 7, 8. | A. | Mexico | . 1824 |
| glaucifolius, 1 | . . | Purple | 8. | Ev. S. | | |
| grandiflorus | . . | Yellow | 6, 8. | B. | Trinidad | . 1818 |
| Kunthii, 2 | . . | Green | 5, 8. | A. | S. Amer. | |
| latifolius | . . | Yellow | 8, 8. | Ev. S. | Jamaica | . 1821 |
| Russellianus | . . | Purple | 7, G. | A. | Mexico | . 1835 |
| umbellatus | . . | Yellow | 7, 8. | Ev. S. | Jamaica | . 1822 |

**LISIANTHUS**, see *Tachia.*

**LISSANTHE**, *R. Brown.* From *lissos*, smooth, and *anthos*, a flower. *Linn.* 5, Or. 1, Nat. Or. *Epacrideæ.* Fine ornamental shrubs, attaining the height of three feet, and producing numerous small white flowers; for culture and propagation, see *Epacris*, to which this genus is nearly allied.

| | | | | | | |
|---|---|---|---|---|---|---|
| ciliata | . . | White | 6, G. | Ev. S | V. D. L. | . 1825 |
| daphnoides | . . | White | 6, G. | Ev. S. | N. Holl. | . 1818 |
| alpida | . . | White | 6, G. | Ev. S. | N. S. W. | . 1824 |
| strigosa | . . | White | 6, G. | Ev. S. | N. S. W. | . 1824 |
| subulata | . . | White | 5, G. | Ev. S. | N. S. W. | . 1823 |

**LISTERA**, *R. Brown.* In honour of Martin Lister, M.D., a famous English physician and naturalist. *Linn.* 20, Or. 1, Nat. Or. *Orchidaceæ.* Curious little plants, growing in peat and loam, and increased by divisions of the roots. *Synonyme*: 1. *Neottia ovata.*

| | | | | | | |
|---|---|---|---|---|---|---|
| cordata | . . | Brown | . 6, H. | Ter. | Britain | |
| ovata, 1 | . . | Green | . 5, H. | Ter. | Britain | |

**LITHONTRIPTIC**, having the power of breaking the stone.

**LITHOSPERMUM**, *Linn.* From *lithos*, a stone, and *sperma*, a seed; the little nuts or seeds are extremely hard, and have a surface as smooth as a polished pebble. *Linn.* 5, Or. 1, Nat. Or. *Boraginaceæ.* The species of this genus are all of the easiest culture. The shrubby kinds are well adapted for growing on rock-work, or on the top of walls, where they will speedily establish themselves if allowed to scatter their seeds; or they may be kept in pots among alpine plants, and increased by cuttings. *Synonymes*: 1. *L. latifolium.* 2. *Anchusa tinctoria.*

| | | | | | | |
|---|---|---|---|---|---|---|
| dispermum | . . | Blue | . 6, H. | A. | Siberia | . 1799 |
| distichum | . . | Yel. wht. | 5, G. | Her. P. | Cuba | . 1806 |
| fruticosum | . . | Blue | . 5, H. De. | S. | S. Eur. | . 1683 |
| graminifolium | . . | Blue | . 5, H. | Ev. S. | Italy | . 1825 |
| lineatum | . . | Purple | . 7, H. | B. | Greece | . 1826 |
| officinale | . . | Yellow | . 6, H. | Her. P. | Britain | |
| latifolium, 1 | . . | Yellow | . 6, H. | Her. P. | N. Amer. | . 1825 |
| orientale | . . | Yellow | . 6, H. | Her. P. | Levant | . 1713 |
| prostratum | . . | Blue | . 6, H. | Ev. Tr. | France | . 1825 |
| purp.-cœruleum | . . | Purple | . 5, H. | Her. P. | England | |
| rosmarinifolium | . . | Blue | . 9, H. | Ev. S. | Italy | . 1833 |
| scabrum | . . | White | . 9, G. | Her. P. | C. G. H. | . 1822 |
| strigosum | . . | Blue | . 7, H. | Her. P. | Tauria | . 1820 |
| tenuiflorum | . . | Blue | . 5, H. | A. | Egypt | . 1796 |
| tinctorium, 2 | . . | Blue | . 7, H. | Her. P. | S. Eur. | . 1596 |
| villosum | . . | Blue | . 7, H. | Her. P. | S. France | . 1817 |

*apulum, arvense.*

**LITTÆA**, *Brignoli.* In honour of the Duke of Lytta, near Milan, a patron of botany. *Linn.* 6, Or. 1, Nat. Or. *Amaryllidaceæ.* This is a handsome plant, and was long confounded with *Bonapartea juncea*, but is now found to be a totally different plant. It grows well in sandy loam, and is increased by suckers. *Synonyme*: 1. *Agave geminiflora.*

| | | | | | | |
|---|---|---|---|---|---|---|
| geminiflora, 1 | . | Green | 7 G. | Ev. P. | America | . 1810 |

**LITTORELLA**, *Linn.* From *littus*, the shore; in allusion to its place of growth. *Linn.* 21, Or. 4, Nat. Or. *Plantaginaceæ.* A pretty little sub-aquatic, with neat white flowers, and long tremulous stamens; it is increased by seeds.

| | | | | | | |
|---|---|---|---|---|---|---|
| lacustris | . . | White | . 7, H. Aq. P. | Britain | . . |

**LIVISTONIA**, *R. Brown.* In honour of Patrick Murray, of Livistone, near Edinburgh. *Linn.* 6, Or. 2, Nat. Or. *Palmaceæ.* This is a splendid genus of palms; they require to be grown in a sandy loam, and strong heat.

| | | | | | | |
|---|---|---|---|---|---|---|
| humilis | . . . | | Palm. N. Holl. | . . 1824 |
| inermis | . . . | | Palm. N. Holl. | . . 1824 |

**LIZARD'S-TAIL**, see *Saururus.*

**LOASA**, *Linn.* The meaning is unknown. *Linn.* 13, Or. 2, Nat. Or. *Loasaceæ.* This is a genus of plants highly interesting from the beauty of their curiously formed flowers. They would all be invaluable in collections were it not for the abominable stinging property of some of the species, as *L. Placei*: on that account it is necessary to be very careful in touching them. Any common loamy soil suits them, and they are easily increased by seeds. *Synonymes*: 1. *ambrosiæfolia.* 2. *tricolor.* 3. *acanthifolia.*

| | | | | | | |
|---|---|---|---|---|---|---|
| alba | . . | White | 7, H. | A. | Chile | . 1831 |
| grandiflora | . . | Yellow | G. | A. | Peru | . 1825 |
| hispida, 1 | . . | Yellow | 7, G. Tr. | A. | Lima | . 1830 |
| incana | . . | White | 10, G. | Ev. Tr. | Peru | . 1820 |
| lateritia | . . | Red | 8, F. Cl. | B. | Tucuman | . 1835 |
| nitida, 2 | . . | Yellow | 7, H. | A. | Chile | . 1822 |
| pallida | . . | Yellow | 7, H. | A. | Chile | . 1827 |
| Placei, 3 | . . | Yellow | 7, H. | A. | Chile | . 1822 |
| volubilis | . . | Yellow | 6, G. | A. | Chile | . 1824 |

**LOBATE**, lobed, divided into a number of segments.

**LOBATELY-CRENATED**, having deep crenatures, or indentations.

**LOBE**, a division.

**LOBELIA**, *Linn.* In honour of Matthew Lobel, author of various botanical works; he was a native of Lisle, became physician and botanist to James I, and died in London in 1616. *Linn.* 5, Or. 1, Nat. Or. *Lobeliaceæ.* This is an extremely interesting genus of plants, on account of the beauty of the blossoms. The greenhouse and stove shrubby and herbaceous kinds grow well in a mixture of peat and sand; the shrubby kinds are readily increased by cuttings in the same kind of soil, and the herbaceous species by dividing, and by seeds. The hardy herbaceous kinds do well in a light rich earth, or peat soil; but in winter most of them require the protection of a frame. The greenhouse annuals and biennials must be sown in pots, and treated as other greenhouse annuals and biennials. The seeds of the hardy kinds have only to be sown in the open border. *L. longiflora* is one of the most venomous of plants. Barton says the Spanish Americans call it *Rebenta Cavallos*, because it proves fatal to horses that eat it, swelling them until they burst. Taken internally, it acts as a violent cathartic, the effects of which no remedy can assuage, and which end in death. *Synonymes*: 1. *L. erinoides.* 2. *L. goodenioides.* 3. *L. spicata.* 3. *L. crispa.* 4. *L. commutata.* 5. *L. maculata.* 6. *Isotoma axillaris.* 7. *L. pedunculata.* 8. *L. micrantha.*

| | | | | | | |
|---|---|---|---|---|---|---|
| acuminata | . . | Gra. yel. | 6, 8. | Ev. S. | W. Ind. | . 1822 |
| alata | . . | Blue | . 6, G. | Her. P. | N. Holl. | . 1804 |
| amœna | . . | Blue | . 7, H. | Her. P. | N. Amer. | . 1812 |
| anceps | . . | Blue | . 6, H. | A. | C. G. H. | . 1818 |
| arguta | . . | Blue | . 9, S. | Her. P. | Chile | . 1824 |
| assurgens | . . | Scarlet | 8, G. | Ev. S. | W. Ind. | . 1787 |
| atro-cœrulea | . . | Dk. blue | 7, H. | Her. P. | Hybrid | . 1836 |
| atrosanguinea | . . | Black | 7, H. | Her. P. | Eng. hyb. | . 1836 |
| bellidifolia | . . | Blue | . 7, G. | Her. P. | C. G. H. | . 1790 |
| bicolor | . . | Pa. blue | 7, G. | A. | C. G. H. | . 1795 |
| Bridgesii | . . | Pink | . 6, G. | Her. P. | Chile | . 1836 |
| cœrulea | . . | Blue | . 6, G. | Her. P. | C. G. H. | . 1824 |
| campanulata | . . | Blue | . 6, H. | A. | C. G. H. | . 1821 |
| campanuloides, 1 | . | White | . 6, 8. | Her. P. | China | . 1820 |
| cardinalis | . . | Scarlet | . 7, H. | Her. P. | Virginia | . 1629 |
| Milleri | . . | Pink | . 7, H. | Her. P. | Eng. hyb. | . 1835 |
| Cavanillesiana | . | Red | . 6, 8. | Her. P. | N. Spain | . 1825 |
| Claytoniana, 2 | . | Blue | . 6, H. | Her. P. | N. Amer. | . 1824 |
| Cliffortiana | . . | Pink | . 7, H. | A. | N. Amer. | |
| coelestis | . . | Blue | . 7, H. | Her. P. | N. Amer. | . 1821 |
| colorata | . . | Orange | 8, F. | Her. P. | N. Amer. | . 1822 |
| coronopifolia | . . | Blue | . 7, G. | Her. P. | C. G. H. | . 1752 |
| crenata | . . | Blue | . 4, G. | Her. P. | C. G. H. | . 1794 |

| | | | | | |
|---|---|---|---|---|---|
| dubĭlis | . . . | Blue | . 7, G. | A. C. G. H. | . 1774 |
| decŭmbens | . . . | Blue | . 10, G. Her. P. | C. G. H. | . 1820 |
| densĭrrĕus | . . . | Purple | . 7, F. Ev. S. | Chile | . 1826 |
| dentātă | . . . | Blue | . 6, G. Her. P. | N. Holl. | . 1824 |
| Erĭnŭs | . . . | Blue | . 7, G. Har. P. | C. G. H. | . 1752 |
| fenestrālis | . . . | Blue | . 7, H. | A. Mexico | . 1824 |
| fŭlgens | . . . | Scarlet | . 7, F. Her. P. | Mexico | . 1809 |
| grācĭlis | . . . | Dk. blue | . 7, G. | A. N. S. W. | . 1801 |
| grandĭs | . . . | Purple | . 6, H. Her. P. | Hybrid | . 1834 |
| heterophȳllă | . . . | Blue | . 9, F. Her. P. | V. D. L. | . 1837 |
| hirsūtă | . . . | Blue | . 7, G. Her. P. | C. G. H. | . 1759 |
| hypocrateriførmis | Blue | . 9, G. | A. N. Holl. | . 1829 |
| ilicifòlia | . . . | Pink | . 6, G. Her. P. | C. G. H. | . 1815 |
| inflātă | . . . | Pa. blue | . 7, H. | A. N. Amer. | . 1759 |
| inundātă | . . . | Blue | . 6, G. Her. P. | N. Holl. | . 1821 |
| Kalmĭi | . . . | Blue | . 7, H. Her. P. | Carolina | . 1820 |
| Krauŭssĭi | . . . | Blue | . 1, G. Her. P. | Dominica | . 1828 |
| laurentĭa | . . . | Blue | . 7, G. | A. Italy | . 1778 |
| lineārĭs | . . . | Blue | . G. Ev. | C. G. H. | . 1791 |
| longiflòră | . . . | White | . 5, S. Her. P. | Jamaica | . 1752 |
| longifòlĭa | . . . | Purple | . H. Her. P. | Hybrid | . 1834 |
| minĭmă | . . . | White | . 7, G. Her. P. | C. G. H. | . 1800 |
| minūtă | . . . | White | . 7, H. Her. P. | C. G. H. | . 1772 |
| mollĭs | . . . | Purple | . 6, H. Her. P. | Dominica | . 1828 |
| nicotianæfòlĭa | . | . 6, G. | B. E. Ind. | . 1823 |
| Nuttallĭi | . . . | Blue | . 7, H. Her. P. | N. Amer. | . 1824 |
| odorātă | . . . | White | . 9, G. Ev. | Tr. B. Ayres | . 1832 |
| pauciflòră, 4 | . . | Blue | . 7, G. Her. P. | Mexico | . 1824 |
| pedunculātă | . . | Blue | . 10, G. Her. P. | N. S. W. | . 1819 |
| persicifòlĭa | . . | Purple | . 6, S. Her. P. | W. Ind. | . 1824 |
| pinifòlĭa | . . . | Blue | . 6, G. Ev. | C. G. H. | . 1782 |
| polyphȳllă | . . . | Purple | . 8, H. Her. P. | Valparaiso | . 1829 |
| propinqua | . . . | Scarlet | . 9, F. Her. P. | Hybrid | . |
| pubērŭlă | . . . | Pa. blue | . 6, H. Her. P. | N. Amer. | . 1800 |
| glabella | . . . | Pur. blue | . 7, H. Her. P. | Louisiana | . 1832 |
| pubescens | . . . | Blue | . 9, G. Her. P. | C. G. H. | . 1780 |
| purpurascens | . . | Blue | . 7, G. Her. P. | N. S. W. | . 1809 |
| pyramidālis | . . | Blue | . 9, G. Her. P. | Nepal | . 1822 |
| racemòsă | . . . | Green | . 7, G. Ev. S. | W. Ind. | . 1818 |
| ramòsă | . . . | Dk. blue | . 8, H. Her. P. | S. River. | . 1838 |
| rhizophȳtă | . . . | White | . 7, G. Her. P. | C. G. H. | . 1800 |
| robŭstă | . . . | Blue | . 8, S. Ev. S. | Hayti | . 1830 |
| rugulòsă, 5 | . . | Blue | . 6, G. Her. P. | N. Zeal. | . 1828 |
| secundă | . . . | White | . 6, G. Her. P. | C. G. H. | . 1790 |
| senecioldēs, 6 | . | Blue | . 7, G. Her. P. | N. Holl. | . 1824 |
| serrulātă | . . . | Blue | . 6, H. | A. Spain | . 1820 |
| setācĕă | . . . | Blue | . 6, G. Her. P. | C. G. H. | . 1816 |
| simplēx | . . . | Blue | . 7, G. | C. G. H. | . 1794 |
| Simsĭi, 7 | . . . | Blue | . 10, G. Her. P. | C. G. H. | . 1819 |
| splendens | . . . | Scarlet | . 6, F. Her. P. | Mexico | . 1814 |
| stellātă | . . . | Crimson | . H. Her. P. | Hybrid | . 1836 |
| syphilitĭcă | . . | Li. blue | . 9, H. Her. P. | Virginia | . 1665 |
| alba | . . . | White | . 8, H. Her. P. | | |
| hȳbrĭdă | . . . | Blue | . 8, H. Her. P. | Hybrid | . |
| tenella | . . . | Pur. vio. | . 5, H. Her. P. | Sicily | . 1821 |
| Thunbergĭi | . . | Blue | . 8, G. Her. P. | C. G. H. | . 1822 |
| tomentòsă | . . . | Blue | . 7, G. Her. P. | C. G. H. | . 1821 |
| trialātă, 8 | . . | Blue | . 7, G. Her. P. | Nepal | . 1822 |
| triquetră | . . . | Blue | . 7, G. Her. P. | C. G. H. | . 1774 |
| umbellātă | . . . | Blue | . 6, G. Har. P. | | . 1818 |
| ūrens | . . . | Blue | . 6, H. | A. England | . |
| violācĕă | . . . | Violet | . H. Her. P. | Hybrid | . |
| zeylānĭcă | . . . | Blue | . 6, G. Her. P. | E. Ind. | . 1821 |

LOBĒLĬA, see *Parastrănthŭs.*
LOBĒLĬA, see *Prattĭă.*
LOBĒLĬA, see *Siphocampȳlŭs.*
LOBĒLĬA, see *Tŭpă.*
LOCĂTED, placed.
LOCŬLAMENTS, partitions or cells of a seed-vessel.
LOCŬLAR; a fruit is called unilocular if it contains but one cell, bilocular if it contains two cells, and so on.
LOCUST-TREE, see *Hymenœă.*
LODDIGĒSĬA, *Sims.* In honour of Conrad Loddiges, the celebrated nurseryman at Hackney near London, and father of the present eminent proprietors. He died in 1820. *Linn.* 16, Or. 6, Nat. Or. *Leguminosæ.* This is an extremely interesting shrub, succeeding well in an equal mixture of sandy loam and peat; and cuttings of the young wood root freely planted in sand, under a glass.

| | | | | | |
|---|---|---|---|---|---|
| oxalidifòlĭa | . . | Pa. pur. | . 6, G. Ev. S. | C. G. H. | . 1802 |

LODOÏCĔA, *Labillardière.* Named after Laodice, the daughter of Priamus and Hecuba. *Linn.* 22, Or. 12, Nat. Or. *Palmaceæ.* For the culture and propagation of this palm, see *Cocos.* Synonyme: 1. *Cocos maldivica.*

| | | | | | |
|---|---|---|---|---|---|
| sechellàrum | . . . | | Palm. Seychelles | . . | |

LŒFLINGĬA. Named by Linnæus, in compliment to his disciple Peter Lœfling, a traveller in Spain and America, who died on his travels in 1756. *Linn.* 3, Or. 1, Nat. Or. *Alsinaceæ.* The seed of these plants need only be sown in the open ground where they are to remain.

| | | | | | |
|---|---|---|---|---|---|
| hispānĭcă | . . . | Green | . 6, H. | A. Spain | . 1770 |
| pentāndră | . . . | Green | . 6, H. | A. S. Eur. | . 1820 |

LOGĂNĬA, *R. Brown.* In honour of J. Logan, a distinguished botanist. *Linn.* 5, Or. 1, Nat. Or. *Loganiaceæ.* Rather small but interesting shrubs, which produce their flowers in axillary or terminal bunches. They grow well in sandy loam and peat, and ripened cuttings root freely in sand, under a glass. Synonymes: 1. *Euosma albiflora.* 2. *Esacum vaginale.*

| | | | | | |
|---|---|---|---|---|---|
| floribūndă, 1 | . | White | . 4, G. Ev. S. N. S. W. | . 1797 |
| latifòlĭa, 2 | . . | White | . G. Ev. S. N. Holl. | . 1816 |
| ligustrìna | . . . | | G. Ev. S. N. Zeal. | . 1837 |
| revolūtă | . . . | White | . G. Ev. S. N. Holl. | . 1826 |

LOGWOOD, see *Hæmatôxȳlon.*
LŌLĬŬM, *Linn.* From the Celtic, *loloa,* which in Latin is rendered *lolium,* Rye-grass. *Linn.* 3, Or. 2, Nat. Or. *Gramineæ.* This is a very valuable genus of grasses. *L. perenne,* or perennial Rye-grass, is one of the most esteemed fodder grasses, and is said to have been the first species that was taken into cultivation in Europe. They grow best in a good rich soil, and increase readily from seeds.

| | | | | | |
|---|---|---|---|---|---|
| arvense | . . . | | Apetal | . 7, Grass. England | . . |
| perenne | . . . | | Apetal | . 5, Grass. Britain | . . |
| compositum | . . | | Apetal | . 5, Grass. Britain | . . |
| humile | . . . | | Apetal | . 5, Grass. Britain | . . |
| monstrôsum | . . | | Apetal | . 5, Grass. Britain | . . |
| multifidum | . . | | Apetal | . 5, Grass. Britain | . . |
| paniculātum | . . | | Apetal | . 5, Grass. Britain | . . |
| ramòsum | . . . | | Apetal | . 5, Grass. Britain | . . |
| Russelliànum | . . | | Apetal | . 5, Grass. Britain | . . |
| Stickneyānum | . . | | Apetal | . 5, Grass. Britain | . . |
| tenue | . . . | | Apetal | . 5, Grass. Britain | . . |
| tivipărum | . . . | | Apetal | . 5, Grass. Britain | . . |
| vulgāre | . . . | | Apetal | . 5, Grass. Britain | . . |
| Whitwòrthĭi | . . | | Apetal | . 5, Grass. Britain | . . |
| temulentum | . . | | Apetal | . 7, Grass. Britain | . . |

*multiflòrum, rigĭdum, speciôsum, tenŭě.*

LOMĂRĬA, *Willdenow.* Derived from *loma,* an edge; in allusion to the marginal position of the indusia. *Linn.* 24, Or. 1, Nat. Or. *Polypodiaceæ.* An interesting genus of ferns; for culture and propagation, see *Lindsæa.* Synonymes: 1. *Stegania falcata.* 2. *Acrostichum longifolium.* 3. *Stegania nuda, Onoclea nuda.* 4. *Stegania procera, Osmunda procera.* 5. *Blechnum boreale.*

| | | | | | |
|---|---|---|---|---|---|
| attenuātă | . . . | Brown | . 8, G. Her. P. | | . 1838 |
| falcātă, 1 | . . | Brown | . 7, G. Her. P. | V. D. L. | . 1823 |
| lanceolātă | . . | Brown | . 9, G. Her. P. | N. Holl. | . 1830 |
| longifòlĭa, 2 | . . | Brown | . 6, S. Her. Cr. W. Ind. | . 1810 |
| nūdă, 3 | . . . | Brown | . 6, G. Her. P. | V. D. L. | . 1822 |
| Patersònĭ | . . . | Brown | . 9, G. Her. P. | N. Holl. | . 1830 |
| procēră, 4 | . . | Brown | . 7, G. Her. P. | N. Zeal. | . 1822 |
| spicānt, 5 | . . | Brown | . 7, H. Her. P. | Britain | . |

LOMĂTĬA, *R. Brown.* From *loma,* a border; in allusion to the winged edge of the seeds. *Linn.* 4, Or. 1, Nat. Or. *Proteaceæ.* This is a genus of very handsome plants, which thrive well in a sandy peat soil, and increase by cuttings in sand, under a glass.

| | | | | | |
|---|---|---|---|---|---|
| dentātă | . . . | | G. Ev. S. Chile | . 1824 |
| ilicifòlĭa | . . . | | . 7, G. Ev. S. N. Holl. | . 1824 |
| longifòlĭa | . . . | Green | . 7, G. Ev. S. N. S. W. | . 1816 |
| silaifòlĭa | . . . | Orange | . 7, G. Ev. S. N. S. W. | . 1792 |
| tinctòrĭa | . . . | | G. Ev. S. N. Holl. | . 1822 |

LŌNĂS, *Gærtner.* The meaning unknown. *Linn.* 19, Or. 1, Nat. Or. *Compositæ.* The seed of this plant has only to be sown in the open ground. Synonyme: 1. *Athanasia annua.*

| | | | | | |
|---|---|---|---|---|---|
| inodòră, 1 | . . | Yellow | . 7, H. | A. Barbary | . 1686 |

LONCHĪTĬS, *Linn.* From *lonche,* a lance; in allusion to the form of the fronds. *Linn.* 24, Or. 1, Nat. Or. *Polypodiaceæ.* This genus consists of two very handsome ferns, which grow best in a mixture of turfy loam and peat, and increase by divisions. Synonyme: 1. *Pteris podophylla.*

| | | | | | |
|---|---|---|---|---|---|
| hirsūtă | . . . | Brown | . 8, S. Her. P. W. Ind. | . 1793 |
| pedātă, 1 | . . | Brown | . 6, S. Her. P. Jamaica | . 1793 |

LONCHOCĂRPŬS, *Humboldt, Bonp. and Kunth.* From *lonche,* a lance, and *karpos,* a fruit; in reference to the lance shape of the pods. *Linn.* 17, Or. 4, Nat. Or. *Leguminosæ.* Ornamental shrubs, growing well in loam and peat, and increased by cuttings of the young wood planted in sand, under a glass, in heat. Synonymes: 1. *Dalbergia domingensis.* 2. *Amerimnum latifolium, Pterocarpus latifolius.* 3.

*A. pubescens.* 4. *Robinia hispida, roses.* 5. *R. sepium.* 6. *R. sericeus.* 7. *R. violacea.*

| | | | | | |
|---|---|---|---|---|---|
| domingénsis, 1 | Red | 8. Ev. T. St. Domin. | 1820 |
| latifólia, 2 | Purple | 8. Ev. T. W. Ind. | 1808 |
| macrophýllus | Purple | 8. Ev. T. S. Amer. | 1818 |
| pubéscens, 3 | Purple | 8. Ev. T. Caraccas | 1824 |
| pyxidátus | Purple | 8. Ev. T. Cuba | 1820 |
| rósea, 4 | Red | 8. Ev. T. S. Amer. | 1700 |
| sepiúm, 5 | Purple | 8. Ev. T. S. Amer. | 1821 |
| sericéus, 6 | Purple | 8. Ev. T. W. Ind. | 1826 |
| violacéus, 7 | Violet | 8. Ev. T. Carthage | 1759 |

LONOCHÁMPSIX, *Willdenow.* In honour of J. L. A. Loiseleur des Longchamps, M.D., a famous French botanist. *Linn.* 19, Or. 2. Nat. Or. *Composita.* The seed of this pretty little annual merely requires sowing in the open ground. *Synonymes:* 1. *Pectis discoidea, Leysera discoidea, Gnaphalium leyseroides.*

| | | | | | |
|---|---|---|---|---|---|
| capillifólia, 1 | Yellow | 6, H. | A. Barbary | 1822 |

LONDON-PRIDE, see *Saxifrāgă umbrósă.*
LONDON-ROCKET, see *Sisymbriūm Irīŏ.*
LONGICOANU, long-spurred.

LONICÉRĂ, *Linn.* Named after Adam Lonicer, a German botanist, who died in 1586. *Linn.* 5, Or. 1, Nat. Or. *Caprifoliaceæ.* This is a genus of very ornamental shrubs, closely allied to the genus *Caprifolium.* The species grow in any common soil, and are readily increased by cuttings taken off in autumn, and planted in a sheltered situation. *Synonymes:* 1. *L. sibirica.* 2. *L. campaniflora.* 3. *Symphoricarpus puniceus.*

| | | | | | |
|---|---|---|---|---|---|
| alpigéná | Yellow | 4, H. De. S. | S. Eur. | 1596 |
| sibírica, 1 | Yellow | 4, H. De. S. | Siberia | 1810 |
| cærúleá | Yellow | 5, H. De. S. | Switzerl. | 1629 |
| canadénsis | Yellow | 5, H. De. S. | Canada | 1812 |
| canéscens | | 4, H. De. Tw. | Europe | |
| ciliáta | Wht. red | 4, H. De. S. | N. Amer. | 1824 |
| álbă | Wht. red | 4, H. De. S. | N. Amer. | 1824 |
| flexuósá | Orange | 7, F. Ev. S. | Japan | 1806 |
| ibérica | Orange | 4, H. De. S. | Iberia | 1824 |
| involucráta | Yellow | 4, H. De. S. | Hud. Bay | 1824 |
| microphýllá | | 4, H. De. S. | Siberia | 1818 |
| nígra | Pa. yel. | 4, H. De. S. | Switzerl. | 1597 |
| campaniflóra, 2 | Yellow | 5, H. De. S. | N. Amer. | |
| oblongifólia | White | 4, H. De. S. | N. Amer. | 1823 |
| orientális | Yellow | 6, H. De. S. | Iberia | 1825 |
| punícea, 3 | Crimson | 4, H. De. S. | N. Amer. | 1822 |
| pyrenáicá | White | 4, H. De. S. | Pyrenees | 1739 |
| tatáricá | Pink | 4, H. De. S. | Russia | 1752 |
| albiflórá | White | 5, H. De. S. | Pyrenees | 1739 |
| rubriflórá | Red | 4, H. De. S. | Russia | 1752 |
| villósá | Yellow | 4, H. De. S. | Canada | 1820 |
| xylostéum | Yellow | 6, H. De. S. | England | |

LOOKING-GLASS PLANT, see *Heritièră.*
LOOSE-STRIFE, see *Lysimachiă.*

LOPÉZIĂ, *Cavanilles.* Named in honour of J. Lopez, a Spanish botanist. *Linn.* 6, Or. 1, Nat. Or. *Onagraceæ.* This is a genus of very elegant plants. The annual species should be raised on a gentle hotbed, and afterwards transplanted out into a warm border. The biennial kinds require to be kept in the greenhouse.

| | | | | | |
|---|---|---|---|---|---|
| cordáta | Purple | 8, H. | A. Mexico | 1821 |
| coronáta | Red | 8, H. | A. Mexico | 1805 |
| hirsúta | Red | 8, G. | B. Mexico | 1796 |
| púmila | Red | 8, H. | A. Mexico | 1824 |
| racemósá | Red | 8, G. | B. Mexico | 1792 |

LOPHÁNTHUS, *Bentham.* From *lophos*, a crest, and *anthos*, a flower; in allusion to the crenated middle lobe of the lower lip of the corolla. *Linn.* 14, Or. 1, Nat. Or. *Labiatæ.* Very pretty plants, growing in common garden soil, and increased by dividing the roots, or by cuttings planted under a glass, or by seeds when those are procured. *Synonymes:* 1. *Hyssopus anisatus.* 2. *H. Lophanthus.* 3. *Nepeta multifida.* 4. *H. nepetoides.* 5. *H. scrophularioides.*

| | | | | | |
|---|---|---|---|---|---|
| anisátus, 1 | Blue | 7, H. Her. P. N. Amer. | 1826 |
| multifídus, 3 | White | 7, H. Her. P. Siberia | 1795 |
| nepetoídes, 4 | Yel. wht. | 7, H. Her. P. N. Amer. | 1692 |
| scrophularioídes, 5 | Pink | 7, H. Her. P. N. Amer. | 1800 |
| urticæfólius, 2 | Blue | 7, H. Her. P. N. Amer. | 1826 |

LOPHIÓLĂ, *Ker.* A diminutive of *lopha*, a crest; in reference to the crest of the sepals. *Linn.* 6, Or. 1, Nat. Or. *Hæmodoraceæ.* This is a rare little herbaceous plant, growing in peat soil in a damp situation. It will also grow and flower well in pots placed in pans of water; it is increased by

dividing the roots. *Synonyme:* 1. *Conostylis americana.*

| | | | | | |
|---|---|---|---|---|---|
| aúrea, 1 | Yellow | 6, H. Her. P. N. Amer. | 1811 |

LOPHÍRĂ, *Banks.* One of the sepals is extended out into a ligulate wing or crest; whence the name from *lophos*, a crest. *Linn.* 12, Or. 1, Nat. Or. *Dipteraceæ.* This is a very fine low-growing tree. It has tap roots, and therefore requires to be planted in a very deep pot, in order to allow the roots to descend. It should be grown in sandy loam and peat, and kept rather dry; cuttings of the ripened wood will root in sand, under a glass, in heat. In Sierra Leone, it is called *Scurby* or *Scrubby Oak.*

| | | | | | |
|---|---|---|---|---|---|
| africáná | White | 6, S. Ev. T. S. Leone | 1822 |

LOPHÍUM, *Fries.* From *lophion*, a little hillock. *Linn.* 24, Or. 9, Nat. Or. *Fungi.* These extremely minute plants are very similar to the valves of a bivalved shell—*elátăm, mytilinăm.*

LOPHOSPÉRMUM, *D. Don.* From *lophos*, a crest, and *sperma*, a seed; the seeds are furnished with a crest-like wing. *Linn.* 14, Or. 2, Nat. Or. *Scrophulariaceæ.* This genus is composed of very elegant plants, with large purple, or rose-coloured flowers; for culture and propagation, see *Maurandya.* *Synonyme:* 1. *Rhodochiton volubile, L. Rhodochiton.*

| | | | | | |
|---|---|---|---|---|---|
| atrosanguíneúm, 1 | Drk. pur. | 6, G. Ev. Cl. Mexico | 1833 |
| erubéscens | Rosy | 8, F. Ev. Cl. Talapa | 1830 |
| scándens | Pur. vio. | 6, G. Ev. Cl. Mexico | 1834 |

LOPIMIĂ, *Marthus.* From *lopimus*, signifying easy of decortication. *Linn.* 14, Or. 3, Nat. Or. *Malvaceæ.* This plant grows well in any rich soil, and is readily increased by young cuttings taken off at a joint, and planted in sand, under a glass, in heat. *Synonyme:* 1. *Sida malacophylla.*

| | | | | | |
|---|---|---|---|---|---|
| malacophýllá, 1 | Red | 8, S. Ev. S. Bahia | 1823 |

LORÁNTHÚs, *Linn.* From *loron*, a thong, and *anthos*, a flower; in allusion to the long linear form of the petals. *Linn.* 6, Or. 1, Nat. Or. *Loranthaceæ.* A genus of parasitical plants, with the habit of the well-known Mistletoe.

| | | | | | |
|---|---|---|---|---|---|
| europǽus | Greenish | Parasite. Europe | 1824 |

LORÁNTHÚs, see *Nýtsiă.*
LORATE, thong or strap shaped.
LORD ANSON'S PEA, see *Lathýrus magellānicus.*
LÓRĕÚs, leathery.
LOTE, see *Zizýphus Lótŭs.*
LÓTŬS. From *lotos* of Theophrastus; the true *Lotus* is *Zizyphus Lotus.* *Linn.* 17, Or. 4, Nat. Or. *Leguminosæ.* An ornamental genus of plants. The greenhouse and frame species grow freely in any light soil, and are increased by cuttings of the young wood planted in sand, under a glass, or they may be increased by seeds. The hardy kinds are well suited for ornamenting rock-work, or dry banks. The seeds of the hardy annual species need only be sown in the open ground in spring. *L. corniculatus* and *L. major* are sometimes sown with white clover and cow-grass, in laying down permanent pastures. *Synonymes:* 1. *L. diffusus.* 2. *Cytisus argenteus.* 3. *L. decumbens.* 4. *Trigonella indica.*

| | | | | | |
|---|---|---|---|---|---|
| angustissimús, 1 | Yellow | 5, H. Tr. A. Britain | |
| anthylloídes | Drk. pur. | 6, G. Ev. S. C. G. H. | 1812 |
| arábicus | Pink | 7, H. Tr. A. Arabia | 1773 |
| arenárius | Yellow | 4, H. Tr. A. Teneriffe | 1831 |
| argéntátus, 2 | Yellow | 6, F. Her. P. | 1827 |
| angustifólius | Yellow | 7, F. Her. P. | 1827 |
| atropurpúreús | Drk. brn. | G. Ev. S. Teneriffe | 1830 |
| austrális | Pink | 7, G. Her. P. N. Holl. | 1806 |
| ciliátus | Yellow | 7, H. Tr. A. Sicily | 1812 |
| coimbrénsis | Wht. red | 6, H. | A. Portugal | 1800 |
| corniculátus | Yellow | 6, H. De. Tr. Britain | |
| alpínus | Yellow | 6, H. De. Tr. Switzerl. | 1819 |
| flóre-plénó | Yellow | 7, H. De. Tr. Gardens | |
| crassifólius | Yellow | 8, H. Her. P. S. Eur. | 1812 |
| créticús | Yellow | 6, G. Ev. Tr. Levant | 1680 |
| cytisoídes | Yellow | 6, H. Tr. A. S. Eur. | 1752 |
| decúmbens | Yellow | 7, H. Tr. A. Europe | 1816 |
| depréssús | | 7, H. De. Tr. Hungary | 1819 |
| Dioscóridis | Yellow | 6, H. | A. Nice | 1658 |
| edúlis | Yellow | 7, H. Tr. A. Italy | 1759 |
| flexuósús | Yellow | 7, H. Tr. Europe | 1816 |
| Forstéri, 3 | Yellow | 7, H. De. Tr. Britain | |
| Gebélia | Yellow | 5, F. Ev. Tr. Aleppo | 1816 |
| glaúcus | Yellow | 7, F. Her. P. Madeira | 1777 |
| glabérrimús | White | 7, H. Tr. A. S. Eur. | 1816 |

grácilis . . . Yellow . 7, H. A. Hungary . 1812
hispidùs . . . Yellow . 7, H. Tr. A. France . 1817
indicùs, 4 . . Yellow . 7, S. Tr. A. E. Ind. . 1793
jacobæùs . . Drk. brn. . 7, G. Ev. S. C. Verd . 1714
luteùs . . . Yellow . 7, G. Ev. S.
màjor . . . Yellow . 6, H. Her. P. Britain .
villòsùs . . Yellow . 6, H. Her. P. Switzer. . 1817
microphýllùs . Yellow . 6, G. Tr. A. C. G. H. . 1827
odoràtùs . . Yellow . 6, F. A. Barbary . 1804
ornithopodioldès Yellow . 6, H. A. Sicily . 1683
palùstris . . Yellow . 6, H. Her. P. Crete . 1821
pedunculatùs . Yellow . 7, H. Her. P. Spain . 1814
peregrinùs . . Yellow . 7, H. A. S. Eur. . 1713
pilosissimùs . Yellow . 7, H. A. France . 1818
portosanctánùs . Yellow . 7, H. Ev. S. Porto San. . 1829
pusillùs . . . Yellow . 7, H. A. S. Eur. . 1816
sessilifòlùs . . Yellow . 7, G. Her. P. Teneriffe . 1820
spectàbilis . . Yellow . G. Ev. S. Teneriffe
suavèolèns . . Yellow . 7, H. Her. P. S. France . 1816
ténùis . . . Yellow . 7, H. A. Hungary . 1816

LOÙRÆÀ, *Necker.* Unquestionably the name of some person. *Linn.* 17, Or. 4, Nat. Or. *Leguminosæ.* These plants are worth cultivating; they require the same treatment as most other biennials. *Synonyme:* 1. *Hedysarum vespertilionis.*

reniformis . . . Violet . 6, S. B. China . 1818
vespertilionis, 1 . White . . 7, S. B. Co. China . 1780

LOURÈÀ, *Cavanilles.* In honour of John de Loureiro, a Portuguese botanical author. *Linn.* 22, Or. 13, Nat. Or. *Euphorbiaceæ.* These plants grow well in a mixture of loam and peat; and cuttings root readily in sand, under a glass, in heat

cuneifòlia . . . White. . 7, S. Ev. S. Mexico . 1824
glandulòsa . . . 8. Ev. S. Mexico . 1799

LOUSEWORT, see *Pediculàris*
LOVAGE, see *Ligùsticùm.*
LOVAGE, see *Achilléa Ligùsticà.*
LOVE-APPLE, see *Lycopèrsicùm esculèntùm.*
LOVE-GRASS, see *Eragrostis.*
LOVE-LIES-BLEEDING, see *Amaranthùs caudàtùs.*
LOWÈÀ, *Lindley.* In compliment to the Rev. Mr. Lowe, Travelling Bachelor of the University of Cambridge. *Linn.* 12, Or. 3, Nat. Or. *Rosaceæ.* This ornamental plant is found in its native country growing in saltish fields. Although it is an old inhabitant of our gardens, it is yet very scarce, being very difficult of cultivation. A mixture of loam, peat, and sand appears to suit it best, and it may be increased by seeds or layers. *Synonyme:* 1. *Rosa berberifòlia.*

berberifòlia . . . Yel. pur. . 6, F. De S. Persia . . 1790

LUBÍNÌÀ, *Ventenat.* In honour of M. de St. Lubin, a French officer and botanist. *Linn.* 5, Or. 1, Nat. Or. *Primulaceæ.* This species grows freely in loam and peat, and young plants are readily obtained from cuttings.

atropurpúreà . . Purple F. Her. P. C. G. H. . 1820

LUBRICATE, slippery.
LUCERN, see *Medicàgò satìvà.*
LÙCIDÙS, shining, glittering.
LUCÙLÌÀ, *Sweet.* *Luculi sra* is the name given to the tree by the Nepalese. *Linn.* 5, Or. 1, Nat. Or. *Cinchonaceæ.* This fine tree is worthy of a place in every collection, as there cannot be a more beautiful object than this tree is when covered with its numerous cymes of pink-coloured, very fragrant, flowers. It grows well in an equal mixture of light turfy loam and peat; and cuttings will root in sand, under a glass, in a little heat. *Synonymes:* 1. *Cinchona gratissima, Mussænda Luculia.*

gratissima . . . Red . . 8, G. Ev. S. Nepal . . 1823

LUCÙMA, *Jussieu.* *Lucuma* is the name of the tree in Peru. *Linn.* 5, Or. 1, Nat. Or. *Sapotaceæ.* Fruit-bearing trees, cultivated in a mixture of rich loam, with a little light soil to keep it open; and cuttings of the ripened wood root in sand, under a glass, in heat. *Synonyme:* 1. *Achras mammosa.* 2. *A. Lucuma.*

Bonplándià . . . White . . 8. Ev. T. Cuba . . 1822
mammòsà, 1 . . White . . 8. Ev. T. S. Amer. . 1739
obovàtà, 2 . . . White . . 8. Ev. T. Peru . . 1822
salicifòlià . . . White . . 8. Ev. T. Mexico . . 1823

LÙDÌÀ, *Lamarck.* From *ludo*, to sport; the leaves of *L. heterophylla* assume various forms. *Linn.* 13, Or. 1, Nat. Or. *Bixaceæ.* Rich loam, and a little peat, suit these plants; and cuttings soon root in

sand, under a glass, in heat. *Synonyme.* 1. *tuberculata.*

heterophýllà . . Yellow . 7, S. Ev. S. Maurit. . . 1823
sessiliflòrà, 1 . . Yellow . 7, S. Ev. S. Maurit. . . 1820

LUDWIGÌÀ, *Linn.* In honour of Christian Gottlieb Ludwig, professor of medicine at Leipsic and botanical author, in 1787. *Linn.* 4, Or. 2, Nat. Or. *Onagraceæ.* Uninteresting plants, not worth cultivating except in general collections—*parviflòrâ, prostrâtâ.*

LÙFFÀ, *Cavanilles.* Derived from *louff*, the Arabic name of *L. ægyptiaca.* *Linn.* 21, Or. 5, Nat. Or. *Cucurbitaceæ.* A remarkable kind of gourd, possessed of a very disagreeable odour; for culture and propagation, see *Cucumis.* *Synonymes:* 1. *Cucumis acutangulus.* 2. *Momordica luffa.*

acutángùla, 1 . . Purple . 7, F. Tr. A. N. Amer. . 1692
ægyptiacà, 2 . . Purple . 7, F. Tr. A. E. Ind. . , 1789
fœtidà . . . . Purple . 7, H. Tr. A. India . . 1812

LUHÈÀ, *Willdenow.* In honour of Charles Vander Luhe, a famous German botanist. *Linn.* 18, Or. 2, Nat. Or. *Tiliaceæ.* This is a very pretty plant, which thrives well in a mixture of peat and loam; and cuttings of the nearly ripened wood root readily in sand, under a glass, in heat. In Brazil, they use the bark of *L. paniculata* for tanning leather.

paniculàtà . . . Rosy . 8. Ev. Cl. Brasil . . 1828

LUÌSÌÀ, *Gaudich.* The meaning of the name not explained. *Linn.* 20, Or. 1, Nat. Or. *Orchidaceæ.* This is a pretty species, very scarce in collections. The sepals and petals are light green, and the labellum is strongly streaked internally with deep purple. The leaves of the plant bear a strong resemblance to those of an *Aerides*, and the plant requires precisely the same treatment as that genus.

alpìnà . . . Grn. pur. . 4, S. Epi. Silhet . . . 1837

LUMNITZERÌÀ, *Willdenow.* In honour of Stephen Lumnitzer, a botanical author. *Linn.* 14, Or. 1, Nat. Or. *Combretaceæ.* A pretty little plant, of common culture.

moschàtà . . . White. . 8, G. A. N Holl. . 1823
tenuiflòrà . . . Pa. pur. . 7, S. Her. P. E. Ind. . . 1708

LUNÀRÌÀ, *Linn.* From *luna*, the moon; in allusion to the appearance of the broad silvery silicles. *Linn.* 15, Nat. Or. *Cruciferæ.* A genus of large, rather pretty plants, with cordate leaves, and purple or white flowers. Any common border soil suits them, and they are increased by seeds. *L. rediviva* may also be increased by dividing. *Synonyme:* 1. *annua.*

biénnis, 1 . . . Li. pur. . 5, H. B. S. Eur. . . 1570
albiflòrà . . . White . . 5, H. B. S. Eur. . . 1570
redivìvà . . . Li. pur. . 5, H. Her. P. S. Eur. . . 1596

LUNATE, shaped like a half-moon.
LUNGWORT, see *Pulmonàrià.*
LUNGWORT, see *Hierácium pulmonàrià.*
LUPINE, see *Lupìnùs.*
LUPÌNÙS, *Linn.* From *lupus*, a wolf; in allusion to its drowning or exhausting land. *Linn.* 16, Or. 6, Nat. Or. *Leguminosæ.* The species of this genus are among the most beautiful of our annual and herbaceous border-flowers. They will flourish in almost any soil, but a rich loam suits them best. They perfect their seeds very freely, from which young plants are easily obtained.

albifrons . . . Blue . 9, F. Ev. S. California . 1833
albus . . . . White . . 7, H. A. Levant . . 1596
angustifòlùs . . Blue . 7, H. A. Spain . 1686
arbòreùs . . . Yellow . 7, F. Ev. S. . . . . . 1793
arbùstùs . . . Pa. pur. . 7, F. Her. P. California . 1826
argentèùs . . . White . . 6, H. Her. P. N. Amer. . 1826
aridùs . . . . Pur. blue . 8, H. Her. P. N. Amer. . 1827
bicolòr . . . . Pa. blue . 7, H. A. N. Amer. . 1826
bimaculàtùs . . Blue . . F. Her. P. Texas . 1835
bracteolàris . . Blue . . 7, H. A. M. Video . 1820
canaliculàtùs . . Blue . . 7, F. Ev. S. B. Ayres . 1828
Cruickshánkii . . Varieg. . 7, F. Ev. S. Peru . 1829
densiflòrùs . . Wht. pnk. 7, H. A. California . 1833
elègàns . . . . Vio. rose . 6, H. A. Mexico . 1831
exaltàtùs . . . . H. A. . . . . 1832
grandifòliùs . . Purple . 7, H. Her. P. N. Amer. .
Hartwegii . . . Bl. pink . 7, H. A. Mexico . 1838
hirsùtùs . . . Blue . 7, H. A. S. Eur. . 1629
hirsutissimùs . . Red . 7, H. A. California . 1833
incànùs . . . Pa. li. . 7, G. Ev. S. B. Ayres . 1830
laxiflòrùs . . . Blue pnk. . H. Her P. Columbia . 1826
latifòliùs . . . . 7, H. Her. P. California . 1834

| | | | | | | | |
|---|---|---|---|---|---|---|---|
| lĕpĭdŭs | Blue pink | 8, | H. Her. | P. | Columbia | 1826 |
| leptophýllŭs | Blue li. | 7, | H. | A. | California | 1833 |
| leucophýllŭs | Pink | 7, | H. Her. | P. | N. Amer. | 1826 |
| liniföliŭs | Blue | 7, | H. | A. | Mt. Video | 1799 |
| littŏrālis | Blue pink | 7, | H. Her. | P. | Columbia | 1826 |
| lūcĭdŭs | Purple | 7, | H. Her. | P. | N. Amer. | |
| lūtĕŭs | Yellow | 7, | H. | A. | Sicily | 1596 |
| macrŏphýllŭs | Blue | 7, | H. Her. | P. | California | 1834 |
| Marshalliānŭs | Blue | 7, | H. De. | S. | Hybrid | 1830 |
| mexicānŭs | Blue | 2, | G. | B. | Mexico | 1819 |
| micrānthŭs | Pur. blue | 7, | H. | A. | N. Amer. | 1826 |
| microcārpŭs | Blue | 4, | H. | A. | Chile | 1821 |
| multiflōrŭs | Blue | 7, | F. Ev. | S. | M. Video | 1810 |
| mutābĭlis | Blue yel. | 7, | F. Ev. | S. | Bogota | 1819 |
| nānŭs | Blue | 7, | H. | A. | California | 1826 |
| nootkatēnsis | Purple | 7, | H. Her. | P. | Nootka So. | 1794 |
| ornātŭs | Blue pink | 5, | H. Her. | P. | Columbia | 1826 |
| perēnnis | Blue | 6, | H. Her. | P. | N. Amer. | 1658 |
| plumōsŭs | Blue | 6, | H. Her. | P. | California | 1820 |
| pilōsŭs | Flesh | 7, | H. | A. | S. Eur. | 1710 |
| polyphýllŭs | Blue | 6, | H. Her. | P. | Columbia | 1826 |
| albiflōrŭs | White | 7, | H. Her. | P. | Columbia | 1826 |
| pallĭdŭs | Pa. blue | 7, | H. Her. | P. | Eng. hyb. | |
| pulchéllŭs | Blue pur. | 7, | F. Ev. | S. | Mexico | 1828 |
| pusĭllŭs | Pa. blue | 7, | H. | A. | N. Amer. | 1817 |
| rivulāris | Wht. pur. | 4, | H. Her. | P. | California | 1831 |
| Sabiniānŭs | Yellow | | H. Her. | P. | N. Amer. | 1827 |
| serĭcĕŭs | Purple | 5, | H. Her. | P. | N. Amer. | 1826 |
| subcarnōsŭs | Blue wht. | 7, | H. Her. | P. | Texas | 1835 |
| texēnsis | Blue | 6, | H. | A. | Santa Fe | |
| Thérmis | White | 6, | H. | A. | Egypt | 1802 |
| tomentōsŭs | Pink wht. | 7, | F. Ev. | S. | Peru | 1825 |
| tristis | Pa. brn. | 7, | H. Her. | P. | N. Amer. | |
| vărĭŭs | Blue wht. | 7, | H. | A. | S. Eur. | 1596 |
| versĭcŏlŏr | Pink blue | 7, | F. Ev. | S. | Mexico | 1825 |
| villōsŭs | Pink | 7, | H. Her. | P. | Carolina | 1787 |

LURID, between a purple, yellow, and grey colour.

LŬZŬLA, *Decandolle*. From the *Gramen Luzulæ* of Bauhin, the Glowworm-grass. *Linn.* 6, Or. 1, Nat. Or. *Juncaceæ*. These plants are nearly related to *Juncus*, from which they are at once distinguished by their flat leaves. They possess but little beauty, and are of the easiest culture. *Synonymes: 1. Juncus arcuatus. 2. J. spadiceus.*

| | | | | | | |
|---|---|---|---|---|---|---|
| Berthelóttii | Apetal | Grass | Teneriffe | 1829 |

*albĭdă, arcuātă 1, campēstris, capēnsis, congēstă, flavēscēns, Fostĕri, glabrātă, lūtĕă, māxĭmă, multiflōră, nĭvĕă, pediförmis, pilōsă, spadĭcĕă 2, spicātă, sudētĭcă, vernālis.*

LÝCHNIS, *Decandolle*. From *lychnos*, a lamp; on account of the brilliancy of the flowers of most of the species. *Linn.* 10, Or. 5, Nat. Or. *Silenaceæ*. An extremely beautiful genus of plants, well meriting extensive cultivation for the brilliancy of their flowers. Among the most showy and esteemed of the border-flowers, is L. Chalcedonica, the double varieties of which require some care to prevent them from returning to a single state. *L. fulgens* and *grandiflora* are truly beautiful; the latter will grow and flower well if planted out in the open border in spring, but it must be taken up in autumn, or the frost will kill it. They all grow freely in light rich loamy soil; but they must be frequently divided, or they will dwindle away, and the best time to do this is early in spring. The seed of the annual species has only to be sown in the open border in spring. *L. Cæli Rosa* is very handsome. *Synonymes: 1. Viscaria alpina. 2. L. brachypetala. 3. Agrostemma coronaria. 4. A. corsica. 5. A. sylvestris. 6. A. Flos-cuculi. 7. Githago segetum. 8. Viscaria helvetica. 9. V. neglecta. 10. Githago nicæensis. 11. Agrostemma pyrenaica. 12. A. sibirica. 13. A. dioica. 14. Viscaria vulgaris.*

| | | | | | | | |
|---|---|---|---|---|---|---|---|
| ălpīnă, 1 | Pink | 4, | H. Her. | P. | Scotland | |
| apetălă | White | 6, | H. Her. | P. | Lapland | 1810 |
| pauciflōră, 2 | White | 6, | H. Her. | P. | Siberia | 1817 |
| Chalcedónĭcă | Scarlet | 6, | H. Her. | P. | Russia | 1596 |
| alba | White | 6, | H. Her. | P. | Russia | |
| alba-plēnă | White | 6, | H. Her. | P. | Gardens | |
| flōrĕ-plānō | Scarlet | 6, | H. Her. | P. | Russia | |
| Cæli-Rŏsă | Flesh | 7, | H. | A. | Levant | 1713 |
| corŏnārĭa, 3 | Red | 7, | H. Her. | P. | Italy | 1596 |
| alba | White | 7, | H. Her. | P. | | |
| plēnă | Red | 7, | H. Her. | P. | | |
| rŭbră | Red | 7, | H. Her. | P. | | |
| córsĭcă, 4 | Red | 6, | H. Her. | P. | Corsica | 1818 |
| diūrnă, 5 | Purple | 6, | H. Her. | P. | Britain | |
| plēnă | Purple | 6, | H. Her. | P. | Britain | |
| Flōs-jŏvis | Red | 7, | H. Her. | P. | Germany | 1796 |
| Flos-cŭcŭli, 6 | Pink | 7, | H. Her. | P. | Britain | |
| albiflōră | White | 7, | H. Her. | P. | Britain | |
| plēnă | Pink | 7, | H. Her. | P. | | |

| | | | | | | | |
|---|---|---|---|---|---|---|---|
| fúlgĕns | Scarlet | 6, | H. Her. | P. | Siberia | 1822 |
| Githăgŏ, 7 | Purple | 7, | H. | A. | Britain | |
| grandiflōră | Red | 7, | G. Her. | P. | China | 1774 |
| helvétĭcă, 8 | Red | 7, | H. Her. | P. | Switzerl. | 1814 |
| lātă | Flesh | | H. Her. | P. | Portugal | 1778 |
| neglēctă, 9 | White | 6, | H. Her. | P. | | |
| nicæēnsis, 10 | Wht. red | 6, | H. | A. | Nice | 1794 |
| pyrenāĭcă, 11 | White | 6, | H. Her. | P. | Pyrenees | 1819 |
| sĭbĭrĭcă, 12 | White | 6, | H. Her. | P. | Siberia | 1817 |
| vespertĭnă, 13 | White | 6, | H. Her. | P. | Britain | |
| multiplēx | White | 6, | H. Her. | P. | Britain | |
| rōsĕă | Wht. red | 6, | H. Her. | P. | Britain | |
| Viscārĭă, 14 | Pink | 5, | H. Her. | P. | Britain | |
| plēnă | Red | 5, | H. Her. | P. | Britain | |

*apétălă, brachypétălă.*

LYCIOSĔRĬSĔĂ, *Ræmer and Schultes*. From *lycium*, and *serisea*, serisea-like lycium. *Linn.* 5, Or. 1, Nat. Or. *Solanaceæ*. A Cape shrub, which grows in peat and loam, and is increased by cuttings—*capénsis*.

LÝCĬŬM, *Linn*. From *lycion*, a name given by Dioscorides to a thorny shrub, and applied to this genus because of its containing some thorny shrubs. *Linn.* 5, Or. 1, Nat. Or. *Solanaceæ*. The stove and greenhouse kinds require the same treatment as other similar plants. *L. afrum*, and some others of the Cape species, thrive and flower well against a south or west wall, and are very handsome when in flower. The hardy species are admirably suited for training against trellis-work, or walls, or for covering arbours. They are all readily increased by cuttings of the ripened wood planted in sand, under a glass. *Synonyme: 1. L. carnosum.*

| | | | | | | | |
|---|---|---|---|---|---|---|---|
| afrŭm | Violet | 6, | H. De. T. | C. G. H. | 1712 |
| bărbārŭm | Violet | 6, | H. De. Cl. | Barbary | 1696 |
| caroliniānŭm | Blue | 7, | H. Ev. S. | Carolina | 1806 |
| chinēnsĕ | Purple | 7, | H. De. Cl. | China | |
| cinĕrĕŭm | Violet | 6, | G. Ev. S. | C. G. H. | 1818 |
| europēŭm | Pink | 6, | H. De. Cl. S. Eur. | | 1730 |
| chrysocārpŭm | | 5, | H. De. Cl. | | |
| sphærocārpŭm | | 5, | H. De. Cl. | | |
| hórrĭdŭm | White | 7, | F. Ev. S. | C. G. H. | 1791 |
| lanceolātŭm | Pink | 6, | H. De. Cl. | S. Eur. | |
| microphýllŭm | Violet | 6, | H. De. S. | C. G. H. | 1795 |
| rĭgĭdŭm, 1 | Violet | 4, | H. De. S. | C. G. H. | 1795 |
| ruthēnĭcŭm | White | | H. De. Cl. | Siberia | 1804 |
| caspĭcŭm | | 7, | H. De. Cl. | Casp. Sea | |
| Shawii | Pink | 7, | G. Ev. Cl. | C. G. H. | 1700 |
| tēnŭĕ | Violet | 6, | F. Ev. S. | C. G. H. | 1819 |
| tetrāndrŭm | Violet | 6, | H. De. Cl. | C. G. H. | 1810 |
| Trewiānŭm | Purple | 6, | H. De. Cl. | China | 1818 |
| turbinātŭm | Violet | 7, | H. De. Cl. | China | 1709 |

LYCŏGĂLĂ, *Michaux*. From *lykos*, a wolf, and *gala*, milk. *Linn.* 24, Or. 9, Nat. Or. *Fungi*. In the early stage of this plant's existence, it appears like a mass of thick cream. It is found upon rotten or decayed leaves—*miniātā*.

LYCŏPĔRDŏN, *Michaux*. The meaning of the name is not explained. *Linn.* 24, Or. 9, Nat. Or. *Fungi*. This is a genus of roundish, tuber-like plants, which, when ripe, explode, and emit their sporules like smoke, and known among country people by the name of Puff-balls. They grow in pastures and on the stumps of trees—*Bovĭstă, excipulĭförmĕ, perlātŭm, pratēnsĕ, pyrĭförmĕ.*

LYCŏPĔRSĬCŏN, *Tournefort*. From *lykos*, a wolf, and *persicon*, a peach; in allusion to its aphrodisiacal qualities. *Linn.* 5, Or. 1, Nat. Or. *Solanaceæ*. The *Lycopersicon*, or Love-apple, consists chiefly of annual plants, several of which are trained against walls for the sake of their fruit, which is used for soups. They are generally raised in frames, or in a stove, and when of sufficient size, they are transplanted into the open border. *Synonymes: 1. Solanum Pseudo Lycopersicum. 2. S. Lycopersicum. 3. S. pimpinellifolium.*

| | | | | | | | |
|---|---|---|---|---|---|---|---|
| cerasĭförmĕ, 1 | Green | 7, | H. | A. | Peru | 1800 |
| lūtĕŭm | Green | 7, | H. | A. S. Amer. | 1596 |
| commutātŭm | Yellow | 7, | H. | A. S. Amer. | 1818 |
| esculēntŭm, 2 | Green | 7, | H. | A. S. Amer. | 1596 |
| chrysocārpŭm | Green | 7, | H. | A. S. Amer. | 1596 |
| erythrocārpŭm | Green | 7, | H. | A. S. Amer. | 1596 |
| leucocārpŭm | Green | 7, | H. | A. S. Amer. | 1596 |
| Humboldtii | Yellow | 8, | H. | A. S. Amer. | 1822 |
| peruviānŭm | Yellow | 5, | S. Her. | P. Peru | 1823 |
| pimpinellifōlĭŭm, 3 | Green | 6, | H. | A. Peru | |
| procūmbēns | Cream | 7, | H. Tr. | A. S. Amer. | 1700 |
| pyrĭförmĕ | Yellow | 8, | H. | A. | 1823 |
| regulārĕ | Green | 6, | H. | A. | |

LYCŏPŎDĬŬM, *Linn*. From *lykos*, a wolf, and *pous*, a foot; because of the resemblance of the roots.

Linn. 24, Or. 3, Nat. Or. *Lycopodiaceæ.* The hardy species of Club-moss require to be cultivated in peat soil, in a moist situation; some of them succeed in pots of water. They are readily increased by suckers.

| | | | | | | |
|---|---|---|---|---|---|---|
| alopecuroídes | . | Brown | . 8, H. Ev. Tr. Britain | . |
| alpínûm | . | Brown | . 8, H. Ev. Tr. Britain | . |
| annótínûm | . | Brown | . 7, H. Ev. Tr. Britain | . |
| ápôdûm | . | Brown | . 8, H. Ev. Tr. N. Amer. | . 1819 |
| carolíniánûm | . | Brown | . 8, H. Ev. Tr. Carolina | . 1812 |
| circínátûm | . | Brown | . 7, S. Her. P. E. Ind. | . 1831 |
| clavátûm | . | Brown | . 8, H. Ev. Tr. Britain | . |
| complanátûm | . | Brown | . 8, H. Her. P. N. Amer. | . 1770 |
| dendroídeûm | . | Brown | . 7, H. Her. P. N. Amer. | . 1770 |
| dénsûm | . | Brown | . 8, G. Ev. Tr. N. Holl. | . 1820 |
| denticulátûm | . | Brown | . 7, H. Ev. Tr. Switzerl. | . 1779 |
| depréssûm | . | Brown | . 8, G. Ev. Tr. C. G. H. | . 1818 |
| helvéticûm | . | Brown | . H. Aq. P. Switzerl. | . 1779 |
| inundátûm | . | Brown | . 6, H. Ev. Tr. Britain | . |
| lucídúlûm | . | Brown | . 8, H. Ev. Tr. N. Amer. | . 1823 |
| ornithopodioídes | . | Brown | . 7, H. Ev. Tr. | . 1812 |
| rupéstré | . | Brown | . 8, H. Ev. Tr. N. Amer. | . |
| selaginoídes | . | Brown | . 8, H. Ev. Tr. Britain | . |
| Selágó | . | Brown | . 8, H. Ev. Tr. Britain | . |
| stoloníferûm | . | Brown | . 7, S. Her. P. Brasil | . 1831 |

**LYCÓPSÍS,** *Linn.* From *lykos*, a wolf, and *opsis*, the face; some resemblance in the flowers. Linn. 5, Or. 1, Nat. Or. *Boraginaceæ.* The seeds of these plants have only to be sown in the open ground in spring. *Synonymes:* 1. *Nonea arvensis.* 2. *Anchusa echioides, N. echioides.* 3. *N. obtusifolia.* 4. *Anchusa ovata.* 5. *A. variegata—arvensis* 1. *calycína* 2, *echioídes* 3, *obtusifólià* 4, *orientális* 5, *variegátá* 6.

**LYCÓPÛS.** From *lykos*, a wolf, and *pous*, a foot; in allusion to the resemblance of the leaves to the foot of that animal. Linn. 2, Or. 1, Nat. Or. *Labiatæ.* They succeed in the open ground, in any light rich soil, preferring a moist situation, and are readily increased by seeds, or divisions of the roots. *Synonyme:* 1. *L. virginicus quercifolius.*

| | | | | | | |
|---|---|---|---|---|---|---|
| australis | . | White | . 5, G. Her. P. N. Holl. | . 1823 |
| europǽus | . | White | . 7, H. Her. P. Britain | . |
| exaltátûs | . | White | . 7, H. Her. P. Italy | . 1739 |
| intermédíûs | . | White | . 7, H. Her. P. Europe | . 1820 |
| macrophýllûs, 1 | . | White | . 8, H. Her. P. N. Amer. | . 1700 |
| virgínicûs | . | White | . 8, H. Her. P. Virginia | . 1760 |

**LYGĚÛM,** *Linn.* From *lygeo*, to bend; on account of its flexibility. Linn. 3, Or. 1, Nat. Or. *Gramineæ.* A species of grass with rushy leaves. It is much used in Spain, Provence, &c., for making ropes, baskets, nets, for filling mattresses, &c. It grows in light loamy soil, and is increased by dividing the roots.

| | | | | | | |
|---|---|---|---|---|---|---|
| Spártûm | . | . | . Apetal | . 5, Gram. Spain | . 1776 |

**LYGÓDÍÛM,** *Swartz.* From *lygodes*, flexible; in allusion to the twining habit of the plants. Linn. 24, Or. 1, Nat. Or. *Osmundaceæ.* The Snake's-tongue is a climbing genus of ferns, which grows freely in a mixture of turfy loam and peat, and is readily increased by dividing of the roots, or by seeds sown in the usual way. *Synonymes:* 1. *Hydroglossum hirsutum.* 2. *Osmunda scandens.*

| | | | | | | |
|---|---|---|---|---|---|---|
| circinátûm | . | Brown | . 8, S. Ev. Cl. E. Ind. | . 1823 |
| hastátûm | . | Brown | . 8, S. Ev. Cl. Maranh. | . 1820 |
| mexicánûm | . | Brown | . G. Her. P. Mexico | . 1831 |
| palmátûm | . | Brown | . 8, S. Ev. Cl. N. Amer. | . |
| polymórphûm, 1 | Brown | . 8, S. Ev. Cl. S. Amer. | . 1820 |
| scándêns | . | Brown | . 5, S. Ev. Cl. E. Ind. | . 1798 |
| volúbíle, 2 | . | Brown | . 8, S. Ev. Tw. W. Ind. | . 1810 |

**LYME-GRASS,** see *Elymus.*

**LYMPHATIC,** belonging to lymph or sap.

**LYNGBÝÁ,** *Agardh.* In honour of the famous Danish botanist H. C. Lyngbye. Linn. 24, Or. 7, Nat. Or. *Algæ.* Curious plants, resembling some species of the genus *Conferva.* They are found on damp earth at all seasons of the year—*crispá, murális, prolífrá.*

**LYÔNÍÁ,** *Nuttall.* In memory of John Lyon, an American collector of plants, who fell a victim to a dangerous epidemic among those savage and romantic mountains which had so often been the theatre of his labours. Linn. 10, Or. 1, Nat. Or. *Ericaceæ.* Very ornamental shrubs, well worth a place in every garden. They grow best when planted in a peat soil, and may be increased by layers, or seeds; if by seeds, they must be sown in pots filled with sandy peat soil, and covered slightly over. *Synonymes:* 1. *Andromeda ferru-*

*ginea.* 2. *A. frondosa.* 3. *A. paniculata.* 4. *A. ferruginea.*

| | | | | | | |
|---|---|---|---|---|---|---|
| capreæfólíis | . | White | . 7, H. Ev. S. N. Amer. | . 1812 |
| ferrugíneá, 1 | . | White | . 6, H. Ev. S. N. Amer. | . 1734 |
| frondósá, 2 | . | White | . 5, H. Ev. S. Virginia | . 1806 |
| multiflóra | . | White | . 7, H. Ev. S. N. Amer. | . |
| paniculátá, 3 | . | White | . 5, H. Ev. S. N. Amer. | . 1748 |
| rígidá, 4 | . | White | . 7, H. Ev. S. N. Amer. | . 1774 |

**LYÔNSÍÁ,** *R. Brown.* In memory of Israel Lyons, author of a botanical work, and from whom Sir Joseph Banks received his earliest instructions in botany. Linn. 5, Or. 1, Nat. Or. *Gentianaceæ.* A pretty plant; for culture and propagation, see *Echites.*

| | | | | | | |
|---|---|---|---|---|---|---|
| stramíneá | . | Striped | . 6, S. Ev. Tw. N. Holl. | . 1820 |

**LYPERANTHÛS,** *R. Brown.* From *lupe*, sadness, and *anthos*, a flower; in allusion to the sombre appearance of the flowers. Linn. 20, Or. 1, Nat. Or. *Orchidaceæ.* A genus of curious, tuberous-rooted plants, thriving well in a mixture of loam and peat, and increased by divisions of the roots.

| | | | | | | |
|---|---|---|---|---|---|---|
| ellípticûs | . | Drk. brn. | . G. Ter. N. Holl. | . 1824 |
| nigricáns | . | Drk. brn. | . G. Ter. N. Holl. | . 1824 |
| suavéólēns | . | Drk. brn. | . G. Ter. N. Holl. | . 1822 |

**LYRATE,** lyre-shaped.

**LYSIMÁCHÍA,** *Linn.* From *lysis*, dissolution, and *mache*, strife. Linn. 5, Or. 1, Nat. Or. *Primulaceæ.* A very pretty genus of plants, with mostly yellow flowers. L. Nummularia is a handsome free-flowering plant, and from its trailing habit, is well fitted for decorating rock-work. All the species are of the easiest culture, and may be propagated by divisions, except L. dubia and L. Linum-stellatum, which must be increased by seeds. *Synonymes:* 1. *atropurpurea.* 2. *stellata.* 3. *quadrifolia.*

| | | | | | | |
|---|---|---|---|---|---|---|
| affínís | . | Yellow | . 7, H. Her. P. | . |
| angustifólíá | . | Yellow | . 7, H. Her. P. N. Amer. | . 1803 |
| atropurpúreá | . | Dk. pur. | . 8, G. Her. P. Levant | . 1820 |
| azórícá | . | Yellow | . 6, H. Her. P. Azores | . 1831 |
| capitátá | . | Yellow | . 6, H. Her. P. N. Amer. | . 1818 |
| ciliátá | . | Yellow | . 7, H. Her. P. N. Amer. | . 1732 |
| dúbíá, 1 | . | Yellow | . 8, H. B. Levant | . 1789 |
| Ephemérûm | . | White | . 8, H. Her. P. Spain | . 1730 |
| hýbrídá | . | Yellow | . 7, H. Her. P. N. Amer. | . 1805 |
| Linûm-stellátûm 2 | Green | . 6, H. A. Italy | . 1658 |
| longifólíá, 3 | . | Yellow | . 7, H. Her. P. N. Amer. | . 1796 |
| maculátá | . | Yellow | . 6, G. Ev. Tr. N. Holl. | . 1822 |
| némórûm | . | Yellow | . 6, H. Her. P. Britain | . |
| Nummulárí | . | Yellow | . 6, H. Ev. Tr. Britain | . |
| punctátá | . | Yellow | . 7, H. Her. P. N. Holl. | . 1658 |
| quadrifólíá | . | Yellow | . 7, H. Her. P. N. Amer. | . 1794 |
| stríctá | . | Yellow | . 7, H. Her. P. N. Amer. | . 1781 |
| thyrsiflórá | . | Yellow | . 6, H. Aq. P. England | . |
| verticillátá | . | Yellow | . 7, H. Her. P. Crimea | . 1820 |
| vulgárís | . | Yellow | . 8, H. Her. P. Britain | . |

**LYSINĚMÁ,** *R. Brown.* From *lysis*, a freeing, and *nema*, a filament; in allusion to the stamens being free from the corolla. Linn. 5, Or. 1, Nat. Or. *Epacridaceæ.* A genus of very pretty plants, which thrive best in a very rough sandy peat soil, and are increased by cuttings of the nearly ripened wood, planted in sand, under a glass. *Synonyme:* 1. *Epacris rosea.*

| | | | | | | |
|---|---|---|---|---|---|---|
| attenuátûm | . | White | . 2, G. Ev. S N. S. W. | . 1812 |
| conspícúûm | . | | . 8, G. Ev. S. N. Holl. | . 1824 |
| lasianthûm | . | Pink | . 3, G. Ev. S. N. Holl. | . 1820 |
| pentapétálûm | . | Pink | . 3, G. Ev. S. N. Holl. | . 1823 |
| púngēns | . | White | . 8, G. Ev. S N. S. W. | . 1804 |
| rúbrûm, 1 | . | Red | . 3, G. Ev. S. N. S. W. | . 1804 |

**LYTHRÛM,** *Linn.* From *lythron*, black-blood; in allusion to the purple colour of most of the flowers. Linn. 11, Or. 1, Nat. Or. *Lythraceæ.* The hardy perennial species of this genus are very handsome. They thrive in any common garden soil, and are readily increased by dividing the plants at the root. The seeds of the annual species should be sown in the open border in spring. *Synonymes:* 1. *L. Kennedianum.* 2. *L. diffusum.*

| | | | | | | |
|---|---|---|---|---|---|---|
| alátûm, 1 | . | Purple | . 7, G. Her. P. America | . 1812 |
| Græffer | . | Purple | . 7, H. A. Italy | . 1800 |
| hyssopifólíûm | . | Purple | . 8, H. A. England | . |
| lanceolátûm, 2 | . | Purple | . 7, H. Her. P. Carolina | . 1800 |
| lineáré | . | White | . 7, H. Her. P. N. Amer. | . 1812 |
| myrtifólíûm | . | Purple | . 7, H. Her. P. N. Amer. | . 1820 |
| Salicária | . | Purple | . 7, H. Her. P. Britain | . |
| thesioídes | . | Lilac | . 8, H. A. S. Eur. | . 1816 |
| thymifólíûm | . | Purple | . 7, H. A. N. Amer. | . 1800 |
| tomentósûm | . | Purple | . 7, H. Her. P. Caucasus | . 1828 |
| virgátûm | . | Purple | . 7, H. Her. P. Austria | . 1776 |

# M.

MĀBĀ, *Forster.* The name applied to it in Tonga-Tabu. *Linn.* 22, Or. 2, Nat. Or. *Ebenaceæ.* These plants are well worthy of cultivation; a mixture of loam and peat suits them, and cuttings of the ripened wood root freely in sand, under a glass. *Synonyme:* 1. *Ferreola buxifolia.*

buxifôliä, 1 . . Yellow . 8. Ev. S. E. Ind. . . 1810
laurinä . . . . 7, G. Ev. Tr. N. Holl. . 1824

MACAW-TREE, see *Acrocōmiä fusifōrmis.*

MACERATE, to decompose by steeping in water, or other liquid.

MACLEĀYA, *R. Brown.* In honour of Alexander M'Leay, F.R.S., L.S., a famous entomologist and colonial secretary in New South Wales. *Linn.* 13, Or. 1, Nat. Or. *Papaveraceæ.* A very beautiful herbaceous plant, succeeding in any rich mould, and increased by dividing the roots in spring; it may also be propagated by seeds. *Synonyme:* 1. *Bocconia cordata.*

cordātä, 1 . . . Red yel. . 6, H. Her. P China . . 1795

MACLŪRĀ, *Nuttall.* In honour of William Maclure, a North American geologist. *Linn.* 21, Or. 4, Nat. Or. *Urticaceæ.* A genus of very ornamental trees, attaining the height of thirty feet. They require to be grown in turfy loam and peat, and are increased from cuttings of the ripened wood planted in sand, under a glass. *M. aurantiaca* should be slightly protected in severe weather. *Synonymes:* 1. *Morus Plumieri, Broussonetia Plumieri.* 2. *M. tinctoria, B. tinctoria.*

aurantiācā . . . Apetal . H. De. T. N. Amer. . 1818
Plumiéri, 1 . . Apetal . S. Ev. T. W. Ind. . 1804
tinctoriä, 2 . . Apetal . S. Ev. T. W. Ind. . 1789

MACRADENĪĀ, *R. Brown.* From *makros*, long, and *aden*, a gland; in allusion to the long caudicula of the pollen-masses. *Linn.* 20, Or. 1, Nat. Or. *Orchidaceæ.* This is rather a pretty genus, requiring a strong moist heat to keep the species healthy. They should be potted in turfy peat broken into small squares, and raised a little above the pot, which must have a good drainage.

lutéscēns . . . Olive . 11, S. Epi. Trinidad . . 1821
mūtīcā . . . . Dingy wht. 2, S. Epi. Trinidad .
triāndrä . . . . Wht. grn. 5, S. Epi. Surinam .

MACROCNĒMŪM, *R. Brown.* From *makros*, long, and *kneme*, a leg; in allusion to the long flower-stalk. *Linn.* 5, Or. 1, Nat. Or. *Cinchonaceæ.* Ornamental plants, succeeding in loam and peat, and propagated by cuttings in sand, under a glass, in heat.

jamaicénsē . . . White . . 8. Ev. T. Jamaica . 1806
tinctôriūm . . . Red . . 9, S. Ev. T. Trinidad . 1820

MACROPŌDĪŪM, *R. Brown.* From *makros*, long, and *pous*, a foot; in allusion to the shape of the seed-vessel. *Linn.* 15, Nat. Or. *Cruciferæ.* A light rich soil suits these plants well, and cuttings of the herbaceous species root readily in sand. *M. laciniatum* is readily increased by seeds. *Synonyme:* 1. *Cardamine nivalis.*

laciniātūm . . . White . 7, H. A. N. Amer. . 1827
nivālē, 1 . . . White . 7, H. Her. P. Siberia . . 1796

MACRORRHĪZĪ, long, or large-rooted,

MACROSTYLĪS, *Bartling.* From *makros*, long, and *stylis*, a style; referring to the length of the style. *Linn.* 5, Or. 1, Nat. Or. *Rutaceæ.* This is an interesting genus of plants; for culture and propagation, see *Diosma.* *Synonymes:* 1. *Agathosma barbata.* 2. *A. obtusa, Diosma ciliata.*

barbātā, 1 . . White . 5, G. Ev. S. C.G. H. . 1810
obtūsä, 2 . . . Purple . 5, G. Ev. S. C.G. H. . 1774
lanceolātä . . . Purple . 5, G. Ev. S. C.G. H. . 1774
oblōngä . . . . Purple . 5, G. Ev. S. C.G. H. . 1774
orātä . . . . . Purple . 5, G. Ev. S. C.G. H. . 1774

MACROTRŌPĪS, *Decandolle.* From *makros*, long, and *tropis*, a keel; alluding to the long keel of the flowers. *Linn.* 10, Or. 1, Nat. Or. *Leguminosæ.*

An ornamental plant; for culture and propagation, see *Anagyris.*

fœtidä . . . . Yellow . 4, G. Ev. S. China . . 1820

MACRŌTYS, *Rafinesque.* From *makros*, long, and *ous*, an ear; resemblance in the long capsules. *Linn.* 13, Or. 1, Nat. Or. *Ranunculaceæ.* A pretty plant, growing freely in any good soil, and increased by divisions. *Synonyme:* 1. *Actæa racemosa.*

racemôsä, 1 . . White . 5, H. Her. P. N. Amer. .

MADAGASCAR NUTMEG, see *Agathophyllūm.*
MADAGASCAR POTATO, see *Solānūm unguāni.*
MAD APPLE, see *Solānūm insānūm.*
MADDER, see *Rūbiä.*

MĀDĪĀ, *Molina.* *Madi* is the name of the original species in Chile. *Linn.* 19, Or. 2, Nat. Or. *Compositæ.* The seeds of these rather handsome plants should be sown in May or June, in a shady situation, in any common garden soil. They grow about two feet high, flower in about two months after being sown, and continue in beauty about six weeks or two months. *Synonymes:* 1. *M. mellosa, M. viscosa.*

elégāns . . . Yellow . 8, H. A. N. W. Amer. 1831
satīvā, 1 . . . Yellow . 7, H. A. Chile . . . 1794

MADWORT, see *Alyssum.*

MĀESĀ, *Forskal.* From *maas*, the Arabic name of one of the species. *Linn.* 5, Or. 1, Nat. Or. *Myrsinaceæ.* These are ornamental plants; for culture and propagation, see *Ardisia.* *Synonymes:* 1. *Bæobotrys indica.* 2. *M. tomentosa.* 3. *B. pubescens.*

argêntēä . . . White . 4, S. Ev. S. E. Ind. . 1818
indicä, 1 . . . White . 11, S. Ev. S. E. Ind. . 1817
macrophyllä, 2 . White . 8, S. Ev. T. E. Ind. . 1818
pubêscēns, 3 . . White . 6, S. Ev. S. E. Ind. . 1824

MAGNŌLĪĀ, *Linn.* After Pierre Magnol, professor of medicine at Montpelier, and author of several botanical works; he died in 1715. *Linn.* 13, Or. 6, Nat. Or. *Magnoliaceæ.* This is a genus of very elegant and showy plants when in flower, and all well worthy of extensive cultivation. The hardy kinds being remarkably handsome shrubs, should be planted in conspicuous situations, where they will flower profusely when they attain a good size. *M. glauca* and some others grow best in a peat soil in a moist situation. They are generally increased by layers put down in spring or autumn, or by seeds; when the layers are first taken off, they should be potted in a mixture of loam and peat, and placed in a close frame till they have taken fresh root. None of the leaves should be taken off or shortened, nor any shoots be cut off, or their tops shortened, as they will not succeed so well; for the more branches and leaves are on, the sooner they will strike fresh root. The Chinese kinds are often inarched or budded on *M. obovata,* which takes readily. The greenhouse kinds thrive best in a mixture of peat and loam, and are also increased by inarching or budding on *M. obovata,* one of the readiest growing kinds. *M. fuscata,* and any of the weak-growing species, increase with facility from cuttings taken off as soon as ripe, and planted in a pot of sand, under a glass. The seeds of the North American species are received annually from that country. They should be sown as soon as possible after their arrival in pots of light rich earth, covering them half an inch deep; these may be placed either in a hotbed or a warm sheltered situation, or they may be sown in the open ground, and when the plants are of sufficient size, they should be planted out singly into pots, and sheltered till they have taken fresh root, and they should be protected from the frost by a frame for two or three successive winters, giving them the benefit of the open air in mild weather. *Synonymes:* 1. *M. gracilis, M. Yulan.* 2. *M. Soulangiana.* 3. *M. tomentosa.* 4. *M. umbrella.*

[ 194 ]

| | | | | | |
|---|---|---|---|---|---|
| acuminata . . | Yel. grn. . | 6, | H. De. T. | N. Amer. . | 1736 |
| Candollii . . | Yelsh. . | 6, | H. De. T. | N. Amer. . | 1736 |
| maxima . . | Yelsh. . | 6, | H. De. T. | N. Amer. . | 1736 |
| auriculata, 1 . | White . | 4, | H. De. T. | Carolina . | 1786 |
| conspicua, 8 . | White . | 8, | F. De. T. | China . | 1789 |
| Alexandrina . | White . | 4, | F. De. T. | China . | 1831 |
| citriodora . . | White . | 4, | F. De. T. | China . | 1831 |
| Soulangeana, 2 | Pur. wht. . | 4, | H. De. S. | Hybrid . | 1826 |
| cordata . . . | Yel. wht. . | 6, | H. De. T. | N. Amer. . | 1801 |
| fuscata . . . | Brown . | 4, | G. Ev. S. | China . | 1789 |
| anonaefolia . | Red . . | 6, | G. Ev. S. | China . | 1789 |
| glauca . . . | White . | 7, | H. De. T. | N. Amer. . | 1688 |
| Burchelliana . | White . | 6, | H. De. T. | | |
| Gordoniana . | White . | 6, | H. De. T. | | 1750 |
| longifolia . . | White . | 7, | H. De. T. | Hybrid . | |
| Thomsoniana . | White . | 7, | H. De. T. | Hybrid . | 1817 |
| gracilis . . . | Purple . | 4, | H. De. S. | Japan . | 1804 |
| grandiflora . | White . | 8, | H. Ev. T. | Carolina . | 1734 |
| angustifolia . | White . | 7, | H. Ev. T. | Paris . | 1825 |
| crispa . . . | White . | 6, | H. Ev. T. | N. Amer. . | |
| elliptica . . | White . | 8, | H. Ev. T. | Carolina . | 1784 |
| exoniensis . . | White . | 8, | H. Ev. T. | N. Amer. . | |
| ferruginea . . | White . | 8, | H. Ev. T. | N. Amer. . | |
| lanceolata . . | White . | 8, | H. Ev. T. | Carolina . | 1784 |
| obovata . . | White . | 8, | H. Ev. T. | Carolina . | 1784 |
| praecox . . | White . | 8, | H. Ev. T. | N. Amer. . | |
| rotundifolia . | White . | 8, | H. Ev. T. | N. Amer. . | |
| Kobus, 3 . . | Pur. wht. . | 7, | H. Ev. S. | Japan . | 1804 |
| macrophylla . | White . | 7, | H. De. T. | N. Amer. . | 1800 |
| obovata . . . | Purple . | 7, | F. De. S. | China . | 1790 |
| discolor . . | Pur. wht. . | 7, | F. De. S. | | 1790 |
| purpurea . . | Purple . | 4, | H. De. S. | Japan . | 1790 |
| pyramidata . | White . | 5, | H. De. T. | Carolina . | 1811 |
| tripetala, 4 . | White . | 5, | H. De. T. | N. Amer. . | 1752 |

MAHERNIA, *Linn.* An anagram of *Hermannia*, signifying affinity. *Linn.* 16, Or. 2, Nat. Or. *Sterculiaceae.* These are extremely pretty plants. The soil best adapted to them is an equal mixture of loam and sandy peat; and young cuttings taken off at a joint, will soon root, if planted in the same kind of soil, under a glass. *Synonymes:* 1. *M. pinnata.* 2. *M. odorata.* 3. *M. Burchellii.*

| | | | | |
|---|---|---|---|---|
| bipinnata, 1 . | Brown . | 7, G. Ev. S. | C. G. H. . | 1752 |
| diffusa . . . | Yellow . | 6, G. Ev. S. | C. G. H. . | 1774 |
| glabrata, 2 . | Yellow . | 6, G. Ev. S. | C. G. H. . | 1789 |
| grandiflora, 3 | Red . . | 6, G. Ev. S. | C. G. H. . | 1812 |
| heterophylla . | Yellow . | 5, G. Ev. S. | C. G. H. . | 1731 |
| incisa . . . | Yel. wht. . | 7, G. Ev. S. | C. G. H. . | 1792 |
| oxalidifolia . | Yellow . | 6, G. Ev. S. | C. G. H. . | 1817 |
| pulchella . . | Reddish . | 7, G. Ev. S. | C. G. H. . | 1792 |
| resedaefolia . | Yellow . | 7, G. Ev. S. | C. G. H. . | 1816 |
| sessilifolia . | Yel. wht. . | 6, G. Ev. S. | C. G. H. . | 1818 |
| verniciata . . | Vermil. . | 7, G. Ev. S. | C. G. H. . | 1816 |
| verticillata . | Yellow . | 7, G. Ev. S. | C. G. H. . | 1820 |
| vesicaria . . | Yellow . | 6, G. Ev. S. | C. G. H. . | 1818 |

MAHOGANY, see *Swietenia Mahagoni.*

MAHONIA, *Nuttall.* In honour of Bernard M'Mahon, of North America, a lover of botanical science. *Linn.* 6, Or. 1, Nat. Or. *Berberaceae.* A mixture of sand, peat, and loam, is the soil best adapted to the growth of these beautiful shrubs. They may be increased by layers, or by cuttings of the ripened wood planted in sand, in autumn, under a glass. *Synonymes:* 1. *Berberis Aquifolium.* 2. *B. pinnata, M. diversifolia.* 3. *B. nervosa, M. glumacea.* 4. *B. repens.*

| | | | | |
|---|---|---|---|---|
| Aquifolium, 1 . | Yellow . | F. Ev. S. | N. Amer. . | 1824 |
| fascicularis, 2 . | Yellow . | 4, F. Ev. S. | California . | 1819 |
| nervosa, 3 . | Yellow . | H. De. S. | N. Amer. . | 1820 |
| repens, 4 . | Yellow . | 4, H. Ev. S. | N. Amer. . | 1824 |

MAIDENHAIR, see *Adiantum.*
MAIDENHAIR, see *Passiflora Adiantum.*
MAIDENHAIR-TREE, see *Salisburia adiantifolia.*
MAIDEN-LIP, see *Echinospermum lappula.*
MAIDEN-PLUM, see *Comocladia.*
MAJORANA, *Mœnch.* An alteration of the Arabic name, *Maryamych.* *Linn.* 14, Or. 1, Nat. Or. *Labiatae.* These plants succeed well in sandy soil and a dry situation. The species are all shrubby if protected during winter, and they are easily increased by slips or cuttings. *Synonymes:* 1. *Origanum Maru.* 2. *O. Majorana.* 3. *O. syriacum.* 4. *O. Onites, O. smyrnaeum.*

| | | | | |
|---|---|---|---|---|
| crassifolia, 1 . | Purplish . | 6, F. Ev. S. | Levant . | |
| hortensis, 2 . | Purplish . | 6, H. . | A. N. Africa . | 1573 |
| nervosa, 3 . | Pink . | 8, F. Ev. S. | Egypt . | 1823 |
| Onites, 4 . . | Whitish . | 8, F. Ev. S. | Mediter. . | 1759 |

MALABAR LEAF, see *Cinnamomum Malabatrum.*
MALABAR NIGHTSHADE, see *Basella.*
MALABAR NUT, see *Justicia Adhatoda.*
MALABAR ROSE, see *Hibiscus Rosa malabarica.*
MALACHODENDRON, *Linn.* From *malachos,* soft, and *dendron,* a tree. *Linn.* 16, Or. 8, Nat. Or. *Sterculi-*

-aceae. This fine ornamental plant is highly deserving a place in every garden, on account of its large cream-coloured blossoms. The plant should be kept in the greenhouse, for though sufficiently hardy to stand our winters in the open air, the young shoots often get injured by frost, the summer not being long enough to ripen the wood, or even to flower it in perfection. The best soil for it is peat, mixed with a little loam; and it is readily increased by layers, or cuttings of the ripened wood, in sand, under a glass.

| | | | | |
|---|---|---|---|---|
| ovatum . . . . | White . | 7, H. De. T. | N. Amer. . | 1785 |

MALACHRA, *Linn.* A name under which Pliny speaks of a Persian tree, which produces a gum. The name is preserved to designate plants analogous to *mallow,* from the similarity of the word *malachra* with that of *malache,* a mallow. *Linn.* 16, Or. 8, Nat. Or. *Malvaceae.* Annuals of no interest; they require to be raised in a hothouse, and, when of sufficient size, to be planted singly into small pots, and placed among the stove plants. *Synonyme:* 1. *M. fasciata*—*alceaefolia, bracteata, capitata, fasciata, heptaphylla 1, radiata, rotundifolia, triloba.*

MALAY APPLE, see *Jambosa malaccensis.*
MALAXIS, *Swartz.* *Malaxis,* delicate; in allusion to the texture of the species. *Linn.* 20, Or. 1, Nat. Or. *Orchidaceae.* A pretty little plant, growing freely in sandy peat.

| | | | | |
|---|---|---|---|---|
| paludosa . . . | Yel. grn. . | 7, H. Ter. | England . | |

MALCOMIA, *R. Brown.* Named after William Malcolm, F.L.S., a celebrated nurseryman and cultivator. *Linn.* 15, Nat. Or. *Cruciferae.* These plants are not possessed of much beauty. They should be sown in the open border in spring; or by sowing at various times, they may be got to flower all the year, except in severe frosty weather. *Synonymes:* 1. *Hesperis africana.* 2. *H. arenaria.* 3. *Cheiranthus lyratus.* 4. *C. maritimus.*

| | | | | |
|---|---|---|---|---|
| africana, 1 . . | Purple . | 6, H. . | A. Africa . | 1747 |
| arenaria, 2 . . | Violet . | 6, H. . | A. Algiers . | 1804 |
| chia . . . . | Purple . | 6, H. . | A. Chio . | 1732 |
| erodea . . . | . | 6, H. . | A. Portugal . | 1814 |
| incrassata . . | Purple . | 6, H. . | A. Tenedos . | 1820 |
| lacera . . . | Wht. yel. . | 6, H. . | A. S. Eur. . | 1718 |
| laxa . . . | Purple . | 6, H. . | A. Siberia . | 1820 |
| littorea . . | Wht. yel. . | 6, H. . | A. S. Eur. . | 1683 |
| lyrata, 3 . . | Purple . | 6, H. . | A. Cyprus . | 1820 |
| maritima, 4 . | Violet . | 6, H. . | A. S. Eur. . | 1713 |
| parviflora . . | Lilac . | 6, H. . | A. S. Eur. . | 1823 |
| taraxacifolia . | Purple . | 6, H. . | A. Siberia . | 1795 |

MALE FERN, see *Aspidium Filix-mas.*
MALESHERBIA, *Ruiz and Pavon.* In honour of Lamoignon de Malesherbes, an illustrious French patriot and agriculturist. *Linn.* 5, Or. 3, Nat. Or. *Malesherbiaceae.* This is a very interesting genus, requiring the treatment common to most greenhouse annuals. *Synonyme:* 1. *M. coronata.*

| | | | | |
|---|---|---|---|---|
| humilis . . . | White . | G. . | A. Chile . | 1832 |
| linearifolia, 1 . | Pur. blue . | 8, G. . | A. Chile . | 1831 |

MALLOW, see *Malva.*
MALLOW ROSE, see *Hibiscus moschatus.*
MALOPE, *Linn.* From *malos,* tender; in allusion to the soft leaves. *Linn.* 16, Or. 8, Nat. Or. *Malvaceae.* These are very beautiful plants. The seed should be sown in the open border about the beginning or middle of April.

| | | | | |
|---|---|---|---|---|
| malacoides . . | Purple . | 6, H. . | A. Barbary . | 1710 |
| sinuata . . . | Pur. vio. . | 7, H. . | A. Mauritan. . | 1710 |
| trifida . . . | Purple . | 7, H. . | A. Barbary . | 1808 |

MALPIGHIA, *Linn.* In honour of Marcello Malpighi, once professor of medicine at Pisa, and author of many valuable works on natural history. He died in 1694. *Linn.* 10, Or. 3, Nat. Or. *Malpighiaceae.* A genus of interesting plants, some of which, as *M. Aquifolia, coccifera,* and one or two others, are especially worth the cultivator's care. They thrive well in any light soil, and cuttings of the ripened wood root readily in sand, under a glass, in heat. *M. glabra* is known by the name of Barbadoes Cherry in the British West Indies. It is cultivated in all the West Indian Islands, and in many parts of South America, for its fruit, which is esteemed there, but is much inferior to our cherries. *Synonyme:* 1. *M. punicifolia.*

| | | | | |
|---|---|---|---|---|
| angustifolia . . | Pink . | 7, S. Ev. S. | W. Ind. . | 1787 |
| Aquifolium . . | Pink . | 8, S. Ev. S. | S. Amer. . | 1759 |
| biflora, 1 . . | Pa. red . | 7, S. Ev. S. | S. Amer. . | 1810 |

| | | | | | |
|---|---|---|---|---|---|
| cocolferá . . | Pink . | 8. Ev. S. | S. Amer. | . 1733 | |
| cubénsis . . | Pa. red . | 7. S. Ev. S. | Havannah | . 1824 | |
| dubiá . . | Yellow . | 7. S. Ev. S. | Jamaica | . 1820 | |
| foglosá . . | Yellow . | 7. S. Ev. S. | S. Amer. | . 1820 | |
| fucatá . . | Pa. pink . | 6. S. Ev. S. | | . 1814 | |
| glabrá . . . | Rose . | 6. S. Ev. T. | W. Ind. | . 1757 | |
| incaná . . | Rose . | 8. S. Ev. T. | Campeachy | 1742 | |
| macrophýllá . | Red pk. . | 7. S. Ev. T. | Brazil | . 1820 | |
| nitidá . . | Pink . | 5. S. Ev. S. | W. Ind. | . 1733 | |
| punicifoliá . | Rose . | 8. S. Ev. S. | W. Ind. | . 1690 | |
| úreos . . | Pink . | 8. S. Ev. S. | S. Amer. | . 1787 | |

**MĀLVĀ, Linn.** Altered from the Greek, *malache*, soft, which comes from *malacho*, to soften; in allusion to the emollient qualities of the species. *Linn.* 16, Or. 8, Nat. Or. *Malvaceæ*. This is an extensive genus of plants. The stove and greenhouse kinds grow well in any rich soil, and are very ornamental, especially some of the greenhouse species; they are readily increased by cuttings planted in any light soil, under a glass. Among the most interesting of the hardy herbaceous species, are *M. moschata*, *Munroana*, and *purpurata*. They should be planted in the flower-border, and increased by divisions of the roots, or by seeds. The annual species should be sown in the open ground, but few of them are worth cultivating. *Synonymes*: 1. *M. alceoides*. 2. *M. scoparia*. 3. *M. reflexa*. 4. *M. glomerata*.

| | | | | | |
|---|---|---|---|---|---|
| Alcea . . | Purple | 8. H. Her. P. | Germany | . 1597 | |
| americaná . | Yellow . | 6. H. | A. St. Domin. | . 1756 | |
| amœná . | Purple | 4. G. Ev. S. | C. G. H. | . 1796 | |
| angulatá . | Purple | 7. G. Her. P. | | . 1820 | |
| aspérrimá . | Red . | 7. G. Ev. S. | C. G. H. | . 1796 | |
| balsamicá . | Pink . | 7. G. Ev. S. | C. G. H. | . 1800 | |
| borbónicá . | Yellow . | 7. S. Ev. S. | Maurit. | . 1816 | |
| bryonifóliá . | Purple . | 7. G. Ev. S. | C. G. H. | . 1781 | |
| calycina . | Pa. red . | 7. G. Ev. S. | C. G. H. | . 1812 | |
| campanuloídés . | Blush | 10. F. Da. | Tr. N. Amer. | . 1825 | |
| capénsis . | Red wht. | 6. G. Ev. S. | C. G. H. | . 1713 | |
| capitatá . | Red . | 4. G. Ev. S. | Peru | . 1798 | |
| chinénsis . | Reddish . | 7. H. | A. China | | |
| coccineá . . | Lilac . | 7. S. Ev. S. | S. Amer. | . 1835 | |
| Creeaná . | Rose . | 6. G. Ev. S. | Hybrid | . 1835 | |
| crispá . . | White . | 6. H. | A. Syria | . 1573 | |
| divaricatá . | Wht. vein. | 7. G. Ev. S. | C. G. H. | . 1792 | |
| domingénsis . | Yellow . | 7. H. Her. P. | St. Domin. | . 1824 | |
| fragráns . . | Scarlet | 6. G. Ev. S. | C. G. H. | . 1759 | |
| grossulariæfóliá | Pink . | 7. G. Ev. S. | C. G. H. | . 1732 | |
| Henningii . | Wht. red | 6. H. Her. P. | Russia | . 1820 | |
| italicá . | Purple | 8. H. Her. P. | Italy | . 1829 | |
| lactéá . | White | 1. G. Ev. S. | Mexico | . 1780 | |
| limenais . | Red . | 7. H. | A. Peru | . 1768 | |
| mareóticá . | Pink . | 8. H. | A. Egypt | . 1822 | |
| mauritiâná . | Pink . | 7. H. | A. S. Eur. | . 1768 | |
| miniatá . | Velny . | 6. G. Ev. S. | S. Amer. | . 1798 | |
| Mouroaná . | Scarlet | 8. H. Her. P. | Columbia | . 1828 | |
| major . | Orange | 8. F. Her. P. | Hybrid | . 1835 | |
| Morénii, l | Red . | 7. H. Her. P. | Italy | . 1820 | |
| moschatá . | Flesh | 6. H. Her. P. | Britain | | |
| undulatá . | White | 7. H. Her. P. | | | |
| Mullerii . | | H. | B. Sardinia | . 1832 | |
| oxyacanthoídés . | White | 4. G. Ev. S. | C. G. H. | . 1818 | |
| purpuratá . | Pa. red . | 7. F. Her. P. | Chile | . 1825 | |
| retúsá . | Pink . | 4. G. Ev. S. | C. G. H. | . 1803 | |
| scabrá, 2 . | Yellow . | 6. S. Ev. S. | Peru | . 1798 | |
| scopariá . | Yellow . | 4. S. Ev. S. | Peru | . 1782 | |
| spicatá . | Orange . | 7. S. Ev. S. | Jamaica | . 1726 | |
| strictá . | White | 4. G. Ev. S. | C. G. H. | . 1805 | |
| sylvéstris . | Purple . | 7. H. Her. P. | Britain | | |
| albiflórá . | White | 7. H. Her. P. | Europe | | |
| tomentosá . | Yellow . | 7. S. Ev. S. | E. Ind. | . 1820 | |
| tricuspidatá . | Yellow . | 7. S. | B. W. Ind. | . 1796 | |
| tridactylitá, 3 | Pink . | 7. G. Ev. S. | C. G. H. | . 1791 | |
| vitifóliá . | White . | 9. F. | B. Mexico | . 1828 | |
| virgatá . | Purple . | 6. G. Ev. S. | C. G. H. | . 1797 | |
| walthæriæfóliá . | Yellow . | 8. Her. P. | Java | . 1824 | |

*agyptiá, althæoídés, bonariénsis, brasiliénsis, créticá, fastigiatá, flexuosá, gangéticá, hispánicá, leprósá, microcárpá, nicæénsis, parviflórá, peruviáná, rotundifóliá, R. pusilla, Sherardiáná, stipulacéá, Tournefortiáná, trachelifóliá, trifidá, verticillatá.*

**MĀLVAVISCŪS, Decandolle.** From *malva*, a mallow, and *viscus*, glue. *Linn.* 16, Or. 8, Nat. Or. *Malvaceæ*. This is a genus of very desirable plants, on account of their rich scarlet flowers. The soil best adapted to them is a mixture of loam and peat, and cuttings root readily in sand, under a glass; these should be taken off as near the stem of the plant as possible, not being so apt to rot as when taken off by the middle of the shoot. None of the leaves should be taken off or shortened above the sand.— *Sweet. Synonymes*: 1. *Achania Malvaviscus*. 2. *A. mollis*. 3. *A. pilosa*.

| | | | | | |
|---|---|---|---|---|---|
| arbóreús, 1 . | . Scarlet . | 8. Ev. S. | W. Ind. | . 1714 | |

| | | | | | |
|---|---|---|---|---|---|
| móllis, 2 . | . Scarlet | 8. S. Ev. S. | Mexico | . 1780 | |
| pilósús, 3 . | Red . | 10. S. Ev. S. | Jamaica | . 1780 | |

**MAMMÆFORM**, nipple-formed.

**MAMMĒĀ, Linn.** *Mamey* is the aboriginal name of the species. *Linn.* 13, Or. 1, Nat. Or. *Guttiferæ*. This is a tall, handsome tree, with a thick, spreading, elegant head, somewhat resembling *Magnolia grandiflora*. In the West Indies it is cultivated for the sake of its fruit, which is much esteemed, and is eaten alone, or cut in slices with wine or sugar, or preserved in sugar. It grows freely in sandy loam, and cuttings of the ripened wood, with the leaves not shortened, will root in sand, under a glass, in a moist heat.

| | | | | | |
|---|---|---|---|---|---|
| americaná . . | . White . | 8. Ev. T. | S. Amer. | . 1780 | |

**MAMMEE-TREE**, see *Mammēá*.

**MAMMILLĀRĪĀ, Haworth.** From *mamma*, the nipple; in allusion to the small tubercles. *Linn.* 12, Or. 1, Nat. Or. *Cactaceæ*. This genus contains some very beautiful plants, and all highly-deserving of a place in every collection of plants, on account of their very curious and interesting habit. To grow them well, they require the following treatment:— About the middle of April they should be fresh potted, in peat and a little sand mixed, and then plunged in tan, in a pit or frame, where the heat must be kept from 85 to 95 degrees by dung linings, not giving them much water until they have started afresh, and then may be added gentle waterings over head, occasionally in the afternoon; they should be closed early, and air given early in the mornings, and shade during sunshine; by treating them in this manner, they will make an amazing growth in the three following months, when they may be gradually hardened before removing them back to the succulent house; they are increased by offsets, and some of the kinds occasionally produce seeds if fertilised. *Synonymes*: 1. *M. densa*. 2. *M. straminea*. 3. *M. stellaris*.

| | | | | | |
|---|---|---|---|---|---|
| acanthophlégmá . | | 8. Ev. S. | | . 1835 | |
| ambigua . | | 8. Ev. S. | Chile | . 1827 | |
| Andreæ . . | | 8. Ev. S. | | . 1835 | |
| angularis . . | | 8. Ev. S. | | . 1835 | |
| atratá . . | Drk. grn. . | 8. Ev. S. | | | |
| bicolor . . | | 8. Ev. S. | | . 1835 | |
| cæspitósá, 1 . | | 8. Ev. S. | S. Amer. | . 1827 | |
| candicáns . . | | 8. Ev. S. | S. Amer. | . 1827 | |
| carneá . . | Flesh . . | 8. Ev. S. | | . 1835 | |
| caudatá . . | | 8. Ev. S. | Chile | . 1827 | |
| chrysacánthá . | | 8. Ev. S. | S. Amer. | . 1827 | |
| chrysánthá . | Yellow . | 8. Ev. S. | S. Amer. | . 1827 | |
| cirrhifera . . | | 8. Ev. S. | | . 1835 | |
| spina fúscá . | | 8. Ev. S. | | . 1835 | |
| coccineá . . | | 8. Ev. S. | Chile | . 1827 | |
| columáris . . | | 8. Ev. S. | | . 1835 | |
| cónicá . . | . 7. | 8. Ev. S. | | . 1808 | |
| corioídés . . | | 8. Ev. S. | | . 1835 | |
| coromária . . | Scarlet . 7. | 8. Ev. S. | S. Amer. | . 1817 | |
| coronatá . . | | 8. Ev. S. | S. Amer. | . 1817 | |
| crinitá . . | Wht. yel. . | 8. Ev. S. | | | |
| ancistroídés . | | 8. Ev. S. | | | |
| rúbrá . . | | 8. Ev. S. | | | |
| cuneiflórá . | Red . . | 8. Ev. S. | | | |
| cylindricá . . | | 8. Ev. S. | | | |
| depréssá . . | Red. grn. 7. | 8. Ev. S. | S. Amer. | . 1800 | |
| dichótómá . | Pink . . | 8. Ev. S. | | | |
| discólor . . | Red . 7. | 8. Ev. S. | S. Amer. | . 1800 | |
| divaricatá . | Pink . . | 8. Ev. S. | | | |
| echinatá . . | Pale . . | 8. Ev. S. | Mexico | . 1830 | |
| elongatá . . | | 8. Ev. S. | Mexico | . 1830 | |
| eriacánthá . . | | 8. Ev. S. | | | |
| flavéscens, 2 . | Yellow . | 8. Ev. S. | | . 1811 | |
| floríbúndá . . | Pink . | 8. Ev. S. | Chile | | |
| fulvispiná . | Red . . | 8. Ev. S. | Brazil | . 1829 | |
| fuscatá . . | | 8. Ev. S. | S. Amer. | . 1827 | |
| geminispiná . | Red . . | 8. Ev. S. | Mexico | . 1832 | |
| grándis . . | | 8. Ev. S. | | | |
| intertéxtá . . | | 8. Ev. S. | Mexico | . 1836 | |
| Karwinskii . . | | 8. Ev. S. | | . 1836 | |
| laniferá . . | Red . . | 8. Ev. S. | Mexico | . 1823 | |
| Lehmânni . . | Yellow . | 8. Ev. S. | Mexico | . 1836 | |
| longimámmá . | | 8. Ev. S. | | . 1835 | |
| loricatá . . | | 8. Ev. S. | | . 1835 | |
| lutéscens . . | | 8. Ev. S. | | . 1835 | |
| macrothéle . . | | 8. Ev. S. | | . 1836 | |
| magnimámmá . | | 8. Ev. S. | Mexico | . 1823 | |
| missouriénsis . | White . 7. | F. Ev. S. | Missouri | . 1818 | |
| negléctá . . | | 8. Ev. S. | | . 1835 | |
| niveá . . | | 8. Ev. S. | | . 1834 | |
| nivósá . . | | 8. Ev. S. | | | |
| parvimámmá . | . 7. | 8. Ev. S. | S. Amer. | . 1817 | |
| polyédrá . . | | 8. Ev. S. | | . 1826 | |
| polythéle . . | | 8. Ev. S. | | . 1835 | |

| | | | | | |
|---|---|---|---|---|---|
| prolifera | Whitish | 7, S. Ev. S. | | S. Amer. | 1800 |
| pulcherrima | Red | 8. Ev. S. | | | |
| pulchra | Yellow | 6, S. Ev. S. | | Mexico | 1826 |
| pusilla | Pa. red | 8. Ev. S. | | S. Amer. | 1820 |
| pycnacantha | | 8. Ev. S. | | | 1835 |
| pyramidalis | | 8. Ev. S. | | Mexico | 1835 |
| quadrata | | 8. Ev. S. | | Chile | 1827 |
| quadrispina | Scarlet | 8. Ev. S. | | | 1835 |
| rhodantha | | 8. Ev. S. | | | 1836 |
| Scitziana | | 8. Ev. S. | | | 1835 |
| simplex | White | 7, S. Ev. S. | | S. Amer. | 1688 |
| solitaria | | 8. Ev. S. | | Chile | 1827 |
| speciosa | Red | 8. Ev. S. | | Chile | 1827 |
| sphacelata | | 8. Ev. S. | | | 1836 |
| spinosa | | 8. Ev. S. | | Chile | 1827 |
| stellata | Pink | 5, S. Ev. S. | | S. Amer. | 1815 |
| stella-aurata | Yellow | 8. Ev. S. | | | 1835 |
| suberosa | | 8. Ev. S. | | Mexico | 1836 |
| subpolyedra | Li. scr. grn. | 8. Ev. S. | | | 1836 |
| supertexta | | 8. Ev. S. | | | 1836 |
| tentaculata | Scarlet | 8. Ev. S. | | | 1836 |
| tenuis | Pa. yel. | 5, S. Ev. S. | | Mexico | 1830 |
| vetula | Li. scar. | 8. Ev. S. | | | 1835 |
| viripara | Red | 8. Ev. S. | | Louisiana | 1811 |
| Wildiana | | 8. Ev. S. | | | |
| xuccariniana | | 8. Ev. S. | | | 1835 |

MANCHINEEL, see *Hippomane Mancinella*.
MANCHINKEL, see *Sapium Hippomane*.
MANDARIN ORANGE, see *Citrus nobilis*.
MANDRAGORA, *Tournefort*. The English name Mandrake, is derived from *mandra*, an ox-stall, something relating to cattle, and *agauros*, cruel; on account of its poisonous effects on cattle when accidentally gathered with their fodder in the countries where the plants abound. Linn. 5, Or. 1, Nat. Or. *Solanaceae*. These plants thrive well in a light soil, in a shaded situation. They can only be increased by seeds. The roots are very apt to rot during winter. Synonymes: 1. *Atropa Mandragora*. 2. *M. officinalis*. 3. *A. mandragora*.

| | | | | |
|---|---|---|---|---|
| autumnalis, 1 | Yel. wht. | 6, H. Her. P. | S. Eur. | |
| neglecta | Yellow | 5. H. Her. P. | | |
| praecox, 2 | Fuscous | 3, H. Her. P. | Switzerl. | 1819 |
| vernalis, 3 | White | 4, H. Her. P. | Levant | 1548 |

MANDRAKE, see *Mandragora*.
MANETTIA, *Mutis*. In honour of Xavier Manetti, prefect of the botanic garden at Florence, and author of Regnum Vegetabile, 1756. Linn. 4, Or. 1, Nat. Or. *Cinchonaceae*. These plants are well worth cultivating for the beauty and elegance of their flowers. The best soil for them is a mixture of loam and peat. They are easily increased by cuttings of the young wood in the same kind of soil, under a glass, in a moderate heat. Synonyme: 1. *M. cordifolia*.

| | | | | |
|---|---|---|---|---|
| coccinea | Scarlet | 6, S. Ev. Tw. | Guiana | 1806 |
| glabra, 1 | Scarlet | 3, S. Ev. Tw. | B. Ayres | |
| Lygistum | Pink | 3, S. Ev. Tw. | Cuba | 1832 |

MANGIFERA, *Linn.* Derived from *mango*, the name of the tree, and *fero*, to bear. Linn. 23, Or. 1, Nat. Or. *Anacardiaceae*. This is a genus of much esteemed tropical fruit trees, thriving well in sandy loam, or a mixture of loam and peat. The species are readily increased by cuttings of the ripened wood planted in sand, under a glass, in heat. Fresh seeds imported from the places of their natural growth, will vegetate freely. Within the tropics, they hardly eat any other fruit besides *M. indica*, or Common Mango, during the hot months; but if wine be not drunk with it, the Mango is apt to throw out boils, which are, however, conducive to health. The fruit of the finest Mangos have a rich sweet-perfumed flavour, accompanied by a grateful acidity.

| | | | | |
|---|---|---|---|---|
| foetida | Red | 8. Ev. T. | E. Ind. | 1824 |
| indica | White | 7, S. Ev. T. | E. Ind. | 1690 |

MANGO GINGER, see *Curcuma Amada*.
MANGOSTAN, see *Garcinia Mangostana*.
MANGOSTAN, see *Amaranthus Mangostanus*.
MANGO-TREE, see *Mangifera*.
MANGROVE, see *Rhizophora Mangle*.
MANICARIA, *Gaertner.* From *manica*, a glove; in allusion to the spathe. Linn. 21, Or. 9, Nat. Or. *Palmaceae*. This is a fine palm, which must be grown in a rich loam, and can only be increased by seeds.

| | | | | |
|---|---|---|---|---|
| saccifera | | | Palm. E. Ind. | 1823 |

MANISURIS, *Swartz.* From *manis*, a scaly lizard, and *oura*, a tail; referring to the appearance of the

spikes. Linn. 3, Or. 2, Nat. Or. *Gramineae*. A curious plant, of simple culture.

| | | | | |
|---|---|---|---|---|
| granularis | Apetal | 7, Grass. | E. Ind. | 1821 |

MANNA, see *Alhagi*.
MANNA ASH, see *Ornus rotundifolia*.
MANTISIA, *Sims.* Name taken from the insect *mantis*; because of the resemblance of the flowers. Linn. 1, Or. 1, Nat. Or. *Scitamineae*. These singular plants thrive well in a mixture of loam, peat, and sand, and are easily increased by dividing the roots.

| | | | | |
|---|---|---|---|---|
| saltatoria | Purple | 6, S. Her. P. | E. Ind. | 1808 |
| spatulata | Blue | 6, S. Her. P. | E. Ind. | 1823 |

MANULEA, *Linn.* From *manus*, the hand; in allusion to the five divisions of the corolla. Linn. 14, Or. 2, Nat. Or. *Scrophulariaceae*. Handsome plants, rarely to be met with in collections; they grow well in a mixture of peat and sand, or vegetable mould, and are propagated with ease either by cuttings or seeds. Synonymes: 1. *Buchnera falida*. 2. *B. capensis*. 3. *B. viscosa*.

| | | | | |
|---|---|---|---|---|
| argentea | Yellow | 7, G. | A. C. G. H. | 1801 |
| Cheiranthus | Orange | 8, G. Her. P. | C. G. H. | 1795 |
| cordata | Red | 7, G. Ev. Tr. | C. G. H. | 1816 |
| foetida, 1 | White | 7, G. | A. C. G. H. | 1794 |
| pedunculata | White | 9, G. Ev. S. | C. G. H. | 1790 |
| rhynchantha | Yellow | 9, S. Her. P. | C. G. H. | 1823 |
| rubra | Red | 6, G. Ev. S. | C. G. H. | 1790 |
| tomentosa | Yellow | 8, G. Ev. S. | C. G. H. | 1774 |
| villosa, 2 | White | 6, G. | A. C. G. H. | 1783 |
| violacea | Violet | 9, S. Her. P. | | 1824 |
| viscosa, 3 | Pink | 9, G. Ev. S. | C. G. H. | 1774 |

*aethiopica, alternifolia, capitata, crystallina, linifolia, oppositifolia.*

MAPLE, see *Acer*
MARANTA, *Linn.* After B. Maranti, a Venetian physician and botanist, who died in 1554. Linn. 10, Or. 1, Nat. Or. *Marantaceae*. A genus of interesting plants, which grow well in any light rich soil; they are readily increased by dividing at the roots. *M. arundinacea* is esteemed in the East for the fecula which abounds in the root, and on that account it is collected as a delicate article of food.

| | | | | |
|---|---|---|---|---|
| angustifolia | Red | 7, S. Her. P. | W. Ind. | 1820 |
| arundinacea | White | 7, S. Her. P. | S. Amer. | 1739 |
| bicolor | White | 7, S. Her. P. | Brasil | 1823 |
| minor | White | 4, S. Her. P. | S. Amer. | 1828 |
| cuspidata | Yellow | 7, S. Her. P. | S. Leone | 1822 |
| divaricata | White | 7, S. Her. P. | Brasil | 1818 |
| purpurascens | White | 8, S. Her. P. | Brasil | 1823 |
| gibba | White | 7, S. Her. P. | E. Ind. | 1818 |
| gracilis | White | 7, S. Her. P. | Guiana | 1823 |
| Iudica | White | 6, S. Her. P. | W. Ind. | 1800 |
| lutea | Grn. wht. | 6, S. Her. P. | Caracas | 1809 |
| malacobola | Grn. wht. | 12, S. Her. P. | E. Ind. | 1820 |
| obliqua | Red | 7, S. Her. P. | Guiana | 1803 |
| petiolata | | 7, S. Her. P. | Guiana | 1818 |
| sylvatica | Yellow | 7, S. Her. P. | W. Ind. | 1800 |
| Tonchat | Red | 7, S. Her. P. | E. Ind. | 1819 |
| variegata | | 7, S. Her. P. | S. Amer. | 1825 |

MARATTIA, *Swartz.* In honour of J. F. Maratti, of Vallombrosa in Tuscany, a writer upon ferns. Linn. 24, Or. 1, Nat. Or. *Danaeaceae*. This ornamental fern grows well in loam and peat, and is increased by dividing the roots, or by seeds.

| | | | | |
|---|---|---|---|---|
| alata | Brown | 8, S. Her. P. | Jamaica | 1793 |

MARCESCENT, permanent, when withered not falling off.
MARCGRAAVIA, *Linn.* In honour of George Marcgraave, a German, who published a Natural History of Brazil in 1718. Linn. 13, Or. 1, Nat. Or. *Marcgraaviaceae*. This is a genus of curious shrubby, creeping plants; they are found adhering by their fibres to the trunks of trees, though they are not strictly parasitical. They are well suited for covering the walls or rafters of stoves. They grow in turfy loam and peat; and cuttings root in sand, under a glass, in heat.

| | | | | |
|---|---|---|---|---|
| coriacea | White | 8. Ev. S. | Guiana | 1820 |
| umbellata | White | 8. Ev. S. | W. Ind. | 1792 |

MARE'S-TAIL, see *Hippuris*.
MARGARITACEOUS, pearl-bearing.
MARCHANTIA, *Corda.* In honour of Nicholas Marchant, a French botanist. Linn. 24, Or. 6, Nat. Or. *Hepaticae*. Creeping plants, with green, cellular, fleshy fronds, spreading over the surface of the ground in moist places—*androgyna, conica, hemispherica, irrigua, polymorpha*.

MARGIN, edge or border.

MARGINATED, having a border.

MARGYRICARPUS, *Ruiz* and *Pavon.* From *margaron*, a pearl, and *karpos*, a fruit; resemblance of the fruit. *Linn.* 2, Or. 1, Nat. Or. *Rosaceæ.* This is rather a pretty plant, growing well in sandy peat, and increased by cuttings in sand, under a glass, in heat.

| | | | | | | |
|---|---|---|---|---|---|---|
| setòsus | . . . | Green | . . | 8. Ev. S. | Peru | . 1829 |

MARICA, *Schreber.* From *maraino*, to become flaccid; in allusion to the flowers. *Linn.* 3, Or. 1, Nat. Or. *Iridaceæ.* Very beautiful and curious plants, delighting in a mixture of loam, peat, and sand, and increased by dividing the roots, or by seed, which ripens in abundance.

| | | | | | | |
|---|---|---|---|---|---|---|
| cœrùlea | . . . | Blue | . . 5, | G. Her. P. | Brasil | . 1818 |
| cœléstis | . . . | Blue | . . 8. | Her. P. | Brasil | . 1829 |
| grácilis | . . . | Yel. blue | . 8, | G. Her. P. | Brasil | . 1830 |
| hùmilis | . . . | Yellow | . 6, | G. Her. P. | Brasil | . 1823 |
| longifòlia | . . . | Striped | . 8, | S. Her. P. | Brasil | . 1830 |
| martinicénsis | . . | Yellow | . 6, | G. Her. P. | Martinico | . 1782 |
| Northiàna | . . . | Yellow | . 6, | G. Her. P. | Brasil | . 1789 |
| paludòsa | . . . | White | . 7, | S. Aq. P. | Guiana | . 1792 |
| Sabini | . . . | Yellow | . 8, | G. Her. P. | St. Thomas | . 1822 |
| sémi-apérta | . . . | Yellow | . 6, | G. Her. P. | Brasil | . 1820 |

MARIGOLD, see *Calêndòlá.*

MARISCUS, *Vahl.* From the Celtic word *mar*, signifying a marsh; in allusion to the plants growing in marshes. *Linn.* 3, Or. 1, Nat. Or. *Cyperaceæ.* Curious stove plants, growing in a loamy soil well supplied with water, and increased by dividing the roots.

| | | | | | |
|---|---|---|---|---|---|
| aggregàtus | . . . | Apetal | . 6, Grass. | | . 1822 |
| conféxus | . . . | Apetal | . 7, Grass. | Brasil | . 1819 |
| elàtus | . . . | Apetal | . 7, Grass. E. Ind. | | . 1805 |
| umbellàtus | . . . | Apetal | . 7, Grass. E. Ind. | | . 1789 |

*lævis, ovalàris, punícëus.*

MARJÒRAM, see *Origànùm.*

MARJÒRUM, see *Majorànà.*

MARLEA, *Roxburgh.* From *Marliya*, the Bengalese name of the plant. *Linn.* 8, Or. 1, Nat. Or. *Alangiaceæ.* A pretty plant, succeeding in peat and loam; and cuttings of the half-ripened wood root readily in sand, under a glass.

| | | | | | |
|---|---|---|---|---|---|
| begonimfòlia | . . | Yellow | . | G. Ev. S. | China | . . |

MARRUBIUM. From *marrob*, a Hebrew word, signifying a bitter juice; in allusion to the extreme bitterness of the plants. *Linn.* 14, Or. 1, Nat. Or. *Labiatæ.* Any common garden soil will suit these plants, and they are readily increased by divisions of the roots, or by seeds. Synonymes: 1. *M. affine.* 2. *M. creticum* 3. *M. apulum.*

| | | | | | | |
|---|---|---|---|---|---|---|
| Alýssum | . . . | Purple | . 7, | H. Her. P. | Spain | . 1597 |
| astracánicùm | . . | Pa. pur. | . 7, | H. Her. P. | Levant | . 1816 |
| candidíssimùm | . . | White | . 7, | H. Her. P. | Levant | . 1782 |
| catariæfòlium | . . | Purple | . 7, | H. Her. P. | Levant | . 1819 |
| leonuroìdës, 1 | . . | Purple | . 7, | H. Her. P. | Caucasus | . 1819 |
| mollissìmùm | . . | White | . 6, | F. Her. P. | Nepal | . 1820 |
| peregrìnùm, 2 | . . | White | . 8, | H. Her. P. | Sicily | . 1640 |
| supìnùm | . . . | Purple | . 9, | H. Her. P. | S. Eur. | . 1714 |
| vulgàrè | . . . | White | . 7, | H. Her. P. | Britain | . . |
| lanàtùm, 3 | . . . | White | . 8, | H. Her. P. | Britain | . . |

MARSDÈNIA, *R. Brown.* In honour of William Marsden, F.R.S., late secretary to the Admiralty, and author of a History of Sumatra. *Linn.* 5, Or. 2, Nat. Or. *Asclepiadaceæ.* A genus of very interesting plants. *M. flavescens* is well suited for covering rafters, pillars, or trellis-work, in stoves or conservatories. They grow in a mixture of loam, peat, and sand; and cuttings root in sand, under a glass, in heat.

| | | | | | | |
|---|---|---|---|---|---|---|
| erécta | . . . | White | . 7, | G. Ev. S. | Syria | . 1597 |
| flavéscens | . . . | Yelsh. | . 8, | S. Ev. Tw. | N. Holl. | . 1830 |
| suavéòlens | . . . | White | . 7, | S. Ev. Cl. | N. Holl. | . 1830 |

MARSHÀLLIA, *Schreber.* In honour of Humphrey Marshall, a botanical author. *Linn.* 19, Or. 1, Nat. Or. *Compositæ.* This is a genus of very handsome plants. They grow very well in a mixture of loam and peat, and are readily increased by cuttings.

| | | | | | | |
|---|---|---|---|---|---|---|
| angustifòlia | . . | Purple | . 7, | F. Her. P. | Carolina | . 1800 |
| cæspitòsa | . . . | Pur. wht. | . 7, | F. Her. P. | Texas | . 1837 |
| lanceolàtà | . . . | Purple | . 6, | F. Her. P. | Carolina | . 1812 |
| latifòlia | . . . | Pa. pur. | . 6, | F. Her. P. | Carolina | . 1806 |

MARSH-CINQUEFOIL, see *Cômàrûm palûstrè.*

MARSH-MALLOW, see *Altheà.*

MARSH-MARIGOLD, see *Cálthà.*

MARSH-PENNYWORT, see *Hydrocótylë vulgàris.*

MARSÍLEA. Linnæus dedicated this genus to the Count L. F. Marsigli, founder of the Academy of Sciences, Bologna. *Linn.* 24, Or. 4, Nat. Or. *Marsileaceæ.* A curious aquatic plant, readily increased by divisions.

| | | | | | | |
|---|---|---|---|---|---|---|
| quadrifòlia | . . . | | . 7, | H. Aq. P. | Europe | . 1820 |

MARSYPIÀNTHUS, *Martius.* From *marsupos*, a purse, and *anthos*, a flower; because of the shape of the flowers. *Linn.* 14, Or. 1, Nat. Or. *Labiatæ.* This is not a plant of much beauty. The seed may be reared on a hotbed, and treated as other tender annuals. Synonyme: 1. *Hyptis inflata.*

| | | | | | |
|---|---|---|---|---|---|
| hyptoìdes, 1 | . . | Blue | . 7, S. | A. America | . 1823 |

MARTYNIA, *Linn.* In honour of John Martyn, F.R.S., professor of botany at Cambridge, who died in 1768. *Linn.* 14, Or. 2, Nat. Or. *Pedaliaceæ.* Handsome annuals. The seed should be raised on a hotbed, and when transplanted singly into pots of light rich soil, they should be kept in the stove or greenhouse. Synonyme: 1. *M. annua.*

| | | | | | |
|---|---|---|---|---|---|
| diándrà | . . . | Red | . 7, S. | A. N. Spain | . 1731 |
| longiflòrà | . . . | Pa. pur. | . 7, S. | A. C. G. H. | . 1781 |
| lùtea | . . . | Yellow | . 7, S. | A. Brazil | . 1825 |
| proboscìdèa, 1 | . | Lgt. blue | . 7, S. | A. America | . 1738 |

MÀRUM, signifying a herb with a strong smell.

MARVEL-OF-PERU, see *Mirábilis.*

MASSÒNIA, *Linn.* In honour of Mr. F. Masson, author of Stapeliæ Novæ. *Linn.* 6, Or. 1, Nat. Or. *Liliaceæ.* A genus of very singular plants, flourishing in an equal mixture of loam, peat, and sand, and requiring no water when in a dormant state. They may be increased by offsets from the bulbs, or by seeds. They will grow very well in a frame. Synonyme: 1. *M. pustulata.*

| | | | | | | |
|---|---|---|---|---|---|---|
| angustifòlia | . . | White | . 4, | G. Bl. P. | C. G. H. | . 1775 |
| cándidà | . . . | White | . 4, | G. Bl. P. | C. G. H. | . |
| cordàtà | . . . | White | . 5, | G. Bl. P. | C. G. H. | . 1826 |
| echinàtà | . . . | White | . 5, | G. Bl. P. | C. G. H. | . 1790 |
| ensifòlia | . . . | Livid | . 4, | G. Bl. P. | C. G. H. | . 1790 |
| grandiflòrà | . . | Wht. grn. | 10, | G. Bl. P. | C. G. H. | . 1825 |
| latifòlia | . . . | White | . 3, | G. Bl. P. | C. G. H. | . 1775 |
| longifòlia | . . . | White | . 3, | G. Bl. P. | C. G. H. | . |
| muricàtà | . . . | White | . 4, | G. Bl. P. | C. G. H. | . 1790 |
| pauciflòrà | . . . | White | . 4, | G. Bl. P. | C. G. H. | . 1790 |
| scàbrà, 1 | . . . | White | . 2, | G. Bl. P. | C. G. H. | . 1790 |
| undulàtà | . . . | White | . 4, | G. Bl. P. | C. G. H. | . 1791 |
| violàceà | . . . | White | . 5, | G. Bl. P. | C. G. H. | . 1800 |

MASTERWORT, see *Imperatòrià.*

MASTERWORT, see *Astrántià.*

MASTIC, see *Majorànà crassifòlià.*

MASTICATION, grinding or chewing with the teeth.

MASTICH, see *Thymùs Mastichìnà.*

MASTICH-TREE, see *Pistàcià Lentíscùs.*

MATAYBA, *Aublet.* From *Matahaiba*, the name of *M. guianensis* in French Guiana. *Linn.* 8, Or. 1, Nat. Or. *Sapindaceæ.* These trees attain the height of sixty feet. They grow in a mixture of loam and peat, and cuttings of the ripened wood, not deprived of any of their leaves, will root in sand, under a glass, in heat. Synonyme: 1. *Ephielis fraxinea.*

| | | | | | |
|---|---|---|---|---|---|
| guianénsis, 1 | . | White | . . 8. Ev. S. | Guiana | . 1803 |
| Patrisiànà | . . | White | . . 8. Ev. S. | Guiana | . 1825 |

MAT-GRASS, see *Nàrdus.*

MAT-GRASS, see *Psàmmèà.*

MATH, an old term for crop.

MATHIÒLA, *R. Brown.* In honour of Peter Andrew Mathioli, a famous Italian physician, and author of a commentary on the works of Dioscorides; he died in 1757. *Linn.* 15, Nat. Or. *Cruciferæ.* This is a genus of old and well-known inhabitants of the garden. In order to obtain good double *Stock-gilliflowers*, *Brompton* and *Queen-stocks*, choice should be made of such single-flowering plants as grow near many double ones. The seed should be sown in May, and after they have reached two or three inches high, they should be thinned at least nine inches asunder, and the plants taken out may be planted at about the same distance apart in the flower-border; if the following winter be severe, they must be protected by mats, and in the following May and June they will flower beautifully. Desirable double varieties may be propagated by cuttings, which root readily by being planted under a hand-glass, and shaded. To have a succession of the *Annual*, or *Ten-week-stock*, the seed should be sown in February, March, April, and May, and the plants from the May sowing will continue to flower till Christmas. In preserving plants of the *Stock-gilliflower*, and *Ten-week-stock*, for seed, select only such single-flowering plants as have fine-coloured flowers. The biennial and hardy shrubby kinds should be treated in the same manner as the *Stock-gilliflower*, and all the annual kinds in the same way as the *Ten-week-stock*. The greenhouse shrubby species grow best in a mixture of light soil and sand, and cuttings root readily under a glass. Fine double stocks may be planted in pots, and kept in a frame during winter.

| | | | | | | |
|---|---|---|---|---|---|---|
| acaúlis | . . | Red . | 6, | H. | A. Egypt | . 1823 |
| ánnúa | . . | Various | 8, | H. | A. S. Eur. | . 1731 |
| álba | . . | White . | 7, | H. | A. S. Eur. | . . |
| flóre-pléno | . | Red . | 7, | H. | A. | |
| coronopifólia | . | Purple . | 6, | H. | B. Sicily | . 1819 |
| fenestrális | . | Purple . | 7, | H. | B. Crete | . 1759 |
| glabráta | . | White . | 8, | F. Ev. | S. | |
| flóre-pléno | . | Wht. pur. | 8, | F. Ev. | S. | |
| purpúreá | . | Purple . | 8, | F. Ev. | S. | |
| græcá | . | White . | 8, | H. | A. S. Eur. | . . |
| incáná | . | Purple . | 8, | H. Ev. | S. England | |
| álba | . | Purple . | 8, | H. Ev. | S. England | |
| coccíneá | . | Scarlet . | 8, | H. Ev. | S. England | |
| múltiplex | . | Varieg. . | 8, | F. Ev. | S. England | |
| lívida | . . | Livid pur. | 7, | H. | A. Egypt | . 1820 |
| longipétála | . | Red yel. . | 6, | H. | A. Bagdad | . 1818 |
| odoratíssimá | . | Livid . | 6, | G. Ev. | S. Persia | . 1795 |
| frágrans | . | Livid . | 6, | G. Ev. | S. Crimea | . 1823 |
| oxycéras | . | Livid . | 7, | H. | A. Damascus | . 1820 |
| parviflóra | . | Purple . | 7, | H. | A. Morocco | . 1799 |
| sténá | . | Lilac . | 7, | H. | B. Sicily | . 1835 |
| simplicicáulis | . | Purple . | 7, | H. | B. | |
| álba | . | White . | 7, | H. | B. | |
| sinuáta | . | Dingy red | 7, | H. | B. England | |
| tatárica | . | Red yel. . | 7, | H. | B. Tartary | . 1820 |
| tenélla | . | Grn. brn. . | 7, | H. | A. Cyprus | . 1820 |
| tortuósa | . | Purple . | 7, | G. Ev. | S. C. G. H. | . 1816 |
| tricuspidáta | . | Purple . | 7, | H. | A. Barbary | . 1739 |
| trístis | . | Livid . | 6, | G. Ev. | S. S. Eur. | . 1768 |
| váriá | . | Livid . | 6, | G. Ev. | S. S. Eur. | . 1820 |

MATRICÁRIA, *Linn.* From *matrix*, the womb. *Linn.* 19, Or. 2, Nat. Or. *Compositæ.* Hardy annuals, of no interest—*capénsis, Chamomílla, C. flóre-pléno, pusílla, suavéólens.*

MÍTRIX, a place where anything is generated or formed.

MÁTTIA, *Schultes.* Supposed to be after some botanist. *Linn.* 5, Or. 1, Nat. Or. *Boraginaceæ.* Ornamental plants, growing well in any common garden soil, and increased by divisions.

| | | | | | | |
|---|---|---|---|---|---|---|
| lanáta | . . . | Reddish . | 6, | H. Her. P. | Levant . | . 1800 |
| umbelláta | . | Red . | 5, | H. Her. P. | Hungary | . 1822 |

MAURÁNDYA, *Jacquin.* In honour of Dr. Maurandy, professor of botany at Carthagena. *Linn.* 14, Or. 2, Nat. Or. *Scrophulariaceæ.* The species of this genus are very elegant, climbing, evergreen, or herbaceous plants, and are therefore well worthy of a place in every garden. During summer, they will grow and flower abundantly planted against a wall in the open air, or at the bottom of trellis-work; but they require the protection of a greenhouse in winter. A light rich soil suits them, and they are easily increased by young cuttings planted under a glass, or by seeds.

| | | | | | | |
|---|---|---|---|---|---|---|
| antirrhiniflóra | . | Purple . | 7, | G. Ev. Tw. | Mexico | . 1814 |
| Barclayáná | . | Blue wht. . | 7, | G. Ev. Tw. | Mexico | . 1825 |
| semperflórens | . | Purple . | 7, | G Ev. Tw. | Mexico | . 1796 |

MAURÍTIA, *Linn.* In honour of the Prince Maurice of Nassau, the patron of the celebrated Piso. *Linn.* 22, Or. 6, Nat. Or. *Palmaceæ.* This is a genus of splendid plants, growing well in a rich sandy loam, in a good strong heat, with a copious supply of water when growing vigorously.

| | | | | | |
|---|---|---|---|---|---|
| armáta | . . . | | Palm. | Brasil | . 1824 |
| flexuósa | . . | Wht. grn. . | Palm. | Surinam | . 1816 |
| vinífera | . . | | Palm. | Marash. | . 1823 |

MAXILLÁRIA, *Ruiz and Pavon.* So named in consequence of the resemblance between the column and labellum and the jaws or maxillæ of some animal. *Linn.* 20, Or. 1, Nat. Or. *Orchidaceæ.* This is an extensive and very elegant genus of plants, all of which are highly deserving of cultivation, either for the beauty or delicious fragrance of the flowers. *M. Steelii* is not only a very remarkable, but a very beautiful plant; the flowers are large, of a fine yellow colour, irregularly spotted with dark purple.

[ 199 ]

This, and several other species, as *M. aciculáris, imbricata, racemosa,* and *M. rufescens,* should be grown on wood, on which a little moss should be placed, then the roots of the plant put on that, with a sufficient quantity of moss, and the whole fastened to the wood with some metallic wire. For the culture of the other species, see *Stanhopea.* Synonymes: 1. *Maxillaria fuscata.* 2. *M. placanthera.*

| | | | | | | |
|---|---|---|---|---|---|---|
| aciculáris | . . | Purplish . | | 8. | Epi. Brasil | . . |
| aromática | . | Yellow . | 5, | 8. | Epi. Mexico | . 1825 |
| atrórúbens | . | Drk. red . | 7, | 8. | Epi. | |
| aúreó-fúlva | . | Gol. brn. . | 6, | 8. | Epi. S. Amer. | . 1836 |
| Barringtónia | . | Yel. brn. . | 4, | 8. | Epi. Jamaica | . 1790 |
| Boóthii | . | Grnsh. yel. | 5, | 8. | Epi. Guatemala | . 1835 |
| chlorántha | . | Yelsh. grn. | | 8. | Epi. Demerara | . 1837 |
| Cólleyi | . | Dingy brn. | 9, | 8. | Epi. Mexico | . 1834 |
| cristáta | . | Wht. pur. | 7, | 8. | Epi. Trinidad | . . |
| eróceá | . | Saffron . | | 8. | Epi. Rio Jan. | . . |
| decólor | . | Yel. wht. | 1, | 8. | Epi. Jamaica | . . |
| dénsa | . | Wht. pink | 11, | 8. | Epi. Mexico | . 1834 |
| Deppíi | . | Yel. grn. . | 6, | 8. | Epi. Xalapa | . 1828 |
| dicryptóídes | . | | | 8. | Epi. | |
| foveáta | . | Straw . | | 8. | Epi. Demerara | . . |
| galeáta | . | Orange . | 9, | 8. | Epi. Xalapa | . 1828 |
| gramíneá | . | Yel. red . | | 8. | Epi. Demerara | . . |
| Harrisónia | . | Yel. red . | | 8. | Epi. Brasil | . . |
| Henchmanni | . | Purple . | 3, | 8. | Epi. Mexico | . 1835 |
| imbricáta | . | | | 8. | Epi. | |
| longifólia | . | | 6, | 8. | Epi. N. Granada | . 1822 |
| macrophýlla | . | Pa. straw . | | 8. | Epi. Columbia | |
| madída | . | Yellow . | | 8. | Epi. Brasil | . . |
| ochroleúca | . | Yelsh. . | 7, | 8. | Epi. Rio Jan. | . . |
| pallidiflóra | . | Yellow . | | 8. | Epi. St. Vin. | . 1826 |
| párvúla | . | Bro. pink . | 4, | 8. | Epi. Brasil | . 1824 |
| Parkéri | . | Buff wht. . | 4, | 8. | Epi. Demerara | . 1826 |
| picta | . | Yel. wht. | 12, | 8. | Epi. Brasil | . . |
| porrécta | . | Pa. buff. . | | 8. | Epi. Rio Jan. | . . |
| psittacína | . | Red yel. . | 10, | 8. | Epi. Mexico | . 1836 |
| púmíla | . | Purple . | | 8. | Epi. Demerara | . 1835 |
| punctáta | . | Wht. spot. | 10, | 8. | Epi. | |
| racemósa | . | Buff yel. . | 6, | 8. | Epi. Rio Jan. | . 1826 |
| Rollissónii | . | Yellow . | 8, | 8. | Epi. Brasil | . 1836 |
| ruféscens, 1 | . | Yel. spot. | 12, | 8. | Epi. Trinidad | . . |
| sinuósa | . | Striped . | 10, | 8. | Epi. Demerara | . 1834 |
| squálens | . | Whitish . | 8, | 8. | Epi. Brasil | . 1822 |
| stapelioídes | . | Orange . | 6, | 8. | Epi. Brasil | . 1837 |
| Stéélii | . | Yel. spot. | 7, | 8. | Epi. Demerara | . 1836 |
| stenopétála | . | | | 8. | Epi. | |
| streptopétála | . | | | 8. | Epi. | |
| tenuifólia | . | Red. yel. . | 6, | 8. | Epi. Vera Cruz. | . 1837 |
| tetragóna | . | Pur. grn. wht. | 7, | 8. | Epi. Brasil | . 1837 |
| uncáta | . | | | 8. | Epi. Demerara | . 183-- |
| variabílis | . | Purple . | 1, | 8. | Epi. Mexico | . . |
| unipunctáta | . | Yellow . | | 8. | Epi. Mexico | . 1836 |
| víridis, 2 | . | Green . | 5, | 8. | Epi. Brasil | . . |
| vitellína | . | Orange . | 6, | 8. | Epi. Brasil | . 1837 |
| Warreáná | . | Wht. pur. | 8, | 8. | Epi. Brasil | . 1829 |
| xanthína | . | Yellow . | | 8. | Epi. Organ Mts. | |

MAXIMILIÁNA, *Martius.* In honour of Maximilian Prince of Wied-Neuwied. *Linn.* 23, Or. 1, Nat. Or. *Palmaceæ.* This is a very beautiful plant, requiring the same treatment as the genus *Mauritia.*

| | | | |
|---|---|---|---|
| régia | . . . | Palm. Brasil | . . 1825 |

MAY-APPLE, see *Podophýllum peltátum.*

MAYTÉNUS, *Feuille. Maiten* is the Chilian name of one of the species. *Linn.* 23, Or. 2, Nat. Or. *Celastraceæ.* The species of this ornamental genus thrive well in a mixture of peat, loam, and sand; and cuttings of the ripened wood root readily in the same kind of soil, under a glass. Synonymes: 1. *Celastris octagonus.* 2. *C. verticillatus.*

| | | | | | | |
|---|---|---|---|---|---|---|
| boária | . . . | White . | | F. Ev. T. | Chile | . 1822 |
| chilénsis | . | Grn. yel. . | 5, | F. Ev. | S. Chile | . 1829 |
| octagóna, 1 | . | White . | 10, | G. Ev. | S. Peru | . 1786 |
| verticilláta, 2 | . | White . | 10, | G. Ev. | S. Peru | . 1823 |

MÁZUS, *Loureiro.* From *mazos,* a teat; in allusion to the mouth of the corolla being closed by tubercles. *Linn.* 14, Or. 2, Nat. Or. *Scrophulariaceæ.* This is a genus of interesting annuals. They require to be raised on a gentle hotbed, and about the end of May to be planted out into a warm sheltered situation in the open ground. Synonyme: 1. *Lindernia japonica.*

| | | | | | | |
|---|---|---|---|---|---|---|
| pumílio . | . . | Pa. pur. . | 6, | H. | A. V. D. L. | . 1823 |
| rugósus, 1 | . | Yel. pur. . | 7, | F. Tr. | A. China | . 1780 |

MEADOW-GRASS, see *Póa.*
MEADOW-RUE, see *Thalictrum.*
MEADOW-SAFFRON, see *Cólchicum.*
MEADOW-SAXIFRAGE, see *Séséli.*
MEADOW-SWEET, see *Spíræa Ulmária.*

Mᴇᴄᴏɴᴏᴘsᴙs, *Decandolle.* From *mekon*, a poppy, and *opsis*, resemblance ; the appearance of the plants. *Linn.* 13, Or. 1, Nat. Or. *Papaveraceæ.* Ornamental plants, growing in any light rich soil, and increased by seed. Synonyme : 1. *Papaver cambrica.*

| | | | | | |
|---|---|---|---|---|---|
| cámbricǎ, 1 | . Yellow | . 6, H. Her. P. England | |
| crassifóliǎ | . Oran. red. | H. Her. P. California | 1833 |
| heterophỹllǎ | . Oran. red. | H. Her. P. California | 1833 |

Mᴇᴅᴇᴏ́ʟǍ, *Linn.* From *Medea*, the sorceress ; supposed medicinal qualities. *Linn.* 6, Or. 3, Nat. Or. *Melanthaceæ.* This is a curious plant, succeeding well in light sandy soil, and increased by dividing the roots. *Synonyme* : 1. *Gyronia virginica.*

| | | | | |
|---|---|---|---|---|
| virgínicǎ | . . Yellow | . 6, H. Her. P. Virginia | . 1759 |

Mᴇᴅɪᴄᴀ̆ɢᴏ̆, *Linn.* From *medike*, a name given by Dioscorides to a Median grass. *Linn.* 17, Or. 4, Nat. Or. *Leguminosæ.* The perennial herbaceous species of this genus will grow in any common garden soil, and are increased by dividing the plants in spring at the roots. The shrubby kinds grow in the same kind of soil, and are readily increased by cuttings. The seeds of the annual species require to be sown in the open border in spring. *Synonymes* : 1. *Medicago littoralis.* 2. *Melilotus brachyloba.* 3. *Medicago pubescens.* 4. *M. Helix.* 5. *M. lupulina unguiculata.* 6. *M. elegans.* 7. *Melilotus sibirica.* 8. *Medicago tricycla.*

| | | | | |
|---|---|---|---|---|
| aculeátǎ | . Yellow | . 7, H. Tr. A. | | 1802 |
| agagróphllǎ | . Yellow | . 7, H. Tr. A. | Italy | 1820 |
| agréstis | . Yellow | . 7, H. Tr. A. | Italy | 1820 |
| apiculátǎ | . Yellow | . 6, H. | A. S. Eur. | 1800 |
| applanátǎ | . Yellow | . 7, H. Tr. A. | | 1810 |
| arbórⱥǎ | . Yellow | . 5, H. Ev. S. | | 1596 |
| arenáriǎ, 1 | . Yellow | . 6, H. Tr. A. | Naples | 1820 |
| brachycárpǎ, 2 | Pa. yel. | 6, H. | A. Tiflis | 1823 |
| cancellátǎ | . Yellow | . 7, H. Tr. A. | Caucasus | 1818 |
| carstiénsls | . Yellow | . 7, H. Her. P. | Carinthia | 1789 |
| catalónicǎ | . Yellow | | A. Catalonia | 1820 |
| ciliáris | . Yellow | . 7, H. Tr. A. S. Eur. | | 1686 |
| coronátǎ | . Yellow | . 6, H. Tr. A. S. Eur. | | 1660 |
| eretáceǎ | . Yellow | . 7, H. De. Tr. | Tauria | 1805 |
| cylindráceǎ | . Yellow | . 7, H. Tr. A. | | 1822 |
| denticulátǎ | . Yellow | . 6, H. | A. France | 1800 |
| disciformis | . Yellow | . | A. S. France | 1822 |
| distáns | . Yellow | . 7, H. Tr. A. S. Eur. | | 1810 |
| echínus | . Yellow | . 6, H. Tr. A. | S. France | 1818 |
| falcátǎ | . Yellow | . 7, H. Her. P. England | | |
| flexuósǎ | . Yellow | . 7, H. Tr. A. | Italy | 1819 |
| Gerárdi | . Yellow | . 7, H. Tr. A. S. Eur. | | 1816 |
| glomerátǎ | . Yellow | . 6, H. Her. P. | Italy | 1817 |
| glutinósǎ | . Yellow | . 6, H. De. Tr. | Caucasus | 1817 |
| grǽcǎ | . Yellow | . 7, H. Tr. A. | Greece | 1804 |
| granadénsis | . Yellow | . 7, H. | A. Spain | 1816 |
| Hornemanniánǎ, 8 | Yellow | . 6, H. Tr. A. | Morocco | 1818 |
| hỹstrix | . Yellow | . 6, H. Tr. A. | Naples | 1820 |
| intermédiǎ | . Yellow | . 7, H. Her. P. | Naples | 1817 |
| intertéxtǎ | . Yellow | . 7, H. Tr. A. S. Eur. | | 1629 |
| laciniátǎ | . Yellow | . 7, H. Tr. A. S. Eur. | | 1683 |
| lǽvis, 4. | . Yellow | . 7, H. Tr. A. S. Eur. | | 1816 |
| lappáceǎ | . Yellow | . 7, H. Tr. A. | Montpelier | 1810 |
| littorális | . Yellow | . 7, H. | A. Europe | 1822 |
| lupulínǎ | . Yellow | . 6, H. Tr. A. | Britain | |
| polyståchỹǎ | . Yellow | . H. Tr. A. | Switzerl. | |
| Willdenówii | . Yellow | . H. Tr. A. | Europe | |
| maculátǎ | . Yellow | . 5, H. Tr. A. | England | |
| marginátǎ | . Yellow | . 7, H. Tr. A. S. Eur. | | 1816 |
| marínǎ | . Yellow | . 7, H. Her. P. S. Eur. | | 1596 |
| médiǎ | . Yellow | . 6, H. Tr. A. | Europe | 1817 |
| mínimǎ | . Yellow | . 5, H. Tr. A. | England | |
| mnisocárpǎ, 5 | . Yellow | . 6, H. Tr. A. | Switzerl. | 1816 |
| mollíssimǎ | . Yellow | . 7, H. Tr. A. | Spain | 1818 |
| mórex | . Yellow | . 7, H. Tr. A. | | 1802 |
| muricátǎ | . Yellow | . 6, H. Tr. A. | England | |
| muricoléptis | . Yellow | . 7, H. Tr. A. | Europe | 1820 |
| nígrǎ | . Yellow | . 7, H. Tr. A. S. Eur. | | 1789 |
| obscúrǎ | . Yellow | . 7, H. Tr. A. | S. France | 1734 |
| orbiculáris | . Yellow | . 7, H. Tr. A. S. Eur. | | 1688 |
| pentacyclǎ | . Yellow | . 7, H. Tr. A. | S. France | 1820 |
| prǽcox | . Yellow | . 7, H. Tr. A. | Provence | 1820 |
| procúmbens | . Yellow | . 6, H. De. Tr. S. Eur. | | 1818 |
| prostrátǎ | . Yellow | . 7, H. De. Tr. | Hungary | 1793 |
| pubéscens | . Yellow | . 7, H. Tr. A. | Montpal. | 1819 |
| réctǎ | . Yellow | . 7, H. | A. Barbary | 1810 |
| rigídulǎ | . Yellow | . 7, H. Tr. A. | S. France | 1780 |
| rugósǎ, 6 | . Yellow | . 7, H. Tr. A. S. Eur. | | 1680 |
| rupéstris | . Yellow | . 6, H. Tr. A. | Tauria | 1820 |
| satívǎ | . Violet | . 6, H. Her. P. | England | |
| versícolor | . Yel. blue | 6, H. Her. P. | Britain | |
| scutellátǎ | . Yellow | . 7, H. Tr. A. S. Eur. | | 1562 |
| sibíricǎ, 7. | . Yellow | . 6, H. Tr. A. | Siberia | 1817 |
| sphærocárpǎ | . Yellow | . 7, H. Tr. A. | Italy | 1818 |
| spínulósǎ | . Yellow | . 7, H. Tr. A. | S. France | 1820 |
| striátǎ, 8 | . Yellow | . 7, H. | A. S. France | 1820 |
| suffruticósǎ | . Vio. yel. | 6, H. Her. P. | Pyrenees | 1820 |

| | | | | | |
|---|---|---|---|---|---|
| Tenoreánǎ | . Yellow | . 7. H. Tr. A. | Italy | . 1820 |
| tentaculátǎ | . Yellow | . 6, H. Tr. A. S. Eur. | | . 1800 |
| terybéllǎm | . Yellow | . 7, H. Tr. A. S. Eur. | | . 1798 |
| tornátǎ | . Yellow | . 7, H. | A. S. Eur. | . 1658 |
| tribuloídǎ | . Yellow | . 7, H. | A. S. Eur. | . 1730 |
| tuberculátǎ | . Yellow | . 7, H. | A. S. Eur. | . 1658 |
| turbinátǎ | . Yellow | . 7, H. | A. S. Eur. | . 1680 |

Mᴇᴅɪᴄᴋ, see *Medicago.*
MᴇᴅɪɴɪʟʟǍ, *Gaudichaud.* The meaning is not explained. *Linn.* 10, Or. 1, Nat. Or. *Melastomaceæ.* This very elegant shrub may be referred to *Melastoma* for culture and propagation. ,

| | | | | |
|---|---|---|---|---|
| erythrophỹllǎ | . Rose | . . 8, S. Ev. S. Khoseⱥⱥ | . 1837 |

Mᴇᴅʟᴀʀ, see *Mespilus.*
Mᴇᴅᴜ́ʟʟǍ, the pith of a plant.
Mᴇᴅᴜsᴀ'ꜱ-ʜᴇᴀᴅ, see *Euphorbia Caput Medusæ.*
MᴇɢᴀᴄᴀʀᴘǼǍ, *Decandolle.* From *megas*, great, and *karpos*, a fruit ; in allusion to the large pods. *Linn.* 15, Nat. Or. *Cruciferæ.* This plant grows best in light sandy soil, and may readily be increased by seeds. *Synonyme* : 1. *Biscutella megacarpa.*

| | | | | |
|---|---|---|---|---|
| laciniátǎ, 1 | . Yellow | . 6, H. Her. P. S. Eur. | | . 1818 |

Mᴇɢᴀᴄʟɪ́ɴɪᴜᴍ, *Lindley.* From *megas*, large, and *kline*, a bed ; in allusion to the broad, sword-shaped bed, or rachis of the flowers. *Linn.* 20, Or. 1, Nat. Or. *Orchidaceæ.* This is a most singular genus of plants, the flowers being produced on a rachis, which is upwards of nine inches long. The lip of *M. falcatum* moves up and down with great rapidity, much in the same way as the head of the Chinese images of mandarins. For culture and propagation, see *Stanhopea.*

| | | | | |
|---|---|---|---|---|
| falcátǔm | . . Yel. red | . 3, S. Epi. S. Leone | . 1824 |
| máximǔm | . . Yel. grn. | . 7, S. Epi. S. Leone | . 1836 |
| oxyptérǔm | . . Green | . 3, S. Epi. S. Leone | |

Mᴇɢᴀsᴛᴀ́ᴄʜʏǍ, *Beauvois.* From *megas*, large, and *stachys*, a spike ; in allusion to the flower-spike. *Linn.* 3, Or. 2, Nat. Or. *Gramineæ.* Rather pretty plants, chiefly annuals. They grow in any kind of soil, and are increased by seeds.

| | | | | |
|---|---|---|---|---|
| amábilis | . . Apetal. | . 7, Gram. E. Ind. | . 1802 |
| brizoídès | . . Apetal. | . 6, Gram. C. G. H. | . 1818 |
| ciliáris | . . Apetal. | . 7, Gram. Jamaica | . 1776 |
| elongátǎ | . . Apetal. | . 7, Gram. E. Ind. | . 1812 |
| Eragróstis | . . Apetal. | . 7, Gram. Italy | . 1699 |
| nigricáns | . . Apetal. | . 6, Gram. S. Amer. | . 1818 |
| pulchéllǎ | . . Apetal. | . 7, Gram. Tauria | . 1819 |
| rupéstris | . . Apetal. | . 6, Gram. E. Ind. | . 1820 |
| spectábilis | . . Apetal. | . 6, Gram. N. Amer. | . 1820 |

Mᴇʟᴀʟᴇᴜ́ᴄǍ, *Linn.* From *melas*, black, and *leukos*, white ; because the trunk is black and the branches white. *Linn.* 18, Or. 2, Nat. Or. *Myrtaceæ.* This is a very desirable genus of greenhouse or conservatory plants, on account of the neatness of their foliage, and their splendid flowers. They thrive best in an equal mixture of loam, peat, and sand ; and cuttings, if not too ripe, will root readily planted in sand, under a glass. *M. Leucadendron* and *Cajuputi* yield the volatile oil of *Cajeputi*, well known as a powerful sudorific, and a useful external application in chronic rheumatism. *Synonymes* : 1. *M. parviflora.* 2. *M. imbricata.* 3. *M. canescens, M. tomentosa.* 4. *M. Cajuputi.* 5. *M. epacridea.* 6. *M. discolor.*

| | | | | |
|---|---|---|---|---|
| acerósǎ | . . Purple | . 6, G. Ev. S. N. Holl. | |
| armilláris | . . Green | . 6, G. Ev. S. N. S. W. | . 1788 |
| calycínǎ | . . Purple | . 7, G. Ev. S. N. Amer. | . 1803 |
| cuticuláris | . . | . G. Ev. S. N. Holl. | |
| decussátǎ, 1 | . . Lilac | . 8, G. Ev. S. N. Holl. | . 1803 |
| dénsǎ | . . Purple | . G. Ev. S. N. Holl. | . 1803 |
| diosmæfóliǎ | . . Reddish | . 6, G. Ev. S. N. Holl. | . 1794 |
| dumósǎ | . . | . G. Ev. S. N. Holl. | |
| ericifóliǎ | . . Green | . 8, G. Ev. S. N. S. W. | . 1788 |
| ericocéphálǎ | . . | . G. Ev. S. N. Holl. | . 1824 |
| erubéscens | . . Yellow | . 6, G. Ev. S. N. Holl. | |
| euphorbioídès | . . | . G. Ev. S. N. Holl. | . 1824 |
| fimbriátǎ | . . | . G. Ev. S. N. Holl. | . 1817 |
| Fraséri | . . Pa. rose | . G. Ev. S. N. S. W. | . 1822 |
| fúlgens | . . Scarlet | . 8, G. Ev. S. N. Holl. | . 1803 |
| genistifóliǎ | . . Reddish | . G. Ev. S. N. S. W. | . 1793 |
| gibbósǎ, 2 | . . | . G. Ev. S. N. Holl. | . 1820 |
| globíferǎ | . . | . G. Ev. S. N. Holl. | . 1803 |
| grándis | . . | . G. Ev. S. N. Holl. | |
| Hugélii | . . | . G. Ev. S. Swan R. | . 1822 |
| hypericifóliǎ | . . Scarlet | . 7, G. Ev. S. N. S. W. | . 1792 |
| incánǎ, 3 | . . Yellow | . 7, G. Ev. S. N. Holl. | . 1822 |
| lanceolátǎ | . . | . 7, G. Ev. S. N. Holl. | . 1817 |
| Leucadéndron | . . White | . 8. Ev. T. E. Ind. | . 1796 |
| linarifóliǎ | . . Cream | . 7, G. Ev. S. N. S. W. | . 1793 |

| | | | |
|---|---|---|---|
| mĭnŏr, 4 | White | 8. Ev. R. E. Ind. | 1800 |
| nodŏsā | Pa. yel. | 6, G. Ev. S. N. S. W. | 1790 |
| paludŏsā | Red | 8, G. Ev. S. N. Holl. | 1803 |
| pendulinā | | G. Ev. S. N. Holl. | 1820 |
| pentagŏnā | | G. Ev. S. N. Holl. | 1820 |
| pulchĕllā | Purple | 7, G. Ev. S. N. Holl. | 1803 |
| rotundifoliā | | 7, G. Ev. S. N. Holl. | 1816 |
| scābrā | Purple | 5, G. Ev. S. N. Holl. | 1803 |
| squāmĕā | Lilac | 6, G. Ev. S. V. D. L. | 1805 |
| squarrŏsā | White | G. Ev. S. N. S. W. | 1794 |
| striātā | Purple | 6, G. Ev. S. N. Holl. | 1803 |
| stypheloidĕs, 5 | White | 6, G. Ev. S. N. S. W. | 1793 |
| taxifoliā | | G. Ev. S. N. Holl. | |
| tetragŏnā | | G. Ev. S. N. Holl. | 1820 |
| theæformis | | G. Ev. S. N. Holl. | 1824 |
| thymifoliā, 6 | Purple | 8, G. Ev. S. N. S. W. | 1792 |
| thymoidĕs | Purple | G. Ev. S. N. Holl. | 1808 |
| trinĕrviā | | G. Ev. S. N. Holl. | 1816 |
| uncinātā | Purple | 7, G. Ev. S. N. Holl. | 1803 |
| virgātā | | G. Ev. S. N. Holl. | 1818 |
| viridiflŏrā | Green | G. Ev. T. N. S. W. | 1777 |

MELAMPŎDĬUM, *Linn.* From *melas*, black, and *pous*, a foot; in allusion to the seeds. *Linn.* 19, Or. 4, Nat. Or. *Compositæ.* Uninteresting plants; they require to be sown and treated as other tender annuals. *Synonymes:* 1. *M. ovalifolium, Wedelia minor, Alcina ovalifolia, Dyssodium divaricatum-americānūm, hispidūm, hamile, longifŏliūm, paludŏsūm* 1.

MELAMPȲRUM, *Linn.* From *melas*, black, and *pyros*, wheat. *Linn.* 14, Or. 2, Nat. Or. *Scrophulariaceæ.* Annual weeds, which require to be sown in the open ground—*arvĕnsĕ, cristātūm, nemorŏsūm, pratĕnsĕ, sylvāticūm.*

MELANĂNTHĔRĂ, *Richard.* From *melas*, black, and *anthera*, an anther; alluding to the colour of the anthers. *Linn.* 19, Or. 1, Nat. Or. *Compositæ.* Uninteresting plants, growing in any common soil, and increased by divisions and seeds. *Synonymes:* 1. *Calea aspera.* 2. *Bidens nivea—deltoidĕd* 1, *hastātā* 2, *h. pandurātā.*

MELANCŎNĬŬM, *Link.* From *melas*, black, and *konis*, dust; in allusion to the black dusty appearance of the species. *Linn.* 24, Or. 9, Nat. Or. *Fungi.* These are very minute plants, found on dead branches of trees—*conglomerātūm, ovātūm.*

MELANOCAŬLŎN, black-stemmed.

MELANORRHŒI, *Wallich.* From *melas*, black, and *rheo*, to flow; when wounded it yields a black juice. *Linn.* 23, Or. 2, Nat. Or. *Anacardiaceæ.* This splendid tree attains the height of a hundred feet; it grows in peat and loam, and cuttings of the ripened wood root freely in sand, under a glass, in heat. The varnish of Martaban is obtained from this tree; it is known in that country by the name of *Theet-see*, or *Kheu*, and is extremely dangerous, as the skin, if rubbed with it, inflames, and becomes covered with pimples, which are difficult to heal.

| | | | |
|---|---|---|---|
| usitatissimā | Red | 8. Ev. T. E. Ind. | 1829 |

MELANOSELINŬM, *Hoffmannsegg.* From *melas*, black, and *selinon*, parsley. *Linn.* 5, Or. 2, Nat. Or. *Umbelliferæ.* This plant grows in any common soil, and is increased by divisions. *Synonyme:* 1. *Selinum decipiens*

| | | | |
|---|---|---|---|
| decipiens | White | 6, H. Her. P. Madeira | 1785 |

MELANŎXȲLŎN, black-wooded.

MELANĂNTHŎN, dark-flowered.

MELĂNTHĬŬM, *Linn.* From *melas*, black, and *anthos*, a flower; in allusion to the dusky colour of the flowers. *Linn.* 6, Or. 3, Nat. Or. *Melanthaceæ.* The plants of this genus deserve a place in every collection; for culture and propagation, see *Massonia.* *Synonyme:* 1. *Tulipa Breyniana.*

| | | | |
|---|---|---|---|
| capĕnsĕ | Yellow | 5, G. Bl. P. C. G. H. | 1768 |
| ciliātūm | Pa. yel. | 6, G. Bl. P. C. G. H. | 1810 |
| gramineūm | White | 5, G. Bl. P. Madagasc | 1823 |
| junceūm | Pink | 9, G. Bl. P. C. G. H. | 1788 |
| phalangioidĕs | White | 6, G. Bl. P. Carolina | 1810 |
| secundūm | White | 9, G. Bl. P. C. G. H. | 1812 |
| sibiricūm | | G. Bl. P. Siberia | 1823 |
| uniflŏrūm, 1 | Wht. yel. | 6, G. Bl. P. C. G. H. | 1787 |

MELASPHÆRŬLĂ, *Ker.* From *melas*, black, and *sphaira*, a globule; dark colour of the bulbs. *Linn.* 3, Or. 1, Nat. Or. *Iridaceæ.* These handsome plants require to be treated similar to the *Ixias.* *Synonyme:* 1. *M. graminea.*

| | | | |
|---|---|---|---|
| graminĕā | Green | 6, G. Bl. P. C. G. H. | 1787 |
| intermĕdiā, 1 | Yel. grn. | 6, G. Bl. P. C. G. H. | 1787 |
| iridifoliā | Grn. yel. | 6, G. Bl. P. C. G. H. | 1787 |
| parviflŏrā | Yellow | 6, G. Bl. P. C. G. H. | |

MELASTŎMĂ, *Burmann.* From *melas*, black, and *stoma*, the mouth; the black berries of some of the species are commonly eaten by children, whose mouths they stain black. *Linn.* 10, Or. 1, Nat. Or. *Melastomaceæ.* These plants are very showy when in flower, especially *M. elongata*: indeed, this plant can hardly be excelled for beauty; in its native habitat its flowers are large, and vary from blue to purple and white. Loam, peat, and sand, mixed, suit all the species best; and cuttings of the young wood root readily planted in pots filled with peat, and placed under a glass, in heat. *Synonymes*: 1. *Osbeckia grandiflora.* 2. *M. malabāthrica.*

| | | | |
|---|---|---|---|
| affinis | | 8. Ev. S. E. Ind. | 1810 |
| Afzeliānā | Red | 8. Ev. S. Leone | 1824 |
| aspĕrā | Purple | 6, 8. Ev. S. E. Ind. | 1815 |
| Bankaii | White | 9, 8. Ev. S. N. Holl. | 1824 |
| cāndidā | Purple | 8. Ev. S. China | 1822 |
| corymbŏsā | Purple | 6, 8. Ev. S. Leone | 1792 |
| cymŏsā | Purple | 6, 8. Ev. S. S. Amer. | 1792 |
| ecostātā | Purple | 7, 8. Ev. S. Jamaica | 1793 |
| elongātā, 1 | Purple | 5, 8. Tu. P. S. Leone | 1823 |
| macrocārpā, 2 | Purple | 6, G. Ev. S. China | 1793 |
| malabāthricā | Purple | 6, 8. Ev. S. E. Ind. | 1793 |
| sanguinĕā | Purple | 9, 8. Ev. S. China | 1818 |

MELASTŎMĂ, see *Pleromā.*

MELEXŎRIS, freckled, speckled.

MELHĂNĬĂ, *Forskahl.* From Mount Melhan, in Arabia Felix, where the original species was first found. *Linn.* 16, Or. 2, Nat. Or. *Sterculiaceæ.* Ornamental trees, growing about twenty feet high. They thrive best in a mixture of sandy loam, and cuttings root readily in the same kind of soil, under a glass, in heat.

| | | | |
|---|---|---|---|
| Burchĕllii | White | G. Ev. T. C. G. H. | 1818 |
| Erythrŏxylŏn | White | 7, 8. Ev. T. St. Helena | 1772 |
| Melanŏxylŏn | White | 7, 8 Ev. T. St. Helena | 1800 |

MELĬĂ, *Linn.* The Greek name of the manna ash; resemblance in the leaves. *Linn.* 14, Or. 10, Nat. Or. *Meliaceæ.* Fine trees, thriving well in a mixture of loam, peat, and sand; and large cuttings of the ripened wood, with the leaves not shortened, will root in sand, under a glass; those of the stove species in heat. The root of *M. Azedarach* is bitter, and is used as an anthelmintic in North America. The fruit of *M. Azadirachta* is oily, acrid, and bitter, as is also the bark.

| | | | |
|---|---|---|---|
| austrālis | Lilac | G. Ev. T. N. Holl. | 1810 |
| Azadirāchtā | White | 7, 8. Ev. T. E. Ind. | 1759 |
| Azedārach | Blue | 7, G. De. T. Syria | 1656 |
| compŏsitā | Wht. red | 7, 8. Ev. T. E. Ind. | 1810 |
| excĕlsā | White | 7, 8. Ev. T. E. Ind. | 1819 |
| guineensis | Wht. red | 7, 8. Ev. T. Guinea | 1824 |
| robŭstā | Wht. red | 7, G. Ev. T. E. Ind. | 1820 |
| sempervirens | Brown | 8. Ev. T. Jamaica | 1656 |
| supĕrbā | Wht. red | 8. Ev. T. E. Ind. | 1820 |

MELIĂNTHŬS, *Linn.* From *mel*, honey, and *anthos*, a flower; the flowers are full of honey. *Linn.* 4, Or. 1, Nat. Or. *Zygophyllaceæ.* Ornamental shrubs, thriving in any light rich soil; and cuttings root freely under a glass.

| | | | |
|---|---|---|---|
| comŏsūs | Yellow | G. Ev. S. C. G. H. | 1820 |
| mājŏr | Brown | 6, H. Ev. S. C. G. H. | 1688 |
| minŏr | Brown | 6, H. Ev. S. C. G. H. | 1696 |

MELĬCĂ, *Linn.* From *mel*, honey; the Italian name of the great millet. *Linn.* 3, Or. 2, Nat. Or. *Gramineæ.* Some species of this genus are worth growing; they are all of the simplest culture.

| | | | |
|---|---|---|---|
| altissimā | Apetal | 7, Grass. Siberia | 1770 |
| ciliātā | Apetal | 7, Grass. Europe | 1771 |
| nūtāns | Apetal | 6, Grass. Britain | |
| uniflŏrā | Apetal | 5, Grass. Britain | |

*Bauhini, glăbrā, pyramidālis, speciŏsā, sylvāticā.*

MELIC-GRASS, see *Melicā.*

MELICHRŬS, *R. Brown.* From *melichros*, honey-coloured; alluding to the colour of the glands of the flowers. *Linn.* 5, Or. 1, Nat. Or. *Epacridaceæ.* These are very pretty shrubs; for culture and propagation, see *Epacris.*

| | | | |
|---|---|---|---|
| mĕdiūs | Scarlet | 5, G. Ev. S. N. S. W. | 1824 |
| rotātūs | Scarlet | 6, G. Ev. S. N. Holl. | 1824 |

MELICŎCCĂ, *Jussieu.* From *mel*, honey, and *coccos*, a berry; the fruit is very sweet. *Linn.* 8, Or. 1, Nat. Or. *Sapindaceæ.* These plants are cultivated to a great extent in the West Indies for their eatable fruits. They grow well in a light loamy soil; and cuttings of the ripened wood will root in sand;

under a glass in heat. Synonyme : 1. Scytalia trijuga.

| | | | | | | |
|---|---|---|---|---|---|---|
| bijūgā | . . | Yellow | . | S. Ev. T. Antilles | . | 1778 |
| olivæfórmls | . . | Yellow | . | S. Ev. T. N. Granada | | 1824 |
| paniculātā | . . | | | S. Ev. T. St. Domin. | . | 1820 |
| trijūgā, 1 | . . | | | S. Ev. T. Ceylon | . | 1820 |

MĒLICŌPĀ, Forster. From mel, honey, and kope, a division ; in allusion to the honey glands at the base of the ovaries. Linn. 8, Or. 1, Nat. Or. Rutaceæ. An ornamental shrub, growing freely in loam and peat ; and cuttings of the young wood root in sand, under a glass.

| | | | | | |
|---|---|---|---|---|---|
| ternātā | . . . . | White | . | O. Ev. S. N. Zeal. | . 1822 |

MELILOT, see Melilōtus.

MELILŌTUS, Tournefort. From mel, honey, and lotus ; honey lotus. The plants are similar to the Lotus, and are the favourite haunt of bees. Linn. 14, Or. 10, Nat. Or. Leguminosæ. Very few of these plants are worth cultivating except in general collections. M. arborea is readily increased by cuttings. The seed of the other kinds only requires to be sown in the open border in spring. Synonymes : 1. M. alba. 2. M. plicata. 3. Trifolium Kochianum. 4. M. vulgaris. 5. Trifolium Melilotus officinalis. 6. M. rugulosa. 7. M. mauritanica.

| | | | | | | |
|---|---|---|---|---|---|---|
| altissima, 1 | . . | White | . 7, | H. | B. France | . 1816 |
| arbōreā | . . | White | . 7, | H. Ev. | S. Turkey | . 1826 |
| officinalls, 5 | . . | Yellow | . 8, | H. | B. Britain | . |
| pallida | . . | Pa. yel. | . 7, | H. | B. Volhinia | . 1816 |
| segetālis | . . | Yellow | . 7, | H. | A. Spain | . 1820 |
| suavēōlēns | . . | Yellow | . 7, | H. Her. | P. Dahuria | . 1824 |

arvēnsis, Baumētti, Besseriānā 2, dentātā, grācilis, indica, itālicā, Kochiānā 3, leucānthā 4, lineāris, macrorhīsā, melanospērmā, messanēnsis, neapolitānā, palūstris, parviflōrā 6, Petitpierrcānā, polōnicā, rotundifōliā, ruthēnicā, sulcātā 7, taūricā.

MĒLISSĀ, Bentham. From melissa, a bee ; the bees obtain a great quantity of honey from the Balm. Linn. 14, Or. 1, Nat. Or. Labiatæ. These plants will grow in common garden soil, and are readily increased by dividing the roots. Synonymes : 1. M. altissima, M. cordifolia. 2. Horminum pyrenaicum.

| | | | | | | |
|---|---|---|---|---|---|---|
| crēticā | . . . | Wht. pur. | 6, H. Her. | P. Candia | . | 1596 |
| officinalls | . . . | White | . 7, H. Her. | P. S. Eur. | . | 1573 |
| variegātā | . . . | White | . 6, H. Her. | P. Gardens | . | |
| villōsā, 1 | . . . | White | . 8, H. Her. | P. Italy | . | 1573 |
| polyānthōs | . . . | White | . 7, H. Her. | P. | . | 1820 |
| pyrenāicā, 2 | . . . | Wht. pur. | 7, H. Her. | P. Pyrenees | . | 1800 |

MĒLITTĀ, Linn. From melitta, a bee ; a name synonymous with Melissa. Linn. 14, Or. 1, Nat. Or. Labiatæ. These are showy plants when in flower, and are, on that account, well fitted for ornamenting flower-borders and shrubberies. They are increased by dividing the roots in spring or autumn. Synonyme : 1. M. grandiflora.

| | | | | | |
|---|---|---|---|---|---|
| Melissophyllum | . Flesh | . 5, H. Her. | P. England | . |
| alpinā | . . | . Flesh | . 5, H. Her. | P. Switserl. | . |
| grandiflōrā, 1 | . Wht. yel. | 5, H. Her. | P. England | . |

MELLIFEROUS, honey-bearing.

MELOCĀCTŪS, C. Bauhin. From melos, a melon, and cactus ; in allusion to the appearance of the plants. Linn. 12, Or. 1, Nat. Or. Cactaceæ. This is a genus of grotesque-looking plants. They are well worthy of a place in every collection of plants, and require precisely the same treatment as the Mammillarias. Synonymes : 1. Cactus Melocactus. 2. C. macracantha. 3. M. Besleri. 4. Echinocactus polyacantha. 5. E. Sellowii.

| | | | | | |
|---|---|---|---|---|---|
| amœnūs | . . | Li. scar. | . | S. Ev. S. | . 1835 |
| commūnis, 1 | . . | Red | . 7, | S. Ev. S. W. Ind. | . 1688 |
| viridis | . . | | . | S. Ev. S. | . 1836 |
| deprēssūs | . . | Scarlet | . | S. Ev. S. Pernambuco | |
| excavātūs | . . | | . | S. Ev. S. | . 1834 |
| Grengēlii | . . | | . | S. Ev. S. St Thos. Is. | . 1836 |
| macracānthā, 2 | . Wht. red | . | S. Ev. S. S. Amer. | . 1820 |
| macranthū | . . | Wht. red | . | S. Ev. S. S. Amer. | . 1820 |
| meonacānthūs | . . | | . | S. Ev. S. Jamaica | . 1835 |
| octagōnūs | . . | | . | S. Ev. S. Mexico | . 1834 |
| placentifōrmis, 3 | . Red | . | S. Ev. S. Brazil | . |
| polyacānthā, 4 | . . | | . | S. Ev. S. Brazil | . |
| pyramidālis | . . | Red | . | S. Ev. S. Curacoa | . 1824 |
| spinis-rūbris | . . | | . | S. Ev. S. | . |
| Salmiānūs | . . | | . | S. Ev. S. | . 1835 |
| Sellōwii, 5 | . . | | . | S. Ev. S. Brazil | . |

MĒLOCĀNNĀ, Kæmpfer. From melon, an apple, and kanna, a reed. Linn. 6, Or. 1, Nat. Or. Gramineæ. This species is nearly allied to Bambusa ; it is readily increased by suckers. Synonyme : 1. Bambusa baccifera.

| | | | | | |
|---|---|---|---|---|---|
| bambusoidēs, 1 | . . | Apetal | . . 7, Grass. E. Ind. | . . 1818 |

MĒLŌCHIĀ, Linn. Altered from Melochich, the Arabic name of Corchorus olitorius, which is used in the East as a salad-plant. Linn. 16, Or. 2, Nat. Or. Sterculiaceæ. Plants of little beauty. Any light rich soil suits them ; and cuttings root freely in the same kind of soil, under a glass, in heat.

| | | | | | |
|---|---|---|---|---|---|
| parviflōrā | . . | Purple | . 7, S. Ev. S. Caraccas | . 1820 |
| parvifōlis | . . | White | . 6, S. Ev. S. Trinidad | . 1819 |
| pyramidātā | . . | Flesh | . 5, S. Ev. S. Brazil | . 1768 |
| tomentōsā | . . | Purple | . 5, S. Ev. S. W. Ind. | . 1768 |

MĒLODĪNŪS, Forster. From melon, an apple, and dineo, to turn round. Linn. 5, Or. 2, Nat. Or. Apocynaceæ. Ornamental plants, well worth cultivation for the sake of their showy flowers. They grow well in a mixture of loam and peat ; and cuttings will root in sand, under a glass, in heat.

| | | | | | |
|---|---|---|---|---|---|
| monōgȳnūs | . . | White | . 7, S. Ev. Tw. E. Ind. | . 1820 |
| scāndēns | . . | White | . 7, S. Ev. Tw. N. Caled. | . 1775 |

MELON, see Cūcūmis Mēlō.

MELON-PUMPKIN, see Cucūrbita Melopēpō.

MELON-THISTLE, see Melocāctūs.

MELON-TURK'S-CAP, see Melocāctūs commūnis.

MĒLOSĒIRĀ, Agardh. From melon, a melon, and seira, a chain ; shape of the filaments. Linn. 24, Or. 7, Nat. Or. Algæ. Very minute species, found in salt marshes, rivulets, &c.—discigērā, lineātā, nummuloidēs.

MĒLŌTHRIX, Linn. From melothron of Theophrastus ; supposed to be Bryony. Linn. 21, Or. 2, Nat. Or. Cucurbitaceæ. A mere weed ; it grows in any rich soil, and is increased by seeds. Synonyme : 1. Trichosanthes fœtidissima—fœtida 1, pendula.

MEMBRANACEOUS, or MEMBRANOUS, having the texture of a membrane.

MĒMĒCȲLON, Linn. From memecylon of Dioscorides ; the Greek name of the fruit of the Arbutus. Linn. 8, Or. 1, Nat. Or. Memecylaceæ. The soil best adapted to the growth of these plants is a mixture of peat, loam, and sand ; and cuttings of the young wood root freely in sand, under a glass, in heat.

| | | | | | |
|---|---|---|---|---|---|
| capitellātūm | . . . | . 7, S. Ev. S. E. Ind. | . 1796 |
| edūlē | . . | Purple | . S. Ev. T. Ceylon | . 1820 |

MĒNIŌCŪS, Desfontaines. From mene, the moon, and okkos, the eye ; supposed to refer to the shape of the seeds. Linn 15, Nat. Or. Cruciferæ. A pretty little annual, well fitted for ornamenting rock-work. The seed may be sown where it is to remain. Synonyme : 1. Alyssum linifolius.

| | | | | | |
|---|---|---|---|---|---|
| linifōliūs, 1 | . . | White | . 6, H. | A. Caucasus | . 1819 |

MĒNISCIŪM, Schreber. From meniskos, a crescent ; alluding to the shape of the fructification. Linn. 24, Or. 1, Nat. Or. Polypodiaceæ. This is a very elegant genus of ferns. They thrive well in loam and peat, and are increased by dividing the roots, or by seeds. Synonymes : 1. Hemionitis prolifera. 2. Polypodium reticulatum. 3. Asplenium sorbifolium.

| | | | | | |
|---|---|---|---|---|---|
| prolifērūm, 1 | . Brown | . 6, S. Her. P. E. Ind. | . 1820 |
| reticulātūm, 2 | . Brown | . 5, S. Her. P. Martinique | 1793 |
| sorbifōliūm, 3 | . Brown | . 6, S. Her. P. Brazil | . 1823 |

MĒNISPĒRMŪM, Linn. From mene, the moon, and spermā, a seed ; the fruit is kidney or half-moon-shaped ; whence the English name, Moon-seed. Linn. 22, Or. 10, Nat. Or. Menispermaceæ. This genus is chiefly composed of hardy plants, well adapted for covering arbours or trellis-work. They grow in any common soil, and may be increased by dividing the roots, or by cuttings planted early in spring in a sheltered situation, or by seeds. Synonymes : 1. M. virginicum. 2. Cissampelos smilacina.

| | | | | | |
|---|---|---|---|---|---|
| canadēnsē | . . | Grn. yel. | 6, H. De. Tw. N. Amer. | . 1691 |
| lobātūm, 1 | . . | Grn. yel. | 6, H. De. Tw. N. Amer. | . 1782 |
| daūricūm | . . | Wht. yel. | 6, H. De. Tw. Dauria | . 1810 |
| Lȳōnii | . . | Purple | . 6, H. De. Tw. N. Amer. | . 1823 |
| planifōliūm | . . | Yellow | . 6, H. De. Tw. E. Ind. | . 1823 |
| smilacīnūm, 2 | . Grn. yel. | . H. Ev. Tw. Carolina | . 1776 |

MĒNONVILLEĀ, Decandolle. In honour of M. Thiery de Menonville, an enterprising French naturalist. Linn. 15, Nat. Or. Cruciferæ. Rather a pretty hardy plant, growing freely in light loamy soil, and is increased by seeds.

| | | | | | |
|---|---|---|---|---|---|
| filifōliā | . . | Grn.-wht | 8, H. | A. Chile | . . 1836 |

MĒNSTRŪŪM, a liquor used as a dissolvent.

**MĬNTHĂ, Linn.** The poets celebrate Minthe, a daughter of Cocytus, as being turned into mint by Proserpine in a fit of jealousy. Linn. 14, Or. 1, Nat. Or. Labiatæ. The Mint is a well-known genus of useful herbs, with the culture and propagation of which every one is familiar. Synonymes: 1. M. pyramidalis. 2. M. crispa. 3. M. hirsuta, M. nepetoides. 4. M. paludosa, M. palustris. 5. M. rivalis. 6. M. agrestis. 7. M. præcox. 8. M. gentilis. 9. M. Badensis. 10. M. rubra. 11. M. acutifolia, M. sativa. 12. M. austriaca. 13. M. borealis. 14. M. odorata. 15. M. gracilis. 16. M. macrostachya, M. rugosa. 17. M. capensis. 18. M. hirta. 19. M. undulata. 20. M. canescens. 21. M. nemorosa, M. Niliaca. 22. M. gratissima. 23. M. brevispicata, M. lævigata. 24. M. crispata.

| | | | | | |
|---|---|---|---|---|---|
| aquatica, 1 | . | Pur. red | . 8, H. Her. P. Britain | . | |
| crispa, 2 | . | Purple | . 7, H. Her. P. Siberia | . | 1640 |
| hirsūtā, 3 | . | Purple | . 8, H. Her. P. Britain | . | |
| subspicatā, 4 | . | Purple | . 8, H. Her. P. Britain | . | |
| arvēnsis, 5 | . | Purplish | . 8, H. Her. P. Britain | . | |
| agrēstis, 6 | . | Purple | . 6, H. Her. P. Britain | . | |
| glabrā, 7 | . | Purple | . 6, H. Her. P. Britain | . | |
| grācilis, 8 | . | Purple | . 7, H. Her. P. Britain | . | |
| nitidā, 9 | . | Purple | . 7, H. Her. P. Britain | . | |
| rūbrā, 10 | . | Purple | . 9, H. Her. P. Britain | . | |
| sativā, 11 | . | Purple | . 7, H. Her. P. England | . | |
| vulgāris, 12 | . | Purple | . 7, H. Her. P. Germany | . | |
| auriculārĭā | . | Purple | . 7, H. Her. P. E. Ind. | . | 1796 |
| balsāmeā | . | Purple | . 7, H. Her. P. Italy | . | 1804 |
| blanda | . | White | . 9, H. Her. P. Nepal | . | 1824 |
| canadēnsis | . | Purple | . 7, H. Her. P. N. Amer. | . | 1800 |
| glabrātā, 13 | . | Purple | . 7, H. Her. P. N. Amer. | . | 1800 |
| citrātā, 14 | . | Red pur. | . 7, H. Her. P. Britain | . | |
| eoccīneā | . | Scarlet | . 7, H. Her. P. E. Ind. | . | 1823 |
| dentātā | . | Purple | . 7, H. Her. P. Germany | . | 1816 |
| divaricātā | . | Purple | . 7, H. Her. P. Spain | . | 1824 |
| glabrātā | . | Purple | . 7, H. Her. P. Egypt | . | 1802 |
| incānā | . | Purple | . 7, H. Her. P. Greece | . | 1790 |
| lavandulaceā | . | Purple | . 7, H. Her. P. Spain | . | 1823 |
| piperītā | . | Purple | . 8, H. Her. P. England | . | |
| pratēnsis, 15 | . | Purple | . 8, H. Her. P. England | . | |
| pubēscens | . | Purple | . 7, H. Her. P. | . | |
| Pulegĭūm | . | Pa. pur. | . 8, H. Her. P. Britain | . | |
| Requiēnī | . | Lilac | . 8, H. Her. P. Corsica | . | 1829 |
| rotundifōlĭā, 16 | . | Whitish | . 8, H. Her. P. Britain | . | |
| salīcinā, 17 | . | | . H. ⅃u. P. C. G. H. | . | |
| suāvis, 18 | . | Red | . 7, H. Her. P. S. France | . | |
| sylvēstris | . | Purplish | . 7, H. Her. P. Britain | . | |
| crispā, 19 | . | Purple | . 7, H. Her. P. | . | 1816 |
| mollissimā, 20 | . | Purple | . 7, H. Her. P. Spain | . | 1800 |
| nemorsā, 21 | . | Purple | . 7, H. Her. P. | . | |
| vulgāris, 22 | . | Purple | . 7, H. Her. P. Germany | . | 1799 |
| tēnŭis | . | Purple | . 7, H. Her. P. N. Amer. | . | |
| villōsā | . | Purple | . 9, H. Her. P. Britain | . | |
| virīdis, 23 | . | Purple | . 8, H. Her. P. Britain | . | |
| crispā, 24 | . | Purple | . 7, H. Her. P. | . | 1807 |

**MĔNTZĔLĬĂ, Linn.** In honour of C. Mentzel, a botanical author of Brandenburg. Linn. 12, Or. 1, Nat. Or. Loasaceæ. These curious plants grow freely in a mixture of sandy loam and peat; and cuttings root freely in sand, under a glass, in heat.

| | | | | | |
|---|---|---|---|---|---|
| ăsperā | . | Yellow | . 7, F. | A. America | . 1733 |
| hĭspĭdā | . | Yellow | . 4, S. Her. P. Peru | . | 1831 |
| oligospermā | . | Yellow | . 5, G. Her. P. Louisiana | . | 1812 |
| stĭpĭtātā | . | Yellow | . 10, H. Her. P. Mexico | . | 1835 |

**MĔNYĂNTHĔS, Linn.** From men, a month, and anthos, a flower; alluding to the duration of the flowers. Linn. 5, Or. 1, Nat. Or. Gentianaceæ. Plants of the simplest culture. M. trifoliata is bitter, tonic, and febrifugal. Synonyme: 1. M. americana.

| | | | | | |
|---|---|---|---|---|---|
| trifoliātā | . | White | . 7, H. Aq. P. Britain | . | |
| americānā, 1 | . | Pa. red | . 7, H. Aq. P. N. Amer. | . | 1818 |

**MĔNZĬĔSĬĂ, Smith.** In honour of Archibald Menzies, F.L.S., &c., surgeon and naturalist to the expedition under Vancouver; he collected many specimens of plants on the North-west coast of America, New Holland, Van Diemen's Land, &c. Linn. 8, Or. 1, Nat. Or. Ericaceæ. A very ornamental genus of plants; for culture and propagation, see Azalea. Synonyme: 1. Erica Dabœci.

| | | | | | |
|---|---|---|---|---|---|
| ferruginēā | . | Brown | . 5, H. De. S. N. Amer. | . | 1811 |
| globulāris | . | Brown | . 5, H. De. S. N. Amer. | . | 1806 |
| polifōlĭā, 1 | . | Purple | . 7, H. Ev. S. Ireland | . | |
| atro-purpūreā | . | Drk. pur. | . H. Ev. S. | | |
| florĕ-albō | . | White | . 6, H. Ev. S. Ireland | . | |
| latifōlĭā | . | Purple | . 7, H. Ev. S. | | |
| longifōlĭā | . | Purple | . 7, H. Ev. S. | | |
| nānā | . | Purple | . 7, H. Ev. S. Ireland | . | |
| pallĭdā | . | Purple | . 7, H. Ev. S. Britain | . | |

**MĔNZĬĔSĬĂ, see Phyllŏdŏcĕ.**

**MĔRCŬRĬĂLĬS, Linn.** After Mercury, who is said to have first discovered the plant. Linn. 22, Or. 8, Nat. Or. Euphorbiaceæ. Weeds of the simplest culture. The juice of M. perennis is emetic, while the seed is purgative, and highly dangerous— ambĭgŭā, ānnŭā, ellĭptĭcā, perĕnnis, tomentōsā.

**MĔRĔNDĔRĂ, Ramond.** A name given to Colchicum by the Spaniards, and applied to this genus because of its affinity. Linn. 6, Or. 3, Nat. Or. Melanthaceæ. This species thrives well in a light loamy soil, and is readily increased by seeds, or offsets from the bulbs. Synonymes: 1. Bulbocodium trigynum, Colchicum caucasicum.

| | | | | | |
|---|---|---|---|---|---|
| caucāsicā, 1 | . | Purple | . 8, H. Bl. P. Caucasus | . | 1823 |

**MĔRĬĂNĬĂ.** In honour of Maria Sybylla Merian, authoress of a work on insects. Linn. 10, Or. 1, Nat. Or. Melastomaceæ. This is a genus of very beautiful stove plants, which grow freely in sandy peat mixed with a little loam; and cuttings of the half-ripened wood root freely in sand, under a glass, in heat.

| | | | | | |
|---|---|---|---|---|---|
| leucānthā | . | White | . 8, Ev. S. Jamaica | . | 1825 |
| purpūreā | . | Purple | . 8, Ev. S. Jamaica | . | 1825 |

**MĔRĬSMĂ, Fries.** From merismos, a division; because of the branched habit. Linn. 24, Or. 9, Nat. Or. Fungi. These plants are found in woods and damp places—cristātā, fœtĭdā-anthocĕphālā, tuberōsā.

**MĔRTĔNSĬĂ, Willdenow.** In honour of F. C. Mertens, professor of medicine at Bremen. Linn. 23, Or. 1, Nat. Or. Urticaceæ. All the species of this genus are highly esteemed by the lovers of border plants for the brilliant colour of their blossoms. M. maritima and parviflora require to be grown in pots, in very sandy peat. The other species will grow in common garden soil, though they succeed much better when kept in a peat border; increased by divisions. Synonymes: 1. Pulmonaria dahurica. 2. P. denticulata. 3. P. lanceolata. 4. P. maritima. 5. P. paniculata. 6. P. parviflora. 7. P. virginica. 8. P. sibirica.

| | | | | | |
|---|---|---|---|---|---|
| dahūricā, 1 | . | Blue | . 5, H. Her. P. Dahuria | . | 1812 |
| denticulātā, 2 | . | Blue | . 6, H. Her. P. N. Amer. | . | 1800 |
| marginātā, 3 | . | Blue | . 6, H. Her. P. Louisiana | . | 1812 |
| maritīmā, 4 | . | Blue | . 7, H. Her. P. Britain | . | |
| paniculātā, 5 | . | Blue | . 6, H. Her. P. Hud.'s Bay | | 1778 |
| parvifōrā, 6 | . | Blue | . 7, H. Her. P. Canada | . | 1827 |
| pulmonarioĭdes, 7 | . | Blue | . 4, H. Her. P. N. Amer. | . | 1699 |
| sibĭricā, 8 | . | Blue | . 6, H. Her. P. Siberia | . | 1801 |

**MĔRŬLĬŬs, Haller.** From meta, a pillar; because of the resemblance in the original fungus metulius. Linn. 24, Or. 9, Nat. Or. Fungi. This is one of the most important of parasitical fungi, being what is called the dry rot, so well known as the pest of wooden constructions—aurantĭacūs, lāchrymāns-obliquūs, tremellōsūs.

**MĔSĔMBRYĂNTHĔMŬM, Linn.** From mesembria, midday, and anthemon, a flower. Linn. 12, Or. 2, Nat. Or. Ficoideæ. This beautiful and well-known genus of succulents is very easily cultivated. If they are intended to remain in pots, a light sandy loam will suit them best; but if they are planted out in a dry hot border, they will flower more profusely. Many of the kinds are very beautiful objects for the flower-garden; for this purpose, cuttings should be struck in the autumn, and allowed to remain in the store-pots all winter. A dry pit or frame, where frost is excluded, is sufficient for their protection in winter. Cuttings of the most succulent kinds should be allowed to dry a little after planting before water is given, after which they root readily. M. edule is the Hottentot-fig, the leaves of which are eaten. M. nodiflorum is used in making Maroquin leather. Synonymes: 1. M. stellatum. 2. M. Candollei. 3. M. purpureo croceum. 4. M. dimidiatum. 5. M. parviflorum. 6. M. magnipunctatum. 7. M. micranthum. 8. M. canescens. 9. M. hirsutum. 10. M. hispidum.

| | | | | | |
|---|---|---|---|---|---|
| abbreviātūm | . | | G. Ev. Tr. N. Holl. | . | 1825 |
| acinaciformĕ | . | Pink | . G. Ev. Tr. C. G. H. | . | 1714 |
| longūm | . | Pink | . 8, G. Ev. Tr. C. G. H. | . | |
| acuminātūm | . | White | . 8, G. Ev. S. C. G. H. | . | 1820 |
| acutāngŭlūm | . | White | . 8, G. Ev. S. C. G. H. | . | 1821 |
| acūtūm | . | Red | . 7, G. Her. P. C. G. H. | . | 1793 |
| adscēndēns | . | Yellow | . 7, G. Her. P. C. G. H. | . | 1805 |
| adūncūm | . | Pink | . 2, G. Ev. S. C. G. H. | . | 1795 |
| æquilaterālĕ | . | Pink | . 6, G. Ev. Tr. N. Holl. | . | 1791 |
| ăgnīnūm | . | Yellow | . 6, G. Her. P. C. G. H. | . | 1824 |

| Species | Colour | No. | | | | Locality | Date |
|---|---|---|---|---|---|---|---|
| erectiusculum | Yellow | 5, | G. Her. | P. | | C.G.H. | 1824 |
| minus | Yellow | 5, | G. Her. | P. | | C.G.H. | 1824 |
| Aitoni | Pink | 8, | G. | B. | | C.G.H. | 1774 |
| albicaule | White | 8, | G. Ev. | S. | | C.G.H. | 1824 |
| albidum | Yellow | 7, | G. Her. | P. | | C.G.H. | 1714 |
| albinotum | Yellow | 9, | G. Her. | P. | | C.G.H. | 1823 |
| albipunctatum | Yellow | 9, | G. Her. | P. | | C.G.H. | 1823 |
| aloides | Yellow | | G. Her. | P. | | C.G.H. | 1819 |
| alsinifolium | | 6, | G. | A. | | N. Holl. | 1827 |
| anatomicum | White | 9, | G. Ev. | S. | | C.G.H. | 1803 |
| fragile | White | 11, | G. Ev. | S. | | C.G.H. | 1803 |
| anceps | Pink | 6, | G. Ev. | S. | | C.G.H. | 1811 |
| pallidum | Pa. pink | 6, | G. Ev. | S. | | C.G.H. | 1819 |
| angustum | Yellow | 7, | G. Her. | P. | | C.G.H. | 1790 |
| heterophyllum | Yellow | 7, | G. Her. | P. | | C.G.H. | 1790 |
| pallidum | Yellow | 7, | G. Her. | P. | | C.G.H. | 1790 |
| apetalum | Apetal | 7, | G. | A. | | C.G.H. | 1774 |
| asperum | | | G. Ev. | S. | | C.G.H. | 1818 |
| caerulescens | | | G. Ev. | S. | | C.G.H. | 1820 |
| attenuatum | White | 7, | G. Ev. | Tr. | | C.G.H. | 1821 |
| aurantium | Orange | 8, | G. Ev. | S. | | C.G.H. | 1793 |
| aureum | Yellow | 6, | G. Ev. | S. | | C.G.H. | 1750 |
| australe | Yellow | 7, | G. Ev. | Tr. | | N. Zeal. | 1773 |
| barbatum | Pink | 8, | G. Ev. | S. | | C.G.H. | 1705 |
| bellidiflorum | Red wht. | 7, | G. Her. | P. | | C.G.H. | 1717 |
| subulatum | Red | 7, | G. Her. | P. | | C.G.H. | 1717 |
| viride | Red | 7, | G. Her. | P. | | C.G.H. | 1717 |
| bibracteatum | Yellow | 7, | G. Ev. | S. | | C.G.H. | 1803 |
| bicolorum | Orange | 7, | G. Ev. | S. | | C.G.H. | 1732 |
| minus | Orange | 7, | G. Ev. | S. | | C.G.H. | |
| petalum | Orange | 7, | G. Ev. | S. | | C.G.H. | |
| bidentatum | Yellow | 8, | G. Ev. | S. | | C.G.H. | 1818 |
| majus | Yellow | 8, | G. Ev. | S. | | C.G.H. | 1818 |
| bifidum | Yellow | 11, | G. Her. | P. | | C.G.H. | 1795 |
| bigibberatum | Yellow | 8, | G. Ev. | S. | | C.G.H. | 1820 |
| blandum | White | 6, | G. Ev. | S. | | C.G.H. | 1810 |
| brachiatum | Yellow | 7, | G. Ev. | S. | | C.G.H. | 1774 |
| bracteatum | Yellow | 7, | G. Ev. | S. | | C.G.H. | 1774 |
| brevicaule | Pa. yel. | 8, | G. Ev. | S. | | C.G.H. | 1820 |
| brevifolium | Pa. yel. | 8, | G. Ev. | S. | | C.G.H. | 1777 |
| bulbosum | Pink | 8, | G. Ev. | S. | | C.G.H. | 1820 |
| caducum | Pink | 7, | G. | A. | | C.G.H. | 1774 |
| calamiforme | White | 8, | G. Ev. | S. | | C.G.H. | 1717 |
| calendulaceum | Yellow | | G. | A. | | C.G.H. | 1819 |
| calycinum | White | 7, | G. Ev. | Tr. | | C.G.H. | 1819 |
| canaliculatum | Pink | 7, | G. Ev. | S. | | C.G.H. | 1794 |
| candens | White | 6, | G. Ev. | S. | | C.G.H. | 1820 |
| viridius | White | 9, | G. Ev. | Tr. | | | |
| caninum | Yellow | 9, | G. Her. | P. | | C.G.H. | 1717 |
| canum | Yellow | 7, | G. Her. | P. | | C.G.H. | 1795 |
| capitatum | Pa. yel. | 8, | G. Her. | P. | | C.G.H. | 1717 |
| ramigerum | Pa. yel. | 8, | G. Her. | P. | | C.G.H. | 1816 |
| carinans | | | G. Her. | P. | | C.G.H. | 1818 |
| caulescens | Pink | 6, | G. Ev. | S. | | C.G.H. | 1781 |
| ciliatum | White | | G. | A. | | C.G.H. | 1774 |
| clandestinum | White | 6, | G. Ev. | S. | | C.G.H. | 1822 |
| clavellatum | Pink | 6, | G. Ev. | Tr. | | N. Holl. | 1803 |
| aggregatum | Pink | 6, | G. Ev. | Tr. | | N. Holl. | 1803 |
| minus | Pink | 6, | G. Ev. | Tr. | | N. Holl. | 1810 |
| coccineum | Scarlet | 7, | G. Ev. | S. | | C.G.H. | 1696 |
| acutus | Scarlet | 7, | G. Ev. | S. | | C.G.H. | |
| minus | Scarlet | 7, | G. Ev. | S. | | C.G.H. | |
| compactum | Yellow | 11, | G. Ev. | S. | | C.G.H. | 1780 |
| compressum | Red | 8, | G. Ev. | S. | | C.G.H. | 1792 |
| confertum | Pink | 8, | G. Ev. | S. | | C.G.H. | 1805 |
| conspicuum | | 9, | G. Ev. | S. | | C.G.H. | 1806 |
| corallinum | Pink | 8, | G. Ev. | S. | | C.G.H. | 1820 |
| cordifolium | Pink | 7, | G. Ev. | S. | | C.G.H. | 1774 |
| corniculatum | Pa. yel. | 4, | G. Her. | P. | | C.G.H. | 1732 |
| isophyllum | Pa. yel. | 4, | G. Her. | P. | | C.G.H. | 1732 |
| coruscans | Pa. yel. | 8, | G. Ev. | S. | | C.G.H. | 1812 |
| crassicaule | Pa. yel. | 8, | G. Ev. | S. | | C.G.H. | 1815 |
| crassuloides | Pink | 8, | G. Ev. | S. | | C.G.H. | 1819 |
| crassifolium | Pink | 6, | G. Ev. | Tr. | | C.G.H. | 1727 |
| cruciatum | Yellow | 8, | G. Ev. | S. | | C.G.H. | 1792 |
| crystallinum | White | 7, | H. Tr. | A. | | Greece | 1775 |
| cultratum | Yellow | 9, | H. Her. | P. | | C.G.H. | 1820 |
| scitum | White | | G. Ev. | S. | | C.G.H. | |
| majus | White | | G. Ev. | S. | | C.G.H. | |
| minus | White | | G. Ev. | S. | | C.G.H. | |
| politum | White | 8, | G. Ev. | S. | | C.G.H. | |
| curvifolium | Pink | 10, | G. Ev. | S. | | C.G.H. | 1799 |
| curviflorum | White | 6, | G. Ev. | S. | | C.G.H. | 1818 |
| cylindricum | Red | 5, | G. Her. | P. | | C.G.H. | 1792 |
| cymbifolium | Yellow | 7, | G. Ev. | S. | | C.G.H. | 1822 |
| cymbiforme | Yellow | | G. Ev. | Tr. | | C.G.H. | 1793 |
| debile | | | G. Ev. | Tr. | | C.G.H. | 1824 |
| decumbens | Pa. red | 7, | G. Her. | P. | | C.G.H. | 1759 |
| decipiens | Pa. yel. | 8, | G. Her. | P. | | C.G.H. | 1820 |
| deflexum | Pink | 8, | G. Ev. | S. | | C.G.H. | 1774 |
| defoliatum | | 7, | G. Ev. | S. | | C.G.H. | 1820 |
| deltoideum | Pink | 5, | U. Ev. | S. | | C.G.H. | 1731 |
| densum | Pink | 6, | G. Ev. | Tr. | | C.G.H. | 1732 |
| denticulatum | Yellow | 4, | G. Her. | P. | | C.G.H. | 1793 |
| candidissimum | Yellow | 4, | G. Her. | P. | | C.G.H. | |
| glaucum | Yellow | 4, | G. Her. | P. | | C.G.H. | |
| depressum | Yellow | 10, | G. Ev. | S. | | C.G.H. | 1795 |
| lividum | Yellow | 10, | G. Ev. | S. | | C.G.H. | 1819 |
| difforme | Yellow | 8, | G. Ev. | S. | | C.G.H. | 1732 |
| digitiforme | | | G. Her. | P. | | C.G.H. | 1775 |
| dilatatum | White | 7, | G. Ev. | S. | | C.G.H. | 1820 |
| diminutum | Red | 4, | G. Her. | P. | | C.G.H. | 1789 |
| cauliculatum | Red | 4, | G. Her. | P. | | C.G.H. | 1789 |
| diversifolium | Pa. yel. | 8, | G. Her. | P. | | C.G.H. | 1726 |
| atro-virens | Pa. yel. | 8, | G. Her. | P. | | C.G.H. | |
| brevifolium | Pa. yel. | 8, | G. Her. | P. | | C.G.H. | |
| glaucum | Pa. yel. | 8, | G. Her. | P. | | C.G.H. | 1726 |
| laete-virens | Pa. yel. | 8, | G. Her. | P. | | C.G.H. | |
| dolabriforme | Yellow | 6, | G. Ev. | S. | | C.G.H. | 1705 |
| dubium | Pa. yel. | 8, | G. Her. | P. | | C.G.H. | 1800 |
| echinatum | Yellow | 8, | G. Ev. | S. | | C.G.H. | 1774 |
| album | White | 8, | G. Ev. | S. | | C.G.H. | 1774 |
| edule | Pink | 7, | G. Ev. | Tr. | | C.G.H. | 1690 |
| elongatum | Pa. yel. | 8, | G. Tu. | P. | | C.G.H. | 1793 |
| fusiforme | Pa. yel. | 5, | G. Tu. | P. | | C.G.H. | 1793 |
| minus | Pa. yel. | 5, | G. Tu. | S. | | C.G.H. | 1793 |
| emarginatum | Pink | 7, | G. Ev. | S. | | C.G.H. | 1732 |
| erinium | Yellow | 5, | G. Her. | P. | | C.G.H. | 1824 |
| expansum | Pa. yel. | 7, | G. Ev. | S. | | C.G.H. | 1705 |
| falcatum | Pink | 7, | G. Ev. | S. | | C.G.H. | 1727 |
| falciforme | Pink | 7, | G. Ev. | S. | | C.G.H. | 1805 |
| fastigiatum | White | 8, | G. Ev. | S. | | C.G.H. | 1794 |
| reflexum | White | 8, | G. Ev. | S. | | C.G.H. | 1792 |
| felinum | Yellow | 9, | G. Her. | P. | | C.G.H. | 1730 |
| fibuliforme | | | G. Her. | P. | | C.G.H. | 1795 |
| filiforme | | 7, | G. Her. | P. | | C.G.H. | 1819 |
| filicaule | Pink | 9, | G. Ev. | S. | | C.G.H. | 1800 |
| filamentosum | Pink | 6, | G. Ev. | Tr. | | C.G.H. | 1732 |
| flaccum | | | G. Her. | P. | | C.G.H. | 1776 |
| flavum | Yellow | 8, | G. Ev. | S. | | C.G.H. | 1890 |
| fixile | Pink | 8, | G. Ev. | S. | | C.G.H. | 1820 |
| flexifolium | Pink | 10, | G. Ev. | S. | | C.G.H. | 1820 |
| laete-virens | Pink | 10, | G. Ev. | S. | | C.G.H. | 1818 |
| flexuosum | White | 7, | G. Ev. | S. | | C.G.H. | 1795 |
| floribundum | Pink | 7, | G. Ev. | Tr. | | C.G.H. | 1704 |
| foliosum | Pink | 9, | G. Ev. | S. | | C.G.H. | 1802 |
| forcatum | Pink | 9, | G. Ev. | S. | | C.G.H. | 1758 |
| formosum | Crimson | 8, | G. Ev. | S. | | C.G.H. | 1890 |
| fragrans | Yellow | | G. Her. | P. | | C.G.H. | |
| fulvum | Fulvous | 7, | G. Ev. | S. | | C.G.H. | 1890 |
| furfureum | Blush | | G. Ev. | Tr. | | C.G.H. | 1830 |
| geminatum | Pink | | G. Her. | P. | | C.G.H. | 1792 |
| geniculiflorum | White | 8, | G. | A. | | C.G.H. | 1727 |
| gibbosum | Red | 2, | G. Her. | P. | | C.G.H. | 1780 |
| glaciale | White | 6, | H. Tr. | A. | | Greece | |
| gladiatum | Pink | 6, | G. Ev. | S. | | C.G.H. | 1792 |
| glaucescens | Pink | 7, | G. Ev. | Tr. | | C.G.H. | 1804 |
| glaucinum | Pink | 7, | G. Ev. | S. | | C.G.H. | |
| crassum | Pink | 7, | G. Ev. | S. | | C.G.H. | |
| glaucum | Orange | 6, | G. Ev. | S. | | C.G.H. | 1696 |
| glomeratum | Pink | 7, | G. Ev. | S. | | C.G.H. | 1732 |
| gracile, 1 | Red | 9, | G. Ev. | S. | | C.G.H. | 1794 |
| gracilis | Red | 9, | G. Ev. | S. | | C.G.H. | |
| grandiflorum | Yellow | 7, | G. Her. | P. | | C.G.H. | 1824 |
| graniforme | Yellow | 7, | G. Ev. | S. | | C.G.H. | 1727 |
| granulicaule | | | G. Ev. | S. | | C.G.H. | 1820 |
| grossum | Pa. yel. | 9, | G. Ev. | S. | | C.G.H. | 1774 |
| Haworthii | Brown | 8, | G. Ev. | S. | | C.G.H. | 1793 |
| helianthoides, 2 | Yellow | 9, | G. | A. | | C.G.H. | 1774 |
| heteropetalum | Pink | 9, | G. Ev. | S. | | C.G.H. | 1794 |
| heterophyllum | Yellow | | G. Her. | P. | | C.G.H. | 1795 |
| hirtellum | Pink | 7, | G. Ev. | Tr. | | C.G.H. | 1792 |
| hispidum | Purple | 7, | G. Ev. | S. | | C.G.H. | 1704 |
| platypetalum | Purple | 7, | G. Ev. | S. | | C.G.H. | 1890 |
| hispifolium | White | 7, | G. Ev. | Tr. | | C.G.H. | 1821 |
| roseum | Pink | 7, | G. Ev. | Tr. | | C.G.H. | 1818 |
| horizontale | Straw | 7, | G. Ev. | S. | | C.G.H. | 1795 |
| humifusum | White | 7, | G. Ev. | S. | | C.G.H. | 1774 |
| hybridum | Yellow | | G. Her. | P. | | C.G.H. | |
| imbricans | Pink | 7, | G. Ev. | S. | | C.G.H. | 1818 |
| imbricatum | White | 7, | G. Ev. | S. | | C.G.H. | 1792 |
| medium | White | 7, | G. Ev. | S. | | C.G.H. | |
| viride | White | 7, | G. Ev. | S. | | C.G.H. | |
| inaequale | Orange | 7, | G. Ev. | S. | | C.G.H. | 1716 |
| incomptum | White | 7, | G. Ev. | S. | | C.G.H. | 1819 |
| inclaudens | Pink | 6, | G. Ev. | S. | | C.G.H. | 1805 |
| inconspicuum | Red | 7, | G. Ev. | S. | | C.G.H. | 1822 |
| incurvum | Pink | 7, | G. Ev. | S. | | C.G.H. | 1802 |
| densifolium | Pink | 6, | G. Ev. | S. | | C.G.H. | 1809 |
| dilatans | Pink | 6, | G. Ev. | S. | | C.G.H. | |
| pallidius | Pink | 6, | G. Ev. | S. | | C.G.H. | |
| roseum | Pink | 6, | G. Ev. | S. | | C.G.H. | |
| inflexum | Pink | 7, | G. Ev. | S. | | C.G.H. | 1819 |
| institium, 3 | Purple | 9, | G. Ev. | S. | | C.G.H. | 1780 |
| flavo-croceum | Yellow | 9, | G. Ev. | S. | | C.G.H. | 1816 |
| minus | Yellow | 9, | G. Ev. | S. | | C.G.H. | |
| intonsum | Pink | 7, | G. Ev. | S. | | C.G.H. | 1824 |
| album | Pink | 7, | G. Ev. | S. | | C.G.H. | 1824 |
| junceum | Pink | 9, | G. Ev. | S. | | C.G.H. | 1800 |
| laceram, 4 | Pink | 7, | G. Ev. | Tr. | | C.G.H. | 1811 |
| laeve | Pink | 8, | G. Ev. | S. | | C.G.H. | 1774 |
| lavigatum | Pink | 6, | G. Ev. | Tr. | | C.G.H. | 1802 |
| lanceolatum | White | 8, | G. Ev. | S. | | C.G.H. | 1795 |
| roseum | Pink | 8, | G. Ev. | S. | | C.G.H. | 1812 |
| latum | Yellow | 7, | G. Her. | P. | | C.G.H. | 1620 |
| breve | Yellow | 7, | G. Her. | P. | | C.G.H. | 1802 |
| laxum | Pink | 6, | G. Ev. | Tr. | | C.G.H. | 1820 |
| lepidium | White | 8, | G. Ev. | S. | | C.G.H. | 1823 |

| | | | | | | | |
|---|---|---|---|---|---|---|---|
| leptaléon | Pink | 8, | G. | Ev. | S. | C. G. H. | 1819 |
| limpidûm | Red | 7, | G. | | A. | C. G. H. | 1774 |
| lineolâtûm | Pink | 8, | G. | Ev. | S. | C. G. H. | 1819 |
| Lāvé | | 7, | G. | Ev. | S. | C. G. H. | 1819 |
| minûs | | 7, | G. | Ev. | S. | C. G. H. | 1819 |
| nîtêns | | 8, | G. | Ev. | S. | C. G. H. | 1819 |
| linguæfôrmě | Yellow | 7, | G. | Her. | P. | C. G. H. | 1732 |
| assûrgēns | Yellow | 7, | G. | Her. | P. | C. G. H. | 1819 |
| prostrâtûm | Yellow | 7, | G. | Her. | P. | C. G. H. | |
| ruféscēns | Yellow | 7, | G. | Her. | P. | C. G. H. | 1732 |
| suberuciâtûm | Yellow | | G. | Her. | P. | C. G. H. | 1820 |
| longispinûlûm | Pa. yel. | 9, | G. | Ev. | S. | C. G. H. | 1820 |
| lôngûm | Yellow | 9, | G. | Her. | P. | C. G. H. | 1725 |
| angûstiûs | Yellow | 9, | G. | Her. | P. | C. G. H. | |
| attôlléns | Yellow | 9, | G. | Her. | P. | C. G. H. | 1819 |
| declîvé | Yellow | 9, | G. | Her. | P. | C. G. H. | |
| deprésaûm | Yellow | 9, | G. | Her. | P. | C. G. H. | |
| purpurâscēns | Yellow | 9, | G. | Her. | P. | C. G. H. | 1819 |
| uncâtûm | Yellow | 9, | G. | Her. | P. | C. G. H. | 1819 |
| lorâtûm | White | 7, | G. | Ev. | S. | C. G. H. | 1819 |
| lôrêûm | Pa. yel. | 9, | G. | Her. | P. | C. G. H. | 1732 |
| congêstûm | Pa. yel. | 9, | G. | Her. | P. | C. G. H. | 1805 |
| lûcîdûm | Yellow | 9, | G. | Her. | P. | C. G. H. | 1732 |
| lunâtûm | Pink | 7, | G. | Ev. | S. | C. G. H. | 1819 |
| lupînûm | Yellow | | G. | Her. | P. | C. G. H. | |
| lutéôlûm | Pa. yel. | 6, | G. | Ev. | S. | C. G. H. | 1820 |
| luteovîridě | Yellow | 1, | G. | Ev. | S. | C. G. H. | 1795 |
| lûtêûm | Pa. yel. | 6, | G. | Ev. | S. | C. G. H. | 1824 |
| maculâtûm | Scarlet | 7, | G. | Ev. | S. | C. G. H. | 1732 |
| macrorhîzûm | White | 5, | G. | Ev. | S. | C. G. H. | 1824 |
| magnipunctâtûm | Yellow | | G. | Her. | P. | C. G. H. | 1822 |
| unciâlě | Yellow | | G. | Her. | P. | C. G. H. | 1822 |
| marginâtûm | White | 5, | G. | Ev. | S. | C. G. H. | 1793 |
| máxîmûm | Pink | 9, | G. | Ev. | S. | C. G. H. | 1787 |
| mêdîûm | Yellow | 6, | G. | Her. | P. | C. G. H. | |
| micâns | Scarlet | | G. | Ev. | S. | C. G. H. | 1704 |
| micrânthōn, 5 | White | 5, | G. | Her. | P. | C. G. H. | 1804 |
| microphýllûm | Pink | 5, | G. | Ev. | S. | C. G. H. | 1795 |
| minîmûm | Pa. yel. | 10, | G. | Her. | P. | C. G. H. | 1796 |
| minûtûm | Pink | 10, | G. | Her. | P. | C. G. H. | 1795 |
| môllě | Pink | 10, | G. | Ev. | S. | C. G. H. | 1774 |
| monillifôrmě | White | 5, | G. | Ev. | S. | C. G. H. | 1791 |
| mucronâtûm | Pink | | G. | Ev. | S. | C. G. H. | 1794 |
| mucronifôrmě | Yellow | 7, | G. | Ev. | S. | C. G. H. | 1821 |
| multîflôrûm | White | 8, | G. | Ev. | S. | C. G. H. | 1792 |
| minûs | White | 8, | G. | Ev. | S. | C. G. H. | |
| nîtêns | | | G. | Ev. | S. | C. G. H. | |
| pátēns | White | 8, | G. | Ev. | S. | C. G. H. | 1820 |
| rûbrûm | Red | 8, | G. | Ev. | S. | C. G. H. | |
| muricâtûm | Pink | 5, | G. | Ev. | S. | C. G. H. | 1731 |
| minûs | Pink | 5, | G. | Ev. | S. | C. G. H. | |
| mûrînûm | Yellow | 9, | G. | Her. | P. | C. G. H. | 1790 |
| musculîûm | Yellow | 6, | G. | Her. | P. | C. G. H. | 1824 |
| mustellînûm | Yellow | 6, | G. | Her. | P. | C. G. H. | 1820 |
| mutâbîlě | Pink | 8, | G. | Ev. | S. | C. G. H. | 1792 |
| nîtîdûm | Yellow | 8, | G. | Ev. | S. | C. G. H. | 1790 |
| nôbîlě, 6 | Yellow | 7, | G. | Ev. | S. | C. G. H. | 1822 |
| noctîflôrûm | White | 7, | G. | Ev. | S. | C. G. H. | 1714 |
| elâtûm | Scarlet | 7, | G. | Ev. | S. | C. G. H. | 1714 |
| stramînêûm | Straw | 7, | G. | Ev. | S. | C. G. H. | 1732 |
| nodîflôrûm | | 9, | G. | Ev. | S. | C. G. H. | 1789 |
| nucîfôrmě | | | G. | Her. | P. | C. G. H. | 1790 |
| obconêllûm | White | 6, | G. | Ev. | S. | C. G. H. | 1786 |
| obcordêllûm | White | 6, | G. | Ev. | S. | C. G. H. | 1776 |
| oblîqûûm | Purple | 8, | G. | Ev. | S. | C. G. H. | 1819 |
| obsubulâtûm | White | | G. | Ev. | S. | C. G. H. | 1796 |
| obtûsûm | Pa. red | 8, | G. | Her. | P. | C. G. H. | 1792 |
| octophýllûm | Yellow | 11, | G. | Her. | P. | C. G. H. | 1819 |
| longìôsculûm | Yellow | 11, | G. | Her. | P. | C. G. H. | 1774 |
| rôsêûm | Red | 11, | G. | Her. | P. | C. G. H. | 1774 |
| pállēns | Pa. yel. | 7, | G. | Ev. | S. | C. G. H. | 1774 |
| palléscēns | White | 8, | G. | Ev. | S. | C. G. H. | 1820 |
| parvîflôrûm, 7 | Purple | 8, | G. | Ev. | S. | C. G. H. | 1800 |
| parvifôlîûm | White | 8, | G. | Ev. | S. | C. G. H. | 1820 |
| pátûlûm | Pink | 10, | G. | Ev. | S. | C. G. H. | 1811 |
| perfoliâtûm | Purple | 7, | G. | Ev. | S. | C. G. H. | 1714 |
| monacânthûm | Purple | 7, | G. | Ev. | S. | C. G. H. | |
| perpusîllûm | Pa. yel. | 10, | G. | Her. | P. | C. G. H. | 1819 |
| pervîridě | Red | 9, | G. | Her. | P. | C. G. H. | 1792 |
| pîlôsûm | Yellow | 7, | G. | | A. | C. G. H. | 1800 |
| pinnâtîfîdûm | Yellow | 7, | G. | Tr. | A. | C. G. H. | 1774 |
| pisîfôrmě | White | | G. | Her. | P. | C. G. H. | 1796 |
| polyânthōn | Pink | 8, | G. | Ev. | S. | C. G. H. | 1803 |
| polyphýllûm | Pink | 6, | G. | Ev. | S. | C. G. H. | 1819 |
| pomeridiânûm | Yellow | 7, | G. | | A. | C. G. H. | 1774 |
| Andréwsîì | Yellow | 7, | G. | | A. | C. G. H. | |
| præpîngûě | Yellow | 9, | G. | Her. | P. | C. G. H. | 1792 |
| procûmbēns | Pa. yel. | 4, | G. | Her. | P. | C. G. H. | 1820 |
| prodûctûm | Rose | 5, | G. | Ev. | S. | C. G. H. | 1822 |
| pubêrûlûm | White | | G. | Tr. | B. | C. G. H. | 1829 |
| pubêscēns | Red | 9, | G. | Her. | P. | C. G. H. | 1792 |
| pugionîfôrmě | Pa. yel. | 8, | G. | Ev. | S. | C. G. H. | 1714 |
| bíênně | Pa. yel. | 8, | G. | Ev. | S. | C. G. H. | 1714 |
| cârnêûm | Pink | 8, | G. | Ev. | S. | C. G. H. | 1714 |
| purpûrêûm | Purple | 8, | G. | Ev. | S. | C. G. H. | 1714 |
| pulchéllûm, 3 | Pink | 4, | G. | Ev. | S. | C. G. H. | 1793 |
| revôlûtûm | Pink | 4, | G. | Ev. | S. | C. G. H. | |
| pulverulêntûm | Pink | 5, | G. | Ev. | S. | C. G. H. | 1792 |
| punctâtûm | Red | 7, | G. | Her. | P. | C. G. H. | 1798 |
| purpûrêô-âlbûm | White | 8, | G. | Her. | P. | C. G. H. | 1824 |
| pustulâtûm | Yellow | 8, | G. | Her. | P. | C. G. H. | 1818 |
| pygmæûm | Pink | | G. | Ev. | S. | C. G. H. | 1805 |
| quadrîfîdûm | Yellow | 11, | G. | Her. | P. | C. G. H. | 1795 |
| radiâtûm | Red | 9, | G. | Ev. | S. | C. G. H. | 1732 |
| ramulôsûm | Yellow | 6, | G. | Ev. | S. | C. G. H. | 1791 |
| rêctûm | White | 7, | G. | Ev. | S. | C. G. H. | 1819 |
| relaxâtûm | Pink | 7, | G. | Ev. | S. | C. G. H. | 1815 |
| rêptāns | Pink | 7, | G. | Ev. | Tr. | C. G. H. | 1774 |
| retroflêxûm | Pink | 7, | G. | Ev. | S. | C. G. H. | 1724 |
| rigidicâulě | Pink | 5, | G. | Ev. | Tr. | C. G. H. | 1819 |
| rîgîdûm | White | 8, | G. | Ev. | S. | C. G. H. | 1793 |
| robûstûm | Yellow | | G. | Her. | P. | C. G. H. | 1795 |
| rôsêûm | Pink | 7, | G. | Ev. | S. | C. G. H. | 1795 |
| âlbûm | White | 7, | G. | Ev. | S. | C. G. H. | 1819 |
| lineârě | White | 7, | G. | Ev. | S. | C. G. H. | 1819 |
| Rôsei | Pink | | G. | Ev. | Tr. | V. D. L. | 1820 |
| rostéllûm | Wht. pink | 6, | G. | Ev. | S. | C. G. H. | 1820 |
| rostrâtûm | Yellow | 4, | G. | Her. | P. | C. G. H. | 1732 |
| rubricâulě | Pa. pur. | 6, | G. | Ev. | Tr. | C. G. H. | 1802 |
| dēnsûs | Pink | | G. | Ev. | Tr. | C. G. H. | 1818 |
| sûbvîrēns | Pink | | G. | Ev. | Tr. | C. G. H. | 1818 |
| rubrocînctûm | Pink | | G. | Ev. | Tr. | C. G. H. | 1811 |
| comprêssûm | Pink | 8, | G. | Ev. | Tr. | C. G. H. | |
| tênerûm | Pink | 8, | G. | Ev. | Tr. | C. G. H. | |
| Sâlmîì | Yellow | 10, | G. | Ev. | S. | C. G. H. | 1818 |
| angustifôlîûm | Yellow | 10, | G. | Ev. | S. | C. G. H. | 1823 |
| semicruciâtûm | Yellow | 10, | G. | Ev. | S. | C. G. H. | 1818 |
| salmônîûm | White | 10, | G. | Ev. | S. | C. G. H. | 1819 |
| sarmentôsûm | Red | 4, | G. | Ev. | Tr. | N. Holl. | 1805 |
| scâbrûm | Pink | 7, | G. | Ev. | S. | C. G. H. | 1731 |
| purpûrêûm | Purple | 7, | G. | Ev. | S. | C. G. H. | 1731 |
| scalprâtûm | Yellow | 8, | G. | Her. | P. | C. G. H. | 1714 |
| scapîgerûm | Yellow | 8, | G. | Her. | P. | C. G. H. | 1823 |
| Schôllîì | Pink | 5, | G. | Ev. | Tr. | C. G. H. | 1810 |
| semidentâtûm | Purple | 8, | G. | Ev. | S. | C. G. H. | |
| semicylindrîcûm | Yellow | | G. | Her. | P. | C. G. H. | 1732 |
| serrâtûm | Pink | 6, | G. | Ev. | S. | C. G. H. | 1707 |
| serrulâtûm | Pink | 11, | G. | Ev. | Tr. | C. G. H. | 1795 |
| vîrîdîûs | Pink | 11, | G. | Ev. | Tr. | C. G. H. | |
| sessilifôrûm | Yellow | 7, | G. | Tr. | A. | C. G. H. | 1774 |
| âlbûm | White | 7, | G. | Tr. | A. | C. G. H. | |
| simîlě | Pink | | G. | Ev. | Tr. | C. G. H. | 1819 |
| speciôsûm | Scarlet | 6, | G. | Ev. | S. | C. G. H. | 1793 |
| spectâbîlě | Crimson | 6, | G. | Ev. | S. | C. G. H. | 1787 |
| spinifôrmě | Pink | 9, | G. | Ev. | S. | C. G. H. | 1793 |
| subadûncûm | Pink | 9, | G. | Ev. | S. | C. G. H. | |
| spinôsûm | Pink | 7, | G. | Ev. | S. | C. G. H. | 1714 |
| spinulîferûm | Pa. yel. | 7, | G. | Ev. | S. | C. G. H. | 1794 |
| splêndēns | White | 7, | G. | Ev. | S. | C. G. H. | 1716 |
| stellâtûm, 9 | Pink | 7, | G. | Ev. | S. | C. G. H. | 1716 |
| stellîgerûm | Pink | 9, | G. | Ev. | S. | C. G. H. | 1793 |
| stênûm | Pink | 8, | G. | Ev. | S. | C. G. H. | 1829 |
| stipulâcêûm | Pink | 5, | G. | Ev. | S. | C. G. H. | 1728 |
| striâtûm | Pink | 7, | G. | Ev. | S. | C. G. H. | 1727 |
| pállēns | White | 7, | G. | Ev. | Tr. | C. G. H. | |
| strictûm | Yellow | | G. | Ev. | S. | C. G. H. | 1795 |
| strumôsûm | Pa. yel. | 8, | G. | Ev. | S. | C. G. H. | 1820 |
| subcomprêssûm | Purple | 7, | G. | Ev. | S. | C. G. H. | 1823 |
| minûs | Purple | 7, | G. | Ev. | S. | C. G. H. | 1823 |
| subglobôsûm | Red | 8, | G. | Ev. | S. | C. G. H. | 1795 |
| subhîspîdûm, 10 | Purple | 7, | G. | Ev. | Tr. | C. G | 1704 |
| subîncânûm | White | 7, | G. | Ev. | S. | C. G. H. | 1820 |
| subulâtûm | Pink | | G. | Ev. | Tr. | C. G. H. | 1768 |
| sulcâtûm | White | 8, | G. | Ev. | S. | C. G. H. | 1819 |
| surréctûm | Yellow | 10, | G. | Ev. | S. | C. G. H. | 1819 |
| brevifôlîûm | Yellow | 10, | G. | Ev. | S. | C. G. H. | 1819 |
| taurînûm | Yellow | 10, | G. | Her. | P. | C. G. H. | 1795 |
| tenêllûm | White | 8, | G. | Ev. | S. | C. G. H. | 1792 |
| tênûě | | | G. | Ev. | S. | C. G. H. | 1819 |
| tenuîflôrûm | Pink | 9, | G. | Ev. | S. | C. G. H. | 1820 |
| tenuifôlîûm | Scarlet | 8, | G. | Ev. | S. | C. G. H. | 1700 |
| eréctûm | Scarlet | 7, | G. | Ev. | S. | C. G. H. | |
| teretifôlîûm | Pink | 6, | G. | Her. | P. | C. G. H. | 1794 |
| teretiûscûlûm | Pink | | G. | Her. | P. | C. G. H. | 1794 |
| testâcêûm | Orange | 8, | G. | Ev. | S. | C. G. H. | 1820 |
| testiculârě | White | 10, | G. | Ev. | S. | C. G. H. | 1774 |
| tîgrînûm | Yellow | 7, | G. | Her. | P. | C. G. H. | 1790 |
| tricôlôr | Red | 7, | G. | Ev. | S. | C. G. H. | 1795 |
| tricôlôrûm | Yel. red | 10, | G. | Her. | P. | C. G. H. | 1795 |
| Tripôlîûm | Pa. yel. | 7, | G. | | S. | C. G. H. | 1700 |
| tortuôsûm | Pa. yel. | 8, | G. | Ev. | S. | C. G. H. | 1705 |
| torquâtûm | Pink | 8, | G. | Ev. | S. | C. G. H. | 1820 |
| truncatéllûm | Pa. yel. | 7, | G. | Her. | P. | C. G. H. | 1795 |
| tuberculâtûm | Yellow | 8, | G. | Ev. | S. | C. G. H. | 1818 |
| tuberôsûm | Orange | 4, | G. | Ev. | S. | C. G. H. | 1714 |
| minûs | Orange | 8, | G. | Ev. | S. | C. G. H. | 1714 |
| tumîdûlûm | Pink | 8, | G. | Ev. | S. | C. G. H. | 1802 |
| minûs | Pink | 8, | G. | Ev. | S. | C. G. H. | 1820 |
| umbellâtûm | White | 7, | G. | Ev. | S. | C. G. H. | 1727 |
| anômâlûm | White | 7, | G. | Ev. | S. | C. G. H. | |
| umbellifôrûm | | 8, | G. | Ev. | S. | C. G. H. | 1820 |
| uncinâtûm | Pa. pur. | 7, | G. | Ev. | S. | C. G. H. | 1795 |
| uncinéllûm | Pa. pur. | 7, | G. | Ev. | S. | C. G. H. | 1819 |
| ûnîdēns | | | G. | Ev. | S. | C. G. H. | 1824 |
| uvæfôrmě | | | G. | Her. | P. | C. G. H. | 1820 |
| vaginâtûm | White | 7, | G. | Ev. | S. | C. G. H. | 1802 |
| parvîflôrûm | White | 7, | G. | Ev. | S. | C. G. H. | |
| vâlîdûm | Pink | 5, | G. | Ev. | Tr. | C. G. H. | 1824 |

| | | | | | | | |
|---|---|---|---|---|---|---|---|
| variābĭlĕ | . . | Yellow | 7, G. Ev. | S. | C. G. H. | | 1796 |
| lǣvĭŏs | . . | Yellow | 7, G. Ev. | S. | C. G. H. | | 1796 |
| vărĭāns | . . | Pa. yel. | 8, G. Ev. | S. | C. G. H. | | 1706 |
| verruculātūra | . . | Yellow | 5, G. Ev. | S. | C. G. H. | | 1731 |
| Candollii | . . | Yellow | 5, G. Ev. | S. | C. G. H. | | |
| versĭcŏlŏr | . . | Pink | 6, G. Ev. | S. | C. G. H. | | 1795 |
| villōsŭm | . . | Apetal | 7, G. Ev. | S. | C. G. H. | | 1759 |
| violāceŭm | . . | Purple | 7, G. Ev. | S. | C. G. H. | | 1820 |
| vīrāns | . . | Pink | 6, G. Ev. | Tr. | C. G. H. | | 1821 |
| virēscēns | . . | Pink | 6, G. Ev. | Tr. | N. Holl. | | 1804 |
| virgātŭm | . . | Pink | 8, G. Ev. | S. | C. G. H. | | 1793 |
| vĭrĭdĕ | . . | Pa. pur. | 7, G. Ev. | S. | C. G. H. | | 1792 |
| viridiflōrŭm | . . | Green | 9, G. Ev. | S. | C. G. H. | | 1774 |
| vulpīnŭm | . . | Yellow | 9, G. Her. | P. | C. G. H. | | 1795 |

**MESHES**, the openings in any tissue.

**MESOGLŎĬA.** From *mesos*, middle, and *gloios*, viscid; the spines of the branches are in a solid mass. *Linn.* 24, Or. 7, Nat. Or. *Algæ.* This genus is entirely composed of marine plants. *Synonymes:* 1. *Rivularia verticillata.* 2. *R. vermiculata—capillaris, coccinēā* 1, *Hudsŏnī, multĭfĭdā, vermiculāris-coriāceā* 2.

**MESPĬLŬS**, *Linn.* From *mesos*, a half, and *pilos*, a bullet; in allusion to the resemblance the fruit bears to half a bullet. *Linn.* 12, Or. 2, Nat. Or. *Rosacea.* The Mespilus, or *Medlar,* is a genus of low-growing trees; they are very ornamental, and are therefore worth a place in every shrubbery. Any common soil suits them, and they are readily increased by budding or grafting on the common Hawthorn, or they may be increased by seeds, which do not vegetate till the second year after sowing. *Synonymes:* 1. *M. grandiflora, M. Smithii.*

| | | | | | |
|---|---|---|---|---|---|
| germānĭcă | . . | White | 6, H. De. | T. | England |
| diffūsă | . . | White | 6, H. De. | T. | Europe |
| strĭctă | . . | White | 6, H. De. | T. | Europe |
| sylvēstrĭs | . . | White | 5, H. De. | T. | Europe |
| lobātă, 1 | . . | White | 5, H. De. | T. | |

**MESSERSCHMĪDĬĂ**, *Linn.* In honour of Dr. Messerschmid, a German botanist. *Linn.* 5, Or. 1, Nat. Or. *Ehretiaceæ.* These plants are of easy cultivation in loam and peat, and cuttings root readily planted in sand, under a glass. *Synonymes:* 1. *Tournefortia hirsutissima.* 2. *T. laurifolia.* 3. *T. scandens.* 4. *T. volubilis.*

| | | | | | | |
|---|---|---|---|---|---|---|
| hirsutĭssĭmă, 1 | . . | Orn. yel. | 6, S. Ev. | T. | W. Ind. | 1818 |
| laurifŏlĭă, 2 | . . | Yellow | 7, S. Ev. | Cl. | W. Ind. | 1819 |
| scandēns, 3 | . . | Orn. yel. | 7, S. Ev. | Cl. | Peru | 1816 |
| volūbĭlĭs, 4 | . . | Orn. yel. | 7, S. Ev. | Tw. | Jamaica | 1752 |

**MESŬĂ**, *Linn.* In honour of Mesue, the father and son, two celebrated Arabian physicians and botanists; they resided at Damascus, and flourished in the eighth and ninth centuries. The works of the son were published at Venice in 1581. *Linn.* 16, Or. 7, Nat. Or. *Guttiferæ.* This tree is well deserving of cultivation on account of its beautiful, orange and white, sweet-scented flowers, which contrast finely with the dark-green foliage. It attains the height of fifty feet, and grows best in a mixture of strong loam, peat, and sand. Young plants are commonly obtained from seeds; cuttings will root in sand, under a glass, but not freely. The wood is used for a variety of purposes in the East Indies, being considered harder and more durable than most other Oriental timber. The dried blossoms may be found under the name of *Nagkesur* in every bazaar in India; they are used in medicine, and universally esteemed for their fragrance.

| | | | | | | |
|---|---|---|---|---|---|---|
| fērrĕā | . . | White | 7, S. Ev. | T. | E. Ind. | 1837 |

**METALĀSĬĂ**, *R. Brown.* From *meta*, a change, and *lasios*, hairy; supposed to refer to the leaves. *Linn.* 19, Or. 2, Nat. Or. *Compositæ.* These are pretty plants, growing about three feet high, in a mixture of three parts sandy peat and one part loam; and cuttings root readily in the same kind of soil, under a glass. *Synonymes:* 1. *Gnaphalium divergens.* 2. *G. fastigiatum.*

| | | | | | | |
|---|---|---|---|---|---|---|
| divērgēns, 1 | . . | White | 7, G. Ev. | S. | C. G. H. | 1816 |
| fastigiātă, 2 | . . | White | 6, G. Ev. | S. | C. G. H. | 1812 |
| mucronātă | . . | White | 6, G. Ev. | S. | C. G. H. | 1824 |
| murĭcātă | . . | White | 7, G. Ev. | S. | C. G. H. | 1816 |
| scriphiŏīdēs | . . | Yellow | | G. Ev. | S. | C. G. H. | 1825 |

**METASTĒLMĂ**, *R. Brown.* From *meta*, instead of, and *stelma*, a crown. *Linn.* 5, Or. 2, Nat. Or. *Asclepiadaceæ.* This is a very ornamental twiner, well suited for covering the rafters or pillars of a stove.

It grows in peat and loam, and cuttings of the young wood root readily in sand, under a glass.

| | | | | | |
|---|---|---|---|---|---|
| parviflōrŭm | . . | Orn. wht. | S. Ev. | Tw. | W. Ind. |

**METROSĬDĔRŎS**, *Gærtner.* From *metra*, the heart of a tree, and *sideros*, iron; on account of the hardness of the wood and pith of the trees. *Linn.* 12, Or. 1, Nat. Or. *Myrtaceæ.* These plants are well worth a place in every collection of greenhouse plants. They grow best in loam, peat, and sand, well incorporated, and young plants are readily obtained from cuttings of the young wood planted in sand, under a glass. *Synonyme:* 1. *Leptospermum ambiguum.*

| | | | | | | |
|---|---|---|---|---|---|---|
| angustifŏlĭŭs | . . | Yellow | G. Ev. | S. | C. G. H. | 1787 |
| ǎsperŭs | . . . | | G. Ev. | S. | C. G. H. | 1824 |
| capitātŭs | . . | Pink | G. Ev. | S. | C. G. H. | 1824 |
| corĭfŏlĭŭs, 1 | . . | White | G. Ev. | S. | N. Holl. | |
| glomulĭfĕr | . . | Yel. grn. | 5, G. Ev. | S. | N. S. W. | 1805 |
| vērŭs | . . | Yel. grn. | 4, S. Ev. | T. | E. Ind. | 1819 |

**MĒŬM**, *Tournefort.* From *mcion*, small; in allusion to the leaves. *Linn.* 5, Or. 2, Nat. Or. *Umbelliferæ.* Hardy herbaceous plants, of no beauty—*athamanticum, Bunius, Mutellina, sibiricum.*

**MEXICAN-MUGWORT**, see *Artemisiā mexicānă.*
**MEXICAN-TEA**, see *Psorālĕā glandulōsā.*
**MEXICAN-TIGER-FLOWER**, see *Tigridiā pavōnĭā.*

**MEYĒRĂ**, *Schreber.* In honour of Gottlieb Andrew Meyer, a German botanist. *Linn.* 19, Or. 2, Nat. Or. *Compositæ.* A little inconspicuous plant, growing about a foot high, and of the easiest culture.

| | | | | | | |
|---|---|---|---|---|---|---|
| sĕssĭlĭs | . . | Yellow | 7, S. Her. | P. | W. Ind. | |

**MICACEOUS**, glittering or shining.
**MICÆ**, glittering particles.
**MICHAELMAS-DAISY**, see *Astĕr.*

**MICHAŬXĬĂ**, *L'Heritier.* In honour of Andrew Michaux, botanist to Louis XVI.; he travelled in Syria, Persia, and North America. *Linn.* 8, Or. 1, Nat. Or. *Campanulaceæ.* This is a genus of handsome plants; the seeds merely require sowing in the open ground, and the plants are treated like other biennials. They should be slightly protected in winter. *Synonyme:* 1. *M. decandra.*

| | | | | | | |
|---|---|---|---|---|---|---|
| campanulŏīdēs | . . | Pa. red | 7, H. | B. | Levant | 1787 |
| lævĭgātă, 1 | . . | White | 7, H. | B. | Persia | 1827 |

**MICHĒLĬĂ**, *Linn.* In honour of Pietro Antonio Micheli, a famous Florentine botanist, who died in 1757. *Linn.* 13, Or. 6, Nat. Or. *Magnoliaceæ.* This handsome tree attains the height of thirty feet, and produces fragrant flowers, and an edible but not an agreeable fruit. It grows well in a light loam; and cuttings root freely planted in sand, under a glass, in heat.

| | | | | | | |
|---|---|---|---|---|---|---|
| Champācă | . . | Yellow | S. Ev. | T. | E. Ind. | 1779 |

**MICŎNĬĂ**, *Ruis and Pavon.* In honour of D. Micon, M.D., a Spanish botanist. *Linn.* 10, Or. 1, Nat. Or. *Melastomaceæ.* The species of this genus are well deserving of a place in every stove. For culture and propagation, see *Meriana.* *Synonymes:* 1. *Melastoma acinodendron.* 2. *M. grandifolia.* 3. *M. lævigata.* 4. *M. lævigata.* 5. *M. purpurea.* 6. *M. tetrandra.* 7. *M. trinervia.*

| | | | | | | |
|---|---|---|---|---|---|---|
| Acinodēndrŏn, 1 | . . | Purple | S. Ev. | S. | Jamaica | 1804 |
| angustātă | . . | White | S. Ev. | S. | Trinidad | 1820 |
| decussātă | . . | White | S. Ev. | S. | Guiana | 1818 |
| grandifŏlĭă, 2 | . . | White | S. Ev. | S. | Trinidad | 1820 |
| impetiolārĭs | . . | White | S. Ev. | S. | W. Ind. | 1822 |
| lævĭgātă, 3 | . . | White | S. Ev. | S. | W. Ind. | 1815 |
| longifŏlĭă | . . | White | S. Ev. | S. | Guiana | 1817 |
| prasĭnă, 4 | . . | White | 7, S. Ev. | S. | Jamaica | 1817 |
| purpurāscēns, 5 | . . | Purple | S. Ev. | S. | Guiana | 1817 |
| rubēscens | . . | White | S. Ev. | S. | Amer. | 1818 |
| semicrenātă | . . | White | S. Ev. | S. | Guadaloupe | 1817 |
| tenuifŏlĭă | . . | White | S. Ev. | S. | Amer. | 1818 |
| tetrāndră, 6 | . . | White | S. Ev. | S. | Jamaica | 1815 |
| trinērvĭă, 7 | . . | White | 7, S. Ev. | S. | Jamaica | 1795 |

**MICRĂNTHĔMŬM**, *Michaux.* From *mikros*, small, and *anthos*, a flower. *Linn.* 2, Or. 1, Nat. Or. *Scrophulariaceæ.* An ornamental plant, growing in sandy peat, and increased by divisions.

| | | | | | | |
|---|---|---|---|---|---|---|
| orbiculātŭm | . . | White | 5, F. Ev. | Tr. | Carolina | 1826 |

**MICROCĂLĂ**, *Link.* From *mikros*, small, and *kalos*, pretty; in allusion to the small, pretty flowers. *Linn.* 4, Or. 1, Nat. Or. *Gentianaceæ.* A pretty little plant, of easy cultivation. *Synonyme:* 1. *Exacum filiforme.*

| | | | | | | |
|---|---|---|---|---|---|---|
| filiförmĕ, 1 | . | . Yellow | . 6, H. | A. Britain | . | . |
| pulchéllům | . | . Rose | . 5, H. | A. N. Jersey | . | 1826 |

MICRŎCHLŎĂ, *R. Brown*. From *mikros*, small, and *chloa*, a grass; in allusion to the minute size of the plants. *Linn.* 3, Or. 2, Nat. Or. *Gramineæ*. A hardy annual. It grows in any common soil.

| | | | | | | |
|---|---|---|---|---|---|---|
| setācĕa | . | . Apetal | . 7, Grass. E. Ind. | . | . | 1816 |

MICROLÆNĂ, *R. Brown*. From *mikros*, small, and *lenos*, wool; in allusion to the small, woolly flower-stalk. *Linn.* 4, Or. 2, Nat. Or. *Gramineæ*. A green-house perennial species, growing in loam and peat, and increased by seed. *Synonyme:* 1. *Ehrhartia stipoides.*

| | | | | | | |
|---|---|---|---|---|---|---|
| stipoídĕa, 1 | . | . . Apetal | . 7, Grass. N. Holl. | . | 1822 |

MICROLŎMĂ, *R. Brown*. From *mikros*, small, and *loma*, a fringe; the flowers are fringed. *Linn.* 5, Or. 2, Nat. Or. *Asclepiadaceæ*. Small climbing plants, growing freely in a mixture of loam and peat; and cuttings will root readily in sand, under a glass. *Synonymes:* 1. *Periploca linearis.* 2. *Ceropegia sagittata.*

| | | | | | | |
|---|---|---|---|---|---|---|
| lineárĕ, 1 | . | . White | . 7, G. Ev. Tw. C. G. H. | . | 1823 |
| sagittātŭm, 2 | . | Grn. pur. | 7, G. Ev. Tw. C. G. H. | . | 1775 |

MICROMÈRIĂ, *Bentham*. From *mikros*, small, and *meris*, a part. *Linn.* 14, Or. 1, Nat. Or. *Labiatæ*. These plants will grow well in common garden soil, and are easily increased by cuttings. *Synonymes:* 1. *Satureia approximata.* 2. *Mentha australis.* 3. *Satureia græca.* 4. *S. tenuifolia, S. congesta.* 5. *S juliana.* 6. *S. hirsuta.* 7. *Nepeta marifolia.* 8. *S. viminea.* 2. *Thymus Teneriffæ.* 10. *T. ericæfolius.*

| | | | | | | |
|---|---|---|---|---|---|---|
| approximātă, 1 | . Purple | . 6, F. Ev. S. Mediter. | . 1822 |
| austrālis, 2 | . | F. Ev. S. N. S. W. | |
| græcă, 3 | . . | Purple | 6, F. Ev. S. Greece | . | 1759 |
| densiflŏră, 4 | . | Purple | 6, F. Ev. S. S. Eur. | . | 1822 |
| juliānă, 5 | . . | Pa. red. | 7, F. Ev. S. Mediter. | . | 1596 |
| hirsūtă, 6 | . | Purple | 6, F. Ev. S. Sicily | . | 1822 |
| marifŏliă, 7 | . | Blue | . 7, F. Ev. S. Spain | . | 1800 |
| obovātă, 8 | . . | Purple | 6, S. Ev. S. Jamaica | . | 1783 |
| Teneriffæ, 9 | . | Purple | 5, F. Ev. S. Teneriffe | . | |
| vāriă, 10 | . | Purple | . 7, F. Ev. S. Canaries | . | 1806 |

MICRŎPŬS, *Linn.* From *mikros*, small, and *pous*, a foot. *Linn.* 19, Or. 4, Nat. Or. *Compositæ*. Uninteresting annuals; the seeds need only be sown in the open ground—*erēctŭs, supīnŭs.*

MICROSPĔRMŬM, small-seeded.

MICRŎSTÝLIS, *Nuttall*. From *mikros*, small, and *stylos*, a column; in allusion to the very small column. *Linn.* 20, Or. 1, Nat. Or. *Orchidaceæ*. A genus of plants possessing little to recommend them. The Mexican species should be kept in the greenhouse, and grown in sandy peat; they come up in spring when they flower, after which, the leaves die down, and the plants remain dormant till the following season; they are increased by dividing the roots.

| | | | | | | |
|---|---|---|---|---|---|---|
| excavātă | . . | Green | . . | G. Ter. Mexico | . | |
| ophioglossoídĕs | . | Yel. grn. | 7. H. Ter. N. Amer. | . | 1824 |
| mexicānă | . | Green | . 7, G. Ter. Mexico | . | 1829 |
| versicŏlŏr | . , | Orange | . 8, G. Ter. Mexico | . | 1830 |

MICRŎTÈĂ, *Swartz*. From *microtes*, smallness; in allusion to the very minute parts of fructification. *Linn.* 5, Or. 2, Nat. Or. *Amarantaceæ*. The seeds should be sown in loam and peat, and treated as other stove annuals. *Synonyme:* 1. *Ancistrocarpus maypurensis.*

| | | | | | | |
|---|---|---|---|---|---|---|
| debīlis | . . | White | . 6, S. | A. Jamaica | . | 1816 |
| maypurénsis, 1 | . White | . 7, S. | A. Trinidad | . | 1817 |

MICRŎTIS, *R. Brown*. From *mikros*, small, and *otos*, an ear; appearance of the anthers. *Linn.* 20, Or. 1, Nat. Or. *Orchidaceæ*. A curious genus of tuberous-rooted plants, which require the same treatment as *Corycium.*

| | | | | | | |
|---|---|---|---|---|---|---|
| alba | . . . | . White | . 6, F. Ter. N. Holl. | . | 1826 |
| mèdiă | . . . | . Green | . F. Ter. N. S. W. | . | 1823 |
| parviflŏră | . . . | Green | . 9, F. Ter. N. S. W. | . | 1824 |

MID-RIB, the middle vein of a leaf, which passes from the petiole to the apex.

MIGNONETTE, see *Rĕsēdă.*

MIKANĬĂ, *Willdenow*. In honour of Joseph Mikan, professor of botany at Prague. *Linn.* 19, Or. 1, Nat. Or. *Compositæ*. These plants grow well in any light rich soil, and are increased by cuttings, in sand, under a glass. In Spanish America, a

valuable antidote against the bite of serpents is obtained from *M. guaco.*

| | | | | | | |
|---|---|---|---|---|---|---|
| amāră | . . . | . White | . 8, S. Ev. Cl. Guiana | . | 1813 |
| Guācŏ | . . . | . Pa. blue | . 8, S. Ev. Tw. S. Amer. | . | 1823 |
| opiferă | . . . | . White | . 8, S. Ev. Tw. Brazil | . | 1823 |
| scándĕns | . . . | . White | . 8, S. Ev Tw. N. Amer. | . | 1714 |
| suaveŏlĕns | . . . | . White | . 8, S. Ev. Tw. S. Amer. | . | 1823 |

*chenopodifŏliă, hastātă, Houstŏnĭ, orinocĕnsis.*

MILFOIL, see *Achillĕă.*

MILIARY, granulated, resembling many seeds.

MILĬŬM, *Linn.* From *mille*, a thousand; in allusion to the immense number of seeds produced by it. *Linn.* 3, Or. 2, Nat. Or. *Gramineæ*. Hardy annuals and perennials, not worth growing, except in botanical collections. Any common soil will suit them—*confertům, effusům, frutēcĕns, gallecĭcům, microspērmům, velutĭnăm, vernālĕ.*

MILK-PARSLEY, see *Selīnŭm.*

MILK-VETCH, see *Astrăgălŭs.*

MILKWORT, see *Polÿgălă.*

MILK-WOOD, see *Brŏsimŭm.*

MILLĂ, *Cavanilles*. In honour of Julian Milla, head gardener in the Royal Garden of Madrid. *Linn.* 6, Or. 1, Nat. Or. *Liliaceæ*. Two very pretty plants highly deserving of cultivation. They grow in light loam, and are increased by seeds.

| | | | | | | |
|---|---|---|---|---|---|---|
| biflŏră | . . | . White | . 5, F. Bl. P. Mexico | . | 1826 |
| uniflŏră | . . | . Wht. li. | . 2, F. Bl. P. B. Ayres | . | 1832 |

MILLERĬĂ, *Linn.* In honour of the celebrated Philip Miller, F.R.S., author of the Gardener's Dictionary. *Linn.* 19, Or. 4, Nat. Or. *Compositæ*. Stove annuals of no beauty. Any common soil suits them—*biflŏră, quinqueflŏră.*

MILLET, see *Pănĭcŭm.*

MILLET-GRASS, see *Milĭům.*

MILLINGTŎNĬĂ, *Roxburgh*. In honour of Sir T. Millington, professor of botany at Oxford. *Linn.* 14, Or. 2, Nat. Or. *Millingtoniaceæ*. An ornamental-growing tree. For culture and propagation, see *Jacaranda.*

| | | | | | | |
|---|---|---|---|---|---|---|
| simplicifŏliă | . . | . Yellow | . 8. Ev. T. E. Ind. | . | 1828 |

MILTŎNĬĂ, *Lindley*. Thus named in compliment to Earl Fitzwilliam, one of the oldest and steadiest friends of Natural Science in this country, and a great lover of Orchidaceæ. *Linn.* 20, Or. 1, Nat. Or. *Orchidaceæ*. The flowers of these plants are strikingly handsome; the sepals and petals of *M. spectabilis* are delicate cream-colour, and the labellum, which is very large, is elegantly marked with various shades of purple, deepest towards the base. In *M. candida*, the sepals and petals are yellow-brown, and the labellum pure white, finely marked with pink. In potting these plants, the peat should be raised, for a well-grown, good-sized plant, two or three inches, in the same way as recommended for *Stanhopeas*; and the creeping stems, from which the pseudo-bulbs grow, ought to be entirely on the surface, and if necessary, they may be fastened to the peat with hooked pegs. The best way of propagating the species of this genus is, first, to cut the stem half through, which will cause young plants to be sent out; and finally, to cut them through a month before dividing. They require a hot part of the house. *Synonyme:* 1. *Macrochilus Fryanus.*

| | | | | | | |
|---|---|---|---|---|---|---|
| cándidă | . . . | . White | . 8, S. Epi. | . | 183.. |
| spectabĭlis, 1 | . . | . Ro. wht. | . 7, S. Epi. Brazil | . | 1835 |

MIMĔTĔS, *Salisbury*. From *mimos*, a mimic; because of its resemblance to several other genera. *Linn.* 4, Or. 1, Nat. Or. *Proteaceæ*. This is a genus of very pretty shrubs. For culture and propagation, see *Protea. Synonymes:* 1. *Protea cucullata.* 2. *Deastella vaccinifolia.*

| | | | | | | |
|---|---|---|---|---|---|---|
| cucullātă, 1 | . . | . Purple | . G. Ev. S. C. G. H. | . | 1789 |
| divaricātă | . . | . White | . 7, G. Ev. S. C. G. H. | . | 1795 |
| Hartŏgĭi | . . | . | 7, G. Ev. S. C. G. H. | . | 1824 |
| hirtă | . . | . Red | . 7, G. Ev. S. C. G. H. | . | 1774 |
| palústris | . . | . Purple | . 7, G. Ev. S. C. G. H. | . | 1802 |
| pauciflŏră | . . | . Red | . 7, G. Ev. S. C. G. H. | . | 1818 |
| purpūreă | . . | . Purple | . 11, G. Ev. S. C. G. H. | . | 1789 |
| vacciniifŏliă, 2 | . | . | G. Ev. S. C. G. H. | . | 1800 |

MIMŎSĂ, *Adanson*. From *mimos*, a mimic; the leaves of many of the species resemble animal sensibility. *Linn.* 23, Or. 1, Nat. Or. *Leguminosæ*. The leaves of several of the species belonging to this genus are more or less sensitive to the touch, but none so much so as *M. pudica*; they are, on that account, well worth cultivating. They grow well in loam and peat, with a little sand; and cuttings of the young wood will root in sand, under a glass. They may also be increased by seeds.

| | | | | | |
|---|---|---|---|---|---|
| abstèrgēns | . . | | 8. Ev. 8. E. Ind. . | . 1820 |
| asperāta | . . | White . | 6, 8. Ev. 8. W. Ind. . | . 1823 |
| Barclayāna | . . | | 8. Ev. 8. | . 1824 |
| canēscēns | . . | White . | 6, 8. Ev. 8. Guinea . | . 1822 |
| cāstā | . . | Pa. yel. | 7, 8. Ev. 8. 8. Amer. | . 1741 |
| dōrmiēns | . . | White . | 6, 8. Ev. 8. 8. Amer. | . 1818 |
| ferrugīnēā | . . | | 8. Ev. 8. E. Ind. . | . 1818 |
| floribūndā | . . | Pink . | 6, 8. Ev. 8. Cumana | . 1824 |
| hispīdūlā | . . | Pa. red | 6, 8. Ev. 8. 8. Amer. | . 1820 |
| latispīnōsā | . . | White . | 9, 8. Ev. 8. Madagascar | . 1823 |
| marginātā | . . | Pink | 8. Ev. 8. Mexico . | |
| microcēphālā | . . | Red . | 6, 8. Ev. 8. Orinoco . | . 1820 |
| obtusifōlia | . . | Purple | 8. Ev. 8. Brazil | . 1816 |
| polydāctylā | . . | Purple | 6, 8. Ev. 8. Guiana . | . 1822 |
| pudibūndā | . . | Pa. red | 8. Ev. 8. Bahia . | . 1818 |
| pudīcā | . . | White . | 6, 8. A. Brazil . | . 1688 |
| rubicaūlis | . . | Pa. yel. | 6, 8. Ev. 8. E. Ind. . | . 1799 |
| sensitīvā | . . | Pink . | 6, 8. Ev. 8. Brazil . | . 1648 |
| stipulātā | . . | | 8. Ev. 8. E. Ind. . | . 1831 |
| strigōsā | . . | Purple . | 6, 8. Ev. 8. 8. Amer. | . 1818 |
| viscīdā | . . | Red . | 8. Ev. 8. Brazil . | . 1825 |
| vīvā | . . | Purple . | 8, 8. Her. P. Jamaica | . 1739 |

**MIMŪLŪS**, *Linn.* From *mimo*, an ape or actor; so named because of the ringent corollas of the species. *Linn.* 14, Or. 2, Nat. Or. *Scrophulariaceæ*. Most of these plants are showy, and worth cultivating, particularly the hardy-herbaceous kinds, which are so well suited for ornamenting flower-borders; they thrive in any common garden soil, and are readily increased by divisions of the roots, or by seeds. The greenhouse and frame species will grow well in light rich soil, and may be increased by cuttings in the same kind of soil, under a glass. The seeds of the annual kinds may be sown where the plants are intended to remain. The leaves of *M. guttatus* are eatable as salad. Synonymes: 1. *M. propinquus.* 2. *M. luteus.* 3. *M. Hodsoni.*

| | | | | | |
|---|---|---|---|---|---|
| alātūs | . . | Ll. blue | 7, H. Her. P. N. Amer. | . 1783 |
| andicōlus | . . | Yellow | 5, H. Her. P. Chile | . 1831 |
| cardinālis | . . | Red . | 6, H. Her. P. California | . 1835 |
| floribūndūs | . . | Yellow | 8, H. A. N. Amer. | . 1826 |
| glabrātūs, 1 | . . | Yellow | 6, H. Her. P. Mexico . | . 1827 |
| guttātūs, 2 | . . | Yellow | 7, H. Her. P. N. Amer. | . 1812 |
| Harrisoniānūs | . . | Yellow | 8, H. Her. P. Eng. hyb. | |
| lanātūs | . . | Yellow | 6, F. Her. P. N. Amer. | . 1826 |
| Lewīsii | . . | Pa. pur. | 8, H. Her. P. Missouri | . 1824 |
| lūteūs | . . | Yellow | 7, H. Her. P. Chile | . 1826 |
| rivulāris | . . | Yellow | 7, H. Her. P. Chile | . 1826 |
| Wilsōni | . . | Yel. spot. | 7, H. Her. P. Hybrid | . 1836 |
| Youngānūs | . . | Yel. spot. | 7, H. Her. P. Chile | . 1833 |
| moschātūs | . . | Yellow | 8, H. Her. Cr. Columbia | . 1826 |
| parviflōrūs | . . | Yellow | 7, H. A. Chile . | . 1824 |
| rīngēns | . . | Ll. blue | 7, H. Her. P. N. Amer. | . 1759 |
| roseo-cardinālis 3 | | Red . | 8, H. A. Hybrid | . 1837 |
| rōseūs | . . | Rose . | 8, F. Her. P. California | . 1831 |
| Smithii | . . | Yellow | 6, H. Her. P. Hybrid | . 1832 |
| variegātūs | . . | Wht. rosy . | 6, H. Her. P. Chile | . 1831 |

**MIMŪSŌPS**, *Linn.* From *mimo*, an ape, and *ops*, the face; the flowers may be fancied to resemble the face of a monkey. *Linn.* 8, Or. 1, Nat. Or. *Sapotaceæ*. Ornamental trees, which grow in a light loamy soil, or in a mixture of loam and peat; and cuttings of the ripened wood root with ease in sand, under a glass. Synonyme: 1. *Achras dissecta.*

| | | | | | |
|---|---|---|---|---|---|
| cyanocārpā | . . | Greenish . | 8. Ev. 8. N. Holl. | . 1821 |
| dissēctā, 1 | . . | | 8. Ev. T. Sea. Ia. | . 1804 |
| Elēngi | . . | White . | 8. Ev. T. E. Ind. . | . 1796 |
| hexāndrā | . . | Yel. wht. | 8. Ev. T. India | . 1804 |
| Kāuki | . . | | 8. Ev. T. E. Ind. . | . 1796 |
| parvifōlia | . . | | 8. Ev. T. N. Holl. | . 1821 |

**MINT**, see *Menthā*.

**MINUĀRTIĀ**, *Læfling.* After John Minuart, a Spanish apothecary and restorer of botany in Spain. *Linn.* 8, Or. 1, Nat. Or. *Alsinaceæ*. The seeds of these plants have only to be sown in the open ground.

| | | | | | |
|---|---|---|---|---|---|
| campēstris | . . | Apetal . | 6, H. A. Spain . | . 1806 |
| dichōtōmā | . . | Apetal . | 6, H. A. Spain . | . 1771 |
| montānā | . . | Apetal . | 6, H. A. Spain . | . 1806 |

**MIRĀBĪLIS**, *Linn.* From *mirabilis*, wonderful; alluding to the flowers. *Linn.* 5, Or. 1, Nat. Or. *Nyctaginaceæ*. Few plants make a more handsome appearance when in flower, either in the greenhouse or open border. They grow well in any light rich soil, and are increased by seeds. They may be planted out in the open border in spring, where they will do as well as in the greenhouse;

at the approach of winter the roots must be taken up, and kept dry and free from frost.

| | | | | | |
|---|---|---|---|---|---|
| dichōtōmā | . . | Yellow | . 7, G. Fu. P. Mexico . | . 1640 |
| hybridā | . . | White . | . 7, G. Fu. P. | . 1818 |
| Jalāpā | . . | Red . | . 7, G. Fu. P. W. Ind. | . 1596 |
| albā | . . | White . | . 7, G. Fu. P. W. Ind. | . 1596 |
| flāvā | . . | Yellow | . 7, G. Fu. P. W. Ind. | . 1596 |
| rūbrō ālbā | . . | Red wht. | . 7, G. Fu. P. W. Ind. | . 1596 |
| rūbrō-flāvā | . . | Red yel. | . 7, G. Fu. P. W. Ind. | . 1596 |
| longiflōrā | . . | White . | . 7, G. Fu. P. Mexico . | . 1759 |
| cārnēā | . . | Pink . | . 8, G. Fu. P. Germany | |
| violācēā | . . | Pink . | . 8, G. Fu. P. Germany | |
| suavēōlēns | . . | White . | . 7, G. Fu. P. Mexico . | . 1824 |

**MIRBĒLIĀ**, *Smith.* In honour of Mons. C. F. Brisseau Mirbel, one of the most distinguished vegetable physiologists of our age, and director of the Jardin du Roi at Paris. *Linn.* 10, Or. 1, Nat. Or. *Leguminosæ*. These are beautiful plants when in flower, and therefore worth a place in every greenhouse. Their culture and propagation is the same as *Pultenæa*, except that the cuttings must be young.

| | | | | | |
|---|---|---|---|---|---|
| Baxtēri | . . | Yellow | G. Ev. 8. N. Holl. | . 1825 |
| dilatātā | . . | Yellow | . 7, G. Ev. 8. N. Holl. | . 1803 |
| grandiflōrā | . . | Yellow | . 6, G. Ev. 8. N. Holl. | . 1825 |
| pūngēns | . . | Yellow | . 6, G. Ev. 8. N. Holl. | . 1824 |
| reticulātā | . . | Yellow | . 6, G. Ev. 8. N. S. W. | . 1792 |
| speciōsā | . . | Purple | . 6, G. Ev. 8. N. Holl. | . 1824 |

**MISTLETOE**, see *Viscūm*.

**MITCHĒLLĀ**, *Linn.* In honour of John Mitchell, M.D., a physician in Virginia, who described many Virginian plants. *Linn.* 4, Or. 1, Nat. Or. *Cinchonaceæ*. This plant grows well in a peat border, or in a pot filled with peat and sand mixed, and placed among alpine plants; it is easily increased by separating the running stem.

| | | | | | |
|---|---|---|---|---|---|
| rēpēns | . . . | White . | 6, H. Her. Cr. N. Amer. | . 1731 |

**MITĒLLĀ**, *Linn.* A diminutive of *mitra*, a mitre; the fruit being somewhat mitre-shaped. *Linn.* 10, Or. 2, Nat. Or. *Saxifragaceæ*. The plants of this genus are pretty, and well adapted for the front of flower-borders, or to grow on rock-work. They grow most luxuriantly in peat, and are easily increased by dividing the roots. Synonyme: 1. *M. reniformis.*

| | | | | | |
|---|---|---|---|---|---|
| cordifōliā | . . | White . | 5, H. Her. P. N. Amer. | . 1812 |
| diphyllā | . . | White . | 4, H. Her. P. N. Amer. | . 1731 |
| nūdā, 1 | . . | White . | 7, H. Her. P. N. Amer. | . 1758 |
| prostrātā | . . | White . | 5, H. Her. Tr. N. Amer. | . 1818 |
| trifīdā | . . | White . | 5, H. Her. P. N. Amer. | . 1827 |

**MITRĒLLĀ**, see *Drummondiā*.

**MITRASĀCMĒ**, *Labillardière.* From *mitra*, a mitre, and *acme*, a point. *Linn.* 4, Or. 1, Nat. Or. *Gentianaceæ*. These plants grow best in about three parts sandy peat, and one of loam; and may be increased by seeds, which should be sown as soon as possible.

| | | | | | |
|---|---|---|---|---|---|
| canēscēns | . . | White . | . 7, G. Her. P. N. S. W. | . 1824 |
| polymōrphā | . . | White . | . 6, G. A. N. S. W. | . 1826 |
| serpyllifōlia | . . | White . | . 7, G. A. N. S. W. | . 1826 |

**MITRIFORM**, formed like a mitre.

**MITRŪLĀ**, *Fries.* From *mitra*, a mitre. *Linn.* 24, Or. 9, Nat. Or. *Fungi*. These plants are found in wet ditches and fir woods. Synonymes: 1. *Leotia Mitrula*—*Abietis* 1, minūtā, uliginōsā.

**MNIARUM**, *Linn.* From *mniaros*, mossy. *Linn.* 1, Or. 2, Nat. Or. *Scleranthaceæ*. This plant grows in sandy peat, and may be increased by seed.

| | | | | | |
|---|---|---|---|---|---|
| biflōrūm | . . | White . | . 6, G. Her. P. N. Zeal. | . 1823 |

**MODĒCCĀ**, *Jacquin.* The East Indian name of one of the species. *Linn.* 22, Or. 5, Nat. Or. *Passifloraceæ*. These plants somewhat resemble *Passiflora* in habit, but are by no means so handsome. Their culture and propagation are the same.

| | | | | | |
|---|---|---|---|---|---|
| dūbiā | . . . | | 8. Ev. Cl. E. Ind. . | . 1826 |
| lobātā | . . . | Green . | 8, 8. Ev. Cl. S. Leone | . 1812 |
| trilobātā | . . . | | 8, 8. Ev. Cl. E. Ind. . | . 1818 |
| tuberōsā | . . . | | 8, 8. Ev. Cl. E. Ind. . | . 1822 |

**MOEHRINGIĀ**. In honour of Paul Henry Gerard Moerbing, a German physician and botanical author, 1736. *Linn.* 8, Or. 2, Nat. Or. *Alsinaceæ*. Very handsome alpine plants, well suited for ornamenting rock-work, or to be grown in pots in a mixture of sand, loam, and peat; and increased by dividing the plants at the root.

| | | | | | |
|---|---|---|---|---|---|
| muscōsā | . . | Li. pur. | . 6, H. Her. P. S. Eur. . | . 1775 |
| sedifōlia | . . | Wht. scar. | 6, H. Her. P. S. Eur. . | . 1823 |

MOGIPHĀNĒS, *Martius.* Name not explained. *Linn.* 5, Or. 1, Nat. Or. *Amarantaceæ.* This species may be successfully grown in sandy loam.

virgātā . . . . Whitish . 9, S.　B. Russia . . 1836

MOLDAVIAN BALM, see *Dracocēphālum moldāvīcūm.*

MOLINĒRIĀ, *Colladon.* After Ignatio Molineria, director of the botanic garden at Turin. *Linn.* 6, Or. 1, Nat. Or. *Amaryllidaceæ.* This little plant thrives well in peat and loam, and is increased by divisions.

plicātā . . . . Scar. yel. . 8, S. H. P. Java . . 1820

MOLINIĀ, *Mœnch.* In honour of J. Molina, a writer upon Chilian plants, in 1782. *Linn.* 3, Or. 2, Nat. Or. *Gramineæ.* Weeds not worth growing in any collection. *Synonyme:* 1. *Melica cærulea—cærūlēā* 1, *depauperātā.*

MŌLLĒ, soft, pliable.

MOLLŪGŌ, *Linn.* A name applied by Pliny to a plant supposed to be the same as our *Galium Mollugo*; given to this genus because of the resemblance of the species. *Linn.* 3, Or. 3, Nat. Or. *Illecebraceæ.* Stove annuals of no beauty. *Synonymes:* 1. *M. dichotoma.* 2. *M. Linkii—hīrtā, oppositifōliā, Schrānkii* 1, *triphȳllā* 2, *verticillātā.*

MOLOSPĒRMŪM, *Koch.* From *molops,* a stripe, and *sperma,* a seed; the fruit has the appearance of being striped. *Linn.* 5, Or. 2, Nat. Or. *Umbelliferæ.* This plant grows in any common soil, and is increased by dividing at the root, or by seeds. *Synonyme.* 1. *Ligusticum peloponnesiacum.*

peloponnesiācūm . Pa. yel. . 6, H. H. P. Switzerl. . 1598

MOLUCCA-BALM, see *Moluccēllā.*

MOLUCCĒLLĀ, *Linn.* The plants were supposed to be natives of the Molucca Islands. *Linn.* 14, Or. 1, Nat. Or. *Labiatæ.* The seed of these plants should be sown on a hotbed in spring, and when the plants are of sufficient size, they may be planted singly into pots, and kept under the glass till the end of May, when they may be planted out in a dry warm border, where they will flower and ripen their seeds freely.

lævis . . . . Pa. pur. . 7, H.　A. Syria . . 1570
Marrubiāstrūm . Purple . 7, H.　A. Siberia . . 1820
tuberōsā . . . Pa. pur. . 7, H. Tu. P. Tartary . 1796

MOMORDICĀ, *Linn.* From *mordeo,* to bite; the seeds have the appearance of being bitten. *Linn.* 21, Or. 10, Nat. Or. *Cucurbitaceæ.* Stove and frame twining annuals and perennials, of neither interest nor beauty—*Balsāmīnā, charāntiā, dioīcā, Elatērīūm, mīxtā, muricātā, operculātā, senegalēnsis, tubiflōrā, umbellātā.*

MONACHĀNTHŪS, *Lindley.* From *monachos,* a monk, and *anthos,* a flower; in allusion to the labellum of *M. viridis,* which is like a cowl: whence the English name of the genus, Monks'-flower. *Linn.* 20, Or. 1, Nat. Or. *Orchidaceæ.* Though not a handsome genus, it is rendered very interesting from the singular form of the flowers. They will grow and flower well when treated as the *Catasetums.*

discōlōr . . . . Pa. yel. . 9, S. Epi. Demerara . 1834
fimbriātūs . . . Orn. wht. 10, S. Epi. Pernamb. . 1837
virīdis . . . . Green . . 9, S. Epi. Brazil . .

MONĀCHNĒ, *Beauvois.* From *monos,* one, and *achne,* a glume. *Linn.* 3, Or. 2, Nat. Or. *Gramineæ.* A stove annual, not worth cultivating—*unilateralis.*

MONADELPHOUS, having the filaments cohering into a tube.

MONANDROUS, having only one stamen.

MONĀNTHĒS, *Haworth.* From *monos,* one, and *anthos,* a flower. *Linn.* 11, Or. 7, Nat. Or. *Crassulaceæ.* This may be referred to *Sempervivum* for culture and propagation. *Synonyme:* 1. *Sempervivum monanthes.*

polyphȳllā, 1 . . Red . . 8, G. H. P. Canaries . 1777

MONĀRDĀ, *Linn.* After N. Monarda, a physician of Seville, in the sixteenth century. *Linn.* 2, Or. 1, Nat. Or. *Labiatæ.* These plants are of easy culture, growing well in any common soil; and readily increased by dividing the roots. *M. aristata* and *M. punctata* should be grown in pots, in a mixture of peat and sand. *Synonymes:* 1. *M. citriodora.* 2. *M. Kalmiana.* 3 *M. affinis, M. altissima, M. media, M. oblongata, M. purpurea, M. rugosa.* 4. *M. menthæfolia.* 5. *M. mollis.*

[ 209 ]

aristāta. 1 . . . Yellow . 8, H. Her. P. S. Amer. . 1825
clinopōdiā . . . Pur. wht. 7, H. Her. P. N. Amer. . 1771
didȳmā, 2 . . . Scarlet . 7, H. Her. P. N. Amer. . 1752
fistulōsā, 3 . . . Purple . 7, H. Her. P. N. Amer. . 1656
flōre-maculātā, 4 Rose spot 6, H. Her. P. N. Orleans . 1832
mōllis, 5 . . . Lilac . 7, H. Her. P. N. Amer. . 1656
grācīlis . . . Purple . 7, H. Her. P. N. Amer. . 1820
punctātā . . . Yel. brn. 8, H. Her. P. N. Amer. . 1714
Russelliānā . . White . 9, H. Her. P. N. Amer. . 1823

MONĒMĀ, *Greville.* From *monos,* one, and *nema,* a filament; filaments simple. *Linn.* 24, Or. 7, Nat. Or. *Algæ.* These plants are only to be found in the sea—*apiculātūm, Dillwȳnii, obtūsūm, quadripunctātūm.*

MONĒRMĀ, *Beauvois.* From *monos,* one, and *herma,* a support. *Linn.* 1, Or. 2, Nat. Or. *Gramineæ.* A curious species, growing in any soil, and increased by seeds. *Synonymes:* 1. *Psillurus nardoides, Rottboellia monandra.*

monāndrūm, 1 . . Apetal . 7, Grass. Spain . . 1804

MONĒTIĀ, *L'Heritier.* In honour of Monet de la Marck, a famous French botanist. *Linn.* 4, Or. 1, Nat. Or. *Aquifoliaceæ.* An ornamental shrub, growing about three feet high, and succeeding in loam and peat, and readily increased by cuttings in sand, under a glass, in a little bottom heat. *Synonyme:* 1 *Azima tetracantha.*

bar'eriotdēs, 1 . Green . . 7, S. Ev. S. E. Ind. . . 1758

MONEYWORT, see *Dioscōrēā nummulārīā.*
MONEYWORT, see *Lysimāchiā nummulārīā.*
MONEYWORT, see *Tavernierā nummulārīā.*

MONILIĀ, *Persoon.* From *monile,* a necklace; the filaments are articulated. *Linn.* 24, Or. 9, Nat. Or. *Fungi.* This fungus is found in autumn on dead wood—*antennātā.*

MONILIFORM, formed like a necklace; that is to say, with alternate swellings and contractions, resembling a string of beads.

MONKEY-FLOWER, see *Mīmūlūs.*
MONK'S-HOOD, see *Acōnītūm.*
MONK'S-HOOD, see *Dielȳtrā cucullārīā.*

MONNIĒRĀ, *Aublet.* In honour of William le Monnier, once professor of botany in the Jardin du Roi, at Paris. *Linn.* 17, Or. 1, Nat. Or. *Rutaceæ.* A stove annual, of no beauty—*trifōliā.*

MONNINĀ, *Ruiz and Pavon.* In honour of Monnino, Count de Florida Blanca, a Spanish promoter of botany. *Linn.* 17, Or. 3, Nat. Or. *Polygalaceæ.* An ornamental shrub, growing in peat and loam, and increased by cuttings or seed.

obtusifōliā . . . Red . . 6, G. Ev. S. Peru . . 1830

MONOCOTYLEDONOUS, having only one seed-leaf or cotyledon.

MONŒCIOUS, having the one sex in one flower, and the other in another, on the same plant.

MONODŌRĀ, *Dunont.* From *monos,* one, and *dora,* a skin; in allusion to the fruit being one-celled. *Linn.* 13, Or. 6, Nat. Or. *Anonaceæ.* This plant thrives in a light sandy loam; and ripened cuttings root in sand, under a glass, in a moist heat. *Synonyme:* 1. *Anona Myristica.*

Myristicā　　　　　　　　　S. Ev. S. Jamaica . .

MONOPETALOUS, having only one petal.

MONOPSĪS, *Salisbury.* From *monos,* one, and *opsis,* a face; the flowers are regular, not bilabiate. *Linn.* 5, Or. 1, Nat. Or. *Lobeliaceæ.* This little plant deserves a place in every garden because of its neat, elegant, deep-blue flowers. The seeds should be raised on a hotbed, and when the plants are about an inch high, planted singly into pots, in a mixture of peat and sand; or they may be planted out in a sheltered situation in the open border in May. *Synonyme:* 1. *Lobelia speculum.*

conspicuā, 1 . . Blue . 7, H.　A. C. G. H. . 1812

MONOSEPALOUS, having only one sepal.
MONOSTĀCHYĀ, one-spiked.

MONŌTŌCĀ, *R. Brown.* From *monos,* one, and *tokos,* a birth; the fruit is one-seeded. *Linn.* 5, Or. 1, Nat. Or. *Epacridaceæ.* Very elegant plants; for culture and propagation, see *Leucopogon.* The pots must be well drained with potsherds. *Synonyme.* 1. *Styphelia glauca.*

alba . . . . . White . 6, G. Ev. S. N. S. W. . 1824
ellīptica . . . . White . 6, G. Ev. S. N. S. W. . 1802
2 E

lineătă, 1 . . . White . . 6, G. Ev. S. V. D. L. . 1804
scopăriă . . . White . . 6, G. Ev. S. N. S. W. . 1825

**MONŌTRŌPX**, *Linn.* From *monos*, one, and *tropeo*, to turn; the flowers are turned one way. *Linn.* 10, Or. 1, Nat. Or. *Ericaceæ.* Curious parasitical plants, growing on the roots of beech and pine trees in shady moist places.

Hypŏpĭtys . . . White . 6, H. Her. P. Britain . .
unĭflŏrā . . . White . 6, H. Her. P. N. Amer. . 1824

**MONSŌNIX**, *Linn.* In honour of Lady Ann Monson, the assistant of Lee in his Introduction to Botany. *Linn.* 16, Or. 7, Nat. Or. *Geraniaceæ.* This is a genus of beautiful plants, delighting in a mixture of turfy loam and leaf-mould. *M. ovata* is increased by seed, and the others may be propagated by cuttings, or by dividing the roots. *Synonyme:* 1. *M. speciosa.*

lobătă . . . Purple . 6, G. Her. P. C. G. H. . 1774
ovătă . . . White . 8, G. . . . . B. C. G. H. . 1774
pilōsă, l . . . White . 7, G. Her. P. C. G. H. . 1778
Collă . . . Pa. red . 7, G. Her. P. C. G. H. . 1820
speciōsă . . . Red . . 6, G. Her. P. C. G. H. . 1774
pallĭdă . . . Pa. red . 6, G. Her. P. C. G. H. .

**MONTANŌX**, *La Lave.* After Montanoa, a Mexican patriot. *Linn.* 19, Or. 4, Nat. Or. *Compositæ.* Greenhouse shrubs of no beauty, growing in any common soil, and increased by cuttings—*grandi-flŏră, tomentōsă.*

**MONTEZŪMX**. Named by Mocino and Sesse, two Mexican botanists, in honour of Montezuma, a sovereign of Mexico. *Linn.* 16, Or. 7; Nat. Or. *Sterculiaceæ.* An ornamental, large-growing tree; loam and peat suit it best, and cuttings of the half-ripened wood will root in sand, plunged in heat.

speciosissimă . . Red . . . 8. Ev. T. Mexico . . 1827

**MŌNTIX**, *Linn.* In honour of Joseph Monti, Ph. D., professor of botany, and a botanical author, 1791. *Linn.* 3, Or. 3, Nat. Or. *Portulaceæ.* This genus is nearly akin to *Claytonia.* The plants are well-known British aquatics—*fontānă, rivulāris.*

**MONTINIX**, *Linn.* In honour of Laurence Montin, a Swedish botanist. *Linn.* 22, Or. 4, Nat. Or. *Ona-graceæ.* This species is not possessed of much beauty; it thrives well in peat and loam, and is increased by cuttings.

caryophyllăcĕă . White . 7, G. Ev. S. C. G. H. . 1774

**MOON-SEED**, see *Menispĕrmŭm.*
**MOON-TREFOIL**, see *Medicăgŏ arbŏrĕă.*
**MOONWORT**, see *Botrgchĭŭm.*
**MOONWORT**, see *Rŭmĕx Lunārĭă.*

**MORÆX**, *Linn.* In honour of R. Moore, a botanist of Shrewsbury. *Linn.* 3, Or. 1, Nat. Or. *Iridaceæ.* This is a very elegant genus of bulbous-rooted plants. For culture and propagation, see *Ixia.* *Synonyme:* 1. *M. edulis lutescens.*

angŭstă . . . Lilac . 6, G. Bl. P. C. G. H. . 1790
barbigĕră . . . Purple . 5, G. Bl. P. C. G. H. . 1587
bitumĭnōsă . . Yellow . 5, G. Bl. P. C. G. H. . 1787
catenulătă . . Wht. blue 5, G. Her. P. Maurit. . 1826
ciliātă . . . Yellow . 9, G. Bl. P. C. G. H. . 1587
crispă . . . Blue . . 5, G. Bl. P. C. G. H. . 1803
edŭlĭs . . . Fulvous 5, G. Bl. P. C. G. H. . 1792
longifŏlĭă, l . Yellow . 5, G. Bl. P. C. G. H. . 1808
longiflŏră . . . Yellow . 5, G. Bl. P. C. G. H. . 1801
minŭtă . . . Blue . . 6, G. Bl. P. C. G. H. . 1825
odŏră . . . Lilac . . 6, G. Bl. P. C. G. H. . 1792
papilionăcĕă . Varieg. . 5, G. Bl. P. C. G. H. . 1795
plumārĭs . . Yellow . 5, G. Bl. P. C. G. H. . 1825
polystăchyă . . Yellow . 6, G. Bl. P. C. G. H. . 1825
ramōsă . . . Yellow . 5, G. Bl. P. C. G. H. . 1789
setăcĕă . . . Yellow . 5, G. Bl. P. C. G. H. . 1825
Sisyrinchĭŭm . Blue . . 5, H. Bl. P. S. Eur. . 1597
Tenorĭānă . . Purple . 6, H. Bl. P. Naples . 1824
tristis . . . Blue . . 6, G. Bl. P. C. G. H. . 1768
viscārĭs . . . Lilac . . 5, G. Bl. P. C. G. H. . 1800

**MORCHĔLLX**, *Dillwyn.* Derived from *morchel*, the German name of the plant. *Linn.* 24, Or. 9, Nat. Or. *Fungi.* A genus of eatable *Fungi*, found upon the ground — *esculĕntă, e. rotŭndă, e. vulgārĭs, hybrĭdă, pătŭlă.*

**MORDANT**, that which enables matter to receive dyes or colouring matter, and to retain them.

**MOREXŌX**, *La Lave.* In honour of P. Moreno, a Mexican patriot. *Linn.* 5, Or. 1, Nat. Or. *Con-volvulaceæ.* Ornamental plants, growing in a mixture of peat and loam; and cuttings root readily in sand, under a glass, in heat.

---

globōsă . . . Scarlet . 8. Ev. Tw. Mexico . 1837
grandiflŏră . . Scarlet . 8. Ev. Tw. Mexico . 1826
pătŭlă . . . Scarlet . 8. Ev. Tw. Mexico . 1826

**MORICĂNDIX**, *Decandolle.* In honour of Stephen Moricand, an Italian botanist and author. *Linn.* 15, Nat. Or. *Cruciferæ.* A very pretty plant; the seed only requires sowing in the open ground early in spring. *Synonyms:* 1. *Brassica arvensis.*

arvĕnsis . . . Violet . 7, H. B. Europe . . 1739

**MORĪNX**, *Linn.* In honour of L. Morin, a French botanist. *Linn.* 2, Or. 1, Nat. Or. *Dipsaceæ.* This is an ornamental plant, but seldom to be met with in collections; it grows well in a light rich soil, and is increased by seed.

pĕrsĭcă . . . Red wht. 7, G. Her. P. Persia . . 1740

**MORĪNDX**, *Ventenat.* Altered from *Morus Indica*, or Indian Mulberry, because of the shape of its fruit, and native country. *Linn.* 5, Or. 1, Nat. Or. *Cinchonaceæ.* Ornamental plants, growing freely in a mixture of loam and peat; and cuttings root readily in the same kind of soil, under a glass, in a moist heat.

angustifŏlĭă . . White . 5, S. Ev. S. E. Ind. . 1816
bracteătă . . . White . 5, S. Ev. S. E. Ind. . 1816
citrifŏlĭă . . . White . 8. Ev. S. E. Ind. . 1793
jasminoĭdĕs . . Pa. buff. 4, G. Ev. Cl. Pt. Jackson 1823
Rŏybe . . . White . 8, S. Ev. S. W. Ind. . 1793

**MORĪNGX**, *Burmann. Muringo* is the name of the species in Malabar. *Linn.* 10, Or. 1, Nat. Or. *Moringaceæ.* This plant thrives well in light loamy soil, and cuttings root freely in sand, under a glass, in heat. The young roots of this tree are scraped, and used by the inhabitants of the places of its natural growth as horse-radish is in Europe, having much the same sharp taste. *Synonyme:* 1. *Hyperanthera Moringa.*

pterygospĕrmă . Yellow . 8. Ev. T. E. Ind. . . 1759

**MORĪSIX**, *Cassini.* In honour of Professor Moris, who discovered the species. *Linn.* 15, Nat. Or. *Cru-ciferæ.* This plant is well fitted for ornamenting rock-work, where its bright yellow flowers contrast well with its deep-green polished leaves; it is increased by seed sown as soon as ripe.

hypogæă . . . Yellow . 6, H. Her. P. Sardinia . 1833

**MORISŌNIX**, *Plumier.* In honour of Robert Morison, a Scotchman, professor of botany at Oxford, who died in 1683. *Linn.* 16, Or. 8, Nat. Or. *Capparidaceæ.* An ornamental plant, which grows well in a mixture of loam and peat; and cuttings of the ripened wood will root in sand, under a glass, in a gentle heat. *Synonyme:* 1. *Capparis Morisoni.*

americānă, 1 . . White . 8. Ev. T. W. Ind. . 1824

**MORMŌDĔS**, *Lindley.* From *mormo*, a frightful-looking object, a goblin; in allusion to the strange appearance of the flowers. *Linn.* 20, Or. 1, Nat. Or. *Orchidaceæ.* These are very singular plants when in flower. For culture and propagation, see *Cata-setum.*

atropurpŭrĕă . . Purple . 10, S. Epi. S. Mexi. . 1834
pardĭnă . . . Redsh. pur. 7, S. Epi. Oaxaca . .

**MŌRNX**, *Lindley.* Morna, a heroine of Northern romances. *Linn.* 19, Or. 1, Nat. Or. *Compositæ.* This is a genus of very beautiful plants, well deserving of cultivation. They are half-hardy annuals, and may be had to flower in the greenhouse from May to the end of August, if sown at two different seasons. Plants intended to flower in May should be sown the preceding September, and plants for autumn flowering should be sown in February. The seeds should be sown in pots, in sandy peat and leaf mould, and placed in the greenhouse; the young plants should be potted off when small into sixties, two plants in each pot close to the side, shifting them into larger ones as they require it, keeping them near the glass in a dry, airy part of the house. They must be very cautiously watered, as too much or too little will, in a few hours, destroy the healthiest plants; the pots should therefore be well drained, and the plants should not receive too great a shift at any time. If they are intended to flower in the open border, the plants must not be planted out before the end of May, as the least frost kills them.

| | | | | | |
|---|---|---|---|---|---|
| alٟidă | . . . . | Yellow | . 2, G. | A. S. River. | . 1835 |
| niveă | . . . . | Wht. yel. | . 7, G. | A. S. River. | . 1836 |

MORRĔNĬĂ, *Lindley*. In honour of Professor Charles Morren, of Liege, one of the most distinguished vegetable anatomists of the present day. *Linn*. 5, Or. 2, Nat. Or. *Asclepiadaceæ*. This is a very curious little plant, requiring the same treatment as the greenhouse species of *Cynanchum*.

| | | | | | |
|---|---|---|---|---|---|
| odorătă | . . . | Green | . 7, G. | Ev. Tw. E. Ayres | . 1837 |

MŌRŬS, *Linn*. From the Celtic word *mor*, signifying black; in allusion to the colour of the fruit. *Linn*. 21, Or. 4, Nat. Or. *Urticaceæ*. The species of Morus or Mulberry, grow from ten to thirty feet high. A moist situation and loamy soil suit them best. *M. nigra* is in general cultivation for the sake of its fruit, which is well known. *M. alba* is extensively cultivated for food for the silk-worms. *Synonymes*: 1. *M. sinensis*. 2. *M. alba ovalifolia*. 3. *M. pumila*, *M. nana*. 4. *M. sinensis*. 5. *M. pennsylvanica*.

| | | | | | |
|---|---|---|---|---|---|
| albă | . . | Apetal | 6, H. De. T. China | | . 1596 |
| Columbăssă | . | Apetal | H. De. T. | | |
| italĭcă, 1 | . . | Apetal | 6, H. De. T. Italy | | . 1817 |
| macrophyllă | . | Apetal | 6, H. De. T. China | | . . |
| membranăceă | . | Apetal | H. De. T. | | |
| Morettiănă | . | Apetal | 6, H. De. T. | | |
| multicaŭlis | . | Apetal | 6, H. De. T. China | | . . |
| pūmĭlă, 3 | . | Apetal | 6, H. De. T. China | | . . |
| rŏseă | . . | Apetal | 6, H. De. T. China | | . . |
| sĭnĕnsĭs, 4 | . | Apetal | 6, H. De. T. | | |
| calcăr gallĭ | . | Apetal | H. Ev. S. N. S. W. | | . 1830 |
| constantinopolĭtănă | Apetal | 6, H. De. T. Turkey | | . 1818 |
| indĭcă | . . | Apetal | S. Ev. T. E. Ind. | | . 1824 |
| mauritiănă | . | Apetal | S. Ev. T. Mauritius | | . 1823 |
| nĭgră | . . | Apetal | 6, H. De. T. Italy | | . 1548 |
| lacinĭătă | . | Apetal | 6, H. De. T. | | |
| rŭbră, 5 | . . | Apetal | 6, H. De. T. N. Amer. | | . 1629 |
| scăbră | . . | Apetal | 6, H. De. T. N. Amer. | | . 1817 |
| tatărĭcă | . . | Apetal | 6, H. De. T. Tartary | | . 1784 |

MOSCHĂRĬĂ, *Ruiz and Pavon*. From *moschos*, musk; on account of the smell of the plant. *Linn*. 19, Or. 1, Nat. Or. *Compositæ*. This pretty annual is found in sandy waste places in Chile; in this country, it requires the treatment common to half-hardy annuals.

| | | | | | |
|---|---|---|---|---|---|
| pinnatifĭdă | . . | | . 7, H. | A. Chile | . 1823 |

MOSCHATEL, see *Adŏxă*.

MOSCHŌSMĂ, *Reichenbach*. From *moschos*, musk, and *osme*, a smell. *Linn*. 14, Or. 1, Nat. Or. *Labiatæ*. Interesting annuals; the seed should be sown in light rich soil on a hotbed, and afterwards planted out in the open ground, or potted, and placed among the stove plants. *Synonymes*: 1. *Lumnitzera ocymoides*. 2. *Ocymum polystachyon*, *Lumnitzera polystachya*.

| | | | | | |
|---|---|---|---|---|---|
| ocymoĭdĕs, 1 | . | White | . 8, S. | A. | 1823 |
| polystachyă, 2 | . | White | . 7, S. | A. E. Ind. | . 1783 |

MOTH, see *Verbascum Blattărĭă*.

MOTHERWORT, see *Leonūrŭs*.

MOTTLED, marked with blotches of colour of unequal intensity, passing insensibly into each other.

MOUGEŌTĬĂ, *Agardh*. After J. B. Mougeot, a cryptogamic botanist. *Linn*. 24, Or. 7, Nat. Or. *Algæ*. These little plants are found in ditches—*cærulescēns*, *genuflexă*.

MOULDINESS, see *Aspergillŭs*.

MOUNTAIN-ASH, see *Pȳrŭs aucupărĭă*.

MOUNTAIN-EBONY, see *Bauhĭnĭă*.

MOUNTAIN-PARSLEY, see *Selĭnŭm oreoselĭnŭm*.

MOUNTAIN-SORREL, see *Oxȳrĭă*.

MOURĬRĬĂ, *Jussieu*. From *Mouriri*, the native name of *M. guianensis*. *Linn*. 10, Or. 1, Nat. Or. *Memecylaceæ*. These plants require to be grown in a mixture of loam and peat; and cuttings of the young wood will root in sand, under a glass, in heat. *Synonymes*: 1. *Petaloma mouriri*. 2. *P. myrtilloides*.

| | | | | | |
|---|---|---|---|---|---|
| guianĕnsĭs, 1 | . | Yellow | . 8, S. Ev. S. Guiana | | . 1817 |
| myrtilloĭdĕs, 2 | . | Wht. yel. | 8. Ev. S. W. Ind. | | . 1823 |

MOUSE-EAR, see *Hierăcĭŭm pilosĕllă*.

MOUSE-EAR CHICKWEED, see *Cerastĭŭm*.

MOUSE-TAIL, see *Myosūrŭs*.

MOUSE-TAIL, see *Mygalūrŭs*.

MOUSE-TAIL, see *Dendrōbĭŭm Myosūrŭs*.

MOUSE-THORN, see *Centaŭrĕă myacănthă*.

MOVING PLANT, see *Desmōdĭŭm gȳrăns*.

MŌXĂ, see *Artemĭsĭă chinĕnsĭs*.

[ 211 ]

MUCILAGE, a turbid slimy fluid.

MUCŎR, *Michaux*. From *muceo*, to be musty. *Linn*. 24, Or. 9, Nat. Or. *Fungi*. The plants grow on musty bread and vegetables—*amethystĕŭs*, *canĭnŭs*, *clavātŭs*, *delicatŭlŭs*, *fusĭgĕr*, *stercŏrĭŭs*.

MUCRONATE, sharp-pointed.

MUCRONE, a small sharp point.

MUCRONULATE, having a little hard sharp point.

MUCŪNĂ, *Adanson*. *Mucuna-guaca* is the Brazilian name of *M. urens*. *Linn*. 17, Or. 4, Nat. Or. *Leguminosæ*. These plants are not possessed of much beauty. A rich soil suits the species of Cow-itch, and they are readily increased by cuttings. The stinging effects of the hairs of the pods of *M. pruriens* are well known. A strong infusion of the roots of the same plant, sweetened with honey, is used by the Indian doctors in cases of cholera-morbus. *Synonymes*: 1. *Stizolobium altissimum*. 2. *Carpopogon giganteus*. 3. *C. imbricatus*. 4. *S. pruriens*. 5. *S. urens*, *Dolichos urens*.

| | | | | | |
|---|---|---|---|---|---|
| altissĭmă, 1 | . | Purple | . | S. Ev. Cl. Martinico | . 1779 |
| anguĭnĕă | . . | | | S. Ev. Cl. E. Ind. | . 1817 |
| atropurpūrĕă | . | Purple | . | S. Ev. Cl. E. Ind. | . 1820 |
| bracteătă | . . | | | S. Ev. Cl. E. Ind. | . 1826 |
| imbricătă, 3 | . | Purple | . | S. Ev. Cl. E. Ind. | . 1815 |
| prūrĭĕns, 4 | . | Purple | . | S. Ev. Cl. E. Ind. | . 1680 |
| ūrĕns, 5 | . | Yellow | . 6, S. Ev. Cl. W. Ind. | | . 1691 |

*gigănteă 2*, *macrocerătĭdĕs*, *mĭtĭs*, *monospĕrmă*, *nĭvĕă*.

MUDWORT, see *Limosĕllă*.

MUGWORT, see *Artemĭsĭă vulgārĭs*.

MULBERRY, see *Mōrŭs*.

MULCH, a gardener's term for the placing manure about the roots of trees, on the surface of the ground.

MULLEIN, see *Verbascŭm*.

MULLĔRĂ, *Linn*. In honour of Otto Frederick Muller, a Dane, and one of the editors of the Flora Danica. *Linn*. 16, Or. 6, Nat. Or. *Leguminosæ*. An ornamental tree, growing in loam and peat mixed; and cuttings of the young wood will root in sand, under a glass, in heat.

| | | | | | |
|---|---|---|---|---|---|
| monilifŏrmĭs | . | Yellow | . | S. Ev. T. Guiana | . 1792 |

MULTICOSPĬS, many-jointed.

MULTIFARIOUS, very numerous, or arranged in many rows.

MULTIFID, cleft into many parts.

MULTIFIDLY-PINNATIFID; a leaf is so called when it is pinnately-lŏbed, and these lobes are again divided into many parts.

MULTIPARTITE, divided into many parts.

MULTIPLEX, much multiplied.

MŬNDĬĂ, *Kunth*. From *mundus*, neat; in allusion to the appearance of the plants. *Linn*. 17, Or. 3, Nat. Or. *Polygalaceæ*. This species, and its variety, are well worth cultivating for the sake of their flowers and fruit, which are very pretty. Sandy peat is the best soil for them; they are readily increased by young cuttings in sand, under a glass. *Synonymes*: 1. *Polygala spinosa*. 2. *P. viminea*.

| | | | | | |
|---|---|---|---|---|---|
| spinŏsă, 1 | . . | White | . 3, G. Ev. S. C. G. H. | | . 1780 |
| angustifolĭă, 2 | . | Purple | . 3, G. Ev. S. C. G. H. | | . 1800 |

MUNTĬNGĬĂ, *Linn*. In honour of Abraham Munting, professor of botany at Groningen; he died in 1683. *Linn*. 13, Or. 1, Nat. Or. *Tiliaceæ*. The flowers of this curious shrub bear a strong resemblance to those of the bramble, while the fruit is as like the cherry; it thrives well in a light loamy soil, and may be increased by cuttings in sand, under a glass, plunged in heat.

| | | | | | |
|---|---|---|---|---|---|
| Calabŭră | . . | White | . 6, S. Ev. S. Jamaica | | . 1690 |

MURĂLTĬĂ, *Necker*. In honour of John Von Muralt, a Swiss botanist. *Linn*. 17, Or. 3, Nat. Or. *Polygalaceæ*. This beautiful genus of furze-like plants are highly deserving every care in cultivating them. A sandy peat soil suits them, and cuttings, taken from the young wood, will root in sand, under a glass. *Synonymes*: 1. *Polygala alopecuroides*. 2. *P. filiformis*. 3. *P. Heisteria*. 4. *P. humilis*. 5. *P. mixta*.

| | | | | | |
|---|---|---|---|---|---|
| alopecuroĭdĕs, 1 | . | Purple | . 6, G. Ev. S. C. G. H. | | . 1800 |
| ciliărĭs | . . | Purple | . 5, G. Ev. S. C. G. H. | | . 1824 |
| diffŭsă | . . | Purple | . G. Ev. S. C. G. H. | | . 1800 |
| filifŏrmĭs | . | Purple | . 8, G. Ev. S. C. G. H. | | . 1812 |
| Heisterĭă, 3 | . | Purple | . 1, G. Ev. S. C. G. H. | | . 1787 |
| hūmĭlĭs, 4 | . | Purple | . 6, G. Ev. S. C. G. H. | | . 1818 |
| juniperifolĭă, 4 | . | Purple | . 6, G. Ev. S. C. G. H. | | . 1810 |

| linophyllă | . . | Purple | . 6, G. Ev. S. C. G. H. | . 1816 |
|---|---|---|---|---|
| maeröcerăs | . . | Purple | . G. Ev. S. C. G. H. | . 1812 |
| micrănthă | . . | Purple | . G. Ev. S. C. G. H. | . 1800 |
| mixtă, 5 | . . | Purple | . G. Ev. S. C. G. H. | . 1791 |
| squarrösă | . . | Purple | . 5, G. Ev. S. C. G. H. | . 1820 |
| stipulăceă | . . | Red | . 6, G. Ev. S. C. G. H. | . 1801 |
| virgătă | . . | Purple | . 7, S. Ev. S. C. G. H. | . 1823 |

MURICĂRIĂ, *Desfontaines.* From *muricatus*, full of prickles; the pods are beset with prickles. *Linn.* 15, Nat. Or. *Cruciferæ.* A hardy annual, not worth a place in any collection. *Synonyme:* 1. *Bunias prostrata—prostrătă* 1.

MURICATE, covered with short, sharp points.

MURICATELY-HISPID, covered with short, sharp, stiff bristles.

MURRĂYĂ, *Konig.* In honour of John Adam Murray, once professor of botany at Gottingen, and editor of some of Linnæus's works. *Linn.* 10, Or. 1, Nat. Or. *Aurantiaceæ.* These shrubs are well worthy of cultivation for the sake of their sweet-scented flowers. They thrive well in a mixture of turfy loam and peat; and cuttings of the ripened wood, not deprived of any of their leaves, will root in sand, under a glass, in a moist heat.

| exötică | . . . | White | . 8, S. Ev. S E. Ind. | . 1771 |
|---|---|---|---|---|
| paniculătă | . . | White | . 7, S. Ev. T. E. Ind. | . 1823 |

MURUCÖYĂ, *Tournefort.* The name of the species in Brazil. *Linn.* 16, Or. 2, Nat. Or. *Passifloraceæ.* This is a genus of plants nearly allied to *Passiflora*, which see for culture and propagation. *Synonymes:* 1. *Passiflora Murucuia.* 2. *P. perfoliata.*

| ocellatŭ, 1 | . . | Scarlet | . 7, S. Ev. Cl. W. Ind. | . 1730 |
|---|---|---|---|---|
| perfoliătă, 2 | . . | Purple | . 7, S. Ev. Cl. W. Ind. | . 1816 |

MÜsă, *Linn.* Altered from the Egyptian Mauz, in honour of Antonius Musa. *Linn.* 5, Or. 1, Nat. Or. *Musaceæ.* To this genus belong those universally-esteemed fruits the *Banana* and *Plantain*, but from these plants growing to twenty-five or thirty feet high, they are rarely seen in perfection in this country on account of the quantity of room required; but the valuable species, *M. Cavendishii*, does not grow more than four or five feet high, so that any one possessing a moderate-sized house may, with a very little trouble, be rewarded by abundance of its excellent fruit, which is much superior to that of any of the other species. They all thrive best in a rich soil, requiring plenty of room and moisture; they are increased by suckers, which the old plants produce in abundance. It is considered that no known plant produces anything like the same quantity of nutriment from the same space of ground, as the *Banana*. It is indigenous to all the tropics, and from the numerous uses to which it is applied we may mention the following. The tops of the young plants are eaten as a delicate vegetable; the fermented juice of the trunks produces an agreeable wine. The fruit is served up both raw and stewed; slices fried are also considered a delicacy; and, finally, the leaves are used for thatching and basket-making.

| Cavendishii | . | Scarlet | . 8. Her. P. China | . 1829 |
|---|---|---|---|---|
| coccineă | . | Scarlet | . 7, S. Her. P. China | . 1792 |
| glaücă | . | Pink | . 8. Her. P. E. Ind. | . 1824 |
| maculătă | . | Pink | . 8. Her. P. Mauritius | . 1818 |
| nepalĕnsis | . | Yellow | . 2, S. Her. P. Nepal | . 1823 |
| ornătă | . | Orange | . 7, S. Her. P. E. Ind. | . 1823 |
| paradisiăcă | . | Pink | . 11, S. Her. P. Tropics | . 1690 |
| rosăceă | . | Pink | . 8, S. Her. P. Mauritius | . 1805 |
| sapiĕntŭm | . | Pink | . 6, S. Her. P. Tropics | . 1729 |
| supĕrbă | . | Purple | . 7, S. Her. P. E. Ind. | . 1820 |

MUSCĂRI, *Desfontaines.* From *moschos*, musk; smell of the flowers. *Linn.* 6, Or. 1, Nat. Or. *Liliaceæ.* Some of the species of this genus are very handsome, and should be planted near the front of flower-beds or borders; they thrive well in sandy loam, and are readily increased by offsets from the bulbs. *Synonymes:* 1. *M. moschatum, flavum.* 2. *Hyacinthus moschatus.*

| botryoïdĕs | . . | Blue | . 4, H. Bl. P. Italy | . 1596 |
|---|---|---|---|---|
| albŭm | . . | White | . 4, H. Bl. P. Italy | . 1596 |
| pallidŭm | . . | Pa. blue | . 4, H. Bl. P. Italy | . 1596 |
| ciliătŭm | . . | Brn. pur. | . 5, H. Bl. P. Crimea | . 1822 |
| commutătŭm | . . | Blue | . H. Bl. P. Italy | . 1836 |
| comösŭm | . . | Blue | . 5, H. Bl. P. S. Eur. | . 1596 |
| monströsŭm | . . | Pa. blue | . 4, H. Bl. P. S. Eur. | . 1596 |
| glaücŭm | . . | Pur. grn. | . 5, H. Bl. P. Persia | . 1825 |
| macrocărpŭm, 1 | . | Grn. yel. | . 4, H. Bl. P. Levant | . 1596 |
| moschătŭm, 2 | . | Blue yel. | . 4, H. Bl. P. Levant | . 1596 |

| pallĕns | . . | Pa. blue | . 5, H. Bl. P. Crimea | . 1822 |
|---|---|---|---|---|
| parviflörŭm | . | Blue | . 4, H. Bl. P. Sicily | . 1827 |
| pedunculărĕ | . | Blue | . 4, H. Bl. P. | |
| racemösŭm | . | Blue | . 4, H. Bl. P. Europe | . 1780 |
| minŭs | . | Blue | . 4, H. Bl. P. Europe | . 1780 |

MUSCĬFERĂ, resembling a fly.

MUSCĬPŬLĂ, mouse or fly trap.

MUSSÆNDĂ, *Linn.* The name of *M. frondosa* in Ceylon. *Linn.* 5, Or. 1, Nat. Or. *Cinchonaceæ.* Some of these plants are very pretty. They all grow well in a mixture of loam and peat; and cuttings root freely in the same kind of soil, under a glass, in heat. *Synonyme:* 1. *Macrocnemum coccineum.*

| arcuătă | . . . | Yellow | . 8. Ev. S. L. France | . 1822 |
|---|---|---|---|---|
| chinĕnsis | . . . | . | 8. Ev. S. China | . 1820 |
| coccinĕă, 1 | . . | Red | . 8. S. Ev. T. Trinidad | . 1825 |
| frondösă | . . | Yellow | . 8, S. Ev. S. E. Ind. | . 1814 |
| glăbră | . . | Orange | . 7, S. Ev. S. E. Ind. | . 1820 |
| Landiă | . . | . | 7, S. Ev. S. I. France | . 1824 |
| pubĕscĕns | . . | Yellow | . 7, S. Ev. S. China | . 1805 |
| speciösă | . . | Red | . 8. S. Ev. S. Trinidad | . 1820 |

MUTABLE, changeable, inconstant.

MUTATE, changed.

MUTĬSIĂ, *Linn.* In honour of Celestine Mutis, a South American botanist, and discoverer of this his genus. *Linn.* 19, Or. 2, Nat. Or. *Compositæ.* Very pretty climbers, requiring to be grown in peat and loam; and cuttings root in sand, under a glass, in a gentle heat. *Synonyme:* 1. *M. speciosa.*

| arachnoïdĕs, 1 | . | Red | . 7, S. Ev. Cl. Brasil | . 1823 |
|---|---|---|---|---|
| iliciföliă | . . . | . | G. Ev. Cl. S. Amer. | . 1832 |
| latiföliă | . . . | Pnk. yel. | . 9, G. Ev. Cl. Valparaiso | . 1832 |

MYĂGRŬM, *Tournefort.* From *myia*, a fly, and *agra*, capture; an ancient plant was so named from its properties of catching flies. *Linn.* 15, Nat. Or. *Cruciferæ.* The seed of this pretty annual has only to be sown in the open ground.

| perfoliătŭm | . . | Pa. yel. | . 6, H. | A. France | . 1648 |
|---|---|---|---|---|---|

MYĂNTHŬS, *Lindley.* From *myia*, a fly; when the flowers are dried they look very much like a fly pressed flat. *Linn.* 20, Or. 1, Nat. Or. *Orchidaceæ.* This is a very curious genus of plants, and like other plants of a similar habit, they are easily cultivated, provided they are placed in a cool house and kept dry for some months, and afterwards vigorously forced in the same manner as the *Catasetums.*

| barbătŭs | . . . | Grn. pur. | . 2, S. Epi. Demerara | |
|---|---|---|---|---|
| immaculătŭs | . . | Grn. pur. | . 3, S. Epi. Demerara | . 1835 |
| cernŭŭs | . . | Grn. pur. | . 5, S. Epi. Brazil | |
| deltoïdĕs | . . | Grn. pink | 10, S. Epi. Demerara | . 1835 |

MYCĬNEMĂ, *Agardh.* From *mykes*, a kind of minute fungus, and *nema*, a thread. *Linn.* 24, Or. 7, Nat. Or. *Algæ.* The plants composing this genus are found on rotten wood—*arachnoïdĕŭm, fŭlvŭm, phosphörĕŭm, pulvĕrĕŭm, rubiginösŭm.*

MYOSŬRŬS, *Link.* From *mygale*, a field-mouse, and *oura*, a tail. *Linn.* 3, Or. 2, Nat. Or. *Gramineæ.* Mere annual weeds. *Synonymes:* 1. *Festuca bromoides.* 2. *F. myurus.* 3. *F. uniglumis—alopecuroïdĕs, bromoïdĕs* 1, *caudătŭs* 2, *delicătŭlăs, stipoïdĕs, uniglŭmis*, 3.

MYGĬNDĂ, *Jacquin.* In honour of Francis Von Mygind, a German botanist. *Linn.* 4, Or. 3, Nat. Or. *Aquifoliaceæ.* These plants grow freely in loam and peat, and cuttings of the ripened wood will root in sand, under a glass; the stove species in heat. *Synonyme:* 1. *Ilex Myrsinitis.*

| integriföliă | . . | White | . 8. Ev. S. Martinique | 1826 |
|---|---|---|---|---|
| latiföliă | . . | White | . 4, S. Ev. S. W. Ind. | . 1795 |
| myrtiföliă, 1 | . . | White | . 6, H. Ev. S. N. Amer. | . 1818 |
| Rhacömă | . . | White | . 8, S. Ev. S. Jamaica | . 1793 |
| uragögă | . . | Purple | . 8, S. Ev. S. S. Amer. | . 1790 |

MYLOCĂRYŬM, *Willdenow.* From *myle*, mill, and *karyon*, a nut; the seeds have four wings. *Linn.* 10, Or. 1, Nat. Or. *Celastraceæ.* An ornamental species, with the habit of *Andromeda*; it may be successfully grown in loam and peat, and cuttings will root in sand, under a glass. *Synonyme:* 1. *Cliftonia ligustrina.*

| ligŭstrinŭm, 1 | . White | . 5, F. Ev. S. Georgia. | |
|---|---|---|---|

MYÖPÖRŬM, *Banks.* From *myo*, to shut, and *poros*, a pore; in reference to the leaves. *Linn.* 14, Or. 2, Nat. Or. *Myoporaceæ.* Pretty shrubs, delighting in a mixture of loam and peat; and cuttings will root readily in sand, under a glass. *Synonyme:* 1 *Pogonia glabra.*

| | | | | |
|---|---|---|---|---|
| acuminatum | . White | . G. Ev. S. N. S. W. | . 1818 |
| adscendens | . White | . G. Ev. S. N. Holl. | . 1820 |
| crassifolium | . White | . G. Ev. S. N. Zeal. | . 1822 |
| debile | . White . | 6, G. Ev. S. N. S. W. | . 1793 |
| diffusum | . White . | 4, G. Ev. S. N. Holl. | |
| ellipticum, l | . White . | 2, G. Ev. S. N. S. W. | . 1789 |
| insulare | . White . | 2, G. Ev. S. N. S. W. | . 1800 |
| montanum | . White | . G. Ev. S. N. Holl. | . 1823 |
| oppositifolium | . White | . G. Ev. S. N. Holl. | . 1803 |
| parvifolium | . White | . G. Ev. S. N. Holl. | . 1803 |
| tuberculatum | . White | . G. Ev. S. N. Holl. | . 1803 |
| viscosum | . White | . G. Ev. S. N. Holl. | . 1803 |

MYOSERIS, *Link*. From *mys*, a mouse, and *seris*, succory. *Linn.* 19, Or. 1, Nat. Or. *Compositæ*. This species will grow in any common soil, and is increased by divisions. *Synonyme*: 1. *Borkhausia purpurea*.

| | | | | |
|---|---|---|---|---|
| purpurea | . . Purple | . 5, H. Her. P. Tauria | . 1824 |

MYOSOTIS, *Linn.* From *mys*, *myos*, a mouse, and *otos*, an ear; fancied resemblance in the leaves. *Linn.* 5, Or. 1, Nat. Or. *Boraginaceæ*. All the perennial species of this genus are very beautiful, especially *M. palustris*, the Forget-me-not. They grow best in moist places, or by the edges of ponds or ditches; they may also be grown in pots among alpine plants. The annual species like a dry sandy soil. Most of the perennial species may be increased by divisions of the roots, and all by seeds. *Synonymes*: 1. *M. lithospermifolia, M. rupicola, M. suaveolens*.

| | | | | |
|---|---|---|---|---|
| alpestris | . . Blue | . 7, H. Her. P. Switzerl. | . 1818 |
| arvensis | | | |
| alba | . White . | 6, H. | A. Britain | . |
| caespitosa | . Blue . | 6, H. Aq. P. Britain | . |
| macrocalyx | . Blue . | 6, H. Aq. P. Britain | . |
| californica | . White . | 8, H. | A. Californ. | . 1837 |
| collina | . Blue . | 5, H. | A. Britain | . |
| intermedia | . Blue . | 4, H. De. Tr. Britain | . |
| nana | . Blue . | 7, H. Her. P. Europe | . 1800 |
| palustris, l | . Blue yel. | 7, H. Aq. P. Britain | . |
| pedunculāris | . Blue . | 6, H. | A. Astracan | . 1824 |
| rupicola | . Blue . | 6, H. Her. P. Scotland | . |
| sparsiflora | . Blue . | 5, H. Her. P. S. France | . 1822 |

*arvensis, involucrata, pusilla, stricta, sylvatica, versicolor*.

MYOSURUS, *Linn.* From *mys*, a mouse, and *oura*, a tail; the seeds are seated on a spiked receptacle, and appear exactly like the tail of a mouse, Mousetail. *Linn.* 5, Or. 1, Nat. Or. *Ranunculaceæ*. This species should be sown in a moist situation.

| | | | | |
|---|---|---|---|---|
| minimus | . . Yellow | . 4, H. | A. Britain | . . |

MYRCIA, *Decandolle*. A surname of Venus. *Linn.* 12, Or. 1, Nat. Or. *Myrtaceæ*. Pretty plants, when in flower they are very much like the common myrtle. Loam, peat, and sand, suit them best, and young cuttings root readily in sand, under a glass, in heat. *Synonymes*: 1. *Myrtus acris*. 2. *M. coriacea*. 3. *M. pimentoides*.

| | | | | |
|---|---|---|---|---|
| acris, 1 | . . . White | . 6, S. Ev. S. W. Ind. | . 1759 |
| coriacea, 2 | . | . S. Ev. S. Carrib. Ia. | . 1759 |
| pimentoides, 3 | . White . | 5, S. Ev. T. W. Ind. | . |

MYRIADENUS, *Desfontaines*. From *myrios*, innumerable, and *aden*, a gland; the leaves are beset with glands. *Linn.* 17, Or. 4, Nat. Or. *Leguminosæ*. The seed of this plant must be raised on a hotbed, and afterwards treated as other stove biennials. *Synonyme*: 1. *Ornithopus tetraphyllus*.

| | | | | |
|---|---|---|---|---|
| tetraphyllus | . Yellow . | 7, S. | B. Jamaica | . 1818 |

MYRICA, *Linn.* From *myrio*, to flow; found on the banks of rivers. *Linn.* 12, Or. 4, Nat. Or. *Myricaceæ*. Ornamental plants. The greenhouse kinds require to be grown in a peat soil, and cuttings root readily under a glass. The hardy kinds are increased by seeds or layers. *M. cerifera* is a powerful astringent, and abundance of wax is obtained from its fruit. *Synonymes*: 1. *M. carolinensis, M. pennsylvanica*. 2. *M. æthiopica*.

| | | | | |
|---|---|---|---|---|
| cerifera | . . Apetal | . 5, H. De. S. N. Amer. | . 1699 |
| latifolia, 1 | . Apetal | . 5, H. Ev. S. N. Amer. | . 1730 |
| cordifolia | . Apetal | . 6, G. Ev. S. C. G. H. | . 1759 |
| esculenta | . Apetal | . 5, G. Ev. T. Nepal | . 1817 |
| Faya | . Apetal | . 9, G. Ev. S. Azores | . 1777 |
| Gale | . Apetal | . 5, H. De. S. Britain | . |
| hirsuta | . Apetal | . 6, G. Ev. S. C. G. H. | . |
| laciniata | . Apetal | . 6, G. Ev. S. C. G. H. | . 1752 |
| mexicana | . Apetal | . 2, G. Ev. S. Mexico | . 1823 |
| quercifolia | . Apetal | . 6, G. Ev. S. C. G. H. | . 1759 |
| segregata | . Apetal | . G. Ev. S. S. Amer. | . 1824 |
| serrata, 2 | . Apetal | . 8, G. Ev. S. C. G. H. | . 1798 |

MYRICARIA, *Desvaux*. From *murike*, the Greek name of the tamarisk. *Linn.* 16, Or. 5, Nat. Or. *Tamaricaceæ*. A genus of tall ornamental shrubs, requiring the same treatment as *Tamarix*. *Synonymes*: 1. *Tamarix dahurica*. 2. *T. germanica*.

| | | | | |
|---|---|---|---|---|
| dahurica, 1 | . . Pink | . 4, H. Ev. S. Dahuria | . 1816 |
| germanica, 2 | . Pink | . 7, H. Ev. S. Germany | . 1582 |

MYRIOCOCCUM, *Fries*. From *myrios*, a myriad, and *kokkos*, a berry. *Linn.* 24, Or. 9, Nat. Or. *Fungi*. Found upon dead leaves in the spring—*præcox*.

MYRIONEMA, *Greville*. From *myrios*, a myriad, and *nema*, a filament. *Linn.* 24, Or. 7, Nat. Or. *Algæ*. This species is only to be met with in the sea—*strangulare*.

MYRIOPHYLLUM, *Linn.* From *myrios*, a myriad, and *phyllon*, a leaf; division of the leaves. *Linn.* 21, Or. 9, Nat. Or. *Onagraceæ*. Aquatics of some beauty, and common culture.

| | | | | |
|---|---|---|---|---|
| spicatum | . . . Red | . 7, H. Aq. P. Britain | . . |
| verticillatum | . Green | . 7, H. Aq. P. England | . . |

MYRIOTRICHIA, *Harvey*. From *myrios*, myriad, and *thrix*, a hair; alluding to the filaments. *Linn.* 24, Or. 7, Nat. Or. *Algæ*. A minute olive-coloured species—*claveformis*.

MYRISTICA, *Linn.* From *myristikos*, sweet-smelling; odour of the fruit. The well-known Nutmeg. *Linn.* 22, Or. 18, Nat. Or. *Myristicaceæ*. These very interesting plants are seldom to be met with in this country, and are considered difficult to cultivate. A sandy loam suits them best, and cuttings of the ripened wood planted in sand, and placed under a glass, in a moist bottom heat, would probably root freely, and the plants be more likely to thrive and make good plants, than the imported ones. All the plants that have come under our notice have been imported ones. *Synonymes*: 1. *M. officinalis, aromatica*. 2. *Virola sebifera*.

| | | | | |
|---|---|---|---|---|
| fatua | . . . Grn. wht. | . 8, Ev. T. Surinam | . 1812 |
| moschata, 1 | . Pa. yel. | . 8, Ev. T. E. Ind. | . 1795 |
| sebifera, 2 | . Yel. grn. | . 8, Ev. S. Guiana | . . |

MYROBALAN PLUM, see *Prūnus domestica myrobalana*.

MYRODIA, *Swartz*. From *myron*, fragrant balsam, and *odme*, a smell. *Linn.* 16, Or. 8, Nat. Or. *Sterculiaceæ*. This plant prefers a light rich soil; and cuttings will root in sand, under a glass.

| | | | | |
|---|---|---|---|---|
| turbinata | . . White | . 8, S. Ev. S. W. Ind. | . 1793 |

MYROSPERMUM, *Jacquin*. From *myron*, myrrh, and *sperma*, a seed; the seeds and cells yield a balsam, which has a strong smell. *Linn.* 10, Or. 1, Nat. Or. *Leguminosæ*. This lofty-growing tree thrives well in loam and peat in equal portions; and young cuttings will root in sand, under a glass, in heat.

| | | | | |
|---|---|---|---|---|
| toluiferum | . . . | . 8. Ev. T. S. Amer. | . |

MYROTHECIUM, *Tode*. From *myro*, to distil, and *theke*, thecium. *Linn.* 24, Or. 9, Nat. Or. *Fungi*. This plant is found on rotten bog matter—*Carmichælii*.

MYRRH, see *Myrrhis*.

MYRRHIS, *Scopoli*. From *myron*, perfume, or myrrh, myrrh; scent of a gland. *Linn.* 5, Or. 2, Nat. Or. *Umbelliferæ*. Formerly this plant was used in a variety of ways, but it has disappeared from our tables a long time ago. Any common soil suits it, and it is readily increased by seeds, or dividing at the root.

| | | | | |
|---|---|---|---|---|
| odorata | . . . White | . 5, H. Her. P. Britain | . . |

MYRSINE, *Linn.* The Greek name of myrrh. *Linn.* 23, Or. 2, Nat. Or. *Myrsinaceæ*. These plants grow freely in a mixture of loam, peat, and sand; and cuttings, if not too ripe, root in sand, under a glass, in a little heat. *Synonymes*: 1. *M. retusa*. 2. *Manglilla canariensis*. 3. *Sideroxylon melanophleum*. 4. *Manglilla Milleriana*. 5. *Samara pentandra*.

| | | | | |
|---|---|---|---|---|
| africana | . . Brown . | 4, G. Ev. S. C. G. H. | . 1691 |
| retusa, 1 | . Wht. grn. | 6, G. Ev. S. C. G. H. | . 1788 |
| bifaria | . Wht. pink | 1, G. Ev. S. Nepal | . 1822 |
| canariensis, 2 | . Whitish . | G. Ev. S. Teneriffe | . 1820 |
| capitellata | . Green . | 1, G. Ev. S. Nepal | . 1822 |
| coriacea | . . . | . 12, S. Ev. T. Jamaica | . 1770 |
| ilicifolia | . | . G. Ev. S. | . 1826 |
| melanophlea, 3 | . Wht. grn. | . G. Ev. S. C. G. H. | . 1788 |
| mitis, 4 | . White | . 7, G. Ev. S. C. G. H. | . 1692 |
| Samara, 5 | . Wht. grn. all | G. Ev. S. C. G. H. | . 1770 |
| semiserrata | . Pink | . 1, G. Ev. T. Nepal | . 1822 |
| subspinosa | . ● | . G. Ev. T. Nepal | . 1823 |
| variabilis | . | . G. Ev. S. N. S. W. | . 1824 |

**MYRSIPHYLLUM**, *Willdenow*. From *myrsine*, a myrtle, and *phyllon*, a leaf; resemblance of the leaves. *Linn.* 6, Or. 3, Nat. Or. *Melanthaceæ*. A genus of pretty twining plants, thriving well in sandy loam and peat, and readily multiplied by dividing at the root. Synonyme: 1. *Medeola asparagoides*.

angustifolium . Grn. wht. 7, G. De. Tw. C. G. H. . 1752
asparagoides, 1 . Grn. wht. 6, G. De. Tw. C. G. H. . 1702

**MYRTLE**, see *Myrtus*.
**MYRTLE BILBERRY**, see *Vaccinium Myrtillus*.

**MYRTUS**, *Linn.* From *myron*, perfume; *myrtos* of the Greeks; *myrtus* of the Dutch, and of almost every other European language. *Linn.* 12, Or. 1, Nat. Or. *Myrtaceæ*. The Myrtle is a favourite and well-known genus of plants, which grow well in sandy loam and peat; and cuttings, if not too ripe, will root freely either in sand or soil, under a glass.

affinis . . . . Purple . 6, G. Ev. S. China . . 1823
biflora . . . . White . . 5, S. Ev. S. Jamaica . 1759

communis . . . White . . 7, G. Ev. S. S. Eur. . . 1597
bætica . . . White . . 7, G. Ev. S. S. Eur. . . 1597
belgica . . . White . . 7, G. Ev. S. S. Eur. . . 1597
flore-pleno . . White . . 7, G. Ev. S. S. Eur. . . 1597
italica . . . White . . 7, G. Ev. S. S. Eur. . . 1597
lusitanica . . White . . 7, G. Ev. S. S. Eur. . . 1597
maculata . . . White . . 7, G. Ev. S. S. Eur. . . 1597
mucronata . . White . . 7, G. Ev. S. S. Eur. . . 1597
romana . . . White . . 7, G. Ev. S. S. Eur. . . 1597
tarentina . . White . . 7, S. Ev. S. S. Eur. . . 1597
variegata . . White . . 7, S. Ev. S. S. Eur. . . 1597
dumosa . . . White . . 6, S. Ev. S. W. Ind. . . 1793
Gregii . . . White . . 8. Ev. S. Dominica . 1776
melastomoides . White . . G. Ev. T. Moreton B.
obscura . . . White . . 7, S. Ev. S. Maranh. . . 1823
tenuifolia . . White . . 7, S. Ev. S. N. Holl. . 1824
tomentosa . . Purple . 6, G. Ev. S. China . . 1776
trinervis . . White . . 7, G. Ev. S. N. Holl. . 1824
virgultosa . . White . . 7, S. Ev. S. Jamaica . 1787

**MYXOTRICHIUM**, *Kunze*. From *myxa*, gluten, and *thrix*, a hair; filaments. *Linn.* 24, Or. 9, Nat. Or. *Fungi*. This species is found on rotten branches—*cæsium*.

# N.

**NÆMASPORA**, *Persoon*. From *nema*, a thread, and *spora*, a sporule. *Linn.* 24, Or. 9, Nat. Or. *Fungi*. Very minute plants, found on dead branches of Hornbeam, &c.—carpini, crocea, filamentosa, Rosæ.

**NÆMATELIA**, *Fries*. From *naima*, gelatine, and *ello*, to contain; in allusion to the nucleus in the receptacle. *Linn.* 24, Or. 9, Nat. Or. *Fungi*. A curious flesh-coloured species, growing on partially decayed pine-wood—encephala.

**NAGEIA**, *Gærtner*. From *Nagi*, the Japanese name of the plant. *Linn.* 22, Or. 4, Nat. Or. *Myricaceæ*. A plant of very little interest, growing best in a good rich loam; and cuttings of the ripened wood root in sand, under a glass, in a strong heat.

Putranjiva . . . Apetal . S. Ev. S. E. Ind. . . 1822

**NAIN FLAGEOLET**, see *Phaseolus tumidus*.

**NAIAS**, *Linn.* From *naias*, a water-nymph; on account of the habitation of the plant. *Linn.* 21, Or. 5, Nat. Or. *Fluviales*. A curious plant, of very simple culture. Synonyme: 1. *monosperma*.

major, 1 . . . . . 7, H. Aq. A. Europe . . 1816

**NAKED**, without hairs, leaves, or branches, &c.
**NAKEDISH**, nearly destitute of hairs, leaves, &c.

**NANDINA**, *Thunberg*. *Nandin*, or *Nand-scokf*, is the name of the shrub in Japan. *Linn.* 6, Or. 2, Nat. Or. *Berberaceæ*. This is a handsome plant, growing in a mixture of loam and peat; and ripened cuttings will root in sand, under a glass, provided the leaves are not shortened.

domestica . . . Orn. brn. . 7, G. Ev. S. China . . 1804

**NANODES**, *Lindley*. From *nanodes*, pigmy; in allusion to the small size of both plant and flowers. *Linn.* 20, Or. 1, Nat. Or. *Orchidaceæ*. This is among the most curious of orchidaceous plants; its flowers are completely embosomed by the leaves, and so similar in colour, that it would scarcely be observed to be in flower, even if every branch were blossoming. It is rather difficult to cultivate, but will be found to succeed best treated after the manner of *Burlingtonia*.

discolor . . . . Purph. grn. 8, S. Epi. Brazil . . 1827

**NAPIFORM**, formed like a turnip, tuberous.
**NAPOLEON'S WEEPING WILLOW**, see *Salix Napoleona*.

**NARAVELIA**, *Decandolle*. From *Naravel*, its name in Ceylon. *Linn.* 13, Or. 6, Nat. Or. *Ranunculaceæ*. A mixture of sandy loam and peat suits this species, and cuttings of the young wood will root readily in sand, under a glass, in heat. Synonyme: 1. *Atragene zeylanica*.

zeylanica . . . Yellow . S. Ev. Cl. Ceylon . . 1796

**NARCISSUS**, *Linn.* From *narke*, stupor; on account of the effects produced by the smell upon the nerves. *Linn.* 6, Or. 2, Nat. Or. *Amaryllidaceæ*. This is an old and very popular flower of great beauty, and some of the species are highly fragrant. They are all of very easy culture, growing well in any light sandy soil, or on glasses of water, and increased by offsets from the bulbs. *N. poeticus*, and one or two more, are well known to be emetic. Synonymes: 1. *radiiflorus*. 2. *triandrus*. 3. *orientalis*, var. 4. *Corbularia conspicua*. 5. *Queltia concolor*. 6. *Narcissus præcox*. 7. *bicolor*. 8. *Ajax maximus*. 9. *Narcissus Tazetta*. 10. *trilobus* 11. *calathinus*. 12. *unicolor*, *nevius*. 13. *poeticus*, *majalis*. 14. *moschatus*. 15. *festalis*. 16. *Phylogyne minor*. 17. *calathinus*, *odorus*, *tripartitus*.

ajax . . . . Yellow . 3, H. Bl. P.
albicans . . . Pa. yel. 3, H. Bl. P. . . . 1789
albus . . . . Wht. yel. 4, H. Bl. P.
plenus . . . Sulphur . 4, H. Bl. P.
angustifolius, 1 . White . 5, H. Bl. P. S. Eur. . . 1570
aputicorona . . Yel. or. 4, H. Bl. P. N. Africa
aurantius . . . Yellow . 3, H. Bl. P. . . . 1629
plenus-luteus . Yellow . 3, H. Bl. P. . . . 1629
bicolor . . . . Wht. yel. 4, H. Bl. P. Spain . 1629
biflorus . . . White . 3, H. Bl. P. Britain .
bifrons . . . . Yellow . 3, H. Bl. P. S. Eur. .
Bulbocodium . . Yellow . 4, H. Bl. P. Portugal . 1629
capax . . . . Pa. yel. 5, H. Bl. P.
cerinus . . . . White . 4, H. Bl. P.
cæruleus, 2 . . Crm. wht. 3, H. Bl. P. Spain . .
corona-plena . Crm. wht. 3, H. Bl. P. Spain . .
citrinus, 3 . . Wht. yel. 4, H. Bl. P.
compressus . . Li. yel. 3, H. Bl. P. Spain . .
concolor . . . Yellow . 4, H. Bl. P. . . . 1820
conspicuus, 4 . White . 4, H. Bl. P.
cernulatus . . White . 4, H. Bl. P. Spain . .
Cypri . . . . Wht. yel. 3, H. Bl. P. Cyprus . .
corona-plena . Wht. yel. 3, H. Bl. P. Gardens .
dubius . . . . White . 3, H. Bl. P. France . .
fistulosus . . . Wht. yel. 4, H. Bl. P.
floribundus . . Wht. yel. 3, H. Bl. P. Spain . .
galanthifolius . White . 5, H. Bl. P.
gracilis . . . Yellow . 4, H. Bl. P.
grandiflorus . . Wht. yel. 4, H. Bl. P.
Haworthii, 5 . . Yellow . 4, H. Bl. P. . . . 1700
plenus-sulphureus Sulphur . 4, H. Bl. P. . . . 1629
hemialis . . . Yellow . 3, H. Bl. P.
incomparabilis . Yellow . 4, H. Bl. P. Portugal . 1629
inflatus . . . Yellow . 4, H. Bl. P.
minor . . . . P. sulphur 3, H. Bl. P. Spain . 1696
infundibularis . Yellow . 4, H. Bl. P.
interjectus . . Yellow . 4, H. Bl. P. . . . 1810
intermedius . . Pa. yel. 3, H. Bl. P. Pyrenees .
italicus, 6 . . Pa. yel. 3, H. Bl. P. S. Eur. . .
plenus . . . Cream . 3, H. Bl. P. Italy . .
semiplenus . Cream . H. Bl. P. Italy . .
Jonquilla . . . Pa. yel. 4, H. Bl. P. Spain . 1596
flore-pleno . Yellow . 4, H. Bl. P. Spain . 1596
latifolius . . . Yellow . 4, H. Bl. P.
lobulatus . . . Yellow . 4, H. Bl. P.
lorifolius, 7 . . Yellow . 3, H. Bl. P.
anceps . . . Yellow . 4, H. Bl. P. . . . 1800
breviflos . . Yellow . 4, H. Bl. P.
Lunæ . . . . White . 4, H. Bl. P.
Macleaii . . . Cream . 3, H. Bl. P. Smyrna . 1815
major . . . . Yellow . 4, H. Bl. P. Spain . 1629
maximus, 8 . . Yellow . 4, H. Bl. P.
minor . . . . Yellow . 3, H. Bl. P. Spain . 1629
montanus . . . White . 4, H. Bl. P. Portugal .
moschatus . . White . 4, H. Bl. P. England .
multiflorus, 9 . Yellow . 4, H. Bl. P.

| | | | | | |
|---|---|---|---|---|---|
| aūrēūs | . . | Yellow | 4, H. Bl. P. | | |
| neglēctūs | . . | Wht. yel. | 4, H. Bl. P. | Naples | . 1830 |
| nivēūs | . . | White | 4, H. Bl. P. | S. Eur. | . |
| nobīlīs | . . | Yellow | 4, H. Bl. P. | | |
| nūtāns, 10 | . . | Yellow | 4, H. Bl. P. | S. Eur. | . 1789 |
| obscūrūs | . . | Yellow | 5, H. Bl. P | Spain | . |
| obsolētūs | . . | White | 8, H. Bl. P | Spain | . 1819 |
| obvallārīs, 11 | . | Yellow | 8, H. Bl. P | Spain | . |
| odōrūs | . . | Yellow | 8, H. Bl. P. | S. Eur. | . 1629 |
| orientālīs | . . | White | 4, H. Bl. P. | Levant | . |
| papyrāceūs, 12 | . | White | 8, H. Bl. P. | | |
| jasminēūs | . | White | 4, H. Bl. P. | | |
| patellārīs, 13 | . | White | 5, H. Bl. P. | England | . |
| exsērtūs | . | White | 5, H. Bl. P. | England | . |
| plēnūs | . | White | 5, H. Bl. P. | England | . |
| pātūlūs, 14 | . | White | 3, H. Bl. P. | Spain | . |
| albūs | . | White | 3, H. Bl. P. | Spain | . |
| poētīcūs | . | White | 5, H. Bl. P. | S. Eur. | . |
| primulīnūs | . | Yellow | 4, H. Bl. P. | | |
| propinquūs | . | Yellow | 8, H. Bl. P. | Spain | . 1629 |
| Pseūdō-Narcissūs, 15 | } | Pa. yel. | 8, H. Bl. P. | England | . |
| plenissimūs | . | Yellow | 8, H. Bl P. | | |
| plēnūs | . | Yellow | 8, H. Bl. P. | France | . |
| scotīcūs | . | Yellow | 5, H. Bl. P. | Scotland | . |
| pulchēllūs | . | Yellow | 4, H. Bl. P. | Spain | . |
| pūmīlūs | . | Yellow | 4, H. Bl. P. | Spain | . |
| pusīllūs, 16 | . | Yellow | 4, H. Bl. P. | | . 1818 |
| plēnūs | . | Yellow | 4, H. Bl. P. | | . 1810 |
| recūrvūs | . | White | 5, H. Bl. P. | S. Eur. | . |
| rugulōsūs | . | Yellow | 4, H. Bl. P. | | . 1818 |
| Sabini | . | Sulphur | 3, H. Bl. P. | | |
| semipartītūs | . | Yellow | 4, H. Bl. P. | | |
| serōtīnūs | . | Pa. yel. | 9, H. Bl. P. | Barbary | . 1629 |
| serrātūs | . | Pa. yel. | 8, H. Bl. P. | S. Eur. | . |
| suāvīs | . | Pa. yel. | 8, H. Bl. P. | S. Eur. | . |
| sīmīlīs | . | Yellow | 4, H. Bl. P. | | |
| spūrīūs | . | Yellow | 8, H. Bl. P. | England | . |
| stēllārīs | . | Wh. crim. | 5, H. Bl. P. | | . 1629 |
| striātūlūs | . | Yellow | 4, H. Bl. P. | | |
| Tazēttā | . | White | 8, H. Bl. P. | Spain | . 1759 |
| Telamōnīūs | . | Yellow | 4, H. Bl. P. | | |
| grandiplēnūs | . | Yellow | 4, H. Bl. P. | | |
| plēnūs | . | Yellow | 4, H. Bl. P. | | |
| tenuifōlīūs | . | White | 4, H. Bl. P. | | |
| tenūīor | . | Li. white | 5, H. Bl. P. | | . 1789 |
| teretīcaūlīs | . | Pa. yel. | 4, H. Bl. P. | Spain | . |
| tortuōsūs | . | White | 8, H. Bl. P. | Spain | . 1629 |
| Trewiānūs | . | Wht. yel. | 8, H. Bl. P. | Spain | . |
| triandrūs | . | White | 4, H. Bl. P. | Portugal | . 1629 |
| trilōbūs, 17 | . | Yellow | 4, H. Bl. P. | S. Eur. | . 1629 |
| tubiflōrūs | . | Wht. yel. | 8, H. Bl. P. | | . |
| viridiflōrūs | . | Green | 9, H. Bl. P. | Barbary | . 1629 |

NARCOTIC, producing sleep or torpor.

NĀRDŪS, *Linn.* From *nardos*, in Greek, and *nard*, in the Hebrew; having a peculiar smell. *Linn.* 3, Or. 1, Nat. Or. *Gramineæ.* An insignificant species, growing on moist heaths in many parts of Britain

| | | | | | |
|---|---|---|---|---|---|
| strictā | . . | Apetal. | . 6, Gram. | Britain | . . |

NARROWED, tapering.

NARTHĒCĪŪM, *Mœhring.* From *narthex*, a rod; referring to the stem. *Linn.* 6, Or. 1, Nat. Or. *Liliaceæ.* Iris-looking plants, which grow in turfy peat, and are multiplied by divisions.

| | | | | | |
|---|---|---|---|---|---|
| americānūm | . | Yellow | 7, H. Her. P. | N. Amer. | . 1811 |
| ossifrāgūm | . | Yellow | 7, H. Her. P. | Britain | . . |

NASEBERRY-TREE, see *Achras Zapotilla.*

NASTŪRTĪŪM, *R. Brown.* From *nasus*, the nose, and *tortus*, tormented; the acridity of *N. officinalis* affects the muscles of the nose. *Linn.* 15, Nat. Or. *Cruciferæ.* Few of these plants are worth cultivating; they are of the simplest culture. The seed of the annual kinds has only to be sown in the open ground in spring. *Synonymes:* 1. *Sisymbrium nasturtium.* 2. *S. terrestre.* 3. *S. sylvestre.*

| | | | | | |
|---|---|---|---|---|---|
| nātāns | . . | Yellow | 7, H. Aq. P. | Siberia | . 1827 |
| officinālē, 1 | . | White | 4, H. Aq. P. | Britain | . . |

amphībīūm, indicūm, variifōlīūm, bengalēnsē, bursifōlīūm, clandestīnūm, coronopifōlīūm, indicūm, lippizēnsē, palūstrē 2, pyrenāicūm, sagittātūm, sylvestrē 3.

NĀXŪS, *Jussieu.* *Naxus* is the Greek name for a kind of reed. *Linn.* 6, Or. 1, Nat. Or. *Gramineæ.* A curious species of grass, requiring the heat of the stove and a good sandy peat soil; it is increased by suckers. *Synonyme:* 1. *Bambusa latifolia.*

| | | | | | |
|---|---|---|---|---|---|
| latifōlīā, 1 | . . . | | Grass. | Cumana | . . 1818 |

NĀSŪTŪS, having a fancied resemblance to the nose.
NĀTĀNS, floating, sounding.
NAŪCLEĀ, *Linn.* From *naus*, a ship, and *kleio*, to

( 215 )

inclose; the half capsule is hull-shaped. *Linn.* 5, Or. 1, Nat. Or. *Cinchonaceæ.* A noble genus of plants, producing their flowers in large round heads. They grow well in a rich loamy soil, and young plants may be obtained from layers or cuttings.

| | | | | | |
|---|---|---|---|---|---|
| Cadambā | . . | Orange | . S. Ev. S. | E. Ind. | . . |
| cordifōlīā | . . | Yellow | . S. Ev. T. | E. Ind. | . . |
| orientālīs | . . | Yellow | . S. Ev. T. | E. Ind. | . . |
| purpūreā | . . | Purple | . S. Ev. T. | E. Ind. | . . |
| undulātā | . . | Yellow | . S. Ev. T. | E. Ind. | . . 1820 |

NAUENBURGĪĀ, *Mœnch.* In honour of John Samuel Nauenburgh, a botanical author. *Linn.* 19, Or. 5, Nat. Or. *Compositæ.* A stove annual, not worth cultivating. *Synonyme:* 1. *Brotera Contrayerva—trinervatā.*

NAVELWORT, see *Cotylēdōn.*

NAVICULAR, boat-shaped.

NEAPOLITAN VIOLET, see *Violā odorātā-pallidā-plēnā.*

NEBULŌSŪS, cloudy, dingy.

NECK; the upper tapering end in bulbs, or other plants, is called the neck.

NECKĒRĀ, *Hedwig.* In honour of N. J. Necker, a famous German botanist. *Linn.* 24, Or. 5, Nat. Or. *Musci.* This is a beautiful genus of mosses; the plants are found in woods, upon trees, and rocks—crispā, pennātā, pūmīlā.

NECTARIAL, of, or belonging to the nectary.

NECTARIFEROUS, bearing honey, or nectaries.

NECTARIFEROUS-TUBE, in *Pelargonium* is the tube or swelled part at the top of the pedicel.

NECTĀRĪŪM, nectary, that part of a flower which produces honey.

NECTAROSCORDŪM, *Lindley.* From *nektar*, honey, and *skorodon*, garlic; in allusion to the honey-pores in its flowers, Honey-garlic. *Linn.* 6, Or. 1, Nat. Or. *Liliaceæ.* This is an ornamental plant, succeeding well in any common soil, and increased by offsets.

| | | | | | |
|---|---|---|---|---|---|
| sicūlūm | . . . | Pur. wht. | 6, H. Bl. P. | Sicily | . . 1832 |

NEGŪNDŌ, *Mœnch.* The meaning is unknown to us. *Linn.* 22, Or. 5, Nat. Or. *Aceraceæ.* Fine ornamental trees, well suited for ornamenting the back of shrubberies. A light soil suits them best, and they are easily propagated by layers or seeds. *Synonymes:* 1. *Acer negundo, Negundium americanum.*

| | | | | | |
|---|---|---|---|---|---|
| fraxinifōlīūm, 1 | . | Green | . 4, H. De. T. | N. Amer. | . 1688 |
| crispūm | . | Green | . 4, H. De. T. | N. Amer. | . 1688 |
| violāceūm | . | . | 4, H. De. T. | | |

NEJĀ, *Don.* Meaning unknown. *Linn.* 19, Or. 2, Nat. Or. *Compositæ.* A worthless greenhouse herbaceous plant, growing in any common soil, and increased by seeds—grācīlīs.

NELITRIS, *Gærtner.* From *ne*, privative, and *elytron*, a seed-vessel; the berry is without any partitions. *Linn.* 12, Or. 1, Nat. Or. *Myrtaceæ.* An ornamental shrub; for culture and propagation, see *Psidium.* *Synonyme:* 1. *Psidium decaspermum.*

| | | | | | |
|---|---|---|---|---|---|
| Jambosēllā, 1 | . | White | . . S. Ev. S. | Society's Is. | 1810 |

NELSONĪĀ, *R. Brown.* In honour of D. Nelson, the botanist who accompanied the circumnavigator Captain Cook. *Linn.* 2, Or. 1, Nat. Or. *Acanthaceæ.* A stove herbaceous plant, not worth cultivating—hirsūtā.

NELŪMBĪŪM, *Jussieu.* From *nelumbo*, the Cingalese name of *N. speciosum.* *Linn.* 13, Or. 6, Nat. Or. *Nelumbiaceæ.* This is a genus of very interesting plants, which require to be grown in a rich loamy soil. The tub or pot in which the plants are grown should be kept full of water while the plants are growing, but may be allowed to get dry when the flowering season is over. They require to be grown in a strong heat, or they will not flower well; they may be increased by dividing the roots, but they are more readily increased by seeds. The fruit of *N. speciosum* is supposed to be the Egyptian bean of Pythagoras.

| | | | | | |
|---|---|---|---|---|---|
| caspicūm | . . | Pink | . S. Aq. P. | Casp. Sea | . 1822 |
| jamaicēnsē | . . | Pa. blue | . S. Aq. P. | Jamaica | . 1824 |
| lūteūm | . . | Yellow | . S. Aq. P. | Carolina | . 1810 |
| speciōsūm | . . | Pink | . 7, S. Aq. P. | India | . 1787 |
| Tamārā | . . | Pink | . S. Aq. P. | Malabar | . 1818 |

NEMESĪĀ, *Ventenat.* A name applied by Dioscorides to a kind of *Antirrhinum.* *Linn.* 14, Or. 2, Nat. Or. *Scrophulariaceæ.* These plants will grow well in any rich light soil. *N. bicornis* may be treated as other tender or half-hardy annuals; the others may be increased by cuttings of the young wood planted under a glass. *Synonyme*: 1. *Antirrhinum macrocarpum.*

| | | | | | |
|---|---|---|---|---|---|
| bicornis . . | . Purple | . 7, H. | A. C. G. H. | . 1774 |
| chamædrifolia, 1 | . Purple | . 6, G. Her. | P. C. G. H. | . 1787 |
| fœtens . . | . Purple | . 6, G. Her. | P. C. G. H. | . 1798 |

**NEMOPÁNTHES**, *Rafinesque*. From *nemos*, a grove, and *anthos*, a flower; habitat of the plant. *Linn.* 22, Or. 5, Nat. Or. *Aquifoliaceæ.* This is an ornamental plant, thriving well in a peat soil, and readily increased by layers or seeds. *Synonymes*: 1. *fascicularis, Ilex canadensis.*

| | | | |
|---|---|---|---|
| canadénsis . . . | | H. De. S. N. Amer. | . 1812 |

**NEMÓPHILA**, *Barton.* From *nemos*, a grove, and *phileo*, to love; the plants delight in a shady situation. *Linn.* 5, Or. 1, Nat. Or. *Hydrophyllaceæ.* This is a genus of very pretty annuals, all of which are well worth cultivating; they grow and flower best in a moist shaded situation, and a peat or vegetable soil. If the plants are wanted to flower early, the seed should be sown on a hotbed, and afterwards transplanted; but if not wanted to flower before late in summer, they may be sown in the open border. *Synonymes*: 1. *Hydrophyllum appendiculatum.* 2. *Phacelia parviflora, Eutoca parviflora.*

| | | | | |
|---|---|---|---|---|
| atomaria . . | . Wht. pur. | 8, H. | A. California | . 1836 |
| aurita . . . | . Purple | . 6, H. | A. California | . 1831 |
| insignis . . | . Blue | . 8, H. | A. California | . 1833 |
| paniculata, 1 . | . Pa. blue | . 5, H. Her. | P. N. Amer. | . 1813 |
| parviflora, 2 . | . Blue | . H. Her. | P. N. Amer. | . 1826 |
| phacelioides | Blue | . 7, H. Her. | P. N. Amer. | . 1822 |

**NEMORÓSUS**, growing in the woods, or among trees.

**NEÓTTIA**, *Linn. Neottia*, a bird's nest; in allusion to the interwoven fibres of the roots. *Linn.* 20, Or. 1, Nat. Or. *Orchidaceæ.* This is a pretty genus of orchidaceous plants. The hardy species will succeed well in chalky soil, or a mixture of loam, peat, and sand. The stove kinds may be referred to *Blettia* for culture; they are all increased by divisions. *Synonymes*: 1. *Spiranthes bicolor.* 2. *S. elata.* 3. *S. picta.* 4. *S. pudica.*

| | | | | |
|---|---|---|---|---|
| æstivalis . . . | . White | . 9, H. Ter. | N. Amer. | . 1822 |
| aphylla . . . | . Red pnk. | 6, S. Ter. | Trinidad | . 1826 |
| australis . . . | . Red | . G. Ter. | N. Holl. | . 1823 |
| autumnalis . . | . White | . 9, H. Her. | Europe . | . 1800 |
| bicolor, 1 . . | . White | . 2, S. Ter. | Trinidad | . 1823 |
| calcarata . . | . White | . 8, S. Ter. | Jamaica | |
| cérnua . . . | . White | . 7, H. Ter. | N. Amer. | . 1796 |
| elata, 2 . . | . Green | . 7, S. Ter. | W. Ind. | . 1790 |
| gemmipára . . | . White | . 7, H. Ter. | Ireland . | |
| glandulósa . . | . Grn. wht. | 1, S. Ter. | W. Ind. | |
| grandiflóra . . | . Wht. grn. | 4, S. Ter. | St. Vin. | . 1829 |
| nidus-ávis . . | . Brown | . 5, H. Ter. | Britain . | |
| orchioídes . . | . Rose | . 11, S. Ter. | Jamaica | . 1826 |
| picta, 3 . . . | . Green | . 4, S. Ter. | Trinidad | . 1805 |
| plantaginea . . | . Red | . 6, S. Ter. | Nepal . | . 1824 |
| procéra . . . | . White | . 6, S. Ter. | Nepal . | |
| pudica, 4 . . | . Pink | . 11, S. Ter. | China . | . 1819 |
| spirális . . . | . White | . 8, H. Ter. | Britain . | |
| tórtilis . . . | . White | . 7, S. Ter. | W. Ind. | . 1822 |

**NEPÉNTHES**, *Linn.* This is a name under which Homer speaks of a substance, probably opium; but in what way it is applied to this plant we do not know. *Linn.* 22, Or. 13, Nat. Or. *Nepenthaceæ. N. distillatoria* is a most extraordinary and singular plant, and well known under the name of Chinese Pitcher Plant; it ought to be in every collection of stove plants. It attains the height of twenty or even thirty feet, when its appearance is inconceivably singular from the fine large pitchers which hang gracefully from the points of the strongest leaves. It is supposed by most cultivators to be extremely difficult of cultivation, but we have not found the least difficulty in cultivating it; indeed, we question whether the plants at Chatsworth are not finer than plants growing in and enjoying all the advantages of their native soil. Experience has clearly taught us that heat at the roots is as necessary to the successful growth of this plant as a heated atmosphere is indispensable to the stem and leaves. The plants should be potted in a compost of a little coarse fibrous peat, mixed with a greater portion of Hypnum Moss, and the pots to be then immersed in moss, the heat of which should not be less than eighty degrees, while the heat of

the house need not be, except in summer, more than seventy. The moss in which the plants are plunged should be kept rather wet, so that a constant but gentle humidity is given off, which rises among the plants, and thus strengthens, while it promotes their growth. Offsets are thrown out from the base of the stem of old plants, which, when a few inches long, or when each offset has made three or four leaves, are taken off, and potted singly into thirty-two-sized pots, using the same kind of compost, and plunging them in the moss, as before directed, and as the plants grow, and the rootlets in the pot become numerous, an additional sized pot should be given to each, using precisely the same materials as before, observing to secure a good open drainage at the bottom of each; young plants may also be obtained from seeds.

| | | | | |
|---|---|---|---|---|
| distillatória | . Orn. yel. | all S. Ev. Cl. | China | . 1789 |
| Phyllámphóra | . Orn. yel. | . 7, S. Ev. Cl. | China | . 1820 |

**NÉPETA**, *Linn.* From *Nepet*, the name of a town in Tuscany, where the plants were first found. *Linn.* 14, Or. 1, Nat. Or. *Labiatæ.* Some of the plants belonging to this genus are very pretty, and well adapted for flower-borders, while others are not worth growing. They prefer to grow in a light dry soil, and are increased by dividing at the root in spring or autumn, or by seeds. *Synonymes*: 1. *arragonensis.* 2. *Melissa alba.* 3. *N. patella.* 4. *grandiflora.* 5. *Melissa cretica, Thymus marifolius.* 6. *N. longiflora.* 7. *amethystina.* 8. *pannonica.* 9. *paniculata.* 10. *Teucrium sibiricum.*

| | | | | |
|---|---|---|---|---|
| amethýstina . | . Blue | . 7, H. Her. | P. S. Eur. . | . 1816 |
| angustifólia, 1 | . Purple | . 6, H. | A. Spain . | . 1798 |
| botryoídes . . | . White | . 6, H. Her. | P. Siberia . | . 1779 |
| cærúlea . . | . Blue | . 5, H. Her. | P. | . 1777 |
| catária . . | . White | . 8, H. Her. | P. Britain . | |
| crispa . . | . Pa. blue | . 7, H. Her. | P. Levant . | . 1800 |
| croática, 2 . | . White | . 7, H. Her. | P. Hungary | . 1821 |
| diffúsa . . | . Purple | . 7, H. Her. | P. Siberia . | . 1824 |
| flava . . | . Blue | . H. Her. | P. Caucasus | . 1831 |
| grandiflóra . | . Blue | . 7, H. Her. | P. Caucasus | . 1817 |
| graveólens, 3 | . Purple | . 7, H. Her. | P. S. Eur. . | . 1804 |
| imbricáta . | . Blue | . 7, H. Her. | P. Spain . | . 1820 |
| incána . . | . White | . 8, H. Her. | P. Levant . | . 1723 |
| itálica . . | . Red wht. | 7, H. Her. | P. Italy . | . 1640 |
| latifólia, 4 . | . Purple | . 7, H. Her. | P. Pyrenees | . 1816 |
| longiflóra . | . Violet | . 7, H. Her. | P. Persia . | . 1802 |
| macroúra . | . Wht. pur. | 7, H. Her. | P. Siberia . | . 1820 |
| marrubioídes | . Red | . 7, H. Her. | P. | |
| multibracteáta | . Purple | . 7, H. Her. | P. Algiers . | . 1817 |
| Mussini, 6 . | . Violet | . 7, H. Her. | P. Siberia . | . 1804 |
| Nepetélla, 7 | . Red | . 7, H. Her. | P. S. Eur. . | . 1758 |
| núda, 8 . . | . White | . 7, H. Her. | P. S. Eur. . | . 1713 |
| pannónica, 9 | . Red | . 9, H. Her. | P. Hungary | . 1683 |
| parviflóra . | . Blue | . 7, H. Her. | P. Caucasus | . 1820 |
| Scordótis . | . Blue | . 7, H. Her. | P. N. Africa | . 1817 |
| serpyllifólia | . | . 7, H. Her. | P. Tauria . | . 1828 |
| sibírica, 10 | . Purple | . 7, H. Her. | P. Siberia . | . 1804 |
| suaveólens . | . Blue | . 7, H. Her. | P. | . 1817 |
| supína . . | . Blue | . 7, H. Her. | P. Caucasus | . 1816 |
| teucrifólia . | . Purple | . 7, H. Her. | P. Armenia | . 1816 |
| teucrioídes . | . White | . 7, H. Her. | P. S. Eur. . | . 1820 |
| tuberósa . . | . Violet | . 7, H. Her. | P. Spain . | . 1683 |
| ucránia . . | . Blue | . 7, H. Her. | P. Ukraine | . 1796 |
| violácea . . | . Blue | . 8, H. Her. | P. Spain . | . 1723 |

*coloráta, lamiifólia, lanáta, malabárica, melissæfólia, reticuláta.*

**NEPHRÓMA**, *Acharius.* From *nephros*, a kidney; in allusion to the form of the apothecia. *Linn.* 24, Or. 8, Nat. Or. *Lichenes.* These plants are found amongst moss in stone quarries, &c.—*parilis, resupináta.*

**NERÍNE**, *Herbert.* After *Nerine*, the daughter of *Nerius. Linn.* 6, Or. 1, Nat. Or. *Amaryllidaceæ.* A genus of pretty bulbous plants. *N. sarniensis*, or Guernsey-lily, is a very popular autumnal flower. They flourish best in a rich sandy mould, and are readily increased by offsets, or by seeds. *Synonymes*: 1. *Lycorus aurea.* 2. *Amaryllis curvifolia.* 3. *Lycorus radiata.*

| | | | | |
|---|---|---|---|---|
| aúrea, 1 . . | . Yellow | . 8, G. Bu. | P. China . | . 1777 |
| corúsca . . | . Scarlet | . 7, G. Bu. | P. C. G. H. | . 1809 |
| curvifólia, 2 . | . Purple | . 7, G. Bu. | P. C. G. H. | . 1777 |
| flexuósa . . | . Pink | . 9, G. Bu. | P. C. G. H. | . 1795 |
| húmilis . . | . Red | . 6, G. Bu. | P. C. G. H. | . 1795 |
| pulchélla . . | . Pink | . 7, G. Bu. | P. C. G. H. | . 1820 |
| radiáta, 3 . | . Pink | . 6, G. Bu. | P. China . | . 1758 |
| rósea . . . | . Pink | . 7, G. Bu. | P. C. G. H. | . 1818 |
| sarniénsis . . | . Red | . 9, G. Bu. | P. Japan . | . 1659 |
| undulata . . | . Pink | . 5, G. Bu. | P. China . | . 1767 |
| venústa . . | . Scarlet | . 6, G. Bu. | P. C. G. H. | . 1806 |
| versícolor . . | . Varieg. | . 8, G. Bu. | P. Hybrid . | . 1815 |

[ 216 ]

NĒRĬŬM, *Linn.* From *nēros*, humid; alluding to the habitat of the plants. *Linn.* 5, Or. 1, Nat. Or. *Apocynaceæ.* This is a genus of noble evergreen shrubs, of easy culture, and flowering freely the greater part of the year. *N. Oleander* and its varieties bear forcing remarkably well, and although treated as greenhouse plants, yet they will not flower well unless they are kept in the stove; they grow well in any rich light soil, and young cuttings root in any soil if kept moist. The leaves of *N. Oleander* contain gallic acid, and the leaves and bark of the root of *N. odorum* are applied externally as powerful repellents by the Indian practitioners.

| | | | | | |
|---|---|---|---|---|---|
| flaveacēns | . | Pa. yel. | 7, G. Ev. S. | | 1816 |
| odorŭm | . | Pa. red | 7, S. Ev. S. E. Ind. | | 1683 |
| cärneŭm | . | Pink | 7, S. Ev. S. E. Ind. | | 1683 |
| plēnŭm | . | Pa. red | 7, S. Ev. S. E. Ind. | | 1683 |
| Oleändēr | . | Red | 8, G. Ev. S. S. Eur. | | 1596 |
| ālbŭm | . | White | 8, G. Ev. S. S. Eur. | | 1596 |
| splēndēns | . | Red | 8, G. Ev. S. S. Eur. | | 1814 |
| variegātŭm | . | Striped | 8, G. Ev. S. S. Eur. | | |
| thyrsiflōrŭm | . | Pink | 7, G. Ev. S. Nepal | | 1830 |

NĒRVĒLĔSS, without nerves.

NĒRVĒS, the strong ribs upon leaves or flowers.

NĒRVŌSA, or NĒRVŌUS, full of nerves.

NĒRVŌSĒLY-FŬRRŌWĒD, or STRĒAKĒD, having nerves like furrows, or streaks.

NĒSĒÆA, *Commerson.* From *Nesea*, a sea-nymph. *Linn.* 11, Or. 1, Nat. Or. *Lythraceæ.* An ornamental plant when in flower, growing best in a mixture of loam, peat, and sand, and readily increased by cuttings in sand, under a glass.

| | | | | | |
|---|---|---|---|---|---|
| triflōrā | . | Blue | 8, S. Her. P. Mauritius | . | 1802 |

NĀSLĬX, *Desfontaines.* The meaning not explained. *Linn.* 15, Nat. Or. *Cruciferæ.* A hardy annual, not worth cultivating. *Synonyme:* 1. *Myagrum paniculatum—paniculátá* 1.

NĒTTĒD, having the veins reticulated.

NĒTTLE, see *Urtica.*

NĒTTLE-TREE, see *Celtis.*

NĒURŌCĀRPŬM, *Desfontaines.* From *neuron*, a nerve, and *karpos*, a fruit; each of the valves of the pod is furnished with a longitudinal nerve. *Linn.* 17, Or. 4, Nat. Or. *Leguminosæ.* These plants require to be treated like other stove plants. *Synonyme:* 1. *Crotalaria guianensis.*

| | | | | | |
|---|---|---|---|---|---|
| guianēnse, 1 | . | Purple | 8, Ev. S. Guiana | . | 1826 |
| simplicifōlĭŭm | . | White | 8, Ev. S. S. Amer. | . | 1824 |

NĒURŌLĀENĀ, *R. Brown.* From *neuron*, a nerve, and *læna*, a cloak; alluding to the calyx. *Linn.* 19, Or. 1, Nat. Or. *Compositæ.* A worthless stove shrub, growing in sandy peat—*lobátá.*

NĒURŌLŌMĀ, *Andrzejowski.* From *neuron*, a nerve, and *loma*, a fringe. *Linn.* 15, Nat. Or. *Cruciferæ.* A plant of some beauty; it grows in any common soil, and is readily increased by divisions. *Synonymes:* 1. *Arabis grandiflora, Hesperis arabidifolia.*

| | | | | | |
|---|---|---|---|---|---|
| arabidiflōrŭm, 1 | . | Purple | 5, H. Her. P. Siberia | . | 1800 |

NĒURŌSPĒRMĀ, *Rafinesque.* From *neuron*, a nerve, and *sperma*, a seed; the seeds are articulated with anastomosing nerves. *Linn.* 21, Or. 1, Nat. Or. *Cucurbitaceæ.* For the culture and propagation of this worthless plant, see *Cucurbita.*

| | | | | | |
|---|---|---|---|---|---|
| cuspidātā | . | Yellow | 7. H. Tr. A. Kentucky | . | 1827 |

NĒUTĒR, neither male nor female.

NEW JĒRSEY TĒA, see *Ceanóthus americânus.*

NEW ZĒALĀND SPĪNACH, see *Tetragonia expánsa.*

NEW ZĒALĀND TĒA, see *Leptospermum scopária.*

NĪCKER-TREE, see *Guilandina.*

NĪCOLSŌNĬA, *Decandolle.* In honour of Mr. Nicolson, author of an "Essay upon the Nat. Hist. of St. Domingo." *Linn.* 17, Or. 4, Nat. Or. *Leguminosæ.* For the culture and propagation of this plant, see *Uraria. Synonyme:* 1. *Hedysarum barbatum.*

| | | | | | |
|---|---|---|---|---|---|
| barbātā, 1 | . | Purple | 6, G. Ev. S. Jamaica | . | 1818 |

NĪCOTĬĀNĀ, *Linn.* In honour of John Nicot, of Nismes, ambassador from the King of France to Portugal, who procured the first seeds from a Dutchman, who had them from Florida. *Linn.* 5, Or. 1, Nat. Or. *Solanaceæ.* The species of this genus generally grown as tobacco, are *N. Tabacum* and *N. macrophylla.* The popular narcotic which it furnishes is probably in more extensive use than any other, and its only rival is the betel of the

East. The herb for smoking was brought to England from Tobago in the West Indies, or from Tobasco in Mexico (and whence the name), by Sir Ralph Lane, in 1586. Seeds were shortly afterwards introduced from the same quarter. Sir Walter Raleigh first introduced smoking; in the house in which he lived at Islington were his arms on a shield, with a tobacco plant on the top. "Tobacco as used by man," says Du Tour, "gives pleasure to the savage and the philosopher, to the inhabitant of the burning desert and the frozen zone; in short, its use either in powder, to chew, or to smoke, is universal, and for no other reason than a sort of convulsive motion (sneezing) produced by the first, and a degree of intoxication by the two last modes of usage."—*Don's Gard. and Bot.* Many of the species are showy when in flower, and are well suited for decorating the flower-borders. The seeds require to be sown on a hotbed in spring, and when the plants have got two or three leaves, they should be planted into small pots, and placed in the frame, and planted out about the end of May, those for the open border in conspicuous situations, and those intended for leaves in rows three feet apart. *Synonyme:* 1. *suaveolens.*

| | | | | | |
|---|---|---|---|---|---|
| ālātā | . | Pink | 9, H. | A. N. Amer. | 1829 |
| angustifōlĬā | . | White | 8, H. | A. Chile | 1819 |
| bonariēnsĬs | . | White | 8, H. | A. B. Ayres | 1821 |
| cerinthoīdēs | . | Grn. yel. | 8, H. | A. | 1821 |
| chinēnsĬs | . | Pink | 8, H. | A. China | 1819 |
| decŭrrēns | . | | 8, H. | A. | 1820 |
| dilatātā | . | Pink | 8, H. | A. | 1820 |
| fruticōsā | . | Pink | 7, G. Ev. S. China | | 1699 |
| glaūcā | . | Yel. grn. | 9, H. | A. B. Ayres | 1827 |
| glutinōsā | . | Scarlet | 8, H. | A. Peru | 1759 |
| hŭmĬlĬs | . | Grn. yel. | 8, H. | A. Egypt | 1819 |
| Langsdōrffĭī | . | Orn. yel. | 8, H. | A. Chile | 1819 |
| longiflōrā | . | White | 8, H. | A. B. Ayres | 1832 |
| macrophyllā | . | Pink | 7, H. | A. America | |
| micranthā | . | Orn. wht. | 7, H. | A. | |
| multivalvĬs | . | White | 8, H. | A. Columbia | 1826 |
| nānā | . | White | 7, H. | A. N. Amer. | 1823 |
| noctiflōrā | . | Pink | 8, H. | A. Chile | 1826 |
| paniculātā | . | Orn. yel. | 8, H. | A. Peru | 1752 |
| persĬcā | . | Wht. grn. | 8, H. | A. Persia | 1831 |
| plumbaginifōlĬā | . | White | 8, H. | A. America | 1816 |
| pusīllā | . | White | 8, H. | B. Vera Cruz | 1733 |
| quadrivalvĬs | . | White | 7, H. | A. N. Amer. | 1811 |
| repändā | . | White | 6, H. | A. Havannah | 1820 |
| rotŭndifōlĬā | . | White | 8, H. | A. Swan River | 1837 |
| rŭstĬcā | . | White | 8, H. | A. America | 1750 |
| Tabācŭm | . | Pink | 7, H. | A. America | 1570 |
| alīpēs | . | Pink | 7, H. | A. S. Amer. | 1570 |
| attēnuātā | . | Pink | 7, H. | A. S. Amer. | 1570 |
| gracilĭpēs | . | Pink | 7, H. | A. S. Amer. | 1570 |
| linguā | . | Pink | 7, H. | A. S. Amer. | 1570 |
| macrophyllā | . | Pink | 7, H. | A. S. Amer. | 1570 |
| pallescēns | . | Pink | 7, H. | A. S. Amer. | 1570 |
| serōtĬnā | . | Pink | 7, H. | A. S. Amer. | 1570 |
| Vērdĭn | . | Pink | 7, H. | A. S. Amer. | 1570 |
| undulātā, 1 | . | White | 7, G. Her. P. N. S. W. | | 1800 |
| vincæflōrā | . | White | 8, G. Her. P. S. Amer. | | 1820 |
| viscōsā | . | Pink | 8, H. | A. B. Ayres | 1824 |
| YbarrēnsĬs | . | Pink | 8, H. | A. S. Amer. | 1823 |

NĪDŬLANT, nestling, as a bird in its nest.

NĪDŬLĀRĬĀ, *Bulliard.* From *nidus*, a nest; on account of the plants consisting of cups, which contain egg-like seeds. *Linn.* 24, Or. 9, Nat. Or. *Fungi.* Interesting plants, found on rotten leaves, shavings of wood, bark, &c.—*campanulátá, Crucibŭlŭm, striátá.*

NĪDŬS, the nest of anything.

NĪEBŬHRĬA, *Decandolle.* After Carslen Niebuhr, a traveller in Arabia. *Linn.* 13, Or. 1, Nat. Or. *Capparidaceæ.* These plants grow well in a mixture of loam and peat; and cuttings of the nearly ripened wood will root in sand, under a glass, the stove species in heat. *Synonymes:* 1. *Crateva cäffra.* 2. *Capparis heteroclita.*

| | | | | | |
|---|---|---|---|---|---|
| cäffrā, 1 | . | White | G. Ev. S. C. G. H. | | 1818 |
| madagascariēnsĬs | . | White | 8. Ev. S. Madagas. | | 1822 |
| oblongifōlĬā, 2 | . | White | G. Ev. Cl. E. Ind. | | 1822 |

NĪEREMBĒRGĬA, *Ruiz and Pavon.* In honour of John Eusebius Nieremberg, a Spanish Jesuit, author of a History of Nature, Antwerp, 1635. *Linn.* 5, Or. 1, Nat. Or. *Solanaceæ.* These very elegant plants may be referred to *Petunia* for culture and propagation. *Synonyme:* 1. *N. linariæfolia.*

| | | | | | |
|---|---|---|---|---|---|
| aristātā | . | Wht. pur. | 7. H. | A. Panama | 1832 |
| calycĬnā | . | White | 7, G. Her. P. Uraguay | | 1834 |

filicaulis, 1 . . Lilac . . 6, G. Her. P. B. Ayres . 1832
grácilis . . . Wht. pur. 7, F. Her. P. Uruguay . 1831

NIGELLA, *Linn.* From *niger*, black; the black seed, which is the part of the plant known in cookery. *Linn.* 13, Or. 5, Nat. Or. *Ranunculaceæ.* The species of Fennel-flower are curious and ornamental; they only require to be sown in the open ground. The seeds of *N. sativa* and *N. arvensis* were formerly used instead of pepper, and are said to be still extensively used in adulterating it.

aristáta . . . Blue . 8, H. B. Athens
arvénsis . . . Brn. wht. 7, H. A. Germany . 1683
ciliáris . . . Yellow . 7, H. A. Levant
coarctáta . . . Wht. grn. 8, H. Her. P. S. Eur. . 1793
corniculáta . . Yellow . 7, H. A. . 1820
damascéna . . Li. blue . 7, H. A. S. Eur. . 1570
floré-pléno . . Li. blue . 7, H. A. S. Eur. . 1570
divaricáta . . Brn. wht. 7, H. A. Egypt
fœniculácea . . Brn. wht. 7, H. B. Tauria . 1835
hispánica . . . Brn. wht. 7, H. A. Spain . 1629
orientális . . . Yellow . 7, H. A. Syria . 1699
satíva . . . Yellow . 7, H. A. Egypt . 1548
citrína . . . Pa. blue . 7, H. A. S. Eur.
crética . . . Pa. blue . 7, H. A. Crete
índica . . . Pa. blue . 7, H. A. E. Ind.

NIGHTSHADE, see *Solánum.*
NIGRITA, partially black.
NIGRITELLA. From *niger*, black; because of the dark colour of the flowers. *Linn.* 20, Or. 1, Nat. Or. *Orchidaceæ.* A curious tuberous-rooted species, growing freely in loam and peat, and increased by divisions of the roots.

angustifólia . . Drk. crim. 7, H. Ter. Austria . . 1795

NIPA, *Thunberg.* The name of the tree in the Moluccas. *Linn.* 21, Or. 10, Nat. Or. *Palmaceæ.* A fine palm, requiring to be grown in a strong loamy soil and a hot, humid atmosphere.

frúticans . . . White . . Palm. E. Ind. . 1822

NIPHOBOLUS, *Kaulfuss.* From *niphobolos*, covered with snow; the indusia appear as if covered with snow. *Linn.* 24, Or. 1, Nat. Or. *Polypodiaceæ.* A genus of very ornamental ferns, which grow well in sandy loam and peat in equal portions, and are increased by dividing the roots, or by seeds. Synonymes: 1. *Polypodium adnascens.* 2. *confluens.* 3. *lineare.* 4. *lingua, Acrostichum lingua.* 5. *P. pertusum.* 6. *P. rupestris.*

adnascens, 1 . . Brown . 5, S. Ev. Cr. E. Ind. . 1824
albicans . . . Brown . 7, S. Her. P. Ceylon
confluens, 2 . . Brown . 5, S. Ev. Cr. N. Holl. . 1820
lineáre, 3 . . . Brown . 5, S. Ev. Cr. Japan . 1822
lingua, 4 . . . Brown . 5, S. Ev. Cr. Japan . 1817
pertúsus, 5 . . Brown . 5, S. Ev. Cr. China . 1821
rupéstris, 6 . . Brown . 5, S. Ev. Cr. N. Holl. . 1824
sinénsis . . . Brown . 5, S. Ev. Cr. China

NIPPLEWORT, see *Lapsána.*
NISSÓLIA, *Jacquin.* In honour of William Nissole, a diligent French botanist. *Linn.* 17, Or. 4, Nat. Or. *Leguminosæ.* Ornamental shrubs, which grow well in a mixture of loam and peat; and cuttings of the ripened wood will root in sand, under a glass, in heat.

aculeáta . . . S. Ev. Cl. Rio Jan. . 1824
fruticósa . . . Yellow . 8, S. Ev. Cl. S. Amer. . 1766
glabráta . . . White . S. Ev. S. . 1823
micróptera . . White . 7, S. Ev. S. Teneriffe . 1820
racemósa . . . White . 7, S. Ev. Cl. W. Ind. . 1800
retúsa . . . S. Ev. Cl. S. Amer. . 1819
robiniæfólia . . S. Ev. S. St. Vinc. . 1824

NITELLA, *Agardh.* From *niteo*, to shine; shining plants. *Linn.* 24, Or. 7, Nat. Or. *Algæ.* Fresh water *Algæ*; the plants are found in pools and rivulets. The stems are composed of simple tubes. Synonyme: 1. *Chara flexilis—flexilis* 1, *grácilis, nidifíca, opáca, translúcens.*

NITIDUS, shining, glossy.
NITRARIA, *Schreber.* From *nitrum*, nitre; first found by Schreber near the nitre works in Siberia. *Linn.* 11, Or. 1, Nat. Or. *Nitraceæ.* Curious dwarf-growing shrubs; they succeed well in a light sandy soil, and may be increased either by cuttings or layers. Synonyme: 1. *N. caspica.*

Schóberi . . . Pur. blue . 6, H. De. S. Siberia . . 1788
cáspica, 1 . . . White . 6, H. De. S. Caspian . 1812
sibírica . . . H. De. S. Siberia
tridentáta . . . H. De. S. Barbary . 1820

NITTA-TREE, see *Párkia.*
NIVEA, covered with a pubescence resembling snow.

NIVENIA, *R. Brown.* In honour of James Niven, an eminent collector of South African seeds. *Linn.* 4, Or. 1, Nat. Or. *Proteaceæ.* These shrubs are possessed of some beauty; they thrive in sandy peat and a little loam mixed, and cuttings of the young wood root freely in sand, under a glass; they may also be increased by seeds. Synonyme: 1. *Protea spatulata.*

crithmifólia . . Pa. pur. . 7, G. Ev. S. C. G. H. . 1797
Lagópus . . . Purple . 7, G. Ev. S. C. G. H. . 1810
média . . . Purple . 7, G. Ev. S. C. G. H. . 1803
parvifó'ia, 1 . . Purple . 7, G. Ev. S. C. G. H. . 1823
scéptrum . . . Pa. pur. . 7, G. Ev. S. C. G. H. . 1790
spathuláta . . . Purple . 7, G. Ev. S. C. G. H. . 1790
spicáta . . . Purple . 7, G. Ev. S. C. G. H. . 1790

NOCCA, *Cavanilles.* In honour of Dominic Nocca, a professor at Pavia. *Linn.* 19, Or. 1, Nat. Or. *Compositæ.* Ornamental plants, growing in any common soil, and increased by cuttings. Synonymes: 1. *Lagasca helianthifolia.* 2. *L. rubra.* 3. *L. suaveolens.*

latifólia . . . White . 8, F. Ev. S. Mexico . 1826
rígida, 1 . . . Pink . 8, S. Ev. S. Mexico . 1825
rúbra, 2 . . . Red . 7, S. Ev. S. Mexico . 1823
suavéolens, 3 . . White . 8, S. Ev. S. Mexico . 1825

NODDING, having a drooping position.
NODI, the swelled articulations of stems, the place where one joint is articulated with another.
NODOSE, having many nodi, or knots.
NODULUS, a small, hard nodus, or knot.
NOISETTIA, *Humb., Bonp., and Kunth.* In honour of Louis Noisette, an eminent French cultivator. *Linn.* 5, Or. 1, Nat. Or. *Violaceæ.* This species grows freely in any light rich soil, and young cuttings root in sand, under a glass, in heat. Synonymes: 1. *Ionidium longifolium, Viola longifolia.*

longifólia, 1 . . Cream . S. Ev. S. Cayenne . 1824

NOLANA, *Linn.* From *nola*, a little bell; because of the form of the corolla. *Linn.* 5, Or. 1, Nat. Or. *Nolanaceæ.* These plants are very showy when in flower, and are therefore well suited for ornamenting flower-borders. The seed ought to be sown on a gentle hotbed in spring, and transplanted to the open ground about the middle of May.

atriplicifólia . . Wht. yel. 7, H. A. Peru . 1834
grandiflóra . . . Blue . 7, H. Tr. A. Chile . 1829
paradóxa . . . Blue . 8, H. Tr. A. Chile . 1825
prostráta . . . Blue . 8, H. Tr. A. Peru . 1761
tenélla . . . Blue . 8, H. Tr. A. Chile . 1824

NOLINA, *Michaux.* After P. C. Nolin, an American botanist. *Linn.* 6, Or. 3, Nat. Or. *Melanthaceæ.* This is a very ornamental plant, succeeding in sandy peat, and increased by offsets. Synonyme: 1. *Phalangium virgatum.*

georgiána, 1 . . White . 7, H. Her. P. Georgia . . 1812

NONATELIA, *Aublet.* The name of one of the species in Guiana. *Linn.* 5, Or. 1, Nat. Or. *Cinchonaceæ.* A genus of ornamental plants; for culture and propagation, see *Hamiltonia.* Synonymes: 1. *Psychotria involucrata.* 2. *P. racemosa.*

lútea . . . Yellow . 6, S. Ev. S. Guiana . 1823
officinalis, 1 . . White . 6, S. Ev. S. Cayenne . 1827
racemósa, 2 . . White . 6, S. Ev. S. Guiana . 1818
violácea . . . White . 6, S. Ev. S. Guiana . 1824

NONNEA, *Decandolle.* In honour of J. P. Nonne, a German botanist. *Linn.* 5, Or. 1, Nat. Or. *Boraginaceæ.* Plants of no great beauty; they grow well in the open border, where the seed has only to be sown. Synonymes: 1. *Lycopsis lutea.* 2. *L. picta, Anchusa picta.* 3. *L. vesicaria.* 4. *Anchusa rosea.* 5. *A. versicolor.* 6. *L. vesicaria.*

ciliáta . . . Yellow . 6, H. A. Levant . 1804
flavéscens . . . Yellow . 6, H. A. Russia . 1835
lútea, 1 . . . Yellow . 6, H. A. Crimea . 1805
nígricans . . . Dark . 5, H. Tr. A. Barbary . 1822
picta, 2 . . . Varieg. . 6, H. Tr. A. Tauria . 1800
pulla, 3 . . . Dark . 6, H. Her. Tr. Germany . 1648
rósea, 4 . . . Pink . 6, H. A. Crimea . 1823
versícolor, 5 . . Varieg. . 6, H. Tr. A. Caucasus . 1820
violácea, 6 . . . Purple . 6, H. Tr. A. S. Eur. . 1686

NORANTEA, *Aublet.* From the Guiana name of *N. guianensis, Gonora-antegri.* *Linn.* 13, Or. 1, Nat. Or. *Marcgraaviaceæ.* These are singular and very beautiful plants; they grow well in a mixture of loam and peat, and cuttings root freely either in sand or mould, under a glass, in heat.

| | | | | | |
|---|---|---|---|---|---|
| brasiliénsis | . . | 8. Ev. S. Brazil | . 1820 |
| guianénsis | . . Violet . . | 8. Ev. S. Guiana | . 1818 |

**NORŌNHÏX**, *Thouars.* In honour of C. Noronha, a traveller in Madagascar. *Linn.* 2, Or. 1, Nat. Or. *Oleaceæ.* For the culture and propagation of these plants, see the genus *Olea.* Synonymes: 1. *Olea cernua.* 2. *O. emarginata.*

| | | | | | |
|---|---|---|---|---|---|
| cérnŭā, 1 | . . . White | 8. Ev. T. Mauritius | . 1816 |
| emargināta, 2 | . . White | 8. S. Ev. T. Madagas. | . 1825 |

**NORWAY-SPRUCE,** see *Pinus canadensis.*

**NŌSTÓC,** *Vauch.* Meaning unknown. *Linn.* 24, Or. 7, Nat. Or. *Algæ.* A genus of curious plants, found in lakes, and on rocks in moist situations —cærūléŭm, commŭnĕ, foliācéŭm, humifŭsŭm, microscŏpicŭm, Muscŏrŭm, prunifŏrmĕ, sphǣricŭm, verrucōsŭm, vesicāriŭm.

**NOTELǢX,** *Ventenat.* From *notos,* south, and *elaia,* an olive; in allusion to the genus being allied to *Olea,* and from its native country. *Linn.* 2, Or. 1, Nat. Or. *Oleaceæ.* These plants grow well in peat and loam, and cuttings of the ripened wood root readily in sand, under a glass.

| | | | | | |
|---|---|---|---|---|---|
| ligustrina | . . . White | . 7, G. Ev. S. V.D.L. | . 1807 |
| longifolia | . . . White | . 4, G. Ev. S. N.S.W. | . 1790 |
| ovata | . . . White | . 6, G. Ev. S. N. S. W. | . 1824 |
| punctata | . . . White | . 6, G. Ev. S. N. Holl. | . 1826 |
| rigida | . . . White | . 7, G. Ev. S. V.D.L. | . 1821 |

**NOTHOCHLǢNX,** *R. Brown.* From *nothos,* spurious, and *chlaina,* a cloak; the sori are frequently only covered over by the paleæ of the frond. *Linn.* 24, Or. 1, Nat. Or. *Polypodiaceæ.* This is a genus of very handsome stove ferns. They grow well in sandy peat soil, in a hot, humid atmosphere, and are increased by divisions, or by seeds, sown and treated in the usual manner. Synonymes: 1. *Acrostichum velleum, lanuginosum.* 2. *A. Maranta.* 3. *Pteris piloselloides.*

| | | | | | |
|---|---|---|---|---|---|
| distans | . . . Brown | . 7, G. Her. P. N. Holl. | . 1823 |
| Eckloniana | . . Brown | . 8, S. Her. P. | . 1838 |
| lanuginosa, 1 | . Brown | . 8, G. Her. P. Madeira | . 1778 |
| Maranta 2 | . . Brown | . 7, G. Her. P. N. Holl. | . 1820 |
| nivea | . . . White | . 7, S. Her. P. Mexico | . |
| piloselloides, 3 | . Brown | . 7, S. Her. P. E. Ind. | . 1822 |
| pumila | . . . Brown | . 8, S. Her. P. N. Holl. | . |
| sinuata | . . . Brown | . 8. Her. P. Peru | . 1831 |
| tenera | . . . Brown | . 8. Her. P. Mendoza | . |

**NOTŎCRĀS,** *R. Brown.* From *notos,* the back, and *keras,* a horn; back of the pods. *Linn.* 15, Nat. Or. *Cruciferæ.* Hardy annuals, not worth cultivating. Synonymes: 1. *Erysimum bicorne.* 2. *E. quadricorne, Nasturtium quadricorne—canariénsĕ 1, hispănicŭm, quadricŏrnĕ 2.*

**NOTYLÏX,** *Lindley.* From *notos,* back, and *tylos,* a hump; in allusion to a singular callosity on the stigma. *Linn.* 20, Or. 1, Nat. Or. *Orchidaceæ.* Pretty little plants, well worthy of a place in every collection; for culture and propagation, see *Burlingtonia.*

| | | | | | |
|---|---|---|---|---|---|
| Barkeri | . . . Straw . . | 8. Epi. Mexico | . 1837 |
| incūrva | . . . Straw yel. | 8. Epi. Trinidad | . |
| micrantha | . . Pa. grn. | 8. Epi. Demerara | . |
| punctata | . . . Yel. grn | 8. Epi. Trinidad | . 1822 |
| tenuis | . . . Pa. straw | 8. Epi. Demerara | . 1836 |

**NŬCLĔŬS,** the kernel of a nut.

**NUCAMENTACEOUS,** producing nuts.

**NŬDICAŬLIS,** naked-stemmed.

**NUMMULĀRÏX,** round, like a piece of coin.

**NŪPHĀR,** *Sibthorp.* From *naufar,* or *nyloufar,* the Arabic name of *Nymphæa.* *Linn.* 13, Or. 1, Nat. Or. *Nymphæaceæ.* This is a genus of very beautiful plants, admirably adapted for growing in ponds, cisterns, or lakes; and they are increased by dividing the roots, or by seeds, which have only to be thrown into the water where they are intended to grow. Synonymes: 1. *Nymphæa advena.* 2. *N. lutea.* 3. *Nuphar minima.*

| | | | | | |
|---|---|---|---|---|---|
| advéna, 1 | . . . Yellow | . 7, H. Aq. P. N. Amer. | . 1772 |
| Kalmiana | . . . Yellow | . 7, H. Aq. P. Canada . | . 1807 |
| lutea, 2 | . . . Yellow | . 6, H. Aq. P. Britain . | . |
| pumila, 3 | . . . Yellow | . 7, H. Aq. P. Scotland | . |
| sagittæfŏlïa | . . Yellow | . 7, H. Aq. P. N. Amer. | . 1824 |

**NŪTXNS,** nodding, drooping.

**NUTMEG,** see *Myristica.*

**NUTMEG,** see *Monodōra myristica.*

**NUTS,** seeds covered with hard shells.

**NUTTXLLÏX,** *Dickson.* In honour of Thomas Nuttall, F.L.S., professor of mineralogy at New Cambridge,

North America, an eminent botanist. *Linn.* 16, Or. 8, Nat. Or. *Malvaceæ.* A genus of very elegant plants when in blossom, and, therefore, well worth cultivating. They grow in a sandy peat soil, and are increased by seeds, and sometimes by dividing at the roots. They require a slight protection in severe weather.

| | | | | | |
|---|---|---|---|---|---|
| cordāta | . . . Pink | . 8, H. Her. P. N. Amer. | . 1835 |
| digitāta | . . . Purple | . 8, H. Her. P. N. Amer. | . 1834 |
| grandiflŏra | . . Pink | . 8, F. Her. P. | . |
| papaveracéa | . . Red. pur. | . 8, H. Her. P. Louisiana | . 1833 |
| pedāta | . . . Purple | . 8, H. Her. P. N. Amer. | . 1834 |

**NUT-TREE,** see *Corglus.*

**NŪYTSÏX,** *R. Brown.* After Peter Nuyts, a famous Dutch navigator. *Linn.* 5, Or. 1, Nat. Or. *Loranthaceæ.* This very singular tree requires to be grown in a mixture of loam, peat, and sand; young plants may probably be obtained from cuttings planted in sand, under a glass. Synonyme: 1. *Loranthus floribundus.*

| | | | | | |
|---|---|---|---|---|---|
| floribūndā | . . . Sulphur | . G. Ev. T. N. Holl. | . 1831 |

**NYCTXNTHĒs,** *Linn.* From *nux, nuctos,* night, and *anthos,* a flower; the flowers expand at night, and fall off at the break of day: whence *arbor-tristis,* the name of the species. *Linn.* 22, Or. 1, Nat. Or. *Jasminaceæ.* This tree is much valued on account of its very fragrant flowers, which are unfortunately seldom to be seen in this country. It grows in loam and peat, and is increased by cuttings, not too ripe, planted in sand, under a glass, in heat.

| | | | | | |
|---|---|---|---|---|---|
| arbor-tristïs | . . White | . 8. Ev. S. E. Ind. . | . 1781 |

**NYCTERISÏTÏÖN,** *Ruiz and Pavon.* From *nykteris,* a bat, and *sition,* food; bats feed on the flowers. *Linn.* 5, Or. 1, Nat. Or. *Sapotaceæ.* This plant grows well in light turfy loam and peat well incorporated, and is increased by cuttings of the ripened wood planted in sand, under a glass, in heat. Synonyme: 1. *Chrysophyllum splendens.*

| | | | | | |
|---|---|---|---|---|---|
| ferruginéŭm, 1 | . White . | 8. Ev. T. S. Amer. | . 1823 |

**NYCTXLÏŬM,** see *Solānŭm.*

**NYMPHǢX,** *Linn.* From *nymphe,* a water-nymph; alluding to the habitation of the plants. *Linn.* 13, Or. 1, Nat. Or. *Nymphæaceæ.* These are beautiful plants, well worthy of cultivating in every collection. The stove species should be grown in tubs of water placed in a warm part of the house, with some rich loamy soil at the bottom. The hardy kinds may be grown in ponds, canals, &c. They are all increased either by seeds, dividing the roots, or separating the tubers. The stems of *N. alba* are superior to oak galls for dyeing grey. Synonymes: 1. *stellata, var.* 2. *cahlara.* 3. *esculenta, Castalia edulis.* 4. *C. mystica.* 5. *N. odorata minor.* 6. *cærulea.* 7. *Lotus.*

| | | | | | |
|---|---|---|---|---|---|
| alba | . . . . White | . 6, H. Aq. P. Britain . | . |
| canadénsis | . . White | . 6, H. Aq. P. Canada . | . 1820 |
| amplā | . . . White | . 7, S. Aq. P. Jamaica | . 1801 |
| blanda | . . . White | . 7, S. Aq. P. Trinidad | . 1820 |
| cærūléā, 1 | . . . Blue | . 7, S. Aq. P. Egypt . | . 1792 |
| cyanéā, 2 | . . . Blue | . 7, S. Aq. P. E. Ind. . | . 1809 |
| edūlïs, 3 | . . . White | . 7, S. Aq. P. E. Ind. . | . |
| Lōtūs, 4 | . . . Pink | . 7, S. Aq. P. Egypt . | . 1802 |
| minŏr, 5 | . . . White | . 7, S. Aq. P. N. Amer. | . 1812 |
| nitida | . . . White | . 7, H. Aq. P. Siberia . | . 1809 |
| odorāta | . . . White | . 7, H. Aq. P. N. Amer. | . 1786 |
| pubéscens | . . White | . 6, S. Aq. P. E. Ind. . | . 1803 |
| pygmǣā | . . . White | . 7, H. Aq. P. China . | . 1805 |
| reniformis | . . White | . 7, G. Aq. P. Carolina | . 1823 |
| rŭbra | . . . Red | . 7, S. Aq. P. E. Ind. . | . 1803 |
| rōséā | . . . Pink | . 7, S. Aq. P. E. Ind. . | . 1803 |
| scutifŏlïā, 6 | . Blue | . 8, S. Aq. P. C. G. H. | . 1792 |
| stellāta | . . . Blue | . 7, S. Aq P. E. Ind. . | . 1803 |
| thermālïs, 7 | . White | . 7, S. Aq. P. Hungary | . 1800 |
| versicŏlŏr | . . Pink wht. | 8, S. Aq. P. Bengal . | . 1807 |

**NYSSX,** *Linn.* Supposed to be from the name of a water-nymph, on account of the habitat of the plants. *Linn.* 23, Or. 2, Nat. Or. *Santalaceæ.* These trees are well suited for large shrubberies; they grow in any common soil, but prefer a damp situation, growing best when planted on an island in a pond or river; they may be propagated by layers or seeds. Synonymes: 1. *N. aquatica.* 2. *N. capitata.* 3. *N. denticulata, tomentosa.* 4. *N. sylvatica.*

| | | | | | |
|---|---|---|---|---|---|
| biflŏrā, 1 | . . . Green | . 5, H. De. T. N. Amer. | . 1789 |
| cāndicāna, 2 | . . Green | . H. De. T. N. Amer. | . 1806 |
| grandidentāta, 3 | . Green | . 5, H. De. T. N. Amer. | . 1735 |
| villōsā, 4 | . . . Green | . 5, H. De. T. N. Amer. | . 1824 |

# O.

OAK, see *Quércus*.

OAT-GRASS, see *Avéna*.

OB is used in the composition of Latin technicals to indicate that the thing is inverted, as *obovate* is inversely *ovate*.

OBRĀTŬS, bottle-shaped.

OBCONICAL, inversely conical.

OBCORDATELY TWO-LOBED, inversely-cordate, with the indentation very deep, so as to appear of two lobes.

OBĒSĬĀ, *Haworth*. From *obesus*, fat; alluding to the flowers. *Linn.* 5, Or. 2, Nat. Or. *Asclepiadaceæ*. This is an interesting genus of little plants; sandy loam suits them, and young cuttings root in sand, under a glass. *Synonymes*: 1. *Stapelia geminata.* 2. *S. serrulata.*

| | | | | | |
|---|---|---|---|---|---|
| decŏrā | . . . | Yel. str. | .8, G. Ev. S. C. G. H. | .1795 |
| gemĭnātă, 1 | . . | Purple | .3, G. Ev. S. C. G. H. | .1795 |
| serrulātă, 2 | . . | Purple | .7, G. Ev. S. C. G. H. | .1805 |

OBLIQUELY-REPAND; a leaf having a margin undulated, and unequally and obliquely dilated, is said to be obliquely-repand.

OBLIQUELY-TRUNCATE, cut off in an oblique manner.

OBLONG, when joined by a hyphen to another word, signifies a form between the two words, as oblong-elliptical, oblong-linear, and so on.

OBLONG-TRIQUETROUS, oblong and three-sided.

OBOVATE, } inversely egg-shaped, with the broadest
OBOVOID, } end uppermost.

OBOVATE, when joined by a hyphen to another word, signifies a shape between the two words, thus, obovate-spatulate, a shape between obovate and spatulate.

OBOVATE-CUNEATED, } between obovate and wedge-shaped, with the broadest end up-permost.
OBOVATELY-WEDGE-SHAPED, }

OBSOLETE, hardly evident.

OBSOLETELY-TOOTHED, scarcely toothed.

OBTUSE-ANGLED, having blunt angles.

ONVOLUTE, having one part rolled on another.

OCCIDENTAL, coming from the west.

OCHNĀ, *Schreber*. From *ochne*, the Greek name of the wild pear-tree; there is some resemblance in the foliage. *Linn.* 13, Or. 1, Nat. Or. *Ochnaceæ*. The species of this genus are said to be very ornamental; they grow from six to eight, and *O. arborea* to twenty, feet high. Sandy loam and peat mixed suit them, and cuttings root in sand, under a glass, in heat. *Synonyme*: 1. *O. squarrosa.*

| | | | | | |
|---|---|---|---|---|---|
| arbŏrĕā | . . . | Yellow | . S. Ev. T. C. G. H. | .1822 |
| atropurpŭrĕā | . . | Purple | . O. Ev. S. C. G. H. | .1816 |
| lūcĭdă | . . . | Yellow | . S. Ev. S. E. Ind. | .1819 |
| mauritiānă | . . | Yellow | . S. Ev. S. Mauritius | .1822 |
| multĭflŏrā | . . | Yellow | . S. Ev. S. S. Leone | .1820 |
| nĭtĭdă | . . . | Yellow | . S. Ev. S. C. G. H. | .1815 |
| obtusātă, 1 | . . | Yellow | . S. Ev. S. E. Ind. | .1790 |

OCHROLEUCOUS, pale yellow, ochre-coloured.

OCHRŌMĀ, *Swartz*. From *ochros*, pale; referring to the flowers, leaves, and wool of the seeds. *Linn.* 16, Or. 2, Nat. Or. *Sterculiaceæ*. Interesting plants, attaining from twelve to twenty feet high; they grow best in sandy loam, and young plants are raised from cuttings in sand, under a glass, in heat.

| | | | | | |
|---|---|---|---|---|---|
| Lagŏpŭs | . . . | White | . S. Ev. T. Jamaica | .1804 |
| tomentōsā | . . . | White | . S. Ev. T. S. Amer. | .1816 |

OCHRŌSĬĀ, *Jussieu*. From *ochros*, pale; alluding to the wood. *Linn.* 5, Or. 1, Nat. Or. *Apocynaceæ*. A rather pretty shrub; for culture and propagation, see *Cerbera*. *Synonyme*: 1. *Cerbera borbonica.*

| | | | | | |
|---|---|---|---|---|---|
| borbōnĭcā, 1 | . . | | . S. Ev. S. Bourbon | .1823 |

OCHRŬS, *Persoon*. From *ochros*, yellow; on account of the colour of the flowers. *Linn.* 17, Or. 4, Nat. Or. *Leguminosæ*. A pretty annual, of easy cultivation in any common garden soil. *Synonyme*: 1. *Pisum Ochrus.*

| | | | | | |
|---|---|---|---|---|---|
| pallĭdă, 1 | . . . | Yellow | .7, H. Cl. A. S. Eur. | |

OCTRŌDĬŬM, *Decandolle*. From *oethodes*, warted ;

alluding to the warted surface of the pods. *Linn.* 15, Nat. Or. *Cruciferæ*. A plant of little beauty and very simple culture. *Synonymes*: 1. *Bunias ægyptiaca*, *Rapistrum ægyptiacum.*

| | | | | | |
|---|---|---|---|---|---|
| ægyptĭācŭm, 1 | . | Yellow | . S. H. A. Egypt | .1787 |

OCTANDROUS, having eight stamens.

OCTOGYNOUS, having eight styles.

OCTOMĒRĬĀ, *R. Brown*. From *okto*, eight, and *meris*, a part; in allusion to the pollen-masses. *Linn.* 20, Or. 1, Nat. Or. *Orchidaceæ*. The species of this genus are not of a very interesting character; for culture and propagation, see *Burlingtonia*.

| | | | | | |
|---|---|---|---|---|---|
| grācĭlĭs | . . . | Yellow | . S. Epi. Rio Jan. | |
| gramĭnĭfŏlĭā | . . | Wht. yel. | 5, S. Epi. W. Ind. | .1793 |
| serratĭfŏlĭā | . . | White | .10, S. Epi. Rio Jan. | |
| tridentātă | . . | Yellow | . S. Epi. Demerara | |

OCY̆MŬM, *Linn.* From *oxo*, a smell; alluding to the powerful scent of the plants. *Linn.* 14, Or. 1, Nat. Or. *Labiatæ*. Some of the species of *Ocymum*, or *Basil*, are much esteemed as herbs, and are of the simplest culture. *Synonymes*: 1. *O. cristatum.* 2. *O. caryophyllatum.* 3. *O. thyrsiflorum.* 4. *O. cordifolium.* 5. *O. americanum.* 6. *O. grandiflorum.* 7. *O. montanum.* 8. *Plectranthus monachorum.* 9. *O. febrifugum.*

| | | | | | |
|---|---|---|---|---|---|
| adscēndēns, 1 | . | White | . 8, H. Her. P. E. Ind. | .1822 |
| albŭm | . . . | White | . H. A. E. Ind. | .1816 |
| basĭlĭcŭm | . . | White | . 8, H. A. E. Ind. | .1548 |
| glabrātŭm, 2 | . | White | . 7, H. A. E. Ind. | .1817 |
| pilōsŭm | . . | White | . 7, H. A. | |
| thyrsĭflŏrŭm, 3 | White | . 6, H. A. E. Ind. | .1806 |
| Bojĕrī, 4 | . . | White | . S. Her. H. Madagas. | .1825 |
| cānŭm, 5 | . . | White | . 7, H. A. China | .1822 |
| filamentōsŭm, 6 | . | White | . 9, S. Ev. S. Africa | .1802 |
| gratissĭmŭm | . . | White | . 7, S. Ev. S. E. Ind. | .1751 |
| menthoĭdēs | . | White | . S. A. | |
| micranthŭm, 7 | . | Pa. pur. | . 7, H. A. S. Amer. | .1816 |
| minĭmŭm | . . | White | . 7, H. A. Chile | .1573 |
| sānctŭm, 8 | . | Purple | . S. A. | .1768 |
| suāvĕ | . . | White | . 8, S. Ev. S. Madagas. | .1816 |
| vĭrĭdĕ, 9 | . . | Wht. grn. | 9, S. Ev. S. Africa | .1816 |

*americānum, cānum, cordĭfŏlĭum, grandĭflŏrum, gratissĭmum, menthoĭdes, micranthum, pilōsum, sānctum, suāvĕ, vĭrĭdĕ.*

ODONTARRHĒNĀ, *Meyer*. From *odous*, a tooth, and *arrhen*, a male; filaments. *Linn.* 15, Nat. Or. *Cruciferæ*. This pretty little trailer may be successfully cultivated in a mixture of loam and peat; cuttings.

| | | | | | |
|---|---|---|---|---|---|
| microphyllă | . | | H. Ev. Tr. | .1822 |

ODONTOGLŌSSŬM, *Humboldt and Kunth*. From *odous*, a tooth, and *glossa*, a tongue; alluding to the labellum. *Linn.* 20, Or. 1, Nat. Or. *Orchidaceæ*. This plant is new to our collections. The flowers are described as very handsome, the sepals and petals being yellowish-green, richly blotched with brown. It will probably succeed well with the treatment given to *Oncidiums*, and the like.

| | | | | | |
|---|---|---|---|---|---|
| cordātŭm | . . | Grn. brn. | . S. Epi. Mexico | .1837 |

ŒCEOCLĀDĒS, *Lindley*. From *oikeo*, to inhabit, and *klados*, a branch. *Linn.* 20, Or. 1, Nat. Or. *Orchidaceæ*. These are fine plants, well deserving a place in every collection; for culture and propagation, see *Vanda*. *Synonymes*: 1. *Angræcum falcatum.* 2. *A. maculatum.*

| | | | | | |
|---|---|---|---|---|---|
| falcātă, 1 | . . | White | . 4, S. Epi. China | .1815 |
| maculātă, 2 | . | Ro. wht. | 10, S. Epi. Africa | .1819 |

ŒDĒRĀ, *Crantz*. In honour of George Œder, a Danish professor of botany at Copenhagen. *Linn.* 19, Or. 5, Nat. Or. *Compositæ*. A pretty shrub, succeeding in sandy loam, mixed with a little peat, and propagated in sand, or sandy soil, under a glass.

| | | | | | |
|---|---|---|---|---|---|
| prolĭfĕră | . . | Yellow | . 5, G. Ev. S. C. G. H. | .1789 |

ŒNANTHĒ, *Lamarck*. From *oinos*, wine, and *anthos*, a flower; odour. *Linn.* 5, Or. 2, Nat. Or. *Umbelliferæ*. These plants are mostly uninteresting, and of simple culture in any common soil. The juice of the leaves and stem of *Œ. crocata* is a violent poison for man and animals. *Synonymes*: 1. Œ. *gymnorhiza*. 2. Œ. *approximata*. 3. Œ. *involucrata*. 4. Œ. *australis*. 5. Œ. *virgata*. 6. Œ. *glauca—apiifolia*, *crocata*, *fistulosa*, *globulosa*, *inēbrians*, *interrupta*, *Lachenalii* 1, *L. approximata* 2, *L. involucrata* 3, *nodiflora*, *peucedanifolia*, *phellandrium*, *pimpinelloides*, *P. chœrophylloides* 4, *P. pimpinellœfolia* 5, *prolifera*, *silaifolia* 6, *tenuifolia*.

ŒNOCĀRPŪS, *Martius*. From *oinos*, wine, and *karpos*, fruit; wine obtained from the fruit. *Linn*. 21, Or. 6, Nat. Or. *Palmaceæ*. A fine palm, attaining twenty feet high, thriving in any rich mould in a strong humid heat, and is increased from suckers.

| | | | | | |
|---|---|---|---|---|---|
| Bataūā . . . . | | Palm. S. Amer. | | | 1820 |

ŒNOTHĒRĀ, *Linn*. From *oinos*, wine, and *thera*, a catching; the roots of Œ. *biennis* were formerly taken after meals as incentives to wine-drinking. *Linn*. 8, Or. 1, Nat. Or. *Onagraceæ*. The Evening Primrose is a genus of truly beautiful plants, well suited for ornamenting flower-borders; they will grow in any common garden soil. The perennial species are increased by dividing the plants at the roots, by seeds, and some by cuttings. The seeds of the annual and biennial kinds merely require to be sown in the open border. *Synonymes*: 1. Œ. *spectabilis*. 2. Œ. *ambigua*. 3. Œ. *suaveolens*. 4. Œ. *concinna*. 5. Œ. *hirta*. 6. Œ. *alata*. 7. Œ. *striata*. 8. Œ. *undulata*. 9. Œ. *pinnatifida*. 10. Œ. *minima*. 11. Œ. *rhizocarpa*.

| acaulis | . . | White | . 7, | F. | Her. | P. | Chile | . | 1821 |
|---|---|---|---|---|---|---|---|---|---|
| albicans | . . | Whitish | . 6, | H. | | B. | Peru | . | 1823 |
| albicaulis | . . | White | . 6, | H. | | B. | N. Amer. | . | 1811 |
| amœna | . . | Purple | . 7, | H. | | A. | N. Amer. | . | 1825 |
| anisolobā | . . | White | . 6, | H. | Her. | P. | Chiloe | . | 1828 |
| biennis | . . | Yellow | . 7, | H. | | B. | N. Amer. | . | 1629 |
| bifrons | . . | Purple | . 8, | H. | | B. | Texas | . | 1835 |
| cespitosa | . . | White | . 6, | H. | Her. | P. | N. Amer. | . | 1811 |
| cheiranthifolia | . | Yellow | . 7, | G. | Ev. | S. | Chile | . | 1823 |
| clavata | . . | White | . 7, | H. | | A. | Mexico | . | 1827 |
| corymbosa, 1 | . | Yellow | . 8, | H. | | B. | Mexico | . | 1816 |
| cruciata | . . | Yellow | . 7, | H. | | B. | N. Amer. | . | 1824 |
| decumbens | . . | Purple | . 8, | H. | | A. | California | . | 1827 |
| densiflora | . . | Purple | . 8, | H. | | A. | California | . | 1830 |
| dentata | . . | Yellow | . 7, | H. | | A. | Peru | . | 1818 |
| Drummondii | . | Yellow | . 8, | F. | Her. | P. | Texas | . | 1833 |
| elata | . . | Pa. yel. | . 7, | H. | | B. | Mexico | . | 1826 |
| eroca | . . | Citron col. | . 7, | H. | | B. | C. G. H. | . | 1828 |
| Fraseri | . . | Yellow | . 6, | H. | Her. | P. | N. Amer. | . | 1811 |
| variegata | . . | Yellow | . 7, | H. | Her. | P. | Gardens | . | |
| fruticosa | . . | Yellow | . 8, | H. | Her. | P. | N. Amer. | . | 1737 |
| ambigua, 2 | . | Yellow | . 7, | H. | Her. | P. | N. Amer. | . | 1813 |
| gauroïdes | . . | Yellow | . 7, | H. | | B. | | . | 1810 |
| glauca | . . | Yellow | . 6, | H. | Her. | P. | N. Amer. | . | 1812 |
| variegata | . . | Yellow | . 7, | H. | Her. | P. | Gardens | . | |
| globularis | . . | Yellow | . 7, | H. | | B. | | . | 1824 |
| gracilis | . . | Yellow | . 7, | H. | Her. | P. | | . | 1833 |
| grandiflora, 3 | . | Yellow | . 7, | H. | | B. | N. Amer. | . | 1778 |
| humifusa, 4 | . | Purple | . 7, | H. | | A. | Florida | . | 1824 |
| hybrida | . . | Yellow | . 7, | H. | Her. | P. | N. Amer. | . | 1813 |
| incana | . . | Yellow | . 7, | H. | | B. | N. Amer. | . | 1820 |
| Lindleyii | . . | Purple | . 8, | H. | | A. | N. Amer. | . | 1826 |
| linearis | . . | Yellow | . 6, | H. | | A. | N. Amer. | . | 1822 |
| longiflora | . . | Yellow | . 7, | H. | | B. | B. Ayres | . | 1776 |
| macrocarpa | . | Yellow | . 6, | H. | Her. | P. | N. Amer. | . | 1811 |
| media | . . | Yellow | . 7, | H. | | B. | N. Amer. | . | 1823 |
| micrantha, 5 | . | Yellow | . 6, | H. | | A. | California | . | 1833 |
| missouriensis, 6 | . | Yellow | . 6, | H. | Her. | P. | N. Amer. | . | 1818 |
| mollissima | . . | Yellow | . 7, | H. | | B. | B. Ayres | . | 1732 |
| muricata | . . | Yellow | . 7, | H. | | B. | N. Amer. | . | 1789 |
| nervosa | . . | Yellow | . 7, | H. | Her. | P. | | . | 1827 |
| nocturna, 7 | . | Yellow | . 7, | H. | | B. | C. G. H. | . | 1790 |
| Nuttallii | . . | White | . 6, | H. | Her. | P. | N. Amer. | . | 1811 |
| odorata, 8 | . | Yellow | . 6, | H. | | B. | S. Amer. | . | 1790 |
| pallida | . . | Wht. red | . 6, | H. | Her. | P. | America | . | 1826 |
| parviflora | . . | Yellow | . 6, | H. | | B. | N. Amer. | . | 1757 |
| pubescens | . . | White | . 7, | H. | | B. | S. Amer. | . | 1825 |
| pumila | . . | Yellow | . 7, | H. | Her. | P. | N. Amer. | . | 1757 |
| purpurea | . . | Purple | . 6, | H. | | A. | N. Amer. | . | 1794 |
| Pūrshii, 9 | . | White | . 7, | H. | | B. | N. Amer. | . | 1811 |
| pusilla | . . | Yellow | . 7, | H. | | A. | N. Amer. | . | 1817 |
| quadrivulnera | . | Pink | . 9, | H. | | A. | N. Amer. | . | 1826 |
| Romanzovii | . | Purple | . 7, | H. | | A. | N. Amer. | . | 1817 |
| rosea | . . | Pink | . 6, | F. | Her. | P. | Peru | . | 1783 |
| rosea-alba | . | Red wht. | . 5, | H. | | A. | Nepal | . | 1827 |
| salicifolia | . . | Yellow | . 7, | H. | | | | . | |
| Sellowii | . . | | . 7, | H. | Her. | P. | M. Video | . | 1831 |
| serrulata | . . | Yellow | . 6, | H. | Her. | P. | N. Amer. | . | 1824 |
| serotina | . . | Yellow | . 9, | H. | Her. | P. | N. Amer. | . | 1820 |
| Simsiana | . . | Yellow | . 7, | H. | | B. | Mexico | . | 1816 |
| sinuata | . . | Yellow | . 7, | H. | | A. | N. Amer. | . | 1770 |
| minima, 10 | . | Yellow | . 7, | H. | | A. | N. Amer. | . | 1825 |
| speciosa | . . | White | . 6, | H. | Her. | P. | N. Amer. | . | 1821 |
| major | . . | White | . 7, | H. | Her. | P. | N. Amer. | . | |
| striata | . . | Yellow | . 7, | H. | | B. | | . | 1822 |

| stricta | . . | Yellow | . 6, | H. | | A. | | . | 1822 |
|---|---|---|---|---|---|---|---|---|---|
| taraxacifolia | . | White | . 6, | H. | Her. | P. | Peru | . | 1825 |
| tenella | . . | Purple | . 6, | H. | | A. | Chile | . | 1822 |
| tenuifolia | . . | Purple | . 8, | H. | | A. | Chile | . | 1828 |
| tetragona | . . | Yellow | . 7, | H. | Her. | P. | N. Amer. | . | 1820 |
| tetraptera | . . | White | . 7, | H. | | A. | Mexico | . | 1796 |
| triloba, 11 | . | Yellow | . 6, | H. | | A. | N. Amer. | . | 1822 |
| villosa | . . | Yellow | . 7, | H. | | B. | C. G. H. | . | 1791 |
| viminea | . . | Purple | . 7, | H. | | A. | California | . | 1826 |
| virgata | . . | Pur. wht. | . 7, | H. | | A. | Peru | . | 1823 |

OFFICINAL, any thing sold in shops.

OGECHEE-LIME, see *Nyssa candicans*.

OIDIUM, *Link*. From *oon*, an egg, and *eidos*, resemblance. *Linn*. 24, Or. 9, Nat. Or. *Fungi*. The species of this genus grow on decayed wood, and the leaves of various plants—*Erysiphoïdes*, *fructigēnum*, *fulvum*, *leucoconium*.

OIL-NUT, see *Hamiltonia*.

OIL-SEED, see *Verbesina sativa*.

OILY GRAIN, see *Sēsamum*.

OILY PALM, see *Elaïs*.

OLĀX. Named by Linnæus from *olax*, a furrow; but how applied to this genus we are not informed. *Linn*. 3, Or. 1, Nat. Or. *Oleaceæ*. Ornamental climbers of simple culture in loam and peat; and young plants may be raised from cuttings in sand, under a glass, in heat.

| imbricata | . . | White | . 12, | S. Ev. Cl. E. Ind. | . . | 1820 |
|---|---|---|---|---|---|---|
| scandens | . . | White | . 12, | S. Ev. Cl. E. Ind. | . . | 1820 |

OLDENLĀNDIĀ, *Linn*. In memory of H. B. Oldenland, a Dane, who collected plants at the Cape of Good Hope in 1695. *Linn*. 4, Or. 5, Nat. Or. *Cinchonaceæ*. An interesting under-shrub, growing in loam and peat, and increased by cuttings in sand, under a glass, in heat.

| Deppiana | . . | White | . 6, | S. Ev. S. Mexico | . . | 1835 |
|---|---|---|---|---|---|---|

OLD-MAN'S-BEARD, see *Geropōgon*.

OLĒĀ, *Linn*. From *elaia*, olive. *Linn*. 2, Or. 1, Nat. Or. *Oleaceæ*. The Olive is a very important genus of plants, on account of the oil, &c., which is obtained, chiefly from some of the varieties of *O. europæa*. They are also much admired for the fragrance of their flowers, which render them worthy of a place in every collection. They grow well in loam and peat; ripened cuttings root readily in sand, under a glass. They may also be increased by grafting on the common privet. *Synonymes*: 1. *O. undulata*. 2. *Phillyrea robusta*. 3. *O. europæa*.

| americana | . . | White | . 6, | G. Ev. S. N. Amer. | . | 1758 |
|---|---|---|---|---|---|---|
| arborea | . . | White | . 8, | G. Ev. T. | | 1825 |
| capensis | . . | White | . 7, | G. Ev. S. C. G. H. | . | 1730 |
| undulata, 1 | . | White | . 7, | G. Ev. T. C. G. H. | . | 1730 |
| dioica | . . | White | . 8, | S. Ev. T. E. Ind. | . | 1818 |
| excelsa | . . | White | . 5, | G. Ev. T. Madeira | . | 1784 |
| fragrans | . . | Yellow | . 7, | G. Ev. T. China | . | 1771 |
| lancea | . . | White | . 8, | S. Ev. T. I. France | . | 1819 |
| Oleaster | . . | White | . 7, | G. Ev. S. Portugal | . | 1821 |
| paniculata | . | White | . 7, | G. Ev. T. N. Holl. | . | 1825 |
| robusta, 3 | . | White | . 6, | S. Ev. T. Nepal | . | 1834 |
| Roxburghiana | . | White | . 8, | S. Ev. T. E. Ind. | . | 1820 |
| sativa, 3 | . | White | . 8, | H. Ev. T. S. Eur. | . | 1570 |
| buxifolia | . . | White | . 7, | F. Ev. T. S. Eur. | . | |
| ferruginea | . | White | . 7, | F. Ev. T. C. G. H. | . | |
| latifolia | . . | White | . 7, | F. Ev. T. S. Eur. | . | |
| longifolia | . | White | . 7, | F. Ev. T. S. Eur. | . | |
| obliqua | . . | White | . 7, | F. Ev. T. S. Eur. | . | |
| verrucosa | . | White | . 4, | G. Ev. S. C. G. H. | . | 1814 |

OLEA, see *Noronhia*.

OLEAGINOUS, having the qualities of oil.

OLEASTER, see *Elæagnus*.

OLERACEOUS, esculent, eatable.

OLIBANUM-TREE, see *Boswellia*.

OLIVE, see *Olēa*.

OLIVE-BARK-TREE, see *Bucida*.

OLIVĒRIĀ, *Ventenat*. In honour of M. G. L. Olivier, a celebrated French naturalist. *Linn*. 5, Or. 2, Nat. Or. *Umbelliferæ*. A plant of little interest; the seed should be sown on a gentle hotbed, and afterwards transplanted.

| decumbens | . . | Purple | . 6, | H. Tr. A. Bagdad | . | 1816 |
|---|---|---|---|---|---|---|

OLIVE-WOOD, see *Elæodendron*.

OLYNTHIĀ, *Lindley*. From *olynthos*, signifying an unripe fig. *Linn*. 12, Or. 1, Nat. Or. *Myrtaceæ*. An ornamental species; for culture and propagation, see *Myrtus*. *Synonyme*: 1. *Myrtus disticha*.

| disticha, 1 | . . . | White | . 5, | S. Ev. T. Jamaica | . | 1793 |
|---|---|---|---|---|---|---|

OLYRĀ, *Linn*. The name of a kind of grain mentioned

by the Greek authors. *Linn.* 21, Or. 3, Nat. Or.
*Gramíneæ.* Worthless plants, of easy cultivation.
*Synonyme:* 1. *O. paniculata—latifolia* 1, *pauci-
flóra.*

OMALÁNTHUS, *Adrien Jussieu.* From *homalos*, smooth,
and *anthos*, a flower. *Linn.* 21, Or. 10, Nat. Or.
*Euphorbiaceæ.* A pretty stove shrub, cultivated in
peat and loam, and propagated from ripened cuttings in sand, under a glass, in heat.

| | | | | | |
|---|---|---|---|---|---|
| populifolia . . . | White . | 8, S. Ev. S. N. Holl. | | | 1825 |

OMIME-PLANT, see *Plectránthus ternátus.*

OMPHALEA, *Linn.* From *omphalos*, navel; umbilicated
anthers. *Linn.* 21, Or. 10, Nat. Or. *Euphorbiaceæ.*
Interesting trees, from twelve to twenty feet high,
cultivated in a mixture of peat and loam, and propagated from cuttings in sand, under a glass, in heat.

| | | | | | |
|---|---|---|---|---|---|
| diándra . . . . | Apetal | 8 | Ev. T. | W. Ind. | 1820 |
| densifolia . . . | Apetal | 8 | Ev. T. | Cuba | 1823 |
| triándra . . . . | Apetal | 6, S. Ev. T. | Jamaica | 1763 |

OMPHALÓBYUM, *Gærtner.* From *omphalos*, a navel,
and *lobus*, a pod. *Linn.* 10, Or. 1, Nat. Or. *Leguminosæ.* A genus of very pretty plants; for culture
and propagation, see *Schotia.* *Synonymes:* 1. *Connarus africánus.* 2. *C. asiaticus, Rhus Rædælijavel.*

| | | | | | |
|---|---|---|---|---|---|
| africánum, 1 . | Pa. red . | 8. Ev. S. | Guinea | 1822 |
| indicum, 2 . . | Pa. red . | 8. Ev. S. | Ceylon | |

OMPHALÓBYUM, see *Schótia.*

OMPHALÓDES, *Tournefort.* From *omphalos*, the navel,
and *eidos*, like; the fruit resembles the navel:
whence the genus has been called Venus's Navelwort. *Linn.* 5, Or. 1, Nat. Or. *Boraginaceæ.* These
plants are very elegant border-flowers, and of the
easiest culture. The perennial kinds grow well
under the shade of trees and shrubs, and are increased by division. The seed of the annual species should be sown in the open border in spring.
*Synonymes:* 1. *Cynoglossum brassicæfolium.* 2. *C.
linifolium.* 3. *C. nitida.* 4. *scorpioides.* 5. *Anchusa sempervirens.* 6. *C. omphalodes.*

| | | | | | |
|---|---|---|---|---|---|
| amplexicaulis, 1 . | White . | 7, H. Her. P. | Spain | 1823 |
| linifolia, 2 . . | White . | 8. | A. | Portugal | 1748 |
| littoralis . . . | White . | 7, H. | A. | France | 1826 |
| myosotoides . . | Brush . | 9, F. Her. P. | Russia | 1838 |
| nitidum 3 . . . | White . | 5, H. Her. P. | Portugal | 1812 |
| scorpioides, 4 . . | Blue . | 7, H. Tr. A. | Bohemia | 1825 |
| sempérvirens, 5 . | Blue . | 6, H. Her. P. | Britain | |
| vérna, 6 . . . | Blue . | 3, H. Her. P. S. Eur. | 1633 |

ONCIDIUM, *Swartz.* Derived from *ogkos*, a tumour;
the plants belonging to this genus have warts,
tumours, or other excrescences at the base of the
labellum. *Linn.* 20, Or. 1, Nat. Or. *Orchidaceæ.*
This is an extensive and very handsome genus of
plants, every one of which is highly deserving a
place in every collection. *O. papilio* bears a striking resemblance to a butterfly on the wing. *O.
altissimum* throws up from fifteen to twenty flower-
spikes, producing as many as *two thousand* flowers,
the colour of which is yellow spotted with brown,
and there is the splendid *O. Lanceanum*, one of the
most prized in this valuable genus; but to par-
ticularise, where all are remarkable either for the
beauty or the singularity of the flowers, would be
invidious. The large-leaved kinds do best when
grown in rustic baskets, which can readily be suspended from the rafters of the house; the basket
should be made of small pieces of oak nailed together, or holes may be bored, and a piece of strong
wire run through near the end of each, and fastened
at the bottom. Some moss and rotten wood should
be placed in the bottom previous to putting the
plant in, in doing which, care must be taken not to
insert the plant too deep. Moss and rotten wood
must surround the roots of the plant, but should
not on any account be raised higher than the roots
of the leaves, or they will be liable to damp off.
The small-growing kinds, as *O. iridifolium*, should
be fastened on wood, and treated as the *Burlingtonias.* The other kinds, as *O. papilio* and *O. altissimum*, require to be potted similarly to the genus
*Stanhopea.* *Synonyme:* 1. *O. juncifolium.*

| | | | | | |
|---|---|---|---|---|---|
| altissimum . . | Yel. brn. | 3, S. Epi. | Panama | 1793 |
| ampliátum . . | Yellow . | 4, S. Epi. | Panama | 1793 |
| barbátum . . . | Yellow . | 4, S. Epi. | Brazil | 1818 |
| Bauëri . . . | Yel. brn. | 4, S. Epi. | | |
| bicornútum . . | Yel. spot. | 6, S. Epi. | Rio Jan. | 1830 |
| bifolium . . . | Yel. pur. | 7, S. Epi. | M. Video | 1811 |

| | | | | | |
|---|---|---|---|---|---|
| carthaginénsé . | Olive . | 6, S. Epi. | Carthage | 1791 |
| Cebolléta, 1 . | Yellow . | 4, S. Epi. | W. Ind. | 1825 |
| ciliátum . . . | Yel. red . | 1, S. Epi. | Brazil | 1818 |
| citrinum . . . | Yellow . | 8, S. Epi. | Trinidad | |
| confragósum . . | Straw . | 8. S. Epi. | Mexico . | |
| cornigérum . . | Yellow . | 7, S. Epi. | Brazil | |
| crispum . . . | Orange . | 6, S. Epi. | | |
| deltoidéum . . | Yellow . | 8, S. Epi. | Lima | 1836 |
| Devonianum . . | Yel. grn. | 1, S. Epi. | Guatemala | 1836 |
| divaricátum . . | Yel. brn. | 12, S. Epi. | Brazil | 1826 |
| flexuósum . . | Yellow . | 6, S. Epi. | Brazil | 1818 |
| Forbésii . . . | Scar. yel. | 9, S. Epi. | Organ M. | 1837 |
| Harrisonianum . | Yellow . | 6, S. Epi. | Brazil | |
| intermédium . . | Orange . | 8, S. Epi. | Cuba | |
| iridifólium . . | Yellow . | 6, S. Epi. | Mexico . | 1835 |
| Lanceánum . . | Grn. pur. | 6, S. Epi. | Mexico . | |
| Lemonianum . . | Yel. spot. | 8, S. Epi. | Havannah | 1836 |
| leucochilum . . | Wht. red. | 6, S. Epi. | Guatemala | 1836 |
| lunátum . . . | Orange . | 6, S. Epi. | Demerara | 1836 |
| lúridum . . . | Olive . | 8, S. Epi. | Jamaica | 1822 |
| guttátum . . | Yel. red | 8, S. Epi. | Jamaica | |
| ornithorynchum . | Pink . | 7, S. Epi. | Mexico . | 1826 |
| papilio . . . | Yel. pur. | 6, S. Epi. | Trinidad | 1823 |
| púbes . . . | Orn. red . | 4, S. Epi. | Brazil | 1824 |
| pulchéllum . . | Wht. spot. | 6, S. Epi. | Jamaica | |
| pulvinátum . . | Yel. brn. | 6, S. Epi. | Brazil | 1836 |
| pûmilum . . . | Yellow . | 5, S. Epi. | Brazil | 1824 |
| raniferum . . | Yellow . | 8, S. Epi. | Brazil | 1838 |
| majór . . . | Yellow . | 8, S. Epi. | Brazil | |
| refléxum . . . | Yellow . | 10, S. Epi. | Mexico . | 1836 |
| Russellianum . . | Pur. grn. | 8. Epi. | Rio Jan. | 1835 |
| sanguineum . . | Stra. crim. | 8. Epi. | La Quayra | |
| stramineum . . | Straw . | 8. Epi. | Vera Cruz | |
| Tayleúri . . . | Brown . | 8. Epi. | Mexico . | 1837 |
| tetrapetálum . . | Yel. brn. | 8. Epi. | Jamaica | |
| triquétrum . . | Wht. pur. | 9, S. Epi. | Jamaica | 1793 |
| unicórne . . . | Pa. yel. | 6, S. Epi. | Rio Jan. | |
| variegátum . . | Yellow . | 7, S. Epi. | W. Ind. | 1824 |
| viperinum . . | Pa. yel. | 8. Epi. | Jamaica | |

ONCORHYNCHUS, *Fischer and Meyer.* Derived from
*onkos*, tumour, and *rhynchus*, beak; alluding to the
lip. Nat. Or. *Scrophulariaceæ.* The seed of this
plant may be sown in any common garden soil.

| | | | | |
|---|---|---|---|---|
| tenéllus . . . | | H. B. | | 1837 |

ONION, see *Allium Cépa.*

ONOBRÓMA, *Decandolle.* From *onos*, an ass, and *broma*,
food; favourite food of the ass. *Linn.* 19, Or. 1,
Nat. Or. *Compositæ.* Ornamental plants, succeeding in any common soil, and increased by cuttings,
divisions, or seeds. *Synonymes:* 1. *Carthamus arborescens.* 2. *C. cæruleus.* 3. *C. cynaroides.* 4. *C.
glaucus.* 5. *C. leucocaulis.*

| | | | | | |
|---|---|---|---|---|---|
| arborescens, 1 . | Yellow . | 7, G. Ev. S. | Spain | 1731 |
| cærúleum, 2 . | Blue . | 6, H. Her. P. | Spain | 1640 |
| cynaroides, 3 . | White . | 6, H. Her. P. | Caucasus | 1820 |
| glaúcum, 4 . . | Purple . | 7, H. | A. | Tauria | 1817 |
| leucocaúlon, 5 . | White . | 6, H. Her. P. | Greece | 1800 |

ONOBRYCHIS, *Tournefort.* From *onos*, an ass, and
*brycho*, to gnaw; plants grateful to the ass. *Linn.*
17, Or. 4, Nat. Or. *Leguminosæ.* All the species of
Saintfoin are very showy, and well suited for
ornamenting rock-work or flower-borders. The
herbaceous kinds grow best in pots, in a mixture
of chalk, sand, and loam; they succeed best when
raised from seed, which should be sown where the
plants are to remain. *Synonymes:* 1. *O. orientalis.*
2. *O. picta.* 3. *Hedysarum Onobrychis.* 4. *H. saxatile.*

| | | | | | |
|---|---|---|---|---|---|
| arenária . . . | Red . | 7, H. Her. P. | Siberia | 1818 |
| alba . . . | White . | 6, H. Her. P. | Hungary | 1804 |
| cápút-galli . . | Flesh . | 7, H. | A. | France | 1781 |
| carpática . . . | Purple . | 7, H. Her. P. | Carpat. | 1818 |
| conférta . . . | Purple . | 7, H. Her. P. | Iberia | 1817 |
| cornúta, 1 . . | Red . | 7, F. Ev. S. | Caucasus | 1816 |
| Crísta-galli . . | Flesh . | 7, H. | A. S. Eur. | 1710 |
| echináta . . . | Flesh . | 6, H. Her. P. | Calabria | 1831 |
| Fontanésii . . | Red . | 7, H. Her. P. | Tunis | 1820 |
| glábra . . . | Purple . | 7, H. Her. P. | Tauria | 1816 |
| grácilis . . . | Pa. red . | 7, H. Her. P. | Podolia | 1820 |
| marotica . . . | Pa. red . | 7, H. Her. P. | Caucasus | 1820 |
| Michaúxii, 2 . | Purple . | 7, H. Her. P. | Levant . | 1820 |
| montána . . . | Purple . | 7, H. De. Tr. S. Eur. | 1817 |
| Pallásii . . . | Pa. yel. | H. Her. P. | Iberia | 1820 |
| petrǽa . . . | Wht. red. | H. Her. P. | Caucasus | 1818 |
| procúmbens . . | Purple . | 7, H. De. Tr. Iberia | 1819 |
| ptolemáica . . | Yellow . | H. Her. P. | Egypt . | 1816 |
| radiáta . . . | Pa. yel. | 7, H. Her. P. | Iberia | 1818 |
| satíva, 3 . . . | Pa. pink . | 7, H. Her. P. | Britain | |
| saxátilis, 4 . . | Ll. yel. | H. Her. P. | S. Eur. | 1790 |
| supína . . . | Pa. red . | H. Her. P. | Switzerl. | 1819 |
| tanaítica . . | Purple . | 7, H. Her. P. | Caucasus | 1817 |

ONOCLEA, *Linn.* From *onos*, a vessel, and *kleio*, to
inclose; referring to the apparent capsules. *Linn.*

24, Or. 1, Nat. Or. *Polypodiaceæ*. These plants grow well in loam and peat, or on rock-work; they are increased by dividing at the roots, or by seeds.

| | | | | | |
|---|---|---|---|---|---|
| obtusilobatā | . Brown | . 7, H. Her. P. N. Amer. | . 1812 |
| sensibilis | . Brown | . 8, H. Her. P. Virginia | . 1799 |

ONŌNĬS, *Linn.* From *onos*, an ass, and *onemi*, to delight; some of these plants are said to be grateful to asses. *Linn.* 16, Or. 6, Nat. Or. *Leguminosæ*. All the plants belonging to this genus are of easy cultivation, and several of them are rather handsome when in flower. *Synonymes:* 1. *hircina*. 2. *spinosa, glabra*. 3. *fruticosa*. 4. *barbata*. 5. *Natrix*. 6. *arvensis*. 7. *reclinata*.

| | | | | |
|---|---|---|---|---|
| alba | . White | . 7, H. | A. Barbary | . 1823 |
| angustissimā | . Pink | . 6, F. Ev. S. Spain | . 1825 |
| apūla | . Yellow | . 9, H. | B. Naples | . 1834 |
| arborēscēus | . Red | . 6, H. Ev. S. Barbary | . 1826 |
| arenāriā | . Yellow | . 7, H. Ev. S. France | . 1819 |
| arragouēusis | . Yellow | . 7, H. De. S. Spain | . 1816 |
| biflōrā | . Yel. pur. | . 7, H. | A. Barbary | . 1818 |
| brachycārpā | . Yellow | . 7, H. | A. Spain | . 1823 |
| brevislōrā | . Yellow | . 8, H. | S. Eur. | . 1800 |
| capēnsis | . Purple | . A. C. G. H. | . 1800 |
| capitātā | . Yellow | . 8, H. Ev. Tr. Spain | . 1820 |
| cuspidātā | . Yellow | . 6, F. Her. B. Naples | . 1818 |
| Denhardtii | . Yellow | . 8, H. | B. Naples | . 1832 |
| diffūsā | . Purple | . 7, H. | A. Italy | . 1820 |
| emarginātā | | . 8. Ev. S. Maurit. | . 1825 |
| falcātā | . Yellow | . 7, F. Ev. S. Eur. | |
| fœtidā | . Pink | . 6, H. | A. Morocco | . 1818 |
| fruticōsā | . Pink | . 5, H. Ev. S. S. Eur. | . 1680 |
| microphyllā, 8 | Pur. red | . 6, H. Ev. S. Arragon | |
| geminiflōrā | . Purple | . 7, H. | A. Spain | . 1817 |
| glabrā | . Yellow | . 7, G. Ev. Tr. C. G. H. | . 1824 |
| hīrtā | . Blue | . 7, H. Her. P. S. Eur. | . 1816 |
| hispānicā | . Yellow | . 7, H. Ev. S. Spain | . 1799 |
| hispidā | | . 7, F. Ev. S. Barbary | . 1818 |
| longifōliā | . Yellow | . 7, F. Ev. S. Teneriffe | . 1816 |
| minutissimā, 4 | . Yellow | . 6, F. | B. S. France | . 1818 |
| oligophyllā | . White | . 7, H. | A. Naples | . 1823 |
| parviflōrā | | . 7, G. | A. C. G. H. | . 1818 |
| peduncularis | . Wht. ro. | . F. Ev. S. Teneriffe | . 1829 |
| pēndūlā | . Purple | . 7, H. | A. S. Eur. | . 1818 |
| pictā | . Pur. yel. | . F. Her. P. Barbary | . 1820 |
| procūrrēns | . Purple | . 7, H. Her. P. Europe | . 1820 |
| ramosissimā | . Yellow | . 7, F. Ev. S. Sicily | . 1819 |
| rotundifōliā | . Pink | . 5, H. Ev. S. Pyrenees | . 1570 |
| arietat. | . Pink | . 6, H. Ev. S. | |
| sicūlā | . Yellow | . 7, H. | A. Sicily | . 1817 |
| tribracteātā | . Pink | . 6, H. Ev. S. S. Eur. | . 1800 |
| tridentātā | . Purple | . 6, H. Ev. S. Spain | . 1752 |
| villōsā | | . 7, G. Her. P. C. G. H. | . 1820 |

*alopecuroīdēs, altissimā* 1, *antiquōrūm* 2, *cenīslā, C. subariatātā, cērnuā, Cherlērii, Columnæ, crispā, millssimā, monophȳllā, nātrix, ornithopodioīdēs, pinguis* 5, *pubēscēns, reclinātā, rēpēns spinōsā* 6, *S. alba, striātā* 7, *vaginālis, variegātā, viscōsā*.

ONOPŎRDŎN, *Linn.* From *onos*, an ass, and *perdo*, to explode; referring to the supposed effects on the ass. *Linn.* 19, Or. 1, Nat. Or. *Compositæ*. Rather interesting plants, of common cultivation.

| | | | | |
|---|---|---|---|---|
| acānthiūm | . Purple | . 7, H. | B. Britain | |
| aculōm | . White | . 7, H. | B. Pyrenees | . 1739 |
| arābicūm | . Purple | . 7, H. | B. S. Eur. | . 1686 |
| cynaroīdēs | . White | . 6, H. | B. Caucasus | . 1823 |
| ēlātūm | . Purple | . 7, H. | B. Greece | . 1816 |
| græcūm | . Purple | . 7, H. | A. Levant | . 1799 |
| heteracānthūm | | . 7, H. | B. | . 1836 |
| illȳricūm | . Purple | . 7, H. | B. S. Eur. | . 1640 |
| macracānthūm | . Purple | . 7, H. | A. Barbary | . 1798 |
| pyrenāicūm | . White | . 8, H. | B. Pyrenees | . 1820 |
| taūricūm | . Purple | . 7, H. | B. Tauria | . 1800 |
| uniflōrūm | . White | . 7, H. | B. Spain | . 1826 |
| virēus | . Purple | . 7, H. | B. Montpel. | . 1818 |
| viscōsūm | . Purple | . 7, H. | B. S. Eur. | . 1818 |

ONŌSMĂ, *Linn.* From *onos*, an ass, and *osme*, smell; said to be grateful to the ass. *Linn.* 5, Or. 1, Nat. Or. *Boraginaceæ*. These are extremely pretty plants when in blossom, and are well adapted for growing on rock-work or wall-tops, in which places they should be sown, where they will afterwards maintain themselves if allowed to scatter their seeds. The stove and greenhouse species must be kept in pots. *Synonyme:* 1. *O. arenarium*.

| | | | | |
|---|---|---|---|---|
| divaricātūm | . Yellow | . 6, H. Her. P. Caucasus | . 1818 |
| echioīdēs | . White | . 5, H. Her. P. S. Eur. | . 1683 |
| arenāriūm, 1 | . Yellow | . 6, H. Her. P. Hungary | . 1804 |
| gigantēūm | . Yellow | . 4, H. Her. P. Tauria | . 1818 |
| Gmelini | . Striped | . 6, H. Her. P. Altai | . 1829 |
| orientālē | . Yellow | . 5, H. Her. P. Levant | . 1752 |
| polyphyllūm | . Yellow | . 7, H. Her. P. Tauria | . 1829 |

| | | | | |
|---|---|---|---|---|
| rigidūm | . Pa. yel. | . 7, H. Her. P. Tauria | . 1826 |
| rupēstrē | . Yellow | . 5, F. Her. P. Iberia | . 1819 |
| sericēūm | . Yellow | . 6, H. Her. P. Iberia | . 1752 |
| setōsūm | . Yellow | . 4, H. Her. P. Russia | . 1838 |
| simplicissimūm | . Yellow | . 4, H. Her. P. Siberia | . 1768 |
| stellulātūm | . Yellow | . 4, H. Her. P. Hungary | . 1819 |
| taūricūm | . Yellow | . 5, H. Her. P. Caucasus | . 1801 |
| tinctōriūm | . Yellow | . 5, H. Her. P. Caucasus | . 1826 |
| tricerospērmūm | . Yellow | . 5, H. Her. P. Spain | . 1824 |
| trinērviūm | . Yellow | . 8. Her. P. S. Amer. | . 1824 |

ONOSMŌDĬŪM, *Michaux.* From *onosma*, and *eidos*, like; from the similarity of the plants to those of *Onosma*. *Linn.* 5, Or. 1, Nat. Or. *Boraginaceæ*. Ornamental plants; for culture and propagation, see *Onosma*. *Synonymes:* 1. *Purshia hispida*. 2. *P. mollis*.

| | | | | |
|---|---|---|---|---|
| hispidūm, 1 | . Yellow | . 6, H. Her. P. N. Amer. | . 1759 |
| mōllē, 2 | . White | . 6, H. Her. P. N. Amer. | . 1812 |

ONȲGĒNĂ, *Persoon.* From *onyx*, a hoof, and *genas*, an offspring. *Linn.* 24, Or. 9, Nat. Or. *Fungi*. This minute autumnal species is found on decaying hoofs and horns of animals—*equini*.

OPAQUE, dark, destitute of transparency.

OPĒGRĂPHĂ, *Persoon.* From *ope*, a chink, and *grapho*, to write; cracks upon the surface of the thallus. *Linn.* 24, Or. 9, Nat. Or. *Fungi*. These plants are found on the bark of trees, on stones, &c., at all seasons of the year—*calcārēā, cerebrīnā, epipātā, microscōpicā, herpēticā, dispartātā, maculāris, nimbōsā, nothā, didphōrā, Persoōnāā, apōrēā, saxigēnā, stenocārpā, denigrātā, sulcātā, tesserātā, venōsā, vulgātā.*

OPERA-GIRLS, see *Manfield saltatoriā*.

OPERCULĂRĬĂ, *Richard.* From *operculum*, a lid; in allusion to the operculate calyx. *Linn.* 5, Or. 1, Nat. Or. *Cinchonaceæ*. Pretty plants, easily cultivated in a mixture of loam, peat, and sand; and young plants are obtained from cuttings under a glass. *Synonymes:* 1. *aspera, diphylla*.

| | | | | |
|---|---|---|---|---|
| aspērā | . White | . 6, G. Her. P. N. Holl. | . 1790 |
| hispidā, 1 | . White | . 7, G. Her. P. N. Holl. | . 1790 |
| ocymifōliā | . White | . 7, S. Her. P. E. Ind. | . 1824 |
| sessiliflōrā | . White | . 6, G. Her. P. C. G. H. | . 1824 |

OPERCULĂRĬĂ, see *Pōmāx*.

OPERCULATE, covered with a lid.

OPĒRCŪLŪM, a lid.

OPERCULATED, covered with a lid.

OPHIOGLŌSSŪM. From *ophis*, a serpent, and *glossa*, a tongue; the resemblance of the leaves. *Linn.* 24, Or. 1, Nat. Or. *Ophioglossaceæ*. These ferns will grow well in a mixture of loam and peat, and may be increased by divisions of the roots, or seeds. The hardy kinds should be planted in a moist situation.

| | | | | |
|---|---|---|---|---|
| bulbōsūm | . Brown | . 7, F. Tu. P. N. Amer. | |
| costātūm | . Brown | . 6, G. Her. P. N. Holl. | . 1820 |
| gramīnēūm | . Brown | . 6, G. Her. P. N. Holl. | . 1820 |
| lusitānicūm | . Brown | . 6, H. Her. P. Portugal | . 1816 |
| petiolātūm | . Brown | . 8, S. Her. P. Jamaica | . 1820 |
| reticulātūm | . Brown | . 6, S. Her. P. W. Ind. | . 1793 |
| vulgātūm | . Brown | . 6, H. Her. P Britain. | |

OPHIOPŌGŎN, *Ker.* From *ophis*, a snake, and *pogon*, a beard. *Linn.* 6, Or. 1, Nat. Or. *Liliaceæ*. An ornamental genus, thriving well in sandy loam and peat, and increased by dividing at the roots. *Synonyme:* 1. *Convallaria japonica*.

| | | | | |
|---|---|---|---|---|
| jabūrān | . White | . 7, F. Her. P. Japan | . 1830 |
| japōnicūs, 1 | . Li. yel. | . 6, F. Her. P. Japan | . 1784 |
| spicātūs | . Violet | . 10, F. Her. P. Nepal | . 1821 |

OPHIORHĪZĂ, *Forskahl.* From *ophis*, a snake, and *rhiza*, a root; Snake-root. *Linn.* 5, Or. 1, Nat. Or. *Cinchonaceæ*. This shrub grows well in light loamy soil, and cuttings of the young wood root in sand, under a glass, in a moist heat; it may also be increased by seeds.

| | | | | |
|---|---|---|---|---|
| Mūngōs | . White | . 8, S. Ev. S. E. Ind. | . 1820 |

OPHIOXȲLŎN, *Burmann.* From *ophis*, a serpent, and *xylon*, wood; alluding to the tortuous root and stems. *Linn.* 23, Or. 2, Nat. Or. *Apocynaceæ*. This plant is rather pretty; for culture and propagation, see *Sti phanthus*.

| | | | | |
|---|---|---|---|---|
| serpentīnūm | . White | . 5, S. Ev. S. E. Ind. | . 1690 |

OPHIŪRŬS, *Gærtner.* From *ophis*, a snake, and *oura*, a tail. *Linn.* 3, Or. 2, Nat. Or. *Gramineæ*. Curious annual grasses, growing in any common garden soil. *Synonymes:* 1. *Rottboellia filiformis*. 2. *R. incurvata*. 3. *R. cylindrica, Monerma subulata, Lepturus cylindricus*.

| | | | | | |
|---|---|---|---|---|---|
| filifórmis, 1 | . Apetal | . 7, Grass. | Portugal | . 1800 |
| incurvátūs, 2 | . Apetal | . 7, Grass. | Britain | . |
| subulātūs, 3 | . Apetal | . 7, Grass. 8. Eur. | . 1806 |

**OPHRYS,** *Linn. Ophrys* is the Greek appellation for eyebrows, and is said to be applied to this genus because of the fringe of the inner sepals. *Linn.* 20, Or. 1, Nat. Or. *Orchideæ.* The species of this genus are highly curious, and worth a place in every collection. They thrive best in a frame in a mixture of loam, peat, and chalk, broken small; the lights should be put on in very wet or frosty weather. It is advisable to have some turfy grass growing where they are planted, as they can only be increased from seeds, which are parasitic when young, and will lay hold of the grass when they first vegetate. They will ripen seed without difficulty if care be taken to rub the pollen on the stigma. The seeds should be sown as soon as ripe, and when come up sufficiently, to be transplanted to where they are to remain.

| | | | | | |
|---|---|---|---|---|---|
| apífera | . . . Purple | . 6, H. Ter. | England | . . |
| arachnítes | . . Brown | . 6, H. Ter. | England | . . |
| aranífera | . . Green | . 5, H. Ter. | England | . . |
| limbáta | . . Brown | . 4, F. Ter. | Rome . | . 1826 |
| atráta | . . . Gra. brn. | . 4, F. Ter. | Gibraltar | . 1825 |
| fucífera | . . Pur. grn. | . 6, H. Ter. | England | . . |
| fūsca | . . . Brown | . 4, F. Ter. | Gibraltar | . 1825 |
| lūtea | . . . Yellow | . 4, F. Ter. | Spain . | . 1818 |
| mucífera | . . Purple | . 5, H. Ter. | England | . . |
| scōlōpax | . . Purple | . 5, F. Ter. | Italy . | . 1825 |
| tenthredinífera | . Yel. brn. | . 4, F. Ter. | Barbary | . 1815 |
| minōr | . . . Yel. brn. | . 4, F. Ter. | N. Africa | . 1824 |

**OPIATE,** having the power of opium.

**OPLOTHÈCA,** *Nuttall.* From *oplon,* armour, and *theca,* a sheath; in allusion to the appearance of the capsules. *Linn.* 5, Or. 1, Nat. Or. *Amarantaceæ.* Ornamental plants, growing in loam and peat, and increased by cuttings. *O. floridana* is readily multiplied by divisions of the roots. *Synonyme:* 1. *Gomphrena interrupta.*

| | | | | | |
|---|---|---|---|---|---|
| floridána | . . White | . 9, H. Her. | P. N. Amer. | . 1824 |
| interrūpta, 1 | . Green | . 7, S. | B. W. Ind. | . 1783 |

**OPŎPĂNĂX,** *Koch.* From *opos,* juice, *pan,* all, and *akos,* a remedy; the juice of the plant is supposed to cure all diseases. *Linn.* 5, Or. 2, Nat. Or. *Umbelliferæ.* A plant of little beauty, and of easy cultivation; it is increased by seeds, or divisions at the roots. *Synonyme:* 1. *Pastinaca Opopanax.*

| | | | | | |
|---|---|---|---|---|---|
| Chirónium, 1 | . Yellow | . 6, H. Her. | P. S. Eur. | . 1640 |

**OPORÌNA,** *Don.* From *oporinos,* autumnal; alluding to the time of flowering. *Linn.* 19, Or. 1, Nat. Or. *Compositæ.* A mere herbaceous weed, growing in meadows, &c. *Synonyme:* 1. *Apargia autumnalis* —autumnalis, 1.

**OPÚNTIA,** *Tournefort.* Some of the species are plentiful near Opus, a city of Locris. *Linn.* 19, Or. 1, Nat. Or. *Cactaceæ.* This is a very interesting genus of plants, well deserving of cultivation in every collection. They require to be treated like the *Mammillarias;* and young plants may be obtained by separating the branches at the joints, and allowing them to dry for a few days before sticking them in the soil, where they soon root. *O. cochinillifera* is valuable on account of its rearing the well-known *coccus cacti,* or cochineal insect. *Synonymes:* 1. *Cactus aurantiacus.* 2. *C. elatior.* 3. *O. humilis.* 4. *O. glomerata.* 5. *C. Opuntia.*

| | | | | | |
|---|---|---|---|---|---|
| albicáns | . . . | . | 8. Ev. 8. | | 1835 |
| alpína | . . . | . | 8. Ev. 8. | | 1836 |
| americána | . . | . | 8. Ev. 8. | S. Amer. | 1835 |
| Amyclāēa | . . | . | 8. Ev. 8. | Naples | 1825 |
| andicóla | . . | . | 8. Ev. 8. | | 1690 |
| articuláta | . . | . | 8. Ev. 8. | | 1836 |
| attílica | . . | . | 8. Ev. 8. | | 1827 |
| aurantíaca, 1 | . Or. yel. | . | 8. Ev. 8. | Chile | 1824 |
| Bonplándi | . . Yellow | . 7, | 8. Ev. 8. | Brazil | 1816 |
| brasiliénsis | . . Yellow | . 7, | 8. Ev. 8. | Brazil | 1816 |
| calacántha, 2 | . | . | 8. Ev. 8. | | 1836 |
| candelabrifórmis | . | . | 8. Ev. 8. | | 1835 |
| ciliósa | . . | . | 8. Ev. 8. | | |
| clavarioídes | . . | . | 8. Ev. 8. | | 1836 |
| cochinillífera | . Red | . 8, | 8. Ev. 8. | S. Amer. | 1688 |
| corrugáta | . . | . | 8. Ev. 8. | Chile | 1824 |
| crinéca | . . Yellow | . | 8. Ev. 8. | Mexico | 1817 |
| curassavíca | . Yellow | . 6, | 8. Ev. 8. | Curassoa | 1690 |
| elongáta | . . | . | 8. Ev. 8. | | |
| lónga | . . Yellow | . 6, | 8. Ev. 8. | Curassoa | 1690 |
| cylindrica | . . Scarlet | . | 8. Ev. 8. | Peru | 1799 |

| | | | | | |
|---|---|---|---|---|---|
| decípiens | . . | . | 8. Ev. 8. | Mexico | 1830 |
| decumána | . . Yellow | . | 8. Ev. 8. | S. Amer. | 1768 |
| decūmbens | . . | . | 8. Ev. 8. | Mexico | 1835 |
| dejécta | . . Yellow | . | 8. Ev. 8. | Havannah | 1836 |
| dichótoma | . . | . | 8. Ev. 8. | B. Ayres | 1836 |
| Dilléni | . . Yellow | . 9, | 8. Ev. 8. | | 1810 |
| dolabrifórmis | . | . | 8. Ev. 8. | | 1835 |
| elatiōr | . . Yellow | . 7, | 8. Ev. 8. | S. Amer. | 1731 |
| exténsa | . . Li. yel. | . | 8. Ev. 8. | | 1824 |
| exuriáta | . . Yellow | . | 8. Ev. 8. | Mexico | 1830 |
| feróx | . . Yellow | . | 8. Ev. 8. | S. Amer. | 1817 |
| Ficus-indíca | . Yellow | . 6, | 8. Ev. 8. | S. Amer. | 1731 |
| flexíbilis | . . | . | 8. Ev. 8. | | 1836 |
| foliósa | . . Yellow | . | 8. Ev. 8. | S. Amer. | 1805 |
| frágilis | . . | . | H. Ev. 8. | N. Amer. | 1814 |
| glaúca | . . | . | 8. Ev. 8. | | 1835 |
| glomeráta | . . | . | 8. Ev. 8. | Brasil | 1829 |
| grándis | . . | . | 8. Ev. 8. | | 1835 |
| Hernandési | . Varieg. | . | 8. Ev. 8. | Mexico | 1827 |
| Hitchéni | . . | . | 8. Ev. 8. | | 1825 |
| horisontális | . . | . | 8. Ev. 8. | | 1814 |
| hórrida, 3 | . Yellow | . 7, | 8. Ev. 8. | S. Amer. | 1795 |
| imbricáta | . . | . | 8. Ev. 8. | | 1820 |
| inérmis | . . Yellow | . 7, | 8. Ev. 8. | S. Amer. | 1796 |
| itálica | . . | . | 8. Ev. 8. | | 1835 |
| Kleìníi | . . | . | 8. Ev. 8. | | 1836 |
| lanceoláta | . . Yellow | . 7, | 8. Ev. 8. | S. Amer. | 1796 |
| lasiacántha | . . | . | 8. Ev. 8. | | 1795 |
| leptocaúlis | . . | . | 8. Ev. 8. | | 1836 |
| leucacánthā | . . White | . | 8. Ev. 8. | S. Amer. | 1825 |
| leucótricha | . . | . | 8. Ev. 8. | Germany | 1836 |
| longispína, 4 | . | . | 8. Ev. 8. | Brazil | 1829 |
| longíssima | . . | . | 8. Ev. 8. | | 1835 |
| máxima | . . Yellow | . | 8. Ev. 8. | S. Amer. | 1830 |
| mádia | . . Yellow | . | F. Ev. 8. | N. Amer. | 1827 |
| megacántha | . . | . | 8. Ev. 8. | Mexico | 1835 |
| mexicána | . . | . | 8. Ev. 8. | Mexico | 1835 |
| microdasys | . . | . | 8. Ev. 8. | | 1810 |
| minōr | . . | . | 8. Ev. 8. | | |
| missouriénsis | . Yellow | . 6, | H. Ev. 8. | N. Amer. | 1814 |
| monacántha | . . Yellow | . | 8. Ev. 8. | S. Amer. | 1816 |
| myriacántha | . . Yellow | . | 8. Ev. 8. | Mexico | 1830 |
| nigricáns | . . Pink | . 8, | 8. Ev. 8. | S. Amer. | 1795 |
| Paróta | . . | . | 8. Ev. 8. | | 1825 |
| párvula | . . | . | 8. Ev. 8. | Chile | 1825 |
| platyacántha | . | . | 8. Ev. 8. | | 1814 |
| polyántha | . . Yellow | . | 8. Ev. 8. | S. Amer. | 1811 |
| polyacántha | . . Yellow | . | F. Ev. 8. | N. Amer. | 1814 |
| Pseúdo-Túna | . Yellow | . | 8. Ev. 8. | | 1811 |
| pubéscens | . . | . | 8. Ev. 8. | | 1836 |
| pusílla | . . Yellow | . | 8. Ev. 8. | S. Amer. | 1805 |
| ramulífera | . . | . | 8. Ev. 8. | Mexico | 1836 |
| rósea | . . Rose | . | 8. Ev. 8. | Mexico | 1830 |
| rubéscens | . . | . | 8. Ev. 8. | Brazil | 1828 |
| Sabíni | . . | . | 8. Ev. 8. | | |
| Salmi | . . | . | 8. Ev. 8. | | 1835 |
| senílis | . . | . | 8. Ev. 8. | | 1837 |
| sericéa | . . Yellow | . | 8. Ev. 8. | Chile | 1827 |
| spinosíssima | . Yellow | . 7, | 8. Ev. 8. | Jamaica | 1732 |
| spinulífera | . . | . | 8. Ev. 8. | Mexico | 1836 |
| stapélia | . . Yellow | . | 8. Ev. 8. | Mexico | 1830 |
| subinérmis | . . | . | 8. Ev. 8. | | 1819 |
| sulphúrea | . . Yellow | . | 8. Ev. 8. | Chile | 1827 |
| tomentósa | . . Yellow | . | 8. Ev. 8. | S. Amer. | 1820 |
| triacántha | . . | . | 8. Ev. 8. | | |
| tuberculáta | . . Yellow | . | 8. Ev. 8. | America | 1818 |
| Túna | . . Pa. yel. | . 7, | 8. Ev. 8. | S. Amer. | 1731 |
| tunicáta | . . | . | 8. Ev. 8. | | 1836 |
| virgáta | . . | . | 8. Ev. 8. | | 1836 |
| vulgáris, 5 | . Yellow | . 7, | F. Ev. 8. | S. Eur. | 1596 |

**ORACHE,** see *Atriplex.*

**ORANGE-TREE,** see *Citrus.*

**ÓRBĒA,** *Haworth.* From *orbis,* an orb; the orb in the centre of the flower is large and elevated. *Linn.* 5, Or. 2, Nat. Or. *Asclepiadaceæ.* A genus of interesting plants; for culture and propagation, see *Stapelia. Synonymes:* 1. *Stapelia clypeata.* 2. *variegata.* 3. *maculosa.* 4. *mutabilis.* 5. *rugosa.*

| | | | | | |
|---|---|---|---|---|---|
| anguína | . . Yel. str. | . 6, | 8. Ev. 8. | C. G. H. | 1812 |
| bisúlca | . . Yel. str. | . 7, | 8. Ev. 8. | C. G. H. | 1805 |
| bufónia | . . Yel. str. | . 7, | 8. Ev. 8. | C. G. H. | 1806 |
| conspurcáta | . Yel. str. | . 7, | 8. Ev. 8. | C. G. H. | 1795 |
| clypeáta, 1 | . | . 7, | 8. Ev. 8. | C. G. H. | 1812 |
| Curtísi, 2 | . Yel. str. | . 7, | 8. Ev. 8. | C. G. H. | 1690 |
| inodóra | . . Yel. str. | . 6, | 8. Ev. 8. | C. G. H. | 1788 |
| lépida | . . Grn. str. | . 7, | 8. Ev. 8. | C. G. H. | |
| maculósa, 3 | . Brn. str. | . 8, | 8. Ev. 8. | C. G. H. | 1804 |
| margináta | . Yel. str. | . 7, | 8. Ev. 8. | C. G. H. | 1805 |
| marmoráta | . Yel. str. | . 7, | 8. Ev. 8. | C. G. H. | 1820 |
| mixta | . . Yel. str. | . 7, | 8. Ev. 8. | C. G. H. | 1800 |
| mutgánica, 4 | . Yel. str. | . 7, | 8. Ev. 8. | C. G. H. | 1823 |
| normális | . . Yel. str. | . 7, | 8. Ev. 8. | C. G. H. | 1821 |
| orbiculáris | . Yel. str. | . 7, | 8. Ev. 8. | C. G. H. | 1799 |
| pícta | . . Yel. str. | . 8, | 8. Ev. 8. | C. G. H. | 1799 |
| planifóra | . . Pa. yel. | . 8, | 8. Ev. 8. | C. G. H. | 1805 |
| quinquenérvis | . Yel. str. | . 6, | 8. Ev. 8. | C. G. H. | 1800 |
| retúsa | . . Yel. str. | . 7, | 8. Ev. 8. | C. G. H. | 1800 |
| rugósa | . . Pa. str. | . 6, | 8. Ev. 8. | C. G. H. | 1805 |

[ 224 ]

| variegāta | . . . | Yel. str. | . 8, 8. Ev. 8. C. G. H. | . 1727 |
| Woodlandiāna, 5 | Yel. str. | . 8, 8. Ev. 8. C. G. H. | . 1818 |
| Woodfordiāna | . | . 8. Ev. 8. C. G. H. | . 1810 |

ORBICULATE, circular, or spherical.
ORBICULATELY-DEPRESSED, spherical, but depressed on the top.
ORCHALL, see Roccéllā.
ORCHIS, Linn. Orchis, testis; frequent shape in the roots. Linn. 20, Or. 1, Nat. Or. Orchidaceæ. Some of the species of this genus are well known, and require the same treatment as the genus Ophrys. O. maculata, and several others, grow best in peat soil. Synonymes: 1. Orchis parviflora. 2. Gymnadenia angustifolia. 3. O. palustris. 4. O. tephrosanthos. 5. O. Rivini. 6. O. sulphurea. 7. O. Cyrilli. 8. O. Schleicheri. 9. Habenaria spectabilis. 10. O. similia. 11. O. tephrosanthos.

| acumināta, 1 | . | . Purple | . 5, F. Ter. Barbary | . 1815 |
| coriophōrā | . . | . Brown | . 6, H. Ter. Switzerl. | . 1825 |
| foliōsa | . . | . Purple | . 5, F. Ter. Madeira | . |
| fūscā | . . | . Brown | . 6, H. Ter. England | . |
| fus-tecdus | . . | . Green | . 6, H. Ter. N. Amer. | . 1831 |
| globō-ā | . . | . Purple | . 6, H. Ter. Austria | . 1792 |
| hircina | . . | . Brown | . 6, H. Ter. England | . |
| ibérica, 2 | . . | . White . | . 6, H. Ter. Caucasus | . 1819 |
| latifolia | . . | . Pink . | . 6, H. Ter. Britain | . |
| laxiflōrā, 3 | . . | . Purple | . 6, H. Ter. Europe | . 1820 |
| longibracteāta | . | . Purple | . 5, F. Ter. Sicily | . 1818 |
| longicōrnis | . . | . Purple | . 5, F. Ter. Barbary | . 1816 |
| mācrā, 4 | . . | . Pa. pur. | . 6, H. Ter. Britain | . |
| maculāta | . . | . Flesh . | . 6, H. Ter. Britain | . |
| mascūlā | . . | . Purple | . 5, H. Ter. Britain | . |
| militāris | . . | . Purple | . 6, H. Ter. Switzerl. | . 1825 |
| vēra, 5 | . . | . Purple | . 5, H. Ter. Switzerl. | . 1825 |
| mōriō | . . | . Purple | . 5, H. Ter. Britain | . |
| pallēus, 6 | . . | . Pa. yel. | . 5, H. Ter. Switzerl. | . 1825 |
| papilionācēā | . . | . Purple | . 4, H. Ter. Rome | . 1788 |
| provinciālis, 7 | . | . Pur. yel. | . 6, H. Ter. Switzerl. | . 1825 |
| pauciflōrā | . . | . Purple | . 7, H. Ter. Italy | . 1825 |
| pseudo-sambucina | . Purple | . 4, H. Ter. Italy | . 1828 |
| quadripunctāta | . | . Purple | . 4, H. Ter. Italy | . 1828 |
| saccāta | . . | . Purple | . 4, H. Ter. Sicily | . 1828 |
| sambucina, 8 | . | . Yellow | . 4, H. Ter. Switzerl. | . 1825 |
| spectābilis, 9 | . | . Pink . | . 6, H. Ter. N. Amer. | . 1801 |
| tephrosanthos, 10 | . Purple | . 4, H. Ter. England | . |
| undulāta | . . | . Pa. pur. | . 12, F. Ter. Sicily | . 1818 |
| undulatifolia, 11 | . Pa. pur. | . 5, H. Ter. Britain | . |
| ustulāta | . . | . Purple | . 5, H. Ter. England | . |
| variegāta | . . | . Pa. pur. | . 5, H. Ter. S. Eur. | . 1818 |

ORIFICE, an opening.
ORIGĀNŪM, Linn. From oros, a mountain, and ganos, joy; in allusion to the habitation of the plants. Linn. 14, Or. 1, Nat. Or. Labiatæ. Marjoram is a genus of well-known and easily cultivated plants; they grow in any light dry soil. The shrubby kinds are increased by cuttings or slips; the herbaceous species by dividing at the roots. O. Dictamnus is said to be tonic and stimulant. Synonymes: 1. O. stoloniferum. 2. O. humile. 3. O. creticum, O. megastachyum. 4. O. oblongatum, O. virens.

| ægyptiācūm | . | . Pink . | . 7, F. Ev. 8. Egypt | . 1731 |
| Dictamnūs . | . | . Pink . | . 7, F. Ev. 8. Candia | . 1551 |
| heracleōticūm | . | . White. | . 8, H. Her. P. S. Eur. | . 1640 |
| Mārū | . . | . Pink . | . 6, F. Ev. 8. | |
| normāle | . . | . Blue . | . 6, H. Her. P. Nepal | . 1819 |
| sipyleūm | . . | . Pink . | . 8, F. Ev. 8. Levant | . 1699 |
| Tournefortū | . | . Pink . | . 8, F. Ev. 8. Amorgos | . 1788 |
| vulgāre, 1 | . | . Pink . | . 8, H. Her. P. Britain | . |
| flore-albō | . | . White . | . 6, H. Her. P. Britain | . |
| humile, 2 | . | . Purple | . 6, H. Her. P. Asia | . 1818 |
| prismaticūm, 3 | White . | . 7, H. Her. P. Mediter. | . |
| virens, 4 | . | . Purple | . 6, H. Her. P. Portugal | . |

ORLĀYA, Hoffmann. In honour of John Orlay, M.D., secretary to the Medico-Chirurgical Society of Moscow. Linn. 5, Or. 2, Nat. Or. Umbelliferæ. Worthless plants. The seed should be sown in the open ground in spring. Synonymes: 1. Caucalis grandiflora. 2. C. maritima. 3. platycarpos—grandiflorā 1, maritimā 2, platycārpōs.

ORMOCĀRPŪM, P. Browne. From ormos, a necklace, and karpos, a fruit; the pods are jointed, and appear like a necklace. Linn 17, Or. 4, Nat. Or. Leguminosæ. For the culture and propagation of this plant, see Pectitia. Synonyme: 1. Hedysarum sennoides—sennoīdēs.

ORMŌSĪĀ, Jackson. From ormos, a necklace; the seeds of O. coccinea are strung for necklaces; they are red, and have a black spot at one end. Linn. 10, Or. 1, Nat. Or. Leguminosæ. Ornamental trees, requiring to be treated the same as the stove species of Edwardsia. Synonyme: 1. Robinia coccinea.

[ 225 ]

| coccinēā, 1 | . . | . Blue . | . 7, 8. Ev. T. Guiana | . 1823 |
| dasycārpā | . . | . Blue . | . 6, 8. Ev. T. W. Ind. | . 1793 |

ORNITHIDIŪM, Salisbury. From ornis, a bird, and eidos, like; the upper lip of the stigma is beak-like. Linn. 20, Or. 1, Nat. Or. Orchidaceæ. This is a genus of rather interesting plants; for culture and propagation, see Burlingtonia.

| albūm | . . . | . White . | . 9, 8. Epi. Trinidad | . 1833 |
| coccinēūm | . . | . Scarlet . | . 6, 8. Epi. Martinique | 1790 |

ORNITHOCĒPHALŪS, Hooker. From ornis, a bird, and kephale, a head; the column resembles a bird's-head. Linn. 20, Or. 1, Nat. Or. Orchidaceæ. A curious little epiphyte, requiring precisely the same treatment as the genus Burlingtonia.

| gladiātūs . | . | . Green . | . 8. Epi. Trinidad | . 1823 |
| trichorhīzūs . | . | . Straw . | . 4, 8. Epi. Trinidad | . 1835 |

ORNITHŌGĀLŪM. From ornis, a bird, and gala, milk. Linn. 6, Or. 1, Nat. Or. Liliaceæ. An ornamental genus of plants, thriving well in sandy loam and peat; they require very little or no water when dormant, and are increased by offsets from the bulbs. When any of the tender kinds are planted out in the open border, they should be taken up in autumn, and placed in a dry room free from frost, and planted out again early in spring. Synonyme: 1. Scilla maritima.

| alliāceūm | . . | . White . | . 9, G. Bl. P. Chile | . 1821 |
| arābicūm | . . | . White . | . 5, F. Bl. P. Egypt | . 1629 |
| aūreūm | . . | . Yellow | . 6, G. Bl. P. C. G. H. | . 1790 |
| barbātūm | . . | . White . | . 6, G. Bl. P. C. G. H. | . 1795 |
| Bārgīī | . . | . Wht. grn. | . 8, G. Bl. P. | . 1816 |
| biflōrūm | . . | . White . | . 4, G. Bl. P. Peru | . 1832 |
| bifolium | . . | . White . | . 8, G. Bl. P. Chile | . 1831 |
| brachystāchys | . | . White . | . 3, G. Bl. P. Dahuria | . 1821 |
| bulbiferūm | . . | . White . | . 4, H. Bl. P. Russia | . 1821 |
| caudātūm | . . | . Wht. grn. | . 6, G. Bl. P. C. G. H. | . 1774 |
| chloroleūcūm | . | . Grn. wht. | . 7, G. Bl. P. Valparaiso | . 1834 |
| ciliātūm | . . | . White . | . 4, G. Bl. P. C. G. H. | . 1819 |
| coarctātūm | . | . Wht. grn. | . 6, G. Bl. P. C. G. H. | . 1804 |
| comōsūm | . . | . White . | . 7, H. Bl. P. Austria | . 1596 |
| concinnūm | . . | . White . | . 5, F. Bl. P. Portugal | . 1797 |
| conicūm | . . | . Wht. grn. | . 6, G. Bl. P. C. G. H. | . 1823 |
| corymbōsūm | . | . Wht. grn. | . 5, F. Bl. P. Chile | . 1823 |
| crenulātūm | . | . White . | . 4, F. Bl. P. C. G. H. | . 1816 |
| elātūm | . . | . White . | . 3, F. Bl. P. Egypt | . 1804 |
| exscāpūm | . . | . White . | . 3, H. Bl. P. Italy | . 1824 |
| fimbriātūm | . | . White . | . 2, H. Bl. P. Crimea | . 1820 |
| flavissimūm | . | . Yellow | . 5, G. Bl. P. C. G. H. | . 1804 |
| fuscātūm | . . | . Light . | . 6, G. Bl. P. C. G. H. | . 1820 |
| geminiflōrūm | . | . Grnsh. wht. | . G. Bl. P. Lima | . |
| hispidūm | . . | . White . | . 6, G. Bl. P. C. G. H. | . 1824 |
| ixioīdēs | . . | . White . | . 5, F. Bl. P. California | . 1796 |
| juncifolium | . | . White . | . 7, F. Bl. P. C. G. H. | . 1794 |
| lacteūm | . . | . White . | . 6, G. Bl. P. C. G. H. | . 1796 |
| latifolium | . . | . White . | . 6, F. Bl. P. Egypt | . 1629 |
| longibracteātūm | . White . | . 5, G. Bl. P. C. G. H. | . 1817 |
| maculātūm | . | . White . | . 5, F. Bl. P. C. G. H. | . 1823 |
| miniātūm | . . | . Yellow | . 6, F. Bl. P. C. G. H. | . 1790 |
| montānūm | . . | . White . | . 5, H. Bl. P. Italy | . 1824 |
| narbonēnsē | . | . White . | . 7, H. Bl. P. S. Eur. | . 1810 |
| nīveūm | . . | . White . | . 6, G. Bl. P. C. G. H. | . 1774 |
| notātūm | . . | . | . 7, G. Bl. P. C. G. H. | . 1825 |
| nūtāns | . . | . White . | . 6, H. Bl. P. Britain | . |
| odorātūm | . . | . Pa. yel. | . 6, G. Bl. P. C. G. H. | . 1795 |
| ovātūm | . . | . White . | . 5, G. Bl. P. C. G. H. | . 1824 |
| pilōsūm | . . | . White . | . 5, G. Bl. P. C. G. H. | . 1826 |
| polyphyllūm | . | . White . | . 6, G. Bl. P. C. G. H. | . 1824 |
| praslnūm | . . | . Green . | . 6, G. Bl. P. C. G. H. | . 1816 |
| pyramidāle | . | . White . | . 6, H. Bl. P. Spain | . 1752 |
| pyrenāicūm | . | . Green . | . 6, G. Bl. P. England | . |
| refrāctūm | . . | . White . | . 5, H. Bl. P. Hungary | . 1820 |
| revolūtūm | . . | . White . | . 5, G. Bl. P. C. G. H. | . 1795 |
| rupēstrē | . . | . White . | . 5, G. Bl. P. C. G. H. | . 1795 |
| secundūm | . . | . White . | . 5, G. Bl. P. C. G. H. | . 1826 |
| scilloīdēs | . . | . White . | . 6, G. Bl. P. C. G. H. | . 1795 |
| Squilla, 1 | . . | . White . | . 5, F. Bl. P. S. Eur. | . 1829 |
| stachyoīdēs | . | . Li. yel. | . 5, H. Bl. P. S. Eur. | . 1771 |
| suavēolens . | . | . White . | . 6, G. Bl. P. C. G. H. | . 1826 |
| tenēllūm | . . | . White . | . 6, G. Bl. P. C. G. H. | . 1818 |
| tenuifolium | . | . White . | . 4, G. Bl. P. C. G. H. | . 1819 |
| thyroīdēs | . . | . Yellow | . 6, G. Bl. P. C. G. H. | . 1757 |
| flavēcēns | . | . Yellow | . 6, F. Bl. P. C. G. H. | . 1800 |
| trigynūm | . . | . Wht. grn. | . 6, F. Bl. P. | . 1825 |
| umbellātūm | . | . White . | . 5, H. Bl. P. England | . |
| unifolium | . . | . Green . | . 6, G. Bl. P. Gibraltar | . 1805 |
| virens | . . | . White . | . 6, G. Bl. P. Del. Bay | . 1823 |

ORNITHOGLŌSSŪM, Salisbury. From ornis, a bird, and glossa, a tongue; resemblance of the petals. Linn. 6, Or. 3, Nat. Or. Melanthaceæ. Ornamental plants; for culture and propagation, see Ornithogalum. Synonyme: 1. Melanthium viride.

| undulātūm | . . | . Green . | . 9, G. Bl. P. C. G. H. | . 1825 |
| viride, 1 | . . | . Green . | . 10, G. Bl. P. C. G. H. | . 1788 |

ORNĬTHŎPŬS, *Linn.* From *ornithos*, a bird, and *pous*, a foot; the pods are like the claws of a bird. *Linn.* 17, Or. 4, Nat. Or. *Leguminosæ.* Plants of very little beauty. The seed should be sown in the open ground in spring. *Synonyme:* 1. *O. perpusillus intermedius.*

| | | | | | |
|---|---|---|---|---|---|
| comprĕssŭs | . | Yellow | . 6, H. | A. S. Eur. . | 1737 |
| perpusillŭs | . | Red wht. | 7, H. | A. Britain . . | |
| nodŏsŭs | . . | Wht. red | 6, H. Tr. | A. Britain . . | |
| satīvŭs, 1 | . . | Violet . | 6, H. | A. Portugal . | 1818 |

ORNŬS, *Scopoli.* Oren, Hebrew, *oreinos*, Greek, *ornus*, Latin; names for the wild ash. *Linn.* 2, Or. 1, Nat. Or. *Oleaceæ.* All the species of Flowering Ash are ornamental and useful; they are easily cultivated, and may be raised from seeds, as those of *Fraxinus*, or they may be increased by budding or grafting on the common ash. *Synonyme:* 1. *Fraxinus striata.*

| | | | | | |
|---|---|---|---|---|---|
| americānā | . . | White | . 5, H. De. T. | N. Amer. | 1820 |
| europēā | . . | White | . 5, H. De. T. | Italy . | 1730 |
| floribundā | . . | White | . H. De. T. | Nepal . | 1822 |
| rotundifōliā | . | White | . 5, H. De. T. | Italy . | 1697 |
| striātā, 1 | . . | Whitish | . 4, H. De. T. | N. Amer. | 1818 |

OROBĂNCHĒ, *Linn.* From *orobos*, vetch, and *ancho*, to strangle; supposed to kill the plants on which it grows. *Linn.* 14, Or. 2, Nat. Or. *Orobanchaceæ.* The Broom Rape is a genus of curious parasitical plants, none of which are properly cultivable. *O. major* is powerfully astringent.

| | | | | | |
|---|---|---|---|---|---|
| caryophyllācĕā | . | | Parasite. | England | . . |
| cærulēā | . . | Blue | . 7, Parasite. | Britain | . . |
| elātĭŏr | . . | Yellow | . 8, Parasite. | Britain | . . |
| mājŏr | . . | Brown | . 6, Parasite. | Britain | . . |
| minŏr | . . | Yel. wht. | 7, Parasite. | Britain | . . |
| ramōsā | . . | Br. pur. | 8, Parasite. | Britain | . . |
| rūbrā | . . | Red | . 8, Parasite. | Britain | . . |

OROBŬS, *Linn.* From *oro*, to excite, and *bous*, an ox; the *Orobos* of Theophrastus was the name of a plant used for fattening oxen. *Linn.* 17, Or. 4, Nat. Or. *Leguminosæ.* The plants of this genus deserve to have a place in every flower-border, on account of their very elegant pea-blossoms. Any light soil suits them, and they are readily increased by dividing the plants at the roots in spring, or by seeds. *Synonyme:* O. Gmelini.

| | | | | | |
|---|---|---|---|---|---|
| albŭs | . . . | White | . 4, H. Her. P. | Austria | 1794 |
| alpēstrĭs | . . | Purple | . 6, H. Her. P. | Hungary | 1817 |
| americānŭs | . | Pa. pur. | G. Ev. S. | Jamaica | 1731 |
| angustifōliŭs | . | White | . 4, H. Her. P. | Siberia . | 1766 |
| atropurpūrĕŭs | . | Purple | . 5, H. Her. P. | Algiers . | 1826 |
| aurāntĭŭs | . . | Yellow | . 6, H. Her. P. | Iberia . | 1818 |
| canēscĕns | . . | Wht. blue | 6, H. Her. P. | France . | 1816 |
| coccĭnĕŭs | . . | Scarlet | . 4, H. Her. P. | Vera Cruz | |
| unijŭgŭs | . . | Scarlet | . 4, H. Her. P. | N. Amer. | |
| divaricātŭs | . . | Purple | . 6, H. Her. P. | Pyrenees | 1816 |
| erēctŭs | . . | Yel. red | . 7, H. Her. P. | | |
| Fischerī | . . | Purple | . 6, H. Her. Cr. | Siberia . | |
| formōsŭs | . . | Purple | . 6, H. Her. P. | Caucasus | 1818 |
| hirsūtŭs | . . | Red | . 5, H. Her. P. | Thrace . | 1822 |
| hūmĭlĭs | . . | Purple | . 7, H. Her. P. | Dahuria | 1825 |
| Jordānī | . . | Blue | . 6, H. Her. P. | Lucania | 1830 |
| lactĕŭs, 1 | . . | White | . 4, H. Her. P. | Caucasus | 1820 |
| lævigātŭs | . . | Yellow | . 6, H. Her. P. | Hungary | 1820 |
| lathyroĭdĕs | . | Blue | . 6, H. Her. P. | Siberia . | 1758 |
| laxiflōrŭs | . . | Violet | . 6, H. Her. P. | Candia . | 1820 |
| lutĕŭs | . . | Li. yel. | . 6, H. Her. P. | Siberia . | 1759 |
| multiflōrŭs | . . | Pa. red | . 6, H. Her. P. | Italy . | 1820 |
| nĭgĕr | . . | Purple | . 6, H. Her. P. | Britain . | |
| ochrolĕŭcŭs | . | Yel. wht. | 4, H. Her. P. | Hungary | 1816 |
| pallēscĕns | . . | White | . 4, H. Her. P. | Tauria . | 1823 |
| pauciflōrŭs | . | Purple | . 6, H. Her. P. | | 1820 |
| platĭfōrmĭs | . | Purple | . 6, H. Her. P. | S. Eur. . | 1822 |
| pyrenāĭcŭs | . . | Purple | . 5, H. Her. P. | Pyrenees | 1699 |
| saxātĭlĭs | . . | Purple | . 7, H. | A. S. France | 1820 |
| sylvātĭcŭs | . . | Cr. pur. | 6, H. Her. P. | Britain . | |
| tenuifōliŭs | . . | Purple | . 6, H. Her. P. | Europe . | 1810 |
| Tournefortī | . | Yel. pur. | 6, H. Her. P. | Hungary | 1821 |
| tuberōsŭs | . . | Purple | . 6, H. Her. P. | Britain . | |
| variegātŭs | . . | Purple | . 7, H. Her. P. | Italy . | 1821 |
| vāriŭs | . . | Yel. red | . 4, H. Her. P. | Italy . | 1759 |
| vēnŏsŭs | . . | Purple | . 4, H. Her. P. | Germany | |
| vernŏsŭs | . . | Blue | . 6, H. Her. P. | Siberia . | 1820 |
| vernŭs | . . | Purple | . 3, H. Her. P. | Europe . | 1629 |
| cārnĕŭs | . . | Flesh | . 3, H. Her. P. | | |
| vicioĭdĕs | . . | Yellow | . 6, H. Her. P. | Hungary | 1819 |

ORŎNTĬŬM. Adopted from the Greek by Linnæus. *Linn.* 6, Or. 1, Nat. Or. *Araceæ.* A curious aquatic, of easy culture.

| | | | | | |
|---|---|---|---|---|---|
| aquātĭcŭm | . . | Apetal | . 6, H. Aq. P. | N. Amer. | 1775 |

ORPĬNE, see *Telēphĭum.*

ORPĬNE, see *Sĕdŭm Telēphĭum.*

ORTĔGĬA, *Linn.* In honour of Casimir Gomez de Ortega, once professor of botany at Madrid. *Linn.* 3, Or. 1, Nat. Or. *Illecebraceæ.* These plants should be grown on rock-work, or in pots well drained, in a mixture of loam, peat, and sand; they may be increased by cuttings or seeds.

| | | | | | |
|---|---|---|---|---|---|
| dichŏtŏmā | . . | Apetal | . 8, H. Her. P. | Italy | . 1820 |
| hispānĭcā | . . | Apetal | . 6, H. Her. P. | Spain | . 1768 |

ORTHŎCĔRĂS, *R. Brown.* From *orthos*, straight, and *keras*, a horn; in allusion to the appearance of the outer sepals. *Linn.* 20, Or. 1, Nat. Or. *Orchidaceæ.* A curious little plant, requiring the same treatment as the genus *Disa.*

| | | | | | |
|---|---|---|---|---|---|
| striātŭm | | | G. Ter. N. Holl. | | . 1826 |

ORTHŎPŎGŌN, *R. Brown.* From *orthos*, straight, and *pogon*, a beard. *Linn.* 3, Or. 2, Nat. Or. *Gramineæ.* These plants require the same treatment as other stove biennials. *Synonymes:* 1. *Oplismenus africanus.* 2. *Orthopogon loliaceus.*

| | | | | | |
|---|---|---|---|---|---|
| hirtēllŭs | . . | Apetal | . 6, Grass. | W. Ind. . | . 1795 |

*africānŭs* 1, *bromoĭdĕs* 2, *Burmānnī*, *compŏsĭtŭs*, *undulatifōlĭŭs.*

ORTHŎTRĬCHŬM, *Hedwig.* From *orthos*, straight, and *thrix*, a hair; teeth of the peristome. *Linn.* 24, Or. 5, Nat. Or. *Musci.* An extensive genus of very minute plants, found on rocks, trunks of trees, &c. *Synonymes:* 1. *O. nudum, O. anomalum.* 2. *O. aristatum—affīnĕ, mājŭs, pŭmĭlŭm, anomālŭm, crĭspŭm, cupulātŭm* 1, *diaphānŭm* 2, *Drummōndī, Hutchinsĭæ, Ludwigĭī, Lyēllĭī, pulchēllŭm, rivulārĕ, rupĭcōlā, speciōsŭm, striātŭm.*

ORTHROSĂNTHŬS, *Sweet.* From *orthros*, morning, and *anthos*, a flower; time of flowering. *Linn.* 16, Or. 1, Nat. Or. *Iridaceæ.* This is a very pretty plant, growing well in an equal mixture of loam and peat, and may be increased by offsets from the roots, or by seeds.

| | | | | | |
|---|---|---|---|---|---|
| multiflōrŭs | . | Blue | . 6, G. Her. P. | N. Holl. | . 1820 |

ORYZĂ, *Linn.* Derived from the Arabic name, *erus.* *Linn.* 6, Or. 2, Nat. Or. *Gramineæ.* The species of *Oryza*, or Rice, should be sown in a pan or cistern of water, and kept in the stove.

| | | | | | |
|---|---|---|---|---|---|
| latifōliā | . . | Apetal | . 8, Grass. | S. Amer. . | . 1820 |
| nepalēnsĭs | . . | Apetal | . 8, Grass. | Nepal . | . 1818 |
| satīvā | . . | Apetal | . 7, Grass. | E. Ind. . | . 1596 |

ORYZŌPSĬS, *Richard.* From *oryza*, rice, and *opsis*, appearance. *Linn.* 3, Or. 1, Nat. Or. *Gramineæ.* This species grows in any common soil, and is increased by divisions.

| | | | | | |
|---|---|---|---|---|---|
| asperifōliā | . . | Apetal | . 7, Grass. | N. Amer. | . 1822 |

OSAGE-APPLE, see *Maclūrā.*

OSBĔCKĬA, *Linn.* In honour of Peter Osbeck, a Swedish clergyman and naturalist. *Linn.* 8, Or. 1, Nat. Or. *Melastomaceæ.* These shrubs are well worth cultivating on account of their beautiful flowers; for culture and propagation, see *Melastoma.* *Synonymes:* 1. *Melastoma osbeckioides.* 2. *Pleroma glomerata.* 3. *Rhexia glomerata.* 4. *Melastoma nepalensis.*

| | | | | | |
|---|---|---|---|---|---|
| canēscĕns | . . | | . 8, De. S. | | . 1838 |
| chinēnsĭs, 1 | . . | Purple | . 7, S. Ev. S. | China . | 1818 |
| glomerātā, 2 | . | Pink | . 7, S. De. S. | Trinidad | 1818 |
| albiflōrā, 3 | . | White | . 1, S. Ev. S. | Brazil . | 1821 |
| nepalēnsĭs, 4 | . | Purple | . 6, S. Ev. S. | Nepal . | 1821 |
| albiflōrā | . . | White | . 8, S. De. S. | Nepal . | 1829 |
| stellātā | . . | Pink | . 7, S. Ev. S. | Nepal . | 1820 |
| zeylānĭcā | . . | Yellow | . 8, S. Ev. S. | Ceylon . | 1799 |

OSCILLATŌRĬA, *Vauch.* Plants having an oscillatory motion. *Linn.* 24, Or. 7, Nat. Or. *Algæ.* Minute plants, found on stones in rivers, pools, &c. *Synonyme:* 1. *rupestris—alātā, autumnālĕ, vaginātā, contēxtā, cōrĭŭm, cyānĕā, decōrtĭcā, limbātā* 1, *limōsā, littorālĭs, nĭgrā, ochrācĕā, spadĭcĕā, spirālĭs, splēndĭdā, subfūscā, tĕnŭĭs, tenuĭssĭmā, turfōsā.*

OSIER, see *Salĭx vimĭnālĭs.*

OSMĪTĔS, *Cassini.* From *osme*, perfume; strong smell of camphor. *Linn.* 19, Or. 3, Nat. Or. *Compositæ.* Ornamental plants, thriving in any rich light soil, and increased by cuttings in sand, under a glass.

| | | | | | |
|---|---|---|---|---|---|
| bellidiāstrŭm | . | White | . 6, G. Ev. S. | C. G. H. | . 1816 |
| camphorīnā | . | White | . 5, G. Ev. S. | C. G. H. | . 1794 |
| dentātā | . . | White | . 5, G. Ev. S. | C. G. H. | . 1820 |

OSMŬNDĂ, *Linn.* From *Osmunder*, one of the names of Thor, a Celtic deity. *Linn.* 24, Or. 1, Nat. Or. *Osmundaceæ.* Ornamental ferns, of easy culture. *Synonyme:* 1. *regalis.*

| Species | Colour | Details | Origin | Date |
|---|---|---|---|---|
| cinnamomea | Brown | 6, H. Her. P. | N. Amer. | 1772 |
| Claytoniana | Brown | 8, H. Her. P. | N. Amer. | 1772 |
| gracilis | Brown | 6, H. Her. P. | | 1827 |
| interrupta | Brown | 6, H. Her. P. | N. Amer. | |
| palustris | Brown | 7, H. Her. P. | | 1831 |
| regalis | Brown | 7, H. Her. P. | Britain | |
| spectabilis, 1 | Brown | 7, H. Her. P. | N. Amer. | 1811 |

OSSIFIED, becoming like bone.

OSTEOSPERMUM, *Linn.* From *osteon*, a bone, and *sperma*, a seed; hardness of the seeds. Linn. 19, Or. 4, Nat. Or. *Compositæ.* Ornamental shrubs; for culture and propagation, see *Osmites.* Synonyme: 1. *Bidens calendulacea.*

| Species | Colour | Details | Origin | Date |
|---|---|---|---|---|
| cæruleum | Blue | 7, G. Ev. S. C. G. H. | | 1774 |
| calendulaceum, 1 | Yellow | 7, G. Ev. S. C. G. H. | | |
| corymbosum | Yellow | 8, G. Ev. S. C. G. H. | | 1822 |
| ilicifolium | Yellow | 7, G. Ev. S. C. G. H. | | 1816 |
| incanum | Yellow | 8, G. Ev. S. C. G. H. | | 1815 |
| moniliferum | Yellow | 7, G. Ev. S. C. G. H. | | 1714 |
| niveum | Yellow | 7, G. Ev. S. C. G. H. | | 1816 |
| perfoliatum | Yellow | 7, G. Ev. S. C. G. H. | | 1820 |
| pisiferum | Yellow | 4, G. Ev. S. C. G. H. | | 1757 |
| polygaloides | Yellow | 7, G. Ev. S. C G. H. | | 1759 |
| rigidum | Yellow | 5, G. Ev. S. C. G. H. | | 1774 |
| spinescens | Yellow | 4, G. Ev. S. C. G. H. | | 1793 |
| spinosum | Yellow | 4, G. Ev. S. C. G. H. | | 1730 |

OSTERICUM, *Hoffmann.* The meaning is not known. Linn. 5, Or. 2, Nat. Or. *Umbelliferæ.* For the culture of this plant, see *Opopanax.* Synonyme: 1. *Angelica pratensis—pratensé.*

OSTRYA, *Michaux.* From *ostryos*, a scale; in allusion to the scaly catkins. Linn. 21, Or. 9, Nat. Or. *Cupuliferæ.* The species of Hop Hornbeam attain a good size, and are increased by layers or seeds. Synonyme: 1 *Carpinus Ostrya.*

| Species | Colour | Details | Origin | Date |
|---|---|---|---|---|
| virginica | Apetal | 4, H. De. T. | N. Amer. | 1692 |
| vulgaris, 1 | Apetal | 5, H. De. T. | Italy | 1724 |

OSWEGO-TEA, see *Monarda didyma.*

OSYRIS, *Linn.* From *ozos*, a branch; numerous pliant branches. Linn. 22, Or. 3, Nat. Or. *Santalaceæ.* This plant grows well in a mixture of loam and peat; and cuttings of the ripened wood root readily in sand, under a glass.

| Species | Colour | Details | Origin | Date |
|---|---|---|---|---|
| alba | White | F. Ev. S. | S. Eur. | 1739 |

OTAHEITE-APPLE, see *Spondias dulcis.*
OTAHEITE-CHESNUT, see *Inocarpus.*
OTAHEITE-MYRTLE, see *Securinega.*

OTANTHUS, *Link.* From *ous*, an ear, and *anthos*, a flower; appendages at the base of the florets. Linn. 19, Or. 1, Nat. Or. *Compositæ.* A pretty plant, growing well in sandy loam; and cuttings planted in a shady border in autumn will soon root. Synonymes: 1. *Diotis candidissima, Santolina maritima.*

| Species | Colour | Details | Origin | Date |
|---|---|---|---|---|
| maritimus, 1 | Yellow | 8, H. Her. P. | England | |

OTHONNA, *Linn.* From *othone*, linen; alluding to the downy clothing of the original plant. Linn. 19, Or. 4. Nat. Or. *Compositæ.* Ornamental plants. *O. Tagetes* must be treated as other greenhouse annuals; the others may all be referred to *Osmites,* for culture, &c. Synonyme: 1. *O. flabellifolia.*

| Species | Colour | Details | Origin | Date |
|---|---|---|---|---|
| abrotanifolia | Yellow | 5, G. Ev. S. C. G. H. | | 1692 |
| arborescens | Yellow | 7, G. Ev. S. C. G. H. | | 1793 |
| Athanasiæ | Yellow | 1, G. Ev. S. C. G. H. | | 1795 |
| bulbosa | Yellow | 5, G. Tu. P. C. G. H. | | 1774 |
| cacalioides | Yellow | 7, G. Tu. P. C. G. H. | | 1774 |
| cheirifolia | Yellow | 5, F. Ev. Cr. Barbary | | 1752 |
| coronopifolia | Yellow | 8, G. Ev. S. C. G. H. | | 1731 |
| crassifolia | Yellow | 9, G. Ev. S. C. G. H. | | 1710 |
| denticulata | Yellow | 6, G. Ev. S. C. G. H. | | 1774 |
| digitata | Yellow | 7, G. Ev. S. C. G. H. | | 1824 |
| ericoides | Yellow | 7, G. Ev. S. C. G. H. | | 1818 |
| filicaulis | Yellow | 4, G. Tu. P. C. G. H. | | 1791 |
| frutescens | Yellow | 7, G. Ev. S. C. G. H. | | 1816 |
| heterophylla | Yellow | 5, G. Ev. S. C. G. H. | | 1812 |
| ilagua | Yellow | 8, G. Her. P. C. G. H. | | 1787 |
| linifolia | Yellow | 7, G. Her. P. C. G. H. | | 1824 |
| parviflora | Yellow | 7, G. Ev. S. C. G. H. | | 1704 |
| pectinata | Yellow | 5, G. Ev. S. C. G. H. | | 1781 |
| perfoliata | Yellow | 6, G. Her. P. C. G. H. | | 1789 |
| pinnata | Yellow | 5, G. Her. P. C. G. H. | | 1759 |
| pinnatifida | Yellow | 7, G. Her. P. C. G. H. | | 1823 |
| retrofracta | Yellow | 6, G. Ev. S. C. G. H. | | 1812 |
| Tagetes | Yellow | 6, G | A. C. G. H. | 1823 |
| tenuissima | Yellow | 5, G. Ev. S. C. G. H. | | 1759 |
| virginea | Yellow | 10, G. Ev. S. | Africa | 1821 |

OUREA, *Aublet. Jouiay* is the name of the species in Guiana. Linn. 3, Or. 1, Nat. Or. *Leguminosæ.* These trees grow in sandy loam; and cuttings of

the ripened wood root in sand, plunged in heat, under a glass. Synonymes: 1. *Macrolobium bijugum.*

| Species | Colour | Details | Origin | Date |
|---|---|---|---|---|
| bijuga, 1 | | 8. Ev. S. | E. Ind. | 1823 |
| guianensis | | 8. Ev. T. | Guiana | 1825 |

OVA, the eggs of anything.
OVAL, having the figure of an ellipse.
OVARIUM, or OVARY, the part of the flower in which the young seeds are contained.
OVATE, egg-shaped.
OVATE, when joined by a hyphen to another word, signifies a form between the two, as ovate-cordate, ovate, and heart-shaped.
OVERLAPPING; when the margin of one thing lies upon that of another, it is said to overlap.
OVOID, egg-like.
OVULES, the young seeds of plants contained in the ovarium.

OXALIS, *Linn.* From *oxys*, acid; the leaves have an acid taste. Linn. 10, Or. 4, Nat. Or. *Oxalidaceæ.* Most of the plants of this genus deserve cultivating on account of their very pretty blossoms, which are produced in great abundance. The stove, greenhouse, and frame species, thrive well in a mixture of loam, peat, and sand; they should not be watered after they have done flowering until they begin to grow afresh. The shrubby kinds may be increased by cuttings or seeds; the herbaceous fibrous-rooted ones by dividing the plants at the roots, or by seeds, the bulbous-rooted species by offsets. Most of those marked greenhouse may be grown in a frame, only they must be protected from frost in winter. The hardy species should be planted in a shady border, where they will grow and flower very freely. The seeds of the hardy annual species should be sown in the open border in spring. *O. Acetosella* contains pure oxalic acid, and several species are used in Brazil against malignant fevers. Synonymes: 1. *caprina.* 2. *arrucacha.* 3. *rubens.* 4. *floribunda.* 5. *Martiana.* 6. *rosea.*

| Species | Colour | Details | Origin | Date |
|---|---|---|---|---|
| Acetosella | White | 5, H. Bl. P. | Britain | |
| alba | White | 5, H. Bl. P. | America | 1836 |
| ambigua | White | 10, G. Bl. P. C. G. H. | | 1790 |
| americana | White | 4, H. Bl. P. | N. Amer. | |
| arcuata | Violet | 9, G. Bl. P. C. G. H. | | 1795 |
| asinina | Yellow | 11, G. Bl. P. C. G. H. | | 1792 |
| Barrelieri | Pa. red | 9, S. Ev. S. | Caracas | 1824 |
| bifida | Violet | 8, G. Bl. P. C. G. H. | | 1791 |
| bipunctata | Lilac | 5, G. Bl. P. | Brazil | 1825 |
| Bowiei | Crimson | 10, G. Bl. P. C. G. H. | | 1823 |
| brasiliensis | Rose | 10, G. Bl. P. | Brazil | 1829 |
| brevicapa | White | 5, G. Bl. P. C. G. H. | | 1823 |
| Burmanni | Purple | 6, G. Bl. P. C. G. H. | | 1820 |
| canescens | Purple | 3, G. Bl. P. C. G. H. | | 1821 |
| caprina | Flesh | 8, G. Bl. P. C. G. H. | | 1757 |
| carnosa | Yellow | 10, G. Bl. P. | Chile | 1826 |
| cernua, 1 | Yellow | 3, G. Bl. P. C. G. H. | | 1757 |
| chinensis | Yellow | 8, G. Ev. Tr. | China | |
| ciliaris | Purple | 10, G. Bl. P. C. G. H. | | 1793 |
| Commersonii | Yellow | 10, G. Bl. P. | Brazil | |
| compressa | Yellow | 12, G. Bl. P. C. G. H. | | 1794 |
| convexula | Pink | 6, G. Bl. P. C. G. H. | | 1789 |
| corniculata | Yellow | 8, H. | A. Britain | |
| crenata, 2 | Yellow | 9, G. Tu. P. | Lima | 1829 |
| crispa | White | 10, G. Bl. P. C. G. H. | | 1793 |
| cruentata | Purple | 10, G. Bl. P. C. G. H. | | 1826 |
| Cummingii | Golden | 9, F. Her. P. | Chile | 1831 |
| cuneata | Yel. wht. | 7, G. Bl. P. C. G. H. | | 1822 |
| cuneifolia | White | 4, G. Bl. P. C. G. H. | | 1793 |
| cuprea | Copper | 5, G. Bl. P. C. G. H. | | 1822 |
| Darwalliana | | F. Bl. P. | | |
| dentata | Flesh | 10, G. Bl. P. C. G. H. | | 1793 |
| Deppei | Red | G. Bl. P. | Mexico | 1827 |
| Dillenii | Copper | H. | A. America | 1798 |
| florida | Yellow | H. | A. America | 1798 |
| disticha | Pa. yel. | 5, G. Bl. P. C. G. H. | | 1818 |
| divergens | White | 7, F. Bl. P. | Mexico | 1829 |
| elongata | White | 6, G. Bl. P. C. G. H. | | 1791 |
| amœna | Copper | 9, G. Bl. P. C. G. H. | | 1810 |
| faberfolia | Red | 10, G. Bl. P. C. G. H. | | 1794 |
| fallax | Yellow | 9, G. Bl. P. C. G. H. | | 1825 |
| ferruginata | Yellow | 6, G. Bl. P. C. G. H. | | 1820 |
| filicaulis | Violet | 9, G. Bl. P. C. G. H. | | 1815 |
| filifolia | Pink | 6, G. Bl. P. C. G. H. | | 1822 |
| flabellifolia | Yel. red | 8, G. Bl. P. C. G. H. | | 1789 |
| flaccida | Wht. red | 9, G. Bl. P. C. G. H. | | 1812 |
| flava | Yellow | 2, G. Bl. P. C. G. H. | | 1775 |
| flore-pleno | Yellow | 3, G. Bl. P. | | |
| floribunda | Red | 7, G. Her. P. | S. Amer. | 1827 |
| fruticosa | Yellow | 12, S. Ev. S. | Rio Jan. | 1817 |
| fulgida | Crimson | 10, G. Bl. P. C. G. H. | | 1820 |
| furcata | Red | 9, G. Bl. P. C. G. H. | | 1823 |
| fuscata | Yellow | 5, G. Bl. P. C. G. H. | | 1795 |

| geniculātā | . Yellow | . 10, G. Bl. | P. | C. G. H. | . |
| glabrā . | . Purple | . 5, G. Bl. | P. | C. G. H. | . 1795 |
| glandulōsā | . White | . 10, G. Bl. | P. | C. G. H. | . 1822 |
| hirtā . | . Lilac | . 10, G. Bl. | P. | C. G. H. | . 1787 |
| hirtellā . | . Red | . 8, G. Bl. | P. | C. G. H. | . 1823 |
| incarnātā . | . Flesh | . 5, G. Bl. | P. | C. G. H. | . 1789 |
| laburnifōliā | . Yellow | . 9, G. Bl. | P. | C. G. H. | . 1793 |
| lævigātā . | . Purple | . 6, H. | A. | C. G. H. | . 1818 |
| lanātā . | . White | . 10, G. Bl. | P. | C. G. H. | . 1791 |
| lanceæfōliā | . Yellow | . 10, G. Bl. | P. | C. G. H. | . 1795 |
| laterifōra . | . Purple | . 8, G. Bl. | P. | C. G. H. | . 1824 |
| laxūla . | . White | . 11, G. Bl. | P. | C. G. H. | . 1820 |
| lēpidā . | . White | . 10, G. Bl. | P. | C. G. H. | . 1823 |
| leporīnā . | . White | . 10, G. Bl. | P. | C. G. H. | . 1795 |
| lineāris . | . Violet | . 10, G. Bl. | P. | C. G. H. | . 1795 |
| līvidā . | . Flesh | . 10, G. Bl. | P. | C. G. H. | . 1793 |
| lobātā . | . Yellow | . 10, G. Bl. | P. | C. G. H. | . 1823 |
| lupinifōliā | . Yellow | . 9, G. Bl. | P. | C. G. H. | . 1791 |
| luteōlā . | . Yellow | . 5, G. Bl. | P. | C. G. H. | . 1823 |
| Lyōnii . | . Yellow | . 8, H. Her. | P. | N. Amer. | . 1816 |
| macrophyllā | . Yellow | . 6, G. Bl. | P. | C. G. H. | . 1820 |
| macrostýlis | . Purple | . 10, G. Bl. | P. | C. G. H. | . 1793 |
| marginātā . | . White | . 11, G. Bl. | P. | C. G. H. | . 1812 |
| Martiāna . | . Yellow | . 7, S. Her. | P. | Brazil | . 1829 |
| mauritiāna . | . Pa. rose | . 9, G. Bl. | P. | l France | . 1810 |
| microphyllā, 3 | . Pa. red | . G. | A. | N. S. W. | . |
| miniātā . | . Vermil. | . 5, G. Bl. | P. | C. G. H. | . 1819 |
| monophyllā | . Yellow | . 10, G. Bl. | P. | C. G. H. | . 1774 |
| multifōrā . | . Lilac . | . 2, G. Bl. | P. | C. G. H. | . 1789 |
| nātans . | . White | . 10, G. Aq. | P. | C. G. H. | . 1795 |
| obtūsā . | . White | . 9, G. Bl. | P. | C. G. H. | . 1812 |
| papiliōnacēā | . Varieg. | . G. Bl. | P. | Brazil | . 1819 |
| pectinātā . | . Yellow | . 10, G. Bl. | P. | C. G. H. | . 1790 |
| pentaphyllā | . Pink . | . 6, F. Bl. | P. | C. G. H. | . 1800 |
| perennāns | . Yellow | . 7, G. Her. | P. | N. S. W. | . |
| Piōttæ . | . Orange | . 6, G. Bl. | P. | C. G. H. | . 1816 |
| Plumiēri . | . Yellow | . 8, Ev. | S. | S. Amer. | . 1823 |
| polyphyllā | . Pa. pur. | . 10, G. Bl. | P. | C. G. H. | . 1791 |
| pulchellā . | . White | . 10, G. Bl. | P. | C. G. H. | . 1795 |
| punctātā . | . Purple | . 5, G. Bl. | P. | | |
| purpurātā . | . Pa. pur. | . 10, G. Bl. | P. | C. G. H. | . 1822 |
| purpūrea . | . Purple | . 10, G. Bl. | P. | C. G. H. | . 1812 |
| pusillā . | . Pa. red | . 5, G. Bl. | P. | C. G. H. | . 1823 |
| reclinātā . | . Pink . | . 10, G. Bl. | P. | | . 1795 |
| rēpens . | . Yellow | . 5, G. Her. | P. | C. G. H. | . 1793 |
| reptātrix . | . Flesh | . 11, G. Bl. | P. | C. G. H. | . 1795 |
| rosācēā . | . Pink . | . 10, G. Bl. | P. | C. G. H. | . 1792 |
| rōsea, 4 | . Rose . | . 2, G. Her. | P. | Chile | . 1826 |
| rostrātā . | . Pur. vio. | . 10, G. Bl. | P. | C. G. H. | . 1795 |
| rubellā . | . Pink . | . 10, G. Bl. | P. | C. G. H. | . 1791 |
| rubro-flāvā | . Red yel. | . 6, G. Bl. | P. | C. G. H. | . 1823 |
| sanguīnea . | . Yellow | . 11, G. Bl. | P. | C. G. H. | . 1795 |
| secūndā . | . Lilac . | . 10, G. Bl. | P. | C. G. H. | . 1790 |
| serīceā . | . Yellow | . 5, G. Bl. | P. | C. G. H. | . 1794 |
| speciōsā . | . Purple | . 10, G. Bl. | P. | C. G. H. | . 1690 |
| strictā . | . Yellow | . 7, H. Her. | P. | N. Amer. | . 1658 |
| strumōsā . | . White | . 12, G. Bl. | P. | C. G. H. | . 1821 |
| sulphūrea . | . Pa. yel. | . 10, G. Bl. | P. | C. G. H. | . 1795 |
| sylvēstris . | . White | . 2, G. Bl. | P. | C. G. H. | . |
| tenellā . | . Lilac . | . 5, G. Bl. | P. | C. G. H. | . 1793 |
| tenērā . | . Yellow | . 5, G. Bl. | P. | Brazil | . 1826 |
| tetraphyllā | . Purple | . 6, G. Bl. | P. | Mexico | . 1823 |
| tenuifōlia . | . Wht. red | 10, G. Bl. | P. | C. G. H. | . 1790 |
| tomentōsā . | . White | . 5, G. Bl. | P. | C. G. H. | . 1791 |
| tortuōsā . | . Yellow | . 6, G. Ev. | S. | Chile | . 1825 |
| tricōlor . | . Wht. red | 11, G. Bl. | P. | C. G. H. | . 1794 |
| tubiflōrā | . Pink . | . 11, G. Bl. | P. | C. G. H. | . 1790 |
| undulātā . | . Lilac . | . 10, G. Bl. | P. | C. G. H. | . 1795 |
| ūrbica, 5 | . White | . 8, G. Her. | P. | Brazil | . 1828 |
| variābilis . | . Wht. red | 11, G. Bl. | P. | C. G. H. | . 1795 |
|   grandiflōra | . White | . 11, G. Bl. | P. | | . 1790 |
|   Simsii, 6 | . White | . 11, G. Bl. | P. | | . 1790 |
| venōsā . | . Vio. yel. | . 10, G. Bl. | P. | C. G. H. | . 1823 |
| versicōlor . | . Crimson | . 2, G. Bl. | P. | C. G. H. | . 1774 |
| violācēā . | . Violet | . 5, H. Bl. | P. | N. Amer. | . 1772 |
| virgīnea . | . White | . 4, G. Bl. | P. | C. G. H. | . 1820 |

OXEYE, see *Bupthālmum.*

OXEYE DAISY, see *Chrysānthēmum leucānthēmum.*

OXLEYA, *Hooker.* In honour of Mr. Oxley, late surveyor-general of New South Wales. *Linn.* 10, Or. 1, Nat. Or. *Cedrelaceæ.* A fine tree, attaining the height of one hundred feet; it should be grown in loam, peat, and sand, and cuttings of the ripened wood will root in sand, under a glass, provided the leaves are not shortened.

| xanthōxylōn | . . | | G. Ev. T. | N. Holl. | . 1828 |

OX-LIP, see *Prīmūlā elātiŏr.*

OXHORN, see *Būcĭdā Būcĕrǎs.*

OXTONGUE, see *Pĭcrĭs.*

OXYĀNTHŬS, *Decandolle.* From *oxys,* acute, and *anthos,* a flower. *Linn.* 5, Or. 1, Nat. Or. *Cinchonaceæ.* An ornamental plant; for culture and propagation, see the stove species of *Gardenia.*

| speciōsŭs | . . White | . 7, S. Ev. | S. | S. Leone | . 1789 |

OXYBĀPHŬS, *Jussieu.* From *oxys,* acid, and *baphe,*

dyer's-colour. *Linn.* 3, Or. 1, Nat. Or. *Nyctaginaceæ.* This is a genus of curious plants, which succeed well in the open border in summer, but they should be taken up in autumn, and laid up in a dry room out of the reach of frost; they are readily increased by seeds, which ripen in abundance. *Synonymes*: 1. *Allionia linearis, Calymenia angustifolia.* 2. *A. nyctaginea.* 3. *A. pilosa.*

| aggregātŭs | . Pink | . 7, F. Her. | P. | N. Spain | . 1811 |
| angustifōliŭs, 1 | . Purple | . 8, H. De. | Cr. | Louisiana | . 1812 |
| Cervantesii | . Purple | . 6, F. Ev. | Tr. | Mexico | . 1823 |
| chilēnsis . | . Lilac | . 9, H. Her. | P. | Chile | . 1832 |
| decūmbēns . | . Purple | . 8, H. De. | Cr. | Missouri | . 1818 |
| expānsŭs . | . Purple | . 7, F. Ev. | Tr. | Peru | . 1819 |
| glabrifōliŭs | . Purple | . 7, F. Her. | P. | N. Spain | . 1811 |
| hirsūtŭs . | . Purple | . 8, H. De. | Cr. | Louisiana | . 1824 |
| nyctaginēŭs, 2 | . Purple | . 8, H. De. | Cr. | Missouri | . 1823 |
| ovātŭs . | . Purple | . 8, H. Ev. | Tr. | Peru | . 1820 |
| pilosŭs, 3 | . Purple | . 8, H. De. | Cr. | Missouri | . 1812 |
| viscōsŭs . | . Purple | . 8, H. Ev. | P. | Peru | . 1793 |

OXYCŎCCŬS, *Richard.* From *oxys,* sharp, and *kokkos,* a berry; sharp acid taste of the berries. *Linn.* 8, Or. 1, Nat. Or. *Ericaceæ.* The Cranberry is a well-known genus of plants. *O. palustris* grows in most turfy mossy bogs in the mountainous parts of Britain, the berries being very much sought after. When the plants are grown for the sake of the fruit, they should be planted on an artificial bog, but when grown only for having specimens, they will do in pots well drained, and filled with peat and sand, with some sphagnum moss about their roots, and placed in pans of water. *Synonymes*: 1. *O. erythrocarpus.* 2. *Vaccinium macrocarpus.* 3. *V. Oxycoccus.*

| erēctŭs, 1 | . . Pink | . 5, H. Ev. | S. | N. Amer. | . 1806 |
| macrocārpŭs, 2 | . Pink | . 5, H. Ev. | Tr. | N. Amer. | . 1760 |
| variegātŭs | . Pink | . 5, H. Ev. | Tr. | Gardens | . |
| palūstris, 3 | . Pink | . 5, H. Ev. | | Britain | . |

OXYLŌBĬŬM, *Botanical Repository.* From *oxys,* sharp, and *lobos,* a pod; the legumes are furnished with a sharp pod. *Linn.* 10, Or. 1, Nat. Or. *Leguminosæ.* Ornamental plants; for culture and propagation, see *Podolobium.*

| arborēscens | . Yellow | . 5, G. Ev. | S. | V. D. L. | . 1805 |
| capitātŭm | . | | G. Ev. | S. | Swan R. | |
| cordifōliŭm | . Yellow | . 6, G. Ev. | S. | N. S. W. | . 1807 |
| ellipticŭm | . Yellow | . 7, G. Ev. | S. | V. D. L. | . 1805 |
| ferrugineŭm | . Yellow | . 5, G. Ev. | S. | N. Holl. | . 1820 |
| obtusifōliŭm | . Scarlet | . 5, G. Ev. | S. | N. Holl. | . 1824 |
| Pultenēæ | . Drk. or. | . 5, G. Ev. | S. | N. Holl. | . 1824 |
| retūsŭm | . Orange | . 5, G. Ev. | S. | N. Holl. | . 1823 |
| spinōsŭm | . Yellow | . 5, G. Ev. | S. | N. Holl. | . 1825 |

OXYPĔTĂLŬM, *R. Brown.* From *oxys,* sharp, and *petalon,* a petal. *Linn.* 5, Or. 2, Nat. Or. *Asclepiadaceæ.* An interesting plant, growing in peat and loam, and increased by cuttings in sand, under a glass, in heat.

| appendiculātŭm | | | 8. Ev. Tw. | | Brazil | . . 1823 |

OXYRĬA, *Hill.* From *oxys,* acid. *Linn.* 6, Or. 2, Nat. Or. *Polygonaceæ.* The Mountain Sorrel grows well in common garden soil, and is increased by dividing at the roots, or by seeds. *Synonymes*: 1. *Rumex digynus.* 2. *O. reniformis.*

| reniformis, 1 | . Green | . 6, H. Her. | P. | Britain | . |
| americānŭs, 2 | . Green | . 6, H. Her. | P. | N. Amer. | . |

OXYSTĚLMA, *R. Brown.* From *oxys,* sharp, and *stelma,* a crown; the foliola of the corona is acute. *Linn.* 5, Or. 2, Nat. Or. *Asclepiadaceæ.* An ornamental plant; for culture and propagation, see *Oxypetalum.*

| esculentŭm | . . Yellow | . 8. Ev. Tw. | | E. Ind. | . . 1816 |

OXYTRŎPIS, *Decandolle.* From *oxys,* sharp, and *tropis,* a keel; flowers ending in a mucrone at the apex of the keel. *Linn.* 17, Or. 4, Nat. Or. *Leguminosæ.* These plants are very handsome when in flower, and are well adapted for ornamenting rock-work, or the front of flower-borders. The seed should be sown where the plants are intended to grow, as they seldom thrive after transplanting. The rarer kinds may be grown in pots well drained, in a mixture of peat, sand, and a little loam, and treated as other alpine plants. *Synonymes*: 1. *Astragalus Halleri.* 2. *O. Gmelini.* 3. *Astragalus montanus.* 4. *A. dahuricus.* 5. *A. uralensis, O. sordida.*

| ambīgŭā . | . Purple | . 6, H. Her. | P. | Siberia | . 1817 |
| argyrophyllā | . Purple | . H. Her. | P. | | . 1831 |
| brevirōstris | . Blue | . 8, H. Her. | P. | Siberia | . 1802 |
| campēstris | . Pa. yel. | . 6, H. Her. | P. | Scotland | . |
| cyānēā . | . Blue | . 7, H. Her. | P. | Caucasus | . 1818 |

| | | | | | |
|---|---|---|---|---|---|
| dealbātā . | . Purple | . 7, H. Her. P. | Caucasus | . 1803 |
| deflexā . | . Purple | . 6, H. Her. P. | Siberia | . 1800 |
| dichoptērā | . Blue | . 6, H. Her. P. | Siberia | . 1815 |
| Fischeri . | . Blue | . 7, H. Her. P. | Altai | . 1817 |
| fœtida, 1 . | . Pa. yel. | . 7, H. Her. P. | Switzerl. | . 1819 |
| glābrā . | . Purple | . 7, H. Her. P. | Dahuria | . 1823 |
| grandiflōrā | . Red | . 6, H. Her. P. | Siberia | . 1820 |
| leptoptērā . | . Blue | . 7, H. Her. P. | Siberia | . 1818 |
| Lambērti . | . Purple | . 8, H. Her. P. | Missouri | . 1811 |
| leptophyllā | . Red | . 7, H. Her. P. | Siberia | . 1818 |
| longirōstrā, 2 | . Purple | . H. Her. P. | Siberia | . 1820 |
| microphyllā | . Pa. yel. | . 7, H. Her. P. | Siberia | . 1819 |
| montānā, 3 | . Purple | . 7, H. Her. P. | Austria | . 1681 |
| myriophyllā | . Pur. wht. | . 7, H. Her. P. | Siberia | . 1818 |
| oxyphyllā | . Purple | . 7, H. Her. P. | Siberia | . 1816 |
| Pallasii . | . Pa. yel. | . 7, H. Her. P. | Siberia | . 1818 |
| pilōsā . | . Pa. yel. | . 7, H. Her. P. | Siberia | . 1789 |
| prostrātā, 4 | . Blue wht. | . 7, H. De. Tr. | Siberia | . 1820 |
| songarica . | . Violet | . 6, H. Her. P. | Altai | . 1824 |
| sulphūreā . | . Cream | . 7, H. Her. P. | Siberia | . 1820 |
| uncātā . | . White | . 7, H. Her. P. | Aleppo | . 1768 |
| uralēnsis, 5 | . Purple | . 7, H. Her. P. | Siberia | . 1800 |
| verticillāris | . Blue wht. | . 7, H. Her. P. | Siberia | . 1819 |
| viscōsā | . White | . 7, H. Her. P. | Switzerl. | . 1817 |

OxYÜRĀ, *Decandolle.* Supposed to be from *oxys*, sharp,

and *oura*, a tail; but the application is not evident. *Linn.* 19, Or. 2, Nat. Or. *Compositæ.* An ornamental plant, having somewhat the appearance of *Chrysanthemum coronarium.* It grows in any common soil.

| | | | | |
|---|---|---|---|---|
| chrysanthemoĭdēs . | Yellow | . 7, H. | A. California | . 1834 |

OzōnĪŪm, *Persoon.* From *ozos*, a branch; the filaments are branched. *Linn.* 24, Or. 9, Nat. Or. *Fungi.* This plant is found during autumn on decayed wood—*auricōmŭm.*

OzoThĀmnŬs, *R. Brown.* From *ozos*, a branch, and *thamnos*, a shrub. *Linn.* 19, Or. 1, Nat. Or. *Compositæ.* Ornamental plants, growing freely in an equal mixture of loam and peat; and cuttings of the young wood will root in a few days planted in sand, under a glass. *Synonymes:* 1. *Chrysocoma cinerea.* 2. *Eupatorium ferrugineum.* 3. *E. rosmarinifolium.*

| | | | | | |
|---|---|---|---|---|---|
| cinerēūs, 1 . | . Yellow | . 7, H. Ev. S. | V. D. L. | . 1820 |
| ferruginēūs, 2 | . Yellow | . 7, G. Ev. S. | V. D. L. | . 1822 |
| rosmarinifolĭūs, 3 | . Yellow | . 7, G. Ev. S. | V. D. L. | . 1822 |

# P.

PĀchĬdĒndrŏn, *Willdenow.* From *pachys*, thick, and *dendron*, a tree. *Linn.* 6, Or. 1, Nat. Or. *Liliaceæ.* A genus of tree Aloes, thriving in a mixture of sandy loam mixed with old lime and brick rubbish; the pots in which they are grown must be well drained, that the moisture may readily pass off. They require but little water in winter, and are increased from suckers, or young side shoots, when they are produced; leaves taken off close from the stem, and laid to dry for a few days, then planted in pots of dry soil, will throw out young plants at their base. *Synonymes:* 1. *Aloe africana.* 2. *A. angustifolia.* 3. *A. ferox.* 4. *A. principis.* 5. *A. pseudo-africana, africana angustior.* 6. *A. pseudo-ferox, subferox.* 7. *A. supralævis.*

| | | | | | |
|---|---|---|---|---|---|
| africānŭm, 1 | . Red | . 7, G. Ev. S. C. G. H. | . 1819 |
| angustifolĭŭm, 2 | . Red | . 7, G. Ev. S. C. G. H. | . 1806 |
| ferōx, 3 | . Yellow | . 5, G. Ev. S. C. G. H. | . 1759 |
| principis, 4 | . Yellow | . 7, G. Ev. S. C. G. H. | . 1821 |
| pseudō-africānŭm, 5 | Orange | . 6, G. Ev. S. C. G. H. | . 1731 |
| pseudō-ferōx, 6 | . Orange | . 5, G. Ev. S. C. G. H. | . 1820 |
| supralēvē, 7 | . Orange | . G. Ev. S. C. G. H. | . 1731 |

PāchnŏcŸbĒ, *Berkley.* From *pachne*, hoar-frost, and *kybe*, a head. *Linn.* 24, Or. 9, Nat. Or. *Fungi.* These substances are found on decaying plants of various sorts—*acicŭlā, albĭdā, ferrugĭnēā, grĭsēā, subŭlātā.*

PāchynĒmā, *R. Brown.* From *pachys*, thick, and *nema*, a filament; filaments very thick. *Linn.* 10, Or. 3, Nat. Or. *Dilleniaceæ.* This little leafless shrub thrives best in a mixture of loam and peat; cuttings strike root freely in sand, under a glass.

| | | | |
|---|---|---|---|
| complanātŭm . | . | G. Ev. S. N. Holl. | . |

PāchyrŏdĪŬm, *Lindley.* From *pachys*, thick, and *podion*, a peduncle; thick footstalks. *Linn.* 5, Or. 1, Nat. Or. *Apocynaceæ.* This succulent and tuberous-rooted genus succeeds in an equal mixture of light turfy loam, peat, and sand; as the plants require scarcely any water in winter, the pots must be well drained, that the moisture may pass off readily; cuttings taken off, and laid to dry till the wound is dried up, then planted in a pot of dry soil in spring, will strike root, and produce tubers before winter. *Synonymes:* 1. *Echites succulenta.* 2. *E. tuberosa.*

| | | | | | |
|---|---|---|---|---|---|
| succulēntŭm, 1 | . Wht. red | . 5, G. De. S. C. G. H. | . 1820 |
| tuberōsŭm, 2 | . Wht. red | . 8, G. De. S. C. G. H. | . 1818 |

PāchyrrhizŬs, *Richard.* From *pachys*, thick, and *rhiza*, a root; alluding to the thick tuberous roots of the plants. *Linn.* 17, Or. 4, Nat. Or. *Leguminosæ.* The plants succeed well in a light rich soil; they may be increased from cuttings in sand, under a glass, by the tubers of the roots, or by seeds. *Synonyme:* 1. *Dolichos bulbosus.*

| | | | | |
|---|---|---|---|---|
| angulātŭs, 1 | . Purple | . 7, S. Ev. Tw. E. Ind. | . 1781 |

PāchysĀndrā, *Michaux.* From *pachys*, thick, and

*aner*, a man; in allusion to the thickness of the stamens. *Linn.* 21, Or. 4, Nat. Or. *Euphorbiaceæ.* This genus of dwarf growing plants thrives in any common soil, and may be planted near the front of flower-borders; it is increased freely by suckers from the roots.

| | | | | | |
|---|---|---|---|---|---|
| coriāceā | . . White | . 6, S. Ev. S. | Nepal | . 1822 |
| procūmbēns | . . White | . 4, H. Her. P. | N. Amer. | . 1800 |

PādĪnā, *Adanson.* Derivation doubtful. *Linn.* 24, Or. 7, Nat. Or. *Fungi.* A small brownish-coloured species, found in the ocean—*devād.*

PĀdĒrĪā, *Linn.* From *pæderos*, opal; in reference to the transparent berries. *Linn.* 5, Or. 1, Nat. Or. *Cinchonaceæ.* The species are remarkably free growers; any kind of light rich soil suits them, and cuttings root readily in the same kind of soil, under a glass.

| | | | | |
|---|---|---|---|---|
| fœtĭdā . | . . Purple | . 8. Ev. S. | China | . 1806 |

PĀdĒrŏtĀ, *Linn.* The ancients applied this name to a species of *Acanthus. Linn.* 2, Or. 1, Nat. Or. *Scrophulariaceæ.* These pretty dwarf alpine plants are well adapted for rock-work; light sandy soil, or an equal mixture of peat, loam, and sand, will suit them very well; if grown in the open border, the situation should be dry and airy; increased from seeds.

| | | | | |
|---|---|---|---|---|
| Agĕrĭā . | . . Yellow | . 5, H. | A. Italy | . 1824 |
| Bonarōtā | . . Blue | . 5, H. | A. Austria | . 1818 |

PÆŏnĪā, *Linn.* The physician Pæon was the first who used it in medicine. *Linn.* 13, Or. 2, Nat. Or. *Ranunculaceæ.* Beautiful flowering plants, mostly hardy enough to endure our winters. *P. Moutan,* and its varieties, though able to bear a moderate degree of frost, do not flower so well as when planted out in the border of the conservatory; they bear forcing well; a rich loamy soil suits them best. The shrubby kinds are increased from cuttings taken off in August or September, with part of the wood of the preceding year attached, and planted in a sheltered situation where they will root freely. The herbaceous species are increased by dividing the plants at the roots, taking care to leave a bud to each slip; the new varieties are obtained from seeds. *Synonymes:* 1. *P. Moutan.* 2. *P. laciniata.* 3. *P. tartarica.* 4. *P. dahurica.* 5. *P. sessiliflora.*

| | | | | | |
|---|---|---|---|---|---|
| albiflōrā | . . White | . 5, H. Hbr. P. | Siberia | . 1548 |
| candĭdā | . . Flesh | . 5, H. Her. P. | Siberia | . |
| festa, 1 | . . Wht. pink | . 6, H. Her. P. | |
| frāgrāns | . . Red | . 5, H. Her. P. | China | . 1805 |
| Humei | . . Red | . 5, H. Her. P. | China | . 1808 |
| Pottali | . . Crimson | . 5, H. Her. P. | China | . 1822 |
| Reevēsii | . . Pink | . 6, F. Her. P. | China | . 1822 |
| Richardsōni | . . White | . 6, F. Her. P. | Seedl. | . 1833 |
| rubēscēns | . . Pink | . 5, H. Her. P. | Siberia | . |
| sibĭrĭcā | . . White | . 5, H. Her. P. | Siberia | . |
| tatarĭcā | . . Flesh | . 5, H. Her. P. | Siberia | . |

| | | | | |
|---|---|---|---|---|
| uniflörä | Pink | 5, H. Her. | P. Siberia | |
| vestälis | White | 5, H. Her. | P. Siberia | |
| Whitleji | Blush | 5, H. Her. | P. China | 1808 |
| anomälä, 2 | Crimson | 5, H. Her. | P. Siberia | 1788 |
| arietinä | Purple | H. Her. | P. Levant | |
| Andersöni | Rose | 6, H. Her. | P. | |
| oxoniänsis | Pa. blush | 6, H. Her. | P. | |
| Brownii | Red | 5, H. Her. | P. N. Amer. | 1826 |
| corallinä | Crimson | 5, H. Her. | P. England | |
| córsicä | Purple | 5, H. Her. | P. Corsica | |
| cretica | White | 5, H. Her. | P. Crete | |
| decörä | Purple | 5, H. Her. | P. Turkey | |
| elätiör | Purple | 5, H. Her. | P. Crimea | |
| Pallasii | Purple | 5, H. Her. | P. Crimea | |
| hümilis | Purple | 5, H. Her. | P. Spain | 1683 |
| hybridä | Red | 5, H. Her. | P. Siberia | |
| lobätä | Purple | 5, H. Her. | P. Spain | 1821 |
| möllis | Purple | 5, H. Her. | P. Siberia | |
| Moūtän | Purple | 5, H. De. | S. China | 1789 |
| albidä-plänä | White | 5, H. De. | S. China | |
| Annéslei | Pink | 5, H. De. | S. China | |
| Banksii | Purple | 5, H. De. | S. China | 1794 |
| cárneä-plénä | Flesh | 5, H. De. | S. China | |
| lacerä | Rosy red | 5, H. De. | S. Hybrid | 1831 |
| Hümei | Purple | 5, H. De. | S. China | 1817 |
| papaveräcëä | White | 5, H. De. | S. China | 1789 |
| punícëä | Carmine | 5, H. De. | S. Hybrid | 1831 |
| Rawësii | Pa. pink | 5, H. De. | S. China | 1820 |
| rösëä | Pink | 5, H. De. | S. China | |
| rösëä-plänä | Red | 5, H. De. | S. China | 1804 |
| rösëä-semiplänä | Red | 5, H. De. | S. China | 1794 |
| specïösä | Pink | 5, H. De. | S. China | 1825 |
| variegätä | Wht. pur. | 5, H. De. | S. Hybrid | |
| officinälis | Red | 5, H. Her. | P. Europe | 1548 |
| albicäns | White | 5, H. Her. | P. | |
| anemonifflörä | Pink | 5, H. Her. | P. | 1830 |
| Baxteri | Crimson | H. Her. | P. Oxford | |
| blandä | White | 5, H. Her. | P. | |
| carnäcëäns | White | 5, H. Her. | P. | |
| polypétäli | Crimson | 6, H. Her. | P. | |
| rösëä | Red | 5, H. Her. | P. | |
| rubrä | Red | 5, H. Her. | P. | |
| Sabini | Crimson | 6, H. Her. | P. Seedl. | |
| variegätä | Crimson | 6, H. Her. | P. | |
| paradöxä | Purple | 5, H. Fu. | P. Levant | |
| fimbriätä, 3 | Purple | 5, H. Her. | P. | |
| peregrinä | Drk. pur. | 5, H. Her. | P. Levant | 1629 |
| compäctä | Purple | 5, H. Her. | P. | |
| Grevillii | Purple | 5, H. Her. | P. | |
| pübëns | Red | 5, H. Her. | P. | |
| Reevesiänä | Crimson | 5, H. Her. | P. China | |
| Rusi | Crimson | 5, H. Her. | P. Sicily | |
| tenuifölïä | Red | 5, H. Her. | P. Siberia | 1765 |
| flörä-plénö | Red | 5, H. Her. | P. Russia | 1831 |
| latifölïä | Crimson | 6, H. Her. | P. | |
| triternätä, 4 | Purple | 5, H. Her. | P. Siberia | 1790 |
| versïcölör | Purple | 6, H. Her. | P. Scotch seedl. | |
| villösä, 5 | Red | 5, H. Her. | P. S. Eur. | 1816 |

PÆONY, see *Pæönïä*.

PALAFŎXIÄ. Named by Lagasca in honour of Palafox, a Spanish general. *Linn.* 19, Or. 1, Nat. Or. *Compositæ.* This is an ornamental species, growing about two feet high, with rather pretty white flowers; it flourishes in any common soil. *Synonyme:* 1. *Stevia linearis.*

| | | | | |
|---|---|---|---|---|
| lineäris, 1 | White | 6, G. Her. | P. Mexico | 1821 |

PALATE, the mouth of a ringent flower.

PALĀVÏÄ, *Cavanilles.* In honour of A. Palau y Verdera, once professor of botany at Madrid. *Linn.* 16, Or. 8, Nat. Or. *Malvaceæ.* Plants only worth cultivating in botanical collections. Seeds sown on a hotbed early in spring, and the plants transplanted into the open border in May, will produce their flowers and seeds in abundance. *Synonyme:* 1. *P. prostrata—malvæfölïä, moschätä* 1, *rhombifölïä.*

PALEACEOUS, abounding with chaffy scales.

PALICOŪRËÄ. Named by Aublet, who does not give the meaning of the word. *Linn.* 5, Or. 1, Nat. Or. *Cinchonaceæ.* A genus of pretty shrubs, from four to six feet high; for culture and propagation, they may be referred to *Psychotria. Synonymes:* 1. *Psychotria lineata.* 2. *P. crocea.* 3. *P. rigida.*

| | | | | |
|---|---|---|---|---|
| apicätä, 1 | Yellow | 7, S. Ev. | S. Caraccas | 1824 |
| cröcëä, 2 | Orange | 7, S. Ev. | S. W. Ind. | 1823 |
| rigïdä, 3 | Yellow | 8, S. Ev. | S. Caraccas | 1820 |

PALIMBÏÄ, *Besser.* Derivation not known. *Linn.* 5, Or. 2, Nat. Or. *Umbelliferæ.* These plants are not possessed of much beauty; for culture and propagation, see *Peucedanum. Synonymes:* 1. *Selinum Chabræi.* 2. *S. podolicum.* 3. *Sison salsum.*

| | | | | |
|---|---|---|---|---|
| Chabræi, 1 | Orn. yel. | 7, H. Her. | P. France | 1791 |
| podolica, 2 | White | 7, H. Her. | P. Podolia | 1791 |
| salsä, 3 | Cream | 6, H. Her. | P. Russia | 1804 |

PALIŪRŬS, *Tournefort.* The name of a town in Africa. *Linn.* 5, Or. 1, Nat. Or. *Rhamnaceæ.* Very handsome plants, well fitted for shrubberies. The fruit of *P. aculeatus* is very singular, appearing something like a head with a broad-brimmed hat on. This is the shrub of which it is by many persons supposed the crown of thorns which was put on our Saviour's head was made; and this assertion is borne out by many travellers of credit, who say that it is one of the most common shrubs in the country of Judæa, and from the pliability of its branches, which may be brought into any figure, it may afford a probability. They will grow in any common soil, and may be increased by layers, cuttings of the roots, or seeds. *Synonymes:* 1. *P. australis.* 2. *Zizyphus incurvus.*

| | | | | |
|---|---|---|---|---|
| aculeätüs, 1 | Orn. yel. | 6, H. De. | S. S. Eur. | 1596 |
| virgätüs, 2 | Orn. yel. | 8, H. De. | S. Nepal | 1817 |

PALMATE, or PALMATED, divided so as to resemble a hand spread open.

PALMATELY-PARTED, parted in a palmate manner.

PALMĚLLÄ, *Lynghye.* From *palmas*, vibration; jelly-like nature of the species. *Linn.* 24, Or. 7, Nat. Or. *Algæ.* Minute species, found in marshy or inundated places; they consist of very small globules, supposed by some naturalists to be the ova of animalcules—*adnätä, botryoïdes, cruëntä, grumösä, hyalïnä, livïdä, montänä, protubërâns, rivuläris, rösëä.*

PANÆTÏÄ, *Lindley.* Meaning not explained. *Linn.* 19, Or. 2, Nat. Or. *Compositæ.* This is described as being a beautiful little annual. The flower-heads are of the red-gold colour of *Elichrysum bracteatum.*

| | | | | |
|---|---|---|---|---|
| fulvä | Yellow | 5, G. | A. Swan R. | 1837 |

PANARY, used for making bread.

PĀNÁX, *Linn.* From *pan*, all, and *akos*, a remedy; in allusion to the miraculous virtues ascribed to *P. quinquefolia. Linn.* 23, Or. 2, Nat. Or. *Araliaceæ.* The species thrive well in a mixture of peat, loam, and sand, and cuttings root readily under a hand-glass. The root of *P. quinquefolium*, or *Ginseng* of the shops, is much esteemed by the Chinese for its beneficial influence upon the nerves, and for other supposed virtues; but our physicians have not discovered any proofs of its efficacy in Europe. *Synonymes:* 1. *P. conchifolia.* 2. *P. chrysophyllum.*

| | | | | |
|---|---|---|---|---|
| aculeätüm | Green | 11, S. Her. | P. China | 1773 |
| arbörëüm | Green | G. Ev. | T. N. Zeal. | 1820 |
| attenuätüm | Green | 8. Ev. | T. W. Ind. | 1823 |
| cochleätüm, 1 | Green | 8. Ev. | S. Moluccas | 1820 |
| frägräns | Green | 8. Ev. | S. E. Ind. | 1816 |
| fruticösüm | Green | 8, S. Ev. | S. Ternate | 1800 |
| Morötöni, 2 | Green | 8. Ev. | T. Cayenne | 1822 |
| quinquefölïüm | Lgt. yel. | 6, H. Her. | P. N. Amer. | 1740 |
| trifölïüm | Green | 5, H. Her. | P. N. Amer. | 1759 |

PANCRÄTÏŬM, *Herbert.* From *pan*, all, and *kratys*, potent; supposed medicinal virtues. *Linn.* 6, Or. 1, Nat. Or. *Amaryllidaceæ.* These are handsome, well-known bulbous plants, requiring to be grown in a composition of three-parts light sandy loam, and one-part vegetable mould; they are increased by offsets from the roots, or by seeds, from which the new varieties are obtained. The bulbs of *P. maritimum* are emetic. *Synonyme:* 1. *P. mexicanum.*

| | | | | |
|---|---|---|---|---|
| acutifölïüm, 1 | White | 6, S. Bl. | P. Mexico | 1824 |
| americänüm | White | 6, S. Bl. | P. Jamaica | 1820 |
| anänüm | White | 6, S. Bl. | P. Guiana | 1790 |
| angustüm | White | 6, S. Bl. | P. | |
| biflörüm | White | 6, S. Bl. | P. E. Ind. | 1820 |
| canariänsé | White | 6, G. Bl. | P. Canaries | 1815 |
| caribäüm | White | 6, S. Bl. | P. W. Ind. | 1730 |
| carolinïänüm | White | 6, F. Bl. | P. Carolina | 1759 |
| crassifölïüm | White | 6, S. Bl. | P. S. Amer. | |
| declinätüm | White | 6, S. Bl. | P. W. Ind. | 1825 |
| distichüm | White | 6, S. Bl. | P. S. Amer. | |
| Dryandri | White | 6, S. Bl. | P. | |
| expänsüm | White | 6, S. Bl. | P. W. Ind. | 1820 |
| frägräns | White | 6, S. Bl. | P. W. Ind. | 1819 |
| guianénsé | White | 11, S. Bl. | P. Guiana | 1815 |
| illyrïcüm | White | 5, H. Bl. | P. S. Eur. | 1615 |
| littorälé | White | 6, S. Bl. | P. S. Amer. | 1758 |
| longiflörüm | White | 6, S. Bl. | P. E. Ind. | 1810 |
| maritïmüm | White | 6, H. Bl. | P. S. Eur. | 1597 |
| mexicänüm | White | 6, S. Bl. | P. Mexico | 1732 |
| ovätüm | White | 6, S. Bl. | P. W. Ind. | |
| pätëns | White | 7, S. Bl. | P. W. Ind. | 1822 |
| pedälé | White | 8, S. Bl. | P. Brasil | 1820 |
| plicätüm | White | 7, S. Bl. | P. Macao | 1827 |
| rotätüm | White | 8, F. Bl. | P. Carolina | 1803 |

| | | | | | |
|---|---|---|---|---|---|
| speciōsūm | . . | White | 7, 8. Bl. P. W. Ind. | . 1759 |
| undulātūm | . . | White | 6, 8. Bl. P. S. Amer. | |
| verecūndūm | . . | White | 7, 8. Bl. P. E. Ind. | . 1776 |
| zeylānĭcūm | . . | White | 6, 8. Bl. P. Ceylon | . 1752 |

PANDĀNŪS, *Linn.* From *pandang*, a word in the Malay language, signifying conspicuous. *Linn.* 22, Or. 1, Nat. Or. *Pandanaceæ.* This stately, fine-looking genus has received the English name, Screw-Pine, on account of the appearance of the plants; they thrive in a light loamy soil. Some of the species produce suckers, by which they may be increased.

| | | | | | |
|---|---|---|---|---|---|
| albūs | . . | White | 8. Ev. T. E. Ind. | . 1818 |
| amaryllifōlĭūs | . | White | 8. Ev. T. E. Ind. | . 1820 |
| candelābrūm | . | White | 8. Ev. T. Guinea | . 1826 |
| edūlis | . . | White | 8. Ev. T. Madagas. | . 1824 |
| fasciculāris | . | White | 8. Ev. T. E. Ind. | . 1822 |
| fœtĭdūs | . . | White | 8. Ev. T. E. Ind. | . 1818 |
| furcātūs | . . | White | 8. Ev. T. E. Ind. | . 1824 |
| hūmĭlis | . . | White | 8. Ev. T. Maurit. | |
| inērmis | . . | White | 8. Ev. T. E. Ind. | . 1818 |
| integrifōlĭūs | . | White | 8. Ev. T. E. Ind. | . 1823 |
| latifōlĭūs | . . | White | 8. Ev. T. E. Ind. | . 1820 |
| longifōlĭūs | . . | White | 8. Ev. T. E. Ind. | . 1829 |
| marginātūs | . | White | 8. Ev. T. E. Ind. | . 1823 |
| odoratissĭmūs | . | White | 8. Ev. T. E. Ind. | . 1771 |
| pedunculātūs | . | White | 8. Ev. T. N. Holl. | . 1825 |
| reflēxūs | . . | White | 8. Ev. T. E. Ind. | . 1818 |
| sessĭlis | . . | White | 8. Ev. T. E. Ind. | . 1820 |
| spirālis | . . | White | 8. Ev. T. N. S. W. | . 1805 |
| turbinātūs | . . | White | 8. Ev. T. E. Ind. | . 1823 |
| ūtĭlis | . . | White | 8. Ev. T. Bourbon | |

PANDURATE, fiddle-shaped.
PANICEOUS, eatable, good for bread.
PANIC-GRASS, see *Pānĭcūm.*
PANIC-GRASS, see *Ehrārtā panicēā.*
PANICLE, a loose disposition of inflorescence, as oats.
PANICLED, or PANICULATE, forming a panicle.
PANICULATELY-BRANCHED, loosely branched.
PANICULATELY-RACEMOSE, a panicle formed by numerous racemes.
PĀNĬCŪM, *Linn.* From *panicula*, a panicle, or *panis*, bread. *Linn.* 3, Or. 2, Nat. Or. *Gramineæ.* A useful genus of grasses. *P. miliaceum* is frequently sown for feeding poultry, and is sometimes used as a substitute for rice. *P. arborescens* is said by Linnæus to equal in height the loftiest trees in the East Indies, though the culm is little thicker than a goose's-quill; it grows in the woods and jungles. In cultivation, the species grow in any common soil, and are increased by dividing at the root, or by seeds.

| | | | | | |
|---|---|---|---|---|---|
| brizoīdēs | . . | Apetal | 7, Grass. E. Ind. | . 1861 |
| colōnūm | . . | Apetal | 8, Grass. E. Ind. | . 1699 |
| fasciculātūm | . | Apetal | 6, Grass. Jamaica | . 1801 |
| frumentācēūm | . | Apetal | 7, Grass. E. Ind. | . 1810 |
| miliācēūm | . . | Apetal | 7, Grass. E. Ind. | . 1596 |
| muricātūm | . . | Apetal | 6, Grass. E. Ind. | . 1805 |
| oryzoīdēs | . . | Apetal | 8, Grass. W. Ind. | . 1822 |
| prolifērūm | . . | Apetal | 7, Grass. N. Amer. | . 1820 |

altissĭmūm, āncĭps, arborēscēns, asperrĭmūm, attenuātūm, bĭcŏlŏr, brevifōlĭūm, capillārē, C. mĭnŏr, carthaginēnsē, clandestīnūm, colorātūm, costātūm, decumbēns, dichŏtŏmūm, diffūsūm, divaricātūm, flavĭdūm, fūscūm, gongylōdēs, hispidūlūm, ĭndĭcūm, interrūptūm, lævē, latifōlĭūm, lāxūm, marginātūm, māxĭmūm, miliārē, mŏllē, nervōsūm, nitidūm, numidiānūm, palmifōlĭūm, pātēns, plicātūm, rēpens, tenēllūm, uliginōsūm, villōsūm, virgātūm.

PAPĀVĒR, *Linn.* From *papa*, pap, or thick milk; the juice of the poppy was formerly used in children's food to make them sleep. *Linn.* 13, Or. 1, Nat. Or. *Papaveraceæ.* *P. somniferum* is cultivated in the vicinity of London; the capsules are sold to the druggists for the opium which is obtained from them. The plants succeed in a light rich soil. The perennial kinds are increased by dividing at the roots. All the species are narcotic. *Synonymes:* 1. *P. Burseri.* 2. *P. pulcherrimum.* 3. *P. aurantiacum.* 4. *P. alpinum.*

| | | | | | |
|---|---|---|---|---|---|
| alpīnūm, 1 | . | White | 7, H. Her. P. Austria | . 1759 |
| amœnūm | . | Vermil. | H. A. N. Ind. | . 183— |
| arenārĭūm | . | Red | 6, H. A. Caucasus | . 1828 |
| Argĕmŏnē | . | Scarlet | 6, H. A. Britain | |
| armenĭācūm | . | Yellow | 8, H. A. Armenia | . 1815 |
| bracteātūm, 2 | . | Red | 5, H. Her. P. Siberia | . 1817 |
| caucasĭcūm | . | Red | 6, H. A. Caucasus | . 1818 |
| croceūm | . | Saffron | 6, H. Her. P. Altai | . 1829 |
| dubĭūm | . | Scarlet | 6, H. A. Britain | |
| flore-albo | . | White | 6, H. A. Tauria | |
| floribūndūm | . | Scarlet | 6, H. B. Levant | . 1816 |

| | | | | | |
|---|---|---|---|---|---|
| fūgax | . . | Pa. carm. | 6, H. | A. Persia | . 1827 |
| gariepīnūm | . | Scarlet | 6, H. | A. Africa | . 1835 |
| hōrrĭdūm | . | Red | 7, H. | A. N. Holl. | . 1825 |
| hўbrĭdūm | . | Scarlet | 6, H. | A. England | |
| lævigātūm | . | Red | 6, H. | A. Caucasus | . 1823 |
| microcārpūm | . | Yellow | 6, H. Her. | P. Kamtsch. | . 1824 |
| nudicaūlē | . | Yellow | 7, H. Her. | P. Siberia | . 1790 |
| coccineūm | . | Red oran. | 4, H. Her. | P. Hybrid | . 1820 |
| glabrātūm | . | Yellow | 7, H. Her. | P. Siberia | . 1800 |
| lutēūm | . | Yellow | 7, H. Her. | P. Siberia | . 1730 |
| radicātūm | . | Yellow | 7, H. Her. | P. Norway | . 1800 |
| orientāle | . | Red | 5, H. Her. | P. Armenia | . 1714 |
| concŏlŏr | . | Scarlet | 6, H. Her. | P. S. Eur. | . 1714 |
| maculātūm | . | Scarlet | 6, H. Her. | P. S. Eur. | . 1714 |
| obtusifōlĭūm | . | Rose | 6, H. | A. Africa | . 1828 |
| persĭcūm | . | Brick | 6, H. Her. | P. Persia | . 1830 |
| pyrenaĭcūm, 3 | . | Yellow | 7, H. | P. Pyrenees | |
| punĭceūm, 4 | . | Red | 6, H. Her. | P. Switzerl. | |
| Rhœas | . | Scarlet | 6, H. | A. Britain | |
| albū | . | White | 6, H. | A. Britain | |
| cārnĕā | . | Flesh | 6, H. | A. Britain | |
| coccĭnĕā | . | Scarlet | 6, H. | A. Britain | |
| maculātā | . | Varieg. | 6, H. | A. Britain | |
| multĭplēx | . | Varieg. | 6, H. | A. Britain | |
| variegātā | . | Varieg. | 6, H. | A. Britain | |
| Roubĭœi | . | Red | 6, H. | A. Montpel. | . 1823 |
| rubrŏ-aurantiācūm | Red | 7, H. Her. | P. Dahuria | . 1822 |
| setigĕrūm | . | White | 7, H. | A. S. Eur. | . 1824 |
| somnifĕrūm | . | White | 7, H. | A. England | |
| albŏ-plēnūm | . | Varieg. | 7, H. | A. Britain | |
| ālbūm | . | White | 7, H. | A. Britain | |
| fimbriātūm | . | Varieg. | 7, H. | A. Britain | |
| nĭgrūm | . | Purple | 7, H. | A. Britain | |
| rūbrŏ-plēnūm | . | Varieg. | 7, H. | A. Britain | |
| variegātūm | . | Varieg. | 7, H. | A. Britain | |
| trilōbūm | . | Red | 6, H. | A. Holland | . 1818 |

PAPAW-TREE, see *Carĭcā Papāyā.*
PAPER-MULBERRY, see *Broussonētĭā papyrācēā.*
PAPILIONACEOUS, butterfly-shaped flowers, as the common pea.
PAPILLÆ, small, soft excrescences.
PAPILLOSE, or PAPILLOUS, having small glandular excrescences, like pimples.
PAPPŎPHŎRŪM, *Schreber.* From *pappos*, down, and *phoreo*, to carry. *Linn.* 3, Or. 2, Nat. Or. *Gramineæ.* Grasses of no interest; increased by seeds —*nigricans, phleoīdes.*
PAPPŪS, crown of the fruit of compositæ, and similar plants.
PAPULÆ, round, soft, watery protuberances.
PAPULOSE, covered with papulæ.
PAPYRACEOUS, resembling paper.
PĀPỸRŪS, *Willdenow.* From the Syrian, *babeer*; whence the Egyptian word *papyrus*, paper. *Linn.* 3, Or. 1, Nat. Or. *Cyperaceæ.* This is a splendid genus, requiring to be grown in a tub or large pot of water, with rich mud at the bottom; increased from divisions, or by seeds. The famed *Papyrus* of the Egyptians was obtained from our *Cyperus Papyrus.* *Synonymes:* 1. *Cyperus elegans.* 2. *C. odoratus.*

| | | | | | |
|---|---|---|---|---|---|
| antiquōrūm | . | Apetal | 8, S. Aq. P. Egypt | . 1803 |
| elĕgans, 1 | . | Apetal | 7, S. Aq. P. W. Ind. | . 1822 |
| laxiflōrūs | . | Apetal | 7, S. Aq. P. Madagascar | . 1822 |
| odorātūs, 2 | . | Apetal | 7, S. Aq. P. W. Ind. | . 1819 |

PARABOLICAL, form of a parabola, longer than broad, tapering gradually to both ends.
PARAGUAY TEA, see *Ĭlēx paraguēnsis.*
PARASTRĀNTHŪS, *Don.* From *parastrepho*, to invert, and *anthos*, a flower; the flowers are upside down compared with those of other genera of the order. *Linn.* 5, Or. 1, Nat. Or. *Lobeliaceæ.* These beautiful plants are easily cultivated in a mixture of loam, peat, and sand; increased by dividing at the root. *Synonymes:* 1. *Lobelia lutea.* 2. *L. unidentata.* 3. *L. variifolia.*

| | | | | | |
|---|---|---|---|---|---|
| simplēx, 1 | . | Yellow | 6, H. Her. P. C. G. H. | . 1774 |
| unidentātā, 2 | . | Blue | 7, H. Her. P. C. G. H. | . 1794 |
| variifōlĭā, 3 | . | Yellow | 6, H. Her. P. C. G. H. | . 1812 |

PARDĀNTHŪS, *Ker.* From *pardos*, a leopard, and *anthos*, a flower; alluding to the spotted flowers. *Linn.* 3, Or. 1, Nat. Or. *Iridaceæ.* A handsome genus, succeeding in light rich soil; when planted in the open border the plants require a little protection in severe weather; increased by divisions, or by seeds.

| | | | | | |
|---|---|---|---|---|---|
| chinēnsis | . . | Orange | 6, H. Her. P. China | . 1759 |
| nepalēnsis | . . | Orange | 6, H. Her. P. Nepal | . 1823 |

PAREIRA BRAVA ROOT, see *Cissampēlos.*
PARENCHYMA, parts of plants consisting of cellular tissue only.

PARIĂNĂ, *Aublet*. Its name in Guiana. *Linn.* 21, Or. 9, Nat. Or. *Gramineæ.* A curious under-shrub, growing in any common soil, and increased by divisions.

campestris . . . Apetal . . 8. Ev. 8. Cayenne . 1803

PARIETARIĂ, *Linn.* From *paries*, a wall; they are commonly found on old walls. *Linn.* 23, Or. 1, Nat. Or. *Urticaceæ.* Mere weeds, found on old walls, stony ground, &c.; they are of no beauty, and the easiest culture. *Synonyme:* 1. *Bœhmeria urticifolia—crética, floridănă, indĭcă, judaĭcă, lusitănĭcă, micrănthă, officinălis, pennsylvănĭcă, polygonoĭdĕs, prostrătă, urticæfoliă* 1.

PARIETAL, attached to the sides of the ovary.

PARIĔTĔs, the sides of the ovary or capsule.

PARINARIĂM, *Jussieu.* From *Parinari*, the Guiana name of one of the species. *Linn.* 7, Or. 1, Nat. Or. *Chrysobalanaceæ.* A noble genus of plants. *P. excelsum* is a fine tree, attaining the height of sixty feet, with long leaves and large terminal bunches of flowers, succeeded by a fruit of plum-like appearance, which is eaten in Sierra Leone under the name of Rough Plum. The plants grow freely in three parts sandy loam and one part peat; ripened cuttings in pots of sand, under a glass, in heat, root readily. *Synonyme:* 1. *Petrocarya campestris.*

campĕstrĕ, 1 . . Yellow . . 8. Ev. 8. Guiana . 1824
excelsŭm . . . White . . 8. Ev. T. 8. Leone . 1822
macrophýllŭm . White . . 8. Ev. 8. 8. Leone . 1822

PĂRIs, *Linn.* From *par*, equal; in allusion to the regularity of the parts. *Linn.* 8, Or. 4, Nat. Or. *Melanthaceæ.* The species of this genus thrive in light sandy loam, in a shady situation; increased from divisions, or by seeds. The juice of the berries of *P. quadrifolia* has been used in inflammation of the eyes.

polyphýllă . . . Green . . 5, H. Her. P. Nepal . 1826
quadrifoliă . . . Green . . 5, H. Her. P. Britain . .
verticillătă . . . Green . . 4, H. Her. P. Caucasus . 1825

PARIVŎĂ, *Aublet.* The Guiana name of the tree. *Linn.* 10, Or. 1, Nat. Or. *Leguminosæ.* A very handsome pinnate-leaved stove tree, delighting in rich loamy soil, and propagated from cuttings. *Synonyme:* 1. *Dimorpha grandiflora.*

grandiflorĕ, 1 . . Purple . . 8. Ev. T. Guiana . . 1821

PARKĔRIĂ, *Hooker.* In honour of C. S. Parker, who first found the plant in Essequibo. *Linn.* 24, Or. 1, Nat. Or. *Polypodiaceæ.* This species of fern grows best in turfy loam and peat mixed; it is increased by dividing the roots, or by seeds.

pteroĭdĕs . . . Brown . 8. 8. Aq. P. Essequibo . 1825

PĂRKĬĂ. Named by Brown in memory of the celebrated African traveller Mungo Park. *Linn.* 16, Or. 6, Nat. Or. *Leguminosæ.* A beautiful genus of plants; for culture and propagation, see *Inga.* *Synonymes:* 1. *Inga biglobosa, P. biglobosa.*

africănă, 1 . . Vermil. . 3, 8. Ev. T. Africa . . 1822
uniglobŏsă . . Vermil. . 3, 8. Ev. T. 8. Leone . 1822

PARKINSŎNĬĂ, *Linn.* In honour of John Parkinson, a London apothecary, and author of Theatrum Botanicum, &c. *Linn.* 10, Or. 1, Nat. Or. *Leguminosæ.* This is a very handsome species, but seldom suffered to grow large enough to flower; a mixture of peat and loam suits it, and cuttings root in sand, under a glass. The imported seeds of it also vegetate freely.

aculeătă . . . Yellow . . 8. Ev. 8. W. Ind. . 1739

PARMELIĂ, *Acharius.* From *parma*, a kind of small shield, and *heilo*, to inclose; the thallus. *Linn.* 24, Or. 8, Nat. Or. *Lichenes.* The species of this genus are found on rocks, trunks of trees, &c.; several of them are used in dyeing—*adglutinătă, ambiguă, aleurĭtĕs, âquĭlă, Borrĕrĭ, cǣsiă, C. dăbiă, caperdătă, Clementiănă, columnărĭs, conspĕrsă, corrugătă, cyclosĕlĭs, diacăpsĭs, diatrĭpă, elæĭnă, encaustă, fahlunĕnsĭs, glomulĭfĕră, herbăceă, horrĕscĕns, lævigătă, lanuginŏsă, olivăceă, omphalŏdĕs, parietĭnă, perforătă, perlătă, physŏdĕs, pitgrĕă, plŭmbeă, pulverulĕntă, recŭrvă, reticulătă, rubiginŏsă, rugŏsă, saxatĭlĭs, scŏrtĕă, sinuŏsă, speciŏsă, stellărĭs, stĭgĭă, sulcătă, tiliăceă.*

PARNĂssĬĂ, *Linn.* From Mount Parnassus, the abode

of grace and beauty; these plants, on account of their elegance, are feigned to have first sprung up there. *Linn.* 5, Or. 3, Nat. Or. *Saxifragaceæ.* The plants do best in a moist peat soil and a shady situation. *P. palustris* is one of our most elegant marsh plants; increased by divisions, or by seeds, which ripen plentifully.

asarifoliă . . . White . 7, H. Her. P. N. Amer. . 1812
carolinĭănă . . . White . 5, H. Her. P. N. Amer. . 1802
palŭstrĭs . . . White . 7, H. Her. P. Britain . .
parviflŏră . . . White . 6, H. Her. P. N. Amer. . 1820
speciŏsă . . . Cream . 7, H. Her. P. N. Amer. .

PARŎCHĔTŭs, *Hamilton.* From *para*, nigh, and *ochetos*, a brook; in allusion to the habitation of the plant. *Linn.* 17, Or. 4, Nat. Or. *Leguminosæ.* A light rich soil will answer this pretty creeper, which is readily increased by dividing.

communĭs . . . Purple . 7, F. Ev. Cr. Nepal . . 1820

PARONYCHIĂ, *Tournefort.* From *para*, near, and *onyx*, a claw; supposed to cure a tumour which rises near the nail. *Linn.* 3, Or. 1, Nat. Or. *Illecebraceæ.* From the dwarf stature of the species, they are all well adapted for ornamenting rock-work; they, however, thrive best in pots, in a mixture of sand and loam, and are easily increased by dividing at the roots, or by cuttings under a glass, or by seeds. *Synonymes:* 1. *Illecebrum capitatum.* 2. *I. echinatum.* 3. *I. Paronychia.*

alsinifoliă . . . White . 7, F. Her. P. Spain . .
bengalĕnsĭs . . White . 7, H. . . . A. Bengal . 1817
brasiliănă . . . White . 6, F. Her. P. Brazil . 1820
canariĕnsĭs . . . White . 9, O. Her. P. Teneriffe . 1829
capitătă, 1 . . . White . 7, F. Her. P. Spain . 1683
echinătă, 2 . . . Greenish . 7, H. . . A. 8. Eur. . 1821
hispănĭcă, 3 . . White . 7, F. Ev. Tr. Spain . 1683
italĭcă . . . . White . 6, F. Ev. Tr. Italy . 1821
maritĭmă . . . White . 7, H. De. Tr. Pyrenees . 1820
nĭvĕă . . . . White . 7, H. Her. P. Spain . 1812
polygonifoliă . . White . 6, H. Ev. Tr. Spain . 1816
pubĕscĕns . . . White . 6, H. De. Tr. Pyrenees . 1820
serpyllifoliă . . White . 7, H. De. Tr. France . 1818
tenuifoliă . . . White . 6, H. . . . A. . . 1820

PĂRRYĂ, *R. Brown.* In honour of Captain William Edward Parry, R.N., commander of the expedition sent to discover a north-west passage. *Linn.* 15, Nat. Or. *Cruciferæ.* A pretty little annual, growing well in the border of the flower-garden.

arctĭcă . . . . Purple . . H. Her. P. Melville Is. 1820

PARSLEY, see *Apium.*
PARSLEY-PIĔRT, see *Alchemillă arvĕnsĭs.*
PARSLEY-PIĔRT, see *Erică aphănĕs.*
PARSNIP, see *Pastinăcă.*

PARSŌNSĬĂ, *R. Brown.* In memory of James Parsons, M.D., a Scotch botanist. *Linn.* 5, Or. 1, Nat. Or. *Apocynaceæ.* Ornamental plants; for culture and propagation, see *Echites.* *Synonymes:* 1. *Echites corymbosa.* 2. *E. floribunda.*

corymbŏsă, 1 . . Red . . 7, 8. Ev. Tw. 8. Amer. . 1820
floribŭndă, 2 . . White . 7, 8. Ev. Tw. Jamaica . 1820

PARTED, divided, but not to the base.

PARTHENĬŎM, *Linn.* From *parthenos*, a virgin; supposed medicinal qualities. *Linn.* 19, Or. 4, Nat. Or. *Compositæ.* Plants of no beauty, growing in any common soil—*Hysterophŏrŭs, incănŭm, integrifoliă.*

PASCĂLIĂ, *Ortega.* In honour of Dedan Pascal, M.D., a professor at Parma. *Linn.* 19, Or. 2, Nat. Or. *Compositæ.* This species should be grown in pots, as it requires the protection of the frame in severe frosts; loam and peat suits it well, and cuttings planted under a glass, soon root.

glaucă . . . . Yellow . 7, H. Her. P. Chile . . 1799

PASPĂLŬM, *Flugge.* From *paspalos*, one of the Greek names for millet. *Linn.* 3, Or. 2, Nat. Or. *Gramineæ.* Curious species of grass, without much beauty, and of easy culture. *Synonymes:* 1. *P. pubescens.* 2. *P. Swartziana.* 3. *P. littorale.* 4. *P. orbiculatum.* 5. *Digitaria pilosa.*

distichŭm . . . Apetal . 7, Gram. Jamaica . 1776
elĕgăns . . . Apetal . 7, Gram. Brazil . 1816
KorĂ, 2 . . . Apetal . 7, Gram. E. Ind. . 1810
paniculătŭm . . Apetal . 6, Gram. Jamaica . 1782
quadrifărĭŭm . . Apetal . 7, Gram. Trinidad . 1820
scrobiculătŭm . . Apetal . 8, Gram. E. Ind. . 1778
serotinŭm, 5 . . Apetal . 7, Gram. N. Amer. . 1804
stoloniferŭm . . Apetal . 7, Gram. Peru . . 1794

ciliatifoliŭm 1, conjugătŭm, debĭlĕ, diffŏrmĕ, dissĕctum,

dūbiûm, filifōrmē 2, glābrûm, inæquālē, lēvis, noti-
tûm, pusillûm 4, setācēûm, tenellûm, vaginātûm,
villōsûm, virgātûm.

PASQUE-FLOWER, see Anemone pulsatilla.

PASSERINA, Linn. From passer, a sparrow; in allusion to the beaked seeds. Linn. 8, Or. 1, Nat. Or.
Thymelaceæ. The plants of this genus flourish
well in a mixture of sandy peat and loam; and
cuttings of the young wood root freely in sand,
under a glass. The seeds of P. annua may be sown
in spring in the open ground. Synonymes: 1. Stel-
lera Passerina. 2. S. Chamæjasme.

| | | | | | | |
|---|---|---|---|---|---|---|
| annūa, 1 | . | White | . | 7, H. | A. | 8. Eur. | 1759 |
| anthylloidēs | . | White | . | 5, G. Ev. 8. | C. G. H. | 1823 |
| capitātā | . | White | . | 7, G. Ev. 8. | C. G. H. | 1789 |
| ciliātā | . | White | . | 5, G. Ev. 8. | C. G. H. | 1818 |
| empetrifōliā | . | Yellow | . | 7, G. Ev. 8. | Spain | 1834 |
| ericoidēs | . | White | . | 5, G. Ev. 8. | C. G. H. | 1810 |
| filifōrmis | . | White | . | 5, G. Ev. 8. | C. G. H. | 1752 |
| grandiflōrā | . | White | . | 5, G. Ev. 8. | C. G. H. | 1789 |
| hirsūtā | . | White | . | 7, G. Ev. 8. | 8. Eur. | 1759 |
| laxā | . | White | . | 6, G. Ev. 8. | C. G. H. | 1804 |
| linearifōliā | . | White | . | 5, G. Ev. 8. | C. G. H. | 1820 |
| rigidā | . | White | . | 5, G. Ev. 8. | C. G. H. | 1817 |
| spicātā | . | White | . | 5, G. Ev. 8. | C. G. H. | 1787 |
| Stellēri, 2 | . | White | . | 6, G. Ev. 8. | Siberia | 1817 |
| tenuiflōrā | . | White | . | 7, G. Ev. 8. | C. G. H. |
| Thunbērgii | . | White | . | 5, G. Ev. 8. | C. G. H. | 1817 |
| uniflōrā | . | White | . | 5, G. Ev. 8. | C. G. H. | 1759 |

PASSIFLORA, Linn. From passio, passion, and flos, a
flower; in allusion to the filamentous appendages or
rays bearing a resemblance to the emblems of the
passion of Christ. Linn. 16, Or. 2, Nat. Or. Passifloraceæ. The species of this interesting and elegant
genus are admirably adapted for stove and greenhouse climbers, being of easy culture, free growers,
and if allowed plenty of room, producing abundance
of beautiful flowers; many of the kinds produce fruit
freely, from which, through impregnation, several
fine hybrids have been raised. The fruit of some,
as P. edulis, laurifolia, and P. quadrangularis, or
Granadilla, are eaten; the succulent pulp which
surrounds the seeds is found to be fragrant, cooling,
and pleasant, agreeably acid, and admirably adapted
for allaying thirst in hot climates. P. edulis and
P. laurifolia will fruit freely in the plant stove.
The quadrangularis bears fruits resembling a large
lime, and to cause it to produce them in abundance,
should be treated as follows:—Plant it in a large
box, or in a partitioned-off corner of a stove, or tan-
pit; if in the latter, holes may be bored in the sides
to admit the egress of the roots into the tan. The
shoots should be trained parallel to the glass as
vines, and treated similar to melons, that is, the
most vigorous shoots removed, as they will be
found not to bear so freely as those of a moderate
growth; it will generally be found necessary to
set the fruit by artificial impregnation, taking care
to give the plant abundance of water. All the
species will thrive well in a mixture of loam and
peat, and are easily increased by cuttings planted
in sand. The hardy kinds should be planted in
sheltered situations. Synonymes: 1. P. heterophylla.
2. P. lunata. 3. P. lyrafolia. 4. P. palmata. 5. P.
hircina. 6. P. hibiscifolia. 7. P. glabrata. 8. P. peltata. 9. P. discolor. 10. P. glauca. 11. P. punctata.

| | | | | | | |
|---|---|---|---|---|---|---|
| Adiantûm | . | Yellow | . | 8. Ev. Cl. | Norfolk Is. | 1792 |
| alātā | . | Gr. blu. red | 6, 8. Ev. Cl. | W. Ind. | 1772 |
| alāto-cœrūlēā | . | White | . | 8, 8. Ev. Cl. | Hybrid | 1823 |
| albicans | . | White | . | 8, 8. Ev. Cl. | Mexico | 1826 |
| albidā | . | White | . | 8, 8. Ev. Cl. | Brazil | 1816 |
| Andersōnii | . | Striped | . | 8, 8. Ev. Cl. | St. Lucia | 1823 |
| angulātā | . | | . | 8. Ev. Cl. | Mexico | 1822 |
| angustifōliā, 1 | . | White | . | 7, 8. Ev. Cl. | W. Ind. | 1773 |
| auriculātā | . | Apetal | . | 7, 8. Ev. Cl. | Orinoco | 1820 |
| biflōrā, 2 | . | White | . | 7, 8. Ev. Cl. | W. Ind. | 1800 |
| bryoniæfōliā | . | Whitish | . | 8. Ev. Cl. | Mexico | 1823 |
| cærūlēā | . | Wht. blue | 8, H. De. Cl. | Brazil | 1699 |
| angustifōliā | . | Wht. blue | 8, F. Ev. Cl. | Hybrid | 1820 |
| Colvillii | . | Varieg. | . | 8, H. De. Cl. | Hybrid | 1824 |
| glaucophyllā | . | Blue | . | 8, H. De. Cl. | Brazil |
| cærūlēā-racemōsā | . | Purple | . | 8, 8. Ev. Cl. | Hybrid | 1820 |
| capsulāris | . | Yel. grn. | 6, 8. Ev. Cl. | W. Ind. | 1820 |
| acutilobā | . | Yel. grn. | 6, 8. Ev. Cl. | Brazil | 1820 |
| geminiflōrā | . | Yel. grn. | 6, 8. Ev. Cl. | Jamaica | 1820 |
| carnescēns | . | Pink | . | 6, 8. Ev. Cl. | Caraccas | 1821 |
| Cavanillēsii | . | Copper | . | 8, 8. Ev. Cl. | W. Ind. | 1822 |
| cephalēmā | . | | . | 8. Ev. Cl. | Brazil | 1826 |
| chinēnsis | . | Wht. blue | 8, G. Ev. Cl. | China |
| ciliātā | . | Pink | . | 8, 8. Ev. Cl. | Jamaica | 1783 |
| coccīneā | . | Scarlet | . | 9, 8. Ev. Cl. | Guiana | 1820 |
| cunēātā, 8 | . | | . | 7, 8. Ev. Cl. | Caraccas | 1816 |

| | | | | | | |
|---|---|---|---|---|---|---|
| cuneifōliā | . | | 7, 8. Ev. Cl. | 8. Amer. | 1825 |
| cuprēā | . | Orange | 7, 8. Ev. Cl. | Bahama Is. | 1724 |
| digitātā | . | Blue | 7, 8. Ev. Cl. | Trinidad | 1820 |
| edūlis | . | White | 7, 8. Ev. Cl. | W. Ind. |
| filamentōsā, 4 | . | Wht. blue | 8, 8. Ev. Cl. | America | 1817 |
| fœtidā, 5 | . | Wht. grn. | 7, 8. Ev. Cl. | W. Ind. | 1731 |
| gossypiifōliā, 6 | . | White | 8, 8. Ev. Cl. | W. Ind. | 1831 |
| gracīlis | . | White | 8, 8. Ev. Cl. | | 1823 |
| hederācēā | . | White | 6, 8. Ev. Cl. | W. Ind. |
| hemicyclā, 7 | . | White | 6, 8. Ev. Cl. | Surinam | 1817 |
| heterophyllā | . | Yellowish | 8. Ev. Cl. | St. Domin. | 1817 |
| hirsūtā | . | White | 7, 8. Ev. Cl. | W. Ind. | 1778 |
| holosericēā | . | Wht. pur. | 9, 8. Ev. Cl. | Vera Cruz. | 1733 |
| incarnātā | . | Pink | 6, F. Ev. Cl. | 8. Amer. | 1699 |
| kermesīnā | . | Crimson | 7, 8. Ev. Cl. | | 1831 |
| laurifōliā | . | Red vio. | 8, 8. Ev. Cl. | W. Ind. | 1690 |
| ligulāris | . | Grn. pur. | 9, 8. Ev. Cl. | Peru | 1819 |
| Loudōni | . | Purple | 8. Ev. Cl. | | 1838 |
| lūtēā | . | Yellow | 5, 8. Ev. Cl. | America | 1714 |
| maculātā, 8 | . | Apetal | 8, G. Ev. Cl. | N. Amer. | 1820 |
| maliförmis | . | Orn. red | 9, 8. Ev. Cl. | W. Ind. | 1731 |
| Maximiliānā, 9 | . | Green | 6, 8. Ev. Cl. | Brazil | 1800 |
| Mayāni | . | | 8. Ev. Cl. | Hybrid | 1833 |
| mexicānā | . | Whitish | 8. Ev. Cl. | Mexico | 1820 |
| minīmā | . | White | 7, 8. Ev. Cl. | Curasav. | 1690 |
| mucronātā | . | | 7, 8. Ev. Cl. | Brasil | 1820 |
| multiflōrā | . | Ornsh. | 7, 8. Ev. Cl. | St. Domin. | 1731 |
| multiförmis | . | | 8. Ev. Cl. | 8. Amer. | 1820 |
| nigelliflōrā | . | Wht. grn. | 9, 8. Ev. Tw. B. Ayres | 1835 |
| normālis | . | White | 6, 8. Ev. Cl. | Vera Cruz. | 1771 |
| oblongātā | . | Apetal | 7, 8. Ev. Cl. | Jamaica | 1816 |
| obscūrā | . | Wht. grn. | 7, 8. Ev. Cl. | 8. Amer. | 1823 |
| onychinā | . | Purplish | 11, 8. Ev. Cl. | B. Ayres | 1827 |
| pallidā | . | Yel. grn. | 8, 8. Ev. Cl. | St. Domin. |
| palmātā | . | White | 8. Ev. Cl. | Brazil | 1817 |
| patūlā | . | | 8. Ev. Cl. | |
| pedātā | . | Wht. grn. | 8. Ev. Cl. | W. Ind. | 1781 |
| peltātā | . | Green | 8, 8. Ev. Cl. | W. Ind. | 1778 |
| perfoliātā | . | Crimson | 7, 8. Ev. Cl. | Jamaica | 1800 |
| phœnicēā | . | Crimson | 8. Ev. Cl. | | 1831 |
| picturātā | . | Red | 9, 8. Ev. Cl. | Brazil | 1820 |
| pubescens | . | Grn. wht. | 8. Ev. Cl. | 8. Amer. |
| punctātā | . | Wht. yel. | 6, 8. Ev. Cl. | Peru | 1784 |
| quadrangulāris | . | Grn. blue | 6, 8. Ev. Cl. | Jamaica | 1763 |
| racemōsā | . | Scarlet | 6, 8. Ev. Cl. | Brazil | 1815 |
| princeps | . | Scarlet | 6, 8. Ev. Cl. | Hybrid |
| Raddiānā | . | White | 6, 8. Ev. Cl. | Brazil | 1825 |
| rotundifōliā | . | White | 6, 8. Ev. Cl. | Antilles | 1779 |
| rūbrā | . | Red | 6, 8. Ev. Cl. | W. Ind. | 1831 |
| sanguīnēā | . | Scarlet | 8, 8. Ev. Cl. | Hybrid |
| serrātā | . | Wht. grn. | 8. Ev. Cl. | Martinique | 1800 |
| serratifōliā | . | Grn. pur. | 7, 8. Ev. Cl. | 8. Amer. | 1731 |
| sexflōrā | . | | 6, 8. Ev. Cl. | Hispaniola | 1826 |
| stipulātā, 10 | . | White | 8, 8. Ev. Cl. | Cayenne | 1779 |
| suberōsā | . | Grn. yel. | 7, 8. Ev. Cl. | W. Ind. | 1759 |
| tiliæfōliā | . | Gr. red blu. | 7, 8. Ev. Cl. | Peru | 1823 |
| tinifōliā | . | | 7, 8. Ev. Cl. | Cayenne | 1824 |
| tuberōsā, 11 | . | Orsh. wht. | 7, 8. Ev. Cl. | 8. Amer. | 1810 |
| tucumanēnsis | . | Wht. grn. | 7, 8. Ev. Cl. | Chile | 1836 |
| ulmifōliā | . | | 8. Ev. Cl. | W. Ind. | 1819 |
| vespertīliō | . | White | 5, 8. Ev. Cl. | W. Ind. | 1732 |
| vitifōliā | . | | 8. Ev. Cl. | 8. Amer. | 1823 |

PASSION FLOWER, see Passiflora.

PASTINACA, Tournefort. From pastinum, a dibble; in
allusion to the form of the root. Linn. 5, Or. 2,
Nat. Or. Umbelliferæ. P. sativa, or Parsnep, is a
well known culinary root: the other species are
unworthy of cultivation. They are only increased
from seed, which should be sown in spring in the
open ground. Synonymes: 1. Ferula faniculacea.
2. Malabaila graveolens. 3. Smyrnium nudicaule.
4. Malabaila pimpinelloides. 5. P. opaca, P. sylvestris. 6. P. dissecta—P. faniculactā 1, divaricātā,
gravēolēns 2, latifōliā, lūcidā, nudicaūlis 3, panaci-
fōliā, pimpinellifōliā 4, sativā 5, Sekākûl 6, stenocārpā, taraxacifōliā, umbrōsā.

PATAGONULA, Linn. From the name of its native
country, Patagonia. Linn. 5, Or. 1, Nat. Or.
Boraginaceæ. This is an ornamental tree, growing
well in an equal mixture of loam and peat; cuttings
planted in the same kind of soil, under a glass, root
readily. Synonyme: 1. Cordia Patagonula.

| | | | | | | |
|---|---|---|---|---|---|---|
| americānā, 1 | . | White | . | 7, 8. Ev. 8. | 8. Amer. | 1732 |

PATELLARIA, Fries. Derived from patella, a saucer;
form of the cup. Linn. 24, Or. 9, Nat. Or. Fungi.
An extremely minute species, found on wood—
P. atrātā.

PATENT, spreading, diffuse.

PATERSONIA, R. Brown. In honour of Colonel William
Paterson, an excellent botanist. Linn. 16, Or. 1,
Nat. Or. Iridaceæ. A handsome genus of plants, in
habit and growth resembling the Iris; they succeed
well in sandy peat, and may be increased by divisions, or seeds. Synonyme: 1. P. glauca.

| | | | |
|---|---|---|---|
| glabrātā | Purple | 6, G. Her. | P. N. S. W. | 1814 |
| glaūcā | Blue | 6, G. Her. | P. N. S. W. | 1890 |
| lanātā | Blue | 6, G. Her. | P. N. S. W. | 1824 |
| longifōlīā | Blue | 6, G. Her. | P. N. S. W. | 1818 |
| longiscāpā, 1 | Blue | 6, G. Her. | P. N. S. W. | |
| mēdīā | Purple | 6, G. Her. | P. N. S. W. | 1816 |
| occidentālis | Blue | 6, G. Her. | P. N. S. W. | 1824 |
| serīceā | Blue | 6, G. Her. | P. N. S. W. | 1803 |

PATIENCE, see *Rūmex patiēntiā*.
PATRINIA, *Jussieu*. Named in compliment to M. Patrin, a Siberian traveller. Linn. 4, Or. 1, Nat. Or. *Valerianaceæ*. Pretty plants, succeeding well in a light rich soil; multiplied from seeds. *Synonymes*: 1. P. *audiuscula*. 2. *Valeriana sibirica*, *Fedia rupestris*. 3. P. *serrutulifolia*. 4. P. *coronata*, *Valeriana ruthenica*, V. *sibirica*.

| | | | | |
|---|---|---|---|---|
| intermēdīā, 1 | Yellow | 6, H. | B. Siberia | 1820 |
| rupēstrīs, 2 | Yellow | 5, H. | B. Siberia | 1801 |
| sc-biennifōlīā, 3 | Yellow | 6, H. | B. Dahuria | 1817 |
| sibīrīcā, 4 | Yellow | 6, H. | B. Siberia | 1751 |

PATULOUS, slightly spreading.
PAUCIFLŌRĀ, few-flowered.
PAULLINIA, *Schumacher*. In honour of S. Paulli, professor of botany at Copenhagen. Linn. 8, Or. 3, Nat. Or. *Sapindaceæ*. These species succeed well in light loamy soil, and ripened cuttings root in sand, under a glass, in heat. Some of them are said to be poisonous.

| | | | |
|---|---|---|---|
| barbadēnsis | Wht. grn. | S. Ev. Tw. | W. Ind. | 1786 |
| bipinnātā | White | S. Ev. Tw. | Brazil | 1816 |
| carlbūā | Wht. grn. | S. Ev. Tw. | W. Ind. | 1818 |
| carthaginēnsis | White | S. Ev. Tw. | Carthag. | 1818 |
| caulifōrā | White | S. Ev. Tw. | Caraccas | 1822 |
| Cupānīā | White | S. Ev. Tw. | Trinidad | 1818 |
| curassavīcā | Wht. grn. | S. Ev. Tw. | S. Amer. | 1739 |
| Curūrū | White | S. Ev. Tw. | Antilles | 1824 |
| hispīdā | White | S. Ev. Tw. | Trinidad | 1825 |
| melisefōlīā | White | S. Ev. Tw. | Brazil | 1819 |
| pinnātā | Wht. grn. | S. Ev. Tw. | W. Ind. | 1752 |
| pubēscēns | White | S. Ev. Tw. | S. Amer. | 1820 |
| senegalēnsis | White | S. Ev. Tw. | Guinea | 1822 |
| sphærocārpā | White | S. Ev. Tw. | Guinea | 1824 |
| tetragōnā | White | S. Ev. Tw. | Cayenne | 1825 |
| vespertilīō | White | S. Ev. Tw. | St. Christ | 1823 |

PAULLINIA, see *Serjānīā*.
PAUPERITIOUS, poor, having a starved appearance.
PAVĒTTĀ, *Linn*. The name of one of the species in Malabar. Linn. 4, Or. 1, Nat. Or. *Cinchonaceæ*. Handsome shrubs, growing best in an equal mixture of sandy loam and peat; increased from cuttings in sand, under a glass, in heat. *Synonymes*: 1. P. *indica*. 2. P. *alba*, *Ixora paniculata*.

| | | | |
|---|---|---|---|
| arenōsā, 1 | White | 6, G. Ev. S. | China | 1799 |
| cāffrā | White | G. Ev. S. | C. G. H. | 1823 |
| indīcā, 2 | White | 9, G. Ev. S. | E. Ind. | 1791 |

PAVIA, *Boerhaave*. In honour of Peter Paw, a Dutch botanist, once professor at Leyden. Linn. 7, Or. 1, Nat. Or. *Æsculaceæ*. Handsome flowering shrubs or trees; increased by layers, or by grafting on the common horse chesnut. When seeds can be obtained, they should be sown in March in common soil, about an inch deep. *Synonymes*: 1. *Æsculus discolor*, *Pavia hybrida*. 2. *Æ. flava*. 3. *Æsculus Pavia macrocarpa*. 4. P. *parviflora*, *Æ. macrostachya*. 5. *Æ. neglecta*. 6. *Æ. Pavia*. 7. P. *humilis*.

| | | | |
|---|---|---|---|
| eārneā | Red | H. De. T. | | 1820 |
| discōlōr, 1 | Red yel. | 6, H. De. S. | N. Amer. | 1812 |
| flāvā, 2 | Yellow | 5, H. De. T. | N. Amer. | 1764 |
| macrocārpā, 3 | Red yel. | 6, H. De. T. | | 1826 |
| macrostāchyā, 4 | White | 6, H. De. T. | N. Amer. | 1820 |
| neglēctā, 5 | Pa. yel. | 5, H. De. S. | | 1823 |
| rūbrā, 6 | Scarlet | 5, H. De. S. | N. Amer. | 1711 |
| argūtā | Red | H. De. S. | Europe | 1820 |
| hūmīlīs, 7 | Red | 5, H. De. S. | N. Amer. | |
| hūmīlīs-pēndūlā | Red | 5, H. De. S. | N. Amer. | |
| sublacinīātā | Red | 5, H. De. S. | N. Amer. | |

PAVŌNIA, *Cavanilles*. In honour of Don Josef Pavon, M.D. of Madrid, a traveller in Peru, and in conjunction with Ruiz, the author of "Flora Peruviana." Linn. 16, Or. 8, Nat. Or. *Malvaceæ*. Mostly species of no merit, growing in any light soil; cuttings root readily in sand, under a glass; they may likewise be increased by seeds. *Synonymes*: 1. *Hibiscus cancellatus*. 2. P. *spicata*. 3. *Lebretonia Schrankii*. 4. *H. spinifex*. 5. *Urena Typhalea*.

| | | | |
|---|---|---|---|
| coccineā | Scarlet | S. Ev. S. | St. Domin. | 1816 |
| Schrankii, 3 | Scarlet | 7, S. Ev. S. | Brazil | 1823 |
| Typhalēā, 5 | Wht. red | 7, S. Ev. S. | Jamaica | 1824 |
| typhaloīdēs | Pa. red | S. Ev. S. | Trinidad | 1824 |

cancellātā 1, Columēllā, corymbōsā, leptocārpā, odorātā, paniculātā, parviflōrā, præmōrsā, racemōsā 2, sidoīdēs, spinīfēx 4, ūrēns, zeylānīcā.
PAVONIOUS, spotted so as to resemble a peacock.
PAXTŌNIA, *Lindley*. In compliment to Joseph Paxton, F.L.S., H.S., gardener to His Grace the Duke of Devonshire, Chatsworth, and conductor of the Magazine of Botany. Linn. 20, Or. 1, Nat. Or. *Orchidaceæ*. This pretty species may be successfully grown in a mixture of very turfy loam, leaf-mould, and sand, with the treatment given to *Bletias*.

| | | | |
|---|---|---|---|
| rōseā | Pink | 7, S. Ter. | Philippines | 1837 |

PEA, see *Pīsum*.
PEACH, see *Amygdālūs*.
PEAR, see *Pyrus*.
PEARLWORT, see *Saginā*.
PECTINARIA, *Haworth*. Derived from *pecten*, a comb. Linn. 5, Or. 2, Nat. Or. *Asclepiadaceæ*. This species requires the same treatment as the genus *Stapelia*. *Synonyme*: 1. *Stapelia articulata*.

| | | | |
|---|---|---|---|
| articulātā, 1 | Purple | 7, S. Ev. S. | C. G. H. | 1800 |

PECTINATE, or PECTINATED, like the teeth of a comb, or rake.
PECTIS, *Less*. From *pecten*, a comb; appearance of the teeth of the pappus. Linn. 19, Or. 2, Nat. Or. *Compositæ*. Stove annuals, of neither interest nor beauty, and the simplest culture—P. *canēscēns*, *ciliāris*, *humifūsā*, *linifōliā*, *prostrātā*.
PECTORAL, relating to the breast.
PEDALIŌM, *Linn*. From *pedalion*, a rudder; in reference to the dilated angles of the fruit. Linn. 14, Or. 2, Nat. Or. *Pedaliaceæ*. A curious annual, remarkable for its hard, nut-like fruit, with sharp points or horns; it prefers a mixture of loam and peat.

| | | | |
|---|---|---|---|
| mūrēx | Wht. pur. | S. S. | A. E. Ind. | 1778 |

PEDATE; when leaves are cut in divisions, and the outer divisions again lobed, they are pedate.
PEDATIFID, cut into lobes, the lateral ones not radiating from the petiole like the rest.
PEDICEL, commonly applied to the partial footstalks of flowers.
PEDICULARIS, *Linn*. From *pediculus*, a louse; supposed effect on sheep eating it. Linn. 14, Or. 2, Nat. Or. *Scrophulariaceæ*. Beautiful little plants, with very regular, finely-cut leaves; they thrive best if planted in a mixture of peat soil, and kept moderately moist. The best way of obtaining an increase is by seeds. *Synonyme*: 1. P. *asplenifolia*.

| | | | |
|---|---|---|---|
| adscendēns | Red | 7, H. Her. | P. Switzerl. | 1819 |
| atrorūbēns, 1 | Dk. red | 7, H. Her. | P. Switzerl. | 1819 |
| canadēnsis | Yellow | 7, H. Her. | P. N. Amer. | 1780 |
| comōsā | Yellow | 7, H. Her. | P. Italy | 1775 |
| compāctā | Yellow | 7, H. Her. | P. Siberia | 1815 |
| euphrasioīdēs | Purple | F. Her. | P. Siberia | 1816 |
| flāmmeā | Yel. scar. | 7, H. Her. | P. Switzerl. | 1775 |
| foliōsā | Cream | 7, F. Her. | P. Austria | 1796 |
| gyroflēxā | Purple | 7, F. Her. | P. Switzerl. | 1819 |
| incarnātā | Pink | 6, H. Her. | P. Austria | 1796 |
| myriophyllā | Yellow | 7, H. Her. | P. Dauria | 1816 |
| palūstris | Purple | 6, H. Her. | P. Britain | |
| recutītā | Purple | 6, F. Her. | P. Austria | 1787 |
| resupinātā | Purple | 7, F. Her. | P. Siberia | 1816 |
| rostrātā | Purple | 6, F. Her. | P. Switzerl. | 1816 |
| scēptrūm carolīnūm | Yellow | 7, F. Her. | P. Sweden | 1793 |
| sylvātīcā | Pink | 5, H. Her. | P. Britain | |
| tuberōsā | Yellow | 7, F. Her. | P. Switzerl. | 1799 |
| uncinātā | Yellow | 7, F. Her. | P. Siberia | 1815 |
| versicolōr | Yellow | 6, F. Her. | P. Switzerl. | 1819 |
| verticillātā | Rose | 7, F. Her. | P. Austria | 1790 |

PEDILANTHUS, *Necker*. From *pedilon*, a slipper, and *anthos*, a flower. Linn. 11, Or. 3, Nat. Or. *Euphorbiaceæ*. Curious plants, resembling *Euphorbia* in habit and general appearance, to which genus they may be referred for cultivation, &c. *Synonymes*: 1. *Euphorbia canaliculata*. 2. *Crepidaria carinata*. 3. C. *cordellata*. 4. P. *myrtifolius*, *Crepidaria myrtifolia*.

| | | | |
|---|---|---|---|
| canaliculātūs, 1 | Apetal | 7, S. Ev. S. | S. Amer. | 1820 |
| carinātūs, 2 | Apetal | 7, S. Ev. S. | | 1817 |
| cordellātūs, 3 | Apetal | 7, S. Ev. S. | S. Amer. | 1699 |
| padifōlīūs | Apetal | 7, S. Ev. S. | S. Amer. | 1699 |
| subcarinātūs | Apetal | 7, S. Ev. S. | S. Amer. | 1795 |
| tithymaloīdēs, 4 | Apetal | 7, S. Ev. S. | S. Amer. | 1820 |

PEDUNCLE, flower-stalk.
PEGANUM, *Linn*. From *paganon*, rue; on account of the resemblance. Linn. 11, Or. 1, Nat. Or. *Zygo-*

[ 234 ]

*phyllaceæ.* Plants of little beauty, thriving in any light soil, and multiplied by division at the roots.

| | | | | | | |
|---|---|---|---|---|---|---|
| daūricūm . . . | White . | 7, | H. Her. | P. | Siberia . | 1816 |
| Harmāla . . . | White . | 7, | H. Her. | P. | Spain . . | 1570 |

Pelargonĭūm, *L'Heritier.* From *pelargos*, a stork; the capsules may be fancied to resemble the head and beak of a stork. *Linn.* 16, Or. 4, Nat. Or. *Geraniaceæ.* The shrubby kinds of this favourite genus will thrive in any rich soil; loam and decayed leaves will be found a good compost for them. The pots should be well drained with potsherds, and the plants receive plenty of air and water whilst in a vigorous growing state; cuttings root freely in soil or sand, under a glass; some of the finer and hard-wooded kinds will be found easier to increase by cuttings from the roots. The tuberous-rooted kinds should be kept quite dry when not in a growing state, and may be increased by small offsets from the roots. No genus is more liable than this to sport into hybrids by promiscuous impregnation. All the fine varieties which are found in gardens have been produced by artificial hybridization, that is, by cutting out the anthers of the plant intended for the female parent before they burst, and impregnating the stigmas with the pollen of another. *Synonymes:* 1. *Geranium Grenvillea.* 2. *P. australe.* 3. *G. capitatum.* 4. *G. stenopetalum.* 5. *G. miniatum, album.* 6. *Phymalanthus tricolor.*

| | | | | | | |
|---|---|---|---|---|---|---|
| abrotanifōlĭūm . | Red . . | 5, | G. Ev. | S. | C. G. H. . | 1791 |
| acerifōlĭūm . . | Pa. pur. . | 4, | G. Ev. | S. | C. G. H. . | 1784 |
| acetōsūm . . . | Pink . . | 7, | G. Ev. | S. | C. G. H. . | 1710 |
| aeugnaticūm . . | Red . . | 6, | G. Ev. | S. | Tris. d'Ac. | 1818 |
| adulterinūm . . | Purple . | 5, | G. Ev. | S. | C. G. H. | 1786 |
| affinē . . . . | Purple . | 6, | G. Tu. | P. | C. G. H. . | 1800 |
| alchemilloīdēs . | Pink . . | 6, | G. Her. | P. | C. G. H. . | 1698 |
| alnifōlĭūm . . . | Pink vein. | 5, | | | | |
| altērnāns . . . | Wht. pur. | 6, | G. Ev. | S. | C. G. H. . | 1791 |
| althæoīdēs . . . | White . . | 5, | G. Her. | P. | C. G. H. . | 1724 |
| amplissimūm . . | Purple . | 5, | G. Ev. | S. | | |
| ānceps . . . . | Pink . . | 6, | G. Ev. | Tr. | C. G. H. . | 1788 |
| Andrēwsĭī . . . | Blush . . | 6, | G. Her. | P. | C. G. H. . | 1802 |
| anemonifōlĭūm . | Pink . . | 7, | G. | B. | C. G. H. . | |
| angulōsūm . . . | Purple . | 8, | G. Ev. | S. | C. G. H. . | 1724 |
| apiifōlĭūm . . . | Wht. red . | 6, | G. Tu. | P. | C. G. H. . | 1800 |
| ārdēns . . . . | Red . . | 6, | G. Ev. | S. | C. G. H. . | 1807 |
| aristātūm . . . | Wht. red . | 6, | G. Tu. | P. | C. G. H. . | 1800 |
| armātūm . . . | Purple | 5, | G. Ev. | S. | C. G. H. . | 1789 |
| artemisiæfōlĭūm . | White . . | 6, | G. Ev. | S. | C. G. H. . | 1817 |
| asarifōlĭūm . . | Drk. pur. | 12, | G. Tu. | P. | C. G. H. . | 1821 |
| āspērūm . . . | Pink . . | 8, | G. Ev. | S. | C. G. H. . | 1795 |
| astragalifōlĭūm . | Wht. pur. | 7, | G. Tu. | P. | C. G. H. . | 1788 |
| ātrūm . . . . | Drk. brn. . | 6, | G. Tu. | P. | C. G. H. . | 1793 |
| auriculātūm . . | Pa. red . | 5, | G. Tu. | P. | C. G. H. . | |
| austrālē . . . . | Rose . . | 6, | G. Ev. | S. | N. Holl. . | 1792 |
| balsamēūm . . | Pink . . | 8, | G. Ev. | S. | C. G. H. . | 1790 |
| Barringtōnĭī . . | Purple . | 5, | G. Ev. | S. | C. G. H. . | |
| barbātūm . . . | Flesh . . | 7, | G. Tu. | P. | C. G. H. . | 1790 |
| Beaufortiānūm . | Lilac . . | 6, | G. Ev. | S. | C. G. H. . | |
| Bellārdĭī . . . | White . . | 6, | G. Ev. | S. | C. G. H. . | |
| Bentinckiānūm . | Scarlet . | 5, | G. Ev. | S. | C. G. H. . | |
| betulinūm . . . | Wht. red . | 7, | G. Ev. | S. | C. G. H. . | 1759 |
| bicŏlŏr . . . . | Pur. wht. . | 7, | G. Ev. | S. | | 1778 |
| blāndūm . . . | Blush . . | | G. Her. | P. | C. G. H. . | 1801 |
| blattarĭūm . . . | Violet . . | 7, | G. Ev. | S. | C. G. H. . | 1720 |
| bubonifōlĭūm . . | Wht. pur. | 5, | G. Tu. | P. | C. G. H. . | 1800 |
| bullātūm . . . | Pink . . | 6, | G. Ev. | S. | C. G. H. . | |
| canariēnsē . . . | Wht. red . | 8, | G. | B. | Canaries . | 1802 |
| canēscēns . . . | White . . | 7, | G. Ev. | S. | C. G. H. . | |
| cānūm . . . . | Pa. pur. . | 8, | G. Ev. | S. | C. G. H. . | 1820 |
| capitātūm . . . | Purple . | 6, | G. Ev. | S. | C. G. H. . | 1690 |
| cardaifōlĭūm . . | Pa. pur. . | 7, | G. Ev. | S. | C. G. H. . | 1816 |
| carinātūm . . . | Wht. pur. | 7, | G. Ev. | S. | C. G. H. . | 1820 |
| cārnēūm . . . | Pink . . | 5, | G. Tu. | P. | C. G. H. . | 1812 |
| carnōsūm . . . | Pur. wht. . | 5, | G. Ev. | S. | C. G. H. . | 1724 |
| caucalifōlĭūm . . | Pink . . | 7, | G. | B. | C. G. H. . | 1812 |
| ceratophyllūm . | White . . | 6, | G. Ev. | S. | Africa . | 1786 |
| chamædrifōlĭūm . | White . . | 5, | G. Her. | P. | C. G. H. . | 1812 |
| ciliātūm . . . | Flesh . . | 5, | G. Tu. | P. | C. G. H. . | 1795 |
| citriodōrūm . . | White . . | 7, | G. Ev. | S. | C. G. H. . | 1800 |
| cochleātūm . . | Purple . | 5, | G. Ev. | S. | | |
| columbinūm . . | Purple . | 8, | G. Her. | P. | C. G. H. . | 1795 |
| coluteæfōlĭūm . | Yel. red . | 6, | G. Tu. | P. | Hybrid . | 1824 |
| conduplicātūm . | Pur. wht. . | 5, | G. Ev. | S. | | 1774 |
| congēstūm . . . | Lilac . . | 6, | G. Tu. | P. | C. G. H. . | 1824 |
| conspicŭūm, 1 . | Drk. pink . | 9, | G. Tu. | P. | Africa . | 1810 |
| consanguinēūm . | Pink . . | 6, | G. Ev. | S. | | |
| cordātūm . . . | Pur. wht. . | 5, | G. Ev. | S. | C. G. H. . | 1774 |
| coriandrifōlĭūm . | Wht. red . | 6, | G. | B. | C. G. H. . | 1724 |
| coronillæfōlĭūm . | Brown . | 6, | G. Tu. | P. | C. G. H. . | 1795 |
| coronopifōlĭūm . | Pa. red . | 8, | G. Ev. | S. | C. G. H. . | 1791 |
| cortusæfōlĭūm . | Pink . . | 7, | G. Ev. | S. | Africa . | 1786 |
| corydaliflōrūm . | Pa. yel. . | 5, | G. Tu. | P. | C. G. H. . | 1821 |
| Cotylēdōnis . . | White . . | 6, | G. Ev. | S. | St. Helena | 1765 |
| crassicaūlē . . . | White . . | 7, | G. Tu. | P. | S. Africa . | 1786 |
| crenātūm . . . | | 7, | G. Ev. | S. | C. G. H. . | 1800 |
| crispūm . . . | Purple . | 9, | G. Ev. | S. | C. G. H. . | 1774 |
| crithmifōlĭūm . | Wht. pur. | 5, | G. Ev. | S. | C. G. H. . | 1790 |
| cucullātūm . . | Purple . | 5, | G. Ev. | S. | C. G. H. . | 1690 |
| grandiflōrūm | Purple . | 5, | G. Ev. | S. | C. G. H. . | 1818 |
| mājŏr . . | Purple . | 5, | G. Ev. | S. | C. G. H. . | 1812 |
| striatiflōrūm | Purple . | 5, | G. Ev. | S. | C. G. H. . | 1810 |
| cuspidātūm . . | Wht. red . | 7, | G. Ev. | S. | C. G. H. . | |
| cynosbatifōlĭūm | Drk. red . | 6, | G. Ev. | S. | | |
| dasycaūlŏn . . | Wht. pur. | 9, | G. Ev. | S. | C. G. H. . | 1795 |
| decōrūm . . . | Lilac . . | 7, | G. Ev. | S. | C. G. H. . | 1825 |
| delphinifōlĭūm . | Pink . . | 6, | G. Ev. | S. | | |
| denticulātūm . . | Pink . . | 6, | G. Ev. | S. | C. G. H. . | 1789 |
| deprēssūm . . . | Cream . . | 5, | G. Tu. | P. | C. G. H. . | 1812 |
| dioicūm . . . | Drk. brn. . | 6, | G. Tu. | P. | C. G. H. . | 1795 |
| dipetālūm . . . | Pa. pur. . | 5, | G. Tu. | P. | C. G. H. . | 1795 |
| discĭpēs . . . . | | | G. Ev. | S. | Africa . | 1808 |
| diversifōlĭūm . . | Wht. red . | 7, | G. Ev. | S. | C. G. H. . | 1794 |
| echinātūm . . . | Wht. red . | 5, | G. Tu. | P. | C. G. H. . | 1789 |
| elātūm . . . . | Wht. pur. | 8, | G. Ev. | S. | C. G. H. . | 1795 |
| elēctūm . . . . | White . . | 7, | G. Ev. | S. | C. G. H. | |
| ēlegāns . . . . | Wht. red . | 4, | G. Ev. | S. | C. G. H. . | 1795 |
| mājŭs . . . | Wht. red . | 6, | G. Ev. | S. | C. G. H. . | 1795 |
| mĭnŭs . . . | Wht. red . | 6, | G. Ev. | S. | C. G. H. . | 1795 |
| eriostēmŏn . . . | White . . | 4, | G. Ev. | S. | C. G. H. . | 1794 |
| exstipulātūm . . | Violet . . | 7, | G. Ev. | S. | C. G. H. . | 1779 |
| filipendulifōlĭūm | Grn. brn. . | 7, | G. Tu. | P. | C. G. H. . | 1812 |
| fissifōlĭūm . . . | Wht. red . | 6, | G. Tu. | P. | C. G. H. . | 1795 |
| flāvūm . . . . | Yel. brn. . | 8, | G. Tu. | P. | C. G. H. . | 1724 |
| floribŭndūm . . | White . . | 4, | G. Tu. | P. | C. G. H. . | 1800 |
| foliōsūm . . . | Yel. red . | 5, | G. Tu. | P. | C. G. H. . | 1800 |
| formosissimūm . | Wht. red . | 7, | G. Ev. | S. | C. G. H. . | 1759 |
| Fothergillĭī . . | Scarlet . | 8, | G. Ev. | S. | C. G. H. . | |
| purpūrēūm . | Purple . | 8, | G. Ev. | S. | C. G. H. . | 1810 |
| frāgrāns . . . | Varieg. . | 7, | G. Ev. | S. | C. G. H. . | |
| fulgidūm . . . | Scarlet . | 5, | G. Ev. | S. | C. G. H. . | 1723 |
| fuscātūm . . . | Pur. red . | 5, | G. Ev. | S. | C. G. H. . | 1812 |
| gibbōsūm . . . | Grn. yel. . | 6, | G. Ev. | S. | C. G. H. . | 1712 |
| glaūcūm . . . | Wht. red . | 7, | G. Ev. | S. | C. G. H. . | 1775 |
| glomerātūm, 2 . | White . . | 7, | G. Ev. | S. | C. G. H. . | |
| glutinōsūm . . | Pa. rose . | 5, | G. Ev. | S. | C. G. H. . | 1777 |
| grandiflōrūm . . | Wht. red . | 5, | G. Ev. | S. | C. G. H. . | 1794 |
| grātūm . . . . | Pink . . | 6, | G. Ev. | S. | | |
| graveŏlēns . . . | Purple . | 5, | G. Ev. | S. | C. G. H. . | 1774 |
| variegātūm, 3 | Purple . | 5, | G. Ev. | S. | C. G. H. . | |
| grossularioīdēs . | Pink . . | 6, | G. Ev. | S. | C. G. H. . | 1731 |
| hepaticifōlĭūm . | Rose . . | 7, | G. Ev. | S. | C. G. H. . | 1791 |
| heracleifōlĭūm . | Grey . . | 7, | G. Her. | P. | C. G. H. . | 1800 |
| hermannifōlĭūm . | Pink . . | 5, | G. Ev. | S. | C. G. H. . | |
| heterogămūm . . | Pink . . | 7, | G. Ev. | S. | | 1786 |
| heterophyllūm . | Wht. red . | 5, | G. Tu. | P. | C. G. H. . | 1800 |
| hirsūtūm . . . | Pink . . | 8, | G. Tu. | P. | C. G. H. . | 1788 |
| hirtūm . . . . | Rose . . | 7, | G. Ev. | S. | C. G. H. . | 1768 |
| hispidūm . . . | Purple . | 6, | G. Ev. | S. | C. G. H. . | 1790 |
| holosericēūm . . | Drk. pur. . | 4, | G. Ev. | S. | C. G. H. . | 1820 |
| humifūsūm . . | Red . . | 6, | G. Tr. | A. | C. G. H. . | 1801 |
| hybrĭdūm . . . | Lilac . . | 7, | G. Ev. | S. | C. G. H. . | 1732 |
| ignēscēns . . . | Scarlet . | 4, | G. Ev. | S. | Hybrid . | 1812 |
| imbricātūm . . | Lil. pur. . | 6, | G. Ev. | S. | C. G. H. . | 1800 |
| incīsūm . . . | Wht. red . | 6, | G. Ev. | S. | C. G. H. . | 1791 |
| incrassātūm . . | Pa. rose . | 5, | G. Tu. | P. | C. G. H. . | 1801 |
| inodōrūm . . . | Pa. pur. . | 7, | G. Ev. | Tr. | N. Holl. . | 1796 |
| inquinans . . . | Scarlet . | 7, | G. Ev. | S. | C. G. H. . | 1714 |
| lācērūm . . . | Pink . . | 7, | G. Her. | P. | C. G. H. . | 1781 |
| laciniātūm . . . | Pink . . | 5, | G. Tu. | P. | C. G. H. . | 1800 |
| lævigātūm . . . | Wht. red . | 6, | G. Ev. | S. | C. G. H. . | |
| lanceolātūm . . | Wht. pur. | 7, | G. Ev. | S. | C. G. H. . | 1775 |
| lateripēs . . . | Pa. pur. . | 7, | G. Ev. | S. | C. G. H. . | 1787 |
| albō-marginātūm | Pa. red . | 8, | G. Ev. | S. | C. G. H. . | 1787 |
| rŏsēūm . . . | Red . . | 8, | G. Ev. | S. | C. G. H. . | 1787 |
| zonātūm . . . | Pa. pur. . | 8, | G. Ev. | S. | C. G. H. . | 1787 |
| lateritĭūm . . . | Red . . | 7, | G. Ev. | S. | C. G. H. . | 1800 |
| lāxūm . . . . | White . . | 5, | G. Ev. | S. | C. G. H. . | 1821 |
| Leeānūm . . . | White . . | 5, | G. Tu. | P. | C. G. H. . | 1823 |
| leptopetălūm, 4 . | Red . . | 6, | G. Ev. | S. | C. G. H. . | 1800 |
| lineārē . . . . | Yellow . | 6, | G. Tu. | P. | C. G. H. . | 1800 |
| littorālē . . . | | | | | S. River . | 1827 |
| lobātūm . . . | Yel. brn. . | 7, | G. Tu. | P. | C. G. H. . | 1710 |
| longicaūlē . . . | Pa. rose . | 6, | G. Ev. | Tr. | C. G. H. . | |
| longiflōrūm . . | Yellow . | 5, | G. Tu. | P. | C. G. H. . | 1812 |
| longifōlĭūm . . | Pink . . | 5, | G. Tu. | P. | C. G. H. . | 1812 |
| lūridūm . . . | Straw . . | 8, | G. Her. | P. | C. G. H. . | 1811 |
| lūtēūm . . . . | Yellow . | 5, | G. Tu. | P. | C. G. H. . | 1802 |
| maculātūm . . | Blush . . | 7, | G. Ev. | S. | C. G. H. . | 1796 |
| malvæfōlĭūm . . | Pa. red . | 7, | G. Ev. | S. | C. G. H. . | 1812 |
| melanānthūm . . | Drk. brn. . | 5, | G. Tu. | P. | C. G. H. . | 1790 |
| micrānthūm . . | Scarlet . | 9, | G. Ev. | S. | C. G. H. . | |
| millefoliātūm . . | Yel. brn. . | 7, | G. Tu. | P. | C. G. H. . | |
| mŏnstrūm . . . | Red . . | 7, | G. Ev. | S. | C. G. H. . | 1784 |
| multicaūlē . . . | Pa. vio. . | 7, | G. Her. | P. | C. G. H. . | 1802 |
| multiradiātūm . | Drk. brn. . | 5, | G. Tu. | P. | C. G. H. . | 1820 |
| myrrhifōlĭūm . . | Wht. red . | 6, | G. Ev. | S. | C. G. H. . | 1696 |
| nervifōlĭūm . . | Varieg. . | 6, | G. Tu. | P. | C. G. H. . | 1812 |
| nigrēscēns . . . | Purple . | 5, | G. Ev. | S. | C. G. H. . | 1777 |
| nivēūm . . . . | White . . | 6, | G. Tu. | P. | | 1821 |
| nŏthūm . . . . | Pink . . | 5, | G. Ev. | S. | | |
| nummularifōlĭūm | Yellow . | 6, | G. Tu. | P. | C. G. H. . | 1801 |
| nūtāns . . . . | Yellow . | 5, | G. Tu. | P. | C. G. H. . | 1788 |

| obtusifolium | Purple | 6, G. Ev. S. | C.G.H. | |
|---|---|---|---|---|
| odoratissimum | Pink | 7, G. Ev. S. | | 1724 |
| Œnotheræ | Rose | 4, G. Her. P. | C.G.H. | 1812 |
| orobifolium | Blood | 6, G. Tu. P. | C.G.H. | 1824 |
| ovale | Purple | 6, G. Her. P. | C.G.H. | 1774 |
| ovalifolium | White | 5, G. Tu. P. | C.G.H. | 1820 |
| oxalidifolium | Yellow | 6, G. Tu. S. | C.G.H. | 1801 |
| oxyphyllum, 5 | White | 8, G. Ev. S. | C.G.H. | 1800 |
| pallens | Pa. yel. | 6, G. Ev. S. | | 1800 |
| pallidum | Pink | 6, G. Ev. S. | | |
| papilionaceum | Pa. wht. | 6, G. Ev. S. | C.G.H. | 1724 |
| parviflorum | Pur. red | 6, G. Her. P. | C.G.H. | 1800 |
| patentissimum | Lt. wht. | 6, G. Ev. S. | C.G.H. | 1820 |
| patulum | Pa. bld. | 6, G. Ev. S. | C.G.H. | 1821 |
| pedicellatum | Grn. brn. | 7, G. Ev. S. | C.G.H. | 1822 |
| peltatum | Purple | 7, G. Tu. P. | C.G.H. | 1701 |
| variegatum | Purple | 7, G. Ev. S. | C.G.H. | 1701 |
| pendulum | Red | 5, G. Ev. Tr. | C.G.H. | |
| penicillatum | Wht. red | 7, G. Ev. S. | C.G.H. | 1794 |
| penniforme | Yellow | 6, G. Tu. S. | C.G.H. | 1800 |
| petroselinum | Blush | 7, G. Her. P. | C.G.H. | 1802 |
| pictum | Wht. red | 6, G. Tu. S. | C.G.H. | 1800 |
| pilosum | Pink | 6, G. Tu. P. | C.G.H. | 1801 |
| primulinum | Violet | 7, G. Ev. S. | C.G.H. | |
| principissæ | Dk. pink | 6, G. Ev. S. | C.G.H. | 1820 |
| procumbens | Purple | 4, G. Her. P. | C.G.H. | 1801 |
| pulchellum | White | 4, G. Tu. S. | C.G.H. | 1795 |
| pulverulentum | Grey bld. | 7, G. Ev. S. | C.G.H. | 1822 |
| pumilum | Pink | 6, G. Ev. S. | C.G.H. | 1800 |
| punctatum | Cream | 5, G. Tu. P. | C.G.H. | 1794 |
| purpurascens | Purple | 5, G. Tu. S. | C.G.H. | 1800 |
| pustulosum | Wht. pink | 6, G. Ev. S. | C.G.H. | 1820 |
| quercifolium | Purple | 6, G. Ev. S. | C.G.H. | 1774 |
| bipinnatifidum | Purple | 5, G. Ev. S. | | 1774 |
| quinatum | Pa. yel. | 5, G. Ev. S. | C.G.H. | 1793 |
| quinquelobum | Red | 5, G. Ev. S. | C.G.H. | 1820 |
| quinquevulnerum | Dk. pur. | 7, G. Ev. S. | C.G.H. | 1796 |
| radiatum | Dk. pur. | 7, G. Ev. S. | C.G.H. | 1790 |
| radicatum | Yellow | 6, G. Tu. S. | C.G.H. | 1802 |
| radula | Yellow | 6, G. Tu. P. | C.G.H. | 1774 |
| rapaceum | Purple | 5, G. Ev. S. | C.G.H. | 1788 |
| recurvatum | White | 7, G. Her. P. | C.G.H. | 1790 |
| reflexum | White | 6, G. Ev. S. | C.G.H. | 1800 |
| reniforme | Purple | 7, G. Ev. S. | C.G.H. | 1791 |
| reticulatum | Pink | 5, G. Tu. S. | C.G.H. | 1820 |
| retusum | Drk. crim. | 6, G. Tu. P. | C.G.H. | 1824 |
| revolutum | Purple | 6, G. Ta. P. | C.G.H. | 1800 |
| rubifolium | White | 5, G. Ev. S. | C.G.H. | 1798 |
| rigidum | Whitish | 7, G. Ev. S. | C.G.H. | |
| roseum | Rose | 4, G. Ev. P. | C.G.H. | 1792 |
| rubens | Purple | 6, G. Ev. S. | | |
| rubrocinctum | Pur. wht. | 5, G. Ev. S. | C.G.H. | 1774 |
| rugosum | Pink lil. | 5, G. Ev. S. | | 1800 |
| rumicifolium | Yellow | 6, G. Tu. P. | | 1823 |
| sanguineum | Scarlet | 5, G. Her. P. | | |
| saniculæfolium | Pa. red | 7, G. Ev. S. | C.G.H. | 1806 |
| scabrum | Wht. red | 6, G. Ev. S. | | 1775 |
| scandens | Rose | 7, G. Ev. S. | | 1800 |
| schizopetalum | Yel. brn. | 6, G. Tu. P. | C.G.H. | 1821 |
| scutatum | White | 6, G. Ev. S. | C.G.H. | 1701 |
| semitrilobatum | Purple | 6, G. Ev. S. | C.G.H. | 1800 |
| senecioides | White | 6, G. A. | C.G.H. | 1775 |
| setosum | Rose | 5, G. Tu. P. | C.G.H. | 1821 |
| sororium | Wht. red | 6, G. Ev. P. | | |
| spatulatum | Yellow | 5, G. Ev. S. | C.G.H. | 1805 |
| affine | Yellow | 4, G. Tu. P. | C.G.H. | 1794 |
| speciosum | Purple | 5, G. Ev. S. | C.G.H. | 1794 |
| spinosum | Pink | 5, G. Ev. S. | C.G.H. | 1795 |
| spurium | Violet | 5, G. Ev. S. | | |
| staphimagrioides | Purple | 7, G. Ev. S. | C.G.H. | 1825 |
| stenopetalum | Scarlet | 6, G. Ev. S. | C.G.H. | 1800 |
| Synnoti | Lilac | 5, G. Ev. S. | C.G.H. | 1825 |
| tabulare | Pa. yel. | 6, G. Her. P. | C.G.H. | 1775 |
| tenellum | Yellow | 6, G. Tu. P. | C.G.H. | 1802 |
| tenuifolium | Purple | 6, G. Tu. S. | C.G.H. | 1768 |
| ternatum | Pink | 5, G. Ev. S. | C.G.H. | 1789 |
| tetragonum | Pink | 7, G. Ev. S. | C.G.H. | 1774 |
| variegatum | Pink | 7, G. Ev. S. | C.G.H. | 1774 |
| tomentosum | White | 6, G. Ev. S. | C.G.H. | 1790 |
| tricolor, 6 | Wht. pur. | 7, G. Ev. S. | C.G.H. | 1791 |
| tricuspidatum | Wht. pur. | 5, G. Ev. S. | C.G.H. | 1780 |
| tripartitum | Pa. yel. | 5, G. Ev. S. | C.G.H. | 1789 |
| triphyllum | Flesh | 5, G. Tu. P. | C.G.H. | 1812 |
| triste | Grn. yel. | 6, G. Tu. P. | C.G.H. | 1632 |
| undulatum | White | 6, G. Tu. P. | C.G.H. | 1795 |
| undulæflorum | Black | 6, G. Tu. S. | C.G.H. | 1821 |
| unicolorum | Crimson | 6, G. Ev. S. | C.G.H. | |
| uniflorum | | 6, G. Ev. S. | C.G.H. | 1800 |
| variegatum | Wht. red | 6, G. Ev. S. | C.G.H. | 1812 |
| verbascifolium | Lilac | 7, G. Ev. S. | | 1811 |
| viciæfolium | Pa. rose | 5, G. Tu. S. | C.G.H. | 1779 |
| violæflorum | White | 5, G. Tu. P. | C.G.H. | 1810 |
| virgineum | Wht. red | 6, G. Tu. S. | C.G.H. | 1795 |
| viscosissimum | Lt. wht. | 5, G. Ev. S. | C.G.H. | 1820 |
| vitifolium | Purple | 7, G. Ev. S. | C.G.H. | 1724 |
| Watsoni | Purple | 5, G. Ev. S. | | |
| Willdenovii | Wht. veiny | 6, G. Ev. S. | C.G.H. | |
| zonale | Scarlet | 8, G. Ev. S. | C.G.H. | 1710 |
| coccineum | Scarlet | 8, G. Ev. S. | C.G.H. | 1710 |
| crystallinum | Scarlet | 8, G. Ev. S. | C.G.H. | 1710 |
| marginatum | Scarlet | 8, G. Ev. S. | | |

PELEXIA, *Poiteau.* From *pelex*, a helmet. *Linn.* 20, Or. 1, Nat. Or. *Orchidaceæ.* An herbaceous plant of no great beauty, growing in a mixture of loam and peat, and increased slowly by division at the roots.

| spiranthoides | Grn. wht. | 8. Ter. | St. Vincent | 1823 |
|---|---|---|---|---|

PELIOSANTHES, *Andrews.* From *pelios*, livid, and *anthos*, a flower. *Linn.* 6, Or. 1, Nat. Or. *Liliaceæ.* Curious plants, with ovate-lanceolate leaves, requiring a mixture of loam, peat, and sand; propagated freely from suckers.

| humilis | Green | 5, S. Her. P. | E. Ind. | 1809 |
|---|---|---|---|---|
| Teta | Brn. grn. | 4, S. Her. P. | E. Ind. | 1807 |

PELLICLE, a thin skin which envelopes certain seeds.
PELLITORY, see *Parietaria.*
PELLITORY, see *Pyrethrum Parthenium.*
PELLITORY OF SPAIN, see *Anthemis Pyrethrum.*
PELLUCID, bright, transparent.

PELTARIA, *Linn.* From *pelte*, a small buckler; in allusion to the form of the silicle. *Linn.* 15, Nat. Or. *Cruciferæ.* Pretty little plants, flourishing in any light soil; readily increased by dividing the roots, or by seed.

| alliacea | White | 6, H. Her. P. | Austria | 1601 |
|---|---|---|---|---|
| glastifolia | White | 6, H. | A. Syria | 1823 |

PELTATE, a leaf is peltate, when the petiole is fixed in the disk instead of the margin.

PELTATE-NERVED, used in reference to the nerves of a leaf, radiating from the centre.

PELTIDEA, *Acharius.* From *pelte*, a target, and *eidos*, resemblance; form of the shields. *Linn.* 24, Or. 8, Nat. Or. *Lichenes.* The species of this genus grow on thatch, the bark of trees, among moss, &c. *P. aphthosa* is used, boiled in milk, by the peasants in Sweden, as a cure for the aphtha, from which it takes its name—*P. aphthosa, canina, horizontalis, membranacea, polydactyla, rufescens, scutata, sparsa, venosa.*

PENÆA, *Linn.* In honour of P. Pena, who, in conjunction with Lobel, published Adversaria Botanica in 1570. *Linn.* 4, Or. 1, Nat. Or. *Penæaceæ.* Handsome shrubs, growing in sandy peat; and young plants may be obtained from ripened cuttings, in sand, under a glass.

| fruticulosa | Red | 6, G. Ev. S. | C.G.H. | 1822 |
|---|---|---|---|---|
| imbricata | Pink | 6, G. Ev. S. | C.G.H. | 1824 |
| latifolia | Red | 6, G. Ev. S. | C.G.H. | 1825 |
| marginata | Red | 6, G. Ev. S. | C.G.H. | 1816 |
| mucronata | Yellow | 6, G. Ev. S. | C.G.H. | 1787 |
| myrtoides | Red | 6, G. Ev. S. | C.G.H. | 1816 |
| sarcocolla | Red | 6, G. Ev. S. | C.G.H. | 1825 |
| squamosa | Red | 6, G. Ev. S. | C.G.H. | 1787 |

PENCILLED, marked in lines, as with a pencil, or having the appearance of hair pencil, as the stigmas of numerous species of *Oxalis.*

PENDULOUS, drooping, hanging down.

PENICILLARIA, *Willdenow.* From *penicillus*, a pencil; in allusion to the spikes. *Linn.* 3, Or. 2, Nat. Or. *Gramineæ.* Mere weeds, thriving in any common soil, and increased by seeds—*P. ciliata, spicata.*

PENICILLIUM, *Link.* From *penicillum*, a painter's pencil; alluding to the form of the filaments. *Linn.* 24, Or. 9, Nat. Or. *Algæ.* The species are found on the decaying stems of herbaceous plants and other rotten substances—*P. candidum, glaucum, sparsum.*

PENNISETUM, *Beauvois.* From *penna*, a feather, and *seta*, a bristle. *Linn.* 3, Or. 1, Nat. Or. *Gramineæ.* A genus of grasses, not worth cultivating except in botanical collections. The seed may be sown in the open border. Synonyme: 1. *Panicum holcoides* —*P. barbatum, cenchroides, compressum, dichotomum, holcoides* 1, *nepalense, orientale, polystachyon, setosum, violaceum.*

PENNATOUS, soft, downy, like a feather.
PENNY-CRESS, see *Thlaspi arvense.*
PENNYROYAL, see *Mentha Pulegium.*
PENNYWORT, see *Hydrocotyle.*

PENTACRYPTA, *Lehmann.* From *pente*, five, and *krypte*, a vault. *Linn.* 23, Or. 1, Nat. Or. *Umbelliferæ.* A parsley-scented plant, requiring protection in winter; increased by seeds only—*P. atropurpurea.*

PENTADESMA, *R. Brown.* From *pente*, five, and *desma*,

a bundle; the stamens are disposed in five bundles. *Linn.* 18, Or. 2, Nat. Or. *Guttiferæ.* A handsome, lofty-growing tree, very difficult to transplant, on account of the long tap-root, which, if injured, will kill it; the tree produces its flowers when about twenty feet high. It requires a strong moist heat. A mixture of loam and peat suits it; and ripened cuttings, with their leaves not shortened, will root in sand, under a glass, in a moist heat.

| | | | | | |
|---|---|---|---|---|---|
| butyrácea | . . . | . 11, S. Ev. T. S. Leone | . 1822 |

**PENTAGONAL,** having five angles.

**PENTAGYNOUS,** having five styles.

**PENTANDROUS,** having five stamens.

**PENTAPETALOUS,** having five petals.

**PENTAPETES,** *Linn.* One of the Greek names for Cinquefoil. From *pente,* five; alluding to the five-celled fruit. *Linn.* 16, Or. 7, Nat. Or. *Sterculiaceæ.* Beautiful flowering plants, growing in any light rich soil; cuttings soon root in mould or sand, under a glass, in heat. Synonyme: 1. *Brotera ovata.*

| | | | | | |
|---|---|---|---|---|---|
| ovàta, 1 | . . . Scarlet | . 7, S. | B. N. Spain | . 1805 |
| phœnicèa | . . . Scarlet | . 7, S. Her. P. India | . 1690 |

**PENTARAPHIA,** *Lindley.* From *pente,* five, and *raphis,* a spike. *Linn.* 14, Or. 2, Nat. Or. *Gesneraceæ.* A handsome West Indian plant; for culture and propagation, it may be referred to *Gesneria.* Synonyme: 1. *Gesnera ventricosa.*

| | | | | | |
|---|---|---|---|---|---|
| longiflòra, 1 | . . | . 7, S. Ev. S. Jamaica | . 1823 |

**PENTHORUM,** *Linn.* From *pente,* five, and *horos,* a boundary; the capsule is terminated by five beaks. *Linn.* 10, Or. 5, Nat. Or. *Crassulaceæ.* A succulent plant of little beauty, growing in light sandy soil, and increased by division at the roots; cuttings also root freely under a glass.

| | | | | | |
|---|---|---|---|---|---|
| sedoídes | . . . Grn. yel. 7, H. Her. P. Virginia | . 1768 |

**PENTSTEMON,** *L'Heritier.* From *pente,* five, and *stemon,* a stamen; there are four perfect, and one imperfect. *Linn.* 14, Or. 2, Nat. Or. *Scrophulariaceæ.* Charming herbaceous plants, worthy of a place in every collection; they all delight in a mixture of loam and peat, and are readily increased by divisions, or by seeds. Synonymes: 1. *Chelone cærulea, hirsuta.* 2. *C. atropurpurea.* 3. *C. cristata.* 4. *C. erianthera.* 5. *P. Bradburii.* 6. *C. angustifolia.* 7. *C. elegans, P. elegans.* 8. *C. rosea, angustifolia.*

| | | | | | |
|---|---|---|---|---|---|
| acuminàtum | . Purple | . 7, H. Her. P. N. Amer. | 1827 |
| albìdum | . White | . 7, H. Her. P. Missouri | . 1823 |
| angustifòlium, 1 | . Li. pur. | . 8, H. Her. P. Louisiana | . 1811 |
| argùtum | . . Blue | . H. Her. P. Columbia | . 1825 |
| atropurpùreùm, 2 | Drk. pur. | 7, H. Her. P. Mexico | . 1827 |
| attenuàtum | . Cream | . 7, H. Her. P. N. Amer. | . 1827 |
| breviflòrum | . Wht. pink | 9, H. Her. P. California | |
| campanulàtum | . Li. pur. | 6, H. Her. P. Mexico | . 1794 |
| Cobéa | . . Pa. pur. | . H. Her. P. Texas | . 1835 |
| confértum | . Pa. yel. | . 7, H. Her. P. N. Amer. | 1827 |
| crassifòlium | . Blue | . 6, H. Her. P. N. Amer. | |
| dentàtum | . Cream | . H. Her. P. N. Amer. | 1827 |
| diffùsum | . Purple | . 9, H. Her. P. N. Amer. | 1826 |
| digitàlis | . White | . 8, H. Her. P. Arkansas | 1824 |
| eriánthèrùm, 3 | . Purple | . 8, H. Her. P. Louisiana | 1811 |
| glàbrum, 4 | . Drk. pur. | . 8, H. Her. P. Louisiana | 1811 |
| glaberrìmùm | . Blue | . H. Her. P. Columbia | 1835 |
| glandulòsùm | . Pa. blue | . 6, H. Her. P. N. Amer. | 1827 |
| glaùcùm | . Pa. lilac | . 7, H. Her. P. N. Amer. | 1827 |
| grácilis | . . Blue | . 8, H. Her. P. N. Amer. | 1824 |
| grandiflòrùm, 5 | . Purple | . 7, H. Her. P. N. Amer. | 1811 |
| heterophýllùm | . Red | . 7, H. Her. P. California | 1834 |
| hirsùtùm | . Pa. pur. | . 8, H. Her. P. N. Amer. | 1758 |
| Kunthii, 6 | . Purple | . F. Her. P. Mexico | . 1825 |
| lævigàtum | . Lilac | . 8, H. Her. P. N. Amer. | 1776 |
| Mackayànùm | . Pur. yel. | 8, H. Her. P. Ohio | . 1834 |
| Murrayànùm | . Scarlet | . 8, H. Her. P. S. Felipe | . 1835 |
| ovàtùm | . . Blue | . 7, H. Her. P. N. Amer. | 1826 |
| procèrùm | . Purple | . 7, H. Her. P. N. Amer. | 1827 |
| pruinòsùm | . Blue | . 6, H. Her. P. N. Amer. | 1827 |
| pubéscens | . Pa. pur. | . 8, H. Her. P. N. Amer. | 1758 |
| pulchéllum, 7 | . Lilac | . 7, F. Her. P. Mexico | . 1827 |
| Richardsòni | . Drk. pur. | 7, H. Her. P. Columbia | . 1825 |
| ròseùm, 8 | . . Rose | . F. Her. P. Mexico | . 1825 |
| Scoulèri | . Purple | . 5, H. Her. P. N. Amer. | 1827 |
| speciòsùm | . Blue | . 8, H. Her. P. N. Amer. | 1827 |
| staticæfòlìùm | . Lilac | . 6, H. Her. P. California | 1833 |
| triphýllùm | . Pa. red | . 7, H. Her. P. California | 1827 |
| venùstùm | . . Purple | . 7, H. Her. P. N. Amer. | 1827 |

**PENTZIA.** Named by Thunberg, in honour of his pupil Charles John Pentz. *Linn.* 19, Or. 1, Nat. Or. *Compositæ.* A bushy, hoary-branching shrub, with corymbs of little yellow flowers; it grows in a

mixture of loam and peat, and ripened cuttings root freely in sand, under a glass. Synonyme: 1. *P. crenata, Tanacetum flabelliforme.*

| | | | | | |
|---|---|---|---|---|---|
| flabellifórmis, 1 | . Yellow | . 6, G. Ev. S. C. G. H. | . 1774 |

**PEPEROMIA,** *Ruiz and Pavon.* Analogous to Piper. *Linn.* 2, Or. 3, Nat. Or. *Piperaceæ.* This is the herbaceous tribe of Pepper. The species grow freely in an equal mixture of sandy loam and peat, and may be increased by cuttings, or divisions of the roots.

| | | | | | |
|---|---|---|---|---|---|
| acuminàta | . . Apetal | . 6, S. Her. P. W. Ind. | . 1812 |
| alàta | . . . Apetal | . 8, S. Her. P. S. Amer. | . 1812 |
| amplexicaùlis | . Apetal | . 7, S. Her. P. W. Ind. | . 1793 |
| amplexifòlia | . Apetal | . 3, S. Her. P. S. Amer. | . 1823 |
| blànda | . . . Apetal | . 8, S. Her. P. Caraccas | . 1802 |
| brachyphýlla | . Apetal | . 7, S. Her. P. S. Amer. | . 1818 |
| capénsis | . . Green | . 5, S. Ev. Cr. C. G. H. | . 1820 |
| clusiæfòlia | . Green | . 5, S. Ev. S. Amer. | . 1817 |
| coriàcéa | . . Apetal | . 5, S. Ev. S. E. Ind. | . 1815 |
| cuneifòlia | . . Apetal | . 6, S. Her. P. Caraccas | 1809 |
| discòlór | . . Apetal | . 7, S. Her. P. S. Amer. | . 1821 |
| distàchyà | . . Apetal | . 6, S. Her. P. S. Amer. | . 1793 |
| hispídùla | . Apetal | . 8, G. B. Jamaica | . 1818 |
| hùmilis | . . Apetal | . 6, S. Her. P. W. Ind. | . 1768 |
| inæqualifòlia | . Apetal | . 7, S. Her. P. Peru | . 1800 |
| incàna | . . Apetal | . 2, S. Her. P. Brasil | . 1815 |
| macrostàchyà | . Green | . 5, S. Ev. Cr. Trinidad | . 1824 |
| magnoliæfòlia | . Apetal | . 2, S. Her. P. W. Ind. | . 1793 |
| maculòsa | . . Apetal | . 9, S. Her. P. St. Domin. | 1790 |
| nummulariæfòlia | Apetal | . 6, S. Her. P. W. Ind. | . 1818 |
| obtusifòlia | . Apetal | . 6, S. Her. P. W. Ind. | . 1789 |
| ovalifòlia | . . Green | . 5, S. Ev. Cr. St. Vincent | 1824 |
| pellùcida | . . Apetal | . 5, S. A. S. Amer. | . 1748 |
| pereskiæfòlia | . Apetal | . 5, S. Her. P. S. Amer. | . 1820 |
| polystàchyà | . Apetal | . 6, S. Her. P. Jamaica | . 1775 |
| pubéscens | . . Apetal | . 8, S. Her. P. S. Amer. | . 1809 |
| pulchélla | . . Apetal | . 6, S. Her. P. Jamaica | . 1778 |
| quadrifòlia | . Apetal | . 6, S. Her. P. S. Amer. | . 1818 |
| renifórmis | . Green | . 5, S. Ev. Cr. St. Vincent | 1824 |
| répens | . . Apetal | . 6, S. Ev. Cr. S. Amer. | . 1823 |
| rotundifòlia | . Apetal | . 6, S. Her. P. W. Ind. | . 1822 |
| rubélla | . . Apetal | . 3, S. Her. P. W. Ind. | . 1820 |
| rubricaùlis | . Apetal | . 5, F. Her. P. | . 1822 |
| sérpens | . . Green | . 5, S. Ev. Cr. Jamaica | . 1820 |
| stellàta | . . Apetal | . 6, S. Her. P. Jamaica | . 1802 |
| subrotùnda | . Apetal | . 2, S. Her. P. | . 1812 |
| tallinifòlia | . Green | . 5, S. Ev. Cr. W. Ind. | . 1820 |
| tenélla | . . Green | . 5, S. Ev. Cr. Jamaica | . 1820 |
| tricarinàta | . . Green | . 5, S. Ev. Cr. W. Ind. | . 1818 |
| trifòlia | . . Apetal | . 7, S. Her. P. S. Amer. | . 1802 |
| tristàchyà | . . Green | . 5, S. Ev. Cr. W. Ind. | . 1826 |

**PEPLIS,** *Linn.* The Greek name of *purslane. Linn.* 6, Or. 1, Nat. Or. *Lythraceæ.* The species of *Water Purslane* grow in any very moist soil, in which also the seeds may be sown.

| | | | | | |
|---|---|---|---|---|---|
| alternifòlia | . . Purple | . 7, H. A. Siberia | . 1816 |
| occidentàlis | . . Green | . 7, S. Aq. A. Guadaloupe | 1829 |
| Portùla | . . Purple | . 8, H. Aq. A. Britain | . |

**PEPPER,** see *Piper.*

**PEPPERMINT,** see *Mentha piperita.*

**PEPPERMINT-TREE,** see *Eucalyptus piperita.*

**PEPPER-VINE,** see *Ampelopsis bipinnata.*

**PEPPERWORT,** see *Lepidium.*

**PERDICIUM,** *Linn.* From *perdix,* a partridge; partridges were fond of the original plant. *Linn.* 19, Or. 2, Nat. Or. *Compositæ.* An uninteresting hardy herbaceous plant, succeeding in any common soil. Synonyme. 1. *Tussilago Anandria—P. Anandria* 1.

**PEREGRINOUS,** wandering, diffuse.

**PERENNIAL,** lasting many years without perishing.

**PERESKIA,** *Plumier.* Named in honour of Nicholas F. Pieresk, of Aix, in Provence, a lover of botany. *Linn.* 12, Or 1, Nat. Or. *Cactaceæ.* Grotesque and ornamental plants, very different from the rest of the genera in *Cactaceæ,* from the branches being woody, as well as furnished with proper leaves. The species grow in any light soil; and cuttings root readily in mould, under a glass, in heat. Synonymes: 1. *Cactus Pereskia.* 2. *C. portulacæfolia.*

| | | | | | |
|---|---|---|---|---|---|
| aculeàta, 1 | . . White | . 10, S. De. S. W. Ind. | . 1696 |
| Bleo | . . . Pa. red | . 11, S. De. S. Mexico | . 1827 |
| grandifòlia | . . | . 8, S. De. S. Brasil | . 1818 |
| longispìna | . . . | . 8, S. De. S. S. Amer. | . 1808 |
| portulacæfòlia, 2 | . White | . 8, S. De. S. W. Ind. | . 1820 |

**PERFORATED,** full of holes.

**PERGULARIA,** *Linn.* From *pergula,* trellis-work; twining plants, fit for arbours, &c. *Linn.* 5, Or. 2, Nat. Or. *Asclepiadaceæ.* A genus much prized for the fragrance of the flowers. All the species prefer a rich mould, and are readily multiplied by cuttings.

minŏr . . . . Yel. grn. . 6, S. Ev. Tw. E. Ind. . 1790
odoratissimă . . Green . . 6, S. Ev. Tw. E. Ind. . 1784
sanguinolentă . . Grn. yel. . 7, S. Ev. Tw. S. Leone . 1822

PERIANTH, or PERIANTHIUM, the envelope which surrounds the flower. This term is applied when the calyx cannot be distinguished from the corolla, as in *Lilium*, &c. &c.

PERIBALLĬA, *Trinius*. From *periballo*, to encompass. *Linn.* 3, Or. 2, Nat. Or. *Gramineæ*. A worthless species of grass, growing in any common soil, and increased by seeds. Synonyme: 1. *Aira involucrata*—*P. hispanicá* 1.

PERICALLĬS, *D. Don*. From *perikalles*, very pretty; radial ligulæ beautiful. *Linn.* 19, Or. 2, Nat. Or. *Compositæ*. A very desirable plant; increased by cuttings or seeds, and treated as the *Cinerarias*. Synonyme: 1. *Cineraria tussilaginis, Senecio tussilaginis*.

tussilaginis, 1 . . Purple . 4, G. Her. P. Teneriffe . 1829

PERICARP, the seed-vessel.

PERICHÆNĂ, *Fries*. From *peri*, around, and *ischano*, to encompass. *Linn.* 24, Or. 9, Nat. Or. *Fungi*. Very minute *Fungi*, found on the cones of *Pinus Abies*, and dead trunks of trees—*P. populină, strobilină*.

PERICHÆTIAL, leaves which in mosses surround the base of the stalk of the theca.

PERIGONE, the calyx and corolla.

PERIGYNOUS, inserted in the calyx, or in the disk which adheres to it.

PERILLĂ, *Linn*. The meaning not explained. *Linn.* 14, Or. 1, Nat. Or. *Labiatæ*. Plants of little merit, flourishing in any light loamy soil.

fruticosă . . . . 7, G. Ev. S. Nepal . .
ocymoides . . . White . 7, H. A. India . . 1770

PERILOMĬA, *Humboldt and Bonpland*. From *peri*, around, and *loma*, a fringe; in allusion to the membranaceously-winged achenia. *Linn.* 14, Or. 1, Nat. Or. *Labiatæ*. For the culture and propagation of this pretty species, see *Prostanthera*.

ocymoides . . . Purple . 8, G. Ev. S. Peru . .

PERIOLĂ, *Fries*. From *peri*, about, and *ioulos*, down; appearance of the species when growing. *Linn.* 24, Or. 9, Nat. Or. *Fungi*. A minute fungus, growing on potato roots, &c.—*P. tomentosă*.

PERIPLOCĂ, *Linn*. From *periploke*, an intertwining; alluding to the habit of the plants. *Linn.* 5, Or. 2, Nat. Or. *Asclepiadaceæ*. Handsome species, growing freely in any common soil. *P. græca* is a valuable hardy plant for covering naked walls, &c. They are readily propagated by layers, or cuttings, under a glass.

angustifolĭă . . Purplish . H. De. Tw. S. Eux. . 1800
græcă . . . . Brown . 7, H. De. Tw. Syria . 1597
lævigată . . . Grn. yel. F. Ev. Tw. Canaries . 1779
mauritiană . . . Brown . 8. Ev. Cl. Malabar . 1823

PERIPTERĂ, *Decandolle*. From *periptera*, a shuttlecock; resemblance in the form of the flower. *Linn.* 16, Or. 8, Nat. Or. *Malvaceæ*. A pretty little shrub, growing about three feet high, in a mixture of loam and peat. The species ripens its seed freely, from which it may be increased, as also from cuttings in sand, under a glass. Synonymes: 1. *Sida Periptera, Anoda punicea*.

punĭceă, 1 . . . Crimson . 5, S. Ev. S. N. Spain . 1814

PERIPHERIC, circular, curved.

PERISTERĬĂ, *Hooker*. From *peristera*, a dove; in allusion to the dove-like appearance of the column. *Linn.* 20, Or. 1, Nat. Or. *Orchidaceæ*. This is a genus of splendid plants, the most remarkable and interesting of which is the *P. elata*; it produces a long spike of yellowish-white waxy flowers, yielding a very peculiar fragrance. In the neighbourhood of Panama, it is known to the natives by the appellation of "el Spirito Santo," and the reason for this name is quite obvious on looking at the flower; the centre of it exhibits a column which, with its summit and the projecting gland of the pollen-masses, together with the erect wings, bears a very striking resemblance to the figure of a Dove: whence the English name of the genus Dove-flower. The species should be grown in pots well drained, in a mixture of fibrous loam, leaf-mould, and sandy peat, and must not be overwatered at any season, more especially when torpid; they are increased by separating the pseudo-bulbs.

Barkeri . . . . Yellow . 6, S. Epi. Mexico . 1837
cerina . . . . Yellow . 6, S. Epi. S. Main . 1835
elata . . . . . White . 7, S. Epi. Panama . 1826
guttata . . . . Red yel. . 6, S. Epi. S. Amer. . 1837
pendula . . . . Wht. spot. 9, S. Epi. Panama . .

PERISTOME, the rim which surrounds the orifice of the theca of a moss.

PERITHECĬUM, PERIDĬUM, different kinds of envelopes of the reproductive organs of *Fungi*.

PERITOMĂ, *Decandolle*. From *peritome*, a cutting round about; base of the calyx. *Linn.* 15, Nat. Or. *Capparidaceæ*. The seeds of this plant require to be sown on a gentle hotbed, and the plants, when large enough, to be turned out into a sheltered situation in the flower-garden. Synonyme: 1. *Cleome serrulata*.

serrulată, 1 . . Purple . 7, H. A. Missouri . 1823

PERIWINKLE, see *Vinca*.

PERMANENT, or PERSISTENT, remaining, not falling off.

PEROTĬS, *Aiton*. From *peros*, deficient; alluding to the flower. *Linn.* 3, Or. 2, Nat. Or. *Gramineæ*. An annual species of grass, succeeding in any common garden soil.

latifolĭă . . . . Apetal . 8, Grass. E. Ind. . . 1777

PERPUSILLUS, very small.

PERSEĂ, *Gærtner*. A name applied by Theophrastus to an Egyptian tree. *Linn.* 9, Or. 1, Nat. Or. *Lauraceæ*. This ornamental species succeeds well in a mixture of turfy loam and peat. The best way of propagating it is by layers, which root freely; ripened shoots, taken off at a joint, and planted in sand, under a glass, in heat, will sometimes root. Synonyme: 1. *Laurus Persea*.

gratissimă, 1 . . Grn. yel. . 8. Ev. S. W. Ind. . 1739

PERSIAN SUN'S-EYE, see *Tulipa oculus solis*.

PERSICĂ, *Tournefort*. So named from the Peach-tree coming originally from Persia. *Linn.* 12, Or. 1, Nat. Or. *Rosaceæ*. To this genus belong the well-known and much-esteemed fruits the Peach and Nectarine. The different kinds are propagated by budding on Damask plum-stocks, and new varieties are raised from the stone, after a mixture of the sorts by impregnation. In this country, they are usually trained on south walls in the fan manner, which is allowed to be the most natural. The soil best suited for them is three-parts mellow loam, enriched with one-part vegetable mould. Synonymes: 1. *Amygdalus Persica Nectarina*. 2. *A. Persica*.

lævis, 1 . . . . Red . . 4, H. De. T. Persia . 1562
vulgaris, 2 . . . Red . . 4, H. De. T. Persia . 1562
alba . . . . . White . 4, H. De. S. Persia . .
compressă . . . . . . 4, H. De. T. .
flore-pleno . . Red . . 4, H. De. T. Persia . .
fol. variegatis . . . . 4, H. De. T. Persia . .

PERSOONĬĂ, *Smith*. In honour of C. H. Persoon, a distinguished botanist, the author of Synopsis Plantarum, and other valuable botanical works. *Linn.* 4, Or. 1, Nat. Or. *Proteaceæ*. An ornamental genus of plants, growing from five to seven feet high, and thriving well in a mixture, of equal parts of loam, peat, and sand; and cuttings of the ripened wood root in sand, under a glass.

chamæpitys . . . Yellow . 6, G. Ev. S. N. Holl. . 1824
ferruginea . . . Yel. red. . 6, G. Ev. S. N. S. W. . 1823
hirsută . . . . Yellow . 6, G. Ev. S. N. S. W. . 1800
flexifolĭă . . . Yellow . 6, G. Ev. S. N. Holl. . 1824
juniperina . . . Yellow . 6, G. Ev. S. N. S. W. . 1826
lanceolată . . . Yellow . 6, G. Ev. S. N. S. W. . 1791
latifolĭă . . . Yellow . 6, G. Ev. S. N. S. W. . 1795
linearis . . . . Yellow . 7, G. Ev. S. N. S. W. . 1794
mollis . . . . Yellow . 7, G. Ev. S. N. S. W. . 1826
myrtilloides . . . . . G. Ev. S. N. S. W. . 1837
nutans . . . . Yellow . G. Ev. S. N. Holl. . 1824
pallida . . . . Orange . 7, G. Ev. S. N. Holl. . 1824
pinifolĭă . . . Yellow . 6, G. Ev. S. N. S. W. . 1822
pruinosă . . . Yellow . 6, G. Ev. S. N. S. W. . 1824
salicina . . . . Pink . 7, G. Ev. S. N. S. W. . 1795
scabra . . . . Yellow . 6, G. Ev. S. N. S. W. . 1824
spatulata . . . Yellow . 6, G. Ev. S. N. Holl. . 1824
tenuifolĭă . . . Yellow . 6, G. Ev. S. N. Holl. . 1822

PERTUSARIA, *Acharius*. Derived from *pertusus*, full of holes. *Linn.* 24, Or. 8, Nat. Or. *Lichenes*. A new genus of cryptogamic plants, nearly allied to *Verrucaria*—*P. isidioides*.

PERVIUS, having a passage through which anything can be transmitted.

PESOMERĬĂ, *Thouars*. From *pipto, peso*, to fall, and

*meros*, a part; the sepals are spontaneously thrown off from the flower shortly after they have expanded, just as leaves are thrown off the stems of many of these plants when they receive a sudden check, and then the petals and labellum only remain to constitute the flower. *Linn.* 20, Or. 1, Nat. Or. *Orchidaceæ*. The plant is nearly related to *Blettia* and *Phaius*, but will probably be found to grow best under the treatment given to *Burlingtonia*.

| | | | | |
|---|---|---|---|---|
| tetragóná | . . . Brown | . 12, S. Epi. Maurit. | . . 1837 |

PETAL-LIKE SCALES in *Alsinaceæ* and *Silenaceæ*, the scales which are fixed to the throat of the petals.

PETALOSTÉMÜM, *Michaux*. From *petalon*, a petal, and *stemon*, a stamen; the stamens are joined to the petals at the base. *Linn.* 16, Or. 2, Nat. Or. *Leguminosa*. Pretty herbaceous plants, growing in any border soil; young plants are readily obtained by divisions. *Synonyme*: 1. *Dalea Kuhnistera*.

| | | | | |
|---|---|---|---|---|
| cándidüm | . . . White | . 7, F. Her. | P. N. Amer. | . 1811 |
| carnéüm | . . . Flesh | . 7, F. Her. | P. N. Amer. | . 1811 |
| corymbósüm, 1 | . White | . 8, H. Her. | P. N. Amer. | . 1811 |
| violácéüm | . . Violet | . 8, H. Her. | P. N. Amer. | . 1811 |

PETALS, divisions of a corolla.

PETIOLATE, or PETIOLED, having footstalks.

PETIOLULATE, having little petioles.

PETIVÉRIA. Named by Linnæus in honour of J. Petiver, F.R.S., a London apothecary. *Linn.* 7, Or. 1, Nat. Or. *Petiveraceæ*. Ornamental plants, growing in a mixture of loam and peat; they propagate readily by cuttings under a glass.

| | | | | |
|---|---|---|---|---|
| alliacéa | . . . White | . 6, S. Ev. S. | Jamaica | . 1759 |
| octándra | . . . White | . 6, S. Ev. S. | W. Ind. | . 1737 |

PETRÉA. Linnæus dedicated this genus to Robert James, Lord Petre, a famous patron of botany, who died in 1742. *Linn.* 14, Or. 2, Nat. Or. *Verbenaceæ*. Beautiful stove plants. *P. volubilis* is one of the most handsome stove twiners we possess. To grow them well, they must be planted in good rich mould, and kept in a strong heat. They may be propagated readily by cuttings under a glass.

| | | | | |
|---|---|---|---|---|
| erécta | . . . Blue | . . S. Ev. S. | S. Amer. | . 1823 |
| rugósa | . . . Blue | . . S. Ev. S. | Caraccas | . 1824 |
| Stapéliä | . . . Lilac | . 6. S. Ev. Cl. | S. Amer. | |
| volubilis | . . . Purple | 7, S. Ev. Tw. | Vera Cruz | . 1733 |

PETROBIÜM, *R. Brown*. From *petros*, a rock, and *bio*, to live; habitation of the species. *Linn.* 19, Or. 1, Nat. Or. *Compositæ*. An ornamental shrub, growing well in sandy loam; and cuttings root without difficulty in the same kind of soil. *Synonymes*: 1. *Bidens arborea, Spilanthes arborea*.

| | | | | |
|---|---|---|---|---|
| arbóreüm, 1 | . . Pa. yel. | . 8. Ev. S. | St. Helena | . 1816 |

PETROCALLIS, *R. Brown*. From *petros*, a rock, and *kalos*, beautiful; the plant adorns the rocks on which it grows. *Linn.* 15, Nat. Or. *Cruciferæ*. This little plant is well fitted for ornamenting rock-work, or it may be grown in pots, in a mixture of sandy loam and peat, and is multiplied by seeds, or divisions at the root. *Synonyme*: 1. *Draba pyrenaica*.

| | | | | |
|---|---|---|---|---|
| pyrenáicá, 1 | . . Pink | . 5, G. Her. | P. Pyrenees | . 1759 |

PETROMARÜLA, *A. Decandolle*. From *petros*, a rock, and *maron*, a bitter herb. *Linn.* 5, Or. 1, Nat. Or. *Campanulaceæ*. This plant requires to be grown in a sheltered situation, and protected by a frame in winter; it may be increased by divisions. *Synonyme*: 1. *Phyteuma pinnata*.

| | | | | |
|---|---|---|---|---|
| pinnáta, 1 | . . Pa. blue | . 8, F. Her. | P. Candia | . 1640 |

PETROPHILA, *R. Brown*. From *petros*, a stone, and *phileo*, to love; in allusion to the places in which the plants are found. *Linn.* 4, Or. 1, Nat. Or. *Proteaceæ*. A genus of ornamental shrubs, nearly related to *Protea*, to which genus they may be referred for culture and propagation. *Synonyme*: 1. *Protea fucifolia*.

| | | | | |
|---|---|---|---|---|
| aciculáris | . . Wht. red | . 5, G. Ev. S. | N. Holl. | . 1830 |
| canéscens | . . | . G. Ev. S. | N. Holl. | . 1830 |
| diversifólia | . . | . G. Ev. S. | N. Holl. | . 1803 |
| fastigiátá | . . | . 7, G. Ev. S. | N. Holl. | . 1820 |
| ilicifólia | . . White | . 6, G. Ev. S. | N. Holl. | . 1824 |
| pedunculátá | . . White | . 7, G. Ev. S. | N. Holl. | . 1824 |
| pulchélla, 1 | . . White | . 7, G. Ev. S. | N. S. W. | . 1790 |
| rigidá | . . . White | . 6, G. Ev. S. | N. Holl. | . 1823 |
| teretifólia | . . White | . 7, G. Ev. S. | N. Holl. | . 1824 |
| trifidá | . . . White | . 7, G. Ev. S. | N. Holl. | . 1820 |

PETROSELINÜM, *Hoffmann*. From *petros*, a rock, and *selinon*, parsley; habitation of the species. *Linn.*

5, Or. 2, Nat. Or. *Umbelliferæ*. *P. sativum*, the common Parsley, is a well-known culinary herb. The seeds of all the species may be sown in spring, in the open ground. *Synonymes*: 1. *Apium Petroselinum*. 2. *Sison segetum*. 3. *Ligusticum peregrinum*.

| | | | | |
|---|---|---|---|---|
| sativüm, 1 | . . Lgt. yel. | . 6, H. | B. Sardinia | . 1548 |
| segetüm, 2 | . . White | . 7, H. | A. Britain | |
| peregrinüm, 3 | . White | . 6, H. | B. Portugal | . 1633 |

PETTY-WHIN, see *Genistá anglicá*.

PETÜNIA, *Jussieu*. The Brazilian name for tobacco is *Petun*; applied to this genus because of its affinity with *Nicotiana*. *Linn.* 5, Or. 1, Nat. Or. *Solanaceæ*. A highly ornamental genus of free-flowering plants, well adapted for turning out in beds or borders during summer. They will grow in any light soil, but prefer a mixture of sandy loam and vegetable mould; cuttings will strike at any season in heat, care being taken to keep them from damp. *Synonymes*: 1. *Salpiglossis linearis, Nierembergia intermedia*. 2. *Nicotiana nyctaginiflora*. 3. *P. phœnicea, Nierembergia phœnicea, Salpiglossis integrifolia*.

| | | | | |
|---|---|---|---|---|
| acumináta | . . White | . 7, F. Her. | P. Chile | . 1827 |
| Atkinsiáná | . Crim. pur. | 7, H. | A. Hybrid | . 1834 |
| intermédia, 1 | . Yrl. pur. | 8, F. Her. | P. B. Ayres | . 1832 |
| nyctaginiflóra, 2 | White | . 8, F. Her. | P. S. Amer. | . 1823 |
| violácéá, 3 | . Rose pur. | 8, F. Her. | P. B. Ayres | . 1831 |

PEUCEDÁNÜM, *Koch*. From *peuke*, a pine, and *danos*, parched; so named because of its strong resinous smell. *Linn.* 5, Or. 2, Nat. Or. *Umbelliferæ*. The species are of no interest, and will grow in any common garden soil. *Synonymes*: 1. *Cnidium alsaticum*. 2. *Selinum venetum*. 3. *S. austriacum*. 4. *S. baicalense*. 5. *S. peucedanoides*. 6. *S. polymorphum*. 7. *S. Oreoselinum*. 8. *S. gallicum*. 9. *S. elegans, P. lineare*. 10. *S. Bellardi*. 11. *P. tauricum*. 12. *P. palustre, Thysselinum palustre*. 13. Heracleum pumilum—*P. álbüm, alpéstré, alsaticüm* 1, *A. albiflórüm* 2, *arenárium, aúréüm, austriacüm* 3, *baicalénsé* 4, *daüricüm, involucrátüm* 5, *iseténsé, longifóliüm, montánüm* 6, *officinálé, O. italicüm, Oreoselínüm* 7, *paniculátüm, parisiénsé* 8, *rablénsé* 9, *R. Bellárdi* 10, *rupéstré, ruthenicüm, R. tauricüm* 11, *seseloídés, sibiricüm, S. sylváticüm* 12, *tenuifóliüm, Vocontiórüm* 13.

PEÜMÜS, *Persoon*. From *Peumo*, its Chilian name. *Linn.* 22, Or. 2, Nat. Or. *Monimiaceæ*. An odoriferous tree, attaining the height of thirty feet; it delights in peaty loam, and ripened cuttings root readily in sand.

| | | | | |
|---|---|---|---|---|
| fragrans | . . . | . S. Ev. T. | Chile | . . 1824 |

PEYROÜSIA, *Decandolle*. In honour of La Peyrouse, the French navigator. *Linn.* 3, Or. 1, Nat. Or. *Iridaceæ*. A genus of fine bulbous plants, requiring the same treatment as *Ixia*. *Synonyme*: 1. *Galaxia plicata*.

| | | | | |
|---|---|---|---|---|
| aculeátá | . . Blu. yel. | . 6, G. Bl. P. | C. G. H. | . 1825 |
| áncéps | . . . Blue | . 9, F. Bl. P. | C. G. H. | . 1824 |
| corymbósá | . . Blue | . 5, F. Bl. P. | C. G. H. | . 1791 |
| Fabricii | . . . Blue | . 6, G. Bl. P. | C. G. H. | . 1825 |
| falcátá | . . . Blue | . 5, G. Bl. P. | C. G. H. | . 1825 |
| fasciculátá, 1 | . Blue | . 5, G. Bl. P. | C. G. H. | . 1825 |
| flexifólia | . . Violet | . 8, G. Bl. P. | C. G. H. | . 1809 |
| silenoídés | . . Violet | . 6, G. Bl. P. | C. G. H. | . 1822 |

PEZIZA, *Dillwyn*. Name derived from *Pesica*, a tribe of fungi in Pliny. *Linn.* 24, Or. 9, Nat. Or. *Fungi*. This is a very extensive genus, containing some of the most beautiful of our fungi, which appear in the end of autumn on decayed wood, or in places where trees have formerly stood; they are in the form of small undulated scarlet cups. *Synonymes*: 1. *P. cyathoides*. 2. *P. epidendra*. 3. *P. albella*—*P. Abbotiáná, acetabúlá, aciculáris, æruginósá, agaricíná, álbó-spadicéá, albo-violascéns, amórphá, anomálá, arenósá, A. salicíná, argilláceá, Aspegrénii, atrátá, atrorúfá, atro-virens, auratiá, axilláris, bádiá, bicólór, boláris, buccíná, cærúlá, cæsiá, calyculús, campanúlá, cérá, ceríná, chrysocómá, cinérá, citríná* 1, *clandestíná, clarsflává, cochleátá, coccíneá* 2, *compréssá, concíná, conigérá, cribrósá, cupuláris, domesticá, epiphériá, erráticá, erúmpens, faginá, fasciculáris, fibuliformis, fírmá, flssá, flexéllá, fructigérá, furfuráceá, fuscá, fuscaríoídés, granulátá, Grevillii, hemisphæricá, herbárüm, hírtá, hispidálá, humósá, hyaliná,* inflātā, leporīnā, leucolōmā, leucostigmā, macrōpus, Marchāntiā, melalōmā, melastōmā, melaxānthā, nidālā, ochrāctā, onotīcā, pallēscens, papillāris, pedicellātā, Persoōnii, phascoīdēs, pinātī, plānō-umbilicātā, plumbēā, punctātā, radiculātā, Rāpūlism, repandnā, reticulātā, rhabarbarīnā, Rōsā, rufo-olivācēā, rutilāns, saniōsā, sclerotioīdēs, serotīnā, stercorēā, subtīlis, sulphūrēā, tricolōr, tūbā, tuberōsā, variecolōr, vesiculōsā, villōsā, vinōsā, virgīntā, vitellīnā, vulgāris 3, V. diaphānā, Wauchii, xanthostīgmā.

**Phaca**, *Linn.* From *phago*, to eat; a name adopted from Dioscorides. *Linn.* 17, Or. 4, Nat. Or. *Leguminosæ*. Ornamental herbaceous plants, growing well in the open borders, in common garden soil; they are all increased by dividing the plants at the root, or by seeds, which is by far the best method of propagating them. *Synonymes*: 1. *P. membranacea*. 2. *Astragalus leontinus, oroboides*.

| | | | | | | |
|---|---|---|---|---|---|---|
| alpīnā | . | . | Pa. yel. | . 7, H. Her. P. | Austria | . 1759 |
| dahurīcā, 1 | . | . | Pa. yel. | . 7, H. Her. P. | Dahuria | . 1820 |
| arenārīā | . | . | Cream | . 7, H. Her. P. | Siberia | . 1798 |
| astragalīnā | . | . | Wht. blu. | . 7, H. Her. P. | Scotland | . |
| austrālis | . | . | Pa. pur. | . 5, H. De. Tr. | S. Eur. | . 1779 |
| bœtīcā | . | . | White | . 5, H. Her. P. | Spain | . 1640 |
| canēscēns | . | . | Pa. rose | . 7, G. Her. P. | Valparaiso | . 1831 |
| densifolīā | . | . | Red | . 7, H. Her. P. | California | . 1822 |
| exaltātā | . | . | | . 7, H. Her. P. | Altai | . 1828 |
| frīgīdā | . | . | Cream | . 7, H. Her. P. | Austria | . 1795 |
| glabrā | . | . | White | . 7, H. De. Tr. | S. France | . 1818 |
| lappōnīcā | . | . | Purple | . 7, H. Her. P. | N. Eur. | . 1816 |
| lūtēā | . | . | Yellow | . 7, H. Her. P. | Siberia | . 1827 |
| oroboīdēs, 2 | . | . | Purple | . 7, H. Her. P. | Norway | . 1820 |
| triangulāris | . | . | Blue | . 7, H. Her. P. | Siberia | . 1824 |

**Phacelia**, *Jussieu.* From *Phakelos*, a bundle; in reference to the disposition of the flowers. *Linn.* 5, Or. 1, Nat. Or. *Hydrophyllaceæ*. Hardy plants of some beauty, flourishing in any common garden soil; young plants may be obtained by divisions or seeds. *Synonyme*: 1. *Hydrophyllum magellanicum*.

| | | | | | | |
|---|---|---|---|---|---|---|
| Aldēā | . | . | Pink | . 6, H. Her. P. | Peru | . 1824 |
| bipinnatifidā | . | . | Blue | . 6, H. Her. P. | N. Amer. | . 1824 |
| circinātā, 1 | . | . | Pink | . 6, H. Her. P. | Magellan | . 1817 |
| congēstā | . | . | Pur. blue | . 6, H. | A. Texas | . 1835 |
| tanacetifolīā | . | . | Blue | . 6, H. | A. California | . 1832 |
| vinifolīā | . | . | Lgt. blue | . 9, H. | A. Texas | . 1834 |

**Phacidīum**, *Fries.* From *phakos*, a lentil, and *eidos*, similar. *Linn.* 24, Or. 9, Nat. Or. *Fungi.* Curious species, found on oak-leaves, both in a living and dead state, raspberry-leaves, &c.—*P. carbondēum, coronātum, densātum, Laurocerāsi, Pīni, repāndum, Rūbi.*

**Phacosperma**, *Haworth.* From *phakos*, a lentil, and *sperma*, seed. *Linn.* 11, Or. 1, Nat. Or. *Portulacaceæ*. An ornamental plant, succeeding in peat and loam. The best way to obtain young plants is from seed, which it ripens freely.

| | | | | | | |
|---|---|---|---|---|---|---|
| peruviānā | . | . | Purple | . 5, S. Her. P. | Peru | . 1820 |

**Phænogamous**, such plants as possess visible sexual organs.

**Phaīus**, *Loureiro.* From *phaios*, shining; in allusion to the beauty of the original species. *Linn.* 20, Or. 1, Nat. Or. *Orchidaceæ*. This is an interesting and valuable genus of plants, especially *P. albus*, which ought to be in every collection of orchidaceous plants; the following is the best way of cultivating it:—When the plant becomes dormant, it should be placed in a cool house, the temperature of which, in winter, should not be more than 45 or 50 degrees. After reposing the proper time, it will begin to push from the base of the stems; and when the young shoots are about half an inch in length, the plants should be repotted into heath soil, well drained at the bottom, and mingled with an abundance of finely-broken potsherds, according to the usual method of cultivating orchidaceous plants. For a moderate-sized plant, the pot should be about six inches in diameter at the top, which will allow of its completing the annual growth without being again potted. It will bear a free supply of water when growing vigorously, and may then be syringed once or twice a day, till it shows signs of flowering, when the syringing must be discontinued. When it has ceased flowering, it should be kept in a cool house, and sparingly watered until the leaves begin to turn yellow, when it must be removed to its winter quarters, and kept dry, merely supplying as much water as will keep the plant alive, and

taking care never to wet the stems; for the culture of the other species, see *Bletia*. *Synonymes*: 1. *Bletia Tankervilliæ.* 2. *B. Woodfordii.*

| | | | | | | |
|---|---|---|---|---|---|---|
| albus | . | . | White | . 7, S. Epi. | Sylhet | . 1836 |
| bicŏlŏr | . | . | Brn. yel. | . 5, S. Epi. | Ceylon | . |
| grandifolīus, 1 | . | . | Wht. brn. | . 4, S. Ter. | China | . 1778 |
| maculātus, 2 | . | . | Grn. yel. | . 5, S. Ter. | Nepal | . 1823 |
| Wallichii | . | . | Oran. yel. | . 4, S. Ter. | Khoosm | . 1837 |

**Phalænopsis**, *Blume.* From *phalaina*, a moth, and *opsis*, resemblance; in allusion to the appearance of the flower, which bears a striking resemblance to that insect: whence the name Indian Butterfly-plant. *Linn.* 20, Or. 1, Nat. Or. *Orchidaceæ*. This is a very rare and extremely beautiful plant. The flowers are produced on a nearly erect spike, and are very elegant, on account of their large size and the brilliant whiteness of the broad leathery petals. It requires a very hot, damp part of the house, and is otherwise treated as the genus *Vanda*. It can only be increased from side shoots, which it does not appear to throw out freely.

| | | | | | |
|---|---|---|---|---|---|
| amabilis | . | . | Wht. yel. | 6, S. Epi. Manilla | . 1836 |

**Phalangium**, *Decandolle.* From *phalanx*, a venomous spider; said to cure the bite. *Linn.* 6, Or. 1, Nat. Or. *Liliaceæ.* The greenhouse and frame species of this ornamental genus grow well in an equal mixture of sandy loam and peat: the hardy species do well in any light rich soil; they may all be increased by division at the root, or by seeds. *Synonymes*: 1. *Anthericum Liliago.* 2. *Anthericum ramosum.*

| | | | | | | |
|---|---|---|---|---|---|---|
| glaucūm | . | . | White | . 7, F. Her. P. | Peru | . 1823 |
| Liliāgo, 1 | . | . | White | . 5, H. Her. P. | S. Eur. | . 1596 |
| minŏr | . | . | White | . 5, H. Her. P. | S. Eur. | . 1596 |
| longifolīūm | . | . | Green | . 9, G. Her. P. | Lima | . 1829 |
| nepalēnsē | . | . | White | . 5, F. Her. P. | Nepal | . 1824 |
| ramōsūm, 2 | . | . | White | . 5, H. Her. P. | S. Eur. | . 1570 |

**Phalaris**, *Linn.* From *phaluros*, brilliant; having shining seeds. *Linn.* 3, Or. 2, Nat. Or. *Gramineæ.* Mostly uninteresting species. *P. commutata* and *appendiculata* are rather pretty; *P. canariensis* is cultivated on account of its seeds (canary-seed), which are given to birds; they merely require to be sown in any common soil.

| | | | | | | |
|---|---|---|---|---|---|---|
| appendiculātā | . | . | Apetal | . 6, Gram. | Egypt | . 1820 |
| canariēnsis | . | . | Apetal | . 7, Gram. | Britain | . |
| commutātā | . | . | Apetal | . 6, Gram. | Italy | . 1823 |

*aquatīcā, bulbōsā, cærulēscens, capēnsis, microstāchgā, minŏr, nĭtĭdā, nodōsā, paradōxā, quadrivālvis.*

**Phalerocarpus**, *G. Don.* From *phaleros*, white, and *karpus*, fruit; because of the colour of the fruit. *Linn.* 8, Or. 1, Nat. Or. *Ericaceæ.* This pretty little plant may be referred to *Oxycoccus* for culture and propagation. *Synonymes*: 1. *Gaultheria serpyllifolia, Oxycoccus hispidulus.*

| | | | | | |
|---|---|---|---|---|---|
| serpyllifolīā, 1 | . | White. | . 4, H. Ev. Cr. N. Amer. | . 1815 |

**Phalilus**, *Michaux.* From *phallos*, signifying a wooden club. *Linn.* 24, Or. 9, Nat. Or. *Fungi.* Fœtid-smelling fungi, found in woods and hedges, on hazel trunks, &c.—*P. canīnus, fœtidus, iōmŏs.*

**Phalocallis**, *Herbert.* Not explained by its author. *Linn.* 3, Or. 1, Nat. Or. *Iridaceæ.* This remarkable plant produces a delicate and beautiful flower on a strong and tall stem. It will, perhaps, be found to succeed well under a warm south wall in the open ground; seeds. *Synonyme*: 1. *Capella plumbea.*

| | | | | | |
|---|---|---|---|---|---|
| plumbēā, 1 | . | . Lead col. | . 7, F. Bl. P. Mexico | . 1837 |

**Pharbitis**, *Choisy.* Meaning not explained. *Linn.* 5, Or. 1, Nat. Or. *Convolvulaceæ.* This is a genus of very showy, tender annuals. The seed should be sown on a hotbed, and when the plants are large enough, they should be planted into pots, in a mixture of sandy loam and decayed leaves; and afterwards treated as other tender annuals. *Synonymes*: 1. *Ipomæa barbata.* 2. *I. barbigera.* 3. *I. cærulescens.* 4. *I. cuspidata.* 5. *I. Dillenii.* 6. *I. hederacea.* 7. *I. hispida.* 8. *I. Nil, I. cærulea.* 9. *I. punctata.* 10. *I. scabra.* 11. *I. varia.*

| | | | | | | |
|---|---|---|---|---|---|---|
| barbātā, 1 | . | . | | . 9, H. Tw. A. | Virginia | . 1729 |
| barbigerā, 2 | . | . | Blue | . 9, H. Tw. A. | N. Amer. | . |
| cærulēscens, 3 | . | . | Pa. blue | . 7, H. Ev. Tw. | E. Ind. | . 1820 |
| cuspidātā, 4 | . | . | Purple | . 9, H. Tw. A. | Peru | . 1732 |
| Dillēnii, 5 | . | . | Blue | . 6, G. Tw. A. | Æthiopia | . |
| diversifolīā | . | . | Blue | . 6, G. Tw. A. | Mexico | . 1836 |
| hederācēā, 6 | . | . | Blue | . 8, H. Tw. A. | N. Amer. | . 1729 |

| | | | | | | |
|---|---|---|---|---|---|---|
| bisplda, 7 | . | Wht. pur. | 8, S. Tw. A. | E. Ind. | . | 1629 |
| Nil, 8 | . | Blue | 8, G. Tw. A. | America | . | 1597 |
| punctàtà, 9 | . | Pur. vio. | 8, G. Tw. A. | India | . | |
| scàbrà, 10 | . | White | 9, S. Tw. A. | | . | 1823 |
| vàrfà, 11 | . | Blue vio. | 9, S. Ev. Tw. | | . | 1816 |

PHAXIOM, see *Bèsèrà*.

PHARMACEUTICAL, relating to the art of pharmacy.

PHARNACEUM, *Linn.* Pharnaces, king of Pontus, is said to have first used it in medicine. *Linn.* 5, Or. 3, Nat. Or. *Illecebraceæ.* Plants of little beauty, hardly worth cultivating except in botanical collections. The stove and greenhouse shrubby species thrive well in sandy loam and peat; and cuttings root readily, in the same kind of soil, if placed under a glass. The annual kinds should be sown in pots in the spring, and placed in a moderate hotbed, where they may remain till they are removed into the greenhouse in June. Synonymes: 1. *Mollugo bellidifolia.* 2. *M. spergula.*

| | | | | | | |
|---|---|---|---|---|---|---|
| bellidifòlium, 1 | . | White | 7, S. | A. W. Ind. | . | 1823 |
| Cerviànum | . | White | 6, H. | A. Russia | . | 1771 |
| cordifòlium | . | White | 7, F. | A. C. G. H. | . | 1823 |
| dichòtòmûm | . | White | 7, F. | A. C. G. H. | . | 1788 |
| glomeràtûm | . | White | 7, G. | A. C. G. H. | . | 1817 |
| Hoffmansèggiànûm | White | 7, S. Cr. | A. Brasil | . | 1829 |
| incànûm | . | White | 7, G. Ev. S. | C. G. H. | . | 1782 |
| linèàrè | . | White | 5, G. Ev. S. | C. G. H. | . | 1795 |
| Mollûgò, 2 | . | White | 7, S. | A. E. Ind. | . | 1752 |
| pruinòsûm | . | | 7, G. Ev. S. | C. G. H. | . | 1819 |
| spergulòîdès | . | | 7, S. | A. E. Ind. | . | 1819 |
| umbellàtûm | . | Brown | 7, H. | A. Egypt | . | 1820 |

PHARUS, *Linn.* From *pharos*, a covering; the long broad leaves are used as wrappers for various articles in Jamaica. *Linn.* 21, Or. 6, Nat. Or. *Gramineæ.* A fine stove species, succeeding in rich loamy soil; young plants may be obtained from seed.

| | | | | | | |
|---|---|---|---|---|---|---|
| latifòlîûs | . | Green | . 7, Grass. | Jamaica | . | 1793 |

PHASCUM, *Linn.* From *phaskon*, an ancient Greek name for a moss. *Linn.* 24, Or. 5, Nat. Or. *Musci.* Minute species of moss, often scarcely discernible to the naked eye, and varying much in appearance from each other; they grow on moist banks, in clay fields, &c. Synonymes: 1. *P. Schreberianum, curvisetum.* 2. *P. strictum.* 3. *P. multicapsulare.* 4. *P. stoloniferum—P. alternifòlîûm, apiculàtûm* 1, *axillàrè* 2, *bryoîdès, crassinerviûm, crispûm* 3, *C. rostellàtûm, curvifòlîûm, cuspidàtûm, muticûm, M. màjûs, P. minûs, pàtèns, M. recurvifòlîûm, pilîfèrûm, rèctûm, serràtûm* 4, *subulàtûm.*

PHASEOLUS, *Linn.* From *phaselus*, a little boat; fancied resemblance in the pods. *Linn.* 17, Or. 4, Nat. Or. *Leguminosæ.* The different varieties of kidney-bean belong to this genus: they all thrive in any rich light soil. The annual kinds are increased by seeds, and the perennials by seeds or cuttings. Synonymes: 1. *P. trilobus.* 2. *P. hirtus.* 3. *Dolichos polystachyos.*

| | | | | | | |
|---|---|---|---|---|---|---|
| aconitifòlîûs | . | Pink | . 7, S. Tw. A. | E. Ind. | . | 1731 |
| amœnûs | . | Red | . 7, H. Tw. A. | Society Is. | . | 1820 |
| angulòsûs | . | Pa. red | . 7, H. Tw. A. | N. Amer. | . | 1820 |
| Caracàllà | . | Lilac | 8, S. De. | Tw. India | . | 1690 |
| chrysànthôs | . | Yellow | . 7, H. | A. | | |
| comprèssûs | . | White | . 7, H. Tw. A. | | | |
| deràtûs | . | Wht. grn. | 7, H. Tw. A. | Brasil | . | 1819 |
| gonospèrmûs | . | Pa. vio. wht. | 7, H. Tw. A. | | | |
| hæmatocàrpûs | . | Pa. vio. | 7, H. Tw. A. | | | |
| helvòlûs | . | Pa. red | . 7, H. Tw. A. | Carolina | . | 1732 |
| heterophyllûs | . | Red | . 6, H. Tw. A. | Mexico | . | 1820 |
| lathyroîdès | . | Scarlet | . 7, H. Tw. A. | Jamaica | . | 1786 |
| lunàtûs | . | Green | . 7, S. Tw. A. | E. Ind. | . | 1779 |
| Max | . | Green | . 6, H. Tw. A. | Moluccas | . | 1758 |
| microspèrmûs | . | Drk. pur. | 6, S. Tw. A. | Cuba | . | 1825 |
| multiflòrûs | . | Scarlet | . 7, H. De. | Tw. S. Amer. | . | 1633 |
| albiflòrûs | . | White | . 8, H. De. | Tw. S. Amer. | . | 1633 |
| Mûngò, 2 | . | Yellow | . 6, H. Tw. A. | India | . | 1790 |
| oblòngûs | . | Pa. vio. | 8, H. Tw. A. | | | |
| perènnîs, 3 | . | Drk. pur. | 7, H. De. | Tw. Carolina | . | 1824 |
| saponàceûs | . | White | . 8, H. Tw. A. | | | |
| scàbèr | . | Yel. grn. | 7, H. Tw. A. | E. Ind. | . | |
| semierèctûs | . | Red | . 7, H. Tw. A. | W. Ind. | . | 1781 |
| speciòsûs | . | Scarlet | . 7, S. De. | Tw. Orinoco | . | 1820 |
| sylvèstrîs | . | Scarlet | . 7, G. De. | Tw. Mexico | . | 1825 |
| tortôsûs | . | Violet | . 7, H. Tw. A. | Nepal | . | 1818 |
| tumidûs | . | White | . 7, H. Tw. A. | | | |
| vexillàtûs | . | Orn. pur. | 7, H. Tw. A. | Carolina | . | 1732 |
| violàceûs | . | Violet | . 7, S. Tw. A. | Africa | . | 1800 |
| vulgàrîs | . | White | . 7, H. De. | Tw. India | . | 1597 |
| fasciàtûs | . | White | . 7, H. De. | Tw. India | . | 1597 |
| variegàtûs | . | White | . 7, H. De. | Tw. India | . | 1597 |
| Xuarèsîî | . | Red | . 7, H. Tw. A. | S. Amer. | . | 1818 |

*alàtûs, diversifòlîûs* 1, *farinòsûs, inamœnûs, nànûs, radiàtûs, stipulàrîs, subtrilobàtûs, trilòbûs.*

[ 241 ]

PHAYLOPSIS, *Willdenow.* From *phaylos*, contemptible, and *opsis*, appearance. *Linn.* 14, Or. 2, Nat. Or. *Acanthaceæ.* Plants of little beauty, growing in light rich soil; young cuttings in the same sort of soil, placed under a glass, in heat, will root in a few days. Synonymes: 1. *Ætheilema imbricata.*

| | | | | | | |
|---|---|---|---|---|---|---|
| glutinòsà | . | White | . 5, S. Her. | P. Guinea | . | 1824 |
| imbricàtà, 1 | . | White | . 5, S. Har. | P. Maurit. | . | 1822 |
| longifòlîà | . | White | . 7, S. Ev. S. | S. Leone | . | 1822 |

PHEASANT'S EYE, see *Adònîs autumnàlîs.*

PHEBALIUM, *Ventenat.* From *phibale*, a myrtle; appearance of the species. *Linn.* 10, Or. 1, Nat. Or *Rutaceæ.* Ornamental species, requiring a mixture of three parts sandy peat, and one part sandy loam; cuttings of the young wood root readily in sand, under a glass.

| | | | | | | |
|---|---|---|---|---|---|---|
| aûreûm | . | Golden | . 5, G. Ev. S. | N. Holl. | . | 1823 |
| elàtûm | . | Yellow | . 5, G. Ev. S. | N. S. W. | . | 1825 |
| lachnoîdès | . | Yellow | . 5, G. Ev. S. | N. Holl. | . | 1824 |
| linèàrè | . | Yellow | . 6, G. Ev. S. | N. Holl. | . | 1825 |
| salicifòlîûm | . | Yellow | . 6, G. Ev. S. | N. Holl. | . | 1825 |
| squamulôsûm | . | Yellow | . 5, G. Ev. S. | N. Holl. | . | 1824 |

PHELLANDRIUM, *Linn.* From *phello*, to deceive, and *aner*, a man. *Linn.* 5, Or. 2, Nat. Or. *Umbelliferæ.* A curious little plant, growing by the sides of rivers, in muddy ditches, or pools. Linnæus says it will render horses paralytic, which is caused by a coleopterous insect which breeds in the stalks.

| | | | | | | |
|---|---|---|---|---|---|---|
| aquaticûm | . | White | . 6, H. | A. Britain | . | |

PHELLOS, signifying a cork.

PHILADELPHUS, *Linn.* The philadelphos of Aristotle is a tree now unknown. *Linn.* 12, Or. 1, Nat. Or. *Philadelphaceæ.* A very handsome and desirable genus of shrubs, producing their elegant blossoms in May and June; they have the appearance, and smell of orange-flowers, only much more powerful. The plants succeed in any common soil, and are readily increased from layers, or suckers. Synonymes: 1. *P. gracilis.* 2. *P. nepalensis.* 3. *P. grandiflorus.*

| | | | | | | |
|---|---|---|---|---|---|---|
| coronàrîûs | . | White | . 5, H. De. S. | S. Eur. | . | 1596 |
| flòre-plèno | . | White | . 5, H. De. S. | S. Eur. | . | |
| foliis-variegàtîs | White | . 5, H. De. S. | S. Eur. | . | |
| nànûs | . | White | . 5, H. De. S. | | | |
| vulgàrîs | . | White | . 5, H. De. S. | | | |
| floribundûs | . | White | . 6, H. De. S. | N. Amer. | . | |
| Gordonianûs | . | White | . 7, H. De. S. | N. Amer. | . | |
| grandiflòrûs | . | White | . 6, H. De. S. | Carolina | . | 1811 |
| hirsûtûs, 1 | . | White | . 6, H. De. S. | N. Amer. | . | 1820 |
| inodòrûs | . | White | . 6, H. De. S. | Carolina | . | 1738 |
| latifòlîûs | . | White | . 6, H. De. S. | N. Amer. | . | |
| làxûs | . | White | . 6, H. De. S. | N. Amer. | . | 1830 |
| speciòsûs | . | White | . 6, H. De. S. | N. Amer. | . | |
| tomentòsûs, 2 | . | White | . 6, H. De. S. | Nepal | . | 1822 |
| triflòrûs | . | White | . H. De. S. | Himalaya | . | |
| verrucòsûs, 3 | . | White | . 6, H. De. S. | N. Amer. | . | |
| Zeyhèrî | . | White | . 6, H. De. S. | N. Amer. | . | |

PHILIBERTIA, *Kunth.* In honour of J. C. Philibert, author of an Elementary Treatise on Botany. *Linn.* 5, Or. 2, Nat. Or. *Asclepiadaceæ.* This interesting plant is admirably adapted to training up rafters, pillars, or trellis-work, in stoves or conservatories. A mixture of loam, peat, and sand, suits it; and cuttings root readily when planted in sand or soil, under a glass, in a little heat. Synonyme: 1. *P. gracilis.*

| | | | | | | |
|---|---|---|---|---|---|---|
| grandiflòrà, 1 | . | Yel. wht. | 6, G. Ev. Tw. | B. Ayres | . | 1836 |

PHILLYREA, *Linn.* From *phyllon*, a leaf; leafy plants. *Linn.* 2, Or. 1, Nat. Or. *Oleaceæ.* Ornamental shrubs, more valuable on account of their deep green foliage than for any beauty in their flowers, which are small and insignificant; they grow in any common soil, and are multiplied with facility, either by cuttings or layers; which last, is the best way of obtaining young plants. Synonymes: 1. *P. virgata.* 2. *P. ilicifolia.*

| | | | | | | |
|---|---|---|---|---|---|---|
| angustifòlîà | . | White | . 5, H. Ev. S. | S. Eur. | . | 1597 |
| brachiàtà | . | White | . 5, H. Ev. S. | S. Eur. | . | 1597 |
| rosmarinifòlîà | . | White | . 5, H. Ev. S. | S. Eur. | . | 1597 |
| lævîs | . | White | . 5, H. Ev. S. | S. Eur. | . | 1597 |
| lanceolàtà | . | White | . 6, H. Ev. S. | | | |
| latifòlîà | . | White | . 5, H. Ev. S. | S. Eur. | . | 1597 |
| ligustrifòlîà, 1 | . | White | . 5, H. Ev. S. | S. Eur. | . | 1596 |
| mèdîà | . | White | . 5, H. Ev. S. | S. Eur. | . | 1597 |
| buxifòlîà | . | White | . 5, H. Ev. S. | S. Eur. | . | 1797 |
| oblîquà | . | White | . 5, H. Ev. S. | S. Eur. | . | 1597 |
| oleæfòlîà | . | White | . 5, H. Ev. S. | S. Eur. | . | 1597 |
| pendûlà | . | White | . 5, H. Ev. S. | S. Eur. | . | 1597 |
| spinòsà, 2 | . | White | . 6, H. Ev. S. | S. Eur. | . | 1597 |

2 I

PHILODĒNDRŎN, *Lindley*. From *phileo*, to love, and *dendron*, a tree; in allusion to the habits of the plants of this genus to overrun trees in the South American forests. *Linn.* 21, Or. 3, Nat. Or. *Araceæ*. This is a curious species, thriving in loam and peat, and increased by divisions of the roots.

| | | | | | |
|---|---|---|---|---|---|
| crassinĕrvĭŭm | . | Grn. wht. 12, S. Ev. Cl. Brasil | . | . 1835 |

PHILOTHĒCĂ, *Rudge*. From *philos*, smooth, and *theke*, a sheath; smooth tube of stamens. *Linn.* 16, Or. 6, Nat. Or. *Rutaceæ*. An ornamental plant, requiring the same treatment as *Phebalium*. Synonyme : 1. *Eriostemon salsoloides*.

| | | | | | |
|---|---|---|---|---|---|
| australis, 1 | . | Pa. red | . 4, G. Ev. S. N. S. W. | . 1822 |

PHILOXĔRŬS, *R. Brown*. From *philos*, a lover, and *xeros*, arid; the plants like an arid situation. *Linn.* 5, Or. 1, Nat. Or. *Amarantaceæ*. Plants of little beauty; and of easy culture and propagation. Synonyme : 1. *Illecebrum vermiculare*.

| | | | | | |
|---|---|---|---|---|---|
| aggregātŭs | . | White | . 8, S. Ev. Tr. Trinidad | . 1820 |
| brasiliēnsis | . | White | . 8, S. Ev. S. Brasil | . 1790 |
| vermiculātŭs, 1 | . | Pink | . 8, S. Ev. Tr. S. Amer. | . |

PHILYDRŬM, *Banks*. From *philos*, a lover, and *hydor*, water. *Linn.* 1, Or. 1, Nat. Or. *Philydraceæ*. A pretty little species, with hairy leaves, and spikes of bright yellow flowers. It delights in a mixture of three parts loam and one part peat, in which it merely requires to be sown.

| | | | | | |
|---|---|---|---|---|---|
| lanuginōsŭm | . | Yellow | . 6, G. | B. China | . 1801 |

PHLĔBĬX, *Fries*. From *phleps*, a vein; veiny branches. *Linn.* 24, Or. 9, Nat. Or. *Fungi*. Three rather interesting species, common in the latter part of the year on Alder trees—*P. merismoides*, *radiāta*, *vāga*.

PHLĔŬM, *Linn.* Supposed to be the Greek name for *Typha*. *Linn.* 3, Or. 2, Nat. Or. *Gramineæ*. *P. pratense* and its varieties are extensively cultivated as spring grass for fodder, and are considered very valuable herbage: they prefer a strong stiff soil; the other species have little to recommend them, being mostly uninteresting. Synonyme : 1. *P. stoloniferum*.

| | | | | |
|---|---|---|---|---|
| alpīnŭm | . | . | Apetal | . 7, Grass. Scotland . |
| Michellī | . | . | Apetal | . 7, Grass. Scotland . |
| pratēnse | . | . | Apetal | . 7, Grass. Britain . |
| mājŭs | . | . | Apetal | . 7, Grass. Britain . |
| mĭnŭs | . | . | Apetal | . 7, Grass. Britain . |

*Bertolinī* 1, *commutātŭm*, *echinātŭm*, *felīnŭm*, *Gerārdī*, *nodōsŭm*.

PHLŎMĬS, *Linn.* From *phlogmos*, a flame; in reference to the down being used for wicks. *Linn.* 14, Or. 1, Nat. Or. *Labiatæ*. Very handsome plants, the greenhouse and hardy kinds all succeeding well in a rich light soil; cuttings, planted under a glass, root freely. The perennial species may be increased by seed, or divisions. Synonymes : 1. *P. samia*. 2. *P. cretica* 3. *P. rotundifolia*. 4. *P. microphylla*. 5. *P. salviæfolia*. 6. *P. lunarifolia Russelliana*. 7. *P. virens*.

| | | | | |
|---|---|---|---|---|
| agrārĭa | . | . | Purplish | . 7, H. Her. P. Siberia . 1830 |
| alpīna | . | . | Purple | . 7, H. Her. P. Siberia . 1802 |
| angustifōlĭa | . | . | Cream | . 7, F. Ev. S. Levant . 1596 |
| armeniācă | . | . | Yellow | . 7, H. Her. P. Armenia . 1834 |
| bīcŏlŏr, 1 | . | . | Yel. pur. | . 6, H. Ev. S. Lybia . 1714 |
| crinīta | . | . | Pa. brn. | . 6, F. Her. P. Spain . 1820 |
| ferrugīnĕă | . | . | Yel. brn. | . 6, H. Ev. S. Naples . 1822 |
| cretĭca, 2 | . | . | Yellow | . 6, H. Ev. S. Crete . 1820 |
| floccōsă | . | . | Yellow | . 8, F. Ev. S. Egypt . 1828 |
| frutĭcōsă | . | . | Yellow | . 6, H. Ev. S. Spain . 1596 |
| herba-vēntī | . | . | Red | . 8, H. Her. P. S. Eur. . 1596 |
| italĭca, 3 | . | . | Purple | . 7, H. Ev. S. Italy . 1661 |
| lacinĭātă | . | . | Purple | . 7, H. Her. P. Levant . 1731 |
| lanātă, 4 | . | . | Yellow | . 6, H. Ev. S. Candia . 1696 |
| lunarifōlĭa | . | . | Yellow | . 6, H. Her. P. Levant . 1818 |
| Lychnītĭs | . | . | Yel. brn. | . 7, H. Ev. S. S. Eur. . 1658 |
| Nīssōlĭī | . | . | Yellow | . 6, F. Her. P. Levant . 1757 |
| orientālĭs | . | . | Pa. brn. | . 7, H. Ev. S. Eur. . 1820 |
| pūngĕns | . | . | Brown | . 7, H. Her. P. Armenia . 1820 |
| purpūrĕă, 5 | . | . | Purple | . 7, H. Ev. S. S. Eur. . 1661 |
| Russelliānă, 6 | . | . | Brown | . 6, H. Her. P. Levant . 1821 |
| sāmĭă | . | . | Purple | . 6, H. Her. P. N. Africa . 1714 |
| tuberōsă | . | . | Purple | . 8, H. Tu. P. Siberia . 1759 |
| vincōsă, 7 | . | . | Yellow | . 6, H. Ev. S. Levant . |

PHLŎX, *Linn.* From *phlox*, a flame; appearance of the flowers. *Linn.* 5, Or. 1, Nat. Or. *Polemoniaceæ*. This is an elegant genus of plants. The species are all rendered more valuable, from their lively red, purple, or white flowers, being produced at a season of the year when the majority of the plants that flower at the same period are syngenesious, and for the most part yellow; the trailing kinds are admirably adapted for growing on rock-work, or in small pots; they grow best in a rich loamy soil. All the species root freely by cuttings, under glass, or by divisions. Synonymes : 1. *P. amœna*. 2. *P. stolonifera*. 3. *P. crassifolia*. 4. *P. scabra*. 5. *P. longiflora*.

| | | | | |
|---|---|---|---|---|
| acuminātă | . | Pa. pur. | 7, H. Her. P. N. Amer. | . 1812 |
| acutifōlĭa | . | Purple | 8, H. Her. P. N. Amer. | . 1825 |
| aristātă | . | White | 4, F. Her. P. Carolina | . 1828 |
| atrocaulĭs | . | Red | 9, H. Her. P. Eng. hyb. | . 1834 |
| canadēnsĭs | . | Blue | 4, H. Her. P. N. Amer. | . 1825 |
| carnĕă | . | Pink | 8, H. Her. P. N. Amer. | . 1816 |
| mājor | . | Flesh | 8, H. Her. P. Gardens | |
| Carolīnă | . | Pa. pur. | 8, H. Her. P. Carolina | . 1728 |
| cordātă | . | Pa. pur. | H. Her. P. Carolina | . 1827 |
| grandiflōră | . | Pa. pur. | H. Her. P. Gardens | |
| rōsĕă | . | Rose | 7, H. Her. P. | |
| distīchă | . | Red | 8, H. Her. P. N. Amer. | . 1826 |
| divaricātă | . | Lgt. blu. | 3, H. Her. P. N. Amer. | . 1746 |
| Drummōndĭ | . | Purple | 7, H. | A. Texas | . 1835 |
| elātă | . | Lilac | 9, H. Her. P. N. Amer. | . 1828 |
| excēlsă | . | Purple | 8, H. Her. P. N. Amer. | . 1824 |
| floridānă | . | Rose | 4, S. Ev. S. N. Amer. | . 1834 |
| glaberrĭmă | . | Red | 7, H. Her. P. N. Amer. | . 1725 |
| fragrmānă | . | Lilac | 7, H. Her. P. Hybrid | . 1834 |
| intermĕdĭă | . | Purple | 7, H. Her. P. N. Amer. | |
| involucrātă | . | Lilac | 6, H. Her. P. N. Amer. | . 1820 |
| lātă | . | White | 8, H. Her. P. | |
| latifōlĭa | . | Purple | 7, H. Her. P. Carolina | . 1812 |
| maculātă | . | Purple | 7, H. Her. P. N. Amer. | . 1740 |
| nĭtĭdă | . | Purple | 7, H. Her. P. N. Amer. | . 1800 |
| nivālĭs | . | White | 4, H. Her. P. N. Amer. | . 1820 |
| odorātă | . | Lilac | 8, H. Her. P. N. Amer. | |
| omniflōră | . | White | 8, H. Her. P. Hybrid | |
| ovātă | . | Purple | 6, H. Her. P. N. Amer. | . 1759 |
| Listoniānă | . | Purple | 7, H. Her. P. N. Amer. | . 1816 |
| paniculātă | . | Pink | 8, H. Her. P. N. Amer. | . 1732 |
| albă | . | White | 8, H. Her. P. N. Amer. | . 1813 |
| penduliflōră | . | Ro. pur. | 10, H. Her. P. N. Amer. | . 1823 |
| pilōsă | . | Purple | 8, H. Her. P. N. Amer. | . 1759 |
| amœnă, 1 | . | Pink | 5, H. Her. P. N. Amer. | . 1809 |
| procūmbēns | . | Flesh | 5, H. Her. P. N. Amer. | . 1827 |
| pulchēllă | . | Wht. pink | 8, H. Her. P. Hybrid | . 1835 |
| pyramidālĭs | . | Flesh | 7, H. Her. P. N. Amer. | . 1800 |
| albă | . | White | 6, H. Her. P. | |
| corymbōsă | . | Purple | 7, H. Her. P. N. Amer. | |
| penduliflōră | . | Purple | 7, H. Her. P. N. Amer. | |
| reflēxă | . | Drk. pur. | 8, H. Her. P. Hybrid | |
| rēptāns, 2 | . | Blue pur. | 7, H. Her. P. N. Amer. | . 1800 |
| crassifōlĭa, 3 | . | Purple | 7, H. Her. P. N. Amer. | . 1825 |
| scābră | . | Lilac | 8, H. Her. P. N. Amer. | |
| setācĕă | . | Flesh | 4, H. Her. P. N. Amer. | . 1786 |
| Shephārdĭ | . | Purple | 7, H. Her. P. Hybrid | . 1824 |
| Sickmānnĭ, 4 | . | White | 8, H. Her. P. N. Amer. | . 1826 |
| speciōsă | . | Flesh | F. Her. P. Columbia | . 1826 |
| suavĕōlēns | . | White | 7, H. Her. P. N. Amer. | . 1766 |
| variegātă | . | White | 7, H. Her. P. N. Amer. | . 1766 |
| subulātă | . | Drk. pur. | 4, H. Her. P. N. Amer. | . 1786 |
| suffruticōsă | . | Drk. pur. | 8, H. Her. P. N. Amer. | . 1790 |
| tardiflōră, 5 | . | White | 9, H. Her. P. N. Amer. | . 1825 |
| purpūrĕă | . | Purple | 8, H. Her. P. Hybrid | . 1836 |
| triflōră | . | Pa. lilac | 8, H. Her. P. Carolina | . 1816 |
| undulātă | . | Purple | 7, H. Her. P. N. Amer. | . 1759 |
| Verzoniānă | . | Purple | 8, H. Her. P. Hybrid | . 1834 |
| virgĭnĭcă | . | Purple | 7, H. Her. P. Virginia | . 1612 |
| albă | . | White | 7, H. Her. P. Hybrid | . 1834 |
| Wheeleriānă | . | Pink | 8, H. Her. P. Hybrid | |

PHŒNĬX, *Linn.* The Greek name of the Date. *Linn.* 22, Or. 3, Nat. Or. *Palmaceæ*. The Date of the ancients is included in this noble genus of palms. *P. dactylifera* is a fine lofty-growing tree, with a rugged trunk, and leaves from six to eight feet long. The inhabitants of Arabia, Upper Egypt, &c., chiefly live upon the fruit of it; the hard stones are even ground up as food for their camels, and of the leaves they make bags and baskets. In Barbary, the boughs are used as fences for their gardens, and they sometimes make use of the trunks in small buildings. The threads of the integuments between the boughs are made into ropes, and the rigging of smaller vessels; a juice is sometimes extracted from the tree by incisions, or scooping holes at the top, which is afterwards made into an agreeable wine. *P. farinifera* contains a farinaceous substance in the heart of the stem, which is said to be as nutritive as sago. The species all delight in a strong rich soil, and the only way of obtaining young plants is by seeds.

| | | | | |
|---|---|---|---|---|
| acaulĭs | . | . | Wht. grn. | Palm. E. Ind. . 1816 |
| dactylifĕră | . | . | Wht. grn. | Palm. Levant . 1597 |
| farinifĕră | . | . | Wht. grn. | Palm. E. Ind. . 1800 |

| | | | | | |
|---|---|---|---|---|---|
| leonénsis | . . . | | Palm. | S. Leone | . 1823 |
| paludósa | . . . | | Palm. | E. Ind. | . 1820 |
| pygmǽa | . . . | | Palm. | Maurit. | . 1823 |
| reclináta | . . . | Wht. grn. | Palm. | C. G. H. | . 1792 |
| sylvéstris | . . . | | Palm. | E. Ind. | . 1823 |

**PHŒNOCÒMA,** *Don.* From *phoinos*, bloody, and *kome*, hair; involucrum. *Linn.* 19, Or. 2, Nat. Or. *Compósitæ*. An ornamental species, requiring the same treatment as *Elichrysum.* Synonyme: 1. *Elichrysum proliferum.*

| | | | | | | |
|---|---|---|---|---|---|---|
| prolífera, 1 | . | Crimson | . 9, S. Ev. S. C. G. H. | . 1789 |

**PHOLIDÒTA,** *Lindley.* From *pholis*, a scale, and *ous*, (*otos*,) an ear; in allusion to the scaly ear-like bractea of the spike. *Linn.* 20, Or. 1, Nat. Or. *Orchidàceæ.* These are very pretty plants, and of easy cultivation; by keeping them constantly moist, they will grow well with the same treatment as the *Burlingtonias.* Synonyme: 1. *P. imbricata.*

| | | | | |
|---|---|---|---|---|
| articuláta | . . . | Wht. yel. | 4, S. Epi. Khossea | . 1837 |
| imbricáta | . . . | Yellowish | 2, S. Epi. E. Ind. | . 1834 |
| pállida, 1 | . . . | White | . 11, S. Epi. E. Ind. | . 1828 |
| unduláta | . . . | | S. Epi. E. Ind. | . 1828 |

**PHOLIÙRUS,** *Trinius.* From *pholis*, a scale, and *oura*, a tail. *Linn.* 3, Or. 2, Nat. Or. *Gramíneæ.* A curious species of grass, growing in any common soil, and increased by seeds, which only require sowing in the open ground. Synonyme: 1. *Ophiurus pannonicus.*

| | | | | | |
|---|---|---|---|---|---|
| pannonicus, 1 | . | Apetal | . 7, Grass. Hungary | . . 1804 |

**PHÒMA,** *Fries.* From *phos*, a pustule; appearance of the plants. *Linn.* 24, Or. 9, Nat. Or. *Fungi.* Minute and curious species of brown-coloured fungi, commonly found on dead willow and poplar leaves.— *P. Dahliæ, Hedéræ, Popúli, pustúla, salígna.*

**PHORMÌUM,** *Thunberg.* From *phormos*, a basket; use made of the plant in its native country. *Linn.* 6, Or. 1, Nat. Or. *Liliàceæ.* In its native country this is a very useful plant, serving the inhabitants of New Zealand, Norfolk Island, &c., with cordage, coarse thread, and linen. Attempts have been made to grow it for manufacturing purposes in New Holland, but without success. It requires to be grown in a rich strong loam, and is multiplied by divisions of the root.

| | | | |
|---|---|---|---|
| ténax | . . . . | Grn. wht. 8, H. Her. P. N. Zeal. | . 1798 |

**PHOTÌNIA,** *Lindley.* From *photeinos*, shining; in reference to the leaves. *Linn.* 12, Or. 2, Nat. Or. *Rosàceæ.* A very handsome genus of trees, with fine, bright, glossy leaves, and corymbs of white flowers. The species require very little protection except in severe weather. They thrive best if planted in a mixture of loam and peat against a wall, in a warm situation; ripened cuttings put in sand, under a glass, will root readily; they may also be grafted or inarched on the different species of *Pyrus,* or *Mespilus.* In Nepal, they use the bark of *P. dubia* for dyeing scarlet. Synonymes: 1. *Mespilus bengalensis.* 2. *Cratægus glabra.*

| | | | | |
|---|---|---|---|---|
| arbutifólia | . . . | White. | . 7, F. Ev. T. California | . 1796 |
| dúbia, 1 | . . . | White. | F. Ev. T. Nepal | . 1821 |
| integrifólia | . . . | White. | F. Ev. T. Nepal | . 1820 |
| serruláta, 2 | . . . | White. | . 5, F. Ev. T. China | . 1804 |

**PHRAGMIDÌUM,** *Link.* From *phragma*, a division, and *eidos*, similar. *Linn.* 24, Or. 9, Nat. Or. *Fungi.* Extremely minute species of black fungi. *P. gracile* is found in autumn on raspberry leaves; the others on the leaves from which they have taken their names—*P. grácile, Potentíllæ, Ròsæ, Rúbi.*

**PHRAGMÌTES,** *Trinius.* From *phragmos*, a hedge; forming hedges. *Linn.* 3, Or. 2, Nat. Or. *Gramíneæ.* This plant is very common in ditches, and is readily increased by divisions. Synonyme: 1. *Arundo Phragmites.*

| | | | | |
|---|---|---|---|---|
| commúnis, 1 | . | Apetal | . 8, H. Aq. P. Britain | . . |

**PRASÌMA,** *Linn.* Meaning unknown. *Linn.* 14, Or. 1, Nat. Or. *Labiàtæ.* A dwarf-growing plant, of no great merit. It succeeds best in a mixture of peat and loam, and cuttings planted under a glass root readily.

| | | | | |
|---|---|---|---|---|
| leptostáchya | . . | Wht. pur. 8, H. Her. P. N. Amer. | . 1802 |

**PHRYNÌUM,** *Willdenow.* From *phrynos*, a frog; plants inhabiting marshes. *Linn.* 1, Or. 1, Nat. Or. *Marantàceæ.* Plants resembling *Calathea* in general appearance. " In China, they use the leaves for

wrapping up cakes in the oven; they are infused before expansion in spirit of rice or sugar, with three times its quantity of water, to make vinegar." —*Loudon's Ency. of Plants.* For culture and propagation, see *Canna.* Synonymes: 1. *Maranta Casupo.* 2. *M. comosa.* 3. *M. spicata.* 4. *Myrosma cannæfolia.*

| | | | | | | |
|---|---|---|---|---|---|---|
| angustifólium | . | Yellow | 6, S. Her. P. E. Ind. | . 1824 |
| capitátum | . | Wht. pur. | 7, S. Her. P. E. Ind. | . 1807 |
| Casúpo, 1 | . | Yellow | 7, S. Her. P. S. Amer. | . 1820 |
| colorátum | . | Orange | 5, S. Her. P. Brazil | . 1823 |
| comósum, 2 | . | Yellow | 7, S. Her. P. Surinam | . 1812 |
| dichótomum | . | White . | 7, S. Her. P. E. Ind. | . 1810 |
| ellípticum, 3 | . | Pa. yel. | 7, S. Her. P. Guiana | . 1822 |
| grandiflòrum | . | Yellow | 7, S. Her. P. Brazil | . 1823 |
| imbricátum | . | Pa. red | 6, S. Her. P. E. Ind. | . 1818 |
| Myrósma, 4 | . | White . | 7, S. Her. P. S. Amer. | . 1820 |
| oblíquum | . | Yellow | 6, S. Her. P. E. Ind. | . 1824 |
| Parkéri | . | Yellow | 7, S. Her. P. Grenada | . 1823 |
| parviflòrum | . | Yellow | 7, S. Her. P. E. Ind. | . 1820 |
| setósum | . | Purple | 6, S. Her. P. Rio Jan. | . 1824 |
| spicátum | . | Yellow | 7, S. Her. P. E. Ind. | . 1825 |
| virgátum | . | White . | 6, S. Her. P. E. Ind. | . 1818 |

**PHYCÈLLA,** *Lindley.* A diminutive of *phykos*, red alkanet; colour of the flowers. *Linn.* 6, Or. 1, Nat. Or. *Amaryllidàceæ.* Very pretty plants, succeeding in a mixture of one part loam, one of sand, and the rest peat. They are sufficiently hardy to grow well if planted in a pit, frame, or warm border, with a slight protection in severe frost; increased by offsets from the bulbs, or by seeds. Synonymes: 1. *Amaryllis cyrtanthoides.* 2. *P. ignea glauca.* 3. *A. ignea.*

| | | | | | |
|---|---|---|---|---|---|
| biflòra | . . . | Scarlet | 4, G. Bl. P. Chile | . . |
| brevitúba | . . . | Scarlet | 7, G. Bl. P. | . 1836 |
| cordáta | . . . | Scarlet | 9, G. Bl. P. Coquimbo | . 1825 |
| cyrtanthoìdes, 1 | . | Crimson | 6, G. Her. P. Chile | . 1824 |
| glaúca, 2 | . . | Red . | 6, G. B. Valparaiso | . 1824 |
| Herbertiána | . | Red yel. | 6, G. Bl. P. Andes | . 1825 |
| ignéa, 3 | . . | Scarlet | 4, G. Bl. P. Chile | . 1824 |
| púlchra | . . | Red | . 10, G. Bl. P. Valparaiso | . |

**PHYLÌCA,** *Linn.* From *phyllikos*, leafy; in allusion to the abundant evergreen foliage. *Linn.* 5, Or. 1, Nat. Or. *Rhamnàceæ.* Ornamental shrubs. *P. ericoides* covers tracts of land about Lisbon in the same manner as heath does in England. They grow best in sandy peat, and young cuttings root readily in sand, under a glass, in heat. Synonymes: 1. *P. reflexa.* 2. *P. pubescens.* 3. *P. eriophora.*

| | | | | | |
|---|---|---|---|---|---|
| acerósa | . . | White | 5, G. Ev. S. C. G. H. | . 1820 |
| acumináta | . . | White | 5, G. Ev. S. C. G. H. | . 1819 |
| austrális | . . | White | 5, G. Ev. S. N. Holl. | . 1818 |
| bícolor | . . | White | 6, G. Ev. S. C. G. H. | . 1817 |
| callósa, 1 | . . | Yel. grn. | 8, G. Ev. S. C. G. H. | . 1774 |
| capitáta, 2 | . . | White | 6, G. Ev. S. C. G. H. | . 1800 |
| Commelíni | . . | White | 5, G. Ev. S. C. G. H. | . 1800 |
| cylindríca | . . | Yel. grn. | 6, G. Ev. S. C. G. H. | . |
| ericoìdes | . . | White | 6, G. Ev. S. C. G. H. | . 1731 |
| excélsa | . . | Yel. grn. | 5, G. Ev. T. C. G. H. | . 1823 |
| glabráta | . . | White | 5, G. Ev. S. C. G. H. | . 1817 |
| globósa | . . | White | 6, G. Ev. S. C. G. H. | . 1800 |
| hirsúta | . . | White | 6, G. Ev. S. C. G. H. | . 1820 |
| horizontális | . . | White | 5, G. Ev. S. C. G. H. | . 1820 |
| imbérbis | . . | White | 6, G. Ev. S. C. G. H. | . 1824 |
| imbricáta | . . | White | 10, G. Ev. S. C. G. H. | . 1801 |
| lanceoláta | . . | White | 5, G. Ev. S. C. G. H. | . 1790 |
| ledifólia | . . | White | 6, G. Ev. S. C. G. H. | . 1820 |
| nítida | . . | White | 11, G. Ev. S. C. G. H. | . 1774 |
| eriophòra, 3 | . | White | 11, G. Ev. S. C. G. H. | . 1774 |
| papillósa | . . | Pa. yel. | 6, G. Ev. S. C. G. H. | . 1820 |
| parviflòra | . . | White | 6, G. Ev. S. C. G. H. | . 1790 |
| pinéa | . . | White | 11, G. Ev. S. C. G. H. | . 1774 |
| pinifólia | . . | White | 7, G. Ev. S. C. G. H. | . 1789 |
| plumósa | . . | White | 4, G. Ev. S. C. G. H. | . 1759 |
| púmila | . . | White | 6, G. Ev. S. C. G. H. | . 1823 |
| rosmarinifólia | . | White | 6, G. Ev. S. C. G. H. | . 1815 |
| secúnda | . . | White | 5, G. Ev. S. C. G. H. | . 1817 |
| squarrósa | . . | White | 9, G. Ev. S. C. G. H. | . 1800 |
| trichótoma | . . | White | 6, G. Ev. S. C. G. H. | . 1818 |
| villósa | . . | White | 5, G. Ev. S. C. G. H. | . 1790 |

**PHYLICA,** see *Souldángia.*
**PHYLÌCA,** see *Trichocephálus.*

**PHYLLÁNTHUS,** *Linn.* From *phyllon*, a leaf, and *anthos*, a flower; flowers produced from the edges of the leaves. *Linn.* 21, Or. 10, Nat. Or. *Euphorbiàceæ.* A very interesting genus of plants. The shrubby kinds thrive well in a mixture of loam and peat, and cuttings of the ripened wood root freely in sand, under a glass, in heat. The annuals and biennials may be sown in a hotbed frame; they require the same treatment as other tender annuals. In India the root, leaves, and young shoots of *P. Niruri*, are considered deobstruent and diuretic. *P. Urinaria* is also powerfully diuretic.

| | | | | | |
|---|---|---|---|---|---|
| calycīnūs | . . | . 5. G. Ev. S. N. Holl. | . 1823 |
| cantonlēnsis | . Orn. yel. | 8, S. A. Canton | . 1820 |
| Conāmi . . | . Green . | 7, S. Ev. S. W. Ind. | . 1791 |
| cuneātūs . . | . Orn. yel. | 8, S. A. China | . 1818 |
| fraxinifolīūs . | . Green . | 8, S. Ev. S. E. Ind. | . 1819 |
| grandifolīūs . | . Apetal | 8. Ev. S. America | . 1771 |
| grācilis . . | . Orn. yel. | 8, S. B. E. Ind. | . 1818 |
| juglandifolīūs . | . Orn. yel. | 8, S. Ev. S. | . 1818 |
| lanceolātūs . | . Orn. yel. | 8, S. Ev. S. I. Bourbon | 1822 |
| longifolīūs . . | . Orn. yel. | 8, S. Ev. S. I. Bourbon | 1822 |
| lūcdūs . . | . Orn. yel. | 8, G. Ev. S. China | . 1820 |
| maderaspatēnsis | . Apetal | 7, S. Ev. S. E. Ind. | . 1783 |
| microphylla | . Orn. yel. | 8, S. Ev. S. Caraccas | . 1817 |
| mimocoīdēs . | . Green . | 8, S. Ev. S. Caribbees | . 1817 |
| Nirūri . . . | . Green . | 7. A. E. Ind. | . 1692 |
| nūtāns . . . | . Orn. yel. | 8, S. Ev. S. Jamaica | . 1820 |
| obcordātūs . | . Orn. yel. | 8, S. B. E. Ind. | . 1817 |
| obovātūs . . | . Apetal | 7, H. A. N. Amer. | . 1803 |
| obscūrūs . . | . Orn. yel. | 8, S. Ev. S. E. Ind. | . 1824 |
| polyphyllūs . | . Green . | 8, S. Ev. S. E. Ind. | . 1805 |
| reticulātūs . | . Red . | 8, S. Ev. S. E. Ind. | . |
| rhamnoīdēs . | . Orn. yel. | 7, S. Ev. S. E. Ind. | . 1820 |
| scāndēns . . | . Orn. yel. | 8, S. Ev. Cl. E. Ind. | . 1822 |
| simplēx . . | . Orn. yel. | 8, S. A. E. Ind. | . 1817 |
| strictūs . . | . Orn. yel. | 8, S. A. E. Ind. | . 1824 |
| thymoīdēs . . | . | G. Ev. S. N. Holl. | . 1835 |
| turbinātūs . . | . Green . | 7, S. Ev. S. China | . |
| Urinārīā . . | . Orn. yel. | 8. A. E. Ind. | . 1819 |
| virōsūs . . . | . Green . | 8. S. Ev. S. E. Ind. | . 1802 |

**Phyllis,** *Linn.* From *phyllon*, a leaf; its chief recommendation. *Linn.* 5, Or. 2, Nat. Or. *Cinchonaceæ.* An ornamental shrub, growing from two to three feet high, and producing axillary corymbs of green flowers in abundance. It succeeds best in a rich strong mould, and cuttings root freely under a glass, in sand.

| | | | | | |
|---|---|---|---|---|---|
| Nobla . . | . Green . | 6, G. Ev. S. Canaries | . 1699 |
| paucifiora | . | 6, G. Ev. S. Canaries | . 1699 |

**Phyllocládus,** *Richard.* From *phyllon*, a leaf, and *klados*, a branch. *Linn.* 21, Or. 10, Nat. Or. *Taxaceæ.* An ornamental tree; for culture and propagation, see *Podocarpus.* Synonyme: 1. *Podocarpus asplenifolius.*

| | | | | | |
|---|---|---|---|---|---|
| rhomboīdālis, 1 | . Apetal | G. Ev. T. V.D. L. | . 1825 |

**Phyllodīūm,** a dilated petiole, with the consistence of a leaf.

**Phyllolobīūm,** *Fischer.* From *phyllon*, a leaf, and *lobos*, a pod; in allusion to the flat membranous pods. *Linn.* 16, Or. 6, Nat. Or. *Leguminosæ.* This species will grow well in a mixture of peat and sand, and cuttings will root in the same kind of soil, with a glass over them, in heat.

| | | | | | |
|---|---|---|---|---|---|
| zanzibarēnse | . | 8. Her. P. Zanguebar | . 1826 |

**Phyllōmā,** *Link.* From *phyllon*, a leaf, and *loma*, a fringe; in reference to the coloured edges of the leaves of *P. aloiflorum.* *Linn.* 6, Or. 1, Nat. Or. *Liliaceæ.* A genus of plants nearly related to the Aloes. They grow well in sandy loam, and are readily increased by suckers; they require to be very cautiously watered. Synonymes: 1. *Dracæna marginata, Lomatophyllum borbonicum.* 2. *Aloe hexapetala, Lomatophyllum Jacquinii.* 3. *A. macra.* 4. *A. rufocincta.*

| | | | | | |
|---|---|---|---|---|---|
| aloiflōrūm, 1 | . Orange | . 4, S. Ev. T. Bourbon | . 1766 |
| Jacquinī, 2 | . Orange | . 6, G. Ev. S. | |
| mācrūm, 3 | . Orange | . 6, G. Ev. S. Maurit. | . 1817 |
| rufocinctūm, 4 | . Orange | . 6, G. Ev. S. E. Ind. | . 1818 |

**Phymatánthūs,** see *Pelargonīum.*

**Physālis,** *Linn.* From *physa*, a bladder; alluding to the calyx. *Linn.* 5, Or. 1, Nat. Or. *Solanaceæ.* A genus principally composed of weeds. The stove and greenhouse species will grow well in any rich light soil; young plants may be obtained from cuttings, which root readily under a glass. The hardy kinds thrive in common garden soil, and are increased from seeds. The annual species merely require sowing in the open ground. Synonymes: 1. *Atropa aristata.* 2. *P. tuberosa.* 3. *P. fœtidissima. P. nodosa.* 4. *Atropa frutescens.* 5. *P. parviflora.* 6. *P. dubia.* 7. *P. Lagasca, P. Rothiana.* 8. *P. edulis.* 9. *P. striplicifolia.* 10. *P. pruinosa, P. barbadensis.* 11. *P. flexuosa.* 12. *P. pennsylvanica.* 13. *P. Jacquini.*

| | | | | | |
|---|---|---|---|---|---|
| Alkekengi . . | . White | . 8, H. Her. P. S. Eur. | . 1548 |
| arborēscēns . | . Yellow | . 7, G. Ev. S. C. G. H. | . 1700 |
| aristātā, 1 . | . Yellow | . 7, G. Ev. S. Canaries | . 1779 |
| frutēscēns, 4 | . Yellow | . 6, G. Ev. S. Spain | . 1787 |
| peruviānā . | . White | . 7, G. Her. P. S. Amer. | . 1772 |
| edūlis, 8 . | . Yellow | . 7, G. Her. P. S. Amer. | . 1772 |

*æquātā, angulātā, chenopodifolīā 2, curassāvīcā, fætēns 3, Indīcā 5, Linkiānā 6, micrānthā, minīmā 7, parviflōrā, philadēlphīcā 9, prostrātā, pubēscēns, P. pruinōsā 10, somnīfērā, S. flexuōsā 11, viscōsā 12, V. Jacquini 13.*

**Physārūm,** *Persoon.* From *physa*, a bladder; appearance of peridium. *Linn.* 24, Or. 9, Nat. Or. *Fungi.* Curious species, found on dead beech-wood, decaying trunks of trees, &c.—*P. aūrēūm, hyalīnūm, leucōpūs, metallīcūm, nigripēs, nūtāns, rubiginōsūm, sulcātūm, virīdē.*

**Physēmatīūm,** *Kaulfuss.* Derivation not certain. *Linn.* 24, Or. 1, Nat. Or. *Polypodiaceæ.* Ornamental plants, growing well in a mixture of peat and loam, and they may be increased by divisions. Synonyme: 1. *Woodsia pubescens.*

| | | | | | |
|---|---|---|---|---|---|
| mōllis . . . | . Brown | . 7, S. Her. P. | |
| pubēscēns, 1 | . Brown | . 8, S. Her. P. Brasil | . 1820 |

**Physiánthūs,** *Martius.* From *physa*, a bladder, and *anthos*, a flower; the corolla is inflated at its base. *Linn.* 5, Or. 2, Nat. Or. *Asclepiadaceæ.* This is a very interesting climber, well adapted for training to the rafters or pillars of a stove. It grows in sandy loam and peat, and is increased by seeds or cuttings.

| | | | | | |
|---|---|---|---|---|---|
| albēns . . . | . White | . 7, S. Ev. Cl. B. Ayres | . 1830 |

**Physic-nut,** see *Jatrōphā.*

**Physinōx,** *Lindley.* Name not explained. *Linn.* 20, Or. 1, Nat. Or. *Orchidaceæ.* This is said to be a plant of no beauty, but very curious; it has the habit of an *Epidendrum*, and will require similar treatment to most other Mexican epiphytes.

| | | | | | |
|---|---|---|---|---|---|
| prostrātā . . | . Purple | . 8. Epi. Demerara | . 182- |

**Physochlaínā,** *Don.* Derived from *physa*, a bladder, and *chlaina*, an outer garment; alluding to the inflated calyx. *Linn.* 5, Or. 1, Nat. Or. *Solanaceæ.* The species of this genus produce their very elegant flowers early in the season, and are therefore desirable plants. They grow well in any soil, and are easily increased by divisions of the root, or by seed. Synonyme: 1. *Hyoscyamus orientalis.* 2. *H. physaloides.*

| | | | | | |
|---|---|---|---|---|---|
| orientālis, 1 | . Pur. blue | . 4, H. Her. P. Iberia | . 1821 |
| physaloīdēs, 2 | . Pur. vio. | . 3, H. Her. P. Siberia | . 1777 |

**Physolōbīūm,** *Bentham.* From *physa*, a bladder, and *lobos*, a pod; alluding to the shape of the seed-vessel. *Linn.* 10, Or. 1, Nat. Or. *Leguminosæ.* This genus is quite unknown to us.

| | | | | | |
|---|---|---|---|---|---|
| alātūm . . . | . | Swan R. . | . 1837 |

**Physosīphōn,** *Lindley.* From *physa*, an inflated containing object, and *siphon*, a tube; the calyx is tubular, and inflated at the base. *Linn.* 20, Or. 1, Nat. Or. *Orchidaceæ.* Curious little plants, with the habit of *Pleurothallis*, and requiring precisely similar treatment to that genus. Synonyme: 1. *Stelis tubata.*

| | | | | | |
|---|---|---|---|---|---|
| carinātūs . . | . Orange | . 8, S. Epi. Mexico | . 1838 |
| emarginātūs . | . | . 8. Epi. Peru | |
| Loddigēsī, 1 | . Orange | . 4, S. Epi. N. Spain | . 1828 |
| spirālis . . | . Purple | . 8. Epi. Brasil | |

**Physospērmūm,** *Vela.* From *physa*, a bladder, and *sperma*, a seed; the teguments do not adhere to the seed in a young state. *Linn.* 5, Or. 2, Nat. Or. *Umbelliferæ.* A rather ornamental genus of plants; for culture and propagation, see *Pleurospermum.* Synonymes: 1. *Ligusticum cornubiense.* 2. *Smyrnium nudicaule.*

| | | | | | |
|---|---|---|---|---|---|
| commutātūm, 1 | . White | . 7, H. Her. P. England | |
| nudicaūle, 2 | . Green | . 5, H. Her. P. Caucasus | . 1817 |

**Physostēgīā,** *Bentham.* From *physa*, a bladder, and *stege*, a covering; alluding to the calyx. *Linn.* 14, Or. 1, Nat. Or. *Labiatæ.* Ornamental plants; for culture and propagation, see *Dracocephalum.* Synonymes: 1. *Dracocephalum cordatum.* 2. *D. denticulatum.* 3. *D. speciosum.* 4. *D. variegatum.* 5. *D. virginianum.*

| | | | | | |
|---|---|---|---|---|---|
| cordātā, 1 | . Purple | . 7, H. Her. P. N. Amer. | . 1824 |
| denticulātā, 2 | . Striped | . 8, H. Her. P. Carolina | . 1787 |
| imbricātā . | . Pa. pur. | . 9, H. Her. P. Texas | . 1833 |
| speciōsa, 3 | . Pink | . 7, H. Her. P. Siberia | . 1822 |
| truncātā . | . Pa. pink | . H. Her. P. S. Felipe | . 1834 |
| variegātā, 4 | . Purple | . H. Her. P. Carolina | . 1812 |
| virginiānā, 5 | . Red | . 8, H. Her. P. N. Amer. | . 1683 |
| alba . . . | . White | . 8, H. Her. P. | |

**Phytelēphās,** *Ruiz et Pavon.* From *phyton*, a plant,

and *elephas*, ivory; buttons are made from the hard albumen of the plant. *Linn.* 22, Or. 12, Nat. Or. *Cyclanthaceæ.* This ornamental shrub succeeds well in sandy loam and peat.

| | | | | |
|---|---|---|---|---|
| macrocárpā . . | | 8. Ev. S. Peru | . . . | 1822 |

**PHYTEUMA.** Linnæus adopted this name from Dioscorides; meaning unknown. *Linn.* 5, Or. 1, Nat. Or. *Campanulaceæ.* Handsome herbaceous plants, well adapted for rock-work, or growing in small pots; they will grow in any common soil, and increase readily by divisions or seeds. *P. spicatum* is occasionally eaten as an article of food. *Synonymes:* 1. *P. strictum, P. virgatum.* 2. *P. cordatum.* 3. *P. brevifolium.* 4. *P. ellipticum.* 5. *P. ovatum.*

| | | | | | |
|---|---|---|---|---|---|
| betonicifolium | . Pa. blue | . 6, H. Her. P. S. Eur. | . | 1818 |
| campanuloides | . Blue | . 7, H. Her. P. Caucasus | . | 1804 |
| Sibthorpiānum | | . 7, H. Her. P. M. Olympus | | 1804 |
| canéscens . . | . Lilac | . 7, H. Her. P. Hungary | . | 1804 |
| Charmélī . . | . Blue | . 6, H. Her. P. Pyrenees | . | 1823 |
| comósūm . . | . Blue | . 6, H. | B. Austria | . | 1752 |
| globularifolium | . Blue | . 6, H. Her. P. S. France | . | 1820 |
| Hallérī . . | . Violet | . 5, H Her. P. S. France | . | 1822 |
| hemisphæricūm | . Blue | . 7, H. Her. P. Switzerl. | . | 1752 |
| hispidūm . . | . Blue | . 6, H. Her. P. Switzerl. | . | 1825 |
| húmīlīs . . | . Blue | . 6, H. Her. P. Switzerl. | . | 1825 |
| inæquatūm . . | . Blue | . 6, H. Her. P. Austria | . | 1820 |
| lanceolatūm . | . White | . 6, H. Her. P. Armenia | . | 1826 |
| limosifolium, 1 | | . H. Ev. S. Switzerl. | . | 1822 |
| Michélī . . | . Red | . 6, H. Her. P. Switzerl. | . | 1822 |
| nigrūm . . | . Red | . 7, H. Her. P. Bohemia | . | 1820 |
| orbiculāre, 2 | . Violet | . 7, H. Her. P. England | . | |
| decipiēns, 3 | . Blue | . 7, H. Her. P. Switzerl. | . | 1819 |
| gigantēum, 4 | . Blue | . 7, H. Her. P. France | . | 1817 |
| pauciflorūm | . Blue | . 5, H. Her. P. Switzerl. | . | 1823 |
| pulchéllum | | . H. Her. P. | . | 1826 |
| Scheuchzérī, 5 | . Blue | . 5, H. Her. P. Switzerl. | . | 1813 |
| scorsonerifolium | . Blue | . 7, H. Her. P. Alps | . | 1819 |
| sibīricūm . . | . Blue | . 7, H. Her. P. Siberia | . | 1817 |
| Siebérī . . | . Blue | . 6, H. Her. P. Pyrenees | . | 1826 |
| spicātum . . | . Blue | . 5, H. Her. P. Europe | . | 1597 |

**PHYTOLACCA,** *Linn.* From *phyton*, a plant, and *lacca*, lac; in allusion to the crimson colour of the fruit. *Linn.* 10, Or. 5, Nat. Or. *Phytolaccaceæ.* The stove species of this ornamental genus grow well in any rich light soil, and may be increased either from cuttings or seeds. *P. decandra* is a fine herbaceous plant, requiring a good deal of room, on account of its wide-spreading branches. Its greatest beauty is in the numerous bunches of black berries, which make a pretty appearance; it grows freely in rich soil, and is increased by seed, or cuttings under a glass. *Synonymes:* 1. *P. icosandra.* 2. *P. heptandra.*

| | | | | | |
|---|---|---|---|---|---|
| abyssinicā . . | . Wht. gra. | 5, S. Ev. S. Africa | . | 1775 |
| bogoténsis . . | . White . | 8. Her. P. Bogota | . | 1824 |
| decándrā . . | . Li. pur. | 8, H. Her. P. Virginia | . | 1615 |
| dioīcā . . | . Wht. grn. | 8. Ev. T. S. Amer. | . | 1768 |
| dodecándrā . | . Red . | . 5, S. Her. P. Africa | . | |
| icosándrā . . | . White . | 9, S. Her. P. E. Ind. | . | 1758 |
| mexicānā, 1 . | . White . | . 7, S. Her. P. Mexico | . | 1824 |
| octándrā . . | . Wht. gra. | 9, S. Her. P. Mexico | . | 1732 |
| strictā, 2 . . | . Wht. grn. | 6, S. Her. P. S. Amer. | . | 1820 |

**PICRAMNIA,** *Swartz.* From *picros*, bitter, and *thamnos*, a shrub; whole plant very nauseous. *Linn.* 22, Or. 5, Nat. Or. *Anacardiaceæ.* Shrubs of little beauty, succeeding in peat and loam; large cuttings will root in sand, under a glass, in heat.

| | | | | | |
|---|---|---|---|---|---|
| Antidésmā . | . Green . | . 8. Ev. S. Jamaica | . | 1793 |
| pentándrā . | . Green . | . 8. Ev. S. W. Ind. | . | 1822 |

**PICRIDIUM,** *Desfontaines.* From *picros*, bitter. *Linn.* 19, Or. 1, Nat. Or. *Compositæ.* The perennial species of this genus thrive well in common garden soil, and are increased by seed or divisions. The annual kinds merely require sowing in the open ground. *Synonymes:* 1. *Crepis albida.* 2. *Sonchus picroides.*

| | | | | | |
|---|---|---|---|---|---|
| albidūm, 1 . | . Wht. yel. 8, H. Her. P. France | . | 1781 |
| ilicifolium . . | . Yellow . 8, F. Her. P. Teneriffe | . | 1829 |
| tingitanūm . | . Yellow . 7, H. | A. Barbary | . | 1713 |
| vulgāre, 2 . . | . Yellow . 7, H. | A. France | . | 1773 |

**PICRIS,** *Linn.* Derivation same as the genus *Picridium.* *Linn.* 19, Or. 1, Nat. Or. *Compositæ.* A genus nearly allied to, and requiring the same treatment, as *Picridium.* *Synonymes:* 1 *Crepis lappacea—P. altissimā* 1, *asperrimā, asplenioīdēs, barbarōrūm, dahuricā, hieracioīdēs, hispidā, Kamtschāticā, lyrātā, nepalénsis, pauciflorā, Rhagadiōlūs, rigidā, Sprengeriānā, strigōsā.*

**PICTA,** painted.

**PICTETIA,** *Decandolle.* In honour of A. Pictet, a celebrated physician. *Linn.* 17, Or. 4, Nat. Or. *Leguminosæ.* Ornamental plants, growing freely in a mixture of loam and peat; young cuttings will root readily in sand, under a glass, in heat. *Synonymes:* 1. *Æschynomene aristata.* 2. *Robinia squamata.*

| | | | | | |
|---|---|---|---|---|---|
| aristātā, 1 . | . Yellow | . 6, S. Ev. S. St. Domin. | . | 1816 |
| squamātā, 2 . | . Yellow | . 8. Ev. S. W. Ind. | . | 1824 |

**PIERARDIA,** *Roxburgh.* In honour of Mr. Pierard, of Kew. *Linn.* 8, Or. 1, Nat. Or. *Sapindaceæ.* An edible-fruited tree. It grows in a mixture of loam, peat, and sand, and ripened cuttings root in sand, under a glass, in heat. *Synonyme:* 1. *Pierardia sapida.*

| | | | | | |
|---|---|---|---|---|---|
| dúlcis, 1 . | . Yellow | . 8. Ev. T. Sumatra | . | 1820 |

**PIGEON-PEA,** see *Cajānus.*

**PILEA,** *Lindley.* From *pilos*, a cap; one of the divisions of the perianth. *Linn.* 21, Or. 4, Nat. Or. *Urticaceæ.* A neat little creeper, making a good cover to hide the earth of large pots, &c.; it will grow in any common soil, and propagates freely from cuttings.

| | | | | | |
|---|---|---|---|---|---|
| muscósā . . | . Green . | . 5, S. Ev. Tr. W. Ind. | . | 1793 |

**PILEATE,** having a cap or lid like the cap of a mushroom.

**PILI,** long stiffish hairs.

**PILIFEROUS,** bearing hairs.

**PILOBOLUS,** *Tode.* Derived from *pilos*, a cap, and *boleo*, to eject. *Linn.* 24, Or. 9, Nat. Or. *Fungi.* A curious little species, of a very fugacious nature, found on dung during the summer and autumn months—*P. crystallinūs, C. roridūs.*

**PILOSE,** covered with long soft hairs.

**PILULARIA,** *Linn.* From *pilula*, a pill; shape of the heads containing the reproductive organs. *Linn.* 24, Or. 5, Nat. Or. *Marsileaceæ.* An obscure little plant, found in damp meadows among grass, especially where they have been overflowed with water during winter.

| | | | | | |
|---|---|---|---|---|---|
| globiférā . . | . Brown . | 7, H. Ev. Tr. Britain | . | . |

**PILULIFERA,** producing little balls.

**PIMELEA,** *Banks.* From *pimele*, fat. *Linn.* 2, Or. 1, Nat. Or. *Thymelaceæ.* A genus of beautiful shrubs, growing three or four feet high, and producing numerous heads of flowers. To flourish well, they must be planted in a mixture of three parts sandy peat and one part loam, the pots being carefully drained; young cuttings will strike in sand, under a glass; they likewise produce seeds, by which they are readily increased.

| | | | | | |
|---|---|---|---|---|---|
| arenāriā . . | . White . | . 7, G. Ev. S. N. Zeal. | . | 1827 |
| ceratā . . | . Yellow | . 7, G. Ev. S. Australia | . | 1835 |
| clavātā . . | . White . | 4, G. Ev. S. N. Holl. | . | 1824 |
| collīnā . . | . White . | 4, G. Ev. S. N. Holl. | . | 1824 |
| crinītā . . | . White . | 8, G. Ev. S. Swan R. | . | 1837 |
| decussātā . . | . Red . | 5, G. Ev. S. N. Holl. | . | 1824 |
| diosmæfolīā . | . Rose . | 7, G. Ev. S. N. Holl. | . | 1826 |
| drupáceā . . | . White . | 5, G. Ev. S. N. Holl. | . | 1817 |
| filamentōsā . | | G. Ev. S. N. Holl. | . | 1826 |
| glaūcā . . | . White . | G. Ev. S. N. Holl. | . | 1824 |
| graciliflorā . | . White . | 6, G. Ev. S. K. G.'s 3d. | . | 1830 |
| Hendersōnī . | . Rose . | 7, G. Ev. S. K. G.'s 3d. | . | 1837 |
| hispidā . . | . Bluish . | 5, G. Ev. S. N. Holl. | . | 1830 |
| húmīlīs . . | . White . | 9, G. Ev. S. N. Holl. | . | 1824 |
| hypericīnā . | . White . | 5, G. Ev. S. K. G.'s 3d. | . | 1830 |
| incānā . . | . White . | 4, G. Ev. S. N. Holl. | . | 1824 |
| intermédīā . | . White . | 5, G. Ev. S. K. G.'s 3d. | . | 1825 |
| lanātā . . | . White . | 5, G. Ev. S. V. D. L. | . | 1834 |
| ligustrīnā . | . White . | 5, G. Ev. S. V. D. L. | . | 1823 |
| linifolīā . . | . White . | 5, G. Ev. S. N. S. W. | . | 1793 |
| linoīdēs . . | . White . | 7, G. Ev. S. N. Holl. | . | 1826 |
| longiflorā . | . White . | 6, G. Ev. S. N. Holl. | . | 1831 |
| nīvéā . . | . White . | G. Ev. S. N. Holl. | . | 1833 |
| pauciflorā . | . White . | 5, G. Ev. S. V. D. L. | . | 1812 |
| prostrātā . . | . White . | G. Ev. S. N. Zeal. | . | |

| | | | | |
|---|---|---|---|---|
| róseä . . . | . Red | . 6, G. Ev. S | N. Holl. | . 1800 |
| spicätä . . . | . White | . 6, G. Ev. S. | N. Holl. | . 1824 |
| sylvéstris . . | . Bluish | . 6, G. Ev. S. | N. Holl. | . 1830 |

PIMĔNTÄ, *Lindley.* Pimento is the Spanish name for Indian-pepper. Linn. 12, Or. 1, Nat. Or. *Myrtaceæ.* This species forms in Jamaica a handsome tree, growing thirty feet high, and producing a fruit well known in this country under the name of Allspice. It delights in a strong loamy soil, and ripened cuttings will root in sand, under a glass, in heat. *Synonyme:* 1. *Myrtus pimenta.*

| | | | | |
|---|---|---|---|---|
| vulgäris, 1. . | . White | . 6, S. Ev. T. | W. Ind. | . 1723 |

PIMPERNEL, see *Anagällis.*

PIMPINĔLLÄ, *Linn.* Altered from *bipinnate*; referring to the leaves being twice pinnate. Linn. 5, Or. 2, Nat. Or. *Umbelliferæ.* Worthless species, growing best in a dry sandy soil, and increased only by seed, which ripen in abundance. *Synonymes:* 1. *Tragium Anisum.* 2. *T. aromaticum.* 3. *T. Broteri.* 4. *P. tenuis.* 5. *T. depressum.* 6. *P. dissecta.* 7. *P. media.* 8. *T. peregrinum.* 9. *P. nigra.* 10. *T. Columnæ.* 11. *T. villosum—P. Anïsä* 1, *aromätïcä* 2, *aūrĕä, bubonoïdĕs* 3, *crĕticä* 4, *deprĕssä* 5, *flävä, intermĕdïä, lätĕä, mägnä, M. dissĕctä* 6, *M. orientälïs* 7, *peregrïnä* 8, *rotundïfolïä, Saxifrägä, S. nïgrä* 9, *Tragïüm* 10, *villösä* 11.

PIMPLED, covered with minute pustules, resembling pimples.

PINCKNĔŸÄ. Named by Michaux in honour of Mr. Pinckney, an American, now forgotten. Linn. 5, Or. 1, Nat. Or. *Cinchonaceæ.* A handsome half-hardy tree, furnished with long downy leaves, and dividing but little into branches. It grows best planted against a south wall, with a little protection in severe weather; sand and peat is the best soil for it, and cuttings will root, if planted in sand, under a glass.

| | | | | |
|---|---|---|---|---|
| pūbens . . . | . Red | . 6, F. Ev. T. | Georgia . | . 1786 |

PINE, see *Pinūs.*

PINE-APPLE, see *Anänäsä.*

PINGUÏCŬLÄ, *Linn.* From *pinguis*, fat; in allusion to the greasiness of the leaves. Linn. 2, Or. 1, Nat. Or. *Lentibulaceæ.* Beautiful little plants, but difficult to keep artificially. *P. grandiflora* will succeed in common bog soil. The other species require a shaded morass to come to any perfection. *P. vulgaris* acts as cow's-milk the same as common rennet. In Sweden and Norway the milk of the Reindeer is poured on the leaves, and set aside for a day or so, when it acquires consistence and tenacity, and then neither the whey nor the cream will separate, forming a very grateful food.

| | | | | |
|---|---|---|---|---|
| alpïnä . . . | . White | . 4, H. Her. P. | Germany | . 1794 |
| edentülä . . | . Yellow | . 4, F. Her. P. | N. Amer. | . 1828 |
| grandiflörä . . | . Blue | . 4, H. Her. P. | Britain . | . |
| lusitánïcä . . | . Lilac | . 6, H. Her. P. | Britain . | . |
| lūtĕä . . . | . Yellow | . 6, F. Her. P. | Carolina | . 1816 |
| vulgäris . . | . Violet | . 5, H. Her. P. | Britain . | . |

PINGUIS, fat, greasy.

PINK, see *Dïänthüs.*

PINNÆ, the leaflets of a pinnate leaf.

PINNATE; when a leaf is divided into numerous small leaflets, as the leaves of the ash.

PINNATELY-TERNATE, having three leaflets disposed in a pinnate manner.

PINNATIFID, when a leaf is divided into lobes from the margin neatly to the mid-rib.

PINNATIFIDLY-SINUATED, scolloped in a pinnatifid manner.

PIN-PILLAR, see *Opüntïä curassävïcä.*

PINŪS, *Linn.* From *pinos*, a Greek word used by Theophrastus to designate a pine-tree; and some authors derive it from the Celtic *pin*, or *pyn*, a mountain or rock; alluding to the habitat of the tree. Linn. 21, Or. 10, Nat. Or. *Coniferæ.* This much-esteemed and well-known genus contains some of the trees of most universal use in civilised society, and forming a very important article of commerce both in Europe and America. Most, if not all, of the species are highly deserving of culture, being very ornamental and beautiful in every stage of their growth. They will succeed on almost any kind of soil, but to bring the timber to its greatest state of perfection, a somewhat loamy and a cool subsoil are requisite. Young plants may be obtained by a variety of methods. All the species may be propagated by layers, by inarching on nearly allied kinds, by herbaceous grafting; many may also be increased by cuttings; but the speediest way is by seed, and which process we shall briefly notice. In some of the species the cones attain their full size the first year, but, in most, not till the end of the second autumn. The cones of *P. sylvestris* and the like, open of themselves shortly after being gathered from the tree, and spread out in the sun; but the cones of *P. Pinaster, P. Pinea*, and similar kinds, do not, though treated in the same manner, open their scales for several months. The seed should be sown on finely-prepared rather sandy soil, in March or April. The seeds of the most common kinds are always sown on beds, and after being gently beaten down, are slightly covered with light soil. The seeds of the rare kinds are sown in pots filled with finely-prepared soil, and when up, treated like other hardy seedlings. For a great mass of other useful information relative to these fine trees, indeed, for every thing that it is necessary to know respecting them, we refer the reader to *Loudon's Arboretum et Fruticetum Britannicum*, a work which ought to be in the hands of every lover of hardy trees and shrubs.

Under *Pinus*, we have included the genera *Abies* and *Picea*, of Don and other authors, believing them to be so nearly akin as to render it unnecessary to keep them generically distinct. We have, however, in this genus departed a little from the original plan of the work, by dividing it into Sections, so that those who differ from us in opinion, will have no difficulty in recognising the species of *Abies* and *Picea* of authors, every species of those genera being retained alphabetically under the respective Sections.

SECT. 1. PĪNŪS, *Linn.* Derivation same as genus. *Synonymes:* 1. *P. palustris.* 2. *P. genuensis.* 3. *P. oocarpa.* 4. *P. Pinaster Ascarina.* 5. *P. Lemoniana.* 6. *P. nova-zelandica.* 7. *P. echinata, P. uncinata.* 8. *P. rubra.*

| | | | | |
|---|---|---|---|---|
| apulcénsis . . | . Apetal | . H. Ev. T. | Mexico . | . 1839 |
| australis, 1 . . | . Apetal | . H. Ev. T. | N. Amer. | . 1730 |
| austrïäcä . . | . Apetal | . 6, H. Ev. T. | Austria | . 1835 |
| Banksïänä . . | . Apetal | . 5, H. Ev. T. | Huds. B. | . 1785 |
| brütïä . . . | . Apetal | . H. Ev. T. | Calabria | . |
| califórnïcä . . | . Apetal | . H. Ev. T. | California | . 1829 |
| canariénsis . . | . Apetal | . H. Ev. T. | Canaries | . 1815 |
| Cĕmbrä . . | . Apetal | . 5, H. Ev. T. | Siberia . | . 1746 |
| helvĕtïcä . . | . Apetal | . 5, H. Ev. T. | Switserl. | . 1819 |
| pygmĕä . . | . Apetal | . 5, H. Ev. T. | Siberia . | . |
| sibīrïcä . . | . Apetal | . 5, H. Ev. T. | Siberia . | . 1746 |
| Coultĕri . . | . Apetal | . 3, H. Ev. T. | California | . 1832 |
| Devonïänä . . | . Apetal | . H. Ev. T. | Mexico . | . 1839 |
| excélsä . . | . Apetal | . H. Ev. T. | Nepal . | . 1823 |
| Gerardïänä . | . Apetal | . F. Ev. T. | E. Ind. . | . |
| halepénsis . . | . Apetal | . 6, H. Ev. T. | Levant . | . 1683 |
| genuénsis, 2 . | . Apetal | . 5, H. Ev. T. | Geneva . | . 1830 |
| marítïmä . . | . Apetal | . 6, H. Ev. T. | | |
| minör . . . | . Apetal | . 5, H. Ev. T. | | |
| Hartwĕgii . . | . Apetal | . H. Ev. T. | Mexico . | . 1839 |
| Inöps . . . | . Apetal | . 5, H. Ev. T. | N. Amer. | . 1739 |
| insígnis . . | . Apetal | . H. Ev. T. | Californ. | . 1833 |
| Lambertïänä . | . Apetal | . H. Ev. T. | N. Amer. | . 1827 |
| Larĭcïö . . | . Apetal | . 5, H. Ev. T. | S. Eur. . | . 1814 |
| caramänïcä . | . Apetal | . 5, H. Ev. T. | S. Eur. . | . 1820 |
| corsïcänä . | . Apetal | . 5, H. Ev. T. | Corsica . | . 1814 |
| subvíridis . | . Apetal | . 5, H. Ev. T. | | |
| leiophýllä . . | . Apetal | . F. Ev. T. | Mexico . | . |
| Llaveänä . . | . Apetal | . H. Ev. T. | Mexico . | . 1830 |
| longifólïä . . | . Apetal | . F. Ev. T. | Nepal . | . 1801 |
| macrophýllä . | . Apetal | . H. Ev. T. | Mexico . | . 1839 |
| mïtis . . . | . Apetal | . 5, H. Ev. T. | N. Amer. | . 1739 |
| Montezümä . | . Apetal | . H. Ev. T. | Mexico . | . |
| monticölä . . | . Apetal | . H. Ev. T. | Californ. | . 1831 |
| occidentälis . | . Apetal | . F. Ev. T. | St. Domin. | . |
| Ocötĕ, 3 . . | . Apetal | . F. Ev. T. | Mexico . | . 1838 |
| Pallasïänä . . | . Apetal | . 5, H. Ev. T. | Siberia . | . 1820 |
| pätülä . . | . Apetal | . 5, H. Ev. T. | Mexico . | . 1826 |
| Pinäster . . | . Apetal | . 6, H. Ev. T. | S. Eur. . | . 1596 |
| Aberdónïä, 4 | . Apetal | . 5, H. Ev. T. | Nice . | . 1825 |
| chinénsis . | . Apetal | . 5, H. Ev. T. | China . | . |
| fol. variegätis | . Apetal | . 5, H. Ev. T. | Gardens | . |
| Lemonïänä, 5 | . Apetal | . 5, H. Ev. T. | | |
| marítïmä . | . Apetal | . 5, H. Ev. T. | | |
| Massonïänä | . Apetal | . 5, H. Ev. T. | China . | . 1824 |
| minör . . | . Apetal | . 5, H. Ev. T. | France . | . |
| nepalénsis . | . Apetal | . 5, H. Ev. T. | Nepal . | . 1824 |
| nova hollandï- cä, 6 | . Apetal | . 5, H. Ev. T. | N. Holl. | . 1816 |
| St. helénïcä . | . Apetal | . 5, H. Ev. T. | St. Helena | . 1816 |
| Pïnĕä . . . | . Apetal | . 6, H. Ev. T. | S. Eur. . | . 1548 |

[ 246 ]

| | | | | |
|---|---|---|---|---|
| americāna | Apetal | 5, H. Ev. T. | America | |
| cretica | Apetal | 5, H. Ev. T. | Crete | |
| fragilis | Apetal | 5, H. Ev. T. | S. Eur. | |
| ponderōsā | Apetal | H. Ev. T. | N. Amer. | 1828 |
| pseudostrōbūs | Apetal | H. Ev. T. | Mexico | 1839 |
| pumīlīo | Apetal | 5, H. Ev. T. | Europe | |
| Fischĕri | Apetal | 5, H. Ev. T. | | 1832 |
| Mūghūs, 7 | Apetal | 5, H. Ev. T. | Austria | |
| nānā | Apetal | 5, H. Ev. T. | Styria | |
| rubriflōrā | Apetal | 5, H. Ev. T. | | |
| pūngēns | Apetal | 5, H. Ev. T. | N. Amer. | 1804 |
| pyrenāīcā | Apetal | 5, H. Ev. T. | Pyrenee | 1834 |
| resinōsā, 8 | Apetal | 5, H. Ev. T. | N. Amer. | 1756 |
| rigīdā | Apetal | 5, H. Ev. T. | N. Amer. | 1759 |
| Russelliāna | Apetal | H. Ev. T. | Mexico | 1839 |
| Sabiniāna | Apetal | 3, H. Ev. T. | Californ. | 1832 |
| serotīnā | Apetal | 5, H. Ev. T. | N. Amer. | 1713 |
| sinēnsis | Apetal | F. Ev. S. | China | 1825 |
| Strōbūs | Apetal | 4, H. Ev. T. | E. Amer. | 1705 |
| alba | Apetal | 4, H. Ev. T. | | |
| brevifōlīā | Apetal | 4, H. Ev. T. | | |
| comprēssā | Apetal | 4, H. Ev. T. | Fleetbeck | |
| sylvēstris | Apetal | 5, H. Ev. T. | Scotland | |
| altāīcā | Apetal | H. Ev. T. | | 1836 |
| genevēnsis | Apetal | 5, H. Ev. T. | Geneva | 1830 |
| haguenēnsis | Apetal | 5, H. Ev. T. | Haguen | 1828 |
| horisontālis | Apetal | 5, H. Ev. T. | Scotland | |
| intermēdīā | Apetal | 5, H. Ev. T. | Russia | |
| monophylla | Apetal | 5, H. Ev. T. | | |
| rigēnsis | Apetal | 5, H. Ev. T. | Livonia | |
| scarīōsā | Apetal | 5, H. Ev. T. | France | 1830 |
| tortuōsā | Apetal | 5, H. Ev. T. | | |
| uncinātā | Apetal | 5, H. Ev. T. | Scotland | |
| vulgāris | Apetal | 5, H. Ev. T. | Scotland | |
| Tæda | Apetal | 5, H. Ev. T. | N. Amer. | 1713 |
| alopecurōidēs | Apetal | 5, H. Ev. T. | | |
| Teocōtā | Apetal | H. Ev. T. | Mexico | 1826 |
| timoriēnsis | Apetal | H. Ev. T. | Timor | |
| variābilis | Apetal | 5, H. Ev. T. | N. Amer. | 1789 |

SECT. II. ĀBĪĒS, *Tourn.* From *abeo*, to rise; in allusion to the aspiring habit of growth of the tree, or from *apios*, a pear-tree; the cones being like its fruit; *Abies* species of most authors. *Synonymes*: 1. *Abies excelsa.* 2. *A. alba.* 3. *A. canadensis.* 4. *A. cephalonica.* 5. *A. Douglasii.* 6. *A. Menziesii.* 7. *A. nigra.* 8. *A. orientalis.* 9. *A. rubra.* 10. *A. Smithiana, A. Morinda.*

| | | | | |
|---|---|---|---|---|
| Abīēs, 1 | Apetal | 4, H. Ev. T. | N. Eur. | 1548 |
| carpatīcā | Apetal | 4, H. Ev. T. | Carp. M. | |
| Clanbrasiliāna | Apetal | 5, H. Ev. S. | Moira | |
| Claub. stricta | Apetal | 5, H. Ev. S. | Florence Ct. | |
| commūnis | Apetal | 4, H. Ev. T. | N. Eur. | 1548 |
| fol. variegātis | Apetal | 4, H. Ev. T. | N. Eur. | |
| gigāntēa | Apetal | H. Ev. T. | | |
| monstrōsā | Apetal | H. Ev. S. | | |
| nigra | Apetal | 4, H. Ev. T. | | |
| pendūlā | Apetal | H. Ev. T. | | |
| pygmæā | Apetal | H. Ev. T. | | |
| tenuifōlīā | Apetal | H. Ev. S. | | |
| alba, 2 | Apetal | 5, H. Ev. T. | N. Amer. | 1700 |
| nānā | Apetal | 5, H. Ev. S. | | |
| canadēnsis, 3 | Apetal | 5, H. Ev. T. | N. Amer. | 1736 |
| cephalōnica, 4 | Apetal | 5, H. Ev. T. | Cephalonia | 1824 |
| Douglāsīi, 5 | Apetal | 5, H. Ev. T. | N. Amer. | 1826 |
| taxifōlīa | Apetal | 5, H. Ev. T. | N. Amer. | |
| Menziēsii, 6 | Apetal | H. Ev. T. | Californ. | 1831 |
| nigra, 7 | Apetal | 5, H. Ev. T. | N. Amer. | 1700 |
| orientālis, 8 | Apetal | 5, H. Ev. T. | Levant | 1825 |
| rūbra, 9 | Apetal | 5, H. Ev. T. | N. Amer. | 1755 |
| Smithiāna, 10 | Apetal | H. Ev. T. | Kamaon | |

SECT. III. PĪCĒA, *D. Don.* From *pix*, pitch; the tree producing abundance of resin—*Picea* and *Abies* species of most authors. *Synonymes*: 1. *Picea amabilis.* 2. *P. balsamea, Abies balsamifera.* 3. *P. Fraseri, A. Fraseri.* 4. *P. grandis, A. grandis.* 5. *P. nobilis, A. nobilis.* 6. *P. pectinata, A. pectinata.* 7. *P. Pichta, A. Pichta.* 8. *P. Pindrow.* 9. *P. Pinsapo.* 10. *P. Webbiana, Pinus spectabilis, A. Webbiana.*

| | | | | |
|---|---|---|---|---|
| amabīlis, 1 | Apetal | H. Ev. T. | Calif. | 1831 |
| balsāmēa, 2 | Apetal | 5, H. Ev. T. | N. Amer. | 1696 |
| longifōlīā | Apetal | 5, H. Ev. T. | | |
| Frasĕri, 3 | Apetal | 5, H. Ev. T. | Pennsylv. | 1811 |
| grandīs, 4 | Apetal | 5, H. Ev. T. | Calif. | 1831 |
| nōbīlis, 5 | Apetal | H. Ev. T. | N. Amer. | 1831 |
| Picēa, 6 | Apetal | 5 H. Ev. T. | Germany | 1603 |
| Pichtā, 7 | Apetal | 5, H. Ev. T. | Siberia | 1820 |
| Pindrow, 8 | Apetal | 5, H. Ev. T. | Kamaon | 1837 |
| Pinsāpō, 9 | Apetal | H. Ev. T. | Spain | 1838 |
| Webbiāna, 10 | Apetal | H. Ev. T. | Nepal | 1822 |

PĪPER, *Linn.* From *pippul*, a Bengalese name, or *pepto*, to digest. *Linn.* 2, Or. 3, Nat. Or. *Piperaceæ.* All the species of this interesting genus flourish in a mixture of loam and peat, requiring but little water; they are multiplied with facility by cut-

tings and suckers. The well-known pepper of the shops is principally produced by *P. nigrum. P. Betle* furnishes the Betle-leaf of the Southern Asiatics, in which they inclose a few slices of the Areca-nut, and a little shell lime; this they chew to sweeten the breath, and to keep off the pangs of hunger, and such is the immense consumption of this luxury in the East, that it nearly forms as extensive an article of commerce as that of tobacco in the West.

| | | | | |
|---|---|---|---|---|
| acutifōlīūm | Apetal | 8. Ev. S. | Peru | 1823 |
| adūncūm | Apetal | 5, 8. Ev. S. | Jamaica | 1748 |
| Amalāgō | Apetal | 7, 8. Ev. S. | Jamaica | 1759 |
| Betle | Apetal | 8. Ev. S. | E. Ind. | 1804 |
| colubrīnūm | Apetal | 8. Ev. S. | Brazil | 1820 |
| decumānūm | Apetal | 8, 8. Ev. S. | Carthage | 1768 |
| discōlōr | Apetal | 7, 8. Ev. S. | W. Ind. | 1821 |
| geniculātūm | Apetal | 8. Ev. S. | Jamaica | 1823 |
| glābrūm | Apetal | 8. Ev. S. | Campeachy | 1768 |
| glaucēscēns | Apetal | 8. Ev. S. | Peru | 1822 |
| hirsūtūm | Apetal | 8. Ev. S. | W. Ind. | 1793 |
| hispīdūm | Apetal | 7, 8. Ev. S. | S. Amer. | 1793 |
| laurifōlīūm | Apetal | 7, 8. Ev. S. | W. Ind. | 1768 |
| lōngūm | Apetal | 6, 8. Ev. S. | E. Ind. | 1788 |
| macrophyllūm | Apetal | 8. Ev. S. | W. Ind. | 1800 |
| marginātūm | Apetal | 8. Ev. S. | S. Amer. | 1811 |
| medīūm | Apetal | 8. Ev. S. | W. Ind. | 1820 |
| nigrūm | Apetal | 8. Ev. Cl. | E. Ind. | 1790 |
| nitīdūm | Apetal | 5, 8. Ev. S. | Jamaica | 1793 |
| peltātūm | Apetal | 8. Ev. S. | W. Ind. | 1748 |
| racemōsūm | Apetal | 8 Ev. S. | Campeachy | 1768 |
| reticulātūm | Apetal | 8, 8. Ev. S. | W. Ind. | 1748 |
| Sirībōa | Apetal | 8, 8. Ev. S. | E. Ind. | 1768 |
| tomentōsūm | Apetal | 8, 8. Ev. S. | W. Ind. | 1768 |
| triūicūm | Apetal | 8. Ev. S. | E. Ind. | 1818 |
| tuberculātūm | Apetal | 8. Ev. S. | S. Amer. | 1816 |
| umbellātūm | Apetal | 6, 8. Ev. S. | W. Ind. | 1748 |

PĪPĒRĪTŪS, hot, pungent.
PĪPEWORT, see *Eriocaūlōn.*
PĪPTĀNTHŪS, *Sweet.* From *pipto*, to fall, and *anthos*, a flower; the flowers are very fugacious. *Linn.* 10, Or. 1, Nat. Or. *Leguminosæ.* A very handsome and ornamental shrub when in flower, and sufficiently hardy to thrive in the open ground without any protection; it grows well in a rich loamy soil, and is increased by layers, or cuttings of the nearly ripened wood, planted in sand, under a glass. *Synonyme*: 1. *Anagyris indica.*

| | | | | |
|---|---|---|---|---|
| nepalēnsis, 1 | Yellow | 5. H. De. S. | Nepal | 1821 |

PĪPTĀTHĒRŪM, *Beauvois.* From *pipto*, to fall, and *ather*, an awn. *Linn.* 3, Or. 2, Nat. Or. *Gramineæ.* Curious species of grass, requiring the same treatment as *Milium. Synonymes*: 1. *Milium cærulescens.* 2. *M. multiflorum, arundinaceum.* 3. *M. paradoxum, Arachne virescens.*

| | | | | |
|---|---|---|---|---|
| cærulēscēns, 1 | Apetal | 6, Grass. | Barbary | 1819 |
| multiflōrūm, 2 | Apetal | 6, Grass. | S. Eur. | 1778 |
| paradōxūm, 3 | Apetal | 6, Grass. | France | 1771 |

PĪPTOCLĀINĀ, *Don.* From *pipto*, to fall, and *klaina*, a cloak; the calyx is deciduous. *Linn.* 5, Or. 1, Nat. Or. *Ehretiaceæ.* The seeds of this annual should be sown on a hotbed, and in May or June the plants should be planted out in the open border. *Synonyme*: 1. *Heliotropium supinum.*

| | | | | |
|---|---|---|---|---|
| supīna, 1 | Yel. wht. | 6, H. | A. S. Eur. | 1640 |

PĪQUĒRĪA, *Cavanilles.* After Andreas Piqueria, a Spanish botanist. *Linn.* 19, Or. 1, Nat. Or. *Compositæ. P. trinervia* is a pretty herbaceous plant; all the species are of easy culture, and are multiplied by divisions.

| | | | | |
|---|---|---|---|---|
| trinervīa | White | 7, H. Her. P. | Mexico | 1798 |

*artemisiōidēs, ovātā, pilōsā.*

PĪSCĪDĪA, *Linn.* The leaves, bark, and twigs are used for the purpose of stupifying fish; whence the name from *piscis*, a fish, and *cædo*, to kill. *Linn.* 16, Or. 6, Nat. Or. *Leguminosæ.* This genus, the Jamaica Dogwood, consists of two ornamental timber-trees, with spreading branches and pinnate leaves. Sandy loam suits them best, and cuttings may be rooted in sand, under a glass, in heat. *Synonyme*: 1. *P. Erythrina.*

| | | | | |
|---|---|---|---|---|
| carthaginēnsis, 1 | Dirty w | 8. Ev. T. | Carthage | 1690 |
| Erythrīnā | Dirty w | 8. Ev. T. | W. Ind. | 1690 |

PĪSIFORME, formed like a pea.
PĪSŌNĪA, *Linn.* In honour of M. Piso, an eminent physician of Amsterdam. *Linn.* 7, Or. 2, Nat. Or. *Nyctaginaceæ.* Stove shrubs, of not much merit.

*P. aculeata* is remarkable for its spiny branches, and for its glutinous and burry seeds, which fasten to whatever touches them. A mixture of peat and loam suits them best, and they are easily propagated by cuttings in the same sort of soil.

| | | | | | | |
|---|---|---|---|---|---|---|
| aculeātā | . | . Green | . . | 8. Ev. T. | Jamaica | . 1739 |
| frāgrāns | . | . | . | 8. Ev. S. | | . 1823 |
| grācīlis | . | . | . | 8. Ev. T. | N. Holl. | . 1806 |
| hirtēlla | . | . | . | 8. Ev. S. | Mexico | . 1825 |
| macrophȳllā | . | . | . | 8. Ev. S. | | . 1823 |
| mexicānā | . | . | . | 8. Ev. S. | Mexico | . 1824 |
| nigrĭcāns | . | . Grn. wht. | . | 8. Ev. S. | W. Ind. | . 1806 |
| nītĭdā | . | . | . | 8. Ev. S. | Madagas. | . 1824 |
| obovātā | . | . | . | 8. Ev. S. | | . 1823 |
| obtusātā | . | . | . | 8. Ev. S. | W. Ind. | . 1824 |
| subcordātā | . | . | . | 8. Ev. S. | Jamaica | . 1821 |

PISTACHIA-TREE, see *Pistācĭā.*

PISTĀCĬA, *Linn.* Altered from *Foustaq*, its Arabic name. *Linn.* 22, Or. 5, Nat. Or. *Terebinthaceæ.* Ornamental plants. The greenhouse kinds thrive in loam and peat, and cuttings of the ripened wood root in sand, under a glass. The hardy species do best planted against a wall, as they are rather tender; common garden soil suits them, and they may be increased by layers, or cuttings in sandy soil under a glass. *Synonymes:* 1. *P. Lentiscus massiliensis.* 2. *P. officinarum.* 3. *P. reticulata.*

| | | | | | | |
|---|---|---|---|---|---|---|
| atlantĭcā | . . | Apetal | | F. De. T. | Barbary | . 1790 |
| Lentiscūs | . . | Apetal | . 5, | G. Ev. T. | S. Eur. | . 1654 |
| angustifōlĭā, 1 | Apetal | . 5, | H. Ev. T. | S. Eur. | |
| chĭā | . . | Apetal | . 5, | H. Ev. T. | Scio | . |
| Terebinthūs | . | Apetal | . 6, | H. De. T. | S. Eur. | . 1656 |
| sphærocārpā | . | Apetal | . 5, | H. Ev. T. | | |
| vērā, 2 | . . | Apetal | . 5, | H. De. T. | Syria | . 1770 |
| narbōnēnsīs, 3 | Apetal | . 4, | H. De. T. | Narbonne | . 1752 |
| triflōrā | . . | Apetal | . 5, | H. De. T. | Syria | . |

PISTILLUM, or PISTIL, the columnar body in the centre of a flower, consisting commonly of three parts; viz., the ovary, styles, and stigmas.

PISTILLARĬA, *Fries.* From *pistillum*, a pestle; form of the plants. *Linn.* 24, Or. 9, Nat. Or. *Fungi.* The species constituting this genus are chiefly found on the decayed leaves of ferns—*P. micāns, muscicōlā, puberŭlā, pusīllā, quisquilĭārīs.*

PISTORĪNĬA, *Decandolle.* The meaning is unknown to us. *Linn.* 10, Or. 5, Nat. Or. *Crassulaceæ.* The seeds merely require sowing in light soil in any dry situation in the open border, or on rock-work, where it has a pretty appearance. *Synonyme:* 1. *Cotyledon hispanica.*

| | | | | | | |
|---|---|---|---|---|---|---|
| hispanĭcā, 1 | . | . Red | . 6, | H. | B. Spain | . 1790 |

PISŬM, *Linn.* From *pis*, the Celtic word for pea; whence the Latin *pisum*. *Linn.* 17, Or. 4, Nat. Or. *Leguminosæ.* This genus affords one of the most valuable and well-known legumes, the Pea, and like most cultivated vegetables, it has produced numerous improved varieties, growing from a foot to twelve feet high. They prefer a rich dry soil, in which they may be sown at any season, according to the time when they are wanted.

| | | | | | | |
|---|---|---|---|---|---|---|
| americānŭm | . | Purple | . 7, | H. Her. P. | S. Amer. | . 1800 |
| arvēnsē | . | Red | . 7, | H. Cl. A. | Eur. | |
| elātŭm | . | Drk. blue | . 7, | H. Cl. A. | Iberia | . 1820 |
| Jomārdĭ | . | White | . 7, | H. Cl. A. | Egypt | . 1820 |
| maritĭmŭm | . | Purple | . 7, | H. Her. P. | England | |
| satīvŭm | . | White | . 7, | H. Cl. A. | S. Eur. | |
| humĭlĕ | . | White | . 7, | H. Cl. A. | |
| macrocārpŭm | White | . 7, | H. Cl. A. | |
| quadrātŭm | White | . 7, | H. Cl. A. | |
| saccharātŭm | White | . 7, | H. Cl. A. | |
| umbellātŭm | . | Purple | . 7 | H. Cl. A. | |
| thebāĭcŭm | . | | . 7, | H. Cl. A. | | . 1825 |

PITCAIRNĬA, *L'Héritier.* In honour of W. Pitcairn, a physician of London. *Linn.* 6, Or. 1, Nat. Or. *Bromeliaceæ.* A handsome genus of plants, remarkable for their long narrow prickly leaves, and regular panicles of flowers; for culture, &c., see *Tillandsia.*

| | | | | | | |
|---|---|---|---|---|---|---|
| albĭflōrā | . | . White | . 9, | S. Her. P. | Brazil | . 1824 |
| angustifōlĭā | . | Scarlet | . 8. | S. Her. P. | Santa Cruz | . 1777 |
| bromeliæfōlĭā | . | Scarlet | . 6, | S. Her. P. | Jamaica | . 1781 |
| bracteātā | . | Scarlet | . 4, | S. Her. P. | W. Ind. | . 1799 |
| chilēnsĭs | . | Scarlet | . 7, | S. Her. P. | Chile | . 1820 |
| flāmmēā | . | Flame | . 11, | S. Her. P. | Rio Jan. | . 1825 |
| furfurācēā | . | Red | . 7, | S. Her. P. | S. Amer. | . 1816 |
| humĭlĭs | . | Scarlet | . 7, | S. Her. P. | S. Amer. | . 1800 |
| integrifōlĭā | . | Red | . 8, | S. Her. P. | W. Ind. | . 1820 |
| intermedĭā | . | Scarlet | . 7, | S. Her. P. | S. Amer. | . 1820 |
| iridĭflōrā | . | Scarlet | . 7, | S. Her. P. | S. Amer. | . 1820 |
| latifōlĭā | . | Scarlet | . 8, | S. Her. P. | W. Ind. | . 1785 |

| | | | | | | |
|---|---|---|---|---|---|---|
| medĭā | . . | . Scarlet | . 7, | 8. Her. P. | S. Amer. | . 1820 |
| stamĭnēā | . . | . Scarlet | . 1, | 8. Her. P. | S. Amer. | . 1823 |
| suaveōlēns | . . | . Yellow | . 7, | 8. Her. P. | Brazil | . 1824 |
| sulphūrēā | . . | . Yellow | . 8, | 8. Her. P. | W. Ind. | . 1797 |

PITCHER-LEAF, see *Nepēnthēs Phyllāmphŏrā.*

PITCHER-PLANT, see *Nepēnthēs.*

PITCHERS, hollow leaves, having the appearance of pitchers.

PITH, medulla, occupying the centre of a stem or shoot.

PITTOSPŎRŬM, *Banks.* From *pitte*, to pitch, and *sporos*, a seed; the seeds are covered with a resinous pulp. *Linn.* 5, Or. 1, Nat. Or. *Pittosporaceæ.* All the species are very handsome shrubs, on account of their glossy foliage and pretty flowers, which render them well adapted for conservatories. *P. Tobira* will succeed against a south wall, with the protection of a mat in severe weather. All the species thrive well in a mixture of peat and loam, and ripened cuttings root in sand, under a glass. *Synonyme:* 1. *P. hirsutum.*

| | | | | | | |
|---|---|---|---|---|---|---|
| Andersōnĭĭ | . | . Yellow | . 5, | G. Ev. S. | N. Holl. | . 1820 |
| angustifōlĭŭm | . | Yellow | . 6, | G. Ev. S. | N. S. W. | . 1830 |
| bracteolātŭm | . | | . | G. Ev. S. | Norfolk Is. | . 1837 |
| capēnsē | . | . | . 5, | G. Ev. S. | | . 1820 |
| coriācēŭm | . | . Blue | . 5, | G. Ev. S. | Madeira | . 1783 |
| cornifōlĭŭm | . | . Brown | . 5, | G. Ev. S. | N. Zeal. | . 1827 |
| ferrugĭnēŭm | . | . Yellow | . 3, | G. Ev. S. | Guinea | . 1787 |
| fūlvŭm | . | . Yellow | . 4, | G. Ev. S. | N. Holl. | . 1820 |
| hirtŭm, 1 | . | . Yellow | . 5, | G. Ev. S. | Canaries | . 1822 |
| ligustrifōlĭŭm | . | | . 9, | G. Ev. S. | N. Holl. | . 1823 |
| maurĭtĭānŭm | . | Yellow | . 5, | G. Ev. S. | Mauritius | . 1825 |
| oleĭfōlĭŭm | . | | . | G. Ev. S. | N. Holl. | . 1823 |
| revolūtŭm | . | . Yellow | . 8, | G. Ev. S. | N. Holl. | . 1795 |
| tenuifōlĭŭm | . | | . 5, | G. Ev. S. | N. Holl. | . 1820 |
| Tobīra | . | . White | . 5, | G. Ev. S. | Japan | . 1804 |
| tomentōsŭm | . | . Yellow | . 7, | G. Ev. S. | N. Holl. | . 1824 |
| undulātŭm | . | . Wht. grn. | . 4, | G. Ev. S. | N. S. W. | . 1789 |
| variegātŭm | . | . Wht. yel. | . 4, | G. Ev. S. | Gardens | . |
| viridĭflōrŭm | . | . Green | . 5, | G. Ev. S. | C. G. H. | . 1806 |

PLACENTA, that part of the capsule to which the seeds are attached.

PLADĒRĀ, *Roxburgh.* From *pladaros*, abounding in juice. *Linn.* 4, Or. 1, Nat. Or. *Gentianaceæ.* The seed of these plants should be sown on a hot-bed, and treated similarly to balsams.

| | | | | | | |
|---|---|---|---|---|---|---|
| decussātā | . | . White | . 8, | G. | B. W. Ind. | . 1816 |
| virgātā | . | . Red | . 7, | G. | B. E. Ind. | . 1820 |

PLAGIĀNTHŪS, *Forster.* From *plagios*, oblique, and *anthos*, a flower; direction of the flowers. *Linn.* 16, Or. 7, Nat. Or. *Euphorbiaceæ.* These plants grow well in any rich light soil, and cuttings of the young wood root freely in sand, under a glass, in heat.

| | | | | | | |
|---|---|---|---|---|---|---|
| divaricātŭs, 1 | . | Red | . 6, | G. Ev. S. | N. Zeal. | . 1822 |
| sidōĭdēs, 2 | . | Yelsh. | . 9, | G. Ev. S. | V. D. L. | |

PLAGIOBŎTRŸS, *Fischer and Meyer.* From *plagios*, transverse, and *bothrys*, a pit; the pits at the base of the carpels are transverse, and not longitudinal. *Linn.* 5, Or. 1, Nat. Or. *Boraginaceæ.* A hardy annual, not worth cultivating except in botanic gardens—*P. ruſéscēns.*

PLAGIOLŌBĬŬM, *Sweet.* From *plagios*, transverse, and *lobos*, a pod; alluding to the shape of the pod. *Linn.* 17, Or. 4, Nat. Or. *Leguminosæ.* A genus of very beautiful greenhouse plants. For culture and propagation, see *Hovea.*

| | | | | | | |
|---|---|---|---|---|---|---|
| chorozemæfōlĭŭm | Purple | . 3, | G. Ev. S. | N. Holl. | . 1824 |
| ilicĭfōlĭŭm | . | . Purple | . 3, | G. Ev. S. | K. G.'s Sd. | . 1824 |

PLANĒRĀ, *Michaux.* In honour of J. Planer, a German botanist. *Linn.* 4, Or. 8, Nat. Or. *Ulmaceæ.* A genus very nearly related to *Ulmus*, growing freely in a loamy soil, in moist situations; they may be multiplied by layers or grafts. *Synonymes:* 1. *Planera aquatica.* 2. *Ulmus nemoralis.*

| | | | | | | |
|---|---|---|---|---|---|---|
| Gmelinĭ, 1 | . | . Brown | . 4, | H. De. T. | N. Amer. | . 1816 |
| Richārdĭ, 2 | . | . Brown | . 4, | H. De. T. | N. Amer. | . 1760 |

PLANE TREE, see *Platānŭs.*

PLANK PLANT, see *Bossĭēā scolopēndrĭā.*

PLANTĀGŌ, *Linn.* Derived from *planta*, the sole of the foot; resemblance in the leaves. *Linn.* 4, Or. 1, Nat. Or. *Plantaginaceæ.* A genus, the greater number of the species of which are mere weeds, of the easiest culture and propagation. *Synonymes:* 1. *P. sphærocephala.* 2. *P. crispa.* 3. *P. rigida.* 4. *P. Cornuti.* 5. *P. Cornuti.* 6. *P. alpina.*

| | | | | | | |
|---|---|---|---|---|---|---|
| Ispaghŭlā | . | . White | . 6, | H. | A. E. Ind. | . 1824 |
| Kentuckēnsĭs | . | White | . 6, | H. Her. P. | N. Amer. | . 1829 |

*afrā, albicāns, alpīnā, altissimā, amplexicaūlis, arenāriā, asiāticā, Bellārdī* 1, *brasiliēnsis, brūtiā, capēnsis, ceratophȳllā, cordātā, coronōpūs, crāssā* 2, *crassifōliā, crēticā, Cȳnōps, deprēssā, divaricātā* 3, *elongātā, eriostāchyā, exaltātā, gargānicā, gentianoīdēs, Goudnī* 4, *gramīnēā, hirsūtā, holosēricēā, Holostēūm, humifūsā, hungāricā, indicā, interrūptā, Jacquīnī* 5, *Kamtchāticā, Lagopūs, lanceolātā, L. variegātā, Læflingīi, lusitānicā, macrorhizā, mājor, M. rōsēā, M. scopāriā, maritimā, M. variegātā, M. vivipārā, māximā, mediā, mexicānā, microcēphālā, minimā, montānā, nōtātā, parviflōrā, patagōnicā, pilōsā, Pōgilliūm, pūmilā, recurvātā, sālsā, saxātilis, scorzonerifōliā, sericēā, serpentinā, Serrāriā, sibiricā, sinuātā, sphærocēphālā* 6, *squarrōsā, strictā, subulātā, tenuiflōrā, teretifōliā, tumidā, vaginātā, vāriā, villōsā, virginicā, Wulfēnī.*

PLANTAIN, see *Alisma Plantāgō.*

PLANTAIN, see *Plantāgō.*

PLANTAIN TREE, see *Mūsā.*

PLATĀNTHĒRĀ, *Richard.* From *platys*, broad, and *anthera*, an anther. Linn. 20, Or. 1, Nat. Or. *Orchidaceæ.* Pretty plants. For culture and propagation, see *Orchis.* Synonymes: 1. *Orchis bifolia.* 2. *Habenaria ciliaris.* 3. *H. cristata.* 4. *H. dilatata.* 5. *H. fimbriata.* 6. *H. flava.* 7. *H. herbiola.* 8. *H. blephariglottis.* 9. *H. orbiculata.* 10. *H. hyperborea.* 11. *H. incisa.* 12. *H. psychodes, H. lacera.* 13. *H. gigantea.*

| | | | | | | | |
|---|---|---|---|---|---|---|---|
| bifōlia, 1 | . | . | . | White | . 6, | H. Ter. | Britain | . . |
| ciliāris, 2 | . | . | . | Yellow | . 6, | H. Ter. | N. Amer. | . 1796 |
| cristātā, 3 | . | . | . | Yellow | . 9, | H. Ter. | N. Amer. | . 1806 |
| dilatātā, 4 | . | . | . | White | . 9, | H. Ter. | Canada | . 1823 |
| fimbriātā, 5 | . | . | . | Purple | . 6, | H. Ter. | Canada | . 1789 |
| flāvā, 6 | . | . | . | Yellow | . 7, | G. Ter. | N. Holl. | . 1823 |
| herbiolā. 7 | . | . | . | Green | . 6, | H. Ter. | N. Amer. | . 1789 |
| holopetālā, 8 | . | . | . | White | . 5, | H. Ter. | Canada | . 1820 |
| Hookēri, 9 | . | . | . | Green | . 6, | H. Ter. | N. Amer. | . 1822 |
| hyperbōrēa, 10 | . | . | . | Green | . 6, | H. Ter. | N. Amer. | . 1805 |
| inclsā, 11 | . | . | . | Pa. yel. | . 6, | F. Ter. | N. Amer. | . 1826 |
| psychōdēs, 12 | . | . | . | Yellow | . 6, | H. Ter. | N. Amer. | . 1826 |
| Susānnæ, 13 | . | . | . | Orn. wht. | . 8. | Ter. | E. Ind. | . 1834 |

PLATĀNŪS, *Linn.* From *platys*, ample; in allusion to the spreading branches and shady foliage. Linn. 21, Or. 9, Nat. Or. *Platanaceæ.* Noble trees, of peculiar grace and elegance, well fitted for large plantations, or to stand singly on a lawn. They are easily increased by layers, or cuttings planted out in autumn, in a sheltered situation. Synonymes: 1. *P. acerifolia.* 2. *P. cuneata.*

| | | | | | | |
|---|---|---|---|---|---|---|
| occidentālis | . | Apetal | . 4, | H. De. | T. N. Amer. | . 1636 |
| orientālis | . | Apetal | . 4, | H. De. | T. Levant | . 1548 |
| acerifōliā, 1 | . | Apetal | . 4, | H. De. | T. Levant | . . |
| cuneātā, 2 | . | Apetal | . 4, | H. De. | T. Levant | . . |
| hispānicā | . | Apetal | . 4, | H. De. | T. Levant | . . |

PLATYCĀRPIŪM, *Humboldt.* From *platys*, broad, and *karpos*, fruit; in reference to the compressed seed-pod. Linn. 5, Or. 1, Nat. Or. *Bignoniaceæ.* This tree thrives in peat and loam; and half-ripened cuttings planted in sand, and placed under a hand-glass, root readily. If the plants are kept rather dry in winter, it will tend to throw them into flower.

| | | | | | | |
|---|---|---|---|---|---|---|
| orinocēnsā | . | . | . | Pa. rose | . 8. | Ev. T. Orinoco | . 1818 |

PLATYCHĪLŪM, *Delaunay.* From *platys*, broad, and *cheilos*, a lip; breadth of corolla. Linn. 16, Or. 6, Nat. Or. *Leguminosæ.* A beautiful plant, requiring the same treatment as the *Hoveas.* Synonyme: 1. *Gompholobium celsianum.*

| | | | | | |
|---|---|---|---|---|---|
| Celsiānūm, 1 | . | . | Yellow | . G. Ev. S. N. Holl. | . 1820 |

PLATYCŌDŌN, *Decandolle.* From *platys*, broad, and *kodon*, a bell; the flowers are broad and bell-shaped. Linn. 5, Or. 1, Nat. Or. *Campanulaceæ.* A neat, elegant plant when in flower; it grows best in sandy loam, and may be increased by seeds or young cuttings. Synonyme: 1. *Campanula grandiflora.*

| | | | | | |
|---|---|---|---|---|---|
| grandiflōrūm | . . | Blue | . 6, H. Her. P. Dahuria | . 1782 |

PLATYLŌBIŪM. *Smith.* From *platys*, broad, and *lobos*, a pod; in reference to the broad legumes. Linn. 16, Or. 6, Nat. Or. *Leguminosæ.* Free-flowering shrubs, of rather difficult culture; they require a mixture of three-parts sandy peat and one part loam; the pots must be carefully drained, to allow the water to pass off freely, and care must be taken not to over-water them. They may be propagated by cuttings in sand, under a glass; or by seeds, which are sometimes produced in abundance.

[ 249 ]

| | | | | | | |
|---|---|---|---|---|---|---|
| formōsūm | . | . | Orange | . 7, | G. Ev. S. N. Holl. | . 1790 |
| Murrayānūm | . | Yel. red | . 5, | G. Ev. S. V. D. L. | . 1832 |
| obtusangūlūm | . | Yel. red | . 5, | G. Ev. S. V. D. L. | . 1832 |
| ovātūm | . | . | Orange | . 7, | G. Ev. S. N. Holl. | . 1792 |
| parviflōrūm | . | Orange | . 7, | G. Ev. S. N. Holl. | . 1792 |
| triangulārē | . | Orange | . 7, | G. Ev. S. V. D. L. | . 1805 |

PLATYLŌPHŪS, *D. Don.* From *platys*, broad, and *lophos*, a crest; the capsule, from being much compressed at the apex, appears as if winged. Linn. 10, Or. 2, Nat. Or. *Cunoniaceæ.* The White Ash of the English colonists is an elegant tree. It succeeds well in a mixture of loam and peat; and cuttings of the ripened wood root freely in sand, under a glass. Synonyme: 1. *Weinmannia trifoliata.*

| | | | | |
|---|---|---|---|---|
| trifoliātūs, 1 | . . | G. Ev. T. C. G. H. | . 1820 |

PLATYPTĒRĪS, *Humboldt and Bonpland.* From *platys*, broad, and *pteron*, a wing; appendage to the seed. Linn. 19, Or. 1, Nat. Or. *Compositæ.* A small plant of little beauty, growing in any peaty soil, and increased by cuttings, in the same kind of soil, under a glass. Synonyme: 1. *Spilanthus crocatus.*

| | | | | | |
|---|---|---|---|---|---|
| crocātā, 1 | . . | Orange | . 3, S. Her. P. S. Amer. | . 1812 |

PLATYSPERMŪM, *Hooker.* From *platys*, broad, and *sperma*, a seed. Linn. 6, Or. 2, Nat. Or. *Cruciferæ.* Mere annual weeds, growing in any garden soil. Synonymes: 1. *Caucalis littoralis.* 2. *C. orientalis.* 3. *Daucus muricatus—P. littoralis* 1, *orientālis* 2, *O. pulcherrimūm, muricātūm* 3.

PLATYSTĒMŌN, *Bentham.* From *platys*, broad, and *stemon*, a stamen. Linn. 13, Or. 1, Nat. Or. *Ranunculaceæ.* A genus of rather pretty annuals, growing freely in sandy loam.

| | | | | | |
|---|---|---|---|---|---|
| californicūs | . | Yellow | . 8, H. | A. California | . 1833 |
| leiocārpūs | . | Yellow | . 7, H. | A. Siberia | . 1837 |

PLATYSTĪGMA, *Bentham.* From *platys*, broad, and *stigma*; the stigma is ovate. Linn. 13, Or. 1, Nat. Or. *Ranunculaceæ.* This plant somewhat resembles *Platystemon californicus*, and requires the same treatment as that plant.

| | | | | | |
|---|---|---|---|---|---|
| lineārē | . | . | Yellow | . F. Her. P. California | . 1833 |

PLATYSTȲLIS, *Sweet.* From *platys*, broad, and *stylos*, a style; in allusion to the dilated style. Linn. 17, Or. 4, Nat. Or. *Leguminosæ.* A very handsome genus of flower-border plants. For culture and propagation see *Orobus.* Synonymes: 1. *Orobus cyaneus.* 2. *O. sessilifolius.* 3. *O. stipulaceus.*

| | | | | | |
|---|---|---|---|---|---|
| cyānēā, 1 | . | . | Purple | . 5, H. Her. P. Caucasus | . 1823 |
| sessilifōliūs, 2 | . | Purple | . 5, H. Her. P. Tauria | . 1823 |
| stipulācēā, 3 | . | Purple | . 5, H. Her. P. Siberia | . . |

PLECTRĀNTHŪS, *L'Heritier.* From *plektron*, a cock's-spur, and *anthos*, a flower; referring to the shape of the flowers. Linn. 14, Or. 2, Nat. Or. *Labiatæ.* Any light rich soil will suit the stove and greenhouse shrubby and herbaceous kinds; and cuttings root readily. The seeds of the annual and biennial species require to be sown on a hotbed, and treated the same as other tender annuals and biennials. Synonymes: 1. *P. secundus.* 2. *Ocymum molle.* 3. *O. scutellarioides.*

| | | | | | |
|---|---|---|---|---|---|
| incānūs | . | . | . | Blue | . 7, G. Her. P. | . 1822 |
| parviflōrūs | . | . | Blue | . 7, G. Ev. S. S. Amer. | 1805 |
| punctātūs | . | . | Blue | . 8, | A. Africa | . 1775 |
| ternātūs | . | . | Purple | . 8, S. Her. P. Madag. | . 1821 |
| ternifōliūs | . | . | Blue | . 8, G. Her. P. Nepal | . 1820 |
| viscōsūs | . | . | Blue | . 8, S. Ev. S. E. Ind. | . 1826 |

*aspēr, austrālis, Coētsā, colorātus, comōsūs, cordifōliūs* 1, *galeātūs, graveolēns, mōllis* 2, *rotundifōliūs, scutellarioīdēs* 3, *secūndūs, strobiliferūs, thymiflōrūs.*

PLECTRĪTIS, *Lindley.* From *plektron*, a cock's-spur; in reference to the flower being gibbous in front. Linn. 3, Or. 1, Nat. Or. *Valerianaceæ.* The seed of this plant only requires to be sown in the open border. Synonyme: 1. *Valerianella congesta.*

| | | | | | |
|---|---|---|---|---|---|
| congēstā, 1 | . | . | Rose | . 7, H. | A. N. Amer. | . 1826 |
| minōr | . | . | Rose | . 7, H. | A. N. Amer. | . 1826 |

PLECTRŌNIĀ, *Linn.* From *plektron*, a cock's-spur; tree with large spines. Linn. 4, Or. 1, Nat. Or. *Cinchonaceæ.* An ornamental tree; for culture and propagation, see *Chiococca.*

| | | | | | |
|---|---|---|---|---|---|
| corymbōsā | . | . | Wht. grn. | G. Ev. T. C. G. H. | . 1816 |

PLĒRĀ, *Michaux.* From *pleias*, the seven stars; disposition of the flowers. Linn. 9, Or. 2, Nat. Or. *Melanthaceæ.* A species succeeding well in peat

2 K

soil, in a moist situation : it also grows well in pots, placed in pans of water; increased by seeds.

| tenuifolia | . . . Brown | . 7, Grass. Carolina . | 1824 |

PLEOPELTIS, *Humboldt and Bonpland.* From *pleos,* full, and *pelte,* a shield ; the form of the indusium. *Linn.* 24, Or. 1, Nat. Or. *Polypodiaceæ.* A genus of *Ferns,* succeeding well in loam and peat, in a shady situation ; readily increased by dividing the roots, or by seeds.

| ensifolia | . . . Brown | . 5, S. Her. P. S. Amer. | . 1823 |
| latifolia | . . . Brown | . 5, S. Her. P. S. Amer. | . 1823 |
| nuda | . . . Brown | . 5, S. Her. P. Nepal . | |

PLEROMA, *Don.* From *pleroma,* fulness ; cells of the capsule. *Linn.* 10, Or. 1, Nat. Or. *Melastomaceæ.* Ornamental shrubs, from three to six feet high. For culture and propagation, see *Melastoma.* Synonymes : 1. *Melastoma heteromalla.* 2. *M. villosum.* 3. *Rhexia viminea.*

| heteromalla, 1 | . Purple | . 7, S. Ev. S. Brasil | . 1819 |
| villosa, 2 | . White | . 7, S. Ev. S. Amer. | . 1820 |
| viminea, 3 | . Purple | . 7, S. Ev. S. Brasil | . 1821 |

PLEURANDRA, *Labillardière.* From *pleuron,* a side, and *aner,* a male ; in allusion to the stamens being on one side of the calyx. *Linn.* 13, Or. 2, Nat. Or. *Dilleniaceæ.* A very pretty genus of plants, growing about two feet high, in a mixture of sandy loam and peat ; and cuttings of the ripened wood root readily in the same sort of soil, under a glass.

| acicularis | . Yellow | . 5, G. Ev. S. N. Holl. | 1822 |
| bractaeta | . Yellow | . 5, G. Ev. S. N. Holl. | 1823 |
| calycina | . Yellow | . 5, G. Ev. S. N. Holl. | 1822 |
| Cneorum | . Yellow | . 6, G. Ev. S. N. Holl. | 1824 |
| ericæfolia | . Yellow | . 5, G. Ev. S. N. Holl. | 1824 |
| nitida | . Yellow | . 5, G. Ev. S. N. Holl. | 1823 |
| stricta | . Yellow | . 5, G. Ev. S. N. Holl. | 1826 |

PLEUROSPERMUM, *Hoffman.* From *pleuron,* a rib, and *sperma,* a seed ; in allusion to the membranes of the pericarps both having ribs. *Linn.* 5, Or. 2, Nat. Or. *Umbelliferæ.* A plant of no interest, growing in any common soil, and readily increased by seeds. Synonyme : 1. *Ligusticum austriacum—P. austriacum.*

PLEUROTHALLIS, *R. Brown.* From *pleuron,* a side or rib, and *thallo,* to flower ; in allusion to the one-sided disposition of the flowers of some of the species. *Linn.* 20, Or. 1, Nat. Or. *Orchidaceæ.* This is a genus of curious little plants, well fitted for cultivating on wood, in the same way as the *Burlingtonias.*

| aphthosa | . . Yellow | . S. Epi. Mexico . . | |
| bicarinata | . Grsh. yel. | . S. Epi. Brasil | |
| ciliata | . . Brown | . S. Epi. Demerara | 1834 |
| circumplexa | . Yelsh. | . S, S. Epi. Mexico . . | |
| Grobyi | . Pur. yel. | . 4, S. Epi. Demerara | 1834 |
| Lanceana | . Orange | . 1, S. Epi. Surinam | 1831 |
| marginata | . Orange | . 6, S. Epi. Guatemala | |
| muscoidea | . . | . S. Epi. . . | 183— |
| occulta | . . | . S. Epi. Brasil | 1837 |
| ophiocephala | . Yelsh. brn. | . S. Epi. Mexico . | |
| pectinata | . Grn. spot. | . S. Epi. Rio Jan. | |
| picta | . Yel. strip. | . 3, S. Epi. Demerara | 1834 |
| prolifera | . Purple | . 6, S. Epi. Brasil | 1826 |
| pulchella | . Purple | . 6, S. Epi. Quito | |
| racemiflora | . Yelsh. | . 9, S. Epi. Jamaica | 1823 |
| ruscifolia | . Grn. yel. | . 4, S. Epi. W. Ind. | 1794 |
| saurocephala | . Grn. spot. | . 9, S. Epi. Rio Jan. | 1829 |
| stenopetala | . Pa. grn. | . S. Epi. Brasil | 183— |
| strupifolia | . Pur. wht. | . S. Epi. Rio Jan. | 183— |
| vittata | . . Purple | . 8, S. Epi. Mexico . | 1837 |

PLICATE, plaited ; 3, 4, or 5, plicate, means 3, 4, or 5 plaited.

PLOCAMA, *Aiton.* From *plokamos,* bent hairs ; alluding to the pendulous branches. *Linn.* 5, Or. 1, Nat. Or. *Cinchonaceæ.* The plant grows best in a mixture of loam and peat ; and it may be readily propagated by cuttings, in sand, under a glass.

| pendula | . . . . White . . | G. Ev. S. Canaries | . 1772 |

PLOUGHMAN'S SPIKENARD, see *Baccharis.*

PLUKENETIA. Named by Plumier in honour of Leonard Plukenet, an English botanist. *Linn.* 21, Or. 10, Nat. Or. *Euphorbiaceæ.* Uninteresting stove climbers, growing in a light loamy soil ; increased by cuttings, under a glass, in sand—*P. verrucosa, volubilis.*

PLUM, see *Prunus.*

PLUMBAGO, *Linn.* From *plumbum,* a disorder in the eyes, which some species were formerly said to cure. *Linn.* 5, Or. 1, Nat. Or. *Plumbaginaceæ.*

Pretty free flowering plants, growing in any common soil, and increased readily by cuttings. The root of *P. europæa,* it is said, when chewed will cure the toothach. Synonymes : 1. *P. zeylanica, scandens.*

| capensis | . Blue | . 11, G. Ev. S. C. G. H. | . 1818 |
| europæa | . Blue | . 9, H. Her. P. S. Eur. | . 1596 |
| lapathifolia | . White | . 6, H. Her. P. Iberia | . 1822 |
| mexicana | . White | . 7, S. Ev. S. Mexico | . 1829 |
| micrantha | . White | . H. Her. P. Siberia | . 1829 |
| occidentalis, 1 | . White | . 6, S. Ev. Cl. W. Ind. | . 1817 |
| rhombifolia | . Blue | . 9, S. . A. S. Amer. | . 1826 |
| rosea | . Red | . 5, S. Ev. S. E. Ind. | . 1777 |
| scandens | . White | . 7, S. Ev. Cl. W. Ind. | . 1699 |
| tristis | . Brown | . 5, G. Ev. S. C. G. H. | . 1792 |
| zeylanica | . White | . 6, S. Ev. S. E. Ind. | . 1731 |

PLUMIERIA, *Linn.* In honour of C. Plumier, a celebrated French botanist. *Linn.* 5, Or. 1, Nat. Or. *Apocynaceæ.* A genus of very fine flowering plants, growing best in a light loamy soil, or a mixture of peat and loam ; large cuttings, with their leaves on, after being dried for a few days, will grow freely in pots of mould, without being watered. The plants, when in a dormant state, must be kept dry, otherwise they do not flower freely. Synonymes : 1. *P. tricolor.* 2. *P. Gouani.*

| acuminata | . Red yel. | . 7, S. Ev. T. E. Ind. | . 1790 |
| alba | . White | . 7, S. Ev. T. Jamaica | . 1733 |
| bicolor | . Wht. yel. | . 8, S. Ev. T. S. Amer. | . 1815 |
| Blandfordiana | . | . 7, S. Ev. S. S. Amer. | . 1825 |
| conspicua | . | . 7, S. Ev. S. S. Amer. | . 1820 |
| incarnata | . Flesh | . 7, S. Ev. S. Peru | . 1820 |
| Karti, 1. | . Yellow | . 7, S. Ev. T. Mexico | . 1815 |
| Lambertiana, 2 | . White | . 7, S. Ev. S. Mexico | . 1819 |
| leucantha | . White | . 7, S. Ev. S. S. Amer. | . 1825 |
| longifolia | . White | . 7, S. Ev. S. Madag. | . 1819 |
| lutea | . Yellow | . 7, S. Ev. S. Peru | . 1815 |
| macrophylla | . White | . 7, S. Ev. S. S. Amer. | . 1825 |
| mexicana | . White | . 6, S. Ev. S. Mexico | . 1810 |
| Milleri | . Flesh | . 7, S. Ev. S. W. Ind. | |
| nivea | . White | . 7, S. Ev. S. S. Amer. | . 1825 |
| Northiana | . | . 7, S. Ev. S. S. Amer. | . 1820 |
| obtusa | . White | . 7, S. Ev. T. W. Ind. | . 1733 |
| pudica | . Yellow | . 7, S. Ev. S. S. Amer. | |
| purpurea | . Purple | . 7, S. Ev. S. Peru | . 1820 |
| rubra | . Red | . 7, S. Ev. T. Jamaica | . 1690 |
| tenuifolia | . White | . 7, S. Ev. S. S. Amer. | . 1820 |
| tuberculata | . White | . 8, S. Ev. S. St. Domin. | . 1812 |

PLUMOSE, resembling feathers.
PLUMOUS, feathery, downy.
PLUMULE, the young leaf in the embryo.
PLURILOCULAR, having many cells.
PLUVIALIS, expanding in wet weather.

POA, *Linn.* From *poa,* signifying grass or herbage. *Linn.* 3, Or. 2, Nat. Or. *Gramineæ.* This genus contains some valuable hay and pasture grasses, succeeding well in rich loamy soil ; some of the species are aquatic, growing in water or very moist situations ; increased by seeds, or divisions of the roots. Synonymes : 1. *Arundo poæformis.* 2. *P. thermalis.* 3. *P. flexuosa.*

| alpina | . . . Apetal | . 6, Grass. Scotland . . | |
| festucæformis | . Apetal | . 8, Grass. Dalmatia . . | 1800 |
| nemoralis | . . Apetal | . 7, Grass. Britain . | |
| pratensis | . . Apetal | . 5, Grass. Britain . | |
| angustifolia | . Apetal | . 7, Grass. Germany . | |
| trivialis | . . . Apetal | . 7, Grass. Britain . | |

*abyssinica, amboynensis, anceps, angustata, annua, aspera, atrovirens, australis* 1, *badensis, brachyphylla, bromoïdes, bulbosa, cæsia, cæspitosa, capillaris, caroliniana, cenisia, chinensis, cilianensis, coarctata, collina* 2, *compressa, concinna, convoluta, debilis, decipiens, depauperata, diandra, digitata, distichophylla* 3, *effusa, elegans, filiformis, flava, flexuosa, Gaudini, glauca, Gmelini, gracilis, Halleri, hirsuta, humilis, hybrida, imbecilla, laxa, meliacea, Molineri, mucronata, nemoralis, N. angustifolia, nervata, pallida, papillosa, peruviana, plebeia, Poiretti, retroflexa, scariosa, serotina, S. palustris, spicata, sterilis, sudetica, sulcata, supina, tenax, tremula, versicolor, viridis, vivipara.*

POCOCKIA, *N. C. Seringe.* In honour of Richard Pococke, a botanical traveller in the Levant. *Linn.* 17, Or. 4, Nat. Or. *Leguminosæ.* The seeds merely require sowing in the open border about the beginning of April. Synonymes : 1. *Trifolium cretica, Melilotus cretica.*

| cretica, 1 | . . Yellow . 7, H. | A. Candia . . | 1713 |

POD, a kind of seed-vessel, such as that of the pea tribe.

**PODALÝRIA**, *Lambert.* Podalyrius, in heathen mythology, was the son of Æsculapius. *Linn.* 10, Or. 1, Nat. Or. *Leguminosa.* A genus of elegant shrubs, with silky leaves. They grow well in an equal quantity of loam and peat; cuttings will root in sand, under a glass, but they are generally raised from seeds. *Synonymes:* 1. *P. biflora.* 2. *P. calyptrata.*

| | | | | | | |
|---|---|---|---|---|---|---|
| argentéa, 1 | . | Wht. red | 4, G. Ev. S. C. G. H. | | . | 1789 |
| Burchellii | . | Purple | 6, G. Ev. S. C. G. H. | | . | 1816 |
| buxifolia | . | Blue | 6, G. Ev. S. C. G. H. | | . | 1790 |
| cordáta | . | Blue | 6, G. Ev. S. C. G. H. | | . | 1794 |
| cuneifolia | . | White | 6, G. Ev. S. C. G. H. | | . | 1804 |
| glaúca | . | Purple | 6, G. Ev. S. C. G. H. | | . | 1810 |
| hirsúta | . | Red | 7, G. Ev. S. C. G. H. | | . | 1774 |
| liparioides | . | Flesh | 4, G. Ev. S. C. G. H. | | . | 1820 |
| myrtillifólia | . | Purple | 6, G. Ev. S. C. G. H. | | . | 1795 |
| oleæfólia | . | Purple | 5, G. Ev. S. C. G. H. | | . | 1804 |
| sericéa | . | Purple | 6, G. Ev. S. C. G. H. | | . | 1778 |
| subbiflóra | . | Purple | 4, G. Ev. S. C. G. H. | | . | 1810 |
| styracifólia, 2 | . | Pink | 5, G. Ev. S. C. G. H. | | . | 1792 |

**PODÁNTHE**, *Haworth.* Pous, a foot, and *anthos,* a flower; in allusion to the flowers being on long pedicels. *Linn.* 5, Or. 1, Nat. Or. *Asclepiadeæ.* For the culture and propagation of the species which form this genus, refer to *Stapelia.* *Synonyme:* 1. *Stapelia verrucosa.*

| | | | | | | |
|---|---|---|---|---|---|---|
| ciliáta | . | Grn. str. | 11, S. Ev. S. C. G. H. | — | . | 1795 |
| inoráta | . | Yel. str. | 8, S. Ev. S. C. G. H. | | . | 1795 |
| pulchélla | . | Yel. str. | 5, S. Ev. S. C. G. H. | | . | 1795 |
| púlchra | . | Yel. str. | 8, S. Ev. S. C. G. H. | | . | 1800 |
| verrucósa, 1 | . | Pa. yel. | 8, S. Ev. S. C. G. H. | | . | 1800 |
| roríflúa | . | Yel. str. | 8, S. Ev. S. C. G. H. | | . | 1802 |
| verrucósa | . | Yel. str. | 8, S. Ev. S. C. G. H. | | . | 1795 |

**PODÁNTHUS**, *Lagasca.* From *pous,* a foot, and *anthos,* a flower; stalked. *Linn.* 19, Or. 5, Nat. Or. *Compositæ.* An ornamental hardy shrub, succeeding well in a mixture of loam and peat, and readily increased by cuttings.

| | | | | | | |
|---|---|---|---|---|---|---|
| Mitiquí | . | Yellow | 9, H. Ev. S. Chile | | . | 1824 |

**POD FERN**, see *Ellobocárpus.*

**PODISÓMA**, *Link.* Pous, a foot, and *soma,* a body. *Linn.* 24, Or. 9, Nat. Or. *Fungi.* Found on juniper leaves.—*P. foliicólum.*

**PODOCÁRPUS**, *L'Heritier.* From *pous,* a foot, and *karpos,* a fruit; length of the footstalks. *Linn.* 21, Or. 10, Nat. Or. *Taxaceæ.* A genus of small trees; loam and peat suits them best, and cuttings of the ripened wood root readily in sand, under a glass. The Chinese species bear our winters when planted in a sheltered situation in the open border. *Synonymes:* 1. *Thalamia asplenifolia.* 2. *Taxus chinensis.* 3. *T. elongatus.* 4. *T. nucifer.*

| | | | | | |
|---|---|---|---|---|---|
| asplenifolius | . | Apetal | G. Ev. S. N. Holl. | . | 1825 |
| chinénsis, 1 | . | Apetal | G. Ev. T. China | . | 1800 |
| elongátus, 2 | . | Apetal | 7, G. Ev. T. C. G. H. | . | 1774 |
| latifólius | . | Apetal | 8, G. Ev. T. Pundua | . | 1828 |
| macrophýllus | . | Apetal | 7, G. Ev. T. China | . | 1804 |
| nerifolius | . | Apetal | 8. Ev. T. E. Ind. | . | 1820 |
| nucifer, 3 | . | Apetal | 8. Ev. T. Japan | . | 1822 |
| spinulósus | . | Apetal | G. Ev. T. N. Holl. | . | 1820 |
| taxifólius | . | Apetal | 8. Ev. T. S. Amer. | . | 1820 |
| verticillátus | . | Apetal | G. Ev. T. Japan | . | |
| Yacca | . | Apetal | 8. Ev. T. W. Ind. | . | 1818 |

**PODOLÉPIS**, *Labillardière.* From *pous,* a foot, and *lepis,* a scale; flower-stalk covered with scales. *Linn.* 19, Or. 2, Nat. Or. *Compositæ.* A mixture of loam and peat suits the species of this genus, which are easily increased by dividing the roots, or by seeds. *Synonymes:* 1. *Scalia jaceoides.* 2. *Stylolepis gracilis.*

| | | | | | |
|---|---|---|---|---|---|
| acumináta, 1 | . | White | 6, G. Her. P. N. S. W. | . | 1803 |
| aristáta | . | | Swan R. | . | 1837 |
| contórta | . | Yellow | 7, H. Her. P. V. D. L. | . | 1837 |
| gracilis, 2 | . | Pink | 8, H. Her. P. N. S. W. | . | 1826 |
| rugáta | . | White | 7, F. Her. P. N. Holl. | . | 1808 |

**PODOLÓBIUM**, *R. Brown.* From *pous,* a foot, and *lobos,* a pod; the legume stands on a stalk within the calyx. *Linn.* 10, Or. 1, Nat. Or. *Leguminosæ.* A very elegant and desirable genus of dwarf shrubs, well adapted for planting out in a conservatory; they require to be grown in an equal mixture of loam, peat, and sand. Cuttings of the young wood, with a glass over them, will root in sand. *Synonymes:* 1. *Chorozema scandens.* 2. *Podolobium aquifolium.*

| | | | | | |
|---|---|---|---|---|---|
| coriaceúm | . | Yellow | 4, G. Ev. S. N. Holl. | . | 1824 |
| heterophýllum | . | Yellow | 6, G. Ev. S. N. Holl. | . | 1824 |
| scándens, 1 | . | Yellow | 4, G. Ev. Cl. N. Holl. | . | 1824 |
| humifúsum | . | Yellow | 4, G. Ev. Tr. N. Holl. | . | 1824 |
| staurophýllum, 2 | . | Yellow | 4, G. Ev. S. N. Holl. | . | 1822 |
| trilobátum | . | Yellow | 4, G. Ev. S. N. S. W. | . | 1791 |

[ 251 ]

**PODOPHÝLLUM**, *Linn.* Abridged from *Anapodophylium,* a word signifying a duck's-foot: the leaves bear some resemblance to that; whence the English name Duck's-foot. *Linn.* 13, Or. 1, Nat. Or. *Podophyllaceæ.* This plant requires a moist shady situation, and to be grown in peat soil; increased by division at the root.

| | | | | | |
|---|---|---|---|---|---|
| peltátum | . | White | 5, H. Her. P. N. Amer. | . | 1664 |

**PODOPTÉRUS**, *Humboldt and Bonpland.* From *pous,* a foot, and *pteris,* a wing. *Linn.* 6, Or. 3, Nat. Or. *Polygonaceæ.* A handsome plant, requiring to be planted in an equal mixture of loam and peat; young cuttings planted in any light mould, under a glass, will root readily.

| | | | | | |
|---|---|---|---|---|---|
| mexicánus | . | | 7, G. Ev. S. Mexico | . | 1825 |

**PODOSPÉRMUM**, *Decandolle.* From *pous,* a foot, and *sperma,* a seed. *Linn.* 19, Or. 1, Nat. Or. *Compositæ.* Pretty plants, producing flowers resembling those of *Scorzonera;* they thrive in any common soil, and plants may be raised from seed. The annual and biennial kinds only require sowing in the open border. *Synonyme:* 1. *Scorzonera taraxacifolia.*

| | | | | | |
|---|---|---|---|---|---|
| angustifólium | . | Yellow | 6, H. | B. S. Eur. | . | 1823 |
| calcitrapifólium | . | Yellow | 6, H. Her. P. Levant | . | 1820 |
| cánum | . | | | Russia | . | 1833 |
| cornuopifólium | . | Yellow | 6, H. Her. P. N. Africa | . | 1818 |
| laciniátum | . | Yellow | 6, H. | B. S. Eur. | . | 1640 |
| octanguláre | . | Yellow | 6, H. | B. S. Eur. | . | 1818 |
| púmilum | . | Yellow | 6, H. | A. Spain | . | 1816 |
| resedifólium | . | Yellow | 6, H. | B. S. Eur. | . | 1818 |
| taraxacifólium, 1 | Yellow | 6, H. Her. P. Bohemia | . | 1820 |

**PODOSPERM**, the stalk on which some seeds are borne.

**POETICUS**, celebrated by the poets.

**POET'S CASSIA,** see *Osyris.*

**POGÓNIA**, *Jussieu.* From *pogon,* a beard: in allusion to the fringed lip of the flowers. *Linn.* 20, Or. 1, Nat. Or. *Orchidaceæ.* Tuberous-rooted plants, growing best in peat soil, and increased by offsets.

| | | | | | |
|---|---|---|---|---|---|
| divaricáta | . | Pink | 6, H. Ter. N. Amer. | . | 1787 |
| ophioglossoídes | . | Ro. pink | H. Ter. N. Amer. | . | 1816 |
| pendúla | . | Pink | 8, H. Ter. N. Amer. | . | 1824 |

**POGOSTÉMON**, *Desfontaines.* From *pogon,* a beard, and *stemon,* a stamen. *Linn.* 14, Or. 1, Nat. Or. *Labiatæ.* These plants grow well in any rich light soil; young cuttings of *P. plectranthoides,* planted in the same kind of soil, root freely. *Synonymes:* 1. *Origanum indicum.* 2. *O. bengalense.*

| | | | | | |
|---|---|---|---|---|---|
| Heyneánum, 1 | . | White | 8. | A. E. Ind. | . |
| plectranthoídes, 2 | White | . | 7, S. Ev. S. E. Ind. | . |

**POINCIÁNA**, *Decandolle.* In honour of M. de Poinci, once governor of the Antilles, and a patron of botany. *Linn.* 10, Or. 1, Nat. Or. *Leguminosæ.* This genus, the Barbadoes Flower-fence, is truly elegant and ornamental. *P. pulcherrima* is a spiny plant, growing about twelve feet high, the bruised leaves of which emit an odour resembling Savin. They require a good rich soil, and a strong heat to make them flower well in our stoves; cuttings will strike readily in sand. They sometimes produce seed, from which they may also be increased.

| | | | | | |
|---|---|---|---|---|---|
| eláta | . | Yellow | 8, S. Ev. S. E. Ind. | . | 1778 |
| Gillièsii | . | Yellow | 7, S. Ev. S. Mendoza | . | 1829 |
| insígnis | . | Copper | 8, S. Ev. S. Amer. | . | 1823 |
| pulchérrima | . | Red yel. | 7, S. Ev. S. E. Ind. | . | 1691 |
| régia | . | Crimson | 8. Ev. T. Madag. | . | 1828 |

**POINSÉTTIA**, *Graham.* In honour of Mr. Poinsette, who discovered the plant in Mexico in 1828. *Linn.* 21, Or. 1, Nat. Or. *Euphorbiaceæ.* This is a truly splendid and very desirable genus, growing well in good open, rather sandy loam, mixed with a little vegetable mould; and in order to keep the plants in a clean, free-growing state, they should have plenty of water at the roots, and be frequently syringed over the leaves and branches. In spring, before the plants are potted, or the buds begin to push, the branches of the previous year should be cut down to within three or four eyes of the old wood. These parts should be laid to dry for a few days, and then made into cuttings, and planted in sand, or sand and loam mixed; if placed in a gentle bottom heat, with a glass over them, they will root very readily, but before the cuttings are planted in the soil, they should be dried for a day or two in an airy part of the house.

| | | | | | |
|---|---|---|---|---|---|
| pulchérrima | . | Brt. scar. | 3, S. Ev. S. Mexico | . | 1834 |
| albída | . | White | 12, S. Ev. S. Mexico | . | 1834 |

**POIRÉTIA**, *Ventenat.* In honour of J. L. M. Poiret, a

French botanist and traveller in Barbary. *Linn.*
16, Or. 6, Nat. Or. *Leguminosa.* A pretty species;
for culture and propagation, see *Pictetia.* Synonymes: 1. *Glycine punctata, Turpinia punctata.*

scándens, 1 . . . 3, S. Ev. Cl. Caraccas . 1823

POISON-BULB, see *Brunsvigia toxicaria.*
POISON-BULB, see *Crinum asiaticum.*
POISON-NUT, see *Strychnos Nux-vomica.*
POISON OAK, see *Rhus Toxicodendron.*

POIVREA, *Commerson.* Named in compliment to N.
Poivre, intendant of the Mauritius, in 1766. *Linn.*
10, Or. 1, Nat. Or. *Combretaceæ.* This is a very
elegant genus of plants, all well worthy of being
cultivated for ornamenting the pillars or back of
the stove. They grow best in a mixture of sandy
loam and peat, and most of them strike with
ease from young cuttings, planted in sand, under a
glass, in heat. Synonymes: 1. *Combretum Afzelii.*
2. *C barbatum.* 3. *C. purpureum.* 4. *C. comosum.*
5. *C. decandrum.* 6. *C. intermedium.*

Afzelii, 1 . . Scarlet . 4, S. Ev. Cl. S. Leone . 1826
barbáta, 2 . . White . S. Ev. Cl. Maranh. 1820
coccínea, 3 . . Scarlet . 9, S. Ev. Cl. Madaga. 1818
comósa, 4 . . Purple . S. Ev. Cl. S. Leone . 1822
decándra, 5 . . White . 4, S. Ev. Cl. E. Ind. . 1826
intermédia, 6 . Scarlet . 4, S. Ev. Cl. S. Leone . 1823

POLANISIA, *Rafinesque.* From *poly*, many, and *anisos*,
unequal; stamens numerous and unequal. *Linn.*
11, Or. 1, Nat. Or. *Capparidaceæ.* A genus of
pretty plants, growing about a foot and a half high.
They require to be sown in a hotbed frame, and
turned out into a sheltered situation in the open
border, about the middle of May. Synonymes: 1.
*Cleome cheladonii.* 2. *C. dodecandra.* 3. *C. dodecandra canadensis.* 4. *C. uniglandulosa.* 5. *C. viscosa.* 6. *C. icosandra.*

Cheladónii, 1 . Rose . 6, H. A. E. Ind. . 1792
dodecándra, 2 . White . 6, H. A. E. Ind. . 1795
gravéolens, 3 . Pinksh. . 6, H. A. Canada . 
uniglandulósa, 4 Wht. red . 6, H. A. Mexico . 1823
viscósa, 5 . . Yellow . 6, H. A. E. Ind. . 1730
icosándra, 6 . Yellow . 6, H. A. Ceylon . 1730

POLEMONIUM, *Linn.* From *polemos*, war; Pliny says
this plant gained its name from having caused a
war between two kings, each of whom claimed the
honour of having first discovered its virtues. *Linn.*
5, Or. 1, Nat. Or. *Polemoniaceæ.* Ornamental
border plants. *P. cæruleum* is one of long standing.
They are all of the easiest culture and propagation.
Synonymes: 1. *P. bursifolium.*

cærúleum . . Blue . 6, H. Her. P. Britain . .
álbum . . . White . 6, H. Her. P. Britain . .
maculátum . . Striped . 6, H. Her. P. Britain . .
pilíferum . . Blue . 6, H. Her. P. N. Amer. .
variegátum . Blue . 6, H. Her. P. Britain . .
grácile . . . Blue . 6, H. Her. P. Dahuria . 1818
húmile . . . Blue . 8, H. Her. P. N. Amer. 1826
lácteum . . . White . 5, H. Her. P. . 1829
mexicánum, 1 . Blue . 4, H. Her. P. Mexico . 1817
monchátum . Black . 6, H. Her. P. N. Amer. 1827
pulchérrimum . Blue . 7, H. Her. P. N. Amer. 1827
réptans . . . Ll. blue . 4, H. Her. Cr. N. Amer. 1758
Richardsóni . Pa. blue . 9, H. Her. P. N. Amer. 1826
sibíricum . . White . 6, H. Her. P. Siberia . 1800
villósum . . . Pa. blue . 8, H. Her. P. Siberia . 1826

POLIANTHES, *Linn.* From *poly*, many, and *anthos*, a
flower; abundance of flowers. *Linn.* 6, Or. 1, Nat.
Or. *Liliaceæ.* Highly odoriferous plants. *P. tuberosa* is the well-known Tuberose. The bulbs are
imported annually, principally from Italy; they
flower well if planted in a mixture of sandy loam and
rotten dung, or leaf-mould, with a moderate supply
of water; they require to be brought forward in a
hotbed frame or pit; when in flower, they may be
placed in a greenhouse or warm room, where they
will remain a considerable time in blossom.

grácilis . . . Pa. yel. . 8, S. Tw. P. Brazil . 1822
tuberósa . . . White . 8, G. Tw. P. E. Ind. . 1629
floré-pléno . . White . 8, G. Tw. P.

POLLEN, powder contained in the anthers, composed
of globules, and containing the fecundating fluid;
also the bloom of leaves.

POLLICHIA, *Linn.* In honour of John Adam Pollich,
M.D., author of a History of the Plants of the
Palatinate of the Rhine. *Linn.* 1, Or. 1, Nat. Or.
*Illecebraceæ.* An obscure plant, of the simplest
culture.

campéstris . . Apetal . 9, F. Her. P. C. G. H. . 1780

POLLINIA, *Linn.* After Cyrus Pollini, a professor of
botany at Verona. *Linn.* 23, Or. 1, Nat. Or. *Gramineæ.* A genus of worthless grasses, growing in
any common soil, and increased by dividing the
root. Synonymes: 1. *Andropogon distachyos.* 2. *A.
striatus.* 3. *A. undatus*—P. distáchya 1, striátá 2,
undátá 3.

POLYANDROUS, having more than twenty stamens inserted in the receptacle.

POLYANGIUM, *Link.* From *poly*, many, and *angium*,
a capsule; many piridiums. *Linn.* 24, Or. 9, Nat.
Or. *Fungi.* A species of *Fungus*, about the size of
a grain of sand, found on damp trunks of trees—
P. vitellínum.

POLYBOTRYA, *Humboldt.* From *poly*, many, and
*botrys*, a raceme; fertile division of frond. *Linn.*
24, Or. 1, Nat. Or. *Polypodiaceæ.* Handsome species of Fern, delighting in a hot humid atmosphere,
and turfy peat soil; increased by division at the
root, or by seeds.

acumináta . . . S. Her. P. . 1831
cervína . . . Brown . 4, S. Her. P. Jamaica . 1823
vivípara . . . Brown . 6, S. Her. P. W. Ind. . 1823

POLYCARPON, *Læffling.* From *poly*, many, and
*karpos*, a fruit; numerous seeds. *Linn.* 3, Or. 3,
Nat. Or. *Illecebraceæ.* Worthless annuals, merely
requiring to be sown in the open border.

diphýllum . . White . 6, H. A. Spain . 1821
tetraphýllum . White . 7, H. A. England . 

POLYCNEMUM, *Linn.* From *poly*, many, and *kneme*,
a knee. *Linn.* 3, Or. 1, Nat. Or. *Chenopodiaceæ.*
The seeds of the different species only require
sowing in the open ground.

arvénse . . . Apetal . 7, H. A. S. Eur. . 1640
malacophýllum . Apetal . 7, H. A. Caucasus . 1823
oppositifólium . Apetal . 7, H. A. Siberia . 1826
recúrvum . . . Apetal . 7, H. A. France . 1820
sclerospérmum . Apetal . 7, H. A. Tauria . 1818
sibíricum . . . Apetal . 7, H. A. Siberia . 1823

POLYGALA, *Linn.* From *poly*, much, and *gala*, milk;
reputed effects of the plant on cattle that feed upon
it. *Linn.* 17, Or. 3, Nat. Or. *Polygalaceæ.* All the
species of this genus are very showy. The greenhouse kinds thrive well in one part turfy loam, and
three parts peat, with a quantity of sand mixed
in it. To obtain cuttings fit for planting, the
shoots should be topped, which will cause them to
push out numerous young ones; these should be
taken off close when in a growing state, about three
inches long, planted in pots of sand under glass,
and placed in the propagating house; the glasses
must be occasionally taken off and wiped. The
hardy perennial kinds thrive in a peat soil, and
increase freely by seeds or divisions of the roots.
The annual kinds require sowing in the open
ground, preferring a peat soil. The root of *P.
Senega* is diuretic, expectorant, purgative, emetic,
and sudorific; it has been used with success in
croup, and as a cure against the bite of venomous
reptiles. According to Barton, *P. sanguinea* possesses similar qualities. Synonymes: 1. *P. oppositifolia.* 2. *P. cordifolia.* 3. *P. grandiflora.* 4. *P.
viridescens.* 5. *P. sanguinea.*

amára . . . . Blue . 6, H. Her. P. Europe . 1775
ambígua . . . Purpsh. . 6, H. A. N. Amer. 1824
attenuáta . . . Purple . 7, G. Ev. S. C. G. H. 1820
austríaca . . . Purple . 6, H. Her. P. Germany .
borboniæfólia, 1 Purple . G. Ev. S. C. G. H. 1790
bracteoláta . . Purple . 7, G. Ev. S. C. G. H. 1718
brevifólia . . . Red . 6, H. A. N. Amer. 1824
Burmanni . . Purple . 6, G. Ev. S. C. G. H. 1800
Chamæbúxus . Yellow . 5, H. Ev. Tr. Austria . 1658
cordifólia . . . Purple . 5, G. Ev. S. C. G. H. 1791
cruciáta . . . Red grn. . 6, H. A. N. Amer. 1739
fastigiáta . . . Red . 6, H. A. N. Amer. 1824
Garcíni . . . Purple . 7, G. Ev. S. C. G. H. 1823
genistoídes . . Purple . 7, G. Ev. S. C. G. H. 1824
graminifólia . . Li. yel. . 6, H. Her. P. Carolina . 1824
incarnáta . . . Pink . 6, H. A. N. Amer. 1812
intermédia . . Purple . 6, G. Ev. S. C. G. H.
lanceoláta . . . Purple . 7, G. Ev. S. C. G. H. 1820
latifólia, 2 . . Purple . 5, G. Ev. S. C. G. H. 1820
ligulária . . . Purple . 6, G. Ev. S. C. G. H. 1820
liliifólia . . . Purple . 7, G. Ev. S. C. G. H. 1823
lútea . . . . Yellow . 6, H. A. N. Amer. 1739
májor . . . . Red . 7, H. Her. P. Austria . 1739
monspelíaca . . Blue . 6, H. A. Mediter. .
myrtifólia . . . Purple . 7, G. Ev. S. C. G. H. 1707
grandiflóra, 3 . Purple . 7, G. Ev. S. C. G. H. 1818

| | | | | | | | |
|---|---|---|---|---|---|---|---|
| nāna, 4 | . | . Grn. yel. | . 6, H. | A. | N. Amer. | . 1815 |
| Nummulāriā | . | . Purple | . | G. Ev. | S. | C. G. H. | . 1812 |
| oppo-itifoliā | . | . Purple | . 6, | G. Ev. | S. | C. G. H. | . 1790 |
| major | . | . Purple | . 7, | G. Ev. | S. | C. G. H. | |
| paniculātā | . | . Pa. pur. | . 7, S. | A. | S. Amer. | . 1823 |
| paucifoliā | . | . Purple | . 6, H. Her. | P. | N. Amer. | . 1812 |
| pinifoliā | . | . Purple | . 7, G. Ev. | S. | C. G. H. | . 1823 |
| purpūreā, 5 | . | . Purple | . 6, H. | A. | N. Amer. | . 1739 |
| rubellā | . | . Pa. red | . 6, H. Her. | P. | N. Amer. | . 1828 |
| sanguineā | . | . Rose | . 8, H. | A. | N. Amer. | . 1789 |
| Senēgā | . | . Red wht. | . 7, F. Her. | P. | N. Amer. | . 1739 |
| simplēx | . | . Purple | . 7, G. Ev. | S. | C. G. H. | . 1816 |
| speciosā | . | . Purple | . 7, G. Ev. | S. | C. G. H. | . 1814 |
| tenuifoliā | . | . Flesh | . 5, G. Ev. | S. | C. G. H. | |
| teretifoliā | . | . Purple | . 8, G. Ev. | S. | C. G. H. | . 1791 |
| tetragōnā | . | . Purple | . | G. Ev. | S. | C. G. H. | . 1820 |
| theoloidēs | . | . Blue | . 7, F. Ev. | S. | Valparaiso | . 1830 |
| umbellātā | . | . Purple | . 7, S. | A. | C. G. H. | |
| verticillātā | . | . White | . 7, H. | A. | N. Amer. | . 1739 |
| vulgāris | . | . Blue | . 5, H. Her. | P. | Britain | . . |

POLYGAMOUS, when some flowers are male, some female, and others hermaphrodite, on the same plant.

POLYGONĀTUM, *Desfontaines*. From *poly*, many, and *gonu*, a knee; referring to the numerous joints of the stem. *Linn.* 6, Or. 1, Nat. Or. *Liliaceæ*. Pretty border plants, growing about two feet high in any rich soil, and readily increased by seed or divisions of the root. *Synonymes* : 1. *P. latifolium*. 2. *Convallaria verticillata*. 3. *C. Polygonatum*.

| | | | | | | |
|---|---|---|---|---|---|---|
| angustifoliūm | . | White | . 5, H. Her. | P. | N. Amer. | . 1824 |
| brachiātūm | . | White | . 7, H. Her. | P. | Switserl. | . 1827 |
| canaliculātūm | . | White | . 6, H. Her. | P. | N. Amer. | . 1812 |
| hirtūm | . | White | . 5, H. Her. | P. | N. Amer. | . 1819 |
| latifoliūm | . | White | . 5, H. Her. | P. | Germany | . 1802 |
| leptophyllūm | . | White | . 6, G. Her. | P. | Nepal | . 1816 |
| macrophyllūm, 1 | . | White | . 5, H. Her. | P. | N. Amer. | . 1800 |
| multiflorūm | . | White | . 6, H. Her. | P. | Britain | . . |
| oppositifoliūm | . | White | . 4, G. Her. | P. | Nepal | . 1822 |
| polyanthemūm | . | White | . 5, H. Her. | P. | Caucasus | . 1826 |
| pubescens | . | White | . 5, H. Her. | P. | N. Amer. | . 1812 |
| verticillātūm, 2 | . | White | . 5, H. Her. | P. | Scotland | . |
| vulgāre, 3 | . | White | . 5, H. Her. | P. | England | . |
| flore-plēnō | . | Wht. grn. | 6, H. Her. | P. | England | . Gard. |
| minōr | . | Wht. grn. | 6, H. Her. | P. | England | . Gard. |

POLYGŌNŪM, *Linn.* Derivation same as that of *Polygonatum*. *Linn.* 8, Or. 3, Nat. Or. *Polygonaceæ*. The species of this genus grow freely in any light rich soil. The perennial kinds are readily increased from seeds, or by divisions of the root. The hardy annual species merely require sowing in the open ground. The tender kinds must be raised on a gentle hotbed, and transplanted into the flower-border. Some species, such as *P. Hydropiper*, are extremely acrid, and said to blister the skin. The seeds of *P. Fagopyrum* and *tataricum* are used as food, and according to Humboldt, the leaves of *P. hispidum* are used in South America as a substitute for tobacco. *Synonymes* : 1. *P. petiolatum*. 2. *P. elegans*. 3. *P. flagellare*.

| | | | | | | |
|---|---|---|---|---|---|---|
| acutātūm | . | Pink | . 7, H. | A. | | . 1828 |
| adprēssūm | . | Red | . 7, G. Ev. | S. | N. Holl. | . 1822 |
| affine | . | Red | . 6, H. Her. | P. | Nepal | . 1822 |
| alpinūm | . | White | . 7, H. Her. | P. | Switzerl. | . 1816 |
| amphibiūm | . | Pink | . 7, H. Aq. | P. | Britain | . . |
| hirsūtūm | . | Red | . 7, H. Her. | P. | Britain | . . |
| amplexicaūlē, 1 | . Red | . 7, H. Her. | P. | India | . 1837 |
| arenariūm | . | Purple | . 6, H. Tv. | A. | Hungary | . 1807 |
| arifoliūm | . | Wht. red | . 4, H. Tw. | A. | N. Holl. | . 1816 |
| articulātūm | . | White | . 7, H. | A. | N. Amer. | . 1817 |
| australē | . | Red | . 7, H. | B. | N. Holl. | . 1818 |
| barbātūm | . | White | . 7, H. De. | Tr. | China | . 1819 |
| Bistōrtā | . | Pink | . 7, H. Her. | P. | Britain | . . |
| chinēnsē | . | Wht. grn. | . 7, H. Tw. | A. | China | . 1795 |
| cilinodē | . | Pink | . 8, H. Cl. | A. | Canada | . 1800 |
| coccineūm | . | Scarlet | . 7, H. Her. | P. | N. Amer. | . 1819 |
| cymōsūm | . | Pink | . 7, H. | A. | Nepal | . 1827 |
| decipiens | . | Red | . 7, G. Her. | P. | N. Holl. | . 1822 |
| diffūsūm | . | White | . 7, H. Her. | Tr. | Siberia | . 1817 |
| Dryandrī, 2 | . Whits. | . 7, H. | A. E. Ind. | . 1800 |
| elēgans | . | Wht. grn. | 6, H. Her. | Tr. | Nepal | . 1824 |
| ellipticūm | . | Pink | . 6, H. Her. | P. | Siberia | . 1807 |
| emarginātūm | . | Pink | . 7, H. | A. | China | . 1806 |
| Fagopyrūm | . | Pink | . 7, H. | A. | England | . |
| floribundūm | . | Red | . 7, H. | A. | Siberia | . 1818 |
| glabrūm | . | Red | . 7, H. | A. | E. Ind. | . 1810 |
| glaucūm | . | | . 7, H. Her. | P. | N. Amer. | . |
| gracilē | . | Red | . 7, G. Her. | P. | N. Holl. | . 1822 |
| herniarioidēs | . | | . 7, G. Ev. | S. | Egypt | . 1827 |
| hirsūtūm | . | White | . 7, H. | A. | N. Amer. | . 1817 |
| Laxmannī | . | White | . 6, H. Her. | P. | Davuria | . 1800 |
| macrophyllūm | . | Purple | . 6, H. Her. | P. | Nepal | . 1820 |
| mitē | . | Red | . 7, H. Aq. | A. | N. Amer. | . 1800 |
| ocreātūm | . | Wht. grn. | 7, H. Her. | P. | Siberia | . 1730 |

| | | | | | | |
|---|---|---|---|---|---|---|
| orientalē | . | . Red | . 8, H. | A. | E. Ind. | . 1707 |
| album | . | . White | . 8, H. | A. | E. Ind. | . 1781 |
| oxyspermūm | . | . | . H. Her. | P. | Russia | . 1831 |
| patens | . | . | . 7, H. Her. | Tr. | Nepal | . 1823 |
| patūlūm | . | . White | . 8, H. | A. | Tauria | . 1820 |
| pennaylvanicūm | . Red | . 7, H. | A. | N. Amer. | . 1800 |
| persicarioidēs | . Pink | . 7, H. | A. | Mexico | . 1816 |
| plebēiūm | . | . Red | . 7, G. Her. | P. | N. Holl. | . 1822 |
| sagittātūm | . | . Wht. grn. | . 7, H. Tw. | A. | N. Amer. | . 1759 |
| salsuginēūm | . | . Pink | . 6, H. Aq. | A. | Caucasus | . 1817 |
| senegalēnsis | . | . Red | . 7, H. Aq. | A. | Guinea | . 1825 |
| sericeūm | . | . White | . 7, H. Her. | Tr. | Siberia | . 1820 |
| setōsūm | . | . White | . 7, H. Her. | P. | A. Minor | . 1817 |
| tinctōriūm | . | . Red | . 7, G. | B. | China | . 1776 |
| virginiānūm | . | . White | . 8, H. Her. | P. | N. Amer. | . 1640 |
| vivipārūm | . | . Wht. grn. | . 7, H. Her. | P. | Britain | . . |

*acetōsūm, acidūlūm, alpinūm, aviculāre, Bellardi, Convolvūlūs, divaricātūm, dumetōrūm, equisetifōrmē, erēctūm, Hydropiper, incānūm, injucūndūm, lapathifoliūm, littorālē 3, maritimūm, minūs, niloticūm, Persicāriā, ramosissimūm, salignūm, scāndēns, tataricūm, undulātūm.*

POLYIDĒS, *Agardh*. From *polyeides*, multifarious; diversity of appearance. *Linn.* 24, Or. 7, Nat. Or. *Algæ*. A very singular worm-like species of *Algæ*, found in the sea during the month of November—*P. lumbricalis*.

POLYMNIĀ, *Linn. Polymnia* was the name of one of the Muses. *Linn.* 19, Or. 4, Nat. Or. *Compositæ*. Species of no great beauty, succeeding well in common garden soil. *P. abyssinica* requires to be raised on a hotbed, and when potted off, set with the stove plants.

| | | | | | | |
|---|---|---|---|---|---|---|
| abyssinicā | . | . Yellow | . 4, S. | B. | Africa | . 1775 |
| canadēnsis | . | . Yellow | . 7, H. Her. | P. | N. Amer. | . 1768 |
| maculātā | . | . Yellow | . 8, H. Her. | P. | Mexico | . 1824 |
| Uvedalēā | . | . Yellow | . 9, H. Her. | P. | N. Amer. | . 1699 |

POLYMORPHOUS, assuming various forms.

POLYPETALOUS, having many petals.

POLYPHORE, an elongated receptacle, which bears many ovaries, but not the petals or stamens.

POLYPODIŪM, *Swartz*. From *poly*, many, and *pous*, a foot; numerous root-like feet. *Linn.* 24, Or. 1, Nat. Or. *Polypodiaceæ*. A genus of very ornamental ferns. The stove and greenhouse species require, to grow them well, a mixture of loam and peat. The hardy kinds are well adapted for ornamenting rock-work, or they may be grown in pots, in light loamy soil. All the species may be readily increased by dividing the roots, or by seeds. *P. crassifolium* is said to be sudorific and anti-rheumatic. In the Sandwich Islands, they use the bruised fronds of *P. phymatodes* to perfume the cocoa nut oil. *Synonymes* : 1. *P. scandens*. 2. *P. latifolium*.

| | | | | | | |
|---|---|---|---|---|---|---|
| alpēstrē | . | . Brown | . 7, H. Her. | P. | | |
| angustifoliūm | . | . Brown | . 5, H. Her. | Cr. | W. Ind. | . 1820 |
| areolātūm | . | . Brown | . 8, H. Her. | P. | Brazil | . 1824 |
| asplenifoliūm | . | . Brown | . 7, S. Her. | P. | Martinico | . 1790 |
| attenuātūm | . | . Brown | . 5, S. Her. | Cr. | N. Holl. | . 1823 |
| aūreūm | . | . Brown | . 8, S. Her. | P. | W. Ind. | . 1742 |
| auriculātūm | . | . Brown | . 7, S. Her. | Cr. | Brazil | . 1824 |
| Billardiēri, 1 | . | . Brown | . 5, S. Her. | Cr. | V. D. L. | . 1823 |
| calcārēūm | . | . Brown | . 7, H. Her. | P. | Britain | . . |
| Catharinē | . | . Brown | . | S. Her. | P. | Brazil | . 1824 |
| connectilē | . | . Brown | . 6, H. Her. | P. | Canada | . 1823 |
| cremātūm | . | . Brown | . 8, S. Her. | P. | Jamaica | . 1823 |
| crassifoliūm | . | . Brown | . 8, S. Her. | P. | W. Ind. | . 1823 |
| curvātūm | . | . Brown | . 8, S. Her. | P. | Jamaica | . 1823 |
| decumānūm | . | . Brown | . 8, S. Her. | P. | Brazil | . 1818 |
| deflexūm | . | . Brown | . 7, S. Her. | P. | | . 1830 |
| dissimilē | . | . Brown | . 7, S. Her. | P. | Brazil | . 1820 |
| drepānūm | . | . Brown | . all | S. Her. | P. | Madeira | . |
| Dryoptēris | . | . Brown | . 7, H. Her. | P. | Britain | . . |
| effūsūm | . | . Brown | . 11, S. Her. | P. | Jamaica | . 1769 |
| fraxinifoliūm | . | . Brown | . 8, S. Her. | P. | Caraccas | . 1817 |
| hastātūm | . | . Brown | . 7, S. Her. | P. | Jamaica | . 1820 |
| heterophyllūm | . | . Brown | . 7, S. Her. | Cr. | W. Ind. | . 1820 |
| hexagonōptērūm | Brown | . 7, H. Her. | P. | N. Amer. | . 1811 |
| incānūm | . | . Brown | . 7, S. Her. | Cr. | S. Amer. | . 1811 |
| incīsūm | . | . Brown | . 7, S. Her. | P. | W. Ind. | . 1810 |
| iridifoliūm | . | . Brown | . 9, S. Her. | P. | | |
| jamaicēnsē | . | . Brown | . 6, S. Her. | P. | Jamaica | . 1820 |
| juglandifoliūm | . | . Brown | . 7, S. Her. | P. | S. Amer. | . 1822 |
| lanceolātūm | . | . Brown | . 8, S. Her. | P. | W. Ind. | . 1812 |
| latipēs | . | . Brown | . 10, S. Her. | P. | Brazil | . |
| longifoliūm | . | . Brown | . 7, S. Her. | P. | Brazil | . 1819 |
| lycopodioidēs | . | . Brown | . 7, S. Her. | Cr. | W. Ind. | . 1793 |
| olivāceūm | . | . Brown | . 8, S. Her. | P. | S. Amer. | . |
| Otitēs | . | . Brown | . 10, S. Her. | P. | Brazil | . 1834 |
| owariēnsē | . | . Brown | . 8, S. Her. | Cr. | S. Leone | . |
| pectinātūm | . | . Brown | . 7, S. Her. | P. | W. Ind. | . 1793 |
| Phagoptēris | . | . Brown | . 6, H. Her. | P. | Britain | . . |

| | | | | |
|---|---|---|---|---|
| Phyllitidis | . Brown | 7, 8. Her. P. | W. Ind. | 1793 |
| phymatōdēs | . Brown | 7, 8. Her. P. | E. Ind. | 1823 |
| piloselloidēs | . Brown | 8, 8. Her. Cr. | W. Ind. | 1793 |
| plantaginēum, 2 | Brown | 7, 8. Her. P. | W. Ind. | 1817 |
| plumūla | . Brown | 7, 8. Her. P. | S. Amer. | 1824 |
| polyanthēum | . Brown | 8. Her. P. | Brasil | 1824 |
| proliferūm | . Brown | all 8. Her. P. | Madeira | |
| pruinātūm | . Brown | 9, 8. Her. P. | Jamaica | 1793 |
| pustulātum | . Brown | 6, G. Her. P. | N. Zeal. | 1820 |
| quercifolium | . Brown | 8, 8. Her. P. | E. Ind. | 1824 |
| repandūm | . Brown | 8, 8. Her. P. | Jamaica | 1820 |
| repēns | . Brown | 5, 8. Her. Cr. | W. Ind. | 1810 |
| salicifolium | . Brown | 8, 8. Her. Cr. | Brasil | |
| sānctūm | . Brown | 7, 8. Her. P. | W. Ind. | 1820 |
| Schkuhrii | . Brown | 7, 8. Her. P. | Brasil | 1824 |
| scolopendrioidēs | Brown | 6, 8. Her. P. | W. Ind. | 1820 |
| serpēns | . Brown | 8. Her. P. | W. Ind. | 1816 |
| simile | . Brown | all 8. Her. Cr. | | |
| stigmōsūm | . Brown | 8. Her. P. | E. Ind. | 1823 |
| taeniōsūm | . Brown | 8, 8. Her. Cr. | S. Amer. | 1815 |
| tenellūm | . Brown | 8. Her. Cr. | N. Holl. | 1823 |
| tetragōnūm | . Brown | 6, 8. Her. P. | Brasil | 1827 |
| trichomanoidēs | . Brown | 8, 8. Her. P. | W. Ind. | 1822 |
| trifurcātūm | . Brown | 7, 8. Her. P. | W. Ind. | 1820 |
| tuberōsūm | . Brown | all 8. Her. P. | W. Ind. | |
| vaccinifolium | . Brown | 9, 8. Her. Cr. | W. Ind. | 1820 |
| virginiānūm | . Brown | 7, H. Her. P. | N. Amer. | |
| vulgāre | . Brown | 7, H. Her. P. | Britain | |
| cambricum | . Brown | 7, H. Her. P. | Britain | |

POLYPODY, see Polypodium.

POLYPOGON, Desfontaines. From poly, many, and pogon, a beard. Linn. 3, Or. 2, Nat. Or. Gramineæ. Grasses, thriving in any common soil, and increased by seeds or divisions of the roots. Synonymes: 1. Agrostis setosa. 2. A. littoralis.

| | | | |
|---|---|---|---|
| littoralis, 2 | . Apetal | . 7, Grass. | Britain |
| monspeliensis | . Apetal | . 7, Grass. | Britain |

glomerātūs 1, maritimūs, tatāricūs.

POLYPORUS, Michaux. Derived from poly, many, and poros, a pore; the under surface is full of pores. Linn. 24, Or. 9, Nat. Or. Fungi. These species of Fungi are found in pastures, trunks of trees, &c. Synonyme: 1. Boletus velutinus.—P. abietinus, adustus, amorphus, armeniacus, betulinus, brumalis, cæsius, Carmichælianus, castaneus, cinctus, cuticularis, ferruginōsūs, fomentarius, fraxinēus, frondōsūs, gigantēus, heteroclitus, hispidus 1, igniarius, incarnātūs, lentus, leptocephalus, lucidus, medulla-panis, molliscus, nigricans, pachypus, P. olivaceus, pallescens, pellucidus, perennis, radiātūs, reticulātūs, Ribis, scoticus, spongiōsūs, spūmāns, squamōsūs, suaveolens, S. salicinus, sulphurēus, strobiliformis, ulmarius, undātūs, varius, V. lateralis, V. nummularis, velutinus, versicolor, vulgaris.

POLYPTERIS, Nuttall. From poly, many, and pteron, a wing. Linn. 19, Or. 1, Nat. Or. Compositæ. A pretty little plant, requiring the same treatment as other rather tender annuals. Synonyme: 1. Hymenopappus integrifolius.

| | | | | |
|---|---|---|---|---|
| integrifolia, 1 | . White | . 7, H. | A. Georgia | . 1823 |

POLYRHIZA, having many roots.

POLYSIPHONIA, Greville. From poly, many, and siphon, a tube; in allusion to the numerous little canals by which the coloured matter is carried through the different parts of the plant. Linn. 24, Or. 7, Nat. Or. Algæ. Very singular plants, found in the ocean, on the sea-shore, rocks, &c.—P. Agardhiana, allochroa, atrorubescens, badia, Brodiæi, byssoidēs, coccinēa, C. denudāta, C. tenēior, cristāta, divaricāta, elongāta, E. denudāta, E. sanguinolenta, elongēllā, fastigiāta, filamentōsa, fruticulōsa, furcellāta, grācilis, macrocārpa, nigrēscēns, N. pectināta, parasitica, recūrva, Richardsōni, spinulōsa, thuyoidēs, urceolāta, violacēa, V. mājor.

POLYSPORA, Sweet. From poly, many, and spora, a seed; many seeds in a capsule. Linn. 16, Or. 8, Nat. Or. Ternstrœmiaceæ. This handsome shrub requires a mixture of loam and peat; and cuttings, when the wood is not too ripe, will root in sand, under a glass, in heat; it may likewise be increased by grafting on the single red Camellia Japonica. Synonyme: 1. Camellia axillaris.

| | | | | |
|---|---|---|---|---|
| axillaria, 1 | . White | . 3, 8. Ev. S. | E. Ind. | 1818 |

POLYSTACHYA, Hooker. From poly, many, and stachys, a spike. Linn. 20, Or. 1, Nat. Or. Orchidaceæ. Rather interesting plants; for culture and propagation, see Burlingtonia.

| | | | |
|---|---|---|---|
| affinis | . . White | . 8. Epi. | S. Leone 1838 |
| grandiflora | . Orn. pur. | 9, 8. Epi. | S. Leone 1837 |
| luteola | . . Yel. grn. | 7, 8. Epi. | Mexico 1818 |

| | | | |
|---|---|---|---|
| pubartila | . . Green | . 8. Epi. | S. Leone . 1822 |
| ramulōsa | . . Green | . 9, 8. Epi. | S. Leone . 1837 |
| zeylanica | . . Yellow | . 9, 8. Epi. | Ceylon |

POLYSTIGMA, Persoon. From poly, many, and stigma, a mark. Linn. 24, Or. 9, Nat. Or. Fungi. Very minute species of brown Fungi, found in autumn on live aloe and bird-cherry leaves—P. fulvūm, rubrūm.

POLYTHRINCIUM, Kunze. From poly, many, and thrikos, a little division. Linn. 24, Or. 9, Nat. Or. Fungi. A very small species, growing on cloverleaves, in the form of numerous black spots of unequal size—P. Trifolii.

POLYTRICHUM, Linn. From poly, many, and thrix, a hair; in allusion to the hairy calyptra. Linn. 24, Or. 5, Nat. Or. Musci. Very pretty species of moss, with rigid leaves, and the theca of a square form, mostly covered with a hairy calyptra; found on moist banks, among heath, &c. Synonymes: 1. P. rubellum. 2. P. gracile. 3. P. strictum. 4. P. subrotundum. 5. P. sexangulare—P. aloidēs, A. Dickēoni, A. mājus 1, alpinūm, commūne, C. attenuātum 2, C. yuccæfolium, hercynicūm, juniperinūm, J. gracilius 3, nānūm 4, piliferūm, septentrionālē 5, undulātūm, urnigērūm.

POMADERRIS, Labillardière. From poma, a lid, and derris, a skin; alluding to the membranous covering of the capsule. Linn. 5, Or. 1, Nat. Or. Rhamnaceæ. A beautiful early-flowering genus, very nearly akin to Willemetia, which genus see for culture and propagation. Synonymes: 1. Ceanothus capsularis. 2. C. globulosus. 3. C. spatulatus. 4. C. Wendlandianus.

| | | | | |
|---|---|---|---|---|
| acumināta | . Pa. yel. | 6, G. Ev. S. | N. Holl. | . 1816 |
| andromedæfolia | . Yellow | 6, G. Ev. S. | N. Holl. | . 1824 |
| apetāla | . . Greenish | 6, G. Ev. S. | N. Holl. | . 1803 |
| aspēra | . . Cream | 6, G. Ev. S. | N. Holl. | . 1825 |
| betulīna | . . Yellow | 5, G. Ev. S. | N. S. W. | . 1823 |
| capsularia, 1 | . Pa. yel. | 4, G. Ev. S. | N. Holl. | . 1820 |
| discolor | . . Whitish | 4, G. Ev. S. | N. Holl. | . 1814 |
| elliptica | . . Pa. yel. | 4, G. Ev. S. | N. Holl. | . 1805 |
| globulōsa, 2 | . Yellow | 7, G. Ev. S. | N. Holl. | . 1803 |
| intermedia | . . | 4, G. Ev. S. | N. Holl. | . 1825 |
| lanigera | . . Pa. yel. | 4, G. Ev. S. | N. Holl. | . 1806 |
| ledifolia | . . Pa. yel. | 4, G. Ev. S. | N. Holl. | . 1824 |
| phillyreoidēs | . Pa. yel. | 4, G. Ev. S. | N. Holl. | . 1818 |
| phylicifolia | . Pa. yel. | 4, G. Ev. S. | N. Holl. | . 1819 |
| spatulāta, 3 | . Pa. yel. | 4, G. Ev. S. | N. Holl. | . 1826 |
| Wendlandiāna, 4 | Pa. yel. | 4, G. Ev. S. | N. Holl. | . 1819 |

POMAX, Solander. From poma, an operculum; alluding to the operculum to the fruit. Linn. 4, Or. 1, Nat. Or. Cinchonaceæ. For the culture and propagation of this species, see Opercularia. Synonyme: 1. Opercularia umbellata.

| | | | | |
|---|---|---|---|---|
| hirta, 1 | . . Wht. grn. | 7, G. Ev. S. | N. Holl. | . 1826 |

POMBALIA, Vandelli. In honour of S. J. de Carvalho, Marquis de Pombal, a famous Portuguese statesman. Linn. 5, Or. 1, Nat. Or. Violaceæ. An interesting plant, growing best in an equal mixture of sandy loam and peat; it may be increased by young cuttings in the same kind of soil, under a glass, in heat, or by seeds. Synonyme: 1. Ionidium Ipecacuanha.

| | | | | |
|---|---|---|---|---|
| ituba, 1 | . . White | . 7, 8. Her. P. | Brasil | . 1822 |

POMEGRANATE, see Punica.

POMIFEROUS, apple-bearing.

PONCELETIA, R. Brown. After Mr. Poncelet, author of a Treatise on Wheat. Linn. 5, Or. 1, Nat. Or. Epacridaceæ. A very pretty plant; for culture and propagation, see Epacris.

| | | | | |
|---|---|---|---|---|
| sprengelioidēs | . . | 5, G. Ev. S. | N. S. W. | . 1826 |

POND-WEED, see Potamogeton.
POND-WEED, see Zannichellia.

PONERA, Lindley. From poneros, miserable; alluding to the wretched appearance of the species. Linn. 20, Or. 1, Nat. Or. Orchidaceæ. This is a plant of no beauty, and will perhaps be found to succeed best when attached to a piece of wood, in the same manner as the species of Pleurothallis. Synonyme: 1. Nemaconia graminifolia.

| | | | |
|---|---|---|---|
| graminifolia, 1 | . . | 8. Epi. | Mexico . 1837 |

PONGAMIA, Lamarck. Pongam is the Malabar name of P. glabra. Linn. 17, Or. 4, Nat. Or. Leguminosæ. Handsome stove trees; for culture and propagation, see Dalbergia. Synonymes: 1. Dalbergia arborea, Robinia media. 2. R. uliginosa, Galedupa uliginosa.

| | | | | |
|---|---|---|---|---|
| glabra, 1 | . . White | . S. Ev. S. | E. Ind. | . 1699 |
| grandiflora | . . White | . S. Ev. S. | E. Ind. | . 1818 |

| | | | | |
|---|---|---|---|---|
| Piscidia | . . White . | . 8. Ev. T. E. Ind. | . 1818 |
| uliginòsa, 2 | . . White . | . 8. Ev. T. W. Ind. | . 1824 |

PONTEDÈRA, *Linn.* In honour of Julius Pontedera, professor of botany at Padua. *Linn.* 6, Or. 1, Nat. Or. *Pontederaceæ.* The species of this genus require to be grown in rich loamy soil, in a tub or cistern of water; increased by division at the roots.

| | | | | |
|---|---|---|---|---|
| angustifòlia | . Blue | . 7, 8. Aq. P. N. Amer. | . 1806 |
| azùrea | . . . Blue | . 7, 8. Aq. P. Jamaica | . 1824 |
| cærùlea | . . . Blue | . 7, H. Aq. P. N. Amer. | . 1830 |
| cordàta | . . . Blue | . 7, 8. Aq. P. N. Amer. | . 1759 |
| crassipès | . . Blue | . 5, 8. Aq. P. Guiana | . 1825 |
| dilatàta | . . . Blue | . 7, 8. Aq. P. E. Ind. | . 1806 |
| lanceolàta | . . Blue | . 7, 8. Aq. P. N. Amer. | . 1815 |

PONTHIÈVA, *R. Brown.* Named in honour of M. de Ponthieu, a French West Indian merchant, who sent a number of plants to Sir Joseph Banks. *Linn.* 20, Or. 1, Nat. Or. *Orchidaceæ.* These curious plants grow well in a mixture of sandy loam and peat, with the pots well drained. They require to be kept dry when not in a growing state.

| | | | | |
|---|---|---|---|---|
| glandulòsa | . . Green | . 2, 8. Ter. W. Ind. | . 1800 |
| petiolàta | . . Brown | . 8, 8. Ter. St. Vincent | 1822 |

POPLAR, see *Populus.*

POPPY, see *Papaver.*

POPÙLUS, *Tournefort.* Some derive the word Populus from *paipallo,* to vibrate or shake; others suppose it obtained its name from being used in ancient times to decorate the public places in Rome, where it was called *arbor populi,* or the tree of the people. *Linn.* 22, Or. 7, Nat. Or. *Salicaceæ.* Most of the species of poplar are very ornamental, more especially in early spring, when the catkins of the males are produced. Their favourite place of growth is in moist soil near a running stream; but they do not thrive in very marshy situations. All the species are readily increased by cuttings or layers, and some by suckers. *Synonymes:* 1. *P. nivea.* 2. *P. suaveolens.* 3. *P. viminalis, P. longifolia.* 4. *P. macrophylla.* 5. *P. acerifolia.* 6. *P. dilatata.* 7. *P. acladesca.* 8. *P. lævigata.* 9. *P. supina.*

| | | | | |
|---|---|---|---|---|
| alba, 1 | . . . Apetal | . 3, H. De. T. Britain | . |
| angulàta | . . Apetal | . 3, H. De. T. Carolina | . 1738 |
| balsamífera | . . Apetal | . 4, H. De. T. N. Amer. | . 1692 |
| fol. variegàtis | . Apetal | . 4, H. De. T. | |
| intermèdia | . . Apetal | . 4, H. De. T. | |
| latifòlia | . . Apetal | . 4, H. De. T. | |
| suavèolens, 2 | . Apetal | . 4, H. De. T. Russia | . 1825 |
| viminàlis, 3 | . Apetal | . 4, H. De. T. Altai | . 1826 |
| betulifòlia | . . Apetal | . 3, H. De. T. N. Amer. | |
| canadénsis | . . Apetal | . 3, H. De. 8. Canada | . |
| cándicans, 4 | . Apetal | . 3, H. De. T. N. Amer. | . 1772 |
| canéscens | . . Apetal | . 3, H. De. T. England | |
| acerifòlia, 5 | . Apetal | . H. De. T. | |
| ægyptìaca | . . Apetal | . H. De. T. Egypt | . |
| arembérgica | . Apetal | . H. De. T. | . 1835 |
| bélgica | . . Apetal | . H. De. T. 8. Eur. | . 1835 |
| cándicans | . Apetal | . H. De. T. | |
| hýbrida | . . Apetal | . 4, H. De. T. Caucasus | . 1816 |
| nívea | . . Apetal | . H. De. T. | |
| péndùla | . . Apetal | . H. De. T. | |
| fastigiàta, 6 | . Apetal | . 3, H. De. T. Italy | . 1758 |
| fœmìna | . . Apetal | . 3, H. De. T. Italy | . 1838 |
| græca | . . Apetal | . 3, H. De. T. Archipel. | . 1779 |
| grandidentàta | . Apetal | . 3, H. De. T. N. Amer. | . 1772 |
| péndùla | . . Apetal | . 3, H. De. T. N. Amer. | . 1820 |
| heterophýlla | . Apetal | . 3, H. De. T. N. Amer. | . 1765 |
| monilífera, 7 | . Apetal | . 5, H. De. T. Canada | . 1772 |
| Lindleyàna | . Apetal | . 4, H. De. T. Canada | . 1772 |
| variegàta | . Apetal | . 5, H. De. T. | |
| nigra | . . Apetal | . 3, H. De. T. Britain | . |
| salicifòlia | . . Apetal | . 4, H. De. T. Floetbeck | . 1834 |
| víridis | . . Apetal | . 4, H. De. T. Britain | Gard. |
| trémùla | . . Apetal | . 3, H. De. T. Britain | . |
| lævigàta, 8 | . Apetal | . 3, H. De. T. N. Amer. | . 1760 |
| péndùla | . . Apetal | . 4, H. De. T. | |
| supìna, 9 | . . Apetal | . 3, H. De. T. N. Amer. | . 1824 |
| trépida | . . Apetal | . H. De. T. N. Amer. | . 1812 |

PORÀNA, *Linn.* From *poreno,* to journey; branches extending to a great distance. *Linn.* 5, Or. 1, Nat. Or. *Convolvulaceæ.* An ornamental plant, requiring a mixture of loam and peat, and increased by seeds.

| | | | | |
|---|---|---|---|---|
| volùbilis | . . . White | . 7, 8. Ev. Tw. E. Ind. | . 1820 |

PORANTHÈRA, *Rudge.* From *poros,* a pore, and *anthera,* an anther. *Linn.* 5, Or. 3, Nat. Or. *Euphorbiaceæ.* This ornamental species grows freely in a mixture of sandy loam and peat, and young cuttings will root readily if planted in sand, under a glass.

| | | | | |
|---|---|---|---|---|
| ericifòlia | . . White | . 7, G. Ev. S. N. Holl. | . 1824 |

PORCUPINE, see *Chætária Agrostis.*

[ 255 ]

PORCUPINE, see *Hordèum Agrostis.*

PORES, apertures in the cuticle, through which transpiration takes place, or apertures in the anthers through which the pollen is ejected.

PORÌNA, *Acharius.* From *porinos,* anything that crumbles away. *Linn.* 24, Or. 9, Nat. Or. *Fungi.* A curious species, found on the bark of trees, &c. —*P. pertùsa.*

PORLIÈRA, *Ruiz and Pavon.* In honour of Andrew de Porlier, a Spanish patron of botany. *Linn.* 8, Or. 1, Nat. Or. *Zygophyllaceæ.* A curious and ornamental shrub, with leaves the linear leaflets of which remain open in serene weather, and contract before rain. It grows in a mixture of loam and peat, and ripened cuttings will root in sand, under a glass, in heat.

| | | | | |
|---|---|---|---|---|
| hygrometrìca | . . | . 8. Ev. S. Peru | . . 1820 |

POROPHÝLLUS, having porous leaves.

PORPHÝRA, *Agardh.* From *porphyra,* purple; the colour of the species. *Linn.* 24, Or. 7, Nat. Or. *Algæ.* Curious purple species, found during summer on the sea-shore. *P. laciniata* is stewed, and considered a great luxury—*P. laciniàta, purpùrèa.*

PORRÈCTUS, stretched out, diffuse.

PORTLÀNDIA, *P. Browne.* Named in honour of the Duchess of Portland, a great patroness of botany. *Linn.* 5, Or. 1, Nat. Or. *Rubiaceæ.* Superb plants, worthy of a place in every collection, on account of their large showy flowers. They require a mixture of sandy loam and peat; and cuttings, with their leaves whole, will root in sand, under a glass, in heat. A strong heat is necessary for them; without that, they will never grow well.

| | | | | |
|---|---|---|---|---|
| coccínea | . . . Scarlet | . 8. Ev. S. Jamaica | . 1812 |
| grandiflòra | . . White | . 8. Ev. S. Jamaica | . 1775 |

PORTUGAL LAUREL, see *Ceràsus lusitànicus.*

PORTULÀCA, *Linn.* From *porto,* to carry, and *lac,* milk; juicy nature of the plants. *Linn.* 11, Or. 1, Nat. Or. *Portulacaceæ.* The seeds of the hardy annual species of this genus may be sown in a sheltered part of the flower-garden in spring. The stove and greenhouse kinds require the same treatment as other stove and greenhouse annuals.

| | | | | |
|---|---|---|---|---|
| foliòsa | . . . Yellow | . 6, H. | A. Guinea | . 1822 |
| Gillièsii | . . Red puk. | . G. Ev. S. Mendoza | . 1827 |
| grandiflòra | . . Yel. pur. | . 6, F. Tu. P. Chile | . 1827 |
| lùtea | . . Yellow | . 6, G. Tu. P. Chile | . 1827 |
| Thellusònii | . Crimson | . 6, G. Tu. P. Mendoza | . 1839 |
| guineénsis | . . Yellow | . 6, H. | A. Guinea | . 1823 |
| halimoìdes | . . Yellow | . 6, F. | A. Jamaica | . 1823 |
| involucràta | . . Pink | . 6, H. | A. | . 1820 |
| meridiàna | . . Yellow | . 5, G. | A. E. Ind. | . 1791 |
| mucronàta | . . Yellow | . 6, H. | A. | . 1822 |
| oleràcea | . . Yellow | . 7, H. | A. Europe | . 1582 |
| parvifòlia | . . Yellow | . 6, 8. | A. Jamaica | . 1799 |
| pilòsa | . . . Pink | . 6, 8. | A. S. Amer. | . 1690 |
| pusìlla | . . . Yellow | . 6, 8. | A. Trinidad | . 1824 |
| quadrifìda | . . Yellow | . 8 8. | A. E. Ind. | . 1773 |
| satìva | . . . Yellow | . 8, H. | A. S. Amer. | . 1652 |
| aùrea | . . . Yellow | . 8, H. | A. S. Amer. | . 1652 |

PORTULACÀRIA, *Jacquin.* Altered from *Portulaca.* *Linn.* 5, Or. 1, Nat. Or. *Portulacaceæ.* This plant, the African Purslane-tree, will grow well in any dry light soil; and young cuttings, taken off and dried for a few days, when potted, will root freely. The plant has never flowered in British gardens.

| | | | | |
|---|---|---|---|---|
| àfra | . . . . | . G. Ev. S. Africa | . . 1732 |

POSOQUÈRIA, *Aublet.* Aymara *posoqueri* is the name of *P. longiflora* among the natives of Guiana. *Linn.* 5, Or. 1, Nat. Or. *Cinchonaceæ.* The species are remarkably pretty when in flower; for culture and propagation, see *Gardenia.* *Synonymes:* 1. *Solena gracilis.* 2. *S. longiflora.*

| | | | | |
|---|---|---|---|---|
| grácilis, 1 | . . White | . 8. Ev. S. Guiana | . 1825 |
| longiflòra, 2 | . . White | . 8. Ev. S. Guiana | . 1822 |

POTAMOGÈTON, *Linn.* From *potamos,* a river, and *geiton,* near; growing in rivers and ponds. *Linn.* 4, Or. 3, Nat. Or. *Fluviales.* The species of this genus mostly grow wholly immersed in water; they are increased by seeds, or by dividing the roots. The roots of *P. natans* are said to be eaten in Siberia.

| | | | | |
|---|---|---|---|---|
| acutifòlium | . . Grn. yel. | . 6, H. Aq. P. Britain | . . |
| compréssum | . . Green | . 6, H. Aq. P. Britain | . . |
| críspum | . . . Red | . 6, H. Aq. P. Britain | . . |
| cuspidàtum | . . Green | . 6, H. Aq. P. Britain | . . |
| dénsum | . . . Red | . 6, H. Aq. P. Britain | . . |

| | | | | | |
|---|---|---|---|---|---|
| fluitāns . . . | . Red | . 7, H. Aq. P. Britain | . . |
| gramineūm | . Green | . 7, H. Aq. P. Britain | . . |
| heterophyllūm | . Green | . 7, H. Aq. P. Britain | . . |
| lanceolātūm | . Olive | . 7, H. Aq. P. England | . . |
| lūcēns . . . | . Green | . 6, H. Aq. P. Britain | . . |
| nātāns . . . | . Green | . 8, H. Aq. P. Britain | . . |
| oblongūm | . Olive | . 7, H. Aq. P. Britain | . . |
| pectinātūm | . Olive | . 6, H. Aq. P. Britain | . . |
| perfoliātūm | . Purple | . 7, H. Aq. P. Britain | . . |
| pusillūm | . Green | . 7, H. Aq. P. Britain | . . |
| setaceūm | . Green | . 7, H. Aq. P. Britain | . . |

POTAMOPHÝLĀ, R. Brown. From *potamos*, a river, and *phileo*, to love. *Linn.* 23, Or. 1, Nat. Or. *Gramineæ.* A worthless species of grass, growing in any wet situation, and increased by divisions— *P. parriflörd.*

POTĀTO, see *Solānūm tuberōsūm.*

POTENTILLĀ, Linn. From *potens*, powerful; supposed medical qualities of some of the species. *Linn.* 12, Or. 3, Nat. Or. *Rosaceæ.* Some of the species are very handsome when in flower. They grow in any common garden soil, and increase freely by dividing the roots, or by seeds. The shrubby kinds are well adapted for the front of shrubberies, and are propagated in autumn by cuttings planted in a sheltered situation. *Synonyms:* 1. *P. aurea, P. Halleri, P. salisburgensis.* 2. *P. leucophylla.* 3. *P. pumila.* 4. *P. thuringiaca.* 5. *P. subauda, filiformis.* 6. *P. nepalensis.* 7. *P. fragariastrum.* 8. *P. dahurica.* 9. *P. floribunda.* 10. *P. Weinmanniana.* 11. *P. vinosa.* 12. *P. hispida.* 13. *P. splendens.* 14. *P. cinerea.*

| | | | | |
|---|---|---|---|---|
| adscendēns | . Yellow | . 6, H. Her. P. Hungary | . 1806 |
| agrimonioidēs | . Yellow | . 7, H. Her. P. Caucasus | . 1817 |
| alba . . . | . White | . 5, H. Her. P. Wales | . . |
| alchemilloidēs | . White | . 6, H. Her. P. Pyrenees | . 1823 |
| alpestris, 1 | . Orange | . 7, H. Her. P. Britain | . . |
| angustifoliā, 2 | . Yellow | . 6, H. Her. P. Siberia | . 1824 |
| Anserinā | . Yellow | . 7, H. Her. P. Britain | . . |
| apenninā | . White | . 5, H. Her. P. Apennines | . 1821 |
| arachnoidēs | . Yellow | . 7, H. Her. P. N. Amer. | . 1826 |
| argentēā | . Yellow | . 7, H. Her. P. Britain | . . |
| argūtā . . | . Yelsh. wht. | 7, H. Her. P. N. Amer. | . 1826 |
| astracanicā | . Yellow | . 7, H. Her. P. Siberia | . 1787 |
| atrosanguineā | . Purple | . 7, H. Her. P. Nepal | . 1822 |
| atrosanguineā- pedātā | } Orange | . 7, H. Her. P. Eng. hyb. | . 1831 |
| coccineā | . Drk. scar. | 7, H. Her. P. Hybrid | . . |
| fulgēns . . | . Crimson | . 7, H. Her. P. Hybrid | . . |
| ignēscēns | . Crimson | . 7, H. Her. P. Hybrid | . . |
| biflorā . . | . Yellow | . 6, H. Her. P. Siberia | . 1820 |
| bifūrcā . . | . Yellow | . 6, H. Her. P. Siberia | . 1773 |
| subsericeā | . Yellow | . 6, H. Her. P. Astracan | . 1827 |
| bipinnatifidā | . Yellow | . 7, H. Her. P. N. Amer. | . 1826 |
| bithynicā . | . Yellow | . 6, H. Her. P. Bithynia | . 1817 |
| Boccōnī . | . White | . 6, H. Her. P. Apennines | . 1823 |
| calābrā . | . Yellow | . 6, H. Her. P. Calabria | . 1820 |
| canadēnsis, 3 | . Yellow | . 6, H. Her. P. N. Amer. | . 1800 |
| candēscēns | . Yellow | . 6, H. Her. P. Europe | . 1817 |
| candicāns | . Yellow | . 6, F. Her. P. Mexico | . 1820 |
| caulescēns | . White | . 7, H. Her. P. Austria | . 1759 |
| chrysānthā, 4 | . Golden | . 6, H. Her. P. Siberia | . 1827 |
| cicutarimfoliā | . Yellow | . 7, H. Her. P. Galacea | . 1818 |
| Clusiānā | . Wht. yel. | 6, H. Her. P. Austria | . 1806 |
| collinā . | . Yellow | . 6, H. Her. P. S. Eur. | . 1816 |
| confertā . | . Yellow | . 7, H. Her. P. | . 1831 |
| crŏceā, 5 | . Copper | . 8, H. Her. P. Switzerl. | . 1816 |
| dealbātā . | . Yellow | . 7, H. Her. P. Altai | . . |
| dēbilis . . | . Yellow | . 5, H. Her. P. Switzerl. | . 1819 |
| declinātā . | . Yellow | . 5, H. Her. P. | . 1817 |
| diffūsā . | . Yellow | . 7, H. Her. P. | . 1817 |
| Egedī . . | . Yellow | . 5, H. Her. P. Denmark | . 1820 |
| effŏsā . . | . Yellow | . 8, H. Her. P. N. Amer. | . 1826 |
| elatiōr . . | . Yellow | . 6, H. Her. P. Siberia | . 1824 |
| ferruginēā | . Or. blue | . 7, H. Her. P. Hybrid | . 1835 |
| Filipendulā | . Yellow | . 6, H. Her. P. Dahuria | . 1823 |
| flagellāris | . Yellow | . 6, H. Her. Cr. Siberia | . 1820 |
| formŏsā, 6 | . Purple | . 6, H. Her. P. Nepal | . 1822 |
| Garnieriānā | . Yel. red | . 7, H. Her. P. Hybrid | . . |
| Mayānā | . Yel. pk. | . 7, H. Her. P. Hybrid | . . |
| Fragāriā, 7 | . White | . 5, H. Her. P. Britain | . . |
| fragarioidēs | . White | . 5, H. Her. P. Siberia | . 1773 |
| fragiformis | . Yellow | . 6, H. Her. P. S. Eur. | . 1800 |
| frigidā . | . Yellow | . 6, H. Her. P. Alp. Delp. | 1819 |
| fruticŏsā . | . Yellow | . 7, H. De. S. England | . . |
| dahūricā, 8 | . Yellow | . 8, H. De. S. Dauria | . 1824 |
| tenuilŏbā, 9 | . Yellow | . 8, H. De. S. N. Amer. | . 1811 |
| geoidēs . | . Yellow | . 6, H. Her. P. Tauria | . 1820 |
| geranioidēs | . Yellow | . 6, H. Her. P. Armenia | . 1820 |
| glabrā . . | . White | . 7, H. De. S. Dahuria | . 1818 |
| glaciālis . | . Yellow | . 5, H. Her. P. Switzerl. | . 1819 |
| glandulŏsā | . Yellow | . 8, H. Her. P. California | . 1830 |
| incīsā | . Yellow | . 7, H. Her. P. California | . 1835 |
| grācilis . | . Yellow | . 7, H. Her. P. N. Amer. | . 1826 |
| grandiflorā | . Yellow | . 6, H. Her. P. Siberia | . 1640 |

| | | | | | |
|---|---|---|---|---|---|
| Guntheri, 10 | . Yellow | . 6, H. Her. P. Europe | . 1818 |
| hæmatŏchrūs | . | . H. Her. P. | . 1832 |
| Hippiānā | . Yellow | . 7, H. Her. P. N. Amer. | . 1826 |
| hirsūtā | . Yellow | . 6, H. Her. P. N. Amer. | . 1820 |
| hirtā | . Yellow | . 6, H. Her. P. S. Eur. | . 1795 |
| Hopwoodiānā | . Varieg. | . 7, H. Her. P. Eng. hyb. | . 1829 |
| hybridā | . White | . 6, H. Her. P. Germany | . 1820 |
| incīsā | . Yellow | . 6, H. Her. P. | . 1818 |
| inclinātā | . Yellow | . 5, H. Her. P. Alp. Del. | . 1818 |
| intermediā | . Yellow | . 6, H. Her. P. Switzerl. | . 1796 |
| laciniŏsā | . Yellow | . 7, H. Her. P. Hungary | . 1816 |
| linearilŏbā | . Yellow | . 7, G. Her. P. Mexico | . 1824 |
| Loddigēsiī, 11 | . Yellow | . 6, H. Her. P. Siberia | . . |
| lupinoidēs | . Wht. yel. | 7, H. Her. P. Alp. Eur. | . 1739 |
| Mackayānā | . Yel. pak. | 5, H. Her. P. Eng. hyb. | . . |
| macrānthā | . Yellow | . 5, H. Her. P. Siberia | . 1820 |
| micranthā | . White | . 6, H. Her. P. Siberia | . 1826 |
| minimā | . Yellow | . 6, H. Her. P. Switzerl | . 1819 |
| missouricā | . Yellow | . 6, H. Her. P. N. Amer. | . 1827 |
| mollissimā | . Yellow | . 6, H. Her. P. Europe | . 1832 |
| monspeliēnsis | . Yellow | . 4, H. Her. P. France | . 1680 |
| multifidā | . Yellow | . 7, H. Her. P. Siberia | . 1759 |
| angustifoliā | . Yellow | . 6, H. Her. P. Siberia | . . |
| nemorāli-furmŏsā | Oran. wht. | 6, H. Her. P. Hybrid | . 1829 |
| nitidā | . Wht. red. | 7, H. Her. P. Switzerl. | . . |
| niveā | . Yellow | . 7, H. Her. P. Siberia | . 1816 |
| macrophylla | . Yellow | . 6, H. Her. P. N. Amer. | . 1827 |
| norvēgicā | . Yellow | . 6, H. Her. P. N. Eur. | . 1764 |
| obscūrā | . Yellow | . 7, H. Her. P. Siberia | . 1806 |
| ontŏpŏdā | . Yellow | . 8, H. Her. P. N. Amer. | . 1826 |
| ornithŏpŏdā | . Yellow | . 7, H. Her. P. Siberia | . 1836 |
| ornithopodioidēs | Yellow | . 6, H. Her. P. | . 1827 |
| opācā | . Yellow | . 7, H. Her. P. S. Eur. | . 1680 |
| pātulā | . Yellow | . 7, H. Her. P. Hungary | . 1818 |
| pectinātā | . Yellow | . 7, H. Her. P. N. Amer. | . 1826 |
| pedātā | . Yellow | . 6, H. Her. P. Europe | . 1819 |
| pennsylvanicā 12 | Yellow | . 7, H. Her. P. N. Amer. | . 1725 |
| petræā | . Yellow | . 6, H. Her. P. France | . 1819 |
| pimpinelloidēs | . Yellow | . 5, H. Her. P. Levant | . 1758 |
| rēctā | . Yellow | . 6, H. Her. P. S. Eur. | . 1648 |
| rēptāns | . Yellow | . 5, H. Her. Cr. Britain | . . |
| florē-plēnŏ | . Yellow | . 7, H. Her. Cr. Britain | gard. |
| variegātā | . Yellow | . 7, H. Her. Cr. Britain | gard. |
| Richardsonī | . Yellow | . 7, H. Her. P. N. Amer. | . 1826 |
| rupestris | . White | . 6, H. Her. P. England | . . |
| ruthenicā | . Yellow | . 7, H. Her. P. Siberia | . 1799 |
| Russeliānā | . Scarlet | . 7, H. Her. P. Hybrid | . . |
| Salesōvī | . White | . 6, H. Her. P. Siberia | . 1823 |
| Sanguisorbā | . Cream | . 7, H. Her. P. Siberia | . 1826 |
| sericeā | . Yellow | . 7, H. Her. P. Siberia | . 1780 |
| Sieversiānā, 13 | . Yellow | . 6, H. Her. P. Nepal | . 1822 |
| speciŏsā | . Yellow | . 7, H. Her. P. Crete | . 1821 |
| stipulāris | . Yellow | . 7, H. Her. P. Siberia | . 1727 |
| stolonifērā | . | . H. Her. P. | . 1831 |
| subacaūlis, 14 | . Yellow | . 5, H. Her. P. S. France | . 1820 |
| suplnā | . Yellow | . 5, H. Her. P. Siberia | . 1696 |
| taūricā | . Yellow | . 7, H. Her. P. Tauria | . 1820 |
| Thomāsī | . Yellow | . 6, H. Her. P. Italy | . 1822 |
| tridentātā | . White | . 6, H. Her. P. Scotland | . . |
| umbrŏsā | . White | . 5, H. Her. P. Tauria | . 1818 |
| uniflorā | . Yellow | . 7, H. Her. P. Dahuria | . 1819 |
| Valderiā | . Sulphur | . 4, H. Her. P. Piedmont | . 1825 |
| velutinā | . Yellow | . 6, H. Her. P. France | . 1819 |
| vērnā | . Yellow | . 6, H. Her. P. Britain | . . |
| verticillāris | . Yellow | . 6, H. Her. P. Siberia | . 1818 |
| villŏsā | . Yellow | . 6, H. Her. P. N. Amer. | . 1820 |
| virgātā | . Yellow | . 7, H. Her. P. | . 1820 |
| viscŏsā | . Yellow | . 7, H. Her. P. Dahuria | . 1797 |

POTĒRIŪM, Linn. From *poterion*, a cup; *P. Sanguisorba* is used in cooling drinks. *Linn.* 21, Or. 9, Nat. Or. *Rosaceæ.* Plants of little beauty. The shrubby species grow well in any light rich soil; and young cuttings root readily under a glass. The herbaceous kinds grow in any common soil, and are increased by seeds. *Synonyms:* 1. *P. hybridum.*

| | | | | |
|---|---|---|---|---|
| agrimonifoliūm | . Green | . 7, H. Her. P. Spain | . 1822 |
| hybridūm, 1 | . Green | . 6, H. Her. P. France | . 1683 |
| caudātūm | . Green | . 8, G. Ev. S. Canaries | . 1779 |
| polygāmūm | . Brown | . 7, H. Her. P. Hungary | . 1803 |
| Sanguisorbā | . Green | . 7, H. Her. P. England | . . |
| spinŏsūm | . Green | . 7, H. Ev. S. Archip. | . 1596 |
| verrucŏsūm | . Green | . 7, H. Her. P. | . 1828 |

PŌTHŌS, Linn. *Pothos*, the name of a species in Ceylon. *Linn.* 4, Or. 1, Nat. Or *Araceæ.* Very singular epiphytal plants: in the West Indies and South America, they grow on trees, as the Ivy does in England. The leaves of *P. palmata* are three feet, and the footstalks four feet long. They all succeed well in peat and loam, and may be increased by dividing the roots. *Synonyms:* 1. *P. grandifolia.*

| | | | | |
|---|---|---|---|---|
| acaūlis . . . | . Apetal | . 5, Epiphy. W. Ind. | . 1790 |
| angustātā . . | . Apetal | . 5, Epiphy. Trinidad | . 1823 |

| | | | | | | | |
|---|---|---|---|---|---|---|---|
| cannæfoliā | . | . | Apetal | . | 5, Epiphy. | W. Ind. | 1789 |
| cordātā | . | . | Apetal | . | 4, Epiphy. | America | 1770 |
| coriáceā | . | . | Apetal | . | 6, Epiphy. | Brazil | 1824 |
| crassinérvia | . | . | Apetal | . | Epiphy. | S. Amer. | 1796 |
| crenātā | . | . | Apetal | . | 5, Epiphy. | W. Ind. | 1823 |
| decurvātā | . | . | Apetal | . | 8, Ev. Cr. | E. Ind. | 1822 |
| digitātā | . | . | Apetal | . | 5, Epiphy. | W. Ind. | 1820 |
| gigántēā | . | . | Apetal | . | 6, S. Ev. Tr. | E. Ind. | 1824 |
| glaūcā | . | . | Apetal | . | Epiphy. | Mexico | 1829 |
| grácilis | . | . | Apetal | . | 5, Epiphy. | Trinidad | 1825 |
| Harrisiī | . | . | Apetal | . | 6, Epiphy. | Brazil | 1824 |
| heterophyllā | . | . | Apetal | . | 8, Ev. Cr. | E. Ind. | 1824 |
| lanceolātā | . | . | Apetal | . | 6, Epiphy. | Barbadoes | 1790 |
| Lāsiā | . | . | Apetal | . | Epiphy. | E. Ind. | 1819 |
| longifoliā | . | . | Apetal | . | Epiphy. | Mexico | 1829 |
| macrophyllā, 1 | . | . | Apetal | . | 5, Epiphy. | W. Ind. | 1794 |
| microphyllā | . | . | Apetal | . | 9, Epiphy. | Brazil | 1829 |
| obtusifoliā | . | . | Apetal | . | 5, Epiphy. | Barbadoes | 1790 |
| officinālis | . | . | Apetal | . | 6, S. Ev. Tr. | E. Ind. | 1820 |
| palmātā | . | . | Apetal | . | 6, Epiphy. | S. Amer. | 1803 |
| Peepleā | . | . | Apetal | . | 6, S. Ev. Cr. | E. Ind. | 1820 |
| pentaphyllā | . | . | Apetal | . | 10, Epiphy. | Cayenne | 1803 |
| pertūsā | . | . | Apetal | . | 6, S. Ev. Cr. | E. Ind. | 1824 |
| pinnātā | . | . | Apetal | . | 8, S. Ev. Cr. | E. Ind. | 1820 |
| reflēxā | . | . | Apetal | . | 9, S. Her. P. | Brazil | 1828 |
| réptāns | . | . | Apetal | . | 9, S. Ev. Cl. | Brazil | 1828 |
| rubéscēns | . | . | Apetal | . | 9, S. Her. P. | Brazil | 1828 |
| rubrinérviā | . | . | Apetal | . | Epiphy. | S. Amer. | 1820 |
| sagittātā | . | . | Apetal | . | 8, Epiphy. | W. Ind. | 1800 |
| scándēns | . | . | Apetal | . | 5, S. Ev. Cr. | E. Ind. | 1821 |
| violāceā | . | . | Apetal | . | 6, S. Ev. | Jamaica | 1793 |

POT-MARIGOLD, see Calendùlā officinālis.

POUCH, a little sack or bag at the base of some petals and sepals.

POUPĀRTIĀ, Commerson. The tree is called Bois de Poupart, in the Island of Bourbon. Linn. 10, Or. 4, Nat. Or. Rhamnàceæ. An ornamental tree. For culture and propagation, see Spondias. Synonymes: 1. Spondias dulcis. 2. S. mangifera.

| | | | | | | | |
|---|---|---|---|---|---|---|---|
| borbōnicā | . | . | Purple | . | 8, Ev. T. | Bourbon | 1825 |
| dúlcis, 1 | . | . | | . | 8, Ev. T. | Java | 1793 |
| mangíferā, 2 | . | White | . | . | 8, Ev. T. | E. Ind. | 1820 |

POURRĒTIĀ, Ruiz and Pavon. In honour of Abbé Pourret, a French botanist and traveller in Spain. Linn. 6, Or. 1, Nat. Or. Bromeliàceæ. An ornamental genus of plants, growing freely in a mixture of sandy loam and peat; they are increased by suckers, or by seeds.

| | | | | | | | |
|---|---|---|---|---|---|---|---|
| coeruleā | . | . | Blue | . | 6, S. Her. P. | Chile | 1827 |
| coarctātā | . | . | Yellow | . | 5, S. Her. P. | Chile | 1822 |
| magnispáthā | . | . | Grn. wht. | 5, Epiphy. | S. Amer. | 1820 |
| pyramidātā | . | . | Yellow | . | 6, S. Her. P. | Peru | 1822 |
| rubricaúlis | . | . | Blue red | . | 6, S. Her. P. | Chile | 1827 |

PRÆGNANS, swollen, protuberant.

PRÆMORSE, appearing as if bitten off.

PRASINATE, of a green colour.

PRASIŌM, Linn. The Greek name for Horehound. Linn. 14, Or. 1, Nat. Or. Labiàtæ. Plants of little beauty, and of the simplest culture.

| | | | | | | | |
|---|---|---|---|---|---|---|---|
| mājūs | . | . | White | . | 7, F. Ev. S. | Spain | 1699 |
| minūs | . | . | White | . | 7, F. Ev. S. | Sicily | 1751 |

PRASOPHYLLŪM, R. Brown. From prason, a leek, and phyllon, a leaf; similarity in the leaves. Linn. 20, Or. 1, Nat. Or. Orchidàceæ. The species of this genus are not possessed of much beauty. A mixture of loam, peat, and sand, in equal quantities, suits them best; they are increased by divisions of the roots. They must be sparingly watered.

| | | | | | | | |
|---|---|---|---|---|---|---|---|
| elātūm | . | . | Brown | . | G. Ter. | N. Holl. | 1824 |
| fimbriātūm | . | . | Brown | . | G. Ter. | N. Holl. | 1824 |
| flāvūm | . | . | Yellow | . | G. Ter. | N. Holl. | 1825 |
| fūscūm | . | . | Brown | . | G. Ter. | N. Holl. | 1824 |
| pátēns | . | . | Brown | . | F. Ter. | N. Holl. | 1823 |
| rūfūm | . | . | Rufous | . | G. Ter. | N. Holl. | 1824 |
| striātūm | . | . | Green | . | G. Ter. | N. Holl. | 1824 |

PRATIĀ, Gaudichaud. In memory of M. Prat Bernon, of the French navy. Linn. 5, Or. 1, Nat. Or. Lobeliàceæ. Pretty plants when in flower. They grow well in a mixture of loam, peat, and sand; and are easily increased by division at the root, or by seed. Synonymes: 1. Lobelia begoniæfolia. 2. L. corymbosa. 3. L. concolor.

| | | | | | | | |
|---|---|---|---|---|---|---|---|
| begoniæfoliā, 1 | . | Blue | . | 7, G. Her. P. | Nepal | . | 1827 |
| corymbōsā, 2 | . | White | . | 6, G. Her. P. | C. G. H. | 1824 |
| eréctā, 3 | . | Blue | . | 6, G. Her. P. | N. Holl. | 1819 |

PRÆCOCITY, becoming ripe before the usual time.

PRÆMNĀ, Linn. From premnon, a stump of a tree, Linn. 14, Or. 2, Nat. Or. Verbenàceæ. Dwarf trees,

[ 257 ]

growing freely in a mixture of loam and peat, and increased by seeds, or cuttings.

| | | | | | | | |
|---|---|---|---|---|---|---|---|
| aspérrimā | . | . | | . | 8, Ev. T. | E. Ind. | 1832 |
| esculéntā | . | . | White | . | 8, Ev. T. | E. Ind. | 1824 |
| integrifoliā | . | . | | . | 8, Ev. T. | E. Ind. | 1824 |
| reticulātā | . | . | | . | 8, Ev. T. | Jamaica | 1819 |

PRENĀNTHĒS, Linn. From prenes, drooping, and anthos, a flower. Linn. 19, Or. 1, Nat. Or. Compósitæ. Mostly uninteresting plants, growing in common garden soil, and increased by divisions, or seeds. Synonyme: 1. P. hispida.

| | | | | | | | |
|---|---|---|---|---|---|---|---|
| áspērā | . | . | | . | 7, H. Her. P. | | 1831 |
| deltoīdēa | . | . | Yellow | . | 7, H. Her. P. | Iberia | 1825 |
| purpūrēa | . | . | Purple | . | 8, H. Her. P. | Germany | 1658 |

chondrilloīdes, hispidā, murālis, racemōsā, rubicūndā, tenuifoliā, tuberōsā 1.

PRESCŌTTIĀ, Lindley. Named in compliment to John Prescott, Esq., a learned and indefatigable English botanist, resident at St. Petersburgh. Linn. 20, Or. 1, Nat. Or. Orchidàceæ. Herbaceous plants, requiring precisely the same treatment as the Ponthievas.

| | | | | | | | |
|---|---|---|---|---|---|---|---|
| colōrāns | . | . | Green | . | 6, S. Ter. | Brazil | 1834 |
| plantagínēa | . | . | Grn. wht. | 6, S. Ter. | Brazil | 1822 |

PRĒSLIĀ, Opiz. In honour of C. B. and I. S. Presl, of Prague; authors of "Flora Sicula," Deliciæ Pragenses," and other works. Linn. 14, Or. 1, Nat. Or. Labiàtæ. This species succeeds well in any moist soil, and is readily increased by divisions. Synonyme: 1. Mentha cervina.

| | | | | | | | |
|---|---|---|---|---|---|---|---|
| cervinā, 1 | . | . | Pa. pur. | 7, H. Her. P. | S. Eur. | . | 1684 |

PRESTŌNIĀ, R. Brown. After C. Preston, M.D., a correspondent of Ray. Linn. 5, Or. 1, Nat. Or. Apocynàceæ. These pretty species grow well in a mixture of sandy loam and peat; and cuttings, thinly planted in a pot of sand, with a glass over them, root readily.

| | | | | | | | |
|---|---|---|---|---|---|---|---|
| glabrātā | . | . | White | . | 7, S. Ev. Tw. | S. Amer. | 1822 |
| tomentōsā | . | . | White | . | 7, S. Ev. Tw. | Brazil | 1820 |

PRICKLY CEDAR, see Cyathòdes Oxycèdrus.

PRIESTLEYĀ, Decandolle. In honour of the great Dr. Priestley. Linn. 17, Or. 4, Nat. Or. Leguminòsæ. Elegant flowering plants, growing well in a mixture of sandy loam and peat. They do not require to be watered so freely as most plants belonging to Leguminòsæ; if they are watered too much over their leaves, it is sure to kill them; cuttings of the very young wood will strike in sand, under a glass, kept free from damp. Synonymes: 1. Borbonia axillaris. 2. Liparia capitata. 3. B. ericæfolia. 4. Liparia graminifolia. 5. L. hirsuta. 6. L. lævigata. 7. L. myrtifolia. 8. L. sericea. 9. L. teres. 10. L. tomentosa. 11. L. umbellifera. 12. L. vestita. 13. L. villosa.

| | | | | | | | |
|---|---|---|---|---|---|---|---|
| axillāris, 1 | . | . | Yellow | . | 6, G. Ev. S. | C. G. H. | 1822 |
| capitātā, 2 | . | . | Yellow | . | 7, G. Ev. S. | C. G. H. | 1812 |
| ellíptica | . | . | Yellow | . | G. Ev. S. | C. G. H. | 1825 |
| ericæfoliā, 3 | . | . | Yellow | . | 6, G. Ev. S. | C. G. H. | 1812 |
| graminifoliā, 4 | . | . | Yellow | . | 6, G. Ev. S. | C. G. H. | 1800 |
| hirsūtā, 5 | . | . | Yellow | . | 8, G. Ev. S. | C. G. H. | 1792 |
| lævigātā, 6 | . | . | Yellow | . | 7, G. Ev. S. | C. G. H. | 1820 |
| myrtifoliā, 7 | . | . | Yellow | . | 6, G. Ev. S. | C. G. H. | 1823 |
| sericēā, 8 | . | . | Yellow | . | 6, G. Ev. S. | C. G. H. | 1794 |
| térēs, 9 | . | . | Yellow | . | 6, G. Ev. S. | C. G. H. | 1816 |
| tomentōsā, 10 | . | . | Yellow | . | 7, G. Ev. S. | C. G. H. | 1812 |
| umbellíferā, 11 | . | . | Yellow | . | 7, G. Ev. S. | C. G. H. | 1826 |
| vestītā, 12 | . | . | Yellow | . | 7, G. Ev. S. | C. G. H. | 1800 |
| villōsā, 13 | . | . | Yellow | . | 6, G. Ev. S. | C. G. H. | 1774 |

PRIMROSE, see Primùlā.

PRIMŪLĀ, Linn. From primus, the first; in allusion to the early flowering of the plants. Linn. 5, Or. 1, Nat. Or. Primulàceæ. This is an extensive genus of small, but very pretty and desirable plants. All the species of Primrose succeed best in a mixture of loam and peat; and increase readily by seeds, or by dividing the plants, which should be done as soon as they have flowered. Synonymes: 1. P. grandiflora. 2. P. intermedia. 3. P. norvegica. 4. P. calycina. 5. P. crenata. 6. P. nivalis. 7. P. sinensis. 8. P. villosa. 9. P. rotundifolia. 10. P. villosa flore-albo. 11. P. Hornemanniana. 12. P. Columna. 13. P. acaulis.

| | | | | | | | |
|---|---|---|---|---|---|---|---|
| Allionī | . | . | Red | . | 4, H. Her. P. | France | 1818 |
| altaīca | . | . | Red | . | 4, H. Her. P. | Altai | 1819 |
| amoēnā | . | . | Purple | . | 4, H. Her. P. | Caucasus | 1823 |
| aurícūlā | . | . | Yellow | . | 4, H. Her. P. | Switzerl. | 1596 |
| calycánthā | . | . | Yellow | . | 4, H. Her. P. | Switzerl. | 1596 |

2 L

| Name | Colour | | | | Locality | Year |
|---|---|---|---|---|---|---|
| hortênsis | Varieg. | 4 | H. Her. | P. | Europe | 1596 |
| integerrimâ | Varieg. | 4 | H. Her. | P. | Switzerl. | 1596 |
| lûtea | Yellow | 5 | H. Her. | P. | Switzerl. | 1596 |
| lutea-plênâ | Yellow | 4 | H. Her. | P. | Gardens | |
| Balbisii | Yellow | 4 | H. Her. | P. S. Eur. | | 1823 |
| brevistylâ | Yellow | 6 | H. Her. | P. | France | 1818 |
| versicôlôr | Yel. red | 6 | H. Her. | P. | France | 1818 |
| carniolica, 1 | Purple | 3 | H. Her. | P. | Carniola | 1826 |
| ciliâtâ | Red | 4 | H. Her. | P. | Switzerl. | 1700 |
| purpurâtâ | Drk. pur. | 5 | H. Her. | P. | Hybrid | 1833 |
| cortusoidês | Red | 6 | H. Her. | P. | Siberia | 1794 |
| davûricâ, 2 | Red | 4 | H. Her. | P. | Siberia | 1806 |
| decôrâ | Pink | 4 | H. Her. | P. S. Eur. | | 1800 |
| denticulâtâ | Purple | 5 | H. Her. | P. | | |
| dentiflôrâ | Red | 6 | H. Her. | P. | Siberia | 1806 |
| elatiôr | Yellow | 5 | H. Her. | P. | Britain | |
| calycânthâ | Varieg. | 4 | H. Her. | P. | Britain | gard. |
| flôrê-plênâ | Brn. crim. | 4 | H. Her. | P. | Britain | gard. |
| polyânthâ | Varieg. | 4 | H. Her. | P. | Britain | gard. |
| farinôsâ | Red | 6 | H. Her. | P. | Britain | |
| finmârchica, 3 | Violet | 4 | H. Her. | P. | Norway | 1798 |
| gigantêâ | Red | 6 | H. Her. | P. | Siberia | 1820 |
| glaucêscens, 4 | Pink | 4 | H. Her. | P. | Switzerl. | 1826 |
| glutinôsâ | Red | 6 | H. Her. | P. S. Eur. | | 1824 |
| helvêticâ | Red | 6 | H. Her. | P. | Switzerl. | |
| alba | White | 5 | H. Her. | P. | | |
| inflâtâ | Yellow | 5 | H. Her. | P. | Hungary | 1825 |
| integrifôliâ | Pink | 6 | H. Her. | P. | Pyrenees | 1792 |
| latifôliâ | Red | 4 | H. Her. | P. | Pyrenees | 1820 |
| longiflôrâ | Red | 6 | H. Her. | P. | Europe | 1825 |
| longifôliâ | Red | 4 | H. Her. | P. | Levant | 1790 |
| marginâtâ, 5 | Pink | 4 | H. Her. | P. | Switzerl. | 1777 |
| majôr | Pink | 4 | H. Her. | P. | | |
| minimâ | Red | 4 | H. Her. | P. S. Eur. | | 1819 |
| mistassinica | Red | 6 | H. Her. | P. N. Amer. | | 1818 |
| nivâlis | Purple | 5 | H. Her. | P. | Dahuria | 1790 |
| nivêâ, 6 | White | 4 | H. Her. | P. | Siberia | |
| Palinûri | Yellow | 4 | H. Her. | P. | Naples | 1816 |
| Pallasii | Yellow | 6 | H. Her. | P. | Altai | 1823 |
| Perrinianâ | Yellow | 6 | H. Her. | P. | Spain | |
| piedmontânâ | Pink | 5 | H. Her. | P. | Piedmont | 1826 |
| prænitens, 7 | Pink | 5 | H. Her. | P. | China | 1820 |
| fimbriâta-alba | White | 6 | G. Her. | P. | Gardens | 1828 |
| fimbriâtâ-rôsêâ | Rose | 6 | G. Her. | P. | Gardens | 1828 |
| flôrê-albô | White | 6 | G. Her. | P. | China | |
| pubêscens, 8 | Red | 4 | H. Her. | P. S. Eur. | | 1800 |
| pusilla | Purple | 4 | H. Her. | P. N. Amer. | | 1822 |
| scotica | Red | 6 | H. Her. | P. | Scotland | |
| sibirica, 9 | Red | 4 | H. Her. | P. | Siberia | 1818 |
| integerrimâ | Rose li. | 4 | H. Her. | P. | Altai | 1823 |
| Simsii, 10 | White | 4 | H. Her. | P. | Switzerl. | 1768 |
| stricta, 11 | Pink | 4 | H. Her. | P. | Denmark | 1823 |
| suavêolens, 12 | Yellow | 4 | H. Her. | P. | Italy | 1824 |
| truncâtâ | Purple | 4 | H. Her. | P. S. Eur. | | |
| venûstâ | Purple | 4 | H. Her. | P. | Hungary | 1823 |
| vêris | Yellow | 4 | H. Her. | P. | Britain | |
| rûbrâ | Red | 5 | H. Her. | P. | Britain | gard. |
| verticillâtâ | Yellow | 3 | G. Her. | P. | Egypt | 1826 |
| villôsâ | Purple | 4 | H. Her. | P. | Switzerl. | 1768 |
| viscôsâ | Purple | 4 | H. Her. | P. | Piedmont | 1792 |
| vulgâris, 13 | Yellow | 6 | H. Her. | P. | Britain | |
| albâ | White | 4 | H. Her. | P. | Britain | gard. |
| plena-albâ | White | 4 | H. Her. | P. | Britain | gard. |
| plena-atropurpûrêâ | Purple | 4 | H. Her. | P. | Britain | gard. |
| plena-cârnêâ | Flesh | 4 | H. Her. | P. | Britain | gard. |
| plena-cûprêâ | Copper | 4 | H. Her. | P. | Britain | gard. |
| plena-rûbrâ | Red | 4 | H | Her. | P. Britain | gard. |
| plena-sulphûrêâ | Pa. yel. | 4 | H. Her. | P. | Britain | gard. |
| plena-violâcêâ | Violet | 4 | H. Her. | P. | Britain | gard. |

PRÎNCEPS, chief, principal.

PRINCE' FEATHER, see *Amarânthûs hypochondriâcûs*.

PRÎNÔS, *Linn*. Prinos is the Greek name of the Holly, which the present genus much resembles. *Linn*. 6, Or. 1, Nat. Or. *Aquifoliaceæ*. Ornamental plants. The stove species will grow in loam and peat; and ripened cuttings root in sand, under a glass, in heat. The hardy kinds are well adapted for shrubberies; they will grow in any soil, but thrive best in peat, and are easily increased by layers, or by seeds, which do not vegetate till the second year. *Synonymes*: 1. *Ilex prinoides*. 2. *I. canadensis*.

| Name | Colour | | | | Locality | Year |
|---|---|---|---|---|---|---|
| ambîgûûs | White | | H. De. S. | Carolina | | 1812 |
| atomârîûs | White | 7 | H. De. S. | N. Amer. | | 1822 |
| coriâcêûs | White | 6 | H. De. S. | N. Amer. | | 1820 |
| decidûûs, 1 | White | 6 | H. De. S. | Virginia | | 1736 |
| dûbîûs | White | 7 | H. De. S. | N. Amer. | | 1736 |
| giâbêr | White | 7 | H. De. S. | Canada | | 1759 |
| lævigâtûs | White | 6 | H. De. S. | N. Amer. | | 1812 |
| lanceolâtûs | White | 7 | H. De. S. | Carolina | | 1811 |
| lucidûs, 2 | White | 6 | H. Ev. S. | N. Amer. | | 1778 |
| montânûs | White | | S. Ev. S. | W. Ind. | | 1820 |
| verticillâtûs | White | | H. De. S. | N. Amer. | | 1736 |

PRÎSMATIC, formed like a prism.

PRISMATOCÂRPÛS, *L'Heritier*. From *prisma*, a prism, and *karpos*, a fruit; long prismatic form of the fruit. *Linn*. 5, Or. 1, Nat. Or. *Campanulaceæ*.

These plants grow well in sand, loam, and peat; and cuttings of the young wood, planted in the same kind of soil, under a glass, will root freely: they are also easily increased by seeds. The species are showy when in flower. *Synonymes*: 1. *Trachelium diffusum*. 2. *Campanula fruticosa*. 3. *C. interrupta*. 4. *C. Prismatocarpus*.

| diffûsâ, 1 | Blue | 3 | G. Ev. S. | C. G. H. | 1787 |
|---|---|---|---|---|---|
| fruticôsâ, 2 | Blue | 3 | H. Ev. S. | C. G. H. | 1787 |
| interrûptâ, 3 | Blue | 6 | G. Her. | P. C. G. H. | 1818 |
| nîtidûs, 4 | White | 6 | G. Her. | P. C. G. H. | 1787 |

PRISMATOCÂRPÛS, see *Speculâriâ*.

PRÎVÂ, *Adanson*. Derivation unknown. *Linn*. 14, Or. 2, Nat. Or. *Verbenaceæ*. A genus composed of small verbena-looking plants, with insignificant flowers; loam and peat suits them well, and cuttings root readily under a glass. *Synonymes*: 1. *P. echinata*. 2. *P. hispida*, Verbena mexicana.

| lappulâcea, 1 | Blue | 7, S. Her. | P. W. Ind. | 1817 |
|---|---|---|---|---|
| mexicânâ, 2 | Violet | 3, S. Her. | P. Mexico | 1726 |

PRÎVET, see *Ligûstrûm*.

PROCESS, protrusions either natural or monstrous.

PRÔCKIÂ, *Linn*. A name of unknown meaning. *Linn*. 13, Or. 1, Nat. Or. *Bixaceæ*. Ornamental shrubs, thriving in a mixture of loam, sand, and peat; cuttings root freely if planted in sand, under a glass, in heat. *Synonyme*: 1. *Ludia heterophylla*.

| crûcis | Yellow | 7, S. Ev. S. | W. Ind. | 1822 |
|---|---|---|---|---|
| serrâtâ | Yellow | 7, S. Ev. S. | Montserrat | 1823 |
| theæformis, 1 | Yellow | 7, S. Ev. S. | Bourbon | 1820 |

PRÔCRÎS, *Commerson*. Procris was the wife of Cephalus. *Linn*. 21, Or. 4, Nat. Or. *Urticaceæ*. Herbaceous plants, of no interest, growing in any common soil, and increased by divisions—*P. integrifôliâ, punctâtâ*.

PROLIFEROUS, when a plant produces young plants about its root in abundance, or when the inflorescence bears shoots instead of flowers, contrary to the usual course of things.

PRONÂIÂ, *Hugel*. In honour of M. Pronay, a French naturalist. *Linn*. 5, Or. 1, Nat. Or. *Pittosporaceæ*. This species will be found to succeed in a mixture of loam, peat, and sand.

| élegâns | | | Swan R. | 1837 |
|---|---|---|---|---|

PRÔNÛS, having the face downwards.

PROPENDENT, hanging forwards and downwards.

PROSERPINÂCÂ, *Linn*. From *proserpo*, to creep; nature of the species. *Linn*. 3, Or. 3, Nat. Or. *Onagraceæ*. These plants should be grown in large pans of water, with a little mould for the roots to run in; or they may be grown in ponds. They require shelter in winter.

| palûstris | White | 7, H. Aq. | A. Canada | 1818 |
|---|---|---|---|---|
| pectinâtâ | White | 7, H. Aq. | A. N. Amer. | 1821 |

PROSÔPIS, *Linn*. From *prosopis*, a mask; but why applied is unknown. *Linn*. 10, Or. 1, Nat. Or. *Leguminosæ*. Fine stove trees. For culture and propagation, see *Inga*. *Synonymes*: 1. *Acacia cumanensis*. 2. *A. edulis*. 3. *A. falcata*, Mimosa piliflora. 4. *Adenanthera aculeata*.

| cumanensis, 1 | Wht. grn. | 8. Ev. T. | Cumana | 1822 |
|---|---|---|---|---|
| domingênsis | Yel. grn. | 8. Ev. T. | St. Domin. | 1818 |
| dûlcis, 2 | Wht. grn. | 8. Ev. T. | N. Spain | 1818 |
| juliflôrâ, 3 | Yellow | 8. Ev. T. | Jamaica | 1800 |
| spiciger̃â | Yel. grn. | 8. Ev. T. | Coromandel | 1812 |
| adenanthêrâ, 4 | Yel. grn. | 8. Ev. T. | Coromandel | 1820 |

PROSTÂNTHÊRÂ, *Labillardière*. From *prostheke*, appendage, and *anthera*, an anther. *Linn*. 14, Or. 1, Nat. Or. *Labiatæ*. Pretty greenhouse plants, requiring a sandy peat soil, and the pots carefully drained, as the plants are apt to damp off; they may be increased by cuttings of the young shoots, in sand, under a glass.

| denticulâtâ | | 7, G. Ev. S. | N. S. W. | 1824 |
|---|---|---|---|---|
| incisâ | | 7, G. Ev. S. | N. S. W. | |
| lasiânthôs | Pur. li. | 6, G. Ev. S. | N. S. W. | 1808 |
| lineâris | | 7, G. Ev. S. | N. S. W. | 1824 |
| rhômbêâ | | 7, G. Ev. S. | N. S. W. | 1823 |
| rotundifôlia | | 7, G. Ev. S. | V. D. L. | 1824 |
| violâcêâ | Violet | 6, G. Ev. S. | N. S. W. | 1820 |

PROSTHEMIÛM, *Kunze*. Derived from *prosthema*, an addition. *Linn*. 24, Or. 9, Nat. Or. *Fungi*. A very minute black fungus, found in autumn on the trunks of trees—*P. betulinûm*.

PRÔTÊÂ, *Linn*. From *Proteus*, a self-transforming sea-god; in allusion to the diversity of appearance of the species. *Linn*. 4, Or. 1, Nat. Or. *Proteaceæ*.

This is an extensive genus of magnificent evergreen shrubs, generally considered difficult of culture; but this supposed difficulty may be removed by attending strictly to the watering of the plants. The soil best suited for them is light turfy loam, mixed with about a third part fine sand; the pots must be well drained, and it is advisable to mix some small pieces of broken free-stone with the soil, in potting, to prevent them from retaining too much moisture; the roots are also fond of running among the free-stone or broken potsherds. Care must also be taken not to let them droop for want of water, as the young roots are of a fleshy substance, and are as liable to suffer from too much drought as they are from too much water, whence the necessity of the waterings being regular and moderate. Ripened cuttings will root when taken off at a joint, planted thinly in sand, and placed under a glass, but not in heat; the glass should occasionally be removed to allow them to dry, as they are liable to damp off. Water them, but not over the leaves, whenever they want it, and let them get a little dry before the glass is placed over them again. *Synonymes:* 1. *P. longifolia.* 2. *P. speciosa.*

| | | | | | |
|---|---|---|---|---|---|
| acutis | . | Purple | 7, G. Ev. 8. | C. G. H. | 1802 |
| acerosa | . | Black | 4, G. Ev. 8. | C. G. H. | 1808 |
| acuminata | . | Purple | 5, G. Ev. 8. | C. G. H. | 1809 |
| amplexicaulis | . | Purple | 2, G. Ev. 8. | C. G. H. | 1802 |
| angustata | . | Purple | 6, G. Ev. 8. | C. G. H. | 1820 |
| canaliculata | . | Pink | 7, G. Ev. 8. | C. G. H. | 1800 |
| coccinea | . | Scarlet | 6, G. Ev. 8. | C. G. H. | 1824 |
| compacta | . | | 7, G. Ev. 8. | C. G. H. | 1810 |
| cordata | . | Purple | 8, G. Ev. 8. | C. G. H. | 1790 |
| cynaroides | . | Purple | 8, G. Ev. T. | C. G. H. | 1774 |
| elongata | . | Purple | 7, G. Ev. 8. | C. G. H. | 1820 |
| formosa | . | Red | 5, G. Ev. 8. | C. G. H. | 1789 |
| glaucophylla | . | Green | 4, G. Ev. 8. | C. G. H. | 1816 |
| grandiflora | . | White | 5, G. Ev. 8. | C. G. H. | 1787 |
| marginata | . | White | 6, G. Ev. 8. | C. G. H. | 1795 |
| hirsuta | . | Pale | 7, G. Ev. 8. | C. G. H. | 1819 |
| humilis | . | Brown | 7, G. Ev. 8. | C. G. H. | 1802 |
| incompta | . | White | 4, G. Ev. 8. | C. G. H. | 1822 |
| lævis, 1 | . | Green | 5, G. Ev. 8. | C. G. H. | 1806 |
| latifolia | . | Purple | 8, G. Ev. 8. | C. G. H. | 1806 |
| coccinea | . | Scarlet | 8, G. Ev. 8. | C. G. H. | 1806 |
| viridiflora | . | Green | 8, G. Ev. 8. | C. G. H. | 1806 |
| lepidocarpon | . | Purple | 8, G. Ev. 8. | C. G. H. | 1806 |
| ligulæfolia | . | Purple | 4, G. Ev. 8. | C. G. H. | 1798 |
| longiflora | . | Pale | 2, G. Ev. 8. | C. G. H. | 1795 |
| longifolia | . | Purple | 5, G. Ev. 8. | C. G. H. | 1798 |
| lorea | . | White | 5, G. Ev. 8. | C. G. H. | 1824 |
| macrophylla | . | White | 5, G. Ev. 8. | C. G. H. | 1824 |
| magnifica | . | White | 4, G. Ev. 8. | C. G. H. | 1789 |
| melaleuca | . | Purple | 5, G. Ev. 8. | C. G. H. | 1786 |
| mellifera | . | Pa. yel. | 9, G. Ev. 8. | C. G. H. | 1774 |
| alba | . | White | 9, G. Ev. 8. | C. G. H. | 1795 |
| mucronifolia | . | White | 9, G. Ev. 8. | C. G. H. | 1803 |
| nana | . | Pink | 5, G. Ev. 8. | C. G. H. | 1787 |
| nerifolia | . | White | 3, G. Ev. 8. | C. G. H. | 1806 |
| obtusa, 2 | . | Red | 8, G. Ev. T. | C. G. H. | 1786 |
| pallens | . | Pale | 4, G. Ev. 8. | C. G. H. | 1819 |
| patens | . | Wht. pur. | 4, G. Ev. 8. | C. G. H. | 1789 |
| pendula | . | | 4, G. Ev. 8. | C. G. H. | 1806 |
| pulchella | . | Red | 6, G. Ev. 8. | C. G. H. | 1795 |
| ciliata | . | Red | 6, G. Ev. 8. | C. G. H. | 1795 |
| glabra | . | Red | 6, G. Ev. 8. | C. G. H. | 1795 |
| speciosa | . | Red | 6, G. Ev. 8. | C. G. H. | 1795 |
| repens | . | | 7, G. Ev. 8. | C. G. H. | 1800 |
| revoluta | . | Purple | 5, G. Ev. 8. | C. G. H. | 1824 |
| scabra | . | Brown | 6, G. Ev. 8. | C. G. H. | 1809 |
| Scolopendrium | . | | 5, G. Ev. 8. | C. G. H. | 1802 |
| Scolymus | . | Purple | 4, G. Ev. 8. | C. G. H. | 1780 |
| speciosa | . | Purple | 4, G. Ev. 8. | C. G. H. | 1786 |
| tenax | . | Yellow | 4, G. Ev. 8. | C. G. H. | 1801 |
| tenuifolia | . | | 4, G. Ev. 8. | C. G. H. | 1795 |
| turbiniflora | . | Pink | 4, G. Ev. 8. | C. G. H. | 1803 |
| umbonalis | . | Wht. black | 5, G. Ev. 8. | C. G. H. | 1798 |
| villifera | . | Purple | 5, G. Ev. 8. | C. G. H. | 1812 |

PROTOCOCCUS, *Agardh.* From *protos*, first, and *kokkos*, a berry. *Linn.* 24, Or. 7, Nat. Or. *Algæ.* This species is found on rocks during summer—*P. nivalis.*

PROTONEMA, *Agardh.* From *protos*, first, and *nema*, a filament; in allusion to the simplicity of structure. *Linn.* 24, Or. 7, Nat. Or. *Algæ.* Singular species of *Algæ*, found in caverns, on the earth, hotbeds, &c.— *P. cryptarum, frágrans, muscicolâ, Orthotrichi, répens, umbrosum, velutinum.*

PRUINOSE, covered with glittering particles, as if fine dew had been congealed upon it.

PRUNELLA, *Linn.* Altered from *Brunella*, derived from the German *die Braune*, a disorder in the jaws and throat, which this plant was supposed to cure. *Linn.* 14, Or. 1, Nat. Or. *Labiatæ.* The species of

[ 269 ]

this genus grow freely in a light rich soil, and are well adapted for ornamenting rock-work, or the front of flower-borders; they are readily increased by divisions. *Synonymes:* 1. *P. australis.* 2. *P. pennsylvanica.* 3. *P. hirta.* 4. *P. alba, P. laciniata.* 5. *P. incisa, P. longifolia.*

| | | | | | | |
|---|---|---|---|---|---|---|
| Browniana, 1 | . | Blue | . | 8, H. | A. N. S. W. | 1826 |
| grandiflora | . | Blue | . | 8, H. Her. | P. Austria. | 1596 |
| hyssopifolia | . | Lgt. blue | 8, H. Her. | P. France | . | 1731 |
| Marryatta | . | Purple | . | 7, H. Her. | P. | |
| ovata | . | Purple | . | 7, H. | A. America | |
| vulgaris | . | Pink | . | 7, H. Her. | P. Britain | . |
| elongata, 2 | . | Violet | . | 7, H. Her. | P. N. Amer. | |
| flore-pleno | . | Pink | . | 7, H. Her. | P. Britain | gard. |
| hispida, 3 | . | Pa. pur. | 7, H. Her. | P. Europe | . | |
| laciniata, 4 | . | White | . | 7, H. Her. | P. Europe | . |
| pinnatifida, 5 | . | Purple | . | 7, H. Her. | P. S. Eur. | . |
| rubra | . | Red | . | 7, H. Her. | P. Britain | gard. |
| Webbiana | . | Lilac | . | 8, H. Her. | P. | |

PRUNUS, *Linn.* From *prune*, its Greek name. *Linn.* 12, Or. 1, Nat. Or. *Rosaceæ.* All the kinds of *Plum* grow well in any common soil, and are increased by seeds or suckers, or by grafting or budding to perpetuate the particular kinds.

| | | | | | | |
|---|---|---|---|---|---|---|
| candicans | . | White | . | H. De. 8. | | 1820 |
| Coccomilla | . | White | . | H. De. 8. | Calabria | 1824 |
| divaricata | . | White | . | 4, H. De. 8. | Caucasus | 1820 |
| domestica | . | White | . | 4, H. De. T. | England | |
| armenioidæ | . | White | . | 4, H. De. T. | | |
| flore-pleno | . | White | . | 4, H. De. T. | | |
| fol. variegatis | . | White | . | 4, H. De. T. | | |
| myrobalana | . | White | . | 4, H. De. T. | | |
| turonensis | . | White | . | 4, H. De. T. | Turia | . |
| insititia | . | White | . | 4, H. De. T. | Britain | . |
| flore-pleno | . | White | . | 4, H. De. T. | | |
| fr. luteo-albo | . | White | . | 4, H. De. T. | | |
| fructu-nigro | . | White | . | 4, H. De. T. | | |
| fructu-rubro | . | White | . | 4, H. De. T. | | |
| maritima | . | White | . | 4, H. De. T. | N. Amer. | 1800 |
| pubescens | . | White | . | 4, H. De. T. | | 1818 |
| spinosa | . | White | . | H. De. T. | Britain | . |
| flore-pleno | . | White | . | 4, H. De. T. | Tarascon | |
| fol. variegatis | . | White | . | 4, H. De. T. | Britain | . |
| macrocarpa | . | White | . | 4, H. De. T. | Britain | . |
| microcarpa | . | White | . | 4, H. De. T. | Britain | . |
| ovata | . | White | . | 4, H. De. T. | Britain | . |

PRURIENT, causing an itching sensation.

PSAMMA, *Roemer and Schultes.* From *psammos*, sand; its place of growth. *Linn.* 3, Or. 2, Nat. Or. *Gramineæ.* A grass with a strong perennial creeping root; on some parts of the coast it is planted to keep the sand from being removed by the wind and tides; it is also used for mats and thatch. *Synonyme:* 1. *Arundo arenaria.*

| | | | | | |
|---|---|---|---|---|---|
| arenaria, 1 | . | Apetal | . | 6, Gram. Britain | . |

PSIADIA, *Jacquin.* From *psias*, a dew-drop; in allusion to the glutinous exudation on the leaves. *Linn.* 19, Or. 5, Nat. Or. *Compositæ.* A species of little beauty, growing in any rich soil; cuttings will root freely under a glass. *Synonyme:* 1. *Conyza glutinosa.*

| | | | | | |
|---|---|---|---|---|---|
| glutinosa, 1 | . | Yellow | . | 6, S. Ev. 8. Maurit. | 1796 |

PSIDIUM, *Linn.* Derived from *psidion*, the Greek name of Pomegranate. *Linn.* 12, Or. 1, Nat. Or. *Myrtaceæ.* The species of *Guava* grow well in a mixture of loam and peat, and cuttings will root in sand, under a glass; they will also root from layers. Some of the species fruit well in our stoves, but they are not considered to be of much value. *P. Cattleyanum* has a fruit of a fine claret colour, and bears some resemblance in consistence and flavour to the strawberry. *Synonymes:* 1. *P. grandiflorum.* 2. *P. chinense.* 3. *P. guianense.* 4. *P. sapidissimum.*

| | | | | | |
|---|---|---|---|---|---|
| aromaticum | . | White | . | 8, S. Ev. 8. Guiana | . 1779 |
| grandiflorum, 1 | White | . | 7, S. Ev. 8. Guiana | . | 1800 |
| Cattleyanum, 2 | . | White | . | 5, S. Ev. T. S. Amer. | 1818 |
| cordatum | . | White | . | 6, S. Ev. 8. Guadal. | 1811 |
| fluviatile, 3 | . | White | . | 8, S. Ev. 8. Cayenne | . |
| fragrans | . | White | . | 6, S. Ev. 8. Guiana | . 1828 |
| guineense | . | White | . | 6, S. Ev. 8. Guinea | . 1822 |
| latifolium | . | White | . | 6, S. Ev. 8. S. Amer. | 1800 |
| montanum | . | White | . | 8, S. Ev. T. Jamaica | . 1779 |
| myrtifolium | . | White | . | 4, S. Ev. 8. | . 1820 |
| eliæospermum | . | White | . | 8, S. Ev. 8. | . 1817 |
| polycarpon | . | White | . | 5, S. Ev. 8. Trinidad | . 1810 |
| pomiferum | . | White | . | 6, S. Ev. 8. W. Ind. | 1692 |
| sapidissimum, 4 | White | . | 6, S. Ev. 8. | . 1824 |
| pyriferum | . | White | . | 6, S. Ev. 8. W. Ind. | 1656 |

PSILONYX, *Fries.* From *psilos*, a spot. *Linn.* 24, Or. 9, Nat. Or. *Fungi.* A reddish-coloured species,

found in masses on the surface of felled oaks—
*P. gilva.*

**PSILŌTUM,** *Swartz.* From *psilos,* naked; destitute of
leaves. *Linn.* 24, Or. 8, Nat. Or. *Lycopodiaceæ.*
A small bushy plant, of little beauty. It is of the
simplest culture, but not worth growing except as
an object of curiosity. *Synonyme:* 1. *Bernhardia
dichotoma.*

| | | | | | | |
|---|---|---|---|---|---|---|
| triquétrum, 1 | . | Brown | . 7, S. Her. | P. | W. Ind. | . 1798 |

**PSOPHOCĀRPŪS,** *Necker.* From *psophos,* a sound, and
*karpos,* a fruit; the seeds, when ripe, make a rattling
noise in the pods if shaken. *Linn.* 17, Or. 4,
Nat. Or. *Leguminosæ.* In the Mauritius they use
the seed of this plant in the same way as we do
peas. For culture, &c., see *Lablavia.* *Synonyme:*
1. *Dolichos tetragonolobus.*

| | | | | | | |
|---|---|---|---|---|---|---|
| tetragonolóbus, 1 | . | Blue | . 10, S. Tw. | A. | Maurit. | . 1816 |

**PSORĀLĒA,** *Linn.* From *psoraleos,* scurfy; in allusion
to the appearance of the calyx, and most parts of
the plants. *Linn.* 17, Or. 4, Nat. Or. *Leguminosæ.*
All the species are rather handsome when in
flower. The stove and greenhouse kinds are best
cultivated in loam and peat, and cuttings root
freely in sand, under a glass. The frame and
hardy sorts do best in peat and sand, or any light
sandy soil, and are increased by cuttings or seeds.
The biennial species must be raised on a hotbed
frame, and when potted off, kept with the greenhouse plants. The seeds of *P. corylifolia* are used
by native doctors in India, and considered stomachic and deobstruent. *Synonymes:* 1. *P. linearis.*
2. *P. americana.* 3. *P. pedunculata.* 4. *P. intermedia.*

| | | | | | | |
|---|---|---|---|---|---|---|
| acaúlis | . | Yellowish | 7, F. Her. P. | | | . 1838 |
| aculeáta | . | Blue | . 6, G. Ev. S. | C. G. H. | | . 1774 |
| aphýlla | . | Blue | . 6, G. Ev. S. | C. G. H. | | . 1790 |
| arbórea | . | Bluish | . 5, G. Ev. S. | C. G. H. | | . 1814 |
| arenária | . | Purple | . 7, F. Her. P. | Missouri | | . 1823 |
| argéntea | . | Blue | . 6, G. Ev. S. | C. G. H. | | . 1816 |
| axilláris, 1 | . | Blue | . 6, G. Ev. S. | C. G. H. | | . 1890 |
| bituminósa | . | Pa. blue | . 6, G. Ev. S. | S. Eur. | | . 1570 |
| brachiáta | . | Wht. blue | 7, G. Ev. S. | Rocky Mts. | | 1828 |
| bracteáta | . | Purple | . 6, G. Ev. S. | C. G. H. | | . 1731 |
| canéscens | . | Blue | . 7, F. Her. P. | Carolina | | . 1821 |
| capitáta | . | Purple | . 7, G. Ev. S. | C. G. H. | | . 1798 |
| cinérea | . | Purple | . 7, H. | A. N. Holl. | | |
| corylifólia | . | Violet | . 6, G. | B. India | | . 1739 |
| cuspidáta | . | Purple | . 6, F. Tu. P. | Louisiana | | 1811 |
| decúmbens | . | Wht. blue | 4, G. Ev. Tr. | C. G. H. | | . 1774 |
| dentáta, 2 | . | Purple | . 7, G. Ev. S. | Madeira | | . 1640 |
| divaricáta | . | Purple | . 8, S. Ev. S. | S. Amer. | | . 1890 |
| esculénta | . | Blue | . 6, F. Tu. P. | Missouri | | . 1811 |
| glandulósa | . | Pa. blue | . 7, G. Her. P. | Peru | | . 1770 |
| hírta | . | Wht. blue | 6, G. Ev. S. | C. G. H. | | . 1713 |
| incána | . | Blue | . 7, F. Tu. P. | Missouri | | . 1824 |
| involucráta | . | Blue | . 6, G. Ev. S. | C. G. H. | | . 1818 |
| lathyrifólia | . | Blue | . 7, G. Ev. S. | | | . 1816 |
| Lupinélla | . | Purple | . 6, H. Her. P. | Carolina | | . 1812 |
| macrostáchya | . | Purple | . 7, H. Her. P. | California | | . 1833 |
| melilotoídes | . | Violet | . 8, F. Her. P. | Carolina | | . 1814 |
| multicaúlis | . | Wht. blue | 9, G. Her. P. | | | . 1798 |
| odoratíssima | . | Pa. blue | . 6, G. Ev. S. | C. G. H. | | . 1725 |
| Onobrýchis | . | Purple | . 6, F. Her. P. | N. Amer. | | . 1818 |
| orbiculáris | . | Purple | . 6, H. Her. P. | California | | 1835 |
| palæstína | . | Violet | . 6, G. Her. P. | Levant | | . 1771 |
| pinnáta | . | Blue | . 6, G. Ev. S. | C. G. H. | | . 1690 |
| pubéscens | . | Pa. blue | . 6, G. Ev. S. | Lima | | . 1825 |
| répens | . | Blue | . 7, G Ev. Cr. | C. G. H. | | . 1774 |
| sericéa, 8 | . | Violet | . 9, G. Ev. S. | C. G. H. | | . 1815 |
| spicáta | . | Blue | . 6, G. Ev. S. | C. G. H. | | . 1774 |
| Stachýdis | . | Brown | . 4, G. Ev. S. | C. G. H. | | . 1798 |
| striáta | . | Blue | . 6, G. Ev. S. | C. G. H. | | . 1816 |
| tenuifólia | . | Wht. blue | 6, G. Ev. S. | C. G. H. | | . 1793 |
| tomentósa | . | Blue | . 6, G. Ev. S. | C. G. H. | | . 1820 |
| verrucósa | . | Blue | . 7, G. Ev. S. | C. G. H. | | . 1820 |
| intermédia, 4 | . | Blue | . 6, G. Ev. S. | C. G. H. | | . 1820 |

**PSYCHĪNE,** *Desfontaines.* From *psyche,* a butterfly;
the pods are furnished with wings like a butterfly.
*Linn.* 15, Nat. Or. *Cruciferæ.* A worthless annual,
merely requiring to be sown in the open ground.
*Synonyme:* 1. *Thlaspi Psychine—P. stylosa* 1.

**PSYCHŌTRIA,** *Linn.* Said to be from *psyche,* life; in
allusion to the powerful medical qualities of some
of the species. *Linn.* 5, Or. 1, Nat. Or. *Cinchonaceæ.* Most of the species are handsome in foliage,
but the flowers of all are rather insignificant.
They are of the easiest cultivation, growing best
in a mixture of loam, peat, and sand; and cuttings
strike root readily in sand, under a glass. Several
species are used as substitutes for Ipecacuanha.

| | | | | | | |
|---|---|---|---|---|---|---|
| brachiáta | . | Wht. yel. | 8. Ev. S. | W. Ind. | | . 1793 |
| citrifólia | . | White | . 8. Ev. S. | W. Ind. | | . 1793 |
| corácea | . | White | . 7, S. Ev. S. | S. Amer. | | . 1810 |
| cumanénsis | . | Yellow | . 8. Ev. S. | Trinidad | | . 1824 |
| daphnoídes | . | White | . 6, G. Ev. S. | Moreton B. | | 1820 |
| elliptica | . | Green | . 8, S. Ev. S. | Brazils | | . 1821 |
| glabráta | . | White | . 6, S. Ev. S. | Jamaica | | . 1810 |
| hirsúta | . | White | . 8. Ev. S. | Jamaica | | . 1826 |
| laurifólia | . | White | . 6, S. Ev. S. | Jamaica | | . 1818 |
| marginála | . | White | . 5, S. Ev. S. | Jamaica | | . 1819 |
| megalospérma | . | White | . 8. Ev. S. | W. Ind. | | . 1824 |
| myrtifólia | . | White | . 8. Ev. S. | Jamaica | | . 1826 |
| parasítica | . | White | . Parasite. | W. Ind. | | . 1802 |
| pedunculáta | . | White | . 8. Ev. S. | Jamaica | | . 1818 |
| pubéscens | . | Yel. grn. | 8. Ev. S. | Jamaica | | . 1812 |
| undáta | . | White | . 5, S. Ev. S. | Bahamas | | . 1823 |

**PSYCHOTRIA,** see *Palicourèa.*

**PTĒLĒA,** *Linn.* From *ptelea,* the Greek name of the
elm, derived from *ptao,* to fly; alluding to the
winged fruit. *Linn.* 4, Or. 1, Nat. Or. *Xanthoxylaceæ.* A hardy North American plant, with
laburnum-like leaves; it will thrive in any common border soil, and increases readily by layers.

| | | | | | | |
|---|---|---|---|---|---|---|
| trifoliáta | . | Green | . 6, H. De. S. | N. Amer. | | . 1704 |

**PTELIDĪUM,** *Linn.* So named by *Thouars,* from its similarity
to *Ptelea.* *Linn.* 4, Or. 1, Nat. Or. *Celastraceæ.*
An ornamental shrub, growing best in a mixture of
loam, peat, and sand; and cuttings of the ripened
wood root readily in sand, under a glass, in heat.
*Synonyme:* 1. *Ptelea ovata, Scringia ovata.*

| | | | | | | |
|---|---|---|---|---|---|---|
| ovátum, 1 | . | | S. Ev. S. | Madagascar | | 1818 |

**PTĒRIS,** *Linn.* From *pteryx,* a wing; in allusion to
the appearance of the leaves. *Linn.* 24, Or. 1, Nat.
Or. *Polypodiaceæ.* An ornamental genus of *Ferns.*
The stove and greenhouse kinds are best cultivated
in a mixture of sandy loam and peat. The hardy
kinds grow best among rock-work, or in a shady
border; a light sandy soil suits them, and they are
all readily increased by divisions, or seeds. *P.
aquilina* is the well known brake of this country,
which has been sometimes used as an anthelmintic.
*P. esculenta* is occasionally used as an article of food
in different countries. *Synonyme:* 1. *P. elegans.*

| | | | | | | |
|---|---|---|---|---|---|---|
| aculeáta | . | Brown | . 8, S. Ev. T. | W. Ind. | | . 1793 |
| allocárus | . | Brown | . 8. Her. P. | | | |
| ámpla | . | Brown | . 7, S. Her. P. | | | |
| aquilína | . | Brown | . 7, H. Her. P. | Britain | | . |
| argéntea | . | Brown | . 7, H. Her. P. | Siberia | | . 1816 |
| argúta | . | Brown | . 8, G. Her. P. | Madeira | | . 1778 |
| atropurpúrea | . | Brown | . 8, H. Her. P. | N. Amer. | | . 1770 |
| calomélanos | . | Brown | . 9, S. Her. P. | C. G. H. | | . 1830 |
| caudáta | . | Brown | . 10, H. Her. P. | N. Amer. | | . 1777 |
| Cervantésii | . | Brown | . 7, S. Her. P. | Mexico | | . 1824 |
| chinénsis | . | Brown | . 7, S. Her. P. | China | | . 1824 |
| collína | . | Brown | . 7, S. Her. P. | Brazil | | . |
| cordáta | . | Brown | . 6, S. Her. P. | Mexico | | . 1820 |
| cretica | . | Brown | . 7, G. Her. P. | Candia | | . 1820 |
| crenuláta | . | Brown | . 7, S. Her. P. | | | . 1827 |
| denticuláta | . | Brown | . 7, S. Her. P. | Brazil | | . 1824 |
| discólor | . | Brown | . 8, S. Her. P. | N. Zeal. | | . 1837 |
| edúlis | . | Brown | . 8. Her. P. | E. Ind. | | . 1824 |
| élegans | . | Brown | . 8, G. Her. P. | N. S. W. | | . 1815 |
| esculénta | . | Brown | . 6, G. Her. P. | N. Holl. | | . 1820 |
| falcáta | . | Brown | . 8. Her. P. | | | . 1831 |
| flexuósa | . | Brown | . 8. Her. P. | | | |
| grandifólia | . | Brown | . 8, S. Her. P. | W. Ind. | | . 1793 |
| hastáta | . | Brown | . 8, G. Her. P. | C. G. H. | | . 1823 |
| heterophýlla | . | Brown | . 7, S. Her. P. | Jamaica | | . 1820 |
| intramarginális | . | Brown | . 9, F. Her. P. | Mexico | | . 1828 |
| láctea | . | Brown | . 11, S. Her. P. | | | |
| lanuginósa | . | Brown | . 7, S. Her. P. | Bourbon | | . 1819 |
| latizóna | . | Brown | . 6, G. Her. P. | Moreton B. | | 1831 |
| leptophýlla | . | Brown | . 8, S. Her. P. | Brazil | | . 1824 |
| longifólia | . | Brown | . 8, S. Her. P. | W. Ind. | | . 1770 |
| nemorális | . | Brown | . 6, S. Her. P. | Bourbon | | . 1823 |
| palmáta | . | Brown | . 7, S. Her. P. | Caraccas | | . 1821 |
| pedáta | . | Brown | . 7, H. Her. P. | Virginia | | . 1820 |
| peruviána | . | Brown | . 10, S. Her. P. | Peru | | . 1830 |
| Plumíeri | . | Brown | . 7, S. Her. P. | S. Amer. | | . 1818 |
| rotundifólia | . | Brown | . 7, S. Her. P. | N. Zeal. | | . 1824 |
| sagittáta | . | Brown | . 6, S. Her. P. | S. Amer. | | . 1826 |
| sagittæfólia | . | Brown | . 7, S. Her. P. | Brazil | | . 1826 |
| serruláta | . | Brown | . 7, S. Her. P. | India | | . 1770 |
| spinulósa | . | Brown | . 9, S. Her. P. | | | . 1834 |
| subverticilláta | . | Brown | . F. Her. P. | Mexico | | . 1831 |
| ternifólia | . | Brown | . 6, S. Her. P. | | | . 1838 |
| tremúla | . | Brown | . 7, G. Her. P. | N. Holl. | | . 1820 |
| umbrósa | . | Brown | . 7, S. Her. P. | N. Holl. | | . 1823 |
| vespertilliónis | . | Brown | . 7, G. Her. P. | N. Holl. | | . 1823 |

**PTEROCĀRPŪS,** *Linn.* From *pteron,* a wing, and *karpos,*
a fruit; the pods are girded with a broad wing.
*Linn.* 16, Or. 7, Nat. Or. *Leguminosæ.* Mostly fine
ornamental trees, attaining the height of from forty

to sixty feet, and growing best in a loamy soil. Cuttings of the young wood not deprived of any of their leaves, will root in sand, under a glass, in heat. The wood of *P. santalinus* yields the officinal Red Sanders-wood; the wood of the tree is dark red with black veins, capable of a good polish, and so heavy as to sink in water.

| | | | | | |
|---|---|---|---|---|---|
| dalbergioides | . | Yellow | . 8. Ev. T. E. Ind. | . | 1817 |
| draco | . . | White . | . 8. Ev. T. W. Ind. | . | 1820 |
| indicus | . . | White . | . 8. Ev. T. E. Ind. | . | 1818 |
| marsupium | . | White . | . 8. Ev. T. E. Ind. | . | 1811 |
| Rohrii | . . | | . 8. Ev. T. Guiana | . | 1816 |
| santalinoides | . | Yellow | . 8. Ev. T. S. Leone | . | 1793 |
| santalinus | . | Yellow . | . 8. Ev. T. E. Ind. | . | 1800 |
| scandens | . . | Yellow | . 8. Ev. Cl. Caraccas | . | 1817 |

PTEROCEPHALUS, *Vaillant.* From *pteron*, a wing, and *kephale*, a head; in allusion to the receptacle of the flowers being villous. *Linn.* 4, Or. 1, Nat. Or. *Dipsaceæ.* *P. dumetorum* will grow well in sandy loam, and increase freely from cuttings, or seeds. The annual kinds merely require sowing in the open border where they are intended to flower. *Synonymes:* 1. *Scabiosa dumetorum.* 2. *P. brachiata.* 3. *C. papposus, P. Vaillantii.* 4. *P. diandrus.* 5. *C. plumosus.*

| | | | | | |
|---|---|---|---|---|---|
| dumetorum, 1 | . | White . | . 6, G. Ev. S. Teneriffe | . | 1820 |
| palmatus, 2 | . | White . | . 7, H.    A. Cyprus | . | 1771 |
| papposus, 3 | . | White . | . 7, H.    A. S. Eur. | . | 1597 |
| diandrus, 4 | . | Purple | . 6, H.    A. Spain | . | 1823 |
| plumosus, 5 | . | Blue . | . 6, H.    A. Spain | . | 1819 |

PTEROGONIUM, *Swartz.* From *pteron*, a wing, and *gonos*, a shoot; referring to the pinnated stems. *Linn.* 24, Or. 5, Nat. Or. *Musci.* These plants are found on trees and sub-alpine rocks. *Synonyme:* 1. *P. cæspitosum—P. filiforme 1, gracile, Smithii.*

PTERONEURON, *Decandolle.* From *pteron*, a wing, and *neuron*, a nerve; because of the winged placentæ. *Linn.* 15, Nat. Or. *Cruciferæ.* Rock plants, requiring a light soil, and increased by seeds, which may be sown where the plants are intended to remain. *Synonymes:* 1. *Cardamine carnosa.* 2. *C. græcum.*

| | | | | | |
|---|---|---|---|---|---|
| carnosum, 1 | . | Pale . | . 6, H. Her. P. Hungary | . | 1824 |
| græcum, 2 | . | White . | . 6, H.    A. S. Eur. | . | 1710 |

PTERONIX, *Linn.* From *pteron*, a wing; the feathery scales of the receptacle. *Linn.* 19, Or. 1, Nat. Or. *Compositæ.* A genus of interesting plants, growing well in loam and peat, and readily increased by cuttings.

| | | | | | |
|---|---|---|---|---|---|
| camphorata | . | Yellow | . 6, G. Ev. S. C. G. H. | . | 1774 |
| echinata | . | Yellow | . 7, G. Ev. S. C. G. H. | . | 1818 |
| fasciculata | . | Yellow | . 6, G. Ev. S. C. G. H. | . | 1818 |
| flexicaulis | . | Yellow | . 7, G. Ev. S. C. G. H. | . | 1812 |
| glomerata | . | Yellow | . 6, G. Ev. S. C. G. H. | . | 1817 |
| oppositifolia | . | Yellow | . 7, G. Ev. S. C. G. H. | . | 1774 |
| pallens | . | Yellow | . 6, G. Ev. S. C. G. H. | . | 1816 |
| scariosa | . | Yellow | . 7, G. Ev. S. C. G. H. | . | 1815 |
| stricta | . | Yellow | . 5, G. Ev. S. C. G. H. | . | 1774 |

PTEROSPERMUM, *Schreber.* From *pteron*, a wing, and *sperma*, a seed; the seeds are winged. *Linn.* 16, Or. 7, Nat. Or. *Sterculiaceæ.* Large-leaved trees. They thrive in a mixture of peat, loam, and sand; and cuttings not deprived of their leaves will root in sand, under a glass, in a moderate heat.

| | | | | | |
|---|---|---|---|---|---|
| acerifolium | . | White . | . 8. S. Ev. T. E. Ind. | . | 1790 |
| canescens | . | White . | . 8. Ev. T. E. Ind. | . | 1823 |
| lanceæfolium | . | White . | . 8. Ev. T. E. Ind. | . | 1820 |
| platanifolium | . | White . | . 8. Ev. T. E. Ind. | . | 1820 |
| semisagittatum | . | White . | . 8. Ev. T. E. Ind. | . | 1820 |
| suberifolium | . | White . | . 9. S. Ev. T. E. Ind. | . | 1788 |

PTEROSTEGIA, *Fischer and Meyer.* From *pteron*, a wing, and *stegos*, covering; involucrum winged. *Linn.* —, Or. —, Nat. Or. *Polygaleæ.* This species may be grown in any common soil.

| | | | | | |
|---|---|---|---|---|---|
| drymarioides | . | Green . | . H.    A. California | . | 1836 |

PTEROSTYLIS, *R. Brown.* From *pteron*, a wing, and *stylos*, a style; in allusion to the column being winged at the top. *Linn.* 20, Or. 1, Nat. Or. *Orchidaceæ.* Interesting plants. For culture and propagation, see *Prasophyllum.*

| | | | | | |
|---|---|---|---|---|---|
| acuminata | . | Pa. yel. | . 5, G. Ter. N. Holl. | . | 1826 |
| Banksii | . | Yel. wht. | 12, G. Ter. N. Zeal. | . | 1827 |
| concinna | . | Pa. yel. | . G. Ter. N. Holl. | . | 1824 |
| cucullata | . | Pa. yel. | . 6, G. Ter. V. D. L. | . | 1823 |
| curta | . | Pa. yel. | . 5, G. Ter. N. Holl. | . | 1822 |
| gibbosa | . | Pa. yel. | . G. Ter. N. Holl. | . | 1824 |
| grandiflora | . | Pa. yel. | . 9. Ter. N. Holl. | . | 1824 |

| | | | | | |
|---|---|---|---|---|---|
| longifolia | . | Pa. yel. | . 7, G. Ter. N. Holl. | . | 1823 |
| nutans | . | Pa. yel. | . G. Ter. N. Holl. | . | 1823 |
| obtusa | . | Pa. yel. | . 7, G. Ter. N. Holl. | . | 1810 |
| ophioglossa | . | Pa. yel. | . G. Ter. N. Holl. | . | 1826 |
| reflexa | . | Pa. yel. | . 7, G. Ter. N. Holl. | . | 1826 |

PTERYGODIUM, *Swartz.* The name is probably derived from *pterygodes*, wing-like; because of the appearance of the sepals. *Linn.* 20, Or. 1, Nat. Or. *Orchidaceæ.* A genus of tuberous-rooted plants, requiring the same treatment as *Corycium.*

| | | | | | |
|---|---|---|---|---|---|
| alatum | . . . | | . 7, G. Ter. C. G. H. | . | 1821 |
| volucris | . . . | | . 7, G. Ter. C. G. H. | . | 1797 |

PTILOSTEPHIUM, *Kunth.* From *ptilon*, a feather, and *stephos*, a crown; from the feathery-like pappus. *Linn.* 19, Or. 2, Nat. Or. *Compositæ.* The seed of these plants should be sown on a gentle hotbed, and the young plants transplanted into the open border.

| | | | | | |
|---|---|---|---|---|---|
| coronopifolium | . | Yellow | . 6, H.    A. Mexico | . | 1828 |
| trifidum | . | Yellow | . 6, H.    A. Mexico | . | 1828 |

PTILOTA, *Agardh.* From *ptilotos*, pinnated; the form of the frond. *Linn.* 24, Or. 7, Nat. Or. *Algæ.* This species and its variety, are found in the ocean—*P. plumosa, P. tenuissima.*

PTYCHOTIS, *Koch.* From *ptyche*, a plait, and *ous*, an ear; the petals have a plait emitting a segment resembling a little ear. *Linn.* 5, Or. 2, Nat. Or. *Umbelliferæ.* Annuals not worth cultivating. *Synonymes:* 1. *Seseli ammoides.* 2. *Trachyspermum copticum.* 3. *S. corsicum.* 4. *S. saxifragum, Carum Bunius, Meum heterophyllum.* 5. *S. verticillatum, pusillum—P. ammoides 1, coptica 2, corsica 3, heterophylla 4, verticillata 5.*

PUBERULA, rather downy.

PUBESCENT, downy, hoary, covered with short soft hairs.

PUCCINIA, *Persoon.* In honour of T. Puccinius, a professor of anatomy at Florence. *Linn.* 24, Or. 9, Nat. Or. *Fungi.* The species of this genus have all the appearance of blackish or brown smut; and are found, as most of the specific names imply, upon the leaves of various plants—*P. Adoxæ, Ægopodii, Anemones, Asparagi, Aviculariæ, Betonicæ, Buxi, Calthæ, Campanulæ, caricina, Centauriæ, Chrysosplenii, Circææ, clandestina, Epilobii, Galiorum, Glechomatis, globosa, glomerata, Graminis, Heraclei, Lychnidearum, Menthæ, Polygoni, Primulæ, Prunorum, pulverulenta, Saniculæ, Scorodoniæ, Syngenesiarum, tumida, Ulmariæ, Umbelliferarum, Valantiæ, variabilis, Veronicarum, Vincæ, Violæ.*

PUCCOON, see *Sanguinaria.*

PUDICA, modest, humble.

PUERARIA, *Decandolle.* In honour of M. M. N. Puerari, a professor at Copenhagen. *Linn.* 16, Or. 6, Nat. Or. *Leguminosæ.* Ornamental plants. For culture and propagation, see *Clitoria.* *Synonyme:* 1. *Hedysarum tuberosum.*

| | | | | | |
|---|---|---|---|---|---|
| tuberosa, 1 | . | Yellow | . G. Ev. Cl. E. Ind. | . | 1806 |
| Wallichii | . | Yellow | . G. Ev. Cl. Nepal | . | 1826 |

PUFF-BALL, see *Lycoperdon.*

PULMONARIA, *Linn.* So named from its supposed medical properties in diseases of the lungs. *Linn.* 5, Or. 1, Nat. Or. *Boraginaceæ.* Very pretty flowering plants, well adapted for ornamenting the front of shrubberies. They thrive in any common soil, and are readily increased by divisions. *Synonyme:* 1. *P. oblongata.*

| | | | | | |
|---|---|---|---|---|---|
| angustifolia | . | Violet | . 4, H. Her. P. Britain | . | |
| oblongata, 1 | . | Pink | . 5, H. Her. P. Germany | . | |
| azurea | . | Blue | . 4, H. Her. P. Poland | . | 1823 |
| grandiflora | . | Pink | . 5, H. Her. P. France | . | 1819 |
| mollis | . | Blue | . 6, H. Her. P. N. Amer. | . | 1805 |
| officinalis | . | Pink | . 4, H. Her. P. England | . | |
| alba | . | White | . 6, H. Her. P. England | . | |
| pubescens | . | Purple | . 4, H. Her. P. Russia | . | 1821 |
| saccharata | . | Pink | . 6, H. Her. P. Europe | . | 1817 |
| tuberosa | . | Pink | . 5, H. Her. P. Hungary | . | 1824 |

PULMONARIA, see *Mertensia.*

PULTENÆA, *Smith.* In honour of W. Pulteney, M.D., a botanical author. *Linn.* 10, Or. 1, Nat. Or. *Leguminosæ.* The beautiful little shrubs of this genus succeed best in a compost of loam, peat, and sand, and placed in an airy part of the greenhouse or conservatory. Cuttings of the half-ripened wood root readily in sand, under a glass.

| | | | | | |
|---|---|---|---|---|---|
| argentea | . | Yellow | . 4, G. Ev. S. N. Holl. | . | 1824 |
| aristata | . | Yellow | . 5, G. Ev. S. N. Holl. | . | 1824 |
| aspera | . | Yellow | . 6, G. Ev. S. N. Holl. | . | 1824 |

| | | | | | |
|---|---|---|---|---|---|
| bilòbà | . . | Yellow | . 4, G. Ev. S. | N. S. W. | . 1817 |
| càndidà | . . | Yellow | . 5, G. Ev. S. | N. Holl. | . 1825 |
| canèscèns | . . | Yellow | . 4, G. Ev. S. | N. Holl. | . 1822 |
| capitellàtà | . . | Yellow | . 4, G. Ev. S. | N. Holl. | . 1823 |
| conòéà | . . | Yellow | . 5, G. Ev. S. | N. Holl. | . 1822 |
| cordàtà | . . | Yellow | . 5, G. Ev. S. | V. D. L. | . 1822 |
| crassifòlìà | . . | Yellow | . 5, G. Ev. S. | N. Holl. | . 1824 |
| cuneàtà | . . | Yellow | . 6, G. Ev. S. | N. Holl. | . 1824 |
| daphnoìdès | . . | Yellow | . 4, G. Ev. S. | N. S. W. | . 1792 |
| dentàtà | . . | Yellow | . 6, G. Ev. S. | N. Holl. | . 1820 |
| ecìfìnùlà | . . | Yellow | . 5, G. Ev. S. | N. Holl. | . 1823 |
| ellìptìcà | . . | Yellow | . 6, G. Ev. S. | N. Holl. | . 1810 |
| eùchìlà | . . | Yellow | . 5, G. Ev. S. | N. Holl. | . 1820 |
| ferrùgìnéà | . . | Yellow | . 5, G. Ev. S. | N. Holl. | . 1810 |
| flexìlìs | . . | Yellow | . 5, G. Ev. S. | Pt. Jack. | . 1801 |
| hypolàmprà | . . | Yellow | . 5, G. Ev. S. | N. Holl. | . 1824 |
| incarnàtà | . . | Yellow | . 5, G. Ev. S. | N. Holl. | . 1824 |
| incurvàtà | . . | Yellow | . 5, G. Ev. S. | N. Holl. | . 1823 |
| junìperìnà | . . | Yellow | . 6, G. Ev. S. | N. Holl. | . 1824 |
| linophìllà | . . | Yellow | . 4, G. Ev. S. | N. S. W. | . 1789 |
| mìcrophyllà | . . | Yellow | . 5, G. Ev. S. | N. Holl. | . 1810 |
| mucronàtà | . . | Yellow | . 5, G. Ev. S. | N. Holl. | . 1826 |
| obcordàtà | . . | Yellow | . 6, G. Ev. S. | V. D. L. | . 1808 |
| oxalìdìfòlìà | . . | Yellow | . 4, G. Ev. S. | N. Holl. | . 1826 |
| paleàceà | . . | Yellow | . 5, G. Ev. S. | N. S. W. | . 1789 |
| parvìflòrà | . . | Yellow | . 6, G. Ev. S. | N. Holl. | . 1824 |
| pedunculàtà | . . | Yellow | . 5, G. Ev. S. | N. Holl. | . 1820 |
| phylicoìdès | . . | Yellow | . 5, G. Ev. S. | N. Holl. | . 1822 |
| plumòsà | . . | Yellow | . 4, G. Ev. S. | N. Holl. | . 1824 |
| polìfòlìà | . . | Yellow | . 5, G. Ev. S. | N. Holl. | . 1824 |
| polygalìfòlìà | . . | Yellow | . 5, G. Ev. S. | N. Holl. | . 1817 |
| procùmbèns | . . | Yellow | . 4, G. Ev. Tr. | N. Holl. | . 1823 |
| racemulòsà | . . | Yellow | . 4, G. Ev. S. | N. Holl. | . 1820 |
| retùsà | . . | Yellow | . 4, G. Ev. S. | N. S. W. | . 1789 |
| rosmarìnifòlìà | . . | Yellow | . 5, G. Ev. S. | N. Holl. | . 1824 |
| scàbrà | . . | Yellow | . 4, G. Ev. S. | N. S. W. | . 1803 |
| squarròsà | . . | Yellow | . 6, G. Ev. S. | N. Holl. | . 1825 |
| staphyleoìdès | . . | Yellow | . 5, G. Ev. S. | N. Holl. | . 1824 |
| stenophyllà | . . | | . G. Ev. S. | | |
| stipulàris | . . | Yellow | . 4, G. Ev. S. | N. S. W. | . 1792 |
| strìctà | . . | Yellow | . 6, G. Ev. S. | N. S. W. | . 1803 |
| subumbellàtà | . . | Yellow | . 5, G. Ev. S. | V. D. L. | . 1831 |
| tenuifòlìà | . . | Yellow | . 4, G. Ev. S. | N. Holl. | . 1817 |
| thymìfòlìà | . . | Yellow | . 5, G. Ev. S. | N. Holl. | . 1810 |
| vestìtà | . . | Yellow | . 4, G. Ev. S. | N. Holl. | . 1803 |
| villìfèrà | . . | Yellow | . 5, G. Ev. S. | N. Holl. | . 1824 |
| villòsà | . . | Yellow | . 5, G. Ev. S. | N. S. W. | . 1790 |

PULVERULENT, powdery, downy.

PULVINATE, convex and flattened, cushion-shaped.

PUMPKIN, see *Cucurbìtà Pèpò*.

PUNCTARÌA, *Greville*. From *punctum*, a dot; numerous dotted fructifications. *Linn.* 24, Or. 7, Nat. Or. *Algæ*. These plants are generally found on marine rocks—*P. latìfòlìà, plantagìnéà, tenuìssìmà*.

PUNCTATE, dotted.

PUNGENT, pricking or stinging.

PUNÌCÀ, *Linn.* From *punicus*, of "Carthage," near which city it is said to have been first found; or from *puniceus*, scarlet: alluding to the colour of the flowers. *Linn.* 12, Or. 1, Nat. Or. *Myrtaceæ*. There is no tree more showy than the Pomegranate. *P. granatum* and its varieties produce their splendid flowers and fruit very plentifully when planted against a south wall. They all grow well in a light rich loam, and strike root freely from cuttings or layers; the rarer varieties are sometimes increased by grafting on the common kinds. *Synonymes*: 1. *P. G. album*. 2. *P. G. plenum*.

| | | | | | |
|---|---|---|---|---|---|
| Granàtum | . . | Red | . 8, H. De. S. | S. Eur. | . 1548 |
| albèscèns | . . | Whitish | . 8, H. De. S. | China . | . |
| albèscèns fl. plènò 1 | | Whitish | . 8, H. De. S. | | |
| flàvum | . . | Yellow | . 8, H. De. S. | | |
| rùbrum fl. plènò, 2 | | Red | . 8, H. De. S. | S. Eur. | . |
| nànà | . . | Red | . 8, G. De. S. | W. Ind. | . 1723 |

PUNICEUS, red, or scarlet.

PÙRSHÌÀ, *Decandolle*. In honour of Frederick Pursh, author of "Flora Americæ Septentrionalis," 1817. *Linn.* 12, Or. 1, Nat. Or. *Rosaceæ*. A dwarf shrub, requiring to be grown in a dry, light, sandy soil. It may be propagated by cuttings, but is easier increased by seeds. *Synonyme*: 1. *Tigarea tridentata*.

| | | | | | |
|---|---|---|---|---|---|
| tridentàtà, 1 | . . | Yellow | . H. Ev. S. | N. Amer. | . 1826 |

PURSLANE, see *Portulàcà*.

PURSLANE-TREE, see *Portulacàrìà*.

PUSCHKÌNÌÀ, *Adams*. Named in honour of Count M. Puschkin, a Russian botanist. *Linn.* 6, Or. 1, Nat. Or. *Liliaceæ*. This plant requires to be cultivated in sandy loam, and is increased by offsets. *Synonyme*: 1. *Adamsia scilloides*.

| | | | | | |
|---|---|---|---|---|---|
| scilloìdès, 1 | . . | Pa. blue | . 5, F. Bl. P. | Siberia . | . 1819 |

PUSILLOUS, weak, diminutive.

PUSTULATE, covered with glandular excrescences.

PYCNANTHEMUM, *Michaux*. From *pyknos*, dense, and *anthemis*, a flower; the flowers are produced in dense whorls. *Linn.* 14, Or. 1, Nat. Or. *Labiatæ*. White-flowering plants of little beauty, but fragrant in a high degree. A peat border suits them best, and they are readily increased by divisions. *Synonymes*: 1. *P. verticillatum*. 2. *Thymus virginicus*. 3. *Monardella caroliniana*.

| | | | | | |
|---|---|---|---|---|---|
| aristàtum, 1 | . . | White | . 8, H. Her. P. | N. Amer. | . 1752 |
| incànum | . . | White | . 8, H. Her. P. | N. Amer. | . 1732 |
| lanceolàtum | . . | White | . 7, H. Her. P. | N. Amer. | . 1812 |
| linifòlìum, 2 | . . | White | . 7, H. Her. P. | N. Amer. | . 1789 |
| Monardella, 3 | . . | White | . 7, H. Her. P. | N. Amer. | . 1816 |
| nùdum | . . | White | . 7, H. Her. P. | Carolina | . 1824 |
| ovàtum | . . | White | . 7, H. Her. P. | N. Amer. | . 1829 |

PYCNOSTACHYS, *Hooker*. From *pyknos*, dense, and *stachys*, a spike; the spikes are dense-flowered. *Linn.* 14, Or. 1, Nat. Or. *Labiatæ*. This plant requires the same treatment as other stove annuals.

| | | | | | |
|---|---|---|---|---|---|
| cærùléà | . . | Blue | . 8, S. | A. Madagas. | . 1825 |

PYGMÆI, dwarf.

PYRAMIDAL, formed like a pyramid.

PYRASTER, see *Pýrùs commùnìs Pyràstèr*.

PYRENÌUM, *Fries*. From *pyren*, a kernel; appearance of the plants. *Linn.* 24, Or. 9, Nat. Or. *Fungi*. This species is found on dead wood—*P. lignàtìle*.

PYRENÙLÀ, *Acharius*. From a diminutive of *pyren*, a kernel; the receptacle is enclosed in the thalamium as a kernel in its shell. *Linn.* 24, Or. 8, Nat. Or. *Lichenes*. These plants are to be met with on rocks, and the bark of beech-trees, at all seasons of the year—*P. nigrèscèns, nìtìdà, tessellàtà, umbonàtà*.

PYRETHRUM, *Smith*. From *pyr*, fire; the roots are hot to the taste. *Linn.* 19, Or. 2, Nat. Or. *Compositæ*. A genus of very interesting plants. The greenhouse kinds grow in any rich light soil, and young cuttings root readily when planted under a glass. The hardy kinds are increased by divisions or seeds; any common soil suits them. *Synonymes*: 1. *Chrysanthemum coccineum*. 2. *P. grandiflorum*. 3. *P. grandiflorum*. 4. *Achillea sambucifolia*.

| | | | | | |
|---|---|---|---|---|---|
| achilleìfòlìum | . . | Yellow | . 7, H. Her. P. | Caucasus | . 1823 |
| alpìnum | . . | White | . 7, H. Her. P. | Switzerl. | . 1759 |
| pubèscèns | . . | White | . 7, H. Her. P. | Switzerl. | . 1819 |
| anethìfòlìum | . . | White | . G. Ev. S. | Teneriffe | . 1815 |
| Balsamìtà | . . | White | . 7, H. Her. P. | Levant . | . 1779 |
| Barrelìèrì | . . | White | . 8, H. Her. P. | S. Eur. | . 1820 |
| bipinnàtum | . . | Yellow | . 6, H. Her. P. | Siberia . | . 1796 |
| Boccòni | . . | Yellow | . 7, H. Her. P. | Spain . | . 1823 |
| brevìradiàtum | . . | Yellow | . 7, H. | A. | . 1818 |
| Broussònètì | . . | White | . 7, G. Ev. S. | Canaries | . 1817 |
| carnèum, 1 | . . | Pink . | . 8, H. Her. P. | Caucasus | . 1804 |
| caucàsìcum | . . | White | . 7, H. Her. P. | Caucasus | . 1804 |
| ceratophylloìdès | . . | White | . 6, H. Her. P. | Piedmont | . 1819 |
| cinerariæfòlìum | . . | White | . 7, H. Her. P. | Dalmatia | . 1826 |
| coronopìfòlìum | . . | White | . G. Ev. S. | Canaries | . |
| corymbòsum | . . | White | . 7, H. Her. P. | Germany | . 1596 |
| crithmìfòlìum | . . | White | . G. Ev. S. | Teneriffe | . 1815 |
| diversìfòlìum | . . | White | . 7, H. Her. P. | N. Holl. | . 1823 |
| élègans | . . | White | . 7, H. Tr. B. | Mt. Baldo | . 1816 |
| fœnìculàceum | . . | White | . G. Ev. S. | Teneriffe | . 1815 |
| frutèscèns | . . | White | . 6, G. Ev. S. | Canaries | . 1699 |
| fuscàtum | . . | White | . 7, H. | A. S. Eur. | . 1821 |
| grandiflòrum | . . | White | . G. Ev. S. | Canaries | . 1815 |
| Hallèri | . . | White | . 6, H. Her. P. | Switzerl. | . 1819 |
| incànum | . . | | . 7, H. Her. P. | Siberia . | . 1831 |
| indìcum | . . | Yellow | . 7, H. | A. E. Ind. | . 1810 |
| inodòrum | . . | White | . 7, H. Her. P. | Britain . | . |
| floribùs plènìs, 2 | | White | . 7, H. Her. Tr. | | . 1825 |
| latìfòlìum, 3 | . . | White | . 6, H. Her. P. | Pyrenees | . 1820 |
| leptophyllum | . . | White | . 7, H. Her. P. | Caucasus | . 1821 |
| macrophyllum, 4 | . . | White | . 7, H. Her. P. | Hungary | . 1803 |
| Mundìànum | . . | White | . 7, H. Her. P. | France . | . 1816 |
| marìtìmum | . . | White | . 8, H. Her. P. | Britain . | . |
| maxìmum | . . | White | . 7, H. Her. P. | S. Eur. | . 1818 |
| millefòlìàtum | . . | Yellow | . 7, H. Her. P. | Siberia . | . 1731 |
| palùstrè | . . | White | . 6, H. Her. P. | Armenia | . 1820 |
| parthenìfòlìum | . . | White | . 7, H. Her. P. | Caucasus | . 1804 |
| Parthenìum | . . | White | . 7, H. Her. P. | Britain . | . |
| flòrè-plènò | . . | White | . 7, H. Her. P. | | |
| parvìflòrum | . . | White | . 7, H. | A. | . 1820 |
| pinnatìfìdum | . . | White | . 7, H. Her. P. | | . 1823 |
| præcòx | . . | White | . 6, H. | A. Caucasus | . 1818 |
| ptarmicæfòlìum | . . | White | . 7, H. Her. P. | Caucasus | . 1803 |
| pulverulèntum | . . | White | . 6, H. Her. P. | Caucasus | . 1806 |
| ròsèum | . . | Pa. red | . 6, H. Her. P. | Caucasus | . 1826 |
| serìceum | . . | White | . 7, H. Her. P. | Iberia . | . 1823 |
| serotìnum | . . | White | . 8, H. Her. Cr. | N. Amer. | . 1731 |
| simplicìfòlìum | . . | White | . 6, S. Ev. Tr. | W. Ind. | . 1817 |
| specìòsum | . . | White | . G. Ev. S. | Canaries | . 1815 |
| tenuìfòlìum | . . | White | . 7, H. Her. P. | Caucasus | . 1806 |
| tomentòsum | . . | White | . 7, H. Her. P. | Corsica . | . 1818 |

| | | | | | | | |
|---|---|---|---|---|---|---|---|
| trifurcătŭm | . . | Yellow | . 7, H. | | A. | Barbary | . 1820 |
| uliginŏsŭm | . . | White | . 8, H. Her. | P. | | Hungary | . 1816 |

Pȳăŏlĭ, *Linn.* From *pyrus*, a pear-tree; similarity in the leaves. *Linn.* 10, Or. 1, Nat. Or. *Pyrolaceæ.* A genus of very pretty plants, rather difficult to cultivate. A shaded peat border appears to suit them best, and they are readily increased by divisions or seeds. Synonymes: 1. *P. chlorantha.* 2. *P. rosea.*

| | | | | | | | |
|---|---|---|---|---|---|---|---|
| amarifŏlĭă | . . | Grn. yel. | . 6, H. Her. | P. | N. Amer. | | . 1810 |
| convolūtă, 1 | . . | Grn. wht. | . 6, H. Her. | P. | N. Amer. | | . 1818 |
| elliptică | . . | White | . 6, H. Her. | P. | N. Amer. | | . 1818 |
| mēdĭă | . . | Wht. red | . 6, H. Her. | P. | England | | |
| minŏr, 2 | . . | Red | . 6, H. Her. | P. | Britain | | |
| rotundifŏlĭă | . . | White | . 6, H. Her. | P. | Britain | | |
| secŭndă | . . | White | . 6, H. Her. | P. | Britain | | |
| uniflŏră | . . | White | . 6, H. Her. | P. | Britain | | |

Pȳrolĭrĭŏn, *Herbert.* Literally *Fire-lily*; from the colour of the flowers. *Linn.* 6, Or. 1, Nat. Or. *Amaryllidaceæ.* Rather a pretty plant, growing in sandy loam, and increased by offsets. Synonyme: 1. *Amaryllis peruviana.*

| | | | | | | | |
|---|---|---|---|---|---|---|---|
| aŭrĕŭm, 1 | . . | Gold clrd. | . 6, G. Bl. | P. | Peru | | . 1833 |

Pȳrŭlărĭă, *Michaux.* The meaning is not known to us. *Linn.* 23, Or. 2, Nat. Or. *Santalaceæ* An ornamental shrub, growing in sandy loam, and increased by cuttings. Synonyme: 1. *Hamiltonia oleifera.*

| | | | | | | | |
|---|---|---|---|---|---|---|---|
| pūbĕră | . . . | Grn. yel. | . F. De. | S. | N. Amer. | | . 1800 |

Pȳrŭs, *Linn.* From *peren*, the Celtic word for pear. *Linn.* 12, Or. 2, Nat. Or. *Rosaceæ.* To this genus belong the Pear and Apple, as well as the Service-tree, and many others, either prized for their fruit or their ornamental appearance. In our shrubberies, they grow in any common soil; but for the more highly cultivated ones a deep loam is necessary. They are increased by seeds, and the established kinds are multiplied by grafting the choicer on the common kinds. Synonymes: 1. *P. malus sylvestris.* 2. *P. salicifolia.* 3. *P. alpina.* 4. *P. sylvestris.* 5. *P. orientalis.* 6. *P. pubens.* 7. *P. edulis.* 8. *Sorbus latifolius.* 9. *Sorbus microcarpa.* 10. *S. hybrida.* 11. *P. Bollwylleriana.* 12. *Sorbus domestica.* 13. *P. hybrida, P spuria sambucifolia.* 14. *Cratægus torminalis.* 15. *P. Pashia.* 16. *P. nepalensis.*

| | | | | | | | |
|---|---|---|---|---|---|---|---|
| acĕrbă, 1 | . . | White | . 4, H. De. | T. | Europe | | |
| americănă | . . | White | . 5, H. De. | T. | Canada | . | 1782 |
| amygdalifŏrmĭs, 2 | | White | . 5, H. De. | T. | S. Eur. | . | 1810 |
| angustifŏlĭă | . . | Pink | . 5, H. De. | T. | N. Amer. | . | 1750 |
| arbutifŏlĭă | . . | White | . 5, H. De. | S. | N. Amer. | . | 1700 |
| intermēdĭă | . . | White | . 5, H. De. | S. | | | |
| pumĭlă | . . | White | . 5, H. De. | S. | | | |
| serotĭnă | . . | White | . 6, H. De. | S. | | | |
| Arĭă | . . | White | . 5, H. De. | T. | Britain | . | |
| acutifŏlĭă, 3 | . . | White | . 5, H. De. | T. | Europa | . | |
| bullătă | . . | White | . 5, H. De. | T. | S. Eur. | . | |
| cretică | . . | White | . 5, H. De. | T. | Crete | . | |
| obtusifŏlĭă | . . | White | . 5, H. De. | T. | Europe | . | |
| rugŏsă | . . | White | . 5, H. De. | T. | S. Eur. | . | |
| undulătă | . . | White | . 5, H. De. | T. | S. Eur. | . | |
| astracănĭcă | . . | White | . 6, H. De. | T. | Astracan | . | 1810 |

| | | | | | | | |
|---|---|---|---|---|---|---|---|
| aucupărĭă | . . | White | . 5, H. De. | T. | Britain | . | |
| fastigiătă | . . | White | . 5, H. De. | T. | | | |
| fol. variegātă | . . | White | . 5, H. De. | T. | Britain | | Gard. |
| frūctū lūtĕŏ | . . | White | . 5, H. De. | T. | Britain | | Gard. |
| auriculātă | . . | White | . 5, H. De. | T. | Egypt | . | 1800 |
| baccătă | . . | Pink | . 4, H. De. | T. | Siberia | . | 1784 |
| Chamæmespĭlŭs | . | White | . 5, H. De. | S. | Pyrenees | . | 1683 |
| commŭnĭs | . . | White | . 4, H. De. | T. | England | . | |
| Achrăs | . . | White | . 4, H. De. | T. | | | |
| florĕ-plēnŏ | . . | White | . 4, H. De. | T. | | | |
| fol. variegātĭs | . . | White | . 4, H. De. | T. | | | |
| frūctū variegătŏ | | White | . 4, H. De. | T. | | | |
| isapĭdeă | . . | White | . 4, H. De. | T. | | | |
| Pyrāstĕr, 4 | . . | White | . 4, H. De. | T. | | | |
| sanguinolentă | . . | White | . 4, H. De. | T. | | | |
| sativă | . . | White | . 4, H. De. | T. | | | |
| cuneārĭă | . . | Pink | . 5, H. De. | T. | Virginia | . | 1724 |
| crenătă | . . | White | . 5, H. De. | T. | Nepal | . | 1820 |
| deprēssă | . . | White | . 5, H. De. | S. | | | |
| dioĭcă | . . | White | . 4, H. De. | T. | | . | 1818 |
| edŭlĭs | . . | White | . 4, H. De. | T. | France | . | 1816 |
| elæagnifŏlĭă, 5 | . | White | . 4, H. De. | T. | Siberia | . | 1806 |
| floribŭndă | . . | White | . 5, H. De. | T. | China | . | 1818 |
| grandifŏlĭă, 6 | . | White | . 4, H. De. | S. | N. Amer. | . | |
| intermēdĭă | . . | White | . 5, H. De. | S. | Sweden | . | 1789 |
| angustifŏlĭă, 7 | . | White | . 5, H. De. | T. | | | |
| latifŏlĭă, 8 | . . | White | . 5, H. De. | T. | Denmark | . | 1789 |
| lanătă | . . | White | . 5, H. De. | T. | Nepal | . | 1818 |
| lanuginŏsă | . . | White | . 4, H. De. | T. | Hungary | . | |
| Mālŭs | . . | White | . 5, H. De. | T. | Britain | . | |
| melanocărpă | . . | White | . 5, H. De. | S. | N. Amer. | . | 1700 |
| subpubēscens | . | White | . 5, H. De. | S. | | | |
| microcărpă, 9 | . | White | . 4, H. De. | T. | N. Amer. | . | |
| nivālĭs | . . | White | . 4, H. De. | T. | Austria | . | |
| pinnatifĭdă, 10 | . | White | . 5, H. De. | T. | England | . | |
| arbŭscŭlă | . . | White | . 5, H. De. | T. | Germany | . | |
| lanuginŏsă | . . | White | . 5, H. De. | T. | England | . | |
| pendŭlă | . . | White | . 5, H. De. | T. | England | . | |
| Pollverĭă, 11 | . | White | . 5, H. De. | T. | Germany | . | 1786 |
| præcŏx | . . | Blush | . 4, H. De. | T. | Russia | . | 1784 |
| prunifŏlĭă | . . | Pink | . 5, H. De. | T. | Siberia | . | 1758 |
| pūbĕns | . . | White | . 5, H. De. | S. | | | |
| salicifŏlĭă | . . | White | . 5, H. De. | T. | Russia | . | 1780 |
| salvifŏlĭă | . . | White | . 5, H. De. | T. | France | . | 1806 |
| sinaĭcă | . . | White | . 5, H. De. | T. | Levant | . | 1820 |
| sinēnsĭs | . . | White | . 5, H. De. | S. | China | . | |
| Sorbŭs, 12 | . . | White | . 5, H. De. | T. | England | . | |
| malifŏrmĭs | . . | White | . 5, H. De. | T. | | | |
| pyrifŏrmĭs | . . | White | . 5, H. De. | T. | | | |
| spectābĭlĭs | . . | White | . 5, H. De. | T. | China | . | 1780 |
| spŭrĭă | . . | White | . 5, H. De. | T. | | . | 1900 |
| pendŭlă, 13 | . | White | . 5, H. De. | T. | | | |
| sambucifŏlĭă | . | White | . 5, H. De. | T. | | . | 1818 |
| tomentŏsă | . . | White | . 5, H. De. | T. | Europe | . | 1810 |
| torminālĭs, 14 | . | White | . 5, H. De. | T. | England | . | |
| trilobātă | . . | White | . 5, H. De. | T. | S. Eur. | . | 1810 |
| variolŏsă, 15 | . | White | . 5, H. De. | T. | Nepal | . | 1825 |
| vestītă, 16 | . . | White | . 4, H. De. | T. | Nepal | . | 1820 |

Pȳxĭdănthĕră, *Michaux.* From *pyxis*, a box, and *anthera*, an anther. *Linn.* 5, Or. 1, Nat. Or. *Diapensiaceæ.* This species thrives in peat soil, treated as other frame plants, and it may be increased by cuttings or divisions. Synonyme: 1. *Diapensia cuneifolia.*

| | | | | | | | |
|---|---|---|---|---|---|---|---|
| barbulātă, 1 | . . | White | . 7, F. Ev. | Tr. | Carolina | . | 1806 |

Pȳxĭdătă, box-shaped.

## Q.

Quadrangular, four-angled.

Quadrate, square.

Quadrĭă, *Ruiz and Pavon.* In honour of Antonio de la Quadra, a Spanish cultivator. *Linn.* 4, Or. 1, Nat. Or. *Proteaceæ.* This tree requires to be grown in peat and loam, and propagated by cuttings, in sand, under a glass.

| | | | | | | |
|---|---|---|---|---|---|---|
| heterophȳllă | . . | | G. Ev. | T. | Chile | . . 1826 |

Quadrifarious, arranged in four rows.

Quadrifid, divided into four parts.

Quaking-grass, see Brīză.

Quapĭlĭă, *Aublet.* The name of the tree among the Guianese Indians. *Linn.* 1, Or. 1, Nat. Or. *Vochyaceæ.* This tree will grow best in peat and loam, and is said to be increased by seeds.

| | | | | | | |
|---|---|---|---|---|---|---|
| violăcĕă | . . | Violet | . | S. Ev. | T. | Brazil | . . 1824 |

Quamash, see Scillă esculentă.

Quamŏclĭt, *Tournefort.* From *kyamos*, a kidney-bean, and *klitos*, dwarf; the species of this genus resemble the kidney-bean in their climbing stems, but are less tall. *Linn.* 5, Or. 1, Nat. Or. *Convolvulaceæ.* This genus, for the most part, consists of very beautiful half-hardy annuals. They require to be reared on a hotbed, and about the end of May they may be planted out in a warm sheltered situation in the open border; some of them may be kept in the greenhouse, where they will flower and ripen their seeds freely. The perennial kinds are well adapted for covering pillars in the stove or greenhouse. Any light rich soil suits them, and cuttings of the young wood root readily in sand, under a glass, in heat. Synonymes: 1. *Ipomœa coccinea.* 2. *I. digitata.* 3. *I. hastigera.* 4. *I. hederifolia.* 5. *I. longiflora.* 6. *I. luteola.* 7. *I. phœnicea.* 8. *I. sanguinea.* 9. *I. triloba.* 10. *I. Quamoclit.*

| | | | | | | | |
|---|---|---|---|---|---|---|---|
| coccĭnĕă, 1 | . | Scarlet | . 8, S. Tw. | A. | S. Amer. | . | 1713 |
| digitātă, 2 | . | Purple | . 9, S. Tw. | A. | W. Ind. | | |
| hastigĕră, 3 | . | Purple | . 6, S. Her. | Tw. | Mexico | . | 1824 |
| hederifŏlĭă, 4 | . | Violet | . 7, S. Tw. | A. | W. Ind. | . | 1773 |

| | | | | | | |
|---|---|---|---|---|---|---|
| longiflōrā, 5 | . White | . 6, S. Her. Tw. | Cuba | . 1808 |
| lutēolā, 6 | . Or. yel. | 8, S. Tw. A. | Guatemala | 1759 |
| phœnīceā, 7 | . Crimson | 7, S. Tw. A. | E. Ind. | . 1806 |
| angulōsā, 8 | . Crimson | 7, S. Ev. Tw. | San. Cruz | 1812 |
| trilōbā, 9 | . Violet | 7, S. Tw. A. | Amer. | . 1752 |
| vulgāris, 10 | . Scarlet | 8, S. Tw. A. | E. Ind. | 1629 |
| albiflōrā | . White | 9, S. Tw. A. | E. Ind. | 1629 |

**QUARTZ**, a kind of stone.

**QUASSIA**, *Linn.* Quassi, the name of a negro slave, who first used the bark as a febrifuge. *Linn.* 10, Or. 1, Nat. Or. *Simarubaceæ.* This valuable tree thrives in loam and peat; and cuttings of the ripened wood, with their leaves left whole, will root in sand, under a glass, in heat. The wood of this tree is well known as one of the most intense bitters, and is considered an effectual remedy in any disorder where pure bitters are required.

| | | | | | |
|---|---|---|---|---|---|
| amāra | . . . Red | . 6, S. Ev. T. | Guiana | . 1790 |

**QUATERNARY**, arranged in fours.

**QUEKETTIA**, *Lindley.* Named after Edwin J. Quekett, F.L.S., an excellent botanical observer, and one of our best vegetable anatomists. *Linn.* 20, Or. 1, Nat. Or. *Orchidaceæ.* Dr. Lindley says, "although this little plant is only a few inches high, and has no attractions for the vulgar eye, it is in some respects one of the most interesting I know, if examined microscopically." It will be found to succeed best on wood, treated precisely as the species of *Pleurothallis.*

| | | | |
|---|---|---|---|
| microscopicā | . Yellow | . 8. Epi. |

**QUERCITRON**, see *Quércus tinctóriā.*

**QUERCUS**, *Linn.* From the Celtic *quer*, fine, and *cuez*, a tree, fine tree; others derive it from the Greek word *choiros*, a pig; because those animals feed on the acorns. *Linn.* 21, Or. 9, Nat. Or. *Cupuliferæ.* All the species of this very important genus have a highly ornamental appearance, either on the lawn or in the forest; the wood is also much superior to that of any other tree, teak alone excepted, for the purpose of naval architecture; indeed, there is no purpose in the arts to which the wood of the oak is not applicable. Q. *Suber* is very valuable on account of its being the only tree which produces in any quantity that very important article, cork. The bark, leaves, and fruit, of all the species abound in astringent matter, and in tannin. The oak succeeds best in a deep loamy soil, and in a somewhat low situation. The species are generally increased from seed; and it is only when particular varieties are to be perpetuated, that grafting is resorted to. The seeds may either be sown when they drop from the tree, or they may be thoroughly dried, and preserved till the following March; previous to sowing, the soil should be well prepared, and after the drills are opened, or the earth drawn off the beds, the acorns may be scattered along the drills or over the beds, keeping them about two inches apart; before covering, the acorns must, if sown in beds, be patted down with the back of a spade, or the back of a wooden headed rake if sown in drills. They should be covered from half an inch, to an inch and a half deep, according to the size of the acorn, with finely broken soil. The after culture of the oak does not require any notice here. *Synonymes :* 1. Q. *Phullata.* 2. Q. *conglomerata.* 3. Q. *hemisphærica.* 4. Q. *nana.* 5. Q. *austriaca.* 6. Q. *Lucombeana crispa.* 7. Q. *L. dentata.* 8. Q. *cerris dentata.* 9. Q. *L. heterophylla.* 10. Q. *L. incisa.* 11. Q. *exoniensis.* 12. Q. *Ragnal.* 13. Q. *L. suberosa.* 14. Q. *frondosa.* 15. Q. *discolor, Q. elongata, Q. triloba.* 16. Q. *humilis, Q. nana.* 17 Q. *lanuginosa.* 18. Q. *aquatic t.* 19. Q. *stellata.* 20. Q. *Banisteri, Q. montana.* 21. Q. *fastigiata.* 22 Q. *laciniata.* 23. Q. *pendula.* 24. Q. *purpurea.* 25. Q. *cinerea.* 26. Q. *sericea.* 27. Q. *Castanea.* 28. Q. *montana.* 29. Q. *prinoides.* 30. Q. *Michauxii.* 31. Q. *Tauxin.* 32. Q. *Robur.* 33 Q. *pubescens.*

| | | | | | |
|---|---|---|---|---|---|
| Ægilops | . . | . Apetal | . H. De. T. | Levant | . 1781 |
| latifōliā | . | . Apetal | . H. De. T. | | |
| pendūlā | . | . Apetal | . H. De. T. | | |
| alba | . . | . Apetal | . 5, H. De. T. | N. Amer. | 1724 |
| pinnatifīdā | . | . Apetal | . 5, H. De. T. | N. Amer. | 1724 |
| repandā | . | . Apetal | . 5, H. De. T. | N. Amer. | |
| ambiguā | . | . Apetal | . 5, H. De. T. | N. Amer. | 1800 |
| annulātā, 1 | . | . Apetal | . H. Ev. T. | Nepal | 1822 |
| apennīnā, 2 | . | . Apetal | . 5, H. D. T. | S. Eur. | . |
| aquāticā | . | . Apetal | . 5, H. De. T. | N. Amer. | 1723 |

---

| | | | | |
|---|---|---|---|---|
| maritīmā, 3 | . Apetal | 5, H. De. T. | N. Amer. | |
| nānā, 4 | . . Apetal | 5, H. De. T. | N. Amer. | . 1738 |
| austrālis | . . Apetal | 5, H. Ev. T. | Portugal | . 1835 |
| Ballōtā | . . Apetal | 5, H. Ev. T. | Barbary | |
| Catesbæī | . . Apetal | 5, H. De. T. | N. Amer. | . 1823 |
| Cērris | . . Apetal | 5, H. De. T. | S. Eur. | . 1735 |
| austrīacā, 5 | . Apetal | 5, H. De. T. | Austria | . 1824 |
| cānā-mājōr | . Apetal | 5, H. De. T. | S. Eur. | |
| cānā-mīnōr | . Apetal | 5, H. De. T. | S. Eur. | |
| crispā, 6 | . . Apetal | 5, H. Ev. T. | Exeter | seed |
| dentātā, 7 | . Apetal | H. Ev. T. | Exeter | seed |
| fulhamēnsis, 8 | . Apetal | 5, H. De. T. | Fulham | |
| heterophyllā, 9 | Apetal | H. Ev. T. | Exeter | seed |
| incīsā, 10 | . Apetal | 5, H. Ev. T. | Exeter | seed |
| Lucombeānā, 11 | Apetal | 5, H. De. T. | Exeter | seed |
| pendūlā | . . Apetal | 5, H. De. T. | S. Eur. | . |
| Ragnal, 12 | . Apetal | 5, H. De. T. | Ragnal | . |
| suberōsā, 13 | . Apetal | 5, H. De. T. | Exeter | seed |
| variegātā | . Apetal | 5, H. De. T. | S. Eur. | |
| vulgāris, 14 | . Apetal | 5, H. De. T. | S. Eur. | . 1735 |
| coccīferā | . Apetal | 5, H. Ev. T. | S. Eur. | . 1683 |
| coccīneā | . Apetal | 5, H. De. T. | N. Amer. | . 1691 |
| Cookii | . . Apetal | H. Ev. T. | Gibraltar | . 1835 |
| Esculūs | . . Apetal | 5, H. De. T. | S. Eur. | . 1739 |
| falcātā, 15 | . . Apetal | 5, H. De. T. | N. Amer. | . 1763 |
| Falkenbergēnsis | Apetal | H. De. T. | Hanover | . 1837 |
| Fontanēsii | . Apetal | H. De. T. | Calabria | |
| gramūntīā | . Apetal | 6, H. Ev. T. | France | . 1736 |
| heterophyllā | Apetal | 5, H. De. T. | N. Amer. | |
| hybrīda-nānā, 16 | Apetal | 5, H. De. T. | Hybrid | . 1825 |
| Ilex | . . Apetal | 6, H. Ev. T. | S. France | . 1581 |
| crispā | . Apetal | 5, H. Ev. T. | France | |
| fagifōliā | . Apetal | 5, H. Ev. T. | S. France | . 1781 |
| integrifōliā | . Apetal | 5, H. Ev. T. | S. France | . 1581 |
| latifōliā | . Apetal | 5, H. Ev. T. | S. France | . 1781 |
| longifōliā | . Apetal | 5, H. Ev. T. | | |
| serratifōliā | . Apetal | 5, H. Ev. T. | S. France | . 1781 |
| variegātā | . Apetal | 5, H. Ev. T. | | |
| illicifōliā | . Apetal | 5, H. Ev. T. | N. Amer. | . 1800 |
| imbricāriā | . . Apetal | 6, H. De. T. | N. Amer. | . 1786 |
| lanātā, 17 | . . Apetal | H. Ev. T. | Nepal | . 1818 |
| laurifōliā | . Apetal | 5, H. De. T. | N. Amer. | . 1786 |
| hybrīdā | . . Apetal | 5, H. De. T. | N. Amer. | . 1786 |
| lusitānīcā | . Apetal | 6, H. Ev. T. | Portugal | . 1824 |
| lūteā | . . Apetal | 5, H. De. T. | Mexico | . 1825 |
| lyrātā | . . Apetal | 5, H. De. T. | N. Amer. | . 1786 |
| macrocārpā | . Apetal | H. De. T. | N. Amer. | |
| montānā | . . Apetal | 5, H. De. T. | N. Amer. | . 1800 |
| myrtifōliā | . Apetal | H. Ev. T. | | |
| nigrā, 18 | . . Apetal | 5, H. De. T. | N. Amer. | . 1739 |
| obtusilōbā, 19 | . Apetal | 5, H. De. T. | N. Amer. | . 1819 |
| olivæfōrmis | . Apetal | 5, H. De. T. | N. Amer. | . 1811 |
| palūstris, 20 | . Apetal | 5, H. De. T. | N. Amer. | . 1800 |
| pedunculātā | . Apetal | 5, H. De. T. | Britain | . |
| fastigiātā, 21 | . Apetal | 5, H. De. T. | S. Eur. | . 1820 |
| fol. variegātā | . Apetal | 5, H. De. T. | Britain | Gard. |
| heterophyllā, 22 | Apetal | 5, H. Ev. T. | Britain | . |
| Hodginsii | . Apetal | 5, H. De. T. | Britain | . |
| pendūlā, 23 | . Apetal | 5, H. De. T. | Britain | . |
| pubēscens | . Apetal | 5, H. De. T. | Britain | |
| purpūreā, 24 | . Apetal | 5, H. De. T. | Britain | . |
| Phellōs | . . Apetal | 5, H. De. T. | N. Amer. | . 1723 |
| cinēreā, 25 | . Apetal | 5, H. De. T. | N. Amer. | . 1739 |
| hūmilis | . Apetal | 5, H. De. T. | N. Amer. | |
| latifōliā | . Apetal | 5, H. De. T. | N. Amer. | |
| sericeā, 26 | . Apetal | 5, H. De. S. | N. Amer. | . 1724 |
| sylvātīcā | . Apetal | 5, H. De. T. | N. Amer. | . 1723 |
| Prīnūs | . . Apetal | 6, H. De. T. | N. Amer. | . 1730 |
| acuminātā, 27 | . Apetal | 5, H. De. T. | N. Amer. | . 1822 |
| monticōlā, 28 | . Apetal | 5, H. De. T. | N. Amer. | . 17:0 |
| palūstris | . Apetal | H. De. T. | N. Amer. | . 1720 |
| pūmilā, 29 | . Apetal | 5, H. De. T. | N. Amer. | . 1823 |
| tomentōsā, 30 | . Apetal | H. De. T. | N. Amer. | . 1800 |
| pseūdō-coccīferā | Apetal | H. Ev. T. | | |
| pseūdō-sūber | . Apetal | 5, H. De. T. | S. Eur. | . 1824 |
| pyrenaīcā, 31 | . Apetal | 5, H. De. T. | Pyrenees | . 1822 |
| rūbrā | . . Apetal | 5, H. De. T. | N. Eur. | . 1739 |
| sessilifōrā, 32 | . Apetal | 5, H. De. T. | Britain | . |
| pubēscens, 33 | . Apetal | 5, H. De. T. | Britain | . |
| Sūber | . . Apetal | 5, H. Ev. T. | Spain | . 1581 |
| tinctōriā | . . Apetal | 5, H. De. T. | N. Amer. | . |
| angulōsā | . Apetal | 5, H. De. T. | N. Amer. | . |
| sinuōsā | . Apetal | 5, H. De. T. | N. Amer. | . |

**QUERIA**, *Lœfling.* In honour of Don J. Query Martinez, M.D., a professor of botany at Madrid. *Linn.* 3, Or. 3, Nat. Or. *Alsinaceæ.* The seed of this plant only requires sowing in the open border.

| | | | | |
|---|---|---|---|---|
| hispānīcā | . . . Apetal | . 6, H. | A. Spain | . 1800 |

**QUILLWORT**, see *Isoëtes.*

**QUINCE**, see *Cydōniā.*

**QUISQUALIS**, *Linn.* From *quis*, who, and *qualis*, what kind; when the genus was named, it was uncertain to what class or order it belonged. *Linn.* 10, Or. 1, Nat. Or. *Combretaceæ.* The species of this genus are all very great favourites with cultivators, on account of the brilliancy of their flowers. For culture and propagation, see *Poivrea.*

| glabrā | . . . | 8. Ev. Cl. Java | . 1815 |
| indica | . . Or. red | 6, 8. Ev. Cl. Java | . 1815 |
| pubëscens | . Or. red | 8. Ev. Cl. Guinea | |

QUIVISIA, *Commerson.* From *Bois de quivi*, the name of one of the unintroduced species in the Isle of France. Linn. 10, Or. 1, Nat. Or. *Meliaceæ.* This shrub succeeds well in a mixture of peat and loam; and ripened cuttings root freely in sand, under a glass, in heat.

| heterophylla | . . White . . | 8. Ev. 8. 1. France | . 1822 |

# R.

RACEME, a term commonly applied to flowers, when they are arranged round a filiform simple axis, each particular flower being stalked.

RACEMOSE, flowering in racemes.

RACEMOSELY-CORYMBOSE, flowers disposed in a manner between a corymb and a raceme, or numerous racemes forming a corymb.

RACHIS, that part of a culm which runs up through the ear of corn, and consequently that part which bears the flowers in other plants; also the common petiole of a pinnate leaf.

RACODIUM, *Link.* From *rakos*, a torn garment; in allusion to the appearance of the plants. Linn. 24, Or. 9, Nat. Or. *Fungi.* This species is found in undisturbed wine-cellars. Synonyme: 1. *Fibrillaria vinaria—R. cellārā.*

RADIATE, RADIANT, RAYED, } a flower is said to be so when, in a cluster or head of florets, those of the circumference or ray are long and spreading, and unlike those of the disk. A stigma is said to be rayed or radiant when its divisions resemble the rays of a star.

RADICAL, belonging to, or proceeding from, the root.

RADICANT, rooting, producing roots from the stem.

RADICLE, the root of an embryo.

RADIOLA, *Gmelin.* From *radiolus*, a little ray; in allusion to the capsule being rayed. Linn. 4, Or. 3, Nat. Or. *Linaceæ.* A little white-flowering, insignificant plant, found in sandy places.

| millegrana | . . . White | . 7 H. | A. Britain . |

RADISH, see *Raphānus.*

RADIUS, the ray of a compound flower.

RAFNIA, *Thunberg.* In honour of C. G. Rafn, of Copenhagen, a botanical author. Linn. 16, Or. 6, Nat. Or. *Leguminosæ.* This is a genus of remarkably pretty plants; they succeed well in peat and loam, and young cuttings root without difficulty in sand, under a glass. Synonymes: 1. *Crotalaria opposita.* 2. *Borbonia corduta.*

| cuneifolia | . . | . Yel. pur. | 6, G. Ev. 8. C. G. H. | . 1816 |
| elliptica | . . | . Yellow | . 6, G. Ev. 8. C. G. H. | . 1819 |
| lancea | . . | . Yellow | . 6, G. Ev. 8. C. G. H. | . 1823 |
| oppo-ita, 1 | . | . Yellow | . 6, G. Ev. 8. C. G. H. | . 1824 |
| triflora, 2 | . | . Yellow | . 6, G. | B. C. G. H. | . 1786 |

RAGGED ROBIN, see *Lychnis Floscūcūli.*

RAGWORT, see *Othōnnā.*

RAGWORT, see *Senēciō Jacobēā.*

RAJANIA, *Linn.* In honour of John Ray, an eminent English naturalist. Linn. 22, Or. 6, Nat. Or. *Dioscoreaceæ.* Stove climbers, of no beauty, growing in peat and loam. They may be readily increased by division of the root—*R. cordātā, hastātā, quinquefolia.*

RAMALINA, *Acharius.* From *ramale*, a withered branch; habitat of the plants. Linn. 24, Or. 8, Nat. Or. *Lichenes.* Greyish-coloured *Lichens*, found on rocks and dead branches of trees—*R. farinacea, fastigiata, F. calicaris, fraxinea, pollinaria, polymorpha, scopulorum.*

RAMENTA, little brown withered scales, with which the stems of some plants, especially ferns, are covered.

RAMIFICATIONS, subdivisions of roots or branches.

RAMONDIA, *Richard.* In honour of M. L. Ramond, a French botanist and traveller. Linn. 5, Or. 1, Nat. Or. *Gesneraceæ.* A genus consisting of one very pretty little alpine plant, well adapted for the front of flower-borders, or for growing in pots. Any light soil suits it, and it is readily increased by division of the root. Synonymes: 1. *Verbascum Myconi, Chaixia Myconi.*

| pyrenaica, 1 | . . Purple | . 5, H. Her. P. Pyrenees | . 1731 |

RAMOON-TREE, see *Trophis.*

RAMOSE, branchy.

[ 283 ]

RAMPION, see *Phyteūmā.*

RAMPION, see *Campānūlā Rapūnculūs.*

RAMPION, see *Cyphiā Phyteūmā.*

RAMULI, twigs, or small branches.

RANDIA, *Houston.* In honour of J. Rand, a London botanist. Linn. 5, Or. 1, Nat Or. *Cinchonaceæ.* This genus is nearly allied to *Gardenia*, and requires precisely the same treatment. Synonymes: 1. *R. aculeata, obovata, Gardenia Randia.* 2. *G. multiflora.* 3 *R. longiflora.* 4. *R. obovata.* 5. *Petunga Roxburghii.*

| Bowieana | . . | . Pa. yel. | . 8. Ev. 8. Brazil | . 1815 |
| latifolia, 1 | . | . White | . 7, 8. Ev. 8. W. Ind. | . 1733 |
| longiflora, 2 | . | . White | . 8, 8. Ev. 8. E. Ind. | . 1818 |
| macrantha, 3 | . | . Cr. col. | . 8, 8. Ev. 8. 8. Leone | . 1596 |
| parviflora | . | . White | . 8, 8. Ev. 8. W. Ind. | . 1818 |
| pubëscens, 4 | . | . White | . 7, 8. Ev. 8. Peru | . 1820 |
| racemōsa, 5 | . | . Grn. wht | . 8. Ev. 8. E. Ind. | . 1820 |
| rotundifolia | . | . White | . 7, 8. Ev. 8. Peru | . 1820 |
| sinënsis | . | . White | . 7, G. Ev. 8. China | . 1818 |

RANUNCULUS, *Linn.* From *rana*, a frog; many of the species are found in moist places frequented by that reptile. Linn. 13, Or. 1, Nat. Or. *Ranunculaceæ.* Many of the plants belonging to this extensive genus are well worth the cultivator's care, and they have long been favourites with the florist. The aquatic kinds require to be grown in water. The grumose-rooted species will thrive in any common soil, and in any situation; they are increased by offsets from the roots, or by seeds. *R. asiaticus* and its varieties should be grown in good fresh loam and well-rotted cow-dung; the tubers should be planted in October or March; if in the former month, they will require to be slightly protected in bad weather. Seeds selected from the best semi-double varieties, sown early in October, and kept growing during the winter, will flower the next season; these latter may also be increased by dividing the roots. These plants are mostly poisonous. Synonymes: 1. *R. polyanthemos.* 2. *aureus, villosus.* 3. *pyrenæus.* 4. *Thomasi.* 5. *sericeus.* 6. *apiifolius.* 7. *monspeliacus.* 8. *polyanthemos.* 9. *aureus, villosus.* 10. *rigidus, circinatus.* 11. *peucedanifolius.* 12. *pyrenæus, plantagineus.* 13. *aconitifolius.* 14. *muricatus, brasilianus.* 15. *Breynianus.*

| aconitifolius | . | . White . | . 5, H. Her. P. Alp. Eur. | . 1596 |
| crassicaulis | . | . White . | . 5, H. Her. P. Europe | |
| hūmilis | . | . White . | . 5, H. Her. P. Europe | |
| acris . . | . | . Yellow | . 6, H. Her. P. Britain | |
| albūs . . | . | . White . | . 6, H. Her. P. | |
| multifidūs, 1 | . | . Yellow | . 6, H. Her. P. Europe | |
| plenūs . | . | . Yellow | . 6, H. Her. P. Britain | |
| sylvaticūs | . | . Yellow | . 6, H. Her. P. France | |
| alpestris | . | . White . | . 5, H. Her. P. Scotland | |
| amplexicaulis | . | . White . | . 5, H. Her. P. Pyrenees | . 1633 |
| angulatus | . | . Yellow | . H. Tu. P. Naples | . 1832 |
| angustifolius | . | . White . | . 5, H. Her. P. Granada | . 1822 |
| apiifolius | . | . Wht. red | . 6, H. Her. P. Bonaria | . 1816 |
| aquatilis | . | . White . | . 6, H. Aq. P. Britain | |
| peltatus | . | . White . | . 6, H. Aq. P. Britain | |
| arcticūs . | . | . Yellow | . 6, H. Her. P. N. Amer. | . 1827 |
| asiaticūs | . | . Varieg. | . 5, H. Tu. P. Levant | . 1596 |
| sanguineūs | . | . Scarlet | . 5, H. Tu. P. Syria | |
| tenuifolia | . | . White . | . 5, H. Tu. P. Greece | |
| auricomūs | . | . Yellow | . 5, H. Her. P. Britain | |
| bonariensis | . | . Yellow | . 6, H. P. N. Amer. | . 1817 |
| bracteātūs | . | . Yellow | . 5, H. Tu. P. Pyrenees | |
| flōrā-plēnō | . | . Yellow | . 5, H. Tu. P. | |
| ochroleucūs | . | . Pa. yel. | . 8, H. Tu. P. England | |
| brevicaulis | . | . Yellow | . 5, H. Her. P. N. Amer. | . 1827 |
| brevifolius | . | . Yellow | . 6, H. Tu. P. Nap. | . 1824 |
| Breynianūs, 2 | . | . Yellow | . 6, H. Her. P. Switzerl. | . 1818 |
| brutiūs | . | . Yellow | . 5, H. Her. P. Italy | . 1823 |
| bulbosūs | . | . Yellow | . 5, H. Tu. P. Britain | |
| bullatūs | . | . Yellow | . 5, H. Tu. P. S. Eur. | . 1640 |
| flōrā-plēnō | . | . Yellow | . 5, H. Tu. P. S. Eur. | . 1640 |
| grandiflorūs | . | . Yellow | . 5, H. Tu. P. S. Eur. | . 1640 |
| bupleuroides | . | . Yellow | . 5, H. Her. P. Portugal | . 1826 |

| | | | | | | |
|---|---|---|---|---|---|---|
| cardiophýllūs | Yellow | 5, | H. Her. | P. | Canada | 1829 |
| casubicūs | Yellow | 6, | H. Her. | P. | Siberia | 1794 |
| caucásicūs | Yellow | 6, | H. Her. | P. | Caucasus | 1820 |
| chærophýllūs | Yellow | 5, | H. Tu. | P. | Portugal | |
| chiūs | Yellow | 6, | H. | A. | Archipel. | 1827 |
| dieutárūs | Yellow | 6, | H. Tu. | P. | Siberia | 1818 |
| cortusæfólīūs | Yellow | 5, | H. Tu. | P. | Teneriffe | 1826 |
| crássicaulīs | Yellow | 6, | H. Her. | P. | Europe | 1827 |
| crenátūs | White | 6, | H. Her. | P. | Hungary | 1818 |
| crèticūs | Yellow | 5, | H. Her. | P. | Candia | 1658 |
| macrophýllūs | Yellow | 5, | H. Her. | P. | Teneriffe | 1658 |
| Cymbalárīa | Yellow | 6, | H. Her. | P. | Siberia | 1824 |
| disséctūs | Yellow | 6, | H. Her. | P. | Caucasus | 1818 |
| Eschschóltzīī | Yellow | 5, | H. Her. | P. | N. Amer. | 1827 |
| fascículárīs | Yellow | 5, | H. Her. | P. | N. Amer. | |
| Flámmūlā | Yellow | 8, | H. Her. | P. | Britain | |
| filifórmīs | Yellow | 6, | H. Ev. | Cr. | N. Amer. | 1823 |
| frígidūs | Pa. yel. | 5, | H. Her. | P. | S. Eur. | 1827 |
| fumáriæfólīūs | Yellow | 5, | H. Tu. | P. | | |
| gargánicūs | Yellow | 8, | H. Tu. | P. | Naples | 1832 |
| glabérrimūs | Yellow | 6, | H. Her. | P. | N. Amer. | 1827 |
| glaciálīs | White | 7, | H. Her. | P. | Lapland | 1775 |
| aconitoídēs | White | 7, | H. Her. | P. | Switzerl. | 1819 |
| Gouáni, 3 | Yellow | 6, | H. Her. | P. | Pyrenees | 1818 |
| grácilīs | Yellow | 5, | H. Tu. | P. | Archipel. | 1818 |
| gramíneūs | Yellow | 5, | H. Her. | P. | Wales | |
| flòre-plèno | Yellow | 5, | H. Her. | P. | | |
| phœnicifólīūs | Yellow | 5, | H. Her. | P. | Europe | |
| grandiflòrūs | Yellow | 6, | H. Her. | P. | Cappad. | |
| gregárīūs, 4 | Yellow | 6, | H. Tu. | P. | Italy | 1817 |
| hederáceūs | White | 6, | H. Aq. | P. | Britain | |
| hírtūs | Yellow | 6, | H. Her. | P. | N. Zeal. | 1820 |
| híspidūs | Yellow | 6, | H. Her. | P. | N. Amer. | 1810 |
| hýbridūs | Yellow | 6, | H. Tu. | P. | Austria | 1820 |
| hyperbòreūs | Yellow | 5, | H. De. | Cr. | N. Eur. | 1820 |
| illýricūs, 5 | Yellow | 5, | H. Her. | P. | S. Eur. | 1596 |
| isopyroídēs | White | 5, | H. Her. | P. | Siberia | 1818 |
| làcerūs | White | 5, | H. Her. | P. | S. France | 1821 |
| lanugiòsūs | Yellow | 5, | H. Her. | P. | S. Eur. | 1683 |
| lappáceūs | Yellow | 6, | G. Her. | P. | N. Holl. | 1822 |
| lappónicūs | Yellow | 5, | H. Ev. | Cr. | Lapland | 1827 |
| Língua | Yellow | 7, | H. Her. | P. | Britain | |
| millefolīátūs | Yellow | 6, | H. Tu. | P. | Sicily | 1820 |
| grandiflòrūs | Yellow | 4, | H. Tu. | P. | Naples | 1833 |
| monspelíacūs | Yellow | 5, | H. Her. | P. | S. France | |
| cuneátūs, 6 | Yellow | 5, | H. Tu. | P. | S. Eur. | |
| rotundifólīūs, 7 | Yellow | 5, | H. Her. | P. | S. Eur. | |
| montánūs | Yellow | 6, | H. Her. | P. | Lapland | 1775 |
| napellifólīūs | Yellow | 7, | H. Her. | P. | Turkey | 1822 |
| nemoròsūs, 8 | Yellow | 5, | H. Her. | P. | Switzerl. | 1810 |
| paucíflòrūs, 9 | Yellow | 6, | H. Her. | P. | Switzerl. | 1819 |
| niválīs | Yellow | 7, | H. Her. | P. | Lapland | 1775 |
| obtusifólīūs | White | 6, | H. Aq. | P. | England | |
| oxyspérmūs | Pa. yel. | 5, | H. Tu. | P. | Caucasus | 1822 |
| pállidūs | Pa. yel. | 6, | H. Her. | P. | Hybrid | |
| pántōthrix | White | 6, | H. Aq. | P. | Britain | |
| cæspitòsūs, 10 | A petal | 7, | H. Aq. | P. | Britain | |
| fluviátilīs, 11 | Yellow | 6, | H. Aq. | P. | Britain | |
| parnassifólīūs | White | 6, | H. Her. | P. | S. Eur. | 1769 |
| pedátūs | Yellow | 5, | H. Tu. | P. | Hungary | 1805 |
| pedatífidūs | Yellow | 4, | H. Her. | P. | Siberia | 1827 |
| Philonòtīs | Yellow | 7, | H. | A. | S. Eur. | 1800 |
| plantagíneūs, 12 | White | 6, | H. Her. | P. | Piedmont | 1819 |
| platanifólīūs | White | 6, | H. Her. | P. | Germany | 1769 |
| flòre-plèno, 13 | White | 6, | H. Her. | P. | Alps. Eur. | 1596 |
| plebèius | Yellow | 6, | G. Her. | P. | N. Holl. | 1820 |
| polyphýllūs | Yellow | 4, | H. Aq. | A. | Hungary | 1819 |
| Purshíī | Yellow | 7, | H. Her. | P. | N. Amer. | 1827 |
| pygmæūs | Yellow | 4, | H. Her. | P. | Lapland | 1810 |
| pyrenæūs | White | 5, | H. Her. | P. | Pyrenees | 1807 |
| bupleurifólīūs | White | 6, | H. Her. | P. | Pyrenees | 1818 |
| recurvátūs | Yellow | 6, | H. Her. | P. | N. Amer. | 1827 |
| rèpens | Yellow | 7, | H. De. | Cr. | Britain | |
| flòre-plèno | Yellow | 7, | H. De. | Cr. | | |
| réptans | Yellow | 8, | H. Ev. | Cr. | Britain | |
| rhomboídeūs | Yellow | 4, | H. Her. | P. | N. Amer. | 1825 |
| ráfiliūs | Yellow | 6, | H. Her. | P. | Portugal | 1825 |
| rutæfólīūs | White | 6, | H. Her. | P. | Austria | 1759 |
| Sabíni | Yellow | 7, | H. Her. | P. | N. Amer. | 1827 |
| salanginòsūs | Yellow | 4, | H. Her. | P. | Siberia | 1822 |
| scelerátūs | Yellow | 6, | H. | A. | Britain | |
| scutátūs | Yellow | 6, | H. Tu. | P. | Hungary | 1817 |
| Seguièri | Yellow | 6, | H. Her. | P. | Piedmont | 1819 |
| sessiliflòrūs | Yellow | 6, | H. | A. | N. Holl. | |
| Stevéni | Yellow | 6, | H. Her. | P. | Volhinia | 1819 |
| Thòrā | Yellow | 5, | H. Tu. | P. | Austria | 1710 |
| tomentòsūs | Yellow | 6, | H. Her. | P. | N. Amer. | 1820 |
| tripártitūs | White | 6, | H. Aq. | P. | Europe | |
| trilóbūs | Yellow | 6, | H. | A. | Greece | 1818 |
| tuberculátūs | Yellow | 6, | H. | A. | Tauria | 1817 |
| tuberòsūs | Yellow | 6, | H. Tu. | P. | Pyrenees | 1820 |
| uliginòsūs | Yellow | 6, | H. | A. | Teneriffe | 1826 |
| ventricòsūs, 14 | Yellow | 7, | H. | A. | Brazil | |
| Villársīī, 15 | Yellow | 6, | H. Her. | P. | S. Eur. | 1819 |

*abórtivūs, affinīs, arvénsīs, Flámmūlā ovátūs, F. serrā-
tūs, hírsūtūs, Hornemánni, laciniátūs, marylándicūs,
muricátūs, M. carolìnūs, M. crèticūs, nodiflòrūs,
N. dentátūs, oldusifólīūs, ophioglossifólīūs, ovàlīs,*

*paludòsūs, parviflòrūs, parvulūs, pennsylvánicūs,
polyanthèmōs, Schlechtēndálīī, trifoliátūs.*

RAPE, see *Brássica Ràpa.*

RAPHÁNŪS, *Linn.* From *ra*, quickly, and *phaínomai*,
to appear; in allusion to the speedy germination of
the seeds. *Linn.* 15, *Nat. Or. Crucíferæ.* The
familiarity of the culture of this truly useful genus
to every person, renders any observation on this
subject unnecessary. *Synonymes:* 1. *R orbicularis.*
2. *R. chinensis.*

| | | | | | | |
|---|---|---|---|---|---|---|
| caudátūs | Wht. pur. | 7, | H. | A. | Java | 1815 |
| Lándra | Yellow | 6, | H. Her. | P. | Italy | 1820 |
| satívūs | Wht. pur. | 5, | H. | A. | China | 1548 |

*álbūs* 1, *grìseūs, niger, oblóngūs, oleiférūs* 2, *radicá-
līs, rotúndūs, vulgárīs.*

| | | | | | | |
|---|---|---|---|---|---|---|
| rostrátūs | Purplish | 7, | H. | A. | Persia | 1823 |

*marítimūs, Raphanistrūm, R. flòrī-álbo, R. flòrī-
flàvo, R. purpuráscens.*

RAPHE, in seeds, the channel of vessels which connects the chalaza with the hilum; in umbelliferous
plants, the line of junction, of the two halves of
which their fruit is composed.

RAPHIÓLEPIS, *Lindley.* From *raphis*, a needle, and
*lepis*, a scale; referring to the narrow subulate
bracteæ. *Linn.* 12, *Or.* 2, *Nat. Or. Pomaceæ.* A
genus of some interest, the species of which will,
we have no doubt, prove tolerably hardy. They
grow freely in a mixture of loam, peat, and sand;
and may be propagated by cuttings, placed in sand,
under a glass. *Synonymes:* 1. *Cratægus indica.* 2.
*R. indica.*

| | | | | | | |
|---|---|---|---|---|---|---|
| índica, 1 | White | 6, | F. Ev. | S. | China | 1806 |
| phæostèmōn, 2 | White | 6, | F. Ev. | S. | China | 1818 |
| rùbra | White | 6, | F. Ev. | S. | China | 1806 |
| salicifólīā | White | 6, | F. Ev. | S. | China | 1820 |

RAPISTRŪM, *Boerhaave.* From *rapa*, the rape; resemblance in the leaves. *Linn.* 15, *Nat. Or. Crucíferæ.*
Plants of no interest; increased by division of the
roots, or by seeds. *Synonymes:* 1. *Myagrum orientale.* 2. *M. perenne, Cakile perennis.* 3. *C. rugosa,
M. rugosum—R. orientále* 1, *perénne* 2, *rugòsum* 3.

RASPÁLLI, *Brongniart.* In honour of M. Raspall, a
French botanist. *Linn.* 5, *Or.* 1, *Nat. Or. Bruniaceæ.* An interesting shrub, requiring to be grown
in a sandy peat soil; and increased by cuttings of
the young wood, planted in sand, under a glass.
*Synonyme:* 1. *Brunia microphylla.*

| | | | | | | |
|---|---|---|---|---|---|---|
| microphýlla, 1 | White | 7, | G. Ev. | S. | C. G. H. | 1804 |

RASPBERRY, see *Rùbus Idæùs.*

RATABIDA, *Rafinesque.* Meaning not known. *Linn.*
19, *Or.* 3, *Nat. Or. Compositæ.* This is a very
desirable genus for the flower border. For culture
and propagation, see Rudbeckia. *Synonyme:* 1.
*Rudbeckia columnaris.*

| | | | | | | |
|---|---|---|---|---|---|---|
| columnárīs, 1 | Yellow | 8, | H. Her. | P. N. Amer. | 1811 |
| pulchérrima | Red yel. | 8, | H. Her. | P. N. Amer. | 1835 |

RAT POISON, see *Chaillètia toxicária.*

RATTLESNAKE FERN, see *Botrychium virgínicum.*

RATTLESNAKE ROOT, see *Polýgala Sénega.*

RAUWÓLFIA, *Linn.* In honour of Leonhard Rauwolf,
M.D., a botanical traveller. *Linn.* 5, *Or.* 1, *Nat.
Or. Apocyneæ.* These plants thrive in a mixture
of loam, peat, and sand; and cuttings will root
readily in sand, under a glass, in heat.

| | | | | | | |
|---|---|---|---|---|---|---|
| canéscens | Pink | 8, | S. Ev. | S. | Jamaica | 1759 |
| nítida | White | 8, | S. Ev. | T. | Spain | 1752 |
| ternifólīā | White | 5, | S. Ev. | S. | W. Ind. | 1823 |
| tomentòsa | White | 7, | S. Ev. | S. | W. Ind. | 1823 |

REAUMÚRIA, *Linn.* In honour of René A. Ferchault
de Reaumur, a famous French entomologist. *Linn.*
13, *Or.* 5, *Nat. Or. Reaumuriaceæ.* Very beautiful
shrubs, of simple culture; they thrive best in
sandy loam and peat, and are readily propagated
by cuttings, taken from the young wood, and placed
under a glass. *Synonymes:* 1. *R. linifolia, Hypericum alternifolium.*

| | | | | | | |
|---|---|---|---|---|---|---|
| hypericoídēs, 1 | Purple | 8, | F. Ev. | S. | Syria | 1800 |
| vermiculáta | Pink | 6, | F. Ev. | S. | Sicily | 1823 |

RECEPTACLE, that part of the fructification which
supports the other parts.

RECESSES, the bays, or sinuses of lobed leaves.

RECUMBENT, prostrate, lying flat.

RED BAY, see *Laùrus caroliněnsis.*

RED CEDAR, see *Juníperus virginiäna.*

RED GUM-TREE, see *Eucalýptus resiníferà.*

RED LAC, see *Rhūs succedānĕā.*
RED NIGHTSHADE, see *Ērĭcā Halicācābā.*
RED OSIER, see *Sālīx rūbrā.*
RADOÚTEÏX. Named by Ventenat, in honour of P. J. Redouté, a celebrated French botanical artist. *Linn.* 16, Or. 8, Nat. Or. *Malvaceæ.* This shrub grows in peat and loam, and may be increased by cuttings planted in sand or loam, under a glass, in heat; it may also be raised from seed sown in the usual way.

heterophyllā  . .  Yellow  . 6, S. Ev. S. W. Ind.  . 1822

RED SAUNDERS-WOOD, see *Pterocārpūs santalĭnŭs.*
RED WATER-TREE, see *Erythrōphlēŭm.*
RED WOOD, see *Ceanōthŭs.*
RED WOOD, see *Rhămnŭs Erythrōxylŏn.*
RED WOOD, see *Melhănĭā Erythrōxylŏn.*
REED, see *Phrāgmĭtēs.*
REED-UPON-REED, see *Calamagrōstĭs effŭsā.*
REEVESÏX. Named by Lindley, in compliment to John Reeves, Esq., F.L.S., of Canton, from whom the botany of China has received material assistance, and to whom our gardens are indebted for many of their fairest ornaments. *Linn.* 16, Or. 8, Nat. Or. *Sterculiaceæ.* This very handsome shrub may be referred to the greenhouse species of *Sterculia,* for culture and propagation.

thyrsoidea  . . .  White  . 1, G. Ev. S. China  . . 1826

REFRIGERANT, producing coolness.
REHMANNÏX, *Libosch.* Not explained. *Linn.* 14, Or. 2, Nat. Or. *Scrophulariaceæ.* The flowers of this plant are large, but their colour so much destroys the effect of their magnitude, that the plant is, on that account, more curious than ornamental. Though hardy, it will succeed best in a cool greenhouse or frame, planted in any common soil, and is propagated by cuttings.

chinēnsis  . . .  Dingy  . .  H. Her. P. China  . . . 1835

REICHARDÏX, *Roth.* In honour of John James Reichard, a celebrated botanist and author. *Linn.* 10, Or. 1, Nat. Or. *Leguminosæ.* For the culture and propagation of this ornamental tree, see *Poinciana.* Synonyme: 1. *Cæsalpinia ligulata.*

hexapétalā, 1  . .  Yellow  .  8. Ev. S. E. Ind.  . . 1824

RELHANÏX, *L'Heritier.* In honour of the Rev. Richard Relhan, author of "Flora Cantabrigiensis." *Linn.* 19, Or. 2, Nat. Or. *Compositæ.* For the culture of these ornamental plants, see *Athanasia.* Synonymes: 1. *Athanasia genistifolia.* 2. *Leysera ericoides.*

| | | | | | |
|---|---|---|---|---|---|
| genistifoliā, 1  . | . | Yellow | . 5, G. Ev. S. C. G. H. | | 1822 |
| lateriflorā  . | . | Yellow | . 9, G. Ev. S. C. G. H. | | 1823 |
| paleácea, 2  . | . | Yellow | . 4, G. Ev. S. C. G. H. | | 1818 |
| püngēns  . | . | Yellow | . 9, G. Ev. S. C. G. H. | | 1820 |
| squārrósā  . | . | Yellow | . 5, G. Ev. S. C. G. H. | | 1774 |

REMÏRÏÏX, *Aublet.* Its name in Guiana. *Linn.* 3, Or. 1, Nat. Or. *Cyperaceæ.* A plant of no value: it is increased by seeds or divisions.—*R. marĭtĭmā.*
RENANTHÈRÏX, *Loureiro.* From *ren,* a kidney, and *anthera,* an anther; in allusion to the kidney or reniform shape of the anthers or pollen-masses. *Linn.* 20, Or. 1, Nat. Or. *Orchidaceæ.* R. coccinea is a truly splendid plant. The flowers are produced on a lateral loose panicle; the sepals are of a pale scarlet, obscurely and irregularly blotched; the petals are marked with yellow bands on a beautiful scarlet ground; the labellum is yellow and scarlet. The plant will succeed in peat mixed with broken potsherds, carefully placed about the roots, so as to ensure a safe drainage. But the best way of growing it, is to plant it in *sphagnum* or *hypnum* moss, cut short and packed close about the roots, with a quantity of broken potsherds to act as a drainage. Any of the young branches taken off and potted in moss will soon make plants, which succeed well in any place where a strong heat and an abundance of moisture is kept up; when the plant has attained a good size, about the height of six feet, it should be placed in a house where the heat is from 65 to 70 degrees, and kept perfectly free from moisture, except what arises from watering and occasional syringing. The whole of the plant should be as near the glass and as much exposed to the sun as possible; and to prevent the leaves from shrivelling too much, it may be occasionally syringed in the afternoon. After being in this house two or three

months, the flower spikes will make their appearance; when the flowers are expanded, the plant should be removed to a cool house, and placed in a light situation: it will there continue in perfection for a great length of time. Synonyme: 1. *Aerides arachnites.*

| | | | | | |
|---|---|---|---|---|---|
| arachnites, 1  . . | Brn. pur. | | 8. Epi. Japan | . | 1793 |
| coccínea  . . . | Scar. or. | | 8, S. Epi. Co. China | . | 1816 |

RENEALMÏX, *R. Brown.* In honour of P. and M. L. Renealme, the first a famous French physician, and the other a botanist. *Linn.* 3, Or. 1, Nat. Or. *Iridaceæ.* These plants may be referred to *Alpinia,* for culture and propagation.

| | | | | | |
|---|---|---|---|---|---|
| grandiflorā  . . | . | White | . 4, G. Her. P. N. Zeal. | . | 1822 |
| paniculátā  . . | . | White | . 6, G. Ev. S. N. Holl. | . | 1823 |
| pulchēllā  . . | . | White | . 6, G. Ev. S. N. Holl. | . | 1823 |

RENIFORM, kidney-shaped.
REPAND, a leaf is said to be repand when its margin is undulated, and unequally dilated.
REPLICATE, folded back.
REPTANT, creeping and rooting.
REQUIÈNÏX, *Decandolle.* In honour of M. Requien, a botanist of Avignon. *Linn.* 16, Or. 6, Nat. Or. *Leguminosæ.* This plant should be grown in a mixture of peat, loam, and sand; and young cuttings will strike if planted in sand, under a glass, in heat. The glass must be occasionally taken off and wiped, to prevent damp. Synonyme: 1. *Podalyria obcordata.*

obcordátā, 1  . .  Yellow  . 7, S. Ev. S. Senegal  . 1825

RESÈDÏX, *Linn.* From *resedo,* to calm or appease; the Latins considered its application useful in external bruises. *Linn.* 11, Or. 3, Nat. Or. *Resedaceæ.* The Mignonette is an old and universal favourite, on account of the very pleasant odour emitted by the flowers. In summer it merely requires the treatment of other hardy annuals; but to obtain flowering plants through the winter and spring months, two other sowings must be made; to obtain flowering plants from December to March, the seeds should be sown about the middle of July upon a light, rich, open border, and the plants potted before the frost sets in, plunged in old tan or ashes, and covered by a frame, which should front the west. Those to flower from March to June, should be sown in pots not later than the third week in August, and treated in a manner similar to the November sowing. The third, or spring crop to succeed the last, may be sown about the middle of February; these should be placed in a frame in a gentle heat, and the plants thus obtained will be in perfection by the end of May. The suffruticose species may be increased by cuttings or seeds.

| | | | | | |
|---|---|---|---|---|---|
| albā  . . . | Apetal | . 7, H. | B. S. Eur. | . | 1596 |
| bipinnátā  . . | Apetal | . 7, F. Ev. S. | Spain | . | 1816 |
| chinēnsis  . . | Yel. grn. | . 6, H. | A. China | . | 1819 |
| fruticulósā  . . | Apetal | . 9, H. Ev. S. | Spain | . | 1794 |
| lævigátā  . . | Yellow | . 7, H. | A. Egypt | . | 1822 |
| linifoliā  . . | Yel grn. | . 7, H. Her. P. | S. Eur. | . | 1819 |
| lūtea  . . . | Apetal | . 7, H. | B. Britain | . | |
| lutéolā  . . | Apetal | . 6, H. | A. Britain | . | |
| mediterránĕā  . | Apetal | . 8, H. | A. Palestine | . | 1791 |
| myriophyllā  . | Wht. yel. | . 7, H. | B. Italy | . | 1823 |
| odorátā  . . | Apetal | . 8, H. | A. Italy | . | 1752 |
| fruttescens  . | Apetal | . 8, G. Ev. S. | Egypt | . | 1752 |
| Phytéumā  . . | Apetal | . 8, H. | A. S. Eur. | . | 1752 |
| pruinósā  . . | Apetal | . 6, H. Her. P. | Egypt | . | 1824 |
| ramosissimā  . | Apetal | . 7, H. Her. P. | Spain | . | 1816 |
| scopáriā  . . | Apetal | . 8, G. Ev. S. | Teneriffe | . | 1815 |
| sesamoídēs  . | Apetal | . 7, H. Her. P. | France | . | 1767 |
| undátā  . . | Apetal | . 7, H. | B. Spain | . | 1789 |

R. canēscens, crispátā, dipsátā, glaucā, saxátilis, virēscēns.
RESOLVENT, having the power to dissolve.
RESTHARROW, see *Onōnis.*
RESTÏÖ, *Linn.* From *restis,* cord; used as cord at the Cape of Good Hope. *Linn.* 22, Or. 3, Nat. Or. *Restiaceæ.* These plants grow in any common soil, and are increased by divisions. Synonyme: 1. *Calorophus elongatus.*

| | | | | | |
|---|---|---|---|---|---|
| austrális  . . . | Apetal | . 5, Grass. N. Holl. | | . | 1824 |
| fastigiátus  . . | Apetal | . 5, Grass. N. Holl. | | . | 1824 |
| grácilis  . . . | Apetal | . 5, Grass. N. Holl. | | . | 1824 |
| lateriflórus, 1  . | Apetal | . 6, Grass. N. Holl. | | . | 1824 |
| paniculátus  . . | Apetal | . 5, Grass. C. G. H. | | . | 1824 |
| tectórum  . . | Apetal | . 6, Grass. C. G. H. | | . | 1793 |
| tetraphyllus  . | Apetal | . 6, Grass. V. D. L. | | . | 1825 |
| vaginátus  . . | Apetal | . 6, Grass. C. G. H. | | . | 1820 |
| virgátus  . . | Apetal | . 6, Grass. C. G. H. | | . | 1824 |

Resupinate, lying on the back.

Restanilla, *Decandolle*. Its Peruvian name. *Linn.* 5, Or. 1, Nat. Or. *Rhamnaceæ.* Small evergreens, thriving in loam and peat, and propagated by cuttings planted in sand, under a glass. *Synonymes*: 1. *Colletia Ephedra.* 2. *Colletia obcordata.*

| | | | | | | |
|---|---|---|---|---|---|---|
| Ephèdra, 1 | . | . | Green | . | F. Ev. S. Chile | . 1823 |
| obcordáta, 2 | . | . | Yellow | . | S. Ev. S. Peru | . 1822 |

Reticularia, *Bulliard*. From *reticulum*, a net; appearance. *Linn.* 24, Or. 9, Nat. Or. *Fungi.* These species are found upon rotten sticks, leaves, &c.—*R. argéntëã, minátã, olivácëã.*

Reticulated, netted, resembling a net.

Retracted, bent backwards.

Retrograde, usually applied to hairs when they are bent back or down, instead of forward, or up.

Retuse, appearing as if bitten off at the end.

Rätziã, *Linn.* In honour of Anders Johan Retzius, professor of natural history in the University of Lund; author of "Observations on Botany." *Linn.* 5, Or. 1, Nat. Or. *Retziaceæ.* This plant thrives in any light soil; and cuttings will root readily in sand, under a glass.

| | | | | | |
|---|---|---|---|---|---|
| spicáta | . . . | . | Brown | . 5, G. Ev. S. C. G. H. | . |

Revolute, rolled back: usually applied to the edges of leaves.

Rhabdochlöã, *Beauvois*. From *rhabdos*, a twig. and *chloa*, grass. *Linn.* 3, Or. 2, Nat. Or. *Gramineæ.* Pretty annuals, growing in any light soil; and increased by seeds. *Synonymes*: 1. *Chloris cruciata.* 2. *Chloris poæformis, Cynosurus virgatus.*

| | | | | | | |
|---|---|---|---|---|---|---|
| cruciáta, 1 | . . | . | Apetal | . 7, Grass. W. Ind. | . . | 1818 |
| mucrönáta | . . | . | Apetal | . 7, Grass. N. Amer. | . | 1820 |
| virgáta, 2 | . . | . | Apetal | . 7, Grass. W. Ind. | . . | 1820 |

Rhagadiölüs, *Tournefort*. From *rhagas*, a slit; in allusion to the divisions of the calyx. *Linn.* 19, Or. 1, Nat. Or. *Compositæ.* Annuals of no interest; increased by seed in any common soil. *Synonymes*: 1. *R. lapsanoides, Lapsana Rhagadiolus.* 2. *Kælpinia linearis—R. ĕdúlis 1, Kælpiniã 2, stēllátüs.*

Rhagödiã, *R. Brown*. From *rhax*, a berry; its principal distinction. *Linn.* 23, Or. 1, Nat. Or. *Chenopodiaceæ.* Interesting plants, growing well in a mixture of loam and peat; and increasing readily by cuttings, placed under a glass.

| | | | | | | |
|---|---|---|---|---|---|---|
| Billardiéri | . | . | Grn. yel. | . 6, G. Ev. S. N. Holl. | . | 1823 |
| hastáta | . . | . | Green | . 6, G. Ev. S. N. S. W. | . | 1808 |
| nútans | . . | . | Grn. yel. | . 6, G. Ev. Tr. N. Holl. | . | 1820 |
| parabólica | . | . | Grn. yel. | . 6, G. Ev. S. N. Holl. | . | 1823 |

Rhamnüs, *Linn.* From the Celtic *ram*, signifying a tuft of branches. *Linn.* 5, Or. 1, Nat. Or. *Rhamnaceæ.* The plants belonging to this genus are mostly valued on account of their foliage. The stove and greenhouse kinds are easily grown in any light soil; and increase readily by cuttings under a glass. The hardy kinds grow in any common soil, and are usually propagated by layers and seeds. The plants and berries possess very strong purgative qualities. The juice of the berries of *R. catharticus* is sold under the name of syrup of buckthorn; the French berries of the shops is the juice of the unripe fruit of the same species, and is used for dyeing Turkey or Morocco leather yellow. The wood of *R. dahuricus* is red, and is known to the Russians by the name of sandal-wood. *Synonymes*: 1. *R. Clusii.* 2. *R. Willdenovianus.* 3. *R. rupestris.* 4. *R. pumilus.* 5. *R. pumilus.*

| | | | | | | |
|---|---|---|---|---|---|---|
| alatérnüs | . | . | Green | . 5, H. Ev. S. S. Eur. | . | 1629 |
| angustifolia, 1 | . | . | Green | . 5, H. Ev. S. S. Eur. | . | 1629 |
| balearica | . | . | Green | . 5, H. Ev. S. S. Eur. | . | |
| fol. argentêã | . | . | Green | . 5, H. Ev. S. S. Eur. | . | |
| fol. aúreis | . | . | Green | . 5, H. Ev. S. S. Eur. | . | |
| fol. maculátis | . | . | Green | . 5, H. Ev. S. S. Eur. | . | |
| hispanicá | . | . | Green | . 5, H. Ev. S. S. Eur. | . | |
| alnifolius | . | . | Green | . 5, H. De. S. N. Amer. | . | 1778 |
| alpinüs | . | . | Green | . 5, H. Ev. S. Switzerl. | . | 1752 |
| buxifolius | . | . | | . 5, H. Ev. S. Numidia | . | 1820 |
| cardiocarpüs | . | . | | . H. Ev. S. | . | 1832 |
| carolinianüs | . | . | Green | . 5, H. De. S. N. Amer. | . | 1819 |
| catharticüs | . | . | Grn. yel. | . 5, H. De. T. England | . | |
| hydriänsis | . | . | Grn. yel. | . 6, H. De. T. C. G. H. | . | |
| celtifolius | . | . | Grn. yel. | . 5, G. Ev. S. C. G. H. | . | |
| crenulátüs | . | . | Grn. yel. | . 4, G. Ev. S. Teneriffe | . | 1778 |
| dahúricüs | . | . | Grn. yel. | . 5, H. De. S. Davuria | . | 1817 |
| Erythröxylön | . | . | Yel. grn. | . 7, H. De. S. Siberia | . | 1823 |
| angustissimüm | . | . | | . H. De. S. Caucasus | . | |
| Frángúla | . | . | White | . 5, H. De. T. Britain | . | |
| angustifolia | . | . | White | . 5, H. De. T. Britain | . | |
| franguloidës | . | . | Green | . 5, H. De. T. N. Amer. | . | 1810 |

| | | | | | | |
|---|---|---|---|---|---|---|
| glandulösüs | . | . | Green | . 6, G. Ev. S. Canaries | . | 1785 |
| hybridüs | . | . | Green | . H. De. S. | . | |
| infectoriüs | . | . | Grn. yel. | . 6, H. De. S. S. Eur. | . | 1683 |
| integrifoliüs | . | . | Green | . 6, G. Ev. S. Teneriffe | . | 1822 |
| lanceolatüs | . | . | Green | . 5, H. De. S. N. Amer. | . | 1812 |
| latifoliüs | . | . | Green | . 7, H. De. S. Azores | . | 1778 |
| lycioidës | . | . | Grn. yel. | . 11, H. De. S. Spain | . | 1752 |
| arragoménsis | . | . | Grn. yel. | . 10, H. De. S. Arragon | . | 1752 |
| longifoliüs, 2 | . | . | Green | . H. De. S. | . | 1823 |
| microphyllüs | . | . | | . S. Ev. S. Mexico | . | 1823 |
| oleoidës | . | . | Grn. yel. | . 6, H. De. S. Spain | . | 1752 |
| Pallasii | . | . | | . H. De. S. Russia | . | 1838 |
| prinoidës | . | . | Yellow | . 6, G. Ev. S. C. G. H. | . | 1778 |
| pubéscens | . | . | Pa. yel. | . 5, H. Ev. S. France | . | 1817 |
| pùmilá, 3 | . | . | Grn. yel. | . 7, H. De. S. Carniola | . | 1752 |
| pùsillüs | . | . | | . 5, H. De. S. Naples | . | 1823 |
| rupéstris | . | . | Green | . 5, H. De. S. S. Eur. | . | 1752 |
| saxátilis | . | . | Grn. yel. | . 5, H. De. T. Europe | . | 1752 |
| spatulæfoliüs | . | . | | . H. De. S. Russia | . | 1838 |
| surinaménsis | . | . | Grn. yel. | . 8. Ev. S. Surinam | . | 1820 |
| tetragönüs | . | . | Green | . G. Ev. S. C. G. H. | . | 1816 |
| Theézans | . | . | Green | . 5, G. Ev. S. China | . | |
| tinctöriüs | . | . | Grn. yel. | . 6, H. De. S. Hungary | . | 1820 |
| valentinüs, 4 | . | . | Green | . 5, H. De. T. S. Eur. | . | 1816 |
| virgátüs | . | . | Green | . 6, H. De. S. Nepal | . | 1820 |
| Wúlfänii, 5 | . | . | Green | . 7, H. De. S. S. Eur. | . | 1758 |

Rhapis, *Linn.* From *rhapis*, a needle; alluding to the acute awns of the corolla. *Linn.* 23, Or. 1, Nat. Or. *Palmaceæ.* Dwarfish palms, thriving well in sandy loam; and increasing by suckers from the roots.

| | | | | | | |
|---|---|---|---|---|---|---|
| arundinácëã | . | . | Green | . 9, Palm. Carolina | . | 1765 |
| flabelliformis | . | . | Green | . 8, Palm. China | . | 1774 |

Rhapontici, *Decandolle*. From *rha*, rhubarb, and *Ponticus*, of Pontus. *Linn.* 19, Or. 3, Nat. Or. *Compositæ.* These plants will grow in any common soil, and may be readily increased by divisions. *Synonymes*: 1. *Centaurea Rhapontica.* 2. *C. Rhapontica.*

| | | | | | | |
|---|---|---|---|---|---|---|
| Pallasii, 1 | . | . | Purple | . 7, H. Her. P. Switzerl. | . | 1818 |
| púlchrá | . | . | | . H. S. Caucasus | . | 1837 |
| scarioeá, 2 | . | . | Purple | . 7, H. Her. P. Switzerl. | . | 1640 |
| lyráta | . | . | Purple | . 7, H. Her. P. Switzerl. | . | 1819 |
| uniflorá | . | . | Purple | . 7, H. Her. P. Siberia | . | 1796 |

Rheêdiã. In honour of Henry Rheede Van Draakenstein, author of Hortus Malabaricus, in ten vols. folio. *Linn.* 12, Or. 3, Nat. Or. *Guttiferæ.* This very handsome, broad-leaved tree, will grow in a mixture of peat, loam, and sand; and ripened cuttings will root in sand, under a glass, in a moist heat.

| | | | | | |
|---|---|---|---|---|---|
| javánicá | . . . | | . 8. Ev. T. Java | . . . | 1826 |

Rheüm, *Linn.* From *rha*, the Wolga: the first plants were brought from its banks. *Linn.* 9, Or. 2, Nat. Or. *Polygonaceæ.* The culture and uses of the Rhubarb are well known. The plants all thrive well in a rich loamy soil; and are increased by divisions of the roots, or by seed. *Synonyme*: 1. *R. Emodi.*

| | | | | | | |
|---|---|---|---|---|---|---|
| australé, 1 | . | . | Purple | . H. Fu. P. Nepal | . | 1823 |
| austriacüm | . | . | White | . 5, H. Fu. P. Austria | . | 1800 |
| cáspicüm | . | . | White | . 5, H. Fu. P. Russia | . | 1817 |
| compactüm | . | . | Wht. grn. | . 5, H. Fu. P. Tartary | . | 1758 |
| crispüm | . | . | White | . 5, H. Fu. P. | . | 1800 |
| fenestrátüm | . | . | White | . 5, H. Fu. P. | . | 1790 |
| hybridüm | . | . | Wht. grn. | . 5, H. Fu. P. Asia | . | 1778 |
| leucorhizüm | . | . | Striped | . 5, H. Her. P. Siberia | . | 1827 |
| nútans | . | . | White | . 5, H. Fu. P. Siberia | . | 1800 |
| palmátüm | . | . | Wht. grn. | . 6, H. Fu. P. Bucharia | . | 1763 |
| Rhapónticüm | . | . | Wht. grn. | . 5, H. Fu. P. Asia | . | 1573 |
| Ribes | . | . | Wht. grn. | . 5, H. Fu. P. Levant | . | 1724 |
| sibiricüm | . | . | White | . 5, H. Fu. P. Siberia | . | 1800 |
| tataricüm | . | . | Wht. grn. | . 5, H Fu. P. Tartary | . | 1798 |
| undulátüm | . | . | Wht. grn. | . 5, H. Fu. P. China | . | 1734 |

Rhexiã, *Linn.* From *rhexis*, a rupture; from its astringent qualities, it is supposed to cure ruptures. *Linn.* 8, Or. 1, Nat. Or. *Melastomaceæ.* This is a genus of very elegant plants when in flower. The plants grow best in a bed of peat soil, but are sometimes grown in pots in the same kind of soil. They are readily increased by division at the root.

| | | | | | | |
|---|---|---|---|---|---|---|
| angustifoliá | . | . | White | . 7, H. Her. P. N. Amer. | . | 1812 |
| ciliósá | . | . | Purple | . 7, H. Her. P. Carolina | . | 1812 |
| mariáná | . | . | Purple | . 7, H. Her. P. N. Amer. | . | 1759 |
| rubélla | . | . | Pink | . 7, H. Her. P. N. Amer. | . | 1823 |
| virginicá | . | . | Purple | . 7, H. Her. P. N. Amer. | . | 1759 |

Rhinanthüs, *Linn.* From *rhin*, a snout, and *anthos*, a flower; alluding to the appearance of the corolla. *Linn.* 14, Or. 2, Nat. Or. *Scrophulariaceæ.* The seeds of the Yellow Rattle have only to be sown in a moist situation. *Synonymes*: 1. *R. Alectorolophus, Bartsia Trixago, Trixago rhinanthina.*

| | | | | | | |
|---|---|---|---|---|---|---|
| Alectorolŏphŭs | . Yellow | . 7, H. | A. Europe | . . 1820 |
| Crĭstā-gallĭ | . . Yellow | . 7, H. | A. Britain | . . |
| mājŏr | . . . Yellow | . 7, H. | A. Britain | . . |
| Trīxāgŏ, 1 | . . . Yellow | . 7, H. | A. Europe | . . 1800 |

RHINOPĔTĂLŬM, *Fischer.* From *rhin,* nose, *petalon,* petal; base of upper sepal. *Linn.* 6, Or. 1, Nat. Or. *Liliaceæ.* For culture and propagation, refer to the hardy species of *Lilium.*

| | | | | | |
|---|---|---|---|---|---|
| Karalini | . . . Pa. pk. spt. 1, H. Tu. P. Ural. | . . 1834 |

RHIPIDODĔNDRŎN, *Willdenow.* From *rhipis,* a fan, and *dendron,* a tree; in allusion to the growth. *Linn.* 6, Or. 1, Nat. Or. *Liliaceæ.* This genus may be referred to the *Aloes* for culture and propagation. *Synonymes:* 1. *R. distichum, Aloe plicatilis.*

| | | | | | |
|---|---|---|---|---|---|
| plicātilĕ, 1 | . . . Rea | . 6, G. Ev. S. Africa | . . 1723 |
| mājŭs | . . . Red | . 6, G. Ev. S. Africa | . . 1723 |

RHIPSĂLĬS, *Haworth.* From *rhips,* a willow branch; in allusion to the flexible branches. *Linn.* 12, Or. 1, Nat. Or. *Cactaceæ.* The plants of this genus are more singular than beautiful. A light vegetable soil, mixed with a little brick rubbish, suits them best; and they are readily increased by cuttings. *Synonymes:* 1. *Cactus pendula.* 2. *C. funalis.*

| | | | | |
|---|---|---|---|---|
| Cassythā, 1 | . . . Yellow | . 9, S. Ev. S. W. Ind. | . . 1758 |
| cereūscŭlā | . . . | S. Ev. T. Brazil | . . 1829 |
| fasciculātā | . . . Grah. wht. | 8. Ev. S. W. Ind. Ia. | 1817 |
| grandiflōrā, 2 | . . White. | 7, S. Ev. S. S. Amer. | . 1818 |
| Hookeriānā | . . . White. | 8, S. Ev. S. W. Ind. | |
| mesembryanthoīdēs | White. | 8. Ev. S. S Amer. | . 1817 |
| parasītică | . . . Yellow | . 8. S. Ev. S. S. Amer. | . 1800 |
| salicornoīdēs | . . . Yellow | . 6, S. Ev. S. E. Ind. | . 1817 |

RHIZOCTŎNĬX, *Decandolle.* From *rhiza,* a root, and *kleino,* to destroy; the name is applied in consequence of its destroying the roots upon which it grows. *Linn.* 24, Or. 9, Nat. Or. *Fungi.* This species is found on *Colchicum* and the roots of the Crocus—*R. Crocorum.*

RHIZŎMA, applied to roots which spread under ground, similar to those of the Iris.

RHIZOMŎRPHĂ, *Roth.* From *rhiza,* a root, and *morphe,* form; the appearance of the plants. *Linn.* 24, Or. 9, Nat. Or. *Fungi.* The species of this genus are found beneath bark and in cellars—*R. divergens, medullaris, subcorticalis, subterranea.*

RHIZŎPHŎRĂ, *Linn.* From *rhiza,* a root, and *phoreo,* to bear; the branches of this tree throw out roots very freely, which descend into the mud; consequently, every branch being supported by its own roots, one tree may, in this manner, extend over a considerable space. *Linn.* 11, Or. 1, Nat. Or. *Rhizophoraceæ.* The Mangrove may be tried in loam and sand, well mixed, and kept moist by the frequent application of salted water. It is difficult, if not altogether impossible, to cultivate it in this country.

| | | | | |
|---|---|---|---|---|
| Manglĕ | . . . . Pa. yel. | . S. Ev. T. E. Ind. | . 1820 |

RHIZOPŎGŎN, *Trinius.* From *rhiza,* a root, and *pogon,* a beard. *Linn.* 24, Or. 9, Nat. Or. *Fungi.* This species is found by the waysides. *Synonyme:* 1. *Lycoperdon gibbosum—R. albus* 1.

RHODĂNTHĔ, *Lindley.* From *rhodon,* a rose, and *anthos,* a flower; in allusion to the colour of the flower-heads. *Linn.* 19, Or. 1, Nat. Or. *Compositæ.* This is one of the most delightful annuals ever introduced to our collections. To obtain flowering plants in March, the seed should be sown in August, in a compost of decayed leaf-soil and light maiden earth, in equal parts, having the pots well drained. The seed-pots should not be placed in a lower temperature than 60 nor ever higher than 80 degrees. The earth should never be allowed to become too dry, taking care to apply water of a temperature nearly equal to that of the house. They will require several shifts previous to flowering; at the two last, viz. those in January and March, decayed manure should be substituted for leaf mould, and a small portion of white sand added to the compost; a second sowing should be made in October and treated as the first, and they will flower beautifully the following May; and if a final sowing is effected in March, the plants will be ready to plant out in the flower-garden in May or June, where they will flower during the autumnal months. After the plants raised from any of the sowings have been potted, they should be removed to a much cooler house, and when properly established, placed on some elevated situation near the glass. Seed should be obtained from the plants grown in the greenhouse.

| | | | | |
|---|---|---|---|---|
| Manglēsĭĭ | . . . Ro. yel. | . 6, G. | A. S. River | . 1832 |

RHODIOLA, see *Sĕdŭm.*

RHODODĔNDRŎN, *Linn.* From *rhodon,* a rose, and *dendron,* a tree; because of the appearance of the terminal bunches of flowers. *Linn.* 10, Or. 1, Nat. Or. *Ericaceæ.* The Rhododendron is decidedly one of the finest of all known genera, containing some of the most handsome, elegant, and showy shrubs; all of which are admirably adapted either for ornamenting the greenhouse or shrubbery, or for planting singly on lawns. Peat soil is most suitable to these plants, but they may also be grown in very sandy loam, or vegetable mould. Propagation may be effected by layers or seeds; if the latter mode be preferred, the seeds must be sown early in spring, in flat pans filled with peat soil, and the seed covered very slightly over; the pans should then be set in a close frame till the plants make their appearance, taking care to water very slightly when the soil appears dry. The seedlings having attained to a sufficient height, so as to admit of their being drawn without fear of injury, should be removed into other pots or pans, using the same kind of mould. After this removal they should be kept in a close frame till fresh roots are produced, and they may then, by degrees, be hardened to the air. The small-wooded kinds may be also increased very freely by young cuttings, planted in sand under a glass. The tender kinds may be easily propagated by young cuttings torn off close to the stem, planted in sand and plunged in heat under a glass. *Synonymes:* 1. *R. aromaticum.* 2. *R. cinnamomeum.* 3. *R. album.* 4. *R. Russellianum.* 5. *R. Nobleanum.* 6. *R. officinale.* 7. *R. azaleoides.* 8. *R. myrtifolium.* 9. *R. obtusum.* 10. *R. indicum Smithii, Azalea indica Smithii.* 11. *R. Smithii.* 12. *Rhodora canadensis.*

| | | | | | |
|---|---|---|---|---|---|
| albiflōrŭm | . . . White | . 6, H. Ev. S. N. Amer. | . 1835 |
| altā-clĕrĕnsĕ | . . . Crimson | . 5, H. Ev. S. Eng. hyb. | |
| anthopŏgŏn, 1 | . . Purple | . 5, F. Ev. S. Nepal | . 1820 |
| arbŏrĕŭm | . . . Scarlet | . 5, F. Ev. S. Nepal | . 1820 |
| cinnamŏmĕŭm, 2 | Purple | . 6, H. Ev. S. Nepal | . 1820 |
| nivĕŭm, 3 | . . . White | . 3, H. Ev. T. Nepal | . 1817 |
| rŏsĕŭm | . . . Rose | . 4, H. Ev. T. Nepal | . 1817 |
| sanguinĕŭm | . . . Scarlet | . 4, H. Ev. T. Nepal | . 1817 |
| undulātŭm | . . . Rich p. | . 4, H. Ev. S. Eng. hyb. | . 1829 |
| venŭstŭm | . . . Pk. spot. | . 3, H. Ev. S. Eng. hyb. | . 1829 |
| barbātŭm | . . . | H. Ev. S. Nepal | . 1829 |
| campanulātŭm | . . Pa. pink | . 5, F. Ev. S. Nepal | . 1825 |
| camtchātĭcŭm | . . Purple | . H. Ev. S. Kamt. | . 1802 |
| catawbiĕnsĕ | . . . Purple | . 7, H. Ev. S. N. Amer. | . 1809 |
| Russelliānŭm, 4 | Bt. ro. | . 3, H. Ev. S. | . 1829 |
| tigrīnŭm | . . . Ro. spot. | . 3, H. Ev. S. Hybrid | |
| Cateabēi | . . . Purple | . 5, H. Ev. S. N. Amer. | . 1810 |
| caucāsĕŭm | . . . Purple | . 8, H. Ev. S. Caucasus | . 1803 |
| Noblĕānŭm, 5 | . Dp. red | . 3, H. Ev. S. Hybrid | . 1832 |
| pulchĕrrimŭm | . . Pa. rose | . 8, H. Ev. S. Hybrid | . 1832 |
| stramĭnĕŭm | . . . Straw | . 4, H. Ev. S. | |
| Chamæcĭstŭs | . . Pa. pur. | . 5, H. Ev. S. Austria | . 1786 |
| chrysanthŭm, 6 | . Yellow | . 6, H. Ev. S. Siberia | . 1796 |
| daŭrĭcŭm | . . . Purple | . 3, H. Ev. S. Siberia | . 1780 |
| atrovĭrĕns | . . . Purple | . 3, H. Ev. S. Siberia | |
| Farrĕrā | . . . Lilac | . 3, H. Ev. S. China | . 1829 |
| ferrugĭnĕŭm | . . Scarlet | . 6, H. Ev. S. Switzerl. | . 1752 |
| albŭm | . . . White | . 6, H. Ev. S. Pyrenees | . 1830 |
| hybrĭdŭm | . . . Pink | . 7, H. Ev. S. | |
| hirsūtŭm | . . . Scarlet | . 6, H. Ev. S. Switzerl. | . 1656 |
| variĕgātŭm | . . Scarlet | . 6, H. Ev. S. | . 1800 |
| lapponĭcŭm | . . . Crimson | . 4, F. Ev. S. Lapland | . 1825 |
| lepidŏtŭm | . . . Rose | . F. Ev. S. Nepal | . 1829 |
| maxĭmŭm | . . . Pink | . 7, H. Ev. S. N. Amer. | . 1756 |
| albŭm | . . . White | . 7, H. Ev. S. | |
| hybrĭdŭm | . . . Wht. pur. | . H. Ev. S. Hybrid | . 1830 |
| pontĭcŭm | . . . Purple | . 5, H. Ev. S. Gibraltar | . 1763 |
| azaleoīdĕs, 7 | . Pink | . 7, H. Ev. S. Hybrid | . 1820 |
| Lŏwĭĭ | . . . White | . H. Ev. S. Eng. hyb. | |
| myrtifŏliŭm, 8 | Purple | . 5, H. Ev. S. Gibraltar | . 1763 |
| obtŭsŭm, 9 | . . Purple | . 5, H. Ev. S. Armenia | |
| odorātŭm | . . . Pink | . 7, H. Ev. S. | . 1820 |
| pŭlchrŭm, 10 | . Rose | . 6, H. Ev. S. Eng. hyb. | . 1827 |
| Smithĭĭ, 11 | . . Crimson | . 9, H. Ev. S. Eng. hyb. | . 1826 |
| punctātŭm | . . . Pink | . 7, H. Ev. S. N. Amer. | . 1786 |
| mājŭs | . . . Pink | . 7, H. Ev. S. | |
| purpŭrĕŭm | . . . Purple | . 7, H. Ev. T. N. Amer. | |
| Pŭrshĭĭ | . . . White. | . 7, H. Ev. S. N. Jersey | . 1811 |
| Rhodŏrā, 12 | . . Pa. pur. | . 5, H. De. S. N. Amer. | . 1767 |
| setŏsŭm | . . . Purple | . F. Ev. S. Nepal | . 1825 |

RHODOMĔLĂ, *Agardh.* From *rhodon,* a rose, and *melos,* a limb, colour of the fronds. *Linn.* 24, Or.

8, Nat. Or. *Algæ.* These plants are found in the ocean, on the sea-shore, &c.—*R. dentátá, lycopodioídéś, pinastroídéś, scorpioídéś, subfúscá.*

RHODOMÉNÍA. From *rhodos,* red, and *hymen,* a membrane. *Linn.* 24, Or. 8, Nat. Or. *Algæ.* The species of this genus, like those of the one immediately preceding, are found in the ocean, &c. *Synonymes:* 1. *Sphærococcus bifidus.* 2. *S. ciliatus.* 3. *S. c. angustus.* 4. *S. c. jubatus.* 5. *S. c. palmatus.* 6. *S. c. spinosus.* 7. *S. cristatus.* 8. *S. laciniatus.* 9. *S. Palmetta.* 10. *S. reniformis*—*R. bifidá* 1, *ciliátá* 2, *C. angustá* 3, *C. jubátá* 4, *C. palmátá* 5, *C. spinósá* 6, *cristátá* 7, *laciniátá* 8, *Palmëttá* 9, *polycárpá, reniförmis* 10, *soboliférá.*

RHODÓRA, see *Rhododéndron.*

RHOMB or RHOMBOID, like a Rhombus.

RHOMB-OVATE, } between rhomboid and egg-<br>
RHOMBOID-OVATE, } shaped.

RHUBARB, see *Rhéum.*

RHÚS, *Linn.* Derived from *rous,* in Greek, which is from *rhudd,* a Celtic word signifying red; alluding to the colour of the fruit and leaves of some species in autumn. *Linn.* 5, Or. 3, Nat. Or. *Anacardiaceæ.* The stove and greenhouse species will grow well in any common soil; and may be readily increased by ripened cuttings planted in sand, under a glass; the stove species must be placed in heat. The hardy kinds are rather ornamental and well fitted for shrubberies; some are propagated by cuttings of the roots, and others by cuttings and layers. The juice of *R. radicans* and *Toxicodendron* is milky, stains black, and is extremely poisonous. *R. Coriaria* is powerfully astringent, and is used in tanning Turkey or Morocco leather. *Synonymes:* 1. *R. Bucku Amela.* 2. *R. lucida.* 3. *Laurus caustica.* 4. *R. lucida.* 5. *spicata.* 6. *oxyacanthoides.* 7. *caroliniana, elegans.* 8. *elongata.* 9. *theezans.* 10. *venenata.* 11. *juglandifolia.*

| | | | | | |
|---|---|---|---|---|---|
| acuminátá | . . | F. Ev. S. | Nepal | . | 1820 |
| Amelá, 1 | . . | H. De. S. | Nepal | . | |
| alátá | . . | G. Ev. S. | C. G. H. | . | 1824 |
| albídá | . . | G. Ev. S. | Mogadore | . | 1816 |
| angustifóliá | . Grnsh. | H. De. S. | C. G. H. | . | 1714 |
| aromáticá | . Yellow | 5, H. De. S. | N. Amer. | . | 1773 |
| atomáriá | . Grn. yel. | G. Ev. S. | C. G. H. | . | 1800 |
| Burmánni, 2 | . Grn. yel. | 7, G. Ev. S. | C. G. H. | . | 1797 |
| canística, 3 | . Grn. wht. | G. Ev. S. | Chile | . | 1828 |
| Cavanillesii, 4 | . White | 7, G. Ev. S. | Mexico | . | 1697 |
| chinénsis | . . | G. Ev. S. | China | . | 1800 |
| ciliátá | . . | G. Ev. S. | C. G. H. | . | 1816 |
| Commersónii | . . | S. Ev. T. | Brasil | . | 1810 |
| concínná | . . | G. Ev. S. | C. G. H. | . | 1820 |
| copallíná | . Grn. yel. | 8, H. De. S. | N. Amer. | . | 1688 |
| leucánthá | . Whitsh. | 8, H. De. S. | N. Amer. | . | |
| Coriáriá | . Grn. yel. | 7, H. De. T. | S. Eur. | . | 1640 |
| Cótinus | . Pa. pur. | 6, H. De. S. | S. Eur. | . | 1656 |
| creáná | . . | G. Ev. S. | C. G. H. | . | |
| cuneifóliá | . Grn. wht. | G. Ev. S. | C. G. H. | . | 1816 |
| dentátá, 5 | . Yelsh. | . G. Ev. S. | C. G. H. | . | 1798 |
| digitátá | . . | G. Ev. S. | C. G. H. | . | 1820 |
| dioíca, 6 | . Grnsh. yel. | G. Ev. S. | Mogadore | . | 1825 |
| disséctá | . . | G. Ev. S. | C. G. H. | . | 1820 |
| élegáns | . Red | 7, H. De. S. | N. Amer. | . | 1726 |
| ellipticá | . . | 7, G. Ev. S. | C. G. H. | . | 1818 |
| exciśá | . . | G. Ev. S. | C. G. H. | . | 1816 |
| frágrans | . . | G. Ev. S. | C. G. H. | . | 1824 |
| fraxinifóliá | . . | G. Ev. T. | Nepal | . | 1820 |
| glábrá | . Grn. yel. | 8, H. De. S. | N. Amer. | . | 1726 |
| coccíneá, 7 | . Red | 7, H. De. S. | N. Amer. | . | |
| dioíca | . Grnsh. | 7, H. De. S. | N. Amer. | . | |
| hermaphrodítá | . Grnsh. | 6, H. De. S. | N. Amer. | . | |
| glaúcá | . Grn. yel. | G. Ev. S. | C. G. H. | . | 1821 |
| heterophýllá | . . | G. Ev. S. | C. G. H. | . | 1800 |
| incíśá | . Grn. yel. | G. Ev. S. | C. G. H. | . | 1789 |
| javánicá | . White | 3, G. Ev. T. | Java | . | 1799 |
| lævigátá, 8 | . Yelsh. w. | G. Ev. S. | C. G. H. | . | 1758 |
| láncéá | . . | G. Ev. S. | C. G. H. | . | 1810 |
| lineatifóliá | . Cream | 8, S. Ev. S. | Cuba | . | 1818 |
| lobátá | . . | G. Ev. S. | Teneriffe | . | 1800 |
| lúcídá | . White | 7, G. Ev. S. | C. G. H. | . | 1697 |
| Metópíum | . . | S. Ev. S. | W. Ind. | . | 1823 |
| micránthá | . Grnsh. w. | G. Ev. S. | C. G. H. | . | 1818 |
| mucronátá | . . | G. Ev. S. | C. G. H. | . | 1824 |
| nervóśá | . Grnsh. yel. | G. Ev. S. | C. G. H. | . | 1800 |
| obliquá | . . | S. Ev. S. | C. G. H. | . | 1825 |
| obscúrá | . . | 8, H. De. S. | Iberia | . | 1820 |
| Oxyacánthá | . Grn. yel. | H. De. S. | Barbary | . | 1823 |
| oxyacanthoídes | . Grn. yel. | H. De. S. | Barbary | . | 1824 |
| paniculátá | . Green | 6, G. Ev. S. | Nepal | . | 1823 |
| paucifórá | . . | G. Ev. S. | C. G. H. | . | |
| pendulíná | . Grn. yel. | G. Ev. S. | C. G. H. | . | |
| pentaphýllá | . Yellow | F. Ev. S. | Barbary | . | 1816 |
| pubéscens | . Grn. yel. | G. Ev. S. | C. G. H. | . | 1800 |

| | | | | | |
|---|---|---|---|---|---|
| pùmílá | . . | Grn. yel. | 7, H. De. S. | N. Amer. | . 1806 |
| pyroídes | . . | | G. Ev. S. | C. G. H. | . 1816 |
| rádícans | . . | Grn. yel. | 6, H. De. Cr. | N. Amer. | |
| microcárpi | . . | Grn. yel. | 6, H. De. Cl. | N. Amer. | |
| volubílis | . . | Grn. yel. | 6, H. De. Cl. | N. Amer. | |
| vulgáris | . . | Grn. yel. | 6, H. De. Cr. | N. Amer. | |
| rígidá | . . | | G. Ev. S. | C. G. H. | . 1700 |
| rosmarinifóliá | . Green | | S. Ev. S. | C. G. H. | . 1800 |
| schinoídes | . . | | S. Ev. S. | Brasil | . 1824 |
| semilátá | . . | | G. Ev. T. | Mexco | . 1780 |
| serráfóliá | . . | | G. Ev. S. | C. G. H. | . 1816 |
| sinuátá | . . | | G. Ev. S. | C. G. H. | . 1820 |
| suavéólens | . Grnsh. yel. | 5, H. De. S. | N. Amer. | |
| succedáneá | . Grn. yel. | 6, G. Ev. S. | China | . 1768 |
| Thunbergiáná | . Grnsh. yel. | G. Ev. S. | C. G. H. | |
| tomentóśá | . Grnsh. yel. | G. Ev. S. | C. G. H. | . 1691 |
| Toxicodéndron | . Grn. yel. | 6, H. De. Cr. | N. Amer. | . 1640 |
| tridáctylis | . Grnsh. yel. | G. Ev. S. | C. G. H. | . 1816 |
| tridentátá | . Grnsh. yel. | G. Ev. Cl. | C. G. H. | . 1816 |
| trijúga | . . | | S. Ev. S. | Brasil | |
| typhíná | . Grn. yel. | 7, H. De. T. | N. Amer. | . 1629 |
| arboréscens | . Grn. yel. | 7, H. De. T. | | |
| frutéscens | . Grn. yel. | 7, H. De. S. | | |
| undulátá, 9 | . Whtsh. yel. | H. De. S. | C. G. H. | . 1816 |
| vérnix, 11 | . Grn. yel. | 7, H. De. T. | N. Amer. | . 1713 |
| vernicíferá | . Grn. yel. | H. De. T. | Nepal | . 1823 |
| villóśá | . Grn. yel. | 7, G. Ev. S. | C. G. H. | . 1714 |
| viminális | . Grn. yel. | G. Ev. S. | C. G. H. | . 1774 |
| viridiflóra | . Grn. yel. | 7, H. De. S. | N. Amer. | |
| Zizyphína | . . | | G. Ev. S. | Sicily | . 1800 |

RHYNCHOSÍA, *Loureiro.* From *rhynchos,* a beak; the keel of the flower is beaked. *Linn.* 17, Or. 4, Nat. Or. *Leguminosæ.* These plants are not possessed of much beauty; any rich light soil suits them; and they are easily increased by cuttings or seeds. *Synonymes:* 1. *Glycine angustifolia.* 2. *Dolichos scarabæoides.* 3. *Glycine caribœa.* 4. *G. tomentosa, volubilis.* 5. *G. erecta.* 6. *Dolichos minimus.* 7. *G. mollis.* 8. *G. phaseoloides.* 9. *G. precatoria.* 10. *G. reniformis.* 11. *G. reticulata.* 12. *G. rhombifolia.* 13. *Dolichos scarabæoides.* 14. *G. suaveolens.* 15. *G. picta, Cytisus violaceus.* 16. *G. viscosa, glutinosa.*

| | | | | | |
|---|---|---|---|---|---|
| caribáá, 3 | . Yellow | 9, S. Ev. Tw. | W. Ind. | . 1742 |
| erécta, 5 | . Sulphur | 7, H. Her. P. | N. Amer. | . 1820 |
| reniformis, 10 | . Yellow | 7, F. De. Tw. | Carolina | . 1806 |
| reticulata, 11 | . White | 8, S. Ev. Tw. | Jamaica | . 1779 |
| suaveólens, 14 | . Yel. red | 8, S. Ev. S. | W. Ind. | . 1816 |

*R. angustifóliá* 1, *biflórá* 2, *difförmis* 4, *Fredericiáná, minímá* 6, *móllis* 7, *phaseoloídes* 8, *precatóriá* 9, *rhombifóliá* 12, *scarabæoídes* 13, *violaceá* 15, *viscóśá* 16.

RHYNCHOSPÓRÁ, *Vahl.* From *rhynchos,* a beak, and *spora,* a seed. *Linn.* 3, Or. 1, Nat. Or. *Cyperaceæ.* Worthless plants, growing in bogs, &c.—*R. albá, comátá, fúscá.*

RHYTISMÁ, *Fries.* From *rhytis,* a wrinkle; appearance of the plants. *Linn.* 24, Or. 9, Nat. Or. *Fungi.* Found upon sycamore leaves and other live plants, as some of the specific appellations imply—*R. acerínum, Andrómèdæ, corrugátum, punctátum, salicínum, Urticæ.*

RIB, the projecting vein of anything.

RÍBES, *Linn.* From *Ribas,* the name of an acid plant mentioned by the Arabian physicians, which is known to be *Rheum Ribes.* *Linn.* 5, Or. 1, Nat. Or. *Grossulaceæ.* This is a valuable genus, and contains the gooseberry and currant, the uses of which every cottager is familiar with; and in addition to these much esteemed fruits, some of the species are well suited for ornamenting shrubberies. The most ornamental species are *R. atropurpureum, aureum, sanguineum,* and *speciosum.* All the species of *Ribes* will grow in any soil, and increase from cuttings, planted in autumn, or early in spring. *Synonymes:* 1. *R. aureum sanguineum.* 2. *R. hybridum.* 3. *R. reclinatum.* 4. *Uvacrispa.* 5. *R. oxyacanthoides.* 6. *R. glandulosum.* 7. *R. laxiflorum.* 8. *R. malvaceum.* 9. *R. stamineum.* 10. *R. missouriense.* 11. *R. stamineum.*

| | | | | | |
|---|---|---|---|---|---|
| acículáré | . White | . | H. De. S. | Siberia | . |
| albinérvium | . Green | . | 4, H. De. S. | N. Amer. | . |
| alpínum | . Green | . | 4, H. De. S. | Britain | . |
| fólis-variegátá | . Green | . | 5, H. De. S. | Britain | . |
| pùmílum | . Green | . | 4, H. De. S. | | |
| auréum | . Yellow | . | 5, H. De. S. | Missouri | . 1812 |
| præcóx | . Yellow | . | 5, H. De. S. | N. Amer. | . 1812 |
| serotínum | . Yellow | . | 6, H. De. S. | N. Amer. | . 1812 |
| villóśum | . Yellow | . | 4, H. De. S. | N. Amer. | . 1812 |
| carpathícum | . Green | . | 4, H. De. S. | Carpathia | . 1818 |
| céréúm | . White | . | 4, H. De. S. | N. Amer. | . 1827 |
| Cynosbáti | . Green | . | 4, H. De. S. | Canada | . 1759 |
| Diacánthá | . Grn. yel. | . | 5, H. De. S. | Siberia | . 1781 |
| divaricátum | . Wht. red | . | 4, H. De. S. | N. Amer. | . 1826 |

| | | | | | |
|---|---|---|---|---|---|
| flāvŭm, 1 | Yellow | 4, H. De. S. | N. Amer. | 1812 |
| flōrĭdŭm | Yellow | 4, H. De. S. | N. Amer. | 1729 |
| grandiflōrŭm | Yellow | 4, H. De. S. | N. Amer. | |
| parviflōrŭm | Yellow | 4, H. De. S. | N. Amer. | |
| glaciālĕ | Yellow | 4, H. De. S. | Nepal | 1823 |
| glandulōsŭm | Grn. yel. | 4, H. De. S. | Peru | 1830 |
| grăcĭlĕ | Grn. white | 4, H. De. S. | N. Amer. | 1812 |
| Grossulāriă | Green | 4, H. De. S. | England | |
| Besserianā, 2 | White | 4, H. De. S. | Cracow | |
| bractēātă | Grn. white | 4, H. De. S. | | |
| macrocārpă | Grn. white | 4, H. De. S. | | |
| reclinātā, 3 | Grn. white | 4, H. De. S. | Germany | 1781 |
| spinosissimā | Grn. white | 4, H. De. S. | Britain | |
| subinērmis | Grn. white | 4, H. De. S. | | |
| Uva-crispā, 4 | Grn. white | 4, H. De. S. | Britain | |
| hirtēllŭm | Grn. white | 4, H. De. S. | Canada | 1812 |
| hudsoniānŭm | White | H. De. S. | Hud's. B. | |
| inēbriāns | Grn. white | 4, H. De. S. | N. Amer. | 1827 |
| irrigŭŭm | Grn. white | 4, H. De. S. | N. Amer. | 1830 |
| lacŭstrĕ, 5 | Yel. grn. | 4, H. De. S. | N. Amer. | 1812 |
| macracānthŭm | Green | 5, H. De. S. | | |
| multiflōrŭm | Green | 4, H. De. S. | Hungary | 1822 |
| nĭgrŭm | Green | 4, H. De. S. | Britain | |
| baccā-flāvidă | | H. De. S. | Hybrid | |
| baccā-vĭridī | | H. De. S. | Russia | |
| fol.-variegātĭs | | H. De. S. | Britain | |
| nĭvĕŭm | White | 4, H. De. S. | N. Amer. | 1826 |
| opulifōliŭm | | H. De. S. | Russia | |
| orientālĕ | Grn. yel. | 5, H. De. S. | Syria | 1824 |
| oxyacanthoīdēs | Grn. white | 4, H. De. S. | N. Amer. | 1763 |
| petrēŭm | Red | 5, H. De. S. | England | |
| procŭmbēns | Purple | 5, H. De. Tr. | Dahuria | 1804 |
| prostrātŭm, 6 | Yellow | 5, H. De. Tr. | N. Amer. | 1812 |
| laxiflōrŭm, 7 | Grn. yel. | 4, H. De. Tr. | N. Amer. | 1812 |
| punctātŭm | Grn. yel. | 4, F. De. S. | Chili | 1826 |
| resinōsŭm | Yel. grn. | 4, H. De. S. | N. Amer. | 1800 |
| rĭgēns | Green | 4, H. De. S. | N. Amer. | 1812 |
| rŭbrŭm | Green | 4, H. De. S. | Britain | |
| albŭm | Green | 4, H. De. S. | Britain | |
| carnĕŭm | Green | 4, H. De. S. | Britain | |
| fol. albŏ | Green | 4, H. De. S. | | |
| fol. lūtĕŏ | Green | 4, H. De. S. | | |
| hortēnsĕ | Green | 4, H. De. S. | Britain | |
| sylvēstrĕ | Green | 4, H. De. S. | Britain | |
| variegātŭm | Green | 4, H. De. S. | Austria | |
| sanguĭnĕŭm | Blood | 4, H. De. S. | N. Amer. | 1826 |
| atrorŭbēns | Drk. red | 4, H. De. S. | N. Amer. | |
| glutinōsŭm | Pa. pink | 4, H. De. S. | N. Amer. | |
| malvācĕŭm, 8 | Drk. pink | 4, H. De. S. | N. Amer. | |
| saxātĭlĕ | Green | 5, H. De. S. | Siberia | 1819 |
| setōsŭm | Grn. white | 4, H. De. S. | N. Amer. | 1810 |
| specĭōsŭm, 9 | Crimson | 5, H. De. S. | California | 1829 |
| spicātŭm | Green | 4, H. De. S. | England | |
| tenuiflōrŭm, 10 | Yellow | 4, H. De. S. | N. Amer. | 1812 |
| fructŭ-lūtĕŏ | Yellow | 4, H. De. S. | | |
| fructŭ-nĭgrŏ | Yellow | 4, H. De. S. | | |
| trĭfĭdŭm | | 4, H. De. S. | Quebec | 1823 |
| triflōrŭm, 11 | Grn. white | 4, H. De. S. | N. Amer. | 1812 |
| trĭstĕ | | 4, H. De. S. | Siberia | 1820 |
| viscosissimŭm | Yellow | 4, H. De. S. | N. Amer. | 1820 |

RIB-GRASS, see *Plantāgŏ lanceolātā*.

RICCIX, *Linn.* In honour of P. Francisco Riccio, a Florentine botanist. *Linn.* 24, Or. 6, Nat. Or. *Hepaticæ.* The species belonging to this genus are found floating in ditches, &c.—*R. flŭitāns, glaūcă, obtūsă, nătāns, spūriă.*

RICE, see *Orȳză.*

RICHĂRDIX, *Kunth.* In honour of L. C. Richard, an eminent French botanist. *Linn.* 7, Or. 1, Nat. Or. *Araceæ.* This desirable plant thrives in any light rich soil, and is readily increased by offsets from the roots; while, on account of its frequent flowering, and large sweet-scented flowers, it is well worthy of a place in every collection. *Synonyme:* 1. *Calla æthiopica.*

| | | | | |
|---|---|---|---|---|
| æthiŏpĭcă, 1 | White | 8, G. Her. P. C. G. H. | 1731 |

RICHARDSŎNIX, *Kunth.* In memory of Richard Richardson, an English botanist. *Linn.* 6, Or. 1, Nat. Or. *Cinchonaceæ.* This genus grows well in loam and peat; and cuttings root readily in the same kind of soil, under a glass, in a little heat. The white Ipecacuanha of the shops, is the root of *R. scabra. Synonymes:* 1. *Richardia scabra, Richardsonia pilosa.*

| | | | | |
|---|---|---|---|---|
| scabră, 1 | White | 9, S. Her. P. Brazil | 1814 |

RICHĬX, *R. Brown.* In memory of Mr. Richie, an African traveller, who died in 1821, at Tripoli. *Linn.* 13, Or. 1, Nat. Or. *Epacridaceæ.* A very handsome stove climber: it grows best in a mixture of loam, peat, and sand; and cuttings root readily in sand, under a glass, in heat. *Synonyme:* 1. *Cratæva fragrans, Cī capparoidēs.*

| | | | | |
|---|---|---|---|---|
| fragrāns, 1 | White | 6, S. Ev. Cl. S. Leone | 1795 |

RICĬNŬS, *Linn.* From *ricinus*, a tick; resemblance

in the seeds. *Linn.* 21, Or. 1, Nat. Or. *Euphorbiaceæ.* The plants belonging to this genus will thrive in any rich soil, and are easily increased by seeds and cuttings. The well known Castor oil is the produce of *R. communis.*

| | | | | |
|---|---|---|---|---|
| africānŭs | Green | 7, G. Ev. S. | Africa | |
| armātŭs | Green | 8, F. A. | Malta | 1807 |
| commŭnis | Green | 7, F. A. | E. Ind. | 1548 |
| globōsŭs | | 8. Ev. S. | Jamaica | 1826 |
| inērmis | Purple | 7, F. A. | India | 1758 |
| lĭvidŭs | Purple | 7, G. Ev. S. C. G. H. | | 1795 |
| tanarĭūs | Green | 8, F. A. | E. Ind. | 1810 |
| vĭridis | Green | 8, F. A. | E. Ind. | 1802 |

RICŌTIX, *Linn.* Probably after some unknown botanist. *Linn.* 15, Nat. Or. *Cruciferæ.* A pretty little annual, well fitted for adorning rock-work, on which the seed may be sown. A light sandy soil suits it best. *Synonyme:* 1. *R. ægyptiaca.*

| | | | | |
|---|---|---|---|---|
| Lunāriă, 1 | Lt. pur. | 6, H. A. | Egypt | 1757 |

RIEDLEIX, *Ventenat.* In honour of M. Riedley, a French naturalist, who accompanied Captain Baudin round the world. *Linn.* 16, Or. 2, Nat. Or. *Sterculiaceæ.* The plants are not worth growing, except for the purpose of making up a collection. They are all of the easiest culture, and are readily increased by seeds. *Synonymes:* 1. *Melochia caracasana.* 2. *M. corchorifolia.* 3. *M. depressa.* 4. *M. supina.* 5. *M. truncata.*

| | | | | |
|---|---|---|---|---|
| caracasānā, 1 | White | 6, S. Ev. S. | Caraccas | 1817 |
| nodiflōră | Yellow | 6, S. Ev. S. | Jamaica | 1800 |

*R. borbōnĭcă, concatenātā, corchorifōliă 2, deprēssă 3, polystāchiă, supīnă 4, truncātă 5, velutīnă.*

RIGID, stiff, untractable.

RIMOSE, having a longitudinal fissure or fissures, chinky.

RINDERX, *Pallas.* In honour of Dr. Rinder, once dean of medicine in Moscow. *Linn.* 5, Or. 1, Nat. Or. *Boraginaceæ.* This plant is of the easiest culture, but of no beauty. *Synonymes:* 1. *R. lævigata, Cynoglossum Rindera.*

| | | | | |
|---|---|---|---|---|
| tetrāspis, 1 | Red | 6, H. Her. P. Siberia | 1818 |

RINGENT, gaping.

RINGING, removing a small strip of bark from around a branch, in the form of a ring.

RIPIDIŬM, *Trinius.* From *rhipidion*, a little fan; in allusion to the inflorescence. *Linn.* 23, Or. 1, Nat. Or. *Gramineæ.* Grasses, growing in any common soil, and increased by divisions. *Synonymes:* 1. *Andropogon Ravenna, Saccharum Ravenna, Erianthus Ravennæ.* 2. *A. strictus, S. adpressum.*

| | | | | |
|---|---|---|---|---|
| Ravēnnæ, 1 | Apetal | 7, Grass. S. Eur. | 1816 |
| strictŭm, 2 | Apetal | 7, Grass. Hungary | 1802 |

RIPOGŌNŬM, *Forster.* From *ripos*, a flexile twig, and *gonos*, a shoot. *Linn.* 6, Or. 1, Nat. Or. *Smilaceæ.* Ornamental climbers, thriving in loam and peat; and increasing by young cuttings, planted in sand, under a glass.

| | | | | |
|---|---|---|---|---|
| albŭm | White | 6, G. Ev. Cl. N. Holl. | 1820 |
| parviflōrŭm | White | 6, G. Ev. Cl. N. Holl. | 1820 |

RIVEX. Dedicated by Choisy, to Auguste de la Rive, a physiologist of Geneva. *Linn.* 5, Or. 1, Nat. Or. *Convolvulaceæ.* For culture, &c. see *Ipomœa. Synonyme:* 1. *Ipomœa gangetica.*

| | | | | |
|---|---|---|---|---|
| tiliæfōliă, 1 | White | 6, S. Ev. Tw. E. Ind. | 1812 |

RIVĬNX, *Linn.* In honour of A. Q. Rivinus, a botanist of Saxony. *Linn.* 4, Or. 1, Nat. Or. *Phytolaccaceæ.* These plants are mostly valued on account of their ornamental appearance when fruiting; they grow in any light soil, and are readily increased by seeds or cuttings.

| | | | | |
|---|---|---|---|---|
| brasiliēnsis | Green | 6, S. Ev. S. | Brazil | 1790 |
| hŭmĭlis | White | 6, S. Ev. S. | W. Ind. | 1699 |
| canēscēns | White | 6, S. Ev. S. | W. Ind. | 1804 |
| lævis | Pink | 5, S. Ev. S. | W. Ind. | 1733 |
| lanceolātā | | 6, S. Ev. S. | Brazil | 1815 |
| octāndră | White | 5, S. Ev. S. | W. Ind. | 1752 |
| purpurāscēns | Pink | 6, S. Ev. S. | W. Ind. | 1815 |
| tinctōriă | White | 5, S. Ev. S. | Caraccas | 1830 |

RIVULĀRIX, *Roth.* From *rivulus*, a rivulet; place of growth. *Linn.* 24, Or. 7, Nat. Or. *Algæ.* These plants are found in lakes, ditches, &c. *Synonyme:* 1. *Linkia durā—R. angulōsă, applanātă, āirā, botryoīdēs, calcārĕā ī, crustācĕā, nĭtidă, plānă, plicātā.*

ROBERGIX, *Schreber.* In honour of Laurent Roberg, professor of medicine at Upsal. *Linn.* 10, Or. 4, Nat. Or. *Connaraceæ.* An ornamental plant, growing in loam and peat; and increased by cuttings in sand, under a glass, in heat.

| frutéscens | . . . | White | . . | 8. Ev. S. | Guiana | . . | 1823 |

**ROBÉRTIA**, *Decandolle.* In honour of M. Robert, a Corsican botanist. *Linn.* 19, Or. 1, Nat. Or. *Compositæ.* Mere weeds, of the most common culture; seeds. *Synonyme:* 1. *Hypochæris pinnatifida—R. pinnatifida* 1, *taraxacoïdes.*

**ROBÍNIA**, *Decandolle.* In honour of Jean Robin, a French botanist, once herbalist to Henry IV. of France. *Linn.* 17, Or. 4, Nat. Or. *Leguminosæ.* The hardy kinds of *Robinia* are remarkably handsome when in flower, and well adapted for ornamenting the shrubbery. They will grow in any common soil; and are increased either by layers or by grafting the rare species upon the common kinds, chiefly on *R. Pseud-acacia.* The stove and greenhouse species should be grown in a mixture of loam, sand, and peat; and young cuttings will root, if planted in sand, under a glass. *R. Pseud-acacia,* if properly seasoned, is equally as strong and as durable as oak. *Synonymes:* 1. *R. hybrida, ambigua, echinata.* 2. *grandiflora, macrophylla.* 3. *amorphæfolia.* 4. *monstrosa.* 5. *pendula.* 6. *procera.* 7. *sophoræfolia.* 8. *stricta.* 9. *inermis.*

| davúrica | . . . | . . | . . | 5, H. De. T. | Davuria | 1820 |
| dúbia, 1 | . . . | Wht. red | . | 5, H. De. T. | N. Amer. | . |
| guineénsis | . . | White | . | 8. Ev. S. | Guinea | . 1822 |
| híspida | . . . | Pink | . | 7, H. De. S. | Carolina | . 1743 |
| macrophýlla, 2 | Red | . | 5, H. De. T. | N. Amer. | . |
| nána | . . . | Pink | . | 6, H. De. S. | Carolina | . |
| rósea | . . . | Red | . | 7, H. De. S. | N. Amer. | . |
| Pseud-Acácia | White | . | 5, H. De. T. | N. Amer. | . 1640 |
| amórphæfólia, 3 | Wht. red | . | 5, H. De. T. | N. Amer. | . |
| crispá | . . . | White | . | 6, H. De. T. | N. Amer. | . |
| flóre lúteö | . . | Yellow | . | 5, H. De. T. | . |
| inérmis | . . . | White | . | 5, H. De. T. | N. Amer. | . |
| latisíliqua | . . | White | . | 5, H. De. T. | . |
| macrophýlla | . . | White | . | 5, H. De. T. | N. Amer. | . |
| microphýlla | . . | White | . | 5, H. De. T. | N. Amer. | . |
| monstrósa, 4 | Wht. red | . | 5, H. De. T. | N. Amer. | . |
| péndúla, 5 | . | Pink | . | 5, H. De. T. | N. Amer. | . |
| procéra, 6 | . | Wht. red | . | 5, H. De. T. | N. Amer. | . |
| sophoræfólia, 7 | Wht. red | . | 5, H. De. T. | N. Amer. | . |
| spectábilis | . . | White | . | 5, H. De. T. | France | . |
| strictá, 8 | . | Wht. red | . | 5, H. De. T. | N. Amer. | . |
| tortuósa | . . | White | . | 5, H. De. T. | . |
| umbraculífera, 9 | White | . | 5, H. De. T. | N. Amer. | . |
| purpúrea | . . | Purple | . | 7, 8. Ev. T. | | 1810 |
| viscósa | . . | Pa. pur. | . | 7, H. De. T. | N. Amer. | . 1797 |

**ROCAMBOLE**, see *Allium Scorodopràsum.*

**ROCCÉLLA**, *Decandolle.* Altered from the Portuguese *Roccha,* signifying a rock; in allusion to its place of growth. *Linn.* 24, Or. 8, Nat. Or. *Lichenes.* *R. tinctoria* is the *Orchall* of the dyers, so famed for the fine purple colour which it yields—*R. fuciformis, tinctória.*

**RÓCHEA**, *Decandolle.* In honour of M. de la Roche, a botanical writer. *Linn.* 5, Or. 5, Nat. Or. *Crassulaceæ.* This is a very elegant genus of succulent plants when in flower. They require to be treated in a manner similar to that recommended for the genus *Globulea.*

| albiflórá, 1 | . . | White | . | 7, G. Ev. S. | C. G. H. | . 1800 |
| falcáta | . . | Scarlet | . | 7, G. Ev. S. | C. G. H. | . 1795 |
| perfoliáta | . . | Scarlet | . | 7, G. Ev. S. | C. G. H. | . 1700 |
| albiflóra | . . | White | . | 7, G. Ev. S. | C. G. H. | . 1800 |

**ROCKET**, see *Erúca.*

**ROCKET**, see *Hésperis.*

**ROCK-ROSE**, see *Cístus.*

**ROCK-ROSE**, see *Convólvulus Dorýcnium.*

**RODÍGIA**, see *Seríóla.*

**RODRIGUÉZIA**, *Ruiz and Pavon.* In honour of Em. Rodriguez, a Spanish physician and botanist. *Linn.* 20, Or. 1, Nat. Or. *Orchídeæ.* These interesting plants may either be grown in peat, in a manner similar to that recommended for the species of *Stanhopea,* or be fastened on a piece of wood, and treated like the genus *Burlingtonia.* *Synonymes:* 1. *Gomeza recurva.* 2. *Pleurothallis coccinea.*

| Barkéri | . . . | Green | . | 1, S. Epi. | Brazil | . . |
| crispá | . . . | Green | . | 8. Epi. | Brazil | . . |
| laxiflóra | . . | Pa. grn. | . | 8. Epi. | Brazil | . . |
| planifólia | . . | . | . | 8. Epi. | Brazil | . . |
| recúrva, 1 | . . | Yellow | . | 6, 8. Epi. | Brazil | . 1824 |
| secúnda, 2 | . . | Red | . | 7, 8. Epi. | Trinidad | . 1820 |

**ROÉLLA**, *Linn.* In honour of William Roell, professor of anatomy at Amsterdam. *Linn.* 5, Or. 1, Nat. Or. *Campanulaceæ.* Elegant plants when in flower. The soil best adapted for them is a mixture

of sandy loam and peat. They are readily increased by seed; or young cuttings will root freely planted in the same kind of soil, with a glass over them. *Synonymes:* 1. *R. filiformis* 2. *Zygophyllum fruticulosum.*

| ciliáta | . . | Wht. pur. | 7, G. Ev. S. | C. G. H. | . 1774 |
| decúrrens | . . | Blue | . | 8, F. | A. C. G. H. | . 1787 |
| élegáns | . . | Purple | . | 2, 8. Ev. S. | C. G. H. | . 1836 |
| fruticulósá | . | Yellow | . | 7, G. Ev. S. | N. Holl. | . 1820 |
| muscósá | . . | Blue | . | 8, G. Her. P. | C. G. H. | . 1802 |
| squarrósá | . . | White | . | 7, G. Ev. S. | C. G. H. | . 1787 |
| Bergíi, 1 | . . | Blue | . | 8, G. Ev. S. | C. G. H. | . 1816 |

**ROÉPERA**, *A. Jussieu.* In honour of J. Rœper, a writer on the Euphorbias of Germany. *Linn.* 8, Or. 1, Nat. Or. *Zygophyllaceæ.* Ornamental little plants, growing freely in loam, peat, and sand; and readily increasing by young cuttings or seeds. *R. aurantiaca* flowers beautifully when planted out in the open border. *Synonyme:* 1. *Zygophyllum fruticulosum.*

| aurantiáca | . . | Or. yel. | 8, | N. Holl. | . 1837 |
| fruticulósa, 1 | . | Yellow | . | 7, G. Ev. S. | N. Holl. | . 1820 |

**ROLÁNDRA**, *Rottboell.* In honour of Daniel Rolander, a pupil of Linnæus, who visited Surinam. *Linn.* 19, Or. 5, Nat. Or. *Compositæ.* This plant thrives in loam and peat, and is readily increased by cuttings.

| argéntéá | . . | White | . | 7, G. Ev. S. | W Ind. | . 1714 |

**RÖHDEA**, see *Tupístra.*

**RÖMÉRIA**, *Medicus.* In honour of John James Rômer, M.D., professor of botany at Landshut; died 1820. *Linn.* 13, Or. 1, Nat. Or. *Papaveraceæ.* Very pretty annuals. The seed has only to be sown in the open border early in spring. *Synonyme:* 1. *Chelidonium hybridum.*

| hybrídá, 1 | . . | Purple | . | 5, H. | A. Britain | . |
| refráctá | . . | Violet | . | 6, H. | A. Tauria | . 1823 |

**RONDELÉTIA**, *Blume.* In honour of William Rondelet, M.D., a famous natural historian of Montpellier. *Linn.* 5, Or. 1, Nat. Or. *Cinchonaceæ.* Shrubs, well worth cultivating. They should be grown in a mixture of loam, peat, and sand; and cuttings will root freely if planted in sand, under a glass, in heat.

| americáná | . . | White | . | 8, 8. Ev. S. | W. Ind. | . 1752 |
| hirsútá | . . | Yellow | . | 7, 8. Ev. S. | Jamaica | . 1820 |
| hírtá | . . | Pink | . | 7, 8. Ev. S. | Jamaica | . 1776 |
| lævigátá | . . | White | . | 7, 8. Ev. S. | W. Ind. | . 1790 |
| laurifóliá | . . | White | . | 7, 8. Ev. S. | Jamaica | . 1824 |
| odorátá | . . | Red | . | 7, 8. Ev. S. | W. Ind. | . 1836 |
| paniculátá | . . | White | . | 7, 8. Ev. S. | E. Ind. | . 1820 |
| racemósá | . . | White | . | 7, 8. Ev. S. | Jamaica | . 1820 |
| speciósá | . . | Scarlet | . | 8. Ev. S. | Havannah | . 1823 |
| thyrsoídeá | . . | White | . | 7, 8. Ev. S. | Jamaica | . 1819 |
| tomentósá | . . | White | . | 7, 8. Ev. S. | Jamaica | . 1819 |

**ROPÁLA**, *Aublet.* From *Roupala,* its aboriginal name. *Linn.* 4, Or. 1, Nat. Or. *Proteaceæ.* Ornamental trees, growing well in a mixture of loam and peat; and increasing by cuttings, in sand, under a glass, in heat.

| dentátá | . . | Green | . | 6, G. Ev. T. | S. Amer. | . 1802 |
| médiá | . . | . | . | 5, G. Ev. T. | Guiana | . 1823 |
| sessilifóliá | . . | Green | . | G. Ev. T. | Guiana | . 1803 |

**ROPE-GRASS**, see *Réstió.*

**RÓSA**, *Linn.* From the Celtic *rhod,* red; in reference to the prevailing colour of the flowers. *Linn.* 12, Or. 3, Nat. Or. *Rosaceæ.* The name of this genus carries with it a charm as well for the beauty as the unrivalled fragrance of its flowers, and it has justly been the theme of writers, from the remotest antiquity, as a favourite and universal object of culture among all civilised nations. The plants vary in size, and the colours are red, white, purple, yellow, striped, or of almost numberless shades and mixtures, from single to semi-double and double. As it would be impossible to give a standard list of the most improved cultivated kinds, owing to the number of superior sorts raised annually from seed, and many of the varieties being annually lost, going out of repute, or entirely changing their appearance from time and local circumstances; we would on that account recommend those who wish to form a selection of these popular plants, to resort to the latest and best catalogue of Roses now actually in cultivation; such as that of Messrs. Rivers and Son, of Sawbridgeworth, Hertfordshire, which is not only the best as a catalogue, but as containing other particulars worthy of the cultivator's consideration. The rose is propagated by every method capable of being applied to ligneous plants; by seeds for new varieties, for obtaining sweet-briar, and for stocks. The Indian, Chinese, and climbing kinds, by cuttings of the young wood placed in a gentle heat. The Moss, and Provence or Cabbage rose, by layers or suckers; also by cuttings of the large fleshy roots, which being planted, and covered with a little light rich earth, will each throw up one or more shoots. This will be found a good and an expeditious mode of obtaining young plants. Budding is chiefly used to produce standard roses, or to increase the number of kinds upon one plant; it is also resorted to to preserve some of the more tender kinds which languish upon their own roots. *Rosa canina*, or common dog-rose, is the best for budding upon; it is asserted by some cultivators, that all roses flower finer and last longer, by being budded on this stock. The Moss and Provence kinds are well adapted for forcing in winter and spring; the Chinese, and other tender kinds, for decorating the greenhouse nearly throughout the year. To keep a succession of flowers of the first named kinds from Christmas, until their natural season of flowering, a quantity should be introduced into the forcing-house every month from the first of October to the first of March; the dung heat at first should not be more than 55 degrees, but it may be gradually raised to 65 or 70 degrees of Fahrenheit. The fruit of *R. canina* is astringent, and employed in medicine in cases of chronic diarrhœa and other maladies. The various preparations from the flowers are rose water, vinegar of roses, attar, or essence of roses, &c. *Synonymes:* 1. *R. hybrida.* 2. *R. rubiginosa inodora.* 3. *R. canina cæsia.* 4. *R. leucantha.* 5. *R. canina dumetorum.* 6. *R. parvifolia.* 7. *R. Fraseriana.* 8. *R. odorata.* 9. *R. floribunda.* 10. *R. laxa.* 11. *R. Eglanteria.* 12. *R. platyphylla, R. Roxburghii.* 13. *R. scabriuscula.*

| | | | | | |
|---|---|---|---|---|---|
| acicularis | . | Blush | 6, | H. De. S. | Siberia . . 1805 |
| alba | . | White | 6, | H. De. S. | S. Eur. . . 1597 |
| alpina | . | Blush | 6, | H. De. S. | S. Eur. . . 1683 |
| globosa | . | | | H. De. S. | |
| helleborina | . | | | H. De. S. | |
| hispidula | . | | | H. De. S. | |
| lævis | . | | | H. De. S. | |
| lagenaria | . | | | H. De. S. | |
| pilosula | . | | | H. De. S. | |
| pimpinellifolia | . | | | H. De. S. | |
| pyriformis | . | | | H. De. S. | |
| setosa | . | | | H. De. S. | |
| sorbinella | . | | | H. De. S. | |
| speciosa | . | Scarlet | 6, | H. De. S. | Hybrid . . |
| turbinata | . | Dbl. red | 6, | H. De. S. | |
| arvensis | . | White | 7, | H. De. Tr. | Britain . . |
| Andersonii | . | Pa. flesh | 6, | H. De. Tr. | Britain . . |
| Ayrshirea | . | White | 8, | H. De. T. | Scotland . . |
| hybrida, 1 | . | Flesh | | H. De. Tr. | Switzerl. . . |
| Banksia | . | White | 6, | H. De. Cl. | China . . 1807 |
| lutea | . | Pa. buff | 6, | H. De. Cl. | China . . 1807 |
| Borreri, 2 | . | Pa. red | | H. De. S. | Britain . . |
| bracteata | . | White | 7, | H. Ev. S. | China . . 1795 |
| scabriuscula | . | White | | H. Ev. S. | China . . |
| bracteescens | . | Pink | 6, | H. Ev. S. | England . . |
| Brunonii | . | White | | H. De. Cl. | Nepal . . 1822 |
| cdalii, 3 | . | Pink wht. | 7, | H. De. S. | Scotland . . |
| canina | . | Pa. red | 6, | H. De. S. | Britain . . |
| aciphylla | . | Pink | 6, | H. De. S. | Britain . . |
| ægyptiaca | . | Pink | 6, | H. De. S. | Egypt . . |
| ambigua | . | | | H. De. S. | |
| borbonica | . | Purple | 6, | H. De. S. | Bourbon . . |
| fastigiata | . | | | H. De. S. | France . . |
| glaucescens | . | | 6, | H. De. S. | France . . |
| hispida | . | | | H. De. S. | |
| Moratiana | . | | | H. De. S. | France . . |
| microcarpa | . | | | H. De. S. | France . . |
| nitens | . | | 6, | H. De. S. | |
| nuda | . | Pink | 6, | H. De. S. | Britain . . |
| obtusifolia | . | | 6, | H. De. S. | |
| pilosiuscula | . | | | H. De. S. | |
| rubiflora | . | | | H. De. S. | |
| Schottiana | . | | 6, | H. De. S. | Podolia . . |
| squarrosa | . | | | H. De. S. | Germany . . |
| surculosa | . | Pink | 6, | H. De. S. | Britain . . |
| carolina | . | Crimson | 6, | H. De. S. | N. Amer. . 1726 |
| caucasea, 4 | . | Red | 6, | H. De. S. | Iberia . . 1796 |
| centifolia | . | Pink | 6, | H. De. S. | Caucasus . 1596 |
| cristata | . | Pink | 6, | H. De. S. | France . . 1833 |
| muscosa | . | Wht. red | 6, | H. De. S. | |
| muscosa cristata | . | Wht. red | 6, | H. De. S. | France . . |
| pompona | . | Wht. red | 6, | H. De. S. | |
| cinnamomea | . | Pink | 5, | H. De. S. | Europe . . |
| dahurica | . | Red | 6, | H. De. S. | Dahuria . 1824 |
| damascena | . | Pink | 6, | H. De. S. | Syria . . 1573 |
| Dicksoni | . | White | 6, | H. De. S. | Ireland . . |
| Doniana | . | Pink | 6, | H. De. S. | Scotland . . |

[ 273 ]

| | | | | | |
|---|---|---|---|---|---|
| horrida | . | Pink | 6, | H. De. S. | |
| dumetorum, 5 | . | Pink | 6, | H. De. S. | England . . |
| færox | . | Red | 7, | H. De. S. | Caucasus . 1596 |
| nitens | . | Pa. crim. | 6, | H. De. S. | . . 1822 |
| Forsteri | . | Pink | 6, | H. De. S. | Britain . . |
| fraxinifolia | . | Red | 6, | H. De. S. | Newfound. . |
| frutetorum | . | Pink | 6, | H. De. S. | Volhynia . 1818 |
| gallica | . | Pink | 6, | H. De. S. | S. Eur. . 1596 |
| Agatha | . | Purple | | H. De. S. | |
| arvina | . | | | H. De. S. | Silesia . . |
| inaperta | . | Wht. red | | H. De. S. | |
| inermis | . | Purple | | H. De. S. | |
| parvifolia, 6 | . | Purple | 6, | H. De. S. | Europe . . |
| pumila | . | Red | 6, | H. De. S. | Austria . 1810 |
| glutinosa | . | Pa. blush | 6, | H. De. S. | Candia . 1821 |
| gracilis | . | Pa. pink | 6, | H. De. S. | Britain . . |
| grandiflora | . | White | 5, | H. De. S. | Siberia . . 1818 |
| hibernica | . | Blush | 8, | H. De. S. | Ireland . . |
| iberica | . | Pink | 6, | H. De. S. | Iberia . 1820 |
| indica | . | Red | all | H. Ev. S. | China . 1789 |
| Blairii | . | Red | 6, | H. Ev. S. | Hybrid . 1830 |
| caryophyllea | . | | | H. Ev. S. | |
| cruenta | . | | | H. Ev. S. | |
| Fraseriana, 7 | . | Pink | 6, | H. Ev. S. | Hybrid . . |
| longifolia | . | Pink | 6, | H. Ev. S. | China . . |
| nivea | . | Wht. red | 7, | H. Ev. S. | Gardens . 1831 |
| Noisettiana | . | Pa. red | 6, | H. Ev. S. | Hybrid . . |
| ochroleuca | . | Cream | 6, | H. Ev. S. | China . 1824 |
| odoratissima, 8 | . | Pa. pink | 6, | H. Ev. S. | China . 1810 |
| pannosa | . | Pur. rose | | H. Ev. S. | |
| pumila | . | Pink | 7, | H. Ev. S. | China . . |
| ruga | . | Bh. white | 7, | H. De. Cl. | Ital. hyb. . 1827 |
| Smithii | . | Yellow | 6, | H. Ev. S. | Eng. hyb. . 1829 |
| involucrata | . | White | 7, | H. De. S. | E. Ind. . 1818 |
| involuta | . | Pa. red | 6, | H. De. S. | Scotland . . |
| Kamtschatica | . | Red | 7, | H. De. S. | Kamtschat. 1791 |
| Klokii, 9 | . | Pink | 7, | H. De. S. | Tauria . 1819 |
| Lawrenceana | . | Blush | all | H. Ev. S. | China . 1810 |
| Lindleyi, 10 | . | Red | 7, | H. De. S. | N. Amer. . |
| lucida | . | Red | 7, | H. De. S. | N. Amer. . 1724 |
| lutea, 11 | . | Yellow | 6, | H. De. S. | Germany . 1596 |
| flore pleno | . | Yellow | | H. De. S. | Seedling . . |
| Hoggii | . | Yellow | 6, | H. De. S. | Amer. hyb. 1832 |
| punicea | . | Yel. scal. | 6, | H. De. S. | Austria . 1596 |
| subrubra | . | Red yel. | 6, | H. De. S. | |
| lutescens | . | Pa. yel. | 6, | H. De. S. | N. Amer. . 1780 |
| macrophylla | . | Red | | H. De. S. | Gossingthan |
| majalis | . | Pa. red | 5, | H. De. S. | Britain . . |
| micrantha | . | Pa. red | 6, | H. De. S. | Britain . . |
| microcarpa | . | White | 7, | H. De. Cl. | China . 1822 |
| microphylla | . | Blush | 9, | H. Ev. S. | China . 1828 |
| alba | . | White | | H. Ev. S. | |
| mollis | . | Red | 6, | H. De. S. | Caucasus . 1818 |
| Montezumæ | . | Pa. red | 6, | H. De. S. | Mexico . 1825 |
| moschata | . | White | 8, | H. De. Tr. | Barbary . 1596 |
| nivea | . | White | 7, | H. De. S. | Hybrid . 1822 |
| multiflora | . | Red | 6, | H. De. Cl. | China . 1822 |
| Boursaltii | . | Pink | 6, | H. De. Cl. | Hybrid . 1821 |
| carnea | . | Pink | 6, | H. De. Cl. | China . 1804 |
| Grevillæ, 12 | . | Purple | 6, | H. De. Cl. | China . 1821 |
| Russelliana | . | | | H. De. Cl. | |
| myriacantha | . | White | 5, | H. De. S. | France . 1820 |
| nitida | . | Red | 7, | H. De. S. | N. Amer. . 1807 |
| oxyacantha | . | Red | 6, | H. De. S. | Siberia . 1820 |
| flore pleno | . | Blush | 7, | H. De. S. | N. Amer. . |
| parviflora | . | Flesh | 7, | H. De. S. | N. Amer. . 1724 |
| pulchella | . | Red | 6, | H. De. S. | . . 1824 |
| rapa | . | Red | 7, | H. De. S. | N. Amer. . |
| reversa | . | Wht. pnk. | 6, | H. De. S. | Hungary . 1816 |
| rubifolia | . | Pa. red | 6, | H. De. S. | N. Amer. . 1830 |
| fenestralis | . | Flesh | 8, | H. De. Tr. | N. Amer. . |
| rubiginosa | . | Pink | 6, | H. De. S. | Britain . . |
| aculeatissima | . | | | H. De. S. | |
| flexuosa | . | | | H. De. S. | |
| grandiflora | . | | | H. De. S. | |
| Lyonii | . | | | H. De. S. | |
| major | . | Sem. d. | | H. De. S. | |
| nemoralis | . | | | H. De. S. | France . . |
| parvifolia | . | Pa. rose | | H. De. S. | |
| pubera | . | Pink | 6, | H. De. S. | |
| rotundifolia | . | | | H. De. S. | Germany . |
| spinulifolia | . | | | H. De. S. | |
| umbellata | . | Pink | 6, | H. De. S. | Germany . |
| Vaillantiana | . | White | | H. De. S. | |
| rubrifolia | . | Red | 6, | H. De. S. | S. Eur. . 1814 |
| hispidula | . | Red | 6, | H. De. S. | . . 1822 |
| inermis | . | Purple | 6, | H. De. S. | Switzerl. . |
| pinnatifida | . | Purple | 6, | H. De. S. | Switzerl. . |
| Redoutea | . | Pa. red | 6, | H. De. S. | |
| Sabini | . | Red | 6, | H. De. S. | Britain . . |
| gracilis | . | Wht. red | | H. De. S. | Britain . . |
| sanguisorbifolia | . | White | 6, | H. De. S. | |
| sarmentacea | . | Pink | 6, | H. De. S. | Britain . . |
| semperflorens | . | Crimson | all | H. Ev. S. | China . 1789 |
| sempervirens | . | White | 6, | H. Ev. Cl. | S. Eur. . 1629 |
| Clarei | . | Dp. red | 6, | H. Ev. Cl. | Eng. hyb. . |
| Leschenaultiana | . | Violet | 6, | H. Ev. Cl. | Neelgherry |
| Russelliana | . | Blush | 6, | H. De. Cl. | Eng. hyb. . |
| sepium | . | Pink | 6, | H. De. S. | Britain . . |

| | | | | | | | |
|---|---|---|---|---|---|---|---|
| Sherardi | . . | Pink | . 6, H. De. S. | England | |
| alaica | . . | White | . 6, H. De. Cl. | China | . 1759 |
| spinosissima | . . | Wht. red | 6, H. De. S. | Britain | |
| suaveolens | . . | Pink | . 6, H. De. S. | N. Amer. | . 1800 |
| suavis | . . | Purple | . 6, H. De. S. | | . 1818 |
| sulphurea | . . | Yellow | . 7, H. De. S. | Levant | . 1629 |
| sylvestris | . . | Red | . 6, H. De. S. | England | |
| syntyla | . . | Pink | . 6, H. De. Cl. | Britain | |
| taurica | . . | Red | . 6, H. De. S. | | |
| tomentosa | . . | Red wht. | 6, H. De. S. | Britain | |
| scabriuscula, 13 | Pink | . 6, H. De. S. | Britain | |
| turbinata | . . | Red | . 6, H. De. S. | Germany | . 1629 |
| francofurtana | . . | Ro. purp. | 6, H. De. S. | Frankfort | |
| orbessanea | . . | Rose old. | 6, H. De. S. | | |
| villosa | . . | Red | . 6, H. De. S. | Britain | |
| pomifera | . . | Red | . 6, H. De. S. | Europe | |
| resinosa | . . | Red | . 6, H. De. S. | Ireland | |
| Woodsii | . . | Pink | . 5, H. De. S. | N. Amer. | |

ROSCOEA, *Smith.* In honour of William Roscoe, the famous historian of the Medici, and the founder of the Liverpool Botanic Garden. *Linn.* 1, Or. 1, Nat. Or. *Zingiberaceæ.* A genus of pretty plants when in flower. A light turfy loam suits them best, and they are readily propagated by divisions.

| | | | | | |
|---|---|---|---|---|---|
| capitata | . . | Purple | . 7, 8. Her. P. | Nepal | . 1819 |
| elatior | . . | Purple | . 7, 8. Her. P. | Nepal | . 1820 |
| gracilis | . . | Purple | . 7, 8. Her. P. | Nepal | . 1821 |
| purpurea | . . | Purple | . 7, 8. Her. P. | Nepal | . 1820 |
| spicata | . . | Purple | . 7, 8. Her. P. | Nepal | . 1820 |

ROSE, see *Rosa.*

ROSE ACACIA, see *Robinia hispida.*

ROSE BAY, see *Epilobium angustifolium.*

ROSE CAMPION, see *Lychnis.*

ROSELLATE, when leaves are disposed like the petals of a rose.

ROSEMARY, see *Athamanta Libanotis.*

ROSEMARY, see *Cachrys Libanotis.*

ROSEMARY, see *Rosmarinus.*

ROSE OF HEAVEN, see *Lychnis Cæli-rosa.*

ROSE OF JERICHO, see *Anastatica.*

ROSE OF THE WORLD, see *Camellia japonica Rosa-mundi.*

ROSE ROOT, see *Sedum Rhodiola.*

ROSE SNOWBALL-TREE, see *Viburnum Opulus roseum.*

ROSMARINUS, *Linn.* From *ros,* dew, *marinus,* of the sea; on account of its maritime habitat. *Linn.* 2, Or. 1, Nat. Or. *Labiatæ.* A genus of pretty shrubs, requiring to be grown in a rather sheltered dry situation; and cuttings of the ripened wood root readily, if planted in spring. *R. officinalis* is the herb employed in the manufacture of Hungary water; tea made from it is also considered very beneficial to persons troubled with nervous headach, and it is one of the most powerful preparations for stimulating and strengthening the nervous system.

| | | | | |
|---|---|---|---|---|
| officinalis | . . | Purple | . 2, H. Ev. S. | S. Eur. . 1548 |
| fol. argenteis | . | Purple | . 3, H. Ev. S. | S. Eur. . 1548 |
| fol. aureis | . . | Purple | . 2, H. Ev. S. | S. Eur. . 1548 |
| latifolius | . . | Purple | . 2, H. Ev. S. | S. Eur. . 1548 |

ROSMARINUS, see *Sphacele.*

ROSTRARIA, *Trinius.* From *rostrum,* a beak. *Linn.* 3, Or. 2, Nat. Or. *Gramineæ.* A grass of no interest. *Synonyme:* 1. *Bromus dactyloides,* or *Dactylis pungens* —*R. pubescens.*

ROTATE, when the limb of a monopetalous corolla is flat, and the tube very short, it is called rotate, or wheel-shaped.

ROTHIA, *Persoon.* In honour of A. W. Roth, of Bremen, a German botanist. *Linn.* 16, Or. 6, Nat Or. *Leguminosæ.* The seeds of this curious little plant should be sown on a warm border, where the plants are intended to flower. *Synonymes:* 1. *Glycine humifusa, Cleome prostrata.*

| | | | | |
|---|---|---|---|---|
| trifoliata, 1 | . | Sulphur | . 7, H. Tr. A. | |

ROTTBOELLIA, *Linn.* In honour of C. F. Rottboell, a Danish botanist. *Linn.* 3, Or. 2, Nat. Or. *Gramineæ.* Stove grasses, growing in any common soil, and increasing by seeds.

| | | | | |
|---|---|---|---|---|
| exaltata | . . | Apetal | . Grass. E. Ind. | . 1806 |
| perforata | . . | Apetal | . Grass. E. Ind. | . 1822 |

ROTTLERA, *Roxburgh.* In honour of Dr. Rottler, a Danish missionary. *Linn.* 22, Or. 11, Nat. Or. *Euphorbiaceæ.* Uninteresting stove plants, which grow freely in loam and peat; and may be increased by cuttings, under a glass. *Synonyme:* 1. *Croton paniculata*—*R. brasiliensis, paniculata* 1, *tinctoria.*

ROUGH CHERVIL, see *Anthriscus.*

ROUNDISH DELTOID, between orbicular and deltoid.

ROXBURGHIA, *Dryander.* In honour of the late William Roxburgh, M.D., director of the botanic garden, Calcutta. *Linn.* 8, Or. 1, Nat. Or. *Roxburghiaceæ.* Interesting plants, thriving in light turfy loam, and readily increasing by suckers.

| | | | | | |
|---|---|---|---|---|---|
| gloriosoides | . | Pk. yel. | . 7, S. Ev. Cl. | E. Ind. | . 1803 |
| viridiflora | . . | Green | . 8, S. Ev. Cl. | E. Ind. | . 1836 |

ROYAL BAY, see *Laurus nobilis.*

ROYENA, *Linn.* In honour of Adrian von Royen, professor of botany at Leyden. *Linn.* 10, Or. 2, Nat Or. *Ebenaceæ.* These plants require to be grown in a mixture of loam, peat, and sand; and ripened cuttings strike freely in sand, under a glass. *Synonyme:* 1. *R. cuneata.*

| | | | | |
|---|---|---|---|---|
| ambigua | . . | White | . 6, G. Ev. S. | C. G. H. . 1815 |
| angustifolia | . . | White | . 6, G. Ev. S. | C. G. H. . 1789 |
| glabra | . . | White | . 9, G. Ev. S. | C. G. H. . 1721 |
| hirsuta | . . | Purple | . 7, G. Ev. S. | C. G. H. . 1752 |
| latifolia | . . | White | . 6, G. Ev. S. | C. G. H. . 1816 |
| lucida | . . | White | . 5, G. Ev. S. | C. G. H. . 1690 |
| myrtifolia | . | | . 6, G. Ev. S. | C. G. H. . 1800 |
| pallens | . . | | . 6, G. Ev. S. | C. G. H. . 1789 |
| polyandra | . | | . 7, G. Ev. S. | C. G. H. . 1774 |
| pubescens, 1 | . | Wht. grn. | . 7, G. Ev. S. | C. G. H. . 1752 |
| villosa | . . | | . 6, G. Ev. S. | C. G. H. . 1774 |

ROYLEA, *Wallich.* In honour of John Forbes Royle, M.D., late superintendant of the botanic garden at Saharumpur; now Professor of Materia Medica in King's College, London. *Linn.* 14, Or. 1, Nat. Or. *Labiatæ.* An interesting little shrub, growing in any light rich soil. Cuttings root readily in the same kind of soil, with a glass over them. *Synonyme:* 1. *Ballota cinerea.*

| | | | | |
|---|---|---|---|---|
| elegans, 1 | . . | Purple | . 7, G. Ev. S. | Nepal . . 1824 |

RUBEFACIENT, any thing which reddens the skin, and raises slight cutaneous inflammation.

RUBIA, *Tournefort.* From *ruber,* red; in allusion to the colour of the roots. *Linn.* 4, Or. 1, Nat. Or. *Galiaceæ.* Interesting plants. Any common garden soil suits them, and they are easily increased by seeds, or divisions of the roots. The root of *R. tinctorum* is one of the most valuable dyes with which we are acquainted; it is known under the name of *madder,* and is a very important article of commerce. *Synonyme:* 1. *R. galioides.*

| | | | | |
|---|---|---|---|---|
| angustifolia | . . | Pa. yel. | . 7, F. Ev. S. | Spain . . 1772 |
| Bocceni | . . | Grn. wht. | 7, H. Her. P. | Italy . . 1823 |
| cordifolia | . . | White | . 7, H. Her. P. | Siberia . 1783 |
| splendens | . . | Yellow | . 7, F. Ev. S. | Spain . . 1812 |
| tinctorum | . . | Yellow | . 7, H. Her. P. | S. Eur. . 1596 |

*R. fruticosa, F. galioides* 1, *lucida, peregrina.*

RUBUS, *Linn.* From the Celtic *rub,* signifying red; in reference to the colour of the fruit of some of the species. *Linn.* 12, Or. 3, Nat. Or. *Rosaceæ.* An extensive and interesting genus of plants. The shrubby kinds of *Bramble* grow best in a rich loam; and are readily increased by suckers from the root, or by cuttings. The herbaceous species thrive best in peat soil, and are likewise propagated by suckers. The well known and much esteemed Raspberry is the fruit of *Rubus Idæus* and its garden varieties. The fruit of *R. Chamæmorus* is acid, and pleasant to the taste. It is known by the name of Cloudberry, from the plants being found in high situations. The Scottish Highlanders and Laplanders esteem it one of their most grateful and useful fruits, more especially on account of its long duration. *Synonymes:* 1. *R. pistillatus.* 2. *R. pedunculosus.* 3 *R. vulgaris.* 4. *R. flavus.* 5. *R. inermis.* 6. *R. discolor, abruptus.* 7. *R. f. plenus.* 8. *R. f. albus.* 9. *R. paniculatus.* 10. *R. pauciflorus.* 11. *R. echinatus.* 12. *R. villosus vulpinus.* 13. *R. ægopodioides.*

| | | | | | |
|---|---|---|---|---|---|
| aculeus, 1 | . | Rose | . 6, H. Her. P. | N. Amer. | . 1802 |
| affinis | . . | White | . 7, H. De. Tr. | Britain | . |
| bracteosus | . | White | . 8, H. De. Tr. | Britain | . |
| agrestis | . . | White | . 6, H. De. Tr. | Hungary | . 1820 |
| apetalus | . . | Purple | . 7, S. Ev. S. | L. France | . 1823 |
| arcticus | . . | Pink | . 6, H. Her. P. | Britain | . |
| argutus | . . | White | . 6, H. De. Tr. | N. Amer. | . 1822 |
| asper | . . | White | . 5, H. De. S. | Nepal | . 1821 |
| biflorus, 2 | . | | . 5, H. De. S. | Nepal | . 1818 |
| cæsius | . . | White | . 6, H. De. Tr. | Britain | . |
| arvensis | . . | White | . 6, H. De. Tr. | Britain | . |
| fol. variegatis | . | White | . 6, H. De. Tr. | Britain | . |
| grandiflorus | . | White | . 6, H. De. Tr. | Britain | . |
| parvifolius | . . | White | . 6, H. De. Tr. | Britain | . |
| canadensis | . . | White | . 6, H. De. Tr. | N. Amer. | . 1811 |
| canescens | . . | White | . 7, H. De. Tr. | Alp. Eur. | . 1820 |
| carpinifolius | . | White | . 7, H. Ev. Tr. | Britain | . |

[ 274 ]

| | | | | | | |
|---|---|---|---|---|---|---|
| Chamæmorūs . . | White | . 5, | H. Her. | P. | Britain | . |
| cordifolīūs . . | White | . 6, | H. De. | Tr. | Germany | . 1816 |
| corylifolīūs, 3 . | White | . 7, | H. De. | Tr. | Britain | . |
| canūs . . . | White | . 7, | H. De. | Tr. | Britain | . |
| glandulōsūs . | White | . 7, | H. De. | Tr. | Britain | . |
| cuneifolīūs . . | White | . 6, | H. De. | Tr. | N. Amer. | . 1811 |
| dilatāns . . | White | . 7, | H. De. | S. | Nepal | . 1818 |
| diversifolīūs . | White | . 8, | H. De. | Tr. | Britain | . |
| dumetōrūm . . | White | . 8, | H. De. | Tr. | Britain | . |
| Eglantārīā . . | White | . 5, | H. Ev. | S. | N. Holl. | . 1825 |
| ellipticūs, 4 . | White | . F. | De. | Tr. | Nepal | . 1827 |
| fastigiātūs . . | White | . 7, | H. De. | Tr. | Britain | . |
| flexūs . . . | | | H. De. | Tr. | | |
| flagellārīs . . | White | . 6, | H. De. | Tr. | N. Amer. | . 1789 |
| inermīs, 5 . | | | H. De. | Tr. | | |
| folīolōsūs . . | White | . 6, | H. De. | Tr. | Nepal | . 1818 |
| fruticōsūs, 6 . | Pink | . 8, | H. De. | Tr. | Britain | . |
| concŏlŏr . . | Pink | . 7, | H. De. | Tr. | Germany | . |
| dalmāticūs . | Rose | . 7, | H. De. | Tr. | Germany | . |
| fl. rōseō plēnō, 7 | Pink | . 7, | H. De. | Tr. | Britain | . |
| fol. variegātīs | Pink | . 7, | H. De. | Tr. | Britain | . |
| glandulōsūs . | Pink | . 7, | H. De. | Tr. | Germany | . |
| inermīs . . | Pink | . 7, | H. De. | Tr. | Britain | . |
| leucocărpūs, 8 | White | . 7 | H. De. | Tr. | Britain | . |
| pompōnīūs . | Wht. pk. | 7, | H. De. | Tr. | Britain | . |
| taurīcūs . . | Pkish. | . 7, | H. De. | Tr. | | |
| fuscō-āter . . | White | . 8, | H. De. | Tr. | Britain | . |
| glandulōsūs . | White | . 8, | H. De. | Tr. | Germany | . 1816 |
| hirtūs . . . | White | . 8, | H. De. | Tr. | Hungary | . 1816 |
| hispidūs . . | White | . 8, | H. De. | Tr. | Canada | . 1768 |
| horridūs . . | White | . 6, | H. De. | Tr. | Germany | . 1817 |
| Idæūs . . . | White | . 5, | H. De. | S. | Britain | . |
| microphyllūs | White | . 5, | H. De. | S. | Britain | . |
| jamaicēnsīs . | White | . | G. Ev. | S. | Jamaica | . 1822 |
| Köhlĕrī . . . | White | . 8, | H. De. | Tr. | Britain | . |
| lacinīātūs . . | Wht. red | 8, | H. De. | Tr. | | |
| lanuginōsūs . | White | . 6, | H. De. | Tr. | Siberia | . 1820 |
| leucostāchys . | White | . 6, | H. De. | Tr. | Britain | . |
| Linkiānūs, 9 . | White | . 6, | H. De. | Tr. | Europe | . 1821 |
| macrophyllūs . | White | . 6, | H. De. | Tr. | Britain | . |
| Mēnkiī . . . | White | . 6, | H. De. | Tr. | Germany | . 1816 |
| micranthūs, 10 | Red | . 7, | H. De. | Tr. | Nepal | . 1822 |
| moluccanūs . | Red | . | G. Ev. | Tr. | Indies | . 1810 |
| nitidūs . . . | White | . 8, | H. De. | Tr. | Britain | . |
| nutkanūs . . | White | . 6, | H. De. | S. | N. Amer. | . 1826 |
| occidentalīs . | White | . 5, | H. De. | S. | N. Amer. | . 1696 |
| odorātūs . . | White | . 6, | H. De. | S. | N. Amer. | . 1700 |
| pallidūs . . | White | . 8, | H. De. | Tr. | Britain | . |
| parvifolīūs . | Pink | . 8, | F. Ev. | S. | China | . 1818 |
| pinnātūs . . | Pink | . 6, | G. Ev. | S. | Madeira | . 1789 |
| plicātūs . . | White | . 6, | H. De. | Tr. | Britain | . |
| reflexūs . . | Red | . 7, | G. Ev. | Tr. | China | . 1817 |
| rhamnifolīūs . | White | . 9, | H. De. | Tr. | Britain | . |
| roridūs . . . | White | . 8, | G. Ev. | S. | Madagas. | . 1831 |
| rosæfolīūs . . | White | . 8, | G. Ev. | S. | Maurit. | . 1811 |
| coronārīūs . | White | . 8, | G. Ev. | S. | Maurit. | . 1811 |
| rubricaulīs . . | White | . 6, | H. De. | Tr. | Germany | . 1818 |
| rūdīs, 11 . . | | | H. De. | Tr. | Britain | . |
| rugōsūs . . . | Red | . 6, | G. Ev. | S. | S. Amer. | . 1819 |
| sănetūs . . . | Pink | . 6, | H. De. | Tr. | Palestine | . 1823 |
| sanguinolentūs | Red | . | G. Ev. | S. | I. France | . 1824 |
| saxatilīs . . | White | . 6, | H. De. | Tr. | Britain | . |
| Schlechtendāhliī | White | . 6, | H. De. | Tr. | Europe | . 1823 |
| Schleichĕrī . . | White | . 6, | H. De. | Tr. | Germany | . 1818 |
| setōsūs . . . | White | . 6, | H. De. | Tr. | N. Amer. | . 1827 |
| spectābilīs . . | Dk. red | . 5, | H. De. | S. | Columbia | . 1827 |
| Sprengelīī, 12 . | Pink | . 8, | H. De. | Tr. | Germany | . 1823 |
| stellātūs . . | White | . 6, | H. Her. | P. | N. Amer. | . 1834 |
| strigōsūs . . | White | . 6, | H. De. | S. | N. Amer. | . |
| auberčctūs . . | White | . 8, | H. De. | S. | Britain | . |
| tiliæfolīūs . . | White | . 6, | H. De. | Tr. | Germany | . 1819 |
| tomentōsūs . | White | . 8, | H. De. | Tr. | Germany | . 1818 |
| trifidūs, 13 . . | White | . 8, | H. De. | Tr. | Canada | . |
| ulmifolīūs . . | White | . 8, | H. De. | Tr. | Spain | . 1823 |
| villōsūs . . . | White | . 8, | H. De. | S. | N. Amer. | . 1777 |

**RUDBECKĪA, _Linn._** In honour of Olaf Rudbec, professor of botany at Upsal. _Linn._ 19, Or. 3, Nat. Or. _Compositæ._ The perennial species will grow in any common soil, and all, except _R. napifolia_, may be grown in the borders of the flower-garden. They are readily increased by division or seeds. _Synonyme:_ 1. _R. amplexicaulis._

| | | | | | | |
|---|---|---|---|---|---|---|
| amplexifolīa, 1 | Yellow | . 7, | H. | A. | Louisiana | . 1793 |
| aspérrīmā . . | Red wht. | 9, | H. Her. | P. | N. Amer. | . 1832 |
| digitātā . . | Yellow | . 7, | H. Her. | P. | N. Amer. | . 1759 |
| Drummŏndī . | Orange | . 8, | H. Her. | P. | N. Amer. | . 1836 |
| fulgīdā . . | Yellow | . 8, | H. Her. | P. | N. Amer. | . 1760 |
| hīrtā . . . | Yellow | . 8, | H. Her. | P. | N. Amer. | . 1714 |
| lacinīātā . . | Yellow | . 8, | H. Her. | P. | N. Amer. | . 1640 |
| lævigātā . . | Yellow | . 7, | H. Her. | P. | Carolina | . 1812 |
| napifolīā . . | Yellow | . 7, | G. Her. | P. | N. Spain | . 1824 |
| pinnātā . . | Yellow | . 7, | H. Her. | P. | N. Amer. | . 1803 |
| radūlā . . . | Yellow | . 8, | H. | B. | Georgia | . 1825 |
| subtomentōsā . | Yellow | . 8, | H. Her. | P. | N. Amer. | . 1802 |
| trilōbā . . . | Yellow | . 8, | H. Her. | P. | N. Amer. | . 1699 |

**RUDIMENT,** an organ imperfectly developed.

**RUDOLPHĪA, _Willdenow._** In honour of Charles Asmund Rudolph, a botanist of Jena. _Linn._ 17, Or. 4, Nat. Or. _Leguminosæ._ Handsome climbers, growing freely in loam and peat; young cuttings root readily if planted in sand, under a glass, in a moist heat. _Synonyme:_ 1. _Glycine sagittata._

| | | | | | | |
|---|---|---|---|---|---|---|
| dūbīa, 1 . . . | Scarlet | . 8 | Ev. Cl. | Havannah | . 1815 |
| rōseā . . . | Red | . 8. | Ev. Cl. | W. Ind. | . 1826 |

**RUE, see _Ruta_.**

**RUELLĪA, _Linn._** In honour of John Ruelle, of Soissons, botanist and physician to Francis I. _Linn._ 14, Or. 2, Nat. Or. _Acanthaceæ._ A genus of very pretty plants when in flower, and of very easy culture in any light rich soil; cuttings root without difficulty in the same kind of soil, if they have a glass over them. _R. elegans_ must be propagated and treated as other stove annuals.

| | | | | | | |
|---|---|---|---|---|---|---|
| australīs . . | Blue | . 7, 8. | Her. | P. | N. Holl. | . 1824 |
| biflōra . . . | Pa. blue | . 7, | G. Her. | P. | Carolina | . 1765 |
| cĕrnŭā . . . | Blue | . 7, 8. | Ev. | S. | E. Ind. | . 1816 |
| cilīātā . . . | Purple | . 7, 8. | Ev. | S. | E. Ind. | . 1806 |
| ciliatiflōrā . . | Pur. blue | . 8, 8. | Her. | P. | B. Ayres | . 1838 |
| clliōsā . . . | Blue | . 7, 8. | Her. | P. | Georgia | . 1824 |
| clandestīnā . | Blue | . 7, 8. | Her. | P. | Barbadoes | . 1728 |
| dependēns . . | Blue | . 7, 8. | Her. | P. | E. Ind. | . 1816 |
| elēgans . . . | Blue | . 8, 8. | A. | E. Ind. | . 1834 |
| fŏulīā . . . | Blue | . 7, 8. | Ev. | S. | S. Amer. | . |
| formōsā . . | Scarlet | . 8, 8. | Ev. | S. | Brazil | . 1808 |
| fŭlgīdā . . | Scarlet | . 7, 8. | Ev. | S. | W. Ind. | . 1804 |
| hīrtā . . . | Blue | . 7, 8. | Her. | P. | E. Ind. | . 1817 |
| lactēā . . . | Pa. vio. | . 7, | G. Her. | P. | Mexico | . 1796 |
| longifolīā . . | Blue | . 7, 8. | Her. | P. | E. Ind. | . 1820 |
| macrophyllā . | Red | . 8, | Her. | P. | S. Martha. | . 1824 |
| oblongifolīūs . | Rose | . 8, 8. | Ev. | S. | Brazil | . 1830 |
| ocymoidēs . . | Blue | . 7, 8. | Ev. | S. | Mexico | . 1815 |
| ovātā . . . | Drk. blue | . 7, 8. | Her. | P. | Mexico | . 1800 |
| panicŭlātā . . | Purple | . 8, 8. | Her. | P. | W. Ind. | . 1768 |
| patŭlā . . . | Pa. vio. | . 7, 8. | Ev. | S. | E. Ind. | . 1774 |
| pictā . . . | Blue | . 6, 8. | Ev. | S. | Domingo | . 1826 |
| pubēscēns . . | Drk. blue | . 7, 8. | Her. | P. | C. G. H. | . 1823 |
| rubricaulīs . . | Blue | . 7, 8. | Her. | P. | Mexico | . 1832 |
| salicifolīā . . | Blue | . 7, 8. | Her. | P. | E. Ind. | . 1830 |
| strēpēns . . | Pa. blue | . 7, | F. Her. | P. | N. Amer. | . 1726 |
| tetragōnā . . | Blue | . 7, 8. | Her. | P. | Brazil | . 1824 |
| tuberōsā . . | Blue | . 7, 8. | Tu. | P. | Jamaica | . 1752 |
| undulātā . . | | . 8. | Her. | P. | E. Ind. | . 1824 |
| violacēā . . | Violet | . 7, 8. | Her. | P. | Guiana | . 1820 |

**RUVESCENT,** rather rusty.
**RUFOUS,** reddish, orange-coloured, rusty.
**RUGOSE,** rough, coarsely wrinkled.
**RUGOSITIES,** protuberances.
**RUGULOSE,** finely wrinkled.

**RUIZĪA, _Cavanilles._** In honour of Don Hippolito Ruiz, a traveller, and, in conjunction with Pavon, author of " Flora Peruviana et Chilensis." _Linn._ 16, Or. 8, Nat. Or. _Sterculiaceæ._ Desirable shrubs, growing in a mixture of loam, peat, and sand; and cuttings root freely if planted in the same kind of soil, under a glass, in heat.

| | | | | | | |
|---|---|---|---|---|---|---|
| lobāta . . . | White | . 8. | Ev. | S. | Bourbon | . 1816 |
| variabīlīs . . | White | . 5, 8. | Ev. | S. | Bourbon | . 1792 |

**RULINGĪA, _R. Brown._** In honour of J. P. Ruling, author of an essay on the Natural Orders. _Linn._ 5, Or. 5, Nat. Or. _Sterculiaceæ._ The plants belonging to this genus are not worth cultivating, except in general collections. A mixture of loam, peat, and sand, suits them; and ripened cuttings will root in either sand or soil, if planted under a glass.

| | | | | | | |
|---|---|---|---|---|---|---|
| cistifolīa . . | White | . | G. Ev. | S. | N. Holl. | . 1824 |
| corylifolīa . . | White | . | G. Ev. | S. | N. Holl. | . 1824 |
| hermannīæfolīa | White | . | G. Ev. | S. | N. Holl. | . 1818 |
| pannōsā . . | White | . | G. Ev. | S. | N. Holl. | . 1819 |

**RUMEX, _Linn._** Rumo, to suck; in allusion to the practice among the Romans of sucking the leaves to allay thirst. _Linn._ 6, Or. 3, Nat. Or. _Polygonaceæ._ All the species of Duck grow in any common soil. The perennial species are easily increased by seeds or divisions of the roots. The annuals by sowing the seed in the open ground. They are mostly all weeds. _R. acetosa_ contains pure oxalic acid. _Synonymes:_ 1. _R. fimbriatus._ 2. _sagittatus._ 3. _tuberosus._ 4. _caudatus._ 5. _cuneifolius._ 6. _tuberosus._

| | | | | | | |
|---|---|---|---|---|---|---|
| Acetosēllā . . | Green | . 6, H. | P. | Britain | . . |
| Acetōsā . . | Green | . 6, H. Her. | P. | Britain | . . |
| aculeātūs . . | Green | . 6, H. Her. | P. | Candia | . . |
| acūtūs . . . | Green | . 7, F. Fu. | P. | Britain | . . |
| alpīnūs . . . | Green | . 6, H. Her. | P. | France | . 1597 |

| | | | | | |
|---|---|---|---|---|---|
| britannicūs | . | Green | . | 6, H. Fu. P. N. Amer. | |
| Brŏwnīī, 1 | . | Green | . | 6, G. Ta. P. N. Holl. | 1823 |
| bucephalophŏrūs | Gr. m | Green | . | 6, H. A. Italy | 1683 |
| frutescens | . | Green | . | 6, H. Ev. S. Tris. d'As. | 1823 |
| graminifŏliūs | . | Green | . | 7, H. Her. P. Russia | 1890 |
| hastulātūs | . | Green | . | 6, F. Her. P. Chile | 1823 |
| lacerūs | . | Green | . | 6, H. A. Egypt | 1810 |
| Lunārīā | . | Green | . | 6, G. Ev. S. Canaries | 1690 |
| Patiēntīā | . | Green | . | 7, F. Fu. P. Italy | 1573 |
| purpūrēūs | . | Green | . | 7, H. Fu. P. Switzerl. | 1819 |
| pyrenāicūs | . | Green | . | 6, H. Her. P. Pyrenees | 1812 |
| sanguinēūs | . | Green | . | 6, H. Fu. P. England | |
| sarcorhizūs, 4 | . | Green | . | 7, G. Tu. P. C. G. H. | 1824 |
| scutātūs | . | Green | . | 6, H. Ev. Cr. France | 1596 |
| triangulārīs, 6 | . | Green | . | 6, H. Tu. P. | 1817 |
| tuberŏsūs | . | Green | . | 7, H. Tu. P. Italy | 1752 |
| vesicārīūs | . | Green | . | 7, H. A. Africa | 1656 |

abyssinīcūs, Acetosēllā, aegyptīācūs, amplexicaūlis, aquātīcūs, arifŏliūs, brasiliēnsis, Burchēllī 2, condylŏdēs, confērtūs, crispātūlūs, crispūs, cristātūs, dentātūs, divaricātūs, domēstīcūs, fimbriātūs, gigantēus, glomerātūs, hastaefŏliūs, heterophȳllūs, Hydrolāpāhūm, intermēdīūs, lancifŏliūs, laevigātūs, longifŏliūs, luxūriāns, maritīmūs, maximūs, montevidēnsis, multīfidūs, Nemolāpāthūm, nemorōsūs, nepalēnsis 3, obtusifŏliūs, palūstris, persicarioīdēs, polygonifŏliūs, pulchēr, reticulātūs, rōsēūs, salicifŏliūs, spatulātūs 5, strictūs, sylvēstris, tingitānūs, ucrānicūs, uncātūs, venōsūs, verticillārīs.

ROMĪĀ, *Hoffman. Rumia*, the name of the goddess who presided over suckling. *Linn.* 5, Or. 2, Nat. Or. *Umbelliferae*. An uninteresting plant, growing in any common soil, and readily increasing by divisions or by seeds.

| | | | |
|---|---|---|---|
| taurīca | . | . . White | . 7, H. Her. P. Crimea . . 1819 |

RUNCINATE, a term applied to the lobes of leaves; a leaf is said to be runcinate when it is irregularly lobed, the lobes gradually diminishing to the base, and hooked back.

RUNNERS, procumbent shoots, which root at their extremity.

RUPESTRIS, growing on rocks.

ROPPĪĀ, *Linn.* In honour of H. B. Ruppius, a German botanist. *Linn.* 4, Or. 3, Nat. Or. *Fluviales*. This species is found in ditches in various parts of Britain.

| | | | |
|---|---|---|---|
| maritīmā | . | . . Green | . 7, H. Aq. P. Britain . . |

RUPTURE-WORT, see *Herniārīā*.

ROSCŪS, *Linn.*; formerly *Bruscus*. From *beus*, box, and *kelen*, holly; the Celtic for box-holly. *Linn.* 22, Or. 13, Nat. Or. *Liliaceae*. Ornamental plants. The greenhouse species will grow well in any rich soil, and are readily increased by dividing the roots. The hardy kinds are very suitable for the front of shrubberies; any common soil suits them, and they are easily increased by suckers.

| | | | | | |
|---|---|---|---|---|---|
| aculeātūs | . . | . | Green | . 5, H. Ev. S. England | . |
| laxūs | . . | . | Green | . 4, H. Ev. S. Portugal | |
| rotundifŏliūs | . | . | Green | . 3, H. Ev. S. | |
| androgȳnūs | . | . | Grn. wht. | 4, G. Ev. Cl. Canaries | 1713 |
| hypoglōssūm | . | . | Pa. yel. | 6, H. Ev. S. Italy | 1596 |
| hypophȳllūm | . | . | Green | . 6, H. Ev. S. Italy | 1640 |
| trifoliātūs | . | . | Green | . H. Ev. S. Zante | |
| racemōsūs | . | . | Grn. yel. | 4, H. Ev. S. Portugal | 1713 |

| | | | | | |
|---|---|---|---|---|---|
| reticulātūs | . . | . | Green | . 4, G. Ev. Cl. C. G. H. | . 1816 |
| volūbilis | . . | . | Green | . 4, G. Ev. Cl. C. G. H. | . 1816 |

RUSH, see *Juncūs*.

RUSH, see *Chondrilla juncēa*.

RUSH BROOM, see *Viminārīā*.

RUSH NUT, see *Cypērūs esculēntūs*.

RUSSELĪĀ, *Jacquin.* In honour of Alexander Russel, M.D., F.R.S., author of a Natural History of Aleppo, 1756. *Linn.* 14, Or. 2, Nat. Or. *Scrophulariaceae*. These plants are very showy when in flower, and are on that account well deserving of a place in every collection. A light rich soil is best adapted to them; and cuttings root freely under a glass, in heat.

| | | | |
|---|---|---|---|
| floribūnds | . . . | Red | . 8. Ev. S. Mexico . 1824 |
| juncēa | . . . | Scarlet | . 7, S. Ev. S. Mexico . 1833 |
| multiflōra | . . . | Red | . 7, S. Ev. S. S. Amer. . 1812 |
| ternifŏlīā | . . . | Red | . 8. Ev. S. Mexico . 1818 |

ROTĀ, *Linn.* From the Greek *rue*, from *ruo*, to flow; probably in reference to some reputed qualities of the plants; hence the English word Rue. *Linn.* 8, Or. 1, Nat. Or. *Rutaceae*. The species of Rue are all of the simplest culture. Any light rich soil suits them, and they are readily increased by cuttings placed under a hand-glass; or by seeds, which are produced in abundance by many of the species. Synonyms: 1. *R. chalepensis.*

| | | | |
|---|---|---|---|
| albiflōrā | . . . | White | . 7, F. Ev. S. Nepal . 1823 |
| gravēolēns | . . | Yel. grn. | . 8, H. Ev. S. S. Eur. . 1562 |

*angustifŏliā* 1, *bracteōsā*, *corsīcā*, *divaricātā*, *macrophȳllā*, *montānā*, *pinnātā*.

RUYSCHĪĀ, *Jacquin.* In honour of Fred. Ruysch, M.D., who published the "Hortus Amstelodamensis," a posthumous work of John Commelin: he died 1731. *Linn.* 5, Or. 1, Nat. Or. *Marcgraaviaceae*. This very desirable shrub will succeed well in a mixture of loam and vegetable mould; and ripened cuttings will root freely in sand, under a glass, in heat. In Guiana and the Caribbee islands, it is a parasitical under-shrub, rooting on trees in moist woods, similarly to the Ivy with us.

| | | | |
|---|---|---|---|
| clusiaefŏliā | . . . | Purple | . 8. Ev. S. W. Ind. . 1823 |

RYANĪĀ, *Decandolle.* In honour of John Ryan, M.D., F.R.S., a correspondent of Vahl. *Linn.* 13, Or. 1, Nat. Or. *Flacourtiaceae*. This is described as a very beautiful stove plant, thriving in peat and loam; and it is propagated by ripened cuttings, planted in sand, under a glass, in heat.

| | | | |
|---|---|---|---|
| speciōsā | . . . | Cream | . 8, S. Ev. S. Trinidad . 1823 |

RYE, see *Secālē*.

RYE GRASS, see *Lōliūm*.

RYTIDOPHȲLLŪM, *Martius.* From *rytis*, a wrinkle, and *phyllon*, a leaf; the surface of the upper side of the foliage is wrinkled. *Linn.* 14, Or. 2, Nat. Or. *Gesneraceae*. An ornamental under-shrub, nearly related to Gesnera; which see, for culture, &c.

| | | | |
|---|---|---|---|
| auriculātūm | . . | Yel. red. | 11, S. Ev. S. Brazil . 1836 |

RYTIPHLAĪ, *Agardh.* From *rytis*, a wrinkle, and *phleo*, to abound in. *Linn.* 24, Or. 7, Nat. Or. *Algae*. A genus of sea-weeds—*R. complanātā*, *tinctōriā*.

---

# S.

SĀBĀL, *Adanson.* Not explained. *Linn.* 6, Or. 3, Nat. Or. *Palmaceae*. This noble genus of Palms grows best in a light loamy soil. Suckers are occasionally produced, by which the species may be multiplied. Synonymes: *Chamaerops acaulis, Corypha minor, Rhaphis acaulis.*

| | | | | | |
|---|---|---|---|---|---|
| Adansŏnī, 1 | . . | . | Green | . 7, Palm. Florida | . 1810 |
| Blackbūrnīānā | . | . | Green | . Palm. Tropics | . |
| graminifŏliā | . | . | Green | . Palm. S. Amer. | . 1825 |
| Palmēttō | . . | . | Green | . Palm. Georgia | . 1825 |
| umbraculifērā | . | . | Green | . Palm. Jamaica | . 1825 |

SABBATĪĀ, *Adanson.* In honour of L. Sabbati, a celebrated Italian botanist. *Linn.* 5, Or. 1, Nat. Or. *Gentianaceae*. The species of this genus are very handsome when in flower, and are, on that account, deserving of a place in every collection. The seeds, as soon as ripe, should be sown thinly in pots, or on a shady border, in peat soil; if grown in pots, they should be placed in shallow pans of water, as the species are natives of marshes or bogs. Synonyms: 1. *Chironia gracilis.*

| | | | |
|---|---|---|---|
| angulārīs | . . . | Purple | . 7, H. B. N. Amer. . 1826 |
| calycōsā | . . . | Dk. red | . 7, H. B. N. Amer. . 1812 |
| chlorōidēs | . . . | Red | . 7, H. B. N. Amer. . 1817 |
| grācĭlis, 1 | . . . | Rose | . 7, H. B. N. Amer. . |
| paniculātā | . . . | White | . 5, H. Her. P. N. Amer. . 1817 |

SACCATE, having a pouch.

SACCHĀRŪM, *Linn.* From *Soukar*, its Arabic name. *Linn.* 3, Or. 2, Nat. Or. *Gramineae*. This genus is of very great importance, on account of its containing the sugar cane, *S. officinarum*. The species are all of very simple culture, in a light rich moist soil, with a good heat; and are increased by suckers, or cuttings of the stem will throw out shoots at their joints.

| | | | | | |
|---|---|---|---|---|---|
| caudátūm . . . | Apetal | | Grass. | W. Ind. . | 1816 |
| contráctūm . . . | Apetal | 7, | Grass. | Trinidad | 1823 |
| dūbiūm . . . | Apetal | 7, | Grass. | Trinidad | 1826 |
| mexicānūm . . . | Apetal | 7, | Grass. | Mexico | 1820 |
| Múnjá . . . | Apetal | | Grass. | E. Ind. | 1805 |
| officinārūm . . . | Apetal | | Grass. | India . | 1597 |
| polystáchyūm . . . | Apetal | 7, | Grass. | Trinidad | 1823 |
| procērūm . . . | Apetal | | Grass. | E. Ind. | 1822 |
| sinénsē . . . | Apetal | | Grass. | China | 1822 |
| violáceūm . . . | Apetal | 7, | Grass. | W. Ind. . | 1824 |

SACCOLÀBIŪM, *Blume.* From *saccus*, a bag, and *labium*, a lip; in allusion to the bagged labellum of all the species. *Linn.* 20, Or. 1, Nat. Or. *Orchidaceæ.* This genus contains some of the most interesting as well as beautiful species of the tribe. Their culture &c. is the same as that recommended for the genus *Vanda.* Synonyme: 1. *Sarcanthus guttatus.*

| | | | | | |
|---|---|---|---|---|---|
| bifidūm . . . | Pk. yel. | 12, S. | Epi. | Manilla | 1837 |
| calceolárē . . | Yel. brn. | 8, S. | Epi. | E. Ind. | 1837 |
| comprèsūm . . | Cr. wht. | 8. | Epi. | Manilla | |
| densiflórūm . . | | 8. | Epi. | Manilla | |
| denticulátūm . | | 8. | Epi. | Sylhet | 1837 |
| gemmátūm . . | Purple | 5, | | Sylhet | 1837 |
| guttátūm, 1 . | Red wht. | 4, | | E. Ind. | 1820 |
| micránthūm . | Orange | 6, | | Sylhet | 1837 |
| pállēns . . . | Lilac | | | Pondooah | 1837 |
| papillōsūm . . | Wht. spot. | | | Malabar | 1837 |

SACRED BEAN, see *Nelùmbīūm.*
SAFFRON, see *Cròcūs satīvūs.*
SAGE, see *Sālviā.*
SAGÌNĀ, *Linn.* From *sagina*, fatness; in allusion to its presumed nourishing qualities for sheep. *Linn.* 4, Or. 3, Nat. Or. *Alsinaceæ.* Hardy annual weeds, growing in any soil. Synonymes: 1. *Mænchia cerastoides.* 2. *M. erecta.*

| | | | | | |
|---|---|---|---|---|---|
| filifórmis . . . | White | . 6, H. | A. | Pyrenees | 1824 |

*apétálā, cerastoídēs* 1, *erèctā* 2, *maritīmā, procûmbēns, P. plénā.*

SAGITTĀRĪĀ, *Linn.* From *sagitta*, an arrow; because of the resemblance to the head of that weapon in the leaves of some species. *Linn.* 21, Or. 9, Nat. Or. *Alismaceæ.* Aquatics, requiring a loamy soil; and readily increasing by divisions. The stove and greenhouse kinds may be planted in a tub or large pot, with a little soil at the bottom, and filled up with water; a coating of pebbles may be laid on the soil to prevent the water from disturbing it, and rendering it muddy. Synonyme: 1. *hastuta.*

| | | | | | |
|---|---|---|---|---|---|
| acutifólia . . . | White | 6, S. | Aq. P. | America | 1816 |
| angu-tifólia . . | White | 7, S. | Aq. P. | Essequibo | 1827 |
| Doniānā, 1 . . | White | 7, F. | Aq. P. | Nepal | 1820 |
| falcátá . . . | White | 7, H. | Aq. P. | Carolina | 1812 |
| graminéá . . . | White | 7, F. | Aq. P. | Carolina | 1812 |
| hastátá . . . | White | 7, F. | Aq. P. | N. Amer. | 1818 |
| heterophýllá . . | White | 7, F. | Aq. P. | N. Amer. | 1822 |
| lancifólia . . . | White | 6, G. | Aq. P. | W Ind. | 1787 |
| latifólia . . . | White | 7, H. | Aq. P. | N. Amer. | 1819 |
| fl. plénó . . . | White | 7, H. | Aq. P. | N. Amer. | |
| nátāns . . . | White | 7, H. | Aq. P. | Carolina | 1812 |
| obtúsá . . . | White | 7, F. | Aq. P. | N. Amer. | 1820 |
| obtusifólia . . | White | 7, S. | Aq. P. | China | 1804 |
| rígidá . . . | White | 6, H. | Aq. P. | N. Amer. | 1806 |
| sagittifólia . . | White | 7, H. | Aq. P. | England | |
| fl. plénó . . | White | 7, H. | Aq. P. | Brit. gard. | |
| sinénsis . . . | White | 10, G. | Aq. P. | China | 1812 |

SAGITTATE, shaped like an arrow-head.
SAGO PALM, see *Rháphis flabellifórmis.*
SÀGŪS, *Rumphius.* From *sagu*, the Malay name of various Palms. *Linn.* 21, Or. 6, Nat. Or. *Palmaceæ.* A fine genus of plants, well deserving of a place in every collection. They succeed best in sandy loam, and a strong moist heat. Sago is chiefly obtained from *S. farinifera.* Synonymes: 1. *Raphia pedunculata.* 2. *Metroxylon Sagus.* 3. *R. vinifera, S. Palma-Pinus.*

| | | | | | |
|---|---|---|---|---|---|
| pedunculátā, 1 . | | | Palm. | Madagas. | 1820 |
| Rúffia . . . | Green | | Palm. | Madagas. | 1820 |
| Rúmphii, 2 . . | Green | | Palm. | E. Ind. | 1800 |
| vinifèrá, 3 . . | Green | | Palm. | Guiana | 1820 |

ST. ANDREW'S CROSS, see *Ascýrūm Crūx Andréä.*
ST. BARNABY'S THISTLE, see *Centaūrēā solstitiālis.*
SAINTFOIN, see *Onobrýchis.*
ST. JOHN'S BREAD, see *Ceratónia silīquā.*
ST. JOHN'S WORT, see *Hypéricūm.*
ST. MARTIN'S FLOWER, see *Alstroemèriā Flos-Mārtīni.*
ST. PETER'S WORT, see *Symphóriā.*
ST. PETER'S WORT, see *Hypéricūm Ascýrōn.*
SALĀCĪĀ, *Linn.* From *Salacia*, in heathen mythology,

the wife of Neptune. *Linn.* 3, Or. 1, Nat. Or. *Celastraceæ.* Plants of no great beauty; succeeding in loam and peat, and increasing by ripened cuttings planted in sand, under a glass. The fruit of *S pyriformis* is eatable. It is about the size of a Bergamot Pear, and of a sweet, rich, flavour. Synonymes: 1. *Tonsella pyriformis.* 2. *T. scandens.*

| | | | | | |
|---|---|---|---|---|---|
| pyrifórmis, 1 . | Green | 8, S. | Ev. Cl. | Guiana . | 1825 |
| scándēns, 2 . | Green | 8, S. | Ev. Cl. | Guiana . | 1824 |

SALEP, see *Tàccā pinnatīfīdā.*
SALICŌRNĪĀ, *Linn.* From *sal*, salt, and *cornu*, a horn. *Linn.* 1, Or. 1, Nat. Or. *Chenopodiaceæ.* These plants will grow in any common soil, and are readily increased by divisions. The plants being natives of the sea-shore, they will thrive better if a little salt be occasionally sprinkled on the surface of the soil. Soda is yielded in great quantities by the species of *Salicornia.*

| | | | | | |
|---|---|---|---|---|---|
| arábicá . . . | Apetal | 6, G. | Ev. S. | Arabia | 1758 |
| fruticósá . . . | Apetal | 8, H. | Ev. S. | Britain | |
| herbáceá . . . | Apetal | 8, H. | A. | Britain | |
| perénnās . . . | Apetal | 8, F. | Her. P. | Siberia | 1823 |
| procûmbēns . . | Apetal | 8, H. | Tr. A. | England | |
| radicāns . . . | Apetal | 9, H. | Ev. | Cr. Britain | |

SALISBÙRĪĀ, *Smith.* In honour of Richard Anthony Salisbury, a distinguished English botanist. *Linn.* 21, Or. 9, Nat. Or. *Taxaceæ.* The Maiden-hair Tree is well worth growing, if only on account of its singular foliage. The male and female flowers being produced on two different trees, the readiest way of obtaining fruit would be to graft or bud both sorts on the same tree, or by growing both trees near each other. Common garden soil suits it, and it is readily increased by layers. The fruit has never been perfected in this country, but in China the tree is extensively cultivated for the purpose of procuring it.

| | | | | | |
|---|---|---|---|---|---|
| adiantifólia . . | Apetal | 4, H. | De. T. | Japan . | 1754 |

SÀLIX, *Linn.* From *sal*, near, and *lis*, water, Celtic; in allusion to its place of growth; or from *salire*, to leap; because of the rapidity of its growth. *Linn.* 22, Or. 2, Nat. Or. *Salicaceæ.* An extensive genus of well known, useful, and ornamental trees and shrubs. They all delight to grow in swampy places, and are increased by cuttings; though some of the more rare alpine kinds root with difficulty. Many of the species of willow are extensively grown for the manufacture of basket-rods. The best sorts for cultivating for hoops are *S. capreæ* and *S. viminalis.* The branches of some of the species are used as stakes, poles, handles to rakes, hoes, and a great variety of economical purposes. Loudon says, "In the north of Europe the bark of *S. alba* is used for tanning leather, and for dyeing yarn of a cinnamon colour, and the leaves and young shoots are given to cattle in a green state, or dried like the twigs of the birch and laid up for winter fodder."—*Arb. Brit.* The leaves of *S. herbacea*, soaked in water, are employed in Iceland for tanning leather. Synonymes: 1. *S. violacea.* 2. *S. cærulea.* 3. *S. uliginosa.* 4. *S. annularis.* 5. *S. Napoleona.* 6. *S. præcox.* 7. *S. argentea.* 8. *S. adscendens, parvifolia.* 9. *S. incubacea.* 10. *S. prostrata.* 11. *S. repens.* 12. *S. malifolia.* 13. *S. serrulata.* 14. *S. riparia.* 15. *S. arbutifolia.* 16. *S. phylicifolia.* 17. *S. Fluggeana.* 18. *S. Hoppeana.*

| | | | | | |
|---|---|---|---|---|---|
| acumínátā . . | Apetal | 4, H. | De. T. | Britain | |
| acutifólia, 1 . | Apetal | 4, H. | De. T. | Casp. Sea | 1823 |
| alternoídēs . . | Apetal | 4, H. | De. T. | Switzerl. | 1824 |
| albá . . . | Apetal | 4, H. | De. T. | Britain | |
| cærúlēā, 2 . | Apetal | 5, H. | De. T. | Britain | |
| albésēns . . | Apetal | 4, H. | De. T. | Switzerl. | 1824 |
| ambíguā . . | Apetal | 4, H. | De. T. | Britain | |
| Ammanīnā . . | Apetal | 5, H. | De. T. | Austria | 1821 |
| amygdalínā . . | Apetal | 4, H. | De. T. | Britain | |
| Andersonīnā . . | Apetal | 4, H. | De. T. | Scotland | |
| angustátá . . | Apetal | 3, H. | De. T. | Pennsylv. | 1811 |
| angustifólia . . | Apetal | 4, H. | De. T. | Caspian | 1823 |
| Ansonīnā . . | Apetal | 3, H. | De. T. | Switzerl. | 1827 |
| aquáticá . . . | Apetal | 4, H. | De. T. | Britain . | |
| arenáriá . . . | Apetal | 6, H. | De. T. | Scotland | |
| atropúrpúréā . . | Apetal | 4, H. | De. T. | Switzerl. | 1824 |
| atrovírēns . . | Apetal | 5, H. | De. T. | Switzerl. | 1824 |
| aurítá, 3 . . | Apetal | 4, H. | De. T. | England | |
| austrális . . | Apetal | 4, H. | De. T. | Switzerl. | 1824 |
| babylónicá . . | Apetal | 5, H. | De. T. | Levant | 1730 |
| crispá, 4 . | Apetal | 5, H. | De. T. | | |
| Napoleónā, 5 | Apetal | | H. De. T. | | |
| vulgáris . . | Apetal | 6, H. | De. T. | England | |

| | | | | |
|---|---|---|---|---|
| berberifòlĭă . . | Apetal | 5, H. De. Tr. | Dauria | 1824 |
| betulifòlĭă . . | Apetal | 5, H. De. S. | Scotland | |
| bicòlŏr . . | Apetal | 4, H. De. S. | Britain | |
| Bonplandiānă | Apetal | G. De. T. | Mexico | |
| Borreriānă | Apetal | 5, H. De. S. | Scotland | |
| cæsĭă . . | Apetal | 5, H. De. S. Eur. | | 1824 |
| cándĭdă . . | Apetal | 4, H. De. T. | N. Amer. | 1811 |
| canéscĕns . . | Apetal | 4, H. De. S. | | |
| cápreă . . | Apetal | 4, H. De. T. | Britain | |
| carinàtĭ . . | Apetal | 4, H. De. S. | Scotland | |
| carpinifòlĭă | Apetal | 4, H. De. S. | Germany | 1824 |
| ceraaifòlĭă . . | Apetal | 4, H. De. S. | Switzerl. | 1824 |
| chrysánthŏs . | Apetal | 4, H. De. S. | Norway | |
| cinéreă . . | Apetal | 4, H. Ev. T. | Britain | |
| confòrmĭs . . | Apetal | 4, H. De. S. | N. Amer. | |
| conìferă . . | Apetal | 6, H. De. S. | N. Amer. | 1820 |
| cordàtă . . | Apetal | 4, H. De. S. | N. Amer. | 1811 |
| cordifòlĭă . . | Apetal | H. De. Tr. | N. Amer. | 1811 |
| coriàceă . . | Apetal | 4, H. De. S. | Switzerl. | 1825 |
| corùscăns . . | Apetal | 4, H. De. S. | Germany | 1818 |
| cotinifòlĭă . . | Apetal | 3, H. De. S. | Britain | |
| craasifòlĭă . . | Apetal | 3, H. De. S. | | |
| crĭspă . . | Apetal | 3, H. De. S. | | |
| Croweānă . . | Apetal | 4, H. De. S. | Scotland | |
| cydoniæfòlĭă . | Apetal | 4, H. De. S. | Switzerl. | 1824 |
| damascénă . . | Apetal | 4, H. De. S. | Scotland | |
| daphnoìdĕs, 6 . | Apetal | 4, H. De. S. | Switzerl. | 1820 |
| Davalliānă | Apetal | 5, H. De. S. | Scotland | |
| decìpĭĕns . . | Apetal | 5, H. De. T. | England | |
| decúmbĕns . . | Apetal | 4, H. De. Tr. | Switzerl. | 1823 |
| Dickeonlànă | Apetal | 4, H. De. S. | Scotland | |
| discŏlŏr . . | Apetal | 4, H. De. S. | N. Amer. | 1811 |
| Doniànă . . | Apetal | 4, H. De. S. | Scotland | |
| dùră . . | Apetal | 4, H. De. T. | | |
| elæagnoìdĕs . . | Apetal | 5, H. De. S. | Europe | 1824 |
| fagifòlĭă . . | Apetal | H. De. S. | Croatia | |
| falcàtă . . | Apetal | 4, H. De. S. | N. Amer. | 1811 |
| ferruginĕă . . | Apetal | 4, H. De. S. | Britain | |
| finmárchĭcă . . | Apetal | 4, H. De. T. | Sweden | 1825 |
| fírmă . . | Apetal | 4, H. De. S. | | |
| foliolòsă . . | Apetal | 4, H. De. S. | Lapland | 1818 |
| Forbesiānă . . | Apetal | 4, H. De. S. | Britain | |
| Forbyānă . . | Apetal | 4, H. De. S. | England | |
| Forsteriānă | Apetal | 4, H. De. T. | Scotland | |
| frágĭlĭs . . | Apetal | 4, H. De. T. | Britain | |
| fúscă . . | Apetal | 5, H. De. Tr. | Britain | |
|   argéntĕă, 7 . . | Apetal | 5, H. De. Tr. | England | |
|   fœtĭdă, 8 . . | Apetal | 5, H. De. Tr. | Britain | |
|   incubàceă, 9 . . | Apetal | 5, H. De. S. | England | |
|   prostràtă, 10 . | Apetal | 5, H. De. Tr. | Britain | |
|   répĕns . . | Apetal | 5, H. De. Tr. | Britain | |
|   vulgàrĭs . . | Apetal | 5, H. De. S. | Britain | |
| fuscàtă . . | Apetal | 5, H. De. S. | N. Amer. | 1811 |
| geminàtă . . | Apetal | 3, H. De. T. | | |
| glaùcă . . | Apetal | 7, H. De. S. | Scotland | |
| grìsĕă . . | Apetal | 4, H. De. S. | Pennaylv. | 1820 |
| grisonénsĭs . . | Apetal | 4, H. De. S. | Grisons | 1824 |
| grisophýllă . . | Apetal | 4, H. De. S. | Switzerl. | 1824 |
| hastàtă . . | Apetal | 5, H. De. T. | Lapland | 1780 |
|   arbùsculă . . | Apetal | 4, H. De. S. | Switzerl. | 1824 |
|   malifòlĭă, 12 . | Apetal | H. De. S. | Britain | |
|   serrulàtă, 13 . . | Apetal | 5, H. De. S. | Lapland | 1810 |
| Hélĭx . . | Apetal | 3, H. De. T. | Britain | |
| helvétĭcă . . | Apetal | 3, H. De. S. | Switzerl. | 1824 |
| herbàceă . . | Apetal | 6, H. De. S. | Britain | |
| hírtă . . | Apetal | 4, H. De. T. | England | |
| Hoffmánnĭă . . | Apetal | 4, H. De. T. | England | |
| holosericĕă . . | Apetal | 4, H. De. S. | Switzerl. | |
| Houstoniànă . . | Apetal | 4, H. De. S. | Virginia | |
| Humboldtiānă | Apetal | F. Ev. T. | Peru | 1823 |
| húmĭlĭs . . | Apetal | 4, H. De. S. | | 1820 |
| incànă, 14 . . | Apetal | 4, H. De. S. | Austria | 1821 |
| incanéscĕns . . | Apetal | 3, H. De. S. | Switzerl. | 1823 |
| Jacquìnĭi . . | Apetal | 4, H. De. S. | Austria | 1818 |
| Kitaibelliànă . | Apetal | 4, H. De. Tr. | Carpath. | 1823 |
| lacústrĭs . . | Apetal | 3, H. De. S. | Switzerl. | 1824 |
| Lambertiànă . . | Apetal | 4, H. De. S. | England | |
| lanàtă . . | Apetal | 5, H. De. S. | Scotland | |
| Lappònŭm . . | Apetal | 5, H. De. Tr. | Lapland | 1812 |
| latifòlĭă . . | Apetal | 3, H. De. S. | | |
| laurìnă . . | Apetal | 4, H. De. T. | England | |
| laxiflòră . . | Apetal | 3, H. De. S. | Scotland | |
| leucophýllă . . | Apetal | 5, H. De. S. | Europe | 1824 |
| lineàrĭs . . | Apetal | 4, H. De. S. | Switzerl. | 1820 |
| lìvĭdă . . | Apetal | 5, H. De. S. | Lapland | 1820 |
| lùcĭdă . . | Apetal | 5, H. De. S. | N. Amer. | 1811 |
| Lyònĭi . . | Apetal | H. De. S. | Switzerl. | |
| macrostipulàceă | Apetal | 5, H. De. S. | Switzerl. | 1824 |
| Meyeriànă . . | Apetal | 4, H. De. T. | Sweden | 1822 |
| Micheliànă | Apetal | 4, H. De. S. | | |
| mollissĭmă . . | Apetal | 4, H. De. T. | Germany | |
| monspeliénsĭs . | Apetal | 5, H. De. T. | Montpelier | 1825 |
| montànă . . | Apetal | 4, H. De. T. | Switzerl. | |
| Muhlenbergiànă | Apetal | 4, H. De. S. | N. Amer. | 1811 |
| mutábĭlĭs . . | Apetal | 3, H. De. S. | Switzerl. | 1824 |
| myricoìdĕs . . | Apetal | 4, H. De. S. | N. Amer. | 1811 |
| Myrsinìtĕs, 15 . | Apetal | 5, H. De. S. | Scotland | |
| myrtilloìdĕs . . | Apetal | 5, H. De. S. | Sweden | 1772 |
| nìgră . . | Apetal | 5, H. De. T. | N. Amer. | 1811 |
| nigrĭcăns . . | Apetal | 4, H. De. S. | England | |
| nìtĕns . . | Apetal | 4, H. De. S. | Scotland | |
| obovàtă . . | Apetal | 5, H. De. Tr. | N. Amer. | |
| obtusifòlĭă . . | Apetal | 4, H. De. S. | Lapland | 1818 |
| oleifòlĭă . . | Apetal | 4, H. De. S. | Britain | |
| pállĭdă . . | Apetal | 4, H. De. S. | Switzerl. | 1823 |
| pannòsă . . | Apetal | 4, H. De. T. | Switzerl. | 1824 |
| pátĕns . . | Apetal | 4, H. De. S. | | |
| pedicellàrĭs . . | Apetal | 3, H. De. S. | N. Amer. | 1811 |
| pennsylvánĭcă . | Apetal | 4, H. De. S. | N. Amer. | 1825 |
| pentándră . . | Apetal | 4, H. De. T. | Britain | |
| petiolàrĭs . . | Apetal | 4, H. De. T. | Scotland | |
| petræă . . | Apetal | 4, H. De. S. | Britain | |
| phyllireifòlĭă . | Apetal | 4, H. De. S. | Scotland | |
| planifòlĭă . . | Apetal | H. De. S. | Labrador | 1811 |
| polàrĭs . . | Apetal | 4, H. De. S. | Lapland | 1820 |
| pomeránĭcă . . | Apetal | 5, H. De. T. | Pomerania | 1822 |
| Pontederānă . . | Apetal | 4, H. De. S. | Switzerl. | 1821 |
| prinoìdĕs . . | Apetal | 3, H. De. S. | N. Amer. | 1811 |
| procúmbĕns . . | Apetal | 6, H. De. Tr. | Scotland | |
| propínquă . . | Apetal | H. De. S. | Britain | |
| protæfòlĭă . . | Apetal | 4, H. De. S. | Switzerl. | 1820 |
| prunifòlĭă . . | Apetal | 5, H. De. S. | Scotland | |
| purpúreă . . | Apetal | 3, H. De. S. | England | |
| Purshiànă . . | Apetal | 5, H. De. T. | N. Amer. | |
| pyrenàĭcă . . | Apetal | 5, H. De. Tr. | Pyrenees | 1823 |
| rádĭcăns, 16 . . | Apetal | 5, H. De. Tr. | Britain | |
| ramifúsă . . | Apetal | 4, H. De. S. | Britain | |
| recurvàtă . . | Apetal | 4, H. De. S. | N. Amer. | 1811 |
| refléxă . . | Apetal | 3, H. De. S. | | |
| reticulàtă . . | Apetal | 6, H. De. S. | Britain | |
| retùsă . . | Apetal | 4, H. De. Tr. | S. Eur. | 1673 |
| rìgĭdă . . | Apetal | 4, H. De. T. | N. Amer. | 1811 |
| rivulàrĭs . . | Apetal | 5, H. De. S. | Switzerl. | 1824 |
| rosmarinifòlĭă . | Apetal | 4, H. De. S. | Britain | |
| rotundàtă . . | Apetal | 4, H. De. S. | Switzerl. | 1824 |
| rùbră . . | Apetal | 5, H. De. S. | England | |
| rupéstrĭs . . | Apetal | 4, H. De. Tr. | Scotland | |
| Russelliānă . . | Apetal | 4, H. De. T. | England | |
| salviæfòlĭă, 17 . | Apetal | H. De. S. | | |
| Schleicheriānă . | Apetal | 4, H. De. S. | Switzerl. | 1824 |
| Schraderiānă . | Apetal | 5, H. De. S. | Germany | 1820 |
| serìcĕă . . | Apetal | 4, H. De. S. | Switzerl. | 1820 |
| serpyllifòlĭă . . | Apetal | 4, H. De. Tr. | Switzerl. | 1818 |
| silesìacă . . | Apetal | 5, H. De. S. | Silesia | 1816 |
| Smithiānă . . | Apetal | 5, H. De. T. | England | |
| sórdĭdă . . | Apetal | 4, H. De. S. | Switzerl. | 1824 |
| spatulàtă . . | Apetal | 5, H. De. S. | Germany | 1818 |
| sphacelàtă . . | Apetal | 4, H. De. S. | Scotland | |
| stipulàrĭs . . | Apetal | 3, H. De. S. | England | |
| strépĭdă . . | Apetal | 4, H. De. S. | Switzerl. | 1820 |
| Stuartiànă . . | Apetal | 7, H. De. S. | Scotland | |
| subalpìnă . . | Apetal | 4, H. De. S. | Switzerl. | 1820 |
| tenuifòlĭă . . | Apetal | 4, H. De. S. | Britain | |
| tenuìŏr . . | Apetal | 5, H. De. S. | Scotland | |
| tetrápĭs . . | Apetal | 3, H. De. S. | Scotland | |
| tetraspérmă . . | Apetal | F. De. T. | E. Ind. | 1796 |
| triándră . . | Apetal | 7, H. De. T. | Britain | |
|   Hoppeànă, 18 . | Apetal | 5, H. De. T. | Austria | 1820 |
| trístĭs . . | Apetal | 4, H. De. S. | N. Amer. | 1765 |
| ulnifòlĭă . . | Apetal | 4, H. De. S. | Switzerl. | 1821 |
| undulàtă . . | Apetal | 4, H. De. S. | England | |
|   lanceolàtă . . | Apetal | 4, H. De. T. | England | |
| Uvă úrsi . . | Apetal | 4, H. De. S. | Labrador | 1811 |
| vaccinifòlĭă . . | Apetal | 4, H. De. S. | Scotland | |
| vaudénsĭs . . | Apetal | 3, H. De. S. | Switzerl. | 1824 |
| venulòsă . . | Apetal | 4, H. Ev. S. | Scotland | |
| versicŏlŏr . . | Apetal | 5, H. De. S. | Switzerl. | |
| Villarsiānă . . | Apetal | 4, H. De. T. | France | 1818 |
| viminàlĭs . . | Apetal | 5, H. De. T. | England | |
| viréscĕns . . | Apetal | 4, H. De. S. | Switzerl. | |
| virgàtă . . | Apetal | 5, H. De. S. | | |
| vitellìnă . . | Apetal | 3, H. De. T. | England | |
| Waldsteiniànă . | Apetal | 4, H. De. S. | Alp. Tyrol | |
| Weigeliānă . . | Apetal | 5, H. De. S. | Britain | |
| Willdenoviānă . | Apetal | 4, H. De. S. | | |
| Woolgariànă . | Apetal | 4, H. De. S. | England | |
| Wulfeniānă . . | Apetal | 5, H. De. S. | Carinthia | 1818 |

SALMĬĂ, *Decandolle.* In honour of Prince Charles, of Salm Dyck, in Holland, an enthusiastic cultivator of plants. Linn. 19, Or. 1, Nat. Or. *Compositæ.* A genus of pretty stove twiners, succeeding best in a light rich soil; and readily increasing by cuttings of the young wood planted in sand, under a glass, in heat. *Synonymes: 1. Bidens scandens, Hopkirkia scandens.*

| | | | | |
|---|---|---|---|---|
| hirsùtă . . | Yellow | 8, S. Ev. Tw. | Jamaica | 1823 |
| scándĕns, 1 . | Yellow | 6, S. Ev. Tw. | Vera Cruz | 1820 |

SALPĬGLÓSSĬS, *Ruiz and Pavon.* From *salpinx*, a tube, and *glossa*, a tongue; alluding to the tongue-like style in the mouth of the corolla. Linn. 14, Or. 2, Nat. Or. *Scrophulariaceæ.* This genus of very showy plants should be in every ornamental collection. For culture, &c., see *Schizanthus.* Synonymes: 1. *S. atropurpurea.* 2. *S. Barclayana.* 3. *S. picta.* 4. *S. straminea.*

[ 278 ]

| sinuata, 1 | Purple | 8, H. | B. | Chile | 1824 |
| Barclayana, 2 | Bro. yel. | 7, G. | B. | Eng. hyb. | |
| picta, 3 | Varieg. | 5, H. | A. | Chile | 1890 |
| straminea, 4 | Red wht. | 7, G. | A. | Chile | 1824 |

SALSIFY, see *Tragopōgŏn porrifōliŭs.*

SALSŎLĂ, *Linn.* From *salsus,* salt; in allusion to the saline properties of the species. Linn. 5, Or. 2, Nat. Or. *Chenopodiaceæ.* A genus of not much beauty. For culture and propagation, see *Salicornia.* Synonymes: 1. *Anabasis foliosa.* 2. *S. spicata.*

| brachiata | Brown | 7, H. | A. | Tauria | 1818 |
| crassa | Wht. yel. | 7, H. | A. | Caucasus | 1820 |
| foliosa, 1 | Pink | 7, H. | A. | Siberia | 1820 |
| glauca, 2 | Yellow | 7, F. Ev. | S. | Caucasus | 1821 |
| Kali | Flesh | 7, H. | A. | Britain | |
| laniflora | Yellow | 7, H. | A. | Siberia | 1797 |
| microphylla | Red | 7, H. | A. | Spain | 1759 |
| oppositifolia | | 7, F. Ev. | S. | Sicily | 1823 |
| rigida | Green | 7, F. Ev. | S. | Siberia | 1824 |
| rosacea | Pink | 7, H. | A. | Asia | 1759 |
| sativa | Pink | 7, H. | A. | Spain | 1783 |
| Soda | White | 7, H. | A. | S Eur. | 1683 |
| tamariscina | Yellow | 7, H. | A. | Tauria | 1820 |
| Tragus | White | 7, H. | A. | S. Eur. | 1817 |
| vermiculata | Green | 7, H. | A. | Siberia | 1759 |
| verrucosa | Green | 7, H. | A. | Siberia | 1817 |

SALTATORIA, having a leaping or dancing motion.

SALT-TREE, see *Halimodĕndrŏn.*

SALTWORT, see *Salsŏlă.*

SĀLVĬĂ, *Linn.* From *salvo,* to save; in allusion to the healing qualities of the sage. Linn. 2, Or. 1, Nat. Or. *Labiatæ.* This is a very extensive genus, consisting chiefly of extremely showy flowering plants, well worthy of cultivation. They are easily grown in a rich light soil. The shrubby kinds increase freely by cuttings of the young wood, under a glass; those of the stove species must be placed in heat; the herbaceous kinds must be multiplied by division of the roots. The seeds of the annual and biennial kinds simply require to be sown in the open ground where they are intended to bloom. The common sage, *Salvia officinalis,* is a well known culinary herb. Synonymes: 1. *S. patula, pyramidalis.* 2. *S. colorata.* 3. *S. polymorpha.* 4. *S. multifida, laciniata.* 5. *S. rosea.* 6. *S. prismatica.* 7. *S. Boosiana.* 8. *S. trichostemoides.* 9. *S. pilantha.* 10. *S. abyssinica, applanata.* 11. *S. betonicæfolia, hastata.* 12. *S. lineatifolia* 13. *S. hæmatodes, Tenorii, variegata.* 14. *S. foliosa.* 15. *S. vulnerariæfolia, Hablitziana.* 16. *S. Sinuiana.* 17. *S. elongata, bullata.* 18. *S. dominica.* 19. *S. campestris, mollis.* 20. *S. ægyptiaca.* 21. *S. nemorosa, valentina.* 22. *S. coarctata.* 23. *S. oblongata.* 24. *S. affinis, amplexicaulis, gigantea.* 25. *S. truncata, Spielmanni.*

| æthiopis | White | 5, H. | B. | Austria | 1570 |
| africana | Violet | 5, G. Ev. | S. | C. G. H. | 1731 |
| amarissima | Blue | 3, G. Her. | P. | Mexico | 1803 |
| amethystina | Blue | 3, S. Ev. | S. | Columbia | 1817 |
| angustifolia | Blue | 5, G. Her. | P. | Mexico | 1816 |
| argentea, 1 | Yellow | 6, H. Her. | P. | Crete | 1759 |
| aurea, 2 | Blue | 7, G. Ev. | S. | C. G. H. | 1731 |
| aurita | Li. yel. | 5, G. Ev. | S. | C. G. H. | 1795 |
| austriaca | Cream | 6, H. Her. | P. | Austria | 1776 |
| azurea | Blue | 8, H. Her. | P. | N. Amer. | 1806 |
| Barrelieri | Blue | 4, H. Her. | P. | Spain | 1821 |
| bicolor | Red wht. | 6, H. Her. | P. | Barbary | 1793 |
| bracteata | Purple | 8, H. Her. | P. | Russia | 1821 |
| byzantina | Blue | 7, H. | B. | Turkey | 1825 |
| cana | Blue | 7, G. Ev. | S. | S. Amer. | 1812 |
| calycina | Pink | 8, H. Ev. | S. | Greece | 1823 |
| canariensis | Purple | 7, G. Ev. | S. | Canaries | 1697 |
| candidissima | White | | H. Her. | P. | Armenia | 1820 |
| canescens | Purple | 7, H. Her. | P. | Caucasus | |
| ceratophylla | Yellow | 7, H. | B. | Persia | 1699 |
| ceratophylloides | Yellow | 7, H. | B. | Egypt | 1771 |
| chamædryoides | Blue | 7, G. Ev. | S. | Mexico | 1795 |
| clandestina, 3 | Blue | 6, H. Her. | P. | Italy | 1739 |
|   multifida, 4 | Blue | 4, H. Her. | P. | Europe | 1822 |
| coccinea, 5 | Scarlet | 7, G. Her. | P. | S. Amer. | 1772 |
| compressa | White | 5, H. Her. | P. | East | 1822 |
| confertiflora | Red | 9, S. Ev. | S. | Rio Jan. | 1838 |
| crassifolia | Blue | 6, H. Her. | P. | S. Eur. | 1804 |
| cretica | Violet | 6, G. Ev. | S. | Crete | 1760 |
| dentata | White | 12, G. Ev. | S. | C. G. H. | 1774 |
| desertorum | Blue | 10, G. Her. | P. | Siberia | 1829 |
| diasmus | White | 7, | | | Syria | 1778 |
| dolichostachya | Scarlet | 8, G. Ev. | S. | Mexico | 1820 |
| erui | Blue | 7, H. | A. | Europe | 1817 |
| formosa | Scarlet | 6, G. Ev. | S. | Peru | 1783 |
| Forskŏhlii | Black | 7, H. Her. | P. | Levant | 1800 |
| fulgens | Scarlet | 7, G. Ev. | S. | Mexico | 1829 |

| glutinosa | Yellow | 7, H. Her. | P. | Germany | 1769 |
| Grahami | Pur. blue | 9, G. Her. | P. | Mexico | 1829 |
| grandiflora | Blue | 7, H. Her. | P. | S. Eur. | 1816 |
| hirsuta | Blue | 5, H. | A. | | 1801 |
| hispanica, 6 | Blue | 7, H. | A. | Spain | 1739 |
| Horminum | Purple | 6, H. | A. | S. Eur. | 1596 |
|   rubra | Red | 7, H. | A. | S. Eur. | 1596 |
|   violacea | Purple | 6, H. | A. | S. Eur. | 1596 |
| indica | Blue | 6, H. Her. | P. | India | 1731 |
| interrupta | White | 7, H. Ev. | S. | Barbary | 1790 |
| involucrata | Red | 8, S. Ev. | S. | Mexico | 1824 |
| lamiifolia, 7 | Blue | 7, G. Ev. | S. | S. Amer. | 1821 |
| lanceolata, 8 | Blue | 7, H. | A. | W. Ind. | 1818 |
| leucantha | White | | G. Her. | P. | Mexico | 1825 |
| limbata | | | H. Her. | P. | Russia | 1838 |
| Linkiana, 9 | Blue | 7, H. Her. | P. | Levant | 1823 |
| lusitanica | Blue | 6, H. Her. | P. | Spain | 1819 |
| lyrata | Purph. | 6, H. Her. | P. | N. Amer. | 1728 |
| mexicana | Scarlet | 6, S. Her. | P. | Mexico | 1724 |
| micrantha | Blue | 5, S. | A. | Cuba | 1823 |
| Moorcroftiana | Pa. blue | 7, H. Her. | P. | India | |
| napifolia | Dk. blue | 16, H. Her. | P. | Italy | 1776 |
| nepetifolia | Blue | 7, H. | A. | Europe | 1823 |
| nilotica, 10 | Blue | 7, H. | A. | Egypt | 1780 |
| nobilis | Blue | 6, G. Her. | P. | Abyssinia | 1784 |
| nubicola | Yellow | 10, F. Her. | P. | Nepal | 1823 |
| nutans, 11 | Violet | 7, H. Her. | P. | E. Eur. | 1780 |
| occidentalis | White | 7, S. Ev. | S. | Jamaica | 1824 |
| odorata | White | 7, G. Ev. | S. | Bagdad | 1804 |
| officinalis | Blue | 6, H. Ev. | S. | S. Eur. | 1597 |
|   tenuior | Blue | 6, H. Ev. | S. | Spain | 1597 |
|   variegata | Blue | 6, H. Ev. | S. | S. Eur. | 1597 |
| paniculata | Violet | 7, G. Ev. | S. | C. G. H. | 1758 |
| patens | Blue | 9, F. Her. | P. | Mexico | 1838 |
| phlomoides | Blue | 5, H. | B. | Spain | 1805 |
| pinnata | Purple | 7, H. | B. | Levant | 1731 |
| polystachys, 12 | Blue | 10, G. Her. | P. | Mexico | 1829 |
| pomifera | Blue | 7, H. Ev. | S. | Candia | 1699 |
| pratensis, 13 | Violet | 5, H. Her. | P. | England | |
| Pseudo-coccinea | Scarlet | 7, H. Her. | P. | S. Amer. | 1797 |
| pulchella | Scarlet | 12, G. Her. | P. | S. Amer. | 1821 |
| purpurea | Purple | 6, G. Her. | P. | Mexico | 1825 |
| pyrenaica | Blue | 7, H. Her. | P. | Pyrenees | 1824 |
| rhombifolia, 14 | Blue | all | S. | A. | Peru | 1827 |
| rugosa | Wht. red | 9, G. Her. | P. | C. G. H. | 1775 |
| runcinata | Blue | 7, G. Ev. | S. | C. G. H. | 1774 |
| scabiosæfolia, 15 | White | 8, H. De. | S. | Siberia | 1818 |
| scabra | Blue | 6, G. Ev. | S. | C. G. H. | 1774 |
| Sclarea, 16 | Wht. pur. | 7, H. | B. | S. Eur. | 1562 |
| sclareoides, 17 | Violet | 7, H. Her. | P. | S. Eur. | 1804 |
| scorodonifolia | White | 7, H. Ev. | S. | | 1825 |
| serotina, 18 | Blue | 6, H. Her. | P. | Ohio | 1803 |
| Sibthorpii, 19 | Blue | 6, H. Her. | P. | Europe | 1812 |
| spinosa, 20 | White | 6, H. | B. | Egypt | 1789 |
| splendens | Scarlet | 12, G. Her. | P. | Mexico | 1822 |
| strictiflora | Brn. red | 12, S. Ev. | S. | Peru | 1831 |
| sylvestris, 21 | Pur. vio. | 8, H. Her. | P. | Germany | 1759 |
| syriaca | White | 7, H. Her. | P. | Levant | 1759 |
| tiliæfolia | Blue | 5, S. Her. | P. | Caraccas | 1793 |
| tingitana, 22 | White | 7, H. | B. | Barbary | 1796 |
| triloba | Red | 6, H. De. | S. | S. Eur. | 1596 |
| tubiflora | Scarlet | 6, S. Her. | P. | Mexico | 1820 |
| urticifolia | Blue | 6, H. Her. | P. | N. Amer. | 1799 |
| verbascifolia | White | 5, H. Her. | P. | Iberia | 1823 |
| verbenaca | Violet | 5, H. | P. | Britain | |
|   oblongifolia, 23 | Blue | 9, H. | A. | Europe | 1820 |
| versicolor | Bl wht. | 7, H. Her. | P. | Spain | 1822 |
| verticillata | Blue | 8, H. Her. | P. | Germany | 1628 |
| virgata, 24 | White | 9, H. Her. | P. | Armenia | 1758 |
| viridis, 25 | Blue | 7, H. | A. | Italy | 1759 |
| viscosa | Violet | 5, H. Her. | P. | Italy | 1778 |

SALVĬNĬĂ, *Guettard.* In honour of Antonio Maria Salvini, a Greek professor at Florence. Linn. 24, Or. 4, Nat. Or. *Salviniaceæ.* A hardy aquatic, growing in light loamy soil; and increasing by divisions.

| natans | | 7, H. Aq. | P. | Italy | 1818 |

SAMBŪCŬS, *Linn.* From *sambuca,* a musical instrument, which is supposed to have been made of elder-wood. Linn. 5, Or. 3, Nat. Or. *Caprifoliaceæ.* The species of Elder are all of the simplest culture, in any soil or situation. The shrubby species are increased by cuttings; the herbaceous species by divisions. The wood of the Elder is remarkable for its hardness; and various kinds of medicine are obtained from the different species, but more especially from *S. nigra.* Synonymes: 1. *S. nigra variegata.* 2. *S. aurea.* 3. *S. laciniata.* 4. *S. nigra albida.* 5. *S. viridis.*

| canadensis | White | 7, H. De. | S. | N. Amer. | 1761 |
| chinensis | White | 9, H. Her. | P. | China | 1823 |
| Ebulus | Wht. red | 6, H. Her. | P. | Britain | |
| humilis | Wht. pk. | 6, H. Her. | P. | | |
| nigra | White | 6, H. De. | S. | Britain | |
|   fol. argentea, 1 | White | 6, H. De. | T. | Britain | |

| fol. lutèis, 2 | . White | . 6, H. De. T. Britain | . . |
| aciniàtà, 8. | . White | . 6, H. De. T. Britain | . . |
| leucocàrpa, 4 | . White | . 6, H. De. T. Britain | . . |
| monstróaà | . White | . 6, H. De. T. Britain | . . |
| pulverulèntà | . White | . 6, H. De. T. Britain | . . |
| rotundifòlià | . White | . 6, H. De. T. Britain | . . |
| viréscens, 5. | . White | . 6, H. De. T. Britain | . . |
| pūbèns . | . White | H. De. N. Amer. | . 1812 |
| racemòsà | . Orn. yel. 5, H. De. S. S. Eur. | . 1596 |
| flavéscens | . Yel. grn. 5, H. De. S. S. Eur. | . 1596 |
| purpūrèà | . Purple . 5, H. De. S. S. Eur. | . 1596 |

SĂMŌLŬS, *Linn.* From *san*, salutary, and *mos*, a pig; which, in Celtic, signifies pigs'-food. *Linn.* 5, Or. 1, Nat. Or. *Primulaceæ*. Pretty little plants, growing freely in common soil, planted in a rather moist situation, and increasing by divisions. *Synonyme*: 1. *Campanula porosa.*

| campanuloidès, 1 | . . | . 7, G. Her. P. C. G. H. | . 1816 |
| littoràlis | . . White | . 6, G. Her. P. N. S. W. | . 1806 |
| Valerándi | . . White | . 7, H. Her. P. Britain | . . |

SĂMPHIRE, see *Crithmŭm.*
SĂMŸDĂ, *Linn.* The Greek name of the *Birch*; applied to this genus because of its resemblance. *Linn.* 10, Or. 1, Nat. Or. *Samydaceæ*. Ornamental plants, thriving well in a mixture of loam and peat; and cuttings root readily if planted in a pot of sand, under a glass, in a little heat. *Synonymes*: 1. *S. viridiflora.* 2. *S. pubescens.*

| decūrrèns | . . Green | . 8. Ev. S. Brasil | . 1820 |
| glabràtà | . . White | . 8, S. Ev. S. W. Ind. | . 1800 |
| macrophýllà, 1 | . White | . 8, S. Ev. S. E. Ind. | . 1820 |
| nitidà | . . Green | . 8. S. Ev. S. W. Ind. | . 1793 |
| rò-sà, 2. | . . Pink | . 6, S. Ev. S. W. Ind. | . 1793 |
| serrulàtà | . . White | . 7, S. Ev. S. W. Ind. | . 1793 |
| villòsà | . . White | . 8, S. Ev. S. W. Ind. | . 1820 |

SĂNDAL-TREE, see *Sandŏrĭcŭm.*
SĂNDAL-WOOD, see *Sãntàlŭm.*
SĂNDBOX-TREE, see *Hūrà.*
SĂNDŎRĬCŬM, *Cavanilles.* From *santoor*, the Malay name of the tree. *Linn.* 10, Or. 1, Nat. Or. *Meliaceæ*. This tree thrives well in a mixture of loam, peat, and sand; and ripened cuttings root in sand, under a glass, in heat.

| indicūm | . . . White | . 8. Ev. T. E. Ind. | . 1820 |

SĂND-WOOD, see *Bremontièrà Ammŏxẏlŏn.*
SĂNDWORT, see *Arenărià.*
SĂNGUINĂRĬĂ, *Linn.* From *sanguis*, blood; all the parts of the plant yield a red juice when cut or broken. *Linn.* 13, Or. 1, Nat. Or. *Papaveraceæ*. Dwarf plants, serving well to ornament the front of the flower-border, in a light sandy loam or peat soil; and they are readily increased by dividing the roots, or by seeds.

| canadénsis | . . White . 3, H. Tu. P. N. Amer. | . 1680 |
| grandiflòrà | . . White . 5, H. Tu. P. N. Amer. | . |

SĂNGUISŎRBĂ, *Linn.* From *sanguis*, blood, and *sorbeo*, to absorb; *S. officinalis* was formerly supposed to be a powerful vulnerary. *Linn.* 4, Or. 1, Nat. Or. *Rosaceæ*. All the species of *Burnet* are of the easiest culture in any common soil; and are readily increased by divisions of the roots, or by seeds. *Synonyme*: 1. *S. rubra.*

| Andersòni | . . Pink | . 7, H. Her. P. Siberia | . . |
| canadénsis | . . White | . 8, H. Her. P. Canada | . 1633 |
| cārnèà, 1 | . . Red | . 7, H. Her. P. Siberia | . 1823 |
| mauritánicà | . . Pink | . 7, H. Her. P. Algiers | . 1810 |
| mèdià | . . Flesh | . 8, H. Her. P. Canada | . 1785 |
| neglèctà | . . White | . 7, H. Her. P. Europe | . 1800 |
| officinàlis | . . Purple | . 7, H. Her. P. Britain | . . |
| auriculàtà | . . Pink | . 7, H. Her. P. Sicily | . . |
| tenuifòlià | . . Pink | . 7, H. Her. P. Dahuria | . 1820 |

SĂNICLE, see *Sanĭcŭlà.*
SĂNĬCŬLĂ, *Tournefort.* From *sano*, to heal; supposed healing effects of *Sanicula europæa*. *Linn.* 5, Or. 2, Nat. Or. *Umbelliferæ.* Mere weeds, multiplied by divisions of the roots—*S. canadénsis, europæà, marilándicà.*
SĂNSEVIÈRĂ, *Thunberg.* In honour of M. Sansevier, a Swedish botanist. *Linn.* 6, Or. 1, Nat. Or. *Liliaceæ*. Interesting plants, growing well in sandy loam; and increasing by suckers. The stove species should be very sparingly watered when dormant. *Synonyme*: 1. *S. sessiliflora.*

| cārnèà, 1 | . . Flesh | . 4, H. Her. P. China | . 1792 |
| ensifòlià | . . White . | . S. Her. P. E. Ind. | . |
| fulvocinctà | . . White | . 8. Her. P. Brasil | . 1820 |
| glaūcà | . . White . | . 8. Her. P. | . |

| grandicéspis | . . White . | . 8. Her. P. | . |
| guineénsis | . . Green . | . 9, 8. Her. P. Guinea | . 1690 |
| lætevirèns | . . Wht. grn. | . 8. Her. P. | . |
| lanugiuòsà | . . | . 8. Her. P. E. Ind. | . |
| longiflòrà | . . White . | . 7, 8. Her. P. Africa | . 1824 |
| polyphýllà | . . White . | . 8. Her. P. | . |
| pŭmilà | . . White . | . 8. Her. P. C. G. H. | . 1796 |
| spicàtà | . . White . | . 8. Her. P. E. Ind. | . 1790 |
| stenophýllà | . . | . 8. Her. P. | . 1818 |
| zeylánicà | . . Wht. grn. | . 9, 8. Her. P. Ceylon | . 1731 |

SĂNTĂLŬM, *Linn.* From its Persian name *sandul*, signifying useful. *Linn.* 4, Or. 1, Nat. Or. *Santalaceæ*. A mixture of loam and peat suits these interesting plants; and cuttings will root in sand, under a glass, in heat. Saunders-wood is the produce of *S. album*, and in India it is considered sedative and cooling; it is also esteemed as a perfume.

| albūm | . . . Purple | . 8. Ev. T. E. Ind. | . 1804 |
| myrtifòliūm | . . Red | . 8. Ev. S. E. Ind. | . 1804 |
| obtusifòliūm | . . Red | . 8. Ev. S. N. Holl. | . 1823 |

SĂNTOLĬNĂ, *Linn.* From *sanctus*, holy, and *linum*, flax; in allusion to its medicinal qualities. *Linn.* 19, Or. 1, Nat. Or. *Compositæ*. These plants thrive well in any common soil; and increase freely by cuttings. They have the same anthelmintic qualities as *Tansy* and *Artemisia.*

| Chamæcyparissūs | Yellow | . 7, H. Ev. S. S. Eur. | . 1573 |
| pectinàtà | . . Yellow | . 7, H. Ev. S Spain | . 1822 |
| rosmarinifòlià | . Yellow | . 8. H. Ev. S. S. Eur. | . 1683 |
| squarròsà | . . Yellow | . 7, H. Ev. S. S. Eur. | . 1570 |
| virìdis | . . Yellow | . 7, H. Ev. S. S. Eur. | . 1727 |

SĂNVITĂLĬĂ, *Cavanilles.* Unknown, probably a man's name. *Linn.* 19, Or. 2, Nat. Or. *Compositæ*. An interesting plant, requiring the same treatment as other half-hardy annuals.

| procūmbèns | . . Yellow | . 7, H. Tr. A. Mexico | . 1798 |

SĂOUARI NUT, see *Caryŏcăr.*
SĂPID, agreeable to the taste.
SĂPINDŬS, *Linn.* Altered from *Sapo-indicus*, Indiansoap; the aril which surrounds the seed of *S. saponaria* is used as soap in S. America. *Linn.* 8, Or. 3, Nat. Or. *Sapindaceæ*. These plants are hardly worth growing, except in general collections. They thrive in a mixture of loam, peat, and sand; and large cuttings will root in sand, under a glass, in heat. According to Browne, the seed-vessels are very acrid; they lather freely in water, and will cleanse more linen than thirty times their weight of soap, but in time they corrode or burn the linen. *Synonyme*: 1. *Moulinsia rubiginosa.*

| arborèscens | . . | . 8. Ev. S. Guiana | . 1824 |
| emarginàtūs | . . Wht. grn. | . 8. Ev. T. E. Ind. | . 1822 |
| Forsȳthii | . . White . | . 8. Ev. T. Granada | . |
| frutéscens | . . Wht. grn. | . 8. Ev. S. Guiana | . 1824 |
| indicūs | . . Wht. grn. | . 8. Ev. T. E. Ind. | . 1800 |
| laurifòliūs | . . Wht. grn. | . 8. Ev. T E. Ind. | . 1820 |
| longifòliūs | . . Wht. grn. | . 8. Ev. T. E. Ind. | . 1820 |
| marginàtūs | . . Wht. grn. | . 8. Ev. T. Carolina | . |
| rigidūs | . . Wht. grn. 8, 8. Ev. T. America | . 1759 |
| rubiginòsūs, 1 | . Wht. grn. | . 8. Ev. T. E. Ind. | . 1821 |
| Saponàrià | . . Wht. grn. | . 8. Ev. T. W. Ind. | . 1697 |
| senegalénsis | . . Wht. grn. | . 8. Ev. T. Senegal | . 1823 |

SĂPĬŬM, *Jacquin.* From *sap*, Celtic, signifying fat; in allusion to the unctuous exudation from the wounded trunk. *Linn.* 21, Or. 10, Nat. Or. *Euphorbiaceæ*. These trees thrive well in loam and peat; and cuttings will root in sand, under a glass, in heat. The juice of *S. aucuparium* is said to be poisonous. *Synonyme*: 1. *Hippomane spinosa.*

| aucupàriūm | . . Green . | . 8. Ev. T. W. Ind. | . 1692 |
| Hippŏmàne | . . | . 8. Ev. T. Guiana | . 1822 |
| ilicifòliūm | . . | . 8. Ev. T. S. Amer. | . 1820 |
| indicūm | . . | . 8. Ev. T. E. Ind. | . 1818 |

SĂPONĂCEOUS, soapy.
SĂPONĂRĬĂ, *Linn.* From *sapo*, soap; the bruised leaves are said to produce a lather, like soap, when agitated in the water. *Linn.* 10, Or. 2, Nat. Or. *Silenaceæ*. This genus contains some truly beautiful plants, well deserving of a place in every garden. *S. ocymoides*, from its trailing habit, and handsome flowers, is well adapted for rock-work. A mixture of sandy loam and peat suits them best, and they are readily increased by division at the roots or by seed; young cuttings of the branching species will also root readily if planted under a glass. The leaves of *S. officinalis* form a lather,

which much resembles that of soap, and is similarly efficacious in removing grease spots.

| | | | | | | | | |
|---|---|---|---|---|---|---|---|---|
| bellidifolia | . | Red | . | 7, F. Her. | P. | Italy | . | 1825 |
| cæspitósä | . | Red | . | 7, H. Her. | P. | Pyrenees | . | 1824 |
| calabrica | . | Rose | . | 8, H. | A. | Calabria | . | 1830 |
| cornutioídēs | . | Pink | . | H. | A. | Russia | . | 1835 |
| glutinósä | . | Pink | . | 6, H. | B. | Tauria | . | 1817 |
| lútea | . | Yellow | . | 7, F. Her. | P. | Switzerl. | . | 1804 |
| ocymoídēs | . | Pink | . | 6, H. Her. | Tr. | France | . | 1768 |
| officinális | . | Pink | . | 7, H. Her. | Cr. | England | | |
| hybrida | . | Pink | . | 7, H. Her. | P. | England | | |
| orientális | . | Pink | . | 7, H. | A. | Levant | . | 1732 |
| perfoliátä | . | Pink | . | 6, H. | A. | N. Ind. | . | 183.. |
| pórrigēns | . | Flesh | . | 7, H. | A. | Levant | . | 1680 |
| Vaccaría | . | Red | . | 7, H. | A. | Germany | . | 1596 |
| viscósä | . | | . | H. | A. | | . | 1836 |

SĀRĀCHĀ, *Ruiz and Pavon.* In honour of Isidore Saracha, a Benedictine monk, much attached to botany, and who enriched the royal gardens at Madrid with many rare plants. *Linn.* 5, Or. 1, Nat. Or. *Solanaceæ.* These plants will grow well in any common garden soil. *S. viscosa* is easily increased by cuttings. The seeds of the annual species should be sown in the open border in spring.

| | | | | | | | |
|---|---|---|---|---|---|---|---|
| procúmbēns | . | Cream | . | 6, H. Tr. | A. | Peru | . | 1822 |
| umbellátä | . | Pa. yel. | . | 6, H. Tr. | A. | Peru | . | 1822 |
| viscósä | . | White | . | 9, H. De. | S. | Peru | . | 1835 |

SARCĀNTHŪS, *Lindley.* From *sarx,* flesh, and *anthos,* a flower; in allusion to the fleshiness of the flowers. *Linn.* 20, Or. 1, Nat. Or. *Orchidaceæ.* The plants of this genus are highly deserving of cultivation. They require to be grown in a hot damp atmosphere, and treated the same as the *Vandas.*

| | | | | | |
|---|---|---|---|---|---|
| oxyphyllūs | . | | 8. Epi. | China. | . | 1837 |
| paniculátūs | . | Yel. brn. | 8. Epi. | China. | | |
| præmórsūs | . | Green | 8. Epi. | E. Ind. | . | 1824 |
| rostrátūs | . | Or. brn. | 4, 8. Epi. | China. | . | 1824 |
| succísūs | . | Green | 8. Epi. | China. | . | 1824 |
| teretifólīūs | . | Orn. brn. | 5, 8. Epi. | China. | . | 1819 |

SARCOCĀPNŌS, *Decandolle.* From *sarx,* flesh, and *capnos,* the Greek name for fumitory; in allusion to the fleshy leaves. *Linn.* 17, Or. 2, Nat. Or. *Papaveraceæ.* This plant thrives well in the open border or on rock-work, and is easily increased by seeds or cuttings. *Synonyme:* 1. *Fumaria enneaphylla.*

| | | | | | |
|---|---|---|---|---|---|
| enneáphyllä, 1 | . | Pa. yel. | . | 6, H. Her. | P. Spain | . | 1714 |

SARCOCARP, the most fleshy part of fruit, under the pericarp.

SARCOCAÚLŌN, *Decandolle.* From *sarx,* flesh, and *caulos,* a stem; fleshy stems. *Linn.* 16, Or. 7, Nat. Or. *Geraniaceæ.* Ornamental under-shrubs, growing best in a mixture of loam, peat, and leaf mould or sand; they are easily increased by planting young cuttings in sand, under a glass, or by cuttings of the root. *Synonymes:* 1. *Geranium spinosum.* 2. *Monsonia spinosa.*

| | | | | | | | |
|---|---|---|---|---|---|---|---|
| Burmánni, 1 | . | Purple | . | 5, S. Ev. S. | C. G. H. | . | 1800 |
| Heritiéri, 2 | . | | . | 5, S. Ev. S. | C. G. H. | . | 1790 |
| Patersóni | . | Purple | . | 5, S. Ev. S. | C. G. H. | . | 1827 |

SARCOCĒPHĀLŪS, *Afzelius.* From *sarx,* flesh, and *kephale,* a head; in allusion to the fruit being combined into a fleshy head. *Linn.* 5, Or. 1, Nat. Or. *Cinchonaceæ.* This interesting plant is seldom seen in collections. It requires to be grown in a mixture of loam, peat, and sand, and kept in a hot part of the house. Cuttings will root in sand, under a glass, in heat. The heads of the fruit are eatable and are much sought after by the negroes.

| | | | | | | | |
|---|---|---|---|---|---|---|---|
| esculéntūs | . | Pink | . | 7, S. Ev. S. | Leone | . | 1822 |

SARCOCHĪLŪs, *R. Brown.* From *sarx,* flesh, and *cheilos,* a lip; in allusion to the fleshy lip. *Linn.* 20, Or. 1, Nat. Or. *Orchidaceæ.* A genus of rather interesting plants. For culture, &c., see *Burlingtonia.*

| | | | | | | | |
|---|---|---|---|---|---|---|---|
| falcátūs | . | White | . | 4, S. Epi. | N. Holl. | . | 1821 |
| oliváceūs | . | Or. grn. | | 8. Epi. | N. Holl. | | |
| parvifórūs | . | Green | | 8. Epi. | N. Holl. | | |

SARCOCŌCCĀ, *Lindley.* From *sarx,* flesh, and *kokkos,* a capsule; fleshy capsules. *Linn.* 21, Or. 4, Nat. Or. *Euphorbiaceæ.* This plant thrives well in a mixture of sandy loam and peat; and cuttings of the half-ripened wood will root readily in sand, under a glass, in a little heat.

| | | | | | | | |
|---|---|---|---|---|---|---|---|
| prunifóliä | . | Pa. yel. | . | 6, G. Ev. S. | Nepal | . | 1820 |

SARCŌLŌBŪS, *R. Brown.* From *sarx,* flesh, and *lobos,* a pod; the seed-vessels are fleshy. *Linn.* 5, Or. 2, Nat. Or. *Asclepiadaceæ.* Ornamental twiners. For culture and propagation, see *Pergularia.*

| | | | | | | | |
|---|---|---|---|---|---|---|---|
| carinátūs | . | Grn. yel. | 8. Ev. Tw. | E. Ind. | . | 1828 |
| globósūs | . | White | 8. Ev. Tw. | E. Ind. | . | 1828 |

SARCOPHYLLŪM, *Thunberg.* From *sarx,* flesh, and *phyllon,* a leaf; alluding to the fleshy leaves. *Linn.* 16, Or. 6, Nat. Or. *Leguminosæ.* This species should be grown in a mixture of loam, peat, and sand; and young cuttings root freely in sand, under a glass. Much water will injure the plant.

| | | | | | | | |
|---|---|---|---|---|---|---|---|
| carnósūm | . | Yellow | . | 7, G. Ev. S. | C. G. H. | . | 1812 |

SARCOSTĒMMĀ, *R. Brown.* From *sarx,* flesh, and *stemma,* a crown; the leaflets of the inner corona are fleshy. *Linn.* 5, Or. 2, Nat. Or. *Asclepiadaceæ.* Ornamental plants, requiring the same treatment as the *Ceropegias. Synonymes:* 1. *Asclepias viminalis.* 2. *Cynanchum viminale.*

| | | | | | | | |
|---|---|---|---|---|---|---|---|
| Swartziánūm, 1 | . | White | . | 8. Ev. Tw. | Jamaica | . | 1820 |
| viminále, 2 | . | White | . | 7, 8. Ev. Tw. | E. Ind. | . | 1731 |

SARMENTOSE, producing runners, or trailing offsets.

SARRACĒNIĀ, *Linn.* In honour of Dr. Sarrasin, a French physician. *Linn.* 13, Or. 1, Nat. Or. *Sarraceniaceæ.* These curious and interesting plants grow well in pots partly filled with rough peat soil, and the rest sphagnum moss. They should be kept in a cool frame and a moist close atmosphere; the mode of propagation is by division. *Synonymes:* 1. *S. psittacina.* 2. *S. adunca.*

| | | | | | | | |
|---|---|---|---|---|---|---|---|
| flávä | . | Yellow | . | 6, F. Her. | P. N. Amer. | . | 1752 |
| minōr | . | Pur. grn. | . | 4, F. Her. | P. Carolina | . | 1829 |
| purpúreä | . | Purple | . | 6, F. Her. | P. N. Amer. | . | 1640 |
| rúbrä, 1 | . | Purple | . | 6, F. Her. | P. N. Amer. | . | 1786 |
| variolaris, 2 | . | Yellow | . | 6, F. Her. | P. N. Amer. | . | 1803 |

SASSAFRAS, see *Laúrūs Sássäfrās.*

SATURĒIĀ, *Linn.* From *SSáttar,* the Arabic name for all labiate plants. *Linn.* 14, Or. 1, Nat. Or. *Labiatæ.* This genus contains the well known herb Savory. For culture and propagation, see *Thymus. Synonymes:* 1. *Thymus Tragoriganum.* 2. *S. obovata.*

| | | | | | | | |
|---|---|---|---|---|---|---|---|
| horténsis | . | Pink | . | 7, H. | A. Italy | . | 1562 |
| montána | . | Purple | . | 6, H. Her. | P. S. Eur. | . | 1562 |
| múticä | . | | . | 6, H. Ev. S. | Caucasus | . | 1836 |
| nervósä | . | Purple | . | F. Ev. S. | Ion. Is. | . | 1820 |
| rupéstris | . | Purple | . | 6, H. Her. | P. Carniola | . | 1798 |
| Thymbrä, 1 | . | Purple | . | 6, H. Ev. S. | Candia | . | 1640 |
| virgátä, 2 | . | Purple | . | 6, H. Ev. S. | Naples | . | 1824 |

SATURĒIĀ, see *Microměriä.*

SATURĒIĀ, see *Thymūs.*

SATÝRIŪM, *Swartz.* Said to be from *satyrus,* a satyr, because of its supposed aphrodisiacal properties. *Linn.* 20, Or. 1, Nat. Or. *Orchidaceæ.* This is a genus of very pretty tuberous-rooted plants. For culture, &c., see *Corycium.*

| | | | | | | | |
|---|---|---|---|---|---|---|---|
| cándidūm | . | White | . | 9, G. Ter. | C. G. H. | . | 1836 |
| cárneūm | . | Pink | . | 6, G. Ter. | C. G. H. | . | 1797 |
| chrysostáchyūm | . | Orange | . | 6, G. Ter. | C. G. H. | . | 1836 |
| coriifólíūm | . | Yellow | . | 10, G. Ter. | C. G. H. | . | 1820 |
| cucullátūm | . | Green | . | 6, G. Ter. | C. G. H. | . | 1786 |
| papillósūm | . | Ro. purp. | . | G. Ter. | C. G. H. | . | 1836 |
| parvifórūm | . | | . | 6, G. Ter. | C. G. H. | . | 1769 |
| pustulátūm | . | Purple | . | G. Ter. | C. G. H. | . | 1800 |

SAURAÚJĀ, *Willdenow.* From *Sauraujo,* the name of a Portuguese botanist known to Willdenow. *Linn.* 12, Or. 5, Nat. Or. *Ternstromiaceæ.* These trees are well worth cultivating on account of their fine leaves and flowers. They grow well in loam and peat; and ripened cuttings root in sand, under a glass, in heat.

| | | | | | | | |
|---|---|---|---|---|---|---|---|
| excélsä | . | White | . | 8. Ev. S. | Caraccas | . | 1820 |
| nepalénsis | . | White | . | 8, S. Ev. S. | Nepal | . | 1824 |

SAUROGLŌSSŪM, *Lindley.* From *saura,* a lizard, and *glossa,* a tongue; many of the parts of the plant bear a striking resemblance to the tongue of some reptile. *Linn.* 20, Or. 1, Nat. Or. *Orchidaceæ.* This very curious species requires the same treatment as is recommended for *Neottia.*

| | | | | | | | |
|---|---|---|---|---|---|---|---|
| elátūm | . | White | . | 4, S. Ter. | Brazil | . | 1832 |

SAURŪRŪS, *Linn.* From *saura,* a lizard, and *oura,* a tail; in allusion to the appearance of the flower-spike. *Linn.* 7, Or. 3, Nat. Or. *Piperaceæ.* These plants should be grown in sandy loam, in a pond or cistern; they are readily increased by divisions or seeds.

| | | | | | |
|---|---|---|---|---|---|
| cernùus . | . Apetal | . 9, H. Aq. P. Virginia | . 1759 |
| chinénsis . | . Apetal | . 6. Aq. P. China | . 1819 |
| lucidus . | . Apetal | . 9, H. Aq. P. China | . 1791 |

**SAUSSÙREX**, *Decandolle*. In honour of Horace Benjamin de Saussure, a Swiss physiologist. *Linn.* 19, Or. 1, Nat. Or. *Compositæ*. Interesting plants, growing in common garden soil, and increasing by division or seeds. Synonymes: 1. *Serratula alpina*. 2. *S. amara*. 3. *S. angustifolia*. 4. *S. discolor*. 5. *S. pygmæa*. 6. *S. salsa*.

| | | | | | |
|---|---|---|---|---|---|
| alàta . . | . Red | . 7, H. Her. P. Siberia | . 1818 |
| alpìna, 1 | . Purple | . 7, H. Her. P. Britain | . |
| amàra, 2 | . Purple | . 7, H. Her. P. Siberia | . 1820 |
| angustifòlia, 3 | . Purple | . 7, H. Her. P. Siberia | . 1816 |
| discolor, 4 | . Purple | . 7, H. Her. P. Switzerl. | . 1818 |
| lapathifòlia | . Purple | . 7, H. Her. P. Europe | . 1816 |
| elongàta | . Purple | . 7, H. Her. P. Caucasus | . 1820 |
| lyràta | . Red | . 7, H. Her. P. Siberia | . 1827 |
| pygmæa, 5 | . Purple | . 7, H. Her. P. Austria | . 1816 |
| pulchélla | . | . H. Her. P. | . 1835 |
| runcinàta | . Red | . 7, H. Her. P. Siberia | . 1819 |
| salicifòlia | . Red | . 7, H. Her. P. Siberia | . 1796 |
| sálsa, 6 | . Red | . 7, H. Her. P. Caucasus | . 1816 |

**SAUVAGÈSIA**, *Jacquin*. In honour of Francis Bossier de Sauvages, a distinguished physician of Montpelier, and a friend and correspondent of Linnæus. *Linn.* 5, Or. 1, Nat. Or. *Violaceæ*. These charming little annuals should be sown thinly in pots of loam and peat soil, in the month of March, and afterwards treated as other stove annuals. Synonyme: 1. *S. nutans*.

| | | | | | |
|---|---|---|---|---|---|
| erécta, 1 | . Pink | . 5, S. | A. S. Amer. | . 1820 |
| geminiflòra | . Pur. red | . 6, S. | A. Mexico | . 1824 |

**SAVIN**, see *Junipèrus Sabìna*.
**SAVORY**, see *Saturèia*.
**SAVOY CABBAGE**, see *Brássica oleràcea màjor*.
**SAWWORT**, see *Serrátula*.
**SAXĬFRĂGA**, *Linn.* From *saxum*, a stone, and *frango*, to break; its reputed medical qualities in that disease. *Linn.* 10, Or. 2, Nat. Or. *Saxifragaceæ*. A very extensive genus of beautiful alpine plants, the greater part of which are particularly suitable for ornamenting rock-work, or for growing on the sides of naked banks. A light sandy soil is best for them; and they are all readily increased by seeds or divisions. Many of the more rare and tender kinds require the protection of a frame in winter, and should therefore be grown in pots. Synonymes: 1. *S. aquatica*. 2. *S. lævis*. 3. *S. grænlandica*. 4. *S. palmata*. 5. *S. crenata*. 6. *S. dentata*. 7. *S. polita*. 8. *S. sphæroidea*. 9. *S. recta*. 10. *Megasea ciliata*. 11. *S. muscoides*. 12. *S. moschata*. 13. *S. congesta* 14. *S. moschata*. 15. *Leptarrhena pyrolæfolia*. 16. *S. cuscutæformis*. 17. *S. dissimilis*. 18. *S. punctata*. 19. *S. serratifolia*.

| | | | | | |
|---|---|---|---|---|---|
| adscéndens, 1 | . White | . 5, H. Her. P. Pyrenees | . 1752 |
| affìnis, 2 | . White | . 5, H. Her. P. | . |
| aizoìdes | . Yellow | . 7, H. Her. P. Britain | . |
| Aizòon | . White | . 6, H. Her. P. Alps | . 1731 |
| ajugæfòlia | . White | . 5, H. Her. P. Pyrenees | . 1770 |
| allìfida | . White | . 7, H. Her. P. | . |
| androsàcea | . White | . 5, H. Her. P. Austria | . 1792 |
| aretioìdes | . Yellow | . 6, H. Her. P. Switzerl. | . 1826 |
| argùta | . White | . 5, H. Her. P. N. Amer. | . 1827 |
| áspera | . Cream | . 8, H. Her. P. Switzerl. | . 1752 |
| biflòra | . Purple | . 5, H. Her. P. Switzerl. | . 1820 |
| bronchiàlis | . Cream | . 5, H. Her. P. Siberia | . 1819 |
| bryoìdes | . Cream | . 5, H. Her. P. Switzerl. | . 1752 |
| bulbìfera | . White | . 6, H. Her. P. S. Eur. | . 1819 |
| Burseriàna | . Cream | . 4, H. Her. P. Carniola | . 1826 |
| cæsìa | . Pa. yel. | . 6, H. Her. P. Switzerl. | . 1752 |
| cespitòsa, 3 | . Cream | . 5, H. Her. P. Wales | . |
| ceratophylla | . White | . 5, H. Her. P. Spain | . 1804 |
| cérnua | . White | . 7, H. Her. P. Scotland | . |
| condensàta | . White | . 5, H. Her. P. Scotland | . |
| controvérsa | . White | . 5, H. | A. S. Eur. | . 1824 |
| cordifòlia | . Purple | . 4, H. Her. P. Siberia | . 1779 |
| Cotylèdon | . White | . 6, H. Her. P. Alp. Eur. | . 1596 |
| crassifòlia | . Purple | . 4, H. Her. P. Siberia | . 1765 |
| crustàta | . White | . 6, H. Her. P. Switzerl. | . 1800 |
| cuneifòlia | . White | . 5, H. Her. P. Switzerl. | . 1768 |
| davùrica | . White | . 6, H. Her. P. Siberia | . 1809 |
| decìpiens, 4 | . White | . 5, H. Her. P. Wales | . |
| denudàta | . White | . 5, H. Her. P. Scotland | . |
| diapensioìdes | . White | . 4, H. Her. P. Switzerl. | . 1825 |
| élegans | . White | . 5, H. Her. P. Ireland | . |
| elongélla | . | . 4, H. Her. P. Scotland | . |
| érosa | . White, yel. | . 5, H. Her. P. Carolina | . 1812 |
| hirsùta | . Wht. yel. | . 6, H. Her. P. N. Amer. | . 1800 |
| exaràta | . White | . 5, H. Her. P. S. Eur. | . 1818 |
| ferruginea | . White | . 9, H. Her. P. N. Amer. | . 1827 |
| flagellàris | . Yellow | . 6, H. Ev. Tr. Greenland | . 1819 |

| | | | | | |
|---|---|---|---|---|---|
| geranioìdes . | . White | . 4, H. Her. P. Pyrenees | . 1770 |
| Geum | . White | . 6, H. Her. P. Ireland | . |
| crenàta, 5 | . White | . 5, H. Her. P. | . |
| dentàta, 6 | . White | . 5, H. Her. P. Ireland | . |
| polìta, 7 | . White | . 5, H. Her. P. Ireland | . |
| granulàta | . White | . 5, H. Her. P. Britain | . |
| plèna | . White | . 5, H. Her. P. Gardens | . |
| hederàcea | . White | . 7, H. Tr. A. Levant | . 1752 |
| hieracifòlia | . White | . 5, H. Her. P. Hungary | . 1789 |
| Hirculus | . Yellow | . 8, H. Her. P. England | . |
| hirsùta | . Flesh | . 5, H. Her. P. Ireland | . |
| sphæroìdes, 8 | . Flesh | . 5, H. Her. P. Pyrenees | . |
| hìrta | . White | . 6, H. Her. P. Scotland | . |
| hýbrida | . White | . 5, H. Her. P. Piedmont | . 1810 |
| hypnoìdes | . White | . 5, H. Her. P. Britain | . |
| angustifòlia | . White | . 5, H. Her. P. Scotland | . |
| muscòsa | . White | . 5, H. Her. P. Scotland | . |
| pulchélla | . White | . 5, H. Her. P. Scotland | . |
| viscòsa | . White | . 5, H. Her. P. Scotland | . |
| incurvifòlia | . White | . 5, H. Her. P. Ireland | . |
| intácta, 9 | . White | . 6, H. Her. P. Tyrol | . |
| minòr | . White | . 5, H. Her. P. Alp. Eur. | . |
| parvifòra | . White | . 5, H. Her. P. Alp. Eur. | . |
| intermèdia | . White | . 7, H. Her. P. | . 1808 |
| irrìgua | . White | . 6, H. B. Tauria | . 1817 |
| lætevìrens | . White | . 5, H. Her. P. Scotland | . |
| lævis | . White | . 8, H. Her. P. Caucasus | . |
| lanceolàta | . White | . 5, H. Her. P. Europe | . 1800 |
| obtùsa | . White | . 5, H. Her. P. Europe | . 1820 |
| leptophylla | . White | . 5, H. Her. P. Wales | . |
| angustifìda | . White | . 5, H. Her. P. Wales | . |
| leucanthemifòlia | . White | . 6, H. Her. P. N. Amer. | . 1812 |
| ligulàta, 10 | . Wht. red | . 5, F. Her. P. Nepal | . 1821 |
| lingulàta | . White | . 7, H. Her. P. Switzerl. | . 1821 |
| mèdia | . White | . 6, H. Her. P. Carniola | . 1800 |
| moschàta, 11 | . Ll. yel. | . 5, H. Her. P. Pyrenees | . |
| muscoìdes, 12 | . Pa. yel. | . 5, H. Her. P. England | . 1819 |
| mutàta | . Li. yel. | . 6, H. Her. P. Switzerl. | . 1779 |
| nivàlis, 13 | . White | . 6, H. Her. P. Britain | . |
| nudicaùlis | . White | . 5, H. Her. P. N. Amer. | . |
| oppositifòlia | . Purple | . 3, H. Her. P. Britain | . |
| paniculàta | . White | . H. Her. P. | . |
| pedatífida | . White | . 5, H. Her. P. Scotland | . |
| pennsylvánica | . Grn. yel. | . 5, H. Her. P. N. Amer. | . 1732 |
| glabra | . Grn. yel. | . 5, H. Her. P. N. Amer. | . 1732 |
| pentadáctylis | . White | . 5, H. Her. P. Pyrenees | . 1815 |
| petræa | . White | . 4, H. A. Norway | . 1732 |
| platypétala | . White | . 5, H. Her. P. Scotland | . |
| pulchélla | . White | . 5, H. Her. P. Germany | . 1818 |
| pygmæa, 14 | . Wht. yel. | . 5, H. Her. P. Scotland | . |
| pyrolæfòlia, 15 | . White | . 5, H. Her. P. N. Amer. | . 1827 |
| quinquéfida | . White | . 5, H. Her. P. Scotland | . |
| retùsa | . Purple | . 5, H. Her. P. Piedmont | . 1826 |
| rivulàris | . White | . 6, H. Her. P. Scotland | . |
| rotundifòlia | . Wht. red | . 5, H. Her. P. Austria | . 1596 |
| repánda | . White | . 5, H. Her. P. Caucasus | . 1800 |
| sarmentòsa | . White | . 6, F. Her. P. China | . 1771 |
| cuscutæfórmis 16 | . White | . 6, F. Her. P. China | . 1815 |
| Schraderi | . White | . 5, H. Her. P. | . 1825 |
| sedoìdes | . Yellow | . 5, H. Her. P. Europe | . 1820 |
| semipubéscens | . Grn. yel. | . 5, H. Her. P. N. Amer. | . 1800 |
| sibìrica | . White | . 7, H. Her. P. Siberia | . 1802 |
| spicàta | . Spotted | . 5, H. Her. P. N. Amer. | . 1827 |
| stellàris | . White | . 6, H. Her. P. Britain | . |
| dissìmilis, 17 | . White | . 6, H. Her. P. Scotland | . |
| Schleichéri | . White | . H. Her. P. Switzerl. | . 1819 |
| Sternbérgii | . White | . 5, H. Her. P. Germany | . |
| tenélla | . White | . 7, H. Her. P. Carinthia | . 1819 |
| ténera | . Cream | . 5, H. Her. P. Switzerl. | . 1819 |
| tricuspidàta | . White | . 5, H. Her. P. N. Amer. | . 1824 |
| tridactylìtes | . White | . 4, H. A. Britain | . |
| tridentàta | . White | . 5, H. Her. P. | . |
| umbròsa | . Flesh | . 5, H. Her. P. Britain | . |
| punctàta, 18 | . White | . 5, H. Her. P. Ireland | . |
| serratifòlia, 19 | . White | . 5, H. Her. P. Ireland | . |
| virginiénsis | . White | . 5, H. Her. P. N. Amer. | . 1790 |
| viscòsa | . White | . 5, H. Her. P. | . |

**SAXIFRAGE**, see *Saxìfraga*.
**SAXIFRAGE**, see *Pimpinélla Saxìfraga*.
**SCABIÒSA**, *Ræmer*. From *scabies*, the itch; the common kind is said to cure that disorder. *Linn.* 4, Or. 1, Nat. Or. *Dipsaceæ*. Some of these plants are well adapted for ornamenting the flower-border. The herbaceous kinds are readily increased by division at the root, or by seed. The seeds of the annual kinds merely require sowing in the open border. Synonymes: 1. *S. pseud-australis*. 2. *S. norica*.

| | | | | | |
|---|---|---|---|---|---|
| austràlis, 1 | . Purple | . 6, H. Her. P. Styria | . 1820 |
| carpática | . White | . 6, H. Her. P. Prussia | . 1819 |
| dichótoma | . Pink | . 7, H. Her. P. Sicily | . 1804 |
| dipsacifòlia | . White | . 6, H. Her. P. Germany | . 1818 |
| pubéscens | . White | . 6, H. Her. P. Hungary | . 1820 |
| Salcedi | . White | . 6, H. Her. P. Spain | . 1823 |
| strìcta, 2 | . Red | . 6, H. Her. P. Hungary | . 1820 |

**SCABIÒSA**, see *Knaùtia*.

SCABIOUS, see *Scabiòsa.*

SCABROUS, rough from little asperities.

SCÆVÒLA, *Linn.* From *scæva,* the left hand; in allusion to the form of the corolla. *Linn.* 5, Or. 1, Nat. Or. *Scævolaceæ.* Ornamental plants, thriving in a mixture of turfy loam, peat, and sand; and cuttings will root readily if planted in the same kind of soil, under a glass, the stove species in heat. *Synonymes:* 1. *Goodenia ramosissima.* 2. *G. albida.* 3. *Scævola Lobelia, Lobelia Plumieri.* 4. *G. calendulacea.*

| | | | | | |
|---|---|---|---|---|---|
| crassifòlia | . . | . White . | . 9, G. Her. P. N. Holl. | . 1805 |
| cuneiformis | . | . Blue . | . 7, G. Her. P. N. Holl. | . 1824 |
| hispida, 1 | . | . Lilac . | . 7, G. Her. P. N. Holl. | . 1827 |
| Konigii . | . | . Pa. red | . 8. Ev. S. E. Ind. | . 1820 |
| microcarpå, 2 | . | . Violet . | . 7, G. Her. P. N. S. W. | . 1790 |
| Plumieri, 3 | . | . White . | . 8. S. Ev. S. W. Ind. | . 1724 |
| suaveòlens, 4 | . | . Blue . | . 8, G. Her. P. N. S. W. | . 1793 |
| Táccada | . | . White . | . 8, S. Ev. S. E. Ind. | . 1810 |

SCALE-FORMED, formed like scales.

SCALES, any small processes, resembling minute leaves.

SCALLION, see *Allium ascalònicum màjus.*

SCAMMONY, see *Convolvulus Scammònia.*

SCANDENT, climbing.

SCANDIX, *Gærtner.* The Greek name of an eatable plant. *Linn.* 5, Or. 2, Nat. Or. *Umbelliferæ.* Uninteresting plants; the seeds may be sown in the open border in spring. *Synonymes:* 1. *Wylia radicans.* 2. *W. grandiflora.* 3. *W. iberica.* 4. *S. Pecten—S. austràlis, brachycàrpå, falcàtå 1, grandiflòrå 2, ibèricå 3, Pèctèn-Vèněris 4, pinnatifìdå.*

SCAPE, a stem rising from the roots and bearing nothing but the flowers.

SCAPHYGLÒTTIS, *Poppig.* From *skaphos,* a boat, and *glotta,* a tongue; in allusion to the form of the labellum. *Linn.* 20, Or. 1, Nat. Or. *Orchidaceæ.* The species of this genus are altogether destitute of beauty. For culture and propagation, see *Burlingtonia.*

| | | | | | |
|---|---|---|---|---|---|
| reflèxa | . . . | . . | . S. Epi. Demerara | . 1838 |
| violàcea | . . . | . Pink | . . 2, S. Epi. Demerara | . 1837 |

SCARIOSE, membranous, and dry.

SCARLET POMPONE, see *Lilium pompònium.*

SCEPTRANTHÈS, *Graham.* From *skeptron,* a sceptre, *anthos,* a flower. *Linn.* 6, Or. 1, Nat. Or. *Amaryllidaceæ.* An ornamental plant, for the culture and propagation of which see *Zephyranthes. Synonyme:* 1. *Zephyranthes Drummondi.*

| | | | | |
|---|---|---|---|---|
| Drummòndi, 1 | . Wht. pink 7, F. Tu. P. Texas | . . 1835 |

SCHÆFFERIA, *Jacquin.* In honour of James Christian Schæffer, a German naturalist. *Linn.* 22, Or. 4, Nat. Or. *Celastraceæ.* This plant thrives well in a mixture of loam, peat, and sand; and half ripened cuttings root freely in sand, under a glass, in heat. *Synonyme:* 1. *S. completa.*

| | | | | |
|---|---|---|---|---|
| frutèscens, 1 | . . White . | . 8, S. Ev. S. W. Ind. | . 1793 |

SCHEDONÒRUS, *Ræmer.* From *schedon,* near to, and *oros,* a mountain. *Linn.* 3, Or. 2, Nat. Or. *Gramineæ.* A genus of perennial grasses, growing in common soil; and increasing by seeds. *Synonymes:* 1. *Festuca calamaria.* 2. *F. decidua.* 3. *F. elatior.* 4. *Bromus inermis.* 5. *Festuca loliacea.* 6. *F. nigrescens.* 7. *F. nutans.* 8. *F. poæformis.* 9. *F. pratensis.* 10. *F. Scheuchzeri.* 11. *F. spadicea.* 12. *F. sylvatica.* 13. *F. tenella, Brachypodium festucoides.* 14. *F. violacea.*

| | | | | | |
|---|---|---|---|---|---|
| decidùus, 2 | . . . | . Apetal . | . 6, Grass. Britain | . |
| elatior, 3 | . . | . Apetal . | . 6, Grass. Britain | . |
| loliàceus, 5 | . . | . Apetal . | . 6, Grass. Britain | . |
| nigrèscens, 6 | . | . Apetal . | . 6, Grass. Switzerl. | . 1819 |
| poæformis, 8 | . | . Apetal . | . 6, Grass. Switzerl. | . 1819 |
| phœnicòides | . | . Apetal . | . 7, Grass. Switzerl. | . 1819 |
| pratènsis, 9 | . | . Apetal . | . 6, Grass. Britain | . |
| spadìceus, 11 | . | . Apetal . | . 4, Grass. Italy | . 1775 |
| sylvàticus, 12 | . | . Apetal . | . 7, Grass. Germany | . 1804 |

*calamàrius* 1, *cærulèscens,* inèrmis 4, nùtans 7, pùmilus, Scheuchzèri 10, tenèllus 13, violàceus 14.

SCHELHÀMMERIA, *R. Brown.* In honour of C. C. Schelhammer, professor at Jena. *Linn.* 6, Or. 1, Nat. Or. *Melanthaceæ.* A mixture of peat and loam suits these pretty flowering plants best; and they are easily increased by divisions. They succeed well in a warm border, but require the protection of the greenhouse in winter.

| | | | | |
|---|---|---|---|---|
| multiflòra | . . | . | . G. Her. P. N. Holl. | . 1824 |
| undulàta | . . | . Purple | . 6, G. Her. P. N. Holl. | . 1824 |

SCHEUCHZERIA, *Linn.* In honour of John and James Scheuchzer, German botanists. *Linn.* 6, Or. 3, Nat. Or. *Juncaginaceæ.* A native species, found in marshes and spongy bogs.

| | | | | |
|---|---|---|---|---|
| palùstris | . . | . Brown . | . 6, H. Her. P. England | . |

SCHÌNUS, *Linn.* From *schinos,* the Greek name of the mastick; a resinous juice exudes from this tree similar to mastick. *Linn.* 22, Or. 9, Nat. Or. *Anacardiaceæ.* Ornamental plants. For culture and propagation, see the greenhouse and stove species of *Rhus. Synonyme:* 1. *Schinus Molle.*

| | | | | |
|---|---|---|---|---|
| Mólle, 1 | . . | . Green . | . 7, S. Ev. S. Peru | . 1597 |
| Arèira | . . | . Yel. grn. | . 7, G. Ev. S. Peru | . |
| terebinthifòlia | . | . Grnsh. wht. | . 8. Ev. T. Brasil | . 1829 |

SCHISMUS, *Beauvois.* From *schisme,* a cleft; alluding to the outer palea. *Linn.* 3, Or. 2, Nat. Or. *Gramineæ.* An annual species of grass, of no interest. *Synonyme:* 1. *Festuca calycina—S. marginàtus* 1.

SCHISTÒSTEGA. From *schistos,* split, and *stege,* a covering; the lid is split at the margin. *Linn.* 24, Or. 5, Nat. Or. *Musci.* This species is found on banks. *Synonyme:* 1. *Gymnostomum pennatum—S. pennàtå* 1.

SCHIVERECKIA, *Andrzejowski.* In honour of Andr. Schivereck, a Russian botanist. *Linn.* 15, Nat. Or. *Cruciferæ.* This species will thrive in common garden soil; and is readily increased by divisions. *Synonyme:* 1. *Alyssum podolicum.*

| | | | | |
|---|---|---|---|---|
| podolìca, 1 | . . | . Yellow . | . 6, H. Her. P. Podolia | . 1821 |

SCHIZÆA, *Swartz.* From *schizo,* to cleave; appearance of the fan-like spikes. *Linn.* 24, Or. 1, Nat. Or. *Oemundaceæ.* A genus of ornamental ferns. For culture and propagation, see *Davallia.*

| | | | | |
|---|---|---|---|---|
| bifìda | . . . | . Brown . | . 6, G. Her. P. N. Holl. | . 1822 |
| èlegans | . . | . Brown . | . 6, S. Her. P. Trinidad | . 1819 |
| penicillàta | . | . Brown . | . 6, S. Her. P. Amer. | . 1816 |
| pusilla | . . | . Brown . | . 6, H. Her. P. N. Amer. | . |
| rupèstris | . | . Brown . | . 6, G. Her. P. N. Holl. | . 1822 |

SCHIZANDRA, *Michaux.* From *schizo,* to cleave, and *aner,* a man; the stamens are split. *Linn.* 21, Or. 5, Nat. Or. *Anonaceæ.* An ornamental plant, thriving in a mixture of sandy loam and peat; ripened cuttings root readily in sand, under a glass.

| | | | | |
|---|---|---|---|---|
| coccìnea | . . | . Scarlet . | . 6, G. Ev. Tr. N. Amer. | . 1806 |

SCHIZANTHUS, *Ruiz and Pavon.* From *schizo,* to cut, and *anthos,* a flower; in allusion to the irregularly divided corolla. *Linn.* 2, Or. 1, Nat. Or. *Scrophulariaceæ.* This is a genus of extremely beautiful and showy annuals. A light fresh soil, not too rich, appears to suit these plants best. They succeed well if the seed be sown in an open border early in spring; they may also be reared on a hotbed in spring, planting a portion in the open border, and growing the remainder in pots in the greenhouse, with a free admission of air and light. To procure flowering plants early in summer, the seed should be sown in pots during the autumn, and the plants kept in a frame or greenhouse throughout the winter.

| | | | | |
|---|---|---|---|---|
| Gràhami | . . | . Varieg. . | . 8, H.   A. Chile | . 1831 |
| Hookèri | . . | . Rn. li. . | . 8, H.   A. Chile | . 1828 |
| pinnàtus | . . | . Wht. pur. | . 8, H.   A. Chile | . 1822 |
| hùmilis | . . | . Crimson | . 7, H.   A. Valparaiso | . 1831 |
| pòrrigens | . . | . Crimson | . 8, H.   A. Chile | . 1822 |
| retùsus | . . | . Varieg. | . 8, H.   A. Chile | . 1831 |

SCHIZOMERIA, *D. Don.* From *schizo,* to cut, and *meris,* a part; alluding to the cut petals. *Linn.* 10, Or. 2, Nat. Or. *Araliaceæ.* An ornamental shrub, succeeding in loam and sandy peat, and increasing by cuttings.

| | | | | |
|---|---|---|---|---|
| ovàta | . . . | . White . | . G. Ev. S. N. Holl. | . 1825 |

SCHIZONEMA, *Agardh.* From *schizo,* to divide, and *nema,* a filament. *Linn.* 24, Or. 7, Nat. Or. *Algæ.* These plants are found upon the sea-coast, and in lakes—*S. lacùstre, Smithii.*

SCHIZOPETALON, *Sims.* From *schizo,* to cut, and *petalon,* a petal; the petals are cut. *Linn.* 15, Nat. Or. *Cruciferæ.* This very singular plant should be raised in pots in the greenhouse during spring, and when of sufficient size, some of the seedlings may be planted out in the open border: others may be kept in pots in an airy part of the house, where they will sparingly produce seeds. A mixture of loam, peat, and sand suits it best.

| | | | | | |
|---|---|---|---|---|---|
| Walkeri | . . White . | 6, F. | A. Chile | . | 1822 |

**SCHIZOPHYLLUM,** *Fries.* From *schizo*, to cut, and *phyllon*, a leaf; in allusion to the appearance of the plants. *Linn.* 24, Or. 9, Nat. Or. *Fungi.* Found upon the trunks of trees—*S. commune.*

**SCHKUHRIA,** *Roth.* In honour of Christian Schkuhr, a German botanist. *Linn.* 19, Or. 2, Nat. Or. *Compositæ.* A Mexican annual of no interest—*S. abrotanoides.*

**SCHMIDELIA,** *Linn.* In honour of C. C. Schmidel, a professor of botany at Erlangen. *Linn.* 8, Or. 1, Nat. Or. *Sapindaceæ.* Ornamental plants, thriving in a mixture of loam and peat; cuttings of the ripened wood will root readily in sand, under a glass, in heat. *Synonymes:* 1. *Ornitrophe Cominia.* 2. *O. serrata.*

| | | | | | |
|---|---|---|---|---|---|
| Cominia, 1 | . . White | . 8. Ev. T. Jamaica | . 1778 |
| integrifolia | . . | 8. Ev. T. Bourbon | . 1804 |
| occidentalis | . . | 8. Ev. T. W. Ind. | . 1828 |
| racemosa | . . White | . 5. 8. Ev. T. E. Ind. | . 1820 |
| serrata, 2 | . . White | . 8. Ev. T. E. Ind. | . 1804 |

**SCHMIDTIA,** *Sternberg.* In honour of M. Schmidt, a German botanist. *Linn.* 2, Or. 2, Nat. Or. *Gramineæ.* A small annual grass. *Synonyme:* 1. *Coleanthus subtilis.*

| | | | | | |
|---|---|---|---|---|---|
| subtilis, 1 | . . Apetal | . 6, Grass. Bohemia | . 1820 |

**SCHŒNUS,** *Beauvois.* From *schoinos*, a cord, made into cordage. *Linn.* 3, Or. 1, Nat. Or. *Cyperaceæ.* Rushes, growing in bogs.

| | | | | | |
|---|---|---|---|---|---|
| imbarbis | . . Apetal | . 4, Grass. N. Holl. | . 1818 |
| melanostachya | . . Apetal | . 7, Grass. N. Holl. | . 1822 |
| stellatus | . . Apetal | . 8, Grass. W. Ind. | . 1822 |

*mucronatus, nigricans.*

**SCHOMBURGKIA,** *Lindley.* In honour of Mr. Robert H. Schomburgk, a zealous naturalist, and a traveller in British Guiana on account of the Royal Geographical Society. *Linn.* 20, Or. 1, Nat. Or. *Orchidaceæ.* This very elegant plant, and another, not yet introduced, were originally discovered by the gentleman to whom the genus is dedicated. *S. marginata* is at present supposed to be rather difficult of culture. It will not grow so as to flower if kept in a pot, but thrives perfectly well when attached to a piece of wood, with a little moss on its roots. It must be kept in a hot, moist part of the house. "In its native state, its flower-stalk is frequently four feet high, branching, and covered with flowers. During the dry season, it will bear intense heat without injury."—*Sertum Orchidaceum.*

| | | | | | |
|---|---|---|---|---|---|
| marginata | . . Red yel. | 8, S. Epi. Surinam | . 1834 |

**SCHOTIA.** Jacquin named this genus in honour of Richard Van der Schot, his companion in his travels. *Linn.* 10, Or. 1, Nat. Or. *Leguminosæ.* The plants of this genus are very beautiful when in flower. For culture and propagation, see *Schmidelia.* *Synonyme:* 1. *Omphalobium Schotii.*

| | | | | | |
|---|---|---|---|---|---|
| alata | . . Crimson | . 6, G. Ev. S. C. G. H. | . 1816 |
| latifolia, 1 | . . Pur. wht. | . 8. Ev. S. C. G. H. | . 1810 |
| speciosa | . . Scarlet | . 8. Ev. S. C. O. H. | . 1759 |
| stipulata | . . Crimson | . 7, S. Ev. S. C. O. H. | . 1794 |
| tamarindifolia | . . Crimson | . 8, S. Ev. S. C. O. H. | . 1795 |

**SCHRADERA,** *Vahl.* In honour of Henry A. D. Schrader, a German botanist. *Linn.* 6, Or. 1, Nat. Or. *Cinchonaceæ.* This plant grows well in a mixture of loam, peat, and sand; and cuttings root in sand, under a glass, in heat.

| | | | | | |
|---|---|---|---|---|---|
| cephalotes | . . Red | . 7, S. Ev. Cl. Jamaica | . 1820 |

**SCHRANKIA,** *Willdenow.* In honour of Francis Paula von Schrank, a famous German botanist, and author of many botanical works. *Linn.* 23, Or. 1, Nat. Or. *Leguminosæ.* These plants are very interesting on account of their leaves, which, like those of the sensitive plant, fall at the slightest touch. A mixture of loam, peat, and sand, is best adapted to them; and they may be increased by young cuttings, planted in sand, under a glass, in heat, or by separating the tubers of the roots.

| | | | | | |
|---|---|---|---|---|---|
| aculeata | . . Red | . 7, S. Her. P. Vera Cruz | . 1733 |
| uncinata | . . Red | . 7, F. Her. P. N. Amer. | . 1789 |

**SCHUBERTIA,** *Martius.* In honour of H. B. Schubert,

a professor at Erlangen. *Linn.* 5, Or. 1, Nat. Or. *Asclepiadaceæ.* To grow this pretty stove-climber well, it should be potted in a mixture of loam, peat, and sand; and cuttings root readily in sand, under a glass, in heat.

| | | | | | |
|---|---|---|---|---|---|
| graveolens | . . Cream | . 8. Ev. Tw. Brazil | . . |

**SCHUBERTIA,** see *Taxodium.*

**SCHULTESIA,** *Martius.* Named in honour of Joseph Augustus Schultes, M.D., professor of botany of Landshut; author of *Systema Vegetabilium.* *Linn.* 4, Or. 1, Nat. Or. *Gentianaceæ.* For culture and propagation, see *Sebæa.* *Synonyme:* 1. *Sebæa guianensis.*

| | | | | | |
|---|---|---|---|---|---|
| Aubletii, 1 | . . Pa. red | . 8. A. Guiana | . 1825 |

**SCHULTZIA,** *Sprengel.* In honour of M. Schultz, an eminent German botanist. *Linn.* 5, Or. 2, Nat. Or. *Umbelliferæ.* A plant of no interest; increased by seeds in the open ground. *Synonyme:* 1. *Sison crinitum—S. crinita* 1.

**SCHWENCKIA,** *Linn.* In honour of J. T. Schwenck, a professor of medicine at Jena. *Linn.* 2, Or. 1, Nat. Or. *Primulaceæ.* This plant grows in any light soil, and may either be increased by cuttings or seeds.

| | | | | | |
|---|---|---|---|---|---|
| americana | . . Lilac | . 8, S. B. Guiana | . 1781 |

**SCILLA,** *Linn.* From *skyllo*, to injure; roots poisonous. *Linn.* 6, Or. 1, Nat. Or. *Liliaceæ.* An extensive genus of interesting bulbous plants. A light soil is most suitable for them; and they are readily increased by offsets from the bulbs. *Synonymes:* 1. *S. monophylla.* 2 *S. bifolia rubra.*

| | | | | | |
|---|---|---|---|---|---|
| amœna | . . Blue | . 3, H. Bl. P. Levant | . 1596 |
| amœnula | . . Blue | . 6, H. Bl. P. Russia | . 1822 |
| autumnalis | . . Pink | . 8, H. Bl. P. England | . |
| alba | . . White | . 8, H. Bl. P. Gardens | . |
| major | . . Pink | . 8, H. Bl. P. Britain | . |
| bifolia | . . Blue | . 3, H. Bl. P. England | . |
| alba | . . White | . 3, H. Bl. P. S. Eur. | . |
| rubra | . . Red | . 3, H. Bl. P. S. Eur. | . |
| brevifolia | . . Pink | . 1, G. H. Bl. P. C. G. H. | . 1811 |
| campanulata | . . Drk. blue | . 5, H. Bl. P. Spain | . 1683 |
| alba | . . White | . 5, H. Bl. P. S. Eur. | . 1683 |
| carnea | . . Pink | . 5, H. Bl. P. S. Eur. | . 1683 |
| cernua | . . Pink | . 3, H. Bl. P. Spain | . 1815 |
| corymbosa | . . Pink | . 10, H. Bl. P. C. G. H. | . 1792 |
| Cupaniana | . . Purple | . 6, H. Bl. P. Sicily | . 1834 |
| esculenta | . . White | . 6, H. Bl. P. N. Amer. | . 1811 |
| hyacinthoides | . . Blue | . 8, F. H. Bl. P. Madeira | . 1585 |
| indica | . . | 8. H. Bl. P. E. Ind. | . 1816 |
| italica | . . Blue | . 5, H. Bl. P. Switzerl. | . 1605 |
| Lilio-Hyacinthus | . . Blue | . 6, H. Bl. P. Europe | . 1597 |
| lusitanica | . . Blue | . 5, H. Bl. P. Portugal | . 1777 |
| mauritanica | . . Blue | . 4, H. Bl. P. Maurit. | . 1812 |
| non-scripta | . . Blue | . 4, H. Bl. P. Britain | . |
| alba | . . White | . 4, H. Bl. P. Britain | . |
| carnea | . . Flesh | . 4, H. Bl. P. Britain | . |
| obtusifolia | . . Blue | . 3, H. Bl. P. S. Eur. | . 1829 |
| odorata | . . Blue | . 5, H. Bl. P. Portugal | . 1818 |
| peruviana | . . Drk. blue | . 5, H. Bl. P. Spain | . 1607 |
| alba | . . White | . 5, H. Bl. P. Spain | . 1607 |
| plumbea | . . Lead | . 5, H. Bl. P. C. G. H. | . 1812 |
| præbracteata | . . Blue | . 5, H. Bl. P. S. Eur. | . |
| præcox | . . Drk. blue | . 3, H. Bl. P. | . 1790 |
| pratensis | . . Blue | . 5, H. Bl. P. Hungary | . 1827 |
| pumila, 1 | . . Blue | . 5, H. Bl. P. | . 1821 |
| rosea, 2 | . . Rose | . H. Bl. P. Numidia | . 1827 |
| sibirica | . . Blue | . 3, K. Bl. P. Siberia | . 1796 |
| umbellata | . . Blue | . 4, H. Bl. P. Pyrenees | . 1822 |
| unifolia | . . White | . 5, H. Bl. P. Portugal | . |
| verna | . . Blue | . 4, H. Bl. P. Britain | . |
| alba | . . White | . 5, H. Bl. P. Gardens | . |
| rosea | . . Rose | . 5, H. Bl. P. Gardens | . |
| villosa | . . Lilac | . H. Bl. P. Tripoli | . 1831 |

**SCIODAPHYLLUM,** *P. Browne.* From *skioeides*, shady, and *phyllon*, a leaf; the leaves are large, and consequently afford much shade. *Linn.* 5, Or. 5, Nat. Or. *Araliaceæ.* The foliage of this genus being very handsome, the species are, on that account, well worth cultivating. Loam, peat, and sand mixed, appears to suit them best; and cuttings root very freely in sand, under a glass, in heat. *Synonymes:* 1. *Carolinea insignis.* 2. *Aralia sciodaphyllum.* 3. *Actinophyllum conicum.* 4. *A. digitatum.*

| | | | | | |
|---|---|---|---|---|---|
| acuminatum | . . Yellow | . G. Ev. Cl. Peru | . |
| anomalum, 1 | . . Wht. grn. | . 8. Ev. T. Trinidad | . 1817 |
| Brownii, 2 | . . White | . 8. Ev. T. Jamaica | . 1793 |
| conicum, 3 | . . Pa. red | . 8. Ev. Cl. Peru | . |
| digitatum, 4 | . . Green | . 8. Ev. S. E. Ind. | . 1820 |
| pedicellatum | . . Purple | . G. Ev. Cl. Peru | . |
| pentandrum | . . Pa. red | . 8. Ev. T. Peru | . 1820 |

SCION, a shoot intended for a graft.

SCIRPUS, *Beauvois.* From the Celtic *cirs*, rushes. Linn. 3, Or. 1, Nat. Or. *Cyperaceæ.* Rushes, generally found in bogs. *Synonymes:* 1. *Schœnus compressus.* 2. *Schœnus rufus—S. articulātūs, atrovīrēns, cæspitōsūs, caricīnūs* l, *carinātūs, elongātūs, glaūcūs, lacūstris, Luzūlæ, marītīmūs, mucronātūs, paucīflōrūs, quinquangulāris, rādīcāns, rūfūs* 2, *sylvātīcūs, triquētēr.*

SCLERANTHUS, *Linn.* From *scleros*, hard, and *anthos*, a flower; in allusion to the dry juiceless calyx. Linn. 10, Or. 2, Nat. Or. *Scleranthaceæ.* Mere weeds, not worth cultivating—*S. ānnūūs, perĕnnis, pŭngēns.*

SCLEROCARPUS, *Jacquin.* From *scleros*, hard, and *karpos*, a fruit; in reference to the hard covering of the grains. Linn. 19, Or. 3, Nat. Or. *Compositæ.* A plant of very little beauty. It grows in any soil.

africānūs . . . Yellow . 7, G.    A. Guinea . . 1812

SCLEROCHLŌĀ, *Beauvois.* From *scleros*, hard, and *chloa*, grass. Linn. 3, Or. 2, Nat. Or. *Gramineæ.* Worthless annuals. *Synonymes:* 1. *Triticum maritimum, Festuca maritima.* 2. *Poa procumbens.* 3. *P. rigida, Megastachya rigida—S. articulātā, dichotōmā* l, *divarīcātā, dūrā, procūmbēns* 2, *rigīdā* 3.

SCLERODERMĀ, *Persoon.* From *scleros*, hard, and *derma*, a skin; the hard coat. Linn. 24, Or. 9, Nat. Or. *Fungi.* Found in plantations, about oak roots, &c. *Synonyme:* 1 *Tuber solidum—S. Cēpā* l, *citrīnūm, spadicēūm, verrucōsūm.*

SCLEROTHAMNUS, *R. Brown.* From *scleros*, hard, and *thamnos*, a shrub; rigid plants, with stiff leaves. Linn. 10, Or. 1, Nat. Or. *Leguminosæ.* A very ornamental shrub. For culture and propagation, see *Dillwynia.*

microphÿllūs . . Yellow . 5, G. Ev. S. N. Holl . 1803

SCLEROTIUM, *Tode.* From *sclerotes*, hardness; in allusion to the texture of the plants. Linn. 24, Or. 9, Nat. Or. *Fungi.* These species are found on various kinds of decayed leaves. *Synonyme:* 1. *S. quercīnūm—S. bullātūm, dūrūm, frūctūm, fungōrūm, herbārūm, medullāre, muscōrūm, neglēctūm, populīnūm, quercīgēnūm* l, *Rūbī, salicīnūm, scutellātūm, sēmēn, S. Brāssicæ.*

SCOLLOPED, having deep and wide indentations.

SCOLOPENDRIUM, *Smith.* From *scolopendra*, a centipede; in allusion to the appearance of the underside of the fronds. Linn. 24, Or. 1, Nat. Or. *Polypodiaceæ.* Interesting ferns, growing well on rock-work; they also succeed in shady situations, where hardly any other plants will live. They are readily increased by seeds, or divisions of the roots. Important medical qualities are ascribed to several of the species. *Synonymes:* 1. *S. palmatum, Asplenium hemionitis.* 2. *A. scolopendrium.*

Hemionītis. 1 . . Brown . 8, H. Her. P. Spain . . 1779
officinārūm, 2 . . Brown . 7, H. Her. P. Britain . .
angustifolīūm . . Brown . 7, H. Her. P. Britain . .
crispūm . . . . Brown . 7, H. Her. P. Britain . .
multifīdūm . . . Brown . 7, H. Her. P. Britain . .
ramōsūm . . . . Brown . 7, H. Her. P. Britain . .
undulātūm . . . Brown . 7, H. Her. P. Britain . .

SCOLYMUS, *Linn.* From *skolos*, a thorn; the plants are spiny. Linn. 19, Or. 1, Nat. Or. *Compositæ.* These plants succeed well in common garden soil; the perennial kinds are readily increased by divisions or seeds. The seeds of *S. maculatus* need only be sown in the open ground. The roots of *S. hispanicus* are equally as good as *Scorzonera*; the leaves and stalks are eaten as Cardoons by the people of Salamanca: the flowers are used for adulterating saffron.

grandiflōrūs . . Yellow . 5, H. Her. P. Barbary . 1820
hispānīcūs . . . Yellow . 8, H. Her. P. S. Eur. . . 1658
maculātūs . . . Yellow . 7, H.    A. S. Eur. . . 1633

SCOPARIA, *Linn.* From *scopa*, a broom; it may be used for similar purposes. Linn. 4, Or. 1, Nat. Or. *Scrophulariaceæ.* This species requires the same treatment as other stove annuals. According to Browne, it is an excellent vulnerary.

dūlcīs . . . . White . 7, S.    A. Jamaica . 1730

SCOPŌLIĀ, *Jacquin.* In honour of John Anthony Scopoli, a celebrated professor, and author of some botanical works. Linn. 5, Or. 1, Nat. Or. *Sola-*

*naceæ.* This is a very desirable plant, on account of its producing its pretty flowers early in spring. It thrives best in a light dry soil, and a shady situation. It may be increased by dividing the roots. *Synonymes:* 1. *S. atropoides, Hyoscyamus scopolia.*

carniōlīcā, 1 . . Drk. pur. . 4, H. Her. P. Carniola . 1780

SCORIA, cinders, ashes.

SCORPION, see *Genistā scōrpīūs.*

SCORPION-GRASS, see *Myosōtis.*

SCORPION-SENNA, see *Coronillā ēmērūs.*

SCORPIURUS, *Linn.* From *scorpios*, a scorpion, and *oura*, a tail, alluding to the twisted form of the legumes. Linn. 17, Or. 4, Nat. Or. *Leguminosæ.* These plants are not possessed of much beauty. The seeds require to be sown in the open border in spring, and thinned as other hardy annuals, if they come up too thick.

acutifōlĭā . . . Yellow . 6, H. Tr. A. Corsica . . 1825
lævigātā . . . . Yellow . 6, H. Tr. A. Archipel. . 1818
muricātā . . . . Yellow . 6, H. Tr. A. S. Eur. . . 1640
subvillōsā . . . Yellow . 6, H. Tr. A. S. Eur. . . 1731
sulcātā . . . . Yellow . 6, H. Tr. A. S. Eur. . . 1596
vermiculātā . . . Yellow . 6, H. Tr. A. S. Eur. . . 1621

SCORZONERĀ, *Linn.* From *scurzon*, the Catalonian name of the viper; in Spain the plants are considered a certain remedy for the bite of the viper. Linn. 19, Or. 1, Nat. Or. *Compositæ.* These plants require the same treatment as carrots. *S. hispanica* is diuretic, stimulant, and sudorific. The root resembles a carrot, and is about the thickness of a man's finger; when the outer rind has been scraped off, it is steeped in water to extract part of its bitter flavour; then boiled or stewed the same as carrots or paraneps. The roots are fit for use from August till the following spring. *Synonymes:* 1. *S. graminifolia.* 2. *S. austriaca.* 3. *S. undulata.* 4. *S. subulata.* 5. *S. villosa.* 6. *S. serrulata.*

angustifōlīā . . . Yellow . 7, H. Her. P. S. Eur. . . 1759
carĭcifōlĭā . . . Yellow . 7, H. Her. P. Siberia . . 1805
ensifōlĭā . . . . Yellow . 5, H. Her. P. Caucasus . 1825
eriospĕrmā . . . Yellow . 7, H. Her. P. Siberia . . 1805
glastĭfōlĭā, 1 . . . Yellow . 7, H. Her. P. Germany . 1816
graminifōlĭā . . . Yellow . 7, H. Her. P. Portugal . 1759
hirsūtā . . . . Yellow . 5, H. Her. P. S. Eur. . . 1818
hispānīcā . . . . Yellow . 7, H. Her. P. Spain . . 1576
hūmīlīs, 2 . . . . Yellow . 8, H. Her. P. Europe . 1597
lanātā . . . . . Yellow . 7, H. Tu. P. Iberia . . 1824
parvĭflōrā . . . . Yellow . 7, H. Tu. P. Austria . 1819
purpūrēā . . . . Yellow . 5, H. Tu. P. Austria . 1759
rōsēā . . . . . Pink . 7, H. Tu. P. Hungary . 1807
taŭrīcā . . . . . Yellow . 7, H. Tu. P. Tauria . 1820
tomentōsā . . . . Yellow . 7, H. Tu. P. Armenia . 1780
tuberōsā . . . . Yellow . 6, H. Tu. P. Volga . 1825
villōsā . . . . . Yellow . 6, H.    B. S. Eur. . . 1818

*chondrilloīdēs, crīspā, fīstulōsā, jūlīā, macrorhīzā, mŏllīs* 3, *pinifōlīā* 4, *radiātā, rumicīfōlīā, strīctā* 5, *trachyspērmā* 6.

SCOTCH ASPHODEL, see *Tofīeldīā alpīnā.*

SCOTCH LABURNUM, see *Cȳtīsūs alpīnūs.*

SCOTTIĀ, *R. Brown.* In honour of R. Scott, M.D., professor of botany in Dublin. Linn. 16, Or. 6, Nat. Or. *Leguminosæ.* A genus of elegant plants, thriving well in sandy loam and peat; cuttings of the young wood root freely in sand, under a glass.

angustifolĭā . . . Grn. yel. . 4, G. Ev. S. N. Holl. . 1825
dentātā . . . . Red grn. . 7, G. Ev. S. N. Holl. . 1803
lævĭs . . . . . Yel. scar. . 6, G. Ev. S. N. Holl. . 1833

SCREW-PINE, see *Pandānūs.*

SCREW-TREE, see *Helīctērēs.*

SCROBICULATE, excavated into little pits, or hollows.

SCROPHULARIA. So named by Linnæus, from its supposed use in the cure of scrofula. Linn. 14, Or. 2, Nat. Or. *Scrophulariaceæ.* The species of Figwort are all of the easiest culture, growing freely in a light soil, preferring a moist situation. The shrubby species require protection in winter. They all increase freely by seeds. *Synonymes:* 1. *S. Balbisii.* 2. *S. chrysanthemifolia.* 3. *S. glandulosa.* 4. *S. arguta.* 5. *S. frutescens.* 6. *S. mellifera.* 7. *S. rugosa.* 8. *S. appendiculata.* 9. *S. laciniata.*

canīnā . . . . Brn. pur. . 8, H Her. P. S. Eur. . . 1683
chrysanthemĭfolīā, 2 . } Bru. pur. . 7, H. Her. P. Tauria . 1817
cordĭfolĭā . . . . . . 6, H. Her. P. Hungary . 1817
grandiflōrā . . . Yel. pur. . 7, H. Her. P. S. Amer. . 1820
orientālis . . . . Brown . 7, H. Her. P. Levant . 1710
sambucĭfolĭā, 6 . . Red grn. . 8, H. Her. P. Spain . 1640
verbenæfolĭā, 9 . . Brn. pur. . 7, H. Her. P. . . 1816
vernālis . . . . Yellow . 4, H.    B. Britain . .

adscéndéns, altáicá, aquática 1, auriculátá, betonicæfóliá, biserrátá, crétáceá, filicifóliá, fruitéscéns, glabrátá, grandidentátá 3, hirsútá, híspidá, lanceolátá, lúcidá, lyrátá, marilándicá, melissæfóliá, mulitifídá, nodósá, peregriná 4, pinnatifídá, ramosíssimá 5, rupéstris, Scopólii 7, scorodóniá, Smithii, tanacetifóliá, trifoliátá 8, variegátá.

SCROTIFORM, shaped like a double bag.

SCRUBBY OAK, see *Lophíra africáná*.

SCUNKWEED, see *Symplocárpús fétidús*.

SCURFY, covered with scales, resembling scurf.

SCURVY GRASS, see *Cochleáriá*.

SCUTATE, shaped like an ancient round buckler.

SCUTELLÁRIA, *Linn.* From *scutella*, a little saucer; alluding to the form of the calyx. *Linn.* 14, Or. 2, Nat. Or. *Labiata*. From the plants being for the most part very handsome when in flower, they are well suited for ornamenting the front of the flower-border. They grow in any common garden soil, and increase readily by seeds and divisions; the shrubby species may be readily multiplied by young cuttings. The greenhouse and frame species require protection only in winter. Synonymes: 1. *S. nigrescens, pallida*. 2. *S. altaica*. 3. *S. lupulina*. 4. *S. decumbens*. 5. *S. Caroliniana, hyssopifolia*. 6. *S. ambigua*. 7. *S. rubicunda*.

| | | | | | |
|---|---|---|---|---|---|
| albídá, 1 | . | Dirty wht. | 6, H. Her. | P. Levant | . 1771 |
| alpíná, 2 | . | Purple | 8, H. Her. | P. Hungary | . 1752 |
| lútéá, 3 | . | Yellow | 8, H. Her. | P. Tartary | . 1789 |
| sanguíneá | . | Red | 7, H. Her. | P. | . 1835 |
| variegátá | . | Pa. yel. | 8, H. Her. | P. Switzerl. | . |
| altíssimá | . | Drk. pur. | 7, H. Her. | P. Crimea | . 1824 |
| Columná | . | Blue | 7, H. Her. | P. S. Eur. | . 1806 |
| commutátá | . | Purple | 8, H. Her. | P. Hungary | . 1688 |
| galericulátá | . | Blue | 7, H. Her. | P. Britain | . |
| grandiflórá | . | Red | 7, H. Her. | P. Siberia | . 1804 |
| hastifóliá | . | Purple | 6, H. Her. | P. Germany | . 1798 |
| havanénsis | . | Blue | 6, S. Her. | P. Havannah | . 1793 |
| hirtá, 4 | . | Drk. pur. | 6, H. Her. | P. Candia | . 1825 |
| húmilis | . | Blue | 6, F. Her. | P. N. S. W. | . 1823 |
| integr fóliá, 5 | . | Blue | 7, H. Her. | P. N. Amer. | . 1781 |
| lateriflórá | . | Blue | 7, H. Her. | P. N. Amer. | . 1752 |
| macrántha | . | Blue | 8, H. Her. | P. Dahuria | . 1827 |
| minór | . | Pink | 7, H. Her. | P. Britain | . |
| nervósá | . | Blue | 7, H. Her. | P. Virginia | . 1826 |
| orientális | . | Yellow | 8, H. Her. | P. Levant | . 1729 |
| párvúlá, 6 | . | Blue | 7, H. Her. | P. N. Amer. | . 1822 |
| peregriná, 7 | . | Violet | 8, H. Her. | P. Tauria | . 1823 |
| pilósá | . | Blue | 7, H. Her. | P. N. Amer. | . 1825 |
| purpuráscéns | . | Blue | 6, H. Her. | P. W. Ind. | . 1820 |
| scordifóliá | . | Blue | 6, H. Her. | P. Siberia | . 1817 |
| serrátá | . | Blue | 8, H. Her. | P. N. Amer. | . 1800 |
| Tournefórtii | . | Purple | 7, H. Her. | P. Persia | . 1837 |
| verná | . | Blue | 6, H. Her. | P. S. Eur. | . 1821 |

SCYPHÁNTHÚS, *Sweet.* From *scyphos*, a cup, and *anthos*, a flower; in reference to the shape of the flower. *Linn.* 18, Or. 2, Nat. Or. *Loasaceæ*. This elegant little plant may be referred to *Loasa* for culture and propagation. Synonyme: 1. *Loasa volubilis*.

| | | | | | |
|---|---|---|---|---|---|
| grandiflórús, 1 | . | Yellow | . 8, H. Tw. | A. Chile | . 1824 |

SCYTHYMÉNIA, *Agardh.* From *scytos*, leather, and *hymen*, a membrane; substance of plant. *Linn.* 24, Or. 7, Nat. Or. *Algæ*. This species is found upon rocks—*S. rupéstris*.

SCYTONÉMA, *Agardh.* From *scytos*, leather, and *nema*, a filament; the nature of the filamentous fronds. *Linn.* 24, Or. 7, Nat. Or. *Algæ*. Some of these species are found on rocks, and others in the ocean —*S. Bángii, byssoídéúm, comoídés, compáctúm, myóchrôús, M. inundátúm, M. ocellátúm, Sowerbyánúm.*

SCYTOSIPHON, *Agardh.* From *scytos*, leather, and *siphon*, a tube; the fonds are coriaceous and tubular. *Linn.* 24, Or. 7, Nat. Or. *Algæ*. These plants are found only in the ocean—*S. fæniculáceús, fílúm, F. thríx, F. tomentósúm.*

SEA BLITE, see *Chenopódiúm maritimúm*.

SEA BUCKTHORN, see *Hippóphaë*.

SEA CHICKWEED, see *Arenáriá peploídés*.

SEAFÓRTHIA, *R. Brown.* In honour of Francis Lord Seaforth, a botanical patron. *Linn.* 23, Or. 1, Nat. Or. *Palmaceæ*. An ornamental Palm, growing in turfy loam and a little sand; and increasing only by seed. A cool part of the stove suits it.

| | | | | |
|---|---|---|---|---|
| élégáns | . . . | . | Palm. N. Holl. | . . 1822 |

SEA HEATH, see *Frankéniá*.

SEA HOLLY, see *Erýngiúm*.

SEA KALE, see *Crámbé maritimá*.

---

SEA LAVENDER, see *Státicé*.

SEA MATGRASS, see *Psámmá arenáriá*.

SEA PARSNEP, see *Echinóphorá*.

SEA RAGWORT, see *Cineráriá maritimá*.

SEA ROCKET, see *Cakílé maritimá*.

SEASIDE BALSAM, see *Crótón Eleutériá*.

SEASIDE GRAPE, see *Coccólóbá*.

SEASIDE LAUREL, see *Xylophýllá latifóliá*.

SEASIDE OAT, see *Uníolá*.

SEA WRACKGRASS, see *Zostérá mariná*.

SEBÆA, *Solander.* In honour of Al. Seba, an apothecary and botanical author, of Amsterdam. *Linn.* 4, Or. 1, Nat. Or. *Gentianaceæ*. These elegant plants require to be raised on a hotbed, and afterwards planted out into a warm sheltered border, towards the end of May.

| | | | | | |
|---|---|---|---|---|---|
| albéns | . . | White | . 8, G. | A. C. O. H. | . 1820 |
| aúreá | . . | Yellow | . 7, G. | A. C. O. H. | . 1824 |
| cordátá | . . | Yellow | . 7, G. | A. C. O. H. | . 1815 |
| ovátá | . . | Red | . 8, G. | A. N. S. W. | . 1820 |

SEBÆA, see *Schultésiá*.

SECÁLE, *Linn.* An ancient name, said to be derived from *seco*, to cut. *Linn.* 3, Or. 2, Nat. Or. *Gramineæ*. The Rye is next to Wheat in value for making bread, and is used for this purpose generally throughout the north of Europe. It is hardier and earlier than wheat. Synonymes: 1. *S. cereale*. 2. *Triticum orientale*.

| | | | | | |
|---|---|---|---|---|---|
| cereálé | . . | Apetal | . 6, Grass. | Crimea | . . |
| compósitúm | . . | Apetal | . 6, Grass. | Tauria | . . |
| hybérnúm | . . | Apetal | . 6, Grass. | Tauria | . . |
| vernúm | . . | Apetal | . 6, Grass. | Tauria | . . |
| fragilé, 1 | . . | Apetal | . 6, Grass. | Tauria | . 1816 |
| orientálé, 2 | . . | Apetal | . 6, Grass. | Levant | . 1817 |

SECAMÓNE, *R. Brown.* Altered from *Squamona*, the Arabic name of *S. ægyptiaca. Linn.* 5, Or. 2, Nat. Or. *Asclepiadaceæ*. Ornamental plants. For culture and propagation, see *Pergularia*.

| | | | | | |
|---|---|---|---|---|---|
| ægyptíacá | . | White | . 7, S. Ev. Tw. | Egypt | . 1752 |
| ellíptica | . | | . 8. Ev. S. | N. Holl. | . 1824 |
| emética | . | White | . 8. Ev. Tw. | India | . 1816 |

SECHIÚM, *Browne.* From *sekiso*, to fatten; the fruit serves to fatten hogs in the mountains and inland parts of Jamaica, where the plant is much cultivated. *Linn.* 21, Or. 10, Nat. Or. *Cucurbitaceæ*. This plant requires the same treatment as the *Cucurbita*. Synonyme: 1. *Sicyos edulis*.

| | | | | | |
|---|---|---|---|---|---|
| édúlé, 1 | . | Yellow | . 6, F. | A. W. Ind. | . 1816 |

SECUND, arranged on one side only.

SECURIDÁCA, *Linn.* From *securis*, a hatchet; in allusion to the form of the wing at the end of the pod. *Linn.* 17, Or. 8, Nat. Or. *Polygalaceæ*. Pretty plants, growing well in loam, peat, and sand; cuttings will root without difficulty in sand, under a glass, in heat.

| | | | | | |
|---|---|---|---|---|---|
| virgátá | . . . | White | . 8. Ev. Tw. | Jamaica | . 1739 |
| volúbilis | . . . | White | . 8. Ev. Tw. | W. Ind. | . 1739 |

SECURIGÉRA, *Decandolle.* From *securis*, a hatchet, and *gero*, to bear; in reference to the shape of the pods. *Linn.* 17, Or. 4, Nat. Or. *Leguminosæ*. The seeds have only to be sown in the open border in spring. Synonymes: 1. *Securidaca lutea, Coronilla securidaca.*

| | | | | | |
|---|---|---|---|---|---|
| Coronílla, 1 | . | Yellow | . 7, H. | A. S. Eur. | . 1562 |

SECURINÉGA, *Jussieu.* From *securis*, a hatchet, and *nego*, to refuse; because of the extreme hardness of the wood. *Linn.* 21, Or. 5, Nat. Or. *Euphorbiaceæ*. These plants succeed well in a mixture of peat and loam; and cuttings of the half-ripened wood root readily in sand, under a glass, in heat.

| | | | | | |
|---|---|---|---|---|---|
| Commersónii | . . | | . 8. Ev. T. | | . 1815 |
| nítida | . . | White | . 6, S. Ev. T. | Maurit. | . 1793 |

SEDUM, *Linn.* From *sedere*, to sit; the plants are found growing upon stones, rocks, walls, and roofs of houses. *Linn.* 10, Or. 4, Nat. Or. *Crassulaceæ*. The hardy species of this interesting succulent genus are admirably suited for ornamenting rock-work. Some of the rarer kinds may be grown in small pots, in light sandy soil, or in loam mixed with brick rubbish. They are readily increased by divisions or cuttings. The greenhouse kinds require the same treatment as the *Globulea*. The annual kinds also succeed best on rock-work, where the seed has merely to be sown. Synonymes: 1. *Rhodiola sibirica*. 2. *Sedum fruticulosum, Jacquini, Sempervivum sediforme*. 3. *Sedum glaucum.* 4. *S.*

*rupestre.* 5. *S. maximum.* 6. *S. album micranthum.*
7. *S. hexapetalum, quinquefidum.* 8. *S. collinum.*
9. *S. recurvatum.* 10. *S. Guettardi, Monregalense.*
11. *Rhodiola rosea.* 12. *S. minus.* 13. *S. annuum.*
14. *S. sempervivoides.* 15. *S. spirale.* 16. *S. argutum, paucidens, triphyilum.* 17. *S. portulacoides.*

| | | | | | |
|---|---|---|---|---|---|
| acre . . . | Yellow | 6, H. Her. P. | Britain | . |
| diminūtum . | Yellow | 6, H. Her. P. | England | . |
| elongātum . | Yellow | 6, H. Her. P. | England | . |
| Aizōōn . . | Yellow | 8, H. Her. P. | Siberia | . 1757 |
| albescēns . | Yellow | 6, H. Her. P. | England | . |
| albicāns . | White . | 8, H. Her. P. | Europe | . 1794 |
| Albūm . . | White . | 6, H. Her. P. | | |
| altilēdm, 1 | Yellow | 6, H. Her. P. | Altai | . 1831 |
| altissimūm, 2 | Yellow | 7, H. Her. P. | S. Eur. | . 1769 |
| anacampserōs | Purple . | 7, H. Her. P. | France ; | . 1596 |
| andegavēnse | Yellow . | 7, H. | A. Andeg. | . 1835 |
| Andersonii, 3 | White . | 9, H. | Hungary | . 1816 |
| anglicūm . | White . | 7, H. Her. P. | Britain | . |
| hibernicūm . | White . | 7, H. Her. P. | Ireland | . |
| microphyllūm | White . | 7, H. Her. P. | Britain | . |
| anopetālūm, 4 | Pa. yel. | 7, H. Her. P. | S. France | . 1818 |
| aurantiācūm | Orange | 6, H. Her. P. | France | . 1820 |
| atrātum . | Purple . | 8, H. | A. | Italy | . 1795 |
| Cepēa . . | White . | 7, H. | A. | France | . 1640 |
| cœrulescēns | Yellow . | 7, H. Her. P. | | . 1890 |
| cœruleūm . | Pa. blue | 7, H. | A. | Africa | . 1822 |
| calabricūm . | Whitish | 7, H. | A. | Calabria | . 1835 |
| dasyphyllūm | White . | 6, H. Her. P. | England | . |
| dentātūm . | Purple . | 6, H. Her. P. | | . 1810 |
| Ewērsii . | | 6, H. Her. P. | Siberia | . 1829 |
| Forsteriānūm | Yellow | 7, H. Her. P. | Wales | . |
| glaucūm . | Yellow | 7, H. Her. P. | England | . |
| hispānicūm . | Pa. yel. | 6, H. Her. P. | Spain | . 1732 |
| hybridūm . | Yellow . | 6, H. Her. P. | Siberia | . 1776 |
| ibericūm . | Pink . | 7, H. Her. P. | Spain | . |
| involucrātūm | Yellow . | 7, H. Her. P. | | . |
| latifōlium, 5 | Grn. wht | 8, H. Her. P. | Switzerl. | . 1794 |
| lividūm . | Wht. grn. | 7, H. Her. P. | | . 1816 |
| micranthūm, 6 | White . | 6, H. Her. P. | England | . |
| minerūm . | Green . | 7, G. | A. | Mexico | . 1837 |
| neglectūm . | White . | 8, H. Her. P. | Naples | . 1835 |
| nūdūm . . | White . | 7, G. Ev. S. | Madeira | . 1777 |
| oblongūm . | White . | 7, H. Her. P. | Britain | . |
| ochroleūcūm | White . | 7, H. Her. P. | Greece | . 1818 |
| oppositifōlīūm | White . | 8, H. Her. P. | Caucasus | . |
| pallēns . | White . | 7, H. | S. Eur. | . 1816 |
| pallidūm . | Pa. red | 7, H. | A. | Caucasus | . 1817 |
| pectinātūm . | White . | 7, H. Her. P. | | . 1818 |
| populifōlium | White . | 8, H. Her. P. | Siberia | . 1780 |
| quadrifidūm, 7 | Yellow . | 7, H. Her. P. | N. Asia | . 1800 |
| reflexūm . | Yellow . | 6, H. Her. P. | England | . |
| collinūm, 8 | Yellow . | H. Her. P. | | . 1815 |
| recurvātūm, 9 | Yellow . | 6, H. Her. P. | Europe | . 1818 |
| rēpens, 10 . | Red . | 6, H. Her. P. | Switzerl. | . 1826 |
| Rhodiōla, 11 . | Yellow . | 6, H. Her. P. | Britain | . |
| rupestrē, 12 . | Yellow . | 7, H. Her. P. | England | . |
| saxātile, 13 . | . | 6, H. Her. P. | S. Eur. | . 1820 |
| sempervivūm, 14 | Dp. pur. | 7, H. Her. P. | Iberia | . 1825 |
| septangulārē . | Yellow . | 7, H. Her. P. | | . 1795 |
| sexangulārē, 15 | Yellow . | 7, H. Her. P. | England | . |
| sexfidūm . | White . | 7, H. | A. | Caucasus | . 1816 |
| Siebōldii . | Blue . | 7, H. Ev. | Cr. | Japan | . |
| spatulātūm . | White . | 7, H. | B. | Hungary | . 1815 |
| spūrīūm . | White . | 8, H. Her. P. | Caucasus | . 1816 |
| stellātūm . | Pink . | 7, H. | A. | S. Eur. | . 1640 |
| stenopetālūm | Golden | 6, H. Her. P. | N. Amer. | . 1826 |
| subclavātūm . | | 7, H. Her. P. | N. Amer. | . 1829 |
| Telephīūm, 16 | Purple . | 8, H. Her. P. | Britain | . |
| telephloidēs . | Purple . | 8, H. Her. P. | N. Amer. | . 1810 |
| teretifōlīūm . | White . | H. Ev. | Cr. | England | . |
| ternātūm, 17 | White . | 7, H. Her. P. | N. Amer. | . 1789 |
| verticillātūm | Pink . | 6, H. Her. P. | S. Eur. | . |
| villōsūm . | Pink . | 6, H. Her. P. | Britain | . |
| virēns . . | Yellow . | 6, H. Her. P. | Portugal | . 1774 |
| virescēns . | Grn. yel. | 7, H. Her. P. | | . 1815 |
| viridūlūm . | Yellow . | 6, H. Ev. S. | Europe | . 1824 |

SEGMENT, a part of anything.
SELAGŌ, *Linn.* From the Celtic *sel,* sight, and *jach,*
salutary ; supposed medicinal qualities. *Linn.* 14,
Or. 2, Nat. Or. *Selaginaceæ.* A genus of very pretty
plants, of easy culture ; a mixture of loam, peat,
and sand suits them ; and cuttings root freely in
sand or soil, under a glass. Synonymes : 1. *S. lucida.* 2. *S. teretifolia.* 3. *S. fulvo-maculata.* 4. *S. diffusa.*

| | | | | |
|---|---|---|---|---|
| angustifōlīā . | . | 8, G. Ev. S. | C. G. H. | . 1819 |
| bracteāta, 1 . | Purple . | 6, G. Ev. S. | C. G. H. | . 1812 |
| candescēns . | Pa. pur. | 9, G. Ev. S. | C. G. H. | . 1812 |
| corymbōsā . | White . | 7, G. Ev. S. | C. G. H. | . 1699 |
| dentātā, 2 . | White . | 7, G. Ev. S. | C. G. H. | . 1823 |
| diffūsā . . | Purple . | 7, G. Ev. S. | C. G. H. | . 1807 |
| fasciculātā . | Blue . | 6, G. Ev. S. | C. G. H. | . 1774 |
| Gilli . . | Pa. rose | 3, G. Ev. S. | S. Africa | . 1829 |
| heterophyllā . | Purple . | 7, G. Ev. S. | C. G. H. | . 1823 |
| ovātā . . | Drk. pur. | 6, G. Ev. S. | C. G. H. | . 1774 |

| | | | | |
|---|---|---|---|---|
| polygaloidēs . | Purple . | 8, G. Ev. S. | C. G. H. | . 1607 |
| ramulōsā . | White . | G. Ev. S. | C. G. H. | . 1824 |
| rapunculoidēs, 3 | Violet . | G. Ev. S. | C. G. H. | . 1824 |
| rotundifōlīā . | Purple . | 6, G. Ev. S. | C. G. H. | . 1816 |
| spicātā . . | Purple . | 8, G. Ev. S. | C. G. H. | . 1824 |
| spūrea, 4 . | Purple . | G. Ev. S. | C. G. H. | . 1824 |
| spūrīā . . | Violet . | 8, G. Ev. S. | C. G. H. | . 1779 |

SELFHEAL, see *Prunélla.*
SELINŪM, *Huffman.* From *selinon,* the Greek name for
parsley ; applied to this genus on account of the resemblance in the leaves. *Linn.* 5, Or. 2, Nat. Or.
*Umbelliferæ.* Hardy plants, of no interest ; increased
by seeds. Synonymes : 1. *Seseli pyrenæum, Angelica
lancifolia.* 2. *Imperatoria caucasica.* 3. *Thysselinum Plinii.* 4. *Angelica pyrenæa* 5. *Seseli pimpinelloides—S. angelicastrūm* 1, *carvifōlium caucasicūm*
2, *latifōlium, Plinii* 3, *pyrenæūm* 4, *rigidūlūm* 5, *scabrūm, sibiricūm, terebinthāceūm.*
SELLŌX, *Humboldt and Bonpland.* In honour of Mr.
Sello, a German botanist. *Linn.* 19, Nat. Or. *Compositæ.* A worthless stove perennial ; increased by
cuttings—*S. glutinōsā.*
SEMECĀRPŪS, *Linn.* From *semecion,* a mark ; and *karpos,* a fruit ; the black, acrid juice of the nut is used
by the natives for marking cotton cloths. *Linn.* 23,
Or. 2, Nat. Or. *Anacardiaceæ.* For the culture and
propagation of this lofty growing tree, see *Anacardium.* Synonyme : *Anacardium longifolium, Cassuvium.*

| | | | | |
|---|---|---|---|---|
| Anacardīūm, 1 | Grn. yel. | 8. Ev. T. E. Ind. | . . 1820 |
| cuneifōlīūm | Grn. yel. | 8. Ev. T. E. Ind. | . . 1824 |

SEMI, half.
SEMINAL, belonging to the seed.
SEMPERVĪVŪM, *Linn.* From *semper vivo,* to live for
ever ; the tenacity of life of the Houseleek is well
known *Linn.* 11, Or. 7, Nat. Or. *Crassulaceæ.* These
interesting plants are worthy of a place in every
collection. The greenhouse species succeed best in
a mixture of sandy loam and brick rubbish ; and
when not in flower, they must be very sparingly
watered. Cuttings taken off, and laid to dry for two
or three days, will root very freely. The readiest
way of obtaining cuttings from *S. tubulæforme* and
some others, is to cut the top out, when lateral shoots
will be immediately produced. The hardy kinds
succeed best on walls or rock-work, and are easily
increased by offsets. The juice of the common
houseleek, *S. tectorum,* applied either by itself or
mixed with cream, gives immediate relief in burns,
and other external inflammations. Synonymes : 1.
*Sedum divaricatum.* 2. *Sempervivum calyciforme.*
3. *S. lineolare.* 4. *S. barbatum, ciliatum.* 5. *S.
laxum.* 6. *S. grandiflorum.* 7. *S. soboliferum.* 8.
*S. villosum.*

| | | | | |
|---|---|---|---|---|
| africānūm . | | G. Her. P. | C. G. H. | . 1766 |
| aizoidēs, 1 . | Yellow . | 6, G. Ev. S. | Madeira | . |
| arachnoideūm | Purple . | H. Her. P. | Italy | . 1699 |
| majūs . . | Red . | 6, F. Her. P. | Italy | . |
| minūs . . | Red . | 6, F. Her. P. | Italy | . |
| arbōreūm . | Golden | 7, G. Ev. S. | Levant | . 1640 |
| variegātūm | Yellow . | 7, G. Ev. S. | Levant | . 1640 |
| aūreūm, 2 . | Yellow . | 7, G. Ev. S. | Canaries | . 1815 |
| spūrīūm . | Yellow . | 7, G. Ev. S. | Canaries | . 1820 |
| barbātūm, 3 . | Yellow . | 8, G. Ev. S. | Canaries | . 1815 |
| bifūreūm . | | G. Ev. S. | Madeira | . |
| cæspitōsūm, 4 | Yellow . | 8, G. Ev. S. | Madeira | . 1815 |
| canariēnse . | White . | 6, G. Ev. S. | Canaries | . 1699 |
| ciliātūm . | Pa. yel. | G. Ev. S. | Teneriffe | . 1815 |
| hybridūm . | Yellow . | 7, G. Ev. S. | Hybrid | . 1820 |
| dichōtomūm, 5 | Yellow . | 7, G. | S. | Canaries | . 1815 |
| dodrantāle . | Flesh . | 7, G. | A. | Teneriffe | . 1815 |
| flagelliformē . | Reddish | 7, H. Her. P. | Siberia | . 1823 |
| frutescēns . | Yellow . | G. Ev. S. | Teneriffe | . 1804 |
| glandulōsūm . | Yellow . | 4, G. Ev. S. | Madeira | . 1777 |
| globīferūm, 6 | Yellow . | 6, H. Her. P. | Germany | . 1731 |
| glutinōsūm . | Yellow . | 7, G. Ev. S. | Madeira | . 1777 |
| hirtūm, 7 . | Cream . | 6, H. Her. P. | Italy | . 1804 |
| micranthēs . | Grn. red | 9, G. Her. P. | Canaries | . |
| montānūm . | Red . | 6, H. Her. P. | Pyrenees | . 1752 |
| pumilūm . | Pa. red | 6, H. Her. P. | Caucasus | . 1824 |
| retūsūm . | Yellow . | 7, G. Ev. S. | Teneriffe | . 1824 |
| Smithii . | Pa. yel. | 7, G. Ev. S. | Teneriffe | . 1815 |
| stellātūm, 8 . | Yellow . | 7, G. | A. | Madeira | . 1790 |
| tabulæformē . | Yellow . | 7, G. Ev. S. | Madeira | . 1817 |
| tectōrūm . | Pursh. . | 7, H. Her. P. | Britain | . |
| tortuōsūm . | Yellow . | 7, G. Ev. S. | Canaries | . 1779 |
| urbicūm . | Yellow . | 7, G. Ev. S. | Teneriffe | . 1815 |
| aviferūm . | Yellow . | G. Ev. S. | Teneriffe | . 1829 |
| villōsūm . | Yellow . | 6, G. Ev. S. | Canaries | . 1777 |

SENACIA, *Commelin.* In honour of John Senac, a distinguished French physician ; he died in 1770. *Linn.*

5, Or. 1, Nat. Or. *Pittosporaceæ*. Interesting plants, thriving well in a mixture of loam and peat, or any rich light soil; cuttings of the ripened wood will root without difficulty in sand, under a glass, in heat. *Synonyme*: 1. *Celastrus verticillatus*.

| | | | | | | |
|---|---|---|---|---|---|---|
| nepalénsis, 1 | . | White | . | 8. Ev. S. Nepal | . | 1820 |
| undulátus | . | White | . | 8. Ev. S. Bourbon | . | 1785 |

**SENEBIÈRA,** *Poiret.* In honour of John de Senebier of Geneva, a vegetable physiologist. *Linn.* 15, Nat. Or. *Cruciferæ.* Plants of no beauty. The seeds have only to be sown in the open ground. *Synonymes*: 1. *Coronopus Ruellii.* 2. *Cochlearia nilotica.* 3. *Coronopus didymus, Lepidium didymum—S. Coronōpus* 1. *nilótica* 2. *pinnatifida* 3.

**SENECÍLLIS,** *Gærtner.* Probably a diminutive of *Senecio. Linn.* 19, Or. 2, *Compositæ.* Interesting plants, thriving in any light, rich soil, and increasing readily by divisions. *Synonymes*: 1. *Cineraria glauca.* 2. *C. purpurata.*

| | | | | | | |
|---|---|---|---|---|---|---|
| glaúca, 1 | . | Yellow | . | 7, H. Her. P. Siberia | . | 1790 |
| purpuráta, 2 | . | Purple | . | 6, H. Har. P. C. G. H. | . | 1816 |

**SENECÍO,** *Linn.* From *senex*, an old man; the receptacle is naked, and resembles a bald head. *Linn.* 19, Or. 2, Nat. Or. *Compositæ.* An extensive genus of plants, many of the species of which are very ornamental. The shrubby kinds grow well in any light soil, and increase freely by cuttings. The hardy species will thrive in common garden soil, and may be increased by dividing the plants. The annuals and biennials are also of the easiest culture. *Synonymes*: 1. *Cineraria alpina.* 2. *S. cinerarioides.* 3. *Cacalia sarracenica.* 4. *S. incanus.* 5. *Cineraria cordifolia.* 6. *Cineraria cruenta.* 7. *S. aquaticus.* 8. *S. glutinosus.* 9. *S. incanus.* 10. *S. canescens.* 11. *Cineraria alpina*, var. 12. *S. paradoxus.* 13. *S. lanceus.* 14. *Cacalia pinnata.* 15. *C. peucedanifolia.* 16. *S. chrysanthemifolius.* 17. *S. graminifolius.* 18. *S. nemorensis, persicæfolius.* 19. *S. leucanthemifolius.*

| | | | | | | |
|---|---|---|---|---|---|---|
| adonidifōlius | . | Yellow | . | 7, H. Her. P. Europe | . | 1800 |
| alpínus, 1 | . | Yellow | . | 7, H. Her. P. S. Eur. | . | 1683 |
| ampullacèus | . | Yellow | . | H. | A. Texas | . | 1834 |
| argútus | . | Yellow | . | 7, G. Ev. S. Mexico | . | 1827 |
| ásper | . | Yellow | . | 9 H. Her. P. France | . | 1772 |
| sacalitáter, 2 | . | Yellow | . | 7, G. Ev. S. C. G. H. | . | 1774 |
| cacalioídes | . | Yellow | . | 8, S. | A. Brasil | . | 1820 |
| canadénsis | . | Yellow | . | 7, H. Her. P. N. Amer. | . | 1820 |
| cærúlèus | . | Violet | . | 7, H. | A. E. Ind. | . | 1780 |
| cinerarioídes | . | Yellow | . | 7, G. Ev. S. Mexico | . | 1826 |
| cordifólius, 5 | . | Yellow | . | 7, H. Her. P. Austria | . | 1749 |
| coriácèus | . | Yellow | . | 7, H. Her. P. Levant | . | 1728 |
| crassifólius | . | Purple | . | 7, H. | A. S. Eur. | . | 1815 |
| eroáticus | . | Yellow | . | 7, H. Her. P. Hungary | . | 1805 |
| cruéntus, 6 | . | Purple | . | 4, G. Her. P. Teneriffe | . | |
| delphinifólius | . | Yellow | . | 7, G. Ev. S. Barbary | . | 1800 |
| divaricátus | . | Purple | . | 7, G. B. China | . | 1801 |
| Dória | . | Yellow | . | 8, H. Her. P. Austria | . | 1570 |
| Doronicum | . | Yellow | . | 8, H. Her. P. S. Eur. | . | 1705 |
| élegans | . | Purple | . | 7, H. Ev. S. C. G. H. | . | 1700 |
| flore albo | . | White | . | 7, G. Ev. S. C. G. H. | . | 1700 |
| plénus albus | . | White | . | 7, G. Ev. S. C. G. H. | . | 1700 |
| plénus rúber | . | Red | . | 7, G. Ev. S. C. G. H. | . | 1700 |
| erubéscens | . | Purple | . | 7, G. B. C. G. H. | . | 1774 |
| hæmatophýllus | . | Yellow | . | 4, S. Ev. S. | | 1789 |
| halimifólius | . | Yellow | . | 7, G. Ev. S. C. G. H. | . | 1728 |
| hieracifólius | . | White | . | 8, H. A. N. Amer. | . | 1699 |
| ilicifólius | . | Yellow | . | 6, G. Ev. S. C. G. H. | . | 1731 |
| japónicus | . | Yellow | . | 8, H. Her. P. Japan | . | 1774 |
| lánceus | . | Yellow | . | 8, G. Ev. S. C. G. H. | . | 1774 |
| lanugínosus | . | Yellow | . | 11, H. | A. | . | 1826 |
| leucophýllus, 9 | . | Yellow | . | 7, H. Her. P. S. Eur. | . | 1816 |
| lilacínus | . | Lilac | . | 6, G. Ev. S. C. G. H. | . | 1826 |
| longifólius | . | Yellow | . | 9, G. Ev. S. C. G. H. | . | 1775 |
| lyratifólius, 11 | . | Yellow | . | 7, H. Her. P. Austria | . | 1749 |
| microphýllus | . | Yellow | . | 7, H. Her. P. Caucasus | . | 1818 |
| nemorénsis | . | Yellow | . | 7, H. Her. P. Austria | . | 1785 |
| odorátus | . | Yellow | . | H. Her. P. N. Holl. | . | |
| sporbúlus, 18 | . | Yellow | . | 11, G. Her. P. | . | 1817 |
| Othónnæ, 14 | . | Pink | . | 7, H. Her. P. Iberia | . | 1816 |
| ovátus | . | Yellow | . | 9, H. Her. P. Germany | . | 1823 |
| paludósus | . | Yellow | . | 7, H. Her. P. England | . | |
| persicæfólius | . | Yellow | . | 7, G. Ev. S. C. G. H. | . | 1820 |
| poucedanifólius, 15 | . | Purple | . | 5, G. Ev. S. C. G. H. | . | 1816 |
| Pseudo-China | . | Yellow | . | 7, H. Her. P. E. Ind. | . | 1732 |
| pubígerus | . | Red | . | 6, G. Ev. S. C. G. H. | . | 1816 |
| purpúrèus | . | Purple | . | 8, G. Her. P. C. G. H. | . | 1774 |
| reclinátus, 17 | . | Purple | . | 7, G. Ev. S. C. G. H. | . | 1774 |
| ripiescens | . | Yellow | . | 7, G. Ev. S. C. G. H. | . | 1815 |
| rigídus | . | Yellow | . | 7, G. Ev. S. C. G. H. | . | 1704 |
| rosmarinifólius | . | Yellow | . | 7, G. Ev. S. C. G. H. | . | |
| sarracenicus | . | Yellow | . | 7, H. Her. P. Britain | . | |
| scáber | . | Yellow | . | 7, G. Ev. S. C. G. H. | . | 1700 |
| solidagíneus | . | Yellow | . | 7, G. Ev. S. C. G. H. | . | 1824 |

| | | | | | | |
|---|---|---|---|---|---|---|
| speciósus | . | Scarlet | . | 7, G. Her. P. China | . | 1789 |
| telephifólius | . | Yellow | . | 7, H. A. C. G. H. | . | 1820 |
| Tournefortii, 18 | . | Yellow | . | 7, H. Her. P. Pyrenees | . | 1810 |
| umbròsus | . | Yellow | . | 7, H. Her. P. Hungary | . | 1815 |
| uniflórus | . | Yellow | . | 7, H. Her. P. Alp. Eur. | . | 1789 |
| valerianæfólius | . | Yellow | . | 7, H. A. Europe | . | 1800 |
| venústus | . | Purple | . | 8, G. Ev. S. C. G. H. | . | 1774 |

*abrotanifólius, ægyptíus, aquáticus, arábicus, arenárius 2, artemisiæfólius, aúrèus, aurítus, Baldénsis, Balsamíta, Barrelíeri, calcárèus, carniólicus 4, chrysanthemifólius, cinerácèus, coronopifólius, dentátus, errátícus 7, erucifólius, gigantèus, glaucéscens, glaúcus, glomerátus, hastátus 8, incánus, Jacobéa, laxiflórus, linifólius, lívidus, lycopifólius 10, lyrátus, montánus 12, nebrodénsis, parviflórus, præáltus 16, rotundifólius, rupéstris, sinuátus, squálidus, squamósus, sylvátícus, tenuifólius, triflórus, trilóbus, verbenæfólius, vernális, vérnus 19, viscósus, vulgáris.*

**SENNA,** see *Cassia lanceolata.*

**SENSITIVE FERN,** see *Onoclea sensibilis.*

**SENSITIVE PLANT,** see *Mimosa sensitiva.*

**SEPALS,** the divisions of the calyx.

**SEPEDÒNIUM,** *Link.* From *sepedon*, putrescence. *Linn.* 24, Or. 9, Nat. Or. *Fungi.* These species are found in autumn growing on decayed substances—*S. mycophilum, róseum.*

**SEPTA,** the partitions which divide the interior parts of a fruit.

**SÉPTAS,** *Linn.* From *septem*, seven; the number seven prevailing in the fructification. *Linn.* 7, Or. 4, Nat. Or. *Crassulaceæ.* Neat little plants, thriving well in a mixture of loam, peat, and sand; and readily increasing by division of the tubers. They must be very sparingly watered when in a state of dormancy. *Synonyme*: 1. *S. globiflora.*

| | | | | | | |
|---|---|---|---|---|---|---|
| capénsis | . | White | . | 8, G. Her. P. C. G. H. | . | 1774 |
| globiflóra, 1 | . | White | . | 3, G. Her. P. C. G. H. | . | 1809 |
| umbélla | . | White | . | 7, G. Her. P. C. G. H. | . | 1800 |

**SEPTFOIL,** see *Tormentilla.*

**SEPTÒRIA,** *Fries.* From *septum*, a division. *Linn.* 24, Or. 9, Nat. Or. *Fungi.* These species appear as stains upon the leaves of the Elm, &c.—*S. Ægopódii, Oxyacánthæ, Ulmi.*

**SERÁPIAS,** *Linn.* After an Egyptian divinity of that name. *Linn.* 20, Or. 1, Nat. Or. *Orchidaceæ.* Curious little plants, succeeding best when planted in light sandy soil, with the protection of a south wall.

| | | | | | | |
|---|---|---|---|---|---|---|
| cordígera | . | Grn. brn. | . | 4, F. Ter. S. Eur. | . | 1806 |
| lingua | . | Brown | . | 6, F. Ter. S. Eur. | . | 1786 |
| longipétala | . | Brown | . | 4, F. Ter. Rome | . | 1826 |

**SERÀCEOUS,** silky, downy.

**SERIES,** a row, or layer.

**SERÍNGIA,** *Gay.* In honour of Nicholas Charles Seringe, a Swiss botanist. *Linn.* 5, Or. 1, Nat. Or. *Sterculiaceæ.* An interesting shrub, thriving in a mixture of sand, loam, and peat; young cuttings planted in the same kind of soil, under a glass, will root readily, or the species may be increased by seeds. *Synonyme*: 1. *Lasiopetalum arborescens.*

| | | | | | | |
|---|---|---|---|---|---|---|
| platyphýlla, 1 | . | White | . | 6, G. Ev. S. N. Holl. | . | 1822 |

**SERIÒLA,** *Linn.* From *seris*, succory; resemblance of the plants. *Linn.* 19, Or. 1, Nat. Or. *Compositæ.* These plants succeed in any common soil, and are readily increased by seeds. *Synonymes*: 1. *Rodigia alliata.* 2. *R. commutata.* 3. *R. lævigata.*

| | | | | | | |
|---|---|---|---|---|---|---|
| albicans | . | Yellow | . | 4, H. Her. P. Sicily | . | 1823 |
| apargioídes | . | Yellow | . | 4, H. Her. P. Sicily | . | 1829 |
| glauca | . | Yellow | . | 4, H. Her. P. Sicily | . | 1828 |
| rubéscens | . | Redsh. | . | 7, H. A. Sicily | . | |

*ætnénsis, alliáta* 1, *commutáta* 2, *lævigáta* 3, *úrens.*

**SERÍSSA,** *Commelin.* Not explained. *Linn.* 5, Or. 1, Nat. Or. *Cinchonaceæ.* This plant succeeds best in a mixture of loam, peat, and sand; and cuttings root if planted in sand, under a glass.

| | | | | | | |
|---|---|---|---|---|---|---|
| fœtida | . | White | . | 7, G. Ev. S. Japan | . | 1787 |

**SERJÀNIA,** *Plumier.* In honour of Paul Sergeant, a French friar and botanist. *Linn.* 8, Or. 3, Nat. Or. *Sapindaceæ.* Plants of little beauty, thriving in a mixture of loam and peat; large cuttings will root in sand, under a glass, in heat. *Synonyme*: 1. *Paullinia polyphylla.*

| | | | | | | |
|---|---|---|---|---|---|---|
| caracasána | . | Wht. grn. | . | 8. Ev. Cl. Caraccas | . | 1816 |
| divaricáta | . | Wht. grn. | . | 8. Ev. Cl. Jamaica | . | 1824 |
| mexicána | . | Wht. grn. | . | 8. Ev. Cl. Mexico | . | 1823 |
| sinuáta | . | Wht. grn. | . | 8. Ev. Cl. S. Amer. | . | |
| triternáta, 1 | . | Wht. grn. | . | 8. Ev. Cl. S. Amer. | . | 1739 |

SERÓTINUS, late, or evening-flowered.

SERPICULA, *Linn.* From *serpo*, to creep; in reference to the habit of the species. *Linn.* 21, Or. 5, Nat. Or. *Onagraceæ*. This plant grows in any common soil, and is readily multiplied by dividing the creeping shoots.

| | | | |
|---|---|---|---|
| répens . . . . | White . | 7, G. Her. Cr. C. G. H. . | 1789 |

SERRATE, cut like the teeth of a saw.

SERRATULA, *Linn.* From *serra*, a saw; the leaves are edged with cutting teeth. *Linn.* 19, Or. 1, Nat. Or. *Compositæ.* All the species of *Serratula* succeed well in any common soil. The herbaceous kinds are increased by seeds or divisions of the roots; the annuals and biennials merely require sowing in the open ground. *Synonymes:* 1. *Centaurea Behen.* 2. *S. alata, Carduus cyanoides.* 3. *Cnicus centaurioides.* 4. *Carduus nitidus.* 5. *S. linearifolia.* 6. *Centaurea nitens.* 7. *Carduus cerinthoides, cerinthifolius, glaucus.* 8. *Carduus pannonicus, serratuloides, Cnicus pannonicus.* 9. *S. ambigua, Carduus polyclonos.* 10. *S. centaurioides.* 11. *S. simplex.*

| | | | | | |
|---|---|---|---|---|---|
| alata . . . . | Purple . | 7, H. | Her. P. | | |
| arguta . . . . | Purple . | 9, H. | Her. P. | Hungary | 1824 |
| aspera . . . . | Purple . | 8, H. | A. | Nepal | 1821 |
| Behen, 1 . . . | Yellow . | 7, H. | B. | Levant | 1797 |
| caspica . . . . | Purple . | 7, H. | Her. P. | Caspia | 1820 |
| centauroides . | Purple . | 7, H. | Her. P. | Siberia | 1804 |
| coronata . . . | Purple . | 7, H. | Her. P. | Siberia | 1789 |
| cyanoides, 2 . . | Red . | 7, H. | Her. P. | Siberia | 1778 |
| cynaroides, 3 . | Purple . | 7, H. | Her. P. | Pyrenees | 1640 |
| depressa . . . | Purple . | 7, H. | Her. P. | Caucasus | 1818 |
| elegans . . . . | Purple . | 7, H. | Her. P. | Caucasus | 1819 |
| glauca . . . . | | | H. Her. P. | Russia | 1831 |
| heterophylla . | Purple . | 7, H. | Her. P. | Dauphiny | 1824 |
| Kitaibelii, 4 . | Purple . | 7, H. | Her. P. | Hungary | 1816 |
| multiflora, 5 . | Purple . | 7, H. | Her. P. | Siberia | 1816 |
| nitens, 6 . . . | Purple . | 7, H. | B. | Caucasus | 1828 |
| nitida . . . . | Purple . | 7, H. | Her. P. | Siberia | 1827 |
| nudicaulis, 7 . | Purple . | 7, H. | Her. P. | S. Eur. | 1789 |
| pannonica, 8 . | Purple . | 7, H. | Her. P. | Hungary | 1810 |
| Picris . . . . | Purple . | 7, H. | Her. P. | Caucasus | 1822 |
| polyclonos, 9 . | Purple . | 7, H. | Her. P. | Caucasus | 1820 |
| pulchella . . . | Purple . | 7, H. | Her. P. | Siberia | 1820 |
| quinquefolia . | Purple . | 7, H. | Her. P. | Persia | 1804 |
| radiata, 10 . . | Purple . | 7, H. | B. | Hungary | 1800 |
| simplex . . . . | Purple . | 7, H. | Her. P. | Nepal | 1821 |
| stoechadifolia . | Purple . | 7, H. | Her. P. | Tauria | 1820 |
| tinctoria . . . | Purple . | 8, H. | Her. P. | Britain | |
| alba . . . . | White . | 8, H. | Her. P. | Britain | |
| transylvanica, 11 | Purple . | 7, H. | B. | Transylv. | 1818 |
| xeranthemoides . | Purple . | 7, H. | Her. P. | Caucasus | 1825 |

SERRATURE, the teeth of a serrated leaf.

SERRULATED, having small serratures on the margin.

SERRURIA, *Salisbury.* In honour of Dr. James Serrurier, professor of botany at Utrecht. *Linn.* 4, Or. 1, Nat. Or. *Proteaceæ.* A genus of very desirable greenhouse shrubs. For culture and propagation, see *Protea. Synonymes:* 1. *S. arenaria.* 2. *Protea decumbens.* 3. *P. abrotanifolia odorata.*

| | | | |
|---|---|---|---|
| abrotanifolia . | Pink . | 7, G. Ev. S. C. G. H. . | 1803 |
| adscendens . . | Purple . | 7, G. Ev. S. C. G. H. . | 1819 |
| æmula . . . . | Purple . | 7, G. Ev. S. C. G. H. . | 1843 |
| arenaria . . . | Purple . | 7, G. Ev. S. C. G. H. . | 1803 |
| artemisiæfolia . | Purple . | 7, G. Ev. S. C. G. H. . | 1789 |
| Burmanni . . . | Purple . | 7, G. Ev. S. C. G. H. . | 1786 |
| ciliata . . . . | Purple . | 7, G. Ev. S. C. G. H. . | 1803 |
| congesta . . . | Purple . | 7, G. Ev. S. C. G. H. . | 1820 |
| crithmifolia . | Red . | 7, G. Ev. S. C. G. H. . | 1818 |
| cyanoides . . . | Purple . | 7, G. Ev. S. C. G. H. . | 1843 |
| decipiens . . . | Purple . | 7, G. Ev. S. C. G. H. . | 1806 |
| decumbens . . | Purple . | 7, G. Ev. S. C. G. H. . | 1818 |
| diffusa . . . . | Purple . | 7, G. Ev. S. C. G. H. . | 1810 |
| elongata . . . | Purple . | 7, G. Ev. S. C. G. H. . | 1810 |
| emarginata, 1 . | Pink . | 7, G. Ev. S. C. G. H. . | 1800 |
| faniculacea . . | Purple . | 7, G. Ev. S. C. G. H. . | 1810 |
| flagellaris . . | Purple . | 7, G. Ev. S. C. G. H. . | 1816 |
| florida . . . . | Purple . | 7, G. Ev. S. C. G. H. . | 1824 |
| glaberrima . . | Purple . | 7, G. Ev. S. C. G. H. . | 1825 |
| glomerata . . . | Purple . | 7, G. Ev. S. C. G. H. . | 1789 |
| millefolia . . | Purple . | 7, G. Ev. S. C. G. H. . | 1803 |
| nitida . . . . | Purple . | 7, G. Ev. S. C. G. H. . | 1828 |
| Nivenii, 2 . . | Purple . | 7, G. Ev. S. C. G. H. . | 1800 |
| odorata, 3 . . | Pink . | 7, G. Ev. S. C. G. H. . | 1803 |
| parilis . . . . | Pink . | 7, G. Ev. S. C. G. H. . | 1803 |
| pedunculata . | Purple . | 7, G. Ev. S. C. G. H. . | 1789 |
| phylicoides . . | Purple . | 7, G. Ev. S. C. G. H. . | 1789 |
| pinnata . . . . | Pink . | 7, G. Ev. S. C. G. H. . | 1803 |
| Roxburghii . . | White . | 7, G. Ev. S. C. G. H. . | 1806 |
| rubricaulis . . | Purple . | 7, G. Ev. S. C. G. H. . | 1812 |
| scoparia . . . | Purple . | 7, G. Ev. S. C. G. H. . | 1809 |
| squarrosa . . . | Purple . | 7, G. Ev. S. C. G. H. . | 1810 |
| triternata . . | Purple . | 7, G. Ev. S. C. G. H. . | 1802 |
| villosa . . . . | Purple . | 7, G. Ev. S. C. G. H. . | 1829 |

[ 289 ]

SERSALISIA, *R. Brown.* In memory of John Baptiste Sersalis, a Neapolitan ecclesiastic, much praised by Fabius Columna. *Linn.* 5, Or. 1, Nat. Or. *Sapotaceæ.* This shrub thrives best in a mixture of loam, peat, and sand; and cuttings root freely in sand, under a glass. *Synonyme:* 1. *Sideroxylon sericeum.*

| | | | |
|---|---|---|---|
| sericea, 1 . . . | White . . | 8. Ev. S. N. Holl. . | 1772 |

SERVICE, see *Pyrus Sorbus.*

SESAMUM, *Linnæus.* From *sempsen*, the Egyptian name of one of the species. *Linn.* 14, Or. 2, Nat. Or. *Pedaliaceæ.* Only worth growing as botanical curiosities. They require the same treatment as other tender annuals. The seeds contain an abundance of oil, which might be substituted for olive oil; it is procured from them in Egypt in great quantities.

| | | | |
|---|---|---|---|
| indicum . . . | Pa. pur. . | 7, 8. A. E. Ind. . . | 1731 |
| orientale . . . | White . | 7, 8. A. E. Ind. . . | 1731 |

SESBANIA, *Persoon.* From *Sesban*, the Arabic name of *S. ægyptiaca. Linn.* 17, Or. 4, Nat. Or. *Leguminosæ.* Interesting plants, requiring to be kept in a strong heat, or they will not thrive. A mixture of loam and peat suits them; and cuttings of the shrubby kinds will root in sand, under a glass, in heat. The annual species are increased by seeds, which they sometimes produce in this country. *Synonymes:* 1. *Æschynomene Sesban.* 2. *Æ. cannabina.*

| | | | | |
|---|---|---|---|---|
| aculeata . . . | Yellow . | 7, 8. | A. E. Ind. . . | 1690 |
| ægyptiaca, 1 . | Yellow . | 7, 8. | Ev. S. Egypt . | 1680 |
| affinis, 2 . . . | Yellow . | 7, 8. | A. E. Ind. . | 1800 |
| cannabina . . . | Yellow . | 7, 8. | A. E. Ind. . | 1800 |
| gracilis . . . . | Yellow . | 7, 8. | A. . | 1820 |
| macrocarpa . . | Yellow . | 7, 8. | A. Louisiana . | 1820 |
| occidentalis . . | Yellow . | 7, 8. | Ev. S. W. Ind. . | 1816 |
| paludosa . . . | Yellow . | 7, 8. | A. E. Ind. . | 1816 |
| picta . . . . . | Yellow . | 7, 8. | B. W. Ind. . | 1823 |
| punctata . . . | Yellow . | 7, 8. | A. Guinea . | 1825 |
| sericea . . . . | Yellow . | 7, 8. | A. E. Ind. . | 1818 |
| uliginosa . . . | Yellow . | 7, 8. | A. E. Ind. . | 1818 |

SESELI, *Linn.* The Greek name of an umbelliferous plant. *Linn.* 5, Or. 2, Nat. Or. *Umbelliferæ.* The species of Meadow-saxifrage are of very little interest. A sandy or chalky soil suits them, and they are readily increased by seeds. *Synonymes:* 1. *Bubon siculum.* 2. *S. Athamanta, Bubon buchtornense.* 3. *S. annuum.* 4. *B. dichotomum.* 5. *Athamanta Libanotis.* 6. *S. glaucum.* 7. *S. crassifolium.* 8. *S. proliferum.* 9. *B. rigidum.* 10. *S. tauricum*—*S. Bocconi* 1, *buchtornense* 2, *campestre, cervariæfolium, chærophylloides, coloratum* 3, *dichotomum* 4, *divaricatum, elatum, fragile, gracile, gummiferum, Hippomarathrum, leucospermum, Libanotis* 5, *Lobelianum, montanum, M. glaucum* 6, *Pallasii* 7, *peucedanifolium* 8, *rigidum* 9, *aridum, strictum, tortuosum, triternatum, varium* 10.

SESLERIA, *Arduini.* In honour of M. Sesler, a physician and botanist of the eighteenth century. *Linn.* 3, Or. 2, Nat. Or. *Gramineæ.* Uninteresting grasses. *Synonyme:* 1. *Cynosurus cæruleus*—*S. cærulea* 1, *cylindrica, disticha, elongata, nitida, tenella, tenuifolia, sphærocephala.*

SESSILE, without stalks.

SESUVIUM, *Linn.* Not explained. *Linn.* 12, Or. 2, Nat. Or. *Tetragoniaceæ.* These succulent plants require to be grown in sandy loam and peat. They increase freely by cuttings, (which should be dried a little,) in the same kind of soil, under a glass. They must be sparingly watered. *Synonymes:* 1. *S. pedunculatum.* 2. *S. sessile, S. Portulacastrum.*

| | | | | |
|---|---|---|---|---|
| longifolium . . | Red wht. | 7, 8. | A. S. Amer. . | 1816 |
| Portulacastrum . | Orn. red | 6, G. Her. P. | W. Ind. . | 1692 |
| pedunculatum, 1 | Red wht. | 6, 8. Her. P. | W. Ind. . | 1692 |
| sessile, 2 . . . | Red wht. | 6, 8. Her. P. | W. Ind. . | |
| répens . . . . | Red wht. | 7, 8. | A. E. Ind. . | 1816 |
| revolutifolium . | Red wht. | 7, 8. Her. P. | S. Amer. . | |

SETACEOUS, shaped like a bristle.

SETÆ, bristles.

SETARIA, *Beauvois.* From *seta*, a bristle; the involucrum is bristly. *Linn.* 3, Or. 2, Nat. Or. *Gramineæ.* These grasses are of no interest. They are nearly all annuals—*S. aspera, auricoma, cenchroides, composita, cylindrica, erubescens, geniculata, germanica, glauca, helvola, intermedia, italica, macrochæta, maritima, muricata, Pennisetum, polystāchyā, pūmilā, purpurāscēns, scāndēns, sericēā, setōsā, tenacissimā, verticillātā, vīridis, Weinmánni.*

**SĒTHIĀ,** *Kunth.* In honour of S. Sethi, author of a work on culinary vegetables. *Linn.* 10, Or. 3, Nat. Or. *Malpighiaceæ.* This plant thrives well in turfy loam and peat, and cuttings will root in sand, under a glass, in a moist heat. *Synonyme:* 1. *Erythroxylon monogynum.*

indicā . . . . Yellow . 8. Ev. T. E. Ind. . . 1824

**SETIFORM,** formed like bristles.
**SETIGEROUS,** bearing bristles.
**SETOSE,** covered with bristles.

**SEYMĒRIĀ,** *Pursh.* In honour of Henry Seymer, an English naturalist. *Linn.* 14, Or. 2, Nat. Or. *Scrophulariaceæ.* The seeds should be sown in a bed of peat soil. The plants are very pretty when in blossom, but rather difficult to cultivate. *Synonymes:* 1. *Afzelia cassioides, Gerardia Afzelia.*

pectinātā . . . Yellow . 7, H.   A. N. Amer. . 1820
tenuifōliā, 1 . . Yellow . 7, H.   A. N. Amer. . 1730

**SHALLOT,** see *Allium ascalōnicūm.*
**SHARP CEDAR,** see *Acācia Oxycēdrūs.*
**SHARP CEDAR,** see *Juniperūs oxycēdrūs.*
**SHEATH,** the lower part of the leaf that surrounds the stem.
**SHEEP LAUREL,** see *Kalmiā angustifōliā.*
**SHEEP'S SCABIOUS,** see *Jasiōnē.*
**SHEEP'S SORREL,** see *Rūmēx Acetosēllā.*

**SHEPHĒRDIĀ,** *Nuttall.* In honour of the late Mr. John Shepherd, curator of the Botanic Garden of Liverpool. *Linn.* 22, Or. 4, Nat. Or. *Elæagnaceæ.* Ornamental trees. For culture, &c., see *Hippophae.* *Synonymes:* 1. *Hippophae argentea.* 2. *H. canadensis.*

argentēā, 1 . . Apetal . 4, H. De. T. Missouri . 1820
canadēnsis, 2 . . Apetal . 4, H. De. T. N. Amer. . 1759

**SHEPHERD'S BEARD,** see *Arnopōgōn.*
**SHEPHERD'S CLUB,** see *Verbāscum Thāpsūs.*
**SHEPHERD'S PURSE,** see *Capsēllā.*
**SHEPHERD'S PURSE,** see *Thláspī.*

**SHERĀRDIĀ.** Named by Dillenius in honour of his patron William Sherard, LL D., consul at Smyrna. *Linn.* 4, Or. 1, Nat. Or. *Galiaceæ.* Uninteresting plants. The seed has only to be sown in the open ground. *Synonyms:* 1. *Galium murale—S. arvensis, murālis* 1.

**SHERDS,** fragments of pots, employed to drain the soil supplied to potted plants.
**SHIELD,** a broad table-like process in the flowers of *Stapēliā.*
**SHIELD FERN,** see *Aspīdiūm.*
**SHOREWEED,** see *Littorēllā.*
**SHORTLY-ACUMINATED,** having a short tapering point.
**SHORTLY-BIFID,** } slightly cleft at the apex into
**SHORTLY-TWO-CLEFT,** } two parts.
**SHRUBBY TREFOIL,** see *Ptēlēā.*

**SHUTĒRIĀ,** *Choisy.* Named in honour of Dr. Shuter, formerly a physician at Madras. This beautiful twiner may be raised from seeds on a hotbed in spring, and the young plants, when of a sufficient size, should be placed in separate pots, and trained to sticks. Unless a very warm sheltered situation can be found, they require to be placed in a stove or greenhouse to blossom and ripen their seeds. *Synonyms:* 1. *Ipomæa bicolor.*

bicolōr, 1 . . Yel. pur. . 8, S. Ev. Tw. E. Ind. . 1812

**SHUTTLECOCK,** see *Periplērā punīcēā.*

**SIBBĀLDIĀ,** *Linn.* In honour of Robert Sibbald, professor of physic at Edinburgh. *Linn.* 5, Or. 5, Nat. Or. *Rosaceæ.* Small alpine plants, succeeding best when grown in pots in a mixture of loam, peat, and sand, and increased by dividing the roots. *Synonymes:* 1. *Chamærhodos erecta.* 2. *Chamærhodos polygyna.*

erēctā, 1 . . . Pink . 7, H. Her. P. Siberia . 1806
parvifōlorā . . . Yellow . 7, H. Her. P. Cappa . .
polygȳnā, 2 . . Yel. grn. . 7, H. Her. P. Siberia . 1824
procūmbēns . . . Yellow . 7, H. Ev. Tr. Britain .
americānā . . . Yellow . 7, H. Ev. Tr. N. Amer. . 1820
helvēticā . . . Yellow . 7, H. Ev. Tr. Switzerl. . 1819

**SIBERIAN CRAB,** see *Pȳrūs prunifōliā.*
**SIBERIAN PEA-TREE,** see *Caragānā.*

**SIBTHŌRPIĀ,** *Linn.* In honour of Humphrey Sibthorp, M.D., formerly professor of botany at Oxford. *Linn.* 14, Or. 2, Nat. Or. *Scrophulariaceæ.* This

---

singular species succeeds best in peat soil and a moist situation, and is readily increased by divisions.

europæā . . . Yellow . 7, H. Her. Cr. England .

**SICYŌS,** *Linn.* Sicyos is the Greek name for cucumber applied to this genus because of the resemblance and affinity of the species. *Linn.* 21, Or. 10, Nat. Or. *Cucurbitaceæ.* Plants of no value except as curiosities. The seeds require to be sown in a hotbed in spring, and treated the same as *Gourds.*

angulātūs . . . Yellow . 8, F. Tr. A. N. Amer. . 1710
laciniātūs . . . Yellow . 8, F. Tr. A. S. Amer. . 1824
microphȳllūs . . Yellow . 8, F. Tr. A. Mexico . 1823
parvifōrūs . . . Whitish . 8, F. Cl. A. Quito . 1823
vitifōliūs . . . Yellow . F. Tr. A.

**SIDĀ,** *Linn.* Theophrastus gave this name to an aquatic plant, supposed to be identical with *Althæa.* *Linn.* 16, Or. 3, Nat. Or. *Malvaceæ.* Mostly free-flowering plants, of no beauty, thriving in any rich soil; and increased by seeds, which they produce in abundance. The shrubby kinds may be increased by cuttings, placed in sand, under a glass. They are for the most part stove plants. *S. cordifolia,* mixed with rice, is used to alleviate the bloody flux. The bark of several of the species is so tenacious as to be manufactured into cordage. *Synonymes:* 1. *Abutilon avicenna.* 2. *A. acerifolium.* 3. *A. albidum.* 4. *A. americanum.* 5. *A. arboreum.* 6. *A. asiaticum.* 7. *A. auritum* 8. *A. crispum.* 9. *Napæa dioica.* 10. *A. ferrugineum.* 11. *S. viscosa.* 12. *A. giganteum.* 13. *A. glaucum.* 14. *A. globiflorum.* 15. *A. hernandioides.* 16. *S. pilosa, A. hirtum.* 17. *A. incanum.* 18. *A. indicum,* 19. *A. Lechenaultianum.* 20. *A. lucianum.* 21. *S. suberosa.* 22. *A. mauritianum.* 23. *S. grandifolia. A. molle.* 24. *A. mollicomum.* 25. *A. mollissimum.* 26. *Napæa levis.* 27. *A. nudiflorum.* 28. *A. orbiculatum.* 29. *A. periplocifolium.* 30. *A. permolla.* 31. *A. polyandrum.* 32. *A. populifolium.* 33. *A. pulchellum, Plagianthus Lampenii.* 34. *A. pulchrum.* 35. *A. reflexum.* 36. *S. philippica.* 37. *S. brasilia.* 38. *A. Sonneratianum.* 39. *A. tiliæfolium.* 40. *A. umbellatum.* 41. *A. vesicarium.* 42. *A. virgatum.*

acūtā . . . . Pa. yel. . 8. Ev. S. Java . 1820
altāicā . . . . Yelsh. . 8, H. Her. P. Altai . 1831
aprīcā . . . . . . H. Her. P. Russia . 1827
atrosanguīneā . . Dk. pur. . 7, H. Her. P. S. Amer. . 1795
aūrēā . . . . Or. red . 8. Ev. S. India . 1820
chlorōphis . . . Yelsh. . 7, H.   R. India . 1822
globifōrā, 14 . . White . 11, S. Ev. S. Maurit. . 1821
juvenīlis . . . White . 8, H.   A. . 1825
mōllis, 23 . . . Yellow . 7, S. Ev. S. Peru . 1816
pyramidātā . . . Yellow . 7, S. Ev. S. St. Dom. . 1820
rēgiā . . . . Scarlet . 6, H. Her. P. N. Amer. . 1811
rōseā . . . . Rose . 10, S. Ev. S. Brazil . 1820
sericēā . . . . . . . . . 1804
versailifōrā . . . Yellow . 8. Ev. S. S. Amer. . 1827
stylōsā . . . . Yelsh. . 7, H. Her. P. . 1831

*Abutilon* 1, *acerifōliā* 2, *acrānthā, acuminātā, ālbā, albidā* 3, *alnifōliā, althæifōliā, americānā* 4, *angustifōliā, arbōreā* 5, *argātā, asiāticā* 6, *aurītā* 7, *betullnā, bracteolātā, brasiliēnsis, brevipēs, calyxrhymfōldā, cariēnsis, carpinifōliā, carpinoīdēs, ciliāris, compāctā, comprēssā, confēriā, contrāctā, cordifōliā, crispā* 8, *dioica* 9, *dumōsā, erōsā, ferrugīneā* 10, *fœtidā* 11, *frutēscēns, gigāntēā* 12, *glaucā* 13, *grandifōrā, graveōlēns, Hernandioīdēs* 15, *hīrtā* 16, *hūmilis, inæquālis, incānā* 17, *indicā* 18, *jamaicēnsis, jatrophoīdēs, lastustēgā, Lechenaultiānā* 19, *linifōliā, lucidā* 20, *maculātā* 21, *malvæfōrā, mauritiānā* 22, *micāns, Millerī, mollicōmā* 24, *mollissimā* 25, *multifōrā, Napæā* 26, *nudifōrā* 27, *occidentālis, orbiculātā* 28, *paniculātā, platycārphā, periplocifōliā* 29, *P. carībéā, P. zeylinicā, permōllis* 30, *pilōsā, polyānthā* 31, *populifōliā* 32, *pulchēllā* 33, *pulchrā* 34, *purpurāscēns, rectā, reflēxā* 35, *retāsā* 36, *rhomboīdēā, rhombifōliā, ricinoīdēs, rōsēā, rotundifōliā, Schrānkiī* 37, *semicrenātā, Sonneratiānā* 38, *spinōsā, spiræifōliā, stipulātā, supīnā, tiliæfōliā* 39, *tridentātā, trilōbā, triquētrā, umbellātā* 40, *ūrēns, verruculātā, verticillātā, vesicāriā* 41, *villōsā, viminēā, virgātā* 42, *virginicā.*

**SIDERĪTIS,** *Linn.* From *sideros,* iron; so named on account of its supposed property of healing flesh-wounds made by iron. *Linn.* 14, Or. 1, Nat. Or. *Labiata.* Many of these plants are admirably adapted for ornamenting rock-work. They prefer a dry sandy or chalky soil; and are readily increased by cuttings, seeds, or divisions. The annual kinds have only to be sown in the open ground in spring. *Synonymes:* 1. *S. cretica.* 2. *S. elegans.* 3. *S. alpina, pyrenaica.* 4. *S. hyssopifolia.* 5. *S. fœtida.*

| | | | | | | |
|---|---|---|---|---|---|---|
| angustifoliā | . | Yellow | 7. | F. Ev. | S. | Spain | 1820 |
| canariānsis | . | Yellow | 7. | G. Ev. | S. | Canaries | 1697 |
| cándicans, 1 | . | Yel. brn. | 6. | G. Ev. | S. | Madeira | 1714 |
| chamædrifóliā | . | Yellow | 7. | F. Ev. | S. | Spain | 1816 |
| crispatā | . | Yellow | 7. | F. Ev. | S. | Gibraltar | 1816 |
| hírsútā | . | Yellow | 6. | F. Ev. | S. Eur. | | 1731 |
| ilicifóliā | . | Yellow | 7. | F. Ev. | S. | Levant | |
| incānā | . | Yellow | 7. | F. Ev. | S. | Spain | 1752 |
| lanātā, 2 | . | Yellow | 7. | F. | A. | Egypt | 1787 |
| leucánthā | . | White | 7. | F. Ev. | S. | Spain | 1823 |
| montānā | . | Yel. brn. | 7. | H. | A. | Austria | 1752 |
| perfoliātā | . | Yellow | 9. | F. Ev. | S. | Levant | 1731 |
| romānā | . | Yelsh. | 7. | H. | A. | Italy | 1740 |
| scordioídēs | . | Yellow | 9. | H. Ev. | S. | France | 1597 |
| alpinā, 3 | . | Yellow | 7. | H. Ev. | S. | Pyrenees | 1827 |
| angustifóliā, 4 | . | Lt. yel. | 7. | H. Ev. | S. | Pyrenees | 1597 |
| elongátā, 5 | . | Yellow | 8. | F. Ev. | S. | Spain | 1822 |
| serrātā | . | Yellow | 8. | H. Her. | P. | Spain | 1818 |
| spínó-ā | . | Yellow | 8. | H. Her. | P. | Spain | |
| syrīācā | . | Yellow | 7. | F. Ev. | S. | Levant | 1597 |
| taúricā | . | Pa. yel. | 7. | H. | S. | Tauria | 1822 |

**SIDERODĒNDRŎN,** *Schreber.* From *sideros*, iron, and *dendron*, a tree; in reference to the hardness of the wood. *Linn.* 4, Or. 1, Nat. Or. *Cinchonaceæ.* A lofty-growing tree, thriving in loam, peat, and sand; cuttings root in sand, under a glass, in heat.

| | | | | | | |
|---|---|---|---|---|---|---|
| triflórūm | . | Pink | . | 8. Ev. T. W. Ind. | | 1793 |

**SIDERŌXŸLŎN,** *Linn.* From *sideros*, iron, and *xylon*, wood; because of the hardness of the wood. *Linn.* 5, Or. 1, Nat. Or. *Sapotaceæ.* These shrubs may be referred to *Sersalisia,* for culture and propagation.

| | | | | | | |
|---|---|---|---|---|---|---|
| inérmē | . | White | . | 7. | G. Ev. | S. C. G. H. | 1692 |
| tomentósūm | . | Dull wht. | . | 8. Ev. S. E. Ind. | | 1818 |

**SIDESADDLE-FLOWER, see *Sarracēniā.***

**SIEGESBĒCKIĀ,** *Linn.* In honour of George Siegesbeck, M.D., a German botanist. *Linn.* 19, Or. 2, Nat. Or. *Compositæ.* A genus of rather pretty annuals; the seed should be sown on a hotbed in spring, and the seedlings, when sufficiently strong, planted into the open border, about the end of May.

| | | | | | | |
|---|---|---|---|---|---|---|
| cordifóliā | . | Yellow | . | 8. H. | A. | Mexico | 1826 |
| droseroídēs | . | Yellow | . | 8. H. | A. | Mexico | 1825 |
| flosculósā | . | Yellow | . | 6. H. | A. | Peru | 1784 |
| ibéricā | . | White | . | 8. H. | A. | Iberia | 1818 |
| orientális | . | Yellow | . | 9. H. | A. | India | 1730 |
| triangulāris | . | Yellow | . | 8. H. | A. | Mexico | 1825 |

**SIEVĒRSIĀ,** *Willdenow.* In honour of M. Sievers, a Russian botanical collector. *Linn.* 12, Or. 3, Nat. Or. *Rosaceæ.* Interesting plants, thriving in any light soil; and readily increased by seeds, or by dividing the root. *Synonymes:* 1. *Adamsia glacialis.* 2. *Geum Peckii.* 3. *G. triflora.*

| | | | | | | |
|---|---|---|---|---|---|---|
| anemonoídēs | . | Yellow | . | 7. H. Her. | P. | Kamtsch. | 1820 |
| glaciālis, 1 | . | Yellow | . | 7. H. Her. | P. | Siberia | 1819 |
| montānā | . | Yellow | . | 7. H. Her. | P. | Austria | 1597 |
| Pēckii, 2 | . | Yellow | . | 7. H. Her. | P. N. Amer. | | 1826 |
| réptāns | . | Yellow | . | 7. H. Her. | P. | Switzerl. | 1597 |
| rósea | . | Yellow | . | 5. H. Her. | P. | Rocky M. | 1827 |
| triflórā, 3 | . | Yellow | . | 7. H. Her. | P. | Louisiana | 1826 |

**SILĀŬS,** *Besser.* A name given to an umbelliferous plant by Pliny. *Linn.* 5, Or. 2, Nat. Or. *Umbelliferæ.* Hardy herbaceous plants, of no interest; increased by divisions or seeds. *Synonymes:* 1. *Sium peucedanoides.* 2. *Ligusticum longifolium* 3. *Peucedanum Silaus, Cnidium Silaus.* 4. *Pastinaca rigida, Sium rigidum* 5. *S. Mathioli—S. carvifolius* ), *longifolius* 2, *pratensis* 3, *rigidus* 4, *tenuifolius* 5.

**SILĒNĒ,** *Linn.* From *sialon*, saliva; in allusion to the viscid moisture on the stalks of many of the species, by which the smaller kinds of flies are entrapped; hence, also, the English name of the genus, *Catchfly.* *Linn.* 10, Or. 3, Nat. Or. *Silenaceæ.* Elegant flowering plants, succeeding best in a light, rich soil. The shrubby kinds are readily increased by young cuttings, planted in sand or soil, under a glass. The hardy herbaceous kinds may be planted in the open border; the dwarfer species thrive well on rock-work, but duplicates should be kept in small pots, as alpines, that they may be sheltered by a frame in winter. The seeds of the hardy annual and biennial kinds only have to be sown, about the beginning of April, where they are intended to

[ 291 ]

remain. They may all be easily multiplied by seeds, and some of the herbaceous sorts by dividing the plants at the root in spring. *Synonymes:* 1. *S. conoidea.* 2. *S. hirsuta.* 3 *Cucubalus chloræfolius.*

| | | | | | | |
|---|---|---|---|---|---|---|
| acaúlis | . | Rose | . | 7. H. Her. | P. | Britain | . |
| albā | . | White | . | 7. H. Her. | P. | Britain | . |
| fœmina | . | Red | . | 7. H. Her. | P. | Scotland | . |
| exucāpā | . | Red | . | 7. H. Her. | P. | Switzerl. | 1819 |
| más | . | Rose | . | 7. H. Her. | P. | Scotland | . |
| ægyptiācā | . | Pink | . | 7. H. | A. | Egypt | 1800 |
| amœná | . | White | . | 7. H. Her. | P. | Tartary | 1779 |
| angustifóliā | . | White | . | 7. H. Her. | P. | Europe | 1817 |
| apétalā | . | Apetal | . | 6. H. | A. | | 1801 |
| Armériā | . | Pink | . | 8. H. | A. | England | . |
| albā | . | White | . | 8. H. | A. | | . |
| ascéndēns | . | Red | . | 6. H. | A. | Spain | 1822 |
| Atōciŏn | . | Pink | . | 6. H. | A. | Levant | 1781 |
| bellidifóliā | . | Pink | . | 6. H. | A. | | 1794 |
| bicolŏr | . | Striped | . | 6. H. | A. | France | 1820 |
| bupleuroídēs | . | Wht. pur. | . | 7. H. Her. | P. | Persia | 1801 |
| cæspitósā | . | Pink | . | 6. H. Her. | P. | Caucasus | 1824 |
| campánulā | . | Grn. wht. | . | 7. H. Her. | P. | Piedmont | 1823 |
| cāná | . | Red | . | 7. H. Her. | P. | | 1824 |
| canariénsis | . | Red | . | 6. H. | A. | Madeira | 1822 |
| cáspica | . | Pink | . | 6. H. Her. | P. | Caucasus | 1823 |
| Catesbǽi | . | Pink | . | 6. H. Her. | P. | Carolina | 1810 |
| cathólica | . | Grn. wht. | . | 8. H. Her. | P. | Italy | 1711 |
| cerastoídēs | . | White | . | 7. H. | A. S. Eur. | | 1732 |
| cheiranthifóliā | . | Red | . | 7. H. | A. | San Rocco | 1821 |
| chloræfóliā | . | Ll. yel. | . | 8. H. Her. | P. | Armenia | 1796 |
| chlorántha | . | Grn. wht | . | 7. H. Her. | P. | Germany | 1732 |
| ciliátā | . | Purple | . | 6. H. Her. | Tr. | Crete | 1804 |
| cinérea | . | White | . | 6. H. | | N. Africa | 1819 |
| coarctátā | . | Pink | . | 6. H. | A. | Valencia | 1825 |
| colorātā | . | Purple | . | 6. H. | A. | Morocco | 1810 |
| compáctā | . | Pink | . | 8. H. | B. | Caucasus | 1823 |
| congéstā | . | Pink | . | 6. H. | A. | Greece | 1818 |
| conoídēa | . | Purple | . | 6. H. | A. S. Eur. | | 1683 |
| cordifóliā | . | Pink | . | 6. H. Her. | P. | Piedmont | 1819 |
| córsica | . | Purple | . | 6. H. Her. | P. | Corsica | 1820 |
| crassifóliā | . | Brown | . | 7. G. | | B. C. G. H. | 1774 |
| crética | . | Grn. wht. | . | 7. H. | B. | Crete | 1732 |
| cylindriflórā | . | Red | . | 6. H. | B. | Levant | 1824 |
| decúmbēns | . | Red | . | 6. H. | A. | Spain | 1823 |
| depréssā | . | White | . | 6. H. Her. | P. | Iberia | 1816 |
| discolŏr | . | Red | . | 4. H. | A. | Greece | 1817 |
| distáchyā | . | Pa. pur. | . | 6. H. | A. | Portugal | 1817 |
| dístichā | . | Red | . | 6. H. | A. | Minorca | 1817 |
| divaricātā | . | Red | . | 6. H. | A. | Sicily | 1818 |
| diversifóliā | . | Purple | . | 6. H. | A. | | 1820 |
| effósā | . | Wht. yel. | . | 7. H. Her. | P. | Volga | 1823 |
| elátā | . | White | . | 6. H. Her. | P. | Tauria | 1819 |
| élegāns | . | White | . | 6. H. Her. | P. | Portugal | 1819 |
| fabāriā | . | White | . | 7. F. Her. | P. | Sicily | 1731 |
| fimbriátā | . | White | . | 6. H. Her. | P. | Caucasus | 1803 |
| flavéscēns | . | Yellow | . | 6. H. Her. | P. | Hungary | 1804 |
| fruticósā | . | Pink | . | 6. F. Ev. | S. | Sicily | 1629 |
| gállica | . | Pink | . | 6. H. | A. | France | 1683 |
| graminiflórā | . | Purple | . | 6. H. | A. | | 1816 |
| gigántēā | . | White | . | 6. G. | B. | Africa | 1788 |
| glaucifóliā | . | Red | . | 6. H. Her. | P. | Spain | 1820 |
| grácilis | . | White | . | 7. H. | A. | | 1823 |
| graminifóliā | . | White | . | 6. H. Her. | P. | Altaia | 1819 |
| Gypsóphilā | . | White | . | 6. H. Her. | P. | | 1822 |
| hirsutíssimā, 2 | . | White | . | 6. H. | A. | Spain | 1821 |
| hispánica | . | Red | . | 6. H. Her. | P. | Spain | 1819 |
| híspida | . | Cream | . | 6. H. | A. | Barbary | 1817 |
| ibérica | . | White | . | 6. H. | A. | Iberia | 1823 |
| imbricátā | . | White | . | 6. H. | A. | N. Africa | 1818 |
| inclúsā | . | Red | . | 6. H. | A. | | 1817 |
| inflátā | . | White | . | 7. H. Her. | P. | Britain | . |
| hirsútā | . | White | . | 7. H. Her. | P. | Britain | . |
| infráctā | . | White | . | 7. H. Her. | P. | Hungary | 1800 |
| itálica | . | White | . | 6. H. | B. | Italy | 1759 |
| jenissénsis | . | Pink | . | 6. H. Her. | P. | Siberia | 1817 |
| lácera | . | White | . | 7. H. Tr. | B. | Caucasus | 1818 |
| laciniátā | . | Scarlet | . | 7. H. Her. | P. S. Amer. | | 1822 |
| lævigátā | . | Red | . | 6. H. | A. | Greece | 1817 |
| latifóliā | . | White | . | 7. H. Her. | P. | Barbary | 1817 |
| latifórā | . | White | . | 6. H. | A. | Spain | 1820 |
| linifóliā | . | Orn. yel. | . | 7. H. | A. | Portugal | 1817 |
| lívida | . | Wht. grn. | . | 6. H. Her. | P. | Carniola | 1816 |
| longicaúlis | . | Red | . | 6. H. | A. | Spain | 1818 |
| longiflórā | . | Li. pur. | . | 6. H. Her. | P. | Hungary | 1793 |
| longipétalā | . | Grn. wht. | . | 7. H. | A. | Aleppo | 1822 |
| lusitánicā | . | Pink | . | 6. H. | A. | Portugal | 1732 |
| marítimā | . | White | . | 8. H. Her. | P. | Britain | . |
| flóre plésō | . | White | . | 8. H. De. Tr. | | England | . |
| Mocinlánā | . | Purple | . | 6. F. Her. | P. | Mexico | 1827 |
| mollíssimā | . | Pink | . | 6. H. | A. | Italy | 1739 |
| multiflórā | . | White | . | 7. H. | B. | Hungary | 1794 |
| muscipúlā | . | Red | . | 7. H. | A. | Spain | 1596 |
| nemorālis | . | White | . | 6. H. | B. | Hungary | 1816 |
| nicæénsis | . | White | . | 6. H. | A. | Nice | 1820 |
| noctiflórā | . | Pink | . | 7. H. | A. | England | . |
| noctúrnā | . | White | . | 7. H. | A. S. Eur. | | 1683 |
| nyctánthā | . | Brown | . | 7. H. | A. | | 1815 |
| obtusifóliā | . | Purple | . | 6. H. | A. | | 1820 |

| | | | | | |
|---|---|---|---|---|---|
| ocymoídes | . . . . | | 4, H. Her. P. | | 1823 |
| Oliveriàna | . Red | . 7, H. | A. | Aleppo | 1818 |
| Orchídéä | . Rose | . 6, H. | A. | Levant | 1781 |
| ornátä | . Purple | . 7, S. | B. | C. G. H. | 1775 |
| Odtäe | . Cream | . 7, H. Her. P. | | England | |
| ovátä | . White | . 6, H. Her. P. | | N. Amer. | 1820 |
| paradóxä | . Pink | . 7, H. Her. P. | | Europe | |
| parvíflörä | . Grn. yel. | . 7, H. Her. P. | | Hungary | 1796 |
| parvifòliä | . Pink | . 6, H. Her. P. | | | 1817 |
| pátúlä | . White | . 7, H. Her. P. | | Barbary | 1823 |
| péndúlä | . Red | . 6, H. | A. | Sicily | 1731 |
| pennsylvánicä | . Red | . 6, H. Her. P. | | N. Amer. | 1806 |
| perfoliàta, 8 | . Red | . 6, H. | B. | Levant | 1817 |
| petrǽä | . White | . 7, H. Her. P. | | Hungary | 1822 |
| píctä | . Pink | . 7, H. | A. | France | 1817 |
| pilòsä | . White | . 8, H. Her. P. | | Europe | 1739 |
| pínguïs | . Brn. red | . 6, H. | A. | Denmark | 1816 |
| polyphýllä | . White | . 6, H. Her. P. | | Austria | 1800 |
| porténsïs | . Pink | . 7, H. | A. | Portugal | 1759 |
| procúmbéns | . Pink | . 6, H. Her. P. | | Siberia | 1823 |
| Psammítïs | . Cream | . 6, H. | B. | | 1818 |
| Pseudo-Atòcïon | . Rose | . 6, H. | A. | N. Africa | 1820 |
| pubéscéns | . Purple | . 6, H. | A. | Corsica | 1818 |
| pumílïo | . Pink | . 6, H. | A. | Germany | 1823 |
| quadridentàtä | . White | . 6, H. Her. P. | | Alps | 1822 |
| quadrífïdä | . White | . 6, H. Her. P. | | Verona | 1818 |
| quinquevúlnérä | . Blood | . 7, H. | A. | England | |
| ramòsä | . White | . 7, H. | A. | Barbary | 1820 |
| ramosíssïmä | . Rose | . 6, H. | B. | Candia | |
| refléxä | . Purple | . 6, H. Her. P. | | S. Eur. | 1726 |
| règïä | . Crimson | . 6, H. Her. P. | | N. Amer. | 1811 |
| répéns | . Pink | . 8, H. Her. P. | | Siberia | 1823 |
| Requienïi | . Wht. red | . 6, H. Her. P. | | Corsica | 1823 |
| reticulàtä | . Rose | . 7, H. | A. | Barbary | 1804 |
| rubéllä | . Flesh | . 6, H. | A. | Portugal | 1732 |
| ruthénïcä | . Grn. yel. | . 6, H. Her. P. | | Russia | 1820 |
| sabulètòrúm | . Purple | . 6, H. | A. | | 1818 |
| saxátïlïs | . Green | . 6, H. Her. P. | | Siberia | 1800 |
| Saxífrägä | . Flesh | . 7, H. Her. P. | | France | 1640 |
| secundíflörä | . Purple | . 6, H. | A. | Spain | 1820 |
| sedòídés | . Grn. wht. | 7, H. | A. | Crete | 1804 |
| serícéä | . Pink | . 7, H. | A. | S. Eur. | 1801 |
| sibíricä | . Rose | . 7, H. Her. P. | | Siberia | 1773 |
| spatulàtä | . Purple | . 6, H. | B. | Caucasus | 1823 |
| spergulífòlïä | . White | . 6, H. Her. P. | | Armenia | 1817 |
| stellàtä | . White | . 7, H. Her. P. | | N. Amer. | 1696 |
| strìctä | . Purple | . 6, H. | A. | Spain | 1802 |
| supìnä | . Pink | . 7, H. Her. P. | | Caucasus | 1804 |
| tatàrïcä | . White | . 7, H. Her. P. | | Russia | 1769 |
| tenuifòliä | . Purple | . 6, H. | A. | Dahuria | 1820 |
| tenùïs | . Cream | . 7, H. Her. P. | | Siberia | 1816 |
| tridentàtä | . Pink | . 5, H. | A. | Barbary | 1823 |
| undulæfòliä | . Red | . 6, H. | A. | Sardinia | 1829 |
| undulàtä | . Red | . 9, G. | B. | C. G. H. | 1775 |
| Vallésïi | . Flesh | . 7, H. Her. P. | | Switzerl. | 1765 |
| vespertìnä | . Rose | . 7, H. | A. | Brittany | 1796 |
| virgínïcä | . Purple | . 7, H. Her. P. | | N. Amer. | 1783 |
| viridíflörä | . Grn. wht. | 7, H. | A. | Spain | 1739 |
| viscaginòídés | . Pink | . 6, H. Her. P. | | Dauria | 1824 |
| víscídä | . Wht. grn. | 6, H. | B. | Carniola | 1820 |
| viscòsä | . White | . 6, H. | B. | Levant | 1731 |
| viscosíssïmä | . . | . 6, H. | A. | Naples | 1824 |
| Wolgénsïs | . Grn. yel. | 7, H. Her. P. | | Volga | 1824 |

*Alpéstrïs, ánglïcä, antirrhínä, Béhén, canéscéns, cérnòsä, cérnúä, clandestìnä, cònïcä, C. ramòsä 1, dichotòmä, inapértä, Índïcä, micránthä, micropétálä, nútáns, pusíllä, rupéstrïs, Stevéni.*

SILÉR, *Scopoli.* Siler, withy, from *salio* to spring; alluding to the rapid growth of the plant. *Linn.* 5. Or. 1, Nat. Or. *Umbelliferæ.* This species is quite worthless, and flourishes in the commonest soil. *Synonymes:* 1. *Laserpitium trilobum, Siler aquilegifolium—S. trilobum* 1.

SILICEOUS, flinty.

SILICLE, the small short pod of *Cruciferæ.*

SILIQUA, the long cylindrical pod of *Cruciferæ.*

SILK COTTON-TREE, see *Bombax.*

SILKEN PUBESCENCE, a very soft kind of pubescence.

SILK TREE, see *Acacia julibrissin.*

SILPHIÜM, *Linn.* From *silphion,* the Greek name applied to an Asafœtida plant. *Linn.* 19, Or. 4, Nat. Or. *Compositæ.* Tall growing plants, of little beauty, and best adapted for the back of flower borders. Any common soil suits them; and they may be increased freely by dividing the plants at the root. *Synonymes:* 1. *Coreopsis latifolia.* 2. *S. tomentosum.*

| | | | | | |
|---|---|---|---|---|---|
| erythrocaulôn | . Yellow | . 8, H. Her. P. | | N. Amer. | |
| glaucûm, 1 | . Yellow | . 8, H. Her. P. | | N. Amer. | 1786 |
| pûmílûm, 2 | . Yellow | . 8, H. Her. P. | | N. Amer. | 1786 |

*Asterìscûs, atropurpúrêûm, compósïtûm, conjúnctûm, connátûm, laciniàtûm, perfoliàtûm, terebinthinàcêûm, ternàtûm, trifoliàtûm.*

SILVER-TREE, see *Leucadéndrôn serícêûm.*

SILVER-WEED, see *Argyreïä.*

SILYBÜM, *Vaillant.* A name applied by Greek writers to a plant now unknown. *Linn.* 19, Or. 1, Nat. Or. *Compositæ.* These plants succeed in any common soil, and are propagated by seeds. *Synonymes:* 1. *Cnicus cernuus.* 2. *Carduus marianus.*

| | | | | | |
|---|---|---|---|---|---|
| cérnúûm, 1 | . Yellow | . 6, H. Her. P. | | Siberia | 1775 |
| Mariànûm, 2 | . Purple | . 7, H. | B. | Britain | |

SIMĀBÄ, *Aublet.* The native name of *S. guianensis.* *Linn.* 10, Or. 1, Nat. Or. *Simarubaceæ.* These shrubs should be grown in a mixture of turfy loam and peat; and cuttings of the ripened wood will root in sand, under a glass, in heat.

| | | | | |
|---|---|---|---|---|
| guianénsïs | . . White | . 8. Ev. S. | Guiana | 1826 |
| orinocénsïs | . . White | . 8. Ev. S. | Orinoco | 1818 |

SIMARŪBÄ, *Aublet.* Simaruba is the Caribbean name of *S. officinalis.* *Linn.* 10, Or. 1, Nat. Or. *Simarubaceæ.* Valuable plants, on account of their medical properties. For culture and propagation, see *Quassia.* The *Simaruba* in *Materia Medica,* is the bark of the root of this tree; it is much used in curing obstinate dysenteries and diarrhœas. Fluxes, induced by warm climates, are speedily cured by this bark. *Synonymes:* 1. *Quassia excelsa.* 2. *Quassia Simaruba.*

| | | | | |
|---|---|---|---|---|
| excélsä, 1 | . Yel. wht. | 8. Ev. T. | Jamaica | 1818 |
| officinàlïs, 2 | . Yel. wht. | 8. Ev. S. | W. Ind. | 1789 |

SIMPLE, not divided.

SINĀPÏS, *Tournefort.* From the Celtic *nap,* a designation applied to all plants resembling the cabbage or turnip. *Linn.* 15, Nat. Or. *Cruciferæ.* Principally annual plants; the seeds of which have only to be sown in the open ground in spring. Mustard (the use of which is familiar to every one) is the ground seed of *S. nigra.* *S. Alba* is extensively cultivated as a small salad. The seeds are also swallowed whole, to the quantity of a table-spoonful, or more, to stimulate the stomach in some cases of dyspepsia, and to excite the peristaltic motion of the intestines, when they are torpid.

| | | | | | |
|---|---|---|---|---|---|
| albä | . Yellow | . 6, H. | A. | Britain | |
| amplexicaùlïs | . Yellow | . 7, H. | A. | Algiers | 1829 |
| chinénsïs | . Yellow | . 7, H. | A. | China | 1783 |
| frutéscéns | . Yellow | . 7, G. Ev. S. | | Madeira | 1777 |
| nudicaùlïs | . Yellow | . 6, H. Her. P. | | Spain | 1818 |
| pekinénsïs | . . | . H. | A. | China | 1838 |

*Allíònïi, ápúlä, arvénsïs, auriculàtä, brassicàtä, cérnúä, disséctä, foliòsä, geniculàtä, hastàtä, heterophýllä, híspïdä, incànä, integrifòliä, júncéä, Kàbér, lævigàtä, nígrä, N. lævigàtä, N. torulòsä, N. túrgïdä, N. villòsä, nudicaùlïs, orientàlïs, pubéscéns, ramòsä, retrohirsûtä, subpinnatífïdä, taùrïcä, túrgïdä.*

SINGLE-SEEDED CUCUMBER, see *Sicyôs.*

SINNÍNGÏÄ, *Nees.* In honour of William Sinning, Gardener to the University of Bonn, on the Rhine. This genus of very pretty plants ought to be in every collection. Their culture and propagation is the same as that recommended for the genus *Gloxinia.*

| | | | | |
|---|---|---|---|---|
| calycìnä | . Red wht. | . 7, S. Ev. S. | Jamaica | 1824 |
| guttàtä | . Yel. red | . 6, S. Ev. S. | Brasil | 1827 |
| Héllérï | . Wht. grn. | 6, S. Ev. S. | Rio Jan. | 1820 |
| velutìnä | . Yellow | . 6, S. Ev. S. | Brasil | 1827 |
| villòsä | . Yel. grn. | 6, S. Ev. S. | Brasil | 1827 |

SINUATE, cut so as to have a broken and wavy margin.

SINUS, the indentation or recess formed by the lobes of leaves, and other bodies.

SIPHOCAMPÝLÜS, *Pohl.* From *siphon,* a tube, and *kampulos,* curved; in allusion to the curved tube of the corolla. *Linn.* 5, Or. 1, Nat. Or. *Lobeliaceæ.* Very beautiful little shrubs, succeeding in a light sandy soil; and readily increased by cuttings. *Synonymes:* 1. *Lobelia gigantea.* 2. *Lobelia surinamensis.*

| | | | | |
|---|---|---|---|---|
| bicôlör | . Red yel. | . 4, H. Ev. S. | Georgia | 1835 |
| gigantéä, 1 | . Yel. red | . 8. Ev. S. | N. Granada | |
| surinaménsïs, 2 | . Orange | . 4, S. Ev. S. | Amer. | 1786 |

SIPHŌNÏÄ, *Richard.* From *siphon,* a pipe; the use made of the exudation, which constitutes Indian rubber. *Linn.* 21, Or. 10, Nat. Or. *Euphorbiaceæ.* This plant grows freely in sandy loam and peat; and cuttings of the half ripened wood will root in sand, under a glass, in heat. The Caoutchouc of Para is obtained from this species. *Synonymes:* 1. *S. elastica, Jatropha elastica.*

| | | | | |
|---|---|---|---|---|
| Cahúchû, 1 | . . . | 8. Ev. S. | Guiana | 1823 |

SIR JOSEPH BANKS' PINE, see *Araucāria imbricātā.*

SISÓN, *Linn.* From the Celtic *sisun,* a running stream; some plants formerly in this genus were found in running streams. *Linn.* 5, Or. 2, Nat. Or. *Umbelliferæ.* The seeds merely require sowing in common garden soil in spring—*S. Amŏmum, arvēnsĕ, capillācĕum, flexuŏsum.*

SISTOTRĒMĂ, *Fries.* From *sisto,* to place, and *trema,* orifice; alluding to the pores being in rows. *Linn.* 24, Or. 9, Nat. Or. *Fungi.* This species is found by the waysides—*S. conflūens.*

SISYMBRĬŬM, *Allioni.* An old Greek name of unknown origin. *Linn.* 15, Nat. Or. *Cruciferæ. S. Millefŏlium* is a pretty shrub, growing freely in any light soil; and readily increased by cuttings. The others are worthless annuals and biennials, flourishing in the open ground, in any soil. *Synonymes:* 1. *S. sinapioides, Sinapis pyrenaica.* 2. *S. altissimum.* 3. *S. orientale.* 4. *S. Loeselii.* 5. *S. gallicum.* 6. *S. glabrum.* 7. *Erysimum officinale.* 8. *S. affine.* 9. *S. contortum.*

| | | | | |
|---|---|---|---|---|
| Millefŏlium | . . | Yellow | . 7, G. Ev. S. Canaries | . 1779 |

*Acutāngulum* 1, *aspĕrum, austrĭăcum, brachycārpum, bursĭfōlium, canēscēns, Colŭmnæ, C. altissĭmum* 2, *C. orientālĕ* 3, *C. villosissĭmum* 4, *contortuplicātum, cornĭculātum, crassĭfōlium, Cummingiānum, eckhartubergēnsĕ, erysimoidĕs, fŭgāx, hirsŭtum, hispānĭcum, incānum, Irio, I. gallĭcum* 5, *I. glăbrum* 6, *jūncĕum, lineārĕ, nitĭdum, obtusāngŭlum, officĭnālĕ* 7, *pannŏnĭcum, pērsĭcum, pinnatĭfĭdum, polycerdĭŭm, pŭmĭlum, rigĭdum, runcinātum, Sophĭă, strictissĭmum, subhastātum, supīnum, tanacetĭfōlium, T. affĭnĕ* 8, *T. contŏrtum* 9, *taraxacĭfōlium, Tilliĕri, torulŏsum, tripinnātum.*

SISYRINCHĬŬM, *Linn.* From *sys,* a pig, and *rygchos,* snout; so called on account of swine grubbing the roots. *Linn.* 8, Or. 1, Nat. Or. *Iridaceæ.* A genus of very pretty plants when in flower. They succeed well in any light soil; and increase freely by seeds or offsets. *Synonymes:* 1. *Marica iridioides.* 2. *M. iridifolia.* 3. *S. bermudianum.* 4. *M. plicata.*

| | | | | |
|---|---|---|---|---|
| ancĕps | . . . | Blue | . 6, H. Her. P. N. Amer. | . 1693 |
| bermudiānum, 1 | . | Blue | . 6, G. Her. P. Bermudas | . 1732 |
| califŏrnĭcum | . . | Yellow | . 7, F. Her. P. California. | . 1796 |
| chilēnsĕ | . . | Blue | . 7, G. Her. P. Chile | . 1826 |
| convolūtum | . . | Yellow | . 5, F. Her. P. S. Amer. | . 1816 |
| CummingII | . . | Cream | . 7, H. Her. P. S. Amer. | . 1832 |
| glaucophȳllum | . | Blue | . 8, H. Her. P. N. Amer. | . 1830 |
| graminĭfōlium | . | Yellow | . 4, F. Her. P. Chile | . 1825 |
| pŭmĭlum | . . | Yellow | . 10, S. Her. P. Chile | . |
| grandĭflōrum | . | White | . 5, H. Her. P. N. Amer. | . 1826 |
| hirtēllum | . . | White | . 7, F. Her. P. N. Amer. | . 1830 |
| iridĭfōlium, 2 | . | Yellow | . 6, F. Her. P. S. Amer. | . 1832 |
| jūncĕum | . . | Lilac | . 6, G. Her. P. Chile | . 1832 |
| laxum | . . . | Yellow | . 6, F. Her. P. S. Amer. | . 1818 |
| lutēscens | . . | Yellish. | . 6, F. Her. P. Chile | . 1830 |
| lūtĕum | . . | Yellow | . 6, F. Her. P. S. Amer. | . 1823 |
| macrocĕphălum | . | Yellish. | . 6, F. Her. P. | |
| maculātum | . | Yel. spot. | . 6, F. Her. P. Chile | . 1830 |
| micrānthum | . | Yellow | . 6, G. Her. P. S. Amer. | . 1815 |
| mucronātum | . | Blue | . 6, H. Her. P. N. Amer. | . 1812 |
| Nuttāllĭĭ, 3 | . | Blue | . 6, H. Her. P. N. Amer. | . 1823 |
| odoratissĭmum | . | White | . 6, F. Her. P. S. Amer. | . 1828 |
| palmĭfōlium | . | White | . 2, S. Her. P. Brasil | . 1823 |
| pedunculātum | . | Yellow | . 9, F. Her. P. Chile | . 1827 |
| plicātum, 4 | . | White | . 2, S. Her. P. W. Ind. | . 1779 |
| speciōsum | . . | Blue | . 6, G. Her. P. Chile | . 1836 |
| striātum | . . | Yellow | . 6, H. Her. P. Mexico | . 1788 |
| tenuĭfōlium | . | Yellow | . 5, F. Her. P. S. Amer. | . 1816 |

SIŬM, *Linn.* From the Celtic *siw,* water; the habitat of most of the species. *Linn.* 5, Or. 2, Nat. Or. *Umbelliferæ.* These plants thrive best in a very moist soil; and are increased readily by dividing the roots, or by seeds. The succulent roots of *S. Sisarum* were formerly much esteemed in cookery under the name of *Skirret. Synonymes:* 1. *Bunium ferulæfolium.*

| | | | | |
|---|---|---|---|---|
| Falcārĭă | . . | White | . 7, H. Her. P. Europe | . 1726 |
| Sisărum | . . | White | . 7, H. Her. P. China | . 1548 |

*Angustĭfōlium, ferulācĕum* 1, *lancĭfōlium, lineārĕ, podŏlĭcum, virĭdĕscēns.*

SKIRRET, see *Siŭm Sisărum.*

SKULLCAP, see *Scutellārĭă.*

SLIPPER PLANT, see *Pedilānthĕs.*

SLIPPERWORT, see *Calceolārĭă.*

SLOĀNĔĂ, *Linn.* In honour of Sir Hans Sloane, once President of the Royal Society, founder of the British Museum, and Chelsea Botanical Garden, died in 1753. *Linn.* 13, Or. 1, Nat. Or. *Tiliaceæ.* A genus of fine lofty growing trees, with large

leaves. They succeed best in a mixture of loam and peat; and cuttings of the ripened wood will root in sand, under a glass, in heat.

| | | | | |
|---|---|---|---|---|
| dentātā | . . . | White | . 8. Ev. T. S. Amer. | . 1752 |
| sinemariēnsĭs | . | White | . 8. Ev. T. Guiana . | . 1823 |

SLOE-TREE, see *Prūnŭs spinōsā.*

SMALL NUT, see *Triumfētta Lappŭlā.*

SMALL BURDOCK, see *Xanthĭum strumārĭă.*

SMALL CARDAMON, see *Amōmum Cardamōmum.*

SMALL LUPINE, see *Lupīnŭs nānŭs.*

SMALL MONARDA, see *Pycnānthĕmum monardēllā.*

SMALL PALM, see *Sābăl Palmētto.*

SMALL PEPPERMINT, see *Thȳmŭs Piperēllā.*

SMEATHMĀNNĬĂ, *Decandolle.* In honour of Smeathman, a naturalist, who travelled in Africa, and collected many botanical specimens. *Linn.* 13, Or. 6, Nat. Or. *Passifloraceæ.* A very beautiful shrub, which ought to be in every stove. A compost of loam, peat, and sand, suits it; and half ripened cuttings root freely in sand, under a glass, in heat.

| | | | | |
|---|---|---|---|---|
| lævigātā | . . . | White | . 2, S. Ev. S. S. Leone | . 1823 |

SMILACĪNĂ, *Desfontaines.* From *smile,* a scraper; alluding to the roughness of the stems. *Linn.* 6, Or. 1, Nat. Or. *Smilaceæ.* Interesting plants, succeeding well in any light soil; and increased readily by divisions.

| | | | | |
|---|---|---|---|---|
| bifolĭă | . . . | White | . 5, H. Her. P. N. Eur. | . 1596 |
| borealis | . . . | Yellow | . 5, H. Her. P. N. Amer. | . 1787 |
| canadēnsĭs | . . | | . 6, H. Her. P. N. Amer. | . 1812 |
| ciliātā | . . . | White | . 5, H. Her. P. N. Amer. | . 1823 |
| racemōsā | . . | Pa. yel. | . 5, H. Her. P. N. Amer. | . 1640 |
| ramōsā | . . | Pa. yel. | . 5, H. Her. P. Siberia . | . 1820 |
| stellātā | . . | White | . 5, H. Her. P. N. Amer. | . 1633 |
| trifolĭă | . . | White | . 6, H. Her. P. N. Amer. | . 1812 |
| umbellātā | . . | White | . 5, H. Her. P. N. Amer. | . 1778 |

SMILĀX, *Linn.* From *smile,* a scraper; the stems are rough from prickles. *Linn.* 22, Or. 6, Nat. Or. *Smilaceæ.* Climbers, of little beauty. They grow well in loam and peat; and increase readily by suckers. *S. Sarsaparilla* is well known as a restorative of health, after the use of mercury. *Synonymes:* 1. *S. mauritanica.* 2. *S. lanceolata, Watsoni.*

| | | | | |
|---|---|---|---|---|
| China | . . | Wht. grn. | . 7. Ev. Cl. China | . 1759 |
| rūbēns | . . | Grn. wht. | . 7. H. Ev. Cl. N. Amer. | . 1812 |
| sagittæfolĭă | . | White | . 9, G. Ev. S. China . | . 1820 |
| Sarsaparilā | . . | Wht. grn. | . 7. H. Ev. Cl. N. Amer. | . 1664 |
| Watsōnĭ | . . | Wht. grn. | . 7. H. De. Cl. N. Amer. | . 1812 |

*Acumĭnātā, alpīnā, aspĕrā, A. auriculātā, A. mauritānĭcă* 1, *austrālĭs, bōnă nŏx, brasiliēnsĭs, cadūcă, canariēnsĭs, catalōnĭcă, cumanēnsĭs, excēlsă, glābră, glaucă, glycyphȳllă, hastātă, H. lanceolātā* 2, *havanēnsĭs, herbācĕă, hŏrrĭdă, lanceolātă, latifōlĭă, laurĭfōlĭă, longĭfōlĭă, maculātă, nĭgră, ovalĭfōlĭă, penduncŭlārĭs, prolĭfĕră, Pseūdŏ-Chīnă, pŭbĕră, quadrangulārĭs, rotundĭfōlĭă, syphilĭtĭcă, tamnoidĕs, virginiānd, Waltĕri, zeylānĭcă.*

SMĬTHĬĂ, *H. Kew.* In honour of the late Sir James Edward Smith, M.D., F.R.S., and P.L.S., founder of the Linnæan society, possessor of the Linnæan herbarium, and author of numerous well-known botanical works; died in 1829. *Linn.* 17, Or. 4, Nat. Or. *Leguminosæ.* The seeds of these plants should be sown in pots, in a mixture of peat, sand, and loam, and placed in heat. They must be potted off singly, and shifted into larger pots as they grow.

| | | | | |
|---|---|---|---|---|
| confērtă | . . | Yellow | . 7, S. Tr. A. N. Holl. | . 1820 |
| geminiflōră | . | Yellow | . 8, S. Tr. A. E. Ind. . | . 1810 |
| sensitīvă | . . | Yellow | . 8, S. Tr. A. E. Ind. . | . 1785 |

SMOOTH, without hairs.

SMȲRNĬŬM, *Linnæus.* From *smyrna,* myrrh; the plants have the odour of Myrrh. *Linn.* 5, Or. 2, Nat. Or. *Umbelliferæ.* These plants succeed in any common garden soil; and are readily increased by seeds.

| | | | | |
|---|---|---|---|---|
| apiifolĭum | . . | Pur. yel. | . 6, H. | B. Candia . | . 1731 |
| cicutārĭum | . | Grn. wht. | . 6, H. Her. P. Caucasus | . 1827 |
| Olusātrum | . . | Green | . 5, H. | B. Britain . | . |

SNAIL-FLOWER, see *Phaseŏlŭs Caracāllă.*

SNAKE-GOURD, see *Trichosānthĕs.*

SNAKE-ROOT, see *Aristolōchĭă serpentārĭă.*

SNAKE-ROOT, see *Ophiorhīzā.*

SNAKE'S-BEARD, see *Ophiopŏgŏn.*

SNAKE'S-TONGUE, see *Ophioglōssum.*

SNAKEWEED, see *Polygŏnum bistŏrtă.*

SNAKEWOOD, see *Cecrŏpĭă.*

SNAKEWOOD, see *Colubrīnă.*

SNAPDRAGON, see *Antirrhīnum.*

SNAPDRAGON, see *Silēnĕ antirrhīnă.*

SNAP-TREE, see *Justicia Hyssopifolia*.

SNEEZEWORT, see *Achillea Ptarmica*.

SNOWBALL-TREE, see *Viburnum Opulus*.

SNOWBERRY, see *Chiococca*.

SNOWDROP, see *Galanthus*.

SNOWDROP, see *Anemone sylvestris*.

SNOWDROP-TREE, see *Halesia*.

SNOWFLAKE, see *Leucojum*.

SOAPBERRY, see *Sapindus*.

SOAPWORT, see *Saponaria*.

SOBOLEWSKIA, *Bieberstein*. In honour of G. Sobolewski, a Russian botanist. *Linn.* 15, Nat. Or. *Cruciferæ*. The seeds of this biennial may be sown on rock-work, in any common soil. ◦ *Synonyme:* 1. *Crambe macrocarpa—S lithophila* 1.

SOBOLIFEROUS, producing young plants from the roots.

SOFT GRASS, see *Holcus*.

SOJA, *Mænch*. From *sooja*, the name given to a sauce prepared from the seeds in Japan. *Linn.* 17, Or. 4, Nat. Or. *Leguminosæ*. The seeds of this plant may be sown in a warm sheltered situation in May, or raised with the tender annuals, and afterwards planted out. *Synonyme:* 1. *Dolichos Soja*.

hispida, 1 . . . Violet . 7, H.    A. E. Ind. . . 1790

SOLANDRA, *Linn.* In honour of Daniel Charles Solander, LL.D , F.R.S , a Swede, companion of Sir Joseph Banks in his voyage round the world, and collector of the botanical notes made during that expedition. They are preserved in the British Museum, and exhibit great learning and deep research. *Linn.* 5, Or. 1, Nat. Or. *Solanaceæ*. This is a splendid genus of plants; the foliage being very fine, and the flowers large, like those of the *Brugmansia*. The best way to induce them to flower is to grow them in two parts turfy loam, and one of peat, liberally applying heat and water till they have perfected a good growth; then gradually withhold water until the leaves drop off from drought, and they will flower profusely. Cuttings, planted in mould or tan, will root without any difficulty. Those taken from the flowering shoots are more likely to produce flowers while small.

grandiflora . . . Pa. yel. . 8, S. Ev. Cl. Jamaica . 1781
guttata . . . . Pa. yel. . . 8. Ev. S. Mexico . 1830
nitida . . . . Yelsh. wht. . 8. Ev. S. E. Ind. . 1820
oppositifolia . . White . . 8. Ev. S. Ceylon . 1820
viridiflora . . . Green . . 8. Ev. S. S. Amer. . 1815

SOLANUM, *Linn.* The derivation of this word is quite uncertain; some derive it from *Sol*, the sun; others say it is *Solanum*, from *Sus*, being serviceable in disorders of swine; and others assert that it is from *Solor* to comfort, referring to its soothing narcotic effects. *Linn.* 5, Or. 1, Nat. Or. *Solanaceæ*. All the more showy species of this extensive genus thrive best in a light, rich soil, and are readily increased by seeds, or by cuttings, in sand, under a glass. A great number of them are highly deserving of cultivation, on account of their ornamental appearance. The seeds of the tender annual species should be raised on a hotbed, and planted out in the open ground about the end of May in a sheltered, dry situation. *S. tuberosum* is that well-known and invaluable root, the potato, which, in a state of putrefaction, is said to give out a most vivid light, sufficient to read by. This was particularly remarked by an officer on guard at Strasburg, who thought the barracks were on fire, in consequence of the light thus emitted from a cellar full of potatoes. *S. nigrum* and some others are highly virulent poisons. *S. Dulcamara* is a very dangerous plant; when first bruised or chewed it is bitter, which quickly gives place to a considerable degree of sweetness, hence its name *Dulcamara* or *Bittersweet*. The berries may be readily taken for currants by children; they excite vomiting and catharsis. Floyer states that thirty of them killed a dog in less than three hours, remaining undigested in the stomach. *Synonymes:* 1. *Nycterium amazonium*. 2. *S. Quitense*. 3. *S. violaceum*. 4. *N. cornutum*. 5. *N. Fontanesianum*. 6. *N. lobatum*. 7. *N. heterodoxum*. 8 *S. undatum*. 9. *S. miniatum*. 10. *S. longifolium*. 11. *S. ovigerum*. 12. *S. insanum*. 13. *S. uniflorum*. 14. *S. melanocerasum*. 15. *S. Cervantesii*. 16. *S. spinosissimum*. 17. *N. rostratum*. 18. *S. oleraceum*. 19. *N. cordifolium*.

aculeatissimum . Pa. blue . 4, G. Ev. S. S. Amer. . 1816
æthiopicum . . White . 8, H.    A. Æthiop. . 1597

| | | | | | |
|---|---|---|---|---|---|
| aggregatum . . | Purple | . 6, S. Ev. | S. | C. G. H. | . 1821 |
| amazonium, 1 . | Blue | . 7, S. Ev. | S. | Mexico | . 1800 |
| angulatum, 2 . | White | . 7, S. Ev. | S. | Lima | . 1825 |
| appendiculatum . | White | . 7, G. Ev. | S. | Mexico | . 1823 |
| arboreum . . | White | . 6, S. Ev. | S. | Cumana | . 1819 |
| argentatum . . | | . 6, S. Ev. | S. | Rio Jan. | . 1824 |
| armatum . . | | . 8, G. Ev. | S. | N. S. W. | . 1818 |
| astroides . . | White | . 6, S. Ev. | S. | | . 1818 |
| auriculatum . . | Violet | . 8, S. Ev. | S. | Madagas. | . 1773 |
| bahamense . . | White | . 6, S. Ev. | S. | Bahama | . 1732 |
| Balbisii . . | Blue | . 7, G. Ev. | S. | S. Amer. | . 1816 |
| betaceum . . | Pink | . 6, S. Ev. | S. | S. Amer. | . 1803 |
| bonbense . . | White | . 6, G. Ev. | S. | Mexico | . 1822 |
| bonariense . . | White | . 7, G. Ev. | S. | B. Ayres | . 1727 |
| brasilianum . . | | . 6, S. Ev. | S. | Brazil | . 1820 |
| Brownii, 3 . . | Violet | . 7, G. Ev. | S. | N. S. W. | . 1820 |
| calycinum . . | Blue | . 6, S. Her. | P. | Mexico | . 1820 |
| campanulatum . | Blue | . 6, G. Her. | P. | N. S. W. | . 1836 |
| castrifolium . . | White | . 6, S. Ev. | S. | | . 1823 |
| cinereum . . | | . 8, G. Ev. | S. | N. Holl. | . 1823 |
| coagulans . . | Purple | . 7, G. Ev. | S. | Arabia | . 1802 |
| coccineum . . | White | . 6, S. Ev. | S. | | . 1810 |
| Commersoni . . | White | . 7, H. Tu. | P. | S. Amer. | . 1822 |
| congense . . | Blue | . 6, S. Ev. | S. | Guinea | . 1821 |
| coriaceum . . | Pur. wht. | . 7, S. Ev. | S. | Mexico | . 1820 |
| cornutum, 4 . | Yellow | . 7, G. Ev. | S. | Mexico | . 1823 |
| corymbosum . . | Violet | . 7, S. Ev. | S. | Peru | . 1786 |
| crispum . . | Blue | . 6, H. Ev. | T. | Chile | . 1824 |
| cuneifolium . . | White | . 6, S. Ev. | S. | Guiana | . 1818 |
| dealbatum . . | Pa. lilac | . 6, G. Ev. | S. | Chile | . 1825 |
| diphyllum . . | White | . 6, S. Ev. | S. | W. Ind. | . 1699 |
| Dulcamara . . | Violet | . 6, H. De. | Cl. | Britain | . |
| alba . . | White | . 6, H. De. | Cl. | Britain | . |
| carnea . . | Flesh | . 6, H. De. | Cl. | Britain | . |
| hirsuta . . | Purple | . 6, H. De. | Cl. | Britain | . |
| rupestris . . | Purple | . 6, H. De. | Cl. | Bohemia | . |
| variegata . . | Violet | . 6, H. De. | Cl. | Britain | . |
| violacea . . | Violet | . 6, H. De. | Cl. | Britain | . |
| elatum . . | White | . 6, S. Ev. | S. | | . 1820 |
| elæagnifolium . . | Blue | . 6, F. Ev. | S. | Chile | . 1823 |
| etuberosum . . | Purple | . 6, H. Her. | P. | Chile | . 1833 |
| fastigiatum . . | Pa. blue | . 6, G. Ev. | S. | S. Eur. | . 1818 |
| ferrugineum . . | Pa. blue | . 7, G. Ev. | S. | | . 1816 |
| flavescens . . | Blue | . 6, G. Ev. | S. | Trinidad | . 1826 |
| Fontanesianum, 5 | Yellow | . 8, H. | A. | Brazil | . 1813 |
| fragrans . . | Green | . 6, S. Ev. | S. | Brazil | . 1825 |
| fugax . . | White | . 6, G. Ev. | S. | Caracces | . 1816 |
| fuscatum . . | Scarlet | . 6, G. | A. | S. Amer. | . 1817 |
| giganteum . . | Violet | . 6, G. Ev. | T. | C. G. H. | . 1792 |
| glutinosum . . | Blue | . 6, S. Ev. | S. | | . 1810 |
| gracile . . | | . 6, G. Her. | P. | | . 1832 |
| guineense . . | Whitish | . 8, H. | A. | Guinea | . 1817 |
| Havanense . . | Blue | . 7, S. Ev. | S. | W. Ind. | . 1793 |
| Herbertianum . . | Pur. yel. | . 7, S. Ev. | S. | | |
| heterandrum, 6 | Yellow | . 7, H. | A. | Missouri | . 1812 |
| heterodoxum . . | Blue | . 7, H. | A. | Mexico | . 1820 |
| heterotrichum . | White | . 6, S. Ev. | S. | S. Amer. | . 1824 |
| hirtum . . | White | . 6, S. Ev. | S. | Trinidad | . 1821 |
| hybridum . . | Pur. blue | . 6, S. Ev. | S. | Guinea | . 1815 |
| igneum . . | White | . 7, S. Ev. | S. | S. Amer. | . 1714 |
| incanum, 8 . | Purple | . 7, S. Ev. | S. | Ceylon | . 1823 |
| incertum . . | White | . 7, H. | A. | India | . 1823 |
| miniatum, 9 . | White | . 6, H. | A. | S. Eur. | . 1823 |
| indicum . . | Purple | . 7, S. Ev. | S. | India | . 1732 |
| jamaicense . . | White | . 6, S. Ev. | S. | Jamaica | . 1818 |
| laciniatum . . | Violet | . 7, G. Ev. | S. | N. Holl. | . 1772 |
| herbaceum . . | Violet | . 7, S. Her. | P. V. D. L. | | . 1772 |
| lanceæfolium . . | White | . 6, S. Ev. | S. | W. Ind. | . 1816 |
| lanceolatum . . | Pa. blue | . 6, S. Ev. | S. | Mexico | . 1800 |
| laurifolium . . | | . 6, S. Ev. | S. | S. Amer. | . 1820 |
| lentum . . | Pur. vio. | . 8, S. Ev. | Cl. | N. Spain | . 1823 |
| ligustrinum . . | Dp. lilac | . 6, F. Ev. | S. | Chile | . 1831 |
| Linkii . . | White | . 6, S. Ev. | S. | | . 1824 |
| littorale . . | White | . 6, H. De. | Cl. | France | . 1819 |
| longiflorum, 10 | Violet | . 7, S. Ev. | S. | Cayenne | . 1828 |
| lycioides . . | Pa. blue | . 6, S. Ev. | S. | Peru | . 1791 |
| macrocarpum . . | Blue | . 8, G. Ev. | S. | Peru | . 1759 |
| mammosum . . | Pa. blue | . 7, S. | A. | W. Ind. | . 1699 |
| marginatum . . | Purple | . 7, G. Ev. | S. | Africa | . 1775 |
| melanoxylum . . | White | . 6, S. Ev. | S. | | . 1821 |
| Melongena . . | Violet | . 6, S. | A. E. Ind. | | . 1597 |
| ovigerum, 11 . | Blue | . 6, G. | A. | Africa | . 1597 |
| fructu albo . | Blue | . 6, G. | A. | Tropics | . 1597 |
| fructu luteo . | Blue | . 6, G. | A. | Tropics | . 1597 |
| fructu rubro . | Blue | . 6, G. | A. | Tropics | . 1597 |
| fructu violaceo | Blue | . 6, G. | A. | Tropics | . 1597 |
| esculentum, 12 | Blue | . 6, G. | A. E. Ind. | | . 1815 |
| mexicanum . . | Violet | . 6, S. Ev. | S. | Mexico | . 1825 |
| Milleri . . | White | . 6, S. Ev. | S. | C. G. H. | . 1762 |
| molle . . | Purple | . 7, S. Ev. | S. | Trinidad | . 1817 |
| monanthum, 13 | Blue | . 6, S. Her. | P. N. Spain | | . 1818 |
| muricatum . . | Violet | . 7, S. Ev. | S. | Peru | . 1785 |
| myriacanthum . | Purple | . 7, S. Ev. | S. | | . 1822 |
| myrtifolium . . | Blue | . 6, G. Ev. | S. | | . |
| neglectum . . | Violet | . 6, S. Ev. | S. | W. Ind. | . 1824 |
| nigrum . . | White | . 7, H. | A. | Britain | . |
| melanocerasum, 14 | White | . 7, H. | A. | Virginia | . 1820 |
| obtusifolium . . | | . 8, H. | A. | | . 1831 |

| | | | | | | |
|---|---|---|---|---|---|---|
| oligánthŭm | White | . | 8. | Ev. | S. | 1824 |
| oporínŭm | Blue | . 6, | S. | Ev. | S. | 1820 |
| pătŭlŭm | Violet | . 8, | H. | A. | India | 1818 |
| pentadactylŭm | Blue | . 7, | S. | Ev. | S. Trinidad | 1808 |
| polyacanthŭm | Red | . 7, | S. | Ev. | S. W. Ind. | 1821 |
| Pseudō-Capsicŭm | White | . 7, | G. | Ev. | S. Madeira | 1596 |
| pubéscēns | Purple | . 6, | G. | Ev. | S. E. Ind. | 1820 |
| pubĭgĕrŭm, 15 | White | . 6, | G. | Ev. | S. Mexico | 1818 |
| pungēns | Blu. vio. | 6, | G. | A. | N. Holl. | 1823 |
| Pyracánthă, 16 | Purple | . 8, | S. | Ev. | S. Madagas. | 1789 |
| inērmis | Purple | . 9, | S. | Ev. | S. Madaga. | 1789 |
| quadrangulărĕ | | . | G. | S. | C. G. H. | 1817 |
| quercifólĭŭm | Violet | . 6, | H. | Her. | P. Peru | 1787 |
| racemĭflôrŭm | Wht. rose | 8, | G. | B. | S. Amer. | 1818 |
| racemôsŭm | White | . 7, | S. | Ev. | S. W. Ind. | 1781 |
| radícāns | Purple | . | G. | Ev. | S. Peru | 1771 |
| reticulátŭm | White | . 6, | S. | Ev. | S. W. Ind. | 1820 |
| rigéscēns | Violet | . 6, | G. | Ev. | S. C. G. H. | 1823 |
| Rōsĕll | Pa. blue | . | G. | | S. Mexico | |
| rostrátŭm, 17 | Yellow | . 7, | H. | A. | Mexico | 1823 |
| rubiginôsŭm | White | . 6, | S. | Ev. | S. Guiana | 1821 |
| rancivátŭm | Violet | . 9, | G. | Her. | P. Chile | 1831 |
| sánctŭm | Purple | . 7, | G. | Ev. | S. Egypt | 1818 |
| saponácĕŭm | White | . 7, | G. | Ev. | T. Chile | 1825 |
| scándēns | | . 7, | S. | Ev. | Cl. Surinam | 1820 |
| Seaforthiánŭm | Pink | . 8, | S. | Ev. | Cl. Barbadoes | 1804 |
| sinuátŭm | Bluish | . 7, | G. | Ev. | S. | 1815 |
| sodómĕŭm | Violet | . 6, | G. | Ev. | S. Africa | 1688 |
| stellátŭm | Blue | . 6, | G. | Ev. | S. | 1805 |
| stellĭgĕrŭm | Pa. pur. | . 7, | G. | Ev. | S. N. Holl. | 1823 |
| stramonifólĭŭm | Purple | . 7, | G. | Ev. | S. E. Ind. | 1778 |
| subarmátŭm | White | . 6, | S. | Ev. | S. | 1820 |
| subinērmĕ | Blue | . 7, | S. | Ev. | S. W. Ind. | 1752 |
| suffruticôsŭm | White | . 7, | G. | Ev. | S. Barbary | 1804 |
| téctŭm | Yellow | . 6, | S. | Ev. | S. Mexico | 1823 |
| Tegŏrĕ | Blue | . 6, | S. | Ev. | S. Guiana | 1822 |
| tomentôsŭm | Blue | . 6, | S. | Ev. | S. C. G. H. | 1662 |
| tórvŭm | Pa. blue | . 7, | S. | Ev. | S. W. Ind. | 1816 |
| triquétrŭm | White | . 6, | S. | Ev. | S. N. Spain | 1820 |
| tristĕ | Violet | . 6, | S. | Ev. | S. W. Ind. | 1820 |
| tuberôsŭm | White | . 7, | H. | Tu. | P. Peru | 1597 |
| Tweediánŭm | Wht. pur. | 9, | G. | Her. | P. B. Ayres | 1832 |
| umbrôsŭm | White | . 7, | S. | Ev. | S. Trinidad | 1825 |
| uncinéllŭm | Pink | . 7, | H. | Tr. | A. | |
| uniflôrŭm | Blue | . 5, | G. | Ev. | T. S. Domingo | 1820 |
| verbascifólĭŭm | White | . 6, | S. | Ev. | S. W. Ind. | 1749 |
| vespertílĭŏ, 19 | Blue | . 6, | S. | Ev. | S. Canaries | 1779 |
| violácĕŭm | Blue | . 6, | S. | Ev. | S. E. Ind. | 1817 |
| virgátŭm | Violet | . 8, | G. | Ev. | S. W. Ind. | 1820 |
| volúbĭlĕ | Blue | . 6, | S. | Ev. | S. W. Ind. | 1823 |
| Zuccágniánŭm | White | . 6, | H. | | A. | 1823 |

*Angulví, Bessĕrí, campechiēnsĕ, carolinēnsĕ, ciliátŭm, Dillēnil, diversifólĭŭm, fĕrōx, flāvŭm, hirsŭtŭm, hámilĕ, Jacquíni, juddálcŭm, Kitaibélli, nodiflôrŭm, platanifólĭŭm, pterocaûlŭm, pygmæŭm, rŭbrŭm, R. olerácĕŭm 18, triangulárĕ, Trôngŭm, vernicálŭm, villôsŭm, virginiánŭm, xanthocárpŭm.*

SOLDANĚLLĂ, *Linn.* A diminutive of *solidus*, a shilling; in allusion to the leaves. *Linn.* 5, Or. 1, Nat. Or. *Primulaceæ.* Pretty alpine plants, succeeding best in a peat border, or in small pots, in peat and loam. They are increased by seeds or division of the root.

| | | | | | | |
|---|---|---|---|---|---|---|
| affînis | . . . | Purple | . 4, | H. Her. | P. Switzerl. | |
| alpínă | . . . | Purple | . 4, | H. Her. | P. Switzerl. | 1656 |
| Cluall | . . . | Purple | . 4, | H. Her. | P. Germany | |
| crenátă | . . . | Purple | . 4, | H. Her. | P. | |
| mínĭmă | . . . | Blue | . 4, | F. Her. | P. Switzerl. | 1823 |
| álbă | . . . | Bluish | . 5, | F. Her. | P. Switzerl. | |
| montánă | . . . | Purple | . 4, | H. Her. | P. Bohemia | 1816 |
| puzílla | . . . | Blue | . 4, | F. Her. | P. Switzerl. | 1820 |

SOLDEVÍLLĂ. *Lagasca* named this genus in honour of one of his friends. *Linn.* 19, Or. 1, Nat. Or. *Compositæ.* This plant is of common culture, and propagated by divisions or seeds.

| | | | | | |
|---|---|---|---|---|---|
| setôsă | . . . | Yellow | . 5, | H. Her. | P. Spain | 1822 |

SOLDIER-WOOD, see *Ingă purpúrĕă.*

SÓLĔĂ, *Sprengel.* In honour of W. Sole, author of an essay on the genus *Mentha.* *Linn.* 5, Or. 1, Nat. Or. *Violaceæ.* A curious little plant, requiring protection during severe frosts. A limestone soil seems to suit it best; and it is increased by divisions or seeds. *Synonyme:* 1. *Viola concolor.*

| | | | | | |
|---|---|---|---|---|---|
| cóncŏlŏr, 1 | . . | Green | . 6, | H. Her. | P. N. Amer. | 1788 |

SOLĔNĬX, *Hoffman.* From *solen*, a tube; on account of the tubular nature of the fronds. *Linn.* 24, Or. 7, Nat. Or. *Algæ.* These plants are found in ditches and in the ocean—*S. clathrátă, C. uncinátă, compréssă, C. crinítă, intestinális, I. máxĭmă, Línză, L. lanceolátă.*

SOLIDĂGŌ, *Linn.* From *solidare*, to unite; on account of the vulnerary qualities of the plants. *Linn.* 19, Or. 2, Nat. Or. *Compositæ.* An extensive genus of

coarse flowering plants, suitable for the back of flower borders. Any common soil suits them; and they are readily increased by divisions of the root. *Synonymes:* 1. *S. montana.* 2. *S. argentea.* 3. *S. retrorsa.* 4. *Conyza rugosa.*

| | | | | | | |
|---|---|---|---|---|---|---|
| alpéstris | . . | Yellow | . 8, | H. Her. | P. Hungary | 1816 |
| altíssĭmă | . . | Yellow | . 8, | H. Her. | P. N. Amer. | 1686 |
| recurvátă | . | Yellow | . 8, | H. Her. | P. N. Amer. | 1686 |
| virginiánă | . | Yellow | . 8, | H. Her. | P. N. Amer. | 1686 |
| ambĭgŭă | . . | Yellow | . 7, | H. Her. | P. | 1759 |
| angustifólĭă | . | Yellow | . 9, | H. Her. | P. N. Amer. | |
| aniátă | . . | Yellow | . 9, | H. Her. | P. N. Amer. | 1815 |
| arenárĭă, 1 | . | Yellow | . 7, | H. Her. | P. S. Eur. | 1816 |
| argútă | . . | Yellow | . 7, | H. Her. | P. N. Amer. | 1758 |
| áspĕră | . . | Yellow | . 8, | H. Her. | P. N. Amer. | 1732 |
| aspĕrátă | . | Yellow | . 9, | H. Her. | P. N. Amer. | 1808 |
| axillárĭs | . | Yellow | . | H. Her. | P. N. Amer. | 1811 |
| cǽsĭă | . . | Yellow | . 9, | H. Her. | P. N. Amer. | 1732 |
| cámbrĭcă | . | Yellow | . 7, | H. Her. | P. Wales | |
| canadénsis | . | Yellow | . 8, | H. Her. | P. N. Amer. | 1648 |
| ciliárĭs | . | Yellow | . 8, | H. Her. | P. N. Amer. | 1811 |
| decúrrēns | . | Yellow | . 9, | H. Her. | P. China | 1823 |
| elátă | . . | Yellow | . 9, | H. Her. | P. N. Amer. | 1811 |
| ellíptĭcă | . | Yellow | . 9, | H. Her. | P. N. Amer. | 1759 |
| eréctă | . . | Yellow | . 9, | H. Her. | P. N. Amer. | |
| flexicaúlis | . | Yellow | . 9, | H. Her. | P. N. Amer. | 1725 |
| frágrāns | . | Yellow | . 8, | H. Her. | P. N. Amer. | |
| gigántĕă | . | Yellow | . 8, | H. Her. | P. N. Amer. | 1758 |
| glomerátă | . | Yellow | . 9, | H. Her. | P. N. Amer. | 1820 |
| hírtă | . . | Yellow | . 9, | H. Her. | P. N. Amer. | |
| híspĭdă | . | Yellow | . 9, | H. Her. | P. N. Amer. | 1800 |
| hūmĭlis | . | Yellow | . 7, | H. Her. | P. N. Amer. | 1811 |
| júncĕă | . | Yellow | . 8, | H. Her. | P. N. Amer. | 1769 |
| lævigátă | . | Yellow | . 9, | H. Her. | P. N. Amer. | 1699 |
| lateriflôră | . | Yellow | . 8, | H. Her. | P. N. Amer. | 1758 |
| latifólĭă | . | Yellow | . 9, | H. Her. | P. N. Amer. | 1725 |
| leucanthemifólĭă | | Yellow | . | F. Her. | P. | 1834 |
| lithospermifólĭă | | Yellow | . 9, | H. Her. | P. N. Amer. | 1811 |
| littorális | . | Yellow | . 7, | H. Her. | P. Etruria | 1827 |
| lívĭdă | . | Yellow | . 9, | H. Her. | P. N. Amer. | |
| macrophýllă | . | Yellow | . 9, | H. Her. | P. N. Amer. | |
| mexicánă | . | Yellow | . 9, | H. Her. | P. N. Amer. | 1683 |
| minútă | . | Yellow | . 7, | H. Her. | P. Pyrenees | 1772 |
| multiradiátă | . | Yellow | . 7, | H. Her. | P. Labrador | 1776 |
| nemorális | . | Yellow | . 9, | H. Her. | P. N. Amer. | 1769 |
| nepalénsis | . | Yellow | . 7, | H. Her. | P. Nepal | |
| novaborácénsis | | Yellow | . 9, | H. Her. | P. N. Amer. | |
| nudiflôră | . | Yellow | . 7, | H. Her. | P. S. Eur. | 1820 |
| odôră | . | Yellow | . 7, | H. Her. | P. N. Amer. | 1699 |
| pátŭlă | . | Yellow | . 9, | H. Her. | P. N. Amer. | 1805 |
| pauciflosculôsă | | Yellow | . 9, | H. Her. | P. N. Amer. | 1811 |
| petiolárĭs | . | Yellow | . 11, | H. Her. | P. N. Amer. | 1758 |
| polifólĭă | . | Yellow | . 9, | H. Her. | P. N. Amer. | 1826 |
| procêră | . | Yellow | . 9, | H. Her. | P. N. Amer. | 1758 |
| pubérŭlă | . | Yellow | . 9, | H. Her. | P. N. Amer. | |
| pulverulántă, 2 | | Yellow | . 9, | H. Her. | P. N. Amer. | |
| pyramidátă | . | Yellow | . 9, | H. Her. | P. | 1790 |
| recurvátă, 3 | . | Yellow | . 10, | H. Her. | P. N. Amer. | |
| refléxă | . | Yellow | . 8, | H. Her. | P. N. Amer. | 1758 |
| rígĭdă | . | Yellow | . 9, | H. Her. | P. N. Amer. | 1710 |
| rugôsă | . | Yellow | . 8, | H. Her. | P. N. Amer. | 1732 |
| scábră | . | Yellow | . 8, | H. Her. | P. N. Amer. | 1811 |
| sempervírēns | . | Yellow | . 9, | H. Her. | P. N. Amer. | 1699 |
| serotínă | . | Yellow | . 7, | H. Her. | P. N. Amer. | 1758 |
| símpléx | . | Yellow | . | H. Her. | P. N. Amer. | 1826 |
| spéciōsă | . | Yellow | . 10, | H. Her. | P. N. Amer. | 1817 |
| spúrĭă, 4 | . | Yellow | . 4, | G. Ev. | S. St. Helena | 1772 |
| squarrôsă | . | Yellow | . 9, | H. Her. | P. N. Amer. | |
| strictă | . | Yellow | . 9, | H. Her. | P. N. Amer. | 1758 |
| ulmifólĭă | . | Yellow | . 9, | H. Her. | P. N. Amer. | 1805 |
| villôsă | . | Yellow | . 8, | H. Her. | P. N. Amer. | 1732 |
| vimínĕă | . | Yellow | . 9, | H. Her. | P. N. Amer. | 1759 |
| virgátă | . | Yellow | . 9, | H. Her. | P. N. Amer. | 1800 |
| Virgaúrĕă | . | Yellow | . 9, | H. Her. | P. Britain | |
| alpína | . | Yellow | . 8, | H. Her. | P. Switzerl. | 1819 |
| americánă | . | Yellow | . 7, | H. Her. | P. N. Amer. | 1800 |

SOLITÁRIUS, alone, distinct.

SOLÍVĂ, *Ruiz and Pavon.* In honour of Salvator Soliva, a Spanish physician and botanist. *Linn.* 19, Or. 4, Nat. Or. *Compositæ.* Annuals of little beauty. *S. anthemifolia* requires the treatment common to half-hardy annuals. *Synonymes:* 1. *Gymnostyles anthemifolia.* 2. *G. stolonifera.*

| | | | | | | |
|---|---|---|---|---|---|---|
| anthemifólĭă, 1 | . | Apetal | . 6, | H. | A. N. Holl. | 1818 |
| stolonífĕră, 2 | . | Apetal | . 6, | H. | A. Portugal | 1816 |

SÓLLYĂ, *Lindley.* In honour of Richard Horsman Solly, a vegetable physiologist and anatomist. *Linn.* 5, Or. 1, *Pittosporaceæ.* Ornamental plants, succeeding in loam and peat; and increased by cuttings, planted in sand, under a glass. *Synonymes:* 1. *Billardiera fusiformis.*

| | | | | | | |
|---|---|---|---|---|---|---|
| angustifólĭă, 1 | . | Blue | . 7, | G. Ev. | Tw. V. D. L. | 1823 |
| heterophýllă | . | Blue | . 7, | G. Ev. | Tw. N. Holl. | 1830 |
| lineárĭs | . | Dp. blue | . | G. Ev. | Cl. Swan R. | |
| salicifólĭă | . | Blue | . | G. Ev. | Cl. | |

SOLOMON'S SEAL, see *Convallāriā*.

SOLORĪNĂ, *Acharius*. From *solos*, solid, and *rhinos*, skin; in allusion to the firm texture of the fronds. *Linn.* 24, Or. 8, Nat. Or. *Lichenes.* Leafy fronds, found on the soil upon the tops of mountains—*S. crŏcĕā, saccātā.*

SOMNIFERUS, causing sleep.

SŎNCHŪS, *Linn.* From *somphos*, hollow; the stems are hollow. *Linn.* 19, Or. 1, Nat. Or. *Compositæ.* Plants of easy culture in any common soil. The shrubby kinds are increased by cuttings, placed in sand, under a glass; the herbaceous species by divisions. The seeds of the annual and biennial kinds only require to be sown in the open ground. *Synonyme:* 1. *S. Jacquinii.*

| | | | | | |
|---|---|---|---|---|---|
| abbreviātŭs | . Yellow | 6, G. Ev. S. | Teneriffe | 1820 |
| acuminātŭs | . Yellow | 8, H. | B. N. Amer. | 1812 |
| caucāsicŭs | . Yellow | 8, H. Her. P. | Caucasus | 1818 |
| chondrilloīdĕs | . Yellow | 6, H. | B. Spain | 1729 |
| dentātŭs | . Yellow | 7, H. Her. P. | Siberia | 1832 |
| divaricātŭs | . Yellow | 7, H. Her. P. | | 1823 |
| fruticōsŭs, 1 | . Yellow | 6, G. Ev. S. | Madeira | 1777 |
| hyoserifōliŭs | . Yellow | 6, G. Ev. S. | Madeira | 1821 |
| lăcerŭs | . Yellow | 8, H. | A. | 1820 |
| lævigātŭs | . Yellow | G. Ev. S. | Madeira | 1816 |
| leucophæŭs | . Purple | 7, H. | B. N. Amer. | 1821 |
| lyrātŭs | . Yellow | G. Ev. S. | Madeira | 1816 |
| macrophyllŭs | . Blue | 7, H. Her. P. | N. Amer. | 1823 |
| maritimŭs | . Yellow | 8, H. Her. P. | S. Eur. | 1748 |
| pallidŭs | . Yellow | 7, H. Her. P. | Canada | 1704 |
| palustrĭs | . Yellow | 7, H. Her. P. | England | |
| pinnātŭs | . Yellow | G. Ev. S. | Madeira | 1777 |
| radicātŭs | . Yellow | 7, G. Ev. S. | Canaries | 1780 |
| uliginōsŭs | . Yellow | 7, H. | A. Caucasus | 1821 |

*Arvēnsis, ăspĕr, olerācĕŭs, racemōsŭs, rŏeĕŭs, taraxacifōliŭs, tenĕrrimŭs.*

SŎPHŎRĂ, *R. Brown.* Altered from *sophera*, the Arabic name of a papilionaceous tree. *Linn.* 10, Or. 1, Nat. Or. *Leguminosæ.* S. chinensis and S. japonica are two of the most handsome species, and well adapted for growing singly on lawns. When young, they require a slight protection in winter. They are sometimes increased by layers, but generally by seeds. The stove and greenhouse kinds thrive well in a light, loamy soil; and cuttings will root, if planted in sand, under a glass. The hardy herbaceous kinds are increased by dividing the roots in spring. *Synonyme:* 1. *Astragalus carnosus.*

| | | | | | |
|---|---|---|---|---|---|
| alopecuroīdĕs | . Yellow | 7, H. Her. P. | Levant | |
| chinēnsis | . White | 8, H. De. T. | China | 1763 |
| crassifōliā | . White | 8. Ev. T. | Guinea | 1818 |
| flavēscēns | . Yellow | 6, H. Her. P. | Siberia | 1785 |
| galegoīdĕs | . Yellow | 6, H. Her. P. | Siberia | 1817 |
| glaūca | . Purple | 8. Ev. S. | E. Ind. | 1818 |
| havanēnsis | . Yellow | 8, S. Ev. S. | Havannah | 1822 |
| japōnicā | . White | 8, H. De. T. | Japan | 1763 |
| fōliis variegātĭs | White | 8, H. De. T. | Japan | |
| pendŭlă | . White | 8, H. De. T. | Japan | |
| littorālĭs | | 8, S. Ev. S. | Brazil | 1820 |
| macrocārpā | . Yellow | 4, G. Ev. S. | Chile | 1822 |
| secundiflorā | . Violet | 8, G. Ev. S. | N. Spain | 1820 |
| sericēa, 1 | . White | 6, H. Her. P. | N. Amer. | 1820 |
| tomentōsā | . White | 8, S. Ev. T. | India | 1739 |
| velutīnā | . Pink | 6, F. Ev. S. | Nepal | |

SŎPHRŎNĪTĬS, *Lindley.* From *sophrona*, modest; in allusion to the pretty little flowers of the original species. *Linn.* 20, Or. 1, Nat. Or. *Orchidaceæ.* S. grandiflora is a very lovely plant, the blossom being large, internally of a uniform red colour, approaching to orange, with darker red streaks; the other species are also well worthy of cultivation, for which, see *Burlingtonia.* *Synonymes:* 1. *Sophronia cernua.* 2. *Cattleya coccinea.*

| | | | | | |
|---|---|---|---|---|---|
| cernŭă, 1 | . Red | 6, S. Epi. | Rio Jan. | 1827 |
| grandiflorā, 2 | . Red | 8. Epi. | Organ Mts. | 1837 |
| violācĕă | . Violet | 2, S. Epi. | | |

SŎRGHŬM, *Persoon.* From *Sorghi*, its Indian name. *Linn.* 23, Or. 1, Nat. Or. *Gramineæ.* Annual plants, growing in any common soil; and increased by seeds. *Synonymes:* 1. *Holcus avenaceus.* 2. *S. arduini.*

| | | | | | |
|---|---|---|---|---|---|
| avenācĕŭm, 1 | . Apetal | 7, Grass. | C. G. H. | 1816 |
| bicŏlŏr | . Apetal | 7, Grass. | Persia | 1731 |
| Caffrōrŭm, 2 | . Apetal | 7, Grass. | C. G. H. | 1816 |
| cērnŭŭm | . Apetal | 7, Grass. | | 1810 |
| nigrŭm | . Apetal | 7, Grass. | India | 1816 |
| rūbēns | . Apetal | 7, Grass. | Africa | 1817 |
| saccharātŭm | . Apetal | 7, Grass. | India | 1759 |
| vulgārĕ | . Apetal | Grass. | India | 1596 |

*Elongātŭm, halepēnsĕ.*

SŎRI, the patches of fructification on the back of the fronds of ferns.

SORINDEĬĂ, *Thouars.* Not explained. *Linn.* 23, Or. 2, Nat. Or. *Burseraceæ.* This shrub may be referred to *Boswellia* for culture and propagation.

| | | | | |
|---|---|---|---|---|
| madagascariēnsis | . Purple | 8. Ev. S. | Madag. | 1828 |

SŎROCĔPHĂLŬS, *R. Brown.* From *soros*, a heap, and *kephale*, a head; in allusion to the clustered heads of flowers. *Linn.* 4, Or. 1, Nat. Or. *Proteaceæ.* This genus of ornamental shrubs ought to be in every collection. For culture and propagation, see *Protea.*

| | | | | | |
|---|---|---|---|---|---|
| diversifōliă | . Purple | 6, G. Ev. S. | C. G. H. | 1803 |
| imbērbis | . Purple | 7, G. Ev. S. | C. G. H. | 1806 |
| imbricātă | . Purple | 6, G. Ev. S. | C. G. H. | 1794 |
| lanātă | . Purple | 8, G. Ev. S. | C. G. H. | 1790 |
| setācĕă | . Purple | 6, G. Ev. S. | C. G. H. | 1823 |
| spatalloīdĕs | . Purple | 7, G. Ev. S. | C. G. H. | 1803 |
| tenuifōliă | . Purple | 7, G. Ev. S. | C. G. H. | 1802 |

SORREL, see *Rūmēx Acetōsā*.

SORREL TREE, see *Andrŏmēdā arbŏrĕā*.

SOULĂNGĬĂ, *Brongniart.* In honour of Soulange Bodin, an eminent nurseryman near Paris. *Linn.* 5, Or. 1, Nat. Or. *Rhamnaceæ.* Interesting plants, which may be referred to *Phylica* for culture and propagation. *Synonymes:* 1. *Phylica arborea.* 2. *P. axillaris.* 3. *P. buxifolia.* 4. *P. cordata.* 5. *P. dioica.* 6. *P. myrtifolia.* 7. *P. oleæfolia.* 8. *P. orientalis.* 9. *P. paniculata.* 10. *P. reclinata.* 11. *P. thymifolia.*

| | | | | | |
|---|---|---|---|---|---|
| arbŏrĕă, 1 | . White | G. Ev. S. | Trist. d'Acun. | 1817 |
| axillāris, 2 | . White | 6, G. Ev. S. | C. G. H. | 1812 |
| buxifōliă, 3 | . White | 7, G. Ev. S. | C. G. H. | 1759 |
| cordātă, 4 | . Pur. yel. | 5, G. Ev. S. | C. G. H. | 1789 |
| dioīcă, 5 | | 7, G. Ev. S. | C. G. H. | 1817 |
| myrtifōliă, 6 | . Drk. yel. | G. Ev. S. | C. G. H. | 1774 |
| oleæfōliă, 7 | . White | 6, G. Ev. S. | C. G. H. | 1800 |
| orientālĭs, 8 | . White | 6, G. Ev. S. | | 1820 |
| paniculātă, 9 | . White | 6, G. Ev. S. | C. G. H. | 1817 |
| reclinātă, 10 | . White | 6, G. Ev. S. | C. G. H. | 1823 |
| rŭbră | . Red | 12, G. Ev. S. | C. G. H. | 1827 |
| thymifōliă, 11 | . White | 6, G. Ev. S. | C. G. H. | 1820 |

SOUR GOURD, see *Adansōniā digitāta*.

SOUR GUM, see *Nȳssā villōsā*.

SOURSOP, see *Anŏnā muricātā*.

SOUTHERNWOOD, see *Artemisiā arbŏrĕā*.

SOUTH SEA TEA, see *Ilex vomitōriā*.

SOWERBÆĬ, *Smith.* In honour of James Sowerby, F.L.S., an eminent botanical artist. *Linn.* 6, Or. 1, Nat. Or. *Liliaceæ.* This species succeeds well in sandy loam and peat; and young plants are readily obtained by divisions.

| | | | | |
|---|---|---|---|---|
| juncĕă | . Pink | 5, G. Her. P. | N. S. W. | 1792 |

SOWTHISTLE, see *Sŏnchŭs*.

SOY, see *Sōjā*.

SPADIX, a spike enveloped in a spatha.

SPANĂNTHĔ, *Jacquin.* From *spanos*, rare, and *anthos*, a flower; few flowers in the umbel. *Linn.* 5, Or. 2, Nat. Or. *Umbelliferæ.* A stove biennial, not worth growing. *Synonyme:* 1. *Hydrocotyle Spananthe—S. paniculātā* 1.

SPANISH BROOM, see *Spărtiŭm juncĕŭm*.

SPANISH CRESS, see *Lepidiŭm cardaminēs*.

SPANISH ELM, see *Cŏrdiā Geraschānthŭs*.

SPANISH NUT, see *Morēā Sisyrinchiŭm*.

SPARĂXĬS, *Ker.* From *sparasso*, to tear; alluding to the lacerated spathes. *Linn.* 3, Or. 1, Nat. Or. *Iridaceæ.* The species of this genus are very pretty when in flower. For culture and propagation, see *Ixia.* *Synonyme:* 1. *Ixia anemonijlora.*

| | | | | | |
|---|---|---|---|---|---|
| anemoniflorā, 1 | . White | 6, G. Bl. P. | C. G. H. | 1825 |
| bicŏlŏr | . Blue yel. | 8, G. Bl. P. | C. G. H. | 1786 |
| bulbiferă | . Violet | 5, G. Bl. P. | C. G. H. | 1758 |
| frāgrāns | . Yellow | 6, G. Bl. P. | C. G. H. | 1825 |
| grandiflorā | . Purple | 4, G. Bl. P. | C. G. H. | 1758 |
| Liliāgŏ | . White | 4, G. Bl. P. | C. G. H. | 1758 |
| striātă | . Varieg. | 4, G. Bl. P. | C. G. H. | 1758 |
| lineātā | . Wht. pk. | 4, G. Bl. P. | C. G. H. | |
| pendŭlă | . Drk. pk. | 6, F. Bl. P. | C. G. H. | 1825 |
| stellārĭs | . Purple | 7, F. Bl. P. | C. G. H. | 1836 |
| tricŏlŏr | . Orange | 5, G. Bl. P. | C. G. H. | 1789 |
| rŏsĕŏ-albā | . Pink | 4, G. Bl. P. | C. G. H. | 1811 |
| sanguinĕŏ-purpurĕā | Red | 4, G. Bl. P. | C. G. H. | 1811 |
| violācĕŏ-purpurĕā | Vl. pur. | 4, G. Bl. P. | C. G. H. | 1811 |
| versicŏlŏr | . Pur. yel. | 9, F. Bl. P. | C. G. H. | 1825 |

SPARGĂNĬŬM, *Linn.* From *sparganon*, a fillet; because of the riband-like leaves. *Linn.* 21, Or. 3, Nat. Or. *Typhaceæ.* The common *Bur Reed*, found in ditches and stagnant waters: increased by seeds—*S. alpīnūm, ūdīns, ramōsūm, sīmplēx.*

**SPARGANŌPHŌRŪS**, *Gærtner.* From *sparganon*, a fillet, and *phoreo*, to bear; shape of the seeds. Linn. 19, Or. 1, Nat. Or. *Compositæ.* Tender annuals, not worth cultivating—*S. Strūchīūm, Vaillāntii, verticillātūs.*

**SPARMĀNNĬĀ**, *Thunberg.* In honour of Andrew Sparmann, M.D., a Swedish botanist, who accompanied Captain Cook in his second voyage round the world. Linn. 13, Or. 1, Nat. Or. *Tiliaceæ.* This beautiful early flowering shrub succeeds best in a mixture of loam and peat; and cuttings root freely in sand, under a glass.

africānă . . . White . 5, G. Ev. T. C. G. H. . 1790

**SPARROW-WORT**, see *Passerīnā.*
**SPARROW-WORT**, see *Erīcă Passerīnā.*
**SPARSA**, scattered.

**SPARTĪNĂ**, *Schreber.* From *spartine*, a rope made from broom. Linn. 3, Or. 1, Nat. Or. *Gramineæ.* Perennial grasses, of very easy culture; and increased by divisions and seeds.

| | | | |
|---|---|---|---|
| alternīflōră | . Apetal | . 7, Grass. France | . 1819 |
| cynosurōīdes | . Apetal | . 8, Grass. N. Amer. | . 1781 |
| genīculātă | . Apetal | . 7, Grass. Java | . 1822 |
| jūncēă | . Apetal | . 7, Grass. N. Amer. | . 1781 |
| pātēns | . Apetal | . 7, Grass. N. Amer. | . 1781 |
| polystāchyă | . Apetal | . 8, Grass. N. Amer. | . 1781 |
| pūmīlă | . Apetal | . 8, Grass. N. Amer. | . 1826 |
| strīctă | . Apetal | . 8, Grass. Britain | . . |

**SPARTĬŪM**, *Linn.* From *sparton*, cordage; use made of the plant in early ages. Linn. 16, Or. 6, Nat. Or. *Leguminosæ.* These plants, from being very ornamental when in flower, are well adapted for planting in shrubberies. They are usually increased by seeds, but cuttings of the young wood will root, if planted under a glass.

| | | | |
|---|---|---|---|
| acutifōliŭm | . Yellow | . 8, H. De. S. Turkey. | . 1836 |
| jūncēŭm | . Yellow | . 8, H. De. S. Eur. | . 1548 |
| flōrē plēnō | . Yellow | . 8, H. De. S. Eur. | . 1548 |
| odorātissĭmŭm | . Yellow | . 7, H. De. S. Persia | . 1834 |

**SPATALĀNTHŪS**, *Sweet.* From *spatalos*, delicate, and *anthos*, a flower. Linn. 16, Or. 1, Nat. Or. *Iridaceæ.* A beautiful-flowering Cape bulb, succeeding in sandy loam and peat; and increased by offsets. Synonyme: 1. *Trichonema monadelpha.*

speciōsŭs, 1 . . H. Bl. P. C. G. H. . 1825

**SPATĀLLĀ**, *Salisbury.* From *spatale*, wantonness. Linn. 4, Or. 1, Nat. Or. *Proteaceæ.* This genus of ornamental plants requires the same treatment as that recommended for *Serruria.*

| | | | | |
|---|---|---|---|---|
| bractēātă | . Purple | . 6, G. Ev. S. C. G. H. | . 1806 |
| brevifōlĭă | . Purple | . 7, G. Ev. S. C. G. H. | . 1823 |
| caudātă | . Purple | . 6, G. Ev. S. C. G. H. | . 1819 |
| incūrvă | . Purple | . 5, G. Ev. S. C. G. H. | . 1789 |
| mōllĭs | . Purple | . 6, G. Ev. S. C. G. H. | . 1826 |
| nĭvēă | . Purple | . 6, G. Ev. S. C. G. H. | . 1806 |
| prolīfĕră | . Purple | . 7, G. Ev. S. C. G. H. | . 1800 |
| ramulōsă | . Purple | . 6, G. Ev. S. C. G. H. | . 1787 |
| Thunbĕrgii | . Purple | . 5, G. Ev. S. C. G. H. | . 1806 |

**SPATHA**, a broad sheathing leaf, enclosing flowers arranged on a spadix.
**SPATHĒLĬĂ**, *Linn.* From *spathe*, a palm-tree; similarity of habit. Linn. 5, Or. 3, Nat. Or. *Amyridaceæ.* This tree succeeds best in a mixture of loam and peat; and ripened cuttings will root in sand, under a glass, in heat.

sīmplēx . . . Red . . 8. Ev. T. Jamaica . 1778

**SPATHŌDĔĂ**, *Beauvois.* From *spathe*, a spatha, in reference to the form of the calyx. Linn. 14, Or. 2, Nat. Or. *Bignoniaceæ.* This is a genus of truly splendid plants when in flower. For culture and propagation, see *Bignonia.* Synonymes: 1. *Bignonia fraxinifolia.* 2. *B. chelonoides.* 3. *B. spathacea.* 4. *B. quadrilocularis.* 5. *B. uncata.*

| | | | | |
|---|---|---|---|---|
| corymbōsă | . Yellow | . 8. Ev. T. Trinidad | . 1824 |
| fraxinifōlĭă, 1 | . | . 8. Ev. Cl. Caraccas | . 1822 |
| lævĭs | . Purple | . 8. Ev. S. Guinea | . 1825 |
| longiflōră, 2 | . Red | . 8. Ev. T. E. Ind. | . 1816 |
| pentāndră | . Yelsh. | . 6, S. Ev. T. India | . |
| Rhēēdii, 3 | . Cream | . 8. Ev. T. E. Ind. | . 1794 |
| Roxbūrghii, 4 | . Pink | . 8. Ev. T. E. Ind. | . 1820 |
| uncātă, 5 | . Yellow | . 8. Ev. Cl. Guiana | . 1804 |

**SPATHŪLĔĂ**, *Fries.* From *spathula*, a spreading knife; so named from the form of the plant. Linn. 24, Or. 9, Nat. Or. *Fungi.* This species is found in autumn upon dead leaves—*S. flāvidă.*
**SPATULA**, a spatulate-shaped process.

[ 247 ]

**SPATULATE**, like a spatula, a knife having the upper end broadest.
**SPEARWORT**, see *Ranūncŭlūs flāmmēă.*
**SPECKLINĬĂ**, *Lindley.* Named after Rudolph Speckin, the artist who drew the woodcuts in Fuchs's Historia Plantarum. Linn. 20, Or. 1, Nat. Or. *Orchidaceæ.* Small plants, with dull green, purple-spotted flowers. For culture and propagation, see *Burlingtonia.*

| | | | | |
|---|---|---|---|---|
| atropurpūrēă | . Dk. pur. | . 8. Epi. Jamaica | . 1834 |
| cilĭārĭs | . Grn. pur. | . 8. Epi. Mexico | . 1836 |
| obŏvātă | . Pa. yel. | . 8. Epi. Brazil | . |
| orbiculārĭs | . Purple | . 8 Epi. Demerara | . 1836 |
| rēpēns | . Grn. pur. | . 8. Epi. Mexico | . 183.. |

**SPECULĀRĬĂ**, *Heister.* From the ancient name *Speculum Veneris.* Linn. 5, Or. 1, Nat. Or. *Campanulaceæ.* For culture and propagation refer to *Prismatocarpus.* Synonymes: 1. *Prismatocarpus falcatus.* 2. *P. hybridus.* 3. *P. pentagonius.* 4. *P. perfoliatus.* 5. *P. speculum.* 6. *P. hirsutus.*

| | | | | |
|---|---|---|---|---|
| biflōră | . Blue | . 6, H. | A. Russia | . 1836 |
| falcātă, 1 | . Rose | . 7, H. | A. Medit. | . 1820 |
| hybrīdă, 2 | . Rose | . 7, H. | A. England | . |
| pentagōnĭă, 3 | . Blue | . 7, H. | A. Levant | . 1686 |
| perfolĭātă, 4 | . Blue | . 7, H. | A. N. Amer. | . 1680 |
| spĕcŭlŭm, 5 | . Grn. wht. | . 7, H. | A. Europe | . 1596 |
| calycīnă | . | . 7, H. | A. Iberia | . |
| Libānĭcă | . | . 7, H. | A. | . |
| pubēscēns, 6 | . | . 7, H. | A. France | . . |

**SPEEDWELL**, see *Verōnĭcă.*
**SPELT**, see *Trītĭcŭm spēltă.*
**SPERGŬLĂ**, *Linn.* From *spargo*, to scatter; because it expels its seeds. Linn. 10, Or. 4, Nat. Or. *Illecebraceæ.* None of these plants are worth cultivating, except in botanical gardens. They grow in any moist situation—*S. glābră, lariciā, nodōsă, pilīfĕră, saginōīdēs, subulātă.*
**SPERGULĀRĬĂ**, *Persoon.* Altered from *Spergula*, which see for explanation. Linn. 10, Or. 4, Nat. Or. *Caryophyllaceæ.* Worthless plants, undeserving of the culturist's care—*S. arvēnsis, pāllīdă, pentāndră.*
**SPERGULĀSTRŬM**, *Michaux.* From *spergula*, spurry, and *astrum*, an affixed term, signifying like. Linn. 10, Or. 3, Nat. Or. *Alsineæ.* This species is of no interest, except in botanical collections. Sandy peat suits it, and young plants may be obtained by dividing the roots or by seeds. Synonyme: 1. *Micropetalon lanuginosum.*

lanuginōsŭm, 1 . Wht. pur. 6, H. Her. P. N. Amer. . 1821

**SPERMACŌCĔ**, *Dillenius.* From *sperma*, a seed, and *akoke*, a point; in allusion to the capsule being crowned by the calycine points. Linn. 4, Or. 1, Nat. Or. *Cinchonaceæ.* The species of *Spermacoce* are of the simplest culture. Any light soil suits them; and cuttings of the shrubby and perennial kinds root freely in the same kind of soil, in a little heat. The annual species require the treatment common to hardy and tender annuals: Synonymes: 1. *S. lævis.* 2. *S. strigosa.*

| | | | | |
|---|---|---|---|---|
| glābră | . . White | . 7, H. | A. N. Amer. | . 1823 |
| lanceolātă | . | . 7, H. | A. W. Ind. | . 1818 |
| Roxbūrghii, 1 | . White | . 7, S. | B. E. Ind. | . 1818 |
| rūbră, 2 | . Red | . 10, S. | A. Mexico | . 1797 |
| tenŭĭōr | . Pink | . 7, H. | A. W. Ind. | . 1792 |

*Ascēndēns, ăspĕră, cornifōlĭă, diodīnă, Fischĕrī, hīrtă, hĭspĭdă, lĕvĭs, latifōlĭă, linifōlĭă, mucronātă, rādīcāns, scābră, stylōsă, suffrutīcōsă, villōsă.*
**SPERMODERM**, the outer covering of a seed.
**SPERMĀXYRŬM**, *Labillardière.* From *sperma*, a seed; and *axyra*, an anchor; the umbilical funicle is shaped like an anchor. Linn. 8, Or. 1, Nat. Or. *Olacaceæ.* This species succeeds best in loam and peat; and cuttings will root in sand, under a glass.

strĭctŭm . . . White . . G. Ev. S. N. Holl. . 1820

**SPERMŌĔDĬĂ**, *Fries.* From *sperma*, a seed, and *anoideo*, to swell; the diseased seeds. Linn. 24, Or. 9, Nat. Or. *Fungi.* This very minute species is found in autumn on the glumes of grasses—*S. clāvūs.*
**SPHACELATE**, withered, or dead.
**SPHACĔLĔ**, *Bentham.* From *sphakos*, sage; similarity. Linn. 14, Or. 1, Nat. Or. *Labiatæ.* Free-flowering plants, of easy culture in any light rich soil. Cuttings root readily in earth, under a glass. Synonyme: 1. *Stachys Salvia.*

| | | | | |
|---|---|---|---|---|
| campanulātă | . Pa. blue | . 7, G. Ev. S. Chile | . 1795 |
| Lindleyī, 1 | . Violet | . 7, G. Ev. S. Chile | . 1825 |

**SPHACELLĂRĬĂ**, *Lyngbye.* From *sphakelos*, gangrene:

2 Q

appearance of the truncate extremities of the fronds. *Linn.* 24, Or. 7, Nat. Or. *Algæ.* These species are found in the ocean, on the sea-shore, &c.—*S. cirrhōsā, C. patentissimā, distichā, Mertēnsii, plumōsā, racemōsā, rādicāns, scopariā.*

SPHÆRLCEA, *St. Hilaire.* From *sphaira,* a globe, and *alcea,* marsh-mallow. The carpels are disposed in a round head. *Linn.* 16, Or. 8, Nat. Or. *Malvaceæ.* Ornamental plants. For culture and propagation, see the greenhouse species of *Malva.* Synonymes: 1. *Malva abutiloides.* 2. *M. angustifolia.* 3. *M. caroliniana, Modiola caroliniana.* 4. *M. decumbens, Modiola decumbens.* 5. *M. elegans.* 6. *M. obtusiloba.* 7. *M. prostrata, Modiola prostrata.* 8. *M. umbellata.*

| | | | | | |
|---|---|---|---|---|---|
| abutiloīdēs, 1 | Purple | 8, G. Ev. S. | Bahamas | 1725 |
| angustifōliā, 2 | Pink | 8, G. Ev. S. | Mexico | 1780 |
| carolinānā, 3 | Dk. red | 8, H. | A. N. Amer. | 1723 |
| decumbēns, 4 | Red | 4, G. Her. P. | S. Amer. | 1815 |
| elēgāns, 5 | Red | 7, G. Ev. S. | C. G. H. | 1791 |
| obtusilōbā, 6 | Purple | 7, G. Ev. S. | Chile | 1827 |
| prostrātā, 7 | Red | 7, H. | A. Brazil | 1806 |
| umbellātā, 8 | Violet | 4, S. Ev. S. | N. Spain | 1814 |

SPHÆRANTHUS, *Linn.* From *sphaira,* a globe, and *anthos,* a flower; alluding to the globular heads of flowers. *Linn.* 19, Or. 1, Nat. Or. *Compositæ.* Stove plants, not worth growing—*S. africānus, hīrtus, indicus.*

SPHÆRIA, *Linn.* From *sphaira,* a globe; their shape. *Linn.* 24, Or. 9, Nat. Or. *Fungi.* An extensive genus of very minute plants, found at all seasons on a variety of decayed substances, as on the leaves and trunks of trees, honeysuckle leaves, fir cones, &c. —*S. acervātā, acuminātā, acūtā, Ægopōdii, affīnis, alutācēā, ambiēns, Angēlicæ, anserīnā, aquifōliā, aquīlā, arbuticōlā, artocrēās, arundinācēā, aspērā, atropurpūrēā, atrovīrēns, Avellānæ, aurāntiā, aūrēā, Berbēridis, biformis, bifrōns, bombārdā, botryōsā, Brāssicæ, brunnēōlā, bullātā, byssisēdā, cālvā, canēscēns, capitātā, carpōphilā, ceratospērmā, ceuthocārpā, ceuthosporoīdēs, cinnabarinā, cirrhōsā, citrīnā, clypeātā, coccīnēā, cohērēns, comātā, complanātā, concentricā, convērgēns, cornicōlā, corniculātā, coronātā, Cōrÿli, crinītā, culmifrāgā, cupulāris, curvirōsērā, Dematīum, deūstā, Diānthi, digitātā, dioīcā, disciformis, discūtiēns, ditōpā, doliolūm, dothīdēā, dūplex, ellipticā, elongātā, Empētri, enteroleūcā, ēntipā, entomorrhīzā, excipuliformis, favācēā, ferrugīnēā, fibrōsā, filicīnā, fimbriātā, fimēti, flavovīrēns, fragiformis, frondicōlā, fuliginōsā, furfurācēā, fūscā, gelatinōsā, gnōmōn, grācilis, Grāminis, gyrōsā, Hedērā, hedericōlā, herbārūm, hirsūtā, hispidā, Hookēri, hypodērmicā, hypoxÿlon, hÿstrix, Ilicis, immērsā, inquīnāns, inquilīnā, irregulāris, juglāndis, Jūnci, Kērriā, Labūrni, lātā, leiphæmiā, leucostōmā, lignāriā, lirēllā, līvidā, longissimā, Lōnicērā, maculæformis, malōrūm, mammæformis, melogrāmmā, microscōpicā, militāris, millepunctātā, milliāriā, moriformis, multiformis, myriocāmpā, nebulōsā, nidūlā, nigrēllā, nīvēā, nuculā, nummulāriā, obdūcēns, obturātā, ocellātā, ochrācēā, ophioglossoīdēs, ostrūthii, ovīnā, pellītā, petiolōrūm, Pexizā, pilisērā, pilōsā, Pināstri, Pisi, Platāscā, polymōrphā, pomiformis, populīnā, profūsā, pruinōsā, Prunāstri, pulchēllā, pulverācēā, pulvis, pÿrinās, punctātā, punctiformis, quaternātā, quercīnā, Racōdīum, ramōsā, recuītērā, relicīnā, Rībis, rosēllā, rostellātā, rubēllā, rubiginōsā, rūdis, rūfā, salicēllā, salicīnā, sanguīnēā, S. cicātricūm, scirpicōlā, scrophulāriæ, semi-immērsā, sepincōlā, sērpēns, sētācēā, Solāni, Sōrbi, sordāriā, spermodēs, sphærocēphalā, spinōsā, stellulātā, stilbostōmā, striæformis, strigōsā, strobilīnā, stygmēā, succenturiātā, Taleōlā, Tamariscinās, Taxi, Tīliæ, Trifōlii, trīstis, tubæformis, ūdā, umbrīnā, undulātā, Vaccīnii, velātā, verrucæformis, verrucōsā, vibratīlis, Yūccæ.*

SPHÆRŌBŌLUS, *Tode.* From *sphaira,* a globe, and *ballo,* to eject; the plant becomes elastic and emits a spherical sporangium. *Linn.* 24, Or. 9, Nat. Or. *Fungi.* Found in autumn, on dead wood, shavings, sawdust, &c.—*S. stellātus.*

SPHÆROCARPŪS, *Michaux.* From *sphaira,* a globe, and *karpos,* a fruit; the seed-vessel is globular. *Linn.* 24, Or. 6, Nat. Or. *Hepaticæ.* This species is found during winter, in damp places—*S. terrēstris.*

SPHÆROCOCCUS, *Agardh.* From *sphaira,* a globe, and *kokkos,* fruit; the theca is round. *Linn.* 24, Or. 7, Nat. Or. *Algæ.* The species of *Sphærococcus* are found in the water, and on the sea-shore. Synonyme: 1. *Chondria pusilla*—*S. aciculāris, Brodlæi, cartilagīnēus, confervoīdēs, C. ālbidūs, C. geniculātūs, C. procērrimūs, cōrnēūs, C. clavātūs 1, C. clavifer, C. nereīdēūs, C. pinnātūs, C. pulchēllūs, coronopifōliūs, crispūs, gigartīnūs, Griffithsiæ, lichenoīdēs, mammillōsūs, membranifōliūs, norvēgicūs, plicātūs, purpurāscēns, rubēns, Teēdii.*

SPHÆROLŌBIUM, *Smith.* From *sphaira,* a sphere, and *lobos,* a pod; the pods are spherical. *Linn.* 10, Or. 1, Nat. Or. *Leguminosæ.* These plants succeed best in a mixture of loam and peat; and young cuttings root freely in sand, under a glass. Synonyme: 1. *S. minus.*

| | | | | | |
|---|---|---|---|---|---|
| mēdiūm | Red | 7, G. Ev. S. | N. Holl. | 1803 |
| viminēūm, 1 | Yellow | 7, G. Ev. S. | N. Holl. | 1802 |

SPHÆRONĒMĀ, *Fries.* From *sphaira,* a sphere, and *naima,* gelatine; in allusion to the mucous receptacle in which the sporules are inclosed. *Linn.* 24, Or. 9, Nat. Or. *Fungi.* Found on dead wood—*S. blephariutōmā, subulātum.*

SPHÆROPHŌRŌN, *Persoon.* From *sphaira,* a globe, and *phoreo,* to bear; form of fructification. *Linn.* 24, Or. 8, Nat. Or. *Lichenes.* A very elegant genus of *Lichens,* easily known by its branched smooth habit. The species are found on rocks—*S. comprēssūm, coralloīdēs, frāgilē.*

SPHÆROPHŸSA, *Decandolle.* From *sphaira,* a sphere, and *physa,* a bladder; the pods are spherical and bladdery. *Linn.* 17, Or. 4, Nat. Or. *Leguminosæ.* This species succeeds in common garden soil; but is difficult to preserve on account of the want of that saline principle in which it grows in its native country; the plants should, therefore, be occasionally watered with salted water: they are increased by seeds, which are sometimes ripened in this country. Synonymes: 1. *Colutea caspica, Phaca salsula.*

| | | | | | |
|---|---|---|---|---|---|
| cáspicā, 1 | Red | 7, H. Her. P. | Siberia | 1816 |

SPHÆROSTĒMĀ, *Blume.* From *sphaira,* a globe, and *stema,* a stamen; the filaments of the stamens are coadunated into a fleshy solid mass, the anthers only being at liberty, and nestling in a number of little excavations of the mass. *Linn.* 22, Or. 12, Nat. Or. *Anonaceæ.* This interesting plant succeeds well in a mixture of sandy peat and loam; and cuttings root in sand, under a glass, in heat.

| | | | | | |
|---|---|---|---|---|---|
| propinquum | Yellow | 7, S. Ev. Cl. | Nepal | 1828 |

SPHÆROSTIGMĀ, *Fischer and Meyer.* From *sphaira,* a globe, and *stigma,* a stigma. *Linn.* 8, Or. 1, Nat. Or. *Onagraceæ.* Same cultivation as for *Œnothera.*

| | | | | | |
|---|---|---|---|---|---|
| Chamissōnis | Yellow | 8, H. | A. Russia | 1837 |
| hirtūm | Yellow | 8, H. | B. Russia | 1836 |
| minutiflōrūm | Yellow | 8, H. | B. Russia | 1837 |

SPHAGNUM, *Linn.* A name used by Pliny for some kind of moss. *Linn.* 24, Or. 5, Nat. Or. *Musci.* The species belonging to this genus are found in bogs at all seasons. The leaves are nerveless, and of a singularly whitish colour. Synonymes: 1. *S. capillifōliūm.* 2. *S. latifōliūm.*—*S. acutifōliūm* 1, *cuspidātum, obtusifōliūm, O. vulgārē* 2, *O. fluitāns, O. mīnūs, squarrōsūm.*

SPHENODĒSMĀ, *Jack.* From *sphen,* a wedge, and *desme,* fascicle; in allusion to the fascicles of flowers. *Linn.* 5, Or. 1, Nat. Or. *Verbenaceæ.* This species succeeds in sandy loam; and is increased by cuttings, planted in sand, under a glass, in heat.

| | | | | | |
|---|---|---|---|---|---|
| pentandrā | | S. Ev. Cl. | E. Ind. | 1823 |

SPHENOGŸNE, *R. Brown.* From *sphen,* a wedge, and *gyne,* a female; in allusion to the wedge shaped stigmas. *Linn.* 19, Or. 3, Nat. Or. *Compositæ.* This is a genus of very elegant under-shrubs, and half-hardy annuals. They succeed best in a mixture of loam and peat; and cuttings of the shrubby kinds root readily in sand, under a glass. Synonymes: 1. *Ursinia faniculacea, Arctotis faniculacea.* 2. *Arctotis leucanthemoides.*

| | | | | | |
|---|---|---|---|---|---|
| abrotanifōliā | Yellow | 7, G. Ev. S. | C. G. H. | 1789 |
| anthemoīdēs | Yellow | 8, H. | A. C. G. H. | 1774 |
| erithmifōliā | Yellow | 7, G. Ev. S. | C. G. H. | 1768 |
| dentātā | Yellow | 6, G. Ev. S. | C. G. H. | 1787 |
| faniculātā, 1 | Yellow | 8, H. | A. C. G. H. | 1825 |
| leucanthemoīdēs, 2 | Yellow | 8, | A. C. G. H. | 1825 |
| odorātā | Yellow | 5, G. Ev. S. | C. G. H. | 1774 |
| pilifērā | Yellow | 12, G. Ev. S. | C. G. H. | 1821 |

| | | | | | |
|---|---|---|---|---|---|
| scarièsā | . . . | Yellow | . 6, G. Ev. S. C. G. H. | . 1774 |
| speciòsā | . . . | Yellow | . 7, H.   A. S. Amer. | . 1836 |

**SPHENŌTŌMĀ,** *R. Brown.* From *sphenoo*, to cleave, and *tome*, a section; in allusion to the deeply divided limb of the corolla. *Linn.* 5, Or. 1, Nat. Or. *Epacridaceæ.* Ornamental shrubs. For culture and propagation, see *Epacris. Synonymes:* 1. *Dracophyllum capitatum.* 2. *D. gracile.*

| | | | | | |
|---|---|---|---|---|---|
| capitātūm, 1 | . | White | . 4, G. Ev. S. N. Holl. | . 1830 |
| grācīlē, 2 | . | White | . 5, G. Ev. S. N. Holl. | . 1823 |

**SPHERICAL,** round like a sphere.

**SPHERULES,** minute spheres, or globules.

**SPICATE,** having a spike.

**SPICKNEL,** see *Athamāntā.*

**SPIDER OPHRYS,** see *Ophrys araniférā.*

**SPIDERWORT,** see *Tradescāntiā.*

**SPIELMĀNNĬĀ,** *Medicus.* In honour of R. S. Spielmann, professor of medicine and botany at Strasburg. *Linn.* 14, Or. 2, Nat. Or. *Verbenaceæ.* This species will thrive in any light rich soil; and young plants are easily obtained from cuttings, planted in sand, under a glass.

| | | | | |
|---|---|---|---|---|
| africānā | . . | White | . 7, G. Ev. S. C. G. H. | . 1710 |

**SPIGĒLĬĀ,** *Linn.* In honour of Adrian Spigellus, professor of anatomy and surgery at Padua; and a botanical author; died 1625. *Linn.* 5, Or. 1, Nat. Or. *Spigeliaceæ.* These plants are showy when in blossom, and therefore worth growing; a compost of loam and peat suits them best, and cuttings of the herbaceous species root freely in the same kind of soil, under a glass. The roots of *S. marilandica* are used in North America as a vermifuge, and if administered in large doses, it acts as a powerful cathartic.

| | | | | | |
|---|---|---|---|---|---|
| Anthelmiā | . . | Red | . 7, 8.   A. S. Amer. | . 1759 |
| marilāndicā | . | Scarlet | . 7, H. Her. P. N. Amer. | . 1694 |

**SPIKE,** a long rachis of sessile flowers.

**SPIKELETS,** in grasses, are collections of florets.

**SPIKE RUSH,** see *Eleochāris.*

**SPILĀNTHES,** *Jacquin.* From *spilos*, a spot, and *anthos*, a flower, in allusion to the original species having yellow flowers and a brown disk. *Linn.* 19, Or. 1, Nat. Or. *Compositæ.* Worthless plants, requiring the treatment commonly given to stove annuals. *Synonyme:* 1. *Acmella lanceolata—S. Acmēllā, ālbā, brasiliēnsis, debĭlis, exasperātā, olerācēā, Psēudō-Acmēllā* 1, *uliginosā.*

**SPILOCĀĀ,** *Fries.* From *spilos*, a spot; *Linn.* 24, Or. 9, Nat. Or. *Fungi.* This plant grows upon apples, whence its specific name—*S. pŏmī.*

**SPILŌMĀ,** *Acharius.* Spiloma, a spot; appearance of the fructification. *Linn.* 24, Or. 8, Nat. Or. *Lichenes.* The species of *Spiloma* are generally found on the bark of trees and decaying wood—*S. aurātūm, decolōrāns, dispērsūm, melanŏpūm, micro-clŏnūm, microscōpicūm, murālē, punctātūm, tubercu-lōsūm, tumĭdūlūm, T. cōncŏlor, T. dĭvĭtātūm, T. dū-bĭūm, T. marginātūm, T. microstigmā, T. rosācēūm, variolōsūm, versĭcŏlor.*

**SPINACH,** see *Spinācĭā.*

**SPINĀCĬĀ,** *Linn.* From *spina*, a prickle, in allusion to the prickly processes of the fruit. *Linn.* 22, Or. 5, Nat. Or. *Chenopodiaceæ.* Valuable herbs, of the commonest culture, and well known by the English name *Spinach.*

| | | | | |
|---|---|---|---|---|
| olerācēā | . . | Green | . 6, H.   A. | . 1568 |
| glābrā | . . | Green | . 6, H.   A. | |
| spinōsā | . . | Green | . 6, H.   A. | |

**SPINDLE-TREE,** see *Euŏnўmūs.*

**SPINES,** indurated and pointed branches or processes, which do not fall off from the part that bears them.

**SPINOUS,** furnished with spines.

**SPIRÆĀ,** *Linn.* From *speirao*, to become spiral; in allusion to the flexile branches being suitable for twisting into garlands. *Linn.* 12, Or. 2. Nat. Or. *Rosaceæ.* An extensive genus of very handsome plants, when in flower. The shrubby kinds are well adapted for planting in ornamental shrubberies; and are increased by layers, or cuttings of the young wood. The herbaceous species look well in the flower border; and are easily increased by dividing the plants at the roots. *Synonymes:* 1. *S. hypericifolia acuta.* 2. *S. media.* 3. *S. oblongi-folia.* 4. *S. sororia.* 5. *S. Besseriana.* 6. *S. Ulmaria denudata.* 7. *S. altaiensis.* 8. *S. hypericifolia cre-*

*nata.* 9. *S. carpinifolia.* 10. *S. salicifolia alba.* 11. *S. hypericifolia savranica.* 12. *S. grandiflora.* 13. *S. triloba.* 14. *S. hypericifolia uralensis, S. crenata.*

| | | | | | | |
|---|---|---|---|---|---|---|
| acutifòliā, 1 | . | White | . 4, H. De. S. Siberia | . 1817 |
| alpīnā | . . | White | . 7, H. De. S. Siberia | . 1806 |
| argentēā | . . | | H. De. S. Nepal | |
| ariæfòliā | . | White | . 6, H. De. S. N. Amer. | . 1827 |
| Arūncūs | . | White | . 6, H. Her. P. Siberia | . 1633 |
| americānā | . | White | . 6, H. Her. P. N. Amer. | |
| barbātā | . | White | . 6, H. Her. P Nepal | . 1835 |
| bēllā | . . | Red | . 7, H. De. S. Nepal | . 1820 |
| betulifòliā | . | Pink | . 6, H. De. S. N. Amer. | . 1812 |
| cānā | . . | White | . 6, H. De. S. Hungary | . 1825 |
| capitātā | . | White | . 6, H. De. S. Columbia | . 1827 |
| ceanothifòliā | . | White | . 6, H. De. S. | . 1823 |
| chamædrifòliā | . | White | . 6, H. De. S. Siberia | . 1789 |
| inciaā | . | White | . 6, H. De. S. Germany | |
| mēdiā, 2 | . | White | . 6, H. De. S. Canada | . |
| oblongifòliā, 3 | . | White | . 6, H. De. S. Hungary | . 1816 |
| subracemòsā | . | | . 6, H. De. S. | |
| vulgāris | . . | . | . 6, H. De. S. | |
| corymbòsā | . | White | . 7, H. De. S. Virginia | . 1819 |
| sorōriā, 4 | . | White | . 8, H. De. S. N. Amer. | . 1829 |
| cratægifòliā | . | White | . 7, H. De. S. Siberia | . 1812 |
| crenātā, 5 | . | White | . 4, H. De. S. Podolia | . 1739 |
| cuneifòliā | . | White | . H. De. S. India | |
| denudātā, 6 | . | White | . 7, H. Her. P. S. Eur. | |
| digitātā | . | Red | . 7, H. Her. P. Siberia | . 1823 |
| Filipēndūlā | . | White | . 9, H. Tu. P. Britain | |
| minōr | . | White | . 8, H. Tu. P. Europe | |
| multiplēx | . | White | . 8, H. Her. P. Brit. gar. | |
| pubēscēns | . | White | . 8, H. Tu. P. France | |
| flexuòsā | . | White | . 6, H. De. S. Europe | . 1820 |
| hypericifòliā | . | White | . 6, H. De. S. N. Amer. | . 1640 |
| Plukenetiānā | . | White | . 4, H. De. S. Canada | |
| japonicā | . | | . H. Her. P. Japan | . 1836 |
| lævigātā, 7 | . | Red | . 5, H. De. S. Siberia | . 1774 |
| lanceolātā | . | White | . H. De. S. Mauritius | |
| laxiflòrā | . | White | . H. De. S. India | |
| lobātā | . | Red | . 7, H. Her. P. N. Amer. | . 1765 |
| obovātā, 8 | . | White | . 6, H. De. S. Hungary | . 1816 |
| opulifòliā | . | White | . 6, H. De. S. N. Amer. | . 1690 |
| tomentēllā | . | White | . 6, H. De. S. N. Amer. | |
| palmātā | . | Red | . 7, H. Her. P. China | . 1823 |
| pickowiēnsis | . | White | . 6, H. De. S. Podolia | . 1807 |
| salicifòliā | . | White | . 7, H. De. S. Britain | |
| alpēstris | . | White | . 7, H. De. S. Russia | . 1820 |
| cārnēā | . | Flesh | . 7, H. De. S. Britain | |
| grandiflòrā | . | Pink | . 7, H. Her. P. Kamtsch. | . 1827 |
| latifòliā, 9 | . | White | . 7, H. De. S. Europe | |
| paniculātā, 10 | . | White | . 7, H. Her. P. N. Amer. | |
| savrānicā, 11 | . | White | . 4, H. De. S. Podolia | . 1819 |
| sorbifòliā | . | White | . 8, H. De. S. Siberia | . 1759 |
| alpīnā, 12 | . | White | . 8, H. De. S. Siberia | . 1817 |
| thalictroidēs | . | White | . 6, H. De. S. Dahuria | . 1806 |
| tobōlskiā | . | White | . 8, H. De. S. Russia | . 1823 |
| tomentòsā | . | White | . 8, H. De. S. N. Amer. | . 1736 |
| trilobātā, 13 | . | White | . 5, H. De. S. Altai | . 1801 |
| Ulmāriā | . | White | . 8, H. Her. P. Britain | |
| multiplēx | . | White | . 8, H. Her. P. Britain | |
| variegātā | . | White | . 7, H. Her. P. Britain | |
| ulmifòliā | . | White | . 6, H. Her. P. Carniola | . 1790 |
| phyllāntha | . | White | . 6, H. De. S. | |
| uralensis, 14 | . | White | . 4, H. Her. P. Uralia | . 1817 |
| vaccinifòliā | . | White | . 6, H. Her. P. India | . 1820 |

**SPIRAL,** twisted like a screw.

**SPIRALĒPIS,** *Don.* From *speira*, a spire, and *lepis*, a scale; scales twisted. *Linn.* 19, Or. 2, Nat. Or. *Compositæ.* Ornamental plants. For culture and propagation, see *Gnaphalium. Synonymes:* 1. *Gna-phalium declinatum.* 2. *G. glomeratum.* 3. *G. mo-destum.* 4. *G. squarrosum.*

| | | | | | |
|---|---|---|---|---|---|
| declinātā, 1 | . | Brown | . 8, G. Her. P. C. G. H. | . 1787 |
| glomerātā, 2 | . | Pur. grn. | . 7, G. Her. P. C. G. H. | . 1774 |
| modēstā, 3 | . | Red | . 9, G. Her. P. C. G. H. | . 1826 |
| squarròsā, 4 | . | Purple | . 9, G. Ev. S. C. G. H. | . 1816 |

**SPIRĀNTHĒRĀ,** *St. Hilaire.* From *speira*, a spire, and *anthera*, an anther; the anthers are spiral shaped. *Linn.* 5, Or. 1, Nat. Or. *Rutaceæ.* A very handsome flowering, sweet-scented shrub, thriving in a mixture of sandy loam and peat; and cuttings of the half ripened wood will root in sand, under a glass; but they must be planted thinly, and the glass occasionally removed to allow them to dry, as they are very liable to damp. *Synonyme:* 1. *Terpnan-thus jasminoides.*

| | | | | |
|---|---|---|---|---|
| odoratissimā, 1 | . Wht. red | . 8, Ev. S. Brazil | . . 1823 |

**SPIRĀNTHES,** *Richard.* From *speira*, a spiral, and *anthos*, a flower; in allusion to the spiral manner in which the flowers are arranged. *Linn.* 20, Or. 1, Nat. Or. *Orchidaceæ.* The species of *Spiranthes* (*Lady's Traces*) require the same treatment as the *Neottia.*

| | | | | | | |
|---|---|---|---|---|---|---|
| bracteòsā | . . . | Wht. yel. | . 5, S. Ter. St. Cather. | . 1835 |
| diurèticā | . . . | Grn. wht. | . 8, G. Ter. Valparaiso | . 1838 |
| grandiflòrā | . . . | Green | . 9, F. Ter. N. Amer. | |

SPLĀCHNŬM, *Linn.* From *splagchnon*, one of the Greek names for moss. *Linn.* 24, Or. 5, Nat. Or. *Musci.* These plants are chiefly found growing on mountains. *Synonymes:* 1. *S. Turnerianum* 2. *S. fastigiatum.* 3. *S. ovatum.* 4. *Grimmia splachnoides—S. ampullàceūm* 1, *angustàtum, mniöldēs, M. màjus* 2, *M. mìnŭs, sphèricūm* 3, *tènŭī* 4, *vasculòsūm, V. rugòsūm.*

SPLEENWORT, see *Asplēnīum.*

SPŎNDĬĀS. *Linn.* The Greek name for a kind of plum; the fruit resembles a plum. *Linn.* 10, Or. 4, Nat. Or. *Spondiaceæ.* The species of *Spondias* succeed best in a mixture of loam and peat; and cuttings of the ripened wood will root in sand, under a glass, in heat. The fruit of some of the species is eatable. *Synonymes:* 1. *S. Myrobalanus.* 2. *S. Mombin.*

| | | | | | | |
|---|---|---|---|---|---|---|
| lùtea, 1 | . . . | Yel. grn. | . B. Ev. T. W. Ind. | . 1789 |
| purpùrea, 2 | . . | Wht. grn. | . B. Ev. T. W. Ind. | . 1817 |

SPONGE-TREE, see *Acàciä farnesiänä.*

SPŎRENDŎNĒMĀ, *Desmazieres.* From *sporos*, a seed, *endon*, within, and *nema*, a thread. *Linn.* 24, Or. 9, Nat. Or. *Fungi.* Minute species; the first is found on cheese, the last on flies—*S. càseī, mùscæ.*

SPORĪDĚSMĬŬM, *Link.* From *sporos*, a sporule, and *desme*, a skin. *Linn.* 24, Or. 9, Nat. Or. *Fungi.* A minute plant, found on some species of *Thelephora —S. àtrŭm.*

SPŎRŎBŎLŬS, *R. Brown.* From *sporos*, a seed, and *ballo*, to cast forth; its seeds are loose and easily scattered. *Linn.* 3, Or. 2, Nat. Or. *Gramineæ.* Annual grasses, of simple culture in any common soil, and propagated by seeds. *Synonymes:* 1. *Agrostis diandra.* 2. *A. purpurascens.*

| | | | | | | |
|---|---|---|---|---|---|---|
| diandrŭs, 1 | . . | Apetal | . 8, Gram. E. Ind. | . 1820 |
| elongàtŭs | . . | Apetal | . 8, Gram. N. Holl. | . 1820 |
| indicŭs | . . | Apetal | . 9, Gram. India | . 1773 |
| purpuràscens, 2 | . | Apetal | . 8, Gram. W. Ind. | . 1806 |
| tenacissimŭs | . | Apetal | . 8, Gram. E. Ind. | . 1801 |

SPŎRŎCHNŬS, *Agardh.* From *sporos*, seed, and *chnous*, wool; because of its reproductive organs being tufted with hair. *Linn.* 24, Or. 7, Nat. Or. *Algæ.* Marine plants—*S. aculeàtŭs, Cabrèræ, ligulàtŭs, pedunculàtŭs, rhizòdēs, R. màjŏr, villòsŭs, vìrĭdĭs.*

SPŎRŎCŬBĒ, *Fries.* From *sporos*, a seed, and *kube*, a head. *Linn.* 24, Or. 9, Nat. Or. *Fungi.* Found on the decaying stems of plants—*S. byssoïdēs, Culicioïdēs.*

SPŎRŎTRĪCHŬM, *Link.* From *spora*, a sporule, and *thrix*, a hair; alluding to the filamentous sporules. *Linn.* 24, Or. 9, Nat. Or. *Fungi.* Very minute species, found in various situations, chiefly on decaying substances—*S. aurèŭm, badiŭm, fenestràlē, latæbràrŭm, macrospòrŭm, minùtŭm, stercoràrĭŭm, sulphùrëŭm, tenuissĭmŭm.*

SPORULES, in cryptogamic plants, those parts which are analogous to the seeds of other plants.

SPRĒNGĚLĬĀ, *Smith.* In honour of Christian Conrad Sprengel, of Brandenburgh, who published, in 1793, an ingenious work on the manner in which insects promote the impregnation of plants. *Linn.* 5, Or. 1, Nat. Or. *Epacridaceæ.* This very elegant little shrub requires the same treatment as is recommended for *Epacris.*

| | | | | | | |
|---|---|---|---|---|---|---|
| incarnàtā | . . | Flesh | . 5, G. Ev. S. N. S. W. | . 1793 |

SPRING GRASS, see *Anthoxanthŭm.*

SPŪMĀRĬĀ, *Persoon.* From *spuma*, froth; appearance of the species. *Linn.* 24, Or. 9, Nat. Or. *Fungi.* This plant is found in autumn on grass, rotten wood, &c.—*S. mucilàgo.*

SPUMOSE, frothy.

SPURS, long processes, like horns, produced by various parts of a flower.

SPURGE, see *Euphòrbĭā.*

SPURGE LAUREL, see *Daphnè Laurèölā.*

SPURIOUS, counterfeit.

SPURLESS VIOLET, see *Erpètlòn.*

SPURREY, see *Spergùlā.*

SQUALIDUS, mean, unseemly.

SQUAMARIA, scaly, covered with scales.

SQUAMĀRĬĀ, *Hooker.* From *squama*, a scale; the thallus is scaly. *Linn.* 24, Or. 8, Nat. Or. *Lichenes.* These plants are found on rocks, stones, and trees—*S. miniàtā, Muscòrŭm, tribàcēā.*

SQUAMIFORM, } formed like scales.
SQUAMOSE, }

SQUARE PARSLEY, see *Mèŭm Bănĭŭs.*

SQUARROSE, spreading rigidly at right angles, or in a yet greater degree.

SQUASH, see *Cucŭrbĭtä Melopèpo.*

SQUILL, see *Scïllä.*

SQUINANCY, an inflammation in the throat.

SQUIRTING CUCUMBER, see *Momŏrdĭcä Elaterĭŭm.*

STAĀvĬĀ, *Dahl.* In honour of Martin Staaf, a correspondent of Linnæus. *Linn.* 5, Or. 1, Nat. Or. *Bruniaceæ.* Elegant little shrubs, succeeding best in a sandy peat soil; cuttings of the young wood will root readily in sand, under a glass. *Synonymes:* 1. *Brunia ciliata.* 2. *B. glutinosa.* 3. *B. radiata, Phylica radiata.*

| | | | | | | |
|---|---|---|---|---|---|---|
| ciliàta, 1 | . . | White | . 6, G. Ev. S. C. G. H. | . 1812 |
| glutinòsa, 2 | . | White | . 4, G. Ev. S. C. G. H. | . 1793 |
| radiàta, 3 | . | White | . 5, G. Ev. S. C. G. H. | . 1787 |

STACHYLĪDĬŬM, *Fries.* From *stachys*, a spike, and *eidos*, similar; in allusion to the manner in which the sporules are fixed on the filaments. *Linn.* 24, Or. 9, Nat. Or. *Fungi.* Found on dead wood—*S. bìcôlŏr, terrēstrē.*

STĂCHŶS, *Linn.* From *stachys*, a spike; mode of flowering. *Linn.* 14, Or. 1, Nat. Or. *Labiatæ.* A genus of rather weedy-looking plants, hardly worth cultivating for ornament. They all succeed in common garden soil. The greenhouse species require to be treated as other greenhouse plants. The perennial kinds are easily increased by dividing the root in spring or autumn. The seeds of the annual kinds should be sown in spring, in the open border. *Synonymes:* 1. *S. cretica, intermedia, orientalis, sibirica.* 2. *S. tenuifolia.* 3. *S. diffusa, Iberica, scordifolia.* 4. *S. arvensis, hispida.* 5. *S. latifolia.* 6. *Hyssopus anisatus.* 7. *S. biennis, lusitanica, polystachya.* 8. *S. phlomoides.* 9. *Ambleia inflata.* 10. *S. salviæfolia.* 11. *Sideritis decumbens.* 12. *Sideritis calycantha.* 13. *Stachys ambigua.* 14. *S. Balbisii.* 15. *Sideritis linearifolia.*

| | | | | | | |
|---|---|---|---|---|---|---|
| æthiòpica | . . | Purple | . 5, G. Her. P. C. G. H. | . 1770 |
| angustifòlia, 2 | . | Purple | . 7, H. Her. P. Tauria | . 1823 |
| aràbica | . . | Violet | . 7, H. A. Arabia | . 1819 |
| arenària, 3 | . | Purple | . 7, H. Her. P. Levant | . 1864 |
| betonicæfòlia | . | Yellow | . 6, H. A. Rochelle | . 1812 |
| coccinèā | . . | Scarlet | . 7, G. Her. P. S. Amer. | . 1798 |
| dèbilis | . | Pa. vio. | . 7, H. Her. P. S. Amer. | . 1825 |
| Fœnĭcŭlŭm, 6 | . | Blue | . 5, H. B. N. Amer. | . 1824 |
| fruticulòsā | . | Purple | . 7, H. Ev. S. Caucasus | . 1818 |
| glaucèscens | . | Purple | . 7, H. Her. P. Caucasus | . 1826 |
| glutinòsā | . | Purple | . 6, H. Her. P. Candia | . 1739 |
| Heraclèā, 8 | . | Purple | . 7, H. Her. P. Italy | . 1822 |
| hirsùtā | . | Red | . F. Her. P. Mexico | . 1829 |
| hìrtā | . | Yellow | . 7, H. A. Spain | . 1725 |
| inflàtā, 9 | . | Pink | . 7, H. Her. P. Africa | . 1832 |
| Itàlicā, 10 | . | Purple | . 6, H. Her. P. Europe | |
| Lamàrckiī, 11 | . | Purple | . 7, G. Ev. S. C. G. H. | . 1820 |
| lanàtā | . | Striped | . 7, H. Her. P. Siberia | . 1782 |
| lavandulæfòliā, 12 | Purple | . 7, H. Ev. S. Caucasus | . 1820 |
| marìtimā | . | Pa. yel. | . 7, H. Her. P. S. Eur. | . 1714 |
| obliquā | . | Yellow | . 6, H. Her. P. Hungary | . 1816 |
| Palæstìnā | . | Purple | . 7, H. Ev. S. Syria | . 1820 |
| pauciflòrā | . | Yelsh. | . G. Ev. S. Egypt | . 1834 |
| pubèscens, 14 | . | Yelsh. | . 7, H. Her. P. Europe | . 1816 |
| rèctā | . | Yellow | . 7, H. Her. P. S. Eur. | . 1683 |
| rugòsā | . | Pa. yel. | . 7, G. Ev. S. C. G. H. | . 1774 |
| scordioïdēs | . | Yellow | . 7, H. Her. S. Morocco | . 1818 |
| serĭcèā | . | Lilac | . 8, H. Her. P. Nepal | . 1820 |
| setìferā | . | Red brn. | . H. Her. P. Caucasus | . 1837 |
| stenophylla, 15 | . | Yellow | . 7, H. Ev. S. Spain | . 1823 |

Albicaùlis, alpìnā 1, A. intermèdiā, annuā, arvènsis, àsperā 4, circinàtā 5, corsĭcā, C. albā, decŭmbēns, germànicā 7, G. pubèscens, grandidentàtā, hyssopĭfòliā, mollissĭmā, nepetæfòliā, palùstris, P. albā, P. hybridā 13, P. variegàtā, spinòsā, sylvàticā.

STĂCHYTĀRPHĒTĀ, *Vahl.* From *stachys*, a spike, and *tarpheios*, dense; manner of flowering. *Linn.* 2, Or. 1, Nat. Or. *Verbenaceæ.* The species of *Stachytarpheta* thrive in a light rich mould. The shrubby kinds are increased by cuttings, planted in sand, under a glass. The annuals and biennials require to be treated as other stove annuals and biennials. *S. mutabilis* is a handsome, ever-flowering shrub, the leaves of which have been imported from South America for the purpose of adulterating tea.

| | | | | | | |
|---|---|---|---|---|---|---|
| angustifòliā | . | Blue | . 7, G. B. S. Amer. | |
| cayennènsis | . | Blue | . 5, S. Ev. S. Cayenne | . 1822 |
| hirsutissĭmā | . | Blue | . 4, S. Her. P. Brazil | . 1822 |
| indĭcā | . . . | White | 8, S. A. Ceylon | . 1732 |

| | | | | | |
|---|---|---|---|---|---|
| jamaicénsis | . | Blue . | 7, 8. | B. W. Ind. | 1714 |
| mutábilis | . | Orange . | 6, 8. Ev. | 8. S. Amer. | 1801 |
| erúbica | . | Violet . | 7, 8. | A. Panama | 1699 |
| prismáticà | . | Blue . | 5, 8. | B. W. Ind. | 1699 |
| urticifòliÀ | . | Blue . | 6, 8. | B. S. Amer. | |

STACKHOÛSIÀ, *Smith*. In honour of Mr. Stackhouse, a British botanist. *Linn.* 5, Or. 2, Nat. Or. *Stackhousiaceæ.* Ornamental plants, of common culture.

| | | | | | |
|---|---|---|---|---|---|
| linarimfòliÀ | . | . | G. Ev. 8. | N. Holl. | 1823 |
| monogýnÀ | . | Pink . | 4, H. Her. | P. V. D. L. | 1835 |

STADMANNIA, *Lamarck.* In honour of M. Stadmann, a German botanical traveller. *Linn.* 8, Or. 1, Nat. Or. *Sapindaceæ.* A lofty-growing tree, with very large showy leaves. It grows in loam and peat; and cuttings of the ripened wood, with the leaves left entire, will root in sand, under a glass, in a moist heat.

| | | | | |
|---|---|---|---|---|
| austràlis | . . Whitish . | G. Ev. T. | N. Holl. | 1823 |

STÆHELÌNÀ, *Linn.* In honour of Benedict Stæhelin, a Swiss botanist. *Linn.* 19, Or. 1, Nat. Or. *Compositæ.* Any light rich soil suits these plants; and cuttings root readily in the same kind of soil. *Synonyme:* 1. *Pteronia Chamæpeuce.*

| | | | | | |
|---|---|---|---|---|---|
| arboréscens | . | Purple . | 8, F. Ev. 8. | Candia | 1739 |
| Chamæpeúce, 1 | . | Purple . | 7, F. Ev. 8. | Candia | 1640 |
| dùbiÀ | . | Purple . | 6, H. De. 8. | S. Eur. | 1640 |

STAFF-TREE, see *Celástrus.*

STALAGMÌTIS, *Murray.* From *stalagnos*, a running out; the trees exude a yellow resinous juice when cut. *Linn.* 18, Or. 2, Nat. Or. *Guttiferæ.* A genus of very fine ornamental trees, thriving well in a mixture of turfy loam and peat, and requiring to be kept in a strong heat. Cuttings of the ripened wood will root in sand, under a glass, in a moist heat. The fruit of some of the species is eatable. The trees yield a yellow viscid juice, hardly distinguishable from gamboge, and used for the same purposes by painters. *Synonymes:* 1. *Xanthochymus edulis.* 2. *X. guineensis.* 3. *X. luteus.* 4. *X. macrophyllus.* 5. *X. ovalifolius.* 6. *X. purpureus.* 7. *X. tinctorius.*

| | | | | | |
|---|---|---|---|---|---|
| aúleÀ, 1 | . | Yellow | 8. Ev. T. | E. Ind. | 1820 |
| guineénsla, 2 | . | Yellow | 8. Ev. T. | Guiana | 1824 |
| lùteÀ, 3 | . | Yellow | 8. Ev. T. | | |
| macrophýllia, 4 | . | Yellow | 8. Ev. T. | | |
| ovalifòlia, 5 | . | Yellow | 8. Ev. T. | Ceylon | 1820 |
| purpùreÀ, 6 | . | | 8. Ev. T. | | |
| tinctóriÙ, 7 | . | | 8. Ev. T. | | |

STALKS, the foot-stalks of leaves or flowers.

STAMEN, the male organ of a flower.

STANDARD, the upper petals in a pea-flower.

STANHÒPEÀ, *Hooker.* In compliment to Earl Stanhope, president of the Medico-botanical Society. *Linn.* 20, Or. 1, Nat. Or. *Orchidaceæ.* The species of Stanhopea are splendid plants when in flower, particularly S. *Devoniensis* and S. *tigrina,* both of which are at present rare in collections. The flowers of all the species are more or less fragrant. The following is the method of cultivating these favourite plants at Chatsworth:—Over the drainage hole of the pot to be used for large plants, is inverted one of a smaller size, generally covering about half the bottom of the pot; above and around this is carefully thrown a quantity of broken pots, sufficient to fill the remaining cavity to within one-third of the top. A sufficient quantity of fibrous, moderately sandy peat is next selected, and placed on the top of the drainage, being first broken into various forms and sizes, but none of them less than a walnut. In placing these, care is taken to dispose of each, so as to leave a passage for the escape of water; this is more effectually secured by introducing, as the process of potting goes on, a few pieces of broken pots between every layer, more or less, according to the size of the plant; indeed, it is an excellent plan to continue a connexion of broken pots all the way up the centre, to the bottom of the pseudo-bulbs. After the peat becomes level with the summit of the pot, the successive external layers are made fast by means of small pegs, varying from four to six inches long: these pegs penetrate the layers of peat, and thus secure the whole firmly together. At eight inches above the edge of the pot the plant is placed on the top, and the roots are carefully laid out, and covered up to the bulbs very carefully with smaller pieces of peat and potsherds,

continuing to fasten the peat as before described, until the whole is finished; when it will be a foot or fifteen inches above the top of the pot;—small plants are not potted so high. When a single pseudo-bulb is first potted, it should be but very slightly raised above the level, and when a small plant of two or three bulbs is potted, it should not, at first, be raised more than two or three inches, but as it grows larger it is progressively elevated. In building up, as is here described, with peat, it does not terminate in the shape of a cone, but is carried up nearly square, being merely rounded a little at the top. Unless the plants are very healthy, water is given but sparingly at the roots, and in winter very little or none is supplied; the great desideratum in the cultivation of Orchidaceæ being *to preserve the roots,* which, by over-watering, especially in winter, are almost sure to be destroyed. The general temperature of the house ranges from 60 to 85 degrees; in the afternoon, during the growing season, it is shut up early, and the paths well watered, and once or twice a week a little water is sprinkled over the plants. It is of great advantage to have a tan bed in the house, for the purpose of plunging the plants, as the heat from the tan circulates through the peat and potsherds, and causes the specimens to grow with great luxuriance. Young plants are obtained by taking off one or more of the bulbs, potting them in proper sized pots, in the above soil, well drained, and placing them on a hot flue; being careful, in watering, not to allow the smallest quantity to rest upon the young buds. After they have formed roots, increase the size of the pots, and in other respects attend to them as before recommended.

| | | | | | |
|---|---|---|---|---|---|
| Devoniénsis | . . | Or. spot. red | 7, 8. Epi. | Mexico | . . |
| ebúrneÀ | . . | White . | G, 8. Epi. | Brasil | . . |
| grandiflórÀ | . . | White . | 6, 8. Epi. | Trinidad | 1824 |
| insígnis | . . | Wht. pur. | 9, 8. Epi. | Quito | . . |
| LindlèyÌ | . . | Brn. red | 8, 8. Epi. | Mexico | . . |
| maculòsÀ | . . | Blue grn. | 8, 8. Epi. | Mexico | 1830 |
| oculàta | . . | Wht. pur. | 6, 8. Epi. | Brasil | 1829 |
| quadricórnis | . . | Wht. spot. | 6, 8. Epi. | 8. Main | . . |
| tìgrìnÀ | . . | Or. spot. red | 7, 8. Epi. | Xalapa | . . |
| WardÌÌ | . . | Yel. brn. | 8, 8. Epi. | Mexico | 1836 |

STÀNLÈYÀ, *Nuttall* named this genus in compliment to Edward Stanley, Earl of Derby, F.R.S.,V.P.L.S., President of the Zoological Society, and a munificent patron of the sciences, especially Botany and Ornithology. *Linn.* 15, Nat. Or. *Cruciferæ.* A pretty little plant, succeeding well in the open border in vegetable mould; and increased by divisions of the root or by seeds. *Synonyme:* 1. *Cleome pinnata.*

| | | | | | |
|---|---|---|---|---|---|
| pinnatífìdÀ, 1 | . | Yellow . | 6, H. Her. | P. Louisiana | 1816 |

STAPÈLIÀ. Named by *Linnæus* after Bodcrus Stapel, a physician of Amsterdam, and commentator on Theophrastus. *Linn.* 5, Or. 2, Nat. Or. *Asclepiadaceæ.* An extensive genus of plants, well worth cultivating for their grotesque appearance, and their singularly beautiful star-like flowers, which have usually a very fetid smell. The soil best suited for them is sandy loam, and old brick or lime rubbish. The pots should be well drained, and the plants at all times carefully watered, especially in winter, when they must be kept in a perpetually dry state. They are readily increased by cuttings, which should, if possible, be only taken off in spring, when the plants are dormant. They should be allowed to dry for a few days after they are taken from the mother plant; after which, they may be planted in separate pots, in the same compost as before recommended, when they will strike root in a very short time. *Synonymes:* 1. *S. deflexa.* 2. *S. grandiflora.*

| | | | | | |
|---|---|---|---|---|---|
| acuminàtà | . | Pur. str. | 8, 8. Ev. 8. | C. G. H. | 1795 |
| ambígùÀ | . | Pur. brn. | 6, 8. Ev. 8. | C. G. H. | 1795 |
| apértÀ | . | Yel. pur. | 7, 8. Ev. 8. | C. G. H. | 1795 |
| AstériÀs | . | Violet . | 5, G. Ev. 8. | C. G. H. | 1795 |
| canéscens | . | Brown | 7, G. Ev. 8. | C. G. H. | 1795 |
| comàtÀ | . | Pa. yel. | 9, G. Ev. 8. | C. G. H. | 1819 |
| concinnÀ | . | Green . | 7, G. Ev. 8. | C. G. H. | 1798 |
| fissiróstris | . | Yel. grn. | G. Ev. 8. | C. G. H. | 1823 |
| flavicomàtÀ | . | Yellow | G. Ev. 8. | C. G. H. | 1810 |
| glandulíferÀ | . | Yellsh. | 8, G. Ev. 8. | C. G. H. | |
| glandulifiórÀ | . | Brown | 8, G. Ev. 8. | C. G. H. | 1795 |
| Gordónì | . | Yel. brn. | G. Ev. 8. | C. G. H. | 1796 |
| grandiflórÀ | . | Dk. pur. | 10, G. Ev. 8. | C. G. H. | 1795 |
| hamàtÀ | . | Bld. red | 7, G. Ev. 8. | C. G. H. | 1820 |

| | | | | |
|---|---|---|---|---|
| hirsūta | Purple | 7, G. Ev. S. C. G. H. | 1710 |
| ātra | Dk. pur. | 7, G. Ev. S. C. G. H. | 1710 |
| hirtella | Brown | 8, G. Ev. S. C. G. H. | 1800 |
| hispidūla | Green | 7, G. Ev. S. C. G. H. | 1824 |
| juvēncūla | Brn. pur. | 7, G. Ev. S. C. G. H. | |
| laxīgēra | Brown | 8, G. Ev. S. C. G. H. | 1800 |
| lūcīda | Purple | 7, G. Ev. S. C. G. H. | 1812 |
| Massoni | | G. Ev. S. C. G. H. | |
| multiflōra | Vio. red | 9, G. Ev. S. C. G. H. | 1817 |
| ophiūncūla | Brown | 7, G. Ev. S. C. G. H. | 1805 |
| pātūla | Orange | 7, G. Ev. S. C. G. H. | 1797 |
| pilīfēra | Dk. pur. | 7, G. Ev. S. C. G. H. | 1790 |
| pulvināta | Dk. vio. | 8, G. Ev. S. C. G. H. | 1795 |
| ramōsa | Dk. pur. | 6, G. Ev. S. C. G. H. | 1795 |
| reflexā, 1 | Orn. pur. | 7, G. Ev. S. C. G. H. | |
| rūfa | Brown | 9, G. Ev. S. C. G. H. | 1795 |
| sorōriā | Dk. pur. | 7, G. Ev. S. C. G. H. | 1797 |
| spectābīlīs, 2 | Dk. pur. | 12, G. Ev. S. C. G. H. | 1802 |
| stellāris | | G. Ev. S. C. G. H. | |

STAPHYLĒA, *Linn.* Abridged from *Staphylodendron,* its ancient name, from *staphyle,* a bunch, and *dendron,* a tree; the flowers and fruit are disposed in clusters. *Linn.* 5, Or. 3, Nat. Or. *Staphylaceæ.* Shrubs of very little beauty. They succeed well in any common soil, and are readily increased by suckers from the roots, by layers, or by cuttings, planted in autumn.

| | | | | |
|---|---|---|---|---|
| occidentalis | White | S. Ev. T. Jamaica | 1824 |
| pinnāta | White | 6, H. De. S. England | |
| trifōlia | White | 5, H. De. S. N. Amer. | 1640 |

STAR APPLE, see *Chrysophÿllum.*
STAR FISH, see *Stapēliā Astērīās.*
STĪARKĒA, *Willdenow.* In honour of the Rev. M. Starke, of Gros Tschirna, in Silesia, a cryptogamic botanist. *Linn.* 19, Or. 2, Nat. Or. *Compositæ.* A stove herbaceous perennial, growing in any light rich soil, and increased by divisions. *Synonyme:* 1. *Amellus umbellatus—S. umbellāta.*
STAR OF BETHLEHEM, see *Ornithōgālum.*
STAR OF THE EARTH, see *Plantāgō Corōnōpūs.*
STARRY, in the manner of a star, radiating.
STAR THISTLE, see *Centaūrēā calcitrāpā.*
STARWORT, see *Aster.*
STĀTICE, *Linn.* From *statizo,* to stop; in allusion to the powerful astringency of some of the species. *Linn.* 5, Or. 6, Nat. Or. *Plumbaginaceæ.* The species of *Statice,* or Sea Lavender, ought to be in every garden, on account of their lively little flowers. The greenhouse and frame kinds succeed best in sandy loam and peat, and may be increased by cutting. The hardy herbaceous species are very suitable for ornamenting the front of flower-borders; they increase freely by division, or seeds, which latter some of them produce in abundance. The root of *S. caroliniana* is one of the most powerful astringents known. *Synonymes:* 1. *Taxanthema australis.* 2. *Statice lyrata.* 3. *S. spatulata.*

| | | | | |
|---|---|---|---|---|
| acerōsa | Pa. pink | 6, F. Her. P. Ararat | 1829 |
| ægyptīāca | White | 6, F. Her. P. Egypt | 1823 |
| alāta | Pur. yel. | 7, F. Her. P. | 1806 |
| altāīca | Blue | 7, H. Her. P. Siberia | 1820 |
| arbōrēa | Blue | 7, G. Ev. S. Teneriffe | 1829 |
| articulāta | Blue | 7, H. Her. P. S. France | 1826 |
| aūrea | Golden | H. Her. P. Siberia | 1832 |
| auriculāta | Blue | 7, H. Her. P. Galicia | 1817 |
| auriculæfōlia | Red | 7, H. Her. P. Barbary | 1781 |
| australis, 1 | | G. Her. P. N. Holl. | 1823 |
| bellidifolia | Pa. blue | 6, H. Her. P. Greece | 1810 |
| binervōsa | Blue | 7, H. Her. P. England | |
| carolīnīāna | Blue | 6, H. Her. P. Carolina | 1820 |
| cāspīca | Pa. blue | 7, H. Her. P. Casp. Sea | |
| cinērēa | Blue | 7, G. Her. P. C. G. H. | 1810 |
| conspīcūa | Pink | 7, F. Her. P. Russia | 1804 |
| cordāta | Blue | 7, H. Her. P. S. Eur. | 1752 |
| Corīārīā | Lilac | 7, H. Her. P. Caucasus | |
| cuneāta | Blue | 7, H. Her. P. Siberia | 1820 |
| dichōtōmā | Blue | 7, H. Her. P. S. Eur. | 1810 |
| Echinūs | Red | 7, H. Her. P. Caucasus | 1813 |
| echioīdēs | Pa. blue | 7, G. B. S. Eur. | 1752 |
| elāta | Blue | 7, H. Her. P. Siberia | 1820 |
| emargināta | Purple | 7, H. Her. P. Gibraltar | |
| ferulācēa | Yellow | 7, H. Her. P. Siberia | 1796 |
| flexuōsa | Purple | 7, H. Her. P. Siberia | 1791 |
| foliōsā | Pur. wht. | 7, F. Her. P. Graciosa | 1830 |
| globulariæfōlia | White | 8, H. Her. P. Mexico | 1822 |
| Gmelini | Blue | 7, H. Her. P. Siberia | 1796 |
| grācā | White | 6, H. Her. P. Greece | 1810 |
| graminifōlia | Red | 6, H. Her. P. Siberia | 1780 |
| grandiflōra | | G. Ev. S. | 1836 |
| imbricāta | | F. H. Her. P. Teneriffe | 1829 |
| incāna | Pink | 7, H. Her. P. Egypt | 1823 |
| latifōlia | Blue | 6, H. Her. P. Siberia | 1791 |
| Limōnium | Blue | 7, F. Her. P. England | |

| | | | | |
|---|---|---|---|---|
| macrophÿlla | White | 5, G. Her. P. Canaries | 1824 |
| mimāta | Red | 6, H. Her. P. Mediter. | 1658 |
| monopētāla | Purple | 5, H. Ev. S. Sicily | 1731 |
| mucronāta | Red | 7, F. Her. P. Barbary | 1784 |
| nāna | Blue | 7, H. Her. P. Britain | |
| oleīfōlia | Red | 7, H. Her. P. Italy | 1688 |
| ovalifōlia | White | 7, G. Her. P. Canaries | 1816 |
| pectināta | Blue | 9, F. Her. P. Canaries | 1780 |
| pruinōsā | White | 7, H. Her. P. S. Eur. | 1823 |
| pubertīs | Violet | 5, G. Her. P. Graciosa | 1830 |
| pubescēns | Red | 7, F. Her. P. S. Eur. | 1824 |
| purpurāta | Purple | 6, G. Her. P. C. G. H. | 1800 |
| reticulāta | Blue | 7, H. Her. P. England | |
| scābra | Blue | 6, G. Her. P. C. G. H. | 1788 |
| Scopārīa | Blue | 7, H. Her. P. Siberia | 1796 |
| sinuāta | Pur. yel. | 7, H. Her. P. Levant | 1629 |
| spatulāta | Purple | 7, H. Her. P. Barbary | 1804 |
| speciōsa | White | 7, H. Her. P. Russia | 1776 |
| spicāta, 2 | White | 7, H. A. Caucasus | 1819 |
| suffruticōsa | Blue | 7, H. Ev. S. Siberia | 1799 |
| tatārīca | Pink | 6, H. Her. P. Russia | 1731 |
| tetragōnā | Red | 7, H. Her. P. C. G. H. | 1820 |
| Thouīnī | Blue | 8, H. Her. P. N. Africa | 1700 |
| viminēa | Blue | 7, H. Her. P. | 1818 |
| virgāta | Blue | 7, H. Her. P. Spain | |
| Willdenovīāna, 3 | Violet | 7, H. Her. P. France | 1800 |

STAURACĀNTHŪS, *Link.* From *stauros,* a cross, and *akantha,* a spine; the spines have each two smaller spines at the side; which give them the appearance of a cross. *Linn.* 16, Or. 5, Nat. Or. *Leguminosæ.* A very beautiful dwarf shrub, well suited for the front of shrubberies; it is easily increased by young cuttings, planted in sand, or by seeds. *Synonyme:* 1. *Ulex genistoides.*

| | | | | |
|---|---|---|---|---|
| aphyllus, 1 | Yellow | 5, H. Ev. S. Portugal | 1823 |

STĒLIS, *Swartz.* Not explained. *Linn.* 20, Or. 1, Nat. Or. *Orchidaceæ.* The species of *Stelis* are small, rather interesting plants. For culture and propagation, see *Pleurothallis.*

| | | | | |
|---|---|---|---|---|
| micrantha | Green | 4, S. Epi. Jamaica | 1805 |
| ophioglossoïdēs | Pur. brn. | 9, S. Epi. Jamaica | 1791 |
| tristÿla | Green | 8, S. Epi. Brazil | |

STELLĀRIA, *Linn.* From *stella,* a star; the flowers are star-like. *Linn.* 10, Or. 3, Nat. Or. *Alsinaceæ.* Weeds, of no known use. *Synonymes:* 1. *S. uliginosa.* 2. *S. multicaulis.* 3. *S. dichotoma—S. aquatica* 1, *arendrīa, bulbōsa, cerastoïdēs, C. triflōrā* 2, *crassifōlia, dahūrīca, ělěgāns, glaūca, graminēa, Holōstēa, humifūsa, latifōlia, Laxmānni, longīpēs, mēdīa* 3, *multicaulis, murālis, nemorūm, scapigēra, velutīna, vīscīda.*

STEM-CLASPING, when applied to a leaf, signifies that its base surrounds the stem.

STEMŌDIA, *Linn.* From *stemon,* a stamen, and *dis,* double; in allusion to each stamen bearing two anthers. *Linn.* 14, Or. 2, Nat. Or. *Scrophulariaceæ.* Plants of little beauty, growing well in any light rich soil, and increased by cuttings or seeds. The annual species are half-hardy. *Synonymes:* 1. *Capraria durantifolia.* 2. *Columnea trifoliata.*

| | | | | |
|---|---|---|---|---|
| chīlensis | Red | 9, F. De. Cr. Chile | 1829 |
| suffruticōsa, 2 | Blue | 7, S. Ev. S. N. Granada | 1820 |

*durantifōlia* 1, *maritīmā, parviflōrā, verticillāris, viscōsā.*

STEMONĪTIS, *Gleditsch.* From *stemon,* the plant may be compared to the male organ of a flower. *Linn.* 24, Or. 9, Nat. Or. *Fungi.* Found upon rotten wood. *Synonyme:* 1. *Trichia nuda—S. faciculāta* 1, *obtusāta, papillāta.*

STENĀCTIS, *Nees.* Probably from *stene,* narrow, and *aktin,* a sunbeam; from the narrow and sunlike rays of the expanded flower. *Linn.* 19, Or. 2, Nat. Or. *Compositæ.* This is a very showy plant, well adapted for planting in beds; it grows in any common garden soil; and is readily increased by dividing the root, or by seeds, which it produces in great abundance.

| | | | | |
|---|---|---|---|---|
| speciōsa | Purple | 7, H. Her. P. Californ. | 1831 |

STENĀNTHĒRA, *R. Brown.* From *stenos,* narrow, and *anthera,* an anther; the filaments are broader than the anthers, which causes the latter to appear narrow. *Linn.* 5, Or. 1, Nat. Or. *Epacridaceæ.* This beautiful greenhouse shrub requires a soil composed of one third sandy loam, and two thirds very sandy peat. The pot should be well drained, as the fine roots of the plants are easily injured by much wet; it should be kept in a shaded part of the house in summer. Cuttings taken from the young shoots, will strike with ease, if planted in sand, under a glass.

| | | | | |
|---|---|---|---|---|
| pinifōlia | Scarlet | 6, G. Ev. S. N. S. W. | 1811 |

STENÎÀ, *Lindley.* From *stenos*, narrow; in allusion to the form of the pollen-masses. *Linn.* 20, Or. 1, Nat. Or. *Orchidaceæ.* This is rather a pretty species, requiring to be treated the same as the species of *Maxillaria.*

| | | | | | |
|---|---|---|---|---|---|
| pallída | . . . . | Yellow | . 8, S. Epi. | Demerara | . 1837 |

STENOCÁRPÙS, *R. Brown.* From *stenos*, narrow, and *karpos*, fruit. *Linn.* 4, Or. 1, Nat. Or. *Proteaceæ.* An equal mixture of sandy loam and peat suits this plant, and cuttings of the ripened wood will root in sand, under a glass.

| | | | | | |
|---|---|---|---|---|---|
| salignùs | . . . | Green | . 6, G. Ev. S. | N. Holl. | . 1819 |

STENOCHILÙS, *R. Brown.* From *stenos*, narrow, and *cheilos*, a lip, in allusion to the narrow lip of the flower. *Linn.* 14, Or. 2, Nat. Or. *Myoporaceæ.* Pretty little greenhouse shrubs, thriving in sandy loam and peat; and readily increased by cuttings, planted in sand, under a glass.

| | | | | | |
|---|---|---|---|---|---|
| glabèr | . . . . | Red | . | G. Ev. S. N. Holl. | . 1803 |
| incánùs | . . . . | Orn. pur. | | | |
| longifòliùs | . . | Scarlet | . 4, G. Ev. S. N. Holl. | | . 1825 |
| maculàtùs | . . | Scarlet | . 4, G. Ev. S. N. Holl. | | . 1830 |
| viscòsùs | . . | Yellow | . 10, G. Ev. S. N. Holl. | | . 1824 |

STENOPETALOUS, narrow petaled.

STEPHÀNÌÀ, *Willdenow.* In honour of S. Stephan, once a professor at Moscow, died 1817. *Linn.* 6, Or. 1, Nat. Or. *Capparidaceæ.* Well worth cultivating, on account of the beauty of the flowers. It thrives in loam, peat, and sand, and cuttings of the young wood will root in sand, under a glass, in heat. Synonyme: 1. *Capparis paradoxa.*

| | | | | | |
|---|---|---|---|---|---|
| cleomoídès, 1 | . . | | S. Ev. S. | Caraccas | . 1823 |

STERCÙLÌÀ, *Linn.* From *Sterculius*, a God, derived from *stercus*; the flowers and leaves of some of the species are fetid. *Linn.* 21, Or. 10, Nat. Or. *Sterculiaceæ.* These plants succeed best in light turfy loam; or a mixture of loam and peat; and cuttings of the ripened wood, with the leaves left entire, will root freely in sand, under a glass, in heat. The seeds of *S. acuminata* afford the *Cola* or *Kola*, of tropical Africa, so much spoken of by African travellers; and which, when chewed or sucked, enhances the flavour of anything that may be eaten afterwards; and is even said to render putrid water agreeable. The seeds are brown, and about the size of a pigeon's egg. Synonymes: 1. *S. heterophylla.* 2. *Helicteres apetala.* 3. *S. crinita.* 4. *S. balanghas.* 5. *S. pubescens.*

| | | | | | |
|---|---|---|---|---|---|
| acerifòliá | . . | | S. Ev. T. N. Holl. | | . 1824 |
| acuminàtà | . . | White | . | S. Ev. T. Guinea | . 1795 |
| angustifòliá | . . | | S. Ev. T. Nepal | | . 1823 |
| Balanghàs | . . | Purplish | . 8, S. Ev. T. E. Ind. | | . 1787 |
| coccíneà | . . | | S. Ev. T. E. Ind. | | . 1817 |
| coloràtà | . . | Scarlet | . | S. Ev. T. E. Ind. | . 1818 |
| diversifòliá, 1 | . . | | G. Ev. T. N. Holl. | | . 1824 |
| fœtídà | . . | Brn. red | . | S. Ev. S. E. Ind. | . 1690 |
| grandiflorá | . . | | S. Ev. S. E. Ind. | | . 1830 |
| guttátà | . . | | S. Ev. T. E. Ind. | | . 1825 |
| Helicterès, 2 | . . | Yel. pur. | . | S. Ev. S. Carthage | . 1830 |
| Ivírà, 3 | . . | Green | . | S. Ev. T. S. Amer. | . 1798 |
| nòbilis, 4 | . . | Pa. buff. | . | S. Ev. T. E. Ind. | . 1787 |
| platanifòliá | . . | Green | . 7, S. Ev. T. China | | . 1757 |
| pubéscens | . . | White | . | S. Ev. T. Guinea | . 1798 |
| tragacánthà, 5 | . . | Red brn. | . 5, S. De. T. S. Leone | | . 1798 |
| ùrens | . . | Yellow | . | S. Ev. T. E. Ind. | . 1798 |
| villòsà | . . | | S. Ev. T. E. Ind. | | . 1805 |

STEREOCAÙLÒN, *Schreber.* From *stereos*, rigid, and *kaulon*, a stem, firm branching fronds. *Linn.* 24, Or. 8, Nat. Or. *Lichenes.* This is the first of its tribe found clothing the lava of volcanoes—*S. botryòsùm, Cereòlùs, paschàle.*

STERIGMÀ, *Decandolle.* From *sterigma*, a fork; the larger stamens are joined at the base, and forked at the top. *Linn.* 15, Nat. Or. *Cruciferæ.* The species of this genus are well adapted for ornamenting rock-work. They require to be treated as other alpine plants. Synonymes: 1. *Cheiranthus tomentosus.* 2. *C. torulosus.*

| | | | | | |
|---|---|---|---|---|---|
| tomentòsùm, 1 | . | Yellow | . 6, H. | B. Astracan | . 1823 |
| torulòsùm, 2 | . | Yellow | . 6, H. | B. Iberia | . 1823 |

STERILE, barren.

STERNBÈRGÌÀ, *Waldstein and Kitaibel.* In honour of Count Caspar Sternberg, a celebrated botanist. *Linn.* 6, Or. 1, Nat. Or. *Amaryllidaceæ.* Handsome hardy bulbs, though seldom met with in ordinary collections. They succeed well with common

treatment, in any rich garden soil; and are increased by offsets.

| | | | | | |
|---|---|---|---|---|---|
| Clusiáná | . . | Pa. yel. | . 8, H. Bl. P. Constant. | | |
| colchiciflorá | . . | Yellow | . 8, H. Bl. P. Hungary | | . 1816 |
| exìgùá | . . | Yellow | . 8, H. Bl. P. N. Africa | | . 1820 |
| lùtèá | . . | Yellow | . 8, H. Bl. P. S. Eur. | | . 1596 |
| angustifòliá | . . | Yellow | . 8, H. Bl. P. S. Eur. | | . 1596 |

STERNUTATORY, possessing qualities which provoke sneezing.

STEVÈNÌÀ, *Adanson.* In honour of Christian Stephen, Counsellor of the University of Moscow, and author of a paper on some new plants from Caucasus, published in the Linnæan Transactions. *Linn.* 15, Nat. Or. *Cruciferæ.* The seeds of these plants should be sown on rock-work, but not sooner than the beginning of April—*S. alyssoídès, cheiranthoídès.*

STEVÌÀ, *Cavanilles.* In honour of Peter James Esteve, M.D., professor of botany at Valencia. *Linn.* 19, Or. 1, Nat. Or. *Compositæ.* Pretty autumnal flowering plants, succeeding well in the flower border during summer; they require the protection of a frame in severe weather, and are increased by cuttings, divisions, or seeds. Synonyme: 1. *S. canescens.*

| | | | | | |
|---|---|---|---|---|---|
| adenophorà | . . | White | . 8, F. Her. | P. Chile | . 1822 |
| angustifòliá | . . | Pink | . 8, F. Her. | P. Mexico | . 1823 |
| breviaristàtà | . . | Rose | . 7, S. Her. | P. Tucuman | . 1836 |
| callòsà | . . | Red | . 8, H. Her. | P. Mexico | . 1826 |
| Eupatòriá | . . | Pink | . 8, H. Her. | P. Mexico | . 1798 |
| fascicularis | . . | White | . 9, G. Her. | P. Mexico | . 183.. |
| fastigiàtà | . . | White | . 8, F. Her. | P. N. Spain | . 1826 |
| hyssopifòliá | . . | Pink | . 8, H. Her. | P. Mexico | |
| incanéscens, 1 | . | White | . 8, F. Her. | P. N. Spain | . 1827 |
| ìvæfòliá | . . | White | . 8, F. Her. | P. Mexico | . 1816 |
| lanceolàtà | . . | Purple | . 8, F. Her. | P. Mexico | . 1822 |
| lùcidà | . . | Pink | . 8, G. Her. | P. N. Spain | . 1824 |
| microphyllá | . . | Blush | . 9, G. Her. | P. Mexico | . 1828 |
| monardæfòliá | . . | Violet | . 8, F. Her. | P. Mexico | . 1826 |
| nepetæfòliá | . . | White | . 8, F. Her. | P. Mexico | . 1824 |
| ovàtà | . . | White | . 8, F. Her. | P. Mexico | . 1816 |
| paniculàtà | . . | White | . 8, F. Her. | P. N. Spain | . 1824 |
| pilòsà | . . | Pink | . 8, F. Her. | P. Mexico | . 1820 |
| pubéscens | . . | Purple | . 8, F. Her. | P. Mexico | . 1823 |
| purpùrèá | . . | Purple | . 8, H. Her. | P. Mexico | . 1812 |
| rhombifòliá | . . | White | . 8, F. Her. | P. Mexico | . 1827 |
| salicifòliá | . . | Pink | . 8, F. Her. | P. Mexico | . 1803 |
| salviæfòliá | . . | White | . 8, F. Her. | P. Mexico | . 1827 |
| serràtà | . . | Flesh | . 8, H. Her. | P. Mexico | . 1799 |
| suavèòlens | . . | White | . 8, F. Her. | P. N. Spain | . 1823 |
| subpubéscens | . . | Pink | . 8, G. Her. | P. N. Spain | . 1830 |
| ternifòliá | . . | White | . 8, F. Her. | P. Mexico | . 1824 |
| tomentòsà | . . | Violet | . 8, F. Her. | P. Mexico | . 1824 |
| trífídà | . . | White | . 8, F. Her. | P. N. Spain | . 1827 |
| violàceà | . . | Violet | . 8, H. Her. | P. Mexico | . 1829 |
| viscòsà | . . | Purple | . 8, F. Her. | P. Mexico | . 1821 |

STEWÀRTÌÀ, *Cavanilles.* In honour of John Stewart, Marquis of Bute, once a distinguished patron of botany. *Linn.* 16, Or. 2, Nat. Or. *Ternströmiaceæ.* This beautiful species deserves a place in every collection of ornamental shrubs. For culture and propagation, see *Malachodendron.* Synonyme: 1. *S. Malachodendron.*

| | | | | | |
|---|---|---|---|---|---|
| virgínícà, 1 | . . | White | . 7, H. De. T. N. Amer. | | . 1742 |

STÍCTÀ, *Schreber.* From *stiktos*, dotted; in allusion to the little pits on the under surface of the fronds. *Linn.* 24, Or. 8, Nat. Or. *Lichenes.* A handsome genus of Lichens, found growing upon trees. *S. pulmonacea* possesses the same qualities as the Iceland moss of the shops—*S. auràtà, ciliàtà, crocàtà, fuliginòsà, limbàtà, macrophyllà, pulmonàcèà, scrobiculàtà, sylvàtìcà.*

STÍCTÌS, *Persoon.* From *stiktos*, dotted; the dot-like appearance of many of the species. *Linn.* 24, Or. 9, Nat. Or. *Fungi.* Very minute species, found on dead branches—*S. abietìnà, lōngà, pàllìdà, radiàtà, microstōmà, sphærālis, versìcolor.*

STIFFTÌÀ, *Mikan.* Named after some unknown botanist. *Linn.* 19, Or. 2, Nat. Or. *Compositæ.* A fine showy plant, requiring the same treatment as the shrubby species of *Baccharis.*

| | | | | | |
|---|---|---|---|---|---|
| insignis | . . | White | . | G. De. S. | . 1838 |

STIGMA, the female organ of a flower.

STIGMAPHYLLÒN, *Jussieu.* From *stigma*, a stigma, and *phyllon*, a leaf; stigma foliaceous. *Linn.* 10, Or. 3, Nat. Or. *Malpighiaceæ.* These handsome plants produce their fine yellow flowers, from three to five together, in an umbel. For culture and propagation, see *Banisteria.* Synonyme: 1. *Banisteria auriculata.*

| | | | | | |
|---|---|---|---|---|---|
| aristàtùm | . . . | Yellow | . 7, S. Ev. Tw. Brazil | | . 1832 |
| auriculàtùm, 1 | . | Yellow | . 8. Ev. Tw. Brazil | | . 1820 |

STIGMATOSE, when the stigma is long, lateral, or on one side of the style.

STIGONÉMA, *Agardh.* From *stigon*, dotted, and *nema*, a filament, alluding to the regular annular dots of the filaments. Linn. 24, Or. 7, Nat. Or. *Algæ*. Small dark green tufts, found on rocks—S. atrovirēns, panniförmē.

STILĀGO, *Linn.* From *stylos*, a style; probably alluding to its length. Linn. 22, Or. 3, Nat. Or. *Stilaginaceæ*. Ornamental trees, thriving in a mixture of sandy loam and peat; cuttings will root in sand, under a glass, in heat.

| | | | | |
|---|---|---|---|---|
| Bunīus . . . . . | Apeta. | 8, S. Ev. T. E. Ind. | . | 1757 |
| diāndra . . . . . | Apetal | 8. Ev. T. E. Ind. | . | 1800 |

STILBOSPŌRA, *Persoon.* From *stilbo*, to shine, and *spora*, a sporule; the naked sporules are imbedded in a black substance, flowing from dead trunks and branches of trees—S. betulīnā, biloculātā, proprīā.

STILBUM, *Tode.* From *stilbos*, shining; the species are found upon old rotten wood, and are at first watery and gelatinous, but become opaque as they ripen. Linn. 24, Or. 9, Nat. Or. *Fungi*—S. aurāntiūm, bicŏlōr, citrīnūm, erythrocĕphālūm, nigrūm, pellūcidūm, piliförmē, tomentōsūm, vulgārē.

STILLINGIĀ, *Gardner.* In honour of Dr. Benjamin Stillingfleet, an eminent English botanist. Linn. 21, Or. 10, Nat. Or. *Euphorbiaceæ*. The species of *Stillingia* should be grown in a mixture of sandy loam and peat, and cuttings will root in sand, under a glass, in heat. S. sebifera is the Tallow-tree of China; its kernel contains an oil, which, when expressed, consolidates through the cold to the consistence of tallow, and by boiling, it becomes as hard as bees-wax.

| | | | | |
|---|---|---|---|---|
| populnea . . . | | S. Ev. T. Ceylon | . | 1823 |
| sebiferā . . . . | Yellow | S. Ev. S. China | . | 1703 |

ligustrīnā, sylvātīcā.

STIMULATING, exciting.

STINKING HOREHOUND, see *Ballōta*.

STIPA, *Linn.* From *stipe*, a silky or feathery substance. Linn. 3, Or. 2, Nat. Or. *Gramineæ*. A genus of beautiful grasses; they are increased by divisions. S. pennata is grown in the flower-garden for the sake of its beautifully feathered beards, which, Gerarde says, the ladies used to wear as feathers.

| | | | | |
|---|---|---|---|---|
| capillātā . . . . | Apetal | 7, Grass. Europe | . | 1815 |
| confērtā . . . . | Apetal | 7, Grass. | | 1819 |
| gigantēā . . . . | Apetal | 7, Grass. Spain | . | 1823 |
| hūmīlis . . . . | Apetal | 7, Grass. S. Amer. | . | 1802 |
| jūncēā . . . . | Apetal | 7, Grass. France | . | 1772 |
| pennātā . . . . | Apetal | 7, Grass. Britain | . | |
| sibīricā . . . . | Apetal | 7, Grass. Siberia | . | 1777 |
| tenacissīmā . . . | Apetal | 7, Grass. Spain | . | 1817 |

aristĕllā, bicŏlōr, Lagāscæ, tŏrtīlis.

STIPE, the stalk of a fern leaf, or of the head of a fungus.

STIPITATE, furnished with a stipe.

STIPULES, small scales at the base of the petioles.

STITCHWORT, see *Plantāgŏ holōstēūm*.

STITCHWORT, see *Stellārīā*.

STOBÆA, *Thunberg.* In honour of Dr. Stobæus, of Lund, one of Linnæus' first patrons. Linn. 19, Or. 1, Nat. Or. *Compositæ*. Any light rich soil suits this interesting plant, and young cuttings root readily in sand, under a glass.

| | | | | |
|---|---|---|---|---|
| pinnātā . . . . | Yellow | 6, G. Ev. S. C.G.H. | . | 1812 |

STOCK, see *Mathiŏla*.

STŒBE, *Leysser.* From *stibas*, a bed of leaves; the original plant was so used. Linn. 19, Or. 5, Nat. Or. *Compositæ*. Interesting plants, succeeding best in a mixture of sandy loam and peat, and increased by young cuttings, planted in sand, under a glass. Synonyme: 1. Seriphium alopecuroides.

| | | | | |
|---|---|---|---|---|
| æthiŏpicā . . . | | S. G. Ev. S. C.G.H. | . | 1759 |
| cinĕrēā . . . . | | S. G. Ev. S. C.G.H. | . | 1784 |
| ericoīdēs . . . | | S. G. Ev. S. C.G.H. | . | 1816 |
| rĕflēxā, 1 . . . | | S. G. Ev. S. C.G.H. | . | 1816 |

STOKESIA, *L'Heritier.* In honour of Jonathan Stokes, M.D., the coadjutor of Withering, in his arrangement of British Plants. Linn. 19, Or. 1, Nat. Or. *Compositæ*. A very handsome herbaceous plant, succeeding well in the open border during the summer months. It is increased by seeds or by division of the roots.

| | | | | |
|---|---|---|---|---|
| cyănēā . . . . | Blue | 8, G. Her. P. Carolina | . | 1766 |

STOLONES, runners, which root at the joints.

STOLONIFEROUS, bearing runners which root at the joints.

STOMACHIC, agreeable to the stomach.

STONECROP, see *Sēdum*.

STONE PINE, see *Pīnūs Pīnēā*.

STORAX, see *Stўrāx*.

STORK'S BILL, see *Pelargōnīūm*.

STRANGURY, a disease produced on plants by tight ligatures.

STRANVÆSIA. Lindley named this genus in honour of the Honourable William Fox Strangways, F.R.S., a learned and indefatigable investigator of the Flora of Europe. Linn. 12, Or. 2, Nat. Or. *Rosaceæ*. This species is better known under the name of *Cratægus glauca*; it is ornamental, and succeeds best when planted against a south wall, with a slight protection in severe weather. It is readily increased by grafting or budding upon the common thorn. Synonyme: 1. Cratægus glauca.

| | | | | |
|---|---|---|---|---|
| glaucēscēns, 1 . . | White. | 6, H. Ev. T. Nepal | . . | 1828 |

STRAPWOOD, see *Corrigiŏla*.

STRATA, layers, beds.

STRATIŌTES, *Linn.* From *stratos*, an army; in allusion to its long sword-like leaves. Linn. 22, Or. 10, Nat. Or. *Hydrocharaceæ*. An ornamental aquatic, increasing so fast in the ponds where it is planted as to become almost a troublesome weed.

| | | | | |
|---|---|---|---|---|
| aloīdēs . . . . | White. | 6, H. Aq. P. England | . | |

STRAVĀDIUM, *Jussieu.* From *Tejeria Samstravadi*, the Malabar name of one of the species. Linn. 16, Or. 8, Nat. Or. *Myrtaceæ*. Fine ornamental trees. For culture and propagation, see *Barringtonia*. Synonymes: 1. Barringtonia aculangula, Eugenia aculangula. 2. B. racemosa, E. racemosa.

| | | | | |
|---|---|---|---|---|
| acutāngūlūm, 1 . | Purple | S. Ev. T. E. Ind. | . . | 1822 |
| racemōsūm, 2 . . | White . | S. Ev. T. W. Ind. | . | 1822 |
| rūbrūm . . . . | Red . . | S. Ev. T. E. Ind. | . | 1822 |

STRAWBERRY, see *Fragārīā*.

STRAWBERRY BLITE, see *Blītūm*.

STRAWBERRY TREE, see *Arbūtūs*.

STREAKS, little furrowed lines.

STRELITZIĀ. Named by Aiton in honour of the Queen of George III., from the house of Mecklenburgh-Strelitz. Linn. 5, Or. 1, Nat. Or. *Musaceæ*. A genus of splendid plants, generally found in our stoves, though they will thrive equally as well in the greenhouse. A very turfy loam suits them, and they may be increased slowly by suckers; but young specimens are more readily obtained by impregnating the stigma when the plants are in bloom.

| | | | | |
|---|---|---|---|---|
| angustifōlīā . . | Yellow | 5, S. Her. P. C.G.H. | . | 1778 |
| augūstā . . . . | White | 3, S. Her. P. C.G.H. | . | 1791 |
| farinōsā . . . . | Yellow | 2, S. Her. P. C.G.H. | . | 1795 |
| hūmīlis . . . . | Yellow | 5, S. Her. P. C.G.H. | . | |
| jūncēā . . . . | Yellow | 5, S. Her. P. C.G.H. | . | |
| ovātā . . . . | Yellow | 3, S. Her. P. C.G.H. | . | 1777 |
| parvifōlīā . . . | Yellow | 6, S. Her. P. C.G.H. | . | 1796 |
| regīnæ . . . . | Yellow | 4, S. Her. P. C.G.H. | . | 1773 |

STREPTANTHĒRĀ, *Sweet.* From *streptos*, twisted, and *anthera*, an anther. Linn. 3, Or. 1, Nat. Or. *Iridaceæ*. Very pretty bulbs when in flower. A mixture of loam and peat suits them best; and young plants are obtained by offsets.

| | | | | |
|---|---|---|---|---|
| cūprēā . . . . | Copper | 6, G. Bl. P. C.G.H. | . | 1825 |
| ĕlĕgāns . . . . | Wht blue | 6, G. Bl. P. C.G.H. | . | 1827 |

STREPTANTHŪS, *Nuttall.* From *streptos*, twisted, and *anthos*, a flower; twisted claws of petals. Linn. 15, Nat. Or. *Cruciferæ*. The seed of these plants may be sown in the open border late in spring; or they may be reared on a gentle hotbed; and afterwards planted out.

| | | | | |
|---|---|---|---|---|
| hyacinthoīdēs . . | Purple | 9, H. A. Texas | . | 1834 |
| obtusifōlīūs . . | Rose . | 6, H. A. Arkansas | . | 1833 |

STREPTIŪM, *Roxburgh.* From *streptos*, twisted; in allusion to the spiral tube of the corolla. Linn. 14, Or. 2, Nat. Or. *Verbenaceæ*. A pretty plant, of very easy culture, and propagated by cuttings. Synonymes: 1. Priva leptostachya, Tortula aspera.

| | | | | |
|---|---|---|---|---|
| aspĕrūm, 1 . . | Violet . | 7, S. Her. P. E. Ind. | . . | 1799 |

STREPTOCARPŪS, *Lindley.* From *streptos*, twisted, and *carpos*, a fruit; the capsule is spirally twisted. Linn. 2, Or. 1, Nat. Or. *Cyrtandraceæ*. A very pretty plant, succeeding in any rich soil or vegetable mould; and readily increased by division. *Synonyme:* 1. *Didymocarpus Rexii.*

| Rexii | . . . | Blue . . | . 6, S. Her. P. C. O. H. | . 1824 |

**Streptopus,** *Michaux.* From *streptos,* twisted, and *pous,* a foot; in allusion to the twisted flower-stalks *Linn.* 6, Or. 1, Nat. Or. *Liliaceæ.* Interesting plants, of common culture in any light soil; and multiplied by seeds or divisions.

| amplexifolius | . . | White | . . 5, H. Her. P. Hungary | . 1752 |
| distortus | . . | Yellow | . 5, H. Her. P. N. Amer. | . 1753 |
| lanuginosus | . . | Yel. grn. | . 6, H. Her. P. N. Amer. | . 1812 |
| roseus | . . | Pink | . 6, H. Her. P. N. Amer. | . 1806 |
| simplex | . . | . . | . 6, O. Her. P. Nepal | . 1822 |

**Striæ,** small streaks.

**Striaria,** *Greville.* From *stria,* a groove, the plant is marked with grooves. *Linn.* 24, Or. 7, Nat. Or. *Algæ.* Found in the ocean—*S. attenuata.*

**Striated,** having streaks.

**Strict,** upright, straight.

**Strigæ,** little upright unequal, stiff hairs, swelled at their bases.

**Strigose,** covered with strigæ.

**Strobilanthes,** *Blume.* From *strobilos,* the cone of a pine, and *anthos,* a flower; the inflorescence in the bud state resembles the cone of a pine. *Linn.* 14, Or. 2, Nat. Or. *Acanthaceæ.* This beautiful stove plant is well deserving of a place in every collection, on account of its very showy purple flowers, and the deep purple colour of the under side of the leaves. For culture and propagation, see *Ruellia. Synonyme:* 1. *Ruellia Sabiniana.*

| Sabiniana, 1 | . | Blue pur. | 3, S. Ev. S. Nepal | . 1826 |

**Strobile,** a fir cone, the fruit of the Magnolia, or a fructiferous organ of a similar form.

**Strophanthus,** *Desvaux.* From *strophos,* a twisted thong, and *anthos,* a flower; the segments of the corolla are long, narrow, and twisted. *Linn.* 5, Or. 1, Nat. Or. *Apocynaceæ.* Very beautiful shrubs, of easy culture in a mixture of sandy loam and peat; and cuttings root readily in sand, under a glass, in a little heat. *Synonymes:* 1. *S. divergens.* 2. *Echites caudata.*

| Chinensis, 1 | . | Yellow | . 6, S. Ev. S. China | . 1816 |
| dichotomus, 2 | . | Rosy | . 6, S. Ev. S. E. Ind. | . 1816 |
| sarmentosus | . | Red | . 6, S. Ev. S. S. Leone | . 1824 |

**Strophiola,** a round protuberance at the base of some seeds.

**Struma,** a wen, or protuberance.

**Strumaria,** *Jacquin.* From *struma,* a tubercle; in allusion to the base of the calyx. *Linn.* 6, Or. 1, Nat. Or. *Amaryllidaceæ.* Interesting plants, succeeding well in sandy loam; and increased by offsets.

| angustifolia | . | Pink | . . 4, O. Bl. P. C. G. H. | . 1795 |
| crispa | . . | Pink | . 6, O. Bl. P. C. G. H. | . 1790 |
| filifolia | . . | White | . 11, O. Bl. P. C. G. H. | . 1774 |
| gemmata | . . | Pa. yel. | . 2, O. Bl. P. C. G. H. | . 1812 |
| linguæfolia | . | White | . 4, O. Bl. P. C. G. H. | . |
| rubella | . . | Pink | . 5, O. Bl. P. C. G. H. | . 1795 |
| spiralis | . . | Pink | . 7, O. Bl. P. C. G. H. | . 1774 |
| stellaris | . . | Pink | . 10, O. Bl. P. C. G. H. | . 1794 |
| truncata | . . | White | . 4, O. Bl. P. C. G. H. | . 1795 |
| undulata | . . | White | . 5, O. Bl. P. C. G. H. | . 1820 |

**Struthiola,** *Linn.* From *strouthion,* a little sparrow; resemblance of the seeds to a beak. *Linn.* 4, Or. 1, Nat. Or. *Thymelaceæ.* A very pretty Cape genus, thriving best in sandy peat; and young cuttings root with facility in sand, under a glass. *Synonyme:* 1. *S. stricta.*

| angustifolia | . . | Yellow | . 7, G. Ev. S. C. G. H. | . 1816 |
| ciliata | . . | White | . 6, G. Ev. S. C. G. H. | . 1779 |
| erecta, 1 | . . | White | . 6, G. Ev. S. C. G. H. | . 1798 |
| glabra | . . | Yellow | . 6, G. Ev. S. C. G. H. | . 1820 |
| imbricata | . . | Yellow | . 6, G. Ev. S. C. G. H. | . 1794 |
| incana | . . | White | . 8, G. Ev. S. C. G. H. | . 1817 |
| juniperina | . . | White | . 6, G. Ev. S. C. G. H. | . 1758 |
| lateriflora | . . | Yellow | . 7, G. Ev. S. C. G. H. | . 1819 |
| longiflora | . . | Yellow | . 7, G. Ev. S. C. G. H. | . 1823 |
| lucens | . . | Yellow | . 6, G. Ev. S. C. G. H. | . 1817 |
| ovata | . . | White | . 4. G. Ev. S. C. G. H. | . 1792 |
| pubescens | . . | Red | . 6, G. Ev. S. C. G. H. | . 1790 |
| striata | . . | Yellow | . 7, G. Ev. S. C. G. H. | . 1820 |
| tomentosa | . . | Yellow | . 8, G. Ev. S. C. G. H. | . 1799 |
| virgata | . . | Red | . 6, G. Ev. S. C. G. H. | . 1779 |

**Struthiopteris,** *Willdenow.* From *strouthios,* an ostrich, and *pteris,* a fern; the fronds bear a resemblance to feathers. *Linn.* 24, Or. 1, Nat. Or.

*Polypodiaceæ.* An ornamental genus of Ferns, of common culture. *Synonyme:* 1. *Osmunda Struthiopteris.*

| germanica, 1 | . | Brown | . 7, H. Her. P. Europe | . 1760 |
| pennsylvanica | . | Brown | . 8, H. Her. P. N. Amer. | . 1812 |

**Strychnos,** *Linn.* The Greek name of the *Solanum. Linn.* 5, Or. 1, Nat. Or. *Apocynaceæ.* Valuable plants, on account of the medicinal properties ascribed to them. They all succeed well in a mixture of loam and sandy peat, and half-ripened cuttings will root in sand, under a glass, in heat. *S. colubrina* is given as an anthelmintic in intermitting fevers. The seeds of *S. Nux-vomica* are well known by the latter name, as possessing a dangerous narcotic property, which depends upon the presence of a peculiar principle called *Strychnia.* It has been administered in a great number of cases with different degrees of success; small quantities have been given for mania, gout, epilepsy, hysteria, and dysentery. It is a most violent poison, and its energy so great, that half a grain blown into the throat of a rabbit, occasions death in five minutes. Its operation is always accompanied with symptoms of locked jaw and other tetanic affections. The seeds of *S. potatorum* are sold in the Indian bazaars for the purpose of clearing muddy water: the vessel containing the water being rubbed for a minute or two round the inside, with one of the seeds; after which, by allowing the water to settle for a short time, however impure and muddy it may have been before, it becomes clear and wholesome.

| axillaris | . . | White | . . 8. Ev. T. E. Ind. | . 1824 |
| colubrina | . . | . | . 8. Ev. Cl. E. Ind. | . 1820 |
| madagascariensis | . . | . | 8. Ev. T. Madaga. | . 1823 |
| Nux-vomica | . . | Grn. wht. | . 8. Ev. T. E. Ind. | . 1788 |
| potatorum | . . | White | . 8. Ev. T. E. Ind. | . 1794 |
| spinosa | . . | White | . 8. Ev. T. Madaga. | . 1818 |

**Stupa,** filamentose matter.

**Stylandra,** *Nuttall.* From *stylos,* a column, and *aner,* a male; the gynostegium is pedicellate. *Linn.* 5, Or. 2, Nat. Or. *Asclepiadaceæ.* For culture and propagation, see *Asclepias. Synonymes:* 1. *Podostigma pubescens, Asclepias pedicellata.*

| pumila, 1 | . . | Grn. yel. | . 7, F. Her. P. N. Amer. | . 1824 |

**Style,** the stalk which bears the stigma, and intervenes between that and the ovary.

**Stylidium,** *Swartz.* From *stylos,* a column; the stamens and style are joined. *Linn.* 20, Or. 2, Nat. Or. *Stylidiaceæ.* Beautiful and rare little plants, succeeding best in sandy loam and peat. Cuttings of the shrubby kinds root very readily in sand, under a glass; a few of the herbaceous kinds are increased by divisions of the root, but chiefly by seeds. *Synonymes:* 1. *S. glandulosum.* 2. *Ventenatia minor.* 3. *S. laricifolium.*

| adnatum | . . | Pink | . 7, G. Her. P. N. Holl. | . 1824 |
| fasciculatum | . | Pink | . 8, G. Ev. S. N. Holl. | . 1822 |
| fruticosum, 1 | . | Pink | . 7, G. Ev. S. N. Holl. | . 1803 |
| graminifolium | . | Pink | . 7, G. Her. P. N. S. W. | . 1803 |
| hirsutum | . . | Rose | . 6, G. Her. P. K. G. S. | . 1830 |
| junceum | . . | Rose | . G. Her. P. N. Holl. | . 1830 |
| lineare, 2 | . | Red | . 6, G. Her. P. N. Holl. | . 1812 |
| scandens | . . | Pink | . 7, G. Her. P. N. Holl. | . 1803 |
| tenuifolium, 3 | . | Pink | . 7, G. Her. P. N. Holl. | . 1818 |

**Stylosanthes,** *Swartz.* From *stylos,* a style, and *anthos,* a flower; in allusion to the flower having a long style. *Linn.* 16, Or. 6, Nat. Or. *Leguminosæ.* Plants of little interest, except in botanical collections. They require to be grown in a mixture of sandy loam and peat; and cuttings of the shrubby kinds root readily in sand, under a glass, in a moist heat. *Synonymes:* 1. *S. hispida.* 2. *Trifolium guianense.*

| elatior, 1 | . . | Yellow | . 7, F. Her. P. N. Amer. | . 1816 |
| erecta | . . | Yellow | . 7, S. | . A. Guinea | . 1825 |
| guianensis, 2 | . | Yellow | . 7, S. | . A. Guiana | . 1820 |
| mucronata | . . | Yellow | . 7, S. Her. P. Ceylon | . 1817 |
| procumbens | . . | Yellow | . 7, S. Ev. Tr. W. Ind. | . 1818 |
| viscosa | . . | Yellow | . 7, S. Ev S. W. Ind. | . 1821 |

**Stypandra,** *R. Brown.* From *stype,* tow, and *aner,* an anther. *Linn.* 6, Or. 1, Nat. Or. *Liliaceæ.* These plants should be grown in a mixture of sandy loam and peat, and increased by divisions. They succeed well in a pit or warm border, if protected in severe weather. *Synonyme:* 1. *Arthropodium glaucum.*

| | | | | | | |
|---|---|---|---|---|---|---|
| cæspitósa . . | White | . 6, | G. Her. P. | N. Holl. | . 1824 |
| frutéscens . . | Violet | . 6, | G. Ev. S. | N. Holl. | . 1836 |
| glaúca, 1 . . | White | . 6, | G. Her. P. | N. Holl. | . 1823 |
| propinqua . . | Azure | . 9, | G. Her. P. | N. S. W. | . 1833 |
| umbellàta . . | White | . 6, | G. Her. P. | N. Holl. | . 1826 |

STYPHELIA, *Smith*. From *styphelos*, hard; in allusion to the habit of the plants. Linn. 5, Or. 1, Nat. Or. *Epacrideæ*. A genus of very beautiful shrubs, succeeding best in a mixture of two parts sandy peat, and one of sandy loam; and increased by young cuttings, planted in sand, under a glass.

| | | | | | | |
|---|---|---|---|---|---|---|
| adscéndens . . | Green | . | G. Ev. S. | N. Holl. | . 1822 |
| epacridóides . . | Crimson | . 7, | G. Ev. S. | N. Holl. | . 1823 |
| læta . . | Green | . | G. Ev. S. | N. Holl. | . 1822 |
| latifòlia . . | Pink | . 6, | G. Ev. S. | N. Holl. | . 1823 |
| longifòlia . . | Green | . 6, | G. Ev. S. | N. Holl. | . 1807 |
| triflòra . . | Pink | . 7, | G. Ev. S. | N. S. W. | . 1796 |
| tubiflòra . . | Scarlet | . 7, | G. Ev. S. | N. S. W. | . 1802 |
| viridiflòra . . | Green | . 5, | G. Ev. S. | N. Holl. | . 1791 |

STYPTIC, having the power to staunch blood.

STYRAX, *Linn*. A mere alteration of *Assthirak*, the Arabic name of *S. officinale*. Linn. 10, Or. 1, Nat. Or. *Ebenaceæ*. The species of *Styrax* are very handsome when in flower, and are, therefore, well suited for ornamenting shrubberies. A light soil suits them best, and they are readily increased by layers, in spring or autumn. *S. officinale* is remarkable for producing the very powerful and fragrant balsam known by the name of storax; it is bitter and pungent to the taste, and possesses a strong, agreeable odour. Synonyme: 1. *S. glabrum*.

| | | | | | | |
|---|---|---|---|---|---|---|
| grandifo'lium . . | White | . 7, | H. De. S. | N. Amer. | . 1765 |
| lævigàtum, 1 . . | White | . 7, | H. De. S. | N. Amer. | . 1765 |
| officinàle . . | White | . 7, | H. De. S. | Levant . | . 1597 |
| pulverulèntum . . | White | . 6, | H. De. S. | N. Amer. | . 1794 |

SUB, in composition, signifies somewhat; as *sub-umbellate*, somewhat umbellate, *sub-rotund*, somewhat round or roundish, &c.

SUBALATE, with a narrow wing, or margin.

SUBEROSE, corky.

SUBULARIA, *Linn*. From *subula*, an awl; shape of the leaves. Linn. 15, Nat. Or. *Cruciferæ*. This little annual is very remarkable from expanding its flowers two or three feet under water, and impregnation taking place in that element. It only requires planting in a pond or rivulet, with a gravelly bottom; or it may be grown in pots filled with sand, and plunged in water.

| | | | | | | |
|---|---|---|---|---|---|---|
| aquàtica . . | White | . 7, | H. Aq. A. | Britain . | |

SUBULATE, awl-shaped, tapering to a point.

SUCCEDANEOUS, taking the place of another.

SUCCISA, *Vaillant*. From *succisus*, lopped; appearance of the roots. Linn. 4, Or. 1, Nat. Or. *Dipsaceæ*. Plants of no great beauty, and of very common culture. Synonymes: 1. *Cephalaria albescens*. 2. *C. alpina*. 3. *C. attenuata*. 4. *C. coriacea, Lepicephalus leucantha*. 5. *C. corniculata*. 6. *C. cretacea*. 7. *Scabiosa glabrata* 8. *Scabiosa decurrens, Cephalaria græca*. 9. *C. lævigata, Succisa centaurioides*. 10. *C. leucantha*. 11. *C. leucanthema, Lepicephalus leucantha*. 12. *Scabiosa succisa*. 13. *Cephalaria rigida*. 14. *C. scabra*. 15. *C. syriaca*. 16. *C. tatarica*. 17. *C. transylvanica*. 18. *C. uralensis*.

| | | | | | | |
|---|---|---|---|---|---|---|
| albéscens, 1 . . | White | . 6, | H. Her. P. | Siberia . | . 1804 |
| alpìna, 2 . . | White | . 6, | H. Her. P. | Switzerl. | . 1570 |
| attenuàta, 3 . . | White | . 6, | G. Ev. | S. C. G. H. | . 1774 |
| coriàcea, 4 . . | Striped | . 6, | H. Her. P. | Tauria . | . 1819 |
| corniculàta, 5 . . | Striped | . 7, | H. Her. P. | Hungary . | . 1801 |
| cretàcea, 6, . . | Striped | . 7, | H. Her. P. | Caucasus . | . 1818 |
| glabràta, 7 . . | Purple | . 6, | H. Her. P. | Austria . | . 1819 |
| græca, 8 . . | Yellow | . 6, | H. Her. P. | S. Eur. . | . 1819 |
| lævigàta, 9 . . | Striped | . 7, | H. Her. P. | Hungary . | . 1805 |
| leucàntha, 10 . . | White | . 9, | H. Her. P. | France . | . 1739 |
| leucanthèma, 11 . | White | . 9, | H. Her. P. | France . | . 1800 |
| praténsis, 12 . . | Violet | . 8, | H. Her. P. | Britain . | |
| rigida, 13 . . | White | . 7, | G. Ev. | S. C. G. H. | . 1781 |
| scàbra, 14 . . | White | . 6, | G. Ev. | S. C. G. H. | . 1825 |
| syrìaca, 15 . . | White | . 6, | H. | A. Syria | . 1752 |
| tatàrica, 16 . . | Li. yel. | . 7, | H. | B. Russia | . 1759 |
| transylvánica, 17. | Lilac | . 7, | H. | A. Transyl. | . 1699 |
| uralènsis, 18 . . | Yellow | . 7, | H. | A. Siberia | . 1789 |

SUCCORY, see *Cichòrium*.

SUCCOWIA, *Medicus*. In honour of Professor Suckow, a botanist of Heidelberg. Linn. 15, Nat. Or. *Cruciferæ*. A light soil suits this plant. The seed has only to be sown in the open border, or on rock-work.

| | | | | | | |
|---|---|---|---|---|---|---|
| baleàrica . . | Yellow | . 6, | H. | A. Minorca | . 1781 |

SUCCULENT, fleshy, filled with juice.

SUDORIFIC, having the power of producing perspiration.

SUFFRUTICOSE, somewhat shrubby.

SUGAR CANE, see *Sacchàrum*.

SULCATE, furrowed, channelled.

SULPHURWORT, see *Peucedànum*.

SUMACH, see *Rhûs*.

SUMMER CYPRESS, see *Kòchia scopària*.

SUNDEW, see *Drosèrd*.

SUN-FERN, see *Polypòdium Phegòptèris*.

SUNFLOWER, see *Heliànthus*.

SUNFLOWER, see *Actinòtis Heliànthi*.

SUN ROSE, see *Heliánthèmum*.

SUPERIOR, this appellation is given to anything that is above the ovarium.

SUPINE, lying with the face upwards.

SUPPLE JACK, see *Serjània triternàta*.

SURCULI, young shoots.

SUTHERLÀNDIA, *R Brown*. In honour of James Sutherland, one of the first superintendents of the Royal Botanical Garden at Edinburgh. Linn. 17, Or. 4, Nat. Or. *Leguminosæ*. This species is very showy when in flower; it succeeds best in loam and peat; and is readily increased by seeds, or young cuttings. Synonyme: 1. *Colutea frutescens*.

| | | | | | | |
|---|---|---|---|---|---|---|
| frutéscens, 1 . . | Scarlet | . 6, | F. Ev. S. | C. G. H. | . 1683 |

SUTURE, the line formed by the cohesion of two parts.

SUWARROW NUT, see *Caryòcar*.

SWAINSONIA, *Salisbury*. In honour of Isaac Swainson, F.R.S., L.S., a celebrated cultivator of plants, about the end of the last century. His garden was at Twickenham in Middlesex. Linn. 17, Or. 4, Nat. Or. *Leguminosæ*. Very elegant shrubs, well worthy of a place in every greenhouse. They succeed best in a mixture of sandy loam and peat; and young cuttings root freely in sand, under a glass; they may also be increased by seeds. Synonyme: 1. *Colutea galegifolia*.

| | | | | | | |
|---|---|---|---|---|---|---|
| coronillæfo'lia . | Purple | . 7, | G. Ev. S. | N. S. W. | . 1802 |
| galegifòlia, 1 . . | Red | . 7, | G. Ev. S. | N. S. W. | . 1800 |
| albiflòra . . | White | . 7, | G. Ev. S. | N. S. W. | . 1826 |
| lessertiæfòlia . . | Purple | . 7, | G. Ev. S. | N. Holl. | . 1824 |

SWALLOW-WORT, see *Asclèpias*.

SWALLOW-WORT, see *Thàpsia Asclèpias*.

SWAMP LOCUST-TREE, see *Gleditschia monospèrma*.

SWAMP-POST, see *Quércus lyràta*.

SWARTZIA, *Willdenow*. In honour of Olof Swartz, M.D., a long time resident in the West Indies, and author of "Flora Indiæ Occidentalis." Linn. 13, Or. 1, Nat. Or. *Leguminosæ*. The species of this genus should be grown in a mixture of sandy loam and peat; and cuttings, not deprived of their leaves, will root in sand, under a glass, in heat.

| | | | | | | |
|---|---|---|---|---|---|---|
| grandiflòra . . | Yellow | . | S. Ev. S. | Trinidad . | . 1821 |
| pinnàta . . | Yelsh. | . | S. Ev. S. | Trinidad . | . 1817 |
| simplicifòlia . . | Pa. yel. | . | S. Ev. S. | W. Ind. . | . 1818 |

SWEDISH BEAM-TREE, see *Pyrus intermèdia*.

SWEDISH TURNIP, see *Brássica campéstris*; var. *rutabaga*.

SWEET BAY, see *Laùrus nòbilis*.

SWEET BRIAR, see *Ròsa rubiginòsa*.

SWEET CALABASH, see *Passiflòra maliformis*.

SWEET FLAG, see *Acòrus Càlamus*.

SWEET GALE, see *Mýrica Gàle*.

SWEET GUM, see *Liquidàmbar styraciflùa*.

SWEETIA, *Decandolle*. In honour of Robert Sweet, F.L.S., author of numerous well-known botanical works. Linn. 17, Or. 4, Nat. Or. *Leguminosæ*. These plants should be kept in a strong heat, and grown in a mixture of loam and sand. They are increased by cuttings, planted in sand, under a glass, or by seeds. Synonymes: 1. *Galega filiformis*. 2. *Glycine lignosa*. 3. *Galega longifolia*.

| | | | | | | |
|---|---|---|---|---|---|---|
| filiformis, 1 . . | Purple | . 7, | S. Ev. Tw. | S. Amer. | . 1820 |
| lignòsa, 2 . . | Purple | . | S. Ev. Tw. | St. Domin. | . 1824 |
| longifòlia, 3 . . | Purple | . | S. Ev. Tw. | S. Amer. | . 1818 |

SWEET MARJORAM, see *Orìganum Majorànà*.

SWEET MAUDLIN, see *Achillèa ageràtum*.

SWEET PEA, see *Làthyrus odoràtus*.

SWEET POTATO, see (Supplement) *Batàtas*.

SWEETSOP, see *Anòna squamòsa*.

SWEET SULTAN, see *Centaùrèa moschàta*.

SWEET WILLIAM, see *Diànthus barbàtus*.

SWEET WILLIAM, see *Silène Armèria*.

SWERTIA, *Linn*. In honour of Iman. Swert, a famous cultivator of bulbs and flowers, in Holland. Linn.

[ 324 ]

5, Or. 2, Nat. Or. *Gentianaceæ.* These plants prefer a marshy or peat soil; and are increased by seeds. *S. perennis,* though a perennial, may likewise be increased by seeds. *Synonyme:* 1. *S. corniculata.*

| | | | | | |
|---|---|---|---|---|---|
| corniculâtă | . . Pa. grn. | . 8, H. | A. Siberia | . 1817 |
| Michauxiàna, 1 . | Orn. yel. | . 7, H. | B. N. Amer. | . 1824 |
| perénnis | . . . Purple | . 7, H. Aq. | P. England | . |

**Swietènia,** *Linn.* In honour of Gerard Van Swieten, a Dutch botanist, and author. *Linn.* 10, Or. 1, Nat. Or. *Cedrelaceæ.* These interesting and valuable plants succeed well in a mixture of loam and sand; and ripened cuttings root in sand, under a hand-glass, in heat, but the leaves must not be shortened. The well-known mahogany is the produce of *S. Mahagoni.*

| | | | | | |
|---|---|---|---|---|---|
| febrifúgă | . . . Wht. yel. | . 8. Ev. T. E. Ind. | . 1796 |
| Mahágoni | . . . Red yel. | . 8. Ev. T. W. Ind. | . 1734 |

**Swine's succory,** see *Hyòsèris.*
**Sword fern,** see *Xiphòptèris.*
**Sword grass,** see *Alsinè segetàlis.*
**Sword grass,** see *Melilòtus segetàlis.*

**Syàgrus,** *Martius.* The first who wrote the history of the Trojan war in verse. *Linn.* 21, Or. 5, Nat. Or. *Palmaceæ.* This Palm succeeds in sandy loam and a moist heat; it is multiplied by seeds.

| | | | | |
|---|---|---|---|---|
| cocoïdès | . . . . | Palm. Brasil | . . 1824 |

**Sycamore,** see *Acèr Pseùdo-Plàtànùs.*

**Symphiàndra,** *A. Decandolle.* From *symphio,* to grow together, and *aner,* an anther; the anthers are connate. *Linn.* 5, Or. 1, Nat. Or. *Campanulaceæ.* For culture and propagation, see *Campanula. Synonyme:* 1. *Campanula pendula.*

| | | | | |
|---|---|---|---|---|
| pèndùlă, 1 | . . . Cream. | . 7, H. | B. Caucasus | . 1823 |

**Symphoricàrpus,** *Dillenius.* From *symphoreo,* to accumulate, and *karpos,* fruit; in allusion to its clustered bunches of fruit. *Linn.* 5, Or. 1, Nat. Or. *Caprifoliaceæ.* The species of St. Peter's Wort are handsome dwarf shrubs, suitable for the fronts of ornamental shrubberies. They are readily increased by cuttings, planted in autumn or spring, or by suckers, which they throw up in abundance. *Synonymes:* 1. *Symphoria montana.* 2. *S. racemosa.* 3. *Lonicera Symphoricarpos, Symphoria glomerata.* 4. *Symphoria glomerata ful. variegatis.*

| | | | | | |
|---|---|---|---|---|---|
| montànă, 1 | . . Pink | . 8, H. De. S. | Mexico | . 1829 |
| racemòsă, 2 | . . Pink | . 8, H. De. S. | N. Amer. | . 1817 |
| vulgàris, 3 | . . White | . 8, H. De. S. | N. Amer. | . 1730 |
| fol. variegàtis, 4 | Pink | . 8, H. De. S. | | |

**Symphytum,** *Linn.* From *symphyo,* to make unite, and *phyton,* a plant; in reference to the healing qualities of the plant. *Linn.* 5, Or. 1, Nat. Or. *Boraginaceæ.* Showy plants, thriving in any soil or situation; some of the kinds are well adapted for the flower border, where they can be much shaded. They succeed well under the shade of trees, and flower throughout the principal part of the summer season; increase is obtained by division. *Synonymes:* 1. *S. bohemicum.* 2. *S. bullatum.*

| | | | | | |
|---|---|---|---|---|---|
| aspérrimûm | . . Red blue | . 7, H. Her. | P. Caucasus | . 1799 |
| hybridûm | . . . Red blue | . 7, H. Her. | P. Hybrid | . 1825 |
| caucásicûm | . . Azure | . 6, H. Her. | P. Caucasus | . 1820 |
| cordàtûm | . . . Cream | . 6, H. Her. | P. Transylv. | . 1813 |
| officinàle | . . . White | . 6, H. Tu. | P. Britain | . |
| bohèmicûm, 1 | . Crimson | . 6, H. Tu. | P. Bohemia | . 1810 |
| pàtèns | . . . Blue | . 6, H. Tu. | P. Britain | . |
| orientàle | . . . White | . 5, H. Her. | P. Turkey | . 1752 |
| peregrinûm | . . . | . 7, H. Her. | P. Podolia | . 1816 |
| taùricûm | . . . White | . 6, H. Her. | P. Tauria | . 1806 |
| bullàtûm, 2 | . Pa. yel. | . 6, H. Her. | P. Caucasus | . 1818 |
| tuberòsûm | . . Yellow | . 7, H. Tu. | P. Scotland | . |

**Sympièză,** *Lichtenstein.* From *sympiezo,* to press; in reference to the stamens, which adhere to the tube of the corolla. *Linn.* 4, Or. 1, Nat. Or. *Ericaceæ.* A pretty little plant, thriving in turfy peat and sand; and readily increased by young cuttings,

placed in sand, under a glass. *Synonyme:* 1. *Blæria bracteata.*

| | | | | | |
|---|---|---|---|---|---|
| capitellàtă, 1 | . | . 7, G. Ev. S. | C. G. H. | . 1812 |

**Symplocàrpus,** *Salisbury.* From *symploke,* connexion, and *karpos,* fruit. *Linn.* 4, Or. 1, Nat. Or. *Araceæ.* This is a curious species, bearing large, handsome leaves. It succeeds in a marshy situation, in peat soil; and is increased by division. The roots and seeds are powerful antispasmodics; they are also expectorant, and useful in phthysical coughs. *Synonymes:* 1. *Pothos fœtidus, Dracontium fœtidum.*

| | | | | | |
|---|---|---|---|---|---|
| fœtidă, 1 | . . | . Apetal | . 5, H. Aq. | P. N. Amer. | . 1735 |

**Symplòcòs,** *Linn.* From *symploke,* a connexion; the stamens are united at the base. *Linn.* 18, Or. 2, Nat. Or. *Rhenaceæ.* These plants thrive well in a mixture of loam, peat, and sand; and cuttings root without difficulty in sand, under a glass; the stove species requiring heat.

| | | | | | |
|---|---|---|---|---|---|
| coccineă | . . . Rose | . 8. Ev. T. | Mexico | . 1825 |
| sínică | . . . White | . 5, G. Ev. S. | China | . 1822 |
| tinctòrià | . . . Yellow | . G. Ev. S. | Carolina | . 1780 |

**Syncarsià,** *Taylor.* Derivation unknown to us. *Linn.* 24, Or. 8, Nat. Or. *Lichenes.* This species is found on rocks, dry shores, &c.—*S. albida.*

**Synedrèlià,** *Gærtner.* From *synedrella,* a little bench, in allusion to the naked receptacle. *Linn.* 19, Or. 2, Nat. Or. *Compositæ.* A stove annual, neither interesting nor beautiful. *Synonyme:* 1. *Verbesina nodiflora—S. nodiflòrà* 1.

**Syngenesious,** belonging to the 19th class in the sexual system.

**Synnòtià,** *Sweet.* In honour of W. Synnet, who collected many plants at the Cape. *Linn.* 3, Or. 1, Nat. Or. *Iridaceæ.* Pretty bulbous plants, requiring the same treatment as the species of *Ixia. Synonymes:* 1. *Ixia bicolor, Sparaxis bicolor, Gladiolus bicolor.* 2. *Gladiolus galeatus.*

| | | | | | |
|---|---|---|---|---|---|
| bicòlor, 1 | . . . Brn. yel. | . 3, G. Bl. P. | C. G. H. | . 1786 |
| galeàtă, 2 | . . Brn. yel. | . 4, G. Bl. P. | C. G. H. | . 1825 |
| variegàtă | . . . Varieg. | . 5, G. Bl. P. | C. G. H. | . 1825 |

**Synthetical,** combining, a term used in an opposite sense to analytical.

**Syphilitic,** of or belonging to Syphilis.

**Syrian rue,** see *Pegànûm Hàrmàlă.*

**Syrinx,** *Linn.* From *syrinx,* a pipe; the branches are long and straight, and are filled with *medulla;* hence the old name of the Lilac, pipe-tree. The English name of the genus is from *liluc* or *lilag,* the Persian word for the flower. *Linn.* 2, Or. 1, Nat. Or. *Oleaceæ.* The species of Lilac are well known elegant shrubs; readily increased by layers, or by suckers from the roots. *Synonyme:* 1. *S. chinensis.*

| | | | | | |
|---|---|---|---|---|---|
| Josikæă | . . . Dp. lil. | . 6, H. De. S. | Germany | . 1833 |
| pèrsică | . . . Purple | . 5, H. De. S. | Persia | . 1640 |
| alba | . . . White | . 5, H. De. S. | Persia | . |
| laciniàtă | . . Purple | . 5, H. De. S. | Persia | . |
| salvifòlià | . . . | . 5, H. De. S. | | |
| rothomagènsis, 1 | Purple | . 6, H. De. S. | Hybrid | . 1795 |
| sanguíneă | . . Red | . 6, H. De. S. | | |
| vulgàris | . . . Blue | . 5, H. De. S. | Persia | . 1597 |
| alba | . . . White | . 5, H. De. S. | Persia | . |
| alba màjor | . . White | . 5, H. De. S. | | |
| alba plenă | . . White | . 5, H. De. S. | | |
| cœrùleă | . . . Blue | . H. De. S. | | |
| rùbră | . . . Red | . 5, H. De. S. | | |
| rùbră màjor | . . Red | . 5, H. De. S. | | |
| violàceă | . . . Purple | . 5, H. De. S. | Persia | . |

**Syringa,** see *Philadèlphus.*

**Syzygium,** *Gærtner.* From *syzygos,* coupled; in allusion to the manner in which the branches and leaves are united by pairs. *Linn.* 12, Or. 1, Nat. Or. *Myrtaceæ.* Interesting plants. For culture and propagation, see *Myrica. Synonymes:* 1. *Calyptranthes caryophyllifolia.* 2. *C. Jambolana.* 3. *Eugenia zeylanica.*

| | | | | | |
|---|---|---|---|---|---|
| caryophyllifòlium, 1 | White | . 8. Ev. T. E. Ind. | . 1822 |
| Jambolàna, 2 | . . White | . 8. Ev. T. E. Ind. | . 1796 |
| zeylanică, 3 | . . White | . 8. Ev. T. S. | Ceylon | . 1798 |

# T.

**TABERNÆMONTÀNÀ**, *Linn.* In honour of James Theodore Tabernæmontanus, a celebrated physician and botanist. *Linn.* 5, Or. 1, Nat. Or. *Apocynaceæ.* A genus of interesting plants, mostly bearing white, sweet-scented flowers. A mixture of loam, peat, and sand, suits them best ; and young plants may be obtained from cuttings, planted in sand, under a glass, in a moist heat. *Synonymes :* 1. *T. citrifolia.* 2. *Nerium coronarium.* 3. *T. multiflora.* 4. *Cameraria lutea, T. Tamaquarina.*

| | | | | | |
|---|---|---|---|---|---|
| albâ, 1 | . | White | 6, S. Ev. T. W. Ind. | . 1780 |
| amygdalifòliâ | . | Yellow | 7, S. Ev. S. S. Amer. | . 1780 |
| arcuâtâ | . | Cream | 8. Ev. T. Peru | . 1824 |
| citrifòliâ | . | Yellow | 8. Ev. S. Jamaica | . 1784 |
| coronâriâ | . | White | 7, S. Ev. S. E. Ind. | . 1770 |
| flôrê plênô, 2 | . | White | 7, S. Ev. S. E. Ind. | . 1770 |
| crispâ | . | White | 7, S. Ev. S. E. Ind. | . 1818 |
| cymôsâ, 3 | . | White | 8. Ev. S. Carthag. | . 1820 |
| densiflôrâ | . | White | 6, S. Ev. S. E. Ind. | . 1824 |
| discolôr | . | Cream | 4, S. Ev. T. Jamaica | . 1822 |
| grandiflôrâ | . | White | 8. Ev. S. Trinidad | . 1823 |
| gratissimâ | . | White | 6, S. Ev. S. E. Ind. | . 1824 |
| laurifòliâ | . | Yellow | 8. Ev. T. W. Ind. | . 1768 |
| odorâtâ, 4 | . | Yellow | 10. S. Ev. S. Cayenne | . 1793 |
| persicariæfòliâ | . | Cream | 8. Ev. T. Mauritius | . 1819 |
| undulâtâ | . | Orange | 8. Ev. T. Trinidad | . 1824 |

**TÀccÀ**, *Forster.* The Malay name of the species. *Linn.* 6, Or. 1, Nat. Or. *Taccaceæ.* Interesting plants, thriving well in a mixture of loam, peat, and sand ; and readily increasing by division of the roots. They must be very sparingly watered whilst in a dormant state. The large fleshy roots, when scraped and frequently washed, yield a nutritive fæcula resembling arrow-root.

| | | | | | |
|---|---|---|---|---|---|
| aspera | . | Brown | 7, S. Bl. P. E. Ind. | . 1816 |
| guineensis | . | Brown | 7, S. Bl. P. E. Ind. | . 1823 |
| integrifòliâ | . | Purple | 6, S. Her. P. E. Ind. | . 1810 |
| lævis | . | Brown | 7, S. Bl. P. E. Ind. | . 1820 |
| phallifera | . | Brown | 7, S. Bl. P. Maurit. | . 1826 |
| pinnatifìdâ | . | Purple | 7, S. Bl. P. E. Ind. | . 1793 |

**TÀcHÌX**, *Aublet.* From *Tachi*, which, it is said, signifies an ant's nest ; a name applied in its native country to *T. Guianensis* on account of its trunk and branches being usually full of ants ; this species, we believe, is not yet introduced to this country. *Linn.* 5, Or. 1, Nat. Or. *Gentianaceæ.* These plants will grow freely in a mixture of peat, sand, and loam ; a small proportion of the last will suffice ; cuttings planted in sand, under a hand-glass, in heat, will strike root readily. The species are rather difficult to keep through the winter, in this country, on acccount of their being liable to damp off ; and in order to prevent this, they should be very sparingly watered in damp weather. *Synonymes :* 1. *Lisianthus cordifolius.* 2. *L. longifolius.* 3. *L. exsertus.*

| | | | | | |
|---|---|---|---|---|---|
| cordifòliâ, 1 | . | Yellow | 8. Ev. S. Jamaica | . 1816 |
| longifòliâ, 2 | . | Yellow | 8. Ev. S. Jamaica | . 1793 |
| Swârtsìî, 3 | . | Yellow | 8. Ev. S. Jamaica | . 1793 |

**TÀcHÌGÀLÌÀ**, *Aublet.* Tachigali is the name of the species in Guiana. *Linn.* 10, Or. 1, Nat. Or. *Leguminosæ.* This plant succeeds best in a light loamy soil ; and large cuttings root readily if planted in sand, with a glass over them ; they must be placed in heat.

| | | | | |
|---|---|---|---|---|
| bijugâ | . | Yellow | 8. Ev. T. Brazil | . 1822 |

**TÀcsônÌÀ**, *Jussieu.* From *Tacso*, the name of one of the species in Peru. *Linn.* 16, Or. 2, Nat. Or. *Passifloraceæ.* Showy plants, with the habit of *Passiflora*, and requiring the same culture as that genus. *Synonyme :* 1. *Passiflora pedun--cularis.*

| | | | | | |
|---|---|---|---|---|---|
| peduncularis, 1 | . | | 8. Ev. Cl. Peru | . 1815 |
| pinnatistipùla | . | Pa. rose | 9, S. Ev. Cl. Chile | . 1828 |

**TÀniosus**, ribbon-like.

**TÆniÎtìs**, *Swartz.* From *tainia*, a fillet ; alluding to the long, narrow frond. *Linn.* 24, Or. 1, Nat. Or. *Polypodiaceæ.* Interesting Ferns, succeeding in sandy loam and peat ; and increased by division at the roots, or by seeds. *Synonymes :* 1. *Pteris angus- tifolia.* 2. *P. lanceolata.*

| | | | | | |
|---|---|---|---|---|---|
| angustifòliâ, 1 | . | Brown | 7. S. Ev. Cr. Jamaica | . 1816 |
| graminifòliâ | . | Brown | 7, S. Ev. Cr. Trinidad | . 1820 |
| lanceolâta, 2 | . | Brown | 8, S. Ev. Cr. W. Ind. | . 1818 |

**TÀGÈTÈS**, *Linn.* From the beauty of its flowers, this genus is named after *Tages*, a Tuscan divinity. *Linn.* 19, Or. 2, Nat. Or. *Compositæ.* A genus of elegant plants when in flower, and, therefore, well deserving a place in every garden. The annual species should be raised on a hotbed in spring, and planted out about the end of May. The herbaceous kinds thrive in any rich, light soil ; and may be increased by cuttings or divisions.

| | | | | | |
|---|---|---|---|---|---|
| angustifòliâ | . | Yellow | 8, H. | A. Mexico | . 1826 |
| caracasânâ | . | Yellow | 8, H. | A. Caraccas | . 1819 |
| clandestinâ | . | Yellow | 7, H. | A. Mexico | . 1823 |
| corymbôsâ | . | Yellow | 8, H. | A. Mexico | . 1825 |
| lùtea | . | Yellow | 8, H. | A. Mexico | . 1825 |
| erêctâ | . | Yellow | 7, H. | A. Mexico | . 1596 |
| filifòliâ | . | Yellow | 8, H. | A. Mexico | . 1826 |
| flôridâ | . | Yellow | 8, F. Her. P. Mexico | . 1827 |
| glandulifera | . | Yellow | 10, H. | A. Mexico | . 1826 |
| glandulôsâ | . | Yellow | 9, H. | A. S. Amer. | . 1819 |
| lùcidâ | . | Yellow | 8, G. Her. P. S. Amer. | . 1798 |
| micrânthâ | . | Yellow | 8, H. | A. Mexico | . 1822 |
| minùtâ | . | Pa. yel. | 8, H. | A. Chile | . 1728 |
| pâtùlâ | . | Yellow | 8, H. | A. Mexico | . 1573 |
| subvillôsâ | . | Yellow | 9, H. | A. Mexico | . 1823 |
| tenuifòliâ | . | Yellow | 8, H. | A. Peru | . 1797 |

**TÀils**, the long feathery or hairy terminations of certain fruits.

**TÀLAÙMÀ**, *Jussieu.* The vernacular name of the South American species. *Linn.* 13, Or. 6, Nat. Or. *Magnoliaceæ.* The species of *Talauma* are well worth cultivating on account of their beautiful and fragrant flowers. A mixture of loam, peat, and sand, suits them well. They may be increased by layers, or by inarching on *Magnolia obovata*, and ripened cuttings will root with difficulty in a pot of sand, under a glass, in heat ; but the leaves must not be shortened. *Synonymes :* 1. *Magnolia odora- tissima.* 2. *M. pumila.*

| | | | | | |
|---|---|---|---|---|---|
| Candòllîì, 1 | . | Striped | 4, S. Ev. S. Java | . 1827 |
| Plumièrì | . | White | 8. Ev. S. Antilles | . 1829 |
| pùmilâ, 2 | . | Cream | all S. Ev. S. Java | . 1786 |

**TÀLÌÈRÀ**, *Martius.* Its aboriginal name. *Linn.* 6, Or. 1, Nat. Or. *Palmaceæ.* An ornamental, lofty-growing tree, requiring to be grown in turfy loam and sand ; increased by seeds. *Synonyme :* 1. *Corypha Taliera.*

| | | | | |
|---|---|---|---|---|
| bengalénsis, 1 | . | | Palm. E. Ind. | . 1822 |

**TÀLìnum**, *Adanson.* Supposed to be from *thalia*, a green branch ; durable verdure. *Linn.* 11, Or. 1, Nat. Or. *Portulaceæ.* Interesting succulent plants, growing best in a mixture of loam, peat, and sand ; and readily increased by cuttings. The biennial species must be raised on a hotbed, and afterwards planted out in a warm, sheltered part of the flower garden. *Synonymes :* 1. *T. patens.* 2. *T. fruticosum.* 3. *Portulaca racemosa.*

| | | | | | |
|---|---|---|---|---|---|
| Andrêwsiî, 1 | . | Pink | 8, S. Ev. S. W. Ind. | . 1800 |
| crassifòliûm | . | Red | 8, S. Ev. S. | . 1800 |
| albiflòrûm, 2 | . | White | 7, G. Ev. S. S. Amer. | . 1816 |
| cuneifòliûm | . | Purple | 7, S. Ev. S. Egypt | . 1820 |
| pâtêns | . | Red | 9, S. Her. P. S. Amer. | . 1776 |
| reflêxûm | . | Yellow | 9, S.    B. S. Amer. | . 1800 |
| teretifòliûm | . | Pink | 8, G. Her. P. N. Amer. | . 1823 |
| triangulâre, 3 | . | Red | 8, S. Ev. S. W. Ind. | . 1739 |

**TÀLÌsìÀ**, *Aublet.* Derived from *Toulichi*, its name in Guiana. *Linn.* 8, Or. 1, Nat. Or. *Sapindaceæ.* This shrub succeeds well in a mixture of turfy loam and peat ; and large cuttings, not deprived of any of their leaves, will root in sand, under a glass, in a moist heat.

| | | | | |
|---|---|---|---|---|
| guianénsis | . | Rose | S. Ev. S. Guiana | . 1824 |

**TÀLLOW-TREE**, see *Stillingìâ sebìfêrâ.*

**TÀMÀRÌND-TREE**, see *Tamarindûs.*

**TÀMÀRÌNDÛS**, *Linn.* *Tamar*, in Arabic, is the name

of the date, and *Indus*, Indian; *Indian-date*. Linn.
16, Or. 6, Nat. Or. *Leguminosæ*. The species of
*Tamarind* thrive in a mixture of sandy loam and
peat; and are readily increased by seeds, which
are annually imported from the East and West
Indies; they should be sown on a hotbed, and
planted singly into pots, when about three inches
high. Cuttings root readily in sand, under a glass,
in heat. The preserved pulp of the tamarind is
well known as a delicious confection.

| | | | | |
|---|---|---|---|---|
| indicâ | . . Yellow | . 6, S. Ev. T. India | . . | 1633 |
| occidentâlis | . . Yelßh. | . 2, S. Ev. T. W. Ind. | . | 1633 |

TAMARISK, see *Tamárix*.

TAMÁRIX, *Linn*. So named on account of the plants
growing on the banks of the Tamaris, now Tambro,
on the borders of the Pyrenees. Linn. 5, Or. 3,
Nat. Or. *Tamaricaceæ*. This is a genus of very
elegant shrubs. The hardy species is well suited
for ornamenting shrubberies; it grows well in any
soil or situation; and increases freely by cuttings,
planted in the open ground, in spring or autumn.
*T. orientalis* succeeds well in a mixture of loam and
peat; and cuttings root readily in sand, under a
glass, in heat. The bark of all the species is
slightly bitter, astringent, and probably tonic.
The manna of Mount Sinai is produced by a variety
of *T. gallica*; it consists wholly of pure mucilaginous
sugar. *Synonyme*: 1. *T. articulata*.

| | | | | |
|---|---|---|---|---|
| dioicâ | . . . . | 8. Ev. S. E. Ind. | . . | 1823 |
| gallicâ | . . . Flesh | . 7, H. De. S. England | . | |
| orientâlis, 1 | . . Pink | . . 8. Ev. T. E. Ind. | . . | |

TAMÓNEX, *Aublet*. Tamone is its name in Guiana.
Linn. 14, Or. 2, Nat. Or. *Verbenaceæ*. Ornamental
biennials. They should be raised on a hotbed, and,
when of sufficient size, planted singly into pots of
sandy soil, and treated as other stove biennials.
*Synonymes*: 1. *T. verbenacea, Ghinia spinosa*. 2. *G.
mutica*.

| | | | | |
|---|---|---|---|---|
| curassâvicâ, 1 | . Blue | . . 7, S. | B. W. Ind. | . 1823 |
| muticâ, 2 | . . Blue | . . 7, S. | B. Guiana | . 1820 |

TÁMUS, *Linn*. A name applied by Columella to a
plant resembling a vine. Linn. 22, Or. 6, Nat. Or.
*Dioscoreaceæ*. Hardy twining plants, of no interest,
succeeding in common garden soil; division of the
roots—*T. communis, critica*.

TANACÉTUM, *Linn*. Said to be altered from *Athanasia*.
Linn. 19, Or. 2, Nat. Or. *Compositæ*. The species
of Tanacetum or Tansy are not possessed of much
beauty. The hardy kinds succeed in any common
soil; and are readily increased by division. The
greenhouse species should be grown in a light, rich
soil. They increase freely by cuttings. Withering
asserts, that if meat be rubbed with the leaves of
tansy, the flesh-fly will not touch it. *Synonymes*:
1. *Achillea filipendula*. 2. *A. bipinnata*.

| | | | | |
|---|---|---|---|---|
| angulâtûm, 1 | . Yellow | . 7, H. Her. P. Levant | . 1820 |
| erispûm | . . Yellow | . 7, H. Her. P. | | |
| globulíferûm | . Yellow | . 9, H. | A. Russia | . 1838 |
| grandiflôrûm | . Yellow | . 5, G. Her. P. C. G. H. | . 1820 |
| incânûm | . . | H. Her. P. Altai | . 1831 |
| myriophÿllûm, 2 Yellow | . 6, H. Her. P. Levant | . 1816 |
| purpúreûm | . . Pa. red | . 6, H. Her. P. Nepal | . 1818 |
| vulgâré | . . Yellow | . 6, H. Her. P. Britain | . . |
| variegâtûm | . Yellow | . 7, H. Her. P. Britain | . . |

*Argénteûm, boreâlé, canariénsé, linifòliûm, orientâlé,
sibíricûm, suffruticôsûm, vestîtûm*.

TANÆCIÛM, *Swartz*. From *tanaekes*, long; stems
elongated. Linn. 14, Or. 2, Nat. Or. *Gesneraceæ*.
This species is described as an ornamental, lofty-
growing tree. For culture and propagation, see.
Bignonia. *Synonymes*: 1. *Crescentia pinnata, Tri-
pinnaria africana*.

| | | | | |
|---|---|---|---|---|
| pinnâtûm, 1 | . . Red | . . . 8. Ev. T. Mozamb. | . 1826 |

TANGHINIA, *Du Petit Thouars*. From *Tanghin*, the
Madagascar name of *T. venenifiua*, the seed of
which is the ordeal nut of that Island. Linn. 5,
Or. 1, Nat. Or. *Apocynaceæ*. These remarkable
plants may be referred to Tabernæmontana for
culture and propagation. *T. venenifiua* is the celebrated ordeal tree of Madagascar. The fruit is
yellow; and incloses a fibrous stone or nut; the
kernel inclosed in this stone, or nut, is said by
some to be the part used for the ordeal, and to be
infused in a liquid of which the accused person is
made to drink; others say the infusion is made of
the entire fruit. In *Don's Dictionary of Gard. and*

*Bot.*, vol. 4, p. 98, is the following passage relative
to this subject:—" The custom of administering
*Tanghin* as an ordeal, in Madagascar, has become
far more universal during the present reign, than
at any former period of the Huwa government.
When her present Majesty, in the beginning of
1830, came to the resolution of cleansing her lands
from sorcerers, an ordeal was commanded in every
town and village; and in Tannanarivoo scarcely
any class of the inhabitants escaped. On the 9th
of May, 1830, in compliance with the sovereign's
mandate, a notable administration of Tanghin took
place. The accused persons amounted to about
thirty, including some of the highest rank in the
kingdom. All the nobility recovered, while the
unknown plebeians, who, according to the common
jugglery, had been compelled to drink with them,
died. The former made the usual triumphant
entry into the town, on the 17th, borne in open
palanquins, amongst the shouting, dancing, and
grimaces of the many thousands of people. In the
following month, about an equal number of Malagassy ladies submitted to the same ordeal; but all
survived, and, in due course, made a grand entry
into town. The Tanghin is administered in private,
as well as in public. A subject so deeply rooted
in the minds of all the Malagassy people, from the
sovereign down to the slave, is the belief in witch-
craft; and so blindly led on by this belief,
that a whole nation may be considered as labouring
under a spell, as powerful as the fascination which
they attribute to the unfortunate sorcerers themselves." *Synonymes*: 1. *Cerbera laurifolia*. 2. *C.
lactaria*. 3. *C. Odollam*. 4. *C. Tanghin*.

| | | | | |
|---|---|---|---|---|
| laurifòliâ, 1 | . . White | . 6, S. Ev. T. E. Ind. | . 1818 |
| Mânghâs, 2 | . . White | . 8, S. Ev. T. Singapore | . 1800 |
| Odollâm, 3 | . . White | . 8, S. Ev. T. India | . 1756 |
| veneníflûâ, 4 | . . Pink | . 5, S. Ev. T. Madagas. | . 1826 |

TANGIER PEA, see *Láthÿrûs tingitânûs*.

TANNA, see *Euphôrbiâ tannênsis*.

TANSY, see *Tanacêtûm*.

TAPERING, becoming gradually narrower.

TAP-ROOT, a root which penetrates deep and perpen-
dicularly into the ground, without dividing.

TARCHONÁNTHÛS, *Linn*. From *tarchon*, the Arabic
word for *taragon*, and *anthos*, a flower. Linn. 19,
Or. 1, Nat. Or. *Compositæ*. Interesting plants,
succeeding well in light rich soil; and readily increased by cuttings, in sand, under a glass.

| | | | | |
|---|---|---|---|---|
| camphorâtûs | . . Purple | . G. Ev. S. C. G. H. | . 1690 |
| ellípticûs | . . . | G. Ev. S. C. G. H. | . 1816 |

TARE, see *Ervûm*.

TARGIÓNIÂ, *Micheli*. In honour of John Anthony
Targioni, a Florentine botanist. Linn. 24, Or. 6,
Nat. Or. *Hepaticæ*. This species is found growing
in broad patches, in wet places—*T. hypophÿllâ*.

TARTAREOUS, consisting of tartar.

TAUSCHERIÂ, *Fischer*. In honour of Ignat. Frederick
Tauscher, Professor of Botany at Prague, author of
several botanical works. Linn. 15, Nat. Or. *Cruciferæ*. Annuals of no beauty. The seed merely
requires to be sown in the open border, or on rock-
work.

| | | | | |
|---|---|---|---|---|
| gymnocârpâ | . . White | . 6, H. | A. Siberia | . 1820 |
| lasiocârpâ | . . White | . 6, H. | A. Siberia | . 1824 |

TAVERNIÉRÂ, *Decandolle*. In honour of J. B. Taver-
nier, a traveller in the Levant. Linn. 17, Or. 4,
Nat. Or. *Leguminosæ*. For culture and propagation,
see *Dicerma*. *Synonymes*: 1. *Hedysarum lappaceum*.
2. *H. nummularifolium*.

| | | | | |
|---|---|---|---|---|
| lappâceâ, 1 | . . Yellow | . 7, G. Ev. Tr. Arabia | . 1820 |
| nummulâriâ, 2 | . Rose | . 6, G. Ev. S. Levant | . 1826 |

TAXÓDIÛM, *Richard*. From *taxus*, the yew, and *eidos*,
like; trees resembling the yew. Linn. 21, Or. 3,
Nat. Or. *Coniferæ*. Ornamental, lofty-growing
trees, well suited for planting singly on lawns.
They grow best in a rich moist soil; and are readily
increased by seeds, layers, or by cuttings, with the
leaves left whole, placed in a vessel of water, where
they will root in a few weeks. The *Deciduous
Cypress* is universally employed, throughout the
United States, for making the best kind of shingles;
and in Louisiana it is used for almost every other
purpose to which timber is applied. *Synonymes*:
1. *Schubertia capensis*. 2. *S. disticha*. 3. *S. d. pendula*.
4. *T. sinense pendulum*. 5. *T. sinense*.

| | | | | | | |
|---|---|---|---|---|---|---|
| capénsè, 1 | . | . Apetal | . 4, | G. Ev. S. | C. G. H. | . |
| distíchūm, 2 | . | . Apetal | . 5, | H. De. | T. N. Amer. | . 1640 |
| excelsūm | . | . Apetal | . 5, | H. De. | T. | |
| nútāns, 3 | . | . Apetal | . 5, | H. De. | T. | |
| pátēns | . | . Apetal | . 5, | H. De. | T. | |
| pendūlūm, 4 | . | . Apetal | . 5, | H. De. | T. | |
| sinénsè, 5 | . | . Apetal | . 5, | H. De. | T. | |

**TÁXŪS,** *Linn.* From *toxon*, a bow; being formerly used in making them; or from *taxis*, arrangement; the leaves are arranged on the branches like the teeth of a comb. Yew is supposed to be from the Celtic word *iw*, signifying verdure; alluding to the yew being an evergreen. *Linn.* 22, Or. 13, Nat. Or. *Taxaceæ*. Ornamental trees, well adapted for underwood, as they thrive under the shade and drip of other trees; they are also very ornamental when planted to form hedges. They will grow in any moist soil, but succeed best in loams and clays. They are chiefly propagated from seeds, which should be sown as soon as ripe; they may also be increased by cuttings, formed of either one or two years' wood, and planted in a shady border in the beginning of April or end of August. *Synonymes:* 1. *T. fastigiata*, *T. hibernica*, *T. baccata hibernica.*

| | | | | | | |
|---|---|---|---|---|---|---|
| baccátā | . | . Apetal | . 2, | H. Ev. | T. Britain | . |
| erictā | . | . Apetal | . | H. Ev. | T. Seedling | . |
| fastigiátā, 1 | . | . Apetal | . 4, | H. Ev. | T. Ireland | . 1780 |
| fructu-lúteō | . | . Apetal | . 4, | H. Ev. | T. Ireland | . |
| procúmbēns | . | . Apetal | . 2, | H. Ev. | S. Europe | . |
| variegátā | . | . Apetal | . 2, | H. Ev. | T. Europe | . |
| canadénsis | . | . Apetal | . 2, | H. Ev. | T. Canada | . 1800 |
| Harringtónīā | . | . Apetal | . 5, | H. De. | T. Penang | . 1837 |
| Makoyā | . | . Apetal | . 5, | H. De. | T. Japan | . 1838 |
| nuciférā | . | . Apetal | . | G. Ev. | T. China | . 1820 |

**TEAK WOOD,** see *Tectóna.*
**TEASEL,** see *Dipsacus.*
**TEATED,** having protuberances which resemble the teats of animals.
**TEA-TREE,** see *Théa.*
**TECÓMA,** *Jussieu.* From *Tecomaxochitl*, the Mexican name of the species. *Linn.* 14, Or. 2, Nat. Or. *Bignoniaceæ*. A genus of very elegant plants, well worth cultivating. *T. radicans* is peculiarly adapted for ornamenting a wall, or front of a house. The other kinds require the same treatment as the species of *Bignonia. Synonymes:* 1. *Bignonia Pandoræ.* 2. *B. capensis.* 3. *B. grandiflora, chinensis, Incarvillea grandiflora.* 4. *B. pentaphylla.* 5. *B. radicans.* 6. *B. stans.* 7. *T. incisa.*

| | | | | | | |
|---|---|---|---|---|---|---|
| austrális, 1 | . | . Orange | . 6, | F. Ev. Cl. | N. S. W. | . 1793 |
| capénsis, 2 | . | . Orange | . 8, | F. Ev. Cl. | C. G. H. | . 1823 |
| digitátā | . | . Yellow | . | S. Ev. | T. S. Amer. | . 1818 |
| diversifóliā | . | . | . | F. De. | Cl. N. Holl. | . 1830 |
| grandiflórā, 3 | . | . Orange | . 7, | G. De. | Cl. China | . 1800 |
| jasminoídes | . | . Pink | . 8, | G. Ev. | Cl. N. S. W. | . |
| mexoánthā | . | . Blush | . 4, | G. Ev. | Cl. N. Holl. | . 1815 |
| móllis | . | . Yellow | . | G. De. | S. Mexico | . 1824 |
| pentaphýllā, 4 | . | . Orange | . 7, | S. Ev. | S. E. Ind. | . |
| radícans, 5 | . | . Orange | . 7, | H. De. | Cl. N. Amer. | . 1640 |
| major | . | . Orange | . 7, | F. De. | Cl. N. Amer. | . 1640 |
| minór | . | . Scarlet | . 7, | H. De. | Cl. N. Amer. | . 1640 |
| rosæfóliā | . | . Yellow | . 8, | S. Ev. | S. Peru | . |
| sambucifóliā | . | . Yellow | . 8, | S. Ev. | S. Peru | . 1824 |
| sorbifóliā | . | . Yellow | . 8, | S. Ev. | S. Amer. | . |
| spléndidā | . | . Yellow | . 8, | S. Ev. | S. Brazil | . 1830 |
| stáns, 6 | . | . Yellow | . 8, | S. Ev. | S. S. Amer. | . 1730 |
| incísā, 7 | . | . Yellow | . 8, | S. Ev. | S. S. Amer. | . 1820 |

**TECTÓNA,** *Linn.* From its name in Malabar, *Tekka. Linn.* 5, Or. 1, Nat. Or. *Verbenaceæ.* This tree thrives well in a mixture of peat and loam, in a strong heat; and ripened cuttings will root in sand, under a glass, in heat. In its native country, it is much valued for the hardness and durability of its wood; of which some of the largest ships have been built, both at Calcutta and Madras.

| | | | | | | |
|---|---|---|---|---|---|---|
| grándis | . | . . White | . | S. Ev. | T. E. Ind. | . 1777 |

**TEEDIA,** *Rudolph.* Meaning not explained. *Linn.* 14, Or. 2, Nat. Or. *Scrophulariaceæ.* Pretty plants when in blossom. A rich light soil suits them best; and they are readily increased by cuttings or seeds.

| | | | | | | |
|---|---|---|---|---|---|---|
| lúcidā | . | . . Purple | . 4, | G. | B. C. G. H. | . 1774 |
| pubéscēns | . | . . Purple | . 5, | G. | B. C. G. H. | . 1816 |

**TEESDÁLIA,** *R. Brown.* In honour of Robert Teesdale, author of a Catalogue of plants growing about Castle Howard. *Linn.* 15, Nat. Or. *Cruciferæ.* Pretty little annuals, well adapted for rock-work, where the seeds have only to be sown, and may afterwards be allowed to scatter themselves. *Synonymes:* 1. *T. nudicaulis.* 2. *T. regularis.*

| | | | | | | |
|---|---|---|---|---|---|---|
| ibérica, 1 | . | . White | . 5, | H. | A. Britain | . |
| lepídium, 2 | . | . White | . 2, | H. | A. S. Eur. | . 1824 |

**TELEKIA,** *Baumgarten.* Not explained. *Linn.* 19, Or. 2, Nat. Or. *Compositæ.* This plant succeeds well in common garden soil; and is readily increased by division of the roots. *Synonymes:* 1. *Bupthalmum cordifolium.*

| | | | | | | |
|---|---|---|---|---|---|---|
| speciósa, 1 | . | . Yellow | . 7, | H. Her. | P. Hungary | . 1739 |

**TELÉPHIUM.** Linnæus named this genus after *Telephus*, son of Hercules by Auge, and, according to some, king of Mysia. *Linn.* 5, Or. 1, Nat. Or. *Illecebraceæ.* A hardy herbaceous plant, not worth cultivating—*T. Imperáti.*

**TELLÍMA,** *R. Brown.* An anagram of Mitella; separated from it. *Linn.* 10, Or. 2, Nat. Or. *Saxifragaceæ.* A very handsome plant. For culture and propagation, see *Mitella.*

| | | | | | | |
|---|---|---|---|---|---|---|
| grandiflórā | . | . Pink | . 4, | H. Her. | P. N. Amer. | . 1826 |

**TELÓPEA,** *R. Brown.* From *Telopos*, seen at a distance; alluding to the great distance from which its crimson-coloured blossoms are discernible in its native country. *Linn.* 4, Or. 1, Nat. Or. *Proteaceæ.* This magnificent plant is considered to be rather difficult of culture. A light soil, composed of equal parts of sandy loam and heath mould, with a good proportion of sand and gritstone, well incorporated, appears to suit it best. The pot in which it is grown must be well drained; and in watering, care must be taken never to allow the plant to flag, nor yet to over-water it. Though it requires very little water in the winter season, it must have a good supply in the summer months, particularly while growing freely. It should always be kept in a light, airy part of the house. It may be propagated by cuttings, in sand, under a glass; but young plants may be obtained readier, and with greater certainty, by layers; as the plants naturally produce an abundance of suckers, which may be easily laid down into small pots, introduced round the one in which the plant is growing. In summer, the *Warratah* succeeds well in an airy part of the greenhouse, but in winter, it subsists better in a cool, airy part of the stove.

| | | | | | | |
|---|---|---|---|---|---|---|
| speciosíssimā | . | . Scarlet | . 6, | G. Ev. | T. N. S. W. | . 1789 |

**TEMPLETÓNIA,** *R. Brown.* In honour of Mr. John Templeton, of Orange Grove, near Belfast, an excellent botanist. *Linn.* 16, Or. 6, Nat. Or. *Leguminosæ.* Interesting plants, thriving well in a mixture of sandy loam and peat; and increased by young cuttings, in sand, under a glass.

| | | | | | | |
|---|---|---|---|---|---|---|
| glaúcā | . | . . Red | . 4, | G. Ev. | S. N. Holl. | . 1818 |
| retúsā | . | . . Red | . 5, | G. Ev. | S. N. Holl. | . 1803 |

**TENAX,** tough, adhesive.
**TENDRILS,** the curling, twining organs by which some plants lay hold of others.
**TENÓRIA,** see *Bupleúrum.*
**TEPHRÓSIA,** *Persoon.* From *tephros*, ash-coloured; in allusion to the colour of the foliage of some of the species. *Linn.* 17, Or. 4, Nat. Or. *Leguminosæ.* The species of *Tephrosia* thrive well in a mixture of loam and peat, and are readily increased by seeds, or by young cuttings planted in sand, under a glass; those of the stove species, in heat. " The leaves and branches of *T. toxicaria*, well pounded, and thrown into a river or pond, very soon affect the water, and cause it to intoxicate the fish, so as to make them float on the surface as if dead; most of the large ones recover after a short time, but the greater part of the small fry perish on those occasions. It has been introduced into Jamaica, and cultivated there on account of its intoxicating qualities."—*Don's Gard. and Bot.*, vol. 2, p. 229. *Synonymes:* 1. *Galega biflora.* 2. *Robinia candida.* 3. *G. caribæa.* 4. *G. grandiflora.* 5. *G. heterophylla.* 6. *G. mucronata.* 7. *G. ochroleuca.* 8. *G. pallens.* 9. *G. piscatoria.* 10. *Indigofera stricta.* 11. *Robinia suberosa.* 12. *Galega virginica.*

| | | | | | | |
|---|---|---|---|---|---|---|
| apollínea | . | . Blue | . 7, | S. Ev. | S. Egypt | . 1815 |
| biflórā, 1 | . | . Purple | . 7, | S. Ev. | S. | . 1816 |
| cándidā, 2 | . | . Pa. red | . 7, | S. Ev. | S. Bengal | . 1816 |
| capénsis | . | . Purple | . 7, | G. Ev. | S. C. G. H. | . 1825 |
| capituláta | . | . Red | . 7, | S. Her. | P. Owhyhee | . 1823 |
| caríbæa, 3 | . | . Red wht. | . 6, | S. Ev. | S. W. Ind. | . 1748 |
| chinénsis | . | . Purple | . 7, | G. Ev. | S. China | . 1822 |
| colorátā | . | . Purple | . 7, | S. Ev. | S. E. Ind. | . 1818 |
| fruticósa | . | . Red | . 7, | S. Ev. | S. E. Ind. | . 1814 |
| grandiflórā, 4 | . | . Pink | . 6, | G. Ev. | S. C. G. H. | . 1774 |

| | | | | | | | |
|---|---|---|---|---|---|---|---|
| Heyneàna | Purple | 6, 8. | Ev. | S. | E. Ind. | 1822 |
| hypargyrèa, 5 | Purple | 6, 8. | Ev. | S. | E. Ind. | 1825 |
| lanceolàtla | Pa. yel. | 7, 8. | Ev. | S. | | 1820 |
| lineàris | Red | 7, 8. | Ev. | S. | W. Ind. | 1823 |
| littoràlis | Purple | 7, 8. | Ev. | Tr. | W. Ind. | 1824 |
| longifòlla | Red | 6, 8. | Ev. | S. | S. Amer. | 1820 |
| mucronàta, 6 | Pale | 6, G. | Ev. | S. | C. G. H. | 1823 |
| ochroleùca, 7 | Cream | | 8. | Ev. | S. | W. Ind. | 1799 |
| pàllens, 8 | Pink | 7, G. | Ev. | S. | C. G. H. | 1787 |
| pentaphýlla | Purple | 6, 8. | Ev. | S. | E. Ind. | 1818 |
| piscatòrla, 9 | Purple | 6, 8. | Ev. | S. | India | 1778 |
| purpúrea, 10 | Purple | 7, 8. | Her. | P. | E. Ind. | 1768 |
| sericea | Red | 7, G. | Ev. | S. | C. G. H. | 1800 |
| strictà, 10 | Pink | 6, G. | Ev. | S. | C. G. H. | 1774 |
| suberòsa, 11 | Rose | 7, 8. | Ev. | S. | E. Ind. | 1818 |
| toxicària | Pa. red | | 8. | Ev. | S. | W. Ind. | 1791 |
| villòsa | White | 7, 8. | Ev. | S. | E. Ind. | 1779 |
| virginiàna, 12 | Pink | 7, F. | Her. | P. | N. Amer. | 1765 |

**TERAMNUS**, *P. Browne.* From *teramnos*, soft; in reference to the pods and leaves of the species being soft. *Linn.* 16, Or. 6, Nat. Or. *Leguminosæ.* For culture and propagation, see *Abrus.*

| | | | | | | |
|---|---|---|---|---|---|---|
| uncinàtus | Red | 8. | Ev. | Tw. | Jamaica | 1822 |
| volùbilis | Red | 8. | Ev. | Tw. | Jamaica | 1824 |

**TEREBINTHINATE**, consisting of turpentine.
**TERETE**, round and long, like a taper.
**TERGEMINATE**, three-paired.
**TERMINAL**, ending, bounding.
**TERMINÀLIA**, *Linn.* The leaves are in bunches at the ends of the branches; hence the name, from *terminus*, end. *Linn.* 23, Or. 1, Nat. Or. *Combretaceæ.* Interesting plants. For culture and propagation, see *Bucida.* The fruit and bark of several of the species are astringent and tonic. The fruit and galls of *T. Chebula* are highly valued by dyers, creating, when mixed with alum, a durable yellow. The bark and leaves of *T. Catappa* yield a black pigment, with which Indian ink is made. A milky juice is said to flow from *T. angustifolia*, which, when dried, is fragrant, and resembling Benzoin is used as a kind of incense in the churches in the Mauritius. *Synonymes* : 1. *T. Benzoin.* 2. *T. subcordata.* 3. *T. madagascariensis, Myrobalanus Fatræa.*

| | | | | | | |
|---|---|---|---|---|---|---|
| angustifòlia, 1 | Wht. grn. | 8. | Ev. | T. | E. Ind. | 1692 |
| arbúscula | Wht. grn. | 8. | Ev. | S. | S. Amer. | 1822 |
| Bellérica | Yel. grn. | 8. | Ev. | T. | E. Ind. | 1818 |
| Biticària | Yel. grn. | 8. | Ev. | T. | E. Ind. | 1823 |
| Catàppa | White | 8. | Ev. | T. | E. Ind. | 1778 |
| subcordàta, 2 | Yel. grn. | 8. | Ev. | T. | S. Amer. | 1816 |
| Chebùla | White | 8. | Ev. | T. | E. Ind. | 1796 |
| citrìna | Yel. grn. | 8. | Ev | T. | E. Ind. | 1823 |
| distìcha | Yel. grn. | 8. | Ev. | T. | E. Ind. | 1824 |
| Fatræà, 3 | Yel. grn. | 8. | Ev. | T. | Madagas. | 1826 |
| gangética | Yel. grn. | 8. | Ev. | T. | E. Ind. | 1820 |
| latifòlia | | 8. | Ev. | T. | W. Ind. | 1800 |
| mauritiàna | Yel. grn. | 8. | Ev. | S. | Maurit. | 1824 |
| moluccàna | Wht. grn. | 8. | Ev. | S. | E. Ind. | 1804 |
| procèra | Yel. grn. | 8. | Ev. | T. | E. Ind. | 1816 |
| rotundifòlla | Yel. grn. | 8. | Ev. | S. | E. Ind. | 1824 |

**TERN**, in threes, or three in a whorl.
**TERNARY**, consisting of threes.
**TERNATE**, applied to a leaf consisting of three leaflets.
**TERNSTRÆMIA**, *Mutis.* In honour of Ternström, a Swedish naturalist and traveller, who died at Pulicandre, in 1745. *Linn.* 13, Or. 1, Nat. Or. *Ternstroemiaceæ.* Interesting plants, succeeding in loam and peat ; and cuttings of the ripened wood will root in sand, under a glass, in heat.

| | | | | | | |
|---|---|---|---|---|---|---|
| brèvipes | Red | 7, 8. | Ev. | S. | S. Amer. | 1816 |
| peduncularis | White | 7, 8. | Ev. | S. | W. Ind. | 1818 |
| punctàta | Yelsh. | 7, 8. | Ev. | S. | E. Ind. | 1820 |
| venòsa | White | 7, 8. | Ev. | S. | Brasil | 1824 |

**TESSELATED**, variegated by squares, chequered.
**TESTA**, the skin or integument of a seed.
**TESTACEOUS**, light brown.
**TESTUDINÀRIA**, *Salisbury.* From *testudo*, a tortoise; resemblance of the outside roots. *Linn.* 22, Or. 6, Nat. Or. *Dioscoreaceæ.* Curious and interesting plants, succeeding well in turfy loam and peat. They should be kept dry when not growing. Roots are frequently received from the Cape of Good Hope. The plants being diœcious, there is no chance of obtaining seeds in this country, unless specimens of both sexes should happen to flower at the same time. *Synonyme* : 1. *Tamus elephantipes.*

| | | | | | | |
|---|---|---|---|---|---|---|
| elephántipes, 1 | Yellow | 7, G. | De. | Cl. | C. G. H. | 1774 |
| montàna | Yellow | 7, G. | De. | Cl. | C. G. H. | 1816 |

**TETANUS**, lockjaw.

**TETRACÈRA**, *Linn.* From *tetra*, four-fold, and *keras*, a horn ; the four capsules are recurved like as many horns. *Linn.* 22, Or. 12, Nat. Or. *Dilleniaceæ.* These handsome climbers are well suited for covering rafters or pillars in stoves. They succeed well in turfy loam and peat ; and cuttings of the ripened wood root freely in sand, under a glass, in heat. *Synonyme* : 1. *Dillenia scandens.*

| | | | | | | |
|---|---|---|---|---|---|---|
| alnifòlia | Yellow | 8. | Ev. | Cl. | Guinea | 1793 |
| obovàta | | 2, 8. | Ev. | Cl. | Guinea | 1822 |
| pointòria | | 8. | Ev. | Cl. | S. Leone | 1822 |
| volùbilis, 1 | Yellow | 8. | Ev. | Cl. | S. Amer. | 1818 |

**TETRACHOTOMOUS**, a stem that ramifies in fours.
**TETRÀDIUM**, *Loureiro.* From *tetradion*, quaternary ; parts of flowers and fruit in fours. *Linn.* 22, Or. 4, Nat. Or. *Connaraceæ.* For culture and propagation, see *Brucea.* *Synonyme* : 1. *Brucea trichotoma.*

| | | | | | |
|---|---|---|---|---|---|
| trichotomum, 1 | | 8. | Ev. | T. | Cochin China 1820 |

**TETRAGONAL**, having four angles.
**TETRAGÒNIA**, *Linn.* From *tetra*, four, and *gonia*, an angle ; in allusion to the fruit being four-angled. *Linn.* 12, Or. 2, Nat. Or. *Tetragoniaceæ.* Plants not worth cultivating, except in general collections. *T. expansa* has been used as a substitute for spinach. *T. crystallina, decumbens, echinàta, expànsa, fruticòsa, herbàcea, lineàris, obovàta, spicàta, Tetràpteris.*
**TETRAGONOLÒBUS**, *Scopoli.* The legumes are furnished with four wings or angles ; whence the name, from *tetra*, four, *gonia*, an angle, and *lobos*, a pod. *Linn.* 17, Or. 4, Nat. Or. *Leguminosæ.* Ornamental plants, succeeding in common garden soil ; and increased by seeds. The perennial kinds are well adapted for ornamenting rock-work, and the annual kinds for flower borders. *Synonymes* : 1. *Lotus conjugatus, biflorus.* 2. *L. conjugatus.* 3. *L. Tetragonolobus.* 4. *L. siliquosus.*

| | | | | | | |
|---|---|---|---|---|---|---|
| biflòrus, 1 | Yellow | 7, H. | Tr. | A. | Barbary | 1818 |
| conjunàtus, 2 | Purple | 7, H. | Tr. | A. | Montpel. | 1759 |
| marìtimus | Yellow | 8. | H. | De. | Tr. | Europe | 1683 |
| purpùreus, 3 | Dk. pur. | 7, H. | Dr. | A. | Sicily | 1769 |
| siliquòsus, 4 | Yellow | 7, H. | De. | Tr. | S. Eur. | 1683 |

**TETRAGONOTHÈCA**, *Dillwyn.* From *tetragonos*, quadrangular, and *theke*, case ; the four-angled grains. *Linn.* 19, Or. 2, Nat. Or. *Compositæ.* An interesting plant, growing well in any rich, light soil ; and increased by divisions or seeds.

| | | | | | | |
|---|---|---|---|---|---|---|
| helianthoïdes | Yellow | 8, H. | Her. | P. | Virgin. | 1726 |

**TETRAGYNOUS**, having four styles.
**TETRAMERIUM**, see *Coffea.*
**TETRAMERIUM**, see *Faramea.*
**TETRANDROUS**, having four stamens.
**TETRANTHÈRA**, *Jacquin.* From *tetra*, four, and *aner*, an anther. *Linn.* 9, Or. 1, Nat. Or. *Lauraceæ.* Ornamental plants, requiring to be grown in a mixture of turfy loam, peat, and sand , and ripened cuttings root readily in sand, under a glass, in heat. *Synonymes* : 1. *Litsea citrifolia.* 2. *L. Cervantesii.* 3. *L. glaucescens.* 4. *L. chinensis.* 5. *T. involucrata.* 6. *L. zeylanica.*

| | | | | | | |
|---|---|---|---|---|---|---|
| apètala, 1 | Orn. yel. | 4, G. | Ev. | S. | N. Holl. | 1824 |
| Cervantesii, 2 | | 8. | Ev. | T. | Mexico | 1823 |
| dealbàta | Yel. grn. | 4, G. | Ev. | S. | N. Holl. | 1825 |
| ferruginèa | | 5, G. | Ev. | S. | N. Holl. | 1824 |
| glaucescens, 3 | Yel. grn. | 5, 8. | Ev. | T. | Mexico | 1825 |
| laurifòlia, 4 | Green | 5, 8. | Ev | S. | China | 1822 |
| sebìfera, 5 | Yel. grn. | 5, 8. | Ev. | S. | E. Ind. | 1820 |
| trinérvis, 6 | Yel. grn. | 5, 8. | Ev. | S. | Ceylon | 1821 |

**TETRÀNTHUS**, *Swartz.* From *tetra*, four, and *anthos*, a flower. *Linn.* 19, Or. 2, Nat. Or. *Compositæ.* A pretty plant, thriving in sandy loam ; and readily increased by division.

| | | | | | | |
|---|---|---|---|---|---|---|
| littoràlis | White | 8, 8. | Ev. | Cr. | W. Ind. | 1820 |

**TETRAPÈLTIS**, *Wallich.* Not explained. *Linn.* 20, Or. 1, Nat. Or. *Orchidaceæ.* This is an interesting and highly fragrant species. For culture and propagation, see *Cælogyne.*

| | | | | | | |
|---|---|---|---|---|---|---|
| fràgrans | White | 8. | Epl. | E. Ind. | 1836 |

**TETRAPETALOUS**, having four petals.
**TETRÀPHIS**, *Hedwig.* From *tetra*, four ; in allusion to the teeth of the peristome being in fours. *Linn.* 24, Or. 5, Nat. Or *Musci.* Broad tufts, found on dry banks. *Synonymes* : 1. *T. ovata, Grimmia Browniana—T. Brownidna* 1, *pellúcida.*
**TETRAPÒGON**, *Desfontaines.* From *tetra*, four, and

*pogon*, a beard. *Linn.* 3, Or. 2. Nat. Or. *Gramineæ*. A curious hardy annual species, of common culture.

| | | | | | | | |
|---|---|---|---|---|---|---|---|
| villòsa | . . . . | Apetal. | . 7, | Gras. | Barbary | . | 1818 |

TETRAPŌMI, *Turcz.* From *tetra*, four, and *poma*, a cover; capsule four-valved. *Linn.* 15, Nat. Or. *Cruciferæ.* We are not acquainted with this plant, but we presume it is of little value—*T. barbareæfolium*.

TETRAPTERYS, *Cavanilles.* From *tetra*, four, and *pteron*, a wing; the carpels are each four-winged. *Linn.* 10, Or. 3, Nat. Or. *Malpighiaceæ.* Interesting plants, seldom seen in blossom. For culture and propagation, see *Malpighia*. Synonymes: 1. *Triopteris buxifolia.* 2. *T. citrifolia.*

| | | | | | | | |
|---|---|---|---|---|---|---|---|
| buxifòlia, 1 | . | Yellow | . | 8. Ev. | S. | St. Domin. | . 1822 |
| citrifòlia, 2 | . | Yellow | . | 8. Ev. | S. | Cayenne | . 1818 |

TETRAQUETROUS, having four angles or sides.

TETRASEPALOUS, having four sepals.

TETRATHĒCA, *Smith.* From *tetra*, four, and *theke*, a cell; alluding to the anthers being four-celled. *Linn.* 8, Or. 1, Nat. Or. *Tremandraceæ.* A genus of very pretty under-shrubs, rather difficult to cultivate. A mixture of loam, peat, and sand, in equal parts, seems to suit them best; and cuttings of the young wood root in sand, under a glass.

| | | | | | | | |
|---|---|---|---|---|---|---|---|
| ericæfòlia | . . | Rose | . 7, | G. Ev. | S. | N. Holl. | . 1820 |
| glandulòsa | . | Purple | . 7, | G. Ev. | S. | V. D. L. | . 1822 |
| júncea | . | Purple | . 7, | G. Ev. | S. | N. Holl. | . 1803 |
| pilòsa | . | Purple | . 7, | G. Ev. | S. | V. D. L. | . 1823 |
| rubiòides | . | Purple | . 7, | G. Ev. | S. | N. Holl. | . 1825 |
| thymifòlia | . | Purple | . 7, | G. Ev. | S. | N. Holl. | . 1824 |

TEUCRIUM, *Linn.* Named after *Teucer*, son of Scamander, and father-in-law of Dardanus, king of Troy. *Linn.* 14, Or. 1, Nat. Or. *Labiatæ.* Interesting plants, of very easy culture. The perennial herbaceous kinds succeed well in common garden soil; and are readily increased by division and by seeds. Most of the shrubby kinds require the protection of a frame or greenhouse in winter; they are easily increased by young cuttings. The seeds of the annual species only require to be sown in the open border in spring. Synonymes: 1. *Scutellaria cretica.* 2. *T. orchideum.* 3. *T. latifolium.* 4. *T. supinum.* 5. *T. capitatum, flavum.* 6. *T. aureum.* 7. *T. pseudo-hyssopus.*

| | | | | | | | |
|---|---|---|---|---|---|---|---|
| abutilòides | . | Yellow | . 4, | G. Ev. | S. | Madeira | . 1777 |
| angustissimum | . | Purple | . 6, | H. Ev. | S. | Spain | . 1818 |
| Arduíni, 1 | . | Yellow | . 7, | F. Ev. | S. | Candia | . 1823 |
| asiàticum | . | Pink | . 8, | F. Ev. | S. | | . 1777 |
| betònicum | . | Lilac | . 7, | G. Ev. | S. | Madeira | . 1775 |
| bicôlor, 2 | . | Yel. red | . 7, | H. Her. | P. | Chile | . 1826 |
| Botrys | . | Red | . 8, | H. | A. | S. Eur. | . 1633 |
| brevifòlium | . | Pink | . 6, | H. Ev. | S. | Crete | . 1824 |
| campanulàtum | . | Blue | . 7, | H. Her. | P. | Levant | . 1798 |
| canadénse | . | Purple | . 8, | H. Her. | P. | N. Amer. | . 1768 |
| cánum | . | Purple | . | F. Ev. | S. | Armenia | . 1836 |
| Chamædrys | . | Purple | . 7, | H. Her. | P. | England | . |
| crèticum | . | Purple | . 7, | F. Ev. | S. | Crete | . 1824 |
| cubénse | . | Purple | . 5, | 8. | B. | Cuba | . 1733 |
| flàvum, 3 | . | Yellow | . 8, | F. Ev. | S. | S. Eur. | . 1640 |
| frùticans | . | Violet | . 8, | F. Ev. | S. | Spain | . 1648 |
| gnaphalòides | . | Purple | . 8, | F. Ev. | S. | Spain | . 1816 |
| heterophýllum | . | Purple | . 6, | F. Ev. | S. | Madeira | . 1759 |
| hyrcànicum | . | Purple | . 9, | H. Her. | P. | Persia | . 1763 |
| inflàtum | . | Red | . 9, | S. | Her. | P. | Jamaica | . 1778 |
| lævigàtum | . | | . | G. Her. | P. | | . 1832 |
| Laxmánni | . | Varieg. | . 7, | H. Her. | P. | Siberia | . 1800 |
| lùcidum | . | Purple | . 8, | H. Her. | P. | S. Eur. | . 1730 |
| lusitànicum | . | Purple | . 8, | H. Her. | P. | Portugal | . 1822 |
| Màrum | . | Pa. pur. | . 8, | F. Ev. | S. | Spain | . 1640 |
| massiliénse | . | Purple | . | H. Her. | P. | France | . 1731 |
| montànum, 4 | . | White | . | F. Ev. | S. | S. Eur. | . 1710 |
| multiflòrum | . | Li. red | . 8, | H. Her. | P. | Spain | . 1731 |
| nissoliànum | . | Purple | . 7, | H. Her. | P. | Spain | . 1752 |
| orientàle | . | Blue | . 7, | H. Ev. | S. | Levant | . 1752 |
| Polium | . | Pale | . 8, | H. Ev. | S. | S. Eur. | . 1562 |
| angustifòlium, 5 | . | Purple | . 7, | F. Ev. | S. | Spain | . 1731 |
| flavéscens, 6 | . | Yellow | . 6, | F. Ev. | S. | S. Eur. | . 1731 |
| vulgàre, 7 | . | White | . 6, | F. Ev. | S. | S. Eur. | . 1820 |
| Pseudo-Chamæpitys | . | Purple | . 7, | H. Her. | P. | S. Eur. | . 1820 |
| Pseudo-Scorodònia | . | Yellow | . 7, | H. Her. | P. | N. Africa | . 1818 |
| pùmilum | . | Purple | . 7, | F. Ev. | S. | Spain | . 1816 |
| pycnophýllum | . | Purple | . 7, | H. Her. | P. | Spain | . 1816 |
| pyrenàicum | . | Pa. wht. | . 6, | H. Her. | P. | Pyrenees | . 1731 |
| régium | . | Purple | . 7, | F. Ev. | S. | Spain | . 1699 |
| resupinàtum | . | Pa. yel. | . 7, | H. | A. | Barbary | . 1801 |
| saxàtile | . | Pa. yel. | . 7, | H. Ev. | Tr. | Valentia | . 1820 |
| scordiòides | . | Purple | . 6, | H. Her. | P. | England | . |
| Scórdium | . | Purple | . 7, | H. Aq. | P. | England | . |
| Scorodònia | . | Yellow | . 7, | H. Her. | P. | Britain | . |
| spinòsum | . | White | . 5, | H. | A. | Spain | . 1648 |
| subspinòsum | . | Purple | . | F. Ev. | S. | Minorca | . 1816 |

| | | | | | | | |
|---|---|---|---|---|---|---|---|
| thymifòlium | . . | Reidich. | . 8. | H. Ev. | S. | Spain | . 1816 |
| trifidum | . . | Purple | . 7, | G. Ev. | S. | C. G. H. | . 1791 |
| virgulèum | . . | Blue | . | H. Her. | P. | N. Amer. | . 1768 |

THALAMUS, that part of the flower which rises from below the ovarium, and sometimes supports the outer envelopes as well as the stamens in all the *Thalamiflora*.

THALÎA, *Linn.* In honour of J. Thalius, a German physician, died in 1588. *Linn.* 1, Or. 1, Nat. Or. *Marantaceæ.* Interesting plants, thriving well in a rich, light soil; and increased by division. T. *dealbata* will withstand the severity of our winters, if planted about two feet beneath the surface of the water.

| | | | | | | | |
|---|---|---|---|---|---|---|---|
| dealbàta | . . | Blue | . 7, | F. Aq. | P. | S. Carolina | 1791 |
| geniculàta | . . | Blue | . 8, | S. Her. | P. | W. Ind. | . 1823 |

THALICTRUM, *Linn.* From *thallo*, to grow green; in allusion to the bright colour of the young shoots. *Linn.* 13, Or. 6, Nat. Or. *Ranunculaceæ.* The greater part of the species are hardy herbaceous plants, adapted for the back of flower borders; any light soil suits them, and they are readily increased by division. Synonymes: 1. *Anemone thalictroides.* 2. T. *rugosum.* 3. *T. minus.* 4. *T. corynellum.* 5. T. *revolutum.* 6. *T. ambiguum.* 7. *T. vaginatum.* 8. *T. styloideum.* 9. *T. speciosum.* 10. *T. diffusum.* 11. *T. acuminatum.* 12. *T. discolor.* 13. *T minus.*

| | | | | | | | |
|---|---|---|---|---|---|---|---|
| acutilòbum | . | Pa. yel. | . 6, | H. Her. | P. | Siberia | . 1820 |
| alpìnum | . | Wht. yel. | . 6, | H. Her. | P. | Britain | . |
| anemonòides, 1 | . | | . 4, | H. Tw. | P. | N. Amer. | . 1768 |
| flòre plèno | . | | . 4, | H. Tw. | P. | N. Amer. | . 1768 |
| angustifòlium | . | Pa. yel. | . 6, | H. Her. | P. | Germany | . 1793 |
| appendiculàtum | . | | . | H. Her. | P. | Russia | . 1832 |
| aquilegifòlium | . | Li. pur. | . 6, | H. Her. | P. | Austria | . 1731 |
| atropurpùreum | . | Dk. pur. | . 6, | H. Her. | P. | Austria | . 1731 |
| formòsum | . | Purple | . 6, | H. Her. | P. | S. Eur. | . 1800 |
| calàbricum | . | Yellow | . 7, | H. Her. | P. | Sicily | . 1800 |
| caroliniànum, 2 | . | White | . 6, | H. Her. | P. | N. Amer. | . 1818 |
| Chelidònii | . | Purplish | . 6, | H. Her. | P. | Nepal | . 1823 |
| cinèreum | . | Yellow | . 6, | H. Her. | P. | | . 1810 |
| clavàtum | . | White | . 6, | H. Her. | P. | N. Amer. | . 1790 |
| collìnum, 3 | . | Pa. yel. | . 6, | H. Her. | P. | Europe | . 1800 |
| concinnum | . | Wht. grn. | . 6, | H. Her. | P. | | . |
| contórtum | . | White | . 6, | H. Her. | P. | Siberia | . 1796 |
| Cornùti, 4 | . | Wht. yel. | . 5, | H. Her. | P. | N. Amer. | . 1806 |
| revolùtum, 5 | . | Lgt. yel. | . 6, | H. Her. | P. | N. Amer. | . 1806 |
| crenàtum | . | Yellow | . 7, | H. Her. | P. | Europe | . 1800 |
| cynapifòlium | . | Pur. yel. | . 6, | H. Her. | P. | Siberia | . 1822 |
| diòicum | . | Li. yel. | . 6, | H. Her. | P. | N. Amer. | . 1759 |
| divaricàtum | . | Yelsh. | . 6, | H. Her. | P. | Europe | . 1819 |
| divérgens | . | Yellow | . 6, | H. Her. | P. | Siberia | . 1819 |
| elàtum | . | Li. yel. | . 8, | H. Her. | P. | Hungary | . 1794 |
| ambiguum, 6 | . | Pa. yel. | . 6, | H. Her. | P. | Switzerl. | . 1819 |
| exaltàtum | . | | . | H. Her. | P. | Siberia | . 1832 |
| flàvum | . | Orange | . 6, | H. Her. | P. | Britain | . |
| vaginàtum, 7 | . | Yellow | . 6, | H. Her. | P. | Siberia | . 1810 |
| flexuòsum | . | Yellow | . 6, | H. Her. | P. | Germany | . 1820 |
| fœtidum, 8 | . | Wht. yel. | . 6, | H. Her. | P. | France | . 1640 |
| foliolòsum | . | Purple | . 6, | H. Her. | P. | Nepal | . 1819 |
| galiòides | . | Yellow | . 6, | H. Her. | P. | Alsace | . 1816 |
| glaucéscens | . | Grn. yel. | . 6, | H. Her. | P. | Russia | . 1818 |
| glaùcum, 9 | . | Yellow | . 6, | H. Her. | P. | Spain | . 1796 |
| laserpitiifòlium | . | Yellow | . 6, | H. Her. | P. | Europe | . 1810 |
| lùcidum, 10 | . | Yellow | . 6, | H. Her. | P. | Spain | . 1789 |
| màjus | . | Grn. yel. | . 6, | H. Her. | P. | England | . |
| mèdium, 11 | . | Grn. yel. | . 7, | H. Her. | P. | Hungary | . 1789 |
| mexicànum | . | Green | . 8, | H. Her. | P. | Mexico | . 1826 |
| microcàrpon | . | | . | H. Her. | P. | Russia | . 1832 |
| minus | . | Pa. yel. | . 6, | H. Her. | P. | Britain | . |
| nigricans | . | Grn. yel. | . 6, | H. Her. | P. | Austria | . 1796 |
| nùtans, 12 | . | Grn. yel. | . 6, | H. Her. | P. | Switzerl. | . 1819 |
| oligospèrmum | . | Pur. yel. | . 6, | H. Her. | P. | Siberia | . 1820 |
| petaloìdeum | . | Wht. yel. | . 6, | H. Her. | P. | Dauria | . 1799 |
| polygàmum | . | Wht. pur. | . 6, | H. Her. | P. | Pennsylv. | . 1812 |
| pubéscens | . | Pa. yel. | . 6, | H. Her. | P. | Switzerl. | . 1819 |
| purpuráscens | . | Li. pur. | . 6, | H. Her. | P. | N. Amer. | . 1699 |
| ranunculìnum | . | Pa. yel. | . 6, | H. Her. | P. | N. Amer. | . 1806 |
| répens | . | | . | H. Her. | P. | Russia | . 1832 |
| rosmarinifòlium | . | Pur. yel. | . 6, | H. Her. | P. | S. Eur. | . 1816 |
| rugòsum | . | Wht. yel. | . 7, | H. Her. | P. | N. Amer. | . 1774 |
| discòlor, 13 | . | Yellow | . 6, | H. Her. | P. | N. Amer. | . 1810 |
| sexatile | . | Wht. red. | . 6, | H. Her. | P. | Europe | . 1819 |
| Schweiggèri | . | Yellow | . | H. Her. | P. | | . |
| sibìricum | . | Li. yel. | . 6, | H. Her. | P. | Siberia | . 1775 |
| simplex | . | Li. yel. | . 6, | H. Her. | P. | Sweden | . 1772 |
| squarròsum | . | Yellow | . 6, | H. Her. | P. | Siberia | . 1806 |
| stipulàceum | . | Wht. yel. | . 6, | H. Her. | P. | Europe | . 1820 |
| trigynum | . | Grn. yel. | . 6, | H. Her. | P. | Dahuria | . 1818 |
| tuberòsum | . | Wht. yel. | . 6, | H. Tw. | P. | Spain | . 1713 |

THALLUS, that part which bears the fructification in *Lichens.*

THAMNIDIUM, *Link.* From *thamnos*, a twig; the appearance of the plant when under the microscope.

Linn. 94, Or. 9, Nat. Or. *Fungi*. A minute plant, found on putrid substances—*T. elégáns*.

THAMNOCHŌRTŬS, *Bergius*. From *thamnos*, a shrub, and *chortos*, grass; habit of the plant. *Linn.* 22, Or. 3, Nat. Or. *Restiaceæ*. This species succeeds well in sandy peat; and is readily increased by division. *Synonyme*: 1. *Restio dichotomus*.

| | | | | | | | |
|---|---|---|---|---|---|---|---|
| dichótomŭs, 1 | . | . | Apetal. | . 6, Grass. N. Holl. | . . 1817 |

THĀPSĬÁ, *Tournefort*. So named from the first species being discovered in the Isle of Thapsus. *Linn.* 5, Or. 2, Nat. Or. *Umbelliferæ*. These plants will grow in any common soil. They can only be increased by seeds, which should be sown in autumn, as soon as ripe. *Synonymes*: 1. *Laserpitium gummiferum*. 2. *L. thapsoides*.

| | | | | | | |
|---|---|---|---|---|---|---|
| asclépĭŭm | . . | Yellow | . 7, H. Her. P. Levant | . |
| fœtĭdá | . . | Yellow | . 7, H. Her. P. Spain | . . 1596 |
| gargánĭcá | . . | Li. yel. | . 7, H. Her. P. Barbary | . 1683 |
| gummĭferá, 1 | . | Yellow | . 6, H. Her. P. Spain | . . 1810 |
| Laserpĭtĭ, 2 | . . | Yellow | . 7, H. Her. P. S. Eur. | . 1826 |
| Silphĭŭm | . . | . | . 7, H. Her. P. Africa | . 1824 |
| villósá | . . | Yellow | . 6, H. Her. P. S. Eur. | . 1710 |

THĀPSĬŬM, *Nuttall*. From the Isle of Thapsus, which gave the name to the *Thapsia* of the ancients; in allusion to its affinity with that genus. *Linn.* 5, Or. 2, Nat. Or. *Umbelliferæ*. These plants will grow in any common soil, and are readily increased by divisions or seeds. *Synonymes*: 1. *Ligusticum actæifolium*. 2. *Thapsia trifoliata*.

| | | | | | | |
|---|---|---|---|---|---|---|
| actæifólĭŭm, 1 | . | White | . 6, H. Her. P. Canada | . 1810 |
| barbĭnódá, 2 | . | Yellow | . 6, H. Her. P. Philadel. | . 1700 |

THĒÁ, *Linn*. Derived from *Teha*, the Chinese name for tea. *Linn.* 16, Or. 3, Nat. Or. *Ternströmiaceæ*. For the culture and propagation of these valuable plants, see *Camellia*. They only require to be protected from severe frost. All the different kinds of tea imported into this country from China, are the produce of *T. viridis*, the differences depending entirely upon soil and climate, and the different ages at which their leaves are gathered, and the modes of drying. Tea is said to be the best of all medicines, moderately and properly taken; it is gently astringent; it strengthens the stomach and bowels; and is efficacious against indigestion. It refreshes the spirits in heaviness and sleepiness, and appears to counteract the effects of inebriating liquors. The immoderate use of it is very prejudicial. From Dr. Smith's experiments, it appears that green tea has the power of destroying the sensibility of the nerves and the irritability of the muscles. For a very valuable account of this plant see *Royle's Illustrations of the Himalayan Mountains*, p. 107. *Synonymes*: 1. *T. chinensis Bohea*. 2. *T. chinensis viridis*.

| | | | | | | |
|---|---|---|---|---|---|---|
| Bohea, 1 | . . | White | . 10, G. Ev. S. China | . . 1768 |
| latĭfólĭs | . . | White | . all G. Ev. S. China | . . 1825 |
| viridĭs, 2 | . . | White | . 6, G. Ev. S. China | . . 1768 |

THĒCÆ, the cases that contain the sporules of cryptogamic plants.

THĒCÁPHORÆ, an elongated receptacle, which bears one ovary only, but not the petals, nor stamens.

THĒBEAN TEA, see RHĀMNŬs Theēzáns.

THĒLĒBÓLŬs, *Tode*. From *thele*, a nipple, and *boleo*, to eject. *Linn.* 24, Or. 9, Nat. Or. *Fungi*. This species is found on cow-dung, after rain, in June and July—*T. stercóréŭs*.

THĒLĒPHORÁ, *Ehrhart*. From *thele*, a nipple, and *phoreo*, to bear; in allusion to the papillose surface of all the species. *Linn.* 24, Or. 9, Nat. Or. *Fungi*. The species of *Thelephora* are common upon old roots and branches of trees. *Synonymes*: 1. *Himantia candida*. 2. *Auricularia nicotiana*—*T. acerĭná, Avellāná, biénnĭs, byssŏídés, cálcĕá, carbonárĭá, caryophyllĕá, cinérĕá, comēdéns, cŏrĭŭm, corglēá, doméstĭcá, elĕgáns, epidérmĕá, fraxĭnĕá, fúscá, gigántĕá, granŭlósá, hepátĭcá, hirsútá, incarnátá, incrŭstáns, intybácĕá, lacinĭátá, láctĕá* 1, *lactéscéns, Laŭró cérásĭ, lĭvĭdá, minĭátá, nŭdá, ochrácĕá, ochrŏlĕŭcá, Pádĭ, pannósá, purpúrĕá, putĕáná, quercĭná, radĭátá, R. rimósá, rŏsĕá, rubĭgĭnósá, Sambúcĭ, sanguĭnolēntá, sinŭáns, spadícĕá, tabacĭná* 2, *terréstrĭs, Tílĭæ, viscósá*.

THĒLOTRĒMÁ, *Acharius*. From *thele*, a nipple, and *trema*, orifice; the protuberances of the thallus are perforated. *Linn.* 24, Or. 8, Nat. Or. *Lichenes*. These plants are found on the bark of trees—*T. exanthemátĭcŭm, Hutchĭnsĭá, hyménĭŭm, lepadĭnŭm, melalĕŭcŭm, variclarĭŏĭdés, V. agélĕŭm*.

THĒLYGŎNŬM, from *thelys*, woman, and *gonu*, a knee; supposed resemblance in the joints. *Linn.* 21, Or. 9, Nat. Or. *Chenopodiaceæ*. Common garden soil suits this species; seeds—*T. cynocrámbé*.

THĒLYMĬTRÁ. Forster, who named the genus, is said to have derived it from *thelis*, a woman, and *mitra*, a cap. *Linn.* 20, Or. 1, Nat. Or. *Orchidaceæ*. This is a tuberous-rooted genus requiring precisely the same treatment as *Disa*.

| | | | | | | |
|---|---|---|---|---|---|---|
| angustifólĭá | . . | Blue | . 4, G. Ter. N. Holl. | . 1825 |
| cárnĕá | . . | Flesh | . 5, G. Ter. N. Holl. | . 1820 |
| Forstérĭ | . . | . | . 5, G. Ter. N. Zeal. | . 1824 |
| ixĭŏídés | . . | Blue | . 5, G. Ter. N. Holl. | . 1810 |
| longĭfólĭá | . . | . | . 5, G. Ter. V. D. L. | . 1824 |
| medĭá | . . | Blue | . 5, G. Ter. N. Holl. | . 1820 |
| paucĭflórá | . . | Blue | . 6, G. Ter. N. Holl. | . 1820 |
| venósá | . . | Blue | . 4, G. Ter. N. Holl. | . 1826 |
| villósá | | | | | |

THĒNĀRDĬÁ. Kunth named this genus in honour of his friend, L. J. Thenard, a Frenchman, who has written on the chemical physiology of plants. *Linn.* 5, Or. 1, Nat. Or. *Apocynaceæ*. An interesting plant. For culture and propagation, see *Echites*.

| | | | | | | |
|---|---|---|---|---|---|---|
| floribúndá | . . | Blue | . 8, Ev. Tw. Mexico. | . 1823 |

THĒOBRŌMA, *Linn*. From *theos*, god, and *broma*, food; celestial food. *Linn.* 18, Or. 1, Nat. Or. *Sterculiaceæ*. The species of *Theobroma* or Chocolate-nut grow well in a mixture of loam and peat; and cuttings root readily in sand, under a glass, in heat. Seeds do not retain their vegetative power for a great length of time. The seeds of *T. Cacao* furnish the chocolate of the shops. The seeds are very nourishing and agreeable to most people, and are, therefore, kept in the majority of the houses in America as a necessary part of the provisions of the family.

| | | | | | | |
|---|---|---|---|---|---|---|
| bicólŏr | . . | Brown | . 8, Ev. T. N. Gran. | . 1820 |
| Cacáŏ | . . | Brown | . 8, Ev. T. S. Amer. | . 1739 |
| guianénsĭs | . . | Yellow | . 8, Ev. T. Guiana | . 1803 |

THĒOPHRĀSTÁ, *Linn*. Named after *Theophrastus*, the father of natural history. *Linn.* 5, Or. 1, Nat. Or. *Myrsinaceæ*. A small, handsome tree, with a tuft of long, evergreen branches at the top of its simple stem, something like a palm-tree. It is well worth cultivating, on account of its long, holly-like leaves. A mixture of peat, loam, and sand, suits it best; and cuttings, with the leaves entire, root readily in sand, under a glass, in heat. Bread is said to be prepared from the pounded seeds of this tree in St. Domingo, where it is called *Le Petit Coco*.

| | | | | | | |
|---|---|---|---|---|---|---|
| Jussiéŭĭ | . . . | White | . . 8, Ev. T. St. Domingo 1818 |

THĒRMŌPSĬÁ, *R. Brown*. From *thermos*, a lupine, and *opsis*, resemblance; because of the resemblance of the species to lupines. *Linn.* 10, Or. 1, Nat. Or. *Leguminosæ*. The species of *Thermopsis* are very elegant, but rather difficult to preserve. They succeed best in a light, rich soil; and the safest way of increasing them is by seed; for when the plants are separated at the roots they are very liable to suffer. *Synonymes*: 1. *Podalyria alpina, Sophora alpina*. 2. *S. fabacea, T. rhombifolia*. 3. *T. Lupinoides, P. lupinoides*.

| | | | | | | |
|---|---|---|---|---|---|---|
| corgonénsĭs, 1 | . | Yellow | . 7, H. Her. P. Altaia | . 1820 |
| fabácĕá, 2 | . . | Yellow | . 6, F. Her. P. N. Amer. | . 1811 |
| lanceolátá, 3 | . | Yellow | . 6, H. Her. P. Siberia | . 1779 |

THĒSĬŬM, *Linn*. From *thes*, a labouring servant; mean appearance of the plants. *Linn.* 5, Or. 1, Nat. Or. *Santalaceæ*. The herbaceous species grow best when planted in a chalky soil, and are increased by division or seeds. *T. amplexicaule* succeeds well in loam and peat, and is readily increased by cuttings, in sand, under a glass. *Synonyme*: 1. *T. humifusum*.

| | | | | | | |
|---|---|---|---|---|---|---|
| alpĭnŭm, 1 | . . | White | . 6, H. Her. P. Germany | . 1814 |
| amplexĭcaŭlĕ | . . | White | . G. Ev. S. C. G. H. | . 1787 |
| ebracteátŭm | . . | White | . 6, H. Her. P. Germany | . 1814 |
| intermedĭŭm | . . | White | . 6, H. Her. P. Germany | . 1818 |
| linophyllŭm | . . | White | . 6, H. Her. P. England | . |
| montánŭm | . . | White | . 6, H. Her. P. Europe | . 1817 |

THĒSPĒSĬÁ, *Correa de Serra*. Within the tropics *T. populnea* is usually planted about churches; whence the name from *thespesios*, divine. *Linn.* 16, Or. 8, Nat. Or. *Malvaceæ*. Ornamental trees, succeeding well in sandy loam; and cuttings of the half-ripened wood will root in sand, under a glass, in heat. *Synonyme*: 1. *Hibiscus populneus*.

| | | | | | | |
|---|---|---|---|---|---|---|
| grandĭflórá | . . | Scarlet | . 8. Ev. T. Pt. Rico | . 1827 |
| populnéá, 1 | . . | White | . 8. Ev. T. E. Ind. | . 1770 |
| guadalupénsĭs | . | | . 8. Ev. T. Guadal. | |

THIBAUDIA, *Pavon.* In honour of Thiebaut de Berneaud, secretary of the Linnæan Society of Paris, and a botanical writer. *Linn.* 10, Or. 1, Nat. Or. *Vaccinaceæ.* This is a genus of extremely elegant plants, well deserving the gardener's care. They grow freely in a mixture of turfy loam, peat, and sand; and cuttings root readily in sand or soil, either with or without a glass over them. *Synonymes*: 1. *Agapetes setigera.* 2. *A. variegata.*

| | | | | | |
|---|---|---|---|---|---|
| macrophylla | . | White. | . 8. Ev. 8. E. Ind. | |
| setigera, 1 | . | Scarlet | . 8. Ev. 8. Khossæa. | 1837 |
| vaccinacea | . | . | . 8. Ev. 8. Khossæa. | 1837 |
| variegata, 2 | . | Scarlet | . 8. Ev. 8. Khossæa. | 1837 |

THISTLE, see *Cárdüüs.*

THLASPI, *Dillenius.* From *thlao*, to compress; the seed-vessels are compressed. *Linn.* 15, Nat. Or. *Cruciferæ.* Not worth cultivating; increased by seed — *T. alliáceüm, alpéstré, arvénsé, ceratocárpüm, collínüm, latifólіüm, montánüm, perfoliátüm, umbellátüm.*

THOMASIA, *Gay.* In memory of Peter and Abraham Thomas, collectors of Swiss plants in the time of Haller. *Linn.* 5, Or. 1, Nat. Or. *Sterculiaceæ.* A genus of very elegant plants, well worth cultivating in every collection. They thrive well in a mixture of loam, peat, and sand; and cuttings of the ripened wood root freely in sand, under a glass. *Synonymes*: 1. *Lasiopetalum purpureum.* 2. *L. triphyllum.*

| | | | | |
|---|---|---|---|---|
| dumosa | . | White. | . 5. G. Ev. 8. N. Holl. | 1826 |
| foliósa | . | Apetal | . 6. G. Ev. 8. N. Holl. | 1823 |
| purpúrea, 1 | . | Purple | . 6. G. Ev. 8. N. Holl. | 1803 |
| quercifolia | . | Purple | . 5. G. Ev. 8. N. Holl. | 1803 |
| solanácea | . | White. | . 6. G. Ev. 8. N. Holl. | 1803 |
| triphylla, 2 | . | Apetal | . 6. G. Ev. 8. N. Holl. | 1824 |

THORN APPLE, see *Datürä.*
THOROUGH WAX, see *Bupleürum rotundifolіüm.*
THOUINIA, *Poiteau.* In honour of André Thouin, a distinguished professor of Agriculture in the Jardin des Plantes of Paris; died in 1830. *Linn.* 8, Or. 1, Nat. Or. *Sapindaceæ.* This shrub grows well in a mixture of sandy loam and peat; and cuttings of the ripened wood will root in sand, under a glass, in heat.

| | | | |
|---|---|---|---|
| pinnáta | . . . White . | . 8. Ev. 8. N. Spain | . 1823 |

THREADS, long hairs like threads.
THRIFT, see *Státícé.*
THRINAX, *Linn.* From *thrinax*, a fan; form of the leaves. *Linn.* 6, Or. 1, Nat. Or. *Palmaceæ.* This species succeeds in turfy loam, and is increased by seeds.

| | | | |
|---|---|---|---|
| parviflóra | . . . Wht. grn. | . Palm. Jamaica | . . 1778 |

THRINCIA, *Roth.* From *thrigkos*, battlement; the seed crown of the marginal florets. *Linn.* 19, Or. 1, Nat. Or. *Compositæ.* Uninteresting plants, succeeding in common garden soil; and increased by seeds. *Synonymes*: 1. *Hyoseris hispida.* 2. *Apargia tuberosa, Leontodon tuberosus, Thrincia pruinosa — T. hirta, hispida, maroccana* 1, *tuberosa* 2.
THROAT, the orifice of a flower.
THROATWORT, see *Campánülä Cervicária.*
THROATWORT, see *Campánülä Trachelіüm.*
THROATWORT, see *Trachelіüm.*
THRYALLIS, *Linn.* A name given by the Greeks to *Verbascum*, which is derived from *thrauo*, to break: however, the present plant has nothing to do with the plant of the Greeks, except in having yellow flowers. *Linn.* 10, Or. 3, Nat. Or. *Malpighiaceæ.* This plant succeeds in a mixture of loam and peat; and ripened cuttings root in sand, under a glass, in heat.

| | | | |
|---|---|---|---|
| brachystáchys | . . Yellow | . 8. S. Ev. Cl. Rio Jan. | . 1823 |

THUJA, *Linn.* From *thyon*, a sacrifice; the resin of the Eastern variety is used instead of incense at sacrifices. Why it is called *Arbor Vitæ* is not known, unless it be on account of the supposed medicinal qualities of its berries. In the East, the cypress is called the tree of life; and its berries are considered a cure for all diseases. *Linn.* 21, Or. 10, Nat. Or. *Coniferæ.* In Britain the species of *Arbor Vitæ* can only be considered as ornamental, low shrubs or trees, well deserving of being cultivated, especially *T. pendula* ; which, on account of its very graceful, long, slender, pendulous shoots, ought to be in every collection. The American and European kinds succeed well in any soil or situation, but prefer low, sheltered, and swampy places. The

more tender species, natives of China, require, when young, the protection of the greenhouse. They are all readily increased by seeds, either imported from the places of their natural growth, or gathered from the trees in this country; some of the rarer kinds, as *T. pendula*, are propagated by cuttings. *Synonymes*: 1. *T. pyramidalis.* 2. *T. tatarica.*

| | | | | | |
|---|---|---|---|---|---|
| articulata | . . | Apetal | . 8. F. Ev. T. Barbary | . 1815 |
| australis | . . | Apetal | . 5, H. Ev. T. 8. Eur. | . 1820 |
| cupressoídes | . | Apetal | . G. Ev. T. C. G. H. | . 1799 |
| nepalénsis | . | Apetal | . 5, H. Ev. T. Nepal | . 1824 |
| occidentális | . | Apetal | . 5, H. Ev. T. N. Amer. | . 1596 |
| variegáta | . | Apetal | . 5, H. Ev. T. | |
| orientális | . | Apetal | . 5, H. Ev. T. China | . 1752 |
| strícta, 1 | . | Apetal | . 5, H. Ev. T. Italy | . 1824 |
| tatárica, 2 | . | Apetal | . 5, H. Ev. T. Tartary | . 1820 |
| péndula | . | Apetal | . 5, H. Ev. T. Tartary | . 1823 |
| plicáta | . | Apetal | . 5, H. Ev. T. Nootka S. | . 1796 |

THUNBERGIA, *Linn.* In honour of Charles P. Thunberg, F.R.S., a celebrated traveller and botanist. *Linn.* 14, Or. 2, Nat. Or. *Acanthaceæ.* A genus of extremely pretty plants when in blossom. They succeed best in a mixture of sandy loam and leaf mould, and are readily increased by cuttings or seeds.

| | | | | |
|---|---|---|---|---|
| aláta | . . | Yellow | . 6, S. Ev. Cl. E. Ind. | . 1823 |
| álba | . . | White . | . 5, S. Ev. Cl. Madagas. | |
| anguláta | . . | . | . 6, S. Ev. Cl. Madagas. | . 1823 |
| aurantíáca | . . | Orange | . 8, G. Her. P. C. G. H. | |
| capénsis | . . | Yellow | . 6, S. Ev. Cl. Nepal . | . 1824 |
| coccínéa | . | Scarlet | . 6, S. Ev. Cl. Trinidad | . 1823 |
| cordáta | . . | White . | . 7, S. Ev. Cl. E. Ind. | . 1820 |
| frágrans | . | White . | . 6, S. Ev. Cl. E. Ind. | . 1796 |
| grandiflóra | . | Blue . | . 6, S. Ev. Cl. E. Ind. | . 1820 |
| Hawtayneána | . | Scarlet | . 6, S. Ev. Cl. Nepal . | . 1826 |

THYMBRA, *Linn.* *Thymbra* is the Greek name of a sweet-scented herb. *Linn.* 14, Or. 1, Nat. Or. *Labiatæ.* This plant is well adapted for rock-work, or growing in pots among alpine plants. A gravelly soil suits it best, and it is readily increased by young cuttings or seeds. *Synonyme*: 1. *T. verticillata.*

| | | | | |
|---|---|---|---|---|
| spicáta, 1 | . . . Pa. pur. | . 6, F. Ev. S. Levant | . . 1699 |

THYME, see *Thýmüs.*
THYMUS, *Linn.* From *thumos*, courage, strength, the smell of thyme being reviving; or from *thuo*, to perfume, being formerly used for incense in the temples. *Linn.* 14, Or. 1, Nat. Or. *Labiatæ.* Well known under-shrubs or herbs, preferring an exposed situation, and a dry, light, sandy soil. They are of very easy culture, and may be increased with facility either by divisions, slips, cuttings, or by seeds sown in March or April. Some of the rarer species may be grown in pots among alpine plants, and protected in winter. The different purposes to which Thyme is applied are so well known, as not to require any notice here. *Synonymes*: 1. *T. acicularis, odoratissimus, Zygis.* 2. *T. creticus, marinosci, Satureia capitata.* 3. *Thymbra ciliata.* 4. *Thymus Marschallianus.* 5. *T. exscrens.* 6. *T. citriodorus.* 7. *T. lanuginosus.* 8. *T. montanus, nummularius.* 9. *T. collinus.*

| | | | | |
|---|---|---|---|---|
| angustifóliüs, 1 | Purple | . 8, H. Ev. T. S. Eur. | . 1771 |
| azoricüs | . | . | . 6, H. Ev. Tr. Azores | . 1820 |
| azúréüs | . | Purple | . 6, H. Ev. 8. Eur. | . 1830 |
| capitátüs, 2 | . | Purple | . 6, H. Ev. 8. S. Eur. | . 1596 |
| cephalótés | . | Purple | . 7, F. Ev. S. Portugal | . 1759 |
| ciliátüs, 3 | . | Violet . | . 7, F. Ev. S. N. Afric. | . 1824 |
| córsicüs | . | Lilac sm. | . H. Her. P. Corsica | . 1831 |
| croáticüs | . | Purple | . 7, H. Ev. 8. Hungary | . 1802 |
| elongátüs | . | Purple | . 8, H. Ev. 8. | . 1816 |
| ericæfólіüs | . | Purple | . 7, H. Ev. 8. Spain | . 1806 |
| fruticulósüs | . | Purple | . 7, H. Ev. 8. Sicily | . 1822 |
| glabrátüs | . | Purple | . 7, H. Ev. 8. S. Eur. | . 1823 |
| hirsútüs | . | Purple | . 7, H. Ev. 8. Spain | . 1821 |
| lanceolátüs | . | Purple | . 7, H. Ev. 8. N. Afric. | . 1823 |
| pannónicüs, 4 | . | Purple | . 7, H. Ev. Tr. Crimea | . 1817 |
| Piperélla | . | Purple | . 7, F. Ev. 8. Spain | . 1810 |
| Serpyllüm, 5 | . | Purple | . 7, H. Ev. Tr. Britain | . |
| albüs | . | White | . 7, H. Ev. Tr. | . |
| citrátüs, 6 | . | Purple | . 7, H. Ev. Tr. | |
| lanuginósüs, 7 | Purple | . 7, H. Ev. Tr. Britain | . |
| montánüs, 8 | . | Striped | . 6, H. Ev. Tr. Hungary | . 1806 |
| variegátüs | . | Purple | . 7, H. Ev. Tr. Britain | . |
| vulgáris, 9 | . | Purple | . 7, H. Ev. Tr. Tauria | . 1820 |
| spicátüs | . | Purple ant | . F. Ev. 8. Pyren. | . 1832 |
| vulgáris | . | Purple | . 6, H. Ev. 8. 8. Eur. | . 1548 |
| latifólіüs | . | Purple | . 6, H. Ev. 8. | |
| variegátüs | . | Purple | . 7, H. Ev. Tr. Britain | . |

THYMUS, see *Zizíphórä.*
THYMUS, see *Satureíä.*

**THYRSE**, a kind of dense panicle.

**THYSANŌTŪS**, *R. Brown.* The three inner sepals are fringed; whence the name, from *thysanotos*, fringed. *Linn.* 6, Or. 1, Nat. Or. *Liliaceæ.* A genus of very elegant plants when in flower. They succeed well in sandy loam, and are readily increased by offsets.

| | | | | | | |
|---|---|---|---|---|---|---|
| elatiŏr | . | Purple | . 8, | G. Tu. | Per. | N. Holl. | 1823 |
| intricātūs | . | Purple | . 7, | G. Her. | P. | Swan R. | 1838 |
| isanthērūs | . | Purple | . 8, | G. Tu. | P. | N. S. W. | 1822 |
| jūncēūs | . | Purple | . 8, | G. Her. | P. | N. S. W. | 1804 |
| prolifĕrūs | . | Purple | . 8, | G. Her. | P. | N. S. W. | |
| tĕnūis . | . | Lilac | . 6, | F. Her. | P. | Swan R. | 1836 |
| tuberŏsūs | . | Purple | . 6, | G. Tu. | P. | N. Holl. | 1825 |

**THYSSELINUM**, see *Selinum*.

**TIARĒLLA**, *Linn.* From *tiara*, a Persian diadem; on account of the shape of the capsules. *Linn.* 10, Or. 2, Nat. Or. *Saxifragaceæ.* The species of *Tiarella* are well fitted for rock-work, or the front of flower borders; they are increased by division of the root.

| | | | | | | |
|---|---|---|---|---|---|---|
| colŏrāns | . | White | . 6, | H. Her. | P. | N. Amer. | 1827 |
| cordifōlīa | . | White | . 4, | H. Her. | P. | N. Amer. | 1731 |
| Mensiēsīi | . | White | . 4, | H. Her. | P. | N. Amer. | 1812 |
| polyphȳllā | . | White | . 4, | H. Her. | P. | Nepal | 1820 |

**TIARIDIŬM**, *Lehmann.* From *tiara*, a Persian diadem, and *eidos*, like; form of the capsule. *Linn.* 5, Or. 1, Nat. Or. *Ehretiaceæ.* Half-hardy annuals, of common culture. *Synonyme:* 1. *Heliotropium indicum.*

| | | | | | | |
|---|---|---|---|---|---|---|
| indicŭm, 1 | . | Blue | . 6, | H. | A. | W. Ind. | 1820 |
| velutinŭm | . | Blue | . 6, | H. | A. | W. Ind. | 1820 |

**TICK SEED**, see *Coriespermum*.

**TIGER FLOWER**, see *Tigridiā*.

**TIGRIDĪA**, *Jussieu.* From *Tigris*, a tiger, and *eidos*, like; in reference to the spotted flowers. *Linn.* 16, Or. 1, Nat. Or. *Iridaceæ.* Splendid bulbs when in blossom. They thrive in a rich, light soil in the open border, but must be taken up when the flowers have withered or the frost will injure them. They should be kept in a dry place, free from frost, until the spring, when they may again be planted out; increased by offsets or seeds. *Synonyme:* 1. *Ferraria Tigridia, pavonia.*

| | | | | | | |
|---|---|---|---|---|---|---|
| conchiflŏrā | . | Dk. yel. | . 6, | H. Bl. | P. | Mexico | 1823 |
| pavōnīa, 1 | . | Or. red | . 6, | H. Bl. | P. | Mexico | 1796 |
| leōnā | . | Or. red | . 6, | H. Bl. | P. | Mexico | 1823 |

**TILE ROOT**, see *Geissorhīzā*.

**TILĪA**, *Linn.* The etymology of this word is entirely unknown; in Dutch it is called *Linden*, in Anglo-Saxon *Lind*, and in English *Lime-tree*. *Linn.* 13, Or. 1, Nat. Or. *Tiliaceæ.* Ornamental, lofty-growing trees, well suited for avenues and parks. They thrive well in any soil, and are increased by layers or seeds: if by layers, the tree may be cut down close to the ground, and from its roots a great number of shoots are produced, in the following year; these will be strong enough to lay down the following autumn. Trees raised from seed are far preferable to those raised from layers. The Russian bass-mats are made from the inner bark of the lime-tree; while the wood, from its being light and white, is much used by the carver, and musical instrument-maker. *Synonymes:* 1. *T. argentea.* 2. *T. glabra, canadensis.* 3. *T. heterophylla.* 4. *T. laxiflora.* 5. *T. pubescens.* 6. *T. pub. leptophylla.* 7. *T. intermedia.* 8. *T. platyphylla laciniata.* 9. *T. microphylla.* 10. *T. platyphylla.* 11. *T. rubra.*

| | | | | | | |
|---|---|---|---|---|---|---|
| albā, 1 | . | Yel. grn. | 7, | H. De. | T. | Hungary | 1767 |
| americānā, 2 | . | Yel. grn. | 6, | H. De. | T. | N. Amer. | 1752 |
| heterophȳllā, 3 | . | Yel. grn. | 7, | H. De. | T. | N. Amer. | 1811 |
| laxiflŏrā, 4 | . | White | . 6, | H. De. | T. | N. Amer. | 1820 |
| pubescēns, 5 | . | Yel. grn. | 7, | H. De. | T. | N. Amer. | 1726 |
| pub. leptophȳllā, 6 | Yellow | 7, | H. De. | T. | N. Amer. | |
| europǣā, 7 | . | Yel. grn. | 7, | H. De. | T. | Britain | |
| aūrēā | . | Yel. grn. | 8, | H. De. | T. | Britain | |
| dasystȳlā | . | Yel. grn. | 7, | H. De. | T. | Tauria | |
| laciniātā, 8 | . | Yel. grn. | 7, | H. De. | T. | Britain | |
| microphȳllā, 9 | . | Yel. grn. | 8, | H. De. | T. | Britain | |
| platyphȳllā, 10 | . | Yel. grn. | 8, | H. De. | T. | Britain | |
| platyph. aūrēā | . | Yel. grn. | 8, | H. De. | T. | Britain | |
| rūbrā, 11 | . | Yel. grn. | 8, | H. De. | T. | Britain | |

**TILIACŌRĀ**, *Colebrook.* Tiliakora is its name in Bengal. *Linn.* 22, Or. 6, Nat. Or. *Menispermaceæ.* This species succeeds well in a mixture of sandy loam and peat; and cuttings root readily in sand, under a glass, in heat. *Synonyme:* 1. *Menispermum polycarpon.*

| | | | | | | |
|---|---|---|---|---|---|---|
| racemōsā, 1 | . | Yellow | . | S. Ev. Cl. | E. Ind. | . | 1820 |

**TILLǢA**, *Linn.* In honour of M. A. Tilli, an Italian botanist. *Linn.* 4, Or. 3, Nat. Or. *Crassulaceæ.* The seeds of these plants have only to be sown in the open ground.

| | | | | | |
|---|---|---|---|---|---|
| aquaticā | . | Pur. red | . 7, | H. | A. S. Eur. | . 1816 |
| muscōsā | . | Purple | . 7, | H. | A. England | . |

**TILLANDSĪA**, *Linn.* In honour of Elias Tillands, professor of Physic at Abo. *Linn.* 6, Or. 1, Nat. Or. *Bromeliaceæ.* These interesting plants being epiphytal, will succeed well in baskets filled with moss, cut small, and mingled with broken pots; or they may be fastened to pieces of wood, with moss round their roots, and supplied regularly with water. The larger growing species may be treated like the *Pitcairniæ* and *Bromelia.* Increased by suckers, or by seeds.

| | | | | | |
|---|---|---|---|---|---|
| acaūlīs | . | White | . 8, | Epiphy. | R. Jan. | 1826 |
| aloifōlīā | . | Pink | . 11, | Epiphy. | Trinidad | 1824 |
| ancĕps | . | Blue | . 4, | Epiphy. | W. Ind. | 1820 |
| angustifōlīā | . | Blue | . 8, | Epiphy. | W. Ind. | 1822 |
| Bartrāmī | . | Blue | . 4, | Epiphy. | Carolina | 1825 |
| bracteātā | . | | . 8, | Epiphy. | W. Ind. | 1824 |
| bulbōsā | . | Blue | . 11, | Epiphy. | Trinidad | 1823 |
| canēscēns | . | Blue | . 6, | Epiphy. | W. Ind. | 1824 |
| coarctātā | . | | . 6, | Epiphy. | Chile | 1823 |
| comprēssā | . | | . 6, | Epiphy. | Chile | 1823 |
| fasciculātā | . | Blue | . 6, | Epiphy. | W. Ind. | 1820 |
| flexuōsā | . | Blue | . 6, | Epiphy. | W. Ind. | 1790 |
| pallidā | . | Yellow | . 6, | Epiphy. | W. Ind. | 1815 |
| gracīlīs | . | | . 6, | Epiphy. | Chile | 1822 |
| nitidā | . | Blue | . 10, | Epiphy. | Jamaica | 1823 |
| nūtāns | . | Blue | . 6, | Epiphy. | Jamaica | 1793 |
| obacūrā | . | | . 7, | Epiphy. | S. Amer. | 1820 |
| paniculātā | . | Blue | . 6, | Epiphy. | W. Ind. | 1820 |
| polystāchyā | . | | . 6, | Epiphy. | S. Amer. | 1825 |
| psittacinā | . | Scarlet | . 7, | Epiphy. | Rio Jan. | 1826 |
| pulchrā | . | Pink | . 10, | Epiphy. | Trinidad | 1823 |
| ramōsā | . | | . 6, | Epiphy. | Chile | 1822 |
| recurvātā | . | Purple | . 7, | Epiphy. | Jamaica | 1793 |
| rigidā | . | | . 6, | Epiphy. | Chile | 1823 |
| rŏsēā | . | Pink | . | Epiphy. | Brasil | |
| serrātā | . | Yellow | . 6, | Epiphy. | Jamaica | 1793 |
| setācēā | . | Blue | . 6, | Epiphy. | W. Ind. | 1824 |
| strictā | . | Blue | . 9, | Epiphy. | Brasil | 1810 |
| tenuifōlīā | . | Blue | . 6, | Epiphy. | W. Ind. | 1825 |
| usneoïdēs | . | Purple | . 7, | Epiphy. | W. Ind. | 1823 |
| utriculātā | . | Pur. yel. | . | Epiphy. | S. Amer. | 1793 |
| xiphioïdēs | . | White | . 7, | Epiphy. | B. Ayres | 1810 |

**TIMMĪA**, *Hedwig.* In honour of J. C. Timm, a German botanist. *Linn.* 24, Or. 5, Nat. Or. *Musci.* This plant is found in broad patches, in moist sandy plains—*T. megapolitānd.*

**TISSUE** is the elementary organization of a plant; it consists of a delicate transparent membrane formed into cells, tubes, vessels, &c.

**TITHŌNĪA**, *Desfontaines.* From *Tithonus*, the favourite of Aurora; the flower is *couleur d'aurore.* *Linn.* 19, Or. 3, Nat. Or. *Compositæ.* This plant succeeds well in light rich soil, and is readily increased by cuttings, in sand, under a glass, in heat.

| | | | | | |
|---|---|---|---|---|---|
| tagetiflŏrā | . | Orange | . 8, | T. Ev. | S. V. Cruz | . 1818 |

**TITTMANNIA**, see *Vandellīā*.

**TOAD FLAX**, see *Linārīā*.

**TOBACCO**, see *Nicotiānā*.

**TOCŌCĀ**, *Aublet.* Tococo is the name of *T. guianensis* in Guiana. *Linn.* 10, Or. 1, Nat. Or. *Melastomaceæ.* The species of *Tococa* are remarkable for bearing bladders on their petioles. For culture and propagation, see *Melastoma.* *Synonymes:* 1. *T. Aubletii, Melastoma physiphora.* 2. *M. lanata.*

| | | | | | |
|---|---|---|---|---|---|
| guianénsīs, 1 | . | Pa. red | . 8, | S. Ev. | S. Guiana | 1826 |
| lanātā, 2 | . | White | . 8, | S. Ev. | S. Trinidad | 1817 |

**TOCOYENĀ**, *Aublet.* Tocoyena is its name in Guiana. *Linn.* 5, Or. 1, Nat. Or. *Cinchonaceæ.* This species succeeds well in sandy peat, mixed with a little loam; it is increased by cuttings of the young wood, in sand, under a glass, in heat. *Synonyme:* 1. *Meriana speciosa.*

| | | | | | |
|---|---|---|---|---|---|
| longiflŏrā, 1 | . | Yellow | . 8, | S. Ev. | S. Guiana | . 1826 |

**TODDALĪA**, *Jussieu.* From *Kaka-Toddali*, the name of *T. aculeata* in Malabar. *Linn.* 21, Or. 5, Nat. Or. *Xanthoxylaceæ.* Interesting shrubs, succeeding best in a mixture of loam, peat, and sand; and cuttings planted in sand will root readily, if placed under a glass, in heat. The bark of the root of *T. aculeata* is said to be employed as a cure for the remittent fevers caught in the jungles of the Indian hills. *Synonymes:* 1. *Scopolia aculeata, Paullinia asiatica.* 2. *Rubentia angustifolia.*

aculeātă, 1 . . . White . . S. Ev. S. E. Ind. . . 1790
angustifōliă, 2 . White . . S. Ev. S. Maurit. . 1824

TODDĂLIĂ, see *Vĕpris.*

TŌDĔĂ, *Swartz.* In honour of Henry Julius Tode, of Mecklenburg, an able and experienced mycologist. *Linn.* 24, Or. 1, Nat. Or. *Osmundaceæ.* Interesting Ferns, growing freely in loam and peat; and increased by division or seeds. *Synonyme:* 1. *Osmunda barbara.*

africānă, 1 . . . Brown . 6, G. Her. P. C. G. H. . 1805
australis . . . Brown . all, G. Her. P. N. Holl. . 1831

TOFIĔLDIĂ, *Hudson* named this genus in compliment to his friend Mr. Tofield. *Linn.* 6, Or. 3, Nat. Or. *Melanthaceæ.* Loam and peat, or any light soil, and a moist situation, suit the species of *Tofieldia.* They are increased by division of the roots. *Synonyme:* 1. *T. palustris.*

alpīnă, 1 . . . Green . . 7, H. Her. P. N. Eur.
glutinōsă . . . White . . H. Her. P. N. Amer. . 1825
palūstris . . . Green . . 7, H. Her. P. Britain .
pubēscens . . . White . . 4, H. Her. P. N. Amer. . 1790
stenopetălă . . Green . . 5, H. Her. P. N. Amer. . 1820

TŎLPĬS, *Adanson.* Meaning not known. *Linn.* 19, Or. 1, Nat. Or. *Compositæ.* A genus of very pretty annuals, well suited for ornamenting flower borders, where the seeds may be sown in spring. *Synonymes:* 1. *Crepis barbata.* 2. *C. coronopifolia.*

altissimă . . . Yellow . 6, H. . . A. Piedmont 1823
barbātă, 1 . . . Yel. pur. 6, H. . . A. France . 1620
coronopifōliă, 2 . Yellow . 6, H. . . A. S. Eur. . 1777
umbellātă . . . Yel. pur. H. . . A. Genoa . 1820
virgātă . . . . Yellow . H. . . A. S. Eur. . 1800

TOMENTOSE, covered with dense white down.

TOMENTUM, dense, close, white hairs, or down.

TONIC, bracing, corroborative.

TONQUIN BEAN, see *Diptĕrix.*

TONSĬLLĂ, see *Salĭcĭd.*

TOOTHACHE-TREE, see *Xanthŏxўlŭm.*

TOOTHED, divided, so as to resemble teeth.

TOOTHLETTED, furnished with little teeth.

TOOTHWORT, see *Lathræ̆ă.*

TOPICAL, local, confined to some particular place.

TORDŸLIŬM, *Tournefort.* An ancient Greek name, of unknown meaning. *Linn.* 5, Or. 2, Nat. Or. *Umbelliferæ.* Uninteresting annuals. The seeds should be sown in the open border—*T. lusitănicŭm, maximŭm, peregrīnŭm, siĭ ŏllăm, syriăcŭm.*

TORĔNIĂ, *Linn.* In honour of Olof Toren, a Swedish clergyman, who discovered *T. asiatica,* and other plants in China. *Linn.* 14, Or. 2, Nat. Or. *Scrophulariaceæ.* For culture, &c., see *Herpestis.*

scābră . . . . Pa. blue . 6, G. Ev. S. Moreton B. 1830

*asiătĭcă, cordifōlĭă.*

TORĔNĬĂ, see *Vandĕlliă.*

TŎRĬLĬS, *Sprengel.* Not explained. *Linn.* 5, Or. 2, Nat. Or. *Umbelliferæ.* The seed of these plants may be sown in the open ground. *Synonymes:* 1. *Caucalis Anthriscus.* 2. *C. arvensis, helvetica.* 3. *Scandix trichosperma*—*T. anthriscŭs* 1, *inflātă* 2, *neglĕctă, nodōsă, trichospĕrmă* 3, *tuberculātă.*

TORMENTĬLLĂ, *Linn.* From *tormentum,* pain; alluding to its supposed efficacy in tooth-ache, as well as to its being supposed to cure diseases of the bowels. *Linn.* 12, Or. 3, Nat. Or. *Rosaceæ.* British herbaceous plants, not worth growing, except in botanical gardens. The roots of *T. erecta* are so astringent as to be used in the western isles of Scotland for tanning leather; for which purpose they are superior even to oak bark. The root is likewise one of the most efficacious of our indigenous aromatic astringents, and may be used with great effect in cases where medicines of this class are proper. It is usually given in decoction. *Synonymes:* 1. *T. officinalis.* 2. *Potentilla humifusa*—*T. erĕctă* 1, *humifŭsă* 2, *rĕptăns.*

TOROSE, uneven, alternately elevated and depressed.

TŎRTŪLĂ, *Hedwig.* From *torqueo,* to twist; in allusion to the singular manner in which the teeth of the peristome are twisted together. *Linn.* 24, Or. 5, Nat. Or. *Musci.* Small plants, generally found in thick tufts. They are common to nearly all situations. The character from which the genus has received its designation will always faithfully indicate the species. *Synonymes:* 1. *Zigotrichia cylindrica.* 2. *T. rigida.* 3. *T. imberbis, unguiculata.* 4. *T. nervosa.* 5. *T. apiculata, aristata, barbata,*

*humilis, mucronulata*—*T. brevirōstris, convolūtă, cuneifōliă, cylīndrică* 1, *enervis* 2, *fallax* 3, *F. brevicaŭlis, linoīdes, grăcilis, G. viridis, murālis, M. brevipĭlă, revolūtă* 4, *rigĭdă, rurālis, R. lævipĭlă, stellātă, subulātă, S. obtūsă, tortuōsă, unguiculātă* 5.

TŎRŬLĂ, *Persoon.* A diminutive of *torus,* a twisted cord; appearance of the filaments. *Linn.* 24, Or. 9, Nat. Or. *Fungi.* Found upon dead stems of plants—*T. cylīndrică, Eriophŏrī, herbārŭm, monilioīdes, ovalispŏră.*

TŎRULOSE, slightly torose.

TŎRUS, the same as *Thalamus*

TOUCH-ME-NOT, see *Impătiens.*

TOURNEFŎRTIĂ, *Linn.* In memory of Joseph Pitton de Tournefort, the distinguished author of an arrangement of plants under the title of " *Institutiones Rei Herbariæ,*" and other botanical works, from 1694 to 1717; his first work " *Institutiones,*" laid the foundation of the arrangement now followed, called the Jussieuan, or Natural System. *Linn.* 19, Or. 1, Nat. Or. *Ehretiaceæ.* The species of *Tournefortia* are hardly worth cultivating for ornament. They are of the easiest management; and are readily increased by cuttings, in sand, those of the stove species in heat. *Synonymes:* 1. *Arguzia montana, Messerschmidia Arguzia. T. Arguzia.*

angustifōliă . . Wht. grn. 8, G. Ev. S. Canaries . 1820
argĕntēă . . . White . . 8, S. Ev. S. E. Ind. . . 1822
bicŏlŏr . . . . Green . . 6, S. Ev. S. Jamaica . 1812
cymōsă . . . . Dull wht. 7, S. Ev. S. Jamaica . 1777
fœtidissimă . . Dull wht. 7, S. Ev. S. Jamaica . 1789
fruticōsă . . . White . . 6, G. Ev. S. Canaries . 1800
heliotropioīdes . Pa. li. . . 5, S. Ev. S. B. Ayres . 1829
laurifōliă . . . Yel wht. . 7, S. Ev. S. S. Amer. .
mutābĭlis . . . Grnsh. wht. 7, G. Ev. S. Java . . 1820
scăbră . . . . Wht. red . 8, S. Ev. S. St. Domingo 1700
sibīrĭcă, 1 . . . White . . 8, F. Her. P. Siberia . 1780
suffruticōsă . . White . . 6, S. . . S. Jamaica . 1759

TOURRETTIĂ, *Dombey.* In honour of Marc Antoine Louis Claret de la Tourrette, a friend of Rousseau, author of some botanical works. *Linn.* 14, Or. 2, Nat. Or. *Bignoniaceæ.* The seed should be sown on a hotbed, early in spring, and when the young plants are sufficiently strong, they may be planted in light soil, against a wall or pillar. *Synonyme:* 1. *Dombeya lappacea.*

lappāceă, 1 . . . Ro. grn. . 7, H. Cl. A. Peru . . 1788

TOWER MUSTARD, see *Turrĭlis.*

TOWER MUSTARD, see *Arăbis Turrĭlă.*

TRACHĔLIŬM, *Linn.* From *trachelos,* the neck; from its supposed efficacy in diseases of the *Trachea;* hence the English name of the genus, *Throatwort. Linn.* 5, Or. 1, Nat. Or. *Campanulaceæ.* This plant is very showy when in flower. It thrives best in light soil, against a south wall; and is easily increased by seeds, or by cuttings, planted under a glass, in spring.

cærūlĕŭm . . . Blue . . 8, H. Her. P. Italy . . 1640

TRACHYMĔNĔ, *Rudge.* From *trachys,* rough, and *hymen,* a membrane; channels of the fruit. *Linn.* 5, Or. 2, Nat. Or. *Umbelliferæ.* All the species will succeed well in a mixture of loam and sandy peat; and they may be increased by young cuttings, in the same kind of soil, under a glass, or by seeds. *T. cærulea* is raised from seed, sown on a gentle hotbed; and afterwards treated like other greenhouse plants. *Synonyme:* 1. *Didiscus cæruleus.*

albĭdă . . . . Brt. cream G. . . A. N. Holl. . 1838
cærūlĕă, 1 . . . Blue . . 7, G. . . A. N. Holl. . 1827
gigantĕă . . . . . . . . . S. Ev. S.
incīsă . . . . . . . . . G. Ev. S. N. Holl. . 1819
lanceolātă . . . White . 7, G. Ev. S. N. Holl. . 1829
lineāris . . . . Yellow . 7, G. Ev. S. N. Holl. . 1824

TRACHYSPĔRMŬM, *Link.* From *trachys,* rough, and *sperma,* a seed; in reference to the muricated fruit. *Linn.* 5, Or. 2, Nat. Or. *Umbelliferæ.* An uninteresting plant, of very simple culture, and increased by seeds. *Synonymes:* 1. *Bunium rigens, Conium rigens*—*T. rigĕns* 1.

TRACHYTĔLLĂ, *Decandolle.* From *trachytes,* roughness; because the leaves, which have a very rough surface, are used for polishing wood, and also metal. *Linn.* 13, Or. 5, Nat. Or. *Dilleniaceæ.* This species succeeds well in a mixture of peat and loam, and ripened cuttings root freely in sand, under a glass.

actăă . . . . White . . . G. Ev. Cl. China . 1823

TRADESCANTIA, *Linn.* In honour of John Tradescant, gardener to Charles I. *Linn.* 6, Or. 1, Nat. Or. *Commelineæ.* Interesting plants, succeeding well in any rich, light soil; and readily increased by division. Synonyme: 1. *T. multiflora.*

| | | | | | | | |
|---|---|---|---|---|---|---|---|
| auriculfòliă | . | . Blue | . | 8, H. | Her. P. | Texas | . 1885 |
| congestă | . | . Blue | . | 8, H. | Her. P. | N. Amer. | . 1896 |
| cordifòliă | . | . Blue | . | 6, S. | Ev. Cr. | Jamaica | . 1819 |
| crassifòliă | . | . Blue | . | 8, F. | Her. P. | Mexico | . 1796 |
| erûsulă | . | . White | . | 7, S. | Her. P. | Brazil | . 1825 |
| discòlor | . | . Blue | . | 7, S. | Her. P. | S. Amer. | . 1783 |
| diurêtică | . | . Blue | . | 6, S. | Her. P. | Brazil | . 1825 |
| divaricătă | . | . Blue | . | 6, S. | Her. P. | Trinidad | . 1818 |
| erêctă | . | . Blue | . | 7, H. | A. | Mexico | . 1794 |
| fuscătă | . | . Blue | . | 9, S. | Her. P. | S. Amer. | . 1820 |
| geniculătă | . | . Blue | . | 7, S. | Her. P. | W. Ind. | . 1788 |
| iridescêns | . | . Purple | . | 6, G. | Her. P. | Mexico | . 1838 |
| latifòliă | . | . Blue | . | 10, H. | A. | Lima | . 1816 |
| malabârică | . | . Purple | . | 7, S. | Her. P. | E. Ind. | . 1776 |
| multiflòră | . | . Blue | . | 6, S. | Her. P. | Jamaica | . 1820 |
| paniculătă | . | . Blue | . | 8, G. | B. | E. Ind. | . 1816 |
| parviflòră | . | . Blue | . | 8, S. | Her. P. | Peru | . 1822 |
| pilôsă | . | . Purple | . | 7, H. | Her. P. | Louisiana | . 1832 |
| procumbênă, 1 | | . Blue | . | 6, S. | Ev. | Tr. Trinidad | . 1824 |
| pulchêllă | . | . Blue | . | 7, G. | Ev. | Tr. Mexico | . 1825 |
| rôsă | . | . Pink | . | 6, H. | Her. P. | Carolina | . 1802 |
| speciôsă | . | . Blue | . | 7, S. | Her. P. | Mexico | . 1825 |
| spicătă | . | . Purple | . | 8. | Her. P. | Mexico | . |
| subaspêră | . | . Purple | . | 6, H. | Her. P. | N. Amer. | . 1812 |
| tuberôsă | . | . Blue | . | 7, S. | Tu. | P. E. Ind. | . 1817 |
| undătă | . | . Blue | . | 6, S. | Her. P. | Trinidad | . 1819 |
| virginîcă | . | . Blue | . | 7, H. | Her. P. | N. Amer. | . 1629 |
| albă | . | . White | . | 7, H. | Her. P. | N. Amer. | . 1629 |
| caerûlă-albă | . | . Blue wht | 7, H. | Her. P. | N. Amer. | . 1629 |
| pilôsă | . | . White. | . | 7, H. | Her. P. | N. Amer. | . 1629 |
| plênă | . | . Blue | . | 7, H. | Her. P. | N. Amer. | . 1629 |
| rûbră | . | . Red | . | 7, H. | Her. P. | N. Amer. | . 1629 |

TRAGÌA, *Plumier.* In honour of Jerome Bock, generally called Tragus, a German botanist. *Linn.* 21, Or. 3, Nat. Or. *Euphorbiaceæ.* Chiefly stove annuals, and uninteresting—*T. cannabìnă, cor culătă, infêstă, involucrătă, Mercurìàlis, pedunculătă, urêns, urticæfòliă, volubìlis.*

TRAGÌUM, see *Pimpinêllă.*

TRAGOPÒGON, *Linn.* From *tragos,* a goat, and *pogon,* a beard; in allusion to the long silky beard of the seeds. *Linn.* 19, Or. 1, Nat. Or. *Compositæ.* Ornamental plants, succeeding in common garden soil. *T. porrifolius* is the *Salsafy* of gardens; it is sown and treated in the same manner as carrots; the flavour of the root is mild and sweetish. Synonymes: 1. *T. parviflorus.* 2. *T. livescens.* 3. *T. ruber.*

| | | | | | | |
|---|---|---|---|---|---|---|
| angustifòlìus, 1 | . Purple | . 7, H. | | B. Italy | . 1823 |
| campêstris | . . Yellow | . 6, H. | | B. Podolia | . 1819 |
| crânus | . . Yellow | . 7, H. | | B. Hungary | . 1824 |
| crocifòlìus | . . Purple | . 6, H. | | B. Italy | . 1739 |
| dûblìus, 2 | . Pa. yel. | . 5, H. | | B. Podolia | . 1818 |
| floccôsus | . . Yellow | . 5, H. | | B. Hungary | . 1816 |
| major | . . Yellow | . 5, H. | | B. Austria | . 1788 |
| mutabìlis | . . Pale | . 5, H. | | B. Siberia | . 1816 |
| orientàlis | . . Yellow | . 6, H. | | B. Levant | . 1787 |
| porrifòlìus | . . Purple | . 5, H. | | B. England | . |
| pratênsis | . . Yellow | . 5, H. | | B. Britain | . |
| pusìllus | . . Yellow | . 6, H. | | B. Iberia | . 1820 |
| rôsêus, 3 | . . Red | . 5, H. | | B. Siberia | . 1826 |
| undulàtus | . . Wht. yel. | . 5, H. | | B. Crimea | . 1790 |
| villôsus | . . Pur. yel. | . 5, H. | | B. Spain | . 1794 |

TRAGOPÝRUM, *Bieberstein.* From *tragos,* a goat, and *pyros,* wheat. *Linn.* 8, Or. 3, Nat. Or. *Polygoneæ.* Ornamental dwarf shrubs, thriving in a mixture of peat and sandy loam; and increased by layers in spring. Synonymes: 1. *Polygonum crispulum, caucasicum.* 2. *P. frutescens.* 3. *P. polygamum, parvifolium.*

| | | | | | | |
|---|---|---|---|---|---|---|
| buxifòlìum, 1 | . White | . 7, H. | De. S. | Siberia | . 1800 |
| lanceolàtum, 2 | . Pink | . 7, H. | De. S. | Siberia | . 1778 |
| polygàmum, 3 | . Pink | . 7, H. | De. S. | Carolina | . 1810 |

TRANSVERSELY-FLEXUOSE, waved in a cross direction.

TRAPA, *Linn.* Abridged from *calcitrapa,* the Latin name of an instrument called *caltrops,* furnished with four spines, formerly used in war to impede the progress of cavalry; the fruit of some of the species is furnished with four spines. *Linn.* 4, Or. 1, Nat. Or. *Onagraceæ.* Aquatic plants, requiring a rich, loamy soil, and to be grown in a cistern, or large pot or tub of water; increased by seeds. The large seeds of *T. bispinosa* are sweet and eatable; they form an extensive article of cultivation. In Cashmere and other parts of the East, they are common food, and known under the name of Singhara nuts.

[ 317 ]

| | | | | | | |
|---|---|---|---|---|---|---|
| bicôrnis | . . White | . 7, G. | Aq. A. | China | . 1790 |
| bispinôsă | . . White | . 7, S. | Aq. A. | E. Ind. | . 1822 |
| nătăns | . . Wht. pur. | 7, H. | Aq. A. | Europe | . 1781 |
| quadrispinôsă | . . White | . 7, S. | Aq. B. | E. Ind. | . 1823 |

TRAPEZIFORM, shaped like a trapezium.

TRAVELLER'S JOY, see *Clêmătis Vitâlbă.*

TRAVELLER'S JOY, see *Clêmătis Viôrnă.*

TREACLE MUSTARD, see *Clypêŏlă.*

TREE CELANDINE, see *Boccônìă frutêscens.*

TREE MALLOW, see *Lavatêră arbôrĕă.*

TREE OF SADNESS, see *Nyctânthĕs arbor trìstis.*

TREE ONION, see *Allìum prolìfĕrum.*

TREE SORREL, see *Rûmĕx Lunârìă.*

TREFOIL, see *Trifòlìum.*

TREMBLING AMERICAN-TREE, see *Pôpŭlus trêmŭlă.*

TREMÊLLĂ, *Dillenius.* From *tremo,* to tremble; in allusion to the gelatinous texture of the plants. *Linn.* 24, Or. 9, Nat. Or. *Fungi.* Found growing on fallen branches of trees—*T. albìdă, biparasìtică, cerebrìnă, clavariæfòrmis, clavâtă, fimbriâtă, foliâcĕă, F. violâcĕă, intumêscĕns, mesentêrică, sarcoìdĕs.*

TRENTEPÒHLIĂ, *Agardh.* In honour of M. Trentepohl, an obscure German botanist. *Linn.* 24, Or. 7, Nat. Or. *Algæ.* Found on rocks, on the sea-coast—*T. aûrĕă, A. ilicicòlă, pulchêllă, P. chalybêă, purpûrĕă.*

TREVIRÀNIĂ, *Willdenow.* In honour of Lud. Christ. Trevìranus, M.D., professor of botany in the university of Bonn. *Linn.* 14, Or. 2, Nat. Or. *Gesnereæ.* This species is extremely handsome when in flower. It requires to be grown in a light, rich soil, and when the blossoms have withered, the plants should not have any more water till the roots begin again to vegetate; when they must be taken out of the pots and divided. After they are potted, they require moisture and heat to make them grow and flower in perfection. Synonyme: 1. *Cyrilla pulchella. T. coccinea.*

| | | | | | | |
|---|---|---|---|---|---|---|
| pulchêllă, 1 | . Scarlet | . 8, S. | Her. P. | Jamaica | . 1778 |

TREVÔĂ, *Hooker.* Trevo, the name of a Spanish botanist. *Linn.* 5, Or. 1, Nat. Or. *Rhamnaceæ.* Interesting plants, thriving in sandy loam and peat; and increased by young cuttings, in sand, under a glass.

| | | | | | | |
|---|---|---|---|---|---|---|
| quinquenêrvìă | . White | . 6, G. | Ev. S. | Chile | . 1827 |
| trinêrvis | . . Grn. yel. | . 6, G. | Ev. S. | Chile | . 1823 |

TREWIĂ, *Linn.* In honour of C. J. Trew, of Nuremberg, a botanical author. *Linn.* 22, Or. 12, Nat. Or. *Trewiaceæ.* This species succeeds well in sandy loam and peat; and is readily increased by cuttings, in sand, under a glass, in heat. Synonyme: 1. *T. macrophylla.*

| | | | | | | |
|---|---|---|---|---|---|---|
| nudiflòră, 1 | . . | . 8. | Ev. S. | E. Ind. | . 1796 |

TRIANDROUS, having three stamens.

TRIÀNTHĔMĂ, *Linn.* From *treis,* three, and *anthos,* a flower; flowers usually disposed in threes. *Linn.* 5, Or. 1, Nat. Or. *Portulaceæ.* Plants of little interest. Any common garden soil suits them; seeds.

| | | | | | | |
|---|---|---|---|---|---|---|
| decândră | . . Green | . 7, S. | | A. E. Ind. | . 1824 |
| monogýnă | . . Pur. grn. | . 7, S. | | A. Jamaica | . 1820 |
| pentândră | . . | . 7, G. | Ev. Tr. | Arabia | . 1820 |
| obcordâtă | . . Green | . 7, S. | Ev. Tr. | E. Ind. | . 1816 |

TRIAS, *Lindley.* From *trias,* growing in threes; the floral envelopes are so arranged. *Linn.* 20, Or. 1, Nat. Or. *Orchidaceæ.* Small plants, growing best when treated as the *Burlingtoniæ.*

| | | | | | | |
|---|---|---|---|---|---|---|
| oblôngă | . . Grn. yel. | . 8. | Epi. | E. Ind. | . 1837 |
| racemôsă | . . Grn. yel. | . 8. | Epi. | E. Ind. | . 1837 |

TRIBRACHIĂ, see *Bolbophýllum.*

TRIBŬLUS, *Linn.* From *treis,* three, and *ballo,* to project; each carpel is armed with three, and sometimes four prickly points. *Linn.* 10, Or. 1, Nat. Or. *Zygophylleæ.* The annual species of this genus may be sown on a moderate hotbed, in spring; and the young plants, when of sufficient size, planted in a sheltered situation in the open border. *T. cistoides* succeeds best in a mixture of loam and peat, and may either be increased by cuttings or seeds.

| | | | | | | |
|---|---|---|---|---|---|---|
| albus | . . White | . 6, S. | | A. Guinea | . 1826 |
| cistoìdĕs | . . Yellow | . 7, S. | Ev. Tr. | S. Amer. | . 1752 |
| lanuginôsus | . . Yellow | . 6, G. | Tr. A. | E. Ind. | . 1822 |
| littoràlis | . . | . 7, S. | Ev. Tr. | N. Holl. | . 1821 |
| maxìmus | . . Yellow | . 6, S. | Tr. A. | Jamaica | . 1728 |
| subinêrmis | . . Yellow | . 6, G. | Tr. A. | Thibet | . 1820 |
| terrêstris | . . Yellow | . 6, H. | Tr. A. | S. Eur. | . 1596 |
| trijugàtus | . . Yellow | . 6, G. | Tr. A. | Georgia | . 1819 |

TRICHÆTA, Link. From *treis*, three, and *chæta*, a bristle. Linn. 3, Or. 2, Nat. Or. *Gramineæ*. A mere weed; increased by seeds. *Synonymes*: 1. *Bromus ovatus, Trisetum ovatum, Avena ovata*—T. *ovata* 1.

TRICHIA, *Hall.* From *thrix*, a hair; in allusion to the internal mass of elastic fibres gradually expanding after the head bursts. Linn. 24, Or. 9, Nat. Or. *Fungi.* Small, pin-headed plants, found upon rotten wood. *Synonyme*: 1. *Sphærocarpus fragilis*—T. *fallax* 1, *nitens, ovata, reticulata.*

TRICHILIA, *Linn.* From *tricha*, ternary; the stigma is three-lobed, and the capsule three-celled and three-valved. Linn. 10, Or. 1, Nat. Or. *Meliaceæ.* These trees succeed in a mixture of loam and peat; and cuttings of the ripened wood, with the leaves entire, will root in sand, under a glass, in heat. *Synonyme*: 1. *T. glabra.*

| glandulosa | Whitish | 7, S. Ev. T. N. Holl. | 1821 |
| havannula, 1 | White | 6, S. Ev. T. Havannah | 1794 |
| hirta | Grn. wht | 6, S. Ev. T. Jamaica | 1800 |
| odorata | Grn. wht | 6, S. Ev. T. W. Ind. | 1801 |
| spondioides | Whitish | 6, S. Ev. T. Jamaica | 1800 |

TRICHOCENTRON, *Poppig.* From *thrix*, a hair, and *centron*, a spur or centre; to what it refers we are not informed. Linn. 20, Or. 1, Nat. Or. *Orchidaceæ.* The species of this genus do not appear to be difficult of culture. They will probably be found to succeed best if attached to a piece of wood, with a little moss upon their roots; and treated after the manner recommended for the *Burlingtonia.* *Synonyme*: 1. *Acoidium fuscum.*

| fuscum, 1 | Grn. wht. | 7, S. Epi. Mexico | 1835 |
| iridifolium | Yellow | 9, S. Epi. Demerara | 183-- |

TRICHOCEPHALUS, *Brongniart.* From *thrix*, hair, and *kephale*, a head; in allusion to the hairy heads of flowers. Linn. 5, Or. 1, Nat. Or. *Rhamnaceæ.* For culture, &c., refer to *Phylica.* *Synonymes*: 1. *Phylica ramosissima.* 2. *P. spicata.* 3. *P. stipularis.*

| ramosissima, 1 | White | G. Ev. S. St. Helena | 1810 |
| spicata, 2 | White | 11, G. Ev. S. C. G. H. | 1774 |
| stipularis, 3 | White | 6, G. Ev. S. C. G. H. | 1786 |

TRICHOCHLOA, *Trinius.* From *thrix*, a hair, and *chloa*, grass. Linn. 3, Or. 2, Nat. Or. *Gramineæ.* A genus of curious grasses, succeeding well in common soil; and increased by seeds. *Synonymes*: 1. *Agrostis filiformis, Cinna filiformis.* 2. *A. tenuiflora, C. tenuiflora.* 3. *A. mexicana, C. mexicana.* 4. *A. microsperma.*

| capillaris | Apetal | 7, Grass. Carolina | 1818 |
| foliosa, 1 | Apetal | 7, Grass. N. Amer. | 1819 |
| longiseta, 2 | Apetal | 7, Grass. N. Amer. | 1820 |
| mexicana, 3 | Apetal | 8, Grass. Mexico | 1780 |
| microsperma, 4 | Apetal | 7, Grass. Mexico | 1820 |
| sobolifera | Apetal | 7, Grass. N. Amer. | 1819 |

TRICHOCLADUS, *Persoon.* From *thrix*, a hair, and *klados*, a branch; the branches are clothed with stellate hairs. Linn. 22, Or. 1, Nat. Or. *Hamamelaceæ.* For culture and propagation, see *Trevoa.*

| crinitus | Green | 8, G. Ev. S. C. G. H. | 1823 |

TRICHODERMA, *Persoon.* From *thrix*, a hair, and *derma*, a skin; downy covering. Linn. 24, Or. 9, Nat. Or. *Fungi.* Powdery masses, found upon dead branches—T. *viride.*

TRICHODESMA, *R. Brown.* From *thrix*, a hair, and *desmos*, a bond; the anthers are bound to each other by hairs. Linn. 5, Or. 1, Nat. Or. *Boraginaceæ.* Worthless half-hardy annuals, of the easiest culture—T. *africanum, indicum, zeylanicum.*

TRICHODIUM, *Schrader.* From *thrix*, a hair, and *eidos*, like; hair-like appearance of inflorescence. Linn. 3, Or. 2, Nat. Or. *Gramineæ.* Worthless plants, readily increased by seeds in common soil—T. *alpinum, caninum, decumbens, diffusum, elegans, flavescens, hybridum, laxiflorum, neglectum, rubrum, rupestre, setaceum.*

TRICHOLÆNA, *Schrader.* From *thrix*, a hair, and *chlaina*, a cassock. Linn. 3, Or. 2, Nat. Or. *Gramineæ.* A pretty grass, succeeding in loam and peat; and increased by seeds. *Synonymes*: 1. *Saccharum Teneriffæ, Panicum Teneriffæ.*

| micrantha, 1 | Apetal | 6, Grass. Teneriffe | 1825 |

TRICHOMANES, *Linn.* From *thrix*, a hair, and *manos*, soft; the shining stems appear like fine hair. Linn. 24, Or. 1, Nat. Or. *Gleicheniaceæ.* A genus of elegant ferns. A mixture of loam and peat suits them best; and they are increased by division or seeds. *Synonyme*: 1. *Hymenophyllum alatum.*

| brevisetum, 1 | Brown | 6, H. Her. P. Britain | |
| membranaceum | Brown | 6, S. Her. P. W. Ind. | 1820 |

TRICHONEMA, *Ker.* From *thrix*, a hair, and *nema*, a filament; the filaments are hairy. Linn. 3, Or. 1, Nat. Or. *Iridaceæ.* A genus of very pretty bulbs when in flower. They should be planted out, in a pit or frame, in a mixture of sandy loam and peat, and increased by offsets. *Synonymes*: 1. *Iris cælestina.* 2. *T. cruciatum.* 3. *Ixia purpurascens.* 4. *I. quadrangula.* 5. *I. ramiflora.*

| Bulbocodium | Red | 3, H. Bl. P. S. Eur. | 1739 |
| caulescens | Yellow | 6, G. Bl. P. C. G. H. | 1810 |
| chloroleucum | Grn. wht. | 6, G. Bl. P. C. G. H. | 1825 |
| coelestinum, 1 | Blue | 3, G. Bl. P. Carolina | 1818 |
| Columnæ | Blue | 3, G. Bl. P. Italy | 1825 |
| cruciatum | Rose | 5, F. Bl. P. C. G. H. | 1758 |
| filifolium | Yellow | 5, H. Bl. P. C. G. H. | 1822 |
| longifolium, 2 | Rose | 5, F. Bl. P. C. G. H. | 1758 |
| pudicum | Red | 3, G. Bl. P. C. G. H. | 1806 |
| purpurascens, 3 | Purple | 5, G. Bl. P. Italy | 1825 |
| quadrangulum, 4 | | 6, G. Bl. P. C. G. H. | 1825 |
| ramiflorum, 5 | Purple | 5, H. Bl. P. Naples | 1830 |
| recurvum | Red | 6, G. Bl. P. C. G. H. | 1812 |
| roseum | Pink | 7, G. Bl. P. C. G. H. | 1818 |
| speciosum | Red | 5, G. Bl. P. C. G. H. | 1808 |
| tortuosum | Yellow | 5, F. Bl. P. C. G. H. | 1822 |

TRICHOPETALUM, *Lindley.* From *thrix*, a hair; and *petalon*, a petal; the inner series of the perianth is fringed. Linn. 6, Or. 1, Nat. Or. *Liliaceæ.* This curious species succeeds best if planted out in a pit, or frame effectively drained, with a southern aspect, and from which the frost is entirely excluded; it will also succeed in pots, well drained, in a light, rich soil; increased by divisions.

| gracile | Ornsh | 7, F. Her. P. Chile | 1822 |

TRICHOPHORUM, *Richard.* From *thrix*, a hair, and *phoreo*, to bear; the inflorescence resembles a bunch of hair. Linn. 3, Or. 1, Nat. Or. *Cyperaceæ.* The species are found in peat bogs. Their seeds are covered with a silky down, of which cloth, paper, and wicks of candles have been made; and with which pillows and cushions are sometimes stuffed. *Synonyme*: 1. *Eriophorum montevidense.*

| alpinum | Apetal | Grass. Scotland | |
| cyperinum | Apetal | 7, Grass. N. Amer. | 1802 |

Lockhartii, *montevidense* 1.

TRICHOPILIA, *Lindley.* From *thrix*, a hair, and *pilion*, a cap; in allusion to the anther being concealed below a cap surmounted by three tufts of hair. Linn. 20, Or. 1, Nat. Or. *Orchidaceæ.* This is a beautiful and very curious species. It appears to succeed best when treated as the *Maxillaria.*

| tortilis | Wht. red | 1, S. Epi. Mexico | 1835 |

TRICHOSANTHES, *Linn.* From *thrix*, a hair, and *anthos*, a flower; the corollas are ciliated. Linn. 21, Or. 10, Nat. Or. *Cucurbitaceæ.* The seeds of the *Snake-Gourd* should be sown on a hotbed in spring, and afterwards treated like cucumbers. *Synonyme*: 1. *Cucumis anguineus.*

| anguina, 1 | White | 6, F. Tr. A. China | 1735 |

colubrina, cordata, cucumerina, lobata.

TRICHOSTEMA, *Linn.* From *thrix*, a hair, and *stema*, a stamen; in allusion to the slender, hair-like stamens. Linn. 14, Or. 1, Nat. Or. *Labiatæ.* The seeds of *Trichostema* should be sown in the open border.

| dichotomum | Blue | 6, H. A. N. Amer. | 1759 |
| lineare | Blue | 7, H. A. N. Amer. | 1759 |

TRICHOSTOMUM, *Hedwig.* From *thrix*, a hair, and *stoma*, the mouth; the divisions of the mouth of the theca are very fine. Linn. 24, Or. 5, Nat. Or. *Musci.* Dark green tufts, found on mountains. *Synonymes*: 1. *Dicranum aciculare.* 2. *T. ericoides.* 3. *D. ellipticum.* 4. *D. patens, obtusum.* 5. *D. polyphyllum, cirrhatum*—T. *aciculare* 1, *canescens* 2, *ellipticum* 3, *fasciculare, heterostichum, lanuginosum, microcarpon, patens* 4, *polyphyllum* 5.

TRICHOTHECIUM, *Link.* From *thrix*, a hair, and *theke*, a seed-case; the thecæ are intermixed among a mass of hair-like filaments. Linn. 24, Or. 9, Nat.

Or. *Fungi*. Found upon decayed wood—*T. heterosporûm, roseûm*.

**Trichotomous**, divided into threes.

**Tricoccus**, a fruit of three one-seeded cells, as that of *Euphorbia*.

**Tricoryne**, *R. Brown*. From *treis*, three, and *koryne*, a club; in allusion to the form of the capsules. *Linn*. 6, Or. 1, Nat. Or. *Liliaceæ*. The species of this genus thrive well in a light rich soil; and are readily increased by division; *T. simplex* by seeds.

| elatiôr | White | 6, G. Her. | P. | N. Holl. | 1824 |
|---|---|---|---|---|---|
| scabra | White | G. Her. | P. | N. Holl. | 1826 |
| simplex | White | 7, G. | B. | N. Holl. | 1823 |

**Tricuspidate**, having three points.

**Tricuspis**, *Beauvois*. From *treis*, three, and *cuspis*, a point; in allusion to the structure of the flowers. *Linn*. 3, Or. 2, Nat. Or. *Gramineæ*. According to Pursh, this is a very valuable grass for mountain meadows. In Pennsylvania it produces two excellent crops every year; and lasts many years without manure, even upon indifferent soils; increased by seeds. *Synonyme*: 1. *Poa cærulescens*.

| quinquefida, 1 | Apetal | 6, Gram. | N. Amer. | 1820 |
|---|---|---|---|---|

**Tridax**, *Linn*. From *tridaknos*, thrice-bitten; the rays of the flower are divided into three. *Linn*. 19, Or. 2, Nat. Or. *Compositæ*. A hardy annual, of no interest. *Synonyme*: 1. *Balbisia elongata—T. procumbens* 1.

**Tridentate**, having three teeth.

**Tridentea**, *Haworth*. From *tridens*, a trident; the segments of the outer corona are tridentate. *Linn*. 5, Or. 2, Nat. Or. *Asclepiadaceæ*. Nearly allied to the genus *Stapelia*; which see, for culture and propagation. *Synonymes*: 1. *Stapelia gemmiflora*. 2. *S. hircosa*. 3. *S. vetula*.

| depressa | Brn. pur. | 7, S. Ev. | S. | C. G. H. | |
|---|---|---|---|---|---|
| gemmiflora, 1 | Dk. pur. | 10, S. Ev. | S. | C. G. H. | 1795 |
| paniculata | Grn. br. pur. | 7, S. Ev. | S. | C. G. H. | 1805 |
| moschata, 2 | Brn. pur. | 7, S. Ev. | S. | C. G. H. | |
| Simsii, 3 | Dk. pur. | 7, S. Ev. | S. | C. G. H. | 1800 |
| stygia | Dk. pur. | 8, S. Ev. | S. | C. G. H. | 1810 |
| vetula | Dk. pur. | 8, S. Ev. | S. | C. G. H. | 1793 |

**Trientalis**, *Linn*. From *triens*, one third, probably in allusion to the humble growth of the species. *Linn*. 7, Or. 1, Nat. Or. *Primulaceæ*. Interesting little plants, thriving in a light rich soil; and readily increased by division or seeds.

| americana | White | 7, H. Her. | P. | N. Amer. | 1816 |
|---|---|---|---|---|---|
| europæa | White | 5, H. Her. | P. | Britain | |

**Trifarious**, arranged in three rows.

**Trifid**, divided into three.

**Trifoliolate**, having three leaflets.

**Trifolium**, *Linn*. From *tres*, three, and *folium*, a leaf; all the species of the genus have trifoliolate leaves. The French call it *trèfle*; and the English *trefoil* or clover. *Linn*. 17, Or. 4, Nat. Or. *Leguminosæ*. The white, red, and yellow clover are among the most valuable herbage plants adopted in European agriculture. *Lucern* has been recommended as superior to clover, and *saintfoin* and various other leguminous plants have been highly extolled; yet the red clover for mowing, and the white for pasturage, far excel all other plants in these respects. All the species thrive in common garden soil, and many of them, being very showy, are well suited for ornamenting the flower borders. The perennial kinds are readily increased by dividing the plants at the root in spring, or by seeds. The seeds of the annual and biennial kinds only require sowing in the open border. Those species marked frame and greenhouse, require protection only in winter. *Synonymes*: 1. *T. Cupani*. 2. *T. gracile*. 3. *T. hispidum*. 4. *T. pictum*. 5. *T. Molinerii*. 6. *T. conicum*. 7. *T. conicum*. 8. *T. obscurum*. 9. *T. aristatum*. 10. *Lupinaster pentaphyllum*. 11. *T. albens*. 12. *T. irregulare*. 13. *Lupinaster macrocephalum*. 14. *T. strictum*. 15. *T. campestre*. 16. *Lupinaster oblongifolium*. 17. *T. squarrosum*. 18. *T. pratense flavicans*. 19. *T. recurvum*.

| agrarium | Yellow | 6, H. | A. | Europe | 1815 |
|---|---|---|---|---|---|
| alatum, 1 | Flesh | 6, H. Her. | Tr. | S. Eur. | 1820 |
| albidum | Cream | 7, H. | A. | | 1796 |
| alexandrinum | Pa. yel. | 6, H. | A. | Egypt | 1798 |
| alpestre | Drk. pur. | 7, H. Her. | P. | Europe | 1789 |
| alpinum | Purple | 7, H. Her. | P. | Europe | 1775 |
| angulatum | Red | 7, H. | A. | Hungary | 1803 |
| angustifolium | Pa. rose | 7, H. | A. | S. Eur. | 1640 |

| anomalum | White | 7, H. De. | Tr. | | |
|---|---|---|---|---|---|
| armeniacum | Red | 7, H. Her. | P. | Armenia | 1830 |
| armenium | Cream | 8, H. Her. | P. | Armenia | 1820 |
| badium | Yellow | 7, H. Her. | P. | Pyrenees | |
| Bocconi | Pa. pur. | 6, H. | A. | Spain | 1820 |
| bracteatum | Purple | 6, H. | B. | Morocco | 1804 |
| cærulescens | Brn. red | 7, H. | A. | Siberia | 1827 |
| cæspitosum | Purple | 7, H. Her. | P. | Switzerl. | 1815 |
| canescens | Cream | 5, H. Her. | P. | Cappadoc. | 1803 |
| cernuum | Pa. pur. | 6, H. | A. | Spain | 1820 |
| Cherleri | White | 5, H. | A. | S. Eur. | 1750 |
| cinctum | Pa. yel. | 7, H. | A. | | 1820 |
| clandestinum | | 6, H. | A. | Spain | 1826 |
| clypeatum | Pa. red | 7, H. | A. | Levant | 1711 |
| comosum | White | 6, H. Her. | P. | America | 1798 |
| congestum | Wht. red | 6, H. Tr. | A. | S. Eur. | 1820 |
| conicum | Cream | 7, H. | A. | | 1816 |
| constantinopolitanum | Yellow | 6, H. | A. | Turkey | 1820 |
| Cussoni | Blue | 7, H. Her. | P. | Sicily | 1826 |
| decipiens | Yellow | 6, H. | A. | | 1820 |
| diffusum | Purple | 7, H. Tr. | A. | Hungary | 1801 |
| divaricatum | Wht. red | 6, H. | A. | S. Eur. | 1816 |
| echinatum | White | 6, H. | A. | Caucasus | 1821 |
| elegans | Pa. red | 7, H. Her. | P. | Europe | 1823 |
| erinaceum | Pa. red | 6, H. | A. | Iberia | 1818 |
| eximium | Purple | 6, H. De. | Tr. | Dahuria | 1820 |
| albiflorum | White | 6, H. De. | Tr. | Altai | |
| expansum | Purple | 7, H. Her. | P. | | 1830 |
| fucatum | Yellow | 7, H. | A. | Californ. | 1834 |
| gemellum | Yellow | 6, H. | A. | Spain | 1818 |
| globosum | Purple | 7, H. | A. | Levant | 1713 |
| Gussoni | Whitish | 7, H. | A. | | 1835 |
| hirtum, 3 | Purple | 7, H. | A. | Barbary | 1817 |
| pictum, 4 | Purple | 7, H. | A. | | 1800 |
| hybridum | Purple | 7, H. De. | Tr. | Europe | 1777 |
| incarnatum | Flesh | 7, H. | A. | Italy | 1596 |
| Molinerii, 5 | Wht. red | 7, H. | A. | S. Eur. | 1820 |
| intermedium | White | 6, H. | A. | Italy | 1820 |
| involucratum | Pa. pur. | 6, H. | A. | Mexico | 1802 |
| Kitaibelianum, 6 | Pa. pur. | 7, H. | A. | Hungary | 1818 |
| Lagascanum, 7 | Pa. yel. | 7, H. | A. | Spain | 1818 |
| Lagopus | Red | 7, H. | A. | S. Eur. | 1827 |
| lappaceum | Pa. red | 7, H. | A. | Montpel. | 1787 |
| lasiocephalum | Purple | 7, H. Her. | P. | C. G. H. | 1823 |
| latinum | Wht. red | 6, H. Her. | P. | Italy | |
| leucanthum, 8 | White | 6, H. | A. | Tauria | 1820 |
| ligusticum, 9 | Wht. red | 6, H. | A. | Spain | 1816 |
| Lupinaster, 10 | Purple | 7, H. Her. | P. | Siberia | 1741 |
| albiflorum, 11 | White | 7, H. Her. | P. | Siberia | 1818 |
| malacanthum | Purple | 7, H. | A. | | 1824 |
| maritimum, 12 | Pa. pur. | 6, H. | A. | Britain | |
| medium | Purple | 6, H. Her. | P. | England | |
| megacephalum, 13 | Yel. wht. | H. Her. | P. | Missouri | |
| Michelianum | Wht. grn. | 7, H. | A. | Italy | 1815 |
| micranthum | Yellow | 7, H. | A. | Cyrene | 1816 |
| microphyllum | Purple | 7, H. | A. | Scandia. | 1819 |
| montanum | White | 7, H. | A. | Europe | 1786 |
| noricum | Cream | 7, H. Her. | P. | Carinthia | 1821 |
| obscurum | Pa. red | 6, H. | A. | Italy | 1824 |
| ochroleucum | Sulphur | 5, H. Her. | P. | England | |
| olympicum | Cream | 6, H. Her. | P. | S. Eur. | 1817 |
| pallescens | Pa. yel. | 7, H. De. | Tr. | Carinthia | 1804 |
| pallidum | White | 6, H. | A. | Hungary | 1803 |
| pannonicum | Wht. yel. | 6, H. Her. | P. | Hungary | 1752 |
| parisiense | Yellow | 6, H. | A. | France | |
| parviflorum, 14 | White | 6, H. | A. | Hungary | 1820 |
| pennsylvanicum | Red | 7, H. Her. | P. | N. Amer. | 1811 |
| phleoides | Wht. pur. | 6, H. | A. | Spain | 1818 |
| physodes | Reddish | 6, H. De. | Tr. | Hungary | 1805 |
| pratense | Purple | 7, H. Her. | P. | Britain | |
| procumbens, 15 | Yellow | 6, H. Tr. | A. | Britain | |
| purpurascens, 16 | Purple | 6, H. Her. | P. | Siberia | 1816 |
| purpureum | Purple | 6, H. | A. | France | 1816 |
| reflexum | Purple | 6, H. | A. | Virginia | 1794 |
| repens | White | 7, H. De. | Tr. | Britain | |
| pentaphyllum | White | 6, H. De. | Tr. | Britain | |
| rubens | Drk. red | H. Her. | P. | S. Eur. | 1633 |
| rupestre | White | 6, H. Her. | P. | Naples | 1820 |
| saxatile | Pa. wht. | 6, H. | B. | Switzerl. | 1816 |
| scabrum | White | 5, H. Tr. | A. | Britain | |
| Sebastianum | Pa. yel. | 6, H. | A. | Italy | 1800 |
| spadiceum | Yellow | 7, H. Her. | P. | Europe | 1778 |
| speciosum | Yellow | 6, H. | A. | Candia | 1752 |
| sphærocephalon | White | 6, H. | A. | N. Afric. | 1820 |
| squarrosum | Pa. pur. | 7, H. | A. | Spain | 1640 |
| flavicans, 17 | Pa. yel. | 7, H. | A. | Pisania | 1817 |
| stellatum | Pa. rose | 7, H. Tr. | A. | England | |
| strictum | White | 7, H. | A. | S. Eur. | 1805 |
| suaveolens | Purph. | 7, H. | A. | Italy | 1820 |
| subterraneum | White | 7, H. | A. | England | |
| supinum | Pa. pur. | 6, H. | A. | S. Eur. | 1816 |
| sylvaticum | Purple | 6, H. | A. | France | |
| tenuiflorum | Pa. red | 7, H. | A. | Italy | 1823 |
| tenuifolium | | 6, H. | A. | Italy | 1826 |
| tomentosum | White | 6, H. | A. | S. Eur. | 1640 |
| trichocephalum | Cream | 6, H. Her. | P. | Caucasus | 1827 |
| uniflorum | Blue | 6, H. De. | Tr. | Italy | 1800 |
| Sternbergianum | White | 6, H. De. | Tr. | S. Eur. | 1822 |

| vaginātŭm, 18 | . | Pa. yel. | . | H. Her. | P. | Switzerl. | 1819 |
| vesiculōsŭm, 19 | . | Red | . 6, | H. | A. | Hungary | 1805 |
| Wormskieldii | . | Purple | . 8, | H. | A. | | 1830 |

*arvênsé*, *A. grăcĭlĕ* 2, *cyathifolĭŭm, filĭfŏrmĕ, fimbriātŭm, fragĭfĕrŭm glomerātŭm, resupinātŭm, spumōsŭm, striātŭm, suffŏcātŭm, tridentātŭm.*

TRIGLŌCHĬN, *Linn.* From *treis*, three, and *glochin*, a point; in allusion to the three angles of the capsule. *Linn.* 6, Or. 3, Nat. Or. *Juncagineæ.* These plants are found in marshy situations. *T. bulbosum* is increased by offsets, all the other species by division.

| Barrelieri | . | . | Green | . 7, | H. Her. | P. | Italy | . | 1820 |
| bulbōsŭm | . | . | Purple | . 10, | G. Bl. | P. C. O. H. | | . | 1806 |
| decĭpiēns | . | . | Green | . 7, | G. Her. | P. N. Holl. | | . | 1820 |
| elātŭm | . | . | Green | . 6, | H. Her. | P. N. Amer. | | . | 1818 |
| marĭtĭmŭm | . | . | Green | . 6, | H. Her. | P. Britain | | . | |
| palūstrĕ | . | . | Green | . 7, | H. Her. | P. Britain | | . | |
| Dicksōnii | . | . | Green | . 7, | H. Her. | P. England | | . | |

TRIGONAL, having three angles.
TRIGONĔLLA, *Linn.* From *treis*, three, and *gonu*, an angle; the vexillum of the flower is flat, while the wings spread and give it a triangular appearance. *Linn.* 17, Or. 4, Nat. Or. *Leguminosæ.* These plants are not very ornamental. They all succeed best in a light sandy soil; the perennial kinds are readily increased by dividing the plants at the root, or by seeds; while the annual kinds only require sowing in the open border in spring. The seeds of *T. Fœnumgræcum* are used in fomentations, for softening, maturing, and dispersing tumours. *Synonymes:* 1. *Melilotus procumbens.* 2. *M. cæruleus.* 3. *Trigonella flexuosa.* 4. *Trifolium ornithopodioides.* 5. *Trigonella media.* 6. *M. hamosa, uncinata.*

| ægyptiăcă | . | . | Yellow | . 7, | H. Tr. | A. | Egypt | . | 1818 |
| Besseriānă, 1 | . | . | Blue | . 7, | H. | A. | Podolia | . | 1810 |
| cærūlĕă, 2 | . | . | Blue | . 7, | H. | A. | Switzerl. | . | 1562 |
| cornicŭlātă | . | . | Yellow | . 6, | H. | A. | S. Eur. | . | 1597 |
| esculēntă | . | . | Yellow | . 7, | S. | A. | E. Ind. | . | 1815 |
| Fischeriānă, 3 | . | . | Yellow | . 7, | H. | A. | Tiflis | . | 1818 |
| Fœnumgræcŭm | . | . | White | . 7, | H. | A. | Montpel. | . | 1597 |
| hybrĭdă | . | . | Yellow | . 7, | H. De. | Tr. | France | . | 1806 |
| littorālis | . | . | Yellow | . 7, | H. | A. | Sicily | . | 1816 |
| monspellĭacă | . | . | Yellow | . 6, | H. Tr. | A. | Montpel. | . | 1710 |
| ornithopodioĭdĕs, 4 | Red | . | . | | H. Tr. | A. | Britain | . | |
| ornithoryncha | . | . | Yellow | . 7, | H. | A. | Russia | . | 1818 |
| platycārpōs | . | . | Yellow | . 7, | H. | A. | Siberia | . | 1741 |
| pinnatĭfĭdă, 5 | . | . | Yellow | . 7, | H. Tr. | A. | Spain | . | 1801 |
| polycĕrātă | . | . | Yellow | . 8, | H. | A. | S. Eur. | . | 1759 |
| prostrātă | . | . | White | . 7, | H. Tr. | A. | S. France | . | 1818 |
| ruthenĭcă | . | . | Yellow | . 6, | H. De. | Tr. | Siberia | . | 1759 |
| uncinātă, 6 | . | . | Yellow | . 7, | H. | A. | Tauria | . | 1798 |

*callĭcĕrăs, cancellātă, flexuōsă, gladiātă, hamōsă, spinōsă, striātă, tĕnŭis.*

TRIGŌNĬA, *Aublet.* From *treis*, three, and *gonu*, an angle, the fruit is three-angled, three-valved, and three-celled. *Linn.* 16, Or. 2, Nat. Or. *Celastraceæ.* For culture and propagation, see *Trewia.*

| mōllis | . | . | . | Yelsh. wht | . | 8. Ev. | S. | Brazil | . | 1823 |
| villōsă | . | . | . | Yel. red | . | 8. Ev. | S. | Cayenne | . | 1820 |

TRIGONĬDĬUM, *Lindley.* From *trigona*, a triangle, and *eidos*, like; in allusion to the triangular form of several parts of the plant. *Linn.* 20, Or. 1, Nat. Or. *Orchidaceæ.* This is rather an interesting genus of easily cultivated, though slow growing plants. They require to be grown in good fibrous peat, raised a little above the pot, which must be thoroughly drained.

| acuminātŭm | . | . | Straw col. | . | 8. Epi. | | Demerara | . | 1834 |
| acūtŭm | . | . | . | | . | 8. Epi. | | Demerara | . | |
| Egertoniānŭm | . | . | Pa. brn. | . | 8. Epi. | | Demerara | . | |
| obtūsŭm | . | . | Orange | . 6, | 8. Epi. | | Demerara | . | 1834 |

TRIGUĔRĂ. Cavanilles named this genus after D. Trigueros, a Spanish botanist who first discovered the plant. *Linn.* 5, Or. 1, Nat. Or. *Malvaceæ.* For culture and propagation, see *Verbascum.* Synonyme: 1. *Verbascum Osbeckia.*

| ambrosiăcă, 1 | . | Pursh. vio. 7, | H. | | A. | Spain | . | . | 1752 |

TRIGYNOUS, having three styles.
TRILLĬUM, *Linn.* From *trilix*, triple; the calyx has three sepals, the corolla three petals, the pistil three styles, and the stem three leaves. *Linn.* 6, Or. 3, Nat. Or. *Melanthaceæ.* Curious little tuberous rooted plants, succeeding best in a bed of peat soil, and rather slowly increased by dividing the roots, or by seeds. The roots of all the species are violently emetic, and their mawkish, rather nauseous

berries, are at least suspicious. *Synonymes:* 1. *T. rhomboideum.* 2. *T. pendulum.* 3. *T. pictum.* 4. *T. erythrocarpum.* 5. *T. erectum var.* 6. *T. pusillum.*

| Catesbæi | . | . | Red | . 5, | H. Tu. | P. | Carolina | . | 1820 |
| cērnŭŭm | . | . | White | . 4, | H. Tu. | P. | N. Amer. | . | 1758 |
| discŏlŏr | . | . | Green | . 5, | H. Tu. | P. | Georgia | . | 1831 |
| erēctŭm, 1 | . | . | Brown | . 4, | H. Tu. | P. | N. Amer. | . | 1759 |
| album | . | . | White | . 4, | H. Tu. | P. | N. Amer. | . | 1700 |
| viridiflōrŭm, 2 | . | Pa. grn. | . 4, | H. Tu. | P. | Canada | . | 1805 |
| erythrocārpŭm, 3 | Red wht. | . 5, | H. Tu. | P. | N. Amer. | . | 1811 |
| grandiflōrŭm, 4 | . | White | . 7, | H. Tu. | P. | N. Amer. | . | 1799 |
| nervōsŭm | . | . | Red | . 4, | H. Tu. | P. | Georgia | . | 1820 |
| obovātŭm | . | . | Red | . 4, | H. Tu. | P. | Canada | . | 1810 |
| ovātŭm | . | . | Pa. pur. | . 5, | H. Tu. | P. | N. Amer. | . | 1812 |
| pendŭlŭm, 5 | . | . | White | . 5, | H. Tu. | P. | N. Amer. | . | 1805 |
| petiolātŭm | . | . | Brown | . 4, | H. Tu. | P. | N. Amer. | . | 1811 |
| pŭmĭlŭm, 6 | . | . | Red | . 5, | H. Tu. | P. | Carolina | . | 1812 |
| sessĭlĕ | . | . | Brown | . 4, | H. Tu. | P. | N. Amer. | . | 1759 |
| stylōsŭm | . | . | Red | . 4, | H. Tu. | P. | Carolina | . | 1823 |
| undulātŭm | . | . | Red | . 4, | H. Tu. | P. | N. Amer. | . | 1818 |

TRILOCULAR, having three cells.
TRINĬA, *Hoffmann.* In honour of Dr. Trinius, a famous Russian botanist. *Linn.* 5, Or. 2, Nat. Or. *Umbelliferæ.* Worthless hardy biennials. *Synonymes:* 1. *Pimpinella dioica.* 2. *P. dichotoma, ramosissima, glauca.* 3. *T. Henningii—T. Hoffmanni* 1, *Kitaibelii* 2, *vulgaris* 3.

TRIŎDĬA, *R. Brown.* From *treis*, three, and *odous*, teeth; the palea. *Linn.* 3, Or. 2, Nat. Or. *Gramineæ.* A perennial hardy grass, increased by seeds. *Synonyme:* 1. *Poa decumbens—T. decumbens.*

TRIOPTĔRĬS, *Linn.* From *treis*, three, and *pteron*, a wing; the carpels are each furnished with three wings. *Linn.* 16, Or. 6, Nat. Or. *Malpighiaceæ.* A genus of very elegant twiners, extremely difficult to bring into flower in this country. They grow well in a mixture of loam and peat; and cuttings of the ripened wood will root in sand, under a glass, in heat.

| jamaicēnsis | . | . | Yellow | . 8. Ev. | Tw. | Jamaica | . | 1822 |
| sericĕă | . | . | Yellow | . 8. Ev. | Tw. | S. Amer. | . | 1823 |

TRIŎSTĔUM, *Linn.* From *treis*, three, and *osteon*, a bone, in allusion to the three hard seeds. *Linn.* 5, Or. 1, Nat. Or. *Caprifoliaceæ.* The species thrive well in a light rich soil; and are increased by cuttings, or by parting at the roots. *T. perfoliatum* is a mild cathartic. Its dried and roasted berries have been used as coffee.

| angustifolĭŭm | . | Yellow | . 6, | H. Her. | P. | Virginia | . | 1699 |
| perfoliātŭm | . | Dk. red | . 6, | H. Her. | P. | N. Amer. | . | 1730 |

TRIPETALOUS, having three petals.
TRIPHĀSĬĂ, *Loureiro.* From *triphasios*, triple; the calyx is three-toothed, and there are three petals. *Linn.* 6, Or. 1, Nat. Or. *Aurantiaceæ.* This plant succeeds well in turfy loam and peat; but it must be carefully watered during winter. Cuttings, ripened at the base, will root in sand, under a glass, in heat. *Synonymes:* 1. *T. aurantiola.* 2. *Limonia trifoliata.*

| trifoliātă, 1 | . | White | . 6, | G. Ev. | S. | China | . | 1798 |

TRIPINNATE, thrice pinnate.
TRIPLĂRIS, *Linn.* From *triplex*, triple; the parts of fructification are disposed in threes. *Linn.* 22, Or. 8, Nat. Or. *Polygonaceæ.* For culture and propagation, see *Trewia.*

| americāna | . | . | Pa. yel. | . | 8. Ev. | T. | S. Amer. | . | 1824 |

TRIPLE-NERVED, throwing out three side nerves a little above the base.
TRIPSĂCUM, *Linn.* From *tribo*, to thresh; in allusion to the purpose to which its grain may be applied. *Linn.* 21, Or. 3, Nat. Or. *Gramineæ.* These plants grow in any rich mould, and are increased by division. They are forage grasses of the West Indies—*T. dactyloides. monostachyon.*

TRIPTILĬŌN, *Ruiz and Pavon.* From *treis*, three, and *ptilon*, a feather; on account of the three divisions of the pappus. *Linn.* 19, Or. 1, Nat. Or. *Compositæ.* A genus of very pretty annuals. The seeds must be raised on a hotbed in spring, and planted out in the open border about the end of May.

| cordifolĭŭm | . | . | White | . 7, | H. | A. | Chile | . | 1824 |
| spinōsŭm | . | . | Blue | . 7, | H. | A. | Chile | . | 1827 |

TRIQUETROUS, having three sides or angles.
TRISECTED, cut into three parts.
TRISĔTUM, *Persoon.* From *treis*, three, and *seta*, a bristle, on account of the three awns of the flower. *Linn.* 3, Or. 2, Nat. Or. *Gramineæ.* According to

the Woburn experiments, *T. pubescens* is well suited for a permanent pasture on light rich soils; it is hardy, early, and more productive than many other kinds in similar soils. *Synonymes*: 1. *Avena planiculmis, alpina.* 2. *A. flavescens.* 3. *A. pubescens.* 4. *A. striata—T. airoïdes, Alopecürüs, alpëstrë, alpïnüm* 1, *argëntëüm, brevifölïüm, carpätïcüm, condensätüm, distichophÿllüm, flavëscëns* 2, *Loeflingiänüm, micränthüm, neglëctüm, parvïflörüm, pennsylvänïcüm, pilösüm, pubëscëns* 3, *rigïdüm, striätüm* 4, *tënüë.*

TRISTĀNIĂ, *R. Brown.* In honour of M. Tristan, a French botanist. *Linn.* 18, Or. 2, Nat. Or. *Myrtaceæ.* Very pretty shrubs, thriving well in loam, peat, and sand, and increased readily by half-ripened cuttings, planted in sand, under a glass. *Synonyme*: 1. *T. laurina.*

| albicāns | | | White . | 6, G. Ev. T. | N. Holl. | 1818 |
|---|---|---|---|---|---|---|
| arborëscëns | | | Yellow | G. Ev. S. | N. Holl. | 1820 |
| confërtă | | | Yellow | 8, G. Ev. S. | N. S. W. | 1805 |
| dëprëssă | | | | 8, G. Ev. S. | N. Holl. | 1820 |
| macrophyllă, 1 | | | White . | 6, G. Ev. T. | Moreton B. | 1800 |
| myrtifölïă | | | | G. Ev. S. | N. Holl. | 1818 |
| nereïfölïă | | | Yellow | 7, G. Ev. S. | N. S. W. | 1804 |
| persïcïfölïă | | | | G. Ev. S. | N. Holl. | 1824 |

TRISTËGĬS, *Ness.* From *treis,* three, and *stege,* a covering; in reference to the three glumes or valves of the calyx. *Linn.* 3, Or. 2, Nat. Or. *Gramineæ.* Growing in common soil; seeds.

| glutinösă | | | Apetal . | 6, Grass. | | 1822 |
|---|---|---|---|---|---|---|

TRITËLEĬĂ, *Lindley.* From *treis,* three, and *teleios,* complete; in allusion to the perfect ternary arrangement of its parts. *Linn.* 3, Or. 1, Nat. Or. *Liliaceæ.* Very handsome plants, of easy culture in a mixture of peat, loam, and sand, and readily increased by offsets from the roots; or by seeds.

| grandiflörä | | | White . | 7, F. Bl. P. | N. Amer. | 1826 |
|---|---|---|---|---|---|---|
| läxă | | | Dk. blue . | 7, F. Bl. P. | Californ. | 1832 |
| unïflörä | | | Blue . | 7, F. Bl. P. | B. Ayres | 1836 |

TRITĬCÜM, *Linn.* From *tritum,* rubbed; in allusion to its being originally rubbed down to make it eatable. *Linn.* 3, Or. 2, Nat. Or. *Gramineæ.* This is undoubtedly the most important genus of the order *Gramineæ,* as it includes the wheats, the properties of which are too well known to require any detailed notice in this work. *Synonymes*: 1. *Secale creticum.* 2. *T. villosum.* 3. *T. Zea.* 4. *Secale villosum.*

| sätïvüm | | | Apetal . | 6, Grass. | Baschkiros | |
|---|---|---|---|---|---|---|
| aträtüm | | | Apetal . | 7, Grass. | Austria | 1820 |
| Bauhïnï | | | Apetal . | 7, Grass. | Spain | 1821 |
| Cevällöä | | | Apetal . | 6, Grass. | | |
| Cianfügöä | | | Apetal . | 7, Grass. | Spain | 1821 |
| cochleärë | | | Apetal . | 7, Grass. | Spain | 1820 |
| compäctüm | | | Apetal . | 7, Grass. | Austria | 1819 |
| compösïtüm | | | Apetal . | 7, Grass. | Egypt | 1799 |
| dicöccüm | | | Apetal . | 6, Grass. | | |
| albüm | | | Apetal . | 6, Grass. | | |
| rüfüm | | | Apetal . | 6, Grass. | | |
| dürüm, 2 | | | Apetal . | 7, Grass. | S. Eur. | 1820 |
| fastuösüm | | | Apetal . | 7, Grass. | Spain | 1820 |
| Gærtnerïänüm | | | Apetal . | 7, Grass. | Spain | 1824 |
| hordeïförmë | | | Apetal . | 7, Grass. | Austria | 1819 |
| hybärnüm | | | Apetal . | 6, Grass. | | |
| Linnæänüm | | | Apetal . | 7, Grass. | Spain | 1820 |
| monocöccüm | | | Apetal . | 6, Grass. | | 1648 |
| platystächyüm | | | Apetal . | 7, Grass. | Spain | 1821 |
| polönïcüm | | | Apetal . | 7, Grass. | | 1692 |
| sibïrïcüm | | | Apetal . | 6, Grass. | Siberia | 1800 |
| strïctüm | | | Apetal . | 6, Grass. | Sicily | 1826 |
| Spëltä, 3 | | | Apetal . | 6, Grass. | | |
| trïcöccüm | | | Apetal . | 6, Grass. | | |
| türgïdüm | | | Apetal . | 6, Grass. | | |
| venulösüm | | | Apetal . | 6, Grass. | Egypt | |
| villösüm, 4 | | | Apetal . | 6, Grass. | S. Eur. | 1790 |

*campëstrë, crëtïcüm* 1, *hispänïcüm, squarrösüm.*

TRITÖMĬĂ, *Ker.* From *treis,* three, and *temno* to cut; in allusion to the three sharp edges of the ends of the leaves. *Linn.* 6, Or. 1, Nat. Or. *Liliaceæ.* Handsome flowering plants, succeeding in a light rich soil, and readily increased by suckers from the root. The species often flower very late in autumn, and even through very mild winters; but they ought to have the protection of a frame.

| Burchellïï | | | Yel. red . | H. Her. P. | C. G. H. | 1816 |
|---|---|---|---|---|---|---|
| mëdïă | | | Orange . | 4, F. Her. P. | C. G. H. | 1789 |
| pümïlă | | | Orange . | 9, F. Her. P. | C. G. H. | 1774 |
| Uvärïă | | | Orange . | 9, F. Her. P. | C. G. H. | 1707 |

TRITÖNĬĂ, *Ker.* From *triton,* a weathercock; in

allusion to the variable direction of the stamens in the various species. *Linn.* 3, Or. 1, Nat. Or. *Iridaceæ.* Very handsome plants when in flower. They require the same treatment as the genus *Ixia* and other similar genera.

| anigozänthäflörä | | | Yellow | 6, G. Bl. P. | C. G. H. | 1825 |
|---|---|---|---|---|---|---|
| capënsïs | | | White . | 9, G. Bl. P. | C. G. H. | 1811 |
| cöncölör | | | Yellow | 5, G. Bl. P. | C. G. H. | 1811 |
| erëctä | | | Orange | 6, G. Bl. P. | C. G. H. | 1758 |
| crispä | | | Flesh . | 4, G. Bl. P. | C. G. H. | 1787 |
| dëüstä | | | Fulvid | 5, G. Bl. P. | C. G. H. | 1774 |
| fenesträtä | | | Yellow | 5, G. Bl. P. | C. G. H. | 1801 |
| flävä | | | Yellow | 2, G. Bl. P. | C. G. H. | 1780 |
| fucätä | | | Red yel. | 5, G. Bl. P. | C. G. H. | 1813 |
| lineätä | | | Varieg. | 5, G. Bl. P. | C. G. H. | 1774 |
| longïflörä | | | White . | 5, G. Bl. P. | C. G. H. | 1774 |
| minïätä | | | Fulvid | 8, G. Bl. P. | C. G. H. | 1795 |
| odörätä | | | Yellow | 6, G. Bl. P. | C. G. H. | 1829 |
| pallïdä | | | White . | 8, G. Bl. P. | C. G. H. | 1806 |
| pectïnätä | | | Yellow | 5, G. Bl. P. | C. G. H. | 1825 |
| refrāctä | | | Yellow | 5, G. Bl. P. | C. G. H. | 1815 |
| rochënsïs | | | Yellow | 5, G. Bl. P. | C. G. H. | 1811 |
| rösëä | | | Pink . | 6, G. Bl. P. | C. G. H. | 1795 |
| securïgërä | | | Brown | 5, G. Bl. P. | C. G. H. | 1774 |
| squalïdä | | | Rufous | 5, G. Bl. P. | C. G. H. | 1774 |
| strïätä | | | Blue . | 5, G. Bl. P. | C. G. H. | 1825 |
| tenuïflörä | | | Yellow | 4, G. Bl. P. | C. G. H. | 1811 |
| virïdïs | | | Green . | 7, G. Bl. P. | C. G. H. | 1788 |
| xanthospïlä | | | Red. yel. | 6, G. Bl. P. | C. G. H. | 1825 |

TRITÜRĀTED, reduced to powder by pounding.

TRIUMFËTTĬĂ, *Linn.* In honour of John Baptist Triumfetti, an Italian botanist and author. *Linn.* 14, Or. 1, Nat. Or. *Tiliaceæ.* Uninteresting plants, chiefly under-shrubs, growing in common garden soil; cuttings and seeds. *Synonyme*: 1. *T. macrophylla—T. althæoïdës* 1, *angulätä, aürëä, glandulösä, grandïflörä, havänënsïs, heterophŷllä, Läppülä, micröpëtälä, oblongätä, pïlösä, rhomboïdëä, rotundïfölïä, semïtrïlöbä, suborbïculätä, trïchoclädä, trïloculärïs.*

TRIXIS, *P. Browne.* From *trixos,* triple; on account of its triangular capsule, with three cells. *Linn.* 19, Or. 4, Nat. Or. *Compositæ.* Interesting plants, of common culture. *Synonymes*: 1. *Perdicium brasiliense.* 2. *Leuceria senecioides.*

| auriculätä, 1 | | | White . | 8, S. Ev. S. | Brasil | 1827 |
|---|---|---|---|---|---|---|
| senecioïdës, 2 | | | White . | 8, H. | A. Chile | 1821 |

TRIZEÜXIS, *Lindley.* From *treis,* three, and *zeuxis,* a union; in allusion to the cohesion of the three sepals. *Linn.* 20, Or. 1, Nat. Or. *Orchidaceæ.* A small plant, of no beauty. It succeeds best if fastened to a piece of wood.

| falcätä | | | Green . | 8, S. Epi. | W. Ind. | 1820 |
|---|---|---|---|---|---|---|

TROCHISCÄNTHËS, *Koch.* From *trochiskos,* a small wheel, and *anthos,* a flower. *Linn.* 5, Or. 2, Nat. Or. *Umbelliferæ.* A hardy herbaceous plant, of no beauty. *Synonyme*: 1. *Ligusticum nodiflorum—T. nodïflörä.*

TROCHLEÄTË, twisted like a pully.

TROCHOCÄRPĂ, *R. Brown.* From *trochos,* a wheel, and *karpos,* fruit: the cells of the fruit diverge from a common centre like the spokes of a wheel. *Linn.* 5, Or. 1, Nat. Or. *Epacridaceæ.* An extremely handsome shrub. For culture and propagation, see *Epacris.*

| laurïnä | | | Yellow . | 6, G. Bl. P. | N. Holl. | 1829 |
|---|---|---|---|---|---|---|

TRÖLLĬÜS, *Linn.* From *trol,* or *trolin,* an old German word signifying something round; in allusion to the shape of the flower; whence, also, the English name Globe-flower. *Linn.* 13, Or. 6, Nat. Or. *Ranunculaceæ.* Pretty border plants, thriving best in a light moist soil, and increasing by division or seeds. *Synonymes*: 1. *T. laxus.* 2. *T. ranunculinus.*

| americänüs, 1 | | | Yellow | 5, H. Her. P. | N. Amer. | 1805 |
|---|---|---|---|---|---|---|
| asïätïcüs | | | Drk. or. | 5, H. Her. P. | Siberia | 1759 |
| caucäsïcüs | | | Yellow | 5, H. Her. P. | Caucasus | 1817 |
| europäüs | | | Yellow | 5, H. Her. P. | Britain | |
| albüs | | | Whitish | 5, H. Her. P. | Britain | |
| humïlïs | | | Yellow | 5, H. Her. P. | Austria | 1800 |
| napellïfölïüs | | | Yellow | 5, H. Her. P. | Europe | |
| pätülüs, 2 | | | Orange | 5, H. Her. P. | Siberia | 1800 |

TROMÖTRĬCHĂ, *Haworth.* From *tromos,* fear, and *thrix,* a hair; in reference to the cilia of the corolla being tremulous. *Linn.* 5, Or. 2, Nat. Or. *Asclepiadaceæ.* Interesting plants. For culture and propagation, see *Stapelia.* *Synonymes*: 1. *Stapelia fuscata.* 2. *S. obliqua.* 3. *S. revoluta.*

| fuscätä, 1 | | | Brn. pur. | 7, S. Ev. S. | C. G. H. | 1814 |
|---|---|---|---|---|---|---|
| glaücä | | | Red pur. | 7, S. Ev. S. | C. G. H. | 1799 |

| | | | | | |
|---|---|---|---|---|---|
| obliquā, 2 | . . . | Dull yel. | 7, S. Ev. S. | C. G. H. | 1805 |
| pruinōsā | . . . | Drk. brn. | 6, S. Ev. S. | C. G. H. | 1795 |
| revolūtā, 3 | . . . | Purple | 7, S. Ev. S. | C. G. H. | 1790 |

**TROPÆOLUM**, *Linn.* From *tropaion*, a trophy; the leaves resemble a buckler, and the flowers an empty helmet. *Linn.* 8, Or. 1, Nat. Or. *Tropæolaceæ.* All the species are very showy when in flower, and are therefore desirable acquisitions to every collection. The greenhouse and frame species thrive in any light rich soil; and are readily increased by cuttings in the same kind of soil, under a glass. The annual species should be sown in the open ground in spring. The tuberous-rooted kinds succeed well in the open air, in a sheltered situation, during summer; in winter they may be taken up and kept in sand until spring, when they may be again planted out into the open ground. The seeds of *T. majus* are pickled, and used as capers, to which they are preferred by some. The roots of *T. tuberosum* are eaten in Peru. *Synonyme:* 1. *T. peregrinum.*

| | | | | | |
|---|---|---|---|---|---|
| aduncūm, 1 | . | Yellow | 8, G. Ev. Cl. | N. Granada | 1810 |
| brachycērās | . | Yellow | F. Tu. P. | Chile | 1830 |
| hybridūm | . | Orange | 7, G. Ev. Tr. | Peru | |
| Jarrăttĭ | . | Scar. yel. | G. Ev. Cl. | Santiago | 1836 |
| majūs | . | Or. yel. | 7, H. Tw. A. | Peru | 1686 |
| atrosanguinēŭm | . | Dk. red | 8, H. Tw. A. | Peru | |
| flōrē plēnō | . | Or. yel. | 8, G. Ev. Tw. | Peru | 1686 |
| minŭs | . | Or. yel. | 8, G. Ev. Tw. | Peru | 1596 |
| flōrē plēnō | . | Or. yel. | G. Ev. Tr. | Peru | 1596 |
| pentaphyllūm | . | Or. yel. | 8, F. Ev. Tw. | M. Video | 1824 |
| pinnātūm | . | Yellow | 6, G. Ev. Cl. | Peru | |
| polyphyllūm | . | Or. yel. | 6, G. Ev. Cl. | Chile | 1827 |
| tricolōrŭm | . | Or. pur. | 7, F. Ev. Cl. | Valparaiso | 1828 |
| tuberōsūm | . | Yel. red | 9, F. Tu. P. | Peru | 1836 |

**TRŎPHĬS**, *Linn.* From *trophe*, fodder; the leaves and twigs are used as fodder for cattle when grass is scarce. *Linn.* 22, Or. 2, Nat. Or. *Urticaceæ.* These plants grow freely in loam and peat; cuttings.

| | | | | |
|---|---|---|---|---|
| americānā | . . | Green | 4, S. Ev. T. W. Ind. | 1789 |
| asperā | . . | Green | S. Ev. T. E. Ind. | 1802 |

**TRŎXĬMŎN**, *Don.* From *troximon*, eatable. *Linn.* 19, Or. 1, Nat. Or. *Compositæ.* Any common soil suits these plants, and they are readily increased by division. *Synonyme:* 1. *T. marginatum.*

| | | | | |
|---|---|---|---|---|
| cuspidātūm, 1 | Yellow | 7, H. Her. P. | Louisiana | 1824 |
| glaūcūm | . | Yellow | 5, H. Her. P. | Missouri | 1811 |

**TRUE DODDER,** see *Cuscūtă Epīthȳmŭm.*

**TRUE PARSLEY,** see *Apīŭm Petroselīnŭm.*

**TRUE SERVICE,** see *Pȳrŭs Sŏrbŭs.*

**TRUFFLE,** see *Tŭbĕr.*

**TRUMPET-FLOWER,** see *Bīgnōnĭā.*

**TRUNCATUS,** blunt, as if cut off.

**TRYMĂLĬŎM**, *Fenzl.* Not explained. *Linn.* 5, Or. 1, Nat. Or. *Rhamnaceæ.* This species is well deserving of a place in every collection of greenhouse plants, on account of its snow-white flowers; which, being produced in numerous loose, drooping panicles, render it a very beautiful object when in blossom; its flowers are also deliciously fragrant. The wood is said to be soft and pithy, and the plant apt to die off in winter, if overpotted, and not kept in a warm and light situation: in other respects, it may be treated as the greenhouse species of *Ceanothus.*

| | | | | |
|---|---|---|---|---|
| odoratissimūm | . | White | 2, G. Ev. S. N. Holl. | 1837 |

**TUBE-FLOWER,** see *Clerodēndrŏn Siphonānthŭs.*

**TUBE OF CALYX,** the tube formed by the cohesion of the sepals.

**TUBE OF STAMENS,** the tube formed by the cohesion of the filaments in *monadelphous* flowers.

**TŬBĔR**, *Michaux.* An ancient Roman name for a fungus. *Linn.* 24, Or. 9, Nat. Or. *Fungi.* T. *cibarium* is the famous truffle, so celebrated in the annals of cookery. It grows under ground, and is found in light dry soils, in some of the southern counties; but it is much more common in Italy, Germany, and the south of France, whence immense quantities are imported. Dogs are taught to find this fungus by the smell, and to scratch it up out of the earth. An instance is recorded of a man having possessed this power. It is brought to the table boiled or stewed. It is reported to have a stimulating aphrodisiacal quality, which perhaps renders it more popular than its flavour, which is trifling. *Loudon's Encyclop. of Plants—T. ălbĭdŭm, cĭbārĭŭm.*

**TUBERCULĀRĬĀ**, *Tode.* From *tuberculum*, a pimple;

warted appearance of the plants. *Linn.* 24, Or. 9, Nat. Or. *Fungi.* Found upon dead branches. *Synonyms:* 1. *Clavaria coccinea—T. ălbĭdā, cōnflūĕns, discoidēā, granulātā, nigrĭcāns, vulgārĭs* 1.

**TUBERCULĀTUS,** covered with knots or tubercles.

**TUBEROSE,** see *Polyānthēs tuberōsā.*

**TUBEROUS,** bearing fleshy, solid, roundish, or longish root like underground stems, as the potato.

**TULBĂGHĬĀ**, *Linn.* In honour of Tulbagh, a Dutch governor at the Cape of Good Hope. *Linn.* 6, Or. 1, Nat. Or. *Liliaceæ.* Interesting plants when in flower. They succeed well in sandy loam and peat, and are increased by offsets or seeds.

| | | | | | |
|---|---|---|---|---|---|
| affīnĭs | . . | Brown | 6, G. Bl. P. | C. G. H. | 1820 |
| alliācēā | . . | Brown | 6, G. Bl. P. | C. G. H. | 1774 |
| cepācēā | . . | Brown | 4, G. Bl. P. | C. G. H. | 1795 |
| Ludwigiānā | . | Green | 10, G. Bl. P. | C. G. H. | 1838 |
| violācēā | . . | Purple | 8, G. Bl. P. | C. G. H. | |

**TULIP,** see *Tŭlĭpā.*

**TŬLĬPĂ**, *Tournefort.* Said to be from *Thoulyban*, its Persian name. *Linn.* 6, Or. 1, Nat. Or. *Liliaceæ.* A genus of very celebrated and much prized florist's flowers. They succeed well in rich loam and sand, and are increased by offsets; new varieties are obtained from seed. The choicer kinds require to be taken up and dried after they have ceased flowering, and planted again in the autumn. They should be slightly protected in very rainy or frosty weather, or they are very liable to rot. *Synonyme:* 1. *T. acuminata.*

| | | | | | |
|---|---|---|---|---|---|
| altaĭcā | . | Yellow | 4, H. Bl. P. | Altai | |
| Bieberstein iānā | . | Yel. pur. | 4, H. Bl. P. | Siberia | 1820 |
| biflōrā | . | Yellow | 4, H. Bl. P. | Russia | 1805 |
| Bonarotiānā | . | Varieg. | 4, H. Bl. P. | Italy | 1827 |
| Celsiānā | . | Yellow | 6, H. Bl. P. | Levant | |
| Clusiānā | . | Wht. pur. | 7, H. Bl. P. | Sicily | 1636 |
| cornūtā, 1 | . | Striped | 4, H. Bl. P. | Levant | 1816 |
| Gesneriānā | . | Striped | 4, H. Bl. P. | Levant | 1577 |
| laciniātā | . | Varieg. | 4, H. Bl. P. | Levant | 1603 |
| lūtēā | . | Yellow | 4, H. Bl. P. | Levant | 1603 |
| plēnā | . | Varieg. | 4, H. Bl. P. | Levant | 1603 |
| versĭcolŏr | . | Varieg. | 4, H. Bl. P. | Levant | 1603 |
| maleolēns | . | Red yel. | 5, H. Bl. P. | Italy | 1827 |
| variegātā | . | Varieg. | 5, H. Bl. P. | Italy | 1827 |
| mēdĭā | . | Scar. wht. | 5, H. Bl. P. | | 1828 |
| montānā | . | Scarlet | 7, H. Bl. P. | Persia | 1826 |
| ŏcŭlŭs-sōlĭs | . | Red blue | 4, H. Bl. P. | Italy | 1816 |
| persĭcā | . | Scar. blk. | 4, H. Bl. P. | Persia | 1826 |
| patēns | . | Wht. grey | 4, H. Bl. P. | Siberia | 1826 |
| præcōx | . | Scarlet | 4, H. Bl. P. | Italy | 1825 |
| pubēscēns | . | Red | 4, H. Bl. P. | | 1824 |
| rēpēns | . | Yellow | 4, H. Bl. P. | Russia | 1819 |
| saxātĭlĭs | . | Yellow | 4, H. Bl. P. | Crete | 1827 |
| scabriscāpā | . | Red yel. | 4, H. Bl. P. | Italy | 1847 |
| stellātā | . | White | 4, H. Bl. P. | Camana | 1827 |
| strangulātā | . | | 4, H. Bl. P. | | |
| suavēolēns | . | Red yel. | 4, H. Bl. P. | S. Eur. | 1603 |
| sylvēstrĭs | . | Yellow | 4, H. Bl. P. | England | |
| tricolŏr | . | Scarlet | 4, H. Bl. P. | Russia | 1817 |
| tūrcĭcā | . | Striped | 4, H. Bl. P. | | |

**TULIP-TREE,** see *Liriodēndrŏn.*

**TULOSTŎMĂ**, *Persoon.* From *tulos*, a wart, and *stoma*, the mouth; in allusion to the nature of the orifice by which the seeds are dispersed. *Linn.* 24, Or. 9, Nat. Or. *Fungi.* Found upon the mossy tops of walls in winter and spring—*T. brumāle.*

**TUMID,** swelling.

**TUNIC,** a coat, or seed cover.

**TŬPĂ**, *D. Don.* *Tupa* is the name of *T. Feuillei* in Chile. *Linn.* 5, Or. 1, Nat. Or. *Lobeliaceæ.* These plants are well worth a place in every collection, on account of the beauty and singularity of their flowers. For culture and propagation, see *Lobelia.* *Synonymes:* 1. *Lobelia arguta.* 2. *L. Tupa.* 3. *L. polyphylla.* 4. *L. purpurea.* 5. *L. gigantea, L. salicifolia.*

| | | | | | |
|---|---|---|---|---|---|
| argūtā, 1 | . | Yellow | 9, F. Her. P. | Chile | 1824 |
| blāndā | . | Pink | 5, F. Her. P. | Chile | |
| Feuillēĭ, 2 | . | Scarlet | 9, F. Her. P. | Chile | 1824 |
| polyphyllā, 3 | . | Purple | 8, F. Her. P. | Valparaiso | 1832 |
| purpūrēā, 4 | . | Purple | 8, F. Her. P. | Valparaiso | 1825 |
| salicĭfōlĭā, 5 | . | Red | 10, F. Her. P. | Valparaiso | |

**TŬPĬSTRĂ**, *Ker.* A diminutive of *typis*, a mallet; in allusion to the peculiar form of the flower. *Linn.* 6, Or. 1, Nat. Or. *Acoraceæ.* These plants succeed well in sandy loam and peat, and are readily increased by dividing the root. *Synonyme:* 1. *Rohdea japonica.*

| | | | | | |
|---|---|---|---|---|---|
| japonĭcā, 1 | . | Apetal | 2, H. Her. P. | Japan | 1783 |
| nūtāns | . | Livid | S. Her. P. E. Ind. | | 1822 |
| squalĭdā | . | Livid | S. Her. P. Amboyna | | 1820 |

[ 322 ]

TURBINATE, having the figure of a top.

TURGENIX, *Hoffmann.* From *turgeo*, to swell: the fruit. *Linn.* 5, Or. 2, Nat. Or. *Umbelliferæ.* An uninteresting plant; seeds. *Synonyme:* 1. *Caucalis latifolia—T. latifoliā* 1.

TURGID, swollen, puffed.

TUROODSIX, see *Crássulā.*

TURMERIC, see *Curcúmā.*

TURNERA. Linnæus dedicated this genus to the memory of William Turner, Prebendary of York, Canon of Windsor, &c., author of a "New Herbal," 1551, fol.; he died in 1568. *Linn.* 5, Or. 3, Nat. Or. *Turneraceæ.* A genus of very elegant plants when in flower. They thrive in any rich soil, and are all readily increased by seeds. The shrubby kinds may also be increased by cuttings. *Synonymes.* 1. *Piriqueta racemosa.* 2. *T. elegans.*

| | | | | | |
|---|---|---|---|---|---|
| brasiliensis | . | Yellow | . 6, S. Ev. S. Brazil | . | 1810 |
| cistoides | . | Yellow | . 7, S. A. America | . | 1774 |
| cuneiformis | . | Yellow | . 6, S. Ev. S. S. Amer. | . | 1821 |
| guianensis | . | Yellow | . 6, S. A. Guiana | . | 1823 |
| hirtā | . | Yellow | . 6, S. A. Brazil | . | 1818 |
| Pumilēā | . | Yellow | . 7, S. A. Jamaica | . | 1796 |
| racemōsā, 1 | . | Yellow | . 7, H. A. Siberia | . | 1789 |
| rupestris | . | Yellow | . 7, S. Ev. S. Guiana | . | 1824 |
| trioniflōrā, 2 | . | Pa. yel. | . 8. Her. P. Brazil | . | 1819 |
| ulmifōliā | . | Yellow | . 7, S. B. Jamaica | . | 1733 |
| angustifōliā | . | Pa. yel. | . 6, S. Ev. S. Jamaica | . | 1733 |

TURNSOLE, see *Heliotrōpium.*

TURPENTINE, see *Silphiūm terebinthāceūm.*

TURPENTINE-TREE, see *Pistácid Terebínthūs.*

TURPINIX, *Ventenat.* In honour of M. Turpin, a distinguished French botanical artist and naturalist. *Linn.* 23, Or. 2, Nat. Or. *Staphyleaceæ.* Trees of little beauty. They thrive well in a mixture of loam and peat, and are increased by cuttings in sand, under a glass, in heat. *Synonymes:* 1. *Staphylea occidentalis.* 2. *Dalrymplea pomifera.*

| | | | | |
|---|---|---|---|---|
| occidentalis, 1 | . White | . 8. Ev. T. Jamaica | . | 1824 |
| pomifera, 2 | . Yelsh. wht. | 5, S. Ev. T. Sylhet | . | 1820 |

TURRÆX, *Linn.* In honour of Geo. Turra, once professor of Botany at Padua, and author of several botanical works; died in 1607. *Linn.* 16, Or. 6, Nat. Or. *Meliaceæ.* These plants succeed well in loam, peat, and sand, and are easily increased by cuttings, planted in sand, under a glass, in heat.

| | | | | |
|---|---|---|---|---|
| pinnātā | . . . | Pink | . 4, S. Ev. T. Sylhet | . 1828 |
| rigida | . . . | Yellow | . 8. Ev. T. Maurit. | . 1816 |
| virens | . . . | White | . 8. Ev. T. E. Ind. | . 1820 |

TURRITIS, *Dillenius.* From *turris*, a tower; the foliage is so disposed on the stems as to give them a pyramidal form; and for the same reason the plants are called *Tower-mustard. Linn.* 15, Nat. Or. *Crucíferæ.* Hardy annuals, not worth growing—*T. glābrā, G. ramōsā, Grāhāmi, mōllis, pātūlā, salsuginōsā, strictā.*

TUSSILLAGŌ, *Tournefort.* From *tussis*, a cough; for curing which the flowers have been employed. *Linn.* 19, Or. 2, Nat. Or. *Compositæ.* Some of the species are very pretty. They succeed well in common soil, and are readily increased by division. *T. Farfara* is a demulcent bitter, and has been used to soothe irritations in the air passages; hence its reputation as a pectoral medicine. *Synonymes:* 1. *T. bohemica.* 2. *T. paradoxa.* 3. *T. lobata.* 4. *T. tomentosa.*

| | | | | |
|---|---|---|---|---|
| alba | . . . | White | . 3, H. Her. P. Europe | . 1683 |
| alpina | . . . | Li. pur. | . 4, H. Her. P. Austria | . 1710 |
| discolōr | . . . | Li. pur. | . 4, H. Her. P. Austria | . 1633 |
| Farfarā | . . . | Yellow | . 3, H. Her. P. Britain | . |
| fōliis variegātis | Yellow | . 3, H. Her. P. Britain | . |
| frāgrāns | . . . | White | . 2, H. Her. P. Italy | . 1806 |
| frigida | . . . | Pale | . 5, H. Her. P. Lapland | . 1710 |
| laevigātā, 1 | . . . | Yellow | . 5, H. Her. P. Bohemia | . 1816 |
| nivēā, 2 | . . . | White | . 4, H. Her. P. Switserl. | . 1713 |
| palmātā, 3 | . . . | White | . 4, H. Her. P. Labrador | . 1778 |
| purpūrēā | . . . | Purple | . 7, F. Her. P. C. G. H. | . 1824 |
| sagittātā | . . . | White | . 4, H. Her. P. N. Amer. | . |
| spūriā, 4 | . . . | White | . 4, H. Her. P. Germany | . 1790 |

*Petasítes,* P. hȳbridā, sylvéstris.

TUTSAN, see *Androsæmūm.*

TWAYBLADE, see *Listérā.*

TWEEDIX, *Hooker.* In compliment to Mr. James Tweedie, an intelligent and indefatigable collector of plants in Buenos Ayres, Tucuman, S. Brazil, &c. *Linn.* 5, Or. 2, Nat. Or. *Asclepiadaceæ.* These very interesting plants succeed well in sandy loam, with a little peat mixed; and they may be readily increased by cuttings or seeds. They will prove to be nearly, if not quite hardy.

| | | | | |
|---|---|---|---|---|
| coerūlēā | . . . | Blue | . 7, H. De. Tw. B. Ayres | . 1836 |
| versicolōr | . . . | Blue | . 7, H. De. Tw. Tucuman | . 1836 |

TYLOPHŌRĀ, *R. Brown.* From *tylos*, a swelling, and *phoreo*, to bear; alluding to the ventricose pollen masses. *Linn.* 5, Or. 2, Nat. Or. *Asclepiadaceæ.* Interesting plants. For culture and propagation, see *Hoya.*

| | | | | |
|---|---|---|---|---|
| barbātā | . . . | . 7, S. Ev. Tw. N. S. W. | . 1822 |
| exilis | . . . Pa. pur. | . 7, S. Ev. Tw. Sylhet | . 1823 |
| grandiflōrā | . . . | . 7, S. Ev. Tw. N. S. W. | . 1822 |

TYMPANIS, *Tode.* From *tympanon*, a drum; the resemblance of the young velum. *Linn.* 24, Or. 9, Nat. Or. *Fungi.* Found upon dead alder branches —*T. alnēā, conspērsā, fráxini.*

TYPHA, *Linn.* From *typhos*, a marsh; habitat of the species. *Linn.* 21, Or. 3, Nat. Or. *Typhaceæ.* The pollen of Typha is inflammable like that of *Lycopodium*, and is used as a substitute for it.

| | | | | |
|---|---|---|---|---|
| angustifōliā | . . . | Brown | . 6, Grass. Britain | . . |
| latifōliā | . . . | Brown | . 7, Grass. Britain | . . |
| minimā | . . . | Brown | . 7, Grass. Switserl. | . 1822 |
| minōr | . . . | Brown | . 7, Grass. England | . . |

TYPHULX, *Fries.* A diminutive of *Typha*, to which the heads bear a miniature resemblance. *Linn.* 24, Or. 9, Nat. Or. *Fungi.* Found on rotten wood and dead leaves—*T. erythrōpūs, filifōrmis, grácilis, Phacorhīzā, ténūis.*

TYTONIX, *G. Don.* In honour of Arthur Tyton, F.L.S., by whom many of the oldest inhabitants of our gardens are preserved, but particularly those which were formerly cultivated by Miller, and which are now only to be found in his collection. *Linn.* 5, Or. 1, Nat. Or. *Balsaminaceæ.* A beautiful aquatic plant, worthy of a place in every collection. It must be grown in large pots of water, in a rich loamy soil, and placed in the stove or on a hotbed. The seeds require to be sown in spring. *Synonyme:* 1. *Impatiens natans.*

| | | | | |
|---|---|---|---|---|
| nātāns, 1 | . . . Various | . 8, S. Aq. A. E. Ind. | . . | 1810 |

# U.

ULEX, *Linn.* Said to be taken from the Celtic *ac*, a point; in allusion to the prickly branches. *Linn.* 16, Or. 6, Nat. Or. *Leguminosæ.* The double variety of *U. Europæa* is a very elegant plant, and is increased by young cuttings, under a handglass; the other kinds are increased by seeds. *Synonyme:* 1. *U. hibernica.*

| | | | | |
|---|---|---|---|---|
| europēā | . . . | Yellow | . 6, H. Ev. S. Britain | . . |
| flōre plēnō | . . . | Yellow | . 5, H. Ev. S. Britain | . . |
| nānā | . . . | Yellow | . 2, H. Ev. S. Britain | . . |
| provinciālis | . . . | Yellow | . 7, H. Ev. S. S. Eur. | . 1823 |
| strictā, 1 | . . . | Yellow | . 10, H. Ev. S. Ireland | . . |

ULLŌX, *Persoon.* In honour of Antonio Ulloa, a Spanish naturalist. *Linn.* 5, Or. 1, Nat. Or. *Solanaceæ.* This species succeeds well in decayed wood,

or vegetable mould; and is increased by cuttings. *Synonyme:* 1. *Juanulloa parasitica.*

| | | | | |
|---|---|---|---|---|
| parasitica, 1 | . Red | . . Parasite. Peru | . . . | 1824 |

ULMUS, *Linn.* Supposed to be from the Saxon word *elm*, or *ulm*, a name which is applied, with very slight alterations, to the trees of this genus in all the dialects of the Celtic tongue. *Linn.* 5, Or. 2, Nat. Or. *Ulmaceæ.* Fine forest trees, succeeding best when grown on strong lands. They are increased by layers, from stools, or by grafting on the *U. montana. Synonymes:* 1. *U. chinensis.* 2. *U. stricta.* 3. *U. humilis, microphylla, parvifolia, pumila.* 4. *U. planifolia.* 5. *U. sarniensis.* 6. *U. viscosa.* 7. *U. ciliata.* 8. *U. pendula.* 9. *U. americana, montana vegeta.* 10. *U. scabra.* 11. *U. crispa.*

| | | | | | | |
|---|---|---|---|---|---|---|
| alátá . . | . Brown | . 4, H. De. T. N. Amer. | . 1890 |
| álbá . . | . Brown | . 4, H. De. T. Hungary | . 1824 |
| americáná . | . Brown | . 4, H. De. T. N. Amer. | . |
| álbá . . | . Brown | . 4, H. De. T. | |
| fol. variegátá | . Brown | . 4, H. De. T. | |
| incísá . . | . Brown | . 4, H. De. T. N. Amer. | . |
| péndúlá . . | . Brown | . 4, H. De. T. N. Amer. | . 1820 |
| rúbrá . . | . Brown | . 4, H. De. T. N. Amer. | . 1824 |
| campéstris . | . Brown | . 4, H. De. T. Britain | . . |
| acutifóliá . | . Brown | . 4, H. De. T. Britain | . . |
| álbá . . | . Brown | . 4, H. De. T. Britain | . . |
| betulæfóliá . | . Brown | . 4, H. De. T. Britain | . . |
| chinénsis, 1 | . Brown | . 4, H. De. T. China | . . |
| concavæfóliá . | . Brown | . 4, H. De. T. Britain | . . |
| cornubiénsis, 2 . | . Brown | . 4, H. De. T. Britain | . . |
| cucullátá . | . Brown | . 4, H. De. T. | |
| fol. aúreis . | . Brown | . 4, H. De. T. Britain | . . |
| fol. variegátá | . Brown | . 4, H. De. T. Britain | . . |
| latifóliá . | . Brown | . 4, H. De. T. Britain | . . |
| náná . . | . Brown | . 4, H. De. S. Britain | . . |
| parvifóliá, 3 | . Brown | . 4, H. De. T. Siberia | . 1822 |
| planifóliá, 4 | . Brown | . 4, H. De. T. | |
| carpinámá, 5 | . Brown | . 4, H. De. T. Britain | . . |
| strictá . . | . Brown | . 4, H. De. T. Britain | . . |
| tortuósá . | . Brown | . 4, H. De. T. Britain | . . |
| viminális . | . Brown | . 4, H. De. T. Britain | . . |
| vírens . . | . Brown | . 4, H. De. T. Britain | . . |
| viscósá, 6 . | . Brown | . 4, H. De. T. Britain | . . |
| vulgáris . | . Brown | . 4, H. De. T. Britain | . . |
| carpinifóliá . | . Brown | . 4, H. De. T. Britain | . . |
| effúsá, 7 . | . Brown | . 4, H. De. T. Britain | . . |
| fruticósá . | . Brown | . 4, H. De. S. Europe | . . |
| fúlvá, 8 . | . Brown | . 4, H. De. T. N. Amer. | . . |
| glábrá . . | . Brown | . 4, H. De. T. Britain | . . |
| glandulósá . | . Brown | . 4, H. De. T. Britain | . . |
| latifóliá . | . Brown | . 4, H. De. T. Britain | . . |
| májor . . | . Brown | . 4, H. De. T. Britain | . . |
| microphýllá . | . Brown | . 4, H. De. T. Britain | . . |
| péndúlá . | . Brown | . 4, H. De. T. Britain | . . |
| ramulósá . | . Brown | . 4, H. De. T. Floetbeck | . . |
| variegátá . | . Brown | . 4, H. De. T. Britain | . . |
| vegétá, 9 . | . Brown | . 4, H. De. T. Britain | . . |
| vulgáris . | . Brown | . 4, H. De. T. Britain | . . |
| integrifóliá . | . Brown | . 8, Ev. T. E. Ind. | . 1822 |
| májor . . | . Brown | . 4, H. De. T. Britain | . . |
| montáná, 10 . | . Brown | . 4, H. De. T. Britain | . . |
| austrális . | . Brown | . 4, H. De. T. | |
| cevennénsis . | . Brown | . 4, H. De. T. | |
| crispá, 11 . | . Brown | . 4, H. De. T. N. Amer. | . |
| fastigiátá . | . Brown | . 4, H. De. T. Exeter | . 1826 |
| májor . . | . Brown | . 4, H. De. T. Britain | . . |
| minor . . | . Brown | . 4, H. De. T. Britain | . . |
| nígrá . . | . Brown | . 4, H. De. T. Ireland | . . |
| péndúlá . | . Brown | . 4, H. De. T. Britain | . . |
| rugósá . | . Brown | . 4, H. De. T. Britain | . . |
| vulgáris . | . Brown | . 4, H. De. T. Britain | . . |
| suberósá . | . Brown | . 4, H. De. T. Britain | . . |
| álbá . . | . Brown | . 4, H. De. T. Britain | . . |
| angustifóliá . | . Brown | . 4, H. De. T. Hertford | . . |
| eréctá . | . Brown | . 4, H. De. T. Britain | . . |
| fol. variegátá . | . Brown | . 4, H. De. T. Britain | . . |
| latifóliá . | . Brown | . 4, H. De. T. Hertford | . . |
| vulgáris . | . Brown | . 4, H. De. T. Holland | . . |

ULOSPÉRMUM, see Krubérá.

ÚLVÁ, Linn. From the Celtic ul, water; place of growth. Linn. 24, Or. 7, Nat. Or. Algæ. Found in the ocean, on marine rocks, and in ditches. The green laver which, stewed with lemon-juice, is so much esteemed in England, is the U. Lactuca—U. bulbósá, críspá, furfurácéá, Lactúcá, latíssimá.

UMBELLATE, having the flowers arranged in round flat heads, with the peduncles originating from a common centre.

UMBELLULATE, disposed in small umbels.

UMBEL, a particular arrangement of the flowers in certain plants, of which the carrot is a familiar example; the peduncles and pedicels spring from a common centre, and rise till they form a flat tuft. The difference between an umbel and a corymb, is, that whilst in the latter the flowers form a flat head, they do not, as in the former, spring from a common centre.

UMBILICATE, hollowed like the navel.

UMBILICUS, the cord which attaches the seed to the placenta.

UMBILICUS, Decandolle. From umbilicus, the navel; the concave leaves of some species. Linn. 10, Or. 4, Nat. Or. Crassulaceæ. Interesting plants, thriving well on rock-work or on old walls; they also grow freely in pots, in a mixture of loam, peat, and sand, and are increased by offsets or seeds. Synonymes: 1. Cotyledon lutea. 2. C. Umbilicus. 3. C. serrata. 4. C. spinosa, Sedum spinosum, Sempervivum cuspidatum.

| | | | | | | |
|---|---|---|---|---|---|---|
| eréctus, 1 . . . Yellow . 6, H. Her. P. England . . |

| | | | | | | |
|---|---|---|---|---|---|---|
| pendulínus, 2 . Yellow . 6, H. Her. P. Britain . . |
| serrátus, 3 . . Purple . 6, H. Her. P. Siberia . 1732 |
| spinósus, 4 . . White . 6, F. Her. P. Siberia . 1790 |

UMBONATE, having a rounded protuberant centre like an ancient shield.

UMBRELLA-TREE, see Hibiscus guineénsis.

UMBRELLA-WORT, see Oxybáphus.

UNARMED, destitute of prickles or spines.

UNCÁRIÁ, Schreber. From uncus, a hook; the old petioles are converted into hooked spines. Linn. 5, Or. 1, Nat. Or. Cinchonaceæ. For culture and propagation, see Nauclea. Synonymes: 1. Nauclea Gambier.

| | | | | | | |
|---|---|---|---|---|---|---|
| Gámbier, 1 . . Pa. red . 8, Ev. Cl. E. Ind. . . 1825 |
| sessilifrúctus . . Pa. red . 8, Ev. Cl. E. Ind. . . 1829 |

UNCINATE, hooked.

UNCÍNIÁ, Persoon. From ogkinos, a hook; alluding to the awn. Linn. 21, Or. 3, Nat. Or. Cyperaceæ. Plants resembling sedge; increased by division. Synonyme: 1. Carex uncinata—U. jamaicénsis 1, phleoídes.

UNCTUOUS, fat, oily.

UNDULATED, waved, rising and falling.

UNEQUAL, applied to petals and sepals, indicates that they or their sides are of unequal size and shape.

UNGUICULATE, furnished with a claw or an unguis.

UNGUIS, the taper base of anything.

UNILABIATE, having only one lip.

UNILOCULAR, having one cell.

UNIÓLÁ, Michaux. From unus, one, alone; united glumes. Linn. 3, Or. 2, Nat. Or. Gramineæ. Hardy perennial species, succeeding in common soil; seeds. They are found chiefly upon the sea-coast; hence the name, Seaside Oat—U. distichophýllá, latifóliá, paniculátá, spicátá.

UNISEXUAL, of one sex.

UNÓNÁ, Linn. From uno, to unite; stamens united with germen. Linn. 13, Or. 6, Nat. Or. Anonaceæ. Interesting plants, succeeding in light turfy loam, and propagated by cuttings of the ripened wood, planted in sand, under a glass, in heat. The dry fruit of U. aromatica is very pungent. From U. Narum, a sweet-smelling, greenish oil is procured by distilling the roots, and is used medicinally as a stimulant. Synonyme: 1. Uvaria lucida.

| | | | | | | |
|---|---|---|---|---|---|---|
| acumináta . . . . 8, Ev. S. Guiana . 1890 |
| aromática . . Brown . 8, Ev. S. Guiana . 1820 |
| esculénta . . Brown . 8, Ev. Cl. Madras . 1818 |
| fasciculátá . . . . 8, Ev. T. E. Ind. . 1823 |
| fuscátá . . . Brown . 8, Ev. S. Guiana . 1820 |
| longiflóra . . . . 8, Ev. T. E. Ind. . 1823 |
| longifóliá . . . . 8, Ev. S. Bengal . 1820 |
| Nárum . . . Brown . 8, Ev. Cl. Malabar . |
| nitidíssimá, 1 . . Blue . 8, Ev. T. N. Caledon. . 1825 |
| odorátá . . . Brown . 8, Ev. E. Ind. . . 1804 |

URÁNIÁ, Schreber. From ouranios, sublime; stateliness of the tree. Linn. 6, Or. 1, Nat. Or. Musaceæ. A splendid plant, well worthy of a place in every collection. It requires a mixture of turfy loam and a little peat, in a moist heat, and a good supply of water to make it grow luxuriantly. Newly imported seeds vegetate freely. Synonyme: 1. Ravenala madagascariensis.

| | | | | | | |
|---|---|---|---|---|---|---|
| speciósa, 1 . . Red . 8, Her. P. Madagas. . |

URÁRIÁ, Desvaux. From oura, a tail; the bracts. Linn. 17, Or. 4, Nat. Or. Leguminosæ. These plants succeed well in a mixture of loam, peat, and sand, and are increased by young cuttings in sand, under a glass, in heat; but they are raised with more facility by seeds. Synonymes: 1. Hedysarum crinitum. 2. H. lagocephalum. 3. H. lagopodioides. 4. H. arboreum. 5. H. pictum.

| | | | | | | |
|---|---|---|---|---|---|---|
| comósá . . . Purple . 7, S. Ev. S. E. Ind. . 1818 |
| crinítá, 1 . . Pink . 7, S. Ev. S. E. Ind. . |
| lagocéphalá, 2 . Yellow . 7, S. Her. P. Brasil . 1824 |
| lagopodioídes, 3 Purple . 7, G. Ev. S. China . 1790 |
| Lagópús, 4 . Purple . 6, G. Ev. S. Nepal . 1824 |
| pictá, 5 . . Purple . 7, S. Ev. S. Guinea . 1788 |

URCEOLAR, of, or belonging to, or having an urceolus.

URCEOLÁRIÁ, Acharius. From urceolus, a little pitcher, alluding to the form of the shields. Linn. 24, Or. 8, Nat. Or. Lichenes. Found on stones and bricks. U. cinerea and U. scruposa are used in dyeing—U. Achárii, A. cyriáspis, calceolárëá, C. Hoffmánni, cinéréá, Gágii, globósá, ruféscens, scrupósá.

URCEOLATE, pitcher-shaped.

URCEOLÍNÁ, Reichenbach. From urceolus, a small cup

or pitcher; in allusion to the membranous cup. *Linn.* 6, Or. 1, Nat. Or. *Amaryllidaceæ.* A curious little plant, said to thrive best in a strong rich loam, and may be increased by offsets. It must not be watered in winter.

pendúlä . . . Yel. grn. . 6, G. Bl. P. Peru . . .

URCEOLUS, the filaments joined into a pitcher-shaped body constitute the urceolus of the stamens, or the name may be applied to any part of a similar form.

UREDO, *Persoon.* From *uro,* to scorch; applied to those plants called mildew or blight. *Linn.* 24, Or. 9, Nat. Or. *Fungi.* The species of this obscure genus are found on the leaves of different plants. Synonyms: 1. Æcidium Cardui—U. æcidiiformis, Alchemillæ, antholtidis, appendiculōsä, Armēriæ, Bētæ, bifrōns, Campanūlæ, cándidä, Caryophyllacearūm, Cerástii, Cichoracearūm, cönflũēns, crustáceä, effūsä, Epilobii, Equisēti, Fābæ, farinōsä, Ficāriæ, Gerānii, gyrōsä, Helioscōpiæ, Heraclēi, Hypericōrum, intrūsä, Iridis, Labiatarūm, lineāris, Lini, oblongātä, olivācēä, ovātä, parallēlä, Petasītes, Polygonōrum, Populnūä, Potentillæ, Potērii, Primũlæ, pustulātä, Pyrōlæ, Quircũs, Rhinanthearūm, Rōsæ, rubōrum, rũmicūm, Sālicis, Saxifragarūm, Scillarūm, Senecionis, Sōnchi, suavēōlēns 1, Tussilāginis, Umbellatarūm, utriculōsum, Vacciniōrum, Vīncæ, vitellīnæ.

URENA, *Linn.* From *uren,* its name in Malabar. *Linn.* 16, Or. 8, Nat. Or. *Malvaceæ.* Uninteresting stove under-shrubs and annuals, growing in peat and loam; cuttings and seeds. Synonymes: 1. U. lobata. 2. U. americana—U. heterophõllä, lobátä, multifidä, muricātä, repándä, reticulátä, scabriuscũlä 1, Siebēri, sinuátä, speciōsä, subtrilōbä, Swārtzii 2, tricũspis.

UROPETĂLŎN, *Ker.* From *oura,* a tail, and *petalon,* a petal; the divisions of the flower are lengthened out. *Linn.* 6, Or. 1, Nat. Or. *Liliaceæ.* Interesting plants, succeeding best in a mixture of loam and leaf mould; they are increased by offsets or seeds. They should not be watered in winter. Synonyms: 1. Scilla serotina.

erispüm . . . Green . G. Bl. P. C. G. H. . 1816
fūlvüm, l . . Orn. red . 7, F. Bl. P. Mogadore . 1808
glaucüm . . . Green . 7, G. Bl. P. C. G. H. . 1816
longifolüm . . Pur. blue . 8, G. Bl. P. Mozamb. . 1825
serotinüm . . . Grn. red . 7, F. Bl. P. Spain . . 1629
viride . . . Green . 8, F. Bl. P. C. G. H. . 1774

URTICA, *Linn.* From *uro,* to burn; in reference to the stinging properties of most of the species. *Linn.* 21, Or. 4, Nat. Or. *Urticaceæ.* Plants of little beauty, and of the easiest culture. They all succeed in any common garden soil; and are increased by cuttings, divisions, and seeds. The effects of the venomous sting of the common Nettle are well known, but are, however, not to be compared with those of some of the Indian species, grown in the gardens of this country; yet all the known species are far surpassed for virulence by one, which in Timor is called *douun setan,* or devil's leaf, the effects of which are said by the natives in many cases to cause death.

cannabinä . . . Apetal . 8, H. Her. P. Siberia . . 1749
divaricātä . . . Yellow . 10, H. Her. P. Canada . . 1816
ferōx . . . . Green . G. Ev. T. N. Zeal. . 1828
gigäs . . . . Green . G. Ev. T. N. Holl. . 1822

heterophÿllä . . Green . 7, 8. Ev. 8. E. Ind. . 1819
microphÿllä . . Green . 8, 8. Her. P. W. Ind. . 1798
moroīdes . . . Green . G. Ev. T. N. Holl. . 1823
photeinophÿllä . . . G. Ev. T. Moret. B. . 1830
scriptä . . . Yellow . 8, F. Her. P. Nepal . . 1819

æstũans, angustifolią, arborēscēns, árdēns, baccifērä, baleārică, canadēnsis, capitellātä, cavacasānä, caravellānä, chamædryoīdēs, ciliātä, convēxä, crassifolią, deprēssä, diffūsä, dioīcä, diversifolią, Doddārtii, elongātä, grácilis, grandifolią, hōrridä, involucrātä, macrostáchÿä, membranácēä, nivēä, nudicaülis, nummularifolią, Parietāriä, pentándrä, pilulifērä, pulchēllä, pũmilä, reticulātä, rũfä, rugōsä, scabrēllä, trēns.

URVILLEA, *Kunth.* In honour of Captain Dumont D'Urville, of the French navy, who was sent out to ascertain the fate of La Peyrouse; an acute botanist. *Linn.* 8, Or. 1, Nat. Or. *Sapindaceæ.* Plants of little beauty. They may be grown in a mixture of loam and peat, and moderate-sized cuttings will root readily in sand, under a glass, in heat.

ferrugiōsä . . . White . 6, 8. Ev. Cl. Brazil . . 1823
ulmácēä . . . White . 8. Ev. Cl. S. Amer. . 1824

USNEA, *Dillenius.* From *achneh,* a name applied to lichens in general by the Arabian physicians. *Linn.* 24, Or. 8, Nat. Or. *Lichenes.* Found in winter, on old trees—U. barbátä, articulátä, flōridä, plicātä, hīrtä.

USTILĂGŎ, *Link.* From *ustus,* scorched; appearance. *Linn.* 24, Or. 9, Nat. Or. *Fungi.* Found upon grasses, &c.—U. antherārūm, cārīēs, flosculōsä, sigītūm, Urceolārum.

USTULATE, blackened.

UTERUS, the womb.

UTRICLE, a little bladder.

UTRICULAR, composed of little bladders.

UTRICULARIA, *Linn.* From *utriculus,* a little bladder; applied to the small inflated appendages of the roots. *Linn.* 2, Or. 1, Nat. Or. *Lentibulaceæ.* Elegant little plants, found in ponds and rivulets.

intermediä . . . Yellow . 5, H. Aq. P. Britain . .
minōr . . . . Yellow . 7, H. Aq. P. Britain . .
vulgāris . . . Yellow . 6, H. Aq. P. Britain . .

UVARIA, *Linn.* From *uva,* a cluster of grapes; resemblance in the fruit. *Linn.* 13, Or. 6, Nat. Or. *Anonaceæ.* Interesting plants, succeeding in a mixture of sandy loam and peat, and increased by cuttings of the ripened wood, in sand, under a glass, in heat.

Gærtnēri . . . Brown . 8. Ev. 8. E. Ind. . 1820
lũtēa . . . . Ornah. yel. 8. Ev. 8. E. Ind. . 1822
tomentōsä . . . Brown . 8. Ev. 8. E. Ind. . 1822
valutinä . . . Brown . 8. Ev. 8. E. Ind. . 1823
villōsä . . . Brown . 8. Ev. 8. E. Ind. . 1821
zeylánicä . . . Scarlet . 8. Ev. Tw. Ceylon . 1794

UVULARIA, *Linn.* The plants were formerly used in diseases of the *uvula.* *Linn.* 6, Or. 1, Nat. Or. *Liliaceæ.* A light sandy soil suits these plants best, and they are readily increased by division at the root.

flāvä . . . . Yellow . 5, H. Her. P. N. Amer. . 1810
grandiflōrä . . . Purple . 5, H. Her. P. N. Amer. . 1802
lanceolātä . . . Yellow . 7, H. Her. P. N. Amer. . 1710
perfoliātä . . . Pa. yel. . 5, H. Her. P. N. Amer. . 1710
pubertlä . . . Yellow . 5, H. Her. P. N. Amer. . 1824
sessilifoliä . . . Lgt. yel. . 6, H. Her. P. N. Amer. . 1790

# V.

VACCINIUM, *Linn.* An ancient Latin name, whether of a berry or a flower, is not satisfactorily known. *Linn.* 8, Or. 1, Nat. Or. *Vacciaceæ.* All the species of this genus are well worth cultivating, some of them for the sake of their fruit, some for curiosity, and others for ornament. The different kinds of *Whortle-berry* and *Bilberry* succeed best in peat soil, or very sandy loam. Some of them grow best in moist situations, and others in dry. Those requiring the heat of the stove must receive the same treatment as the generality of stove plants; and are readily increased by cuttings, planted in sand, under a glass, in heat; they may also, like the hardy species, be raised from root-suckers,

creeping roots, trailing rooting stems, or from seeds treated as follows:—In autumn, as soon as the seeds are ripe, they should be sown in shallow pans, filled with very sandy peat soil, and covered slightly over; when about an inch high, they must be pricked out thinly into other pans, filled with the same kind of soil. After being well rooted in these pans, they must be planted out in spring in proper places, taking care to keep a ball of earth about the roots. If finally planted out in autumn, the worms are apt to throw them out of the ground during winter. Synonymes: 1. V. myrtilloides. 2. V. diffusum. 3. V. brachycerum. 4. V. album, amænum, dicomorphum. 5. V. virgatum angusti-

*folium.* 6. *V. fuscatum, formosum.* 7. *V. virgatum.*
8. *V. hirtellum, frondosum.* 9. *V. glaucum.* 10. *V. venustum.* 11. *V. maderense.* 12. *V. tenellum.* 13.
*V. parviflorum.* 14. *V. album, elevatum.*

| | | | | | | |
|---|---|---|---|---|---|---|
| albiflōrûm . | . | White . | 5, | H. De. S. | N. Amer. | 1833 |
| angustifoliûm, 1 | . | Pa. yel. . | 5, | H. De. S. | N. Amer. | 1776 |
| arbōreûm, 2 . | . | Wht. red . | 5, | H. De. S. | N. Amer. | 1765 |
| buxifoliûm, 3 | . | White . | 5, | H. Ev. S. | N. Amer. | |
| canadénse . | . | Wht. red . | 5, | H. De. S. | Canada | 1825 |
| caracasānûm . | . | White . | 7, | S. Ev. S. | Caraccas . | 1825 |
| cæspitōsûm . | . | White . | 5, | H. De. S. | Huds. Bay | 1823 |
| corymbōsûm, 4 . | . | White . | 5, | H. De. S. | N. Amer. | 1765 |
| angustifoliûm, 5 | White . | . | | H. De. S. | N. Amer. | 1767 |
| fuscatûm, 6 . | . | Wht. pink | 6, | H. De. S. | N. Amer. | 1770 |
| virgatûm, 7 . | . | Wht. red . | 4, | H. De. S. | N. Amer. | 1767 |
| crassifoliûm . | . | White . | 6, | H. De. S. | Carolina | 1787 |
| dumōsûm, 8 . | . | White . | 5, | H. De. S. | N. Amer. | 1774 |
| hûmîlê . | . | White . | 5, | H. De. S. | N. Amer. | 1774 |
| elongatûm . | . | White . | 7, | H. De. S. | N. Amer. | 1812 |
| frondōsûm, 9 . | . | Wht. grn. | 5, | H. De. S. | N. Amer. | 1761 |
| venustûm, 10 . | . Pink . | . | 6, | H. De. S. | N. Amer. | 1770 |
| galēûm . | . | White . | 5, | H. De. S. | N. Amer. | 1806 |
| glābrûm . | . | Pink . | 7, | H. De. S. | N. Amer. | 1812 |
| grandiflōrûm . | . | White . | 7, | H. De. S. | N. Amer. | 1812 |
| humifûsûm . | . | White . | | H. Ev. Tr. | N. Amer. | 1827 |
| ligustrinûm . | . | Purple . | 5, | H. De. S. | | |
| meridionālê . | . | Red wht. | 4, | S. Ev. S. | Jamaica . | 1778 |
| minutiflōrûm . | . | White . | 5, | H. De. S. | N. Amer. | 1812 |
| Myrsinîtes . | . | Purple . | 5, | H. De. S. | Carolina | |
| lanceolātûm . | . | Purple . | 5, | H. De. S. | Florida | |
| obtûsûm . | . | Purple . | 5, | H. De. S. | Carolina | |
| myrtifoliûm . | . | White . | 6, | F. Ev. Tr. | Carolina | 1812 |
| myrtillōdes . | . | Pink . | 6, | H. De. S. | N. Amer. | 1776 |
| Myrtillûs . | . | Pink . | 5, | H. De. S. | Britain | |
| baccis albis . | . | Green . | 5, | H. De. S. | Britain | |
| nitidûm . | . | Pink . | 5, | H. De. S. | Carolina | 1794 |
| decûmbens . | . | Pink . | 5, | H. De. Tr. | Carolina | 1794 |
| ovātûm . | . | Pink . | 5, | H. De. S. | N. Amer. | 1826 |
| padifoliûm, 11 . | . | Pa. grn. . | 7, | H. De. S. | Madeira | 1777 |
| pallidûm . | . | White . | 5, | H. De. S. | N. Amer. | 1774 |
| pensylvanicûm, 12 | Wht. bh. . | . | 6, | H. De. S. | N. Amer. | 1772 |
| resinōsûm . | . | Pur. grn. . | 5, | H. De. S. | N. Amer. | 1782 |
| lutescêns, 13 . | . | Redish. grn. | 6, | H. De. S. | N. Amer. | 1804 |
| rubêscêns . | . | Yel. grn. . | 5, | H. De. S. | N. Amer. | 1773 |
| staminēûm, 14 . | . | White . | 5, | H. De. S. | N. Amer. | 1772 |
| albûm . | . | White . | | H. De. S. | Mexico | |
| uliginōsûm . | . | Flesh . | 4, | H. De. S. | Britain | |
| Vitis Idæa . | . | Pink . | 5, | H. De. S. | Britain | |

**VAILLANTIA**, *Decandolle.* In honour of Sebastian Vaillant, an eminent French botanist and author in the early part of the last century. *Linn.* 22, Or. 1, Nat. Or. *Stellatæ,* or *Galiaceæ.* Plants of little interest, growing in common soil, on rock-work, old walls, or in any dry situation; division and seeds. *Synonymes:* 1. *Galium articulatum.* 2. *G. cruciatum.* 3. *G. Bauhini.* 4. *G. pedemontanum.* 5. *V. glabra, Galium vernum.*

| | | | | | | |
|---|---|---|---|---|---|---|
| chersonénsis . | . | Yellow . | 6, | H. De. Tr. | China . | 1817 |
| cruciāta, 2 . | . | Yellow . | 5, | H. De. Tr. | Britain . | |
| humifūsa . | . | Yellow . | 6, | H. De. Tr. | A. Minor . | 1816 |
| pedemontāna, 4 . | . | Orn. yel. . | 7, | H. | A. | Hungary | 1799 |
| vērna, 5 . | . | Yellow . | 5, | H. De. Tr. | Switzerl. . | 1819 |

*articulāta* 1, *filiformis, glābra* 3, *hispida, murālis.*

**VALERIAN**, see *Valeriāna.*

**VALERIANA**, *Necker.* Said by some to be named after Valerius, who first used it in medicine; others assert that it is derived from *valere,* to be in health, on account of the medicinal qualities of *V. officinalis. Linn.* 3, Or. 1, Nat. Or. *Valerianaceæ.* Most of the species are very ornamental in flower borders. The perfectly hardy kinds succeed well in common garden soil; those from warmer climates should be grown in pots in a mixture of loam, sand, and peat, and placed in a frame or greenhouse in winter. They are all readily increased by division at the root. The root of *V. officinalis* is eminently antispasmodic. It is very frequently prescribed with success in hysterical cases. In habitual costiveness, it is an excellent medicine. The unpleasant flavour of *Valerian* is best counteracted by a small addition of mace. *Synonymes:* 1. *S. heterophylla.* 2. *V. Cardamines.*

| | | | | | | |
|---|---|---|---|---|---|---|
| alliariæfoliā . | . | Red . | 6, | H. Her. P. | Caucasus | 1826 |
| asarifoliā . | . | Red . | 6, | H. Her. P. | Crete . | 1824 |
| capénsis . | . | Red . | 6, | G. Her. P. | C. G. H. . | 1816 |
| celtica . | . | White . | 6, | H. Her. P. | Switzerl. . | 1748 |
| dioica . | . | Flesh . | 6, | H. Her. P. | Britain . | |
| elongāta . | . | Yellow . | 6, | H. Her. P. | Austria . | 1812 |
| globulariæfoliā, 1 . | Red . | . | 6, | H. Her. P. | Pyrenees . | |
| intermēdia . | . | White . | 6, | H. Her. P. | Pyrenees . | 1818 |
| montāna . | . | Lgt. red . | 7, | H. Her. P. | Switzerl. . | 1748 |
| officinalis . | . | Flesh . | 6, | H. Her. P. | Britain . | |
| Phū . | . | White . | 8, | H. Her. P. | Germany | 1597 |

| | | | | | | |
|---|---|---|---|---|---|---|
| pyrenāîcā . | . | Pink . | 8, | H. Her. P. | Scotland | |
| Salīûnca . | . | Red . | 6, | H. Her. P. | France . | 1824 |
| sambucifoliā . | . | White . | 6, | H. Her. P. | Germany . | 1819 |
| saxātīlis . | . | White . | 7, | H. Her. P. | Austria . | 1740 |
| sibērica . | . | Red . | 6, | H. | S. S. Eur. . | 1824 |
| supīnā . | . | Wht. red . | 7, | H. Her. P. | Switzerl. | 1822 |
| tripterīs . | . | White . | 5, | H. Her. P. | Switzerl. . | 1752 |
| tuberōsā . | . | Lgt. red . | 6, | H. Her. P. | S. Eur. . | 1629 |

**VALERIANELLA**, *Mœnch.* From a diminutive of *Valeriana,* which see. *Linn.* 3, Or. 1, Nat. Or. *Valerianaceæ.* The species only require to be sown in early spring, in the open border. They answer well for a spring salad, and are generally known by the name of *Lamb's-lettuce. Synonymes:* 1. *V. dasycarpa, dentata.* 2. *V. tridentata.*

| | | | | | | |
|---|---|---|---|---|---|---|
| campanulāta . | . | . | | H. | A. S. Eur. . | |
| echinātā . | . | Pink . | 7, | H. | A. S. Eur. . | 1807 |
| olitōria . | . | Blue . | 4, | H. | A. Britain . | |

*auriculāta, carinātā, coronātā, discoidēā, eriocarpā, excapā, mixtā, Morisōnii* 1, *platylobā, pumilā* 2, *radiātā, uncinātā, vesicāriā.*

**VALLARIS**, *Brown.* From *vallo,* to inclose; used for fences in Java. *Linn.* 5, Or. 1, Nat. Or. *Apocynaceæ.* This species grows well in sandy loam and peat, and is increased by cuttings, in sand, under a glass, in heat. *Synonyme:* 1. *Pergularia glabra.*

| | | | | | | |
|---|---|---|---|---|---|---|
| pergulāna, 1 . | . | White . | | S. Ev. Tw. | E. Ind. . | 1818 |

**VALLESIA**, *Ruiz and Pavon.* In honour of F. Vallesio, physician to Philip II. of Spain. *Linn.* 5, Or. 1, Nat. Or. *Apocynaceæ.* For culture and propagation, see *Vallaris.*

| | | | | | | |
|---|---|---|---|---|---|---|
| cymbifoliā . | . | White . | 6, | S. Ev. S. | N. Spain . | 1821 |
| dichotōma . | . | White . | 5, | S. Ev. S. | Peru . | 1822 |

**VALLISNERIA**, *Micheli.* In honour of Antonio Vallisneri, an Italian botanist. *Linn.* 22, Or. 2, Nat. Or. *Hydrocharaceæ.* This aquatic plant requires to be grown in a large pot or tub of water, in the conservatory or greenhouse; it should be planted deeply in the water, since it grows at the bottom of ditches in its native country.

| | | | | | | |
|---|---|---|---|---|---|---|
| spirālis . | . | Brown . | 7, | G. Aq. P. | S. Eur. . | 1818 |

**VALLOTA**, *Herbert.* In honour of Pierre Vallot, a French botanist. *Linn.* 6, Or. 1, Nat. Or. *Amaryllidaceæ.* For culture and propagation, see *Amaryllis. Synonyme:* 1. *Amaryllis purpurea.*

| | | | | | | |
|---|---|---|---|---|---|---|
| purpūrea, 1 . | . | Scarlet . | 5, | G. Bl. P. | C. G. H. . | 1774 |
| minor . | . | Scarlet . | 5, | G. Bl. P. | C. G. H. . | 1774 |

**VALVATE**, opening like a valve.

**VALVÆFORM**, shaped as a valve.

**VALVES**, the divisions of the capsule.

**VALVULAR**, consisting of valves.

**VALVULAR-DISSEPIMENTS**, partitions in the centre of the valves.

**VANDA**, *R. Brown. Vanda* is the Sanscrit name of the original species of this genus. *Linn.* 20, Or. 1, Nat. Or. *Orchidaceæ.* The species of this genus, as well as those elegant and interesting plants referred to it for culture, &c., are all well deserving of the cultivator's best care and attention. The beauty of their deliciously fragrant flowers is quite sufficient to recommend them to all lovers of orchidaceous plants, besides their being in general such admirably free flowerers. Some of the species of *Saccolabium* and *Sarcanthus* produce from thirty to one hundred spikes of flowers each; indeed, we know from the best authority, that there are single plants of *Saccolabium guttatum,* growing upon trees in the Botanic Garden, Calcutta, which produce every year from fifty to one hundred spikes or flowers. In their native districts, all, or the greater part of the plants referred to this genus, grow upon trees in dense forests, and consequently derive their chief support from the atmosphere; therefore their cultivation in this country is rendered very simple and easy, as the greater part of them require nothing more than a piece of wood to attach themselves to, or an ornamental wire basket filled with moss and broken pots, and suspended from the pillars or roof of the house. There are, however, exceptions to this rule; as, for instance, some of the stronger and more robust growing kinds, such as *Vanda Roxburghii,* and *V. multiflora.* These should be grown in wide shallow pots, carefully filled with cut *sphagnum* moss, and potsherds broken small. We would recommend oak branches for those intended to be grown upon wood. They all require a good strong moist heat, and a plentiful supply of water during the growing season, which ought to commence about the beginning or middle of June, and continue to the end of September, from which time they should be kept cool and dry until the beginning of March, when they should be placed in a strong dry heat to induce them to flower. They will, if thus treated, flower most abundantly; whereas, if kept in a continued moist atmosphere, they will do nothing but grow from year to year, and of course never produce flowers, because they are not allowed a proper season to elaborate and perfect their flower-buds, neither have they a proper season for the development of those buds. Propagation is effected by carefully detaching the lateral shoots after they have grown to the length of about six inches, and fastening them to another block of wood in a similar manner to the old ones; but great caution is necessary to preserve them from excision by moisture till they have recovered from the effects of being severed from the parent plant, and commenced growing.

| | | | | | |
|---|---|---|---|---|---|
| eruentā | Red | 8, S. Epi. | China | | 1819 |
| lamellātā | Pa. yel. | 8, S. Epi. | Manilla | | 1837 |
| multiflōrā | Yellow | 6, S. Epi. | China | | 1800 |
| Roxburghiī | Wht. pur. | 7, S. Epi. | China | | 1810 |
| tessellātā | Wht. pur. | 7, S. Epi. | China | | 1816 |
| unicōlor | Ch. brn. | 8, Epi. | | | |
| tērēs | Red yel. | 8, S. Epi. | Silhet | | 1828 |

VANDELLIĀ, Linn. In honour of Dominico Vandelli, professor of botany at Lisbon. Linn. 14, Or. 2, Nat. Or. Scrophulariaceæ. These plants require the same treatment as other tender annuals. Synonymes: 1. Hornemannia ovata, Tittmannia ovata. 2. H. viscosa, T. viscosa. 3. Torenia diffusa.

| | | | | | |
|---|---|---|---|---|---|
| crustacea, 1 | Blue | 6, S. | A. India | | 1816 |
| diffusā | White | 7, S. | A. Santa Cruz | | 1824 |
| hirsūtā, 2 | Blue | 6, H. | A. India | | 1823 |
| Roxburghiī, 3 | Purple | 7, S. | A. Coroman. | | 1818 |

VANGUERIĀ, Commelin. Altered from Voa-Vanguer, the name of V. edulis in Madagascar. Linn. 5, Or. 1, Nat. Or. Cinchonaceæ. These plants succeed best in a mixture of loam and peat, and are readily increased by cuttings, in the same kind of soil, under a glass, in heat. The fruit of V. edulis, as the name implies, is succulent and eatable.

| | | | | | |
|---|---|---|---|---|---|
| edūlis | Green | S. Ev. S. | India | | 1809 |
| spinōsā | Green | 6, S. Ev. S. | Madagas. | | 1816 |
| velutīnā | Lgt. grn. | 6, S. Ev. S. | Madagas. | | 1829 |

VANILLĀ, Plumier. An alteration of Vaynilla, which is a diminutive of Vaina, a Spanish word signifying a sheath; in reference to the cylindrical pod being like the sheath of a knife. Linn. 20, Or. 1, Nat. Or. Vanillaceæ. These plants thrive best in a mixture of moss and turfy peat, in a moist warm atmosphere. They should have the rough bark of a piece of wood, or a wall for their long roots, which issue from every joint, to cling to; and they are readily increased by cuttings. The fruit is one of the most delightful aromatics known, and is extensively used in the manufacture of liqueurs, chocolate, and various articles of confectionary, and also for perfuming snuffs.

| | | | | | |
|---|---|---|---|---|---|
| aromātica | White | 7, S. Ev. Cl. S. | Eur. | | 1739 |
| bicolor | Dull red | 8, Ev. | Guiana | | |
| planifōliā | White | 5, S. Ev. Cl. | W. Ind. | | 1800 |

VARICOSE, swollen here and there.

VARIOLARIĀ, Persoon. From variola, measles; the shields of these plants resemble the eruptive spots of the measles. Linn. 24, Or. 8, Nat. Or. Lichenes. Crustaceous plants, found on rocks, walls, and the bark of trees—V. amāra, A. discoīdeā, chlorothācīā, cinēreā, communis, C. aspergillā, constellātā, dealbātā, globulifērā, grisēo-virēns, lāctēā, L. arenārīā, multipunctā, M. lavigātā, polythācīā, terricōlā, tortā, veldtā.

VARRONIĀ, see Cordiā.

VASCOĀ, Decandolle. In honour of Vasco de Gama, the celebrated Portuguese circumnavigator. Linn. 16, Or. 6, Nat. Or. Leguminosæ. Showy plants when in blossom. They grow well in a mixture of loam and peat; and young cuttings root readily in sand, under a glass. Synonymes: 1. Rafnia amplexicaulis, Crotalaria amplexicaulis. 2. Borbonia perfoliata, C. amplexicaulis.

| | | | | | |
|---|---|---|---|---|---|
| amplexicaulis, 1 | Yellow | 7, G. Ev. S. | C. G. H. | | 1816 |
| perfoliātā, 2 | Yellow | 7, G. Ev. S. | C. G. H. | | 1812 |

VASCULAR, composed of tubes or vessels.

VAUANTHES, see Grammanthes.

VAUCHERIĀ, Decandolle. In honour of the Rev. M. Vaucher of Geneva, a botanical author. Linn. 24, Or. 7, Nat. Or. Algæ. Found in ditches, &c.—V. dichotōmā, D submarīnā, Dillwgnii, gemīnātā, multicapsulāris, racemōsā, radicātā, terrēstris.

VAULTED, formed like a vault.

VEINLESS, without veins.

VELEZIĀ, Linn. In honour of C. Velez, a physician and botanist at Madrid. Linn. 5, Or. 2, Nat. Or. Silenaceæ. The seeds may be sown in any light soil.

| | | | | | |
|---|---|---|---|---|---|
| rigidā | Wht. pur. 7, H. | A. Spain | | 1683 |

VELLĀ, Decandolle. From velar, the Celtic name of the Cress. Linn. 15, Nat. Or. Cruciferæ. This shrub is commonly grown as a greenhouse plant, but it is sufficiently hardy to endure the winter when planted in a dry, warm, south border: it is increased by young cuttings, in sand, under a glass.

| | | | | | |
|---|---|---|---|---|---|
| Pseudō-cytisus | Yellow | 4, G. Ev. S. | Spain | | 1759 |

VELLEIĀ, Smith. In honour of Major Velley, a gentleman who paid much attention to marine Algæ. Linn. 5, Or. 1, Nat. Or. Goodeniaceæ. Interesting plants, succeeding best in a mixture of loam, peat, and sand, and increased by division, or by seeds, which are sometimes produced in this country. The plants must be sparingly watered in winter.

| | | | | | |
|---|---|---|---|---|---|
| lyrātā | Yellow | 4, G. Her. P. N. Holl. | | | 1819 |
| paradōxā | Yellow | 7, G. Her. P. N. Holl. | | | 1824 |
| spatulātā | Yellow | 4, G. Her. P. N. Holl. | | | 1825 |

VELTHEIMIĀ, Gleditsch. In honour of F. A. Veltheim, a German botanist. Linn. 6, Or. 1, Nat. Or. Liliaceæ. The species of Veltheimia thrive best in a light loamy soil; and are readily increased by offsets from the bulbs; the leaves pulled off close to the bulb, and planted in pots of soil, will produce bulbs at their base.

| | | | | | |
|---|---|---|---|---|---|
| glaucā | Flesh | 3, G. Bl. P. C. G. H. | | | 1781 |
| rubescenti pur. pūrēā | Red pur. | 7, G. Bl. P. C. G. H. | | | 1834 |
| intermedia | Flesh | 4, G. Bl. P. C. G. H. | | | 1800 |
| viridifōliā | Flesh wht. | 8, G. Bl. P. C. G. H. | | | 1768 |

VELVETY, covered with down resembling velvet.

VENTRICOSE, inflated.

VENUS's COMB, see Scandix Pecten-Veneris.

VENUS's FLYTRAP, see Dionæa muscipula.

VENUS's HAIR, see Adiantum Capillus-Veneris.

VENUS's LOOKING-GLASS, see Specularia speculum.

VENUS's NAVELWORT, see Omphalodes.

VEPRIS, Commelin. From vepres, a briar or bramble. Linn. 21, Or. 2, Nat. Or. Rutaceæ. For culture and propagation, see Toddalia. Synonyme: 1. Toddalia paniculata.

| | | | | | |
|---|---|---|---|---|---|
| obovātā | White | 8. Ev. S. | Maurit. | | 1824 |

VERATRUM, Linn. From vere, truly, and ater, black; in allusion to the colour of the root. Linn. 22, Or. 1, Nat. Or. Melanthaceæ. A genus of elegant plants when in flower. They thrive best in a rich soil, and are increased by division or seeds. "The dangerous medicinal properties of the root of Veratrum are owing to a peculiar alkaline principle, called Veratrin, which acts with singular energy on the membrane of the nose, exciting violent sneezings, though taken in very minute quantity. When taken internally in very small doses, it produces excessive irritation of the mucous coat of the stomach and intestines, and a few grains are found fatal to the lower animals. V. viride is an acrid, emetic, and powerful stimulant, followed by sedative effects." Lindley's Nat. Syst. of Bot., 2d Ed. p. 368.

| | | | | | |
|---|---|---|---|---|---|
| album | White | 7, H. Her. P. Europe | | | 1548 |
| angustifōlium | Green | 6, H. Her. P. N. Amer. | | | 1823 |
| Lobeliānum | White | 6, H. Her. P. S. Eur. | | | 1818 |
| nigrum | Drk. pur. | 6, H. Her. P. Siberia | | | 1596 |
| parviflōrum | Green | 6, H. Her. P. Carolina | | | 1809 |
| viride | Green | 7, H. Her. P. N. Amer. | | | 1742 |

VERBASCUM, Linn. Said to be from barbascum, bearded; in allusion to the bearded filaments. Linn. 5, Or. 1, Nat. Or. Scrophulariaceæ. The species of Verbascum are strong, robust growing plants, producing an abundance of showy, yellow flowers, and on that account they are well adapted for planting at the back of flower borders, or in shrubberies. They

grow freely in any soil, and are readily increased by
seeds; some of the perennial kinds by divisions of
the root. *Synonymes:* 1. *V. ferrugineum.*

| | | | | | |
|---|---|---|---|---|---|
| Alopecūrūs | . Yellow | 7, H. Her. | P. | France | 1890 |
| angustifolīūm | . Yellow | 7, H. | B. | Naples | 1824 |
| austrāle | . Yellow | 7, H. | B. | S. Eur. | 1815 |
| austrīacūm | . Yellow | 7, H. Her. | P. | Austria | 1818 |
| Bastārdī | . Yellow | 7, H. Her. | P. | France | 1824 |
| betonicæfolīūm | . Yellow | 7, H. Her. | P. | Armenia | 1825 |
| Blattārīa | . Pink | 7, H. | B. | Britain | |
| blattariōīdēs | . Yellow | 7, H. | B. | France | 1805 |
| Boerhaāvīī | . Yellow | 7, H. | A. | S. Eur. | 1731 |
| candidissimā | . Pa. yel. | 5, H. | B. | Naples | 1823 |
| Chaixīī | . Yellow | 7, H. | B. | France | 1821 |
| collīnūm | . Yellow | 7, H. Her. | P. | Germany | 1890 |
| compāctūm | . Yellow | 7, H. | B. | Tauria | 1890 |
| condensātūm | . Yellow | 7, H. | B. | Austria | 1890 |
| crassifolīūm | . Yellow | 7, H. | B. | Portugal | 1818 |
| cūprēūm | . Brown | 7, H. Her. | P. | Caucasus | 1798 |
| cuspidātūm | . Yellow | 5, H. | B. | Vienna | 1817 |
| ferrugīnēūm | . Brown | 7, H. | B. | S. Eur. | 1683 |
| floccōsūm | . Yellow | 7, H. | B. | Hungary | 1805 |
| formōsūm | . Yellow | 7, H. | B. | Russia | 1818 |
| glābrūm | . Yellow | 7, H. | B. | Europe | 1605 |
| gnaphalōīdēs | . Yellow | 7, H. | B. | Caucasus | 1825 |
| gossypīnūm | . Yellow | 7, H. | B. | Caucasus | 1820 |
| grandiflōrūm | . Yellow | 7, H. | B. | Europe | 1890 |
| hæmorrhoidāle | . Wht. pur. | 7, G. | B. | Madeira | 1777 |
| indīcūm | . Yellow | 7, H. | B. | Nepal | |
| lanātūm | . Yellow | 7, H. Her. | P. | Italy | 1825 |
| leptostāchȳūm | . Yellow | 7, H. | B. | S. France | 1825 |
| longifolīūm | . Yellow | 7, H. | B. | Naples | 1824 |
| Lychnītīs | . Yellow | 7, H. | B. | Britain | |
| lyrātūm | . Yellow | 6, H. | B. | Spain | 1819 |
| macrānthūm | . Yellow | 7, H. | B. | Portugal | 1890 |
| majāle | . Yellow | 7, H. | B. | Montpel. | 1817 |
| montānūm | . Yellow | 7, H. | B. | France | 1819 |
| mucronātūm | . Yellow | 7, H. | B. | Greece | 1814 |
| nemorōsūm | . Yellow | 6, H. | B. | Austria | 1820 |
| nīgrūm | . Yellow | 7, H. Her. | P. | England | |
| nīvēūm | . Yellow | 5, H. | B. | Naples | 1823 |
| orientāle | . Yellow | 7, H. Her. | P. | Caucasus | 1821 |
| ovalifolīūm | . Orange | 7, H. Her. | P. | Caucasus | 1804 |
| ovātūm | . Yellow | 7, H. | B. | Spain | 1824 |
| phœnicēūm | . Purple | 7, H. Her. | P. | S. Eur. | 1796 |
| phlomoīdēs | . Yellow | 7, H. | B. | S. Eur. | 1789 |
| pinnatīfīdūm | . Yellow | 7, H. | B. | Archipel. | 1788 |
| pulverulēntūm | . Yellow | 7, H. | B. | England | |
| punīcēūm | . Brown | 7, H. Her. | P. | S. Eur. | 1820 |
| pyramidātūm | . Yellow | 7, H. | B. | Caucasus | 1804 |
| ramīgērūm | . Yellow | 7, H. | B. | S. Eur. | 1824 |
| ramosissimūm | . Yellow | 7, H. | B. | France | 1824 |
| repāndūm | . Yellow | 7, H. | B. | Europe | 1813 |
| rotundifolīūm | . Yellow | 7, H. | B. | Italy | 1823 |
| rubigīnōsūm | . Yel. red | 7, H. | B. | Hungary | 1817 |
| sinuātūm | . Yellow | 8, H. | B. | S. Eur. | 1570 |
| speciōsūm | . Yellow | 7, H. | B. | Austria | 1818 |
| spectābīle | . Yel. pur. | 7, H. | B. | Tauria | 1820 |
| spinōsūm | . Purple | 7, F. Ev. | S. | Crete | 1824 |
| Stevenī | . Yellow | 7, H. | B. | Siberia | 1821 |
| thapsiforme | . Orn. yel. | 7, H. | B. | Europe | 1817 |
| thapsoīdēs | . Yellow | 7, H. Her. | P. | Portugal | 1819 |
| Thāpsūs | . Yellow | 7, H. | B. | | |
| elongātūm | . Yellow | 7, H. | B. | Europe | 1813 |
| triste, 1 | . Yel. red | 7, H. Her. | P. | S. Eur. | 1788 |
| undulātūm | . Yellow | 7, H. | B. | S. Eur. | 1819 |
| versiflōrūm | . Purple | 7, H. | B. | Bohemia | 1823 |
| virgātūm | . Yellow | 8, H. | B. | Britain | |

VERBĒNĀ, *Linn.* Said to be from its Celtic name,
*Ferfaen. Linn.* 14, Or. 2, Nat. Or. *Verbenaceæ.*
This is a genus of extremely beautiful and ornamental plants while in flower, either when grown
in pots in the greenhouse, or when planted out in
the flower-garden; and they will all succeed well
in the open ground during the summer months.
The flowers of *V. teucrioides* have a delightful jas-
mine-like odour. They all succeed well in a light
loamy soil, with careful drainage when kept in
pots. The herbaceous perennial kinds increase
rapidly by cuttings, planted in sand, under a glass;
the greenhouse kinds in a little heat. The annuals
and biennials should be raised on a gentle hotbed.
*Synonymes:* 1. *V. Melindres.* 2. *V. Drummondii.* 3.
*V. erinoides.*

| | | | | | |
|---|---|---|---|---|---|
| alātā | . Rosy | 8, F. Her. | P. | M. Video | 1828 |
| amœnā | . Pksh. pur. | 7, G. Her. | P. | Mexico | |
| Araniānā | . Purple | 8, G. Her. | P. | | 1836 |
| Aublētīā | . Purple | 8, F. | B. | N. Amer. | 1774 |
| Drummōndī | . Lilac | 7, H. Her. | P. | Texas | |
| barbātā | . Pink | 8, F. Her. | P. | Mexico | 1826 |
| bractēōsā | . Pink | 7, H. | B. | Mexico | 1890 |
| canēscēns | . Blue | 7, H. | A. | Mexico | 1824 |
| chamædrifolīā, 1 | Scarlet | 8, F. Her. | P. | B. Ayres | 1827 |
| diffūsā | . Blue | 7, F. Her. | P. | N. Amer. | 1818 |
| elēgāns | . Blue | 7, H. | B. | Mexico | 1826 |
| glandulōsā | . Pale | 7, G. Her. | P. | | 1832 |

---

| | | | | | |
|---|---|---|---|---|---|
| hispīda | . Purple | 7, H. | A. | Peru | 1816 |
| incīsā | . Red | 8, G. Her. | P. | Panama | 1835 |
| intermēdīā | . Purple | 7, H. Her. | P. | Hybrid | 1828 |
| Lambērtī | . Purple | 7, H. Her. | P. | S. Amer. | |
| rōsēā, 2 | . Pink | 7, H. Her. | P. | Carolina | |
| lasiostāchȳs | . Purple | 7, H. | B. | Califor. | 1826 |
| littorālīs | . Cinereous | 6, H. | A. | S. Amer. | 1832 |
| multīfīdā, 3 | . Blue | 7, H. | A. | Peru | 1818 |
| Sabīnī | . Purplish | 7, G. Her. | P. | Chile | 1834 |
| officināli-venōsā | . Bluish | 8, H. Her. | P. | Oxford | 1837 |
| pinnatīfīdā | . Purple | 7, H. | B. | N. Amer. | 1810 |
| polystāchȳā | . Red | 7, H. Her. | P. | Mexico | 1890 |
| pulchēllā | . Purple | 7, F. | B. | B. Ayres | 1827 |
| corōllā-ālbīdā | . Whitish | 7, G. Her. | P. | | 1834 |
| rādīcāns | . Lilac | 7, G. Her. | P. | Chile | 1832 |
| rugōsā | . Violet | 7, H. Her. | P. | B. Ayres | 1833 |
| scābrā | . Red | 7, H. Her. | P. | Mexico | 1825 |
| sorōrīā | . Purple | 7, H. Her. | P. | Nepal | 1824 |
| sulphūrēā | . Sulphur | 7, G. Her. | P. | Chile | 1832 |
| teucrioīdēs | . Purplish | 7, H. Her. | P. | M. Video | 1837 |
| trifīdā | . Purple | 8, H. | A. | Mexico | 1818 |
| Tweedīānā | . Scarlet | 8, F. Her. | P. | Brazil | 1834 |
| venōsā | . Rosy | 7, H. Her. | P. | B. Ayres | 1830 |
| veronicæfolīā | . Blue | 7, H. | A. | Mexico | 1825 |

*angustifolīā, bonariēnsis, caroliniānā, hastātā, offici-
nālis, paniculātā, prostrātā, spūrīā, strictā, supīnā,
urticæfolīā.*

VERBĒSĪNĀ, *Linn.* A name of the same meaning as
*Verbena. Linn.* 19, Or. 2, Nat. Or. *Compositæ.*
These plants succeed well in any light rich soil,
and are increased by division of the root, or by
seeds. *Synonymes:* 1. *Galinsogea discolor.* 2. *Siege-
beckia laciniata.* 3. *S. occidentalis.*

| | | | | | |
|---|---|---|---|---|---|
| alātā | . Orange | 8, G. Her. | P. | S. Amer. | 1699 |
| striplicifolīā, 1 | . Yellow | 7, G. Ev. | S. | | 1823 |
| Boswāllīā | . Yellow | 7, G. | A. | E. Ind. | 1818 |
| helianthoīdēs | . Yellow | 8, H. Her. | P. | N. Amer. | 1897 |
| lacinīātā, 2 | . Yellow | 7, G. Her. | P. | Carolina | 1821 |
| pinnatīfīdā | . Yellow | 8, G. Her. | P. | Mexico | 1825 |
| salicifolīā | . Yellow | 7, G. Her. | P. | Mexico | 1825 |
| virginīcā | . White | 8, H. Her. | P. | N. Amer. | 1818 |

*calendulācēā, dichōtōmā, fruticōsā, gigāntēā, satīvā,
serrātā, Siegesbēckīā 3.*

VERMICULAR, having the appearance of a worm.

VERMICULĀRĪA, *Tode.* From *vermiculus,* a little worm;
the arrangement of the seeds. *Linn.* 94, Or. 9, Nat.
Or. *Fungi.* Found upon dead ivy leaves—*V. tri-
chēllā.*

VERMIFUGE, that which expels worms.

VERNACULAR, native.

VERNAL, spring.

VERNŌNĪA, *Schreber.* In honour of William Vernon,
a botanical traveller in North America. *Linn.* 19,
Or. 1, Nat. Or. *Compositæ.* The stove and greenhouse species thrive well in a light rich soil, and
are readily increased by seeds and young cuttings.
The hardy herbaceous kinds are fine stately plants,
well adapted for the back of flower borders, and are
increased by division.

| | | | | | |
|---|---|---|---|---|---|
| acutifolīā | . Pa. pur. | 12, G. Ev. | S. | S. Amer. | |
| altissimā | . Purple | 10, H. Her. | P. | Ohio | 1820 |
| angustifolīā | . Purple | 10, H. Her. | P. | N. Amer. | 1817 |
| arborēscēns | . Purple | 11, S. Ev. | S. | Jamaica | 1788 |
| axilliflōrā | . Lilac | 9, S. | B. | Bahia | |
| flexuōsā | . Purple | 9, S. Her. | P. | Brazil | 1828 |
| fruticōsā | . Purple | 10, S. Ev. | S. | W. Ind. | 1818 |
| glaūcā | . Purple | 7, H. Her. | P. | N. Amer. | 1710 |
| linēārīs | . Purple | 8, H. | A. | S. Amer. | 1825 |
| noveboracēnsis | . Purple | 8, H. Her. | P. | N. Amer. | 1710 |
| odoratissimā | . Purple | 10, S. Ev. | S. | Caraccas | 1817 |
| pandurātā | . Purple | 10, H. Her. | P. | | 1825 |
| præāltā | . Purple | 10, H. Her. | P. | N. Amer. | 1732 |
| scabērrimā | . Purple | 10, H. Her. | P. | N. Amer. | 1824 |
| serīcēā | . Pa. pur. | 12, S. Her. | P. | Brazil | 1823 |

VERŌNĪCĀ, *Linn.* The derivation of the word is not
known. *Linn.* 2, Or. 1, Nat. Or. *Scrophulariaceæ.*
The hardy herbaceous species of this extensive
genus are admirably adapted for ornamenting the
flower borders, on account of their pleasing habit and
beautiful flowers. They are all of the easiest
culture, and are readily increased by division at
the root. The greenhouse shrubby kinds are readily
increased by cuttings. The annual species are
hardly worth cultivating, except in botanical collections; the seeds of them merely require to be
sown in the open ground. *Synonymes:* 1. *V. polymorpha.* 2. *V. lamiifolia.* 3. *V. pulchra.* 4. *V. incarnata.* 5. *V. gentianoides.* 6. *V. Barrelieri.* 7. *V.
angustifolia.* 8. *V. acuta, ambigua, rigens.* 9. *V.
grossa.* 10. *V. falcata.* 11. *V. corymbosa.* 12. *V.
hirsuta.* 13. *V. amethystina.* 14. *V. Hostii.* 15. *V.
pilocarpa.* 16. *V. circæoides.*

| | | | | |
|---|---|---|---|---|
| abrotanifòlìã | Blue | 8, H. Hær. P. | Siberia | 1830 |
| acinifòlìã | Lgt. blue | 5, H. | A. S. Eur. | 1788 |
| acutiflòrã | Red | 5, H. Hær. P. | France | 1821 |
| Allionìì | Blue | 5, H. Ev. | Cr. S. Eur. | 1740 |
| alpìnã | Blue | 5, H. De. | T. Europe | |
| heterophýllã | Blue | 5, H. De. | Tr. Europe | |
| integrifòlìã | Blue | 5, H. De. | Tr. Silesia | 1814 |
| obtusifòlìã | Blue | 7, H. De. | T. Scotland | |
| pùmìlã | Blue | 8, H. De. | T. Piedmont | 1819 |
| rotundifòlìã | Blue | 5, H. De. | T. Europe | 1816 |
| amœnã | Red | 5, H. | A. Iberia | 1824 |
| Anagàllìs | Blue | 7, H. Aq. P. | Britain | |
| aphýllã | Blue | 5, H. Hær. P. | Italy | 1775 |
| argùtã | Blue | 7, H. Hær. P. | S. Eur. | 1812 |
| austràlis | Blue | 8, H. Hær. P. | S. Eur. | 1812 |
| austrìãcã, 1 | Blue | 7, H. Hær. P. | Austria | 1748 |
| azùrëã | Blue | 5, H. Hær. P. | | 1821 |
| Beccabùngã | Blue | 5, H. Aq. P. | Britain | |
| bellidioìdës | Blue | 5, H. Hær. P. | Switzerl. | 1775 |
| bilòbã | Blue | 6, H. | A. Iberia | 1819 |
| brachyphýllã | Blue | 7, H. Hær. P. | | 1822 |
| brevifòlìã | Blue | 5, H. Hær. P. | | 1822 |
| Buxbaùmìì | White | 6, H. | A. S. Eur. | 1800 |
| callistàchyã | Blue | 6, H. Hær. P. | Podolia | 1829 |
| caroliniànã | Blue | 6, H. Aq. P. | Carolina | 1821 |
| caucàsìcã | Pa. red | 6, H. Hær. P. | Caucasus | 1816 |
| latifòlìã | Pa. red | 6, H. Hær. P. | Caucasus | 1820 |
| Chàixì | Blue | 6, H. Hær. P. | S. Eur. | 1825 |
| Chamædrys | Blue | 6, H. Hær. P. | Britain | |
| lamiifòlìã, 2 | Blue | 6, H. Hær. P. | | 1825 |
| variëgàtã | Blue | 8, H. Hær. P. | Gardens | |
| Clùsìì | Blue | 8, H. Hær. P. | Hungary | 1822 |
| complicàtã | Blue | 5, H. Hær. P. | Europe | 1812 |
| confùsã | Blue | 6, H. Hær. P. | | 1819 |
| crassifòlìã | Violet | 5, H. Hær. P. | Europe | 1822 |
| crenulàtã | Blue | 8, H. Hær. P. | S. Eur. | 1814 |
| crètìcã | Blue | 5, F. Hær. P. | Crete | 1819 |
| crinìtã | Blue | 7, H. Hær. P. | Hungary | 1822 |
| crispã | Blue | 5, H. Hær. P. | | |
| cymbalàrìã | White | 4, H. Tr. | A. S. Eur. | 1821 |
| decussàtã | Blue | 7, F. Ev. | S. Falkl. Is. | 1776 |
| dentàtã | Blue | 5, H. Hær. P. | Europe | 1818 |
| depauperàtã | Blue | 5, H. Hær. P. | Hungary | 1823 |
| dianthifòlìã, 3 | Blue | 5, G. Hær. P. | N. Holl. | 1823 |
| diosmæfòlìã | Lilac | 7, H. Hær. P. | V. D. L. | 1835 |
| distàns | Blue | 4, G. Hær. P. | N. Holl. | 1825 |
| elàtìôr | Blue | 8, H. Hær. P. | S. Eur. | 1808 |
| élégans, 4 | Pink | 5, H. Hær. P. | S. France | 1822 |
| exaltàtã | Blue | 6, H. Hær. P. | Siberia | 1816 |
| filifòrmìs | Blue | 5, H. Hær. P. | Levant | 1780 |
| foliòsã | Blue | 8, H. Hær. P. | Hungary | 1805 |
| formòsã | White | | | |
| fruticulòsã | Flesh | 7, H. Ev. | S. Scotland | |
| gentianifòlìã, 5 | Pa. blue | 5, H. Hær. P. | Levant | 1748 |
| gentianoìdës | Violet | 6, H. Hær. P. | Levant | 1748 |
| glàbrã | Blue | 8, H. Hær. P. | S. Eur. | 1804 |
| àlbã | White | 8, H. Hær. P. | | |
| gràcilis | Blue | 5, G. Hær. P. | N. S. W. | 1820 |
| gràndis | White | 8, H. Hær. P. | Siberia | 1826 |
| hýbrìdã, 6 | Blue | 6, H. Hær. P. | England | |
| incànã | Blue | 5, H. Hær. P. | Russia | 1759 |
| incìsã | Blue | 7, H. Hær. P. | Siberia | 1739 |
| Jacquìnì | Blue | 5, H. Hær. P. | Austria | 1748 |
| labiàtã | Lgt. blue | 6, G. Hær. P. | N. Holl. | 1802 |
| laciniàtã | Blue | 7, H. Hær. P. | Siberia | 1780 |
| latifòlìã | Wht. blue | 5, H. Hær. P. | Austria | 1748 |
| leucànthã | White | 7, H. Hær. P. | Siberia | 1817 |
| limariæfòlìã, 7 | Blue | 5, H. Hær. P. | Siberia | 1822 |
| longibracteàtã | Blue | 5, H. Hær. P. | | 1817 |
| latifòlìã | Blue | 7, H. Hær. P. | | 1818 |
| longiflòrã | Lilac | 6, H. Hær. P. | | 1824 |
| longifòlìã | Blue | 8, H. Hær. P. | S. Eur. | 1731 |
| abbreviàtã, 8 | Blue | 5, H. Hær. P. | | 1823 |
| àlbã | White | 8, H. Hær. P. | | |
| incarnàtã | Flesh | 8, H. Hær. P. | | |
| latifòlìã, 9 | Blue | 6, H. Hær. P. | Crimea | 1821 |
| marìtìmã | Blue | 5, H. Hær. P. | Sweden | 1570 |
| variëgàtã | Blue | 7, H. Hær. P. | Gardens | |
| màximã | Blue | 8, H. | A. Caucasus | 1824 |
| mèdìã | Blue | 8, H. Hær. P. | Germany | 1804 |
| melancòlìcã | Blue | 5, H. Hær. P. | | 1820 |
| melissæfòlìã | Blue | 5, H. Hær. P. | | 1826 |
| menthæfòlìã | Blue | 8, H. Hær. P. | Austria | 1823 |
| | Blue | 7, H. Hær. P. | | 1834 |
| Michaùxìì | Blue | 7, H. Hær. P. | Portugal | 1819 |
| micrànthã | White | 8, H. Hær. P. | | |
| microphýllã | Blue | 6, H. Hær. P. | Hungary | 1822 |
| montànã | Blue | 7, H. Hær. P. | Britain | |
| Mülleriànã | Blue | 6, H. Hær. P. | Syria | 1825 |
| multifìdã | Lgt. blue | 6, H. De. | Tr. Siberia | 1748 |
| neglèctã | Blue | 6, H. Hær. P. | Siberia | 1797 |
| nìtëns | Blue | 7, H. Hær. P. | Europe | 1817 |
| falcàtã, 10 | Blue | 8, H. Hær. P. | | 1830 |
| nìtìdã | Blue | 7, H. Hær. P. | Europe | 1817 |
| nummulàrìã | Blue | 6, H. De. | Tr. Pyrenees | 1830 |
| officinàlis | Blue | 6, H. Ev. | Cr. Britain | |
| orchidëã | Blue | 8, H. Hær. P. | Europe | 1819 |
| orientàlis | Blue | 7, H. De. | Tr. Levant | 1748 |
| pàllìdã | Blue | 8, H. Hær. P. | Tauria | 1821 |
| paniculàtã | Blue | 6, H. Hær. P. | Russia | 1797 |

| | | | | |
|---|---|---|---|---|
| parmulàrìã | Red | 7, H. Aq. P. | Austria | 1824 |
| parviflòrã | Blue | 5, G. Ev. | S. N. Zeal. | 1822 |
| pectinàtã | Blue | 5, H. Hær. P. | Italy | 1819 |
| pedunculàrìs | Blue | 8, H. Hær. P. | Caucasus | 1826 |
| peregrìnã | Blue | 7, H. | A. N. Eur. | 1680 |
| perfoliàtã | Blue | 8, G. Hær. P. | N. S. W. | 1815 |
| persicifòlìã | Blue | 8, H. Hær. P. | | 1823 |
| petræã | Blue | 5, H. Hær. P. | Caucasus | 1821 |
| pilòsã | Blue | 7, H. Hær. P. | Bohemia | 1819 |
| pinnàtã | Blue | 5, H. Hær. P. | Siberia | 1776 |
| pinnatìfìdã | Blue | 6, H. Hær. P. | | 1817 |
| plebèìã | Blue | 6, G. Hær. P. | N. Holl. | 1820 |
| plicàtã | Blue | 6, H. Hær. P. | Bohemia | 1817 |
| polystàchyã, 11 | Blue | 7, H. Hær. P. | | 1817 |
| Pònæ | Blue | 9, H. Hær. P. | Pyrenees | 1822 |
| præàltã | Blue | 8, H. Hær. P. | | 1817 |
| præcôx | Blue | 6, H. Hær. P. | S. Eur. | 1775 |
| prostràtã | Blue | 6, H. De. | Tr. Germany | 1774 |
| maturelæfòlìã | Blue | 7, H. De. | Tr. S. Eur. | |
| pulchèllã | White | 7, H. | A. | 1819 |
| rèpèns | White | 9, H. Ev. | Cr. Europe | 1829 |
| rìgëns | Blue | 7, H. | A. | 1823 |
| ruthènìcã | Blue | 4, H. Hær. P. | Russia | 1821 |
| saxàtìlis | Blue | 6, H. De. | Tr. Scotland | |
| Schmidtìì | Blue | 6, H. De. | Tr. Bohemia | 1820 |
| scutellàtã | Flesh | 5, H. Aq. P. | Britain | |
| serpyllifòlìã | Blue | 5, H. De. | Tr. Britain | |
| humifùsã | Blue | 5, H. De. | Tr. Europe | |
| neglèctã | Blue | 5, H. De. | Tr. Europe | |
| nummulàrìã | Blue | 5, H. De. | Tr. Europe | |
| quaternàtã | Blue | 5, H. De. | Tr. Europe | |
| tenèllã | Blue | 5, H. De. | Tr. Europe | |
| setìgèrã, 12 | Blue | 5, H. Hær. P. | Scotland | |
| speciòsã | | F. Ev. | S. V. D. L. | 1835 |
| spicàtã | Blue | 8, H. Hær. P. | England | |
| spùrìã, 13 | Lgt. blue | 5, H. Hær. P. | Siberia | 1731 |
| Stephaniànã | Blue | 6, H. Hær. P. | Persia | 1821 |
| stoloniferã | Blue | 6, H. De. | Cr. | |
| taùrìcã | Blue | 6, H. De. | Tr. Siberia | 1820 |
| tenèllã | Blue | 6, H. Hær. P. | France | 1820 |
| tenuifòlìã | Blue | 6, H. Hær. P. | Pyrenees | 1821 |
| Teucrìum | Lgt. blue | 7, H. Hær. P. | Germany | 1596 |
| Ticinènsis, 14 | Blue | 5, H. Hær. P. | Ticin. | 1819 |
| Tournefòrtìì | Blue | 5, H. Ev. | Cr. France | 1824 |
| trichocàrpã, 15 | Blue | 6, H. Hær. P. | Levant | 1820 |
| urticæfòlìã, 16 | Pink | 6, H. Hær. P. | Austria | 1776 |
| villòsã | Blue | 8, H. Hær. P. | S. Eur. | 1824 |
| Wormskioldìì | Blue | 6, H. Hær. P. | Greenland | 1819 |

agrèstis, A. opàcã, A. versìcôlôr, arvènsis, digitàtã, hederæfòlìã, polìtã, triphýllòs, vèrnã.

VÈRPÃ, Swartz. An old Roman name, synonymous with *Phallus*. Linn. 24, Or. 9, Nat. Or. *Fungi*. Found upon the ground—*V. cònìcã, digitàlis*.

VERRUCÀRÌÃ, Persoon. From verruca, a wart; on account of the verrucose nature of the shields. Linn. 24, Or. 8, Nat. Or. *Lichenes*. Found upon rocks, and the bark of trees—*V. analèptã, alphànës, bifòrmìs, ceuthocàrpã, circumscrìptã, concìnnã, confèrtã, dermatòdës, Dufoùrìì, epidèrmìdìs, epìgêã, epipolèã, erysìbòdã, fìssã, gemmàtã, gemmiferã, Harrimànnì, Hookèrì, immèrsã, irrìgùã, lævàtã, leucocèphàlã, L. amphìbòlã, lithìnã, lùcêns, maùrã, mòllis, muràlis, nìvèo-àtrã, olivàcëã, periphèrìcã, plùmbèã, polystìctã, punctifòrmìs, rhypòntã, rubigìnòsã, rùdis, Schraderì, stigmatèllã, striàtùlã, S. acrotèllã, submèrsã, trachònã, umbròsã*.

VÈRSATILE, swinging lightly on a stalk, so as to be continually changing direction.

VÈRTEX, the uppermost point.

VÈRTICAL, perpendicular.

VÈRTICÌLLATE, disposed in a whorl.

VÈRTILINEAR, having straight lines.

VÈRVAIN, see *Verbèna*.

VÈSICÀRÌÃ, Lamarck. From vesica, a bladder or blister; in allusion to the inflated pods. Linn. 15, Nat. Or. *Cruciferæ*. These plants are well adapted for ornamenting rock-work. They are of the easiest culture and propagation. Synonymes: 1. *Alyssum arcticum*. 2. *A. creticum*. 3. *A. Vesicaria*. 4. *A. Utricularia*.

| | | | | |
|---|---|---|---|---|
| arctìcã, 1 | Yellow | 8, H. Ev. | S. N. Amer. | 1828 |
| arenòsã, 2 | Yellow | 8, H. Ev. | S. N. Amer. | 1826 |
| crètìcã, 3 | Yellow | 7, F. Ev. | S. Crete | 1739 |
| gràcìlis | Yellow | 6, H. | A. Texas | 1834 |
| grandiflòrã | Yellow | 7, H. | A. Texas | 1835 |
| Ludoviciànã | Yellow | 6, H. Hær. P. | Louisiana | 1825 |
| reticulàtã, 4 | Yellow | 5, H. Hær. P. | S. Eur. | 1700 |
| sinuàtã | Lgt. yel. | 5, H. | B. Spain | 1596 |
| utriculàtã, 5 | Yellow | 5, H. Ev. | S. Levant | 1780 |

VÈSICLÈS, hollow excrescences, like bladders.

VÈSTÌÃ, Willdenow. In honour of Dr. Vest, of Clagenfurth. Linn. 5, Or. 1, Nat. Or. *Cestraceæ*. An interesting shrub. For culture and propagation, see *Cestrum*. *Synonyme:* 1. *Cantua ligustri-folia.*

lycioídes, 1 . . . Yellow . 6, G. De. S. Chile . . 1815

VETCH, see *Vicia*.

VETCH, see *Astrágalus Cícer*.

VETCHLING, see *Láthyrus Aphàca*.

VEXILLUM, standard, the upper petal of a pea flower.

VIBÓRGIA, *Ortega*. In honour of Eric Viborg, a Danish botanist. *Linn.* 16, Or. 6, Nat. Or. *Leguminosæ*. Pretty plants. For culture, &c., see *Loddigesia*. *Synonyme:* 1. *Crotalaria floribunda, obcordata.*

obcordàta, 1 . . Yellow . 7, G. Ev. S. C.G.H. . 1810
sericèa . . . . Yellow . 7, G. Ev. S. C.G.H. . 1810

VIBRÍSSEA, *Fries*. From *vibro*, to vibrate. *Linn.* 24, Or. 9, Nat. Or. *Fungi*. This species is found on the branches and trunks of trees lying in water—*V. truncòrum.*

VIBÚRNUM, *Linn.* Said to be from *vieo*, to tie; because of the pliability of some of the branches. *Linn.* 5, Or. 3, Nat. Or. *Caprifoliaceæ*. The species of *Vi-burnum* are all very elegant, rather early-flowering shrubs. The hardy kinds are well fitted for planting in ornamental shrubberies. They are increased by layers, or by cuttings, planted under a glass, in a shady situation. The fruit becomes eatable after fermentation, and is made into a sort of cake by the North American Indians. *Synonymes:* 1. *V. squa-matum.* 2 *V. Opulus roseum.* 3. *V. lucidum.* 4. *V. strictum virgatum.* 5. *V. strictum.*

acerifòlium . . . White . 6, H. De. S. N. Amer. 1736
cassinoídes . . . White . 6, H. Ev. S. N. Amer. 1761
cotinifòlium . . . White . 6, H. De. S. Himal. Mts. 1830
dahúricum . . . Yelsh. wht. 6, H. De. S. Dahuria 1785
dentàtum . . . White . 6, H. De. S. N. Amer. 1763
edùle . . . . . White . 6, H. De. S. N. Amer. 1812
Lantàna . . . . White . 5, H. De. S. Britain .
  fòlis variegàtis White . 5, H. De. S. Britain .
  grandifòlium . White . 6, H. De. S. Britain .
lantanoídes . . . White . 6, H. De. S. N. Amer. .
lævigàtum . . . White . 5, H. Ev. S. N. Amer. 1724
Lentàgo . . . . White . 7, H. De. S. Spain . 1761
mòlle . . . . . White . 5, G. Ev. S. N. Amer. 1812
monogýnum . . . . . . F. Ev. S. Java .
nítidum . . . . White . 6, H. De. S. N. Amer. 1758
nùdum . . . . Pa. yel. 6, H. De. S. N. Amer. 1752
  squamàtum, 1 . White . 7, H. De. S. N. Amer. 1822
obovàtum . . . White . 4, H. De. S. N. Amer. 1812
  punicifòlium . White . 5, H. De. S. N. Amer. 1812
odoratíssimum . White . 5, F. De. S. China . 1818
Opùlus . . . . White . 7, H. De. S. Britain .
  fol. variegàtis . White . 6, H. De. S. Britain .
  nànum . . . . . . . H. De. S. .
  stérile, 2 . . . White . 7, H. De. S. Britain .
orientàle . . . White . 5, H. De. S. Caucasus 1827
Oxycóccos . . . White . 6, H. De. S. N. Amer. .
  subintegrifòlium White . 7, H. De. S. Columbia .
prunifòlium . . . White . 5, H. De. S. N. Amer. 1731
pubèscens . . . White . 6, H. De. S. N. Amer. 1736
pyrifòlium . . . White . 6, H. De. S. N. Amer. 1812
rugòsum . . . . White . 5, F. Ev. S. Canaries 1796
tinoídes . . . . . . . 8. Ev. S. S. Amer. 1820
Tìnus . . . . . White . 7, H. Ev. S. S. Eur. 1596
  hírtum, 3 . . . White . 7, H. Ev. S. S. Eur. .
  lúcidum . . . . White . 8, H. Ev. S. Algiers .
  variegàtum . . White . 8, H. Ev. S. .
  virgàtum, 4 . . White . 8, H. Ev. S. Italy .
  strictum, 5 . . . White . 8, H. Ev. S. S. Eur. .
  variegàtum . . White . 8, H. Ev. S. S. Eur. .
tomentòsum . . . White . G. Ev. S. Japan .
villòsum . . . . White . F. Ev. S. Jamaica . 1824

VICIA, *Tournefort*. From *vincio*, to bind together; because the species have tendrils by which they bind other plants. *Linn.* 17, Or. 4, Nat. Or. *Legu-minosæ*. Some of the species of this genus are well worth cultivating in the flower border for the beauty of their flowers. They are of the easiest culture in any common garden soil. The perennial kinds may be readily increased by dividing the root or by seeds. The seeds of the annual kinds only require to be sown in the open border in spring. *V. sativa* and its varieties are extensively cultivated, and well known by the common name of vetch or tares; they are used as food for all kinds of cattle, and are allowed to be more nutritive and profitable than hay or any other herbage. *Synonymes:* 1. *V. luganensis.* 2. *V. sordida.* 3. *Lathyrus Bithynicus.* 4. *V. monantha.* 5. *V. Cracca.* 6. *V. parviflora.* 7. *Ervum soloniense.* 8. *V. alba.* 9. *V. atropurpurea.* 10. *V. tenuifolia.*

abbreviàta . . . Pa. blue . 6, H. De. Cl. Caucasus . 1818
altíssima . . . . Pa. blue . 8, H. De. Cl. Barbary . 1820

americàna . . . White . 6, H. De. Cl. N. Amer. . 1800
amœna . . . . Purple . 6, H. De. Cl. Siberia . 1818
amphicàrpos . . Purple . 5, H. Cl. A. France . 1815
angustifòlia, 1 . Red . 5, H. Cl. A. Britain .
argentàta . . . Pink . 6, H. Her. P. Pyrenees 1827
atropurpùrea . . Purple . 6, H. Cl. A. Algiers . 1815
bætica . . . . . Purple . 7, H. Cl. A. Algiers . 1820
benghalénsis . . Dk. pur. . 6, H. Cl. A. E. Ind. . 1792
bícolor . . . . Pur. wht. 7, H. Cl. A. . 1820
Biebersteinii, 2 . Yellow . 7, H. Cl. A. Podolia . 1820
biénnis . . . . Purple . 8, H. Cl. B. Siberia . 1753
biflòra . . . . Blue . 7, H. Cl. A. Algiers . 1801
Bithýnica, 3 . . Pur. vio. 7, H. Her. P. Britain .
calcaràta, 4 . . Red blue . 7, H. Cl. A. Barbary . 1790
canéscens . . . Blue . 7, H. Cl. A. Libanus . 1800
capénsis . . . . Purple . 7, H. Her. P. C.G.H. . 1802
carolinàna, 5 . . White . 6, H. De. Cl. Carolina . 1820
canúbica . . . . Lgt. blue . 7, H. De. Cl. Germany 1711
consentìna . . . Blue . 6, H. Cl. A. Italy . 1818
cordàta . . . . Purple . 5, H. . A. Germany 1816
Cracca . . . . Violet . 7, H. De. Cl. Britain .
  flóribus albis . White . 7, H. De. Cl. Britain .
  flóribus rùbris Red . 7, H. De. Cl. Britain . 1819
dentàta . . . . Violaceous 7, H. De. Cl. Siberia . 1819
disperma, 6 . . White . 7, H. Cl. A. S. France 1820
dòlia . . . . . Purple . 7, H. Cl. A. . 1820
dumetòrum . . . Purple . 6, H. De. Cl. France . 1752
Gerárdi . . . . Violet . 7, H. De. Cl. S. Eur. 1810
glàbra . . . . . Purple . 7, H. Cl. A. Switzerl. 1819
globòsa . . . . Blue . 7, H. Cl. A. . 1804
grandiflòra . . . Yellow . 7, H. Cl. A. S. Eur. 1818
hirsùta . . . . Purple . 7, H. Cl. A. Siberia . 1818
hírta . . . . . Pa. cream 6, H. Cl. A. Europe . 1816
hýbrida . . . . Yellow . 7, H. Cl. A. England .
incìsa . . . . . Purple . 6, H. Cl. A. Caucasus 1820
intermèdia . . . Purple . 7, H. Cl. A. Europe . 1818
lævigàta . . . . Pa. yel. 6, H. De. Cl. England .
lathyroídes, 7 . Purple . 6, H. Cl. A. Britain .
leucospérma, 8 . Purple . 6, H. Cl. A. Europe . 1810
longifòlia . . . Cream . 7, H. Cl. A. Syria . 1818
lùtea . . . . . Yellow . 7, H. Cl. A. Britain .
megalospérma . . Purple . 7, H. Cl. A. . 1798
Michaúxii . . . White . 7, H. . A. . 1803
monadélpha . . . Purple . 7, H. . A. N. Amer. 1820
multicaùlis . . . . . . . H. Her. P. Russia . 1832
Musquínea . . . Purple . 7, H. Cl. A. Europe . 1818
narbonénsis . . . Purple . 7, H. Cl. A. France . 1596
Nissoliàna, 9 . . Dk. pur. . 7, H. Cl. A. Levant . 1778
ochroleùca . . . Pa. yel. . 7, H. De. Cl. Italy . 1835
onobrychioídes . Purple . 6, H. Cl. P. S. Eur. 1759
pannónica . . . White . 7, G. De. Cl. C.G.H. 1638
pellùcida . . . . Purple . 7, H. Cl. A. Hungary 1773
peregrìna . . . . Purple . 7, H. Cl. A. S. Eur. 1779
perénnis . . . . Purple . 7, H. De. Cl. S. Eur. .
pilòsa . . . . . Purple . 7, H. Cl. A. Tauria . 1818
pimpinelloídes . Purple . 7, H. . A. Rome . 1832
pisifórmis . . . Cream . 7, H. De. Cl. Austria . 1739
platycàrpa . . . Purple . 7, H. Cl. A. Germany 1723
polyphýlla . . . Pa. pur. . 7, H. De. Cl. Algiers . 1816
polyspérma . . . Purple . 6, H. Cl. A. . 1833
Pseúdo-cracca, 10 Yellow . 7, H. Cl. A. S. Eur. 1820
punctàta . . . . Purple . 7, H. Cl. A. Switzerl. 1819
pyrenàica . . . Purple . 5, H. Her. P. Pyrenees 1818
satìva . . . . . Purple . 5, H. Cl. A. Britain .
  nemoràlis . . Purple . 5, H. Cl. A. Britain .
  segetàlis . . . Violet . 5, H. Cl. A. Britain .
sepìum . . . . . Violet . 5, H. Cl. A. Britain .
serratifòlia . . . Purple . 6, H. Cl. A. Hungary 1723
sórdida . . . . Yellow . 6, H. Cl. A. Hungary 1802
striàta . . . . . Purple . 7, H. Cl. A. Tauria . 1823
sylvàtica . . . . Wht. blue 7, H. De. Cl. Britain .
syrìaca . . . . . Violet . 6, H. Cl. A. Syria . 1816
tenuifòlia . . . . Violet . 6, H. De. Cl. Germany 1799
Thouíni . . . . Purple . 6, H. Cl. A. Europe . 1800
tricòlor . . . . Pur. yel. 7, H. Cl. A. Italy . 1818
triflòra . . . . Purple . 7, H. Cl. A. Italy . 1820
truncàtula . . . Pa. yel. . 7, H. Cl. A. Caucasus 1818
variegàta . . . . Pa. pur. . 6, H. De. Cl. Caucasus 1816
villòsa . . . . . Dk. pur. . 6, H. Cl. A. Germany 1815

VIEUSSÉUXIA, *Laroche*. In honour of M. Vieusseux, a physician of Geneva. *Linn.* 3, Or. 1, Nat. Or. *Iridaceæ*. Ornamental plants when in flower, and requiring precisely the same treatment as the genus *Homeria*. *Synonymes:* 1. *Moræa tricuspis lutea.* 2. *Iris pavonia.* 3. *M. lurida.* 4. *M. pavonia, Iris pavonia.* 5. *M. tenuis.* 6. *Iris tricuspis, Moræa tricuspis, Ferraria tricuspis.* 7. *M. tripetala, I. tripetala.* 8. *M. unguiculata.* 9. *Iris villosa, M. villosa.*

Bellendéni, 1 . . Yellow . 6, G. Bl. P. C.G.H. . 1803
fùgax . . . . . Purple . 6, G. Bl. P. C.G.H. . 1825
glaucòpis, 2 . . Red brn. . 6, F. Bl. P. C.G.H. . 1776
lùrida, 3 . . . . Crimson . 6, G. Bl. P. C.G.H. . 1817
pavonìna, 4 . . . Red blue . 5, G. Bl. P. C.G.H. . 1790
spiràlis . . . . White . 6, G. Bl. P. C.G.H. . 1824
tenùis, 5 . . . . Purple . 6, G. Bl. P. C.G.H. . 1807
tricúspis, 6 . . . Green . 5, G. Bl. P. C.G.H. . 1776

tripetaloídes, 7 . Violet . 6, G. Bl. P. C. G. H. . 1802
unguiculárìs, 8 . Varieg. . 6, G. Bl. P. C. G. H. . 1802
villósā, 9 . . . Purple . 7, G. Bl. P. C. G. H. . 1789

VÍGNĀ, *Savi.* In memory of Dominic Vigni, a commentator on Theophrastus. *Linn.* 17, Or. 4, Nat. Or. *Leguminosæ.* The seeds of this species may be sown in a warm sheltered situation in the open ground. *Synonyme:* 1. *Dolichos luteolus.*

glábrā, 1 . . . Yellow . 7, H. Tr. A. N. Amer. . 1685

VIGUIĒRĀ, *Kunth.* In honour of L. G. A. Viguier, a botanist of Montpelier. *Linn.* 19, Or. 8, Nat. Or. *Compositæ.* Interesting plants, succeeding well in a mixture of sandy peat and loam, and increased by cuttings in sand, under a glass. *Synonyme:* 1. *Helianthus dentatus.*

dentátā, 1 . . . Yellow . 7, S. Her. P. Mexico . . 1826
helianthoídes . . Yellow . 7, S. Her. P. Cuba . . 1825

VILLĀRSĪĀ, *Ventenat.* Named in honour of D. Villars, a famous French botanist. *Linn.* 5, Or. 1, Nat. Or. *Gentianaceæ.* A genus of very elegant plants when in blossom. The stove and greenhouse aquatic species should be grown in tubs or cisterns of water. The hardy kinds succeed well in a pond. The marshy kinds, as *V. geminata,* require to be grown in pots, in a mixture of peat and sand, and the pots to be placed in water. They are all readily increased by divisions, or by seed. *Synonymes:* 1. *Menyanthes indica.* 2. *V. cordata.* 3. *M. nymphoides.*

chīlénsìs . . . Yellow . 6, F. Aq. P. Chile . . 1832
geminátā . . . Yellow . 6, G. Her. P. N. Holl. . 1828
índìcā, 1 . . . White . 7, S. Aq. P. C. G. H. . 1792
lacunósā, 2 . . White . 6, G. Aq. P. N. Amer. . 1812
nymphoídes, 3 . Yellow . 6, H. Aq. P. England .
ovátā . . . Orange . 6, G. Aq. P. C. G. H. . 1786
parnassifóliā . . Yellow . 8, G. Aq. P. N. S. W. . 1825
renifórmìs . . . Yellow . 6, G. Aq. P. N. Holl. . 1820
sarmentósā . . Yellow . 6, G. Her. P. N. Holl. . 1800
Símsìì . . . Yellow . 7, S. Her. P. Nepal . . 1792

VILLI, long, close, rather soft hairs.
VILLOUS, covered with soft, close, long, loose hairs.
VILMORÍNĪĀ, *Decandolle.* In compliment to M. Vilmorin, a famous French cultivator, and Member of the Agricultural Society of Paris. *Linn.* 17, Or. 4, Nat. Or. *Leguminosæ.* For culture and propagation, see *Clitoria.* *Synonyme:* 1. *Clitoria multiflora.*

multiflórā, 1 . . Purple . 8. Ev. S. W. Ind. . 1826

VIMINĀRĪĀ, *Smith.* From *vimen,* a twig; the appearance of the species is that of a bundle of twigs, being destitute of leaves. *Linn.* 10, Or. 1, Nat. Or. *Leguminosæ.* For culture and propagation, see *Jacksonia.*

denudátā . . . Yellow 8, G. Ev. S. N. Holl. . 1780
laterìflórā . . . Yellow . 7, G. Ev. S. N. Holl. . 1824

VÍNCA, *Linn.* Probably from *vinculum,* a band; in allusion to the suitableness of the shoots for making bands. *Linn.* 5, Or. 1, Nat. Or. *Apocynaceæ.* These plants are well adapted for covering naked ground in shaded situations. Any common soil suits them, and they are readily increased by separating the rooted trailing shoots. *Synonymes:* 1. *V. media flore pleno.* 2. *V. media.*

herbáceā . . . Pur. blue . 6, H. Ev. Tr. Hungary . 1816
majòr . . . . Pur. blue . 8, H. Ev. Tr. England .
  flòrè plénô, 1 . Blue . . 8, H. Ev. Tr. Gardens .
  intermédīā, 2 . Blue . . 8, H. Ev. Tr. Gardens .
  variegátā . . Blue . . 7, H. Ev. Tr. England .
minòr . . . . Blue . . 8, H. Ev. Tr. Britain .
  flòrè albô . . White . 7, H. Ev. Tr. Gardens .
  flòrè plénô . . Violet . 5, H. Ev. Tr. Gardens .
  flòrè puníceô . Red . . H. Ev. Tr. Gardens .
  fol. argéntìs . Violet . 7, H. Ev. Tr. Gardens .
  fol. aúrèìs . . Violet . 6, H. Ev. Tr. Gardens .

VÍNCA, see *Catharánthus.*
VINE BOWER, see *Clematìs Viticéllā.*
VINE LEEK, see *Allìum ampelóprásūm.*
VÍOLA, *Linn.* Latin name of the flowers. *Linn.* 5, Or. 1, Nat. Or. *Violaceæ.* All the species of this genus deserve to be cultivated, either for the beauty or the scent of their flowers. The hardy perennial kinds are well fitted for ornamenting the front of flower-borders or rock-work, but the smaller species succeed best when grown in pots, in a mixture of loam, peat, and sand. The species, natives of America, thrive best in vegetable mould or peat, and are readily increased by parting the roots, or by seeds. The greenhouse and stove species should be grown in a mixture of loam and peat; the her-

[ 331 ]

baceous kinds of them are increased by seed, or dividing the roots, and the shrubby kinds by cuttings, which root readily when planted under a glass. The annual species may be sown in the open borders or on rock-work. The Neapolitan violet, *V. odorata pallido-plena,* may be made to flower throughout the winter and early spring, by placing it in a stove or warm pit. *V. canina* is said to be a famous agent in removing cutaneous diseases. *Synonymes:* 1. *V. sororia.* 2. *V. Pallasii, chrysantha.* 3. *V. Allioni.* 4. *V. lanceolata.* 5. *V. Patrinii nepalensis, primulæfolia.* 6. *V. multifida.* 7. *V. dentata.* 8. *V. sibirica.* 9. *V. odorata.* 10. *V. stagnina.* 11. *V. Hornemanniana.* 12. *V. primulæfolia.* 13. *V. prunellæfolia.* 14. *V. digitata.* 15. *V. ranunculifolia.* 16. *V. ericetorum.* 17. *V. lancifolia.* 18. *V. littoralis.* 19. *V. Broussonetiana.* 20. *V. saxalilis.* 21. *V. arvensis.* 22. *V. Kitaibeliana.* 23. *V. calcarata.*

affínìs, 1 . . . Blue . . 4, H. Her. P. N. Amer. . 1802
alleghanénsìs . . Blue . . 5, H. Her. P. N. Amer. . 1824
alpínā . . . . Purple . 6, H. Ev. Cr. Austria . 1823
altáìcā, 2 . . . Dk. pur. 5, H. Her. P. Siberia . 1808
  purpúrèā . . Purple . 5, H. Her. P. Siberia . 1810
ambígūā . . . Bluish . 5, H. Her. P. Hungary . 1823
amœ́nā . . . . Purple . 6, H. Her. P. Scotland .
arboréscèns . . Pa. blue . 5, G. Ev. S. Spain . . 1779
arenárìā, 3 . . Blue . . 6, H. Her. P. France . 1823
assarifólìā . . . Blue . . 5, H. Her. P. N. Amer. . 1820
áspérā . . . . Pa. yell. 5, H. Her. P. Nepal . 1824
attenuátā, 4 . . White . 7, H. Her. P. N. Amer. . 1759
bannátìcā . . . Yel. pur. 8, H. . A. Germany . 1820
betonicæfóliā . . Blue . . 8, G. Her. P. N. Holl. . 1820
bicólòr . . . . White . 5, H. . A. N. Amer. . 1818
biflórā . . . . Yellow . 6, H. Her. P. Alp. Eur. 1752
blándā . . . . White . 5, H. Her. P. N. Amer. . 1802
cæspitósā, 5 . . Violet . 3, F. Her. P. Nepal . 1825
calcarátā . . . Lgt. blue 5, H. Her. P. Switzerl. 1752
campéstrìs . . . Purple . 5, H. Her. P. Tauria . 1824
canadénsìs . . White . 5, H. Her. P. N. Amer. . 1783
  discólor . . Blue wht. 6, H. Her. P. N. Amer. . 1783
canínā . . . . Blue . . 5, H. De. Tr. Britain .
  álbā . . . White . 5, H. De. Cr. Gardens .
  rúbrā . . . Red . . 5, H. De. Cr. Gardens .
cenísìā . . . . Blue . . 6, H. Her. P. Mt. Cenis . 1759
clandestínā . . Brown . 4, H. Her. P. Pennsylv. . 1800
collínā . . . . Blue . . 5, H. Her. P. Poland . 1822
cornútā . . . . Blue . . 5, H. Her. P. Pyrenees . 1776
cucullátā . . . Blue . . 5, H. Her. P. N. Amer. . 1762
dactyloídes . . Blue . . 5, H. Her. P. Siberia . 1820
débìlìs . . . . Pa. blue . 4, H. Her. P. N. Amer. . 1820
declinátā . . . Pa. blue . 6, H. Her. P. Pannonia . 1818
decúmbèns . . . Pa. blue . 6, F. Her. P. C. G. H. . 1819
digitátā . . . . Pa. blue . 6, H. Her. P. Virginia .
disséctā, 6 . . . Violet . 5, H. Her. P. Altaian Mts.
emarginátā, 7 . Blue . . 5, H. Her. P. N. Amer. .
epipélā . . . . Yellow . 6, H. Her. P. Livonia . 1822
eriocárpā . . . Yellow . 6, H. Her. P. N. Amer. . 1823
flabellifólìā . . . Blue . . 6, H. Her. P. N. Amer. . 1823
flavicórnìs . . . Yell. blue 6, H. Her. P. Britain .
glaúcā . . . . Pa. blue . 5, H. Her. P. Poland . 1822
Gmelínìánā, 8 . Blue . . 5, H. Her. P. Siberia . 1820
grácìlìs . . . . Purple . 6, H. Her. P. Greece . 1817
grandìflórā . . . Yellow . 7, H. Her. P. Switzerl. .
hastátā . . . . Yellow . 5, H. Her. P. Carolina . 1823
hirsútā . . . . Blue . . 5, H. Her. P. Bohemia . 1820
hírtā . . . . . Greyish . 5, H. Her. P. England .
húmìlìs . . . . White . 5, F. Her. P. Mexico . 1824
japónìcā, 9 . . Blue . . 5, H. Ev. Cr. Japan . 1818
Kröckérì . . . Pa. red . 5, H. Her. P. Siberia . 1820
láctéā, 10 . . . Crimson . 5, H. Her. P. England .
lanceolátā . . . White . 6, H. Her. P. N. Amer. . 1759
Langsdórfìì . . Blue . . 6, H. Her. P. Siberia . 1823
lútèā . . . . Yellow . 6, H. Her. P. Britain .
mirábìlìs . . . Lgt. blue 7, H. Her. P. Germany . 1752
montánā . . . Lgt. blue 5, H. Her. P. Alp. Eur. 1683
  strícta, 11 . . Cream . 5, H. Her. P. England . 1819
negléctā . . . . Pur. blue 5, H. Her. P. Crimea . 1817
nummularifólìā . Blue . . 5, H. Her. P. S. France . 1820
Nuttálìì . . . . Yellow . 5, H. Her. P. Missouri . 1812
oblíquā . . . . Yel. blue 5, H. Her. P. N. Amer. . 1762
ochroleúcā . . . Cream . 5, H. Her. P. N. Amer. . 1800
occúltā . . . . Veiny . 5, H. . A. . . 1832
odorátā . . . . Purple . 6, H. Ev. Tr. Britain .
  álbā . . . White . 4, H. Ev. Tr. Britain .
  albó-plénā . . White . 4, H. Ev. Tr. Britain .
  cœrúleā . . . Blue . . 4, H. Ev. Tr. Britain .
  cœrúlèo-plénā . Blue . . 4, H. Ev. Tr. Britain .
  pállìdo-plénā . Pa. blue . 4, H. Ev. Tr. Britain .
  purpúreā . . . Purple . 5, H. Ev. Tr. Britain .
  purpúrèo-plénā Purple . 4, H. Ev. Tr. Britain .
oreádes . . . . Purple . 6, H. Her. P. Tauria . 1818
ovátā, 12 . . . Pur. blue . 6, H. Her. P. N. Amer. . 1783
palmánsìs . . . Purple . 6, F. Ev. S. S. Eur. . 1836
palmárìs . . . . Yellow . 6, H. De. Tr. Nepal . 1824
palmátā . . . . Blue . . 5, H. Her. P. N. Amer. . 1759
  variegátā . . Pur. wht. 6, H. Her. P. N. Amer. .
palústrìs . . . . Blue . . 5, H. Her. P. Britain .

| | | | | | | |
|---|---|---|---|---|---|---|
| pennsylvánica | Drk. blue | 6, | H. Her. P. | N. Amer. | |
| papilionácea | Blue | 6, | H. Her. P. | N. Amer. | 1800 |
| Patrinii, 13 | Pa. blue | 6, | H. Her. P. | Siberia | 1822 |
| pedáta | Blue | 6, | H. Her. P. | N. Amer. | 1759 |
| flabelláta, 14 | Lgt. pur. | 6, | H. Her. P. | Georgia | |
| ranunculifòlia,15 | Whitish | 6, | H. Her. P. | N. Amer. | 1818 |
| pedatífida | Blue | 6, | H. Her. P. | N. Amer. | 1826 |
| pennsylvánica | Yellow | 6, | H. Her. P. | N. Amer. | 1772 |
| persicifòlia | Cream | 6, | H. Her. P. | Germany | 1817 |
| pinnáta | Violet | 6, | H. Her. P. | S. Eur. | 1752 |
| præmórsa | Yellow | 6, | H. Her. P. | Columbia | 1828 |
| primulæfòlia | Pa. blue | 6, | H. Her. P. | Carolina | 1783 |
| prostráta | Cream | 6, | H. Da. Tr. | Teneriffe | 1824 |
| pubéscens | Yellow | 6, | H. Her. P. | France | 1772 |
| pùmila | Pa. blue | 6, | H. Her. P. | France | 1818 |
| ericetòrum, 16. | Blue | 5, | H. Her. P. | Germany | 1826 |
| lancifòlia, 17 | Blue | 6, | H. Her. P. | Germany | |
| littoràlia, 18 | Blue | 6, | H. Her. P. | Baltic | |
| pygmæa | Pur. blue | 8, | G. Her. P. | Peru | 1822 |
| pyrenáica | Blue | 5, | H. Her. P. | Pyrenees | 1817 |
| rádicans | Blue | 6, | H. Ev. Cr. | Carolina | 1823 |
| rothomagénsis | Blue | 7, | H. Her. P. | France | 1781 |
| rotundifòlia | Pa. yel. | 5, | H. Her. P. | N. Amer. | 1800 |
| Rüppii, 19. | Blue | 5, | H. Her. P. | Italy | 1822 |
| sagittáta | Wht. blue | 7, | H. Her. P. | N. Amer. | 1775 |
| sarmentòsa | Blue | 5, | H. Ev. Cr. | Caucasus | 1824 |
| Schmidtiána | Blue | 5, | H. Her. P. | Austria | 1821 |
| Selkirkii | Blue | 6, | H. Her. P. | N. Amer. | 1822 |
| striáta | Striped | 6, | H. Her. P. | N. Amer. | 1772 |
| suàvis | Pa. blue | 6, | H. Ev. Cr. | Ukraine | 1823 |
| sudética, 20 | Yellow | 7, | H. Her. P. | Germany | 1805 |
| sylvéstris | Blue | 5, | H. Her. P. | Hungary | 1826 |
| tricólor | Yel. pur. | 8, | H. Her. P. | Britain | |
| arvénsis, 21 | Yel. pur. | 6, | H. | A. | Britain |
| élegans | Veiny sum | H. | B. | Altai | 1832 |
| hírta, 21 | Pa. blue | 6, | H. Her. P. | Pannonia | 1820 |
| tripartíta | Yellow | 6, | H. Her. P. | N. Amer. | 1823 |
| uliginósa | Purple | 4, | H. Her. P. | Carinthia | 1823 |
| uniflòra | Yellow | 6, | H. Her. P. | Siberia | 1774 |
| valdéria | Purple | 5, | H. Her. P. | Mt. Cenis | 1759 |
| variegáta | Pa. vio. | 5, | H. Her. P. | Dahuria | 1817 |
| Villarsiána, 22 | Blue | 6, | H. Her. P. | Vallesia | 1826 |
| Zòysii | Yellow | 3, | H. Her. P. | Carinthia | |

VIOLACEOUS, violet-coloured.

VIOLET, see *Vìòla*.

VIOLET THLASPI, see *Clypeòla Iòn Thláspi*.

VIORNA, see *Clèmàtis Viòrna*.

VIPER'S BUGLOSS, see *Echìum*.

VIPER'S GRASS, see *Scorzonèra*.

VIRENS, green, flourishing.

VIRESCENT, greenish.

VIRGÌLIA. Lamarck dedicated this genus to the poet Virgil, whose Georgics contain many things interesting to botanists. *Linn.* 10, Or. 1, Nat. Or. *Leguminòsæ.* The greenhouse species are very elegant when in blossom; they succeed well in a mixture of loam, peat, and sand, and are increased by young cuttings, in sand, under a glass. *V. lùtea* is an elegant hardy tree, well suited for shrubberies or pleasure grounds. It is commonly propagated by laying down the shoots in autumn or spring. *Synonymes:* 1. *Robinia capensis.* 2. *Sophora sylvatica.*

| | | | | | |
|---|---|---|---|---|---|
| aùrea | Yellow | 7, | G. Ev. S. | Abyssinia | 1777 |
| capénsis | Pur. wht. | 7, | G. Ev. S. | C. G. H. | 1767 |
| intrùsa | Pa. yel. | 7, | G. Ev. S. | C. G. H. | 1790 |
| lùtea | Yellow | 7, | H. Da. T. | N. Amer. | 1812 |
| robinioìdes, 1 | Yellow | 8, | G. Ev. S. | C. G. H. | 1818 |
| sylvática, 2 | Yellow | 8, | G. Ev. S. | C. G. H. | 1816 |

VIRGINIAN CREEPER, see *Ampelópsis hederácea.*

VIRGINIAN HEMP, see *Acnìda.*

VIRGINIAN POKE, see *Phytolácca decándra.*

VIRGIN'S BOWER, see *Clèmàtis Viticélla.*

VIRILIS, stout, strong, vigorous.

VIROSUS, rank, poisonous.

VISCÀRIA, *Roehler.* From *viscus*, birdlime; in allusion to the glutinous stems of the species. *Linn.* 10, Or. 5, Nat. Or. *Silenàceæ.* For culture and propagation, see *Lychnis.*

| | | | | | |
|---|---|---|---|---|---|
| grácilis | Yellow | 6, | H. | A. Texas | 1834 |
| grandiflòra | Yellow | 7, | H. | A. Texas | 1835 |

VISCOSUS, clammy, like bird-lime.

VISCUM, *Tournefort.* From *viscus*, bird-lime; on account of the sticky nature of the berries. *Linn.* 22, Or. 4, Nat. Or. *Loranthàceæ.* The Mistletoe is a well-known parasite, readily propagated by sticking the berries on thorn or apple-trees, after a little of the outer bark has been cut off, and tying a shade or mat over them, to protect them from the birds. Its branches are much sought after at Christmas to hang up in houses along with other evergreens.

| | | | |
|---|---|---|---|
| álbum | Green | 5, Parasite | England |

VISMÌA, *Vandelli.* In honour of M. de Visme, a Lisbon merchant. *Linn.* 18, Or. 4, Nat. Or. *Hypericàceæ.* These plants succeed well in a mixture of loam and peat, and are increased by young cuttings, planted in sand, under a glass, in heat. *Synonyme:* 1. *Hypericum guianense.*

| | | | | | |
|---|---|---|---|---|---|
| brasiliénsis | Yellow | 6, | S. Ev. S. | Brasil | 1824 |
| glàbra | Red | 7, | S. Ev. S. | S. Amer. | 1824 |
| guianénsis, 1 | Yellow | 6, | S. Ev. S. | Guiana | 1824 |

VISNÈA, *Linn.* Origin unknown. *Linn.* 11, Or. 3, Nat. Or. not yet ascertained. This imperfectly known plant may be grown in loam and peat, and increased by cuttings, in sand, under a glass, probably in a little heat.

| | | | | | |
|---|---|---|---|---|---|
| Mocanèra | White | | G. Ev. S. | Canaries | 1815 |

VITEX, *Linn.* From *vieo*, to bind; in allusion to the flexible branches. *Linn.* 14, Or. 2, Nat. Or. *Verbenàceæ.* Interesting plants. The stove and greenhouse species succeed best in a mixture of loam and peat, and are increased by cuttings, in sand, under a glass; those of the stove species in heat. The hardy kinds succeed in any common, tolerably dry soil, and are increased by cuttings, planted in autumn, under a glass. *Synonymes:* 1. *V. Negundo.* 2. *Wallrothia leucoxylon.* 3. *V. rotundifolia.*

| | | | | | |
|---|---|---|---|---|---|
| Agnus-Cástus | Wht. blue | | H. Da. S. | Sicily | 1570 |
| latifòlia | Wht. blue | 9, | H. Da. S. | Sicily | 1570 |
| alàta | Purple | 9, | S. Ev. S. | E. Ind. | 1820 |
| altíssima | Purple | | S. Ev. S. | Ceylon | 1802 |
| arbòrea | Purple | | S. Ev. T. | | |
| bicólor | Purple | | S. Ev. S. | E. Ind. | 1810 |
| incisa, 1 | Purple | 8, | G. Ev. S. | China | 1758 |
| Leucóxylon, 2 | Purple | | S. Ev. S. | Ceylon | 1793 |
| Negúndo | Purple | | S. Ev. S. | E. Ind. | 1812 |
| ováta, 3 | Purple | 7, | G. Ev. S. | China | 1796 |
| triflòra | Purple | | S. Ev. S. | Cayenne | 1819 |
| trifòlia | Purple | | S. Ev. S. | E. Ind. | 1759 |
| umbròsa | Purple | | S. Ev. T. | Jamaica | 1823 |

VÌTIS, *Linn.* From the Celtic *gwid*, signifying the best of trees. Wine is derived from the Celtic word *gwin.* *Linn.* 5, Or. 1, Nat. Or. *Vitàceæ.* A very valuable genus of plants. *V. vinifera*, or common grape-vine, with its very numerous garden varieties, is in general cultivation for its much esteemed fruit. It must be grown in a strong, very rich soil, to have it in perfection. It is readily increased by cuttings or layers. None of the other species are worth cultivating. The acid of grapes is chiefly tartaric; malic acid, however, exists in them. *Synonymes:* 1. *V. vulpina.* 2. *V. indica.* 3. *V. æstivalis sinuata.* 4. *V. laciniosa.*

| | | | | | |
|---|---|---|---|---|---|
| æstivàlis, 1 | Green | | H. Da. Cl. | N. Amer. | 1656 |
| caribbæa, 2 | Green | | F. Da. Cl. | W. Ind. | 1800 |
| cordifòlia | Green | | H. Da. Cl. | N. Amer. | 1806 |
| dentàta | | | H. Da. Cl. | | 1820 |
| glabráta | | | S. Ev. Cl. | E. Ind. | 1819 |
| índica | Green | | S. Ev. Cl. | E. Ind. | 1692 |
| Labrúsca | Green | | H. Da. Cl. | N. Amer. | 1656 |
| bácca álbis | Green | | H. Da. Cl. | N. Amer. | 1805 |
| Puráni | | | H. Da. Cl. | Nepal | 1820 |
| ripària | | 5, | H. Da. Cl. | N. Amer. | 1806 |
| rotundifòlia | Green | | H. Da. Cl. | N. Amer. | 1806 |
| sinuàta, 3 | Green | | H. Da. Cl. | N. Amer. | |
| vinífera | Green | 6, | H. Da. Cl. | Various | |
| apifòlia, 4 | Green | 6, | H. Da. Cl. | | 1648 |
| fol. incàna | Green | 6, | H. Da. Cl. | Seedling | |
| fol. rubescéntibus | Green | 6, | H. Da. Cl. | Seedling | |

VITTÀRIA, *Smith.* From *vitta*, a riband; shape of narrow fronds. *Linn.* 24, Or. 1, Nat. Or. *Polypodiàceæ.* Interesting species of Fern, succeeding in loam and peat, and increased by division or seeds.

| | | | | | |
|---|---|---|---|---|---|
| graminifòlia | Brown | 7, | S. Her. P. | Brazil | 1820 |
| lineàta | Brown | 6, | S. Her. P. | America | 1793 |

VIVIPAROUS, bearing young plants in the place of flowers and seed.

VOANDZÈIA, *Thouars.* Voandzou is the name of the plant in Madagascar. *Linn.* 23, Or. 1, Nat. Or. *Leguminòsæ.* For culture and propagation, see *Arachis.* *Synonyme:* 1. *Glycine subterranea.*

| | | | | | |
|---|---|---|---|---|---|
| subterrànea, 1 | Yellow | 7, | S. Cr. A. | Africa | 1823 |

VOLKAMÈRIA, *Linn.* In honour of J. G. Volkamer, a German botanist. *Linn.* 14, Or. 2, Nat. Or. *Verbenàceæ.* Interesting plants, succeeding well in sandy loam and peat, and increased by cuttings, in sand, under a glass, in heat.

| | | | | | |
|---|---|---|---|---|---|
| aculeáta | White | 9, | S. Ev. S. | W. Ind. | 1739 |
| japónica | Purple | | G. Ev. T. | Japan | 1820 |

VOMIT-NUT, see *Strychnos Nux-vomica*.
VOUAPI, *Aublet*. *Vouapa* is the name of the species in Guiana. *Linn.* 3, Or. 1, *Nat. Or. Leguminosæ.* This plant succeeds in sandy loam and a little peat, and is increased by ripened cuttings, in sand, under a glass, in heat.

| bifolia | . . . . Violet | . . S. Ev. S. Guiana . . 1823 |

VOYRA, *Aublet*. From *Voyra*, the name of a species in Guiana. *Linn.* 5, Or. 1, *Nat. Or. Gentianaceæ.* This species may be grown in a mixture of sandy loam and peat; seeds.

| rosea | . . . . Red | . . 7, S. Her. P. Guiana . . 1822 |

VULNERARY, useful in the cure of wounds.
VULVIFORM, like a cleft, with projecting edges.

# W.

WACHENDORFIA, *Linn.* In honour of J. E. Wachendorf, a Dutch botanist. *Linn.* 3, Or. 1, *Nat. Or. Hæmodoraceæ.* The species of *Wachendorfia* succeed well in a mixture of very sandy loam and a little peat, taking care to supply them with little or no water when dormant. If planted out in a pit or frame, where they can be protected from frost, they will flower much stronger than if kept in pots. They are increased by offsets, or by seeds. *Synonyme:* 1. W. paniculata.

| brevifolia | . . . Purple | . 4, G. Bl. P. C. G. H. | . 1795 |
| Breyniana | . . . | . 4, G. Bl. P. C. G. H. | . 1825 |
| graminea | . . . Yellow | . 4, G. Bl. P. C. G. H. | . |
| Hibbertii, 1 | . . Yellow | . 4, G. Bl. P. C. G. H. | . 1823 |
| hirsuta | . . . Violet | . 4, G. Bl. P. C. G. H. | . 1687 |
| paniculata | . . . Yellow | . 4, G. Bl. P. C. G. H. | . 1700 |
| tenella | . . . Yellow | . 4, G. Bl. P. C. G. H. | . 1816 |
| thyrsiflora | . . . Yellow | . 5, G. Bl. P. C. G. H. | . 1759 |

WAHLENBERGIA, *Schrader*. In honour of George Wahlenberg, M.D., author of "Flora Lapponica," &c. *Linn.* 5, Or. 1, *Nat. Or. Campanulaceæ.* Interesting plants. The herbaceous species succeed best when grown in pots, in a mixture of loam and peat, and kept rather moist; they are increased by division or seeds. The annuals should be raised on a slight hotbed, and afterwards planted in a warm sheltered border. *Synonymes:* 1. *Campanula elongata*, W. elongata. 2. *C. grandiflora*. 3. *Wahlenbergia pendula*.

| capensis, 1 | . . Blue | . . 7, H. | . A. | . . 1819 |
| grandiflora, 2 | . Blue | . . 7, H. Her. P. Siberia | . 1782 |
| lobellioides, 3 | . Pa. red | . 7, H. | . A. Madeira | . 1777 |
| repens | . . . Whtsh. | . 7, H. Ev. Cr. | . . 1830 |

WALDSTEINIA, *Willdenow*. In honour of Count Francis Von Waldstein, a German botanist and author. *Linn.* 12, Or. 2, *Nat. Or. Rosaceæ.* This plant thrives in any common garden soil, and is readily increased by division or seeds.

| geoides | . . . . Yellow | . 6, H. Her. P. Hungary . 1804 |

WALKERA, *Schreber*. In honour of Richard Walker, D.D., founder of the Cambridge Botanic Garden. *Linn.* 5, Or. 1, *Nat. Or. Ochnaceæ.* Ornamental plants, succeeding in a mixture of sandy loam and peat, and cuttings of the ripened wood will root in sand, under a glass, in heat. The root and leaves of *W. serrata* are bitter, and employed in Malabar in a decoction of milk or water as a tonic, stomachic, and anti-emetic.

| integrifolia | . . . Yellow | . S. Ev. S. Guiana . |
| serrata | . . . . Yellow | . S. Ev. S. Malabar . 1824 |

WALL CRESS, see *Arabis*.
WALL-FLOWER, see *Cheiranthus*.
WALL-FLOWER, see *Brassica Cheiranthus*.
WALLICHIA, *Roxburgh*. In honour of Nathaniel Wallich, M.D., F.R.S. and L.S., superintendant of the Botanic Garden, Calcutta. *Linn.* 21, Or. 6, *Nat. Or. Palmaceæ.* This genus of Palms should be grown in a strong, rich soil, and a warm temperature; they can only be increased by seeds.

| caryotoides | . . . Palm. E. Ind. . . 1825 |
| spectabilis | . . . Palm. E. Ind. . . 1831 |

WALLROTHIA, *Sprengel*. In honour of F. Wallroth, M.D., a German botanist. *Linn.* 5, Or. 2, *Nat. Or. Umbelliferæ.* Worthless, hardy, herbaceous plants; seeds. *Synonymes:* 1. *Ligusticum splendens*, W. splendens. 2. *Bunium alpinum*, L. alpinum—W. tenuifolia 1, tuberosa 2.
WALL RUE, see *Asplenium Ruta muraria*.
WALSURA, *Roxburgh*. Altered from *Wallursi*, its Telinga name. *Linn.* 10, Or. 1, *Nat. Or. Meliaceæ.* For culture and propagation, see *Walkera*.

| robusta | . . . . S. Ev. T. E. Ind. . . 1827 |

WALNUT, see *Juglans*.
WALTHERIA, *Linn.* In honour of A. F. Walther, professor of medicine at Leipsic. *Linn.* 16, Or. 2, *Nat. Or. Sterculiaceæ.* Uninteresting stove shrubs, of simple culture. *W. americana*, being biennial, is increased by seeds; the other species by cuttings. *Synonyme:* 1. *W. lævis*—W. americana, elliptica, glabra 1, indica, microphylla.
WAMPEE-TREE, see *Cookia*.
WANGENHEIMIA, *Mœnch*. In honour of F. A. J. Wangenheim, a German botanist. *Linn.* 3, Or. 2, *Nat. Or. Gramineæ.* A worthless, hardy, annual grass. *Synonyme:* 1. *Dinebra lima*—W. lima 1.
WARRATAH, see *Camellia japonica* var.
WARRATAH, see *Telopea*.
WART CRESS, see *Senebiera*.
WARTED, covered with wart-like protuberances.
WARTWORT, see *Euphorbia heliscopia*.
WATER CALTROPS, see *Trapa*.
WATER CHICKWEED, see *Montia fontana*.
WATER-CRESS, see *Nasturtium officinale*.
WATER DOCK, see *Rumex Hydrolapathum*.
WATER DROPWORT, see *Œnanthe*.
WATER GERMANDER, see *Teucrium Scordium*.
WATER HEMLOCK, see *Phellandrium*.
WATER HOREHOUND, see *Lycopus*.
WATER LEAF, see *Hydrophyllum*.
WATER LEMON, see *Passiflora laurifolia*.
WATER LILY, see *Nymphæa*.
WATER MELON, see *Cucumis Citrullus* var.
WATER MILFOIL, see *Myriophyllum*.
WATER PARSNIP, see *Sium*.
WATER PEPPER, see *Polygonum mite*.
WATER PEPPER, see *Elatine Hydropiper*.
WATER PLANTAIN, see *Alisma Plantago*.
WATER PURSLANE, see *Peplis*.
WATER REED, see *Arundo*.
WATER SOLDIER, see *Stratiotes*.
WATER STARWORT, see *Callitriche*.
WATER VINE, see *Tetracera potatoria*.
WATER VIOLET, see *Hottonia*.
WATSONIA, *Ker*. In honour of W. Watson, a celebrated London apothecary. *Linn.* 3, Or. 1, *Nat. Or. Iridaceæ.* All the species of this genus are very handsome when in flower. For culture and propagation, see *Wachendorfia*.

| aletroides | . . . Scarlet | . 6, G. Bl. P. C. G. H. | . 1774 |
| variegata | . . . Varieg. | . 6, G. Bl. P. C. G. H. | . 1774 |
| angusta | . . . Scarlet | . 6, G. Bl. P. C. G. H. | . 1825 |
| brevifolia | . . . Pink | . 5, G. Bl. P. C. G. H. | . 1794 |
| compacta | . . . Purple | . 5, G. Bl. P. C. G. H. | . 1821 |
| fulgida | . . . Red | . 5, G. Bl. P. C. G. H. | . 1795 |
| humilis | . . . Lake | . 5, G. Bl. P. C. G. H. | . 1754 |
| iridifolia | . . . Flesh | . 5, G. Bl. P. C. G. H. | . 1795 |
| marginata | . . . Pink | . 7, G. Bl. P. C. G. H. | . |
| minor | . . . Pink | . 8, G. Bl. P. C. G. H. | . 1812 |
| Meriana | . . . Flesh | . 5, G. Bl. P. C. G. H. | . 1750 |
| plantaginea | . . . White | . 6, G. Bl. P. C. G. H. | . 1774 |
| punctata | . . . Purple | . 6, G. Bl. P. C. G. H. | . 1800 |
| rosea | . . . Pink | . 7, G. Bl. P. C. G. H. | . 1803 |
| roseo-alba | . . . Pink wht. | . 7, G. Bl. P. C. G. H. | . |
| variegata | . . . Varieg. | . 7, G. Bl. P. C. G. H. | . |
| spicata | . . . Pink | . 5, G. Bl. P. C. G. H. | . 1791 |
| strictiflora | . . . Red | . 6, G. Bl. P. C. G. H. | . 1810 |

WATTLED, having processes, like the wattles of a cock.
WAVY, undulated.
WAYFARING-TREE, see *Viburnum Lantana*.
WEBERA, see *Cupia*.
WEDELIA, *Jacquin*. In honour of George Wolfgang Wedel, a German botanist. *Linn.* 19, Or. 4, *Nat. Or. Compositæ.* Uninteresting plants, of very easy culture and propagation.

| acapulcensis | . . Yellow | . 7, S. Her. P. Acapulco | . 1826 |
| aurea | . . . . Yellow | . 9, F. Tu. P. Mexico | . 1829 |
| bengalensis | . . Yellow | . 6, H. Cr. A. E. Ind. | . . |

| | | | | | |
|---|---|---|---|---|---|
| carnŏsā | . . | Yellow | . 6, S. De. Cr. W. Ind. | . 1820 |
| helianthoĭdēs | . | Yellow | . 11, H. | A. Guisto | . 1827 |
| hispĭdā | . . | Yellow | . 6, F. Her. P. N. Spain | . 1819 |
| radicāl | . . | Yellow | . 6, S. Ev. S. Brazil | . 1820 |

WEINMĂNNĬA, *Linn.* In honour of John William Weinmann, apothecary at Ratisbon, author of " Phytanthoza Iconographica." *Linn.* 8, Or. 2, Nat. Or. *Cunoniaceæ.* These plants thrive in any light rich soil, and are readily increased by cuttings, under a glass, in heat. The bark of some of the species has been used in Peru for tanning leather, and it has also been employed in the adulteration of Peruvian Bark. *Synonymes*: 1. *W. pinnata.* 2. *Acrophyllum venosum.*

| | | | | | |
|---|---|---|---|---|---|
| australis | . . . | | . G. Ev. S. N. Holl. | . 1836 |
| elliptica | . . | White | . 5, S. Ev. S. S. Amer. | . 1824 |
| glabra, 1 | . . | White | . 5, S. Ev. S. Jamaica | . 1815 |
| hirta | . . | White | . 5, S. Ev. S. Jamaica | . 1820 |
| ovāta | . . | White | . 8, S. Ev. S. Peru | . 1824 |
| venŏsa, 2 | . . | Red | . 5, G. Ev. S. N. Holl. | . 1836 |

WEISSĬA, *Hedwig.* In honour of F. W. Weis, a German botanist. *Linn.* 24, Or. 5, Nat. Or. *Musci.* Greenish mosses, found in wet places, on rocks, and alpine banks. *Synonymes*: 1. *Grimmia acuta.* 2. *Brium calcareum.* 3. *Grimmia cirrhata.* 4. *G. controversa.* 5. *G. crispula.* 6. *G. recurvirostra.* 7. *G. lanceolata.* 8. *G. nigrita.* 9. *G. nuda.* 10. *G. pusilla.* 11. *G. recurvata.* 12. *G. Starkeana.* 13. *Funaria Templetoni.* 14. *G. trichodes.* 15. *G. verticillata*—W. acūta 1, affīnis, calcārĕā 2, cirrhātā 3, controvĕrsā 4, crispŭlā 5, curvirŏstrā 6, elongātā, lanceolātā 7, latifŏlĭā, nĭgrĭtā 8, nŭdā 9, pusĭllā 10, recurvātā 11, Starkĕānā 12, striātā, S. mājŏr, S. mĭnŏr, Templetŏnĭ 13, tenuirŏstrĭs, trichŏdēs 14, verticillātā 15.

WELSH ONION, see *Allium fistulŏsum.*

WENDLĂNDĬA, *Bartling.* In honour of Henry Lndovicus Wendland, Curator of the botanic garden at Hanover. *Linn.* 6, Or. 4, Nat. Or. *Cinchonaceæ.* An ornamental plant, succeeding well in a mixture of loam, peat, and sand, and increased by cuttings, in sand, under a glass, in heat. *Synonymes*: 1. *Rondeletia paniculata.* 2. *Cocculus carolinus.*

| | | | | | |
|---|---|---|---|---|---|
| paniculāta, 1 | . | White | . 7, S. Ev. T. Malay Is. | . 1820 |
| populifŏlĭā, 2 | . | White | . 6, G. Ev. Tw. Florida | . 1759 |

WERNERĬA, *Kunth.* In honour of A. G. Werner, the celebrated mineralogist. *Linn.* 19, Or. 2, Nat. Or. *Compositæ.* This species thrives well in a light soil, and is increased by division of the roots. *Synonyme*: 1. *Doronicum peruvianum.*

| | | | | | |
|---|---|---|---|---|---|
| rigĭdā | . . . | | . 2, G. Her. P. Quito | . 1828 |

WESTRINGĬA, *Smith.* In honour of J. P. Westring, physician to the king of Sweden. *Linn.* 14, Or. 1, Nat. Or. *Labiatæ.* A light rich soil suits all the species well, and young cuttings, planted under a glass, soon strike root.

| | | | | | |
|---|---|---|---|---|---|
| angustifŏlĭā | . . | White | . 7, G. Ev. S. N. Holl. | . 1823 |
| cinĕrĕā | . . | White | . 6, G. Ev. S. N. Holl. | . 1821 |
| Dampiĕrĭ | . . | White | . 9, G. Ev. S. N. Holl. | . 1803 |
| eremicŏlā | . . | Pa. blue | . 6, G. Ev. S. N. S. W. | . 1823 |
| glabrā | . . | White | . 6, G. Ev. S. N. Holl. | . 1824 |
| longifŏlĭā | . . | White | . 6, G. Ev. S. N. Holl. | . 1823 |
| rigĭdā | . . | White | . 6, G. Ev. S. N. Holl. | . 1823 |
| rosmarinifŏrmis | . | Pa. blue | . 7, G. Ev. S. N. S. W. | . 1791 |
| rubiæfŏlĭā | . . | Pa. blue | . 6, G. Ev. S. N. Holl. | . 1820 |
| triphylla | . . | Pa. blue | . 9, G. Ev. S. N. S. W. | . 1823 |

WHEAT, see *Trĭtĭcum.*
WHIRLING PLANT, see *Desmŏdĭum gyrans.*
WHITE BEAN-TREE, see *Pyrus Ariă.*
WHITE CEDAR, see *Cupressus thyoĭdēs.*
WHITE CLOVER, see *Trifolĭum rēpēns.*
WHITE FIORIN, see *Agrŏstis ālbā.*
WHITE SPRUCE, see *Pinūs ālbā.*
WHITE TREE, see *Melaleucā Leucadēndrŏn.*
WHITE VINE, see *Clemātīs vitālbā.*
WHITE WOOD, see *Petrŏblum.*
WHITLOW GRASS, see *Lepĭdĭum Drābā.*
WHOLE SCHÆNUS, see *Isolēpĭs holoschænus.*
WHORLS, leaves arranged in a regular circumference round a stem.
WHORTLE BERRY, see *Vaccinĭum.*
WIDOW-WAIL, see *Cneŏrum.*

WIGĂNDĬA. Named by Kunth in honour of John Wigand, a bishop of Pomerania. *Linn.* 5, Or. 2, Nat. Or. *Hydroleaceæ.* " If well grown, and formed into a bush, feathered to the surface of the ground, this plant must have a very beautiful appearance

with its large clusters of delicate lilac flowers, which continue to open in succession for a long time. But if formed into a sort of stake, with a few leaves and flowers at the top, as is too frequently the case with stove plants, it will be found to possess little claims to attractiveness." *Lindley in Bot. Reg.* For the culture and propagation, we can give no certain directions.

| | | | | | |
|---|---|---|---|---|---|
| caracasāna | . . | Lilac | . 8, De. S. Caracas | . 1836 |

WILD BASIL, see *Clinopŏdĭum.*
WILD BEET, see *Sĭlĕnĕ Limŏnĭum.*
WILD BLITE, see *Amarănthŭs Blĭtum.*
WILD BUGLOSS, see *Lycŏpsĭs.*
WILD CHAMOMILE, see *Matricărĭă chamomĭllă.*
WILD CLOVE-TREE, see *Myrcĭă ācrĭs.*
WILD CUMIN, see *Lagæcĭă cuminoĭdēs.*
WILD LIQUORICE, see *Abrŭs.*
WILD OAT, see *Avēnă fătŭă.*
WILD OLIVE, see *Rhŭs Cŏtĭnŭs.*
WILD OLIVE, see *Dăphnē Thymĕlæă.*
WILD PURSLANE, see *Euphŏrbĭă Pēplĭs.*
WILD RADISH, see *Raphănŭs Raphanĭstrum.*
WILD ROSEMARY, see *Andrŏmĕdă polifŏlĭă,* var.
WILD SERVICE, see *Pyrŭs termĭnălĭs.*
WILD TAMARIND, see *Codărĭum.*
WILD TANSY, see *Potentĭllă anserĭnă.*
WILD THYME, see *Thymŭs Serpyllum.*
WILD VINE, see *Vĭtĭs Labrŭscă.*

WILLDENOVĬA, *Thunberg.* In honour of Charles Louis Willdenow, a celebrated professor of botany at Berlin. *Linn.* 22, Or. 3, Nat. Or. *Restiaceæ.* Interesting plants, succeeding well in loam and peat, and increased by dividing at the root.

| | | | | | |
|---|---|---|---|---|---|
| striātā | . . . | | . Apetal . 6, Grass. C. G. H. | . 1818 |
| tĕrĕs | . . . | | . Apetal . 6, Grass. C. G. H. | . 1790 |

WILLEMĕTĬA, *Necker.* In honour of P. R. Willemet, author of Herbarium Mauritianum. *Linn.* 5, Or. 1, Nat. Or. *Rhamnaceæ.* A pretty shrub, succeeding in a mixture of sandy loam and peat, and increased by young cuttings, planted in sand, under a glass. *Synonyme*: 1. *Ceanothus africanus.*

| | | | | | |
|---|---|---|---|---|---|
| africāna, 1 | . . | Blue | . 5, G. Ev. S. C. G. H. | . 1712 |

WILLOW, see *Sălĭx.*
WILLOW, see *Lythrum salicārĭă.*
WILLOW HERB, see *Epilŏbĭum.*
WILLUGHBEĬA, *Roxburgh.* In honour of Francis Willughby, F.R.S., a friend and pupil of Ray. *Linn.* 5, Or. 1, Nat. Or. *Apocynaceæ.* This shrub succeeds well in a mixture of loam, peat, and sand, and is increased by cuttings, planted in sand, under a glass, in heat. The fruit, as the name implies, is eatable.

| | | | | | |
|---|---|---|---|---|---|
| edŭlĭs | . . . | | . Pa. pink . 7, S. Ev. S. E. Ind. | . . 1818 |

WIND FLOWER, see *Gentiănă Pneumonānthē.*
WINE PALM, see *Manicărĭă saccĭfĕră.*
WING, in Botany, signifies a membranous border, wherewith many seeds are supported in the air, when floating from place to place.
WING, the side petals of a pea-flower.
WINGED PEA, see *Tetragonŏlŏbŭs purpŭrĕŭs.*
WINTER ACONITE, see *Erănthĭs.*
WINTER BERRY, see *Prĭnŏs.*
WINTER CHERRY, see *Physălĭs.*
WINTER CHERRY, see *Cardiospĕrmŭm Halicăcăbŭm.*
WINTER CRESS, see *Barbărĕă.*
WINTER GRAPE, see *Vĭtĭs cordifŏlĭă.*
WINTER GREEN, see *Pyrŏlă.*
WINTER GREEN, see *Trientălĭs.*
WINTER SWEET, see *Origănum heracleŏtĭcum.*
WISE MEN'S BANANA-TREE, see *Mŭsă sapiēntum.*

WISTĂRĬA, *Nuttall.* In honour of Caspar Wistar, once professor of anatomy in the university of Pennsylvania. *Linn.* 17, Or. 4, Nat. Or. *Leguminosæ.* Hardy climbers, bearing flowers of great beauty, and on that account they ought to be in every collection of plants. They thrive best in a light rich soil, trained against a south wall, where they will flower in great profusion. They are commonly increased by layers, but cuttings root very freely if planted in either sand or soil, under a glass. *Synonymes*: 1. *Glycine sinensis,* W. *Consequana.* 2. *G. frutescens,* W. *speciosa,* *Apios frutescens.*

| | | | | | |
|---|---|---|---|---|---|
| sinĕnsĭs, 1 | . | Bluish pur. 5, H. De. Cl. China | . 1818 |
| frutescĕns, 2 | . | Bluish pur. 7, H. De. Cl. N. Amer. | . 1724 |

WITCH HAZEL, see *Hamamělis*.

WITHERINGIA, *L'Heritier*. In honour of William Withering, M.D., author of a " Botanical Arrangement of the Vegetables of Great Britain," Birmingham, 1776. Linn. 5, Or. 1, Nat. Or. *Solanaceæ*. Interesting plants, thriving well in a light rich soil, and readily increasing by cuttings, under a glass, or by seeds. *W. phyllantha* should be raised on a gentle hotbed in spring, and, when of sufficient size, planted in the open border.

| | | | | | |
|---|---|---|---|---|---|
| crassifoliă | . | Yellow | . 6, G. Ev. S. | C. G. H. | . 1706 |
| montānă | . | White | . 6, G. Her. P. | Peru | . 1822 |
| phyllanthă | . | Yellow | . 7, G. | A. Peru | . 1822 |
| pinnatifīdă | . | Blue | . 7, G. Her. P. | Peru | . 1822 |
| purpūreă | . | Pa. pur. | . 7, G. Tu. P. | Chile | . 1829 |
| solanăceă | . | Yellow | . 7, S. Her. P. | S. Amer. | . 1742 |
| stramonifoliă | . | Yellow | . 6, S. Ev. S. | Mexico | . 1823 |

WITHY, see *Laserpitium Siler*.

WITSENIA, *Linn*. In honour of M. Witsen, a Dutch patron of Botany. Linn. 3, Or. 1, Nat. Or. *Iridaceæ*. Ornamental plants, succeeding best in a sandy peat soil, and increased by offsets from the roots, or by seeds.

| | | | | | |
|---|---|---|---|---|---|
| corymbosă | . . | Pur. blue | . 6, G. Her. P. | C. G. H. | . 1803 |
| maură | . . | Yel. blue | . 12, G. Her. P. | C. G. H. | . 1790 |
| ramosă | . . | Pur. blue | . 4, G. Her. P. | C. G. H. | . 1819 |

WOAD, see *Isătis*.

WOLF'S-BANE, see *Aconītum lupulīnum*.

WOODBINE, see *Caprifolium Periclymĕnum*.

WOODBINE, see *Polygōnum Convolvŭlus*.

WOOD EVERLASTING PEA, see *Lăthўrus sylvěstris*.

WOODROOF, see *Asperŭlă*.

WOOD SAGE, see *Teŭcrium Scorodōnium*.

WOODSIA, *R. Brown*. In honour of Joseph Woods, a British botanist. Linn. 24, Or. 1, Nat. Or. *Polypodiaceæ*. Ferns, growing best in peat and loam mixed, and increased by division, or by seeds.

| | | | | | |
|---|---|---|---|---|---|
| hyperbōreă | . | Brown | . 7, H. Her. P. Scotland | . |
| ilveněis | . | Brown | . 6, H. Her. P Britain | . |
| Perriniānă | . | Brown | . 6, H. Her. P. N. Amer. | . |

WOOD SORREL, see *Oxălis*.

WOODWARDIA, *Smith*. In honour of Thomas Jenkinson Woodward, an English botanist. Linn. 24, Or. 1, Nat. Or. *Polypodiaceæ*. For culture and propagation, see *Woodsia*. Synonymes: 1. *W. onocleoides, Osmunda caroliniana*. 2. *Blechnum virginicum*.

angustifoliă, 1 . Brown . 8, H. Her. Cr. N. Amer. . 1812
rădĭcāns . . Brown . 7, G. Her. P. Madeira . 1779
virginĭcă, 2 . Brown . 8, H. Her. P. N. Amer. . 1724

WORM GRASS, see *Spigēliă*.

WORMIA, *Rottboll*. In honour of Olaus Wormius, M.D., a famous Danish philosopher and naturalist. Linn. 13, Or. 5, Nat. Or. *Dilleniaceæ*. This is a very elegant stove plant. For culture and propagation, see *Dillenia*. Synonyme: 1. *Dillenia dentata*.

dentātă, 1 . . Yellow . 8. Ev. T. Ceylon . . 1818

WORMWOOD, see *Artemĭsiă*.

WOUNDWORT, see *Anthýllis vulnerāriă*.

WRACK GRASS, see *Zostērā*.

WRIGHTIA, *R. Brown*. After the late William Wright, M.D., F.R.S., L. and E., F.L.S., a Scotch physician and botanist, resident in Jamaica. Linn. 5, Or. 1, Nat. Or. *Apocynaceæ*. Ornamental plants. For culture and propagation, see *Strophanthus*. Synonymes: 1. *Nerium antidysentericum*. 2. *N. coccineum*.

antidysenterică, 1 White . 8. Ev. S. Ceylon . . 1778
coccineă, 2 . . Scarlet . 7, S. Ev. T. E. Ind. . 1822
pubescĕns . . Grn. yel. . 8, S. Ev. S. N. Holl. . 1829
tinctōriă . . White . 8, S. Ev. S. E. Ind. . 1812

WULFENIA, *Jacquin*. In honour of the Rev. Francis Xavier Wulfen, a botanical author. Linn. 2, Or. 1, Nat. Or. *Scrophulariaceæ*. This is a very showy plant when in blossom; and is well adapted for ornamenting flower-borders. A light rich soil suits it, and it is readily increased by division or seeds. It requires the protection of a frame in winter, as it is very apt to rot at that season, if allowed to remain in the open air.

carinthiăcă . . Blue . 7, H. Her. P. Carinthia . 1817

WURMBEA, *Thunberg*. In honour of F. Van Wurmb, Secretary to the Academy of Sciences at Batavia. Linn. 6, Or. 3, Nat. Or. *Melanthaceæ*. Pretty plants when in flower. They grow well in sandy peat, mixed with a little loam, and are readily increased by offsets. Synonymes; 1. *Melanthium monopetalum*. 2. *M. spicatum*.

campanulātă, 1 . White . 6, G. Bl. P. C. G. H. . 1819
longiflōră . . White . 5, G. Bl. P. C. G. H. . 1788
pūmilă . . . White . 5, F. Bl. P. C. G. H. . 1800
purpūreă, 2 . Purple . 5, G. Bl. P. C. G. H. . 1788

WYCH ELM, see *Ulmŭs montānă*.

# X.

XANTHIUM, *Tournefort*. From *xanthos*, yellow; the plants being formerly used by the Greeks to dye their hair. Linn. 21, Or. 5, Nat. Or. *Compositæ*. Plants of no great beauty. The seed may be sown in the open border.

| | | | | | |
|---|---|---|---|---|---|
| canadĕnse | . . | Green | . . 7, H. | A. N. Amer. | . 1700 |
| cathărticum | . . | Green | . . 7, H. | A. S. Amer. | . 1824 |
| macrocărpum | . . | Green | . . 7, H. | A. France | . 1817 |

echinātum, orientālě, spinōsum, *Strumāriŭm*.

XANTHOCHYMUS, see *Stalagmītis*.

XANTHORHIZA, *Marsh*. From *xanthos*, yellow, and *rhiza*, a root; the roots being of a deep yellow colour. Linn. 5, Or. 6, Nat. Or. *Ranunculaceæ*. An interesting dwarf shrub, succeeding well in common garden soil, and increased by suckers. The wood contains both a gum and a resin, each of which is intensely bitter.

apiifoliă . . . Pur. grn. . 2, H. Ev. S. N. Amer. . 1766

XANTHORRHŒA, *Swartz*. From *xanthos*, yellow, and *rheo*, to flow; yellow resinous exudation. Linn. 6, Or. 1, Nat. Or. *Liliaceæ*. These plants thrive well in a mixture of peat and loam, and are increased by offsets from the roots. Synonyme: 1. *X. pumilio*.

| | | | | | |
|---|---|---|---|---|---|
| austrālis | . . | White | . 4, G. Ev. S. | N. Holl. | . 1824 |
| bracteātă | . . | White | . 4, G. Her. P. | N. S. W. | . 1810 |
| hăstilis | . . | White | . 4, G. Ev. S. | N. S. W. | . 1803 |
| hūmilis, 1 | . . | White | . G. Her. P. | N. Holl. | . 1825 |
| mediă | . . | White | . 4, G. Ev. S. | N. Holl. | . 1803 |
| minŏr | . . | White | . 4, G. Her. P. | N. S. W. | . 1804 |

XANTHOSIA, *Decandolle*. From *xanthos*, yellow; in allusion to the yellow down with which some species belonging to this genus are clothed. Linn. 5, Or. 2, Nat. Or. *Umbelliferæ*. A very curious

under-shrub, succeeding well in a mixture of loam, peat, and sand, and readily increased by cuttings, or seeds.

rotundifoliă . . Wht. red . 6, G. Ev. S. Pt. Jackson 1836

XANTHOXYLUM, *Linn*. From *xanthos*, yellow, and *xylon*, wood; the roots are yellow. Linn. 22, Or. 5, Nat. Or. *Xanthoxylaceæ*. Ornamental trees and shrubs. The hardy species, from their beauty, are well adapted for planting in shrubberies. They grow freely in any common garden soil, and are readily increased by cuttings of the ripened wood, planted under a glass. The stove and greenhouse kinds are of easy culture, and are increased by cuttings, in sand, under a glass. The bark and capsules of *X. fraxineum* have a hot, acrid taste, and are used for easing the toothache; hence the name *Toothache tree*. *X. Avicennæ* and *Piperitum* are used in China and Japan as an antidote against all poisons, and in Japan the capsules of the latter species are used as a substitute for pepper. Synonymes: 1. *Fagara Budrunga*. 2. *F. Piperita*. 3. *F. Pterota*. 4. *F. tragodes*.

| | | | | | |
|---|---|---|---|---|---|
| acuminātum | . . | | 8. Ev. S. | Jamaica | . 1818 |
| armātum | . . | | 8. Ev. S. | E. Ind. | . 1816 |
| aromaticum | . . | | 8. Ev. S. | W. Ind. | . 1824 |
| Avicennă | . . | | G. Ev. S. | China | . 1823 |
| Budrūngă, 1 | . | White . | 8, S. Ev. T. | E. Ind. | . 1825 |
| clavă Herculis | . | Orn. wht. | G. Ev. S. | W. Ind. | . 1739 |
| emarginātum | . | Orn. wht. | 8. Ev. S. | Jamaica | . 1789 |
| fraxineum | . . | Orn. wht. | 8, H. De. S. | N. Amer. | . 1759 |
| mite | . . | | Yellowish | 8, H. De. S. | N. Amer. | . 1818 |
| nitidum | . . | Orn. wht. | 8. Ev. S. | China | . 1823 |
| Piperītum, 2 | . | White . | 9, G. Ev. S. | Japan | . 1773 |
| Pterota, 3 | . | White . | 8, S. Ev. T. | Jamaica | . 1768 |

| | | | | | |
|---|---|---|---|---|---|
| tragōdēs, 4 | . . Whitish | . | 8. Ev. 8t. Domin. | 1759 |
| tricárpum | . . . Grn. wht. | 7, H. De. 8. N. Amer. | 1806 |

**XERÁNTHEMUM**, *Tournefort*. From *xeros*, dry, and *anthemon*, a flower; alluding to the dry nature of the flower, which retains its form and colour for years. *Linn.* 19, Or. 2, Nat. Or. *Compositæ*. Plants of the easiest culture in any rich light soil.

| | | | | | |
|---|---|---|---|---|---|
| annūūm | . . . Purple | . 7, H. | A. 8. Eur. | 1570 |
| inapértum | . . . Purple | . 7, H. | A. 8. Eur. | 1690 |
| orientālē | . . . White | . 7, H. | A. Levant | 1713 |

**XEROPHÝLLUM**, *Michaux*. From *xeros*, dry, and *phyllon*, a leaf; in reference to the dry grassy leaves. *Linn.* 6, Or. 3, Nat. Or. *Melanthaceæ*. Handsome plants when in flower, and, therefore, well worth cultivating. They succeed best in a peat border, and will, if treated with care, ripen their seeds, from which they may be increased, as also by dividing the roots. *Synonymes:* 1. *X. setifolium, Helonias asphodeloides.* 2. *H. graminea.* 3. *Veratrum Sabadilla, Velloxia squamata.* 4. *Helonias tenax.*

| | | | | | |
|---|---|---|---|---|---|
| asphodeloīdes, 1 | . White | . 5, H. Her. P. N. Amer. | 1765 |
| gramīnēum, 2 | . White | . 5, H. Her. P. N. Amer. | 1812 |
| Sabadilla, 3 | . . White | . H. Her. P. Vera Cruz | 1830 |
| tēnāx, 4 | . . White | . H. Her. P. N. Amér. | 1811 |

**XERŌTES**, *R. Brown*. From *xerotes*, dryness; because of the aridity of the herbage. *Linn.* 22, Or. 6, Nat. Or. *Juncaceæ*. A genus of herbaceous plants. They succeed well in light rich soil, and are readily propagated by dividing the plants at the root. *Synonyme:* 1. *Lomaria longifolia.*

| | | | | | |
|---|---|---|---|---|---|
| arenāria | . . Wht. grn. | . G. Her. P. N. Holl. | 1820 |
| denticulātā | . . Wht. grn. | . G. Her. P. N. Holl. | 1825 |
| echinātā | . . Wht. grn. | . G. Her. P. N. Holl. | 1824 |
| filifōrmis | . . Wht. grn. | . G. Her. P. N. Holl. | 1824 |
| flexifōliā | . . Wht. grn. | . G. Her. P. N. Holl. | 1824 |
| grácilis | . . Wht. grn. | . G. Her. P. N. Holl. | 1822 |
| hystrix | . . Wht. grn. | . G. Her. P. N. Holl. | 1824 |
| laxā | . . Wht. grn. | . G. Her. P. N. Holl. | 1823 |
| longifōlia, 1 | . Grn. wht. | . G. Her. P. N. Holl. | 1796 |
| montānā | . . Grn. wht. | . G. Her. P. N. Holl. | 1824 |
| mucronātā | . . Grn. wht. | . G. Her. P. N. Holl. | 1824 |
| rigīdā | . . . Grn. wbt. | . G. Her. P. N. Holl. | 1791 |

**XIMENĒSIĀ**, *Cavanilles*. In honour of Joseph Ximenes, a Spanish apothecary. *Linn.* 19, Or. 2, Nat. Or. *Compositæ*. Interesting plants, of common culture. *Synonymes:* 1. *Coreopsis heterophylla.* 2. *Simsia ficifolia.*

| | | | | | |
|---|---|---|---|---|---|
| Cavanillésiī, 1 | . Yellow | . 8, H. | B. Mexico | 1820 |
| cordātā | . . . Yellow | . 9, G. Her. P. Mexico | 1826 |
| enceloīdes | . . Yellow | . 8, G. Her. P. Mexico | 1795 |
| fœtidā, 2 | . . Yellow | . 8, H. | A. Mexico | 1824 |
| heterophýllā | . . Yellow | . A. Mexico | 1827 |

**XIMĒNIĀ**, *Linn.* In honour of Francis Ximenes, a Spanish monk, who wrote a work upon medicinal plants. *Linn.* 8, Or. 1, Nat. Or. *Olacaceæ*. A mixture of loam and peat suits these plants, and cuttings root readily in sand, under a glass, in heat. The drupes of *X. americana* have a sweet, aromatic taste, but are a little rough to the palate. They are eaten in Senegal; the flowers are very sweet.

| | | | | | |
|---|---|---|---|---|---|
| americānā | . . Grnsh. yel. | 8. Ev. T. W. Ind. | 1759 |
| inérmis | . . . White | . 8. Ev. T. Jamaica | 1810 |

**XIPHIDIUM**, *Loeffling*. From *xiphos*, a sword; the leaves are sword-shaped. *Linn.* 3, Or. 1, Nat. Or. *Hæmodoraceæ*. An equal mixture of loam, peat, and sand, suits these species, and they are readily increased by division of the root.

| | | | | | |
|---|---|---|---|---|---|
| albūm | . . . White | . 8. Her. P. W. Ind. | 1787 |
| cærūlēum | . . . Blue | . 8. Her. P. Guiana | 1793 |

**XIPHÓPTERIS**, *Kaulfuss*. From *xiphos*, a sword, and *pteris*, fern; form of the fronds; hence *Sword Fern*. *Linn.* 24, Or. 1, Nat. Or. *Polypodiaceæ*. Ornamental plants. For culture and propagation, see *Polypodium*. *Synonymes:* 1. *Grammitis heterophylla, Polypodium grammitoides.* 2. *Grammitis serrulata.*

| | | | | | |
|---|---|---|---|---|---|
| heterophýllā, 1 | . Brown | . 6, G. Her. P. N. Holl. | 1824 |
| serrulātā, 2 | . . Brown | . 6, 8. Her. P. W. Ind. | 1823 |

**XYLOMĒLUM**, *Smith*. From *xylon*, wood, and *melon*, an apple; appearance of the fruit of the plant. *Linn.* 4, Or. 1, Nat. Or. *Proteaceæ*. For culture and propagation, see *Hakea*. *Synonyme:* 1. *Hakea pyriformis.*

| | | | | | |
|---|---|---|---|---|---|
| pyrifórmis, 1 | . . | G. Ev. T. N. S. W. | 1789 |

**XYLOPHÝLLĀ**, *Linn.* From *xylon*, wood, and *phyllon*, a leaf; rigidity of the leaves. *Linn.* 21, Or. 10, Nat. Or. *Euphorbiaceæ*. Ornamental shrubs, growing about three feet high. For culture and propagation, see *Phyllanthus*. *Synonymes:* 1. *Phyllanthus angustifolius, epiphyllanthus.* 2. *P. falcatus.* 3. *P. latifolius.* 4. *P. linearis.* 5. *P. ceramicus.* 6. *P. arbuscula.*

| | | | | | |
|---|---|---|---|---|---|
| angustifōliā, 1 | . Yel. red | . 7, 8. Ev. 8. Jamaica | 1789 |
| elongātā | . . Yel. red | . 8, 8. Ev. 8. Jamaica | 1820 |
| falcātā, 2 | . . Yel. red | . 7, 8. Ev. 8. Baham. Is. | 1699 |
| latifōliā, 3 | . . Yel. red | . 8, 8. Ev. 8. Jamaica | 1783 |
| linearīa, 4 | . . Yel. red | . 9, 8. Ev. 8. Jamaica | 1819 |
| longifōliā, 5 | . Yel. red | . 9, 8. Ev. 8. E. Ind. | 1816 |
| mēdiā | . . . Yel. red | . 8, 8. Ev. 8. Jamaica | 1825 |
| montānā | . . . Yel. red | . 8, 8. Ev. 8. Jamaica | 1819 |
| obovātā | . . . Yel. red | . 8, 8. Ev. 8. Siberia | 1806 |
| ramiflōrā | . . Yel. red | . 8, 8. Ev. 8. Siberia | 1785 |
| speciōsā, 6 | . . Yel. red | . 9, 8. Ev. 8. Jamaica | 1818 |

**XYLÓPIX**, *Linn.* Abridged from *xylopicron*, which is from *xylon*, wood, and *picros*, bitter; the wood of some of the species is extremely bitter. *Linn.* 13, Or. 6, Nat. Or. *Anonaceæ*. Ornamental plants; for culture and propagation, see *Phyllanthus*. The wood of *X. glabra* is so intensely bitter, that a quantity of sugar made from it, and sent from Jamaica in hogsheads, was so bitter that purchasers could not be found for it. A decoction of the wood is said to be of service in colics, and to be used for the purpose of creating an appetite.

| | | | | | |
|---|---|---|---|---|---|
| frutéscēns | . . . | 8. Ev. 8. Guiana | 1823 |
| glabrā | . . . | 8. Ev. 8. Jamaica | 1820 |
| muricātā | . . . | 8. Ev. 8. W. Ind. | 1779 |

**XÝRIS**, *Linn.* From *xyros*, acute; the leaves terminate in points. *Linn.* 3, Or. 1, Nat. Or. *Xyridaceæ*. Curious rush-like plants. For culture and propagation, see *Xerotes.*

| | | | | | |
|---|---|---|---|---|---|
| altíssimā | . . . Yellow | . 9, G. Her. P. N. Holl. | 1826 |
| americānā | . . . Blue | . 8, H. Her. P. Guiana | 1825 |
| bracteātā | . . . Yellow | . 7, G. Her. P. N. Holl. | 1825 |
| brevifōlis | . . . Yellow | . 7, H. Her. P. Carolina | 1812 |
| grácilis | . . . Yellow | . 6, G. Her. P. N. Holl. | 1821 |
| juncēā | . . . Yellow | . 7, G. Her. P. N. Holl. | 1822 |
| lævis | . . . Yellow | . 7, 8. Her. P. N. Holl. | 1819 |
| operculātā | . . . Yellow | . 6, 8. Her. P. N. S. W. | 1804 |

**XYSMALÓBIUM**, *Brown*. From *xysma*, a thread, and *lobos*, a pod; in reference to the follicles being clothed with ramenta. *Linn.* 5, Or. 2, Nat. Or. *Asclepiadaceæ*. For culture and propagation, see *Asclepias*. *Synonyme:* 1. *Asclepias undulata.*

| | | | | | |
|---|---|---|---|---|---|
| undulātum, 1 | . . Green | . 7, G. Ev. 8. C. G. H. | 1783 |

# Y.

YAM, see *Dioscōrēā.*
YARROW, see *Achillēā millefōliūm.*
YELLOW BIRD'S NEST, see *Monotrōpā.*
YELLOW CHESTNUT, see *Quércus Castānēā.*
YELLOW DEAD NETTLE, see *Galeóbdōlōn lútēum.*
YELLOW RATTLE, see *Rhinánthus.*
YELLOW ROOT, see *Xanthorhīzā.*
YELLOW SULTAN, see *Centaūrēā suavēōlēns.*
YELLOW VETCHLING, see *Láthýrus Aphácā.*
YELLOW-WORT, see *Chlōrā.*
YEW-TREE, see *Tāxūs.*
YÚCCĀ, *Linn.* The name of the plant in Peru. *Linn.* 6, Or. 1, Nat. Or. *Liliaceæ*. The species are mostly evergreen shrubs, with the habit of palm-trees. They are all of great beauty, and are, on that account, highly deserving of culture in every collection of plants. A light rich soil suits the whole of them, and they are all increased by suckers from the root. *Synonyme:* 1. *Y. gloriosa.*

| | | | | | |
|---|---|---|---|---|---|
| acuminātā | . . . White | . 8, H. Ev. 8. | 1800 |
| aletrifōrmis | . . . | 8. Ev. 8. C. G. H. | 1823 |
| aloifōliā | . . . White | . 8, G. Ev. 8. S. Amer. | 1696 |
| pendūlā | . . . Wht. grn. | 8, H. De. T. | |
| variegātā | . . . Wht. grn. | 8, G. Ev. 8. | |

| angustifòliä | . | . Wht. grn. | 7, H. Ev. | S. Missouri | . 1811 |
|---|---|---|---|---|---|
| arcuàtä | . . | . Wht. grn. | 7, H. Ev. | S. | . 1817 |
| concàvä | . . | . Wht. grn. | 8, H. Her. | P. | . 1816 |
| conspìcuä | . . | . G. Ev. | S. | | . 1818 |
| crenulàtä | . . | . Wht. grn. | 8, H. Ev. | S. | . 1818 |
| dracònis | . . | . Wht. grn. | 8, G. Ev. | S. S. Amer. | . 1732 |
| filamentòsä | . | . Wht. grn. | 9, H. Her. | P. Virginia | . 1675 |
| variegàtä | . | . Wht. grn. | 9, H. Ev. | S. | |
| flàccidä | . . | . Wht. grn. | H. Her. | P. | . 1816 |
| glaucéscéns | . | . Wht. grn. | 7, H. Ev. | S. N. Amer. | . 1819 |
| gloriòsä | . . | . Wht. grn. | 7, H. Ev. | S. America | . 1596 |

| fol. variegàtis | . | . Wht. grn. | 7, H. Ev. | S. | |
|---|---|---|---|---|---|
| gracìlis | . . | . Wht. grn. | 7, S. Her. | P. Mexico | . 1829 |
| obliquä | . . | . Wht. grn. | H. Her. | P. | . 1808 |
| màjor | . . | . Wht. grn. | H. Her. | P. | . 1808 |
| puberùlä | . . | . Wht. grn. | 8, H. Her. | P. | |
| recùrvä | . . | . Wht. grn. | 8, H. Ev. | S. Georgia | . 1794 |
| rùfo-cìnctä | . | . Wht. grn. | 7, H. Her. | P. | . 1816 |
| serrulàtä | . . | . Wht. grn. | G. Ev. | S. Carolina | . 1808 |
| strìctä | . . | . Wht. grn. | 7, H. Ev. | S. Carolina | . 1817 |
| supérbä, 1 | . | . Wht. grn. | 8, G. Ev. | S. | |
| tenuifòliä | . . | . Wht. grn. | H. Ev. | S. Malta | . 1817 |

# Z.

**ZACĪNTHĀ**, *Gærtner*. The species was first found in the Island of Zante, formerly Zacinthus. *Linn.* 19, Or. 1, *Nat. Or. Compositæ.* An uninteresting hardy annual, of easy culture. *Synonyme :* 1. *Lapsana Zacintha—Z. verrucōsä.*

**ZALĂCCÄ**, see *Cälämŭs Zalăccä.*

**ZALUZĀNIÄ**, *Persoon.* In honour of Zaluzianski, a Polish botanist. *Linn.* 19, Or. 2, Nat. Or. *Compositæ.* A frame herbaceous plant, not worth growing. *Synonyme :* 1. *Acmella trilobata—Z. trilōbä* 1.

**ZĀMIÄ**, *Linn.* From *zamia*, loss; alluding to the sterile appearance of the male fructification. *Linn.* 22, Or. 12, Nat. Or. *Cycadaceæ.* A genus of very remarkable plants, nearly related to both Ferns and Palms. The species thrive well in a light sandy soil, and are increased by suckers.

| angustifòliä | . | . Apetal | . 7, S. Her. | P. C. G. H. | . |
|---|---|---|---|---|---|
| càffrä | . . | . Apetal | . 8. Her. | P. C. G. H. | . |
| cycadifòliä | . . | . Apetal | . G. Her. | P. C. G. H. | . 1775 |
| Cycàdis | . . | . Apetal | . G. Her. | P. C. G. H. | . 1775 |
| dèbilis | . . | . Apetal | . 7, S. Her. | P. W. Ind. | . 1777 |
| furfuràceä | . | . Apetal | . 7, S. Her. | P. W. Ind. | . 1691 |
| hòrrïdä | . . | . Apetal | . Apetal | P. C. G. H. | . 1800 |
| integrifòliä | . | . Apetal | . 7, S. Her. | P. W. Ind. | . 1768 |
| lanuginòsä | . | . Apetal | . O. Her. | P. C. G. H. | . 1812 |
| latifòliä | . . | . Apetal | . 8. Her. | P. | |
| longifòliä | . | . Apetal | . G. Her. | P. C. G. H. | . 1818 |
| mèdiä | . . | . Apetal | . 7, S. Her. | P. W. Ind. | . |
| prunìferä | . | . Apetal | . 8. Her. | P. | |
| pùmilä | . . | . Apetal | . S. Her. | P. C. G. H. | . 1812 |
| pùngéns | . . | . Apetal | . S. Her. | P. C. G. H. | . 1775 |
| pygmaeä | . . | . Apetal | . 5, S. Her. | P. W. Ind. | . |
| repàndä | . . | . Apetal | . S. Her. | P. | |
| spinòsä | . . | . Apetal | . 8. Her. | P. | |
| spiràlis | . . | . Apetal | . 7, G. Her. | P. N. S. W. | . 1796 |
| tènuïs | . . | . Apetal | . 8. Her. | P. Bahama I. | . |
| tridentàtä | . . | . Apetal | . G. Her. | P. C. G. H. | . 1814 |

**ZANNICHĒLLIÄ**, *Linn.* In honour of John Jerome Zannichelli, a Venetian botanist. *Linn.* 21, Or. 1, Nat. Or. *Fluviales.* A hardy aquatic annual, found in ditches—*Z. palustris.*

**ZAPPĀNIÄ**, *Scopoli.* In honour of P. A. Zappa, an Italian botanist. *Linn.* 14, Or. 2, Nat. Or. *Verbenaceæ.* These plants succeed well in any light soil, and are readily increased by cuttings, under a glass. *Synonymes :* 1. *Verbena nodiflora, Lippia nodiflora.* 2. *Lippia stæchadifolia—Z. nodiflōrä* 1, *N. rōsèä, stæchadifòliä* 2.

**ZĒÄ**, *Linn.* From *zao*, to live; in reference to the nutritive properties of the plants. *Linn.* 21, Or. 3, Nat. Or. *Gramineæ.* Z. *Mays* is the common, well-known Indian Corn, some of the numerous varieties of which are hardy enough to endure the open air in this country.

| Ouràgüä | . . . | . Apetal | . 6, Grass. Chile. | . . 1824 |
|---|---|---|---|---|
| Màys | . . . | . Apetal | . 6, Grass. America. | . . 1562 |

**ZEBRA PLANT**, see *Calàthèä zebrīnä.*

**ZEPHYRĀNTHĒS**, *Herbert.* From *zephyros*, west wind, and *anthos*, a flower. *Linn.* 6, Or. 1, Nat. Or. *Amaryllidaceæ.* Very pretty plants when in flower. Their culture, &c., is the same as that recommended for *Amaryllis.* *Synonymes :* 1. *Amaryllis Atamasco.* 2. *A. candida.* 3. *A. tubispatha.*

| Atamàscö, 1 | . | . White | . . 5, H. Her. | P. N. Amer. | . 1629 |
|---|---|---|---|---|---|
| càndidä, 2 | . | . White | . . 9, H. Her. | P. Peru | . 1822 |
| carinàtä | . . | . Pink | . . 5, F. Her. | P. Mexico | . 1824 |
| chlorolèücä | . | . Pa. grn. | . . 7, H. Bl. | P. | |
| Drummōndiï | . | . Wht. pink | 7, G. Bl. | P. Texas | . 1835 |
| mesochlòä | . . | . Wht. grn. | 6, F. Bl. | P. B. Ayres | . 1825 |
| ròsèä | . . | . Red | . . 5, F. Bl. | P. Havannah | . 1823 |

[ 337 ]

| Spofforthiànä | . | . Rose | . . 4, G. Bl. | P. Hybrid | . . 1833 |
|---|---|---|---|---|---|
| striàtä | . . | . White | . . 4, F. Bl. | P. Mexico | . 1824 |
| tubispàthä, 3 | . | . White | . . 5, S. Bl. | P. S. Amer. | |
| verecùndä | . . | . Pa. red | . . 4, F. Bl. | P. Mexico | . 1824 |

**ZEXMĒNIÄ**, *La Lave.* An anagram of *Ximenesia.* *Linn.* 19, Or. 4, Nat. Or. *Compositæ.* An interesting plant, succeeding in any common soil, and increased by seeds.

| tagetiflòrä | . . | . Yellow | . 9, F. Her. | P. Mexico | . . 1829 |
|---|---|---|---|---|---|

**ZICHÝÄ**, *Baron C. De Hugel.* In honour of Countess Molly Zichy, a noble Austrian lady, fond of botany. *Linn.* 17, Or. 4, Nat. Or. *Leguminosæ.* Pretty climbing plants, resembling *Kennedya*, and requiring precisely the same treatment as that genus.

| Mòllÿ | . . . | . | G. Ev. Tw. | Swan R. | . 1837 |
|---|---|---|---|---|---|
| tricòlör | . . | . Red yel. pur. | G. Ev. Tw. | Swan R. | . 1837 |

**ZIĒRIÄ**, *Smith.* In honour of Mr. John Zier, an industrious Polish botanist, who assisted Mr. Dickson in his Cryptogamia. *Linn.* 4, Or. 1, Nat. Or. *Rutaceæ.* This is a genus of remarkably pretty plants, thriving best in an equal mixture of sandy loam and peat, and young cuttings root readily, if planted in sand, under a glass. *Synonyme :* 1. *Z. Smithii.*

| hiràtä | . . . | . White | . . 6, G. Ev. | S. N. Holl. | |
|---|---|---|---|---|---|
| laevigàtä | . . | . White | . . 6, G. Ev. | S. N. Holl. | . 1822 |
| lanceolàtä, 1 | . | . White | . . 6, G. Ev. | S. N. Holl. | . 1808 |
| macrophÿllä | . | . White | . . 6, G. Ev. | S. N. Holl. | . 1820 |
| microphÿllä | . | . White | . . 6, G. Ev. | S. N. Holl. | . 1822 |
| obcordàtä | . . | . White | . . 6, G. Ev. | S. N. Holl. | . 1824 |
| octàndrä | . . | . Green | . . 4, G. Ev. | T. N. Holl. | . 1825 |
| pauciflòrä | . . | . White | . . 6, G. Ev. | S. N. Holl. | . 1822 |
| pilòsä | . . | . White | . . 6, G. Ev. | S. N. Holl. | . 1822 |
| revolùtä | . . | . White | . . 6, G. Ev. | S. N. Holl. | . 1824 |

**ZIETĒNIÄ**, see *Stàchÿs.*

**ZIGADĒNÚS**, *Michaux.* From *zygnuo*, I join, and *aden*, a gland; in allusion to the double glands on the perianth. *Linn.* 6, Or. 1, Nat. Or. *Melanthaceæ.* A genus of pretty plants when in flower. They succeed best in a moist peat soil, and are readily increased by dividing the plants at the root, or by seeds. *Synonymes :* 1. *Helonias bracteata.* 2. *H. glaberrima.*

| bracteàtä, 1 | . | . Cream | . . 5, H. Her. | P. N. Amer. | . 1811 |
|---|---|---|---|---|---|
| commutàtüs, 2 | . | . Cream | . . 6, H. Her. | P. N. Amer. | . 1811 |
| élégäns | . . | . White | . . 5, H. Her. | P. N. Amer. | . 1828 |
| glabérrimüs | . | . Cream | . . 6, H. Her. | P. N. Amer. | . 1811 |
| glaücüs | . . | . Green | . . 7, H. Her. | P. N. Amer. | . |

**ZIGOTRĪCHIÄ**, see *Tòrtülä.*

**ZIGZAG**, a stem is zigzag when it bends from side to side.

**ZILLÄ**, *Forskahl.* The name of an Egyptian plant. *Linn.* 15, Nat. Or. *Cruciferæ.* Interesting plants, growing best in a light rich soil, and readily increased by cuttings.

| macrocàrpä | . . | . | F. Ev. | S. Egypt | . . 1820 |
|---|---|---|---|---|---|
| Myagrøìdès | . | . Lilac | . . | F. Ev. | S. Egypt | . . 1822 |

**ZINGĪBĚR**, *Gærtner.* The Indian name. *Linn.* 1, Or. 1, Nat. Or. *Zingiberaceæ.* The species of *Zingiber* or ginger succeed best when grown in a mixture of loam, peat, and sand, and they are readily increased by division of the roots. Ginger is the root of *Z. officinale*, and is much valued for the sake of its aromatic, stimulating properties.

| capitàtüm | . . | . Yellow | . 2, S. Her. | P. E. Ind. | . . 1825 |
|---|---|---|---|---|---|
| Casumùnär | . | . Wht. yel. | 2, S. Her. | P. E. Ind. | . 1807 |
| chrysànthüm | . | . Yellow | . 7, S. Her. | P. E. Ind. | . 1821 |
| elàtüm | . . | . Yellow | . 7, S. Her. | P. E. Ind. | . 1820 |

| | | | | | |
|---|---|---|---|---|---|
| ligulātūm | Pink | 6, S. Her. P. E. Ind. | 1823 |
| Miōga | Pink | 5, G. Her. P. Japan | 1796 |
| officinālis | Red | 7, S. Her. P. E. Ind. | 1605 |
| pandurātūm | Pink | 6, S. Her. P. E. Ind. | 1812 |
| purpūrēūm | Purple | 9, S. Her. P. E. Ind. | 1822 |
| rōsēūm | Ro. yel. | 6, S. Her. P. E. Ind. | 1822 |
| rūbēns | Red | 10, S. Her. P. E. Ind. | 1822 |
| squarrōsūm | Pink | 8, S. Her. P. E. Ind. | 1822 |
| Zerūmbēt | Yel. grn. | 8, S. Her. P. E. Ind. | 1690 |

**ZĪNNĪA**, *Linn.* In honour of John Godfrey Zinn, professor of botany at Gottingen. *Linn.* 19, Or. 2, Nat. Or. *Compositæ.* A genus of very pretty annuals, well deserving extensive cultivation. The seeds require to be raised upon a gentle hotbed in spring, and afterwards planted in warm sheltered situations of the flower-garden. *Synonyme:* 1. *Z. violacea.*

| | | | | | |
|---|---|---|---|---|---|
| angustifōliā | Red | 7, H. | A. Mexico. | 1824 |
| ēlēgāns, 1 | Scarlet | 7, H. | A. Mexico. | 1796 |
| coccinēā | Scarlet | 8, H. | A. Mexico. | 1829 |
| rādīīs albīs | White | 8, H. | A. Hybrid. | 1832 |
| hybridā | Scarlet | 6, H. | A. S. Amer. | 1818 |
| multiflōrā | Red | 8, H. | A. N. Amer. | 1770 |
| pauciflōrā | Yellow | 7, H. | A. Peru | 1753 |
| revolūtā | Scarlet | 7, H. | A. Mexico. | 1817 |
| tenuiflōrā | Scarlet | 7, H. | A. Mexico. | 1799 |
| verticillātā | Red | 7, H. | A. Mexico. | 1789 |

**ZIZĀNĪA**, *Linn.* The Greek name of *darnel.* The modern plants have no relation to the ancient, being natives of America. *Linn.* 21, Or. 6, Nat. Or. *Gramineæ.* Z. aquatica has been acclimated in Middlesex and Ross-shire; it grows on the margin of ponds, and is exceedingly prolific of bland, farinaceous seeds, which afford a very good meal. It abounds in all the shallow streams of North-West America, where its seeds contribute essentially to the support of the wandering tribes of Indians, and feed immense flocks of wild swans, geese, and other water-fowl. Pinkerton says, " this plant seems intended by nature to become the bread-corn of the north."—*Loudon's Encyclopædia of Plants.*

| | | | | |
|---|---|---|---|---|
| aquaticā | Green | 8, H. Aq. A. N. Amer. | 1790 |
| flūitāns | Green | 7, H. Aq. A. N. Amer. | 1824 |
| miliācēā | Green | 7, H. Aq. A. Carolina | 1816 |

**ZIZĪA**, *Koch.* In honour of J. B. Zizi, a German botanist. *Linn.* 5, Or. 2, Nat. Or. *Umbelliferæ.* The species of this genus succeed best in a moist soil, and they are easily increased by dividing the roots, or by seeds. *Synonymes:* 1. *Smyrnium aureum.* 2. *S. cordatum,* *S. trifoliatum.* 3. *S. integerrimum.*

| | | | | |
|---|---|---|---|---|
| aūrēā, 1 | Yellow | 5, H. Her. P. N. Amer. | 1699 |
| cordātā, 2 | Yellow | 6, H. Her. P. N. Amer. | 1597 |
| integērrimā, 3 | Yellow | 8, H. Her. P. N. Amer. | 1758 |

**ZIZĪPHŌRA**, *Linn.* Said to be from *zizi* of the Indians, and *phoreo,* to bear. *Linn.* 2, Or. 1, Nat. Or. *Labiatæ.* The species of this genus are very pretty, and the perennial kinds well suited for growing on rock-work, or in pots well drained, in light sandy soil; they are increased by seeds and cuttings. The seeds of the annual species should be sown in the open border in April. *Synonymes:* 1. *Z. serpyllacea,* *Thymus lucidus.* 2. *Z. media,* *Z. serpyllacea.* 3. *Z. Pouschkini.*

| | | | | |
|---|---|---|---|---|
| acinoīdēs | Red | 7, H. De. Tr. Siberia | 1786 |
| capitātā | Red | 7, H. | A. Syria | 1752 |
| clinopodioīdēs | Pink | 6, F. Ev. S. Siberia | 1821 |
| canēscēns, 1 | Red | 7, F. Ev. S. | 1803 |
| mēdīā, 2 | Red | 7, F. Ev. S. Caucasus | 1822 |
| dasyānthā, 3 | Red | 7, F. Ev. S. Siberia | 1803 |
| hispānicā | Red | 6, H. | A. Spain | 1759 |
| taūricā | Red pur. | 8, H. | A. Tauria | 1816 |
| tenuiōr | Purplish | 6, H. | A. Levant | 1752 |

**ZIZYPHŪS**, *Tournefort.* *Zizouf,* in Arabic, is the name of the *Lotus.* *Linn.* 5, Or. 1, Nat. Or. *Rhamnaceæ.* The species of *Zizyphus* are all very pretty, and deserve to be grown in every collection of plants. The stove and greenhouse species thrive well in loam, peat, and sand, and ripened cuttings root readily in sand, under a glass. The hardy kinds are well fitted for shrubberies, and are easily increased by ripened cuttings, planted in soil, with a glass over them, or by slips of the roots. The fruit of *Z. Jujuba* and *Lotus* is very excellent, and is partaken of by all classes of people, in the countries to which these species are indigenous. It is sweet and mealy. *Synonymes:* 1. *Rhamnus*

*Jujuba.* 2. *R. Lotus.* 3. *Z. bubalina.* 4. *Z. sororia.* 5. *Rhamnus Zizyphus.*

| | | | | | |
|---|---|---|---|---|---|
| albēns | Grn. yel. | G. Ev. S. China | 1822 |
| Caracūttā | Grn. yel. | 5, S. Ev. S. Mysore | 1823 |
| flexuōsā | Yelsh. | H. De. S. Nepal | 1820 |
| incūrvā | Grn. yel. | H. De. T. Nepal | 1823 |
| Jujūbā, 1 | Pur. grn. | 4, G. Ev. S. E. Ind. | 1759 |
| Lōtūs, 2 | Grn. yel. | F. Ev. S. Africa | 1731 |
| mucronātā, 3 | Yel. grn. | G. Ev. S. C. G. H. | 1810 |
| Napēcā | Yellowish | S. Ev. S. Ceylon | 1816 |
| nitīdā | Yellow | 6, S. Ev. S. China | 1822 |
| Œnōplīā | Grn. yel. | S. Ev. S. Ceylon | |
| sinēnsīs | White | 5, F. Ev. S. China | 1818 |
| spinā-Christī | Grn. yel. | 8, H. Ev. S. Egypt | |
| inērmīs | Grey | 8, H. Ev. S. | |
| trinērvīs, 4 | Grn. yel. | S. Ev. S. E. Ind. | 1821 |
| vulgārīs, 5 | Pur. grn. | 8, H. De. S. S. Eur. | 1640 |
| Xylopyrūs | Grn. yel. | 8, S. Ev. S. E. Ind. | 1824 |

**ZŌEGĒA**, *Linn.* In honour of J. Zoega, author of a " Flora Islandica." *Linn.* 19, Or. 3, Nat. Or. *Compositæ.* A worthless hardy annual—*Z. Leptaūreā.*

**ZONĀRĪA**, *Agardh.* From *zona,* a girdle; transverse lines. *Linn.* 24, Or. 7, Nat. Or. *Algæ.* Marine plants—*Z. atomāriā, dichōtōmā, D. intricātā, multifīdā, pavōniā.*

**ZONATE**, having a dark belt in the shape of a horseshoe.

**ZONES**, stripes or belts.

**ZŌRNĪA**, *Gmelin.* In honour of John Zorn, once an apothecary at Kempten, in Bavaria, a botanical author. *Linn.* 16, Or. 6, Nat. Or. *Leguminosæ.* Interesting plants. For culture and propagation, see *Myriadenus.* *Synonymes:* 1. *Z. diphylla.* 2. *Hedysarum tetraphyllum.* 3. *Z. diphylla ciliata.* 4. *Anonymos bracteata, Hedysarum tetraphyllum.*

| | | | | | |
|---|---|---|---|---|---|
| angustifōliā, 1 | Purple | 7, S. | A. India | 1733 |
| capēnsīs, 2 | Yellow | 7, G. Her. P. C. G. H. | 1824 |
| dictyocārpā | Yellow | 7, S. | A. N. Holl. | 1820 |
| glochidiātā | Yellow | 7, S. | A. Guiana | 1823 |
| reticulātā, 3, | Yellow | 7, S. | A. W. Ind. | 1810 |
| tetraphyllā, 4 | Yellow | 7, G. Her. P. Carolina | 1824 |
| zeylonēnsīs | Yellow | 7, S. | A. Ceylon | 1825 |

**ZOSTĒRĀ**, *Linn.* From *zoster,* a riband; the leaves. *Linn.* 1, Or. 1, Nat. Or. *Fluviales.* This pretty aquatic is found in ditches.

| | | | |
|---|---|---|---|
| marīnā | Apetal | 8, H. Aq. P. Britain | |

**ZOZĪMIA**, *Hoffman.* In honour of A. N. and Z. Zozima, distinguished editors of the Greek classics. *Linn.* 5, Or. 2, Nat. Or. *Umbelliferæ.* A mere weed. *Synonyme:* 1. *Heracleum absinthifolium—Z. absinthifōliā.*

**ZYGNĒMA**, *Agardh.* From *zygos,* a yoke, and *nema,* a filament; filaments jointed together in pairs. *Linn.* 24, Or. 7, Nat. Or. *Algæ.* The species of this genus are found in rivulets, ditches, &c.—*Z. bicōlōr, cruciātūm, C. brēvī-articulātūm, C. lōngī-articulātūm, curvātūm, decimīnūm, decussātūm, epigēūm, nitīdūm, pectinātūm, punctātūm, quinīnūm.*

**ZYGŌDŌN**, *Hooker.* From *zygos,* a yoke, and *odous,* a tooth, the teeth are yoked together in pairs. *Linn.* 24, Or. 5, Nat. Or. *Musci.* A pale-green species of moss, found on the trunks of trees. *Synonyme:* 1. *Mnium conoideum—Z. conoīdēūm.*

**ZYGOPĒTĀLŪM**, *Hooker.* From *zygos,* a yoke, and *petalon,* a petal; in allusion to the adhesion of the segments of the perianth by their bases in the original species. *Linn.* 20, Or. 1, Nat. Or. *Orchidaceæ.* This is a genus of extremely beautiful and fragrant plants when in flower. They are easily cultivated in a damp heat, and must in all respects be treated similarly to the genus *Stanhopea.* *Synonyme:* 1. *Z. crinitum, Eulophia crinita.*

| | | | | |
|---|---|---|---|---|
| cochlearē | Wht. pur. | 8, S. Epi. Demerara | |
| Mackayī | Grn. lil. | 3, S. Epi. Brazil | 1825 |
| crinītūm, 1 | Wht. grn. | 9, S. Epi. Brazil | 1829 |
| maxillārē | Brn. grn. | 9, S. Epi. S. Amer. | 1829 |
| Murrayānūm | Grn. wht. | 7, S. Epi. Brazil | 1837 |
| rostrātūm | Wht. brn. | 9, S. Epi. Demerara | 1837 |
| stenōchīlūm | Wht. yel. | 9, S. Epi. Brazil | 1828 |

**ZYGOPHYLLŪM**, *Linn.* From *zygos,* a yoke, and *phyllon,* a leaf; the leaves are in pairs. *Linn.* 10, Or. 1, Nat. Or. *Zygophyllaceæ.* The species of this genus are all very handsome when in flower. The stove and greenhouse species should be grown in a mixture of loam, peat, and sand, and are readily increased by cuttings, in sand, under a glass, or by

[ 353 ]

seeds, when these can be obtained. *Z. Fabago* grows well in any light soil, in a dry situation; it can only be increased by seeds, which should be sown in a pot, and placed in a frame, and when the plants are large enough, they may be planted out in the open border, in a warm, dry, sheltered situation.

| | | | | | | | |
|---|---|---|---|---|---|---|---|
| album . . . . | . White | . 10, | S. Ev. | S. | Canaries | . 1779 |
| coccineûm . | . Scarlet | . | G. Ev. | S. | Egypt | . 1823 |
| cordifolîûm . | . Orange | . 10, | G. Ev. | S. | C. G. H. | . 1774 |

| | | | | | | | |
|---|---|---|---|---|---|---|---|
| fœtidûm . . | . Or. yel. | 6, | G. Ev. | S. | C. G. H. | . 1790 |
| insuâvé | . Yellow | . 7, | G. Ev. | S. | C. G. H. | . 1790 |
| maculâtûm . | . Yellow | . 10, | G. Ev. | S. | C. G. H. | . 1782 |
| microphyllûm | . Yellow | . 7, | G. Ev. | S. | C. G. H. | . 1816 |
| Morgsânâ | . Yellow | . 8, | G. Ev. | S. | C. G. H. | . 1732 |
| prostrâtûm . | . Yellow | . 7, | G. Ev. | Tr. | C. G. H. | . 1810 |
| sessilifolîûm . | . Yellow | . 7, | S. Ev. | S. | C. G. H. | . 1713 |
| simpléx . . | . Yellow | . 7, | F. | A. | St. Jago | . 1825 |
| spatulâtûm . | . Yellow | . 6, | S. Her. | P. | C. Verd. I. | . 1824 |
| spinôsûm . . | . Yellow | . 7, | G. Ev. | S. | C. G. H. | . 1830 |

# SUPPLEMENT.

[THE lapse of time consequent on the passage through the press of a work of this description and extent, has necessarily caused the omission of many plants that have been discovered or described since its commencement. All of these that have hitherto (June 1840) been made known, are now inserted in due alphabetical order. Those new genera upon which no remarks are supplied, have not yet fallen beneath our observation, and we are unwilling to furnish any unauthenticated accounts.]

ABŪTĬLŎN, *Mœnch.* Arabic name of a plant analogous to the marsh-mallow. *Linn.* 16, Or. 8, Nat. Or. *Malvaceæ.* "It is a greenhouse shrub of the easiest culture, and of great beauty."—*Bot. Reg.*

| | | | | |
|---|---|---|---|---|
| striátūm | . . . Orange | all, G. Ev. S. Brazil | . . | |

ACĀCĬA.

| | | | | |
|---|---|---|---|---|
| astringens | . . | G. Ev. S. N. S. W. | . 1823 |
| cultrátā | . . | G. Ev. S. N. Holl. | . 1820 |
| cuneátā | . . Yellow | G. Ev. S. Swan R. | . 1837 |
| cyanophyllā | . Yellow | G. Ev. S. Swan R. | |
| dolabrátā | . . | G. Ev. S. N. Holl. | . 1820 |
| depéndens | . . | G. Ev. S. V. D. L. | . 1819 |
| holoserícea | . . | G. Ev. S. N. Holl. | . 1820 |
| humifúsā | . . | G Ev. Tr. N. Holl. | . 1820 |
| Kermesínā | . . Purple | S. De. S. | |
| Lawsóni | . . | G. Ev. S. N. S. W. | |
| leptocárpā | . . | G. Ev. S. N. Holl. | . 1821 |
| ligulátā | . . | G. Ev. S. N. S. W. | . 1818 |
| neurocárpā | . . | G. Ev. S. N. Holl. | . 1820 |
| persoonioídes | . . | G. Ev. S. N. Holl. | |
| pulchéllā | . . | | |
| magnā | . . Yellow | . G. Ev. S. | |
| Riceánā | . . Yellow | . 3, G. De. S. V. D. L. | . 1835 |
| sericátā | . . | G. Ev. S. N. Holl. | . 1820 |
| Simsii | . . | G. Ev. S. N. Holl. | . 1819 |
| spectábilis | . . | G. Ev. S. N. S. W. | . 1837 |
| stenophyllā | . . | G. Ev. S. N. S. W. | . 1818 |
| umbellátā | . . | G. Ev. S. N. Holl. | . 1819 |
| viminális | . . | G. Ev. S. N. Holl. | . 1820 |
| vomeriformis | . . | G. Ev. S. N. S. W. | . 1818 |
| xylocárpā | . . | G. Ev. S. N. Holl. | . 1820 |

ACÆNĀ.

| | | | |
|---|---|---|---|
| spléndens | . . . | G. Ev. S. | . 1838 |

ĀCĔR.

campéstrĕ

| | | | | |
|---|---|---|---|---|
| austríacūm | . Grn. yel. | . 6, H. De. T. Austria | . . |
| hebecárpūm | . Grn. yel. | . 6, H. De. T. Britain | . . |
| lævigátūm | . Grn. yel. | . 6, H. De. T. | |
| nánūm | . . Grn. yel. | . 6, H. De. S. | |

ACHILLĔA. *Synonyme:* 1. *A. amœna.*

Millefólium

| | | | |
|---|---|---|---|
| variegátā | . White | . 8, H. Her. P. Gardens | |
| vermiculária, 1 | . Yellow | . 8, H. Her. P. Russia | . 1835 |

ACONĪTŪM.

| | | | |
|---|---|---|---|
| ochránthūm | . Yellow | . 8, H. De. P. Russia | . 1834 |

ACREMÓNIŬM—*alternátūm.*

ACRŎSTĬCHŪM.

| | | | |
|---|---|---|---|
| asplenifólium | . . | 8. Her. P. Brazil | . . |
| citrifólium | . . Brown | . 9, S. Her. P. W. Ind. | . . |
| juglandifólium | . . | 8. Her. P. Surinam | . 1832 |
| latifólium | . . Blue | . 8. Her. P. Jamaica | |
| nicotianifólium | . Brown | . 10, S. Her. P. W. Ind. | |
| Scolopéndrium | . Brown | . 8, S. Her. P. W. Ind. | |

ACTINŌTŬS.

| | | | |
|---|---|---|---|
| leucocéphalŭs | . . | Swan R. | . 1837 |

ADIĀNTŪM.

| | | | |
|---|---|---|---|
| æthiopícūm | . . Brown | . 9, S. Her. P. | . 1838 |
| concinnūm | . . Brown | . 6, S. Her. P. N. Holl. | |
| flabellifólium | . . Brown | . 9, S. Her. P. Jamaica | |
| foliósūm | . . Brown | . 8, G. Her. P. | |
| Fovánūm | . . Brown | . 5, S. Her. P. W. Ind. | |
| lúcidūm | . . Brown | . 8, S. Her. P. S. Amer. | . 1824 |
| Moritziánūm | . . Brown | . 9, S. Her. P. | . 1838 |
| oblíquūm | . . Brown | . S. Her. P. W. Ind. | |

ÆCHMĔA, *Ruiz and Pavon.* From *aichme*, a point; in allusion to the rigid points on the calyces. *Linn.*

6, Or. 1, Nat. Or. *Bromeliaceæ.* These plants require to be grown in a compost of loam, peat, and sand.

| | | | | |
|---|---|---|---|---|
| Merténsii | . . Grn. red | . 3, S. Epi. Demerara | . 1830 |
| suavéolens | . . Pink | . 4, S. Her. P. Brazil | . 1838 |

ÆCĬDĬŬM—*Arī, Behénis, cancellátūm, Euphórbiæ, Gerānii, Oróbi, quadrĭfídūm, Soldanéllæ, Valerianaceārūm.*

ÆGŎCHLŎA, *Bentham.* From *aix*, a goat, and *chloa*, a green herb; alluding to the fetid smell of some of the species. *Linn.* 5, Or. 1, Nat. Or. *Polemoniaceæ.* For culture and propagation refer to the genus *Gilia.*

| | | | | |
|---|---|---|---|---|
| atractyloídés | . Blue | . . H. | A. California | . 1833 |
| cotulæfóliā | . Blue | . . H. | A. California | . 1833 |
| eryngioídés | . . | . . H. | A. Chile | . 1833 |
| intertéxtā | . Blue | . . H. | A. California | . 1833 |
| pubéscens | . Blue | . . H. | A. California | . 1833 |

ÆSCHYNĀNTHŬS.

| | | | | |
|---|---|---|---|---|
| ramosíssimūs | . . Scarlet | . 6, S. Epi. Khossea | . 1837 |

ÆSCŬLŬS.

Hippocástanūm

| | | | |
|---|---|---|---|
| flóre-plénō | . White | . 3, H. De. T. | |
| fol. argéntéis | . White | . 3, H. De. T. Gardens | |

ÆTHĔRĬA. *Linn.* 20, Or. 1, Nat. Or. *Orchidaceæ.* *Synonymes:* 1. *Goodyera occulta, Platylepis Goodyeroides.*

| | | | |
|---|---|---|---|
| occúlta, 1 | . . . Wht. grn. 10, S. Ter. Mauritius | . |

AGANĬSĬA, *Lindley.* From *aganos*, quiet, or desirable; in allusion to the pretty, neat appearance of the plant. *Linn.* 20, Or. 1, Nat. Or. *Orchidaceæ.* In speaking of the cultivation of this superlatively pretty plant, Dr. Lindley remarks: "In order to cultivate this plant successfully it should be suspended upon a block of wood from the rafters of the stove, and its thick fleshy roots allowed to hang in the air and imbibe its moisture. A damp atmosphere, syringing its roots and leaves freely when in a growing state, and shade during bright sunshine, are the principal requisites in its cultivation. In other respects it may receive the same treatment as the rest of this tribe."—*Bot. Reg.*

| | | | |
|---|---|---|---|
| pulchéllā | . . . Cream | . . 6, S. Epi. Demerara | |

AGĀRĬCŬS—*adipósūs, areolátūs, atomátūs, balanínūs, bífrōns, blándūs, boláris, bulláceūs, calyptræfórmis, camptophýllus, Candolleánūs, Centunculūs, cerāsínūs, cérnūūs, chiōnēūs, constríctūs, corrūgis, cydœnēūs, cyphellifórmis, decolōrans, deflūēns, D. rúbidūs, elátūs, erubéscens, erythrópūs, excélsūs, fœnisecii, fibrillōsūs, flocculōsūs, fuliginōsūs, fumōsūs, hæmatophýllus, Hookĕri, hypnóphilūs, iliopódīus, imbricátūs, inamænūs, Iris, lasclvūs, lentūs, limōnīūs, livido-ochracēūs, Loveiánūs, mammōsūs, Mārīæ, mastoídēūs, médīūs, miniátūs, mitis, nigréscens, pachyphýllus, pauperculūs, pelianthínūs, phyllōphilūs, polystíctūs, Rúbi, rúfo-cárnēūs, speciōsūs, sphagnícolā, stipátūs, solitárīūs, S. graminēūs, striátūlūs, striátūs, lentérrimūs, trechispōrūs, undátūs, unguinōsūs, vālidūs, vitellīnūs.*

AGĀVĔ.

| | | | | |
|---|---|---|---|---|
| élegáns | . . . | S. Her. P. | |
| glaucéscens | . . | G. Her. P. Mexico | . . 1835 |
| polycanthoídes | . | G. Her. P. Mexico | . . 1835 |

pulchérrimā . . . G. Her. P. Mexico . . 1835
saponāriā . . . Grn. yel. . G. Her. P. Mexico . .

**AGROSTĔMMĀ.**
suecica . . . . Pink . . 8, H. Her. P. Sweden . 1824

**AGRŌSTĬS.**
élegāns . . . . Apetal . . 6, Grass. Russia . . 1834

**AĪRŎPSĬS.**
pulchéllā . . . Apetal . . 3, Grass . . . . 1831

**AJŪGĀ.**
réptāns
variegātā . . Blue . . 4, H. De. Cr. Britain . .

**ALEURĪTĔS.**
cordātā . . . . Apetal . 8. Ev. T. Japan . . 1818

**ALLANTŎDĬĀ.**
strigōsā . . . Brown all, S. Her. P. Madeira .

**ĀLLĬŪM.**
pūlchrūm . . . Yellow . 6, H. Bl. P. S. Eur. . .

**ĀLNŬS.**
barbātā . . . . H. De. S. Russia . . 1838
jorullénsis . . . H. De. T. Mexico . .
suocordātā . . . H. De. S. Russia . . 1838

**AĪSĬNĔ.**
laricifōliā . . . H. Her. P. Siberia . . 1834

**ALSTRŒMĔRĬĀ.**
acutifōliā
aūreā . . Yellow . 9, F. De. Tw.
Barclayānā . . Orange . 7, F. Tu. P.
Berteroānā . . Pa. pk. . 7, F. Tu. P. Chile . .
bicôlōr . . . . 9, S. Tu. P. Chile . . 1826
chilénsis . . . Pink . 7, F. Tu. P. Chile . . 1834
Errembaūltii . . Wht. spot 8, F. Tu. P. Hybrid . 1835

**ALTĔRNANTHĔRĀ.**
filifórmis
nodiflōrā . . .

**ALŸssŎM.**
micránthūm . . Yellow . 8, H. Ev. Tr. Russia . . 1836
orientāle
variegātūm . . Yellow . 4, H. Ev. S. Gardens .
procúmbēns . . . H. Ev. S.

**AMARŸLLĬS.**
psittacīnā
hybrīdā . . . Red. grn. . 4, S. Bl. P. Hybrid . . 1820

**AMELĀNCHĬĔR.**
flōrĭdā . . . . White . 5, H. De. T. N. Amer. . 1826
parvifōliā . . White . 5, H. De. S.
ovālis
semi-integrifōliā White . 5, H. De. T. N. Amer. .
subcordātā . . White . 5, H. De. T. N. Amer. .

**AMŌRPHĀ.**
fruticōsā
angustifōliā . Purple . 6, H. De. S.
cærūleā . . Blue . 6, H. De. S.

**AMPELŸGŌNŬM**, *Lindley.* From *ampelos*, a vine, and *gonu*, a joint; in allusion to the stems. *Linn.* —, Or. —, Nat. Or. *Polygonaceæ.* This plant has lately flowered in the garden of the Horticultural Society, where it has been raised from seed received from Dr. Falconer of Saharunpur. It forms a spreading herbaceous plant, from one and a half to two feet high, with ovate-lanceolate, acuminate, stalked leaves, and with small heads of yellowish-white, fleshy flowers, which are succeeded by a black, succulent fruit. This latter circumstance has led to the establishment of a new genus, to which a name indicating its grape-like fruit has been assigned.
chinénse . . Yeh. wht. 8, G. Her. P. Saharunpur

**AMPHĬCŌMĔ**, *Royle.* From *amphi*, around, and *kome*, hair; in allusion to the seeds. *Linn.* 14, Or. 2, Nat. Or. *Bignoniaceæ.* An elegant perennial, probably hardy enough to stand out, if planted in any dry situation, or on rock-work, and protected during winter from the wet and most severe frost by a hand-glass. It is very impatient of wet even in summer, and requires to be kept particularly dry during winter; it thrives best in a loamy soil, with a small portion of sandy peat added, and may be increased by seeds or cuttings. The seeds should be sown in February, in a loamy soil, and placed in the greenhouse. Cuttings of the young shoots strike at any time from March to September, but rather slowly.
argūtā . . . . Lilac . . 8, H. Ev. Cl. Himalayas .

**AMSĬNCKĬĀ**, *Lehmann.* Meaning unknown. *Linn.* 5, Or. 1, Nat. Or. *Boraginaceæ.* The seeds of these plants only require to be sown in the open ground, about the beginning of May, in a dry, warm, sheltered situation. They are not worthy of cultivation, except in botanical gardens—*A. angustifōliā, lycopsĭōidēs.*

**AMŸGDĀLŬS.**
pedunculātā . . H. De. S. . 1833

**ANACŸCLŬS.**
pyréthrūm . . . H. Her. P. . 1837

**ANAGĀLLĬS.**
Monéllii
lilacīnā . . . Lilac . . 5, G. Her. P. . 1836

**ANEĪLĒMĀ.**
crispātā . . . G. Her. P. N. Holl. . 1822

**ANEĪMĬĀ.**
longifōliā . . . Brown . 8, S. Her. P. Brazil . .
rādicāns . . . S. Her. P. Brazil . .

**ANĔMŎNĔ.**
horténsis
miniātā . . . Brt. red . 5, H. Tu. P. Gardens .
nemorōsā
cærūleā . . Lgt. blue . 5, H. Tu. P. Gardens .
Pulsatillā
albĭdā . . . Whitish . 4, H. Her. P. Germany . 1834
rūbrā . . . Redsh. pur. 5, H. Her. P. Germany . 1834
virginiānā
grandiflōrā . . White . . 6, H. Her. P. Gardens .

**ANGELŌNĬĀ.**
Gardnéri . . . Wht. pur. 5, S. Her. P. Pernambuco 1838

**ANGRĒCŬM.**
armeniācūm . . . Apricot . 8. Epi. S. Leone .
gladiifōliūm . . . White . . 8. Epi. Mauritius .

**ANICTĀNGĬŪM—** *striātūm, S. subincānūm, S. unicôlōr.*

**ANIGOZĀNTHŎS.**
coccinēūs . . . Crimson . 7, G. Her. P. Swan R. . 1837
flāvĭdūs
bicôlōr . . . Scar. grn. . F. Her. P. Swan R. . 1837
hūmĭlĭs, 1 . . . Browu . . F. Her. P. Swan R. . .
Manglésii
angustifōlĭūs . . Grn. red . 6, G. Her. P. N. Holl. . 1836

**ANŌTĬS**, *Decandolle.* From *a*, privative, and *ous*, an ear; teeth to calyx. *Linn.* 4, Or. 1, Nat. Or. *Rubiaceæ.* "A pretty little plant, which will flower from June to September, in the open border, or on rock-work, for which it is remarkably well adapted."—*Gard. Mag.* It requires the protection of a frame or greenhouse during winter, and may be increased by dividing the root. *Synonymes*: 1. *Hedyotis ciliolosa, Houstonia ciliolosa.*
ciliolōsā, 1 . . Pa. lilac . 7, F. Her. P. N. Amer. . 1832

**ANTHĔMĬS.** *Synonyme*: 1. *A. porrigens.*
mucronulātā, 1 . . . H. A. Italy . . 1836

**ANTHŸLLĬS.** *Synonyme*: 1. *A. italica.*
Vulnerāriā
hirsutissimā, 1 Red . . 7, H. Her. P. Europe . . 1816

**ANTĬRRHĪNŬM.**
mājūs
caryophyllōidēs Scar. striped 8, H. Her. P. Hybrid .
ochroleūcūm . . Pa. yel. . . 7, H. Her. P.

**AŌTŬS.**
grácĭlis . . . . G. Ev. S. N. Holl. . 1820

**APLOTĀXĬS.** "A handsome herbaceous plant which has lately been introduced by the East India Company. It forms a bush about three feet high, with long, lanceolate, deep green leaves, hoary with down on the under side. The flower-heads are arranged in a panicled manner, and are narrow, with pale, bright, purple blossoms."—*Bot. Reg.*
albéscēns . . . Purple . 7, H. Her. P. India . . 1837

**AQUILĔGĬĀ.**
arcticā . . . . Red yel. . 6, H. Her. P. Siberia . .
canadénsis
lūteā . . . Pa. yel. . 5, H. Her. P. N. Amer. . 1835
glandulōsā
discôlōr . . . . 6, H. Her. P. Siberia . . 1789
leptocérās . . . H. Her. P. Russia . . 1838
vulgāris
élegāns . . Purple . 6, H. Her. P. Europe . .

**ĀRĀBĬS.**
albĭdā
variegātā . . White . . H. Ev. Tr. Gardens .

flexuósá . . . H. B. Naples . . 1832
lilacīná . . . Lilac . . 8, H. - B.

**ARCTOSTĂPHỸLŎS.**
nitīdá . . . Swan R. .
tomentósá . . . White . 4, G. Ev. S. California . 1826

**ARĒNĀRIĂ.**
biflorá . . . White . H. Her. P. Switzerl. . 1818
nemorósá . . White . 6, H. Ev. S. S. Amer. . 1832

**AROŸRĒ̆Ă.** Synonymes: 1. Ipomœa capitata. 2. I. malabarica.
capitātá, 1 . . Purple . 7, S. Ev. Tw. E. Ind. . 1823
Malabáricá, 2 . Cream . 7, S. Ev. Tw. E. Ind. . 1823

**ARISÆ̆MĂ, Bentham.** "A small, stemless plant, with tuberous roots like those of the common Arum, purple stalked pedate leaves, and a pink or purple spathe from five to six inches long. It will probably form a greenhouse herbaceous plant. Mr. Hartweg found it in shady woods near Morelia flowering in July, and sent it to the Horticultural Society, with whom it has been raised."—*Bot. Reg.*
macrospāthá . . . 7, G. Tu. P. Morelia . 1839

**ARISTOLŎCHIĂ.**
ciliāta . . . Pur. yel. . G. Ev. Tw. B. Ayres .
ciliósá . . . Pur. grn. . 9, S. Ev. Cl. N. Patag. . 1836
hyperbōréá . . . 5, S. De. Tw. India . .

**ARMENIĂCĂ.** Synonyme: 1. A. pedunculata.
vulgāris
  florē plenó, 1 . White . . 4, H. De. T.
  fol. variegāta . White . 4, H. De. T.

**ARMĒRIĂ.**
hybrīdă . . . Red . . H. Her. P. Hybrid .
Popeāná . . . Red . . H. Her. P. Hybrid
vulgāris
  albá . . . White . 9, H. Her. P. Gardens .
  coccīnéá . . Red . 9, H. Her. P. Gardens .

**ARPOPHỸLLŬM, La Llave.** Linn. 20, Or. 1, Nat. Or. Orchidaceæ. "One of the most graceful and beautiful of the Mexican Orchidaceæ; recently introduced. The stem is slender and a foot or a foot and half high, with the sheaths as rough as shagreen leather; it is terminated by one long, curved leaf, from the axil of which there curves, in an opposite direction, a dense spike of pink, or pale purple flowers. It is a species of great rarity even in Mexico, where it has hitherto been only seen at Sultepec and near Arimbaro, growing upon trees."—*Bot. Reg.* The genus belongs to *Epidendreæ*, and may therefore, probably, be referred to the other genera of this sub-order for cultivation, &c.
spicātúm . . . Pink . . 8. Epi. Mexico . 1838

**ARTEMISIĂ.**
Abrŏtānúm
  hūmīlé . . Yel. grn. . 9, H. De. S. S. Eur. . .
  tobolskiānúm Yel. grn. . 9, H. De. S.
aprīcá . . . H. Ev. Tr.
vulgāris
  variegātá . Purple . 8, H. Her. P. Gardens .

**ARTHŎNYĂ**—illicīná, lūrīdá.

**ARŬM.**
sarmentósúm . . 8. Her. P. Brasil . 1835

**ARUNDINĂ, Blume.** From arundo, a reed; resemblance. Linn. 20, Or. 1, Nat. Or. Orchidaceæ.
bambusifōliá . . Purple . . 8. Epi. Nepal .

**ASAGRÆ̆Ă, Lindley.** In compliment to Dr. Asa Gray, the author of a treatise upon North American Melanthaceæ. Linn. 6, Or. 3, Nat. Or. Melanthaceæ. A plant of not much beauty, the culture and propagation of which is, we believe, similar to that of Tigridia. Synonymes: 1. Helonias officinalis, Veratrum officinale.
officinalis, 1 . . White . 9, F. Bl. P. Vera Cruz .

**ASCŎBŎLŬS**—ciliātús, glăbĕr, Trifŏlii, vinōsús.
**ASPEROCŎCCŬS, Lamour.** From asper, rough, kokkos, seed; rough surfaced. Linn. 24, Or. 7, Nat. Or. Algæ. This species is found on rocks—A. compressus.
**ASPERŎILLŬS**—aūréús, cāndīdús, mōllís, rōséús.

**ASPĒRŬLĂ.**
scutellāris . . . H. Her. P. Russia . 1838
tyráīcá . . . White . 6, H. Her. P. Levant . 1829

**ASPHŎDĒLŬS.**
capillāris . . Pa. yel. . 6, H. Her. P. S. Eur. .
macrocárpús . . . H. Bl. P. Dalmatia . 1831

**ASPIDISTRĂ.**
elātīŏr . . . Brown . 10, S. Her. P. Japan . . 1835
variegātá . . Brown . 10, S. Her. P. Japan . . 1835

**ASPĬDIŬM.**
crinītúm . . . Brown . 8, S. Her. P. Maurit. . . 1831
Cunninghāmí . . Brown . 7, G. Her. P. N. Zeal. .
drēpānúm . . . Brown . 9, G. Her. P. Madeira . 1831
Goldiānúm . . . Brown . 8, H. Her. P. N. Amer. .
Hippocrēpis . . . Brown . 4, S. Her. P. Jamaica .
lætevīrēns . . . Brown . G. Her. P. Madeira .
Lonchītis
  aspērrīmá . . Brown . 7, H. Her. P. N. Amer. .
lūcéns . . . Brown . 8, S. Her. P. Maurit. . 1831
pennīgérúm . . Brown . G. Her. P. W. Ind. .
prolīférúm . . Brown . 8. Her. P. Brasil .
pūngéns . . . Brown . G. Her. P. W. Ind. .
tuberósúm . . Brown . G. Her. P. W. Ind.

**ASPLĒNIŬM.**
alātúm . . . Brown . 8. Her. P. W. Ind. .
ambīgúúm . . Brown . G. Her. P. W. Ind. .
aurītúm . . . Brown . 9, S. Her. P. S. Amer. . 1829
biaurītúm . . Brown . 7, S. Her. P. W. Ind. .
cuneātúm . . Brown . 9, S. Her. P. W. Ind. . 1832
depréssúm . . Brown . 8, S. Her. P. .
obtusifōliúm . . Brown . 8. Her. P. . 1838
pulchrúm . . . Brown . 7, S. Her. P. Jamaica .
salicifōliúm . . Brown . 7, S. Her. P. W. Ind.

**ASTĒLIĂ, R. Brown.** From a, without, stelechos, a stem. Linn. —, Or. —, Nat. Or. Asphodeleæ. A curious plant, with the flowers of which we are unacquainted. It thrives in the greenhouse, in a light loamy soil, and produces an abundance of offsets. These, if detached, and planted either in sawdust or very porous earth, with a slight bottom heat, will speedily form roots.
Banksíí . . . N. Zeal. . 1837

**ASTĒR.**
bessarábicús . . Purple . 9, H. Her. P. Russia . . 1834

**ASTERACĀNTHĂ.** From aster, a star, and akantha, a spine. "This is a handsome, greenhouse, herbaceous perennial, seeds of which were sent to the Horticultural Society by Mr. M'Culloch, one of the gardeners to His Highness the Pacha of Egypt. If care is taken to reduce the vigour of leaves, by not giving the plant too much shade and moisture, it becomes very handsome, but if it is permitted to run ' to leaf' too much, its beauty is considerably impaired."—*Bot. Reg.*
longifōliá . . . G. Her. P. Egypt . .

**ASTEROCĒPHĂLŬS.**
bannátīcús
  albús . . . White . 7, H. Her. P. Gardens .

**ASTEROMĂ—reticulātúm.**
**ASTRĂGĂLŬS.**
calycīnús . . . 8, H. Her. P. Caucasus . 1819
dasyánthús . . . 6, H. Her. P. Hungary . 1819
hymenocárpús . . Yellow . 7, H. Her. P. Russia . . 1835
hypoglóttís
  albá . . . White . 6, H. De. Tr. Gardens .
lactiflórús . . . H. Her. P. Siberia . . 1832
macrocéphálús . . . H. De. Tr. Caucasus . 1831
Schanginiānús . . . H. Her. P. Siberia . . 1832
strobilīférús . . .
sylvicōlús . . . H. De. Tr. Armenia . 1831

**ATELĬNDRĂ.** Derivation unknown. Linn. 14, Or. —, Nat. Or. Labiatæ. A pretty shrubby plant, not yet thoroughly known in this country, but doubtless requiring a compost of loam and peat, and propagating by cuttings.
incāná . . . Slate . G. Ev. S. Swan R. .

**ATHAMĂNTĂ—strīctá.**
**ATRĂGĒ̆NĂ.**
macropétalá . . . H. De. Cl. Russia . . 1831

**AVĒNĂ—latifōliá.**
**AZĀLĒĂ.**
indīcá
  laterītĭá . . Brick . G. Ev. S. China . . 1833
  Rawsōní . . Crimson . 5, H. Ev. S. Hybrid . 1833
  speciósá . . Purple . 5, G. Ev. S. Hybrid . 1830
  splēndéns . . Red . 2, G. Ev. S. Hybrid . 1835
nudiflórá
  exīmiá . . Crimson . 4, H. Ev. S. Hybrid . 1839
pōntīcá
  ardéns . . Brt. red . 5, H. Ev. S. Hybrid .
  cāndīdá . . White . 5, H. Ev. S. Hybrid . 1834
  coronāriá . . Yellow . 6, H. Ev. S. Holland . 1838

BABIĀNĀ.
plicātā
   mūltīplex . . Purple . 6, G. Bl. P. C. G. H. . 1834

BACTRĪDĪŬM, *Kunze.* From *baktron*, a staff, and *eidos*, resemblance. *Linn.* 24, Or. 9, Nat. Or. *Fungi.* Found on the horizontal surface of stumps—*B. atrovirens.*

BAĒRĪĀ, *Fischer and Meyer.* In honour of Professor Baer, of the university of Dorpat. *Linn.* 19, Or. —, Nat. Or. *Compositæ.*

chrysostōmā . . Yellow . 5, H.    A. California . 1835

BAEŌMŸCĒS—*microcěphālūs, placophŷllūs.*

BALSAMĪNĀ.
Masteriānā . . Purple . 7, S.   A. Khosses Hills 1837

BĀNĀLĀ—*cilīārīs, lacūstrīs, lætevīrens.*

BĀNKSĪĀ.
Hŭgelīī . . . .    G. Ev. S. N. S. W. . 1837
ilicifŏlīā . . .    G. Ev. S. K. G. S. . 1837
Menziěsīī . . .    G. Ev. S. Swan R. . 1837

BAPTĪSĪĀ.
versicŏlŏr . . . Lt. pur. . 7, H. Her. P. N. Amer. . 1824

BARBĀRĒĀ—*arcuātā, orthocěrūs.*

BARKĒRĪĀ, *Knowles and Westcott.* In honour of G. Barker, Esq., of Birmingham. *Linn.* 20, Or. —, Nat. Or. *Orchideæ.* " An elegant little Mexican Orchidaceous plant, with tapering fleshy stems like those of a meagre Cycnoches, narrow-lanceolate, acuminate, membranous leaves, and a terminal inflorescence, in the form of a raceme of a few large bright pink flowers. It is well figured in the Floral Cabinet, and is one of the few plants which rival the Cattleyas in gaiety of appearance. It is, however, said to be difficult of cultivation, and is at present of great rarity. The genus is well distinguished from Cattleya, to which it approaches most nearly, by its lip being flat and undivided, instead of cucullate, and more or less completely three-lobed, as well as by its peculiar habit.—*Bot. Reg.*
ělěgāns . . . . Lgt. pink. S. Epi. Mexico . 1836

BATĀTĀS, *Choisy.* According to Rumphius, a Malay, and to Neiremberg, a Mexican word. *Linn.* 5, Or. 1, Nat. Or. *Convolvulaceæ.* The species of this genus are strong, free-growing plants, requiring room to spread; and, being tuberous-rooted, they should be kept dry when in a dormant state. Light rich soil suits them, and young cuttings strike readily under a hand-glass, in heat. *Synonymes*: 1. *Ipomœa bignonioides.* 2. *I. Cavanillesii.* 3. *I. Batatas.* 4. *I. glaucifolia.* 5. *I. heterophylla.* 6. *I. eriosperma, I. gossypifolia, I. insignis.* 7. *I. pentaphylla.* 8. *I. senegalensis.* 9. *I. ternata.* 10. *I. venosa.* 11. *I. Willdenovii.*

betācēā . . . Pa. vio. . G. De. Tw. Demerara
bignonioĭdes, 1 . Drk. pur. . 7, S. De. Tw. Cayenne . 1824
Cavanillěsīī, 2 . Wht. red . 8, S. De. Tw. . 1815
edŭlīs, 3 . . . Wht. & pur. . 8, S. De. Tw. E. Ind. . 1797
glaucifŏlīā, 4 . Purplish . 6, S. De. Tw. Mexico . 1732
heterophŷllā, 5 . Pa. pur. . 7, S. De. Tw. Cuba . 1817
paniculātā, 6 . . Purple . 7, S. Tw. P. E. Ind. . 1799
pentaphŷllā, 7 . White . 8, S. De. Tw. E. Ind. . 1739
senegalěnsīs, 8 . White . 7, S. De. Tw. Guinea . 1823
ternātā, 9 . . . White . 7, S. De. Tw. Brasil . 1733
venŏsā, 10 . . . Purple . 7, S. De. Tw. Mauritius 1820
Willdenŏvīī, 11 . Purple . 7, S. De. Tw. . 1818

BEGŌNĪĀ.
acerifŏlīā . . . .    S. Ev. S. Brasil . 1829
Barkěrī . . . White . 1, G. Her. P. Mexico . 1837
castaneifŏlīā . . .    S. Ev. S. . 1838
Dregīī . . . .    S. Ev. S. . 1838
fagifŏlīā . . . .    S. Ev. S. . 1838
Meyěrī . . . .    S. Ev. S. . 1838
parvifŏlīā . . . White . 5, S. Ev. S. . 1836
Sellŏvīī . . . White . 9, S.
sinuātā . . . White . 6, S. Ev. S. . 1836
vitifŏlīā . . . White . 8.

BELLĪS.
integrifŏlīā . . Wht. pksh. 7, H.    A. Texas . 1834

BELLĪŬM.
intermēdīūm . . White . 8, H. Her. P.

BELŌNĪĀ, *Carmichael.* From *belone*, a needle; in allusion to the acicular filaments. *Linn.* 24, Or. 7, Nat. Or. *Algæ.* Found on decaying marine Algæ —*torulōsā.*

BERBĒRĪS.
floribūndā . . . .    H. Ev. S. Nepal . .

---

mītīs . . . .    H. Ev. S. N. Amer. . 1834
virgātā . . . Yellow . H. Ev. S. Peru . . 1836
vulgārīs
  dŭlcīs . . . Yellow . 5, H. Ev. S. Austria . .

BESSĒRĀ, *Schults.* Named after Dr. Besser, Professor of Botany at Brody, and author of an enumeration of the plants of Volhynia, Podolia, &c. *Linn.* 17, Or. 3, Nat. Or. *Liliaceæ.* These plants require to be grown in a mixture of peat and sand, to be liberally supplied with water, and kept perfectly dry and cool when the leaves wither and fall off, until next season. They are propagated by offsets. *Synonyme*: 1. *Pharium fistulosum.*

ělěgāns . . . Scarlet . 9, G. Bl. P. Mexico . .
fistulōsūm, 1 . Pur. wht. 9, G. Bl. P. Mexico . 1831

BETCKĒĀ, *Decandolle.* In honour of M. Betcke, who has described many species of *Valerianella. Linn.* 3, Or. 1, Nat. Or. *Valerianaceæ.* The seeds only require to be sown in the open ground in May, in a sheltered situation.

mājŏr . . . . . 8, H.    A. . 1836
samolifŏlīā . . . . 7, H.    A. Chile . .

BETŌNĪCĀ.
serŏtīnā . . . Red . 8, H. Her. P. Austria . 1832

BETŬLĀ. *Synonymes*: 1. *Betula urticifolia.* 2. *B. laciniata.* 3. *B. pendula.*

albā
  fŏlīīs variegātīs Apetal . 5, H. De. T.
  urticifŏlīā, 1 . Apetal . 5, H. De. T.
grandīs . . . . Apetal . H. De. T. N. Amer. . 1834
pallěscēns . . . Apetal . H. De. S.
papyrācēā
  platyphŷllā . . Apetal . 6, H. De. T.
  trichocládā . . Apetal . 6, H. De. T.
populifŏlīā
  laciniātā, 2 . . Apetal . 7, H. De. T.
  pěndŭlā, 3 . . Apetal . 7, H. De. T.
Scopŏlīī . . . Apetal . H. De. S.

BIDĒNS.
coronātā . . . . . 8, H.    B. . 1829
serrulātā . . . . . 8, H.    B. . 1829

BIFRENĀRĪĀ.
longicŏrnīs . . . Or. brn. . 8. Epi. Demerara . .

BIGNŌNĪĀ.
adenophŷllā . . . .    8. Ev. T. E. Ind. . 1832
serrulātā . . . .    8. Ev. T. E. Ind. . 1832

BILLARDIĒRĀ.
daphnoĭdēs . . Yel. pur. . G.   S.

BISCUTELLĀ—*longifŏlīā.*

BLĒCHNŬM.
angustifŏlīūm . . Brown . 7, S. Her. P. W. Ind. . .
hastātūm . . . Brown . 7, S. Her. P. Chile . .

BLĒTĪĀ.
Parkinsōnī . . . Rose . 1, S. Ter. Mexico . 1838

BOERHAĀVĪĀ.
mutābīlīs . . . . . 10, S.    P. N. Holl. . 1821

BOLBOPHŸLLŬM.
apifěrūm . . . Drk. red. . 5, S. Epi. Gambia R. . 1835
fūscūm . . . . Chocol. . 8. Epi. S. Leone . .

BOLĒTŬS—*cālōpūs, laricīnūs.*

BŎNĀ.
scirpoĭdēs . . .

BOSSIĒĀ, *Ventenat.* In honour of M. Bossieu Lamartinière, a French botanist, who accompanied the unfortunate La Peyrouse round the world. *Linn.* 16, Or. 6, Nat. Or. *Leguminosæ.* The species are neat, elegant plants when in flower, and will thrive best in a mixture of turfy loam, peat, and sand; but care must be taken that the pots are well drained, as nothing injures them more than too much water. Cuttings of the half-ripened wood will strike, if planted in a pot of sand, under a glass.

buxifŏlīā . . . Yellow . 5, G. Ev. Tr. N. Holl. . 1824
ciněrēā . . . . Yellow . 6, G. Ev. S. V. D. L. . 1802
cordifŏlīā . . . Yellow . 5, G. Ev. S. N. Holl. . 1820
ensātā . . . . Yellow . 5, G. Ev. S. N. Holl. . 1824
eriocārpā . . . .    K. G. S. . 1837
foliŏsā . . . . Yellow . 5, G. Ev. S. N. Holl. . 1824
heterophŷllā . . Yellow . 9, G. Ev. S. N. S. N. . 1792
lenticulārīs . . Yellow . 6, G. Ev. S. N. Holl. . 1823
linophŷllā . . . Yellow . 8, G. Ev. S. N. Holl. . 1803
microphŷllā . . Orange . 8, G. Ev. S. N. Holl. . 1803
prostrātā . . . Yellow . 7, G. Ev. S. N. S. W. . 1803

| | | | | | |
|---|---|---|---|---|---|
| rhombifóliă | . | Yellow | . 5, G. Ev. S. | N. Holl. | . 1820 |
| rotundifóliă | . | Yellow | . 5, G. Ev. S. | N. Holl. | . 1824 |
| rúfă | . | Orange | . 8, G. Ev. S. | N. Holl. | . 1803 |
| Scolopēndriŭm | . | Yellow | . 6, G. Ev. S. | N. S. W. | . 1792 |

BOTRYADĒNIĂ, *Fischer and Meyer.* From *botrys*, a cluster, and *aden*, an acorn. *Linn.* 19, Or. —, Nat. Or. *Compositæ.*

| | | | |
|---|---|---|---|
| Gmēlini | . . . | H. Her. P. Russia . | . 1836 |

BŌTRŸTĬS—*cānă, cinērĕă, crustōsă, grisĕă, lateritiă, vēră, vulgāris.*
BOUVĀRDIĂ.

| | | | | |
|---|---|---|---|---|
| angustifóliă | . | Red | . 9, S. Ev. S. | Mexico . . 1838 |
| splēndēns | . . | Scarlet | . 9, G. Ev. S. | |

BOVĪSTĂ—*plŭmbĕă.*
BRACHYGLŌTTĬS, *Forster.* From *brachys*, short, and *glottis*, a tongue. *Linn.* 19, Or. —, Nat. Or. *Compositæ.*

| | | | |
|---|---|---|---|
| repāndă | . ., . | | F. Ev. S. N. Zeal. . 1834 |

BRACHYPŌDIŬM—*māximŭm, mexicānŭm.*
BRASSĀVŌLĂ.

| | | | | |
|---|---|---|---|---|
| cuspidātă | . . | White | . . S. Epi. | Trinidad . 1838 |
| glaŭcă | . . | | . . S. Epi. | Vera Cruz . |
| grandiflōră | . . | White | . . S. Epi. | Honduras . |
| Martiāuă | . . | White | . . S. Epi. | Berbice . |
| venōsă | . . | White | . . S. Epi. | Honduras . |

BRĀSSIĂ.

| | | | | |
|---|---|---|---|---|
| cochleātă | . . | Grn. brn. | . 5, S. Epi. | Demerara . 1834 |
| Lanceānă | | | | |
| viridiflōră | . | Green | . 9, S. Epi. | Demerara . |
| verrucōsă | . | Grn. yel. | . S. Epi. | |

BRĀSSĬCĂ—*chinēnsis.*
BRAVŌĂ, *Llex. Linn.* —, Or. —, Nat. Or. ? *Zingiberaceæ.* W. B. Booth, whom Dr. Lindley quotes in describing this plant, makes the following remarks with regard to it. "The plant, from which the above description was made, was cultivated in the stove, but I have since found that others grown in a warm greenhouse succeeded equally well, and had their flowers quite as high-coloured. They seem to thrive in a light rich loam, and not too much water. I suspect it will ripen seeds, and by them be easily increased." It is a beautiful quasi-bulbous plant.

| | | |
|---|---|---|
| geminiflōră | . . . | Mexico . . |

BRŌMŬS—*Schrādēri, Willdenōvii.*
BRŌSIMŬM.

| | | | |
|---|---|---|---|
| microcārpŭm | . . | S. Ev. S. | . 1838 |

BROUGHTŌNIĂ.

| | | | |
|---|---|---|---|
| aūreă | . . . | Yel. red . | Mexico . . |

BROUSSONĒTIĂ.

| | | | |
|---|---|---|---|
| papyrífĕră | | | |
| frūctŭ-ālbŏ | . | Apetal | . 8, H. De. T. |

BRUGMĀNSIĂ.

| | | | |
|---|---|---|---|
| suavēŏlēns | | | |
| flāvă | . . . | Sulphur | . 8, S. Ev. T. |

BRYŌPSĬS—*hypnoīdēs.*
BRŸŬM—*affinĕ, albicāns, Ludwigĭi, punctātŭm, aquāticŭm.*
BUCHNĒRĂ.

| | | | | |
|---|---|---|---|---|
| cuneifóliă | . . . | | . 9, G. Ev. S. | C. G. H. . 1821 |

BULBĪNĔ.

| | | | | |
|---|---|---|---|---|
| floribūndă | . . | Yel. grn. | . 9, G. Bl. P. | . 1836 |

BUPLEŬRŬM.

| | | | |
|---|---|---|---|
| multinērvĕ | . . | Yellsh. | . H. Her. P. Altai. . . |
| prostrātŭm | . . | Yellsh. | . 7, H. Tw. A. |

*altāicŭm.*
BURLINGTŌNIĂ.

| | | | | |
|---|---|---|---|---|
| maculātă | . . | Yel. red | . 5, S. Epi. | Brazil . 1837 |
| venŭstă | . . | White | . 3, S. Epi. | Brazil . . |

BURRIĒLIĂ, *Decandolle.* So named by him in honour of John Mark Burriel, who published, in 1758, the journey of Venegas into California. *Linn.* 19, Or. 2, Nat. Or. *Compositæ.* "It is a hardy annual, flowering in the summer months, and recommending itself by its copious yellow blossoms."—*Bot. Mag.*

| | | | |
|---|---|---|---|
| grācĭlis | . . . | Yellow | . 7, H. A. Californ. . |

BŬXŬS.

| | | | | |
|---|---|---|---|---|
| sempervírēns | | | | |
| arborēscēns | . | Yel. grn. | . 5, H. Ev. T. | Britain . . |
| argēntĕă | . | Yel. grn. | . 5, H. Ev. T. | Britain . . |

| | | | | |
|---|---|---|---|---|
| aūreă | . . | Yel. grn. | . 5, H. Ev. T. | Britain . . |
| myrtifóliă | . . | Yel. grn. | . 5, H. Ev. S. | |
| variegātă | . . | Yel. grn. | . 5, H. Ev. T. | Britain . . |

CÆNŌPTĔRĬS.

| | | | | |
|---|---|---|---|---|
| myriophylla | . | Brown | . 12, S. Her. P. | W. Ind. . |
| rhizophylla | . | | . S. Her. P. | |
| thalictroīdēs | . | Brown | . 9, S. Her. P. | Jamaica . |

CALADĒNIĂ.

| | | | |
|---|---|---|---|
| clavígĕră | . . . | S. Tu. P. | N. S. W. . |
| dilatātă | . . . | S. Tu. P. | N. S. W. . |
| grācĭlis | . . . | S. Tu. P. | N. S. W. . |
| longicaŭdă | . . | Yellow | S. Ter. Swan R. . |
| Patersōnii | . . . | S. Tu. P. | N. S. W. . |

CALĀDIŬM.

| | | | | |
|---|---|---|---|---|
| petiolātŭm | . . | White | . 6, S. Tu. P. | Fernando . 1832 |

CALĀNTHĔ.

| | | | | |
|---|---|---|---|---|
| australĭs | . . . | | S. Her. P. | N. S. W. . 1823 |
| flāvicāns | . . | Wht. blue | 4, S. Ter. | . 1838 |

CALICIŬM—*æruginōsŭm, cærulēscēns, sphærocĕphālŭm crustāsŭm, stigonēllŭm, marginātŭm.*
CALLIŌPSĬS.

| | | | | |
|---|---|---|---|---|
| Drummōndii | . . | Yel. red | . 9, H. | A. . 1835 |

CALOSTĒMMĂ.

| | | | | |
|---|---|---|---|---|
| cārneŭm | . . | Flesh | . G. Bl. P. | Australia . |
| Cunninghāmi | . . | | . 6, G. Bl. P. | Moreton B. . |

CALŌTHRĬX—*Berkeleyānă, cæspĭtōsă, hypnoīdēs, interrūpĭă, Mūcŏr, rufēscēns.*
CALYCĀNTHŬS.

| | | | |
|---|---|---|---|
| flōrĭdŭs | | | |
| asplenifóliŭs | . | Brown | . 7, H. De. S. |
| fērāx | . . . | Brown | . 7, H. De. S. |
| glaŭcŭs | . . . | Brown | . 7, H. De. S. |
| inodōrŭs | . . | Brown | . 7, H. De. S. |
| longifóliŭs | . . | Brown | . 7, H. De. S. |
| oblōngŭs | . . | Brown | . 7, H. De. S. |
| ovātŭs | . . | Brown | . 7, H. De. S. |
| variegātŭs | . . | Brown | . 7, H. De. S. |

CALŸTHRĬX.

| | | | |
|---|---|---|---|
| aūreă | . . . | Brt. yel. | . G. Ev. S. Swan R. . |

CAMARŌTĬS, *Lindley.* Probably from *camera*, a vault; in reference to the chambered lip. *Linn.* 20, Or. 1, Nat. Or. *Orchidaceæ.* This pretty and interesting plant formed a part of the collection brought to this country by Mr. Gibson in 1837, and may be successfully cultivated in a warm and humid atmosphere, placed on a sound, rough block of wood, with the bases of its lower roots protected by moss. Shading must be duly attended to.

| | | | | |
|---|---|---|---|---|
| purpūreă | . . | Pa. pur. | . 5, S. Epi. | Khoseea . 1837 |

CAMELĪNĂ.

| | | | | |
|---|---|---|---|---|
| lāxă | . . . | Yellow | . 6, H. | A. Caucasus . 1837 |

CAMĒLLIĂ.

| | | | |
|---|---|---|---|
| japōnică | | | |
| elātă | . . | Brt. crim. | . G. Ev. S. |
| Epsomēnsis | . | Deep red | . 5, G. Ev. S. Seedling . |
| Knightii | . | Scarlet | . 5, G. Ev. S. Seedling . |
| Mārthă | . | Bh. pk. stri. | 5, G. Ev. S. Seedling . |
| Susānnă | . | Wht. pk. stri. | 5, G. Ev. S. Seedling . |
| Wadisānă | . | White | . 5, G. Ev. S. Seedling . |

CAMPĀNŬLĂ.

| | | | | |
|---|---|---|---|---|
| glomerātă | | | | |
| alba elātă | . | White | . 6, H. Her. P. | Hybrid . . |
| cærūleă elātă | . | Blue | . 6, H. Her. P. | Hybrid . . |
| flōrĕ plēnŏ pur-<br>pūreŏ | } | Pa. pur. | . 6, H. Her. P. | Gardens . |
| lilacĭnă | . . | Lilac | . 6, H. Her. P. | Hybrid . . |
| pallĭdă | . . | Pa. yel. | . 6, H. Her. P. | Hybrid . . |
| latifóliă | | | | |
| macrānthă | . | Lilac | . 7, H. Her. P. | Hybrid . . 1834 |
| mēdiă | | | | |
| purpūreă | . | Purple | . 7, H. Her. P. | Germany . |
| rhomboīdĕă | | | | |
| rūbră | . | Rdsh. lil. | 7, H. Her. P. | Switzerl. . |
| rotundifóliă | | | | |
| flōrĕ plēnŏ | . | Blue | . 7, H. Her. P. | Gardens . |

CANDŌLLEĂ.

| | | | |
|---|---|---|---|
| Brunōnis | . . . | | Swan R. . 1837 |
| Hugĕlii | . . . | | Swan R. . 1837 |

CĀNNĂ.

| | | | | |
|---|---|---|---|---|
| glaŭcă | | | | |
| rūbrŏ-lūteă | . | Yel. red | . 8, S. Her. P. | Jamaica . 1834 |

CANTHARĪLLŬs—*lǣvis.*
CAPRIFŌLIŬM. *Synonyme:* 1. *C. balearicum.*

implexûm
  baleáricûm . . Cream . 8, S. Ev. Tw. Minorca .

CÁPSICÛM.
tomatifórmê . . .Whitish . 8. B.

CARAGÁNÂ.
frutéscêns
  angustifóliâ . Yellow . 5, H. Dʰ. S. Odessa . .
  latifóliâ . . . Yellow . 5, H. Dʰ. S.
pygmǽâ
  arenáriâ . . Yellow . 5, H. Ev. S.
Redôwsʰ II
  prǽcox . . . Yellow . 4, H. Ev. S.

CÁRÊX—frigidâ, nigrâ.

CÁSSIÂ.
Flindérsii . . . G. Ev. S. N. S. W. . 1818

CASSINÍÂ.
speciósâ . . . G. Her. P. N. S. W.

CASTÁNÊÂ.
vêscâ
  cochleátâ . .Green . 6, H. Dʰ. T.
  glaúcâ . . . Green . 6, H. Dʰ. T.

CASTILLÊJÂ.
serrátâ . . . Blue . 6, S. Ev. S. . 1829

CATASÊTÛM.
longifóliûm . . Brt. oran. . S. Epi. Demerara .
proboscidêûm . . . S. Epi. Sertao .
Russeliánûm . Green . S. Epi. Guatemal. .
tridentátûm
  viridiflórûm . Green . . S. Epi. Demerara .

CATHARÁNTHÛS. Synonyme: 1. Vinca rosea fol. variegatis.
rósêûs
  fol. variegátis, 1 Red wht. . 8, S. Ev. S. Gardens .

CÁTTLÊYÂ.
citrínâ . . . Citron . 4, S. Epi. Mexico . 1838
odoratíssimâ . . Rose pur. . S. Epi. Demerara . 1836
Skinnéri . . . Rose . 8, S. Epi. Guatemal. 1836
supérbâ . . . Purple . S. Epi. Guiana . 1838

CEANÔTHÛS.
azúrêûs
  flóre albô . White . 4, F. Ev. S.
pállidûs . . . Pa. blue . F. Ev. S.

CEDRÊLÂ.
austrális . . . S. Ev. T. N. S. W. . 1823

CÊDRÛS.
Libáni
  fol. argéntêis . Apetal . 6, H. Ev. T.
  nánâ . . . Apetal . 6, H. Ev. S.

CENÁNGIÛM—fuliginôsûm, pulverácêûm.
CENOCÓCCÛM, Fries. From kenos, empty, and kokkos,
  a berry. Linn. 24, Or. 9, Nat. Or. Fungi. Found
  in woods—C. geôphilûm.

CENTAÛRÊÂ.
púlchrâ . . . Blue vio. . H. A. N. India . 183-.

CENTROCÁRPHÂ. Synonyme: 1. Rudbeckia moschata.
moschátâ, 1 . . Yellow . 8. H. Her. P. N. Amer. .

CERÁMIÛM—affínê, cruciátûm, fasciculátûm, gracíl-
  limûm, granulátûm, lanôsûm, mesocárpûm, plûmûlâ
  mínûs, polyspêrmûm, pûmilûm, seminûdûm, spi-
  nôsûm, spongiôsûm, tripinnátûm, virgátûlûm.

CERÁSTIÛM. Synonyme: 1. C. collínûm.
glomerátûm . . . H. A.
Ledeboûrii . . White . 6, . . 1837
macrocárpûm . . . H. A. Siberia .
microspérmûm . . . H. A.
purpuráscêns, 1 White . 7, H. Ev. Tr. . 1831
Scaráni . . . White . 7, H. Ev. Tr. Naples .

CÊRASÛS.
Laurocérasûs
  angustifóliâ . White . 5, H. Ev. S.
  variegátâ . . White . 5, H. Ev. S.
serótínâ
  retûsâ . . . 6, H. Dʰ. T. S. Amer. .

CÊRCIS.
canadénsis
  pubéscêns . Pa. red . 6, H. Dʰ. T.
Siliquástrum
  rósêûm . . . Red . 6, H. Dʰ. T. Seedling .

CÊRÊÛS. Synonymes: 1. Epiphyllum splendidum, E.
  Hitchens.
Mallisóni . . . S. Ev. Tr. Eng. hyb. . 1830
speciosíssimûs
  laterítîûs . . Brick red. 8, S. Ev. S. Eng. hyb. . 1831
splendidûs, 1 . Scarlet . 9, G. Ev. S. Mexico . 1831

CEROPÊGIÂ.
vineæfóliâ . . Grnh. wht. 9, S. Ev. Tw. Bombay .

CHÆTÓPHÔRÂ—Berkelêyi, longǽvâ.
CHÁRÂ—Hedwigii, híspidâ, grácilis.

CHEILÁNTHÊS.
dicksoniôidês . . Brown . 8, S. Her. P.
macrophýllâ . . Brown . 8, S. Her. P. W. Ind.
micróptêris . . Brown . 9, S. Her. P. . 1838
profúsâ . . . Brown . 9, S. Her. P.
rúfâ . . . . Reh. brn. . S. Her. P. W. Ind.
ruféscêns . . Brown . 9, S. Her. P. . 1838
sinuôsâ . . . Brown . 8, S. Her. P. W. Ind.
tenuifóliâ . . Brown . 9, S. Her. P. Ceylon . .

CHEIRÁNTHÛS.
Cheiri
  hæmánthûs variegátûs Blood 6, F. Ev. S. S. Eur. . gard.
  purpúrêûs . . . . Purple 6, S. Ev. S. S. Eur. . gard.
  purp. variegátûs . . Purple 6, F. Ev. S. S. Eur. . gard.

CHEIRÔSTÝLIS, Lindley. Linn. 20, Or. 1, Nat. Or.
  Orchidaceæ. "This interesting, but inconspicuous
  plant, was obtained by Messrs. Loddiges from
  Ceylon." In general aspect it is said to be like a
  minute Goodyera, but differs from that genus in
  several particulars.
parvifóliâ . . . White . . S. Epi. Ceylon . . 1837

CHELIDÔNIÛM.
mâjûs
  flóre plênô . Yellow . 9, H. Her. P. Gardens .

CHELÔNE.
barbátâ
  mâjôr . . . Oran. scar. 7, H. Her. P.
speciósâ . . . Pa. red . 8, H. Her. P. N. Amer. .

CHIONÁNTHÛS.
virgínicâ
  angustifóliâ . White . 6, H. Dʰ. T.
  latifóliâ . . White . 6, H. Dʰ. T. Carolina . 1736

CHLÔRÂ.
serótínâ . . . Yellow . 11, H. A. . 1832

CHLORǼÂ, Lindley. From chloros, green; in allusion
  to the hue of the flower. Linn. 20, Or. 1, Nat. Or.
  Orchidaceæ. "This species is the first of this interesting genus that has been introduced into England.
  It was brought from Valparaiso by Mr. Crook in
  1837, and flowered for the first time in the stove of
  W. I. Myers, Esq., of Aigburgh, near Liverpool."
  —Gard. Mag.
longibracteátâ . . Wht. yel. . 9, S. Epi. Chile . . 1837

CHLORÁNTHÛS.
elátiôr . . . . Yellow . 7, S. Ev. S. China . . 1804

CHÔNDRIÂ—pinnatífidâ angûstâ, Osmûndâ.
CHORÊTIS, Herbert. From choretes, rustic. Linn. 6,
  Or. 1, Nat. Or. Amaryllidaceæ. "This is a very
  beautiful, bulbous-rooted plant, with a flower
  greatly resembling that of Ismene, from which
  genus Choretis has been lately divided by the
  Hon. and Rev William Herbert. C. glauca is a
  native of Oaxaca in Mexico, whence it was imported by George Barker, Esq., of Springfield, near
  Birmingham."—Gard. Mag.
glaúcâ . . . . White . 8, S. Bl. P. Mexico . . 1837

CHOROZÊMÂ.
Dicksónii . . . Scar. yel. 7, G. Ev. S. Swan R. . 1836
váriûm . . . . Or. crim. . 6, G. Ev. S. Swan R. . 1837

CHROÔLÊPÛS—Arnôttii, mesômêlâs.
CHRYSÊIS. Synonyme: 1. Eschscholtzia fumariæfolia.
fumariæfóliâ, 1 . Yellow . 9, H. Tu. P. Mexico . . 1837

CÍCÊR.
punctátûm . . . . 7, H. A. . 1830

CINERÁRIÂ. Synonyme: 1. Senecio racemosus.
auriculátâ, 1 . . Yellow . 8, H. Her. P. . 1831

CIRRHǼÂ. Synonyme: 1. C. fusco-lutea.
saccátâ, 1 . . . Yel. grn. . 8, S. Epi. Brazil . . 1834

CIRRHOPÊTÂLÛM.
fimbriátûm . . . Grn. pur. . S. Epi. Bombay . .
nútâns . . . Pa. straw . S. Epi. Manilla . .
Wallichii . . . . S. Epi. Nepal . .

CÍRSIÛM.
Gmélini . . . Purple . 8, H. Her. P. Russia . .
mexicánûm . . . White . 9, G. B. Mexico . 1837
rhizocéphalûm . Pa. yel. . . H. Her. P. Caucasus . 1836

CISTŬS.
lusitānĭcŭs . . Yellow . 9, H. Ev. S. Portugal . 1830
salvĭfōlĭŭs
erectĭŭscūlŭs . White . 6, H. Ev. S.
ochroleŭcŭs . Yellͦh . 6, H. Ev. S.

CLĀRKĬĀ.
ēlĕgāns
flōrē plēnō . . Pa. rose . 9, H. A. Gardens .

CLAVĀRĬĀ—grĭsĕă, rōsĕă.

CLAYTŌNĬĀ.
cālĭfōrnĭcă

CLEISOSTŌMĂ.
maculōsă . . Yelͦh. pk. . S. Epi. Ceylon . .

CLĔMĀTĬS. Synonymes: 1. C. cœspitosa, Flammula.
2. C. bicolor. 3. C. Hendersoni. 4. C. tenuifolia
lusitanica.
Flāmmŭlă
cœspĭtōsă, 1 . White . 9, H. De. Cl.
rŭbĕllă . . Reddish . 9, H. De. Cl.
flōrĭdă
Sĭebōldĭī, 2 . Pur. grn. 6, H. De. Cl. Japan . 1836
ĭntĕgrĭfōlĭă
lātĭfōlĭă . . Purple . 7, H. Her. P.
lathyrĭfōlĭă . White . 7, H. Her. P.
nĕpalēnsĭs, 3 . . 5, H. Ev. Cl. Nepal . 1835
Vītĭcĕllă
tĕnŭĭfōlĭă, 4 . Crimson . 8, G. Ev. Cl.

CLĔŎMĒ.
dendroīdēs . . Purple . G. Ev. S. Brazil . 1823

CLĒTHRĂ.
mexicānă . . . H. Ev. S. Mexico .

CLĬTĂNTHĔS, Herbert. From klitus, a mountainous
declivity, and anthos, a flower. A new genus of
Amaryllidaceœ.
hūmĭlĭs . . . Cordilleras .
lātĕă
Maclĕānĭcă

COHĀĒ.
macrostēmmă . Grn. yel. G. Ev. Cl. Guayaquil 1839
stĭpulārĭs . . Yellow . F. Ev. Cl. Mexico

CODONŎPSĬS, Wallich. From kodon, a bell, and opsis,
resemblance; in reference to the shape of the
flowers. Linn. 5, Or. 1, Nat. Or. Campanulaceœ.
A mixture of sand and loam will probably suit this
plant, and propagation may be effected by cuttings
or seeds.
lūrĭdă . . . Grn. pur. H. A. India . 1837

CŎLCHĬCŬM.
autumnālĕ
atropurpūrĕŭm . . Dk. pur. 9, H. Bl. P. Brit. gard. .
purpūrĕŭm strĭātŭm Pur. strͪ. 9, H. Bl. P. Brit. gard. .
strĭātŭm plēnō . . Lil. strͪ. 9, H. Bl. P. Brit. gard. .

COLĔONĔMĂ.
pūlchrŭm . . Rose . 6, G. Ev. S. C. G. H. .

COLLĒMĂ—ceranoīdēs, dermātīnŭm, frăgĭlē, līmōsŭm,
microphȳllŭm, synallæsŭm, tunæfōrmĕ, tūrgĭdŭm.

COLLŎMĬĂ.
gĭlĭoīdēs . . Pink . 8, H. A. California 1833
glutĭnōsă . . . 9, H. A. California 1833

COLOGĀNĬĂ.
pulchĕllă . . Rose . 9, G. De. Tw. Mexico . 1837

CŎMĂRŬM.
palūstrĕ
variegātŭm . Purple . 7, H. Her. P. Brit. gard. .

COMMĔLĪNĂ—clandestīnă, orchioīdēs.

COMMĬPHŎRĂ, Jacquin. From kommi, gum, and phero,
to bear. Linn. 20, Or. 1, Nat. Or. Orchidaceœ.
madagascărĭēnsĭs . . . Madagas. . 1820

COMPARĔTTĬĂ.
falcātă . . . Rose . S. Epi. Mexico . 1836

CONFĔRVĂ—arenōsă, grăcĭlĭs, nūdă, purpurāscēns.
CONŎSTȲLĬĂ.
jūncĕă . . . . G. Her. P. N. Holl.
setōsă . . . Yellow . F. Her. P. Swan R. .

CONȲZĂ.
chĭlēnsĭs . . . H. A. Chile . 1828

COOPĔRĬĂ. Synonymes: 1. Zephyranthes Drummondi,
Sceptranthus Drummondi.
peduncŭlātă, 1 . White . . S. Bl. P. Texas . 1835

COPRĪNŬS—Hendersōnĭ, macrocĕphălŭs, macrorhīzĕs.
CORDYLĪNĒ.
austrālĭs . . . Norf. Ia. . 1837

CŎRNŬS. Synonymes: 1. Cornus stricta asperifolia,
asperifolia. 2. C. oblongifolia.
albă
sĭbīrĭcă . . White . 8, H. De. S. Siberia . 1824
grāndĭs . . . Mexico . .
mă̄cŭlă
fr. cĕrĕă . . Yellow . 8, H. De. S.
sĕrĭcĕă
asperĭfōlĭă, 1 . White . H. De. S. S. Carol.
oblongĭfōlĭă, 2 . White . H. De. S.
strĭctă
asperĭfōlĭă . White . 8, H. De. S. N. Amer.
sempervīrēns . White . 6, H. De. S.

CORRĒĂ.
bĭcŏlŏr . . Wht. cr. G. Ev. S. Hybrid .
Harrĭsĭī . . Crimson . 5, G. Ev. S. Hybrid .
longĭflōră . . Rose cld. G. Ev. S. Hybrid .

CORYĂNTHĔS.
spĕcĭōsă
albă . . . White . S. Epi. Demerara . 1840

CORȲDĀLĬS.
flavŭlă

CŎRȲLŬS. Synonymes: 1. Corylus Lamberti. 2. C.
sativa alba, C. alba. 3. C. intermedia.
Avellānă
Lambĕrtī, 1 . Apetal . 8, H. De. S.
purpūrĕă . . Apetal . 8, H. De. S.
tĕnŭĭs . . Apetal . 8, H. De. S.
tubulōsă ălbă, 2 Apetal . 8, H. De. S.
Colūrnă
intermĕdĭă, 3 . Apetal . 4, H. De. T. Hybrid . .

CORȲNĔŬM—macrospōrĭŭm.
CŎSMĒĂ.
dĭversĭfōlĭă . . Pink . 8, F. Tu. P. Mexico . 1835

COTONĔĂSTĔR.
buxĭfōlĭă . . . H. Ev. S. Neelgh. . 1824
denticŭlātă . White . . H. Ev.? T. Mexico .
unĭflōră . . . H. De. S.

CŎTŬLĂ.
fĭlĭfōlĭă . . . 8, G. A. C. G. H. . 1831
pusĭllă.

COTYLĔDŎN. Synonymes: 1. Umbilicus Lievenii. 2. U.
sempervivum.
Lĭevĕnĭī, 1 . Red . 5, F. Her. P. Altaia . 1832
Sempervīvŭm, 2 . . 6, F. Her. P. Caucasus . 1836

COUSĬNĬĂ, Meyer. In honour of Cousin, a French
botanist. Linn. 19, Or. —, Nat. Or. Compositœ.
cynaroīdēs . . White . H. B. Caucasus .
hystrĭx . . . 6, H. Her. P. Russia . 1838
macrocĕphălă . Pa. yel.

CRĂMBĒ.
jūncĕă . . . White . 5, H. Tu. P. Iberia . 1828

CRATĒŎŬS. Synonymes: 1. Cratœgus apiifolia. 2.
Mespilus constantinopolitana. 3. Cratœgus macracantha. 4. C. subvillosa. 5. C. orientalis. 6. C.
sibirica, C. monogyna. 7. C. edulis. 8. C. stricta.
9. C. virginiana.
apĭĭfōlĭă
mĭnŏr, 1 . . White . 5, H. De. S.
coccĭnĕă
neapolĭtānă, 2 . . 5, H. Ev. T. Naples .
glandŭlōsă . . White . 6, H. De. T. N. Amer. . 1750
macracănthă, 3 White . 6, H. De. T. N. Amer. . 1819
mĭnŏr . . White . 5, H. De. T. N. Amer.
subvĭllōsă, 4 . White . . H. De. T. . 1832
succŭlēntă . . . H. De. T. Germany .
orientālĭs
sanguĭnĕă, 5 . White . 5, H. De. T. Crimea . 1810
oxyacănthă
apĕtălă . . Apetal . 5, H. De. T.
aurantĭăcă . White . 5, H. De. T.
capĭtătă . . White . 5, H. De. T.
Celsĭānă . . White . 5, H. De. T.
flexŭōsă . . White . 5, H. De. T.
fol. argentĕă . White . 5, H. De. T.
fol. aūrĕĭs . . White . 5, H. De. T.
leucocarpă . White . 5, H. De. T. Britain .
lūcĭdă . . White . 5, H. De. T.
pēndŭlă . . White . 5, H. De. T. Hybrid .
purpūrĕă . . . H. De. T. Eng. hyb.
quercĭfōlĭă . White . 6, H. De. T. Hamb. . 1834
regĭnæ . . White . 5, H. De. T. Scotland .
sĭbīrĭcă, 6 . . White . 5, H. De. T. Siberia .

transylvánicā . White . . ð, H. De. T. Transylv. .
punctātā
  brevispinā . . White . . ð, H. Ev. T. N. Amer. .
  rūbrā, 7. . . White . . ð, H. De. T. N. Amer. .
  rūbrā strictā, 8 White . . ð, H. De. T. N. Amer. .
  virginiēā, 9. . White . . ð, H. De. S. Virginia . . 1812
CRATĒRIŪM—mutābīlē, pyrifōrmē.
CRĒPĪS—multicaūlīs, pōntīcā.
CRIBRĀRIĀ—intermēdiā.
CROTALĀRIĀ.
undulātā . . . Yellow . . G. Ev. S. Mexico . .
CRUCIANĒLLĀ.
  aspērā . . . Grnsh. yel. . H. Her. P. Iberia . . 1837
  gilānīcā . . . . . H. Her. P. Persia . .
  suaveolēns . . . . H. Her. P. Russia . . 1838
CRYPTĀNDRĀ.
  arbutiflōrā . . . . S. River . 1837
CŪPHĒĀ.
  silenoīdēs . . Bluish . 9, H. . A. . . 1836
CUPRĒSSŪS.
  Coultērī . . . Apetal . ð, H. De. S. Mexico . . 1838
  thyoīdēs
    fol. variegātā Apetal . ð, H. Ev. T. Ireland . . 1831
CURCŪMĀ.
  Roscoeānā . . Red yel. . S. Her. P. E. Ind. . 1837
CỸCLĀMĒN.
  persīcūm
    lilacēūm . . Lilac . . 3, G. Tu. P.
    punctātūm . . Wht. lil. . 3, G. Tu. P.
CYCNŌCHĒS.
  chlorochīlōn . . Green . . 6, S. Epi. Demerara . 1838
  maculātā . . . Yel. brn. . S. Epi.
CYCLOGỸNĒ, Bentham. Linn. —, Or. —, Nat. Or.
  Leguminosæ. A profuse flowering Swan River
  plant, whose blooms are highly beautiful. It is
  worthy of a place in every collection.
  canēscēns . . . Purple . ð, . Swan R. .
CYDŌNIĀ.
  japōnīcā
    fl. semī-plēnō . Red . . 8, H. De. S.
CYMBĒLLĀ, Agardh. From cymba, a boat; in reference
  to the shape of the pustules. Linn. 24, Or. 7, Nat.
  Or. Algæ. Small yellowish plants, inhabiting
  marshy places—cymbifōrmīs, hyalīnā, minōr.
CYMBĪDIŪM.
  bicōlōr . . . Brn. crim. . S. Epi. Ceylon . .
  iridifōliūm . . Fuscous . S. Epi.
  pendūlūm . . . Velsh. brn. . S. Epi. Sylhet . 183-.
CYNOGLŌssŪM.
  cælestinūm . . Wht. blue 8, H. . B. India . . 1837
  glochidiātūm . . Blue . . H. . A. India . . 1837
CYPĒRŪS.
  pygmǣīs . . . Apetal . 9, S. Grass. E. Ind. . . 1829
CYPHĒLLĀ, Fries. From kyphellon, a cup. Linn. 24,
  Or. 9, Nat. Or. Fungi. This species is found on
  decayed grass—C. cuticulōsā.
CYPHONĒMĀ. Linn. —, Or. —, Nat. Or. Amaryllidaceæ.
  " A remarkable new genus, of which a live speci-
  men in flower has been sent to Spofforth by Mr.
  Loddiges, imported, as he states, from Valparaiso,
  being the first Cyrtanthiform plant found elsewhere
  than in South Africa."—Bot. Mag. A shade of
  doubt has been cast upon the fact of its being a
  native of the above-mentioned country, Messrs.
  Loddiges having had many Cape bulbs in the same
  house with those imported from Chili.
  Loddigesiānūm . Grn. strip. . S. Bl. P.
CYRTOCHILŪM.
  stellātūm . . . Grn. wht. 10, S. Epi. Brazil . .
CYRTOPŌDIŪM.
  Willmōrī . . . Grn. yel. . 6, S. Epi. Venez. . . 1834
CYTISPŌRĀ—carphospērmā, fūgāx, orbiculārīs, rūbēs-
  cēns.
CYTISŪS. Synonyme; 1. C. L. incīsūm.
  mōllēus
    flōrē plēnō . White . . ð, H. De. S. England .
    fol. variegātā . Yellow . . ð, H. De. S. Gardens .
  alpīnūs
    odorātūs . . . Yellow . . 6, H. De. T. Hybrid .
    pendūlūs . . . Yellow . . 6, H. De. T. Gardens .

[ 347 ]

Labūrnūm
  fol. variegātā . . Yellow . . ð, H. De. T.
  frāgrāns . . . . Yellow . . ð, H. De. T. Gardens .
  pendūlūm . . . Yellow . . ð, H. De. T.
  quercifōliūm, 1 Yellow . . ð, H. De. T.
  uralēnsīs . . . . . ð, H. De. S. Russia . . 1832
Weldēnī . . . Yellow . . H. De. T.

DACRỸMỸCĒS—violācēns.
DACTỸLIŪM, Nees. From daktylos, a finger. Linn.
  24, Or. 9, Nat. Or. Fungi. Found on the moulder-
  ing stems of herbaceous plants—D. pyrifērūm.
DÆDĀLĒĀ—Bulliārdī.
DĀHLIĀ.
  Barkērīā . . . Bluish . 8, H. Tu. P.
  excelsā
    anemonæflōrā . Light . . 9, G. De. S. Mexico . . 1830
  glabrātā . . . Lilac . . 7, H. Her. P. Mexico . .
  scapigērā . . . White . . 6, H. Her. P. Mexico . . 1837
DĀPHNĒ.
  Cneōrūm
    fol. variegātā . Grn. yel. . ð, H. Ev. S.
  indīcā
    rūbrā . . . . Pur. pink . G. Ev. S.
  pōntīcā
    fol. variegātā . Pink . . 8, H. Ev. S.
  viridiflōrā . . . Green . . H. Ev. S. Nepal . . 1829
DAUBĒNYĀ.
  fulvā . . . . Yellow . . S. Bl. P. Africa . .
DAŪCŪS—sīcūlūs.
DAVIĒSIĀ.
  genistoīdēs . . . . G. Ev. S. N. Holl. .
DELESsĒRIĀ—Gmelīnī, lacerātā, uncīnātā.
DELPHINIŪM.
  decōrūm . . . . H. Her. P. Russia . . 1838
  discōlōr . . . Bl. wht. . 8, H. Her. P. Siberia . . 1834
  grandiflōrūm
    Hōlmī . . . Blue . . 8, H. Her. P. England .
    rūbrūm . . . Red pur. . 8, H. Her. P.
  moschātūm . . . Drk. blue 8, H. Her. P. Switzerl. . 1834
DENDRŌBIŪM.
  aūrēūm
    pallīdūm . . . White . . 8, S. Epi. Ceylon . .
  bicameratūm . . Yel. pur. . 8, S. Epi. Khosees . . 1837
  Cambridgeānūm . Yellow . . S. Epi. Khosees . . 1837
  easythoīdēs . . . Golden . . 9, G. Epi. P. Jacka. .
  Devoniānūm . . . . . . ð, S. Epi. E. Ind. . . 1837
  Heyneānūm . . . Wht. grn. . 8, S. Epi. Bombay . . 1838
  macrophyllūm . . Rose . . 8, S. Epi. Manilla . . 1838
  Paxtōnī . . . . Or. brn. . . 4, S. Epi. Khosees . . 1837
  plicatīlē . . . . Yel. red . 8, S. Epi. Manilla .
DENTĀRIĀ.
  dasylōbā . . . . H. Her. P. Russia . . 1838
DESVAŪXIĀ, R. Brown. In honour of N. Desvaux, a
  French botanist. Linn. —, Or. —, Nat. Or. Des-
  vauxiaceæ.
  Billardiēri . . . . S. A. N. Holl. . 1823
DEŪTZIĀ.
  corymbōsā . . . White . . H. Ev. S. Himalaya .
DIĀNTHŪS.
  barbātūs
    flōrē-plēnō . Wht. rose . 7. H. Her. P. Gardens .
DIATŌMĀ—aurītūm, brachygōnūm.
DICHÆĀ.
  ochracēā . . . . Yellow . . S. Epi. Demerara .
DICKSŌNIĀ.
  davallioīdēs . . . Brown . 9, S. Her. P. New Holl. .
  rubiginōsā . . . . . S. Her. P. Brazil . .
  scāndēns . . . . . S. Her. P.
DICRĀNŪM—flagellārē.
DICTYTĀ.
  bicōlōr . . . . Yel. blk. . 8, S. Epi. Demerara . 1834
  discōlōr . . . . Orange . . 8, S. Epi. Demerara .
  iridifōliā . . . . Yel. sp. . 8, S. Epi. Trinidad . 1835
DIDĒRMĀ, Persoon. From dis, double, and derma.
  skin; in allusion to the double peridium. Linn.
  24, Or. 9, Nat. Or. Fungi. Found on bark, moss,
  dead oak-leaves, &c.—D. Carmichaelīnūm, cyanēs-
  cēns, deplanātūm, nītēns, spumarioīdēs, umbilicātūm,
DIDYMIŪM—lobātūm, perīfūsūm, sērpūlā.
DIDYMOCHLÆNĀ, Desvaux. From didymos, double, and
  chlaina, cloak; indusium. Linn. 24, Or. 1, Nat. Or.

*Filices.* A very pretty fern, requiring the same treatment as other stove plants of its class.

pulchérrimă . . Brown . 7, S. Her. P. Brazil . .

DĬDỸMÓDŎN — *brachydŏntiŭs, capillācĕŭs, ĭthyphŷllŭs, crĭspŭlŭs, cỹlĭndrĭcŭs.*

DIGITALIS. *Synonyme:* 1. *Digitalis hybrida.*

Campbelliănă, 1 . Blue yel. 7, H. Her. P. England .

DĬLLWỸNĬĂ.

elavătă . . . Yellow . G. Ev. S. Swan R. .
glycinifòliă . . Or. rose . 4, G. Ev. S. N. Holl. . 1830
speciósă . . . Or. yel. . 6, G. Ev. S. Austral. . 1838

DĬPLĂZĬŬM.

acuminătŭm . . G. Her. P. Brazil . .

DĬPLOLĂENĂ, *Desfontaines.* From *diploos,* double, and *læna,* a cloak; in allusion to the double involucrum. *Linn.* —, Or. —, Nat. Or. *Rutaceæ.*

Dampiĕrĭ . . . G. Ev. S. Swan R. . 1837

DĬPLOPĔLTĬS, *Endlicher.* From *diploos,* double, and *pelte,* a buckler; the application is unknown to us. *Linn.* 23, Or. 1, Nat. Or. *Sapindaceæ.* This plant will probably require a similar treatment to Cape plants, such as *Hebenstreitius,* striking freely from cuttings of the young wood, and will bear to be planted in the open border during the summer season.

Hugelĭĭ . . . White . G. Her. P. Swan R. . 1837

DĬŬRĬĂ.

filifòliă . . . . Yellow . 8. Ter. Swan R. . .

DŎDŎNĂEĂ.

ceratocarpă . . G. Ev. S. K.G.S. . 1837

DŎŎDĬĂ.

máximă . . Brown . 8, S. Her. P. N. Holl.

DŎRŎNĬCŬM.

cordifòliŭm . . H. Her. P. Russia . 1838
macrophỹllŭm . Yellow . 7, H. Her. P. . 1828

DŎTHĬDĔĂ — *Fumāgŏ, Herāclĕĭ, Potentillæ, P. reptāntis, P. vērnæ, Ranūncŭlĭ.*

DRĂBĂ.

grandiflòră . . White . H. Her. P. Altai . 1832
stylaris . . . . H. Her. B. . 1832
tridentătă . . Yellow . 8, H. Her. P. Russia . 1838

DRACĂENĂ.

salicifòliă . . . S. Ev. T.

DRACOCĔPHĂLŬM.

mexicánŭm . . Blue . 7, H. Her. P. Mexico . 1832
pinnătŭm . . . Blue . . H. Her. P. Siberia . 1832

DRỸĂS.

octopĕtălă
   minŏr . . . White . 7, H. Ev. Tr.

ECHĔĂNDĬĂ, *Ortega.* "This singular plant was among a collection received by Sir Charles Lemon in 1837, from Mr. John Rule, superintendant of the Real del Monte Mines, Mexico, in the neighbourhood of which it is probably a native. It flowered in the greenhouse at Carclew in June 1839, and continued during July and August to send out a succession of five or six flowers daily. It promises to produce seeds, by which there is every chance of its being increased."—*Bot. Reg.*

terniflòră . . . Golden . 7, G. Her. P. Mexico . 1837

ECHĬNĂCĔĂ.

dúbiă . . . . Lilac . . 9, F. Tu. P. Mexico . 1837

ECHĬNĔLLĂ — *oblŏngă, rotātă.*

ECHĬNŎPS.

bannăticŭs
   albŭs . . . White . . 5, H. Her. B. Hungary . 1832
dahúricŭs . . Blue . . 8, H. Her. P. Dahuria . 1828
Gmelĭnĭ . . . Wht blue H. B. . 1835
platỹlĕpĭs . . . H. B. . 1835
púngĕns . . . H. B. Russia . 1835
Tournefórtiĭ . . H. B. Caucasus . 1835

ECTOCĂRPŬS — *distŏrtŭs.*

EDWĂRDSĬĂ.

Macnabiănă . . Yellow . G. Ev. S.

ELĂEĂGNŬS. *Synonyme:* 1. *Elæagnus spinosa.*

angustifòliă
   dactyliformĭs . . H. De. T.

spinòsă, 1 . .    H. De. T.
hortĕnsĭs . . . Yellow . 7, H. De. T. S. Eur. . . 1633

ELAPHŎMỸCĔĂ, *Nees.* From *elaphos,* a stag, and *mukes,* a fungus. *Linn.* 24, Or. 9, Nat. Or. *Fungi.* Found on dry heathy ground, &c.—*E. granulātŭs, muricātŭs.*

ELICHRỸSŬM. *Synonyme:* 1. *Gnaphalium arenarium.*

affĭnĕ, 1 . . . Pa. yel. . 8, S. Ev. S. C. G. H. .
macrănthŭm . . Blush . H. Her. P. Swan R. . 1837

EMPĔTRŬM.

nĭgrŭm
   scŏticŭm . . Apetal . 5, H. Ev. S. Scotland .

ENARTHROCĂRPŬS.

lyrătŭs . . . Yel. pur. 7, H. A. Alexand. . 1836

ENDOCĂRPŎN — *euplŏcŭm, lætevĭrĕns, macrocărpŏn, psoromoĭdĕs, pulchĕllŭm, rufo-virĕscĕns, rugòsŭm, sorediătŭm, sulphúrĕŭm.*

ENTEROMŎRPHĂ, *Link.* From *enteron,* entrail, and *morphe,* form; in reference to the appearance. *Linn.* 24, Or. 9, Nat. Or. *Fungi.* Found in pools and oceans—*E. cornucŏpĭæ, Linkiănă.*

EPĂCRĬS.

coccĭnĕă . . . Scarlet . 4, G. Ev. S. Seedling .
imprĕssă
   parviflòră . . Red . . 9, G. Ev. S. N. Holl. .

EPIDĔNDRŬM.

Candŏllĕĭ . . . . S. Epi.
cepifórmĕ . . Brn. yel. . 8, S. Epi. Mexico . 1838
cinnabarinŭm . Vermil. . 6, S. Epi. Pernambuco
coriácĕŭm . . Grn. pur. . 8, S. Epi. Demerara .
crispătŭm . . . 8, S. Epi. Mexico .
densiflòrŭm . . . 8, S. Epi. Mexico . 1839
glumácĕŭm . . Wht. pink. . 8, S. Epi. Brazil . 1838
incŭmbĕns . . . 8, S. Epi.
invĕrsŭm . . . Strw. cold. . 8, S. Epi. Brazil .
Parkinsoniănŭm . Grn. yel. . 8, S. Epi. Mexico .
Stamfordiănŭm . . 8, S. Epi. S. Amer. . 1840
virĭdi-purpŭrĕŭm . Pur. grn. . 9, S. Epi. Jamaica .
vitellinŭm . . Orange . 9, S. Epi. Mexico . 1839

EPILŎBĬŬM.

minútŭm . . . White . 8, H. Her. P. Russia . 1838

EPIMĔDĬŬM.

Musschiănŭm . White . 8, H. Her. P. Japan . 1836

EPIPHỸLLŬM.

Russelliănŭm . . Dp. pink . 5, S. Ev. S. Organ Mts. 1838
speciòsŭm
   Jenkinsŏnĭ . . Crimson . 5, S. Ev. S. Eng. hyb. .
   laterĭtiă . . . Red . . 6, S. Ev. S. Eng. hyb. .

EPITHĔCĬĂ, *Knowles and Westcott.* From *epitheke,* an appendage; in allusion to the shape of the flower. *Linn.* 20, Or. 1, Nat. Or. *Orchidaceæ.*

glaucă . . . . Grn. pur. . 6, S. Epi. Mexico . 1837

ĔRĬĂ.

bicòlŏr . . . White . . S. Epi. Ceylon .
ferruginĕă . . Pink grn. . 8, S. Epi. E. Ind. . 1837
planicaúlĭs . . . S. Epi. . 1838

ERĬCĂ.

arbŏrĕă
   minĭmă . . White . . 4, F. Ev. S. .
cinĕrĕă
   pallĭdă . . . Pa. pur. . 8, H. Ev. S. Britain . .
dichromătă . . Yel. pink 8, G. Ev. S. C. G. H. . 1800

ERĬGĔRŎN — *Synonyme:* 1. *Conyza altaica*—E. cilĭātŭs 1, *elongātŭs.*

ERIOCAÚLŎN.

sexangulărĕ . . White . 9, G. Aq. P. E. Ind. . 1819

ERIOSTĔMŎN.

glaucĕscĕns . . . G. Ev. S.

ERŎDĬŬM.

geifòliŭm . . . Lilac . . H. B. . 1835
pulverulĕntŭm . . Lilac . . H. B. Spain . .

ERUCĂRĬĂ.

pĕrsĭcă . . . . H. A. Persia . 1834

ERỸNGĬŬM.

macrophỹllŭm . . H. Her. P. . 1831

ERỸSĬMŬM.

Perofskiănŭm . . Brt. oran. 7, H. . 1838

ERỸSĬPHĔ — *maculārĭs, tŏrtĭlĭs.*

ERYTHRŌNĬŬM.
gigantēŭm . . .     H. Bl. P. N. Amer. .
EŬCALȲPTŬS.
alpīnā . . . .    H. De. S. V. D. L. . 1834
EŬŌNȲMŬS.
europēŭs
   latifolĭŭs . . White . . 6, H. De. S.
garciniæfolĭŭs . Pa. yel. . H. De. T. Nepal . . 1820
japōnĭcŭs
   maculātŭs . . Pink . 7, F. Ev. S. Japan . . 1836
   variegātŭs . . Pink . 7, F. Ev. S. Japan . . 1836
EŬPHŌRBĬA.
amygdal·ĭdēs
   variegātā . . Apetal . 4, H. Ev. S. Britain . .
dictyocārpŏn.
EŬRȲBĬA.
glutinōsā . . . Pa. vio. . G. Ev. S. V. D. L. .
EŬTŌCĂ.
viscĭdā . . . . Brn. rose . 7, H. . A. California . 1834
EXCĬPŬLĂ—strigōsā.
EYSENHĀRDTĬA, Kunth. In honour of Charles William
Eysenhardt, M.D., a professor in the University of
Königsberg, in Prussia. Linn 17, Or. 4, Nat. Or.
Leguminosæ. This shrub will thrive in a mixture
of loam and peat, and young cuttings will strike
root in sand, under a bell-glass, in heat.
amorphoīdēs . . Pa. yel. . G. Ev. S. Mexico . . 1837

FABĬĀNĂ, Ruiz and Pavon. In honour of Francisco
Fabiano, of Valencia in Spain, a promoter of botany.
Linn. 5, Or. 1, Nat Or. Solanaceæ. The soil adapted
to this pretty little shrub is peat and sand, and it
may be multiplied by cuttings or seed, in the same
manner as Cape heaths.
imbricātā . . . White . . G. Ev. S. Chili . .
FĀGŬS.
ferrugīnēā
   carolinĭānā . Apetal . H. De. T. Carolina .
sylvatĭcā
   cristātā . . . Apetal . 5, H. De. T.
   cŭprēā . . . Apetal . 5, H. De. T.
   fol. argentēā . Apetal . 5, H. De. T.
   fol. aŭrēā . . Apetal . 6, H. De. T.
   pēndŭlā . . . Apetal . 5, H. De. T.
FĒDĬA.
gibbōsā . . . . . 5, H. . A. . 1834
FĒNZLĬA, Bentham. In honour of Dr. Fenzl, author
of a monograph of Alsineæ. Linn. 5, Or. 1, Nat.
Or. Polemoniaceæ. For culture and propagation,
refer to Leptosiphon.
dianthiflōrā . . Pur. yel. . H. . A. Californ. . 1833
FERNĀNDĒZĬA.
lunīferā . . . . . S. Epi. Brazil . .
FĒRŬLĂ.
ammonĭācă . . White . 6, H. Her. P. Persia . . 1831
seacloīdēs.
FESTŬCĂ—geniculātā.
FRAGĬLĀRĬA—aūrēā, confervoīdēs, diatomoīdēs.
FRĀXĬNŬS. Synonyme: 1. Fraxinus nana.
americānā
   latifolĭā . . . Green . . 5, H. De. T.
excelsĭŏr
   aūrēā pēndŭlā Green . 4, H. De. T. Britain . .
   Kincairnĭæ . . Green . 4, H. De. T. Kincairney
heterophȳllā
   variegātā . . Green . 4, H. De. T. Ireland . . 1836
juglandĭfolĭā
   subintegērrĭmā Green . 5, H. De. T.
polemonĭfolĭā, 1 Green . 4, H. De. S. N. Amer. . 1812
pubēscens
   longĭfolĭā . . Green . 5, H. De. T.
quadrangulātā
   nervōsā . . . Green . 5, H. De. T.
FRITĬLLĀRĬA.
imperialĭs
   aurāntĭā . . Or. red . 4, H. Bl. P. Gardens .
   flavā-plēnō . Yellow . 4, H. Bl. P. Gardens .
   rūbrā-plēnō . Red . . 4, H. Bl. P. Gardens .
   variegātā . . Red . . 4, H. Bl. P. Gardens .
FROLŌVĬA. In honour of Frolow, a Russian botanist.

Linn. 19, Or. —, Nat. Or. Compositæ. Synonyme:
1. Saussurea Frolovii.
lyrātā, 1 . . . Sulphur. 9, H. Her. P. Altaia . . 1834
FRŪSTŬLĬA, Agardh. From frustula, fragments; of
which this genus is composed. Linn. 24, Or. 7,
Nat. Or. Algæ. These species are found in fresh
water—F. fasciātā, Ulvā.
FŪCHSĬA.
cylindrācēā . . Scarlet . 8, F. De. S. Mexico . . 1837
globōsā
   Devonĭā . . . Red . . 1, G. Ev. S. Hybrid . .
FŪNKĬA.
lanceæfolĭā
   fol. variegātĭs . Lilac . . 7, H. Her. P. Gardens .
undulātā . . . Lilac . . 8, F. Her. P. Japan . . 1834
   variegātā . . Lilac . . 8, F. Her. P. Japan . . 1834
FŪRCRÆĂ.
longævā . . . . . 5, Palm. . . 1833
FŪSĀRĬŬM—rosēŭm.
FŪSĬPŌRĬŬM, Link. From fusus, a spindle, and sporos,
a seed; referring to the fusiform sporidia. Linn.
24, Or. 9, Nat. Or. Fungi. Found on onions,
decayed cucumbers, &c.—F. atrovīrēns, aurantīā-
cŭm, Bŭxī.

GĀHNĬA, R. Brown. In honour of H. Gahn, a Swedish
botanist. Linn. 3, Or. —, Nat. Or. Gramineæ—G.
procērā.
GALĒŌBDŌLŎN.
lūtēŭm
   variegātŭm . Yellow . 6, H. Her. P. Britain . .
GĀLĬŬM—arenārĭŭm, Barrelĭĕrī, capillĭpēs, pallēscĕns,
rugōsŭm.
GARDŌQUĬA.
multiflōrā . . . Drk. pur. . 8, G. Ev. S. Chile . .
GĀRRȲA.
laurifolĭā . . . . . Mexico . .
GASTROLŌBĬŬM.
cordātŭm . . . Yellow . G. Ev. S. Swan R. .
GEĀSTRŬM—Bryāntĭī, striātŭm, S. minŭs.
GEBLĒRĂ, Fischer and Meyer. In honour of Gebler, a
German botanist. Linn. —, Or. —, Nat. Or. Euphorbiaceæ.
suffruticōsā . . . H. De. S. Russia . . 1835
GELASĬNĔ, Herbert. From gelasinos, a smiling dimple.
Linn. 6, Or. 1, Nat. Or. Iridaceæ. A bulbous rooted
plant, with rather small dark-blue flowers. It was
found by Mr. Tweedie in stony places near Rio
Grande. "Seedlings grow rapidly, and will probably flower at a year and a half old. The speci-
men figured flowered in the greenhouse at Spofforth,
but Mr. Herbert thinks the species will prove very
nearly hardy, and will retain its leaves, in part at
least, through the winter."—Gard. Mag.
azūrēā . . . . Blue . . G. Bl. P. S. Amer. . 1838
GENĬSTĂ. Synonyme: 1. Spartium interruptum.
germanĭcā
   inērmĭs . . . Yellow . 7, H. Ev. S.
sagittalĭs
   minŏr . . . Yellow . 5, H. Ev. Tr.
tinctorĭā
   florē plēnō . Yellow . 7, H. Ev. S. Gardens .
   hirsūtā . . . Yellow . 7, H. Ev. S. Britain .
   latifolĭā . . . Yellow . 8, H. Ev. S. Auvergne .
   pratēnsĭs . . Yellow . 7, H. Ev. S. Italy .
triacanthŏs
   interruptā, 1 . Yellow . 6, H. Ev. S. Tangier .
GENTĬĀNĂ.
asclepiādēā
   majŏr . . . Blue . . 7, H. Her. P.
   ochroleūcā . . Cream . 7, H. Her. P.
Gehlērĭ . . . . . H. Her. P. Russia . . 1832
plebēĭā . . . . Drk. blue . 7, H. Her. P. Germany . 1834
Pneumonanthē
   florē albō . . Wht. grn. 8, H. Her. P. Germany . 1834
vērnā
   florē albō . . White . 5, H. Ev. Tr. Gardens .
GEOGLŌSSŬM—difformĕ, glutinōsŭm.
GERĀNĬŬM.
affīnē . . . . . H. Her. P. . . 1832
asphodeloīdēs . . . H. Her. P. Levant . . 1828

lanuginosum j. . . 7, H. . A. . 1817
mexicanum . Light . 3, F. . P. Mexico . 1832

**GESNERA.**
bibracteata . . Scarlet 8, S. Tu. P. . 1835
cochlearis . . Red . 6, S. Her. P. Organ Mts 1837
latifolia . . Scarlet 8, S. Tu. P. Brazil . 1835
magnifica . . Scarlet 8, S. Tu. P. . 1835
Marchii . . Scarlet 10, S. Her. P. Organ Mts 1837
reflexa . . . 8. Her. P.
sceptrum . . Scarlet . 8. Ev. P. Brazil .
  Ignea . . Redsh. yel. 9, S. Ev. P. Brazil . 1835
stricta . . . Scarlet 7, S. Her. P. Brazil . 1835

**GEUM.**
chiloense
  atrosanguineum . Drk. bld. . H. Her. P. Gardens .
nivale
  alba . . . White . 6, H. Her. P. Gardens .

**GILIA.**
arenaria . . . Blue . H. . A. Californ. 1833
capitata . . H.
  corolla alba . White . H. A. Gardens 1829
crassifolia . . Yellsh. H. A. Chile 1832
liniflora . . White . H. A. Californ. 1833
pharnaceoides . . H. A. Californ. 1833
pusilla . . . H. A. Chile 1833
tenuiflora . . Ro. viol. 8, H. A. Californ. 1833

**GILLENIA.**
trifoliata
major . . . Red wht. 7, H. Her. P. N. Amer.

**GLADIOLUS.**
communis
  albus . . White . 6, H. Bl. P.
pudibundus . . Bluish . F. Bl. P. Eng. hyb.

**GLAUX.**
maritima
  alba . . . White . 5, H. Ev. Tr. Britain .

**GLEDITSCHIA.** Synonymes: 1. Gleditschia horrida major.
2. G. A. nana.
sinensis
  major, 1 . Green . H. De. T.
  nana, 2 . . Green . H. De. T.

**GLOXINIA.**
speciosa
  caulescens
    Menziesii . Blue wht. 8, S. Her. P. Eng. hyb.
  pallida . . Pn. blue 9, S. Her. P. Eng. hyb.
  violacea . . Violet . 8, S. Her. P. Hybrid .

**GOLDFUSSIA.**
glomerata . . Purple 10, S. Her. P. Silhet . 1838

**GOMPHOLOBIUM.**
aduncum . . N. S. W. 1837
angustifolium . . G. Ev. S. N. Holl. 1825
aristatum . . Swan R. 1837
tenue . . Yellow 8, G. Ev. S. N. Holl. 1830
versicolor . . Redsh. yel. G. Ev. S. Swan R. 183-.

**GOMPHONEMA**—ampullaceum.
**GONGORA.**
fulva . . . Yel. spot. 8. Epi. Demerara .
nigrita . . . Drk. pur. 8. Epi. Demerara .

**GONOLOBUS.**
hispidus . . . Black . 7, H. Ev. Tw. Brazil . 1837

**GOODYERA.**
rubicunda . . Cinnamon . 8. Ter. Manilla .

**GOUFFEIA,** Robl. Named after Gouffé de la Cour, a botanist of Marseilles. Linn. 10, Or. 2, Nat. Or. Caryophyllaceæ. This plant is probably unworthy of much regard.

holosteoides . . White . 7, H. A. Russia . 1836

**GOVENIA.**
Gardneri . . Orn. yel. 12, S. Her. P. Organ Mts 1837
lagenophora . . 8. Epi. Mexico .

**GRAMMATOPHYLLUM.** Synonymes: 1. Angræcum scriptum, Epidendrum scriptum, Cymbidium scriptum.

speciosum, 1 . Yel. brn. 8. Epi. E. Ind. . 1837

**GRATELOUPIA,** Agardh. Named in honour of Dr. Grateloup, a French algologist. Linn. 24, Or. 7, Nat. Or. Algæ. This plant is found in the ocean— G. filicina.

**GREVILLEA.**
aquifolia . . G. Ev. S. N. Holl. 1820
bipinnatifida . . G. Ev. S. Swan R. 1837

ferruginea . . . G. Ev. S. N. S. W. 1837
gibbosa . . . G. Ev. S. N. Holl. 1821
longifolia . . Redsh. yel. 5, G. Ev. S. Swan R. .
Manglesii . . . G. Ev. S. N. Holl.
Thelemanniana . Crimson . G. Ev. S. N. Holl.

**GRIFFITHSIA**—multifida pilifera, simplicifilum.
**GRIMMIA**—atrata.
**GYMNOGRAMMA.**
chærophylla . . Brown . 6, S. Her. P. Brazil .
cordata . . . Brown . 8, S. Her. P. C. G. H. 1838
Massonii . . Brown . 9, S. Her. P. Hybrid . 1838

**GYMNOSPORANGIUM,** Decandolle. From gymnos, naked, and sporangium, a seed vessel. Linn. 24. Or. 9, Nat. Or. Fungi. Found on the Juniperus communis —juniperi.

**GYMNOSTOMUM**—cæspititium, conicum minutulum, tortile.

**GYRENIA,** Knowles and Westcott. From gyros, a circle. Linn. 6, Or. 1, Nat. Or. Asphodeleæ.
biflora . . . Grnsh. 9, F. Bl. P. Mexico . 1837

**HABENARIA.**
gigantea . . Grah. wht. 8. Her. P. Bombay . 1834
goodyeroides . White . 12, S. Her. P. Bombay . 1834

**HÆMATOCOCCUS,** Agardh. From haima, blood, and kokkos, a berry; in allusion to the colour of many species. Linn. 24, Or. 7, Nat. Or. Algæ. Found on irrigated cliffs, caverns, &c.

**HAKEA.**
arborescens . . . G. Ev. T. N. Holl. 1820
cristata . . . G. Ev. S. Swan R. 1837
denticulata . . . G. Ev. S. K. Geo.'s Sd. 1837
myricæfolia . . . G. Ev. S. N. Holl. 1823

**HEDERA.**
Helix
  digitata . . Green . 10, H. Ev. S. Britain .
  fol. argentea . Green . 10, H. Ev. Cl. Britain .
  foliis aureis . Green . 10, H. Ev. Cl. Britain .

**HELIANTHEMUM.**
umbellatum
  erectum . . White . 7, F. Ev. S.
  subdecumbens . White . 7, F. Ev. S.

**HELMINTHOSPORIUM,** Link. Linn. 24, Or. —, Nat. Or. —. These species are found on oak branches, rotten sticks, &c.—fusisporium, nanum, simplex, subulatum.

**HEMEROCALLIS.**
fulva
  variegata . . Copper . 7, H. Her. P. Gardens .
  flore-pleno . . Copper . 7, H. Her. P. Gardens .
speciosa . . . Yellow . H. Her. P.

**HEMIANDRA,** Bentham. From hemi, half, and aner, an anther; in allusion to the dimidiate anthers. Linn. 14, Or. 1, Nat. Or. Labiatæ.
rupestris . . . Swan R. . 1837

**HEPATICA.**
americana
  alba . . . White . 3, H. Her. P. N. Amer. 1835
  rubra . . . Red . 3, H. Her. P. N. Amer. 1835

**HERACLEUM**—dissectum, setosum.
**HERMIONE,** Salisbury. Named after Hermione, the daughter of Helen. Linn. —, Or. —, Nat. Or. Amaryllidaceæ.
aperticorona . . . Yel. oran. 4, H. Bl. P. N. Africa .

**HETEROTROPA,** Morren. From heteros, various, trope, a change; the plant is variable. Linn. —, Or. —, Nat. Or. Asarineæ.
asaroides . . . Pur. wht. 4, G. Her. P. Japan . 1836

**HEXOPIA,** Bateman From hex, six, and ope, a cell; alluding to the six pollen masses in six cells. Linn. 20, Or. 1, Nat. Or. Orchidaceæ.
crucigera . . . White . 5, S. Epi. Guatemala 1836

**HIBISCUS.**
collinus . . . Yel. brn. 2, S. Ev. S. . 1836
multifidus . . . Azure . 9, G. De. S. N. Holl. 1837

**HIERACIUM**—Jacquini, Ledebourii.
**HIPPEASTRUM.**
ambiguum
  longiflorum . . Wht. red . 8. Bl. P. Lima . 1836

**HOITZIA.**
mexicana . . . Scarlet . G. Ev. S. Mexico . 1824

[ 350 ]

HOLARRHĒNA, *R. Brown.* From *holos*, entire, and *arrhen*, a male; alluding to the anthers. *Linn.* 5, Or. 1, Nat. Or. *Apocynaceæ.* This plant may be referred to *Echites* for culture and propagation.

| | | | | | |
|---|---|---|---|---|---|
| villōsā . . . . | | 8. Ev. S. E. Ind. . . | 1820 |

HORMĬNŪM—*virgĭnĭcŭm.*
HOSĀCKĬĀ.

| | | | | | |
|---|---|---|---|---|---|
| stolonĭfērā . | . Red . | . 6, H. Her. P. N. Amer. . | 1830 |

HOUSTŌNĬĀ.

| | | | | | |
|---|---|---|---|---|---|
| ciliātā . . . | . Whitish . | 7, F. Her. P. N. Amer. . |

HUGĚLĬĀ, *Bentham.* Named in honour of Baron Charles de Hügel of Vienna. *Linn.* 5, Or. 1, Nat. Or. *Polemoniaceæ.* For culture and propagation, see *Gilia.*

| | | | | | |
|---|---|---|---|---|---|
| densiflorā . . | . Blue . | . H. | A. California . | 1833 |
| elongātā . . | . Dp. blue . | . H. | A. California | 1833 |
| lūtēā . . . | . Yellow . | . H. | A. California | 1833 |
| virgātā . . | . Dp. blue . | . H. | A. California | 1833 |

HŪMŪLŪs.

Lŭpŭlŭs

| | | | | | |
|---|---|---|---|---|---|
| variegātŭs | . Yellow . | 7, H. De. Tw. Britain | gard. |

HŪNTLĔYĀ, *Bateman.* In compliment to the Rev. Mr. Huntley, a zealous collector of rare plants. *Linn.* 20, Or. 1, Nat. Or. *Orchidaceæ.* These rare and charming species require to be grown in a humid atmosphere either in pots placed on the stage or plunged in the bark-bed, or to be hung up, as those kinds with thick fleshy roots frequently succeed well in the latter way. They may be propagated by taking off the young shoots.

| | | | | | |
|---|---|---|---|---|---|
| meleāgris . . | . Yel. brn. . | 7, S. Epi. S. Amer. . | 1838 |
| violācēā . . | . Violet . | S. Epi. Guiana . | 1837 |

HȲDNŬM—*farĭnācēŭm, F. byssoīdēŭs, fĭmbrĭātŭm, fŭscŭm, ŭdŭm.*
HȲDRĀNGĔA.

arborescēns

| | | | | | |
|---|---|---|---|---|---|
| discŏlŏr . . | . Wht. grn. | 8, H. De. S. |

nĭvēā

| | | | | | |
|---|---|---|---|---|---|
| glabellā . . | . Wht. grn. | 7, H. De. S. Gardens . |

HȲDRŌPHŌRĀ, *Tode.* Derived from *hydor*, water, and *phoreo*, to bear; in allusion to the watery peridiolum. *Linn.* 24, Or. 9, Nat. Or. *Fungi.* Found on rats' dung—*H. murīnā.*

HȲMĔNŎCALLĬs, *Herbert.* "This species, very unlike any yet known, was imported from Mexico by T. Harris, Esq., of the Grove, Kingsbury; and three bulbs of it, sent through his liberality to Spofforth, flowered there with their first shoot in the stove at the beginning of April. The seeds of this genus are apt to burst the capsule, and become fully exposed to view in their progress to maturity; but in this species the singular phenomenon has appeared of one of the ovules, which are erect and fill the cell of the germen, splitting it, and forcing itself out, twelve hours after the impregnation of the stigma, while the flower was still fresh."—*Bot. Reg.*

| | | | | | |
|---|---|---|---|---|---|
| Harrisiānā . . . |

HȲMĔNŎPȲRĀMĬs, *Wallich.* From *hymen*, a membrane, and *pyramis*, a pyramid; alluding to its substance and growth. *Linn.* —, Or. —, Nat. Or. *Verbenaceæ.* A mixture of loam, leaf-mould, and sand, will suit this plant, and it may probably be increased by cuttings.

| | | | | | |
|---|---|---|---|---|---|
| brachiātā . . . | | 8. De. S. E. Ind. . | 1832 |

HȲPĔRĬCŬM. Synonyme : 1. *H. fasciculatum.*

| | | | | | |
|---|---|---|---|---|---|
| axillāré, 1 . | . Yellow . | 7, H. Ev. S. Georgia . |
| galloidés . | . Yellow . | 8, H. Ev. S. N. Amer. . |
| macrocārpŭm . | . | 8, H. Her. P. N. Amer. . | 1828 |

HȲPNŬM—*alopecŭrŭm aquātĭcŭm, confĕrtŭm subsecundĭfŏlĭŭm, cordĭfŏlĭŭm purpŭrēŭm, crassinĕrvĭŭm, denticŭm, flavescens, larĭcĭnŭm, mĭcāns, strĭātŭm mĭnŭs.*

HȲPŎXĬs.

| | | | | | |
|---|---|---|---|---|---|
| gracillis . | . Yellow . | 6, S. Bl. P. Mexico . | 1829 |

HȲssŌPŬs.

officinālis

| | | | | | |
|---|---|---|---|---|---|
| flore rubrō | . Red . | . 7, H. Ev. S. Gardens . |
| variegātŭs | . Blue . | . 7, H. Ev. S. Gardens . |

HȲsTĔRĬŬM—*Vaccĭnĭī.*

ĪLĔx.

Aquĭfŏlĭŭm

| | | | | | |
|---|---|---|---|---|---|
| altaclerēnsē . | . White . | . 5, H. Ev. T. Britain . . |
| angustĭfŏlĭŭm . | . White . | . 5, H. Ev. T. Britain . . |
| aūrēŏ pĭctŭm . | . White . | . 5, H. Ev. T. Britain . . |
| cilĭātŭm . . | . White . | . 5, H. Ev. T. Britain . . |
| cil. mĭnŭs . . | . White . | . 5, H. Ev. T. Britain . . |
| crĭspŭm . . | . White . | . 5, H. Ev. T. Britain . . |
| fērōx argentēŭm | White . | . 5, H. Ev. T. Britain . . |
| fērōx aurēŭm . | . White . | . 5, H. Ev. T. Britain . . |
| frŭctū albō . | . White . | . 5, H. Ev. T. Britain . . |
| frŭctū nĭgrō . | . White . | . 6, H. Ev. T. Britain . . |
| latĭfŏlĭŭm . . | . White . | . 5, H. Ev. T. Britain . . |
| laurĭfŏlĭŭm . . | . White . | . 5, H. Ev. T. Britain . . |
| margĭnātŭm . | . White . | . 5, H. Ev. T. Britain . . |
| senēcēns . . | . White . | . 5, H. Ev. T. Britain . . |
| serratĭfŏlĭŭm . | . White . | . 5, H. Ev. T. Britain . . |

ĪMPĀTĬĔNs.

| | | | | | |
|---|---|---|---|---|---|
| glandulĭgĕrā . | . Purple . | 8, G. | A. India . | 1839 |
| macrochĭlā . . | . Pa. pur. . | H. | A. India . | 1839 |
| pĭctā . . . | . Pink . | 6, S. | B. E. Ind. . | 1837 |
| tricŏrnĭs . . | . Yellow . | | India . . |

INGĀ.

| | | | | | |
|---|---|---|---|---|---|
| Harrisiī . . . | . Crimson . | 2, S. Ev. Cl. Mexico . . |

ĪNŪLĀ.

| | | | | | |
|---|---|---|---|---|---|
| glabrā . . . | | H. Her. P. | . 1831 |

IPŎMĒA. Synonyme. 1. *Batatas bonariensis.*

| | | | | | |
|---|---|---|---|---|---|
| bonariēnsis, 1 | . Purple . | 8, S. Tu. P. | B. Ayres . | 1826 |
| Learī . . . | . Blue . | 6, S. Ev. Tw. | Ceylon . |
| longĭfŏlĭā . . | . White . | 8, S. Tu. P. | Mexico . | 1838 |
| Pŭrgā . . . | . Crimson . | S. Ev. Cl. | Mexico . |
| rŭbrō-cærŭlēā . | . Rdsh. blue . | 8. Tw. P. | Mexico . | 1833 |
| Schiedĭānā . . | . Blue . | 10, S. Tw. P. | |

ĪRĬs. Synonyme : 1. *Iris missouriensis pleno.*

| | | | | | |
|---|---|---|---|---|---|
| Blondōwiī . . | | H. Her. P. | Altai . | 1832 |
| ensātā . . | . Blue pur. . | 6, H. Her. P. | Austria . | 1786 |
| florentĭnā | |
| mĭnŏr . . | . lgt. grey . | 5, H. Her. P. | Gardens . |
| frāgrāns . . | . Bl. pur. . | 6, H. Her. P. | India . | 1835 |
| germānĭcā | |
| flōre albō . | . White . | . 5, H. Her. P. | Gardens . |
| lævĭgātā . . | | H. Her. P. | . 1836 |
| Pseud-Acŏrŭs | |
| variegātŭs . | . Yellow . | 6, H. Her. P. |
| pŭmĭlā . . | |
| albā . . . | . White . | . 5, H. Her. P. |
| albā cærŭlēā | . Wht. pa. bl. 5, H. Her. P. |
| cærŭlēā . . | . Pa. blue . | 5, H. Her. P. |
| sĭbĭrĭcā . . | |
| flōre plēnō, 1 | . Purple . | . 5, H. Her. P. |
| variegātā . . | |
| De Berg . . | . Yel. brn. . | 5, H. Her. P. | Belgian hyb. |
| Van de Will . | . Yel. brn. . | 6, H. Her. P. | Belgian hyb. |

ĪRPĔX, *Fries.* From *irpex*, a rake, or harrow; alluding to the hymenium, which somewhat resembles that instrument. *Linn.* 24, Or. 9, Nat. Or. *Fungi.* These species are found on pine and beech wood—*I. lactēŭs, pendŭlŭs.*

IsĬDĬŬM—*microstictĭcŭm ālbŭm, paradōxŭm.*
IsMĔNĔ.

| | | | | | |
|---|---|---|---|---|---|
| deflēxā . . . | | G. Bl. P. |

IsŎTRŌPĬs. "This is a very pretty little greenhouse shrub. The stem is soft, and slightly downy, the leaves oval, the flowers papilionaceous, clear orange yellow, with rich, deep crimson, forked veins, even more distinctly marked than those of *Abutilon striatum.* It was communicated by Robert Mangles, Esq., of Sunning Hill."—*Bot. Reg.*

| | | | | | |
|---|---|---|---|---|---|
| striātā . . . | . Or. yel. crim. | G. Ev. S. | Swan R. . | 183- |

JACKSŌNĬĀ.

| | | | | | |
|---|---|---|---|---|---|
| grandiflōrā . | . Pa. yel. . | G. Ev. S. | Swan R. . |
| Sternbergiānā . | | G. Ev. S. | Swan R. . | 1837 |
| thesioīdés . . | | G. Ev. S. | N. Holl. . | 1830 |

JASMĬNŬM.

| | | | | | |
|---|---|---|---|---|---|
| multiflōrŭm . | . White . | | 8. Ev. S. |

JUNGERMĀNNĬĀ. Synonymes: 1. *Jungermannia epiphylla furcigera.* 2. *J. endiviæfolia.* 3. *J. affinis—J. barbāta mĭnŏr, bidentātā obtusātā, calycĭnā 1, epiphŷllā longĭfŏlĭā 2, hamatĭfŏlĭā echĭnātā, H. exstipulātā, microscŏpĭcā, plataphŷllā mājŏr, P. Thŭgā, reptāns bipinnātā, setĭfŏrmis britānnĭcā, Tamariscī apicŭlātā, turbĭnātā 3.*

JUNĬPĔRŬs. Synonymes: 1. *Juniperus vulgaris fruticosa, J. communis erecta.* 2. *J. lusitanica.*

commúnis
   oblónga péndùlă  Apetal  . 5, H. Ev. S.  .
   vulgáris, 1  .  Apetal  . 5, H. Ev. S. Britain  .
Sabínă
   cupressifóliă, 2  Apetal  . 5, H. Ev. S. S. Eur.  . 1548
virginiánă
   caroliniáná  . .  Apetal  . 5, H. Ev. S. Carolina  .

KĔRRĬĂ.  Synonyme: 1. Corchorus japonicus flore pleno.
japónică
   flóré plénō, 1  . Yellow  . 6, H. Ev. S. Japan  . 1700
KNAÚTĬĂ.
arvénsis
   flóré albō  . . White . 8, H. Her. P. Britain  .

LABĬCHĔĂ, Gaudichaud. In memory of M. Labiche, an officer of the French ship Uranie, who accompanied Freycinet in his voyage round the world; he died on his passage to the Moluccas. Linn. 2, Or. 1, Nat. Or. Leguminosæ. This shrub will probably thrive in a mixture of loam and peat, and cuttings will root, if planted in a pot of sand, with a bell-glass placed over them.
lanceolátă  . .  .  G. Ev. S. Swan R. . 1837
LĂ€LĬĂ.
cinnabarínă  . . . Vermil. . 5, S. Epi. Brazil  . 1836
Perrínĭī  . . . Lilac  . 9, S. Epi. Brazil  . 1835
supérbiens  . . .  S. Epi. S. Amer.  . 1840
LAGENÓPHŎRĂ, Endlicher. From lagenos, a flask, and phoros, bearing. Linn. 19, Or. —, Nat. Or. Compositæ.
Forstérī  . . . Yel. pur.  . G. Her. P. N. Zeal.  . 1837
LAMBĔRTĬĂ.
ovalifóliă  . . .  G. Ev. S.
LĂMĬŬM. Synonyme: 1. Lamium maculatum album.
longiflórùm
   albùm, 1  . White . 5, H. Her. P. Gardens  .
rugósùm
   albùm  . . . White . 7, H. Her. P. Gardens  .
LANTĂNĂ.
multiflóră  . . .  S. Ev. S.  . 1834
Selloviáná  . . .  S. Ev. S. Montevid. 1822
LASĬĂNDRĂ.
petioláta  . . . Blue  . 6, S. De. S.  . 1836
LAXMĂNNĬĂ.
grandiflórà  . . . Wht. brn.  G. Her. P. Swan R. .
LEPTOCĂLLĬs, Don. From leptos, slender, and kallos, beauty; the plant being slender and very pretty. Linn. 5, Or. 1, Nat. Or. Convolvulaceæ. This plant may be referred to Ipomæa for culture, &c. Synonymes: 1. Ipomæa muricata, I. armata.
guinátă, 1  . . . Violet . 7, G. Her. P. Mexico  .
LEPTODĔRMĬs, Wallich. From leptos, slender, and derma, the skin; the branches are covered with separating fibrous bark. Linn. 5, Or. 1, Nat Or. Rubiaceæ. For cultivation, &c., refer to Hamiltonia. Synonyme: 1. Hamiltonia fruticosa.
lanceolátă, 1  . Yellow  . G.  . S. Nepal  . .
LEPTOSĬPHŎN.
grandiflórùs  . Blue gol. . 9, H.  A. Californ. . 1833
luteùs  . . . Dp yel. . 9, H.  A. Californ. . 1833
pállidùs  . . . Pa. yel. . 9, H.  A. Californ. . 1833
parviflórùs  . . Yellow  . 9, H.  A. Californ. . 1833
LIBANŌTĬs, Scopoli. From libanos, incense. Linn. 5, Or. 2, Nat. Or. Umbelliferæ. This plant is of easy culture, requiring a sandy, or chalky soil, and it is readily increased by seeds. Synonyme: 1. Ligusticum athamantoides.
athamantoídes, 1. White . 7, H. Her. P.  . 1817
LĬLĬŬM.
speciósùm
   albiflórùm  . . White  . F. Bl. P. Japan  . .
LISSĂNTHĔ.
stellátă  . . . White . .  N. Holl.
verticilláta  . . Purple . .  N. Holl.
LISSŎCHĬLŬs, R. Brown. From lissos, smooth, and cheilos; in allusion to the lip of the flower. Linn.

---

20, Or. 1, Nat. Or. Orchidaceæ. For culture, &c. see Bletia.
lúteùs  . . . Yellow . 5, S. Ter. C. G. H. . 1822
parviflórùs  . . Pa. red. . 1½. Epi. Algoa B. .
speciósùs  . . Yellow . 6, S. Ter. C. G. H. . 1818
LOBĔLĬĂ.
ignéă  . . . . Flame . 6, F. Her. P.  . 1838
multiflóră  . . . Purple .
LOPĔZĬĂ.
lineátă  . . . .  G.  S. Mexico . .
LUPĬNŬs.
Barkérī  . . . Blue pk. . 7, H.  A. Mexico . .
LYCOPÓDĬŬM. Synonyme: 1. Selaginilla cordata.
brasiliénsě  . . Brown . 11, S. Ev. Cr. Brazil .
cordátùm, 1  . .  S. Her. P.  . 1838
LYSĬMĂCHĬĂ.
nemórùm
   variegátùm  . Yellow  . 6, H. Ev. Tr.

MACRONĚLDĬĂ. Linn. 20, Or. 1, Nat. Or. Orchidaceæ.
antenniféră  . .  Swan R.  .
Smithiáná  . .  Swan R.  .
MACROSPÓRĬŬM, Fries. From makros, long, and sporos, a seed. Linn. 24, Or. 9, Nat. Or. Fungi. The first of the under-mentioned is found on decaying leaves of cabbage, and the latter on those of Cheiranthus —M. Brássicæ, Cheiránthi.
MALACHĔNĬĂ, —— Linn. 20, Or. 1, Nat. Or. Orchidaceæ. "This very singular plant was given to Mr. Bateman by Mr. William Hooper of Lambeth, who received it from Rio in 1836. It is a remarkable genus, resembling Megaclinium in some respects, but belonging in reality to Vandeæ, among which it is marked by the nearly total absence of petals, the cirrhate column, and the soft fleshy cinnamon-coloured gland, to which a pair of reniform pollen masses are slightly attached. In this division of Orchidaceæ it is uncertain where it must stand; probably other genera still undiscovered will connect it with the system better than can at present be done."—Bot. Reg.
clavátă  . . . Grn. pur.  . S. Epi. Rio Jan. . 1836
MĂLVĂ.
campanulátă  . . Pa. pink lil. . G. Ev. P.
concinnă  . . . Light . 5, S. Ev. S. S. Amer. . 1835
lucidă  . . . .  H.  A.
MANDEVĬLLĂ, Lindley. Named after Henry John Mandeville, Esq., H.B.M. Minister at Buénos Ayres, to whom we are indebted for the introduction of this and many interesting plants. Linn. 5, Or. 1, Nat. Or. Apocynaceæ. This new climber, according to Lindley, is remarkable for its deliciously sweet, snowy white, and very beautiful flowers "It will," says he, "probably form an abundant flowerer; but, like all seedling shrubs, its first stage of growth is more productive of foliage than blossoms."—Bot. Reg. It appears that, in order to grow this plant to perfection, it should be planted out in the border of the conservatory. If cultivated during summer in the open air, or in pots in the greenhouse, it grows freely, but does not flower. After the flowering season is over, the plants should be pruned similarly to vines, or other plants which bear their flowers and fruit upon the wood of the same year. It may be propagated by cuttings or seeds, sown in a pit, with a little heat.
suavéolens  . . . White  . G. Ev. Cl. B. Ayres .
MANGLĔSĬĂ, Lindley. "This plant has found its way into gardens, having been raised from Swan River seed by Robert Mangles, Esq., of Sunning Hill. It is a Proteaceous plant, allied to Grevillea, with neat toothed, long-stalked leaves, and very small, white flowers, of no beauty. It is for its foliage alone that it will be cultivated."—Bot. Reg.
glabrátă  . . . White . . G. Ev. S. Swan R. .
MARÁTTĬĂ.
lævis  . . . .  S. Her. P. Jamaica .
MĂNDĔVĂLLĬĂ, Ruiz and Pavon. In honour of Joseph

Masdevall, a Spanish botanist. *Linn.* 20, Or. 1, Nat. Or. *Orchidaceæ.*

| | | | | | |
|---|---|---|---|---|---|
| infractā | . . . | . Whtsh. yel. | 8. Epi. Brazil | . . | |

**MAXILLĀRĪĀ.**

| | | | | | |
|---|---|---|---|---|---|
| acutifolīā | . . | . Brnsh. . | . 8. Epi. Demerara | . | |
| cucullātā | . . | . Yellow . | . 9, 8. Epi. America | . . | 1837 |
| lentiginōsā | . . | . Grn. pur. | 8. Epi. Brazil | . | |
| platanthērā | . . | . Gra. yel. | . 8. Epi. Brazil | . . | 1831 |

**MĒDICĀOŌ.**

| | | | | |
|---|---|---|---|---|
| clypeātā | . . . | | H. Her. P. India | . . |

**MĒNISCYŪM.**

| | | | | |
|---|---|---|---|---|
| palūstrē | . . | . Brown | . 5, 8. Her. P. W. Ind. | . |
| triphyllūm | . . | . Brown | . 8. Her. P. Ceylon | . |

**MICROPĒRĀ,** *Lindley.* From *micros,* small, and *pera,* a pouch. *Linn.* 20, Or. 1, Nat. Or. *Orchidaceæ.* Synonymes: 1. *Micropera pyrifolia.* 2. *Microtis pallida.*

| | | | | | |
|---|---|---|---|---|---|
| Banksiī, 1 | . . | | G. Tu. P. N. Zeal. | . . | |
| pallīdā, 2 | . . | . Pa. yel. | . 8. Epi. | Sylhet | . . |

**MILTŌNĪĀ.**

| | | | | |
|---|---|---|---|---|
| cāndīdā | | | | |
| flavēscēns | . . | . Yellow. | . 9, 8. Epi. Brazil | . . |

**MONACHĀNTHŪS.**

| | | | | | |
|---|---|---|---|---|---|
| discōlōr | | | | | |
| viridiflōrā | . . | . Green | . 8, 8. Epi. Demerara | . | 1835 |
| rōsēō albīdūs | . . | . Rose grn. | . 4, 8. Epi. Brazil | . | 1839 |

**MONOCHĪLŪs,** *Fischer and Meyer.* Derived from *monos,* one, and *cheilos,* a lip; alluding to the flower. *Linn.* —, Or. —, Nat. Or. *Verbenaceæ.*

| | | | | |
|---|---|---|---|---|
| gloxinifolīā | . . | | 8. Tu. P. | . 1838 |

**MONOTĀXĪs,** *Brongniart.* From *monos,* one, and *taxis,* a series; in allusion to the male and female flowers. *Linn.* —, Or. —, Nat. Or. *Euphorbiaceæ.*

| | | | |
|---|---|---|---|
| simplēx | . . . | | G. Ev. 8. N. Holl. . |

**MORĪNĀ.**

| | | | | |
|---|---|---|---|---|
| longifolīā | . . | . Purple | . F. Her. P. E. Ind. | . . |

**MORMŌDĒs.**

| | | | |
|---|---|---|---|
| buccinātōr | . . | . Pa. grn. | . 8. Epi. |

**MŌRŪs.**

| | | | | |
|---|---|---|---|---|
| albā | | | | |
| nervōsā | . . | . Apetal | . 6, H. De. T. | |

**MYĀNTHŪS.**

| | | | | | |
|---|---|---|---|---|---|
| barbātūs | | | | | |
| labēllō albō | . . | . Drk. grn. | . 5, 8. Epi. Demerara | . | 1835 |
| spinōsūs | . . | . Grn. spot. | . 8. Epi. Brazil | . | |

**NEMĒSĪĀ.**

| | | | | |
|---|---|---|---|---|
| floribūndā | . . | . Wht. yel. | . 7, H. | A. C. G. H. . . |

**NEPĒTĀ.**

| | | | | |
|---|---|---|---|---|
| salviæfolīā | . . | . White | . H. Her. P. Himalay. | . |

**NUTTĀLLĪĀ.**

| | | | | |
|---|---|---|---|---|
| malvæflōrā | . . | . Lgt. rose | . 8, F. Her. P. Texas | . . 1838 |

**OBĒRŌNĪĀ,** *Lindley. Linn.* 20, Or. 1, Nat. Or. *Orchidaceæ.* Two species of this remarkable genus have been figured in Lindley's splendid work entitled " Sertum Orchidaceum," where he makes, among other, the following remarks.—" The genus Oberonia consists principally of small, fleshy-leaved epiphytes, inhabiting the branches of trees in the woods of India, and having the most tiny of flowers. Fourteen species have been described, of which one only, and that the least interesting, *O. Iridifolia,* has been seen alive in Europe. The resemblance to insects and other animal forms, which have been perceived in the orchidaceous plants of Europe, and which have given rise to such names as Fly Orchis, &c., may be traced so plainly in the genus *Oberonia,* in every species, that it alone would furnish a magazine of new ideas for the grotesque pencil of a German admirer of the wild and preternatural. If the Brahmins had been botanists, one might have fancied they took their doctrine of metempsychosis from these productions; in the genera *Oberonia* and *Drymoda,* Pythagoras would have found a living evidence of animals transmuted into plants."

| | | | | |
|---|---|---|---|---|
| cylindricā | . . | . Green . . | 8. Epi. Manilla | . . |

[ 853 ]

**OCTOMĒRĪĀ.**

| | | | | |
|---|---|---|---|---|
| diaphānā | . . . | . White . | . 8. Epi. Brazil | . . |

**ODONTOGLŌssŪM.**

| | | | | | |
|---|---|---|---|---|---|
| Clowēsiī | . . | . Yel. brn. | . 8. Epi. Brazil | . . | |
| grāndē | . . | | 8. Epi. Guatemala | . . | |
| maculātūm | . . | . Yel. brn. | . 8. Epi. Mexico | . . | |
| Rōssiī | . . | . Wht. grn. | . 8. Epi. Mexico | . . | 183- |

**ONCĪDYŪM.**

| | | | | | |
|---|---|---|---|---|---|
| Batemaniānūm | . . | . Yellow | . 8. Epi. Mexico | . . | 1838 |
| carinātūm | . . | | 8. Epi. Xalapa | . | |
| concōlōr | . . | . Lemon | . 8. Epi. Organ Mts. | . | 1837 |
| excavātūm | . . | . Yellow | . 8. Epi. | | |
| Forbēsiī | . . | . Yel. brn. | . 8. Epi. | | |
| hīāns | . . | . Brn. yel. | . 8. Epi. | | |
| Huntiānūm | . . | . Yel. red | . 9, 8. Epi. Brazil | . . | |
| Insleāyī | . . | . Drk. brn. | . 8. Epi. Mexico | . . | |
| rōseūm | . . | . Rose | . . 8. Epi. | . | |
| trullifērūm | . . | . Brn. yel. | . 9, 8. Epi. Brazil | . . | 1838 |

**PASSIFLŌRĀ.**

| | | | | |
|---|---|---|---|---|
| hispidūlā | . . | . Yel. wht . | | |
| Moreānā | . . | . Whtsh. . | . 7, H. De. Cl. B. Ayres | . 1837 |

**PATERSŌNĪĀ.**

| | | | | |
|---|---|---|---|---|
| sapphirīnā | . . | . Sapphire | . G. Her. P. Swan R. | . |

**PENTLĀNDĪĀ,** *Herbert.* In honour of I. B. Pentland, Esq., consul-general in Peru. *Linn.* 6, Or. 1, Nat. Or. *Amaryllidaceæ.* " There are two forms of this species, differing very slightly from each other. The first was found in Cusco in Peru, and was sent to Spofforth under the name of the red Narcissus, by I. B. Pentland, Esq., in compliment to whom the genus is named; and the other was found by Commodore Sullivan, during his command on the west coast of South America, in 1837. Both varieties flowered for the first time in England, in August, 1839."—*Bot. Reg.*

| | | | | | |
|---|---|---|---|---|---|
| miniātā | . . | . Red | . 9, H. Tw. P. Peru | . | 1839 |
| lacunōsā | . . | | | | |
| Sulivānicā | . . | | | | |

**PENTSTĒMŌN.**

| | | | | |
|---|---|---|---|---|
| gentianoīdēs | . . | . Drk. pur. | . 8, H. Ev. P. N. Amer. | . . |

**PHILADĒLPHŪs.**

| | | | | |
|---|---|---|---|---|
| mexicānūs | . . | . White . | . | Mexico . . |

**PHLOGOCĀNTHŪs,** *Nees.* From *phlox,* a flame, and *akanthus,* the type of this family; in allusion to the long spike of yellow or flame-coloured flowers. *Linn.* 2, Or. 1, Nat. Or. *Acanthaceæ.* For this magnificent shrub, British collections are mainly indebted to Dr. Wallich. Its common height is from four to six feet, and it may most likely be grown in rather a rich soil.

| | | | | |
|---|---|---|---|---|
| curviflōrūs | . . | . Red yel. | . 6, 8. Ev. 8. Sylhet | . 1839 |

**PLEUROTHĀLLĪs.**

| | | | | | |
|---|---|---|---|---|---|
| scābrīpēs | . . | . Yel. pur. | . 8. Epi. Brazil | . | 1837 |
| villōsā | . . | . Pur. spot. | . | Mexico | . |

**POLYSTĀCHYĀ.**

| | | | | |
|---|---|---|---|---|
| bracteōsā | . . | . Orange | . | 8. Leone . |

**PORTULĀCĀ.**

| | | | |
|---|---|---|---|
| Thelluaōnīī | . . | . Drk. red . | F. A. |

**POLEMŌNYŪM.**

| | | | | |
|---|---|---|---|---|
| cærūlēūm | | | | |
| grandiflōrūm | . Blue | . . | H. | B. India . |

**PRIMŪLĀ.**

| | | | |
|---|---|---|---|
| prænītēns | | | |
| plēnā | . . . | . Cream . | |

**QUĒRCŪs.**

| | | |
|---|---|---|
| Brāntiī | . . | . . |
| mannifērā | . . | . . |
| rēgīā | . . | . . |

**RIGIDĒLLĀ,** *Lindley.* From *rigidus,* rigid; in allusion to the rigidity of the flower-stalk, when supporting the seed-vessel. *Linn.* 16, Or. 1, Nat. Or. *Iridaceæ.* This very pretty plant was found lately by Mr. Hartweg, and it is remarkable for its dissimilarity to any other genus yet known. For culture and propagation it may be referred to *Tigridia.*

| | | | | |
|---|---|---|---|---|
| flāmmēā | . . . | . Flame, | . 5, 8. Tu. P. Mexico | . . 1839 |

SILVIA.

linarioides . . . . Pa. blue . 6, G. Ev. S. S. Amer. .
patula . . . .

SINNINGIA.

Youngeana . . Purple . 7, S. Ev. S. Hybrid . .

SPIRONEMA. " A Mexican herbaceous plant, introduced by Mr. Barker, with something of the appearance of a Sanseviera, but very fragrant; it has lately flowered with Messrs. Low and Co., of Clapton."—*Bot. Reg.*

fragrans . . . S. Her. P. Mexico . .

SPREKELIA.

cybister . . . . Red . . S. Bl. P. Bolivia . .
brevis . . . . Grn. red . S. Bl. P. Bolivia . .

STENOMESSON.

latifolium . . . Yellow . G. Bl. P. Lima . . 1837

THALICTRUM.

cultratum . . . Grn. yel. . H. Her. P. Himalayas .

TANACETUM.

longifolium . . Yellow . Himalayas .

THE END.

BRADBURY AND EVANS, PRINTERS, WHITEFRIARS.

Lightning Source UK Ltd.
Milton Keynes UK
UKOW041905140212

187305UK00006B/73/P